READINGS FOR LIBERAL EDUCATION

EDITED BY

LOUIS G. LOCKE
Mary Baldwin College

WILLIAM M. GIBSON
New York University

GEORGE ARMS
The University of New Mexico

REVISED EDITION

RINEHART & COMPANY · NEW YORK

Printed in the United States of America

Designed by Stefan Salter

Library of Congress Catalog Card Number: 52–5593

READINGS FOR LIBERAL EDUCATION

I. TOWARD LIBERAL EDUCATION

II. INTRODUCTION TO LITERATURE

". . . Some will then be chosen for higher privilege. The studies which they pursued without order in their early years will now be brought together, and the students will see the relationship of these studies to one another and to truth."

"Yes," he said. "That is the only kind of knowledge which takes lasting root."

PLATO, *The Republic*

PREFACE

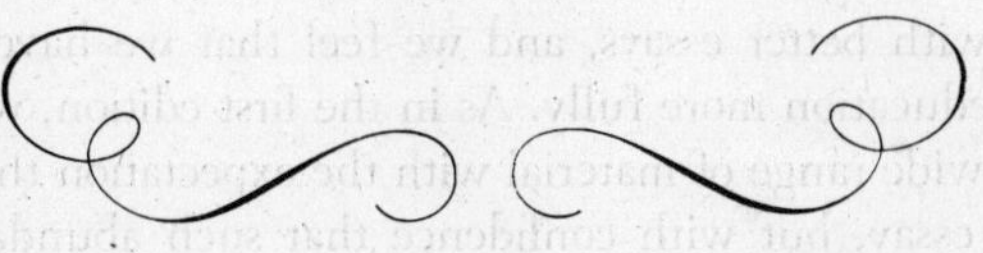

THE idea for this book began several years ago when we were thinking and reading and arguing with our colleagues about liberal education in America. Since then, with starts and stops, with enthusiasm and with a few regrets that we ever began the project, we have tried to shape the idea into a book. Our constant purpose has been to make an anthology that would help first-year college students understand what liberal education can mean to them.

As it seemed to us, the reading provided in most freshman courses went a good way toward realizing this purpose. But the effort was often partial and sometimes fitful. The principal differences between *Readings for Liberal Education* and earlier collections of readings are those of development rather than of radical change. First, this collection points steadily in the direction indicated by its title. Without deviating into models at one time or mere entertainment at another, it seeks systematically to explore the skills and disciplines of our humanistic culture. Second, it makes this exploration by the use of writing chosen for its intrinsic worth. It does not talk down to its readers.

In the first volume, *Toward Liberal Education,* the first three parts are concerned with the skills of a liberal education: learning, reading and writing, and thinking. The four parts that follow these represent the great areas of liberal learning: the arts, science, society, and philosophy and religion. The second volume, *Introduction to Literature,* turns to that discipline which is particularly cherished by teachers of English: literature of the imagination. Plainly we do believe that literature is an efficient means to the self-examined life, and that no small part of its efficiency to this end lies in the unique pleasure which it affords its readers. It is not the keenest of the pleasures, as A. E. Housman has said, but it is yet the least perishable, "the least subject to external things, and the play of chance, and the wear of time."

The development of all eight parts of *Readings for Liberal Education* aims at presenting the material to the student with force and meaning. In arranging the parts in their final order, we thus feel that we have provided a sound framework for a course which uses the anthology. Yet we recognize that each school and each teacher may properly wish to rearrange the order for special needs.

We have chosen writing that bears the stamp of permanent value. This standard has not meant that we stayed in the past. But it has meant the exclusion of superficial journalizing and disregard for the timeliness of yesterday's newspaper. Freshmen, we believe, not only are capable of hard, solid reading, but are happier when they are expected to do it. Such reading is not dull, as we hope this book demonstrates; for certainly not wisdom alone, but the sweetness and joy of wisdom, determines a classic.

In revising the original edition, we have not changed the purpose or plan. Though we do not regret the use of essays now omitted, we believe we have replaced them with better essays, and we feel that we have entered certain areas of liberal education more fully. As in the first edition, we have provided teachers with a wide range of material with the expectation that few will want to assign every essay, but with confidence that such abundance of readings provides a latitude of choice which gives an individuality and a richness to the course.

The revision of the second volume includes most of the literature that appeared formerly; but many new poems, stories, and plays appear that we hope will both strengthen and enhance the earlier selection. It will be apparent that we have discarded the categories of the original edition because they presented the material less advantageously than we had supposed they would.

Many teachers who used the original edition in their classes have generously made their experience and wisdom available to us, and we wish to make full acknowledgment to them. Particularly we should like to thank Professors Morris Bein, Wallace C. Brown, Alan S. Downer, Richard Eastman, J. Stuart Goodman, Hyatt H. Waggoner, Howard A. Wilson, and James L. Wortham; we also appreciate the assistance of Professors Frank Adams, E. W. Baughman, Samuel N. Bogorad, George C. Booth, Frederick Bracher, C. A. Brown, Irving L. Churchill, Fletcher Collins, Jr., J. Hal Connor, Ethel C. Cox, Norton B. Crowell, Grace Donaldson, Ethel A. Fleming, Signi Falk, Eleanor J. Gibson, James J. Gibson, L. P. Goggin, Robert M. Gorrell, Willis D. Jacobs, William R. Keast, John P. Kirby, Jane Kluckhohn, Arthur Kreisman, David G. Kroft, Daniel Kroll, Joseph M. Kuntz, Juanita Kytle, Vernon Lichtenstein, Richard C. R. Louder, Edward G. Lueders, Catherine Mims, Mary E. Osborn, Herbert B. Nelson, Paul Roberts, Macha Rosenthal, Ernest Samuels, Dane F. Smith, F. Smoyer, E. W. Tedlock, Jr., Margaret Trotter, Herbert J. Turner, R. G. Webster, Alfred Westfall, and Horace Williston. We are further aware of indebtedness extending back over many years to teachers, students, and acquaintances of the past.

March, 1952

L. G. L.
W. M. G.
G. A.

TOWARD LIBERAL EDUCATION

CONTENTS

I · *LEARNING*

THE CAMPUS

University Days — *James Thurber* — 1
Kittredge of Harvard — *Rollo Walter Brown* — 6
How Agassiz Taught Shaler — *Nathaniel Southgate Shaler* — 16
Neilson of Smith — *Hubert Herring* — 19
Gate Receipts and Glory — *Robert M. Hutchins* — 32
Freshman Adviser — *George Boas* — 41

EDUCATION

Honors Courses at Swarthmore — *Frank Aydelotte* — 45
Education at Bennington — *Hubert Herring* — 52
General and Special Education — *The Harvard Committee* — 63
On the Need for a Quiet College — *Stephen Leacock* — 68
The Saber-Tooth Curriculum — *J. Abner Peddiwell* — 72
Introductory Lecture — *A. E. Housman* — 79

II · *READING AND WRITING*

READING

Of Studies — *Francis Bacon* — 83
The Library — *Chauncey B. Tinker* — 84
Unrequired Reading — *Irwin Edman* — 87
Reading — *Henry David Thoreau* — 95
Mr. K*a*p*l*a*n and Shakespeare — *Leonard Q. Ross* — 101

WRITING

The Art of Plain Talk: Live Words and Crowded Words — *Rudolf Flesch* — 106
The Language of Business — *The Editors of* Fortune — 115

Notes and Comment — *from* The New Yorker 126
Politics and the English Language — *George Orwell* 128
Interlude: On Jargon — *Arthur Quiller-Couch* 138
On "On Jargon" — *Robert J. Geist* 150
Pleasant Agony — *John Mason Brown* 153
The American Language — *H. L. Mencken* 158
Of the Vanity of Words — *Michel Eyquem de Montaigne* 165

III · *THINKING*

Four Kinds of Thinking — *James Harvey Robinson* 168
The Case for the Daydreamer — *James Thurber* 179
Language and Thought — *Suzanne K. Langer* 182
The Four Stages of Thought — *Graham Wallas* 186
Contexts — *S. I. Hayakawa* 199
Emotional Meanings — *Robert H. Thouless* 207
Logical Fallacies — *Robert Gorham Davis* 215
Of the Conduct of the Understanding — *John Locke* 224
Reasoning — *William James* 228
Idols of the Mind — *Francis Bacon* 237

IV · *THE ARTS*

THE FINE ARTS

Why Abstract? — *Hilaire Hiler* 245
Botticelli's *Primavera* — *Frank Jewett Mather, Jr.* 252
Modern Architecture: The Cardboard House — *Frank Lloyd Wright* 257
The Imperial Façade — *Lewis Mumford* 267
Music for the Man Who Enjoys *Hamlet* — *B. H. Haggin* 277
The Listener — *Roger Sessions* 284

THE MODERN FOLK ARTS

Direction — *Alfred Hitchcock* 295
Soapland — *James Thurber* 302
Washboard Weepers: A Small Case for Radio — *Max Wylie* 308
Strictly from Mars, or, How to Philander in Five Easy Colors — *S. J. Perelman* 315
Ooff!! (Sob!) Eep!! (Gulp!) Zowie!!! — *E. J. Kahn, Jr.* 319

LITERATURE AND CRITICISM

Dover Beach — *Matthew Arnold* 332
Dover Beach Revisited: A New Fable for Critics — *Theodore Morrison* 333
The Essence of Tragedy — *Maxwell Anderson* 346
Fenimore Cooper's Literary Offenses — *Mark Twain* 352
Manners, Morals, and the Novel — *Lionel Trilling* 361
Poetry and Advertising — *S. I. Hayakawa* 372
On Reading Poetry — *John Ciardi* 378
Man Will Prevail — *William Faulkner* 385

V · *SCIENCE*

THE NATURE OF SCIENCE

Concerning Electricity and Combustion — *James B. Conant* 387
The Usefulness of Useless Knowledge — *Abraham Flexner* 406

THE SCIENCES

What Makes the Weather: The Seven American Airs — *Wolfgang Langewiesche* 412
A Primer of Atomic Energy — *William L. Laurence* 424
The Evolution of the Physical World — *Arthur Stanley Eddington* 439
Chlorophyll: The Sun Trap — *Donald Culross Peattie* 442
Of the Quantity of Blood Passing through the Heart — *William Harvey* 448
Carbon Monoxide Poisoning — *Claude Bernard* 450
The Reading Machine — *Morris Bishop* 452
The Ivory Lab — *Jacques Barzun* 454
The Anatomy of the Mental Personality — *Sigmund Freud* 464
Looking Forward — *Lewis Mumford* 480

VI · *SOCIETY*

SOCIAL ATTITUDES

An Anthropologist Looks at the United States — *Clyde Kluckhohn* 489
Trends in Personal Life — *Margaret Mead* 511
Common Women — *Philip Wylie* 516
A Tale of a Tub — *Bergen Evans* 523
Pecuniary Canons of Taste — *Thorstein Veblen* 533
The Bitter Drink — *John Dos Passos* 544

FREEDOM AND SECURITY

The Illusion of Individuality — *Erich Fromm* 551
Approaches to Economic Reform — *Eli Ginzberg* 560
Of the Wages of Labour — *Adam Smith* 564
Gold-Mining — *John Maynard Keynes* 569
Civil Disobedience — *Henry David Thoreau* 571
The Apology of Socrates — *Plato* 585
The Declaration of Independence — *Thomas Jefferson* 605

PROBLEMS OF THE SOCIAL SCIENCES

The Significance of the Frontier in American History — *Frederick Jackson Turner* 609
Does History Repeat Itself? — *Arnold J. Toynbee* 618
The First and the Second Industrial Revolution — *Norbert Wiener* 625
Modern Man Is Obsolete — *Norman Cousins* 640

VII · *PHILOSOPHY AND RELIGION*

THE GOOD LIFE

Virtue — *Aristotle* 649
The Sermon on the Mount — *St. Matthew* 656
The Stoic Code — *Marcus Aurelius* 660
The Enjoyment of Living — *Michel Eyquem de Montaigne* 664
Is Happiness Still Possible? — *Bertrand Russell* 677

RELIGION

A Free Man's Worship — *Bertrand Russell* 683
The Necessity of the Wager — *Blaise Pascal* 689
The Providence of God — 696
Meditation XVII — *John Donne* 698
In His Will Is Our Peace — *John Woolman* 699
The Reasonableness of Christianity — *Theodore M. Greene* 701
Religion and Science — *Alfred North Whitehead* 717
Living Religions and a World Faith — *William Ernest Hocking* 726

THE NATURE OF REALITY

The Allegory of the Cave — *Plato* 742
A Discourse on Method — *René Descartes* 745
An Essay Concerning Human Understanding — *John Locke* 753
What Pragmatism Is — *William James* 756

CAN PHILOSOPHY SAVE CIVILIZATION?

The Breakdown of Modern Philosophy — *Etienne Gilson* 762
The Basis of Renewal — *Lewis Mumford* 766

QUESTIONS 787

BIOGRAPHICAL NOTES 814

INDEX 825

I

LEARNING

· *THE CAMPUS* ·

UNIVERSITY DAYS [1]

JAMES THURBER

I PASSED all the other courses that I took at my University, but I could never pass botany. This was because all botany students had to spend several hours a week in a laboratory looking through a microscope at plant cells, and I could never see through a microscope. I never once saw a cell through a microscope. This used to enrage my instructor. He would wander around the laboratory pleased with the progress all the students were making in drawing the involved and, so I am told, interesting structure of flower cells, until he came to me. I would just be standing there. "I can't see anything," I would say. He would begin patiently enough, explaining how anybody can see through a microscope, but he would always end up in a fury, claiming that I could *too* see through a microscope but just pretended that I couldn't. "It takes away from the beauty of flowers anyway," I used to tell him. "We are not concerned with beauty in this course," he would say. "We are concerned solely with what I may call the *mechanics* of flars." "Well," I'd say, "I can't see anything." "Try it just once again," he'd say, and I would put my eye to the microscope and see nothing at all, except now and again, a nebulous milky substance—a phenomenon of maladjustment. You were supposed to see a vivid, restless clockwork of sharply defined plant cells. "I see what looks like a lot of milk," I would tell him. This, he claimed, was the result of my not having adjusted

1. From *My Life and Hard Times* (New York: Harper & Brothers, 1933). Reprinted by permission of the author. Copyright, 1933, James Thurber. Originally published in *The New Yorker* under the title "College Days."

the microscope properly; so he would readjust it for me, or rather, for himself. And I would look again and see milk.

I finally took a deferred pass, as they called it, and waited a year and tried again. (You had to pass one of the biological sciences or you couldn't graduate.) The professor had come back from vacation brown as a berry, bright-eyed, and eager to explain cell-structure again to his classes. "Well," he said to me, cheerily, when we met in the first laboratory hour of the semester, "we're going to see cells this time, aren't we?" "Yes, sir," I said. Students to right of me and to left of me and in front of me were seeing cells; what's more, they were quietly drawing pictures of them in their notebooks. Of course, I didn't see anything.

"We'll try it," the professor said to me, grimly, "with every adjustment of the microscope known to man. As God is my witness, I'll arrange this glass so that you see cells through it or I'll give up teaching. In twenty-two years of botany, I—" He cut off abruptly for he was beginning to quiver all over, like Lionel Barrymore, and he genuinely wished to hold onto his temper: his scenes with me had taken a great deal out of him.

So we tried it with every adjustment of the microscope known to man. With only one of them did I see anything but blackness or the familiar lacteal opacity, and that time I saw, to my pleasure and amazement, a variegated constellation of flecks, specks, and dots. These I hastily drew. The instructor, noting my activity, came back from an adjoining desk, a smile on his lips and his eyebrows high in hope. He looked at my cell drawing. "What's that?" he demanded, with a hint of a squeal in his voice. "That's what I saw," I said. "You didn't, you didn't, you *did*n't!" he screamed, losing control of his temper instantly, and he bent over and squinted into the microscope. His head snapped up. "That's your eye!" he shouted. "You've fixed the lens so that it reflects! You've drawn your eye!"

Another course that I didn't like, but somehow managed to pass, was economics. I went to that class straight from the botany class, which didn't help me any in understanding either subject. I used to get them mixed up. But not as mixed up as another student in my economics class who came there direct from a physics laboratory. He was a tackle on the football team, named Bolenciecwcz. At that time Ohio State University had one of the best football teams in the country, and Bolenciecwcz was one of its outstanding stars. In order to be eligible to play it was necessary for him to keep up in his studies, a very difficult matter, for while he was not dumber than an ox he was not any smarter. Most of his professors were lenient and helped him along. None gave him more hints, in answering questions, or asked him simpler ones than the economics professor, a thin, timid man named Bassum. One day when we were on the subject of transportation and distribution, it came Bolenciecwcz's turn to answer a question. "Name one means of transportation," the professor said to him. No light came into the big tackle's eyes. "Just any means of transportation," said the professor. Bolenciecwcz sat staring at him. "That is," pursued the professor, "any medium, agency, or method of going from one place to another." Bolenciecwcz had the look of a man who is being led into a trap. "You may choose among steam, horse-drawn, or electrically propelled vehicles," said the instructor. "I might suggest the one which we commonly take in making long journeys across land." There was a profound silence in which everybody stirred uneasily, including Bolenciecwcz and Mr. Bassum. Mr. Bassum abruptly broke this silence in an amazing manner. "Choo-choo-choo," he said, in a low voice, and turned instantly scarlet. He glanced appealingly around the room. All of us, of course, shared Mr. Bassum's desire that Bolenciecwcz should stay abreast of the class in economics, for the Illinois game, one of the hardest and most important of the season, was only a week off. "Toot, toot, too-tooooooot!" some student with a deep voice moaned; and we all looked encouragingly at Bolenciecwcz. Somebody else gave a fine imitation of a locomotive letting off steam. Mr. Bassum himself rounded off the little show. "Ding, dong, ding, dong," he said, hopefully. Bolenciecwcz was staring at the floor now, trying to think, his great brow furrowed, his huge hands rubbing together, his face red.

"How did you come to college this year, Mr. Bolenciecwcz?" asked the professor. "*Chuffa* chuffa, *chuffa* chuffa."

"M'father sent me," said the football player.

"What on?" asked Bassum.

"I git an 'lowance," said the tackle, in a low, husky voice, obviously embarrassed.

"No, no," said Bassum. "Name a means of transportation. What did you *ride* here on?"

"Train," said Bolenciecwcz.

"Quite right," said the professor. "Now, Mr. Nugent, will you tell us——"

If I went through anguish in botany and economics—for different reasons—gymnasium work was even worse. I don't even like to think about it. They wouldn't let you play games or join in the exercises with your glasses on and I couldn't see with mine off. I bumped into professors, horizontal bars, agricultural students, and swinging iron rings. Not being able to see, I could take it but I couldn't dish it out. Also, in order to pass gymnasium (and you had to pass it to graduate) you had to learn to swim if you didn't know how. I didn't like the swimming pool, I didn't like swimming, and I didn't like the swimming instructor, and after all these years I still don't. I never swam but I passed my gym work anyway, by having another student give my gymnasium number (978) and swim across the pool in my place. He was a quiet, amiable blonde youth, number 473, and he would have seen through a microscope for me if we could have got away with it, but we couldn't get away with it. Another thing I didn't like about gymnasium work was that they made you strip the day you registered. It is impossible for me to be happy when I am stripped and being asked a lot of questions. Still, I did better than a lanky agricultural student who was cross-examined just before I was. They asked each student what college he was in—that is, whether Arts, Engineering, Commerce, or Agriculture. "What college are you in?" the instructor snapped at the youth in front of me. "Ohio State University," he said promptly.

It wasn't that agricultural student but it was another a whole lot like him who decided to take up journalism, possibly on the ground that when farming went to hell he could fall back on newspaper work. He didn't realize, of course, that that would be very much like falling back full-length on a kit of carpenter's tools. Haskins didn't seem cut out for journalism, being too embarrassed to talk to anybody and unable to use a typewriter, but the editor of the college paper assigned him to the cow barns, the sheep house, the horse pavilion, and the animal husbandry department generally. This was a genuinely big "beat," for it took up five times as much ground and got ten times as great a legislative appropriation as the College of Liberal Arts. The agricultural student knew animals, but nevertheless his stories were dull and colorlessly written. He took all afternoon on each of them, because he had to hunt for each letter on the typewriter. Once in a while he had to ask somebody to help him hunt. "C" and "L," in particular, were hard letters for him to find. His editor finally got pretty much annoyed at the farmer-journalist because his pieces were so uninteresting. "See here, Haskins," he snapped at him one day, "why is it we never have anything hot from you on the horse pavilion? Here we have two hundred head of horses on this campus—more than any other university in the Western Conference except Purdue—and yet you never get any real low-down on them. Now shoot over to the horse barns and dig up something lively." Haskins shambled out and came back in about an hour; he said he had something. "Well, start it off snappily," said the editor. "Something people will read." Haskins set to work and in a couple of hours brought a sheet of typewritten paper to the desk; it was a two-hundred word story about some disease that had broken out among the horses. Its opening sentence was simple but arresting. It read: "Who has noticed the sores on the tops of the horses in the animal husbandry building?"

Ohio State was a land grant university and therefore two years of military drill was compulsory. We drilled with old Springfield rifles and studied the tactics of the Civil War even though the World War was going on at the time. At 11 o'clock each morning thousands of freshmen and sophomores used to deploy over the campus, moodily creeping up on the old chemistry building. It was good training for the kind of warfare that was waged at Shiloh but it had no connection with what was going on in Europe. Some people used to think there was German money behind it, but they didn't dare say so or they would have been thrown in jail as German spies. It was a period of muddy thought and marked, I believe, the decline of higher education in the Middle West.

As a soldier I was never any good at all. Most of the cadets were glumly indifferent soldiers, but I was no good at all. Once General Littlefield, who was commandant of the cadet corps, popped up in front of me during regimental drill and snapped, "You are the main trouble with this university!" I think he meant that my type was the main trouble with the university but he may have meant me individually. I was mediocre at drill, certainly—that is, until my senior year. By that time I had drilled longer than anybody else in the Western Conference, having failed at military at the end of each preceding year so that I had to do it all over again. I was the only senior still in uniform. The uniform which, when new, had made me look like an interurban railway conductor, now that it had become faded and too tight made me look like Bert Williams in his bell-boy act. This had a definitely bad effect on my morale. Even so, I had become by sheer practise little short of wonderful at squad manoeuvres.

One day General Littlefield picked our company out of the whole regiment and tried to get it mixed up by putting it through one movement after another as fast as we could execute them: squads right, squads left, squads on right into line, squads right about, squads left front into line, etc. In about three minutes one hundred and nine men were marching in one direction and I was marching away from them at an angle of forty degrees, all alone. "Company, halt!" shouted General Littlefield, "That man is the only man who has it right!" I was made a corporal for my achievement.

The next day General Littlefield summoned me to his office. He was swatting flies when I went in. I was silent and he was silent too, for a long time. I don't think he remembered me or why he had sent for me, but he didn't want to admit it. He swatted some more flies, keeping his eyes on them narrowly before he let go with the swatter. "Button up your coat!" he snapped Looking back on it now I can see that he meant me although he was looking at a fly, but I just stood there. Another fly came to rest on a paper in front of the general and began rubbing its hind legs together. The general lifted the swatter cautiously. I moved restlessly and the fly flew away. "You startled him!' barked General Littlefield, looking at me severely. I said I was sorry. "That won't help the situation!" snapped the General, with cold military logic. I didn't see what I could do except offer to chase some more flies toward his desk, but I didn't say anything. He stared out the window at the faraway figures of co-eds crossing the campus toward the library. Finally, he told me I could go. So I went. He either didn't know which cadet I was or else he forgot what he wanted to see me about. It may have been that he wished to apologize for having called me the main trouble with the university; or maybe he had decided to compliment me on my brilliant drilling of the day before and then at the last minute decided not to. I don't know. I don't think about it much any more.

KITTREDGE OF HARVARD[1]

ROLLO WALTER BROWN

THERE could be no doubt about the matter: George Lyman Kittredge consisted of more than one man. Just how many men were required to constitute him, nobody seemed able to say. But that he was not less than two, everybody who knew him was ready to admit.

The first of these two—the one he was most widely thought of as being—was the "Kitty" of Harvard Hall. Undergraduates with vivid imaginations made sketches of the old building on the point of blowing up, with zigzag electric fragments of Shakespeare shooting from windows and roof, whenever "Kitty" held forth. To many of them for a lifetime the total meaning of Harvard Hall was "Kitty."

The sight of him as he came to the ten-o'clock class was in itself something that had to be recognized as dramatic. In the pleasant autumn or spring, men stood high on the steps or out on the turf in front and watched in the direction of Christ Church to see who could catch the first glimpse of him.

"There he comes!" somebody called, and then everybody who was in a position to see watched him as he hurried breezily along—a graceful, tallish man in very light gray suit and gray fedora hat, with a full square beard at least as white as his suit, who moved with energy, and smoked passionately at a big cigar. Students used to say that he smoked an entire cigar while he walked the short distance along the iron fence of the old burying ground and across the street to Johnston Gate. But as he came through the gate he tossed the remnant of his cigar into the shrubbery with a bit of a flourish, and the students still outside hurried in and scrambled up the long stairway in order to be in their places—as he liked—before he himself entered. If any of them were still on the stairway when he came in at the outer door like a gust, they gave way and he pushed up past them, and into the good-sized room and down the aisle to the front, threw his hat on the table in the corner, mounted the two steps to the platform, looked about with a commanding eye, and there was sudden silence and unrestrained expectancy.

"Any questions?" he asked—meaning questions about matters considered at the last meeting of the course. After five minutes of these questions, he was ready to begin.

The play under consideration was *Macbeth*—let us say; and he was ready to take up Act III. Always his method was a meticulously careful examination of every line, every significant word, with a running commentary on problems of drama and theatre. At the end of the year we were supposed to know five plays—sometimes a sixth—so thoroughly that in the final examination we could spot any line or piece of line that he quoted (usually about sixty), tell what came just

1. From *Harvard Yard in the Golden Age,* by Rollo Walter Brown. Copyright, 1948, by permission of Current Books, Inc., A. A. Wyn, Publisher, New York.

before and after, tell who said the words and to whom, and be able to comment on whatever was significant in the passage. Then there were somewhat more than six hundred lines of memory passages. And there were books of assigned reading. Even the least wise in the course filled the margins of his copy of the text, and pages of gummed interleaving paper, with notes against an oncoming evil day.

"Now," he said, after he had read and commented upon Banquo's opening speech, and had reminded us once more that *Macbeth* is a swift-moving play, "there are three very important questions on this next page. They are neatly imbedded, yet for the purposes of the play, they stand out in red ink. What are they?"—and he glanced up and down the class list—"Mr. Howard."

Mr. Howard—it might have been Cabot or Flynn or Jones—did not seem to be present.

"Mr. Howard?" "Kitty" repeated, with the slightest trace of irritation in his voice.

When there was still no response he suddenly exploded. "The college office had two ghost men on my list for two or three weeks before I could get them off! Is this Mr. Howard another?"

There was no response.

"Is there anybody in this room who knows anything about this spook Mr. Howard?"

There was not a murmur, seemingly not even a breath, among the hundred or more students.

He slapped the book down on his desk so sharply that some of the men in the front row jumped. "By heavens, this is not to be endured! I asked a perfectly decent question, and I am going to have an answer if I have to take a poll of the entire class!"

A man in the middle of the room hesitantly lifted a hand. "I am Mr. Howard."

"Then why didn't you answer?"

"I was not prepared."

"Kitty" flew into so vast a rage that even the top of his head was ruddy. "Well, couldn't you at least have identified yourself? Stand up, Mr. Howard"—and he made a movement as if to step down off the platform—"so that this class can see who you are. And"—after Mr. Howard had very promptly stood up—"you are to come over to Sever 3 at twelve o'clock and expostulate with me—in the Elizabethan sense."

He picked up the book and in a twinkling went on, quite as if nothing unusual had happened, to point out that the three questions down the page were the ones that Macbeth asked Banquo:

Ride you this afternoon?

Is't far you ride?

Goes Fleance with you?

And then in an engaging smoothness of temper and in flowing brilliance he commented on one passage after another, made compact explanation of linguistic details, reminded us that it was not the words that had become obsolete that made the most trouble for us in understanding Shakespeare, but the words that had not become obsolete, and otherwise rounded out the whole scene until we felt as if we must be knowing the play somewhat as the audience knew it when it was originally produced.

He came to a very brief stage direction. "Note that Shakespeare is usually brief. If Mr. George Bernard Shaw had been writing that stage direction, he would have filled a page, at least."

There was a flutter of mirthfulness. It was the style then to laugh at any mention of this new playwright, as though of course he could not be much.

"Incidentally," he said, as he paced the platform, "there are other differences between William Shakespeare and Mr. Shaw."

There was greater mirthfulness still; and time flowed on harmoniously.

Some professor of economics had great charts and maps on rollers all over the front of the room, and there were two or three long, gracefully sloping pointers at hand. "Kitty" picked up one of these and used it as a stafflike cane as he paced back and forth and commented. He was magnificent. He was an Anglo-Saxon king speaking to his people.

Once in his march as he socked the royal staff down, it came in two where there was a knot in the wood, and he made a somewhat unkingly lurch. A few students snickered very cautiously.

He glowered upon them. "You have a fine sense of humor!" Then without taking his eyes off the humbled faces, he drew his arm back as if he were hurling a javelin, and drove the long remnant of the pointer into the corner of the room. "Now laugh!" he dared them.

When "Kitty" was having a run of bad days, an hour might be highly electric from beginning to end.

One wintry morning when he was late and the legitimate seven minutes of grace had ticked away, somebody called bravely, "All out!" There was much shuffling of feet and there were echoing cries all over the room, "Time up!" "Let's go!" But nobody moved. Finally one man arose and marched defiantly toward the door, to the accompaniment of whoops and cheers.

Soon there was a solid procession pushing out through the doorway. Just when the Arnolds and Bonbrights from down in front were approaching the door and the room suddenly looked deserted, somebody called from downstairs: "Here he is!"

There was a mad scramble to get back into the room. But he was moving faster than any crowd could move. On the long semicircular stairway he pushed through with his green bookbag and smart gray hat held high, and let everyone give way in the manner possible. He was in the front of the room, and had his hat and overcoat and bookbag on the table, and was mounting the platform all in readiness to begin before the last of the returning students were in their chairs.

He waited for a moment of silence before he spoke—with something of scorn in his voice. "When I was an undergraduate in this college, by thunder we never went back for a professor."

Then for an hour he treated us as if we were a bunch of softies. He commented on words, on lines, on entire speeches with lightning speed. He assumed vast historical and linguistic knowledge on our part which we did not possess. He fired questions in every direction. One of these he addressed to a thirty-eight-year-old graduate student—a professor on leave from a well-known institution—and gave him such a cross-examination that he never came back to the course.

And then, just before bell time when even the laziest student in the course had been stimulated by the charged atmosphere to make notes and otherwise try to keep up, "Kitty" broke off in the middle of a sentence with a terrifying shout that was also a roar, slapped his copy of the play down on the desk, hurried toward the door, nervously pushing his hand back through his white hair, and disappeared into the hallway.

A moment later he reappeared at the door, bowing a man in with extraordinary graciousness. The man was frightened almost beyond speech.

"I b-beg your pardon," he stammered, "I am not a member of the course; I am a visitor."

"That does not excuse you from the rules of courtesy. You were disrespectful to me and to the young gentlemen of the class. Nobody leaves this room till the bell rings."

By the time he was back at his desk and had found the interrupted sentence in the play, the bell was ringing and he made a gesture of dismissal. As the men crowded toward the door they somehow felt sheepish, like schoolboys.

It was always a double experience. "Kitty" might suddenly step out of the Elizabethan world and pounce upon some man and scare him until he was unable to define the diaphragm—it once happened—and require him to come to the next meeting "prepared to discuss the diaphragm" as a preliminary to an hour of *King Lear*. No man might feel altogether sure that he would escape. Once "Kitty" read with such a poetic impression of reality that a man who was later to be widely known as a magazine editor sat lost in rapturous enjoyment. Suddenly "Kitty" stopped. "Now what is the commanding word in that passage"—and he picked up the printed class list and let his eye run down over the names—"Mr. . . . Smith?" Mr. Smith had been so rapturously lost that he did not even know where the passage was. A neighbor whispered the number of the line to him and he answered correctly: "Why—'God.'" "Don't you 'Why—God' me!" "Kitty" stormed back at him, and then gave him such a dressing down for using the unnecessary word as he had never known, so that he always had that to carry along with his memory of the perfect reading. On another occasion

"Kitty" picked up the class list, started on the *R*'s, became interested in one man's brilliant answers to his rapid-fire cross-examination, and left the rest of the *R*'s dangling in suspense throughout the three remaining months of the year.

Men knew that he was a miracle man, and thought it worth accepting all hazards in order to possess some part of his basic richness of life. They completed the year, grumbled a little about the marks he gave them—there were few *A*'s—and very probably came back the next year to study the alternating group of plays. In that case they had the thorough knowledge of ten or eleven plays, instead of five or six; they knew eleven or twelve hundred lines of good passages by heart; they had vast information about drama and theatre and sources and language and Elizabethan life, and they had interesting fragments of such a store of miscellaneous knowledge and wisdom as they had not supposed until last year could be the possession of any one human being.

That was one of the men in the total George Lyman Kittredge. That part of him could not be brushed aside as if it were not an essential part. It was. But it was the more external part. Many of the men in the course in Shakespeare knew this well enough. They saw that it was their irresponsibility, or laziness, or grotesque ignorance, that touched him off into his tantrums. His disgust and amazement and scorn were release for a sensitive mind—usually in need of sleep—whose everyday high level made it impossible for him not to suffer in the presence of unlimited imperfections. And his graduate students who had never taken the course in Shakespeare found it difficult to believe the wild stories about him. For to them he was a courteous gentleman who begged them to smoke some of his good cigars and know that they were potential scholars about to be admitted to the most honorable company of men on earth.

His courtesy did not prevent him from exercising the dominant mind. When a student explained somewhat fearfully that he had noticed in the dictionary that a certain word was accented on the second syllable, "Kitty" said, as he put the word down on the back of an envelope, "That's wrong; I'll see that that is changed." Through generations of Shakespeare students—and his place on the board of editors of one dictionary—he caused a shift in preference to the pronunciation of "Elizabethan" with an accented long *e*. But he could never establish "Shakspere" as a preferred spelling. Sometimes, too, his overpositiveness came back upon him in ironic ways. He insisted on withholding a degree from a man for insufficient acquaintance with the drama who later became a national figure in play-writing. He once prevented a man from receiving honors in English with whom ten years later he marched down the aisle at a university commencement where both received honorary degrees—the young author and the white-haired professor.

Men who were chiefly concerned with the literature of the eighteenth and nineteenth centuries very justly felt that he placed heavy emphasis on the early centuries. But he insisted that the early centuries were of the utmost importance, and that they were full of interest. The age of Chaucer, he contended, was closer to us than the age of Pope. Always there were students who had looked upon Chaucer as some vague accident back there on the edge of the pure night of the Dark Ages, and for a time they sat skeptical, although they assumed that Chaucer was somebody about whom they should know a little.

But when they listened to Professor Kittredge—or "Mr. Kittredge"—they saw the age of Chaucer coming to such vividness of view that they had to admit that it outshone the nearer centuries in brightness. He invited them to see that

> the spirit of radicalism was abroad in the land. To describe as an era of dumb submissiveness the age of Wyclif, and John Huss, and the Great Schism, of the Jacquerie in France and Tyler and Ball in England, is to read both literature and history with one's eyes shut. . . . It was a scambling and unquiet time when nobody was at rest but the dead. In a word, it was a good age to live in, and so Chaucer found it.[2]

And so they found it—and the heroic world of Beowulf, and the world of English and Scottish popular ballads, and all the other less familiar worlds to which he introduced them. Something of his own vividness had gone into his original exploring, and now something of it went into the revelation of what he had discovered.

But whatever the area in which he for the moment was occupied, he was engaged in perhaps the most difficult—and most desperately needed—of all educational endeavors in the United States; that is, in having pure scholarship recognized as a source of life for all men. Scholarship is the final high honesty. Men worked with Professor Kittredge—always the least bit awesomely—and came to feel how great was the disgrace of a human mind that let itself be content with anything short of the completest disinterested understanding.

From his fortunate position he all the while was sending out great numbers of men to important college and university posts. They were such men as John M. Manly, of the University of Chicago, one of his earliest students; Walter Morris Hart, of the University of California; John Samuel Kenyon, of Hiram College; Karl Young, of Yale; Carleton Brown, chiefly of Bryn Mawr; John A. Lomax, of the field of American ballads and folk songs; John Livingston Lowes, who came back from Washington University to teach in the Yard for the rest of his active life—and write *The Road to Xanadu.*

At times the objection made its way back to Cambridge that some of his disciples were not important men of this kind, but only "little Kittredges." And sometimes the reports were true. If men are basically small they are sure to adopt the accessible mannerisms of anyone whose superior qualities are out of reach. But Professor Kittredge's distinguished former students constituted a great company. In Texas, in Iowa, in Pennsylvania, in California, men accustomed to the ax-to-grind sort of thinking in what they called the practical world looked upon

2. *Chaucer and His Poetry.* 1915. Harvard University Press. By permission.

these honest scholars as an ultimate standard of excellence to be applied in matters of every perplexing sort.

And in Professor Kittredge it was more than honesty; it was high faith in honesty. His former students often traveled a thousand miles—sometimes farther—to have his counsel when they were in doubt. A young professor in a Midwestern college had confided in an older man in one of the chief universities of America about an original project that he had in mind for the next year, and then found that the older man had immediately hurried off a young colleague to work at the idea and be first in the field. Sleepless, the young professor went to consult someone who was wise.

Professor Kittredge sat erect and smoked at a great fragrant cigar and listened in silence until the man was through. Then he said without a moment's hesitation: "Don't let the matter trouble you for one minute. And don't modify your plans—not by as much as a hair. Scurvy business of that kind doesn't work out—in the end. It is not the other man's idea; he is working at it because his chief suggested it to him. He will make little of it. The idea is yours, from the inside of you, and consequently you will be aware of all sorts of possibilities in it that the other man, whoever he is, will never see." And when it turned out precisely so, Professor Kittredge said with a trace of a smile round his eyes and down into his white beard, "We have to count on its being like that."

He gave his complete self to the world of the teacher. He required nothing else. In it he had labor and recreation and profound joy—without end. For forty-eight years (1888–1936) he taught at Harvard. He never took a year of leave, nor a half year. He did not like to have breaks in his work. He did not like to go off to other universities to lecture in term time. He made a number of trips to Europe, but with one exception he made them in the summer-vacation period. England was his great fascination east of the Atlantic. When he was made an honorary fellow of Jesus College, Cambridge, he was delighted and proud. When Oxford wished to confer on him an honorary degree he felt highly honored, of course. But the great joy of work was at home.

In this world of the teacher to which he was devoted, he carried on endless research. When he was confronted by the teacher's much-discussed choice between teaching and research, he said: "Thank you, I'll take both."

In his own explorations the range that he covered was so wide that some persons actually believed that there were at least two persons named G. L. Kittredge writing at the time. He was interested in such matters as Increase Mather's views on smallpox, the ballads of Kentucky, the vocabulary of the Australasians, the history of witchcraft, the history of words for popular reading, cowboy songs, the early Teutonic notions of immortality, the toad in folklore, Chaucer on marriage, the history of religion, and scores of subjects thought of as more strictly within the field of language and literature. And his books ranged from *Chaucer and His Poetry* to *The Old Farmer and His Almanack*—and manuals of grammar and composition for high school.

It was at Barnstable, down on the Cape, that he was able to do much of his own work. For there he had long summer weeks that were little interrupted. If one chanced to be at the house on Hilliard Street in Cambridge just when he was about to go away for the summer, one might well decide that he was leaving for all time, so completely did he seem to be transferring his scholarly effects. Eventually he built a study a little away from the house in Barnstable so that he might work in entire seclusion, with only the cheerful voices of his children and their friends on the tennis court to remind him pleasantly—if he heard them at all—that he was not completely isolated in time and space.

On the Cape, too, he could be elementally refreshed. On the Cape, he was happy to say, he—or his son—had come upon the perfect pessimist, a native who grew chickens. When it was suggested that a few chicks just outside a coop were sturdy youngsters, the native replied, "Yes, but the trouble is, the old hen hatched out six, and by God all of them have died on me but five."

The Cape was heaven for work; yet back in Cambridge in the autumn he carried his own work right along with his teaching—and thereby constantly gave his teaching enrichment. He moved briskly from his classroom to Gore Hall, and very quickly disappeared. Then one came upon him somewhere deep in the stacks, lost to the immediate world over a puzzling text or fat galleys of proofs. The library was nothing musty and dead for him. It was man recorded. When the great new Widener Memorial Library was spoken of as an elephant among the other buildings in the Yard, he asked, "What if it is? You could destroy all the other Harvard buildings to the northward, and with Widener left standing, still have a university."

If days were not long enough, always there were nights. Like Charles Péguy, he considered night as the part of existence that holds everything together that is sacred to man, "wherein he accomplishes his being." But for Professor Kittredge this was not to be done through sleep; it was to be done through work.

For many years one of his intimate friends walked from Boston to Cambridge on Sunday afternoon, had supper with the Kittredges, and then the two read Greek together till eleven o'clock—as relaxation. But that still left the body of the night ahead. So, too, was it when his "ballad course" met at his house in the evening, and some of the most enthusiastic lingered a little in the big study. It was when his own house had become quiet, and the lights in houses everywhere were beginning to disappear, and the roar of the city had lost its nearness, and the world was otherwise losing the last signs of its daytime confusion, that he knew freedom. In the enveloping quiet he could give himself to work without fear of distraction. If he felt the need of diversion, he could read one more detective story.

When Mrs. Kittredge chanced to know at two or two-thirty or three in the morning that he was still at work, she would slip down and remind him that it was time for him to be getting some sleep. Very obediently he would go off to bed for the rest of the night. In the course of years, Mrs. Kittredge wearied a little of making the trip downstairs and had an electric bell installed with a button by her bed. But he did not like it. In the perfect quiet of night it made him jump. Sometimes nobody reminded him that he ought to be in bed, and he did not think of the matter himself; and when Thomas the chore man slipped into the study at six in the morning to build a new fire, there sat Professor Kittredge peacefully asleep in his comfortable chair before the empty fireplace, with one hand clutching a book on the arm of the chair as firmly as if he were awake. On such a night he did not get to bed at all.

When a vivid man does a sufficient number of things that are unfailingly characteristic, legend begins to attach itself to his name. And when he lives on and on through one college generation after another until men who were in his classes almost a half century before come back to visit their grandsons in the freshman class and find him still teaching with the same old fire, the contributions of legendary instance mount till they constitute a kind of running supplemental biography.

Men argued over the original color of his hair and beard, for he was gray—or white—so early that nobody could quite remember him when he was not gray or white. They liked to speak, too, of the fact that Kitty never bothered with any degree except an A.B. They laughed over the gushing woman who asked in disappointment why he had never taken a Ph.D. and his supposed reply: "Who would have examined me?" Or they repeated the story of the famous woman college president who wished a Harvard man as an instructor in English, but said she could not consider anyone who lacked a Ph.D., and of Charles Townsend Copeland's stentorian reply to her: "Thank God, then we'll not lose Kittredge!"

Legend was helped, too, by the fact that in his highly charged life there was always unpredictable heartening for the less positive, the less courageous. When a frightened young candidate for honors in English had to say in reply to a question: "I'm afraid I can't answer; I have not read all of Wordsworth," Professor Kittredge brought him quickly to life and confidence by replying: "Neither have I! I couldn't be hired to!" When the efficiency experts were rising up everywhere in institutions, and one of them asked Professor Kittredge just how many hours and minutes it took him to prepare one of his "lectures" on Shakespeare, he replied: "I refuse to answer. It's one of my trade secrets." Then he relented and said, "Just a lifetime—can't you see that?" When graduate students in the field of English made their way to Professor K. G. T. Webster's house at Gerry's Landing for a relaxing great dinner and then a joyous session on the third floor in a room that some of the guests thought of as an Anglo-Saxon mead hall, Professor Kittredge was always so full of wit and generosity of spirit that the guests were stirred to believe they could face anything.

So there he was, about to be seventy-five, full of fiery power, and seemingly without a thought that he had already taught ten years past the usual retiring age. He walked energetically through the traffic of Harvard Square and the policeman said bravely but so that Professor Kittredge would be sure not to hear:

"Be a little careful there, Santa Claus!" In the Yard the general assumption seemed to be that nobody quite dared to tell him that he must retire.

On his seventy-fifth birthday, when he went to his class at Radcliffe the girls had put seventy-five magnificent crimson roses on his desk.

What was this they had done? Often enough he had scolded them. Sometimes he had walked out on them when they did not come up to his expectations in brilliance. And now they had remembered him in this fashion. They had almost taken an unfair advantage of him—so startling was it all. He told them—and suddenly he was deeply touched—that he found it difficult to express his great appreciation. "If it would help, I'd declare a holiday. And I do hereby declare a holiday." Then quite as suddenly he recovered his usual manner, looked up, and said with a self-defiant kind of smile: "Now if only some of you will tell me how to get them home without looking like a bridegroom!"

At home he admitted modestly to his wife that not every man received that many roses from his girl students on his seventy-fifth birthday. In the afternoon when one of his former students and his wife dropped in to offer best wishes, he was in the happiest of moods. He told them how near he had come to being born on the twenty-ninth of February. He admitted in great joviality that undergraduates had at times led him to make "characteristic remarks" and do "characteristic things," and he drew out of the past a few instances himself. Yes, he supposed he would be giving up teaching sooner or later, for he had in mind finishing that annotated edition of such plays of Shakespeare as had interested him most, and that would keep him busy for a number of years ahead.

And so it did.

HOW AGASSIZ TAUGHT SHALER[1]

NATHANIEL SOUTHGATE SHALER

At the time of my secession from the humanities, Agassiz was in Europe; he did not return, I think, until the autumn of 1859. I had, however, picked up several acquaintances among his pupils, learned what they were about, and gained some notion of his methods. After about a month he returned, and I had my first contact with the man who was to have the most influence on my life of any of the teachers to whom I am indebted. I shall never forget even the lesser incidents of this meeting, for this great master by his presence gave an importance to his surroundings, so that the room where you met him and the furniture stayed with the memory of him.

When I first met Louis Agassiz, he was still in the prime of his admirable manhood; though he was then fifty-two years old, and had passed his constructive period, he still had the look of a young man. His face was the most genial and engaging that I had ever seen, and his manner captivated me altogether. But as I had been among men who had a free swing, and for a year among people who seemed to me to be cold and super-rational, hungry as I doubtless was for human sympathy, Agassiz's welcome went to my heart—I was at once his captive. It has been my good chance to see many men of engaging presence and ways, but I have never known his equal. . . .

As my account of Agassiz's quality should rest upon my experiences with him, I shall now go on to tell how and to what effect he trained me.[2] In that day there were no written examinations on any subjects to which candidates for the Lawrence Scientific School had to pass. The professors in charge of the several departments questioned the candidates, and determined their fitness to pursue the course of study they desired to undertake. Few or none who had any semblance of an education were denied admission to Agassiz's laboratory. At that time, the instructors had, in addition to their meagre salaries—his was then $2,500 per annum,—the regular fees paid in by the students under his charge. So I was promptly assured that I was admitted. Be it said, however, that he did give me an effective oral examination, which, as he told me, was intended to show whether I could expect to go forward to a degree at the end of four years of study. On this matter of the degree he was obdurate, refusing to recommend some who had been with him for many years, and had succeeded in their special work, giving as reason for his denial that they were "too ignorant."

The examination Agassiz gave me was directed first to find that I knew enough Latin and Greek to make use of those languages; that I could patter

---

1. From *Autobiography of Nathaniel Southgate Shaler* (Boston: Houghton Mifflin Company, 1907), 93-100, with omissions. Reprinted by permission of Gabriella Shaler Webb.

2. At this time Shaler was nineteen years old.

a little of them evidently pleased him. He didn't care for those detestable rules for scanning. Then came German and French, which were also approved: I could read both, and spoke the former fairly well. He did not probe me in my weakest place, mathematics, for the good reason that, badly as I was off in that subject, he was in a worse plight. Then asking me concerning my reading, he found that I had read the *Essay on Classification,* and had noted in it the influence of Schelling's views. Most of his questioning related to this field, and the more than fair beginning of our relations then made was due to the fact that I had some enlargement on that side. So, too, he was pleased to find that I had managed a lot of Latin, Greek, and German poetry, and had been trained with the sword. He completed this inquiry by requiring that I bring my foils and masks for a bout. In this test he did not fare well, for, though not untrained, he evidently knew more of the *Schläger* than of the rapier. He was heavy-handed, and lacked finesse. This, with my previous experience, led me to the conclusion that I had struck upon a kind of tutor in Cambridge not known in Kentucky.

While Agassiz questioned me carefully as to what I had read and what I had seen, he seemed in this preliminary going over in no wise concerned to find what I knew about fossils, rocks, animals, and plants; he put aside the offerings of my scanty lore. This offended me a bit, as I recall, for the reason that I thought I knew, and for a self-taught lad really did know, a good deal about such matters, especially as to the habits of insects, particularly spiders. It seemed hard to be denied the chance to make my parade; but I afterward saw what this meant—that he did not intend to let me begin my tasks by posing as a naturalist. The beginning was indeed quite different, and, as will be seen, in a manner that quickly evaporated my conceit. It was made and continued in a way I will now recount.

Agassiz's laboratory was then in a rather small two-storied building, looking much like a square dwelling-house, which stood where the College Gymnasium now stands . . . Agassiz had recently moved into it from a shed on the marsh near Brighton bridge, the original tenants, the engineers, having come to riches in the shape of the brick structure now known as the Lawrence Building. In this primitive establishment Agassiz's laboratory, as distinguished from the storerooms where the collections were crammed, occupied one room about thirty feet long and fifteen feet wide—what is now the west room on the lower floor of the edifice. In this place, already packed, I had assigned to me a small pine table with a rusty tin pan upon it . . . .

When I sat me down before my tin pan, Agassiz brought me a small fish, placing it before me with the rather stern requirement that I should study it, but should on no account talk to any one concerning it, nor read anything relating to fishes, until I had his permission so to do. To my inquiry, "What shall I do?" he said in effect: "Find out what you can without damaging the specimen; when I think that you have done the work I will question you." In the course of an hour I thought I had compassed that fish; it was rather an unsavory object, giving forth the stench of old alcohol, then loathsome to me, though in time I came to like it. Many of the scales were loosened so that they fell off. It appeared to me to be a case for a summary report, which I was anxious to make and get on to the next stage of the business. But Agassiz, though always within call, concerned himself no further with me that day, nor the next, nor for a week. At first, this neglect was distressing; but I saw that it was a game, for he was, as I discerned rather than saw, covertly watching me. So I set my wits to work upon the thing, and in the course of a hundred hours or so thought I had done much—a hundred times as much as seemed possible at the start. I got interested in finding out how the scales went in series, their shape, the form and placement of the teeth, etc. Finally, I felt full of the subject, and probably expressed it in my bearing; as for words about it then, there were none from my master except his cheery "Good morning." At length, on the seventh day, came the question, "Well?" and my disgorge of learning to him as he sat on the edge of my table puffing his cigar. At the end of the hour's telling, he swung off and away, saying: "That is not right." Here I began to think that, after all, perhaps the rules for scanning Latin verse were not the worst infliction in the world. Moreover, it was clear that he was playing a game with me to find if I were capable of doing hard, continuous work without the support of a teacher, and this stimulated me to labor. I went at the task anew, discarded my first notes, and in another week of ten hours a day labor I had results which astonished myself and satisfied him. Still there was no trace of praise in words or manner. He signified that it would do by placing before me about a half a peck of bones, telling me to see what I could make of them, with no further directions to guide me. I soon found that they were the skeletons of half a dozen fishes of different species; the jaws told me so much at a first inspection. The task evidently was to fit the separate bones together in their proper order. Two months or more went to this task with no other help than an occasional looking over my grouping with the stereotyped remark: "That is not right." Finally, the task was done, and I was again set upon alcoholic specimens—this time a remarkable lot of specimens representing, perhaps, twenty species of the side-swimmers or Pleuronectidae.

I shall never forget the sense of power in dealing with things which I felt in beginning the more extended work on a group of animals. I had learned the art of comparing objects, which is the basis of the naturalist's work. At this stage I was allowed to read, and to discuss my work with others about me. I did both eagerly, and acquired a considerable knowledge of the literature of ichthyology, becoming especially interested in the system of classification, then most imperfect. I tried to follow Agassiz's scheme of division into the order of ctenoids and ganoids, with the result that I found one of my species of side-swimmers had cycloid scales on one side and ctenoid on the other. This not only shocked my sense of the value of classification in a way that permitted of no full recovery of my original respect for the process, but for a time shook my confidence in my master's knowledge. At the same time I had a malicious pleasure in exhibiting my "find" to him, expecting to repay in part the humiliation which he had evidently tried to inflict on my conceit. To my question as to how the nondescript should be classified he said: "My boy, there are now two of us who know that."

This incident of the fish made an end of my novitiate. After that, with a suddenness of transition which puzzled me, Agassiz became very communicative; we passed indeed into the relation of friends of like age and purpose, and he actually consulted me as to what I should like to take up as a field of study. Finding that I wished to devote myself to geology, he set me to work on the Brachiopoda as the best group of fossils to serve as data in determining the Palaeozoic horizons. So far as his rather limited knowledge of the matter went, he guided me in the field about Cambridge, in my reading, and to acquaintances of his who were concerned with earth structures. I came thus to know Charles T. Jackson, Jules Marcou, and, later, the brothers Rogers, Henry and James. At the same time I kept up the study of zoology, undertaking to make myself acquainted with living organic forms as a basis for a knowledge of fossils.

NEILSON OF SMITH [1]

HUBERT HERRING

THERE is a story, cherished on the campus of Smith College, which tells of a bounding freshman of seventeen off for Christmas vacation who deposited a bowl of goldfish on the steps of the President's house, with a scrawled note: "Dear Mr. Neilson, please take care of my fish until I return."

Mr. Neilson did.

A college president who knows what to do with visiting goldfish presents peculiar problems to intending biographers. I wrote five hundred Smith alumnae and received five hundred answers describing a man half-Aristotle, half-Puck. I journeyed to Northampton and talked with undergraduates who bubbled like a soda fountain out of control. I talked with professors and instructors and gained a vivid impression of a faculty in which confidence prevails. Neilson of Smith must have boarded many goldfish during the past twenty-one years.

William Allan Neilson, who retires from Smith next year at the age seventy, has been teaching most of the time since he was thirteen. The death of his father, the schoolmaster in the Scotch village of Doune in Perthshire, left the frail, shy, small boy to make his own way. He became a "monitor," a pupil-teacher at a stipend of ten pounds for the year, free to acquire his own Latin

1. "Neilson of Smith," *Harper's Magazine*, CLXXVII (June, 1938), 50–61, with omissions. Reprinted by permission of the author.

and Greek before nine o'clock and after four. We catch a glimpse of a solemn little boy to whom tears came quickly, set against the dour background of the rigid Calvinism of his home and village. We see him, later, trudging to the preparatory school at Montrose, reading as he walked, acquiring the stoop which he has carried through life, restlessly searching that truth which is beauty, that beauty which is truth. And then a fleeting picture of the adolescent at the University of Edinburgh, catching life as he could, taking honors as he went, restive under the barren classicism of the time, rebellious against the Scotch religionists who ruled education. But he broke through, thanks in part to an uncle who was termed a free-thinker and who introduced the boy to Matthew Arnold, thanks also to the ferment of the first Fabians. It was a somber lad of twenty-two who graduated from Edinburgh with honors in philosophy in 1891, and set out for a new world, to teach English in Upper Canada College in Toronto. The old world had conferred learning, the new was to yield him a house of freedom, in which abided fear neither of the gods nor of the Greeks.

His four years in Canada were followed by three years in Harvard, where he received his doctorate in 1898, then two years of teaching in Bryn Mawr, four years as an instructor in Harvard, two in Columbia. Then in 1906 he returned to a Harvard professorship in English which he held until 1917. These were years of fulfillment, happy for him, happy for his students, as he made Shakespeare live and Burns sing. He had found release in a balanced sense of life's verities, illuminated by a sure perception of the humor which life holds. A faculty comrade of those days tells of the hours after work was done, of "Neilson perched on the windowseat" in his room, reading Burns and old ballads or arguing about the world's affairs. "When we left his room after an hour or two, with Scotch wit ringing in our ears and a bit of Scotch on our palates, thoughts of the next day's lectures had vanished and we went to bed in perfect peace of mind. . . . It was not merely the merry fellowship . . . it was the extraordinary insight and wisdom . . . which was so stimulating. . . . It was also the immense human sympathy and interest which he brought to every question."

At Harvard Neilson became a close friend of Charles W. Eliot. When Eliot made a speech half in jest announcing that all the needs of an educated man could be met by a "five-foot shelf" and a publisher had invited Eliot to prepare such a shelf, Eliot turned to Neilson and asked his aid in choosing and editing the "Harvard Classics." They worked together for eighteen months, months in which Neilson could learn the secrets of one of the great university presidents of our time. From Eliot he had the definition of the prime requisite for a college president: "Some people say courage, I say patience."

In 1917, Sidney B. Fay, who had taught with Neilson in Harvard and had gone to Smith, decided to bring Neilson and the Smith trustees together. He persuaded Neilson to visit Northampton, showed him the college and the campus, introduced him to the trustees. Shortly after Mr. Lamont invited

Mr. Neilson to take the presidency of Smith College. Two obstacles intervened. Mrs. Neilson must have a house adequate for the entertaining which she must inevitably do. Mr. Neilson, fearful of the ecclesiastical precedents at Smith, did not propose to conduct formal religious services and would not lead in extemporaneous prayer. Lively memories of Scotch churches stuck. Mr. Lamont laid both fears. Mrs. Neilson would have a house. Mr. Neilson could define prayer as he pleased. Mr. Neilson was appointed.

II

There are as many varieties of college presidents as of tulips, and each reveals his peculiar markings in due season. There is the president who is rated like a share of common stock—by his yield. He delivers endowments, buildings, and art collections, and his trustees pronounce him a great educator, raise his salary and send him to Europe. There is the president who is a born manager, and, his trustees admiringly say, he might have been president of the First National Bank. There is the president who is a natural advertiser, with that divine gift of making the worse appear the better cause, and his admirers affirm that had he turned his gift to publicity he might have been as great as Bruce Barton. There is the president whose impressive front serves the same function as the heavy columns of the buildings which line Constitution Avenue, supporting nothing but reassuring the taxpayers. And then of course there is the president who has ideas on educating. He belongs to one of the rarer species.

In the fall of 1917 the students and faculty of Smith asked themselves what manner of president had been sent them. An alumna of that time describes Mr. Neilson's first appearance on the campus. "He seemed a mild and genial scholar," she writes, "of whom there was little to fear . . . but I was Scotch by inheritance . . . and there was a glint in the President's eye which gave me pause. . . . Within a month the college was on its toes and walking lightly."

"Have you a daughter?" desperately put a frantic father whose daughter would not quite behave. "Yes," said Neilson, "two thousand of them." A visit to Smith Chapel confirms this statement. When he is to speak, and it is known, the room is filled. He reads a bit of Scripture or of poetry, he reads the Lord's Prayer, and he talks. His talk ranges all the way from the troubled international situation to the personal habits of the girls. He never talks down, he takes the girls' intelligence for granted, but it is the talk of a wise and witty father with his daughters.

"You slump," he tells them one day. "Sitting on your shoulder blades to read" will lead to lumbago and sciatica. Another day he gives swift comment on the moving events in Spain. Then, again, he will describe the way in which students march down the streets of Northampton, four abreast, "jostling feeble members of the faculty, like myself, and honorable citizens into the gutter." Another day there will be simple words on the meaning of human liberty, and then he will describe the train from New York on which they returned from vacation, and his "impression that the train was owned by Smith College—yet you certainly had not paid for all of it." When some students frame a petition for more entertainment on the campus, he reminds them of "the spoiled brats of Park Avenue bored by nurses who are trying to entertain them. . . . If you don't know how to entertain yourselves, cut out all entertainment until you have acquired a fresh appetite. This all seems to me a clear symptom of overfeeding. If you really have so much more time than you know what to do with, I shall advise the faculty to give you more work."

His straight talk is sometimes barbed. When the library reports that books disappear he uses the word "thieves." Again, facing the student body freshly returned from Christmas vacation, "I wish you all a very good New Year and a much healthier one than I am really hopeful about with all the coughing in this hall. The college now sets about trying to repair the damage done to you by your parents and the vacation. We shall fill up the infirmary and try to take care of the rest of you in the houses. The advice I gave you before you went away about moderation in your pleasures and plenty of sleep has apparently been ignored." When the Boston papers told of scandalized Northamptonites being forced to watch Smith girls roaming about in shorts, he told them to quit their roaming.

He wins the students because he can meet them in every mood. His infectious gaiety sets into higher relief his utmost solemnity. They know that they can count on him. "Never once did he let us down," writes an alumna.

He makes the students' cause his own. When Northampton neighbors complained that girls did not lower their shades when undressing, he suggested to the townspeople, "Pull down your own shades." When a ribald student paper of a neighboring college announced in loud headlines that Smith girls were easily kissed, angry Smith students eagerly discussed what form revenge should take. But they had no need to plan. Smith's president did the revenging, in just one sentence in chapel. "My advice to a daughter would be, kiss only gentlemen, for gentlemen don't tell."

But when tragedy comes he has other tones. When there was a ghastly automobile accident in which several Smith girls and Amherst boys were killed and injured he faced a full chapel with words which were not taken down, but which every student of that time remembers. "He told us," writes one of these, "that we were cowards, that we did not have the moral courage to refuse to go with men who had been drinking. . . . The campus was hushed all that day." . . .

A college president must always be something of a disciplinarian. Neilson has not shirked discipline, although he knows full well that "it is through freedom and not through compulsion that the human spirit gains in power and reach."

"You are here," he told the college on assembling one fall, "to grow into women. We do not believe you can do so without having a large measure of freedom to control your own time and your own actions—a large possibility of going wrong. And the strength of mind that is demanded of the administration of a college like this is to stand by while the risk of your going wrong is operating and to keep hands off. The art of governing here as elsewhere is in knowing at what point a student ought to be temporarily saved from herself by compulsion. I say temporarily, because compulsion can never save her from herself permanently. She alone can do that, but from time to time one has to intervene to prevent irreparable damage."

As a disciplinarian, he must deal with venial and mortal sinning. He had come to a college in which "Christian influences" had long prevailed, and that usually means a fantastic multiplication of sins. Smith had not yet shaken free of those endless rules by which student conduct is regulated. Smith students, for example, might not smoke. As president, Neilson had to uphold the rule so long as it was on the books. He did it in his own way. "Smoking," he told the students, "is a dirty, expensive, and unhygienic habit—to which I am devoted." When an ashtray filled with cigarette butts was found in a dormitory the culprit told the President, "Each butt is the souvenir of a perfect evening." She won. When the smoking rule was finally lifted, Neilson's advice was explicit, "Smoke if you must—but smoke like gentlemen."

He can inject gaiety into discipline. When two girls, in an excess of hospitality, took their two Yale visitors for a swim in the Northampton reservoir, he had to dismiss one of them, for she was a senior and should have known better; but the other, being a freshman, was allowed to remain. He disposed of the whole matter in one chapel sentence: "I prefer my drinking water unflavored by either Smith or Yale."

And, like the wisest disciplinarian, he knows how to close his eyes. There is a story, perhaps apocryphal, of the girl who returned after closing hours, and was struggling to pull herself up on to the fire escape without making much progress. Suddenly she felt herself effectively boosted from below. Safe on the fire escape, she turned round to find that her rescuer was the President.

But college discipline is not all the enforcing of rules on smoking and late hours. There is plenty of room for major as well as minor wickedness in a college of two thousand. The Judicial Board, the students' self-government court, handles the cases which come before it; but a member of that board in other years reports that Mr. Neilson repeatedly "tamed down our judgments . . . we might recommend expelling a girl . . . he would give her a second chance." Another alumna reports on such an experience. A classmate had been caught—in sin. The sin was definite and proved. The Student Council was obdurate; the Dean firmly refused to intercede; but the President persuaded the Council and the Dean, and the girl stayed.

Mr. Neilson as a disciplinarian has picked the difficult middle path between the college where every turn of the hand is controlled and the college whose chief pride is its entire absence of all restraint. Through it all one feels his distaste for rules, and the sense that they are ignoble things at best. For, after all, students "who wish to waste their time and opportunities must be allowed to cheat themselves until such time as we find it necessary to separate them from the college." He is possessed by a sense of noblesse oblige, he knows what sacrifices are behind the girls in college, and he can urge them "retain your self-respect in not being wasters in a world of hardship."

III

It is whispered among some educators that, while Neilson is wise and witty, he is no great educator. One expects such reactions in every craft. His misfortune as an educator is that he has no bags of tricks. One gathers that he suspects bags of tricks. While one youthful president discovers that education will be saved by a return to Plato, while another invents the thesis that education will be revived by the holding of conferences on grassy lawns, and still another, impatient with older disciplines, throws off all the fetters, Neilson has gone his way without any visible breaking of tradition.

Mr. Neilson's method is the old one. He seems, in effect, to say: First, let us collect students susceptible to ideas. Second, let us collect teachers with ideas, and capable of imparting them. Third, let us provide a setting which will encourage the contagion of ideas. It is difficult to make such a course appear revolutionary. Mr. Neilson has made no effort to make it appear revolutionary.

He proceeds upon the assumption that women can be educated, an assumption which still needs proving to those who give money with which to endow colleges. Neilson sees no reason for tempering the educational winds to the hitherto shorn woman's mind, for "we have to provide for all degrees of masculinity in female minds and all degrees of femininity in male minds, as for all the other varieties of human nature." But, while arguing the just claims of woman upon education, he cannot resist giving the women a special scolding for their "docility." He avers that it is a "tendency of women to be satisfied with half-knowledge. You don't think of education as a continuous stream, but as little parcels of knowledge, to be forgotten after examinations are over. You're concerned only with getting by . . . but the teachers are to blame too. So many of us have been dull and dry, unable to arouse the interest of our students. Although I blame the teachers mostly, some of the blame is on you for putting up with us. It is your fault for putting up with the 'stuffed owls in the Assembly Hall.'"

Neilson's chief device in education is the creation of an atmosphere in which curiosity, excitement, discussion, dissent tumble over one another. Smith's atmosphere is a ferment, with Neilson as the continuous catalytic agent. His own tumultuousness pervades the campus, and a sense of life is transmitted to all who come under his eye.

The atmosphere which he creates is the clear air in which growing things thrive. He has deep distaste for the esoteric vocabulary of self-conscious scholarship. "Unnecessary hocus-pocus" he calls it. The medical men have their lingo, and now "the sociologists are building up a terrible jargon, though I have yet to find in their books an idea which is not capable of being explained in standard English."

It is an aura in which the bearing of all learning to life becomes clear. "The ranks of scholarship," he says, "are still crowded with fearful souls who are mining facts in dark galleries, and lack courage and imagination to seek their significance." He drives home this emphasis to his students, stressing "the close bond between the intellectual life and the moral life," the virtue of "straight and honest thinking," the corrosion of "wishful thinking." He seeks a synthesis of the scientific and the classical, arguing that the quarrel between the scientific group and the classical "persists partly because each has at times been untrue to itself, partly because each has misrepresented the other. . . . The scientist sometimes forgets the honor of his calling and dogmatizes . . . he sometimes degenerates into the mere collector." But, he continues, "the classical party . . . have come nearer wrecking their own cause than the scientists . . . the foundation of the revolt against the classics is a widespread indignation at being cheated. Hundreds of thousands of students have spent the major part of their studying time for years upon two languages with the implicit understanding that they would finally have access to two great civilizations through reading the records in the original tongues. They paid the price in time and energy and at the end they did not get what they paid for." He assures the exponents of classical education that "the deadly enemy of the classics is not science or mathematics or modern literature or vocational utilitarianism; it is linguistic fanaticism, the insistence that no one shall enter these fair domains save through the one door of language. . . . It will take several academic generations before we can equip our schools and colleges with teachers who will make classical studies again deserve the name of the humanities."

He is instant in warning against the "too exclusive cultivation of the receptive attitude," remarks that the non-academic occupations of students are described as "student activities . . . as if the classrooms were merely the scene of student passivities." He finds in that tendency roots for the "criticism that the American scholar of today is more distinguished for what he knows than what he thinks." "In a woman's college especially," adds Neilson, "it is necessary to guard against excessive docility . . . from the earliest stages of education, the effort should be made to call forth active curiosity as to the meaning and relation of every fact that is taught." . . .

Neilson was one of the first college presidents to adopt the "honors" system, under which the gifted student is freed from much required routine during her last two years and is encouraged to develop in those areas in which she reveals individual excellence.

Another of Neilson's enthusiasms is the "Junior year abroad." Under the workings of this plan small groups of qualified students spend a year in France, Italy, Spain, or Mexico, thereby gaining practice in the languages of those countries and appreciation of the cultural gifts of their several peoples. His international sympathy reveals itself also in his numerous choices for the faculty of scholars from overseas. He likes to have men and women who bring the cultural gifts and the spiritual understanding of other nations, and many of his most inspiring teachers have come from France, Germany, Italy, and other countries. He believes that thereby the intellectual and spiritual life of the college is enlarged. These international appointments elicit mixed reactions from the other faculty members. Some have been known to murmur, Yes, Mr. Neilson thinks any foreigner better than any American. And another, without rancor, remarks, "I haven't heard so much broken English since Weber and Fields."

Neilson's enthusiasm for scholarship is revealed in every page of the Smith record. He has succeeded in rare degree in transmitting to his faculty and to his students his own passion for the gathering and assessing of ideas. He is a scholar in his own right. He does not, as so many college presidents must, take out his scholarship in his faculty's name. The quality of his research on Shakespeare is recognized, his writing on poetry is respected, and he is awaiting retirement to finish his work on Medieval Allegory. In making additions to the faculty he has a record of bringing productive scholars to his campus. But he is fully as assiduous in searching out those who can teach. "The great teacher," he says, "is almost as rare as the great scholar, and for the undergraduate student is of even greater immediate importance . . . good teachers can usually be found by searching; great teachers are the gift of heaven. All we can do is to cherish those we have and hope for more."

IV

A college is known by the faculty it keeps. There are divers sorts of faculties. There is the "housebroken" variety in which the several members know what exact corners they belong in, when to sit up and beg, when to play dead. Fear rules such faculties, and there are many of them. Then there is the insurgent faculty, in which men and women of intellectual flavor are in tumult against an autocratic and small-minded president. And then there is the faculty in which teachers of fire and resourcefulness achieve unity through strong leadership. That last is Smith's.

It is possible to detect a certain quizzicalness in Neilson's attitude toward his faculty. He knows that they are good—he picked them. He also knows how ignorant an intelligent professor can be, how ludicrous an art teacher can appear when he essays opinions on economics, and how oblivious an economist can be of the finer shadings of the subjunctive. He knows the riotous pigheadedness of the protagonists of each particular cause of education in a faculty, and how each set would gladly close up all the rest of the school and devote the entire endowment to experimentation with white mice or to the teaching of Chaucer. . . .

Neilson's conduct of faculty meetings is characteristic. He has a mind which flashes and races. He sees the end of the argument when the issue is stated. He does not hold back his own judgment until others have talked themselves out, nor does he hold decision until others are persuaded. There are some of his faculty who suggest that his course can be and sometimes is on the dictatorial side. But there are few, if any, who carry over any resentment.

It takes a man of unusual stature to carry off the parental role as Neilson does with his faculty at Smith. It exacts its peculiar toll of the man who assumes that role. The parent may spank and praise, but he must remain to counsel. And Neilson does. His office is a consulting room—and a confessional. His secretary, try as she will, cannot protect him. His counsel is sought on such questions as the relative merits of galvanized iron and copper boilers, and where—and how—to send sons to college. And, upon occasion, his office becomes an informal court of domestic relations. So it is that, no matter how some professors may differ with him on problems of education, no matter what criticism they may have of his genial father-knows-best autocracy, there remains little, if any, resentment toward the man.

There has never been any question as to Neilson's stand on academic freedom. "Our tradition," he wrote in 1927, "is in favor of complete freedom, and our experience seems to show that such freedom produces loyalty to the college and consideration for its interests. With the writing and speaking of the faculty outside, the College has not concerned itself at all. The question as it has arisen during the present administration has always seemed to me to be not, 'Are the views of Professor X as proclaimed in his lectures or his books in all respects correct?' but 'Assuming that Professor X's views may be in part erroneous and to some people offensive, can the College afford to suppress him or his views at the cost of creating an atmosphere of censorship and hampering free thought and free discussion by fear of dismissal?' The history of attempts to limit academic freedom leaves no doubt as to the answer. The greatest universities have been the most tolerant." . . .

The conspicuous test of Neilson's faith on this score was the case of Harry Elmer Barnes. Barnes was no wild radical, but he was a master of the picturesque phrase. As such, he caught the delighted ear of young women from the sober ranges of the United States. They loved to be shocked, and he shocked them deliciously. And worse, he shocked their parents. His firing range was wide. In 1926 he published a book on the World War and let Germany off with less blame than was considered orthodox in those unhappy days. Indignant letters poured in upon the president and the trustees. He was accused of pro-Germanism. He was charged with "ignorance of real historical facts," and of inspiring "disgust among our best classes of citizens," and it was suggested that Mr. Barnes had received "payment from Germany."

Barnes' facile pen and ready tongue yielded a stream of quotable—and misquoted—sentences upon every subject from the Virgin Birth to the length of skirts. Many of the things reported had never been said, but enough was said and graphically said to keep Barnes forever in the headlines, and Barnes' enemies forever in the President's office. But Neilson did not budge. He did not ask Barnes for confirmation or denial. He took his stand that Barnes was a member of the faculty, and that as such he could think what he pleased and say what he pleased—as Barnes did. When in 1929 Barnes was offered a journalistic post with the Scripps-Howard papers, Neilson put no pressure on him. If Neilson breathed a sigh of anticipatory relief when Barnes left, he never voiced it publicly. And Harry Barnes retired gracefully, and perhaps gratefully, saying, "If President Neilson would like a little peace of mind during the remainder of his presidency, I would be the last person in the world to challenge his right to it."

There have been other cases when teachers have been under fire and Neilson has stood by. There was Frank Hankins, professor of sociology, in one of whose senior classes a questionnaire relating to marriage and premarital relations was prepared by a student, and used by the members of the class. One scared girl showed it to her mother, and the mother shared it with the press. The questionnaire, launched as an honest effort to help a class of serious girls think through an important sociological question, made the headlines. One newspaper announced that Smith professors favored the "nationalization of women." Neilson dismissed the matter with his board in one sentence, "This is a question of confidence in the administration and does not need to be discussed."

There have been other instances when the real or fancied radicalism of a faculty member has caused passing disturbance, but Smith's record is clean. No one has been fired for his opinions. There are today on the faculty a full quota of those adjudged radical by one or another of the quaint tests which super-patriots provide, and these "radicals" are the first to assert that never has a hand been raised to limit their freedom of expression.

Of course the genuine red-baiter includes Mr. Neilson himself in the list of undesirables. He has full mention in the redoubtable Mrs. Dilling's "Red Network," from which one learns that Neilson has trifled with Russia, blessed sundry organizations standing for civil liberties, and indulged in sundry other "communistic" deeds. Referring to the volume, Mr. Neilson said, "I feel proud to have been honored with a place."

A college president is known by the honorary degrees which he grants—and does not grant. Smith's honorary degrees over a period of twenty years are few in number and chiefly reserved to women. Not one name on the list can be checked, with the mental note added—Degree given in hope or in payment deferred. If there are a few names which recall memories of family fortune, they are names of those who are persons in their own right, their claim not related to inherited wealth. Rather, the list is of women who from the bench, from the stage, from the concert platform, in the laboratory, in the field of social exploration, with the pen, have made themselves felt in American and world life. An examination of the list gives one an eloquent sense of what Neilson asks of life.

He has a way all his own with alumnae. Alumnae, like alumni, belong on the profit and loss ledger—a little of each. "Alumni," says Mr. Neilson, "exist for two purposes—to give money and to raise trouble when football matches are lost—fortunately a phenomenon unknown to the college for women—we never lost a football match." But, on the other hand, alumnae present problems peculiarly their own. They tend to mother their college, and mothering sometimes takes the form of smothering. With these mothering alumnae Mr. Neilson takes much the same course that he takes with the daughters. He scolds them. He tells them that after making sacrifices to send the girls to college they then encourage the same girls to get away from college just as much as possible. He reminds them that "college is not a place to rest up between weekends." At a dinner in New York, in December, 1937, attended by nine hundred alumnae and their husbands, he turned from his discussion of Smith's problems for an aside on mother love. He assured them that he had no troubles with the students, with the faculty, with the trustees, but that he had no end of trouble with parents. "Mother love," said Neilson, "I used to regard as one of the beautiful things in the world, but now I am tempted to say, I do not believe in mother love. I think in nine cases out of ten, mother love is self love. Mothers do not want their daughters to fail because it reflects on mother and is socially awkward." The press gave the story a big spread. This was news. Indignant editorials sprouted. Letters piled in. His friends explained that of course he was joking. He was just having his Scotch fun. But he was scolding too. And, with inevitable exceptions, the alumnae liked it.

There must be alumnae who do not share in the general adulation. I sought long and found just one. Her testimony must be recorded. She cites three incidents to explain her distaste for Mr. Neilson. First, he criticized the girls in her house because "there was no visible number on the front door." Second, "He remarked that our library table held only such magazines as *Redbook* and *Cosmopolitan,* whereas we should read *Harper's* and *The Atlantic Monthly*." And third, "At my fifth reunion, Dr. Neilson . . . made a jolly little speech about making out wills which would leave money to Smith College."

V

When William Allan Neilson went to Smith it was with the understanding that he would have nothing to do with the finances of the college, and especially that he would not raise money.

Mr. Neilson, one suspects, had observed the ways of college presidents. He had watched their melancholy course as they sniffed out well-filled purses and their divers ways of insinuating themselves into the good graces of bewildered widows. He did not relish that sort of salesman's job. He had always met the world with candor and did not propose henceforth to walk abroad with the blue-print of a dormitory in his eye.

Neilson has kept his word. He has not raised money. He likes to report that only once in twenty-one years has he asked for money. That one time, under pressure, he signed a hundred letters. When signing them he noted one name of a brother college president, and he added a postscript, "This doesn't apply to you. Don't pay any attention to it." He gleefully reports that the only gift which resulted was from the man whom he had thus warned. That is Neilson's money-raising record.

So Neilson can welcome an alumna to the Smith campus without wondering whether her husband is making money. He can invite people to dinner without consulting Dun and Bradstreet. But Neilson wanted money for Smith. He wanted dormitories for his girls, a room for every girl. He wanted better buildings. He wanted a more adequate endowment, so that teachers might have better salaries, enough to afford peace of mind, books, travel. He wanted money for scholarships, so that the daughter of poor parents might have a chance in Smith.

Neilson early decided that the financial problem of the college had two sides. First, there was the job of getting more money. Second, there was the job of making the money on hand go as far as possible. The first he turned over to the alumnae. The second he assigned to himself.

The alumnae have raised money. During the past twenty-one years the endowment has been increased from less than two million to something over six million, and almost five millions have been invested in buildings and grounds. But compared with other colleges of equal standing, Smith has received relatively little money. The substantial gifts which go to men's colleges are denied the women's colleges. Neilson finds the explanation for this niggardly treatment of women's colleges in the fact that "men do not like women to stand up to them and measure them as they are; they prefer to be on a pedestal; they prefer to be the possessors of a great deal of wonderful esoteric information. They don't have much of course; we know it is mainly bluff—but it won't work any more, and they don't like it. So the thing to do of course is to be grudging to the women's colleges." And they have continued to be grudging. Smith, for all its gains in endowment, makes a modest exhibit beside other colleges of equal standing. There is an excellent men's college near-by which has more than twice Smith's endowment—and less than half the students. Neilson did not go after money—and he didn't get it.

But Neilson took on the other side of financial management with avidity. He has seen to it that Smith gets at least two dollars' worth of value for every dollar spent. Not for nothing had he been born in Perthshire, the son of a poor schoolmaster. And he exhibits an almost hilarious glee that he, a mere teacher of English, has known how to balance a budget. Not only that, but in the twenty years 1917–37 the College has had recurring surpluses totaling one and a quarter millions, which have gone into buildings.

As a manager Neilson knows each doorknob and bathtub. He hates waste like a Highland farmer. The sight of lights burning in dormitories during dinner hour elicits some of his finer chapel chastisements. Each building down to every hinge reflects his planning. He knows what will wear and what will return the greatest comfort and usefulness. He knows each flower bed, grass plot, and flagstone walk. Every carpenter, mason, and gardener respects this knowledge. When a bricklayer on the grounds once fell sick he would not stop working. "Why," he argued, "no one else could do this job, except perhaps the President." . . .

Neilson's modesty, his candor, and his light touch stem from a vigorous rooting in certain basic attitudes toward life. He is first and last a liberal. In his educational course he has exemplified the disciplines of liberty. He has been a stalwart liberal in his outreach into national and international affairs. Born a British citizen, he is the most stalwart of Americans; but his sympathies are wide. He was among the first to plead for recognition of Soviet Russia, and has been a persuasive spokesman for the imperiled rights of minorities everywhere. When Massachusetts was pushing Sacco and Vanzetti to the electric chair he was one of the active pleaders in their behalf. When the State required a teachers' loyalty oath he was quick to protest. He has long been an ardent protagonist of civil liberties and an enemy of those measures of coercion and bigotry which are inimical to the American ideal.

Neilson's democracy is ardent and obstinate. When he came to Smith he found more than half the students living off the campus. There were favored houses which lent distinction to those who lived in them, constituting a "gold coast" of social superiority. He set himself to end this situation. He would have no "artificial barrier around some corner, residence in which will bestow on one a glamour which does not belong to one as a person." He knew that a college should offer the fairest chance for democracy, that in college students "can meet and see each other for four years unhampered by the artificialties of organized society. . . . Friendship has a free course in that way." Such an ideal was negated by the system which he found. He did not blame the girls as seriously as he blamed their elder sisters, the alumnae, and their mothers. He would end the situation by providing dormitories, in which all students paid much the same rates, enjoyed the same privileges, and in which it would be more difficult to create favored cliques. By 1933 every girl lived on the campus. It was his practical victory for democracy. . . .

Much is written on the failures of education, of the shabby, shoddy things done in education's name, of the way in which college presidents are picked and behave, of the quirks of college athletics, fraternities, and other strange trivia of the campus scene.

Perhaps it will be forgiven if we picture the college as it might be: as a warm-blooded living organism in which the life currents flow at the pumping of a strong and eager heart, reaching the last capillary in the last extremity. Such a college will have unity which does not crush individuality, teamwork without servility, mutual regard without obsequiousness, forbearance without denial of candor. In such a college jealousies will be over-topped by the excitements of learning and teaching, and personal piques will be devoured by the enthusiasms of common tasks.

Such a college is mirrored only on the retina of hope. But it is for the creation of such a college that presidents must be born. They cannot be made. But the tracing of the lines of William Allan Neilson on the story of Smith College gives substance to the faith that education can yet become a regenerative force for democracy in our own times.

GATE RECEIPTS AND GLORY [1]

ROBERT M. HUTCHINS

THE football season is about to release the nation's colleges to the pursuit of education, more or less. Soon the last nickel will be rung up at the gate, the last halfback will receive his check, and the last alumnus will try to pay off those bets he can recall. Most of the students have cheered themselves into insensibility long ago.

This has been going on for almost fifty years. It is called "overemphasis on athletics," and everybody deplores it. It has been the subject of scores of reports, all of them shocking. It has been held to be crass professionalism, all the more shameful because it masquerades as higher education. But nobody has done anything about it. Why? I think it is because nobody wants to. Nobody wants, or dares, to defy the public, dishearten the students, or deprive alma mater of the loyalty of the alumni. Most emphatically of all, nobody wants to give up the gate receipts. The trouble with football is the money that is in it, and every code of amateurism ever written has failed for this reason.

Money is the cause of athleticism in the American colleges. Athleticism is not athletics. Athletics is physical education, a proper function of the college if carried on for the welfare of the students. Athleticism is not physical education but sports promotion, and it is carried on for the monetary profit of the colleges through the entertainment of the public. This article deals with athleticism, its cause, its symptoms and its cure.

Of all the crimes committed by athleticism under the guise of athletics, the most heinous is the confusion of the country about the primary purpose of higher education. The primary purpose of higher education is the development of the mind. This does not mean that colleges and universities should

1. From *The Saturday Evening Post*, Dec. 3, 1938. Reprinted by permission of the author.

neglect the health of their students or should fail to provide them with every opportunity for physical development. The question is a question of emphasis. Colleges and universities are the only institutions which are dedicated to the training of the mind. In these institutions, the development of the body is important, but secondary.

The apologists of athleticism have created a collection of myths to convince the public that biceps is a substitute for brains. Athletics, we are told, produces well-rounded men, filled with the spirit of fair play. Athletics is good for the health of the players; it is also good for the morals of the spectators. Leadership on the playing fields means leadership in life. The Duke of Wellington said so. Athletes are red-blooded Americans, and athletic colleges are bulwarks against Communism. Gate receipts are used to build laboratories and to pay for those sports that can't pay for themselves. Football is purely a supplement to study. And without a winning team a college cannot hope to attract the students or the gifts which its work requires.

These myths have about them a certain air of plausibility. They are widely accepted. But they are myths. As the Carnegie Foundation has said, "The fact that all these supposed advantages are tinged at one point or another with the color of money casts over every relaxation of standards a mercenary shadow." The myths are designed, consciously or unconsciously, to conceal the color of money and to surround a financial enterprise with the rosy glow of Health, Manhood, Public Spirit and Education.

Since the primary task of colleges and universities is the development of the mind, young people who are more interested in their bodies than in their minds should not go to college. Institutions devoted to the development of the body are numerous and inexpensive. They do not pretend to be institutions of learning, and there is no faculty of learned men to consume their assets or interfere with their objectives.

Athleticism attracts boys and girls to college who do not want and cannot use a college education. They come to college for "fun." They would be just as happy in the grandstand at the Yankee Stadium, and at less expense to their parents. They drop out of college after a while, but they are a sizable fraction of many freshman classes, and, while they last, they make it harder for the college to educate the rest. Even the earnest boys and girls who come to college for an education find it difficult, around the middle of November, to concentrate on the physiology of the frog or the mechanics of the price structure.

Worse yet, athleticism gives the student a mistaken notion of the qualities that make for leadership in later life. The ambition of the average student who grew up reading Stover at Yale is to imitate as closely as possible the attitude and manners of the current football hero. Since this country, like all others, needs brains more than brawn at the moment, proposing football heroes as models for the rising generation can hardly have a beneficial effect on the national future.

The exponents of athleticism tell us that athletics is good for a boy. They are right. But athleticism focuses its attention on doing good for the boys who least need it. Less than half of the undergraduate males—800 out of 1900 at the University of Chicago, for instance—are eligible for intercollegiate competition. But where athleticism reigns, as happily it does not at Chicago, 75 per cent of the attention of the physical-education staff must be lavished on that fraction of the student body who make varsity squads. The Carnegie Foundation found that 37 per cent of all undergraduates engage in no athletic activity, not even in intramural games. Since graduate and professional students are also eliminated from competition, we have more than half the college and university population of the country neglected because we devote ourselves, on the pretext that athletics is good for a boy, to overdeveloping a handful of stars.

And athletics, as it is conducted in many colleges today, is not even good for the handful. Since the fate of the coach sometimes depends on victory, players have sometimes been filled with college spirit through caffein tablets and strychnine. At least one case reached the public in which a coach removed a plaster cast from a star's ankle and sent him in "to win." The Carnegie Foundation found that 17.6 per cent of all football players in twenty-two colleges suffered serious injuries. The same report asserts that college athletes have about the same life expectancy as the average college man and not so good an expectancy as men of high scholarship rank.

Most athletes will admit that the combination of weariness and nervousness after a hard practice is not conducive to study. We can thus understand why athleticism does not contribute to the production of well-rounded men destined for leadership after graduation. In many American colleges it is possible for a boy to win twelve letters without learning how to write one. I need only suggest that you conjure up the name of the greatest college football star of fifteen years ago and ask yourself, "Where is he now?" Many of his contemporaries who made no ninety-yard runs enjoy at least as good health as our hero and considerably more esteem. The cheers that rock the stadium have a rapid depreciation rate.

The alleged connection between athletic experience and moral principles is highly dubious. At worst, the college athlete is led to believe that whatever he does, including slugging, is done for the sake of alma mater. He does not learn that it is sometimes better, both on and off the playing field, to lose than to win. At best, the college athlete acquires habits of fair play, but there is no evidence that he needs to join the football squad to acquire them; he can get them from the studies he pursues and from living in a college community which, since it is a community of comparatively idealistic people, is less tolerant of meanness than most. The football players who threw the campus "radicals" into the lake at the University of Wisconsin knew little of fair play, and incidents in which free speech in the colleges is suppressed have frequently shown the athletic group lined up on the side of suppression.

Even if it were true that athletics developed courage, prudence, tolerance and justice, the commercialism that characterizes amateur sport today would be sufficient to harden the purest young man. He is made to feel that his primary function in college is to win football games. The coach demands it, because the coach wants to hold his job. The college demands it, because the college wants the gate receipts. And the alumni demand it, because the test of a college is the success of its teams and they want to be alumni of a good college.

The university with which I am connected has a different kind of college and a different kind of alumni. I can make this statement because I am in no way responsible for its happy condition. When John D. Rockefeller founded the University of Chicago forty-five years ago, he told William Rainey Harper to run it as he pleased. It pleased Mr. Harper to appoint men of character and distinction. One of the men he appointed was Amos Alonzo Stagg. To the amazement of the country, Mr. Harper made Mr. Stagg a professor on life appointment. It was the first time such a thing had happened.

Secure in his position, whether he produced winning teams or not, Mr. Stagg for forty years kept Chicago an amateur university. Some of his teams were champions. Chicago still has the second best won-and-lost record in the Big Ten, although we are using it up pretty fast. But through all those years Chicago students learned that athletics is only one aspect, and a secondary one, of college education. The result is that today Chicago's alumni are loyal to their university and generous with their moral and financial support.

The prestige that winning teams confer upon a university, and the profits that are alleged to accompany prestige, are the most serious obstacles to reform. Alumni whose sole interest in their alma mater is its athletic standing lose their interest when its teams run on bad years. The result, which horrifies college presidents, is that the alumni do not encourage their children or their neighbors' children to attend the old college. The American public believes that there is a correlation between muscle and manliness. Poor teams at any college are supposed to mean that the character of its student body is in decay.

The myth that donors, like alumni and the public, are impressed by football victories collapses on examination of the report recently issued by the John Price Jones Corporation, showing gifts and bequests to colleges and universities between 1920 and 1937. Among the universities, Harvard, Yale and Chicago led the list, each having received more than $50,000,000. The records of these universities on the gridiron were highly irregular, to say the least; that of one of them was positively bad. Among the colleges, Williams, Wesleyan and Bowdoin led the list, each having received more than $5,000,000. Men of wealth were undeterred by the inconsequential athletic status of these colleges; it does not appear that philanthropists were attracted to their rivals by the glorious victories they scored over them.

If athleticism is bad for students, players, alumni and the public, it is even worse for the colleges and universities themselves. They want to be educational institutions, but they can't. The story of the famous halfback whose only regret, when he bade his coach farewell, was that he hadn't learned to read and write is probably exaggerated. But we must admit that pressure from trustees, graduates, "friends," presidents and even professors has tended to relax academic standards. These gentry often overlook the fact that a college should not be interested in a fullback who is a half-wit. Recruiting, subsidizing and the double educational standard cannot exist without the knowledge and the tacit approval, at least, of the colleges and universities themselves. Certain institutions encourage susceptible professors to be nice to athletes now admitted by paying them for serving as "faculty representatives" on the college athletic board.

We have the word of the famous Carnegie Report that the maxim "every athlete is a needy athlete" is applied up and down the land. Hard times have reduced the price of football players in conformity with the stock-market index. But when we get back to prosperity we may hope to see the resurrection of that phenomenon of the Golden Era, a corporation which tried to corner the market by signing up high-school athletes and auctioning them off to the highest bidder. The promoter of this interesting venture came to a bad end, and I regretted his fate, for he was a man of imagination and a friend of the football tramp, who has always been a victim of cutthroat competition.

Enthusiastic alumni find it hard to understand why a fine young man who can play football should be deprived of a college education just because he is poor. No young man should be deprived of an education just because he is poor. We need more scholarships, but athletic ability should have nothing to do with their award. Frequently the fine young man the alumnus has in mind can do nothing but play football. The alumnus should try hiring the young man and turning him loose in his factory. From the damage that would result he could gain some insight into the damage done his alma mater through admitting students without intellectual interests or capacity.

If the colleges and universities are to commend themselves to the public chiefly through their athletic accomplishments, it seems to me that they ought to be reorganized with that aim in view. Instead of looking for college presidents among educators, we should find them among those gentlemen who have a solid record of sports promotion behind them. Consider what Tex Rickard could have done for Harvard. I am rapidly approaching the retirement age, and I can think of no worthier successor, from the standpoint of athleticism, than Mr. Mike Jacobs, the sage of the prize ring. Mr. Jacobs has demonstrated his genius at selecting young men and developing them in such a way as to gather both gold and glory for the profession of which he is the principal ornament.

Another suggestion for elevating Chicago to the level of some of its sister institutions was advanced last year by Mr. William McNeill, editor of the student paper. Mr. McNeill proposed that instead of buying football players, the colleges should buy race horses. Alumni could show their devotion to alma mater by giving their stables to alma mater. For the time being, Yale would be way out in front, for both Mr. Jock Whitney and Mr. Cornelius Vanderbilt Whitney graduated there. But by a judicious distribution of honorary degrees horse fanciers who never went to college might be induced to come to the assistance of institutions which had not attracted students who had become prosperous enough to indulge in the sport of kings. Chicago could, for instance, confer the doctorate of letters upon that prominent turfman, Alderman Bathhouse John Coughlin, and persuade The Bath to change the color of his silks from green to maroon. The alumni could place their money on Chicago across the board. The students could cheer. Most important of all, the horses would not have to pass examinations.

The center of football strength has been moving, since the turn of the century, from the East to the Middle West, from the Middle West to the Pacific Coast, and from the Pacific Coast to the South and Southwest. According to a recent analysis by Professor Eells, of Stanford, the leading educational institutions of the country are, in order of their eminence, Harvard, Chicago, Columbia, Yale, California, Johns Hopkins, Princeton, Michigan and Wisconsin. None of these universities, except California, is close to the top of Professor Dickinson's annual athletic ranking, and California's success has something to do with the fact that it has a male undergraduate enrollment of 7500 compared with Harvard's 3700 and Chicago's 1900. We used to say that Harvard enjoyed its greatest years as an educational institution when Ted Coy was playing at Yale. If football continues to move to the poorer colleges, the good ones may be saved. Meanwhile it is only fair to say that some inferior colleges are going broke attempting to get rich—and famous—at football.

Athleticism, like crime, does not pay. Last summer St. Mary's College, home of the Galloping Gaels, was sold at auction and bought in by a bondholders' committee. This was the country's most sensational football college. Since 1924 it has won eighty-six and tied seven of its 114 games. Its academic efforts were inexpensive and its gate receipts immense. The bondholders were surprised to learn that it was running $72,000 a year behind in its budget. They were even more surprised to find that football expenses were almost equal to football income.

To make big money in athletics you have to spend big money. Winning coaches come high. The head coaches in our larger colleges and universities receive, on the average, $611 a year more than the highest-ranking professors in the same institutions. One famous coach of a small college was found, not long ago, receiving $25,000 in a year, between his salary and his percentage of the receipts. This situation is not without its advantages to the members of my hard-pressed profession. The president of one celebrated university was paid $8000 a year. A coach qualified to direct the football destinies of the institution could not be found for less than $15,000. Since the trustees had to have the coach, and since they couldn't pay the president less than the coach, they raised the president's salary to $15,000 too.

Subsidizing is expensive. Equipment, travel, advertising and publicity are expensive. These things have been known to run to $10,000 or $15,000, even in the smaller colleges, for football alone. Some of the more glorious teams carry a Pullman full of newspapermen across the country with them, paying the reporters' expenses.

The myth that football receipts support research, education, or even other sports has just been exploded by President Wilkins, of Oberlin. His analysis of football costs in twenty-two typical colleges shows that only two have a surplus of football income over football expense. The twenty others spend on football all they get from football and $1743 apiece a year additional. This is the income on $45,000 of their endowment.

President Wilkins' investigation of the colleges raises an interesting question. If most of the colleges lose money at football, is it not likely that most of the universities, with their proportionately heavy expense, are also playing a losing game? I know of only one university that ever claimed to have built a laboratory out of excess gate receipts, but many of our larger institutions claim that football finances their so-called minor sports. Perhaps it does in a few universities and in the years of their great teams. But I should like to see a study made of the universities along the lines of President Wilkins' investigation of the colleges; and I might suggest to those who make the study that they scrutinize the accounting methods of some of our educators to see if they are charging up coaches and even trainers as "professors," the purchase of players to "contingent expense," and the debt on the stadium to "real estate."

In 1925 the American Association of University Professors expressed the hope that colleges would in time publish the cost of stadiums. This hope has not been fulfilled, and for the most part the cost of stadiums remains one of the dark secrets of the athletic underworld. I understand that there are only two stadiums in the Big Ten which were not built with borrowed money, and that two have not yet been paid for. One cost $1,700,000.

Last fall I met a university president the day before his team was to play its opening game. All he could say was, "We've got to win tomorrow. We've got to pay off that $35,000 on the stadium this year." The necessity of packing these arenas has led colleges to schedule as many big games as possible. In order to establish the team's value as a spectacle as soon as possible, a big game must be played to open the season. The old scheme of playing easy games until the team is in shape has had to be abandoned. Consequently, practice must begin earlier to get the team in shape earlier. Harvard and Princeton have just extended pre-season practice and have given a bad example to the country.

The reason that college stadiums can't be paid off is plain. They are built for one sport, football. A great team year after year might, in fifteen or twenty years, pay off the bond issue. But there are no great teams year after year. Athletic eminence is cyclical. College A has a great team and decides to build a great stadium, so that the entire population can watch it. But the alumni of

College B, which is the traditional rival of College A, are irritated because their alma mater is being beaten by those thugs across the river.

So the alumni go out and buy a great team for College B. Colleges C and D also have alumni who also like to win.

In a few years College A is being beaten regularly and the stadium, except for those local citizens who can't afford to get away to watch B, C, and D, is empty. Then College B builds a great new stadium to cash in on its great new record, and goes through the same routine.

There are several factors already operating to reduce athleticism, whether or not we decide to do anything about it. The rise of the junior colleges, which educate freshmen and sophomores only, is reducing the supply of athletic material for the four-year colleges and universities.

Professional football, which is attracting larger and larger crowds, may ultimately do for college football what professional baseball has done for college baseball. And the United States Supreme Court, in a case involving the taxation of gate receipts, has clarified the national mind to some extent by indicating that intercollegiate football is business.

But neither the Supreme Court, nor professional football, nor the junior colleges can be depended upon to reform us. We must reform ourselves. How?

The committees which have studied the subject—and their name is legion—have suggested stricter eligibility rules, reduction of training periods, elimination of recruiting and subsidizing, easier schedules, limitation of each student's participation to one sport, and abandonment of the double scholastic standard for athletes. President-Emeritus Lowell, of Harvard, once proposed the Oxford and Cambridge system of limiting each sport to one game a season, and that one with the college's natural rival. Mr. Lowell's scheme might have the merit of enabling students and the public to work off their seasonal frenzy in one big saturnalia.

These reforms will never achieve reform. They may serve to offset athleticism at those few institutions which are already trying to be colleges instead of football teams. But it is too much to hope that they will affect the colleges and universities at large.

Since money is the cause of athleticism, the cure is to take the money out of athletics. This can be done only in defiance of the students, the alumni, the public, and, in many cases, the colleges themselves. The majority of the colleges and universities will not do it, because in the aggregate they dare not. Johns Hopkins, in Maryland, and Reed College, in Oregon, have dared, but nobody cares, athletically speaking, what Johns Hopkins or Reed does.

The task of taking the money out of athletics must be undertaken by those institutions which are leaders, institutions which can afford the loss of prestige and popularity involved. I suggest that a group of colleges and of universities composed, say, of Amherst, Williams, Dartmouth, Harvard, Yale, Chicago, Michigan, Stanford and California agree to take the following steps, to take them in unison and to take them at once:

1. Reduce admission to ten cents. This will cover the handling costs. For years prominent educators, all the way from Harper, of Chicago, to Butler, of Columbia, have insisted that college athletics should be supported from endowment like any other educational activity. Colleges should support athletics out of their budgets, or get out of athletics, or get out of education.

2. Give the director of athletics and the major coaches some kind of academic tenure, so that their jobs depend on their ability as instructors and their character as men and not on the gates they draw.

While these two steps are being taken, it might be well, for the sake of once more putting students instead of athletes on the college playing fields, to try to stimulate the urge to play for fun and health, instead of the urge to win at any cost. There are two ways to do this, and many colleges and universities are trying both with considerable satisfaction to their students:

1. Broaden the base of athletic participation, so that all students, graduate and undergraduate, big fellows and little fellows, can play. The development of intramural athletics, which costs less than the maintenance of present programs, is a step in this direction. The English system of selecting a varsity from the intramural teams toward the end of the season and then playing a limited number of intercollegiate games suggests itself at this point.

2. Emphasize games which students will play in later life, when they need recreation and physical fitness as much as in college. Such sports are tennis, handball, skating, swimming, softball, bowling, rackets, golf and touch football. Few college graduates are able to use football, baseball or basketball, except as topics of conversation.

In a word: More athletics, less athleticism.

I think that after the steps I have suggested have been taken by the colleges and universities I have named, the rest of the country's educational institutions will not long be able to ignore their example.

Nor will the public, once the break has been made, attempt for long to prevent reform. The public, in the last analysis, pays for the colleges and the universities. It wants something for its money. It has been taught to accept football. It can, I am confident, be taught to accept education.

The public will not like ten-cent football, because ten-cent football will not be great football. The task of the colleges and the universities, then, is to show the country a substitute for athleticism.

That substitute is light and learning. The colleges and universities, which taught the country football, can teach the country that the effort to discover truth, to transmit the wisdom of the race, and to preserve civilization is exciting and perhaps important too.

FRESHMAN ADVISER[1]

GEORGE BOAS

WE ARE sitting pencil in hand, surrounded by college catalogues, rules and regulations, directories, handbooks, mimeographed slips with last-minute changes of courses on them, folders with big cards for the students' records, pads with two carbons on which to write out schedules. We are all washed and clean, fresh from a summer in which we were supposed to rest and which we spent making enough money to fill out the gap between our salaries and a living wage. We are all resigned to the winter that is before us, teaching, coal bills, committee meetings, those tonsils of Susie's, academic freedom, subscription to the Symphony, student activities, what price a decent pair of shoes. . . . We smile at each other and sigh at the mass of paper. We have never learned all the rules. How can anyone learn them? Different ones for students in the college of arts and sciences, pre-meds, engineers. But what are rules anyway?

Here they come. . . .

His name is Rosburgh Van Stiew. One can see he is one of the Van Stiews—and if one can't, he'll let one know soon enough. That suit of fuzzy tweed, that regimental cravat, that custom-made shirt. Right out of *Vanity Fair*. Already he has the Phi Pho Phum pledge button in his buttonhole.

He speaks with a drawl. It is the voice of his mother's *face-à-main*. He has slightly wavy blond hair—his mother still has a crinkly white pompadour, like Queen Mary's. He has weary eyes.

No use to smile.

"Very well, Mr. Van Stiew. Have you any idea of the courses you'd like to take?"

"No . . . aren't there some things you sort of have to take?"

"Freshman English and Gym."

"Well, I may as well take them."

"History?"

"Do you have to?"

"No. You can take Philosophy, Political Science, or Economics instead."

Mr. Van Stiew tightens his cravat.

"Guess I'll take History."

"Ancient or Modern?"

"Well—when do they come?"

"Modern at 8:30, Wednesdays, Thursdays, and Saturdays; Ancient at 9:30, Mondays, Tuesdays, and Wednesdays."

"Oh, Ancient."

Mr. Van Stiew looks shocked that one should have asked.

---

1. From *Harper's Magazine*, July, 1930. Reprinted by permission of the author and the publishers.

One shouldn't have.

"Very well, Ancient History."

That leaves three more courses.

"One of the fellows said to take Art Appreciation."

"Yes, you could do that. But sooner or later you are required to take French and German and a laboratory science."

"Couldn't I put them off until next year?"

"You can until you're a senior."

"I think I'll put them off then. I don't want too heavy a schedule."

"Mathematics?"

"Do I have to?"

"It all depends. What are you going to major in?"

"Do I have to major?"

"More or less."

"When do I have to decide?"

"Next year."

So it goes with Mr. Van Stiew. He is using his right of election, his free will. His personality must not be crushed. He will have a Liberal Education, be a member of the Tennis Team, the Dramatic Club, and manager of the Glee Club. And as a prominent alumnus, he will see to it that the Football Team is never oppressed by a fastidious faculty.

Enter Mr. William Hogarth.

Hogarth is from the city Technical High School. Engineer. Red hair, freckles. Ready-made blue serge.

"Math, Physics, Philosophy, German—why can't I take Chemistry too? I'll make up my French this summer. . . . No, can't take any Saturday classes, working at the University Clothing Outlet Saturdays."

"English Literature?"

"Do I have to? . . . All right, Professor, put it down. Where do I get my text-books? Don't they have any second-hand ones? . . . Classes begin to-morrow? All right. . . . Yes, I know about the Physical Exam. Had it already. . . . No, I guess I know everything now."

"If you need any information, Mr. Hogarth, I'm in my——"

"Thanks, don't believe I will."

He's gone.

Woof! One lights a cigarette.

A presence is before one, grinning. Lots of yellow hair parted in the middle, rising on each side of the part and falling like too ripe wheat. Head slightly to one side. Very red face.

Timidly shoves forward receipted bill from the Treasurer's Office.

Fred Wilkinson.

Mr. Wilkinson doesn't know what he's going to major in as yet—"you see, I may not stay here four years." A glance at his high-school record makes that more than probable.

"English and Physical Training, that is, Gym."

"Can't I be excused from that?"

"Have you a physical disability?"

"I'm not sure . . ."

"Well, we'll put it down anyway and you can talk it over with the doctor. French? German?"

"I'm not very good on languages."

"Mathematics?"

"Heavens, no!"

"Philosophy?"

"What's that?"

"It's—it's part of the business of philosophy to find out, Mr. Wilkinson."

One stops in time.

"I don't believe you'd like Philosophy. Physics? You have to take one science."

"Isn't there one where you take a trip in the spring?"

"Geology?"

"Is that where you study rocks and things?"

"Yes." God forgive me.

"I guess I'll take that."

"History?"

Quick response. The eyes actually grow bright.

"Oh, yes, History. My brother said to take History."

"Good, that's that anyway. . . . Ancient or Modern?"

"A—what?"

"Ancient or Modern?"

Mr. Wilkinson looks as if he were going to cry. His lower lip seems to swell. His eyes blink. But he is only thinking.

"Which do you study Keats and Shelley in?"

"Which History course?"

"Yes. My brother studied Keats and Shelley. That's the course I want. Don't they come in History?"

"They are undoubtedly a part of history" (one grows pontifical) "but I don't believe they usually are discussed in the History courses."

"I'm sure my brother studied them here."

"Maybe it was the History of English Literature."

"Would that have Keats and Shelley?"

"I imagine so."

Mr. Wilkinson is dubious.

"Well, I tell you, Professor. Couldn't you put it down, and then if it isn't all right maybe I could change it afterwards. I could change it, couldn't I, you know, if I didn't like it, if they didn't teach Keats and Shelley in it? I could change it, couldn't I?"

Why not? Mr. Wilkinson will flunk out at mid-term anyway.

So we go.

The pad of the three carbons grows thinner and thinner. The atmosphere grows thicker and thicker. The advisers grow stupider and stupider. The day grows shorter and shorter. By night all schedules are made. Tomorrow classes will begin. And after tomorrow Mr. Van Stiew, Mr. Hogarth, Mr. Wilkinson, and the rest will begin dropping courses, adding courses, shifting courses about until they have left of their original schedules only English Literature and Gym which are required in the Freshman year.

· EDUCATION ·

HONORS COURSES AT SWARTHMORE[1]

FRANK AYDELOTTE

THOSE who are most concerned about American higher education are in these days waking up to the importance of doing two things which hitherto we have done inadequately or not at all: the first is to select those students who by their intellectual abilities, their qualities of character, and their ambition are most worthy of education; the second is to give to such students a training which alike by its freedom and its severity will develop them to the utmost.

Our conventional academic system is planned for the average student. We have in the past been more concerned with minimum than with maximum standards. Our special efforts have been expended more frequently upon those who were below the average than upon those who were above. We have been unjust to the best. We have not made sufficient allowance for the wide gap which separates those who are really fitted for the intellectual life from those who are not. We have failed to develop adequate methods for selecting the best from the average and for giving to those best a discipline worthy of their abilities. The result has been that academic standards in our institutions of higher education have been inferior to those of Europe, and one of the happiest signs of the times is the widespread dissatisfaction with our conventional standardized academic system and the efforts which are being made to substitute something better. . . .

I do not mean to say that the system is a bad one for the average man for whom it is planned. It may not be ideal, but it has demonstrated its value as a preparation for business and for many other occupations. It takes care of the average student adequately if not ideally, but it is unjust to the best and the most ambitious. We have in every college and university a smaller or larger group who are capable of going faster than the average, who do not need the routine exercises which are necessary for those of mediocre ability, who do not need the compulsion which is necessary for those who are not

1. Reprinted from *Five College Plans*. Copyright 1931 by Columbia University Press.

interested in intellectual things. The academic system as ordinarily administered is, for these better and more ambitious students, a kind of lock step: it holds them back, wastes their time, and blunts their interest by submitting them to exercises which they do not need. It causes, furthermore, the atrophy of the qualities of independence and initiative in those individuals who possess them by furnishing too little opportunity for their exercise.

Our extracurricular activities are organized on a different theory. In them undergraduates have a chance to do something on their own account, a chance to develop their independence and their originality, a chance to succeed or fail on their own responsibility. In studies, on the other hand, the virtue most in demand is docility. It is not surprising that many students feel that they get the best part of their education outside the classroom and that employers of college graduates often look more keenly at the young graduate's record in activities than they do at his record in his studies. The man who will do what he is told when he is told to do it has a certain value in the world, but the man who will do it without being told is worth infinitely more. Consequently when one faces the problem of providing a more severe course of instruction for our abler students, it immediately becomes apparent that it will not solve the problem merely to provide more of the same kind of work, but that they need a training which will not only be harder but also offer more scope for the development of intellectual independence and initiative.

The English universities have long ago faced and solved this problem. They make a frank distinction between those students who are interested in the intellectual life and those who are not. They give the mediocre student a degree on easier terms than we do, but they require of those who are intellectually ambitious a more severe standard than we have ever, until recently, dared to require, and they give to those students more freedom than we have ever dared to give. They do not tell the honors man what he must do in order to get an education; they tell him what he must know. Their requirements are expressed in the form of examinations. The book at Oxford which corresponds to an American catalogue is the "Examination Statutes." There is a very sound basis for all of this. Our academic requirements are too much concerned with processes, assuming that if the student goes through the motions, he will get an education.

The system of honors courses at Swarthmore College was inaugurated ten years ago as an attempt to avoid this regimentation which is the most serious defect of the conventional curriculum. It applies as yet only to the Junior and Senior years. The first two years are arranged according to the usual plan and are filled up by so-called "required" subjects (English, Foreign Languages, Natural Science, and for scientific students, Mathematics), and by the courses prerequisite for Honors work in the various fields.

At the end of the Sophomore year a student may volunteer to read for Honors instead of taking his degree in the ordinary course. Each field of Honors work has a committee which passes upon such applicants. Admission to

Honors work is not determined on the basis of the student's average grades in all his subjects but rather on the quality of his work in the subject in which he proposes to specialize or in related fields. For instance, if a student wished to read for Honors in some literary subject no account would be taken of the fact that he might have failed in a mathematics course. In the case of a student who wished to read for Honors in one of the sciences no particular account would be taken of deficiencies in literary courses. In general he is expected to reach a standard of at least B in the subjects of his choice.

Our experience is that students who do well in the regular courses of their first two years will usually do well in Honors work. There are, however, some interesting exceptions. Honors work requires certain qualities of character as well as scholastic ability. It demands independence, initiative, and self-reliance, very much the qualities which are necessary for success in extra-curricular activities. Some students who make A's in ordinary courses, where they are told day by day just what to do and when to do it, will be less successful in working on their own account. On the other hand, some students who are impatient of the requirements and restrictions of the ordinary academic course do very much better under the freedom of the Honors method.

For success in Honors work we have found that intellectual interests are absolutely essential and that ambition and determination may readily compensate for lack of cleverness. The problem, therefore, of choosing from among the volunteers those who are likely to make a success under the Honors method is rather a complex one and involves personal as well as intellectual factors. In cases of doubt students may be admitted to Honors work on trial and may be required to return to regular courses at the end of their Junior year if they have not demonstrated their capacity for success.

An Honors course at Swarthmore is never confined to a single department but includes instead two or three subjects in a closely related field. The different departments of the Faculty are grouped together for this purpose into Divisions, which cooperatively conduct the different Honors courses. As a general rule the student pursues three closely related subjects, spending half his time on one, and one-fourth of his time on each of the others. Some of the most common combinations are English Literature, English History, and Philosophy; Economics, History, and Political Science; Mathematics, Astronomy, and Physics; Physiology, Zoology, and Chemistry; etc.

When a student is admitted to read for Honors he is given at once an outline statement of the ground which he will be expected to cover in his final two years. This includes periods, topics, experiments, and set books, if any are required. The same statement will be given to his examiners at the end of his Senior year for the preparation of his final examinations. As compared with the prospectuses of various courses as printed in college catalogues, a statement of the field which a student must cover in his Honors work looks modest, although actually the degree of industry necessary for success is much greater than in the ordinary course.

The various fields in which Honors work can be done are pretty definitely fixed, but some choices are allowed. The problem is so to organize and focus the different subjects as to make the student's education a unified whole and so as to have a group of students working at the same material for the sake of common discussion, which forms a very important part of their work. At the same time we try to arrange enough choice to keep the work from being unduly rigid.

Strictly speaking, the sole duty of the Honors student is in two years to master the field which has been outlined. He is not expected to take courses; he may make whatever use he chooses of the different classes and lectures in the college, but this is entirely voluntary. Attendance is not taken; he gets no credit for being regular and no punishment for neglecting them altogether. The only exercises for which he is rigidly held are two seminars per week in the two subjects which he will normally be studying at the same time.

Our Faculty decided for several reasons that Honors instruction could more feasibly be given at Swarthmore in seminars than in individual tutorials. For one thing, the American professor knows how to conduct a seminar and he has not ordinarily had experience in the fine art of individual tutorial work. Furthermore, the informal discussions in the seminar we have found enormously stimulating to the students concerned. The seminar, in addition, is a convenient means of training young members of the Faculty to conduct Honors work, and it tends to some extent to protect the student against a poor tutor.

The work of the seminar is organized somewhat as follows. The reading which a student will do in his two years of Honors work is divided roughly into four parts corresponding to the four semesters. The work of one semester is then divided into weekly topics. The four or five students in a given seminar will do a certain amount of common reading on the topic scheduled for discussion that week. In addition, each of them will write a paper on some phase of the topic, these being carefully arranged to bring out different aspects of the subject and at the same time to be closely enough related to make discussion interesting and profitable. In the course of the seminar, which meets for two hours, each student reads his paper and it is then discussed by the whole group together. These discussions, which frequently run on for three hours or more and are sometimes continued in the undergraduates' rooms in the evening, are an extremely valuable part of the work. The assembling of information and covering of the ground each student does for himself in his room or in the library. The function of the seminar is to guide him, to stimulate his keenness, and to bring out different phases of the subject which he may have neglected or missed in his own reading. An Honors seminar skillfully conducted presents the spectacle of academic teaching in its most delightful and interesting aspect. It is informal, no point need ever be labored, as in a lecture; there are enough people present to ensure variety of opinion, and not so many as to make a frank and severe criticism uncomfortable. The students present will have done enough work to give them a basis for real and solid discussion, and it is always possible to bring in as visitors other students or professors who may have something to contribute to the particular topic under consideration.

In addition to the seminar, members of our Faculty find that some individual guidance and advice are necessary. This is arranged in the most informal manner according to the needs of the situation and the convenience of the individuals concerned. Aside from this, students make a certain amount of use of the classes and lectures in the College. There is a wide variety in this respect, but my rough guess would be that the average is one hour per day. Quite early in the development of Honors work at Swarthmore, students began the custom of carrying books home and reading in their vacations. While by no means universal, this habit has become increasingly common, and the more ambitious accomplish a very substantial amount in this way.

No examinations or tests are required of an Honors student until the end of his Senior year. No records are kept concerning him in the Registrar's office other than a mere note of the fields in which he is working. It is nevertheless true that the contact between instructor and student in the discussion groups is so intimate as to make it easy to tell whether or not a given individual is making satisfactory progress.

The degree of his success, however, is determined by the final examinations at the end of his course. These consist usually of eight three-hour papers followed by an oral conducted by the examiners after they have read the student's written work. The examinations are given by external examiners, professors from other universities who have come to Swarthmore for that purpose. The examinations are, and are meant to be, a severe ordeal. It is the belief of our Faculty that the freedom of Honors work is justified only if it produces better intellectual results than a more rigid system, and the function of these examinations is to test each student by that standard.

This system of external examiners is considered by most of our professors to be fundamental to the success of the Honors plan. The result of it is to make the relation between the professor and the student totally different from the conventional one. They become collaborators in meeting an ordeal in which they are equally interested to secure a creditable result. Furthermore it is inevitable that the student should take somewhat more seriously an examination which is set up by a professor whom he has never seen before, who will not be swayed by any personal knowledge, but only by the individual's grasp of the subject. Each student will have as a rule three examiners in the three subjects in which he has been doing Honors work, and these will then collaborate in deciding whether he is to have his degree with Honors, with High Honors or with Highest Honors. If not qualified for Honors, but still not so poor as to deserve a failure, he may be awarded a pass degree.

The tonic effect of comprehensive examinations at the end of the course is felt by our Faculty to be so valuable that they were a few years ago instituted for the pass degree as well, in this case only in the major subject. These examinations are given, however, not by external examiners but by members of our own Faculty.

Upon our students the most important effect of a decade of Honors work has been to increase enormously their interest in academic work and to make them look upon studies, athletics, and extracurricular activities with a truer sense of proportion. It has seemed to all of us to have great effect in encouraging undergraduates to cultivate specific intellectual interests and to think about their education as a matter of individual concern. It has in addition a most marked effect in increasing the number of students who go on to post-graduate and professional work.

The demands which Honors work makes on members of the Faculty are heavy. They must improve their grasp of the subjects they are teaching. They must keep their scholarship keen and growing. Honors work increases a professor's interest in research and is done best by a man with the research attitude. One marked effect is to increase the desire of the members of the Faculty for leave of absence to pursue their own studies, and we have felt that the success of the plan demands that the College make provision for such leave.

The danger, which had been feared by many of our friends, of the large amount of freedom which is allowed undergraduates under this plan has proved to be negligible. The fact is that the ordinary course and hour system, under which a student is responsible for preparing twelve or fifteen assignments each week, is so distracting as to destroy a great deal of his interest in his work. The concentration under the Honors plan, on the other hand, tends constantly to build up the interest of the student in his work and to supply a very much better motive than any punishments which could be meted out for failure to do his duty.

Honors work has proved to be more expensive than the conventional academic system. So far as the amount of teaching is concerned, running both systems in a small college, as we are compelled to do, demands about 20 per cent more instruction and hence 20 per cent more expense than the ordinary academic plan. This, however, is not the whole story. The effect of Honors work has been to improve very much in the course of ten years the quality of our student body, and this in turn has made us feel the need not merely for more professors but for better ones, with a consequent very large increase in our salary roll. If we were to abandon Honors work but kept a Faculty of the same quality as we have at present, the saving in cost would be negligible.

Ten years' experience has left us with many unsolved problems in connection with what is under American conditions a new academic plan. The problem of definiteness of program versus liberty of choice is one which can be solved only by careful and delicate adjustments. The common intellectual interests of a large number of students pursuing practically the same program are a very important part of the value of the work. At the same time, it is desirable to have as much flexibility as is possible without sacrificing these values. The solution is a matter of adjustment, and we can never feel certain that we have reached the ideal plan.

Nor are the members of our Faculty satisfied with the program of the first two years. The elements of that problem are fixed. Undergraduates must complete certain requirements which are essentially of a secondary-school character, the study of English, foreign languages, science, and elementary mathematics; the elements of the subjects in which they propose to specialize, and certain elective courses which they wish to follow for the sake of their intellectual or practical value. Into these first two years must thus be packed a certain number of rather diverse elements. It is difficult to give them such unity as would make it possible to treat them by the Honors plan. On the other hand, it is absolutely essential that none of them be neglected if a student is going to be in a position to do his best work in the last two years. The best students are a little restive under these disconnected demands, but we have as yet not been able to arrive at what seems any better solution than the plan under which we are working.

Another of our unsolved problems is the question of individual tutorial instruction versus the seminar. Each has certain values which cannot be obtained from the other. To maintain both would be expensive both of time and of money. Whether we shall be able in the future to hit upon some combination of the two, I do not know.

These and other problems we have not yet succeeded in solving, but I think it fair to say that the Honors plan has definitely passed the experimental stage. It has carried us at Swarthmore into a new study of the fine art of teaching. Visitors at the College comment on the fact that here more than at most places the professors are given to talking shop, precisely because their shop is a matter of such intense common interest. Honors work has passed through many stages and variations of student opinion. I think its final result has been a more settled concentration on the part both of students and of professors upon those intellectual purposes for which a college primarily exists.

During the ten years of its development our plan of Honors work at Swarthmore has been subject to many criticisms both within the College and without. I shall mention only one of those criticisms here: that is, the objection that such a system is not democratic. All the students who enter the College, it is argued, have a right to the same training; it is unfair to select out a few and to give them advantages which are denied to the others. Such an objection seems to me to imply a desire, not for intellectual democracy, but for intellectual communism. The fact that all men are equal before the law does not mean that they are equal in Greek or Mathematics. The coaches of our athletic teams feel no such scruples and would not think of trying to put the poorest athletes through the same training that they give to the best. Equality of opportunity is all that a university can be expected to provide:

the responsibility for measuring up to that opportunity or failing to do so must rest upon the individual.

To hold the best back to the standards of the average in the interests of democracy means to condemn democracy to mediocrity. It has sometimes been argued that this is the inevitable consequence of the wide extension of the privilege of higher education. It is my opinion that democracy cannot afford to pay that price. If democracy meant the necessity of leveling down the best to the mediocre standard attainable by the average, then democracy would be foredoomed to failure. But true democracy means not that, but rather the development of every man to the full extent of his ability in order that the state may be provided with the trained servants who are indispensable to its success.

EDUCATION AT BENNINGTON[1]

HUBERT HERRING

When Bennington College opened its doors in the fall of 1932 it engaged the lively attention of those who nursed a tempered grudge against the colleges of their own youth. There was widespread dissatisfaction with American college education—a gnawing sense that reality had been buried in routine, that our colleges did not meet the needs of the individual or respond to the spirit of the times. In various parts of the country experimenters were tinkering with collegiate machinery in the hope of making it work more acceptably. Here in Vermont a group of men and women proposed to open a new college for women which would make a clean break with tradition. They proposed to write on a cleared slate their translation of "progressive" principles into practical terms.

II

. . . This college had been talked about and planned for since 1923. A little money had been collected, a few blueprints drawn, but it was not until the trustees asked Robert D. Leigh, professor of government at Williams, to accept the presidency in 1928, that the institution took form. In 1931 ground was broken for a few buildings; old barns and chicken houses were refurnished; and a year later Bennington College opened with a freshman class of eighty-six, a faculty of nineteen, a generous armful of books, a few test-tubes, microscopes, and pianos, and unlimited enthusiasm. Now, after eight years, there are twelve buildings, two hundred and fifty students, and forty-six teachers, and the enthusiasm is undiminished. The neighbors continue to be

1. "Education at Bennington," *Harper's Magazine*, CLXXXI (September, 1940), 408–418, with omissions. Reprinted by permission of the author.

puzzled. Educators near and afar regard Bennington with mingled question and applause.

This particular visitor to Bennington, assured by a Vermont friend that here was a college "without a past, a present, or a future," set himself to discover the educational impieties which prompted the judgment. He read the catalogues, blue-penciled the curricula, talked with teachers and students, and decided that at least this college had a past. Aliens named Froebel and Pestalozzi had said many of the things which Bennington repeats. A certain Franciscan friar, Pedro de Gante, had had an Indian school on Lake Texcoco in the early sixteenth century which yoked learning and action. As for the present, Bennington is not the only college whose contrivers have sat at the feet of John Dewey.

But Bennington obviously has a well-defined creed which it believes is well adapted both to the present and to the future. It avers that the test of education is preparation for continued learning through life; that the only learning which sticks is that which is voluntary, that no one can be tricked or coerced into thinking; that the learning process does not begin until the student is captured by an authentic interest; that the ability to learn awaits the gaining of a sense of power; that it is high time educational institutions abjure such false tests of attainment as marks, prizes, and decisive examinations; that one learns by doing, that the line between "curricular" and "extra-curricular" activities should be done away with; that sharp differentiation must be made between fundamental disciplines and the mere "tools" of learning; that the curriculum must always be highly personal, fitted to the student, not the student to the curriculum; that education must reckon with the whole of personality, emotions, adjustments, ambitions; and that true education must relate the student to the world in which he lives.

This creed is not new. Educational pioneers have been saying those things for several centuries. It represents the body of faith, if not always of practice, of modern education. Bennington's aim has been to make a fresh start, freed from the necessity of apologetic concessions to tradition and expediency.

Bennington has not had to beg for students. The first class of eighty was picked from two hundred applicants. The latest class represents the choice of one out of five. Bennington broke with conventional policies of admission. There is no automatic key to Bennington. A girl may shine in Latin, have an uncanny genius for memorizing dates, and be refused by Bennington. Another girl may show a mediocre record of high school marks, but have an eye which dances at the sight of an impaled beetle, and be welcomed if she persuades Bennington that her interest is genuine and sustained. Bennington seeks the girl with a record of intelligent work, with promise of creative energy, and does not greatly care whether her ardor is kindled in the arts, the natural or the social sciences. Bennington is not the only college to break with traditional entrance requirements, but her break is perhaps more complete.

The dazed freshman, freshly laundered and delivered on the Bennington campus, is met with a reception at variance with practices prevailing in most colleges.

Bennington's notion is that a girl of seventeen has only the haziest of ideas as to what she wants, or how she will get it—and that a college must reckon with that fact. The girl is going to rattle about, hunting for herself, and the college's business is to furnish room in which to rattle. The girl arrives all bundled up, and she must first get herself unbundled. Detached from the accustomed policing of home and school, faced with the necessity of making her own good or bad decisions, she needs time to find herself. More likely than not, she has been under the spell of a mother who would make her a Maude Adams or an aunt who would make her a Jane Addams. Bennington, denying itself the luxury of playing destiny, sets itself the more arduous task of helping the girl discover her own destiny.

The new arrival is given no list of required courses. Instead she is assigned a counsellor, with whom she sits down and talks. Her first week is spent in such talk, with her counsellor, with other faculty members, with fellow-students. It is the girl's open season for tracking down her real interest. At the end of the week she plunges, picks her "trial major" in one of Bennington's divisions—art, drama, dance, music, literature, science, social studies. She chooses about half of her courses within the lines of her "major," picks the rest in other fields. She is now ready to dig in. The joys—or sorrows—of uncertainty are not thus lightly settled. Let us suppose that she elects science. A month with test-tubes and guinea pigs may convince her that her peculiar gift is for relations between people—so she shifts from science to social studies. Then a month with labor unions, race questions, and statistics may persuade her that her real genius is for the French drama—so she flees social studies for the haven of the drama department. These things happen, although actual changes of trial majors seldom exceed three in a semester. No stigma attaches to such caprice. Bennington makes no fetich of consistency and knows that it is better to have nine false motions, if happily the tenth reveals direction. Bennington suspects that the more straitlaced schooling, which roughly discourages such whimsy, may simply serve to postpone the rattling process until college is over, thereby swelling the company of misfits.

Bennington, by its frank allotment of two years to the stumbling process, feels that it is actually making less room for fumbling than prevails on more conventional campuses. In many colleges a student may beat out his lonely track with little or no personal guidance. In Bennington, from matriculation to graduation, the student has an hour each week with her counsellor, for guidance, diagnosis, criticism, and check upon accomplishment.

Whether Bennington is wise or unwise in its provision for two years of floundering must be determined by a statistician with ten years' experience upon which to draw. That miracles happen, that girls suddenly come to life as they are captured by authentic enthusiasm—that is clear. One girl is discovered sitting up at night in the laboratory with the mysteries of allergy and ragweed; another is feverishly turning out a criticism of Thomas Mann; another, having investigated nursery schools, is formulating her conclusions. This process goes on the first year, the second year. One by one, students fall out of the ranks of the stumblers and are off on trails of their own. Not all; some are still rattling about when the second year is up, and these Bennington firmly passes back to their parents or on to other institutions of higher learning. About sixty-five per cent of those who enroll in Bennington reach the "Senior Division," which covers the third and fourth years. Here the girl is expected to have proved her competence in some one field, to have won the right to some increased specialization, and to give continuing evidence of creative capacity.

The casual visitor to the Bennington campus is impressed by the freedom of the atmosphere. From the beginning, Leigh and his associates vowed that there was to be no strait-jacketing. The girls were to be treated as responsible adults. College regulations would take form out of the experience of the community. . . .

But liberty underwent its own disciplines. The immoderate freedom of some threatened the liberties of others. Students and faculty speedily set up regulations on college traffic. The dogs, cats, goats, and winged creatures were banished, for after all they were waging war upon one another and the battles destroyed the campus calm. Common prudence indicated the advisability of having someone know where an absentee had taken herself, so now one signs up before starting for Boston, New York, or Quebec. She need not ask permission, she simply tells where she has gone. Then the students tired of tripping over other girls' strange males at odd hours, so they fixed limits for such visits. Automobiles appeared as a problem, since they were borrowed and lent generously, so students and faculty decided that thenceforth no cars were to be permitted without the college's license and no cars were to be loaned. These were student regulations, on no account to be given the vulgar name of rules. They were simply a set of self-imposed traffic directions to avert jams.

The true discipline upon Bennington exuberance turned out to be not rules and regulations, but the pressure of work. Theoretically, a student is free to take days off as she pleases, to enjoy unlimited week-ends. Figures reveal that Bennington students without pressure of rules took as little time off from college last year as did students at other institutions. The reason was that the Bennington scheme of education makes the class a highly personal relation between an instructor and a few students. The typical course is a running series of discussions, each hanging upon the last. It is not like a lecture, with notes to be borrowed from a helpful friend. Interest has proved as effective as coercion in assuring regular attendance.

III

But what of Robert D. Leigh, Bennington's contriver? I put the question to a student, my friend since her pigtail days, and she answered in surprise, "Why, Mr. Leigh is all right, but what has he to do with Bennington?" It is a remark calculated to delight the heart of Bennington's president. Robert Leigh is never discovered in front-row-center when the shutter flashes. Bennington, Leigh avers, is the product of teamwork, in which no individual deserves predominant credit. This insistence, devoid of pose, makes one like Leigh. Amiably humorless, innocent of the tricks of the advertiser, he has a shyness which bars him from that warm camaraderie which resolves human relations. Students respect him, few know him.

Robert Leigh took his undergraduate lessons at Bowdoin, managed the football team, and graduated with top honors. Then he was off for graduate work in Columbia, then to Reed College for three years with William Trufant Foster in one of the first pioneering ventures in higher education, one which shaped Leigh's later thought. A stretch of war work in Washington and six years of teaching at Williams completed his preparation for the presidency of Bennington, a college without buildings, without faculty, but with an idea. That idea, rooted in the educational philosophy of such men as John Dewey and William H. Kilpatrick, was given form by Robert Leigh. From the turning of the first furrow to the laying of the latest brick, it has been Leigh who has vicariously measured each load of sand and lime, weighed each length of sewerpipe, chosen each student, picked each member of the faculty, and given direction to the institution. Leigh disclaims credit. Institutions thrive, he contends, as responsibility and ideas are shared. He would see Bennington a body sound in all its parts, each contributing to the health of the whole, a living organism of trustees, faculty, students, and alumnae. . . .

Bennington has its own notions as to the care and feeding of trustees. Leigh would put an end to that prevalent pattern in which a group of preoccupied men and women meet fitfully, dine amiably, approve the *faits accomplis* of a genial president, take fervid interest in athletic records, are severally coaxed into paying for such buildings as their loyalty or zeal for immortality may dictate, and dig down to meet accumulated deficits. Bennington's trustees are not only asked to assume charge of college finances but to furnish continuous lay collaboration in the educational program. Conversations with some trustees reveal that they know the faculty, spend substantial time on the campus, and exert a continuing influence upon the program. The founders of the college, aware of the perils from an unchanging board, established the principle that trustees retire, for a year at least, at the end of a seven-year term.

Bennington teachers know themselves as a part of the growing organic life of the institution. In the Bennington scheme of things there is less room for the virtuoso than in more orthodox surroundings. A teacher who expects to give individual attention to his students cannot take to his tower and shut out the world. A chemist is compelled by the nature of the Bennington plan to admit that a piano has a place on the campus as well as a Bunsen burner. When visiting lecturers come to Bennington to speak on economics, the music and art and drama teachers attend as a matter of course—not because they have to, but because they want to. Under Leigh's hand there is a sharing of responsibilities often relegated elsewhere to trustees and president. The faculty has a definitely assigned share in building plans, in the election of a president, in the naming of new faculty members.

Students also take a hand in the making of decisions. Student organizations, akin to those prevailing elsewhere, are assigned clear responsibilities. The "Community Council" of elected representatives from the student houses, together with faculty members, legislates on community life, administers a measure of discipline, and makes rules for dining rooms and campus activities. The "Student Educational Policies Committee," named by the students, advises the faculty on curriculum and educational methods, and makes regular periodical reports on the quality of the instruction given by individual teachers. Suggestions and criticisms are given frankly, and received seriously. Teachers and administrators really expect to learn from students, and students respond with heartening responsibility. "They think that they own the place," I have heard in criticism. If any representative number of students decided that a given instructor was failing in intelligence and zest they would not hesitate to say so. Even a visiting lecturer is not exempt—I have known such a one to be taken in hand by a nineteen-year-old social scientist and told in precise terms where he failed. Such candor reflects concern. Bennington students, in high degree, consider themselves responsible for the college. Bennington, they tell you gravely, is an experiment. Experiments, one infers, require special nurture.

The alumnae, still a slight company, share in the sense of proprietorship. This is not unique, else whence would come the memorial plaques and class gifts of other institutions? But Bennington's alumnae have a special maternal solicitude. The college is so young, so new, so fluid. It has taken shape under their eyes. They know it as their own: each building, each corner of each building; each tree on the campus, for they had a hand in planting them; almost each book in the library .

The net impression of Bennington upon the visitor is of an honest unity, to which the several members contribute with fidelity and affection. If discordant notes catch his ear, what would one expect in a company of three hundred? If there are little affectations and vanities, if not all evince equal wisdom and skill, if there are serious gaps in the educational scheme of things—well, again, what would you expect? But of the comradeship, of the imaginativeness, of the sober discipline in which the several parties to the compact work at their task, of these one feels no lack.

IV

A teacher has a stiff assignment at Bennington. He cannot deliver (and redeliver) his six or eight lectures each week, read occasional papers, ward off personal encounters, and retreat to his study. He sets out with six or eight students to explore the mysteries of economics, European history, the French drama, or the fundamental concepts of biology. He does not lay out an inflexible program or stick to a specified text. The students will have ideas as to where the search will lead. He must shape the course to the abilities and zeals of the group. Such teaching takes a sterner toll than lecturing.

Teaching and counselling go together. Each teacher is assigned as counsellor to six or seven students, to each of whom he gives an hour a week. The teachers in the several divisions divide responsibility for the students in their divisions. The counsellor meets his *counsellee* week after week, discussing work done, books read, experiences in field work, problems of study. Office hours are disregarded, for genuine interest breaks schedules. It tests the stuff of teachers.

Counselling is at the heart of Bennington's scheme. It is a revolt against machine education, in which a student is thrust into the gears, and given minimum personal attention. Bennington stresses the need for continued guidance. Such guidance must reckon with the entire personality, with a girl's relations to her family, her fellow-students, her teachers. It cannot ignore her fears, hopes, or loves. A bad record in work-shop, laboratory, or classroom may indicate faulty digestion, lack of ability or of interest; it may mean brooding resentments, lack of exercise, or an unhappy love affair. The counsellor serves as a safety valve. The student is free to talk herself out, about courses, books, problems, interests—and to blurt out resentments or hopes. The wise counsellor abjures the role of confessor, and sticks to that of friendly instructor. He will labor to maintain the objectivity which lends weight to counsel; to combine detachment with authentic interest; to make the student's problems so honestly his own as to give integrity to his judgment. If he is wise he will strengthen self-respect by judicious praise, encourage self-criticism for the over-confident, and stir ambition. Having placed counselling at the center of instruction, Bennington stakes everything on the character of its faculty. In a faculty of forty-six not all will be equally wise.

Bennington's physician serves as counsellor to the counsellors. Trained in medicine and psychology, this physician takes account of the physical and psychological factors which impede learning. A student will do good work when the inner house is in order; bad work when something is askew. The physician, very much in the background, knowing full well what a jangling concatenation of nerves, glands, emotions, and digestive juices life is, stands ready to counsel the student threatened with failure. In any group of two hundred and fifty some will be retarded or defeated by their emotional tumults. Bennington takes cognizance of such factors and through its counsellors and physician seeks to furnish the robust catharsis of new incentives.

Bennington's campus is off the main roads of American life. The gain in serenity is obvious, but there is danger lest isolation cut faculty and students off from contact with the country. The College takes steps to overcome this disability. Bennington has its own calendar. The orthodox three-months' vacation is cut to two; the usual Christmas and Easter recesses are expanded into a winter recess of two months. The summer vacation is ample for rest and recreation. The winter period is reckoned in the educational year, affording opportunity for independent field work or study in the student's chosen field.

Each girl picks her winter project with the advice of her counsellor. She may elect two months' reading at home or in the stacks of the Library of Congress; she may spend her time studying co-operatives in Pennsylvania; get a job in a Boston settlement; secure a temporary assignment in a New York bacteriological laboratory; or journey to Mexico to study the murals of Orozco and Rivera. Upon her return she makes a written report to her counsellor. The advantages of the arrangement are obvious—it shortens the cold winter in Vermont and lengthens the spring and fall when New England is at its best; it offers the faculty time for study; it affords students opportunity for practical exploration and the testing of theories.

The winter device is frankly experimental. The results are difficult to appraise. Many students have experiences which lend vitality to their study. Others, through lack of direction or indolence, fail to benefit by the experience. But no student is admitted to the Senior Division who has not used at least one winter period to advantage. The winter period in the Bennington calendar must be put down as one of Bennington's educational novelties which will bear further exploration.

V

The visitor attracted to Bennington finds himself hard pressed to maintain the critical attitude demanded by those who know all about education. His report collects superlatives. So it must be set down in cold 10-point type that there are questions to be raised concerning Bennington's way in education.

A serious question concerns the issue of democracy in a college as expensive as Bennington. Fees total $1,675 for the year—a figure determined by the actual *per capita* cost of each student to the college, and made necessary by meager endowment. That figure automatically shuts out the daughters of many physicians, lawyers, college professors, and business men—and of carpenters and masons. Bennington, concerned to make its student body thoroughly representative, provides scholarships in varying amounts to two-fifths of the students. Some girls earn substantial amounts by waiting on table and at other odd tasks. The fact remains that at least three-fifths of the students must be recruited from families whose incomes are subject to one or two of Mr. Morgenthau's surcharges. . . . Only an increased endowment can eliminate this disproportion. To admit that cliques exist, to cite individuals who parade their social pretension, to name others who are resentful, is simply to confess that Bennington shares markings which disfigure human relations in Spring Valley, Leadville, and Minneapolis.

Bennington is condemned by others on the ground that the students do not work. These delight in describing the college as a rich girls' country club, where the students live in nice houses, dash off to New York for house parties and to Canada for skiing; ride horses, play hockey, study a little music, dabble in a little art, do a little freakish dancing—but do not work. This account of Bennington is given currency by the photographic reporting of certain "picture" magazines. This version fits some in each entering class, but is scarcely an adequate description of those who survive the first two years. Bennington teachers admit that Bennington affords opportunity to some for loafing on a grand scale, but add that it excites others to tenacious work of a fine order. The loafers (and what college has none?) eliminate themselves or are eliminated. The workers remain. About 65 per cent of those who enter reach the Senior Division. The impression of intellectual vigor is confirmed by the quality of random conversation, by the lively and intelligent debate on ideas, on national affairs, on books old and new. Such talk, one infers, is the backwash of solid exercise. The impression is strengthened by leafing over the theses of the seniors. More than one visitor has remarked that these theses in their originality and evidence of research are on the level of theses required elsewhere for a master's degree. The impression of solid work is confirmed by the citing of Bennington's graduates who have gone on into graduate and professional schools, 47 of them out of a total of 199 graduates. "We have our problems," admits Leigh, "but keeping our students at work is not one of them."

Others argue that Bennington's curriculum is faddish, that too large place is given to painting, music, the dance, and the drama. Bennington offers no apology for dignifying the arts in the curriculum of a liberal arts college and takes pride in recognition won in this field. Her musicians, professional and students, work. Her painters spread their mural imagination on college walls (fortunately perhaps on removable panels). Her dramatists and dancers evidence sustained zeal. Whether such skills merit the place assigned them will have to be fought out by the pundits. The skeptical may find comfort in the fact that, in recent classes, not more than one or two specialize on the dance, about twelve devote themselves to art, five to the drama, and six to music, while social studies enlist fifteen to eighteen students, and literature ten to fifteen. It must also be noted that majoring in any of the arts does not mean exclusion of other disciplines. Drama inevitably spills over into literature; and the dramatist who would deal with life commonly discovers that the study of society's patterns falls within her ken. The faculty applies pressure and persuasion against any tendency to over-specialization.

Others charge that Bennington neglects religion. A recent graduate writes me that "in the working philosophy of Bennington too little place is given to the recognition of Christianity." There is no chapel, no chapel service, no orthodox course on religion. There are churches in Bennington and students are invited to participate. A few do. No cross or spire dominates the Bennington campus, and some dread the day when an impulsive donor will offer a chapel, and hope the offer will be refused. Such distaste of formal religious expression is rooted in the experience of other campuses (where a disproportionate slice of the building budget has gone into a gothic or colonial chapel), of college chaplains of uncertain functions, and of a stream of tendentious clergymen preaching to rebellious audiences where attendance is required, or to empty benches where attendance is voluntary. Some describe Bennington as "irreligious." The label does not fit. A graduate of Bennington, who taught in a Midwestern college of fervid church affiliations, writes me that "Bennington was more religious by any decent test." If the religious attitude consists of a lively and sustained concern for human values, of spiritual sensitivity toward truth and beauty, of regard for the health and wealth of the human spirit, many would call Bennington religious. It is all a matter of definition.

Some argue that Bennington permits a degree of specialization not consonant with the genius of a liberal arts college. They cite the case of one student who was so intent upon zoölogy that she gained no awareness of the broader sweep of the social sciences, of another whose zeal for French literature crowded out all interest in the natural sciences. Such specialization, critics aver, defeats the chief purpose of a college, to turn out women with a well-rounded education. Bennington answers that majoring must be done in the broader field of science, not in zoology; in literature, not in French literature; that with the major go the minors, and that she cannot graduate from Bennington without giving some attention to other disciplines; and that the conscious effort of the college community is to encourage awareness of a broad range of human interests through lectures, recitals, play shared by all.

Other critics contend that Bennington shares the common weakness of all schools called progressive in failing to furnish that systematic drill in the solid body of fact essential to the intellectual furnishing of an educated man or woman. They argue that it is idle to stress the independent approach, the play of individual initiative, without solid drill in the corporate body of factual material which must be acquired no matter what it costs in boredom. These critics aver that understanding of the contemporary world hangs upon a considerable knowledge of events, men, theories, and achievements, and question whether such a curriculum as Bennington's affords drill in such detailed knowledge. This criticism is voiced by some graduates, some students, and a few teachers. Their anxiety is lest Bennington's education should turn out a bit spotty. If there is ground for the fear it is equally clear that in the maturing of Bennington increased emphasis is placed upon diversification in election, and upon more intensive drill.

The protagonists for coeducation deplore the creation of another college for women, insisting that the segregation of boys and girls at the mating season is educationally unsound, that they should learn to work together as a preparation for living together. Bennington students and faculty are well-nigh unanimous in agreement. Leigh insists that Bennington is the first unit of a co-educational college in the making.

The classicists turn an unhappy eye upon Bennington, regarding its reputed preoccupation with the contemporary world as a slight upon the Greeks, and inquiring with asperity how a college can turn out educated women who are unaware of the broader sweep of thought. These critics are reminded that drama cannot be explored without reckoning with Aeschylus, Aristophanes, and Euripides; that the study of literature involves recognition that Proust must be read in the light of the romanticists, the romanticists against the background of Racine and Molière, that these lead back to Ronsard, and Ronsard to Horace; that comprehension of Descartes and Hume waits upon Plato; that analysis of the industrial revolution hangs upon comprehension of feudalism, and that feudalism is inexplicable without reference to the Roman world. Whether the Bennington scheme of education makes adequate place for such reckoning with classical backgrounds must be left to the classicists to fight out with Bennington's faculty. The visitor after a cursory glance confesses that he misses that familiar figure on every proper campus, the withered but active patriarch who never fails to affirm that nothing new or notable has befallen the race since the days of Pericles.

How then shall one report on Bennington College? It must be to each according to his taste. This is a report of gratitude to men and women who have cut new patterns with honesty and imaginativeness. Many questions remain. Whether French is a subject or a tool; whether the dance belongs in the college curriculum or in Carnegie Hall; whether girls should be coerced or enticed into learning; whether they should be allowed to specialize on beetles or be told to study Chaucer and calculus; whether there is too much drama and not enough Greek; whether there is too much emphasis on learning to think, and too little upon the body of fact about which to think—these and other items must be relegated to those composers of incredible prose who draw their pay from Teachers' College on Morningside Heights. The visitor has been looking into colleges these twenty-five years. He has dipped into colleges which have rediscovered Plato and suffered others which claim to have discovered Christ. He has been in football colleges, fraternity colleges, and college-spirit colleges. He has seen students driven in platoons down the high-fenced runway called education; seen the cramming and the jamming, watched the lecturing and exhorting. He has known the students who were bored, angry, and indifferent, and he has come upon those rare colleges in which ideas flourish, teachers teach, and students learn.

When a company of alert teachers get a hilltop, remodel a barn or so, gather a few eager students, and set out upon a new experiment in the co-operative search for truth, there is ground for celebration. When this assay in education is carried on with the honesty which is Bennington's there is basis for the hope that education, the bulwark of American democracy, may still be touched with coals from off the altar. If such a college can escape the complacency which readily besets journeyers into new lands; if it can remain aware that its genius is its fluidity; if it can combine due deference to the opinion of others with wholesome indifference to their judgments, then will faith in the renewal of education be confirmed. If such a college can have money enough to pay its bills and never enough to build gothic spires; if it can keep its corporate sense of humor and resist the regularizers and the pedants—then, it might be pleasant to have a granddaughter who would resist all doddering counsel and "go to Bennington, wear pants, and stay up all night."

GENERAL AND SPECIAL EDUCATION[1]

THE HARVARD COMMITTEE

Education is broadly divided into general and special education; our topic now is the difference and the relationship between the two. The term, general education, is somewhat vague and colorless; it does not mean some airy education in knowledge in general (if there be such knowledge), nor does it mean education for all in the sense of universal education. It is used to indicate that part of a student's whole education which looks first of all to his life as a responsible human being and citizen; while the term, special education, indicates that part which looks to the student's competence in some occupation. These two sides of life are not entirely separable, and it would be false to imagine education for the one as quite distinct from education for the other—more will be said on this point presently. Clearly, general education has somewhat the meaning of liberal education, except that, by applying to high school as well as to college, it envisages immensely greater numbers of students and thus escapes the invidium which, rightly or wrongly, attaches to liberal education in the minds of some people. But if one cling to the root meaning of liberal as that which befits or helps to make free men, then general and liberal education have identical goals. The one may be thought of as an earlier stage of the other, similar in nature but less advanced in degree.

The opposition to liberal education—both to the phrase and to the fact—stems largely from historical causes. The concept of liberal education first appeared in a slave-owning society, like that of Athens, in which the community was divided into freemen and slaves, rulers and subjects. While the slaves carried on the specialized occupations of menial work, the freemen were primarily

---

Reprinted by permission of the publishers from Paul H. Buck and others. *General Education in a Free Society:* The Report of the Harvard Committee, Cambridge, Mass.: Harvard University Press, 1945.

concerned with the rights and duties of citizenship. The training of the former was purely vocational; but as the freemen were not only a ruling but also a leisure class, their education was exclusively in the liberal arts, without any utilitarian tinge. The freemen were trained in the reflective pursuit of the good life; their education was unspecialized as well as unvocational; its aim was to produce a rounded person with a full understanding of himself and of his place in society and in the cosmos.

Modern democratic society clearly does not regard labor as odious or disgraceful; on the contrary, in this country at least, it regards leisure with suspicion and expects its "gentlemen" to engage in work. Thus we attach no odium to vocational instruction. Moreover, in so far as we surely reject the idea of freemen who are free in so far as they have slaves or subjects, we are apt strongly to deprecate the liberal education which went with the structure of the aristocratic ideal. Herein our society runs the risk of committing a serious fallacy. Democracy is the view that not only the few but that all are free, in that everyone governs his own life and shares in the responsibility for the management of the community. This being the case, it follows that all human beings stand in need of an ampler and rounded education. The task of modern democracy is to preserve the ancient ideal of liberal education and to extend it as far as possible to all the members of the community. In short, we have been apt to confuse accidental with fundamental factors, in our suspicion of the classical idea. To believe in the equality of human beings is to believe that the good life, and the education which trains the citizen for the good life, are equally the privilege of all. And these are the touchstones of the liberated man: first, is he free; that is to say, is he able to judge and plan for himself, so that he can truly govern himself? In order to do this, his must be a mind capable of self-criticism; he must lead that self-examined life which according to Socrates is alone worthy of a free man. Thus he will possess inner freedom, as well as social freedom. Second, is he universal in his motives and sympathies? For the civilized man is a citizen of the entire universe; he has overcome provincialism, he is objective, and is a "spectator of all time and all existence." Surely these two are the very aims of democracy itself.

But the opposition to general education does not stem from causes located in the past alone. We are living in an age of specialism, in which the avenue to success for the student often lies in his choice of a specialized career, whether as a chemist, or an engineer, or a doctor, or a specialist in some form of business or of manual or technical work. Each of these specialties makes an increasing demand on the time and on the interest of the student. Specialism is the means for advancement in our mobile social structure; yet we must envisage the fact that a society controlled wholly by specialists is not a wisely ordered society. We cannot, however, turn away from specialism. The problem is how to save general education and its values within a system where specialism is necessary.

The very prevalence and power of the demand for special training makes doubly clear the need for a concurrent, balancing force in general education.

Specialism enhances the centrifugal forces in society. The business of providing for the needs of society breeds a great diversity of special occupations; and a given specialist does not speak the language of the other specialists. In order to discharge his duties as a citizen adequately, a person must somehow be able to grasp the complexities of life as a whole. Even from the point of view of economic success, specialism has its peculiar limitations. Specializing in a vocation makes for inflexibility in a world of fluid possibilities. Business demands minds capable of adjusting themselves to varying situations and of managing complex human institutions. Given the pace of economic progress, techniques alter speedily; and even the work in which the student has been trained may no longer be useful when he is ready to earn a living or soon after. Our conclusion, then, is that the aim of education should be to prepare an individual to become an expert both in some particular vocation or art and in the general art of the free man and the citizen. Thus the two kinds of education once given separately to different social classes must be given together to all alike.

In this epoch in which almost all of us must be experts in some field in order to make a living, general education therefore assumes a peculiar importance. Since no one can become an expert in all fields, everyone is compelled to trust the judgment of other people pretty thoroughly in most areas of activity. I must trust the advice of my doctor, my plumber, my lawyer, my radio repairman, and so on. Therefore I am in peculiar need of a kind of sagacity by which to distinguish the expert from the quack, and the better from the worse expert. From this point of view, the aim of general education may be defined as that of providing the broad critical sense by which to recognize competence in any field. William James said that an educated person knows a good man when he sees one. There are standards and a style for every type of activity—manual, athletic, intellectual, or artistic; and the educated man should be one who can tell sound from shoddy work in a field outside his own. General education is especially required in a democracy where the public elects its leaders and officials; the ordinary citizen must be discerning enough so that he will not be deceived by appearances and will elect the candidate who is wise in his field.

Both kinds of education—special as well as general—contribute to the task of implementing the pervasive forces of our culture. Two complementary forces are at the root of our culture: on the one hand, an ideal of man and society distilled from the past but at the same time transcending the past as a standard of judgment valid in itself, and, on the other hand, the belief that no existent expressions of this ideal are final but that all alike call for perpetual scrutiny and change in the light of new knowledge. Specialism is usually the vehicle of this second force. It fosters the open-mindedness and love of investigation which are the wellspring of change, and it devotes itself to the means by which change is brought about. The fact may not always be obvious. There is a sterile specialism which hugs accepted knowledge and ends in the bleakest conservatism. Modern life also calls for many skills which, though specialized, are repetitive and certainly do not conduce to inquiry. These minister to change but unconsciously. Nevertheless, the previous statement is true in the sense that specialism is concerned primarily with knowledge in action, as it advances into new fields and into further applications.

Special education comprises a wider field than vocationalism; and correspondingly, general education extends beyond the limits of merely literary preoccupation. An example will make our point clearer. A scholar—let us say a scientist (whether student or teacher)—will, in the laudable aim of saving himself from narrowness, take a course in English literature, or perhaps read poetry and novels, or perhaps listen to good music and generally occupy himself with the fine arts. All this, while eminently fine and good, reveals a misapprehension. In his altogether unjustified humility, the scientist wrongly interprets the distinction between liberal and illiberal in terms of the distinction between the humanities and the sciences. Plato and Cicero would have been very much surprised to hear that geometry, astronomy, and the sciences of nature in general, are excluded from the humanities. There is also implied a more serious contempt for the liberal arts, harking back to the fallacy which identifies liberal education with the aristocratic ideal. The implication is that liberal education is something only genteel. A similar error is evident in the student's attitude toward his required courses outside his major field as something to "get over with," so that he may engage in the business of serious education, identified in his mind with the field of concentration.

Now, a general education is distinguished from special education, not by subject matter, but in terms of method and outlook, no matter what the field. Literature, when studied in a technical fashion, gives rise to the special science of philology; there is also the highly specialized historical approach to painting. Specialism is interchangeable, not with natural science, but with the method of science, the method which abstracts material from its context and handles it in complete isolation. The reward of scientific method is the utmost degree of precision and exactness. But, as we have seen, specialism as an educational force has its own limitations; it does not usually provide an insight into general relationships.

A further point is worth noting. The impact of specialism has been felt not only in those phases of education which are necessarily and rightly specialistic; it has affected also the whole structure of higher and even of secondary education. Teachers, themselves products of highly technical disciplines, tend to reproduce their knowledge in class. The result is that each subject, being taught by an expert, tends to be so presented as to attract potential experts. This complaint is perhaps more keenly felt in colleges and universities, which naturally look to scholarship. The undergraduate in a college receives his teaching from professors who, in their turn, have been trained in graduate schools. And the latter are dominated by the ideal of specialization. Learning now is diversified and parceled into a myriad of specialties. Correspondingly, colleges and universities are divided into large numbers of departments, with further specialization within the departments. As a result, a student in search of a general course is commonly frustrated. Even an elementary course is devised as an introduction to a specialism within a department; it is significant only as the beginning of a series of courses of advancing complexity. In short, such introductory courses are planned for the specialist, not for the student seeking a general education. The young chemist in the course in literature and the young writer in the course in chemistry find themselves in thoroughly uncomfortable positions so long as the purpose of these courses is primarily to train experts who will go on to higher courses rather than to give some basic understanding of science as it is revealed in chemistry or of the arts as they are revealed in literature.

It is most unfortunate if we envisage general education as something formless—that is to say, the taking of one course after another; and as something negative, namely, the study of what is not in a field of concentration. Just as we regard the courses in concentration as having definite relations to one another, so should we envisage general education as an organic whole whose parts join in expounding a ruling idea and in serving a common aim. And to do so means to abandon the view that all fields and all departments are equally valuable vehicles of general education. It also implies some prescription. At the least it means abandoning the usual attitude of regarding "distribution" as a sphere in which the student exercises a virtually untrammeled freedom of choice. It may be objected that we are proposing to limit the liberty of the student in the very name of liberal education. Such an objection would only indicate an ambiguity in the conception of liberal education. We must distinguish between liberalism in education and education in liberalism. The former, based as it is on the doctrine of individualism, expresses the view that the student should be free in his choice of courses. But education in liberalism is an altogether different matter; it is education which has a pattern of its own, namely, the pattern associated with the liberal outlook. In this view, there are truths which none can be free to ignore, if one is to have that wisdom through which life can become useful. These are the truths concerning the structure of the good life and concerning the factual conditions by which it may be achieved, truths comprising the goals of the free society.

Finally, the problem of general education is one of combining fixity of aim with diversity in application. It is not a question of providing a general education which will be uniform through the same classes of all schools and colleges all over the country, even were such a thing possible in our decentralized system. It is rather to adapt general education to the needs and intentions of different groups and, so far as possible, to carry its spirit into special education. The effectiveness of teaching has always largely depended on this willingness to adapt a central unvarying purpose to varying outlooks. Such adaptation is as much in the interest of the quick as of the slow, of the bookish as of the unbookish, and is the necessary protection of each. What is wanted, then, is a general education capable at once of taking on many different forms and yet of representing in all its forms the common knowledge and the common values on which a free society depends.

ON THE NEED FOR A QUIET COLLEGE[1]

STEPHEN LEACOCK

IF SOMEBODY would give me about two dozen very old elm trees and about fifty acres of wooded ground and lawn—not too near anywhere and not too far from everywhere—I think I could set up a college that would put all the big universities of today in the shade. I am not saying that it would be better. But it would be different.

I would need a few buildings, but it doesn't take many—stone, if possible—and a belfry and a clock. The clock wouldn't need to go; it might be better if it didn't. I would want some books—a few thousand would do—and some apparatus. But it's amazing how little apparatus is needed for scientific work of the highest quality: in fact "the higher the fewer."

Most of all, I should need a set of professors. I would need only a dozen of them—but they'd have to be real ones—disinterested men of learning, who didn't even know they were disinterested. And, mind you, these professors of mine wouldn't sit in "offices" dictating letters on "cases" to stenographers, and only leaving their offices to go to "committees" and "conferences." There would be no "offices" in my college and no "committees," and my professors would have no time for conferences, because the job they would be on would need all eternity and would never be finished.

My professors would never be findable at any fixed place except when they were actually giving lectures. Men of thought have no business in an office. Learning runs away from "committees." There would be no "check up" on the time of the professors: there would be no "hire and fire" or "judge by results" or "standards" or "norms" of work for them: or any fixed number of hours.

But, on the other hand, they would, if I got the ones I want, be well worth their apparent irresponsibility: and when they lectured each one would be, though he wouldn't know it, a magician—with such an interest and absorption that those who listened would catch the infection of it, and hurry from the lecture to the library, still warm with thought.

It must be understood that the work of professors is peculiar. Few professors, real ones, ever complete their work: what they give to the world is fragments. The rest remains. Their contributions must be added up, not measured singly. Every professor has his "life work" and sometimes does it, and sometimes dies first.

I can recall—I say it by way of digression—one such who was working on Machiavelli. When I first met him he had worked fourteen years. He worked in a large room covered a foot deep with Machiavelli—notes, pamphlets, remains. I asked him—it seemed a simple question—what he thought of Machiavelli. He

1. Reprinted by permission of Dodd, Mead & Company, Inc., from *Model Memoirs* by Stephen Leacock. Copyright, 1938, by Dodd, Mead & Company, Inc.

shook his head. He said it was too soon to form an opinion. Later, ten years later, he published his book, *Machiavelli.* One of the great continental reviews—one of the really great ones (you and I never hear of them: they have a circulation of about 300) said his work was based on premature judgments. He was hurt, but he felt it was true. He had rushed into print too soon.

Another such devoted himself—he began years ago—to the history of the tariff. He began in a quiet lull of tariff changes when for three or four years public attention was elsewhere. He brought his work up to within a year or so of actual up-to-date completeness. Then the tariff began to move: two years later he was three years behind it. Presently, though he worked hard, he was five years behind it.

He has never caught it. His only hope now is that the tariff will move back towards free trade, and meet him.

Not that I mean to imply that my professors would be a pack of nuts or freaks. Not at all: their manners might be dreamy and their clothes untidy but they'd be—they'd have to be—the most eminent men in their subjects. To get them would be the main effort of the college: to coax them, buy them, if need be, to kidnap them. Nothing counts beside that. A college is made of men, not by the size of buildings, number of students and football records. But trustees don't know this, or, at best, catch only a glimmer of it and lose it. Within a generation all the greatest books on the humanities would come from my college.

The professors bring the students. The students bring, unsought, the benefactions. The thing feeds itself like a flame in straw. But it's the men that count. A college doesn't need students: it's the students who need the college.

After twenty years my college would stand all alone. There are little colleges now but they ape bigness. There are quiet colleges but they try to be noisy. There are colleges without big games but they boom little ones. Mine would seem the only one, because the chance is there, wide open, and no one takes it. After twenty years people would drive in motor cars to see my college: and wouldn't be let in.

Round such a college there must be no thought of money. Money ruins life: I mean, to have to think of it, to take account of it, to know that it is there. Men apart from money, men in an army, men on an expedition of exploration, emerge to a new life. Money is gone. At times and places whole classes thus lift up, or partly: as in older countries like England the class called "gentry" that once was. These people lived on land and money from the past—stolen, perhaps, five hundred years ago—and so thought no more of it. They couldn't earn more; they didn't know how. They kept what they had, or dropped out, fell through a trestle bridge of social structure and were gone in the stream. This class, in America, we never had. They grow rare everywhere. Perhaps we don't want them. But they had the good luck that, in their lives, money in the sense here meant, didn't enter. Certain money limits circumscribed their life, but from day to day they never thought of it. A cow in a pasture, a fairly generous pasture, doesn't know it's in. It thinks it's outside. So did they.

So I would have it in my college. Students not rich and not poor—or not using their wealth and not feeling their poverty—an equality as unconscious as that where Evangeline lived.

Nor would their studies lead to, or aim at, or connect with wealth. The so-called practical studies are all astray. Real study, real learning must, for the individual, be quite valueless or it loses its value. The proper studies for my college are history and literature and philosophy and thought and poetry and speculation, in the pursuit of which each shall repeat the eager search, the unending quest, of the past. Looking for one thing he shall find another. Looking for ultimate truth, which is unfindable, they will learn at least to repudiate all that is false.

I leave out at one sweep great masses of stuff usually taught: all that goes under such a name as a university faculty of Commerce. There is no such thing. The faculty of Commerce is down at the docks, at Wall Street, in the steel mills. A "degree" in Commerce is a salary of ten thousand a year. Those who fail to pass go to Atlanta—and stay there. Certain things in Commerce are teachable: accountancy, corporate organization and the principles of embezzlement. But that's not a university.

Out goes economics, except as speculation: not a thing to teach in instalments and propositions like geometry. You *can't* teach it. No one knows it. It's the riddle of the Sphinx. My graduates will be just nicely fitted to think about it when they come out. A first-year girl studying economics is as wide of the mark as an old man studying cosmetics. The philosophical speculative analysis of our economic life is the highest study of all, next to the riddle of our existence. But to cut it into classes and credits is a parody. Out it goes.

Out—but to come back again—goes medicine. Medicine is a great reality: it belongs in a *school,* not a college. My college fits people to study medicine, study it in crowded cities among gas-lights and ambulances and hospitals and human suffering, and keep their souls alive while they do it. Then later, as trained men in the noblest profession in the world, the atmosphere of the college, which they imbibed among my elm trees, grows about them again. The last word in cultivation is, and always has been, the cultivated "medicine man."

The engineers?—that's different. Theirs is the most "manly" of all the professions—among water power and gold mines and throwing bridges half a mile at a throw. But it's a *school* that trains them, not a college. They go to my college but they don't like it. They say it's too damn dreamy. So they kick out of it into engineering. For a time they remember the Latin third declension. Presently they forget it. Doctors grow cultivated as they grow older. Engineers get rougher and rougher.

What I mean is that our studies have drifted away, away from the single-minded absorption of learning. Our students of today live in a whirl and clatter of "student activities." They have, in any large college, at least a hundred organizations and societies. They are "all up!" for this today and "all out!" for that tomorrow. Life is a continuous rally! a rah, rah! a parade! They play no games:

they use teams for that. But exercise, and air, is their life. They *root,* in an organized hysteria, a code of signals telling them what to feel. They root, they rush, they organize, they play politics, run newspapers—and when they step from college into life, they fit it absolutely, having lived already.

No one is denying here what fine men and women college makes, physically fine and mentally alert. Any one of them could run an elevator the day he steps out of college.

But there's something wanting: do they *think?* Or is there anything after all to think about? And yet, surely, in the long run the world has lived on its speculative minds. Or hasn't it?

Some who think of course there must be. You can't submerge humanity in two generations. But mostly, I believe, the little poets fade out on their first-year benches, and the wistful intelligence learns to say *"Rah! Rah!"* and is lost.

Not so in my college. There will be no newspaper, except a last week's paper from the back counties of New England. There will be no politics because there will be no offices to run for. My students will control nothing. The whole movement of student control is a mistake. They're so busy controlling that they're not students.

They shall play games all they want to, but as games, not as a profession, not as college advertising—and no gate receipts. Till only a few years ago the country that taught the world its games, played them as apart from money—as far apart as sheer necessity allowed. If Waterloo was won on the playing fields of Eton (it wasn't, really: it was won in Belgium), there was at least no stadium at two dollars a seat.

One asks, perhaps, about the endowments, about the benefactors of my ideal college. The benefactors are all dead: or at least they must act as if they were. Years ago on the prairies many authorities claimed that the only good Indian was a dead Indian. It may not have been true. But it is certainly true that the best college benefactor is a dead one. After all, the reward in the long run is his, those sculptured letters graven in the stone, "To the greater glory of God and in memory of Johannes Smith." That, in a college among elm trees—that's worth a lifetime of gifts, given and given gladly. Such things should best be graven in Latin. In my college they will be; Latin and lots of it, all over the place, with the mystic conspiracy of pretence, the wholesome humbug, that those who see it know what it means. Latin lasts. English seems to alter every thousand years or so. It's like the tariff that I named above—too mobile for academic use.

As with the benefactors, so with the managing trustees who look after the money and never lose it. Not dead, these, but very silent: solid men who don't need to talk and don't, but who can invest a million dollars over three depressions, and there it still is, like gold in a pot in the Pyramids. You find them chiefly in New England, at least I seem to have seen them there, more than anywhere else. They are at the head of huge investment businesses, so big that you never hear of them. Mostly, if they don't talk, it means that they are thinking where to place fifty million dollars. You see, they hate to break it.

And women? The arrangements in my college for the women students, and the women's dormitories? Oh, no—no, thank you. There aren't any women. Coeducation is a wonderful thing for women: college girls under coeducation leave college more fit to leave college than any others. College girls are better companions, better wives (as your own or as someone else's) than any others. It's the women who have made our college life the bright, happy thing it is—too bright, too happy.

But men can't *study* when women are around. And it's not only the students. If I let the women in, they'd get round some of my dusty old professors, and marry them—and good-bye to Machiavelli, and the higher thought.

THE SABER-TOOTH CURRICULUM [1]

J. ABNER PEDDIWELL

THE FIRST great educational theorist and practitioner of whom my imagination has any record was a man of Chellean times whose full name was New-Fist Hammer-Maker but whom, for convenience, I shall hereafter call New-Fist.

New-Fist was a doer, in spite of the fact that there was little in his environment with which to do anything very complex. You have undoubtedly heard of the pear-shaped chipped-stone tool which archaeologists call the *coup-de-poing* [*sic*] or fist hammer. New-Fist gained his name and a considerable local prestige by producing one of these artifacts in a less rough and more useful form than any previously known to his tribe. His hunting clubs were generally superior weapons, moreover, and his fire-using techniques were patterns of simplicity and precision. He knew how to do things his community needed to have done, and he had the energy and will to go ahead and do them. By virtue of these characteristics he was an educated man.

New-Fist was also a thinker. Then, as now, there were few lengths to which men would not go to avoid the labor and pain of thought. More readily than his fellows, New-Fist pushed himself beyond these lengths to the point where cerebration was inevitable. The same quality of intelligence which led him into the socially approved activity of producing a superior artifact also led him to engage in the socially disapproved practice of thinking. When other men gorged themselves on the proceeds of a successful hunt and vegetated in dull stupor for many hours thereafter, New-Fist ate a little less than his comrades to sit [*sic*] by the fire and think. He would stare moodily at the flickering flames and wonder

1. By permission from *The Saber-Tooth Curriculum and Other Essays,* by J. Abner Peddiwell. Copyright 1939. McGraw-Hill Book Company, Inc.

about various parts of his environment until he finally got to the point where he became strongly dissatisfied with the accustomed ways of his tribe. He began to catch glimpses of ways in which life might be made better for himself, his family, and his group. By virtue of this development, he became a dangerous man.

This was the background that made this doer and thinker hit upon the concept of a conscious, systematic education. The immediate stimulus which put him directly into the practice of education came from watching his children at play. He saw these children at the cave entrance before the fire engaged in activity with bones and sticks and brightly colored pebbles. He noted that they seemed to have no purpose in their play beyond immediate pleasure in the activity itself. He compared their activity with that of the grown-up members of the tribe. The children played for fun; the adults worked for security and enrichment of their lives. The children dealt with bones, sticks, and pebbles; the adults dealt with food, shelter, and clothing. The children protected themselves from boredom; the adults protected themselves from danger.

"If I could only get these children to do the things that will give more and better food, shelter, clothing, and security," thought New-Fist, "I would be helping this tribe to have a better life. When the children grew up, they would have more meat to eat, more skins to keep them warm, better caves in which to sleep, and less danger from the striped death with the curving teeth that walks these trails by night."

Having set up an educational goal, New-Fist proceeded to construct a curriculum for reaching that goal. "What things must we tribesmen know how to do in order to live with full bellies, warm backs, and minds free from fear?" he asked himself.

To answer this question, he ran various activities over in his mind. "We have to catch fish with our bare hands in the pool far up the creek beyond that big bend," he said to himself. "We have to catch them in the same way in the pool just this side of the bend. And so we catch them in the next pool and the next and the next. Always we catch them with our bare hands."

Thus New-Fist discovered the first subject of the first curriculum: fish-grabbing-with-the-bare-hands.

"Also we club the little woolly horses," he continued with his analysis. "We club them along the bank of the creek where they come down to drink. We club them in the thickets where they lie down to sleep. We club them in the upland meadow where they graze. Wherever we find them we club them."

So woolly-horse-clubbing was seen to be the second main subject of the curriculum.

"And finally we drive away the saber-tooth tigers with fire," New-Fist went on in his thinking. "We drive them from the mouths of our caves with fire. We drive them from our trails with burning branches. We wave firebrands to drive them from our drinking-hole. Always we have to drive them away, and always we drive them with fire."

Thus was discovered the third subject: saber-tooth-tiger-scaring-with-fire.

Having developed a curriculum, New-Fist took his children with him as he went about his activities. He gave them an opportunity to practice these three subjects. The children liked to learn. It was more fun for them to engage in these purposeful activities than to play with colored stones just for the fun of it. They learned the new activities well, and so the educational system was a success.

As New-Fist's children grew older, it was plain to see that they had an advantage over other children who had never been educated systematically. Some of the more intelligent members of the tribe began to do as New-Fist had done, and the teaching of fish-grabbing, horse-clubbing, and tiger-scaring came more and more to be accepted as the heart of real education.

For a long time, however, there were certain more conservative members of the tribe who resisted the new, formal educational system on religious grounds. "The Great Mystery who speaks in thunder and moves in lightning," they announced impressively, "the Great Mystery who gives men life and takes it from them as he wills—if that Great Mystery had wanted children to practice fish-grabbing, horse-clubbing, and tiger-scaring, he would have taught them these activities himself by implanting in their natures instincts for fish-grabbing, horse-clubbing, and tiger-scaring. New-Fist is not only impious to attempt something the Great Mystery never wanted to have done; he is also a damned fool for trying to change human nature."

Whereupon approximately half of these critics took up the solemn chant, "If you oppose the will of the Great Mystery, you must die," and the remainder sang derisively in unison, "You can't change human nature."

Being an educational statesman as well as an educational administrator and theorist, New-Fist replied politely to both arguments. To the more theologically minded he said that, as a matter of fact, the Great Mystery had ordered this new work done, that he even did the work himself by causing the children to want to learn, that children could not learn by themselves without divine aid, that they could not learn at all except through the power of the Great Mystery, and that nobody could really understand the will of the Great Mystery concerning fish, horses, and saber-tooth tigers unless he had been well grounded in these fundamental subjects. To the human-nature-cannot-be-changed-shouters, New-Fist pointed out the fact that paleolithic culture had attained its high level by changes in human nature, and that it seemed almost unpatriotic to deny the very process which had made the community great.

"I know you, my fellow tribesmen," the pioneer educator ended his argument gravely, "I know you as humble and devoted servants of the Great Mystery. I know that you would not for one moment consciously oppose yourselves to his will. I know you as intelligent and loyal citizens of this great cave-realm, and I know that your pure and noble patriotism will not permit you to do anything which will block the development of that most cave-realmish of all our institutions—the paleolithic educational system. Now that you understand the true nature and purpose of this institution, I am serenely confident that there are no reasonable lengths to which you will not go in its defense and its support."

By this appeal the forces of conservatism were won over to the side of the new school, and in due time everybody who was anybody in the community knew that the heart of a good education lay in the three subjects of fish-grabbing, horse-clubbing, and tiger-scaring. New-Fist and his contemporaries grew old and were gathered by the Great Mystery to the Land of the Sunset far down the creek. Other men followed their educational ways more and more until at last all the children of the tribe were practiced systematically in the three fundamentals. Thus the tribe prospered and was happy in the possession of adequate meat, skins, and security.

It is to be supposed that all would have gone well forever with this good educational system if conditions of life in that community had remained forever the same. But conditions changed, and life which had once been so safe and happy in the cave-realm valley became insecure and disturbing.

A new ice age was approaching in that part of the world. A great glacier came down from the neighboring mountain range to the north. Year after year it crept closer and closer to the headwaters of the creek which ran through the tribe's valley, until at length it reached the stream and began to melt into the water. Dirt and gravel which the glacier had collected on its long journey were dropped into the creek. The water grew muddy. What had once been a crystal-clear stream in which one could easily see the bottom was now a milky stream into which one could not see at all.

At once the life of the community was changed in one very important respect. It was no longer possible to catch fish with the bare hands. The fish could not be seen in the muddy water. For some years, moreover, the fish in this creek had been getting more timid, agile, and intelligent. The stupid, clumsy, brave fish, of which originally there had been a great many, had been caught with the bare hands for fish generation after fish generation, until only fish of superior intelligence and agility were left. These smart fish, hiding in the muddy water under the newly deposited glacial boulders, eluded the hands of the most expertly trained fish-grabbers. Those tribesmen who had studied advanced fish-grabbing in the secondary school could do no better than their less well-educated fellows who had taken only an elementary course in the subject, and even the university graduates with majors in ichthyology were baffled by this problem. No matter how good a man's fish-grabbing education had been, he could not grab fish when he could not find fish to grab.

The melting waters of the approaching ice-sheet also made the country wetter. The ground became marshy far back from the banks of the creek. The stupid woolly horses, standing only five or six hands high and running on four-toed front feet and three-toed hind feet, although admirable objects for clubbing, had one dangerous characteristic. They were ambitious. They all wanted to learn how to run on their middle toes. They all had visions of becoming powerful and aggressive animals instead of little and timid ones. They dreamed of a far distant day when some of their descendants would be sixteen hands high, weigh more than half a ton, and be able to pitch their would-be riders into the dirt. They knew they could never attain these goals in a wet, marshy country, so they all went east to the dry, open plains, far from the paleolithic hunting grounds. Their places were taken by little antelopes who came down with the ice sheet and were so shy and speedy and had so keen a scent for danger that no one could approach them closely enough to club them.

The best-trained horse-clubbers went out day after day and employed the most efficient techniques taught in the schools, but day after day they returned empty-handed. A horse-clubbing education of the highest type could get no results when there were no horses to club.

Finally, to complete the disruption of paleolithic life and education, the new dampness in the air gave the saber-tooth tigers pneumonia, a disease to which the animals were peculiarly susceptible and to which most of them succumbed. A few moth-eaten specimens crept south to the desert, it is true, but they were pitifully few and weak representatives of a once numerous and powerful race.

So there were no tigers to scare in the paleolithic community, and the best tiger-scaring techniques became only academic exercises, good in themselves, perhaps, but not necessary for tribal security. Yet this danger to the people was lost only to be replaced by another and even greater danger, for with the advancing ice-sheet came ferocious glacial bears which were not afraid of fire, which walked the trails by day as well as by night, and which could not be driven away by the most advanced methods developed in the tiger-scaring courses of the schools.

The community was now in a very difficult situation. There was no fish or meat for food, no hides for clothing, and no security from the hairy death that walked the trails day and night. Adjustment to this difficulty had to be made at once if the tribe was not to become extinct.

Fortunately for the tribe, however, there were men in it of the old New-Fist breed, men who had the ability to do and the daring to think. One of them stood by the muddy stream, his stomach contracting with hunger pains, longing for some way to get a fish to eat. Again and again he had tried the old fish-grabbing technique that day, hoping desperately that at last it might work, but now in black despair he finally rejected all that he had learned in the schools and looked about him for some new way to get fish from that stream. There were stout but slender vines hanging from trees along the bank. He pulled them down and began to fasten them together more or less aimlessly. As he worked, the vision of what he might do to satisfy his hunger and that of his crying children back in the cave grew clearer. His black despair lightened a little. He worked more rapidly and intelligently. At last he had it—a net, a crude seine. He called a companion and explained the device. The two men took the net into the water, into pool after pool, and in one hour they caught more fish—intelligent fish in muddy water—than the whole tribe could have caught in a day under the best fish-grabbing conditions.

Another intelligent member of the tribe wandered hungrily through the woods where once the stupid little horses had abounded but where now only the elusive antelope could be seen. He had tried the horse-clubbing technique on the antelope until he was fully convinced of its futility. He knew that one would starve who relied on school learning to get him meat in those woods. Thus it was that he, too, like the fish-net inventor, was finally impelled by hunger to new ways. He bent a strong, springy young tree over an antelope trail, hung a noosed vine therefrom, and fastened the device in so ingenious a fashion that the passing animal would release a trigger and be snared neatly when the tree jerked upright. By setting a line of these snares, he was able in one night to secure more meat and skins than a dozen horse-clubbers in the old days had secured in a week.

A third tribesman, determined to meet the problem of the ferocious bears, also forgot what he had been taught in school and began to think in a direct and radical fashion. Finally, as a result of this thinking, he dug a deep pit in a bear trail, covered it with branches in such a way that a bear would walk on it unsuspectingly, fall through to the bottom, and remain trapped until the tribesmen could come and despatch him with sticks and stones at their leisure. The inventor showed his friends how to dig and camouflage other pits until all the trails around the community were furnished with them. Thus the tribe had even more security than before and in addition had the great additional store of meat and skins which they secured from the captured bears.

As the knowledge of these new inventions spread, all the members of the tribe were engaged in familiarizing themselves with the new ways of living. Men worked hard at making fish nets, setting antelope snares, and digging bear pits. The tribe was busy and prosperous.

There were a few thoughtful men who asked questions as they worked. Some of them even criticized the schools.

"These new activities of net-making and operating, snare-setting, and pit-digging are indispensable to modern existence," they said. "Why can't they be taught in school?"

The safe and sober majority had a quick reply to this naive question. "School!" they snorted derisively. "You aren't in school now. You are out here in the dirt working to preserve the life and happiness of the tribe. What have these practical activities got to do with schools? You're not saying lessons now. You'd better forget your lessons and your academic ideals of fish-grabbing, horse-clubbing, and tiger-scaring if you want to eat, keep warm, and have some measure of security from sudden death."

The radicals persisted a little in their questioning. "Fish-net making and using, antelope-snare construction and operation, and bear-catching and killing," they pointed out, "require intelligence and skills—things we claim to develop in schools. They are also activities we need to know. Why can't the schools teach them?"

But most of the tribe, and particularly the wise old men who controlled the schools, smiled indulgently at this suggestion. "That wouldn't be *education*," they said gently.

"But why wouldn't it be?" asked the radicals.

"Because it would be mere training," explained the old men patiently. "With all the intricate details of fish-grabbing, horse-clubbing, and tiger-scaring—the standard cultural subjects—the school curriculum is too crowded now. We can't add these fads and frills of net-making, antelope-snaring and—of all things—bear-killing. Why, at the very thought, the body of the great New-Fist, founder of our paleolithic educational system, would turn over in its burial cairn. What we need to do is to give our young people a more thorough grounding in the fundamentals. Even the graduates of the secondary schools don't know the art of fish-grabbing in any complete sense nowadays; they swing their horse clubs awkwardly, too; and as for the old science of tiger-scaring—well, even the teachers seem to lack the real flair for the subject which we oldsters got in our teens and never forgot."

"But how can any person with good sense be interested in such useless activities?" exploded one of the radicals. "What is the point of trying to catch fish with the bare hands when it just can't be done any more? How can a boy learn to club horses when there are no horses left to club? And why should children try to scare tigers with fire when the tigers are dead and gone?"

"Don't be foolish," said the wise old men, smiling most kindly smiles. "We don't teach fish-grabbing to grab fish; we teach it to develop a generalized agility which can never be developed by mere training. We don't teach horse-clubbing to club horses; we teach it to develop a generalized strength in the learner which he can never get from so prosaic and specialized a thing as antelope snare-setting. We don't teach tiger-scaring to scare tigers; we teach it for the purpose of giving that noble courage which carries over into all the affairs of life and which can never come from so base an activity as bear-killing."

All the radicals were silenced by this statement, all except the one who was most radical of all. He felt abashed, it is true, but he was so radical that he made one last protest.

"But—but anyway," he suggested, "you will have to admit that times have changed. Couldn't you please try these more up-to-date activities? Maybe they have some educational value, after all."

Even the man's fellow radicals felt that this was going a little too far.

The wise old men were indignant. Their smiles faded. "If you had any education yourself," they said severely, "you would know that the essence of true education is timelessness. It is something that endures through changing conditions like a solid rock standing squarely and firmly in the middle of a raging torrent. You must know that there are some eternal verities, and the saber-tooth curriculum is one of them!"

INTRODUCTORY LECTURE[1]

A. E. HOUSMAN

THE acquisition of knowledge needs no formal justification: its true sanction is a much simpler affair, and inherent in itself. People are too prone to torment themselves with devising far-fetched reasons: they cannot be content with the simple truth asserted by Aristotle: "all men possess by nature a craving for knowledge." πάντες ἄνθρωποι τοῦ εἰδέναι ὀρέγονται φύσει. This is no rare endowment scattered sparingly from heaven that falls on a few heads and passes others by: curiosity, the desire to know things as they are, is a craving no less native to the being of man, no less universal through mankind, than the craving for food and drink. And do you suppose that such a desire means nothing? The very definition of the good, says Aristotle again, is that which all desire. Whatever is pleasant is good, unless it can be shewn that in the long run it is harmful, or, in other words, not pleasant but unpleasant. Mr. Spencer himself on another subject speaks thus: "So profound an ignorance is there of the laws of life, that men do not even know that their sensations are their natural guides, and (when not rendered morbid by long continued disobedience) their trustworthy guides." The desire of knowledge does not need, nor could it possibly possess, any higher or more authentic sanction than the happiness which attends its gratification.

Perhaps it will be objected that we see, every day of our lives, plenty of people who exhibit no pleasure in learning and experience no desire to know; people, as Plato agreeably puts it, who wallow in ignorance with the complacency of a brutal hog. We do; and here is the reason. If the cravings of hunger and thirst are denied satisfaction, if a man is kept from food and drink, the man starves to death, and there is an end of him. This is a result which arrests the attention of even the least observant mind; so it is generally recognised that hunger and thirst cannot be neglected with impunity, that a man ought to eat and drink. But if the craving for knowledge is denied satisfaction, the result which follows is not so striking to the eye. The man, worse luck, does not starve to death. He still preserves the aspect and motions of a living human being; so people think that the hunger and thirst for knowledge can be neglected with impunity. And yet, though the man does not die altogether, part of him dies, part of him starves to death: as Plato says, he never attains completeness and health, but walks lame

1. From A. E. Housman, *Introductory Lecture,* 1937, pp. 26–36. Copyright by The Macmillan Company. By permission of The Macmillan Company, publishers.

to the end of his life and returns imperfect and good for nothing to the world below.

But the desire of knowledge, stifle it though you may, is none the less originally born with every man; and nature does not implant desires in us for nothing, nor endow us with faculties in vain. "Sure," says Hamlet,

> Sure, He that made us with such large discourse,
> Looking before and after, gave us not
> That capability and godlike reason
> To fust in us unused.

The faculty of learning is ours that we may find in its exercise that delight which arises from the unimpeded activity of any energy in the groove nature meant it to run in. Let a man acquire knowledge not for this or that external and incidental good which may chance to result from it, but for itself; not because it is useful or ornamental, but because it is knowledge, and therefore good for man to acquire. "Brothers," says Ulysses in Dante, when with his old and tardy companions he had left Seville on the right hand and Ceuta on the other, and was come to that narrow pass where Hercules assigned his landmarks to hinder man from venturing farther: "Brothers, who through a hundred thousand dangers have reached the West, deny not, to this brief vigil of your senses that remains, experience of the unpeopled world behind the sunset. Consider of what seed ye are sprung: ye were not formed to live like brutes, but to follow virtue and knowledge." For knowledge resembles virtue in this, and differs in this from other possessions, that it is not merely a means of procuring good, but is good in itself simply: it is not a coin which we pay down to purchase happiness, but has happiness indissolubly bound up with it. Fortitude and continence and honesty are not commended to us on the ground that they conduce, as on the whole they do conduce, to material success, nor yet on the ground that they will be rewarded hereafter: those whose office it is to exhort mankind to virtue are ashamed to degrade the cause they plead by proffering such lures as these. And let us too disdain to take lower ground in commending knowledge: let us insist that the pursuit of knowledge, like the pursuit of righteousness, is part of man's duty to himself, and remember the Scripture where it is written: "He that refuseth instruction despiseth his own soul."

I will not say, as Prof. Tyndall has somewhere said, that all happiness belongs to him who can say from his heart "I covet truth." Entire happiness is not attainable either by this or by any other method. Nay it may be urged on the contrary that the pursuit of truth in some directions is even injurious to happiness, because it compels us to take leave of delusions which were pleasant while they lasted. It may be urged that the light shed on the origin and destiny of man by the pursuit of truth in some directions is not altogether a cheerful light. It may be urged that man stands to-day in the position of one who has been reared from his cradle as the child of a noble race and the heir

to great possessions, and who finds at his coming of age that he has been deceived alike as to his origin and his expectations, that he neither springs of the high lineage he fancied, nor will inherit the vast estate he looked for, but must put off his towering pride, and contract his boundless hopes, and begin the world anew from a lower level: and this, it may be urged, comes of pursuing knowledge. But even conceding this, I suppose the answer to be that knowledge, and especially disagreeable knowledge, cannot by any art be totally excluded even from those who do not seek it. Wisdom, said Aeschylus long ago, comes to men whether they will or no. The house of delusions is cheap to build, but draughty to live in, and ready at any instant to fall; and it is surely truer prudence to move our furniture betimes into the open air than to stay indoors until our tenement tumbles about our ears. It is and it must in the long run be better for a man to see things as they are than to be ignorant of them; just as there is less fear of stumbling or of striking against corners in the daylight than in the dark.

Nor again will I pretend that, as Bacon asserts, "the pleasure and delight of knowledge and learning far surpasseth all other in nature." This is too much the language of a salesman crying his own wares. The pleasures of the intellect are notoriously less vivid than either the pleasures of sense or the pleasures of the affections, and therefore, especially in the season of youth, the pursuit of knowledge is likely enough to be neglected and lightly esteemed in comparison with other pursuits offering much stronger immediate attractions. But the pleasure of learning and knowing, though not the keenest, is yet the least perishable of pleasures; the least subject to external things, and the play of chance, and the wear of time. And as a prudent man puts money by to serve as a provision for the material wants of his old age, so too he needs to lay up against the end of his days provision for the intellect. As the years go by, comparative values are found to alter: Time, says Sophocles, takes many things which once were pleasures and brings them nearer to pain. In the day when the strong men shall bow themselves, and desire shall fail, it will be a matter of yet more concern than now, whether one can say "my mind to me a kingdom is"; and whether the windows of the soul look out upon a broad and delightful landscape, or face nothing but a brick wall.

Well then, once we have recognised that knowledge in itself is good for man, we shall need to invent no pretexts for studying this subject or that; we shall import no extraneous considerations of use or ornament to justify us in learning one thing rather than another. If a certain department of knowledge specially attracts a man, let him study that, and study it because it attracts him; and let him not fabricate excuses for that which requires no excuse, but rest assured that the reason why it most attracts him is that it is best for him. The majority of mankind, as is only natural, will be most attracted by those sciences which most nearly concern human life; those sciences which, in Bacon's phrase, are drenched in flesh and blood, or, in the more elegant language of the *Daily Telegraph,* palpitate with actuality. The men who are attracted to the drier and the less palpitating sciences, say logic or pure mathematics or textual criticism, are likely to be fewer in number; but they are not to suppose that the comparative unpopularity of such learning renders it any the less worthy of pursuit. Nay they may if they like console themselves with Bacon's observation that "this same *lumen siccum* doth parch and offend most men's watery and soft natures," and infer, if it pleases them, that their natures are less soft and watery than other men's. But be that as it may, we can all dwell together in unity without crying up our own pursuits or depreciating the pursuits of others on factitious grounds. We are not like the Ottoman sultans of old time, who thought they could never enjoy a moment's security till they had murdered all their brothers. There is no rivalry between the studies of Arts and Laws and Science but the rivalry of fellow-soldiers in striving which can most victoriously achieve the common end of all, to set back the frontier of darkness.

It is the glory of God, says Solomon, to conceal a thing: but the honour of kings is to search out a matter. Kings have long abdicated that province; and we students are come into their inheritance: it is our honour to search out the things which God has concealed. In Germany at Easter time they hide coloured eggs about the house and the garden that the children may amuse themselves in hunting after them and finding them. It is to some such game of hide-and-seek that we are invited by that power which planted in us the desire to find out what is concealed, and stored the universe with hidden things that we might delight ourselves in discovering them. And the pleasure of discovery differs from other pleasures in this, that it is shadowed by no fear of satiety on the one hand or of frustration on the other. Other desires perish in their gratification, but the desire of knowledge never: the eye is not satisfied with seeing nor the ear filled with hearing. Other desires become the occasion of pain through dearth of the material to gratify them, but not the desire of knowledge: the sum of things to be known is inexhaustible, and however long we read we shall never come to the end of our story-book. So long as the mind of man is what it is, it will continue to exult in advancing on the unknown throughout the infinite field of the universe; and the tree of knowledge will remain for ever, as it was in the beginning, a tree to be desired to make one wise.

II
READING AND WRITING

·READING·

OF STUDIES[1]

FRANCIS BACON

Studies serve for delight, for ornament, and for ability. Their chief use for delight is in privateness and retiring; for ornament, is in discourse; and for ability, is in the judgment and disposition of business; for expert men can execute, and perhaps judge of particulars, one by one; but the general counsels, and the plots and marshaling of affairs come best from those that are learned. To spend too much time in studies is sloth; to use them too much for ornament is affectation; to make judgment wholly by their rules is the humor of a scholar. They perfect nature, and are perfected by experience; for natural abilities are like natural plants, that need pruning by study; and studies themselves do give forth directions too much at large, except they be bounded in by experience. Crafty men contemn studies, simple men admire them, and wise men use them; for they teach not their own use; but that is a wisdom without them and above them, won by observation. Read not to contradict and confute, nor to believe and take for granted, nor to find talk and discourse, but to weigh and consider. Some books are to be tasted, others to be swallowed, and some few to be chewed and digested; that is, some books are to be read only in parts; others to be read but not curiously, and some few to be read wholly, and with diligence and attention. Some books also may be read by deputy, and extracts made of them by others; but that would be only in the less important arguments and the meaner sort of books; else distilled books are, like common dis-

1. From *The Essayes or Counsels, Civill and Morall* (enlarged ed., London, 1625), No. 50. The text has been somewhat modernized.

tilled waters, flashy things. Reading maketh a full man; conference a ready man; and writing an exact man. And, therefore, if a man write little, he had need have a great memory; if he confer little, he had need have a present wit; and if he read little, he had need have much cunning, to seem to know that he doth not. Histories make men wise; poets, witty; the mathematics, subtle; natural philosophy, deep; moral, grave; logic and rhetoric, able to contend; *Abeunt studia in mores.*[2] Nay, there is no stand or impediment in the wit but may be wrought out by fit studies; like as diseases of the body may have appropriate exercises. Bowling is good for the stone and reins, shooting for the lungs and breast, gentle walking for the stomach, riding for the head and the like. So if a man's wit be wandering, let him study the mathematics; for in demonstrations, if his wit be called away never so little, he must begin again. If his wit be not apt to distinguish or find differences, let him study the schoolmen; for they are *cymini sectores.*[3] If he be not apt to beat over matters, and to call up one thing to prove and illustrate another, let him study the lawyers' cases; so every defect of the mind may have a special receipt.

2. Studies form manners.
3. Dividers of cuminseed, i.e., hairsplitters.

THE LIBRARY[1]

CHAUNCEY B. TINKER

Soon after the members of the Freshman Class are admitted to college, they are addressed by a series of upper-classmen who represent the various activities with which the place abounds. The post of honour is usually given to the captain of the football team, who pleads for a large squad and attendance at the games. The football player is succeeded by those who advertise the other sports; and they, in turn, by the representatives of the literary world: students are not to forget the importance of the college newspaper (be it daily or weekly is a matter of no consequence). There are often social and fraternity appeals added to the confusion; and, lastly, religious and scholarly activities—the class deacon and the president of Phi Beta Kappa—are given a belated hearing. But even then, when the newly-enrolled college-man has been shown all the rewards that may come from giving his allegiance to the world, it is doubtful whether any of the speakers will have mentioned the College Library.

This of course is because the Library has no outward and visible reward to offer to its devotees. Even to many who might become devotees it seems like a cold and dusty place, where the books are locked away in distant "stacks"

1. From *On Going to College: A Symposium,* 1938, pp. 293–298. By permission of Oxford University Press, New York.

which the student cannot visit, and which are too often presided over by male or female dragons whose obvious aim seems to be to protect them from those who wish to use them. There is an old story told of a triumphant librarian who, on a famous occasion, boasted that all the books save one were on the shelves, and, added he, "I know where that is, and to-morrow the library will be complete." In opposition to such a theory as this it would be wiser to contend that the ideal library is one in which the shelves are empty, since the books are all in circulation. Between these two contrary states, the College Library preserves a precarious life. The circulation of its books is like the circulation of the blood, passing constantly back and forth from the heart to the members of the body.

The frequent assertion that the Library is the heart and center of the College is the simple truth. All scholarly work, and all undergraduate study as well, consists either of the reading and interpretation of the recorded thought of the past or of the setting down of new information for the guidance of posterity. This is true of science as well as of the "humanities." Experiments made in laboratories are recorded, first of all, in note-books and later in the learned publications of the science concerned. The results of all such work are promptly given to the world, so that others may use and profit by them. If the power of recording thought in writing, or print, which is only another form of writing, were taken from us,—by divine *fiat,* let us say,—all civilization would cease at once, and we should relapse into the state of beasts.

The average devotee of a library passes, commonly, through three stages. A man's first notion regarding a public library is that it is filled with books to amuse our leisure. It is very probable that the student coming to college has been in the habit of drawing from the town-library such fiction as he has read. If that library has been wisely administered, he has gradually learned that there are many other uses to which it may be put, if only he is so disposed. And this is, in general, a healthy notion at that time of life. A boy has gained a great deal if he merely realizes that sources of intellectual amusement are to be found within public library walls, and he should continue to derive such entertainment from the college library.

Meanwhile in his classes the student will have been required to purchase certain books for study, and the mastery of them will be demanded by his teachers; but, in addition to this, he will be sent to the college library to consult other books without any intimation from his instructors that he should purchase them. He is only to learn how to consult these books, how to bring the information that he will find there into relation with the subject as set forth in his text-book. He will then learn that no book can be adequately understood by itself alone, but will yield up its treasure only when its words are compared with those of other books, and its truths tested by the experience of other men. The student will find that some of the books to which his attention has been directed are to be quickly consulted and quickly laid aside, as containing but little—though that little may be of great importance—that is related to the subject which he is investigating. Others may well seem to him more important than his text-book, and he may indeed in certain cases come to realize that his text-book has been quarried out of some larger and grander treatise on the subject. Gradually he will come to understand the truth of Bacon's words, "Some books are to be tasted, others to be swallowed, and some few to be chewed and digested; that is some books are to be read only in parts; others to be read, but not curiously; and some few to be read wholly, and with diligence and attention." Such counsel as this of Bacon's implies the guidance of a teacher and the existence of a library to which the student may be sent. No teacher will be content if his instruction ends in his class-room, and a student will have begun the educational process only when he carries away the lessons which he has received in the class-room, not as a body of dogma, to be received as *de fide,* but as an organic and growing thing to be constantly nourished by human intercourse and by private study.

After a student has thus used the library for many months, he will discover that his work there has constituted a kind of initiation into scholarship, or what is more narrowly described as "research." He will find that in his restless pursuit of elusive facts, his examination of sources, and his comparison of one man's view with another's, he has come into possession of information and of ideas which may fairly be termed *new*—in short, that he has entered the very narrow group of those who have a right to an opinion on the matter. He may even come to possess more knowledge of the subject than anybody else. His knowledge may be humble and remote from human interest; it may even be trifling information which he has uncovered; but the experience of thus acquiring it is not trifling, for in it he may see reflected the whole process and progress of learning. He will come to understand why scholars enclose themselves in libraries and scientists in laboratories; why lawyers must be perpetually concerned with precedents—the history—of their profession; and why physicians who aspire to excel must be always studying the latest developments of the art of healing. For every true exponent of a profession is interested not only in learning but in the progress of learning. And the student will come to see that the library or laboratory is a temple dedicated to a faith.

When he has been fully initiated as a scholar, he will also understand why professional practitioners are always talking of documents and of "original sources." He will understand why a scholar is peculiarly excited by written evidence coming to him out of the remote past, in words written long ago by a hand that has now crumbled to dust. *Litera scripta manet.*[2] Here is something that bears testimony to conditions of life which have long since passed away, and are to be rescued and made to live again only by the efforts of scholars. I cannot here do better than to quote the words of a collector of autograph letters, whose name I do not know, but who summarized very well what I am trying to put before the college student:

2. The written word remains.

An autograph is not only a rarity, but it is a unique rarity. You cannot duplicate it. And it is not only a unique rarity; it is, in a real sense, the embodiment of a human personality. One touches hands, so to speak, with the writer himself; and if the writer be a famous person who, by his genius, has won our hearts, the autograph becomes a veritable living thing. It speaks for the man in a way that no printed page can.

That is, I think, a happy expression of the delight which a scholar feels when, at last, he holds in his hand the written evidence on which a recorded fact reposes. Happy is the student who, while yet in college, has such an experience. It is only in a library that he can have it.

I must not conclude these remarks without some word regarding the value of a student's *private* library. Nothing can ever take the place of that. Not the British Museum, not the Bibliothèque Nationale can take the place of the books which the student has bought and read for their own beloved sake. They are like the twenty books clad in black or red, which were prized by Chaucer's Clerk above all the pleasures of the world. To live in the daily presence of a few great books is itself an education. There is something in their very physical presence which invites us to turn and to return to them, till at last old acquaintance begets in us a likeness to our ancient associates, the worthies of the world.

No personal library can ever discharge the function of a great college library, as no college library can ever be to a man what his own humble collection of well-worn books may be; but love of one begets a love of the other, and as there is distinction in a great college library, so there may be distinction in a private assemblage of books, however small.

There is an old and perhaps foolish query about the books which one would wish to take with him if he were to sojourn upon a desert island. But like some other foolish questions, the problem which it sets us is worth pondering. Upon the voyage of life there are few books of which we may hope to make lifelong companions; and, as in the other relations of life, it behoves us, if we hope to avoid calamity on our voyage, to choose our mates with discretion.

UNREQUIRED READING[1]

IRWIN EDMAN

THE title of this essay may strike you as a typographical error. You may be saying to yourself that the writer really means required reading, and the phrase

1. *Saturday Review of Literature,* Nov. 4, 1950, pp. 9–10, 36–38. Copyright, The Saturday Review Associates, 25 W. 45th St., New York City. Reprinted by permission of the author and the publisher.

conjures up for you, I suspect, lists distributed on the first days of college courses: Volume One of this distinguished scholar's work on the Byzantine empire in the fourth century, that brochure on the economic interpretation of the Constitution, this pundit's principles of economics, that pedant's source book.

Or, perhaps, still under the apprehension that I mean required reading, you are reminded of what by now is one of the more maddening insolences of criticism, or at any rate of book reviewing. "This," says Mr. Notability, "is a *must* book." This in the atomic age is compulsory reading. In a world of anxiety this uneasy novel is not to be passed by.

I beg of you to forget such obligations and responsibilities. To this day you have to forget that you *had* to read "Macbeth" in order to begin to remember how perturbingly moving a play it is. Hardly anyone would reread Burke's "Speech on Conciliation" if he recalled how he had to make an abstract of it in high school. For one forgets the delight in the obligation, the eloquence in the remembered pressure. In one way or another even the nonprofessional reader reads from some felt or alleged obligation, some illusion of responsibility. He reads to know or to be in the know, to acquire a mature mind, to insure peace of soul, to understand what to do when the bomb drops, or when peace breaks out. We read because we feel we must know what's what, who is who, why is why. We read because in some way it seems compulsory to know Gide and Proust and Kafka and Sartre, because existentialism is being talked about, first in the small worlds of the little reviews, and then in the larger domains of the gossip columns, the digests, the library forums at the women's clubs.

In the sociology of our culture reading has, in so far as it has at all survived television and the comic strip, survived as a form of obligation. The student, the publisher, the editor, the scholar, even those, including the ladies who feel only the obligation to be *au courant, à la page,* or knowledgeable, read, for the most part, because they have to or think they have to. Not that anyone in any of these groups has necessarily actually read all that the mandarins of literate society expect or enjoin. At college even the most industrious or conforming of us did not do, as we used to put it, all the assigned reading, despite the ominous final examinations as reasons for doing so.

Nor as adults do we read all the books we are supposed to read. We compromise by reading with care the leading book reviews. For purposes of dinner-party conversation the latter method is not without its virtues. One's mind is not cluttered up with the actual details, one's imagination is not haunted by the actual flavor of the book, and one has a good lead and a good authority on what one is supposed to say and think. This obligation to read fashionable current works, to know this year's Hemingway and next year's Toynbee, to know —or to know about—cybernetics, all this makes it almost impossible even for those who have no professional commitments and concerns with books to retain the quality and status of amateurs and to read books for pleasure, to peruse a volume for pure enjoyment, to read not for food but for love.

The inability, including that of lack of time, to read for pleasure, is perhaps especially to be noticed among those whose professional concern *is* with books. The student, the scholar, the teacher, the editor, the publisher all have to do a good deal of reading for special purposes, in special areas, for special reasons. Even when a student enjoys his required reading in a course he still has in mind, if only half consciously, his responsibilities to a teacher and to an examination. An advanced scholar may enjoy a new monograph in his own field, but he cannot read it simply as a delighted dilettante. The chances are that if it is by a rival scholar his delight would in any case not be unqualified. Even, or particularly, if it is good he may not like it. The brochure is an instrument in his work and also a challenge to his own hypotheses and standards of criticism. He is alerted for errors, inconsistencies, and exaggerations. Even if it is good he cannot read it merely as a pastime. And to the specialist there is usually no time to read books outside the specialty.

The editor and the publisher are in much the same dilemma, even the most imaginative editor, and the type of publisher—not, I am told, too current—who likes books even when he doesn't like authors. He may, like Maxwell Perkins, be adventurously alert for new talent. He may be solicitously on the lookout for genius, but in reading a manuscript he has to read with the hunter's eye, the collector's zeal, rather than with the freedom of pleasure.

And yet somehow reading for the love of it persists, both among those who have to deal with books all the time and among those who read largely to keep up with the Joneses intellectually or earnestly to know the best that is being said and thought in the contemporary world or because they feel they have fallen into a rut of illiteracy, what with the demands of their children, canasta, and television. The man or woman who has to read professionally steals time, sometimes late at night, to recover the youthful and delicious pleasure of reading for its own sake. He has just read a novel of lust and pillage in the Deep South, or of neurosis in Newtown, Conn. His eyes are tired and his mind dulled. And suddenly on his shelves he sees a volume of George Borrow, and he is off selling Bibles in Spain, meeting a liberal mayor in a provincial town, who releases him from arrest because he comes from the land of the great Jeremy Bentham. He picks up Jane Austen and is in the Grand Pump Room at Bath.

To what books does one turn, what pleasures does one rediscover when one is too tired or too indolent or too rebellious to read what one must? I remember as a college student being somewhat shocked to learn that Woodrow Wilson—and, what to me at the time was worse, John Dewey—turned for relaxation to detective stories. Since that time so many eminent persons, including my own valued colleagues, have turned to detective stories, too (and written treatises on their hobby), that I have ceased to be shocked, although I have not arrived at being converted. The detective stories that are simply puzzles seem to me weariness compounded, or those tricked out with a whimsey of culture, pure drivel. There are other avenues of literature to turn to more liberating and enchanting.

The curious fact is that quite difficult books are a relaxation and a pleasure, and complex tomes a delight when one has no immediate responsibility whatever for them. I discovered this very early as have thousands of those who began their reading young. For me the insight came in a branch library of the New York Public Library, where a librarian, Miss Lawrence by name, seeing me somewhat nearsightedly exploring the shelves, came to help me. "Are you looking for anything special?" she asked. Somewhat ashamed, I said that I was not. I was wandering in what to me was a fresh and wonderful wilderness. But I began to discover that there it was a well-organized forest, in which trees of the same family stood beside each other and which some forester had labeled with mystical numbers that indicated relationship. It was naturally the Eight Hundreds that I first wandered among. Even in a small branch library in 1910 New York there were a surprising number of books classified under literature. Close by were the biographies, and the number of novels and lives-and-times I read while I was in my early teens is astonishing to myself now that I look back on it. It is the endlessness of the number of books that both appealed to me and appalled me. At the same age when one has a good appetite physically in a parallel way one is stimulated by quantity in print, and frightened that one may cease to be before one has read everything. I think that was one of the things that impressed me about the novels of William de Morgan and Arnold Bennett, not to add Dickens and Thackeray. These were wonderful vast realms to enter into, to lose one's self in. It was here, too, that one discovered quite by accident, as Henry Adams said he discovered Beethoven by accident in a German beer garden, volumes of history and biography often simply by their title.

It is difficult to know what is so attractive about the title "The Rise of the Dutch Republic" or why it should fascinate a fourteen-year-old boy. "The Oregon Trail" was another matter; any American boy would have his mind stirred by any glance at a page of that stunning work of imaginative history. Next to quantity and variety was the joy of discovering things that because I had heard no one mention them came to me with the force of discovery. I think Hamlin Garland was for me a genuine find. I don't know that I had ever heard anyone refer to him and suddenly I came across a dusty brown book about dusty country. It was called "Main-Travelled Roads," and it gave me a sense of the Middle West more profound, accurate, and touching, I think, than I was to get from "Main Street" years later. Was it (I am quite certain it was) in the same library that I came across "Looking Backward"? It made me a Socialist at the age of fifteen and gave me my first boy's dream of Utopia. But, best of all, I discovered the books in the One Hundreds: philosophy, which dealt with first and last things (there was actually H. G. Wells's book by that title), and psychology, with its books on the working of the human mind. To this day I can never pass a branch library without a thrill of memory. This is where I learnt to read for pleasure and where I discovered the lineaments of nature and life.

I continued to learn thus in college, too, for it is in wandering around the shelves and later among the stacks that one acquires the sense that at almost any random number of library classification one may run across something unexpected in the way of beauty and truth. For the pleasure in reading is far from being that simply of nibbling literary hors d'oeuvres. De Quincey divided books into those of knowledge and those of power, power over our hearts and imagination. But there are books of knowledge that have that power. There happened to be published in this country just at the time I was a freshman the series of volumes written mostly by Britons called the Home University Library. The little yellow volumes contained small masterpieces of exposition of important things, presented without either dulness or pomposity. Bertrand Russell's "Problems of Philosophy," Whitehead's "Introduction to Mathematics," Marett's "Anthropology"—all opened up vistas of unexplored possibility for me, and from H. N. Brailsford's "Shelley, Godwin, and Their Circle" I got more of a sense of the romantic movement in English poetry than from the more pretentious works of scholarship I was asked to read. Not that the book was better than those, but it was small, modest, intimate, *and* I had found it for myself. On the reading lists were always books that were merely suggested, and those seemed ever so much more inviting than those that were commanded. Conybeare's "Myth, Magic, and Morals"—I don't know whether it was as good as it then seemed—but I am sure Fustel de Coulanges's "The Ancient City" was.

As it turned out Fate or accident brought me into a life of professional dealing with books. I read them as a professional student of philosophy, I review them as a professional reviewer, occasionally I read them in manuscript to tell publishers with an intended mixture of shrewdness and academic responsibility whether they are worth publishing for themselves or for profit or for both. But all that reading I do not think really counts, not as entertainment, not as education. It is the unrequired reading one steals time for that is the reader's lifeblood.

The great thing about a book is having it in one's home like a medicine or an analgesic, a stimulus or a soporific when the drugstores are all closed. Late at night one's private library is like a medicine chest. One cannot tell what one will be in the mood for or what one's spirit will most urgently crave. Or if the analogy seems too medicinal, perhaps the refrigerator or the cookie jar will do. Who knows when suddenly, late at night when libraries and bookstores are tight shut, there will come into one's head the sudden passionate need to re-read some Dickens? Or, if the truth be told, to read some of him for the first time? Somewhere one day, in a critic I greatly respected, I found a parenthetic clause which said, "'Our Mutual Friend,' which is, of course, Dickens's masterpiece." I bridled a little at the "of course." I tried to think back to the book itself and to my discomfiture I realized I had never read it. That night I was happy that a year ago I had purchased a set of Dickens in big, clear type on a spacious page. After about fifty pages I began to see the plausibility of the easy dogmatism of my critical friend.

Again there may pop into one's head a passage which had bemused one many years ago, like the opening chapter on the London fog in "Bleak House" or the death of the Bishop's wife in Trollope's "Last Chronicles of Barset," that definitive portrait of a dominating woman in whose death scene, at once ironic and pathetic, one may find one of the places where it is impossible to condescend to Trollope. There are any number of books I should, I think, never have read had I not prudently bought them against the time I should have the time to read them, the letters of Edward Fitzgerald, for example, or those of Lady Mary Wortley Montagu or Kilvert's Diary, the journal of that gifted and obscure provincial English cleric whose tender and acute notes on life and nature, and on his life and nature, came to light only a few years ago. And there are works born to be read perennially like the essays of Emerson, the sermons of Donne.

Raiding the icebox is not half so much fun as raiding one's shelves, and sometimes one is surprised to find what books one has bought or received through the kind (or calculated thoughtfulness) of some publisher heaven knows when. When on earth and where did one pick up Henry James's "Notes of a Son and Brother" with its emotions recollected from boyhood of New York of a century ago? One recalls perhaps where one found "A Little Tour in France." There is the familiar paper-covered Tauchnitz edition of prewar memory found in a little bookshop at Nimes, along with other apparatus, like guide-books for English-speaking tourists visiting the magical landscape of Provence for the first time.

And that by a natural association leads me to consider the reading one has done, not only unrequiredly but unexpectedly largely because of the distributive enterprise of American publishers. The twenty-five-cent, now more likely the thirty-five-cent, book and the Modern Library found in small stationery shops or drugstores in remote prairie towns—what a boon these are to the traveler, how much they provide pleasure and enlightenment for hours that would otherwise be fretfully or dully passed in airports or railway stations waiting for delayed planes or trains. Often it is true that one can go through a whole sheaf of reprints to find nothing save "Blood on the Moon" or "Thunderbird on the Trail," but, especially lately, the foraging is better. Sometimes, because the choices worth consideration are few, one is happily constrained to light upon something that is not exactly in the mood one had been looking for but establishes another mood and opens another realm of gold or truth. What I was hoping for one day, marooned for hours in Great Falls, Montana, was a novel, say, by Virginia Woolf. What I found was George Gamow's "Life and Death of the Sun," a book calculated to give one a more stable sense of proportion, even of orientation on the Korean or any other crisis than could the most comprehensive picture weekly or the most thorough review of the week. These reprint series afford wonderful chances, at odd moments and at minimal expense, to take a look—often at the outset a prejudiced look—at books that have had an undignified popularity, and to discover that even if it isn't true in the phrase of a once-famous advertising slogan that such popularity must be deserved, at least there are reasons popularity is attained, reasons not altogether of high-pressure publicity.

I have written for the most part as if unrequired meant necessarily scattered or relatively trivial reading. There must be earnest souls among my readers who feel that it ought to be said that reading even for pleasure includes the pleasures of knowledge and of thought as well as those of imagination and of fancy. It does. I have been stressing the interest of the general or the common reader. But the general reader is with respect to specific fields always in some mild respect a specialist, even if only in the matter of taste; when Samuel Johnson used the term common reader he meant it as a compliment, and the common reader is often uncommonly serious in his literary pleasures. There are books of knowledge that give twin delights: first that of pleasure in exposition lucidly and persuasively done, and the larger joy of vision of the world—a wider and a more exact vision of the universe around us or some crucial, timely, or timeless aspect of it. There are volumes of the gravest history, the most severe speculative philosophy, poetry, the most concentrated and reflective, so long as they are read not because one feels one must fill in this gap in one's knowledge of medieval history or that hole in one's knowledge of the byways of metaphysics or that era or school of poetry. It is clear that the line between reading and study is not a sharp one. But there is a distinction. One does not just *read* Spinoza's "Ethics" (it is a work demanding the severest concentration) but also one does not always read late at night or when one is quite tired. It is possible to read for fun when one is full of energy and health, on a summer day at a mountain altitude, and on vacation, and it is at such times that such intellectually muscular exercise is a true pleasure. In music there are *divertimenti*, serenades, and bagatelles which are enjoyed simply for their delicious minor selves. In music, too, there are requiem masses, sonatas, and symphonies, and there are the late quartets of Beethoven that at least one serious writer has held to disclose whole other worlds or aspects of *our* whole world not expressible in any other way. Most of this article I have been discussing the *divertimenti* of literature. But there is no essential reason why the most demanding and profound of books should not provide along with the tension of effort the pleasures that one may, I think, without professional bias call philosophical.

The analogy with music is not merely fanciful. In music, too, especially when one is only half and dreamily listening or listening with the unthinking ear, it is in smaller incidental works that one may most acutely be aware of the delicacies of counterpoint and rhythms, of melody, color, and orchestration. But in listening to works on a scale grander both in size and in reference one is not listening simply to the surface of sounds but to the meaning and structure of a world, perhaps, as Schopenhauer thought, of *the* world. It is in the printed word and by way of it that these wider and more comprehensive delights, that the joys of contemplative insight as well as the athletic virtuosities of thought may be experienced. For centuries men have climbed mountains for the sheer arduous enterprising pleasure of it, as well as for the ultimate rewarding view. There are books the very reading of which by slow, ascending, total comprehension constitutes stringent but genuine joy. But to take Spinoza's "Ethics" again as an example. Through the careful mastery of it it comes to be enjoyable; the final joy is the achieved vision, the perspective opened upon the eternally glowing serenity that such a perspective yields.

I do not mean to imply that serious works in philosophy are always hard reading though they may demand, even to enjoy them as writing, intense and wakeful alertness. There is a spurious superstition, fortified I fear by the practice of many American scholars, that profound books must be difficult, that serious works must be written with awkward want of grace. It is true that nobody reads Aristotle's "Metaphysics" for its prose style nor, for that matter, works by John Dewey. But there is a long and splendid tradition in philosophy of books at once serious as to matter, distinguished and beguiling as to style; one has but to remember David Hume and Bishop Berkeley. There are in all conscience ultimate ambiguities about life and nature, but even the difficulties of understanding the world can be clearly stated, and it was Aristotle himself who suggested that to know anything was to be able to state it.

It therefore turns out that there are occasions in our reading when the joys of unrequired reading are matched by the profit of wisdom. Books read for pleasure turn out to be liberators of imagination, transmitters of insight, disclosures of life seen steadily and whole; books written out of the most serious concerns of existence turn out to be entrancing literature. There is an aftermath of Puritanism, of moral asceticism among us that makes us suspicious of reading done for the spontaneity or the devil of it. Especially in times of crisis (crisis now seems to have become the normal weather of the world) reading for fun seems to have the immorality of a holiday at the wrong time, an escape from things that urgently need doing. Such spare time as we have we are frequently asked to turn to useful reading. We must find out more about civil defense, about soil erosion, about the welfare or, as its opponents think, the illfare of the state. We need to be briefed at once concerning the history and culture of Korea. We have to know all about Indo-China, and now. Doubtless we do, if only to become armchair strategists.

But at the risk of being thrown to the Congressional Committees as a saboteur I would like to plead not only the intrinsic enjoyments but the timely social usefulness of unrequired reading. As we are often reminded (even at the wrong moment) there is slave labor in Russia. We need to beware lest, out of hysterical fear, we make standard among ourselves the habit of a slave labor of the mind. The freedom of joy, including the freedom to enjoy reading, the liberty for play of imagination, for roving over the whole domain of time and space and humanity—these will help keep freedom alive among us politically. It is not slaves who will be concerned about freedom, and it is only free minds that will keep the values of civilization fresh and growing among us. One of those values is the unrequired adventuring among books, the lifeblood of our civilization.

READING[1]

HENRY DAVID THOREAU

WITH a little more deliberation in the choice of their pursuits, all men would perhaps become essentially students and observers, for certainly their nature and destiny are interesting to all alike. In accumulating property for ourselves or our posterity, in founding a family or a state, or acquiring fame even, we are mortal; but in dealing with truth we are immortal, and need fear no change nor accident. The oldest Egyptian or Hindoo philosopher raised a corner of the veil from the statue of the divinity; and still the trembling robe remains raised, and I gaze upon as fresh a glory as he did, since it was I in him that was then so bold, and it is he in me that now reviews the vision. No dust has settled on that robe; no time has elapsed since that divinity was revealed. That time which we really improve, or which is improbable, is neither past, present, nor future.

My residence was more favorable, not only to thought, but to serious reading, than a university; and though I was beyond the range of the ordinary circulating library, I had more than ever come within the influence of those books which circulate round the world, whose sentences were first written on bark, and are now merely copied from time to time on to linen paper. Says the poet Mîr Camar Uddîn Mast, "Being seated, to run through the region of the spiritual world; I have had this advantage in books. To be intoxicated by a single glass of wine; I have experienced this pleasure when I have drunk the liquor of the esoteric doctrines." I kept Homer's Iliad on my table through the summer, though I looked at his page only now and then. Incessant labor with my hands, at first, for I had my house to finish and my beans to hoe at the same time, made more study impossible. Yet I sustained myself by the prospect of such reading in future. I read one or two shallow books of travel in the intervals of my work, till that employment made me ashamed of myself, and I asked where it was then that *I* lived.

---

1. From *Walden*, ed. by Norman Holmes Pearson (New York: Rinehart & Company, Inc., 1948), pp. 81–90. First printed in 1849.

The student may read Homer or Æschylus in the Greek without danger of dissipation or luxuriousness, for it implies that he in some measure emulate their heroes, and consecrate morning hours to their pages. The heroic books, even if printed in the character of our mother tongue, will always be in a language dead to degenerate times; and we must laboriously seek the meaning of each word and line, conjecturing a larger sense than common use permits out of what wisdom and valor and generosity we have. The modern cheap and fertile press, with all its translations, has done little to bring us nearer to the heroic writers of antiquity. They seem as solitary, and the letter in which they are printed as rare and curious, as ever. It is worth the expense of youthful days and costly hours, if you learn only some words of an ancient language, which are raised out of the trivialness of the street, to be perpetual suggestions and provocations. It is not in vain that the farmer remembers and repeats the few Latin words which he has heard. Men sometimes speak as if the study of the classics would at length make way for more modern and practical studies; but the adventurous student will always study classics, in whatever language they may be written and however ancient they may be. For what are the classics but the noblest recorded thoughts of man? They are the only oracles which are not decayed, and there are such answers to the most modern inquiry in them as Delphi and Dodona never gave. We might as well omit to study Nature because she is old. To read well, that is, to read true books in a true spirit, is a noble exercise, and one that will task the reader more than any exercise which the customs of the day esteem. It requires a training such as the athletes underwent, the steady intention almost of the whole life to this object. Books must be read as deliberately and reservedly as they were written. It is not enough even to be able to speak the language of that nation by which they were written, for there is a memorable interval between the spoken and the written language, the language heard and the language read. The one is commonly transitory, a sound, a tongue, a dialect merely, almost brutish, and we learn it unconsciously, like the brutes, of our mothers. The other is the maturity and experience of that; if that is our mother tongue, this is our father tongue, a reserved and select expression, too significant to be heard by the ear, which we must be born again in order to speak. The crowds of men who merely *spoke* the Greek and Latin tongues in the Middle Ages were not entitled by the accident of birth to *read* the works of genius written in those languages; for these were not written in that Greek or Latin which they knew, but in the select language of literature. They had not learned the nobler dialects of Greece and Rome, but the very materials on which they were written were waste paper to them, and they prized instead a cheap contemporary literature. But when the several nations of Europe had acquired distinct though rude written languages of their own, sufficient for the purposes of their rising literatures, then first learning revived, and scholars were enabled to discern from that remoteness the treasures of antiquity. What the Roman and Grecian multitude could not *hear*, after the lapse of ages a few scholars *read*, and a few scholars only are still reading it.

However much we may admire the orator's occasional bursts of eloquence, the noblest written words are commonly as far behind or above the fleeting spoken language as the firmament with its stars is behind the clouds. *There* are the stars, and they who can may read them. The astronomers forever comment on and observe them. They are not exhalations like our daily colloquies and vaporous breath. What is called eloquence in the forum is commonly found to be rhetoric in the study. The orator yields to the inspiration of a transient occasion, and speaks to the mob before him, to those who can *hear* him; but the writer, whose more equable life is his occasion, and who would be distracted by the event and the crowd which inspire the orator, speaks to the intellect and heart of mankind, to all in any age who can *understand* him.

No wonder that Alexander carried the Iliad with him on his expeditions in a precious casket. A written word is the choicest of relics. It is something at once more intimate with us and more universal than any other work of art. It is the work of art nearest to life itself. It may be translated into every language, and not only be read but actually breathed from all human lips;—not be represented on canvas or in marble only, but be carved out of the breath of life itself. The symbol of an ancient man's thought becomes a modern man's speech. Two thousand summers have imparted to the monuments of Grecian literature, as to her marbles, only a maturer golden and autumnal tint, for they have carried their own serene and celestial atmosphere into all lands to protect them against the corrosion of time. Books are the treasured wealth of the world and the fit inheritance of generations and nations. Books, the oldest and the best, stand naturally and rightfully on the shelves of every cottage. They have no cause of their own to plead, but while they enlighten and sustain the reader his common sense will not refuse them. Their authors are a natural and irresistible aristocracy in every society, and, more than kings or emperors, exert an influence on mankind. When the illiterate and perhaps scornful trader has earned by enterprise and industry his coveted leisure and independence, and is admitted to the circles of wealth and fashion, he turns inevitably at last to those still higher but yet inaccessible circles of intellect and genius, and is sensible only of the imperfection of his culture and the vanity and insufficiency of all his riches, and further proves his good sense by the pains which he takes to secure for his children that intellectual culture whose want he so keenly feels; and thus it is that he becomes the founder of a family.

Those who have not learned to read the ancient classics in the language in which they were written must have a very imperfect knowledge of the history of the human race; for it is remarkable that no transcript of them has ever been made into any modern tongue, unless our civilization itself may be regarded as such a transcript. Homer has never yet been printed in English, nor Æschylus, nor Virgil even,—works as refined, as solidly done, and as beautiful almost as the morning itself; for later writers, say what we will of their genius, have rarely, if ever, equalled the elaborate beauty and finish and the lifelong and heroic literary labors of the ancients. They only talk of forgetting them who never knew them. It will be soon enough to forget them when we have the learning and the genius which will enable us to attend to and appreciate them. That age will be rich indeed when those relics which we call Classics, and the still older and more than classic but even less known Scriptures of the nations, shall have still further accumulated, when the Vaticans shall be filled with Vedas and Zendavestas and Bibles, with Homers and Dantes and Shakespeares, and all the centuries to come shall have successively deposited their trophies in the forum of the world. By such a pile we may hope to scale heaven at last.

The works of the great poets have never yet been read by mankind, for only great poets can read them. They have only been read as the multitude read the stars, at most astrologically, not astronomically. Most men have learned to read to serve a paltry convenience, as they have learned to cipher in order to keep accounts and not be cheated in trade; but of reading as a noble intellectual exercise they know little or nothing; yet this only is reading, in a high sense, not that which lulls us as a luxury and suffers the nobler faculties to sleep the while, but what we have to stand on tip-toe to read and devote our most alert and wakeful hours to.

I think that having learned our letters we should read the best that is in literature, and not be forever repeating our a-b-abs, and words of one syllable, in the fourth or fifth classes, sitting on the lowest and foremost form all our lives. Most men are satisfied if they read or hear read, and perchance have been convicted by the wisdom of one good book, the Bible, and for the rest of their lives vegetate and dissipate their faculties in what is called easy reading. There is a work in several volumes in our Circulating Library entitled "Little Reading," which I thought referred to a town of that name which I had not been to. There are those who, like cormorants and ostriches, can digest all sorts of this, even after the fullest dinner of meats and vegetables, for they suffer nothing to be wasted. If others are the machines to provide this provender, they are the machines to read it. They read the nine thousandth tale about Zebulon and Sophronia, and how they loved as none had ever loved before, and neither did the course of their true love run smooth,—at any rate, how it did run and stumble, and get up again and go on! how some poor unfortunate got up on to a steeple, who had better never have gone up as far as the belfry; and then having needlessly got him up there, the happy novelist rings the bell for all the world to come together and hear, O dear! how he did get down again! For my part, I think that they had better metamorphose all such aspiring heroes of universal noveldom into man weather-cocks, as they used to put heroes among the constellations, and let them swing round there till they are rusty, and not come down at all to bother honest men with their pranks. The next time the novelist rings the bell I will not stir though the meeting-house burn down. "The Skip of the Tip-Toe-Hop, a Romance of the Middle Ages, by the celebrated author of 'Tittle-Tol-Tan,' to appear in monthly parts; a great rush; don't all come together." All this they read with saucer eyes, and erect and primitive curiosity, and with unwearied gizzard, whose corrugations even yet need no sharpening, just as some little four-year-old bencher his two-cent gilt-covered edition of Cinderella,—without any improvement, that I can see, in the pronunciation, or accent, or emphasis, or any more skill in extracting or inserting the moral. The result is dulness of sight, stagnation of the vital circulations, and a general deliquium and sloughing off of all the intellectual faculties. This sort of gingerbread is baked daily and more sedulously than pure wheat or rye-and-Indian in almost every oven, and finds a surer market.

The best books are not read even by those who are called good readers. What does our Concord culture amount to? There is in this town, with a very few exceptions, no taste for the best or for very good books even in English literature, whose words all can read and spell. Even the college-bred and so-called liberally educated men here and elsewhere have really little or no acquaintance with the English classics; and as for the recorded wisdom of mankind, the ancient classics and Bibles, which are accessible to all who will know of them, there are the feeblest efforts anywhere made to become acquainted with them. I know a woodchopper, of middle age, who takes a French paper, not for news as he says, for he is above that, but to "keep himself in practice," he being a Canadian by birth; and when I ask him what he considers the best thing he can do in this world, he says, beside this, to keep up and add to his English. This is about as much as the college-bred generally do or aspire to do, and they take an English paper for the purpose. One who has just come from reading perhaps one of the best English books will find how many with whom he can converse about it? Or suppose he comes from reading a Greek or Latin classic in the original, whose praises are familiar even to the so-called illiterate; he will find nobody at all to speak to, but must keep silence about it. Indeed, there is hardly the professor in our colleges, who, if he has mastered the difficulties of the language, has proportionally mastered the difficulties of the wit and poetry of a Greek poet, and has any sympathy to impart to the alert and heroic reader; and as for the sacred Scriptures, or Bibles of mankind, who in this town can tell me even their titles? Most men do not know that any nation but the Hebrews have had a scripture. A man, any man, will go considerably out of his way to pick up a silver dollar; but here are golden words, which the wisest men of antiquity have uttered, and whose worth the wise of every succeeding age have assured us of;—and yet we learn to read only as far as Easy Reading, the primers and class-books, and when we leave school, the "Little Reading," and story-books, which are for boys and beginners; and our reading, our conversation and thinking, are all on a very low level, worthy only of pygmies and manikins.

I aspire to be acquainted with wiser men than this our Concord soil has produced, whose names are hardly known here. Or shall I hear the name of Plato and never read his book? As if Plato were my townsman and I never saw him, —my next neighbor and I never heard him speak or attended to the wisdom of his words. But how actually is it? His Dialogues, which contain what was immortal in him, lie on the next shelf, and yet I never read them. We are underbred and low-lived and illiterate; and in this respect I confess I do not make any very broad distinction between the illiterateness of my townsman who cannot read at all and the illiterateness of him who has learned to read only what is for children and feeble intellects. We should be as good as the worthies of antiquity, but partly by first knowing how good they were. We are a race of tit-men, and soar but little higher in our intellectual flights than the columns of the daily paper.

It is not all books that are as dull as their readers. There are probably words addressed to our condition exactly, which, if we could really hear and understand, would be more salutary than the morning or the spring to our lives, and possibly put a new aspect on the face of things for us. How many a man has dated a new era in his life from the reading of a book! The book exists for us, perchance, which will explain our miracles and reveal new ones. The at present unutterable things we may find somewhere uttered. These same questions that disturb and puzzle and confound us have in their turn occurred to all the wise men; not one has been omitted; and each has answered them, according to his ability, by his words and his life. Moreover, with wisdom we shall learn liberality. The solitary hired man on a farm in the outskirts of Concord, who has had his second birth and peculiar religious experience, and is driven as he believes into silent gravity and exclusiveness by his faith, may think it is not true; but Zoroaster, thousands of years ago, travelled the same road and had the same experience; but he, being wise, knew it to be universal, and treated his neighbors accordingly, and is even said to have invented and established worship among men. Let him humbly commune with Zoroaster then, and through the liberalizing influence of all the worthies, with Jesus Christ himself, and let "our church" go by the board.

We boast that we belong to the Nineteenth Century and are making the most rapid strides of any nation. But consider how little this village does for its own culture. I do not wish to flatter my townsmen, nor to be flattered by them, for that will not advance either of us. We need to be provoked,—goaded like oxen, as we are, into a trot. We have a comparatively decent system of common schools, schools for infants only; but excepting the half-starved Lyceum in the winter, and latterly the puny beginning of a library suggested by the State, no school for ourselves. We spend more on almost any article of bodily aliment or ailment than on our mental aliment. It is time that we had uncommon schools, that we did not leave off our education when we begin to be men and women. It is time that villages were universities, and their elder inhabitants the fellows of universities, with leisure—if they are, indeed, so well off—to pursue liberal studies the rest of their lives. Shall the world be confined to one Paris or one Oxford forever? Cannot students be boarded here and get a liberal education under the skies of Concord? Can we not hire some Abélard to lecture to us? Alas! what with foddering the cattle and tending the store, we are kept from school too long, and our education is sadly neglected. In this country, the village should in some respect take the place of the nobleman of Europe. It should be the patron of the fine arts. It is rich enough. It wants only the magnanimity and refinement. It can spend money enough on such things as farmers and traders value, but it is thought Utopian to propose spending money for things which more intelligent men know to be of far more worth. This town has spent seventeen thousand dollars on a town-house, thank fortune or politics, but probably it will not spend so much on living wit, the true meat to put into that shell, in a hundred years. The one hundred and twenty-five dollars annually subscribed for a Lyceum in the winter is better spent than any other equal sum raised in the town. If we live in the Nineteenth Century, why should we not enjoy the advantages which the Nineteenth Century offers? Why should our life be in any respect provincial? If we will read newspapers, why not skip the gossip of Boston and take the best newspaper in the world at once?—not be sucking the pap of "neutral family" papers, or browsing "Olive-Branches" here in New England. Let the reports of all the learned societies come to us, and we will see if they know anything. Why should we leave it to Harper & Brothers and Redding Co. to select our reading? As the nobleman of cultivated taste surrounds himself with whatever conduces to his culture,—genius—learning—wit—books—paintings—statuary—music—philosophical instruments, and the like; so let the village do,—not stop short at a pedagogue, a parson, a sexton, a parish library, and three selectmen, because our Pilgrim forefathers got through a cold winter once on a bleak rock with these. To act collectively is according to the spirit of our institutions; and I am confident that, as our circumstances are more flourishing, our means are greater than the nobleman's. New England can hire all the wise men in the world to come and teach her, and board them round the while, and not be provincial at all. That is the *uncommon* school we want. Instead of noblemen, let us have noble villages of men. If it is necessary, omit one bridge over the river, go round a little there, and throw one arch at least over the darker gulf of ignorance which surrounds us.

MR. K*A*P*L*A*N AND SHAKESPEARE [1]

LEONARD Q. ROSS

It was Miss Higby's idea in the first place. She had suggested to Mr. Parkhill that the students came to her class unaware of the *finer* side of English, of its beauty and, as she put it, "the glorious heritage of our literature." She suggested that perhaps poetry might be worked into the exercises of Mr. Parkhill's class. The beginner's grade had, after all, been subjected to almost a year of English and might be presumed to have achieved some linguistic sophistica-

1. From *The Education of Hyman Kaplan,* by Leonard Q. Ross, pp. 129–140. Copyright, 1937, by Harcourt, Brace & Company, Inc. Originally published in *The New Yorker.*

tion. Poetry would make the students conscious of precise enunciation; it would make them read with greater care and an ear for sounds. Miss Higby, who had once begun a master's thesis on Coventry Patmore, *loved* poetry. And, it should be said in all justice, she argued her cause with considerable logic. Poetry *would* be excellent for the enunciation of the students, thought Mr. Parkhill.

So it was that when he faced the class the following Tuesday night, Mr. Parkhill had a volume of Shakespeare on his desk, and an eager, almost an expectant, look in his eye. The love that Miss Higby bore for poetry in general was as nothing compared to the love that Mr. Parkhill bore for Shakespeare in particular. To Mr. Parkhill, poetry meant Shakespeare. Many years ago he had played Polonius in his senior class play.

"Tonight, class," said Mr. Parkhill, "I am going to try an experiment."

The class looked up dutifully. They had come to regard Mr. Parkhill's pedagogical innovations as part of the natural order.

"I am going to introduce you to poetry—great poetry. You see—" Mr. Parkhill delivered a modest lecture on the beauty of poetry, its expression of the loftier thoughts of men, its economy of statement. He hoped it would be a relief from spelling and composition exercises to use poetry as the subject matter of the regular Recitation and Speech period. "I shall write a passage on the board and read it for you. Then, for Recitation and Speech, you will give short addresses, using the passage as the general topic, telling us what it has brought to your minds, what thoughts and ideas."

The class seemed quite pleased by the announcement. Miss Mitnick blushed happily. (This blush was different from most of Miss Mitnick's blushes; there was aspiration and idealism in it.) Mr. Norman Bloom sighed with a business-like air: you could tell that for him poetry was merely another assignment, like a speech on "What I Like to Eat Best" or a composition on "A Day at a Picnic." Mrs. Moskowitz, to whom any public performance was unpleasant, tried to look enthusiastic, without much success. And Mr. Hyman Kaplan, the heroic smile on his face as indelibly as ever, looked at Mr. Parkhill with admiration and whispered to himself: "Poyetry! Now is poyetry! My! Mus' be progriss ve makink awreddy!"

"The passage will be from Shakespeare," Mr. Parkhill announced, opening the volume.

An excited buzz ran through the class as the magic of that name fell upon them.

"Imachine!" murmured Mr. Kaplan. "Jakesbeer!"

"*Shake*speare, Mr. Kaplan!"

Mr. Parkhill took a piece of chalk and, with care and evident love, wrote the following passage on the board in large, clear letters:

Tomorrow, and tomorrow, and tomorrow
Creeps in this petty pace from day to day,
To the last syllable of recorded time;

And all our yesterdays have lighted fools
The way to dusty death. Out, out, brief candle!
Life's but a walking shadow, a poor player
That struts and frets his hour upon the stage,
And then is heard no more; it is a tale
Told by an idiot, full of sound and fury,
Signifying nothing.

A reverent hush filled the classroom, as eyes gazed with wonder on this passage from the Bard. Mr. Parkhill was pleased at this.

"I shall read the passage first," he said. "Listen carefully to my enunciation—and—er—let Shakespeare's thoughts sink into your minds."

Mr. Parkhill read: "'Tomorrow, and tomorrow, and tomorrow . . .'" Mr. Parkhill read very well and this night, as if some special fire burned in him, he read with rare eloquence. "Out, out, brief candle!" In Miss Mitnick's eyes there was inspiration and wonder. "Life's but a walking shadow . . ." Mrs. Moskowitz sat with a heavy frown, indicating cerebration. "It is a tale told by an idiot . . ." Mr. Kaplan's smile had taken on something luminous; but his eyes were closed: it was not clear whether Mr. Kaplan had surrendered to the spell of the Immortal Bard or to that of Morpheus.

"I shall—er—read the passage again," said Mr. Parkhill, clearing his throat vociferously until he saw Mr. Kaplan's eyes open. "'Tomorrow, and tomorrow, and tomorrow. . . .'"

When Mr. Parkhill had read the passage for the second time, he said: "That should be quite clear now. Are there any questions?"

There were a few questions. Mr. Scymzak wanted to know whether "frets" was "a little kind excitement." Miss Schneiderman asked about "struts." Mr. Kaplan wasn't sure about "cripps." Mr. Parkhill explained the words carefully, and several illustrative uses of each word. "No more questions? Well, I shall allow a few minutes for you all to—er—think over the meaning of the passage. Then we shall begin Recitation and Speech."

Mr. Kaplan promptly closed his eyes again, his smile beatific. The students sank into that revery miscalled thought, searching their souls for the symbols evoked by Shakespeare's immortal words.

"Miss Caravello, will you begin?" asked Mr. Parkhill at last.

Miss Caravello went to the front of the room. "Da poem isa gooda," she said slowly. "Itsa have—"

"It *has.*"

"It hasa beautiful wordsa. Itsa lak Dante, Italian poet—"

"Ha!" cried Mr. Kaplan scornfully. "Shaksbeer you metchink mit Tante? *Shaksbeer*? Mein Gott!"

It was obvious that Mr. Kaplan had identified himself with Shakespeare and would tolerate no disparagement of his *alter ego.*

"Miss Caravello is merely expressing her own ideas," said Mr. Parkhill pacifically. (Actually, he felt completely sympathetic to Mr. Kaplan's point of view.)

"Hau Kay," agreed Mr. Kaplan, with a generous wave of the hand. "But to me is no comparink a high-cless man like Shaksbeer mit a Tante, dat's all."

Miss Caravello, her poise shattered, said a few more words and sat down.

Mrs. Yampolsky's contribution was brief. "This is full deep meanings," she said, her eyes on the floor. "Is hard for a person not so good in English to unnistand. But I like."

"*'Like!'*" cried Mr. Kaplan with a fine impatience. "*'Like?'* Batter *love,* Yampolsky. Mit Shaksbeer mus' be *love!*"

Mr. Parkhill had to suggest that Mr. Kaplan control his aesthetic passions. He did understand how Mr. Kaplan felt, however, and sensed a new bond between them. Mrs. Yampolsky staggered through several more nervous comments and retired.

Mr. Bloom was next. He gave a long declamation, ending: "So is passimistic ideas in the poem, and I am optimist. Like should be happy—so we should remember this is only a poem. Maybe is Shakespeare too passimistic."

"You wronk, Bloom!" cried Mr. Kaplan with prompt indignation. "Shaksbeer is passimist because is de *life* passimist also!"

Mr. Parkhill, impressed by this philosophical stroke, realized that Mr. Kaplan, afire with the glory of the Swan of Avon, could not be suppressed. Mr. Kaplan was the kind of man who brooked no criticism of his gods. The only solution was to call on Mr. Kaplan for his recitation at once. Mr. Parkhill was, indeed, curious about what fresh thoughts Mr. Kaplan would utter after his passionate defences of the Bard. When Mr. Parkhill had corrected certain parts of Mr. Bloom's speech, emphasizing Mr. Bloom's failure to use the indefinite article, he said: "Mr. Kaplan, will *you* speak next?"

Mr. Kaplan's face broke into a glow; his smile was like a rainbow. "Soitinly," he said, walking to the front of the room. Never had he seemed so dignified, so eager, so conscious of a great destiny.

"Er—Mr. Kaplan," added Mr. Parkhill, suddenly aware of the possibilities which the situation (Kaplan on Shakespeare) involved: "Speak *carefully.*"

"*Spacially* careful vill I be," Mr. Kaplan reassured him. He cleared his throat, adjusted his tie, and began: "Ladies an' gantleman, you hoid all kinds minninks abot dis piece poyetry, an'—"

"*Po*etry."

"—abot dis piece *po*etry. But to me is a difference minnink altogadder. Ve mus' tink abot Julius Scissor an' how *he* falt!"

Mr. Parkhill moved nervously, puzzled.

"In dese exact voids is Julius Scissor sayink—"

"Er—Mr. Kaplan," said Mr. Parkhill once he grasped the full import of Mr. Kaplan's error. "The passage is from 'Macbeth.'"

Mr. Kaplan looked at Mr. Parkhill with injured surprise. "*Not* fromm 'Julius Scissor'?" There was pain in his voice.

"No. And it's—er—'Julius *Cae*sar.'"

Mr. Kaplan waited until the last echo of the name had permeated his soul. "Podden me, Mr. Pockheel. Isn't '*see*zor' vat you cottink somting op mit?"

"That," said Mr. Parkhill quickly, "is 'scissor.' You have used 'Caesar' for 'scissor' and 'scissor' for 'Caesar.'"

Mr. Kaplan nodded, marveling at his own virtuosity.

"But go on with your speech, please." Mr. Parkhill, to tell the truth, felt a little guilty that he had not announced at the very beginning that the passage was from "Macbeth." "Tell us *why* you thought the lines were from 'Julius Caesar.'"

"Vell," said Mr. Kaplan to the class, his smile assuming its normal serenity. "I vas positif, becawss I can *see* de whole ting." He paused, debating how to explain this cryptic remark. Then his eyes filled with a strange enchantment. "I see de whole scinn. It's in a tant, on de night bafore dey makink Julius de Kink fromm Rome. So he is axcited an' ken't slip. He is layink in bad, tinking: 'Tomorrow an' tomorrow an' tomorrow. How slow dey movink! Almost cripps! Soch a pity de pace!'"

Before Mr. Parkhill could explain that "petty pace" did not mean "Soch a pity de pace!" Mr. Kaplan had soared on.

"De days go slow, fromm day to day, like leetle tsyllables on phonograph racords fromm time."

Anxiety and bewilderment invaded Mr. Parkhill's eyes.

"'An' vat abot yestidday?' tinks Julius Scissor. Ha! 'All our yestiddays are only makink a good light for fools to die in de dost!'"

"'Dusty death' doesn't mean—" There was no interrupting Mr. Kaplan.

"An' Julius Scissor is so tired, an' he vants to fallink aslip. So he hollers, mit fillink, 'Go ot! Go ot! Short candle!' So it goes ot."

Mr. Kaplan's voice dropped to a whisper. "But he ken't slip. Now is bodderink him de idea fromm life. 'Vat is de life altogadder?' tinks Julius Scissor. An' he gives enswer, de pot I like de bast. 'Life is like a bum actor, strottink an' hollerink arond de stage for only vun hour bafore he's kicked ot. Life is a tale told by idjots, dat's all, full of fonny sonds an' phooey!'"

Mr. Parkhill could be silent no longer. "'Full of sound and fury!'" he cried desperately. But inspiration, like an irresistible force, swept Mr. Kaplan on.

"'Life is monkey business! It don' minn a ting. It signifies nottink!' An' den Julius Scissor closes his ice fest—" Mr. Kaplan demonstrated the Consul's exact ocular process in closing his "ice"— "an' falls dad!"

The class was hushed as Mr. Kaplan stopped. In the silence, a tribute to the fertility of Mr. Kaplan's imagination and the power of his oratory, Mr. Kaplan went to his seat. But just before he sat down, as if adding a postscript, he sighed: "Dat vas mine idea. But ufcawss is all wronk, becawss Mr. Pockheel said de voids ain't abot Julius Scissor altogadder. It's all abot an Irishman by de name Macbat."

Then Mr. Kaplan sat down.

It was some time before Mr. Parkhill could bring himself to criticize Mr. Kaplan's pronunciation, enunciation, diction, grammar, idiom, and sentence structure. For Mr. Parkhill discovered that he could not easily return to the world of reality. He was still trying to tear himself away from that tent outside Rome, where "Julius Scissor," cursed with insomnia, had thought of time and life—and philosophized himself to a strange and sudden death.

Mr. Parkhill was distinctly annoyed with Miss Higby.

THE ART OF PLAIN TALK: LIVE WORDS AND CROWDED WORDS[1]

RUDOLF FLESCH

You now know the recipe for simplicity: Talk about people in short sentences with many root words. Here is an easy trick for killing these three birds with one stone: Use verbs. Let me repeat that: *Use verbs.*

Nothing is as simple as a brief three-word sentence that follows the pattern: somebody *does* something. It is the verb that gives life to any sentence; it literally makes the sentence go.

But we have seen that in Chinese, the simplest of all languages, there is no such thing as a verb (or noun or adjective, for that matter). How, then, do the Chinese make their sentences go? Well, the explanation is simple: one word in each sentence serves, so to speak, as its motor; for this particular sentence, it works as a verb. If a Chinese says "Man bite dog," the word *bite,* otherwise unclassified, serves as a verb; that's why it has been put after *man* and before *dog.*

In modern English, which gets more and more "Chinese," we do that all the time and "appoint" a word to do verb service by putting it in a certain place in a sentence. We can say *Raise your face* or *Face your raise; Ship a book*

1. From *The Art of Plain Talk,* by Rudolf Flesch, pp. 66–80. Copyright, 1946, by Rudolf Flesch. Reprinted by permission of Harper & Brothers.

or *Book a ship; Spot the cover* or *Cover the spot.* There is no question that each of these sentences has a verb in it, and no question which is the verb.

The point of all this is, of course, that I am talking here only of those words that are used as verbs in a sentence. They are what the grammarians call the "finite active verb forms" and they are the only ones that have life in them. Hearing of verbs, you probably think of passive participles and infinitives and gerunds and all the other fancy varieties that have plagued your grammar-school days. Well, forget about them: for all practical purposes they are not verbs, but nouns or adjectives—lifeless words that won't make your sentences move. The verbs you want to use are those that are in active business doing verb work; if you use a verb in the passive voice or make a participle or noun out of it, you have lost the most valuable part in the process: it's like cooking vegetables and throwing away the water with all the vitamins in it.

If you go through any newspaper or magazine and look for active, kicking verbs in the sentences, you will realize that this lack of well used verbs is the main trouble with modern English writing. Almost all nonfiction nowadays is written in a sort of pale, colorless sauce of passives and infinitives, motionless and flat as paper. Listen to this, for instance (from an essay by Paul Schrecker in the *Saturday Review of Literature*) :

Maybe the gradual actualization of this solidarity was the result of scientific and hence technological progress which caused distances to shrink and required ever-expanding markets. But it is a preconceived and entirely unwarranted idea to believe this technological unification to have been a primary cause, and hence to overlook the fact that its triumphant appearance on the world scene would not have been possible without the prior existence of a potential world-civilization. The ever-expanding sphere of influence of literature, science, and works of art, which rarely respects any national or regional boundaries, cannot be accounted for by the introduction of faster and easier means of communication or by the improved technological methods of mass reproduction. The phenomenon reveals mankind's preparedness to respond promptly to incentives emerging from the fields of knowledge and the arts, irrespective of their national and regional origin.

Or how about this (from "Mary Haworth's Mail"):

Morbid preoccupation with thoughts of sex gratification, after one has attained the age of reason, is not a sign of emotional precocity, as some may suppose; but just the opposite, namely: evidence of a definitely infantile type of emotional egocentricity; what the psychologists call a state of arrested development. The uncomprehending inarticulate infant's sense of well being is wholly related to bodily feelings,—of being well fed, comfortably clothed and bedded, fondly caressed, etc. His sole concern, insistently registered, is with physical gratification, because instinct tells him that pleasurable sensations, at his helpless level of development, are synonymous with a reassuring sufficiency of creature care and healthy survival.

Now, if you look closely, you will notice that the only active, finite verbs in the first passage are *caused, required, respects,* and *reveals:* four mildly active verbs matched by 27 passive forms, infinitives, participles, verbs made into nouns, and forms of the auxiliary verb *to be.* In the second passage, we have *suppose, call,* and *tells,* against 32 inactive verb forms of various types.

And now let us look at the language of Shakespeare or the Bible, for contrast. Here is a speech by Brutus:

> No, not an oath; if not the face of men,
> The sufferance of our souls, the time's abuse,—
> If these be motives weak, break off betimes,
> And every man hence to his idle bed;
> So let high-sighted tyranny range on,
> Till each man drop by lottery. But if these,
> As I am sure they do, bear fire enough
> To kindle cowards, and to steel with valour
> The melting spirits of women, then, countrymen,
> What need we any spur, but our own cause
> To prick us to redress? what other bond,
> Than secret Romans, that have spoke the word,
> And will not palter? and what other oath,
> Than honesty to honesty engag'd,
> That this shall be, or we will fall for it?
> Swear priests, and cowards, and men cautelous,
> Old feeble carrions and such suffering souls
> That welcome wrongs; unto bad causes swear
> Such creatures as men doubt; but do not stain
> The even virtue of our enterprise,
> Nor the insuppressive mettle of our spirits,
> To think that or our cause or our performance
> Did need an oath; when every drop of blood
> That every Roman bears, and nobly bears,
> Is guilty of a several bastardy,
> If he do break the smallest particle
> Of any promise that hath pass'd from him.

And these are words of Job:

> Wherefore do the wicked live, become old, yea, are mighty in power?
> Their seed is established in their sight with them, and their offspring before their eyes.
> Their houses are safe from fear, neither is the rod of God upon them.
> Their bull gendereth, and faileth not; their cow calveth, and casteth not her calf.
> They send forth their little ones like a flock, and their children dance.
> They take the timbrel and harp, and rejoice at the sound of the organ.

They spend their days in wealth, and in a moment go down to the grave.
Therefore they say unto God, Depart from us; for we desire not the knowledge of thy ways.
What is the Almighty, that we should serve him? and what profit should we have, if we pray unto him?
Lo, their good is not in their hand: the counsel of the wicked is far from me.
How oft is the candle of the wicked put out! and how oft cometh their destruction upon them! God distributeth sorrows in his anger.
They are as stubble before the wind, and as chaff that the storm carrieth away.

Clearly, most of the power, movement, and beauty of these passages comes from the succession of active verbs: Shakespeare makes tyranny *range,* men *drop,* and a cause *prick us to redress;* the Bible makes a bull *gender,* a cow *calve,* and children *dance.* There are 19 live verbs in the Shakespeare passage against 11 passive verb forms, verbal nouns, etc.; in the Bible passage the ratio is 20 to 11.

Maybe you will say that I am unfair in using the Bible and Shakespeare as examples. After all, newspapers and magazine articles are written to meet a deadline, by writers who don't dream of being literary geniuses; so why compare their style with all-time masterpieces? I admit I am a little biased here; but anybody can try to use active, working verbs wherever possible. It won't make him a Shakespeare but it will make him write good, plain English. Here is, for instance, one modern example from Ernie Pyle:

The company I was with got its orders to rest about 5 one afternoon. They dug foxholes along the hedgerows, or commandeered German ones already dug. Regardless of how tired you may be, you always dig in the first thing.

Then they sent some men with cans looking for water. They got more K rations up by jeep, and sat on the ground eating them.

They hoped they would stay there all night, but they weren't counting on it too much. Shortly after supper a lieutenant came out of a farmhouse and told the sergeants to pass the word to be ready to move in 10 minutes. They bundled on their packs and started just before dark.

Within half an hour they had run into a new fight that lasted all night. They had had less than four hours' rest in three solid days of fighting. That's the way life is in the infantry.

There are 16 working verbs there and not a single verb form or noun that could, or should, be turned into an active, finite verb. And now compare it with this sentence from a popular article on economics:

In somewhat over-simplified technical terms, inflation is caused by the existence, at any given time in an economic system, of an aggregate of *effective* purchasing power greater than the aggregate of the goods and services for sale.

What a definition! "Inflation" is caused by the *existence* of an *aggregate* that is *greater* than another *aggregate*. This shows clearly how impossible it is to describe a process—something happening—without using a single active verb. Obviously the writer realized that himself, because the next sentence reads like this:

> . . . When we add up the amounts of cash and credit of all kinds at the disposal of everybody who is ready to buy something, and find that the sum is larger than the sum of all the things to be bought at existing prices, then prices are likely to go up.

Now the verbs are in their proper places, and everything becomes crystal-clear: First we *add* something, then we *find* that it is larger than something else, and then prices will *go up*. This is the classic type of scientific explanation: If you do X and Y, what happens is Z. (Or, in the De Kruif manner: The great scientist did X and Y, and what happened was Z.)

And now, let's get down to work and try to rewrite a "verbless" passage ourselves. Here is another bit from the literary essay I quoted on page 91:

> Integrated into the circulation of national life much more completely than any other modern literature, American belles-lettres also give a much more faithful and adequate picture of the entire civilization to which they belong than literature abroad, whose very compliance with—or willful opposition to—traditions that have long lost their anchorage in the depths of their respective national civilizations, renders them unable to keep abreast of the rejuvenated spirit of their epoch.

Here is the same sentence with the nouns made into verbs:

> American belles-lettres circulate in the national life much more than other modern literatures do; they picture the entire civilization to which they belong more faithfully and adequately. The spirit of the times has become young again, and literatures abroad cannot keep abreast with it because of certain traditions they comply with or willfully oppose. These traditions were once anchored in the depths of their national civilizations, but have lost that anchorage long ago.

And now I expect you to go ahead and pepper your speech and writing with active verbs. But before you start using this rule of thumb, let me warn you. There is one place where it does not work: in written dialogue. You know the sort of thing I mean:

> "She is, I think, a lady not known to Monsieur," murmured the valet . . .
> "Show her out here, Hippolyte," the Comte commanded . . .
> "My descent upon you is unceremonious," she began . . .
> "But seat yourself, I beg of you, Mademoiselle," cried the Comte . . .
> "But yes," she insisted . . .
> "Certainly people are wrong," agreed the Comte . . .
> "Perhaps," he murmured . . .
> "The jewels!" she breathed . . .

Fowler, in his *Dictionary of Modern English Usage,* says that this mannerism was started by George Meredith; wherever it comes from, it is nowadays an excellent means to tell a bad novel from a good one. Apparently all bad writers do it and all good writers don't. Look at the fearless way in which John Hersey repeats the word *said* in *A Bell for Adano:*

Zito said: "What is this Liberty Bell?"

Major Joppolo said: "It is the bell the Americans rang when they declared themselves free from the English."

Zito said: "The idea is good. But would America be willing to part with this bell for Adano?"

Major Joppolo said: "We would have to get a replica, Zito."

Zito said: "Describe this bell."

Major Joppolo said: "Well, it hangs in a tower in Philadelphia, I think . . ."

Imagine this with *Zito ventured* and *Major Joppolo reminisced.* . . .

II

Voltaire once said: "The adjective is the enemy of the noun." This sentence is one of the most famous epigrams about language; many young journalists have been started off with it and taught to hunt adjectives in their copy.

It's a good rule, but a little confusing. The fact is, grammarians still can't agree on what an adjective is. If you say, for instance, *A ravishing math teacher,* some of them will tell you that *ravishing* and *math* are adjectives; some will say that *ravishing* is a verb form; some others will insist that *math* is a noun (if they admit it is a word at all). The best thing for us is to leave grammatical labels behind and see what the words do in and to a sentence. Then, at once, we see that *math* defines *teacher,* and that *ravishing* is a comment on the math teacher. In other words, there are two kinds of so-called adjectives: commenting and defining. Now we can see what Voltaire meant: obviously he didn't mean that a defining adjective is the enemy of the noun, because it really belongs to the noun (*What is she teaching?—Math*); in fact it is a part of the noun and you could just as well write *math-teacher,* with a hyphen. On the other hand, the commenting adjective is hostile to and literally kills the following noun: what we remember is that she is ravishing, not that she teaches math. If we want to "save" the noun from the commenting adjective, we have to write this description in two sentences: *She is ravishing. She is teaching math.*

As you see, the trouble with comment—whether adjective, adverb, or anything else—is that it raises havoc with a sentence where it doesn't belong. In really simple language all sentences are just subject-predicate sentences: *Man bite dog. Man short. Dog tall.* If you make one sentence out of three and stick two comments into the first simple sentence (*Short man bite tall dog*), you are already on your way toward difficulty and sophistication. You force the reader, or listener, to take in three ideas in one sentence and you make understanding just so much harder. (James Joyce went even further and packed several ideas into one word, like *brooder-in-low* or *I was just thinkling upon that.*)

So our rule for plain talk is: Don't try to save a sentence by sticking a comment into another. Reason: Two short sentences are easier to understand than one long one, with extra stuff in it.

I said in the beginning that newspapermen are now being taught that adjectives are Bad. The trouble is, they are also being taught to save words and so, after a while, they forget all about adjective hunting and become sentence stuffers. Here is a mild case:

Married, he lives with his wife and three sons in New Jersey.

What he means is: *He is married and . . .*

Sometimes the two ideas don't match:

The 53-year-old commentator left high school to carry copy on the *Brooklyn Times.*

Or:

Kyser, bespectacled, was born thirty-eight years ago in Rocky Mountain, N. C.

Some writers habitually fill their sentences up to the brim. Here is an extract from a book review by Harrison Smith in the *Saturday Review of Literature* (I have put all the comments in italics):

The two sisters, *island aristocrats, whose lifelong fate was sealed when they saw one morning in Saint Pierre a handsome boy of thirteen, whose father, an untidy but a heart-of-gold physician, had just returned a widower to his native town.* Marguerite, *the younger of the sisters, a happy, blue-eyed, blonde child,* wins his love; Marianne, *dark, passionate, self-willed, determinedly* molds his life until he leaves the island, *a lieutenant in the Royal British Navy, bound for the China coast.* The young ladies sit behind and wait *frigidly* for over ten years for word from him. William, in the meantime, had been lured by a *half-caste* girl in a Chinese port into losing his ship and one morning, *penniless, half-naked, and drugged,* finds himself aboard a *clipper* ship, *bound for New Zealand, an exile.*

Sorted out, this reads:

Marguerite and Marianne were sisters. They were island aristocrats. Marguerite was the younger; she was a happy, blue-eyed, blonde child. Marianne was dark, passionate and self-willed.

One morning, in Saint Pierre, they saw a handsome boy of thirteen. His name was William and he was the son of an untidy physician with a heart of gold. His father had just become a widower and returned to his native town.

That moment sealed the lifelong fate of the sisters: Marguerite won the boy's love, Marianne molded his life.

Then, one day, William left the island. He had joined the Royal British Navy and become a lieutenant. Now he was bound for the China coast . . . etc. etc.

Or let's have a look at our friend from the last chapter, Mary Haworth:

Is it *fine philosophic* restraint or is it *craven* expediency to *tacitly* assent, as you have done so far, to your wife's *outre* performance, when you are confident it is part of a pattern of infidelity? If it were in truth the *large* reaction of a *nobly magnanimous* mind, would it be accompanied on the other hand by the *primitive male-egoist* emotional attitude that the marriage is wrecked for you, if she is indulging in a *passing* fancy, as you believe?

Have you feared *subconsciously* to force and face a showdown lest the *resultant* dissection of the marital relationship and her *possible* counter-charges confront you with a *shrewd and merciless* delineation of yourself as one *pallidly* devoid of *salient traits* of *thorough* masculinity?

Nearly all the key ideas have been put into commenting adjectives and adverbs. Here is another, more sophisticated example (from a film review by James Agee in the *Nation*):

Very belatedly I want to say that "The Watch on the Rhine" seemed much better on the screen than it did, *almost identically,* on the stage—*though I still wished Henry James might have written it;* and that *I join with anyone whose opinion of* Paul Lukas' performance is superlative. Also that *a simple-hearted* friendliness *generated between audience and screen* at "This Is the Army" made that film happy *to see even when it was otherwise boring; though* I am among an *apparent* minority which feels that Warner Brothers' *cuddly-reverential* treatment of President Roosevelt—in "Mission to Moscow," "This Is the Army," and *the forthcoming* "Princess O'Rourke"—is subject to charges *certainly* of indecent exposure and, *quite possibly,* of alienation of affection.

If you read this without the italicized words, you will see that it still makes sense; but the real point of the whole passage is expressed in those casually tucked-in adjectives like *simple-hearted* or *cuddly-reverential.* Mind you, I don't say that this is bad writing; but it isn't plain talk either, by a long shot.

But how about descriptions, you say: How can you describe anything—a city, a landscape—without using descriptive commenting adjectives? How can you get away from the pattern of "the flowery summer meadows, the lush cow-pastures, the quiet lakes and the singing streams, the friendly accessible mountains"? Simple: put your description in verbs, in predicates, in defining adjectives; don't comment but describe what happens, report, don't analyze.

Here is a description of America (from a *New York Times* editorial):

It is small things remembered, the little corners of the land, the houses, the people that each one loves. We love our country because there was a little tree on a hill, and grass thereon, and a sweet valley below; because the hurdy-gurdy man came along on a sunny morning in a city street; because a beach or a farm or a lane or a house that might not seem much to others was once, for each of us, made magic. It is voices that are remembered only, no longer heard. It is parents, friends, the lazy chat of street and store and office, and the ease of mind that makes life tranquil. . . .

It is stories told. It is the Pilgrims dying in their first dreadful winter. It is the Minute Man standing his ground at Concord Bridge, and dying there. It is the army in rags, sick, freezing, starving at Valley Forge. It is the wagons and the men on foot going westward over Cumberland Gap, floating down the great rivers, rolling over the great plains. It is the settler hacking fiercely at the primeval forest on his new, his own lands. It is Thoreau at Walden Pond, Lincoln at Cooper Union, and Lee riding home from Appomattox. . . .

In short, if you want to give descriptive detail in plain language, describe what you see, even using adjectives if you must; but don't stuff your descriptions down the reader's throat, whether he wants them or not, by filling all the odd corners and empty spots in your sentences with little dabs of observation.

Which brings us, of course, to *Time* magazine. As you know, the little descriptive adjectives—*beady-eyed, thin-lipped*—are the hallmark of *Time;* its editors say that they help the reader get a better picture of what's going on in the world. Well, let's have a look:

Bevin v. Bevan

Ernest Bevin, *the bull elephant* of British labor, last week sat *bulkily silent, beadily watchful,* in the back row at a caucus of Parliament's Laborite members. The proposal: to expel from the Party *his homonym—pink, grizzled Welshman* Aneurin Bevan. The crime: Laborite Bevan's revolt against Labor Minister Bevin in the House of Commons.

At the *tense and troubled* meeting, Aneurin Bevan refused to recant. He argued that if he were bounced, 15 other Laborites who sided with him would also have to go. All over Britain, he warned, labor unions were rising against *tough, truculent* Ernie Bevin's Defense Regulation 1-AA (five years in prison for strike fomenters)

As Aneurin Bevan talked, Ernie Bevin *restlessly* shifted *his weight, impatiently* flung his *farm-hardened* hands about *in gestures he had long used to brush aside opponents, soundlessly* worked his *pudgy* lips. . . .

This is the first part of a story about a British antistrike regulation. But, because of the *Time* formula, the reader is allowed only a quick glimpse at the topic in a brief parenthesis. What he really learns from this first third of the story is that Bevin and Bevan have similar names (this is made the heading) and that Bevin, in contrast to Bevan, is a heavy man (this he gets from four comments, with slight variations upon the theme, plus two photographs of Bevin and Bevan to show what they look like). What the trouble is about, or what the arguments are on each side, he cannot even guess at this point.

Now, psychologists have found that one of the main troubles in reading is the "overpotency" of certain words. Since we always read a few words at a time, those that are specially effective or colorful tend to blot out the others. The result is often that we get a wrong impression or, at least, read an emphasis into the text that isn't there. So it's quite obvious that *Time* readers are apt to learn a lot about the faces, figures, hands, lips and eyes of world leaders, but are liable to misread or skip what these people do.

So, for plain talk, here is a special rule about *Time*style adjectives: Don't use any. People will get you better without them.

THE LANGUAGE OF BUSINESS[1]

THE EDITORS OF *Fortune*

NOT so long ago, the businessman used to take his language pretty much for granted. He could afford to. His place was respected and his authority unquestioned. And so he bought, he sold, he collected his bills, made an occasional speech perhaps—and if the public, the workers, or the government didn't quite understand what he was up to, well, so much the better for all concerned.

But no longer. Acknowledging the fact—and the necessity—of others' scrutiny, he has made the interchange of facts and ideas with them one of his principal jobs. The house organ, the interoffice memo, the press release, the press conference, the annual report—the range of his efforts has grown enormous. So widespread, indeed, that business has become almost as extensive a publisher as the government itself.

Is the language of business up to the job? The news—and refreshing news it is—is that the American businessman himself has begun to conclude that it is not. Some, in fact, have gone so far as to assert that the pomposity of management prose is the "root ill of our communication troubles." While that may be an overexcited judgment, management's surveys have demonstrated that a large amount of its language has been not only incomprehensible to the people it is trying to reach, but enormously expensive in money, time, and misunderstanding as well. "It is high time the American businessman discovered the English language—it would be very useful to him" . . . "We've turned our offices into paper mills" . . . "We love curt clear correspondence—but damned few of us know how to write it." Everywhere the chorus of self-criticism is growing.

The positive results of this self-examination have been impressive. In company after company, executives have been setting up "writing clinics" to

1. Reprinted from the November 1950 issue of *Fortune* Magazine by special permission of the Editors. Copyright, 1950, Time, Inc.

scour management copy, staging correspondence-improvement courses, holding school in conference and public-speaking techniques, and, at the very least, peppering subordinates with "For-God's-sake-won't-you-people-learn-to-use-English-around-here" memos. All of which is clearly to the good. At the same time—and not so clearly to the good—a school of experts has come forward to help the businessman by redesigning the language of industry. To accomplish this, the experts have developed a scientific method that, as we shall see later, has some disturbing implications. Meanwhile, a look at the anatomy of this language that is to be redesigned.

First, the written variety—and that infamous jargon, which, for want of a better term, we'll call businesese. Its signal characteristic, as the reader and all other critics of businesese will recognize, is its uniformity. Almost invariably, businesese is marked by the heavy use of the passive construction. Nobody ever *does* anything. Things *happen*—and the author of the action is only barely implied. Thus, one does not refer to something, reference is made to; similarly, while prices may rise, nobody *raises* them. To be sure, in businesese there is not quite the same anonymity as is found in federal prose, for "I" and "we" do appear often. Except when the news to be relayed is good, however, there is no mistaking that the "I" and "we" are merely a convenient fiction and that the real author isn't a person at all but that great mystic force known as the corporation.

Except for a few special expressions, its vocabulary is everywhere quite the same. Midwesterners are likely to dispute the latter point, but a reading of approximately 500,000 words of business prose indicates no striking differences —in the Midwest or anywhere else. Moreover, in sounding out a hundred executives on the subject, *Fortune* found that their views coincided remarkably, particularly so in the matter of pet peeves (principally: "please be advised," "in reference to yours of . . .", "we wish to draw attention," "to acknowledge your letter"). The phrases of businesese are everywhere so uniform, in fact, that stenographers have a full set of shorthand symbols for them.

Because of this uniformity, defenders of businesese can argue that it doesn't make for misunderstanding. After all, everybody knows the symbols, and, furthermore, wouldn't a lot of people be offended by the terseness of more concise wording? There is something to this theory. Since businesese generally is twice as wordy as plain English, however, the theory is rather expensive to uphold. By the use of regular English the cost of the average letter—commonly estimated at 75 cents to $1—can be cut by about 20 cents. For a firm emitting a million letters a year, this could mean an annual saving of $200,000. Probably it would be even greater; for, by the calculations of correspondence specialist Richard Morris, roughly 15 per cent of the letters currently being written wouldn't be necessary at all if the preceding correspondence had been in regular English in the first place.

Where do the terms of businesese come from? Most, of course, are hand-me-downs from former generations of businessmen, but many are the fruit of cross-fertilization with other jargons. A businessman who castigates government bureaucrats, for example, is at the same time apt to be activating, expediting, implementing, effectuating, optimizing, minimizing, and maximizing—and at all levels and echelons within the framework of broad policy areas. Similarly, though he is amused by the long-hairs and the social scientists, he is beginning to speak knowingly of projective techniques, social dynamics, depth interviewing, and sometime soon, if he keeps up at this rate, he will probably appropriate that hallmark of the sound sociological paper, "insightful." Businesese, in fact, has very nearly become the great common meeting ground of the jargons.

Why do people who in private talk so pungently often write so pompously? There are many reasons: tradition, the demands of time, carelessness, the conservative influence of the secretary. Above all is the simple matter of status. Theorem: the less established the status of a person, the more his dependence on jargon. Examine the man who has just graduated from pecking out his own letters to declaiming them to a secretary and you are likely to have a man hopelessly intoxicated with the rhythm of businesese. Conversely, if you come across a blunt yes or no in a letter, you don't need to glance further to grasp that the author feels pretty firm in his chair.

The application of euphemism, a favored device of businesese, further illustrates this status principle. Take the field of selling. At the top of the ladder you will find a great many people in it: *sales* managers, vice presidents for *sales,* etc. As you go down the ranks, however, it becomes difficult to find people in this line of work. Field underwriters, estate planners, merchandising apprentices, social engineers, distribution analysts, and representatives of one kind or another, yes. But *sales*men? Rarely.

Not only does businesese confer status, it protects it as well, by its magnificent usefulness for buck passing and hedging. "All you have to remember," one executive says, "is the one basis which characterizes all such intracommunication: let the language be ambiguous enough that if the text be successfully carried out, all credit may be claimed; but if the text be unsuccessfully carried out, a technical alibi can be set up out of the text itself."

For this purpose there is a regular subglossary of businesese. Most notable terms: "in the process of," "at this time," "under consideration," "in the not-too-distant future," "company policy," and, when one is unable to explain something properly, "obviously." People who have to submit periodic reports to their superiors are particularly dependent on such terms—salesmen, for example, would have a hard time if they couldn't report of some prospects that they were "very impressed." ("I am allergic to that word," says one sales manager. "It results in so few orders.")

The full application of businesese to hedging occurs when more than two heads are put to work on a problem. As the members of top management sit around the table, a relatively simple policy statement is introduced for discussion. This is kicked around a bit, as the saying goes, for though it certainly is a fine statement, couldn't agree with it more, there are just a few little angles and suggestions that maybe ought to be noted. Thereupon each executive, much as a baseball captain grasps a bat in choosing up sides, adds his qualification, until finally the original statement has been at once pointed up, toned down, given more dignity, made more forceful, altered to anticipate possible objections, concretized, amended, and resolved. Now no longer a mere statement but a philosophy, or collection of philosophies, it is turned over to the Public Relations Department to give to the waiting public. There is nothing, as so many people say, quite like what you get when everybody on the team works together.

Besides written businesese, there is another and far more influential category of business English. Generally, it is found in the spoken language of business—in particular, that brand to be heard at the banquet table, the convention, and the conference table.

It might best be called *reverse* gobbledegook, for in almost every outward respect it is the opposite of written jargon. Where written jargon is multisyllabic, the other is filled with short terse words; its sentences are short and their construction so much more active than passive that exclamation marks occur almost as frequently as periods. It is English that is on the beam, English with its feet on the ground; in short, *shirt-sleeve* English.

Thanks to reverse gobbledegook, the less you have to say, the more emphatically you can say it. All one has to do is use certain hard-hitting expressions, and refer as frequently as possible to the fact that these expressions are being used. A sure forewarning of its onrush, accordingly, is a prefatory announcement by the speaker that he is not going to beat around the bush, pull any punches, pussyfoot, use two-dollar words, or the like. The rest is inevitable; so standardized are the expressions of reverse gobbledegook that an audience would be stunned to attention were a single one of them altered by so much as a word. (One of these days a clever speaker is going to capitalize on this. "Gentlemen," he will say, "I offer a panacea.")

As a result, reverse gobbledegook can be self-defeating; that is, since its whole effect lies in the dynamic quality the words convey, their constant use tends to neutralize them. This can be overcome, however, by adding strengtheners—so that, in a very real sense of the word, it cannot be overemphasized that you sincerely, and unquestionably, meant what you said in the first place.

Like written businesese, reverse gobbledegook also confers status. For this purpose, it provides a sort of slang that, skillfully applied—particularly at the conference table—will impart to the user an appearance of savviness, cooniness, and general know-how. Want to mark yourself as a comer in the advertising field? Speak, then, of fun stories, sweet guys, the hard sell, straw men you set up to back into, and points you can hang your hat on.[2] For each field you will find a subglossary, and, common to all of them, such universal terms as "play

2. Other current advertising favorites: "let's pull all the stops out on this one"; "let's noodle this one"; "let's sneak the message across"; "we'll touch all bases on this one"; "means abso-

it by ear," "the pitch," "the deal," and the many expressions built on the suffix "wise." ("Budget-wise, Al, the pitch shapes up like this . . .")

Another characteristic of reverse gobbledegook is its dependence on analogy and metaphor. During a single banquet you may find business problems equated with an airplane, a broad highway, a boat being rocked, a river, a riverbank, a stream, a bridge, a train, a three-legged stool, and, sometimes, three or four of these things at once in which case the passage is generally summed up with something like "It's as simple as that," or "That's all there is to the problem." (From a recent speech: "So business enterprise of America is trying to hone a sales force into the cutting edge of an economy and there is a virus running rampant in the flock. Security-mindedness is a log across the stream when it comes to developing the optimistic salesman outlook.")

Outstanding is the great American football analogy. No figure of speech is a tenth as seductive to the businessman. Just why this should be so—baseball, curiously, is much less used—is generally explained by its adaptability to all sorts of situations. Furthermore, the football analogy is *satisfying*. It is bounded by two goal lines and is thus finite. There is always a solution. And that is what makes it so often treacherous.

For analogy and metaphor can be insidiously attractive substitutes for thought. They are not, of course, when fleetingly used, when, as H. W. Fowler puts it (in *Modern English Usage*), they "flash out for the length of a line or so and are gone," but this is rarely the case in reverse gobbledegook. The user starts innocuously enough; his policy is *like* a thingamajig in one respect. But only the stanchest mind can resist the analogy further. Before long he is entwined, and unconsciously operating on the premise that his policy *is* a thingamajig. The language, in short, has molded thinking, and the results can be a good bit more serious than a poor speech.

The mishaps of one consumer-goods corporation illustrate this hazard. Not so long ago, the men who owned the company were casting about for a Goal. Up to then it had been money. But now they had acquired a lot of it, they were getting on in years, and anyway it didn't sound good. And so, on this enlightened-goal problem, the Chief fell to pondering at the conference table. When you get right down to it, the company was just like a big football team. You don't win unless you have a good team, do you? You could say that again. Well, before he gets a good team, what does the coach have to do? Very simple. He has to go out and find good players. Just thinking out loud, mind you, but wasn't the big job then to get the right recruits?

---

lutely nothing to the lay mind"; "we'll get a plus value on this one"; "it was quite a hassle"; "let's not hassle over this."

Journalists laugh and laugh at this sort of thing. Just why, it is difficult to say, except possibly that being less inventive, they prefer to hang on to the old expressions rather than coin new ones. Terms now nearing the end of the run (including some of *Fortune's*): ambivalence, dichotomy, schizophrenic, "two hours and four martinis (beers, etc.) later"; "it's as difficult (easy, etc.) as it is complex (difficult, etc.)"; "their profits (feelings, etc.) are showing."

Almost automatically, this was mimeographed as the company's rationale—"The Touchdown Play" it was called—and before long executives were spending almost as much time on the new trainees as they were on their regular jobs, and when they weren't doing this, they were scouring the colleges for more. Everything went swimmingly; the policy was soon the wonder of the merchandising world; the top executives were suffused with a sense of enlightenment—and the place was jammed with eager young men.

In only one respect did the analogy break down. A year later practically all of the competition came out with a new product embodying a notable technical advance. Our company didn't. It was still getting the team ready.

Now with almost every use of the cliché and stereotype mentioned so far, a better case could be made out for the use of simple, unhackneyed English. It is a mistake, however, to be too rigorously critical on this score. Since the symbols of language convey emotion as well as communicate facts and ideas, many a prefabricated phrase has become inextricably tied with certain emotional responses. This infuriates the semanticists—"intensional thinking" is their cuss word for it—but a good part of business has been built on it. The American sales meeting, certainly, would be quite impossible otherwise.

Furthermore business, like many another occupation, is governed by a ritual as rigid as the steps of ballet, and while the efficient executive makes fun of all this, he has the good sense to know when to put it to use himself. The dinner for the retiring employee, for example; for years this has been prime fodder for short-story writers. But what if the toastmaster were to dispense with the timeworn expressions and thus tacitly concede what everyone knows to be nothing less than the truth: that old Charlie has been getting in everybody's hair for the last fifteen years and it'll be wonderful to see him go. Everyone, Charlie's worst enemies included, would be shocked, morale would suffer, and the usefulness of the executive to the organization would be lessened.

So with the interoffice memo about the man being horizontally promoted to some branch office. Again the ceremonial is unvarying: pillar of strength . . . larger responsibilities . . . Ed's invaluable experience in this field makes him the logical . . . know the whole staff will join me in wishing Ed good luck in his new job . . . Nobody is fooled in the slightest, of course, but what could have been a disagreeable, and for Ed a shattering, experience is smoothed over by the blessed analgesic of businesese. There is *something* of a case for timeworn expressions. But it is a case that needs no further making.

For all its faults, business language is the subject of plenty of good news. Over a third of top U.S. corporations, a *Fortune* sampling indicates, have set up some sort of program to improve it. Monsanto Chemical and Glidden Co. are working on both letters and interoffice memos. "In our campaign to simplify communications," reports Glidden's President Dwight Joyce, "we encourage 'Yes' and 'No' answers, which in turn makes for briefer, clearer questions." Montgomery Ward uses slide films to show its people how to write good-will-building letters. Numerous banks, insurance companies, and department stores have engaged experts to simplify and personalize their letters. And over the past two years the "Cy" Frailey business-correspondence courses sponsored by the Dartnell Corp. in major cities of the U.S. have attracted 25,000 executives.

Public-speaking courses are provided by such companies as SKF, Jones & Laughlin, and Johnson & Johnson. In the last two years General Motors has encouraged 2,000 of its management and supervisory people to express themselves better by taking Dale Carnegie speech courses. Business and management associations (e.g., National Association of Manufacturers, American Management Association, American Institute of Banking, National Association of Foremen) publish material on speech training. In one notable instance, at Bridgeport, Connecticut, an informal group of businessmen became so absorbed in the problem that they chipped in and hired a Yale professor to teach them how to address groups and conduct meetings. And evidently the crusade is more than a nine-to-five concern of businessmen. To judge from recent book sales, they are reading more "practical English" and vocabulary-building books than ever before.

Paralleling these better-business-English efforts has been a movement of even greater significance. It has been called the "plain talk" movement, but it is, in fact, a sort of prose-engineering program, for its core is the use of some newly refined scientific techniques to achieve readability. In only four years it has already produced a measurable effect on the English of business and, if it continues to thrive, it will have a profound effect not only on the English of business but on the English of advertising, journalism, and literature as well.

How did it happen? Such phenomena are usually hard to account for. This one, however, is not.

"My own contribution . . . has been quite modest," readability expert Dr. Rudolf Flesch recently told a convention of P.R. men, "but I think I can truthfully say that it has already had some effect." Dr. Flesch was unduly modest. Rarely have the man and the moment collided so effectively. Almost from the moment in 1946 when he turned his Columbia Ph.D. thesis on readability into the best-selling *The Art of Plain Talk,* Flesch's impact has been tremendous.

The scientific basis was not new; it was evolved by psychologists in the 1920's for the grading and writing of children's textbooks. But as developed by Flesch it gave a new form—and justification—to a movement that had been overtaking American prose. "It was as if," recalls one enthusiast, "we had just been waiting for someone to break the ice."

What Flesch teaches, briefly, is a scientific method of achieving plain, understandable prose. To this end we should write as we talk; eschew irony, rhythm, rhetorical sentences; substitute concrete for abstract words. Equally important, we should surcharge our prose with as much human interest as possible. Then, to measure how we are succeeding, we can apply two formulas. One, based on syllable and sentence count per 100 words, measures the "reading ease" of our writing. The other, based on the percentage of "personal" words and sentences, measures its "human interest." The reading-ease index is tied to the different levels of the U.S. adult population. Thus we can scientifically make sure that we are writing to the level of our particular audience—or better yet, as Flesch advises, somewhat below it.[3]

The first impact of this doctrine was on newspaper writing, but soon it was making itself felt in another field. For years industrial psychologists had been champing to apply scientific methods to employee-management communication material, but, what with cultural-lag troubles, they hadn't been able to get very far. And now here at last was the ideal wedge; "the effectiveness . . . [of] the Flesch formula," as one put it, "forces the issue." Enthusiastically they fell to work measuring house-organ prose, reconstructing information bulletins, and in general showing business just how terrible its stuff was and how much better it could be.

Before long another readability expert, Robert Gunning, was making studies for Borden's, the B. & O. Railroad, and other large companies. John McElroy (formerly head of Gunning's industrial division) set up Readability Associates, and was soon holding seminars on his "fog-count" system for such firms as Ford, Detroit Edison, and American Airlines. General Motors, making a broad attack on the readability problem, has at times employed all three experts, Gunning, McElroy, and Flesch.[4] The Psychological Corp. began four-day workshops, where, at $500 a head, company representatives could be instructed in the readability techniques so that they in turn could go back and teach them to others. Even the military joined in; in the most notable of such efforts the Air Matériel Command got out an official—and highly readable—manual on the Flesch approach and put psychologist A. O. England to work indoctrinating all hands in it.

What's been the effect of all this? The readability formulas have dramatized, as no subjective critique ever could, the needless obscurity and pomposity of much everyday language. Furthermore, the readability texts have been full of so much good sense on such matters as grammar and punctuation that they have served to encourage the timid away from outworn do's and dont's of writing. Where the readability doctrines have been taught, there has been not only a decrease in the use of jargon, but a new enthusiasm and respect for the rhythm of colloquial speech.

So far, so good. But how much further, and then how good? The implications of the readability approach warrant careful thought. For if American

3. The reading-ease formula—statisticians call it "regression equation"—is 206.835 minus (1.015 times the average number of words per sentence) plus (.846 times the number of syllables per 100 words). Using this (simplified in chart form for quick use), we find that the reading-ease score of the two preceding text paragraphs is 53. This puts them on the "fairly difficult"—i.e., high school—reading level, and thus readable by 54 per cent of the adult population. Human-interest score: 30 ("interesting").

4. G.M. has devised a "Reading-Ease Calculator"—a kind of wheel by which, with a minimum of mathematics, the prose in its twenty-seven employee publications can be measured. Also it has Purdue psychologists compiling a list of the words most frequently used by G.M. personnel, and is measuring the reading-ability levels of some of its employee groups.

"functional" English is to be homogenized more and more along these new lines, we should at least, before it all becomes official, have a hard look at what it is leading us to. In purest businesese, is there a danger that we'll jump out of a Pandora's box into a fire?

First, a look at some of the new rules. Most important, the advice that is the core of the movement: to write as we talk. Part of the "secret" of readable writing, we are told, lies in repetition and loosely built sentences—because that is the way we talk. Well, at least that's the way some people talk—haltings, backtrackings, and that sort of thing—they talk on forever sometimes—a lot of excelsior, that's what it adds up to—and it's not difficult at all, because it's certainly easier than the old-fashioned way of organizing your thoughts. In fact, there is only one real question to be raised. Are talking and writing the same thing? They are not—and to say that they should be allows and encourages us to rationalize sloppiness and faulty thinking.

In this colloquializing we are also adjured to make everything into a human-interest story. (Flesch: "There's nothing on earth that cannot be told through a hero or heroine who's trying to solve a problem in spite of a series of obstacles.") It is true, of course, that one who describes a problem in terms of the simple love of a man for his dog, a tale as old as time, will have a more *readable* piece than one who tends to somewhat more abstract treatment. But there are quite a number of things that *cannot* be explained by a human-interest tale, and to treat them as if they could be is to mislead the reader by oversimplifying.

Emphasis on the short word, naturally enough, is another feature of the plain-talk movement, and while the readability experts themselves caution people against applying this prescription too rigidly, it has reached a rather extreme point of veneration. Short words, certainly, need no defense. But there are times when the longer one is the *right* word, and if it were not used the writer would have to take up more space saying it another way. And even if the long word were unknown to such and such a percentage of the audience, it might be perfectly clear—or stimulating—to them in a context of sound, lucid English. The Elizabethans knew this well—and so, for that matter, do the pulp writers (e.g., the gibbous moon, the lambent rays, diaphanous dresses, etc.).

By now, if we have followed the above rules, our style should be understandable enough. Just to make sure, however, Flesch has a few more rules:

Do not use rhythm (maybe your reader won't catch on).
Do not use periodic sentences.
Do not use rhetorical questions.
Do not use metaphors without an explanation.
Do not use contrast without an explanation.
Do not use irony (half the people won't get it).

Now we are not to forswear these devices because they are bad; we are to discard them because somebody *might* possibly misunderstand us. The blood-toil-tears-and-sweat metaphor of Churchill, for example: "The reader gets a vague notion," says Flesch, "that Churchill used a little word picture of three wet things instead of saying *war*; and that's that." Flesch goes on to ask a rhetorical question: would "you must expect great suffering and hard work" have been a better way to put it? "Nobody, of course," he says, "can answer such a question." Nobody? We'll take a crack at it. NO!

If we have followed these rules, we are now able to talk the level of language the audience will be able to understand "without effort." But even this is not enough. *We must go one step below that level.* We must "shoot beneath the target"; we must "translate down the scale." And for this we don't even need the formulas, for, as Flesch correctly points out, this writing down should by now have become instinctive to us.

Let us imagine that over the next hundred years everyone followed this advice and deliberately wrote beneath the capabilities of his audience. What would happen? Theoretically, we would get ourselves into a sort of ever decreasing circle, and, as layer after layer of our language atrophied, eventually spiral our way back to the schoolbook level that got the whole readability doctrine under way in the first place. The "regression" equation would be complete.

And haven't we gone quite far enough as it is? Already we have turned the man in the street into a Frankenstein. We hand him an electric recorder to edit our movies; we watch his radio dial to predetermine what we will put on the air—and now we are to ape him to learn how to write.

We should long since have delivered ourselves of this oaf, for in reality he does not even exist. He is a self-perpetuating stereotype, the reflection of the lowest common denominators we have been looking for. In creating him we have done not only ourselves but our audiences a disservice, for though they will respond to the tawdry, they will also respond—as many a book, speech, ad, and movie has demonstrated—to the best we give them. But they cannot if we abdicate our moral obligation to give the best that is in us.

So what of the formulas? What do they really measure? Understandability? (And, if so, of what?) Simplicity? Or merely the number of things they are supposed to measure? For a practical experiment, *Fortune* selected thirteen out of a collection of 100 business speeches. The eight most fatuous of the speeches were put in one group; the five most lucid were put in another. Each speech was then evaluated by means of the two formulas to find its reading-ease and human-interest scores. The result: there was practically no *significant difference* between the average scores of the two groups. (Average reading-ease score: 61—eighth- and ninth-grade reading level; average human-interest score: 40—"very interesting.") All, then, represented good "plain talk"—and there was nothing in the scores to indicate the tremendous disparity between the two types.

In thus ignoring the relationship between style and content, the formulas have ignored the fundamentals of language. Language is not something we can disembody; it is an ethical as well as mechanical matter, inextricably bound up in ourselves, our positions, and our relations with those about us. When a businessman doubletalks, for example, it is often for reasons deeper than mishandled prose—hypersensitivity to criticism, fear of the competition, fear of getting out of line with trade-association policy, fear of a government suit, a serious split in corporation policy—or, as is occasionally the case, the lack of any policy to begin with. Is "plain talk" the answer here? It is not. It is a fraud on the listener.

For it is only the illusion of simplicity that the manipulation of language can win for us. Simplicity is an elusive, almost complex thing. It comes from discipline and organization of thought, intellectual courage—and many other attributes more hard won than by short words and short sentences. For plain talk—honest plain talk—is the reward of simplicity, not the means to it. The distinction may seem slight, but it is tremendously important.

In a sense, this whole prose-engineering movement is a measure of the growing specialization of our society—for it is an attempt to provide a sort of pidgin English by which we can intercommunicate over the gaps. So let us give the readability people their due. At least they have tried to bridge the gaps and, perhaps more important, they have called our attention to the necessity for doing so. We owe them, then, a debt—and if their solution falls short in many respects, the very avidity with which people have seized on it is proof enough that there is a void to fill.

Thus the readability movement is also the measure of the failure of our schools and colleges. Patently, something is very wrong with the teaching of English when graduates so fail to grasp the fundamentals of good English that they feel they must learn a separate kind of everyday life—and a rather bobtail one at that. The fault may be, as some have claimed, that our academic English courses are still set up on the implicit assumption that their function is to provide a schooling for those who are to be novelists, poets, and scholars. Perhaps it is for this reason that the word "literary" is increasingly used as a term of opprobrium.

Meanwhile the teaching of English in the non-liberal-arts courses has been geared more and more to the "functional" kind of writing the graduate will perform. "In my opinion," says Professor Edward Kilduff of N.Y.U.'s School of Commerce, "the most effective kind of English composition being taught today . . . is the realistic, practical non-literary American type that we find in such courses as business writing, engineering writing, newspaper writing, publicity writing, and advertising writing."

True or not, is a further extension of this trend necessarily the answer? Specialization in our colleges has already gone so far that it is hard to see how a further breakdown of the humanities would be anything but harmful. We do not need more "applied" English courses; what we need, first of all, is better basic ones. How this is to be achieved in our schools and colleges is a difficult problem, but it is time we were about it.

For somewhere, certainly, between the extremes of the "functional" and the "literary" there is a happy middle ground. Those firms who have pioneered in improving the language of their people seem to have reached the same conclusion. The great majority of their courses, seminars, and "clinics" have been concentrated not on supplying rules to be slavishly followed—but on provoking an *awareness* of good English. Their example is one that all of U.S. business can follow with great profit.

In the meantime let us not forswear all the richness of our language. Its misuse is not the root ill of our communication problem; it is only the signal of it. And if we make a real effort to win mutual understanding, we need have no fear of the infinite variety of our language—or the ability of our listeners to respond to it. All of which applies to businessmen no less than to everyone else in our society. When businessmen have something to say, and mean it, and feel it, their audience will understand.

NOTES AND COMMENT [1]

FROM *The New Yorker*

A PUBLISHER in Chicago has sent us a pocket calculating machine by which we may test our writing to see whether it is intelligible. The calculator was developed by General Motors, who, not satisfied with giving the world a Cadillac, now dream of bringing perfect understanding to men. The machine (it is simply a celluloid card with a dial) is called the Reading-Ease Calculator and shows four grades of "reading ease"—Very Easy, Easy, Hard, and Very Hard. You count your words and syllables, set the dial, and an indicator lets you know whether anybody is going to understand what you have written. An instruction book came with it, and after mastering the simple rules we lost no time in running a test on the instruction book itself, to see how *that* writer was doing. The poor fellow! His leading essay, the one on the front cover, tested Very Hard.

Our next step was to study the first phrase on the face of the calculator: "How to test Reading-Ease of written matter." There is, of course, no such thing as reading ease of written matter. There is the ease with which matter can be read, but that is a condition of the reader, not of the matter. Thus the inventors and distributors of this calculator get off to a poor start, with a Very Hard instruction book and a slovenly phrase. Already they have one foot caught in the brier patch of English usage.

Not only did the author of the instruction book score badly on the front cover, but inside the book he used the word "personalize" in an essay on how to improve one's writing. A man who likes the word "personalize" is entitled to

1. *The New Yorker*, XXVII (Mar. 7, 1951), 21–22. Reprinted by permission. Copyright, 1951, The New Yorker Magazine, Inc.

his choice, but we wonder whether he should be in the business of giving advice to writers. "Whenever possible," he wrote, "personalize your writing by directing it to the reader." As for us, we would as lief Simonize our grandmother as personalize our writing.

In the same envelope with the calculator, we received another training aid for writers—a booklet called "How to Write Better," by Rudolf Flesch. This, too, we studied, and it quickly demonstrated the broncolike ability of the English language to throw whoever leaps cocksurely into the saddle. The language not only can toss a rider but knows a thousand tricks for tossing him, each more gay than the last. Dr. Flesch stayed in the saddle only a moment or two. Under the heading "Think Before You Write," he wrote, "The main thing to consider is your *purpose* in writing. Why are you sitting down to write?" And echo answered: Because, sir, it is more comfortable than standing up.

Communication by the written word is a subtler (and more beautiful) thing than Dr. Flesch or General Motors imagines. They contend that the "average reader" is capable of reading only what tests Easy, and that the writer should write at or below this level. This is a presumptuous and degrading idea. There is no average reader, and to reach down toward this mythical character is to deny that each of us is on the way up, is ascending. ("Ascending," by the way, is a word Dr. Flesch advises writers to stay away from. Too unusual.)

It is our belief that no writer can improve his work until he discards the dulcet notion that the reader is feeble-minded, for writing is an act of faith, not a trick of grammar. Ascent is at the heart of the matter. A country whose writers are following a calculating machine downstairs is not ascending—if you will pardon the expression—and a writer who questions the capacity of the person at the other end of the line is not a writer at all, merely a schemer. The movies long ago decided that a wider communication could be achieved by a deliberate descent to a lower level, and they walked proudly down until they reached the cellar. Now they are groping for the light switch, hoping to find the way out.

We have studied Dr. Flesch's instructions diligently, but we return for guidance in these matters to an earlier American, who wrote with more patience, more confidence. "I fear chiefly," he wrote, "lest my expression may not be *extra-vagant* enough, may not wander far enough beyond the narrow limits of my daily experience, so as to be adequate to the truth of which I have been convinced. . . . Why level downward to our dullest perception always, and praise that as common sense? The commonest sense is the sense of men asleep, which they express by snoring."

Run that through your calculator! It may come out Hard, it may come out Easy. But it will come out whole, and it will last forever.

POLITICS AND THE ENGLISH LANGUAGE[1]

GEORGE ORWELL

Most people who bother with the matter at all would admit that the English language is in a bad way, but it is generally assumed that we cannot by conscious action do anything about it. Our civilization is decadent, and our language—so the argument runs—must inevitably share in the general collapse. It follows that any struggle against the abuse of language is a sentimental archaism, like preferring candles to electric light or hansom cabs to aeroplanes. Underneath this lies the half-conscious belief that language is a natural growth and not an instrument which we shape for our own purposes.

Now, it is clear that the decline of a language must ultimately have political and economic causes: it is not due simply to the bad influence of this or that individual writer. But an effect can become a cause, reinforcing the original cause and producing the same effect in an intensified form, and so on indefinitely. A man may take to drink because he feels himself to be a failure, and then fail all the more completely because he drinks. It is rather the same thing that is happening to the English language. It becomes ugly and inaccurate because our thoughts are foolish, but the slovenliness of our language makes it easier for us to have foolish thoughts. The point is that the process is reversible. Modern English, especially written English, is full of bad habits which spread by imitation and which can be avoided if one is willing to take the necessary trouble. If one gets rid of these habits one can think more clearly, and to think clearly is a necessary first step towards political regeneration: so that the fight against bad English is not frivolous and is not the exclusive concern of professional writers. I will come back to this presently, and I hope that by that time the meaning of what I have said here will have become clearer. Meanwhile, here are five specimens of the English language as it is now habitually written.

These five passages have not been picked out because they are especially bad —I could have quoted far worse if I had chosen—but because they illustrate various of the mental vices from which we now suffer. They are a little below the average, but are fairly representative samples. I number them so that I can refer back to them when necessary:

(1) I am not, indeed, sure whether it is not true to say that the Milton who once seemed not unlike a seventeenth-century Shelley had not become, out of an experience ever more bitter in each year, more alien (*sic*) to the founder of that Jesuit sect which nothing could induce him to tolerate.

Professor Harold Laski (Essay in *Freedom of Expression*)

(2) Above all, we cannot play ducks and drakes with a native battery of idioms

1. From *Shooting An Elephant* by George Orwell, copyright, 1945, 1946, 1949, 1950, by Sonia Brownell Orwell. Reprinted by permission of Harcourt, Brace and Company, Inc.

which prescribes such egregious collocations of vocables as the Basic *put up with* for *tolerate* or *put at a loss* for *bewilder*.

Professor Lancelot Hogben (*Interglossa*)

(3) On the one side we have the free personality; by definition it is not neurotic, for it has neither conflict nor dream. Its desires, such as they are, are transparent, for they are just what institutional approval keeps in the forefront of consciousness; another institutional pattern would alter their number and intensity; there is little in them that is natural, irreducible, or culturally dangerous. But *on the other side,* the social bond itself is nothing but the mutual reflection of these self-secure integrities. Recall the definition of love. Is not this the very picture of a small academic? Where is there a place in this hall of mirrors for either personality or fraternity?

Essay on psychology in *Politics* (New York)

(4) All the "best people" from the gentlemen's clubs, and all the frantic fascist captains, united in common hatred of Socialism and bestial horror of the rising tide of the mass revolutionary movement, have turned to acts of provocation, to foul incendiarism, to medieval legends of poisoned wells, to legalize their own destruction of proletarian organizations, and rouse the agitated petty-bourgeoisie to chauvinistic fervor on behalf of the fight against the revolutionary way out of the crisis.

Communist pamphlet

(5) If a new spirit *is* to be infused into this old country, there is one thorny and contentious reform which must be tackled, and that is the humanization and galvanization of the B.B.C. Timidity here will bespeak canker and atrophy of the soul. The heart of Britain may be sound and of strong beat, for instance, but the British lion's roar at present is like that of Bottom in Shakespeare's *Midsummer Night's Dream*—as gentle as any sucking dove. A virile new Britain cannot continue indefinitely to be traduced in the eyes, or rather ears, of the world by the effete languors of Langham Place, brazenly masquerading as "standard English." When the Voice of Britain is heard at nine o'clock, better far and infinitely less ludicrous to hear aitches honestly dropped than the present priggish, inflated, inhibited, school-ma'amish arch braying of blameless bashful mewing maidens.

Letter in *Tribune*

Each of these passages has faults of its own, but quite apart from avoidable ugliness, two qualities are common to all of them. The first is staleness of imagery; the other is lack of precision. The writer either has a meaning and cannot express it, or he inadvertently says something else, or he is almost indifferent as to whether his words mean anything or not. This mixture of vagueness and sheer incompetence is the most marked characteristic of modern English prose, and especially of any kind of political writing. As soon as certain topics are raised, the concrete melts into the abstract and no one seems able to think of turns of speech that are not hackneyed: prose consists less and less of *words* chosen for the sake of their meaning, and more and more of *phrases* tacked together like the sections of a prefabricated hen-house. I list below, with notes and examples, various of the tricks by means of which the work of prose-construction is habitually dodged:

Dying metaphors. A newly-invented metaphor assists thought by evoking a visual image, while on the other hand a metaphor which is technically "dead" (e.g., *iron resolution*) has in effect reverted to being an ordinary word and can generally be used without loss of vividness. But in between these two classes there is a huge dump of worn-out metaphors which have lost all evocative power and are merely used because they save people the trouble of inventing phrases for themselves. Examples are: *Ring the changes on, take up the cudgels for, toe the line, ride roughshod over, stand shoulder to shoulder with, play into the hands of, an axe to grind, grist to the mill, fishing in troubled waters, on the order of the day, Achilles' heel, swan song, hotbed.* Many of these are used without knowledge of their meaning (what is a "rift," for instance?), and incompatible metaphors are frequently mixed, a sure sign that the writer is not interested in what he is saying. Some metaphors now current have been twisted out of their original meaning without those who use them even being aware of the fact. For example, *toe the line* is sometimes written *tow the line.* Another example is *the hammer and the anvil,* now always used with the implication that the anvil gets the worst of it. In real life it is always the anvil that breaks the hammer, never the other way about: a writer who stopped to think what he was saying would be aware of this, and would avoid perverting the original phrase.

Operators, or *verbal false limbs.* These save the trouble of picking out appropriate verbs and nouns, and at the same time pad each sentence with extra syllables which give it an appearance of symmetry. Characteristic phrases are: *render inoperative, militate against, prove unacceptable, make contact with, be subjected to, give rise to, give grounds for, have the effect of, play a leading part (role) in, make itself felt, take effect, exhibit a tendency to, serve the purpose of, etc., etc.* The keynote is the elimination of simple verbs. Instead of being a single word, such as *break, stop, spoil, mend, kill,* a verb becomes a phrase, made up of a noun or adjective tacked on to some general-purposes verb such as *prove, serve, form, play, render.* In addition, the passive voice is wherever possible used in preference to the active, and noun constructions are used instead of gerunds (*by examination of* instead of *by examining*). The range of verbs is further cut down by means of the *-ize* and *de-* formations, and banal statements are given an appearance of profundity by means of the *not un-* formation. Simple conjunctions and prepositions are replaced by such phrases as *with respect to, having regard to, the fact that, by dint of, in view of, in the interests of, on the hypothesis that;* and the ends of sentences are saved from anti-climax by such resounding commonplaces as *greatly to be desired, cannot be left out of account, a development to be expected in the near future, deserving of serious consideration, brought to a satisfactory conclusion,* and so on and so forth.

Pretentious diction. Words like *phenomenon, element, individual* (as noun), *objective, categorical, effective, virtual, basis, primary, promote, constitute, exhibit, exploit, utilize, eliminate, liquidate,* are used to dress up simple statements and give an air of scientific impartiality to biased judgments. Adjectives like *epoch-making, epic, historic, unforgettable, triumphant, age-old, inevitable, inexorable, veritable,* are used to dignify the sordid processes of international politics, while writing that aims at glorifying war usually takes on an archaic color, its characteristic words being: *realm, throne, chariot, mailed fist, trident, sword, shield, buckler, banner, jackboot, clarion.* Foreign words and expressions such as *cul de sac, ancien régime, deus ex machina, mutatis mutandis, status quo, gleichschaltung, weltanschauung,* are used to give an air of culture and elegance. Except for the useful abbreviations *i.e., e.g.,* and *etc.,* there is no real need for any of the hundreds of foreign phrases now current in English. Bad writers, and especially scientific, political and sociological writers, are nearly always haunted by the notion that Latin or Greek words are grander than Saxon ones, and unnecessary words like *expedite, ameliorate, predict, extraneous, deracinated, clandestine, subaqueous* and hundreds of others constantly gain ground from their Anglo-Saxon opposite numbers.[2] The jargon peculiar to Marxist writing (*hyena, hangman, cannibal, petty bourgeois, these gentry, lackey, flunkey, mad dog, White Guard, etc.*) consists largely of words and phrases translated from Russian, German or French; but the normal way of coining a new word is to use a Latin or Greek root with the appropriate affix and, where necessary, the *-ize* formation. It is often easier to make up words of this kind (*de-regionalize, impermissible, extramarital, non-fragmentary* and so forth) than to think up the English words that will cover one's meaning. The result, in general, is an increase in slovenliness and vagueness.

Meaningless words. In certain kinds of writing, particularly in art criticism and literary criticism, it is normal to come across long passages which are almost completely lacking in meaning.[3] Words like *romantic, plastic, values, human, dead, sentimental, natural, vitality,* as used in art criticism, are strictly meaningless, in the sense that they not only do not point to any discoverable object, but are hardly even expected to do so by the reader. When one critic writes, "The outstanding feature of Mr. X's work is its living quality," while another writes, "The immediately striking thing about Mr. X's work is its peculiar deadness," the reader accepts this as a simple difference of opinion. If words like *black* and *white* were involved, instead of the jargon words *dead* and *living,* he would see at once that language was being used in an improper way. Many political words are similarly abused. The word *Fascism* has now no meaning except in so far as it signifies "something not desirable." The words *democracy, socialism, freedom, patriotic, realistic, justice,* have each of

2. An interesting illustration of this is the way in which the English flower names which were in use till very recently are being ousted by Greek ones, *snap-dragon* becoming *antirrhinum, forget-me-not* becoming *myosotis,* etc. It is hard to see any practical reason for this change of fashion: it is probably due to an instinctive turning-away from the more homely word and a vague feeling that the Greek word is scientific.

3. Example: "Comfort's catholicity of perception and image, strangely Whitmanesque in range, almost the exact opposite in aesthetic compulsion, continues to evoke that trembling atmospheric accumulative hinting at a cruel, an inexorably serene timelessness . . . Wrey Gardiner scores by aiming at simple bullseyes with precision. Only they are not so simple, and through this contented sadness runs more than the surface bittersweet of resignation." (*Poetry Quarterly.*)

them several different meanings which cannot be reconciled with one another. In the case of a word like *democracy,* not only is there no agreed definition, but the attempt to make one is resisted from all sides. It is almost universally felt that when we call a country democratic we are praising it: consequently the defenders of every kind of régime claim that it is a democracy, and fear that they might have to stop using the word if it were tied down to any one meaning. Words of this kind are often used in a consciously dishonest way. That is, the person who uses them has his own private definition, but allows his hearer to think he means something quite different. Statements like *Marshal Pétain was a true patriot, The Soviet Press is the freest in the world, The Catholic Church is opposed to persecution,* are almost always made with intent to deceive. Other words used in variable meanings, in most cases more or less dishonestly, are: *class, totalitarian, science, progressive, reactionary, bourgeois, equality.*

Now that I have made this catalogue of swindles and perversions, let me give another example of the kind of writing that they lead to. This time it must of its nature be an imaginary one. I am going to translate a passage of good English into modern English of the worst sort. Here is a well-known verse from *Ecclesiastes:*

> I returned, and saw under the sun, that the race is not to the swift, nor the battle to the strong, neither yet bread to the wise, nor yet riches to men of understanding, nor yet favor to men of skill; but time and chance happeneth to them all.

Here it is in modern English:

> Objective consideration of contemporary phenomena compels the conclusion that success or failure in competitive activities exhibits no tendency to be commensurate with innate capacity, but that a considerable element of the unpredictable must invariably be taken into account.

This is a parody, but not a very gross one. Exhibit (3), above, for instance, contains several patches of the same kind of English. It will be seen that I have not made a full translation. The beginning and ending of the sentence follow the original meaning fairly closely, but in the middle the concrete illustrations —race, battle, bread—dissolve into the vague phrase "success or failure in competitive activities." This had to be so, because no modern writer of the kind I am discussing—no one capable of using phrases like "objective consideration of contemporary phenomena"—would ever tabulate his thoughts in that precise and detailed way. The whole tendency of modern prose is away from concreteness. Now analyze these two sentences a little more closely. The first contains 49 words but only 60 syllables, and all its words are those of everyday life. The second contains 38 words of 90 syllables: 18 of its words are from Latin roots, and one from Greek. The first sentence contains six vivid images, and only one phrase ("time and chance") that could be called vague. The second contains not a single fresh, arresting phrase, and in spite of its 90 syllables it gives only a shortened version of the meaning contained in the first. Yet without a doubt it is the second kind of sentence that is gaining ground in modern English. I do not want to exaggerate. This kind of writing is not yet universal, and outcrops of simplicity will occur here and there in the worst-written page. Still, if you or I were told to write a few lines on the uncertainty of human fortunes, we should probably come much nearer to my imaginary sentence than to the one from *Ecclesiastes.*

As I have tried to show, modern writing at its worst does not consist in picking out words for the sake of their meaning and inventing images in order to make the meaning clearer. It consists in gumming together long strips of words which have already been set in order by someone else, and making the results presentable by sheer humbug. The attraction of this way of writing is that it is easy. It is easier—even quicker, once you have the habit—to say *In my opinion it is a not unjustifiable assumption that* than to say *I think.* If you use ready-made phrases, you not only don't have to hunt about for words; you also don't have to bother with the rhythms of your sentences, since these phrases are generally so arranged as to be more or less euphonious. When you are composing in a hurry—when you are dictating to a stenographer, for instance, or making a public speech—it is natural to fall into a pretentious, Latinized style. Tags like *a consideration which we should do well to bear in mind* or *a conclusion to which all of us would readily assent* will save many a sentence from coming down with a bump. By using stale metaphors, similes and idioms, you save much mental effort at the cost of leaving your meaning vague, not only for your reader but for yourself. This is the significance of mixed metaphors. The sole aim of a metaphor is to call up a visual image. When these images clash—as in *The Fascist octopus has sung its swan song, the jackboot is thrown into the melting pot*—it can be taken as certain that the writer is not seeing a mental image of the objects he is naming; in other words he is not really thinking. Look again at the examples I gave at the beginning of this essay. Professor Laski (1) uses five negatives in 53 words. One of these is superfluous, making nonsense of the whole passage, and in addition there is the slip *alien* for akin, making further nonsense, and several avoidable pieces of clumsiness which increase the general vagueness. Professor Hogben (2) plays ducks and drakes with a battery which is able to write prescriptions, and, while disapproving of the everyday phrase *put up with,* is unwilling to look *egregious* up in the dictionary and see what it means. (3), if one takes an uncharitable attitude towards it, is simply meaningless: probably one could work out its intended meaning by reading the whole of the article in which it occurs. In (4), the writer knows more or less what he wants to say, but an accumulation of stale phrases chokes him like tea leaves blocking a sink. In (5), words and meaning have almost parted company. People who write in this manner usually have a general emotional meaning—they dislike one thing and want to express solidarity with another—but they are not interested in the detail of what they are saying. A scrupulous writer, in every sentence that he writes, will ask himself at least four questions, thus: What am I trying to say? What words will express it? What image or idiom will make it clearer? Is this image fresh enough to have an effect? And he will probably ask himself two more: Could I put it more shortly? Have I said anything that is avoidably ugly? But you are not obliged to go to all this trouble. You can shirk it by simply throwing your mind open and letting the ready-made phrases come crowding in. They will construct your sentences for you—even think your thoughts for you, to a certain extent—and at need they will perform the important service of partially concealing your meaning even from yourself. It is at this point that the special connection between politics and the debasement of language becomes clear.

In our time it is broadly true that political writing is bad writing. Where it is not true, it will generally be found that the writer is some kind of rebel, expressing his private opinions and not a "party line." Orthodoxy, of whatever color, seems to demand a lifeless, imitative style. The political dialects to be found in pamphlets, leading articles, manifestoes, White Papers and the speeches of under-secretaries do, of course, vary from party to party, but they are all alike in that one almost never finds in them a fresh, vivid, home-made turn of speech. When one watches some tired hack on the platform mechanically repeating the familiar phrases—*bestial atrocities, iron heel, bloodstained tyranny, free peoples of the world, stand shoulder to shoulder*—one often has a curious feeling that one is not watching a live human being but some kind of dummy: a feeling which suddenly becomes stronger at moments when the light catches the speaker's spectacles and turns them into blank discs which seem to have no eyes behind them. And this is not altogether fanciful. A speaker who uses that kind of phraseology has gone some distance towards turning himself into a machine. The appropriate noises are coming out of his larynx, but his brain is not involved as it would be if he were choosing his words for himself. If the speech he is making is one that he is accustomed to make over and over again, he may be almost unconscious of what he is saying, as one is when one utters the responses in church. And this reduced state of consciousness, if not indispensable, is at any rate favorable to political conformity.

In our time, political speech and writing are largely the defense of the indefensible. Things like the continuance of British rule in India, the Russian purges and deportations, the dropping of the atom bombs on Japan, can indeed be defended, but only by arguments which are too brutal for most people to face, and which do not square with the professed aims of political parties. Thus political language has to consist largely of euphemism, question-begging and sheer cloudy vagueness. Defenseless villages are bombarded from the air, the inhabitants driven out into the countryside, the cattle machine-gunned, the huts set on fire with incendiary bullets: this is called *pacification*. Millions of peasants are robbed of their farms and sent trudging along the roads with no more than they can carry: this is called *transfer of population* or *rectification of frontiers*. People are imprisoned for years without trial, or shot in the back of the neck or sent to die of scurvy in Arctic lumber camps: this is called *elimination of unreliable elements*. Such phraseology is needed if one wants to name things without calling up mental pictures of them. Consider for instance some comfortable English professor defending Russian totalitarianism. He cannot say outright, "I believe in killing off your opponents when you can get good results by doing so." Probably, therefore, he will say something like this:

While freely conceding that the Soviet régime exhibits certain features which the humanitarian may be inclined to deplore, we must, I think, agree that a certain curtailment of the right to political opposition is an unavoidable concomitant of transitional periods, and that the rigors which the Russian people have been called upon to undergo have been amply justified in the sphere of concrete achievement.

The inflated style is itself a kind of euphemism. A mass of Latin words falls upon the facts like soft snow, blurring the outlines and covering up all the details. The great enemy of clear language is insincerity. When there is a gap between one's real and one's declared aims, one turns, as it were instinctively, to long words and exhausted idioms, like a cuttlefish squirting out ink. In our age there is no such thing as "keeping out of politics." All issues are political issues, and politics itself is a mass of lies, evasions, folly, hatred and schizophrenia. When the general atmosphere is bad, language must suffer. I should expect to find—this is a guess which I have not sufficient knowledge to verify—that the German, Russian and Italian languages have all deteriorated in the last ten or fifteen years as a result of dictatorship.

But if thought corrupts language, language can also corrupt thought. A bad usage can spread by tradition and imitation, even among people who should and do know better. The debased language that I have been discussing is in some ways very convenient. Phrases like *a not unjustifiable assumption, leaves much to be desired, would serve no good purpose, a consideration which we should do well to bear in mind,* are a continuous temptation, a packet of aspirins always at one's elbow. Look back through this essay, and for certain you will find that I have again and again committed the very faults I am protesting against. By this morning's post I have received a pamphlet dealing with conditions in Germany. The author tells me that he "felt impelled" to write it. I open it at random, and here is almost the first sentence that I see: "[The Allies] have an opportunity not only of achieving a radical transformation of Germany's social and political structure in such a way as to avoid a nationalistic reaction in Germany itself, but at the same time of laying the foundations of a cooperative and unified Europe." You see, he "feels impelled" to write—feels, presumably, that he has something new to say—and yet his words, like cavalry horses answering the bugle, group themselves automatically into the familiar dreary pattern. This invasion of one's mind by ready-made phrases (*lay the foundations, achieve a radical transformation*) can only be prevented if one is constantly on guard against them, and every such phrase anesthetizes a portion of one's brain.

I said earlier that the decadence of our language is probably curable. Those who deny this would argue, if they produced an argument at all, that language merely reflects existing social conditions, and that we cannot influence its development by any direct tinkering with words and constructions. So far as the general tone or spirit of a language goes, this may be true, but it is not true in detail. Silly words and expressions have often disappeared, not through any evolutionary process but owing to the conscious action of a minority. Two recent examples were *explore every avenue* and *leave no stone unturned,* which were killed by the jeers of a few journalists. There is a long list of flyblown metaphors which could similarly be got rid of if enough people would interest themselves in the job; and it should also be possible to laugh the *not un-* formation out of existence,[4] to reduce the amount of Latin and Greek in the average sentence, to drive out foreign phrases and strayed scientific words, and, in general, to make pretentiousness unfashionable. But all these are minor points. The defense of the English language implies more than this, and perhaps it is best to start by saying what it does *not* imply.

To begin with, it has nothing to do with archaism, with the salvaging of obsolete words and turns of speech, or with the setting-up of a "standard English" which must never be departed from. On the contrary, it is especially concerned with the scrapping of every word or idiom which has outworn its usefulness. It has nothing to do with correct grammar and syntax, which are of no importance so long as one makes one's meaning clear, or with the avoidance of Americanisms, or with having what is called a "good prose style." On the other hand it is not concerned with fake simplicity and the attempt to make written English colloquial. Nor does it even imply in every case preferring the Saxon word to the Latin one, though it does imply using the fewest and shortest words that will cover one's meaning. What is above all needed is to let the meaning choose the word, and not the other way about. In prose, the worst thing one can do with words is to surrender them. When you think of a concrete object, you think wordlessly, and then, if you want to describe the thing you have been visualizing, you probably hunt about till you find the exact words that seem to fit it. When you think of something abstract you are more inclined to use words from the start, and unless you make a conscious effort to prevent it, the existing dialect will come rushing in and do the job for you, at the expense of blurring or even changing your meaning. Probably it is better to put off using words as long as possible and get one's meaning as clear as one can through pictures or sensations. Afterwards one can choose—

4. One can cure oneself of the *not un-* formation by memorizing this sentence: *A not unblack dog was chasing a not unsmall rabbit across a not ungreen field.*

not simply *accept*—the phrases that will best cover the meaning, and then switch round and decide what impressions one's words are likely to make on another person. This last effort of the mind cuts out all stale or mixed images, all prefabricated phrases, needless repetitions, and humbug and vagueness generally. But one can often be in doubt about the effect of a word or a phrase, and one needs rules that one can rely on when instinct fails. I think the following rules will cover most cases:

(i) Never use a metaphor, simile or other figure of speech which you are used to seeing in print.

(ii) Never use a long word where a short one will do.

(iii) If it is possible to cut a word out, always cut it out.

(iv) Never use the passive where you can use the active.

(v) Never use a foreign phrase, a scientific word or a jargon word if you can think of an everyday English equivalent.

(vi) Break any of these rules sooner than say anything barbarous.

These rules sound elementary, and so they are, but they demand a deep change of attitude in anyone who has grown used to writing in the style now fashionable. One could keep all of them and still write bad English, but one could not write the kind of stuff that I quoted in these five specimens at the beginning of this article.

I have not here been considering the literary use of language, but merely language as an instrument for expressing and not for concealing or preventing thought. Stuart Chase and others have come near to claiming that all abstract words are meaningless, and have used this as a pretext for advocating a kind of political quietism. Since you don't know what Fascism is, how can you struggle against Fascism? One need not swallow such absurdities as this, but one ought to recognize that the present political chaos is connected with the decay of language, and that one can probably bring about some improvement by starting at the verbal end. If you simplify your English, you are freed from the worst follies of orthodoxy. You cannot speak any of the necessary dialects, and when you make a stupid remark its stupidity will be obvious, even to yourself. Political language—and with variations this is true of all political parties, from Conservatives to Anarchists—is designed to make lies sound truthful and murder respectable, and to give an appearance of solidity to pure wind. One cannot change this all in a moment, but one can at least change one's own habits, and from time to time one can even, if one jeers loudly enough, send some worn-out and useless phrase—some *jackboot, Achilles' heel, hotbed, melting pot, acid test, veritable inferno* or other lump of verbal refuse—into the dustbin where it belongs.

INTERLUDE: ON JARGON[1]

ARTHUR QUILLER-COUCH

We parted, Gentlemen, upon a promise to discuss the capital difficulty of Prose, as we have discussed the capital difficulty of Verse. But, although we shall come to it, on second thoughts I ask leave to break the order of my argument and to interpose some words upon a kind of writing which, from a superficial likeness, commonly passes for prose in these days, and by lazy folk is commonly written for prose, yet actually is not prose at all; my excuse being the simple practical one that, by first clearing this sham prose out of the way, we shall the better deal with honest prose when we come to it. The proper difficulties of prose will remain; but we shall be agreed in understanding what it is, or at any rate what it is not, that we talk about. I remember to have heard somewhere of a religious body in the United States of America which had reason to suspect one of its churches of accepting spiritual consolation from a colored preacher—an offense against the laws of the Synod—and despatched a Disciplinary Committee with power to act; and of the Committee's returning to report itself unable to take any action under its terms of reference, for that while a person undoubtedly colored had undoubtedly occupied the pulpit and had audibly spoken from it in the Committee's presence, the performance could be brought within no definition of preaching known or discoverable. So it is with that infirmity of speech—that flux, that determination of words to the mouth, or to the pen—which, though it be familiar to you in parliamentary debates, in newspapers, and as the staple language of Blue Books, Committees, Official Reports, I take leave to introduce to you as prose which is not prose and under its real name of Jargon.

You must not confuse this Jargon with what is called Journalese. The two overlap, indeed, and have a knack of assimilating each other's vices. But Jargon finds, maybe, the most of its votaries among good douce people who have never written to or for a newspaper in their life, who would never talk of "adverse climatic conditions" when they mean "bad weather"; who have never trifled with verbs such as "obsess," "recrudesce," "envisage," "adumbrate," or with phrases such as "the psychological moment," "the true inwardness," "it gives furiously to think." It dallies with Latinity—"sub silentio," "de die in diem," "cui bono?" (always in the sense, unsuspected by Cicero, of "What is the profit?")—but not for the sake of style. Your journalist at the worst is an artist in his way; he daubs paint of this kind upon the lily with a professional zeal; the more flagrant (or, to use his own word, arresting) the pigment, the happier is his soul. Like the Babu he is trying all the while to embellish our poor language, to make it more floriferous, more poetical—like the Babu for

1. From *On the Art of Writing,* by Sir Arthur Quiller-Couch, pp. 120–126. Courtesy of G. P. Putnam's Sons.

example who, reporting his mother's death, wrote, "Regret to inform you, the hand that rocked the cradle has kicked the bucket."

There is metaphor; *there* is ornament; *there* is a sense of poetry, though as yet groping in a world unrealised. No such gusto marks—no such zeal, artistic or professional, animates—the practitioners of Jargon, who are, most of them (I repeat), douce respectable persons. Caution is its father; the instinct to save everything and especially trouble; its mother, Indolence. It looks precise, but is not. It is, in these times, *safe:* a thousand men have said it before and not one to your knowledge had been prosecuted for it. And so, like respectability in Chicago, Jargon stalks unchecked in our midst. It is becoming the language of Parliament; it has become the medium through which Boards of Government, County Councils, Syndicates, Committees, Commercial Firms, express the processes as well as the conclusions of their thought and so voice the reason of their being.

Has a Minister to say "No" in the House of Commons? Some men are constitutionally incapable of saying no; but the Minister conveys it thus: "The answer to the question is in the negative." That means "no." Can you discover it to mean anything less, or anything more except that the speaker is a pompous person?—which was no part of the information demanded.

That is Jargon, and it happens to be accurate. But as a rule Jargon is by no means accurate, its method being to walk circumspectly around its target; and its faith, that having done so it has either hit the bull's-eye or at least achieved something equivalent, and safer.

Thus the clerk of a Board of Guardians will minute that:

In the case of John Jenkins deceased the coffin provided was of the usual character.

Now this is not accurate: "In the case of John Jenkins deceased," for whom a coffin was supplied, it is wholly superfluous to tell us that he is deceased. But actually John Jenkins never had more than one case, and that was the coffin. The clerk says he had two—a coffin in a case; but I suspect the clerk to be mistaken, and I am sure he errs in telling us that the coffin was of the usual character, for coffins have no character, usual or unusual.

For another example (I shall not tell you whence derived):

In the case of every candidate who is placed in the first class [So you see the lucky fellow gets a case as well as a first-class. He might be a stuffed animal: perhaps he is]—In the case of every candidate who is placed in the first class the class-list will show by some convenient mark (1) the Section or Sections for proficiency in which he is placed in the first class and (2) the Section or Sections (if any) in which he has passed with special distinction.

"The Section or Sections (if any)"—But how, if they are not any, could they be indicated by a mark however convenient?

The Examiners will have regard to the style and method of the candidate's answers, and will give credit for excellence in *these respects.*

Have you begun to detect the two main vices of Jargon? The first is that it uses circumlocution rather than short straight speech. It says: "In the case of John Jenkins deceased, the coffin" when it means "John Jenkins's coffin"; and its yea is not yea, neither is its nay nay; but its answer is in the affirmative or in the negative, as the foolish and superfluous "case" may be. The second vice is that it habitually chooses vague, woolly abstract nouns rather than concrete ones. I shall have something to say by-and-by about the concrete noun, and how you should ever be struggling for it whether in prose or in verse. For the moment I content myself with advising you, if you would write masculine English, never to forget the old tag of your Latin Grammar:

Masculine will only be
Things that you can touch and see.

But since these lectures are meant to be a course in First Aid to writing, I will content myself with one or two extremely rough rules; yet I shall be disappointed if you do not find them serviceable.

The first is: Whenever in your reading you come across one of these words, *case, instance, character, nature, condition, persuasion, degree*—whenever in writing your pen betrays you to one or another of them—pull yourself up and take thought. If it be "case" (I choose it as Jargon's dearest child—"in Heaven yclept Metonomy") turn to the dictionary, if you will, and seek out what meaning can be derived from *casus,* its Latin ancestor; then try how, with a little trouble, you can extricate yourself from that case. The odds are, you will feel like a butterfly who has discarded his chrysalis.

Here are some specimens to try your hand on:

(1) All those tears which inundated Lord Hugh Cecil's head were dry in the case of Mr. Harold Cox.

Poor Mr. Cox! left gasping in his aquarium!

(2) [From a cigar-merchant.] In any case, let us send you a case on approval.

(3) It is contended that Consols have fallen in consequence: but such is by no means the case.

"Such," by the way, is another spoilt child of Jargon, especially in Committee's Rules—"Co-opted members may be eligible as such; such members to continue to serve for such time as"—and so on.

(4) Even in the purely Celtic areas only in two or three cases do the Bishops bear Celtic names.

For "cases" read "dioceses."

Instance. In most instances the players were below their form.

But what were they playing at? Instances?

Character—Nature. There can be no doubt that the accident was caused through the dangerous nature of the spot, the hidden character of the by-road, and the utter absence of any warning or danger signal.

Mark the foggy wording of it all! And yet the man hit something and broke his neck! Contrast that explanation with the verdict of the coroner's jury in the west of England on a drowned postman: "We find that deceased met his death by an act of God, caused by sudden overflowing of the river Walkham and helped out by the scandalous neglect of the way-wardens."

The Aintree course is notoriously of a trying nature.

On account of its light character, purity, and age, Usher's whiskey is a whiskey that will agree with you.

Order. The mésalliance was of a pronounced order.

Condition. He was conveyed to his place of residence in an intoxicated condition.

"He was carried home drunk."

Quality and *Section.* Mr. ——, exhibiting no less than five works, all of a superior quality, figures prominently in the oil section.

This was written of an exhibition of pictures.

Degree. A singular degree of rarity prevails in the earlier editions of this romance.

This is Jargon. In prose it runs simply "The earlier editions of this romance are rare"—or "are very rare"—or even (if you believe what I take leave to doubt), "are singularly rare"; which should mean that they are rarer than the editions of any other work in the world.

Now what I ask you to consider about these quotations is that in each the writer was using Jargon to shirk prose, palming off periphrases upon us when with a little trouble he could have gone straight to the point. "A singular degree of rarity prevails," "the accident was caused through the dangerous nature of the spot," "but such is by no means the case." We may not be capable of much; but we can all write better than that, if we take a little trouble. In place of, "the Aintree course is of a trying nature" we can surely say "Aintree is a trying course" or "the Aintree course is a trying one"—just that and nothing more.

Next, having trained yourself to keep a look-out for these worst offenders (and you will be surprised to find out how quickly you get into the way of it), proceed to push your suspicions out among the whole cloudy host of abstract terms. "How excellent a thing is sleep," sighed Sancho Panza; "it wraps a man round like a cloak"—an excellent example, by the way, of how to say a thing concretely; a Jargoneer would have said that "among the beneficent qualities of sleep its capacity for withdrawing the human consciousness from the contemplation of immediate circumstances may perhaps be accounted not the least remarkable." How vile a thing—shall we say?—is the abstract noun! It wraps a man's thoughts round like cotton wool.

Here is a pretty little nest of specimens, found in *The Times* newspaper by Messrs. H. W. and F. G. Fowler, authors of that capital little book *The King's English:*

One of the most important reforms mentioned in the rescript is the unification of the organization of judicial institutions and the guarantee for all the tribunals of the independence necessary for securing to all classes of the community equality before the law.

I do not dwell on the cacophony; but, to convey a straightforward piece of news, might not the editor of *The Times* as well employ a man to write:

One of the most important reforms is that of the Courts, which need a uniform system and to be made independent. In this way only can men be assured that all are equal before the law.

I think he might.

A day or two ago the musical critic of the *Standard* wrote this:

MR. LAMOND IN BEETHOVEN

Mr. Frederick Lamond, the Scottish pianist, as an interpreter of Beethoven has few rivals. At this second recital of the composer's works at Bechstein Hall on Saturday afternoon he again displayed a complete sympathy and understanding of his material that extracted the very essence of aesthetic and musical value from each selection he undertook. The delightful intimacy of his playing and his unusual force of individual expression are invaluable assets, which, allied to his technical brilliancy, enable him to achieve an artistic triumph. The two lengthy Variations in E flat major (Op. 35) and in D major, the latter on the Turkish March from *The Ruins of Athens,* when included in the same programme, require a master hand to provide continuity of interest. *To say that Mr. Lamond successfully avoided moments that might at times, in these works, have inclined to comparative disinterestedness, would be but a moderate way of expressing the remarkable fascination with which his versatile playing endowed them,* but *at the same time* two of the sonatas given included a similar form of composition, and no matter how intellectually brilliant may be the interpretation, the extravagant use of a certain mode is bound in time to become somewhat ineffective. In the Three Sonatas, the E major (Op. 109), the A Major (Op. 2), No. 2, and the C minor (Op. 111), Mr. Lamond signalized his perfect insight into the composer's varying moods.

Will you not agree with me that here is no writing, here is no prose, here is not even English, but merely a flux of words to the pen?

Here again is a string, a concatenation—say, rather, a tiara of gems of purest ray serene from the dark unfathomed caves of a Scottish newspaper:

> The Chinese viewpoint, as indicated in this letter, may not be without interest to your readers, because it evidently is suggestive of more than an academic attempt to explain an unpleasant aspect of things which if allowed to materialize, might suddenly culminate in disaster resembling the Chang-Sha riots. It also ventures to illustrate incidents having their inception in recent premature endeavors to accelerate the development of Protestant missions in China; but we would hope for the sake of the interests involved that what my correspondent describes as "the irresponsible ruffian element" may be known by their various religious designations only within very restricted areas.

Well, the Chinese have given it up, poor fellows! and are asking the Christians—as today's newspapers inform us—to pray for them. Do you wonder? But that is, or was, the Chinese "viewpoint"—and what a willow-pattern viewpoint! Observe its delicacy. It does not venture to interest or be interesting; merely "to be not without interest." But it does "venture to illustrate incidents" —which, for a viewpoint, is brave enough; and this illustration "is suggestive of something more than an academic attempt to explain an unpleasant aspect of things which, if allowed to materialize, might suddenly culminate." *What* materializes? The unpleasant aspect? or the things? Grammar says the "things," "things which if allowed to materialize." But things are materialized already, and as a condition of their being things. It must be the aspect, then, that materializes. But, if so, it is also the aspect that culminates, and an aspect, however unpleasant, can hardly do that, or at worst cannot culminate in anything resembling the Chang-Sha riots. . . . I give it up.

Let us turn to another trick of Jargon; the trick of Elegant Variation, so rampant in the sporting press that there, without needing to attend these lectures, the undergraduate detects it for laughter:

> Hayward and C. B. Fry now faced the bowling, which apparently had no terrors for the Surrey crack. The old Oxonian, however, took some time in settling to work. . . .

Yes, you all recognize it and laugh at it. But why do you practice it in your essays? An undergraduate brings me an essay on Byron. In an essay on Byron, Byron is (or ought to be) mentioned many times. I expect, nay exact, that Byron shall be mentioned again and again. But my undergraduate has a blushing sense that to call Byron Byron twice on one page is indelicate. So Byron, after starting bravely as Byron, in the second sentence turns into "that great but unequal poet" and thenceforward I have as much trouble with Byron as ever Telemachus with Proteus to hold and pin him back to his proper self. Halfway down the page he becomes "the gloomy master of Newstead"; overleaf he is reincarnated into "the meteoric darling of society"; and so proceeds through successive avatars—"this arch-rebel," "the author of *Childe Harold,*" "the apostle of scorn," "the ex-Harrovian, proud, but abnormally sensitive of his club-foot," "the martyr of Missolonghi," "the pageant-monger of a bleeding heart." Now this again is Jargon. It does not, as most Jargon does, come of laziness; but it comes of timidity, which is worse. In literature as in life he makes himself felt who not only calls a spade a spade but has the pluck to double spades and redouble.

For another rule—just as rough and ready, but just as useful: Train your suspicions to bristle up whenever you come upon "as regards," "with regard to," "in respect of," "in connection with," "according as to whether," and the like. They are all dodges of Jargon, circumlocutions for evading this or that simple statement; and I say that it is not enough to avoid them nine times out of ten, or nine-and-ninety times out of a hundred. You should never use them. That is positive enough, I hope? Though I cannot admire his style, I admire the man who wrote to me, "Re Tennyson—your remarks anent his *In Memoriam* make me sick"; for though *re* is not a preposition of the first water, and "anent" has enjoyed its day, the finish crowned the work. But here are a few specimens far, very far, worse:

The special difficulty in Professor Minocelsi's case [our old friend "case" again] arose *in connexion with* the view he holds *relative to* the historical value of the opening pages of Genesis.

That is Jargon. In prose, even taking the miserable sentence as it stands constructed, we should write "the difficulty arose over the views he holds about the historical value," etc.

From a popular novelist:

I was entirely indifferent *as to* the results of the game, caring nothing at all *as to* whether *I had losses or gains.*

Cut out the first "as" in "as to," and the second "as to" altogether, and the sentence begins to be prose—"I was indifferent to the results of the game, caring nothing whether I had losses or gains."

But why, like Dogberry, have "had losses"? Why not simply "lose"? Let us try again. "I was entirely indifferent to the results of the game, caring nothing at all whether I won or lost."

Still the sentence remains absurd; for the second clause but repeats the first without adding one jot. For if you care not at all whether you win or lose, you must be entirely indifferent to the results of the game. So why not say, "I was careless if I won or lost," and have done with it?

A man of simple and charming character, he was fitly *associated with* the dictinction of the Order of Merit.

I take this gem with some others from a collection made three years ago by the *Oxford Magazine;* and I hope you admire it as one beyond price. "He was associated with the distinction of the Order of Merit" means "he was given the Order of Merit." If the members of that Order make a society then he was associated with them; but you cannot associate a man with a distinction. The inventor of such fine writing would doubtless have answered Canning's Needy Knife-grinder with:

I associate thee with sixpence! I will see thee in another association first!

But let us close our *florilegium* and attempt to illustrate Jargon by the converse method of taking a famous piece of English (say Hamlet's soliloquy) and remolding a few lines of it in this fashion:

To be, or the contrary? Whether the former or the latter be preferable would seem to admit of some difference of opinion; the answer in the present case being of an affirmative or of a negative character according as to whether one elects on the one hand to mentally suffer the disfavor of fortune, albeit in an extreme degree, or on the other to boldly envisage adverse conditions in the prospect of eventually bringing them to a conclusion. The condition of sleep is similar to, if not indistinguishable from that of death; and with the addition of finality the former might be considered identical with the latter: so that in this connection it might be argued with regard to sleep that, could the addition be effected, a termination would be put to the endurance of a multiplicity of inconveniences, not to mention a number of down-right evils incidental to our fallen humanity, and thus a consummation achieved of a most gratifying nature.

That is Jargon: and to write Jargon is to be perpetually shuffling around in the fog and cotton-wool of abstract terms; to be forever hearkening, like Ibsen's Peer Gynt, to the voice of the Boyg exhorting you to circumvent the difficulty, to beat the air because it is easier than to flesh your sword in the thing. The first virtue, the touchstone of masculine style, is its use of the active verb and the concrete noun. When you write in the active voice, "They gave him a silver teapot," you write as a man. When you write "He was made the recipient of a silver teapot," you write Jargon. But at the beginning set even higher store on the concrete noun. Somebody—I think it was FitzGerald—once posited the question, "What would have become of Christianity if Jeremy Bentham had had the writing of the Parables?" Without pursuing that dreadful enquiry I ask you to note how carefully the Parables—those exquisite short stories—speak only of "things which you can touch and see"—"A sower went forth to sow," "The Kingdom of Heaven is like unto leaven, which a woman took,"—and not the Parables only, but the Sermon on the Mount, and almost every verse of the Gospel. The Gospel does not, like my young essayist, fear to repeat a word, if the word be good. The Gospel says "Render unto Caesar the things that are Caesar's"—not "Render unto Caesar the things that appertain to that potentate." The Gospel does not say "Consider the growth of the lilies," or even "Consider how the lilies grow." It says, "Consider the lilies, how they grow."

Or take Shakespeare. I wager you that no writer of English so constantly chooses the concrete word, in phrase after phrase forcing you to touch and see. No writer so insistently teaches the general through the particular. He does it even in *Venus and Adonis* (as Professor Wendell, of Harvard, pointed out in a brilliant little monograph on Shakespeare, published some ten years ago). Read any page of *Venus and Adonis* side by side with any page of Marlowe's *Hero and Leander* and you cannot but mark the contrast: in Shakespeare the definite, particular, visualized image, in Marlowe, the beautiful generalization, the abstract term, the thing seen at a literary remove. Take the two openings, both of which start out with the sunrise. Marlowe begins:

Now had the Morn espied her lover's steeds:
Whereat she starts, puts on her purple weeds,
And, red for anger that he stay'd so long,
All headlong throws herself the clouds among.

Shakespeare wastes no words on Aurora and her feelings, but gets to his hero and to business without ado:

Even as the sun with purple-colour'd face—

(You have the sun visualized at once),

Even as the sun with purple-colour'd face
Had ta'en his last leave of the weeping morn,
Rose-cheek'd Adonis hied him to the chase;
Hunting he loved, but love he laugh'd to scorn.

When Shakespeare has to describe a horse, mark how definite he is:

Round-hoof'd, short-jointed, fetlocks shag and long,
Broad breast, full eye, small head and nostril wide,
High crest, short ears, straight legs and passing strong;
Thin mane, thick tail, broad buttock, tender hide.

Or again, in a casual simile, how definite:

Upon this promise did he raise his chin,
Like a dive-dipper peering through a wave,
Which, being look'd on, ducks as quickly in.

Or take, if you will, Marlowe's description of Hero's first meeting Leander:

It lies not in our power to love or hate,
For will in us is over-ruled by fate . . .

and set against it Shakespeare's description of Venus' last meeting with Adonis, as she came on him lying in his blood:

Or as a snail whose tender horns being hit
Shrinks backward in his shelly cave with pain,
And there, all smother'd up, in shade doth sit,
Long after fearing to creep forth again;
So, at his bloody view . . .

I do not deny Marlowe's lines (if you will study the whole passage) to be lovely. You may even judge Shakespeare's to be crude by comparison. But you cannot help noting that whereas Marlowe steadily deals in abstract, nebulous terms, Shakespeare constantly uses concrete ones, which later on he learned to pack into verse, such as:

Sleep that knits up the ravell'd sleeve of care.

Is it unfair to instance Marlowe, who died young? Then let us take Webster for the comparison; Webster, a man of genius or of something very like it, and commonly praised by the critics for his mastery over definite, detailed, and what I may call *solidified sensation*. Let us take this admired passage from his *Duchess of Malfi:*

Ferdinand. How doth our sister Duchess bear herself
In her imprisonment?
Basola. Nobly: I'll describe her.
She's sad as one long wed to 't, and she seems
Rather to welcome the end of misery
Than shun it: a behaviour so noble
As gives a majesty to adversity.[2]
You may discern the shape of loveliness
More perfect in her tears than in her smiles;
She will muse for hours together;[3] and her silence
Methinks expresseth more than if she spake.

Now set against this the well-known passage from *Twelfth Night* where the Duke asks and Viola answers a question about some one unknown to him and invented by her—a mere phantasm, in short: yet note how much more definite is the language:

Viola. My father had a daughter lov'd a man;
As it might be, perhaps, were I a woman,
I should your lordship.
Duke. And what's her history?
Viola. A blank, my lord. She never told her love,
But let concealment, like a worm i' the bud,
Feed on her damask cheek; she pined in thought,

2. Note the abstract terms.
3. Here we come on the concrete: and how beautiful it is.

And with a green and yellow melancholy
She sat like Patience on a monument
Smiling at grief. Was not this love indeed?

Observe (apart from the dramatic skill of it) how, when Shakespeare *has* to use the abstract noun "concealment," on an instant it turns into a visible worm "feeding" on the visible rose; how, having to use a second abstract word "patience," at once he solidifies it in tangible stone.

Turning to prose, you may easily assure yourselves that men who have written learnedly on the art agree in treating our maxim—to prefer the concrete term to the abstract, the particular to the general, the definite to the vague—as a canon of rhetoric. Whately has much to say on it. The late Mr. E. J. Payne, in one of his admirable prefaces to Burke (prefaces too little known and valued, as too often happens to scholarship hidden away in a schoolbook), illustrated the maxim by setting a passage from Burke's speech *On Conciliation with America* alongside a passage of like purport from Lord Brougham's *Inquiry into the Policy of the European Powers.* Here is the deadly parallel:

BURKE

In large bodies the circulation of power must be less vigorous at the extremities. Nature has said it. The Turk cannot govern Egypt and Arabia and Curdistan as he governs Thrace; nor has he the same dominion in Crimea and Algiers which he has in Brusa and Smyrna. Despotism itself is obliged to truck and huckster. The Sultan gets such obedience as he can. He governs with a loose rein, that he may govern at all; and the whole of the force and vigour of his authority in his centre is derived from a prudent relaxation in all his borders.

BROUGHAM

In all the despotisms of the East, it has been observed that the further any part of the empire is removed from the capital, the more do its inhabitants enjoy some sort of rights and privileges: the more inefficacious is the power of the monarch; and the more feeble and easily decayed is the organisation of the government.

You perceive that Brougham has transferred Burke's thought to his own page; but will you not also perceive how pitiably, by dissolving Burke's vivid particulars into smooth generalities, he has enervated its hold on the mind?

"This particularising style," comments Mr. Payne, "is the essence of poetry; and in prose it is impossible not to be struck with the energy it produces. Brougham's passage is excellent in its way: but it pales before the flashing lights of Burke's sentences." The best instances of this energy of style, he adds, are to be found in the classical writers of the seventeenth century. "When South says, 'An Aristotle was but the rubbish of an Adam, and Athens but the rudiments of Paradise,' he communicates more effectually the notion of the difference between the intellect of fallen and of unfallen humanity than in all the philosophy of his sermons put together."

You may agree with me, or you may not, that South in this passage is expounding trash; but you will agree with Mr. Payne and me that he uttered it vividly.

Let me quote to you, as a final example of this vivid style of writing, a passage from Dr. John Donne far beyond and above anything that ever lay within South's compass:

> The ashes of an Oak in the Chimney are no epitaph of that Oak, to tell me how high or how large that was; it tells me not what flocks it sheltered while it stood, nor what men it hurt when it fell. The dust of great persons' graves is speechless, too; it says nothing, it distinguishes nothing. As soon the dust of a wretch whom thou wouldest not, as of a prince whom thou couldest not look upon will trouble thine eyes if the wind it blow thither; and when a whirlewind hath blown the dust of the Churchyard into the Church, and the man sweep out the dust of the Church into the Churchyard, who will undertake to sift those dusts again and to pronounce, This is the Patrician, this is the noble flowre [flour], this the yeomanly, this the Plebeian bran? So is the death of *Iesabel* (*Iesabel* was a Queen) expressed. They shall not say *This is Iesabel;* not only not wonder that it is, nor pity that it should be; but they shall not say, they shall not know, *This is Iesabel.*

Carlyle noted of Goethe, "his emblematic intellect, his never-failing tendency to transform into *shape,* into *life,* the feeling that may dwell in him. Everything has form, has visual excellence: the poet's imagination bodies forth the forms of things unseen, and his pen turns them into shape."

Perpend this, Gentlemen, and maybe you will not hereafter set it down to my reproach that I wasted an hour of a May morning in a denunciation of Jargon, and in exhorting you upon a technical matter at first sight so trivial as the choice between abstract and definite words.

A lesson about writing your language may go deeper than language; for language (as in a former lecture I tried to preach to you) is your reason, your *λόγος*. So long as you prefer abstract words, which express other men's summarized concepts of things, to concrete ones which lie as near as can be reached to things themselves and are the first-hand material for your thoughts, you will remain, at the best, writers at second-hand. If your language be Jargon, your intellect, if not your whole character, will almost certainly correspond. Where your mind should go straight, it will dodge: the difficulties it should approach with a fair front and grip with a firm hand it will be seeking to evade or circumvent. For the style is the man, and where a man's treasure is there his heart, and his brain, and his writing, will be also.

ON "ON JARGON"[1]

ROBERT J. GEIST

As A freshman I frequently wrote awkward sentences in my themes, sentences I knew to be awkward before the instructor scrawled a huge "Awkward" or "Clumsy" across them. Completely baffled in my attempts to revise them, I found Sir Arthur Quiller-Couch's "Interlude: On Jargon" a revelation; at last I could get hold of something definite in those sentences, something that was a key to the needed revision. Six years later, full of enthusiasm for the essay, I first set out to teach it to a freshman class—in fact, four freshman classes. My enthusiasm so far exceeded my understanding that, when those four classes finished with me, I could find nothing wrong with the word *case* except that it sounded like the German word for cheese.

Conversations with other instructors have convinced me that I was not and am not alone in finding Quiller-Couch's essay full of pitfalls for the unwary instructor. A distinguished Oxford professor finds his reputation and the lecture platform sufficient guaranty against objections from his audience; an undistinguished American instructor has no such safeguard from his handful of unselected listeners. Convinced that "Jargon" is the greatest single essay on the art of writing, I would like to point out some of the objections.

In general, most students, if they react at all, react antagonistically; and for this antagonism Quiller-Couch is at least in part responsible. He is not, of course, responsible for the natural antagonism many students feel toward criticism of so essential a part of their makeup as style; they sometimes feel too strongly that the style is the man, and hence the man is being criticized; but Quiller-Couch is responsible for the antagonism wrought by one who is too positive in his statements, one who does not practice what he preaches, one who loses track of his real point in order to be humorous. Of *with regard to* and *in respect of,* Quiller-Couch says, "I say it is not enough to avoid them nine times out of ten, or ninety-nine times out of a hundred. You should never use them." The average freshman is likely to resent this unyielding condemnation of some of his favorite locutions. Furthermore, when the freshman reads that elegant variation is a favorite trick of jargon, he wonders just what he has hold of when Quiller-Couch says, "Here again is a string, a concatenation—say, rather, a tiara of gems of purest ray serene from the dark unfathomed caves of a Scottish newspaper." Thomas Gray means little enough to the student; for him Quiller-Couch is merely indulging in a flux of words to the pen. Again, the student reads that jargon "dallies with Latinity," only to find, a few pages later, that Quiller-Couch suggests closing "our *florilegium.*" Nor is Latinity all. *Logos,* in Greek characters, leaves the student cold, or infuriated at this professor who has constantly used the jargon of his profession—poetical quo-

1. *College English,* XII (April, 1951), 393–396. By permission of the author and the Editor of *College English.*

tation and foreign words. Most antagonizing of all perhaps is Quiller-Couch's obscuring the real point in order to be humorous. The second vice of jargon, we are told, is the use of "vague woolly abstract nouns"—like *case, instance, character, nature, condition, persuasion, degree.* It is essential for the student to keep in mind that these words are objectionable because they are vague woolly abstract nouns, but Quiller-Couch immediately leads the reader away from vagueness and woolliness by saying, or implying, that *case,* jargon's dearest child, is objectionable because its Latin ancestor did not mean what vague woolly abstract *case* does mean—*situation, circumstance, instance.* Obviously, the ancestral meaning of a word is not the criterion by which we judge its present meaning, but, by inaccurately supposing that *case* can only mean *container,* Quiller-Couch achieves the mildly amusing: "then try how, with a little trouble, you can extricate yourself from that case," and the hilarious: "Poor Mr. Cox! left gasping in his aquarium." I do not object to the undeniable humor in the gasping Mr. Cox, though students frequently fail to find it funny; but it is essential to recognize that the humor is actually beside the point and detracts from the idea that *case* is objectionable because it is a vague woolly abstract noun. The person who wrote "in the case of Mr. Harold Cox" did not mean or say that Mr. Cox was in a container; and the reader does not interpret that Mr. Cox was in one, aquarium or otherwise. The writer did say that Mr. Cox was in a case, a situation—which in effect says nothing and leaves the reader to interpret whether Mr. Cox did not weep or was not wept for. I should certainly not wish to delete Sir Arthur's antagonizing sins from the essay; they give the essay flavor. I believe, however, that these sins should be written large for the student; in fact, I happily agree with the students in finding fault with Quiller-Couch and make our agreement a means to understand his essential point.

The instructor must, of course, seek to counteract the student's antagonism whenever it interferes with the essential point. Thus upon reading, "The first [vice of jargon] is that it uses circumlocution rather than *short straight* speech," some antagonized student inevitably doesn't want to use short, straight, simple speech all the time; it's childish. Well, what is the difference between the simplicity of childhood and the simplicity of maturity, the simplicity of writing like Swift's? Like Quiller-Couch, we fall back on illustration. A first-class jargoneer once wrote in a theme on modern methods of teaching:

> Now let us ask what the effects of the emphasis upon the influence of environment are.

About one in fifty freshmen fathoms the meaning of the sentence; yet the writer had a definite idea, and each word adds meaning. The sentence very clearly has the simplicity of childhood—and the incomprehensibility. The verbs *let, ask,* and especially *are* could hardly be simpler; and the series of prepositional phrases has the simplicity of a chain—perhaps a concatenation. The revised sentence reads:

Now let us ask how emphasizing the influence of environment affects modern teaching.

The sentence is immediately clear—short, straight, simple—but the grammatical simplicity of the childish sentence has given way to grammatical complexity. Since a gerund (*emphasizing*) used as subject and taking an object is in the language, not to be analyzed by grammarians, but to express more precisely the logical relation between sentence elements, the grammatical complexity of the revised sentence creates a simplicity and directness not found in the original sentence, the simplicity and directness of the mature writer.

Regarding the second vice of jargon—the use of the already-mentioned vague woolly abstract nouns—we can avoid trouble with Quiller-Couch's illustrations only if we keep clearly in mind that *case* and the others are objectionable as general abstract nouns that cover the intended meaning without stating it precisely. We have already cited the misleading reference to Latin *casus;* Quiller-Couch's second example is also somewhat beside the point:

[From a cigar-merchant.] In any case, let us send you a case on approval.

Slight analysis is sufficient to make clear that the fault lies in the repetition of a word in two entirely different meanings. Here the word repeated happens to be *case;* but repetition, not meaning, is at fault. Even Quiller-Couch would not object to the second *case,* a container for cigars. The first *case* is obviously the vague woolly abstract *case,* but it is precisely what the writer wants. He wishes to be as vague, broad, and general as possible in order that you will let him send you cigars on approval. If one tries to avoid this *case,* one can only resort to synonymous expressions: *under any circumstances, in any event, no matter what, whatever the situation.* One may prefer these synonyms, but one must recognize that whenever a writer wishes to be general or vague, he may legitimately use a vague woolly abstract noun. It seems to me essential that this legitimate use of *case* be pointed out.

Perhaps a word of caution is in order regarding Quiller-Couch's suggested correction for his fourth illustration:

Even in the purely Celtic areas only in two or three cases do the Bishops bear Celtic names.

For "cases" read "dioceses."

This correction, fitting enough in the sentence, suggests the hunt for synonyms, but a vague woolly abstract noun like *case* rarely lends itself to so concrete a synonym as *diocese*. Rather, as Fowler points out:

There is some danger that, as writers become aware of the suspicions to which they lay themselves open by perpetually using *case,* they may take refuge with *instance,* not realizing that most instances in which *case* would have damned them are also cases in which *instance* will damn them.

Hunting synonymns for vague woolly abstract nouns, then, is dangerous, and I rather suspect that when the writer of this fourth example wrote *cases* he did not intend or mean *dioceses.* He pretty clearly meant two or three bishops. "Even in the purely Celtic areas only two or three Bishops bear Celtic names." This use of general abstract nouns as mere padding without necessarily destroying meaning is, of course, extremely common. "In most cases working students get help from home," to take a recent freshman example. Quiller-Couch's next example: "In most instances the players were below their form," probably illustrates the same point.

Students often object to the censure cast upon the amusing sentence: "He was conveyed to his place of residence in an intoxicated condition." One will do well to recognize that this expansiveness does lend itself to humor, but, to carry a straightforward message, "He was carried home drunk." In order to be humorous, moreover, an expansive passage is best set off against a simple direct background, as Quiller-Couch's concatenation—say, rather, a tiara—itself illustrates.

The essay ends fittingly with a forceful idea forcefully expressed—but marred in the freshman mind by *perpend* and *logos.* Let me end with the reminder that I criticize Quiller-Couch's essay only because I consider it invaluable to the student who understands it.

PLEASANT AGONY[1]

JOHN MASON BROWN

AT A season's end, when the country is calling, it may be permissible to talk shop before shutting it up, however temporarily. For four and a half years now, mine has been the privilege, hence the pleasant agony, of filling these pages each week, or almost every week. I say pleasant agony because I know of no other words with which to describe what writing is to me.

I claim no singularity in this. There may be, there must be, writers to whom writing comes as effortlessly as breathing. There may even be (though I doubt it) writers whose happiness is complete while they are actually writing. But most of us who live by putting words together are not so fortunate. We are tortured while we write and would be tortured were we not allowed to do so. Although when we are done we feel "delivered," as Sainte-Beuve put it, this delirium of delivery is not accomplished without labor pains for which medicine has, as yet, provided no soothing drugs. If all attempts to coerce words into doing what we would have them do are at best painful pleasures, the pains and

1. *Saturday Review of Literature,* XXXII (June 25, 1949), 36–38. Copyright, The Saturday Review Associates, 25 W. 45th St., New York City. Reprinted by permission of the author and publisher.

pleasures of summoning the right words to meet a weekly deadline are of a special kind.

A cook faced with getting dinner when lunch is over knows something of the routine, if not all the anguishes, of a columnist. No mortals, however, have appetites as insatiable as a column's. A column is an omnivorous beast. Its hunger is never appeased. Feed it, and almost at once it demands to be fed again.

Though he used a different image to express this same idea, even Shaw, seemingly the most easeful of writers, knew this. When he abandoned the job of drama critic on London's *Saturday Review,* he protested against the weekly deadlines which had confronted him for nearly four years. He likened himself to a man fighting a windmill. "I have hardly time," wrote he, "to stagger to my feet from the knock-down blow of one sail, when the next strikes me down."

His successor in the same job on that same fortunate magazine shared an identical dislike of deadlines. For twelve years, Max Beerbohm admitted in his valedictory article, Thursdays had been for him the least pleasant day of the week. Why Thursday? Because that was the day, the latest possible one, he set aside each week to get his writing done. On every Wednesday, therefore, he would be engulfed by "a certain sense of oppression, of misgiving, even of dread." It was only on Friday, when once the danger was passed, that the sun would shine again. Then he would move on dancing feet.

I quote my betters to console myself by the reminder that they, too, knew the pangs of weekly columnizing. Yet the consolation I seek is denied me when I discover, for example, that it took Beerbohm one, and only one, short day of pain to turn out the delectable copy which he could write. Shaw, I am certain, was also a one-day man. I wish I were. I wish even more ardently that I could claim any of the merits which glorify their reviews for what it takes me two, three, or sometimes five days of ceaseless sweating to produce as fodder for these columns.

Beerbohm ascribed his disrelish for the act of writing to "the acute literary conscience" with which he had been cursed. It was this conscience, he maintained, which kept his pen from ever running away with him. I know what he means. Unblessed with any of his gifts, I am none the less cursed with something of his conscience. Beerbohm insisted that "to seem to write with ease and delight is one of the duties which a writer owes to his readers." If he worked hard at his sentences, it was because Beerbohm hoped they would read easily. In other words, he was in complete agreement with Sheridan's "easy writing's vile hard reading." One statement of Beerbohm's I could truthfully apply to my own efforts for the *SRL.* It runs, "I may often have failed in my articles here, to disguise labor. But the effort to disguise it has always been loyally made."

There is a passage in "The Goncourt Journals" which has haunted me since I read it. Envy has kept it green for me, and wonder (or is it disbelief?) has kept it alive. I have in mind Gautier's boast that he never thought about what he was going to write. "I take up my pen," he explained, "and write. I am a man of letters and am presumed to know my job. . . . I throw my sentences into the air and I can be sure that they will come down on their feet, like cats. . . . Look here: here's my script: not a word blotted."

When I think of the one-legged kittens that land on my pages; when I remember the false starts, illegible scribblings, unfinished sentences, discarded drafts, changed constructions, and altered words which mark my beginnings, my continuings, and my endings, I blush with shame and, like the voyagers in Dante's realm, abandon all hope.

In these journalistic days the first word that pops into an author's mind is held to be the acceptable, if not the best, word. We are supposed to smile because Wordsworth, at a day's end, was wearied from his quest for the exact word. But where Wordsworth the man may win a smile, Wordsworth the writer, fatiguing himself by doing what is a writer's duty, is far from laughable. The *mot juste* is not just any word. Even if it eludes its pursuer, the search for it seems to me to remain among the obligations of authorship. Indeed, the true hope of anyone who loves the language and respects it is to stumble upon, not the correct word or phrase, but the word or phrase which is so right that it seems inevitable.

The word and the phrase are not the only hurdles—and joys—of authorship. The sentence and the paragraph, by means of which points are made, thoughts communicated, emotions transferred, pictures painted, personalities caught, rhythms established, and cadences varied, offer other challenges and should supply their own sources of delight and pride. When so much hurried writing is done for hurried reading, I find it comforting to have Shaw, a veritable geyser with words and ideas, admit in his "Sixteen Self Sketches" how depleting he found his labors as a weekly feuilletonist for ten years. Why? Because, says he, of "taking all the pains I was capable of to get to the bottom of every sentence I wrote."

One of the modern world's luckier occurrences was what happened at Harrow when a boy named Winston Churchill was being "menaced with Education." Three times, he tells us in "A Roving Commission," his backwardness as a classical scholar forced him to remain in the same form and hence repeat the same elementary course in English. "Thus," writes he (and who can question him?), "I got into my bones the essential structure of the ordinary British sentence—which is a noble thing. . . . Naturally I am biased in favor of boys learning English. I would make them all learn English: and then I would let the clever ones learn Latin as an honor, and Greek as a treat. But the only thing I would whip them for would be for not knowing English. I would whip them hard for that." One trembles to think how many of us whose profession is writing would be flogged today if lapses in English, or American, were whippable offenses.

Later on in that same grand book, Churchill has his more precise say on the subtleties, intricacies, and possibilities of the writer's craft. It is his opinion, and one worth heeding, that, "just as the sentence contains one idea in all its fulness, so the paragraph should embrace a distinct episode; and as sentences should follow one another in harmonious sequence, so the paragraphs must fit on to one another like the automatic couplings of railway carriages."

I quote Churchill and these others belonging to the peerage of prose-writers because, for any author with a memory, one of the disheartening and humbling aspects of writing is the recollection, as his own pen moves, of how those whom he admires have faced and solved identical problems. This recollection of what has been done, this sensing of what could and should be done, this awareness of what one hopes to do regardless of whether one can or cannot do it—these are parts of that literary conscience, mentioned by Beerbohm, which keeps a writer's pen from running away with him. I know they are factors in retarding my own pen (meaning my typewriter, pencil, or dictation) even on those happy days when a subject seems to write itself, when sentences come easily, and one paragraph gives way to another.

Style is a strange and mysterious thing. Some contemporary writers appear to get along without it and to want to do so, and most of us rightly disparage it when it shows the effort that has gone into it. Few of us, for example, can read Pater today without being irritated and put off by the deliberate intricacies and involutions of his sentences. His style, once held to be a model, remains a model, although as we see it it is one to be avoided rather than followed. Pater could not bring himself to say a simple thing simply. His orchestration is so elaborate that the melody of his thought is lost.

Hazlitt comes closer to present-day tastes. More than being the enemy of the gaudy and "Occult" schools of writing, Hazlitt was not only a champion but at his best a matchless practitioner of "The Familiar Style." Although he had the art to make a long sentence seem short, he knew the value of short sentences. "I hate anything," wrote he, "that occupies more space than it is worth. I hate to see a load of band-boxes go along the street, and I hate to see a parcel of big words without any meaning in them."

The perpetual challenge of writing, the challenge presented by each new sentence is to say exactly what one wants to say exactly as one wants to say it. This is where the anguish of composition mixes with the delights. This is where, too, style, as I see it, comes into the picture. Style is merely the means, chosen or instinctive (doubtless both), by which a writer has his precise say.

Certainly, style is not affectation. Conscious though it may be, when self-conscious it is an obstruction. Its purpose, to my way of thinking, is to give the reader pleasure by sparing him the work which the writer is duty-bound to have done for him. Writers, notwithstanding their hopes or ambitions, may or may not be artists. But there is no excuse for their not being artisans. The style is the man, we are told. True, in the final and spiritual sense as this is, style is more than that. It is the writing man *in print*. It is, so to speak, his written voice and, if it is truly his voice, even in print it should be his and his alone. The closer it comes to the illusion of speech, perhaps the better. Yet the closeness of the written word to the spoken can, and in fact should, never be more than an illusion. For the point of the written word is planning, as surely as the charm of the spoken one is its lack of it.

Without shame I confess that, regardless of how unsatisfactory the results may be, I labor when writing these weekly pieces to lighten the labor of those who may read them. That I fail again and again I know to my own chagrin, but I can honestly say I try. I not only rewrite; I often rewrite and rewrite again. I do this though I am well aware that the result is sentences and paragraphs which do not bear rereading. I rewrite partly in longhand, partly by dictation, occasionally sitting down, sometimes walking, but most often snaking my way across the floor on my stomach. My desk, a migratory one, is the small piece of beaverboard I push before me. On it are sheets of typewriter paper darkened with hieroglyphics which must be deciphered immediately to be read at all.

Endeavoring to square my writing with my writing conscience, and having to live with the difference between what I would like to have done and am able to do, is one of the reasons why writing is to me an agony, however pleasant. There are other contributors to the pleasures and the agonies of trying to keep these columns fed. Upon these I shall touch next time. Since there is no earthly reason why anyone should be interested, this can be taken as a threat, not a promise. I can delve into these personal problems of authorship only at a season's end. What is more, I find I want to do so. Surely this is as good a reason for writing as any, and a better one than so regular an offender as the conductor of a weekly column can always claim.

THE AMERICAN LANGUAGE[1]

H. L. MENCKEN

THE first Englishman to notice an Americanism sneered at it aloofly, thus setting a fashion that many of his countrymen have been following ever since. He was one Francis Moore, a ruffian who came out to Georgia with Oglethorpe in 1735, and the word that upset him was *bluff*, in the sense of "a cliff or headland with a broad precipitous face." He did not deign to argue against it; he simply dismissed it as "barbarous," apparently assuming that all Englishmen of decent instincts would agree with him. For nearly a century they seem to have done so, and *bluff* lingered sadly below the salt. When it was printed at all in Great Britain it was set off by sanitary quotation marks, or accompanied by other hints of deprecation, as *rubberneck, hot spot* and *nerts* are accompanied today. But then, in 1830, the eminent Sir Charles Lyell used it shamelessly in the first volume of his monumental "Principles of Geology," and from that day to this it has been a perfectly respectable if somewhat unfamiliar word in England, with a place in every dictionary.

Its history is the history of almost countless other Americanisms. They have been edging their way into English since early colonial times, and, for more than a century past, in constantly increasing volume, but I can't recall one that didn't have to run a gauntlet of opposition in the motherland, at times verging upon the frantic. After the Revolution, that opposition took on the proportions of a holy war. Never an American book came out that the English reviewers did not belabor its vocabulary violently. The brunt of the attack, of course, had to be borne by the poetasters of the era—for example, Joel Barlow, whose "Columbiad" (1807) loosed a really terrifying geyser of abuse. But even the most serious writers got their share—among them, Jefferson, John Marshall, Noah Webster, and John Quincy Adams. Jefferson's crime was that he had invented the verb *to belittle*. It was, one may argue plausibly, a very logical, useful, and perhaps even nifty word, and seventy-five years later the prissy Anthony Trollope was employing it without apology. But when Jefferson ventured to use it in his "Notes on Virginia" (1787) "The London Review" tossed and raged in a manner befitting the discovery of a brace of duelling pistols beneath the cope of the Archbishop of Canterbury, and for several years following its dudgeon was supported virtuously by most of the other reviews. "What an expression!" roared the "London." "It may be an elegant one in Virginia, but for our part, all we can do is to *guess* at its meaning. For shame, Mr. Jefferson! Freely, good sir, will we forgive all your attacks, impotent as they are illiberal, upon our national character; but for the future spare—O spare, we beseech you, our mother-tongue!"

1. "The American Language," *Yale Review*, XXV (March. 1936), 538–552, with omissions.

The underscoring of *guess* was a fling in passing at another foul Americanism. It was the belief of most Englishmen then, as it is today, that the use of the verb in the sense of *to suppose* or *assume* originated in this country. It is actually to be found, in that meaning precisely, in "Measure for Measure" and "Henry VI"; nay, in Chaucer, Wycliffe, and Gower. But such historical considerations have never daunted the more ardent preservers of the King's English. When a word acquires an American flavor it becomes anathema to them, even though it may go back to Boadicea. *To advocate* offers an instructive example. It appeared in English in the dark backward and abysm of time, but during the eighteenth century it seems to have dropped out of general use, though Burke used it. Towards the end of the century it came into vogue in this country, and soon it made its way back to the land of its birth. It was received with all the honors proper to an invasion of Asiatic cholera. The reviews donounced it as loutish, "Gothic," and against God, and lumped it with *to compromit* and *to happify* as proof that civilization was impossible in America, and would be so forevermore. Even Benjamin Franklin, returning from England in 1789, was alarmed into begging Noah Webster to "reprobate" it, along with *to notice, to progress,* and *to oppose.* There is no record of Noah's reply, but it is most unlikely that he did any reprobating, for when he began to make dictionaries he included all four verbs, and they have been listed in every considerable dictionary published since, whether in this country or in England.

The leader of the heroic struggle to keep Americanisms out of Britain, in its early stages, was the celebrated William Gifford, editor of "The Quarterly Review." Gifford was a killer in general practice, and his savage assaults on Wordsworth, Shelley, and Keats are still unpleasantly remembered. He was the first magazine editor in history to make the trade pay, and when he died in 1828 he left £25,000 and was buried in Westminster Abbey. One of his major specialties was the villainousness of everything American, from politics to table manners and from theology to speechways. Among the allegations that he either made himself or permitted his contributors to make were these: (*a*) that the Americans employed naked colored women to wait upon them at table, (*b*) that they kidnapped Scotsmen, Irishmen, Hollanders, and Welshmen and sold them into slavery, and (*c*) that they were planning to repudiate the English language altogether, and adopt Hebrew in its place. This last charge, as it flew from tongue to tongue, acquired variorum readings. One of them made the new American language an Indian dialect, another made it Greek, and a third was to the effect that the people of Britain would be forced to acquire Greek, thus leaving English to the wicked will of the barbaric Yankees. It all sounds idiotic today, but in 1814 it was taken quite seriously by many Englishmen. Gifford was a tyrannical editor and so vastly enjoyed slashing his contributors' copy that Southey once denounced him as "a butcherly review-gelder." But anything that was against the damyankee passed his eye unscathed, and he piled up accusations in a manner so shameless that "The North American Review" was moved to protest that if the tirade went on it would "turn into bitterness the last drops of good-will towards England that exist in the United States."

In the early Twenties of that century there was some amelioration, and when Gifford retired from the "Quarterly" in 1824, voices that were almost conciliatory began to be heard. They heaped praises on Niagara Falls, found something to commend in Cooper's "Spy," and even had kind words for the speed and luxuriousness of American canalboats. But my most diligent researches have failed to unearth anything complimentary to the American language. It continued to be treated as a grotesque and immoral gibberish, full of uncouth terms and at war with all the canons of English. Every British traveller who came to these shores between the War of 1812 and the Civil War had something to say about the neologisms his ears and eyes encountered on his tour, and nearly all were constrained to deplore them. Captain Basil Hall, who was here in 1827 and 1828, went about in a palpitating daze, confounded and outraged by the signs on American places of business. *Clothing Store* he interpreted after long thought, and *Flour and Feed Store* after prayer and soul-searching, but what on earth was a *Leather and Finding Store?* Captain Thomas Hamilton, who followed five years later, found it impossible to penetrate to "the precise import" of *Dry-Goods Store,* and when he encountered an establishment offering *Hollow Ware, Spiders, and Fire-Dogs* he gave up in despair.

Hall was not one to take it lying down. He decided to call upon Noah Webster, whose American Dictionary of the English Language had just come out, to find out what the Yankees meant by using the mother tongue so cruelly. Webster shocked him by arguing stoutly that "his countrymen had not only a right to adopt new words, but were obliged to modify the language to suit the novelty of the circumstances, geographical and political, in which they were placed." The great lexicographer "who taught millions to spell but not one to sin" went on to observe judicially that it was "quite impossible to stop the progress of language—it is like the course of the Mississippi, the motion of which, at times, is scarcely perceptible; yet even then it possesses a momentum quite irresistible. Words and expressions will be forced into use in spite of all the exertions of all the writers in the world."

"But surely," persisted Hall, "such innovations are to be deprecated?"

"I don't think that," replied old Noah. "If a word becomes universally current in America, where English is spoken, why should it not take its station in the language?"

"Because," declared Hall with magnificent pertinacity, "there are words enough already."

This heroic dogma is still heard in England, where even native novelties are commonly opposed violently, and not infrequently strangled at birth. There seems to be, in the modern Englishman, very little of that ecstasy in word-making which so prodigiously engrossed his Elizabethan forebears

Shakespeare alone probably put more new words into circulation than all the English writers since Carlyle, and they were much better ones. The ideal over there today is not picturesque and exhilarating utterance, but correct and reassuring utterance, and one of its inevitable fruits is that bow-wow jargon which Sir Arthur Quiller-Couch describes in "On the Art of Writing" as "the medium through which boards of government, county councils, syndicates, committees, commercial firms, express the processes as well as the conclusions of their thought, and so voice the reason of their being." It is, at its worst, at least in accord with what are taken to be the principles of English grammar, and at its best it shows excellent manners and even a kind of mellifluous elegance; indeed, the English, taking one with another, may be said to write much better than we do—at all events by the standards of the schoolmaster. But what they write is seldom animated by anything properly describable as bounce. It lacks novelty, variety, audacity. There is little juice in it. The reader confronted by it is treated politely and lulled pleasantly, but he seldom enjoys the enchantment of surprise. That diligent search for new and racy locutions which occupied so much of the work day of Walt Whitman and William Dean Howells alike, and is practised so assiduously by scores of saucy Andersons and Hemingways, Sandburgs and Saroyans today, is carried on across the ocean by only a few extravagant eccentrics, virtually all of whom—for example, James Joyce and Ezra Pound—are non- and even anti-Englishmen. The hundred-per-cent English writers, save when they stoop to conscious wickedness, seldom depart very far from the jargon of Quiller-Couch. It is by no means a monopoly of the classes he named, nor is it reserved for solemn occasions. I find it also in my favorite English weekly, the "News of the World," which is devoted principally to sports, the theatres, and the more scabrous varieties of crime, and is probably a far better mirror of England than the "Times." When the "News of the World" reports the downfall of a rural dean or a raid on a Mayfair night club, the thing is done in a style so tight and brittle that nothing to match it is discoverable in this country, at least outside the pages of "The Homiletic Review." "When we want to freshen our speech," Mrs. Virginia Woolf was lately saying, "we borrow from American—*poppycock, rambunctious, flip-flop, booster, good mixer.* All the expressive, ugly, vigorous slang which creeps into use among us, first in talk, later in writing, comes from across the Atlantic." . . .

Whenever an Americanism comes publicly into question in England, there are efforts to track down its etymology, and sometimes the theories offered are extremely bizarre. In January, 1935, for example, the London "Morning Post" opened its columns to a furious and fantastic discussion of the verb-phrase, *to get his goat.* I content myself with one of the explanations: "Among the Negroes in Harlem it is the custom for each household to keep a goat to act as general scavenger. Occasionally one man will steal another's goat, and the household débris then accumulates to the general annoyance." The truth is that *to get his goat* seems to be of French origin, and in the form of *prendre sa chèvre,* philological genealogists have traced it back to the year 1585. But whatever is strange and upsetting is put down, in England, to the hellish ingenuity of Americans—save, of course, when genuine Americanisms are claimed as really English. This last happens often enough to give what may be called a cockeyed aspect to the perennial pother. In 1934 even the learned Dr. C. T. Onions, one of the editors of the great Oxford Dictionary, succumbed to the madness by offering to find in the dictionary any alleged Americanism that a reporter for the London "Evening News" could name. The reporter began discreetly with *fresh* (in the sense of *saucy*), *to figure* (in the sense of *to believe* or *conclude*), and *to grill* (in the sense of *to question*), and Dr. Onions duly found them all. But when the reporter proceeded to *bunkum,* the learned editor had to forget conveniently that its progenitor was the thoroughly American *buncombe,* when *rake-off* followed he had to admit that the earliest example in the dictionary was from an American work, and when *boloney* and *nerts* were hurled at him he blew up with a bang.

Here, of course, Dr. Onions and his interlocutor ended on the level of slang, but there is no telling where they would be if they could be translated to the year 2036. *Boloney,* like *to belittle,* has the imprimatur of an eminent tribune of the people, and is quite as respectable, philologically speaking, as *buncombe, gerrymander, pork barrel, filibuster, carpetbagger, gag rule,* or *on the fence.* All these came into American from the argot of politics, and got only frowns from the schoolmarm, but they are all quite sound American today, and most of them have gone into English. As for *nerts,* it seems to be but one more member of an endless dynasty of euphemisms, beginning with *zounds* and coming down to *son-of-a-gun, gee,* and *darn. Darn,* like *nerts,* is an Americanism, and Dr. Louise Pound has demonstrated that it descends from *eternal,* which first turned into *tarnal* and then lost its tail and borrowed the head of *damn.* I have heard a bishop use it freely in private discourse, with a waggish sprinkling of actual *damns. Son-of-a-gun* is now so feeble and harmless that the Italians in America use it as a satirical designation for native Americans, who seem to them to fall far behind the Italian talent for profanity and objurgation. It is, I believe, a just criticism. Some time ago I was engaged by a magazine to do an article on American and English swearwords. After two or three attempts I had to give it up, for I found that neither branch of our ancient Frisian tongue could show anything worthy of serious consideration. The antinomians of England stick to two or three banal obscenities, one of which, *bloody,* is obscene only formally, and we Americans seldom get beyond variations of *hell* and *damn.* A single Neapolitan boatman could swear down the whole population of Anglo-Saxondom.

Bloody is perfectly innocuous in the United States, and it may be innocuous in England also on some near tomorrow—or even more disreputable than it is today. There is no predicting the social career of words. Dr. Leonard Bloomfield says that even "our word *whore,* cognate with the Latin *carus* (dear), must have been at one time a polite substitute for some term now lost." Prophecy fails just as dismally when propriety does not come into question. Shakespeare's numerous attempts to introduce new words, some of them his own inventions and others borrowed from the slang of the Bankside, failed almost as often as they succeeded. He found ready takers for *courtship, lonely, sportive, multitudinous, hubbub* and *bump,* but his audiences would have none of *definement,* in the sense of description, or of *citizen* as an adjective, and both seem strange and uncouth to us today, though all the others are as familiar and as decorous as *cat* or *rat.* When John Marston used *strenuous* in 1599 it was attacked by Ben Jonson as barbarous, but a dozen years later it had got into Chapman's Homer, and by 1670 it was being used by Milton. It remained perfectly respectable until 1900, when Theodore Roosevelt announced the Strenuous Life. Both the idea and the term struck the American fancy, and in a little while the latter passed into slang, and was worn so threadbare that all persons of careful speech sickened of it. To this day it carries a faintly ridiculous connotation, and is seldom used seriously. But by 1975 it may be restored to the dignity of *psychopath* or *homoousian.* No one can say yes with any confidence, and no one can say no. "Even the greatest purist," observes Robert Lynd, "does not object to the inclusion of *bogus* in a literary English vocabulary, though a hundred years ago it was an American slang word meaning an apparatus for coining false money. *Carpetbagger* and *bunkum* are other American slang words that have naturalized themselves in English speech, and *mob* is an example of English slang that was once as vulgar as *photo.*" . . .

One finds in current American all the characters and tendencies that marked the rich English of Shakespeare's time—an eager borrowing of neologisms from other languages, a bold and often very ingenious use of metaphor, and a fine disdain of the barricades separating the parts of speech. The making of new words is not carried on only, or even principally, to fill gaps in the vocabulary; indeed, one may well agree with Captain Hall that "there are words enough already." It is carried on because there survives in the American something that seems to have faded out of the Englishman: an innocent joy in word-making for its own sake, a voluptuous delight in the vigor and elasticity of the language. The search for the *mot juste* is an enterprise that is altogether too pedantic for him; he much prefers to solve his problem by non-Euclidian devices. *Hoosegow* was certainly not necessary when it appeared, for we already had a large repertory of synonyms for *jail.* But when the word precipitated itself from the Spanish *juzgado* somewhere along the Rio Grande it won quick currency, and in a little while it was on the march through the country, and soon or late, I suppose, it will produce its inevitable clipped forms, *hoose* and *gow,* and its attendant adjective and verb. *Corral,* which entered by the same route in the Forties of the last century, had hatched a verb before the Civil War, and that verb, according to Webster's New International (1934), now has four separate and distinct meanings. *Bummer,* coming in from the German, is now clipped to *bum,* and is not only noun, verb, and adjective but also adverb. *Buncombe,* borrowed by the English as *bunkum,* has bred *bunco* and *bunk* at home, both of which rove the parts of speech in a loose and easy way, and the last of which has issue in the harsh verb *to debunk,* still under heavy fire in England.

The impact of such lawless novelties upon the more staid English of the motherland is terrific. The more they are denounced as heathen and outlandish, the quicker they get into circulation. Nor do they prosper only on the level of the vulgate, and among careless speakers. There are constant complaints in the English newspapers about their appearance in the parliamentary debates, and even in discourses from the sacred desk, and they begin to show themselves also in *belles-lettres,* despite the English dislike of new ways of writing. Their progress, in fact, is so widespread and so insidious that they often pop up in the diatribes that revile them; the Englishman, conquered at last, can no longer protest against Americanisms without using them. Moreover, they are now supported actively by a definitely pro-American party of writers and scholars, and though it is still small in numbers, at least compared to the patriot band, it shows some distinguished names. The late Robert Bridges, Poet Laureate, was an active member of it, and among its other adherents are Wyndham Lewis, Edward Shanks, Richard Aldington, and Sir John Foster Fraser. Sir William Craigie, perhaps the first of living lexicographers, is so greatly interested in the American form of English that he has spent the years since 1925 in a scientific examination of it, and will presently begin the publication of an elaborate dictionary. If only because of the greater weight of the population behind it, it seems destined to usurp the natural leadership of British English, and to determine the general course of the language hereafter. But its chief advantage in this struggle is really not the numerical one, but the fact that its daring experiments and iconoclasms lie in the grand tradition of English, and are signs of its incurable normalcy and abounding vigor.

How far it will move away from the theorizing of grammarians and the policing of schoolmarms remains to be seen. They still make valiant efforts to curb its wayward spirit, but with gradually diminishing success. When, a few years ago, the late Sterling A. Leonard of the University of Wisconsin submitted a long series of their admonitions to a committee of educated Americans, including many philologians, he found that opinion was against them on that high level almost as decidedly as it was on lower ones. His judges favored scores of forms that the school grammars and popular handbooks of usage still condemn. Since then a more direct attack upon the conservative position has been made by Dr. Robert C. Pooley of the same university. He shows that some of the rules laid down with most assurance by pedants have no support in either history or logic, and are constantly violated by writers of unquestionable authority. There have even been rumblings of revolt in the conservative camp. The late George Philip Krapp of Columbia, who was surely anything but a radical, was of the opinion that English would undergo profound changes in the United States, and that many of them would be of such a character that its very grammatical structure would be shaken. Dr. George O. Curme of Northwestern University is another eminent grammarian who warns his colleagues that the rules they cherish have no genuine authority, and must be overhauled from time to time. Once they steel themselves to that sacrifice of their professional dignity, he says, "it will give a thrill to English-speaking students to discover that the English language does not belong to the schoolteacher but belongs to them, and that its future destiny will soon rest entirely in their hands."

Dr. Curme is always careful to think and speak of American as no more than a variation of English. But it must be obvious that, in late years, the tail has begun a vigorous wagging of the dog. "The facts that we ought to realize," says Edward Shanks to his fellow Britons, "and that we ignore when we talk loftily about Americanisms, are that America is making a formidable contribution to the development of our language, and that all our attempts to reject that contribution will in the long run be vain."

OF THE VANITY OF WORDS[1]

MICHEL EYQUEM DE MONTAIGNE

A RHETORICIAN of old said his trade was "To make little things appear and be thought great." There you have a shoemaker who can make big shoes for little feet. In Sparta he would have been given the whip for professing a lying and deceitful art. And I believe that Archidamus, who was king of that country, heard not without astonishment the reply of Thucydides,[2] when he asked him which was the stronger wrestler, Pericles or he: "That," he said, "would be difficult to decide; for when I have thrown him in wrestling, he will persuade the onlookers that he has had no fall, and will carry off the prize."

They who paint and mask the women do less harm, for little is lost by not seeing them in their natural state; whilst those make a profession of deceiving, not our eyes, but our judgment, and of corrupting and adulterating the essence of things. The states that maintained themselves in a well-ordered and well-governed condition, like those of Crete and Lacedemon, made little account of orators.

Aristo wisely defines rhetoric as "a science to persuade the people"; Socrates

1. *The Essays of Montaigne,* translated by E. J. Trechmann (London: Oxford University Press, 1927), I, 297–300. Reprinted by permission of the publishers.

2. Not the historian, but one of the leaders of the aristocratic party opposed to Pericles and exiled by him.

and Plato as "the art of deceiving and flattering." And they who deny the general definition verify it throughout in their precepts.

The Mohammedans forbade their children to be instructed in the art, on account of its uselessness.

And the Athenians, having perceived how pernicious was the practice of it, though it was held in high esteem in their city, ordained that the principal part, the appeal to the passions, should be abolished, together with the exordiums and perorations.

It is a tool invented for handling and stirring up a mob and an unruly community; and it is a tool that is only employed for sick states, like medicine. In those where the vulgar, where the ignorant, where all were all-powerful, as in Athens, Rhodes, and Rome, and where things have been in a perpetual turmoil, there orators have abounded. And indeed we see few persons in those republics who have pushed themselves to high honours without the aid of eloquence. Pompey, Caesar, Crassus, Lucullus, Lentulus, Metellus, made it their principal ladder for mounting to that authoritative eminence to which they at last attained, and found it of greater help than arms; contrary to the opinion of the best times, for L. Volumnius, speaking publicly in favour of Q. Fabius and P. Decius, who had been nominated for the consulship, said, "These men are born commanders, great in action, unskilled in wordy contest, truly consular minds. The clever, the eloquent, and learned are good for the city, to administer justice as Praetors."

Eloquence was most flourishing at Rome when affairs were in the worst condition, and agitated by the storm of civil wars; as a free and untamed field bears the most lusty herbs. From which it would appear that monarchal governments are less in need of it than others: for the stupidity and credulity we find in the common people, which renders them liable to be handled and twisted by the ears by the sweet sound of this harmony, without weighing and knowing the truth of things by the force of reason: this credulity, I say, is not so readily found in an individual, who is more easily safeguarded, by good education and advice, against the influence of that poison. There was never any orator of renown known to come out of Macedon or Persia.

What I have here said was suggested to me by a talk I had lately with an Italian who was in the service of the late Cardinal Caraffa until his death, in the capacity of major domo. I made him tell me about his office. He entertained me with a dissertation on the science of the gullet with the gravity and demeanour of a schoolmaster, as if he were discussing some important point in theology. He minutely explained that there was a difference in appetites: that which we have when fasting, that which comes after the second and third course; the means, now of simply gratifying it, now of arousing and stimulating it; the organization of sauces: firstly in general, then particularizing the qualities of the ingredients and their effects; the different salads according to the season, that which should be warmed, that which requires to be served cold, the manner of adorning and embellishing them to make them pleasing to the sight also. After that he entered upon the order of the courses, full of beautiful and important considerations:

> For, believe me, 'tis no light affair
> To carve a fowl or dissect a hare. (JUVENAL.)

And all this with such a mouthful of rich and magnificent words, as one might use in discussing the government of an empire. It reminded me of my Terence:

> This is too salt, this overdone, this not too clean:
> This is just right, bear that in mind; then I,
> According to my lights, admonish him:
> To make the dish as bright as mirror's face,
> And all the feast serve up in proper style.

And after all even the Greeks highly commended the order and disposition which Paulus Emilius observed in the feast he gave them on his return from Macedon. But I am now speaking, not of deeds, but of words.

I know not whether others feel as I do, but when I hear architects filling their mouths with big words like Pilasters, Architraves, Cornices, Corinthian, and Dorian work, and suchlike jargon, I cannot help my imagination being forthwith possessed with the palace of Apollidon; [3] and after all I find that they are the paltry parts of my kitchen-door.

Just listen to people talking of Metonymy, Metaphor, Allegory, and other such grammatical names; does it not seem as if they were using some rare and exotic form of language? And yet they do no more than describe your housemaid's chatter.

It is a trickery of a like kind to call the offices of our state by the superb titles of the Romans, although they have no resemblance in respect of function, and still less of authority and power. And this too, which will one day, I doubt not, be regarded as evidence of singular conceit in our age, to bestow undeservedly, upon whom we think fit, the most glorious surnames with which antiquity honoured one or two persons in several centuries. Plato has carried off that epithet of *Divine,* by universal consent, which no one has thought of begrudging him; and the Italians, who boast, and rightly so, of usually having a more lively wit and a sounder judgement than the other nations of their time, have lately made a present of that title to Aretino, in whom, saving a turgid style, boiling over with conceits, ingenious indeed but far-fetched and fantastic, and his eloquence, such as it may be, I can see nothing superior to the ordinary authors of his time; so far is he from approaching that ancient divinity.

And the surname of *Great* we apply to princes in whom there is nothing transcending the greatness of the common people.

3. A palace built by the art of the necromancer Apollidon in the old romance of *Amadis of Gaul,* beloved by Don Quixote.

III

THINKING

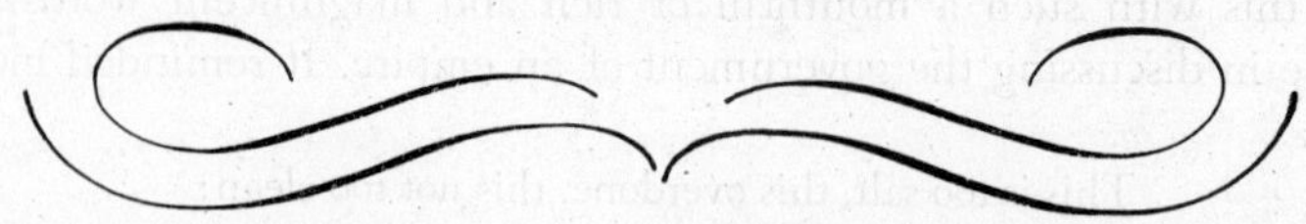

FOUR KINDS OF THINKING[1]

JAMES HARVEY ROBINSON

We do not think enough about thinking, and much of our confusion is the result of current illusions in regard to it. Let us forget for the moment any impressions we may have derived from the philosophers, and see what seems to happen in ourselves. The first thing that we notice is that our thought moves with such incredible rapidity that it is almost impossible to arrest any specimen of it long enough to have a look at it. When we are offered a penny for our thoughts we always find that we have recently had so many things in mind that we can easily make a selection which will not compromise us too nakedly. On inspection we shall find that even if we are not downright ashamed of a great part of our spontaneous thinking it is far too intimate, personal, ignoble or trivial to permit us to reveal more than a small part of it. I believe this must be true of everyone. We do not, of course, know what goes on in other people's heads. They tell us very little and we tell them very little. The spigot of speech, rarely fully opened, could never emit more than driblets of the ever renewed hogshead of thought—*noch grösser wie's Heidelberger Fass*. We find it hard to believe that other people's thoughts are as silly as our own, but they probably are.

We all appear to ourselves to be thinking all the time during our waking hours, and most of us are aware that we go on thinking while we are asleep, even more foolishly than when awake. When uninterrupted by some practical issue we are engaged in what is now known as a *reverie*. This is our spontaneous and favorite kind of thinking. We allow our ideas to take their own course and this course is determined by our hopes and fears, our spontaneous desires, their fulfillment or frustration; by our likes and dislikes, our loves and hates and resentments. There is nothing else anything like so interesting to ourselves as ourselves. All thought that is not more or less laboriously controlled and directed will inevitably circle about the beloved Ego. It is amusing

1. From *The Mind in the Making*, by James Harvey Robinson. Copyright, 1921, by Harper & Brothers. Reprinted by permission of the publishers.

and pathetic to observe this tendency in ourselves and in others. We learn politely and generously to overlook this truth, but if we dare to think of it, it blazes forth like the noontide sun.

The reverie or "free association of ideas" has of late become the subject of scientific research. While investigators are not yet agreed on the results, or at least on the proper interpretation to be given to them, there can be no doubt that our reveries form the chief index to our fundamental character. They are a reflection of our nature as modified by often hidden and forgotten experiences. We need not go into the matter further here, for it is only necessary to observe that the reverie is at all times a potent and in many cases an omnipotent rival to every other kind of thinking. It doubtless influences all our speculations in its persistent tendency to self-magnification and self-justification, which are its chief preoccupations, but it is the last thing to make directly or indirectly for honest increase of knowledge.[2] Philosophers usually talk as if such thinking did not exist or were in some way negligible. This is what makes their speculations so unreal and often worthless.

The reverie, as any of us can see for himself, is frequently broken and interrupted by the necessity of a second kind of thinking. We have to make practical decisions. Shall we write a letter or no? Shall we take the subway or a bus? Shall we have dinner at seven or half-past? Shall we buy U. S. Rubber or a Liberty Bond? Decisions are easily distinguishable from the free flow of the reverie. Sometimes they demand a good deal of careful pondering and the recollection of pertinent facts; often, however, they are made impulsively. They are a more difficult and laborious thing than the reverie, and we resent having to "make up our mind" when we are tired, or absorbed in a congenial reverie. Weighing a decision, it should be noted, does not necessarily add anything to our knowledge, although we may, of course, seek further information before making it.

A third kind of thinking is stimulated when any one questions our belief and opinions. We sometimes find ourselves changing our minds without any resistance or heavy emotion, but if we are told that we are wrong we resent the imputation and harden our hearts. We are incredibly heedless in the formation of our beliefs, but find ourselves filled with an illicit passion for them when anyone proposes to rob us of their companionship. It is obviously not the ideas

2. The poet-clergyman, John Donne, who lived in the time of James I, has given a beautifully honest picture of the doings of a saint's mind: "I throw myself down in my chamber and call in and invite God and His angels thither, and when they are there I neglect God and His angels for the noise of a fly, for the rattling of a coach, for the whining of a door. I talk on in the same posture of praying, eyes lifted up, knees bowed down, as though I prayed to God, and if God or His angels should ask me when I thought last of God in that prayer I cannot tell. Sometimes I find that I had forgot what I was about, but when I began to forget it I cannot tell. A memory of yesterday's pleasures, a fear of tomorrow's dangers, a straw under my knee, a noise in mine ear, a light in mine eye, an anything, a nothing, a fancy, a chimera in my brain troubles me in my prayer."—Quoted by Robert Lynd, *The Art of Letters,* pp. 46–47.

themselves that are dear to us, but our self-esteem, which is threatened. We are by nature stubbornly pledged to defend our own from attack, whether it be our person, our family, our property, or our opinion. A United States Senator once remarked to a friend of mine that God Almighty could not make him change his mind on our Latin-America policy. We may surrender, but rarely confess ourselves vanquished. In the intellectual world at least peace is without victory.

Few of us take the pains to study the origin of our cherished convictions; indeed, we have a natural repugnance to so doing. We like to continue to believe what we have been accustomed to accept as true, and the resentment aroused when doubt is cast upon any of our assumptions leads us to seek every manner of excuse for clinging to them. *The result is that most of our so-called reasoning consists in finding arguments for going on believing as we already do.*

I remember years ago attending a public dinner to which the Governor of the state was bidden. The chairman explained that His Excellency could not be present for certain "good" reasons; what the "real" reasons were the presiding officer said he would leave us to conjecture. This distinction between "good" and "real" reasons is one of the most clarifying and essential in the whole realm of thought. We can readily give what seem to us "good" reasons for being a Catholic or a Mason, a Republican or a Democrat, an adherent or opponent of the League of Nations. But the "real" reasons are usually on a quite different plane. Of course the importance of this distinction is popularly, if somewhat obscurely, recognized. The Baptist missionary is ready enough to see that the Buddhist is not such because his doctrines would bear careful inspection, but because he happened to be born in a Buddhist family in Tokio. But it would be treason to his faith to acknowledge that his own partiality for certain doctrines is due to the fact that his mother was a member of the First Baptist church of Oak Ridge. A savage can give all sorts of reasons for his belief that it is dangerous to step on a man's shadow, and a newspaper editor can advance plenty of arguments against the Bolsheviki. But neither of them may realize why he happens to be defending his particular opinion.

The "real" reasons for our beliefs are concealed from ourselves as well as from others. As we grow up we simply adopt the ideas presented to us in regard to such matters as religion, family relations, property, business, our country, and the state. We unconsciously absorb them from our environment. They are persistently whispered in our ear by the group in which we happen to live. Moreover, as Mr. Trotter has pointed out, these judgments, being the product of suggestion and not of reasoning, have the quality of perfect obviousness, so that to question them

> . . . is to the believer to carry skepticism to an insane degree, and will be met by contempt, disapproval, or condemnation, according to the nature of the belief in question. When, therefore, we find ourselves entertaining an opinion about the basis of which there is a quality of feeling which tells us that to inquire into it

would be absurd, obviously unnecessary, unprofitable, undesirable, bad form, or wicked, we may know that that opinion is a nonrational one, and probably, therefore, founded upon inadequate evidence.[3]

Opinions, on the other hand, which are the result of experience or of honest reasoning do not have this quality of "primary certitude." I remember when as a youth I heard a group of business men discussing the question of the immortality of the soul, I was outraged by the sentiment of doubt expressed by one of the party. As I look back now I see that I had at the time no interest in the matter, and certainly no least argument to urge in favor of the belief in which I had been reared. But neither my personal indifference to the issue, nor the fact that I had previously given it no attention, served to prevent an angry resentment when I heard *my* ideas questioned.

This spontaneous and loyal support of our preconceptions—this process of finding "good" reasons to justify our routine beliefs—is known to modern psychologists as "rationalizing"—clearly only a new name for a very ancient thing. Our "good" reasons ordinarily have no value in promoting honest enlightenment, because, no matter how solemnly they may be marshaled, they are at bottom the result of personal preference or prejudice, and not of an honest desire to seek or accept new knowledge.

In our reveries we are frequently engaged in self-justification, for we cannot bear to think ourselves wrong, and yet have constant illustrations of our weaknesses and mistakes. So we spend much time finding fault with circumstances and the conduct of others, and shifting on to them with great ingenuity the onus of our own failures and disappointments. *Rationalizing is the self-exculpation which occurs when we feel ourselves, or our group, accused of misapprehension or error.*

The little word *my* is the most important one in all human affairs, and properly to reckon with it is the beginning of wisdom. It has the same force whether it is *my* dinner, *my* dog, and *my* house, or *my* faith, *my* country, and *my* God. We not only resent the imputation that our watch is wrong, or our car shabby, but that our conception of the canals of Mars, of the pronunciation of "Epictetus," of the medicinal value of salicine, or the date of Sargon I, is subject to revision.

Philosophers, scholars, and men of science exhibit a common sensitiveness in all decisions in which their *amour propre* is involved. Thousands of argumentative works have been written to vent a grudge. However stately their reasoning, it may be nothing but rationalizing, stimulated by the most commonplace of all motives. A history of philosophy and theology could be written in terms of grouches, wounded pride, and aversions, and it would be far more instructive than the usual treatments of these themes. Sometimes, under Providence, the lowly impulse of resentment leads to great achievements. Milton wrote his treatise on divorce as a result of his troubles with his seven-

3. *Instincts of the Herd,* p. 44.

teen-year-old wife, and when he was accused of being the leading spirit in a new sect, the Divorcers, he wrote his noble *Areopagitica* to prove his right to say what he thought fit, and incidentally to establish the advantage of a free press in the promotion of Truth.

All mankind, high and low, thinks in all the ways which have been described. The reverie goes on all the time not only in the mind of the mill hand and the Broadway flapper, but equally in weighty judges and godly bishops. It has gone on in all the philosophers, scientists, poets, and theologians that have ever lived. Aristotle's most abstruse speculations were doubtless tempered by highly irrelevant reflections. He is reported to have had very thin legs and small eyes, for which he doubtless had to find excuses, and he was wont to indulge in very conspicuous dress and rings and was accustomed to arrange his hair carefully.[4] Diogenes the Cynic exhibited the impudence of a touchy soul. His tub was his distinction. Tennyson in beginning his "Maud" could not forget his chagrin over losing his patrimony years before as the result of an unhappy investment in the Patent Decorative Carving Company. These facts are not recalled here as a gratuitous disparagement of the truly great, but to insure a full realization of the tremendous competition which all really exacting thought has to face, even in the minds of the most highly endowed mortals.

And now the astonishing and perturbing suspicion emerges that perhaps almost all that had passed for social science, political economy, politics, and ethics in the past may be brushed aside by future generations as mainly rationalizing. John Dewey has already reached this conclusion in regard to philosophy.[5] Veblen [6] and other writers have revealed the various unperceived presuppositions of the traditional political economy, and now comes an Italian sociologist, Vilfredo Pareto, who, in his huge treatise on general sociology, devotes hundreds of pages to substantiating a similar thesis affecting all the social sciences.[7] This conclusion may be ranked by students of a hundred years hence as one of the several great discoveries of our age. It is by no means fully worked out, and it is so opposed to nature that it will be very slowly accepted by the great mass of those who consider themselves thoughtful. As a historical student I am personally fully reconciled to this newer view. Indeed, it seems to me inevitable that just as the various sciences of nature were, before the opening of the seventeenth century, largely masses of rationalizations to suit the religious sentiments of the period, so the social sciences have continued

4. Diogenes Laertius, book v.
5. *Reconstruction in Philosophy.*
6. *The Place of Science in Modern Civilization.*
7. *Traité de Sociologie Générale, passim.* The author's term *"derivations"* seems to be his precise way of expressing what we have called the "good" reasons, and his *"residus"* correspond to the "real" reasons. He well says, *"L'homme éprouve le besoin de raisonner, et en outre d'étendre un voile sur ses instincts et sur ses sentiments"*—hence, rationalization. (P. 788.) His aim is to reduce sociology to the "real" reasons. (P. 791.)

even to our own day to be rationalizations of uncritically accepted beliefs and customs.

It will become apparent as we proceed that the fact that an idea is ancient and that it has been widely received is no argument in its favor, but should immediately suggest the necessity of carefully testing it as a probable instance of rationalization.

This brings us to another kind of thought which can fairly easily be distinguished from the three kinds described above. It has not the usual qualities of the reverie, for it does not hover about our personal complacencies and humiliations. It is not made up of the homely decisions forced upon us by everyday needs, when we review our little stock of existing information, consult our conventional preferences and obligations, and make a choice of action. It is not the defense of our own cherished beliefs and prejudices just because they are our own—mere plausible excuses for remaining of the same mind. On the contrary, it is that peculiar species of thought which leads us to *change* our mind.

It is this kind of thought that has raised man from his pristine, subsavage ignorance and squalor to the degree of knowledge and comfort which he now possesses. On his capacity to continue and greatly extend this kind of thinking depends his chance of groping his way out of the plight in which the most civilized peoples of the world now find themselves. In the past this type of thinking has been called Reason. But so many misapprehensions have grown up around the word that some of us have become suspicious of it. I suggest, therefore, that we substitute a recent name and speak of "creative thought" rather than of Reason. *For this kind of meditation begets knowledge, and knowledge is really creative inasmuch as it makes things look different from what they seemed before and may indeed work for their reconstruction.*

In certain moods some of us realize that we are observing things or making reflections with a seeming disregard of our personal preoccupations. We are not preening or defending ourselves; we are not faced by the necessity of any practical decision, nor are we apologizing for believing this or that. We are just wondering and looking and mayhap seeing what we never perceived before.

Curiosity is as clear and definite as any of our urges. We wonder what is in a sealed telegram or in a letter in which some one else is absorbed, or what is being said in the telephone booth or in low conversation. This inquisitiveness is vastly stimulated by jealousy, suspicion, or any hint that we ourselves are directly or indirectly involved. But there appears to be a fair amount of personal interest in other people's affairs even when they do not concern us except as a mystery to be unraveled or a tale to be told. The reports of a divorce suit will have "news value" for many weeks. They constitute a story, like a novel or play or moving picture. This is not an example of pure curiosity, however, since we readily identify ourselves with others, and their joys and despair then become our own.

We also take note of, or "observe," as Sherlock Holmes says, things which have nothing to do with our personal interests and make no personal appeal either direct or by way of sympathy. This is what Veblen so well calls "idle curiosity." And it is usually idle enough. Some of us when we face the line of people opposite us in a subway train impulsively consider them in detail and engage in rapid inferences and form theories in regard to them. On entering a room there are those who will perceive at a glance the degree of preciousness of the rugs, the character of the pictures, and the personality revealed by the books. But there are many, it would seem, who are so absorbed in their personal reverie or in some definite purpose that they have no bright-eyed energy for idle curiosity. The tendency to miscellaneous observation we come by honestly enough, for we note it in many of our animal relatives.

Veblen, however, uses the term "idle curiosity" somewhat ironically, as is his wont. It is idle only to those who fail to realize that it may be a very rare and indispensable thing from which almost all distinguished human achievement proceeds, since it may lead to systematic examination and seeking for things hitherto undiscovered. For research is but diligent search which enjoys the high flavor of primitive hunting. Occasionally and fitfully idle curiosity thus leads to creative thought, which alters and broadens our own views and aspirations and may in turn, under highly favorable circumstances, affect the views and lives of others, even for generations to follow. An example or two will make this unique human process clear.

Galileo was a thoughtful youth and doubtless carried on a rich and varied reverie. He had artistic ability and might have turned out to be a musician or painter. When he had dwelt among the monks at Valambrosa he had been tempted to lead the life of a religious. As a boy he busied himself with toy machines and he inherited a fondness for mathematics. All these facts are of record. We may safely assume also that, along with many other subjects of contemplation, the Pisan maidens found a vivid place in his thoughts.

One day when seventeen years old he wandered into the cathedral of his native town. In the midst of his reverie he looked up at the lamps hanging by long chains from the high ceiling of the church. Then something very difficult to explain occurred. He found himself no longer thinking of the building, worshipers, or the services; of his artistic or religious interests; of his reluctance to become a physician as his father wished. He forgot the question of a career and even the *graziosissime donne*. As he watched the swinging lamps he was suddenly wondering if mayhap their oscillations, whether long or short, did not occupy the same time. Then he tested this hypothesis by counting his pulse, for that was the only timepiece he had with him.

This observation, however remarkable in itself, was not enough to produce a really creative thought. Others may have noticed the same thing and yet nothing came of it. Most of our observations have no assignable results. Galileo may have seen that the warts on a peasant's face formed a perfect isosceles triangle, or he may have noticed with boyish glee that just as the officiating priest was uttering the solemn words, *ecce agnus Dei,* a fly lit on the end of his nose. To be really creative, ideas have to be worked up and then "put over," so that they become a part of man's social heritage. The highly accurate pendulum clock was one of the later results of Galileo's discovery. He himself was led to reconsider and successfully to refute the old notions of falling bodies. It remained for Newton to prove that the moon was falling, and presumably all the heavenly bodies. This quite upset all the consecrated views of the heavens as managed by angelic engineers. The universality of the laws of gravitation stimulated the attempt to seek other and equally important natural laws and cast grave doubts on the miracles in which mankind had hitherto believed. In short, those who dared to include in their thought the discoveries of Galileo and his successors found themselves in a new earth surrounded by new heavens.

On the 28th of October, 1831, two hundred and fifty years after Galileo had noticed the isochronous vibrations of the lamps, creative thought and its currency had so far increased that Faraday was wondering what would happen if he mounted a disk of copper between the poles of a horseshoe magnet. As the disk revolved, an electric current was produced. This would doubtless have seemed the idlest kind of experiment to the stanch business men of the time who, it happened, were just then denouncing the child-labor bills in their anxiety to avail themselves to the full of the results of earlier idle curiosity. But should the dynamos and motors which have come into being as the outcome of Faraday's experiment be stopped this evening, the business man of to-day, agitated over labor troubles, might, as he trudged home past lines of "dead" cars, through dark streets to an unlighted house, engage in a little creative thought of his own and perceive that he and his laborers would have no modern factories and mines to quarrel about if it had not been for the strange, practical effects of the idle curiosity of scientists, inventors, and engineers.

The examples of creative intelligence given above belong to the realm of modern scientific achievement, which furnishes the most striking instances of the effects of scrupulous, objective thinking. But there are, of course, other great realms in which the recording and embodiment of acute observation and insight have wrought themselves into the higher life of man. The great poets and dramatists and our modern story-tellers have found themselves engaged in productive reveries, noting and artistically presenting their discoveries for the delight and instruction of those who have the ability to appreciate them.

The process by which a fresh and original poem or drama comes into being is doubtless analogous to that which originates and elaborates so-called scientific discoveries; but there is clearly a temperamental difference. The genesis and advance of painting, sculpture, and music offer still other problems. We really as yet know shockingly little about these matters, and indeed very few people have the least curiosity about them.[8] Nevertheless, creative intelligence

8. Recently a re-examination of creative thought has begun as a result of new knowledge

in its various forms and activities is what makes man. Were it not for its slow, painful, and constantly discouraged operations through the ages man would be no more than a species of primate living on seeds, fruit, roots, and uncooked flesh, and wandering naked through the woods and over the plains like a chimpanzee.

The origin and progress and future promotion of civilization are ill understood and misconceived. These should be made the chief theme of education, but much hard work is necessary before we can reconstruct our ideas of man and his capacities and free ourselves from innumerable persistent misapprehensions. There have been obstructionists in all times, not merely the lethargic masses, but the moralists, the rationalizing theologians, and most of the philosophers, all busily if unconsciously engaged in ratifying existing ignorance and mistakes and discouraging creative thought. Naturally, those who reassure us seem worthy of honor and respect. Equally naturally, those who puzzle us with disturbing criticisms and invite us to change our ways are objects of suspicion and readily discredited. Our personal discontent does not ordinarily extend to any critical questioning of the general situation in which we find ourselves. In every age the prevailing conditions of civilization have appeared quite natural and inevitable to those who grew up in them. The cow asks no questions as to how it happens to have a dry stall and a supply of hay. The kitten laps its warm milk from a china saucer, without knowing anything about porcelain; the dog nestles in the corner of a divan with no sense of obligation to the inventors of upholstery and the manufacturers of down pillows. So we humans accept our breakfasts, our trains and telephones and orchestras and movies, our national Constitution, our moral code and standards of manners, with the simplicity and innocence of a pet rabbit. We have absolutely inexhaustible capacities for appropriating what others do for us with no thought of a "thank you." We do not feel called upon to make any least contribution to the merry game ourselves. Indeed, we are usually quite unaware that a game is being played at all.

We have now examined the various classes of thinking which we can readily observe in ourselves and which we have plenty of reasons to believe go on, and always have been going on, in our fellow-men. We can sometimes get quite pure and sparkling examples of all four kinds, but commonly they are so confused and intermingled in our reverie as not to be readily distinguishable. The reverie is a reflection of our longings, exultations, and complacencies, our fears, suspicions, and disappointments. We are chiefly engaged in struggling to maintain our self-respect and in asserting that supremacy which we all crave and which seems to us our natural prerogative. It is not strange, but rather

---

which discredits many of the notions formerly held about "reason." See, for example, *Creative Intelligence,* by a group of American philosophic thinkers; John Dewey, *Essays in Experimental Logic* (both pretty hard books); and Veblen, *The Place of Science in Modern Civilization.* Easier than these and very stimulating are Dewey, *Reconstruction in Philosophy,* and Woodworth, *Dynamic Psychology.*

quite inevitable, that our beliefs about what is true and false, good and bad, right and wrong, should be mixed up with the reverie and be influenced by the same considerations which determine its character and course. We resent criticisms of our views exactly as we do of anything else connected with ourselves. Our notions of life and its ideals seem to us to be *our own* and as such necessarily true and right, to be defended at all costs.

We very rarely consider, however, the process by which we gained our convictions. If we did so, we could hardly fail to see that there was usually little ground for our confidence in them. Here and there, in this department of knowledge or that, some one of us might make a fair claim to have taken some trouble to get correct ideas of, let us say, the situation in Russia, the sources of our food supply, the origin of the Constitution, the revision of the tariff, the policy of the Holy Roman Apostolic Church, modern business organization, trade unions, birth control, socialism, the League of Nations, the excess-profits tax, preparedness, advertising in its social bearings; but only a very exceptional person would be entitled to opinions on all of even these few matters. And yet most of us have opinions on all these, and on many other questions of equal importance, of which we may know even less. We feel compelled, as self-respecting persons, to take sides when they come up for discussion. We even surprise ourselves by our omniscience. Without taking thought we see in a flash that it is most righteous and expedient to discourage birth control by legislative enactment, or that one who decries intervention in Mexico is clearly wrong, or that big advertising is essential to big business and that big business is the pride of the land. As godlike beings, why should we not rejoice in our omniscience?

It is clear, in any case, that our convictions on important matters are not the result of knowledge or critical thought, nor, it may be added, are they often dictated by supposed self-interest. Most of them are *pure prejudices* in the proper sense of that word. We do not form them ourselves. They are the whispering of "the voice of the herd." We have in the last analysis no responsibility for them and need assume none. They are not really our own ideas, but those of others no more well informed or inspired than ourselves, who have got them in the same careless and humiliating manner as we. It should be our pride to revise our ideas and not to adhere to what passes for respectable opinion, for such opinion can frequently be shown to be not respectable at all. We should, in view of the considerations that have been mentioned, resent our supine credulity. As an English writer has remarked:

> If we feared the entertaining of an unverifiable opinion with the warmth with which we fear using the wrong implement at the dinner table, if the thought of holding a prejudice disgusted us as does a foul disease, then the dangers of man's suggestibility would be turned into advantages.[9]

9. Trotter, *op. cit.*, p. 45. The first part of this little volume is excellent.

The purpose of this essay is to set forth briefly the way in which the notions of the herd have been accumulated. This seems to me the best, easiest, and least invidious educational device for cultivating a proper distrust for the older notions on which we still continue to rely.

The "real" reasons, which explain how it is we happen to hold a particular belief, are chiefly historical. Our most important opinions—those, for example, having to do with traditional, religious, and moral convictions, property rights, patriotism, national honor, the state, and indeed all the assumed foundations of society—are, as I have already suggested, rarely the result of reasoned consideration, but of unthinking absorption from the social environment in which we live. Consequently, they have about them a quality of "elemental certitude," and we especially resent doubt or criticism cast upon them. So long, however, as we revere the whisperings of the herd, we are obviously unable to examine them dispassionately and to consider to what extent they are suited to the novel conditions and social exigencies in which we find ourselves to-day.

The "real" reasons for our beliefs, by making clear their origins and history, can do much to dissipate this emotional blockade and rid us of our prejudices and preconceptions. Once this is done and we come critically to examine our traditional beliefs, we may well find some of them sustained by experience and honest reasoning, while others must be revised to meet new conditions and our more extended knowledge. But only after we have undertaken such a critical examination in the light of experience and modern knowledge, freed from any feeling of "primary certitude," can we claim that the "good" are also the "real" reasons for our opinions.

I do not flatter myself that this general show-up of man's thought through the ages will cure myself or others of carelessness in adopting ideas, or of unseemly heat in defending them just because we have adopted them. But if the considerations which I propose to recall are really incorporated into our thinking and are permitted to establish our general outlook on human affairs, they will do much to relieve the imaginary obligation we feel in regard to traditional sentiments and ideals. Few of us are capable of engaging in creative thought, but some of us can at least come to distinguish it from other and inferior kinds of thought and accord to it the esteem that it merits as the greatest treasure of the past and the only hope of the future.

THE CASE FOR THE DAYDREAMER [1]

JAMES THURBER

All the books in my extensive library on training the mind agree that realism, as against fantasy, reverie, daydreaming, and woolgathering, is a highly important thing. "Be a realist," says Dr. James L. Mursell, whose "Streamline Your Mind" I have already discussed. "Take a definite step to turn a dream into a reality," says Mrs. Dorothea Brande, the "Wake-Up-and-Live!" woman. They allow you a certain amount of reverie and daydreaming (no woolgathering), but only when it is purposeful, only when it is going to lead to realistic action and concrete achievement. In this insistence on reality I do not see as much profit as these Shapers of Success do. I have had a great deal of satisfaction and benefit out of daydreaming which never got me anywhere in their definition of getting somewhere. I am reminded, as an example, of an incident which occurred this last summer.

I had been travelling about the country attending dog shows. I was writing a series of pieces on these shows. Not being in the habit of carrying press cards, letters of introduction, or even, in some cases, the key to my car or the tickets to a show which I am on my way to attend, I had nothing by which to identify myself. I simply paid my way in, but at a certain dog show I determined to see if the officials in charge would give me a pass. I approached a large, heavy-set man who looked somewhat like Victor McLaglen. His name was Bustard. Mr. Bustard. "You'll have to see Mr. Bustard," a ticket-taker had told me. This Mr. Bustard was apparently very busy trying to find bench space for old Miss Emily Van Winkle's Pomeranians, which she had entered at the last minute, and attending to a number of other matters. He glanced at me, saw that he outweighed me some sixty pounds, and decided to make short shrift of whatever it was I wanted. I explained I was writing an article about the show and would like a pass to get in. "Why, that's impossible!" he cried. "That's ridiculous! If I gave you a pass, I'd have to give a pass to everyone who came up and asked me for a pass!" I was pretty much overwhelmed. I couldn't, as is usual in these cases, think of anything to say except "I see." Mr. Bustard delivered a brief, snarling lecture on the subject of people who expect to get into dog shows free, unless they are showing dogs, and ended with "Are you showing dogs?" I tried to think of something sharp and well-turned. "No, I'm not showing any dogs," I said, coldly. Mr. Bustard abruptly turned his back on me and walked away.

As soon as Mr. Bustard disappeared, I began to think of things I should have said. I thought of a couple of sharp cracks on his name, the least pointed of which was Buzzard. Finely edged comebacks leaped to mind. Instead of

1. From *Let Your Mind Alone* (New York: Harper & Brothers, 1937), pp. 19–25. Reprinted by permission of the author. Copyright, 1936, James Thurber. Originally published in *The New Yorker.*

going into the dog show—or following Mr. Bustard—I wandered up and down the streets of the town, improving on my retorts. I fancied a much more successful encounter with Mr. Bustard. In this fancied encounter, I, in fact, enraged Mr. Bustard. He lunged at me, whereupon, side-stepping agilely, I led with my left and floored him with a beautiful right to the jaw. "Try that one!" I cried aloud. "Mercy!" murmured an old lady who was passing me at the moment. I began to walk more rapidly; my heart took a definite lift. Some people, in my dream, were bending over Bustard, who was out cold. "Better take him home and let the other bustards pick his bones," I said. When I got back to the dog show, I was in high fettle.

After several months I still feel, when I think of Mr. Bustard, that I got the better of him. In a triumphant daydream, it seems to me, there is felicity and not defeat. You can't just take a humiliation and dismiss it from your mind, for it will crop up in your dreams, but neither can you safely carry a dream into reality in the case of an insensitive man like Mr. Bustard who outweighs you by sixty pounds. The thing to do is to visualize a triumph over the humiliator so vividly and insistently that it becomes, in effect, an actuality. I went on with my daydreams about Mr. Bustard. All that day at the dog show I played tricks on him in my imagination, I outgeneralled him, I made him look silly, I had him on the run. I would imagine myself sitting in a living room. It was late at night. Outside it was raining heavily. The doorbell rang. I went to the door and opened it, and a man was standing there. "I wonder if you would let me use your phone?" he asked. "My car has broken down." It was, of all people, Mr. Bustard. You can imagine my jibes, my sarcasm, my repartee, my shutting the door in his face at the end. After a whole afternoon of this kind of thing, I saw Mr. Bustard on my way out of the show. I actually felt a little sorry about the tossing around I had given him. I gave him an enigmatic, triumphant smile which must have worried him a great deal. He must have wondered what I had been up to, what superior of his I had seen, what I had done to get back at him—who, after all, I was.

Now, let us figure Dr. Mursell in my place. Let us suppose that Dr. Mursell went up to Mr. Bustard and asked him for a pass to the dog show on the ground that he could streamline the dog's intuition. I fancy that Mr. Bustard also outweighs Dr. Mursell by sixty pounds and is in better fighting trim; we men who write treatises on the mind are not likely to be in as good shape as men who run dog shows. Dr. Mursell, then, is rebuffed, as I was. If he tries to get back at Mr. Bustard right there and then, he will find himself saying "I see" or "Well, I didn't know" or, at best, "I just asked you." Even the streamlined mind runs into this Blockage, as the psychologists call it. Dr. Mursell, like myself, will go away and think up better things to say, but, being a realist dedicated to carrying a dream into actuality, he will perforce have to come back and tackle Mr. Bustard again. If Mr. Bustard's patience gives out, or if he is truly stung by some crack of the Doctor's he is likely to begin shoving, or snap his fingers, or say "'*Raus!*," or even tweak the Doctor's nose. Dr. Mursell, in that case, would get into no end of trouble. Realists are always getting into trouble. They miss the sweet, easy victories of the daydreamer.

I do not pretend that the daydream cannot be carried too far. If at this late date, for instance, I should get myself up to look as much like Mr. Bustard as possible and then, gazing into the bathroom mirror, snarl "Bustard, you dog!," that would be carrying the daydream too far. One should never run the risk of identifying oneself with the object of one's scorn. I have no idea what complexes and neuroses might lie that way. The mental experts could tell you—or, if they couldn't they would anyway.

Now let us turn briefly to the indomitable Mrs. Brande, eight of whose precious words of advice have, the ads for her book tell us, changed the lives of 860,000 people, or maybe it is 86,000,000—Simon & Schuster published her book. (These words are "act as if it were impossible to fail," in case your life hasn't been changed.) Discussing realistic action as against the daydream, she takes up the case of a person, any person, who dreams about going to Italy but is getting nowhere. The procedure she suggests for such a person is threefold: (1) read a current newspaper in Italian, buy some histories, phrase books, and a small grammar; (2) put aside a small coin each day; (3) do something in your spare time to make money—"if it is nothing more than to sit with children while their parents are at parties." (I have a quick picture of the parents reeling from party to party, but that is beside the point.)

I can see the newspaper and the books intensifying the dream, but I can't somehow see them getting anybody to Italy. As for putting a small coin aside each day, everybody who has tried it knows that it does not work out. At the end of three weeks you usually have $2.35 in the pig bank or the cooky jar, a dollar and a half of which you have to use for something besides Italy, such as a C.O.D. package. At that rate, all that you would have in the bank or the jar at the end of six years would be about $87.45. Within the next six years Italy will probably be at war, and even if you were well enough to travel after all that time, you couldn't get into the country. The disappointment of a dream nursed for six years, with a reality in view that did not eventuate, would be enough to embitter a person for life. As for this business of sitting with children while their parents are at parties, anybody who has done it knows that no trip to anywhere, even Utopia, would be worth it. Very few people can sit with children, especially children other than their own, more than an hour and a half without having their dispositions and even their characters badly mauled about. In fifteen minutes the average child whose parents are at a party can make enough flat statements of fact about one's personal appearance and ask enough pointed questions about one's private life to send one away feeling that there is little, if any, use in going on with anything at all, let alone a trip to Italy.

The long and hard mechanics of reality which these inspirationalists suggest are, it seems to me, far less satisfactory than the soft routine of a dream.

The dreamer builds up for himself no such towering and uncertain structure of hope; he has no depleted cooky jar to shake his faith in himself. It is significant that the line "Oh, to be in England now that April's there," which is a definite dream line, is better known than any line the poet wrote about actually being in England. (I guess *that* will give the inspirationalists something to think about.) You can sit up with children if you want to, you can put a dime a day in an empty coffee tin, you can read the Fascist viewpoint in an Italian newspaper, but when it comes to a choice between the dream and the reality of present-day Italy, I personally shall sit in a corner by the fire and read "The Ring and the Book." And in the end it will probably be me who sends you a postcard from Italy, which you can put between the pages of the small grammar or the phrase book.

LANGUAGE AND THOUGHT[1]

SUSANNE K. LANGER

A SYMBOL is not the same thing as a sign; that is a fact that psychologists and philosophers often overlook. All intelligent animals use signs; so do we. To them as well as to us sounds and smells and motions are signs of food, danger, the presence of other beings, or of rain or storm. Furthermore, some animals not only attend to signs but produce them for the benefit of others. Dogs bark at the door to be let in; rabbits thump to call each other; the cooing of doves and the growl of a wolf defending his kill are unequivocal signs of feelings and intentions to be reckoned with by other creatures.

We use signs just as animals do, though with considerably more elaboration. We stop at red lights and go on green; we answer calls and bells, watch the sky for coming storms, read trouble or promise or anger in each other's eyes. That is animal intelligence raised to the human level. Those of us who are dog lovers can probably all tell wonderful stories of how high our dogs have sometimes risen in the scale of clever sign interpretation and sign using.

A sign is anything that announces the existence or the imminence of some event, the presence of a thing or a person, or a change in a state of affairs. There are signs of the weather, signs of danger, signs of future good or evil, signs of what the past has been. In every case a sign is closely bound up with something to be noted or expected in experience. It is always a part of the situation to which it refers, though the reference may be remote in space and time. In so far as we are led to note or expect the signified event we are making correct use of a sign. This is the essence of rational behavior, which animals

1. From Susanne K. Langer, "The Lord of Creation." Reprinted from the January 1944 issue of *Fortune* Magazine by special permission of Editors copyright, 1944, Time, Inc.

show in varying degrees. It is entirely realistic, being closely bound up with the actual objective course of history—learned by experience, and cashed in or voided by further experience.

If man had kept to the straight and narrow path of sign using, he would be like the other animals, though perhaps a little brighter. He would not talk, but grunt and gesticulate and point. He would make his wishes known, give warnings, perhaps develop a social system like that of bees and ants, with such a wonderful efficiency of communal enterprise that all men would have plenty to eat, warm apartments—all exactly alike and perfectly convenient—to live in, and everybody could and would sit in the sun or by the fire, as the climate demanded, not talking but just basking, with every want satisfied, most of his life. The young would romp and make love, the old would sleep, the middle-aged would do the routine work almost unconsciously and eat a great deal. But that would be the life of a social, superintelligent, purely sign-using animal.

To us who are human, it does not sound very glorious. We want to go places and do things, own all sorts of gadgets that we do not absolutely need, and when we sit down to take it easy we want to talk. Rights and property, social position, special talents and virtues, and above all our ideas, are what we live for. We have gone off on a tangent that takes us far away from the mere biological cycle that animal generations accomplish; and that is because we can use not only signs but symbols.

A symbol differs from a sign in that it does not announce the presence of the object, the being, condition, or whatnot, which is its meaning, but merely *brings this thing to mind*. It is not a mere "substitute sign" to which we react as though it were the object itself. The fact is that our reaction to hearing a person's name is quite different from our reaction to the person himself. There are certain rare cases where a symbol stands directly for its meaning: in religious experience, for instance, the Host is not only a symbol but a Presence. But symbols in the ordinary sense are not mystic. They are the same sort of thing that ordinary signs are; only they do not call our attention to something necessarily present or to be physically dealt with—they call up merely a conception of the thing they "mean."

The difference between a sign and a symbol is, in brief, that a sign causes us to think or act *in face of* the thing signified, whereas a symbol causes us to think *about* the thing symbolized. Therein lies the great importance of symbolism for human life, its power to make this life so different from any other animal biography that generations of men have found it incredible to suppose that they were of purely zoological origin. A sign is always embedded in reality, in a present that emerges from the actual past and stretches to the future; but a symbol may be divorced from reality altogether. It may refer to what is *not* the case, to a mere idea, a figment, a dream. It serves, therefore, to liberate thought from the immediate stimuli of a physically present world; and that liberation marks the essential difference between human and nonhuman mentality. Animals think, but they think *of* and *at* things; men think primarily *about* things. Words, pictures, and memory images are symbols that may be combined and varied in a thousand ways. The result is a symbolic structure whose meaning is a complex of all their respective meanings, and this kaleidoscope of *ideas* is the typical product of the human brain that we call the "stream of thought."

The process of transforming all direct experience into imagery or into that supreme mode of symbolic expression, language, has so completely taken possession of the human mind that it is not only a special talent but a dominant, organic need. All our sense impressions leave their traces in our memory not only as signs disposing our practical reactions in the future but also as symbols, images representing our *ideas* of things; and the tendency to manipulate ideas, to combine and abstract, mix and extend them by playing with symbols, is man's outstanding characteristic. It seems to be what his brain most naturally and spontaneously does. Therefore his primitive mental function is not judging reality, but *dreaming his desires.*

Dreaming is apparently a basic function of human brains, for it is free and unexhausting like our metabolism, heartbeat, and breath. It is easier to dream than not to dream, as it is easier to breathe than to refrain from breathing. The symbolic character of dreams is fairly well established. Symbol mongering, on this ineffectual, uncritical level, seems to be instinctive, the fulfillment of an elementary need rather than the purposeful exercise of a high and difficult talent.

The special power of man's mind rests on the evolution of this special activity, not on any transcendently high development of animal intelligence. We are not immeasurably higher than other animals; we are different. We have a biological need and with it a biological gift that they do not share.

Because man has not only the ability but the constant need of *conceiving* what has happened to him, what surrounds him, what is demanded of him—in short, of symbolizing nature, himself, and his hopes and fears—he has a constant and crying need of *expression.* What he cannot express, he cannot conceive; what he cannot conceive is chaos, and fills him with terror.

If we bear in mind this all-important craving for expression we get a new picture of man's behavior; for from this trait spring his powers and his weaknesses. The process of symbolic transformation that all our experiences undergo is nothing more nor less than the process of *conception,* which underlies the human faculties of abstraction and imagination.

When we are faced with a strange or difficult situation, we cannot react directly, as other creatures do, with flight, aggression, or any such simple instinctive pattern. Our whole reaction depends on how we manage to conceive the situation—whether we cast it in a definite dramatic form, whether we see it as a disaster, a challenge, a fulfillment of doom, or a fiat of the Divine Will. In words or dreamlike images, in artistic or religious or even in cynical form, we must *construe* the events of life. There is great virtue in the figure of speech,

"I can *make* nothing of it," to express a failure to understand something. Thought and memory are processes of *making* the thought content and the memory image; the pattern of our ideas is given by the symbols through which we express them. And in the course of manipulating those symbols we inevitably distort the original experience, as we abstract certain features of it, embroider and reinforce those features with other ideas, until the conception we project on the screen of memory is quite different from anything in our real history.

Conception is a necessary and elementary process; what we do with our conceptions is another story. That is the entire history of human culture—of intelligence and morality, folly and superstition, ritual, language, and the arts—all the phenomena that set man apart from, and above, the rest of the animal kingdom. As the religious mind has to make all human history a drama of sin and salvation in order to define its own moral attitudes, so a scientist wrestles with the mere presentation of "the facts" before he can reason about them. The process of *envisaging* facts, values, hopes, and fears underlies our whole behavior pattern; and this process is reflected in the evolution of an extraordinary phenomenon found always, and only, in human societies—the phenomenon of language.

Language is the highest and most amazing achievement of the symbolistic human mind. The power it bestows is almost inestimable, for without it anything properly called "thought" is impossible. The birth of language is the dawn of humanity. The line between man and beast—between the highest ape and the lowest savage—is the language line. Whether the primitive Neanderthal man was anthropoid or human depends less on his cranial capacity, his upright posture, or even his use of tools and fire, than on one issue we shall probably never be able to settle—whether or not he spoke.

In all physical traits and practical responses, such as skills and visual judgments, we can find a certain continuity between animal and human mentality. Sign using is an ever evolving, ever improving function throughout the whole animal kingdom, from the lowly worm that shrinks into his hole at the sound of an approaching foot, to the dog obeying his master's command, and even to the learned scientist who watches the movements of an index needle.

This continuity of the sign-using talent has led psychologists to the belief that language is evolved from the vocal expressions, grunts and coos and cries, whereby animals vent their feelings or signal their fellows; that man has elaborated this sort of communion to the point where it makes a perfect exchange of ideas possible.

I do not believe that this doctrine of the origin of language is correct. The essence of language is symbolic, not signific; we use it first and most vitally to formulate and hold ideas in our own minds. Conception, not social control, is its first and foremost benefit.

Watch a young child that is just learning to speak play with a toy; he says the name of the object, e.g.: "Horsey! horsey! horsey!" over and over again, looks at the object, moves it, always saying the name to himself or to the world at large. It is quite a time before he talks to anyone in particular; he talks first of all to himself. This is his way of forming and fixing the *conception* of the object in his mind, and around this conception all his knowledge of it grows. *Names* are the essence of language; for the *name* is what abstracts the conception of the horse from the horse itself, and lets the mere idea recur at the speaking of the name. This permits the conception gathered from one horse experience to be exemplified again by another instance of a horse, so that the notion embodied in the name is a general notion.

To this end, the baby uses a word long before he *asks for* the object; when he wants his horsey he is likely to cry and fret, because he is reacting to an actual environment, not forming ideas. He uses the animal language of *signs* for his wants; talking is still a purely symbolic process—its practical value has not really impressed him yet.

Language need not be vocal; it may be purely visual, like written language, or even tactual, like the deaf-mute system of speech; but it *must be denotative.* The sounds, intended or unintended, whereby animals communicate do not constitute a language, because they are signs, not names. They never fall into an organic pattern, a meaningful syntax of even the most rudimentary sort, as all language seems to do with a sort of driving necessity. That is because signs refer to actual situations, in which things have obvious relations to each other that require only to be noted; but symbols refer to ideas, which are not physically there for inspection, so their connections and features have to be represented. This gives all true language a natural tendency toward growth and development, which seems almost like a life of its own. Languages are not invented; they grow with our need for expression.

In contrast, animal "speech" never has a structure. It is merely an emotional response. Apes may greet their ration of yams with a shout of "Nga!" But they do not say "Nga" between meals. If they could *talk about* their yams instead of just saluting them, they would be the most primitive men instead of the most anthropoid of beasts. They would have ideas, and tell each other things true or false, rational or irrational; they would make plans and invent laws and sing their own praises, as men do.

THE FOUR STAGES OF THOUGHT[1]

GRAHAM WALLAS

WHAT I wish to investigate is at what stages in the thought-process the thinker should bring the conscious and voluntary effort of his art to bear. Here we at once meet the difficulty that unless we can recognize a psychological

1. From *The Art of Thought* (New York: Harcourt, Brace & Company, Inc., 1926), pp. 79–107. Copyright, 1926, and reprinted by permission of Harcourt, Brace & Company, Inc.

event, and distinguish it from other events, we cannot bring conscious effort to bear directly upon it; and that our mental life is a stream of intermingled psychological events, all of which affect each other, any of which, at any given moment, may be beginning or continuing or ending, and which, therefore, are extremely hard to distinguish from each other.

We can, to some degree, avoid this difficulty if we take a single achievement of thought—the making of a new generalization or invention, or the poetical expression of a new idea—and ask how it was brought about. We can then roughly dissect out a continuous process, with a beginning and a middle and an end of its own. Helmholtz, for instance, the great German physicist, speaking in 1891 at a banquet on his seventieth birthday, described the way in which his most important new thoughts had come to him. He said that after previous investigation of the problem "in all directions . . . happy ideas come unexpectedly without effort, like an inspiration. So far as I am concerned, they have never come to me when my mind was fatigued, or when I was at my working table. . . . They came particularly readily during the slow ascent of wooded hills on a sunny day."[2] Helmholtz here gives us three stages in the formation of a new thought. The first in time I shall call Preparation, the stage during which the problem was "investigated . . . in all directions"; the second is the stage during which he was not consciously thinking about the problem, which I shall call Incubation; the third, consisting of the appearance of the "happy idea" together with the psychological events which immediately preceded and accompanied that appearance, I shall call Illumination.

And I shall add a fourth stage, of Verification, which Helmholtz does not here mention. Henri Poincaré, for instance, in the book *Science and Method,* describes in vivid detail the successive stages of two of his great mathematical discoveries. Both of them came to him after a period of Incubation (due in one case to his military service as a reservist, and in the other case to a journey), during which no conscious mathematical thinking was done, but, as Poincaré believed, much unconscious mental exploration took place. In both cases Incubation was preceded by a Preparation stage of hard, conscious, systematic, and fruitless analysis of the problem. In both cases the final idea came to him "with the same characteristics of conciseness, suddenness, and immediate certainty." Each was followed by a period of Verification, in which both the validity of the idea was tested, and the idea itself was reduced to exact form. "It never happens," says Poincaré, in his description of the Verification stage, "that unconscious work supplies *ready-made* the result of a lengthy calculation in which we have only to apply fixed rules. . . . All that we can hope from

2. See Rignano, *Psychology of Reasoning* (1923), pp. 267–268. See also Plato, *Symposium* (210): "He who has been instructed thus far in the things of love, and has learned to see beautiful things in due order and succession, when he comes to the end, will suddenly perceive a beauty wonderful in its nature"; and Rémy de Goncourt: "My conceptions rise into the field of consciousness like a flash of lightning or the flight of a bird" (quoted by H. A. Bruce, *Psychology and Parenthood,* 1919, p. 89).

these inspirations, which are the fruit of unconscious work, is to obtain points of departure for such calculations. As for the calculations themselves, they must be made in the second period of conscious work which follows the inspiration, and in which the results of the inspiration are verified and the consequences deduced. The rules of these calculations are strict and complicated; they demand discipline, attention, will, and consequently, consciousness." In the daily stream of thought these four different stages constantly overlap each other as we explore different problems. An economist reading a Blue Book, a physiologist watching an experiment, or a business man going through his morning's letters, may at the same time be "incubating" on a problem which he proposed to himself a few days ago, be accumulating knowledge in "preparation" for a second problem, and be "verifying" his conclusions on a third problem. Even in exploring the same problem, the mind may be unconsciously incubating on one aspect of it, while it is consciously employed in preparing for or verifying another aspect. And it must always be remembered that much very important thinking, done for instance by a poet exploring his own memories, or by a man trying to see clearly his emotional relation to his country or his party, resembles musical composition in that the stages leading to success are not very easily fitted into a "problem and solution" scheme. Yet, even when success in thought means the creation of something felt to be beautiful and true rather than the solution of a prescribed problem, the four stages of Preparation, Incubation, Illumination, and the Verification of the final result can generally be distinguished from each other.

If we accept this analysis, we are in a position to ask to what degree, and by what means, we can bring conscious effort, and the habits which arise from conscious effort, to bear upon each of the four stages. I shall not deal at any length with the stage of Preparation. It includes the whole process of intellectual education. Men have known for thousands of years that conscious effort and its resulting habits can be used to improve the thought-processes of young persons, and have formulated for that purpose an elaborate art of education. The "educated" man can, in consequence, "put his mind on" to a chosen subject, and "turn his mind off" in a way which is impossible to an uneducated man. The educated man has also acquired, by the effort of observation and memorizing, a body of remembered facts and words which gives him a wider range in the final moment of association, as well as a number of those habitual tracks of association which constitute "thought-systems" like "French policy" or "scholastic philosophy" or "biological evolution," and which present themselves as units in the process of thought.

The educated man has, again, learned, and can, in the Preparation stage, voluntarily or habitually follow out, rules as to the order in which he shall direct his attention to the successive elements in a problem. Hobbes referred to this fact when in the *Leviathan* he described "regulated thought," and contrasted it with that "wild ranging of the mind" which occurs when the thought process is undirected. Regulated thought is, he says, a "seeking." "Sometimes," for instance, "a man seeks what he has lost. . . . Sometimes a man knows a place determinate, within the compass whereof he is to seek; and then his thoughts run over all the parts thereof, in the same manner as one would sweep a room to find a jewel; or as a spaniel ranges the field, till he find a scent; or as a man should run over the alphabet, to start a rhyme." A spaniel with the brain of an educated human being could not, by a direct effort of will, scent a partridge in a distant part of the field. But he could so "quarter" the field by a preliminary voluntary arrangement that the less-voluntary process of smelling would be given every chance of successfully taking place.

Included in these rules for the preliminary "regulation" of our thought, are the whole traditional art of logic, the mathematical forms which are the logic of the modern experimental sciences, and the methods of systematic and continuous examination of present or recorded phenomena which are the basis of astronomy, sociology and the other "observational" sciences. Closely connected with this voluntary use of logical methods is the voluntary choice of a "problem-attitude" (*Aufgabe*). Our mind is not likely to give us a clear answer to any particular problem unless we set it a clear question, and we are more likely to notice the significance of any new piece of evidence, or new association of ideas, if we have formed a definite conception of a case to be proved or disproved. A very successful thinker in natural science told me that he owed much of his success to his practice of following up, when he felt his mind confused, the implications of two propositions, both of which he has hitherto accepted as true, until he had discovered that one of them *must* be untrue. Huxley on that point once quoted Bacon, "Truth comes out of error much more rapidly than it comes out of confusion," and went on, "If you go buzzing about between right and wrong, vibrating and fluctuating, you come out nowhere; but if you are absolutely and thoroughly and persistently wrong you must some of these days have the extreme good fortune of knocking your head against a fact, and that sets you all right again." This is, of course, a production, by conscious effort, of that "dialogue form" of alternate suggestion and criticism which Varendonck describes as occurring in the process of uncontrolled thought. It is, indeed, sometimes possible to observe such an automatic "dialogue" at a point where a single effort of will would turn it into a process of preparatory logical statement. On July 18, 1917, I passed on an omnibus the fashionable church of St. Margaret's, Westminster. Miss Ashley, the richest heiress of the season, was being gorgeously married, and the omnibus conductor said to a friend, "Shocking waste of money! But, there, it does create a lot of labour, I admit that." Perhaps I neglected my duty as a citizen in that I did not say to him, "Now make one effort to realize that inconsistency, and you will have prepared yourself to become an economist."

And though I have assumed, for the sake of clearness, that the thinker is preparing himself for the solution of a single problem, he will often (particularly if he is working on the very complex material of the social sciences) have several kindred problems in his mind, on all of which the voluntary work of preparation has been, or is being done, and for any of which, at the Illumination stage, a solution may present itself.

The fourth stage, of Verification, closely resembles the first stage, of Preparation. It is normally, as Poincaré points out, fully conscious, and men have worked out much the same series of mathematical and logical rules for controlling Verification by conscious effort as those which are used in the control of Preparation.

There remain the second and third stages, Incubation and Illumination. The Incubation stage covers two different things, of which the first is the negative fact that during Incubation we do not voluntarily or consciously think on a particular problem, and the second is the positive fact that a series of unconscious and involuntary (or foreconscious and forevoluntary) mental events may take place during that period. It is the first fact about Incubation which I shall now discuss, leaving the second fact—of subconscious thought during Incubation, and the relation of such thought to Illumination—to be more fully discussed in connection with the Illumination stage. Voluntary abstention from conscious thought on any particular problem may, itself, take two forms: the period of abstention may be spent either in conscious mental work on other problems, or in a relaxation from all conscious mental work. The first kind of Incubation economizes time, and is therefore often the better. We can often get more result in the same time by beginning several problems in succession, and voluntarily leaving them unfinished while we turn to others, than by finishing our work on each problem at one sitting. A well-known academic psychologist, for instance, who was also a preacher, told me that he found by experience that his Sunday sermon was much better if he posed the problem on Monday, than if he did so later in the week, although he might give the same number of hours of conscious work to it in each case. It seems to be a tradition among practising barristers to put off any consideration of each brief to the latest possible moment before they have to deal with it, and to forget the whole matter as rapidly as possible after dealing with it. This fact may help to explain a certain want of depth which has often been noticed in the typical lawyer-statesman, and which may be due to his conscious thought not being sufficiently extended and enriched by subconscious thought.

But, in the case of the more difficult forms of creative thought, the making, for instance, of a scientific discovery, or the writing of a poem or play or the formulation of an important political decision, it is desirable not only that there should be an interval free from conscious thought on the particular problem concerned, but also that that interval should be so spent that nothing should interfere with the free working of the unconscious or partially conscious processes of the mind. In those cases, the stage of Incubation should include a large amount of actual mental relaxation. It would, indeed, be interesting to examine, from that point of view, the biographies of a couple of hundred original thinkers and writers. A. R. Wallace, for instance, hit upon the theory of evolution by natural selection in his berth during an attack of malarial fever at sea; and Darwin was compelled by ill-health to spend the greater part of his waking hours in physical and mental relaxation. Sometimes a thinker has been able to get a sufficiency of relaxation owing to a disposition to idleness, against which he has vainly struggled. More often, perhaps, what he has thought to be idleness, is really that urgent craving for intense and uninterrupted day-dreaming which Anthony Trollope describes in his account of his boyhood.

One effect of such a comparative biographical study might be the formulation of a few rules as to the relation between original intellectual work and the virtue of industry. There are thousands of idle "geniuses" who require to learn that, without a degree of industry in Preparation and Verification, of which many of them have no conception, no great intellectual work can be done, and that the habit of procrastination may be even more disastrous to a professional thinker than it is to a man of business. And yet a thinker of good health and naturally fertile mind may have to be told that mere industry is for him, as it was for Trollope in his later years, the worst temptation of the devil. Cardinal Manning was a man of furious industry, and the suspension of his industry as an Anglican archdeacon during his illness in 1847 was, for good or evil, an important event in the history of English religion. Some of those who, like myself, live in the diocese of London, believe that we have reason to regret an insufficiency of intellectual leadership from our present bishop. The bishop himself indicated one of the causes of our discontent in a letter addressed, in September, 1922, to his clergy. "I come back to an autumn of what, from a human point of view, is unrelieved toil. October 1st to Christmas Day is filled every day, except for the one day off every week, from 10 a.m. to 6 p.m." Then comes a long list of administrative and pastoral engagements, including "three days interviewing 110 Harrow boys to be confirmed," "a critical Bill to see through the House of Lords," and "some sixty sermons and addresses already arranged in the diocese, besides the daily letters and interviews." "All this," he says, "might justify the comment of a kindly man of the world, 'Why, Bishop, you live the life of a dog! But this is precisely, though on a larger scale, the life of every one of you.'" It is clear that the bishop considers that he and his clergy ought to be admired for so spending their time; and that he conceives the life of a turn-spit dog to be the most likely to enable them to be successful in the exercise of their office. One sometimes, however, wonders what would be the result if our bishop were kept for ten weeks in bed and in silence, by an illness neither painful nor dangerous, nor inconsistent with full mental efficiency.

Mental relaxation during the Incubation stage may of course include, and sometimes requires, a certain amount of physical exercise. I have already quoted Helmholtz's reference to "the ascent of wooded hills on a sunny day.' A. Carrel, the great New York physiologist, is said to receive all his eally important thoughts while quietly walking during the summer vacation in his native Brittany. Jastrow says that "thinkers have at all times resorted to the restful inspiration of a walk in the woods or a stroll over hill and dale." When I once discussed this fact with an athletic Cambridge friend, he expressed his gratitude for any evidence which would prove that it was the duty of all intellectual workers to spend their vacations in Alpine climbing. Alpine climbing has undoubtedly much to give both to health and to imagination, but it would be an interesting quantitative problem whether Goethe, while riding a mule over the Gemmi Pass, and Wordsworth, while walking over the Simplon, were in a more or in a less fruitful condition of Incubation than are a modern Alpine Club party ascending, with hands and feet and rope and ice-axe, the Finster-Aarhorn. In this, however, as in many other respects, it may be that the human organism gains more from the alternation of various forms of activity than from a consistent devotion to one form. In England, the administrative methods of the older universities during term-time may, I sometimes fear, by destroying the possibility of Incubation, go far to balance any intellectual advantages over the newer universities which they may derive from their much longer vacations. At Oxford and Cambridge, men on whose powers of invention and stimulus the intellectual future of the country may largely depend, are made personally responsible for innumerable worrying details of filling up forms and sending in applications. Their subconscious minds are set on the duty of striking like a clock at the instant when Mr. Jones's fee must be paid to the Registrar. In the newer English universities, the same duties are rapidly and efficiently performed by a corps of young ladies, with card-catalogues, typewriters, and diaries.

But perhaps the most dangerous substitute for bodily and mental relaxation during the stage of Incubation is neither violent exercise nor routine administration, but the habit of industrious passive reading. Schopenhauer wrote that "to put away one's own original thoughts in order to take up a book is the sin against the Holy Ghost." During the century from 1760 to 1860, many of the best brains in England were prevented from acting with full efficiency by the way in which the Greek and Latin classics were then read. It is true that Shelley's imagination was stung into activity by Plato and Æschylus, and that Keats won a new vision of life from Chapman's translation of Homer; but even the ablest of those who then accepted the educational ideals of Harrow and Eton and Oxford and Cambridge did not approach the classical writers with Shelley's or Keats's hunger in their souls. They plodded through Horace and Sophocles and Virgil and Demosthenes with a mild conscious aesthetic feeling, and with a stronger and less conscious feeling of social, intellectual and moral superiority; any one who was in the habit of reading the classics with his feet on the fender must certainly, they felt, be not only a gentleman and a scholar but also a good man.

Carlyle once told Anthony Trollope that a man, when travelling, "should not read, but sit still and label his thoughts." On the other hand, Macaulay, before he went out to India in 1834 to be Legislative Member of the Supreme Council, wrote to his sister: "The provision which I design for the voyage is Richardson, Voltaire's works, Gibbon, Sismondi's *History of the French,* Davila, *Orlando* in Italian, *Don Quixote* in Spanish, Homer in Greek, Horace in Latin. I must also have some books of jurisprudence, and some to initiate me in Persian and Hindustanee"; and, at the end of the four months' voyage, he wrote: "Except at meals, I hardly exchanged a word with any human being. . . . During the whole voyage I read with keen and increasing enjoyment. I devoured Greek, Latin, Spanish, Italian, French, and English; folios, quartos, octavos, and duodecimos." If he had followed Carlyle's advice, he would have had a better chance of thinking out a juristic and educational policy for India which would not have been a mere copy of an English model. One understands why Gladstone's magnificent enthusiasm and driving force was never guided by sufficient elasticity or originality of mind, when one reads, in Mrs. Gladstone's *Life* how she and her sister married the two most splendid Etonians of their time—Gladstone and his friend Lord Lyttelton—and spent a honeymoon of four in Scotland. "Any little waiting time as at the railway stations," says her daughter, Mrs. Drew, "was now spent in reading—both husbands carrying the inevitable little classics in their pockets." During the days when new knowledge, new forms of thought, new methods in industry and war and politics, and the rise of new nations were transforming Western civilization, "Lord Lyttelton was to be seen at cricket-matches in the playing field at Eton, lying on his front, reading between the overs, but never missing a ball."

So far I have inquired how far we can voluntarily improve our methods of thought at those stages—Preparation, Incubation (in its negative sense of abstention from voluntary thought on a particular problem), and Verification —over which our conscious will has comparatively full control. I shall now discuss the much more difficult question of the degree to which our will can influence the less controllable stage which I have called Illumination. Helmholtz and Poincaré, in the passages which I quoted above, both speak of the appearance of a new idea as instantaneous "flash," it is obvious that we cannot influence it by a direct effort of will; because we can only bring our will to bear upon psychological events which last for an appreciable time. On the other hand, the final "flash," or "click," is the culmination of a successful train of association, which may have lasted for an appreciable time, and which has probably been preceded by a series of tentative and unsuccessful trains. The series of unsuccessful trains of association may last for periods varying from a few seconds to several hours. H. Poincaré, who describes the tentative and unsuccessful trains as being, in his case, almost entirely unconscious, believed that they occupied a considerable proportion of the whole Incubation stage. "We might," he wrote, "say that the conscious work [i.e., what I have called the Preparation stage] proved more fruitful because it was interrupted [by the Incubation stage], and that the rest restored freshness to the mind. But it is more probable that the rest was occupied with unconscious work, and that the result of this work was afterwards revealed." [3]

Different thinkers, and the same thinkers at different times, must, of course, vary greatly as to the time occupied by their unsuccessful trains of association; and the same variation must exist in the duration of the final and successful train of association. Sometimes the successful train seems to consist of a single leap of association, or of successive leaps which are so rapid as to be almost instantaneous. Hobbes's "Roman penny" train of association occurred between two remarks in an ordinary conversation, and Hobbes, as I have said, ends his description of it with the words, "and all this in a moment of time, for thought is quick" (*Leviathan,* Chap. III). Hobbes himself was probably an exceptionally rapid thinker, and Aubrey may have been quoting Hobbes's own phrase when he says that Hobbes used to take out his note-book "as soon as a thought darted."

But if our will is to control a psychological process, it is necessary that that process should not only last for an appreciable time, but should also be, during that time, sufficiently conscious for the thinker to be at least aware that something is happening to him. On this point, the evidence seems to show that both the unsuccessful trains of association, which might have led to the "flash" of success, and the final and successful train are normally either unconscious, or take place (with "risings" and "fallings" of consciousness as success seems to approach or retire), in that periphery or "fringe" of consciousness which surrounds our "focal" consciousness as the sun's "corona" surrounds the disk of full luminosity. This "fringe-consciousness" may last up to the "flash" instant, may accompany it, and in some cases may continue beyond it. But, just as it is very difficult to see the sun's corona unless the disk is hidden by a total eclipse, so it is very difficult to observe our "fringe-consciousness" at the instant of full Illumination, or to remember the preceding "fringe" after full Illumination has taken place. As William James says, "When the conclusion is there, we have always forgotten most of the steps preceding its attainment" (*Principles,* Volume I, p. 260).

It is obvious that both Helmholtz and Poincaré had either not noticed, or had forgotten any "fringe-conscious" psychological events which may have preceded and have been connected with the "sudden" and "unexpected" appearance of their new ideas. But other thinkers have observed and afterwards remembered their "fringe-conscious" experiences both before and even at the moment of full Illumination. William James himself, in that beautiful and touching, though sometimes confused introspective account of his own think-

3. H. Poincaré, *Science and Method* (trans., pp. 54 and 55). On the other hand, one of the ablest of modern mathematical thinkers told me that he believed that his Incubation period was, as a rule, spent in a state of actual mental repose for all or part of his brain, which made the later explosion of intense and successful thought possible. His belief may have been partly due to the fact that his brain started fewer unsuccessful and more successful association-trains than the brains of other men.

ing which forms Chapter IX of his *Principles,* says: "Every definite image in the mind is steeped and dyed in the free water that flows round it. With it goes the sense of its relations, near and remote, the dying echo of whence it came to us, the dawning sense of whither it is to lead. The significance, the value, of the image is all in this halo or penumbra that surrounds and escorts it" (*Principles,* Vol. I, p. 255).

I find it convenient to use the term "Intimation" for that moment in the Illumination stage when our fringe-consciousness of an association-train is in the state of rising consciousness which indicates that the fully conscious flash of success is coming. A high English civil servant described his experience of Intimation to me by saying that when he is working at a difficult problem, "I often know that the solution is coming, though I don't know what the solution will be," and a very able university student gave me a description of the same fact in his case almost in the same words. Many thinkers, indeed, would recognize the experience which Varendonck describes when he says that on one occasion: "When I became aware that my mind was simmering over something, I had a dim feeling which is very difficult to describe; it was like a vague impression of mental activity. But when the association had risen to the surface, it expanded into an impression of joy." His phrase "expanded into an impression of joy," clearly describes the rising of consciousness as the "flash" approaches.

Most introspective observers speak, as I have done, of Intimation as a "feeling," and the ambiguity of that word creates its usual crop of difficulties. It is often hard to discover in descriptions of Intimation whether the observer is describing a bare awareness of mental activity with no emotional colouring, or an awareness of mental activity coloured by an emotion which may either have originally helped to stimulate the train of thought, or may have been stimulated by the train of thought during its course. Mr. F. M. McMurry seems to refer to little more than awareness when he says, in his useful text-book, *How to Study,* "Many of the best thoughts, probably most of them, do not come, like a flash, fully into being but find their beginnings in dim feelings, faint intuitions that need to be encouraged and coaxed before they can be surely felt and defined." Dewey, on the other hand, is obviously describing awareness coloured by emotion when he says that a problem may present itself "as a more or less vague feeling of the unexpected, of something queer, strange, funny, or disconcerting." Wundt was more ambiguous when he said (in perhaps the earliest description of Intimation) that feeling is the pioneer of knowledge, and that a novel thought may come to consciousness first of all in the form of a feeling. My own students have described the Intimation preceding a new thought as being sometimes coloured by a slight feeling of discomfort arising from a sense of separation from one's accustomed self. A student, for instance, told me that his first recognition that he was reaching a new political outlook came from a feeling, when, in answer to a question, he was stating his habitual political opinions, that he "was listening to himself." I can just remember that a good many years ago, in a period preceding an important change of my own political position, I had a vague, almost physical, recurrent feeling as if my clothes did not quite fit me. If this feeling of Intimation lasts for an appreciable time, and is either sufficiently conscious, or can by an effort of attention be made sufficiently conscious, it is obvious that our will can be brought directly to bear on it. We can at least attempt to inhibit, or prolong, or divert, the brain-activity which Intimation shows to be going on. And, if Intimation accompanies a rising train of association which the brain accepts, so to speak, as plausible, but would not, without the effort of attention, automatically push to the "flash" of conscious success, we can attempt to hold on to such a train on the chance that it may succeed.

It is a more difficult and more important question whether such an exercise of will is likely to improve our thinking. Many people would argue that any attempt to control the thought-process at this point will always do more harm than good. A schoolboy sitting down to do an algebra sum, a civil servant composing a minute, Shakespeare re-writing a speech in an old play, will, they would say, gain no more by interfering with the ideas whose coming is vaguely indicated to them, before they come, than would a child by digging up a sprouting bean, or a hungry man in front of a good meal, by bringing his will to bear on the intimations of activity in his stomach or his salivary glands. A born runner, they would say, achieves a much more successful co-ordination of those physiological and psychological factors in his organism which are concerned in running, by concentrating his will on his purpose of catching the man in front of him, than by troubling about the factors themselves. And a born orator will use better gestures if, as he speaks, he is conscious of his audience than if he is conscious of his hands. This objection might be fatal to the whole conception of an art of thought if it did not neglect two facts, first that we are not all "born" runners or orators or thinkers, and that a good deal of the necessary work of the world has to be done by men who in such respects have to achieve skill instead of receiving it at birth; and, secondly, that the process of learning an art should, even in the case of those who have the finest natural endowment for it, be more conscious than its practice. Mr. Harry Vardon, when he is acquiring a new grip, is wise to make himself more conscious of the relation between his will and his wrists than when he is addressing himself to his approach-shot at the decisive hole of a championship. The violinist with the most magnificent natural temperament has to think of his fingers when he is acquiring a new way of bowing; though on the concert-platform that acquirement may sink beneath the level of full consciousness. And, since the use of our upper brain for the discovery of new truth depends on more recent and less perfect evolutionary factors than does the use of our wrists for hitting small objects with a stick, or for causing catgut to vibrate in emotional patterns, conscious art may prove to be even more important, as compared to spontaneous gift, in thought than in golf or violin-playing. Here, again, individual thinkers, and the same thinker at different times and when engaged on different tasks, must differ greatly. But my general conclusion is that there are few or none among those whose work in life is thought who will not gain by directing their attention from time to time to the feeling of Intimation, and by bringing their will to bear upon the cerebral processes which it indicates.

On this point the most valuable evidence that I know of is that given by the poets. Poets have, more constantly than other intellectual workers, to "make use" (as Varendonck says) "of foreconscious processes for conscious ends." The production of a poem is a psychological experiment, tried and tested under severer conditions than those of a laboratory, and the poet is generally able to describe his "fringe-consciousness" during the experiment with a more accurate and sensitive use of language than is at the command of most laboratory psychologists. Several of the younger living English poets have given admirable descriptions of Intimation, often using metaphors derived from our experience in daily life of a feeling that there is something which we have mislaid, and which we cannot find because we have forgotten what it is. Mr. John Drinkwater, for instance says:

> Haunting the lucidities of life
> That are my daily beauty, moves a theme
> Beating along my undiscovered mind.

And Mr. James Stephens says:

> I would think until I found
> Something I can never find,
> Something lying on the ground
> In the bottom of my mind.

Mr. J. Middleton Murry, in his *Problem of Style* (1922, p. 93), points out the psychological truth of Shakespeare's well-known description of the poet's work:

> . . . as imagination bodies forth
> The forms of things unknown, the poet's pen
> Turns them to shapes and gives to airy nothings
> A local habitation and a name.

"Forms of things unknown" and "airy nothings" are vivid descriptions of the first appearance of Intimation; and "local habitation and a name" indicates the increasing verbal clearness of thought as Intimation approaches the final moment of Illumination; and may also indicate that Shakespeare was a much more conscious artist than many of his admirers believe.

Some English poets and students of poetry have given descriptions not only of the feeling of Intimation, but also of the effort of will by which a poet may attempt to influence the mental events indicated by Intimation, and the dangers to the thought itself involved in such an effort. In these descriptions they often use metaphors drawn from a boy's attempts to catch in his hand an elusive fish, or a bird which will dart off if the effort is made a fraction of a second too soon or too late. . . .

In this respect, the most obvious danger against which the thinker has to guard is that the association-train which the feeling of Intimation shows to be going on may either drift away of itself, as most of our dreams and day-dreams do, into mere irrelevance and forgetfulness, or may be interrupted by the intrusion of other trains of association. All thinkers know the effect of the ringing of the telephone bell, or the entrance of some one with a practical question which must be answered, during a promising Intimation. Aristophanes, when in the Clouds he makes Socrates complain that his disciple by asking him a question had caused a valuable thought to "miscarry," was probably quoting some saying of Socrates himself, whose mother was a midwife, and who was fond of that metaphor. If, therefore, the feeling of Intimation presents itself while one is reading, it is best to look up from one's book and so avoid the danger that the next printed sentence may "start a new hare." Varendonck describes how, in one of his day-dreams, "The idea that manifested itself ran thus: '*There is something going on in my foreconsciousness which must be in direct relation to my subject. I ought to stop reading for a little while, and let it come to the surface.*'" And, besides such negative precautions against the interruption of an association-train, it is often necessary to make a conscious positive effort of attention to secure success. Vincent d'Indy, speaking of musical creation, said that he "often has on waking, a fugitive glimpse of a musical effect which—like the memory of a dream—needs a strong immediate concentration of mind to keep it from vanishing." But even the effort of attention to a train of association may have the effect of interrupting or hindering it. Schiller is reported by Vischer to have said that when he was fully conscious of creation his imagination did not function "with the same freedom as it had done when nobody was looking over my shoulder."

To a modern thinker, however, the main danger of spoiling a train of association occurs in the process of attempting—perhaps before the train is complete—to put its conclusion into the words. Mr. Henry Hazlitt, in his *Thinking as a Science* (1916), p. 82, says, "Thoughts of certain kinds are so elusive that to attempt to articulate them is to scare them away, as a fish is scared by the slightest ripple. When these thoughts are in embryo, even the infinitesimal attention required for talking cannot be spared"; and a writer on Montaigne in *The Times Literary Supplement* for January 31, 1924, says, "We all indulge in the strange pleasant process called thinking, but when it comes to saying, even to some one opposite, what we think, then how little we are able to convey! The phantom is through the mind and out of the window before we can lay salt on its tail, or slowly sinking and returning to the profound darkness which it has lit up momentarily with a wandering light." In the case of a poet, this danger is increased by the fact that for the poet the finding of expressive words is an integral part of the more or less automatic thought-process indicated by Intimation. The little girl had the making of a poet in her who, being told to be sure of her meaning before she spoke, said, "How can I know what I think till I see what I say?" A modern professed thinker must, however, sooner or later in the process of thought, make the conscious effort of expression, with all its risks. A distant ancestor of ours, some Aurignacian Shelley, living in the warm spell between two ice ages, may have been content to lie on the hillside, and allow the songs of the birds and the loveliness of the clouds to mingle with his wonder as to the nature of the universe in a delightful uninterrupted stream of rising and falling reverie, enjoyed and forgotten as it passed. But the modern thinker has generally accepted, willingly or unwillingly, the task of making permanent his thought for the use of others, as the only justification of his position in a society few of whose members have time or opportunity for anything but a life of manual labour.

The interference of our will should, finally, vary—with the variations of the subject-matter of our thought—not only in respect of the point in time at which it should take place, but also in respect to the element in a complex thought-process with which we should interfere. A novelist who had just finished a long novel, and who must constantly have employed his conscious will while writing it, to make sure of a good idea or phrase, or to improve a sentence, or rearrange an incident, told me that he had spoilt his book by interfering with the automatic development of his main story and of its chief characters, in order to follow out a preconceived plot. Dramatists and poets constantly speak of the need of allowing their characters to "speak for themselves"; and a creative artist often reaches maturity only when he has learned so to use his conscious craftsmanship in the expression of his thought as not to silence the promptings of that imperfectly co-ordinated whole which is called his personality. It is indeed at the stage of Illumination with its fringe of Intimation that the thinker should most constantly realize that the rules of his art will be of little effect unless they are applied with artistic delicacy of apprehension.

CONTEXTS[1]

S. I. HAYAKAWA

Dictionary definitions frequently offer verbal substitutes for an unknown term which only conceal a lack of real understanding. Thus a person might look up a foreign word and be quite satisfied with the meaning "bullfinch" without the slightest ability to identify or describe this bird. Understanding does not come through dealings with words alone, but rather with the things for which they stand. Dictionary definitions permit us to hide from ourselves and others the extent of our ignorance.—H. R. HUSE

1. From *Language in Action* by S. I. Hayakawa, copyright, 1941, by Harcourt, Brace and Company, Inc.

HOW DICTIONARIES ARE MADE

It is an almost universal belief that every word has a "correct meaning," that we learn these meanings principally from teachers and grammarians (except that most of the time we don't bother to, so that we ordinarily speak "sloppy English"), and that dictionaries and grammars are the "supreme authority" in matters of meaning and usage. Few people ask by what authority the writers of dictionaries and grammars say what they say. The docility with which most people bow down to the dictionary is amazing, and the person who says, "Well, the dictionary is wrong!" is looked upon with smiles of pity and amusement which say plainly, "Poor fellow! He's really quite sane otherwise."

Let us see how dictionaries are made and how the editors arrive at definitions. What follows applies, incidentally, only to those dictionary offices where first-hand, original research goes on—not those in which editors simply copy existing dictionaries. The task of writing a dictionary begins with the reading of vast amounts of the literature of the period or subject that it is intended to cover. As the editors read, they copy on cards every interesting or rare word, every unusual or peculiar occurrence of a common word, a large number of common words in their ordinary uses, *and also the sentences in which each of these words appears,* thus:

> pail
>
> The dairy *pails* bring home increase of milk
>
> Keats, *Endymion*
> I, 44-45

That is to say, the *context* of each word is collected, along with the word itself. For a really big job of dictionary writing, such as the *Oxford English Dictionary* (usually bound in about twenty-five volumes), millions of such cards are collected, and the task of editing occupies decades. As the cards are collected, they are alphabetized and sorted. When the sorting is completed, there will be for each word anywhere from two or three to several hundred illustrative quotations, each on its card.

To define a word, then, the dictionary editor places before him the stack of cards illustrating that word; each of the cards represents an actual use of the word by a writer of some literary or historical importance. He reads the cards carefully, discards some, re-reads the rest, and divides up the stack according to what he thinks are the several senses of the word. Finally, he writes his definitions, following the hard-and-fast rule that each definition *must* be based on what the quotations in front of him reveal about the meaning of the word. The editor cannot be influenced by what *he* thinks a given word *ought* to mean. He must work according to the cards, or not at all.

The writing of a dictionary, therefore, is not a task of setting up authoritative statements about the "true meanings" of words, but a task of *recording*, to the best of one's ability, what various words *have meant* to authors in the distant or immediate past. *The writer of a dictionary is a historian, not a lawgiver.* If, for example, we had been writing a dictionary in 1890, or even as late as 1919, we could have said that the word "broadcast" means "to scatter," seed and so on; but we could not have decreed that from 1921 on, the commonest meaning of the word should become "to disseminate audible messages, etc., by wireless telephony." To regard the dictionary as an "authority," therefore, is to credit the dictionary writer with gifts of prophecy which neither he nor anyone else possesses. In choosing our words when we speak or write, we can be *guided* by the historical record afforded us by the dictionary, but we cannot be *bound* by it, because new situations, new experiences, new inventions, new feelings, are always compelling us to give new uses to old words. Looking under a "hood," we should ordinarily have found, five hundred years ago, a monk; today, we find a motorcar engine.

VERBAL AND PHYSICAL CONTEXTS

The way in which the dictionary writer arrives at his definitions is merely the systematization of the way in which we all learn the meanings of words, beginning at infancy, and continuing for the rest of our lives. Let us say that we have never heard the word "oboe" before, and we overhear a conversation in which the following sentences occur:

> He used to be the best *oboe* player in town. . . . Whenever they came to that *oboe* part in the third movement, he used to get very excited. . . . I saw him one day at the music shop, buying a new reed for his *oboe*. . . . He never liked to play the clarinet after he started playing the *oboe*. He said it wasn't so much fun, because it was too easy.

Although the word may be unfamiliar, its meaning becomes clear to us as we listen. After hearing the first sentence, we know that an "oboe" is "played," so that it must be either a game or a musical instrument. With the second sentence the possibility of its being a game is eliminated. With each succeeding sentence the possibilities as to what an "oboe" may be are narrowed down until we get a fairly clear idea of what is meant. This is how we learn by *verbal context*.

But even independently of this, we learn by *physical and social context*. Let us say that we are playing golf and that we have hit the ball in a certain way with certain unfortunate results, so that our companion says to us, "That's a bad *slice*." He repeats this remark every time our ball fails to go straight. If we are reasonably bright, we learn in a very short time to say, when it happens again, "That's a bad slice." On one occasion, however, our friend says to us, "That's not a *slice* this time; that's a *hook*." In this case we consider what has happened, and we wonder what is different about the last stroke from those previous. As soon as we make the distinction, we have added still another word to our vocabulary. The result is that after nine holes of golf, we can use both these words accurately—and perhaps several others as well, such as "divot," "number-five iron," "approach shot," *without ever having been told what they mean.* Indeed, we may play golf for years without ever being able to give a dictionary definition of "to slice": "To strike (the ball) so that the face of the club draws inward across the face of the ball, causing it to curve toward the right in flight (with a right-handed player)" (*Webster's New International Dictionary*). But even without being able to give such a definition, we should still be able to use the word accurately whenever the occasion demanded.

We learn the meanings of practically all our words (which are, it will be remembered, merely complicated noises), not from dictionaries, not from definitions, but from hearing these noises as they accompany actual situations in life and learning to associate certain noises with certain situations. Even as dogs learn to recognize "words," as for example by hearing "biscuit" at the same time as an actual biscuit is held before their noses, so do we all learn to interpret language by being aware of the happenings that accompany the noises people make at us—by being aware, in short, of contexts.

The "definitions" given by little children in school show clearly how they associate words with situations; they almost always define in terms of physical and social contexts: "Punishment is when you have been bad and they put you in a closet and don't let you have any supper." "Newspapers are what the paper boy brings and you wrap up the garbage with it." These are good definitions. The main reason that they cannot be used in dictionaries is that they are *too* specific; it would be impossible to list the myriads of situations

in which every word has been used. For this reason, dictionaries give definitions on a high level of abstraction; that is, with particular references left out for the sake of conciseness. This is another reason why it is a great mistake to regard a dictionary definition as "telling us all about" a word.

EXTENSIONAL AND INTENSIONAL MEANING

From this point on, it will be necessary to employ some special terms in talking about meaning: *extensional meaning,* which will also be referred to as *denotation,* and *intensional meaning*—note the *s*—which will also be referred to as *connotation.*[2] Briefly explained, the extensional meaning of an

2. The words *extension* and *intension* are borrowed from logic; *denotation* and *connotation* are borrowed from literary criticism. The former pair of terms will ordinarily be used, therefore, when we are talking about people's "thinking habits"; the latter, when we are talking about words themselves.

utterance is that which it *points to* or denotes in the extensional world. . . . That is to say, the extensional meaning is something that *cannot be expressed in words,* because it is that which words stand for. An easy way to remember this is to put your hand over your mouth and point whenever you are asked to give an extensional meaning.

The *intensional meaning* of a word or expression, on the other hand, is that which is *suggested* (connoted) inside one's head. Roughly speaking, whenever we express the meaning of words by uttering more words, we are giving intensional meaning, or connotations. To remember this, put your hand over your eyes and let the words spin around in your head.

Utterances may have, of course, both extensional and intensional meaning. If they have no intensional meaning at all—that is, if they start no notions whatever spinning about in our heads—they are meaningless noises, like foreign languages that we do not understand. On the other hand, it is possible for utterances to have no extensional meaning at all, in spite of the fact that they may start many notions spinning about in our heads. Since this point will be discussed more fully . . ., perhaps one example will be enough: the statement, "Angels watch over my bed at night," is one that has intensional but no extensional meaning. This does not mean that there are no angels watching over my bed at night. When we say that the statement has no extensional meaning, we are merely saying that we cannot see, touch, photograph, or in any scientific manner detect the presence of angels. The result is that, if an argument begins on the subject whether or not angels watch over my bed, *there is no way of ending the argument to the satisfaction of all disputants,* the Christians and the non-Christians, the pious and the agnostic, the mystical and the scientific. Therefore, whether we believe in angels or not, knowing in advance that any argument on the subject will be both endless and futile, we can avoid getting into fights about it.

When, on the other hand, statements have extensional content, as when we say, "This room is fifteen feet long," arguments can come to a close. No matter how many guesses there are about the length of the room, all discussion ceases when someone produces a tape measure. This, then, is the important difference between extensional and intensional meanings: namely, when utterances have extensional meanings, discussion can be ended and agreement reached; when utterances have intensional meanings only and no extensional meanings, arguments may, and often do, go on indefinitely. Such arguments can result only in irreconcilable conflict. Among individuals, they may result in the breaking up of friendships; in society, they often split organizations into bitterly opposed groups; among nations, they may aggravate existing tensions so seriously as to become contributory causes of war.

Arguments of this kind may be termed "non-sense arguments," because they are based on utterances about which no sense data can be collected. Needless to say, there are occasions when the hyphen may be omitted—that depends on one's feelings toward the particular argument under consideration. The reader is requested to provide his own examples of "non-sense arguments." Even the foregoing example of thc angels may give offense to some people, in spite of the fact that no attempt is made to deny or affirm the existence of angels. He can imagine, therefore, the uproar that might result from giving a number of examples, from theology, politics, law, economics, literary criticism, and other fields in which it is not customary to distinguish clearly sense from non-sense.

THE "ONE WORD, ONE MEANING" FALLACY

Everyone, of course, who has ever given any thought to the meanings of words has noticed that they are always shifting and changing in meaning. Usually, people regard this as a misfortune, because it "leads to sloppy thinking" and "mental confusion." To remedy this condition, they are likely to suggest that we should all agree on "one meaning" for each word and use it only with that meaning. Thereupon it will occur to them that we simply cannot make people agree in this way, even if we could set up an ironclad dictatorship under a committee of lexicographers who could place censors in every newspaper office and dictaphones in every home. The situation, therefore, appears hopeless.

Such an impasse is avoided when we start with a new premise altogether—one of the premises upon which modern linguistic thought is based: namely, *that no word ever has exactly the same meaning twice.* The extent to which this premise fits the facts can be demonstrated in a number of ways. First, if we accept the proposition that the contexts of an utterance determine its meaning, it becomes apparent that since no two contexts are ever *exactly* the same, no two meanings can ever be exactly the same. How can we "fix the meaning" even for as common an expression as "to believe in" when it can be used in such sentences as the following?

I *believe in* you (I have confidence in you).
I *believe in* democracy (I accept the principles implied by the term democracy).
I *believe in* Santa Claus (It is my opinion that Santa Claus exists).

Secondly, we can take for example a word of "simple" meaning like "kettle." But when John says "kettle," its intensional meanings to him are the common characteristics of all the kettles John remembers. When Peter says "kettle," however, its intensional meanings to him are the common characteristics of all the kettles he remembers. *No matter how small or how negligible the differences may be between John's "kettle" and Peter's "kettle," there is some difference.*

Finally, let us examine utterances in terms of extensional meanings. If John, Peter, Harold, and George each say "my typewriter," we would have to point to *four different typewriters* to get the extensional meaning in each case: John's new Underwood, Peter's old Corona, Harold's L. C. Smith, and the undenotable intended "typewriter" that George plans some day to buy:

"My typewriter, when I buy one, will be a noiseless." Also, if John says "my typewriter" today, and again "my typewriter" tomorrow, the extensional meaning is different in the two cases, because the typewriter is not *exactly* the same from one day to the next (nor from one minute to the next): slow processes of wear, change, and decay are going on constantly. Although we can say, then, that the differences in the meanings of a word on one occasion, on another occasion a minute later, and on still another occasion another minute later, are *negligible,* we cannot say that the meanings are *exactly* the same.

To say dogmatically that we "know what a word means" *in advance of its utterance* is nonsense. All we can know in advance is *approximately* what it *will* mean. After the utterance, we interpret what has been said in the light of both verbal and physical contexts, and act according to our interpretation. An examination of the verbal context of an utterance, as well as the examination of the utterance itself, directs us to the intensional meanings; an examination of the physical context directs us to the extensional meanings. When John says to James, "Bring me that book, will you?" James looks in the direction of John's pointed finger (physical context) and sees a desk with several books on it (physical context); he thinks back over their previous conversation (verbal context) and knows which of those books is being referred to.

Interpretation *must* be based, therefore, on the totality of contexts. If it were otherwise, we should not be able to account for the fact that even if we fail to use the right (customary) words in some situations, people can very frequently understand us. For example:

A. Gosh, look at that second baseman go!
B (looking). You mean the shortstop?
A. Yes, that's what I mean.
A. There must be something wrong with the oil line; the engine has started to balk.
B. Don't you mean "gas line"?
A. Yes—didn't I say gas line?

Contexts sometimes indicate so clearly what we mean that often we do not even have to say what we mean in order to be understood.

THE IGNORING OF CONTEXTS

It is clear, then, that the ignoring of contexts in any act of interpretation is at best a stupid practice. At its worst, it can be a vicious practice. A common example is the sensational newspaper story in which a few words by a public personage are torn out of their context and made the basis of a completely misleading account. There is the incident of an Armistice Day speaker, a university teacher, who declared before a high-school assembly that the Gettysburg Address was "a powerful piece of propaganda." The context clearly revealed that "propaganda" was being used according to its dictionary meanings rather than according to its popular meanings; it also revealed that the speaker was a very great admirer of Lincoln's. However, the local newspaper, completely ignoring the context, presented the account in such a way as to convey the impression that the speaker had called Lincoln a liar. On this basis, the newspaper began a campaign against the instructor. The speaker remonstrated with the editor of the newspaper, who replied, in effect, "*I don't care what else you said.* You said the Gettysburg Address was propaganda, didn't you?" This appeared to the editor complete proof that Lincoln had been maligned and that the speaker deserved to be discharged from his position at the university. Similar practices may be found in advertisements. A reviewer may be quoted on the jacket of a book as having said, "A brilliant work," while reading of the context may reveal that what he really said was, "It just falls short of being a brilliant work." There are some people who will always be able to find a defense for such a practice in saying, "But he did use the words, 'a brilliant work,' didn't he?"

People in the course of argument very frequently complain about words meaning different things to different people. Instead of complaining, they should accept it as a matter of course. It would be startling indeed if the word "justice," for example, were to have the same meaning to the nine justices of the United States Supreme Court; we should get nothing but unanimous decisions. It would be even more startling if "justice" meant the same to Fiorello La Guardia as to Josef Stalin. If we can get deeply into our consciousness the principle that no word ever has the same meaning twice, we will develop the habit of automatically examining contexts, and this enables us to understand better what others are saying. As it is, however, we are all too likely to have signal reactions to certain words and read into people's remarks meanings that were never intended. Then we waste energy in angrily accusing people of "intellectual dishonesty" or "abuse of words," when their only sin is that they use words in ways unlike our own, as they can hardly help doing, especially if their background has been widely different from ours. There are cases of intellectual dishonesty and of the abuse of words, of course, but they do not always occur in the places where people think they do.

In the study of history or of cultures other than our own, contexts take on special importance. To say, "There was no running water or electricity in the house," does not condemn an English house in 1570, but says a great deal against a house in Chicago in 1941. Again, if we wish to understand the Constitution of the United States, it is not enough, as our historians now tell us, merely to look up all the words in the dictionary and to read the interpretations written by Supreme Court justices. We must see the Constitution in its *historical context:* the conditions of life, the current ideas, the fashionable prejudices, and the probable interests of the people who drafted the Constitution. After all, the words "The United States of America" stood for quite a different-sized nation and a different culture in 1790 from what they stand for today. When it comes to very big subjects, the range of contexts to be examined, verbal, social, and historical, may become very large indeed.

THE INTERACTION OF WORDS

All this is not to say, however, that the reader might just as well throw away his dictionary, since contexts are so important. Any word in a sentence—any sentence in a paragraph, any paragraph in a larger unit—whose meaning is revealed by its context, *is itself part of the context of the rest of the text.* To look up a word in a dictionary, therefore, frequently explains not only that word itself, but the rest of the sentence, paragraph, conversation, or essay in which it is found. *All words within a given context interact upon one another.*

Realizing, then, that a dictionary is a historical work, we should understand the dictionary thus: "The word *mother* has most frequently been used in the past among English-speaking people to indicate *a female parent.*" From this we can safely infer, "If that is how it has been used, that is what it probably means in the sentence I am trying to understand." This is what we normally do, of course; after we look up a word in the dictionary, *we re-examine the context to see if the definition fits.*

A dictionary definition, therefore, is an invaluable guide to interpretation. Words do not have a single "correct meaning"; they apply to *groups* of similar situations, which might be called *areas of meaning.* It is for definition in terms of areas of meaning that a dictionary is useful. In each use of any word, we examine the particular context and the extensional events denoted (if possible) to discover the *point* intended within the area of meaning.

EMOTIONAL MEANINGS [1]

ROBERT H. THOULESS

When we use a word in speech and writing, its most obvious purpose is to point to some thing or relation or property. This is the word's "meaning." We see a small four-footed animal on the road and call it a "dog," indicating that it is a member of the class of four-footed animals we call dogs. The word "dog" as we have used it there has a plain, straightforward, "objective" meaning. We have in no way gone beyond the requirements of exact scientific description.

Let us suppose also that one grandparent of the dog was a collie, another was an Irish terrier, another a fox terrier, and the fourth a bulldog. We can express these facts equally scientifically and objectively by saying that he is a dog of mixed breed. Still we have in no way gone beyond the requirements of exact scientific description.

Suppose, however, that we had called that same animal a "mongrel." The

1. From *How to Think Straight.* Copyright, 1939, by Simon and Schuster, Inc. Reprinted by permission of Simon and Schuster, Inc.

matter is more complicated. We have used a word which objectively means the same as "dog of mixed breed," but which also arouses in our hearers an emotional attitude of disapproval toward the particular dog. A word, therefore, can not only indicate an object, but can also suggest an emotional attitude toward it. Such suggestion of an emotional attitude does go beyond exact and scientific discussion because our approvals and disapprovals are individual—they belong to ourselves and not to the objects we approve or disapprove of. An animal which to the mind of its master is a faithful and noble dog of mixed ancestry may be a "mongrel" to his neighbor, whose chickens are chased by it.

Similarly, a Negro may be indicated objectively as a "colored man" or he may be indicated with strong emotional disapproval and contempt as a "nigger." The use of the latter word debases any discussion in which it is used below the level of impartial and objective argument.

Once we are on the lookout for this difference between "objective" and "emotional" meanings, we shall notice that words which carry more or less strong suggestions of emotional attitudes are very common and are ordinarily used in the discussion of such controversial questions as those of politics, morals, and religion. This is one reason why such controversies cannot yet be settled.

There is a well-known saying that the word "firm" can be declined as follows: I am *firm,* thou art *obstinate,* he is *pigheaded.* That is a simple illustration of what is meant. "Firm," "obstinate," and "pigheaded" all have the same objective meaning—that is, following one's own course of action and refusing to be influenced by other people's opinions. They have, however, different emotional meanings: "firm" has an emotional meaning of strong approval, "obstinate" of mild disapproval, "pigheaded" of strong disapproval. . . .

Such thinking in wartime may do much harm by leading humane people to condone cruelty. When the ordinarily liberal-minded Swinburne wrote a poem during the Boer War on the death of a British officer who had been blamed for the bad condition of the camps in which the Boer women and children were interned, he said:

> Nor heed we more than he what liars dare say
> Of mercy's holiest duties left undone
> Toward *whelps* and *dams* of *murderous* foes, whom none
> Save we had spared or feared to starve and slay.

Whelps and *dams* clearly mean in objective fact *children* and *wives,* with the added meaning of the emotional attitude adopted toward the females and young of wild beasts, while *murderous* means no more in objective fact than that our foes killed us when they could (as we also killed them), with the added emotional meaning of an attitude toward them which is our attitude to those who are guilty of murder.

The use of emotionally toned words is not, of course, always to be condemned. They are always harmful when we are trying to think clearly on a disputable point of fact. In poetry, on the other hand, they have a perfectly proper place, because in poetry (as in some kinds of prose) the arousing of suitable emotions is an important part of the purpose for which the words are used.

In "The Eve of St. Agnes," Keats has written:

> Full on this casement shone the wintry moon,
> And threw warm gules on Madeline's fair breast.

These are beautiful lines. Let us notice how much of their beauty follows from the proper choice of emotionally colored words and how completely it is lost if these words are replaced by neutral ones. The words with strikingly emotional meanings are *casement, gules, Madeline, fair,* and *breast. Casement* means simply a kind of window with emotional and romantic associations. *Gules* is the heraldic name for red, with the suggestion of romance which accompanies all heraldry. *Madeline* is simply a girl's name, but one calling out favorable emotions absent from a relatively plain and straightforward name. *Fair* simply means, in objective fact, that her skin was white or uncolored—a necessary condition for the colors of the window to show—but also *fair* implies warm emotional preference for an uncolored skin rather than one which is yellow, purple, black, or any of the other colors which skin might be. *Breast* has also similar emotional meanings, and the aim of scientific description might have been equally well attained if it had been replaced by such a neutral word as *chest.*

Let us now try the experiment of keeping these two lines in a metrical form, but replacing all the emotionally colored words by neutral ones, while making as few other changes as possible. We may write:

> *Full on this window shone the wintry moon,*
> *Making red marks on Jane's uncolored chest.*

No one will doubt that all of its poetic value has been knocked out of the passage by these changes. Yet the lines still mean the same in external fact; they still have the same objective meaning. It is only the emotional meaning which has been destroyed.

Now if Keats had been writing a scientific description for a textbook on physics instead of a poem, it would have been necessary for him to have used some such coldly objective terms as the ones into which we have just translated his lines. Such emotionally charged phrases as *warm gules* and *fair breast* would only have obscured the facts to which the scientist exactly but unbeautifully refers when he speaks of "the selective transmission of homogeneous light by pigmented glass."

The purpose of the present essay is to deal with the kind of problem in which cold and scientific thinking is required. Most of the practical problems of life are of this order. The fact that I shall abuse the use of emotional thinking in connection with such problems as tariffs, social ownership, revolution, and war does not mean that there is no place for emotional thinking. Poetry, romantic prose, and emotional oratory are all of inestimable value, but their place is not where responsible decisions must be made. The common (almost universal) use of emotional words in political thinking is as much out of place as would be a chemical or statistical formula in the middle of a poem. Real democracy will come only when the solution of national and international problems is carried out by scientific methods of thought, purged of all irrelevant emotion. Into the action which follows decision we can put all the emotion which we have refused to allow in our thinking. Let us think calmly and scientifically about war, and then actively oppose it with all the passion of which we are capable.

The growth of the exact thinking of modern science has been largely the result of its getting rid of all terms suggesting emotional attitudes and using only those which unemotionally indicate objective facts. It was not always so. The old alchemists called gold and silver "noble" metals, and thought that this emotionally colored word indicated something belonging to the metals themselves from which their properties could be deduced. Other metals were called "base." Although these terms have survived as convenient labels for the modern chemist, they carry none of their old emotional significance.

In popular biological discussions, on the other hand, such words are still used with their full emotional meaning, as when the "nobility" of man is contrasted with his alleged "base" origin. In this respect, popular biological discussion differs from that of the textbook and the laboratory, in which are used terms almost as devoid of emotional meaning as those of physics or chemistry.

Psychology is still younger in the ranks of the sciences, and the clearing away from it of emotional words has not gone very far. "Passion," "emotion," "sex" are all terms of our science which carry strong emotional meanings, so that it is difficult to discuss a controversial matter in psychology without using words which rouse strong emotions and confuse all issues. A beginning is being made. "Intelligence" was a subject on which it was difficult to think clearly because it carried so much emotional meaning. Now Professor Spearman has replaced it by what he calls "g" (or the "general factor"), which is a conception derived from the statistical analysis of a large collection of figures, and yet which is in its essence all that was really scientific in the old conception of intelligence. Some day a psychological genius will give us X or Z to replace the old emotional conception of sex, and we shall be able to discuss psychoanalysis as objectively as a mathematical physicist can discuss the quantum theory.

When we turn to politics and international questions, we are still further from straight scientific thinking. Such words as "Bolshevik," "Fascist," "reactionary," "revolutionary," "constitutional," "national honor," etc., are all words used in national and international political thinking which carry more of emotional than of any other meaning. So long as such words are the ordinary terms of rival politicians, how can we hope to think straight in national and international affairs? If a chemist doing an experiment depended on such thought processes as a nation uses in selecting its rulers or in deciding on peace or war with other nations, he would blow up his laboratory. This, however, would be a trivial disaster in comparison with what may result from emotional thinking in politics. Better have a hundred chemical laboratories blown up than the whole of civilization!

We must look forward to and try to help on the day when the thinking about political and international affairs will be as unemotional and as scientific as that about the properties of numbers or the atomic weights of elements. The spirit of impartial investigation of facts unswayed by irrelevant emotions has given us great advances in the sciences. Its triumphs will be even greater when it is applied to the most important affairs of life. We look forward to the day when we shall be able to discuss and settle such questions as Tariffs, Public *vs.* Private Ownership, and Disarmament Treaties as successfully as physicists have discussed and settled Einstein's theory of relativity.

Let us try to study a few more examples of the use of words with emotional meanings taken from various sources. Accounts of wars are rich sources of such material, so we are not surprised to find in a book on the French Commune the statement that large numbers of the regular troops were *assassinated* during the street fighting by the Communards, while a much larger number of the latter were *summarily executed* by the regulars. In order to reduce this to a statement of objective fact it is clear that the one word "killed" should be used in place both of *assassinated* and *summarily executed.* We have already noticed how such a choice of words with the same objective but opposite emotional meaning can be used to make us feel sympathetic to one and hostile to the other of two sides in warfare. During the Spanish Civil War, the supporters of the Government referred to themselves as the "Loyalists" and called Franco a "Rebel" or an "Insurgent." The supporters of Franco, on the other hand, called themselves "Nationalists" and referred to their opponents as "Reds." During the conflicts between Red and White forces in Russia and in China, our newspapers told us of the *atrocities* of the Bolsheviks and the *wise severity* of the White commanders. Examination of the details (often possible only long afterwards) shows that the objective facts of an *atrocity* and of *wise severity* are much the same, and that they are not the kind of objective facts which will call out an emotion of approval in a humane person.

A similar choice of words will be noticed in political discussion. A fluent and forcible speech delivered by one of our own party is *eloquent,* a similar speech by one of the opposite party is *fanatical;* again two words with the same objective meaning but with the opposite emotional meanings of approval and strong disapproval. The practical proposals of the opposition, moreover, are *panaceas*—a highly emotional word calling out the strongly disapproving emotions which we feel for those quack patent medicines which make extravagant claims. Those who show enthusiasm in support of proposals with which a speaker disagrees are *crackpots;* while those showing similar enthusiasm on his own side are called *sound.* If a politician wishes to attack some new proposal he has a battery of these and other words with emotional meanings at his disposal. He speaks of "this suggested *panacea* supported only by *fanatical crackpots";* and the proposal is at once discredited in the minds of the majority of people, who like to think of themselves as moderate, distrustful of panaceas, and uninfluenced by windy eloquence. Also, we may notice that it has been discredited without the expenditure of any real thought, for of real objective argument there is none—only the manipulation of words calling out emotion.

It is not, however, only in warfare and politics that such words are used in order to influence opinion more easily than can be done by words embodying real thought. Art criticism is also a good source for this kind of material. Ruskin said of Whistler's Nocturnes: "I have heard and seen much of *Cockney impudence* before now, but never expected to hear a *coxcomb* ask two hundred guineas for *flinging a pot of paint in the public's face."* As in earlier passages, I have italicized the words or phrases with strongly emotional meanings. Stripped of these and reduced to a statement of objective fact, the passage would have to be paraphrased in some such way as follows: "I have heard and seen much of the behavior of Londoners before now, but never expected to hear a painter ask two hundred guineas for painting a picture which seemed to me to have no meaning." Plainly not much is left of Ruskin's criticism after this operation has been performed on it.

As a last example, we may take a part of an attack made by a newspaper on a novel. This runs: "Its *vicious* plea for the acknowledgment and *condonation* of *sexual perversity,* and the grounds on which it is based, loosen the very *sheet anchor of conduct."* This passage calls out such strong emotions of abhorrence that most readers will be content to condemn the novel without further inquiry. Yet the effect is gained entirely by the choice of words with emotional meanings. It happens to deal with a subject on which emotions are strong, so a dispassionate examination is all the more necessary. We note that a *plea* is simply an argument, plus a suggestion of a repugnance for the kind of argument used; that *condonation* is tolerance plus an emotional suggestion that such toleration is indefensible; that *sexual* means something in the life of love of which we disapprove, and that a *perversity* is an unusualness plus an emotional suggestion of abhorrence. The loosening of a *sheet anchor* is a metaphor implying change and suggesting to a landsman the emotion of fear, while *conduct* is simply behavior of which we approve.

So reduced to its bare bones of statement of objective fact (ignoring for a moment the special difficulties raised by the word *vicious*), the passage becomes: "Its argument for the acknowledgment and tolerance of unusualness in the life of love, and the grounds on which it is based, change the principles of behavior." This clearly is an important statement if it is true, but is not enough in itself to condemn the book, because undoubtedly our principles of behavior do need changing from time to time. We can only decide intelligently whether or not they need changing in the particular case under discussion, when we have made a dispassionate statement of what the proposed changes are and why they are defended. As in all other cases, discussion of the question with emotionally charged words obscures the problem and makes a sensible decision difficult or impossible.

The word *vicious* has some special difficulties of its own. It arouses emotions of disapproval, but there is no word with the same objective meaning which would not. If we call the book bad, corrupt, or evil, the same emotions would be aroused. So we cannot perform the simple operation of replacing *vicious* by an emotionally neutral word with the same objective meaning. Can we then leave it out altogether, on the ground that it has no objective meaning, but that it is used merely to arouse emotion?

Here we are up against a problem about which there has been much dispute. Some people consider that all such words as "good," "bad," "beautiful," "ugly," only indicate one's own emotional reactions toward actions or things and in no sense properties of the actions or things themselves. But when we see a man steal a penny from a child and we call his action "bad," we are in fact saying something meaningful about the action itself and not merely about our own feelings. As to what that something is we may leave the philosophers to dispute; it may only be that the man's action has subtracted from the total amount of human happiness. So to say a book is *vicious* is not the same kind of thing as contrasting the *slaughter* of regular troops by Communards with the *execution* of the Communards by regular soldiers. The statement that the book is *vicious* has a meaning which is not merely emotional, although, of course, the statement may not be true.

On the other hand, it is clearly not quite the same kind of meaning as a simple statement of outside fact such as "This is a book." Whether the book is good or bad is a real question, but it is a question peculiarly difficult to decide. Our own statement one way or the other is likely to be nothing but a reflection of our own personal prejudices and to have, therefore, no sort of scientific exactness. At the same time, such words certainly arouse strong emotions and should, therefore, be used sparingly in honest argument. The use of words implying moral judgments in the course of argument is very generally an attempt to distort the hearers' view of the truth by arousing emotions.

If we are trying to decide a simple question of fact, such words should be left out, because it is easier to settle one question at a time. If a man is accused of poisoning his wife, the prosecuting attorney should not say, "This *scoundrel* who hounded his wife to her grave." The question to be decided is whether the man did poison his wife. If he did, he is a "scoundrel" undoubtedly, but calling him a scoundrel does not help to decide the question of fact. On the contrary, it makes a correct decision more difficult by rousing emotions of hatred for the accused in the minds of the jury. Another obvious objection to the use of the word "scoundrel" before the man is convicted, which puts it in the ranks of "crooked thinking," is that it "begs the question" or assumes what is to be proved. The man is only a scoundrel if he is guilty, and yet the word has been used in the course of an argument to prove that he is guilty.

These two objections can be urged against the word "vicious" in the condemnation of a book quoted above. It calls up strong emotions making a just decision of the nature of the book difficult, and it assumes exactly what the article professes to prove—that the book is a bad one.

The aim of this essay has been to distinguish one kind of crooked thinking, in the hope that those who recognize how their opinions can be twisted away from the truth by the use of words with emotional meanings may be able to recognize this source of error and to guard themselves against it. Those of its readers who have found anything new to them in the ideas of this chapter should not, I suggest, be content simply to read the essay, but should try to do some practical work on its subject matter. If you were studying botany, you would not be content merely to read books on botany. If you were, that would not carry you far in botanical knowledge. Instead you would gather plants from the hedges and weeds from your garden, dissecting them, examining them with a microscope or magnifying glass, and drawing them in your notebook. Psychology too should be studied by practical methods. Emotional thinking (like most of the other kinds of crooked thinking we shall be studying) is as common as a weed. It is to be found in the leading articles of newspapers, in the words of people carrying on discussions on political, religious, or moral questions, and in the speeches made by public men when these deal with controversial matters. In order to understand it, we should collect specimens by putting them down on paper and then we should dissect them. Current political and social controversy in the United States abounds in such words and phrases as "crackpots," "economic royalists," "the abundant life," "bureaucracy"—or, on the street level—"scabs," "finks," "nigger-lovers." The New York *Herald Tribune* habitually referred to the child labor bill for New York State as the "youth control bill"; the Hearst press dubbed the New Deal the "Raw Deal"; Communists use the words "Trotzkyite" and "Fascist" to cover a multitude of sinners; Secretary Ickes managed to get some powerful emotional undertones from Ferdinand Lundberg's phrase, "America's Sixty Families."

With these ideas and phrases in mind, it is not difficult to set forth on a practical search for truth. I suggest that readers should copy out controversial phrases from newspapers, books, or speeches which contain emotionally colored words. Then they should underline all the emotional words, afterwards rewriting the passages with the emotional words replaced by neutral ones. Examine the passage then in its new form in which it merely states objective facts without indicating the writer's emotional attitude toward them, and see whether it is still good evidence for the proposition it is trying to prove. If it is, the passage is a piece of straight thinking in which emotionally colored words have been introduced merely as an ornament. If not, it is crooked thinking, because the conclusion depends not on the objective meaning of the passage but on the emotions roused by the words.

When we condemn such a use of emotional words in writings and speeches, we must remember that this is a symptom of a more deep-seated evil—their prevalence in our own private, unexpressed thinking. Many of our highly colored political speakers whose speeches stir us as we are stirred by romantic poetry show themselves unable to think calmly and objectively on any subject. They have so accustomed themselves to think in emotionally toned words that they can no longer think in any other way. They should have been poets or professional orators, but certainly not statesmen.

It really does not matter much if we sometimes use emotional words. We all do when we are trying to produce conviction. What does matter is that we should not lose the power to think without them. So a more important exercise than any we can perform on written material is one we can perform on our own minds. When we catch ourselves thinking in emotional phraseology, let us form a habit of translating our thoughts into emotionally neutral words. So we can guard ourselves from ever being so enslaved by emotional words and phrases that they prevent us from thinking objectively when we need to do so—that is, whenever we have to come to a decision on any debatable matter.

LOGICAL FALLACIES [1]

ROBERT GORHAM DAVIS

UNDEFINED TERMS

The first requirement for logical discourse is knowing what the words you use actually mean. Words are not like paper money or counters in a game. Except for technical terms in some of the sciences, they do not have a fixed face value. Their meanings are fluid and changing, influenced by many considerations of context and reference, circumstance and association. This is just as true of common words such as *fast* as it is of literary terms such as *romantic*. Moreover, if there is to be communication, words must have approximately the same meaning for the reader that they have for the writer. A speech in an unknown language means nothing to the hearer. When an adult speaks to a small child or an expert to a layman, communication may be seriously limited by lack of a mature vocabulary or ignorance of technical terms. Many arguments are meaningless because the speakers are using important words in quite different senses.

1. From *Handbook for English A,* Harvard University, 1941, pp. 58–66. Reprinted by permission of Theodore Morrison and Robert Gorham Davis.

Because we learn most words—or guess at them—from the contexts in which we first encounter them, our sense of them is often incomplete or wrong. Readers sometimes visualize the Assyrian who comes down like the wolf on fold as an enormous man dressed in cohorts (some kind of fancy armor, possibly) gleaming in purple and gold. "A rift in the lute" suggests vaguely a cracked mandolin. Failure to ascertain the literal meaning of figurative language is a frequent reason for mixed metaphors. We are surprised to find that the "devil" in "the devil to pay" and "the devil and the deep blue sea" is not Old Nick, but part of a ship. Unless terms mean the same thing to both writer and reader, proper understanding is impossible.

ABSTRACTIONS

The most serious logical difficulties occur with abstract terms. An abstraction is a word which stands for a quality found in a number of different objects or events from which it has been "abstracted" or taken away. We may, for instance, talk of the "whiteness" of paper or cotton or snow without considering qualities of cold or inflammability or usefulness which these materials happen also to possess. Usually, however, our minds carry over other qualities by association. See, for instance, the chapter called "The Whiteness of the Whale" in *Moby Dick*.

In much theoretic discussion the process of abstraction is carried so far that although vague associations and connotations persist, the original objects or events from which the qualities have been abstracted are lost sight of completely. Instead of thinking of words like *sincerity* and *Americanism* as symbols standing for qualities that have to be abstracted with great care from examples and test cases, we come to think of them as real things in themselves. We assume that Americanism is Americanism just as a bicycle is a bicycle, and that everyone knows what it means. We forget that before the question, "Is Father Coughlin sincere?" can mean anything, we have to agree on the criteria of sincerity.

When we try to define such words and find examples, we discover that almost no one agrees on their meaning. The word *church* may refer to anything from a building on the corner of Spring Street to the whole tradition of institutionalized Christianity. *Germany* may mean a geographical section of Europe, a people, a governing group, a cultural tradition, or a military power. Abstractions such as *freedom, courage, race, beauty, truth, justice, nature, honor, humanism, democracy,* should never be used in a theme unless their meaning is defined or indicated clearly by the context. Freedom for whom? To do what? Under what circumstances? Abstract terms have merely emotional value unless they are strictly defined by asking questions of this kind. The study of a word such as *nature* in a good unabridged dictionary will show that even the dictionary, indispensable though it is, cannot determine for us the sense in which a word is being used in any given instance. Once the student understands the importance of definition, he will no longer be betrayed into fruitless arguments over such questions as whether free verse is "poetry" or whether you can change "human nature."

NAME-CALLING

It is a common unfairness in controversy to place what the writer dislikes or opposes in a generally odious category. The humanist dismisses what he dislikes by calling it *romantic;* the liberal, by calling it *fascist;* the conservative, by calling it *communistic*. These terms tell the reader nothing. What is *piety* to some will be *bigotry* to others. *Non-Catholics* would rather be called *Protestants* than *heretics.* What is *right-thinking* except a designation for those who agree with the writer? Labor leaders become *outside agitators;* industrial organizations, *forces of reaction;* the Child Labor Amendment, the *youth control bill;* prison reform, *coddling;* progressive education, *fads and frills.* Such terms are intended to block thought by an appeal to prejudice and associative habits. Three steps are necessary before such epithets have real meaning. First, they must be defined; second, it must be shown that the object to which they are applied actually possesses these qualities; third, it must be shown that the possession of such qualities in this particular situation is necessarily undesirable. Unless a person is alert and critical both in choosing and in interpreting words, he may be alienated from ideas with which he would be in sympathy if he had not been frightened by a mere name.

GENERALIZATION

Similar to the abuse of abstract terms and epithets is the habit of presenting personal opinions in the guise of universal laws. The student often seems to feel that the broader the terms in which he states an opinion, the more effective he will be. Ordinarily the reverse is true. An enthusiasm for Thomas Wolfe should lead to a specific critical analysis of Wolfe's novels that will enable the writer to explain his enthusiasm to others; it should not be turned into the argument that Wolfe is "the greatest American novelist," particularly if the writer's knowledge of American novelists is somewhat limited. The same questions of *who* and *when* and *why* and under what *circumstances* which are used to check abstract terms should be applied to generalizations. Consider how contradictory proverbial wisdom is when detached from particular circumstances. "Look before you leap," but "he who hesitates is lost."

Superlatives and the words *right* and *wrong, true* and *untrue, never* and *always* must be used with caution in matters of opinion. When a student says flatly that X is true, he often is really saying that he or his family or the author of a book he has just been reading, persons of certain tastes and background and experience, *think* that X is true. Unless these people are identified and their reasons for thinking so explained, the assertion is worthless. Because many freshmen are taking survey courses in which they read a single work by an author or see an historical event through the eyes of a single historian whose bias they may not be able to measure, they must guard against this error.

SAMPLING

Assertions of a general nature are frequently open to question because they are based on insufficient evidence. Some persons are quite ready, after meeting one Armenian or reading one medieval romance, to generalize about Armenians and medieval romances. One ought, of course, to examine objectively as many examples as possible before making a generalization, but the number is less important that the representativeness of the examples chosen. The Literary Digest Presidential Poll, sent to hundreds of thousands of people selected from telephone directories, was far less accurate than the Gallup Poll which questioned far fewer voters, but selected them carefully and proportionately from all different social groups. The "typical" college student, as portrayed by moving pictures and cartoons, is very different from the "representative" college student as determined statistically. We cannot let uncontrolled experience do our sampling for us; instances and examples which impress themselves upon our minds do so usually because they are exceptional. In propaganda and arguments extreme cases are customarily treated as if they were characteristic.

If one is permitted arbitrarily to select some examples and ignore others, it is possible to find convincing evidence for almost any theory, no matter how fantastic. The fact that the mind tends naturally to remember those instances which confirm its opinions imposes a duty upon the writer, unless he wishes to encourage prejudice and superstition, to look carefully for exceptions to all generalizations which he is tempted to make. We forget the premonitions which are not followed by disaster and the times when our hunches failed to select the winner in a race. Patent medicine advertisements print the letters of those who survived their cure, and not of those who died during it. All Americans did not gamble on the stock exchange in the twenties, and all Vermonters are not thin-lipped and shrewd. Of course the search for negative examples can be carried too far. Outside of mathematics or the laboratory, few generalizations can be made airtight, and most are not intended to be. But quibbling is so easy that resort to it is very common, and the knowledge that people can and will quibble over generalizations is another reason for making assertions as limited and explicitly conditional as possible.

FALSE ANALOGY

Illustration, comparison, analogy are most valuable in making an essay clear and interesting. It must not be supposed, however, that they prove anything or have much argumentative weight. The rule that what is true of one thing in one set of circumstances is not necessarily true of another thing in another set of circumstances seems almost too obvious to need stating. Yet constantly nations and businesses are discussed as if they were human beings with human habits and feelings; human bodies are discussed as if they were machines; the universe, as if it were a clock. It is assumed that what held true for seventeenth century New England or the thirteen Atlantic colonies also holds true for an industrial nation of 130,000,000 people. Carlyle dismissed the arguments for representative democracy by saying that if a captain had to take a vote among his crew every time he wanted to do something, he would never get around Cape Horn. This analogy calmly ignores the distinction between the lawmaking and the executive branches of constitutional democracies. Moreover, voters may be considered much more like the stockholders of a merchant line than its hired sailors. Such arguments introduce assumptions in a metaphorical guise in which they are not readily detected or easily criticized. In place of analysis they attempt to identify their position with some familiar symbol which will evoke a predictable, emotional response in the reader. The revival during the 1932 presidential campaign of Lincoln's remark, "Don't swap horses in the middle of the stream," was not merely a picturesque way of saying keep Hoover in the White House. It made a number of assumptions about the nature of depressions and the function of government. This propagandist technique can be seen most clearly in political cartoons.

DEGREE

Often differences in degree are more important than differences in kind. By legal and social standards there is more difference between an habitual drunkard and a man who drinks temperately, than between a temperate drinker and a total abstainer. In fact differences of degree produce what are regarded as differences of kind. At known temperatures ice turns to water and water boils. At an indeterminate point affection becomes love and a man who needs a shave becomes a man with a beard. The fact that no men or systems are perfect makes rejoinders and counter-accusations very easy if differences in degree are ignored. Newspapers in totalitarian states, answering American accusations of brutality and suppression, refer to lynchings and gangsterism here. Before a disinterested judge could evaluate these mutual accusations, he would have to settle the question of the degree to which violent suppression and lynching are respectively prevalent in the countries under consideration. On the other hand, differences in degree may be merely apparent. Lincoln Steffens pointed out that newspapers can create a "crime wave" any time they wish, simply by emphasizing all the minor assaults and thefts commonly ignored or given an inch or two on a back page. The great reported increases in insanity may be due to the fact that in a more urban and institutionalized society cases of insanity more frequently come to the attention of authorities and hence are recorded in statistics.

CAUSATION

The most common way of deciding that one thing causes another thing is the simple principle: *post hoc, ergo propter hoc,* "After this, therefore because of this." Rome fell after the introduction of Christianity; therefore Christianity was responsible for the fall of Rome. Such reasoning illustrates another kind of faulty generalization. But even if one could find ten cases in which a nation "fell" after the introduction of Christianity, it still would not be at all certain that Christianity caused the fall. Day, it has frequently been pointed out, follows night in every observable instance, and yet night cannot be called the cause of day. Usually a combination of causes produces a result. Sitting in a draught may cause a cold, but only given a certain physical condition in the person sitting there. In such instances one may distinguish between necessary and sufficient conditions. Air is a necessary condition for the maintenance of plant life, but air alone is not sufficient to produce plant life. And often different causes at different times may produce the same result. This relation is known as plurality of causes. If, after sitting in a stuffy theatre on Monday, and then again after eating in a stuffy restaurant on Thursday, a man suffered from headaches, he might say, generalizing, that bad air gave him headaches. But actually the headache on Monday may have been caused by eye-strain and on Thursday by indigestion. To isolate the causative factor it is necessary that all other conditions be precisely the same. Such isolation is possible, except in very simple instances, only in the laboratory or with scientific methods. If a picture falls from the wall every time a truck passes, we can quite certainly say that the truck's passing is the cause. But with anything as complex and conditional as a nation's economy or human character, the determination of cause is not easy or certain. A psychiatrist often sees a patient for an hour daily for a year or more before he feels that he understands his psychosis.

Ordinarily when we speak of cause we mean the proximate or immediate cause. The plants were killed by frost; we had indigestion from eating lobster salad. But any single cause is one in an unbroken series. When a man is murdered, is his death caused by the loss of blood from the wound, or by the firing of the pistol, or by the malice aforethought of the murderer? Was the World War "caused" by the assassination at Sarajevo? Were the Navigation Acts or the ideas of John Locke more important in "causing" the American Revolution? A complete statement of cause would comprise the sum total of the conditions which preceded an event, conditions stretching back indefinitely into the past. Historical events are so interrelated that the isolation of a causative sequence is dependent chiefly on the particular preoccupations of the historian. An economic determinist can "explain" history entirely in terms of economic developments; an idealist, entirely in terms of the development of ideas.

SYLLOGISTIC REASONING

The formal syllogism of the type,

> All men are mortal
> John is a man
> Therefore John is mortal,

is not so highly regarded today as in some earlier periods. It merely fixes an individual as a member of a class, and then assumes that the individual has the given characteristics of the class. Once we have decided who John is, and what "man" and "mortal" mean, and have canvassed all men, including John, to make sure that they are mortal, the conclusion naturally follows. It can be seen that the chief difficulties arise in trying to establish acceptable premises. Faults in the premises are known as "material" fallacies, and are usually more serious than the "formal" fallacies, which are logical defects in drawing a conclusion from the premises. But although directly syllogistic reasoning is not much practiced, buried syllogisms can be found in all argument, and it is often a useful clarification to outline your own or another writer's essay in syllogistic form. The two most frequent defects in the syllogism itself are the undistributed and the ambiguous middle. The middle term is the one that appears in each of the premises and not in the conclusion. In the syllogism,

> All good citizens vote
> John votes
> Therefore John is a good citizen,

the middle term is not "good citizens," but "votes." Even though it were true that all good citizens vote, nothing prevents bad citizens from voting also, and John may be one of the bad citizens. To distribute the middle term "votes" one might say (but only if that is what one meant),

> All voters are good citizens
> John is a voter
> Therefore John is a good citizen.

The ambiguous middle term is even more common. It represents a problem in definition, while the undistributed middle is a problem in generalization. All acts which benefit others are virtuous, losing money at poker benefits others, therefore losing at poker is a virtuous act. Here the middle term "act which benefits others" is obviously used very loosely and ambiguously.

NON-SEQUITUR

This phrase, meaning "it does not follow," is used to characterize the kind of humor found in pictures in which the Marx Brothers perform. It is an amusing illogicality because it usually expresses, beneath its apparent incongruity, an imaginative, associative, or personal truth. "My ancestors came over on the Mayflower; therefore I am naturally opposed to labor unions." It is not logically necessary that those whose ancestors came over on the Mayflower should be opposed to unions; but it may happen to be true as a personal fact in a given case. Contemporary psychologists have effectively shown us that there is often such a wide difference between the true and the purported reasons for an attitude that, in rationalizing our behavior, we are often quite unconscious of the motives that actually influence us. A fanatical antivivisectionist, for instance, may have temperamental impulses toward cruelty which he is suppressing and compensating for by a reasoned opposition to any kind of permitted suffering. We may expect, then, to come upon many conclusions which are psychologically interesting in themselves, but have nothing to do with the given premises.

IGNORATIO ELENCHI

This means, in idiomatic English, "arguing off the point," or ignoring the question at issue. A man trying to show that monarchy is the best form of government for the British Empire may devote most of his attention to the character of George V and the affection his people felt for him. In ordinary conversational argument it is almost impossible for disputants to keep to the point. Constantly turning up are tempting side-issues through which one can discomfit an opponent or force him to irrelevant admissions that seem to weaken his case.

BEGGING THE QUESTION; ARGUING IN A CIRCLE

The first of these terms means to assume in the premises what you are pretending to prove in the course of your argument. The function of logic is to demonstrate that because one thing or group of things is true, another must be true as a consequence. But in begging the question you simply say in varying language that what is assumed to be true is assumed to be true. An argument which asserts that we shall enjoy immortality because we have souls which are immaterial and indestructible establishes nothing, because the idea of immortality is already contained in the assumption about the soul. It is the premise which needs to be demonstrated, not the conclusion. Arguing in a circle is another form of this fallacy. It proves the premise by the conclusion and the conclusion by the premise. The conscience forbids an act because it is wrong; the act is wrong because the conscience forbids it.

ARGUMENTS AD HOMINEM AND AD POPULUM

It is very difficult for men to be persuaded by reason when their interest or prestige is at stake. If one wishes to preach the significance of physiognomy, it is well to choose a hearer with a high forehead and a determined jaw. The arguments in favor of repealing the protective tariff on corn or wheat in England were more readily entertained by manufacturers than by landowners. The cotton manufacturers in New England who were doing a profitable trade with the South were the last to be moved by descriptions of the evils of slavery. Because interest and desire are so deeply seated in human nature, arguments are frequently mingled with attempts to appeal to emotion, arouse fear, play upon pride, attack the characters of proponents of an opposite view, show that their practice is inconsistent with their principles; all matters which have, strictly speaking, nothing to do with the truth or falsity, the general desirability or undesirability, of some particular measure. If men are desperate enough they will listen to arguments proper only to an insane asylum but which seem to promise them relief.

After reading these suggestions, which are largely negative, the student may feel that any original assertion he can make will probably contain one or several logical faults. This assumption is not true. Even if it were, we know from reading newspapers and magazines that worldly fame is not dimmed by the constant and, one suspects, conscious practice of illogicality. But generalizations are not made only by charlatans and sophists. Intelligent and scrupulous writers also have a great many fresh and provocative observations and conclusions to express and are expressing them influentially. What is intelligence but the ability to see the connection between things, to discern causes, to relate the particular to the general, to define and discriminate and compare? Any man who thinks and feels and observes closely will not want for something to express.

And in his expression a proponent will find that a due regard for logic does not limit but rather increases the force of his argument. When statements are not trite, they are usually controversial. Men arrive at truth dialectically; error is weeded out in the course of discussion, argument, attack, and counterattack. Not only can a writer who understands logic show the weaknesses of arguments he disagrees with, but also, by anticipating the kind of attack likely to be made on his own ideas, he can so arrange them, properly modified with qualifications and exceptions, that the anticipated attack is made much less effective. Thus, fortunately, we do not have to depend on the spirit of fairness and love of truth to lead men to logic; it has the strong support of argumentative necessity and of the universal desire to make ideas prevail.

OF THE CONDUCT OF THE UNDERSTANDING[1]

JOHN LOCKE

BESIDES the want of determined ideas, and of sagacity, and exercise in finding out, and laying in order intermediate ideas, there are three miscarriages that men are guilty of in reference to their reason, whereby this faculty is hindered in them from that service it might do and was designed for. And he that reflects upon the actions and discourses of mankind, will find their defects in this kind very frequent, and very observable.

1. The first is of those who seldom reason at all, but do and think according to the example of others, whether parents, neighbours, ministers, or who else they are pleased to make choice of to have an implicit faith in, for the saving of themselves the pains and trouble of thinking and examining for themselves.

2. The second is of those who put passion in the place of reason, and being resolved that shall govern their actions and arguments, neither use their own, nor hearken to other people's reason, any farther than it suits their humour, interest, or party; and these one may observe commonly content themselves with words which have no distinct ideas to them, though, in other matters that they come with an unbiassed indifferency to, they want[2] not abilities to talk and hear reason, where they have no secret inclination that hinders them from being tractable to it.

3. The third sort is of those who readily and sincerely follow reason, but for want of having that which one may call *large, sound, round-about sense,* have not a full view of all that relates to the question, and may be of moment to decide it. We are all shortsighted, and very often see but one side of a matter; our views are not extended to all that has a connection with it. From this defect I think no man is free. We see but in part, and we know but in part, and therefore it is no wonder we conclude not right from our partial views. This might instruct the proudest esteemer of his own parts,[3] how useful it is to talk and consult with others, even such as come short of him in capacity, quickness and penetration: for, since no one sees all, and we generally have different prospects of the same thing, according to our different, as I may say, positions to it, it is not incongruous to think, nor beneath any man to try, whether another may not have notions of things which have escaped him, and which his reason would make use of if they came into his mind. The faculty of reasoning seldom or never deceives those who trust to it; its consequences from what it builds on are evident and certain, but that which it oftenest, if not only, misleads us in, is, that the principles from which we conclude, the

1. From *Of the Conduct of the Understanding.* First published in 1706.
2. I.e., lack.
3. I.e., mental endowments.

grounds upon which we bottom our reasoning, are but a part; something is left out which should go into the reckoning to make it just and exact. Here we may imagine a vast and almost infinite advantage that angels and separate spirits may have over us; who, in their several degrees of elevation above us, may be endowed with more comprehensive faculties, and some of them perhaps having perfect and exact views of all finite beings that come under their consideration, can as it were, in the twinkling of an eye, collect together all their scattered and almost boundless relations. A mind so furnished, what reason has it to acquiesce in the certainty of its conclusions!

In this we may see the reason why some men of study and thought, that reason right, and are lovers of truth, do make no great advances in their discoveries of it. Error and truth are uncertainly blended in their minds; their decisions are lame and defective, and they are very often mistaken in their judgments: the reason whereof is, they converse but with one sort of men, they read but one sort of books, they will not come in the hearing but of one sort of notions; the truth is they canton out to themselves a little Goshen in the intellectual world, where light shines, and as they conclude, day blesses them; but the rest of that vast *expansum* they give up to night and darkness, and so avoid coming near it. They have a pretty traffic with known correspondents in some little creek; within that they confine themselves, and are dexterous managers enough of the wares and products of that corner with which they content themselves, but will not venture out into the great ocean of knowledge, to survey the riches that nature hath stored other parts with, no less genuine, no less solid, no less useful, than what has fallen to their lot in the admired plenty and sufficiency of their own little spot, which to them contains whatsoever is good in the universe. Those who live thus mewed up within their own contracted territories, and will not look abroad beyond the boundaries that chançe, conceit, or laziness has set to their inquiries, but live separate from the notions, discourses, and attainments of the rest of mankind, may not amiss be represented by the inhabitants of the Marian Islands, who being separated by a large tract of sea from all communion with the habitable parts of the earth, thought themselves the only people of the world. And though the straitness of the conveniences of life amongst them had never reached so far as to the use of fire, till the Spaniards not many years since in their voyages from Acapulco to Manila, brought it amongst them: yet in the want[4] and ignorance of almost all things, they looked upon themselves, even after that the Spaniards had brought amongst them the notice of variety of nations abounding in sciences, arts, and conveniences of life, of which they knew nothing, they looked upon themselves, I say, as the happiest and wisest people of the universe. But for all that, nobody, I think, will imagine them deep naturalists, or solid metaphysicians; nobody will deem the quickest-sighted among them to have very enlarged views in ethics or politics, nor can any one

4. I.e., lack.

allow the most capable amongst them to be advanced so far in his understanding, as to have any other knowledge but of the few little things of his and the neighbouring islands within his commerce; but far enough from that comprehensive enlargement of mind which adorns a soul devoted to truth, assisted with letters, and a free generation of the several views and sentiments of thinking men of all sides. Let not men, therefore, that would have a sight of what every one pretends to be desirous to have a sight of, truth in its full extent, narrow and blind their own prospect. Let not men think there is no truth but in the sciences that they study, or the books that they read. To prejudge other men's notions before we have looked into them, is not to show their darkness, but to put out our own eyes. *Try all things, hold fast that which is good,* is a divine rule, coming from the Father of light and truth; and it is hard to know what other way men can come at truth, to lay hold of it, if they do not dig and search for it as for gold and hid treasure: but he that does so must have much earth and rubbish before he gets the pure metal; sand, and pebbles, and dross usually lie blended with it, but the gold is nevertheless gold, and will enrich the man that employs his pains to seek and separate it. Neither is there any danger he should be deceived by the mixture. Every man carries about him a touchstone, if he will make use of it, to distinguish substantial gold from superficial glitterings, truth from appearance. And indeed the use and benefit of this touchstone, which is natural reason, is spoiled and lost only by assuming prejudices, over-weening presumption, and narrowing our minds. The want of exercising it in the full extent of things intelligible, is that which weakens and extinguishes this noble faculty in us. Trace it, and see whether it be not so. The day-labourer in a country village has commonly but a small pittance of knowledge, because his ideas and notions have been confined to the narrow bounds of a poor conversation and employment: the low mechanic of a country town does somewhat outdo him; porters and cobblers of great cities surpass them. A country gentleman who, leaving Latin and learning in the university, removes thence to his mansion-house, and associates with neighbours of the same strain, who relish nothing but hunting and a bottle; with those alone he spends his time, with those alone he converses, and can stay with no company whose discourse goes beyond what claret and dissoluteness inspire. Such a patriot formed in this happy way of improvement, cannot fail, as we see, to give notable decisions upon the bench at quarter-sessions, and eminent proofs of his skill in politics when the strength of his purse and party have advanced him to a more conspicuous station. To such a one truly an ordinary coffee-house gleaner of the city is an errant statesman, and as much superior to, as a man conversant about Whitehall and the court is to an ordinary shopkeeper. To carry this a little farther. Here is one muffled up in the zeal and infallibility of his own sect, and will not touch a book, or enter into debate with a person that will question any of those things which to him are sacred. Another surveys our differences in religion with an equitable and fair indifference, and so finds probably that none of them are in every thing unexceptionable. These divisions and systems were made by men, and carry the mark of fallible on them; and in those whom he differs from, and till he opened his eyes had a general prejudice against, he meets with more to be said for a great many things than before he was aware of, or could have imagined. Which of these two, now, is most likely to judge right in our religious controversies, and to be most stored with truth, the mark all pretend to aim at? All these men that I have instanced in, thus unequally furnished with truth, and advanced in knowledge, I suppose of equal natural parts; all the odds between them has been the different scope that has been given to their understandings to range in, for the gathering up of information, and furnishing their heads with ideas and notions and observations, whereon to employ their mind and form their understandings.

It will possibly be objected, "who is sufficient for all this?" I answer, more than can be imagined. Every one knows what his proper business is, and what, according to the character he makes of himself, the world may justly expect of him; and, to answer that, he will find he will have time and opportunity enough to furnish himself, if he will not deprive himself, by a narrowness of spirit, of those helps that are at hand. I do not say, to be a good geographer that a man should visit every mountain, river, promontory, and creek, upon the face of the earth, view the buildings, and survey the land everywhere, as if he were going to make a purchase; but yet every one must allow that he shall know a country better, that makes often [5] sallies into it, and traverses up and down, than he that, like a mill-horse, goes still round in the same track, or keeps within the narrow bounds of a field or two that delight him. He that will inquire out the best books in every science, and inform himself of the most material authors of the several sects of philosophy and religion, will not find it an infinite work to acquaint himself with the sentiments of mankind concerning the most weighty and comprehensive subjects. Let him exercise the freedom of his reason and understanding in such a latitude as this, and his mind will be strengthened, his capacity enlarged, his faculties improved; and the light, which the remote and scattered parts of truth will give to one another, will so assist his judgment that he will seldom be widely out, or miss giving proof of a clear head and a comprehensive knowledge. At least this is the only way I know to give the understanding its due improvement to the full extent of its capacity, and to distinguish the two most different things I know in the world, a logical chicaner from a man of reason. Only he that would thus give the mind its flight, and send abroad his inquiries into all parts after truth, must be sure to settle in his head determined ideas of all that he employs his thoughts about, and never fail to judge himself, and judge unbiassedly, of all that he receives from others, either in their writings or discourses. Reverence or prejudice must not be suffered to give beauty or deformity to any of their opinions.

---

5. I.e., frequent.

REASONING[1]

WILLIAM JAMES

We talk of man being the rational animal; and the traditional intellectualist philosophy has always made a great point of treating the brutes as wholly irrational creatures. Nevertheless, it is by no means easy to decide just what is meant by reason, or how the peculiar thinking process called reasoning differs from other thought sequences which may lead to similar results.

Much of our thinking consists of trains of images suggested one by another, of a sort of spontaneous reverie of which it seems likely enough that the higher brutes should be capable. This sort of thinking leads nevertheless to rational conclusions, both practical and theoretical. The links between the terms are either "contiguity" or "similarity," and with a mixture of both these things we can hardly be very incoherent. As a rule, in this sort of irresponsible thinking, the terms which fall to be coupled together are empirical concretes, not abstractions. A sunset may call up the vessel's deck from which I saw one last summer, the companions of my voyage, my arrival into port, etc.; or it may make me think of solar myths, of Hercules' and Hector's funeral pyres, of Homer and whether he could write, of the Greek alphabet, etc. If habitual contiguities predominate, we have a prosaic mind; if rare contiguities, or similarities, have free play, we call the person fanciful, poetic, or witty. But the thought as a rule is of matters taken in their entirety. Having been thinking of one, we find later that we are thinking of another, to which we have been lifted along, we hardly know how. If an abstract quality figures in the procession, it arrests our attention but for a moment and fades into something else; and is never very abstract. Thus, in thinking of the sun myths, we may have a gleam of admiration at the gracefulness of the primitive human mind, or a moment of disgust at the narrowness of modern interpreters. But, in the main, we think less of qualities than of whole things, real or possible, just as we may experience them.

The upshot of it may be that we are reminded of some practical duty: we write a letter to a friend abroad, or we take down the lexicon and study our Greek lesson. Our thought is rational and leads to a rational act, but it can hardly be called reasoning in a strict sense of the term.

There are other shorter flights of thought, single couplings of terms which suggest each other by association, which approach more to what would commonly be classed as acts of reasoning proper. Those are where a present sign suggests an unseen, distant, or future reality. Where the sign and what it suggests are both concretes which have been coupled together on previous occasions, the inference is common to both brutes and men, being really nothing more than association by contiguity. A and B, dinner bell and dinner, have

1. From *The Principles of Psychology* (New York: Henry Holt and Company, Inc., 1890), II, 325–371, abridged.

been experienced in immediate succession. Hence A no sooner falls upon the sense than B is anticipated, and steps are taken to meet it. The whole education of our domestic beasts, all the cunning added by age and experience to wild ones, and the greater part of our human knowingness consists in the ability to make a mass of inferences of this simplest sort. Our "perceptions" or recognitions of what objects are before us are inferences of this kind. We feel a patch of color, and we say "a distant house"; a whiff of odor crosses us, and we say "a skunk"; a faint sound is heard, and we call it "a railroad train." Examples are needless, for such inferences of sensations not presented form the staple and tissue of our perceptive life, and our Chapter XIX was full of them, illusory or veracious. They have been called *unconscious inferences.* Certainly we are commonly unconscious that we are inferring at all. The sign and the signified melt into what seems to us the object of a single pulse of thought. *Immediate inferences* would be a good name for these simple acts of reasoning requiring but two terms, were it not that formal logic has already appropriated the expression for a more technical use. . . .

II

There are two great points in reasoning: *First, an extracted character is taken as equivalent to the entire datum from which it comes; and second, the character thus taken suggests a certain consequence more obviously than it was suggested by the total datum as it originally came. . . .*

1. Suppose I say, when offered a piece of cloth, "I won't buy that; it looks as if it would fade," meaning merely that something about it suggests the idea of fading to my mind—my judgment, though possibly correct, is not reasoned, but purely empirical; but if I can say that into the color there enters a certain dye which I know to be chemically unstable and that *therefore* the color will fade, my judgment is reasoned. The notion of the dye which is one of the parts of the cloth is the connecting link between the latter and the notion of fading. So, again, an uneducated man will expect from past experience to see a piece of ice melt if placed near the fire, and the tip of his finger look coarse if he views it through a convex glass. In neither of these cases could the result be anticipated without full previous acquaintance with the entire phenomenon. It is not a result of reasoning.

But a man who should conceive heat as a mode of motion, and liquefaction as identical with increased motion of molecules; who should know that curved surfaces bend light rays in special ways, and that the apparent size of anything is connected with the amount of the "bend" of its light rays as they enter the eye—such a man would make the right inferences for all these objects, even though he had never in his life had any concrete experience of them; and he would do this because the ideas which we have above supposed him to possess would mediate in his mind between the phenomena he starts with and the conclusions he draws. But these ideas or reasons for his conclusions are all mere extracted portions or circumstances singled out from the mass of characters which make up the entire phenomena. The motions which form heat, the bending of the light waves, are, it is true, excessively recondite ingredients. . . . But each and all agree in this, that they bear a *more evident relation* to the conclusion than did the immediate data in their full totality.

The difficulty is, in each case, to extract from the immediate data that particular ingredient which shall have this very evident relation to the conclusion. Every phenomenon or so-called "fact" has an infinity of aspects or properties, as we have seen, amongst which the fool, or man with little sagacity, will inevitably go astray. But no matter for this point now. The first thing is to have seen that every possible case of reasoning involves the extraction of a particular partial aspect of the phenomena thought about, and that whilst Empirical Thought simply associates phenomena in their entirety, Reasoned Thought couples them by the conscious use of this extract.

2. And now to prove the second point: Why are the couplings, consequences, and implications of extracts more evident and obvious than those of entire phenomena? For two reasons. First, the extracted characters are more general than the concretes, and the connections they may have are, therefore, more familiar to us, having been more often met in our experience. Think of heat as motion, and whatever is true of motion will be true of heat; but we have had a hundred experiences of motion for every one of heat. Think of the rays passing through this lens as bending toward the perpendicular, and you substitute for the comparatively unfamiliar lens the very familiar notion of a particular change in direction of a line, of which notion every day brings us countless examples.

The other reason why the relations of the extracted characters are so evident is that their properties are so *few* compared with the properties of the whole from which we derived them. In every concrete total the characters and their consequences are so inexhaustibly numerous that we may lose our way among them before noticing the particular consequence it behooves us to draw. But, if we are lucky enough to single out the proper character, we take in, as it were, by a single glance all its possible consequences. Thus the character of scraping the sill has very few suggestions, prominent among which is the suggestion that the scraping will cease if we raise the door; whilst the entire refractory door suggests an enormous number of notions to the mind.

Take another example. I am sitting in a railroad car, waiting for the train to start. It is winter, and the stove fills the car with pungent smoke. The brakeman enters, and my neighbor asks him to "stop that stove smoking." He replies that it will stop entirely as soon as the car begins to move.

"Why so?" asks the passenger.

"It *always* does," replies the brakeman.

It is evident from this "always" that the connection between car moving and smoke stopping was a purely empirical one in the brakeman's mind, bred of habit. But if the passenger had been an acute reasoner he, with no experience of what the stove always did, might have anticipated the brakeman's reply and spared his own question. Had he singled out, of all the numerous points involved in a stove's not smoking, the one special point of smoke pouring freely out of the stovepipe's mouth, he would, probably, owing to the few associations of that idea, have been immediately reminded of the law that a fluid passes more rapidly out of a pipe's mouth if another fluid be at the same time streaming over that mouth; and then the rapid draught of air over the stovepipe's mouth, which is one of the points involved in the car's motion, would immediately have occurred to him.

Thus a couple of extracted characters, with a couple of their few and obvious connections, would have formed the reasoned link in the passenger's mind between the phenomena, smoke stopping and car moving, which were only linked as wholes in the brakeman's mind. Such examples may seem trivial, but they contain the essence of the most refined and transcendental theorizing. The reason why physics grows more deductive the more the fundamental properties it assumes are of a mathematical sort, such as molecular mass or wave length, is that the immediate consequences of these notions are so few that we can survey them all at once and promptly pick out those which concern us.

III

To reason, then, we must be able to extract characters—not *any* characters, but the right characters for our conclusion. If we extract the wrong character, it will not lead to that conclusion. Here, then, is the difficulty: *How are characters extracted, and why does it require the advent of a genius in many cases before the fitting character is brought to light?* Why cannot anybody reason as well as anybody else? Why does it need a Newton to notice the law of the squares, a Darwin to notice the survival of the fittest? To answer such questions we must begin a new research and see how our insight into the facts naturally grows.

All our knowledge at first is vague. When we say that a thing is vague, we mean that it has no subdivisions *ab intra* nor precise limitations *ab extra,* but still all the forms of thought may apply to it. It may have unity, reality, externality, extent, and what not—*thinghood,* in a word, but thinghood only as a whole. In this vague way, probably, does the room appear to the babe who first begins to be conscious of it as something other than his moving nurse. It has no subdivisions in his mind, unless, perhaps, the window is able to attract his separate notice. In this vague way, certainly, does every entirely new experience appear to the adult. A library, a museum, a machine shop, are mere confused wholes to the uninstructed, but the machinist, the antiquary, and the bookworm perhaps hardly notice the whole at all, so eager are they to pounce upon the details. Familiarity has in them bred discrimination. Such vague terms as "grass," "mold," and "meat" do not exist for the botanist or the anatomist. They know too much about grasses, molds, and muscles. A certain person said to Charles Kingsley, who was showing him the dissection of a caterpillar, with its exquisite viscera, "Why, I thought it was nothing but skin and squash!" A layman present at a shipwreck, a battle, or a fire is helpless. Discrimination has been so little awakened in him by experience that his consciousness leaves no single point of the complex situation accented and standing out for him to begin to act upon. But the sailor, the fireman, and the general know directly at what corner to take up the business. They "see into the situation"—that is, they analyze it—with their first glance. It is full of delicately differenced ingredients which their education has little by little brought to their consciousness, but of which the novice gains no clear idea. . . .

We dissociate the elements of originally vague totals by attending to them or noticing them alternately, of course. But what determines which element we shall attend to first? There are two immediate and obvious answers: first, our practical or instinctive interests, and second, our aesthetic interests. The dog singles out of any situation its smells, and the horse its sounds, because they may reveal facts of practical moment and are instinctively exciting to these several creatures. The infant notices the candle flame or the window, and ignores the rest of the room, because those objects give him a vivid pleasure. So the country boy dissociates the blackberry, the chestnut, and the wintergreen, from the vague mass of other shrubs and trees, for their practical uses, and the savage is delighted with the beads, the bits of looking glass brought by an exploring vessel, and gives no heed to the features of the vessel itself, which is too much beyond his sphere. These aesthetic and practical interests, then, are the weightiest factors in making particular ingredients stand out in high relief. What they lay their accent on, that we notice; but what they are in themselves we cannot say. We must content ourselves here with simply accepting them as irreducible ultimate factors in determining the way our knowledge grows.

Now a creature which has few instinctive impulses or interests, practical or aesthetic, will dissociate few characters and will at best have limited reasoning powers, whilst one whose interests are very varied will reason much better. Man, by his immensely varied instincts, practical wants, and aesthetic feelings, to which every sense contributes, would, by dint of these alone, be sure to dissociate vastly more characters than any other animal; and accordingly we find the lowest savages reason incomparably better than the highest brutes. . . .

IV

But, now, since nature never makes a jump, it is evident that we should find the lowest men occupying in this respect an intermediate position between the brutes and the highest men. And so we do. Beyond the analogies which their own minds suggest by breaking up the literal sequence of their experience, there is a whole world of analogies which they can appreciate when imparted to them by their betters, but which they could never excogitate alone. This answers the question why Darwin and Newton had to be waited for so long. The flash of similarity between an apple and the moon, between the rivalry for food in nature and the rivalry for man's selection, was too recondite to have occurred to any but exceptional minds. *Genius, then,* as has already been said, *is identical with the possession of similar association to an extreme degree.* Professor Bain says: "This I count the leading fact of genius. I consider it quite impossible to afford any explanation of intellectual originality except on the supposition of unusual energy on this point." Alike in the arts, in literature, in practical affairs, and in science, association by similarity is the prime condition of success.

But as, according to our view, there are two stages in reasoned thought, one where similarity merely *operates* to call up cognate thoughts, and another further stage where the bond of identity between the cognate thoughts is *noticed,* so *minds of genius may be divided into two main sorts, those who notice the bond and those who merely obey it.* The first are the abstract reasoners, properly so called, the men of science and philosophers—the analysts, in a word; the latter are the poets, the critics—the artists, in a word, the men of intuitions. These judge rightly, classify cases, characterize them by the most striking analogic epithets, but go no further. At first sight it might seem that the analytic mind represented simply a higher intellectual stage and that the intuitive mind represented an arrested stage of intellectual development, but the difference is not so simple as this. Professor Bain has said that a man's advance to the scientific stage (the stage of noticing and abstracting the bond of similarity) may often be due to an *absence* of certain emotional sensibilities. The sense of color, he says, may no less determine a mind away from science than it determines it toward painting. There must be a penury in one's interest in the details of particular forms in order to permit the forces of intellect to be concentrated on what is common to many forms. In other words, supposing a mind fertile in the suggestion of analogies, but at the same time keenly interested in the particulars of each suggested image, that mind would be far less apt to single out the particular character which called up the analogy than one whose interests were less generally lively. A certain richness of the aesthetic nature may, therefore, easily keep one in the intuitive stage. All the poets are examples of this. Take Homer:

Ulysses, too, spied round the house to see if any man were still alive and hiding, trying to get away from gloomy death. He found them all fallen in the blood and dirt, and in such number as the fish which the fishermen to the low shore, out of the foaming sea, drag with their meshy nets. These all, sick for the ocean water, are strewn around the sands, while the blazing sun takes their life from them. So there the suitors lay strewn round on one another.

Or again:

And as when a Maeonian or a Carian woman stains ivory with purple to be a checkpiece for horses, and it is kept in the chamber, and many horsemen have prayed to bear it off; but it is kept a treasure for a king, both a trapping for his horse and a glory to the driver—in such wise were thy stout thighs, Menelaos, and legs and fair ankles stained with blood.

A man in whom all the accidents of an analogy rise up as vividly as this may be excused for not attending to the ground of the analogy. But he need not on that account be deemed intellectually the inferior of a man of drier mind, in whom the ground is not as liable to be eclipsed by the general splendor. Rarely are both sorts of intellect, the splendid and the analytic, found in conjunction. Plato among philosophers, and M. Taine, who cannot quote a child's saying without describing the *"voix chantante, étonnée, heureuse"* in which it is uttered, are only exceptions whose strangeness proves the rule.

An often-quoted writer has said that Shakespeare possessed more *intellectual power* than anyone else who ever lived. If by this he meant the power to pass from given premises to right or congruous conclusions, it is no doubt true. The abrupt transitions in Shakespeare's thought astonish the reader by their unexpectedness no less than they delight him by their fitness. Why, for instance, does the death of Othello so stir the spectator's blood and leave him with a sense of reconcilement? Shakespeare himself could very likely not say why, for his invention, though rational, was not ratiocinative. Wishing the curtain to fall upon a reinstated Othello, that speech about the turbaned Turk suddenly simply flashed across him as the right end of all that went before. The dry critic who comes after can, however, point out the subtle bonds of identity that guided Shakespeare's pen through that speech to the death of the Moor. Othello is sunk in ignominy, lapsed from his height at the beginning of the play. What better way to rescue him at last from this abasement than to make him for an instant identify himself in memory with the old Othello of better days and then execute justice on his present disowned body, as he used then to smite all enemies of the state? But Shakespeare, whose mind supplied these means, could probably not have told why they were so effective.

But though this is true, and though it would be absurd in an absolute way to say that a given analytic mind was superior to any intuitional one, yet it is none the less true that the former *represents* the higher stage. Men, taken historically, reason by analogy long before they have learned to reason by abstract characters. Association by similarity and true reasoning may have identical results. If a philosopher wishes to prove to you why you should do a certain thing, he may do so by using abstract considerations exclusively; a savage will prove the same by reminding you of a similar case in which you notoriously do as he now proposes, and this with no ability to state the *point* in which the cases are similar. In all primitive literature, in all savage oratory, we find persuasion carried on exclusively by parables and similes, and travelers in savage countries readily adopt the native custom. Take, for example, Dr. Livingstone's argument with the Negro conjurer. The missionary was trying to dissuade the savage from his fetchistic ways of invoking rain.

"You see," he said, "that, after all your operations, sometimes it rains and sometimes it does not, exactly as when you have not operated at all."

"But," replied the sorcerer, "it is just the same with you doctors; you give your remedies, and sometimes the patient gets well and sometimes he dies, just the same as when you do nothing at all."

To that the pious missionary replied: "The doctor does his duty, after which God performs the cure if it pleases Him."

"Well," rejoined the savage, "it is just so with me. I do what is necessary to procure rain, after which God sends it or withholds it according to His pleasure."

This is the stage in which proverbial philosophy reigns supreme. "An empty sack can't stand up straight" will stand for the reason why a man with debts may lose his honesty, and "a bird in the hand is worth two in the bush" will serve to back up one's exhortations to prudence. Or we answer the question: "Why is snow white?" by saying: "For the same reason that soapsuds or whipped eggs are white"—in other words, instead of giving the *reason* for a fact, we give another *example* of the same fact. This offering a similar instance instead of a reason has often been criticized as one of the forms of logical depravity in men. But manifestly it is not a perverse act of thought, but only an incomplete one. Furnishing parallel cases is the necessary first step toward abstracting the reason imbedded in them all.

As it with reason, so it is with words. The first words are probably always names of entire things and entire actions, of extensive coherent groups. A new experience in the primitive man can only be talked about by him in terms of the old experiences which have received names. It reminds him of certain ones from among them, but the *points* in which it agrees with them are neither named nor dissociated. Pure similarity must work before the abstraction can work which is based upon it. The first adjectives will therefore probably be total nouns embodying the striking character. The primeval man will say, not "the bread is hard" but "the bread is stone"; not "the face is round," but "the face is moon"; not "the fruit is sweet," but "the fruit is sugar cane." The first words are thus neither particular nor general, but *vaguely* concrete; just as we speak of an "oval" face, a "velvet" skin, or an "iron" will, without meaning to connote any other attributes of the adjective-noun than those in which it *does* resemble the noun it is used to qualify. After a while certain of these adjectively-used nouns come only to signify the particular quality for whose sake they are most often used; the *entire thing* which they originally meant receives another name, and they become true abstract and general terms. "Oval," for example, with us suggests *only* shape. The first abstract qualities thus formed are, no doubt, qualities of one and the same sense found in different objects—as big, sweet; next analogies between different senses, as sharp (of taste), high (of sound), etc.; then analogies of motor combinations or form of relation, as simple, confused, difficult, reciprocal, relative, spontaneous, etc. The extreme degree of subtlety in analogy is reached in such cases as when we say certain English art critics' writing reminds us of a close room in which pastilles have been burning or that the mind of certain Frenchmen is like old Roquefort cheese. Here language utterly fails to hit upon the basis of resemblance.

Over immense departments of our thought we are still, all of us, in the savage state. Similarity operates in us, but abstraction has not taken place. We know what the present case is like, we know what it reminds us of, we have an intuition of the right course to take, if it be a practical matter. But analytic thought has made no tracks, and we cannot justify ourselves to others. In ethical, psychological, and aesthetic matters, to give a clear reason for one's judgment is universally recognized as a mark of rare genius. The helplessness of uneducated persons to account for their likes and dislikes is often ludicrous. Ask the first Irish girl why she likes this country better or worse than her home, and see how much she can tell you. But if you ask your most educated friend why he prefers Titian to Paul Veronese, you will hardly get more of a reply; and you will probably get absolutely none if you inquire why Beethoven reminds him of Michelangelo or how it comes that a bare figure with unduly flexed joints, by the latter, can so suggest the moral tragedy of life. His thought obeys a *nexus,* but cannot name it. And so it is with all those judgments of *experts,* which even though unmotived are so valuable. Saturated with experience of a particular class of materials, an expert intuitively feels whether a newly reported fact is probable or not, whether a proposed hypothesis is worthless or the reverse. He instinctively knows that, in a novel case, this and not that will be the promising course of action. The well-known story of the old judge advising the new one never to give reasons for his decisions—"The decisions will probably be right, the reasons will surely be wrong"—illustrates this. The doctor will feel that the patient is doomed, the dentist will have a premonition that the tooth will break, though neither can articulate a reason for his foreboding. The reason lies imbedded, but not yet laid bare, in all the countless previous cases dimly suggested by the actual one, all calling up the same conclusion, which the adept thus finds himself swept on to, he knows not how or why.

IDOLS OF THE MIND[1]

FRANCIS BACON

XXXVIII

THE idols and false notions which are now in possession of the human understanding, and have taken deep root therein, not only so beset men's minds that truth can hardly find entrance, but even after entrance obtained, they will again in the very instauration of the sciences meet and trouble us, unless men being forewarned of the danger fortify themselves as far as may be against their assaults.

XXXIX

There are four classes of Idols which beset men's minds. To these for distinction's sake I have assigned names,—calling the first class *Idols of the Tribe;* the second, *Idols of the Cave;* the third, *Idols of the Marketplace;* the fourth, *Idols of the Theatre.*

XL

The formation of ideas and axioms by true induction is no doubt the proper remedy to be applied for the keeping off and clearing away of idols. To point them out, however, is of great use; for the doctrine of Idols is to the Interpretation of Nature what the doctrine of the refutation of Sophisms is to common Logic.

XLI

The Idols of the Tribe have their foundation in human nature itself, and in the tribe or race of men. For it is a false assertion that the sense of man is the measure of things. On the contrary, all perceptions as well of the sense as of the mind are according to the measure of the individual and not according to the measure of the universe. And the human understanding is like a false mirror, which, receiving rays irregularly, distorts and discolours the nature of things by mingling its own nature with it.

XLII

The Idols of the Cave are the idols of the individual man. For every one (besides the errors common to human nature in general) has a cave or den of his own, which refracts and discolours the light of nature; owing either to his own proper and peculiar nature; or to his education and conversation with others; or to the reading of books, and the authority of those whom he esteems and admires; or to the differences of impressions, accordingly as they take place in a mind preoccupied and predisposed or in a mind indifferent and settled; or the like: So that the spirit of man (according as it is meted out to different individuals) is in fact a thing variable and full of perturbation, and

1. From *The Works of Francis Bacon,* ed. by James Spedding, Robert Ellis, and Douglas Heath (New York: Hurd and Houghton, 1869), VIII, 76–90, "Novum Organum" (London, 1620).

governed as it were by chance. Whence it was well observed by Heraclitus that men look for sciences in their own lesser worlds, and not in the greater or common world.

XLIII

There are also Idols formed by the intercourse and association of men with each other, which I call Idols of the Market-place, on account of the commerce and consort of men there. For it is by discourse that men associate; and words are imposed according to the apprehension of the vulgar. And therefore the ill and unfit choice of words wonderfully obstructs the understanding. Nor do the definitions or explanations wherewith in some things learned men are wont to guard and defend themselves, by any means set the matter right. But words plainly force and overrule the understanding, and throw all into confusion, and lead men away into numberless empty controversies and idle fancies.

XLIV

Lastly, there are Idols which have immigrated into men's mind from the various dogmas of philosophies, and also from wrong laws of demonstration. These I call Idols of the Theatre; because in my judgment all the received systems are but so many stage-plays, representing worlds of their own creation after an unreal and scenic fashion. Nor is it only of the systems now in vogue, or only of the ancient sects and philosophies, that I speak; for many more plays of the same kind may yet be composed and in like artificial manner set forth; seeing that errors the most widely different have nevertheless causes for the most part alike. Neither again do I mean this only of entire systems, but also of many principles and axioms in science, which by tradition, credulity, and negligence have come to be received.

But of these several kinds of Idols I must speak more largely and exactly, that the understanding may be duly cautioned.

XLV

The human understanding is of its own nature prone to suppose the existence of more order and regularity in the world than it finds. And though there be many things in nature which are singular and unmatched, yet it devises for them parallels and conjugates and relatives which do not exist. Hence the fiction that all celestial bodies move in perfect circles; spirals and dragons being (except in name) utterly rejected. Hence too the element of Fire with its orb is brought in, to make up the square with the other three which the sense perceives. Hence also the ratio of density of the so-called elements is arbitrarily fixed at ten to one. And so on of other dreams. And these fancies affect not dogmas only, but simple notions also.

XLVI

The human understanding when it has once adopted an opinion (either as being the received opinion or as being agreeable to itself) draws all things else to support and agree with it. And though there be a greater number and weight of instances to be found on the other side, yet these it either neglects and despises, or else by some distinction sets aside and rejects; in order that by this great and pernicious predetermination the authority of its former conclusions may remain inviolate. And therefore it was a good answer that was made by one who when they showed him hanging in a temple a picture of those who had paid their vows as having escaped shipwreck, and would have him say whether he did not now acknowledge the power of the gods,—"Aye," asked he again, "but where are they painted that were drowned after their vows?" And such is the way of all superstition, whether in astrology, dreams, omens, divine judgments, or the like; wherein men, having a delight in such vanities, mark the events where they are fulfilled, but where they fail, though this happen much oftener, neglect and pass them by. But with far more subtlety does this mischief insinuate itself into philosophy and the sciences; in which the first conclusion colours and brings into conformity with itself all that come after, though far sounder and better. Besides, independently of that delight and vanity which I have described, it is the peculiar and perpetual error of the human intellect to be more moved and excited by affirmatives than by negatives; whereas it ought properly to hold itself indifferently disposed towards both alike. Indeed in the establishment of any true axiom, the negative instance is the more forcible of the two.

XLVII

The human understanding is moved by those things most which strike and enter the mind simultaneously and suddenly, and so fill the imagination; and then it feigns and supposes all other things to be somehow, though it cannot see how, similar to those few things by which it is surrounded. But for that going to and fro to remote and heterogeneous instances, by which axioms are tried as in the fire, the intellect is altogether slow and unfit, unless it be forced thereto by severe laws and overruling authority.

XLVIII

The human understanding is unquiet; it cannot stop or rest, and still presses onward, but in vain. Therefore it is that we cannot conceive of any end or limit to the world; but always as of necessity it occurs to us that there is something beyond. Neither again can it be conceived how eternity has flowed down to the present day; for that distinction which is commonly received of infinity in time past and in time to come can by no means hold; for it would thence follow that one infinity is greater than another, and that infinity is wasting away and tending to become finite. The like subtlety arises touching the infinite divisibility of lines, from the same inability of thought to stop. But this inability interferes more mischievously in the discovery of causes; for although the most general principles in nature ought to be held merely positive, as they are discovered, and cannot with truth be referred to a cause; nevertheless the human understanding being unable to rest still seeks something prior in the order of nature. And then it is that in struggling towards that which is further off it falls back upon that which is more nigh at hand; namely, on final causes: which have relation clearly to the nature of man rather than to the nature of the universe; and from this source have strangely defiled philosophy. But he is no less an unskilled and shallow philosopher who seeks causes of that which is most general, than he who in things subordinate and subaltern omits to do so.

XLIX

The human understanding is no dry light, but receives an infusion from the will and affections; whence proceed sciences which may be called "sciences as one would." For what a man had rather were true he more readily believes. Therefore he rejects difficult things from impatience of research; sober things, because they narrow hope; the deeper things of nature, from superstition; the light of experience, from arrogance and pride, lest his mind should seem to be occupied with things mean and transitory; things not commonly believed, out of deference to the opinion of the vulgar. Numberless in short are the ways, and sometimes imperceptible, in which the affections colour and infect the understanding.

L

But by far the greatest hindrance and aberration of the human understanding proceeds from the dullness, incompetency, and deceptions of the senses; in that things which strike the sense outweigh things which do not immediately strike it, though they be more important. Hence it is that speculation commonly ceases where sight ceases; insomuch that of things invisible there is little or no observation. Hence all the working of the spirits inclosed in tangible bodies lies hid and unobserved of men. So also all the more subtle changes of form in the parts of coarser substances (which they commonly call alteration, though it is in truth local motion through exceedingly small spaces) is in like manner unobserved. And yet unless these two things just mentioned be searched out and brought to light, nothing great can be achieved in nature, as far as the production of works is concerned. So again the essential nature of our common air, and of all bodies less dense than air (which are very many), is almost unknown. For the sense by itself is a thing infirm and erring; neither can instruments for enlarging or sharpening the senses do much; but all the truer kind of interpretation of nature is effected by instances and experiments fit and apposite; wherein the sense decides touching the experiment only, and the experiment touching the point in nature and the thing itself.

LI

The human understanding is of its own nature prone to abstractions and gives a substance and reality to things which are fleeting. But to resolve nature into abstractions is less to our purpose than to dissect her into parts; as did the school of Democritus, which went further into nature than the rest. Matter rather than forms should be the object of our attention, its configurations and changes of configuration, and simple action, and law of action or motion; for forms are figments of the human mind, unless you will call those laws of action forms.

LII

Such then are the idols which I call *Idols of the Tribe;* and which take their rise either from the homogeneity of the substance of the human spirit, or from its preoccupation, or from its narrowness, or from its restless motion, or from an infusion of the affections, or from the incompetency of the senses, or from the mode of impression.

LIII

The *Idols of the Cave* take their rise in the peculiar constitution, mental or bodily, of each individual; and also in education, habit, and accident. Of this kind there is a great number and variety; but I will instance those the pointing out of which contains the most important caution, and which have most effect in disturbing the clearness of the understanding.

LIV

Men become attached to certain particular sciences and speculations, either because they fancy themselves the authors and inventors thereof, or because they have bestowed the greatest pains upon them and become most habituated to them. But men of this kind, if they betake themselves to philosophy and contemplations of a general character, distort and colour them in obedience to their former fancies; a thing especially to be noticed in Aristotle, who made his natural philosophy a mere bond-servant to his logic, thereby rendering it contentious and well nigh useless. The race of chemists again out of a few experiments of the furnace have built up a fantastic philosophy, framed with reference to a few things; and Gilbert also, after he had employed himself most laboriously in the study and observation of the loadstone, proceeded at once to construct an entire system in accordance with his favourite subject.

LV

There is one principal and as it were radical distinction between different minds, in respect of philosophy and the sciences; which is this: that some minds are stronger and apter to mark the differences of things, others to mark their resemblances. The steady and acute mind can fix its contemplations and dwell and fasten on the subtlest distinctions: the lofty and discursive mind recognises and puts together the finest and most general resemblances. Both kinds however easily err in excess, by catching the one at gradations the other at shadows.

LVI

There are found some minds given to an extreme admiration of antiquity, others to an extreme love and appetite for novelty; but few so duly tempered that they can hold the mean, neither carping at what has been well laid down by the ancients, nor despising what is well introduced by the moderns. This however turns to the great injury of the sciences and philosophy; since these affectations of antiquity and novelty are the humours of partisans rather than judgments; and truth is to be sought for not in the felicity of any age, which is an unstable thing, but in the light of nature and experience, which is eternal. These factions therefore must be abjured, and care must be taken that the intellect be not hurried by them into assent.

LVII

Contemplations of nature and of bodies in their simple form break up and distract the understanding, while contemplations of nature and bodies in their composition and configuration overpower and dissolve the understanding: a distinction well seen in the school of Leucippus and Democritus as compared with the other philosophies. For that school is so busied with the particles that it hardly attends to the structure; while the others are so lost in admiration of the structure that they do not penetrate to the simplicity of nature. These kinds of contemplation should therefore be alternated and taken by turns; that so the understanding may be rendered at once penetrating and comprehensive, and the inconveniences above mentioned, with the idols which proceed from them, may be avoided.

LVIII

Let such then be our provision and contemplative prudence for keeping off and dislodging the *Idols of the Cave,* which grow for the most part either out of the predominance of a favourite subject, or out of an excessive tendency to compare or to distinguish, or out of partiality for particular ages, or out of the largeness or minuteness of the objects contemplated. And generally let every student of nature take this as a rule,—that whatever his mind seizes and dwells upon with peculiar satisfaction is to be held in suspicion, and that so much the more care is to be taken in dealing with such questions to keep the understanding even and clear.

LIX

But the *Idols of the Market-place* are the most troublesome of all: idols which have crept into the understanding through the alliances of words and names. For men believe that their reason governs words; but it is also true that words react on the understanding; and this it is that has rendered philosophy and the sciences sophistical and inactive. Now words, being commonly framed and applied according to the capacity of the vulgar, follow those lines of division which are most obvious to the vulgar understanding. And whenever an understanding of greater acuteness or a more diligent observation would alter those lines to suit the true divisions of nature, words stand in the way and resist the change. Whence it comes to pass that the high and formal discussions of learned men end oftentimes in disputes about words and names; with which (according to the use and wisdom of the mathematicians) it would be more prudent to begin, and so by means of definitions reduce them to order. Yet even definitions cannot cure this evil in dealing with natural and material things; since the definitions themselves consist of words, and those words beget others: so that it is necessary to recur to individual instances, and those in due series and order; as I shall say presently when I come to the method and scheme for the formation of notions and axioms.

LX

The idols imposed by words on the understanding are of two kinds. They are either names of things which do not exist (for as there are things left unnamed through lack of observation, so likewise are there names which result from fantastic suppositions and to which nothing in reality corresponds), or they are names of things which exist, but yet confused and ill-defined, and hastily and irregularly derived from realities. Of the former kind are Fortune, the Prime Mover, Planetary Orbits, Element of Fire, and like fictions which owe their origin to false and idle theories. And this class of idols is more easily expelled, because to get rid of them it is only necessary that all theories should be steadily rejected and dismissed as obsolete.

But the other class, which springs out of a faulty and unskilful abstraction, is intricate and deeply rooted. Let us take for example such a word as *humid;* and see how far the several things which the word is used to signify agree with each other; and we shall find the word *humid* to be nothing else than a mark loosely and confusedly applied to denote a variety of actions which will not bear to be reduced to any constant meaning. For it both signifies that which easily spreads itself round any other body; and that which in itself is indeterminate and cannot solidise; and that which readily yields in every direction; and that which easily divides and scatters itself; and that which easily unites and collects itself; and that which readily flows and is put in motion; and that which readily clings to another body and wets it; and that which is easily reduced to a liquid, or being solid easily melts. Accordingly when you come to apply the word,—if you take it in one sense, flame is humid; if in another, air is not humid; if in another, fine dust is humid; if in another, glass is humid. So that it is easy to see that the notion is taken by abstraction only from water and common and ordinary liquids, without any due verification.

There are however in words certain degrees of distortion and error. One of the least faulty kinds is that of names of substances, especially of lowest species and well-deduced (for the notion of *chalk* and of *mud* is good, of *earth* bad); a more faulty kind is that of actions, as *to generate, to corrupt, to alter;* the most faulty is of qualities (except such as are the immediate objects of the sense) as *heavy, light, rare, dense,* and the like. Yet in all these cases some notions are of necessity a little better than others, in proportion to the greater variety of subjects that fall within the range of the human sense.

LXI

But the *Idols of the Theatre* are not innate, nor do they steal into the understanding secretly, but are plainly impressed and received into the mind from the play-books of philosophical systems and the perverted rules of demonstration. To attempt refutations in this case would be merely inconsistent with what I have already said: for since we agree neither upon principles nor upon demonstrations there is no place for argument. And this is so far well, inasmuch as it leaves the honour of the ancients untouched. For they are no wise disparaged—the question between them and me being only as to the way. For as the saying is, the lame man who keeps the right road outstrips the runner who takes a wrong one. Nay it is obvious that when a man runs the wrong way, the more active and swift he is the further he will go astray.

But the course I propose for the discovery of sciences is such as leaves but little to the acuteness and strength of wits, but places all wits and understandings nearly on a level. For as in the drawing of a straight line or a perfect circle, much depends on the steadiness and practice of the hand, if it be done by aim of hand only, but if with the aid of rule or compass, little or nothing: so is it exactly with my plan. But though particular confutations would be of no avail, yet touching the sects and general divisions of such systems I must say something; something also touching the external signs which show that they are unsound; and finally something touching the causes of such great infelicity and of such lasting and general agreement in error; that so the access to truth may be made less difficult, and the human understanding may the more willingly submit to its purgation and dismiss its idols.

IV

THE ARTS

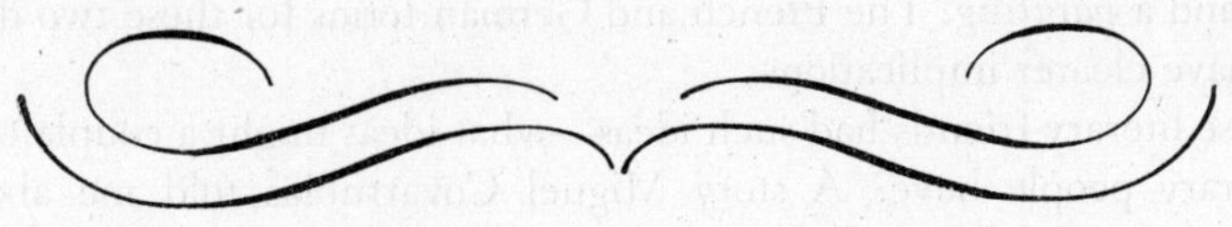

·THE FINE ARTS·

WHY ABSTRACT? [1]

HILAIRE HILER

One night I was sitting in a barroom with a couple of young Canadians who were very much interested in literature. They said that painting was a childish way of wasting one's time and that there were no first rate minds or even second rate minds interested in painting today. I had had a few drinks, and their attitude irritated me pretty considerably. I said, "Let's chew this business over a little." I took another brandy and soda and told them that they were a couple of damned little *parvenus*. Men were painting, I said, before any alphabets were thought of. Before they were farming, probably before they ever got self-conscious enough to get up and shout poetry. Perhaps there were no first rate minds but some very first rate feelings mixed up in the thing. In my opinion there was too much thinking, or what passed for thinking, going on now, and entirely too little feeling. Moreover . . . the wonderful haptic language of painting was still perfectly comprehensible by everyone who could understand it at all, after tens of thousands of years. We needed no glossary, no dictionary, no translation. Whereas . . . that after a few years it was difficult to understand the real meaning of a man of our own tongue like Shakespeare, and almost impossible to understand such relatively recent writings as those of Chaucer.

I could also study my subject freely as to space as well as time. I could feel

1. From *Why Abstract?* (Norfolk, Conn.: New Directions, 1945), pp. 15–29, with omissions. Reprinted by permission of the publisher.

and understand the design of ancient Persia or ancient China without benefit of university, language courses, or clergy. I had made sufficient progress in graphic language to understand and appreciate the design of the Ming vase which stood in the Louvre and quietly laughed off a few more generations.

I must say here that it seems tragic to me that this beautiful non-verbal language so universally human as to time and space should ever be cramped into regional forms or local or yokel confused idioms.

Thus we get to a point where we can begin to see the difference between a *picture* and a *painting*. The French and German terms for these two different things have clearer implications.

If these literary friends had such ideas—what ideas might a couple of much less literary people have? A story Miguel Covarrubias told me about the Mexican painter, Manuel Zarraga, might give us some idea.

Zarraga was working on a mural in the street or in a patio. While he was working he felt someone looking at his back, or over his shoulder. He continued painting for some time, and then looking around saw that two Indians were squatting down silently watching him paint.

After a long time one of them said in their own dialect, which Zarraga happened to understand very well, "Why does he make the machete so big?"

There was another lapse of time and then the other one said, "To go with the sombrero."

These two unverbalized fellows had not lost their feeling or knowledge of design. They expressed themselves in terms of design and were not worried about the picture but about the *painting*. They were not worried about the literary side of it for they could neither read nor write. They could feel.

The machete had to balance the sombrero. The Mexican mural went with the house, and the wall, and the hats, and the bowls, and the saddles, and the blankets. The basic design feeling for all these things was the same.

Form has something to do with style. Not stylization, which as I mentioned somewhere was a self-conscious and superficial thing, not prompted by any inner necessity or plastic necessity.

Form has a plastic significance. The word plastic, as I may have said before —and feel that I have to say again, means, as it is used here, the interrelationships of form and of color *as design* in a painting.

Form is a shape which has meaning, one might say design meaning, in a given plastic set up. Every form in a design must have a definite geometric relationship to every other form in that design. This is what my friend Danz calls its "geomathic" quality. If we don't feel that fitness and relationship, it's no form at all but only a shape. The sort of relationship mentioned by the peons about the curve and the size of the machete and the curve and the size of the sombrero.

Form may be compared to the quality of rhythm in music and color to the quality of harmony. Form and color are definitely related, a fact which is not only accepted by contemporary artists, but also pretty well by psychologists.

It seems to me that certain types of color and certain types of form are interdependent, and that only the sort of freedom and the sort of discipline inherent in abstract design make it possible to utilize this profound and interesting consonance.

Another thought comes up quite naturally here and that is the one which must be used as the basic premise for all form in design: Everything that man constructs is based on the right angle. This angle is constant and static and classic, and influences fundamentally every design which I do.

In the house in which I am at present living, I must have the sort of painting that I like. It so happens that this painting is of and for, now.

I have a painting of Carl Holty's which fits into the living room. That painting can't live with certain furniture, rugs, draperies, or wallpaper, or, to put it a much better way, the sort of order which it represents can't stand the company of a different order of a different epoch. The painting of the last two or three decades determines the design of my house and everything in it. The architect agrees with me. The cabinet makers, and ceramists, and weavers who have to do with this contemporary thing agree with me. We're getting a little nearer to Emerson. Change your house and you change your thought and life.

Dr. Ernest Jones of London, who cured George VI of stammering, says that the important timeless element in a painting is not to be translated into literary or verbal terms. It speaks directly to and from the unapprehended subverbal portions of the mind in another symbolic language. The language of geometric form—design, is what I feel he must mean.

This is as good a time as any to explain another element in pictures which can be disposed of now and lead us further towards abstraction. This element, which is at present very popular, is known as "stylization." It usually, if not always, takes the form of exaggeration of one sort or another. Extra rough, extra smooth, extra straight, or extra rounded. The thick is made thicker or the thin thinner; or the whole thing is "streamlined."

Stylization has been tried at one time or another in some form or another in the life of almost every serious painter. It is not a solution. It is only skin deep. If I had an architect for my house who would build it in "modern style" without a thorough knowledge of why—(and so many architects here do just that with modern style or any other style)—I would have, not a modern or contemporary house intended as a "machine for living" because of contemporary limitations, materials and functions; I would have a "modernistic" house which I don't think either you or I would like any better than we like the word itself.

Now the paintings and everything else in the house would have to be constructed geometrically just as soundly and mathematically as the house itself. The geometry of our mechanical time would be the only way, since actually we are unable to genuinely feel or use any other one. To think this is possible, to try to do so, is in my opinion a somewhat pathetic form of wishful thinking. We see the results of this on all sides. At best, a little self-consciously inoffensive; at worst, pretty hideously tragic-comic.

I hope that these considerations may make the next thing I'm about to try to say a little clearer. It has to do with compromise.

The pictures you saw and admired at the Perls' Gallery were all more or less in the nature of serious, perhaps almost desperate, attempts to compromise. . . .

In the case of *Mediterranée,* the design is pretty easy to see. It is based on what is justly called the "folded envelope." If you care to look at the reproduction of the picture in the little book by Waldemar George, you'll see that the picture is based on a double pyramid (the one at the base with the point up and the one at the top with the point down) just about the way they are on the back of an envelope.

In the picture of the Chinamen and Negroes the design is a little more difficult to see but the color relationships are much more obvious. The third picture, the *Domino Players,* is still more obviously geometrical. It was painted with three colors, red ochre, cobalt blue, and yellow ochre—an unfortunate combination. An Indo-Chinese noble who happened to visit my studio described it well when he said "very interesting attempt to make cubism comprehensible." It is about the most successful compromise that I ever achieved.

These pictures were all painted somewhat over ten years ago. They were done with an approach which I called "Neonaturism," a word I was forced to coin when people asked me what sort of painting it was. I called it "Neonaturism" because I thought that I could combine design with representation when I made the objects perceived subservient to the basic design of the painting. This I tried to do by committing any required violences on their natural forms which I deemed necessary to force them into the design. Franz Marc must have had some such idea in mind when he did his famous, but I believe unsuccessful, picture with the blue horse.

That blue horse of his brings us to the crux of the reason why I now paint abstractly. You could tell me that geometrical design and composition are not incompatible with more or less representational painting. You could cite masterpieces from Giotto and before him, or from Picasso, to bolster your case. I would have a very hard time getting around such evidence. It's better therefore that I shouldn't try it, or risk boring you by a technical and somewhat involved discussion of the rules and means of design and composition as I see them. I feel that I'll still be able to explain to you why I now paint abstractly and leave these things, basically important though they may be, out of the discussion. . . .

Let me retrace my steps a little and tell you about the time I really began to paint abstractly and why I had to.

I was working in the Aquatic Park Building in San Francisco, where I had charge of the decoration of the interior of the building. There were a number of house painters working there and my work naturally brought me into contact with them. First I found out that they knew a lot more about their trade than most artists know about theirs. This was no news, nor is it very sensational, because after all house painting is a much simpler activity than picture painting. Still it's by no means as simple as most people think.

We talked a lot about color. I associated house painters and color in my mind. One day I saw a couple of them eating their lunch. They'd been painting a wall which was about half finished and they were putting on the second coat and hadn't finished a great deal of that. The first coat was white: the second coat was whiter. As you know, they dress in white overalls and wear white caps. They had a white drop cloth spread out under them to protect the floor. Two or three buckets of white paint were standing on the white drop cloth where they were sitting on a couple of boxes and very unhygienically eating sandwiches. The paper these lunches had been wrapped in was lying where they'd thrown it on the drop cloth.

This is the thing that caught me and intrigued me and the thing that I got such a kick out of. House painters use a great deal of very light colors which they properly call "tints." That is to say, for most painting they use mostly white, which is colored a very little bit by the addition of some pigment or other, depending on whether they want a very light gray, light blue, cream, etc.

These two painters were all in white and surrounded by white and all these whites were different! The first coat on the wall was not as white as was the white of the second coat. The overalls were a different white from the drop cloth, and the white paint was the whitest white where it was still in the pot or running down the sides of it. The paper was a little, not much, on the cream side. The drop cloth was a little on the gray side.

If you catch the picture you'll see how delicate and how interesting it was and what a problem for an artist it presented.

I went home as soon as I could and tried to paint it. I painted the whole thing just as I described it here and naturally put in the two house painters. They spoiled it. The thing about them that spoiled it was the natural color of their hands and faces.

Flesh color is not by any means white. The little areas of it broke up my color sequence and relationship. They had nothing to do with the particular thing I was interested in putting over. When I took the most obvious solution and painted the hands and faces white also, that was even more disturbing.

People who saw the picture with the house painters sitting there eating their lunch with their white hands and faces said:

a. "The poor men contracted painters' colic from not washing their hands before eating lunch. Very informative!"

b. "He's making out the proletariat as clowns!"

c. "Modern working conditions lead to T.B."

In short I found out in the long run that the only way I could use these different whites and not completely distract attention from what I considered and still consider their beautiful and subtle relationship to one another, was to leave out the hands and faces, and the painters, and there I was—as abstract as hell!

Or, to put it still another way! I found out that if I was so interested in all this wonderful color and wanted to handle it for its own sake, and in its relation to form, I'd better let myself be as free as possible from the associations and limitations of representation. The white face won't work any better than the blue horse or the pink tree.

Ten years or so ago I'd made a similar discovery, partially by accident and partially by knowledge which I came by somehow in a way I no longer remember. Maybe a good friend of mine, now deceased, hinted to me about it.

Suddenly, or so it seems now, I thought that I'd put some green into all the colors on the picture. I got very excited. I took Viridian, a green pigment we used, and put it into the blue of the sky, and the pond, and into the white walls of the houses, and the brown of the tree trunks, and the grayish brown of the paths, and I did nothing but this all that day. ("Adjusting," I now call it.) I was very excited. Just before I had to go and keep a date with a nice French girl I knew, I got the thing far enough along to know that I'd pulled it together and that as far as I was concerned there was no longer any question of destroying it. That it had taken on a sort of green glow and it looked pretty good.

I rushed out to my date and told Laurette all about it and she shared my excitement, and my enthusiasm, when she saw the picture (which, by the way, is now in Chicago)

Of course the trouble ten years ago was that the trunks of the trees were still psychologically brown, and the houses still white and so forth, even with the green pigment mixed in pretty liberally. The sky, because it was less green, was still blue.

The Park painting then, although probably the most successful thing from a standpoint of color I had accomplished up to that time, did not exploit the full possibilities of color because I still was unable to take that final step, which would enable me to have freedom from the aesthetic chaos of my surroundings and consequent plastic independence in the problem bounded by the four edges of my canvas—the microcosmic problem of creating a painting as an autonomous entity with its own exigencies, its own rules, its particular construction, etc., in and of itself.

Sometimes a happy combination of circumstances permits the full realization of the plastic problem, while leaving the possibility, I might say the natural possibility, of more or less representation. The rock may still resemble a rock. The forms of two dancers may still be recognizably two dancers. How often this may happen. I don't as yet know. Not often enough to be of very much importance, I should say.

The point to be stressed here is simply that when these forms do not happen to fit into the design, they must be modified from rocks or dancers and made to fit into the painting as form-color, for it is only as form-color that they are of any importance in and of the painting. In other words, as they're related to the other forms and colors in the concept of it.

So we're back to design again, and to repeat, I find that if a form which happens to be recognizable as an object does not interfere with the design—O.K.; if it does interfere with it, plastically or psychologically, it must be rebuilt, whittled down, appropriately colored, or fittingly modified in any way necessary to preserve the plastic unity of the painting. This is supposed to explain why some of the paintings are abstract, some partially abstract, and some quite representational. In other words, they are not abstract just for the sake of the word, but in direct ratio to the inherent design requirements.

Hitherto, I didn't know and I didn't care. I used to sell pictures . . . as long as they looked like things people liked or were interested in or had pleasant associations with. Ashamed as I may feel to admit it, this fact had an effect on my painting for a long time. Naturally, like everyone else I also had certain responsibilities to a number of other people. I liked to remain as comfortable mentally and physically as possible and to be as well thought of as possible.

Now for a number of reasons I'm more interested in painting for its own sake than I was then.

So many things have come up that I don't give a damn about a lot of things I used to care about, and I do give more of a damn about a lot of things I didn't dare care about.

These are the kind of reasons why I now paint abstractly and I hope that you'll understand, at least partially, why it can't be helped. It seems that that's the sort of thing that happens to some people who have reached certain points in their pokings about and their investigations. The sort of things which direct that feeling I was discussing and bring it into contact with factors which seem to make a new illusion and a new reality. These at least have the virtue of being fresher and less redundant than the ones they went through before.

Some of the conclusions implied here were reached, as seen upon examination, many years ago. For instance, I might claim the distinction, if distinction it is, of never having painted a nude, portrait, still life, landscape, or marine, in the classic sense of these terms.

Having looked at thousands of paintings (during and between the wars), most of which were certainly bad ones, a strong suspicion made itself felt that by and large the whole affair was getting pretty boring. A great many of my colleagues seemed not only to bore the public quite exquisitely, but even themselves, as they would freely admit in their more lucid or uninhibited moments.

Painting as an exercise of skill or dexterity à la Munich, an implication of refined "good taste," atmospheric, poetic or literary ideas in the passing mood, or prettily executed realisms of some one's tortured or suffering unconscious mind, seemed isolated from life and self-respecting construction in general.

Some of it was illustration, some of it—I was repeatedly informed—was pure painting, though it looked to me as though this viewpoint might really mean "pure brush stroke" or sometimes, merely, pure sloppiness. Whatever it was, I was no longer interested in it. I could no longer understand it very well or appreciate it in a lively fashion even when I thought I understood it. In fact, whether it was painting or not mattered little.

Color first and then design have come to interest me to the exclusion of practically all the considerations which are apparently taken as premises for the great majority of pictures hung in exhibitions at this time. It no longer seems relevant whether these two elements are accepted as painting or not. It seems that they're of sufficient interest and importance to stand for their own sakes in whatever field their exploitation happens to lead one.

Carl Holty wrote me a letter the other day about a visit he had with Piet Mondrian. Piet paints more abstractly than I do (in case you don't happen to know it). I was a little shocked to learn that Mondrian is now in his seventies. He paints so much younger than a lot of our "young painters." Well, anyway, he and Holty were discussing abstract painting and Mondrian very calmly said to Holty:

"To us this approach to painting is the only realistic one so that we can't change even if we wanted to, no matter how much our well-wishers think we should."

BOTTICELLI'S *PRIMAVERA*[1]

FRANK JEWETT MATHER, JR.

In the year 1477, Lorenzo di Pierfrancesco de' Medici having bought a villa at Castello, on the Prato road, commissioned a young Florentine painter, Sandro Botticelli, to paint a decorative panel for his villa. The dimensions, about seven by ten feet, and the subject, the "Coming of Spring," were prescribed. Lorenzo, not to be confused with his cousin and more illustrious namesake, was himself a minor poet and in touch with the great humanist poet Angelo Poliziano. Thus he was a patron of a kind to feel the loveliness of a Tuscan springtime. Botticelli accepted the theme with enthusiasm and cast about for its embodiment.

Instantaneously the general decorative arrangement flashed into Botticelli's mind, for a pattern is already there, waiting for a subject. He has admired the

1. *Concerning Beauty* (Princeton: Princeton University Press, 1935), pp. 70–76. Copyright, 1935, Princeton University Press.

great new engraving of ten fighting men by one of his masters, Antonio Pollaiolo—a fine arabesque of tensely constructed white bodies effectively contrasting with the formal verticals of a grove in the background. Sometime Sandro meant to use the motive more exquisitely. This is his opportunity. His figures shall show a greater variety in drapery and semi-nudity.

It was perhaps at this stage some humanist friend called Sandro's attention to the beautiful lines in which Lucretius described the coming of spring.

> It ver et Venus, et Veneris praenuntius ante
> Pennatus graditur, zephyri vestigia propter
> Flora quibus mater praespargens ante viai
> Cuncta coloribus egregiis et odoribus opplet.

Spring and Venus move by, and the winged herald of Venus goes before; and close upon the track of the West Wind Flora, their mother, strews flowers ahead, covering all the paths with fairest colors and odors.

A group of five figures begins to order itself in Botticelli's mind; the composition now has found its main theme, but he consciously transforms the processional order of Lucretius. Spring no longer leads with Venus, but is blown and chased in by Zephyr at the rear of the line. And the trees shall bend as Zephyr passes, admitting his gentle power. As for Zephyr, Poliziano, in the *"Stanze"* is better than Lucretius. He represents Zephyr as lustful and flying behind Flora. Such shall be his relation to Spring. Flora does not follow Zephyr, but treads daintily ahead of him, behind Venus. Cupid's place as herald is above Venus and a little before her, and since he has wings, shall he not fly rather than walk? In its essentials the group at the right-hand side of the panel, the group that carries the meaning, is now established.

The carpet of spring flowers is obvious. Does not Lucretius suggest it? The flowers shall be so truthful that you could pluck them. They will contrast effectively with the formality of the paling of orange trees which he will pick out decoratively and conventionally with gold. But he will not stand on the somewhat monotonous verticalities of Pollaiolo's paling of trees. His paling shall be interspersed with olive branches delicately sharp against the sky. Everything shall be as fine and precise as any goldsmith's work.

So far everything has gone swimmingly. Presumably sketches have been made of the five figures, the group has taken on organization, at least mentally. Enrichments and refinements have occurred. Out of Spring's lovely mouth roses shall grow; the flowers woven in Flora's frock shall proclaim her function; Venus shall be gravid and heavily draped, for contrast with the semi-nude figures and because spring is the birthday of the year. But now comes an unforeseen difficulty; on the small scale customary at the time, the five figures will never make out a composition for the big, oblong panel. Some filling figures of a congruous kind are indispensable. What figures?

Sandro is reasonably educated, but no scholar. He consults a humanist friend who has the ready answer. Of course Mercury and the Three Graces are the fitting attendants for Venus. Did not Horace, Book I, Ode xxx, when he bid Venus visit the home of his mistress Glycera, summon also the Graces with girdles loosed and Mercury, who withal is a minor cloud-dispeller? Witness *Aeneid,* IV, 245. As for the Graces, Sandro's own fellow Florentine, Leonbattista Alberti, in his treatise *Della Pittura,* which Sandro has doubtless duly read, tells us that their hands should be intertwined, and they themselves clothed in ungirt and transparent veils—quoting Seneca, "implexis inter se manibus, ridentes, solutaque, perlucida veste ornatas." So the humanist counsellor.

Sandro thinks it over. Here are the needed filling figures, and excellent figures for the purpose. Mercury shall be fanning the mists from an orange tree with his caduceus. That will carry the processional rhythm across the picture up to a high finish. He shall then be the terminal figure of the group. But the Graces shall be treading a solemn measure and not smiling. Only the hoyden Spring with the rose in her mouth shall be joyous.

The rest shall be pensive, or like Flora, enigmatically detached, for if spring is the beginning of new life in the world, is it not also the beginning of new death? The flowers and love itself are but for a moment between budding and withering.

Something like this is in Sandro's mind as he sketches the four new figures and considers the organization of the two groups into one. Here the general cadence is clear. The onrush of Zephyr and Spring shall be retarded into the dainty treading of Flora, shall come to a monitory full pause in the heavily clad figure of gravid Venus, shall be resumed in a moderate and more subtle fashion in the dance of the Graces, shall end with the resolutely poised figure of Mercury with his back turned while his hand and magic wand make on high a closing repetend of the right to left motion.

The composition of the picture is now mentally complete. Remains a task of some days to set it down in all its details in a working drawing—a drawing unhappily lost, for which any sensible collector would mortgage his house to the limit. Remained still a task of many months to paint it through on the panel. Rapturous work, work under highest tension, nothing lost of the freshness of the primal vision, much added by way of fit enrichment; fastidiousness in choice of shapes and tints never relaxing, never overasserting itself; a marvel of taste, a miracle of executive prowess.

When it was set in the wall at Castello, Botticelli, unless he was entirely unlike any other painters, relatively lost interest in it. He was now at work on his nobly tragic "St. Augustine" for Ognissanti in competition with the formidably popular Ghirlandaio's "St. Jerome," he was already thinking of great frescoes to be made in Pope Sixtus's new chapel at Rome. Botticelli's part of the esthetic transaction connected with the "Allegory of Spring" was completed and well completed. That the transaction should continue was now the responsibility of others.

The painting is now ready to play its part in the esthetic transaction. Let

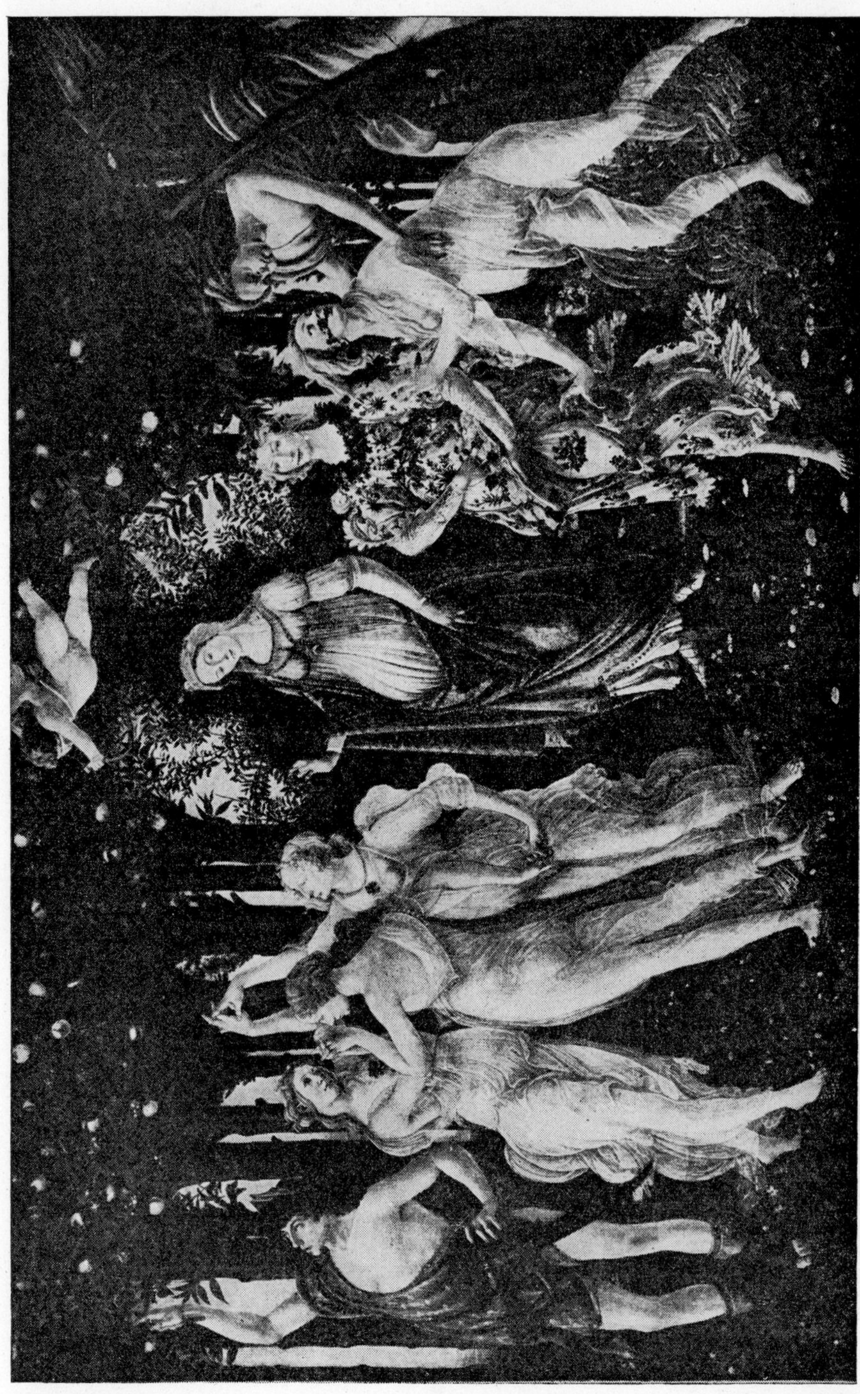

me imagine myself before it. First at a distance I perceive the general design—a very varied processional advance of clothes and lightly draped forms from right to left across a quite formal paling of orange trees. Here I have repeated the primal vision of Botticelli as elaborated by trial and error. Of this trial and error virtually nothing comes to my attention, though I may note that the four figures on the left are out of the main action, may divine that they were an afterthought.

On nearer approach I grasp the exquisiteness of the detail without losing the sense of the whole picture. This detail, the ripe oranges on the trees, the iris, larkspurs, daisies, wild orchid, wood-strawberry daintily balancing in the grass tell me that it is early springtime. Herewith comes the meaning of the figures. Gravid Venus is identified by her winged son. The fantastic figure with a beflowered frock, and strewing flowers must be Flora. An associational item confirms and extends the identifications. I have read Herbert Horne's happy citation of the lines from Lucretius which names all five figures for me. This literary association is legitimately part of my appreciation, for it guided Botticelli in creation. Since it was important for him, it is important for me.

As I identify the main figures I sense their fastidiously distinguished character and the loveliness of the postures, actions and details which represent and delicately emphasize their functions. What a cadence it is, rising from the solemn boisterousness of Zephyr, through the adorable awkward twist of escaping Spring, to the mincing elegance of Flora's measured stride, and the full stop where Venus stands in undulating repose. It is also an undulation in depth, coming forward with Flora and the Graces at the ends, receding with Venus at the center. My sense of the whole picture is being constantly deepened and enriched as I make these explorations of details, and continue then through the flowery sward, the grove, the group of Mercury and the Graces. Here in appreciation I am perceiving that infinite delicate elaboration and richness which arising in Botticelli's imagination commanded his nervous and fastidious hand. These observations gradually tell me of the language in which Botticelli's meaning is expressed. While there is a lovely accompaniment of muted color, it is primarily a language of line—line that races, slows, darts, turns, stops, resumes, always giving assurance of form in implied motion. My soul has echoed the controlled sweep of Botticelli's hand. The sense of the pervading wistful, tranquil melancholy that surrounds and almost denies the high spirits of romping Spring grows deeper as I look.

The experiences which words can only enumerate as successive, have actually overlapped, interwoven, blended, and have uninterruptedly built up that psychical volume which is my appreciation of this lively picture, my virtual if also approximate repetition of what was essential in Botticelli's creative processes—my complete *geniessen,*[2] my partial but sufficient *nachschaffen.*[3]

2. Enjoying. 3. Re-creating.

MODERN ARCHITECTURE: THE CARDBOARD HOUSE[1]

FRANK LLOYD WRIGHT

LET us take for text on this, our fourth afternoon, the greatest of all references to simplicity, the inspired admonition: *"Consider the lilies of the field—they toil not, neither do they spin, yet verily I say unto thee—Solomon in all his glory was not arrayed like one of these."* An inspired saying—attributed to an humble Architect in ancient times, called Carpenter, who gave up Architecture nearly two thousand years ago to go to work upon its Source.

And if the text should seem to you too far away from our subject this afternoon—

"The Cardboard House"

—consider that for that very reason the text has been chosen. The cardboard house needs an antidote. The antidote is far more important than the house. As antidote—and as practical example, too, of the working out of an ideal of organic simplicity that has taken place here on American soil, step by step, under conditions that are your own—could I do better than to take apart for your benefit the buildings I have tried to build, to show you how they were, long ago, dedicated to the Ideal of Organic Simplicity? It seems to me that while another might do better than that, I certainly could not—for that is, truest and best, what I know about the Subject. What a man *does, that* he has.

When, "in the cause of Architecture," in 1893, I first began to build the houses, sometimes referred to by the thoughtless as "The New School of the Middle West" (some advertiser's slogan comes along to label everything in this our busy woman's country), the only way to simplify the awful building in vogue at the time was to conceive a finer entity—a better building—and get it built. The buildings standing then were all tall and all tight. Chimneys were lean and taller still, sooty fingers threatening the sky. And beside them, sticking up by way of dormers through the cruelly sharp, saw-tooth roofs, were the attics for "help" to swelter in. Dormers were elaborate devices, cunning little buildings complete in themselves, stuck to the main roof slopes to let "help" poke heads out of the attic for air.

Invariably the damp sticky clay of the prairie was dug out for a basement under the whole house, and the rubblestone walls of this dank basement always stuck up above the ground a foot or more and blinked, with half-windows. So the universal "cellar" showed itself as a bank of some kind of masonry running around the whole house, for the house to sit up on—like a chair. The lean, upper house-walls of the usual two floors above this stone or brick base-

1. *Modern Architecture, Being the Kahn Lecture for 1930* (Princeton: Princeton University Press, 1931), pp. 68–80. Copyright, 1931, by Frank Lloyd Wright. Reprinted by permission of author and the Princeton University Press.

ment were wood, set on top of this masonry-chair, clapboarded and painted, or else shingled and stained, preferably shingled and mixed, up and down, all together with mouldings crosswise. These overdressed wood house-walls had, cut in them—or cut out of them, to be precise—big holes for the big cat and little holes for the little cat to get in and out or for ulterior purposes of light and air. The house-walls were be-corniced or bracketed up at the top into the tall, purposely profusely complicated roof, dormers plus. The whole roof, as well as the roof as a whole, was scalloped and ridged and tipped and swanked and gabled to madness before they would allow it to be either shingled or slated. The whole exterior was be-deviled—that is to say, mixed to puzzle-pieces, with corner boards, panel-boards, window-frames, corner-blocks, plinth-blocks, rosettes, fantails, ingenious and jigger work in general. This was the only way they seemed to have, then, of "putting on style." The scroll-saw and turning-lathe were at the moment the honest means of this fashionable mongering by the wood-butcher and to this entirely "moral" end. Unless the householder of the period were poor indeed, usually an ingenious corner-tower on his house eventuated into a candle-snuffer dome, a spire, an inverted rutabaga or radish or onion or—what is your favorite vegetable? Always elaborate bay-windows and fancy porches played "ring around a rosy" on this "imaginative" corner feature. And all this the building of the period could do equally well in brick or stone. It was an impartial society. All material looked pretty much alike in that day.

Simplicity was as far from all this scrap-pile as the pandemonium of the barn-yard is far from music. But it was easy for the Architect. All he had to do was to call: "Boy, take down No. 37, and put a bay-window on it for the lady!"

So—the first thing to do was to get rid of the attic and, therefore, of the dormer and of the useless "heights" below it. And next, get rid of the unwholesome basement, entirely—yes, absolutely—in any house built on the prairie. Instead of lean, brick chimneys, bristling up from steep roofs to hint at "judgment" everywhere, I could see necessity for one only, a broad generous one, or at most, for two, these kept low down on gently sloping roofs or perhaps flat roofs. The big fireplace below, inside, became now a place for a real fire, justified the great size of this chimney outside. A real fireplace at that time was extraordinary. There were then "mantels" instead. A mantel was a marble frame for a few coals, or a piece of wooden furniture with tiles stuck in it and a "grate," the whole set slam up against the wall. The "mantel" was an insult to comfort, but the *integral* fireplace became an important part of the building itself in the houses I was allowed to build out there on the prairie. It refreshed me to see the fire burning deep in the masonry of the house itself.

Taking a human being for my scale, I brought the whole house down in height to fit a normal man; believing in no other scale, I broadened the mass out, all I possibly could, as I brought it down into spaciousness. It has been said that were I three inches taller (I am 5 feet 8½ inches tall), all my houses would have been quite different in proportion. Perhaps.

House-walls were now to be started at the ground on a cement or stone water-table that looked like a low platform under the building, which it usually was, but the house-walls were stopped at the second story window-sill level, to let the rooms above come through in a continuous window-series, under the broad eaves of a gently sloping, overhanging roof. This made enclosing screens out of the lower walls as well as light screens out of the second story walls. Here was true *enclosure of interior space*. A new sense of building, it seems.

The climate, being what it was, a matter of violent extremes of heat and cold, damp and dry, dark and bright, I gave broad protecting roof-shelter to the whole, getting back to the original purpose of the "Cornice." The undersides of the roof projections were flat and light in color to create a glow of reflected light that made the upper rooms not dark, but delightful. The over-hangs had double value, shelter and preservation for the walls of the house as well as diffusion of reflected light for the upper story, through the "light screens" that took the place of the walls and were the windows.

At this time, a house to me was obvious primarily as interior space under fine shelter. I liked the sense of *shelter*. I liked the sense of shelter in the "look of the building." I achieved it, I believe. I then went after the variegated bands of material in the old walls to eliminate odds and ends in favor of one material and a single surface from grade to eaves, or grade to second story sill-cope, treated as simple enclosing screens,—or else made a plain screen band around the second story above the window-sills, turned up over on to the ceiling beneath the eaves. This screen band was of the same material as the under side of the eaves themselves, or what architects call the "soffit." The planes of the building parallel to the ground were all stressed, to grip the whole to earth. Sometimes it was possible to make the enclosing wall below this upper band of the second story, from the second story window-sill clear down to the ground, a heavy "wainscot" of fine masonry material resting on the cement or stone platform laid on the foundation. I liked that wainscot to be of masonry material when my clients felt they could afford it.

As a matter of form, too, I liked to see the projecting base, or water-table, set out over the foundation walls themselves—as a substantial preparation for the building. This was managed by setting the studs of the walls to the inside of the foundation walls, instead of to the outside. All door and window tops were now brought into line with each other with only comfortable head-clearance for the average human being. Eliminating the sufferers from the "attic" enabled the roofs to lie low. The house began to associate with the ground and become natural to its prairie site. And would the young man in architecture ever believe that this was all "new" then? Not only new, but destructive heresy —or ridiculous eccentricity. So New that what little prospect I had of ever earning a livelihood by making houses was nearly wrecked. At first, "they" called the houses "dress-reform" houses, because Society was just then excited about that particular "reform." This simplification looked like some kind of "reform" to them. Oh, they called them all sorts of names that cannot be repeated, but "they" never found a better term for the work unless it was "Horizontal Gothic," "Temperance Architecture" (with a sneer), etc., etc. I don't know how I escaped the accusation of another "Renaissance."

What I have just described was all on the *outside* of the house and was there chiefly because of what had happened *inside*. Dwellings of that period were "cut-up," advisedly and completely, with the grim determination that should go with any cutting process. The "interiors" consisted of boxes beside or inside other boxes, called *rooms*. All boxes inside a complicated boxing. Each domestic "function" was properly box to box. I could see little sense in this inhibition, this cellular sequestration that implied ancestors familiar with the cells of penal institutions, except for the privacy of bed-rooms on the upper floor. They were perhaps all right as "sleeping boxes." So I declared the whole lower floor as one room, cutting off the kitchen as a laboratory, putting servants' sleeping and living quarters next to it, semi-detached, on the ground floor, screening various portions in the big room, for certain domestic purposes—like dining or reading, or receiving a formal caller. There were no plans like these in existence at the time and my clients were pushed toward these ideas as helpful to a solution of the vexed servant-problem. Scores of doors disappeared and no end of partition. They liked it, both clients and servants. The house became more free as "space" and more liveable, too. Interior spaciousness began to dawn.

Having got what windows and doors that were left lined up and lowered to convenient human height, the ceilings of the rooms, too, could be brought over on to the walls, by way of the horizontal, broad bands of plaster on the walls above the windows, the plaster colored the same as the room ceilings. This would bring the ceiling-surface down to the very window tops. The ceilings thus expanded, by extending them downward as the wall band above the windows, gave a generous overhead to even small rooms. The sense of the whole was broadened and made plastic, too, by this expedient. The enclosing walls and ceilings were thus made to flow together.

Here entered the important element of Plasticity—indispensable to successful use of the Machine, for true expression of Modernity. The outswinging windows were fought for because the casement window associated the house with out-of-doors—gave free openings, outward. In other words the so-called "casement" was simple and more human. In use and effect, more natural. If it had not existed I should have invented it. It was not used at that time in America, so I lost many clients because I insisted upon it when they wanted the "guillotine" or "double-hung" window then in use. The Guillotine was not simple nor human. It was only expedient. I used it once in the Winslow House —my first house—and rejected it thereafter—forever. Nor at that time did I entirely eliminate the wooden trim. I did make it "plastic," that is, light and continuously flowing instead of the heavy "cut and butt" of the usual carpenter work. No longer did the "trim," so called, look like carpenter work. The machine could do it perfectly well as I laid it out. It was all after "quiet." This plastic trim, too, with its running "back-hand" enabled poor workmanship to be concealed. It was necessary with the field resources at hand at that time to conceal much. Machinery versus the union had already demoralized the workmen. The Machine resources were so little understood that extensive drawings had to be made merely to show the "mill-man" what to leave off. But the "trim" finally became only a single, flat, narrow, horizontal wood-band running around the room, one at the top of the windows and doors and another next to the floors, both connected with narrow, vertical, thin wood-bands that were used to divide the wall-surfaces of the whole room smoothly and flatly into folded color planes. The trim merely completed the window and door openings in this same plastic sense. When the interior had thus become wholly plastic, instead of structural, a New element, as I have said, had entered Architecture. Strangely enough an element that had not existed in Architectural History before. Not alone in the trim, but in numerous ways too tedious to describe in words, this revolutionary sense of the plastic whole, an instinct with me at first, began to work more and more intelligently and have fascinating, unforeseen consequences. Here was something that began to organize itself. When several houses had been finished and compared with the house of the period, there was very little of that house left standing. Nearly every one had stood the house of the period as long as he could stand it, judging by appreciation of the change. Now all this probably tedious description is intended to indicate directly in bare outline how thus early there *was* an ideal of organic simplicity put to work, with historical consequences, here in your own country. The main motives and indications were (and I enjoyed them all):

First—to reduce the number of necessary parts of the house and the separate rooms to a minimum, and make all come together as enclosed space—so divided that light, air and vista permeated the whole with a sense of unity.

Second—To associate the building as a whole with its site by extension and emphasis of the planes parallel to the ground, but keeping the floors off the best part of the site, thus leaving that better part for use in connection with the life of the house. Extended level planes were found useful in this connection.

Third—To eliminate the room as a box and the house as another by making all walls enclosing screens—the ceilings and floors and enclosing screens to flow into each other as one large enclosure of space, with minor subdivisions only.

Make all house proportions more liberally human, with less wasted space in structure, and structure more appropriate to material, and so the whole more liveable. *Liberal* is the best word. Extended straight lines or streamlines were useful in this.

Fourth—To get the unwholesome basement up out of the ground, entirely above it, as a low pedestal for the living-portion of the home, making the foundation itself visible as a low masonry platform, on which the building should stand.

Fifth—To harmonize all necessary openings to "outside" or to "inside" with good human proportions and make them occur naturally—singly or as a series in the scheme of the whole building. Usually they appeared as "light-screens" instead of walls, because all the "Architecture" of the house was chiefly the way these openings came in such walls as were grouped about the rooms as enclosing screens. The *room* as such was now the essential architectural expression, and there were to be no holes cut in walls as holes are cut in a box, because this was not in keeping with the ideal of "plastic." Cutting holes was violent.

Sixth—To eliminate combinations of different materials in favor of mono-material so far as possible; to use no ornament that did not come out of the nature of materials to make the whole building clearer and more expressive as a place to live in, and give the conception of the building appropriate revealing emphasis. Geometrical or straight lines were natural to the machinery at work in the building trades then, so the interiors took on this character naturally.

Seventh—To incorporate all heating, lighting, plumbing so that these systems became constituent parts of the building itself. These service features became architectural and in this attempt the ideal of an organic architecture was at work.

Eighth—To incorporate as organic Architecture—so far as possible—furnishings, making them all one with the building and designing them in simple terms for machine work. Again straight lines and rectilinear forms.

Ninth—Eliminate the Decorator. He was all curves and all efflorescence, if not all "period."

This was all rational enough so far as the thought of an organic architecture went. The particular forms this thought took in the feeling of it all could only be personal. There was nothing whatever at this time to help make them what they were. All seemed to be the most natural thing in the world and grew up out of the circumstances of the moment. Whatever they may be worth in the long run is all they are worth.

Now *simplicity* being the point in question in this early constructive effort, organic simplicity I soon found to be a matter of true coordination. And Beauty I soon felt to be a matter of the sympathy with which such coordination was affected. Plainness was not necessarily simplicity. Crude furniture of the Roycroft-Stickley-Mission Style, which came along later, was offensively plain, plain as a barn door—but never was simple in any true sense. Nor, I found, were merely machine-made things in themselves simple. To think "in simple," is to deal in simples, and that means with an eye single to the altogether. This, I believe, is the secret of simplicity. Perhaps we may truly regard nothing at all as simple in itself. I believe that no one thing in itself is ever so, but must achieve simplicity (as an Artist should use the term) as a perfectly realized part of some organic whole. Only as a feature or any part becomes an harmonious element in the harmonious whole does it arrive at the estate of simplicity.

Any wild flower is truly simple, but double the same wild flower by cultivation, it ceases to be so. The *scheme* of the original is no longer clear. Clarity of design and perfect significance both are first essentials of the spontaneously born simplicity of the lilies of the field who neither toil nor spin, as contrasted with Solomon who had "toiled and spun"—that is to say, no doubt had put on himself and had put on his temple, properly "composed," everything in the category of good things but the cook-stove.

Fives lines where three are enough is stupidity. Nine pounds where three are sufficient is stupidity. But to eliminate expressive words that intensify or vivify meaning in speaking or writing is not simplicity; nor is similar elimination in Architecture simplicity—it, too, may be stupidity. In Architecture, expressive changes of surface, emphasis of line and especially textures of material, may go to make facts eloquent, forms more significant. Elimination, therefore, may be just as meaningless as elaboration, perhaps more often so. I offer any fool, for an example.

To know what to leave out and what to put in, just where and just how—Ah, *that* is to have been educated in knowledge of SIMPLICITY.

As for Objects of Art in the house even in that early day they were the "bête noir" of the new simplicity. If well chosen, well enough in the house, but only if each was properly digested by the whole. Antique or modern sculpture, paintings, pottery, might become objectives in the Architectural scheme and I accepted them, aimed at them, and assimilated them. Such things may take their places as elements in the design of any house. They are then precious things, gracious and good to live with. But it is difficult to do this well. Better, if it may be done, to design all features together. At that time, too, I tried to make my clients see that furniture and furnishings, not built in as integral features of the building, should be designed as attributes of whatever furniture was built in and should be seen as minor parts of the building itself, even if detached or kept aside to be employed on occasion. But when the building itself was finished, the old furniture the clients already possessed went in with them to await the time when the interior might be completed. Very few of the houses were, therefore, anything but painful to me after the clients moved in and, helplessly, dragged the horrors of the old order along after them.

But I soon found it difficult, anyway, to make some of the furniture in the "abstract"; that is, to design it as architecture and make it "human" at the same time—fit for human use. I have been black and blue in some spot, somewhere, almost all my life from too intimate contacts with my own furniture. Human beings must group, sit or recline—confound them—and they must dine, but dining is much easier to manage and always was a great artistic opportunity. Arrangements for the informality of sitting comfortably, singly or in groups, where it is desirable or natural to sit, and still to belong in disarray to the scheme as a whole—that is a matter difficult to accomplish. But it can be done now, and should be done, because only those attributes of human comfort and convenience, made to belong in this digested or integrated sense to the architecture of the home as a whole, should be there at all, in Modern Architecture. For that matter about four-fifths of the contents of nearly every home could be given away with good effect to that home. But the things given away might go on to poison some other home. So why not at once destroy undesirable things . . . make an end of them?

Here then, in foregoing outline, is the gist of America's contribution to Modern American Architecture as it was already under way in 1893. But the gospel of elimination is one never preached enough. No matter how much preached, Simplicity is a spiritual ideal seldom organically reached. Nevertheless, by assuming the virtue by imitation—or by increasing structural makeshifts to get superficial simplicity—the effects may cultivate a taste that will demand the reality in course of time, but it may also destroy all hope of the real thing.

Standing here, with the perspective of long persistent effort in the direction of an organic Architecture in view, I can again assure you out of this initial experience that Repose is the reward of true simplicity and that organic simplicity is sure of Repose. Repose is the highest quality in the Art of Architecture, next to integrity, and a reward for integrity. Simplicity may well be held to the fore as a spiritual ideal, but when actually achieved, as in the "lilies of the field," it is something that comes of itself, something spontaneously born out of the nature of the doing whatever it is that is to be done. Simplicity, too, is a reward for fine feeling and straight thinking in working a principle, well in hand, to a consistent end. Solomon knew nothing about it, for he was only wise. And this, I think, is what Jesus meant by the text we have chosen for this discourse—"Consider the lilies of the field," as contrasted, for beauty, with Solomon.

Now, a chair *is* a machine to sit in.
A home *is* a machine to live in.
The human body *is* a machine to be worked by will.
A tree *is* a machine to bear fruit.
A plant *is* a machine to bear flowers and seeds.
And, as I've admitted before somewhere, a heart *is* a suction-pump. Does that idea thrill you?

Trite as it is, it may be as well to think it over because the *least* any of these things may be, *is* just that. All of them are that before they are anything else. And to violate that mechanical requirement in any of them is to finish before anything of higher purpose can happen. To ignore the fact is either sentimentality or the prevalent insanity. Let us acknowledge in this respect, that this matter of mechanics is just as true of the work of Art as it is true of anything else. But, were we to stop with that trite acknowledgment, we should only be living in a low, rudimentary sense. This skeleton rudiment accepted, *understood,* is the first condition of any fruit or flower we may hope to get from ourselves. Let us continue to call this flower and fruit of ourselves, even in this Machine Age, Art. Some Architects ,as we may see, now consciously acknowledge this "Machine" rudiment. Some will eventually get to it by circuitous mental labor. Some *are* the thing itself without question and already in need of "treatment." But "Americans" (I prefer to be more specific and say "Usonians") have been educated "blind" to the higher human uses of it all—while actually in sight of this higher human use all the while.

Therefore, now let the declaration that "all is machinery" stand nobly forth for what it is worth. But why not more profoundly declare that "Form follows Function" and let it go at that? Saying, "Form follows Function," is not only deeper, it is clearer, and it goes further in a more comprehensive way to say the thing to be said, because the implication of this saying includes the heart of the whole matter. It may be that Function follows Form, as, or if, you prefer, but it is easier thinking with the first proposition just as it is easier to stand on your feet and nod your head than it would be to stand on your head and nod your feet. Let us not forget that Simplicity of the Universe is very different from the Simplicity of a Machine.

New significance in Architecture implies new materials qualifying form and textures, requires fresh feeling, which will eventually qualify both as "ornament." But "Decoration" must be sent on its way or now be given the meaning that it has lost, if it is to stay. Since "Decoration" became acknowledged as such, and ambitiously set up for itself as Decoration, it has been a make-shift, in the light of this ideal of Organic Architecture. Any House Decoration, as such, is an architectural makeshift, however well it may be done, unless the decoration, so called, is part of the Architect's design in both concept and execution.

Since Architecture in the old sense died and Decoration has had to shift for itself more and more, all so-called Decoration has become *ornamental,* therefore no longer *integral.* There can be no true simplicity in either Architecture or Decoration under any such condition. Let Decoration, therefore, die for Architecture, and the Decorator become an Architect, but not an "Interior Architect."

Ornament can never be applied to Architecture any more than Architecture should ever be applied to Decoration. All ornament, if not developed within the nature of Architecture and as organic part of such expression, vitiates the whole fabric no matter how clever or beautiful it may be as something in itself.

Yes—for a century or more Decoration has been setting up for itself, and in our prosperous country has come pretty near to doing very well, thank you. I think we may say that it is pretty much all we have now to show as Domestic Architecture, as Domestic Architecture still goes with us at the present time. But we may as well face it. The Interior Decorator thrives with us because we have no Architecture. Any Decorator is the natural enemy of organic simplicity in Architecture. He, persuasive Doctor-of-Appearances that he *must* be when he becomes Architectural substitute, will give you an imitation of anything, even an imitation of imitative simplicity. Just at the moment, May 1930, he is expert in this imitation. France, the born Decorator, is now engaged with

"Madame," owing to the good fortune of the French market, in selling us this ready-made or made-to-order simplicity. Yes, Imitation Simplicity is the latest addition to imported "stock." The Decorators of America are now equipped to furnish *especially* this. Observe. And how very charming the suggestions conveyed by these imitations sometimes are!

Would you have again the general principles of the spiritual-ideal of organic simplicity at work in our Culture? If so, then let us reiterate: First, Simplicity is Constitutional Order. And it is worthy of note in this connection that 9 times 9 equals 81 is just as simple as 2 plus 2 equals 4. Nor is the obvious more simple necessarily than the occult. The obvious is obvious simply because it falls within our special horizon, is therefore easier for us to *see;* that is all. Yet all simplicity near or far has a countenance, a visage, that is characteristic. But this countenance is visible only to those who can grasp the whole and enjoy the significance of the minor part, as such, in relation to the whole when in flower. This is for the critics.

This characteristic visage may be simulated—the real complication glossed over, the internal conflict hidden by surface and belied by mass. The internal complication may be and usually is increased to create the semblance of and get credit for—simplicity. This is the Simplicity-lie usually achieved by most of the "surface and mass" architects. This is for the young architect.

Truly ordered simplicity in the hands of the great artist may flower into a bewildering profusion, exquisitely exuberant, and render all more clear than ever. Good William Blake says exuberance is *beauty,* meaning that it is so in this very sense. This is for the Modern Artist with the Machine in his hands. False Simplicity—Simplicity as an affectation, that is Simplicity constructed as a Decorator's outside put upon a complicated, wasteful engineer's or carpenter's "Structure," outside or inside—is not good enough Simplicity. It cannot be simple at all. But that is what passes for Simplicity, now that startling Simplicity-effects are becoming the *fashion.* That kind of Simplicity is *violent.* This is for "Art and Decoration."

Soon we shall want Simplicity inviolate. There is one way to get that Simplicity. My guess is, there is *only* one way really to get it. And that way is, on principle, by way of *Construction* developed as Architecture. That is for us, one and all.

THE IMPERIAL FAÇADE[1]

LEWIS MUMFORD

The decade between 1890 and 1900 saw the rise of a new period in American architecture. This period had, it is true, been dimly foreshadowed by the grandiose L'Enfant, but if the superficial forms resembled those of the early republic, and if the precedents of classic architecture again became a guide, the dawning age was neither a revival nor a continuation.

In the meanwhile, fresh influences had entered. The generation of students who had studied in the Ecole des Beaux Arts after the Civil War was ready, at last, to follow the lone trail which Richard H. Hunt had blazed. Richardson's most intimate disciples reacted against the stamp of his personality and sought a more neutral mode of expression, consecrated by established canons of good taste. On top of this, the introduction of steel-cage construction removed the necessity for solid masonry, and placed a premium upon the mask. The stage was set for a new act of the drama.

All these influences shaped the style of our architecture when it arose; but the condition that gave it a substantial base was the rise of a new order in America's economic life. Up to this time, the chief industrial problem had been to improve the processes of mechanical production and to stake out new areas for exploitation. One may compare these economic advances to the separate sorties of an army operating on a wide front: any lone adventurer might take his courage in his hands and exploit an invention, or sink an oil well, if he could find it. By 1890 the frontier had closed; the major resources of the country were under the control of the monopolist; it became more important to consolidate gains than freshly to achieve them. Separate lines of railroads were welded into systems; separate steel plants and oil plants were wrought into trusts; and where monopoly did not rest upon a foundation of natural advantage, the "gentleman's agreement" began its service as a useful substitute. The popular movements which sought to challenge the forces of this new regime—the labor movement, socialism, populism—had neither analyzed the situation with sufficient care nor attracted the adherence of the majority. The defeat of Henry George as a local political candidate was symbolic: by 1888 a humane thinker like Edward Bellamy had already accepted the defeat, had embraced the idea of the trust, and had conceived a comprehensive utopia on the basis of letting the process of monopoly go the limit, so that finally, by a mere yank of the levers, the vast economic organizations of the country would become the "property" of the people.

The drift to the open lands came to a full pause. The land-empire had been conquered, and its overlords were waxing in power and riches: the name "millionaire" became the patent of America's new nobility. With the shift

1. From *Sticks and Stones* (New York: Boni & Liveright, 1924), pp. 123–151, with minor changes in the text made by the author. Reprinted by permission of the author.

from industry to finance went a shift from the producing towns to the spending towns: architecture came to dwell in the stock exchanges, the banks, the shops, and the clubs of the metropolis; if it sought the countryside at all, it established itself in the villas that were newly laid out on hill and shore in the neighborhood of the great cities. The keys to this period are opulence and magnitude: "money to burn."

These years witnessed what the Roman historian, Ferrero, has called a *"véritable recommencement d'histoire."* In the new centers of privilege there arose a scale of living and a mode of architecture which, with all its attendant miseries, depletions, and exploitations, recalled the Rome of the first and second centuries after Christ. It is needless to say that vast acres of buildings, factories, shops, homes, were erected which had no relation at all to the imperial regime; for not everyone participated in either the benefits or the depressions that attended the growth of monopoly; but the accent of this period, the dominant note, was an imperial one. While the commonplace building of the time cannot be ignored, it remains, so to say, out of the picture.

Hardly had the process of concentration and consolidation begun before the proper form manifested itself. The occasion for its appearance was the World's Columbian Exposition, opened in 1893. In creating this fair, the enterprise and capacity for organization which the architects of Chicago had applied to the construction of the skyscraper transformed the unkempt wilderness of Jackson Park into the Great White City in the space of two short years. Here the architects of the country, particularly of New York and Chicago, appeared for the first time as a united profession, or, to speak more accurately, as a college. Led by the New Yorkers, who had come more decisively under European influence, they brought to this exposition the combination of skill and taste in all the departments of the work that had, two centuries earlier, created the magnificent formalities of Versailles. There was unity of plan in the grouping of the main buildings about the lagoon; there was unity of tone and color in the gleaming white façades; there was unity of effect in the use of classic orders and classic forms of decoration. Lacking any genuine unity of ideas and purposes—for Root had initially conceived of a variegated oriental setting—the architects of the exposition had achieved the effects of unity by subordinating their work to an established precedent. They chanted a Roman litany above the Babel of individual styles. It was a capital triumph of the academic imagination. If these main buildings were architecture, America had never seen so much of it at one time before. Even that belated Greco-Puritan, Mr. Charles Eliot Norton, was warm in praise.

It would be foolish to quarrel with the style that was chosen for these exposition buildings, or to deny its propriety. Messrs. McKim, White, Hunt, and Burnham divined that they were fated to serve Renaissance despots and emperors with more than Roman power, and unerringly they chose the proper form for their activities. Whereas Rome had cast its spell over the architects of the early Renaissance because they wished once more to enter into its life, the life of its sages and poets and artists, it attracted the architects of the White City because of its external features—because of its stereotyped canons and rules—because of the relatively small number of choices it offered for a lapse in taste—because of its skill in conspicuous waste, and because of that very noncommittal quality in its massive forms which permitted the basilica to become a church, or the temple to become a modern bank.

Of all the Renaissance architects, their impulses and interests were nearest, perhaps, to Robert Adam, whose church at West Wycombe could be turned into a ballroom by the simple act of removing the pews, and permitting the gay walls and decorations to speak for themselves. Behind the white stiff façade of the World's Fair buildings was the steel and glass structure of the engineer: the building spoke one language and the "architecture" another. If the coming of the skyscraper had turned masonry into veneer, here was a mode of architecture which was little but veneer.

In their place, at the Fair, these classic buildings were all that could be demanded: Mr. Geoffrey Scott's defense of the Baroque, in The Architecture of Humanism, applies particularly to its essential manifestations in the Garden and the Theater—and why not in the Fair? Form and function, ornament and design, have no inherent relation, one with the other, when the mood of the architect is merely playful: there is no use in discussing the anatomy of architecture when its only aim is fancy dress. As a mask, as a caprice, the classic orders are as justifiable as the icing on a birthday cake: they divert the eye without damaging the structure that they conceal. Unfortunately, the architecture of the Renaissance has a tendency to imitate the haughty queen who advised the commons to eat cake. Logically, it demands that a Wall Street clerk shall live like a Lombardy prince, that a factory should be subordinated to esthetic contemplation; and since these things are impossible, it permits "mere building" to become illiterate and vulgar below the standards of the most debased vernacular. Correct in proportion, elegant in detail, courteous in relation to each other, the buildings of the World's Fair were, nevertheless, only the simulacra of a living architecture: they were the concentrated expression of an age which sought to produce "values" rather than goods. In comparison with this new style, the romanticism of the Victorian Age, with its avid respect for the medieval building traditions, was honesty and dignity itself.

The Roman precedent, modified by the work of Louis XIV and Napoleon III, by Le Nôtre and Haussmann, formed the basis not merely for the World's Fair, but for the host of city plans that were produced in the two decades that followed. It seemed for a while as if the architect might take the place of the engineer as city planner, and that the mangled regularity of the engineer's gridiron plan, laid down without respect to topographic advantage or to use, might be definitely supplanted in the remodeled central districts and in the new extensions and suburbs of the American city. The evil of the World's Fair triumph was that it suggested to the civic enthusiast that every city might become a fair: it introduced the notion of the City Beautiful as a sort of municipal cosmetic, and reduced the work of the architect to that of putting a pleasing front upon the scrappy building, upon the monotonous streets and the mean houses, that characterized vast areas in the newer and larger cities.

If the engineer who had devoted himself to sewers and street-plans alone had been superficial, the architectural city planner who centered attention upon parkways alone, grand avenues alone, and squares like the Place de l'Etoile alone, was equally superficial. The civic center and the parkway represented the better and more constructive side of this effort: in Cleveland, in Pittsburgh, in Springfield, Mass., harmonious groups of white buildings raised their heads above the tangle of commercial traffic, and in the restoration of L'Enfant's plan for Washington, the realities of the imperial regime at length caught up with the dreamer born out of his due time. A good many of these plans, however, were pathetically immature. One of the reports for Manhattan, for example, devoted pages and pages to showing the improvement that would follow the demolition of the wall around Central Park—and the importance of clipped trees in the design of grand avenues!

Plainly, the architect did not face with sufficient realism the colossal task with which he was confronted in the renovation of the city. He accepted his improvements too much at the value placed upon them by the leaders of Big Business—as a creator of land-values, as an element in increasing the commercial attractiveness of the city. Did not Mr. Daniel Burnham himself point to the improvements in Periclean Athens, not as the embodiment of Athenian citizenship and religion at its highest point, but as a measure for increasing the attractiveness of the city to visitors from abroad? Cut off from his true function to serve and beautify the community, made an accessory of business itself, like the merest salesman or advertising agent, it is no wonder that the architect speedily lost his leadership; and that the initiative went once again into the hands of the engineer.

The main merit of all these efforts to perpetuate the World's Fair is that they sought to achieve some of the dignity and decisiveness of the formal plan. Their weakness was that they neglected new elements, like the billboard, the skysign, the subway, the tall building, which undermined the effects of the plan even when it was achieved. In their efforts to escape from the welter of misguided commercial enterprise, the advocates of the city beautiful placed too great reliance upon spots of outward order and decency; they took refuge in the paper symmetry of axial avenues and round-points, as one finds them in Haussmann's Paris, and neglected the deeper and more genuine beauties of, let us say, the High Street in Oxford or Chipping Camden, or of many another European town that had achieved completion in its essentials before the nineteenth century.

In short, the advocates of the city beautiful sought a remedy on paper which could be purchased only by a thorough reorganization of the community's life. If all this applies to the better side of the World's Fair, it touches even more emphatically the worse.

The twenty years between 1890 and 1910 saw the complete rehabilitation of the Roman mode, as the very cloak and costume of imperial enterprise. The main effort of architecture was to give an effect of dignity and permanence to the façades of the principal thoroughfares: the public buildings must dominate the compositions, numerous boulevards and avenues must concentrate the traffic at certain points and guide the stranger to the markets and amusements: where possible, as in the Chicago plan, by Messrs. Burnham and Bennett, avenues must be cut through the gridiron pattern of blocks in order to achieve these effects. If this imperial street system is somewhat arbitrary, and if the necessary work of grading, filling, demolishing, and purchasing existing property rights is extremely costly, the end, nevertheless, justifies the means—the architecture impresses and awes a populace that shares vicariously in its glories. Should the effect prove a little too austere and formidable, the monuments will be offset with circuses and hippodromes.

In all this, the World's Fair was a precise and classic example, for it reproduced in miniature the imperial order. When the panic of 1893 kept people away from the exhibitions of art, industry, and culture, sideshows were promptly introduced by the astute organizers. Beyond the serene classic façades, which recalled the elevation of a Marcus Aurelius, sprawled the barkers, the freaks, and the tricksters, whose gaudy booths might have reminded the spectator of the other side of the imperial shield—the gaminism of Petronius Arbiter. The transformation of these white façades into the Gay White Ways came during the next decade; whilst the sideshows achieved a separate existence as "Coney Island." On top of this came the development of the mildly gladiatorial spectacles of football and baseball: at first invented for playful exercise, they became a standard means of exhibition by more or less professional performers. The erection of numerous amphitheaters and arenas, such as the Yale Bowl, the Harvard Stadium, the Lewisohn Stadium, and their counterparts in the West, rounded out the imperial spectacle.

By a happy congruence of forces, the large-scale manufacture of Portland cement, and the reintroduction of the Roman method of concrete construction, came during the same period. Can anyone contemplate this scene and still fancy that imperialism was nothing more than a move for foreign markets and territories of exploitation? On the contrary, it was a tendency that expressed itself in every department of Western civilization, and if it appears most naked, perhaps, in America, that is only because, as in the earlier periods, there was so little here to stand in its way. Mr. Louis Sullivan might well complain, in The Autobiography of an Idea, that imperialism stifled the more creative modes of architecture which might have derived from our fine achievements in science, from our tentative experiments in democracy. It seems inevitable, however, that the dominant fact in our civilization should stamp the most important monuments and buildings with its image. In justice to the great professors of the classic style, Messrs. McKim and Burnham and Carrere and Hastings, one must admit that the age shaped them and chose them and used them for its ends. Their mode of building was almost unescapably determined by the milieu in which they worked.

The change in the social scene which favored an imperial setting was not without its effects upon the industries that supplied the materials for architecture, and upon the processes of building itself. Financial concentration in the stone quarries, for example, was abetted by the creation of a national system of rail transportation, and partly, perhaps, by the elaboration of the mechanical equipment for cutting and trimming stone beyond a point where a small plant could work economically. The result was that during this period numerous small local quarries, which had been called into existence by Richardson's fine eye for color contrasts, were allowed to lapse. Vermont marble and Indiana limestone served better the traditions that had been created in the White City.

The carrying of coals to Newcastle is always a pathetic practice; it remained for the imperial age to make it a subject for boasting. Just as many Connecticut towns whose nearby fields are full of excellent granite boulders, boast a bank or a library of remote marble, so New York City, which has a solid foundation of schist, gneiss, and limestone, can point to only a handful of buildings, notably the College of the City of New York and Mr. Goodhue's Church of the Intercession, in which these excellent local materials were used. The curious result of being able by means of railway transportation to draw upon the ends of the earth for materials has been, not variety, but monotony. Under the imperial order the architect was forced to design structures that were identical in style, treatment, and material, though they were placed thousands of miles apart and differed in every important function. This ignorance of regional resources is not incompatible with grand effects, or even on occasion with decently good architecture. But it does not profit by that fine adaptation to site, that justness of proportion in the size of window and slope of roof, which is an earnest of the architect's mastery of the local situation. Substitute Manila for the military colony of Timgad, or Los Angeles for Alexandria, and it is plain that we have here another aspect of Ferrero's generalization. Even architects whose place of work was nearer to the site of their buildings were, nevertheless, compelled to copy the style of the more successful practitioners in New York and Chicago.

In government, in industry, in architecture, the imperial age was one. The underlying policy of imperialism is to exploit the life and resources of separate regions for the benefit of the holders of privilege in the capital city. Under this rule, all roads lead literally to Rome. While, as the German historian, W. H. Riehl, points out, the provincial highroads served to bring the city out into the countryside, the railroads served to bring the major cities together and to drain the products of rural regions into the metropolis. It was no accident that the great triumphs of American architecture during the imperial period were the railroad stations; particularly the Pennsylvania and the Grand Central in New York, and the Union Station in Washington. Nor is it by mere chance that the Washington and the Pennsylvania stations are the monuments to two architects, McKim and Burnham, who worshiped most whole-heartedly at the imperial shrine. With capital insight, these men established the American Academy at Rome: they recognized their home.

Esthetically considered, it is true, perhaps, that the finest element in the Pennsylvania station is the train hall, where the architect has dealt sincerely with his steel elements and has not permitted himself to cast a fond, retrospective eye upon the Roman baths. When all allowances are made, however, there remains less for criticism in the railway stations and the stadiums—those genuinely Roman bequests—than in any of the other imperial monuments. Indeed, so well does Roman architecture lend itself to the railroad station that one of the prime virtues of such a building, namely ease of circulation, was even communicated to the New York Public Library, where it is nothing but a nuisance, since it both increases the amount of noise and diminishes the amount of space for reading rooms that are already overcrowded.

Here, indeed, is the capital defect of an established and formalized mode: it tends to make the architect think of a new problem in terms of an old solution for a different problem. Mr. Charles McKim, for example, found himself hampered in the competition over the New York Public Library because the demands of the librarian for a convenient and expeditious administration of his business interfered with the full-blown conception which Mr. McKim had in mind. All this happened after years of demonstration in the Boston Library of Messrs. McKim and White's failure to meet that problem squarely; and it apparently was not affected by Mr. McKim's experience with the great Columbia Library, which has ample space for everything except books. In short, the classic style served well enough only when the building to be erected had some direct relation to the needs and interests of the Roman world—the concourse of idlers in the baths or the tiers of spectators in the circuses and hippodromes. When it came face to face with our own day, it had but little to say, and it said that badly, as anyone who will patiently examine the superimposed orders on the American Telegraph Building in New York will discover for himself.

With the transition from republican to imperial Rome, numerous monuments were erected to the Divine Cæsar. Within a much shorter time than marked the growth of the imperial tradition in America, a similar edification of patriotic memories took place.

In the restoration of the original plan of Washington, which began in 1901, the axis of the plan was so altered as to make it pass through the Washington Monument; and at the same time the place of the Lincoln Memorial, designed by the late Mr. Henry Bacon, a pupil of Mr. McKim's, was assigned. This was the first of a whole series of temples devoted to the national deities. In the Lincoln Memorial, in the McKinley Memorial at Niles, Ohio, in the Hall of Fame at New York University, and in their prototype, Grant's Tomb, one feels not the living beauty of our American past, but the mortuary air of archæology. The America that Lincoln was bred in, the homespun and humane and humorous America that he wished to preserve, has nothing in common with the sedulously classic monument that was erected to his memory. Who lives in that shrine, I wonder—Lincoln, or the men who conceived it: the leader who beheld the mournful victory of the Civil War, or the generation that took pleasure in the mean triumph of the Spanish-American exploit, and placed the imperial standard in the Philippines and the Caribbean?

On the plane of private citizenship, a similar movement took place: while before 1890 one can count the tombs in our cemeteries that boast loudly of the owner's earthly possessions and power, from that time onward the miniature temple-mausoleum becomes more and more frequent. In fact, an entire history of architecture could be deduced from our cemeteries; all that has so far been described could be marked in the progress from the simple slab, carved in almost Attic purity with a weeping willow or a cubistic cherub, that characterized the eighteenth century, to the bad lettering and the more awkward headstones of the early nineteenth century; and from this to the introduction of polished granite and iron ornament in the post-Civil War cemetery, down to the mechanically perfect mausoleum, where the corpses are packed like the occupants of a subway train, that some of our more effusively progressive communities boast of today. As we live, so we die: no wonder Shelley described Hell as a place much like London.

The Roman development of New York, Chicago, Washington, and the lesser metropolises, had an important effect upon the homes of the people. Historically, the imperial monument and the slum-tenement go hand in hand. The same process that creates an unearned increment for the landlords who possess favored sites, contributes a generous quota—which might be called the unearned excrement—of depression, overcrowding, and bad living, in the dormitory districts of the city. This had happened in imperial Rome; it had happened again in Paris under Napoleon III, where Haussmann's sweeping reconstructions created new slums in the districts behind the grand avenues, quite as bad, if far less obvious, as those that had been cleared away; and it happened once again in our American cities. Whereas in Rome a certain limit, however, was placed upon the expansion of the city because of the low development of vehicular traffic, the rise of mechanical transportation placed no bounds at all on the American city. If Rome was forced to create huge engineering projects like aqueducts and sewers in order to cleanse the inhabitants and remove the offal of its congested districts, the American city followed the example of the modern Romes like London and Paris by devising man-sewers, in which the mass of plebeians could be daily drained back and forth between their dormitories and their factories.

So far from relieving congestion, these colossal pieces of engineering only made more of it possible: by pouring more feeder lines into the central district of New York, Boston, Chicago, or where you will, rapid transit increased the housing congestion at one end and the business-congestion at the other. As for the primary sewer system devised for the imperial metropolis, it could scarcely even claim, with rapid transit, that it was a valuable commercial investment. The water outlets of New York are so thoroughly polluted that not merely have the shad and the oyster beds vanished from the Hudson River, where both once flourished, but it is a serious question whether the tides can continue to transport their vast load of sewage without a preliminary reduction of its content. Like the extension of the water conduits into the Adirondacks, all these necessary little improvements add to the per capita cost of living in an imperial metropolis, without providing a single benefit that a smaller city with no need for such improvements does not enjoy. In the matter of public parks, for example, the Committee on Congestion in New York, in 1911, calculated that the park space needed for the East Side alone, on the scale provided by the city of Hartford, would be greater than the entire area of Manhattan Island. In short, even for its bare utilitarian requirements, the mass-city, as the Germans call it, costs more and gives less than communities which have not had imperial greatness inflicted upon them.

As to the more positive improvements under the imperial regime, history leaves no doubt as to their dubious character, and current observation only reinforces history's lesson. In discussing the growth of the tenement in Rome after the Great Fire, Friedlander says:

"The motives for piling up storeys were as strong as ever: the site for Cæsar's Forum had cost over £875,000 compensation to tenants and ground landlords. Rome had loftier houses than modern capital. A disproportionately large part of the area available for building was monopolized by the few, in consequence of the waste of space in the plethoric architecture of the day, and a very considerable portion was swallowed up by the public places, such as the imperial forums, which took up six hectares, as well as by the traffic regulations and extensions of the streets. The transformation and decoration of Rome by the Cæsars enhanced the scarcity of housing, as did Napoleon III's improvements in Paris. A further adjutory cause of the increase in the price of dwellings was the habit of speculation in house property (which Crassus had practiced in great style) and the monopoly of the proprietors, in consequence of which houses were let and sublet."

It would be tedious to draw out the parallel: given similar social conditions in America we have not been able to escape the same social results, even down to the fact that the palliatives of private philanthropy flourish here again as they had not flourished anywhere on the same scale since the Roman Empire. So much for imperial greatness. When an architect like Mr. Edward Bennett can say, as he did in The Significance of the Fine Arts: "House the people densely, if necessary, but conserve great acres for recreation," we need not be in doubt as to who will profit by the density and who will profit, at the other end, by the recreation. It is not merely that the park must be produced to remedy the congestion: it is even more that the congestion must be produced in order to provide for the park. To profit by both the disease and the remedy is one of the masterstrokes of imperialist enterprise. Mr. Daniel Burnham said of the World's Fair, according to Mr. Bennett and Mr. Charles Moore, "that it is what the Romans would have wished to create in permanent form." One may say of our imperial cities that they are what the Romans did create—but whether the form will be permanent or not is a matter we may leave to the sardonic attentions of history.

For my own part, I think we have at last acquired a criterion which will enable us to sum up the architecture of the imperial age, and deal justly with these railroad stations and stadiums, these sewers and circuses, these aqueducts and parkways and grand avenues. Our imperial architecture is an architecture of compensation: it provides grandiloquent stones for people who have been deprived of bread and sunlight and all that keeps man from becoming vile. Behind the monumental façades of our metropolises trudges a landless proletariat, doomed to the servile routine of the factory system; and beyond the great cities lies a countryside whose goods are drained away, whose children are uprooted from the soil on the prospect of easy gain and endless amusements, and whose remaining cultivators are steadily drifting into the ranks of an abject tenantry. This is not a casual observation: it is the translation of the last three census reports into plain English. Can one take the pretensions of this architecture seriously; can one worry about its esthetics or take delight in such forms as Mr. Pope's Temple of the Scottish Rite in Washington, or Mr. Bacon's Lincoln Memorial? Yes, perhaps—if one refuses to look beyond the mask.

Even in some of its proudest buildings, the imperial show wears thin; and one need not peer into the slums beyond in order to realize its defects. The rear of the Metropolitan Museum or the Brooklyn Museum, for example, might be the rear of a row of Bronx tenements or Long Island City factories, so gaunt and barren and hideous is their aspect. If the imperial age was foreshadowed in the World's Fair, it has received its apotheosis in the museum. In contrast to the local museums one still finds occasionally in Europe, which are little more than extensions of the local curio cabinet, the imperial museum is essentially a loot-heap, a comprehensive repository for plunder. The sage Viollet-le-Duc once patly said that he preferred to see his apples hanging on a tree, rather than arranged in rows in the fruit shops; but the animus of the museum is to value the plucked fruit more than the tree that bore it.

Into the museum come the disjecta membra of other lands, other cultures, other civilizations. All that had once been a living faith and practice is here reduced to a separate specimen, pattern, or form. For the museum, the world of art has already been created: the future is restricted to a duplication of the perfected past. This animus is identic with that which made the Romans so skillful in copying Greek statues and so dull in carving their own; a desirable habit of humility were it not for the fact that the works of art in the past could not have been created had our ancestors been so punctual in respect to finished designs. The one thing the museum cannot attempt to do is to supply a soil for living art: all that it can present is a pattern for reproduction. To the extent that an insincere or imitative art is better than no art at all, the Imperial Age marked an advance: to the extent, however, that a living art is a fresh gesture of the spirit, the museum confessed all too plainly that the age had no fresh gestures to make; on that score, it was a failure, and the copying of period furniture and the design of period architecture were the livid proofs of that failure.

The museum is a manifestation of our curiosity, our acquisitiveness, our essentially predatory culture; and these qualities were copiously exhibited in the architecture of imperialism. It would be foolish to reproach the great run of architects for exploiting the characteristics of their age; for even those who in belief and design have remained outside the age—such resolute advocates of a medieval polity as Dr. Ralph Adams Cram—have not been able to divert its currents. In so far as we have learned to care more for empire than for a community of freemen living the good life, more for dominion over palm and pine than for the humane discipline of ourselves, the architect has but enshrined our desires. The opulence, the waste of resources and energies, the perversion of human effort represented in this architecture are but the outcome of our general scheme of working and living. Architecture, like government, is about as good as a community deserves. The shell that we create for ourselves marks our spiritual development as plainly as that of a snail denotes its species. If sometimes architecture becomes frozen music, we have ourselves to thank when it is a pompous blare of meaningless sounds.

MUSIC FOR THE MAN WHO ENJOYS *HAMLET* [1]

B. H. HAGGIN

You reach home, let us say, with expectations of a quiet dinner, of slippers, easy chair, a much read copy of *Hamlet* to take your mind far from the wearying details, arguments, and vexations of the long day at the office. And you learn with dismay that this is the night of the third concert of the city's major series, that your wife is going, and you are going with her.

"Schnabel is playing!"—and it is evident that your eyes should light up in anticipation; but instead you groan in recollection. Later, after a hurried change of clothes, a rushed dinner, seated uncomfortably beside your wife in the concert hall while a gray-haired man plays something called Sonata in

1. Reprinted from *Music for the Man Who Enjoys Hamlet* by B. H. Haggin, by permission of Alfred A. Knopf, Inc. Copyright 1944 by B. H. Haggin.

B flat major by Schubert, you think, as you fold and unfold your program: "It seems to mean a lot to Schnabel; and I suppose it means something to all these other people; but it doesn't make sense to me." But by the time Schnabel is playing Beethoven's Sonata Opus 111 your boredom has given way to irritation; and savagely throwing away the shreds of your program you think: "I'll bet it doesn't mean any more to the others or to the old boy on the stage than it means to me. It *doesn't* make sense; and they're only pretending it does."

Some of them may be pretending; but the music Schnabel is playing does make sense—to him, and to others; it makes as much sense, and the same kind of sense, as *Hamlet* makes to you. You don't see that; but you will, I think, if you consider what *Hamlet* is and what it does.

To begin with, *Hamlet* is an example of the employment, on a very large scale, of an artistic medium. The nature of this employment we may see more easily in a small-scale example—in one of the *Sonnets:*

Full many a glorious morning have I seen
Flatter the mountain-tops with sovereign eye,
Kissing with golden face the meadows green,
Gilding pale streams with heavenly alchymy;
Anon permit the basest clouds to ride
With ugly rack on his celestial face,
And from the forlorn world his visage hide,
Stealing unseen to west with this disgrace:
Even so my sun one early morn did shine,
With all-triumphant splendour on my brow:
But, out! alack! he was but one hour mine,
The region cloud hath mask'd him from me now.
    Yet him for this my love no whit disdaineth;
    Suns of the world may stain when heaven's sun staineth.

Other men have had thoughts and emotions about the love they have possessed and lost; what they have not done is to elaborate these thoughts and emotions into the complex form of words, rich in rhythmed sound, in images, in overtones of sense and feeling, in which Shakespeare makes *his* thoughts and emotions on the subject articulate. The articulateness in words in metrical patterns is common enough: it produces huge quantities of worthless poetry by children, adolescents, adults. In Shakespeare's sonnet, however, the quality of the mere articulateness in the medium is itself uncommon; and its complexities and splendors represent in addition the workings of an uncommonly complex and rich mind and personality. Involved, that is, with the articulateness, operating through it, crystallized in the completed poem, are Shakespeare's personal resources—what he is in character, mind, feeling, what he has lived through, what his experience has done to him, what insights it has given him. This is true even of the sonnet; and it is true more obviously, more richly, more excitingly, of *Hamlet.*

If you are moved, excited, exalted by *Hamlet,* if for a time afterwards the real world appears to you wonderfully changed, that is because for several hours you have been looking through Shakespeare's eyes at an imagined world created between the covers of a book or on the stage of a theatre—a world in which the natures of the human beings who inhabit it, the situations in which they are placed, the things they do and say, all express significances which life has come to have for this man with perceptions and insights that you and I do not possess. If *Hamlet* leaves you with an impression of greatness, that impression is one of the greatness of mind and spirit which Shakespeare reveals in his play. And if the insights of that mind and spirit impress you as much as they do, that is because of the richness of the poetic form in which they are embodied and presented to you.

Which brings us to this important fact: that if you are affected by *Hamlet* it is, first of all, because you have the personal resources which enable you to appreciate the insights it conveys; but it is also—and this is the important thing for our discussion—because you have the susceptibility to the poetic medium which enables you to be affected by the poetic form in which these insights are conveyed. I say this is the important thing for our discussion because similar insights are conveyed in Schubert's B flat Sonata and Beethoven's Opus 111, but through a different artistic medium; and if they do not get through to your mind it is because the *medium* is one to which, at the moment, you are not susceptible.

"Perhaps even Shakespeare never reached that final state of illumination that is expressed in some of Beethoven's late music," says Sullivan in his excellent book about Beethoven. If the state of illumination that is conveyed to you by Shakespeare is not conveyed by Beethoven in his second movement of the Sonata Opus 111, the reason is that you are susceptible to Shakespeare's medium of artistic communication but not to Beethoven's; and you will understand how this might be so, if you consider how long and how much you have read Shakespeare, who uses the words that are your own medium of communication and expression, and how few encounters you have had with Beethoven, whose musical idiom is not that of the folk songs or school songs or Broadway songs which you may be familiar with.

Understanding this, you may be disposed to try an experiment—which is to listen to the opening passage of that movement of Opus 111 at least once every evening for a couple of weeks, in order to become thoroughly familiar with it, and to see whether, as you come to know it, you begin to get from it some communication of what a man like Beethoven might feel at the end of his life—the sense of experience mastered, of profound lessons learned, of resignation, inner illumination achieved. You can hear the passage on side 3 of the Columbia recording of Egon Petri's performance (play it to the point about one and a half inches from the first groove; and for the present resist the temptation to go further than that point).

You will be serving the purpose of the experiment and increasing its chance of success if you listen in the same way to another passage—the opening statement up to the faint rumble in the bass, in the first movement of Schubert's Sonata in B flat, which in a different way also communicates the sense of profound lessons learned, inner illumination achieved. By this time Victor may have issued the English recording of Schnabel's performance.

And listen also to two other passages for what they may communicate to you. One is the beginning of the third movement of Beethoven's Trio Opus 97—the two statements of the piano that are echoed by the violin and cello, which you can hear on side 6 of Victor's recording of the Rubinstein-Heifetz-Feuermann performance or on side 5 of the old Victor recording of the Cortot-Thibaud-Casals performance. The other is the statement of the piano with which the first movement of Beethoven's Piano Concerto No. 4 begins; and hear it as it is played by Schnabel on the Victor record, not as it is played by Gieseking on the Columbia record.

I have suggested a couple of weeks; but obviously the experiment doesn't have to stop after two weeks. Give yourself all the time you may need to find those passages of music acquiring significance for you, or on the other hand to satisfy yourself that music is not for you the medium of artistic communication which you are willing to believe it is for others.

II

If now those passages convey significance to you, we can go on—first of all to get a more precise idea of this significance and how it is conveyed.

In the sonnet I quoted, or in one of Hamlet's soliloquies, we see a complex form of words embody and communicate a complex synthesis of thought and emotion. And if anyone were to ask "What thought, what emotion?" the answer would be "The thought and emotion expressed and defined by that form of words." One can say that the sonnet is concerned with the love which is given and then withheld; one can say further that this love is compared with the sun which lights the earth and then is hidden by clouds; but to do this is not to convey the rich overtones of sense and feeling that are expressed by

> Full many a glorious morning have I seen
> Flatter the mountain-tops with sovereign eye,
> Kissing with golden face the meadows green,
> Gilding pale streams with heavenly alchymy;

and the rest of the poem. The only way of conveying those overtones is to state the precise form of words that Shakespeare himself devised for this purpose.

A painter, too, may be aware only of choosing a bit of paint and placing it on the canvas in relation to a number of other bits; but the choice, the placing, the relation involve exercise of judgment—which is to say that they involve the whole man, the sum at that moment of his experience, thought, emotion, insight. What is involved in the choices and uses of the bits of paint reveals itself through them; and in the end the completed integrated arrangement of lines, colors, planes, masses, and forms is a visual embodiment and communication of a particular synthesis of that experience, thought, emotion, insight.

Roger Fry has described the process of a Cézanne still-life, in which bottles, pears, and apples, so commonplace as to have no emotional associations in themselves, are "deprived of all those specific characters by which we ordinarily apprehend their concrete existence," and are "reduced to pure elements of space and volume" which are then "coordinated and organized by the artist's sensual intelligence." He refers to Cézanne's own conception that it was out of these relations of formal elements that emotion was to emanate; and he says: "One may wonder whether painting has ever aroused graver, more powerful, more massive emotions than those to which we are compelled by some of Cézanne's masterpieces in this genre." And these emotions to which we are compelled—not by the subjects of the paintings, but by the pictorial treatment of the subjects—these grave, powerful, massive emotions are something we have no way of knowing or defining or conveying, other than by those relations of formal elements on the canvas that were Cézanne's way.

So with the piece of music that is a formal organization of sound—or sounds—in time. The sounds have no external references to objects or ideas; what they have is the internal coherence of a kind of grammar of their own; and the relations in which they are placed—in a texture of horizontal lines of sounds in sequence (melody) and vertical sounds in simultaneous combination (harmony), articulated by duration and stress (rhythm), and colored by the timbres of instruments or voices—are governed basically by this grammar, which is used in an individual style by each composer, in obedience to the laws of his own being. He too, that is, may be aware only of choosing a sound and placing it in relation to a number of others; but the choice, the placing, the relation, involving exercise of judgment as they do, involve the sum at that moment of his experience, thought, emotion, insight—of which a particular synthesis is finally embodied and communicated in the completed formal arrangement of sounds. If anyone were to ask about the second movement of Beethoven's Sonata Opus 111 "What thought, what emotion, what insight?" one could say, as I did earlier, "The sense of experience mastered, lessons learned, resignation, inner illumination achieved." But one would have to use the same words about the opening of Schubert's B flat Sonata, to describe experience mastered, lessons learned, resignation and illumination achieved that are different from Beethoven's and expressed in different musical terms. This demonstrates the inadequacy of the words, and the fact that here again we have no way of knowing or defining or conveying the synthesis of experience and emotion that is embodied in each piece of music, other than by the formal construction in sound that each man used for the purpose.

One might, for that matter, find no other words than "experience mastered, lessons learned, resignation and illumination achieved" for other pieces of music by Beethoven himself—that is, for the same synthesis of experience and emotion that embodies itself in different constructions of sound. From this we realize that in dealing with a work of art we are concerned not with meaning but with meaning as embodied in form. We read Shakespeare not merely for his profound insights, but for these insights as made explicit and affecting in his rich poetic forms; and so with Cézanne's powerful emotions, and the inner illumination and exaltation of Beethoven in his last years. We are, then, interested in each different formal construction on canvas from which we get the impact of the same powerful emotions, each different construction of sound which conveys to us the same inner illumination and exaltation.

III

I have gone into all this to get you to see that just as the way to understand Shakespeare's poem is to read it, and the way to understand Cézanne's still-life is to look at it, so the way—the only way—to understand Beethoven's or Schubert's sonata movement is the one you have already used successfully with its opening passage—to listen to it. It was natural for you, when the music made no sense, to ask to be told what its sense was, and to ask to be told in words, since you were accustomed to think of sense as expressible in words. And it was necessary for you to learn to apprehend from a phrase of music a sense which was not definable by words—which was defined solely by the particular organization of sounds in that phrase of music. You may say that I did use words to describe it and help you apprehend it; but they did not really describe what in the end you had to apprehend from the music and would have apprehended even without my words; and you will discover, when you are accustomed to the medium, that the meaning of a phrase of Beethoven or Schubert is grasped immediately with the sounds, and that if there is any difficulty, what is needed is not explanation of the phrase in words but repeated hearing of it. And you cannot get a wrong idea by listening to Beethoven or Schubert himself, but you will get some very wrong ideas by listening to the people who undertake to speak for him.

It was natural for you also, when the music made no sense, to think that you might understand it if you were told things about it—about the man who wrote it, the period in which he lived, the ideas, tendencies, forces, which influenced him. But when you have experienced the joyousness, buoyancy, and exuberant playfulness embodied in Beethoven's Eighth Symphony you may be surprised to discover the vexations and turmoil that filled his daily life at the time he was writing this work; and you will learn from this that the biographical and historical background of a work of art may be quite irrelevant to it. For it is the inner core of personal qualities, emotions, and insights created by a lifetime of experience that governs the artist's selection and arrangement of words or paints or sounds in a poem or picture or symphony; and although this inner core is constantly altered and developed by his continuing experience, it is not affected by any and every happening of the day. When this inner development in Beethoven had reached the emotions and attitudes we are made aware of by the Eighth Symphony, they pressed for expression in the sounds of this symphony, unaffected by the external turmoil that was irrelevant to them. Earlier, too, it was the heroic emotions and attitudes that Beethoven had developed in the face of disaster which operated through his articulateness in his medium to produce the *Eroica* Symphony; if there had been no French Revolution there would have been no dedication to Napoleon to tear up when he made himself emperor, but there would have been the same *Eroica* Symphony. And Ernest Newman once pointed to the striking differences in the three great symphonies that Mozart wrote in those two months of wretchedness and despair in the summer of 1788, as evidence of the fact that "the creative imagination of a great artist functions too deep down within him to be greatly affected by anything that may happen on the surface of his life or his being." It is not, then, the biographical or historical background that gives us a clue to the meaning of the music; it is instead the music that often gives us our only clue to what was going on inside the composer.

But to know even relevant biographical and historical details *about* a work of art would not make the relations of elements *in* the work of art clearer and more significant. It is true, as we have seen, that the whole man was involved in the process which produced the Cézanne still-life; and it is further true that with the man there must have been involved, more remotely, the influences which had operated on him—the general ideas, the social and political conditions of the time. But when you knew these things that were involved in the process you would still have to perceive and feel the impact of the formal relations of space and volume that are the result of the process; and for this the things you knew about Cézanne's life would be neither necessary nor helpful. And so with Beethoven's or Schubert's sonata.

Nor do you need the technical knowledge of the professional musician. A piece of music is, to begin with, an organization of sounds; experiencing it begins with hearing the sounds and the way they are related in each phrase, the relation of one phrase to the next in the progression; and learning to hear these relations is at the same time a process by which you learn to follow the grammar and logic of musical thought, the operations by which it proceeds; but you can do all this without knowing the technical facts and names of what you are hearing. For one of those opening passages to acquire significance for you it was necessary to hear the sounds and their relations, for which you did not have to know that the tonic of C major was followed by a second inversion of the dominant seventh—any more than you have to know that a particular brown which you see in a painting is called burnt umber, and another which is placed in relation to it is called yellow ochre. What is true is that when you have heard something you will find the name of it convenient to use in referring to it; and someone else will find the name convenient to use to refer to it when talking to you about it. But a great many matters which the professional musician is concerned with, and the terms which he uses in discussing them—these you don't have to know anything about.

And now go on to hear what comes after those opening passages.

THE LISTENER[1]

ROGER SESSIONS

We are all very much concerned, these days, with the listener—the person who neither makes music nor performs it, but simply listens to it. The market is flooded with books of all sorts, fulfilling all sorts of functions for all sorts of listeners, from the child to "the man who enjoys *Hamlet*" and even "the intelligent listener"—analyses to edify him, critical chit-chat to flatter him, and gossip to amuse him. We have grade school, high school, and university courses designed to inform him and, if possible, to educate him in "appreciation," in "intelligent listening," and even "creative listening." On the radio he may find quiz programs, interviews with personalities, broadcast orchestra rehearsals, and spoken program notes, which have been known on occasion to be so long that there is not enough time for the broadcast of the music. Surely we are leaving no stone unturned in the effort to prepare the listener fully for the strenuous task of listening to music.

This is actually a peculiar state of affairs. Music, and in fact art in general, is not one of the so-called necessities of life, nor does it yield us any of the creature comforts associated with the standard of living of which we are so proud. Why then should we be so concerned about the listener? Is not music available to him, if he wants it? Should we not rather demand simply that the listener be given the best products available? Should we not rather concern ourselves with the quality of our music, and with ways of producing the highest quality, with providing the best possible education for our young musicians, and with creating opportunities for them to function according to their merits? In truth, should we not rather devote ourselves to improving the quality of our music, and to seeing that music of the highest quality is available for all that wish to hear it?

Of course, we have no such choice of alternatives; and the concern that is felt for the listener today is no chance development but the result of the

1. From *The Musical Experience of Composer, Performer, Listener* (Princeton: Princeton University Press, 1950), pp. 87–106. Copyright, 1950, Princeton University Press.

situation in which music finds itself in our contemporary world. Possibly still more than this it is the result of these conditions as they have developed in the United States. In saying that it is "a peculiar state of affairs" I certainly do not wish to imply that it is one to be, if possible, abolished or even, in any fundamental sense, corrected. It is rather a phenomenon to be noted and one which, I think, must be thoroughly understood if our culture is to achieve, as we all wish, a healthy growth. It is not a condition in any basic respect characteristic only of our musical or even our artisric life; it lies at the very core of the situation created by technology and all of its various ramifications; by repercussions, that is, of technology upon the economic, the political, the social and therefore upon the whole cultural world. This situation is a fact to be dealt with, intelligently, let us hope. And while we may smile at some of its manifestations and raise our eyebrows at others, we will certainly be wasting both time and energy if we spend them deploring it. We should also be pursuing cultural mirages if we either ignored it or remained unaware of the questions it poses.

The point is that we are trying with all our means to increase the number of listeners to music, and that not just because we believe culture to be a good thing which should be made available to all members of a democratic society, though we believe this too, of course. It is a part of our tradition, and we have been at pains to educate ourselves. We have even covered a great deal of ground very rapidly; and though we sometimes let ourselves be unduly impressed by mere statistics which mean actually less than we think they do, there is nevertheless a residue of quite genuine achievement not to be gainsaid.

But the condition I have been speaking of—that is, our preoccupation with the listener, and our solicitude for his problems—has quite other causes. The crucial fact is that within a space of approximately twenty-five years the musical public has grown in size from some thousands, mostly in the larger centers, to a so-called "mass audience" numbering many millions. The development of the radio, plus the expansion of the gramophone business, more than any other factors, have brought this about and have undoubtedly played a major role in stimulating interest, not only in concerts and operatic performances, but in musical activity of all sorts.

Thus a far greater quantity of music must be furnished, for so large a public, than was ever dreamed of before. I am of course speaking of performances rather than compositions, and am taking into account the facts both of recorded broadcasts and the nation-wide broadcasts of the large networks. The point is that both the entrepreneurs and the musicians, those who purvey and those who produce, become thus necessarily involved in business enterprise on a large scale. Even before the radio and the gramophone had begun to play the decisive part they do in our musical economy today, various factors, economic and otherwise, had already greatly restricted the role of private patronage in our public musical life. The purveyors of music, however disinterested, found themselves obliged to count costs and to concern themselves with profits. I say "however disinterested," and indeed I feel that in order to understand the situation as it has developed it is necessary to assume this disinterestedness. For the situation I am describing has not been made by individuals at all. It is the result of economic facts the like of which have never existed before; and the facts in question are far too large in scope, too intricately interwoven with the very bases of contemporary life, to be influenced one way or the other by the decisions of individuals.

When music or any other product is furnished to millions of individuals, it is bound to become necessary to consider the tastes of those individuals in relation to the product offered them. Those who furnish the product are obliged to produce as efficiently and as cheaply as possible the goods which they can sell to the most people; they are obliged, furthermore, to try to persuade the people to whom they sell that it is preferable to buy the goods that are most cheaply produced; it is furthermore necessary to do everything possible to enhance the value of the goods sold. If they fail to do these things they are taking foolish economic risks. The larger the quantities involved, the greater the potential profits; but while this is true, it is also true that the risks of possible catastrophic loss are greater. These facts are elementary; not only do they apply vitally to the situation of music today, but I believe that an understanding of them is absolutely indispensable if we are to understand any economic, political, or social aspects whatever of the contemporary world.

In brief, the "listener" has become, in relation to these facts, the "consumer," and however unaware we as individuals are of this, it is nevertheless the basic explanation of our interest in him. Though neither he nor we have chosen this role for him, circumstances have made it inevitable. In relation to the same facts (and please note the phrase carefully, for I shall try to show later that these are not the only facts), the status of the artist in our society has undergone a remarkable change. He has become (in relation to the same facts) no longer a cultural citizen, one of the cultural assets of the community with purely cultural responsibilities, but what is sometimes called a cog in the economic machine. He is asked and even in a sense required to justify his existence as a plausible economic risk; to, as we say, "sell" himself as a possible source of economic profit. Then, having done so, he must produce what is required of him in this sense. He, too, has an interest in the listener; it is the listener who buys his wares and therefore justifies his continued existence as an efficient cog. He has to be constantly aware, in fact, of the requirements of the machinery in approximately the terms I have outlined above. For the aims of business are essentially short-range aims, and it is doubtful whether business, as such, can conceivably operate on any other basis. It can allow itself the luxury of the long-range view only to the extent that it builds up enormous surpluses which make risks economically possible, and even then only under circumstances offering reasonable hope of long-range rewards.

Let me say once again that I do not consider this the entire picture of our cultural situation or of our cultural prospects. I shall later try to show why I do not believe it to be so. Furthermore, these remarks are generalizations, and subject to elaboration, with intricate scoring and with many subtleties of nuance. I do not intend to score them for you here. But we cannot understand the listener unless we know who he is in terms of the conditions actually prevalent. We must see him, in other words, not as an abstraction but as an existing and concrete figure in our musical society.

But it is not mainly in his role of consumer that I wish to speak of the listener. The question for us is rather his own experience of music—what hearing and understanding consist in, and, finally, what discrimination involves. What, in other words, is his relationship to music? How can he get the most from it? How can music mean the most to him? In what does his real education consist? Finally, how can he exercise his powers of discrimination in such a way as to promote valid musical experience in others and, so to speak, in the world in general?

I think we can distinguish four stages in the listener's development. First, he must hear; I have already indicated what I mean by this. It is not simply being present when music is performed, nor is it even simply recognizing bits of the music—leit-motifs, or themes, or salient features in a score. It is rather, as it were, opening one's ears to the sounds as they succeed each other, discovering whatever point of contact one can find, and in fact following the music as well as one can in its continuity. We perhaps tend to ignore the fact that listeners are, like composers and performers, variously endowed, and also that they differ very widely in experience. But this initial stage in listening to music is an entirely direct one; the listener brings to the music whatever he can bring, with no other preoccupation than that of hearing. This is of course what is to be desired; it is the condition of his really hearing. He will hear the music only to the extent that he identifies himself with it, establishing a fresh and essentially naïve contact with it, without preconceived ideas and without strained effort.

The second stage is that of enjoyment, or shall we say the primary response. It is perhaps hardly discernible as a "second stage" at all: the listener's reaction is immediate and seems in a sense identical with the act of hearing. Undoubtedly this is what many listeners expect. And yet, on occasion, one may listen to music attentively, without any conscious response to it until afterwards; one's very attention may be so absorbed that a vivid sense of the sound is retained but a sense of communication is experienced only later. It is this sense of communication to which I refer under the term "enjoyment"; obviously, one may not and often does not, in any real sense, "enjoy" what is being communicated. There is certainly some music that we never "enjoy"; experience inevitably fosters discrimination, and there is certainly some truth even in the frequent, seemingly paradoxial, statement that "the more one loves music, the less music one loves." The statement is true in a sense if we understand it as applying to the experience of the individual, and not as a general rule. But if our relation to music is a healthy one—that is to say, a direct and a simple one—our primary and quite spontaneous effort will be to enjoy it. If this effort becomes inhibited it will be by reason of experience and the associations that inevitably follow in its train. We shall in that case have acquired a sense of musical values, and our specific response will be curtailed in deference to the more general response which our musical experience has given us.

The third of the four phases I have spoken of consists in what we call "musical understanding." I must confess that I am not altogether pleased with this term. To speak quite personally if not too seriously, a composer will certainly have every right to feel pleased, but he may not feel entirely flattered, when he is told "I love your music, but of course I have no right to an opinion—I don't really understand it." In what does "musical understanding" consist? The difficulty, I think, comes from the fact that while, as I tried to show in the first chapter, the instinctive bases of music, the impulses which constitute its raw materials, are essentially of the most primitive sort, yet the organization of these materials, the shaping of them into a means of communication and later into works of art, is, and historically speaking has been, a long and intricate process and one which has few obvious contacts with the world of ordinary experience. The technique of every art has, of course, its esoteric phases; but in the case of visual art even these phases are relatively accessible to the layman, since he can, if he is really interested, grasp them in terms of quite ordinary practical activity. He will have learned early in his life to be aware of the basic facts of size, contour, color, and perspective on very much the same terms as are required for his perception of visual art. He can to a certain extent appreciate the artist's problems in these terms and can define his response, at least on an elementary level, in terms satisfactory to himself. This is even truer in the case of literary art, since he constantly uses words and to a greater or a lesser degree expresses himself by their means. Like Molière's "bourgeois gentlemen," he has talked in prose all his life. His feeling for the values of both visual and literary art consists therefore in a high degree of refinement, and an extension, of experiences which are thoroughly familiar to him, through analogies constantly furnished by his ordinary life.

In the case of music there are no such clear analogies. The technical facts which are commonplace to the composer, and even many of those proper to the performer, have no clear analogies in the ordinary experience of the nonmusician. The latter finds them quite mysterious and, as I have already pointed out, tends to exaggerate both their uniqueness and their inaccessibility to the layman. And if the latter finds it difficult to conceive of the mere fact of inner hearing and auditory imagination, how much more difficult will he find such a conception as, for instance, tonality, or the musical facts on which the principles of what we call "musical form" are based. He is likely not only to regard music *per se* as a book in principle closed to him, but, through the impressive unfamiliarity of whatever technical jargon he chances to hear, to misunderstand both the nature and the role of musical technique. It is likely to seem to him something of an abstraction, with an existence of its own, to which the sensations and impressions he receives from music are only remotely related, as by-products. How often, for instance, have I been asked whether the study and mastery of music does not involve a knowledge of higher mathematics! The layman is only too likely to react in either one of two ways, or in a combination of both. He is likely, that is, either to regard music as something to which he is essentially a stranger, or else to regard its generally accepted values as arbitrary, pretentious, and academic, and both to give to it and to receive from it far less than his aptitudes warrant.

The surprising thing is that all of these conclusions are based on a mistaken idea as to the real meaning of musical "understanding." Technique is certainly useful, not to say indispensable, to the composer or the performer; a knowledge of musical theory is certainly an advantage to the performer and practically inescapable for the composer. But theory, in the sense of generalization, is not of the least use to the listener; in practice it is a veritable encumbrance if he allows preoccupation with it to interfere with his contact with the music as such. He can certainly derive both interest and help from whatever can be pointed out to him in connection with the specific content of a piece of music; but he will be only misled if he is persuaded to listen in an exploratory rather than a completely receptive spirit. Any effort to help him must be in the direction of liberating, not of conditioning, his ear; and the generalizations of which musical theory consists demonstrably often lead him to strained efforts which are a positive barrier to understanding. The "technique" of a piece of music is essentially the affair of the composer; it is largely even subconscious, and composers frequently are confronted by perfectly real technical facts, present in their music, of which they had no conscious inkling. And do we seriously believe that understanding of Shakespeare, or James Joyce, or William Faulkner has anything to do with the ability to parse the sentences and describe the functions of the various words in *Hamlet* or *Ulysses*?

Of course not. Understanding of music, as relevant for the listener, means the ability to receive its full message. . . . In the primary sense, the listener's real and ultimate response to music consists not in merely hearing it, but in inwardly reproducing it, and his understanding of music consists in the ability to do this in his imagination. This point cannot be too strongly emphasized. The really "understanding" listener takes the music into his consciousness and remakes it actually or in his imagination, for his own uses. He whistles it on the street, or hums it at his work, or simply "thinks" it to himself. He may even represent it to his consciousness in a more concentrated form—as a condensed memory of sounds heard and felt, reproduced for his memory by a vivid sensation of what I may call character in sound, without specific details but in terms of sensations and impressions remembered.

It is for this reason that I am somewhat skeptical of the helpfulness of the kind of technical tid-bits and quasi-analyses sometimes offered to the listener as aids to understanding. The trouble with them, as so often presented, seems to me that the essential facts of musical technique cannot really be conveyed in this way. To give one instance, musicians talk, for convenience, about what we call the "sonata form." But they know, or should know, that the conception "sonata form" is a rough generalization and that in practice sonatas, at least those written by masters, are individual and that each work has its own form. To speak of "sonata form" without making clear what constitutes "form" in music, as such, is to falsify, not to illuminate. It is to imply that the composer adapts his ideas to a mold into which he then pours the music. It is also to lay far too much emphasis on what are called "themes," to the detriment of the musical flow in its entirety. What the layman needs is not to acquire facts but to cultivate senses: the sense of rhythm, of articulation, of contrast, of accent. He needs to be aware of the progression of the bass as well as the treble line; of a return to the principal or to a subsidiary key, of a far-flung tonal span. He needs to be aware of all these things as events which his ear witnesses and appreciates as a composition unfolds. Whether or not it is a help to have specific instances pointed out to him, it is certain in any case that his main source of understanding will be through hearing music in general, and specific works in particular, repeatedly, and making them his own through familiarity, through memory, and through inner re-elaboration.

I hardly need point out the fact that this is as true in regard to so-called "modern" music as it is to old. Where the music is radically unfamiliar the three processes I have described are slower. It must therefore be heard more often than the older music needs to be heard. At the beginning the impressions will be chaotic—much more chaotic than impressions produced by purely fortuitous sounds. The impression of chaos comes simply from the fact that the sounds and relationships are unfamiliar; their very consistency since it, too, is based on contexts which are unfamiliar—seems like a denial of logic. As long as this impression prevails the listener has not yet made contact with the music. In connection with contemporary music, I have often observed the first sensations of real contact, while the musical language in question is still essentially unfamiliar but beginning to be intelligible. These first sensations may be acutely pleasurable; the work becomes highly exciting, conveying a kind of superficial excitement which disappears when the stage of real understanding is reached and gives way to an appreciation for the real "message" of the work. Once more, the key to the "understanding" of contemporary music lies in repeated hearing; one must hear it till the sounds are familiar, until one begins to notice false notes if they are played. One can make the effort to retain it in one's head, and one will always find that the accurate memory of sounds heard coincides with the understanding of them. In fact, the power to retain sounds by memory implies that they have been mastered. For the ear by its nature seeks out patterns and relationships, and it is only these patterns that we can remember and that make music significant for us.

The listener's final stage is that of discrimination. It is important that it should be the final stage since real discrimination is possible only with understanding; and both snobbery and immaturity at times foster prejudices which certainly differ from discrimination in any real sense. Actually it is almost impossible not to discriminate if we persist in and deepen our musical experience. We will learn to differentiate between lasting impressions and those which are fleeting, and between the musical experiences which give full satisfaction and those which only partly satisfy us. We will learn to differentiate between our impressions, too, in a qualitative sense. In this way, we cultivate a sense of values to which to refer our later judgment. We will learn that music is unequal in quality; we will possibly learn that instead of speaking of "immortality" in the case of some works and of the ephemeral quality of others, we must conceive of differences in the life span of works—that some works last in our esteem longer than others without necessarily lasting forever. We will learn finally to differentiate in the matter of character, to be aware of the differences between works in ways which have no relation to intrinsic worth. In other words, we will become critics.

The critic is, in fact, the listener who has become articulate, who has learned to put his judgments and his values into words. I am not, for the moment, speaking of him in his professional capacity but as what I may call the end-product of the listening process. It is important that we understand that he is the end-product, because otherwise we will, I think, understand correctly neither the listener nor the critic. I spoke earlier of the speed with which we, in the United States, have developed our culture and of the constant danger of producing a type of artistic culture in which the critic rather than the productive artist is the central figure. Lest this particular turn of phrase seem to indicate a prejudice against critics, which I do not feel, let me put it a little differently. The danger, and a very real one, is that we allow ourselves to cultivate, on the first level, a predominantly critical attitude toward art in precedence over a love for it; that in our overeagerness to produce what we consider mature results, we make of judgment an end in itself instead of the natural and full-grown by-product of a total artistic experience.

For as a growing culture, and possibly in regard to music more than anything else, we still have a strong residue of the diffidence and the self-distrust which results from the consciousness that we have not a thousand-year-old tradition behind us. In cultural matters we tend to question ourselves, our feelings, and our judgment, at every turn. This is, I believe, a deep-seated attitude, and one not always apparent on the surface of things. It expresses itself in a variety of attitudes, each of them potentially dangerous to our musical development, and still present in spite of the achievements of the past half-century. These achievements are real, even after we have dismissed all of the spurious claims resulting from the fact that we have money to buy goods produced elsewhere, and the fact that we often buy not wisely but too well, and that we possess not only the technique of salesmanship but a tremendous territory in which sales are possible. After we have looked beyond these claims and tried conscientiously to appraise the situation in an objective manner, our achievements are still impressive. But they will be in the last analysis sterile unless we overcome our tendency to self-questioning and learn to give ourselves freely to musical experience, and to recognize that mature artistic judgment can result only from the love of art; that any judgment in the absence of love is sterile and therefore false.

A healthy musical culture is one in which the creative function, the function arising from a strong and prevalent love for music, is the primary one, and in which the activities of the composer, the performer, and the listener (and in the category of listener I include the critic) are in their several ways embodiments of that love. It is obvious that real love for music, as for anything else, depends on inner security; but it is also true that inner security depends on the strength of love. What I have described as the critical attitude, the attitude which implies a forced or premature attempt to arrive at artistic judgment, is in reality only the result of basic insecurity; and there is some evidence that such insecurity threatens to become endemic to our culture. Are we not all familiar with the type of pseudo-sophistication that gives more importance to aversions than to preferences, that is more afraid of loving what is bad than of disliking what is good? Do we not all know too well the type of artistic talent which we see embodied in an essentially divided or imperfectly integrated personality—a personality which, like all mature personalities, contains both creative and critical elements, but in this instance divided through the fact that the two faculties are distrustful both of each other and of themselves? In such cases the creator-personality is inhibited through fears for the soundness of his artistic judgment, and the critic-personality is inhibited through fears that its mere existence may indicate a lack of creative force. Finally, there is always the danger that the young and gifted composer may be thrown into self-doubt, and his development seriously threatened, by excessive self-consciousness at exactly the moment when he should rightly be finding his own inner security, through the discovery of his own creative nature by means of constant and untroubled experimentation and productiveness.

The critic, then, finds his true function as an experienced listener, one who has made a vital contact with music and who has developed powers of discrimination through following up this contact to the point where he becomes conscious of values in a generalized sense. His importance in our total musical economy is obvious. I mean our musical economy, and not the economics of our musical life, where his professional role is considerable but more problematical in effect. For in accordance with his gifts he has the power to contribute strongly to musical life, through illumination of the real issues which are vital in any particular time and place. What these issues are for our contemporary world, I shall discuss more fully later. I wish to emphasize here simply that the true role of the critic is precisely to throw these issues into the clearest possible relief. His true role is that of collaborator, so to speak, in a common cultural effort in which composer and performer and listener all participate.

His role is, in a limited sense, a particularly crucial one, owing to our special history and the conditions under which music developed here. For many years, as it were, we imported all our music. It was a product of a tradition developed elsewhere, and our problem was to gain for ourselves the fruits of this tradition. The critic had the task of interpreting the tradition to the American public, and in consequence there was very little he could do except to take due note of judgments and values that had already reached maturity elsewhere. Today, with the ever-increasing development of a rich musical life of our own, he is forced to swim in more perilous waters and to discover values of his own. It is small wonder that he often shows a certain reluctance to do this, and takes refuge in writing long columns on the season's sixth performance of Tristan, or indulging, to cite a ghastly example I shall never forget, in vituperation of Critic B because the latter had written an unfavorable review of a book by Critic C, of whom Critic A (the author of the review in question) approved because he (Critic C) had written disparagingly of Critic D's book on Mozart. A veritable tangle of critics, with poor Mozart, in this case representing the only actual music involved in the whole matter, four steps away! All this is the result of an inherited habit of regarding music as a commodity to be bought and enjoyed, but in the production of which we have no part. I would like to suggest that this is not criticism at all; it is basically irrelevant chit-chat which can have no constructive consequence whatever. Because criticism, like composing, like performance, must spring out of a genuine culture; that is, a pervasive musical impulse, a living and shared relationship to music, which communicates itself within the framework of some kind of common experience. Our musical culture cannot exist, in fact, on any other terms; and the critic will properly fulfill his function only in energetic awareness of the issues and personalities immediate to the cultural situation in which he, too, lives and of which he, too, is inexorably a part. For even what we call the past is for us a part of our present experience, and our relationship to it is false unless we derive living experience from contact with it; and we cannot have that unless we are aware of ourselves and the forces that have gone into our own making. I am not suggesting that the critic should invariably praise contemporary music or even that he should necessarily ever do so. But it seems to me clear that his central task, as a critic, is to be aware of it and to understand it, and to become fully conscious of the issues that have brought it into being. These bring into play his real powers as a critic, make the greatest demands on his powers of discrimination and offer a truly exciting challenge to his gifts. They are certainly, as I have said, the most dangerous, and yet they are also the most stimulating, waters in which he is called upon to swim.

Finally, to conclude our discussion of the listener, let us ask what he demands of the composer. The question has been asked frequently in our time; it has been given tragic power in dictatorships where the effort has been made, sometimes as in Nazi Germany with ruthless force, to coordinate the artist to the purposes of those in power. Less ruthless, less consistently, and even less consciously applied, but nonc the less real, are the pressures which arise in such large-scale economy as I described at the beginning of this chapter—pressures such as those summarized for the theatrical world in the words "Broadway" or "Hollywood." The slogan, sometimes couched in more refined and even quasi-intellectual terms, is "Give the public what it wants;" but as I have pointed out, there is strong pressure on the public, too, to want what it is cheapest and most generally economical to give.

Let us phrase the question in more general terms: What does the listener demand from music? The answer will inevitably be that a variety of listeners want a variety of things. But on any level it may be taken for granted that the listener wants vital experience, whether of a deeply stirring, brilliantly stimulating, or simply entertaining type. If we understand this we should understand, too, that the composer can effectively furnish it only on his own terms. He can persuade others to love only what he loves himself, and can convince only by means of what fully convinces him. It is for this reason that the artist must be completely free, that such a question as I have stated here can ultimately have no importance to him. His obligation is to give the best he can give, wherever it may lead, and to do so without compromise and with complete conviction. This is in fact natural to him; if he is a genuine artist he cannot do otherwise. He can be sure that if he fully achieves his artistic goals, he will find listeners, and that if he has something genuine to say, the number of his listeners will increase, however slowly. This, in any case, will never be for him an artistic preoccupation, however much it may prove to be a practical one.

Composers, like poets, are born, not made; but once born, they have to grow. It is in this sense that a culture will, generally speaking, get the music that it demands. The question, once more, is what we demand of the composer. Do we demand always what is easiest, music that is primarily and invariably entertainment, or do we seriously want from him the best that he has to give? In the latter case, are we willing to come to meet him, to make whatever effort is demanded of us as listeners, in order to get from his music what it has to give us? Once more, it is for the listener and not for the composer, as an individual, that the answer is important. On the answer we ultimately give depends the future of music in the United States.

· THE MODERN FOLK ARTS ·

DIRECTION [1]

ALFRED HITCHCOCK

Many people think a film director does all his work in the studio, drilling the actors, making them do what he wants. That is not at all true of my own methods, and I can write only of my own methods. I like to have a film complete in my mind before I go on the floor. Sometimes the first idea one has of a film is of a vague pattern, a sort of haze with a certain shape. There is possibly a colorful opening developing into something more intimate; then, perhaps in the middle, a progression to a chase or some other adventure; and sometimes at the end the big shape of a climax, or maybe some twist or surprise. You see this hazy pattern, and then you have to find a narrative idea to suit it. Or a story may give you an idea first and you have to develop it into a pattern.

Imagine an example of a standard plot—let us say a conflict between love and duty. This idea was the origin of my first talkie, *Blackmail*. The hazy pattern one saw beforehand was duty—love—love versus duty—and finally either duty or love, one or the other. The whole middle section was built up on the theme of love versus duty, after duty and love had been introduced separately in turn. So I had first to put on the screen an episode expressing duty.

I showed the arrest of a criminal by Scotland Yard detectives, and tried to make it as concrete and detailed as I could. You even saw the detectives take the man to the lavatory to wash his hands—nothing exciting, just the routine of duty. Then the young detective says he's going out that evening with his girl, and the sequence ends, pointing on from duty to love. Then you start showing the relationship between the detective and his girl: they are middle-class people. The love theme doesn't run smoothly; there is a quarrel and the girl goes off by herself, just because the young man has kept her waiting a few minutes. So your story starts; the girl falls in with the villain—he tries to

1. From Charles Davy (ed.), *Footnotes to the Film* (1937). Reprinted by permission of Peter Davies, Ltd., London, publishers.

seduce her and she kills him. Now you've got your problem prepared. Next morning, as soon as the detective is put on to the murder case, you have your conflict—love versus duty. The audience know that he will be trying to track down his own girl, who has done the murder, so you sustain their interest: they wonder what will happen next.

The blackmailer was really a subsidiary theme. I wanted him to go through and expose the girl. That was my idea of how the story ought to end. I wanted the pursuit to be after the girl, not after the blackmailer. That would have brought the conflict on to a climax, with the young detective, ahead of the others, trying to push the girl out through a window to get her away, and the girl turning round and saying: "You can't do that—I must give myself up." Then the rest of the police arrive, misinterpret what he is doing, and say, "Good man, you've got her," not knowing the relationship between them. Now the reason for the opening comes to light. You repeat every shot used first to illustrate the duty theme, only now it is the girl who is the criminal. The young man is there ostensibly as a detective, but of course the audience know he is in love with the girl. The girl is locked up in her cell and the two detectives walk away, and the older one says, "Going out with your girl to-night?" The younger one shakes his head. "No. Not to-night."

That was the ending I wanted for *Blackmail*, but I had to change it for commercial reasons. The girl couldn't be left to face her fate. And that shows you how the films suffer from their own power of appealing to millions. They could often be subtler than they are, but their own popularity won't let them.

But to get back to the early work on a film. With the help of my wife, who does the technical continuity, I plan out a script very carefully, hoping to follow it exactly, all the way through, when shooting starts. In fact, this working on the script is the real making of the film, for me. When I've done it, the film is finished already in my mind. Usually, too, I don't find it necessary to do more than supervise the editing myself. I know it is said sometimes that a director ought to edit his own pictures if he wants to control their final form, for it is in the editing, according to this view, that a film is really brought into being. But if the scenario is planned out in detail, and followed closely during production, editing should be easy. All that has to be done is to cut away irrelevancies and see that the finished film is an accurate rendering of the scenario.

Settings, of course, come into the preliminary plan, and usually I have fairly clear ideas about them; I was an art student before I took up with films. Sometimes I even think of backgrounds first. *The Man Who Knew Too Much* started like that; I looked in my mind's eyes at snowy Alps and dingy London alleys, and threw my characters into the middle of the contrast. Studio settings, however, are often a problem; one difficulty is that extreme effects —extremes of luxury or extremes of squalor—are much the easiest to register on the screen. If you try to reproduce the average sitting-room in Golders Green or Streatham it is apt to come out looking like nothing in particular, just nondescript. It is true that I have tried lately to get interiors with a real lower-middle-class atmosphere—for instance, the Verlocs' living-room in *Sabotage*—but there's always a certain risk in giving your audience humdrum truth.

However, in time the script and the sets are finished somehow and we are ready to start shooting. One great problem that occurs at once, and keeps on occurring, is to get the players to adapt themselves to film technique. Many of them, of course, come from the stage; they are not cinema-minded at all. So, quite naturally, they like to play long scenes straight ahead. I am willing to work with the long uninterrupted shot: you can't avoid it altogether, and you can get some variety by having two cameras running, one close up and one farther off, and cutting from one to the other when the film is edited. But if I have to shoot a long scene continuously I always feel I am losing grip on it, from a cinematic point of view. The camera, I feel, is simply standing there, *hoping* to catch something with a visual point to it. What I like to do always is to photograph just the little bits of a scene that I really need for building up a visual sequence. I want to put my film together on the screen, not simply to photograph something that has been put together already in the form of a long piece of stage acting. This is what gives an effect of life to a picture—the feeling that when you see it on the screen you are watching something that has been conceived and brought to birth directly in visual terms. The screen ought to speak its own language, freshly coined, and it can't do that unless it treats an acted scene as a piece of raw material which must be broken up, taken to bits, before it can be woven into an expressive visual pattern.

You can see an example of what I mean in *Sabotage*. Just before Verloc is killed there is a scene made up entirely of short pieces of film, separately photographed. This scene has to show how Verloc comes to be killed—how the thought of killing him arises in Sylvia Sidney's mind and connects itself with the carving knife she uses when they sit down to dinner. But the sympathy of the audience has to be kept with Sylvia Sidney; it must be clear that Verloc's death, finally, is an accident. So, as she serves at the table, you see her unconsciously serving vegetables with the carving knife, as though her hand were keeping hold of the knife of its own accord. The camera cuts from her hand to her eyes and back to her hand; then back to her eyes as she suddenly becomes aware of the knife making its error. Then to a normal shot—the man unconcernedly eating; then back to the hand holding the knife. In an older style of acting Sylvia would have had to show the audience what was passing in her mind by exaggerated facial expression. But people to-day in real life often don't show their feelings in their faces: so the film treatment showed the audience her mind through her hand, through its unconscious grasp on the knife. Now the camera moves again to Verloc—back to the knife—back again to his face. You see him seeing the knife, realizing its implication. The tension between the two is built up with the knife as its focus.

Now when the camera has immersed the audience so closely in a scene such as this, it can't instantly become objective again. It must broaden the movement of the scene without loosening the tension. Verloc gets up and walks round the table, coming so close to the camera that you feel, if you are sitting in the audience, almost as though you must move back to make room for him. Then the camera moves to Sylvia Sidney again, then returns to the subject—the knife.

So you gradually build up the psychological situation, piece by piece, using the camera to emphasize first one detail, then another. The point is to draw the audience right inside the situation instead of leaving them to watch it from outside, from a distance. And you can do this only by breaking the action up into details and cutting from one to the other, so that each detail is forced in turn on the attention of the audience and reveals its psychological meaning. If you played the whole scene straight through, and simply made a photographic record of it with the camera always in one position, you would lose your power over the audience. They would watch the scene without becoming really involved in it, and you would have no means of concentrating the characters are feeling.

This way of building up a picture means that film work hasn't much need for the virtuoso actor who gets his effects and climaxes himself, who plays directly on to the audience with the force of his talent and personality. The screen actor has got to be much more plastic; he has to submit himself to be used by the director and the camera. Mostly he is wanted to behave quietly and naturally (which, of course, isn't at all easy), leaving the camera to add most of the accents and emphases. I would almost say that the best screen actor is the man who can do nothing extremely well.

One way of using the camera to give emphasis is the reaction shot. By the reaction shot I mean any close-up which illustrates an event by showing instantly the reaction to it of a person or a group. The door opens for some one to come in, and before showing who it is you cut to the expressions of the persons already in the room. Or, while one person is talking, you keep your camera on some one else who is listening. This over-running of one person's image with another person's voice is a method peculiar to the talkies, it is one of the devices which help the talkies to tell a story faster than a silent film could tell it, and faster than it could be told on the stage.

Or, again, you can use the camera to give emphasis whenever the attention of the audience has to be focussed for a moment on a certain player. There is no need for him to raise his voice or move to the center of the stage or do anything dramatic. A close-up will do it all for him—will give him, so to speak, the stage all to himself.

I must say that in recent years I have come to make much less use of obvious camera devices. I have become more commercially-minded; afraid that anything at all subtle may be missed. I have learnt from experience how easily small touches are overlooked.

The other day a journalist came to interview me and we spoke about film technique. "I always remember," he said, "a little bit in one of your silent films, *The Ring*. The young boxer comes home after winning his fight. He is flushed with success—wants to celebrate. He pours out champagne all round. Then he finds that his wife is out, and he knows at once that she is out with another man. At this moment the camera cuts to a glass of champagne; you see a fizz of bubbles rise off it and there it stands untasted, going flat. That one shot gives you the whole feeling of the scene." Yes, I said, that sort of imagery may be quite good: I don't despise it and still use it now and then. But is it always noticed? There was another bit in *The Ring* which I believe hardly any one noticed.

The scene was outside a boxing-booth at a fair, with a barker talking to the crowd. Inside the booth a professional is taking on all comers. He has always won in the first round. A man comes running out of the booth and speaks to the barker: something unexpected has happened. Then a cut straight to the ringside: you see an old figure 1 being taken down and replaced by a brand new figure 2. I meant this single detail to show that the boxer, now, is up against some one he can't put out in the first round. But it went by too quickly. Perhaps I might have shown the new figure 2 being taken out of a paper wrapping—something else was needed to make the audience see in a moment that the figure for the second round had never been used before.

The film always has to deal in exaggerations. Its methods reflect the simple contrasts of black and white photography. One advantage of color is that it would give you more intermediate shades. I should never want to fill the screen with color: it ought to be used economically—to put new words into the screen's visual language when there's a need for them. You could start a color film with a board-room scene: sombre panelling and furniture, the directors all in dark clothes and white collars. Then the chairman's wife comes in, wearing a red hat. She takes the attention of the audience at once, just because of that one note of color. Or suppose a gangster story: the leader of the gang is sitting in a café with a man he suspects. He has told his gunman to watch the table. "If I order a glass of port, bump him off. If I order green chartreuse, let him go."

This journalist asked me also about distorted sound—a device I tried in *Blackmail* when the word "knife" hammers on the consciousness of the girl at breakfast on the morning after the murder. Again, I think this kind of effect may be justified. There have always been occasions when we have needed to show a phantasmagoria of the mind in terms of visual imagery. So we may want to show some one's mental state by letting him listen to some sound—let us say church bells—and making them clang with distorted insistence in his head. But on the whole nowadays I try to tell a story in the simplest possible way, so that I can feel sure it will hold the attention of any audience and won't puzzle them. I know there are critics who ask why lately I have made only thrillers. Am I satisfied, they say, with putting on the screen the equivalent merely of popular novelettes? Part of the answer is that I am out to get the best stories I can which will suit the film medium, and I have usually found it necessary to take a hand in writing them myself.

There is a shortage of good writing for the screen, and is that surprising? A playwright may take a year or more writing a play, but in a year the film industry has to make hundreds of films. More and more pictures, one after the other incessantly, with a certain standard to keep up—it throws a great strain on the creative faculties of every one who has to supply the industry with ideas. Of course there must be co-operation, division of labor, all the time. The old saying, "No one man ever made a picture," is entirely true. And the only answer found so far to the writing problem has been to employ a number of writers to work together on the same picture. Metro-Goldwyn, we are told, employ altogether a staff of eighty or ninety writers, so they can draw at any time on a whole group of writers to see a story through. I don't say there aren't drawbacks in this collective method, but it often makes things easier when time is at stake, as it always is in film production. In this country we can't usually afford to employ large writing staffs, so I have had to join in and become a writer myself. I choose crime stories because that is the kind of story I can write, or help to write, myself—the kind of story I can turn most easily into a successful film. It is the same with Charles Bennett, who has so often worked with me; he is essentially a writer of melodrama. I am ready to use other stories, but I can't find writers who will give them to me in a suitable form.

Sometimes I have been asked what films I should make if I were free to do exactly as I liked without having to think about the box-office. There are several examples I can give very easily. For one thing, I should like to make travel films with a personal element in them: that would be quite a new field. Or I should like to do a verbatim of a celebrated trial—of course there would have to be some editing, some cutting down. The Thompson-Bywaters case, for instance. You can see the figures at Madame Tussaud's and the newspapers gave long reports of the trial. The cinema could reconstruct the whole story. Or there is the fire at sea possibility—that has never been tackled seriously on the screen. It might be too terrifying for some audiences but it would make a great subject, worth doing.

British producers are often urged to make more films about characteristic phases of English life. Why, they are asked, do we see so little of the English farmer or the English seaman? Or is there not plenty of good material in the great British industries—in mining or shipbuilding or steel? One difficulty here is that English audiences seem to take more interest in American life—I suppose because it has a novelty value. They are rather easily bored by everyday scenes in their own country. But I certainly should like to make a film of the Derby, only it might not be quite in the popular class. It would be hard to invent a Derby story that wasn't hackneyed, conventional. I would rather do it more as a documentary—a sort of pageant, an animated modern version of Frith's "Derby Day." I would show everything that goes on all round the course, but without a story.

Perhaps the average audience isn't ready for that, yet. Popular taste, all the same, does move; to-day you can put over scenes that would have been ruled out a few years ago. Particularly towards comedy, nowadays, there is a different attitude. You can get comedy out of your stars, and you used not to be allowed to do anything which might knock the glamour off them.

In 1926 I made a film called *Downhill,* from a play by Ivor Novello, who acted in the film himself, with Ian Hunter and Isabel Jeans. There was a sequence showing a quarrel between Hunter and Novello. It started as an ordinary fight; then they began throwing things at one another. They tried to pick up heavy pedestals to throw and the pedestals bowled them over. In other words I made it comic. I even put Hunter into a morning coat and striped trousers because I felt that a man never looks so ridiculous as when he is well dressed and fighting. This whole scene was cut out; they said I was guying Ivor Novello. It was ten years before its time.

I say ten years, because you remember that in 1936 M.G.M. showed a comedy called *Libelled Lady.* There is a fishing sequence in it: William Powell stumbles about in the river, falls flat and gets soaked and catches a big fish by accident. Here you have a star, not a slapstick comedian, made to do something pretty near slapstick. In *The Thirty-nine Steps,* too, a little earlier, I was allowed to drag Madeleine Carroll over the moors handcuffed to the hero; I made her get wet and untidy and look ridiculous for the purpose of the story. I couldn't have done that ten years ago.

I foresee the decline of the individual comedian. Of course there may always be specially gifted comedians who will have films written round them, but I think public taste is turning to like comedy and drama more mixed up; and this is another move away from the conventions of the stage. In a play your divisions are much more rigid; you have a scene—then curtain, and after an interval another scene starts. In a film you keep your whole action flowing; you can have comedy and drama running together and weave them in and out. Audiences are much readier now than they used to be for sudden changes of mood; and this means more freedom for a director. The art of directing for the commercial market is to know just how far you can go. In many ways I am freer now to do what I want to do than I was a few years ago. I hope in time to have more freedom still—if audiences will give it to me.

SOAPLAND[1]

JAMES THURBER

During the nineteen-thirties, radio daytime serials were occasionally sniped at by press and pulpit, and now and then women's clubs adopted halfhearted resolutions, usually unimplemented by research, disapproving of the "menace of soap opera." Husbands and fathers, exacerbated by what they regarded as meaningless yammering, raised their voices against the programs, and some of them, pushed too far, smashed their sets with their fists, like Mr. Ezra Adams, in Clinton, Iowa. But it wasn't until 1942 that the opponents of the daytime monster discovered in their midst a forceful and articulate crusader to lead the assault on the demon of the kilocycles. He was Dr. Louis I. Berg, of New York, psychiatrist and physician, author, and, according to *Who's Who,* medico-legal expert. In a report published in March, 1942, and widely quoted in the press, Dr. Berg confessed that he had been unaware of the menace of the radio serial until late in 1941. His examination of several female patients undergoing change of life had convinced him that radio serials were a main cause of relapses in the women. He thereupon made a three-week study of two of the aggravations, "Woman in White" and "Right to Happiness." He found these serials guilty of purposefully inducing anxiety, dangerous emotional release, and almost everything else calculated to afflict the middle-aged woman, the adolescent, and the neurotic. "Pandering to perversity and playing out destructive conflicts," Dr. Berg wrote, "these serials furnish the same release for the emotionally distorted that is supplied to those who derive satisfaction from a lynching bee, who lick their lips at the salacious scandals of a *crime passionnel,* who in the unregretted past cried out in ecstasy at a witch burning." Hitting his stride, Dr. Berg referred to "the unwitting sadism of suppurating serials." The Doctor then admitted, "There are several excellent ones," and added, somewhat to my bewilderment, since he had set himself up as a critic, "Naturally, an analysis of them has no place in a study of this kind." In a later report, Dr. Berg set down such a list of serial-induced ailments, physiological and psychological, as would frighten the strongest listener away from the daytime air. It began with tachycardia and arrhythmia and ended with emotional instability and vertigo.

Dr. Berg's onslaught was not unlike the cry of "Fire!" in a crowded theatre, and a comparable pandemonium resulted. The uneasy radio industry decided to call in experts to make a study of the entire field. Professors, doctors, psychologists, research statisticians, and network executives were all put to work on the problem. In the last five years, their findings have run to at least half a million words. This vast body of research covers all types of programs, and

1. Part V of an article in *The New Yorker,* XXIV (July 24, 1948), 63–68, reprinted by permission. Copyright, 1948, James Thurber.

an explorer could wander for weeks just in the section devoted to soap opera. Among the outstanding investigators are Dr. Paul S. Lazarsfeld, of Columbia University, whose Bureau of Applied Social Research has the dignified backing of the Rockefeller Foundation, and Dr. Rudolf Arnheim, professor of psychology at Sarah Lawrence College, who, for *his* three-week study of serials, had the fascinated assistance of forty-seven students at Columbia University. C.B.S. appointed Mrs. Frances Farmer Wilder, a former public-relations director in radio, as program consultant with special reference to the investigation of daytime serials. Both N.B.C. and C.B.S., the only national networks that broadcast soap opera, appointed research committees, and were cheered up by their reports, which admitted that soap opera could be greatly improved, but decided that its effect on the listening women was more likely to be benign than malignant. The cry of "whitewash" went up from the enemy camp, but the networks were able to prove that the data of their specialists agreed in general with studies made by independent researchers in the field. It is not always easy to distinguish between independent investigators and the ladies and gentlemen whose work is stimulated by the networks, and I am not even going to try.

In 1945, Mrs. Wilder summarized the findings of the C.B.S. experts in a pamphlet called "Radio's Daytime Serial." If you have been worried about America's womanhood left home alone at the mercy of the daytime dial, you will be relieved to know that forty-six out of every hundred housewives did not listen to soap opera at all. This figure was approximately confirmed a year later by checkers working for the United States Department of Agriculture, which had presumably become worried about the effect the serials were having on the women in small towns and rural areas of the country. Estimates differ as to how many serials the average addict listens to each day. Mrs. Wilder puts the figure at 5.8. She also points out that a housewife listens to a given serial only about half the time, or five programs out of every ten. On the other hand, a survey by an advertising agency indicates that the ladies listen to only three broadcasts out of every ten.

There have been all kinds of measurements of the social stratification of the listening women, and all kinds of results. There is a popular notion that only ladies of a fairly low grade of intelligence tune in soap operas, but some of the surveys would have us believe that as many as forty per cent of the women in the upper middle class, or the higher cultural level, listen to soap opera. The most interesting specimen that the scientists have examined in their laboratories is the habitual listener who has come to identify herself with the heroine of her favorite serial. Many examples of this bemused female have been tracked down by Dr. Arnheim and other workers, and a comprehensive analysis of the type was completed last year by Professor W. Lloyd Warner and Research Associate William E. Henry, both of the University of Chicago, at the instigation of the Columbia Broadcasting System. They made a study of a group of listeners to "Big Sister," using as subjects mostly women of the lower middle class, and found that almost all of them were "identifiers," if I may coin a pretty word. Let us take a look at the summary of their conclusions about the nature of the serial and its impact on its audience. "The 'Big Sister' program arouses normal and adaptive anxiety in the women who listen," wrote Warner and Henry. "The 'Big Sister' program directly and indirectly condemns neurotic and non-adaptive anxiety and thereby functions to curb such feelings in its audience. This program provides moral beliefs, values, and techniques for solving emotional and interpersonal problems for its audience and makes them feel they are learning while they listen (thus: 'I find the program is educational'). It directs the private reveries and fantasies of the listeners into socially approved channels of action. The 'Big Sister' program increases the women's sense of security in a world they feel is often threatening, by reaffirming the basic security of the marriage ties (John's and Ruth's); by accentuating the basic security of the position of the husband (Dr. John Wayne is a successful physician); by 'demonstrating' that those who behave properly and stay away from wrong-doing exercise moral control over those who do not; and by showing that wrong behavior is punished. The 'Big Sister' program, in dramatizing the significance of the wife's role in basic human affairs, increases the woman's feeling of importance by showing that the family is of the highest importance and that she has control over the vicissitudes of family life. It thereby decreases their feeling of futility and makes them feel essential and wanted. The women aspire to, and measure themselves by, identification with Ruth, the heroine; however, the identification is not with Ruth alone, but with the whole program and the other characters in the plot. This permits sublimated impulse satisfaction by the listeners', first, unconsciously identifying with the bad woman and, later, consciously punishing her through the action of the plot. Unregulated impulse life is condemned, since it is always connected with characters who are condemned and never related to those who are approved."

"Big Sister" is written by two men, Robert Newman and Julian Funt, and they have made it one of the most popular of all serials. For more than two years it has dealt with a moony triangle made up of Ruth Wayne, the big sister of the title, her estranged husband, Dr. John Wayne, and another doctor named Reed Bannister. The authors, I am told, plan to tinker with the popular old central situation, but they are aware that they must proceed with caution. The identifiers are strongly attached to the status quo of plot situation, and to what psychologists call the "symbols" in soap opera—serial authors call them "gimmicks"—and they do not want them tampered with. Thus, the soap-opera males who go blind or lose the use of both legs or wander around in amnesia are, as the psychologists put it, symbols that the listening women demand. As long as the symbols are kept in the proper balance and the woman is in charge and the man is under her control, it does not seem to make a great deal of difference to the female listeners whether the story is good or not.

We come next to that disturbing fringe of the soap-opera audience made up of listeners who confuse the actors with the characters they play. These naïve folk believe that Bill Davidson, the kindly Hartville barber of "Just Plain Bill," is an actual person (he is, of course, an actor, named Arthur Hughes), and they deluge him with letters in the fond belief that he can solve their problems as successfully as he does those of the people in the serial. James Meighan and Ruth Russell, who play the husband and wife in "Just Plain Bill," have had to lead a curious extra-studio life as Mr. and Mrs. Kerry Donovan. When it became apparent to the listening audience, some thirteen years ago, that Mrs. Donovan was going to have her first child, the network and local stations received hundreds of gifts from the devoted admirers of the young couple—bonnets, dresses, bootees, porringers, and even complete layettes were sent by express to the mythical expectant mother—and when, several years later, the child was killed in an automobile accident, thousands of messages of sympathy came in. Such things as this had happened before, and they still happen, to the bewilderment and embarrassment of network executives. In 1940, when Dr. John Wayne married the heroine of "Big Sister," truckloads of wedding presents were received at the C.B.S. Building on Madison Avenue. This flux of silver, cut glass, and odds and ends presented the exasperated broadcasting system with a considerable problem. Gifts for babies had always been disposed of by sending them to children's hospitals and orphanages, but the wedding gifts were another matter. Since network men are a little sheepish about the entire business, they are inclined to change the subject when the question of the misguided largess of listeners is brought up.

The quandary is enlarged when, in addition to gifts for the nursery, parlor, and dining room, checks, paper money, and even coins arrive for this serial hero or that who has let it out over the air that he is in financial difficulties. The money, like the presents, cannot very well be returned to the senders, for fear of breaking their naïve hearts, and the sponsors have adopted the policy of giving it to the Red Cross and other charities. In addition to the newly married, the pregnant, and the broke, soap-opera characters who are single and in the best of health and circumstances receive tokens of esteem, in a constant, if somewhat more moderate, stream. One young actress who plays in a Procter & Gamble serial estimates that she is sent about three hundred pounds of soap every year, much of it the product of her sponsor's rivals. The year 1947 was the Big Year for live turtles and alligators, and radio listeners from all over the country bombarded the studios with gifts of hundreds of these inconvenient creatures.

Mrs. Carrington's "Pepper Young's Family" used to have a recurring scene in which a man and his wife were heard talking in bed—twin beds, naturally. When the man playing the husband quit and was replaced by another actor, indignant ladies wrote in, protesting against these immoral goings on. Equally outraged was the woman who detected that Kerry Donovan, the husband in

"Just Plain Bill," and Larry Noble, the husband in "Backstage Wife," were one and the same man. This pixilated listener wrote Kerry Donovan a sharp letter revealing that she was on to his double life and threatening to expose the whole nasty mess unless the bigamous gentleman gave up one of his wives. The key to this particular scandal is simple. One actor, James Meighan, plays both husbands. A woman in the Middle West once wrote to N.B.C. asserting that the wrong man was suspected of murder in her favorite serial. She said she was tuned in the day the murder took place and she knew who the real culprit was. She offered to come to New York and testify in court if the network would pay her expenses.

Even the listening women who are shrewd enough, God bless them, to realize that serial characters are not real people but are played by actors and actresses expect superhuman miracles of their idols. They never want them to take vacations, but usually the weary players manage to get away for a few weeks in the summer. Sometimes they are replaced by other performers, but often the characters they play are "written out" of the script for the periods of their absence. Thus, the housewives who love Mary Noble, the heroine of "Backstage Wife," are not told that Claire Niesen, who plays that role, is taking her annual vacation. Instead, the script arranges for Mary Noble to visit her sick mother in San Diego for a while or travel to Bangkok to consult a swami who has the secret of the only known cure for that plaguy summer rash of hers. Now and then, a serial audience hears one of its favorite characters complain of a severe headache. This is almost always a symptom of brain tumor. It means that the part is going to be written out of the soap opera forever, perhaps because the player wants to go to Hollywood, or the author is bored with the character, or the producer has to cut the budget. In any case, the listeners become slowly adjusted to the inevitable, and when the character finally dies, many of them write letters of condolence, often bordered in black.

The gravest real crisis in years came a few months ago when Lucille Wall, who plays Portia in "Portia Faces Life," was critically hurt in a fall in her Sutton Place apartment. Until her accident, Miss Wall had taken only one vacation in eight years, and her devoted audience was alarmed when her replacement, Anne Seymour, went on playing Portia week after week. The news that Miss Wall was in the hospital in a serious condition spread swiftly among her followers, and letters, telegrams, flowers, and gifts poured in. Because of this evidence of her popularity, Miss Wall improved rapidly, to the amazement and delight of her doctors, who had told her that she could not go back to work for a year. When she got home from the hospital, Miss Wall spoke to her listeners at the end of a "Portia" broadcast one day over a special hookup at her bedside, thanking them for their kindness and promising to be back soon. She repeated this message on the Thursday before Mother's Day, and again, some time later, while she was still recuperating. On June 14th, after being away less than four months, she began to play Portia again.

This reporter is too tired, after more than a year of travel in Soapland, and too cautious in matters of prophecy, to make any predictions about the future of soap opera. One thing, though, seems certain. The audience of twenty million women has taken over control of the daytime serial. The producers must give them what they want and demand. The formula has been fixed. The few serious writers who have tried to improve on it are gradually giving up the unequal struggle. It is probable that superior serials, like "Against the Storm," winner of a Peabody Award for excellence, are gone from the air forever, and that only the old familiar symbols and tired plots will survive.

Your guess is as good as mine about the effect that television will have on the daytime serial. The creeping apparition called video has already made several experiments with continuous narratives. Two of them have been dropped, but one called "The Laytons," the story of a family, though off the air at the moment, will be back next month. It differs from soap opera in that it is a half-hour nighttime show once a week, but the agent I sent to watch a performance at the WABD studio at Wanamaker's reports that it has the basic stuff of the daytime serials, even if the producer is horrified at the mention of such a thing. Just how television could manage to put on a fifteen-minute program five times a week, I have no idea, but from what I know of American technological skill, I wouldn't bet that it can't be done. There is a problem, however, that the wizards of television may find insurmountable if they attempt to transpose any of the current radio serials to the screen. The researchers have discovered that the listening women have a strong tendency to visualize the serial heroine and her family. Some of them even go so far as to describe to their interviewers what the different women characters wear. If their favorites did not come out to their satisfaction on television (imagine their dismay if they find that the tall, handsome hero of their daydreams is really a mild little fellow, five feet four), the ladies might desert the video versions by the million. The way around that, of course, would be to invent entirely new soap operas for telecasting, and "The Laytons" may well be the first lasting adventure in this field.

It is hard for one who has understood the tight hold of "Just Plain Bill," "Big Sister," and some of the others to believe that their intense and far-flung audience would ever give them up easily. If soap opera did disappear from the air (and I see no signs of it), the wailing of the housewives would be heard in the land. I doubt that it could be drowned out even by the cheers and laughter of the househusbands dancing in the streets.

I took the train from Hartville one day last week, waving goodbye to Bill Davidson and his family, and vowing—I hope they will forgive me—to put my radio away in the attic and give myself up to the activities and apprehensions of the so-called real world. I have also put away the books and pamphlets dealing with the discoveries of the serial researchers. In closing, though, I think you ought to know that Benton & Bowles, an advertising agency, recently employed a system invented by Dr. Rudolph Flesch, of New York University, to determine mathematically the comparative understandability, clarity, and simplicity of various kinds of prose and poetry. The agency wanted to find out just how easy it was to understand that old and popular serial of Elaine Carrington's called "When a Girl Marries." The results of Dr. Flesch's formula showed that this soap opera is as easy to understand as the Twenty-third Psalm and a great deal clearer than what Abraham Lincoln was trying to say in the Gettysburg Address. I don't know about you, but when the final delirium descends upon my mind, it is my fervent hope that I will not trouble the loved ones gathered at my bedside by an endless and incoherent recital of the plot of "When a Girl Marries." It will be better for everyone if my consciousness selects that other clear and famous piece of English prose, and I babble of green fields.

WASHBOARD WEEPERS: A SMALL CASE FOR RADIO [1]

MAX WYLIE

Radio is accused of a multitude of sins, by a multitude of persons. Senators, cranks, and congressmen attack it. Lawyers, psychiatrists, doctors, educators, editors, and clergymen all take swipes at it. Many of these people are important and their views are often given wide publicity. Many of these people are brave and unselfish and really believe what they say. Many, alas, are neither informed nor fair.

By far the greatest amount of abuse—and some of the least justified—is directed at the lowly serials, better known as soap operas or washboard weepers.

1. From *Harper's Magazine*, CLXXXV (November, 1942), 633–638. Copyright, 1942, by Max Wylie. Reprinted by permission of Harold Ober.

This is not surprising, since there are so many of them; many more than enough in the opinion of radio's critics. I have been up to my ears in these weird wonders for quite a time, and I believe I can set down a fair statement of what we in radio think is behind them and why we believe there is justification for their more or less dismal continuance. These super-hardy sunflowers of backyard fiction have crowded the daylight radio hours on weekdays for more than ten years. At night they crawl back in the ditto machines; on weekends they relax entirely after a flamboyant Friday outburst; and many of them estivate all summer. They can be moved from the Red Network to the Blue without turning purple, often without knowing they were transplanted. They can go unnourished for weeks without losing their Hooper. They can stick their roots in a bar of soap and bloom as if it were Wheaties. Aspirin revives them. So does anything in a tube. As flowers go, they are tough babies, but if they are hard to classify, they are harder to kill.

Strangely enough, most of the arguments against daytime serials are based on charges that are entirely justified. Here are the charges: the stories are depressing; the stories are badly written; the stories drag; one story follows another in weary and continuous sequence; one network does what the other does; serial stories dominate program schedules all day for most of the week; the stories, most of them, are dreadful and some are salacious.

The argument then proceeds to tell us that these shows are detrimental to listeners; that they are undermining the American home; that they are thereby undermining America; and that they should therefore be stopped.

Broadcasters do not see it this way. In general they admit the charges. They knew all about it first; they knew about it before the facts became charges. But they flatly deny two things: first, that the charges constitute an argument, and second, that there is any validity in the conclusion.

Broadcasters not only deny that the shows are detrimental to listeners. They insist that they are necessary to them, that they have been constructed for them, and that they would not be on the air unless audience response demanded it. To a very generous extent I share this opinion because I can see nothing wrong in the reasoning. I have been more hotly pursued by backstage wives, orphans of divorce, and women in white than most men. I have made my living from these forlorn females. In some cases I have even determined when and whom they should marry and when they should cease to be married, and I once had the problem of supervising a case of literary parthenogenesis on sixty-eight stations for a large coast-to-coast network. I can modestly say that I know what some of these girls are up to, and some of the writers who put them up to it.

Four characteristics are present in nearly all the criticisms of daytime radio that broadcasters have to contend with. Here they are:

Most of those who criticize daytime radio do so because they can find there no entertainment values *for themselves*.

Most of those who sit down to the task of preparing statements that will improve radio end up by scolding radio. They are on a hunt for evil and they immediately find evil.

Most of those who criticize daytime shows either do not listen to enough shows, or do not listen to any given show long enough, to arrive at any constructive opinion as to what the serials may be doing culturally or psychologically to the listener who follows them all the time.

Few of the critics are steady listeners or general listeners. The great majority are most casual in their listening habits, and some even advise us in their opening sentence that they never listen at all. They tell us they "gave up."

Concluding paragraphs of their attacks usually wind up in a shell-burst of challenge and dismay. "Why aren't there shows about happy homes and happy people?" they ask. "Where are the great American themes?" "With the world afire, why can't writers find inspiration in the courageous performance of our soldiers?" "Is Democracy so sick it can get nourishment from this sort of hokum?"

II

We may as well take care of the primary complaint right away—"Why don't you have shows about happy homes and happy people?"

We have a few—a very few—and they are comedy shows. Most of the shows are about unhappy homes and unhappy people. The main reason of course why radio has so many stories about trouble-ridden families is that the picture of the well-adjusted family presents no problem and hence no story. It is a well-adjusted, comfortable American family, minding its own business, paying its rent, sending its normal children to normal school, going to church, and living at all times, despite the day's weather or the year's season, at room temperature. A writer would lose interest in it in a day's visit, and a listener in a single show. That is the flat answer to a question that any man or woman could answer for himself if he considered it for long. But this is only half of radio's reasoning. Radio knows a handful of sociological verities so unpleasant that the critics hesitate to mention them. Radio not only mentions them. It buys them and sells them and insists upon them, and puts them on live networks so that they can be heard all over the country and then puts them on acetate recordings so that they can be heard in New Zealand and Hawaii. It even translates them so that they can be heard in Polish, Yiddish, Portuguese, and Italian.

What are these verities, if verities they be? They are more fundamental than the adage about misery loving company. They actually presume that most people are more preoccupied with the unhappy aspects of their present lives and past recollections, and more preoccupied about the uncertainty of their futures, than they are with the endurable or, in rare cases, the downright happy *status quo* of the moment. They presuppose that not only the secret and subconscious mind of womankind, but the conscious mind itself, is packed with more memories of loneliness and frustration and unrealized romantic reverie than memories of past delight or present fulfillment. They presuppose that the great mass of all mankind—with the women worse off than the men—is cramped and poor and troubled and tired; ungifted, without a future, and insecure; adventuresome, vain, and seeking.

Women of the daytime audiences are having physical and psychic problems that they themselves cannot understand, that they cannot solve. Being physical, they feel the thrust of these problems. Being poor, they cannot buy remedies in the form of doctors, new clothes, or deciduous coiffures; being unanalytical, they cannot figure out what is really the matter with them; and being inarticulate, they cannot explain their problem even if they know what it is. "There isn't anything the matter with me that a million dollars wouldn't cure" is no passing gag, and no sincere psychiatrist will call it a gag.

Radio doesn't think it's a gag either and does one of two things. It takes them into their own problems or into problems worse than their own (which is the same thing, only better). Or it takes them away from their problems. It gives listeners two constant and frequently simultaneous choices—participation or escape. Both work.

III

Radio's critics like to think of themselves as the true and suitable norm, and in all the arts save radio this is not only a safe presumption; it is a necessary one. The book critic talks to book readers and book lovers. In so far as he can, he reads and criticizes what his instinct and past experience tell him is the most important or most significant or most promising book in any given day or week. He writes for people who read books or who wish to seem to have read them.

The same holds true for the critic of art exhibits, the dance, serious music, statuary, drama, architecture, poetry, epicureanism, flower arrangement, landscape gardening, and street planning. All such critics must concentrate on a field whose limits are pretty well known and accepted. As specialists, they have less to cover and fewer to cover for. Chotzinoff does not have to know what Fadiman knows and he is not expected to. Richard Watts does not have to know much of what Fadiman knows, and nothing at all of what Chotzinoff knows. But the radio critic should know what all these men know. And in addition to this he must be an expert in forensics, elocution, debate, and psychology, and he must also be a sound newspaperman. A radio critic would have to be omniscient.

That is why radio is almost without competent critics. That is why it has had to be its own critic. That is why it is vulnerable to criticism from any outsider who wants to come in with criticism. That is why it cannot protect itself from these outsiders, and therefore why outsiders proliferate without disturbance.

For mass-consumption purposes, in order to carry a case against daytime radio, it would seem to be necessary for the critics to demonstrate that these shows are worse than other avenues of mass entertainment in the matter of violence, or misery, or vulgarity, or in their suggestion and intention.

Let us set up an average man of twenty and see what he has read, heard, and looked at in the course of a normal American education. Before he learned how to read he could recite thirty or forty Mother Goose rhymes. He knew "Goosey, Goosey, Gander," in which he found an old man who wouldn't say his prayers, and being a correct young man of four, he did the only thing possible. He took that old man by his left leg and threw him down the stairs. He saw a spider frighten a Miss Muffett off her tuffet. He saw a farm woman cut off the tails of three blind mice with a carving knife. He saw London Bridge fall and Scotland burn. He knew a kid named Simon who couldn't buy anything from a pieman because he was flat broke. He knew a girl with bonny brown hair who was being stood up for the first time because a fellow named Johnny didn't come home from the fair. Our young friend is now sophisticated enough to know some babes. These seemed to be lost in a wood. Nothing happened to them except that they sobbed and they cried and they lay down and died. And he was the intimate of the children who got spanked soundly and sent to bed because their old lady didn't know what else to do, living in a shoe the way she did.

Except for a merry old soul who liked fiddle players, our young friend has seen little enough that is pleasant. It looks like a troubled world to him, full of lost and impoverished youngsters, homeless and whimpering in the dark; a world of homely parents, most of whom are ancient and cruel; a place of shadows, ridiculous economic structures, and cows with crumpled horns. This wearies him a great deal and he goes to bed in a tree top comforted by the news that the whole works is likely to come crashing to earth any minute.

Presently he learns how to read, and his storybooks introduce him to a man who hangs his wives to rafters by their hair; to a little match girl freezing in the snow; to a boy bumping around Germany in the fire box of a big stove; to a boy who kills giants with a pickax; to wolves, devils, pirates, kidnappers, and people who can unscrew their eyes. Children disappear into a mountain cleft and never come back to Hamelin. Children disappear into a Crusade and never come back to England. A boy gets shot out of a tree and falls dead before Garibaldi. A boy gets his legs shot off, hangs his drum to a bough, and beats the charge till his blood runs out. A French maiden is burned alive. A queen is beheaded.

Comic strips begin to feature more prominently in his development, and he devours panel after panel of the fastest-moving four-color melodrama that man's ingenuity can devise. He does this, it is to be presumed, to relax from the urbane suavity of Poe, the eupeptic exuberance of Hawthorne, Thomas Hardy's irrepressible wise-cracking, and the glyptic inertias of Jack London, Ambrose Bierce, and Bret Harte; Conrad, Wells, Kipling, Scott, and Dickens —all of whom he has been reading in small daily doses for a year or two because they were part of his syllabus. When he is only sixteen our young student is obliged to memorize great sections of a story which when slightly compressed and rephrased might read like this:

Joe's girl, a gun moll, suspects that he's too soft for the killings he's got to undertake. So the next night she pours liquor into the victim's bodyguards, gets them drunk, takes their guns, gives them to Joe, and tells him to go in and do the killing—which he does. But the next night there is good reason to kill the gang leader's lieutenant, and Joe is so scared that he pays a couple of local boys to do the job with clubs. By this time Joe keeps seeing the lieutenant, probably because he isn't there. His nerves are shot. He decides that if he doesn't kill everybody in his way, they'll kill him. But the mob turns on him, kills him, and cuts his head off to make sure.

There is no sex in this story at all. It is the sort of story that you have read in the newspapers in one form or another, and it will be going on in the papers as long as there are men living who do not have what they want, or who do not have what their wives want, which is usually more newsworthy.

I have paraphrased the story just recounted because I wished to conceal its authorship. I think it is a story of violence, a yarn not far removed in many of its features from the very sort of story that has been lambasted all over the four networks. (In May of this year five daytime shows on the Red Network alone were dealing with murder.)

Nobody knows who wrote this story. Some say Holinshed and some say George Buchanan. It doesn't matter in the least. What does matter is that an alert and busy Englishman stumbled upon it, was fascinated by it, rewrote it, and called it "Macbeth."

I do not see any reason to go on with this. The point is clear. All our childhoods were sadistic. Our formative years were explosive, reckless, and packed with excitement. Lyricism, if any, we managed to catch on the fly. By the time the normal American is eighteen he has seen men killed every way it can be done. By the time he is twenty there is almost nothing in the category of classical misconduct he doesn't know. Much of this he has learned by reading, and much of it by reading what was put into his hands by those responsible for his education. I grant of course that he has also read much that was light and easy on the nerves, but his reading thrills were thrilling because they treated of violence or of a promise of violence. (We won't even mention the movies.)

Critics of radio will insist that these stories of exalted adventure are classic stories and therefore improving. This is true. But radio answers this by pointing out that less than one per cent have gone on reading the classics after their limited compulsory exposure to them in school.

That is the thing radio men know. They know other things. They know that most members of American radio homes don't give a hoot for a symphony. Only about six and a half million individual listeners really enjoy symphonic music. About twice this many may pretend to like it, which splits the normal symphony audience into two parts, at a ratio of two fakers for every fan. Culturally this may not be flattering, but factually, though it may be of no interest to critics, it is of compelling interest to broadcasters. It limits the amount of good music this country shall hear. But radio has more harrowing evidence than this. Radio is in 14 million homes where there are no magazines. It is in 8 million homes where there are no cars. It is in 13 million homes where there are no telephones. It is in 6 million homes where there are no bathtubs. These are the homes of America's poor.

Radio believes that these people are limited in a way not understood by radio critics, or it would have been mentioned by them. The critics have criticized radio because there are major aspects of radio they do not like *for themselves*. It is they themselves who do not like soap operas. Wittingly or not, they all speak for themselves or for a plane of privilege and discrimination and social criteria totally unknown to the multitudes. They would exchange the bad taste of these multitudes for their personal idea of good taste. This might get better programs on the air and poor programs off the air, but it would sink radio inside of a year. It would pull the sea-cocks out of her, and she would subside in a wail of woodwinds, bow-heavy with artistic mash, logy with prose.

IV

Here is the fatal flaw running through all the criticism of radio to date, irrespective of source, corrective, or intention. Radio, to be free, must be radio *for all the people*. That is why it is so strong and open-throated in America. Everybody has a piece of it here. That is why it is dead in Europe. It doesn't belong to the listeners.

To-day radio is being badgered and squeezed by the neck. Its eyes are beginning to start. It needs help. Up to now it has handled its fights by itself. Alone it cannot win them all and has already lost some big ones. It has consistently refused to pre-empt its own power to win any converts to its cause, for radio really believes that American broadcasting is owned and operated by its public.

You are its public, and if you like radio stick up for it. If you don't like it complain about it. But complain in the charitable terms that bespeak your recognition of the tastes and the rights of others.

No man in American radio has ever said that everything in radio is right, and no radio man ever will. But they will all tell you this: if you make radio a public issue, radio will bring it to the public. Broadcasters have never flinched from a public issue and as long as democracy exists they never will.

Public trust is radio's only security, public response its mold.

STRICTLY FROM MARS, OR, HOW TO PHILANDER IN FIVE EASY COLORS[1]

S. J. PERELMAN

SOME love Van Johnson, some van Gogh; for every youth who pins up a photograph of Alexis Smith, there is another who does the same for Betty. Sneer if you will at the veal-faced adolescent haunting Grand Central for a glimpse of Perry Como; one of these evenings you will claw your way through the lobby at a first-night intermission to genuflect before Evelyn Waugh or Shostakovich. Everyone, no matter how case-hardened, has his joss. I know a poised and cultivated woman whose contempt for her husband is infinite because he spent two years maneuvering an introduction to Bill Dickey. Last summer, she crouched for a whole afternoon in a bog on Martha's Vineyard to beg an autograph of Katharine Cornell. I, too, have my idol, and if he is neither toreador nor tenor, philosopher nor clown, he is nonetheless romantic for being a plain businessman. Paradoxically enough, I have never heard his name, and I wouldn't be at all sure he exists, except for the indisputable evidence of his handiwork. He is the man who dreams up the dialogue in those advertising comic strips.

The general story pattern of these strips, while elementary, has the rugged simplicity of a piece of pre-Columbian sculpture or the Jupiter Symphony. The hero, a small boy or a creature from outer space, stumbles on various simple or compound disasters and averts them through superhuman strength derived from eating a given cereal or sandwich spread. Though never conveyed in so many words, there is usually a sly implication that the purchaser will acquire similar prowess the instant he lays his money on the barrelhead.

A convenient specimen appeared in a recent Sunday *Herald Tribune.* It shows Peter Pan, a strangely mammiferous teen-ager in a Lincoln green jerkin, stepping out of the trademark on a jar of peanut butter and beguiling a boy to the circus. The pair breathlessly watches the star trapeze act, in which a girl aerialist shuttles between her own flimsy perch and the hands of her catcher. Suddenly, a rope frays and the girl dangles perilously beyond the catcher's reach. "Hang on!" encourages the ringmaster, who evidently has seen peanut butter save the day in many a crisis. "Peter Pan's on the way!" His faith is vindicated forthwith, when Peter, her ankles gripped by the catcher, swings out and snatches the girl back to safety. "Thanks for saving my life, Peter Pan," the latter observes somewhat lymphatically. "Yes," adds the ringmaster, a man obviously accustomed to deal with any social situation. "And I'm treating everybody to these swell peanut-butter sandwiches. Take all you want, folks!" By my limited standards, such munificence is roughly

1. Permission of the author. Copyright 1946 The New Yorker Magazine, Inc. (Formerly The F-R. Publishing Corporation.)

synonymous with a left to the kidneys, but circus people have their own curious code. With the final terse announcement *"It does not stick to the roof of your mouth!,"* Peter Pan steps back in the label and the reader presumably rushes to the nearest grocer. I started to, but my head was wedged between a couple of sofa pillows, and as it would have meant cutting it away with an acetylene torch, I decided to string out the autumn on margarine.

"How Thom McAn Foiled the Flood," a strip decorating the back cover of a comic book called "Wonder Woman," also has its moments of rare verbal beauty. Thom, a red-headed lad of Herculean vitality, is introduced lounging with three friends "outside the clubhouse of the Thom McAn Shoes-True Pals," surely the most neuralgic collection of words ever yoked together in English. Informed by a radio flash that the town dam has broken, he hastily dons a pair of weird red Juliets, which he refers to as "bazooka-shoes," and whizzes to the scene. "Wow!" he shudders as he sees the torrent about to engulf the town. "Not a second to spare! And I can't move the town—so I have to move the flood!" Employing his shoes as a bulldozer, Thom rips a channel through the mountain, thus enabling the river to bypass the town, and returns to the club to receive the plaudits of his friends. "These 'bazooka-shoes' are O.K. for emergencies," he comments wryly. "But for everyday comfort and fun, I'll take good ol' Thom McAn shoes!" His jubilant comrades suggest a feast to celebrate his exploit, but Thom suddenly stands on protocol: "Wait, Jimmy here can't enter. He's not 'shoe-true to Thom McAn!' " After humiliating Jimmy so thoroughly that they lay the foundation for a whopping psychic trauma, his chums agree to let the outlaw participate, on condition he dig up a pair of Thom McAns. An hour later, Thom greets him at the clubhouse door. "Enter, pal," he says with greasy affability. "Your shoes are the key. Now you are officially a 'Thom McAn Shoe-True Pal!' " This piquant hash of child psychology and salesmanship, incidentally, appeared in a publication whose advisory board includes an assistant professor of education at Columbia, a professor of psychiatry and one of English literature at New York University, Pearl Buck, and Gene Tunney. The names of Captain Bligh and Torquemada were missing from the masthead, but I guess they happened to be out of town.

The most captivating example of this sort of moonshine I have met, however, is the strip called "Volto, He Comes from Mars Possessing Strange Magnetic Powers!," in a journal named *Star Spangled Comics,* which I found stashed in my son's bed a few days ago. We first encounter Volto, an interplanetary version of the late Lou Tellegen, on a roller coaster with a small boy. Suddenly, down the incline toward them hurtles another car. "What a way to run a roller coaster!" exclaims Volto pettishly. "I better get busy!" He extends his left hand, repelling the car, but the ensuing jolt dislodges one of the passengers, a reasonably well-stacked brunette. As she falls headlong,

Volto extends his right hand and she is magically swept into his arms. A concessionaire hurries up to offer Volto a hundred dollars for the secret of his stunt. "It's no trick for Volto!" announces his young companion. "He's from Mars, where everybody gets that magnetism from eating whole-grain cereals!" Volto, plainly reluctant, looses his hold on the maiden. "And I must have some right now to recharge my power!" he chimes in with a wolfish grin. Simpering, the brunette tucks back a stray wisp of hair. "Then," she proposes, "let me repay you with the tastiest whole-grain cereal in this world—Grape-Nuts Flakes!" In the final tableau, Volto has apparently whisked the girl away to a quiet little cafeteria for a few rounds of flakes, and the strip concludes with the boy exalting the virtues of the cereal.

An electric climax to a thrilling episode—and yet, somehow, the whole affair leaves one frustrated. What *did* become of Volto and his little pigeon after they left the park? What about Volto's home life—did Mrs. Volto know where he was? Why was he bumming around an amusement park on Earth when he should have been tending to business on Mars? Obviously, Grape-Nuts is playing its cards very close to the vest indeed, and if we are to have an explanation, we shall have to evolve it ourselves. I'll go first:

Alice Volto stirred sleepily on her chaise longue, her ear cocked at the sound of her husband's tread in the corridor. She heard him fumble unsteadily at the keyhole; after a moment the door slammed and a penetrating odor of oatmeal wafted out of the foyer, punctuated by a stifled belch. "Oh, damnation," she thought hopelessly. "Another toot. And after all his promises, too." She held up her wristwatch to the back of her head, where the best of her eyes was located, and peered at the time. Nine-fifteen—two hours late. He would probably have some overplausible yarn about being detained by a client from Betelgeuse or Charles's Wain. She arose with weary resignation, flicked a suède buffer across her nose to accent its patrician metallic gleam, and issued into the living room.

"Hi, sweet," Volto mumbled from behind his evening paper. He was aware that he was holding it upside down, but he didn't care; he felt ghastly. If only he hadn't let that little tramp cajole him into a final dish of Crispies.

"Everything all right at the office?" asked Alice, casually levitating herself to the mantelpiece and lighting a cigarette. She had long since learned the value of forbearance and cunning with her husband.

"Oh, tiptop!" said Volto, assuming a grimace intended to convey sunny insouciance. "I blew out a sprocket this morning, but the nurse at the infirmary welded it."

"Better stop around at the plumber's in the morning and have a checkup," his wife advised. "You may still have a little steam in your gauge from last winter."

"No, I—I feel great," Volto assured her, nimbly brushing an ashtray to the floor and strewing the rug with butts. His red-lacquered neck turned a deeper shade. Alice, her lip curling in amused contempt, extended her right hand and the ashtray leaped back to the table. In the short, meaningful silence that followed, a fine perspiration mantled her husband's forehead.

"You must be famished, darling," remarked Alice, at last. "Your dinner's in the alcove."

"Why—er—uh, I don't think I want anything right now," said Volto, with a sickly grin. "I had a rather late lunch—"

"But it's your favorite dish!" Alice objected. "I made you a great big bowl of Wheaties mixed with Kix and shredded bran. You adore it."

"I know," Volto admitted unhappily. "But you see, I—well, this small goy I met on the midway—er, I mean to say *boy*—"

"What midway?" Alice interrupted.

"Why, the amusement park," he faltered. "The one down there on the Earth. Say, you wouldn't believe the way they run their roller coasters! Irresponsible—yes, sir, absolutely insane!"

"Really?" Alice's voice abruptly turned glacial. "What were you doing on the roller coaster?"

"Who, me?" asked Volto innocently. "Nothing. I was just riding in the front seat with this boy."

"I thought you were at the office all afternoon," said Alice.

"What's the matter with you—don't you understand Martian?" shouted Volto. "I told you I was down on Earth, didn't I?"

"I'm sorry," said Alice. "Well, go on."

"I *am* going on!" he screamed. "Only, for God's sake, stop yelling 'Go on, go on' at me! It's enough to drive a man crazy." He paused, drew some steel wool from his pocket, and sponged his brow. "Well, we were zooming along like anything, when a girl fell out of the other car—"

"Oh," said Alice. "Was she pretty?"

"What's that got to do with it?" demanded Volto savagely.

"Nothing," said Alice. "I was just curious."

"Well, don't start reading double meanings into everything," snapped her husband. "When I see a party in mortal peril, I don't ask if they're a Conover model before I go to their aid."

"No, but it comes in handy afterward," commented Alice. "What happened then?"

"Nothing," replied Volto. "I used my strange magnetic powers, that's all."

"I bet you did," said his wife. "Was she grateful?"

"How do you mean?" asked Volto cautiously.

"Well, you saved her life, if I interpret your story correctly."

"Too damn grateful," returned Volto. "You never saw such a nuisance. I wanted to come home, but she made me go and have some whole-grain cereals with her."

"Where—in a restaurant?" inquired Alice.

"Well—uh, not exactly." Volto hesitated. "You see, all the restaurants down there close by three in the afternoon. We tried 'em."

"But then she remembered she had some cereal up at her place, I suppose," suggested Alice.

"Why, how did you know?" asked Volto, taken aback.

"Oh, I just guessed," smiled his wife. "I always kept some on hand for emergencies before I knew you."

"Well, it was pretty white of her, all the same," said Volto defensively. "If I hadn't found some way to recharge, I might never have come back to this planet."

"My goodness," said Alice with a certain degree of composure. "Whatever would have become of me?"

"That's what I was afraid of," explained Volto. "It had me plenty worried for a spell."

"Well, dear," said Alice, descending from her perch, "you've had a full day, haven't you? Why don't you run along to bed?"

"Think I will," yawned her husband. "You going to sit up and read awhile?"

"No, I believe I'll take a spin," said Alice thoughtfully. "Did you leave the rocket out?"

Volto nodded. "Going over to your mother's?" he asked.

"Uh-uh," smiled Alice. "Coney Island."

OOFF!! (SOB!) EEP!! (GULP!) ZOWIE!!![1]

E. J. KAHN, JR.

A FEW years ago, the Boston *Globe,* perhaps hoping to evoke a handsome testimonial to the influence of its editorial page, asked some of its readers who were attending college, and were thus possibly a cut above the intellectual average, to tell why they preferred the *Globe* to its competitors. Ninety per cent of the students said that they favored the *Globe* because it carried "Li'l Abner," a comic strip that is more or less concerned with the diverting antics of a singular tribe of hillbillies native to Dogpatch, a community situated somewhere in the mountains of the southeastern United States. The results of the *Globe's* survey were conveyed, in due course, to Al Capp, the man who draws and writes "Li'l Abner." Capp is a dark, heavy-set, brash, exuberant, witty, rowdy, and inventive man of thirty-eight, who sometimes professes to despise comic strips and might take a firmer stand against them than he does were it not for the

1. Reprinted by permission from *The New Yorker,* XXIII (Nov. 29, 1947), 45–57. Copyright, 1947, The New Yorker Magazine, Inc.

fact that they earn him, before taxes, nearly a quarter of a million dollars a year, a sum that he cannot bring himself to despise. His first reaction to the *Globe's* findings, when a friend told him the news, was commendably objective. "This is deplorable," said Capp. "Is the younger generation utterly without taste?" A moment later, partly disengaging his teeth from the hand that so royally feeds him, he added, "Still, think how much more deplorable it would have been if those imbeciles had said they read the *Globe* because of 'Jane Arden.'"

Capp's full name is Alfred Gerald Caplin, but since the summer of 1934, when he introduced "Li'l Abner" to what he has grown fond of describing as a horrified public, he has been using the sawed-off version, being convinced that many readers of comics are apt to become restless and irritable when confronted with polysyllabic words. Last year, at the invitation of the Encyclopædia Britannica, Capp wrote a critical essay about the American comic strip for a four-volume supplement called "Ten Eventful Years." Capp noticed delightedly that he had been identified as "A. Cp.," a signature far outdoing in economy his own effort. He was about to write the Britannica editors a congratulatory note when a learned acquaintance explained that these scholars abbreviate all their contributors' names, even those never previously cropped. According to Capp's article, "The comic strip during the decade 1937–1946 became, in terms of the constancy of the devotion of its followers, the most popular U.S. entertainment, surpassing radio and the motion picture." In any terms, the comics are thriving. Every month, nearly forty million comic books are bought and presumably read. Every day, seventy million people, or half the population of the country, are reputed to read, openly or furtively, comic strips in the newspapers. It is difficult to arrive at the exact number of readers of any given strip, since the syndicates that distribute these profitable features are partial to dealing in round, if not downright puffy, figures. The United Feature Syndicate, which transmits Capp's work to a waiting world, computed recently, with exceptional precision, that "Li'l Abner" was printed in 30,189,151 copies of daily newspapers in this country, as well as in a large but indeterminable quantity abroad. Any analysis of such statistics is apt to bring on a headache. In the fall of 1944, for instance, United Feature, then dealing in conventional globular figures, announced that Capp had twenty-seven million readers and that he had acquired them at the rate of seventy-five hundred a day. In the fall of 1945, the syndicate announced that in the preceding twelve months he had picked up 77,923 readers. This amounted to a daily gain for that year of a mere two hundred and thirteen and a half readers, but the syndicate, instead of apologizing for this sudden diminution of converts per day, deftly shifted its ground and let it be known that Capp habitually ensnared new readers at the rate of four and a half a minute. It is agreed by people who ponder such matters that the field is led today by five comic strips—"Blondie," "Dick Tracy," "Joe Palooka," "Little Orphan Annie," and "Li'l Abner," though not necessarily in that order. Each one appears in over twenty-five million copies of newspapers a week, and each copy probably has at least one reader, or, in round figures, each strip has fifty readers per second, day or night, rain or shine, dead or alive.

Partisans of each of the five most illustrious serials, including the men who turn them out, are inclined to think that their own favorite is coincidentally the national favorite. "More Americans give me a piece of their day," Capp recently told a friend, "than anyone else in the country." He is not alone in viewing himself as top dog. The *Illinois State Journal,* published in Springfield, observed last year that "Al Capp, more than any other comic strip artist, has won the complete confidence and genuine affection of the American people. . . . Li'l Abner [has] become an American institution." The Charlotte, North Carolina, *News,* further defining the strip's institutional status, called it "as much a part of the national life as ice cream cones and taxes." These periodicals are among the four hundred and twenty-seven daily and one hundred and seventy-nine Sunday papers in the United States that carry "Li'l Abner." They pay, depending on their size and other factors, from seventy-five cents to six hundred dollars a week for the privilege. Tributes to Capp's eminence have not come only from publications that contentedly serve as the oysters for his pearls. A federal law-enforcement officer in San Antonio once wrote Capp that in the course of his duties he had met up with people suffering from the stings of scorpions, from overdoses of marijuana, and from hydrophobia, but that he had never encountered anybody "who spouted more varied and distorted ideas than you do."

When Capp started "Li'l Abner," comic strips were around forty years old. The early comics were unpretentious illustrated gags; they were comical, or tried to be. By the thirties, according to the Britannica's Mr. Cp., "The clowns had been pushed off the comic page by the misery-vendors, the horror-vendors, the blood-merchants. The hilarious 'Bam!!!' or 'Zowie!!!!' ending of the comic simpleton overcome by the brutality, misunderstanding, avariciousness, or bad temper of his fellowman had been supplanted by the 'Help!! The rattlesnake is strangling me, Mother, dear!!!'—or—'Take dat, you copper—right t'roo de head!!!' type of ending wherein the comic simpleton was supplanted by a pathetic, golden-haired little girl simpleton or a blue-eyed, white-lipped, red-blooded detective simpleton, whose perils never ended—in fact, increased each day in violence and intricacy. . . . The comic strips, with a few die-hard, hard-fighting exceptions, were no longer comic. . . . The word went out from circulation departments that anxiety about the fate of Orphan Annie's dog sold far more papers than did joy over the foolishness of Boob McNutt." Capp is the hardest-fighting exception to the trend he disapproves of. His principal character, a young man named Li'l Abner Yokum, is a simpleton of inimitable foolishness, and practically everybody he meets up with is brutal, misunderstanding, avaricious, or bad-tempered. Abner is a handsome youth with an impressive physique, and he is constantly being troubled by the advances of highly attractive young ladies, but he admits to being in love only with such things as a dressmaker's dummy and a cockroach. Male readers of "Li'l Abner," contemplating this grotesque state of affairs, presumably indulge in a smug, self-satisfied smile, fairly certain that if *they* were ever to be pursued by a host of beautiful women, they would know what to do about it. Capp, working on the popular assumption that people of either sex derive immense satisfaction from laughing at the misadventures of creatures to whom they feel superior, has endowed his characters with such nonsensical traits that it is impossible for the most backward citizen of this country not to consider them inferior to himself. Capp's hillbillies are not all in love with cockroaches, but they are thoroughly individualistic in one way or another. They are uneducated, uninhibited, unsanitary, unconventional, and uncompromising, and it always surprises them that the rest of the world is out of step. By continually enmeshing these rural folk in the complexities of organized society, Capp produces the same kind of laughter aroused, in other fields, by the nonconformist struggles of Charlie Chaplin and Groucho Marx. Capp, an exceptionally worldly fellow, has a low opinion of the present state of organized society, and the fantasies he creates often touch upon current events and are heavily flavored with satire. "It's hard to know just how to sum up Al," a friend of Capp's said recently. "If you rule out the possibility that he is a madman, I guess I would call him an outrageously talented author of terribly funny illustrated topical fairy tales—with social significance."

Capp is perhaps without an equal among contemporary fairy-tale composers in his ability to proceed with engaging plausibility from a ludicrous premise to a preposterous conclusion. "My readers have a hard time," he said a while ago. "They have to learn to accept the incredible as the normal run of things." His readers can be divided into three categories, corresponding to the three levels upon which "Li'l Abner" is constructed. The base level is in the Bam!!!-and-Zowie!!!! tradition, a broad, slapstick foundation of frenzied adventure, such as hair-raising chases, violent fights, and people hanging by their fingertips from the edges of precipitous cliffs. Readers of all ages who like to browse on this level are apt to be quite concerned about the outcome of Capp's elaborate and giddy plots, and those who get a chance always ask him whether Li'l Abner is ever going to marry the heroine of the strip, a handsome but vacuous young lady named Daisy Mae Scragg, whose love for Abner is equalled only by his distaste for her entire sex. Capp is sometimes tolerant of, but always bored with, people who make this inquiry about this foolish young couple, and he refers to them brusquely as "Abner fans." Readers who indicate to him that they are especially pleased with the middle, or socially significant, level of his work, and who ask him when he is going to take another poke at radio commercials or the United States Senate, are, he thinks, much more estimable citizens, and he calls them, approvingly, "disgusting Abner fans." The third level, sometimes of microscopic dimensions, consists of bits of Rabelaisian humor, often so adroitly covered up that, like rare archeological treasures, they are less likely to be spotted by children at play than by people who set out looking for them. These mischievous escapades in print amuse Capp more than anything else about his work, and the thought that few of his readers share this enjoyment with him depresses him. If, however, he were to make these touches more obvious, it is possible that his strip might be banned not only in Boston but in Springfield, Charlotte, and San Antonio as well.

When Capp encounters a reader who enjoys not only the two lower levels but the nuances on Level Three, he confers on the fellow the highest possible token of his esteem, the designation of "slobbering Abner fan." People who have thus been honored realize that the title is a compliment, since "slob" is one of Capp's favorite nouns. "To me, the word 'slob' has a great deal of force and humor," he has said. "It's one of those really choice and charming words." It is not regarded with the same fervor by the United Feature Syndicate, whose editors feel obliged to tone down Capp's material when they detect something that particularly worries them. (A United Feature man was once described by a sympathetic friend as a "quivering Abner fan," and a piece of promotional literature that the syndicate issued a couple of years ago said, with perhaps unconscious wistfulness, "You never know what's coming next when it comes off the pen of the creator of 'Li'l Abner.' ") One of Capp's favorite characters is a Dogpatch girl called Moonbeam McSwine, whose name indicates her paradoxical nature, since although she is uncommonly good-looking, she detests bathing and prefers the company of hogs to that of men. Six years ago, Capp had her say, "Ah is a lazy good-fo'-nothin' slob!" Somebody in the United Feature offices gave this confessional a scrubbing on its way to the public, and when it finally appeared in print it read, "Ah is a lazy good-fo'-nothin'!" Capp was distressed by the disappearance of what to him had been the only really charming word in the sentence, but he cheered up a few years later when he succeeded in having Daisy Mae, a girl of profound delicacy, call Moonbeam McSwine a slob.

Capp is not a self-effacing man, but he has stubbornly resisted the temptation to consider himself, as many of his fellow-citizens do, the world's greatest contemporary comic-strip artist. He feels that he is merely one of the two greatest, the other being Milton Caniff, the gifted inventor of "Terry and the Pirates" (now being done by another man) and at present the shepherd of "Steve Canyon." Capp's estimate seems to be shared by the School of Education of New York University, which, when it revealed, not long ago, that it planned to conduct a study of "the cartoon narrative as a medium of communication," said that Caniff and Capp were the only two cartoon narrators who were slated to take part in the inquiry. Caniff does not share Capp's shy reluctance to put one man at the top of the list; Caniff puts Capp there. "Al's the best of us all," he said recently. "To me, he is the only really funny man in the funnies business." Capp's professional honors are numerous. For one thing, he was the first comic-strip creator (a noun used in the business to describe anyone who both writes and draws a strip) to introduce parodies of other comic strips into his own. For another, he was the first comic-strip man to effect a profitable tieup, in his strip, with commercial broadcasting. Last year, he collaborated on a song about Li'l Abner and, after persuading several important radio vocalists to plug it, worked them into the plot of his strip. Then, on whatever day they were scheduled to sing the number, caricatures of them appeared in "Li'l Abner" and mentioned their broadcasts. Considering that comic strips have to be put together several weeks before publication and that radio programs are often torn apart at the last minute, the fact that Capp managed to synchronize events in the two media was impressive.

Capp has done a great many things other comic-strip artists might well be afraid to attempt. "The funnies have always avoided the enormous comic gold mine of sex," he once said. He was not referring to his own strip. When a song entitled "Six Lessons from Madame La Zonga," which he did not help compose, was at its height, Capp introduced into "Li'l Abner" an engaging and romantic character named Adam Lazonga. "He was a perilous experiment," Capp wrote to a friend, "because he was the master of how to woo, Dogpatch style—a kinda wooing the details of which were never very clear to the reader or to me, but which was superior to all other styles—and because he had won loving cups in exhibitions of Dogpatch-style wooing the world over. It was a nervous moment when I let him loose in the nation's family newspapers. Readers were shocked as it dawned on them what he was famous for doing, but delighted by his courtly and genteel way of doing it, and his dignified attitude toward his work."

Capp has many distinctions besides that of digging pay dirt out of the gold mine of sex. Most comic-strip creators are sedentary folk. Capp is wildly peripatetic. He lives with his wife and their three children on a farm in New Hampshire, has a studio apartment in Boston, and spends from ten days to two weeks of every month relaxing, with indefatigable intensity, in New York. Moreover, he is the only major practitioner of his art involved in two richly rewarding strips. He does the plotting and writes the dialogue for "Abbie an' Slats," which appears in a hundred and thirty daily and eighty Sunday papers in this country. "Abbie" is officially the handiwork of Raeburn Van Buren, who draws it and signs it, but Capp thought up the idea for it eleven years ago, sold it to United Feature, has done all the writing for it ever since, and receives half the net proceeds from it. Neither Capp nor United Feature has ever publicly admitted his connection with "Abbie," perhaps out of consideration for the feelings of comic-strip creators who have barely enough imagination and energy to keep one serial going. Capp enjoys pretending that he has no stake in "Abbie," and when asked by interviewers from high-school papers, as he often is, to name his favorite strip next to "Li'l Abner," he usually pauses, seems to think hard for a moment, and then solemnly plumps for "Abbie an' Slats." In his Britannica article, he modestly mentions "Abner" only once, but he twice praises "Abbie." Just a week ago, Capp established some kind of precedent by reviving, in "Abbie," a character who had been unequivocally killed off several months before. "In comic strips," Capp wrote in a note to his readers that was signed "R.V.B.," "if *you* want it hard enough and if the cartoonist has *nerve* enough, we can get together, remake the make-believe world in which, for a few moments each day, we all meet." Having the continuities of two major comic strips at his mercy, Capp has been able to indulge in a good deal of horseplay. Among the characters who have turned up in "Li'l Abner" are Raeburn Van Huron, an Indian chief, and Bullseye Van Suren, a champion dart-thrower; "Abbie an' Slats" was once given over for several weeks to the story of a conceited, gluttonous, drunken, disorderly, and untalented comic-strip artist named Hal Yapp, the creator of a strip called "Li'l Ebenezer." Yapp worked—at a time when the late George Carlin was managing United Feature—for a syndicate run by George Garlic. Capp often ridicules public figures, and he receives a lot of indignant letters of protest from people who admire his victims. When the Hal Yapp continuity appeared in "Abbie an' Slats," a great many alert Al Capp fans addressed vituperative letters to Raeburn Van Buren, who has since been regarded in the profession as the most stoical member of the human race since Sparta.

Capp's best-known victim is Chester Gould, creator of "Dick Tracy." Three years ago, in "Li'l Abner," Capp unveiled a cartoonist named Lester Gooch, creator of a gory strip entitled "Fearless Fosdick." The title character of this strip-within-a-strip is a detective of immense stupidity and is the idol of Li'l Abner Yokum, whom Capp has described as an individual of average comic-strip-reading mentality. "When Yokum speaks," Capp once wrote in "Li'l Abner," in a further explanation of his hero's mentality, "he speaks for millions of morons." In the lampoons of "Dick Tracy" that Capp has turned out, he has made some sharp observations upon the effect of comics on the American mind. A year and a half ago, Capp began a "Fearless Fosdick" sequence with a letter to Gooch written by Yokum, who was probably speaking not only for millions but for Capp, too. "Yore drawrins cood allus be dependid on to frigten li'l chillun an ole ladys into fitts on account they was so ugly yore drawrins I meen," wrote Abner, the only member of his family, aside from a small pig, who is literate. "Yo has allus bin the leeder of yore profeshun naimly skeerin the liver out of yore fateful reeders. But, laitly, things has changed, Gooch. Lately, *other* comical stripp cree-ay-ters bin cree-ay-tin even *more* horibul cree-ay-shuns then *yo!* Like ladys wif gravel in thar hare, mudd in thar eyes and who smells badd. Natcherly, the Americun public injoys this vurry much, Gooch. The trubble, Gooch, is all *yo* drawrs is horribul *gennulmin!!* Oh, Gooch, don't lett yore galentry hold yo back! Yo kin drawr worse than any of 'em. Go to it, Gooch, whomp up a lady thet is *so* itchy, *so* shakey, *so* smelly, and *so* onbarubbly disgustin that once agin you will be the king of the funny page."

Shortly thereafter, Capp, who, naturally, aspires to be the king of the funny page himself, took his own advice and whomped up a lady named Lena the

Hyena, an inhabitant of a country he called, to show what he thought of it, Lower Slobbovia. Lena had a face so unbearably disgusting that a coal-black shark, happening to glimpse and then to swallow a photograph of it, shrieked, turned white, and sank to the bottom of the sea. Capp did not, however, plan to frighten little children and old ladies into fits by letting them see Lena's face—or so he insists today. He left the space above her neck blank and wrote "Deleted by Editor" across it. Immediately, some of his readers, eager to have the livers scared out of them, wrote to him pleading for a look at the lady's features. Capp then announced, in "Li'l Abner," that only a morbid horror seeker could be interested in the sight. This provoked more letters from confessed morbid horror seekers. Capp, delighted, decided to open a contest for drawings of the worst-looking woman in the world, the winning picture to be used in the strip and the winning artist to receive a prize of five hundred dollars. Three hundred and eighty-one of the newspapers that run "Li'l Abner" joined in, and most of them offered additional awards. Close to a million entries were submitted. On the periphery of the big contest, people all over the country—including a group of adult members of the First Congregational Church of Toledo—banded together to hold elimination contests of their own. A schoolboy who said he owned an authentic likeness of Lena grew rich, by charging his classmates a nickel a peek, before his teacher took it away from him. The annual Homecoming Queen beauty contest of the University of Colorado was disrupted by a write-in movement for Lena, who did so much better than any of the six attractive live candidates that the president of the university hastily called off the competition. Just before Election Day, a California paper that was participating in the contest asked its readers to send in questions they wished to have answered by prospective office holders. The paper got a total of thirty political questions and seven thousand drawings of Lena the Hyena.

There has been only the one Lena contest. For the last ten years, however, every November has been brightened by the celebration, on hundreds of campuses and in other arenas, of an as yet unofficial holiday known as Sadie Hawkins Day, which, according to the Birmingham, Alabama, *Post,* a paper that publishes "Li'l Abner," has become so firmly entrenched as part of the American way of life that it would take an act of Congress to wipe it off the books." In Dogpatch, Sadie Hawkins Day provides unmarried women with an opportunity to obtain husbands by catching the community's eligible men in a foot race. In the rest of the country, the day is a less forthright variation of the leap-year idea. At many academies where it is observed, it is simply an excuse for the temporary reversal of normal social relationships: girls date boys. On some campuses the holiday lasts for a week or more, usually ending with a costume party, for which the guests dress in the fashion of "Li'l Abner" characters, a most scantily clad crew. Every year, Capp is invited to take in a couple of thousand of these parties. Last November, after consenting to look in on eighteen of them, he said to a friend, "Aren't they a wonderful idea? A girl can look charming for nothing!" Halfway through his tour, when he entered an armory where twelve thousand young people, dressed charmingly in rags, had gathered to do him homage, he appeared to have lost some of his enthusiasm. "What have I wrought!" he was heard to mutter. After the eighteenth party, he retired to his studio, sat down, and dashed off a snarling "Li'l Abner" sequence about the kind of people who go to Sadie Hawkins Day parties. Half the girls who attend these functions come dressed as Daisy Mae, and usually they participate in a beauty contest, the winner of which is designated the Daisy Mae of her community. Capp is often invited to serve as a judge. A year ago, he was chief judge and guest of honor at a Sadie Hawkins Day frolic at a large state university. The governor of the state was also present. For several weeks, there had been primary elections to winnow out hundreds of aspiring Daisy Maes. Finally, one chilly night, ten attractive survivors were lined up in a gymnasium for Capp's scrutiny. He is often lax about keeping appointments, and in this instance he was a full hour late. "There were the ten Daisy Maes," he told a friend afterward, "waiting for me, shivering. Usually, when I handle the finals, I spot a couple of standouts right away, either one of whom would be all right to pick. But every now and then it's just no contest. This was one of those cases. One little girl in the line was the loveliest thing I had ever seen. As I was looking them all over, I couldn't help grinning at her. She smiled back. She knew she'd win. Well, there were a lot of photographers hanging around, as always, and I thought I'd be polite and let the governor, who was also hanging around, into the act. I gave him a loving cup and whispered to him, 'The third from the left.' I should have known better than to entrust something like that to a politician. The governor stepped forward and handed the cup to the second from the left, and before I could do anything about it, flash bulbs began popping all over the place and the audience was clapping and cheering. I was stupefied with horror. That poor little third from the left! I couldn't even tell her later about the mistake. It would have created too much of a furor on the campus."

Capp's success in arousing interest in the subject matter of his strip has been thoughtfully noted by many people with axes to grind, and press agents buzz around him as enthusiastically as if he were a syndicated columnist instead of a syndicated cartoonist. When the American Heritage Foundation, sponsor of the Freedom Train, wanted some extra-special publicity for the beginning of its journey, an appeal was made to Capp. He obliged by turning "Li'l Abner," for two weeks, into a dramatization of the Bill of Rights. Some weeks ago, he received a request from Albert Einstein for assistance in disseminating the solemn propaganda of the Emergency Committee of Atomic Scientists. "Will handle in Slobbovia sequence," Capp wrote on the margin of Einstein's letter, and there is no reason to believe that he will not. Capp does not have to be nudged to espouse a cause. Entirely on his own, he has worked up spirited campaigns against, for instance, zoot suits, Southern congressmen, big business, intolerance, and outdoor advertising signs. Once he put Li'l Abner and Daisy

Mae in an automobile and sent them off on a sightseeing trip during which, to view the scenery, Abner was compelled to uproot a hundred and fifty obstructive billboards along a ten-mile stretch of otherwise scenic highway. "Gosh!!" said Daisy Mae afterward. "Hain't America a *bootiful* country—it's even more *bootiful* than billboards advertisin' pork, beans, girdles, shoes, cheese, an' crackers!!" Advertising men have tried to dissuade Capp from this particular crusade. "The implications of such an act," the president of the Outdoor Advertising Association of North Carolina wrote him after Abner's prodigious feats of upheaving, "can hardly remain unnoticed by . . . law-abiding citizens of the United States. . . . If, in the immediate future, a wave of vandalism or property destruction of panels occurs typifying your hero's actions, it will not be a difficult matter to place the blame in the proper quarter." The wave never broke, perhaps because most Americans cannot pull up billboards barehanded. Sometimes, when Capp gets mad, he merely threatens people or institutions with notoriety. During the war, he made a short journey in a day coach and didn't care for it. "I'd never seen anything like the stinking, screaming horror of the whole set-up," he said to an acquaintance. "The poor passengers were treated like prisoners of war. I wrote a letter to the president of the railroad saying that I was planning to have some Dogpatchers take that same trip and that I was going to have them insulted and reviled and knocked about like Polish Jews on a German train on the way to a crematorium. 'I'm going to make it like Dante's "Inferno,"' I told him, 'and I want no protest out of you!' I hadn't drawn a line of any such sequence and didn't intend to, but that railroad president called me up every half hour for four days, conducted a long investigation, discharged two employees, suspended fourteen others, and undoubtedly hasn't had a good night's sleep since."

Some citizens are as eager to get into Capp's strip as others are to stay out. Four years ago, he started using his space on Christmas Day to extend holiday greetings to his friends. Along Broadway, it is now considered even more desirable to get on Capp's December honors list than to be wished happy birthday by Nick Kenny. "You made me the happiest man in the world," a prominent comedian who got mentioned wired Capp last December 26th. As early as the Fourth of July, Capp begins receiving telegrams from press agents reminding him how friendly he feels towards their clients. "It's getting so that if I leave off anybody who was on the year before, he fires his press agent," Capp says. "Why, a music publisher I know called me up the other day and said, 'Al, if you don't include Dick Haymes the way I promised him, I may lose him entirely as a plugger of my songs.'" Capp likes to live well, and he includes on his Christmas list the names of the managers of whatever hotels and night clubs he expects to be spending a substantial amount of time in. Last year he ended his list with the Hampshire House, where he has never since had any trouble reserving a suite. The year before, he extended seasonal wishes to "Halifax." A friend asked him whether he meant the British Ambassador or the city. "I wasn't sure at the time I put it in," Capp replied, "but I got a nice letter of thanks from both." Throughout the year, Capp is offered small gifts if he will make even a casual mention in "Li'l Abner" of something or somebody with a commercial angle, but he has always refused. Once, he was oddly penalized for giving a free plug. The occasion was the opening in New York, in April, 1944, of a musical comedy, "Allah Be Praised!," whose producer, Alfred Bloomingdale, is a friend of Capp's. The cartoonist regards himself as an astute theatrical critic, especially of musical comedies. He attended several rehearsals of "Allah Be Praised!," was delighted with what he saw, and decided to give the show a helping hand. In the strips to be published during the month after the show opened, he decorated a number of walls and fences with placards saying, "Allah Bloomingdale Presents 'Allah Bloomingdale Be Praised.'" The show folded after twenty performances, by which time Capp's outdoor advertising on its behalf had long since been distributed to his newspapers, so it kept coming out for another ten days. Capp was annoyed that "Allah Be Praised!" closed with such inconvenient celerity, and he immediately began writing the book of a musical comedy of his own, an adaptation of "Li'l Abner," which he is still working on.

Outspoken admirers of Capp's work have hailed him as a writer comparable to Lewis Carroll, Mark Twain, Dickens, and Dostoevski, and as an artist comparable to Hogarth, Daumier, and Low. Capp is embarrassed by such accolades. He prefers to think of himself as a simple, incomparable entertainer who specializes in the art of imaginative storytelling. "Practically any artist is better than I am," he once said. "As an artist, I'm just capable." He had such doubts about his capabilities as a writer that three years after starting "Li'l Abner," he took a short-story course at Harvard. His instructor told him that he was not without promise and gave him a B-minus. Technological improvements in communications have given Capp many advantages over earlier storytellers. Homer, for instance, was unable to make himself heard beyond the range of his voice. Capp, without having to raise his voice, can almost simultaneously tell the story of "Li'l Abner" in five languages, in eighteen countries, including Sweden and Venezuela. For telling a black-and-white Monday-through-Saturday continued story and a four-color Sunday-to-Sunday story, he receives around thirty-five hundred dollars a week. His yarns have become so popular in the thirteen years he has been spinning them that he takes in an additional twelve thousand or so a year from royalties on the sales of comic books, toys, costume jewelry, ladies' blouses, cosmetics, and music that have something to do with his comic strip. On behalf of Cream of Wheat, he does six "Li'l Abner" advertisements a year, for which he gets two thousand dollars apiece. "Abbie an' Slats" is good for another twenty thousand annually. Capp has a couple of assistants who do some of his drawing, but even before he took the course at Harvard he declined all offers of assistance in writing. "Li'l Abner" requires an average of a hundred words a day. A fellow-author, arbitrarily assigning half of Capp's gross income from the syndication of "Abner" to its text, has computed that each word, including "Eep" and "Ooff," brings its author three dollars. Capp is not satisfied with this word rate. Most syndicated comic-strippers receive fifty per cent of the gross. Capp now gets sixty-five per cent and is due to get an increase to seventy in 1949. Nevertheless, he is suing United Feature for fourteen and a half million dollars, which he contends the syndicate has deprived him of, in one way or another, since 1934. This may well be the largest claim ever filed by a single literary man against a corporate patron of the arts. The case is an extremely complex one, and unless it is settled out of court, as it may well be, it could drag on for two or three years, like some comic-strip sequences. In the meantime, Capp and United Feature are still working together, in a tight-lipped way.

The success of any storyteller can be measured at least in part by the extent to which his inventions become idiom. Who can utter the words "wine-dark sea" without recalling Homer? Capp's literary achievements, although they have yet to appear in an anthology of quotations, have become a part of the language. He has persuaded a great many of his fellow-citizens that "gulp" and "sob" are expressions that can be legitimately inserted at any point in any sentence. He is responsible for the fact that "oh, happy day!," "amoozin' but confoozin'," "writ by hand," and "as any fool can plainly see" are now used with merciless persistence by millions of Americans. The current enormous popularity of the adverb "naturally" and its variants "natcherly" and "natch" may well be the result of his devotion to them. His nonchalant approach to grammar, punctuation, and spelling has been a stimulating challenge to teachers of English composition, many of whose pupils have indicated a determination to pattern their prose after Al Capp's rather than Dr. Samuel Johnson's. A high-school junior in Lake Bluff, Illinois, assigned to three weeks of earnest study of "some great poet, author, or other writer who symbolizes American literature," chose Capp. In halls of higher learning, too, Capp is a man to reckon with. A year ago, at the College of William and Mary, a debate was held on the subject "Resolved: That 'Dick Tracy' means more to the American public than 'Li'l Abner.'" Two teams, each made up of an undergraduate and a professor, declaimed their arguments. A jury of three other faculty members unanimously returned a verdict in favor of "Li'l Abner."

Some, though by no means all, educators have come to assume that comic strips are read mostly by children and that it is harmful for young and impressionable minds to be continually exposed to characters like Moonbeam McSwine, whose distaste for soap, except as food, has never visibly impaired her physical well-being. The creators of comics, however, long ago abandoned the notion that their readers are all, or even predominantly, children. In a recent survey of adult readers of a number of metropolitan papers that print "Li'l Abner," seventy per cent of the men and sixty per cent of the women questioned said that they followed the strip. Most of the members of our war-time armed forces were of voting age, and their allegiance to "Li'l Abner" seemed at times second only to the one they had pledged to the flag. When the Paris edition of *Stars & Stripes* was unable, for a brief spell, to publish "Abner," it ran an apologetic note saying, "We admit that no newspaper is much good without 'Li'l Abner,' but you'll have to read the rest of the paper for a few days." When "Li'l Abner" failed to appear for three days running in the Vancouver *Sun,* its editors made a great to-do over its absence, which they treated as a news event. Actually, the *Sun* could have published the strip on the second and third day—a delay in the mails had caused a week's worth of "Abner" to arrive twenty-four hours late—but the editors withheld the strip, on the theory, which proved correct, that the despair and then the relief of their readers would be enormously increased. Like many prominent providers of mass-distributed entertainment in an era notable for the affection consumers of this commodity lavish upon its manufacturers, Capp has a vast supply of fervent admirers who aspire to touch or at least to ogle him, and he enjoys his celebrity. He does not, however, receive all the adulation stored up for him, because, unlike most celebrities, his face is not known to all his fans. Some of them aren't even sure of his name: to them he is only that fellow who does "Li'l Abner." At that, his face and name are perhaps better known than are the faces and names of most comic-strip creators, owing to his repeated use of caricatures of the face and variations of the name in the body of his strip. He has always been fond of devising names such as J. P. Gorganfeller, for a millionaire, and Southbrook Juggler, for a columnist, and he is particularly happy when he concocts something like Al Capricorn, for an astrologist, or George Cappley, for a late Bostonian. Connoisseurs of "Li'l Abner" are inclined to the belief that Capp has never got a bigger laugh out of anybody's name than he did out of his own in the fall of 1945, when he had one Westbrook P. Buckingham, the wealthy distiller of a soft drink called Burpsi-Booma, discuss the financing of a proposed new elixir, Eleven Urp, with a pair of Indians belonging to the Seegarstor tribe. "I need capital," said Buckingham. "Capital in Washin'ton. No can move um. Too big," said one of the Indians. "Me once scalp paleface name of 'Al Capital,'" remarked the other Indian triumphantly. There is no evidence that Dickens, Twain, Carroll, or Dostoevski ever contrived anything comparable.

Capp is also working on the project of enabling his admirers to recognize him in the flesh. His calling cards, of which he always carries a bountiful supply, bear on them not merely his name but Li'l Abner's easily recognizable features. When Capp travels, it is usually in a brand-new Cadillac convertible coupé, with the words "Al Capp," in a reproduction of the script in which he signs the strip, painted on the door. At present, he has two 1947 Cadillac convertible coupés, both painted in eye-catching colors and both autographed. While he is riding in either of them, his movements are characterized by a refreshing disdain for the traffic regulations devised by a hundred and forty million other people simply to inconvenience him, and also for policemen churlish enough to wish to enforce them. Some of his friends think that he is, in the vulgar phrase, a cop-hater, but he disagrees. Once, though, he depicted Li'l Abner being mauled by five loutish policemen simply for having picked a flower near a "Keep Off the Grass" sign; this assault occurred immediately after the same officers had unconcernedly watched a couple of thugs spend half an hour beating up an old man. Another time, while Abner and his parents were in London, Capp had them severely dress down a bobby for being polite to them, an attitude that, they told him, was, in a policeman, un-American. Capp himself rarely has any trouble with the police. Whenever a cop does wander across the street to argue with him as he sits in his car, the officer is usually disarmed either by the signature on the car door or, if he doesn't notice that, by the illustrated calling card Capp thrusts upon him. Practically all policemen, it seems, are "Li'l Abner" fans and cannot bring themselves, even after seeing Abner's creator execute a double U turn on a crowded parkway, to be Capp-haters. Capp is usually glad that his prominence can save him from difficulties, but there are moments when he wonders whether it might not be nice to be—instead of a widely acclaimed, splendidly motorized funny man—plain Alfred G. Caplin, a travelling salesman, say, in an unsigned Chevrolet. "My God," he once said, "if only you could imagine the sheer, soul-racking horror of knowing that whenever you are introduced to a stranger as the creator of—gulp—'Li'l Abner,' he'll respond by saying not 'How do you do' but 'Ha ha.'"

· *LITERATURE AND CRITICISM* ·

DOVER BEACH

MATTHEW ARNOLD

The sea is calm to-night.
The tide is full, the moon lies fair
Upon the straits; on the French coast, the light
Gleams and is gone; the cliffs of England stand,
Glimmering and vast, out in the tranquil bay.
Come to the window, sweet is the night-air!
Only, from the long line of spray
Where the sea meets the moon-blanched land,
Listen! you hear the grating roar
Of pebbles which the waves draw back, and fling,

At their return, up the high strand,
Begin and cease, and then again begin,
With tremulous cadence slow, and bring
The eternal note of sadness in.

Sophocles long ago
Heard it on the Aegean, and it brought
Into his mind the turbid ebb and flow
Of human misery: we
Find also in the sound a thought,
Hearing it by this distant northern sea.

The sea of faith
Was once, too, at the full, and round earth's shore
Lay like the folds of a bright girdle furled.
But now I only hear
Its melancholy, long, withdrawing roar,
Retreating, to the breath
Of the night-wind, down the vast edges drear
And naked shingles of the world.

Ah, love, let us be true
To one another! for the world, which seems
To lie before us like a land of dreams,
So various, so beautiful, so new,
Hath really neither joy, nor love, nor light,
Nor certitude, nor peace, nor help for pain;
And we are here as on a darkling plain
Swept with confused alarms of struggle and flight,
Where ignorant armies clash by night.

DOVER BEACH REVISITED: A NEW FABLE FOR CRITICS [1]

THEODORE MORRISON

EARLY in the year 1939 a certain Professor of Educational Psychology, occupying a well-paid chair at a large endowed university, conceived a plot. From his desk in the imposing Hall of the Social Sciences where the Research Insti-

1. "Dover Beach Revisited: A New Fable for Critics," *Harper's Magazine,* CLXXX (February, 1940), 235–244. Reprinted by permission of the author.

tute in Education was housed he had long burned with resentment against teachers of literature, especially against English departments. It seemed to him that the professors of English stood square across the path of his major professional ambition. His great desire in life was to introduce into the study, the teaching, the critical evaluation of literature some of the systematic method, some of the "objective procedure" as he liked to call it, some of the certainty of result which he believed to be characteristic of the physical sciences. "You make such a fetish of science," a colleague once said to him, "why aren't you a chemist?"—a question that annoyed him deeply.

If such a poem as Milton's "Lycidas" has a value—and most English teachers, even to-day, would start with that as a cardinal fact—then that value must be measurable and expressible in terms that do not shift and change from moment to moment and person to person with every subjective whim. They would agree, these teachers of literature, these professors of English, that the value of the poem is in some sense objective; they would never agree to undertake any objective procedure to determine what that value is. They would not clearly define what they meant by achievement in the study of literature, and they bridled and snorted when anyone else attempted to define it. He remembered what had happened when he had once been incautious enough to suggest to a professor of English in his own college that it might be possible to establish norms for the appreciation of Milton. The fellow had simply exploded into a peal of histrionic laughter and then had tried to wither him with an equally histrionic look of incredulity and disgust.

He would like to see what would happen if the teachers of English were forced or lured, by some scheme or other, into a public exposure of their position. It would put them in the light of intellectual charlatanism, nothing less . . . and suddenly Professor Chartly (for so he was nicknamed) began to see his way.

It was a simple plan that popped into his head, simple yet bold and practical. It was a challenge that could not be refused. A strategically placed friend in one of the large educational foundations could be counted on: there would be money for clerical expenses, for travel if need be. He took his pipe from his pocket, filled it, and began to puff exultantly. To-morrow he must broach the scheme to one or two colleagues; to-night, over cheese and beer, would not be too soon. He reached for the telephone.

The plan that he unfolded to his associates that evening aroused considerable skepticism at first, but gradually they succumbed to his enthusiasm. A number of well-known professors of literature at representative colleges up and down the land would be asked to write a critical evaluation of a poem prominent enough to form part of the standard reading in all large English courses. They would be asked to state the criteria on which they based their judgment. When all the answers had been received the whole dossier would be sent to a moderator, a trusted elder statesman of education, known everywhere for his dignity, liberality of intelligence, and long experience. He would be asked to make a preliminary examination of all the documents and to determine from the point of view of a teacher of literature whether they provided any basis for a common understanding. The moderator would then forward all the documents to Professor Chartly, who would make what in his own mind he was frank to call a more scientific analysis. Then the jaws of the trap would be ready to spring.

Once the conspirators had agreed on their plot their first difficulty came in the choice of a poem. Suffice it to say that someone eventually hit on Arnold's "Dover Beach," and the suggestion withstood all attack. "Dover Beach" was universally known, almost universally praised; it was remote enough so that contemporary jealousies and cults were not seriously involved, yet near enough not to call for any special expertness, historical or linguistic, as a prerequisite for judgment; it was generally given credit for skill as a work of art, yet it contained also, in its author's own phrase, a "criticism of life."

Rapidly in the days following the first meeting the representative teachers were chosen and invited to participate in the plan. Professional courtesy seemed to require the inclusion of an Arnold expert. But the one selected excused himself from producing a value judgment of "Dover Beach" on the ground that he was busy investigating a fresh clue to the identity of "Marguerite." He had evidence that the woman in question, after the episode hinted at in the famous poems, had married her deceased sister's husband, thus perhaps affecting Arnold's views on a social question about which he had said a good deal in his prose writings. The expert pointed out that he had been given a half-year's leave of absence and a research grant to pursue the shadow of Marguerite through Europe, wherever it might lead him. If only war did not break out he hoped to complete this research and solve one of the vexing problems that had always confronted Arnold's biographers. His energies would be too much engaged in this special investigation to deal justly with the more general questions raised by Professor Chartly's invitation. But he asked to be kept informed, since the results of the experiment could not fail to be of interest to him.

After a few hitches and delays from other quarters, the scheme was ripe. The requests were mailed out, and the Professor of Educational Psychology sat back in grim confidence to await the outcome.

II

It chanced that the first of the representative teachers who received and answered Professor Chartly's letter was thought of on his own campus as giving off a distinct though not unpleasant odor of the ivory tower. He would have resented the imputation himself. At forty-five Bradley Dewing was handsome in a somewhat speciously virile style, graying at the temples, but still well-knit and active. He prided himself on being able to beat most of his students at tennis; once a year he would play the third or fourth man on the varsity and go down to creditable defeat with some elegiac phrases on the ravages of time. He thought of himself as a man of the world; it was well for his contentment, which was seldom visibly ruffled, that he never heard the class mimic reproducing at a fraternity house or beer parlor his manner of saying: "After all, gentlemen, it is pure poetry that lasts. We must never forget the staying power of pure art." The class mimic never represents the whole of class opinion but he can usually make everyone within earshot laugh.

Professor Dewing could remember clearly what his own teachers had said about "Dover Beach" in the days when he was a freshman in college himself, phrases rounded with distant professorial unction: faith and doubt in the Victorian era; disturbing influence of Darwin on religious belief; Browning the optimist; Tennyson coming up with firm faith after a long struggle in the waters of doubt; Matthew Arnold, prophet of skepticism. How would "Dover Beach" stack up now as a poem? Pull Arnold down from the shelf and find out.

Ah, yes, how the familiar phrases came back. The sea is calm, the tide is full, the cliffs of England stand. . . . And then the lines he particularly liked:

> Come to the window, sweet is the night air!
> Only, from the long line of spray
> Where the ebb meets the moon-blanch'd sand,
> Listen! you hear the grating roar
> Of pebbles which the waves draw back, and fling,
> At their return, up the high strand,
> Begin, and cease, and then again begin,
> With tremulous cadence slow . . .

Good poetry, that! No one could mistake it. Onomatopoeia was a relatively cheap effect most of the time. Poe, for instance: "And the silken sad uncertain rustling of each purple curtain." Anyone could put a string of s's together and make them rustle. But these lines in "Dover Beach" were different. The onomatopoeia was involved in the whole scene, and it in turn involved the whole rhythmical movement of the verse, not the mere noise made by the consonants or vowels as such. The pauses—only, listen, draw back, fling, begin, cease—how they infused a subdued melancholy into the moonlit panorama at the same time that they gave it the utmost physical reality by suggesting the endless iteration of the waves! And then the phrase "With tremulous cadence slow" coming as yet one more touch, one "fine excess," when it seemed that every phrase and pause the scene could bear had already been lavished on it: that was Miltonic, Virgilian.

But the rest of the poem?

> The sea of Faith
> Was once, too, at the full, and round earth's shore
> Lay like the folds of a bright girdle furl'd . . .

Of course Arnold had evoked the whole scene only to bring before us this metaphor of faith in its ebb-tide. But that did not save the figure from triteness and from an even more fatal vagueness. Everything in second-rate poetry is compared to the sea: love is as deep, grief as salty, passion as turbulent. The sea may look like a bright girdle sometimes, though Professor Dewing did not think it particularly impressive to say so. And in what sense is *faith* a bright girdle? Is it the function of faith to embrace, to bind, to hold up a petticoat, or what? And what is the faith that Arnold has in mind? The poet evokes no precise concept of it. He throws us the simple, undifferentiated word, unites its loose emotional connotations with those of the sea, and leaves the whole matter there. And the concluding figure of "Dover Beach":

> we are here as on a darkling plain
> Swept with confused alarms of struggle and flight,
> Where ignorant armies clash by night.

Splendid in itself, this memorable image. But the sea had been forgotten now; the darkling plain had displaced the figure from which the whole poem tacitly promised to evolve. It would not have been so if John Donne had been the craftsman. A single bold yet accurate analogy, with constantly developing implications, would have served him for the whole poem.

Thus mused Professor Dewing, the lines of his verdict taking shape in his head. A critic of poetry of course was not at liberty to pass judgment on a poet's thought; he could only judge whether, in treating of the thought or sensibility he had received from his age, the poet had produced a satisfactory work of art. Arnold, Professor Dewing felt, had not been able to escape from the didactic tone or from a certain commonness and vagueness of expression. With deep personal misgivings about his position in a world both socially and spiritually barbarous, he had sought an image for his emotion, and had found it in the sea—a natural phenomenon still obscured by the drapings of conventional beauty and used by all manner of poets to express all manner of feelings. "Dover Beach" would always remain notable, Professor Dewing decided, as an expression of Victorian sensibility. It contained lines of ever memorable poetic skill. But it could not, he felt, be accepted as a uniformly satisfactory example of poetic art.

III

It was occasionally a source of wonder to those about him just why Professor Oliver Twitchell spent so much time and eloquence urging that man's lower nature must be repressed, his animal instincts kept in bounds by the exertion of the higher will. To the casual observer, Professor Twitchell himself did not seem to possess much animal nature. It seemed incredible that a desperate struggle with powerful bestial passions might be going on at any moment within his own slight frame, behind his delicate white face in which the most prominent feature was the octagonal glasses that focused his eyes on the outside world. Professor Twitchell was a good deal given to discipleship but not much to friendship. He had himself been a disciple of the great Irving Babbitt, and he attracted a small number of disciples among his own more earnest students. But no one knew him well. Only one of his colleagues, who took a somewhat sardonic interest in the mysteries of human nature, possessed a possible clue to the origin of his efforts to repress man's lower nature and vindicate his higher. This colleague had wormed his way sufficiently into Oliver Twitchell's confidence to learn about his family, which he did not often mention. Professor Twitchell, it turned out, had come of decidedly unacademic stock. One of his brothers was the chief salesman for a company that made domestic fire-alarm appliances. At a moment's notice he would whip out a sample from his bag or pocket, plug it into the nearest electric outlet, and while the bystanders waited in terrified suspense, would explain that in the dead of night, if the house caught fire, the thing would go off with a whoop loud enough to warn the soundest sleeper. Lined up with his whole string of brothers and sisters, all older than he, all abounding in spirits, Professor Twitchell looked like the runt of the litter. His colleague decided that he must have had a very hard childhood, and that it was not his own animal nature that he needed so constantly to repress, but his family's.

Whatever the reasons, Professor Twitchell felt no reality in the teaching of literature except as he could extract from it definitions and illustrations of man's moral struggle in the world. For him recent history had been a history of intellectual confusion and degradation, and hence of social confusion and degradation. Western thought had fallen into a heresy. It had failed to maintain the fundamental grounds of a true humanism. It had blurred the distinction between man, God, and nature. Under the influence of the sciences, it had set up a monism in which the moral as well as the physical constitution of man was included within nature and the laws of nature. It had, therefore, exalted man as naturally good, and exalted the free expression of all his impulses. What were the results of this heresy? An age, complained Professor Twitchell bitterly, in which young women talked about sexual perversions at the dinner table; an age in which everyone agreed that society was in dissolution and insisted on the privilege of being dissolute; an age without any common standards of value in morals or art; an age, in short, without discipline, without self-restraint in private life or public.

Oliver Twitchell when he received Professor Chartly's envelope sat down with a strong favorable predisposition toward his task. He accepted wholeheartedly Arnold's attitude toward literature: the demand that poetry should be serious, that it should present us with a criticism of life, that it should be measured by standards not merely personal, but in some sense *real*.

"Dover Beach" had become Arnold's best-known poem, admired as his masterpiece. It would surely contain, therefore, a distillation of his attitude. Professor Twitchell pulled down his copy of Arnold and began to read; and as he read he felt himself overtaken by surprised misgiving. The poem began well enough. The allusion to Sophocles, who had heard the sound of the retreating tide by the Ægean centuries ago, admirably prepared the groundwork of high seriousness for a poem which would culminate in a real criticism of human experience. But did the poem so culminate? It was true that the world

> Hath really neither joy, nor love, nor light, . . .
> Nor certitude, nor peace, nor help for pain

if one meant the world as the worldling knows it, the man who conducts his life by unreflective natural impulse. Such a man will soon enough encounter the disappointments of ambition, the instability of all bonds and ties founded on nothing firmer than passion or self-interest. But this incertitude of the world, to a true disciple of culture, should become a means of self-discipline. It should lead him to ask how life may be purified and ennobled, how we may by wisdom and self-restraint oppose to the accidents of the world a true human culture based on the exertion of a higher will. No call to such a positive moral will, Professor Twitchell reluctantly discovered, can be heard in "Dover Beach." Man is an ignorant soldier struggling confusedly in a blind battle. Was this the culminating truth that Arnold the poet had given men in his masterpiece? Professor Twitchell sadly revised his value-judgment of the poem. He could not feel that in his most widely admired performance Arnold had seen life steadily or seen it whole; rather he had seen it only on its worldly side, and seen it under an aspect of terror. "Dover Beach" would always be justly respected for its poetic art, but the famous lines on Sophocles better exemplified the poet as a critic of life.

IV

As a novelist still referred to in his late thirties as "young" and "promising," Rudolph Mole found himself in a curious relation toward his academic colleagues. He wrote for the public, not for the learned journals; hence he was spared the necessity of becoming a pedant. At the same time the more lucrative fruits of pedantry were denied to him by his quiet exclusion from the guild. Younger men sweating for promotion, living in shabby genteel poverty on yearly appointments, their childless wives mimicking their academic shop-talk in bluestocking phrases, would look up from the stacks of five-by-three cards on which they were constantly accumulating notes and references, and would say to him, "You don't realize how lucky you are, teaching composition. You aren't expected to know anything." Sometimes an older colleague, who had passed through several stages of the mysteries of preferment, would belittle professional scholarship to him with an elaborate show of graciousness and envy. "We are all just pedants," he would say. "You teach the students what they really want and need." Rudolph noticed that the self-confessed pedant went busily on publishing monographs and being promoted, while he himself remained, year by year, the English Department's most eminent poor relation.

He was not embittered. His dealings with students were pleasant and interesting. There was a sense of reality and purpose in trying to elicit from them a better expression of their thoughts, trying to increase their understanding of the literary crafts. He could attack their minds on any front he chose, and he could follow his intellectual hobbies as freely as he liked, without being confined to the artificial boundaries of a professional field of learning.

Freud, for example. When Professor Chartly and his accomplices decided that a teacher of creative writing should be included in their scheme and chose Rudolph Mole for the post, they happened to catch him at the height of his enthusiasm for Freud. Not that he expected to psychoanalyze authors through their works; that, he avowed, was not his purpose. You can't deduce the specific secrets of a man's life, he would cheerfully admit, by trying to fit his works into the text-book patterns of complexes and psychoses. The critic, in any case, is interested only in the man to the extent that he is involved in his work. But everyone agrees, Rudolph maintained, that the man is involved in his work. Some part of the psychic constitution of the author finds expression in every line that he writes. We can't understand the work unless we can understand the psychic traits that have gained expression in it. We may never be able to trace back these traits to their ultimate sources and causes, probably buried deep in the author's childhood. But we need to gain as much light on them as we can, since they appear in the work we are trying to apprehend, and determine its character. This is what criticism has always sought to do. Freud simply brings new light to the old task.

Rudolph was fortunate enough at the outset to pick up at the college bookstore a copy of Mr. Lionel Trilling's recent study of Matthew Arnold. In this volume he found much of his work already done for him. A footnote to Mr. Trilling's text, citing evidence from Professors Tinker and Lowry, made it clear that "Dover Beach" may well have been written in 1850, some seventeen years before it was first published. This, for Rudolph's purposes, was a priceless discovery. It meant that all the traditional talk about the poem was largely null and void. The poem was not a repercussion of the bombshell that Darwin dropped on the religious sensibilities of the Victorians. It was far more deeply personal and individual than that. Perhaps when Arnold published it his own sense of what it expressed or how it would be understood had changed. But clearly the poem came into being as an expression of what Arnold felt to be the particular kind of affection and passion he needed from a woman. It was a love poem, and took its place with utmost naturalness, once the clue had been given, in the group of similar and related poems addressed to "Marguerite." Mr. Trilling summed up in a fine sentence one strain in these poems, and the principal strain in "Dover Beach," when he wrote that for Arnold "fidelity is a word relevant only to those lovers who see the world as a place of sorrow and in their common suffering require the comfort of constancy."

Ah, love, let us be true
To one another! for the world . . .
Hath really neither joy, nor love, nor light . . .

The point was unmistakable. And from the whole group of poems to which "Dover Beach" belonged, a sketch of Arnold as an erotic personality could be derived. The question whether a "real Marguerite" existed was an idle one, for the traits that found expression in the poems were at least "real" enough to produce the poems and to determine their character.

And what an odd spectacle it made, the self-expressed character of Arnold as a lover! The ordinary degree of aggressiveness, the normal joy of conquest and possession, seemed to be wholly absent from him. The love he asked for was essentially a protective love, sisterly or motherly; in its unavoidable ingredient of passion he felt a constant danger, which repelled and unsettled him. He addressed Marguerite as "My sister!" He avowed and deplored his own womanish fits of instability:

I too have wish'd, no woman more,
This starting, feverish heart, away.

He emphasized his nervous anguish and contrary impulses. He was a "teas'd o'erlabour'd heart," "an aimless unallay'd Desire." He could not break through his fundamental isolation and submerge himself in another human soul, and he believed that all men shared this plight:

Yes: in the sea of life enisl'd,
With echoing straits between us thrown,
Dotting the shoreless watery wild,
We mortal millions live *alone.*

He never "without remorse" allowed himself

To haunt the place where passions reign,

yet it was clear that whether he had ever succeeded in giving himself up wholeheartedly to a passion, he had wanted to. There could hardly be a more telltale phrase than "Once-long'd-for storms of love."

In short much more illumination fell on "Dover Beach" from certain other verses of Arnold's than from Darwin and all his commentators:

Truth—what is truth? Two bleeding hearts
Wounded by men, by Fortune tried,
Outwearied with their lonely parts,
Vow to beat henceforth side by side.

The world to them was stern and drear;
Their lot was but to weep and moan.
Ah, let them keep their faith sincere,
For neither could subsist alone!

Here was the nub. "Dover Beach" grew directly from and repeated the same emotion, but no doubt generalized and enlarged this emotion, sweeping into one intense and far-reaching conviction of insecurity not only Arnold's personal fortunes in love, but the social and religious faith of the world he lived in. That much could be said for the traditional interpretation.

Of course, as Mr. Trilling did not fail to mention, anguished love affairs, harassed by mysterious inner incompatibilities, formed a well-established literary convention. But the fundamental sense of insecurity in "Dover Beach" was too genuine, too often repeated in other works, to be written off altogether to that account. The same sense of insecurity, the same need for some rock of protection, cried out again and again, not merely in Arnold's love poems but in his elegies, reflective pieces, and fragments of epic as well. Whenever Arnold produced a genuine and striking burst of poetry, with the stamp of true self-expression on it, he seemed always to be in the dumps. Everywhere dejection, confusion, weakness, contention of soul. No adequate cause could be found in the events of Arnold's life for such an acute sense of incertitude; it must have been of psychic origin. Only in one line of effort this fundamental insecurity did not hamper, sadden, or depress him, and that was in the free play of his intelligence as a critic of letters and society. Even there, if it did not hamper his efforts, it directed them. Arnold valiantly tried to erect a barrier of culture against the chaos and squalor of society, against the contentiousness of men. What was this barrier but an elaborate protective device?

The origin of the psychic pattern that expressed itself in Arnold's poems could probably never be discovered. No doubt the influence that Arnold's father exercised over his emotions and his thinking, even though Arnold rebelled to the extent at least of casting off his father's religious beliefs, was of great importance. But much more would have to be known to give a definite clue—more than ever could be known. Arnold was secure from any attempt to spy out the heart of his mystery. But if criticism could not discover the cause, it could assess the result, and could do so (thought Rudolph Mole) with greater understanding by an attempt, with up-to-date psychological aid, to delve a little deeper into the essential traits that manifested themselves in that result.

V

In 1917 Reuben Hale, a young instructor in a Western college, had lost his job and done time in the penitentiary for speaking against conscription and for organizing pacifist demonstrations. In the twenties he had lost two more academic posts for his sympathies with Soviet Russia and his inability to forget his Marxist principles while teaching literature. His contentious, eager, lovable, exasperating temperament tried the patience of one college administration after another. As he advanced into middle age, and his growing family suffered repeated upheavals, his friends began to fear that his robust quarrels with established order would leave him a penniless outcast at fifty. Then he was invited to take a flattering post at a girls' college known for its liberality of views. The connection proved surprisingly durable; in fact it became Professor Hale's turn to be apprehensive. He began to be morally alarmed at his own security, to fear that the bourgeois system which he had attacked so valiantly had somehow outwitted him and betrayed him into allegiance. When the C.I.O. made its initial drive and seemed to be carrying everything before it, he did his best to unseat himself again by rushing joyfully to the nearest picket lines and getting himself photographed by an alert press. Even this expedient failed, and he reconciled himself, not without wonder, to apparent academic permanence.

On winter afternoons his voice could be heard booming out through the closed doors of his study to girls who came to consult him on all manner of subjects, from the merits of Plekhanov as a Marxist critic to their own most personal dilemmas. They called him Ben; he called them Smith, Jones, and Robinson. He never relaxed his cheerful bombardment of the milieu into which they were born, and of the larger social structure which made bourgeois wealth, bourgeois art, morals, and religion possible. But when a sophomore found herself pregnant it was to Professor Hale that she came for advice. Should she have an abortion or go through with it and heroically bear the social stigma? And it was Professor Hale who kept the affair from the Dean's office and the newspapers, sought out the boy, persuaded the young couple that they were desperately in love with each other, and that pending the revolution a respectable marriage would be the most prudent course, not to say the happiest.

James Joyce remarks of one of his characters that she dealt with moral problems as a cleaver deals with meat. Professor Hale's critical methods were comparably simple and direct. Literature, like the other arts, is in form and substance a product of society, and reflects the structure of society. The structure of society is a class structure: it is conditioned by the mode of production of goods, and by the legal conventions of ownership and control by which the ruling class keeps itself in power and endows itself with the necessary freedom to exploit men and materials for profit. A healthy literature, in a society so constituted, can exist only if writers perceive the essential economic problem and ally themselves firmly with the working class.

Anyone could see the trouble with Arnold. His intelligence revealed to him the chaos that disrupted the society about him; the selfishness and brutality of the ruling class; the ugliness of the world which the industrial revolution had created, and which imperialism and "liberalism" were extending. Arnold was at his best in his critical satire of this world and of the ignorance of those who governed it. But his intelligence far outran his will, and his defect of will finally blinded his intelligence. He was too much a child of his class to disown it and fight his way to a workable remedy for social injustice. He caught a true vision of himself and of his times as standing between "two worlds, one dead, one powerless to be born." But he had not courage or stomach enough to lend his own powers to the birth struggle. Had he thrown in his sympathies unreservedly with the working class, and labored for the inescapable revolution, "Dover Beach" would not have ended in pessimism and confusion. It would have ended in a cheerful, strenuous, and hopeful call to action. But Arnold could not divorce himself from the world of polite letters, of education, of culture, into which he had been born. He did his best to purify them, to make them into an instrument for the reform of society. But instinctively he knew that "culture" as he understood the term was not a social force in the world around him. Instinctively he knew that what he loved was doomed to defeat. And so "Dover Beach" ended in a futile plea for protection against the hideousness of the darkling plain and the confused alarms of struggle and flight.

Professor Chartly's envelope brought Reuben Hale his best opportunity since the first C.I.O. picket lines to vindicate his critical and social principles. He plunged into his answer with complete zest.

VI

When Peter Lee Prampton agreed to act as moderator in Professor Chartly's experiment he congratulated himself that this would be his last great academic chore. He had enjoyed his career of scholarship and teaching, no man ever more keenly. But now it was drawing to an end. He was loaded with honors from two continents. The universities of Germany, France, and Britain had first laid their formative hands on his learning and cultivation, then given their most coveted recognition to its fruits. But the honor and the glory seemed a little vague on the June morning when the expressman brought into his library the sizable package of papers which Professor Chartly had boxed and shipped to him. He had kept all his life a certain simplicity of heart. At seventy-four he could still tote a pack with an easy endurance that humiliated men of forty. Now he found himself giving in more and more completely to a lust for trout. Half a century of hastily snatched vacations in Cape Breton or the Scottish Highlands had never allowed him really to fill up that hollow craving to find a wild stream and fish it which would sometimes rise in his throat even in the midst of a lecture.

Well, there would be time left before he died. And meanwhile here was this business of "Dover Beach." Matthew Arnold during one of his American lecture tours had been entertained by neighbors of the Pramptons. Peter Lee Prampton's father had dined with the great man, and had repeated his conversation and imitated his accent at the family table. Peter himself, as a boy of nineteen or so, had gone to hear Arnold lecture. That, he thought with a smile, was probably a good deal more than could be said for any of these poor hacks who had taken Professor Chartly's bait.

At the thought of Arnold he could still hear the carriage wheels grate on the pebbly road as he had driven, fifty odd years ago, to the lecture in town, the prospective Mrs. Prampton beside him. His fishing rod lay under the seat. He chuckled out loud as he remembered how a pound-and-a-half trout had jumped in the pool under the clattering planks of a bridge, and how he had pulled up the horse, jumped out, and tried a cast while Miss Osgood sat scolding in the carriage and shivering in the autumn air. They had been just a little late reaching the lecture, but the trout, wrapped in damp leaves, lay safely beside the rod.

It was queer that "Dover Beach" had not come more recently into his mind. Now that he turned his thoughts in that direction the poem was there in its entirety, waiting to be put on again like a coat that one has worn many times with pleasure and accidentally neglected for a while.

> The sea of faith was once, too, at the full.

How those old Victorian battles had raged about the Prampton table when he was a boy! How the names of Arnold, Huxley, Darwin, Carlyle, Morris, Ruskin had been pelted back and forth by the excited disputants! *Literature and Dogma, God and the Bible, Culture and Anarchy*. The familiar titles brought an odd image into his mind: the tall figure of his father stretching up to turn on the gas lamps in the evening as the family sat down to dinner; the terrific pop of the pilot light as it exploded into a net of white flame, shaped like a little beehive; the buzz and whine of a jet turned up too high.

> Ah, love, let us be true
> To one another! for the world, which seems
> To lie before us like a land of dreams,
> So various, so beautiful, so new,
> Hath really neither joy, nor love, nor light,
> Nor certitude, nor peace, nor help for pain . . .

Peter Lee Prampton shivered in the warmth of his sunny library, shivered with that flash of perception into the past which sometimes enables a man to see how all that has happened in his life, for good or ill, turned on the narrowest edge of chance. He lived again in the world of dreams that his own youth had spread before him, a world truly various, beautiful, and new; full of promise, adventure, and liberty of choice, based on the opportunities which his father's wealth provided, and holding out the prospect of a smooth advance into a distinguished career. Then, within six months, a lavish demonstration that the world has neither certitude, nor peace, nor help for pain: his mother's death by cancer, his father's financial overthrow and suicide, the ruin of his own smooth hopes and the prospect instead of a long, hampered, and obscure fight toward his perhaps impossible ambition. He lived again through the night hours when he had tramped out with himself the youthful question whether he could hold Miss Osgood to her promise in the face of such reversals. And he did not forget how she took his long-sleepless face between her hands, kissed him, and smiled away his anxiety with unsteady lips. Surely everyone discovers at some time or other that the world is not a place of certitude; surely everyone cries out to some other human being for the fidelity which alone can make it so. What more could be asked of a poet than to take so profound and universal an experience and turn it into lines that could still speak long after he and his age were dead?

The best of it was that no one could miss the human feeling, the cry from the heart, in "Dover Beach"; it spoke so clearly and eloquently, in a language everyone could understand, in a form classically pure and simple. Or did it? Who could tell what any job-lot of academicians might be trusted to see or fail to see? And this assortment in Chartly's package might be a queer kettle of fish! Peter Lee Prampton had lived through the *Yellow Book* days of Art for Art's sake; he had read the muckrakers, and watched the rise of the Marxists and the Freudians. Could "Dover Beach" be condemned as unsympathetic with labor? Could a neurosis or a complex be discovered in it? His heart sank at the sharp sudden conviction that indeed these and worse discoveries about the poem might be seriously advanced. Well, he had always tried to go on the principle that every school of criticism should be free to exercise any sincere claim on men's interest and attention which it could win for itself. When he actually applied himself to the contents of Professor Chartly's bale he would be as charitable as he could, as receptive to light from any quarter as he could bring himself to be.

But the task could wait. He felt the need of a period of adjustment before he could approach it with reasonable equanimity. And in the meanwhile he could indulge himself in some long-needed editorial work on his dry-fly book.

THE ESSENCE OF TRAGEDY[1]

MAXWELL ANDERSON

ANYBODY who dares to discuss the making of tragedy lays himself open to critical assault and general barrage, for the theorists have been hunting for the essence of tragedy since Aristotle without entire success. There is no doubt that playwrights have occasionally written tragedy successfully, from Aeschylus on, and there is no doubt that Aristotle came very close to a definition of what tragedy is in his famous passage on catharsis. But why the performance of tragedy should have a cleansing effect on the audience, why an audience is willing to listen to tragedy, why tragedy has a place in the education of men, has never, to my knowledge, been convincingly stated. I must begin by saying that I have not solved the Sphinx's riddle which fifty genera-

1. From *Off Broadway, Essays about the Theater* (New York: William Sloane Associates, Inc., 1947), pp. 55–66. Copyright, 1939, Anderson House, and, 1947, Maxwell Anderson.

tions of skillful brains have left in shadow. But I have one suggestion which I think might lead to a solution if it were put to laboratory tests by those who know something about philosophical analysis and dialectic.

There seems no way to get at this suggestion except through a reference to my own adventures in playwriting, so I ask your tolerance while I use myself as an instance. A man who has written successful plays is usually supposed to know something about the theory of playwriting, and perhaps he usually does. In my own case, however, I must confess that I came into the theater unexpectedly, without preparation, and stayed in it because I had a certain amount of rather accidental success. It was not until after I had fumbled my way through a good many successes and an appalling number of failures that I began to doubt the sufficiency of dramatic instinct and to wonder whether or not there were general laws governing dramatic structure which so poor a head for theory as my own might grasp and use. I had read the *Poetics* long before I tried playwriting, and I had looked doubtfully into a few well-known handbooks on dramatic structure, but the maxims and theories propounded always drifted by me in a luminous haze—brilliant, true, profound in context, yet quite without meaning for me when I considered the plan for a play or tried to clarify an emotion in dialogue. So far as I could make out every play was a new problem, and the old rules were inapplicable. There were so many rules, so many landmarks, so many pitfalls, so many essential reckonings, that it seemed impossible to find your way through the jungle except by plunging ahead, trusting to your sense of direction and keeping your wits about you as you went.

But as the seasons went by and my failures fell as regularly as the leaves in autumn I began to search again among the theorists of the past for a word of wisdom that might take some of the gamble out of playwriting. What I needed most of all, I felt, was a working definition of what a play is, or perhaps a formula which would include all the elements necessary to a play structure. A play is almost always, probably, an attempt to recapture a vision for the stage. But when you are working in the theater it's most unsatisfactory to follow the gleam without a compass, quite risky to trust "the light that never was on sea or land" without making sure beforehand that you are not being led straight into a slough of despond. In other words, you must make a choice among visions, and you must check your chosen vision carefully before assuming that it will make a play. But by what rules, what maps, what fields of reference can you check so intangible a substance as a revelation, a dream, an inspiration, or any similar nudge from the subconscious mind?

I shan't trouble you with the details of my search for a criterion, partly because I can't remember it in detail. But I reread Aristotle's *Poetics* in the light of some bitter experience, and one of his observations led me to a comparison of ancient and modern playwriting methods. In discussing construction he made a point of the recognition scene as essential to tragedy. The recognition scene, as Aristotle isolated it in the tragedies of the Greeks, was generally an artificial device, a central scene in which the leading character saw through a disguise, recognized as a friend or as an enemy, perhaps as a lover or a member of his own family, some person whose identity had been hidden. Iphigeneia, for example, acting as priestess in an alien country, receives a victim for sacrifice and then recognizes her own brother in this victim. There is an instant and profound emotional reaction, instantly her direction in the play is altered. But occasionally, in the greatest of the plays, the recognition turned on a situation far more convincing, though no less contrived. Oedipus, hunting savagely for the criminal who has brought the plague upon Thebes, discovers that he is himself that criminal—and since this is a discovery that affects not only the physical well-being and happiness of the hero, but the whole structure of his life, the effect on him and on the direction of the story is incalculably greater than could result from the more superficial revelation made to Iphigeneia.

Now scenes of exactly this sort are rare in the modern drama except in detective stories adapted for the stage. But when I probed a little more deeply into the memorable pieces of Shakespeare's theater and our own I began to see that though modern recognition scenes are subtler and harder to find, they are none the less present in the plays we choose to remember. They seldom have to do with anything so naïve as disguise or the unveiling of a personal identity. But the element of discovery is just as important as ever. For the mainspring in the mechanism of a modern play is almost invariably a discovery by the hero of some element in his environment or in his own soul of which he has not been aware—or which he has not taken sufficiently into account. Moreover, nearly every teacher of playwriting has had some inkling of this, though it was not until after I had worked out my own theory that what they said on this point took on accurate meaning for me. I still think that the rule which I formulated for my own guidance is more concise than any other, and so I give it here: A play should lead up to and away from a central crisis, and this crisis should consist in a discovery by the leading character which has an indelible effect on his thought and emotion and completely alters his course of action. The leading character, let me say again, must make the discovery; it must affect him emotionally; and it must alter his direction in the play.

Try that formula on any play you think worthy of study, and you will find that, with few exceptions, it follows this pattern or some variation of this pattern. The turning point of *The Green Pastures,* for example, is the discovery by God, who is the leading character, that a God who is to endure must conform to the laws of change. The turning point of *Hamlet* is Hamlet's discovery, in the play scene, that his uncle was unquestionably the murderer of his father. In *Abe Lincoln in Illinois* Lincoln's discovery is that he has been a coward, that he has stayed out of the fight for the Union because he was afraid. In each case, you will note, the discovery has a profound emotional effect on the hero, and gives an entirely new direction to his action in the play.

I'm not writing a disquisition on playwriting and wouldn't be competent to write one, but I do want to make a point of the superlative usefulness of this one touchstone for play structure. When a man sets out to write a play his first problem is his subject and the possibilities of that subject as a story to be projected from the stage. His choice of subject matter is his personal problem, and one that takes its answer from his personal relation to his times. But if he wants to know a possible play subject when he finds it, if he wants to know how to mold the subject into play form after he has found it, I doubt that he'll ever discover another standard as satisfactory as the modern version of Aristotle which I have suggested. If the plot he has in mind does not contain a playable episode in which the hero or heroine makes an emotional discovery, a discovery that practically dictates the end of the story, then such an episode must be inserted—and if no place can be found for it the subject is almost certainly a poor one for the theater. If this emotional discovery is contained in the story, but is not central, then it must be made central, and the whole action must revolve around it. In a three-act play it should fall near the end of the second act, though it may be delayed till the last; in a five-act play it will usually be found near the end of the third, though here also it can be delayed. Everything else in the play should be subordinated to this one episode—should lead up to or away from it.

Now this prime rule has a corollary which is just as important as the rule itself. The hero who is to make the central discovery in a play must not be a perfect man. He must have some variation of what Aristotle calls a tragic fault; and the reason he must have it is that when he makes his discovery he must change both in himself and in his action—and he must change for the better. The fault can be a very simple one—a mere unawareness, for example—but if he has no fault he cannot change for the better, but only for the worse, and for a reason which I shall discuss later, it is necessary that he must become more admirable, and not less so, at the end of the play. In other words, a hero must pass through an experience which opens his eyes to an error of his own. He must learn through suffering. In a tragedy he suffers death itself as a consequence of his fault or his attempt to correct it, but before he dies he has become a nobler person because of his recognition of his fault and the consequent alteration of his course of action. In a serious play which does not end in death he suffers a lesser punishment, but the pattern remains the same. In both forms he has a fault to begin with, he discovers that fault during the course of the action, and he does what he can to rectify it at the end. In *The Green Pastures* God's fault was that he believed himself perfect. He discovered that he was not perfect, that he had been in error and must make amends. Hamlet's fault was that he could not make up his mind to act. He offers many excuses for his indecision until he discovers that there is no real reason for hesitation and that he has delayed out of cowardice. Lincoln, in *Abe Lincoln in Illinois,* has exactly the same difficulty. In the climactic scene it is revealed to him that he had hesitated to take sides through fear of the consequences to himself, and he then chooses to go ahead without regard for what may be in store for him. From the point of view of the playwright, then, the essence of a tragedy, or even of a serious play, is the spiritual awakening, or regeneration, of his hero.

When a playwright attempts to reverse the formula, when his hero makes a discovery which has an evil effect, or one which the audience interprets as evil, on his character, the play is inevitably a failure on the stage. In *Troilus and Cressida* Troilus discovers that Cressida is a light woman. He draws from her defection the inference that all women are faithless—that faith in woman is the possession of fools. As a consequence he turns away from life and seeks death in a cause as empty as the love he has given up, the cause of the strumpet Helen. All the glory of Shakespeare's verse cannot rescue the play for an audience, and save in *Macbeth* Shakespeare nowhere wrote so richly, so wisely, or with such a flow of brilliant metaphor.

For the audience will always insist that the alteration in the hero be for the better—or for what it believes to be the better. As audiences change the standards of good and evil change, though slowly and unpredictably and the meanings of plays change with the centuries. One thing only is certain: that an audience watching a play will go along with it only when the leading character responds in the end to what it considers a higher moral impulse than moved him at the beginning of the story, though the audience will of course define morality as it pleases and in the terms of its own day. It may be that there is no absolute up or down in this world, but the race believes that there is, and will not hear of any denial.

And now at last I come to the point toward which I've been struggling so laboriously. Why does the audience come to the theater to look on while an imaginary hero is put to an imaginary trial and comes out of it with credit to the race and to himself? It was this question that prompted my essay, and unless I've been led astray by my own predilections there is a very possible answer in the rules for playwriting which I have just cited. The theater originated in two complementary religious ceremonies, one celebrating the animal in man and one celebrating the god. Old Greek Comedy was dedicated to the spirits of lust and riot and earth, spirits which are certainly necessary to the health and continuance of the race. Greek tragedy was dedicated to man's aspiration, to his kinship with the gods, to his unending, blind attempt to lift himself above his lusts and his pure animalism into a world where there are other values than pleasure and survival. However unaware of it we may be, our theater has followed the Greek patterns with no change in essence, from Aristophanes and Euripides to our own day. Our more ribald musical comedies are simply our approximation of the Bacchic rites of Old Comedy. In the rest of our theater we sometimes follow Sophocles, whose tragedy is always an exaltation of the human spirit, sometimes Euripides, whose tragicomedy follows the same pattern of an excellence achieved through suffering. The forms of both tragedy and comedy have changed a good deal in nonessentials, but in essentials—and especially in the core of meaning which they must have for audiences—they are in the main the same religious rites which grew up around the altars of Attica long ago.

It is for this reason that when you write for the theater you must choose between your version of a phallic revel and your vision of what mankind may or should become. Your vision may be faulty, or shallow, or sentimental, but it must conform to some aspiration in the audience, or the audience will reject it. Old Comedy, the celebration of the animal in us, still has a place in our theater, as it had in Athens, but here, as there, that part of the theater which celebrated man's virtue and his regeneration in hours of crisis is accepted as having the more important function. Our comedy is largely the Greek New Comedy, which grew out of Euripides' tragicomedy, and is separated from tragedy only in that it presents a happier scene and puts its protagonist through an ordeal which is less than lethal.

And since our plays, aside from those which are basically Old Comedy, are exaltations of the human spirit, since that is what an audience expects when it comes to the theater, the playwright gradually discovers, as he puts plays before audiences, that he must follow the ancient Aristotelian rule: he must build his plot around a scene wherein his hero discovers some mortal frailty or stupidity in himself and faces life armed with a new wisdom. He must so arrange his story that it will prove to the audience that men pass through suffering purified, that, animal though we are, despicable though we are in many ways, there is in us all some divine, incalculable fire that urges us to be better than we are.

It could be argued that what the audience demands of a hero is only conformity to race morality, to the code which seems to the spectators most likely to make for race survival. In many cases, especially in comedy, and obviously in the comedy of Molière, this is true. But in the majority of ancient and modern plays it seems to me that what the audience wants to believe is that men have a desire to break the molds of earth which encase them and claim a kinship with a higher morality than that which hems them in. The rebellion of Antigone, who breaks the laws of men through adherence to a higher law of affection, the rebellion of Prometheus, who breaks the law of the gods to bring fire to men, the rebellion of God in *The Green Pastures* against the rigid doctrine of the Old Testament, the rebellion of Tony in *They Knew What They Wanted* against the convention that called on him to repudiate his cuckold child, the rebellion of Liliom against the heavenly law which asked him to betray his own integrity and make a hypocrisy of his affection, even the repudiation of the old forms and the affirmation of new by the heroes of Ibsen and Shaw, these are all instances to me of the groping of men toward an excellence dimly apprehended, seldom possible of definition. They are evidence to me that the theater at its best is a religious affirmation, an age-old rite restating and reassuring man's belief in his own destiny and his ultimate hope. The theater is much older than the doctrine of evolution, but its one faith, asseverated again and again for every age and every year, is a faith in evolution, in the reaching and the climb of men toward distant goals, glimpsed but never seen, perhaps never achieved, or achieved only to be passed impatiently on the way to a more distant horizon.

FENIMORE COOPER'S LITERARY OFFENSES [1]

MARK TWAIN

> *The Pathfinder* and *The Deerslayer* stand at the head of Cooper's novels as artistic creations. There are others of his works which contain parts as perfect as are to be found in these, and scenes even more thrilling. Not one can be compared with either of them as a finished whole.
>
> The defects in both of these tales are comparatively slight. They were pure works of art.—PROF. LOUNSBURY.
>
> The five tales reveal an extraordinary fullness of invention.
>
> . . . One of the very greatest characters in fiction, Natty Bumppo. . . .
>
> The craft of the woodsman, the tricks of the trapper, all the delicate art of the forest, were familiar to Cooper from his youth up.—PROF. BRANDER MATTHEWS.
>
> Cooper is the greatest artist in the domain of romantic fiction yet produced by America.—WILKIE COLLINS.

IT SEEMS to me that it was far from right for the Professor of English Literature in Yale, the Professor of English Literature in Columbia, and Wilkie Collins to deliver opinions on Cooper's literature without having read some of it. It would have been much more decorous to keep silent and let persons talk who have read Cooper.

Cooper's art has some defects. In one place in *Deerslayer,* and in the restricted space of two-thirds of a page, Cooper has scored 114 offenses against literary art out of a possible 115. It breaks the record.

There are nineteen rules governing literary art in the domain of romantic fiction—some say twenty-two. In *Deerslayer* Cooper violated eighteen of them. These eighteen require:

1. That a tale shall accomplish something and arrive somewhere. But the *Deerslayer* tale accomplishes nothing and arrives in the air.

2. They require that the episodes of a tale shall be necessary parts of the tale, and shall help to develop it. But as the *Deerslayer* tale is not a tale, and

1. From *In Defense of Harriet Shelley and Other Essays,* by Mark Twain. Copyright, 1918, by The Mark Twain Company; copyright, 1945, by Clara Clemens Samossoud.

accomplishes nothing and arrives nowhere, the episodes have no rightful place in the work, since there was nothing for them to develop.

3. They require that the personages in a tale shall be alive, except in the case of corpses, and that always the reader shall be able to tell the corpses from the others. But this detail has often been overlooked in the *Deerslayer* tale.

4. They require that the personages in a tale, both dead and alive, shall exhibit a sufficient excuse for being there. But this detail also has been overlooked in the *Deerslayer* tale.

5. They require that when the personages of a tale deal in conversation, the talk shall sound like human talk, and be talk such as human beings would be likely to talk in the given circumstances, and have a discoverable meaning, also a discoverable purpose, and a show of relevancy, and remain in the neighborhood of the subject in hand, and be interesting to the reader, and help out the tale, and stop when the people cannot think of anything more to say. But this requirement has been ignored from the beginning of the *Deerslayer* tale to the end of it.

6. They require that when the author describes the character of a personage in his tale, the conduct and conversation of that personage shall justify said description. But this law gets little or no attention in the *Deerslayer* tale, as Natty Bumppo's case will amply prove.

7. They require that when a personage talks like an illustrated, gilt-edged, tree-calf, hand-tooled, seven-dollar Friendship's Offering in the beginning of a paragraph, he shall not talk like a negro minstrel in the end of it. But this rule is flung down and danced upon in the *Deerslayer* tale.

8. They require that crass stupidities shall not be played upon the reader as "the craft of the woodsman, the delicate art of the forest," by either the author or the people in the tale. But this rule is persistently violated in the *Deerslayer* tale.

9. They require that the personages of a tale shall confine themselves to possibilities and let miracles alone; or, if they venture a miracle, the author must so plausibly set it forth as to make it look possible and reasonable. But these rules are not respected in the *Deerslayer* tale.

10. They require that the author shall make the reader feel a deep interest in the personages of his tale and in their fate; and that he shall make the reader love the good people in the tale and hate the bad ones. But the reader of the *Deerslayer* tale dislikes the good people in it, is indifferent to the others, and wishes they would all get drowned together.

11. They require that the characters in a tale shall be so clearly defined that the reader can tell beforehand what each will do in a given emergency. But in the *Deerslayer* this rule is vacated.

In addition to these large rules there are some little ones. These require that the author shall

12. *Say* what he is proposing to say, not merely come near it.

13. Use the right word, not its second cousin.
14. Eschew surplusage.
15. Not omit necessary details.
16. Avoid slovenliness of form.
17. Use good grammar.
18. Employ a simple and straightforward style.

Even these seven are coldly and persistently violated in the *Deerslayer* tale.

Cooper's gift in the way of invention was not a rich endowment; but such as it was he liked to work it, he was pleased with the effects, and indeed he did some quite sweet things with it. In his little box of stage-properties he kept six or eight cunning devices, tricks, artifices for his savages and woodsmen to deceive and circumvent each other with, and he was never so happy as when he was working these innocent things and seeing them go. A favorite one was to make a moccasined person tread in the tracks of the moccasined enemy, and thus hide his own trail. Cooper wore out barrels and barrels of moccasins in working that trick. Another stage-property that he pulled out of his box pretty frequently was his broken twig. He prized his broken twig above all the rest of his effects, and worked it the hardest. It is a restful chapter in any book of his when somebody doesn't step on a dry twig and alarm all the reds and whites for two hundred yards around. Every time a Cooper person is in peril, and absolute silence is worth four dollars a minute, he is sure to step on a dry twig. There may be a hundred handier things to step on, but that wouldn't satisfy Cooper. Cooper requires him to turn out and find a dry twig; and if he can't do it, go and borrow one. In fact, the Leatherstocking Series ought to have been called the Broken Twig Series.

I am sorry there is not room to put in a few dozen instances of the delicate art of the forest, as practised by Natty Bumppo and some of the other Cooperian experts. Perhaps we may venture two or three samples. Cooper was a sailor—a naval officer; yet he gravely tells us how a vessel, driving toward a lee shore in a gale, is steered for a particular spot by her skipper because he knows of an *undertow* there which will hold her back against the gale and save her. For just pure woodcraft, or sailorcraft, or whatever it is, isn't that neat? For several years Cooper was daily in the society of artillery, and he ought to have noticed that when a cannon-ball strikes the ground it either buries itself or skips a hundred feet or so; skips again a hundred feet or so—and so on, till finally it gets tired and rolls. Now in one place he loses some "females"—as he always calls women—in the edge of a wood near a plain at night in a fog, on purpose to give Bumppo a chance to show off the delicate art of the forest before the reader. These mislaid people are hunting for a fort. They hear a cannon-blast, and a cannon-ball presently comes rolling into the wood and stops at their feet. To the females this suggests nothing. The case is very different with the admirable Bumppo. I wish I may never know peace again if he doesn't strike out promptly and *follow the track* of that cannon-ball across the plain through the dense fog and find the fort. Isn't it a daisy? If

Cooper had any real knowledge of Nature's way of doing things, he had a most delicate art in concealing the fact. For instance: one of his acute Indian experts, Chingachgook (pronounced Chicago, I think), has lost the trail of a person he is tracking through the forest. Apparently that trail is hopelessly lost. Neither you nor I could ever have guessed out the way to find it. It was very different with Chicago. Chicago was not stumped for long. He turned a running stream out of its course, and there, in the slush in its old bed, were that person's moccasin tracks. The current did not wash them away, as it would have done in all other like cases—no, even the eternal laws of Nature have to vacate when Cooper wants to put up a delicate job of woodcraft on the reader.

We must be a little wary when Brander Matthews tells us that Cooper's books "reveal an extraordinary fullness of invention." As a rule, I am quite willing to accept Brander Matthews's literary judgments and applaud his lucid and graceful phrasing of them; but that particular statement needs to be taken with a few tons of salt. Bless your heart, Cooper hasn't any more invention than a horse; and I don't mean a high-class horse, either; I mean a clothes-horse. It would be very difficult to find a really clever "situation" in Cooper's books, and still more difficult to find one of any kind which he has failed to render absurd by his handling of it. Look at the episodes of "the caves"; and at the celebrated scuffle between Maqua and those others on the table-land a few days later; and at Hurry Harry's queer water-transit from the castle to the ark; and at Deerslayer's half-hour with his first corpse; and at the quarrel between Hurry Harry and Deerslayer later; and at—but choose for yourself; you can't go amiss.

If Cooper had been an observer his inventive faculty would have worked better; not more interestingly, but more rationally, more plausibly. Cooper's proudest creations in the way of "situations" suffer noticeably from the absence of the observer's protecting gift. Cooper's eye was splendidly inaccurate. Cooper seldom saw anything correctly. He saw nearly all things as through a glass eye, darkly. Of course a man who cannot see the commonest little everyday matters accurately is working at a disadvantage when he is constructing a "situation." In the *Deerslayer* tale Cooper has a stream which is fifty feet wide where it flows out of a lake; it presently narrows to twenty as its meanders along for no given reason, and yet when a stream acts like that it ought to be required to explain itself. Fourteen pages later the width of the brook's outlet from the lake has suddenly shrunk thirty feet, and become "the narrowest part of the stream." This shrinkage is not accounted for. The stream has bends in it, a sure indication that it has alluvial banks and cuts them; yet these bends are only thirty and fifty feet long. If Cooper had been a nice and punctilious observer he would have noticed that the bends were oftener nine hundred feet long than short of it.

Cooper made the exit of that stream fifty feet wide, in the first place, for no particular reason; in the second place, he narrowed it to less than twenty to accommodate some Indians. He bends a "sapling" to the form of an arch over this narrow passage, and conceals six Indians in its foliage. They are "laying" for a settler's scow or ark which is coming up the stream on its way to the lake; it is being hauled against the stiff current by a rope whose stationary end is anchored in the lake; its rate of progress cannot be more than a mile an hour. Cooper describes the ark, but pretty obscurely. In the matter of dimensions "it was little more than a modern canal-boat." Let us guess, then, that it was about one hundred and forty feet long. It was of "greater breadth than common." Let us guess, then, that it was about sixteen feet wide. This leviathan had been prowling down bends which were but a third as long as itself, and scraping between banks where it had only two feet of space to spare on each side. We cannot too much admire this miracle. A low-roofed log dwelling occupies "two-thirds of the ark's length"—a dwelling ninety feet long and sixteen feet wide, let us say—a kind of vestibule train. The dwelling has two rooms—each forty-five feet long and sixteen feet wide, let us guess. One of them is the bedroom of the Hutter girls, Judith and Hetty; the other is the parlor in the daytime, at night it is papa's bedchamber. The ark is arriving at the stream's exit now, whose width has been reduced to less than twenty feet to accommodate the Indians—say to eighteen. There is a foot to spare on each side of the boat. Did the Indians notice that there was going to be a tight squeeze there? Did they notice that they could make money by climbing down out of that arched sapling and just stepping aboard when the ark scraped by? No, other Indians would have noticed these things, but Cooper's Indians never notice anything. Cooper thinks they are marvelous creatures for noticing, but he was almost always in error about his Indians. There was seldom a sane one among them.

The ark is one hundred and forty feet long; the dwelling is ninety feet long. The idea of the Indians is to drop softly and secretly from the arched sapling to the dwelling as the ark creeps along under it at the rate of a mile an hour, and butcher the family. It will take the ark a minute and a half to pass under. It will take the ninety-foot dwelling a minute to pass under. Now, then, what did the six Indians do? It would take you thirty years to guess, and even then you would have to give it up, I believe. Therefore, I will tell you what the Indians did. Their chief, a person of quite extraordinary intellect for a Cooper Indian, warily watched the canal-boat as it squeezed along under him, and when he had got his calculations fined down to exactly the right shade, as he judged, he let go and dropped. *And missed the house!* That is actually what he did. He missed the house, and landed in the stern of the scow. It was not much of a fall, yet it knocked him silly. He lay there unconscious. If the house had been ninety-seven feet long he would have made the trip. The fault was Cooper's, not his. The error lay in the construction of the house. Cooper was no architect.

There still remained in the roost five Indians. The boat has passed under and is now out of their reach. Let me explain what the five did—you would not be able to reason it out for yourself. No. 1 jumped for the boat, but fell in the water astern of it. Then No. 2 jumped for the boat, but fell in the water still farther astern of it. Then No. 3 jumped for the boat, and fell a good way astern of it. Then No. 4 jumped for the boat, and fell in the water *away* astern. Then even No. 5 made a jump for the boat—for he was a Cooper Indian. In the matter of intellect, the difference between a Cooper Indian and the Indian that stands in front of the cigar-shop is not spacious. The scow episode is really a sublime burst of invention; but it does not thrill, because the inaccuracy of the details throws a sort of air of fictitiousness and general improbability over it. This comes of Cooper's inadequacy as an observer.

The reader will find some examples of Cooper's high talent for inaccurate observation in the account of the shooting-match in *The Pathfinder*.

> A common wrought nail was driven lightly into the target, its head having been first touched with paint.

The color of the paint is not stated—an important omission, but Cooper deals freely in important omissions. No, after all, it was not an important omission; for this nail-head is *a hundred yards from* the marksmen, and could not be seen by them at that distance, no matter what its color might be. How far can the best eyes see a common house-fly? A hundred yards? It is quite impossible. Very well; eyes that cannot see a house-fly that is a hundred yards away cannot see an ordinary nail-head at that distance, for the size of the two objects is the same. It takes a keen eye to see a fly or a nail-head at fifty yards—one hundred and fifty feet. Can the reader do it?

The nail was lightly driven, its head painted, and game called. Then the Cooper miracles began. The bullet of the first marksman chipped an edge of the nail-head; the next man's bullet drove the nail a little way into the target—and removed all the paint. Haven't the miracles gone far enough now? Not to suit Cooper; for the purpose of this whole scheme is to show off his prodigy, Deerslayer-Hawkeye-Long-Rifle-Leatherstocking-Pathfinder-Bumppo before the ladies.

> "Be all ready to clench it, boys!" cried out Pathfinder, stepping into his friend's tracks the instant they were vacant. "Never mind a new nail; I can see that, though the paint is gone, and what I can see I can hit at a hundred yards, though it were only a mosquito's eye. Be ready to clench!"
>
> The rifle cracked, the bullet sped its way, and the head of the nail was buried in the wood, covered by the piece of flattened lead.

There, you see, is a man who could hunt flies with a rifle, and command a ducal salary in a Wild West show to-day if we had him back with us.

The recorded feat is certainly surprising just as it stands; but it is not surprising enough for Cooper. Cooper adds a touch. He has made Pathfinder do this miracle with another man's rifle; and not only that, but Pathfinder did not have even the advantage of loading it himself. He had everything against him, and yet he made that impossible shot; and not only made it, but did it with absolute confidence, saying, "Be ready to clench." Now a person like that would have undertaken that same feat with a brickbat, and with Cooper to help he would have achieved it, too.

Pathfinder showed off handsomely that day before the ladies. His very first feat was a thing which no Wild West show can touch. He was standing with the group of marksmen, observing—a hundred yards from the target, mind; one Jasper raised his rifle and drove the center of the bull's-eye. Then the Quartermaster fired. The target exhibited no result this time. There was a laugh. "It's a dead miss," said Major Lundie. Pathfinder waited an impressive moment or two; then said, in that calm, indifferent, know-it-all way of his, "No, Major, he has covered Jasper's bullet, as will be seen if any one will take the trouble to examine the target."

Wasn't it remarkable? How *could* he see that little pellet fly through the air and enter that distant bullet-hole? Yet that is what he did; for nothing is impossible to a Cooper person. Did any of those people have any deep-seated doubts about this thing? No; for that would imply sanity, and these were all Cooper people.

The respect for Pathfinder's skill and for his *quickness and accuracy of sight* [the italics are mine] was so profound and general, that the instant he made this declaration the spectators began to distrust their own opinions, and a dozen rushed to the target in order to ascertain the fact. There, sure enough, it was found that the Quartermaster's bullet had gone through the hole made by Jasper's, and that, too, so accurately as to require a minute examination to be certain of the circumstance, which, however, was soon clearly established by discovering one bullet over the other in the stump against which the target was placed.

They made a "minute" examination; but never mind, how could they know that there were two bullets in that hole without digging the latest one out? for neither probe nor eyesight could prove the presence of any more than one bullet. Did they dig? No; as we shall see. It is the Pathfinder's turn now; he steps out before the ladies, takes aim, and fires.

But, alas! here is a disappointment; an incredible, an unimaginable disappointment—for the target's aspect is unchanged; there is nothing there but that same old bullet-hole!

"If one dared to hint at such a thing," cried Major Duncan, "I should say that the Pathfinder has also missed the target!"

As nobody had missed it yet, the "also" was not necessary; but never mind about that, for the Pathfinder is going to speak.

"No, no, Major," said he, confidently, "that *would* be a risky declaration. I didn't load the piece, and can't say what was in it; but if it was lead, you will find the bullet driving down those of the Quartermaster and Jasper, else is not my name Pathfinder."

A shout from the target announced the truth of this assertion.

Is the miracle sufficient as it stands? Not for Cooper. The Pathfinder speaks again, as he "now slowly advances toward the stage occupied by the females":

"That's not all, boys, that's not all; if you find the target touched at all, I'll own to a miss. The Quartermaster cut the wood, but you'll find no wood cut by that last messenger."

The miracle is at last complete. He knew—doubtless *saw*—at the distance of a hundred yards—that his bullet had passed into the hole *without fraying the edges.* There were now three bullets in that one hole—three bullets embedded processionally in the body of the stump back of the target. Everybody knew this—somehow or other—and yet nobody had dug any of them out to make sure. Cooper is not a close observer, but he is interesting. He is certainly always that, no matter what happens. And he is more interesting when he is not noticing what he is about than when he is. This is a considerable merit.

The conversations in the Cooper books have a curious sound in our modern ears. To believe that such talk really ever came out of people's mouths would be to believe that there was a time when time was of no value to a person who thought he had something to say; when it was the custom to spread a two-minute remark out to ten; when a man's mouth was a rolling-mill, and busied itself all day long in turning four-foot pigs of thought into thirty-foot bars of conversational railroad iron by attenuation; when subjects were seldom faithfully stuck to, but the talk wandered all around and arrived nowhere; when conversations consisted mainly of irrelevancies, with here and there a relevancy, a revelancy with an embarrassed look, as not being able to explain how it got there.

Cooper was certainly not a master in the construction of dialogue. Inaccurate observation defeated him here as it defeated him in so many other enterprises of his. He even failed to notice that the man who talks corrupt English six days in the week must and will talk it on the seventh, and can't help himself. In the *Deerslayer* story he lets Deerslayer talk the showiest kind of book-talk sometimes, and at other times the basest of base dialects. For instance, when some one asks him if he has a sweetheart, and if so, where she abides, this is his majestic answer:

"She's in the forest—hanging from the boughs of the trees, in a soft rain—in the dew on the open grass—the clouds that float about in the blue heaven—the birds that sing in the woods—the sweet springs where I slake my thirst—and in all the other glorious gifts that come from God's Providence!"

And he preceded that, a little before, with this:

"It consarns me as all things that touches a fri'nd consarns a fri'nd."

And this is another of his remarks:

"If I was Injun born, now, I might tell of this, or carry in the scalp and boast of the expl'ite afore the whole tribe; or if my inimy had only been a bear"—[and so on].

We cannot imagine such a thing as a veteran Scotch Commander-in-Chief comporting himself in the field like a windy melodramatic actor, but Cooper could. On one occasion Alice and Cora were being chased by the French through a fog in the neighborhood of their father's fort:

"Point de quartier aux coquins!" cried an eager pursuer, who seemed to direct the operations of the enemy.

"Stand firm and be ready, my gallant 60ths!" suddenly exclaimed a voice above them; "wait to see the enemy; fire low, and sweep the glacis."

"Father! father!" exclaimed a piercing cry from out the mist; "it is I! Alice! thy own Elsie! spare, O! save your daughters!"

"Hold!" shouted the former speaker, in the awful tones of parental agony, the sound reaching even to the woods, and rolling back in solemn echo. " 'Tis she! God has restored me my children! Throw open the sally-port; to the field, 60ths, to the field! pull not a trigger, lest ye kill my lambs! Drive off these dogs of France with your steel!"

Cooper's word-sense was singularly dull. When a person has a poor ear for music he will flat and sharp right along without knowing it. He keeps near the tune, but it is *not* the tune. When a person has a poor ear for words, the result is a literary flatting and sharping; you perceive what he is intending to say, but you also perceive that he doesn't *say* it. This is Cooper. He was not a word-musician. His ear was satisfied with the *approximate* word. I will furnish some circumstantial evidence in support of this charge. My instances are gathered from half a dozen pages of the tale called *Deerslayer*. He uses "verbal" for "oral"; "precision" for "facility"; "phenomena" for "marvels"; "necessary" for "predetermined"; "unsophisticated" for "primitive"; "preparation" for "expectancy"; "rubuked" for "subdued"; "dependent on" for "resulting from"; "fact" for "condition"; "fact" for "conjecture"; "precaution" for "caution"; "explain" for "determine"; "mortified" for "disappointed"; "meretricious" for "factitious"; "materially" for "considerably"; "decreasing" for "deepening"; "increasing" for "disappearing"; "embedded" for "enclosed"; "treacherous" for "hostile"; "stood" for "stooped"; "softened" for "replaced"; "rejoined" for "remarked"; "situation" for "condition"; "different" for "differing"; "insensible" for "unsentient"; "brevity" for "celerity"; "distrusted" for "suspicious"; "mental imbecility" for "imbecility"; "eyes" for "sight"; "counteracting" for "opposing"; "funeral obsequies" for "obsequies."

There have been daring people in the world who claimed that Cooper could write English, but they are all dead now—all dead but Lounsbury. I don't remember that Lounsbury makes the claim in so many words, still he makes it, for he says that *Deerslayer* is a "pure work of art." Pure, in that connection, means faultless—faultless in all details—and language is a detail. If Mr. Lounsbury had only compared Cooper's English with the English which he writes himself—but it is plain that he didn't; and so it is likely that he imagines until this day that Cooper's is as clean and compact as his own. Now I feel sure, deep down in my heart, that Cooper wrote about the poorest English that exists in our language, and that the English of *Deerslayer* is the very worst that even Cooper ever wrote.

I may be mistaken, but it does seem to me that *Deerslayer* is not a work of art in any sense; it does seem to me that it is destitute of every detail that goes to the making of a work of art; in truth, it seems to me that *Deerslayer* is just simply a literary *delirium tremens.*

A work of art? It has no invention; it has no order, system, sequence, or result; it has no life-likeness, no thrill, no stir, no seeming of reality; its characters are confusedly drawn, and by their acts and words they prove that they are not the sort of people the author claims that they are; its humor is pathetic; its pathos is funny; its conversations are—oh! indescribable; its love-scenes odious; its English a crime against the language.

Counting these out, what is left is Art. I think we must all admit that.

MANNERS, MORALS, AND THE NOVEL[1]

LIONEL TRILLING

THE INVITATION that was made to me to address you this evening was couched in somewhat uncertain terms. Time, place, and cordiality were perfectly clear, but when it came to the subject our hosts were not able to specify just what they wanted me to talk about. They wanted me to consider literature in its relation to manners—by which, as they relied on me to understand, they did not really mean *manners.* They did not mean, that is, the rules of personal intercourse in our culture; and yet such rules were by no means irrelevant to what they did mean. Nor did they quite mean manners in the sense of *mores,* customs, although, again, these did bear upon the subject they had in mind.

I understood them perfectly, as I would not have understood them had they been more definite. For they were talking about a nearly indefinable subject.

Somewhere below all the explicit statements that a people makes through its art, religion, architecture, legislation, there is a dim mental region of intention of which it is very difficult to become aware. We now and then get a strong sense of its existence when we deal with the past, not by reason of its

1. From *The Liberal Imagination,* by Lionel Trilling. Copyright, 1948, 1950, by Lionel Trilling. Reprinted by permission of The Viking Press, Inc., New York.

presence in the past but by reason of its absence. As we read the great formulated monuments of the past, we notice that we are reading them without the accompaniment of something that always goes along with the formulated monuments of the present. The voice of multifarious intention and activity is stilled, all the buzz of implication which always surrounds us in the present, coming to us from what never gets fully stated, coming in the tone of greetings and the tone of quarrels, in slang and humor and popular songs, in the way children play, in the gesture the waiter makes when he puts down the plate, in the nature of the very food we prefer.

Some of the charm of the past consists of the quiet—the great distracting buzz of implication has stopped and we are left only with what has been fully phrased and precisely stated. And part of the melancholy of the past comes from our knowledge that the huge, unrecorded hum of implication was once there and left no trace—we feel that because it is evanescent it is especially human. We feel, too, that the truth of the great preserved monuments of the past does not fully appear without it. From letters and diaries, from the remote, unconscious corners of the great works themselves, we try to guess what the sound of the multifarious implication was and what it meant.

Or when we read the conclusions that are drawn about our own culture by some gifted foreign critic—or by some stupid native one—who is equipped only with a knowledge of our books, when we try in vain to say what is wrong, when in despair we say that he has read the books "out of context," then we are aware of the matter I have been asked to speak about tonight.

What I understand by manners, then, is a culture's hum and buzz of implication. I mean the whole evanescent context in which its explicit statements are made. It is that part of a culture which is made up of half-uttered or unuttered or unutterable expressions of value. They are hinted at by small actions, sometimes by the arts of dress or decoration, sometimes by tone, gesture, emphasis, or rhythm, sometimes by the words that are used with a special frequency or a special meaning. They are the things that for good or bad draw the people of a culture together and that separate them from the people of another culture. They make the part of a culture which is not art, or religion, or morals, or politics, and yet it relates to all these highly formulated departments of culture. It is modified by them; it modifies them; it is generated by them; it generates them. In this part of culture assumption rules, which is often so much stronger than reason.

The right way to begin to deal with such a subject is to gather together as much of its detail as we possibly can. Only by doing so will we become fully aware of what the gifted foreign critic or the stupid native one is not aware of, that in any complex culture there is not a single system of manners but a conflicting variety of manners, and that one of the jobs of a culture is the adjustment of this conflict.

But the nature of our present occasion does not permit this accumulation of detail and so I shall instead try to drive toward a generalization and an hypothesis which, however wrong they turn out to be, may at least permit us to circumscribe the subject. I shall try to generalize the subject of American manners by talking about the attitude of Americans toward the subject of manners itself. And since in a complex culture there are, as I say, many different systems of manners and since I cannot talk about them all, I shall select the manners and the attitude toward manners of the literate, reading, responsible middle class of people who are ourselves. I specify that they be reading people because I shall draw my conclusions from the novels they read. The hypothesis I propose is that our attitude toward manners is the expression of a particular conception of reality.

All literature tends to be concerned with the question of reality—I mean quite simply the old opposition between reality and appearance, between what really is and what merely seems. "Don't you *see?*" is the question we want to shout at Oedipus as he stands before us and before fate in the pride of his rationalism. And at the end of *Oedipus Rex* he demonstrates in a particularly direct way that he now sees what he did not see before. "Don't you *see?*" we want to shout again at Lear and Gloucester, the two deceived, self-deceiving fathers: blindness again, resistance to the clear claims of reality, the seduction by mere appearance. The same with Othello—reality is right under your stupid nose, how *dare* you be such a gull? So with Molière's Orgon—my good man, my honest citizen, merely *look* at Tartuffe and you will know what's what. So with Milton's Eve—"Woman, watch out! Don't you see—anyone can see—that's a *snake!*"

The problem of reality is central, and in a special way, to the great forefather of the novel, the great book of Cervantes, whose four-hundredth birthday was celebrated in 1947. There are two movements of thought in *Don Quixote,* two different and opposed notions of reality. One is the movement which leads toward saying that the world of ordinary practicality *is* reality in its fullness. It is the reality of the present moment in all its powerful immediacy of hunger, cold, and pain, making the past and the future, and all ideas, of no account. When the conceptual, the ideal, and the fanciful come into conflict with this, bringing their notions of the past and the future, then disaster results. For one thing, the ordinary proper ways of life are upset—the chained prisoners are understood to be good men and are released, the whore is taken for a lady. There is general confusion. As for the ideal, the conceptual, the fanciful, or romantic—whatever you want to call it—it fares even worse: it is shown to be ridiculous.

Thus one movement of the novel. But Cervantes changed horses in midstream and found that he was riding Rosinante. Perhaps at first not quite consciously—although the new view is latent in the old from the very beginning—Cervantes begins to show that the world of tangible reality is not the real reality after all. The real reality is rather the wildly conceiving, the madly fantasying mind of the Don: people change, practical reality changes, when they come into its presence.

In any genre it may happen that the first great example contains the whole potentiality of the genre. It has been said that all philosophy is a footnote to Plato. It can be said that all prose fiction is a variation on the theme of *Don Quixote*. Cervantes sets for the novel the problem of appearance and reality: the shifting and conflict of social classes becomes the field of the problem of knowledge, of how we know and of how reliable our knowledge is, which at that very moment of history is vexing the philosophers and scientists. And the poverty of the Don suggests that the novel is born with the appearance of money as a social element—money, the great solvent of the solid fabric of the old society, the great generator of illusion. Or, which is to say much the same thing, the novel is born in response to snobbery.

Snobbery is not the same thing as pride of class. Pride of class may not please us but we must at least grant that it reflects a social function. A man who exhibited class pride—in the day when it was possible to do so—may have been puffed up about what he *was*, but this ultimately depended on what he *did*. Thus, aristocratic pride was based ultimately on the ability to fight and administer. No pride is without fault, but pride of class may be thought of as today we think of pride of profession, toward which we are likely to be lenient.

Snobbery is pride in status without pride in function. And it is an uneasy pride of status. It always asks, "Do I belong—do I really belong? And does he belong? And if I am observed talking to him, will it make me seem to belong or not to belong?" It is the peculiar vice not of aristocratic societies which have their own appropriate vices, but of bourgeois democratic societies. For us the legendary strongholds of snobbery are the Hollywood studios, where two thousand dollars a week dare not talk to three hundred dollars a week for fear he be taken for nothing more than fifteen hundred dollars a week. The dominant emotions of snobbery are uneasiness, self-consciousness, self-defensiveness, the sense that one is not quite real but can in some way acquire reality.

Money is the medium that, for good or bad, makes for a fluent society. It does not make for an equal society but for one in which there is a constant shifting of classes, a frequent change in the personnel of the dominant class. In a shifting society great emphasis is put on appearance—I am using the word now in the common meaning, as when people say that "a good appearance is very important in getting a job." To appear to be established is one of the ways of becoming established. The old notion of the solid merchant who owns far more than he shows increasingly gives way to the ideal of signalizing status by appearance, by showing more than you have: status in a democratic society is presumed to come not with power but with the tokens of power. Hence the development of what Tocqueville saw as a mark of democratic culture, what he called the "hypocrisy of luxury"—instead of the well-made peasant article and the well-made middle-class article, we have the effort of all articles to appear as the articles of the very wealthy.

And a shifting society is bound to generate an interest in appearance in the philosophical sense. When Shakespeare lightly touched on the matter that so largely preoccupies the novelist—that is, the movement from one class to another—and created Malvolio, he immediately involved the question of social standing with the problem of appearance and reality. Malvolio's daydreams of bettering his position present themselves to him as reality, and in revenge his enemies conspire to convince him that he is literally mad and that the world is not as he sees it. The predicament of the characters in *A Midsummer Night's Dream* and of Christopher Sly seems to imply that the meeting of social extremes and the establishment of a person of low class in the privileges of a high class always suggested to Shakespeare's mind some radical instability of the senses and the reason.

The characteristic work of the novel is to record the illusion that snobbery generates and to try to penetrate to the truth which, as the novel assumes, lies hidden beneath all the false appearances. Money, snobbery, the ideal of status, these become in themselves the objects of fantasy, the support of the fantasies of love, freedom, charm, power, as in *Madame Bovary*, whose heroine is the sister, at a three-centuries' remove, of Don Quixote. The greatness of *Great Expectations* begins in its title: modern society bases itself on great expectations which, if ever they are realized, are found to exist by reason of a sordid, hidden reality. The real thing is not the gentility of Pip's life but the hulks and the murder and the rats and decay in the cellerage of the novel.

An English writer, recognizing the novel's central concern with snobbery, recently cried out half-ironically against it. "Who cares whether Pamela finally exasperates Mr. B. into marriage, whether Mr. Elton is more or less than moderately genteel, whether it is sinful for Pendennis nearly to kiss the porter's daughter, whether young men from Boston can ever be as truly refined as middle-aged women in Paris, whether the District Officer's fiancée ought to see so much of Dr. Aziz, whether Lady Chatterly ought to be made love to by the gamekeeper, even if he was an officer during the war? Who cares?"

The novel, of course, tells us much more about life than this. It tells us about the look and feel of things, how things are done and what things are worth and what they cost and what the odds are. If the English novel in its special concern with class does not, as the same writer says, explore the deeper layers of personality, then the French novel in exploring these layers must start and end in class, and the Russian novel, exploring the ultimate possibilities of spirit, does the same—every situation in Dostoevski, no matter how spiritual, starts with a point of social pride and a certain number of rubles. The great novelists knew that matters indicate the largest intentions of men's souls as well as the smallest and they are perpetually concerned to catch the meaning of every dim implicit hint.

The novel, then, is a perpetual quest for reality, the field of its research being always the social world, the material of its analysis being always manners as the indication of the direction of man's soul. When we understand this we can understand the pride of profession that moved D. H. Lawrence to say,

"Being a novelist, I consider myself superior to the saint, the scientist, the philosopher and the poet. The novel is the one bright book of life."

Now the novel as I have described it has never really established itself in America. Not that we have not had very great novels but that the novel in America diverges from its classic intention, which, as I have said, is the investigation of the problem of reality beginning in the social field. The fact is that American writers of genius have not turned their minds to society. Poe and Melville were quite apart from it; the reality they sought was only tangential to society. Hawthorne was acute when he insisted that he did not write novels but romances—he thus expressed his awareness of the lack of social texture in his work. Howells never fulfilled himself because, although he saw the social subject clearly, he would never take it with full seriousness. In America in the nineteenth century, Henry James was alone in knowing that to scale the moral and aesthetic heights in the novel one had to use the ladder of social observation.

There is a famous passage in James's life of Hawthorne in which James enumerates the things which are lacking to give the American novel the thick social texture of the English novel—no state; barely a specific national name; no sovereign; no court; no aristocracy; no church; no clergy; no army; no diplomatic service; no country gentlemen; no palaces; no castles; no manors; no old country houses; no parsonages; no thatched cottages; no ivied ruins; no cathedrals; no great universities; no public schools; no political society; no sporting class—no Epsom, no Ascot! That is, no sufficiency of means for the display of a variety of manners, no opportunity for the novelist to do his job of searching out reality, not enough complication of appearance to make the job interesting. Another great American novelist of very different temperament had said much the same thing some decades before: James Fenimore Cooper found that American manners were too simple and dull to nourish the novelist.

This is cogent but it does not explain the condition of the American novel at the present moment. For life in America has increasingly thickened since the nineteenth century. It has not, to be sure, thickened so much as to permit our undergraduates to understand the characters of Balzac, to understand, that is, life in a crowded country where the competitive pressures are great, forcing intense passions to express themselves fiercely and yet within the limitations set by a strong and complicated tradition of manners. Still, life here has become more complex and more pressing. And even so we do not have the novel that touches significantly on society, on manners. Whatever the virtues of Dreiser may be, he could not report the social fact with the kind of accuracy it needs. Sinclair Lewis is shrewd, but no one, however charmed with him as a social satirist, can believe that he does more than a limited job of social understanding. John Dos Passos sees much, sees it often in the great way of Flaubert, but can never use social fact as more than either backdrop or "condition." Of our novelists today perhaps only William Faulkner deals with society as the field of tragic reality and he has the disadvantage of being limited to a provincial scene.

It would seem that Americans have a kind of resistance to looking closely at society. They appear to believe that to touch accurately on the matter of class, to take full note of snobbery, is somehow to demean themselves. It is as if we felt that one cannot touch pitch without being defiled—which, of course, may possibly be the case. Americans will not deny that we have classes and snobbery, but they seem to hold it to be indelicate to take precise cognizance of these phenomena. Consider that Henry James is, among a large part of our reading public, still held to be at fault for noticing society as much as he did. Consider the conversation that has, for some interesting reason, become a part of our literary folklore. Scott Fitzgerald said to Ernest Hemingway, "The very rich are different from us." Hemingway replied, "Yes, they have more money." I have seen the exchange quoted many times and always with the intention of suggesting that Fitzgerald was infatuated by wealth and had received a salutary rebuke from his democratic friend. But the truth is that after a certain point quantity of money does indeed change into quality of personality: in an important sense the very rich *are* different from us. So are the very powerful, the very gifted, the very poor. Fitzgerald was right, and almost for that remark alone he must surely have been received in Balzac's bosom in the heaven of novelists.

It is of course by no means true that the American reading class has no interest in society. Its interest fails only before society as it used to be represented by the novel. And if we look at the commercially successful serious novels of the last decade, we see that almost all of them have been written from an intense social awareness—it might be said that our present definition of a serious book is one which holds before us some image of society to consider and condemn. What is the situation of the dispossessed Oklahoma farmer and whose fault it is, what situation the Jew finds himself in, what it means to be a Negro, how one gets a bell for Adano, what is the advertising business really like, what it means to be insane and how society takes care of you or fails to do so—these are the matters which are believed to be most fertile for the novelist, and certainly they are the subjects most favored by our reading class.

The public is properly not deceived about the quality of most of these books. If the question of quality is brought up, the answer is likely to be: no, they are not great, they are not imaginative, they are not "literature." But there is an unexpressed addendum: and perhaps they are all the better for not being imaginative, for not being literature—they are not literature, they are reality, and *in a time like this* what we need is reality in large doses.

When, generations from now, the historian of our times undertakes to describe the assumptions of our culture, he will surely discover that the word *reality* is of central importance in his understanding of us. He will observe that for some of our philosophers the meaning of the word was a good deal in doubt, but that for our political writers, for many of our literary critics, and for most of our reading public, the word did not open discussion but, rather, closed it. Reality, as conceived by us, is whatever is external and hard, gross, unpleasant. Involved in its meaning is the idea of power conceived in a particular way. Some time ago I had occasion to remark how, in the critical estimates of Theodore Dreiser, it is always being said that Dreiser has many faults but that it cannot be denied that he has great power. No one ever says "a kind of power." Power is assumed to be always "brute" power, crude, ugly, and undiscriminating, the way an elephant appears to be. It is seldom understood to be the way an elephant actually is, precise and discriminating; or the way electricity is, swift and absolute and scarcely embodied.

The word *reality* is an honorific word and the future historian will naturally try to discover our notion of its pejorative opposite, appearance, mere appearance. He will find it in our feeling about the internal; whenever we detect evidences of style and thought we suspect that reality is being a little betrayed, that "mere subjectivity" is creeping in. There follows from this our feeling about complication, modulation, personal idiosyncrasy, and about social forms, both the great and the small.

Having gone so far, our historian is then likely to discover a puzzling contradiction. For we claim that the great advantage of reality is its hard, bedrock, concrete quality, yet everything we say about it tends toward the abstract and it almost seems that what we want to find in reality is abstraction itself. Thus we believe that one of the unpleasant bedrock facts is social class, but we become extremely impatient if ever we are told that social class is indeed so real that it produces actual differences of personality. The very people who talk most about class and its evils think that Fitzgerald was bedazzled and Hemingway right. Or again, it might be observed that in the degree that we speak in praise of the "individual" we have contrived that our literature should have no individuals in it—no people, that is, who are shaped by our liking for the interesting and memorable and special and precious.

Here, then, is our generalization: that in proportion as we have committed ourselves to our particular idea of reality we have lost our interest in manners. For the novel this is a definitive condition because it is inescapably true that in the novel manners make men. It does not matter in what sense the word manners is taken—it is equally true of the sense which so much interested Proust or of the sense which interested Dickens or, indeed, of the sense which interested Homer. The Duchesse de Guermantes unable to delay departure for the dinner party to receive properly from her friend Swann the news that he is dying but able to delay to change the black slippers her husband objects to; Mr. Pickwick and Sam Weller; Priam and Achilles—they exist by reason of their observed manners.

So true is this, indeed, so creative is the novelist's awareness of manners, that we may say that it is a function of his love. It is some sort of love that Fielding has for Squire Western that allows him to note the great, gross details which bring the insensitive sentient man into existence for us. If that is true, we are forced to certain conclusions about our literature and about the particular definition of reality which has shaped it. The reality we admire tells us that the observation of manners is trivial and even malicious, that there are things much more important for the novel to consider. As a consequence our social sympathies have indeed broadened, but in proportion as they have done so we have lost something of our power of love, for our novels can never create characters who truly exist. We make public demands for love, for we know that broad social feeling should be infused with warmth, and we receive a kind of public product which we try to believe is not cold potatoes. The reviewers of Helen Howe's novel of a few years ago, *We Happy Few,* thought that its satiric first part, an excellent comment on the manners of a small but significant segment of society, was ill-natured and unsatisfactory, but they approved the second part, which is the record of the heroine's self-accusing effort to come into communication with the great soul of America. Yet it should have been clear that the satire had its source in a kind of affection, in a real community of feeling, and told the truth, while the second part, said to be so "warm," was mere abstraction, one more example of our public idea of ourselves and our national life. John Steinbeck is generally praised both for his reality and his warmheartedness, but in *The Wayward Bus* the lower-class characters receive a doctrinaire affection in proportion to the suffering and sexuality which define their existence, while the ill-observed middle-class characters are made to submit not only to moral judgment but to the withdrawal of all fellow-feeling, being mocked for their very misfortunes and almost for their susceptibility to death. Only a little thought or even less feeling is required to perceive that the basis of his creation is the coldest response to abstract ideas.

Two novelists of the older sort had a prevision of our present situation. In Henry James's *The Princess Casamassima* there is a scene in which the heroine is told about the existence of a conspiratorial group of revolutionaries pledged to the destruction of all existing society. She has for some time been drawn by a desire for social responsibility; she has wanted to help "the people," she has longed to discover just such a group as she now hears about, and she exclaims in joy, "Then it's real, it's solid!" We are intended to hear the Princess's glad cry with the knowledge that she is a woman who despises herself, "that in the darkest hour of her life she sold herself for a title and a fortune. She regards her doing so as such a terrible piece of frivolity that she can never for the rest of her days be serious enough to make up for it." She seeks out poverty, suffering, sacrifice, and death because she believes that these things alone are real; she comes to believe that art is contemptible; she withdraws her awareness and love from the one person of her acquaintance who most deserves them, and she increasingly scorns whatever suggests variety and modulation, and is more and more dissatisfied with the humanity of the present in her longing for the more perfect humanity of the future. It is one of the great points that the novel makes that with each passionate step that she takes toward what she calls the real, the solid, she in fact moves further away from the life-giving reality.

In E. M. Forster's *The Longest Journey* there is a young man named Stephen Wonham who, although a gentleman born, has been carelessly brought up and has no real notion of the responsibilities of his class. He has a friend, a country laborer, a shepherd, and on two occasions he outrages the feelings of certain intelligent, liberal, democratic people in the book by his treatment of this friend. Once, when the shepherd reneges on a bargain, Stephen quarrels with him and knocks him down; and in the matter of the loan of a few shillings he insists that the money be paid back to the last farthing. The intelligent, liberal, democratic people know that this is not the way to act to the poor. But Stephen cannot think of the shepherd as the poor nor, although he is a country laborer, as an object of research by J. L. and Barbara Hammond; he is rather a reciprocating subject in a relationship of affection—as we say, a friend—and therefore liable to anger and required to pay his debts. But this view is held to be deficient in intelligence, liberalism, and democracy.

In these two incidents we have the premonition of our present cultural and social situation, the passionate self-reproachful addiction to a "strong" reality which must limit its purview to maintain its strength, the replacement by abstraction of natural, direct human feeling. It is worth noting, by the way, how clear is the line by which the two novels descend from *Don Quixote*—how their young heroes come into life with large preconceived ideas and are knocked about in consequence; how both are concerned with the problem of appearance and reality, *The Longest Journey* quite explicitly, *The Princess Casamassima* by indirection; how both evoke the question of the nature of reality by contriving a meeting and conflict of diverse social classes and take scrupulous note of the differences of manners. Both have as their leading characters people who are specifically and passionately concerned with social injustice and both agree in saying that to act against social injustice is right and noble but that to choose to act so does not settle all moral problems but on the contrary generates new ones of an especially difficult sort.

I have elsewhere given the name of moral realism to the perception of the dangers of the moral life itself. Perhaps at no other time has the enterprise of moral realism ever been so much needed, for at no other time have so many people committed themselves to moral righteousness. We have the books that point out the bad conditions, that praise us for taking progressive attitudes. We have no books that raise questions in our minds not only about conditions but about ourselves, that lead us to refine our motives and ask what might lie behind our good impulses.

There is nothing so very terrible in discovering that something does lie behind. Nor does it need a Freud to make the discovery. Here is a publicity release sent out by one of our oldest and most respectable publishing houses.

Under the heading "What Makes Books Sell?" it reads, "Blank & Company reports that the current interest in horror stories has attracted a great number of readers to John Dash's novel . . . because of its depiction of Nazi brutality. Critics and readers alike have commented on the stark realism of Dash's handling of the torture scenes in the book. The publishers originally envisaged a woman's market because of the love story, now find men reading the book because of the other angle." This does not suggest a more than usual depravity in the male reader, for "the other angle" has always had a fascination, no doubt a bad one, even for those who would not themselves commit or actually witness an act of torture. I cite the extreme example only to suggest that something may indeed lie behind our sober intelligent interest in moral politics. In this instance the pleasure in the cruelty is protected and licensed by moral indignation. In other instances moral indignation, which has been said to be the favorite emotion of the middle class, may be in itself an exquisite pleasure. To understand this does not invalidate moral indignation but only sets up the conditions on which it ought to be entertained, only says when it is legitimate and when not.

But, the answer comes, however important it may be for moral realism to raise questions in our minds about our motives, is it not at best a matter of secondary importance? Is it not of the first importance that we be given a direct and immediate report on the reality that is daily being brought to dreadful birth? The novels that have done this have effected much practical good, bringing to consciousness the latent feelings of many people, making it harder for them to be unaware or indifferent, creating an atmosphere in which injustice finds it harder to thrive. To speak of moral realism is all very well. But it is an elaborate, even fancy, phrase and it is to be suspected of having the intention of sophisticating the simple reality that is easily to be conceived. Life presses us so hard, time is so short, the suffering of the world is so huge, simple, unendurable—anything that complicates our moral fervor in dealing with reality as we immediately see it and wish to drive headlong upon it must be regarded with some impatience.

True enough: and therefore any defense of what I have called moral realism must be made not in the name of some highflown fineness of feeling but in the name of simple social practicality. And there is indeed a simple social fact to which moral realism has a simple practical relevance, but it is a fact very difficult for us nowadays to perceive. It is that the moral passions are even more willful and imperious and impatient than the self-seeking passions. All history is at one in telling us that their tendency is to be not only liberating but also restrictive.

It is probable that at this time we are about to make great changes in our social system. The world is ripe for such changes and if they are not made in the direction of greater social liberality, the direction forward, they will almost of necessity be made in the direction backward, of a terrible social niggardliness. We all know which of those directions we want. But it is not enough to want it, not even enough to work for it—we must want it and work for it with intelligence. Which means that we must be aware of the dangers which lie in our most generous wishes. Some paradox of our natures leads us, when once we have made our fellow men the objects of our enlightened interest, to go on to make them the objects of our pity, then of our wisdom, ultimately of our coercion. It is to prevent this corruption, the most ironic and tragic that man knows, that we stand in need of the moral realism which is the product of the free play of the moral imagination.

For our time the most effective agent of the moral imagination has been the novel of the last two hundred years. It was never, either aesthetically or morally, a perfect form and its faults and failures can be quickly enumerated. But its greatness and its practical usefulness lay in its unremitting work of involving the reader himself in the moral life, inviting him to put his own motives under examination, suggesting that reality is not as his conventional education has led him to see it. It taught us, as no other genre ever did, the extent of human variety and the value of this variety. It was the literary form to which the emotions of understanding and forgiveness were indigenous, as if by the definition of the form itself. At the moment its impulse does not seem strong, for there never was a time when the virtues of its greatness were so likely to be thought of as weaknesses. Yet there never was a time when its particular activity was so much needed, was of so much practical, political, and social use—so much so that if its impulse does not respond to the need, we shall have reason to be sad not only over a waning form of art but also over our waning freedom.

POETRY AND ADVERTISING[1]

S. I. HAYAKAWA

ONE does not often mention poetry and advertising in the same breath. Poetry is universally conceded to be the loftiest attainment of the verbal arts; its merits are attested to by the wise of all ages. Advertising, on the other hand, is not even an autonomous art; it is the handmaiden of commercial motives; its name carries connotations (well earned, one might add) of half-truths, deception, and outright fraud, of appeals to vanity, fear, snobbery, and false pride, of radio programs hideous with wheedling voices.

There are many more contrasts. The best poetry seems to be fully appreciated only by the few and to be beyond the comprehension of the many.

1. "Poetry and Advertising," *Poetry: A Magazine of Verse,* LXVII (January, 1946), 204–212. A Paper given at the Sixth Conference on Science, Philosophy, and Religion. Reprinted by permission of the author.

Advertising, however, is considered best when it is laughed over, thought about, and acted upon by multitudes. Poetry is, in the general apprehension, something special to be studied in schools, to be enjoyed by cultivated people who have time for that sort of thing, to be read on solemn or momentous occasions. Advertising is a part of everyday life.

But poetry and advertising have much in common. They both make every possible use of rhyme and rhythm, of words chosen for their connotative rather than their denotative values, of ambiguities that strike the level of unconscious responses as well as the conscious. Furthermore, they both strive to give meaning and overtones to the innumerable data of everyday experience; they both attempt to make the objects of experience symbolic of something beyond themselves. A primrose by the river's brim ceases to be "nothing more" because the poet invests it with meanings; it comes to symbolize the insensitiveness of Peter Bell, the benevolence of God, or anything else he wants it to symbolize. The advertiser is concerned with the primrose only if it happens to be for sale. Once it is on the national market, the advertiser can increase its saleability by making it thrillingly reminiscent of gaiety, romance, and aristocratic elegance, or symbolic of solid, traditional American virtues, or suggestive of glowing health and youth, depending upon his whim. This is what the writer of advertising does with breakfast food, toothpaste, laxatives, whisky, perfume, toilet bowl cleaners. Indeed almost all advertising directed to the general public is the *poeticizing of consumer goods.*

Poetry and advertising are similar too in that they invite the reader to put himself in a role other than his own. In reading poetry we identify ourselves with the characters that a poet creates or with the poet himself. In the course of the experiences that a poet puts us through during these identifications, we feel as others have felt, we see as others have seen, we discover new ways of looking upon ourselves in our relationships with fellow human beings. Advertisers also invite us to make identifications of ourselves in new roles, although the roles are simpler, pleasanter, and more easily within reach. Readers are invited to look upon themselves as "smart housewives and hostesses" (who serve Spam), as "men of distinction" (who drink Calvert's), as responsible and prudent fathers (who protect their dependents with Metropolitan insurance policies), as well-regulated families (who take Ex-Lax).

The identifications to which poets invite us require some imaginative strenuousness on the part of the reader; those to which advertisers invite us require no more than a disposition to daydream and the ability to remember a brand-name that is repeated eight times in sixty-five seconds in spot announcements at half-hour intervals sixteen hours a day. In spite of this marked contrast in the demands made upon the audience, both have the common function of entering into our imaginations and shaping those idealizations of ourselves that determine, in large measure, our conduct. "Life," said Oscar Wilde, "is an imitation of art," and in so far as both poetry and advertising exact this tribute of imitation, they are both, in a real sense, "creative."

Let us call this use of verbal magic (or skulduggery) for the purpose of giving an imaginative, or symbolic, or "ideal" dimension to life and all that is in it, *poetry.* If we speak separately of what are ordinarily called poetry and advertising, let us speak of the former as *disinterested poetry,* of the latter as *venal poetry,* the word *venal* being used in the sense of being available for hire.

Using our terms in this way, we see that our age is by no means deficient in poetry as is often charged. We have more access to poetry (or perhaps we should say poetry has more access to us) than has been the case at any other time in history. One hundred and thirty out of the two hundred pages of each issue of *Harper's Bazaar* are devoted to venal poetry; a similar proportion of poetry to text occurs in most mass circulation magazines. This poetry is written by the highest paid writers in the country, organized into companies of poets, rhapsodists, sub-poets, and sub-rhapsodists, known as "agencies." It is supplemented and reinforced by vast amounts of illustration on which the most expensive and most advanced methods of color reproduction are lavished. It is chanted into national hook-ups night and day at the cost of thousands of dollars an hour, and there it is tied into drama, music, satire, humor, social and political discussion, and news. Product and producer it sings—in unending paeans of praise.

None of the corrupt and vain emperors of history exacted of the sycophant poets in their retinues anything like the discipline imposed upon the poets of Procter and Gamble and Ford Motors. The copy-writer is immeasurably more restricted in his choice of subject-matter than a court poet ever was. Moreover, the merit of his poetry is not measured by the pleasure it gives a single patron; it is measured by its influence on sales statistics. Like the court poet, the copy-writer must praise not only his patron, but also the entire socio-economic system which keeps his patron rich and powerful. Milton was eloquent in his contempt for the "trencher fury of the riming parasite." A contemporary prophet able to look into the twentieth century might well have said to him, "You haven't seen anything yet. Wait until you see the institutional ads of the great corporations during World War II!"

Let us turn from venal poetry to disinterested poetry. Mr. Robert Hillyer in a recent article in *Saturday Review of Literature* entitled "Modern Poetry *versus* the Common Reader" speaks of modern poets as being in a "welter of confusion and frustration." He is distressed by the obscurity of their language —"the flight from clarity," as he calls it. He is certain that both the unintelligibility and the general tone of despair characteristic of much modern verse are due to the moral defects of poets. "Their confusion," says he, "is a sign of artistic effeminacy and egotism."

Mr. Douglas Bush has said in his paper for the Sixth Conference on Science, Philosophy and Religion, that "the modern poet is not altogether fulfilling his traditional function. From antiquity up through the nineteenth century, the poet was regarded as a teacher and leader of his age, and nearly all the greatest poets have been more or less popular; they have counted in the general spiritual life of their times." "Since the romantic age and the industrial revolution," he adds, "the artist has been given to conceiving of himself, not as a normal active member of society, but as a detached, lonely, and hostile observer; and the breach was never wider than it is today, in spite of the poet's concern with the world's ills."

What is responsible for this condition? It is customary, I should say too customary, to blame the shortcomings of modern disinterested poetry on the poets. A great deal of the critical literature of our times is devoted to scolding poets for their excessive compression of images, their oddities of syntax, and their unhappy states of mind. They are constantly being told to buck up and be men, to utter brave and positive affirmations. Very few poets respond to the call, and those who do are seldom praised, even by those who do the calling.

The difficulties of modern poetry, although often exaggerated, are real. As we have been told, it is due in part to the complexity of the modern consciousness; it is due in part to the lack of a widely accepted and recognized poetic tradition; it is no doubt due in part also to the special threats to individuality offered in an industrial age. In addition to the reasons others have given, I should like to add another, namely, that in a world so filled with the clamor of venal writing (of which venal poetry is only the most offensive example), all poetry has come to sound suspicious, so that disinterested poets are practically compelled not to sound poetic (as people ordinarily understand the term poetic) lest suggestions of venal purpose creep into their writing.

In other words, never in history has it been so difficult to say anything with enthusiasm or joy or conviction without running into the danger of sounding as if you were trying to sell something. I shall not say that it is impossible today to make affirmations in verse about the more or less universal facts of human experience that poetry has traditionally been concerned with. But of the vastly increased difficulty of doing so there can be no doubt, and the difficulty continues to increase with the increasing skill, talent, and ingenuity that are constantly being enlisted into advertising, publicity, and public relations as a result of the material rewards offered in those professions.

It is difficult to describe scenery without sounding as if you were promoting a summer-resort, although past ages have done it without compunction:

> To one who has been long in city pent
> 'Tis very sweet to look into the fair
> And open face of heaven,—to breathe in prayer
> Full in the smile of the blue firmament . . .

It is difficult to take delight in a woman's beauty without sounding like an advertisement, although it used to be possible:

Whenas in silks my Julia goes,
Then, then, methinks, how sweetly flows
The liquefaction of her clothes . . .

She was a Phantom of delight
When first she gleamed upon my sight . . .

It is difficult to become inspired by those facets of American life familiar and dear to all of us without sounding as if you were leading into a message from the National Association of Manufacturers on the necessity of maintaining the free enterprise system. Indeed, it is even difficult to speak reverently of the courage of our soldiers and the debt we owe the dead without sounding as if you were shortly going to remind the reader how much he also owes to Nash-Kelvinator's contribution to the war effort.

In 1940, Mr. Archibald MacLeish in his controversial essay, "Post-War Writers and Pre-War Readers" (*New Republic,* June 10, 1940), described the younger generation as being "distrustful of all words, distrustful of all moral judgments of better and worse." He continued, "If all words are suspect, all judgments phony, all conviction of better and worse fake, then there is nothing real and permanent for which men are willing to fight, and the moral and spiritual unpreparedness of the country is worse than its unpreparedness in arms." The condition he described was not as bad as he feared, but there is no denying that to a large degree it still exists—perhaps, after the experience of war, youthful cynicism is even more intense now than then.

But Mr. MacLeish was entirely wrong, it seems to me, in ascribing this youthful scepticism to the influence of the disillusioned authors who followed the first World War: such men as Dos Passos, Hemingway, Barbusse, and Remarque. For every one person reached by such authors, advertisers and publicity men and economic propagandists with goods or ideas to sell reached tens of thousands. The distrust of words does not come from reading writers who honestly state their feelings and convictions, even if those feelings and convictions are extremely gloomy. The distrust arises from long experience with an unending stream of venal poetry, venal speech, venal writing. People are hardly to be blamed, when they encounter so much of it, if they begin to wonder if there is any other kind. The pre-emption by the venal poet of the common value-symbols of our culture, the symbols of courage, of beauty, of domesticity, of patriotism, of happiness, and even of religion, for the purposes of *selling,* that is, of *advantaging the speaker at the expense of the hearer,* has left the disinterested poet with practically no unsullied symbols to work with other than obscure ones hauled up out of *The Golden Bough* or the *Upanishads,* and practically nothing in common human experience to write about except those negative moods that the ghastly cheerfulness of the advertising pages of the *Ladies' Home Journal* has no use for.

The restoration of poetry to its traditional state as one of the most important of the communicators and creators of the values a civilization lives by awaits, therefore, a time when something less than 98 percent of radio time and 85 percent of space in mass-circulation magazines is devoted to selling something.[2] It awaits an economic change profound enough to relieve advertisers of the necessity of invoking all the symbols of home, of mother, of the American way of life, of morality, and of the Christian religion in order to sell a box of soap-flakes. It awaits the dissemination of semantic wisdom, which can be equally well given by departments of history, political science, chemistry, English, or home economics as by teachers of semantics, sufficient to restore insight into the often subtle differences between venal and disinterested utterance, between statements rich with meaning and other statements, equally resonant, containing only sound and fury. It awaits a vision large enough on the part of students of poetry to see that the problems of modern poetry are inextricably interwoven with the character of the *semantic environment* in which the disinterested poet is compelled to work, which in turn compels an examination of the technological, the sociological, the economic beliefs and practices that create that environment. In short, it awaits the time when students of poetry cease to treat their subject as a separate and isolated discipline and begin to look about them at the worlds of science, of commerce, of journalism, of public affairs, and find out what is going on. Then they will be able to do something more than deplore the state of modern poetry.

---

2. Eighty-five percent is perhaps a conservative estimate of the amount of venal writing in many popular magazines, since advertising by no means stops with the advertising pages. Indeed, *Cosmopolitan,* a Hearst publication, appears quite proud of the fact that its editorial content, including its fiction, is as venal in its intent as its paid advertising. The following is quoted from *Cosmopolitan's* advertisement in a trade journal, *Advertising Age*: "Paul Gallico has just told her a dramatic tale. Pepsi Cola is reaching her at the right moment! Because she's young—she's emotional! She responds easily, quickly, wholeheartedly. . . . And Gallico's fiction is just one example of the kind of brilliant entertainment that crowds the pages of *Cosmopolitan.* Great writing makes great reading. It exercises the emotions. It whets the appetite for gracious living. . . . Good going, Pepsi Cola! You've caught her in an emotional mood. She's just been through the make-believe world of Paul Gallico. She's been living the glamorous life so temptingly traced by Ursula Parrott, Sinclair Lewis and the other great *Cosmopolitan* writers. Emotion makes wars. Emotion makes marriages. Emotion makes SALES!"

ON READING POETRY[1]

JOHN CIARDI

What does it take to read a poem?

I am thinking now of poetry not simply as a literary form but as a kind of human behaviour. By human behaviour I mean the reactions of a largely irrational nervous system under a sometimes dreadful and sometimes inspiring compulsion to rationalize itself. It may be argued that this is an undignified view of man, but I doubt that it is. I am not sure but what poetry may be postulated as the final dignity of that irrationality. In any case my premise is that the vital part of the poem begins in the unconscious mind of the poet. It follows that until the reader receives it with more than his conscious mind, the process of communication is not complete. The failure of that communication may be the result of poor writing and it may be the fault of poor reading, of a frog in the speaker's throat or of a buzzing in the listener's ear. At the present time one hears a great deal about the frog, but not much about the buzzing. If only out of didactic habit, therefore, I should like to discuss some of the specific ways in which I have observed readers to misbehave towards the poem.

Let us begin with a really difficult piece of symbolism:

> Hickory, dickory, dock,
> The mouse ran up the clock.
> The clock struck one,
> And down he run.
> Hickory, dickory, dock.

Not really complicated you say? Consider these questions: What does it mean? Why a clock? Why a mouse? Isn't it fairly unusual for mice to run up clocks? What is the point of inventing this esoteric incident? And since the mouse ran up it and down again, the chances are it's a grandfather clock: what does that signify? And isn't it a fairly obsolete notion? Why did the clock strike one? To rhyme with "run"? Why didn't the poem make the clock strike three and the mouse turn to flee? It didn't, but why? What is the origin and significance of all these unexplained symbols? (A symbol is something that stands for something else: what is the something else?) Or is this simply nonsense verse? (I find that hard to believe.) And even as nonsense, what is there in this particular combination of sounds and actions (symbolic actions?) that makes this jingle survive a long word-of-mouth transmission in the English voice-box Why mightn't the poem as easily have read:

1. From *Mid-Century American Poets*, ed. by John Ciardi (New York: Twayne Publishers, Inc., 1950), pp. xiv–xxiii. Copyright, 1950, by John Ciardi.

Thickery, thackery, tea,
An owl flew into the tree.
The tree's down,
The owl's flown.
Thickery, thackery, tea.

I submit: (a) That my parody is a bad poem, that the original is a good one, and that a serious and learned series of lectures might be devoted to the reasons why each is so; (b) That none of the questions I have raised is meaningless and that in fact many critics have made a career of asking this sort of question; and (c) That neither you nor I know what the poem "means." I further submit that such considerations have frightened many readers away from good poems.

But—and this is the point—the child in whose babble the poem is immediate and alive has no critical theories and no troubles. He is too busy enjoying the pleasures of poetry. The moral is obvious: Do not demand that the poem be more rational than you are. The way to read a poem is with pleasure—with the child's pleasure in tasting the syllables on his tongue, with the marvel of the child's eye that can really see the mouse run up the clock, be panic-stricken, and run down again, with the child's hand-clapping rhythmic joy. In short, to read a poem, come prepared for delight.

But if a child can do it why can't you?

That question deserves attention, but before considering it, I should like to say one thing of which I am fairly certain: everyone writes poetry sometime in his life. Bad poetry is what we all have in common. Such poetry generally occurs in three categories: as invective, as obscenity, and as love-yelps.

The obscenity I assume everyone to be capable of documenting. Here is an example of invective:

Billy, Billy, dirty coat
Stinks like a nanny goat.

and here is a fair example of the love-yelp:

Have you ever been in love?
I ask you: have you ever been in love?
Have you?
I have . . . I know!

Billy, Billy, you will recognize of course as a kind of *Georgie Porgie Puddin' and Pie,* but if you think it peculiar to your childhood or to grandfathers, I urge you to look into the encyclopedia under Fescennine for an inkling of the antiquity of man's pleasure in jingling taunts at other men. Billy, Billy, as nearly as I know, was composed in our fourth-grade schoolyard by a former young poet now in the coal business, and was used to taunt our local sloven who has since washed up, cleaned up, grown up, and joined the police force. Almost inevitably, it earned its young author a punch in the nose—a fair example of the way criticism operates in our society to kill the poetic impulse. The love-yelp, a reasonably deplorable specimen of its class, was submitted for the Tufts College literary magazine when I was an undergraduate assistant editor. Anyone who will take the trouble to be reasonably honest can almost certainly summon from himself examples of at least one of these forms which he has attempted at one time or another, and enjoyed attempting.

If, then, the impulse to bad poetry is so widespread (though I insist that *Billy, Billy,* is not at all bad), why is it so few people enjoy reading what passes as good poetry? Why is it, for example, that in a nation of 146 million presumably literate people, the average sale for a book of poems is about 500 copies? Is it that the pleasures and outlets one finds in composing are purely private—that only one's own creation, good or bad, is interesting? Considering the variety of egos which have banded together to pass as the human race, that seems one reasonably good guess, but there is obviously more to it that is worth some speculation:

First, it seems fairly obvious that the process of growing up in a nuts-and-bolts world inhibits the poetry impulse in most people. Somewhere along the line, they learn to say, "Let's face it; we must be practical." Dickens' School of Hard Facts is with us all, and poetry, like poor Sissy Jupe, is still required to blush because it cannot define a horse as "Quadruped. Gramnivorous. Forty teeth, namely twenty-four grinders, four eye-teeth, and twelve incisive." So the literalist on his rostrum demands the rational: "What *does* hickory-dickory-dock *mean*? It *has to* mean *something*." It does indeed, but not anything you can paraphrase, not anything you can prove. It means only what every child knows—delight. And delight is not a function of the rational mind. As Archibald MacLeish has written, "A poem must not mean, but be." Whereby, of course, it does mean, but not nuts-and-bolts. To see what it does mean, you need only go and read Mother Goose to a child: you will then be observing a natural audience busy with the process of receiving poetry as it was intended to be received.

Point one, then, is delight: if you mean to enjoy the poem as a poem, stop cross-examining it, stop trying to force it to "make sense." The poem *is* sense. Or if you must cross-examine, remember at least that the third degree is not the poem. Most poems do reveal themselves most richly after close examination, but the examination is, at best, only a preparation for reading the poem. It is never the reading itself.

More precisely put, an understanding of the rational surfaces of the poem (the prose part of the poem) may, in some cases, point a direction toward the poem. The poem is never experienced, however, until it is felt in the same complex of mind and nerve from which it arose—the subconscious. That experience sometimes happens immediately, and is sometimes helped along by our conscious (rational) perceptions. But to substitute rational analysis for the larger contact of the subconscious is to reject the poem. The kind of communication that happens in a poem is infinitely closer to that of music than to that of prose.

Second, poetry must never be read as an exercise in "reading speed," that deplorable mental-mangle for increasing the rate of destruction of textbook English. The fastest reader is not the best reader any more than the best conductor of Beethoven is the man who gets the orchestra through the *Eroica* in the shortest elapsed time. Music declares its own pace. But so does good poetry. By rhyme, by rhythm, by the word-values of the poem, by the sequence of syllables, and by all these taken together, good poetry contains its own notation, and "We broke the brittle bright stubble like chaff" can no more be read at the same rate as "Bury the great duke with an Empire's lamentation" than *allegro vivace* can intelligently be played *adagio*.

Point two, then: Look for the notation within the poem. Every poem is in part an effort to reconstruct the poet's speaking voice. Listen for it. Listen to the poet on records and at public readings (but know the poems well before you do). You may discover more than you could have foreseen. In any case, when reading a book of poems you must be prepared to linger. That thin volume will take at least as much reading as a detective story.

Third (and of course related to our second consideration), read it aloud. Few poems will come whole at one hearing. Few piano pieces will. But once you have *learned* either, their pleasure is always ready to repeat and to augment itself. Even difficult poems are meant to go into the voice-box.

Fourth, there are still readers who must be specifically cautioned that twentieth-century poetry is not nineteenth-century poetry. That fact may seem rather obvious, but the point is not frivolously made. Your teachers and mine were products of nineteenth-century culture, and almost certainly the first poems you were given to read in school were nineteenth-century poems. I hasten to add that the nineteenth century was a great literary achievement, but it began with one dreadful flaw: it tended to take itself much too seriously. The mind of man seemed to suffer the illusion that it lived in a cathedral, and when man spoke he was not only too likely to pontificate, but he was preinclined to select from experience only the vast, the lofty, the divine-in-nature. The result was what Cleanth Brooks has called "the poetry of high-seriousness." Opposed to that tradition is the poetry of "wit," poetry in which the mind most definitely does not live in a cathedral but in the total world, open to the encounter of all sorts of diverse elements and prepared to take them as they come, fusing fleas and sunsets, love and charley-horses, beauty and trivia, into what is conceived to be a more inclusive range of human experience. Judge the poet of wit by the standards of high-seriousness, and he will likely appear crass and obnoxious; judge the poet of high-seriousness by the standards of wit, and he will likely appear a rather pompous and myopic ass.

The point, then, is quite simple: Judge the poet by his intent; if you tend to the illusion that you are on your way to church when you pick up a poem, stop off at the super-market and watch man against his background of groceries for a while. The church is still next door, and I am quite sure that one of the things "modern" poetry is trying to say, is that the cities of our life contain *both* church spires and wheaties, and that both of them, for better or worse, impinge upon man's consciousness, and are therefore the material of poetry.

A fifth consideration I can best present by asking a question: How do you, reader, distinguish between your responses to a very bad portrait of dear old Aunt Jane, and a very good one of Old Skinflint, the gentleman who holds your mortgage? The question is one that splits the reading audience straight down the middle. The tenacity with which the ladies of the poetry societies will hold on to Aunt Jane with a bluebird in her hair, and the persistence with which they reject all-that-is-not-bluebirds, reaches so far into the problem of a satisfactory approach to poetry (both reading and writing) that it has been necessary to evolve two terms: *poetry* for that which exists as an art form, *poesy* for that which exists as the sentimental bluebird in Aunt Jane's hair. Confusion is inevitable when these terms are not properly applied. The writers and readers of *poesy* always refer to their matter as *poetry* or *true poetry,* and defend it with as much violence as possible from "the ugly." Here is a fair example of *poesy*—a sonnet of course:

THRENODY

Truth is a golden sunset far away
Above the misty hills. Its burning eye
Lights all the fading world. A bird flies by
Alive and singing on the dying day.
Oh mystic world, what shall the proud heart say
When beauty flies on beauty beautifully
While blue-gold hills look down to watch it die
Into the falling miracle of clay?

Say: "I have seen the wing of sunset lift
Into the golden vision of the hills
And truth come flooding proud through the cloud rift,
And known that souls survive their mortal ills."
Say: "Having seen such beauty in the air
I have seen truth and will no more despair."

This is a specimen of what I will call "prop-room poesy." It fills the stage as a poem might, but it fills it with pieces discarded from other poems and left to gather dust in the prop-room of tradition. It makes a stage of the stage, and brings the stage's own dust on as the play, rather than bring on the life outside the theater.

The result may look like a poem, but is really no more than a collection of poetic junk. For example: "golden sunsets far away" (question: Have you ever seen a non-golden one near by?), "misty hills," "burning eye," "fading world," "a bird flies by alive and singing" (question: Have you ever seen a non-live one fly by?), "dying day," "the proud heart." . . .

I have tried many times to explain to the enthusiasts of this school that any reasonably competent craftsman could concoct such a poem in a matter of minutes, and with his tongue in his cheek. I said exactly that from a public platform once and claimed I could turn out such an illusion-of-the-sonnet in three minutes flat. I was challenged and given a first line to start with, but I failed: I discovered it is impossible, simply mechanically, to write off fourteen lines in three minutes. It took four minutes and eighteen seconds. The "sonnet" I have quoted above was the poem produced in answer to that challenge, and by way of further experimentation I sent it off to a magazine for "traditional poetry" and had it accepted for publication. In a moment of cowardice, I withdrew the poem for fear someone I respected might see my name attached to it. I was wrong, of course; no one whose poetic opinion I could respect would have been reading that magazine.

The fact remains beyond all persuasion, however, that the devotees of *poesy* are violent in their charges against Modern Poetry (their capitals) as ugly, coarse, immoral, and debased (their adjectives). My good friend Geraldine Udell, business manager of *Poetry, A Magazine of Verse,* the oldest magazine of good poetry in America, once showed me thirty-four letters received in one day's mail, accusing the magazine of debasing the pure tradition of English Poetry, and enclosing sample pages of *poesy* from a magazine for "traditional poetry" as specimens of what should be printed.

It is, you see, Aunt Jane and Old Skinflint with a vengeance. Poesy, which is always anti-poetry, wants it pretty. It wants well-worn props to which comfortable and vague reactions are already conditioned. Everyone understands the bluebird in Aunt Jane's hair; the response to it is by now so stereotyped that it will do for a birthday card. Poetry, on the contrary, insists on battering at life, and on making the poem capture the thing seen and felt in its own unique complex. It does not repeat; it creates. Therefore, some willingness to dismiss preconception from the reader's mind is necessary if one is to partake of that vital process. One is also required to get himself and his own loose-afflatus out of the way of the poem.

The fifth point then is simple: Poesy is not poetry.

A sixth and related consideration follows almost immediately. It concerns the preconception that demands moral affirmation of oneself from a poem, just as poesy demands a loose emotional affirmation of oneself. Consistently adhered to, this application of one's own morality as a test of the poem can lead to ridiculous ends. It would require, for example, the rejection of Milton by all who do not agree with his theology. It might reject beforehand all poems containing the word harlot, since harlots are immoral, and by that test we should have to reject such great lines as Blake's:

> The harlot's cry from street to street
> Shall weave Old England's winding sheet.

Or, shifted to political concern, it might require a new Communist Manifesto against any poem in which the lover is rich in his love, since it is bourgeois, decadent, and just plain indecent to be rich.

Similarly, I have known many present-day reviewers to reject a poem because it seems cheerful ("withdrawal from reality"), because it does not ("defeatist and negativist"), because it is immediately understandable ("facile and slight"), and because it requires re-reading ("obscurantist"). These are cartoons, of course, but they are cartoons of a real trend. The simple fact is that none of us can hope to be wholly free of preconceptions of one sort or another. I must confess, for example, that I still find Milton's theology a bit silly, and that my feeling prevents me from experiencing *Paradise Lost* as richly as I might. Even Milton's language creates blocks for me that he could not have intended and for which I am solely responsible. For whatever reason, I cannot read of Satan mounted on his "bad eminence" without an impulse to smile. I don't know why I want to smile at such a phrase, but I am sure the reason is within me and that it has nothing to do with the poem. I am being blocked in this case by a pre-set subjective response. I must, therefore, recognize the obstruction and try to allow for it. Unless I can do so, I am not permitting the poet his right to his own kind of vision and existence.

Point six then: the poem does not exist to confirm moral, political, or religious pre-judgments. The poem as a poem is in fact amoral. The poem, I say, not the poet. The poet may be the most moral of men, but when he writes poetry he is performing a ritual dance. He may even sermonize, but if the poem is to succeed as a poem, it must be a dancing sermon. What the poem says is always hickory-dickory-dock, that ineffable, wonderful, everlasting dance of joyous syllables that moves the mouse and winds the clock over and over again, and sends the child to sleep among the swinging nebulae. Or perhaps it is hickory-dickory-God, but still what the poem says is what the child dreams: "Look, Universe, I'm dancing." There is no immorality more wretched than the habit of mind which will insist on moralizing that dance.

The last necessity for good reading that I shall discuss here is tradition. If you will grant me the existence of an unintellectualized basis for poetry upon which the responses of all readers may meet, we can probably agree that a fair example of such a response may be found in, say, Juliet on her balcony swooning into moonlight at the sound of Romeo's song rising from the shrubbery. Hers is certainly a non-intellectualized response. It is certainly a living response. And a world-wide one: Black Jade in her moony garden in Peiping will respond in an almost identical way to Pao-yü's serenade from beyond the garden wall.

But wait: let us switch singers. Now Pao-yü is in Verona beneath Juliet's balcony, and Romeo is in Peiping outside Black Jade's garden. Both strike up a song. Why is it that each girl now hears not a swooning love-cry, but something more nearly a cat fight? The answer is—Tradition.

For the fact is, we are being educated when we know it least. We learn simply by living, and what we learn most automatically is the tradition in which we live. But the responses acquired effortlessly in one tradition will not serve us in another, any more than speaking pure Tuscan will help us in Peiping. Poetry, like all the great arts, exists in a tradition. Some of that tradition comes to us effortlessly, but the greater part of it must be consciously acquired by reading. Without it, you may find yourself in Black Jade's garden listening to Romeo and hearing a cat fight when what is being sung is love.

The final point, then, is that to read poetry you must read poetry. You must acquire by degrees and pleasurably (it's no good if there's no pleasure in it) the tradition of the English-American voice-box. You must come to the poem with the memory of great singing in your inner ear, for that memory haunts the second voice of all good poetry. This, you will recognize, is basically the critical theory that Matthew Arnold put forth as "the touchstone method." It says simply that all poetry is judged by great poetry. It requires, naturally, that you be acquainted with some great poetry.

On the other hand, I cannot lose the belief that it is more important to experience the poem than to judge it. Certainly there is real pleasure to be had from poems no one will ever consider great or near-great. Certainly, too, every mental action implies a kind of judgment. The question is one of emphasis, and generally it seems more desirable for the reader to conceive of himself as a participant in the action of the poem, rather than as a trial judge sitting in judgment upon its claim to immortality.

Time, of course, will hand down that verdict, and in a way from which there is no appeal. It may then happen that the verdict will be against modern poets, and against the principles on which they write. But until that verdict has been achieved it would be well to bear in mind that the reader is as liable to error as the poet, and that when the poem fails to communicate, the failure may as reasonably be charged against the one as against the other.

MAN WILL PREVAIL[1]

Speech of Acceptance upon the award of the Nobel Prize for Literature, delivered in Stockholm on the tenth of December, nineteen hundred fifty.

WILLIAM FAULKNER

I FEEL that this award was not made to me as a man, but to my work—a life's work in the agony and sweat of the human spirit, not for glory and least of all for profit, but to create out of the materials of the human spirit something

1. Reprinted by courtesy of Random House, Inc.

which did not exist before. So this award is only mine in trust. It will not be difficult to find a dedication for the money part of it commensurate with the purpose and significance of its origin. But I would like to do the same with the acclaim too, by using this moment as a pinnacle from which I might be listened to by the young men and women already dedicated to the same anguish and travail, among whom is already that one who will some day stand here where I am standing.

Our tragedy today is a general and universal physical fear so long sustained by now that we can even bear it. There are no longer problems of the spirit. There is only the question: When will I be blown up? Because of this, the young man or woman writing today has forgotten the problems of the human heart in conflict with itself which alone can make good writing because only that is worth writing about, worth the agony and the sweat.

He must learn them again. He must teach himself that the basest of all things is to be afraid; and, teaching himself that, forget it forever, leaving no room in his workshop for anything but the old verities and truths of the heart, the old universal truths lacking which any story is ephemeral and doomed—love and honor and pity and pride and compassion and sacrifice. Until he does so, he labors under a curse. He writes not of love but of lust, of defeats in which nobody loses anything of value, of victories without hope and, worst of all, without pity or compassion. His griefs grieve on no universal bones, leaving no scars. He writes not of the heart but of the glands.

Until he relearns these things, he will write as though he stood among and watched the end of man. I decline to accept the end of man. It is easy enough to say that man is immortal simply because he will endure: that when the last ding-dong of doom has clanged and faded from the last worthless rock hanging tideless in the last red and dying evening, that even then there will still be one more sound: that of his puny inexhaustible voice, still talking. I refuse to accept this. I believe that man will not merely endure: he will prevail. He is immortal, not because he alone among creatures has an inexhaustible voice, but because he has a soul, a spirit capable of compassion and sacrifice and endurance. The poet's, the writer's, duty is to write about these things. It is his privilege to help man endure by lifting his heart, by reminding him of the courage and honor and hope and pride and compassion and pity and sacrifice which have been the glory of his past. The poet's voice need not merely be the record of man, it can be one of the props, the pillars to help him endure and prevail.

V

SCIENCE

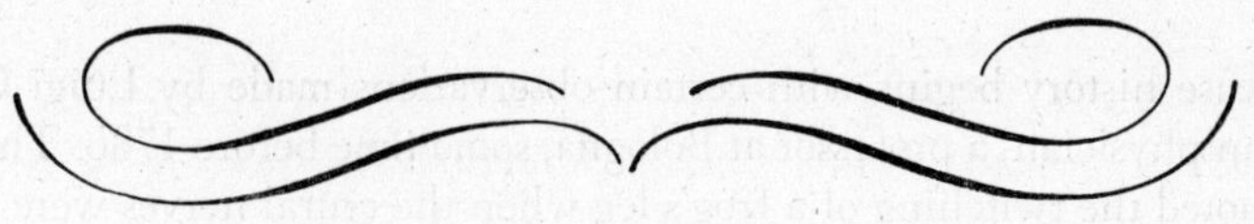

·THE NATURE OF SCIENCE·

CONCERNING ELECTRICITY AND COMBUSTION [1]

JAMES B. CONANT

THIS BOOK is in no sense a presentation of the history of science or of any branch of science. The objective is to indicate how certain principles might be taught by illustrations drawn from the development of science. . . . In this chapter two case histories are presented both drawn from the end of the eighteenth century. The first concerns the discovery of the electric battery, the second concerns the chemical revolution which placed our knowledge of combustion on a sound basis. . . .

THE ROLE OF THE ACCIDENTAL DISCOVERY

The layman is frequently confused in regard to the role of the accidental discovery on the one hand and the planned experiment on the other. This is particularly true in connection with the development of new techniques and the evolution of new concepts from experiment. The case history which I recommend for a study of these topics is the work of Galvani and Volta on the electric current. This case history illustrates the fact that an accidental discovery may lead by a series of experiments (which must be well planned) to a new technique or a new concept or both; it also shows that in the exploration of a new phenomenon the experiments may be well planned without any

1. From James B. Conant, *On Understanding Science: An Historical Approach* (New Haven: Yale University Press, 1947), pp. 65–97, with omissions. Reprinted by permission of the publishers.

"working hypothesis" as to the nature of the phenomenon, but that shortly an explanation is sure to arise. A new conceptual scheme will be evolved. This may be on a grand scale and have wide applicability, or may be strictly limited to the phenomenon in question. A test of the new concept or group of concepts in either instance will probably lead to new discoveries and the eventual establishment, modification, or overthrow of the conceptual scheme in question.

GALVANI'S DISCOVERIES

The case history begins with certain observations made by Luigi Galvani, an Italian physician, a professor at Bologna, some time before 1786. This investigator noted the twitching of a frog's leg when the crural nerves were touched by a metallic scalpel in the neighborhood of an electrostatic machine from which sparks were drawn. *He followed up his observation.* At this point in a course on the Tactics and Strategy of Science the instructor would wax eloquent. He would remind the class that time and time again throughout the history of science the consequences of following up or not following up accidental discoveries have been very great. The analogy of a general's taking advantage of an enemy's error or a lucky break, like the capture of the Remagen bridge, could hardly fail to enter the discussion. Pasteur once wrote that "chance favors only the prepared mind." This is excellently illustrated by the case history at hand. The Dutch naturalist, Swammerdam, had previously discovered that if you lay bare the muscle of a frog in much the same way as Galvani did, grasp a tendon in one hand and touch the frog's nerve with a scalpel held in the other hand, a twitching will result. But Swammerdam never followed up his work. Galvani did. In his own words, "I had dissected and prepared a frog . . . and while I was attending to something else, I laid it on a table on which stood an electrical machine at some distance. . . . Now when one of the persons who were present touched accidentally and lightly the inner crural nerves of the frog with the point of a scalpel all the muscles of the legs seemed to contract again and again. . . . Another one who was there, who was helping us in electrical researches, thought that he had noticed that the action was excited when a spark was discharged from the conductor of the machine. Being astonished by this new phenomenon he called my attention to it, who at that time had something else in mind and was deep in thought. Whereupon I was inflamed with an incredible zeal and eagerness to test the same and to bring to light what was concealed in it."

Galvani did not succeed in bringing to light all that was concealed in the new phenomenon. But he proceeded far enough to make the subsequent discoveries inevitable. In a series of well-planned experiments he explored the obvious variables, but without a clear-cut, over-all hypothesis. This is the usual situation when a new phenomenon is encountered by a gifted experimenter. A series of working hypotheses spring to mind, are tested and either discarded or incorporated into a conceptual scheme which gradually develops.

For example, Galvani first determined whether or not sparks had to be drawn from the electrical machine in order to occasion twitching. He found "Without fail there occurred lively contractions . . . at the same instant as that in which the spark jumped. . . ."

The nerves and muscles of the frog's leg constituted a sensitive detector of an electric charge. Galvani found that not only must a spark be passing from the electrostatic machine but the metallic blade of the scalpel must be in contact with the hand of the experimenter. In this way a small charge originating from the electrical disturbance, namely the spark, passed down the conducting human body through the scalpel to the nerve. So far the physician was on sound and fruitful ground. There now occurred one of those coincidences which more than once has initially baffled an investigator but eventually led to great advances. The frog's leg could under certain circumstances act not only as a sensitive electrical detector but as a source of electricity as well. When this happened, the electricity self-generated so to speak actuated the detector. One can readily see that the superposition of these two effects could be most bewildering and misleading. This was particularly so since the conditions under which the frog's leg became a source of electricity were totally unconnected with any electrical phenomena then known. The variable was the nature of the metal or I should say metals used. For Galvani discovered and duly recorded that the electrostatic machine could be dispensed with if the leg and the nerve were connected together by two *different* metals. Under these conditions the twitching occurred. (The experiment was usually performed as follows: a curved rod was made to touch simultaneously both a hook passing through the spinal cord of the frog and the "muscles of the leg or the feet.") "Thus, for example," wrote Galvani, "if the whole rod was iron or the hook was iron . . . the contractions either did not occur or were very small. But if one of them was iron and the other brass, or better if it was silver (silver seems to us the best of all the metals for conducting animal electricity) there occur repeated and much greater and more prolonged contractions."

Galvani had discovered the principle of the electric battery without knowing it. His two metals separated by the moist animal tissue were a battery, the frog's leg the detector. Every reader can perform the equivalent of Galvani's experiment himself. A copper coin and a silver one placed above and below the tongue when touched together produce in the tongue a peculiar "taste." A very small electric current flows and our tongue records the fact through a series of interactions of electricity and nerves much in the same way as did Galvani's "prepared" frogs. Not having a suspicion of all this, however, Galvani developed a conceptual scheme (an hypothesis on the grand scale, we might say) to account for all the phenomena in terms of what was then known about electricity which was derived entirely from experiment with electrostatic machines. Having found outside electrical disturbances unnecessary (when he unwittingly used the *right* metallic combination!) the experiments, he says, "cause us to think that possibly the electricity was present in the animal itself." Galvani's following up of an accidental discovery by a series of controlled experiments had led to a recording of the significant facts, but it was to be another Italian who developed the fruitful concept. It was Volta who in the late 1790's, continuing the study of the production of electricity by the contact of two different metals, invented the electric battery as a source of what we now often call Galvanic electricity.

VOLTA'S INVENTION OF THE ELECTRIC BATTERY

Alessandro Volta (1745–1827) of Padua had earlier invented a new form of instrument for detecting small charges of electricity. He began by agreeing with Galvani about animal electricity and went about studying it. With his new instrument, a sensitive condensing electrometer, Volta explored various combinations of variables related to Galvani's early experiments and found that the frog could be eliminated in favor of almost any moist material. This discovery might be considered an example of the accidental discovery, but if so it is of a different order from that of Galvani. Explorations with new techniques and tools, if undertaken in a more or less orderly fashion, almost always turn up unexpected facts. In this sense a great majority of new facts of science are accidental discoveries. But the difference between this sort of experience and the example afforded by Galvani's work is obvious. Volta's new discovery amounted, of course, to the invention of the electric battery; for he showed that electricity was produced when two different metals were separated by water containing salt or lye. This was most conveniently done by using moistened paper. In a letter to the President of the Royal Society of London in 1800 Volta wrote "30, 40, 60 or more pieces of copper, or rather of silver, each in contact with a piece of tin, or of zinc, which is much better, and as many layers of water or of some other liquid which is a better conductor than pure water, such as salt-water or lye and so forth, or pieces of pasteboard or of leather, etc. well soaked with these liquids; . . . such an alternative series of these three sorts of conductors always in the same order, constitutes my new instrument; which imitates . . . the effects of Leyden jars. . . ." (see Figure 1). This new battery was a source of electricity different from the electrostatic generator already known in 1800; it was the first source of continuous current. The battery produced electricity of low potential but of considerable quantity (low voltage, relatively high amperage); the sparks from a frictional machine are brief spasms of current of high potential but very low amperage.

There was a hot controversy between Galvani's disciples (Galvani died in 1798) and Volta about whether or not there was such a thing as animal electricity, and what caused the twitching of the frog's leg in the first experiments. Volta soon lost interest in the quarrel and devoted his attention to the study of his new battery. Today we have a rather complete and highly satisfactory conceptual scheme in which all the facts about electric batteries find their place. This is not the case, however, with observations about muscles, nerves, and

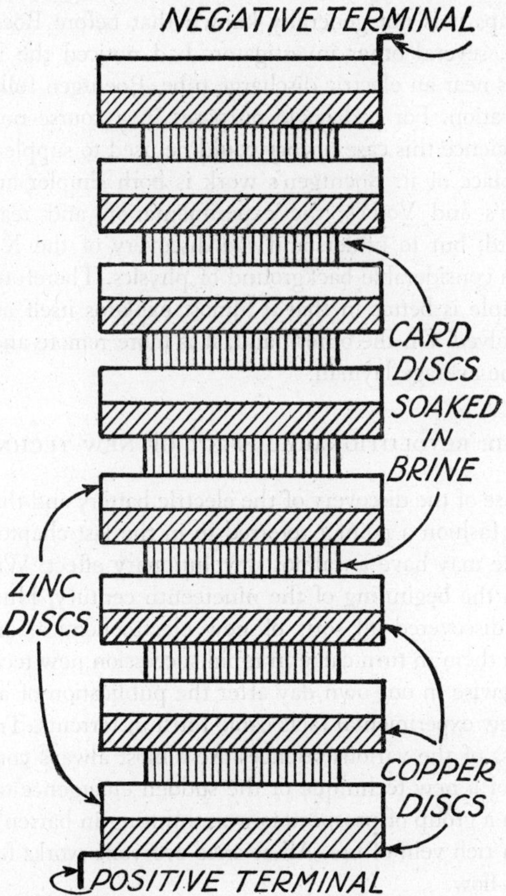

FIG. 1. One form of Volta's battery or pile.

electric currents in animal tissue. In this field one working hypothesis still replaces another and new experiments are still throwing new light on an ancient phenomenon. In a sense, we have not yet finished with Galvani's very first observation, but have finished with Volta's discovery. The original controversy centered on the question, is there animal electricity? This has now become largely a meaningless question, but in attempting to find an answer Volta discovered the electric battery. Such is often the course of scientific history. We end by solving a problem other than the one first at issue.

Another case history which illustrates the role of the accidental discovery, the well-planned experiments by which it may be followed up, the role of the working hypothesis, the development of an hypothesis on the grand scale, and the rapid emergence of both a new technique and a new concept is furnished by a study of the discovery of X rays. The story is familiar to all scientists though perhaps it is not generally known that before Roentgen announced his discovery, several other investigators had noticed the fogging of photographic plates near an electric discharge tube. Roentgen followed up his accidental observation. For pedagogic purposes in a course on the Tactics and Strategy of Science this case history could be used to supplement the one just given or in place of it. Roentgen's work is both simpler and more complex than Galvani's and Volta's; the experimentation and reasoning are more straightforward, but to understand the discovery of the X rays the student should have a considerable background of physics. Therefore, the eighteenth-century example is better in that it almost explains itself as far as technical terms are involved. On the other hand, it is more remote and perhaps less interesting to the average layman.

THE REVOLUTIONARY EFFECT OF NEW TECHNIQUES

Both the case of the discovery of the electric battery and that of X rays show in a dramatic fashion a point I referred to in the last chapter, namely, that a new technique may have an almost revolutionary effect. With the new electric battery in the beginning of the nineteenth century, Humphry Davy and many others discovered all sorts of new electrochemical and physical phenomena; from them in turn came in rapid succession new techniques and new concepts. Likewise in our own day after the publication of an account of the X-ray tube, new experimental facts came forth in torrents. Tremendous spurts in the progress of the various sciences are almost always connected with the development of a new technique or the sudden emergence of a new concept. It is as though a group of prospectors were hunting in barren ground and suddenly struck a rich vein of ore. All at once everyone works feverishly and the gold begins to flow.

TWO FURTHER PRINCIPLES IN THE TACTICS AND STRATEGY OF SCIENCE

Let us now turn to the second case history to be considered in this chapter. It is an example drawn from the history of chemistry in the second half of the eighteenth century, and, it is only fair to warn the reader, a most complicated case. Perhaps too much effort is required to master the facts involved to make this a good example for the layman. But I believe it should be included in the course I am proposing because in it two important principles in the Tactics and Strategy of Science are illustrated in a peculiarly striking fashion. These principles are as follows:

First, a useful concept may be a barrier to the acceptance of a better one if long-intrenched in the minds of scientists.

Second, experimental discoveries must fit the time; facts may be at hand for years without their significance being realized; the total scientific situation must be favorable for the acceptance of new views.

THE OVERTHROW OF THE PHLOGISTON THEORY

The case history which illustrates excellently these two important points might be entitled "the overthrow of the phlogiston theory" or "Lavoisier's work on combustion in the 1770's." As indicated by the first phrase the case also affords a classic example of the mustering of evidence pro and con when two rival concepts are in collision. This phenomenon though frequent is usually so transient in the history of science as to be hard to capture for purposes of historical study. In the investigation of combustion the normal progress of science was, so to speak, delayed; this fact, in a sense, accounts for why a study of this difficult passage in scientific history is of special significance to those interested in the Tactics and Strategy of Science.

The easiest way to understand the revolution in chemistry associated with the name of Lavoisier is first to describe the phenomena in question in terms of modern concepts; then to show how for nearly a hundred years everyone was thoroughly confused. This pedagogic device would have to be used by the instructor in the course I am suggesting. It involves the dogmatic statement of a certain amount of popularized physics and chemistry, but I doubt if the presentation would be much more arbitrary in this respect than most freshman courses. Indeed, some of the material might be said to be common knowledge today.

Almost every high-school graduate "knows" (I put quotation marks around the word) that air is primarily a mixture of oxygen gas and nitrogen gas; furthermore, when a candle or a match or a cigarette "burns," heat and light are being evolved by a chemical reaction involving oxygen. This is called "combustion." If we burn enough material in a closed space, the combustion stops because the oxygen is used up. What burns? Some but not all of the students will say that in the cases mentioned it is a group of carbon compounds, and some will add that the products of combustion are carbon dioxide, CO_2 and water, H_2O. Anyone who has an elementary knowledge of chemical symbols usually loves to share the information! Suppose you heat molten tin in air at a high temperature for a long time, and the bright metal becomes covered with a scum, obviously not a metal. What has happened? A combination with oxygen—an oxide is formed—the bright boys and girls answer. Correct. Suppose we heat this non-metallic substance, an oxide, with carbon. What would happen? The carbon would combine with the oxygen, giving an oxide of carbon and leaving the metal. This is what happens in making iron from iron ore, the very bright boy tells you.

All very simple and plain. And you can set students to work in high-school laboratories to prove it. Yet it is an historic fact that at the time of the American Revolution not one philosopher or experimentalist out of one hundred could have given you an inkling of this explanation which we now designate as "correct." Instead, they would have talked learnedly of "phlogiston," a name probably totally unfamiliar to all but the chemists who read this book. Nearly a hundred years after Newton, and still everyone was thoroughly bewildered by such a simple matter as combustion! This fact needs to be brought home to all who would understand science and who talk of the "scientific method."

The chemical revolution was practically contemporary with the American Revolution and, of course, just preceded the French Revolution. Lavoisier, the man who singlehanded but building on the work of others made the revolution, lost his head at the hands of the Revolutionary Tribune in 1794 (though he was by no means hostile to the basic aims of the great social and political upheaval). Whether or not he was betrayed by a scientific colleague (Fourcroy) who at least was an ardent supporter of the extreme party then in power, is an intriguing historical question; its study would be a by-product of this case history in which certain students would take great interest. Likewise, the fact that another prominent figure in the final controversy was Priestley, a Unitarian clergyman, who was made an honorary citizen by the French Assembly and then fled to America in the very year of Lavoisier's execution to escape a reactionary English mob, adds zest to the story. There is no lack of material to connect science with society in the late eighteenth century, though the connection I think is more dramatic than significant; at all events, for keeping up students' interest it can hardly be surpassed.

THE CLASSIC EXPERIMENT ON THE ROLE OF OXYGEN IN COMBUSTION

The chemical revolution took place during the years 1772–78. By the later date Lavoisier had made clear to the scientific world the role of oxygen in combustion. His classic experiment, often described in elementary textbooks, was as follows: Mercury heated in common air produces a red material (an oxide we would say, a "calx" to the chemists of the eighteenth century). In a closed space about one fifth of the air disappears. The red material weighs more than the metal from which it was formed. Therefore, something has disappeared from the air and combined with the metal. The red material, the oxide or calx, is next strongly heated in an enclosed space with the sun's rays brought to a focus by a large lens or "burning glass," a gas is evolved and the metal regenerated. The new gas is the "something" which disappeared from the original air, for the amount is the same, and the calx has lost weight in the right amount. The new gas (oxygen) mixed with the residue from the first experiment yields a mixture which is identical with common air. (Figures 2 and 3.)

The experiments are simple, the proof appears to be complete. (Lavoisier, of course, generalized far beyond the case of mercury.) But the new concep-

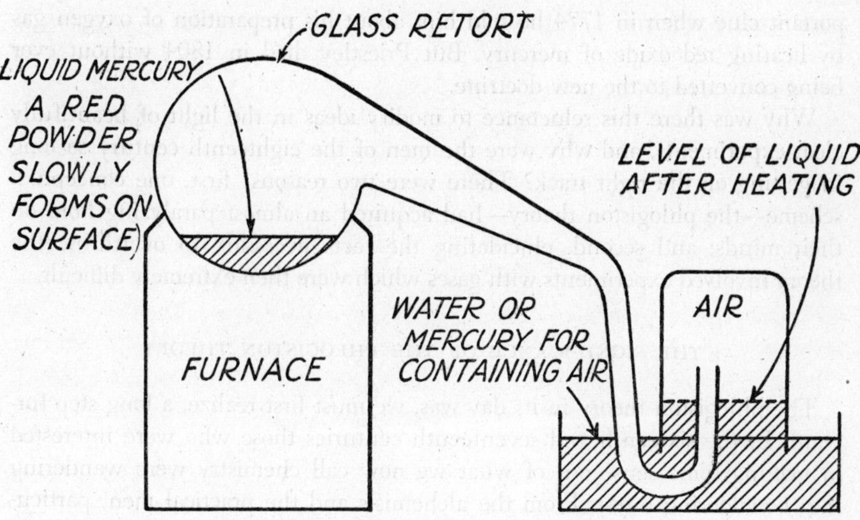

FIG. 2. Mercury heated in air absorbs oxygen.

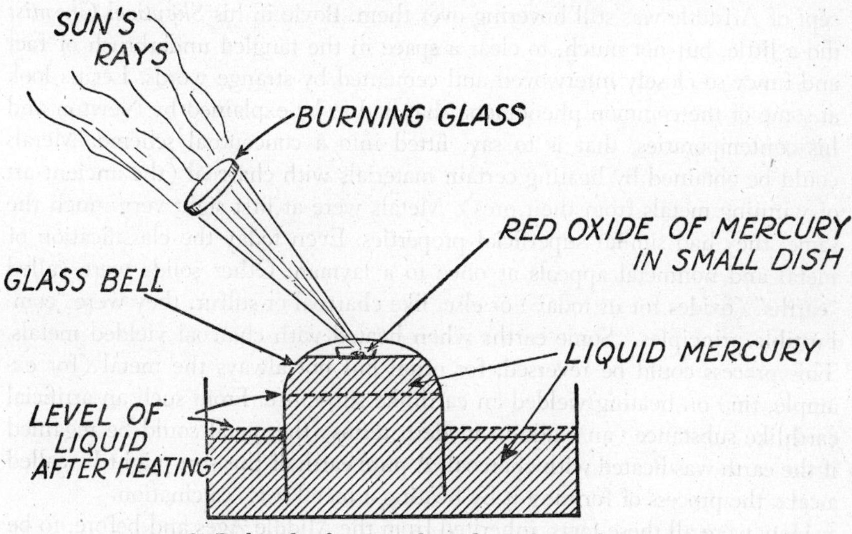

FIG. 3. Red oxide of mercury heated very hot evolves oxygen.

(The temperature in this experiment must be very much higher than in the formation of the oxide.)

tual scheme was by no means accepted at once with great acclaim. Quite the contrary. Lavoisier had to drive home his points with telling arguments. Slowly his French contemporaries were won over, but Priestley and Watt of the steam-engine fame and Cavendish and scores of others continued to cling to the phlogiston theory for a decade. Priestley's case is particularly interesting. This English experimenter had actually provided Lavoisier with an important clue when in 1774 he told him about his preparation of oxygen gas by heating red oxide of mercury. But Priestley died in 1804 without ever being converted to the new doctrine.

Why was there this reluctance to modify ideas in the light of beautifully clear experiments, and why were the men of the eighteenth century so long in getting on the right track? There were two reasons: first, one conceptual scheme—the phlogiston theory—had acquired an almost paralyzing hold on their minds; and second, elucidating the facts necessary to overthrow the theory involved experiments with gases which were then extremely difficult.

THE SIGNIFICANCE OF THE PHLOGISTON THEORY

The phlogiston theory in its day was, we must first realize, a long step forward. In the sixteenth and seventeenth centuries those who were interested in making some sense out of what we now call chemistry were wandering in a bewildering forest. From the alchemists and the practical men, particularly the metal makers, they had acquired a mass of apparently unrelated facts and strange ideas about "elements." The earth, air, fire, and water concept of Aristotle was still hovering over them. Boyle in his *Skeptical Chymist* did a little, but not much, to clear a space in the tangled underbrush of fact and fancy so closely interwoven and cemented by strange words. Let us look at some of the common phenomena that had to be explained by Newton and his contemporaries, that is to say, fitted into a conceptual scheme. Metals could be obtained by heating certain materials with charcoal (the ancient art of winning metals from their ores). Metals were at first sight very much the same; they had similar superficial properties. Even today the classification of metal and nonmetal appeals at once to a layman. Other solids were called "earths" (oxides for us today) or else, like charcoal or sulfur, they were "combustible principles." Some earths when heated with charcoal yielded metals. This process could be reversed, for often but not always the metal (for example, tin) on heating yielded an earthlike substance. From such an artificial earthlike substance (an oxide in modern terms) the metal could be regained if the earth was heated with charcoal. A pure earth of this sort might be called a calx, the process of forming it by heating a metal was "calcination."

How were all these facts, inherited from the Middle Ages and before, to be fitted together? By the introduction of a principle called phlogiston, closely related to Aristotle's old element, fire—closely related, yet the relationship was never clear. To those who sought for clarity it seemed evident that there must be some common principle involved in the process of making various metals from their calces and vice versa. Therefore, let us call this something phlogiston, they in effect declared. When phlogiston was added to a calx you had a metal, when you removed it from a metal a calx was formed; phlogiston was in a sense a metalizing principle. Note there is a common-sense assumption more or less implied in this line of reasoning: except for gold, and occasionally a few other metals, calces *not* metals occur in nature. Therefore, these calces were the simpler materials, something must be added to them to make them metals. Since metals were so alike, the "something" was obviously the same in all cases. We shall call it phlogiston, said Becher, and his pupil Stahl in a series of books published in 1703–31.

Here was a key to unlock a maze, and it was immediately accepted. Here was a concept which provided a pattern into which a mass of otherwise unrelated phenomena could be fitted. Substances were rich or poor in phlogiston, this seemed easy to establish. What was phlogiston itself? It probably was never to be seen. Substances rich in phlogiston easily took fire and, indeed, fire was perhaps a manifestation of phlogiston, or worked with it at least. For some, fire was still an element. Charcoal was a phlogiston-rich material and on heating with a metallic calx gave up its phlogiston to the calx, making a metal. By itself charcoal burned, the phlogiston appearing as fire or combined with the air. Sulfur, using the word in its modern sense, was found free in nature; it burned when heated and yielded an acid, vitriolic acid (sulfuric acid in modern terms). Clearly, this sulfur was only vitriolic acid highly "phlogisticated"; the burning set the phlogiston free and yielded the acid.

We can write these changes in diagrammatic form to illustrate how the chemists of the eighteenth century thought:

Calx + phlogiston (from charcoal) ——→ metal.
Metal heated in air ——→ calx + phlogiston (to the air).
Charcoal burned yields phlogiston to the air accompanied by fire.
Phlogisticated vitriolic acid (sulfur to us) burns yielding phlogiston (to the air) + vitriolic acid (sulfuric acid).

There was one very simple flaw in all this argument and the interesting fact is that this flaw was known and talked about for fifty years before the phlogiston theory was even shaken, much less overthrown. This is a beautiful illustration of the principle in the Tactics and Strategy of Science referred to at the beginning of this section, namely, that a scientific discovery must fit the times. As early as 1630 (note the date—before Boyle was born) a Frenchman, Jean Rey, studied the calcination of tin and showed that the calx weighed more than the tin from which it was formed. More than that, he gave an explanation closely in accord with Lavoisier's ideas of 150 years later. For he said, "this increase in weight comes from the air, which in the vessel has been rendered denser, heavier, and in some measure adhesive . . . which air mixes with the calx . . . and becomes attached to its most minute particles. . . ." Boyle confirmed the increase in weight of metals in calcination in 1673 but added no support to Rey's shrewd guess (it was little more) as to the reason. In fact, if anything, he led subsequent investigators down the wrong path. At least in retrospect it seems that if he had followed up only a little more boldly his own experiments, the phlogiston theory might never have been proposed or, if proposed, never accepted seriously. Yet it is all too easy to imagine that even a still greater genius than Boyle could have discovered oxygen and revealed its role in combustion and calcination in the seventeenth century. Too much physics as well as chemistry lay under wraps which were only slowly removed by the labors of many men.

At all events, Boyle put forward the hypothesis that fire, the Aristotelian principle, had passed through the walls of the glass vessel used and combined with the metal, thereby giving it weight. This was, of course, not the same as the phlogiston theory formulated a generation later; in a sense it was the opposite because according to Boyle something was *added* to the metal in calcination, namely, fire. While in the phlogiston theory something, namely, phlogiston, was *removed.* But Boyle's writings did focus attention on the heat and flame (a characteristic of fire and calcination) rather than on the air which had figured in Rey's explanation.

A SCIENTIFIC DISCOVERY MUST FIT THE TIMES

Rey's ideas about the air seem to have been lost in the subsequent 150 years, but not the facts of calcination. That a calx weighed more than the metal was well known throughout the eighteenth century, but this fact was *not* recognized as being fatal to the phlogiston theory. Here is an important point. Does it argue for the stupidity of the experimental philosophers of the day as a few writers once would have us think? Not at all; it merely demonstrates that in complex affairs of science, one is concerned with trying to account for a variety of facts and with welding them into a conceptual scheme; one fact is not by itself sufficient to wreck the scheme. In discussing Galileo's failure and Torricelli's successful interpretation of lift pumps, I referred to the principle that a conceptual scheme is never discarded merely because of a few stubborn facts with which it cannot be reconciled; a concept is either modified or replaced by a better concept, never abandoned with nothing left to take its place.

Not only was it known in 1770 that a calx weighed more than the metal from which it was formed (which means to us that something must have been taken up in its formation), but Boyle himself back in the 1660's showed that air was necessary for fire. John Mayow and Robert Hooke at about the same date had written about burning and the respiration of animals in terms of air being "deprived of its elastic force by the breathing of animals very much in the same way as by the burning of flame." Stephen Hales, fifty years later, spoke the same language. But these men were all ahead of their times. As we reread their papers we see in spite of strange words and ill-defined ideas they had demonstrated that air in which material had been burned or animals had respired would no longer sustain fire or life; furthermore, they showed that there was an actual diminution of the volume of the air in such cases. All of which seems to force the right explanation to our eyes; not so to the chemists of the eighteenth century.

Air which would no longer support combustion had merely become so rich in phlogiston it could take up no more, the "phlogistonists" declared. Indeed, when Priestley discovered how to prepare essentially pure nitrogen, it was quite natural for him to regard it as completely "phlogisticated air," because nitrogen will not support combustion. Likewise, when he discovered how to prepare essentially pure oxygen gas by heating red oxide of mercury, he called it "dephlogisticated air." He found this gas to be like common air, though a candle burned in it more brightly than even in common air. Upon the whole, said Priestley, it may safely be concluded, "that the purest air is that which contains the least phlogiston: that air is impure (by which I mean that it is unfit for respiration, and for the purpose of supporting flame) in proportion as it contains more of that principle." This letter was read to the Royal Society on May 25, 1775. And in the same year in another letter he spoke of his newly discovered oxygen as "[an air] that is five or six times better than common air, for the purposes of respiration, inflammation and, I believe, every other use of common atmospherical air. As I think I have sufficiently proved that the fitness of air for respiration depends on its capacity to receive the *phlogiston* exhaled from the lungs this species of air may not improperly be called, *dephlogisticated air*."

EXPERIMENTAL DIFFICULTIES WITH GASES

A chemist reading the papers of the phlogistonists clutches his head in despair; he seems to be transported to an Alice-through-the-looking-glass world! But if he is patient and interested he soon recognizes that much of the difficulty stemmed from the experimenters' inability to handle and characterize different gases. This fact illustrates once again the third point of the principles outlined in the last chapter, the difficulty of experimentation. Metals and calxes, inflammable substances like sulfur, charcoal, and phosphorus, the chemists of the eighteenth century could recognize and manipulate since they were solids. Even some liquids like vitriolic acid, water, and mercury were quite definite individuals. But two gases, neither of which would support fire, like nitrogen and carbon dioxide, were often hopelessly confused; or two which burned, like hydrogen and carbon monoxide. Nearly all gases look alike except for the few which are colored. They are compressible and subject to thermal expansion to about the same degree. Their densities, i.e., the weight of a unit volume, differ but that was something not easy to determine in those days. Indeed, in the eighteenth century the distinction between weight and density (i.e., weight per unit volume) even for solids and liquids was often confused. The chemical properties of each gas are characteristic and the way each gas is prepared is different; and it was these differences that finally led to a straightening out of some of the tangled skein.

To understand the difficulties of the chemists of 175 years ago, imagine yourself an elementary student in a laboratory given glass bottles of air, of oxygen, of nitrogen, and one containing air saturated with ether vapor, and asked to tell whether or not all the "airs" or gases in the bottles are identical. The air containing the ether vapor (actually still largely air) will be the only one at first recognized as distinct. A student does not know how to proceed to examine these gases except by looking at them, smelling them, or testing their solubility in water. And from Boyle's day to Priestley's the experimenters were largely in the same predicament. They spoke of different "airs," but hardly knew whether the differences were real or due to the presence of some impurity. Thus, Priestley, writing in 1777, said:

"Van Helmont and other chymists who succeeded him, were acquainted with the property of some *vapours* to suffocate, and extinguish flame, and of others to be ignited. . . . But they had no idea that the substances (if, indeed they knew that they were *substances,* and not merely *properties,* and *affections* of bodies which produced those effects) were capable of being separately exhibited in the form of a *permanently elastic vapour* . . . any more than the thing that constitutes *smell.* In fact they knew nothing at all of any air besides *common air,* and therefore they applied the term to no other substances whatever. . . ."

The history of the study of gases covers a hundred years from Boyle's day. A number of important improvements in techniques were made. They were brought to a focus by Priestley who in 1772 carried out extensive and very original experiments with "airs." He improved still further several techniques of handling these airs or gases which enormously simplified the experimental procedures. Before Priestley's work only three "different airs" were known. In a few years he had discovered eleven more, including oxygen. Here is another illustration of the importance of techniques, though here we meet with an evolutionary rather than a revolutionary change.

Though Priestley was the chief figure in extending the knowledge of gases, his stubborn refusal to accept the consequences of his own discoveries has already been mentioned. It is not necessary in this chapter to discuss either Priestley or Lavoisier as individuals, though the instructor using the case history of combustion would certainly wish to do so. Nor do I propose to digress by examining the priority problems involved in the work of these two men and the Swedish chemist, Scheele, who also discovered oxygen. Such matters fall within the province of the historian of science. For the purposes of the present exposition the important questions are: Why did it take the scientists of the eighteenth century so long to get on the right road? And why were there so many stubborn travelers on the wrong road after the right one had been discovered?

THE PHLOGISTON THEORY, A BLOCK TO A NEW CONCEPT

It is sometimes said that the experimenters before Lavoisier's day did not carry out quantitative experiments, that is, they did not use the balance. If they had, we are told, they would have discovered that combustion involves an increase in weight and would have rejected the phlogiston theory. This is nonsense. Rey, as I have already explained, long before the beginning of the phlogiston period showed that a calx weighed more than a metal. Quantitative experiments, though, of course, not very accurate ones, were repeatedly made. Everyone knew that a calx weighed more than the metal from which it was formed. No straightforward statement of the phlogiston theory could accommodate this fact. Yet the phlogiston theory was so useful that few if any in the mid-eighteenth century were looking to overthrow it or disprove it. Rather, they were interested in reconciling one inconvenient set of facts with what seemed from their point of view an otherwise admirable conceptual scheme. How they twisted and squirmed to accommodate the quantitative facts of calcination with the phlogiston theory makes an interesting chapter in the history of science. The eighteenth-century accounts are often confusing. Fortunately their many details need not concern the readers of this book; nor except in broad outline need they concern one teaching the principles of the Tactics and Strategy of Science with the aid of the eighteenth-century studies on combustion.

The principle which emerges is one already encountered, namely, that it takes a new conceptual scheme to cause the abandonment of an old one: when only a few facts appear to be irreconcilable with a well established conceptual scheme, the first attempt is *not* to discard the scheme but to find some way out of the difficulty and keep it. Likewise the proponents of new concepts are rarely shaken by a few alleged facts to the contrary. They seek at first to prove them wrong or to circumvent them. Thus Lavoisier persisted with his own new concept in spite of the fact that certain experiments seemed to be completely inexplicable in its terms. It was later found that the interpretation of the experiments was in error. Not so in the case of the calcination of metals: there could be no doubt in the mind of anyone by 1770 that the increase in weight during calcination was real. There was also no doubt that there should be a loss in weight according to the phlogiston theory. Or at best no change in weight if phlogiston were an imponderable substance like fire.

ATTEMPTS TO RECONSTRUCT THE PHLOGISTON THEORY

One attempt to get out of the dilemma of calcination took refuge in a confusion between weight and density (calxes are less dense than metals, but the total weight in the calcination increased). This was soon put right by clear thinking. Another attempt involved assigning a negative weight to phlogiston. This illustrates how desperately men may strive to modify an old idea to make it accord with new experiments. But in this case the modification represented not a step forward but several steps to the rear! What was gained by accommodating the quantitative aspect of calcination was lost by following the consequences of negative weight to a logical conclusion. What manner of substance or principle could phlogiston be that when it was added to another material the total mass or weight diminished? The idea that phlogiston had negative weight strained the credulity, and for the most part this logical extension of the phlogiston theory (logical in one sense, highly illogical in another) was never widely accepted. But before we laugh too hard at the investigators of the eighteenth century, let us remember that before the nineteenth century heat was considered a corporeal substance and the whole concept of the atomic and molecular theory of matter lay over the distant horizon.

To some of the chemical experimenters, the dilemma presented by the quantitative facts of calcination seems to have been accepted as just one of those things which cannot be fitted in. And this attitude is much more common in the history of science than most historians would have you believe. Indeed, it is in a way a necessary attitude at certain stages of development of any concept. The keen-minded scientist, the real genius, is the man who keeps in the forefront of his thoughts these unsolved riddles. He then is ready to relate a new discovery or a new technique to the unsolved problems. He is the pioneer, the revolutionist. And it is this combination of strategy and tactics in the hands of a master which is well worthy of study if one would try to understand science through the historical approach.

LAVOISIER'S CLUE

To recount the history of Lavoisier's development of his new theory, and the way in which the new discoveries of the time were fitted into his scheme would mean the recital of a long story. Such an account would be out of place in this volume, though a considerable portion of it would be involved in a thorough study of the case histories at hand. Let me take a few moments of the reader's time, however, to point out how Lavoisier first seems to have taken the right turn in the road. In a famous note of 1772, he wrote as follows:

"About eight days ago I discovered that sulphur in burning, far from losing weight, on the contrary gains it; . . . it is the same with phosphorus; this increase of weight arises from a prodigious quantity of air that is fixed during the combustion and combines with the vapours.

"This discovery, which I have established by experiments that I regard as decisive, has led me to think that what is observed in the combustion of sulphur and phosphorus may well take place in the case of all substances that gain in weight by combustion and calcination: and I am persuaded that the increase in weight of metallic calces is due to the same cause. . . ."

Here we seem to see the mental process at work to which I referred a few moments ago: the perception that a new fact properly interpreted enables one to explain an old dilemma, an outstanding unsolved problem. In a sense, in this note Lavoisier outlined the whole new chemistry, as he always later claimed. (The note was deposited sealed with the Secretary of the French Academy on November 1, 1772.) To be sure, at first Lavoisier mistook the gas evolved in the reduction of a calx with charcoal (carbon dioxide, the "fixed air" of that day) with the gas absorbed in calcination. The study we can now make of his notebooks as well as his later publications makes it plain that it was not until after Priestley's discovery of oxygen and Lavoisier's repetition of some of Priestley's experiments with the new gas that the nature of the gas absorbed in calcination became clear. It was only then that all the pieces of the puzzle fitted together, with the newly discovered oxygen occupying the central position in the picture. But at the outset Lavoisier recognized that something was absorbed from the air. Unconsciously he was retracing the steps Jean Rey had taken nearly 150 years earlier and which had never been followed up. Rey's almost forgotten book was called to Lavoisier's attention shortly after his first publications of his new theory.

An interesting question that will at once come to the mind of many is the following: why did the study of sulfur and phosphorus lead Lavoisier to the right type of explanation? Why after experiments with those substances did he set out full of confidence on a set of planned experiments along a new line? This is one of those historical riddles which can never be answered, but concerning which it is not entirely profitless to speculate. I suggest that the key word in Lavoisier's note of November 1, 1772, is "prodigious"—"this increase of weight arises from a prodigious quantity of air that is fixed." If this is so, we have again another illustration of how experimental difficulties or the lack of them condition the evolution of new concepts. To determine whether air is absorbed or not during the calcination of a metal is not easy; the process takes a long time, a high temperature, and both the increase in weight and the amount of oxygen absorbed are small. But with phosphorus and sulfur the experiment was relatively easy to perform (the materials burn at once on ignition with a burning glass); furthermore, the effect observed is very large. The reason for this in terms of modern chemistry is that sulfur and phosphorus have low atomic weights of 32 and 31 (oxygen is 16), and in the combustion 1 atom of phosphorus combines with 5 of oxygen; 1 atom of sulfur with 3 of oxygen. The atomic weight of the metals is high, the number of atoms of oxygen combining with them, fewer. Thus 62 weights of phosphorus will yield $62 + (5 \times 16) = 142$ parts of combustion product; while in the case of tin, the atomic weight is 118 and only 2 atoms of oxygen are involved. Thus 118 weights of tin would yield only $118 + (2 \times 16) = 150$ weights of calx or an increase of only about 25 per cent. Note that with phosphorus the increase is more than double. The corresponding differences would be reflected in the volume of oxygen absorbed, and furthermore, since the calcination of tin was a long process at a high temperature in a furnace, no entirely satisfactory way of measuring the volume of air absorbed was at hand in 1770.

QUANTITATIVE MEASUREMENTS AND ACCIDENTAL ERRORS

As a matter of fact, until Lavoisier was put on the track of the gas prepared by heating mercuric oxide by Priestley, he had a hard time proving that metallic calxes did gain in weight *because* of absorption of something from the air. The method he used was to repeat certain experiments of Boyle with a slight modification. Both the modification and the difficulties are of interest and point an obvious moral to the tale. Boyle had sealed tin in a glass vessel and heated the vessel a long time on a charcoal fire (which he says is a very dangerous operation as the glass may well explode). Boyle then removed the vessel from the fire and after cooling opened the glass, reweighed the vessel and noted the increase in weight. This was one of the many well-known experiments showing that the calx weighed more than the metal. (Boyle, the reader will recall, believed the increase to be due to the fire particles which passed through the glass). Now, said Lavoisier, where Boyle went wrong was in not weighing the vessel *before* opening it. For if his explanation were right and the fire had passed through the glass and combined with the tin, the increase would have occurred before the air was admitted. While if oxygen were involved, the increase in weight would occur *after* the air was admitted. The results obtained by Lavoisier on repeating this experiment were as expected, but were far from being as striking as those obtained with phosphorus for the reasons just explained. The increase was 10 parts in a total of 4,100 in one experiment and 3 parts in about the same amount in another! We now know that the difficulties of weighing a large glass vessel with a high degree of accuracy are great, due to film moisture and electrical charges. It is, therefore, not surprising that the glass retort, after heating, varied in weight from day to day almost as much as the total gain in weight in one of the two experiments.

These tough facts of experimentation are of great importance. To me, they indicate strongly that even if Boyle had weighed his vessel before and after admitting the air, the uncertainties of his figures would probably have been so great as to confuse him and subsequent investigators. *Important advances in science are based on quantitative measurements only if the measured quantity is large as compared with possible systematic and accidental errors.* The principle of significant figures which plays so large a part in later scientific history is foreshadowed in a crude way by this episode involving the combustion of phosphorus and the calcination of tin. Therefore, in considering the case history at hand the instructor would undoubtedly wish to enlarge at some length on the whole problem of the controlled variable and the role of quantitative measurements.

LAVOISIER AND PRIESTLEY'S STUBBORN FACTS

For students who had some prior knowledge of chemistry, say a good high-school course, the study of the last days of the phlogiston theory might be rewarding. For the controversy between Lavoisier and Priestley not only illustrates with what tenacity an able man may cling to a hopeless position, but also the boldness with which the innovator pushes forward. Even if a few facts appear to be to the contrary, he still pushes his new ideas just as his conservative opponent stoutly maintains his own tenets in spite of contradictory evidence. In such tugs of war which are the commonest experience in science, though usually in highly restricted areas and with limited significance, the innovator is by no means always right. This point needs to be made perfectly clear. Several case histories to this end would be worth recounting. A few dramatic instances would be in order where some bold man put forward a new idea based on alleged facts which turned out to be erroneous or erroneously interpreted.

The record of Lavoisier was the opposite. For the facts he ignored were indeed not facts at all. Priestley's main points against Lavoisier's views were based on a mistaken identification of two different gases. This fact again emphasizes the difficulties of experimentation. Two gases, both inflammable, carbon monoxide and hydrogen, were at that period confused, even by the great experimenters with gases. Assuming their identity Priestley could ask Lavoisier to account for phenomena which were indeed inexplicable according to the new chemistry, but could be accommodated in the phlogiston theory, now being twisted more each day to conform to new discoveries. Not until long after Lavoisier's execution in 1794 was the relationship between the two gases straightened out. Therefore, Lavoisier was never able to respond to the most weighty of Priestley's arguments against his doctrine. He merely ignored the alleged facts, much as Priestley ignored the unexplained gain in weight or calcination. Each undoubtedly believed that some way would be found around the difficulty in question. Lavoisier's hopes, not Priestley's, proved well founded. So proceeds the course of science. Sometimes it turns out that difficulties with a concept or conceptual scheme are wisely ignored, sometimes unwisely. To suppose, with some who write about the "scientific method," that a scientific theory stands or falls on the issue of one experiment is to misunderstand science indeed.

A study of the overthrow of the phlogiston theory is thus seen to be more than a single case history; it is a related series of case histories. The student's knowledge of chemistry or willingness to take time to obtain this knowledge would be the limiting factor on the use of this material. Even without prior study of chemistry, I believe, a profitable excursion into this complicated bit of scientific history could be undertaken. From such an excursion would come a deeper appreciation of the two principles to which I earlier referred in this chapter. Having studied the phlogiston theory no one would fail to realize that old concepts may present barriers to the development of new ones; having traced the course of the history of experiments with gases and calcination, no one could fail to realize that scientific discoveries must fit the times if they are to be fruitful. In addition, other principles of the Tactics and Strategy of Science are constantly recurring throughout the somewhat lengthy story: the influence of new techniques, the difficulties of experimentation, the value of the controlled experiment, the evaluation of new concepts from experiment—all these are to be found illustrated more than once by those who have patience to study a strange and often neglected chapter in the history of science.

THE USEFULNESS OF USELESS KNOWLEDGE [1]

ABRAHAM FLEXNER

Is it not a curious fact that in a world steeped in irrational hatreds which threaten civilization itself, men and women—old and young—detach themselves wholly or partly from the angry current of daily life to devote themselves to the cultivation of beauty, to the extension of knowledge, to the cure of disease, to the amelioration of suffering, just as though fanatics were not simultaneously engaged in spreading pain, ugliness, and suffering? The world has always been a sorry and confused sort of place—yet poets and artists and scientists have ignored the factors that would, if attended to, paralyze them. From a practical point of view, intellectual and spiritual life is, on the surface, a useless form of activity, in which men indulge because they procure for themselves greater satisfactions than are otherwise obtainable. In this paper I shall concern myself with the question of the extent to which the pursuit of these useless satisfactions proves unexpectedly the source from which undreamed-of utility is derived.

We hear it said with tiresome iteration that ours is a materialistic age, the main concern of which should be the wider distribution of material goods and worldly opportunities. The justified outcry of those who through no fault of their own are deprived of opportunity and a fair share of worldly goods therefore diverts an increasing number of students from the studies which their fathers pursued to the equally important and no less urgent study of social, economic, and governmental problems. I have no quarrel with this tendency. The world in which we live is the only world about which our senses can testify. Unless it is made a better world, a fairer world, millions will continue to go to their graves silent, saddened, and embittered. I have myself spent many years pleading that our schools should become more acutely aware of the world in which their pupils and students are destined to pass their lives. Now I sometimes wonder whether that current has not become too strong and whether there would be sufficient opportunity for a full life if the world were emptied of some of the useless things that give it spiritual significance; in other words, whether our conception of what is useful may not have become too narrow to be adequate to the roaming and capricious possibilities of the human spirit.

1. "The Usefulness of Useless Knowledge," *Harper's Magazine,* CLXXIX (October, 1939), 544–550, with omissions. Reprinted by permission of the author.

We may look at this question from two points of view: the scientific and the humanistic or spiritual. Let us take the scientific first. I recall a conversation which I had some years ago with Mr. George Eastman on the subject of use. Mr. Eastman, a wise and gentle farseeing man, gifted with taste in music and art, had been saying to me that he meant to devote his vast fortune to the promotion of education in useful subjects. I ventured to ask him whom he regarded as the most useful worker in science in the world. He replied instantaneously: "Marconi." I surprised him by saying, "Whateve pleasure we derive from the radio or however wireless and the radio may have added to human life, Marconi's share was practically negligible."

I shall not forget his astonishment on this occasion. He asked me to explain. I replied to him somewhat as follows:

"Mr. Eastman, Marconi was inevitable. The real credit for everything that has been done in the field of wireless belongs, as far as such fundamental credit can be definitely assigned to anyone, to Professor Clerk Maxwell, who in 1865 carried out certain abstruse and remote calculations in the field of magnetism and electricity. Maxwell reproduced his abstract equations in a treatise published in 1873. At the next meeting of the British Association Professor H. J. S. Smith of Oxford declared that 'no mathematician can turn over the pages of these volumes without realizing that they contain a theory which has already added largely to the methods and resources of pure mathematics.' Other discoveries supplemented Maxwell's theoretical work during the next fifteen years. Finally in 1887 and 1888 the scientific problem still remaining—the detection and demonstration of the electromagnetic waves which are the carriers of wireless signals—was solved by Heinrich Hertz, a worker in Helmholtz's laboratory in Berlin. Neither Maxwell nor Hertz had any concern about the utility of their work; no such thought ever entered their minds. They had no practical objective. The inventor in the legal sense was of course Marconi, but what did Marconi invent? Merely the last technical detail, mainly the now obsolete receiving device called coherer, almost universally discarded."

Hertz and Maxwell could invent nothing, but it was their useless theoretical work which was seized upon by a clever technician and which has created new means for communication, utility, and amusement by which men whose merits are relatively slight have obtained fame and earned millions. Who were the useful men? Not Marconi, but Clerk Maxwell and Heinrich Hertz. Hertz and Maxwell were geniuses without thought of use. Marconi was a clever inventor with no thought but use.

The mention of Hertz's name recalled to Mr. Eastman the Hertzian waves, and I suggested that he might ask the physicists of the University of Rochester precisely what Hertz and Maxwell had done; but one thing I said he could be sure of, namely, that they had done their work without thought of use and that throughout the whole history of science most of the really great discoveries which had ultimately proved to be beneficial to mankind had been made by men and women who were driven not by the desire to be useful but merely the desire to satisfy their curiosity.

"Curiosity?" asked Mr. Eastman.

"Yes," I replied, "curiosity, which may or may not eventuate in something useful, is probably the outstanding characteristic of modern thinking. It is not new. It goes back to Galileo, Bacon, and to Sir Isaac Newton, and it must be absolutely unhampered. Institutions of learning should be devoted to the cultivation of curiosity and the less they are deflected by considerations of immediacy of application, the more likely they are to contribute not only to human welfare but to the equally important satisfaction of intellectual interest which may indeed be said to have become the ruling passion of intellectual life in modern times."

II

What is true of Heinrich Hertz working quietly and unnoticed in a corner of Helmholtz's laboratory in the later years of the nineteenth century may be said of scientists and mathematicians the world over for several centuries past. We live in a world that would be helpless without electricity. Called upon to mention a discovery of the most immediate and far-reaching practical use we might well agree upon electricity. But who made the fundamental discoveries out of which the entire electrical development of more than one hundred years has come?

The answer is interesting. Michael Faraday's father was a blacksmith; Michael himself was apprenticed to a bookbinder. In 1812, when he was already twenty-one years of age, a friend took him to the Royal Institution where he heard Sir Humphry Davy deliver four lectures on chemical subjects. He kept notes and sent a copy of them to Davy. The very next year, 1813, he became an assistant in Davy's laboratory, working on chemical problems. Two years later he accompanied Davy on a trip to the Continent. In 1825, when he was thirty-four years of age, he became Director of the Laboratory of the Royal Institution where he spent fifty-four years of his life.

Faraday's interest soon shifted from chemistry to electricity and magnetism, to which he devoted the rest of his active life. Important but puzzling work in this field had been previously accomplished by Oersted, Ampère, and Wollaston. Faraday cleared away the difficulties which they had left unsolved and by 1841 had succeeded in the task of induction of the electric current. Four years later a second and equally brilliant epoch in his career opened when he discovered the effect of magnetism on polarized light. His earlier discoveries have led to the infinite number of practical applications by means of which electricity has lightened the burdens and increased the opportunities of modern life. His later discoveries have thus far been less prolific of practical results. What difference did this make to Faraday? Not the least. At no period of his unmatched career was he interested in utility. He was absorbed in disentangling the riddles of the universe, at first chemical riddles, in later periods, physical riddles. As far as he cared, the question of utility was never raised. Any suspicion of utility would have restricted his restless curiosity. In the end, utility resulted, but it was never a criterion to which his ceaseless experimentation could be subjected.

In the atmosphere which envelops the world to-day it is perhaps timely to emphasize the fact that the part played by science in making war more destructive and more horrible was an unconscious and unintended by-product of scientific activity. Lord Rayleigh, president of the British Association for the Advancement of Science, in a recent address points out in detail how the folly of man, not the intention of the scientists, is responsible for the destructive use of the agents employed in modern warfare. The innocent study of the chemistry of carbon compounds, which has led to infinite beneficial results, showed that the action of nitric acid on substances like benzene, glycerine, cellulose, etc., resulted not only in the beneficent aniline dye industry but in the creation of nitro-glycerine, which has uses good and bad. Somewhat later Alfred Nobel, turning to the same subject, showed that by mixing nitro-glycerine with other substances, solid explosives which could be safely handled could be produced—among others, dynamite. It is to dynamite that we owe our progress in mining, in the making of such railroad tunnels as those which now pierce the Alps and other mountain ranges; but of course dynamite has been abused by politicians and soldiers. Scientists are, however, no more to blame than they are to blame for an earthquake or a flood. The same thing can be said of poison gas. Pliny was killed by breathing sulphur dioxide in the eruption of Vesuvius almost two thousand years ago. Chlorine was not isolated by scientists for warlike purposes, and the same is true of mustard gas. These substances could be limited to beneficent use, but when the airplane was perfected, men whose hearts were poisoned and whose brains were addled perceived that the airplane, an innocent invention, the result of long disinterested and scientific effort, could be made an instrument of destruction, of which no one had ever dreamed and at which no one had ever deliberately aimed.

In the domain of higher mathematics almost innumerable instances can be cited. For example, the most abstruse mathematical work of the eighteenth and nineteenth centuries was the "Non-Euclidian Geometry." Its inventor, Gauss, though recognized by his contemporaries as a distinguished mathematician, did not dare to publish his work on "Non-Euclidian Geometry" for a quarter of a century. As a matter of fact, the theory of relativity itself with all its infinite practical bearings would have been utterly impossible without the work which Gauss did at Göttingen.

Again, what is known now as "group theory" was an abstract and inapplicable mathematical theory. It was developed by men who were curious and whose curiosity and puttering led them into strange paths; but "group theory" is to-day the basis of the quantum theory of spectroscopy, which is in daily use by people who have no idea as to how it came about. . . .

III

I am pleading for the abolition of the word "use," and for the freeing of the human spirit. To be sure, we shall thus free some harmless cranks. To be sure, we shall thus waste some precious dollars. But what is infinitely more important is that we shall be striking the shackles off the human mind and setting it free for the adventures which in our own day have, on the one hand, taken Hale and Rutherford and Einstein and their peers millions upon millions of miles into the uttermost realms of space and, on the other, loosed the boundless energy imprisoned in the atom. What Rutherford and others like Bohr and Millikan have done out of sheer curiosity in the effort to understand the construction of the atom has released forces which may transform human life; but this ultimate and unforeseen and unpredictable practical result is not offered as a justification for Rutherford or Einstein or Millikan or Bohr or any of their peers. Let them alone. No educational administrator can possibly direct the channels in which these or other men shall work. The waste, I admit again, looks prodigious. It is not really so. All the waste that could be summed up in developing the science of bacteriology is as nothing compared to the advantages which have accrued from the discoveries of Pasteur, Koch, Ehrlich, Theobald Smith, and scores of others—advantages that could never have accrued if the idea of possible use had permeated their minds. These great artists—for such are scientists and bacteriologists—disseminated the spirit which prevailed in laboratories in which they were simply following the line of their own natural curiosity.

I am not criticising institutions like schools of engineering or law in which the usefulness motive necessarily predominates. Not infrequently the tables are turned, and practical difficulties encountered in industry or in laboratories stimulate theoretical inquiries which may or may not solve the problems by which they were suggested, but may also open up new vistas, useless at the moment, but pregnant with future achievements, practical and theoretical.

With the rapid accumulation of "useless" or theoretic knowledge a situation has been created in which it has become increasingly possible to attack practical problems in a scientific spirit. Not only inventors, but "pure" scientists have indulged in this sport. I have mentioned Marconi, an inventor, who, while a benefactor to the human race, as a matter of fact merely "picked other men's brains." Edison belongs to the same category. Pasteur was different. He was a great scientist; but he was not averse to attacking practical problems—such as the condition of French grapevines or the problems of beer-brewing—and not only solving the immediate difficulty, but also wresting from the practical problem some far-reaching theoretic conclusion, "useless" at the moment, but likely in some unforeseen manner to be "useful" later. Ehrlich, fundamentally speculative in his curiosity, turned fiercely upon the problem of syphilis and doggedly pursued it until a solution of immediate practical use—the discovery of salvarsan—was found. The discoveries of insulin by Banting for use in diabetes and of liver extract by Minot and Whipple for use in pernicious anemia belong in the same category; both were made by thoroughly scientific men, who realized that much "useless" knowledge had been piled up by men unconcerned with its practical bearings, but that the time was now ripe to raise practical questions in a scientific manner.

Thus it becomes obvious that one must be wary in attributing scientific discovery wholly to any one person. Almost every discovery has a long and precarious history. Some one finds a bit here, another a bit there. A third step succeeds later and thus onward till a genius pieces the bits together and makes the decisive contribution. Science, like the Mississippi, begins in a tiny rivulet in the distant forest. Gradually other streams swell its volume. And the roaring river that bursts the dikes is formed from countless sources.

I cannot deal with this aspect exhaustively, but I may in passing say this: over a period of one or two hundred years the contributions of professional schools to their respective activities will probably be found to lie, not so much in the training of men who may to-morrow become practical engineers or practical lawyers or practical doctors, but rather in the fact that even in the pursuit of strictly practical aims an enormous amount of apparently useless activity goes on. Out of this useless activity there come discoveries which may well prove of infinitely more importance to the human mind and to the human spirit than the accomplishment of the useful ends for which the schools were founded.

The considerations upon which I have touched emphasize—if emphasis were needed—the overwhelming importance of spiritual and intellectual freedom. I have spoken of experimental science; I have spoken of mathematics; but what I say is equally true of music and art and of every other expression of the untrammeled human spirit. The mere fact that they bring satisfaction to an individual soul bent upon its own purification and elevation is all the justification that they need. And in justifying these without any reference whatsoever, implied or actual, to usefulness we justify colleges, universities, and institutes of research. An institution which sets free successive generations of human souls is amply justified whether or not this graduate or that makes a so-called useful contribution to human knowledge. A poem, a symphony, a painting, a mathematical truth, a new scientific fact, all bear in themselves all the justification that universities, colleges, and institutes of research need or require. . . .

This is not a new idea. It was the idea which animated von Humboldt when, in the hour of Germany's conquest by Napoleon, he conceived and founded the University of Berlin. It is the idea which animated President Gilman in the founding of the Johns Hopkins University, after which every university in this country has sought in greater or less degree to remake itself. It is the idea to which every individual who values his immortal soul will be true whatever the personal consequences to himself.

WHAT MAKES THE WEATHER: THE SEVEN AMERICAN AIRS[1]

WOLFGANG LANGEWIESCHE

You wake up one morning and you are surprised: the weather, which had been gray and dreary for days and seemed as if it were going to stay that way forever, with no breaks in the clouds and no indication of a gradual clearing, is now all of a sudden clear and sunny and crisp, with a strong northwest wind blowing, and the whole world looks newly washed and newly painted.

"It" has become "fine." Why? How?

"Something" has cleared the air, you might say. But what? You might study out the weather news in the back of your newspaper, and you would get it explained to you in terms of barometric highs and lows; but just why a rise of barometric pressure should clear the air would still leave you puzzled. The honest truth is that the weather has never been explained. In school they told you about steam engines or electricity or even about really mysterious things, such as gravitation, and they could do it so that it made sense to a boy. They told you also about the weather, but their explanations failed to explain, and you knew it even then. The lows and highs, cyclones and anti-cyclones, the winds that blew around in circles—all these things were much more puzzling than the weather itself. That is why weather has always made only the dullest conversation: there simply was no rhyme nor reason to it.

But now there is. A revolutionary fresh view has uncovered the rhyme and reason in the weather. Applied to your particular surprise of that morning, it has this to say:

The air which was warm, moist, and gray last night is still warm, moist, and gray this morning; but it has been pushed fifty or one hundred miles to the south and east of where you live, and has been replaced by a mass of cold, clear, dry air coming from the north or west. It is as simple as that; there is no mysterious "It" in it; just plain physical sense. It is called Air Mass Analysis.

It is based upon the researches and experiments of a physicist named Vilhelm Bjerknes, of Norway, and though in this particular case it seems almost childishly simple, it is Norway's greatest contribution to world culture since

1. From "What Makes the Weather," *Harper's Magazine,* CLXXXV (October, 1942), 478–488. Reprinted by permission of the author.

Ibsen. Or perhaps because it is simple—the rare example of a science which in becoming more sophisticated also becomes more common sense and easier to understand. It is so new that it hasn't yet reached the newspapers, nor the high school curricula, much less the common knowledge of the public in general. But the weather bureaus of the airlines have worked by it for years, and pilots have to learn it. It is indispensable both in commercial flying and in air war; we could fly without gasoline, without aluminum, perhaps without radio, but we could never do without Bjerknes's Air Mass Analysis.

You might inquire next where that morning's new air came from, and just how it got to be cold, dry, and clear. And there you get close to the heart of the new weather science, where meteorology turns into honest, common-sense geography.

That air has come from Canada, where it has been quite literally air-conditioned. Not all parts of the world have the power to condition air, but Canada has. Especially in the fall and winter and early spring, the northern part of this continent becomes an almost perfectly designed mechanical refrigerator. The Rocky Mountains in the west keep currents of new air from flowing into the region. And for weeks the air lies still. The cool ground, much of it snow-covered; the ice of the frozen lakes; plus the perennial stored-up coldness of Hudson's Bay—all cool the layer of air immediately above them. This means a stabilizing and calming of the whole atmosphere all the way up; for cool air is heavy, and with a heavy layer bottommost, there is none of that upflowing of air, that upwelling of moisture-laden heat into the cooler, high altitude which is the mechanism that makes clouds. Thus there may be some low ground fogs there, but above them the long nights of those northern latitudes are clear and starry, wide open toward the black infinite spaces of the universe; and into that black infinity the air gradually radiates whatever warmth it may contain from its previous sojourns over other parts of the world. The result, after weeks of stagnation, is a huge mass of air that is uniformly ice-cold, dry, and clear. It stretches from the Rocky Mountains in the west to Labrador in the east, from the ice wastes of the Arctic to the prairies of Minnesota and North Dakota; and—the third dimension is the most important—it is ice-cold from the ground all the way up to the stratosphere. It is, in short, a veritable glacier of air.

That is an air mass. In the jargon of air-faring men, a mass of Polar Canadian Air.

When a wave of good, fresh Polar Canadian air sweeps southward into the United States—it happens almost rhythmically every few days—you don't need a barometer to tell you so. There is nothing subtle, theoretical, or scientific about it. You can see and feel the air itself and even hear it. It comes surging out of a blue-green sky across the Dakotas, shaking the hangar doors, whistling in the grass, putting those red-checkered thick woolen jackets on the men, and lighting the stoves in the houses. It flows southward down the Mississippi Valley as a cold wave in winter, or as relief from a heat wave in summer, blowing as a northwest wind with small white hurrying clouds in it. In winter it may sweep southward as far as Tennessee and the Carolinas, bringing frosts with brilliantly clear skies, making the darkies shiver in their drafty cabins, and producing a wave of deaths by pneumonia. Sometimes it even reaches the Texas Gulf Coast; then it is locally called a norther, and the cows at night crowd for warmth around the gas flares in the oil fields. A duck hunter dies of exposure in the coastal swamps. A lively outbreak of Polar Canadian air may reach down into Florida, damage the orange crops, and embarrass local Chambers of Commerce. And deep outbreaks have been observed to drive all the way down to Central America, where they are feared as a fierce wind called the Tehuantepecer.

Polar Canadian is only one of many sorts of air. To put it in the unprecise language of the layman, the great Norwegian discovery is that air must always be of some distinct type: that it is never simply air but always conditioned and flavored. What we call weather is caused by gigantic waves in the air ocean which flood whole countries and continents for days at a stretch with one sort of air or another. And there is nothing theoretical about any of these various sorts of air.

Each kind is easily seen and felt and sniffed, and is, in fact, fairly familiar even to the city dweller, although he may not realize it. Each has its own peculiar characteristics, its own warmth or coolness, dampness or dryness, milkiness or clearness. Each has its own quality of light. In each, smoke behaves differently as it pours from the chimneys: in some kinds of air it creeps lazily, in some it bubbles away, in some it floats in layers. That is largely why the connoisseur can distinguish different types of air by smell.

Each type of air combines those qualities into an "atmosphere" of its own. Each makes an entirely different sort of day. In fact, what sort of day it is—raw, oppressive, balmy, dull, a "spring" day—depends almost entirely upon the sort of air that lies over your particular section of the country at that particular time.

And if you tried to describe the day in the old-fashioned terms—wind direction and velocity, humidity, state of the sky—you could never quite express its particular weather; but you can by naming the sort of air. An airplane pilot, once he is trained in the new weather thinking, can get quite impatient with the attempts of novelists, for instance, to describe weather. "Why don't you *say* it was Polar Canadian air and get on with your story?"

And if you are a connoisseur of airs just about the first thing you will note every morning is something like, "Ah, Caribbean air today"; or if you are really a judge you can make statements as detailed as, "Saskatchewan air, slightly flavored by the Great Lakes."

For just as wines do, the airs take their names and their flavors from the regions where they have matured. Of the seven airs that make up the American weather, one is quite rare and somewhat mysterious. It is known by the peculiarly wine-like name of Sec Superieur. It is believed to be of tropical origin, but it comes to this continent after spending weeks in the stratosphere somewhere above the Galápagos Islands. It is usually found only high aloft, and interests pilots more than farmers. But once in a while a tongue of it reaches the ground as hot, extremely dry, very clear weather; and wherever it licks there is a drought.

The other six airs all come from perfectly earthly places, though far-away ones. The easiest to recognize, the liveliest, is Polar Canadian. Its opposite number in the American sky is Tropical Gulf or Tropical Atlantic air—the steamy, warm air of the Eastern and Midwestern summer, the kind that comes as a southwest wind and starts people to talking about heat and humidity, the kind that is sometimes so steamy that it leaves you in doubt as to whether the sky means to be blue or overcast. This air is brewed of hot sun and warm sea water in the Caribbean region. The mechanism that does the air conditioning in this case is mostly the daily afternoon thunderstorm which carries moisture and heat high aloft in it.

Not quite so obvious is the origin of the moist, silvery, cool-in-summer, cool-in-winter air that dominates the weather of Seattle. It is called Polar Pacific, and it is a trick product. Its basic characteristics have been acquired over Siberia and it is cold and dry; but on its way across the Pacific its lower five to ten thousand feet have been warmed up and moistened. Sometimes such air comes straight across, reaching land in a couple of days. Sometimes it hangs over the water for a week, and it takes a good weatherman to predict just what sort of weather it will produce.

Its counterpart is a flavor known as Tropical Pacific. That is the air they sell to tourists in Southern California. It is really just plain South Seas air, though the story here too is not as clear-cut as it might be.

A clear-cut type is Polar Atlantic air. It sometimes blows down the New England coast as a nor'easter, cold, rainy, with low clouds. It is simply a chunk of the Grand Banks off Newfoundland gone traveling, and you can almost smell the sea.

And one air that every tourist notices in the Southwest is Tropical Continental. Its source region is the deserts of Arizona and Mexico. It is dry and hot and licks up moisture so greedily that it makes water feel on your skin as chilly as if it were gasoline. It is not an important one for America, though its European counterpart, Saharan air, is important for Europe. Oklahoma, Colorado, and Kansas are as far as it ever gets; but even so, a few extra outbreaks of it per year, and we have a dustbowl.

II

The air mass idea is simple. As great ideas often do, the air mass idea makes you feel that you have known it right along. And in a vague way, you have. Take, for example, that half-brag, half-complaint of the Texans that there is nothing between Texas and the North Pole to keep out those northers but a barbed wire fence: it contains the kernel of the whole idea—the invading air mass—but only in a fooling way. Or take the manner in which the Mediterranean people have always given definite names to certain winds (boreas, sirocco, mistral) that blow hot or cold, dry or moist, across their roofs. They are names, however, without the larger view. In creative literature such things as a cold front passage—the sudden arrival of a cold air mass—have been described several times quite accurately, but always as a local spectacle, with the key thought missing.

Actually it took genius to see it. For air is a mercurial fluid, bubbly, changeable; it is as full of hidden energies as dynamite; it can assume the most unexpected appearances. There are days, to be sure, when the air virtually advertises its origin. Offhand, you might say that on perhaps half the days of the year it does. But there are also days when its appearance is altogether misleading.

Take, for example, the amazing metamorphosis that happens to Tropical Gulf air when it flows northward across the United States in winter. It starts out from among the Islands looking blue and sunny and like an everlasting summer afternoon. When it arrives over the northern United States that same air appears as a dark-gray shapeless, drizzling overcast, and in the office buildings of New York and Chicago the electric lights are on throughout what is considered a shivery winter day. It *is* still the same air; if we could mix a pink dye into the air, as geographers sometimes mix dyes into rivers to trace the flow of water, a cloud of pink air would have traveled from Trinidad to New York. It has hardly changed at all its actual contents of heat and water; but as far as its appearance and its feel are concerned—its "weather" value—a few days of northward traveling have reversed it almost into a photographic negative of itself.

What happens in this particular case—and it accounts for half our winter days—is simply that the cool ground of the wintry continent chills this moist, warm air mass—chills it just a little, not enough to change its fundamental character, and not all the way up into its upper levels, but in its bottommost layer and that only just enough to make it condense out some of its abundant moisture in the form of visible clouds; it is quite similar to the effect of a cold window pane on the air of a well-heated, comfortable room—there is wetness and cooling right at the window, but the bulk of the room's air is not affected.

Perhaps the oddest example of this is the trick by which Polar Pacific air, striking the United States at Seattle, cool and moist, arrives in eastern Montana and the Dakotas as a chinook, a hot, dry, snow-melting wind.

As Polar Pacific air flows up the slopes of the Sierras and the Cascades it is lifted ten thousand feet into the thinner air of higher altitude. By one law of physics the lifting should chill the air through release of pressure. If you have ever bled excess pressure out of your tires you know this cooling by release of pressure—you know how ice-cold the air comes hissing out. But in this case, by a different law of physics, Polar Pacific reacts by cooling only moderately; then it starts condensing out its moisture and thereby protecting its warmth; hence the tremendous snowfalls of the sierras, the giant redwoods, the streams that irrigate California ranches.

Once across the Cascades and the Sierras, the air flows down the eastern slopes. In descending it comes under pressure and therefore heats up, just as air heats up in a tire pump. Warmed, the air increases its capacity to hold moisture; it becomes relatively drier—thus this air sucks back its own clouds into invisible form. When it arrives over the Columbia Basin, or the country round Reno, or Owens Valley, it is regular desert air—warm, very clear, and very dry. That is why the western deserts are where they are. Flowing on eastward, it comes against another hump, the Continental Divide and the Rockies. Here the whole process repeats itself. Again the air is lifted and *should* become ice-cold; again it merely cools moderately, clouds up, and drops its remaining moisture to protect its warmth; hence the lush greenery of Coeur d'Alene, the pine forests of New Mexico. Finally, as the air flows down the eastern slope of the Rockies, compression heats it once more, as in the bicycle pump. Twice on the way up it has dropped moisture and thus failed to cool; twice on the way down it has been heated: it is now extremely dry, and twenty degrees warmer than it was at Seattle. *That* is the chinook, a wind manufactured of exactly the sort of principles that work in air-conditioning machinery, and a good example of the trickery of air masses. But it is *still* a simple thing; it is still one actual physically identical mass of air that you are following. If you had put pink smoke into it at Seattle, pink smoke would have arrived in South Dakota.

That is how the air mass concept explains all sorts of weather detail: the various kinds of rain—showery or steady; the many types of cloud—low or high, solid or broken, layered or towering; thunderstorms; fog. An air mass, thus-and-thus conditioned, will react differently as it flows over the dry plains, the freshly plowed cotton fields, the cool lakes, the hot pavements, the Rocky Mountains of the United States.

An airplane pilot's weather sense consists largely of guessing the exact manner in which a given sort of air will behave along his route. Tropical Gulf in summer over Alabama? Better not get caught in the middle afternoon with a low fuel reserve. We shall have to detour around many thunderstorms. The details are as multifarious as geography itself, but much of it has by now been put into the manuals, and the pilot memorizes such items as these:

Canadian air that passes over the Great Lakes in winter is moistened and warmed in its lower layers and becomes highly unstable. When such air hits the rolling country of western Pennsylvania and New York and the ridges of the Appalachians, the hills have a sort of "trigger action" and cause snow flurries or rain squalls with very low ceilings and visibility.

In summer, Canadian air that flows into New England, dried, without passing over the Great Lakes, will be extremely clear and extremely bumpy.

Tropical Gulf over the South forms patchy ground fog just before sunrise that will persist for two or three hours.

As Polar Pacific air moves southward along the Pacific Coast it forms a layer of "high fog."

In Colorado and Nebraska fresh arriving Canadian air frequently shows as a dust storm.

Given two types of country underneath, one kind of air can produce two sorts of weather only a few miles apart. Tropical Atlantic air, for instance, appears over the hills of New England as hot and summery weather, slightly hazy, inclined toward afternoon thunderstorms. A few miles off the coast the same air appears as low banks of fog. That is because the granite and the woods are warmed all through, and actually a little warmer than Tropical Gulf air itself, at least during the day; while the ocean is much colder than the air, and cools it.

Again, one kind of country can have opposite effects on two different types of air. For example, the farms of the Middle West in the spring when the frost is just off the ground: that sort of country feels cool to Tropical Gulf air that has flowed up the Mississippi Valley. The bottom layers of that warm moist air are chilled and thus the whole air mass is stabilized. It will stay nicely in layers; the clouds will form a flat, level overcast; smoke will spread and hover as a pall. But to a mass of freshly broken-out Canadian air that sort of country feels warm. The air in immediate contact with the ground is warmed, and the whole mass becomes bottom-light and unstable.

And that means action: a commotion much like the boiling of water on a huge scale and in slow motion. The warmed air floats away upward to the colder air aloft, forming bubbles of rising air, hundreds of feet in diameter, that are really hot-air balloons without a skin.

Those rising chunks of air are felt by fliers as bumps. When the ship flies into one it gets an upward jolt; when it flies out again it gets a downward jolt. They are what makes it possible to fly a glider, even over flat country; all you have to do is to find one of those bubbles, stay in it by circling in a tight turn, and let it carry you aloft.

The clear air, the tremendous visibility of such a day is itself the result of instability: the rising bubbles carry away the dust, the haze, the industrial smoke. The air is always roughest on one of those crisp, clear, newly washed days. If the rising air gets high enough it makes cumulus clouds, those characteristic, towering, puffy good-weather clouds. That sort of cloud is nothing but a puff of upward wind become visible. The rise has cooled the air and made its water vapor visible. Soaring pilots seek to get underneath a cumulus cloud—there is sure to be a lively upflow there. Sometimes, in really unstable air, the rising of the air reaches hurricane velocities. We call that a thunderstorm, but the lightning and thunder are only by-products of the thing. The thing itself is simply a vicious, explosive upsurging of air: the wind in thunderstorms blows sixty to one hundred miles per hour—straight up! The most daring of soaring pilots have flown into thunderstorms and have been sucked up almost to the stratosphere.

The weatherman, unlike the pilot, need not guess. He has got a slide rule; he has got the laws of gases, Charles's Law, Boyle's Law, Buys Ballot's Law at his fingertips. He has studied thermodynamics, and he has got a new device that is the biggest thing in weather science since Torricelli invented the barometer—the radio sonde with which he can take soundings of the upper air, find out just how moisture and temperature conditions are aloft, just how stable or unstable the air will be, at what level the clouds will form, and of what type they will be.

Radio sondes go up in the dead of night from a dozen airports all over the continent. The radio sonde looks like a box of candy, being a small carton wrapped in tinfoil; but it is actually a radio transmitter coupled to a thermometer and a moisture-meter. It is hung on a small parachute which is hitched to a balloon. It takes perhaps an hour for the balloon to reach the stratosphere, and all the time it signals its own readings in a strange, quacky voice, half Donald Duck, half voice from the beyond. Then it stops. You know that the balloon has burst, the parachute is letting the instrument down gently.

The next morning some farm boy finds the shiny thing in a field, with a notice attached offering a reward for mailing it back to the weather bureau.

Also the next morning a man in Los Angeles paces up and down his office, scanning the wall where last night's upper-air soundings are tacked up. Emitting heavy cigar smoke and not even looking out of the window, he dictates a weather forecast for the transcontinental airway as far east as Salt Lake City, a forecast that goes into such detail that you sometimes think he is trying to show off.

III

With the air mass idea as a key, you can make more sense out of the weather than the professional weatherman could before Bjerknes; and even if you don't understand Boyle's Law and all the intricate physics of the atmosphere, you can do a quite respectable job of forecasting.

It goes like this: suppose you are deep in Caribbean air. You will have "air mass weather": a whole series of days of the typical sort that goes with that particular type of air when it overlies your particular section of the country in that particular season. There will be all sorts of minor changes; there will be a daily cycle of weather, clouds, perhaps thunderstorms, or showers; but essentially the weather will be the same day after day. Any *real* change in weather can come only as an incursion of a new air mass—probably Polar Canadian.

And when that air mass comes you will know it. New air rarely comes gently, gradually, by imperceptible degrees; almost always the new air mass advances into the old one with a clear-cut, sharply defined forward front. Where two air masses adjoin each other you may in half an hour's driving—in five minutes' flying—change your entire weather, travel from moist, muggy, cloudy weather into clear, cool, sunny weather. That clear-cut boundary is exactly what makes an air mass a distinct entity which you can plot on a map and say, "Here it begins; here it ends"; these sharp boundaries of the air masses are called "fronts" and are a discovery as important as the air mass itself.

You are watching, then, for a "cold front," the forward edge of an advancing mass of cold air. You will get almost no advance warning. You will see the cold air mass only when it is practically upon you. But you know that sooner or later it must come, and that it will come from the northwest. Thus, an occasional long-distance call will be enough. Suppose you are in Pittsburgh, with a moist, warm southwest wind: the bare news that Chicago has a northerly wind might be enough of a clue. If you knew also that Chicago was twenty degrees cooler you could be certain that a cold air mass had swamped Chicago and was now presumably on its way to Pittsburgh, traveling presumably at something like 30 m.p.h. You could guess the time of arrival of its forward front within a few hours. . . .

Knowing that a cold front is coming, you know what kind of weather to expect; though some cold fronts are extremely fierce, and others quite gentle (noticeable only if you watch for them), the type is always the same. It is all in the book—Bjerknes described it and even drew pictures of it. It was the advance of such a cold front which occurred while you slept that night before you awoke to find the world fresh and newly painted.

Cold air is heavy; as polar air plows into a region occupied by tropical air it underruns; it gets underneath the warm air and lifts it up even as it pushes it back. A cold front acts physically like a cowcatcher.

Seen from the ground, the sequence of events is this: an hour or two before the cold front arrives the clouds in the sky become confused, somewhat like a herd of cattle that smells the coyotes; but you observe that by intuition rather than by measurable signs. Apart from that, there are no advance signs. The wind will be southerly to the last, and the air warm and moist.

Big cumulus clouds build up all around, some of them with dark bases, showers, and in summer thunder and lightning—that is the warm moist air going aloft. A dark bank of solid cloud appears in the northwest, and though the wind is still southerly, this bank keeps building up and coming nearer: it is the actual forward edge of the advancing cold air. When it arrives there is a cloudburst. Then the cold air comes sweeping in from the northwest with vicious gusts. This is the squall that capsizes sailboats and uproots trees, flattens forests and unroofs houses.

The whole commotion probably is over in half an hour. The wind eases up, though it is still cool and northwesterly, the rain ceases, the clouds break and new sky shows; the front has passed, the cold air mass has arrived.

The weatherman can calculate these things too. He has watched and sounded out each of the two air masses for days or even weeks, ever since it moved into his ken somewhere on the outskirts of the American world. Thus an airline weatherman may look at a temperature-moisture graph and say, "This is dynamite. This air will be stable enough as long as it isn't disturbed. But wait till some cold air gets underneath this and starts lifting it. This stuff is going to go crazy."

In making your own guess you would take the same chance that the weatherman takes every morning—that you might be right and yet get an error chalked up against you. Suppose the Chicago weatherman, seeing a cold front approach, forecasts thunderstorms. One thunderstorm passes north of the city, disturbing the 30,000 inhabitants of Waukegan. Another big one passes south of Chicago, across farms just south of Hammond, Ind., affecting another 30,000 people. None happens to hit Chicago itself, with its 3 million people.

On a per capita basis, the weatherman was 98 per cent wrong! Actually he was right.

Now you are in the cold air mass, and you can reasonably expect "air mass weather" for a while rather than "frontal" weather; *i.e.*, a whole series of whatever sort of day goes with Canadian air in your particular section of the country at that particular season.

Any real change in the weather *now* can again come only with an incursion of a new and different air mass—and now that will probably mean tropical maritime air of the Gulf kind. To forecast that invasion is no trick at all: you can see the forward front of the warm air mass in the sky several days before it sweeps in on the ground. Warm air is light. As Caribbean air advances into a region occupied by Canadian air it produces a pattern that is the exact opposite of the cold front. The warm front overhangs forward, overruns the cold air; the warm air mass may appear high above Boston when at ground level it is just invading Richmond, Va.

Again the sequence of events is predictable—Bjerknes drew the picture. It is the approaching warm front that makes for "bad" weather, for rain of the steady, rather than the showery kind, for low ceilings.

Consider a warm front on the morning when its foot is near Richmond and its top over Boston. Boston that morning sees streaks of cirrus in its sky—"mares' tails," the white, feathery, diaphanous cloud arranged in filaments and bands, that is so unsubstantial that the sun shines clear through it and you are hardly conscious of it as a cloud—and actually it doesn't consist of water droplets, as do most clouds, but of ice crystals. New Haven the same morning has the same kind of cloud, but slightly thicker, more nearly as a solid, milky layer. New York that same morning sees the warm air as a gray solid overcast at 8,000 feet. Philadelphia has the same sort of cloud at 5,000, with steady rain. Washington has 1,500 feet, rain. Quantico and Richmond report fog, and all airplanes are grounded. Raleigh, N.C., has clearing weather, the wind has shifted that morning to the southwest, and it is getting hot and humid there. Raleigh would be definitely behind the front, well in the warm air mass itself.

By nightfall Boston has the weather that was New Haven's in the morning. The moon, seen through a milk sheet of cirrus clouds, has a halo: "There is going to be rain." New Haven that night has New York's weather of that morning; New York has Philadelphia's; and so on down the line—the whole front has advanced one hundred miles. In forecasting the weather for Boston it is safe to guess that Boston will get in succession New Haven weather, New York weather, Philadelphia, Washington, Richmond weather—and finally Raleigh weather—in a sequence that should take two or three days: steady lowering clouds, rainy periods, some fog—followed finally by a wind shift to the southwest, and rapid breaking of clouds, and much warmer, very humid weather.

And then the cycle begins all over. You are then deep in Caribbean air again. You will have Caribbean air mass weather, and your weather eye had better be cocked northwest to watch for the first signs of polar air.

IV

There *is* a rhythm, then, in the weather, or at least a sort of rhyme, a repetitive sequence. All those folk rules that attribute weather changes to the phases of the moon, or to some other simple periodicity ("If the weather is O.K. on Friday, it is sure to rain over the week-end") are not so far from the mark after all. The rhythm does not work in terms of rain or shine; but it does work in terms of air masses; and thus, indirectly and loosely, through the tricky physics of the air, it governs also the actual weather.

What makes the air masses move, and what makes them move rhythmically—that is the crowning one of the great Norwegian discoveries. Some of it had long been known. It was understood that the motive power is the sun. By heating the tropics and leaving the polar region cold, it sets up a worldwide circulation of air, poleward at high altitude, equatorward at lower levels. It was understood that this simple circulation is complicated by many other factors such as the monsoon effect: continents heat up in summer and draw air in from over the ocean, in winter they cool and air flows out over the ocean; there was the baffling Coriolis Force that makes all moving things (on the Northern Hemisphere) curve to the right. In everyday life we don't notice it, but some geographers hold that it affects the flow of rivers, and artillerymen make allowance for it: a long-range gun is always aimed at a spot hundreds of yards to the left of the target. The monsoons and the Coriolis Force between them break up the simple pole-to-equator-to-pole flow of the air into a worldwide complicated system of interlocking "wheels"—huge eddies that show variously as tradewinds, calm belts, prevailing westerlies. Charts have been drawn of the air ocean's currents showing how air is piled up over some parts of the world, rushed away from others.

But it remained for the Norwegians to discover the polar front—perhaps the last-discovered geographical thing on this earth. Bjerknes himself first saw it—that the worldwide air circulation keeps piling up new masses of polar air in the north and pressing them southward; it keeps piling up new masses of tropical air in the south, pressing them northward; and thus forever keeps forcing tropical and polar air masses against each other along a front; that the demarcation line between tropical air masses, pressing northward, and polar air masses, pressing southward, runs clear around the world: through North America and across the Atlantic, through Europe and across Siberia, through Japan and across the Pacific. The polar front is clear-cut in some places, tends to wash out in others; but it always reëstablishes itself.

In summer, the polar front runs across North America north of the Great Lakes; in winter, it takes up a position across the United States. Wherever it is, it keeps advancing southward, retreating northward, much like a battlefront. And all the cold fronts and warm fronts are but sections of this greater front.

The rhythmical flowing of the air masses, the Norwegians discovered, is simply this wave action along the polar front. Like all the rest of the modern weather concepts, this one becomes common sense, almost self-evident—the moment you realize that air is stuff, a real fluid that has density and weight. Except that it occurs on a scale of unhuman magnitude, wave action along the polar front is almost exactly the same thing as waves on a lake.

In a lake, a dense, heavy fluid—the water—lies underneath a thin, light fluid—the air—and the result is that rhythmical welling up and down of the lake-surface that we call waves. Along the polar front, a dense, heavy fluid, the polar air, lies to the north of a thin, lighter fluid, the tropical air; the result is a rhythmical welling southward and northward of the two kinds of air. When a water wave rolls across a lake its first manifestation is a downward bulging of the water, then an upward surging. When a wave occurs in the polar front it appears first as a northward surging of warm air, and that means all the phenomena of a warm front. Then, in the rhythmical backswing, comes the southward surging of cold air, and that means all the phenomena of a cold front.

These waves are bigger than the imagination can easily encompass. They measure 500 to 1,000 miles from crest to crest. When tropical air surges northward it will wash to the edge of the Arctic; when Polar air surges southward it reaches down into the tropics. Such a wave will travel along the polar front all the way from somewhere out in the Pacific, across the United States and out to the Atlantic; that is the meterological action which underlies the recent novel *Storm* by George Stewart: the progress of a wave along the polar front.

So similar are these air waves to the air-water waves of a lake that there are even whitecaps and breakers. What we call a whitecap or a breaker is a whirling together of air and water into a white foam. In the great waves along the polar front the same toppling-over can occur: warm and cold air sometimes wheel around each other, underrun and overrun each other, in a complicated, spiral pattern.

And that is where the old papery weather science of the schoolbooks merges with the realistic observations of the Norwegians. You remember about those Lows that were traveling across the weather map and brought with them bad weather. You know how a dropping barometer has always indicated the coming of bad weather—though we have never quite known why.

Now it turns out that the barometric low is nothing but one of those toppling-over waves in the polar front—or rather, it is the way in which the spiral surging of the air masses affects the barometers. Look at the Middle West when it is being swept by one of those waves, take a reading of everybody's barometer, and you get the typical low. Look at it when a low is centered, watch the kinds of air that are flowing there, the wind directions, the temperatures and humidities and you find that a low has a definite internal structure: the typical wave pattern, with a warm air mass going north and a cold air mass going south, both phases of the same wave.

Barometric pressures turn out to be not the cause of the weather, but simply a result, a rather unimportant secondary symptom of it. What weather actually is the Norwegians have made clear. It is the wave action of the air ocean.

A PRIMER OF ATOMIC ENERGY[1]

WILLIAM L. LAURENCE

THE material universe, the earth and everything in it, all things living and non-living, the sun and its planets, the stars and the constellations, the galaxies and the supergalaxies, the infinitely large and the infinitesimally small, manifests itself to our senses in two forms, matter and energy. We do not know, and probably never can know, how the material universe began, and whether, indeed, it ever had a beginning, but we do know that it is constantly changing and that it did not always exist in its present form. We also know that in whatever form the universe may have existed, matter and energy have always been inseparable, no energy being possible without matter, and no matter without energy, each being a form of the other.

While we do not know how and when matter and energy came into being, or whether they ever had a beginning in time as we perceive it, we do know that while the relative amounts of matter and energy are constantly changing, the total amount of both, in one form or the other, always remains the same. When a plant grows, energy from the sun, in the form of heat and light, is converted into matter, so that the total weight of the plant is greater than that of the elementary material constituents, water and carbon-dioxide gas, out of which its substance is built up. When the substance of the plant is again broken up into its original constituents by burning, the residual ashes and gases weigh less than the total weight of the intact plant, the difference corresponding to the amount of matter that had been converted into energy, liberated once again in the form of heat and light.

All energy as we know it manifests itself through motion or change in the physical or chemical state of matter, or both, though these changes and motions may be so slow as to be imperceptible. As the ancient Greek philosopher Heraclitus perceived more than two thousand years ago, all things are in a constant state of flux, this flux being due to an everlasting conversion of matter into energy and energy into matter, everywhere over the vast stretches of the material universe, to its outermost and innermost limits, if any limits there be.

Each manifestation of energy involves either matter in motion or a change in its physical state, which we designate as physical energy; a change in the chemical constitution of matter, which we know as chemical energy; or a combination of the two. Physical energy can be converted into chemical energy and vice versa. For example, heat and light are forms of physical energy, each consisting of a definite band of waves of definite wave lengths in violent, regular, rhythmic oscillations. A mysterious mechanism in the plant, known as photosynthesis, uses the heat and light energy from the sun to create complex substances, such as sugars, starches, and cellulose, out of simpler sub-

---

1. Reprinted from *The Hell Bomb* by William L. Laurence, by permission of Alfred A. Knopf, Inc. Copyright 1950 by William L. Laurence.

stances, such as carbon dioxide and water, converting physical energy, heat and light into the chemical energy required to hold together the complex substances the plant produces. When we burn the cellulose in the form of wood or coal (coal is petrified wood), the chemical energy is once again converted into physical energy in the form of the original heat and light. As we have seen, the chemical energy stored in the plant manifested itself by an increase in the plant's weight as compared with that of its original constituents. Similarly, the release of the energy manifests itself through a loss in the total weight of the plant's substance.

It can thus be seen that neither matter nor energy can be created. All we can do is to manipulate certain types of matter in a way that liberates whatever energy had been in existence, in one form or another, since the beginning of time. All the energy that we had been using on earth until the advent of the atomic age had originally come from the sun. Coal, as already said, is a petrified plant that had stored up the energy of the sun in the form of chemical energy millions of years ago, before man made his appearance on the earth. Oil comes from organic matter that also had stored up light and heat from the sun in the form of chemical energy. Water power and wind power are also made possible by the sun's heat, since all water would freeze and no winds would blow were it not for the sun's heat energy keeping the waters flowing and the air moving, the latter by creating differences in the temperature of air masses.

There are two forms of energy that we take advantage of which are not due directly to the sun's radiations—gravitation and magnetism—but the only way we can utilize these is by employing energy derived from the sun's heat. In harnessing Niagara, or in the building of great dams, we utilize the fall of the water because of gravitation. But as I have already pointed out, without the sun's heat water could not flow. To produce electricity we begin with the chemical energy in coal or oil, which is first converted into heat energy, then to mechanical energy, and finally, through the agency of magnetism, into electrical energy.

The radiations of the sun, of the giant stars millions of times larger than the sun, come from an entirely different source, the greatest source of energy in the universe, known as atomic or, more correctly, nuclear energy. But even here the energy comes as the result of the transformation of matter. The difference between nuclear energy and chemical energy is twofold. In chemical energy, such as the burning of coal, the matter lost in the process comes from the outer shell of the atoms, and the amount of matter lost is so small that it cannot be weighed directly by any human scale or other device. In nuclear energy, on the other hand, the matter lost by being transformed into energy comes from the nucleus, the heavy inner core, of the atom, and the amount of matter lost is millions of times greater than in coal, great enough to be weighed.

An atom is the smallest unit of any of the elements of which the physical universe is constituted. Atoms are so small that if a drop of water were magnified to the size of the earth the atoms in the drop would be smaller than oranges.

The structure of atoms is like that of a minuscule solar system, with a heavy nucleus in the center as the sun, and much smaller bodies revolving around it as the planets. The nucleus is made up of two types of particles: protons, carrying a positive charge of electricity, and neutrons, electrically neutral. The planets revolving about the nucleus are electrons, units of negative electricity, which have a mass about one two-thousandth the mass of the proton or the neutron. The number of protons in the nucleus determines the chemical nature of the element, and also the number of planetary electrons, each proton being electrically balanced by an electron in the atom's outer shells. The total number of protons and neutrons in the nucleus is known as the mass number, which is very close to the atomic weight of the element but not quite equal. Protons and neutrons are known under the common name "nucleons."

There are two important facts to keep constantly in mind about protons and neutrons. The first is that the two are interchangeable. A proton, under certain conditions, loses its positive charge by emitting a positive electron (positron) and thus becomes a neutron. Similarly, a neutron, when agitated, emits a negative electron and becomes a proton. As we shall see, the latter process is taken advantage of in the transmutation of nonfissionable uranium into plutonium, and of thorium into fissionable uranium 233. The transmutation of all other elements, age-old dream of the alchemists, is made possible by the interchangeability of protons into neutrons, and vice versa.

The second all-important fact about protons and neutrons, basic to the understanding of atomic energy, is that each proton and neutron in the nuclei of the elements weighs less than it does in the free state, the loss of weight being equal to the energy binding the nucleons. This loss becomes progressively greater for the elements in the first half of the periodic table, reaching its maximum in the nucleus of silver, element 47. After that the loss gets progressively smaller. Hence, if we were to combine (fuse) two elements in the first half of the periodic table, the protons and the neutrons would lose weight if the newly formed nucleus is not heavier than that of silver, but would gain weight if the new nucleus thus formed is heavier than silver. The opposite is true with the elements in the second half of the periodic table, the protons and neutrons losing weight when a heavy element is split into two lighter ones, and gaining weight if two elements are fused into one.

Since each loss of mass manifests itself by the release of energy, it can be seen that to obtain energy from the atom's nucleus requires either the fusion of two elements in the first half of the periodic table or the fission of an element in the second half. From a practical point of view, however, fusion is possible only with two isotopes (twins) of hydrogen, at the beginning of the periodic table, while fission is possible only with twins of uranium, U-233 and U-235, and with plutonium, at the lower end of the table.

The diameter of the atom is 100,000 times greater than the diameter of the nucleus. This means that the atom is mostly empty space, the volume of the atom being 500,000 billion times the volume of the nucleus. It can thus be seen that most of the matter in the universe is concentrated in the nuclei of the atoms. The density of matter in the nucleus is such that a dime would weigh 600 million tons if its atoms were as tightly packed as are the protons and neutrons in the neucleus.

The atoms of the elements (of which there are ninety-two in nature, and six more man-made elements) have twins, triplets, quadruplets, etc., known as isotopes. The nuclei of these twins all contain the same number of protons and hence all have the same chemical properties. They differ, however, in the number of neutrons in their nuclei and hence have different atomic weights. For example, an ordinary hydrogen atom has a nucleus of one proton. The isotope of hydrogen, deuterium, has one proton plus one neutron in its nucleus. It is thus twice as heavy as ordinary hydrogen. The second hydrogen isotope, tritium, has one proton and two neutrons in its nucleus and hence an atomic mass of three. On the other hand, a nucleus containing two protons and one neutron is no longer hydrogen but helium, also of atomic mass three.

There are hundreds of isotopes, some occurring in nature, others produced artificially by shooting atomic bullets, such as neutrons, into the nuclei of the atoms of various elements. A natural isotope of uranium, the ninety-second and last of the natural elements, contains 92 protons and 143 neutrons in its nucleus, hence its name U-235, one of the two atomic-bomb elements. The most common isotope of uranium has 92 protons and 146 neutrons in its nucleus and hence is known as U-238. It is 140 times more plentiful than U-235, but cannot be used for the release of atomic energy.

Atomic, or rather nuclear, energy is the cosmic force that binds together the protons and the neutrons in the nucleus. It is a force millions of times greater than the electrical repulsion force existing in the nucleus because of the fact that the protons all have like charges. This force, known as the coulomb force, is tremendous, varying inversely as the square of the distance separating the positively charged particles. Professor Frederick Soddy, the noted English physicist, has figured out that two grams (less than the weight of a dime) of piotons placed at the opposite poles of the earth would repel each other with a force of twenty-six tons. Yet the nuclear force is millions of times greater than the coulomb force. This force acts as the cosmic cement that holds the material universe together and is responsible for the great density of matter in the nucleus.

We as yet know very little about the basic nature of this force, but we can measure its magnitude by a famous mathematical equation originally presented by Dr. Einstein in his special theory of relativity in 1905. This formula, one of the great intellectual achievements of man, together with the discovery of the radioactive elements by Henri Becquerel and Pierre and Marie Curie, provided the original clues as well as the key to the discovery and the harnessing of nuclear energy.

Einstein's formula, $E = mc^2$, revealed that matter and energy are two different manifestations of one and the same cosmic entity, instead of being two different entities, as had been generally believed. It led to the revolutionary concept that matter, instead of being immutable, was energy in a frozen state, while, conversely, energy was matter in a fluid state. The equation revealed that any one gram of matter was the equivalent in ergs (small units of energy) to the square of the velocity of light in centimeters per second—namely, 900 billion billion ergs. In more familiar terms, this means that one gram of matter represents 25,000,000 kilowatt-hours of energy in the frozen state. This equals the energy liberated in the burning of three billion grams (three thousand tons) of coal.

The liberation of energy in any form, chemical, electrical, or nuclear, involves the loss of an equivalent amount of mass, in accordance with the Einstein formula. When 3,000 metric tons of coal are burned to ashes, the residual ashes and the gaseous products weigh one gram less than 3,000 tons; that is, one three-billionth part of the original mass will have been converted into energy. The same is true with the liberation of nuclear energy by the splitting or fusing (as will be explained later) of the nuclei of certain elements. The difference is merely that of magnitude. In the liberation of chemical energy by the burning of coal, the energy comes from a very small loss of mass resulting from the rearrangement of electrons on the surface of the atoms. The nucleus of the coal atoms is not involved in any way, remaining exactly the same as before. The amount of mass lost by the surface electrons is one thirtieth of one millionth of one per cent.

On the other hand, nuclear energy involves vital changes in the atomic nucleus itself, with a consequent loss of as high as one tenth to nearly eight tenths of one per cent in the original mass of the nuclei. This means that from one to nearly eight grams per thousand grams are liberated in the form of energy, as compared with only one gram in three billion grams liberated in the burning of coal. In other words, the amount of nuclear energy liberated in the transmutation of atomic nuclei is from 3,000,000 to 24,000,000 times as great as the chemical energy released by the burning of an equal amount of coal. In terms of TNT the figure is seven times greater than for coal, as the energy from TNT, while liberated at an explosive rate, is about one seventh the total energy content for an equivalent amount of coal. This means that the nuclear energy from one kilogram of uranium 235, or plutonium, when released at an explosive rate, is equal to the explosion of twenty thousand tons of TNT.

Nuclear energy can be utilized by two diametrically opposed methods. One is fission—the splitting of the nuclei of the heaviest chemical elements into two uneven fragments consisting of nuclei of two lighter elements. The other is fusion—combining, or fusing, two nuclei of the lightest elements into one nucleus of a heavier element. In both methods the resulting elements are lighter than the original nuclei. The loss of mass in each case manifests itself in the release of enormous amounts of nuclear energy.

When two light atoms are combined to form a heavier atom, the weight of the heavier is less than the total weight of the two light atoms. If the heavier atom could again be split into the two lighter ones, the latter would resume their original weight. As explained before, however, this is true only with the light elements, such as hydrogen, deuterium, and tritium, in the first half of the periodic table of the elements. The opposite is true with the heavier elements of the second half of the periodic table. For example, if krypton and barium, elements 36 and 56, were to be combined to form uranium, element 92, the protons and the neutrons in the uranium nucleus would each weigh about 0.1 per cent more than they weighed in the krypton and barium nuclei. It can thus be seen that energy could be gained either through the loss of mass resulting from the fusion of two light elements, or from the similar loss of mass resulting from the fission of one heavy atom into two lighter ones.

In the fusion of two lighter atoms, the addition of one and one yields less than two, and yet half of two will be more than one. In the case of the heavy elements the addition of one and one yields more than two, yet half of two makes less than one. This is the seeming paradox of atomic energy.

Three elements are known to be fissionable. Only one of these is found in nature: the uranium isotope 235 (U-235). The other two are man-made. One is plutonium, transmuted by means of neutrons from the nonfissionable U-238, by the addition of one neutron to the 146 present in the nucleus, which leads to the conversion of two of the 147 neutrons into protons, thus creating an element with a nucleus of 94 protons and 145 neutrons. The second man-made element (not yet in wide use, as far as is known) is uranium isotope 233 (92 protons and 141 neutrons), created out of the element thorium (90 protons, 142 neutrons) by the same method used in the production of plutonium.

When the nucleus of any one of these elements is fissioned, each proton and neutron in the two resulting fragments weighs one tenth of one per cent less than it weighed in the original nucleus. For example, if U-235 atoms totaling 1,000 grams in weight are split, the total weight of the fragments will be 999 grams. The one missing gram is liberated in the form of 25,000,000 kilowatt-hours of energy, equivalent in explosive terms to 20,000 tons of TNT. But the original number of protons and neutrons in the 1,000 grams does not change.

The fission process, the equivalent of the "burning" of nuclear fuels, is maintained by what is known as a chain reaction. The bullets used for splitting are neutrons, which, because they do not have an electric charge, can penetrate the heavily fortified electrical wall surrounding the positively charged nuclei. Just as a coal fire needs oxygen to keep it going, a nuclear fire needs the neutrons to maintain it.

Neutrons do not exist free in nature, all being tightly locked up within the nuclei of atoms. They are liberated, however, from the nuclei of the three fissionable elements by a self-multiplication process in the chain reaction. The process begins when a cosmic ray from outer space, or a stray neutron, strikes one nucleus and splits it. The first atom thus split releases an average of two neutrons, which split two more nuclei, which in turn liberate four more neutrons, and so on. The reaction is so fast that in a short time trillions of neutrons are thus liberated to split trillions of nuclei. As each nucleus is split, it loses mass, which is converted into great energy.

There are two types of chain reactions: controlled and uncontrolled. The controlled reaction is analogous to the burning of gasoline in an automobile engine. The atom-splitting bullets—the neutrons—are first slowed down from speeds of more than ten thousand miles per second to less than one mile per second by being made to pass through a moderator before they reach the atoms at which they are aimed. Neutron-"killers"—materials absorbing neutrons in great numbers—keep the neutrons liberated at any given time under complete control in a slow but steady nuclear fire.

The uncontrolled chain reaction is one in which there is no moderator—and no neutron-absorbers. It is analogous to the dropping of a match in a gasoline tank. In the uncontrolled chain reaction the fast neutrons, with nothing to slow them down or to devour them, build up by the trillion and quadrillion in a fraction of a millionth of a second. This leads to the splitting of a corresponding number of atoms, resulting in the release of unbelievable quantities of nuclear energy at a tremendously explosive rate. One kilogram of atoms split releases energy equivalent to that of 20,000,000 kilograms (20,000 metric tons) of TNT.

It is the uncontrolled reaction that is employed in the explosion of the atomic bomb. The controlled reaction is expected to be used in the production of vast quantities of industrial power. It is now being employed in the creation of radioactive isotopes, for use in medicine and as the most powerful research tool since the invention of the microscope for probing into the mysteries of nature, living and non-living.

In the controlled reaction the material used is natural uranium, which consists of a mixture of 99.3 per cent U-238 and 0.7 of the fissionable U-235. The neutrons from the U-235 are made to enter the nuclei of U-238 and convert them to the fissionable element plutonium, for use in atomic bombs. The large quantities of energy liberated by the split U-235 nuclei in the form of heat is at too low a temperature for efficient utilization as power, and is at present wasted. To be used for power, nuclear reactors capable of operating at high temperatures are now being designed.

In the atomic bomb only pure U-235, or plutonium, is used.

In both the controlled and the uncontrolled reactions a minimum amount of material, known as the "critical mass," must be used, as otherwise too many neutrons would escape and the nuclear fire would thus be extinguished, as would an ordinary fire for lack of oxygen. In the atomic bomb two masses, each less than a critical mass, which together equal or exceed it, are brought in contact at a predetermined instant. The uncontrolled reaction then comes automatically, since, in the absence of any control, the neutrons, which cannot escape to the outside, build up at an unbelievable rate.

Whereas the fission process for the release of nuclear energy entails making little ones out of big ones, the fusion process involves making big ones out of little ones. In both processes the products weigh less than the original materials, the loss of mass coming out in the form of energy. According to the generally accepted hypothesis, the fusion process is the one operating in the sun and the stars of the same family. The radiant energy given off by them, it is believed, is the result of the fusion of four hydrogen atoms into one atom of helium, two of the protons losing their positive charge, thus becoming neutrons. Since a helium atom weighs nearly eight tenths of one per cent less than the total weight of the four hydrogen atoms, the loss of mass is thus nearly eight times that produced by fission, with a corresponding eight-fold increase in the amount of energy liberated. This process, using light hydrogen, is not feasible on earth.

The nuclei of all atoms are thus vast storage depots of cosmic energy. We must think of them as cosmic safe-deposit vaults, in which the Creator of the universe, if you will, deposited at the time of creation most of the energy in the universe for safekeeping. The sun and the other giant stars that give light have, as it were, drawing accounts in this "First National Bank and Trust Company of the Universe," whereas we on this little planet of ours in the cosmic hinterland are much too poor to have such a bank account. So we have been forced all these years we have been on earth to subsist on small handouts from our close neighbor the sun, which squanders millions all over space, but can spare us only nickels, dimes, and quarters (depending on the seasons of the year) for a cup of coffee and a sandwich. We are thus in the true sense of the word cosmic beggars, living off the bounty of a distant relative.

The discovery of fission in 1939 meant that after a million years of exclusive dependence on the sun we had suddenly managed to open a modest drawing account of our own in this bank of the cosmos. We were enabled to do it by stumbling upon two special master keys to five of the cosmic vaults. One of these keys we call fission; the other, which allows us entry into a much richer chamber of the vault, we call fusion. We can get a lot of the stored-up cosmic treasure by using the key to the fission vaults alone, but, as with our terrestrial bank vaults, which generally require two keys before they can be opened, it is not possible to use the key to the fusion vault unless we first use the fission key.

Except for the payment of our heat and light bill, the sun gives us nothing directly in cash. Instead it deposits a very small pittance in the plants, which serve as its major terrestrial banks. The animals then rob the plants and we rob them both. When we eat the food we live by we thus actually eat sunshine.

The sun makes its deposits in the plant through an agent named chlorophyll, the stuff that makes the grass green. Chlorophyll has the uncanny ability to catch sunbeams and to hand them over to the plant. A chemical supergenius inside the plant changes the sunlight energy into chemical energy, just as a bank teller changes bills into silver. With this chemical energy at their disposal, a great number of devilishly clever chemists in the plants' chemical factory go to work building up many substances to serve as vaults in which to store up a large part of the energy, using only part of it for their own subsistence.

The building materials used by these chemists inside the plants consist mainly of carbon-dioxide gas from the atmosphere, and water from the soil, plus small amounts of minerals either supplied by the good earth or by fertilizers. Carbon dioxide, by the way, composed of one atom of carbon and two atoms of oxygen, is the stuff you exhale. In solid form it is what we know as dry ice, used in efforts to make rain. It is present in the atmosphere in large amounts.

Out of the carbon dioxide and water the chemists in the plants build cellulose, starch, sugar, fat, proteins, vitamins, and scores of other substances, all of which serve as vaults for the sun's rays caught by the chlorophyll. The biggest vaults of all, storing most of the energy, are the cellulose, sugars and starches, fats and proteins. There the stored energy remains until it is released by processes we call burning or digestion, both of which, as we shall see, are different terms for the same chemical reaction. When we burn wood, or the petrified ancient wood we know as coal, we burn largely the cellulose, the chief component of the solid part of plants. When we eat the plants, or the animals in whom the plant tissues are transformed into flesh by the solar energy stored within them, it is the sugars, starches, fats, and proteins that give us the energy we live by.

In the process of burning wood or coal the large cellulose vaults, composed of carbon, hydrogen, and oxygen, are broken up, thus allowing the original solar energy, stored up within them as chemical energy, to escape in the form of heat and light. This is the same heat and light deposited there by the sun many years before—in the case of coal, some two hundred million years back. The process of burning thus transforms the chemical energy in the plants back to its original form of light and radiant heat energy. The complex carbon and hydrogen units in the cellulose are broken up, each freed carbon atom uniting within two oxygen atoms in the air to form carbon dioxide again, while two hydrogen atoms unite with one of oxygen to form water. Thus we see that the cellulose vaults are broken up once more into the original building bricks out of which the chemists in the plants had fashioned them.

When we eat plant or animal food to get the energy to live by, exactly the same process takes place except at a lower temperature. The sunlight deposit vaults of sugar, starch, and fat, also composed, like cellulose, of carbon, hydrogen, and oxygen, are broken up by the digestive system into their component parts, thus allowing the original solar energy stored within them to get free in the form of chemical energy, which our body uses in its essential processes. Here, too, the end products are carbon dioxide, which we exhale, and water. About half the energy we thus obtain is used by us for the work we do. The other half is used by the body for building up the tissues burned up as part of the regular wear and tear of life.

We thus burn food for our internal energy as we burn cellulose for our external energy. The interesting thing here is that, in both types of burning, fission as well as fusion processes take place. The fission is the splitting of the cellulose, sugar, fats, starches, and proteins into carbon and hydrogen atoms. The fusion part is the union of the carbon and the hydrogen with oxygen to form carbon dioxide and water. The fusion part is just as necessary to release the stored-up solar energy in the wood or coal as is the fission part, for, as everyone knows, unless there is oxygen for the carbon to fuse with, no combustion (burning) can take place and hence no release of energy. The plant vaults would remain closed absolutely tight.

At this point two things become clear. We see, in the first place, that whenever we get any kind of energy in any form we do not in any way create any of it. All we do is merely draw on something that is already stored up; in the case of coal and wood by the sun, in the case of uranium and hydrogen by the same power that created the sun and all energy. We draw water from the spring, but we do not make the water. On the other hand, we cannot draw the water unless we first find the spring, and even then we cannot draw it unless we have a pitcher.

And we also see, in the second place, that fission and fusion are common everyday phenomena that occur any time you burn anything. Both are essential whenever energy is released, whether it is the chemical energy from coal or the atomic energy from the nuclei of uranium, deuterium, or tritium. When you light a cigarette you employ both fission and fusion or you don't smoke. The first fission and fusion take place in the lighting of the match, the cellulose in the match (whether it is wood or paper) being fissioned (that is, split into its component atoms of carbon and hydrogen). These atoms are then fusioned with the oxygen in the air. The same thing happens when the tobacco catches fire. In each case the fusion with the oxygen makes possible the fission of cellulose. When we burn U-235, or plutonium, we again get both fission and fusion, except that, instead of oxygen, the nuclei of these elements first fuse with a neutron before they are split apart. Thus we see that the process of burning U-235, or plutonium, requires not only fission but fusion as well, without which they could not burn. This is true also in hydrogen fusion.

When you burn deuterium by fusing two deuterons (nuclei of deuterium) to form helium of atomic weight three, plus a neutron, one of the two deuterons is split in half in the process. Similarly, when you burn tritium by fusion two tritons (nuclei of tritium), one of the tritons splits into two neutrons and a proton, the one proton joining the other triton to form helium of atomic weight four.

Thus we see that fission and fusion are the cosmic firebrands that are always present whenever a fire is lighted, chemical or atomic, whether the fuel is wood, coal, or oil, or uranium, plutonium, deuterium, or tritium. Both, with some variations, are essential for opening the cosmic safe where the energy of the universe is kept in storage. The only reason you get much more energy in the fission and fusion of atomic nuclei is that so much more had been stored in them than in the cellulose vaults on this planet.

The same reason that limits our ability to obtain stored chemical energy to a few fuels also limits our ability to obtain atomic energy. Coal, oil, and wood are the only dividend-paying chemical-energy stocks. Similarly only five elements, uranium 233 and 235, plutonium, deuterium, and tritium are the only dividend-paying atomic-energy stocks, and of these only two (U-235 and deuterium) exist in nature. The other three are re-created from other elements by modern alchemical legerdemain. What is more, we know for a certainty that it will never be possible to obtain atomic energy from any other element, by either fission or fusion.

This should put to rest once and for all the notion of many, including some self-styled scientists, that the explosion of a hydrogen bomb would set the hydrogen in the waters, and the oxygen and the nitrogen in the air, on fire and thus blow up the earth. The energy in common hydrogen is locked up in one of those cosmic vaults which only the sun and the stars that shine can open and which no number of H-bombs could blow apart. Oxygen and nitrogen are locked even for the sun. As for the deuterium in the water, it cannot catch fire unless it is highly concentrated, condensed to its liquid form, and heated to a temperature of several hundred million degrees. Hence all this talk about blowing up the earth is pure moonshine.

But while we know that we have reached the limit of what can be achieved either by fission or by fusion, that by no means justifies the conclusion that we have reached the ultimate in discovery and that fission and fusion are the only possible methods for tapping the energy locked up in matter. We must remember that fifty years ago we did not even suspect that nuclear energy existed and that until 1939 no one, including Dr. Einstein, believed that it would ever become possible to use it on a practical scale. We simply stumbled upon the phenomenon of fission, which in its turn opened the way to fusion.

If science tells us anything at all, it tells us that nature is infinite and that the human mind, driven by insatiable curiosity and probing ever deeper into nature's mysteries, will inevitably find ever greater treasures, treasures that are at present beyond the utmost stretches of the imagination—as far beyond fission and fusion as these are beyond man's first discovery of how to make a fire by striking a spark with a laboriously made flint. The day may yet come, and past history makes it practically certain that it will come, when man will look upon the discovery of fission and fusion as we look today upon the crudest tools made by primitive man.

A great measure of man's progress has been the result of serendipity, the faculty of making discoveries, by chance or sagacity, of things not sought for. Many an adventure has led man to stumble upon something much better than he originally set out to find. Like Columbus, many an explorer into the realms of the unknown has set his sights on a shorter route to the spices of India only to stumble upon a new continent. Unlike Columbus, however, the explorers in the field of science, instead of being confined to this tiny little earth of ours, have the whole infinite universe as the domain of their adventures, and many a virgin continent, richer by far than any yet discovered, still awaits its Columbus.

Roentgen and Becquerel were exploring what they thought was an untrodden path in the forest and came upon a new road that led their successors to the very citadel of the material universe. Young Enrico Fermi was curious to find out what would happen if he fired a neutron into the nucleus of uranium, hoping only to create a heavier isotope of uranium, or at best a new element. His rather modest goal led five years later to the fission of uranium, and in another six years to the atomic bomb.

Yet, as we have seen, in both fission and fusion only a very small fraction of the mass of the protons and neutrons in the nuclei of the elements used is liberated in the form of energy, while 99.3 to 99.9 per cent of their substance remains in the form of matter. We know of no process in nature which converts 100 per cent of the matter in protons and neutrons into energy, but scientists are already talking about finding means for bringing about such a conversion. They are seeking clues for such a process in the mysterious cosmic rays that bombard the earth from outer space with energies billions of times greater than those released by fission or fusion, great enough to smash atoms of oxygen or nitrogen, or whatever other atoms they happen to hit in the upper atmosphere, into their component protons and neutrons. Luckily, their number is small and most of their energy is spent long before they reach sea level.

But we have already learned how to create secondary cosmic-ray particles of relatively low energies (350,000,000 electron-volts) with our giant cyclotrons. The creation of these particles, known as mesons, which are believed to be the cosmic cement responsible for the nuclear forces, represents the actual conversion of energy into matter. This is the exact reverse of the process taking place in fission and fusion, in which, as we have seen, matter is converted into energy. And we are now about to complete multibillion-volt atom-smashers that will hurl atomic bullets of energies of from three to ten billion volts at the nuclei of atoms. With these gigantic machines, known as the cosmotron (at the Brookhaven National Laboratory of the Atomic Energy Commission) and the bevatron (at the University of California), we shall be able to smash nuclei into their individual component protons and neutrons and thus get a much more intimate glimpse of the forces that hold the nuclei together. What is more, instead of creating only mesons, particles with only 300 electron masses, we shall be able for the first time to convert energy into protons and neutrons, duplicating, as far as is known, an act of creation that has not taken place since the beginning of the universe. Man at last will be creating the very building blocks out of which the universe is made, as well as the cosmic cement that holds them together.

What new continents will our first glimpse into the mechanism of the very act of creation of matter out of energy reveal? What new secrets will be uncovered before the dazzled eyes and mind of man when he takes the nucleus of the atom completely apart at last? Not even Einstein could tell us. But, as Omar Khayyam divined, "a single Alif" may provide "the clue" that, could we but find it, leads "to the Treasure-House, and peradventure to the Master too." The fact is that we already have opened the door to the anteroom of the treasure-house, and we are about to unlock the door to one of its inner chambers. What shall we find there? No one as yet knows. But we do know that every door man has opened so far has led to riches beyond his wildest dreams, each new door bringing greater rewards than the one before. On the other hand, we also know that the treasure-house has many mansions, and that no matter how many chambers he may enter, he will always find new doors to unlock. For we have learned that the solution of any one secret always opens up a thousand new mysteries.

We have also learned, to our sorrow, that any new insight gained into nature's laws and forces can be used for great good and for equally great evil. The greater the insight, the greater the potentialities for good or evil. The new knowledge he is about to gain by his deeper insight into the heart of matter, and by his ability to create it out of energy, may offer man the means to make himself complete master of the world he lives in. It is equally true, alas, that he could use it to destroy that world even more thoroughly than with the hydrogen bomb.

As already stated, scientists are even now discussing the possibility of finding means for the complete annihilation of matter by the conversion of the entire mass of protons and neutrons into energy, instead of only 0.1 to 0.7 per cent. And while the total annihilation of protons and neutrons still seems highly speculative, we already know that such a process actually does take place in the realm of the electron. This is the phenomenon already achieved numerous times on a small scale in the laboratory, in which a positive electron (positron) and an electron with a negative charge completely destroy each other, their entire mass being converted into energy. Luckily, this is at present only a laboratory experiment, in which each positron must be individually produced, since there are hardly any positive electrons in our part of the universe. But suppose the new knowledge we are about to pry loose from the inner citadel of matter reveals to us a new process, at present not even suspected, that would release positrons in large numbers, just as the fission and fusion processes made possible for the first time the liberation of large quantities of neutrons. Such an eventuality, by no means beyond the realm of the possible, would open potentialities of horror alongside which those of the H-bomb, even the rigged one, would be puny. For any process that would release large numbers of positrons in the atmosphere, in a chain reaction similar to the one now liberating neutrons, may envelop the earth in one deadly flash of radio-active lightning that would instantly kill all sensate things. And although this is admittedly purely speculative, no one dare say that such a discovery will not be made, not when one remembers how remote and unlikely a process such as fission seemed to be just before it was made.

Though many of the great discoveries came about as the result of chance, they came because, as Pasteur said, "chance favors the prepared mind." Actually they came largely through the intellectual synthesis of what had originally appeared as unrelated phenomena or concepts. When Faraday discovered the principle of electromagnetic induction, he established for the first time that electricity and magnetism, looked upon since prehistoric times as two separate and distinct phenomena, were actually only two aspects of one basic natural force, which we know today as electromagnetism. This great intellectual synthesis led directly to the age of electricity and all its wonders. About thirty years later the great Scottish physicist James Clerk Maxwell demonstrated that electromagnetic action traveled through space in the form of transverse waves similar to those of light and having the same velocity. This revealed the existence in nature of electromagnetic waves, better known to us today as radio waves. About a quarter century later the great German-Jewish physicist Heinrich Hertz not only produced these electromagnetic waves but showed that they are propagated just as waves of light are, possessing all other properties of light, such as reflection, refraction, and polarization. This led directly to wireless telegraphy and telephony, radio and television, radiophotography and radar.

When Einstein, in his special theory of relativity of 1905, united matter and energy in one basic cosmic entity, the road was opened to the atomic age. Yet Einstein was never satisfied and has devoted more than forty-five years of his life to the search for a greater, all-embracing unity underlying the great diversity of natural phenomena. In his general theory of relativity of 1915 he formulated a concept that encompasses the universal law of gravitation in his earlier synthesis of space and time, of which matter and energy were an integral part. This synthesis, wrote Bertrand Russell in 1924, "is probably the greatest synthetic achievement of the human intellect up to the present time. It sums up the mathematical and physical labors of more than two thousand years. Pure geometry from Pythagoras to Riemann, the dynamics and astronomy of Galileo and Newton, the theory of electromagnetism as it resulted from the researches of Faraday, Maxwell, and their successors, all are absorbed, with the necessary modifications, in the theories of Einstein, Weyl, and Eddington.

"So comprehensive a synthesis," he continued, "might have represented a dead end, leading to no further progress for a long time. Fortunately, at this moment quantum theory [the theory applying to the forces within the atom] has appeared, with a new set of facts outside the scope of relativity physics [which applies to the forces governing the cosmos at large]. This has saved us, in the nick of time, from the danger of supposing that we know everything."

Yet Einstein, working away in majestic solitude, has been trying all these years to construct a vast intellectual edifice that would embrace all the laws of the cosmos known so far, including the quantum, in one fundamental concept, which he designates as a "unified field theory." Early in 1950 he published the results of his arduous labors since 1915. This he regards as the crowning achievement of his life's work, a unified theory that bridges the vast gulf that had existed between relativity and quantum, between the infinite universe of the stars and galaxies and the equally infinite universe within the nucleus of the atom. If he is right, and he has always been right before, his latest contribution will prove to be a greater synthetic achievement of the human intellect than ever before, embracing space and time, matter and energy, gravitation and electromagnetism, as well as the nuclear forces within the atom, in one all-encompassing concept. In due time this concept should lead to new revelations of nature's mysteries, and to triumphs even greater than those which followed as a direct consequence of all earlier intellectual syntheses.

If the synthesis of matter and energy led to the atomic age, what may we expect of the latest, all-inclusive synthesis? When Einstein was asked about it he replied: "Come back in twenty years!" which happens to coincide with the end of the hundred-year period recorded by the brothers Goncourt: God swinging a bunch of keys, and saying to humanity: "Closing time, gentlemen!"

The search for new intellectual syntheses goes on, and no doubt new relationships between the diverse phenomena of nature will be found, regardless of whether Einstein's latest theory stands or falls in the light of further discovery. Physicists, for example, are speculating about a fundamental relationship between time and the electronic charge, one of the most basic units of nature, and there are those who believe that this relationship will turn out to be much more fundamental than that between matter and energy. Should this be found to be true, then the discovery of the relationship between time and charge may lead to finding a way for starting a self-multiplying positron-electron chain reaction, just as the relationship between matter and energy led inevitably to the self-multiplying chain reaction with neutrons. If this comes about, then closing time will come much closer.

Yet the sound of the swinging keys need not necessarily mean closing time for man at the twilight of his day on this planet. It could also mean the opening of gates at a new dawn, to a new earth—and a new heaven.

THE EVOLUTION OF THE PHYSICAL WORLD [1]

ARTHUR STANLEY EDDINGTON

LOOKING back through the long past we picture the beginning of the world —a primeval chaos which time has fashioned into the universe that we know. Its vastness appals the mind; space boundless though not infinite, according to the strange doctrine of science. The world was without form and almost void. But at the earliest stage we can contemplate the void is sparsely broken by tiny electric particles, the germs of the things that are to be; positive and negative they wander aimlessly in solitude, rarely coming near enough to seek or shun one another. They range everywhere so that all space is filled, and yet so empty that in comparison the most highly exhausted vacuum on earth is a jostling throng. In the beginning was vastness, solitude and the deepest night. Darkness was upon the face of the deep, for as yet there was no light.

The years rolled by, million after million. Slight aggregations occurring casually in one place and another drew to themselves more and more particles. They warred for sovereignty, won and lost their spoil, until the matter was collected round centers of condensation leaving vast empty spaces from which it had ebbed away. Thus gravitation slowly parted the primeval chaos. These first divisions were not the stars but what we should call "island universes" each ultimately to be a system of some thousands of millions of stars. From our own island universe we can discern the other islands as spiral nebulæ lying one beyond another as far as the telescope can fathom. The nearest of them is such that light takes 900,000 years to cross the gulf between us. They acquired rotation (we do not yet understand how) which bulged them into flattened form and made them wreathe themselves in spirals. Their forms,

1. From Arthur Stanley Eddington, *Science and the Unseen World*, 1930, pp. 11–21.

diverse, yet with underlying regularity, make a fascinating spectacle for telescopic study.

As it had divided the original chaos, so gravitation subdivided the island universes. First the star clusters, then the stars themselves were separated. And with the stars came light, born of the fiercer turmoil which ensued when the electrical particles were drawn from their solitude into dense throngs. A star is not just a lump of matter casually thrown together in the general confusion; it is of nicely graded size. There is relatively not much more diversity in the masses of new-born stars than in the masses of new-born babies. Aggregations rather greater than our Sun have a strong tendency to subdivide, but when the mass is reduced a little the danger quickly passes and the impulse to subdivision is satisfied. Here it would seem the work of creation might cease. Having carved chaos into stars, the first evolutionary impulse has reached its goal. For many billions of years the stars may continue to shed their light and heat through the world, feeding on their own matter which disappears bit by bit into ætherial waves.

Not infrequently a star, spinning too fast or strained by the radiant heat imprisoned within it, may divide into two nearly equal stars, which remain yoked together as a double star; apart from this no regular plan of further development is known. For what might be called the second day of creation we turn from the general rule to the exceptions. Amid so many myriads there will be a few which by some rare accident have a fate unlike the rest. In the vast expanse of the heavens the traffic is so thin that a star may reasonably count on travelling for the whole of its long life without serious risk of collision. The risk is negligible for any individual star, but ten thousand million stars in our own system and more in the systems beyond afford a wide playground for chance. If the risk is one in a hundred millions some unlucky victims are doomed to play the role of "one." This rare accident must have happened to our Sun—an accident to the Sun, but to us the cause of our being here. A star journeying through space casually overtook the Sun, not indeed colliding with it, but approaching so close as to raise a great tidal wave. By this disturbance jets of matter spurted out of the Sun; being carried round by their angular momentum they did not fall back again but condensed into small globes—the planets.

By this and similar events there appeared here and there in the universe something outside Nature's regular plan, namely a lump of matter small enough and dense enough to be cool. A temperature of ten million degrees or more prevails through the greater part of the interior of a star; it cannot be otherwise so long as matter remains heaped in immense masses. Thus the design of the first stage of evolution seems to have been that matter should ordinarily be endowed with intense heat. Cool matter appears as an afterthought. It is unlikely that the Sun is the only one of the starry host to possess a system of planets, but it is believed that such development is very rare. In these exceptional formations Nature has tried the experiment of finding what strange effects may ensue if matter is released from its usual temperature of millions of degrees and permitted to be cool.

Out of the electric charges dispersed in the primitive chaos ninety-two different kinds of matter—ninety-two chemical elements—have been built. This building is also a work of evolution, but little or nothing is known as to its history. In the matter which we handle daily we find the original bricks fitted together and cannot but infer that somewhere and somewhen a process of matter-building has occurred. At high temperature this diversity of matter remains as it were latent; little of consequence results from it. But in the cool experimental stations of the universe the differences assert themselves. At root the diversity of the ninety-two elements reflects the diversity of the integers from one to ninety-two; because the chemical characteristics of element No. 11 (sodium) arise from the fact that it has the power at low temperatures of gathering round it eleven negative electric particles; those of No. 12 (magnesium) from its power of gathering twelve particles; and so on.

It is tempting to linger over the development out of this fundamental beginning of the wonders studied in chemistry and physics, but we must hurry on. The provision of certain cool planetary globes was the second impulse of evolution, and it has exhausted itself in the formation of inorganic rocks and ores and other materials. We must look to a new exception or abnormality if anything further is to be achieved. We can scarcely call it an accident that among the integers there should happen to be the number 6; but I do not know how otherwise to express the fact that organic life would not have begun if Nature's arithmetic had overlooked the number 6. The general plan of ninety-two elements, each embodying in its structural pattern one of the first ninety-two numbers, contemplates a material world of considerable but limited diversity; but the element carbon, embodying the number 6, and because of the peculiarity of the number 6, rebels against limits. The carbon atoms love to string themselves in long chains such as those which give toughness to a soap-film. Whilst other atoms organise themselves in twos and threes or it may be in tens, carbon atoms organise themselves in hundreds and thousands. From this potentiality of carbon to form more and more elaborate structures, a third impulse of evolution arises.

I cannot profess to say whether anything more than this prolific structure-building power of carbon is involved in the beginning of life. The story of evolution here passes into the domain of the biological sciences for which I cannot speak, and I am not ready to take sides in the controversy between the Mechanists and the Vitalists. So far as the earth is concerned the history of development of living forms extending over nearly a thousand million years is recorded (though with many breaks) in fossil remains. Looking back over the geological record it would seem that Nature made nearly every possible mistake before she reached her greatest achievement Man—or perhaps some would say her worst mistake of all. At one time she put her trust in armaments and gigantic size. Frozen in the rock is the evidence of her failures to provide a form fitted to endure and dominate—failures which we are only too ready to imitate. At last she tried a being of no great size, almost defenceless, defective in at least one of the more important sense-organs; one gift she bestowed to save him from threatened extinction—a certain stirring, a restlessness, in the organ called the brain.

And so we come to Man.

CHLOROPHYLL: THE SUN TRAP[1]

DONALD CULROSS PEATTIE

WHAT we love, when on a summer day we step into the coolness of a wood, is that its boughs close up behind us. We are escaped, into another room of life. The wood does not live as we live, restless and running, panting after flesh, and even in sleep tossing with fears. It is aloof from thoughts and instincts; it responds, but only to the sun and wind, the rock and the stream—never, though you shout yourself hoarse, to propaganda, temptation, reproach, or promises. You cannot mount a rock and preach to a tree how it shall attain the kingdom of heaven. It is already closer to it, up there, than you will grow to be. And you cannot make it see the light, since in the tree's sense you are blind. You have nothing to bring it, for all the forest is self-sufficient; if you burn it, cut, hack through it with a blade, it angrily repairs the swathe with thorns and weeds and fierce suckers. Later there are good green leaves again, toiling, adjusting, breathing—forgetting you.

For this green living is the world's primal industry; yet it makes no roar. Waving its banners, it marches across the earth and the ages, without dust around its columns. I do not hold that all of that life is pretty; it is not, in purpose, sprung for us, and moves under no compulsion to please. If ever you fought with thistles, or tried to pull up a cattail's matted root-stocks, you will know how plants cling to their own lives and defy you. The pond-scums gather in the cistern, frothing and buoyed with their own gases; the storm waves fling at your feet upon the beach the limp sea-lettuce wrenched from its submarine hold—reminder that there too, where the light is filtered and refracted, there is life still to intercept and net and by it proliferate. Inland from the shore I look and see the coastal ranges clothed in chaparral—dense shrubbery and scrubbery, close-fisted, intricately branched, suffocating the unrash rambler in the noon heat with its pungency. Beyond, on the deserts, under a fierce sky, between the harsh lunar ranges of unweathered rock, life still, somehow, fights its way through the year, with thorn and succulent cell and indomitable root.

1. From *Flowering Earth*, copyright, 1939, by Donald Culross Peattie. Courtesy of G. P. Putnam's Sons.

Between such embattled life and the Forest of Arden, with its ancient beeches and enchanter's nightshade, there is no great biologic difference. Each lives by the cool and cleanly and most commendable virtue of being green. And though that is not biological language, it is the whole story in two words. So that we ought not speak of getting at the root of a matter, but of going back to the leaf of things. The orator who knows the way to the country's salvation and does not know that the breath of life he draws was blown into his nostrils by green leaves, had better spare his breath. And before anyone builds a new state upon the industrial proletariat, he will be wisely cautioned to discover that the source of all wealth is the peasantry of grass.

The reason for these assertions—which I do not make for metaphorical effect but maintain quite literally—is that the green leaf pigment, called chlorophyll, is the one link between the sun and life; it is the conduit of perpetual energy to our own frail organisms.

For inert and inorganic elements—water and carbon dioxide of the air, the same that we breathe out as a waste—chlorophyll can synthesize with the energy of sunlight. Every day, every hour of all the ages, as each continent and, equally important, each ocean rolls into sunlight, chlorophyll ceaselessly creates. Not figuratively, but literally, in the grand First Chapter Genesis style. One instant there are a gas and water, as lifeless as the core of earth or the chill of space; and the next they are become living tissue—mortal yet genitive, progenitive, resilient with all the dewy adaptability of flesh, ever changing in order to stabilize some unchanging ideal of form. Life, in short, synthesized, plant-synthesized, light-synthesized. Botanists say photosynthesized. So that the post-Biblical synthesis of life is already a fact. Only when man has done as much, may he call himself the equal of a weed.

Plant life sustains the living world; more precisely, chlorophyll does so, and where, in the vegetable kingdom, there is not chlorophyll or something closely like it, then that plant or cell is a parasite—no better, in vital economy, than a mere animal or man. Blood, bone and sinew, all flesh is grass. Grass to mutton, mutton to wool, wool to the coat on my back—it runs like one of those cumulative nursery rhymes, the wealth and diversity of our material life accumulating from the primal fact of chlorophyll's activity. The roof of my house, the snapping logs upon the hearth, the desk where I write, are my imports from the plant kingdom. But the whole of modern civilization is based upon a whirlwind spending of the plant wealth long ago and very slowly accumulated. For, fundamentally, and away back, coal and oil, gasoline and illuminating gas had green origins too. With the exception of a small amount of water power, a still smaller of wind and tidal mills, the vast machinery of our complex living is driven only by these stores of plant energy.

We, then, the animals, consume those stores in our restless living. Serenely the plants amass them. They turn light's active energy to food, which is potential energy stored for their own benefit. Only if the daisy is browsed by the cow, the maple leaf sucked of its juices by an insect, will that green leaf become of our kind. So we get the song of a bird at dawn, the speed in the hoofs of the fleeing deer, the noble thought in the philosopher's mind. So Plato's Republic was builded on leeks and cabbages.

Animal life lives always in the red; the favorable balance is written on the other side of life's page, and it is written in chlorophyll. All else obeys the thermodynamic law that energy forever runs down hill, is lost and degraded. In economic language, this is the law of diminishing returns, and it is obeyed by the cooling stars as by man and all the animals. They float down its Lethe stream. Only chlorophyll fights up against the current. It is the stuff in life that rebels at death, that has never surrendered to entropy, final icy stagnation. It is the mere cobweb on which we are all suspended over the abyss.

And what then is this substance which is not itself alive but is made by life and makes life, and is never found apart from life?

I remember the first time I ever held it, in the historic dimness of the old Agassiz laboratories, pure, in my hands. My teacher was an owl-eyed master, with a chuckling sense of humor, who had been trained in the greatest laboratory in Germany, and he believed in doing the great things first. So on the first day of his course he set us to extracting chlorophyll, and I remember that his eyes blinked amusement behind his glasses, because when he told us all to go and collect green leaves and most went all the way to the Yard for grass, I opened the window and stole from a vine upon the wall a handful of Harvard's sacred ivy.

We worked in pairs, and my fellow student was a great-grand-nephew or something of the sort, of Elias Fries, the founder of the study of fungi. Together we boiled the ivy leaves, then thrust them in alcohol. After a while it was the leaves which were colorless while the alcohol had become green. We had to dilute this extract with water, and then we added benzol, because this will take the chlorophyll away from the alcohol which, for its part, very conveniently retains the yellow pigments also found in leaves. This left us with a now yellowish alcohol and, floating on top of it, a thick green benzol; you could simply decant the latter carefully off into a test tube, and there you had chlorophyll extract, opaque, trembling, heavy, a little viscous and oily, and smelling, but much too rankly, like a lawn-mower's blades after a battle with rainy grass.

Then, in a darkened room where beams from a spectroscope escaped in painful darts of light as from the cracks in an old-fashioned magic lantern, we peered at our extracted chlorophyll through prisms. Just as in a crystal chandelier the sunlight is shattered to a rainbow, so in the spectroscope light is spread out in colored bands—a long narrow ribbon, sorting the white light by wave lengths into its elemental parts. And the widths, the presence or the absence, of each cross-band on the ribbon, tell the tale of a chemical element present in the spectrum, much as the bands on a soldier's insignia ribbon show service in Asia, in the tropics, on the border, in what wars. When the astronomer has fixed spectroscope instead of telescope upon a distant star, he reads off the color bands as easily as one soldier reads another's, and will tell you whether sodium or oxygen, helium or iron is present.

Just so our chlorophyll revealed its secrets. The violet and blue end of the spectrum was almost completely blacked out. And that meant that chlorophyll absorbed and used these high-frequency waves. So, too, the red and orange were largely obliterated, over at the right hand side of our tell-tale bar. It was the green that came through clearly. So we call plants green because they use that color least. It is what they reject as fast as it smites the upper cells; it is what they turn back, reflect, flash into our grateful retinas.

It was only routine in a young botanist's training to make an extraction and spectrum analysis of chlorophyll. My student friends over in the chemistry laboratories were more excited than I about it. They were working under Conant, before he became president of Harvard and had to sneak into his old laboratory at night with a key he still keeps. For chlorophyll was Conant's own problem. His diagram of its structure, displayed to me by his students, was closely worked over with symbols and signs, unfolded to something like the dimensions of a blue print of Boulder Dam, and made clear—to anyone who could understand it!—how the atoms are arranged and deployed and linked in such a tremendous molecule as $MgN_4C_{55}H_{72}O_5$.

To Otto and Alfred and Mort every jot and joint in the vast Rube Goldberg machinery of that structural formula had meaning, and more than meaning—the geometrical beauty of the one right, inevitable position for every atom. To me, a botanist's apprentice, a future naturalist, there was just one fact to quicken the pulse. That fact is the close similarity between chlorophyll and hemoglobin, the essence of our blood.

So that you may lay your hand upon the smooth flank of a beech and say, "We be of one blood, brother, thou and I."

The one significant difference in the two structural formulas is this: that the hub of every hemoglobin molecule is one atom of iron, while in chlorophyll it is one atom of magnesium.

Iron is strong and heavy, clamorous when struck, avid of oxygen and capable of corruption. It does not surprise us by its presence in our blood stream. Magnesium is a light, silvery, unresonant metal; its density is only one seventh that of iron, it has half of iron's molecular weight, and melts at half the temperature. It is rustless, ductile and pliant; it burns with a brilliant white light rich in actinic rays, and is widely distributed through the upper soil, but only, save at mineral springs, in dainty quantities. Yet the plant succeeds always in finding that mere trace that it needs, even when a chemist might fail to detect it.

How does the chlorophyll, green old alchemist that it is, transmute the dross of earth into living tissue? its hand is swifter than the chemist's most sensitive analyses. In theory, the step from water and carbon dioxide to the formation of sugar (the first result readily discerned) must involve several syntheses;

yet it goes on in a split hundredth of a second. One sunlight particle or photon strikes the chlorophyll, and instantaneously the terribly tenacious molecule of water, which we break down into its units of hydrogen and oxygen only with difficulty and expense, is torn apart; so too is the carbon dioxide molecule. Building blocks of the three elements, carbon, hydrogen and oxygen, are then whipped at lightning speed into carbonic acid; this is instantly changed over into formic acid—the same that smarts so in our nerve endings when an ant stings us. No sooner formed than formic acid becomes formaldehyde and hydrogen peroxide. This last is poisonous, but a ready enzyme in the plant probably splits it as fast as it is born into harmless water and oxygen, while the formaldehyde is knocked at top speed into a new pattern—and is grape sugar, glucose. And all before you can say Albert Einstein. Indeed, by the time you have said Theophrastus Bombastus Aureolus Paracelsus von Hohenheim, the sugar may have lost a modicum of water—and turned into starch, the first product of photosynthesis that could be detected by the methods of fifty years ago.

At this very instant, with the sun delivering to its child the earth, in the bludgeoning language of mathematics, 215×10^{15} calories per second, photosynthesis is racing along wherever the leaf can reach the light. (All else goes to waste.) True, its efficiency is very low—averaging no better than one per cent, while our machines are delivering up to twenty-five per cent of the fuel they combust. But that which they burn—coal and gas, oils and wood—was made, once, by leaves in ancient geologic times. The store of such energy is strictly finite. Chlorophyll alone is hitched to what is, for earthly purposes, the infinite.

Light, in the latest theory, is not waves in a sea of ether, or a jet from a nozzle; it could be compared rather to machine gun fire, every photo-electric bullet of energy traveling in regular rhythm, at a speed that bridges the astronomical gap in eight minutes. As each bullet hits an electron of chlorophyll it sets it to vibrating, at its own rate, just as one tuning fork, when struck, will cause another to hum in the same pitch. A bullet strikes—and one electron is knocked galley west into a dervish dance like the madness of the atoms in the sun. The energy splits open chlorophyll molecules, recombines their atoms, and lies there, dormant, in foods.

The process seems miraculously adjusted. And yet, like most living processes it is not perfect. The reaction time of chlorophyll is not geared as high as the arrival of the light-bullets. Light comes too fast; plants, which are the very children of light, can get too much of it. Exposure to the sunlight on the Mojave desert is something that not a plant in my garden, no, nor even the wiry brush in the chaparral, could endure. Lids against the light plants do not have; but by torsions of the stalk some leaves may turn their blades edge-on to dazzling radiation, and present them again broadside in failing light. Within others the chlorophyll granules too, bun or pellet-shaped as they are, can roll for a side or frontal exposure toward the light.

In others they can crowd to the top of a cell and catch faint rays, or sink or flee to the sides to escape a searing blast. . . .

When I began to write these pages, before breakfast, the little fig tree outside my window was rejoicing in the early morning light. It is a special familiar of my work, a young tree that has never yet borne fruit. It is but a little taller than I, has only two main branches and forty-three twigs, and the brave if not impressive sum of two hundred and sixteen leaves—I have touched every one with a counting finger. Though sparse, they are large, mitten-shaped, richly green with chlorophyll. I compute, by measuring the leaf and counting both sides, that my little tree has a leaf surface of about eighty-four square feet. This sun-trap was at work today long before I.

Those uplifted hand-like leaves caught the first sky light. It was poor for the fig's purpose, but plant work begins from a nocturnal zero. When I came to my desk the sun was full upon those leaves—and it is a wondrous thing how they are disposed so that they do not shade each other. By the blazing California noon, labor in the leaves must have faltered from very excess of light; all the still golden afternoon it went on; now as the sun sets behind a sea fog the little fig slackens peacefully at its task.

Yet in the course of a day it has made sugar for immediate burning and energy release, put by a store of starch for future use; with the addition of nitrogen and other salts brought up in water from the roots it has built proteins too—the very bricks and mortar of the living protoplasm, and the perdurable stuff of permanent tissue. The annual growth ring in the wood of stem and twigs has widened an infinitesimal but a real degree. The fig is one day nearer to its coming of age, to flowering and fruiting. Then, still leafing out each spring, still toiling in the sunlight that I shall not be here to see, it may go on a century and more, growing eccentric, solidifying whimsies, becoming a friend to generations. It will be "the old fig" then. And at last it may give up the very exertion of bearing. It will lean tough elbows in the garden walks, and gardeners yet unborn will scold it and put up with it. But still it will leaf out till it dies.

Dusk is here now. So I switch on the lamp beside my desk. The powerhouse burns its hoarded tons of coal a week, and gives us this instant and most marvelous current. But that light is not new. It was hurled out of the sun two hundred million years ago, and was captured by the leaves of the Carboniferous tree-fern forests, fell with the falling plant, was buried, fossilized, dug up and resurrected. It is the same light. And, in my little fig tree as in the ancient ferns, it is the same unchanging green stuff from age to age, passed without perceptible improvement from evolving plant to plant. What it is and does, so complex upon examination, lies about us tranquil and simple, with the simplicity of a miracle.

OF THE QUANTITY OF BLOOD PASSING THROUGH THE HEART[1]

WILLIAM HARVEY

THUS far I have spoken of the passage of the blood from the veins into the arteries, and of the manner in which it is transmitted and distributed by the action of the heart; points to which some, moved either by the authority of Galen or Columbus, or the reasonings of others, will give in their adhesion. But what remains to be said upon the quantity and source of the blood which thus passes, is of so novel and unheard-of character, that I not only fear injury to myself from the envy of a few, but I tremble lest I have mankind at large for my enemies, so much doth wont and custom, that become as another nature, and doctrine once sown and that hath struck deep root, and respect for antiquity influence all men: Still the die is cast, and my trust is in my love of truth, and the candour that inheres in cultivated minds. And sooth to say, when I surveyed my mass of evidence, whether derived from vivisections, and my various reflections on them, or from the ventricles of the heart and the vessels that enter into and issue from them, the symmetry and size of these conduits,—for nature doing nothing in vain, would never have given them so large a relative size without a purpose,—or from the arrangement and intimate structure of the valves in particular, and of the other parts of the heart in general, with many things besides, I frequently and seriously bethought me, and long revolved in my mind, what might be the quantity of blood which was transmitted, in how short a time its passage might be effected, and the like; and not finding it possible that this could be supplied by the juices of the ingested aliment without the veins on the one hand becoming drained, and the arteries on the other getting ruptured through the excessive charge of blood, unless the blood should somehow find its way from the arteries into the veins, and so return to the right side of the heart; I began to think whether there might not be a MOTION, AS IT WERE, IN A CIRCLE. Now this I afterwards found to be true; and I finally saw that the blood, forced by the action of the left ventricle into the arteries, was distributed to the body at large, and its several parts, in the same manner as it is sent through the lungs, impelled by the right ventricle into the pulmonary artery, and that it then passed through the veins and along the vena cava, and so round to the left ventricle in the manner already indicated. Which motion we may be allowed to call circular, in the same way as Aristotle says that the air and the

1. From William Harvey, *On the Motion of the Heart and Blood in Animals,* Robert Willis trans., revised by Alexander Bowie in *Scientific Papers, Physiology, Medicine, Surgery, Geology* (New York: P. F. Collier & Son Corporation, 1910), p. 382. Reprinted by permission of the publishers.

rain emulate the circular motion of the superior bodies; for the moist earth, warmed by the sun, evaporates; the vapours drawn upwards are condensed, and descending in the form of rain, moisten the earth again; and by this arrangement are generations of living things produced; and in like manner too are tempests and meteors engendered by the circular motion, and by the approach and recession of the sun.

And so, in all likelihood, does it come to pass in the body, through the motion of the blood; the various parts are nourished, cherished, quickened by the warmer, more perfect, vaporous, spirituous, and, as I may say, alimentive blood; which, on the contrary, in contact with these parts becomes cooled, coagulated, and, so to speak, effete; whence it returns to its sovereign the heart, as if to its source, or to the inmost home of the body, there to recover its state of excellence or perfection. Here it resumes its due fluidity and receives an infusion of natural heat—powerful, fervid, a kind of treasury of life, and is impregnated with spirits, and it might be said with balsam; and thence it is again dispersed; and all this depends on the motion and action of the heart.

The heart, consequently, is the beginning of life; the sun of the microcosm, even as the sun in his turn might well be designated the heart of the world; for it is the heart by whose virtue and pulse the blood is moved, perfected, made apt to nourish, and is preserved from corruption and coagulation; it is the household divinity which, discharging its function, nourishes, cherishes, quickens the whole body, and is indeed the foundation of life, the source of all action. But of these things we shall speak more opportunely when we come to speculate upon the final cause of this motion of the heart.

Hence, since the veins are the conduits and vessels that transport the blood, they are of two kinds, the cava and the aorta; and this not by reason of there being two sides of the body, as Aristotle has it, but because of the difference of office; nor yet, as is commonly said, in consequence of any diversity of structure, for in many animals, as I have said, the vein does not differ from the artery in the thickness of its tunics, but solely in virtue of their several destinies and uses. A vein and an artery, both styled vein by the ancients, and that not undeservedly, as Galen has remarked, because the one, the artery to wit, is the vessel which carries the blood from the heart to the body at large, the other or vein of the present day bringing it back from the general system to the heart; the former is the conduit from, the latter the channel to, the heart; the latter contains the cruder, effete blood, rendered unfit for nutrition; the former transmits the digested, perfect, peculiarly nutritive fluid.

CARBON MONOXIDE POISONING [1]

CLAUDE BERNARD

About 1846, I wished to make experiments on the cause of poisoning with carbon monoxide. I knew that this gas had been described as toxic, but I knew literally nothing about the mechanism of its poisoning; I therefore could not have a preconceived opinion. What, then, was to be done? I must bring to birth an idea by making a fact appear, i.e., make another experiment to see. In fact I poisoned a dog by making him breathe carbon monoxide and after death I at once opened his body. I looked at the state of the organs and fluids. What caught my attention at once was that its blood was scarlet in all the vessels, in the veins as well as the arteries, in the right heart as well as in the left. I repeated the experiment on rabbits, birds and frogs, and everywhere I found the same scarlet coloring of the blood. But I was diverted from continuing this investigation, and I kept this observation a long time unused except for quoting it in my course *a propos* of the coloring of blood.

In 1856, no one had carried the experimental question further, and in my course at the Collège de France on toxic and medicinal substances, I again took up the study of poisoning by carbon monoxide which I had begun in 1846. I found myself then in a confused situation, for at this time I already knew that poisoning with carbon monoxide makes the blood scarlet in the whole circulatory system. I had to make hypotheses, and establish a preconceived idea about my first observation, so as to go ahead. Now, reflecting on the fact of scarlet blood, I tried to interpret it by my earlier knowledge as to the cause of the color of blood. Whereupon all the following reflections presented themselves to my mind. The scarlet color, said I, is peculiar to arterial blood and connected with the presence of a large proportion of oxygen, while dark coloring belongs with absence of oxygen and presence of a larger proportion of carbonic acid; so the idea occurred to me that carbon monoxide, by keeping venous blood scarlet, might perhaps have prevented the oxygen from changing into carbonic acid in the capillaries. Yet it seemed hard to understand how that could be the cause of death. But still keeping on with my inner preconceived reasoning, I added: If that is true, blood taken from the veins of animals poisoned with carbon monoxide should be like arterial blood in containing oxygen; we must see if that is the fact.

Following this reasoning, based on interpretation of my observation, I tried an experiment to verify my hypothesis as to the persistence of oxygen in the venous blood. I passed a current of hydrogen through scarlet venous blood taken from an animal poisoned with carbon monoxide, but I could not liber-

1. From Claude Bernard, *An Introduction to the Study of Experimental Medicine*, translated by Henry Copley Greene (New York: The Macmillan Company, 1927), pp. 159–161. Reprinted by permission of the General Education Board.

ate the oxygen as usual. I tried to do the same with arterial blood; I had no greater success. My preconceived idea was therefore false. But the impossibility of getting oxygen from the blood of a dog poisoned with carbon monoxide was a second observation which suggested a fresh hypothesis. What could have become of the oxygen in the blood? It had not changed with carbonic acid, because I had not set free large quantities of that gas in passing a current of hydrogen through the blood of the poisoned animals. Moreover, that hypothesis was contrary to the color of the blood. I exhausted myself in conjectures about how carbon monoxide could cause the oxygen to disappear from the blood; and as gases displace one another I naturally thought that the carbon monoxide might have displaced the oxygen and driven it out of the blood. To learn this, I decided to vary my experimentation by putting the blood in artificial conditions that would allow me to recover the displaced oxygen. So I studied the action of carbon monoxide on blood experimentally. For this purpose I took a certain amount of arterial blood from a healthy animal; I put this blood on the mercury in an inverted test tube containing carbon monoxide; I then shook the whole thing so as to poison the blood sheltered from contact with the outer air. Then, after an interval, I examined whether the air in the test tube in contact with the poisoned blood had been changed, and I noted that the air thus in contact with the blood had been remarkably enriched with oxygen, while the proportion of carbon monoxide was lessened. Repeated in the same conditions, these experiments taught me that what had occurred was an exchange, volume by volume, between the carbon monoxide and the oxygen of the blood. But the carbon monoxide, in displacing the oxygen that it had expelled from the blood, remained chemically combined in the blood and could no longer be displaced either by oxygen or by other gases. So that death came through death of the molecules of blood, or in other words by stopping their exercises of a physiological property essential to life.

This last example, which I have very briefly described, is complete; it shows from one end to the other, how we proceed with the experimental method and succeed in learning the immediate cause of phenomena. To begin with I knew literally nothing about the mechanism of the phenomenon of poisoning with carbon monoxide. I undertook an experiment to see, i.e., to observe. I made a preliminary observation of a special change in the coloring of blood. I interpreted this observation, and I made an hypothesis which proved false. But the experiment provided me with a second observation about which I reasoned anew, using it as a starting point for making a new hypothesis as to the mechanism, by which the oxygen in the blood was removed. By building up hypotheses, one by one, about the facts as I observed them, I finally succeeded in showing that carbon monoxide replaces oxygen in a molecule of blood, by combining with the substance of the molecule. Experimental analysis, here, has reached its goal. This is one of the cases, rare in physiology, which I am happy to be able to quote. Here the immediate cause of the phenomenon of poisoning is found and is translated into a theory which accounts for all the facts and at the same time includes all the observations and experiments. Formulated as follows, the theory posits the main facts from which all the rest are deduced: Carbon monoxide combines more intimately than oxygen with the hemoglobin in a molecule of blood. It has quite recently been proved that carbon monoxide forms a definite combination with hemoglobin. So that the molecule of blood, as if petrified by the stability of the combination, loses its vital properties. Hence everything is logically deduced: because of its property of more intimate combination, carbon monoxide drives out of the blood the oxygen essential to life; the molecules of blood become inert, and the animal dies, with symptoms of hemorrhage, from true paralysis of the molecules.

THE READING MACHINE [1]

MORRIS BISHOP

"I HAVE invented a reading machine," said Professor Entwhistle, a strident energumen whose violent enthusiasms are apt to infect his colleagues with nausea or hot flashes before the eyes.

Every head in the smoking room of the Faculty Club bowed over a magazine, in an attitude of prayer. The prayer was unanswered, as usual.

"It is obvious," said Professor Entwhistle, "that the greatest waste of our civilization is the time spent in reading. We have been able to speed up practically everything to fit the modern tempo—communication, transportation, calculation. But today a man takes just as long to read a book as Dante did, or—"

"Great Caesar!" said the Professor of Amphibology, shutting his magazine with a spank.

"Or great Caesar," continued Professor Entwhistle. "So I have invented a machine. It operates by a simple arrangement of photoelectric cells, which

1. Reprinted by permission of the author. Copyright, 1947, The New Yorker Magazine, Inc. (Formerly The F-R. Publishing Corp.)

scan a line of type at lightning speed. The operation of the photoelectric cells is synchronized with a mechanical device for turning the pages—rather ingenious. I figure that my machine can read a book of three hundred pages in ten minutes."

"Can it read French?" said the Professor of Bio-Economics, without looking up.

"It can read any language that is printed in Roman type. And by an alteration of the master pattern on which the photoelectric cells operate, it can be fitted to read Russian, or Bulgarian, or any language printed in the Cyrillic alphabet. In fact, it will do more. By simply throwing a switch, you can adapt it to read Hebrew, or Arabic, or any language that is written from right to left instead of from left to right."

"Chinese?" said the Professor of Amphibology, throwing himself into the arena. The others still studied their magazines.

"Not Chinese, as yet," said Professor Entwhistle. "Though by inserting the pages sidewise . . . Yes, I think it could be done."

"Yes, but when you say this contrivance reads, exactly what do you mean? It seems to me—"

"The light waves registered by the photoelectric cells are first converted into sound waves."

"So you can listen in to the reading of the text?"

"Not at all. The sound waves alter so fast that you hear nothing but a continuous hum. If you hear them at all. You can't, in fact, because they are on a wave length inaudible to the human ear."

"Well, it seems to me—"

"Think of the efficiency of the thing!" Professor Entwhistle was really warming up. "Think of the time saved! You assign a student a bibliography of fifty books. He runs them through the machine comfortably in a weekend. And on Monday morning he turns in a certificate from the machine. Everything has been conscientiously read!"

"Yes, but the student won't remember what he has read!"

"He doesn't remember what he reads now."

"Well, you have me there," said the Professor of Amphibology. "I confess you have me there. But it seems to me we would have to pass the machine and fail the student."

"Not at all," said Professor Entwhistle. "An accountant today does not think of doing his work by multiplication and division. Often he is unable to multiply and divide. He confides his problem to a business machine and the machine does his work for him. All the accountant has to know is how to run the machine. That is efficiency."

"Still, it seems to me that what we want to do is to transfer the contents of the book to the student's mind."

"In the mechanized age? My dear fellow! What we want is to train the student to run machines. An airplane pilot doesn't need to know the history of aerodynamics. He needs to know how to run his machine. A lawyer doesn't want to know the development of theories of Roman law. He wants to win cases, if possible by getting the right answers to logical problems. That is largely a mechanical process. It might well be possible to construct a machine. It could begin by solving simple syllogisms, you know—drawing a conclusion from a major premise and a minor premise—"

"Here, let's not get distracted. This reading machine of yours, it must *do* something, it must make some kind of record. What happens after you get the sound waves?"

"That's the beauty of it," said Professor Entwhistle. "The sound waves are converted into light waves, of a different character from the original light waves, and these are communicated to an automatic typewriter, working at inconceivable speed. This transforms the light impulses into legible typescript, in folders of a hundred pages each. It tosses them out the way a combine tosses out sacked wheat. Thus, everything the machine reads is preserved entire, in durable form. The only thing that remains is to file it somewhere, and for this you would need only the services of a capable filing clerk."

"Or you could read it?" persisted the Professor of Amphibology.

"Why, yes, if you wanted to, you could read it," said Professor Entwhistle.

An indigestible silence hung over the Faculty Club.

"I see where the Athletic Association has bought a pitching machine," said the Assistant Professor of Business Psychology (Retail). "Damn thing throws any curve desired, with a maximum margin of error of three centimetres over the plate. What'll they be thinking of next?"

"A batting machine, obviously," said Professor Entwhistle.

THE IVORY LAB[1]

JACQUES BARZUN

> I degrade Physics into an implement of culture, and this is my deliberate design.—JOHN TYNDALL, *Fragments of Science*

MOST of the excitement about "higher education" in the last three years has been about the teaching of history, languages, and "great books." But the most serious and pressing need in colleges today seems to me to be the teaching of science. It may appear paradoxical that I speak of a "need" which everyone

1. From *Teacher in America* by Jacques Barzun. Copyright, 1944–1945, by Jacques Barzun. Reprinted by permission of Little, Brown & Company and the Atlantic Monthly Press.

believes to be adequately met, but paradox disappears when the point of view changes. From one point of view, science is taught in every American college; from another point of view, it is taught in none, or very few. Looked at in a certain light, science teaching today is the most efficient, up to date, and worldly-wise. In another light, it is backward, wasteful and "escapist." Let me explain these contrasts.

Fifty or sixty years ago, science was a new academic subject. People mistrusted its power to educate, and many of its proponents seemed as if they could never be educated themselves. The tradition of liberal studies had always included mathematics, because mathematics was supposed to train the mind; but the new physical sciences were first seen as manual arts, messy and expensive, and with no more "discipline" to them than a pair of elastic-sided boots. At the time of the fight for adding science to the curriculum, the defensive position was held by Greek and Latin, which unfortunately adopted a "scorched earth" policy. I mean that they allowed themselves to be invaded by the "scientific spirit" and in trying to compete with it reduced their field to a wasteland of verbal criticism, grammar, and philology. Literature was relegated to a second place and studying the classics came to mean research into the uses of *utor, fruor,* and *fungor.*

Naturally the classics were exterminated, for science could beat them at their own game. A young man trained in science could on graduation get any of a hundred desirable jobs in industry. A young "scientific" classicist could only hope to teach his own subject to a dwindling number of students. That is what invariably comes of trying to put belles-lettres into utilitarian envelopes. As Dean Briggs of Harvard said when the Bachelor of Science degree was established: "It does not guarantee that the holder knows any science, but it does guarantee that he does *not* know any Latin." When the study of classical literature in translation was reintroduced for freshmen at Columbia College a few years ago, the undergraduate department of classics was surprised to find its enrollment in beginning Greek increased 150 per cent: they now had ten students.

But the bitter joke is not on the Classics alone. Having stepped into Greek's vacated place, Science now occupies its position, not with respect to size of enrollment, but with respect to educational attitude. It is now in power and it acts disdainful, holier-than-thou, and prudish. Someone once asked, "What is it that our men of science are guarding like a threatened virginity?" "Oh," was the answer, "they have a Vestal interest in their subject." Considered—somewhat unfairly—in the mass, science teachers may be said to contribute the greatest proportion of backward-looking, anti-intellectual, mechanic-minded members to the faculty. Characteristically, single departments of physical science have in certain institutions tried to set up separate schools, where only their one science would be taught for four years and rewarded with some kind of Bachelor's degree. The intention was to monopolize the student's time, cram him full of "practical" knowledge, and sell him to the highest bidder the moment he had clutched his diploma and redeemed his ten-dollar deposit for apparatus.

Doubtless there is a demand for such prefabricated industrial robots and I see no reason why such schools should not function in a manner useful to the commonwealth—off the campus. But departments that once clamored for admission to university status and have had it for fifty years are unwilling to give up all the *douceurs* of the association. They would still like to profit from the university connection, to color their degree with a faint tincture of liberal teaching—perhaps they would require a year of English and a year of history and economics—and to boast that their own subject, be it chemistry or geology, is also one of the "humanities." They want to eat their cake as many times over as a cow does her cud.

A crowd of evils springs from this ambiguous mood in the present college curriculum. There is an undignified scramble for the student's time, with broad hints on the part of the scientist that the rest of the program is folderol. Repressed antagonisms divide teachers of the humanities (vague, pointless, unpractical subjects—except economics) from teachers of the real stuff represented by science. Moreover, departments of physics and chemistry require mathematical preparation in strict amount and order of time, with the result that all scheduling revolves around their claims. Since most young Americans discover their vocational bent while undergraduates, the wish to qualify for a profession is a powerful lever to make everyone study science for one or two years under these barbaric conditions. The doctor, the engineer, the research man in any science must gobble up as many courses as he can; and the man uninterested in science must "fulfill the requirement." Both are often judged on their science record, in the belief that it unmistakably reveals "real brains" or the lack of them.

The worst of all this is that neither group of students learns much about science but goes to swell the ranks of the two great classes of modern men—the single-track expert and the scientific ignoramus. Could anything more plainly demonstrate the failure of science to become a subject fit for college teaching? What makes a subject fit for the higher curriculum is surely no novelty: it is that it shall enlighten all the corners of the mind and teach its own uses. The humble three R's begin in strict utility and end up in poetry, science, and the search for the Infinite. They can and should therefore be taught indefinitely. Men have known for three thousand years that other matters of knowledge naturally divide themselves into special and general, that both are needful, but that whereas the special *add* to one's powers, the general *enhance the quality* of all of them.

At a recent educational conference, the Dean of a Midwestern university complained humorously that he was always being asked to give credits for impossible subjects—subjects that, he said, deserved to be called *in-credible.* A transfer student, for example, wanted "points" for seven hours of saw filing. Undeniably saw filing is a necessary art, but its merits as a general enhancer of power and personality stop accruing so soon after study is begun that it is not properly a branch of academic learning. The same is true of still more complex matters like shorthand, typewriting, and dress designing. Farther on in the series, it becomes harder to draw the line: stamp collecting is sub-educational but numismatics is a province of history.

Fortunately there is no doubt whatever about the place of the sciences: they *are* humanities and they belong in the college curriculum. Accordingly, they should be introduced into it *as humanities,* at the earliest possible moment. How? I have some tentative suggestions to make, but first I want to stress the danger of further delay and of the continuance of our present malpractice.

The worst danger is the creation of a large, powerful, and complacent class of college-trained uneducated men at the very heart of our industrial and political system. We may be too near to judge, but it strikes me that one of the conditions that made possible the present folly in Germany was the split among three groups: the technicians, the citizens, and the irresponsible rabble. This becomes persuasively plain if you consider the professional army caste as a group of unthinking technicians. The rabble together with the technicians can cow the citizenry; the technicians—wedded solely to their work-bench—will work for any group that hires; and the rabble, worshiping "science" to the exclusion of less tangible necessaries, are perfectly willing to sacrifice the citizen. They probably think that, if necessary, "science" could manufacture German citizens—out of wolfram.

Such principles will hardly give long life and happiness to a democracy. The only hope for a democratic state is to have more citizens than anything else. Hence technicians must not be allowed to hibernate between experiments, but must become conscious, responsible, politically and morally active men. Otherwise they will find not only that representative government has slipped out of their fingers, but that they have also lost their commanding position. They will be paid slaves in the service of some rabble, high or low. Meanwhile our present stock of citizens must not simply gape at the wonders of science, but must understand enough of its principles to criticize and value the results. As for the rabble, it must be transmuted as fast as it forms, by science and morals both.

All this clearly depends on teaching our easygoing, rather credulous college boys and girls what science is. If they leave college thinking, as they usually do, that science offers a full, accurate, and literal description of man and Nature; if they think scientific research by itself yields final answers to social problems; if they think scientists are the only honest, patient, and careful workers in the world; if they think that Copernicus, Galileo, Newton, Lavoisier, and Faraday were unimaginative plodders like their own instructors; if they think theories spring from facts and that scientific authority at any time is infallible; if they think that the ability to write down symbols and read manometers is fair grounds for superiority and pride, and if they think that science steadily and automatically makes for a better world—then they have wasted their time in the science lecture room; they live in an Ivory Laboratory more isolated than the poet's tower [2] and they are a plain menace to the society they belong to. They are a menace whether they believe all this by virtue of being engaged in scientific work themselves or of being disqualified from it by felt or fancied incapacity.

I return to what might might perhaps be done preventively and constructively. To begin with, a change of direction must be imparted to the teaching of science. The fact must be recognized that most students still do not make science their profession.[3] Consequently, for future lay citizens the compulsory science requirement in force nearly everywhere must be justified by a course explicitly designed for them. Such a course must not play at making physicists or biologists, but must explain the principles of the physical sciences in a coherent manner. A "survey" of all the sciences is out of the question. It would be at once superficial and bewildering. But an intelligent introduction to principles can be given. The assumptions that connect and that differentiate the sciences of matter, of living beings, and of logical relation can be taught; the meaning and the grounds of great unifying theories can be explained, and significant demonstrations and experiments can be shown to and made by the students.

Out of such a course there would surely come a changed attitude on the part of teachers and indeed a change in teaching personnel. At present, side by side with wise men and ripe teachers in the sciences, one finds many highly trained and absolutely uneducated practitioners. One also finds fanatics of the order that Dickens described in Professor Dingo, who, being caught defacing houses with his geological hammer, replied that "he knew of no building save the Temple of Science." Many university scientists openly scorn teaching and use their appointment to boil the pot of individual research. Now a life of research is a worthy one, but no amount of worthy motive justifies false pretenses and fraudulent impersonation—in this case the pretense of imparting knowledge and the impersonation of a teacher.

In the classroom, such men usually are neither civil, nor literate, nor even scientific, for their knowledge of science is purely from inside—a limitation equally bad but more misleading than the limitation of knowing it purely from outside. "What do they know of science who only science know?" They teach it as a set of rules, and speak of the profession as a "game." Drill in manual dexterity they entrust to laboratory assistants, who are only younger editions of themselves, and for whom a good notebook or speed in performing

2. To judge by results, it would seem that the poet climbs to the top of his tower to look out on the world and write about it. Why cavil at the building material—at once durable and attractive and requiring no upkeep?

3. Statistics for the Middle West, based on large freshman enrollments, show that 50 per cent of those taking Chemistry 1, 60 percent of those taking Geology 1, 73 percent of those taking Physics 1, 75 percent of those taking Biology 1, and 82 percent of those taking Botany 1, never go further into the science.

repetitious experiments is the passport to approval. There is seldom any consideration of the students as thinking minds, of the proper allocation of effort among the many interests legitimate at their time of life, nor of the philosophical implications which the words, the history, and the processes of the particular science disclose.

To offset this lamentable state of things, it must be said that two of the professions most concerned with scientific training—engineering and medicine—have lately amended their outlook and made overtures to the humanities. The medical schools have declared that cramming the student with science in college was a poor thing. He had better study other, less "practical," more formative subjects and postpone advanced chemistry and biology until medical school, where they will be taught him again in a fashion better tailored to his needs. This new policy is excellent, but it is not yet sufficiently enforced. The lesser medical schools—and some others—do not trust their own belief in the principle; they still appeal to "practical" views and judge applicants by A's in science.

Similarly, the Society for the Promotion of Engineering Education has passed splendid resolutions approving what they call the "social-humanistic stem"—by which they mean a few branches of non-engineering study; more accurately then, the "social-humanistic faggots." But here again, engineering thought is ahead of the engineer's emotions. When it comes to the test, the student or the program is pushed around to suit engineering subject matter.

If you add to this the important fact that many young Americans choose "engineering" in the belief that this means a career of research in pure science, you may form some notion of the present anarchical mess. The would-be engineer of seventeen finds that what he really wants to work at is pure research in electricity, that is, to be a physicist. He must therefore back water, change his course, and take some new prerequisites. Meanwhile his upbringing as a man and citizen goes by the board. He is caught between two grindstones, each indifferent to the effect of its motion, just as if the boy being put through this mill were not a human being, a student of the university, and a future citizen of the nation. Who is being "practical" now?

Some would probably still maintain that the professional schools in contact with "the world" know best what is the practical view, and that the college is as ever utopian. But there is one curious fact to be added. It is that the scientic professional schools have a way of relaxing their jaws into a smile whenever the market demand for their product decreases: it is a reflex action. They fall in love with the humanities all over again and raise the amount they require for admission, until outside pressure once again lowers the floodgates and the frown succeeds the smile. This self-regulating action is a feat of engineering in itself—or shall I say of doctoring the supply for public consumption?

The question is not whether this is the easy way to go about marketing young men, but whether it is a responsible grown-up way of replenishing the professional class of society. Granted that practice is the test of all schemes and ideals, is this the most practical scheme that American ingenuity can devise? I concede that in the present state of mind of the American public, desire for vocational training takes the lead over anything else. But are the directing members of the university world to follow other people's untutored impulses or to guide and redirect them? We may well ask when we reflect that the first victims of the system are the children of the unthinking public and the public itself. For it is the oldest fallacy about schooling to suppose that it can train a man for "practical" life. Inevitably, while the plan of study is being taught, "practical life" has moved on. "They did it this way three months ago, now they do it this way." No employer who knows anything about men will value a beginner because he knows the ropes of a particular changeable routine. It would be as sensible to require that newcomers know the floor plan of the factory ahead of time.[4]

The corporations employing the largest numbers of engineers and scientific research men are on this matter way ahead of the colleges. One such firm conducted a survey last year to find out where and how its first-rate executives had been prepared. They came from the most unexpected places—including small liberal arts colleges, the teaching profession, the stage, and the Baptist ministry. It was found that the engineering schools—particularly those sensible ones that make no pretense at intellectual *cachet*—turned out a good average product, but few leaders. The company's own institutes and night courses raised the chance of foremen and district managers—but only up to a point. The survey concluded that what it wanted as material to shape future executives was graduates of liberal arts colleges, trained in history and economics, in philosophy and in good English, and likewise possessed of *an intelligent interest in science and technology*. Gentlemen, the path lies open.

II

My friend Dean Finch, of the Columbia University School of Engineering, might not agree with all I have just said, but I think he would approve of one element in my suggestions which I casually threw in. I mean the utility of history in the teaching of science. He himself is an historian of technology and offers in Columbia College a most valuable course in the subject for the use of "lay" students. What is surprising is that similar courses, accompanied by others in the history of pure science, are not given—indeed required—on every American campus.

4. The S.P.E.E. reports: "From its very nature, engineering education operates under changing conditions which constantly challenge its processes and test its results . . . so as to adapt itself to changing needs." (*Draft of a Report*, etc. November 16, 1939, p. 1). This is fine and good, but it holds true of every other professional subject and most academic ones. The old belief that only a few schools are in touch with the "real world" is untrue, even if the newer belief should prove true that it is best for the world to have the school conform to every change outside.

The very idea, it must be said, is shrouded in the smoke of battle. When I mention it, some of my scientific colleagues slap me on the back and say "more power to you." They may express doubts about persuading their fellows, or finding good instructors, but they want to see it tried. Moreover they do not feel robbed when in my own teaching of nineteenth-century history I discuss Dalton and Darwin, Liebig and Faraday, Mayer and Clerk Maxwell. Though scientists, these colleagues of mine can see that to complain of general ignorance about the role of science in modern history, and to prevent historians from mentioning it, is to love monopoly above riches.

Others take the view that science has no history because every new achievement supersedes previous ones. The history of science, they feel, is nothing but biographical chitchat about scientists. Or else they admit that it is useful to find out what the Middle Ages thought of natural science, but only in order to point the lesson of freedom from church authority and fight anew the old battle of science against religion.

This angry confusion about the history of science is dense but not impenetrable. Three things may be distinguished. First there is historical research into the beginnings of science—Greek or Arabic or Medieval. This goes on as advanced study and concerns undergraduates only in the form of broad tested conclusions. Then there is the biography of scientists, which is of immense educational importance—whatever laboratory men may say. Biography does not mean recounting Newton's imaginary embroilments with women or Lavoisier's perfectly real ones with public finance. It means finding out from the lives of great scientific creators what they worked at and how their minds functioned. How tiresome it is to hear nothing from our scientific departments but Sunday-school homilies on the gameness of Galileo, the patience of Pasteur, and the carefulness of Madame Curie. And how uninstructive! Any man who accomplishes anything in any field is as patient as he has to be, and even little boys know that glass being breakable, you have to be careful.[5]

What would be far more significant and novel, though true, would be to teach that Copernicus gambled on insufficient evidence; that Kepler was chiefly a horoscope-caster; that Faraday probably believed more wrong theories than any man alive—and turned them to good use in experiment; that Darwin, on his own admission, made awful blunders and admired the art of wriggling out of them; that T. H. Morgan's laboratory was rather messy; that Newton could not see how his own astronomy contradicted the Bible; that scientific men have suppressed and persecuted opponents of their theories, and that the best scientific truth can end in a rigid and mistaken orthodoxy—as happened after Newton and Darwin. The point is that science is made by man, in the light of interests, errors, and hopes, just like poetry, philosophy, and human history itself.

5. The self-righteousness of the man of science is universal enough to sustain advertising appeals: "Like the scientist, NEWSWEEK . . . makes it its business to search out truth by continual research, relentless checking and re-checking of the facts." A grim grind!

To say this is not to degrade science, as naïve persons might think; it is on the contrary to enhance its achievements by showing that they sprang not from patience on a monument but from genius toiling in the mud. I leave unexplained here all that accrues from studying how we came to use atoms or devise Absolute Zero or to state the Law of Conservation of Energy (including the reasons why energy is a better word than the earlier "force") or what steps led first to the abandonment and then to the later salvaging of Avogadro's hypothesis. A good scientist-historian would exhibit the assumptions and habits which affected scientific opinion at important turning points. He would unite science to other thought by discussing the nature of its evidence at various periods. And he would show the role of the pure imagination in all great scientific work. I know Bacon promised that science would level all the minds of its devotees to average size, and he is right insofar as drilling can make ordinary men into patient, careful laboratory workers. But science has not yet managed to get along without ideas, and these come only from men of special, powerful, and irreducible aptitudes. The chronological study of these men and ideas is the proper subject matter for an undergraduate course in the history of science.[6]

I know the common objection offered to all this—to an historical and a synoptic account of scientific principles in place of the "regular" science courses: it is that the substitutes would be merely talk about science and not science itself. Grant this for argument's sake. The objectors miss the point if they do not see that talk about science has a place in the curriculum and that such talk may be good or bad, quite all right or all quite wrong, exactly like talk about art. If science is one of the humanities it must be capable of being looked at and thought about apart from direct doing—at least until we require every concertgoer to write a symphony before being allowed to take his seat at Carnegie Hall. Besides, the synoptic course I have in view would include laboratory work, and it would rest with the scientists themselves whether the students mastered enough of the operative side of true science to keep them from irresponsible talk about it. If science teachers think that a year's drudgery in physics as now given prevents silly notions in those who take it in college, they are either inobservant or illogical.

Doubtless it is bad logic they suffer from—the usual weakness of scientists . . . and of the rest of mankind, who generally want to have things both ways. Take as an example a comment made on the relation of science and history in the excellent study of Lavoisier by J. A. Cochrane. The author complains that "although Lavoisier was at the time of his death and for at least fifteen years before it one of the most eminent men in France, the general

6. Some very useful works already exist which exemplify the historical and inductive method of teaching science; among others: Ostwald's *Schule der Chemie* (translated by E. C. Ramsay), Ida Freund's *The Study of Chemical Composition* and *The Experimental Basis of Chemistry,* Norman Campbell's *Physics: The Elements,* and H. T. Pledge's *Science Since 1500.*

historian does not think it worth while to make any mention of him. . . . Science has undoubtedly changed the face of the world, and yet practically the only credit given to it by the historian is the Industrial Revolution . . . and even then the facts are not always accurate."

This is very sound criticism, but the scientist at once reasserts his monopoly: "No doubt the historian, having no qualifications to discuss the progress of science, feels that he had best leave it severely alone, but he can scarcely claim to trace the evolution of the modern world if he omits one of the most important factors in that evolution." Which will the author have—treatment with inevitable errors or leaving the sacred objects "severely alone"? So long as we act like watchdogs over our little plots, it is obvious that we cannot have the comprehensive views that all profess to desire. Somebody has to take the first step—and suffer for his pains.

But it would be unfair if I gave the impression that the opposition to teaching the history of science to college students was universal or came only from certain scientists. At one great university near New York there was a thriving enterprise of this sort, popular with students and science departments alike. It was given by a young man, equally gifted in the humanities and in his chosen physical science—a budding *uomo universale,* whom fellow scientists were willing to aid, guide, and correct—if need be—on the remoter details of their science. After a few years this course built up a tradition, exerted an influence, reached a kind of perfection in the fulfillment of its aim.

With the war, changes came in staff and direction; the instructor left and the opposition rallied to abolish the course. It will scarcely be believed when I say that the prime mover in this *Putsch* was a philosopher. What inspired him, the Absolute only knows. The science course did not teach any philosophy contrary to his own; it only taught the historical fact that great men of science have employed varying philosophical assumptions to gain their ends. It taught, besides, that the several sciences do not look at the world all in the same way and that so far as science has a unified point of view, it is not exclusive of others—the ways, namely, of art, philosophy, religion, and common sense. Lastly, the course imparted a fair amount of matters of fact and showed how wrong was the man who said: "You don't have to teach the history of science to make a man understand that water is H_2O." It is precisely what you have to teach, unless you are willing to barter understanding for mere voodoo formulas.

What more could any philosophy department want? Their students were lucky enough to be taught to think. Is there any other use to make of the four years of college? The world being full of a number of things, it takes practice to think easily about the chief ones. Does philosophy pretend to monopolize cogitation because Descartes said, "Don't doubt I'm thinking!"

The fact is that philosophy has suffered emotionally, like Greek and Latin, from the triumph of science. Philosophy was a minor partner in the defeat of the classics, and that has left it laboring under the same sense of wrong, the same fancied need to be haughty—and even hoity-toity. In the '80s science said: "We bring you the answers. Philosophy will gradually be pushed out as we extend our certainty." Many philosophers agreed and looked for their retirement at the first outrush of some naked Archimedes shouting "Eureka." Other philosophers, courageously holding their ground, fought as critics of science's faulty logic or extreme arrogance, just as a few classicists kept saying, "Poison gas marks a great step forward but have you taken in the meaning of Thucydides's 'Peloponnesian War'?"

The time has now come for the three-cornered duel on the campus to cease. The classics, philosophy, and science are at once overlapping and complementary disciplines. No need even to adjust boundary differences. The students are well able to take care of seeming conflicts, and in truth profit from them, since opposition reinforces attention by heightening the drama of human thought. Science must be taught, and historically, too, or the people will perish. Philosophy likewise must have a voice in all courses throwing light on the history of ideas. It will save philosophy as a subject and save the students from caddishness and provincialism. But philosophy has other obvious collegiate duties. It must read its great masterpieces with the new generation, expound ethical and metaphysical theory, help teach logic, and do liaison work with historians, scientists, and theologians. Once in a while an original philosopher will arise, unsought, in the midst of his colleagues, and the world will know him to its own profit.

The classics, too, must enter the dance. They hold the key to the meaning of our long journey from the cave to—precisely—the laboratory.

THE ANATOMY OF THE MENTAL PERSONALITY[1]

SIGMUND FREUD

LADIES AND GENTLEMEN—I am sure you all recognise in your dealings, whether with persons or things, the importance of your starting-point. It was the same with psycho-analysis: the course of development through which it has passed, and the reception which it has met with have not been unaffected by the fact that what it began working upon was the symptom, a thing which is more foreign to the ego than anything else in the mind. The symptom has its origin in the repressed, it is as it were the representative of the repressed in relation to the ego; the repressed is a foreign territory to the ego, an internal foreign territory, just as reality is—you must excuse the unusual expression—an external foreign territory. From the symptom the path of psycho-analysis led to the

1. From *New Introductory Lectures in Psycho-Analysis* by Sigmund Freud, by permission of W. W. Norton & Company, Inc. Copyright 1933 by Sigmund Freud. Translated by W. J. H. Sprott.

unconscious, to the life of the instincts, to sexuality, and it was then that psycho-analysis was met by illuminating criticisms to the effect that man is not merely a sexual being but has nobler and higher feelings. It might have been added that, supported by the consciousness of those higher feelings, he often allowed himself the right to think nonsense and to overlook facts.

You know better than that. From the very beginning our view was that men fall ill owing to the conflict between the demands of their instincts and the internal resistance which is set up against them; not for a moment did we forget this resisting, rejecting and repressing factor, which we believed to be furnished with its own special forces, the ego-instincts, and which corresponds to the ego of popular psychology. The difficulty was that, since the progress of all scientific work is necessarily laborious, psycho-analysis could not study every part of the field at once or make a pronouncement on every problem in one breath. At last we had got so far that we could turn our attention from the repressed to the repressing forces, and we came face to face with the ego, which seemed to need so little explanation, with the certain expectation that there, too, we should find things for which we could not have been prepared; but it was not easy to find a first method of approach. That is what I am going to talk to you about to-day.

Before I start, I may tell you that I have a suspicion that my account of the psychology of the ego will affect you differently than the introduction into the psychological underworld that preceded it. Why that should be the case, I cannot say for certain. My original explanation was that you would feel that, whereas hitherto I have been telling you in the main about facts, however strange and odd they might appear, this time you would be listening chiefly to theories, that is to say, speculations. But that is not quite true; when I weighed the matter more carefully I was obliged to conclude that the part played by intellectual manipulation of the facts is not much greater in our ego-psychology than it was in the psychology of the neuroses. Other explanations turned out to be equally untenable, and I now think that the character of the material itself is responsible, and the fact that we are not accustomed to dealing with it. Anyhow I shall not be surprised if you are more hesitant and careful in your judgment than you have been hitherto.

The situation in which we find ourselves at the beginning of our investigation will itself suggest the path we have to follow. We wish to make the ego the object of our study, our own ego. But how can we do that? The ego is the subject *par excellence,* how can it become the object? There is no doubt, however, that it can. The ego can take itself as object, it can treat itself like any other object, observe itself, criticise itself, and do Heaven knows what besides with itself. In such a case one part of the ego stands over against the other. The ego can, then, be split; it splits when it performs many of its functions, at least for the time being. The parts can afterwards join up again. After all that is saying nothing new; perhaps it is only underlining more than usual something that every one knows already. But on the other hand we are familiar with the view that pathology, with its magnification and exaggeration, can make us aware of normal phenomena which we should otherwise have missed. Where pathology displays a breach or a cleft, under normal conditions there may well be a link. If we throw a crystal to the ground, it breaks, but it does not break haphazard; in accordance with the lines of cleavage it falls into fragments, whose limits were already determined by the structure of the crystal, although they were invisible. Psychotics are fissured and splintered structures such as these. We cannot deny them a measure of that awe with which madmen were regarded by the peoples of ancient times. They have turned away from external reality, but for that very reason they know more of internal psychic reality and can tell us much that would otherwise be inaccessible to us. One group of them suffer what we call delusions of observation. They complain to us that they suffer continually, and in their most intimate actions, from the observation of unknown powers or persons, and they have hallucinations in which they hear these persons announcing the results of their observations: "now he is going to say this, now he is dressing himself to go out," and so on. Such observation is not the same thing as persecution, but it is not far removed from it. It implies that these persons distrust the patient, and expect to catch him doing something that is forbidden and for which he will be punished. How would it be if these mad people were right, if we all of us had an observing function in our egos threatening us with punishment, which, in their case, had merely become sharply separated from the ego and had been mistakenly projected into external reality?

I do not know whether it will appeal to you in the same way as it appeals to me. Under the strong impression of this clinical picture, I formed the idea that the separating off of an observing function from the rest of the ego might be a normal feature of the ego's structure; this idea has never left me, and I was driven to investigate the further characteristics and relations of the function which had been separated off in this way. The next step is soon taken. The actual content of the delusion of observation makes it probable that the observation is only a first step towards conviction and punishment, so that we may guess that another activity of this function must be what we call conscience. There is hardly anything that we separate off from our ego so regularly as our conscience and so easily set over against it. I feel a temptation to do something which promises to bring me pleasure, but I refrain from doing it on the ground that "my conscience will not allow it." Or I allow myself to be persuaded by the greatness of the expectation of pleasure into doing something against which the voice of my conscience has protested, and after I have done it my conscience punishes me with painful reproaches, and makes me feel remorse for it. I might simply say that the function which I am beginning to distinguish within the ego is the conscience; but it is more prudent to keep that function as a separate entity and assume that conscience is one of its activities, and that the self-observation which is necessary as a preliminary to the judicial aspect of conscience is another. And since the process of recognizing a thing as a separate entity involves giving it a name of its own, I will henceforward call this function in the ego the "super-ego."

At this point I am quite prepared for you to ask scornfully whether our ego-psychology amounts to no more than taking everyday abstractions literally, magnifying them, and turning them from concepts into things—which would not be of much assistance. My answer to that is, that in ego-psychology it will be difficult to avoid what is already familiar, and that it is more a question of arriving at new ways of looking at things and new groupings of the facts than of making new discoveries. I will not ask you, therefore, to abandon your critical attitude but merely to await further developments. The facts of pathology give our efforts a background for which you will look in vain in popular psychology. I will proceed. No sooner have we got used to the idea of this super-ego, as something which enjoys a certain independence, pursues its own ends, and is independent of the ego as regards the energy at its disposal, than we are faced with a clinical picture which throws into strong relief the severity, and even cruelty, of this function, and the vicissitudes through which its relations with the ego may pass. I refer to the condition of melancholia, or more accurately the melancholic attack, of which you must have heard often enough, even if you are not psychiatrists. In this disease, about whose causes and mechanism we know far too little, the most remarkable characteristic is the way in which the super-ego—you may call it, but in a whisper, the conscience—treats the ego. The melancholiac during periods of health can, like any one else, be more or less severe towards himself; but when he has a melancholic attack, his super-ego becomes over-severe, abuses, humiliates, and ill-treats his unfortunate ego, threatens it with the severest punishments, reproaches it for long forgotten actions which were at the time regarded quite lightly, and behaves as though it had spent the whole interval in amassing complaints and was only waiting for its present increase in strength to bring them forward, and to condemn the ego on their account. The super-ego has the ego at its mercy and applies the most severe moral standards to it; indeed it represents the whole demands of morality, and we see all at once that our moral sense of guilt is the expression of the tension between the ego and the super-ego. It is a very remarkable experience to observe morality, which was ostensibly conferred on us by God and planted deep in our hearts, functioning as a periodical phenomenon. For after a certain number of months the whole moral fuss is at an end, the critical voice of the super-ego is silent, the ego is reinstated, and enjoys once more all the rights of man until the next attack. Indeed in many forms of the malady something exactly the reverse takes place during the intervals; the ego finds itself in an ecstatic state of exaltation, it triumphs, as though the super-ego had lost all its power or had become merged with the ego, and this liberated, maniac ego gives itself up in a really uninhibited fashion, to the satisfaction of all its desires. Happenings rich in unsolved riddles!

You will expect me to do more than give a mere example in support of my statement that we have learnt a great deal about the formation of the super-ego, that is of the origin of conscience. The philosopher Kant once declared that nothing proved to him the greatness of God more convincingly than the starry heavens and the moral conscience within us. The stars are unquestionably superb, but where conscience is concerned God has been guilty of an uneven and careless piece of work, for a great many men have only a limited share of it or scarcely enough to be worth mentioning. This does not mean, however, that we are overlooking the fragment of psychological truth which is contained in the assertion that conscience is of divine origin! but the assertion needs interpretation. Conscience is no doubt something within us, but it has not been there from the beginning. In this sense it is the opposite of sexuality, which is certainly present from the very beginning of life, and is not a thing that only comes in later. But small children are notoriously a-moral. They have no internal inhibitions against their pleasure-seeking impulses. The rôle, which the super-ego undertakes later in life, is at first played by an external power, by parental authority. The influence of the parents dominates the child by granting proofs of affection and by threats of punishment, which, to the child, mean loss of love, and which must also be feared on their own account. This objective anxiety is the forerunner of the later moral anxiety; so long as the former is dominant one need not speak of super-ego or of conscience. It is only later that the secondary situation arises, which we are far too ready to regard as the normal state of affairs; the external restrictions are introjected, so that the super-ego takes the place of the parental function, and thenceforward observes, guides and threatens the ego in just the same way as the parents acted to the child before.

The super-ego, which in this way has taken over the power, the aims and even the methods of the parental function, is, however, not merely the legatee of parental authority, it is actually the heir of its body. It proceeds directly from it, and we shall soon learn in what way this comes about. First, however, we must pause to consider a point in which they differ. The super-ego seems to have made a one-sided selection, and to have chosen only the harshness and severity of the parents, their preventive and punitive functions, while their loving care is not taken up and continued by it. If the parents have really ruled with a rod of iron, we can easily understand the child developing a severe super-ego, but, contrary to our expectations, experience shows that the super-ego may reflect the same relentless harshness even when the up-bringing has been gentle and kind, and avoided threats and punishment as far as possible. We shall return to this contradiction later, when we are dealing with the transmutation of instincts in the formation of the super-ego.

I cannot tell you as much as I could wish about the change from the parental function to the super-ego, partly because that process is so complicated that a description of it does not fit into the framework of a set of introductory lectures such as these, and partly because we ourselves do not feel that we have fully understood it. You will have to be satisfied, therefore, with the following indications. The basis of the process is what we call an identification, that is to say, that one ego becomes like another, one which results in the first ego behaving itself in certain respects in the same way as the second; it imitates it, and as it were takes it into itself. This identification has been not inappropriately compared with the oral cannibalistic incorporation of another person. Identification is a very important kind of relationship with another person, probably the most primitive, and is not to be confused with object-choice. One can express the difference between them in this way: when a boy identifies himself with his father, he wants to *be like* his father; when he makes him the object of his choice, he wants to *have* him, to possess him; in the first case his ego is altered on the model of his father, in the second case that is not necessary. Identification and object-choice are broadly speaking independent of each other; but one can identify oneself with a person, and alter one's ego accordingly, and take the same person as one's sexual object. It is said that this influencing of the ego by the sexual object takes place very often with women, and is characteristic of femininity. With regard to what is by far the most instructive relation between identification and object-choice, I must have given you some information in my previous lectures. It can be as easily observed in children as in adults, in normal as in sick persons. If one has lost a love-object or has had to give it up, one often compensates oneself by identifying oneself with it; one sets it up again inside one's ego, so that in this case object-choice regresses, as it were, to identification.

I am myself not at all satisfied with this account of identification, but it will suffice if you will grant that the establishment of the super-ego can be described as a successful instance of identification with the parental function. The fact which is decisively in favour of this point of view is that this new creation of a superior function within the ego is extremely closely bound up with the fate of the Oedipus complex, so that the super-ego appears as the heir of that emotional tie, which is of such importance for childhood. When the Oedipus complex passes away the child must give up the intense object-cathexes which it has formed towards its parents, and to compensate for this loss of object, its identifications with its parents, which have probably long been present, become greatly intensified. Identifications of this kind, which may be looked on as precipitates of abandoned object-cathexes, will recur often enough in the later life of the child; but it is in keeping with the emotional importance of this first instance of such a transformation that its product should occupy a special position in the ego. Further investigation also reveals that the super-ego does not attain to full strength and development if the overcoming of the Oedipus complex has not been completely successful. During the course of its growth, the super-ego also takes over the influence of those persons who have taken the place of the parents, that is to say of persons who have been concerned in the child's upbringing, and whom it has regarded as ideal models. Normally the super-ego is constantly becoming more and more remote from the original parents, becoming, as it were, more impersonal. Another thing that we must not forget is that the child values its parents differently at different periods of its life. At the time at which the Oedipus complex makes way for the super-ego, they seem to be splendid figures, but later on they lose a good deal of their prestige. Identifications take place with these later editions of the parents as well, and regularly provide important contributions to the formation of character; but these only affect the ego, they have no influence on the super-ego, which has been determined by the earliest parental imagos.

I hope you will by now feel that in postulating the existence of a super-ego I have been describing a genuine structural entity, and have not been merely personifying an abstraction, such as conscience. We have now to mention another important activity which is to be ascribed to the super-ego. It is also the vehicle of the ego-ideal, by which the ego measures itself, towards which it strives, and whose demands for ever-increasing perfection it is always striving to fulfil. No doubt this ego-ideal is a precipitation of the old idea of the parents, an expression of the admiration which the child felt for the perfection which it at that time ascribed to them. I know you have heard a great deal about the sense of inferiority which is said to distinguish the neurotic subject. It crops up especially in the pages of works that have literary pretensions. A writer who brings in the expression "inferiority-complex" thinks he has satisfied all the demands of psycho-analysis and raised his work on to a higher psychological plane. As a matter of fact the phrase "inferiority-complex" is hardly ever used in psycho-analysis. It does not refer to anything which we regard as simple, let alone elementary. To trace it back to the perception in oneself of some organic disability or other, as the school of so-called Individual Psychologists like to do, seems to us a short-sighted error. The sense of inferiority has a strong erotic basis. The child feels itself inferior when it perceives that it is not loved, and so does the adult as well. The only organ that is really regarded as inferior is the stunted penis—the girl's clitoris. But the major part of the sense of inferiority springs from the relationship of the ego to its super-ego, and, like the sense of guilt, it is an expression of the tension between them. The sense of inferiority and the sense of guilt are exceedingly difficult to distinguish. Perhaps we should do better if we regarded the former as the erotic complement to the sense of moral inferiority. We have paid but little attention to such questions of conceptual differentiation in psycho-analysis.

Seeing that the inferiority-complex has become so popular, I shall venture to treat you to a short digression. A historical personage of our own time, who is still living but who for the present has retired into the background, suffers from the mal-development of a limb caused by an injury at birth. A very well-known contemporary writer who has a predilection for writing the biographies of famous persons, has dealt with the life of the man to whom I am referring. Now if one is writing a biography, it is naturally very difficult to suppress the urge for psychological understanding. The author has therefore made an attempt to build up the whole development of his hero's character on the basis of a sense of inferiority, which was caused by his physical defect. While doing this he has overlooked a small but not unimportant fact. It is usual for mothers to whom fate has given a sickly or otherwise defective child to try to compensate for this unfair handicap with an extra amount of love. In the case we are speaking of, the proud mother behaved quite differently; she withdrew her love from the child on account of his disability. When the child grew up into a man of great power, he proved beyond all doubt by his behaviour that he had never forgiven his mother. If you will bear in mind the importance of mother-love for the mental life of the child, you will be able to make the necessary corrections in the inferiority-theory of the biographer.

But let us get back to the super-ego. We have allocated to it the activities of self-observation, conscience, and the holding up of ideals. It follows from our account of its origin that it is based upon an overwhelmingly important biological fact no less than upon a momentous psychological fact, namely the lengthy dependence of the human child on its parents and the Oedipus complex; these two facts, moreover, are closely bound up with each other. For us the suger-ego is the representative of all moral restrictions, the advocate of the impulse towards perfection, in short it is as much as we have been able to apprehend psychologically of what people call the "higher" things in human life. Since it itself can be traced back to the influence of parents, teachers, and so on, we shall learn more of its significance if we turn our attention to these sources. In general, parents and similar authorities follow the dictates of their own super-egos in the up-bringing of children. Whatever terms their ego may be on with their super-ego, in the education of the child they are severe and exacting. They have forgotten the difficulties of their own childhood, and are glad to be able to identify themselves fully at last with their own parents, who in their day subjected them to such severe restraints. The result is that the super-ego of the child is not really built up on the model of the parents, but on that of the parents' super-ego; it takes over the same content, it becomes the vehicle of tradition and of all the age-long values which have been handed down in this way from generation to generation. You may easily guess what great help is afforded by the recognition of the super-ego in understanding the social behaviour of man, in grasping the problem of delinquency, for example, and perhaps, too, in providing us with some practical hints upon education. It is probable that the so-called materialistic conceptions of history err in that they underestimate this factor. They brush it aside with the remark that the "ideologies" of mankind are nothing more than resultants of their economic situation at any given moment or superstructures built upon it. That is the truth, but very probably it is not the whole truth. Mankind never lives completely in the present; the ideologies of the super-ego perpetuate the past, the traditions of the race and the people, which yield but slowly to the influence of the present and to new developments, and, so long as they work through the super-ego, play an important part in man's life, quite independently of economic conditions.

In 1921 I tried to apply the distinction between the ego and the super-ego to the study of group psychology. I reached a formula, which ran like this: A psychological group is a collection of individuals, who have introduced the same person into their super-ego, and on the basis of this common factor have identified themselves with one another in their ego. This naturally only holds for groups who have a leader. If we could find more applications of this kind, the hypothesis of the super-ego would lose all its strangeness for us, and we should be entirely relieved of the embarrassment which we cannot help feeling when, used as we are to the atmosphere of the underworld, we make excursions into the more superficial and higher planes of the mental apparatus. Of course we do not for a moment think that the last word on ego-psychology has been spoken with the demarcation of the super-ego. It is rather the beginning of the subject, but in this case it is not only the first step that is difficult.

But now another task awaits us, as it were at the opposite end of the ego. This question is raised by an observation which is made during analytic work, an observation which is, indeed, an old one. As so often happens, it has taken a long time for its true value to be appreciated. As you are aware, the whole of psycho-analytic theory is in fact built up on the perception of the resistance exerted by the patient when we try to make him conscious of his unconscious. The objective indication of resistance is that his associations stop short or wander far away from the theme that is being discussed. He may also become subjectively aware of the resistance by experiencing painful feelings when he approaches the theme. But this last indication may be absent. In such a case we say to the patient that we conclude from his behaviour that he is in a state of resistance, and he replies that he knows nothing about it and is only aware of a difficulty in associating. Experience shows that we were right, but, if so, his resistance too must have been unconscious, just as unconscious as the repressed material which we were trying to bring to the surface. Long ago we should have asked from which part of the mind such an unconscious resistance could operate. The beginner in psycho-analysis will be ready at once with the answer that it must be the resistance of the unconscious. An ambiguous and useless answer! If it means that the resistance operates from the repressed, then we must say: "Certainly not!" To the repressed we must rather ascribe a strong upward-driving force, an impulsion to get through to consciousness. The resistance can only be a manifestation of the ego, which carried through the repression at one time or other and is now endeavouring to keep it up. And that too was our earlier view. Now that we have posited a special function within the ego to represent the demand for restriction and rejection, *i.e.* the super-ego, we can say that repression is the work of the super-ego,—either that it does its work on its own account or else that the ego does it in obedience to its orders. If now we are faced with the case where the patient under analysis is not conscious of his resistance, then it must be either that the super-ego and the ego can operate unconsciously in quite important situations, or, which would be far more significant, that parts of both ego and super-ego themselves are unconscious. In both cases we should have to take account of the disturbing view that the ego (including the super-ego) does not by any means completely coincide with the conscious, nor the repressed with the unconscious.

Ladies and Gentlemen—I feel I must have a little breathing space, which I expect you will welcome with relief, and before I go on I must make an apology. Here am I giving you a supplement to the introduction to psycho-analysis which I started fifteen years ago, and I am behaving as though you yourselves had been doing nothing but psycho-analysis all that time. I know it is a monstrous supposition, but I am helpless, I have no alternative. The reason is that it is exceedingly difficult to give an insight into psycho-analysis to any one who is not himself a psycho-analyst. I assure you that we do not like to give the effect of being members of a secret society carrying on a secret science. And yet we have been obliged to recognise and state as our considered opinion that no one has a right to a say in psycho-analysis unless he has been through certain experiences which he can only have by being analysed himself. When I delivered my lectures to you fifteen years ago I tried to let you off certain speculative parts of our theory, but it is with those very parts that are connected the new discoveries which I am going to speak of to-day.

Now let me return to my theme. With regard to the two alternatives—that the ego and the super-ego may themselves be unconscious, or that they may merely give rise to unconscious effects—we have for good reasons decided in favour of the former. Certainly, large portions of the ego and super-ego can remain unconscious, are, in fact, normally unconscious. That means to say that the individual knows nothing of their contents and that it requires an expenditure of effort to make him conscious of them. It is true, then, that ego and conscious, repressed and unconscious do not coincide. We are forced fundamentally to revise our attitude towards the problem of conscious and unconscious. At first we might be inclined to think very much less of the importance of consciousness as a criterion, since it has proved so untrustworthy. But if we did so, we should be wrong. It is the same with life: it is not worth much, but it is all that we have. Without the light shed by the quality of consciousness we should be lost in the darkness of depth-psychology. Nevertheless we must try to orientate ourselves anew.

What is meant by "conscious," we need not discuss; it is beyond all doubt. The oldest and best meaning of the word "unconscious" is the descriptive one; we call "unconscious" any mental process the existence of which we are obliged to assume—because, for instance, we infer it in some way from its effects—but of which we are not directly aware. We have the same relation to that mental process as we have to a mental process in another person, except that it belongs to ourselves. If we want to be more accurate, we should modify the statement by saying that we call a process "unconscious" when we have to assume that it was active *at a certain time,* although *at that time* we knew nothing about it. This restriction reminds us that most conscious processes are conscious only for a short period; quite soon they become *latent,* though they can easily become conscious again. We could also say that they had become unconscious, if we were certain that they were still something mental when they were in the latent condition. So far we should have learnt nothing, and not even have earned the right to introduce the notion of the unconscious into psychology. But now we come across a new fact which we can already observe in the case of errors. We find that, in order to explain a slip of the tongue, for instance, we are obliged to assume that an intention to say some particular thing had formed itself in the mind of the person who made the slip. We can infer it with certainty from the occurrence of the speech-disturbance, but it was not able to obtain expression; it was, that is to say, unconscious. If we subsequently bring the intention to the speaker's notice, he may recognise it as a familiar one, in which case it was only temporarily unconscious, or he may repudiate it as foreign to him, in which case it was permanently unconscious. Such an observation as this justifies us in also regarding what we have called "latent" as something "unconscious." The consideration of these dynamic relations puts us in a position to distinguish two kinds of unconscious: one which is transformed into conscious material easily and under conditions which frequently arise, and another in the case of which such a transformation is difficult, can only come about with a considerable expenditure of energy, or may never occur at all. In order to avoid any ambiguity as to whether we are referring to the one or the other unconscious, whether we are using the word in the descriptive or dynamic sense, we make use of a legitimate and simple expedient. We call the unconscious which is only latent, and so can easily become conscious, the "preconscious," and keep the name "unconscious" for the other. We have now three terms, "conscious," "preconscious," and "unconscious," to serve our purposes in describing mental phenomena. Once again, from a purely descriptive point of view, the "preconscious" is also unconscious, but we do not give it that name, except when we are speaking loosely, or when we have to defend in general the existence of unconscious processes in mental life.

You will, I hope, grant that so far things are not so bad and that the scheme is a convenient one. That is all very well; unfortunately our psycho-analytic work has compelled us to use the word "unconscious" in yet another, third, sense; and this may very well have given rise to confusion. Psycho-analysis has impressed us very strongly with the new idea that large and important regions of the mind are normally removed from the knowledge of the ego, so that the processes which occur in them must be recognized as unconscious in the true dynamic sense of the term. We have consequently also attributed to the word "unconscious" a topographical or systematic meaning; we have talked of *systems* of the preconscious and of the unconscious, and of a conflict between the ego and the Ucs. system; so that the word "unconscious" has more and more been made to mean a mental province rather than a quality which mental things have. At this point, the discovery, inconvenient at first sight, that parts of the ego and super-ego, too, are unconscious in the dynamic sense, has a facilitating effect and enables us to remove a complication. We evidently have no right to call that region of the mind which is neither ego nor super-ego the Ucs. system, since the character of unconsciousness is not exclusive to it. Very well; we will no longer use the word "unconscious" in the sense of a system, and to what we have hitherto called by that name we will give a better one, which will not give rise to misunderstandings. Borrowing, at G. Groddeck's suggestion, a term used by Nietzsche, we will call it henceforward the "id." This impersonal pronoun seems particularly suited to express the essential character of this province of the mind—the character of being foreign to the ego. Super-ego, ego and id, then, are the three realms, regions or provinces into which we divide the mental apparatus of the individual; and it is their mutual relations with which we shall be concerned in what follows.

But before we go on I must make a short digression. I have no doubt that you are dissatisfied with the fact that the three qualities of the mind in respect to consciousness and the three regions of the mental apparatus do not fall together into three harmonious pairs, and that you feel that the clarity of our conclusions is consequently impaired. My own view is that we ought not to deplore this fact but that we should say to ourselves that we had no right to expect any such neat arrangement. Let me give you an analogy; analogies prove nothing, that is quite true, but they can make one feel more at home. Let us picture a country with a great variety of geographical configurations, hills, plains and chains of lakes, and with mixed nationalities living in it, Germans, Magyars and Slovaks, who, moreover, are engaged upon a number of different occupations. Now the distribution might be such that the Germans lived in the hills and kept cattle, the Magyars on the plains and grew corn and vines, while the Slovaks lived by the lakes and caught fish and plaited reeds. If this distribution were neat and exact it would no doubt give great satisfaction to a President Wilson; it would also be convenient for giving a geography lesson. It is probable, however, that you would find a less orderly state of affairs if you visited the region. Germans, Magyars and Slovaks would be living everywhere mixed up together, and there would be cornfields too in the hills, and cattle would be kept on the plains as well. One or two things would be as you expected, for one cannot catch fish on the mountains, and wine does not grow in water. The picture of the region which you had brought with you might on the whole fit the facts, but in details you would have to put up with departures from it.

You must not expect me to tell you much that is new about the id, except its name. It is the obscure inaccessible part of our personality; the little we know about it we have learnt from the study of dream-work and the formation of neurotic symptoms, and most of that is of a negative character, and can only be described as being all that the ego is not. We can come nearer to the id with images, and call it a chaos, a cauldron of seething excitement. We suppose that it is somewhere in direct contact with somatic processes, and takes over from them instinctual needs and gives them mental expression, but we cannot say in what substratum this contact is made. These instincts fill it with energy, but it has no organisation and no unified will, only an impulsion to obtain satisfaction for the instinctual needs, in accordance with the pleasure-principle. The laws of logic—above all, the law of contradiction—do not hold for processes in the id. Contradictory impulses exist side by side without neutralising each other or drawing apart; at most they combine in compromise formations under the overpowering economic pressure towards discharging their energy. There is nothing in the id which can be compared to negation, and we are astonished to find in it an exception to the philosophers' assertion that space and time are necessary forms of our mental acts. In the id there is nothing corresponding to the idea of time, no recognition of the passage of time, and (a thing which is very remarkable and awaits adequate attention in philosophic thought) no alteration of mental processes by the passage of time. Conative impulses which have never got beyond the id, and even impressions which have been pushed down into the id by repression, are virtually immortal and are preserved for whole decades as though they had only recently occurred. They can only be recognised as belonging to the past, deprived of their significance, and robbed of their charge of energy, after they have been made conscious by the work of analysis, and no small part of the therapeutic effect of analytic treatment rests upon this fact.

It is constantly being borne in upon me that we have made far too little use of our theory of the indubitable fact that the repressed remains unaltered by the passage of time. This seems to offer us the possibility of an approach to some really profound truths. But I myself have made no further progress here.

Naturally, the id knows no values, no good and evil, no morality. The economic, or, if you prefer, the quantitative factor, which is so closely bound up with the pleasure-principle, dominates all its processes. Instinctual cathexes seeking discharge,—that, in our view, is all that the id contains. It seems, indeed, as if the energy of these instinctual impulses is in a different condition from that in which it is found in the other regions of the mind. It must be far more fluid and more capable of being discharged, for otherwise we should not have those displacements and condensations, which are so characteristic of the id and which are so completely independent of the qualities of what is cathected. (In the ego we should call it an idea.) What would one not give to understand these things better? You observe, in any case, that we can attribute to the id other characteristics than that of being unconscious, and you are aware of the possibility that parts of the ego and super-ego are unconscious without possessing the same primitive and irrational quality. As regards a characterisation of the ego, in so far as it is to be distinguished from the id and the super-ego, we shall get on better if we turn our attention to the relation between it and the most superficial portion of the mental apparatus; which we call the Pcpt-cs (perceptual-conscious) system. This system is directed on to the external world, it mediates perceptions of it, and in it is generated, while it is functioning, the phenomenon of consciousness. It is the sense-organ of the whole apparatus, receptive, moreover, not only of excitations from without but also of such as proceed from the interior of the mind. One can hardly go wrong in regarding the ego as that part of the id which has been modified by its proximity to the external world and the influence that the latter has had on it, and which serves the purpose of receiving stimuli and protecting the organism from them, like the cortical layer with which a particle of living substance surrounds itself. This relation to the external world is decisive for the ego. The ego has taken over the task of representing the external world for the id, and so of saving it; for the id, blindly striving to gratify its instincts in complete disregard of the superior strength of outside forces, could not otherwise escape annihilation. In the fulfilment of this function, the ego has to observe the external world and preserve a true picture of it in the memory traces left by its perceptions, and, by means of the reality-test, it has to eliminate any element in this picture of the external world which is a contribution from internal sources of excitation. On behalf of the id, the ego controls the path of access to motility, but it interpolates between desire and action the procrastinating factor of thought, during which it makes use of the residues of experience stored up in memory. In this way it dethrones the pleasure-principle, which exerts undisputed sway over the processes in the id, and substitutes for it the reality-principle, which promises greater security and greater success.

The relation to time, too, which is so hard to describe, is communicated to the ego by the perceptual system; indeed it can hardly be doubted that the mode in which this system works is the source of the idea of time. What, however, especially marks the ego out in contradistinction to the id, is a tendency to synthesise its contents, to bring together and unify its mental processes which is entirely absent from the id. When we come to deal presently with the instincts in mental life, I hope we shall succeed in tracing this fundamental characteristic of the ego to its source. It is this alone that produces that high degree of organisation which the ego needs for its highest achievements. The ego advances from the function of perceiving instincts to that of controlling them, but the latter is only achieved through the mental representative of the instinct becoming subordinated to a larger organisation, and finding its place in a coherent unity. In popular language, we may say that the ego stands for reason and circumspection, while the id stands for the untamed passions.

So far we have allowed ourselves to dwell on the enumeration of the merits and capabilities of the ego; it is time now to look at the other side of the picture. The ego is after all only a part of the id, a part purposively modified by its proximity to the dangers of reality. From a dynamic point of view it is weak; it borrows its energy from the id, and we are not entirely ignorant of the methods—one might almost call them "tricks"—by means of which it draws further amounts of energy from the id. Such a method, for example, is the process of identification, whether the object is retained or given up. The object-cathexes proceed from the instinctual demands of the id. The first business of the ego is to take note of them. But by identifying itself with the object, it recommends itself to the id in the place of the object and seeks to attract the libido of the id on to itself. We have already seen that, in the course of a person's life, the ego takes into itself a large number of such precipitates of former object-cathexes. On the whole the ego has to carry out the intentions of the id; it fulfils its duty if it succeeds in creating the conditions under which these intentions can best be fulfilled. One might compare the relation of the ego to the id with that between a rider and his horse. The horse provides the locomotive energy, and the rider has the prerogative of determining the goal and of guiding the movements of his powerful mount towards it. But all too often in the relations between the ego and the id we find a picture of the less ideal situation in which the rider is obliged to guide his horse in the direction in which it itself wants to go.

The ego has separated itself off from one part of the id by means of repression-resistances. But the barrier of repression does not extend into the id; so that the repressed material merges into the rest of the id.

The proverb tells us that one cannot serve two masters at once. The poor ego has a still harder time of it; it has to serve three harsh masters, and has to do its best to reconcile the claims and demands of all three. These demands are always divergent and often seem quite incompatible; no wonder that the ego so frequently gives way under its task. The three tyrants are the external world, the super-ego and the id. When one watches the efforts of the ego to satisfy them all, or rather, to obey them all simultaneously, one cannot regret having personified the ego, and established it as a separate being. It feels itself hemmed in on three sides and threatened by three kinds of danger, towards which it reacts by developing anxiety when it is too hard pressed. Having originated in the experiences of the perceptual system, it is designed to represent the demands of the external world, but it also wishes to be a loyal servant of the id, to remain upon good terms with the id, to recommend itself to the id as an object, and to draw the id's libido on to itself. In its attempt to mediate between the id and reality, it is often forced to clothe the Ucs. commands of the id with its own Pcs. rationalisations, to gloss over the conflicts between the id and reality, and with diplomatic dishonesty to display a pretended regard for reality, even when the id persists in being stubborn and uncompromising. On the other hand, its every movement is watched by the severe super-ego, which holds up certain norms of behaviour, without regard to any difficulties coming from the id and the external world; and if these norms are not acted up to, it punishes the ego with the feelings of tension which manifest themselves as a sense of inferiority and guilt. In this way, goaded on by the id, hemmed in by the super-ego, and rebuffed by reality, the ego struggles to cope with its economic task of reducing the forces and influences which work in it and upon it to some kind of harmony; and we may well understand how it is that we so often cannot repress the cry: "Life is not easy." When the ego is forced to acknowledge its weakness, it breaks out into anxiety: reality anxiety in face of the external world, normal anxiety in face of the super-ego, and neurotic anxiety in the face of the strength of the passions in the id.

I have represented the structural relations within the mental personality, as I have explained them to you, in a simple diagram, which I here reproduce.

You will observe how the super-ego goes down into the id; as the heir to the Oedipus complex it has, after all, intimate connections with the id. It lies further from the perceptual system than the ego. The id only deals with the external world through the medium of the ego, at least in this diagram. It is certainly still too early to say how far the drawing is correct; in one respect I know it is not. The space taken up by the unconscious id ought to be incomparably greater than that given to the ego or to the preconscious. You must, if you please, correct that in your imagination.

And now, in concluding this certainly rather exhausting and perhaps not very illuminating account, I must add a warning. When you think of this dividing up of the personality into ego, super-ego and id, you must not imagine sharp dividing lines such as are artificially drawn in the field of political geography. We cannot do justice to the characteristics of the mind by means

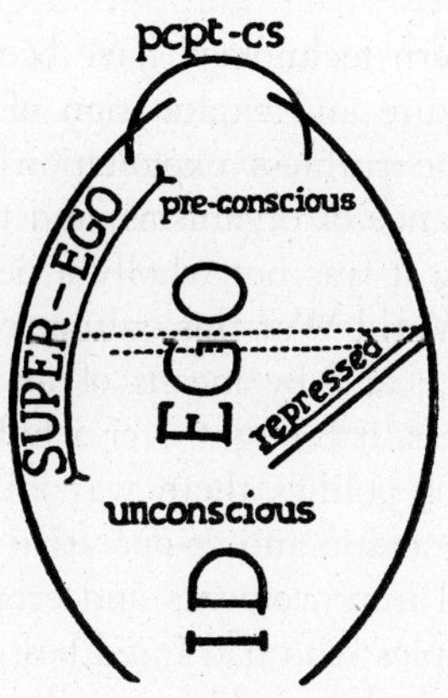

of linear contours, such as occur in a drawing or in a primitive painting, but we need rather the areas of colour shading off into one another that are to be found in modern pictures. After we have made our separations, we must allow what we have separated to merge again. Do not judge too harshly of a first attempt at picturing a thing so elusive as the human mind. It is very probable that the extent of these differentiations varies very greatly from person to person; it is possible that their function itself may vary, and that they may at times undergo a process of involution. This seems to be particularly true of the most insecure and, from the phylogenetic point of view, the most recent of them, the differentiation between the ego and the super-ego. It is also incontestable that the same thing can come about as a result of mental disease. It can easily be imagined, too, that certain practices of mystics may succeed in upsetting the normal relations between the different regions of the mind, so that, for example, the perceptual system becomes able to grasp relations in the deeper layers of the ego and in the id which would otherwise be inaccessible to it. Whether such a procedure can put one in possession of ultimate truths, from which all good will flow, may be safely doubted. All the same, we must admit that the therapeutic efforts of psycho-analysis have chosen much the same method of approach. For their object is to strengthen the ego, to make it more independent of the super-ego, to widen its field of vision, and so to extend its organisation that it can take over new portions of the id. Where id was, there shall ego be.

It is reclamation work, like the draining of the Zuyder Zee.

LOOKING FORWARD[1]

LEWIS MUMFORD

The achievements of modern technology have been part of a culture whose central theme was the seizure and exploitation of power. But although the quest for power led to the ruthless exploitation of natural resources, the breakup of the natural balance of organisms, and the extermination of many valuable cultural traditions, it was not wholly a negative and destructive impulse. For up to the first World War this culture embraced people who lived in every part of the planet; and by means of an increasing interchange of trade, investments, and ideas, it brought over a billion people into a working partnership. In the field of politics there was a steady diffusion of power, through the spread of democratic and co-operative methods of control.

Unfortunately, technical improvements and economic facilities outran the moral capacities of the peoples who had fared best under this culture, and in particular of their governing classes. The very illusion of moral progress that was fostered by the prevailing optimistic philosophy of the nineteenth century tended to conceal the vast hiatus between technological and social achievements.

The underlying axiom of this power culture was that the increased use of non-human sources of energy, and the increase of wealth through the mechanization of the means of production, must automatically increase the possibilities of human well-being. This axiom, as Mr. Arnold Toynbee has amply

1. From *Science and Man* edited by Ruth Nanda Anshen, copyright, 1942, by Harcourt, Brace and Company, Inc.

shown in his *Study of History*, has no factual basis. Though there is a close relation between technics and every other aspect of human culture, material abundance often goes hand in hand with social decay.

As a corollary to this prime assumption about the desirability of material expansion went the notion that the increase of "power and wealth" had no limits, because human desires were boundless and insatiable. This corollary was as baseless as the axiom itself: it was merely an illusion which assumed as given the very fact that remained to be established, the notion that human satisfaction increased in proportion to the number of human desires and to society's capability of satisfying them. That vulgar notion has been responsible for a great deal of human misery. For the experience of the race has abundantly shown that moderation and restriction are essential to human well-being in every aspect of man's existence. This is true on the physiological level, since three dinners at a time are not three times as satisfactory as one; and it is true on the moral level, where the moderation and equilibration of desire have proved organically satisfactory, whereas its inordinate expression, or inordinate contraction, leads to conditions of social and personal maladjustment.

When Lord Acton said, "All power corrupts and absolute power corrupts absolutely," he was referring mainly to political power. But what he said likewise applies to power in all its manifestations. The more energy that man commands the more important it is that this energy should be at the service of his whole personality and his whole culture, and not merely at the command of some narrow ambition or some limited goal. Now the fact is that science and technology, for the last three hundred years, have been at the service of narrow, and often, one must add, quite primitive notions of human development and human well-being. They have given power to the military and political and financial despots: they have fed their egos and justified their ambitions; they have further brutalized the brutal and corrupted the corrupt. As a result they have made mankind the victim of the machine rather than its benign commander and controller. Although many high and humane achievements remain, the animus of this civilization has been a predatory one.

The familiar doctrines of technological materialism are without a sound sociological or psychological basis; and that by itself would be enough to condemn them from a human standpoint. But there is still another way in which their insufficiency may be demonstrated; and this is by reference to the facts of historic development. Technological materialism itself represents a passing phase of human history. The great age of expansion which it fostered is now coming to an end; the conditions that turned men's attention exclusively to the conquest and exploitation of the material environment have been subverted by the very success of Western man's enterprise and invention. We are now probably living through the last great crisis in this power civilization. This crisis will either ruin Western Society entirely—and with it the very advanced technics of science and invention—or it will permit this culture to establish itself on a much broader human basis. In the second instance, the process of materialization, by which one may characterize our culture during the last three centuries, will give way to a process of "etherealization" to use a term coined by Toynbee: quantitative interests will become secondary to qualitative interests; and the great advances that were once made in the physical sciences almost exclusively will now be paralleled by progress in the domain of sociology and personology—sciences which themselves will no longer be dominated by the categories and methods of the physical sciences.

This change within the domain of thought is the counterpart of a wider social process; as it is, no less, one of the means by which further social developments will be guided and applied. If we are to understand both its significance and its necessity, we must understand first of all how completely our technological achievements in the past have been conditioned by the historic movement of expansion: the land expansion of the conquistador and pioneer, the mechanical expansion of the inventor, the industrialist, and the financier, and finally, the population expansion which was the source of the vital energy of Europe during the nineteenth century.

The first thing to note about modern technics is that it is associated with the period of land expansion in the Western world, which began in the fifteenth century, when Europe had reached the limits of its own frontiers. This period of discovery was accompanied by a steady pushing back of the physical horizons; and it was marked by the quick spread of the European from his original habitat to the remotest shores of Asia, Africa, and America. Here was an attempt to break away from the bounded and walled horizons of the medieval city; an attempt to treat the whole world as the habitat of Western man and as the object of his curiosity as well as of his cupidity.

This world-wide immigration and colonization was itself the complex product of economic interests, seeking to widen the area of trade, of a missionary impulse to spread Christian doctrine, which grew up again with the new preaching orders, and of new technical instruments for commanding space and time. The compass, the three-masted sailing ship, the sailing chart, the accurate ship's chronometer—the latter not invented till the eighteenth century—made possible the era of exploration and colonization. It would be impossible to exaggerate the effect of the new spatial horizons upon men's minds. Samuel Morse's impulse to invent the electric telegraph dates from the moment when the lonely young American painter, in London, felt the gap between himself and his family, filled only by letters, to be an unbearably long one.

But the technical results of exploration and colonization were not one-sided ones. Though the Western European, by the nineteenth century, had distributed his firearms and his friction matches, his iron hardware and his missionary pocket-handkerchiefs all over the map, he rapidly acquired, from the primitive peoples he conquered by his "superior" civilization, a greater abundance of resources and technical methods, which could be utilized by his advancing industry, than had been diffused by slower processes during the previous few milleniums. This account has never been accurately reckoned up, as far as I know: perhaps because its results would diminish Western man's self-satisfaction and conceit.

If, however, one goes no farther back than the fifteenth century and takes nothing more away than printing from movable types from Korea, cotton fabrication from India, porcelain manufacture from China, rubber culture from the Amazons, and the new food crops that came from the Americas, the effect would be to bring the whole Western world to a literal standstill and to the verge of outright starvation. At all events, it is extremely doubtful whether anything that could be compared with modern technics could have resulted by the twentieth century out of Western man's unaided imagination. The mechanical conquest of the planet, by means of the sailing vessel, the steamship, the railroad, the cable, the telegraph, the radio—and above all, perhaps, by gunpowder—was a means by which the technological contributions of hitherto isolated cultures were enabled to influence the whole Western world. This happened at a moment when Western man's interests were becoming almost exclusively technological and materialistic; and it therefore had an overwhelming effect.

Now, this period of land expansion has finally come to an end. What was true of the United States around 1890, as Frederick Jackson Turner pointed out, became true of the whole planet during the fifty years that followed: Siberia, Manchuria, and a few scattered outposts around the rest of the globe were the last regions to undergo the invasion and exploitation of modern man. The period of one-sided conquest now has come to its own natural terminus: the process of surface exploitation, of wholesale migration and colonization, with its careless wastage of capital resources and its greed for quick return belongs to the past.

We are now entering a period of settlement or rather of resettlement; and this involves the attempt to find a stable basis for living in the environments that have proved most favorable to human life. There are vast damages to be repaired: deforested areas to be restored to woodland, eroded soils to be built up, more organic patterns of living that are to be reinstated; and if science and technics are to benefit by the stimulus of other cultures, there must be a world-wide give-and-take, as between equals. Political skill must keep open the world-wide channels of intercourse and interco-operation, once established crudely at the point of a gun for the benefit of the Western exploiters.

But at this point it becomes obvious that the conditions for further technical advance, through the stimulus of other cultures and ways of life, rest not upon technicians and scientists, but upon political actions that lie far outside their immediate sphere of control. Once, the political instruments of cultural intercourse could be taken for granted: foreign scientists and explorers traveled freely in the remotest parts of the world, even without passports; unless they aroused purely local animosity they could come and go in safety and freedom.

For the last twenty-five years the common vehicles of such intercourse have been one by one disappearing. The totalitarian states are even in times of peace closed regimes: the democratic states themselves have shared this vice in some degree, as compared with the open world which existed generally before 1914.

The danger should be plain. If each great state or empire becomes a rigid, self-contained unit, immune to outside influences and foreign ideas, the social basis for technological advance, which historically involves world-wide intercourse at all levels, will have disappeared. Doctrines of political and cultural isolationism—which are sometimes heretically preached even by men of science—are based upon historic ignorance as to the actual foundations of our present culture.

Now, world travel and intercourse rest ultimately on world trade. It is the passage of surpluses and specialties across frontiers that makes available the means of exchange that enables other people, besides the merchants involved, to travel freely and exchange their intellectual products. Where no such medium is available, the investigator who wishes to become familiar with foreign thought or technics must either imitate Alexander, and come with an army, or he must follow Plato's reputed example when he went to Egypt and covered his expenses by taking with him a cargo of oil which he sold to the Egyptians. Otherwise only beggars can be travelers. Already there are states in existence where Plato's method would be impossible, even if he were not denied a visa or stopped at the frontier because he was not a believer in "Aryan" anthropology or in "Marxian" genetics.

If the closed totalitarian states should remain in existence for as much as another generation, the international structure of scientific thought would probably collapse. For even before the present war passed into its active phase, the tactics of the Russian, German, and Italian governments had made the procedures of so-called International Congresses almost a farce, for they were either used as a vehicle for fascist propaganda or decimated of some of their most valued contributors by these totalitarian governments.

To mark the change that has taken place here one need only compare the treatment accorded to the Belgian historian, Henri Pirenne, during the World War with that accorded to representative scientists and scholars in the totalitarian states during the last ten years. When Pirenne was taken in custody by the German government, after the occupation of Belgium, that fact was quickly known to the rest of the world; and the expression of outrage was universal. Danish and Dutch scholars dared to denounce it, no less than Americans. As the result of a world-wide protest, headed by President Wilson and the Pope, he was taken out of a prison camp and sequestered in a quiet German village, with no other duty than that of reporting to the Mayor once a day. That was in war time. Outrages a thousand times worse have been committed by the totalitarian governments against world-respected scientists, sometimes without the news coming out, frequently without arousing a single organized protest, always without world opinion being able to effect the slightest improvement in their position.

The problems raised by the termination of the period of land expansion have not yet been widely grasped; for uncontrolled colonization, immigration, trade—all the methods whereby the exploited resources were put ultimately at the disposal of a world community—have now to be replaced by a rational world organization empowered to redistribute the resources and to widen the economic and political basis of international cooperation. The need of the new age is to create balanced regional communities, which will be capable of operating within a world-wide framework: no longer sealed behind the military frontiers of the bellicose state. *Every movement toward regional or self-sufficiency is a betrayal of the positive achievements of the age of conquest, unless it is accompanied by an equal movement toward planetary organization.* Similarly every attempt to resume the age of conquest, on the Nazi pattern, by re-introducing the principle of dominance and by restoring inequalities and slaveries, goes deeply against the grain of civilized effort. This last movement is not the wave of the future but the treacherous undertow of the past.

Extensive exploration and conquest must now yield to intensive cultivation and regional development; not for the purpose of achieving an illusory self-sufficiency but for the purpose of making the fullest contribution ultimately to the life of mankind.

One could trace a similar movement toward stabilization and balance within the domain of the machine itself, as a result of the purely mechanical and economic factors that are in operation. In *Technics and Civilization* (1934) I called attention to some of these factors. But here I prefer to dwell on another development; or rather, on two current changes that must have a bearing on the future of technics and science. The first is the increasing importance of the biological and social sciences. Before 1850 it would be hard to point to a single important invention that rested directly upon a knowledge of the structure and function of organisms; but during the last two generations some of the most critical advances have come about through the direct application of the biological sciences. The telephone grew out of an interest in the mechanism of human voice production, and the telephone receiver was modeled directly upon the structure of the human ear; experiments with heavier than air flying machines resulted directly from Pettigrew's and Marey's study of the locomotion of animals.

Meanwhile, the application of biological knowledge to the raising of food and to the planning of the human diet has effectively altered the whole problem of man's health and his survival: genetics and the new discoveries on the physiology of nutrition have done far more to assure mankind of an adequate food supply than all the gangplows and automatic reapers and binders that the nineteenth century boasted. We are now aware of many processes where chemical, biological, or social science will enable us to provide alternatives for the purely mechanical solutions that were chiefly available during the paleotechnical period. Most of these applications of biology are still in an early stage.

Let me give a simple illustration. By the use of costly apparatus and machinery it is possible to build a house without windows, in which the air shall be filtered, warmed or cooled, and circulated, and in which sun-lamps, applied at intervals, will make up for the need for natural sunlight: such a house will work almost as well in a crowded slum as anywhere else. Unfortunately, such an "advanced" technical form is compatible with hideous social disorder and economic waste—just as mechanical advances in war are, as in Germany, compatible with political barbarism. But with the full employment of other arts and sciences, such a house is actually a monstrosity. By utilizing current knowledge of meteorology, a house can be oriented and designed so that it utilizes to the full all available sunshine; by utilizing the political art of town-planning, the house can be assured permanent open spaces, pure air, freedom from noxious gases or effluvia without any provision of special machinery; by saving on the cost of mechanical equipment interior space and exterior gardens can be provided whose utilization and pleasure will help keep the occupants in health and psychological balance. In short, by employing all the knowledge at his command, the architect and planner of a modern community can reduce the expenditure on mechanical utilities, and create a far more effective human environment.

This simple example has a much wider bearing. The progress of the biological and social sciences will result in a shrinking of the province of the machine. Here, I believe, is a fact of deep significance: its implications have still to be grasped.

The coming utilization of social and political skills rests upon another condition, which held true even before the development of modern science; and that is, there is some relation between the degree of personal culture that prevails in a community and the quantity of physical goods it desires and commands. One can put this in a crude and comic form by saying that if all men were honest there would be no need for locksmiths and safes: if all men were co-operative there would be no need for handcuffs. In such simple relations it is easy to see that the achievement of a higher degree of moral culture would not result in a new form of machine: it would result in the elimination of a particular mechanical contraption.

What does this mean in the broader picture? It means that an effective transfer of interest to the realm of ethics and esthetics will result in a diminished demand for the machine and its products. If the use of speedy motor cars is the chief means of utilizing leisure, it is obvious that the output of motor cars, highroads, steel and concrete, and all the accessory supplies and services will increase: but if other means of utilizing leisure become popular, if more people paint and write and model and carpenter and garden, if more people study the stars or observe the behavior of children or become outdoor naturalists, there will be a lessened demand for swift agents of locomotion purely for the purposes of recreation. A transference of interest from the mechanical to the organic and human may be properly regarded either as a labor-saving device or as a brake upon production. At all events it introduces a new factor not embraced by the crude doctrine of "increasing wants." Such a change is one of the real possibilities that follows from a better scientific knowledge of the human personality.

Plainly, the process of etherealization has always been possible. There is plenty of historic evidence to show that it actually took place in Roman civilization, from the first century B.C. onwards, and that it contributed quite as much as the invasion of the barbarians to overthrow that society. Perhaps the chief problem of our society is to make allowance for these submerged and blockaded human impulses, left out of the mechanical world picture, without permitting them to undermine and disrupt our whole civilization through their uncontrolled eruption.

The facts, at all events, should be plain. Those who have put their faith in mechanical inventions and in the power theme have failed to see that only a modicum of our constant human needs is encompassed by the machine or included in the territory it conquers. We know pretty definitely that men do not live by machines alone, and that the power impulse, however deep and ineradicable, is not a self-sustaining or a self-sufficient one. This is not to deny the importance of the machine in its place; it is merely to acknowledge the fact that it is not a substitute for art and love and fellowship and beauty and contemplative understanding. Many vital human needs have been frustrated by our one-sided overemphasis on the quantitative and the mechanical: this is true both in thought and in social and personal development. Indeed, as Karl Mannheim has pointed out, the hiatus that now exists between those parts of our life that have been rationalized by the machine and those parts that lie outside its scope, constitutes one of the gravest problems of present-day society. There has been, he points out, an uneven development of the human faculties. A diversification and balance of interests will itself be one of the elements that will save science from its own vices: the vices of isolation, non-communicability.

Beyond what is needed to provide what Aristotle called the material basis of the good life, our absorption in the machine deprives us of leisure, of the means of cultivating the arts and sciences for our personal illumination and enjoyment, and of the possibility of taking active parts as citizens in the shaping and direction of our polity. The machine today often serves as a substitute for activities that should be translated directly into biological, social, and personal terms. Our power and leisure are, in fact, empty of significance unless our leisure is used to build up those elements in the human personality and in social relations which are thrust aside or perverted by the one-sided pursuit of power.

The lesson of balance, which comes both from physiology and ecology, is one that has wide applications throughout our culture; it carries with it a demand for co-ordination, for interrelationship, and for intercommunication between the various domains which were once considered free, independent, and sovereign. (Dr. Walter Cannon has very ably elaborated this theme.) Need I point out that there is a close relationship here between the underlying political and social motives of the opening age and the framework of thought in which all our new tasks must be achieved? In both domains power politics and belligerent national sovereignty have produced immediate gains at the expense of the life and integrity of the whole. The age of balance will be one of world-wide federation and interlinkage—in thought no less than in political action.

The real question today is not whether stabilization will take the place of expansion, and symbiosis will replace a more or less predatory economy. The process of stabilization cannot be avoided. The real question is whether this will take place, in disorderly fashion, by a relapse to a more primitive underworld culture, like that envisaged by the Nazis, or whether the change will take place rationally and purposefully: in a fashion that will conserve all of man's great achievements in science and technics during the last three centuries, and bring them to a far richer fruition. But the future of science and technics cannot, in the nature of things, be an automatic continuation of the processes, methods, and beliefs that served the period of expansion. The age of cultivation has new needs and makes new claims. To satisfy these needs every part of our culture must be revitalized and re-oriented; and success here will demand political skill no less than philosophic vision; for thought itself bears an organic relation to life.

VI

SOCIETY

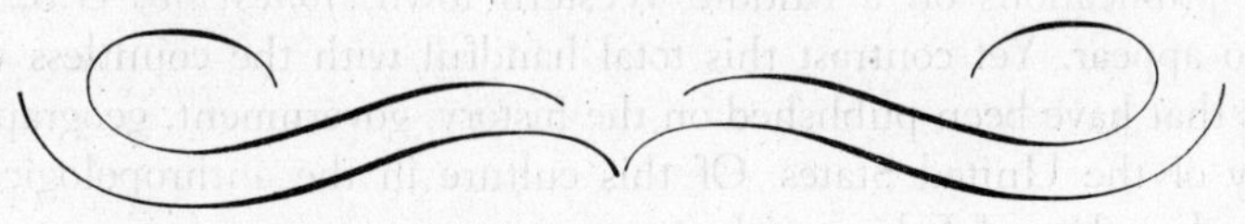

· SOCIAL ATTITUDES ·

AN ANTHROPOLOGIST LOOKS AT THE UNITED STATES[1]

CLYDE KLUCKHOHN

Suppose that archaeologists five hundred years hence were to excavate the ruins of settlements of various sizes in Europe, in America, in Australia, and in other regions. They would properly conclude that American culture was a variant of a culture of world-wide occurrence, distinguished by elaboration of gadgets and especially by the extent to which these were available to all sorts and conditions of men. Careful studies of distribution and diffusion would indicate that the bases of this civilization had been developed in northern Africa, western Asia, and Europe. The shrewd archaeologist would, however, infer that twentieth-century American culture was no longer colonial. He would see that distinctive features in the physical environment of the United States had made themselves perceptible in the warp of the American cultural fabric and that large-scale cultural hybridization and native inventions were continuing to produce a new texture and new patterns in the weft.

Unfortunately, the social anthropologist of 1948 cannot develop this picture much farther and remain in the realm of demonstrated fact. The anthropological study of American communities was initiated in *Middletown* (1928) and

1. From *Mirror for Man* (New York: McGraw Hill Book Company, Inc., 1949), pp. 228–261. Copyright, 1949, McGraw Hill Book Company, Inc.

Middletown in Transition (1937). Since then we have had a series of monographs on *Yankee City;* two books on *Southerntown; Plainville, U.S.A.;* brief studies of six different communities by the Department of Agriculture; Margaret Mead's popular book *And Keep Your Powder Dry;* and a score of scattered papers. Very recently Warner and Havighurst have published a study of class structure and education, *Who Shall be Educated?* Walter Goldschmidt has given us *As You Sow,* a report on California agricultural communities; and the publications on a Middle Western town, *Jonesville, U.S.A.*, have begun to appear. Yet contrast this total handful with the countless valuable volumes that have been published on the history, government, geography, and economy of the United States. Of this culture in the anthropological sense we know less than of Eskimo culture.

In treating American culture one must resort to an analysis that goes only a shade beyond impressionism. There is the special danger, considering the small quantity of recent field work, of describing American culture more as it has been than as it is. Yet a sketch of characteristic thought patterns, values, and assumptions may help us a little to understand ourselves and thus to understand other peoples better. One can assemble points of agreement in the anthropological studies that have been made, in the testimony of astute European and Asiatic observers, in personal observations. This has been a business civilization—not a military, ecclesiastical, or scholarly one. The brevity of our national history has made for this dominance of the economic as well as for the stress upon the potential as opposed to the actual society. Lacking the inertia of a deeply rooted culture pattern and given the high standard of living, American customs have changed rapidly under the influence of automobiles, radio, and moving pictures. There are many culture traits which are too obvious to require a massing of evidence: love of physical comfort, a cult of bodily cleanliness, finance capitalism. Certain values, such as fair play and tolerance, are generally agreed to but represent modifications of our British heritage rather than anything distinctively American. Rather than cataloguing traits exhaustively, however, this chapter will treat selectively some related traits that appear best to bring out the underlying organization of the culture.

American culture has been called a culture of paradoxes. Nevertheless national advertising and a national moving-picture industry would be impossible were there not certain terms in which one can appeal to the vast majority of this capturable people. Though sectional, economic, and religious differences are highly significant in some respects, there are certain themes that transcend these variations. Some life goals, some basic attitudes tend to be shared by Americans of every region and of all social classes.

To start with the commonplace: even the most bitter critics of the United States have conceded us material generosity. In spite of the romanticism of "public-spirited disinterestedness" most Americans are outgoing and genuinely benevolent. Sometimes, to be sure, American humanitarianism is linked with the missionary spirit—the determination to help others by making the world over on the American model.

Perhaps no huge society has ever had such generalized patterns for laughter. In older civilizations it is commonly the case that jokes are fully understood and appreciated only by class or regional groups. It is true that it is some distance from the sophisticated humor of *The New Yorker* to the slapstick of popular radio programs. But the most widespread formulas reach all Americans. Some of the most characteristic of these are related to the cult of the average man. No one becomes so great that we cannot make fun of him. Humor is an important sanction in American culture. Probably the ridicule of Hitler did more than all the rational critiques of Nazi ideology to make the man in the street contemptuous of Nazism.

All European travelers are struck by American attitudes toward women. They often note that "Americans spoil their women," or that "America is dominated by petticoats." The truth is more complicated. On the one hand, it is clear that a very large number of American women of privileged economic position are freed by labor-saving devices from much household drudgery—particularly after their few children have entered school. Their abundant leisure goes into women's clubs, community activities, "cultural" organizations, unhealthy devotion to their children, other mildly or seriously neurotic activities. It is also true that many American men are so wrapped up in pursuit of the success goal that they largely abdicate control over their children's upbringing to their wives. The responsibility of American women for moral and cultural questions is tremendous. On the other hand, it is too often forgotten that in 1940, 26 out of every 100 women of working age worked outside the home, that almost every girl who graduates from high school or college has had some job training. We interest women in careers but make it difficult for them to attain a full life in one. In a culture where "prestige" is everything we have felt it necessary to set aside Mother's Day as a symbolic atonement for the lack of recognition ordinarily given to domestic duties.

In Japan a year ago Japanese of many classes complained to me that it was difficult to understand American democracy because Americans seemed to lack an explicit ideology that they could communicate. The Japanese contrasted the Russians who could immediately give a coherent account of their system of beliefs. Various Americans have remarked that what the United States needed more than a good five-cent cigar was a good five-cent ideology. Such explicit ideology as we have derives largely from the political radicalism of the late eighteenth century. We repeat the old words, and some of the ideas are as alive now as then. But much of this doctrine is dated, and a new latent ideology inherent in our actual sentiments and habits is waiting for popular expression.

Particularly since the drastic disillusionment that followed the fine Wilsonian phrases of World War I, Americans have been shy at expressing their deepest convictions and have been verbally cynical about Fourth of July oratory. Yet devotion to the American Way has been none the less passionate. It is significant that aviators in this past war who were under narcotics in the course of psychotherapy would not only talk freely about personal emotional problems but were equally articulate on the ideological reasons for American participation in the war.

The pattern of the implicit American creed seems to embrace the following recurrent elements: faith in the rational, a need for moralistic rationalization, an optimistic conviction that rational effort counts, romantic individualism and the cult of the common man, high valuation of change—which is ordinarily taken to mean "progress," the conscious quest for pleasure.

Mysticism and supernaturalism have been very minor themes in American life. Our glorification of science and our faith in what can be accomplished through education are two striking aspects of our generalized conviction that secular, humanistic effort will improve the world in a series of changes, all or mainly for the better. We further tend to believe that morality and reason must coincide. Fatalism is generally repudiated, and even acceptance seems to be uncongenial—though given lip service in accord with Christian doctrine.

The dominant American political philosophy has been that the common man would think and act rationally. The same premises are apparent in typical attitudes toward parental responsibility. The individual, if "let alone" and not "corrupted by bad company" will be reasonable. If a child does not turn out well, the mother or both parents tend to blame themselves or to explain the failure by "bad blood"—as if action-guided-by-reason could of itself always produce well-adjusted children when the biological inheritance was adequate.

While many Americans are in some senses profoundly irreligious, they still typically find it necessary to provide moral justifications for their personal and national acts. No people moralizes as much as we do. The actual pursuit of power, prestige, and pleasure for their own sakes must be disguised (if public approval is to be obtained) as action for a moral purpose or as later justified by "good works." Conversely, a contemplative life tends to be considered "idleness."

The American mother offers her love to her child on the condition of his fulfilling certain performance standards. No conversational bromides are more characteristically American than "Let's get going"; "Do something"; "Something can be done about it." Although during the thirties there was widespread devaluation of present and future and though pessimism and apathy about the atomic bomb and other international problems are certainly strong currents in contemporary national thinking, the dominant American reaction is still—against the perspective of other cultures—that this is a world in which effort triumphs. A recent public opinion study showed that only 32 per cent of Americans were concerned about social security—for themselves.

Countless European observers have been impressed by "enthusiasm" as a typically American quality. During the war military analysts noted repeatedly that the British were better at holding a position but the Americans at taking one. As Margaret Mead has observed, the British cope with a problem; Americans start from scratch and build completely anew.

Americans are not merely optimistic believers that "work counts." Their creed insists that anyone, anywhere in the social structure, can and should "make the effort." Moreover, they like to think of the world as man-controlled. This view about the nature of life is thus intimately linked with that conception of the individual's place in society which may be called "romantic individualism."

In the English-speaking world there are two principal ideologies of individualism. The English variety (which may be tagged with the name of Cobden) is capitalistic in its basic outlook. American individualism has agrarian roots and may be associated with Jefferson. To this day Americans hate "being told what to do." They have always distrusted strong government. The social roles most frequently jibed at in comic strips are those that interfere with the freedom of others: the dog-catcher, the truant officer, the female social climber (Mrs. Jiggs) who forces her husband and family to give up their habitual satisfactions. "My rights" is one of the commonest phrases in the American language. This historically conditioned attitude toward authority is constantly reinforced by child-training patterns. The son must "go farther" than his father, and revolt against the father in adolescence is expected.

However, as de Tocqueville pointed out, Americans are characteristically more interested in equality than in liberty. "I'm as good as the next man," seems at first a contradiction of the American emphasis upon success and individual achievement within a competitive system. It is true that there are relatively few places at the top in a social pyramid—*at any one time*. But the American faith that "there is always another chance" has its basis in the historical facts of social mobility and the fluidity (at least in the past) of our economic structure. "If at first you don't succeed, try, try again." The American also feels that if he himself does not "get a break," he has a prospect for vicarious achievement through his children.

American individualism centers upon the dramatization of the individual. This is reflected in the tendency to personalize achievement, good or bad. Americans prefer to attack men rather than issues. Corporations are personified. Public power projects were advertised as much as a means of beating the Utility Devil as a way of getting better and cheaper service.

The less opportunity the greater the merit of success. "You can't keep a good man down." Conversely, failure is a confession of weakness, and status distinctions and even class lines are rationalized on such grounds as, "he got there by hard work," "it's his own fault that he didn't get on." Such attitudes —and the idealization of the "tough guy" and the "red-blooded American" and the fear of "being a sucker"—derive both from the Puritan ethic and from the American pioneer era. Aggressive activity and rapid mobility were effectual in the rapid development of a new country, and it made sense then that the rewards in money and status should be high.

The worship of success has gone farther than in any known culture, save possibly prewar Japan. This is reflected in countless staple phrases such as "bettering yourself," "getting ahead," and "how are you getting on?" The opposition to Roosevelt's proposal for a taxation program that would limit net income to $25,000, attests to the depth of feeling for slogans like "the sky's the limit." But the striving for money is not simply the pursuit of purposeless materialism. Money is primarily a symbol. The deeper competition is for power and prestige. "Aggressive" is, in American culture, a descriptive adjective of high praise when applied to an individual's personality or character. "You have to be aggressive to be a success." The obvious crudities of aggression are, as Lynd says, explained away by identifying them with the common good.

But there is a defensive note in this aggressiveness which is also symptomatic. Competitive aggressiveness against one's fellows is not just playing a part in a drama. The only way to be safe in American life is to be a success. Failure to "measure up" is felt as deep personal inadequacy. In a phrase, the American creed is equality of opportunity, not equality of man.

The cult of the average man might seem to imply disapproval of outstanding individuals of every sort. Certainly it is true that a great deal of hostility is directed upward. However, under the influence of the dramatic and success aspects of the "romantic individualism" orientation, the typical attitude toward leaders may best be described as one of mixed feelings. On the one hand, there is a tendency to snipe at superior individuals with a view to reducing them to the level of their fellows. On the other hand, their very success is a dramatic vindication of the American way of life and an invitation to identification and emulation.

The cult of the average man means conformity to the standards of the current majority. To de Tocqueville this was "enfeeblement of the individual." A more recent observer, Fromm, who also looked at the American scene from a European viewpoint, likewise finds this conformity repressive to self-expression. But he fails to see that the American is not a passive automaton submitting to cultural compulsives like European provincials. The American voluntarily and consciously seeks to be like others of his age and sex—without in any way becoming an anonymous atom in the social molecule. On the contrary, all the devices of the society are mobilized to glamorize the individual woman and to dramatize every achievement of men and women that is unusual —but still within the range of approved aspirations of the conforming majority. "Miss America" and "the typical American mother" are widely publicized each year, but an announced atheist (no matter of what brilliance and accomplishment) cannot be elected President.

American devotion to the underdog must be linked to this attitude. As Lynd points out, we worship bigness yet we idealize "the little man." "Griping" is a characteristic American trait, but the griping of American soldiers against the officer caste system is to be understood in terms of American egalitarian notions and especially of the cult of the average man. The fact that officers and enlisted men did not have equal access to various facilities for recreation and transportation enraged what were felt to be the most basic sentiments in the American code. To some extent this aspect of the cult of the average man doubtless represents a refuge for those who fail "to rise," a justification for envy of those who do.

Because of the cult of the average man, superficial intimacy is easy in America. People of every social class can talk on common topics in a way that is not so easy in Europe where life is based more on repetition of patterns of early family routines that are differentiated by class. However, American friendships tend to be casual and transitory.

Thanks to our expanding economy and to national folklore created by various historical accidents, the nineteenth-century faith in "progress" became intrenched in the United States as nowhere else. As Lovejoy and Boas have pointed out, America's golden age has been located mainly in the future rather than in the past. To some extent, to be sure, the future has been brought into the present by installment plan buying, the philosophy of "spend, don't save," etc. But the basic underlying notions have been well made explicit by Carl Becker.

> By locating perfection in the future and identifying it with the successive achievements of mankind, the doctrine of progress makes a virtue of novelty and disposes men to welcome change as in itself a sufficient validation of their activities.

Western Europeans and Americans tend to be fundamentally different in their attitudes toward conforming. Americans believe in conforming only to the standards of one's own age group and change-in-time is a strong value; Europeans believe—or have believed—in conforming to a past society and have found security in traditional behavior; yet conformity to a contemporary society is only incidental and not a value. There are, to be sure, wide disparities in American hospitality to change. We take pride in material change but are, on the whole, more hostile than contemporary Europeans to changes in our institutions (say the Constitution or the free enterprise system). In some ways the conformity of middle-class Englishmen, for instance, is more rigid than that of Americans—but in other ways it is less so. American attitudes toward change make generational conflicts more serious. These very generational conflicts, however, make certain types of social change possible. As Mead points out, children can be more "successful" than their parents, hence "better."

Americans publicly state that having a good time is an important part of life and admit to craving "something new and exciting." In terms of this ideology we have created Hollywood, our Forest of Arden type of college life, our National Parks, Monuments, and Forests. Leaders of our entertainment industry are the best paid men and women in the United States. In 1947 the

American people spent nearly twenty billion dollars for alcoholic beverages, theater and movie tickets, tobacco, cosmetics, and jewelry. We spend as much for moving pictures as for churches, more for beauty shops than for social service. However, because of the Puritan tradition of "work for work's sake," this devotion to recreation and material pleasure is often accompanied by a sense of guilt—another instance of the bipolarity of many features of American culture. The pleasure principle attains its fullest development in American youth culture. Youth is the hero of the American Dream. Most especially, the young girl ready for marriage is the cynosure of American society.

We have borrowed ideas and values from countless sources. If one takes single features, one can match almost every instance in a dozen or more cultures, including the primitive. For example, during the last war many of our soldiers carried magic amulets, such as a miniature wooden pig which was said to have raised fogs, smoothed out a high sea, commuted an execution, or cured assorted cases of illness. But if one looks at the total combination of premises and attitudes one sees a pattern that has its own special flavor, even though this description is too brief to take account of regional, class, ethnic group, and generational variations.

An anthropological snapshot of the American way of life cannot catch all the details, but, with other cultures in the background, it should highlight some meaningful interplay of light and shadow. And the attempt is needed. No amount of knowledge of Russian or Chinese culture will avail in the solution of our international problems unless we know ourselves also. If we can predict our own reactions to a probable next move in the Russian gambit and have some clues as to why we shall react in that manner, the gain to self-control and toward more rational action will be tremendous. Because of our tradition of assimilating immigrants and because of our overweening pride in our own culture it is particularly difficult to get Americans to understand other cultures.

Seen in the perspective of the range of human institutions, the following combination of outstanding features define the American scene: consciousness of diversity of biological and cultural origins; emphasis upon technology and upon wealth; the frontier spirit; relatively strong trust in science and education and relative indifference to religion; unusual personal insecurity; concern over the discrepancy between the theory and the practice of the culture.

"The melting pot" is one of the surest catchwords that has ever been applied to the United States. Probably much of the vitality of American life and the increased stature and other evidences of physical superiority for new generations of Americans must be attributed to the mingling of diverse cultural and biological strains as well as to dietary and environmental factors. The "Ballad for Americans" triumphantly proclaims our manifold origins. Newspapers during the war proudly referred to the fact that Eisenhower was a German name but he was an American, to the fact that another general was an Indian, to the variety of names in American platoons and in American graveyards overseas. The distinguished record of Japanese-Americans in the armed services was used to document the success of the American Way.

Heterogeneity has, in fact, become one of the organizing principles of American culture. Ripley's "Believe it or Not," "Quiz Kids" programs, "Information Please," and other formal and informal educational devices are evidence that Americans value disconnected pieces of information and feel that people must be prepared to live in a world in which generalizations are hard to apply.

If one looks at a culture as a system in which traits mainly received by borrowing are being patterned in response to situational factors and organic needs our American position at present bears a few compelling resemblances to that of Europe in perhaps the twelfth century. It was only then that a quasi-permanent integration had been attained in the European cultural melting pot. Pagan and Christian, Greco-Roman and Germanic culture elements had seethed in troubled opposition during the centuries of the movements of people. Our mass movements stopped only a generation ago with the closing of the frontier. During the tenth and eleventh centuries in Europe forests were cleared and swamps were drained; cities were built in large numbers in Northern Europe, and there came to be some fixity in the distribution and density of population.

Because of the very fact that diversity is an explicit theme of American culture one must be careful not to overemphasize the threats of the admitted contradictions in our way of life. Those who look longingly back to the good old days of a fancied homogeneity in American values forget that the Tories almost equaled the Patriots in number, do not remember the details of the situation that demanded the Federalist papers, neglect the two radically opposed sets of values that led to the War between the States. Actually, we must agree with Frank Tannenbaum that the harmony best suited to a democratic society "is one which comes from many-sided inner tensions, strains, conflicts, and disagreements." Though the stability of a culture depends on how much the conflicts it engenders can be supplied adequate outlets, still the strength of the democratic process is that it not only tolerates but welcomes difference. Democracy is based not upon a single value but upon a subtle and intricate multiple of values. Its strength rests in the balance of social institutions.

Although the definition of an American as a person who is endlessly catching trains is a caricature, the phrase of G. Lowes Dickinson "contemptuous of ideas but amorous of devices" remains uncomfortably correct as a characterization of all save a tiny minority of Americans. And while we indignantly met the Fascist label of "plutocracy!" by pointing to our humanitarian organizations, our numerous foundations dedicated to the spending of untold millions for lofty aims, and the generosity of individual citizens, it remains true that not only are we the wealthiest nation in the world but that money comes closer with us than with any other people to being the universal standard of value.

This is why the level of intellectual ability is very much higher in the Harvard Law School than in the Harvard Graduate School of Arts and Sciences. The ablest undergraduates in Harvard College do not always receive the highest honors. The energies of many are often, realistically enough, consecrated to "making contacts" through "activities," through a sedulous campaign to acquire membership in a "final club." This is not necessarily because they are congenitally uninterested in ideas, but because they have been effectually conditioned by family pressure and by certain schools. They have considerable intuitive insight into the structure of our culture. They know that intellectual endeavor will lead them to little "recognition" and less salary. They know how vital is "success" to security in our society. Brilliant young men voluntarily condemn themselves to lives of cutthroat competition and narrow slavery.

Our economy is a prestige economy to a pathological extent. The wife must buy fur coats and drive an expensive automobile because she too is an item of conspicuous consumption. Even in the supposedly uncommercial halls of learning the awed whisper is heard, "Why, he is a $15,000-a-year professor." The numerical system of grading, an unmistakably American invention, is simply another projection of our conviction that all attainments can be expressed in figures.

Suppose that an intellectual Australian aborigine, who was also a trained anthropologist, were to write a monograph on our culture. He would unequivocally assert that machines and money are close to the heart of our system of symbolic logics. He would point out that the two are linked in a complex system of mutual interdependence. Technology is valued as the very basis of the capitalistic system. Possession of gadgets is esteemed as a mark of success to the extent that persons are judged not by the integrity of their characters or by the originality of their minds but by what they seem to be—so far as that can be measured by the salaries they earn or by the variety and expensiveness of the material goods which they display. "Success" is measured by two automobiles—not by two mistresses as in some cultures.

Could our aboriginal anthropologist introduce some time perspective into his study, he would note that this value system has shown some signs of alteration during the last two decades. However, against the background of all known cultures, American culture would still stand out for its quantitative and materialistic orientations.

Americans love bigness—so far as things and events are concerned. Their constant overstatement appears to others as boasting. Americans love to speak in numbers. They like to "get down to brass tacks" and "want the lowdown." Europeans are usually content to rate students according to categories corresponding to "high honors," "honors," "pass." Only Americans think that the relative standing of students in a course can be measured on a continuous scale from zero to 100. This emphasis on the quantitative must not be too easily taken as proof of a thoroughgoing materialism. But Americans do tend to get very excited about things as opposed to ideas, people, and aesthetic creations. "Virtuous materialism" has tended to be part of the American creed.

Status in the United States is determined more by the number and price of automobiles, air-conditioning units, and the like owned by a family than by the number of their servants or the learning and aesthetic skills of family members. In fact, Americans usually are scared out of being artists. There is reverence only for the man who "does *things* in a big way." Most Americans do subscribe to the current Einstein legend, but *Time* has recently pointed out that many did not take this very seriously until they were told that Einstein's "theories" had made the atomic bomb possible. It is significant that Edison is a household name, whereas only the professors have heard of Willard Gibbs.

John Dewey says that American thinking is characterized by a "lust after absolutes." By this he does not, of course, mean a hankering for the "absolutes" of religion and philosophy. He refers to the tendency to think that, because simple questions can be posed, there exist simple answers, which classify ideas and individuals as all black or all white. For this reason "compromise" has an unfavorable connotation in American English. Worship of the external and quantitative leaves little patience for the infinite shadings and variations of direct experience. Doubtless the vastness of the American scene and the impermanence of social place create a need to generalize. Europeans are ordinarily more sensitive to the complexity of situations.

Our phrase "pioneer of industry" is not a haphazard combination of words. The patterns of the American Way were set during that period when the United States was on the skirmish line of civilization. The frontier has been a predominant influence in the shaping of American character and culture, in the molding of American political life and institutions; the frontier is the principal, the recurring theme in the American symphony. Whatever distinction we have as a people, whatever differentiates us from the other branches of Western European civilization we owe in large part to the presence of the frontier—its unappropriated wealth, its dangers and challenges.

Unfortunately, many of the responses which made for survival under those conditions are singularly unsuited to our present situation. To some considerable degree, frontier virtues are the intolerable vices of contemporary America. To extemporize and not to plan "paid off" then. Unhappily, we have tended to see these qualities as absolutes rather than from the perspective of cultural relativity. Aggressive and childish young Mickey Rooney was recently the hero of a population which ought to have grown up. A reactionary comic strip which portrays the triumphs Orphan Annie and Daddy Warbucks attain by stubborn clinging to pioneer attitudes and habits is still the inspirational reading of millions of Americans. Egoistic individualism remains long after the economic place for it has passed.

This same frontier spirit, however, affords the spiritual sources which can swiftly bring about potential reforms. If we Americans are restless, unanchored in our ideas as in our habitations, if also we may boast a certain freedom, a flexibility in our thinking and a vigor and independence in our action, it is in some degree traceable to the constant flux of American life, always westward, always away from old and permanent things. The American tempo has not become a sophisticated dignified one, measured in harmony with the persisting splendor of ancient palaces, and the symmetry of great parks carpeted with lawns such as only centuries of tending could produce. We have not evolved a splendid system of common law out of the crude folk code of the German forest by a millennium of patient and slow change. Our political institutions did not grow deep in the shadow which the *imperium Romanum,* the *pax Romana,* the *instituta Gaii* have always cast over the ideas of the men of Western Europe. We on this continent have not upreared under the goad of a common ecstasy and mighty aspiration a sky-striving shrine for Our Lady of Chartres, nor a great temple for the Three Kings of Cologne. We share, to be sure, in all the achievements of Western Europe because we have a common ancestry in blood and in ideas with the men of Western Europe, but we share more distantly, more and more differently. The common ecstasy of our great-grandfathers went toward the conquest of a vast and magnificent, a sometimes pitiless and terrible land; our grandfathers were born beside covered wagons in mountain passes, on the prairie, on the desert; the Vigilantes administered the laws in many of our early communities. If our whole economic development as a nation was conditioned by the fact that for more than a century there was always free land in the West for the man who had lost his job in the East, it is equally true that this terrible struggle for survival against the Indian and against the land itself begot in our forefathers not a slow, ordered, conventionalized response to a given stimulus but a quick tense reaction to fit each differing need: the temper of American life to this day.

Assembly-line factories and skyscrapers must, in part, be understood in terms of the frontier. Our so rapid development in invention and technique, our gigantic financial and industrial systems—in general, the fact that we adjusted so completely and quickly, albeit so inharmoniously, to the Technical Age is to be traced to the absence of an ancient order of society and the presence of the frontier where we had to adapt ourselves to vastness with decision, speed, and skill. In an old culture there is a belief in the established order, a rooted opposition to change, a constitutional imperviousness to new ideas which would involve radical alteration in the mode of life. The frontier liberated the American spirit. It developed generosity and radiant vitality, together with a restlessness which was both good and ill, but did certainly bring with it a resiliency of mind, fluidity of idea and of society, a willingness for bold experiment.

Mass education, like mass suffrage and mass production, is a leading trait of our code. During the last generation education has supplanted the frontier as a favorite means of social mobility, for we have continued to define success in terms of mobility rather than in terms of stability. Our educational system has recently been built upon a kind of watery intellectualism. We have too often naïvely assumed that, if people were "well informed" and taught to reason in accord with accepted canons of logic, their characters would take care of themselves, and they would automatically acquire the point of view requisite in the citizen of a great society. Meanwhile, the toughening influences of frontier conditions were becoming steadily more dilute. Children of the economically dominant classes were being brought up in relative luxury. Parents failed to condition their offspring to rigorous standards of conduct because they were themselves confused. Actually many educative functions formerly carried out by the family have been surrendered to the school. The existing educational system is hopelessly irresolute on many fronts. It vacillates between training girls to be housewives or career women; it is torn between conditioning children for the theoretically desirable cooperative objectives or to the existing competitive realities. In spite of the terrific demands made upon them, elementary and high-school teachers are underpaid and lack social status. Psychiatrists are agreed that the elimination of social disorganization, as well as of personal disorganization, can be furthered only by more consistent educational practices both in the home and in the school because automatic actions based on the habits of early life are the most stable.

The anthropologist must also characterize our culture as profoundly irreligious. More than half of our people still occasionally go through the forms, and there are rural and ethnic islands in our population where religion is still a vital force. But very few of our leaders are still religious in the sense that they are convinced that prayer or the observance of church codes will affect the course of human events. Public figures participate in public worship and contribute financially to a church for reasons of expediency or because they know that churches represent one of the few elements of stability and continuity in our society. But belief in God's judgments and punishments as a motive for behavior is limited to a decreasing minority. Feelings of *guilt* are common but the sense of *sin* is rare.

The legend of Jesus lives in men's hearts and the Christian ethic is far from dead. As Bridges reminds us: "They who understand not cannot forget, and they who keep not His commandments call Him Master and Lord." But, in the opinion of many acute observers, American Protestantism is vital today primarily as an agency of benign social work. Relatively few Protestants, except in a few sects and in some rural areas, manifest deep religious feeling. The Roman Church certainly retains vigor, and parts of the encyclicals of recent Popes are not the least impressive of utterances upon contemporary life. To more than a few intellectuals of recent years the Catholic Church has appeared as the one firm rock in a sea of chaos and decay. To others it seems that the authoritarian Church, for all the social wisdom she has shown, for all the subtlety of her doctors, has purchased peace of mind in their time for her communicants by identifying ephemeral cultural expedients with immutable human nature. A system of beliefs, profoundly felt, is unquestionably necessary to the survival of any society, but an increasing number of Americans debate the extent to which the dogmas of any organized Christian Church are compatible with contemporary secular knowledge.

Much of this debate reflects the shallowness of certain aspects of American culture. The alternative of science *or* religion is fictitious once it be granted that the functions of religion are primarily symbolic, expressive, and orientative. Every culture must define its ends as well as perfect its means. The logical and symbolic expressions of the ultimate values of a civilization cannot arise directly from scientific investigation, though it is fair to demand that they should not rest upon premises contrary to known fact or proven theory. A mechanistic, materialistic "science" hardly provides the orientations to the deeper problems of life that are essential for happy individuals and a healthy social order. Nor does a political philosophy such as "democracy." Men need tenets that do not outrage the brain but are meaningful to the viscera and the aesthetic sensibilities. They must be symbolized in rites that gratify the heart, please the ear and eye, fulfill the hunger for drama.

Observers agree on the poverty of American ceremonial life. American ceremonialism is too overwhelmingly that of Shriner conventions and labor rallies. If such national sentiments as we possess are to be maintained at a degree of intensity sufficient to preserve them, they must be given collective expression on suitable occasions. If the conduct of the individual is to be regulated in accord with the needs and purposes of the society, the society's sentiments must be periodically reinforced in the individual by gatherings in which all classes assert in symbolic form: "we are one people."[2]

Mass economic upheaval following upon unprecedented economic growth; lack of attention to the human problems of an industrial civilization; the impersonality of the social organization of cities; the melting pot, transitory geographical residence, social mobility, weakening of religious faith—all of these trends have contributed to make Americans feel unanchored, adrift upon a meaningless voyage. The American family system is in process of settling into a new type of organization and such a phase does not make for psychic ease. Why are Americans a nation of joiners? In part this is a defense mechanism against the excessive fluidity of our social structure. Weary of the tension of continual struggle for social place, people have tried to gain a degree of

2. These statements may seem to imply an exaltation of nationalism or at least an acceptance of its inevitability for all time. Nothing of the sort is intended. I am primarily interested in calling attention to the empirical fact of the connection between means and ends. Also, I believe that certain American sentiments have a value to us and to the world—at least until the millennium of a world society arrives.

routinized and recognized fixity by allying themselves with others in voluntary associations.

The smooth working of all societies depends upon individuals not having to think about many of their acts. They can carry out their specialized functions better if much of their behavior is a more or less automatic reaction to a standardized situation in a socially appropriate fashion. A man meets a woman acquaintance on the street. He raises his hat. Such small acts bind a society together by making one's behavior intelligible to one's neighbors and give the participants a sense of security. Because one knows what to do and knows what the other person will do everything seems to be under control. Such patterns likewise release energy for the activities in which the individual is really interested. The trouble in our society is that the cluster of meanings upon which such an expective, repetitive way of behaving must depend is sadly disorganized. The cultural dislocation of emigrant groups, the rapid and disorderly expansion of cities, and many other factors have all contributed to the disorientation of individuals from a cohesive social matrix. Technicians have applied science to industry without either management, unions, or the state making more than feeble attempts at the indispensable compensatory adjustments in social structure.

A disproportionate technological development has given tempo to American life but denied it rhythm. It has provided the constant overstimulation necessary to throw many of us into a perpetual state of neurotic indecision. The disparity between our ingenuity in solving mechanical as opposed to human problems is a grave question. It would be infantile, of course, to say "away with the machine!" Obviously, it is not machines but our lack of scientific attention to the problems they raise which is evil. It is a legitimate hope that machines may free the majority of humans from drudgery and thus afford an escape from industrial feudalism. Further, as Mumford has urged, machines and the rapid transportation and distribution of goods which they make possible, create an international reciprocity and dependency such as to make the peace and order of nations more nearly a condition which *must* be attained rather than a pious desirability.

In rural areas and small towns, quick and direct response of neighbors can make for great personal security and for other values enriching to life. In cities, however, the economy is so finely organized and specialized that the dependency of one individual upon another, though actually more acute, is not felt in warm personal terms. People miss a network of relationships linking the job, the family, the church and other institutions. They feel the lack of personal appreciation of the products of their labors and of nonutilitarian creativity. Edward Sapir has well contrasted our psychological position with that of the primitive:

> So long as the individual retains a sense of control over the major goods of life, he is able to take his place in the cultural patrimony of his people. Now that the major

goods of life have shifted so largely from the realm of immediate to that of remote ends, it becomes a cultural necessity for all who would not be looked upon as disinherited to share in the pursuit of these remoter ends. Nor harmony and depth of life . . . is possible when activity is well-nigh circumscribed by the sphere of immediate ends and when functioning within that sphere is so fragmentary as to have no inherent intelligibility or interest. Here lies the grimmest joke of our present American civilization. The vast majority of us, deprived of any but an insignificant and culturally abortive share in the satisfaction of the immediate wants of mankind, are further deprived of both opportunity and stimulation to share in the production of non-utilitarian values. Part of the time we are dray horses; the rest of the time we are listless consumers of goods which have received no least impress of our personality. In other words, our spiritual selves go hungry, for the most part, pretty much all of the time.

Most thoughtful Americans are concerned about the fact that the theory and the practice of our culture are hopelessly out of line. It is well established that while cultural content often changes rapidly, cultural forms often have extraordinary permanency. Thus it is only the *tradition* of economic independence which truly survives. For all our talk of free enterprise we have created the most vast and crushing monopolies in the world. Although the fable that every boy can become president has been repeatedly scoffed at in recent years, parents and children still act upon the ruling motivation that hard work, training, and aggressiveness can overcome almost all limitations. The result is, of course, countless disgruntled or bitter men and women, for as Veblen has shown, in a capitalistic economy the number of places at the top is disappointingly few. A cramping constriction will be felt by individuals so long as our ideal pattern is proclaimed as equality of opportunity for all. "Freedom" likewise has become fertile of disillusioned cynicism because of increasing realization of the truth of Durkheim's words, "I can be free only to the extent that others are forbidden to profit from their physical, economic, or other superiority to the detriment of my liberty." And much of the exultation in our "high standard of living" is, as Norman Thomas contends, "ludicrously beside the point. What the workers have a right to demand of the machine age is not that it will give them more bath tubs than Henry VIII had for his troublesome domestic establishment; they have a right to ask that machinery will conquer poverty rather than increase insecurity."

A society may indeed be viewed as a structure of expectancies. Neuroses have been produced experimentally in laboratory animals by causing the relation between stimulus and proper response to be irregular and haphazard. It follows that if the expectancies which are generated by the cultural ideology are notably unrealistic, mass frustration and mass neurosis are the inescapable consequences.

The diversity of ethnic origins in our forming nation provided strong psychological reinforcement of the doctrines of human equality which were the gospel of the Age of Enlightment and of the Romantic Movement. Had not a belief in mystic equality become part of the official ideology of American culture and offered psychological security to non-Anglo-Saxons, these divergent groups might well have remained tight little islands of transplanted Europeans. But the contrast between this legal and political theory and the private theories and practices of too many American citizens (as symbolized in labels like "wops" and "greasers," in Jim Crow laws and lynchings) constitutes one of the severest strains undermining the equilibrium of the American social systen. The Negroes and, to only a slightly lesser extent, the Spanish-speaking Americans constitute caste groups—that is, normal intermarriage does not occur between them and the rest of the population. Segregation in housing and discriminatory practices in our armed services stand out as intolerable contradictions in the institutions of a free society.

In the last fifteen years anthropologists have presented evidence that, in contrast to our official beliefs, a class structure has even now considerably crystallized in at least some parts of the United States. Lloyd Warner and his associates distinguish a six-class system: upper-upper, lower-upper, upper-middle, lower-middle, upper-lower, lower-lower. These groupings are not solely economic. In fact, members of the top class ordinarily have less money than those of the lower-upper group. Nor does stratification correspond entirely to occupational lines. Physicians, for example, are found in all of the first four classes. In Warner's sense a class consists of persons who visit in one another's home, belong to the same social clubs, exchange gifts, and show awareness of themselves as a group set apart from others, and in a subordinate or superior position to others.

Whether the six-class system is generally valid or whether a larger or smaller subdivision better represents the facts in some communities is a factual question that cannot be answered until there have been more studies. The division of labor in a complex society makes some form of class stratification almost inevitable. It just so happens that in American culture recognition of the facts is repugnant to the American creed. Public-opinion polls indicate that 90 per cent of Americans insist that they are "middle class" despite wide variations in income level, occupation, and social habits. One study shows that 70 per cent of low-income groups claim middle-class social position. Warner, however, places 59 per cent of the people in one New England town in the two lower classes.

Under the influence of the depression and of Marxian theories discussion of class in the United States has increased greatly in the past twenty years. When class position is grudgingly recognized, it is often with anger—as something un-American and hence wrong. Some students of American class structure have failed to examine the significance of values—adhered to by almost all Americans—which operate to deny and tear down class divisions. Except possibly in limited areas of the eastern seaboard, the South, and the San Francisco area, the lines are still relatively fluid and everyone hopes to rise. The statement that American culture is dominantly a middle-class culture is something more than an acceptance of popular ideology which glosses over the sometimes ugly facts of differentiation. Hence "class," though a real phenomenon, does not have precisely the sense that it does in Europe. Certainly Americans are increasingly conscious of status, but the ranking of individuals and their immediate families is often still divorced from that of their close relatives. And the place of the whole body of kin in the smaller communities is frequently based primarily on length of residence there. Our society remains in important respects an open society.

Nevertheless the facts indicate that rapid rise through sheer ability and industry is much more difficult than it was a generation or two ago. Status is harder to achieve by one's own initiative and easier to acquire through family connections. In Washington during the war it was noted that considerable communication and power flowed through channels that were not only nonofficial but not those of political or other normal American interest groups. For the first time since the Age of Jackson an upper class appeared to be operating without much reference to regional or political lines. The class problem is also manifesting itself in the schools. Teachers, themselves usually of middle-class position, discriminate against lower-class children. The children sense that they are punished for following the cultural patterns of their parents. If effort and ability are not rewarded, the way to delinquency or stolid escapism is inviting. In short, class typing rather than individual typing has become one American mode of granting or denying recognition to other people.

Americans are at present seeing social change of a vastness difficult to comprehend. Concretely, social change has its origins in the strains and dissatisfactions felt by specific individuals. When personal insecurity is sufficiently intense and sufficiently widespread, new patterns are germinated in the few creative individuals, and there will be willingness to try them out on the part of larger numbers. Such is the present condition of American society. If a society be regarded as a system in equilibrium, it may be said that in the decade following 1918 the prewar equilibrium was precariously reattained. But the depression and World War II appear to have destroyed the old equilibrium beyond repair. At the moment Americans are in the tortures of attempting to reach a new and differently based equilibrium. The devastating appropriateness of the phrase, "the neurotic personality of our time," is both the condition and the result of this circumstance.

The basis of social life is the sensitivity of human beings to the behavior of other human beings. In a complex society the need for correct interpretation and response to the demands of others is especially great. But in American culture the first experiences of the growing child tend so to emphasize prestige (especially economic prestige) needs that the ego requirements of our adults are often too tremendous for them to follow any other pattern. As Horney says, "the striving for prestige as a means of overcoming fears and inner emptiness is certainly culturally prescribed." Such a device, however, like the intemperate devotion to the pleasure principle, is but a feeble palliative. The popular motto, "every man for himself," was less socially dangerous when firm and generally held beliefs in the afterworld provided some check upon rampant individualism.

The frontier code of sturdy individualism needs tempering and modification the more because it is seldom possible of attainment in the present situation. As Sirjamaki says, "The culture posits individualism as a basic social value but places overwhelming burdens upon its realization." In most aspects of social life American demands for conformity are too great. After the passing of the frontier, individualism was expressed mainly in the economic part of the culture. Today the United States is almost the only country in the world in which large numbers of people cling to laissez-faire principles in economics and government. In its extreme form this is utterly unrealistic, a fixation upon a vain phantasm of our past.

Some acceptance of planning and of stability as a value would decrease the envy and strife that go with incessant mobility. In a society where everybody is either going up or going down there is an excessive psychological necessity to cherish the familiar. This exaggerated stress upon conformity plus our business externalism has created what Fromm has recently termed "the personality of the market place" as the most frequent type in our culture. Given the pressures to conformity, personality fulfillment is denied to many, perhaps most, of our citizens.

America's claim to greatness thus far is not through its Whitmans and Melvilles, nor its Woods and Bentons, nor its Michelsons and Comptons. Still less does it consist in its having added to the contemplative or religious treasures of mankind. Emerson, Thoreau, James, and Dewey are distinguished thinkers, but that they are of the stature of many other ancient and modern philosophers is doubtful. Mary Baker Eddy, Joseph Smith, and other leaders of cultist or revivalistic sects represent all that is characteristically American in religion.

Americans have, however, been inventive in more than one sphere. Admirable and useful as are those material inventions which have made "the American standard of living" an international byword, American social inventions are the most distinctive contributions made by the United States to world culture. The cult of the average man is an even more characteristically American invention than the assembly line. Philosophers of many nations had dreamed of a state guided by a skillfully trained but small group of the good and wise. The United States, however, was the first country to dedicate itself to the conception of a society where the lot of the common man would be made easier, where the same opportunities would be available to all, where the lives of all men and women would be enriched and ennobled. This was something new under the sun.

We cannot rest upon the laurels of past achievement. E. H. Carr has bluntly stated the alternatives:

The impact of the Soviet Union has fallen on a western world where much of the framework of individualism was already in decay, where faith in the self-sufficiency of individual reason had been sapped by the critique of relativism, where the democratic community was in urgent need of reinforcement against the forces of disintegration latent in individualism, and where the technical conditions of production on the one hand, and the social pressures of mass civilization on the other, were already imposing far-reaching measures of collective organization. . . . The fate of the western world will turn on its ability to meet the Soviet challenge by a successful search for new forms of social and economic action in which what is valid in individualist and democratic tradition can be applied to the problems of mass civilization.[3]

All advocates of government by an élite, from Plato to Hitler and Stalin, have ridiculed the competence of average citizens to form rational opinions upon complex issues. There is no doubt that many nineteenth-century utterances absurdly exalted rationality. Yet the best anthropological evidence, as Franz Boas pointed out, is that the judgment of the masses is sounder than the judgment of the classes on broad questions of policy where sentiments and values are concerned. This doctrine must not be perverted into a claim for the common man's expertness on technical or artistic matters. Nor does contemporary thought refer to the individual citizen's judgments. Rather, it refers to collective decisions arrived at in group interaction and dealing with "matters of common concern which depend upon estimates of probability." As Carl Friedrich continues:

This concept of the common man salvages from the onslaught of the irrationalist revolt those elements in the older doctrine which are essential to democratic politics. It seeks a middle ground between the extreme rationalistic ideas of an earlier day and the denial of all rationality by those who were disappointed over its limitations. . . . Enough common men, when confronted with a problem, can be made to see the facts in a given situation to provide a working majority for a reasonable solution, and such majorities will in turn provide enough continuing support for a democratic government to enforce such common judgments concerning matters of common concern.

What is the prospect for American culture? Let one anthropologist, though bearing in mind the principles of his science, speak unashamedly in terms of his own American sentiments. Given our biological and material wealth, given

3. From E. H. Carr, *The Soviet Impact on the Western World*. Copyright 1947 by The Macmillan Company and used with their permission and that of the author.

the adaptive genius which is the constructive heritage of our peculiarly American frontier spirit, it will be the fault not of angels but of ourselves if our problems are not in large part resolved. The decisive factor will be the extent to which individual Americans feel a personal responsibility. This, in turn, depends upon an intangible: their total philosophic attitude. James Truslow Adams in *The Epic of America* urges that the meaningful contribution which the United States has made to the totality of human culture is "the American Dream," "a vision of a society in which the lot of the common man will be made easier and his life enriched and ennobled." It was in the ideological field that America made its first and can still make its greatest contribution to the world. In the New World, peopled by robust men and women who had the courage to emigrate and many of whom were impelled by the active vision of a nobler society, Americans enlarged the meaning of freedom and gave it many new expressions.

It is this prospect for American culture which we must cherish and believe in. Nor is there anything in science which indicates that the dreams of man do not influence, nay sometimes determine his behavior. While choice is most often a flattering illusion, while antecedent and existent hard-sense data usually shape our destinies, there are moments in the careers of nations, as well as in the careers of individuals, when opposing external forces are about equally balanced, and it is then that intangibles like "will" and "belief" throw the scales. Cultures are not altogether self-contained systems which inevitably follow out their own self-determined evolution. Sorokin and other prophets of doom fail to see that one of the factors which determines the next step in the evolution of a system is precisely the dominant attitudes of people. And these are not completely determined by the existent culture. John Dewey has shown us that in "judgments of practice" the hypothesis itself has a crucial influence upon the course of events: "to the extent that it is seized and acted upon, it weights events in its favor."

Even that erstwhile pessimist, Aldous Huxley, has seen that the discoveries of modern psychology have been perverted to bolster a false determinism. If responses can be conditioned, they can by the same token be deconditioned and reconditioned—though neither individuals nor peoples change suddenly and completely. We are now released from the dominantly external and material demands which frontier conditions made upon our society. Intelligent planning can ease the hostile tensions of national anarchy by providing both security and socialized freedom for the individual. Ideals of flourishing freshness that adapt to changed conditions and to what is sound and creative in the distinctive American Way are the only sure antidote for our social ills. Only those ideals will spread and be accepted which correspond to the culturally created emotional needs of the people. Scientific humanism is such an ideal. Rooted in the tradition of Americans to value scientific achievement highly, scientific humanism can actualize the American Dream. As our culture has come from all the world, so must we give back to all the world not that technological materialism which is science cheapened and debased but the scientific attitude woven into the stuff of people's daily lives. This is a vision of humility in the face of the complexity of things, of the joyous pursuit of ideas of which there is no exclusive possession. This is science not as the provider of the agencies of barbarism but science as revealing the order in experience, as heightening the sense of our precarious dependence one upon the other, as the surest and most powerful of internationalizing forces.

Scientific humanism should be the sturdy creed of the future. Despite uncritical worship of invention and technology, the masses are still, in Carlson's expression, "innocent of science, in the sense of the spirit and the method of science as part of their way of life. . . . Science in this sense has as yet hardly touched the common man or his leaders." An effective working majority of our citizens need no longer base their personal security upon expectation of future life or adult dependency upon the projected images of parent-persons. The scientific vision is the vision which Plato saw in the *Symposium,* a security system which is depersonalized but humanized rather than dehumanized. To try to make such a vision real, offers American men and women that common nobility of purpose which is the vitalizing energy of any significant culture. The venture demands a courage analogous to religious faith, a courage undismayed by the failure of any specific experiment, a courage ready to offer the renunciations of waiting long, a courage which recognizes that even negative knowledge means growth, a courage realizing that the general hypotheses underlying the venture will be proved only if diminished anxiety and greater gusto in day-to-day living transform the lives of us all.

TRENDS IN PERSONAL LIFE [1]

MARGARET MEAD

WHEN we, as Americans, ask such questions as: What is happening to personal relations in the United States? we are looking, at least half the time, through European eyes. Our memories are laden with the lovely words with which English and French, even Greek and Latin, have defined human relationships between lovers, between parents and children and between friends. If asked to supply quickly a quotation on any known human relationship, the words that slip easily from our lips are old-world words, begotten in a status society where the Middle Ages still linger in art and in life.

And if we are not quoting, we are at least listening a good half the time to the strictures of our European friends who point to what America lacks in the field of personal relations. "There is no intimacy in America," complains one. "Americans have no expectation of forming deep, intense personal ties," says the noted psychiatrist. "You Americans, you take us to your hearts with both arms—and promptly forget us," says the traveled English lady. "In Germany," muses the exile, "a girl does not have to get drunk before she will make love." "Why do you keep all your lights so low?" asks the male visitor. "We may be shy, but we are not frightened; we can make love with the lights on." "No American woman ever completely gives herself to anyone." "Where is your 'skin' anyway in America—the place where if we could touch you, you would really react?" "Americans are coming to believe in the interchangeability of human beings," your newspaper columnists say. "Your husband bores you, madam, get another husband." So it goes on, from visiting poet to resident psychoanalyst, from the young man who can't see why, if American women are what he has been led to believe, he has so little luck, to the young man who, after listening to the conversation of young American men, feels that every American woman will expect him to make love to her—and therefore flees. Through our minds their evaluation continually echoes, until we find ourselves judging ourselves through their eyes. We have become actors for an audience which is half ourselves soaked in a European tradition, and half the Europeans among us who find their American adventures in love and friendship so very hard to understand.

All this might not matter so much if it were not that the same problem is posed even to the young American who reads no poetry, has barely heard of Dante and knows no recently arrived European literati. He, too, must see his personal relationships—lived American style—through a misty haze of tradition which is no longer relevant or appropriate. The boy and girl who meet for an evening, who perhaps will spend the night together, perhaps will marry and part in a month, or perhaps rear five children and eventually

1. *The New Republic,* CXV (September 23, 1946), 346–348.

buy a farm—do not have a language for each of these situations. They have only one language, that of monogamous and eternal love, a language which is tattered by the cynical overtones which must be present when it is used inappropriately, language which sounds flat when it is true because it has been untrue so often.

A STANDARD WITHOUT LANGUAGE

This confusion of standards is more serious than the trend toward the slight and situational style in our human relationships, for we really have no standard yet by which to judge whether or not these are rewarding. You cannot judge a style in relationships until it has what any style deserves, a language, a poetry of its own. The effects which T. S. Eliot produced in his famous poem: "When lovely woman stoops to folly, and paces about her room again, alone, she smooths her hair with automatic hand, and puts a record on the gramophone," reflect a double tragedy, a form of action which no longer meets the older words but is smothered in their memory.

Thus there is a very real dilemma for the average young American boy or girl. They may know their acts, know the opening and the closing lines of a date or an affair, a romance or a marriage; they may know when to shift the voice but keep the words the same, or when to shift the words but keep the voice the same. They may know how to tell a wolf and they may actually be quite sure in their personal interchanges, but still they are burdened with the patterns of a different kind of a society, at a different period in history; their tongues are clotted with inappropriate words, and the clear line of their movement toward and away from one another is partially obscured by vows which are meaningless on their lips. What indeed is happening to personal relationships in America? They are in fact becoming more and more American, which means they are developing a distinctive style and tempo of their own. And an ethic, too—for the scorn of American young people for those who do not obey the rules is authentic scorn, only cast in a new mold the contours of which our eyes are unpracticed in following.

This new style, which we understand so little, can be understood better, perhaps, when it is referred to the great contrast in the lives of the majority of Americans between the pattern of human relationships which they learn at home and the pattern they learn at school and out in the world. In many cases this contrast is a contrast between cultures, between homeways which are Polish or Italian or Irish, or at least stem from a completely different part of the United States, and school and outer-world ways which represent the more standard American culture. Even where this overt contrast does not occur, there is still an expectation of conflict between the standards of the home and the standards of the social group, with an increasing demand that the home must yield, that mothers must let their daughters "wear what the other girls wear" and "do what the other girls do."

THE FAMILY V. THE GROUP

When mothers cease to say, "When I was a girl I was not allowed . . ." and substitute the question, "What are the other girls doing?" something very fundamental has happened to the whole culture. This expectation of difference and acceptance of a gradual relinquishing of the home style for the group style carry over into personal relations as well. A man does not, when he is an immigrant or the son of an immigrant, expect to marry a girl who either looks or cooks like his mother. Nor, if he is the descendant of several generations of Americans, does he expect his wife to dress or act like his mother. His mother was old, his wife must be young indefinitely. Both cultural difference and the reinforcements of steadily changing fashions help to break the direct resemblances between mother, wife and daughter, and, less explicitly perhaps, between father, husband and son. Relinquishing the image of the parent is balanced by withdrawing all demands upon the child that the parental image be reflected. Discontinuities in the direct family line and an extra-anxious sensitivity to the demands of the age group are pre-eminently characteristic of American culture and are becoming more and more common in other parts of the world, as old stable populations migrate and become urbanized, secularized and uprooted.

So the American can be described as both culturally uprooted and able to take root quickly, the break between home and school severing roots which increasingly—because that home partakes more and more of the general tone of American life—do not go very deep, and the eager acceptance of the outside world developing a rapid facility in putting short roots down very quickly. Where European personal relationships, in their typical forms, seem to follow directly on the family pattern, American relationships follow, instead, patterns characteristic of the school class, the age group, the gang, the team, the office, the outfit, the club—associations formed not in the passionate intensity of a close family circle, but in the give and take of fortuitously assembled groups of contemporaries.

This pattern was highly developed in the army, where loyalty to members of one's outfit was admittedly the strongest incentive to bravery and self-sacrifice and led to bitter self-reproach and even to breakdown if another perished while one oneself survived. Within the outfit, whether it is a school, military or work unit, the average American—especially the American male—for girls have never quite so completely passed from the pattern of relationship based on close home ties to the patterns based on shared goals—makes just one basic distinction. He classifies the other members as either "good joes" or not. If he classifies them as good, it means he will treat them with an effervescent sort of backslapping warmth, stifle his desire to gibe at their weaknesses and jeer at their idiosyncrasies, and accept them. To them he will give a loyalty such as in many societies is reserved for members of one family and which wholly overrides preferences cast in terms of temperament or bent.

This loyalty is strong enough to take men through the darkest days of battle, to keep men working on long shifts or striking outside closed plant doors; on the strength of it one grimly assumes responsibility for the death of a member of the group and takes over the job of comforting his widow. And yet these are not personal friendships, in the sense that they re-enact stronger, personal choices which echo the home ties of childhood. They are not ties to Bill or Joe, but to Bill-on-the-team, to Joe-in-the-office. And because it is a strain, even to the American, who did after all grow up in a home where the relationships were among a very few people with strong contrasts in age and sex and role, to accept so many people, uncritically, as members of the "crowd," various typical compensations develop. Any group that can legitimately be labeled foreign or *other* is rejected in the same wholesale way as the own group is accepted, and there is a nostalgic idealization of past groups in which the intimacy and warmth which all groups simulate are imagined really to have occurred.

IMPERSONAL WARMTH

Here we have a rationale of the seeming contradiction of the American, who is so good-humoredly uncritical of his pals and so unfairly and undiscriminatingly intolerant of outsiders, and of the ever recurrent institution of the reunion, in which people try to recapture a glamor which they solemnly believe lies always in former associations rather than in present ones. The American is compelled to take an enormous slice of mankind to his heart or have it wither altogether. Inevitably he protects the inner core of his heart against the horde whose backs he slaps and whose nicknames fall so enthusiastically from his lips. The situation, not he, has selected them. True to what he learned so young, he buys acceptance by the group with acceptance of it.

Relations between men and women inevitably mirror these same patterns. Beginning with the *date,* significantly an occasion in time rather than a relationship to a person, boys and girls practice a style of social intercourse whose content is personal and sexual but whose form is impersonal and asexual. Each date stands alone, one incident in a series whose number and character determine one's popularity rating. One has dates because it is the thing to do. The popular boy goes with the popular girl, because by so doing each enhances his own popularity. The evening is spent in a conversational and postural game as patterned as a minuet, in which the boy claims the girl's favors as his right, and she refuses them, because she is secure enough in her popularity to do so. All refusals lie with her, and she learns to discipline her responsiveness so that she will never go farther than she wishes.

Only the unpopular girl has to carry petting to the limits where the reward the boy receives is grossly physical rather than a delicate flattery of his good judgment in having taken out a girl who knows her way around. The girl who has to pet excessively or sit at home alone is identified in the boy's mind with the kind of girl who never keeps the seams of her stockings straight, as opposed to the girls whose stocking seams run straight and true and whom you would take out "even if you had to maybe take her *mother* along." Small wonder that American women later feast their imaginations on the Sheik and his recurrent contemporary images—a male who is irresistible because he is foreign and so misses her restrictive cues. While the popular boy and girl go on dating for several years, the unpopular, the frightened, the relatively unchosen, slip away in pairs and "go steady," accepting a permanent and definite relationship with one person in lieu of a gayer world in which they have failed.

HAPPILY EVER AFTER

But when the shift comes to courtship—a shift made so imperceptibly that the foreign ear is very slow in picking up its nuances—the whole original contradiction between a style of personal relationships which have been bequeathed from a world in which family patterns were paramount, and a world in which young people have learned to feel in terms of situations and occasions rather than in reference to persons, comes into play. So young Americans fall in love in terms of an extreme romanticizing of the old values, with the "only girl in the world," with "Mr. Right," with an ideal of the kind of love which Dante had for Beatrice and of a way of life which is only possible when marriages are made between those whose every word evokes deeply shared cultural values. So they pass, through the open gate of coincident physical passion—a passion which is rendered less poignant and more easily repeatable because they have toyed with it all through adolescence—and generalized social approval, into a state which tradition bids them define as eternal.

Grasping at straws: "His grandfather and my uncle had cottages right next to each other in Florida." "My mother and his mother were both born on the 29th of February," pitifully inadequate substitutes for a common culture, they build up a sense of a past which destined them for each other. Taught to use sex as a counter rather than value it as either a means of self-expression or communication, they make rather less of connubial bliss than the members of many other societies, but a surprising number devote their whole lives to a successful attempt to prove that because they married for love, and of their own choice, they are happy. For those who fail, the situational definition of human relationships is immediately available. A new girl becomes the only girl in the world, a new man, Mr. Right. But the great majority who surprisingly enough do not fail, find in the course of improving the cherished proposition that they were in love and so are happy, that they have come to believe it, so for them it is true.

COMMON WOMEN[1]

PHILIP WYLIE

Mom Is the End Product of She

SHE is Cinderella . . . the shining-haired, the starry-eyed, the ruby-lipped virgo æternis, of which there is presumably one, and only one, or a one-and-only for each male, whose dream is fixed upon her deflowerment and subsequent perpetual possession. This act is a sacrament in all churches and a civil affair in our society. The collective aspects of marriage are thus largely compressed into the rituals and social perquisites of one day. Unless some element of mayhem or intention of divorce subsequently obtrudes, a sort of privacy engulfs the union and all further developments are deemed to be the business of each separate pair, including the transition of Cinderella into mom, which, if it occasions any shock, only adds to the huge, invisible burthen every man carries with him into eternity. It is the weight of this bundle which, incidentally, squeezes out of him the wish for death, his last positive biological resource.

Mom is an American creation. Her elaboration was necessary because she was launched as Cinderella. Past generations of men have accorded to their mothers, as a rule, only such honors as they earned by meritorious action in their individual daily lives. Filial *duty* was recognized by many sorts of civilizations and loyalty to it has been highly regarded among most peoples. But I cannot think, offhand, of any civilization except ours in which an entire division of living men has been used, during wartime, or at any time, to spell out the word "mom" on a drill field, or to perform any equivalent act.

The adoration of motherhood has even been made the basis of a religious cult, but the mother so worshipped achieved maternity without change in her virgin status—a distinction worthy of contemplation in itself—and she thus in no way resembled mom.

Hitherto, in fact, man has shown a considerable qui vive to the dangers which arise from momism and freely perceived that his "old wives" were often vixens, dragons, and Xanthippes. Classical literature makes a constant point of it. Shakespeare dwelt on it. Man has also kept before his mind an awareness that, even in the most lambent mother love, there is always a chance some extraneous current will blow up a change, and the thing will become a consuming furnace. The spectacle of the female devouring her young in the firm belief that it is for their own good is too old in man's legends to be overlooked by any but the most flimsily constructed society. . . .

Megaloid momworship has got completely out of hand. Our land, sub-

1. From *Generation of Vipers,* copyright 1942 by Philip Wylie, and reprinted by permission of Rinehart & Company, Inc., New York.

jectively mapped, would have more silver cords and apron strings crisscrossing it than railroads and telephone wires. Mom is everywhere and everything and damned near everybody, and from her depends all the rest of the U. S. Disguised as good old mom, dear old mom, sweet old mom, your loving mom, and so on, she is the bride at every funeral and the corpse at every wedding. Men live for her and die for her, dote upon her and whisper her name as they pass away, and I believe she has now achieved, in the hierarchy of miscellaneous articles, a spot next to the Bible and the Flag, being reckoned part of both in a way. . . .

Mom is something new in the world of men. Hitherto, mom has been so busy raising a large family, keeping house, doing the chores, and fabricating everything in every home except the floor and the walls that she was rarely a problem to her family or to her equally busy friends, and never one to herself. Usually, until very recently, mom folded up and died of hard work somewhere in the middle of her life. Old ladies were scarce and those who managed to get old did so by making remarkable inner adjustments and by virtue of a fabulous horniness of body, so that they lent to old age not only dignity but metal.

Nowadays, with nothing to do, and tens of thousands of men . . . to maintain her, every clattering prickamette in the republic survives for an incredible number of years, to stamp and jibber in the midst of man, a noisy neuter by natural default or a scientific gelding sustained by science, all tongue and teat and razzmatazz. The machine has deprived her of social usefulness; time has stripped away her biological possibilities and poured her hide full of liquid soap; and man has sealed his own soul beneath the clamorous cordillera by handing her the checkbook and going to work in the service of her caprices. . . .

Satan, we are told, finds work for idle hands to do. There is no mistaking the accuracy of this proverb. Millions of men have heaped up riches and made a conquest of idleness so as to discover what it is that Satan puts them up to. Not one has failed to find out. But never before has a great nation of brave and dreaming men absent-mindedly created a huge class of idle, middle-aged women. Satan himself has been taxed to dig up enterprises enough for them. But the field is so rich, so profligate, so perfectly to his taste, that his first effort, obviously, has been to make it self-enlarging and self-perpetuating. This he has done by whispering into the ears of girls that the only way they can cushion the shock destined to follow the rude disillusionment over the fact that they are not really Cinderella is to institute momworship. Since he had already infested both male and female with the love of worldly goods, a single step accomplished the entire triumph: he taught the gals to teach their men that dowry went the other way, that it was a weekly contribution, and that any male worthy of a Cinderella would have to work like a piston after getting one, so as to be worthy, also, of all the moms in the world. . . .

Mom got herself out of the nursery and the kitchen. She then got out of the house. She did not get out of the church, but, instead, got the stern stuff out of *it,* padded the guild room, and moved in more solidly than ever before. No longer either hesitant or reverent, because there was no cause for either attitude after her purge, she swung the church by the tail as she swung everything else. In a preliminary test of strength, she also got herself the vote and, although politics never interested her (unless she was exceptionally naïve, a hairy foghorn, or a size forty scorpion), the damage she forthwith did to society was so enormous and so rapid that even the best men lost track of things. Mom's first gracious presence at the ballot-box was roughly concomitant with the start toward a new all-time low in political scurviness, hoodlumism, gangsterism, labor strife, monopolistic thuggery, moral degeneration, civic corruption, smuggling, bribery, theft, murder, homosexuality, drunkenness, financial depression, chaos and war. Note that.

The degenerating era, however, marked new highs in the production of junk. Note that, also.

Mom, however, is a great little guy. Pulling pants onto her by these words, let us look at mom.

She is a middle-aged puffin with an eye like a hawk that has just seen a rabbit twitch far below. She is about twenty-five pounds overweight, with no sprint, but sharp heels and a hard backhand which she does not regard as a foul but a womanly defense. In a thousand of her there is not sex appeal enough to budge a hermit ten paces off a rock ledge. She none the less spends several hundred dollars a year on permaments and transformations, pomades, cleansers, rouges, lipsticks, and the like—and fools nobody except herself. If a man kisses her with any earnestness, it is time for mom to feel for her pocketbook, and this occasionally does happen.

She smokes thirty cigarettes a day, chews gum, and consumes tons of bonbons and petit fours. The shortening in the latter, stripped from pigs, sheep and cattle, shortens mom. She plays bridge with the stupid voracity of a hammerhead shark, which cannot see what it is trying to gobble but never stops snapping its jaws and roiling the waves with its tail. She drinks moderately, which is to say, two or three cocktails before dinner every night and a brandy and a couple of highballs afterward. She doesn't count the two cocktails she takes before lunch when she lunches out, which is every day she can. On Saturday nights, at the club or in the juke joint, she loses count of her drinks and is liable to get a little tiddly, which is to say, shot or blind. But it is her man who worries about where to acquire the money while she worries only about how to spend it, so he has the ulcers and colitis and she has the guts of a bear; she can get pretty stiff before she topples.

Her sports are all spectator sports.

She was graduated from high school or a "finishing" school or even a college in her distant past and made up for the unhappiness of compulsory education by sloughing all that she learned so completely that she could not pass the final examinations of a fifth grader. She reads the fiction in three women's magazines each month and occasionally skims through an article, which usually angers her so that she gets other moms to skim through it, and then they have a session on the subject over a canister of spiked coffee in order to damn the magazine, the editors, the author, and the silly girls who run about these days. She reads two or three motion-picture fan magazines also, and goes to the movies about two nights a week. If a picture does not coincide precisely with her attitude of the moment, she converses through all of it and so whiles away the time. She does not appear to be lecherous toward the movie photographs as men do, but that is because she is a realist and a little shy on imagination. However, if she gets to Hollywood and encounters the flesh-and-blood article known as a male star, she and her sister moms will run forward in a mob, wearing a joint expression that must make God rue his invention of bisexuality, and tear the man's clothes from his body, yea, verily, down to his B.V.D.'s.

Mom is organization-minded. Organizations, she has happily discovered, are intimidating to all men, not just to mere men. They frighten politicians to sniveling servility and they terrify pastors; they bother bank presidents and they pulverize school boards. Mom has many such organizations, the real purpose of which is to compel an abject compliance of her environs to her personal desires. With these associations and committees she has double parking ignored, for example. With them she drives out of the town and the state, if possible, all young harlots and all proprietors of places where "questionable" young women (though why they are called that—being of all women the least in question) could possibly foregather, not because she competes with such creatures but because she contrasts so unfavorably with them. With her clubs (a solid term!) she causes bus lines to run where they are convenient for her rather than for workers, plants flowers in sordid spots that would do better with sanitation, snaps independent men out of office and replaces them with clammy castrates, throws prodigious fairs and parties for charity and gives the proceeds, usually about eight dollars, to the janitor to buy the committee some beer for its headache on the morning after, and builds clubhouses for the entertainment of soldiers where she succeeds in persuading thousands of them that they are momsick and would rather talk to her than take Betty into the shrubs. All this, of course, is considered social service, charity, care of the poor, civic reform, patriotism, and self-sacrifice. . . .

Knowing nothing about medicine, art, science, religion, law, sanitation, civics, hygiene, psychology, morals, history, geography, poetry, literature, or any other topic except the all-consuming one of momism, she seldom has any especial interest in *what,* exactly, she is doing as a member of any of these endless organizations, so long as it is *something*. . . .

In churches, the true purpose of organized momhood is to unseat bishops, snatch the frocks off prelates, change rectors just for variety, cross-jet community gossip, take the customary organizational kudos out of the pot each for each, bestow and receive titles, and short-circuit one another.

Mom also has patriotism. If a war comes, this may even turn into a genuine feeling and the departure of her son may be her means to grace in old age. Often, however, the going of her son is only an occasion for more show. She has, in that case, no deep respect for him. What he has permitted her to do to him has rendered him unworthy of consideration—and she has shown him none since puberty. She does not miss him—only his varletry—but over that she can weep interminably. . . .

But, peace or war, the moms have another kind of patriotism that, in the department of the human spirit, is identical to commercialized vice, because it captures a good thing and doles it out for the coin of unctuous pride—at the expense of deceased ancestors rather than young female offspring. By becoming a Daughter of this historic war or that, a woman makes herself into a sort of madam who fills the coffers of her ego with the prestige that has accrued to the doings of others. A frantic emptiness of those coffers provides the impulse for the act. There are, of course, other means of filling them, but they are difficult, and mom never does anything that is difficult—either the moving of a piano or the breaking of a nasty habit. . . .

In the matter of her affiliation of herself with the Daughters of some war the Hitler analogue especially holds, because these sororities of the sword often constitute her Party—her shirtism. Ancestor worship, like all other forms of religion, contained an instinctual reason and developed rituals thought to be germane to the reason. People sedulously followed those rituals, which were basically intended to remind them that they, too, were going to be ancestors someday and would have to labor for personal merit in order to be worthy of veneration. But mom's reverence for her bold forebears lacks even a ritualistic significance, and so instructs her in nothing. She is peremptory about historical truth, mandates, custom, fact, and point. She brushes aside the ideals and concepts for which her forebears perished fighting, as if they were the crumbs of melba toast. Instead, she attributes to the noble dead her own immediate and selfish attitudes. She "knows full well what they would have thought and done," and in that whole-cloth trumpery she goes busting on her way.

Thus the long-vanished warriors who liberated this land from one George in order to make another its first president guide mom divinely as she barges along the badgering boulevard of her life, relaying fiats from the grave on birth control, rayon, vitamins, the power trust, and a hundred other items of which the dead had no knowledge. To some degree most people, these days, are guilty of this absurd procedure. There has been more nonsense printed lately detailing what Jefferson would say about matters he never dreamed of than a sensible man can endure. (I do not have any idea, for instance, and I am sure nobody has any idea, what Jefferson would think about the giddy bungle of interstate truck commerce; but people, columnists especially, will tell you.)

Mom, however, does not merely quote Thomas Jefferson on modern topics: she *is* Thomas Jefferson. This removes her twice from sanity. Mom wraps herself in the mantle of every canny man and coward who has drilled with a musket on this continent and reproduced a line that zigzagged down to mom. In that cloak, together with the other miters, rings, scepters, and power symbols which she has swiped, she has become the American pope.

People are feebly aware of this situation and it has been pointed out at one time or another that the phrase "Mother knows best" has practically worn out the staircase to private hell. Most decriers of matriarchy, however, are men of middle age, like me.

Young men whose natures are attuned to a female image with more feelings than mom possesses and different purposes from those of our synthetic archetype of Cinderella-the-go-getter bounce anxiously away from their first few brutal contacts with modern young women, frightened to find their shining hair is vulcanized, their agate eyes are embedded in cement, and their ruby lips case-hardened into pliers for the bending males like wire. These young men, fresh-startled by learning that She is a chrome-plated afreet, but not able to discern that the condition is mom's unconscious preparation of somebody's sister for a place in the gynecocracy—are, again, presented with a soft and shimmering resting place, the bosom of mom. . . .

"Her boy," having been "protected" by her love, and carefully, even shudderingly, shielded from his logical development through his barbaric period, or childhood (so that he has either to become a barbarian as a man or else to spend most of his energy denying the barbarism that howls in his brain—an autonomous remnant of the youth he was forbidden), is cushioned against any major step in his progress toward maturity. Mom steals from the generation of women behind her (which she has, as a still further defense, also sterilized of integrity and courage) that part of her boy's personality which should have become the love of a female contemporary. Mom transmutes it into sentimentality for herself. . . .

As men grow older, they tend to become more like women, and vice versa. Even physically, their characteristics swap; men's voices rise, their breasts grow, and their chins recede; women develop bass voices and mustaches. This is another complementary, or opposite, turn of nature. It is meant to reconcile sexuality and provide a fountainhead of wisdom uncompromised by it, in the persons of those individuals who are hardy enough and lucky enough to survive to old age in a natural environment. But survival, as I have said, no longer depends on any sort of natural selection, excepting a great basic one which our brains are intended to deal with, and which, if allowed to go brainlessly on, will have to reduce our species to savagery in order to get back to a level on which instinct itself can rule effectively. . . .

I have explained how the moms turned Cinderellaism to their advantage and I have explained that women possess some eighty per cent of the nation's money (the crystal form of its energy) and I need only allude, I think, to the statistical reviews which show that the women are the spenders, wherefore the controlling consumers of nearly all we make with our machines. The steel puddler in Pittsburgh may not think of himself as a feminine tool, but he is really only getting a Chevrolet ready for mom to drive through a garden wall. I should round out this picture of America existing for mom with one or two more details, such as annual increase in the depth of padding in vehicles over the past thirty years due to the fact that a fat rump is more easily irritated than a lean one, and the final essential detail of mom's main subjective preoccupation, which is listening to the radio. The radio is mom's soul; a detail, indeed.

It is also a book in itself, and one I would prefer to have my reader write after he has learned a little of the art of catching overtones as a trained ear, such as mine, catches them. But there must be a note on it.

The radio has made sentimentality the twentieth century Plymouth Rock. As a discipline, I have forced myself to sit a whole morning listening to the soap operas, along with twenty million moms who were busy sweeping dust under carpets while planning to drown their progeny in honey or bash in their heads. This filthy and indecent abomination, this trash with which, until lately, only moron servant girls could dull their credulous minds in the tawdry privacy of their cubicles, is now the national saga. Team after team of feebleminded Annies and Davids crawl from the loudspeaker into the front rooms of America. The characters are impossible, their adventures would make a saint spew, their morals are lower than those of ghouls, their habits are uncleanly, their humor is the substance that starts whole races grinding bayonets, they have no manners, no sense, no goals, no worthy ambitions, no hope, no faith, no information, no values related to reality, and no estimate of truth. They merely sob and snicker—as they cheat each other. . . .

The radio is mom's final tool, for it stamps everybody who listens with the matriarchal brand—its superstitions, prejudices, devotional rules, taboos, musts, and all other qualifications needful to its maintenance. Just as Goebbels has revealed what can be done with such a mass-stamping of the public psyche in his nation, so our land is a living representation of the same fact worked out in matriarchal sentimentality, goo, slop, hidden cruelty, and the foreshadow of national death.

That alone is sinister enough, but the process is still more vicious, because it fills in every crack and cranny of mom's time and mind—and pop's also, since he has long ago yielded the dial-privilege to his female; so that a whole nation of people lives in eternal fugue and never has to deal for one second with itself or its own problems. Any interior sign of worry, wonder, speculation, anxiety, apprehension—or even a stirring of an enfeebled will to plan sanely—can be annihilated by an electrical click whereby the populace puts itself in the place, the untenable place—of somebody called Myrt—and never has even to try to *be* itself alone in the presence of this real world.

This is Nirvana at last. It is also entropy. For here the spirit of man, absorbed, disoriented, confused, identified with ten thousand spurious personalities and motives, has utterly lost itself. By this means is man altogether lost.

The radio, in very truth, sells soap. We could confine it to music, intelligent discourse, and news—all other uses being dangerous—but mom will not let us. Rather than study herself and her environment with the necessary honesty, she will fight for this poisoned syrup to the last. Rather than take up her democratic responsibility in this mighty and tottering republic, she will bring it crashing down simply to maintain to the final rumble of ruin her personal feudalism. Once, sentimentalism was piecework, or cost the price of a movie or a book; now it is mass produced and not merely free, but almost compulsory.

I give you mom. I give you the destroying mother. I give you her justice—from which we have never removed the eye bandage. I give you the angel—and point to the sword in her hand. I give you death—the hundred million deaths that are muttered under Yggdrasill's ash. I give you Medusa and Stheno and Euryale. I give you the harpies and the witches, and the Fates. I give you the woman in pants, and the new religion: she-popery. I give you Pandora. I give you Proserpine, the Queen of Hell. The five-and-ten-cent-store Lilith, the mother of Cain, the black widow who is poisonous and eats her mate, and I designate at the bottom of your program the grand finale of all the soap operas: the mother of America's Cinderella.

We must face the dynasty of the dames at once, deprive them of our pocketbooks when they waste the substance in them, and take back our dreams which, without the perfidious materialism of mom, were shaping up a new and braver world. We must drive roads to Rio and to Moscow and stop spending all our strength in the manufacture of girdles: it is time that mom's sag became known to the desperate public; we must plunge into our psyches and find out there, each for each, scientifically, about immortality and miracles. To do such deeds, we will first have to make the conquest of momism, which grew up from male default.

A TALE OF A TUB[1]

BERGEN EVANS

In the *New York Evening Mail* for December 28, 1917, Mr. H. L. Mencken diverted himself by greeting what he called "A Neglected Anniversary." On that day seventy-five years before, he averred, one Adam Thompson, an adventurous cotton broker in Cincinnati, had created quite a splash by lowering his naked form into the first bathtub installed in America. His act had precipitated a storm of protest. Bathing was universally condemned as an affectation and a menace to health and morals. Medical societies expressed their disapprobation, state legislatures imposed prohibitive taxes to prevent the custom from

1. Reprinted from *The Natural History of Nonsense,* by Bergen Evans, by permission of Alfred A. Knopf, Inc. Copyright 1946 by Bergen Evans.

spreading, and the city of Boston—then as now zealous to protect its citizens from harmful contacts—passed a special ordinance forbidding it. There was strong public resentment when President Fillmore had a tub installed in the White House, but ultimately his example carried the day and bathing came to be tolerated if not practiced by our grandfathers.

This story, in its author's words, "of spoofing all compact," was "a tissue of heavy absurdities, all of them deliberate and most of them obvious," but it was seized upon with avidity by all sorts of people and related as one of the most sacred facts of our history. Quacks used it as evidence of the stupidity of doctors. Doctors used it as proof of medical progress. Bathtub manufacturers used it as proof of their foresight, and assorted reformers used it as proof of the public's lack of it. Editors used it as proof of their own knowledge. It appeared as a contribution to public welfare in thick government bulletins. The standard reference works incorporated it. It was solemnly repeated by master thinkers, including the president of the American Geographical Society and the Commissioner of Health for the City of New York. Dr. Hans Zinsser communicated it to his readers as one of the esoteric facts of medical annals, and Alexander Woollcott shared it with the radio public as one of those quaint bits of lore with which his whimsical mind was so richly stored.

By 1926 Mencken, "having undergone a spiritual rebirth and put off sin," felt that the joke had gone far enough. He confessed publicly that his story had been a hoax and pointed out what he felt should have warned the critical reader against accepting it as a fact. His confession was printed in thirty newspapers "with a combined circulation, according to their sworn claim, of more than 250,000,000," and the gullibility of the public (which had consisted largely in believing these same papers) received many an editorial rebuke.

But the original yarn would not die. Within a month of its exposure it was being reprinted in the very papers that had carried the confession. Mencken printed a second confession, but that too was swept aside. His bathtub had become a juggernaut that was not to be stopped by so slight an impediment as the truth. Congressmen had vouched for it, preachers had woven it into their homilies, and professors had rewritten their textbooks to include it. What chance had the mere disavowal of one whom they regarded as a notorious buffoon against the affirmations of such ponderous respectability?

And so the tale of his tub goes on. Not a week passes but it is repeated in the press or from the pulpit. Mencken has tried once or twice again to undo the damage, but he has been called a meddler and a liar for his pains and has withdrawn from the unequal struggle. The story has taken its place in our national mythology beside Washington's cherry tree and Lincoln's conversion. It is now above argument and beyond evidence. Five minutes in any library would be enough to refute it, but it has ceased to be a question of fact and has become an article of faith.

Certain reasons for this are fairly obvious. It is one of those stories—like the theory that Bacon wrote Shakespeare—that make their narrators seem very learned without putting them to the trouble of having to acquire knowledge. It has earned many an easy dollar for sage and commentator and has added enough "fresh material" to textbooks to justify forcing a new edition on the students.

But such temporary individual advantages would not fully account for its vitality. Better canards have been shorter lived. The bathtub story plainly touches something deep in our national psyche, and if we could know why it has spread so vigorously we might know a great deal more about vulgar errors.

One element in its success is that it supports the great idea of progress and particularly the American conviction that progress is to be measured by the increase of material conveniences and creature comforts, an idea that is very important in our national life. An insistent and expensive advertising campaign has connected it with the calendar; the average American is apparently convinced that all mechanical contrivances automatically improve every three hundred and sixty-five days, and under the spell of this delusion he has bought hundreds of millions of cars and radios and refrigerators that he did not need, to the profit of those who fostered the delusion.

The idea of progress is one of our great national investments. The amount of money spent in the schools, in the newspapers, and on the radio to protect it exceeds computation. It is part and parcel of "boosting," of that mass optimism which has made us, for good and evil, what we are today. Nothing is more treasonable to the basic American spirit than to doubt that we have improved and are improving—every day and in every way.

And, for reasons that the social historian can perhaps explain, the bathtub has become a special symbol not only of our material progress but of our spiritual progress as well. For we set great store by things of the spirit. Nothing is more warmly rejoiced in than our superiority to the grimy Europeans in the matter of bathtubs. Cleanliness is far ahead of godliness. State that a man mistreats his bathtub and—as far as most well-to-do Americans are concerned—you have put him beyond the pale of consideration. No argument against public housing has been used more consistently and, one suspects, more effectively than the assertion that even if you give bathtubs to the poor they will only dump coal in them. To point out that most housing projects are centrally heated and supplied with gas and electricity, so that their occupants have no need of coal, is to earn the reproach of being frivolous. It is absolutely "known" that all occupants of housing projects put coal in their bathtubs. And their so doing indicates such depravity that to build houses for them is practically contributing to moral delinquency. The poor have been weighed in the bathtub and found wanting.

It begins to be a little clearer why Mencken's hoax has flourished so. It flatters provincial smugness. It implies that comfortable folk did not come by their comforts without a struggle. They deserve what they have. After all, they pioneered with running hot water. They are heroes, with their thick mats and heavy towels. Their scented soap was gained only through foresight and endurance.

A similar myth, which has had a smaller circulation but has done fairly well and promises to do better, is that the umbrella is a recent innovation and that its early users had to brave public scorn before they could persuade their obtuse fellows to follow their example. One of our largest life insurance companies informs the public in an advertisement that when umbrellas were first introduced they were attacked as a "rediculos effemenacy," and were generally accepted "only when physicians urged their use 'to keep off vertigoes, sore eyes and fevers.'" The *Encyclopædia Britannica,* which seems to have taken its information from *The Dictionary of National Biography,* says that Jonas Hanway "is said to have been the first Londoner habitually to carry an umbrella, and he lived to triumph over all the hackney coachmen who tried to hoot and hustle him down."

Here, again, we have the idea of progress, and here again the glorification of Milquetoast, a suggestion—not inappropriate for a life insurance company —that there is something brave in seeking your own comfort. Policy holders must all have moments of wondering whether they are not perhaps being a little timid about life, and it must be a great satisfaction to learn that they are in a heroic tradition. The only thing wrong with the analogy, however, is that it is based on error. Umbrellas had been in general use for a hundred and fifty years before the scene depicted in the advertisement, long before Jonas Hanway was born, and for anything we know those who carried them were regarded then as they are now—with envy when it was raining and contempt when it was not.[2]

Mere mistakes in point of fact, however, do not in themselves make vulgar errors. They are often the starting point, but the fallacy is always the product of certain processes in popular thinking: of arguing from negatives and analogies, of making false generalizations, of worshipping coincidence, of taking rhetoric for fact, of never questioning or even perceiving the underlying conceptions that make for prejudice, and, above all, of a romantic delight in the wonderful for its own sake. And once made, the error, as has been suggested, is likely to owe its vitality to intellectual currents and social forces with which, superficially regarded, it has no seeming connection.

---

2. For the National Life Insurance Company's advertisement, see *Life,* January 29, 1945, p. 2.

The *Encyclopædia Britannica,* 14th ed., 1943 revision, vol. 11, p. 166; *The Dictionary of National Biography,* vol. VIII, p. 1197.

"The tuck'd-up semstress walks with hasty strides
While streams run down her oil'd umbrella's sides."
—Jonathan Swift, *Description of a City Shower* (1710)

And see "umbrella" in *The Oxford English Dictionary* for references as early as 1610.

It will be remembered that an umbrella was one of the first conveniences of civilization that Robinson Crusoe made for himself.

Popular logic is Erewhonian logic. Whereas the trained mind accords belief to plausible evidence only and grants a possibility solely on the basis of a sound inference from established facts, the untrained mind insists that a proposition must be true if it cannot be *dis*proved. "You can't prove it *isn't* so!" is as good as Q.E.D. in folk logic—as though it were necessary to submit a piece of the moon to chemical analysis before you could be sure that it was not made of green cheese.

Analogical argument—the inferring of a further degree of resemblance from an observed degree—is one of the greatest pitfalls of popular thinking. In medicine it formerly led to what was known as the doctrine of signatures, by which walnuts were prescribed for brain troubles because walnut meats look something like miniature brains, foxes' lungs were prescribed for asthma because foxes were thought to have unusual respiratory powers, and bear's grease was rubbed on the head for baldness because bears have hairy coats. Hundreds of futile remedies were based on such false analogies, and they have not all been cleared off druggists' shelves yet, though the survivors are no doubt "scientifically" prepared and packaged.

Nor was this form of reasoning confined to medicine. It invaded every department of life. It led our grandfathers to wear red flannel underwear because heat is associated with the color of fire. It endowed various gems with properties suggested by their colors, and it has led modern telepathists to insist that the radio justifies their metaphysical assumptions.

Many popular fallacies are rooted in verbal confusions. How few people who dismiss unwelcome evidence by saying that "the exception proves the rule" have any idea of what the saying actually means, and how fewer still have any idea of what they mean by using it! So enmeshed is error in words that a whole new science, semantics, has sprung up which offers, with little danger of being challenged, to produce the millennium just as soon as people know for sure what they are talking about. But since much of the vagueness and confusion is in the words themselves, since all words are in a sense abstractions, the semanticists will probably not get anywhere until (as Swift suggested two hundred years ago) they abandon language altogether and carry about with them the objects to which they wish to allude. This solution of the problems of logic, however, raises even greater problems in logistics and so may fail for lack of a proper trial.

The common mind is intensely literal. The public loves rhetoric, yet it is continually taking rhetoric for fact, often with far-reaching and unpleasant consequences. It would be impossible to estimate, for example, how many lives have been blighted and how much human misery has been augmented by the concept of "blood" as a transmitter of heredity. Yet the term is merely a trope. It has no reality whatever.

The power of this tendency to create myths has recently been demonstrated in the famous assurance that "there are no atheists in foxholes." As nearly as the origin of the formula can be traced, it was first uttered by Lieutenant-

Colonel Warren J. Clear in a story of Bataan's final weeks, delivered during the "Army Hour" program over the NBC Red Network in 1942. Colonel Clear attributed the immortal observation to an unnamed sergeant who had shared a foxhole with him during a Japanese bombing raid. No pretense was made that there had been an official catechism of every man or that the sergeant was a trained theologian. It was simply meant to be an emphatic way of saying that all men in the moment of peril seek the support of religion.

Whether they do or not is as much a question as whether it is creditable to religion to claim that they do, but neither question was widely agitated. As far as the populace was concerned the rhetorical flourish was a military fact, and as far as the papers were concerned it was always news, however frequently repeated. At first it was only the foxholes of Bataan that were distinguished for their conversional powers, but as the war spread the *mana* was found in any sheltering declivity, and the trenches of Port Moresby and Guadalcanal delivered their quota of converts. There was no reason, of course, why Divine favor should be confined to the infantry, and other branches of the services were soon touched with similar grace. By December 1943, according to an article in the *Reader's Digest,* atheists had been pretty well cleaned out of cockpits (where God, it will be remembered, had been retained in the inferior position of co-pilot); and Rickenbacker's celestial seagull drove them even from rubber rafts. A few skeptics may have gone on lurking in the glory holes of the Merchant Marine, but their enlightenment merely awaited the first torpedo.[3]

There were, of course, dissenting voices. Poon Lim, a Chinese steward, who existed for one hundred and thirty-three days alone on a raft in the South Atlantic, stated, on being rescued, that nothing in the experience had led him to believe in a merciful Providence, even though he too had had a seagull. But then he was a heathen to begin with.

The American Association for the Advancement of Atheism felt that the phrase was a reflection on the patriotism of their members and did their best to refute it. They managed to find at least one sturdy doubter in the army who had had his dog tag stamped "Atheist"; but unfortunately, though he had once been run over by a tank, he had never been in a foxhole, and hence could not technically qualify. A better candidate, whom the A.A.A.A. overlooked, was E. J. Kahn, Jr., who in one of his articles in the *New Yorker* confessed that he was not a religious man and in another that he had dived into a latrine trench when Jap planes were overhead. Of course an unbeliever in

3. See the *Reader's Digest,* December 1943, pp. 26–28.

Spectacular conversions in times of stress are claimed not only for the common man but for the hero. Thus Lincoln was said to have been converted on the battlefield of Gettysburg, though the widow of Henry Ward Beecher insisted that Brooklyn was the locale of, and the battle of Bull Run the motivation for, this alleged illumination. See Lloyd Lewis: *Myths after Lincoln* (New York: Harcourt, Brace and Company; 1940), pp. 382–85.

a latrine is not exactly an atheist in a foxhole, but the faithful would probably have been willing to accept it as a reasonable facsimile.

Not that it would have done the Association any good to have found a whole regiment of atheists encamped in a thousand foxholes—as they probably could, had they gone to our Russian allies for assistance. The phrase was intended to confirm prejudice, not to describe combat conditions, and prejudice is not open to conviction.

On the other hand, fortunately, it is not very convincing either. Prejudices are never shaken by counterprejudices because we never perceive our prejudices to be such. We take them either for reasoned conclusions or for revealed truths, and the most serious prejudices of all, those that affect our thinking most, are generally below the level of consciousness. We think within the framework of concepts of which we are often unaware. Our most earnest thoughts are sometimes shaped by our absurdest delusions. We see what we want to see, and observation conforms to hypothesis. Thus it has been suggested that Darwin's theory of sexual selection was owing not to his observations as a naturalist but to his convictions as a gentleman that certain courtesies were due a lady, though five minutes spent in watching chickens ought to have dispelled the assumption that Nature shared his code.

The manner in which our thinking is shaped by our unconscious attitudes and assumptions is strikingly illustrated by our reference to China and Japan as "the East," when in America they would be more properly described as "the West." Of course they are east if you go far enough, but by that logic Chicago is east of New York. The real explanation is that we are Europe-minded—or, more specifically, England-minded. And still more striking is it that Japan, at least, also conceives of herself as the East. She too is Europe-minded, and probably just as unconsciously so. Yet her flag shows her point of view. The menace of the Rising Sun was lost on our complacent fathers, who failed to observe its implication—namely that Japan conceived of herself as a new power, of unparalleled brilliance and glory, rising *on the European horizon.*

The popular mind, irrational and prejudiced, makes some effort to examine evidence, but it has very little knowledge of the true nature of what it is looking for or of the forces at work to frustrate and confuse it in its search. It generalizes from exceptions, and from a mass of experience selects only those elements that confirm its preconceptions—without the faintest awareness of what it is doing. Most of what is called thinking—even up to and including much of what goes on in the brains of college faculties—is actually a seeking for confirmation of previous convictions. The true scientific spirit that leads men to be particularly suspicious of all beliefs they hold dear is utterly incomprehensible to most people. To the naïve, skepticism often seems malicious perversity: only "some secret enemy in the inward degenerate nature of man," said Topsell, could lead anyone to doubt the existence of the unicorn.

And in the eternal search for verification of supernaturalism which engrosses so much of popular "philosophy," nothing passes for more cogent evidence than coincidence. The marveling over unexpected juxtapositions is at once the mark and the diversion of banal minds, and most of them do not require very remarkable happenings to constitute coincidences. Those who for lack of knowledge or imagination expect nothing out of the ordinary are always encountering the unexpected. One of the commonest of "coincidences," as Professor Jastrow has pointed out, is the crossing of letters in the mail. It happens a thousand times a day, yet thousands of men and women whip themselves into amazement every time it happens. As far as they are concerned, it is complete and final proof of the supernatural, whether it be telepathy or Divine guidance or merely soul calling to soul. There it is, sealed, stamped, and delivered. Yet of all human happenings, what is more likely than that lovers or relatives should simultaneously decide to write to each other?

The wonder of most coincidence is subjective. As far as sheer unlikelihood goes, an unsolicited advertisement in the mail is a greater marvel than a letter from someone to whom we have just written. But since we have no emotional interest in the advertisement we rarely meditate upon the "miracle" of its arrival, and, even where some occurrence is unusual enough to justify comment, a desire to exalt ourselves or a complete preoccupation with our own affairs usually prevents us from evaluating its true nature. That the working of the law of averages has no effect whatever on individual instances is a fact that even trained observers sometimes seem reluctant to face. The chances against almost anything's happening just the way it did are almost infinite, and it is very easy to see marvels if you are looking for them. It has been estimated, for example, that a bridge hand consisting of all the spades in the pack can be expected, according to the law of averages, only once in approximately eight hundred billion deals. Apprised of this, any man dealt such a hand could very easily permit himself to be awestruck, and it would be impossible to convince him that there was nothing remarkable about the hand except that it happened to be a desirable one—since exactly the same odds prevail for any hand whatever.

Attempts to point this out, however, would probably be met with resentment, since they would detract from the importance of the individual concerned. He would prefer, most likely, to go on believing that the normal order of things had been suspended for his advantage. For the popular love of the marvelous is, at bottom, egotism. That is why it is so easy to encourage it, as the popular press does, inflating every commonplace into a wonder or manufacturing marvels outright. Half the "miracles" of modern times are pure journalistic fabrications. The success they can achieve was shown in November 1929, when the Boston *Globe* sent a million and a quarter people stampeding into the cemetery at Malden, Massachusetts, by playing up sensational "cures" that were said to have taken place there. A hysterical woman who had been unable to walk for a year, although her hospital record showed no organic trouble, leaped with joy under the healing influence of the flashbulbs. A blind boy was said to have regained his sight; his own pathetic insistence that he was no better was suppressed, despite his father's indignant efforts to get the papers to retract the story of his "cure." Crippled children were stripped of their braces and photographed quickly before they sprawled, crying, in the mud. Meanwhile extras sold like hot cakes and the Mayor knelt in reverence for the rotogravure.

Deliberate misrepresentations and creations of the incidents they "report" are a staple activity of all but half a dozen papers and news magazines in the country. Consider the unwearied zeal with which they have labored to sustain "the curse of Tut-ankh-amen." No one in any remote way connected with the discovery or opening of the tomb can die, at any age whatever, but his death is seen as the working of the "curse." Edgar Wallace, writing in *McCall's Magazine,* said that the very day the tomb was opened a cobra ate the chief explorer's canary, and, from that day to this, Egyptian vengeance has stalked the entire party. In the papers, that is. As a matter of prosaic record, the members of the expedition seem to have enjoyed remarkable health and to have been blessed with longevity far beyond actuarial expectancy.

The retelling of the myth, of course, has earned many a penny and added to the success of many a raconteur. People dearly love the old lies, while truth, as Milton said, "never comes into the world but like a bastard, to the ignominy of him that brought her birth."

Irrationality must come close to being the largest single vested interest in the world. It has a dozen service stations in every town. There are twenty-five thousand practicing astrologers in America who disseminate their lore through a hundred daily columns, fifteen monthly, and two annual publications—and this does not include the half-dozen "confidential" news letters that keep business executives so consistently misinformed about the future. It is even said that there is a movement on foot to have a Federal astrologer appointed as an officer of the government, and, considering the official recognition given to other forms of superstition, the movement may succeed.

But astrologers and crystal gazers are not alone. More men than Bertrand Russell's "bishops and bookies" live off the irrational hopes of mankind. Journalists, stockbrokers, realtors, advertisers, lawyers, professors, promoters, doctors, druggists, and politicians also derive a part of their income from the same source. In fact, everyone in our society not directly engaged in the production and distribution of necessities, transportation, artistic creation, elementary teaching, or the maintenance of public order, to some extent, and more or less consciously, preys upon ignorance and delusion.

A great deal of this exploitation is open and shameless. The supply house, for example, that sold nearly half a million steel-jacketed Testaments and prayer books, at exorbitant prices, to the pathetic and gullible relatives of service men, with the vague assurance that they were "capable of deflecting bullets," was, as the Federal Trade Commission implied, obtaining money under false pretenses. The metal shields, for all the "God Bless You" stamped on them and the sacred literature under them, would, if struck by a bullet, produce almost certainly fatal wounds.

There is a lot of this sort of thing going on, and those who practice it in a small way frequently end up in jail. But those who practice it in a big way frequently end up in *Who's Who* and *The Social Register*. They are our prophets and publicists. They do not actually do the stealing; they supply the sanctions for those who do, and they function chiefly by sonorously repeating clichés. They do not have to prove that this or that proposed reform is wrong; all they have to do is to say that "soft living weakens a nation." They do not labor to defend racial discrimination; they support "innate differences."

One of their most effective catchwords of late has been "science." "Scientists say," or "Scientists agree," or "Science has proved" is a formula of incantation that is thought to place any statement that follows it above critical examination. They love to recall the doubt and scorn that were heaped on scientists in an earlier day, not as a rebuke to those particular doubters—they are still doing a brisk business at the old stands—but as a rebuke to doubt itself.

For the thing they must defend is not this or that belief, but the spirit of credulity. To this end they propagate a vague sort of supernaturalism. They have no profound religious beliefs. Most of them, indeed, would deride their own metaphysical professions if they were presented to them in any but the accustomed phrases; but they are convinced that such beliefs are "good for the people," and they repel any specific questioning of any specific belief as "bad taste." They seem to assume that there is some abstraction called "religion" which is apart from any particular religious belief, yet which is of so sacred a nature that it throws a taboo of silence over all religions. Religion, they say, is a subject that "one doesn't discuss"—though truly religious people do not agree with them.

No error is harmless. "Men rest not in false apprehensions without absurd and inconsequent deductions." Some of the deductions seem inconsequential as well as inconsequent, but in their larger aspects they are not. It cannot do much harm to believe that hair turns white over night, or that birds live a happy family life, or that orientals have slanting eyes; but it can do a great deal of harm to be ignorant of physiology or zoology or anthropology, and the harm that may result from forming an opinion without evidence, or from distorting evidence to support an opinion, is incalculable.

Obscurantism and tyranny go together as naturally as skepticism and democracy. It is very convenient for anyone who profits by the docility of the masses to have them believe that they are not the masters of their fate and that the evils they must endure are beyond human control. It was not surprising to find the author of *Man the Unknown* collaborating with the Nazis. The mist of mysticism has always provided good cover for those who do not want their actions too closely looked into.

From the time of the Peasants' Rebellion on, all true democratic movements have been branded as anti-religious. In part this has been an effort to discredit them, and in part it has been a perception that democracy is essentially antiauthoritarian—that it not only demands the right but imposes the responsibility of thinking for ourselves. And belief is the antithesis to thinking. A refusal to come to an unjustified conclusion is an element of an honest man's religion. To him the call to blind faith is really a call to barbarism and slavery. In being asked to believe without evidence, he is being asked to abdicate his integrity. Freedom of speech and freedom of action are meaningless without freedom to think. And there is no freedom of thought without doubt. The civilized man has a moral obligation to be skeptical, to demand the credentials of all statements that claim to be facts. An honorable man will not be bullied by a hypothesis. For in the last analysis all tyranny rests on fraud, on getting someone to accept false assumptions, and any man who for one moment abandons or suspends the questioning spirit has for that moment betrayed humanity.

PECUNIARY CANONS OF TASTE [1]

THORSTEIN VEBLEN

THE caution has already been repeated more than once, that while the regulating norm of consumption is in large part the requirement of conspicuous waste, it must not be understood that the motive on which the consumer acts in any given case is this principle in its bald, unsophisticated form. Ordinarily his motive is a wish to conform to established usage, to avoid unfavourable notice and comment, to live up to the accepted canons of decency in the kind, amount, and grade of goods consumed, as well as in the decorous employment of his time and effort. In the common run of cases this sense of prescriptive usage is present in the motives of the consumer and exerts a direct constraining force, especially as regards consumption carried on under the eyes of observers. But a considerable element of prescriptive expensiveness is observable also in consumption that does not in any appreciable degree become known to outsiders—as, for instance, articles of underclothing, some articles of food, kitchen utensils, and other household apparatus designed for service rather than for evidence. In all such useful articles a close scrutiny will discover certain features which add to the cost and enhance the commercial value of the goods in question, but do not proportionately increase the serviceability of these articles for the material purposes which alone they ostensibly are designed to serve.

1. From *The Theory of the Leisure Class* by Thorstein Veblen. By permission of The Viking Press, Inc., New York.

Under the selective surveillance of the law of conspicuous waste there grows up a code of accredited canons of consumption, the effect of which is to hold the consumer up to a standard of expensiveness and wastefulness in his consumption of goods and in his employment of time and effort. This growth of prescriptive usage has an immediate effect upon economic life, but it has also an indirect and remoter effect upon conduct in other respects as well. Habits of thought with respect to the expression of life in any given direction unavoidably affect the habitual view of what is good and right in life in other directions also. In the organic complex of habits of thought which make up the substance of an individual's conscious life the economic interest does not lie isolated and distinct from all other interests. Something, for instance, has already been said of its relation to the canons of reputability.

The principle of conspicuous waste guides the formation of habits of thought as to what is honest and reputable in life and in commodities. In so doing, this principle will traverse other norms of conduct which do not primarily have to do with the code of pecuniary honour, but which have, directly or incidentally, an economic significance of some magnitude. So the canon of honorific waste may, immediately or remotely, influence the sense of duty, the sense of beauty, the sense of utility, the sense of devotional or ritualistic fitness, and the scientific sense of truth.

It is scarcely necessary to go into a discussion here of the particular points at which, or the particular manner in which, the canon of honorific expenditure habitually traverses the canons of moral conduct. The matter is one which has received large attention and illustration at the hands of those whose office it is to watch and admonish with respect to any departures from the accepted code of morals. In modern communities, where the dominant economic and legal feature of the community's life is the institution of private property, one of the salient features of the code of morals is the sacredness of property. There needs no insistence or illustration to gain assent to the proposition that the habit of holding private property inviolate is traversed by the other habit of seeking wealth for the sake of the good repute to be gained through its conspicuous consumption. Most offences against property, especially offences of an appreciable magnitude, come under this head. It is also a matter of common notoriety and byword that in offences which result in a large accession of property to the offender he does not ordinarily incur the extreme penalty or the extreme obloquy with which his offence would be visited on the ground of the naïve moral code alone. The thief or swindler who has gained great wealth by his delinquency has a better chance than the small thief of escaping the rigorous penalty of the law; and some good repute accrues to him from his increased wealth and from his spending the irregularly acquired possessions in a seemly manner. A well-bred expenditure of his booty especially appeals with great effect to persons of a cultivated sense of the proprieties, and goes far to mitigate the sense of moral turpitude with which his dereliction is viewed by them. It may be noted also—and it is more immediately to the point—that we are all inclined to condone an offence against property in the case of a man whose motive is the worthy one of providing the means of a "decent" manner of life for his wife and children. If it is added that the wife has been "nurtured in the lap of luxury," that is accepted as an additional extenuating circumstance. That is to say, we are prone to condone such an offence where its aim is the honorific one of enabling the offender's wife to perform for him such an amount of vicarious consumption of time and substance as is demanded by the standard of pecuniary decency. In such a case the habit of approving the accustomed degree of conspicuous waste traverses the habit of deprecating violations of ownership, to the extent even of sometimes leaving the award of praise or blame uncertain. This is peculiarly true where the dereliction involves an appreciable predatory or piratical element.

This topic need scarcely be pursued farther here; but the remark may not be out of place that all that considerable body of morals that clusters about the concept of an inviolable ownership is itself a psychological precipitate of the traditional meritoriousness of wealth. And it should be added that this wealth which is held sacred is valued primarily for the sake of the good repute to be got through its conspicuous consumption. . . .

Obviously, the canon of conspicuous waste is accountable for a great portion of what may be called devout consumption; as, *e.g.*, the consumption of sacred edifices, vestments, and other goods of the same class. Even in those modern cults to whose divinities is imputed a predilection for temples not built with hands, the sacred buildings and the other properties of the cult are constructed and decorated with some view to a reputable degree of wasteful expenditure. And it needs but little either of observation or introspection —and either will serve the turn—to assure us that the expensive splendour of the house of worship has an appreciable uplifting and mellowing effect upon the worshipper's frame of mind. It will serve to enforce the same fact if we reflect upon the sense of abject shamefulness with which any evidence of indigence or squalor about the sacred place affects all beholders. The accessories of any devout observance should be pecuniarily above reproach. This requirement is imperative, whatever latitude may be allowed with regard to these accessories in point of æsthetic or other serviceability.

It may also be in place to notice that in all communities, especially in neighbourhoods where the standard of pecuniary decency for dwellings is not high, the local sanctuary is more ornate, more conspicuously wasteful in its architecture and decoration, than the dwelling-houses of the congregation. This is true of nearly all denominations and cults, whether Christian or Pagan, but it is true in a peculiar degree of the older and maturer cults. At the same time the sanctuary commonly contributes little if anything to the physical comfort of the members. Indeed, the sacred structure not only serves the physical well-being of the members to but a slight extent, as compared with their humbler dwelling-houses; but it is felt by all men that a right and enlightened sense of the true, the beautiful, and the good demands that in all expenditure on the sanctuary anything that might serve the comfort of the worshipper should be conspicuously absent. If any element of comfort is admitted in the fittings of the sanctuary, it should at least be scrupulously screened and masked under an ostensible austerity. In the most reputable latter-day houses of worship, where no expense is spared, the principle of austerity is carried to the length of making the fittings of the place a means of mortifying the flesh, especially in appearance. There are few persons of delicate tastes in the matter of devout consumption to whom this austerely wasteful discomfort does not appeal as intrinsically right and good. Devout consumption is of the nature of vicarious consumption. This canon of devout austerity is based on the pecuniary reputability of conspicuously wasteful consumption, backed by the principle that vicarious consumption should conspicuously not conduce to the comfort of the vicarious consumer.

The sanctuary and its fittings have something of this austerity in all the cults in which the saint or divinity to whom the sanctuary pertains is not conceived to be present and make personal use of the property for the gratification of luxurious tastes imputed to him. The character of the sacred paraphernalia is somewhat different in this respect in those cults where the habits of life imputed to the divinity more nearly approach those of an earthly patriarchal potentate—where he is conceived to make use of these consumable goods in person. In the latter case the sanctuary and its fittings take on more of the fashion given to goods destined for the conspicuous consumption of a temporal master or owner. On the other hand, where the sacred apparatus is simply employed in the divinity's service, that is to say, where it is consumed vicariously on his account by his servants, there the sacred properties take the character suited to goods that are destined for vicarious consumption only. . . .

These canons of reputability have had a similar, but more far-reaching and more specifically determinable, effect upon the popular sense of beauty or serviceability in consumable goods. The requirements of pecuniary decency have, to a very appreciable extent, influenced the sense of beauty and of utility in articles of use or beauty. Articles are to an extent preferred for use on account of their being conspicuously wasteful; they are felt to be serviceable somewhat in proportion as they are wasteful and ill adapted to their ostensible use.

The utility of articles valued for their beauty depends closely upon the expensiveness of the articles. A homely illustration will bring out this dependence. A hand-wrought silver spoon, of a commercial value of some ten to twenty dollars, is not ordinarily more serviceable—in the first sense of the word—than a machine-made spoon of the same material. It may not even be more serviceable than a machine-made spoon of some "base" metal, such as aluminum, the value of which may be no more than some ten to twenty cents. The former of the two utensils is, in fact, commonly a less effective contrivance for its ostensible purpose than the latter. The objection is of course ready to hand that, in taking this view of the matter, one of the chief uses,

if not the chief use, of the costlier spoon is ignored; the hand-wrought spoon gratifies our taste, our sense of the beautiful, while that made by machinery out of the base metal has no useful office beyond a brute efficiency. The facts are no doubt as the objection states them, but it will be evident on reflection that the objection is after all more plausible than conclusive. It appears (1) that while the different materials of which the two spoons are made each possesses beauty and serviceability for the purpose for which it is used, the material of the hand-wrought spoon is some one hundred times more valuable than the baser metal, without very greatly excelling the latter in intrinsic beauty of grain or colour, and without being in any appreciable degree superior in point of mechanical serviceability; (2) if a close inspection should show that the supposed hand-wrought spoon were in reality only a very clever imitation of hand-wrought goods, but an imitation so cleverly wrought as to give the same impression of line and surface to any but a minute examination by a trained eye, the utility of the article, including the gratification which the user derives from its contemplation as an object of beauty, would immediately decline by some eighty or ninety per cent, or even more; (3) if the two spoons are, to a fairly close observer, so nearly identical in appearance that the lighter weight of the spurious article alone betrays it, this identity of form and colour will scarcely add to the value of the machine-made spoon, nor appreciably enhance the gratification of the user's "sense of beauty" in contemplating it, so long as the cheaper spoon is not a novelty, and so long as it can be procured at a nominal cost.

The case of the spoons is typical. The superior gratification derived from the use and contemplation of costly and supposedly beautiful products is, commonly, in great measure a gratification of our sense of costliness masquerading under the name of beauty. Our higher appreciation of the superior article is an appreciation of its superior honorific character, much more frequently than it is an unsophisticated appreciation of its beauty. The requirement of conspicuous wastefulness is not commonly present, consciously, in our canons of taste, but it is none the less present as a constraining norm selectively shaping and sustaining our sense of what is beautiful, and guiding our discrimination with respect to what may legitimately be approved as beautiful and what may not.

It is at this point, where the beautiful and the honorific meet and blend, that a discrimination between serviceability and wastefulness is most difficult in any concrete case. It frequently happens that an article which serves the honorific purpose of conspicuous waste is at the same time a beautiful object; and the same application of labour to which it owes its utility for the former purpose may, and often does, go to give beauty of form and colour to the article. The question is further complicated by the fact that many objects, as, for instance, the precious stones and metals and some other materials used for adornment and decoration, owe their utility as items of conspicuous waste to an antecedent utility as objects of beauty. Gold, for instance, has a high degree of sensuous beauty; very many if not most of the highly prized works of art are intrinsically beautiful, though often with material qualification; the like is true of some stuffs used for clothing, of some landscapes, and of many other things in less degree. Except for this intrinsic beauty which they possess, these objects would scarcely have been coveted as they are, or have become monopolised objects of pride to their possessors and users. But the utility of these things to the possessor is commonly due less to their intrinsic beauty than to the honour which their possession and consumption confers, or to the obloquy which it wards off.

Apart from their serviceability in other respects, these objects are beautiful and have a utility as such; they are valuable on this account if they can be appropriated or monopolised; they are, therefore, coveted as valuable possessions, and their exclusive enjoyment gratifies the possessor's sense of pecuniary superiority at the same time that their contemplation gratifies his sense of beauty. But their beauty, in the naïve sense of the word, is the occasion rather than the ground of their monopolisation or of their commercial value. "Great as is the sensuous beauty of gems, their rarity and price adds an expression of distinction to them, which they would never have if they were cheap." There is, indeed, in the common run of cases under this head, relatively little incentive to the exclusive possession and use of these beautiful things, except on the ground of their honorific character as items of conspicuous waste. Most objects of this general class, with the partial exception of articles of personal adornment, would serve all other purposes than the honorific one equally well, whether owned by the person viewing them or not; and even as regards personal ornaments it is to be added that their chief purpose is to lend éclat to the person of their wearer (or owner) by comparison with other persons who are compelled to do without. The æsthetic serviceability of objects of beauty is not greatly nor universally heightened by possession.

The generalisation for which the discussion so far affords ground is that any valuable object in order to appeal to our sense of beauty must conform to the requirements of beauty and of expensiveness both. But this is not all. Beyond this the canon of expensiveness also affects our tastes in such a way as to inextricably blend the marks of expensiveness, in our appreciation, with the beautiful features of the object, and to subsume the resultant effect under the head of an appreciation of beauty simply. The marks of expensiveness come to be accepted as beautiful features of the expensive articles. They are pleasing as being marks of honorific costliness, and the pleasure which they afford on this score blends with that afforded by the beautiful form and colour of the object; so that we often declare that an article of apparel, for instance, is "perfectly lovely," when pretty much all that an analysis of the æsthetic value of the article would leave ground for is the declaration that it is pecuniarily honorific.

This blending and confusion of the elements of expensiveness and of beauty is, perhaps, best exemplified in articles of dress and of household furniture.

The code of reputability in matters of dress decides what shapes, colours, materials, and general effects in human apparel are for the time to be accepted as suitable; and departures from the code are offensive to our taste, supposedly as being departures from æsthetic truth. The approval with which we look upon fashionable attire is by no means to be accounted pure make-believe. We readily, and for the most part with utter sincerity, find those things pleasing that are in vogue. Shaggy dress-stuffs and pronounced colour effects, for instance, offend us at times when the vogue is goods of a high, glossy finish and neutral colours. A fancy bonnet of this year's model unquestionably appeals to our sensibilities to-day much more forcibly than an equally fancy bonnet of the model of last year; although when viewed in the perspective of a quarter of a century, it would, I apprehend, be a matter of the utmost difficulty to award the palm for intrinsic beauty to the one rather than to the other of these structures. So, again, it may be remarked that, considered simply in their physical juxtaposition with the human form, the high gloss of a gentleman's hat or of a patent-leather shoe has no more of intrinsic beauty than a similarly high gloss on a threadbare sleeve; and yet there is no question but that all well-bred people (in the Occidental civilised communities) instinctively and unaffectedly cleave to the one as a phenomenon of great beauty, and eschew the other as offensive to every sense to which it can appeal. It is extremely doubtful if any one could be induced to wear such a contrivance as the high hat of civilised society, except for some urgent reason based on other than æsthetic grounds.

By further habituation to an appreciative perception of the marks of expensiveness in goods, and by habitually identifying beauty with reputability, it comes about that a beautiful article which is not expensive is accounted not beautiful. In this way it has happened, for instance, that some beautiful flowers pass conventionally for offensive weeds; others that can be cultivated with relative ease are accepted and admired by the lower middle class, who can afford no more expensive luxuries of this kind; but these varieties are rejected as vulgar by those people who are better able to pay for expensive flowers and who are educated to a higher schedule of pecuniary beauty in the florist's products; while still other flowers, of no greater intrinsic beauty than these, are cultivated at great cost and call out much admiration from flower-lovers whose tastes have been matured under the critical guidance of a polite environment. . . .

It is not only with respect to consumable goods—including domestic animals—that the canons of taste have been coloured by the canons of pecuniary reputability. Something to the like effect is to be said for beauty in persons. In order to avoid whatever may be matter of controversy, no weight will be given in this connection to such popular predilection as there may be for the dignified (leisurely) bearing and portly presence that are by vulgar tradition associated with opulence in mature men. These traits are in some measure accepted as elements of personal beauty. But there are certain elements of feminine beauty, on the other hand, which come in under this head, and which are of so concrete and specific a character as to admit of itemised appreciation. It is more or less a rule that in communities which are at the stage of economic development at which women are valued by the upper class for their service, the ideal of female beauty is a robust, large-limbed woman. The ground of appreciation is the physique, while the conformation of the face is of secondary weight only. A well-known instance of this ideal of the early predatory culture is that of the maidens of the Homeric poems.

This ideal suffers a change in the succeeding development, when, in the conventional scheme, the office of the high-class wife comes to be a vicarious leisure simply. The ideal then includes the characteristics which are supposed to result from or to go with a life of leisure consistently enforced. The ideal accepted under these circumstances may be gathered from descriptions of beautiful women by poets and writers of the chivalric times. In the conventional scheme of those days ladies of high degree were conceived to be in perpetual tutelage, and to be scrupulously exempt from all useful work. The resulting chivalric or romantic ideal of beauty takes cognizance chiefly of the face, and dwells on its delicacy, and on the delicacy of the hands and feet, the slender figure, and especially the slender waist. In the pictured representations of the women of that time, and in modern romantic imitators of the chivalric thought and feeling, the waist is attenuated to a degree that implies extreme debility. The same ideal is still extant among a considerable portion of the population of modern industrial communities; but it is to be said that it has retained its hold most tenaciously in those modern communities which are least advanced in point of economic and civil development, and which show the most considerable survivals of status and of predatory institutions. That is to say, the chivalric ideal is best preserved in those existing communities which are substantially least modern. Survivals of this lackadaisical or romantic ideal occur freely in the tastes of the well-to-do classes of Continental countries.

In modern communities which have reached the higher levels of industrial development, the upper leisure class has accumulated so great a mass of wealth as to place its women above all imputation of vulgarly productive labour. Here the status of women as vicarious consumers is beginning to lose its place in the affections of the body of the people; and as a consequence the ideal of feminine beauty is beginning to change back again from the infirmly delicate, translucent, and hazardously slender, to a woman of the archaic type that does not disown her hands and feet, nor, indeed, the other gross material facts of her person. In the course of economic development the ideal of beauty among the peoples of the Western culture has shifted from the woman of physical presence to the lady, and it is beginning to shift back again to the woman; and all in obedience to the changing conditions of pecuniary emulation. The exigencies of emulation at one time required lusty slaves; at another time they required a conspicuous performance of vicarious leisure and consequently an obvious disability; but the situation is now beginning to outgrow this last requirement, since, under the higher efficiency of modern industry, leisure in women is possible so far down the scale of reputability that it will no longer serve as a definitive mark of the highest pecuniary grade.

Apart from this general control exercised by the norm of conspicuous waste over the ideal of feminine beauty, there are one or two details which merit specific mention as showing how it may exercise an extreme constraint in detail over men's sense of beauty in women. It has already been noticed that at the stages of economic evolution at which conspicuous leisure is much regarded as a means of good repute, the ideal requires delicate and diminutive hands and feet and a slender waist. These features, together with the other, related faults of structure that commonly go with them, go to show that the person so affected is incapable of useful effort and must therefore be supported in idleness by her owner. She is useless and expensive, and she is consequently valuable as evidence of pecuniary strength. It results that at this cultural stage women take thought to alter their persons, so as to conform more nearly to the requirements of the instructed taste of the time; and under the guidance of the canon of pecuniary decency, the men find the resulting artificially induced pathological features attractive. So, for instance, the constricted waist which has had so wide and persistent a vogue in the communities of the Western culture, and so also the deformed foot of the Chinese. Both of these are mutilations of unquestioned repulsiveness to the untrained sense. It requires habituation to become reconciled to them. Yet there is no room to question their attractiveness to men into whose scheme of life they fit as honorific items sanctioned by the requirements of pecuniary reputability. They are items of pecuniary and cultural beauty which have come to do duty as elements of the ideal of womanliness. . . .

. . . among objects of use the simple and unadorned article is æsthetically the best. But since the pecuniary canon of reputability rejects the inexpensive in articles appropriated to individual consumption, the satisfaction of our craving for beautiful things must be sought by way of compromise. The canons of beauty must be circumvented by some contrivance which will give evidence of a reputably wasteful expenditure, at the same time that it meets the demands of our critical sense of the useful and the beautiful, or at least meets the demand of some habit which has come to do duty in place of that sense. Such an auxiliary sense of taste is the sense of novelty; and this latter is helped out in its surrogateship by the curiosity with which men view ingenious and puzzling contrivances. Hence it comes that most objects alleged to be beautiful, and doing duty as such, show considerable ingenuity of design and are calculated to puzzle the beholder—to bewilder him with irrelevant suggestions and hints of the improbable—at the same time that they give evidence of an expenditure of labour in excess of what would give them their fullest efficiency for their ostensible economic end. . . .

This process of selective adaptation of designs to the end of conspicuous waste, and the substitution of pecuniary beauty for æsthetic beauty, has been especially effective in the development of architecture. It would be extremely difficult to find a modern civilised residence or public building which can claim anything better than relative inoffensiveness in the eyes of any one who will dissociate the elements of beauty from those of honorific waste. The endless variety of fronts presented by the better class of tenements and apartment houses in our cities is an endless variety of architectural distress and of suggestions of expensive discomfort. Considered as objects of beauty, the dead walls of the sides and back of these structures, left untouched by the hands of the artist, are commonly the best feature of the building. . . .

The position here taken is enforced in a felicitous manner by the place assigned in the economy of consumption to machine products. The point of material difference between machine-made goods and the hand-wrought goods which serve the same purposes is, ordinarily, that the former serve their primary purpose more adequately. They are a more perfect product—show a more perfect adaptation of means to end. This does not save them from disesteem and depreciation, for they fall short under the test of honorific waste. Hand labour is a more wasteful method of production; hence the goods turned out by this method are more serviceable for the purpose of pecuniary reputability; hence the marks of hand labour come to be honorific, and the goods which exihibit these marks take rank as of higher grade than the corresponding machine product. Commonly, if not invariably, the honorific marks of hand labour are certain imperfections and irregularities in the lines of the hand-wrought article, showing where the workman has fallen short in the execution of the design. The ground of the superiority of hand-wrought goods, therefore, is a certain margin of crudeness. This margin must never be so wide as to show bungling workmanship, since that would be evidence of low cost, nor so narrow as to suggest the ideal precision attained only by the machine, for that would be evidence of low cost.

The appreciation of those evidences of honorific crudeness to which hand-wrought goods owe their superior worth and charm in the eyes of well-bred people is a matter of nice discrimination. It requires training and the formation of right habits of thought with respect to what may be called the physiognomy of goods. Machine-made goods of daily use are often admired and preferred precisely on account of their excessive perfection by the vulgar and the underbred who have not given due thought to the punctilios of elegant consumption. The ceremonial inferiority of machine products goes to show that the perfection of skill and workmanship embodied in any costly innovations in the finish of goods is not sufficient of itself to secure them acceptance and permanent favour. The innovation must have the support of the canon of conspicuous waste. Any feature in the physiognomy of goods, however pleasing in itself, and however well it may approve itself to the taste for effective work, will not be tolerated if it proves obnoxious to this norm of pecuniary reputability.

The ceremonial inferiority or uncleanness in consumable goods due to "commonness," or in other words to their slight cost of production, has been taken very seriously by many persons. The objection to machine products is often formulated as an objection to the commonness of such goods. What is common is within the (pecuniary) reach of many people. Its consumption is therefore not honorific, since it does not serve the purpose of a favourable invidious comparison with other consumers. Hence the consumption, or even the sight of such goods, is inseparable from an odious suggestion of the lower levels of human life, and one comes away from their contemplation with a pervading sense of meanness that is extremely distasteful and depressing to a person of sensibility. . . .

The position of machine products in the civilised scheme of consumption serves to point out the nature of the relation which subsists between the canon of conspicuous waste and the code of proprieties in consumption. Neither in matters of art and taste proper, nor as regards the current sense of the serviceability of goods, does this canon act as a principle of innovation or initiative. It does not go into the future as a creative principle which makes innovations and adds new items of consumption and new elements of cost. The principle in question is, in a certain sense, a negative rather than a positive law. It is a regulative rather than a creative principle. It very rarely initiates or originates any usage or custom directly. Its action is selective only. Conspicuous wastefulness does not directly afford ground for variation and growth, but conformity to its requirements is a condition to the survival of such innovations as may be made on other grounds. In whatever way usages and customs and methods of expenditure arise, they are all subject to the selective action of this norm of reputability; and the degree in which they conform to its requirements is a test of their fitness to survive in the competition with other similar usages and customs. Other things being equal, the more obviously wasteful usage or method stands the better chance of survival under this law. The law of conspicuous waste does not account for the origin of variations, but only for the persistence of such forms as are fit to survive under its dominance. It acts to conserve the fit, not to originate the acceptable. Its office is to prove all things and to hold fast that which is good for its purpose.

THE BITTER DRINK[1]

JOHN DOS PASSOS

Veblen,

a greyfaced shambling man lolling resentful at his desk with his cheek on his hand, in a low sarcastic mumble of intricate phrases subtly paying out the logical inescapable rope of matteroffact for a society to hang itself by,

dissecting out the century with a scalpel so keen, so comical, so exact that the professors and students ninetenths of the time didn't know it was there, and the magnates and the respected windbags and the applauded loudspeakers never knew it was there.

Veblen

asked too many questions, suffered from a constitutional inability to say yes.

Socrates asked questions, drank down the bitter drink one night when the first cock crowed,

but Veblen

drank it in little sips through a long life in the stuffiness of classrooms, the dust of libraries, the staleness of cheap flats such as a poor instructor can afford. He fought the boyg all right, pedantry, routine, timeservers at office desks, trustees, collegepresidents, the plump flunkies of the ruling businessmen, all the good jobs kept for yesmen, never enough money, every broadening hope thwarted. Veblen drank the bitter drink all right.

The Veblens were a family of freeholding farmers.

The freeholders of the narrow Norwegian valleys were a stubborn hardworking people, farmers, dairymen, fishermen, rooted in their fathers' stony fields, in their old timbered farmsteads with carved gables they took their names from, in the upland pastures where they grazed the stock in summer.

During the early nineteenth century the towns grew; Norway filled up with landless men, storekeepers, sheriffs, moneylenders, bailiffs, notaries in black with stiff collars and briefcases full of foreclosures under their arms. Industries were coming in. The townsmen were beginning to get profits out of the country and to finagle the farmers out of the freedom of their narrow farms.

The meanspirited submitted as tenants, daylaborers; but the strong men went out of the country

as their fathers had gone out of the country centuries before when Harald the Fairhaired and St. Olaf hacked to pieces the liberties of the northern men, who had been each man lord of his own creek, to make Christians and serfs of them,

---

1. From John Dos Passos, *The Big Money* (Boston: Houghton Mifflin Company, 1936), pp. 93–105. Reprinted by permission of the author.

only in the old days it was Iceland, Greenland, Vineland the northmen had sailed west to; now it was America.

Both Thorstein Veblen's father's people and his mother's people had lost their farmsteads and with them the names that denoted them free men.

Thomas Anderson for a while tried to make his living as a traveling carpenter and cabinetmaker, but in 1847 he and his wife, Kari Thorsteinsdatter, crossed in a whalingship from Bremen and went out to join friends in the Scandihoovian colonies round Milwaukee.

Next year his brother Haldor joined him.

They were hard workers; in another year they had saved up money to preempt a claim on 160 acres of uncleared land in Sheboygan County, Wisconsin; when they'd gotten that land part cleared they sold it and moved to an all-Norway colony in Manitowoc County, near Cato and a place named Valders after the valley they had all come from in the old country;

there in the house Thomas Anderson built with his own tools, the sixth of twelve children, Thorstein Veblen was born.

When Thorstein was eight years old, Thomas Anderson moved west again into the blacksoil prairies of Minnesota that the Sioux and the buffalo had only been driven off from a few years before. In the deed to the new farm Thomas Anderson took back the old farmstead name of Veblen.

He was a solid farmer, builder, a clever carpenter, the first man to import merino sheep and a mechanical reaper and binder; he was a man of standing in the group of Norway people farming the edge of the prairie, who kept their dialects, the manner of life of their narrow Norway valleys, their Lutheran pastors, their homemade clothes and cheese and bread, their suspicion and stubborn dislike of townsmen's ways.

The townspeople were Yankees mostly, smart to make two dollars grow where a dollar grew before, storekeepers, middlemen, speculators, moneylenders, with long heads for politics and mortgages; they despised the Scandihoovian dirtfarmers they lived off, whose daughters did their wives' kitchenwork.

The Norway people believed as their fathers had believed that there were only two callings for an honest man, farming or preaching.

Thorstein grew up a hulking lad with a reputation for laziness and wit. He hated the irk of everrepeated backbreaking chores round the farm. Reading he was happy. Carpentering he liked or running farmmachinery. The Lutheran pastors who came to the house noticed that his supple mind slid easily round the corners of their theology. It was hard to get farmwork out of him, he had a stinging tongue and was famous for the funny names he called people; his father decided to make a preacher out of him.

When he was seventeen he was sent for out of the field where he was working. His bag was already packed. The horses were hitched up. He was being sent to Carleton Academy in Northfield, to prepare for Carleton College.

As there were several young Veblens to be educated their father built them a house on a lot near the campus. Their food and clothes were sent to them from the farm. Cash money was something they never saw.

Thorstein spoke English with an accent. He had a constitutional inability to say yes. His mind was formed on the Norse sagas and on the matteroffact sense of his father's farming and the exact needs of carpenterwork and threshingmachines.

He could never take much interest in the theology, sociology, economics of Carleton College where they were busy trimming down the jagged dogmas of the old New England bibletaught traders to make stencils to hang on the walls of commissionmerchants' offices.

Veblen's collegeyears were the years when Darwin's assertions of growth and becoming were breaking the set molds of the Noah's Ark world,

when Ibsen's women were tearing down the portieres of the Victorian parlors,

and Marx's mighty machine was rigging the countinghouse's own logic to destroy the countinghouse.

When Veblen went home to the farm he talked about these things with his father, following him up and down at his plowing, starting an argument while they were waiting for a new load for the wheatthresher. Thomas Anderson had seen Norway and America; he had the squarebuilt mind of a carpenter and builder, and an understanding of tools and the treasured elaborated builtupseasonbyseason knowledge of a careful farmer,

a tough whetstone for the sharpening steel of young Thorstein's wits.

At Carleton College young Veblen was considered a brilliant unsound eccentric; nobody could understand why a boy of such attainments wouldn't settle down to the business of the day, which was to buttress property and profits with anything usable in the debris of Christian ethics and eighteenth-century economics that cluttered the minds of collegeprofessors, and to reinforce the sacred, already shaky edifice with the new strong girderwork of science, Herbert Spencer was throwing up for the benefit of the bosses.

People complained they never knew whether Veblen was joking or serious.

In 1880 Thorstein Veblen started to try to make his living by teaching. A year in an academy at Madison, Wisconsin, wasn't much of a success. Next year he and his brother Andrew started graduate work at Johns Hopkins. Johns Hopkins didn't suit, but boarding in an old Baltimore house with some ruined gentlewomen gave him a disdaining glimpse of an etiquette motheaten now but handed down through the lavish leisure of the slaveowning planters' mansions straight from the merry England of the landlord cavaliers.

(The valleyfarmers had always been scornful of outlanders' ways.)

He was more at home at Yale where in Noah Porter he found a New England roundhead granite against which his Norway granite rang in clear dissent. He took his Ph.D. there. But there was still some question as to what department of the academic world he could best make a living in.

He read Kant and wrote prize essays. But he couldn't get a job. Try as he could he couldn't get his mouth round the essential yes.

He went back to Minnesota with a certain intolerant knowledge of the amenities of the higher learning. To his slight Norwegian accent he'd added the broad a.

At home he loafed about the farm and tinkered with inventions of new machinery and read and talked theology and philosophy with his father. In the Scandihoovian colonies the price of wheat and the belief in God and St. Olaf were going down together. The farmers of the Northwest were starting their long losing fight against the parasite businessmen who were sucking them dry. There was a mortgage on the farm, interest on debts to pay, always fertilizer, new machines to buy to speed production to pump in a halfcentury the wealth out of the soil laid down in a million years of buffalograss. His brothers kept grumbling about this sardonic loafer who wouldn't earn his keep.

Back home he met again his college sweetheart, Ellen Rolfe, the niece of the president of Carleton College, a girl who had railroadmagnates and money in the family. People in Northfield were shocked when it came out that she was going to marry the drawling pernickety bookish badlydressed young Norwegian ne'erdowell.

Her family hatched a plan to get him a job as economist for the Santa Fe Railroad but at the wrong moment Ellen Rolfe's uncle lost control of the line. The young couple went to live at Stacyville where they did everything but earn a living. They read Latin and Greek and botanized in the woods and along the fences and in the roadside scrub. They boated on the river and Veblen started his translation of the *Laxdœlasaga.* They read *Looking Backward* and articles by Henry George. They looked at their world from the outside.

In '91 Veblen got together some money to go to Cornell to do postgraduate work. He turned up there in the office of the head of the economics department wearing a coonskin cap and grey corduroy trousers and said in his low sarcastic drawl, "I am Thorstein Veblen,"

but it was not until several years later, after he was established at the new University of Chicago that had grown up next to the World's Fair, and had published *The Theory of the Leisure Class,* put on the map by Howells' famous review, that the world of the higher learning knew who Thorstein Veblen was.

Even in Chicago as the brilliant young economist he lived pioneerfashion.

(The valleyfarmers had always been scornful of outlanders' ways.) He kept his books in packingcases laid on their sides along the walls. His only extravagances were the Russian cigarettes he smoked and the red sash he sometimes sported. He was a man without smalltalk. When he lectured he put his cheek on his hand and mumbled out his long spiral sentences, reiterative like the eddas. His language was a mixture of mechanics' terms, scientific latinity, slang and Roget's Thesaurus. The other profs couldn't imagine why the girls fell for him so.

The girls fell for him so that Ellen Rolfe kept leaving him. He'd take summer trips abroad without his wife. There was a scandal about a girl on an ocean liner.

Tongues wagged so (Veblen was a man who never explained, who never could get his tongue around the essential yes; the valleyfarmers had always been scornful of the outlanders' ways, and their opinions) that his wife left him and went off to live alone on a timberclaim in Idaho and the president asked for his resignation.

Veblen went out to Idaho to get Ellen Rolfe to go with him to California when he succeeded in getting a job at a better salary at Leland Stanford, but in Palo Alto it was the same story as in Chicago. He suffered from woman trouble and the constitutional inability to say yes and an unnatural tendency to feel with the workingclass instead of with the profittakers. There were the same complaints that his courses were not constructive or attractive to big money bequests and didn't help his students to butter their bread, make Phi Beta Kappa, pick plums off the hierarchies of the academic grove. His wife left him for good. He wrote to a friend: "The president doesn't approve of my domestic arrangements; nor do I."

Talking about it he once said, "What is one to do if the woman moves in on you?"

He went back up to the shack in the Idaho woods.

Friends tried to get him an appointment to make studies in Crete, a chair at the University of Pekin, but always the boyg, routine, businessmen's flunkeys in all the university offices . . . for the questioner the bitter drink.

His friend Davenport got him an appointment at the University of Missouri. At Columbia he lived like a hermit in the basement of the Davenports' house, helped with the work round the place, carpentered himself a table and chairs. He was already a bitter elderly man with a grey face covered with a net of fine wrinkles, a vandyke beard and yellow teeth. Few students could follow his courses. The college authorities were often surprised and somewhat chagrined that when visitors came from Europe it was always Veblen they wanted to meet.

These were the years he did the most of his writing, trying out his ideas on his students, writing slowly at night in violet ink with a pen of his own designing. Whenever he published a book he had to put up a guarantee with the publishers. In *The Theory of Business Enterprise, The Instinct of Workmanship, The Vested Interests and the Common Man,*

he established a new diagram of a society dominated by monopoly capital,

etched in irony

the sabotage of production by business,

the sabotage of life by blind need for money profits,

pointed out the alternatives: a warlike society strangled by the bureaucracies of the monopolies forced by the law of diminishing returns to grind down more and more the common man for profits.

or a new matteroffact commonsense society dominated by the needs of the men and women who did the work and the incredibly vast possibilities for peace and plenty offered by the progress of technology.

These were the years of Debs's speeches, growing laborunions, the I.W.W. talk about industrial democracy: these years Veblen still held to the hope that the workingclass would take over the machine of production before monopoly had pushed the western nations down into the dark again.

War cut across all that: under the cover of the bunting of Woodrow Wilson's phrases the monopolies cracked down. American democracy was crushed.

The war at least offered Veblen an opportunity to break out of the airless greenhouse of academic life. He was offered a job with the Food Administration, he sent the Navy Department a device for catching submarines by trailing lengths of stout bindingwire. (Meanwhile the government found his books somewhat confusing. The postoffice was forbidding the mails to *Imperial Germany and the Industrial Revolution* while propaganda agencies were sending it out to make people hate the Huns. Educators were denouncing *The Nature of Peace* while Washington experts were clipping phrases out of it to add to the Wilsonian smokescreen.)

For the Food Administration Thorstein Veblen wrote two reports: in one he advocated granting the demands of the I.W.W. as a wartime measure and conciliating the workingclass instead of beating up and jailing all the honest leaders; in the other he pointed out that the Food Administration was a businessman's racket and was not aiming for the most efficient organization of the country as a producing machine. He suggested that, in the interests of the efficient prosecution of the war, the government step into the place of the middleman and furnish necessities to the farmers direct in return for raw materials;

but cutting out business was not at all the Administration's idea of making the world safe for democracy,

so Veblen had to resign from the Food Administration.

He signed the protests against the trial of the hundred and one wobblies in Chicago.

After the armistice he went to New York. In spite of all the oppression of the war-years, the air was freshening. In Russia the great storm of revolt had broken, seemed to be sweeping west, in the strong gusts from the new world in the east the warsodden multitudes began to see again. At Versailles allies and enemies, magnates, generals, flunkey politicians were slamming the shutters against the storm, against the new, against hope. It was suddenly clear for a second in the thundering glare what war was about, what peace was about.

In America, in Europe, the old men won. The bankers in their offices took a deep breath, the bediamonded old ladies of the leisure class went back to clipping their coupons in the refined quiet of their safedeposit vaults.

the last puffs of the ozone of revolt went stale
in the whisper of speakeasy arguments.

Veblen wrote for the *Dial*,
lectured at the New School for Social Research.

He still had a hope that the engineers, the technicians, the nonprofiteers whose hands were on the switchboard might take up the fight where the workingclass had failed. He helped form the Technical Alliance. His last hope was the British general strike.

Was there no group of men bold enough to take charge of the magnificent machine before the pigeyed speculators and the yesmen at office desks irrevocably ruined it
and with it the hopes of four hundred years?

No one went to Veblen's lectures at the New School. With every article he wrote in the *Dial* the circulation dropped.

Harding's normalcy, the new era was beginning;
even Veblen made a small killing on the stockmarket.
He was an old man and lonely.

His second wife had gone to a sanitarium suffering from delusions of persecution.

There seemed no place for a masterless man.

Veblen went back out to Palo Alto
to live in his shack in the tawny hills and observe from outside the last grabbing urges of the profit system taking on, as he put it, the systematized delusions of dementia præcox.

There he finished his translation of the *Laxdœlasaga*.

He was an old man. He was much alone. He let the woodrats take what they wanted from his larder. A skunk that hung round the shack was so tame he'd rub up against Veblen's leg like a cat.

He told a friend he'd sometimes hear in the stillness about him the voices of his boyhood talking Norwegian as clear as on the farm in Minnesota where he was raised. His friends found him harder than ever to talk to, harder than ever to interest in anything. He was running down. The last sips of the bitter drink.

He died on August 3, 1929.

Among his papers a penciled note was found:

It is also my wish, in case of death, to be cremated if it can conveniently be done, as expeditiously and inexpensively as may be, without ritual or ceremony of any kind; that my ashes be thrown loose into the sea or into some sizeable stream running into the sea; that no tombstone, slab, epitaph, effigy, tablet, inscription or monument of any name or nature, be set up to my memory or name in any place or at any time; that no obituary, memorial, portrait or biography of me, nor any letters written to or by me be printed or published, or in any way reproduced, copied or circulated;

but his memorial remains
riveted into the language:
the sharp clear prism of his mind.

· *FREEDOM AND SECURITY* ·

THE ILLUSION OF INDIVIDUALITY[1]

ERICH FROMM

But what about ourselves? Is our own democracy theatened only by Fascism beyond the Atlantic or by the "fifth column" in our own ranks? If that were the case, the situation would be serious but not critical. But although foreign and internal threats of Fascism must be taken seriously, there is no greater mistake and no graver danger than not to see that in our own society we are faced with the same phenomenon that is fertile soil for the rise of Fascism anywhere: the insignificance and powerlessness of the individual.

This statement challenges the conventional belief that by freeing the individual from all external restraints modern democracy has achieved true in-

1. From *Escape from Freedom,* copyright 1941 by Erich Fromm and reprinted by permission of Rinehart & Company, Inc., New York.

dividualism. We are proud that we are not subject to any external authority, that we are free to express our thoughts and feelings, and we take it for granted that this freedom almost automatically guarantees our individuality. *The right to express our thoughts,* however, *means something only if we are able to have thoughts of our own;* freedom from external authority is a lasting gain only if the inner psychological conditions are such that we are able to establish our own individuality. Have we achieved that aim, or are we at least approaching it? . . . In discussing the two aspects of freedom for modern man, we have pointed out the economic conditions that make for increasing isolation and powerlessness of the individual in our era; in discussing the psychological results we have shown that this powerlessness leads either to the kind of escape that we find in the authoritarian character, or else to a compulsive conforming in the process of which the isolated individual becomes an automaton, loses his self, and yet at the same time consciously conceives of himself as free and subject only to himself.

It is important to consider how our culture fosters this tendency to conform, even though there is space for only a few outstanding examples. The suppression of spontaneous feelings, and thereby of the development of genuine individuality, starts very early, as a matter of fact with the earliest training of a child. This is not to say that training must inevitably lead to suppression of spontaneity if the real aim of education is to further the inner independence and individuality of the child, its growth and integrity. The restrictions which such a kind of education may have to impose upon the growing child are only transitory measures that really support the process of growth and expansion. In our culture, however, education too often results in the elimination of spontaneity and in the substitution of original psychic acts by superimposed feelings, thoughts, and wishes. (By original I do not mean, let me repeat, that an idea has not been thought before by someone else, but that it originates in the individual, that it is the result of his own activity and in this sense is *his* thought.) To choose one illustration somewhat arbitrarily, one of the earliest suppressions of *feelings* concerns hostility and dislike. To start with, most children have a certain measure of hostility and rebelliousness as a result of their conflicts with a surrounding world that tends to block their expansiveness and to which, as the weaker opponent, they usually have to yield. It is one of the essential aims of the educational process to eliminate this antagonistic reaction. The methods are different; they vary from threats and punishments, which frighten the child, to the subtler methods of bribery or "explanations," which confuse the child and make him give up his hostility. The child starts with giving up the expression of his feeling and eventually gives up the very feeling itself. Together with that, he is taught to suppress the awareness of hostility and insincerity in others; sometimes this is not entirely easy, since children have a capacity for noticing such negative qualities in others without being so easily deceived by words as adults usually are. They still dislike somebody "for no good reason"—except the very good one that they feel the hostility, or insincerity, radiating from that person. This reaction is soon discouraged; it does not take long for the child to reach the "maturity" of the average adult and to lose the sense of discrimination between a decent person and a scoundrel, as long as the latter has not committed some flagrant act.

On the other hand, early in his education, the child is taught to have feelings that are not at all "his"; particularly is he taught to like people, to be uncritically friendly to them, and to smile. What education may not have accomplished is usually done by social pressure in later life. If you do not smile you are judged lacking in a "pleasing personality"—and you need to have a pleasing personality if you want to sell your services, whether as a waitress, a salesman, or a physician. Only those at the bottom of the social pyramid, who sell nothing but their physical labor, and those at the very top do not need to be particularly "pleasant." Friendliness, cheerfulness, and everything that a smile is supposed to express, become automatic responses which one turns on and off like an electric switch.[2]

To be sure, in many instances the person is aware of merely making a gesture; in most cases, however, he loses that awareness and thereby the ability to discriminate between the pseudo feeling and spontaneous friendliness.

It is not only hostility that is directly suppressed and friendliness that is killed by superimposing its counterfeit. A wide range of spontaneous emotions are suppressed and replaced by pseudo feelings. Freud has taken one such suppression and put it in the center of his whole system, namely the suppression of sex. Although I believe that the discouragement of sexual joy is not the only important suppression of spontaneous reactions but one of many, certainly its importance is not to be underrated. Its results are obvious in cases of sexual inhibitions and also in those where sex assumes a compulsive quality and is consumed like liquor or a drug, which has no particular taste but makes you forget yourself. Regardless of the one or the other effect, their suppression, because of the intensity of sexual desires, not only affects the sexual sphere but also weakens the person's courage for spontaneous expression in all other spheres.

In our society emotions in general are discouraged. While there can be no doubt that any creative thinking—as well as any other creative activity—is inseparably linked with emotion, it has become an ideal to think and to

2. As one telling illustration of the commercialization of friendliness I should like to cite *Fortune's* report on "The Howard Johnson Restaurants." (*Fortune*, September, 1940, p. 96.) Johnson employs a force of "shoppers" who go from restaurant to restaurant to watch for lapses. "Since everything is cooked on the premises according to standard recipes and measurements issued by the home office, the inspector knows how large a portion of steak he should receive and how the vegetable should taste. He also knows how long it should take for the dinner to be served and he knows the exact degree of friendliness that should be shown by the hostess and the waitress."

live without emotions. To be "emotional" has become synonymous with being unsound or unbalanced. By the acceptance of this standard the individual has become greatly weakened; his thinking is impoverished and flattened. On the other hand, since emotions cannot be completely killed, they must have their existence totally apart from the intellectual side of the personality; the result is the cheap and insincere sentimentality with which movies and popular songs feed millions of emotion-starved customers.

There is one tabooed emotion that I want to mention in particular, because its suppression touches deeply on the roots of personality: the sense of tragedy. As we saw in an earlier chapter, the awareness of death and of the tragic aspect of life, whether dim or clear, is one of the basic characteristics of man. Each culture has its own way of coping with the problem of death. For those societies in which the process of individuation has progressed but little, the end of individual existence is less of a problem since the experience of individual existence itself is less developed. Death is not yet conceived as being basically different from life. Cultures in which we find a higher development of individuation have treated death according to their social and psychological structure. The Greeks put all emphasis on life and pictured death as nothing but a shadowy and dreary continuation of life. The Egyptians based their hopes on a belief in the indestructibility of the human body, at least of those whose power during life was indestructible. The Jews admitted the fact of death realistically and were able to reconcile themselves with the idea of the destruction of individual life by the vision of a state of happiness and justice ultimately to be reached by mankind in this world. Christianity has made death unreal and tried to comfort the unhappy individual by promises of a life after death. Our own era simply denies death and with it one fundamental aspect of life. Instead of allowing the awareness of death and suffering to become one of the strongest incentives for life, the basis for human solidarity, and an experience without which joy and enthusiasm lack intensity and depth, the individual is forced to repress it. But, as is always the case with repression, by being removed from sight the repressed elements do not cease to exist. Thus the fear of death lives an illegitimate existence among us. It remains alive in spite of the attempt to deny it, but being repressed it remains sterile. It is one source of the flatness of other experiences, of the restlessness pervading life, and it explains, I would venture to say, the exorbitant amount of money this nation pays for its funerals.

In the process of tabooing emotions modern psychiatry plays an ambiguous role. On the one hand its greatest representative, Freud, has broken through the fiction of the rational, purposeful character of the human mind and opened a path which allows a view into the abyss of human passions. On the other hand psychiatry, enriched by these very achievements of Freud, has made itself an instrument of the general trends in the manipulation of personality. Many psychiatrists, including psychoanalysts, have painted the picture of a "normal" personality which is never too sad, too angry, or too excited. They use words like "infantile" or "neurotic" to denounce traits or types of personalities that do not conform with the conventional pattern of a "normal" individual. This kind of influence is in a way more dangerous than the older and franker forms of name-calling. Then the individual knew at least that there was some person or some doctrine which criticized him and he could fight back. But who can fight back at "science"?

The same distortion happens to original *thinking* as happens to feelings and emotions. From the very start of education original thinking is discouraged and ready-made thoughts are put into people's heads. How this is done with young children is easy enough to see. They are filled with curiosity about the world, they want to grasp it physically as well as intellectually. They want to know the truth, since that is the safest way to orient themselves in a strange and powerful world. Instead, they are not taken seriously, and it does not matter whether this attitude takes the form of open disrespect or of the subtle condescension which is usual towards all who have no power (such as children, aged or sick people). Although this treatment by itself offers strong discouragement to independent thinking, there is a worse handicap: the insincerity—often unintentional—which is typical of the average adult's behavior toward a child. This insincerity consists partly in the fictitious picture of the world which the child is given. It is about as useful as instructions concerning life in the Arctic would be to someone who has asked how to prepare for an expedition to the Sahara Desert. Besides this general misrepresentation of the world there are the many specific lies that tend to conceal facts which, for various personal reasons, adults do not want children to know. From a bad temper, which is rationalized as justified dissatisfaction with the child's behavior, to concealment of the parents' sexual activities and their quarrels, the child is "not supposed to know" and his inquiries meet with hostile or polite discouragement.

The child thus prepared enters school and perhaps college. I want to mention briefly some of the educational methods used today which in effect further discourage original thinking. One is the emphasis on knowledge of facts, or I should rather say on information. The pathetic superstition prevails that by knowing more and more facts one arrives at knowledge of reality. Hundreds of scattered and unrelated facts are dumped into the heads of students; their time and energy are taken up by learning more and more facts so that there is little left for thinking. To be sure, thinking without a knowledge of facts remains empty and fictitious; but "information" alone can be just as much of an obstacle to thinking as the lack of it.

Another closely related way of discouraging original thinking is to regard all truth as relative.[3] Truth is made out to be a metaphysical concept, and if

3. Cf. to this whole problem Robert S. Lynd's *Knowledge for What?* Princeton University Press, Princeton, 1939. For its philosophical aspects cf. M. Horkheimer's *Zum Rationalismusstreit in der Gegenwärtigen Philosophie,* Zeitschrift für Sozialforschung, Vol. 3, 1934, Alcan, Paris.

anyone speaks about wanting to discover the truth he is thought backward by the "progressive" thinkers of our age. Truth is declared to be an entirely subjective matter, almost a matter of taste. Scientific endeavor must be detached from subjective factors, and its aim is to look at the world without passion and interest. The scientist has to approach facts with sterilized hands as a surgeon approaches his patient. The result of this relativism, which often presents itself by the name of empiricism or positivism or which recommends itself by its concern for the correct usage of words, is that thinking loses its essential stimulus—the wishes and interests of the person who thinks; instead it becomes a machine to register "facts." Actually, just as thinking in general has developed out of the need for mastery of material life, so the quest for truth is rooted in the interests and needs of individuals and social groups. Without such interest the stimulus for seeking the truth would be lacking. There are always groups whose interest is furthered by truth, and their representatives have been the pioneers of human thought; there are other groups whose interests are furthered by concealing truth. Only in the latter case does interest prove harmful to the cause of truth. The problem, therefore, is not that there is *an* interest at stake, but *which kind* of interest is at stake. I might say that inasmuch as there is some longing for the truth in every human being, it is because every human being has some need for it.

This holds true in the first place with regard to a person's orientation in the outer world, and it holds especially true for the child. As a child, every human being passes through a state of powerlessness, and truth is one of the strongest weapons of those who have no power. But the truth is in the individual's interest not only with regard to his orientation in the outer world;

his own strength depends to a great extent on his knowing the truth about himself. Illusions about oneself can become crutches useful to those who are not able to walk alone; but they increase a person's weakness. The individual's greatest strength is based on the maximum of integration of his personality, and that means also on the maximum of transparence to himself. "Know thyself" is one of the fundamental commands that aim at human strength and happiness.

In addition to the factors just mentioned there are others which actively tend to confuse whatever is left of the capacity for original thinking in the average adult. With regard to all basic questions of individual and social life, with regard to psychological, economic, political, and moral problems, a great sector of our culture has just one function—to befog the issues. One kind of smokescreen is the assertion that the problems are too complicated for the average individual to grasp. On the contrary it would seem that many of the basic issues of individual and social life are very simple, so simple, in fact, that everyone should be expected to understand them. To let them appear to be so enormously complicated that only a "specialist" can understand them, and he only in his own limited field, actually—and often intentionally—tends to discourage people from trusting their own capacity to think about those problems that really matter. The individual feels helplessly caught in a chaotic mass of data and with pathetic patience waits until the specialists have found out what to do and where to go.

The result of this kind of influence is a twofold one: one is a scepticism and cynicism towards everything which is said or printed, while the other is a childish belief in anything that a person is told with authority. This combination of cynicism and naïveté is very typical of the modern individual. Its essential result is to discourage him from doing his own thinking and deciding.

Another way of paralyzing the ability to think critically is the destruction of any kind of structuralized picture of the world. Facts lose the specific quality which they can have only as parts of a structuralized whole and retain merely an abstract, quantitative meaning; each fact is just *another* fact and all that matters is whether we know more or less. Radio, moving pictures, and newspapers have a devastating effect on this score. The announcement of the bombing of a city and the death of hundreds of people is shamelessly followed or interrupted by an advertisement for soap or wine. The same speaker with the same suggestive, ingratiating, and authoritative voice, which he has just used to impress you with the seriousness of the political situation, impresses now upon his audience the merits of the particular brand of soap which pays for the news broadcast. Newsreels let pictures of torpedoed ships be followed by those of a fashion show. Newspapers tell us the trite thoughts or breakfast habits of a debutante with the same space and seriousness they use for reporting events of scientific or artistic importance. Because of all this we cease to be genuinely related to what we hear. We cease to be excited, our emotions and our critical judgment become hampered, and eventually our attitude to what is going on in the world assumes a quality of flatness and indifference. In the name of "freedom" life loses all structure; it is composed of many little pieces, each separate from the other and lacking any sense as a whole. The individual is left alone with these pieces like a child with a puzzle; the difference, however, is that the child knows what a house is and therefore can recognize the parts of the house in the little pieces he is playing with, whereas the adult does not see the meaning of the "whole," the pieces of which come into his hands. He is bewildered and afraid and just goes on gazing at his little meaningless pieces.

What has been said about the lack of "originality" in feeling and thinking holds true also of the act of *willing*. To recognize this is particularly difficult; modern man seems, if anything, to have too many wishes and his only problem seems to be that, although he knows what he wants, he cannot have it. All our energy is spent for the purpose of getting what we want, and most people never question the premise of this activity: that they know their true wants. They do not stop to think whether the aims they are pursuing are something they themselves want. In school they want to have good marks, as adults they want to be more and more successful, to make more money, to have more prestige, to buy a better car, to go places, and so on. Yet when they do stop to think in the midst of all this frantic activity, this question may come to their minds: "If I do get this new job, if I get this better car, if I can take this trip—what then? What is the use of it all? Is it really I who wants all this? Am I not running after some goal which is supposed to make me happy and which eludes me as soon as I have reached it?" These questions, when they arise, are frightening, for they question the very basis on which man's whole activity is built, his knowledge of what he wants. People tend, therefore, to get rid as soon as possible of these disturbing thoughts. They feel that they have been bothered by these questions because they were tired or depressed —and they go on in the pursuit of the aims which they believe are their own.

Yet all this bespeaks a dim realization of the truth—the truth that modern man lives under the illusion that he knows what he wants, while he actually wants what he is *supposed* to want. In order to accept this it is necessary to realize that to know what one really wants is not comparatively easy, as most people think, but one of the most difficult problems any human being has to solve. It is a task we frantically try to avoid by accepting ready-made goals as though they were our own. Modern man is ready to take great risks when he tries to achieve the aims which are supposed to be "his"; but he is deeply afraid of taking the risk and the responsibility of giving himself his own aims. Intense activity is often mistaken for evidence of self-determined action, although we know that it may well be no more spontaneous than the behavior of an actor or a person hypnotized. When the general plot of the play is handed out, each actor can act vigorously the role he is assigned and even make up his lines and certain details of the action by himself. Yet he is only playing a role that has been handed over to him.

The particular difficulty in recognizing to what extent our wishes—and our thoughts and feelings as well—are not really our own but put into us from the outside, is closely linked up with the problem of authority and freedom. In the course of modern history the authority of the Church has been replaced by that of the State, that of the State by that of conscience, and in our era, the latter has been replaced by the anonymous authority of common sense and public opinion as instruments of conformity. Because we have freed ourselves of the older overt forms of authority, we do not see that we have become the prey of a new kind of authority. We have become automatons who live under the illusion of being self-willing individuals. This illusion helps the individual to remain unaware of his insecurity, but this is all the help such an illusion can give. Basically the self of the individual is weakened, so that he feels powerless and extremely insecure. He lives in a world to which he has lost genuine relatedness and in which everybody and everything has become instrumentalized, where he has become a part of the machine that his hands have built. He thinks, feels, and wills what he believes he is supposed to think, feel, and will; in this very process he loses his self upon which all genuine security of a free individual must be built.

The loss of the self has increased the necessity to conform, for it results in a profound doubt of one's own identity. If I am nothing but what I believe I am supposed to be—who am "I"? We have seen how the doubt about one's own self started with the breakdown of the medieval order in which the individual had had an unquestionable place in a fixed order. The identity of the individual has been a major problem of modern philosophy since Descartes. Today we take for granted that we are we. Yet the doubt about ourselves still exists, or has even grown. In his plays Pirandello has given expression to this feeling of modern man. He starts with the question: Who am I? What proof have I for my own identity other than the continuation of my physical self? His answer is not like Descartes'—the affirmation of the individual self—but its denial: I have no identity, there is no self excepting the one which is the reflex of what others expect me to be: I am "as you desire me."

This loss of identity then makes it still more imperative to conform; it means that one can be sure of oneself only if one lives up to the expectations of others. If we do not live up to this picture we not only risk disapproval and increased isolation, but we risk losing the identity of our personality, which means jeopardizing sanity.

By conforming with the expectations of others, by not being different, these doubts about one's own identity are silenced and a certain security is gained. However, the price paid is high. Giving up spontaneity and individuality results in a thwarting of life. Psychologically the automaton, while being alive biologically, is dead emotionally and mentally. While he goes through the motions of living, his life runs through his hands like sand. Behind a front of satisfaction and optimism modern man is deeply unhappy; as a matter of fact, he is on the verge of desperation. He desperately clings to the notion of individuality; he wants to be "different," and he has no greater recommendation of anything than that "it is different." We are informed of the individual name of the railroad clerk we buy our ticket from; handbags, playing cards, and portable radios are "personalized," by having the initials of the owner put on them. All this indicates the hunger for "difference" and yet these are almost the last vestiges of individuality that are left. Modern man is starved for life. But since, being an automaton, he cannot experience life in the sense of spontaneous activity he takes as surrogate any kind of excitement and thrill: the thrill of drinking, of sports, of vicariously living the excitements of fictitious persons on the screen.

What then is the meaning of freedom for modern man?

He has become free from the external bonds that would prevent him from doing and thinking as he sees fit. He would be free to act according to his own will, if he knew what he wanted, thought, and felt. But he does not know. He conforms to anonymous authorities and adopts a self which is not his. The more he does this, the more powerless he feels, the more is he forced to conform. In spite of a veneer of optimism and initiative, modern man is overcome by a profound feeling of powerlessness which makes him gaze toward approaching catastrophes as though he were paralyzed.

Looked at superficially, people appear to function well enough in economic and social life; yet it would be dangerous to overlook the deep-seated unhappiness behind that comforting veneer. If life loses its meaning because it is not lived, man becomes desperate. People do not die quietly from physical starvation; they do not die quietly from psychic starvation either. If we look only at the economic needs as far as the "normal" person is concerned, if we do not see the unconscious suffering of the average automatized person, then we fail to see the danger that threatens our culture from its human basis: the readiness to accept any ideology and any leader, if only he promises excitement and offers a political structure and symbols which allegedly give meaning and order to an individual's life. The despair of the human automaton is fertile soil for the political purposes of Fascism.

APPROACHES TO ECONOMIC REFORM[1]

ELI GINZBERG

ALTHOUGH it is well known that economics as a formal discipline dates from the second half of the eighteenth century the question has seldom been posed

1. From *Perspectives of a Troubled Decade* (New York: Harper & Brothers, 1950), pp. 367–371. Reprinted with permission of the publisher.

why the birth of economics was so long delayed. The answer is really very simple: As long as the conditions of economic life remain substantially static, not only from year to year but from decade to decade and from century to century—except for the misery of famine and the speculation incident to war—there is little point to scholars speculating about alternative objectives or alternative means of achieving particular objectives. The opening of the trade routes to the Americas and the Indies and the application of modern scientific principles to agriculture and industry laid the foundations for economic progress. And it was this progress that provided the preconditions for the discipline of economics, for now discussions about objectives and methods assumed a realistic hue.

The early economists were preoccupied with two basic questions: How could one redesign the existing institutional patterns so as to enhance the total productivity of the country; secondly, what steps should be taken to establish an equitable distribution of the country's products, not only because equity was good in itself but because the pattern of distribution was likely to influence the size of the total output.

The vocabulary used by the discussants has changed greatly during the past two hundred years but it is questionable whether there has been more than a minor change in their fundamental approaches. Contemporary argument is couched in terms of welfare states, deficit financing, incentives for profits, pressure groups, concepts that one could search for in vain in Adam Smith's *Wealth of Nations* or in the writing of the Physiocrats. But it would be venturesome to conclude without much more evidence that differences in terminology reflect fundamental differences in approach.

No one who seeks to penetrate the meaning that lies back of the public pronouncements of the parties of the right, the center, and the left; no one who studies the speeches and writings of the spiritual descendants of the New Deal or the anniversary addresses of the Republican leaders, can fail to note that to the extent that prejudices do not usurp all the attention, the ideas which find prominence are few and simple. One may go further and contend that even if one peruses the writings of the sophisticated a very few simple ideas hold the center of the stage. It may prove helpful in seeking one's bearings amidst the welter of claims and counter-claims as to the best roads to economic salvation to review the approaches of the great masters of old, as well as the more distinguished contemporary theoreticians.

Although Adam Smith covered a tremendous range of subjects in his eignt hundred pages of description and analysis of economies ancient and modern, he was primarily concerned with four basic considerations. First and foremost, he was concerned with analyzing the conditions which would encourage people to utilize to the maximum their resources for productive work. Placing his major emphasis on the productivity of labor, he next raised the question what government could do to improve the quality of the labor supply and thereby indirectly contribute to enhancing the total output of the country. He was further concerned with those legal and social institutions which stood in the way of the most efficient distribution of the labor supply and therefore restricted the total output, such as the Settlement Acts which made it difficult for a man to remove his domicile from the place of his birth. Finally, he criticized severely the monopolistic powers of special groups, particularly merchants and manufacturers, for he held that these powers not only gave the monopolists unjustified returns but also had an adverse effect upon total productivity of the economy.

Karl Marx approached his problem in the first instance from the side of the inequitable distribution of the products of labor, emphasizing the fact that it was possible for the owners of the means of production to secure a disproportionate return at the expense of the working man. He saw in this basic maldistribution the cause for the periodic breakdown of the economy. Depressions, according to Marx, were brought about largely by inadequacies in the purchasing power of the masses who were "exploited" by the capitalists who kept their wages low. Marx saw no possibility of corrective action within the framework of the existing structure of industrial capitalism and placed his entire faith in the new system which was to rise on the ruins of the old. In this new system he denied that there would be opportunity for inequities in distribution or obstacles to maximum production.

The major classical tradition, represented by Ricardo in its early period and by Alfred Marshall in its later period, pursued an interesting approach, which was more implicit than explicit. To a considerable extent it analyzed situations in which there were obstacles to the free movement of labor and capital and demonstrated that the removal of such obstacles would add to the national welfare. It had no concern with the equities of distribution other than a conviction that any effort to limit the laissez-faire approach would make bad worse. The possibility that there would be an insufficiency of purchasing power to keep the economy at full production—a proposition seriously entertained by Malthus—was brushed aside by the others.

The depressed conditions which prevailed in Great Britain after World War I and the major depression which engulfed the United States in 1929–1933 led John Maynard Keynes to conclude that there was an inherent defect in the structure of latterday capitalism which led to insufficient investment and therefore to a lesser than maximum amount of employment and output. He saw little point in concentrating on the inequities in distribution which he felt were insignificant, when compared to the losses resulting from the marked underutilization of the community's resources. Unlike Marx, he did not believe that corrective action was impossible. He was sure that this defect could be remedied by government's spending to fill in the gaps in private spending.

John Maurice Clark holds with Keynes that one cannot assume, as did the classicists, that the system will keep itself at a maximum level. But unlike

Keynes he does not view the problem of maximum output solely in terms of a mechanical defect which can be remedied by large scale governmental spending. He is convinced that the behavior of strategic groups—industry, labor, and agriculture—which is determined largely by their efforts to improve their immediate economic position exercises a significant influence on the total results which the economy is able to achieve. He sees little prospect for continuing progress and prosperity unless the several groups develop approaches which will lead them when necessary to subordinate their narrow private interests to the broader public interest.

The following observations emerge from this selective review of the approaches of distinguished economists to the problem of economic reform. The classical tradition of Ricardo-Marshall has little to contribute other than a warning not to overestimate the potentialities of state action and to bear in mind that state action is more likely to confuse and complicate the situation than to clarify it. Marx tells us that we can look for no relief until we destroy ourselves and are reborn; and he offers us nothing but his own authority that the new world will be better than the old. Brushing aside the reformers' preoccupation with the equities of distribution, Keynes insists that we concentrate on improving the machinery of modern capitalism which he points out needs periodic adjustment by government in the form of large scale investments. Clark feels that the problem must be approached simultaneously from both levels—the province of public action (government) and the province of group action (classes), for he is convinced that the methods pursued by the several classes to increase their share of the distribution is a major determinant of the total capabilities of the economy.

Apparently we are back to the point where Adam Smith began. He was concerned, as we must be, with the various approaches that lead people to make a maximum effort, for economic progress is primarily a function of work. He was concerned, as we must be, with the contributions that government can make to improving the quality of the people who do the work. And he knew that the equities of distribution were important considerations not only on ethical grounds but because of the impact of the distributive pattern on production; this, too, we should not forget.

If these be in fact the important considerations, as they seem to be, then we had best admit that we are in a sad way, for our knowledge is so much less than our need. This may help to explain why prejudices rather than ideas loom so large in current controversy.

But even if the current controversy leaves so much to be desired, it can make two important contributions. Unless we lose faith in the value of knowledge, we cannot fail to be spurred to new inquiry to fill at least the more grievous gaps. Equally important is the warning contained in the strength of the emotions displayed in current debate. This suggests that the answer to the question how we can best insure that our economy progresses and that every man be dealt with justly can never be found within the discipline of economics itself. The amount and type of production which we desire and the principles for determining how this production should be distributed is only in part a problem in economics. We cannot decide these issues without first deciding what kind of world is worthwhile and what are the desired relations between man and government, and man and fellow man. Adam Smith, the pupil of Francis Hutcheson, knew that economics was one of the moral sciences, something that we must relearn after two hundred years. But learning can be both pleasant and profitable, even when it involves learning anew what the old knew so well.

OF THE WAGES OF LABOUR [1]

ADAM SMITH

THE produce of labour constitutes the natural recompense or wages of labour.

In that original state of things, which precedes both the appropriation of land and the accumulation of stock, the whole produce of labour belongs to the labourer. He has neither landlord nor master to share with him.

Had this state continued, the wages of labour would have augmented with all those improvements in its productive powers to which the division of labour gives occasion. All things would gradually have become cheaper. They would have been produced by a smaller quantity of labour; and as the commodities produced by equal quantities of labour would naturally in this state of things be exchanged for one another, they would have been purchased likewise with the produce of a smaller quantity. . . .

But this original state of things, in which the labourer enjoyed the whole produce of his own labour, could not last beyond the first introduction of the appropriation of land and the accumulation of stock. It was at an end, therefore, long before the most considerable improvements were made in the productive powers of labour, and it would be to no purpose to trace further what might have been its effects upon the recompense or wages of labour.

As soon as land becomes private property, the landlord demands a share of almost all the produce which the labourer can either raise, or collect from it. His rent makes the first deduction from the produce of the labour which is employed upon land.

1. *The Wealth of Nations* (New York: E. P. Dutton & Co., Inc., 1937, Everyman's Library), pp. 57–67, 69–72, with omissions. First printed in 1776.

It seldom happens that the person who tills the ground has wherewithal to maintain himself till he reaps the harvest. His maintenance is generally advanced to him from the stock of a master, the farmer who employs him, and who would have no interest to employ him, unless he was to share in the produce of his labour, or unless his stock was to be replaced to him with a profit. This profit makes a second deduction from the produce of the labour which is employed upon land.

The produce of almost all other labour is liable to the like deduction of profit. In all arts and manufactures the greater part of the workmen stand in need of a master to advance them the materials of their work, and their wages and maintenance till it be completed. He shares in the produce of their labour, or in the value which it adds to the materials upon which it is bestowed; and in this share consists his profit. . . .

What are the common wages of labour, depends everywhere upon the contract usually made between those two parties, whose interests are by no means the same. The workmen desire to get as much, the masters to give as little as possible. The former are disposed to combine in order to raise, the latter in order to lower the wages of labour.

It is not, however, difficult to foresee which of the two parties must, upon all ordinary occasions, have the advantage in the dispute, and force the other into a compliance with their terms. The masters, being fewer in number, can combine much more easily; and the law, besides, authorises, or at least does not prohibit their combinations, while it prohibits those of the workmen. We have no acts of parliament against combining to lower the price of work; but many against combining to raise it. In all such disputes the masters can hold out much longer. A landlord, a farmer, a master manufacturer, a merchant, though they did not employ a single workman, could generally live a year or two upon the stocks which they have already acquired. Many workmen could not subsist a week, few could subsist a month, and scarce any a year without employment. In the long-run the workman may be as necessary to his master as his master is to him; but the necessity is not so immediate.

We rarely hear, it has been said, of the combinations of masters, though frequently of those of workmen. But whoever imagines, upon this account, that masters rarely combine, is as ignorant of the world as of the subject. Masters are always and everywhere in a sort of tacit, but constant and uniform combination, not to raise the wages of labour above their actual rate. . . . Masters, too, sometimes enter into particular combinations to sink the wages of labour even below this rate. These are always conducted with the utmost silence and secrecy, till the moment of execution, and when the workmen yield, as they sometimes do, without resistance, though severely felt by them, they are never heard of by other people. Such combinations, however, are frequently resisted by a contrary defensive combination of the workmen; who sometimes too, without any provocation of this kind, combine of their own accord to raise the price of their labour. Their usual pretences are, sometimes the high price of provisions; sometimes the great profit which their masters make by their work. But whether their combinations be offensive or defensive, they are always abundantly heard of. In order to bring the point to a speedy decision, they have always recourse to the loudest clamour, and sometimes to the most shocking violence and outrage. They are desperate, and act with the folly and extravagance of desperate men, who must either starve, or frighten their masters into an immediate compliance with their demands. The masters upon these occasions are just as clamorous upon the other side, and never cease to call aloud for the assistance of the civil magistrate, and the rigorous execution of those laws which have been enacted with so much severity against the combinations of servants, labourers, and journeymen. The workmen, accordingly, very seldom derive any advantage from the violence of those tumultuous combinations, which, partly from the interposition of the civil magistrate, partly from the superior steadiness of the masters, partly from the necessity which the greater part of the workmen are under of submitting for the sake of present subsistence, generally end in nothing, but the punishment or ruin of the ringleaders.

But though in disputes with their workmen, masters must generally have the advantage, there is, however, a certain rate below which it seems impossible to reduce, for any considerable time, the ordinary wages even of the lowest species of labour.

A man must always live by his work, and his wages must at least be sufficient to maintain him. They must even upon most occasions be somewhat more; otherwise it would be impossible for him to bring up a family, and the race of such workmen could not last beyond the first generation. . . .

There are certain circumstances, however, which sometimes give the labourers an advantage, and enable them to raise their wages considerably above this rate; evidently the lowest which is consistent with common humanity.

When in any country the demand for those who live by wages, labourers, journeymen, servants of every kind, is continually increasing; when every year furnishes employment for a greater number than had been employed the year before, the workmen have no occasion to combine in order to raise their wages. The scarcity of hands occasions a competition among masters, who bid against one another, in order to get workmen, and thus voluntarily break through the natural combination of masters not to raise wages.

The demand for those who live by wages, it is evident, cannot increase but in proportion to the increase of the funds which are destined for the payment of wages. These funds are of two kinds; first, the revenue which is over and above what is necessary for the maintenance; and, secondly, the stock which is over and above what is necessary for the employment of their masters. . . .

It is not the actual greatness of national wealth, but its continual increase, which occasions a rise in the wages of labour. It is not, accordingly, in the richest countries, but in the most thriving, or in those which are growing rich the fastest, that the wages of labour are highest. England is certainly, in the present times, a much richer country than any part of North America. The wages of labour, however, are much higher in North America than in any part of England. . . . The price of provisions is everywhere in North America much lower than in England. A dearth has never been known there. In the worst seasons they have always had a sufficiency for themselves, though less for exportation. If the money price of labour, therefore, be higher than it is anywhere in the mother country, its real price, the real command of the necessaries and conveniencies of life which it conveys to the labourer must be higher in a still greater proportion.

But though North America is not yet so rich as England, it is much more thriving, and advancing with much greater rapidity to the further acquisition of riches. The most decisive mark of the prosperity of any country is the increase of the number of its inhabitants. In Great Britain, and most other European countries, they are not supposed to double in less than five hundred years. In the British colonies in North America, it has been found that they double in twenty or five-and-twenty years. Nor in the present times is this increase principally owing to the continual importation of new inhabitants, but to the great multiplication of the species. . . . The value of children is the greatest of all encouragements to marriage. We cannot, therefore, wonder that the people in North America should generally marry very young. Notwithstanding the great increase occasioned by such early marriages, there is a continual complaint of the scarcity of hands in North America. The demand for labourers, the funds destined for maintaining them, increase, it seems, still faster than they can find labourers to employ.

Though the wealth of a country should be very great, yet if it has been long stationary, we must not expect to find the wages of labour very high in it. The funds destined for the payment of wages, the revenue and stock of its inhabitants, may be of the greatest extent; but if they have continued for several centuries of the same, or very nearly of the same extent, the number of labourers employed every year could easily supply, and even more than supply, the number wanted the following year. There could seldom be any scarcity of hands, nor could the masters be obliged to bid against one another in order to get them. The hands, on the contrary, would, in this case, naturally multiply beyond their employment. There would be a constant scarcity of employment, and the labourers would be obliged to bid against one another in order to get it. If in such a country the wages of labour had ever been more than sufficient to maintain the labourer, and to enable him to bring up a family, the competition of the labourers and the interest of the masters would soon reduce them to this lowest rate which is consistent with common humanity. China has been long one of the richest, that is, one of the most fertile, best cultivated, most industrious, and most populous countries in the world. It seems, however, to have been long stationary. Marco Polo, who visited it more than five hundred years ago, describes its cultivation, industry, and populousness, almost in the same terms in which they are described by travellers in the present times. It had perhaps, even long before his time, acquired that full complement of riches which the nature of its laws and institutions permits it to acquire. The accounts of all travellers, inconsistent in many other respects, agree in the low wages of labour, and in the difficulty which a labourer finds in bringing up a family in China. . . .

China, however, though it may perhaps stand still, does not seem to go backwards. Its towns are nowhere deserted by their inhabitants. The lands which had once been cultivated are nowhere neglected. The same or very nearly the same annual labour must therefore continue to be performed, and the funds destined for maintaining it must not, consequently, be sensibly diminished. The lowest class of labourers, therefore, notwithstanding their scanty subsistence, must some way or another make shift to continue their race so far as to keep up their usual numbers.

But it would be otherwise in a country where the funds destined for the maintenance of labour were sensibly decaying. Every year the demand for servants and labourers would, in all the different classes of employments, be less than it had been the year before. Many who had been bred in the superior classes, not being able to find employment in their own business, would be glad to seek it in the lowest. The lowest class being not only over-stocked with its own workmen, but with the overflowings of all the other classes, the competition for employment would be so great in it, as to reduce the wages of labour to the most miserable and scanty subsistence of the labourer. Many would not be able to find employment even upon these hard terms, but would either starve, or be driven to seek a subsistence either by begging, or by the perpetration perhaps of the greatest enormities. Want, famine, and mortality would immediately prevail in that class, and from thence extend themselves to all the superior classes, till the number of inhabitants in the country was reduced to what could easily be maintained by the revenue and stock which remained in it, and which had escaped either the tyranny or calamity which had destroyed the rest. . . .

The liberal reward of labour, therefore, as it is the necessary effect, so it is the natural symptom of increasing national wealth. The scanty maintenance of the labouring poor, on the other hand, is the natural symptom that things are at a stand, and their starving condition that they are going fast backwards. . . .

The real recompense of labour, the real quantity of the necessaries and conveniencies of life which it can procure to the labourer, has, during the course of the present century, increased perhaps in a still greater proportion than its money price. Not only grain has become somewhat cheaper, but many other things from which the industrious poor derive an agreeable and wholesome variety of food have become a great deal cheaper. . . . The common complaint that luxury extends itself even to the lowest ranks of the people, and that the labouring poor will not now be contented with the same food, clothing, and lodging which satisfied them in former times, may convince us that it is not the money price of labour only, but its real recompense, which has augmented.

Is this improvement in the circumstances of the lower ranks of the people to be regarded as an advantage or as an inconveniency to the society? The answer seems at first sight abundantly plain. Servants, labourers, and workmen of different kinds, make up the far greater part of every great political society. But what improves the circumstances of the greater part can never be regarded as an inconveniency to the whole. No society can surely be flourishing and happy, of which the far greater part of the members are poor and miserable. It is but equity, besides, that they who feed, clothe, and lodge the whole body of the people, should have such a share of the produce of their own labour as to be themselves tolerably well fed, clothed, and lodged. . . .

GOLD-MINING[1]

JOHN MAYNARD KEYNES

When involuntary unemployment exists, the marginal disutility of labour is necessarily less than the utility of the marginal product. Indeed it may be much less. For a man who has been long unemployed some measure of labour, instead of involving disutility, may have a positive utility. If this is accepted, the above reasoning shows how "wasteful" loan expenditure may nevertheless enrich the community on balance. Pyramid-building, earthquakes, even wars may serve to increase wealth, if the education of our statesmen on the principles of the classical economics stands in the way of anything better.

It is curious how common sense, wriggling for an escape from absurd conclusions, has been apt to reach a preference for *wholly* "wasteful" forms of loan expenditure rather than for *partly* wasteful forms, which, because they are not wholly wasteful, tend to be judged on strict "business" principles. For example, unemployment relief financed by loans is more readily accepted than the financing of improvements at a charge below the current rate of interest; whilst the form of digging holes in the ground known as gold-mining,

1. From *The General Theory of Employment, Interest, and Money* by John Maynard Keynes. Reprinted by permission of Harcourt, Brace and Company, Inc.

which not only adds nothing whatever to the real wealth of the world but involves the disutility of labour, is the most acceptable of all solutions.

If the Treasury were to fill old bottles with banknotes, bury them at suitable depths in disused coal-mines which are then filled up to the surface with town rubbish, and leave it to private enterprise on well-tried principles of *laissez-faire* to dig the notes up again (the right to do so being obtained, of course, by tendering for leases of the note-bearing territory), there need be no more unemployment and, with the help of the repercussions, the real income of the community, and its capital wealth also, would probably become a good deal greater than it actually is. It would, indeed, be more sensible to build houses and the like; but if there are political and practical difficulties in the way of this, the above would be better than nothing.

The analogy between this expedient and the gold-mines of the real world is complete. At periods when gold is available at suitable depths experience shows that the real wealth of the world increases rapidly; and when but little of it is so available, our wealth suffers stagnation or decline. Thus gold-mines are of the greatest value and importance to civilisation. Just as wars have been the only form of large-scale loan expenditure which statesmen have thought justifiable, so gold-mining is the only pretext for digging holes in the ground which has recommended itself to bankers as sound finance; and each of these activities has played its part in progress—failing something better. To mention a detail, the tendency in slumps for the price of gold to rise in terms of labour and materials aids eventual recovery, because it increases the depth at which gold-digging pays and lowers the minimum grade of ore which is payable.

In addition to the probable effect of increased supplies of gold on the rate of interest, gold-mining is for two reasons a highly practical form of investment, if we are precluded from increasing employment by means which at the same time increase our stock of useful wealth. In the first place, owing to the gambling attractions which it offers it is carried on without too close a regard to the ruling rate of interest. In the second place the result, namely, the increased stock of gold, does not, as in other cases, have the effect of diminishing its marginal utility. Since the value of a house depends on its utility, every house which is built serves to diminish the prospective rents obtainable from further house-building and therefore lessens the attraction of further similar investment unless the rate of interest is falling *pari passu*. But the fruits of gold-mining do not suffer from this disadvantage, and a check can only come through a rise of the wage-unit in terms of gold, which is not likely to occur unless and until employment is substantially better. Moreover, there is no subsequent reverse effect on account of provision for user and supplementary costs, as in the case of less durable forms of wealth.

Ancient Egypt was doubly fortunate, and doubtless owed to this its fabled wealth, in that it possessed *two* activities, namely, pyramid-building as well as the search for the precious metals, the fruits of which, since they could not serve the needs of man by being consumed, did not stale with abundance. The Middle Ages built cathedrals and sang dirges. Two pyramids, two masses for the dead, are twice as good as one; but not so two railways from London to York. Thus we are so sensible, have schooled ourselves to so close a semblance of prudent financiers, taking careful thought before we add to the "financial" burdens of posterity by building them houses to live in, that we have no such easy escape from the sufferings of unemployment. We have to accept them as an inevitable result of applying to the conduct of the State the maxims which are best calculated to "enrich" an individual by enabling him to pile up claims to enjoyment which he does not intend to exercise at any definite time.

CIVIL DISOBEDIENCE [1]

HENRY DAVID THOREAU

I HEARTILY accept the motto,—"That government is best which governs least"; and I should like to see it acted up to more rapidly and systematically. Carried out, it finally amounts to this, which also I believe,—"That government is best which governs not at all;" and when men are prepared for it, that will be the kind of government which they will have. Government is at best but an expedient; but most governments are usually, and all governments are sometimes, inexpedient. The objections which have been brought against a standing army, and they are many and weighty, and deserve to prevail, may also at last be brought against a standing government. The standing army is only an arm of the standing government. The government itself, which is only the mode which the people have chosen to execute their will, is equally liable to be abused and perverted before the people can act through it. Witness the present Mexican war, the work of comparatively a few individuals

1. From Norman Holmes Pearson, Ed., *Walden* (New York: Rinehart, 1948), pp. 281–304, with omissions. "Rinehart Editions." First printed in 1849.

using the standing government as their tool; for, in the outset, the people would not have consented to this measure.

This American government,—what is it but a tradition, though a recent one, endeavoring to transmit itself unimpaired to posterity, but each instant losing some of its integrity? It has not the vitality and force of a single living man; for a single man can bend it to his will. It is a sort of wooden gun to the people themselves. But it is not the less necessary for this; for the people must have some complicated machinery or other, and hear its din, to satisfy that idea of government which they have. Governments show thus how successfully men can be imposed on, even impose on themselves, for their own advantage. It is excellent, we must all allow. Yet this government never of itself furthered any enterprise, but by the alacrity with which it got out of its way. *It* does not keep the country free. *It* does not settle the West. *It* does not educate. The character inherent in the American people has done all that has been accomplished; and it would have done somewhat more, if the government had not sometimes got in its way. For government is an expedient by which men would fain succeed in letting one another alone; and, as has been said, when it is most expedient, the governed are most let alone by it. Trade and commerce, if they were not made of India-rubber, would never manage to bounce over the obstacles which legislators are continually putting in their way; and, if one were to judge these men wholly by the effects of their actions and not partly by their intentions, they would deserve to be classed and punished with those mischievous persons who put obstructions on the railroads.

But, to speak practically and as a citizen, unlike those who call themselves no-government men, I ask for, not at once no government, but *at once* a better government. Let every man make known what kind of government would command his respect, and that will be one step toward obtaining it.

After all, the practical reason why, when the power is once in the hands of the people, a majority are permitted, and for a long period continue, to rule is not because they are most likely to be in the right, nor because this seems fairest to the minority, but because they are physically the strongest. But a government in which the majority rule in all cases cannot be based on justice, even as far as men understand it. Can there not be a government in which majorities do not virtually decide right and wrong, but conscience?—in which majorities decide only those questions to which the rule of expediency is applicable? Must the citizen ever for a moment, or in the least degree, resign his conscience to the legislator? Why has every man a conscience, then?

I think that we should be men first, and subjects afterward. It is not desirable to cultivate a respect for the law, so much as for the right. The only obligation which I have a right to assume is to do at any time what I think right. It is truly enough said, that a corporation has no conscience; but a corporation of conscientious men is a corporation *with* a conscience. Law never made men a whit more just; and, by means of their respect for it, even the well-disposed are daily made the agents of injustice. A common and natural result of an undue respect for law is, that you may see a file of soldiers, colonel, captain, corporal, privates, powder-monkeys, and all, marching in admirable order over hill and dale to the wars, against their wills, ay, against their common sense and consciences, which makes it very steep marching indeed, and produces a palpitation of the heart. They have no doubt that it is a damnable business in which they are concerned; they are all peaceably inclined. Now, what are they? Men at all? or small movable forts and magazines, at the service of some unscrupulous man in power? Visit the Navy-Yard, and behold a marine, such a man as an American government can make, or such as it can make a man with its black arts,—a mere shadow and reminiscence of humanity, a man laid out alive and standing, and already, as one may say, buried under arms with funeral accompaniments, though it may be,—

"Not a drum was heard, not a funeral note,
As his corpse to the rampart we hurried;
Not a soldier discharged his farewell shot
O'er the grave where our hero we buried."

The mass of men serve the state thus, not as men mainly, but as machines, with their bodies. They are the standing army, and the militia, jailors, constables, posse comitatus, etc. In most cases there is no free exercise whatever of the judgment or of the moral sense; but they put themselves on a level with wood and earth and stones; and wooden men can perhaps be manufactured that will serve the purpose as well. Such command no more respect than men of straw or a lump of dirt. They have the same sort of worth only as horses and dogs. Yet such as these even are commonly esteemed good citizens. Others—as most legislators, politicians, lawyers, ministers, and office-holders—serve the state chiefly with their heads; and, as they rarely make any moral distinctions, they are as likely to serve the Devil, without *intending* it, as God. A very few, as heroes, patriots, martyrs, reformers in the great sense, and *men,* serve the state with their consciences also, and so necessarily resist it for the most part; and they are commonly treated as enemies by it. A wise man will only be useful as a man, and will not submit to be "clay," and "stop a hole to keep the wind away," but leave that office to his dust at least:—

"I am too high-born to be propertied,
To be a secondary at control,
Or useful serving-man and instrument
To any sovereign state throughout the world."

He who gives himself entirely to his fellow-men appears to them useless and selfish; but he who gives himself partially to them is pronounced a benefactor and philanthropist.

How does it become a man to behave toward this American government to-day? I answer, that he cannot without disgrace be associated with it. I cannot for an instant recognize that political organization as *my* government which is the *slave's* government also.

All men recognize the right of revolution; that is, the right to refuse allegiance to, and to resist, the government, when its tyranny or its inefficiency are great and unendurable. But almost all say that such is not the case now. But such was the case, they think, in the Revolution of '75. If one were to tell me that this was a bad government because it taxed certain foreign commodities brought to its ports, it is most probable that I should not make an ado about it, for I can do without them. All machines have their friction; and possibly this does enough good to counterbalance the evil. At any rate, it is a great evil to make a stir about it. But when the friction comes to have its machine, and oppression and robbery are organized, I say, let us not have such a machine any longer. In other words, when a sixth of the population of a nation which has undertaken to be the refuge of liberty are slaves, and a whole country is unjustly overrun and conquered by a foreign army, and subjected to military law, I think that it is not too soon for honest men to rebel and revolutionize. What makes this duty the more urgent is the fact that the country so overrun is not our own, but ours is the invading army. . . .

> "A drab of state, a cloth-o'-silver slut,
> To have her train borne up, and her soul trail in the dirt."

Practically speaking, the opponents to a reform in Massachusetts are not a hundred thousand politicians at the South, but a hundred thousand merchants and farmers here, who are more interested in commerce and agriculture than they are in humanity, and are not prepared to do justice to the slave and to Mexico, *cost what it may*. I quarrel not with far-off foes, but with those who, near at home, coöperate with, and do the bidding of, those far away, and without whom the latter would be harmless. We are accustomed to say, that the mass of men are unprepared; but improvement is slow, because the few are not materially wiser or better than the many. It is not so important that many should be as good as you, as that there be some absolute goodness somewhere; for that will leaven the whole lump. There are thousands who are *in opinion* opposed to slavery and to the war, who yet in effect do nothing to put an end to them; who, esteeming themselves children of Washington and Franklin, sit down with their hands in their pockets, and say that they know not what to do, and do nothing; who even postpone the question of freedom to the question of free-trade, and quietly read the prices-current along with the latest advices from Mexico, after dinner, and, it may be, fall asleep over them both. What is the price-current of an honest man and patriot to-day? They hesitate, and they regret, and sometimes they petition; but they do nothing in earnest and with effect. They will wait, well disposed, for others to remedy the evil, that they may no longer have it to regret. At most, they give only a cheap vote, and a feeble countenance and God-speed, to the right, as it goes by them. There are nine hundred and ninety-nine patrons of virtue to one virtuous man. But it is easier to deal with the real possessor of a thing than with the temporary guardian of it.

All voting is a sort of gaming, like checkers or backgammon, with a slight moral tinge to it, a playing with right and wrong, with moral questions; and betting naturally accompanies it. The character of the voters is not staked. I cast my vote, perchance, as I think right; but I am not vitally concerned that that right should prevail. I am willing to leave it to the majority. Its obligation, therefore, never exceeds that of expediency. Even voting *for the right* is *doing* nothing for it. It is only expressing to men feebly your desire that it should prevail. A wise man will not leave the right to the mercy of chance, nor wish it to prevail through the power of the majority. There is but little virtue in the action of masses of men. When the majority shall at length vote for the abolition of slavery, it will be because they are indifferent to slavery, or because there is but little slavery left to be abolished by their vote. *They* will then be the only slaves. Only *his* vote can hasten the abolition of slavery who asserts his own freedom by his vote.

I hear of a convention to be held at Baltimore, or elsewhere, for the selection of a candidate for the Presidency, made up chiefly of editors, and men who are politicians by profession; but I think, what is it to any independent, intelligent, and respectable man what decision they may come to? Shall we not have the advantage of his wisdom and honesty, nevertheless? Can we not count upon some independent votes? Are there not many individuals in the country who do not attend conventions? But no: I find that the respectable man, so called, has immediately drifted from his position, and despairs of his country, when his country has more reason to despair of him. He forthwith adopts one of the candidates thus selected as the only *available* one, thus proving that he is himself *available* for any purposes of the demagogue. His vote is of no more worth than that of any unprincipled foreigner or hireling native, who may have been bought. O for a man who is a *man,* and, as my neighbor says, has a bone in his back which you cannot pass your hand through! Our statistics are at fault: the population has been returned too large. How many *men* are there to a square thousand miles in this country? Hardly one. Does not America offer any inducement for men to settle here? The American has dwindled into an Odd Fellow,—one who may be known by the development of his organ of gregariousness, and a manifest lack of intellect and cheerful self-reliance; whose first and chief concern, on coming into the world, is to see that the Almshouses are in good repair; and, before yet he has lawfully donned the virile garb, to collect a fund for the support of the widows and orphans that may be; who, in short, ventures to live only by the aid of the Mutual Insurance company, which has promised to bury him decently.

It is not a man's duty, as a matter of course, to devote himself to the eradication of any, even the most enormous wrong; he may still properly have other concerns to engage him; but it is his duty, at least, to wash his hands of it, and, if he gives it no thought longer, not to give it practically his support. If I devote myself to other pursuits and contemplations, I must first see, at least, that I do not pursue them sitting upon another man's shoulders. I must get off him first, that he may pursue his contemplations too. See what gross inconsistency is tolerated. I have heard some of my townsmen say, "I should like to have them order me out to help put down an insurrection of the slaves, or to march to Mexico;—see if I would go;" and yet these very men have each, directly by their allegiance, and so indirectly, at least, by their money, furnished a substitute. The soldier is applauded who refuses to serve in an unjust war by those who do not refuse to sustain the unjust government which makes the war; is applauded by those whose own act and authority he disregards and sets at naught; as if the state were penitent to that degree that it hired one to scourge it while it sinned, but not to that degree that it left off sinning for a moment. Thus, under the name of Order and Civil Government, we are all made at last to pay homage to and support our own meanness. After the first blush of sin comes its indifference; and from immoral it becomes, as it were, *un*moral, and not quite unnecessary to that life which we have made.

The broadest and most prevalent error requires the most disinterested virtue to sustain it. The slight reproach to which the virtue of patriotism is commonly liable, the noble are most likely to incur. Those who, while they disapprove of the character and measures of a government, yield to it their allegiance and support are undoubtedly its most conscientious supporters, and so frequently the most serious obstacles to reform. Some are petitioning the state to dissolve the Union, to disregard the requisitions of the President. Why do they not dissolve it themselves—the union between themselves and the state,—and refuse to pay their quota into its treasury? Do not they stand in the same relation to the state that the state does to the Union? And have not the same reasons prevented the state from resisting the Union which have prevented them from resisting the state?

How can a man be satisfied to entertain an opinion merely, and enjoy *it*? Is there any enjoyment in it, if his opinion is that he is aggrieved? If you are cheated out of a single dollar by your neighbor, you do not rest satisfied with knowing that you are cheated, or with saying that you are cheated, or even with petitioning him to pay you your due; but you take effectual steps at once to obtain the full amount, and see that you are never cheated again. Action from principle, the perception and the performance of right, changes things and relations; it is essentially revolutionary, and does not consist wholly with anything which was. It not only divides states and churches, it divides families; ay, it divides the *individual*, separating the diabolical in him from the divine.

Unjust laws exist: shall we be content to obey them, or shall we endeavor to amend them, and obey them until we have succeeded, or shall we transgress them at once? Men generally, under such a government as this, think that they ought to wait until they have persuaded the majority to alter them. They think that, if they should resist, the remedy would be worse than the evil. But it is the fault of the government itself that the remedy *is* worse than the evil. *It* makes it worse. Why is it not more apt to anticipate and provide for reform? Why does it not cherish its wise minority? Why does it cry and resist before it is hurt? Why does it not encourage its citizens to be on the alert to point out its faults, and *do* better than it would have them? Why does it always crucify Christ, and excommunicate Copernicus and Luther, and pronounce Washington and Franklin rebels?

One would think, that a deliberate and practical denial of its authority was the only offense never contemplated by government; else, why has it not assigned its definite, its suitable and proportionate penalty? If a man who has no property refuses but once to earn nine shillings for the state, he is put in prison for a period unlimited by any law that I know, and determined only by the discretion of those who placed him there; but if he should steal ninety times nine shillings from the state, he is soon permitted to go at large again.

If the injustice is part of the necessary friction of the machine of government, let it go, let it go: perchance it will wear smooth,—certainly the machine will wear out. If the injustice has a spring, or a pulley, or a rope, or a crank, exclusively for itself, then perhaps you may consider whether the remedy will not be worse than the evil; but if it is of such a nature that it requires you to be the agent of injustice to another, then, I say, break the law. Let your life be a counter friction to stop the machine. What I have to do is to see, at any rate, that I do not lend myself to the wrong which I condemn.

As for adopting the ways which the state has provided for remedying the evil, I know not of such ways. They take too much time, and a man's life will be gone. I have other affairs to attend to. I came into this world, not chiefly to make this a good place to live in, but to live in it, be it good or bad. A man has not everything to do, but something; and because he cannot do *everything*, it is not necessary that he should do *something* wrong. It is not my business to be petitioning the Governor or the Legislature any more than it is theirs to petition me; and if they should not hear my petition, what should I do then? But in this case the state has provided no way: its very Constitution is the evil. This may seem to be harsh and stubborn and unconciliatory; but it is to treat with the utmost kindness and consideration the only spirit that can appreciate or deserves it. So is all change for the better, like birth and death, which convulse the body.

I do not hesitate to say, that those who call themselves Abolitionists should at once effectually withdraw their support, both in person and property, from the government of Massachusetts and not wait till they constitute a majority of one, before they suffer the right to prevail through them. I think that it is enough if they have God on their side, without waiting for that other one. Moreover, any man more right than his neighbors constitutes a majority of one already.

I meet this American government, or its representative, the state government, directly, and face to face, once a year—no more—in the person of its tax-gatherer; this is the only mode in which a man situated as I am necessarily meets it; and it then says distinctly, Recognize me; and the simplest, most effectual, and, in the present posture of affairs, the indispensablest mode of treating with it on this head, of expressing your little satisfaction with and love for it, is to deny it then. My civil neighbor, the tax-gatherer, is the very man I have to deal with,—for it is, after all, with men and not with parchment that I quarrel,—and he has voluntarily chosen to be an agent of the government. How shall he ever know well what he is and does as an officer of the government, or as a man, until he is obliged to consider whether he shall treat me, his neighbor, for whom he has respect, as a neighbor and well-disposed man, or as a maniac and disturber of the peace, and see if he can get over this obstruction to his neighborliness without a ruder and more impetuous thought or speech corresponding with his action. I know this well, that if one thousand, if one hundred, if ten men whom I could name,—if ten *honest* men only,—ay, if *one* HONEST man, in this State of Massachusetts, *ceasing to hold slaves,* were actually to withdraw from this copartnership, and be locked up in the county jail therefor, it would be the abolition of slavery in America. For it matters not how small the beginning may seem to be: what is once well done is done forever. But we love better to talk about it: that we say is our mission. Reform keeps many scores of newspapers in its service, but not one man. If my esteemed neighbor, the State's ambassador, who will devote his days to the settlement of the question of human rights in the Council Chamber, instead of being threatened with the prisons of Carolina, were to sit down the prisoner of Massachusetts, that State which is so anxious to foist the sin of slavery upon her sister,—though at present she can discover only an act of inhospitality to be the ground of a quarrel with her,—the Legislature would not wholly waive the subject the following winter.

Under a government which imprisons any unjustly, the true place for a just man is also a prison. The proper place to-day, the only place which Massachusetts has provided for her freer and less desponding spirits, is in her prisons, to be put out and locked out of the State by her own act, as they have already put themselves out by their principles. It is there that the fugitive slave, and the Mexican prisoner on parole, and the Indian come to plead the wrongs of his race should find them; on that separate, but more free and honorable ground, where the State places those who are not *with* her, but *against* her,—the only house in a slave State in which a free man can abide with honor. If any think that their influence would be lost there, and their voices no longer afflict the ear of the State, that they would not be as an enemy within its walls, they do not know by how much truth is stronger than error, nor how much more eloquently and effectively he can combat injustice who has experienced a little in his own person. Cast your whole vote, not a strip of paper merely, but your whole influence. A minority is powerless while it conforms to the majority; it is not even a minority then; but it is irresistible when it clogs by its whole weight. If the alternative is to keep all just men in prison, or give up war and slavery, the State will not hesitate which to choose. If a thousand men were not to pay their tax-bills this year, that would not be a violent and bloody measure, as it would be to pay them, and enable the State to commit violence and shed innocent blood. This is, in fact, the definition of a peaceable revolution, if any such is possible. If the tax-gatherer, or any other public officer, asks me, as one has done, "But what shall I do?" my answer is, "If you really wish to do anything, resign your office." When the subject has refused allegiance, and the officer has resigned his office, then the revolution is accomplished. But even suppose blood should flow. Is there not a sort of blood shed when the conscience is wounded? Through this wound a man's real manhood and immortality flow out, and he bleeds to an everlasting death. I see this blood flowing now.

I have contemplated the imprisonment of the offender, rather than the seizure of his goods,—though both will serve the same purpose,—because they who assert the purest right, and consequently are most dangerous to a corrupt State, commonly have not spent much time in accumulating property. To such the State renders comparatively small service, and a slight tax is wont to appear exorbitant, particularly if they are obliged to earn it by special labor with their hands. If there were one who lived wholly without the use of money, the State itself would hesitate to demand it of him. But the rich man—not to make any invidious comparison—is always sold to the institution which makes him rich. Absolutely speaking, the more money, the less virtue; for money comes between a man and his objects, and obtains them for him; and it was certainly no great virtue to obtain it. It puts to rest many questions which he would otherwise be taxed to answer; while the only new question which it puts is the hard but superfluous one, how to spend it. Thus his moral ground is taken from under his feet. The opportunities of living are diminished in proportion as what are called the "means" are increased. The best thing a man can do for his culture when he is rich is to endeavor to carry out those schemes which he entertained when he was poor. Christ answered the Herodians according to their condition. "Show me the tribute-money," said he;—and one took a penny out of his pocket;—if you use money which has the image of Cæsar on it and which he has made current and valuable, that is, *if you are men of the State,* and gladly enjoy the advantages of Cæsar's government, then pay him back some of his own when he demands it. "Render therefore to Cæsar that which is Cæsar's, and to God those things which are God's,"—leaving them no wiser than before as to which was which; for they did not wish to know. . . .

I have paid no poll-tax for six years. I was put into a jail once on this account, for one night; and, as I stood considering the walls of solid stone, two or three feet thick, the door of wood and iron, a foot thick, and the iron grating which strained the light, I could not help being struck with the foolishness of that institution which treated me as if I were mere flesh and blood and bones, to be locked up. I wondered that it should have concluded at length that this was the best use it could put me to, and had never thought to avail itself of my services in some way. I saw that, if there was a wall of stone between me and my townsmen, there was a still more difficult one to climb or break through before they could get to be as free as I was. I did not for a moment feel confined, and the walls seemed a great waste of stone and mortar. I felt as if I alone of all my townsmen had paid my tax. They plainly did not know how to treat me, but behaved like persons who are underbred. In every threat and in every compliment there was a blunder; for they thought that my chief desire was to stand the other side of that stone wall. I could not but smile to see how industriously they locked the door on my meditations, which followed them out again without let or hindrance, and *they* were really all that was dangerous. As they could not reach me, they had resolved to punish my body; just as boys, if they cannot come at some person against whom they have a spite, will abuse his dog. I saw that the State was half-witted, that it was timid as a lone woman with her silver spoons, and that it did not know its friends from its foes, and I lost all my remaining respect for it, and pitied it.

Thus the State never intentionally confronts a man's sense, intellectual or moral, but only his body, his senses. It is not armed with superior wit or honesty, but with superior physical strength. I was not born to be forced. I will breathe after my own fashion. Let us see who is the strongest. What force has a multitude? They only can force me who obey a higher law than I. They force me to become like themselves. I do not hear of *men* being *forced* to live this way or that by masses of men. What sort of life were that to live? When I meet a government which says to me, "Your money or your life," why should I be in haste to give it my money? It may be in a great strait, and not know what to do: I cannot help that. It must help itself; do as I do. It is not worth the while to snivel about it. I am not responsible for the successful working of the machinery of society. I am not the son of the engineer. I perceive that, when an acorn and a chestnut fall side by side, the one does not remain inert to make way for the other, but both obey their own laws, and spring and grow and flourish as best they can, till one, perchance, overshadows and destroys the other. If a plant cannot live according to its nature, it dies; and so a man. . . .

When I came out of prison,—for some one interfered, and paid that tax,—I did not perceive that great changes had taken place on the common, such as he observed who went in a youth and emerged a tottering and gray-headed man; and yet a change had to my eyes come over the scene,—the town, and State, and country,—greater than any that mere time could effect. I saw yet more distinctly the State in which I lived. I saw to what extent the people among whom I lived could be trusted as good neighbors and friends; that their friendship was for summer weather only; that they did not greatly propose to do right; that they were a distinct race from me by their prejudices and superstitions, as the Chinamen and Malays are; that in their sacrifices to humanity they ran no risks, not even to their property; that after all they were not so noble but they treated the thief as he had treated them, and hoped, by a certain outward observance and a few prayers, and by walking in a particular straight though useless path from time to time, to save their souls. This may be to judge my neighbors harshly; for I believe that many of them are not aware that they have such an institution as the jail in their village.

It was formerly the custom in our village, when a poor debtor came out of jail, for his acquaintances to salute him, looking through their fingers, which were crossed to represent the grating of a jail window. "How do ye do?" My neighbors did not thus salute me, but first looked at me, and then at one another, as if I had returned from a long journey. I was put into jail as I was going to the shoemaker's to get a shoe which was mended. When I was let out the next morning, I proceeded to finish my errand, and, having put on my mended shoe, joined a huckleberry party, who were impatient to put themselves under my conduct; and in half an hour,—for the horse was soon tackled,—was in the midst of a huckleberry field, on one of our highest hills, two miles off, and then the State was nowhere to be seen. . . .

I have never declined paying the highway tax, because I am as desirous of being a good neighbor as I am of being a bad subject; and as for supporting schools, I am doing my part to educate my fellow-countrymen now. It is for no particular item in the tax-bill that I refuse to pay it. I simply wish to refuse allegiance to the State, to withdraw and stand aloof from it effectually. I do not care to trace the course of my dollar, if I could, till it buys a man or a musket to shoot with,—the dollar is innocent,—but I am concerned to trace the effects of my allegiance. In fact, I quietly declare war with the State, after my fashion, though I will still make what use and get what advantage of her I can, as is usual in such cases.

If others pay the tax which is demanded of me, from a sympathy with the State, they do but what they have already done in their own case, or rather they abet injustice to a greater extent than the State requires. If they pay the tax from a mistaken interest in the individual taxed, to save his property, or prevent his going to jail, it is because they have not considered wisely how far they let their private feelings interfere with the public good.

This, then, is my position at present. But one cannot be too much on his guard in such a case, lest his action be biased by obstinacy or an undue regard for the opinions of men. Let him see that he does only what belongs to himself and to the hour.

I think sometimes, Why, this people mean well, they are only ignorant; they would do better if they knew how: why give your neighbors this pain to treat you as they are not inclined to? But I think again, This is no reason why I should do as they do, or permit others to suffer much greater pain of a different kind. Again, I sometimes say to myself, When many millions of men, without heat, without ill will, without personal feeling of any kind, demand of you a few shillings only, without the possibility, such is their constitution, of retracting or altering their present demand, and without the possibility, on your side, of appeal to any other millions, why expose yourself to this overwhelming brute force? You do not resist cold and hunger, the winds and the waves, thus obstinately; you quietly submit to a thousand similar necessities. You do not put your head into the fire. But just in proportion as I regard this as not wholly a brute force, but partly a human force, and consider that I have relations to those millions as to so many millions of men, and not of mere brute or inanimate things, I see that appeal is possible, first and instantaneously, from them to the Maker of them, and, secondly, from them to themselves. But if I put my head deliberately into the fire, there is no appeal to fire or to the Maker of fire, and I have only myself to blame. If I could convince myself that I have any right to be satisfied with men as they are, and to treat them accordingly, and not according, in some respects, to my requisitions and expectations of what they and I ought to be, then, like a good Mussulman and fatalist, I should endeavor to be satisfied with things as they are, and say it is the will of God. And, above all, there is this difference between resisting this and a purely brute or natural force, that I can resist this with some effect; but I cannot expect, like Orpheus, to change the nature of the rocks and trees and beasts.

I do not wish to quarrel with any man or nation. I do not wish to split hairs, to make fine distinctions, or set myself up as better than my neighbors. I seek rather, I may say, even an excuse for conforming to the laws of the land. I am but too ready to conform to them. Indeed, I have reason to suspect myself on this head; and each year, as the tax-gatherer comes round, I find myself disposed to review the acts and position of the general and State governments, and the spirit of the people, to discover a pretext for conformity.

"We must affect our country as our parents,
And if at any time we alienate
Our love or industry from doing it honor,
We must respect effects and teach the soul
Matter of conscience and religion,
And not desire of rule or benefit."

I believe that the State will soon be able to take all my work of this sort out of my hands, and then I shall be no better a patriot than my fellow-countrymen. Seen from a lower point of view, the Constitution, with all its faults, is very good; the law and the courts are very respectable; even this State and this American government are, in many respects, very admirable, and rare things, to be thankful for, such as a great many have described them; but seen from a point of view a little higher, they are what I have described them; seen from a higher still, and the highest, who shall say what they are, or that they are worth looking at or thinking of at all?

However, the government does not concern me much, and I shall bestow the fewest possible thoughts on it. It is not many moments that I live under a government, even in this world. If a man is thought-free, fancy-free, imagination-free, that which *is not* never for a long time appearing *to be* to him, unwise rulers or reformers cannot fatally interrupt him.

I know that most men think differently from myself; but those whose lives are by profession devoted to the study of these or kindred subjects content me as little as any. Statesmen and legislators, standing so completely within the institution, never distinctly and nakedly behold it. They speak of moving society, but have no resting-place without it. They may be men of a certain experience and discrimination, and have no doubt invented ingenious and even useful systems, for which we sincerely thank them; but all their wit and usefulness lie within certain not very wide limits. They are wont to forget that the world is not governed by policy and expediency. Webster never goes behind government, and so cannot speak with authority about it. His words are wisdom to those legislators who contemplate no essential reform in the existing government; but for thinkers, and those who legislate for all time, he never once glances at the subject. I know of those whose serene and wise speculations on this theme would soon reveal the limits of his mind's range and hospitality. Yet, compared with the cheap professions of most reformers, and the still cheaper wisdom and eloquence of politicians in general, his are almost the only sensible and valuable words, and we thank Heaven for him. Comparatively, he is always strong, original, and, above all, practical. Still, his quality is not wisdom, but prudence. The lawyer's truth is not Truth, but consistency or a consistent expediency. Truth is always in harmony with herself, and is not concerned chiefly to reveal the justice that may consist with wrong-doing. He well deserves to be called, as he has been called, the Defender of the Constitution. There are really no blows to be given by him but defensive ones. He is not a leader, but a follower. His leaders are the men of '87. "I have never made an effort," he says, "and never propose to make an effort; I have never countenanced an effort, and never mean to countenance an effort, to disturb the arrangement as originally made, by which the various States came into the Union." Still thinking of the sanction which the Constitution gives to slavery, he says, "Because it was a part of the original compact,—let it stand." Notwithstanding his special acuteness and ability, he is unable to take a fact out of its merely political relations, and behold it as it lies absolutely to be disposed of by the intellect,—what, for instance, it behooves a man to do here in America to-day with regard to slavery,—but ventures, or is driven, to make some such desperate answer as the following while professing to speak absolutely, and as a private man,—from which what new and singular code of social duties might be inferred? "The manner," says he, "in which the governments of those States where slavery exists are to regulate it is for their own consideration, under their responsibility to their constituents, to the general laws of propriety, humanity, and justice, and to God. Associations formed elsewhere, springing from a feeling of humanity, or other cause, have nothing whatever to do with it. They have never received any encouragement from me, and they never will."

They who know of no purer sources of truth, who have traced up its stream no higher, stand, and wisely stand, by the Bible and the Constitution, and drink at it there with reverence and humility; but they who behold where it comes trickling into this lake or that pool, gird up their loins once more, and continue their pilgrimage toward its fountainhead.

No man with a genius for legislation has appeared in America. They are rare in the history of the world. There are orators, politicians, and eloquent men, by the thousand; but the speaker has not yet opened his mouth to speak who is capable of settling the much-vexed questions of the day. We love eloquence for its own sake, and not for any truth which it may utter, or any heroism it may inspire. Our legislators have not yet learned the comparative value of free-trade and of freedom, of union, and of rectitude, to a nation. They have no genius or talent for comparatively humble questions of taxation and finance, commerce and manufactures and agriculture. If we were left solely to the wordy wit of legislators in Congress for our guidance, uncorrected by the seasonable experience and the effectual complaints of the people, America would not long retain her rank among the nations. For eighteen hundred years, though perchance I have no right to say it, the New Testament has been written; yet where is the legislator who has wisdom and practical talent enough to avail himself of the light which it sheds on the science of legislation?

The authority of government, even such as I am willing to submit to,—for I will cheerfully obey those who know and can do better than I, and in many things even those who neither know nor can do so well,—is still an impure one: to be strictly just, it must have the sanction and consent of the governed. It can have no pure right over my person and property but what I concede to it. The progress from an absolute to a limited monarchy, from a limited monarchy to a democracy, is a progress toward a true respect for the individual. Even the Chinese philosopher was wise enough to regard the individual as the basis of the empire. Is a democracy, such as we know it, the last improvement possible in government? Is it not possible to take a step further towards recognizing and organizing the rights of man? There will never be a really free and enlightened State until the State comes to recognize the individual as a higher and independent power, from which all its own power and authority are derived, and treats him accordingly. I please myself with imagining a State at last which can afford to be just to all men, and to treat the individual with respect as a neighbor; which even would not think it inconsistent with its own repose if a few were to live aloof from it, not meddling with it, nor embraced by it, who fulfilled all the duties of neighbors and fellow-men. A State which bore this kind of fruit, and suffered it to drop off as fast as it ripened, would prepare the way for a still more perfect and glorious State, which also I have imagined, but not yet anywhere seen.

THE APOLOGY OF SOCRATES[1]

PLATO

Socrates' Defence

WHAT effect my accusers had upon you, Men of Athens, I know not. As for me, they well-nigh made me forget who I was, so telling were their speeches! And yet, so to say, not one atom of truth did they utter. But that which astonished me most among all their fabrications was this, that they said you must be on your guard, and not be deceived by me, as I was a masterly speaker. That they should not be ashamed when they were promptly going to be caught by me in a lie, through the fact, since I shall show myself to be no orator at all, therein methought they reached the very height of their effrontery; unless perchance what they call masterly speaker means the one who tells the truth. If that is what they are saying, then I will admit I am an orator, though not of the sort they describe.

Well then, as I say, these men have uttered nothing, or next to nothing, that is true. From me, however, you shall hear the simple truth. But, by Heaven! fellow citizens, it will not be in language like theirs, decked out with epithets and phrases, nor beautifully ordered; rather you shall hear such utterances as come to me, in any words that offer, for of the justice of what I say I am convinced, and from me you need none of you expect aught else. No, Gentlemen! it would hardly befit a man of my age to come into your presence moulding phrases like a youngster. And nevertheless, my fellow citizens, and above all, I do request and beg of you this thing: if you should hear me pleading my cause with the same expressions I habitually have used in speaking, whether at the market by the counters, where many of you have heard me, or elsewhere, do not for that reason marvel and make a disturbance. The facts stand thus. At the age of seventy years I now for the first time have come up before a tribunal, and so I am an absolute stranger to the language of this place. Let it be as if I really were a foreigner here, since then you surely would excuse me if I used the accent and manner of speech in which I was reared. And so I now make this request of you, a matter of justice as it seems to me, that you let me use my way of speaking; it may be better, it may be worse, but the only thing you have to consider is this, and this is what you

1. *Plato on the Trial and Death of Socrates,* Lane Cooper trans. (Ithaca: Cornell University Press, 1941), pp. 49–77. Reprinted by permission of the publishers.

have to put your mind on, whether that which I say is right or not. That is the merit of a judge; the merit of a speaker is to tell the truth.

To begin with, fellow citizens, it is right for me to answer the earliest charges falsely brought against me, and my first accusers, and then I must answer the charges and accusers that come later.

Many, in fact, were they who formerly brought charges against me, yes many years ago, and spoke not a word of truth. And them I fear more than I do the group of Anytus, dangerous as these are too. No, Gentlemen, those others are more dangerous, for they have prejudiced the major part of you since your childhood, convincing you of an utterly false charge against me; to wit, 'There is a person, Socrates by name, a "wise man," who speculates about the heavens above, and also searches into everything below the earth, and in argument can make the worse case win.' [2] Those persons who have spread this charge abroad, they, fellow citizens, are my dangerous accusers; for people who listen to them think that men who make the said investigations do not believe in any gods. Add that these accusers are many in number, have brought their charges for a long time now, and, moreover, made them to you when you most readily believed things, when some of you were children or striplings; sheer accusation of an absent person without anybody to defend him. And what is most baffling of all, it is impossible to identify and name them, unless perchance in the case of a certain comic poet. For the rest, for all who through jealousy and malice misled you, and those who, once they were misled, got others to believe the same—with all these it is impossible to deal. There is no means of bringing one of them here to court, or putting a single one to cross-examination. No, in making my defense I am simply forced to fight, as it were, with shadows, and to question with nobody to make reply. Accordingly, I ask you to assume with me that, as I say, my accusers fall into these two classes, one group who are accusing me at present, the other those who of old accused me as aforesaid; and understand that it is these I must reply to first, for it is they whom you heard bringing charges earlier, and far more than this group who now come after.

Well then, fellow citizens, I must now make my defence, and must try to clear away in this brief time that calumny which you have entertained so long. I would that this might come to pass, if so it should be better for both you and me, and if it profits me to plead. But I think the task to be a hard one, and what its nature is I am by no means unaware. Still, let the outcome be as it pleases God; the law must be obeyed, and the defence be made.

Let us, then, go back and look at the original accusation from which the slander arose, the slander that gave Meletus his ground for this indictment he has lodged against me. Let us see. Precisely what did the slanderers say when they slandered? We must read their complaint as if it were a legal accusation: 'Socrates is wicked; overdoes inquiry into what occurs below the

2. The proverbial translation is: 'To make the worse appear the better reason.'

earth and in the heavens; in arguing makes the worse case win; and teaches others to do the same as he.' Such is in substance the accusation—what you actually saw in the comedy [the *Clouds*] of Aristophanes, where a man called 'Socrates' is swung about, declaring that he treads the air, and sputtering a deal of other nonsense on matters of which I have not one bit of knowledge either great or small. And I do not say so in disparagement of any science such as that, if any one is learned in such matters; I should not wish to be attacked by Meletus upon so grave a charge. But actually, fellow citizens, to me these matters are of absolutely no concern. I call the greater part of you yourselves to witness, and beg all who ever heard me in discussion to tell one another and declare it; many of you are in a position to do this. Declare to one another, therefore, whether any of you ever heard me dealing with such matters either briefly or at length. In that way you will see what all the rest amounts to of what the generality of people say concerning me.

No, there is nothing in it whatsoever. And if you have heard anybody say that I profess to give instruction, and get money in that way, neither is that true; although to my mind it is very fine indeed if any one is able to instruct his fellows, as are Gorgias of Leontini, and Prodicus of Ceos, and Hippias of Elis. Each one of them is able, Gentlemen, to go to city after city and attract young men; youths who might without expense consort with any one they chose among their own fellow citizens, these they persuade to give up that fellowship, to consort with them, to pay them money, and to be grateful to them besides. And indeed there is another man of learning here, from Paros, who, I learned, was staying in the City, for I happened to be calling on a man, Callias son of Hipponicus, who has paid more money to the Sophists than have all the others put together. And so I questioned him, he having, in fact, two sons:

'Callias,' said I, 'if your two sons had been colts or calves, we should have no trouble in finding some one to look after them, who for pay would make them fine and good according to the standard of their kind. We should pick some trainer of horses, say, or farmer. But now that they are human beings, whom have you in mind to put in charge of them? Who is there with a knowledge of their proper quality, the excellence of a human being and a citizen? I fancy you have given thought to this since you have sons. Is there any one,' said I, 'or not?'

'Yes, certainly,' said he.

'Who?' said I. 'Whence comes he? What does he charge for teaching?'

'Socrates,' he said, 'it is Evenus; comes from Paros; charge, five minae.'

So I thought Evenus was a lucky man if he really had this art, and would teach it at so reasonable a rate. For myself, I should be very proud and self-conceited if I knew all that. But the truth is, fellow citizens, I have no such knowledge.

Then perhaps some one of you may be inclined to ask: 'But, Socrates, what *is* the matter with you? What is the origin of these charges that are made against you? Unless you acted very differently from everybody else, surely no such story and repute would have arisen—if you did not do something other than most people do. Tell us what it is, in order to keep us from rushing to our own conclusion about you.'

That, I take it, would be fairly spoken; and I shall try to show you what it is that has given me this name and ill repute. Pray listen. Some of you, perhaps, will take me to be joking, but be assured that I shall tell you the simple truth. The fact is, fellow citizens, that I have got this name through my possession of a certain wisdom. What sort of wisdom is it? A wisdom, doubtless, that appertains to man. With respect to this, perhaps, I actually am wise; whereas those others whom I just now mentioned may possibly be wise with a wisdom more than human, or else I do not know what to say of it; as for me, I certainly do not possess it, and whoever says I do is lying, and seeks to injure me.

And, fellow citizens, do not interrupt me even if I say what seems extravagant, for the statement I shall make is not my own; instead, I shall refer you to a witness whose word can be accepted. Your witness to my wisdom, if I have any, and to its nature, is the god at Delphi. You certainly knew Chaerephon. He was a friend of mine from our youth, and a friend of your popular party as well; he shared in your late exile, and accompanied you on your return. Now you know the temper of Chaerephon, how impulsive he was in everything he undertook. Well so it was when once he went to Delphi, and made bold to ask the oracle this question—and, Gentlemen, please do not make an uproar over what I say; he asked if there was any one more wise than I. Then the Pythian oracle made response that there was no one who was wiser. To this response his brother here will bear you witness, since Chaerephon himself is dead.

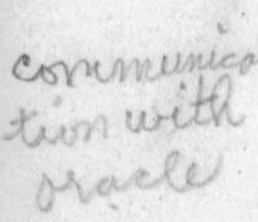

Now bear in mind the reason why I tell you this. It is because I am going on to show you whence this calumny of me has sprung; for when I heard about the oracle, I communed within myself: 'What can the god be saying, and what does the riddle mean? Well I know in my own heart that I am without wisdom great or small. What is it that he means, then, in declaring me to be most wise? It cannot be that he is lying; it is not in his nature.' For a long time I continued at a loss as to his meaning, then finally decided, much against my will, to seek it in the following way.

I went to one of those who pass for wise men, feeling sure that there if anywhere I could refute the answer, and explain to the oracle: 'Here is a man that is wiser than I, but you said I was the wisest.' The man I went to see was one of our statesmen; his name I need not mention. Him I thoroughly examined, and from him, as I studied him and conversed with him, I gathered, fellow citizens, this impression. This man appeared to me to seem to be wise to others, and above all to himself, but not to be so. And then I tried to show him that he thought that he was wise, but was not. The result was that I gained his enmity and the enmity as well of many of those who were present. So, as I went away, I reasoned with myself: 'At all events I am wiser than this man is. It is quite possible that neither one of us knows anything fine and good. But this man fancies that he knows when he does not, while I, whereas I do not know, just so I do not fancy that I know. In this small item, then, at least, I seem to be wiser than he, in that I do not fancy that I know what I do not.' Thereafter I went to another man, one of those who passed for wiser than the first, and I got the same impression. Whereupon I gained his enmity as well as that of many more.

Thereafter I went from one man to another, perceiving, with grief and apprehension, that I was getting hated, but it seemed imperative to put the service of the god above all else. In my search for the meaning of the oracle I must go to all who were supposed to have some knowledge. And, fellow citizens, by the Dog, since I have to tell you the truth, here is pretty much what I encountered. The persons with the greatest reputation seemed to me to be the ones who were well-nigh the most deficient, as I made my search in keeping with the god's intent; whereas others of inferior reputation I found to be men superior in regard to their possession of the truth. I needs must tell you all about my wandering course, a veritable round of toils heroic, which I underwent to prove that the oracle was not to be refuted.

After the statesmen, I went to the poets, tragic, dithyrambic, and the rest. There, I thought, my ignorance would be self-evident in comparison with them. So I took those poems of theirs which seemed to me to have been most carefully wrought by them, and asked the authors what they meant, in order that I might at the same time learn from them. Well, Gentlemen, I am ashamed to tell you the truth; and yet it must be done. The fact is, pretty nearly everybody, so to say, who was present could have spoken better than the authors did about the poems they themselves had written. So here again in a short time I learned this about the poets too, that not by wisdom do they make what they compose, but by a gift of nature and an inspiration similar to that of the diviners and the oracles. These also utter many beautiful things, but understand not one of them. And such, I saw, was the experience of the poets. At the same time I perceived that their poetic gift led them to fancy that in all else, too, they were the wisest of mankind, when they were not. So I went away from them as well, believing that I had the same advantage over them as over the statesmen.

To make an end, I went, then, to the artisans. Conscious that I did not, so to say, know anything myself, I was certain I should find that they knew many things and fine. Nor in that was I deceived; they did indeed know things which I did not, and in that they were wiser than I. But, fellow citizens, these excellent workmen seemed to me to have the same defect as the poets. Because they were successful in the practice of their art, each thought himself most wise about all other things of the highest import, and this mistake of theirs beclouded all that wisdom. So I asked myself the question, for the oracle, whether I preferred to be just what I was, neither wise as they were wise nor ignorant as they were ignorant, or to be both wise and ignorant like them. And my response to myself and the oracle was that it paid me to be as I was.

Such, fellow citizens, was the quest which brought me so much enmity, hatreds so utterly harsh and hard to bear, whence sprang so many calumnies, and this name that is given me of being 'wise'; for every time I caught another person in his ignorance, those present fancied that I knew what he did not. But, Gentlemen, in all likelihood it really is the god who is wise, and by that oracle he meant to say that human wisdom is of little worth, or none. And it appears that when he picked out 'Socrates,' he used my name to take me for an example; it was as if he said: 'O race of men, he is the wisest among you, who, like Socrates, knows that in truth his knowledge is worth nothing.' So even now I still go about in my search, and, in keeping with the god's intent, question anybody, citizen or stranger, whom I fancy to be wise. And when it seems to me that he is not, in defence of the god I show that he is not. And this activity has left me without leisure either to take any real part in civic affairs or to care for my own. Instead, I live in infinite poverty through my service to the god.

In addition, the young men who of their own accord are my companions, of the class who have most leisure, sons of the very rich—they listen with joy to the men who are examined; they often imitate me, and in turn attempt to test out others. And thereupon, I take it, they find a great abundance of men who imagine they have some knowledge, and yet know little or nothing. And then these men whom they examine get angry, not at them, but at me, and say there is one Socrates, a perfect blackguard, who corrupts the young. Yet when anybody asks them how he does it, and by teaching what, they have nothing to tell, nor do they know. But in order not to seem quite at a loss, they make the usual attacks that are leveled at philosophers, namely, about 'things occurring in the heavens and below the earth,' 'not believing in the gods,' and 'making the worse case win.' What they do not care to utter, I imagine, is the truth: that they have been shown up in their pretense to knowledge when they actually knew nothing. Accordingly, since they are proud, passionate, and numerous, and organized and effective in speaking about me, they have long since filled your ears with their violent calumnies.

From among them have come Meletus, Anytus, and Lycon to attack me; Meletus aggrieved on behalf of the poets, Anytus on behalf of the artists and the politicians, Lycon on behalf of the rhetoricians. Consequently, as I said at the beginning, I shall be surprised if I succeed, within so short a time, in ridding you of all this swollen mass of calumny.

There, fellow citizens, you have the truth. I hide nothing from you, either great or small, nor do I dissimulate. And yet I know that even by this I stir up hatred, which itself proves that I tell the truth, and that it is precisely this that constitutes the charge against me, and is the cause of it. And whether now or later you investigate the matter, you will find it to be so.

Therewith let me close my defence to you on the charges made agains by my first accusers. As for Meletus, that honest man and good friend o City, as he styles himself, to him and my more recent foes I will now deavor to reply.

Here again, since the present charges vary from the former, let us take the actual text of the complaint. It runs, in effect, as follows: 'Socrates,' it declares, 'offends against the law since he corrupts the young, does not believe in the gods the State believes in, and believes in novel deities [spirits, *daimonia*] instead.' Such is the accusation. Let us examine it point by point.

First, it holds that I offend by corrupting the young. But I, fellow citizens, I hold that Meletus offends in that he makes a jest of a serious matter, when he lightly brings men to trial on questions in which he pretends to be deeply interested and concerned, whereas he never took the slightest interest in any of them. That this is so, I will try to prove to you.

Your attention, Meletus! Answer! Do you not attach the utmost importance to the moral improvement of our youth?

[Meletus.] I do indeed.

Well then, tell the assembly here, who makes the young men better? You obviously know, for it is your special concern. You have discovered, so you state, who it is that corrupts them: I, whom you bring hither and accuse. Come now, tell who the person is who makes them better, and name him to these judges.

See, Meletus, you are silent. Have you nothing to say? Doesn't that seem shameful to you, and proof enough of my assertion that you have had no interest in the matter? But come, friend, say who makes them better?

[Meletus.] The laws.

No, my good fellow, that is not what I ask. I mean, what man? for, obviously, first of all he will have to know this very thing, the laws.

[Meletus.] These judges, Socrates.

What say you, Meletus? These judges here are competent to instruct the young, and make them better?

[Meletus.] Most certainly.

All are able? Or some are, and some are not?

[Meletus.] All of them!

By Hera, that is welcome news! We have an ample store of men who benefit their kind! What next? What about the audience here, do these too make them better?

[Meletus.] Yes, they too.

What about the Council?

[Meletus.] Yes, the Council also.

But, Meletus, what about the men in the Assembly, the members of it, do they corrupt the young, or do they one and all make young men better?

[Meletus.] Yes, they do it too.

So it seems that every one in Athens except me makes them fine and good, and I alone corrupt them. Is that your meaning?

[MELETUS.] Precisely that.

You detect me in a most unlucky situation. Answer me, though. Does the same thing seem to you to hold for horses too? Do you think all other men make horses better, and only one man ruins them? Or is it just the opposite of this, that some one man, or a very few, the horsemen, can improve them, whereas most people, if they have to deal with horses, and to make use of them, will spoil them? Is that not so, Meletus, both with horses and all other animals? It surely is, whether Anytus and you deny it or admit it. And what wonderful luck it would be for the young people if there were only one who did them harm, and all others did them good! But no, Meletus, you give ample proof that you never cared at all about the young; and your indifference is clearly shown—that you had no interest whatever in the things for which you bring me into court.

Now, Meletus, another question. In the name of Zeus, tell us whether it is better to live with honest citizens or with bad ones. Answer, friend; I ask you nothing difficult. Don't the wicked always do some evil to their neighbors, and the good some good?

[MELETUS.] Certainly.

Well, is there anybody who would rather be harmed than helped by those he lives with? Answer, my friend; the law requires you to do so. Does anybody like to be injured?

[MELETUS.] Certainly not.

Come now. When you bring me into court for corrupting the younger generation and making them worse, do you charge that I do so purposely or without design?

[MELETUS.] Purposely, say I.

What's that, Meletus? Are you at your age so much wiser than I am at mine? And thus, while you know that the wicked always do some injury to their nearest neighbors, and the good some good, I, you think, am come to such a state of ignorance as not to know that if I make some one I live with bad, I run the risk of getting injured by him? So according to you I do myself all this harm on purpose! That, Meletus, you will not get me to believe, nor, I fancy, anybody else in all the world. No, either I do not corrupt them, or if I do corrupt them, it is not by design. So either way you lie. If I ruin them unwittingly, the case is that of an involuntary error which does not legally bring me before this court; the proper thing would be to take me privately, and to instruct and warn me; for obviously when I learn better I shall stop doing what I do unwittingly. But you avoided joining me in order to instruct me; you chose not to do it. You bring me to this court where it is legal to try those who stand in need of punishment, not of learning.

There, fellow citizens, you have evidence enough of what I said, that Meletus has not taken the slightest interest in these matters.

Yet tell us, Meletus: in what way do you say I corrupt the younger men? Or is it not clear from the text of your complaint that you mean I teach them not to believe in the gods the State believes in, but in other new divinities? Isn't that the way you mean I corrupt them by my teaching?

[MELETUS.] Yes, that is just what I assert.

In that case, Meletus, in the name of those very gods we are discussing, explain your meaning still more clearly to these gentlemen here and me, for there is a point I am unable to make out. If you mean that I teach them to believe in the existence of certain gods, then I myself believe that there are gods, and so I am not out and out an atheist, and do not break the law in that respect. Or do you mean that they are not the gods the State believes in, but other gods instead, and is this the point of your complaint, that they are different? Or do you say that I myself do not believe in any gods at all, and that I teach this disbelief to others?

[MELETUS.] Yes, that is what I maintain, that you do not believe in any gods at all.

You amaze me, Meletus. How can you say so? Do you mean that I do not, like other men, regard the sun and moon as gods?

[MELETUS.] By Heaven, Gentlemen of the Jury, he does not; he holds that the sun is a stone, and the moon an earth.

You must think you are accusing Anaxagoras, my dear Meletus. Have you such a poor opinion of these men here, and do you think them so illiterate as not to know that the works of Anaxagoras of Clazomenae are full of these ideas? And so you think that the young men learn these things from me, when on occasion they could buy the books for a drachma at most in the orchestra, and then laugh at Socrates if he pretended that these theories were his—apart from the fact that they are so bizarre! But, by Heaven, is that the way you think of me, that I don't believe in any god whatever?

[MELETUS.] No, by Heaven, not a single one.

Now that, Meletus, is incredible, and something that I take it you do not believe yourself. In my opinion, fellow citizens, this man is an utterly overweening and unbridled person, who has brought this accusation simply out of insolence, intemperance, and youthful rashness. It looks as if he had made up a riddle with which to try me out: 'See whether Socrates, the wise man, will know that I am jesting and self-contradictory, or whether I shall fool him and all the rest who listen; for to me he clearly contradicts himself in the complaint, where in effect he says: 'Socrates offends by not believing in gods, but by believing in gods.' And that is simply joking.

Examine with me, Gentlemen, my way of showing that he says this. And, Meletus, you answer us. But, Gentlemen, remember the request I made at the outset, and do not interrupt if I pursue the argument in my customary fashion.

Is there any living man, Meletus, who believes that there are human things, but does not believe that there are human beings? Let him answer, Gentlemen, and not make noisy protests beside the point. Does any one believe in horsemanship, and not in horses? Or does any one believe there is an art of piping, but that there are no pipers? No, honorable sir, there isn't any one who does it. If you do not choose to answer, I will speak for you and these others here as well. But give the answer to this. Is there anybody who believes in the doings of spirits [*daimonia*], but thinks there are no spirits [*daimones*]?

[Meletus.] No.

How you oblige me by the grudging answer these gentlemen force you to make! Well then, you admit, I believe and teach that there are doings of spirits, whether recent or of old. At all events I do believe in them according to your statement; you have even sworn to this in your complaint. But if I believe in them, then quite necessarily, I suppose, I must believe in spirits. Isn't it so? It must be. I put you down as in agreement since you make no reply.

Now, must we not consider spirits as either gods or the offspring of gods? Say yes or no.

[Meletus.] Yes, certainly.

If, then, I think that there are spirits, as you assert, and if the spirits are in some way gods, am I not right in saying that you talk in riddles and are jesting? First you say that I do not believe in gods, and next that I do believe in them inasmuch as I believe in spirits. Or again: if the spirits [*daimones*] are illegitimate children of the gods, whether by nymphs or other mothers as report will have it, who on earth will ever think that there are children of the gods, but that there are no gods? It would be as queer as to think that mules were the offspring of horses and asses, but that horses and asses did not exist. No, Meletus, there is no way out of it; either you formulated this complaint in order to try us out, or else you could find no real crime with which to charge me. That you could get a living person with the least intelligence to admit that a given man believed in the doings of spirits but not of gods, and that the same man, again, believed in neither spirits, gods, nor heroes, is quite beyond the bounds of possibility.

No, fellow citizens, that I am guiltless with respect to Meletus' indictment seems to me to call for no long defence; rather, let this argument suffice. But what I have said before, that much antagonism has arisen against me in the minds of many, rest assured that it is true. And this it is that will undo me, if I am undone, not Meletus nor Anytus, but the slander of the many, and their malice. Many another man, and good ones, has it undone, and, methinks, it will yet undo. There is no danger that the thing may stop with me.

Perhaps some one will say: 'Well, Socrates, aren't you ashamed that you pursued a course from which you now are in danger of death?' To that it would be right for me to reply: 'Good sir, it is not well said if you think that a man of any worth at all ought to calculate his chances of living or dying, and not rather look to this alone, when he acts, to see if what he does is right or wrong, and if his are the deeds of a good man or a bad. By your account, the demigods who fell at Troy would be sorry fellows, all of them, and notably the son of

Thetis, who so despised all danger in comparison with any disgrace awaiting him, and with what result? When his mother saw him eager to slay Hector, she, the goddess, addressed him, as I recall, approximately thus: "My child, if you avenge the death of your comrade Patroclus by slaying Hector, then you yourself will die. For you the lot of death," she said, "comes straightway after Hector's." But he, on hearing that, made light of death and danger, fearing far more to live a coward and not avenge his loved ones. "Straightway let me die," said he, "once I give the villain his reward, and not continue here, a laughing-stock, beside the hollow ships, a burden to the earth." Do you think that he took heed of death or danger?

That, fellow citizens, is the way things really stand. If any one is stationed where he thinks it is best for him to be, or where his commander has put him, there, as it seems to me, it is his duty to remain, no matter what the risk, heedless of death or any other peril in comparison with disgrace.

It would have been dreadful conduct, fellow citizens, had I acted otherwise. When the leaders you had chosen to command me assigned a post to me at Potidaea, at Amphipolis, and at Delium, in the face of death itself I was as steadfast as any one could be in holding the position where they placed me; and when the god, as I believed and understood, assigned to me as my duty that I should live the life of a philosopher, and examine myself and others, it would have been dreadful had I through fear of death, or of anything else whatever, deserted my post. Dreadful indeed would it be, and verily any one would then be justified in bringing me to trial for not believing in gods, when I had disobeyed the oracle, feared death, and thought that I was wise when I was not.

For, Gentlemen, to be afraid of death is nothing else than thinking that one is wise when one is not, since it means fancying that one knows what one does not. Nobody knows, in fact, what death is, nor whether to man it is not perchance the greatest of all blessings; yet people fear it as if they surely knew it to be the worst of evils. And what is this but the shameful ignorance of supposing that we know what we do not? It is there and in that perhaps that I differ, Gentlemen, from the majority of mankind; and if I might call myself more wise than another, it would be in this, that as I do not know enough about what goes on in Hades, so too I do not think that I know. But doing wrong, and disobeying the person who is better than myself, be it god or man, that I know is base and wicked. Therefore never for the sake of evils which I know to be such will I fear or flee from what for all I know may be a good.

Accordingly, suppose you were now to acquit me, and went against Anytus; he who says that either I ought not to have been summoned hither to begin with, or, once I appeared I must inevitably be put to death; for he tells you that, if I am freed, your sons, who already put in practice what Socrates teaches, will all be utterly ruined. Suppose with reference to that you were to say to me: 'Socrates, at present we shall not give Anytus our assent, but will acquit you, yet upon one condition, namely, that hereafter you shall not pass your time in this investigation nor pursue philosophy; if you are caught doing it again, you die.' Well, as I said, if you were ready to let me go upon these conditions, my reply to you would be:

'Fellow citizens, I respect and love you, but I must obey the god rather than you, and so long as I draw breath, and can pursue philosophy, I will not cease from it nor from exhorting you, and ever pointing out the way to any one of you I meet, saying to him as I have been wont: "Good friend, you are a citizen of Athens, the greatest of all cities and the most renowned for power and learning, and yet you feel no shame at giving your mind to money so that you may get as much as possible, and to your reputation and to honor; but for insight, for the truth, for your soul and how it shall be at its best, you do not care nor trouble." '

And if any one of you disputes it, and says that he does care, I shall not forthwith dismiss him and go away, but will question him, and sift him, and put him to the test; and if he seems to me to have no fund of virtue, while professing to have it, I shall reproach him with attaching little value to what has most importance, and taking paltry things for what is larger. So will I do with young and old, whatever he be that I meet with, foreigner or native, yet rather with you citizens since you are nearer to me by kin; for this, you may rest assured, is what the god demands of me. And I think that there never came to you a greater good in the City than the service I render the god. All I do is to go about persuading you, both young and old, not to think first of your bodies or your property, nor to be so mightily concerned about them as about your souls, how the spirit shall be at its best; it is my task to tell you that virtue does not spring from wealth, but that wealth and every other good that comes to men in private life or in public proceed from virtue. If it is by saying this that I corrupt the young, then this must be injurious; but any one who holds that I say anything save this says nothing. On that head, fellow citizens, I may assure you that whether you trust Anytus or not, and whether you acquit me or do not acquit me, I shall not alter my course, no matter if I have to die a hundred times.

Now, fellow citizens, do not interrupt, but continue granting my request of you not to cry out at what I may say, but to listen; I do believe that you will profit if you listen. I am, in fact, about to tell you certain other things at which you might possibly protest. Yet please do not. No; for you may rest assured that if you condemn me to death, I being such a person as I say, you will do yourselves more harm than you do me. As for me, Meletus will no more hurt me than will Anytus. It does not lie in his power, for in my belief the eternal order does not permit a better man to be harmed by a worse. Oh yes! quite possibly he might kill or banish me, or rob me of my civic rights; and doubtless this man and the next will think that these are major evils. I do not think them such; no, I think it a far greater evil for a man to do what this man now is doing, namely trying to get a man condemned to death unjustly.

So, fellow citizens, at present I am far from making my defence upon my own account, as one might think; I make it for your sake, in order that you may not, by condemning me, do wrong about the gift of the god to you; for if you have me put to death, you will not easily find another of the sort, fastened upon the City by the god, for all the world (if I may use a rather ludicrous comparison) like a gadfly on a great and noble horse that is somewhat sluggish on account of his size and needs the fly to wake him up. So, it seems to me, the god has fastened me like that upon the City, to rouse, exhort, and rebuke each one of you, everywhere besetting you, and never once ceasing all day long. Another one like that, Gentlemen, you will not come by so easily; but if you listen to me, you will take good care of me. You may, however, quite possibly be annoyed, like people awakened from their slumbers, and, striking out at me, may listen readily to Anytus and condemn me to death. Then you would finish out the rest of your life in sleep, unless the god were in mercy to send you some one else to take my place. That it is the deity by whom I, such as I am, have been given to the City you may see from this: it is not like human nature for me to neglect all my own concerns, to put up with a neglected household all these years, and to attend to your affair, ever going to you individually in private, like a father or an elder brother, urging you to care for your moral welfare. And if I got any profit from it all, if these exhortations brought me any pay, there would seem to be some reason in my conduct. As it is, you see for yourselves that my accusers, who, unashamed, have brought so many other charges against me, have yet not had the effrontery to present a witness to allege that I ever took any sort of fee or sought one. Why not? Because, methinks, the witness I present to show that I speak the truth is quite enough—my poverty.

Possibly it may look odd that I should busily go about in private with my counsels, but in public dare not approach the mass of you with counsel for the City. The reason for that is something you have often heard me speak of in many a place; it is that there comes to me a thing divine and spiritual, what Meletus has mockingly referred to in his indictment. From childhood on, this sign has come to me; it is a voice, which, when it comes, always deters me from what I am about to do, but never urges me to act. It is this that fights against my entering political affairs; and the opposition strikes me as being altogether good; for, fellow citizens, you may rest assured that if I, long ago, had tried to take up politics, I should long ago have perished, and been of no service whatever either to you or to myself. And do not be aggrieved at me for telling the truth: there is not a man on earth that is safe if he nobly puts himself in opposition to you or to any other crowd, and strives to stop all sorts of wrong and lawlessness in the State. But if any one is really going to battle for the right, and to be safe for some short time in doing it, he must perforce remain a private citizen; he must not appear in public life.

Of that I will furnish you with telling evidence, not arguments, but what you value, facts. Listen to what happened in my case, and you will see that I am not a man to yield to any one unjustly for fear of death, not even if by my not yielding I were at once to perish. The tale I shall tell you is of the legal sort and uninspiring, but is true.

I never held any public office, fellow citizens, but one: I was a member of the Council. And it happened that our tribe, Antiochis, had the executive function [*prytany*] at the time you wished to sentence in a body the ten commanders who failed to pick up the survivors of the naval action [at Arginusae]. The procedure was illegal, as after a while you all admitted. But at the time I was the only one of the prytanes who stood out against your doing an illegal act and voted against you; and although the orators were ready to indict me and arrest me, while you urged them on and made an uproar, I thought that I ought to risk all danger on the side of law and justice rather than side with you in an unjust decree for fear of imprisonment or death.

This took place while Athens still was a democracy. But again, when the oligarchy was established, the Thirty had me and four others summoned to the Rotunda, and ordered us to go get Leon of Salamis, and bring him thence to have him put to death; they gave such orders frequently to many other persons in order to involve as many as they could in their crimes. But there again I showed, by deeds, and not by words, that death, if I may speak quite baldly, meant nothing at all to me, while not to do an unjust or an impious act, this meant everything; for that power, however huge its sway, did not terrify me into doing what was wrong. No, when we came out of the Rotunda, the other four went off to Salamis and brought back Leon, and as for me I went to my home. And for that I might well have paid with my life, had the government not promptly fallen. Of these facts many persons will bear witness to you.

Well then, do you think I could have survived through all these years if I had taken part in state affairs, and, acting properly as a good citizen, had fought for justice, making this perforce of paramount importance? Far from it, fellow citizens; nor could any other living man have done it. As for me, all my life long, if ever I did anything in an official way, I showed myself to be that sort of person, and in private just the same; never once did I yield to any one in any point against the right, not even to one of those whom my slanderers declare to be my pupils.

But I never have been anybody's teacher. If any one cares to listen to me as I speak and carry on my special function, be he young or old, I never have begrudged it. I am not one who will engage in discussion if he gets money, and if not refuses. No, rich and poor alike I am prepared to question, and whoever will may listen to what I say when I make reply. And for my part, if any of them turns out well or ill, I cannot rightly be held responsible when I never offered to give any one instruction, nor gave it. If any one asserts that he ever learned or heard a thing from me other than what all the others heard as well, rest assured that he who says so does not tell the truth.

Well then, why do certain persons like to spend so much of their time with me? I told you, fellow citizens, what the reason is. The truth of the matter is just what I said: they like to hear the sifting out of those who think that they are wise, but are not. The thing, in fact, is not unpleasant. But for me, as I aver, it is a task enjoined upon me by the deity, through oracles, through dreams, and in every single way that ever a divine injunction was laid upon a man to do a thing. These statements, fellow citizens, are true and are easily proved. Suppose I am at present ruining some of the young people, and already have perverted others; then necessarily, no doubt, a number of them, when they grew older, would have seen that on occasion, when they were young, I gave them evil advice, and would now appear in court to accuse and punish me. Or, if they themselves were unwilling to do it, then some of their relations, fathers, brothers, or others of their kin—if it were true that members of the family had received some injury from me—would now remember it, and have me punished. Certainly there are many of them present whom I see: first Crito here, a man of my own generation and my deme, father of yon Critobulus; next, Lysanias of Sphettus, father of yon Aeschines; add Antiphon here of Kephisia, father of Epigenes. Among others, men whose brothers have attended at the pastime, Nicostratus son of Theozotides and brother of Theodotus—as for Theodotus, he is dead, and therefore could not plead for me against him; so also Paralus here whose father is Demodocus and whose brother is Theages, Adeimantus son of Ariston whose brother is Plato here, and Aiantodorus, whose brother is yon Apollodorus. And many others I could name to you, of whom Meletus surely ought to have offered somebody as witness in his accusation. If he forgot it then, let him present it now—I yield the point—and let him say if he has any evidence of the sort. But, Gentlemen, you will find the case to be the very opposite of that; will find them all prepared to help me, the ruiner, the man who has done injury to their kin, as Meletus and Anytus aver. The ruined themselves, of course, might have some reason for coming to my aid. But those who are not ruined, men already mature, the relatives of these, what other reason could they have for coming to my aid except the straight and just one, that they know that Meletus is lying, and that I am telling the truth?

There you have it, Gentlemen. That is pretty much what I might have to say in my defence, that with possibly some additions to the like effect. Perhaps, however, one or another of you will be angry when he recalls his own experience, in some trial he was engaged in of less gravity than this; if he besought and with many tears implored the judges, and, in order to arouse the greatest pity, brought in his children along with others of his kin and many friends; while, as for me, I shall do nothing of the sort, although I am in danger, as I might suppose, to the last degree of peril. Perhaps, then, as he thinks of this, he will bear himself with the less remorse towards me, and, irritated by these very things, will cast his vote in anger. Now if any of you feels so, though for my part I do not impute it—but if anybody feels that way, then it seems to me the proper thing for me to say to him would be: 'Good friend, I too have friends and relatives; in fact, my case is just as Homer says. "I did not spring from either oak or rock," but from mankind, and so I have a family and sons; three sons, my fellow citizens, one a youth, and the other two are little boys.' Nevertheless not one of them will I bring hither imploring you to let me off. And why shall I do nothing of all that? Not, fellow citizens, out of hardihood, nor in disdain of you. And whether I fear death or not is another question; but for my own honor, and yours, and the honor of the entire City, it does not seem proper for me at my age, and with the name I have, to do any of these things. The opinion may be true, or may be false; at all events the view is held that Socrates is somehow different from the mass of men. Well, if those of you who are regarded as distinguished in point of wisdom, or of courage, or of any other quality, behaved like that, it would be shameful. And yet, often enough, I have seen persons of such sort, persons of some reputation, behaving in extraordinary fashion when they were to hear the verdict, as if they thought they must be going to suffer something terrible if they had to die—as if they thought that they would be immortal in case you did not condemn them. To my mind, they brought shame upon the City; anybody from another city would infer that the Athenians who were eminent for their virtue, those whom their fellows selected as their rulers and for other places of distinction, were in no way better than women. These things, fellow citizens, it behoves us not to do if we have any reputation whatsoever; and if we do them, you should not allow it. No; you should make this very thing quite clear, that you will far more readily give your vote against the person who drags in these tearful dramas, and makes the City ridiculous, than against the man who argues quietly.

But apart from the question of propriety, Gentlemen, it does not seem right to me to beg the judge for mercy, or, by doing it, to get away, when one ought rather to enlighten and convince him. He does not take his seat for this, the judge, to render justice as a favor, but to decide on what is just. Indeed he took an oath that he would not favor people according to his notion of them, but that he would give judgment in accordance with the laws. And so we should not get you into the habit of perjuring yourselves, nor should you get into it; neither of us should commit impiety. So do not ask me, fellow citizens, to treat you in a way which I take to be dishonorable, wrong, and impious; above all, by Zeus! when I am under accusation of impiety by this Meletus here present; for obviously, if I swayed you and by begging forced you to act against your oath, I would be teaching you not to believe that there are gods, and by my defence would simply accuse myself of not believing in them. But that be far from me! I do believe in them, my fellow citizens, as none of my accusers does; and to you I commend myself, and to the Deity, to judge concerning me what shall be best at once for me and for you.

After the vote against him.

If I am not distressed, my fellow citizens, at what has happened in that you voted to convict me, there are many reasons for it, and in particular that the outcome was to me not unexpected. What is to me far more surprising is the actual division of the votes. I thought for my part that the vote would go not by this small majority, but by a large one. As it is, apparently, if only thirty votes had gone the other way, I should have been acquitted. Accordingly, so far as Meletus is concerned, it seems to me I do now stand acquitted, and not only that, but it must be clear to every one that if Anytus and Lycon had not come hither to accuse me, he would have had to pay one thousand drachmas as a fine for not obtaining a fifth part of the votes.

Meanwhile the man proposes for me the penalty of death. So be it. What penalty, fellow citizens, am I to offer you instead? Evidently what I ought to get? What is it, then? What do I deserve to get or pay? I who, when I had learned a thing, did not lead my life in peace, but neglecting what the many care for—wealth, household matters, military leadership and civic and the other high positions, coalitions, factions that arise in the State—thought myself in fact too good a man to enter into these affairs with safety. I did not enter there where if I came I was not to be of any use either to you or to myself, but going to you one by one in private, I did you, I aver, the greatest service possible. There I went trying to persuade each one of you not to care first for his own possessions before caring for himself and how he might be at his best and wisest, nor to set the affairs of the City above the City itself, and to give attention to all other things in just that way. Being a man of that description, what ought I to get? Something good, my fellow citizens, if the award must truly square with the desert; and the good ought further to be something that fits my case. What, then, befits a poor man, a benefactor, who needs leisure for the office of exhorting you? Nothing is so proper as the maintenance of such a man in the Prytaneum, a reward far more befitting him than for any one of you who may have won a victory at Olympia with a horse or a pair of them or four. He makes you think that you are happy; I cause you to be so. He, moreover, has no need of maintenance; I stand in need of it. And so if I must get what I deserve, there is my proposal: maintenance in the Prytaneum.

Perhaps when I say that to you, you will think that I am talking with the same bravado as about the tears and supplications. It is not, fellow citizens, as you think; no, it is more like this. I am persuaded that I never willingly wronged any man, but I have not persuaded you, since we have had small time to reach an understanding; whereas if the law with you were what it is with others, if a case involving the penalty of death could not be settled in a day, but took a number, I believe I would have won you over. As matters stand, it is not easy in a limited time to refute a mass of slanders.

Persuaded that I do no wrong to any one, I am far from ready to do injustice to myself, and will not say of myself that I merit some evil, and should allot myself that sort of penalty. In fear of what? For fear that otherwise I shall suffer the thing which Meletus proposes, that of which I say I know not whether it is good or evil? Instead of that ought I to choose one of the things that I know for certain to be ills, and penalize myself with that? Imprisonment? Why should I live in prison, a slave to a recurrent board of governors, the Eleven? Or say a fine, and to be jailed until I pay it? But that would be no different for me from what I just now mentioned, since I have no money to pay with. Well, suppose I offered to go into exile. Perhaps you would accept that. But truly, fellow citizens, the love of life must have a powerful hold on me, and make me heedless, if I cannot reason thus: You who are my fellow citizens could not endure my doings and discussions; no, they were too much for you, and so irritating that now you seek to be rid of them. Well, will others bear them easily? Far from it, fellow citizens. And what a fine existence that would be, for a man of my age to go away and live a wanderer and a waif driven from city to city; for well I know that wherever I went the young would listen to me just as they do here. And if I drove them off, they would get the older men's permission, and themselves expel me. And if I did not, their fathers and relations would expel me on the sons' account.

Well, perhaps some one will say: 'Why can't you go away from us, and then keep quiet, Socrates, and live in peace?' But that is the thing that is hardest of all to make some of you see. If I say that this means disobedience to the god, and for that very reason I cannot keep still, you will not believe me, but will think I speak in irony. If, on the other hand, I say it is perhaps the greatest good that can befall a man, daily to argue about virtue, and to discuss the other subjects about which you have heard me debating and examining myself as well as others, if I add that for mankind the unexamined life is not worth living, still less will you believe me when I tell you that. These matters stand, however, Gentlemen, precisely as I say, only it is not easy to convince you. And meanwhile, for my part, I am not in the habit of thinking that I merit ill at all. If I had wealth, I would suggest a sum that I was in a position to pay, for in that case I should do myself no harm. But now the fact is that I haven't, unless you chose to set a fine for me at a rate that I could pay. Perhaps I could pay you a silver mina; so that is what I offer.

But Plato here, my fellow citizens, and Crito, Critobulus, and Apollodorus, bid me offer thirty minæ upon their security. Well then, I offer that; these men will be adequate security to you for the amount.

After he is condemned to death.

For no great thrift in time, my fellow citizens, you will have from those who wish to vilify the City the name and blame of having put to death the wise man, Socrates; for they will call me wise, even if I am not, they who would defame you. If only you had waited for a little while, the thing would have occurred for you in the course of nature; for you can see my age, that I am far along in life, and near to death. I say this, not to all of you, but only to those who voted for my death. And to them I have also to say this as well. It may be, Gentlemen, that you think I lost my cause for lack of arguments of the sort with which I might have won you over, if I had thought that I ought to say and do all things in order to escape the verdict. Far from it. I lost for a lack, but not of arguments; it was for lack of impudence and daring, and for not being ready to say to you the sort of thing it would have given you most pleasure to hear—me weeping and wailing, and doing and saying any and every sort of thing that I hold to be unworthy of me, but you are accustomed to hear from the rest. No, I did not then believe that, to avoid a danger, I ought to do anything unseemly in a freeman, nor do I now regret my manner of defence. No, far rather would I choose this manner of defence, and die, than follow that, and live. Whether in a court of justice or in war neither I nor any other man should seek by using every means conceivable to escape from death; for in battle you very often see that if you throw away your weapons and beg those who are pursuing you for mercy, you may get out of dying. Indeed, in every sort of danger there are various ways of winning through, if one is ready to do and say anything whatever. No, Gentlemen, that is not the hard thing, to escape from death; ah no, far harder is it to escape from sin, for sin is swifter than death. And so I, being old and slow, am overtaken by the slower enemy; while my accusers, who are strong and swift, have been caught by the swifter, namely wickedness. And so I now depart, by you condemned to pay the penalty of death; and they, by the truth convicted of a base injustice. And as I abide the payment, so do they. Who knows? Perhaps it had to be so, and I think that things are as they ought to be.

Touching the future, I desire to make for you who voted to condemn me, a prediction; for I am at the point where men foresee the future best—when they are soon to die. Let me tell you then, you men who have condemned me, that after I am gone there will straightway come upon you a chastisement far heavier, by Zeus, than the death you have set for me. You have now done this in the belief that you have freed yourselves from giving any reckoning for your life; but I tell you the result will be the very opposite for you. There will be more inquisitors to sift you, men whom I now hold in check without your knowing it. And they will be more critical as they are younger, and will annoy you more; for if you think that by putting men to death you will prevent the slur from being cast at you that you do not live aright, you are in error. This way of getting freedom is neither very sure nor fine; no, the finest and readiest way is this, not to interfere with other people, but to render oneself as good a man as possible. There is the prophecy I make for you who voted to condemn me. And of them I take my leave.

With those of you who voted to acquit me I should be glad to talk about this thing that has occurred, while the magistrates are busy and it is not time for me to go to the place where I must die. So, Gentlemen, please wait with me as long as that. There is nothing to keep us from talking to each other as long as it is allowed. To you as to friends I wish to explain the real meaning of what has just happened to me.

Justices, for when I call you that I am naming you aright, the thing that has come to me is wonderful.

My customary warning, by the spirit, in previous times has always, up to now, come to me very often to oppose me, even when a matter was quite unimportant, if ever I was going to do something amiss. But to-day, as you yourselves have witnessed, that thing has happened to me which anybody might suppose, and which is considered, to be the uttermost of evils. Yet neither did the sign from god oppose me when I left my house this morning, nor at the point when I ascended here to the tribunal, nor in my speech at anything I was about to say; though often when I have been talking elsewhere it has stopped me in the middle of a speech. But to-day, with reference to the whole procedure, not once did it oppose me in a thing I did or said. What, then, do I take to be the cause of this? No doubt this thing that has happened to me is good, and it cannot be that our supposition is correct when any of us think that death is a misfortune. For me, the proof of this is telling: it cannot be but that the customary sign would have opposed me, if I had not been about to do a thing that was good.

Let us view in another way how ample are the grounds for our hope that death is good. To be dead is one of two things. Either it is a sort of nonexistence, and the dead man has no feeling about anything whatever, or else, as people say, the soul experiences a shift and a migration from here into another place. Now if there is no feeling, if death is like a sleep in which one does not even dream, what a wonderful gain it would be! I believe if a man were to take that night in which he slept so deeply that he did not have a single dream, and compared it with the other nights and days of his life; if he had to say, upon reflection, how many days and nights, all told, in his life, he had passed better and more sweetly than that night; I believe that every one, not merely any private citizen, but the Great King himself, would find them easy to count up in comparison with all the others. So if death is a sleep like that, I say it is a gain; for thus all time appears to be no more than a single night. If, on the other hand, death is like a journey from here to another place, and if what they say is true, that everybody who has died is there, then, Justices, what greater good than this could there be? If, on arriving in Hades, one could be freed from those who here pretend that they are Justices, and there find those who by report deal real justice, Minos, Rhadamanthus, Aæcus, and Triptolemus, and all the rest of the demigods who were just in their lives here, what a small thing would that journey seem! Or, again, to be with Orpheus and Musæus, with Hesiod and Homer, what price would not any of you pay for that? I would gladly die repeatedly, if all that is true. To me it would be a wonderful way to pass my time, there where I could meet with Palamedes and with Ajax son of Telamon, and any one else among the ancients who died through an unjust decision. To compare my lot with theirs, methinks, would not be so unpleasant; and most important of all would be to go on sifting people there, as here, and finding out who is wise, and who thinks he is so, but is not. What would not anybody give to examine, Justices, the leader of that mighty expedition against Troy, or else Odysseus, or Sisyphus, or a myriad of others one might mention, men and women too? There to talk with them, consort with them, examine them, would be a happiness beyond compare! Surely there, I take it, they do not put a man to death for doing that; for, happy in all else, people are happier there than here in that henceforth they are immortal, at all events if what is said is true.

But, Justices, you also it behoves to have good hope with reference to death, and this one thing you must bear in mind as true, that, living or dead, to a good man there can come no evil, nor are his affairs a matter of indifference to the gods. Nor has my destiny now come about by chance; rather, it is clear to me that it was better for me now to die and to be released from my troubles. That is why the sign did not at any point deter me, and why I am not very bitter at those who voted to condemn me, or at my accusers. It is true they did not have this notion in condemning and accusing me; no, they thought to injure me, and therein they merit blame.

One thing, however, I do beg of them. When my sons grow up, then, Gentlemen, I ask you to punish them, you hurting them the same as I hurt you, if they seem to you to care for money, or aught else, more than they care for virtue. And if they pretend to be somewhat when they are nothing, do you upbraid them as I upbraided you, for not regarding as important what they ought to think so, and for thinking they have worth when they do not. If you do that, I shall have received just treatment from you, and my sons as well.

And now the time has come for our departure, I to die, and you to live. Which of us goes to meet the better lot is hidden from all unless it be known to God.

DECLARATION OF INDEPENDENCE

The unanimous declaration of the thirteen United States of America, in Congress, July 4, 1776

THOMAS JEFFERSON

WHEN, in the course of human events, it becomes necessary for one people to dissolve the political bands which have connected them with another, and to assume among the powers of the earth the separate and equal station to which the laws of nature and of nature's God entitle them, a decent respect to the opinions of mankind requires that they should declare the causes which impel them to the separation.

We hold these truths to be self-evident: That all men are created equal; that they are endowed by their Creator with certain inalienable rights; that among these are life, liberty, and the pursuit of happiness. That, to secure these rights, governments are instituted among men, deriving their just powers from the consent of the governed; that, whenever any form of government becomes destructive of these ends, it is the right of the people to alter or to abolish it, and to institute a new government, laying its foundation on such principles, and organizing its powers in such form, as to them shall seem most likely to effect their safety and happiness. Prudence, indeed, will dictate that governments long established should not be changed for light and transient causes; and accordingly all experience hath shown that mankind are more disposed to suffer, while evils are sufferable, than to right themselves by abolishing the forms to which they are accustomed. But when a long train of abuses and usurpations, pursuing invariably the same object, evinces a design to reduce them under absolute despotism, it is their right, it is their duty, to throw off such government and to provide new guards for their future security. Such has been the patient suffering of these colonies, and such is now the necessity which constrains them to alter their former systems of government. The history of the present king of Great Britain is a history of repeated injuries and usurpations, all having in direct object the establishment of an absolute tyranny over these states. To prove this, let facts be submitted to a candid world.

He has refused his assent to laws the most wholesome and necessary for the public good.

He has forbidden his governors to pass laws of immediate and pressing importance, unless suspended in their operation till his assent should be obtained, and, when so suspended, he has utterly neglected to attend to them.

He has refused to pass other laws for the accommodation of large districts of people, unless those people would relinquish the right of representation in the legislature—a right inestimable to them and formidable to tyrants only.

He has called together legislative bodies, at places unusual, uncomfortable, and distant from the repository of their public records, for the sole purpose of fatiguing them into compliance with his measures.

He has dissolved representative houses repeatedly for opposing with manly firmness his invasions on the rights of the people.

He has refused for a long time after such dissolutions to cause others to be elected; whereby the legislative powers, incapable of annihilation, have returned to the people at large for their exercise: the state remaining, in the meantime, exposed to all the dangers of invasion from without and convulsions within.

He has endeavored to prevent the population of these states; for that purpose obstructing the laws for naturalization of foreigners; refusing to pass others to encourage their migration hither, and raising the conditions of new appropriations of lands.

He has obstructed the administration of justice by refusing his assent to laws for establishing his judiciary powers.

He has made judges dependent on his will alone for the tenure of their offices and the amount and payment of their salaries.

He has erected a multitude of new offices and sent hither swarms of officers to harass our people and eat out their substance.

He has kept among us, in times of peace, standing armies without the consent of our legislatures.

He has affected to render the military independent of and superior to the civil power.

He has combined with others to subject us to a jurisdiction foreign to our constitutions and unacknowledged by our laws, giving his assent to their acts of pretended legislation:

For quartering large bodies of armed troops among us;

For protecting them by a mock trial from punishment for any murders which they should commit on the inhabitants of these states;

For cutting off our trade with all parts of the world;

For imposing taxes on us without our consent;

For depriving us in many cases of the benefits of trial by jury;

For transporting us beyond seas to be tried for pretended offenses;

For abolishing the free system of English laws in a neighboring province, establishing therein an arbitrary government, and enlarging its boundaries so as to render it at once an example and fit instrument for introducing the same absolute rule into these colonies;

For taking away our charters, abolishing our most valuable laws, and altering fundamentally the forms of our governments;

For suspending our own legislatures and declaring themselves invested with power to legislate for us in all cases whatsoever.

He has abdicated government here by declaring us out of his protection and waging war against us.

He has plundered our seas, ravaged our coasts, burnt our towns and destroyed the lives of our people.

He is at this time transporting large armies of foreign mercenaries to complete the work of death, desolation, and tyranny already begun, with circumstances of cruelty and perfidy scarcely parallelled in the most barbarous ages and totally unworthy the head of a civilized nation.

He has constrained our fellow citizens taken captive upon the high seas to bear arms against their country, to become the executioners of their friends and brethren, or to fall themselves by their hands.

He has excited domestic insurrection amongst us, and has endeavored to bring on the inhabitants of our frontiers the merciless Indian savages, whose known rule of warfare is an undistinguished destruction of all ages, sexes, and conditions.

In every stage of these oppressions we have petitioned for redress, in the most humble terms; our repeated petitions have been answered only by repeated injury. A prince whose character is thus marked by every act which may define a tyrant is unfit to be the ruler of a free people.

Nor have we been wanting in attention to our British brethren. We have warned them, from time to time, of attempts by their legislature to extend an unwarrantable jurisdiction over us. We have reminded them of the circumstances of our emigration and settlement here. We have appealed to their native justice and magnanimity; and we have conjured them by the ties of our common kindred, to disavow these usurpations, which would inevitably interrupt our connections and correspondence. They, too, have been deaf to the voice of justice and consanguinity. We must, therefore, acquiesce in the necessity which denounces our separation, and hold them, as we hold the rest of mankind, enemies in war; in peace, friends.

We, therefore, the representatives of the United States of America, in general congress assembled, appealing to the Supreme Judge of the World for the rectitude of our intentions, do, in the name and by the authority of the good people of these colonies, solemnly publish and declare that these united colonies are, and of right ought to be, free and independent states; that they are absolved from all allegiance to the British crown, and that all political connection between them and the state of Great Britain is, and ought to be, totally dissolved; and that as free and independent states they have full power to levy war, conclude peace, contract alliances, establish commerce, and to do all other acts and things which independent states may of right do. And for the support of this declaration, with a firm reliance on the protection of Divine Providence, we mutually pledge to each other our lives, our fortunes, and our sacred honor.

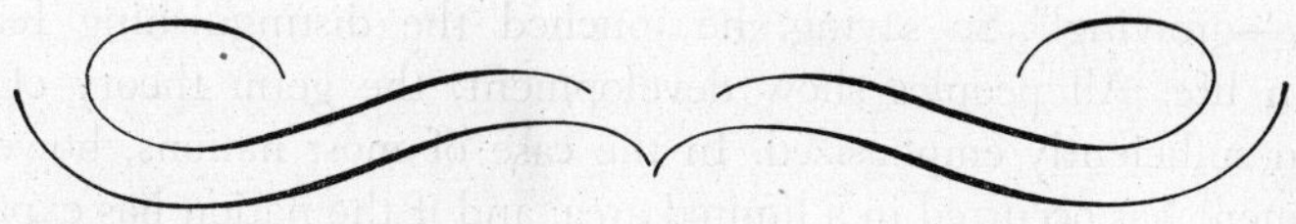

· PROBLEMS OF THE SOCIAL SCIENCES ·

THE SIGNIFICANCE OF THE FRONTIER IN AMERICAN HISTORY[1]

FREDERICK JACKSON TURNER

IN A RECENT bulletin of the Superintendent of the Census for 1890 appear these significant words: "Up to and including 1880 the country had a frontier of settlement, but at present the unsettled area has been so broken into by isolated bodies of settlement that there can hardly be said to be a frontier line. In the discussion of its extent, its westward movement, etc., it can not, therefore, any longer have a place in the census reports." This brief official statement marks the closing of a great historic movement. Up to our own day American history has been in a large degree the history of the colonization of the Great West. The existence of an area of free land, its continuous recession, and the advance of American settlement westward, explain American development.

Behind institutions, behind constitutional forms and modifications, lie the vital forces that call these organs into life and shape them to meet changing conditions. The peculiarity of American institutions is the fact that they

1. From *The Frontier in American History* (with omissions) by Frederick Jackson Turner by permission of the publishers, Henry Holt and Company, Inc. Copyright, 1920, by Frederick J. Turner.

have been compelled to adapt themselves to the changes of an expanding people—to the changes involved in crossing a continent, in winning a wilderness, and in developing at each area of this progress out of the primitive economic and political conditions of the frontier into the complexity of city life. Said Calhoun in 1817, "We are great, and rapidly—I was about to say fearfully—growing!" So saying, he touched the distinguishing feature of American life. All peoples show development; the germ theory of politics has been sufficiently emphasized. In the case of most nations, however, the development has occurred in a limited area; and if the nation has expanded, it has met other growing peoples whom it has conquered. But in the case of the United States we have a different phenomenon. Limiting our attention to the Atlantic coast, we have the familiar phenomenon of the evolution of institutions in a limited area, such as the rise of representative government; the differentiation of simple colonial governments into complex organs; the progress from primitive industrial society, without division of labor, up to manufacturing civilization. But we have in addition to this a recurrence of the process of evolution in each western area reached in the process of expansion. Thus American development has exhibited not merely advance along a single line, but a return to primitive conditions on a continually advancing frontier line, and a new development for that area. American social development has been continually beginning over again on the frontier. This perennial rebirth, this fluidity of American life, this expansion westward with its new opportunities, its continuous touch with the simplicity of primitive society, furnish the forces dominating American character. The true point of view in the history of this nation is not the Atlantic coast, it is the Great West. Even the slavery struggle, which is made so exclusive an object of attention by writers like Professor von Holst, occupies its important place in American history because of its relation to westward expansion.

In this advance, the frontier is the outer edge of the wave—the meeting point between savagery and civilization. Much has been written about the frontier from the point of view of border warfare and the chase, but as a field for the serious study of the economist and the historian it has been neglected.

The American frontier is sharply distinguished from the European frontier—a fortified boundary line running through dense populations. The most significant thing about the American frontier is, that it lies at the hither edge of free land. In the census reports it is treated as the margin of that settlement which has a density of two or more to the square mile. The term is an elastic one, and for our purposes does not need sharp definition. We shall consider the whole frontier belt, including the Indian country and the outer margin of the "settled area" of the census reports. This paper will make no attempt to treat the subject exhaustively; its aim is simply to call attention to the frontier as a fertile field for investigation, and to suggest some of the problems which arise in connection with it.

In the settlement of America we have to observe how European life entered the continent, and how America modified and developed that life and reacted on Europe. Our early history is the study of European germs developing in an American environment. Too exclusive attention has been paid by institutional students to the Germanic origins, too little to the American factors. The frontier is the line of most rapid and effective Americanization. The wilderness masters the colonist. It finds him a European in dress, industries, tools, modes of travel, and thought. It takes him from the railroad car and puts him in the birch canoe. It strips off the garments of civilization and arrays him in the hunting shirt and the moccasin. It puts him in the log cabin of the Cherokee and Iroquois and runs an Indian palisade around him. Before long he has gone to planting Indian corn and plowing with a sharp stick; he shouts the war cry and takes the scalp in orthodox Indian fashion. In short, at the frontier the environment is at first too strong for the man. He must accept the conditions which it furnishes, or perish, and so he fits himself into the Indian clearings and follows the Indian trails. Little by little he transforms the wilderness, but the outcome is not the old Europe, not simply the development of Germanic germs, any more than the first phenomenon was a case of reversion to the Germanic mark. The fact is, that here is a new product that is American. At first, the frontier was the Atlantic coast. It was the frontier of Europe in a very real sense. Moving westward, the frontier became more and more American. As successive terminal moraines result from successive glaciations, so each frontier leaves its traces behind it, and when it becomes a settled area the region still partakes of the frontier characteristics. Thus the advance of the frontier has meant a steady movement away from the influence of Europe, a steady growth of independence on American lines. And to study this advance, the men who grew up under these conditions, and the political, economic, and social results of it, is to study the really American part of our history. . . .

The Atlantic frontier was compounded of fisherman, fur-trader, miner, cattle-raiser, and farmer. Excepting the fisherman, each type of industry was on the march toward the West, impelled by an irresistible attraction. Each passed in successive waves across the continent. Stand at Cumberland Gap and watch the procession of civilization, marching single file—the buffalo following the trail to the salt springs, the Indian, the fur-trader and hunter, the cattle-raiser, the pioneer farmer—and the frontier has passed by. Stand at South Pass in the Rockies a century later and see the same procession with wider intervals between. The unequal rate of advance compels us to distinguish the frontier into the trader's frontier, the rancher's frontier, or the miner's frontier, and the farmer's frontier. When the mines and the cow pens were still near the fall line the traders' pack trains were tinkling across the Alleghenies, and the French on the Great Lakes were fortifying their posts, alarmed by the British trader's birch canoe. When the trappers scaled the Rockies, the farmer was still near the mouth of the Missouri.

Why was it that the Indian trader passed so rapidly across the continent? What effects followed from the trader's frontier? The trade was coeval with American discovery. The Norsemen, Vespucius, Verrazani, Hudson, John Smith, all trafficked for furs. The Plymouth pilgrims settled in Indian cornfields, and their first return cargo was of beaver and lumber. The records of the various New England colonies show how steadily exploration was carried into the wilderness by this trade. What is true for New England is, as would be expected, even plainer for the rest of the colonies. All along the coast from Maine to Georgia the Indian trade opened up the river courses. Steadily the trader passed westward, utilizing the older lines of French trade. The Ohio, the Great Lakes, the Mississippi, the Missouri, and the Platte, the lines of western advance, were ascended by traders. They found the passes in the Rocky Mountains and guided Lewis and Clark, Frémont, and Bidwell. The explanation of the rapidity of this advance is connected with the effects of the trader on the Indian. The trading post left the unarmed tribes at the mercy of those that had purchased fire-arms—a truth which the Iroquois Indians wrote in blood, and so the remote and unvisited tribes gave eager welcome to the trader. "The savages," wrote La Salle, "take better care of us French than of their own children; from us only can they get guns and goods." This accounts for the trader's power and the rapidity of his advance. Thus the disintegrating forces of civilization entered the wilderness. Every river valley and Indian trail became a fissure in Indian society, and so that society became honeycombed. Long before the pioneer farmer appeared on the scene, primitive Indian life had passed away. The farmers met Indians armed with guns. The trading frontier, while steadily undermining Indian power by making the tribes ultimately dependent on the whites, yet, through its sale of guns, gave to the Indian increased power of resistance to the farming frontier. French colonization was dominated by its trading frontier; English colonization by its farming frontier. There was an antagonism between the two frontiers as between the two nations. Said Duquesne to the Iroquois, "Are you ignorant of the difference between the king of England and the king of France? Go see the forts that our king has established and you will see that you can still hunt under their very walls. They have been placed for your advantage in places which you frequent. The English, on the contrary, are no sooner in possession of a place than the game is driven away. The forest falls before them as they advance, and the soil is laid bare so that you can scarce find the wherewithal to erect a shelter for the night."

And yet, in spite of this opposition of the interests of the trader and the farmer, the Indian trade pioneered the way for civilization. The buffalo trail became the Indian trail, and this became the trader's "trace"; the trails widened into roads, and the roads into turnpikes, and these in turn were transformed into railroads. The same origin can be shown for the railroads of the South, the Far West, and the Dominion of Canada. The trading posts reached by these trails were on the sites of Indian villages which had been placed in positions suggested by nature; and these trading posts, situated so as to command the water systems of the country, have grown into such cities as Albany, Pittsburgh, Detroit, Chicago, St. Louis, Council Bluffs, and Kansas City. Thus civilization in America has followed the arteries made by geology, pouring an ever richer tide through them, until at last the slender paths of aboriginal intercourse have been broadened and interwoven into the complex mazes of modern commercial lines; the wilderness has been interpenetrated by lines of civilization growing ever more numerous. It is like the steady growth of a complex nervous system for the originally simple, inert continent. If one would understand why we are to-day one nation, rather than a collection of isolated states, he must study this economic and social consolidation of the country. . . .

The exploitation of the beasts took hunter and trader to the west, the exploitation of the grasses took the rancher west, and the exploitation of the virgin soil of the river valleys and prairies attracted the farmer. Good soils have been the most continuous attraction to the farmer's frontier. The land hunger of the Virginians drew them down the rivers into Carolina, in early colonial days; the search for soils took the Massachusetts men to Pennsylvania and to New York. As the eastern lands were taken up migration flowed across them to the west. Daniel Boone, the great backwoodsman, who combined the occupations of hunter, trader, cattle-raiser, farmer, and surveyor—learning, probably from the traders, of the fertility of the lands of the upper Yadkin, where the traders were wont to rest as they took their way to the Indians, left his Pennsylvania home with his father, and passed down the Great Valley road to that stream. Learning from a trader of the game and rich pastures of Kentucky, he pioneered the way for the farmers to that region. Thence he passed to the frontier of Missouri, where his settlement was long a landmark on the frontier. Here again he helped to open the way for civilization, finding salt licks, and trails, and land. His son was among the earliest trappers in the passes of the Rocky Mountains, and his party are said to have been the first to camp on the present site of Denver. His grandson, Col. A. J. Boone, of Colorado, was a power among the Indians of the Rocky Mountains, and was appointed an agent by the government. Kit Carson's mother was a Boone. Thus this family epitomizes the backwoodsman's advance across the continent. . . .

Omitting those of the pioneer farmers who move from the love of adventure, the advance of the more steady farmer is easy to understand. Obviously the immigrant was attracted by the cheap lands of the frontier, and even the native farmer felt their influence strongly. Year by year the farmers who lived on soil whose returns were diminished by unrotated crops were offered the virgin soil of the frontier at nominal prices. Their growing families demanded more lands, and these were dear. The competition of the unexhausted, cheap, and easily tilled prairie lands compelled the farmer either to go west and continue the exhaustion of the soil on a new frontier, or to adopt intensive culture. Thus the census of 1890 shows, in the Northwest, many counties in which there is an absolute or a relative decrease of population. These States have been sending farmers to advance the frontier on the plains, and have themselves begun to turn to intensive farming and to manufacture. A decade before this, Ohio had shown the same transition stage. Thus the demand for land and the love of wilderness freedom drew the frontier ever onward.

Having now roughly outlined the various kinds of frontiers, and their modes of advance, chiefly from the point of view of the frontier itself, we may next inquire what were the influences on the East and on the New World. . . .

First, we note that the frontier promoted the formation of a composite nationality for the American people. The coast was preponderantly English, but the later tides of continental immigration flowed across to the free lands. This was the case from the early colonial days. The Scotch-Irish and the Palatine Germans, or "Pennsylvania Dutch," furnished the dominant element in the stock of the colonial frontier. With these peoples were also the freed indented servants, or redemptioners, who at the expiration of their time of service passed to the frontier. . . . Very generally these redemptions were of non-English stock. In the crucible of the frontier the immigrants were Americanized, liberated, and fused into a mixed race, English in neither nationality nor characteristics. The process has gone on from the early days to our own. . . .

In another way the advance of the frontier decreased our dependence on England. The coast, particularly of the South, lacked diversified industries, and was dependent on England for the bulk of its supplies. In the South there was even a dependence on the Northern colonies for articles of food. . . . Before long the frontier created a demand for merchants. As it retreated from the coast it became less and less possible for England to bring her supplies directly to the consumer's wharfs, and carry away staple crops, and staple crops began to give way to diversified agriculture for a time. The effect of this phase of the frontier action upon the northern section is perceived when we realize how the advance of the frontier aroused seaboard cities like Boston, New York, and Baltimore, to engage in rivalry for what Washington called "the extensive and valuable trade of a rising empire."

The legislation which most developed the powers of the national government, and played the largest part in its activity, was conditioned on the frontier. Writers have discussed the subjects of tariff, land, and internal improvement, as subsidiary to the slavery question. . . . This is a wrong perspective. The pioneer needed the goods of the coast, and so the grand series of internal improvement and railroad legislation began, with potent nationalizing effects. Over internal improvements occurred great debates, in which grave constitutional questions were discussed. Sectional groupings appear in the votes, profoundly significant for the historian. Loose construction increased as the nation marched westward. But the West was not content with bringing the farm to the factory. Under the lead of Clay—"Harry of the West"—protective tariffs were passed, with the cry of bringing the factory to the farm. The disposition of the public lands was a third important subject of national legislation influenced by the frontier.

The public domain has been a force of profound importance in the nationalization and development of the government. The effects of the struggle of the landed and the landless States, and of the Ordinance of 1787, need no discussion. Administratively the frontier called out some of the highest and most vitalizing activities of the general government The purchase of Louisiana was perhaps the constitutional turning point in the history of the Republic, inasmuch as it afforded both a new area for national legislation and the occasion of the downfall of the policy of strict construction. But the purchase of Louisiana was called out by frontier needs and demands. As frontier States accrued to the Union the national power grew. In a speech on the dedication of the Calhoun monument Mr. Lamar explained: "In 1789 the States were the creators of the Federal Government; in 1861 the Federal Government was the creator of a large majority of the States."

When we consider the public domain from the point of view of the sale and disposal of the public lands we are again brought face to face with the frontier. The policy of the United States in dealing with its lands is in sharp contrast with the European system of scientific administration. Efforts to make this domain a source of revenue, and to withhold it from emigrants in order that settlement might be compact, were in vain. The jealousy and the fears of the East were powerless in the face of the demands of the frontiersmen. John Quincy Adams was obliged to confess: "My own system of administration, which was to make the national domain the inexhaustible fund for progressive and unceasing internal improvement, has failed." The reason is obvious; a system of administration was not what the West demanded; it wanted land. Adams states the situation as follows: "The slaveholders of the South have bought the cooperation of the western country by the bribe of the western lands, abandoning to the new Western States their own proportion of the public property and aiding them in the design of grasping all the lands into their own hands." . . .

It is safe to say that the legislation with regard to land, tariff, and internal improvements—the American system of the nationalizing Whig party—was conditioned on frontier ideas and needs. But it was not merely in legislative action that the frontier worked against the sectionalism of the coast. The economic and social characteristics of the frontier worked against sectionalism. The men of the frontier had closer resemblances to the Middle region than to either of the other sections. Pennsylvania had been the seed-plot of frontier emigration, and, although she passed on her settlers along the Great Valley into the west of Virginia and the Carolinas, yet the industrial society of these Southern frontiersmen was always more like that of the Middle region than like that of the tide-water portion of the South, which later came to spread its industrial type throughout the South.

The Middle region, entered by New York harbor, was an open door to all Europe. The tide-water part of the South represented typical Englishmen, modified by a warm climate and servile labor, and living in baronial fashion on great plantations; New England stood for a special English movement—Puritanism. The middle region was less English than the other sections. It had a wide mixture of nationalities, a varied society, the mixed town and county system of local government, a varied economic life, many religious sects. In short, it was a region mediating between New England and the South, and the East and the West. It represented that composite nationality which the contemporary United States exhibits, that juxtaposition of non-English groups, occupying a valley or a little settlement, and presenting reflections of the map of Europe in their variety. It was democratic and nonsectional, if not national; "easy, tolerant, and contented"; rooted strongly in material prosperity. It was typical of the modern United States. . . .

It was this nationalizing tendency of the West that transformed the democracy of Jefferson into the national republicanism of Monroe and the democracy of Andrew Jackson. The West of the War of 1812, the West of Clay, and Benton and Harrison, and Andrew Jackson, shut off by the Middle States and the mountains from the coast sections, had a solidarity of its own with national tendencies. On the tide of the Father of Waters, North and South met and mingled into a nation. Interstate migration went steadily on—a process of cross-fertilization of ideas and institutions. The fierce struggle of the sections over slavery on the western frontier does not diminish the truth of this statement; it proves the truth of it. Slavery was a sectional trait that would not down, but in the West it could not remain sectional. It was the greatest of frontiersmen who declared: "I believe this Government can not endure permanently half slave and half free. It will become all of one thing or all of the other." Nothing works for nationalism like intercourse within the nation. Mobility of population is death to localism, and the western frontier worked irresistibly in unsettling population. The effect reached back from the frontier and affected profoundly the Atlantic coast and even the Old World.

But the most important effect of the frontier has been in the promotion of democracy here and in Europe. As has been indicated, the frontier is productive of individualism. Complex society is precipitated by the wilderness into a kind of primitive organization based on the family. The tendency is anti-social. It produces antipathy to control, and particularly to any direct control. The tax-gatherer is viewed as a representative of oppression. Prof. Osgood, in an able article, has pointed out that the frontier conditions prevalent in the colonies are important factors in the explanation of the American Revolution, where individual liberty was sometimes confused with absence of all effective government. The same conditions aid in explaining the difficulty of instituting a strong government in the period of the confederacy. The frontier individualism has from the beginning promoted democracy.

The frontier States that came into the Union in the first quarter of a century of its existence came in with democratic suffrage provisions, and had reactive effects of the highest importance upon the older States whose peoples were being attracted there. An extension of the franchise became essential. It was *western* New York that forced an extension of suffrage in the constitutional convention of that State in 1821; and it was *western* Virginia that compelled the tide-water region to put a more liberal suffrage provision in the constitution framed in 1830, and to give to the frontier region a more nearly proportionate representation with the tide-water aristocracy. The rise of democracy as an effective force in the nation came in with western preponderance under Jackson and William Henry Harrison, and it meant the triumph of the frontier—with all of its good and with all of its evil elements. . . .

So long as free land exists, the opportunity for a competency exists, and economic power secures political power. But the democracy born of free land, strong in selfishness and individualism, intolerant of administrative experience and education, and pressing individual liberty beyond its proper bounds, has its dangers as well as its benefits. Individualism in America has allowed a laxity in regard to governmental affairs which has rendered possible the spoils system and all the manifest evils that follow from the lack of a highly developed civic spirit. . . .

From the conditions of frontier life came intellectual traits of profound importance. The works of travelers along each frontier from colonial days onward describe certain common traits, and these traits have, while softening down, still persisted as survivals in the place of their origin, even when a higher social organization succeeded. The result is that to the frontier the American intellect owes its striking characteristics. That coarseness and strength combined with acuteness and inquisitiveness; that practical, inventive turn of mind, quick to find expedients; that masterful grasp of material things, lacking in the artistic but powerful to effect great ends; that restless, nervous energy; that dominant individualism, working for good and for evil, and withal that buoyancy and exuberance which comes with freedom—these are traits of the frontier, or traits called out elsewhere because of the existence of the frontier. Since the days when the fleet of Columbus sailed into the waters of the New World, America has been another name for opportunity, and the people of the United States have taken their tone from the incessant expansion which has not only been open but has even been forced upon them. He would be a rash prophet who should assert that the expansive character of American life has now entirely ceased. Movement has been its dominant fact, and unless this training has no effect upon a people, the American energy will continually demand a wider field for its exercise. But never again will such gifts of free land offer themselves. For a moment, at the frontier, the bonds of custom are broken and unrestraint is triumphant. There is not *tabula rasa.* The stubborn American environment is there with its imperious summons to accept its conditions; the inherited ways of doing things are also there; and yet, in spite of environment, and in spite of custom, each frontier did indeed furnish a new field of opportunity, a gate of escape from the bondage of the past; and freshness, and confidence, and scorn of older society, impatience of its restraints and its ideas, and indifference to its lessons, have accompanied the frontier. What the Mediterranean sea was to the Greeks, breaking the bond of custom, offering new experiences, calling out new institutions and activities, that, and more, the ever retreating frontier has been to the United States directly, and to the nations of Europe more remotely. And now, four centuries from the discovery of America, at the end of a hundred years of life under the Constitution, the frontier has gone, and with its going has closed the first period of American history.

DOES HISTORY REPEAT ITSELF? [1]

ARNOLD J. TOYNBEE

Does history repeat itself? In our Western world in the eighteenth and nineteenth centuries, this question used to be debated as an academic exercise. The spell of well-being which our civilization was enjoying at the time had dazzled our grandfathers into the quaint pharisaical notion that they were "not as other men are"; they had come to believe that our Western society was exempt from the possibility of falling into those mistakes and mishaps that have been the ruin of certain other civilizations whose history, from beginning to end, is an open book. To us, in our generation, the old question has rather suddenly taken on a new and very practical significance. We have awakened to the truth (how, one wonders, could we ever have been blind to it?) that Western man and his works are no more invulnerable than the now extinct civilizations of the Aztecs and the Incas, the Sumerians and the Hittites. So today, with some anxiety, we are searching the scriptures of the past to find out whether they contain a lesson that we can decipher. Does history give us any information about our own prospects? And, if it does, what is the burden of it? Does it spell out for us an inexorable doom, which we can merely await with folded hands—resigning ourselves, as best we may, to a fate that we cannot avert or even modify by our own efforts? Or does it inform us, not of certainties, but of probabilities, or bare possibilities, in our own future? The practical difference is vast, for, on this second alternative, so far from being stunned into passivity, we should be roused to action. On this second alternative, the lesson

1. From *Civilization on Trial* (New York: Oxford University Press, 1948), pp. 29–41.

of history would not be like an astrologer's horoscope; it would be like a navigator's chart, which affords the seafarer who has the intelligence to use it a much greater hope of avoiding shipwreck than when he was sailing blind, because it gives him the means, if he has the skill and courage to use them, of steering a course between charted rocks and reefs.

It will be seen that our question needs defining before we plunge into an attempt to answer it. When we ask ourselves "Does history repeat itself?" do we mean no more than "Does history turn out to have repeated itself, on occasions, in the past?" Or are we asking whether history is governed by inviolable laws which have not only taken effect in every past case to which they have applied but are also bound to take effect in every similar situation that may arise in the future? On this second interpretation, the word "does" would mean "must"; on the other interpretation it would mean "may." On this issue, the writer of the present article may as well put his cards on the table at once. He is not a determinist in his reading of the riddle of human life. He believes that where there is life there is hope, and that, with God's help, man is master of his own destiny, at least to some extent in some respects.

But as soon as we have taken our stand on this issue between freedom and necessity that is raised by the ambiguous word "does," we find ourselves called upon to define what we mean by the word "history." If we have to limit the field of history to events that are wholly within the control of human wills, then, to be sure, for a non-determinist no difficulty would arise. But do such events ever actually occur in real life? In our personal experience, when we are making a decision, do we not always find ourselves only partly free and partly bound by past events and present facts in our own life and in our social and physical environment? Is not history itself, in the last analysis, a vision of the whole universe on the move in the four-dimensional framework of space-time? And, in this all-embracing panorama, are there not many events that the most staunch believer in the freedom of the human will would admit, as readily as the most thoroughgoing determinist, to be inexorably recurrent and precisely predictable?

Some events of this undisputedly recurrent predictable order may have little apparent bearing upon human affairs—as, for example, the repetitions of history in nebulae outside the system of the Milky Way. There are, however, some very obvious cyclic movements in physical nature that do affect human affairs in the most intimate fashion—as, for example, the recurrent predictable alternations of day and night and of the seasons of the year. The day-and-night cycle governs all human work; it dictates the schedules of the transportation systems of our cities, sets the times of their rush hours, and weighs on the minds of the commuters whom it shuttles to and fro, twice in every twenty-four hours, between "dormitory" and "workshop." The cycle of the seasons governs human life itself by governing our food supply.

It is true that man, by taking thought, can win a measure of freedom from these physical cycles that is beyond the reach of birds and beasts. Though the individual cannot break the tyranny of the day-and-night cycle by leading a waking life for twenty-four hours in the day, like the legendary Egyptian Pharaoh Mycerinus, human society can achieve Mycerinus' mythical feat collectively by a planned co-operation and a division of labour. Industrial plants can be operated for twenty-four hours in the day by successive shifts of workers, and the labours of workers who work by day can be prepared for and be followed up by the labours of other workers who rest by day and work by night. The tyranny of the seasons, again, has been broken by a Western society that has expanded from the northern temperate zone into the tropics and the southern temperate zone and has devised a technique of refrigeration. Nevertheless, these triumphs of man's mind and will over the tyranny of the two physical cycles of the day and the year are comparatively small gains for human freedom, remarkable though these triumphs are. On the whole, these recurrent predictable events in physical nature remain masters of human life—even at the present level of Western man's technology—and they show their mastery by subduing human affairs, as far as their empire over them extends, to their own recurrent predictable pattern.

But are there, perhaps, human acts, in other fields of action, that are not—or at any rate not so completely—under physical nature's control? Let us examine this question in a familiar concrete case. When, in the last days of April 1865, the horses that, in the first days of that month, had been the cavalry and artillery horses of the Army of Northern Virginia, were being driven behind the plough by the men who, at the beginning of that April, had been General Lee's cavalrymen and artillerymen, those men and horses were once again performing an annually recurrent agricultural operation which they themselves had performed a number of times before in their lives and which predecessors of theirs, in the Old World before Europeans discovered the New World, and in other societies before our Western society's birth, had been performing, year by year, for some five or six thousand years past. The invention of ploughing is coeval with the species of society that we call civilizations, and pre-plough methods of agriculture—likewise governed by the year cycle—were already in use for perhaps an equal length of time before that, during the neolithic dawn by which the sunrise of civilization was heralded. In the spring of 1865, agriculture in the ex-Confederate States of North America was governed by the seasons very rigidly. A few weeks' delay, and the season would have been too late—with the disastrous consequence that the food-producing capacities of those horses and men would have been lost to the community for a whole year longer.

Thus, in the last days of April 1865, the horses and men of the former Army of Northern Virginia were performing a historical act—the spring ploughing—which had repeated itself, by that date, some five or six thousand times at least, and was still repeating itself in 1947. (In that year the writer of this article witnessed the spring ploughing in Kentucky, and noted the farmers' anxiety when, in the middle of that April, their work was interrupted by heavy rainfall.)

But what about the history that General Lee's horses and men were making, not at the end of April, but at the beginning? Is the kind of history that is represented by the last act of the Civil War a kind that repeats itself—as ploughing and commuting repeat themselves owing to their close and obvious dependence on recurrent predictable cycles in physical nature? Are we not confronted here with a kind of human action that is more or less independent of physical cycles and is capable of overriding them? Suppose that General Lee had not found himself constrained to capitulate till June 1865? Or suppose that, General Lee having capitulated when he did, General Grant had not been moved to make his celebrated concession of allowing the Confederate soldiers who had just laid down their arms to take their horses back with them to their farms, notwithstanding the contrary provision in the terms of surrender that had just been agreed upon. Would not either of these hypothetical man-made variations on the actual course of historical events have prevented history from repeating itself in the Southern States in the spring ploughing of 1865?

The province of history that we are considering now is one that used to be treated as the whole field of history before the provinces of economic and social history were opened up. In this old-fashioned field of battles and policies, captains and kings, does history turn out to have repeated itself as it does in fields of human activity that are manifestly governed by cycles in the movement of physical nature? Was the Civil War, for instance, a unique event, or do we find other historical events that display sufficient similarity and affinity to it to warrant us in treating it and them as so many representatives of a class of events in which history has repeated itself at least to some extent? The present writer inclines to this latter view.

The crisis represented in American history by the Civil War was, surely, repeated in a significant sense in the contemporary crisis in German history that is represented by the Bismarckian wars of 1864–71. In both cases, an imperfect political union had threatened to dissolve altogether. In both cases, the issue between the dissolution of the union and its effective establishment was decided by war. In both cases, the partisans of effective union won, and, in both, one of the causes of their victory was their technological and industrial superiority over their opponents. In both, finally, the victory of the cause of union was followed by a great industrial expansion which turned both the post-bellum United States and the Second German Reich into formidable industrial competitors of Great Britain. And here we have hit upon another repetition of history; for, throughout the century ending about 1870, the industrial revolution in Great Britain might have appeared to be a unique historical event, whereas, since 1870, it has come to appear, in its true light, as simply the earliest instance of an economic transformation which was eventually to occur likewise in a number of other Western countries and in some non-Western countries too. Moreover, if we shift our attention from the economic common feature of industrialization to the political common feature of federal union, we shall see the history of the United States and Germany at this point repeating itself once again in the history of a third country—in this case not Great Britain but Canada, whose constituent provinces entered into their present federation in 1867, two years after the *de facto* re-establishment of the unity of the United States in 1865 and four years before the foundation of the Second German Reich in 1871.

In the formation, in the modern Western world, of a number of federal unions, and in the industrialization of these and other countries, we see history repeating itself in the sense of producing a number of more or less contemporary examples of the same human achievement. The contemporaneity of the different instances is, however, no more than approximate. The industrial revolution occurred as an apparently unique event in Great Britain at least two generations before its occurrence in America, and Germany proved it to be a repetitive phenomenon. The insecurely welded pre-Civil-War United States had existed for "four score and seven years," and the ramshackle post-Napoleonic German Confederation for half a century, before the crucial events of the eighteen-sixties proved that federal union was a repetitive pattern which was to recur not only in Canada but in Australia, South Africa, and Brazil. Contemporaneity is not an essential condition for the repetition of history on the political and cultural plane of human affairs. The historical events that repeat themselves may be strictly contemporary or they may overlap in time or they may be entirely non-contemporaneous with one another.

The picture remains the same when we turn to the consideration of the greatest human institutions and experiences that are known to us: the civilizations in their births and growths, their breakdowns, declines, and falls; the higher religions in their foundation and evolution. Measured by our subjective personal measuring rod of the average span of the memory of a single human being who lives to a normal old age, the time interval that divides our present generation from the date of the emergence of the Sumerian civilization in the fourth millennium B.C. or from the date of the beginning of the Christian era itself seems, no doubt, a very long one. Yet it is infinitesimally small on the objective time scale that has recently been given to us by the discoveries of our geologists and astronomers. Our modern Western physical science tells us that the human race has been in existence on this planet for at least 600,000 and perhaps a million years, life for at least 500 million and perhaps 800 million years, and the planet itself for possibly 2000 million years. On this time scale the last five or six thousand years that have seen the births of civilizations, and the last three or four thousand years that have seen the births of higher religions are periods of such infinitesimal brevity that it would be impossible to show them, drawn to scale, on any chart of the whole history of this planet up to date. On this true time scale, these events of "ancient history" are virtually contemporary with our own lifetime, however remote they may appear to be when viewed through the magnifying lens of the individual human midget's subjective mental vision.

The conclusion seems to be that human history does turn out, on occasions, to have repeated itself up to date in a significant sense even in spheres of human activity in which the human will is at its nearest to being master of the situation and is least under the domination of cycles in physical nature. Must we go on to conclude that, after all, the determinists are right and that what looks like free will is an illusion? In the present writer's opinion, the correct conclusion is just the opposite. As he sees it, this tendency towards repetition, which thus asserts itself in human affairs, is an instance of one of the well-known devices of the creative faculty. The works of creation are apt to occur in bunches: a bunch of representatives of a species, a bunch of species of a genus. And the value of such repetitions is, after all, not difficult to discern. Creation could hardly make any headway at all if each new form of creature were not represented by numerous eggs distributed among numerous baskets. How else could a creator, human or divine, provide himself with sufficient materials for bold and fruitful experiment and with effective means of retrieving inevitable failures? If human history repeats itself, it does so in accordance with the general rhythm of the universe; but the significance of this pattern of repetition lies in the scope that it gives for the work of creation to go forward. In this light, the repetitive element in history reveals itself as an instrument for freedom of creative action, and not as an indication that God and man are the slaves of fate.

What is the bearing of these conclusions about history in general on the particular question of the prospects of our Western civilization? As we observed at the beginning of this paper, the Western world has become rather suddenly very anxious about its own future, and our anxiety is a natural reaction to the formidableness of the situation in which we now find ourselves. Our present situation is formidable indeed. A survey of the historical landscape in the light of our existing knowledge shows that, up to date, history has repeated itself about twenty times in producing human societies of the species to which our Western society belongs, and it also shows that, with the possible exception of our own, all these representatives of the species of society called civilizations are already dead or moribund. Moreover, when we study the histories of these dead and moribund civilizations in detail, and compare them with one another, we find indications of what looks like a recurring pattern in the process of their breakdowns, declines, and falls. We are naturally asking ourselves today whether this particular chapter of history is bound to repeat itself in our case. Is that pattern of decline and fall in store for us in our turn, as a doom from which no civilization can hope to escape? In the writer's opinion, the answer to this question is emphatically in the negative. The effort to create a new manifestation of life—be it a new species of mollusc or a new species of human society—seldom or never succeeds at the first attempt. Creation is not so easy an enterprise as that. It wins its ultimate successes through a process of trial and error; and accordingly the failure of previous experiments, so far from dooming subsequent experiments to fail in their turn in the same way, actually offers them their opportunity of achieving success through the wisdom that can be gained from suffering. Of course a series of previous failures does not guarantee success to the next comer, any more than it condemns him to be a failure in his turn. There is nothing to prevent our Western civilization from following historical precedent, if it chooses, by committing social suicide. But we are not doomed to make history repeat itself; it is open to us, through our own efforts, to give history, in our case, some new and unprecedented turn. As human beings, we are endowed with this freedom of choice, and we cannot shuffle off our responsibility upon the shoulders of God or nature. We must shoulder it ourselves. It is up to us.

What shall we do to be saved? In politics, establish a constitutional co-operative system of world government. In economics, find working compromises (varying according to the practical requirements of different places and times) between free enterprise and socialism. In the life of the spirit, put the secular super-structure back onto religious foundations. Efforts are being made in our Western world today to find our way towards each of these goals. If we had arrived at all three of them, we might fairly feel that we had won our present battle for our civilization's survival. But these are, all of them, ambitious undertakings, and it will call for the hardest work and the highest courage to make any progress at all towards carrying any one of them through to achievement.

Of the three tasks, the religious one is, of course, in the long run by far the most important, but the other two are the more urgent, because, if we were to fail in these in the short run, we might lose forever our opportunity of achieving a spiritual rebirth which cannot just be whistled for at our convenience, but will only come, if it comes at all, at the unhurrying pace at which the deepest tides of spiritual creation flow.

The political task is the most urgent of all. The immediate problem here is a negative one. Faced, as we are, with the prospect that—given our present interdependence and present weapons—the world is now on the eve of being unified politically by one means or another, we have to stave off the disastrous dénouement of unification by force of arms: the familiar method of the forcible imposition of a *Pax Romana* which is probably the line of least resistance for the resolution of the formidable political forces in whose grip our own world finds itself today. Can the United States and the other Western countries manage to co-operate with the Soviet Union through the United Nations? If the United Nations organization could grow into an effective system of world government, that would be much the best solution of our political crux. But we have to reckon with the possibility of this enterprise's failing, and to be ready, should it fail, with an alternative to fall back upon. Could the United Nations split, *de facto,* into two groups without a breach of the peace? And, supposing that the whole face of the planet could be partitioned peacefully into an American and a Russian sphere, could two worlds on one planet live side by side on a footing of "non-violent non-co-operation" for long enough to give a chance for a gradual mitigation of the present differences in their social and ideological climates? The answer to this question would depend on whether, on these terms, we could buy the time needed to carry out our economic task of finding a middle way between free enterprise and socialism.

These riddles may be hard to read, but they do tell us plainly what we most need to know. They tell us that our future largely depends upon ourselves. We are not just at the mercy of an inexorable fate.

THE FIRST AND THE SECOND INDUSTRIAL REVOLUTION[1]

NORBERT WIENER

ONCE before in history, the machine has impinged upon human culture with an effect of the greatest moment. This previous impact is known as the Industrial Revolution, and it concerns the machine purely as an alternative to human muscle. In order to study the present crisis, which we shall term the second industrial revolution, it is perhaps wise to discuss the history of the earlier crisis as something of a model to which we may go back.

The first industrial revolution had its roots in the intellectual ferment of the eighteenth century, which found the scientific techniques of Newton and Huygens already well developed, but with applications which had yet scarcely transcended astronomy. It had, however, become manifest to all intelligent scientists that the new techniques were going to have a profound effect on the other sciences. The first field in which this came to pass was that of navigation and of clockmaking.

Navigation is an art which dates to ancient times, but it had one conspicuous weakness until the seventeen-thirties. The problem of determining latitude has always been an easy one even in the days of the Greeks. It is simply the problem of determining the angular height of the celestial pole. This may be done roughly by taking the pole star as the actual pole of the heavens and it may be done very precisely by further refinements which locate the center of the apparent circular path of the pole star. On the other hand, the problem of longitudes is always more difficult. Short of a geodetic survey, it can only be solved by a comparison of local time with some standard time such as that of Greenwich. In order to do this, we must either carry the Greenwich time

1. From *The Human Use of Human Beings* (New York: Houghton Mifflin Company, 1950), pp. 164–189. Reprinted by permission of the Houghton Mifflin Company.

with us on a chronometer or we must find some heavenly clock other than the sun to take the place of a chronometer.

Before either of these two methods had become available for the practical navigator, he was very considerably hampered in his techniques of navigation. He was accustomed to sail along the coast until he reached the latitude he wanted. Then he would strike out on an east or west course, along a parallel of latitude, until he made a landfall. Except by an approximate dead-reckoning, he could not tell how far he was along the course. It was therefore a matter of great importance to him that he should not come unawares onto a dangerous coast. Having made his landfall, he again sailed along the coast until he came to his destination. It will be seen that under these circumstances every voyage was very much of an adventure. Nevertheless, this was the pattern of voyages for many centuries. It can be recognized in the course taken by Columbus, in that of the Silver Fleet, and that of the Acapulco galleons.

This slow and risky procedure was not satisfactory for the admiralties of the eighteenth century. In the first place, the overseas interests of England and France, unlike those of Spain, lay in high latitudes, where the advantage of a direct great-circle course over an east-and-west course is most conspicuous. In the second place, there was a great competition between the two northern powers for the supremacy of the seas, and the advantage of a better navigation was a serious one. It is not a surprise that both governments offered large rewards for an accurate technique of finding longitudes.

The history of these prize contests is complicated and not too edifying. More than one able man was deprived of his rightful triumph, and went bankrupt. In the end, these prizes were awarded in both countries for two very different achievements. One was the design of an accurate ship's chronometer —that is of a clock sufficiently well constructed and compensated to be able to keep the time within a few seconds over a voyage in which it was subject to the continual violent motion of the ship. The other was the construction of good mathematical tables of the motion of the moon, which enabled the navigator to use that body as the clock with which to check the apparent motion of the sun. These two methods have dominated all navigation until the recent development of radio and radar techniques.

Accordingly, the advance guard of the craftsmen of the industrial revolution consisted on the one hand of clockmakers, who used the new mathematics of Newton in the design of their pendulums and their balance wheels; and on the other hand, of optical-instrument makers, with their sextants and their telescopes. The two trades had very much in common. They both demanded the construction of accurate circles and accurate straight lines, and the graduation of these in degrees or in inches. Their tools were the lathe and the dividing engine. These machine tools for delicate work are the ancestors of our whole machine-tool industry of the present day.

It is an interesting reflection that every tool has a genealogy, and that it is descended from the tools by which it has itself been constructed. The clockmakers' lathes of the eighteenth century have led through a clear historical chain of intermediate tools to the great turret lathes of the present day. The series of intervening steps might conceivably have been foreshortened somewhat, but it has necessarily had a certain minimum length. In order to construct a great turret lathe, it is clearly impossible to depend on the unaided human hand for the pouring of the metal, for the placing of the castings on the instruments to machine them, and above all for the power needed in the task of machining them. These must be done through machines that have themselves been manufactured by other machines, and it is only through many stages of this that one reaches back to the original hand or foot lathes of the eighteenth century.

It is thus entirely natural that those who were to develop new inventions were either clockmakers or scientific-instrument makers themselves, or called on people of these crafts to help them. For instance, Watt was a scientific-instrument maker. To show how even a man like Watt had to bide his time before he could extend the precision of clockmaking techniques to larger undertakings, we must remember, as I have said earlier, that his standard of the fit of a piston in a cylinder was that it should be barely possible to insert and move a thin sixpence between them.

We must thus consider navigation and the instruments necessary for it as the locus of an industrial revolution before the main industrial revolution. The main industrial revolution begins with the steam engine. The first form of the steam engine was the crude and wasteful Newcomen engine, which was used for pumping mines. In the middle of the eighteenth century there were abortive attempts to use it for generating power, by making it pump water into elevated reservoirs, and employing the fall of this water to turn waterwheels. Such clumsy devices became obsolete with the introduction of the perfected engines of Watt, which were employed quite early in their history for factory purposes as well as for mine pumping. The end of the eighteenth century saw the steam engine thoroughly established in industry, and the promise of the steamboat on the rivers and of steam traction on land was not far away.

Let us notice that the first place where steam power came into practical use was in replacing one of the most brutal forms of human or animal labor: the pumping of water out of mines. At best, this had been done by draft animals or by crude machines turned by horses. At worst, as in the silver mines of New Spain, it was done by the labor of human slaves. It is a work that is never finished and which can never be interrupted without the possible closing-down of the mine forever. The use of the steam engine to replace this servitude must certainly be regarded as a great humanitarian step forward.

However, slaves do not only pump mines: they also drag loaded riverboats upstream. A second great triumph of the steam engine was the invention of the steamboat, and in particular of the river steamboat. The steam engine at sea was for many years but a supplement of questionable value to the sails carried by every seagoing steamboat; but it was steam transportation on the

Mississippi which opened up the interior of the United States. Like the steamboat, the steam locomotive started where it seems now about to die, as a means of hauling heavy freight.

The next place where the Industrial Revolution made itself felt, perhaps a little later than in the field of the heavy labor of mine workers, and simultaneously with the revolution in transportation, was in the textile industry. This was already a sick industry. Even before the power spindle and the power looms, the condition of the spinners and the weavers left much to be desired. The bulk of production which they could perform fell far short of the demands of the day. It might thus appear to have been scarcely possible to conceive that the transition to the machine could have worsened their condition; but worsen it, it most certainly did.

The beginnings of textile-machine development go back of the steam engine. The stocking frame has existed in a form worked by hand ever since the time of Queen Elizabeth. Machine spinning first became necessary in order to furnish warps for hand looms. The complete mechanization of the textile industry, covering weaving as well as spinning, did not occur until the beginning of the nineteenth century. The first textile machines were for hand operation, although the use of horsepower and water power followed very quickly. Part of the impetus behind the development of the Watt engine, as contrasted with the Newcomen engine, was the desire to furnish power in the rotary form needed for textile purposes.

The textile mills furnished the model for almost the whole course of the mechanization of industry. On the social side, they began the transfer of the workers from the home to the factory and from the country to the city. There was an exploitation of the labor of children and women to an extent, and of a brutality, scarcely conceivable at the present time; that is, if we forget the South African diamond mines and ignore the new industrialization of China and India and the general terms of plantation labor in every country. A great deal of this was due to the fact that new techniques had produced new responsibilities, at a time at which no code had yet arisen to take care of these responsibilities. There was, however, a phase which was more technical than moral. This lay in the very nature of early steam power and its transmission. The steam engine was very uneconomical of fuel by modern standards, although this is not as important as it might seem, considering the fact that early engines had none of the more modern type with which to compete. However, among themselves they were much more economical to run on a large scale than on a small one. In contrast with the prime mover, the textile machine, whether it be loom or spindle, is a comparatively light machine, and uses little power. It was therefore economically necessary to assemble these machines in large factories, where many looms and spindles could be run from one steam engine.

At that time the only available means of transmission of power were mechanical. The first among these were the line of shafting, supplemented by the belt and the pulley. Even as late as the time of my own childhood, the typical picture of a factory was that of a great shed with long lines of shafts suspended from the rafters, and pulleys connected by belts to the individual machines. This sort of factory still exists; although in very many cases it has given way to the modern arrangement where the machines are driven individually by electric motors.

Indeed this second picture is the typical one at the present time. The trade of the millwright has taken on a totally new form. Here there is an important fact relevant to the whole history of invention. It was exactly these millwrights and other new craftsmen of the machine age who were to develop the inventions lying at the foundation of our patent system. Now, the mechanical connection of machines involves difficulties that are quite serious, but not easy to cover by any simple mathematical formulation. In the first place, long lines of shafting either have to be well aligned, or to employ ingenious modes of connection, such as universal joints or parallel couplings, which allow for a certain amount of freedom. In the second place, the long lines of bearings needed for such shafts are very high in their power consumption. In the individual machine, the rotating and reciprocating parts are subject to similar demands of rigidity, and to similar demands that the number of bearings must be reduced as far as possible for the sake of low power consumption and simple manufacture. These prescriptions are not easily filled on the basis of general formulas, and they offer an excellent opportunity for ingenuity and inventive skill of the old-fashioned artisan sort.

It is in view of this fact that the change-over in engineering between mechanical connections and electrical connections has had so great an effect. The electrical motor is a mode of distributing power which it is very convenient to construct in small sizes, so that the individual machine may have its own motor. The transmission losses in the wiring of a factory are relatively low, and the efficiency of the motor itself is relatively high. The connection of the motor with its wiring is not necessarily rigid, nor does it consist of many parts. There are still motives of traffic and convenience which may induce us to continue the custom of mounting the different machines of an industrial process in a single factory; but the need of connecting all the machines to a single source of power is no longer a serious reason for geographical proximity. In other words, we are now in a position to return to cottage industry, in places where it would otherwise be suitable.

Moreover, if it should be so desired, a single piece of machinery may contain several motors, each introducing power at the proper place. This relieves the designer of much of the need for the ingenuity in mechanical design which he would otherwise have been compelled to use. In an electrical design, the mere problem of the connection of the parts seldom involves much difficulty of a nature which does not lend itself to easy mathematical formulation and solution. This is an example of the way in which the art of invention is conditioned by the existing means.

In the third quarter of the last century, when the electric motor began to be employed in industry, it was at first supposed to be nothing more than an alternative device for carrying out existing industrial techniques. It was probably not foreseen that its final effect would be to give rise to a new concept of the factory.

That other great electrical invention, the vacuum tube, has had a similar history. Before the invention of the vacuum tube, it was a matter of a large number of separate tasks of design to develop the regulation of systems of great power. Indeed, most of the regulatory means employed did not involve a particularly low level of power. There were exceptions to this lack of development of methods of control, but they were in specific fields, such as the steering of ships.

As late as 1915, I crossed the ocean on one of the old ships of the American Line. It belonged to the transitional period when ships still carried sails and the masts on which to stretch them, as well as a pointed bow to carry a bowsprit. In a well-deck not far aft of the main superstructure, there was a formidable engine, consisting of four or five six-foot wheels with hand-spokes. These wheels were supposed to be the method of controlling the ship when its automatic steering engine had broken down. In a storm, it would have taken ten men or more, exerting their full strength, to keep that great ship on its course.

This was not the usual method of control of the ship, but an emergency replacement, or as sailors call it, a "jury steering wheel." For normal control, the ship carried, as had all other large ships for years, a steering engine which translated the relatively small forces of the quartermaster at the wheel into the movement of the massive rudder. Thus even on a purely mechanical basis, some progress had been made toward the solution of the problem of amplification of forces or torques. Nevertheless, at that time, this solution of the amplification problem did not range over extreme differences between the levels of input and of output, nor was it embodied in a convenient universal type of apparatus.

The most flexible universal apparatus for amplifying small energy-levels into high energy-levels is the vacuum tube, or electron valve. The history of this is interesting, though it is too complex for us to discuss here. It is however amusing to reflect that the invention of the electron valve goes back to the greatest scientific discovery of Edison, and perhaps the only one which he did not capitalize into an invention.

He observed that when an electrode was placed inside an electric lamp, and was taken as electrically positive with respect to the filament, then a current would flow, if the filament were heated, but not otherwise. Through a series of inventions by other people, this led to a more effective way than any known before of controlling a large current by a small voltage. This is the basis of the modern radio industry, but it is also an industrial tool which is spreading widely into new fields. It is thus no longer necessary to control a process at high energy-levels by a mechanism in which the important details of control are carried out at these levels. It is quite possible to form a certain pattern of behavior response at levels even much lower than those found in usual radio sets, and then to employ a series of amplifying tubes to control by this apparatus a machine as heavy as a steel-rolling mill. The work of discriminating and of forming the pattern of behavior for this is done under conditions under which the power losses are insignificant, and yet the final employment of this discriminatory process is at arbitrarily high levels of power.

It will be seen that this is an invention which alters the fundamental postulational conditions of industry, quite as vitally as the transmission and subdivision of power through the use of the small electric motor. The study of the pattern of behavior is transferred to a special part of the instrument in which power-economy is of very little importance. We have thus deprived of much of their importance the dodges and devices previously used to insure that a mechanical linkage should consist of the fewest possible elements, as well as the devices used to minimize friction and loss motion. The design of machines involving such parts has been transferred from the domain of the skilled shopworker to that of the research-laboratory man; and in this he has all the available tools of circuit theory to replace a mechanical ingenuity by the old sort. Invention in the old sense has been supplanted by the intelligent employment of the laws of nature. The step from the laws of nature to their employment has been reduced a hundred times.

I have previously said that when an invention is made, it is generally a considerable period before its full implications are understood. It was long before people became aware of the full impact of the airplane on international relations and on the conditions of human life. The effect of atomic energy on mankind and the future is yet to be assessed, although many stupid people of the present day assess it merely as a new weapon like all older weapons.

The situation with the vacuum tube was similar. In the beginning, it was regarded merely as an extra tool to supplement an already existing technique of telephone communication. The electrical engineers first mistook its real importance to such an extent that for years the vacuum tubes were relegated to a particular part of the communication network. This part was connected up with other parts consisting only of the traditional so-called inactive circuit elements—the resistance, the capacitances and the inductances. Only since the war have engineers felt free enough in their employment of vacuum tubes to insert them where necessary, with the same freedom with which they have previously inserted passive elements of these three kinds.

The vacuum tube was first used to replace previously existing components of long-distance telephone circuits and of the wireless telegraphy of the time. It was not long, however, until it had become clear that the radio-telephone had achieved the stature of the radio-telegraph, and that broadcasting was possible. Let not the fact that this great triumph of invention has been given over to the soap-opera and the hillbilly singer blind one to the excellent work which was done in developing it, and to the great civilizing possibilities which have been perverted into a national medicine-show.

Thus the vacuum tube received its début in the communications industry. The boundaries and extent of this industry were not fully understood for a long period. There were sporadic uses of the vacuum tube and of its sister invention, the photo-electric cell, for scanning the products of industry; as for example, for regulating the thickness of a web coming out of a paper machine, or for inspecting the color of a can of pineapples. These uses did not as yet form a reasoned new technique, nor were they associated in the engineering line with the task of communication.

All this changed in the war. One of the few things to be salvaged from the great conflict was the rapid development of invention, under the stimulus of necessity and the unlimited employment of money; and above all, the new blood called in to industrial research. At the beginning of the war, our greatest need was to keep England from being knocked out by an overwhelming air attack. Accordingly, the anti-aircraft cannon was one of the first objects of our scientific war effort, especially when combined with the airplane-detecting device of radar or ultra-high-frequency Hertzian waves. The technique of radar used the same modalities as the existing technique of radio besides inventing new ones of its own. It was thus natural to consider radar as a branch of communication theory. The speed of the airplane made it necessary to give the predicting machine itself communication functions which had previously been assigned to human beings. Thus the problem of anti-aircraft fire control made familiar the notion of a communication addressed to a machine rather than to a person.

During the pre-war period other uses were found for the vacuum tube coupled directly with the machine rather than with the human agent. The concept of the large-scale computing machine as developed by Vannevar Bush among others was originally a purely mechanical one. The integration was done by rolling disks engaging one another in a frictional manner; and the interchange of outputs and inputs between these disks was the task of a classical train of shafts and gears.

The mother idea of these first computing machines is much older than the work of Vannevar Bush. In certain respects it goes back to the work of Babbage early in the last century. Babbage had an idea of the computing machine which is surprisingly modern, but his mechanical means fell far behind his ambitions. The first difficulty he met, and with which he could not cope, was that a long train of gears requires a considerable energy to run it, so that its output of power and torque very soon becomes too small to actuate the remaining parts of the apparatus. Bush saw this difficulty and overcame it in a very ingenious way. Besides the electrical amplifiers depending on vacuum tubes and on similar devices, there are certain mechanical torque-amplifiers which are familiar to everyone acquainted with ships and the unloading of cargo. The stevedore raises the cargo-slings by taking a purchase of his load around the drum of a donkey-engine or cargo-hoist. In this way, the tension which he exerts mechanically is increased by a factor which grows extremely rapidly with the angle of contact between his rope and the rotating drum. Thus one man is able to control the lifting of a load of many tons.

This device is fundamentally a force- or torque-amplifier. By an ingenious bit of design, Bush inserted such mechanical amplifiers between the stages of his computing machine; and was thereby able to do effectively the sort of thing which Babbage had only dreamed of theoretically.

In one of the earlier models of the Bush Differential Analyzer, this sort of mechanical device performed all the principal amplification functions. The only use of electricity was to give power to the motors running the machine as a whole. This state of computing-mechanisms was intermediate and transitory. It very soon became clear that amplifiers of an electric nature, connected by wires rather than by shafts, were both less expensive and more flexible than mechanical amplifiers and mechanical connections. Accordingly, the later forms of Bush's machine made an adequate use of vacuum-tube devices. This has been continued in all their successors; whether they were what is called now analogy machines, which work primarily by the measurement of physical quantities, or digital machines, which work primarily by counting and the operations of arithmetic.

The development of these computing machines has been very rapid since the war. For a large range of computational work, they have shown themselves vastly more rapid and vastly more accurate than the human computer. Their speed has long since reached such a level that any intermediate human intervention in their work is out of the question. Thus they offer the same need to replace human capacities by machine capacities as those in the anti-aircraft computer. The parts of the machine must speak to one another through an appropriate language, without speaking to any person or listening to any person, except in the terminal and initial stages of the process. Here again we have an element which has contributed to the general acceptance of the extension to machines of the idea of communication.

In this conversation between the parts of a machine, it is often necessary to take cognizance of what the machine has already said. Here there enters the notion of feedback, which is older than its exemplification in the ship's steering engine, and is as old, in fact, as the governor which regulates the speed of Watts' steam engine. This governor is needed to keep the engine from running wild when its load is removed. If it starts to run wild, the balls of the governor fly upward from centrifugal action, and in their upward flight they move a lever which partly cuts off the admission of steam. Thus the tendency to speed up produces a partly compensatory tendency to slow down. This method of regulation received a thorough mathematical analysis at the hands of Clerk Maxwell in 1868.

Here feedback is used to regulate the velocity of a machine. In the ship's steering engine it regulates the position of the rudder. The man at the wheel operates a light transmission system, employing chains or hydraulic transmission, which moves a member in the room containing the steering engine. There is some sort of apparatus which notes the distance between this member and the tiller; and this distance controls the admission of steam to the ports of a steam steering-engine, or some similar electrical admission in the case of an electrical steering-engine. Whatever the particular connections may be, this change of admission is always in such a direction as to bring into coincidence the tiller and the member actuated from the wheel. Thus one man at the wheel can do with ease what a whole crew could only do with difficulty at the old man-power wheel.

We have so far given examples where the feedback process takes primarily a mechanical form. However, a series of operations of the same structure can be carried out through electrical and even vacuum-tube means. These means promise to be the future standard method of designing control apparatus.

Quite apart from the vacuum tube and the method of feedback, there has long been a tendency to render factories and machines automatic. Except for some special purpose, one would no longer think of producing screws by the use of the ordinary lathe, in which a mechanic must watch the progress of his cutter and regulate it by hand. The production of screws in quantity without serious human intervention is now the normal task of the ordinary screw machine. Although this does not make any special use of the process of feedback nor of the vacuum tube, it accomplishes a somewhat similar end. What the feedback and the vacuum tube have made possible is not the sporadic design of individual automatic mechanisms, but a general policy for the construction of automatic mechanisms of the most varied type. In this they have been reinforced by our new theoretical treatment of communication, which takes full cognizance of the possibilities of communication between machine and machine. It is this conjunction of circumstances which now renders possible the new automatic age.

The existing state of industrial techniques includes the whole of the results of the first industrial revolution, together with many inventions which we now see to be precursors of the second industrial revolution. What the precise boundary between these two revolutions may be, it is still too early to say. In its potential significance, the vacuum tube certainly belongs to an industrial revolution different from that of the age of power; and yet it is only at present that the true significance of the invention of the vacuum tube has been sufficiently realized to allow us to attribute the present age to a new and second industrial revolution.

Up to now we have been talking about the existing state of affairs. We have not covered more than a small part of the aspects of the previous industrial revolution. We have not mentioned the airplane, nor the bulldozer, together with the other mechanical tools of construction, nor the automobile, nor even one-tenth of those factors which have converted the form of modern life to something totally unlike the life of any other period. It is fair to say, however, that except for a considerable number of isolated examples, the industrial revolution up to the present has displaced man and the beast as a source of power, without making any great impression on other human functions. The best that a pick-and-shovel worker can do to make a living at the present time is to act as a sort of gleaner after the bulldozer. In all important respects, the man who has nothing but his physical power to sell has nothing to sell which it is worth anyone's money to buy.

Let us now go on to a picture of a more completely automatic age. Let us consider what for example the automobile factory of the future will be like; and in particular the assembly line, which is that one of the component parts of that sort of factory which employs the most labor. In the first place, the sequence of operations will be controlled by something like a modern high-speed computing machine. I have often said that the high-speed computing machine is primarily a logical machine, which confronts different propositions with one another and draws some of their consequences. It is possible to translate the whole of mathematics into the performance of a sequence of purely logical tasks. If this representation of mathematics is embodied in the machine, the machine will be a computing machine in the ordinary sense. Nevertheless, such a computing machine, besides ordinary mathematical tasks, will involve the logical task of channeling a series of orders concerning mathematical operations. Therefore, as present high-speed computing machines in fact do, it will contain at least one large assembly which is purely logical.

The instructions to such a machine, and here too I am speaking of present practice, are given by what we have called a taping. The orders given the machine may be fed into it by a taping which is completely predetermined. It is also possible that the actual contingencies met in the performance of the machine may be handed over as a basis of further regulation to a new control tape constructed by the machine itself, or to a modification of the old one.

It may be thought that the present great expense of computing machines bars them from use in industrial processes; and furthermore that the delicacy of the work needed in their construction and the variability of their functions precludes the use of the methods of mass production in constructing them. Neither of these charges is correct. In the first place, the enormous computing machines now used for the highest level of mathematical work cost something of the order of hundreds of thousands of dollars. Even this price would not be forbidding for the control machine of a really large factory, but it is not the relevant price. The present computing machines are developing so rapidly that practically every one constructed is a new model. In other words, a large part of these apparently exorbitant prices goes into new work of design, and into new parts, which are produced by a very high quality of labor under the most expensive circumstances. If one of these computing machines were therefore established in price and model, and put to use in quantities of tens or twenties, it is very doubtful whether its price would be in a higher range than that of tens of thousands of dollars. A similar machine of less capacity, not suited for the most difficult computational problems, but nevertheless quite adequate for factory control, would probably cost no more than a few thousand dollars in any sort of moderate-scale production.

Now let us consider the problem of mass production. If the only opportunity for mass production were the mass production of completed machines, it is quite clear that for a considerable period the best we could hope for would be a moderate-scale production. However, in each machine the parts are largely repetitive in very considerable numbers. This is true, whether we consider the memory apparatus, the logical apparatus, or the arithmetical subassembly. Thus production of a few dozen machines only, represents a potential mass production of the parts, and is accompanied with the same economic advantages.

It may still seem that the delicacy of the machines must mean that each job demands a special new model. This is also false. Given even a rough similarity in the type of mathematical and logical operations demanded of the mathematical and logical units of the machine, the over-all performance is regulated by the taping, or at any rate by the *original* taping. The taping of such a machine is a highly skilled intellectual task for a professional man of a very specialized type; but it is largely or entirely a once-for-all job, and need only be partly repeated when the machine is modified for a new industrial setup. Thus the cost of such a skilled technician will be distributed over a tremendous output, and will not really be a significant factor in the use of the machine.

The computing machine represents the center of the automatic factory, but it will never be the whole factory. On the one hand, it receives its detailed instructions from elements of the nature of sense organs. I am thinking of sense organs such as photo-electric cells, condensers for the reading of the thickness of a web of paper, thermometers, hydrogen-ion-concentration meters, and the general run of apparatus now built by instrument companies for the manual control of industrial processes. These instruments are already built to report electrically at remote stations. All they need to enable them to introduce their information into an automatic high-speed computor is a reading apparatus which will translate position or scale into a pattern of consecutive digits. Such apparatus already exists, and offers no great difficulty, either of principle or of constructional detail. The sense-organ problem is not new, and it is already effectively solved.

Besides these sense organs, the control system must contain effectors, or components which act on the outer world. Some of these are of a type already familiar, such as valve-turning motors, electric clutches, and the like. Some of them will have to be invented, to duplicate more nearly the functions of the human hand as supplemented by the human eye. It is altogether possible in the machining of automobile frames to leave on certain metal lugs, machined into smooth surfaces as points of reference. The tool, whether it be drill or riveter or whatever else we want, may be led to the rough neighborhood of these surfaces by a photo-electric mechanism, actuated for example by spots of paint. The final positioning may bring the tool up against the reference surfaces, so as to establish a firm contact, but not a destructively firm one. This is only one way of doing the job. Any competent engineer can think of a dozen more.

Of course, we assume that the instruments which act as sense organs to the system record not only the original state of the work, but also the result of the functioning of all previous processes. Thus the machine may carry out feedback operations, either those of the simple type now so thoroughly understood, or those involving more complicated processes of discrimination, regulated by the central control as a logical or mathematical system. In other words, the all-over system will correspond to the complete animal with sense organs, effectors and proprioceptors, and not, as in the ultra-rapid computing machine, to an isolated brain, dependent for its experiences and for its effectiveness on our intervention.

The speed with which these new devices are likely to come into industrial use will vary greatly with the different industries. Automatic devices, which may not be precisely like those described here, but which perform roughly the same functions, have already come into extensive use in continuous-process industries like canneries, steel-rolling mills, and especially wire and tin-plate factories. They are also familiar in paper factories, which likewise produce a continuous output. Another place where they are indispensable is in that sort of factory which is too dangerous for any considerable number of workers to risk their lives in its control, and in which an emergency is likely to be so serious and costly that its possibilities should have been considered in advance, rather than left to the excited judgment of somebody on the spot. If a policy can be thought out in advance, it can be committed to a taping which will regulate the conduct to be followed in accordance with the readings of the instrument. In other words, such factories should be under a régime rather like that of the interlocking signals and switches of the railroad signal-tower. This régime is already followed in oil-cracking factories, in many other chemical works, and in the handling of the sort of dangerous materials found in the exploitation of atomic energy.

We have already mentioned the assembly line as a place for applying the same sorts of technique. In the assembly line, as in the chemical factory or the continuous-process paper mill, it is necessary to exert a certain statistical control on the quality of the product. This control depends on a sampling process.

These sampling processes have now been developed by Wald and others into a technique called *sequential analysis,* in which the sampling is no longer taken in a lump, but is a continuous process going along with the production. That which can be done then by a technique so standardized that it can be put in the hands of a statistical computer who does not understand the logic behind it, may also be executed by a computing machine. In other words, except again at the highest levels, the machine takes care of the routine statistical controls, as well as of the production process.

In general, factories have an accounting procedure which is independent of the production. As far as the data which occur in cost-accounting are concerned, that part which comes from the machine or assembly line may be fed directly into the computing machine. Other data may be fed in from time to time by human operators, but the bulk of necessary clerical work will be cut to that not of a completely routine nature. For example, girls will be needed to take care of outside correspondence and the like. Even a large part of this may be received from the correspondents on punched cards, or transferred to punched cards by extremely low-grade labor. From this stage on, everything may go by machine. This mechanization also may apply to a not inappreciable part of the library and filing facilities of an industrial plant.

In other words, the machine plays no favorites as between overall labor and white collar labor. Thus the possible fields into which the new industrial revolution is likely to penetrate are very extensive; and include all labor performing judgments of a low level, in much the same way as the displaced labor of the earlier industrial revolution included every aspect of human power. There will, of course, be trades into which the new industrial revolution of judgment will not penetrate: either because the new control machines are not economical in industries on so small a scale as not to be able to carry the considerable capital costs involved, or because their work is so varied that a new taping will be necessary for almost every job. I cannot see automatic machinery of the judgment-replacing type coming into use in the corner grocery, or in the corner garage, although I can very well see it employed by the wholesale grocer and the automobile manufacturer. The farm laborer too, although he is beginning to be pressed by automatic machinery, is protected from the full pressure of it, because of the ground he has to cover, the variability of the crops he must till, and the special conditions of weather and the like that he must meet. Even here, the large-scale or plantation farmer is becoming increasingly dependent on cotton-picking and weed-burning machinery, as the wheat farmer has long been dependent on the McCormick reaper. Where such machines may be used, some use of machinery of judgment is not inconceivable.

The introduction of the new devices and the dates at which they are to be expected are, of course, largely economic matters, on which I am not an expert. Short of any violent political changes or another great war, I should give a rough estimate that it will take the new tools ten to twenty years to come into their own. A war would change all this overnight. If we should engage in a war with a major power like Russia, which would make serious demands on the infantry, and consequently on our man-power, we may be hard put to it to keep up our industrial production. Under these circumstances, the matter of replacing human production by other modes may well be a life-or-death matter to the nation. We are already as far along in the process of developing a unified system of automatic control machines as we were in the development of radar in 1939. Just as the emergency of the Battle of Britain made it necessary to attack the radar problem in a massive manner, and to hurry up the natural development of the field by what may have been decades, so too, the needs of labor replacement are likely to act on us in a similar way in the case of another war. The personnel of skilled radio amateurs, mathematicians, and physicists, who were so rapidly turned into competent electrical engineers for the purposes of radar design, is still available for the very similar task of automatic-machine design. There is a new and skilled generation coming up, which they have trained.

Under these circumstances, the period of about two years which it took for radar to get onto the battlefield with a high degree of effectiveness is scarcely likely to be exceeded by the period of evolution of the automatic factory. At the end of such a war, the "know-how" needed to construct such factories will be common. There will even be a considerable backlog of equipment manufactured for the government, which is likely to be on sale or available to the industrialists. Thus a new war will almost inevitably see the automatic age in full swing within less than five years.

I have spoken of the actuality and the imminence of this new possibility. What can we expect of its economic and social consequences? In the first place, we can expect an abrupt and final cessation of the demand for the type of factory labor performing purely repetitive tasks. In the long run, the deadly uninteresting nature of the repetitive task may make this a good thing, and the source of the leisure which is necessary for the full cultural development of man on all sides. It may also produce cultural results as trivial and wasteful as the greater part of those so far obtained from the radio and the movies.

Be that as it may, the intermediate period of the introduction of the new means, especially if it comes in the fulminating manner to be expected from a new war, will lead to an immediate transitional period of disastrous confusion. We have a good deal of experience as to how the industrialists regard a new industrial potential. Their whole propaganda is to the effect that it must not be considered as the business of the government but must be left open to whatever entrepreneurs wish to invest money in it. We also know that they have very few inhibitions when it comes to taking all the profit out of an industry that there is to be taken, and then letting the public pick up the pieces. This is the history of the lumber and mining industries, and is part of the traditional American philosophy of progress.

Under these circumstances, industry will be flooded with the new tools to the extent that they appear to yield immediate profits, irrespective of what long-time damage they can do. We shall see a process parallel to the way in which the use of atomic energy for bombs has been allowed to compromise the very necessary potentialities of the long-time use of atomic power to replace our oil and coal supplies, which are within centuries, if not decades, of utter exhaustion. Note well that atomic bombs do not compete with power companies.

Let us remember that the automatic machine, whatever we think of any feelings it may have or may not have, is the precise economic equivalent of slave labor. Any labor which competes with slave labor must accept the economic conditions of slave labor. It is perfectly clear that this will produce an unemployment situation, in comparison with which the present recession and even the depression of the thirties will seem a pleasant joke. This depression will ruin many industries—possibly even the industries which have taken advantage of the new potentialities. However, there is nothing in the industrial tradition which forbids an industrialist to make a sure and quick profit, and to get out before the crash touches him personally.

Thus the new industrial revolution is a two-edged sword. It may be used for the benefit of humanity, assuming that humanity survives long enough to enter a period in which such a benefit is possible. If, however, we proceed along the clear and obvious lines of our traditional behavior, and follow our traditional worship of progress and the fifth freedom—the freedom to exploit—it is practically certain that we shall have to face a decade or more of ruin and despair.

MODERN MAN IS OBSOLETE[1]

NORMAN COUSINS

In the most primitive sense, war in man is an expression of his extreme competitive impulses. Like everything else in nature, he has had to fight for existence; but the battle against other animals, once won, gave way in his evolution to battle against his own kind. Darwin called it natural selection; Spencer called it the survival of the fittest; and its most overstretched interpretation is to be found in *Mein Kampf,* with the naked glorification of brute force and the complete worship of might makes right. In the political and national sense, it has been the attempt of the "have-nots" to take from the "haves," or the attempt of the "haves" to add further to their lot at the expense of the "have-nots." Not always was property at stake; comparative advantages were measured in terms of power, and in terms of tribal or national

1. Condensed from the book *Modern Man Is Obsolete,* by Norman Cousins. Originally published in *The Saturday Review of Literature.* Copyright, 1945, by Norman Cousins. Reprinted by permission of The Viking Press, New York.

superiority. The good luck of one nation became the hard luck of another. The good fortune of the Western powers in obtaining "concessions" in China at the turn of the century was the ill fortune of the Chinese. The power that Germany stripped from Austria, Czechoslovakia, Poland, and France at the beginning of World War II she added to her own.

What does it matter, then, if war is not in the nature of man so long as man continues through the expression of his nature to be a viciously competitive animal? The effect is the same, and therefore the result must be as conclusive—war being the effect, and complete obliteration of the human species being the ultimate result.

If this reasoning is correct, then modern man is obsolete, a self-made anachronism becoming more incongruous by the minute. He has exalted change in everything but himself. He has leaped centuries ahead in inventing a new world to live in, but he knows little or nothing about his own part in that world. He has surrounded and confounded himself with gaps—gaps between revolutionary technology and evolutionary man, between cosmic gadgets and human wisdom, between intellect and conscience. The struggle between science and morals that Henry Thomas Buckle foresaw a century ago has been all but won by science.

Given ample time, man might be expected eventually to span those gaps normally; but by his own hand, he is destroying even time. Decision and execution in the modern world are becoming virtually synchronous. Thus, whatever gaps man has to span he will have to span immediately.

This involves both biology and will. If he lacks the actual and potential biological equipment to build those bridges, then the birth certificate of the atomic age is in reality a *memento mori*.[2] But even if he possesses the necessary biological equipment, he must still make the decision which says that he is to apply himself to the challenge. Capability without decision is inaction and inconsequence.

Man is left, then, with a crisis in decision. The main test before him involves his *will* to change rather than his *ability* to change. That he is capable of change is certain. For there is no more mutable or adaptable animal in the world. We have seen him migrate from one extreme clime to another. We have seen him step out of backward societies and join advanced groups within the space of a single generation. This is not to imply that the changes were necessarily always for the better; only that change was and is possible. But change requires stimulus; and mankind today need look no further for stimulus than its own desire to stay alive. The critical power of change, says Spengler, is directly linked to the survival drive. Once the instinct for survival is stimulated, the basic condition for change can be met.

That is why the power of total destruction as potentially represented by modern science must be dramatized and kept in the forefront of public opinion. The full dimensions of the peril must be seen and recognized. Only then

2. Reminder of death.

will man realize that the first order of business is the question of continued existence. Only then will he be prepared to make the decisions necessary to assure that survival. . . .

At present he is a world warrior; it is time for him to grow up and to become a world citizen. This is not vaporous idealism, but sheer driving necessity. It bears directly on the prospects of his own survival. He will have to recognize the flat truth that the greatest obsolescence of all in the Atomic Age is national sovereignty. Even back in the old-fashioned Rocket Age before August 6, 1945, strict national sovereignty was an anomalous hold-over from the tribal instinct in nations. If it was anomalous then, it is preposterous now.

It is preposterous because we have invested it with non-existent powers. We assume that national sovereignty is still the same as it always was, that it still offers security and freedom of national decision. We assume it still means national independence, the right to get into war or stay out of it. We even debate the question of "surrendering" some of our sovereignty—as though there is still something to surrender. There is nothing left to surrender. There is only something to gain. A common world sovereignty.

At the heart of sovereignty throughout history there has been security based on the advantages of geography or military might. For sovereignty has been inseparable from power. But by the end of World War I, the validity of national sovereignty had sharply changed. The development of air power alone, apart from all other aspects of the world's inexorable trend toward close interrelationship, outdated traditional concepts of independence among nations. Yet we preferred to believe that there was no connection between a world being locked into a single piece and its over-all organization. Unfortunately, our unreadiness or unwillingness to see this connection did not cause the connection to disappear.

So much did this connection exist that it led to World War II. Despite six years of that new war, despite jet planes, rocket planes, despite the abrupt telescoping of a thousand years of human history in the release of atomic energy, despite the loss of millions of lives, we still act as though sovereignty can function as it did two thousand years ago.

Can it be that we do not realize that in an age of atomic energy and rocket planes the foundations of the old sovereignties have been shattered? That no longer is security to be found in armies and navies, however large and mighty? That no longer is there security based on size and size alone? That any nation, however small, with atomic energy, is potentially as powerful as any other nation, however large? That in an Atomic Age all nations are now directly accessible to each other—for better or worse? That in the erasure of man-made barriers and boundaries all the peoples of the world stand virtually unarmed in the presence of one another? That they are at the mercy of one another, and will have to devise a common security or suffer a common cataclysm? That the only really effective influence between peoples is such influence as they are able to exert morally, politically, ideologically upon each other? That the use of disproportionate wealth and abundance of resources by any nation, when applied for bargaining purposes, does not constitute influence but the type of coercion against which severe reaction is inevitable?

All these questions have been in the making for centuries, but the triumph over the invisible and mighty atom has given them an exactness and an immediacy about which there can be no mistake. The need for world government was clear long before August 6, 1945, but Hiroshima and Nagasaki raised that need to such dimensions that it can no longer be ignored. And in the glare brighter than sunlight produced by the assault on the atom, we have all the light we need with which to examine this new world that has come into being with such clicking abruptness. Thus examined, the old sovereignties are seen for what they are—vestigial obstructions in the circulatory system of the world.

Much of the attachment to old concepts of sovereignty, as well as the reluctance to face squarely its severe limitations in the modern world, grows out of apprehension over the control a world authority might have over the internal affairs of the individual state. There is the fear, for example, that the individual Constitutions would be subject to central control. There is the fear that institutions built up over centuries would exist only at the pleasure and discretion of a super-state.

Natural and understandable though these concerns may be, they have their source in confusion over a distinction that should be made between world *sovereignty* and state *jurisdiction*. A common world sovereignty would mean that no state could act unilaterally in its foreign affairs. It would mean that no state could have the instruments of power to aggress against other states. It would mean that no state could withdraw from the central authority as a method of achieving its aims. But it would *not* mean that the individual state would lose its *jurisdiction* over its internal affairs. It would *not* mean the arbitrary establishment of a uniform ideology all over the world. It would not mean the forcible imposition of non-democratic systems on democratic states, any more than it would mean the forcible imposition of democratic systems on non-democratic states.

Though the idea of bestowing democracy on all other peoples throughout the world seems both magnanimous and attractive, the fact remains that democracy is not to be had just for the giving or the taking. It cannot be donated or imposed from without. It is an intricate and highly advanced mechanism capable of existing, like man himself, under certain conditions. It depends not only on the love of freedom, but on the ability to carry the responsibilities of freedom. It requires enduring respect for numberless principles, not all of them incorporated into formal law. It requires adherence to the principle of majority rule with preservation of minority rights. It is as much a way of living and a philosophy of life as it is a form of political organization.

This does not mean, however, that peoples not now democratic must be restrained from moving toward democracy. Nor does it mean that the conditions under which democracy can come into being cannot be nurtured and developed. So far as a central authority is concerned, one way to help in that development can be by providing a greater external harmony that will permit a greater internal harmony. . . .

The world has at last become a geographic unit, if we measure geographic units not according to absolute size but according to access and proximity. All peoples are members of this related group, just as the thirteen American colonies belonged to a related group, and just as the city-states of Greece belonged to a related group. The extent of this relationship need only be measured by the direct access nations have to each other for purposes of war. And the consequences of disunion are as applicable to the world group today as they were to individual groupings of states in the past. The unorganized geographic units of the past have given way to the unorganized unit of the present. It is a unit without unity, an order without any order.

In a world where it takes less time to get from New York to Chungking than it took to get from New York to Philadelphia in 1787, the nature and extent of this geographic entity becomes apparent. All natural distances and barriers vanish. Never before in history has the phrase, the human family, had such a precise meaning. This much all of us—American, European, African, Asiatic, Australian—have in common: Whether we like it or not, we have been brought together or thrust together as members of a world unit, albeit an unorganized world unit. Within that unit, to be sure, are divisions and subdivisions, but they are all heavily interdependent. There is little point in musing or speculating whether this unit is desirable or whether it deserves our support. The fact is that it exists.

Here we must meet the argument that even though the world may be a geographical unit, it is too large, too unwieldy, for the creation and operation of a governmental unit. But size alone does not limit the area in which government can function. Unwieldiness is entirely relative to the instruments of control. For harmony among states depends upon relationships; and relationships among states depend upon law and respect for law.

No less an authority on international organization than *The Federalist* tells us that "the larger the society, provided it be within a practical sphere, the more duly capable will it be of self-government." By "practical," *The Federalist* meant both necessity and workability. Thus a state could be as large as the need behind it, so long as it possesses effective machinery for its administration. And two thousand years before *The Federalist,* Aristotle considered the limitations upon the size of a state and decided that it could be determined by the range of a man's voice. Accessibility seemed to Aristotle to be the prime requisite of a governmental unit. According to this definition, radio has converted the entire world into a small enclosure capable of central government. But radio is only one of the instruments available for drawing the peoples of the world together under a common sovereignty. The revolution in transportation can given them a mutuality such as even the people of any one nation a hundred or more years ago never knew among themselves.

This mutuality—a mutuality built on present and future needs—is more important than physical dimensions. A common ground of destiny is not too large a site for the founding of any community.

But reject all other arguments for world government—reject the geographic, economic, the ideological, the sociological, the humanitarian arguments, valid though they may be. Consider only the towering job of policing the atom—the job of keeping the smallest particle of matter from destroying all matter. This means control. But control is no natural phenomenon. It does not operate of and by itself. Control is impossible without power—the power of investigation, the power of injunction, the power of arrest, the power of punishment.

But power, like control, cannot be isolated, nor is it desirable except under carefully defined circumstances. Power must be subordinate to law, unless it is to take the form of brute, irresponsible force. Here, too, we are involved in an important interrelationship, because law can be derived only through government. Law is a product of moral, judicial, executive, legislative, and administrative sanction—all of which adds up to government. And government means what it says: the process of governing. It is not decentralization, it is not informal organization, it is not the right of veto or the right of secession by any state or states. It is a central body none of whose members has the right or the means of aggression or withdrawal. It is the source of legitimate action and legitimate redress.

Approach the problem in reverse. We are all agreed that war must be "outlawed." If that is what we really mean, then we shall have to apply law. Law based on what? On general agreement? With or without sanctions? With or without protective as well as punitive power? With or without a judiciary? To the extent that the answers to these questions are subtractive, we shall fail in our agreed purpose. Outlawry of war is a noble phrase but its translation into tangible effectiveness requires, by its very nature, the existence of the basis and the instruments of legality, by which we mean government.

We are left, then, with three basic principles necessarily related to an effective system of international control:

No control without power.
No power without law.
No law without government.

Are there no other practicable methods of control? Is atomic power such a menace that nothing less than world government may be able to deal with it? What less drastic plans have been suggested?

Before examining these questions, bear in mind that the atom bomb dropped on Nagasaki represented a substantial improvement over the Hiroshima model. Bear in mind that the first atomic bomb, admittedly still in the experimental stage and said to weigh only a few pounds, was the equivalent of 20,000 tons of the most effective TNT explosive ever previously developed. Bear in mind that more than eighty per cent of the world's supply of uranium is located outside the United States, Canada, and Great Britain, which share the distinction and the responsibility for unleashing atomic energy. Bear in mind that other nations, Japan included, have already experimented successfully with plutonium, a derivative of uranium.

Bear in mind that United States territory is no longer safe from bombing attack. Bear in mind that more than four hundred Japanese balloons carrying not atomic but incendiary bombs were able to perform their explosive missions over the western portion of the United States, some being carried as far east as Michigan—although only a small number caused effective damage. Bear in mind that Japan was getting ready to launch long-range, one-way heavy bombers for a direct attack on the United States when the atomic bombs ended the war. Bear in mind that it is possible *today* to develop pilotless rocket planes, carrying huge explosive atomic cargoes; and that these planes, from their launching stations, will be capable of hitting any specified target area in the world within the radius of a single mile.

Bear in mind that it would require only an infinitesimal percentage of the number of bombing missions in World War II for rocket planes to lay waste every city in the world—not in a matter of months or weeks or even days, but hours. Bear in mind that most military experts predict that within three years —five years at the most—knowledge of utilization of atomic energy may be as commonplace as present-day knowledge of aviation itself.

Bear all this in mind and then consider what would be required to safeguard the world from destructive atomic energy. Consider various suggestions advanced as possible methods of control. Begin by considering the fairly popular theory that every weapon produces a counter-weapon, and that in the course of time the atomic bomb will meet its match in some sort of super-atomic defense. This is by far the coziest, most convenient, approach to the problem. It requires almost no physical and mental exertion and doubtless has its origin in the pleasant belief that everything will come out all right in the end— atomic bombs and rocket planes not excluded. Absurd as the theory seems, it nevertheless requires a sober and serious answer; every shred of hope must be fully and carefully appraised at a time when all hope sorely needs definition and direction.

The obvious answer to the counter-weapon argument is that we can take nothing for granted. We cannot assume the automatic development of such a device, and among those who are the least sanguine in this respect are the scientists themselves. Nor is it true that every new weapon in history has been equated by another weapon. Air power was far ahead of anti-aircraft not only after World War I but after World War II. The only effective answer to air power was more air power, but this did not prevent cities from being leveled during the struggle for air supremacy. Nor did it prevent robots and rocket bombs from taking lives until the invasion of the European Continent overran the launching stations. But the cardinal fallacy of the counter-weapon theory is that it assumes there may be enough time in which to bring the negating devices into play—even granting the possibility of their development.

Modern warfare's only effective counter-weapon is retaliation, and there may not even be time for that, once an attack begins, for the beginning may be the ending as well.

It is said that man can go underground in an atomic war, that he can carve out large cities under the surface of the earth and at the first sign of danger can retire to subterranean shelters and stay there indefinitely if need be. Ingenious cut-away and cross-section sketches have been published, revealing vast improvements over the crude World War II underground shelters. The new shelters will have all conveniences, including hot and cold running water, refrigeration, and moving-picture theaters. But the sketches failed to explain how it would be possible to burrow far enough into the earth to avoid the shattering concussive power of atomic violence. They failed to tell what would happen to those underground cities once the exploded atom left an inextinguishable fire on the crust of the earth. If any imaginative sketches are in order at all, let us see some which can speculate upon the amount of fire and bombarding and atom-splitting a weary planet can absorb without being thrown off its axis or without reverting to its original incandescent mass blazing at millions of degrees. . . .

This is the multiple nature of the challenge to modern man—to bring about world government and to keep it pure; to keep his social, economic, and political institutions apace with his scientific achievements; to make whatever adjustments are needed in his own make-up, conditioning, and outlook on life in order to exist in an Atomic Age.

This is a large order, perhaps the largest order man has had to fill in his fifty thousand-odd years on earth, but he himself has set up the conditions which have made the order necessary. We can put on blinders; we can laugh it all off as just a false alarm; we can claim that talk of an Atomic Age is sheer fancy; we can protest that the threat of the destructive use of atomic energy is exaggeration, overstatement, hysteria, panic.

But all the manufactured calm and scorn in the world cannot alter the precise fact that the atomic bomb plus another war equals global disaster. Nor that the crisis is fast approaching and may be upon us within a few years unless we act now to avert it. Nor that this crisis is created not only by the explosive atom but by inadequate means of controlling international lawlessness. Nor that control is inoperative without power, that power is dangerous without law, and that law is impossible without government.

And if we reject the multiple challenge before us? And if we decide that we are not yet ready for world government? What then? Then there is yet another way, an alternative to world government, an alternative to change in man. This way is the second course. Absurd as this second course may seem, we describe it in all seriousness, for it is possible that through it man may find a way to stay alive—which is the central problem before us.

This second course is fairly simple. It requires that man eliminate the source of the trouble. Let him dissociate himself, carefully and completely, from civilization and all its works. Let him systematically abolish science and the tools of science. Let him destroy all machines and the knowledge which can build or operate those machines. Let him raze his cities, smash his laboratories, dismantle his factories, tear down his universities and schools, burn his libraries, rip apart his art. Let him murder his scientists, his lawmakers, his statesmen, his doctors, his teachers, his mechanics, his merchants, and anyone who has anything to do with the machinery of knowledge or progress. Let him punish literacy by death. Let him eradicate nations and set up the tribe as sovereign. Let him, in short, revert to his condition in society in 10,000 B.C. Thus emancipated from science, from progress, from government, from knowledge, from thought, he can be reasonably certain of prolonging his existence on this planet.

This can be a way out—if "modern" man is looking for a way out from the modern world.

VII

PHILOSOPHY AND RELIGION

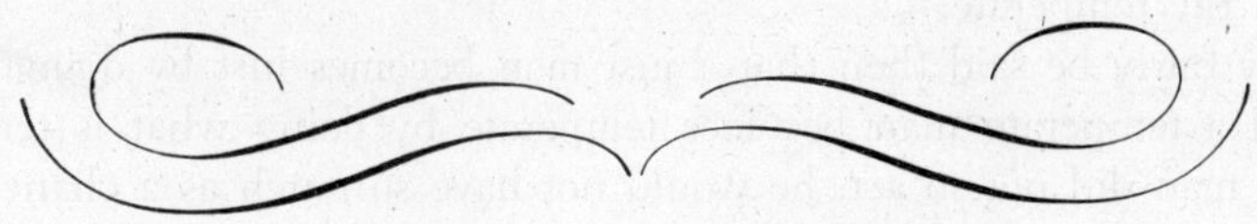

· THE GOOD LIFE ·

VIRTUE[1]

ARISTOTLE

But it may be asked what we mean by saying that people must become just by doing what is just and temperate by doing what is temperate. For if they do what is just and temperate, they are *ipso facto* proved, it will be said, to be just and temperate in the same way as, if they practise grammar and music, they are proved to be grammarians and musicians.

But is not the answer that the case of the arts is not the same? For a person may do something that is grammatical either by chance or at the suggestion of somebody else; hence he will not be a grammarian unless he not only does what is grammatical but does it in a grammatical manner, i.e. in virtue of the grammatical knowledge which he possesses.

There is another point too of difference between the arts and the virtues. The productions of art have their excellence in themselves. It is enough therefore that, when they are produced, they should be of a certain character. But actions in accordance with virtue are not e.g. justly or temperately performed because they are in themselves just or temperate. It is necessary that the agent at the time of performing them should satisfy certain conditions, i.e. in the first place that he should know what he is doing, secondly that he should deliberately choose to do it and to do it for its own sake, and thirdly that he should do it as an instance of a settled and immutable moral state. If it be a question whether a person possesses any art, these conditions, except

1. From *The Nichomachean Ethics of Aristotle,* translated by J. E. C. Welldon (London: Macmillan & Co., Ltd., 1920), Book II, with omissions. Reprinted by permission of Macmillan & Co., Ltd.

indeed the condition of knowledge, are not taken into account; but if it be a question of possessing the virtues, the mere knowledge is of little or no avail, and it is the other conditions, which are the results of frequently performing just and temperate actions, that are not of slight but of absolute importance. Accordingly deeds are said to be just and temperate, when they are such as a just or temperate person would do, and a just and temperate person is not merely one who does these deeds but one who does them in the spirit of the just and the temperate.

It may fairly be said then that a just man becomes just by doing what is just and a temperate man becomes temperate by doing what is temperate, and if a man did not so act, he would not have so much as a chance of becoming good. But most people, instead of doing such actions, take refuge in theorizing; they imagine that they are philosophers and that philosophy will make them virtuous; in fact they behave like people who listen attentively to their doctors but never do anything that their doctors tell them. But it is as improbable that a healthy state of the soul will be produced by this kind of philosophizing as that a healthy state of the body will be produced by this kind of medical treatment.

We have next to consider the nature of virtue.

Now, as the qualities of the soul are three, viz. emotions, faculties and moral states, it follows that virtue must be one of the three. By the emotions I mean desire, anger, fear, courage, envy, joy, love, hatred, regret, emulation, pity, in a word whatever is attended by pleasure or pain. I call those faculties in respect of which we are said to be capable of experiencing these emotions, e.g. capable of getting angry or being pained or feeling pity. And I call those moral states in respect of which we are well or ill disposed towards the emotions, ill-disposed e.g. towards the passion of anger, if our anger be too violent or too feeble, and well-disposed, if it be duly moderated, and similarly towards the other emotions.

Now neither the virtues nor the vices are emotions; for we are not called good or evil in respect of our emotions but in respect of our virtues or vices. Again, we are not praised or blamed in respect of our emotions; a person is not praised for being afraid or being angry, nor blamed for being angry in an absolute sense, but only for being angry in a certain way; but we are praised or blamed in respect of our virtues or vices. Again, whereas we are angry or afraid without deliberate purpose, the virtues are in some sense deliberate purposes, or do not exist in the absence of deliberate purpose. It may be added that while we are said to be moved in respect of our emotions, in respect of our virtues or vices we are not said to be moved but to have a certain disposition.

These reasons also prove that the virtues are not faculties. For we are not called either good or bad, nor are we praised or blamed, as having an abstract capacity for emotion. Also while Nature gives us our faculties, it is not Nature that makes us good or bad, but this is a point which we have already discussed.

If then the virtues are neither emotions nor faculties, it remains that they must be moral states.

The nature of virtue has been now generically described. But it is not enough to state merely that virtue is a moral state, we must also describe the character of that moral state.

It must be laid down then that every virtue or excellence has the effect of producing a good condition of that of which it is a virtue or excellence, and of enabling it to perform its function well. Thus the excellence of the eye makes the eye good and its function good, as it is by the excellence of the eye that we see well. Similarly, the excellence of the horse makes a horse excellent and good at racing, at carrying its rider and at facing the enemy.

If then this is universally true, the virtue or excellence of man will be such a moral state as makes a man good and able to perform his proper function well. We have already explained how this will be the case, but another way of making it clear will be to study the nature or character of this virtue.

Now in everything, whether it be continuous or discrete,[2] it is possible to take a greater, a smaller, or an equal amount, and this either absolutely or in relation to ourselves, the equal being a mean between excess and deficiency. By the mean in respect of the thing itself, or the absolute mean, I understand that which is equally distinct from both extremes; and this is one and the same thing for everybody. By the mean considered relatively to ourselves I understand that which is neither too much nor too little; but this is not one thing, nor is it the same for everybody. Thus if 10 be too much and 2 too little we take 6 as a mean in respect of the thing itself; for 6 is as much greater than 2 as it is less than 10, and this is a mean in arithmetical proportion. But the mean considered relatively to ourselves must not be ascertained in this way. It does not follow that if 10 pounds *of meat* be too much and 2 be too little for a man to eat, a trainer will order him 6 pounds, as this may itself be too much or too little for the person who is to take it; it will be too little e.g. for Milo,[3] but too much for a beginner in gymnastics. It will be the same with running and wrestling; *the right amount will vary with the individual.* This being so, everybody who understands his business avoids alike excess and deficiency; he seeks and chooses the mean, not the absolute mean, but the mean considered relatively to ourselves.

Every science then performs its function well, if it regards the mean and refers the works which it produces to the mean. This is the reason why it is usually said of successful works that it is impossible to take anything from them or to add anything to them, which implies that excess or deficiency is fatal to excellence but that the mean state ensures it. Good artists too, as we say, have an eye to the mean in their works. But virtue, like Nature herself, is more accurate and better than any art; virtue therefore will aim at the mean;

2. In Aristotelian language, as Mr. Peters says, a straight line is a "continuous quantity" but a rouleau of sovereigns a "discrete quantity."

3. The famous Crotoniate wrestler.

—I speak of moral virtue, as it is moral virtue which is concerned with emotions and actions, and it is these which admit of excess and deficiency and the mean. Thus it is possible to go too far, or not to go far enough, in respect of fear, courage, desire, anger, pity, and pleasure and pain generally, and the excess and the deficiency are alike wrong; but to experience these emotions at the right times and on the right occasions and towards the right persons and for the right causes and in the right manner is the mean or the supreme good, which is characteristic of virtue. Similarly there may be excess, deficiency, or the mean, in regard to actions. But virtue is concerned with emotions and actions, and here excess is an error and deficiency a fault, whereas the mean is successful and laudable, and success and merit are both characteristics of virtue.

It appears then that virtue is a mean state, so far at least as it aims at the mean.

Again, there are many different ways of going wrong; for evil is in its nature infinite, to use the Pythagorean [4] figure, but good is finite. But there is only one possible way of going right. Accordingly the former is easy and the latter difficult; it is easy to miss the mark but difficult to hit it. This again is a reason why excess and deficiency are characteristics of vice and the mean state a characteristic of virtue.

"For good is simple, evil manifold." [5]

Virtue then is a state of deliberate moral purpose consisting in a mean that is relative to ourselves, the mean being determined by reason, or as a prudent man would determine it.

It is a mean state *firstly as lying* between two vices, the vice of excess on the one hand, and the vice of deficiency on the other, and secondly because, whereas the vices either fall short of or go beyond what is proper in the emotions and actions, virtue not only discovers but embraces the mean.

Accordingly, virtue, if regarded in its essence or theoretical conception, is a mean state, but, if regarded from the point of view of the highest good, or of excellence, it is an extreme.

But it is not every action or every emotion that admits of a mean state. There are some whose very name implies wickedness, as e.g. malice, shamelessness, and envy, among emotions, or adultery, theft, and murder, among actions. All these, and others like them, are censured as being intrinsically wicked, not merely the excesses or deficiencies of them. It is never possible then to be right in respect of them; they are always sinful. Right or wrong in such actions as adultery does not depend on our committing them with the

4. The Pythagoreans, starting from the mystical significance of number, took the opposite principles of "the finite" (τὸ πέρασ or τὸ πεπερασμένον) and "the infinite" (τὸ απειρον) to represent good and evil.

5. A line—perhaps Pythagorean—of unknown authorship.

right person, at the right time or in the right manner; on the contrary it is sinful to do anything of the kind at all. It would be equally wrong then to suppose that there can be a mean state or an excess or deficiency in unjust, cowardly or licentious conduct; for, if it were so, there would be a mean state of an excess or of a deficiency, an excess of an excess and a deficiency of a deficiency. But as in temperance and courage there can be no excess or deficiency because the mean is, in a sense, an extreme, so too in these cases there cannot be a mean or an excess or deficiency, but, however the acts may be done, they are wrong. For it is a general rule that an excess or deficiency does not admit of a mean state, nor a mean state of an excess or deficiency.

But it is not enough to lay down this as a general rule; it is necessary to apply it to particular cases, as in reasonings upon actions, general statements, although they are broader, are less exact than particular statements. For all action refers to particulars, and it is essential that our theories should harmonize with the particular cases to which they apply.

We must take particular virtues then from the catalogue [6] of *virtues.*

In regard to feelings of fear and confidence, courage is a mean state. On the side of excess, he whose fearlessness is excessive has no name, as often happens, but he whose confidence is excessive is foolhardy, while he whose timidity is excessive and whose confidence is deficient is a coward.

In respect of pleasures and pains, although not indeed of all pleasures and pains, and to a less extent in respect of pains than of pleasures, the mean state is temperance, the excess is licentiousness. We never find people who are deficient in regard to pleasures; accordingly such people again have not received a name, but we may call them insensible.

As regards the giving and taking of money, the mean state is liberality, the excess and deficiency are prodigality and illiberality. Here the excess and deficiency take opposite forms; for while the prodigal man is excessive in spending and deficient in taking, the illiberal man is excessive in taking and deficient in spending.

(For the present we are giving only a rough and summary account *of the virtues,* and that is sufficient for our purpose; we will hereafter determine their character more exactly.)

In respect of money there are other dispositions as well. There is the mean state which is magnificence; for the magnificent man, as having to do with large sums of money, differs from the liberal man who has to do only with small sums; and the excess *corresponding to it* is bad taste or vulgarity, the deficiency is meanness. These are different from the excess and deficiency of liberality; what the difference is will be explained hereafter.

In respect of honour and dishonour the mean state is highmindedness, the

---

6. It would seem that a catalogue of virtues (διαγραφή or ὑπογραφή) must have been recognized in the Aristotelian school. Cp. *Eud. Eth.* ii, ch. 3.

excess is what is called vanity, the deficiency littlemindedness. Corresponding to liberality, which, as we said, differs from magnificence as having to do *not with great but* with small sums of money, there is a moral state which has to do with petty honour and is related to highmindedness which has to do with great honour; for it is possible to aspire to honour in the right way, or in a way which is excessive or insufficient, and if a person's aspirations are excessive, he is called ambitious, if they are deficient, he is called unambitious, while if they are between the two, he has no name.

Anger, like other emotions, has its excess, its deficiency, and its mean state. It may be said that they have no names, but as we call one who observes the mean gentle, we will call the mean state gentleness. Among the extremes, if a person errs on the side of excess, he may be called passionate and his vice passionateness, if on that of deficiency, he may be called impassive and his deficiency impassivity.

There are also three other mean states with a certain resemblance to each other, and yet with a difference. For while they are all concerned with intercourse in speech and action, they are different in that one of them is concerned with truth in such intercourse, and the others with pleasantness, one with pleasantness in amusement and the other with pleasantness in the various circumstances of life. We must therefore discuss these states in order to make it clear that in all cases it is the mean state which is an object of praise, and the extremes are neither right nor laudable but censurable. It is true that these mean and extreme states are generally nameless, but we must do our best here as elsewhere to give them a name, so that our argument may be clear and easy to follow.

In the matter of truth then, he who observes the mean may be called truthful, and the mean state truthfulness. Pretence, if it takes the form of exaggeration, is boastfulness, and one who is guilty of pretence is a boaster; but if it takes the form of depreciation it is irony, and he who is guilty of it is ironical.

There are also mean states in the emotions and in the expression of the emotions. For although modesty is not a virtue, yet a modest person is praised as if he were virtuous; for here too one person is said to observe the mean and another to exceed it, as e.g. the bashful man who is never anything but modest, whereas a person who has insufficient modesty or no modesty at all is called shameless, and one who observes the mean modest.

Righteous indignation, again, is a mean state between envy and malice. They are all concerned with the pain and pleasure which we feel at the fortunes of our neighbours. A person who is righteously indignant is pained at the prosperity of the undeserving; but the envious person goes further and is pained at anybody's prosperity, and the malicious person is so far from being pained that he actually rejoices *at misfortunes*. . . .

There are then three dispositions, two being vices, viz. one the vice of excess and the other that of deficiency, and one virtue, which is the mean state between them; and they are all in a sense mutually opposed. For the extremes are opposed both to the mean and to each other, and the mean is opposed to the extremes. For as the equal if compared with the less is greater but if compared with the greater is less, so the mean states, whether in the emotions or actions, if compared with the deficiencies, are excessive, but if compared with the excesses are deficient. Thus the courageous man appears foolhardy as compared with the coward, but cowardly as compared with the foolhardy. Similarly, the temperate man appears licentious as compared with the insensible but insensible as compared with the licentious, and the liberal man appears prodigal as compared with the illiberal, but illiberal as compared with the prodigal. The result is that the extremes mutually repel and reject the mean; the coward calls the courageous man foolhardy, but the foolhardy man calls him cowardly, and so on in the other cases.

But while there is this mutual opposition between the extremes and the mean, there is greater opposition between the two extremes than between either extreme and the mean; for they are further removed from each other than from the mean, as the great from the small and the small from the great than both from the equal. Again, while some extremes exhibit more or less similarity to the mean, as foolhardiness to courage and prodigality to liberality, there is the greatest possible dissimilarity between the extremes. But things which are furthest removed from each other are defined to be opposites; hence the further things are removed, the greater is the opposition between them.

It is in some cases the deficiency and in others the excess which is the more opposed to the mean. Thus it is not foolhardiness the excess, but cowardice the deficiency which is the more opposed to courage, nor is it insensibility the deficiency, but licentiousness the excess which is the more opposed to temperance. There are two reasons why this should be so. One lies in the nature of the thing itself; for as one of the two extremes is the nearer and more similar to the mean, it is not this extreme, but its opposite, that we chiefly set against the mean. For instance, as it appears that foolhardiness is more similar and nearer to courage than cowardice, it is cowardice that we chiefly set against courage; for things which are further removed from the mean seem to be more opposite to it. This being one reason which lies in the nature of the thing itself, there is a second which lies in our own nature. It is the things to which we ourselves are naturally more inclined that appear more opposed to the mean. Thus we are ourselves naturally more inclined to pleasures *than to their opposites,* and are more prone therefore to licentiousness than to decorum. Accordingly we speak of those things, in which we are more likely to run to great lengths, as being more opposed to the mean. Hence it follows that licentiousness which is an excess is more opposed to temperance than insensibility.

It has now been sufficiently shown that moral virtue is a mean state, and in what sense it is a mean state; it is a mean state as lying between two vices, a vice of excess on the one side and a vice of deficiency on the other, and as aiming at the mean in the emotions and actions.

THE SERMON ON THE MOUNT[1]

AND seeing the multitudes, he went up into a mountain; and when he was set, his disciples came unto him: and he opened his mouth, and taught them, saying, Blessed are the poor in spirit: for theirs is the kingdom of heaven. Blessed are they that mourn: for they shall be comforted. Blessed are the meek: for they shall inherit the earth. Blessed are they which do hunger and thirst after righteousness: for they shall be filled. Blessed are the merciful: for they shall obtain mercy. Blessed are the pure in heart: for they shall see God. Blessed are the peacemakers: for they shall be called the children of God. Blessed are they which are persecuted for righteousness' sake: for theirs is the kingdom of heaven. Blessed are ye, when men shall revile you, and persecute you, and shall say all manner of evil against you falsely, for my sake. Rejoice, and be exceeding glad: for great is your reward in heaven: for so persecuted they the prophets which were before you.

Ye are the salt of the earth: but if the salt have lost his savour, wherewith shall it be salted? it is thenceforth good for nothing, but to be cast out, and to be trodden under foot of men. Ye are the light of the world. A city that is set on an hill cannot be hid. Neither do men light a candle, and put it under a bushel, but on a candlestick; and it giveth light unto all that are in the house. Let your light so shine before men, that they may see your good works, and glorify your Father which is in heaven. Think not that I am come to destroy the law, or the prophets; I am not come to destroy, but to fulfil. For verily I say unto you, Till heaven and earth pass, one jot or one tittle shall in no wise pass from the law, till all be fulfilled. Whosoever therefore shall break one of these least commandments, and shall teach men so, he shall be called the least in the kingdom of heaven: but whosoever shall do and teach them, the same shall be called great in the kingdom of heaven. For I say unto you, That except your righteousness shall exceed the righteousness of the scribes and Pharisees, ye shall in no case enter into the kingdom of heaven.

Ye have heard that it was said by them of old time, Thou shalt not kill; and whosoever shall kill shall be in danger of the judgment: but I say unto you, That whosoever is angry with his brother without a cause shall be in danger of the judgment: and whosoever shall say to his brother, Raca, shall be in danger of the council: but whosoever shall say, Thou fool, shall be in danger

1. From *The Gospel According to Saint Matthew* (King James Version of *The Bible*), Chapters 5, 6, 7.

of hell fire. Therefore if thou bring thy gift to the altar, and there rememberest that thy brother hath ought against thee; leave there thy gift before the altar, and go thy way; first be reconciled to thy brother, and then come and offer thy gift. Agree with thine adversary quickly, whiles thou art in the way with him; lest at any time the adversary deliver thee to the judge, and the judge deliver thee to the officer, and thou be cast into prison. Verily I say unto thee, Thou shalt by no means come out thence, till thou hast paid the uttermost farthing.

Ye have heard that it was said by them of old time, Thou shalt not commit adultery; but I say unto you, That whosoever looketh on a woman to lust after her hath committed adultery with her already in his heart. And if thy right eye offend thee, pluck it out, and cast it from thee: for it is profitable for thee that one of thy members should perish, and not that thy whole body should be cast into hell. And if thy right hand offend thee, cut it off, and cast it from thee: for it is profitable for thee that one of thy members should perish, and not that thy whole body should be cast into hell. It hath been said, Whosoever shall put away his wife, let him give her a writing of divorcement: but I say unto you, That whosoever shall put away his wife, saving for the cause of fornication, causeth her to commit adultery: and whosoever shall marry her that is divorced committeth adultery.

Again, ye have heard that it hath been said by them of old time, Thou shalt not forswear thyself, but shalt perform to the Lord thine oaths: but I say unto you, Swear not at all; neither by heaven; for it is God's throne: nor by the earth; for it is his footstool: neither by Jerusalem; for it is the city of the great King. Neither shalt thou swear by thy head, because thou canst not make one hair white or black. But let your communication be, Yea, yea; Nay, nay: for whatsoever is more than these cometh of evil.

Ye have heard that it hath been said, An eye for an eye, and a tooth for a tooth: but I say unto you, That ye resist not evil: but whosoever shall smite thee on thy right cheek, turn to him the other also. And if any man will sue thee at the law, and take away thy coat, let him have thy cloke also. And whosoever shall compel thee to go a mile, go with him twain. Give to him that asketh thee, and from him that would borrow of thee turn not thou away.

Ye have heard that it hath been said, Thou shalt love thy neighbor, and hate thine enemy. But I say unto you, Love your enemies, bless them that curse you, do good to them that hate you, and pray for them which despitefully use you, and persecute you; that ye may be the children of your Father which is in heaven; for he maketh his sun to rise on the evil and on the good, and sendeth rain on the just and on the unjust. For if ye love them which love you, what reward have ye? do not even the publicans the same? And if ye salute your brethren only, what do ye more than others? do not even the publicans so? Be ye therefore perfect, even as your Father which is in heaven is perfect.

Take heed that ye do not your alms before men, to be seen of them: otherwise ye have no reward of your Father which is in heaven. Therefore when thou doest thine alms, do not sound a trumpet before thee, as the hypocrites do in the synagogues and in the streets, that they may have glory of men. Verily I say unto you, They have their reward. But when thou doest alms, let not thy left hand know what thy right hand doeth: that thine alms may be in secret: and thy Father which seeth in secret himself shall reward thee openly. And when thou prayest, thou shalt not be as the hypocrites are: for they love to pray standing in the synagogues and in the corners of the streets, that they may be seen of men. Verily I say unto you, They have their reward. But thou, when thou prayest, enter into thy closet, and when thou hast shut thy door, pray to thy Father, which is in secret; and thy Father which seeth in secret shall reward thee openly. But when ye pray, use not vain repetitions, as the heathen do: for they think that they shall be heard for their much speaking. Be not ye therefore like unto them: for your Father knoweth what things ye have need of, before ye ask him. After this manner therefore pray ye: Our Father which art in heaven, Hallowed by thy name. Thy kingdom come. Thy will be done in earth, as it is in heaven. Give us this day our daily bread. And forgive us our debts, as we forgive our debtors. And lead us not into temptation, but deliver us from evil: for thine is the kingdom, and the power, and the glory, for ever. Amen. For if ye forgive men their trespasses, your heavenly Father will also forgive you: but if ye forgive not men their trespasses, neither will your Father forgive your trespasses.

Moreover when ye fast, be not, as the hypocrites, of a sad countenance: for they disfigure their faces, that they may appear unto men to fast. Verily I say unto you, They have their reward. But thou, when thou fastest, anoint thine head, and wash thy face; that thou appear not unto men to fast, but unto thy Father which is in secret; and thy Father, which seeth in secret, shall reward thee openly.

Lay up not for yourselves treasures upon earth, where moth and rust doth corrupt, and where thieves break through and steal: but lay up for yourselves treasures in heaven, where neither moth nor rust doth corrupt, and where thieves do not break through nor steal: for where your treasure is, there will your heart be also. The light of the body is the eye: if therefore thine eye be single, thy whole body shall be full of light. But if thine eye be evil, thy whole body shall be full of darkness. If therefore the light that is in thee be darkness, how great is that darkness! No man can serve two masters: for either he will hate the one, and love the other; or else he will hold to the one, and despise the other. Ye cannot serve God and mammon. Therefore I say unto you, Take no thought for your life, what ye shall eat, or what ye shall drink; nor yet for your body, what ye shall put on. Is not the life more than meat, and the body than raiment? Behold the fowls of the air: for they sow not, neither do they reap, nor gather into barns; yet your heavenly Father feedeth them. Are ye not much better than they? Which of you by taking thought can add one cubit unto his stature? And why take ye thought for raiment? Consider the lilies of the field, how they grow; they toil not, neither do they spin: and yet I say unto you, That even Solomon in all his glory was not arrayed like one of these. Wherefore, if God so clothe the grass of the field, which to day is, and to morrow is cast into the oven, shall he not much more clothe you, O ye of little faith? Therefore take no thought, saying, What shall we eat? or, What shall we drink? or, Wherewithal shall we be clothed? (For after all these things do the Gentiles seek:) for your heavenly Father knoweth that ye have need of all these things. But seek ye first the kingdom of God, and his righteousness; and all these things shall be added unto you. Take therefore no thought for the morrow: for the morrow shall take thought for the things of itself. Sufficient unto the day is the evil thereof.

Judge not, that ye be not judged. For with what judgment ye judge, ye shall be judged: and with what measure ye mete, it shall be measured to you again. And why beholdest thou the mote that is in thy brother's eye, but considerest not the beam that is in thine own eye? Or how wilt thou say to thy brother, Let me pull out the mote out of thine eye; and, behold, a beam is in thine own eye? Thou hypocrite, first cast out the beam out of thine own eye; and then shalt thou see clearly to cast out the mote out of thy brother's eye.

Give not that which is holy unto the dogs, neither cast ye your pearls before swine, lest they trample them under their feet, and turn again and rend you. Ask, and it shall be given you; seek, and ye shall find; knock, and it shall be opened unto you: for every one that asketh receiveth; and he that seeketh findeth; and to him that knocketh it shall be opened. Or what man is there of you, whom if his son ask bread, will he give him a stone? Or if he ask a fish, will he give him a serpent? If ye then, being evil, know how to give good gifts unto your children, how much more shall your Father which is in heaven give good things to them that ask him? Therefore all things whatsoever ye would that men should do to you, do ye even so to them: for this is the law and the prophets.

Enter ye in at the strait gate: for wide is the gate, and broad is the way, that leadth to destruction, and many there be which go in thereat: because strait is the gate, and narrow is the way, which leadeth unto life, and few there be that find it. Beware of false prophets, which come to you in sheep's clothing, but inwardly they are ravening wolves. Ye shall know them by their fruits. Do men gather grapes of thorns, or figs of thistles? Even so every good tree bringeth forth good fruit; but a corrupt tree bringeth forth evil fruit. A good tree cannot bring forth evil fruit, neither can a corrupt tree bring forth good fruit. Every tree that bringeth not forth good fruit is hewn down, and cast into the fire. Wherefore by their fruits ye shall know them. Not every one that saith unto me, Lord, Lord, shall enter into the kingdom of heaven; but he that doeth the will of my Father which is in heaven. Many will say to me in that day, Lord, Lord, have we not prophesied in thy name? And in thy name have cast out devils? and in thy name done many wonderful works? And then will I profess unto them, I never knew you: depart from me, ye that work iniquity. Therefore whosoever heareth these sayings of mine, and doeth them, I will liken him unto a wise man, which built his house upon a rock: and the rain descended, and the floods came, and the winds blew, and beat upon that house; and it fell not: for it was founded upon a rock. And every one that heareth these sayings of mine, and doeth them not, shall be likened unto a foolish man, which built his house upon the sand: and the rain descended, and the floods came, and the winds blew, and beat upon that house; and it fell: and great was the fall of it. And it came to pass, when Jesus had ended these sayings, the people were astonished at his doctrine: For he taught them as one having authority, and not as the scribes.

THE STOIC CODE [1]

MARCUS AURELIUS

BEGIN the morning by saying to thyself, I shall meet with the busybody, the ungrateful, arrogant, deceitful, envious, unsocial. All these things happen to them by reason of their ignorance of what is good and evil. But I who have seen the nature of the good that it is beautiful, and of the bad that it is ugly, and the nature of him who does wrong, that it is akin to me, not [only] of the same blood or seed, but that it participates in [the same] intelligence and [the same] portion of the divinity, I can neither be injured by any of them, for no one can fix on me what is ugly, nor can I be angry with my kinsman, nor hate him. For we are made for co-operation, like feet, like hands, like eyelids, like the rows of the upper and lower teeth. To act against one another, then, is contrary to nature; and it is acting against one another to be vexed and to turn away.

2. Whatever this is that I am, it is a little flesh and breath, and the ruling part. Throw away thy books; no longer distract thyself: it is not allowed; but as if thou wast now dying, despise the flesh; it is blood and bones and a network, a contexture of nerves, veins, and arteries. See the breath also, what kind of a thing it is; air, and not always the same, but every moment sent out and again sucked in. The third, then, is the ruling part; consider thus: Thou art an old man; no longer let this be a slave, no longer be pulled by the strings like a puppet to unsocial movements, no longer be either dissatisfied with thy present lot, or shrink from the future.

3. All that is from the gods is full of providence. That which is from fortune is not separated from nature or without an interweaving and involution with the things which are ordered by providence. From thence all things flow; and there is besides necessity, and that which is for the advantage of

1. From *The Thoughts of the Emperor Marcus Aurelius,* translated by George Long (Boston: Little, Brown & Company, 1897), Book II.

the whole universe, of which thou art a part. But that is good for every part of nature which the nature of the whole brings, and what serves to maintain this nature. Now the universe is preserved, as by the changes of the elements so by the changes of things compounded of the elements. Let these principles be enough for thee; let them always be fixed opinions. But cast away the thirst after books, that thou mayest not die murmuring, but cheerfully, truly, and from thy heart thankful to the gods.

4. Remember how long thou hast been putting off these things, and how often thou hast received opportunity from the gods, and yet dost not use it. Thou must now at last perceive of what universe thou art a part, and of what administrator of the universe thy existence is an efflux, and that a limit of time is fixed for thee, which if thou dost not use for clearing away the clouds from thy mind, it will go and thou wilt go, and it will never return.

5. Every moment think steadily as a Roman and a man to do what thou hast in hand with perfect and simple dignity, and feeling of affection, and freedom, and justice, and to give thyself relief from all other thoughts. And thou wilt give thyself relief if thou doest every act of thy life as if it were the last, laying aside all carelessness and passionate aversion from the commands of reason, and all hypocrisy, and self-love, and discontent with the portion which has been given to thee. Thou seest how few the things are, the which if a man lays hold of, he is able to live a life which flows in quiet, and is like the existence of the gods; for the gods on their part will require nothing more from him who observes these things.

6. Do wrong to thyself, do wrong to thyself, my soul; but thou wilt no longer have the opportunity of honoring thyself. Every man's life is sufficient. But thine is nearly finished, though thy soul reverences not itself, but places thy felicity in the souls of others.

7. Do the things external which fall upon thee distract thee? Give thyself time to learn something new and good, and cease to be whirled around. But then thou must also avoid being carried about the other way; for those too are triflers who have wearied themselves in life by their activity, and yet have no object to which to direct every movement, and, in a word, all their thoughts.

8. Through not observing what is in the mind of another a man has seldom been seen to be unhappy; but those who do not observe the movements of their own minds must of necessity be unhappy.

9. This thou must always bear in mind, what is the nature of the whole, and what is my nature, and how this is related to that, and what kind of a part it is of what kind of a whole, and that there is no one who hinders thee from always doing and saying the things which are according to the nature of which thou art a part.

10. Theophrastus, in his comparison of bad acts—such a comparison as one would make in accordance with the common notions of mankind—says, like a true philosopher, that the offences which are committed through desire are more blamable than those which are committed through anger. For he

who is excited by anger seems to turn away from reason with a certain pain and unconscious contraction; but he who offends through desire, being overpowered by pleasure, seems to be in a manner more intemperate and more womanish in his offences. Rightly, then, and in a way worthy of philosophy, he said that the offence which is committed with pleasure is more blamable than that which is committed with pain; and on the whole the one is more like a person who has been first wronged and through pain is compelled to be angry; but the other is moved by his own impulse to do wrong, being carried towards doing something by desire.

11. Since it is possible that thou mayest depart from life this very moment, regulate every act and thought accordingly. But to go away from among men, if there are gods, is not a thing to be afraid of, for the gods will not involve thee in evil; but if indeed they do not exist, or if they have no concern about human affairs, what is it to me to live in a universe devoid of gods or devoid of providence? But in truth they do exist, and they do care for human things, and they have put all the means in man's power to enable him not to fall into real evils. And as to the rest, if there was anything evil, they would have provided for this also, that it should be altogether in a man's power not to fall into it. Now that which does not make a man worse, how can it make a man's life worse? But neither through ignorance, nor having the knowledge but not the power to guard against or correct these things, is it possible that the nature of the universe has overlooked them; nor is it possible that it has made so great a mistake, either through want of power or want of skill, that good and evil should happen indiscriminately to the good and the bad. But death certainly, and life, honor and dishonor, pain and pleasure,—all these things equally happen to good men and bad, being things which make us neither better nor worse. Therefore they are neither good nor evil.

12. How quickly all things disappear,—in the universe the bodies themselves, but in time the remembrance of them. What is the nature of all sensible things, and particularly those which attract with the bait of pleasure or terrify by pain, or are noised abroad by vapory fame; how worthless, and contemptible, and sordid, and perishable, and dead they are,—all this it is the part of the intellectual faculty to observe. To observe too who these are whose opinions and voices give reputation; what death is, and the fact that, if a man looks at it in itself, and by the abstractive power of reflection resolves into their parts all the things which present themselves to the imagination in it, he will then consider it to be nothing else than an operation of nature; and if any one is afraid of an operation of nature, he is a child. This, however, is not only an operation of nature, but it is also a thing which conduces to the purposes of nature. To observe too how man comes near to the Deity, and by what part of him, and when this part of man is so disposed.

13. Nothing is more wretched than a man who traverses everything in a round, and pries into the things beneath the earth, as the poet says, and seeks by conjecture what is in the minds of his neighbors, without perceiving that

it is sufficient to attend to the daemon within him, and to reverence it sincerely. And reverence of the daemon consists in keeping it pure from passion and thoughtlessness, and dissatisfaction with what comes from gods and men. For the things from the gods merit veneration for their excellence; and the things from men should be dear to us by reason of kinship; and sometimes even, in a manner, they move our pity by reason of men's ignorance of good and bad; this defect being not less than that which deprives us of the power of distinguishing things that are white and black.

14. Though thou shouldest be going to live three thousand years, and as many times ten thousand years, still remember that no man loses any other life than this which he now lives, nor lives any other than this which he now loses. The longest and shortest are thus brought to the same. For the present is the same to all, though that which perishes is not the same; and so that which is lost appears to be a mere moment. For a man cannot lose either the past or the future: for what a man has not, how can any one take this from him? These two things then thou must bear in mind; the one, that all things from eternity are of like forms and come round in a circle, and that it makes no difference whether a man shall see the same things during a hundred years, or two hundred, or an infinite time; and the second, that the longest liver and he who will die soonest lose just the same. For the present is the only thing of which a man can be deprived, if it is true that this is the only thing which he has, and that a man cannot lose a thing if he has it not.

15. Remember that all is opinion. For what was said by the Cynic Monimus is manifest: and manifest too is the use of what was said, if a man receives what may be got out of it as far as it is true.

16. The soul of man does violence to itself, first of all, when it becomes an abscess, and, as it were, a tumor on the universe, so far as it can. For to be vexed at anything which happens is a separation of ourselves from nature, in some part of which the natures of all other things are contained. In the next place, the soul does violence to itself when it turns away from any man, or even moves towards him with the intention of injuring, such as are the souls of those who are angry. In the third place, the soul does violence to itself when it is overpowered by pleasure or by pain. Fourthly, when it plays a part, and does or says anything insincerely and untruly. Fifthly, when it allows any act of its own and any movement to be without an aim, and does anything thoughtlessly and without considering what it is, it being right that even the smallest things be done with reference to an end; and the end of rational animals is to follow the reason and the law of the most ancient city and polity.

17. Of human life the time is a point, and the substance is in a flux, and the perception dull, and the composition of the whole body subject to putrefaction, and the soul a whirl, and fortune hard to divine, and fame a thing devoid of judgment. And, to say all in a word, everything which belongs to the body is a stream, and what belongs to the soul is a dream and vapor, and

life is a warfare and a stranger's sojourn, and after-fame is oblivion. What then is that which is able to conduct a man? One thing, and only one, philosophy. But this consists in keeping the daemon within a man free from violence and unharmed, superior to pains and pleasures, doing nothing without a purpose, nor yet falsely and with hypocrisy, not feeling the need of another man's doing or not doing anything; and besides, accepting all that happens, and all that is allotted, as coming from thence, wherever it is, from whence he himself came; and, finally, waiting for death with a cheerful mind, as being nothing else than a dissolution of the elements of which every living being is compounded. But if there is no harm to the elements themselves in each continually changing into another, why should a man have any apprehension about the change and dissolution of all the elements? For it is according to nature, and nothing is evil which is according to nature.

THE ENJOYMENT OF LIVING[1]

MICHEL EYQUEM DE MONTAIGNE

I AM NOT excessively fond of salads or fruit, with the exception of melons. My father hated every kind of sauce; I like them all. Eating too much makes me uncomfortable; but in respect of its properties I am not yet very certain that any kind of food disagrees with me. Nor have I noticed that I am affected by full or new moons, by autumn or spring.

We are subject to fickle and inexplicable changes. For example, radishes, which I first found to agree with me, afterwards disagreed, and now they agree again. In several things I have found my stomach and palate to vary in the same way: I have changed more than once from white wine to claret, and back again from claret to white wine.

I have a dainty tooth for fish, and the meatless days are my meat-days; my fasts are my feasts. Besides, I believe that it is, as some people say, more easily digested than meat. As it goes against my conscience to eat meat on fish-days, so my taste rebels against mixing meat and fish; the difference seems to me too wide.

From my youth up I have occasionally skipped a meal; either to sharpen my appetite for the next day (for, as Epicurus used to fast and make lean meals in order to accustom his greed to dispense with plenty. I do so, on the contrary, in order to train my greed to take better advantage of plenty and to enjoy it more cheerfully); or I used to fast to keep my strength for the performance of some mental or bodily action; for both my body and mind are made cruelly sluggish by repletion. (And especially do I hate the foolish

1. From *The Essays of Montaigne,* translated by E. J. Trechmann (London: Oxford University Press, 1927), II, 584–601. Reprinted by permission of the publishers.

idea of coupling so healthy and active a goddess with that little pot-bellied, belching god, all swelled up with the fumes of his liquor.) Or again, to cure my ailing digestion; or for want of congenial company; for with that same Epicurus I say that we should not so much look to what we eat as to whom we eat with. And I applaud Chilo, who would not promise to accept Periander's invitation to a feast until he was informed who were the other guests.

To me no dressing is so acceptable, and no sauce so appetising, as that derived from good company.

I think it is more wholesome to eat more at leisure, and less, and to eat oftener. But I would give hunger and appetite their due; I should take no pleasure in dragging through three or four wretched repasts a day, restricted by doctors' orders. Who will assure me that I can recover at supper-time the good appetite I had this morning? Let us old men especially take the first opportunity that comes our way. Let us leave the making of dietaries to doctors and almanac-makers.

The best fruit of my health is sensual pleasure; let us seize the first that is present and known. I avoid consistency in these laws of fasting. He who wishes to benefit by a habit, let him avoid continuing it. We become hardened, our powers are dulled by it; six months after your stomach will be so inured to it, that all the advantage you have gained will be to have lost the freedom of doing otherwise except to your prejudice.

I do not cover my legs and thighs more in winter than in summer: simple silk hose. For the relief of my colds I gave way to the habit of keeping my head warmer, and my belly on account of the colic. But in a few days my ailments became accustomed to them and scorned my ordinary precautions: from a cap I advanced to a kerchief, and from a bonnet to a lined hat. The wadding of my doublet is now only ornamental. All that would be of no avail unless I added a hare's skin or a vulture's plumage, with a skull-cap for the head. Continue this gradual progress and you will go a long way. I shall take care not to do so, and would gladly go back to where I began, if I dared.

"Have you developed a new ailment? Is the remedy no longer of any avail? You have grown accustomed to it? Then try another." In this way they ruin their health who allow themselves to be fettered by enforced rules, and superstitiously adhere to them; they need more and more, and after that more again. There is no end.

To suit our occupations, and for pleasure, it is much more convenient to lose one's dinner, as the ancients did, and defer making good cheer till the time of retirement and rest, instead of cutting up the day: that is what I used to do. For health's sake, on the other hand, I have since found by experience that it is better to dine, and that I digest better when awake.

I am not very subject to thirst, whether I am well or ill; in the latter case I very often have a dry mouth, but without thirst, and as a rule I only drink from the desire which comes with eating, and when the meal is well advanced. I drink pretty well for a man of ordinary build; in summer, and with an appetizing repast, I not only exceed the limits of Augustus, who drank only three times and no oftener, but, in order not to violate Democritus' rule, which forbade stopping at four as an unlucky number, I slide on, if need be, to the fifth: about three half-pints. For little glasses are my favourites, and I like to drain them, a thing which others avoid as unbecoming.

As a rule I dilute my wine with half, sometimes a third part of water. And when at home, following an old custom which my father's doctor recommended to him and himself followed, the wine I need is mixed in the buttery, two or three hours before it is served.

It is said that Cranaus, King of the Athenians, first introduced the custom of mixing wine with water; whether beneficially or not has been a matter for debate. I think it more seemly and more wholesome for children not to take wine before they are sixteen or eighteen years of age.

The best mode of life is that which is most usual and common; I think all singularity should be avoided. And I should hate to see a German putting water into his wine as I should to see a Frenchman drinking his pure. General use lays down the law in such things.

I fear a confined atmosphere, and have a mortal dread of smoke (the first repairs I set about in my house were those of the chimneys and the privies which are commonly defective in old buildings, and not to be tolerated); and among the discomforts of war I include the thick clouds of dust in which we are buried in the hot weather for a whole day's march.

My breathing is free and easy, and my colds generally pass off without a cough, and without injury to the lungs.

The rigour of summer is more hostile to me than that of winter; for, besides the discomfort caused by the heat, which is less easily to be remedied than that of cold, and the force of the sunbeams that strike upon my head, my eyes are afflicted by any dazzling light. I cannot even now sit down to dinner opposite a brightly burning fire.

To counteract the whiteness of the paper, when I used to read more than I do now, I laid a piece of glass upon my book, and felt great relief from it. To this moment I am ignorant of the use of spectacles, and can see as far as I ever did, and as any other person. As the day declines my eyes certainly begin to feel a little dim and weak when reading, an exercise that has always tried them, but especially at night-time.

That is a step backwards, but very hardly perceptible. I shall be retiring another step, from the second to the third, from the third to the fourth, so softly that I must needs become really blind before I feel the age and decay of my sight. So cunningly do the Fates unwind our life's thread!

And so I doubt whether my hearing is hesitating on its way to hardness, and you will see that, before I have half lost it, I shall still blame the voices of those who are speaking to me. We must, indeed, put great pressure on the soul to make it feel how it ebbs away.

My step is quick and firm; and I know not which of the two, my mind or my body, I have had most difficulty in arresting at the same point. The preacher who can hold my attention during a whole sermon is very much my friend. On solemn occasions, when the faces of all are so rigid, and when I have seen ladies keep even their eyes so steady, I could never succeed in keeping some part or other of me from ever wandering; though I may be seated, I am anything but settled.

As the house-slave of Chrysippus the philosopher said of her master that he was only drunk in his legs (for he had the habit of moving them about, in whatever position he was in; and she said it when the others were excited by wine and he felt no effects from it), it might have been said of me too that from my childhood I had madness in my feet, or quicksilver, so restless and fidgety are they, wherever I place them.

It is unmannerly, besides being prejudicial to health and even to one's pleasure, to eat greedily as I do. I often bite my tongue in my haste, and sometimes my fingers. Diogenes, meeting a boy who was eating in that way, gave his tutor a box on the ear. There were people at Rome who taught others to masticate, as well as to walk,[2] gracefully. This habit leaves me no time for talking, which gives so agreeable a relish to the dinner-table, provided that the conversation be in keeping, agreeable, and brief.

There is jealousy and envy between our pleasures; they clash and counteract one another. Alcibiades, a man who understood the art of entertainment, banished even music from his tables, lest it should disturb the pleasure of conversation, for the reason that Plato ascribes to him, "that it is the custom of vulgar men to call singers and instrumentalists to their feasts, for want of good conversation and agreeable entertainment, with which intelligent men know how to regale each other."

Varro makes the following requirements for a banquet:

"A company of persons of handsome presence and pleasing conversation, who must be neither dumb nor loquacious; cleanliness and daintiness in the food and in the chamber; and fine weather." It needs no little skill to provide good entertainment, and it is attended with no little pleasure. Neither great generals nor great philosophers have disdained the knowledge and practice of good eating. My imagination has given three repasts to my memory's keeping, which chanced to be particularly pleasant to me, at different times of my greater prime. For each of the guests brings the principal charm with him, according to the good temper of body and mind in which he happens to be at the time. My present condition excludes me from those pleasures.

I who am but of the earth earthy, dislike that inhuman sapience which would have us despise and hate the care of the body. I think it equally wrong to be out of love with natural pleasures and to be too much in love with them.

---

2. *A mascher comme à marcher*. Montaigne cannot keep away from his *jeux de mots*.

Xerxes was a coxcomb who, lapped in all human delights, offered a prize to the man who should invent others; but not much less of a coxcomb is a man who cuts himself off from those that Nature has invented for him. We must neither pursue nor flee them; we must accept them. I accept them a little more generously and graciously, and allow myself more readily to follow the bent of Nature.

We have no need to exaggerate their emptiness; it makes itself sufficiently felt and manifest, thanks to our morbid, kill-joy mind, which disgusts us with them as well as with itself. It treats both itself and all that it takes in, now well, now ill, according to its insatiable, erratic and versatile nature.

> Unless the vessel you would use be sweet,
> 'Twill sour whatever you may pour therein. (HORACE.)

I who boast of embracing so eagerly and particularly all amenities of life, find in them, when I look at them thus closely, little more than wind. But what would you have? We are all wind throughout. And the wind too, more wisely than we, loves to bluster and shift about, and is content with its own functions, with no desire for stability and solidity, which are none of its properties.

The unmixed pleasures of the imagination, as well as its unmixed pains, are, as some say, greater than all others, as hinted at by Critolaus and his scales.[3] It is not to be wondered at, since she composes them at her own sweet will, and cuts them out of the whole cloth. Of this I see every day notable and perhaps desirable examples. But I, who am of a mixed and coarse grain, cannot so fully bite at this single and so simple object presented by the imagination, but that I let myself go, in all my grossness, after the present pleasures prescribed by human and universal laws, intellectually perceptible and perceptibly intellectual.

The Cyronaic philosophers hold that, like bodily pains, so also bodily pleasures are the more powerful, as being both twofold[4] and more rational.

There are some who with savage stupidity, as Aristotle says, express disgust of pleasures; I know some who do so from ambition. Why do they not also forswear breathing? Why do they not live on their own breath, and refuse the light, because it shines gratis, and costs them neither invention nor strength? Let them try to find sustenance in Mars or Pallas or Mercury, and see what happens, instead of Venus, Ceres, and Bacchus. Are not those the sort of people who will try to square the circle when perched on their wives?

I hate to be told that my spirit should be in the clouds whilst my body

3. "Supposing all the goods of the mind to be put into one scale, and the goods of the body into the other, Critolaus thought the goods of the mind would outweigh the others so far, that they would require the whole earth and sea to equalize the balance."—Cicero, *Tusc. Quaes,* v. 17.

4. i.e., both physical and mental.

is at table. I would have the spirit not nailed down to it, nor sprawling upon it, but attending to it; it should sit at it, and not lie upon it.

Aristippus stood up for the body alone, as if we had no soul; Zeno embraced only the soul, as if we had no body. Both of them mistakenly. They say that Pythagoras followed a philosophy that was all contemplation, Socrates one that was all conduct and action; Plato found the adjustment of it between the two. But they say that to make up a tale. And the true adjustment is found in Socrates, and Plato is much more Socratic than Pythagorean; and it becomes him better.

When I dance, I dance; when I sleep, I sleep. Aye, and when I take a solitary stroll in a beautiful garden, if some part of the time my thoughts dwell on outside events, for some other part I recall them to my walk, to the garden, to the sweetness of the solitude and to myself.

Nature has, with motherly care, observed this rule, that the actions she has laid upon us for our need should give us pleasure; and she invites us to them, not only through our reason but also through our desire. It is wrong to infringe her rules.

When I see both Caesar and Alexander, in the thick of their great labours, so fully enjoying natural, and therefore necessary and reasonable pleasures, I do not call it a relaxing of their minds; I call it a stiffening of their minds to subordinate, by strength of spirit, their strenuous occupations and heavy thoughts to the usages of everyday life. Wise they would have been if they could have believed that the latter was their ordinary, the former their extraordinary vocation.

What fools we are! "He has spent his life in idleness," we say; "I have done nothing to-day." What, have you not lived? That is not only the fundamental but the most honourable of your occupations. "If I had been given an opportunity to manage great affairs, I might have shown what I can do." Have you been able to meditate and manage your own life? Then you have performed the greatest work of all. In order to show herself and get to work, Nature has no need of a great destiny; she will show herself equally in all ranks, both behind a curtain and without one.

It is our duty to compose our character, not to compose books, and to win, not battles and provinces, but order and tranquillity for our conduct of life.

Our great and glorious masterpiece is to live to the purpose; all other things, ruling, laying up treasures, building, are at the most but appendicles and adminicles.

I delight in contemplating an army-general, at the foot of a breach he is about to attack, devoting himself entirely and free from cares to his dinner and to his table-talk among his friends. And Brutus, with heaven and earth conspiring against him and Roman liberty, stealing an hour or two from his nightly rounds, to read and epitomize Polybius in all security. It is the part of a little soul, buried under the weight of business, not to be able to get clean away from it, to lay it aside and take it up again:

Now ye brave hearts that have weathered
Many a sorer strait with me,
Chase your cares with wine—to-morrow
We shall plough the mighty sea! (HORACE.)

Whether it be in jest or in earnest that the wine of the Divines[5] and the Sorbonne has become proverbial, like their banquets, I think it reasonable that they should dine more agreeably and cheerfully for having been usefully and seriously employed in the morning teaching their classes. The consciousness of having made good use of the other hours is the right savoury sauce for the table.

Thus did the Sages live. And that inimitable straining after virtue which excites our admiration in both of the Catos, that austere turn of mind that is carried to obtrusiveness, has thus tamely and complacently submitted to the laws of human nature, and of Venus and Bacchus; in accordance with the teachings of their school, which require the perfect sage to be as skilled and experienced in the enjoyment of natural pleasures, as in any other of life's duties. *A wise palate should go with a wise judgement* (Cicero).

The power to relax and assume easy manners is highly honourable, I think, and the most becoming trait in a strong and generous soul. Epaminondas never imagined it to be derogatory to the honour of his glorious victories and the perfect purity of his morals to mingle with the dance of the boys in his town, and to sing, play an instrument, and give his whole mind to these recreations.

And among the many admirable actions of Scipio, the grandfather,[6] a man worthy to be reputed of celestial origin, there is none that shows him in such a charming light as to see him strolling along the beach with Laelius, playing the fool like a careless boy, picking up and selecting shells and playing ducks and drakes; and in bad weather amusing and tickling himself with reproducing in written comedies the commonest and most vulgar actions of the people;[7] and, with his thoughts taken up with that wonderful expedition against Hannibal and Africa, visiting the schools in Sicily and attending lectures in Philosophy, thus arming the teeth of the blind envy of his enemies at Rome.

And there is nothing more remarkable in the life of Socrates than that he

5. *Vin Théologal:* notable good and strong wine; or the best wine, of what kind soever. —Cotgrave.

6. The original reading of the 1588 edition was "of the younger Scipio (when all is considered, the first of the Romans)." Montaigne seems to have forgotten that it was the younger Scipio who was contemporary with Laelius and Terence.

7. Montaigne was quite convinced that Scipio and Laelius wrote the comedies of Terence; see Book I, ch. 4. The 1588 edition had this passage, afterwards deleted. "I am exceedingly vexed that the lives of those two great men, Epaminondas and the younger Scipio, by common consent of the world, the one the first of the Greeks, the other the first of the Romans, the finest pair of lives that Plutarch wrote, should have been among the first to be lost."

found time in his old age to learn to dance and play on instruments, and thought it was time well spent.

This same man was once seen standing for a whole day and night in a trance, in the presence of the whole Greek army, his mind caught and carried away by some deep thought. He first, among so many valiant men of the army, ran to the help of Alcibiades, when the latter was overwhelmed by the enemy, covered him with his body and by main force of arms extricated him from the throng. And he first, among all the Athenians, who, like him, were incensed by so shameful a sight, came forward to rescue Theramenes, who was being led to his death by the satellites of the Thirty Tyrants. And, although he was joined by only two other men, all told, only at the instance of Theramenes himself did he desist from this bold undertaking. Although he was run after by a fair lady with whom he was in love, he was known, in spite of pressing need, to observe strict chastity. At the battle of Delium he was seen to pick up and save Xenophon, who had been thrown by his horse. He was always seen to march to war and tread the ice barefoot, to wear the same gown winter and summer, to surpass all his comrades in enduring hardships, and to eat no more at a banquet than at his ordinary. He was seen for twenty-seven years to endure, with unchanged countenance, hunger, poverty, the perverseness of his children, his wife's clawings, and in the end, calumny, tyranny, imprisonment, fetters, and poison.

But if ever he was challenged to a drinking-bout, he accepted as a matter of civility, and of all the army he was the man who came off best. And he never disdained to play at knuckle-bones with the boys or to ride with them on a hobby-horse, and he did it all gracefully; for all actions, says Philosophy, are equally becoming and honourable in a sage. We have material enough, and we should never weary of presenting the picture of this great man as a pattern and ideal of perfection in all things.

There are very few examples of a pure and perfect life, and our education is all wrong when every day we are shown such crazy and defective models, scarce to be commended for any quality, which rather pull us backward; corrupters rather than correctors.

People generally go wrong: it is much easier to go along the side-path, where the boundary serves as a check and guide, than by the broad and open middle way to be guided by art rather than by Nature; but also much less noble and less commendable.

Greatness of soul consists not so much in soaring high and in pressing forward, as in knowing how to adapt and limit oneself. It regards as great all that is sufficient, and shows its distinction in choosing the mean things rather than the eminent.

There is nothing so noble and so right as to play the man well and fitly, nor anything so difficult to learn as how to live this life well and according to Nature; and the most inhuman of our diseases is to despise our being.

If you would send your soul abroad, do so by all means, if you can, when your body is in a bad way, in order to escape the contagion. At other times, however, let her be kind and helpful to the body, and, with wifely sympathy, not disdain to share his natural pleasures; bringing moderation to them, if she be the wiser of the two, for fear lest, through want of discretion, they be confounded with pain.

Intemperance is the bane of sensual pleasure, and temperance is not its scourge but its seasoning. Eudoxus, for whom pleasure was the sovereign good, and his fellow philosophers, who set so high a value upon it, savoured it in all its charm and sweetness, by reason of their temperance, which they practised in an uncommon and exemplary degree.

I bid my soul to look upon pleasure and pain with a sight equally well-balanced—*for the dilation of the soul in joy is as blameworthy as its contraction in sorrow* (Cicero)—and equally firm; but to regard the one gaily, the other severely, and, as far as in her lies, to be as anxious to extinguish the one as to extend the other.

To take a sane view of good naturally means to take a sane view of evil. And pain has something unavoidable in its gentle beginnings, as pleasure has something to be avoided in its excessive end. Plato couples them together and holds that it is equally the duty of courage to fight against pain and against the immoderate charms and blandishments of pleasure. They are two springs at which all who draw, whence, when and how much they need, whether they be city, man or beast, are very fortunate. The first must be taken in the way of physic and when needed, but more sparingly; the other for thirst, but not to intoxication.

Pain, pleasure, love, hatred, are the first things a child feels; and if they conform to Reason, when she comes, that is Virtue.

I have a vocabulary all my own. I "pass the time" when it is wet and disagreeable.[8] When it is fine I do not wish to pass it; I ruminate it and hold on to it. We should hasten over the bad, and settle upon the good. Those ordinary phrases "pastime" and "pass the time" reflect the habit of those wiseacres who think they cannot make a better use of their life than to let it slide and to escape from it, to while it away, to dodge it, and as far as in them lies to ignore it and run away from it, as if it were an irksome and contemptible thing.

But I know it to be otherwise, and find it agreeable and worthy to be prized, yea even in its last stage, in which I now enjoy it. Nature has given it into our hands, trimmed with so many and such happy surroundings, that we have only ourselves to blame if we feel it a burden, and if we waste it unprofitably. *The life of the fool is joyless, agitated, and wholly given to the future* (Seneca).

8. *Je passe le temps quand il est mauvais, &c.* The word *temps* means both "time" and "weather."

And yet I am resigned to lose it without regret; but as a thing that is by its nature losable, not as if it were a troublesome burden.

Not to hate the idea of death is properly becoming only in those who enjoy life.

It needs good management to enjoy life. I enjoy it doubly as much as others, for the measure of enjoyment depends upon the more or less attention we give to it. Especially now that I feel mine to be so brief in time I try to increase it in weight; I try to arrest the speed of its flight by speedily laying hold of it, and, by the zest of my enjoyment to make up for its hasty ebbing. The shorter my possession of life the fuller and deeper must I live it.

Others feel the sweetness of contentment and well-being; I feel it as well as they, but not in letting it pass by and slip away. Rather should we study, relish and ruminate it, in order to give adequate thanks to him who bestows it upon us.

They enjoy other pleasures, as they do that of sleep, unconsciously. I used to enjoy being disturbed in my sleep in order to get a glimpse of it, and not allow it so senselessly to slip away.

I meditate over a thing that gives me pleasure; I do not skim over it, I go to the bottom of it and force my reason, now grown peevish and hard to please, to welcome it. Am I in some situation where I feel at rest? Is there some sensual pleasure that tickles me? I do not allow my senses to cheat me of it. I make my soul to share in it, not in order to be drawn into it, but to find it acceptable; not to lose, but to find herself in it. And I induce her, for her part, to mirror herself in this fortunate state, to weigh and appreciate its happiness, and to magnify it. She will estimate how far she owes it to God that she is at peace with her conscience, free from other inner passions, that her body is in its natural healthy state, fitly and properly enjoying the exercise of the agreeable and soothing functions with which he of his grace is pleased to compensate her for the afflictions with which his justice chastises us in its turn; how much it means to her to be so situated that, whithersoever she casts her eyes, the heavens around her are serene; that no desire, no fear or doubt disturbs her atmosphere; that there is no difficulty, past, present, or future, over which her imagination may not roam without harm.

Much light is thrown upon this consideration by comparison of my state with that of others. Thus, I can picture to myself in a thousand aspects those who are carried away and tossed about by Fortune or their own errors, as well as those who, more like me, so languidly and indifferently accept their good fortune. Those are the people who really "pass their time"; they overpass the present and what they possess, to be slaves to hope, and for the shadows and vain images that their imagination dangles before their eyes,

> Like phantoms that, folk say, flit after death,
> Or visions that befool the slumbering sense; (VIRGIL.)

which speed and prolong their flight the more they are pursued. The fruit and aim of their pursuit is to pursue; as Alexander said the end of his labour was to labour;

Thinking naught is done, if aught is left to do. (LUCAN.)

For my part then, I love life and cultivate it such as it has pleased God to grant it to me. I do not go about wishing that it might be relieved of the necessity of eating and drinking, and I should think it no less pardonable a sin to wish that necessity to be doubled—*the wise man eagerly desires the treasures of Nature* (Seneca);—or that our life could be sustained by merely putting into our mouth a little of that drug with which Epimenides took away his appetite, and kept himself alive; or that we could obtusely beget children by the fingers or heels (nay, in reverence be it spoken, that we could rather beget them voluptuously by the fingers and heels); or that the body should be without desire and incapable of being titillated.

Those would be ungrateful and wicked complaints. I accept heartily and gratefully what Nature has done for me; and I am proud and well pleased with myself that I do so. For we wrong that great and all-powerful giver when we reject, destroy, and disfigure her gift. Being all good, she has made all things good. *All things that are according to Nature are worthy of esteem* (Cicero).

Of philosophical opinions I more readily embrace those which are most solid, that is to say, most human and most our own; my words, in keeping with my actions, are mean and humble.

Philosophy appears to me very childish when she rides the high horse, and preaches to us that it is a barbarous alliance to marry the divine with the earthly, the reasonable with the unreasonable, the severe with the indulgent, the honest with the dishonest, that sensual pleasure is a brutish thing, unworthy to be enjoyed by the sage; that the only pleasure to be derived from the enjoyment of a fair young bride is the conscientious pleasure of performing an orderly action, like putting on one's boots for a business ride. May her followers have no more right or nerve or sap in ravishing their wives than in learning her lessons!

That is not what Socrates, her master and ours, says. He prizes, as he should, the pleasures of the body; but he prefers those of the mind, as being more powerful, more enduring, more easy to come by, more varied and dignified. The latter by no means go alone, according to him (he is not so fanciful), but only come first. With him temperance is the moderator, not the enemy of pleasures.

Nature is a gentle guide, but not more gentle than she is wise and just. *We must penetrate into the nature of things, and see exactly what it demands* (Cicero). I try to follow her footsteps in all things; we have confounded the traces by artificial means. And the sovereign good of the

Academics and the Peripatetics, which is to "live according to her," becomes for that reason difficult to limit and explain; as does also that of the Stoics, which, related to the other, is to "acquiesce in Nature."

Is it not a mistake to regard some actions as less worthy because they are necessary? Yet they will not knock it out of my head that the marriage of pleasure with necessity (with which, as an ancient says,[9] the Gods always conspire) is a very proper marriage. Why do we dismember by divorce a fabric woven of so close and brotherly a correspondence? Rather, let us knit it again by mutual offices. Let the mind rouse and quicken the dulness of the body, and the body check and steady the levity of the mind. *He who exalts the nature of the soul as the sovereign good, and condemns the nature of the flesh as an evil thing, truly both carnally desires the soul and carnally flees the flesh; since he is inspired by human vanity, not by divine truth* (Saint Augustine).

In this gift of God there is no part that is unworthy of our attention; we must account for it even to the last hair. And it is not a merely formal charge to man to direct man according to his nature; it is positive, simple, and of prime importance, and the Creator has given it to us seriously and sternly.

Authority alone has any weight with an ordinary intellect, and weighs still more heavily in a foreign tongue. Let us here renew the attack. *Who will not say that it is the nature of the fool to do lazily and reluctantly what is to be done; to urge the body one way and the soul another; to be divided between wholly different movements* (Seneca).

Come now, to prove it, let such a man some day tell you the diversions and fancies he fills his head with, for which he diverts his thoughts from a good meal, and regrets the hour he spends over his eating. You will find that there is nothing so insipid in all the dishes on your table as the fine things with which he is entertaining his mind (for the most part it would be better fairly to go to sleep than to keep awake for the thoughts of our waking hours); and you will find that all his talk and all his aspirations are not worth your savoury stew.

Though they were the raptures of Archimedes himself, what of it? I am not here concerned with that riff-raff of men that we are, or those aimless desires and thoughts that divert us from more serious things, nor am I confounding them with those venerable souls, lifted by pious and religious ardour to a constant and conscientious meditation on divine things, who, anticipating, by dint of a lively and passionate hope, the enjoyment of the heavenly food, the final aim and last step of Christian desires, the only constant and incorruptible pleasure, scorn to give their minds to our beggarly, fleeting, doubtful goods, and readily leave it to the body to provide and enjoy sensual and temporal fodder. It is a study for the privileged.

9. Simonides.

Between ourselves, I have ever observed that supercelestial ideas and subterrestrial conduct are singularly suited to each other.

Aesop, that great man, saw his master making water as he walked. "What!" he said, "must we void ourselves as we run?" Use our time as best we may, yet a great part of it will still be idly and ill spent. Our mind has probably not enough other time to spare in which to do its business, unless it dissociates itself from the body for that brief space that it requires for its needs.

People try to get outside of themselves, and escape from the man. That is foolishness: instead of transforming themselves into angels, they transform themselves into beasts. Instead of raising they degrade themselves.

Those transcendental fancies overawe me, like high and inaccessible places; and nothing is for me so hard to swallow in the life of Socrates, as his trances and his possessions by his dæmon; and nothing in Plato is so human as that for which they say he was called Divine.

And of our sciences those appear to me most terrestrial and low which have soared to the greatest heights. And I can see nothing more contemptible and mortal in the life of Alexander than his fancies about his immortalization. Philotas taunted him wittily in his rejoinder. He had congratulated him by letter on his elevation to the Gods by an oracle of Jupiter Ammon. "For your sake I am glad; but those people have reason to be pitied who will have to live with and obey a man who exceeds and is not satisfied with human proportions."

You rule the world because that you
Confess the God's supremacy. (HORACE.)

I quite agree with the pretty inscription with which the Athenians welcomed Pompey on his entering their city:

So far you may be deemed a God
As you confess yourself a man. (PLUTARCH.)

A man who can rightly and truly enjoy his existence is absolutely and almost divinely perfect.

We seek other conditions because we know not how to enjoy our own; and go outside of ourselves for want of knowing what it is like inside of us. So it is no use raising ourselves on stilts, for even on stilts we have to walk on our own legs. And sitting on the loftiest throne in the world we are still sitting on our behind.

The most beautiful lives, in my opinion, are those which conform to the model of common humanity, with order, but with nothing wonderful or extravagant.

Now old age needs to be treated a little more tenderly. Let us commend it to that tutelary God [10] of health and wisdom, but a gay and sociable wisdom.

10. Apollo.

Give me but health, Latona's son,
To enjoy what I possess;
Give me but this, I ask no more,
This and a mind entire—
An old age not unhonoured, nor
Unsolaced by the lyre! (HORACE.)

IS HAPPINESS STILL POSSIBLE?[1]

BERTRAND RUSSELL

HAPPINESS is of two sorts, though, of course, there are intermediate degrees. The two sorts I mean might be distinguished as plain and fancy, or animal and spiritual, or of the heart and of the head. The designation to be chosen among these alternatives depends, of course, upon the thesis to be proved. I am at the moment not concerned to prove any thesis, but merely to describe. Perhaps the simplest way to describe the difference between the two sorts of happiness is to say that one sort is open to any human being, and the other only to those who can read and write. When I was a boy I knew a man bursting with happiness whose business was digging wells. He was of enormous height and of incredible muscles; he could neither read nor write, and when in the year 1885 he got a vote for Parliament, he learned for the first time that such an institution existed. His happiness did not depend upon intellectual sources; it was not based upon belief in natural law, or the perfectability of the species, or the public ownership of public utilities, or the ultimate triumph of the Seventh Day Adventists, or any of the other creeds which intellectuals consider necessary to their enjoyment of life. It was based upon physical vigor, a sufficiency of work, and the overcoming of not insuperable obstacles in the shape of rock. The happiness of my gardener is of the same species; he wages a perennial war against rabbits, of which he speaks exactly as Scotland Yard speaks of Bolsheviks; he considers them dark, designing and ferocious, and is of opinion that they can only be met by means of a cunning equal to their own. Like the heroes of Valhalla who spent every day hunting a certain wild boar, which they killed every evening but which miraculously came to life again in the morning, my gardener can slay his enemy one day without any fear that the enemy will have disappeared the next day. Although well over seventy, he works all day and bicycles sixteen hilly miles to and from his work, but the fount of joy is inexhaustible, and it is "they rabbits" that supply it.

But, you will say, these simple delights are not open to superior people like ourselves. What joy can we experience in waging war on such puny creatures as rabbits? The argument, to my mind, is a poor one. A rabbit is very much

1. From *The Conquest of Happiness* by Bertrand Russell (Chapter 10). Published by Liveright Publishing Corp., N.Y. Copyright: 1930—Horace Liveright, Inc.

larger than a yellow fever bacillus, and yet a superior person can find happiness in making war upon the latter. Pleasures exactly similar to those of my gardener so far as their emotional content is concerned are open to the most highly educated people. The difference made by education is only in regard to the activities by which these pleasures are to be obtained. Pleasures of achievement demand difficulties such that beforehand success seems doubtful although in the end it is usually achieved. This is perhaps the chief reason why a modest estimate of one's own powers is a source of happiness. The man who underestimates himself is perpetually being surprised by success, whereas the man who overestimates himself is just as often surprised by failure. The former kind of surprise is pleasant, the latter unpleasant. It is therefore wise to be not unduly conceited, though also not too modest to be enterprising.

Of the more highly educated sections of the community, the happiest in the present day are the men of science. Many of the most eminent of them are emotionally simple, and obtain from their work a satisfaction so profound that they can derive pleasure from eating, and even marrying. Artists and literary men consider it *de rigueur* to be unhappy in their marriages, but men of science quite frequently remain capable of old-fashioned domestic bliss. The reason of this is that the higher parts of their intelligence are wholly absorbed by their work and are not allowed to intrude into regions where they have no functions to perform. In their work they are happy because in the modern world science is progressive and powerful, and because its importance is not doubted either by themselves or by laymen. They have therefore no necessity for complex emotions, since the simpler emotions meet with no obstacles. Complexity in emotions is like foam in a river. It is produced by obstacles which break the smoothly flowing current. But so long as the vital energies are unimpeded, they produce no ripple on the surface, and their strength is not evident to the unobservant.

All the conditions of happiness are realized in the life of the man of science. He has an activity which utilizes his abilities to the full, and he achieves results which appear important not only to himself but to the general public, even when it cannot in the smallest degree understand them. In this he is more fortunate than the artist. When the public cannot understand a picture or a poem, they conclude that it is a bad picture or a bad poem. When they cannot understand the theory of relativity they conclude (rightly) that their education has been insufficient. Consequently Einstein is honored while the best painters are (or at least were) left to starve in garrets, and Einstein is happy while the painters are unhappy. Very few men can be genuinely happy in a life involving continual self-assertion against the skepticism of the mass of mankind, unless they can shut themselves up in a coterie and forget the cold outer world. The man of science has no need of a coterie, since he is thought well of by everybody except his colleagues. The artist, on the contrary, is in the painful situation of having to choose between being despised and being despicable. If his powers are of the first order, he must incur one or the other of these misfortunes—the former if he uses his powers, the latter if he does not. This has not been the case always and everywhere. There have been times when even good artists, even when they were young, were thought well of. Julius II, though he might ill-treat Michael Angelo, never supposed him incapable of painting pictures. The modern millionaire, though he may shower wealth upon elderly artists after they have lost their powers, never imagines that their work is as important as his own. Perhaps these circumstances have something to do with the fact that artists are on the average less happy than men of science.

In India, China and Japan, external circumstances of a political sort interfere with the happiness of the young intelligentsia, but there is no such internal obstacle as exists in the West. There are activities which appear important to the young, and, in so far as these activities succeed, the young are happy. They feel that they have an important part to play in the national life, and aims to pursue which, though difficult, are not impossible to realize. Cynicism such as one finds very frequently among the most highly educated young men and women of the West results from the combination of comfort with powerlessness. Powerlessness makes people feel that nothing is worth doing, and comfort makes the painfulness of this feeling just endurable. Throughout the East the university student can hope for more influence upon public opinion than he can have in the modern West, but he has much less opportunity than in the West of securing a substantial income. But, neither powerless nor comfortable, he becomes a reformer or a revolutionary, not a cynic. The happiness of the reformer or revolutionary depends upon the course of public affairs, but probably even while he is being executed he enjoys more real happiness than is possible for the comfortable cynic. I remember a young Chinese visitor to my school who was going home to found a similar school in a reactionary part of China. He expected the result to be that his head would be cut off. Nevertheless he enjoyed a quiet happiness that I could only envy.

I do not wish to suggest, however, that these high-flown kinds of happiness are the only possible ones. They are in fact open only to a minority, since they require a kind of ability and a width of interest which cannot be very common. It is not only eminent scientists who can derive pleasure through work, nor is it only leading statesmen who can derive pleasure through advocacy of a cause. The pleasure of work is open to any one who can develop some specialized skill, provided that he can get satisfaction from the exercise of his skill without demanding universal applause. I knew a man who had lost the use of both legs in early youth, but he had remained serenely happy throughout a long life; he had achieved this by writing a work in five volumes on rose blight, on which I always understood he was the leading expert. I have not had the pleasure of knowing any large number of conchologists, but from those who have I have always understood that the study of shells brings contentment to those who engage in it. I knew a man once who was the best compositor in the world, and was sought out by all those who devoted themselves to inventing artistic types; he derived joy, not so much from the very genuine respect in which he was held by persons whose respect was not lightly bestowed as from the actual delight in the exercise of his craft, a delight not wholly unlike that which good dancers derive from dancing. I have known also compositors who were experts in setting up mathematical type, or script, or cuneiform, or anything else that was out of the way and difficult. I did not discover whether these men's private lives were happy, but in their working hours their constructive instincts were fully gratified.

It is customary to say that in our machine age there is less room than formerly for the craftsman's joy in skilled work. I am not at all sure that this is true: the skilled workman nowadays works, it is true, at quite different things from those that occupied the attention of the medieval guilds, but he is still very important and quite essential in the machine economy. There are those who make scientific instruments and delicate machines, there are designers, there are aeroplane mechanics, chauffeurs, and hosts of others who have a trade in which skill can be developed to almost any extent. The agricultural laborer and the peasant in comparatively primitive communities are not, so far as I have been able to observe, nearly as happy as a chauffeur or an engine driver. It is true that the work of the peasant who cultivates his own land is varied; he plows, he sows, he reaps. But he is at the mercy of the elements, and is very conscious of his dependence, whereas the man who works a modern mechanism is conscious of power, and acquires the sense that man is the master, not the slave, of natural forces. It is true, of course, that work is very uninteresting to the large body of mere machine minders who repeat some mechanical operation over and over again with the minimum of variation, but the more uninteresting the work becomes, the more possible it is to get it performed by a machine. The ultimate goal of machine production—from which, it is true, we are as yet far removed—is a system in which everything uninteresting is done by machines, and human beings are reserved for the work involving variety and initiative. In such a world the work will be less boring and less depressing than it has been at any time since the introduction of agriculture. In taking to agriculture mankind decided that it would submit to monotony and tedium in order to diminish the risk of starvation. When men obtained their food by hunting, work was a joy, as one can see from the fact that the rich still pursue these ancestral occupations for amusement. But with  the introduction of agriculture mankind entered upon a long period of meanness, misery, and madness, from which they are only now being freed by the beneficent operation of the machine. It is all very well for sentimentalists to speak of contact with the soil and the ripe wisdom of Hardy's philosophic peasants, but the one desire of every young man in the countryside is to find work in towns where he can escape from the slavery of wind and weather and the solitude of dark winter evenings into the reliable and human atmosphere of the factory and the cinema. Companionship and cooperation are essential elements in the happiness of the average man, and these are to be obtained in industry far more fully than in agriculture.

Belief in a cause is a source of happiness to large numbers of people. I am not thinking only of revolutionaries, socialists, nationalists in oppressed countries, and such; I am thinking also of many humbler kinds of belief. The men I have known who believed that the English were the lost ten tribes were almost invariably happy, while as for those who believed that the English were only the tribes of Ephraim and Manasseh, their bliss knew no bounds. I am not suggesting that the reader should adopt this creed, since I cannot advocate any happiness based upon what seem to me to be false beliefs. For the same reason I cannot urge the reader to believe that men should live exclusively upon nuts, although, so far as my observation goes, this belief invariably ensures perfect happiness. But it is easy to find some cause which is in no degree fantastic, and those whose interest in any such cause is genuine are provided with an occupation for their leisure hours and a complete antidote to the feeling that life is empty.

Not so very far removed from the devotion to obscure causes is absorption in a hobby. One of the most eminent of living mathematicians divides his time equally between mathematics and stamp-collecting. I imagine that the latter affords consolation at the moments when he can make no progress with the former. The difficulty of proving propositions in the theory of numbers is not the only sorrow that stamp-collecting can cure, nor are stamps the only things that can be collected. Consider what a vast field of ecstasy opens before the imagination when one thinks of old china, snuffboxes, Roman coins, arrowheads, and flint implements. It is true that many of us are too "superior" for these simple pleasures. We have all experienced them in boyhood, but have thought them, for some reason, unworthy of a grown man. This is a complete mistake; any pleasure that does no harm to other people is to be valued. For my part, I collect rivers: I derive pleasure from having gone down the Volga and up the Yangtse, and regret very much having never seen the Amazon or the Orinoco. Simple as these emotions are, I am not ashamed of them. Or consider again the passionate joy of the baseball fan: he turns to his newspaper with avidity, and the radio affords him the keenest thrills. I remember meeting for the first time one of the leading literary men of America, a man whom I had supposed from his books to be filled with melancholy. But it so happened that at that moment the most crucial baseball results were coming through on the radio; he forgot me, literature, and all the other sorrows of our sublunary life, and yelled with joy as his favorites achieved victory. Ever since this incident, I have been able to read his books without feeling depressed by the misfortunes of his characters.

Fads and hobbies, however, are in many cases, perhaps most, not a source of fundamental happiness, but a means of escape from reality, of forgetting for the moment some pain too difficult to be faced. Fundamental happiness depends more than anything else upon what may be called a friendly interest in persons and things.

A friendly interest in persons is a form of affectionateness, but not the form which is grasping and possessive and seeking always an emphatic response. This latter form is very frequently a source of unhappiness. The kind that makes for happiness is the kind that likes to observe people and finds pleasure in their individual traits, that wishes to afford scope for the interests and pleasures of those with whom it is brought into contact without desiring to acquire power over them or to secure their enthusiastic admiration. The person whose attitude towards others is genuinely of this kind will be a source of happiness and a recipient of reciprocal kindness. His relations with others, whether slight or serious, will satisfy both his interests and his affections; he will not be soured by ingratitude, since he will seldom suffer it and will not notice when he does. The same idiosyncrasies which would get on another man's nerves to the point of exasperation will be to him a source of gentle amusement. He will achieve without effort results which another man, after long struggles, will find to be unattainable. Being happy in himself, he will be a pleasant companion, and this in turn will increase his happiness. But all this must be genuine; it must not spring from an idea of self-sacrifice inspired by a sense of duty. A sense of duty is useful in work, but offensive in personal relations. People wish to be liked, not to be endured with patient resignation. To like many people spontaneously and without effort is perhaps the greatest of all sources of personal happiness.

I spoke also a moment ago of what I call a friendly interest in things. This phrase may perhaps seem forced; it may be said that it is impossible to feel friendly to things. Nevertheless there is something analogous to friendliness in the kind of interest that a geologist takes in rocks or an archaeologist in ruins, and this interest ought to be an element in our attitude to individuals or societies. It is possible to have an interest in things which is hostile rather than friendly. A man might collect facts concerning the habitats of spiders because he hated spiders and wished to live where they were few. This kind of interest would not afford the same satisfaction as the geologist derives from his rocks. An interest in impersonal things, though perhaps less valuable as an ingredient in everyday happiness than a friendly attitude towards our fellow creatures, is nevertheless very important. The world is vast and our own powers are limited. If all our happiness is bound up entirely in our personal circumstances it is difficult not to demand of life more than it has to give. And to demand too much is the surest way of getting even less than is possible. The man who can forget his worries by means of a genuine interest in, say, the Council of Trent, or the life history of stars, will find that, when he returns from his excursion into the impersonal world, he has acquired a poise and calm which enable him to deal with his worries in the best way, and he will in the meantime have experienced a genuine even if temporary happiness.

The secret of happiness is this: let your interests be as wide as possible, and let your reactions to the things and persons that interest you be as far as possible friendly rather than hostile.

· RELIGION ·

A FREE MAN'S WORSHIP[1]

BERTRAND RUSSELL

To Dr. Faustus in his study Mephistopheles told the history of the Creation, saying:

"The endless praises of the choirs of angels had begun to grow wearisome; for, after all, did he not deserve their praise? Had he not given them endless joy? Would it not be more amusing to obtain undeserved praise, to be worshipped by beings whom he tortured? He smiled inwardly, and resolved that the great drama should be performed.

"For countless ages the hot nebula whirled aimlessly through space. At length it began to take shape, the central mass threw off planets, the planets cooled, boiling seas and burning mountains heaved and tossed, from black masses of cloud hot sheets of rain deluged the barely solid crust. And now the first germ of life grew in the depths of the ocean, and developed rapidly in the fructifying warmth into vast forest trees, huge ferns springing from the damp mould, sea monsters breeding, fighting, devouring, and passing away. And from the monsters, as the play unfolded itself, Man was born, with the power of thought, the knowledge of good and evil, and the cruel thirst for worship. And Man saw that all is passing in this mad, monstrous world, that all is struggling to snatch, at any cost, a few brief moments of life before Death's inexorable decree. And Man said: 'There is a hidden purpose, could we but fathom it, and the purpose is good; for we must reverence something, and in the visible world there is nothing worthy of reverence.' And Man stood aside from the struggle, resolving that God intended harmony to come out of chaos by human efforts. And when he followed the instincts which God had transmitted to him from his ancestry of beasts of prey, he called it Sin, and asked God to forgive him. But he doubted whether he could be justly forgiven, until he invented a divine Plan by which God's wrath was to have been appeased. And seeing the present was bad, he made it yet worse, that thereby the future might be better. And he gave God thanks for the strength that enabled him to forgo even the joys that were

1. Reprinted from *Mysticism and Logic,* pp. 46–57, by Bertrand Russell, by permission of W. W. Norton & Company, Inc. Copyright 1929 by the publishers.

possible. And God smiled; and when he saw that Man had become perfect in renunciation and worship, he sent another sun through the sky, which crashed into Man's sun; and all returned again to nebula.

"'Yes,' he murmured, 'it was a good play; I will have it performed again.'"

Such, in outline, but even more purposeless, more void of meaning is the world which Science presents for our belief. Amid such a world, if anywhere, our ideals henceforward must find a home. That Man is the product of causes which had no prevision of the end they were achieving; that his origin, his growth, his hopes and fears, his loves and his beliefs, are but the outcome of accidental collocations of atoms; that no fire, no heroism, no intensity of thought and feeling, can preserve an individual life beyond the grave; that all the labours of the ages, all the devotion, all the inspiration, all the noonday brightness of human genius, are destined to extinction in the vast death of the solar system, and that the whole temple of Man's achievement must inevitably be buried beneath the débris of a universe in ruins—all these things, if not quite beyond dispute, are yet so nearly certain, that no philosophy which rejects them can hope to stand. Only within the scaffolding of these truths, only on the firm foundation of unyielding despair, can the soul's habitation henceforth be safely built.

How, in such an alien and inhuman world, can so powerless a creature as Man preserve his aspirations untarnished? A strange mystery it is that Nature, omnipotent but blind, in the revolutions of her secular hurryings through the abysses of space, has brought forth at last a child, subject still to her power, but gifted with sight, with knowledge of good and evil, with the capacity of judging all the works of his unthinking Mother. In spite of Death, the mark and seal of the parental control, Man is yet free, during his brief years, to examine, to criticise, to know, and in imagination to create. To him alone, in the world with which he is acquainted, this freedom belongs; and in this lies his superiority to the resistless forces that control his outward life.

The savage, like ourselves, feels the oppression of his impotence before the powers of Nature; but having in himself nothing that he respects more than Power, he is willing to prostrate himself before his gods, without inquiring whether they are worthy of his worship. Pathetic and very terrible is the long history of cruelty and torture, of degradation and human sacrifices endured in the hope of placating the jealous gods: surely, the trembling believer thinks, when what is most precious has been freely given, their lust for blood must be appeased, and more will not be required. The religion of Moloch—as such creeds may be generically called—is in essence the cringing submission of the slave, who dare not, even in his heart, allow the thought that his master deserves no adulation. Since the independence of ideals is not yet acknowledged, Power may be freely worshipped, and receive an unlimited respect, despite its wanton infliction of pain.

But gradually, as morality grows bolder, the claim of the ideal world begins to be felt; and worship, if it is not to cease, must be given to gods of another kind than those created by the savage. Some, though they feel the demands of the ideal, will still consciously reject them, still urging that naked Power is worthy of worship. Such is the attitude inculcated in God's answer to Job out of the whirlwind: the divine power and knowledge are paraded, but of the divine goodness there is no hint. Such also is the attitude of those who, in our own day, base their morality upon the struggle for survival, maintaining that the survivors are necessarily the fittest. But others, not content with an answer so repugnant to the moral sense, will adopt the position which we have become accustomed to regard as specially religious, maintaining that, in some hidden manner, the world of fact is really harmonious with the world of ideals. Thus Man creates God, all-powerful and all-good, the mystic unity of what is and what should be.

But the world of fact, after all, is not good; and, in submitting our judgment to it, there is an element of slavishness from which our thoughts must be purged. For in all things it is well to exalt the dignity of Man, by freeing him as far as possible from the tyranny of non-human Power. When we have realised that Power is largely bad, that Man, with his knowledge of good and evil, is but a helpless atom in a world which has no such knowledge, the choice is again presented to us: Shall we worship Force, or shall we worship Goodness? Shall our God exist and be evil, or shall he be recognised as the creation of our own conscience?

The answer to this question is very momentous, and affects profoundly our whole morality. The worship of Force, to which Carlyle and Nietzsche and the creed of Militarism have accustomed us, is the result of failure to maintain our own ideals against a hostile universe: it is itself a prostrate submission to evil, a sacrifice of our best to Moloch. If strength indeed is to be respected, let us respect rather the strength of those who refuse that false "recognition of facts" which fails to recognise that facts are often bad. Let us admit that, in the world we know, there are many things that would be better otherwise, and that the ideals to which we do and must adhere are not realised in the realm of matter. Let us preserve our respect for truth, for beauty, for the ideal of perfection which life does not permit us to attain, though none of these things meet with the approval of the unconscious universe. If Power is bad, as it seems to be, let us reject it from our hearts. In this lies Man's true freedom: in determination to worship only the God created by our own love of the good, to respect only the heaven which inspires the insight of our best moments. In action, in desire, we must submit perpetually to the tyranny of outside forces; but in thought, in aspiration, we are free, free from our fellow-men, free from the petty planet on which our bodies impotently crawl, free even, while we live, from the tyranny of death. Let us learn, then, that energy of faith which enables us to live constantly in the vision of the good; and let us descend in action, into the world of fact, with that vision always before us.

When first the opposition of fact and ideal grows fully visible, a spirit of fiery revolt, of fierce hatred of the gods, seems necessary to the assertion of freedom. To defy with Promethean constancy a hostile universe, to keep its evil always in view, always actively hated, to refuse no pain that the malice of Power can invent, appears to be the duty of all who will not bow before the inevitable. But indignation is still a bondage, for it compels our thoughts to be occupied with an evil world; and in the fierceness of desire from which rebellion springs there is a kind of self-assertion which it is necessary for the wise to overcome. Indignation is a submission of our thoughts, but not of our desires; the Stoic freedom in which wisdom consists is found in the submission of our desires, but not of our thoughts. From the submission of our desires springs the virtue of resignation; from the freedom of our thoughts springs the whole world of art and philosophy, and the vision of beauty by which, at last, we half reconquer the reluctant world. But the vision of beauty is possible only to unfettered contemplation, to thoughts not weighted by the load of eager wishes; and thus Freedom comes only to those who no longer ask of life that it shall yield them any of those personal goods that are subject to the mutations of Time.

Although the necessity of renunciation is evidence of the existence of evil, yet Christianity, in preaching it, has shown a wisdom exceeding that of the Promethean philosophy of rebellion. It must be admitted that, of the things we desire, some, though they prove impossible, are yet real goods; others, however, as ardently longed for, do not form part of a fully purified ideal. The belief that what must be renounced is bad, though sometimes false, is far less often false than untamed passion supposes; and the creed of religion, by providing a reason for proving that it is never false, has been the means of purifying our hopes by the discovery of many austere truths.

But there is in resignation a further good element: even real goods, when they are unattainable, ought not to be fretfully desired. To every man comes, sooner or later, the great renunciation. For the young, there is nothing unattainable; a good thing desired with the whole force of a passionate will, and yet impossible, is to them not credible. Yet, by death, by illness, by poverty, or by the voice of duty, we must learn, each one of us, that the world was not made for us, and that, however beautiful may be the things we crave, Fate may nevertheless forbid them. It is the part of courage, when misfortune comes, to bear without repining the ruin of our hopes, to turn away our thoughts from vain regrets. This degree of submission to Power is not only just and right; it is the very gate of wisdom.

But passive renunciation is not the whole of wisdom; for not by renunciation alone can we build a temple for the worship of our own ideals. Haunting foreshadowings of the temple appear in the realm of imagination, in music, in architecture, in the untroubled kingdom of reason, and in the golden sunset magic of lyrics, where beauty shines and glows, remote from the touch of sorrow, remote from the fear of change, remote from the failures and disenchantments of the world of fact. In the contemplation of these things the vision of heaven will shape itself in our hearts, giving at once a touchstone to judge the world about us, and an inspiration by which to fashion to our needs whatever is not incapable of serving as a stone in the sacred temple.

Except for those rare spirits that are born without sin, there is a cavern of darkness to be traversed before that temple can be entered. The gate of the cavern is despair, and its floor is paved with the gravestones of abandoned hopes. There Self must die; there the eagerness, the greed of untamed desire must be slain, for only so can the soul be freed from the empire of Fate. But out of the cavern the Gate of Renunciation leads again to the daylight of wisdom, by whose radiance a new insight, a new joy, a new tenderness, shine forth to gladden the pilgrim's heart.

When, without the bitterness of impotent rebellion, we have learnt both to resign ourselves to the outward rule of Fate and to recognise that the non-human world is unworthy of our worship, it becomes possible at last so to transform and refashion the unconscious universe, so to transmute it in the crucible of the imagination, that a new image of shining gold replaces the old idol of clay. In all the multiform facts of the world—in the visual shapes of trees and mountains and clouds, in the events of the life of Man, even in the very omnipotence of Death—the insight of creative idealism can find the reflection of a beauty which its own thoughts first made. In this way mind asserts its subtle mastery over the thoughtless forces of Nature. The more evil the material with which it deals, the more thwarting to untrained desire, the greater is its achievement in inducing the reluctant rock to yield up its hidden treasures, the prouder its victory in compelling the opposing forces to swell the pageant of its triumph. Of all the arts, Tragedy is the proudest, the most triumphant; for it builds its shining citadel in the very centre of the enemy's country, on the very summit of his highest mountain; from its impregnable watch-towers, his camps and arsenals, his columns and forts, are all revealed; within its walls the free life continues, while the legions of Death and Pain and Despair, and all the servile captains of tyrant Fate, afford the burghers of that dauntless city new spectacles of beauty. Happy those sacred ramparts, thrice happy the dwellers on that all-seeing eminence. Honour to those brave warriors who, through countless ages of warfare, have preserved for us the priceless heritage of liberty, and have kept undefiled by sacrilegious invaders the home of the unsubdued.

But the beauty of Tragedy does but make visible a quality which, in more or less obvious shapes, is present always and everywhere in life. In the spectacle of Death, in the endurance of intolerable pain, and in the irrevocableness of a vanished past, there is a sacredness, an overpowering awe, a feeling of the vastness, the depth, the inexhaustible mystery of existence, in which, as by some strange marriage of pain, the sufferer is bound to the world by bonds of sorrow. In these moments of insight, we lose all eagerness of temporary desire, all struggling and striving for petty ends, all care for the little trivial things, that, to a superficial view, make up the common life of day by day; we see, surrounding the narrow raft illumined by the flickering light of human comradeship, the dark ocean on whose rolling waves we toss for a brief hour; from the great night without, a chill blast breaks in upon our refuge; all the loneliness of humanity amid hostile forces is concentrated upon the individual soul, which must struggle alone, with what of courage it can command, against the whole weight of a universe that cares nothing for its hopes and fears. Victory, in this struggle with the powers of darkness, is the true baptism into the glorious company of heroes, the true initiation into the overmastering beauty of human existence. From that awful encounter of the soul with the outer world, renunciation, wisdom, and charity are born; and with their birth a new life begins. To take into the inmost shrine of the soul the irresistible forces whose puppets we seem to be—Death and change, the irrevocableness of the past, and the powerlessness of Man before the blind hurry of the universe from vanity to vanity—to feel these things and know them is to conquer them.

This is the reason why the Past has such magical power. The beauty of its motionless and silent pictures is like the enchanted purity of late autumn, when the leaves, though one breath would make them fall, still glow against the sky in golden glory. The Past does not change or strive; like Duncan, after life's fitful fever it sleeps well; what was eager and grasping, what was petty and transitory, has faded away, the things that were beautiful and eternal shine out of it like stars in the night. Its beauty, to a soul not worthy of it, is unendurable; but to a soul which has conquered Fate it is the key of religion.

The life of Man, viewed outwardly, is but a small thing in comparison with the forces of Nature. The slave is doomed to worship Time and Fate and Death, because they are greater than anything he finds in himself, and because all his thoughts are of things which they devour. But, great as they are, to think of them greatly, to feel their passionless splendour, is greater still. And such thought makes us free men; we no longer bow before the inevitable in Oriental subjection, but we absorb it, and make it a part of ourselves. To abandon the struggle for private happiness, to expel all eagerness of temporary desire, to burn with passion for eternal things—this is emancipation, and this is the free man's worship. And this liberation is effected by a contemplation of Fate; for Fate itself is subdued by the mind which leaves nothing to be purged by the purifying fire of Time.

United with his fellow-men by the strongest of all ties, the tie of a common doom, the free man finds that a new vision is with him always, shedding over every daily task the light of love. The life of Man is a long march through the night, surrounded by invisible foes, tortured by weariness and pain, towards a goal that few can hope to reach, and where none may tarry long. One by one, as they march, our comrades vanish from our sight, seized by the silent orders of omnipotent Death. Very brief is the time in which we can help them, in which their happiness or misery is decided. Be it ours to shed sunshine on their path, to lighten their sorrows by the balm of sympathy, to give them the pure joy of a never-tiring affection, to strengthen failing courage, to instil faith in hours of despair. Let us not weigh in grudging scales their merits and demerits, but let us think only of their need—of the sorrows, the difficulties, perhaps the blindnesses, that make the misery of their lives; let us remember that they are fellow-sufferers in the same darkness, actors in the same tragedy with ourselves. And so, when their day is over, when their good and their evil have become eternal by the immortality of the past, be it ours to feel that, where they suffered, where they failed, no deed of ours was the cause; but wherever a spark of the divine fire kindled in their hearts, we were ready with encouragement, with sympathy, with brave words in which high courage glowed.

Brief and powerless is Man's life; on him and all his race the slow, sure doom falls pitiless and dark. Blind to good and evil, reckless of destruction, omnipotent matter rolls on its relentless way; for Man, condemned to-day to lose his dearest, to-morrow himself to pass through the gate of darkness, it remains only to cherish, ere yet the blow falls, the lofty thoughts that ennoble his little day; disdaining the coward terrors of the slave of Fate, to worship at the shrine that his own hands have built; undismayed by the empire of chance, to preserve a mind free from the wanton tyranny that rules his outward life; proudly defiant of the irresistible forces that tolerate, for a moment, his knowledge and his condemnation, to sustain alone, a weary but unyielding Atlas, the world that his own ideals have fashioned despite the trampling march of unconscious Power.

THE NECESSITY OF THE WAGER[1]

BLAISE PASCAL

. . . LET them at least learn what is the religion they attack, before attacking it. If this religion boasted of having a clear view of God, and of possessing it open and unveiled, it would be attacking it to say that we see nothing in the world which shows it with this clearness. But since, on the contrary, it says that men are in darkness and estranged from God, that He has hidden Himself from their knowledge, that this is in fact the name which He gives Himself in the Scriptures, *Deus absconditus;*[2] and finally, if it endeavours equally to establish these two things: that God has set up in the Church visible signs to make Himself known to those who should seek Him sincerely, and that He

1. From the *Pensées* of Blaise Pascal, Nos. 194 and 233, originally published at Paris, 1669/1670; translated by W. F. Trotter, Everyman's Library, E. P. Dutton & Co., Inc., New York. By permission of E. P. Dutton & Co., Inc., and J. M. Dent & Sons, Ltd., London.

2. The hidden God.

has nevertheless so disguised them that He will only be perceived by those who seek Him with all their heart; what advantage can they obtain, when, in the negligence with which they make profession of being in search of the truth, they cry out that nothing reveals it to them; and since that darkness in which they are, and with which they upbraid the Church, establishes only one of the things which she affirms, without touching the other, and, very far from destroying, proves her doctrine?

In order to attack it, they should have protested that they had made every effort to seek Him everywhere, and even in that which the Church proposes for their instruction, but without satisfaction. If they talked in this manner, they would in truth be attacking one of her pretensions. But I hope here to show that no reasonable person can speak thus, and I venture even to say that no one has ever done so. We know well enough how those who are of this mind behave. They believe they have made great efforts for their instruction, when they have spent a few hours in reading some book of Scripture, and have questioned some priest on the truths of the faith. After that, they boast of having made vain search in books and among men. But, verily, I will tell them what I have often said, that this negligence is insufferable. We are not here concerned with the trifling interests of some stranger, that we should treat it in this fashion; the matter concerns ourselves and our all.

The immortality of the soul is a matter which is of so great consequence to us, and which touches us so profoundly, that we must have lost all feeling to be indifferent as to knowing what it is. All our actions and thoughts must take such different courses, according as there are or are not eternal joys to hope for, that it is impossible to take one step with sense and judgment, unless we regulate our course by our view of this point which ought to be our ultimate end.

Thus our first interest and our first duty is to enlighten ourselves on this subject, whereon depends all our conduct. Therefore among those who do not believe, I make a vast difference between those who strive with all their power to inform themselves, and those who live without troubling or thinking about it.

I can have only compassion for those who sincerely bewail their doubt, who regard it as the greatest of misfortunes, and who, sparing no effort to escape it, make of this inquiry their principal and most serious occupation.

But as for those who pass their life without thinking of this ultimate end of life, and who, for this sole reason that they do not find within themselves the lights which convince them of it, neglect to seek them elsewhere, and to examine thoroughly whether this opinion is one of those which people receive with credulous simplicity, or one of those which, although obscure in themselves, have nevertheless a solid and immovable foundation, I look upon them in a manner quite different.

This carelessness in a matter which concerns themselves, their eternity, their all, moves me more to anger than pity; it astonishes and shocks me; it is to me monstrous. I do not say this out of the pious zeal of a spiritual devotion. I expect, on the contrary, that we ought to have this feeling from principles of human interest and self-love; for this we need only see what the least enlightened persons see.

We do not require great education of the mind to understand that here is no real and lasting satisfaction; that our pleasures are only vanity; that our evils are infinite; and, lastly, that death, which threatens us every moment, must infallibly place us within a few years under the dreadful necessity of being for ever either annihilated or unhappy.

There is nothing more real than this, nothing more terrible. Be we as heroic as we like, that is the end which awaits the noblest life in the world. Let us reflect on this, and then say whether it is not beyond doubt that there is no good in this life but in the hope of another; that we are happy only in proportion as we draw near it; and that, as there are no more woes for those who have complete assurance of eternity, so there is no more happiness for those who have no insight into it.

Surely then it is a great evil thus to be in doubt, but it is at least an indispensable duty to see when we are in such doubt; and thus the doubter who does not seek is altogether completely unhappy and completely wrong. And if besides this he is easy and content, professes to be so, and indeed boasts of it; if it is this state itself which is the subject of his joy and vanity, I have no words to describe so silly a creature.

How can people hold these opinions? What joy can we find in the expectation of nothing but hopeless misery? What reason for boasting that we are in impenetrable darkness? And how can it happen that the following argument occurs to a reasonable man?

"I know not who put me into the world, nor what the world is, nor what I myself am. I am in terrible ignorance of everything. I know not what my body is, nor my senses, nor my soul, not even that part of me which thinks what I say, which reflects on all and on itself, and knows itself no more than the rest. I see those frightful spaces of the universe which surround me, and I find myself tied to one corner of this vast expanse, without knowing why I am put in this place rather than in another, nor why the short time which is given me to live is assigned to me at this point rather than at another of the whole eternity which was before me or which shall come after me. I see nothing but infinites on all sides, which surround me as an atom, and as a shadow which endures only for an instant and returns no more. All I know is that I must soon die, but what I know least is this very death which I cannot escape.

"As I know not whence I come, so I know not whither I go. I know only that, in leaving this world, I fall for ever either into annihilation or into the hands of an angry God, without knowing to which of these two states I shall be for ever assigned. Such is my state, full of weakness and uncertainty. And from all this I conclude that I ought to spend all the days of my life without caring to inquire into what must happen to me. Perhaps I might find some solution to my doubts, but I will not take the trouble, nor take a step to seek it; and after treating with scorn those who are concerned with this care, I will go without foresight and without fear to try the great event, and let myself be led carelessly to death, uncertain of the eternity of my future state."

Who would desire to have for a friend a man who talks in this fashion? Who would choose him out from others to tell him of his affairs? Who would have recourse to him in affliction? And indeed to what use in life could one put him?

In truth, it is the glory of religion to have for enemies men so unreasonable; and their opposition to it is so little dangerous that it serves on the contrary to establish its truths. For the Christian faith goes mainly to establish these two facts: the corruption of nature, and redemption by Jesus Christ. Now I contend that if these men do not serve to prove the truth of the redemption by the holiness of their behaviour, they at least serve admirably to show the corruption of nature by sentiments so unnatural.

Nothing is so important to man as his own state, nothing is so formidable to him as eternity; and thus it is not natural that there should be men indifferent to the loss of their existence, and to the perils of everlasting suffering. They are quite different with regard to all other things. They are afraid of mere trifles; they foresee them; they feel them. And this same man who spends so many days and nights in rage and despair for the loss of office, or for some imaginary insult to his honour, is the very one who knows without anxiety and without emotion that he will lose all by death. It is a monstrous thing to see in the same heart and at the same time this sensibility to trifles and this strange insensibility to the greatest objects. It is an incomprehensible enchantment, and a supernatural slumber, which indicates as its cause an all-powerful force.

There must be a strange confusion in the nature of man, that he should boast of being in that state in which it seems incredible that a single individual should be. However, experience has shown me so great a number of such persons that the fact would be surprising, if we did not know that the greater part of those who trouble themselves about the matter are disingenuous, and not in fact what they say. They are people who have heard it said that it is the fashion to be thus daring. It is what they call shaking off the yoke, and they try to imitate this. But it would not be difficult to make them understand how greatly they deceive themselves in thus seeking esteem. This is not the way to gain it, even I say among those men of the world who take a healthy view of things, and who know that the only way to succeed in this life is to make ourselves appear honourable, faithful, judicious, and capable of useful service to a friend; because naturally men love only what may be useful to them. Now, what do we gain by hearing it said of a man that he has now thrown off the yoke, that he does not believe there is a God who watches our actions, that he considers himself the sole master of his conduct, and that he thinks he is accountable for it only to himself? Does he think that he has thus brought us to have henceforth complete confidence in him, and to look to him for consolation, advice, and help in every need of life? Do they profess to have delighted us by telling us that they hold our soul to be only a little wind and smoke, especially by telling us this in a haughty and self-satisfied tone of voice? Is this a thing to say gayly? Is it not, on the contrary, a thing to say sadly, as the saddest thing in the world?

If they thought of it seriously, they would see that this is so bad a mistake, so contrary to good sense, so opposed to decency, and so removed in every respect from that good breeding which they seek, that they would be more likely to correct than to pervert those who had an inclination to follow them. And indeed, make them give an account of their opinions, and of the reasons which they have for doubting religion, and they will say to you things so feeble and so petty, that they will persuade you of the contrary. The following is what a person one day said to such a one very appositely: "If you continue to talk in this manner, you will really make me religious." And he was right, for who would not have a horror of holding opinions in which he would have such contemptible persons as companions!

Thus those who only feign these opinions would be very unhappy, if they restrained their natural feelings in order to make themselves the most conceited of men. If, at the bottom of their heart, they are troubled at not having more light, let them not disguise the fact; this avowal will not be shameful. The only shame is to have none. Nothing reveals more an extreme weakness of mind than not to know the misery of a godless man. Nothing is more indicative of a bad disposition of heart than not to desire the truth of eternal promises. Nothing is more dastardly than to act with bravado before God. Let them then leave these impieties to those who are sufficiently ill-bred to be really capable of them. Let them at least be honest men, if they cannot be Christians. Finally, let them recognise that there are two kinds of people one can call reasonable; those who serve God with all their heart because they know Him, and those who seek Him with all their heart because they do not know Him.

But as for those who live without knowing Him and without seeking Him, they judge themselves so little worthy of their own care, that they are not worthy of the care of others; and it needs all the charity of the religion which they despise, not to despise them even to the point of leaving them to their folly. But because this religion obliges us always to regard them, so long as they are in this life, as capable of the grace which can enlighten them, and to believe that they may, in a little time, be more replenished with faith than we are, and that, on the other hand, we may fall into the blindness wherein they are, we must do for them what we would they should do for us if we were in their place, and call upon them to have pity upon themselves, and to take at least some steps in the endeavour to find light. Let them give to reading this some of the hours which they otherwise employ so uselessly; whatever aversion they may bring to the task, they will perhaps gain something, and at least will not lose much. But as for those who bring to the task perfect sincerity and a real desire to meet with truth, those I hope will be satisfied and convinced of the proofs of a religion so divine, which I have here collected, and in which I have followed somewhat after this order. . . .

Infinite–nothing.—Our soul is cast into a body, where it finds number, time, dimension. Thereupon it reasons, and calls this nature necessity, and can believe nothing else.

Unity joined to infinity adds nothing to it, no more than one foot to an infinite measure. The finite is annihilated in the presence of the infinite, and becomes a pure nothing. So our spirit before God, so our justice before divine justice. There is not so great a disproportion between our justice and that of God, as between unity and infinity.

The justice of God must be vast like His compassion. Now justice to the outcast is less vast, and ought less to offend our feelings than mercy towards the elect.

We know that there is an infinite, and are ignorant of its nature. As we know it to be false that numbers are finite, it is therefore true that there is an infinity in number. But we do not know what it is. It is false that it is even, it is false that it is odd; for the addition of a unit can make no change in its nature. Yet it is a number, and every number is odd or even (this is certainly true of every finite number). So we may well know that there is a God without knowing what He is. Is there not one substantial truth, seeing there are so many things which are not the truth itself?

We know then the existence and nature of the finite, because we also are finite and have extension. We know the existence of the infinite, and are ignorant of its nature, because it has extension like us, but not limits like us. But we know neither the existence nor the nature of God, because He has neither extension nor limits.

But by faith we know His existence; in glory we shall know His nature. Now, I have already shown that we may well know the existence of a thing, without knowing its nature.

Let us now speak according to natural lights.

If there is a God, He is infinitely incomprehensible, since, having neither parts nor limits, He has no affinity to us. We are then incapable of knowing either what He is or if He is. This being so, who will dare to undertake the decision of the question? Not we, who have no affinity to Him.

Who then will blame Christians for not being able to give a reason for their belief, since they profess a religion for which they cannot give a reason? They declare, in expounding it to the world, that it is a foolishness, *stultitiam;* and then you complain that they do not prove it! If they proved it, they would not keep their word; it is in lacking proofs that they are not lacking in sense. "Yes, but although this excuses those who offer it as such, and takes away from them the blame of putting it forward without reason, it does not excuse those who receive it." Let us then examine this point, and say, "God is, or He is not." But to which side shall we incline? Reason can decide nothing here. There is an infinite chaos which separated us. A game is being played at the extremity of this infinite distance where heads or tails will turn up. What will you wager? According to reason, you can do neither the one thing nor the other; according to reason, you can defend neither of the propositions.

Do not then reprove for error those who have made a choice; for you know nothing about it. "No, but I blame them for having made, not this choice, but a choice; for again both he who chooses heads and he who chooses tails are equally at fault, they are both in the wrong. The true course is not to wager at all."

Yes; but you must wager. It is not optional. You are embarked. Which will you choose then? Let us see. Since you must choose, let us see which interests you least. You have two things to lose, the true and the good; and two things to stake, your reason and your will, your knowledge and your happiness; and your nature has two things to shun, error and misery. Your reason is no more shocked in choosing one rather than the other, since you must of necessity choose. This is one point settled. But your happiness? Let us weigh the gain and the loss in wagering that God is. Let us estimate these two chances. If you gain, you gain all; if you lose, you lose nothing. Wager, then, without hesitation that He is.—"That is very fine. Yes, I must wager; but I may perhaps wager too much."—Let us see. Since there is an equal risk of gain and of loss, if you had only to gain two lives, instead of one, you might still wager. But if there were three lives to gain, you would have to play (since you are under the necessity of playing), and you would be imprudent, when you are forced to play, not to chance your life to gain three at a game where there is an equal risk of loss and gain. But there is an eternity of life and happiness. And this being so, if there were an infinity of chances, of which one only would be for you, you would still be right in wagering one to win two, and you would act stupidly, being obliged to play, by refusing to stake one life against three at a game in which out of an infinity of chances there is one for you, if there were an infinity of an infinitely happy life to gain. But there is here an infinity of an infinitely happy life to gain, a chance of gain against a finite number of chances of loss, and what you stake is finite. It is all divided; wherever the infinite is and there is not an infinity of chances of loss against that of gain, there is no time to hesitate, you must give all. And thus, when one is forced to play, he must renounce reason to preserve his life, rather than risk it for infinite gain, as likely to happen as the loss of nothingness.

For it is no use to say it is uncertain if we will gain, and it is certain that we risk, and that the infinite distance between the *certainty* of what is staked and the *uncertainty* of what will be gained, equals the finite good which is certainly staked against the uncertain infinite. It is not so, as every player stakes a certainty to gain an uncertainty, and yet he stakes a finite certainty to gain a finite uncertainty, without transgressing against reason. There is not an infinite distance between the certainty staked and the uncertainty of the gain; that is untrue. In truth, there is an infinity between the certainty of gain and the certainty of loss. But the uncertainty of the gain is proportioned to the certainty of the stake according to the proportion of the chances of gain and loss. Hence it comes that, if there are as many risks on one side as on the other, the course is to play even; and then the certainty of the stake is equal to the uncertainty of the gain, so far is it from fact that there is an infinite distance between them. And so our proposition is of infinite force, when there is the finite to stake in a game where there are equal risks of gain and of loss, and the infinite to gain. This is demonstrable; and if men are capable of any truths, this is one.

"I confess it, I admit it. But, still, is there no means of seeing the faces of the cards?"—Yes, Scripture and the rest, etc. "Yes, but I have my hands tied and my mouth closed; I am forced to wager, and am not free. I am not released, and am so made that I cannot believe. What, then, would you have me do?"

True. But at least learn your inability to believe, since reason brings you to this, and yet you cannot believe. Endeavour then to convince yourself, not by increase of proofs of God, but by the abatement of your passions. You would like to attain faith, and do not know the way; you would like to cure yourself of unbelief, and ask the remedy for it. Learn of those who have been bound like you, and who now stake all their possessions. These are people who know the way which you would follow, and who are cured of an ill of which you would be cured. Follow the way by which they began; by acting as if they believed, taking the holy water, having masses said, etc. Even this will naturally make you believe, and deaden your acuteness.—"But this is what I am afraid of."—And why? What have you to lose?

But to show you that this leads you there, it is this which will lessen the passions, which are your stumbling-blocks.

The end of this discourse.—Now, what harm will befall you in taking this side? You will be faithful, honest, humble, grateful, generous, a sincere friend, truthful. Certainly you will not have those poisonous pleasures, glory and luxury; but will you not have others? I will tell you that you will thereby gain in this life, and that, at each step you take on this road, you will see so great certainty of gain, so much nothingness in what you risk, that you will at last recognise that you have wagered for something certain and infinite, for which you have given nothing.

"Ah! This discourse transports me, charms me," etc.

If this discourse pleases you and seems impressive, know that it is made by a man who has knelt, both before and after it, in prayer to that Being, infinite and without parts, before whom he lays all he has, for you also to lay before Him all you have for your own good and for His glory, that so strength may be given to lowliness.

THE PROVIDENCE OF GOD[1]

LORD, thou hast been our dwelling place in all generations.

Before the mountains were brought forth, or ever thou hadst formed the earth and the world, even from everlasting to everlasting, thou art God.

1. From *The Book of Psalms* (King James Version of *The Bible*), 90, 91.

Thou turnest man to destruction; and sayest, Return, ye children of men.

For a thousand years in thy sight are but as yesterday when it is past, and as a watch in the night.

Thou carriest them away as with a flood; they are as a sleep: in the morning they are like grass which groweth up.

In the morning it flourisheth, and groweth up; in the evening it is cut down, and withereth.

For we are consumed by thine anger, and by thy wrath are we troubled.

Thou hast set our iniquities before thee, our secret sins in the light of thy countenance.

For all our days are passed away in thy wrath: we spend our years as a tale that is told.

The days of our years are threescore years and ten; and if by any reason of strength they be fourscore years, yet is their strength labour and sorrow; for it is soon cut off, and we fly away.

Who knoweth the power of thine anger? even according to thy fear, so is thy wrath.

So teach us to number our days, that we may apply our hearts unto wisdom.

Return, O LORD, how long? and let it repent thee concerning thy servants.

O satisfy us early with thy mercy; that we may rejoice and be glad all our days.

Make us glad according to the days wherein thou hast afflicted us, and the years wherein we have seen evil.

Let thy work appear unto thy servants, and thy glory unto their children.

And let the beauty of the LORD our God be upon us: and establish thou the work of our hands upon us; yea, the work of our hands establish thou it.

He that dwelleth in the secret place of the most High shall abide under the shadow of the Almighty.

I will say of the LORD, He is my refuge and my fortress: my God; in him will I trust.

Surely he shall deliver thee from the snare of the fowler, and from the noisome pestilence.

He shall cover thee with his feathers and under his wings shalt thou trust: his truth shall be thy shield and buckler.

Thou shalt not be afraid for the terror by night; nor for the arrow that flieth by day;

Nor for the pestilence that walketh in darkness; nor for the destruction that wasteth at noonday.

A thousand shall fall at thy side, and ten thousand at thy right hand; but it shall not come nigh thee.

Only with thine eyes shalt thou behold and see the reward of the wicked.

Because thou hast made the LORD, which is my refuge, even the most High, thy habitation;

There shall no evil befall thee, neither shall any plague come nigh thy dwelling.

For he shall give his angels charge over thee, to keep thee in all thy ways.

They shall bear thee up in their hands, lest thou dash thy foot against a stone.

Thou shalt tread upon the lion and adder: the young lion and the dragon shalt thou trample under feet.

Because he hath set his love upon me, therefore will I deliver him: I will set him on high, because he hath known my name.

He shall call upon me, and I will answer him: I will be with him in trouble; I will deliver him, and honour him.

With long life will I satisfy him, and shew him my salvation.

MEDITATION XVII[1]

JOHN DONNE

Nunc lento sonitu dicunt, morieris[2]

PERCHANCE he for whom this bell tolls may be so ill as that he knows not it tolls for him; and perchance I may think myself so much better than I am as that they who are about me and see my state may have caused it to toll for me, and I know not that. The church is catholic, universal, so are all her actions; all that she does belongs to all. When she baptizes a child, that action concerns me; for that child is thereby connected to that body which is my head too and ingrafted into that body whereof I am a member. And when she buries a man, that action concerns me. All mankind is of one author, and is one volume; when one man dies, one chapter is not torn out of the book, but translated into a better language; and every chapter must be so translated. God employs several translators; some pieces are translated by age, some by sickness, some by war, some by justice; but God's hand is in every translation, and his hand shall bind up all our scattered leaves again for that library where every book shall lie open to one another. As therefore the bell that rings to a sermon calls not upon the preacher only but upon the congregation to come, so this bell calls us all; but how much more me who am brought so near the door by this sickness! There was a contention as far as a suit—in which piety and dignity, religion and estimation, were mingled—which of the religious orders should ring to prayers first in the morning; and it was determined that they should ring first that rose earliest. If we understand aright the dignity of this bell that tolls for our evening prayer, we would be glad to make it ours by rising early, in that application, that it might be ours as well as his, whose indeed it is. The

1. From *Devotions upon Emergent Occasions* by John Donne (London, 1624).
2. Now this bell tolling softly says, you must die.

bell doth toll for him that thinks it doth; and though it intermit again, yet from that minute that that occasion wrought upon him he is united to God. Who casts not up his eye to the sun when it rises? but who takes off his eye from a comet when that breaks out? Who bends not his ear to any bell which upon any occasion rings? but who can remove it from that bell which is passing a piece of himself out of this world? No man is an island entire of itself; every man is a piece of the continent, a part of the main. If a clod be washed away by the sea, Europe is the less, as well as if a promontory were, as well as if a manor of thy friend's or of thine own were. Any man's death diminishes me, because I am involved in mankind, and therefore never send to know for whom the bell tolls; it tolls for thee. Neither can we call this a begging of misery or a borrowing of misery, as though we were not miserable enough of ourselves but must fetch in more from the next house, in taking upon us the misery of our neighbors. Truly it were an excusable covetousness if we did, for affliction is a treasure, and scarce any man hath enough of it. No man hath affliction enough that is not matured and ripened by it and made fit for God by that affliction. If a man carry treasure in bullion or in a wedge of gold and have none coined into current money, his treasure will not defray him as he travels. Tribulation is treasure in the nature of it, but it is not current money in the use of it, except we get nearer and nearer our home, heaven, by it. Another man may be sick too, and sick to death, and this affliction may lie in his bowels as gold in a mine and be of no use to him; but this bell that tells me of his affliction digs out and applies that gold to me, if by this consideration of another's danger I take mine own into contemplation and so secure myself by making my recourse to my God, who is our only security.

IN HIS WILL IS OUR PEACE[1]

JOHN WOOLMAN

TWENTY-SIXTH of eighth month [1772].—Being now at George Crosfield's, in the county of Westmoreland, I feel a concern to commit to writing the following uncommon circumstance.

In a time of sickness, a little more than two years and a half ago, I was brought so near the gates of death that I forgot my name. Being then desirous to know who I was, I saw a mass of matter of a dull gloomy color between the south and the east, and was informed that this mass was human beings in as great misery as they could be, and live, and that I was mixed with them, and that henceforth I might not consider myself as a distinct or separate being. In this state I remained several hours. I then heard a soft melodious voice,

1. From the *Journal* of John Woolman. First printed in 1774.

more pure and harmonious than any I had heard with my ears before; I believed it was the voice of an angel who spake to the other angels; the words were, "John Woolman is dead." I soon remembered that I was once John Woolman, and being assured that I was alive in the body, I greatly wondered what that heavenly voice could mean. I believed beyond doubting that it was the voice of an holy angel, but as yet it was a mystery to me.

I was then carried in spirit to the mines where poor oppressed people were digging rich treasures for those called Christians, and heard them blaspheme the name of Christ, at which I was grieved, for his name to me was precious. I was then informed that these heathens were told that those who oppressed them were the followers of Christ, and they said among themselves, "If Christ directed them to use us in this sort, then Christ is a cruel tyrant."

All this time the song of the angel remained a mystery; and in the morning, my dear wife and some others coming to my bedside, I asked them if they knew who I was, and they telling me I was John Woolman, thought I was lightheaded, for I told them not what the angel said, nor was I disposed to talk much to any one, but was very desirous to get so deep that I might understand this mystery.

My tongue was often so dry that I could not speak till I had moved it about and gathered some moisture, and as I lay still for a time I at length felt a Divine power prepare my mouth that I could speak, and I then said, "I am crucified with Christ, nevertheless I live; yet not I, but Christ liveth in me. And the life which I now live in the flesh I live by the faith of the Son of God, who loved me and gave himself for me." Then the mystery was opened and I perceived there was joy in heaven over a sinner who had repented, and that the language "John Woolman is dead," meant no more than the death of my own will. . . .

After this sickness I spake not in public meetings for worship for nearly one year, but my mind was very often in company with the oppressed slaves as I sat in meetings; and though under his dispensation I was shut up from speaking, yet the spring of the gospel ministry was many times livingly opened in me, and the Divine gift operated by abundance of weeping, in feeling the oppression of this people. It being so long since I passed through this dispensation, and the matter remaining fresh and lively in my mind, I believe it safest for me to commit it to writing.

THE REASONABLENESS OF CHRISTIANITY[1]

THEODORE M. GREENE

1. THE SUPERNATURAL

NATURALISTS and humanists are about equally critical of the "supernatural." They either insist that they can attach no meaning to this term or else give it a meaning which makes belief in it utterly irrational. It is safe to say that no informed Christians—and few professing Christians are informed—believe in the supernatural which these naturalists and humanists repudiate. What, then, do Christians mean by the supernatural? It is quite easy to give a verbal answer to this question but not at all easy to comprehend its true impact.

By the "natural" Christians mean, first of all, whatever has been created by God and what the Bible refers to as a "creature" or the "creaturely." This includes the physical world and man as a psycho-physical being subject to the laws of the universe. God, as the Creator of this creaturely world, is accordingly conceived of as "supernatural."

But the God of Christianity is not the God of eighteenth-century deism, that is, a God who, having created the world, turns it loose and pays no further attention to it. On the contrary, He is the abiding Ground of all being, the continuing Source of all finite existence, the Sustainer of the world as well as its original Creator. Nor is His relation to the world mechanical or impersonal. He is conceived of as a Person who loves the world with a love which resembles, but infinitely transcends, human love. It is this love which has impelled Him to create man in His own image, that is, with a capacity to respond to His love and to enter into communion with Him.

This interpretation of God's relation to man and of human nature distinguishes man from all other creatures and puts him in a unique relation to the supernatural. He has special God-given endowments and is therefore able, and duty bound, to respond to the Divine Initiative in trust and gratitude. The term "soul," of which many psychologists today are so contemptuous, signifies precisely this spiritual capacity and obligation. The soul is not an isolated entity in man, what Professor E. B. Holt has called a "stellar point soul," unrelated to man's psycho-physical nature and complex personality. It is the whole of man, as we know him in this life, in his capacity for spiritual aspiration and achievement, for love of God and obedience to Him. This is what the poetic phrase "resurrection of the body" in the Apostles' Creed emphasizes. The immortality of which Christianity assures us is a spiritual achievement of the whole man in this life and of man as a total personality after death. Man

1. Reprinted from "Christianity and Its Secular Alternatives" by Theodore M. Greene in *The Christian Answer,* edited by Henry P. Van Dusen; copyright 1945 by Charles Scribner's Sons; used by permission of the publishers.

thus partakes of the supernatural by being "inspirited" by the Divine Spirit; he grows in spiritual stature as a son of God by being "possessed" by God. His "soul" is therefore his entire being in its potential and actual orientation to God, his Creator.

To grasp the full Christian meaning of this concept of the supernatural and man's relation to it, we would have to explore the rich Christian concepts of God as a Divine Person, of man as a finite person created "in the image" of God, and of the unique Thou-I relation of God to the human soul. But even on the basis of this brief statement we can ask whether such a concept of the supernatural is either quite meaningless or wholly incredible.

It is meaningless only to those whose initial conception of meaning makes it meaningless. If, for example, only that is meaningful which is ultimately reducible to sensation, or verifiable through sensation, God and the soul are certainly meaningless terms—but so is thought, personality, value and, indeed, everything to which humanists and many naturalists attach supreme importance. Similarly, if only that is meaningful which is completely understood, or even understandable, by the human mind, it follows that what Christians refer to as supernatural is again not meaningful, for Christians are unanimous in believing that man cannot completely fathom God's nature or fully understand the human soul and its ultimate destiny. Yet both naturalists and humanists make use of such concepts as "nature" and "man" without thereby claiming that man does, or perhaps ever will, fully understand the "objects" to which they refer. It seems clear, then, that the supernatural, as the Christian conceives of it, is not a wholly meaningless concept. If it were, the atheist's disbelief and the agnostic's doubt would be as meaningless as the Christian's faith, for one cannot meaningfully even deny or doubt what is wholly meaningless.

Is, then, the reality of God and the soul necessarily and by definition incredible? Only a secular dogmatist would be so bold as to assert that it is. On what reasonable basis could one possibly be sure that the world of nature comprises the whole of reality, unless one equates "nature" with "reality" by definition, or that man is merely a spatio-temporal being incapable of spirituality unless again one sets dogmatic limits to man's potentialities? It surely does not take very much imagination to conceive of the possibility that reality may have aspects or dimensions which are not evident to sense or even wholly comprehensible by human reason. Pascal's dictum, "Not all that is incomprehensible ceases to exist," would seem to be far more reasonable than the rationalistic dogma that only the rational is real and that the whole of reality is at least theoretically comprehensible by human reason.

The Christian concepts of God and the soul are therefore neither meaningless nor necessarily untrue. This does not suffice, however, to give us any reasonable assurance that the God of Christianity and the human spirit are real. What, then, is the positive basis for the Christian belief in God and the human soul?

2. REVELATION

The general Christian answer to this question is that God has revealed Himself to man in many different ways—in the world of nature, in man's basic human experience of being a finite self-transcending creature, in the distinctive religious experiences of mystics, saints, and prophets, and, more particularly, in the individual and corporate experiences recorded in the Bible, culminating in man's encounter with the historical Jesus and continuing in the recorded testimony of the Christian Church. Is there anything initially incredible in this claim?

If the Christian's apprehension of God is true and if in fact He does possess the attributes assigned to Him by Christianity, it is certainly not incredible that He should have revealed Himself to man in various ways, or in distinctive ways to a certain people, or even uniquely in a single historical individual, or with special clarity to the members of a continuing Christian community. What is there in science, history or philosophy to preclude this possibility? The only reasonable response to this claim would seem to be to study the alleged religious experiences and the Christian interpretations of these experiences as open-mindedly as possible, for if the claim has any validity at all it is, indeed, of momentous import to man.

Such a study would make it evident that the religious experience in general, and the Christian experience in particular, is uniformly described by those who have had it as an encounter with a *real* Being whose nature has partially manifested itself in this encounter. What are the criteria of the reality of any "object" of experience? They are, in brief, (a) coerciveness, (b) coherence, and (c) publicity.

(a) We accept as "objectively real" whatever, first of all, intrudes itself upon our consciousness with a character of its own which we ourselves cannot change but must accept for what it is. It is the coerciveness of sense experience, for example, which compels us to take this experience seriously as, in some sense, an experience of reality.

(b) But mere coerciveness is not enough, for dreams, illusions and hallucinations may be coercive and none the less misleading. What is misleading in these cases, however, is not the coercive "given" but the interpretation placed upon it. Only that is accepted by us as objectively real which we can make coherent with some order of reality. Thus, "veridical" (i.e., reliable) sense experiences are judged to be trustworthy clues to what we regard as "real" physical objects, whereas other equally vivid and coercive experiences are called dreams, illusions or hallucinations.

(c) Finally, there is no reason why any given individual should not have a perfectly valid experience of the real which is quite unique, wholly private, and unshared or even unsharable by other men. Indeed, all new discoveries are, at the outset, the private and unique insights of single individuals, and the fact that some of these insights are hard to communicate to others does not in itself invalidate them. None the less, men are not only incorrigibly social; their knowledge of themselves and their environment is essentially the product of human coöperation and communication. Solitary confinement is the most cruel of all punishments; the inability to communicate with others and to share one's experiences with others is a recognized cause and criterion of insanity. The first desire of a scientist who believes himself to have made a new discovery is to await the confirmation of other competent scientists. The first impulse of any man who has an unusual experience is to ask someone he trusts, "Do you see, or hear, or feel what I do?" The third criterion of reality, therefore, which complements the criteria of coerciveness and coherence, is publicity: only that is judged to be undeniably real which others, at least those who are qualified to do so, can also experience and interpret in the same way.

The phrase, "who are qualified to do so," is important in every type of experience. The negative testimony of the blind and the deaf does not make us distrust the reliability of our senses. The inability of non-scientists to repeat the experiments or to understand the interpretations of modern science does not discredit these experiments or interpretations. The same is true in such realms as technology, law, or art; in each realm some men are more expert and wise than others. We realize that man's knowledge of reality is always an aristocratic enterprise in which not all men can share equally. Competent scientists, artists, lawyers and engineers speak with an authority which their peers accept on the basis of first-hand verification and which others accept with a humility which is proportionate to their own sense of limitation in the field in question. Authority has, in secular life, a dual meaning; it signifies, on the one hand, the compulsion to assent which characterizes whatever is, to any given individual, simultaneously coercive, coherent, and sharable; it signifies, on the other hand, what is more or less blindly accepted at second-hand. A scientist accepts as authoritative in the first sense what he himself has verified and confirmed. The common man accepts the pronouncements of scientists as authoritative in the second sense. He does so, despite the fact that he cannot verify or even understand them, partly because he has indirect evidence, e.g., in the practical applications of science, that these scientists know what they are talking about, and partly because he is convinced that, as a group, they are both honest and able.

The authority of Christian Revelation should be interpreted along these same lines, despite the contrary belief of dogmatic naturalists. In direct proportion as Christians have shared at first-hand in the Christian experience and have thought through the Christian interpretation of this experience, this interpretation is accepted as authoritative in the first sense. The large measure of agreement among the prophets, evangelists and saints of the Hebraic-Christian tradition is impressive. They confirm one another's testimony again and again. They agree that the God whom they claim to have encountered presented Himself coercively to them with a character of His own; they agree in broad outline in their interpretation of these coercive experiences. In short, their religious experiences, though necessarily private in the sense in which all experiences are private, are sharable, communicable and verifiable. But in religion, as in science, some men are more sensitive, imaginative and informed than others; Christianity is, in its own way, as "aristocratic" as science. But its "aristocratic" character must be conceived in appropriate terms and not by reference to irrelevant standards. We are here dealing not with a social or intellectual aristocracy but with a spiritual aristocracy—the aristocracy of those, of however humble a social origin, and with however limited scientific or philosophical capacity and training, who possess the humility, the earnestness, the sense of awe, and the capacity for utter devotion to God and man which are simultaneously the condition and the criterion of religious insight.

On the other hand, in proportion as men, both within and outside the Church, are unable to participate in this distinctive experience or to comprehend its Christian interpretation, they must initially either accept or reject the authority of Christian Revelation at second hand.[2] Secularists who reject it simply because it is not reducible to, or verifiable in, purely secular terms do so at their own peril. The simple Christian is less dogmatic and more humble. He is willing to believe that the Bible is indeed the record of God's revelation to man even though he very inadequately comprehends this revelation. He is willing to credit the testimony of the prophets and saints even though he cannot fully verify this testimony in his own experience and reflection. His acceptance of what Mr. Blackmur calls "asserted" authority, whether Biblical or ecclesiastical or a combination of the two, *is* blind in proportion as it is, for him, merely asserted and not confirmed first-hand experience. Such blind faith is as unsatisfactory, and as hazardous, in religion as elsewhere. But the faith of sincere Christians is never wholly blind; it is always rooted, to some extent at least, in their personal encounter with the Jesus of history and the spirit of Christ in the Church, and in their own experience of prayer and religious meditation.

God's revelation of Himself to man need not, therefore, be interpreted superstitiously, though it often has been and still is so interpreted by many Christians. It is not incredible. It has been profoundly meaningful and utterly convincing to the religiously sensitive in the entire Hebraic-Christian tradition, and it has been more or less shared by countless Christians through the centuries of our Christian era.

3. REASON, FAITH, AND DOGMA

It can still be asked whether what has just been said about revelation is a fair account of the Christian attitude toward the authority of the Bible and the Church. To answer this question we must first distinguish between the Roman Catholic and the Protestant positions. The former, in general, gives priority to

2. The Christian Church at its best has always regarded such second-hand acceptance as a second-best course of action, vastly inferior to acceptance on the basis of understanding and first-hand experience.

the Church over the Bible in the sense that it regards the Church, and particularly the Pope, as the ultimate interpreter of Scripture, though the Bible is of course also accepted as the record of God's revelation of Himself to man. The Protestant doctrines of the "priesthood of all believers" and the centrality of the Word make the Bible the Christian's ultimate authority and the individual Christian ultimately responsible for his interpretation of it. The fear that such reliance on each individual Christian would lead to disagreement and heresy has led Protestant fundamentalists to try to exclude the factor of individual interpretation by insisting on the literal truth of every word in the Bible. It is a similar fear that has led Roman Catholics to attribute absolute authority to the Church's interpretation of Christian doctrine.

Both these positions represent, in effect, a determination to safeguard the authority of Christian revelation and the absolute correctness of theological interpretation. Both positions insist that true Christian faith involves the absence of all possible doubt regarding God's existence, nature, and revelation of Himself to man. It must be admitted that these positions have been, and still are, very widely held by orthodox Christians, Catholic and Protestant alike.

There is, however, another conception of Christian faith for which there is good authority in the Bible and in the thought of eminent Christians since New Testament times. It is suggested in Paul's statement, "Now we see through a glass, darkly . . . now we know in part," and it is stated explicitly by Pascal when he says, "If we must not act save on a certainty, we ought not to act on religion, for it is not certain. But how many things do we act on uncertainly . . . ! I say then we must do nothing at all, for nothing is certain, and that there is more certainty in religion than there is as to whether we may see tomorrow." [3]

This view of Christian faith assumes that it has all the essential characteristics of faith in general. Faith may be defined as wholehearted belief on the basis of evidence, but not wholly conclusive evidence, and of interpretation which is reasonable, but which falls short of absolute proof. On this view, faith is never wholly blind, since it can be evoked only by what is at least to some extent experienced and apprehended. Nor is it ever completely enlightened, since that is the prerogative of omniscience, not of finite man. It is always somewhere between these two extremes—more or less informed, more or less blind and credulous. So defined, faith is essential to all human existence. For life necessitates continual decision and action, a continual taking of sides, in the absence of complete evidence and absolute proof. Insofar as man is a rational being he would of course prefer never to decide and act save in the light of perfect knowledge, since, in an orderly world, every action and decision has its inevitable and inescapable consequences. But this is not given to finite man; he must decide and act on faith, in every secular sphere as well as in religion. The scientist cannot prove with absolute certainty that the ob-

3. *Pensées,* Fragment 234.

served regularities of nature will prevail in the future; he has to accept natural order on faith in order to investigate it. The humanist cannot be absolutely sure that man can improve his lot on earth; only a faith in the possibility of such improvement can inspire him to continued humanistic effort.[4] Faith, secular or religious, involves "psychological" certainty when it is accompanied by no conscious doubts. It amounts to "moral" certainty when it is sufficient "for all practical purposes" and if it is resolute and unswerving. But it is never "logically" absolutely certain because faith and knowledge are not identical or co-terminous and because man's knowledge is so incorrigibly finite that complete understanding is forever beyond his grasp.

Christian faith differs, on the view here defended, from secular faith primarily in the nature of the "object" to which it is directed and the resultant trust in and love for this "object." The "object" of Christian faith is not nature, or man, but God. God is not one among other objects if by "object" is meant a created "thing" or any part or all of our created universe. But God is the "object" of religious and Christian faith in the sense that such faith is a faith in God. Christian faith, insofar as it is enlightened, is based on evidence and interpretation of this evidence. But the evidence is distinctive and the proper interpretation of it is appropriate to its distinctive character. The relevant experiences are correctly described as "encounters" with the Deity in direct communion with Him and through His revelation of Himself to man in Jesus Christ. The relevant interpretation of these encounters is theological interpretation. In theology, reason goes as far as it can to give the most reasonable interpretation of God's nature and His relation to man. God's self-revelation is believed by Christians to be absolute in the sense of being wholly adequate to human needs. But men can understand this revelation only as finite beings, therefore only inadequately, never absolutely—sufficiently, Christians believe, to evoke their faith in God, to elicit their proper response to Him, and to lead them to express their proper attitude of love for their fellowmen with assurance—but, none the less, only with such assurance as is within the grasp of finite mortals. To deny this is to commit the fallacy of misplaced absoluteness.

There is, indeed, a philosophical sense in which God's reality can be said to be indubitable, namely, if He is defined from the outset as the ground of all being, the source and basis of all reality. No one, save an extreme solipsist, can deny the reality of God conceived of as the underlying condition of all existence and the "That" to which all human inquiry is ultimately directed. It is also appropriate to call this ultimate being "God" because Christianity, at least,

4. Thus, John Dewey quite properly raises the question as to "whether there are adequate grounds for faith [sic!] in the potentialities of human nature and whether they can be accompanied by the intensity and ardor once awakened by religious ideas upon a theological basis." He continues, "Is human nature intrinsically such a poor thing that the idea is *absurd*? I do not attempt to give any answer, but the word *faith* is intentionally used. For in the long run democracy will stand or fall with the possibility of maintaining the faith and justifying it by works." *Freedom and Culture,* Putnam, 1939, p. 126.

conceives of God as absolute reality as well as in other ways. The factor of uncertainty enters in only when the further attempt is made to apprehend God's nature more specifically and to determine more concretely His relation to the universe and to man. This uncertainty, however, is of great importance for Christian faith, since the God of religious worship is never merely the "ground of all being" but a Person worthy of our reverence, a God who so loves men as to evoke their responsive love. Christian faith in such a God is assured enough to enable Christians to live by it with complete confidence, but it must always fall short of absolute logical certitude.

Similarly, Christian faith, like all concrete religious decisions, is in one sense utterly convincing, but in another sense subject to the hazards and insecurities of any venturing faith. It involves, on the one hand, not only an utter commitment but a commitment that seems to the sincere Christian to be inescapable. For his experience of God is a compulsive experience; he describes it as coercive, as a confrontation, as an experience so overwhelming, luminous, and meaningful that doubt regarding its spiritual validity and significance is unthinkable, an experience with such inner authority that no additional evidence could strengthen the faith which it generates. The assurance which characterizes this faith is of such a character as to make inappropriate such quantitative qualifications as "more" and "less." Yet the fact remains that the criterion of "coerciveness" is, philosophically considered, not a sufficient criterion of reality or objectivity; and the minute the other criterion of "coherence" is applied in the attempt to interpret the coercive religious experience meaningfully, the uncertainties inherent in all finite apprehension and decision are unavoidable. This is why Christian faith, however assured, *must* be a *venture* and why it must always fall short of absolutely certain knowledge, strictly defined.

The Bible and the Church are, for informed Christians, authoritative because they are man's chief objective sources for an understanding of God. The real authority of both is the spiritual authority of luminous and compelling insight. But man's interpretation of the Bible, as the chief record of God's Self-revelation, and the Church's interpretation of Christian doctrine remain finite and inadequate, however much of these interpretations are inspired, or guided by, the Holy Spirit.

Dogmatism, as opposed to dogma, can then be defined as the denial of human finitude, the loss of proper humility, and the improper, indeed blasphemous, ascription to one's own beliefs, or to those of one's Church, of a degree of certainty which can actually characterize only the omniscience of God Himself. It is a manifestation of pride, both intellectual and spiritual, for it involves the deification of man and the absolutizing of his finite and relative knowledge. A Christian can believe that God is absolute without regarding his own conception of God as absolute or final. He can accept the authority of the Bible as the record of God's Self-revelation to man without regarding as finally authoritative his interpretation, or his Church's interpretation, of it.

This sense of humility is desperately needed today, as always, in the Christian Church.

On the other hand, dogmas may, but need not, differ from religious dogmatism, for a dogma is a belief basic to a given community, secular or religious. People cannot band together, share their experiences and work for a common end save on the basis of certain major presuppositions. In this sense, every community, including the Christian community, has its basic dogmas which constitute its credal frame of reference. Science has its dogmas or its creed—its basic faith, for example, in the uniformity of nature, and its unquestioned loyalty to scientific truth. Democracy presupposes the intrinsic value of man as man and the importance of justice and fair play. Similarly, Christianity, in each of the major and minor branches of the Christian Church, has its distinguishing dogmas. Inability to subscribe to the dogmas of any community, secular or religious, necessarily disqualifies one from membership in that community. This does not mean, however, that such dogmas cannot and should not be reëxamined and revised from time to time by the community itself, since only thus is progress possible. This applies to the Christian Church. The steady development of Christian theology through the centuries shows that such reëxamination and revision have actually taken place.

This interpretation of Christian dogmas, which Professor Thomas calls the "central affirmations" of Christianity, is not rationalistic but it is eminently reasonable. It does justice to man's finitude and sense of mystery, to God's Infinity, and to the Christian's faith in the adequacy of God's Self-disclosure. It also does justice to the principle of rationality in man and in the universe. Christian faith, it must be insisted, is not irrational, either in the sense of requiring man to suppress his reason or in the sense that God Himself is an irrational force. On the contrary, such rationality or order as exists in the universe is believed by Christians to be the creation of God and to reflect His character, and human reason is conceived of as having been created by God for use. What Professor Tillich has called "autonomous reason" is reason fully aware of the ultimate rationality of man and the world. What may be called "theonomous reason" is this same reason conceived of and operative in the Christian perspective of God as the Source and Ground of all reality. Christianity is profoundly committed to reason, *provided* it be used aright. What, then, constitutes its abuse?

4. ORIGINAL SIN

No Christian dogma is more obnoxious to the secular mind, whether naturalistic or humanistic, than that of original sin. It is particularly repellent when stated in a mechanistic or legalistic form, as, for example, that we have all inherited at birth the sin incurred by Adam. But it is hardly more acceptable when stated in more reasonable terms, namely, that there is in men, in all men by virtue of their human and finite nature, a fundamental egoism which impels them to value the lower rather than the higher satisfactions of life, themselves rather than their fellowmen, mankind rather than God. On this view, sin is essentially idolatry, the ascription of supreme value to man and his works rather than to God. It is, in essence, alienation from God. "Sin is primarily the wrong attitude taken toward God Himself. . . . It is the practical denial of the fact that apart from personal communion with God, human life is meaningless. By sin the things a person does, and the objectives he strives for, are regarded as being of equal rank with communion with God, and practically they take precedence over them."[5] This sin is "original" because it is a deepseated tendency in all men, and the ultimate cause of their misery. It is so fundamental that it cannot be extirpated by a mere effort of will or by any merely human agency. It is also so fundamental that it perverts all human motives, directs reason to the wrong objectives, and thus progressively leads man further and further away from God. In terms of Professor Tillich's analysis, this misuse of reason is most evident in the irrationalism of Nazi totalitarianism, but it is also evident in the dedication of reason to technological advances as ends in themselves, and in the purely humanistic endeavor to make man as self-sufficient and autonomous as possible. For such striving for complete autonomy is, from the religious and Christian point of view, idolatrous. Reason is, in itself, good and not evil, but its use is good only if it is wisely used, and it is used wisely only within the ultimate religious and Christian perspective in which God is acknowledged to be supreme and communion with God is regarded as man's highest duty and felicity.

Is this an unreasonable analysis of human nature and destiny? It is, of course, if there be no God to whom man can dedicate his supreme devotion. But if the Christian apprehension of God is true it is hard to see how this Christian conclusion can be avoided. There is also much in secular experience, particularly today, that offers secular confirmation of this account of human sin. Is it not true that men, even in the best of health and in the happiest social environment, experience the loneliness of not being fully understood by any human being—a loneliness which an omniscient and loving Person alone could satisfy? Is it not true that there is something diabolical in men which makes them hurt what they most love, which gives them satisfaction in the misfortunes of others, however much they may despise themselves for this satisfaction whenever they become aware of it? Is it not true that, in the face of human hatred, violence, misery and injustice, the best of men, who in one sense are blameless for all these disasters, feel none the less a sense of responsibility for them and a corresponding sense of gnawing guilt and a craving for forgiveness, somehow, from some quarter which they cannot specify?

This sense of need does not, of course, prove in and of itself that there is a God who is able to satisfy the need. It does, however, establish man's need for God; it makes man's search for Him meaningful and urgent, and it confirms

5. Otto A. Piper, "The Biblical Understanding of Man," in *Theology Today,* I: 2, p. 194.

the Christian account of sinful human nature. If Christianity is true, as Christians firmly believe it is, the doctrine of original sin, properly interpreted, explains man's secular feelings of guilt more adequately than any purely psychological or sociological theory.

5. THE CHURCH

There is one other aspect of Christianity which is a great stumbling-block to many sincere humanists who are religiously minded and even sympathethic to the central Christian beliefs. This is the institution of the Christian Church. . . . Here we can deal only with some general preliminary objections and criticisms.

(a) One of these is that a man's religion is his own private affair, that he can best worship God in his own way and in solitude, and that membership in a Church and participation in public worship is far more of a hindrance than an aid. There is, of course, an important element of truth in this contention. Each individual's relation to God is indeed ultimately his own concern; worship is ultimately communion between the individual and God. To stop here, however, is to forget that man is essentially a social being, that all his significant human experiences are informed and nourished by the experiences and insights of others, and that man can benefit from the past and avoid the necessity of forever starting *de novo* only by standing on the shoulders of his predecessors and making the fullest use of his contemporaries.

Every other human enterprise arouses in man a need and desire for corporate action and expressive corporate symbolism. This is true in war and peace, in sport and education and politics and even in scientific research. In all these activities men need each other and they need to come together from time to time to celebrate and express publicly their common objectives and loyalties. It would be strange indeed if man's religious life were the one exception to this universal rule. In point of fact, the history of all religions, including Christianity, demonstrates man's need for a sense of spiritual community and for corporate expression of such communal life.

Hence, if there is anything to Christianity at all, we can hope to make it available to ourselves only through close contact with it as a living tradition; and it is a living tradition today primarily in the Christian Church. Corporate worship, moreover, enables man to participate in a unique type of religious experience. It is not superior to private worship, or an alternative to it, or in conflict with it. On the contrary, Christians have testified again and again that it is an ideal complement to, and setting for, private worship. To believe in the God of Christianity is to believe that all men are indeed brothers; and what could be more natural than for brothers to wish to worship their common Father together, as well as in solitude? At its best, public worship is simultaneously the highest expression of men's sense of Christian community and common devotion, and the ideal setting for man's most sincere private communion with God. It is the sincere belief of Christians that the only wholly adequate community is the Christian community, and that the Church is the institutional expression of this Christian community.

(b) A second objection points to the multiplicity of Christian Churches and the dogmatic insistence of some that they alone provide the true institutional expression of Christianity. The dogmatism of Christian Churches and their inclination to brand other Churches as more or less heretical must be admitted and bitterly deplored. Many Church people talk as though, if Jesus were to return to earth today, He would select the Church to which they belong as the only truly Christian Church. This attitude bespeaks an appalling lack of genuine Christian humility, a lack which sincere Christians should combat with all their strength.

On the other hand, a liberal humanist should be the first to honor the sanctity of man's conscience, particularly in matters of ultimate belief. He should also recognize the possibility of subscribing to a set of beliefs so whole-heartedly that he is willing to live for them and if necessary die for them, while acknowledging, in true humility, the inevitable inadequacy of his own beliefs and those of his Church, and the great likelihood that other Churches have achieved and preserved important Christian insights. A Christian can be loyal to his own Church without renouncing loyalty to the universal Church or looking with contempt or hatred upon those who, with equal sincerity, feel compelled to interpret and worship God in their own way. He can go further. In complete loyalty to the Christian Church, and to his own Church, he can and should also prize the spirit of religious humility and dedication in many who do not associate themselves with any Church and who may even oppose the Christian Church as such. He cannot agree with them, and he must remain convinced of their individual loss and their failure to make their humanistic endeavors more effective than they now are. But he can and should maintain toward them that respect to which all men are entitled as men and as the children of God.

(c) A third objection to the Church is occasioned partly by its use of language, partly by its ritualistic forms and practices. Again it must be admitted that Christians are, like other men, deplorably prone to employ words and phrases that have been worn threadbare, not by over-use but by abuse. The language they use is all too often a conventional jargon, a thoughtless parroting of phrases that have lost, for them and for their hearers, all significant meaning. It must also be admitted that any ritual tends to lose its significance through sheer repetition, and that its symbolic meanings, which once endowed it with expressive value, tend to be forgotten. In proportion as this happens, ritual becomes a type of mechanistic behavior destructive of spirituality, or, even worse, behavior regarded as productive of magical effects. These thoroughly unChristian abuses of language and rite in our Churches call today as always for recognition and reform.

Yet this secular objection may be the result of a lack of understanding of Christian thought and worship. It may, for example, reflect a failure to realize that all distinctive insights and truths can be expressed precisely only in an appropriate and adequate language, and that such a language must often include technical terms or common terms used in a distinctive way. No one today dreams of denying scientists the right to use a highly technical language. Why should a similar right be denied theologians? It may also be occasioned by a failure to appreciate the nature and function of religious ritual and by ignorance of the symbolic and expressive meaning of Christian rites.

But this only partly states and answers the difficulty. The real difficulty is that the secular mind has drifted so far from the Church, and the Church from contemporary interests and needs, that theological language and religious rites which were intelligible and meaningful to earlier generations have become, even when intelligently used, nearly meaningless to most people, including many Christians who attend church services fairly regularly. Even within the Christian Church there is a widespread failure today to recognize the fact that religious belief and dedication are expressed in many different languages, in the language of poetry and the arts as well as in the conceptual language of theology. Hence the stupid insistence of narrow fundamentalists that the Bible be read as though its many poetic and prophetic passages were mere prose, to be taken as literalistically as possible. Hence also the common Protestant prejudice against ritual, as though it were necessarily inexpressive and magical.

The solution of this difficulty is not easy to find. Christian theologians must try to find fresh ways, meaningful to the modern world, to express old Christian truths and the relevance of these truths to the contemporary scene. They must also try to salvage and revivify well-established theological terms and symbolic rites which cannot be abandoned without serious loss. One of the great tasks of Christian education, within the Church and in Church-affiliated schools and colleges, is to promote a better understanding of the ways in which Christianity has been and can be expressed—in theology, in poetry, and in the visual and auditory arts.

(d) A final objection to the Church is the unChristian character and behavior of professing Christians. They are, so goes the criticism, hardly distinguishable from non-Christians in their attitudes toward their fellowmen and their preoccupation with secular pursuits and pleasures. Even the clergy are, with rare exceptions, condemned by the critical secularist as apparently lacking, to a deplorable degree, in that spirituality or essential piety which they, above all others, should manifest. The salt *has* lost its savor; Christian faith seems no longer to produce that saintliness which informed sensitive humanists recognize and respect when they encounter it. In short, the worst enemies of the Christian Church are its own feeble and unfaithful members who so inadequately exemplify the Christian Gospel in their own lives.

It is this type of criticism, taken in conjunction with the admitted failure of the Christian Church to reach or touch the vast majority of folk even in Christian lands, which makes men like Laski and Mumford despair of the present or future effectiveness of the Christian Church. Mumford, for example, fully recognizes that science alone will not save us, that naturalism is a threat to human values, and that we stand in urgent need of a great spiritual revival. But he obviously has little confidence that this revival will come through the agency of the Church.

> With all the talk of reunion between the Churches and sects, which has occupied the leaders of Christianity during the last half century, there are few real signs of the deeper spiritual effort required for Christianity's renewal—its admission of the local and relative nature of its original mission and its willingness to merge, for the sake of the universal values all men should share, with the faiths of other races and peoples which Western man too long spurned. An unChristian pride, disguising itself as a unique revelation of a truth not granted to other peoples, still blocks that essential sacrifice.

Similarly, Laski recognizes the great social benefits of Christianity in the past and the great contemporary need for a faith that will revitalize the human mind. But he feels compelled to turn to Communism, not to Christianity, for this vitalizing faith.

> The Christian faith, in its period of power, . . . offered to the common man the secret consolation of heaven. But now that the basis upon which that faith was built has crumbled before critical examination, neither the Churches nor any other religious organization can hope to effect the work of renovation.

These pessimistic estimates of the Church are the result, in part, of secular beliefs which Christians cannot share—Mumford's apparent belief that religious people throughout the world should ignore the credal differences which now separate them and subscribe to some kind of eclectic world religion, and Laski's outspoken humanistic convictions and deep-seated religious scepticism. But their assessment of the vitality, or lack of vitality, of the Christian Church is impressive. What can be said in answer to these charges?

Our first answer must be a contrite *mea culpa.* We are indeed miserable Christians, clergy and laity alike. We are indeed our Church's worst enemies. Our faith should indeed express itself in Christian works which even the secular mind could recognize and respect.

But our critics are not wholly fair. For some of them seem to believe that membership in a Christian community should automatically transform sinners into saints, or, alternatively, that only those who are already saintly should be eligible for such membership. What they forget is that it is man's bitter sense of sin that drives him to Christianity, and that, though Christ has promised us forgiveness, he has not promised to transform us so radically that we will never sin again. The Church ministers to sinners, and its ministry should be far more effective than it actually is; but it has never pretended to relieve men of their sinful finitude. It is easy for us Christians to demand far too little of ourselves and of each other. It is equally easy for non-Christians to demand too much of us, indeed, to demand the impossible.

Our answer to those who remain aloof from the Christian Church because of its tragic faults must therefore be: Join us in the effort to correct these faults, not by criticism from the outside, valuable as such criticism is, but from the inside, where it can be constructive and healing. Think how immeasurably stronger and healthier the Church would be today if men and women like you—sincere, intelligent, courageous—were active members of the Church, loyal to its ideals and critical of its malpractices, determined to champion in it all that is truly Christian and to condemn with prophetic fury all that is pharisaical and idolatrous, zealous at whatever cost to purify Christian worship, clarify Christian thought, vitalize and redirect Christian practice—comrades with us in the common task of Christianizing Christendom.

But we must also say to them: Join us in order to receive as well as to give, to learn as well as to instruct, to confess your sins and repent and experience within yourselves the healing power of the Christian Gospel. For the Church is not *merely* a human association of men banded together to promote human ends; it is also and essentially the association of men who acknowledge a common need, submit to a common judgment, and worship together a common Lord. It is, for all its faults, the vehicle of a great tradition in which are incorporated many spiritual insights to which you are still blind, the channel through which flow spiritual forces which are not now available to you. There are in the Church today many professing Christians as sincere, intelligent and courageous as you, who constitute a truly Christian community of believers and who derive from this communal life something of the joy and the peace of Christian faith, worship and endeavor. If you join us in the right spirit, critically but humbly, contritely but hopefully, you will yourselves progressively enter into that experience which is the condition and the reward of Christian faith. You will learn to understand more profoundly the human values which you already cherish and to promote far more effectively the human ends to which you are already dedicated, because you will have new sources of illumination and power which you now lack.

No one can say with assurance how much inner vitality still remains in the Christian Church or what it can do to help an anguished world in a period of supreme crisis. There is certainly more genuine piety and spiritual vitality in the Church today than many secularists realize. There is certainly far less than there should be or might be. What Christians must assert is that, if Christianity be true, as they believe it is with all their hearts, they at least have no choice but to remain loyal to it and to redouble their efforts to make it more truly a Christian community. They must acknowledge the enormous difficulty of the task which they have set themselves and which they beg their secular brethren to share with them.

To apprehend
The point of intersection of the timeless
With time, is an occupation for the saint—

No occupation either, but something given
And taken, in a lifetime's death in love,
Ardour and selflessness and self-surrender.[6]

They must admit the actuality of what St. John of the Cross described as the "dark night of the soul," confess the inadequacy of their best apprehension of God and of God's revelation to man, and acknowledge the feebleness and fitfulness of their own spiritual life. Eliot expresses this aspect of spiritual aspiration and frustration, hope and endeavor in poetic language which the sensitive secularist should be able to understand.

For most of us, there is only the unattended
Moment, the moment in and out of time,
The distraction fit, lost in a shaft of sunlight,
The wild thyme unseen, or the winter lightning
Or the waterfall, or music heard so deeply
That it is not heard at all, but you are the music
While the music lasts. These are only hints and guesses,
Hints followed by guesses; and the rest
Is prayer, observance, discipline, thought and action.
The hint half guessed, the gift half understood, is Incarnation.

They have no choice but to subscribe to Christianity's ruthless judgment upon our secular society which, while paying lip service to Christianity, has ignored or repudiated what the Christian Church symbolizes in the service of Holy Communion—a judgment which Eliot has condensed into five savage lines.

The dripping blood our only drink,
The bloody flesh our only food:
In spite of which we like to think
That we are sound, substantial flesh and blood—
Again, in spite of that, we call this Friday good.

But they can also testify, in company with the prophets and the saints and in the light of their own experience, to that peace of God which passeth all secular understanding, to that joy and thanksgiving which fill men's hearts and refresh them when, weary and heavy-laden, they turn to Christ for forgiveness, comfort, and strength. At such moments they too are impelled to cry with the Psalmist:

Make a joyful noise unto the Lord, all ye lands.
Serve the Lord with gladness: come before his presence with singing.
Know ye that the Lord he is God: it is he that hath made us and not we ourselves; we are his people, and the sheep of his pasture.

6. T. S. Eliot, *Four Quartets,* p. 27.

Enter into his gates with thanksgiving, and into his courts with praise: be thankful unto him, and bless his name.

For the Lord is good; his mercy is everlasting; and his truth endureth to all generations. (Psalm 100)

They too can say what St. Paul was able to say in the anguish of his spiritual conflict:

For I am persuaded, that neither death, nor life, nor angels, nor principalities, nor powers, nor things present, nor things to come, nor height, nor depth, nor any other creature, shall be able to separate us from the love of God, which is Christ Jesus our Lord. (Romans 8: 38–9)

RELIGION AND SCIENCE[1]

ALFRED NORTH WHITEHEAD

THE difficulty in approaching the question of the relations between Religion and Science is, that its elucidation requires that we have in our minds some clear idea of what we mean by either of the terms, "religion" and "science." Also I wish to speak in the most general way possible, and to keep in the background any comparison of particular creeds, scientific or religious. We have got to understand the type of connection which exists between the two spheres, and then to draw some definite conclusions respecting the existing situation which at present confronts the world.

The *conflict* between religion and science is what naturally occurs to our minds when we think of this subject. It seems as though, during the last half-century, the results of science and the beliefs of religion had come into a position of frank disagreement, from which there can be no escape, except by abandoning either the clear teaching of science, or the clear teaching of religion. This conclusion has been urged by controversialists on either side. Not by all controversialists, of course, but by those trenchant intellects which every controversy calls out into the open.

The distress of sensitive minds, and the zeal for truth, and the sense of the importance of the issues, must command our sincerest sympathy. When we consider what religion is for mankind, and what science is, it is no exaggeration to say that the future course of history depends upon the decision of this generation as to the relations between them. We have here the two strongest general forces (apart from the mere impulse of the various senses) which

1. From *Science and the Modern World,* copyright 1925 by The Macmillan Company. Reprinted by permission of The Macmillan Company.

influence men, and they seem to be set one against the other—the force of our religious intuitions, and the force of our impulse to accurate observation and logical deduction.

A great English statesman once advised his countrymen to use large-scale maps, as a preservative against alarms, panics, and general misunderstanding of the true relations between nations. In the same way in dealing with the clash between permanent elements of human nature, it is well to map our history on a large scale, and to disengage ourselves from our immediate absorption in the present conflicts. When we do this, we immediately discover two great facts. In the first place, there has always been a conflict between religion and science; and in the second place, both religion and science have always been in a state of continual development. In the early days of Christianity, there was a general belief among Christians that the world was coming to an end in the lifetime of people then living. We can make only indirect inferences as to how far this belief was authoritatively proclaimed; but it is certain that it was widely held, and that it formed an impressive part of the popular religious doctrine. The belief proved itself to be mistaken, and Christian doctrine adjusted itself to the change. Again in the early Church individual theologians very confidently deduced from the Bible opinions concerning the nature of the physical universe. In the year A.D. 535, a monk named Cosmas wrote a book which he entitled, *Christian Topography*. He was a travelled man who had visited India and Ethiopia; and finally he lived in a monastery at Alexandria, which was then a great centre of culture. In this book, basing himself upon the direct meaning of Biblical texts as construed by him in a literal fashion, he denied the existence of the antipodes, and asserted that the world is a flat parallelogram whose length is double its breadth.

In the seventeenth century the doctrine of the motion of the earth was condemned by a Catholic tribunal. A hundred years ago the extension of time demanded by geological science distressed religious people, Protestant and Catholic. And today the doctrine of evolution is an equal stumbling-block. These are only a few instances illustrating a general fact.

But all our ideas will be in a wrong perspective if we think that this recurring perplexity was confined to contradictions between religion and science; and that in these controversies religion was always wrong, and that science was always right. The true facts of the case are very much more complex, and refuse to be summarized in these simple terms.

Theology itself exhibits exactly the same character of gradual development, arising from an aspect of conflict between its own proper ideas. This fact is a commonplace to theologians, but is often obscured in the stress of controversy. I do not wish to overstate my case; so I will confine myself to Roman Catholic writers. In the seventeenth century a learned Jesuit, Father Petavius, showed that the theologians of the first three centuries of Christianity made use of phrases and statements which since the fifth century would be condemned as heretical. Also Cardinal Newman devoted a treatise to the discussion of the development of doctrine. He wrote it before he became a great Roman Catholic ecclesiastic; but throughout his life, it was never retracted and continually reissued.

Science is even more changeable than theology. No man of science could subscribe without qualification to Galileo's beliefs, or to Newton's beliefs, or to all his own scientific beliefs of ten years ago.

In both regions of thought, additions, distinctions, and modifications have been introduced. So that now, even when the same assertion is made today as was made a thousand, or fifteen hundred years ago, it is made subject to limitations or expansions of meaning, which were not contemplated at the earlier epoch. We are told by logicians that a proposition must be either true or false, and that there is no middle term. But in practice, we may know that a proposition expresses an important truth, but that it is subject to limitations and qualifications which at present remain undiscovered. It is a general feature of our knowledge, that we are insistently aware of important truths; and yet that the only formulations of these truths which we are able to make presuppose a general standpoint of conceptions which may have to be modified. I will give you two illustrations, both from science: Galileo said that the earth moves and that the sun is fixed; the Inquisition said that the earth is fixed and the sun moves; and Newtonian astronomers, adopting an absolute theory of space, said that both the sun and the earth move. But now we say that any one of these three statements is equally true, provided that you have fixed your sense of "rest" and "motion" in the way required by the statement adopted. At the date of Galileo's controversy with the Inquisition, Galileo's way of stating the facts was, beyond question, the fruitful procedure for the sake of scientific research. But in itself it was not more true than the formulation of the Inquisition. But at that time the modern concepts of relative motion were in nobody's mind; so that the statements were made in ignorance of the qualifications required for their more perfect truth. Yet this question of the motions of the earth and the sun expresses a real fact in the universe; and all sides had got hold of important truths concerning it. But with the knowledge of those times, the truths appeared to be inconsistent.

Again I will give you another example taken from the state of modern physical science. Since the time of Newton and Huyghens in the seventeenth century there have been two theories as to the physical nature of light. Newton's theory was that a beam of light consists of a stream of very minute particles, or corpuscles, and that we have the sensation of light when these corpuscles strike the retinas of our eyes. Huyghens' theory was that light consists of very minute waves of trembling in an all-pervading ether, and that these waves are travelling along a beam of light. The two theories are contradictory. In the eighteenth century Newton's theory was believed, in the nineteenth century Huyghens' theory was believed. Today there is one large group of phenomena which can be explained only on the wave theory, and another large group which can be explained only on the corpuscular theory. Scientists have to leave it at that, and wait for the future, in the hope of attaining some wider vision which reconciles both.

We should apply these same principles to the questions in which there is a variance between science and religion. We would believe nothing in either sphere of thought which does not appear to us to be certified by solid reasons based upon the critical research either of ourselves or of competent authorities. But granting that we have honestly taken this precaution, a clash between the two on points of detail where they overlap should not lead us hastily to abandon doctrines for which we have solid evidence. It may be that we are more interested in one set of doctrines than in the other. But, if we have any sense of perspective and of the history of thought, we shall wait and refrain from mutual anathemas.

We should wait: but we should not wait passively, or in despair. The clash is a sign that there are wider truths and finer perspectives within which a reconciliation of a deeper religion and a more subtle science will be found.

In one sense, therefore, the conflict between science and religion is a slight matter which has been unduly emphasized. A mere logical contradiction cannot in itself point to more than the necessity of some readjustments, possibly of a very minor character on both sides. Remember the widely different aspects of events which are dealt with in science and in religion respectively. Science is concerned with the general conditions which are observed to regulate physical phenomena; whereas religion is wholly wrapped up in the contemplation of moral and aesthetic values. On the one side there is the law of gravitation, and on the other the contemplation of the beauty of holiness. What one side sees, the other misses; and vice versa.

Consider, for example, the lives of John Wesley and of Saint Francis of Assisi. For physical science you have in these lives merely ordinary examples of the operation of the principles of physiological chemistry, and of the dynamics of nervous reactions: for religion you have lives of the most profound significance in the history of the world. Can you be surprised that, in the absence of a perfect and complete phrasing of the principles of science and of the principles of religion which apply to these specific cases, the accounts of these lives from these divergent standpoints should involve discrepancies? It would be a miracle if it were not so.

It would, however, be missing the point to think that we need not trouble ourselves about the conflict between science and religion. In an intellectual age there can be no active interest which puts aside all hope of a vision of the harmony of truth. To acquiesce in discrepancy is destructive of candour, and of moral cleanliness. It belongs to the self-respect of intellect to pursue every tangle of thought to its final unravelment. If you check that impulse, you will get no religion and no science from an awakened thoughtfulness. The important question is, In what spirit are we going to face the issue? There we come to something absolutely vital.

A clash of doctrines is not a disaster—it is an opportunity. I will explain my meaning by some illustrations from science. The weight of an atom of nitrogen was well known. Also it was an established scientific doctrine that the average weight of such atoms in any considerable mass will be always the same. Two experimenters, the late Lord Rayleigh and the late Sir William Ramsay, found that if they obtained nitrogen by two different methods, each equally effective for that purpose, they always observed a persistent slight difference between the average weights of the atoms in the two cases. Now I ask you, would it have been rational of these men to have despaired because of this conflict between chemical theory and scientific observation? Suppose that for some reason the chemical doctrine had been highly prized throughout some district as the foundation of its social order:—would it have been wise, would it have been candid, would it have been moral, to forbid the disclosure of the fact that the experiments produced discordant results? Or, on the other hand, should Sir William Ramsay and Lord Rayleigh have proclaimed that chemical theory was now a detected delusion? We see at once that either of these ways would have been a method of facing the issue in an entirely wrong spirit. What Rayleigh and Ramsay did was this: They at once perceived that they had hit upon a line of investigation which would disclose some subtlety of chemical theory that had hitherto eluded observation. The discrepancy was not a disaster: it was an opportunity to increase the sweep of chemical knowledge. You all know the end of the story: finally argon was discovered, a new chemical element which had lurked undetected, mixed with the nitrogen. But the story has a sequel which forms my second illustration. This discovery drew attention to the importance of observing accurately minute differences in chemical substances as obtained by different methods. Further researches of the most careful accuracy were undertaken. Finally another physicist, F. W. Aston, working in the Cavendish Laboratory at Cambridge in England, discovered that even the same element might assume two or more distinct forms, termed *isotopes,* and that the law of the constancy of average atomic weight holds for each of these forms, but as between the different isotopes differs slightly. The research has effected a great stride in the power of chemical theory, far transcending in importance the discovery of argon from which it originated. The moral of these stories lies on the surface, and I will leave to you their application to the case of religion and science.

In formal logic, a contradiction is the signal of a defeat: but in the evolution of real knowledge it marks the first step in progress towards a victory. This is one great reason for the utmost toleration of variety of opinion. Once and forever, this duty of toleration has been summed up in the words, "Let both grow together until the harvest." The failure of Christians to act up to this precept, of the highest authority, is one of the curiosities of religious history. But we have not yet exhausted the discussion of the moral temper required for the pursuit of truth. There are short cuts leading merely to an illusory success. It is easy enough to find a theory, logically harmonious and with important applications in the region of fact, provided that you are content to disregard half your evidence. Every age produces people with clear logical intellects, and with the most praiseworthy grasp of the importance of some sphere of human experience, who have elaborated, or inherited, a scheme of thought which exactly fits those experiences which claim their interest. Such people are apt resolutely to ignore, or to explain away, all evidence which confuses their scheme with contradictory instances. What they cannot fit in is for them nonsense. An unflinching determination to take the whole evidence into account is the only method of preservation against the fluctuating extremes of fashionable opinion. This advice seems so easy, and is in fact so difficult to follow.

One reason for this difficulty is that we cannot think first and act afterwards. From the moment of birth we are immersed in action, and can only fitfully guide it by taking thought. We have, therefore, in various spheres of experience to adopt those ideas which seem to work within those spheres. It is absolutely necessary to trust to ideas which are generally adequate, even though we know that there are subtleties and distinctions beyond our ken. Also apart from the necessities of action, we cannot even keep before our minds the whole evidence except under the guise of doctrines which are incompletely harmonized. We cannot think in terms of an indefinite multiplicity of detail; our evidence can acquire its proper importance only if it comes before us marshalled by general ideas. These ideas we inherit—they form the tradition of our civilization. Such traditional ideas are never static. They are either fading into meaningless formulae, or are gaining power by the new lights thrown by a more delicate apprehension. They are transformed by the urge of critical reason, by the vivid evidence of emotional experience, and by the cold certainties of scientific perception. One fact is certain, you cannot keep them still. No generation can merely reproduce its ancestors. You may preserve the life in a flux of form, or preserve the form amid an ebb of life. But you cannot permanently enclose the same life in the same mold.

The present state of religion among the European races illustrates the statements which I have been making. The phenomena are mixed. There have been reactions and revivals. But on the whole, during many generations, there has been a gradual decay of religious influence in European civilization. Each revival touches a lower peak than its predecessor, and each period of slackness a lower depth. The average curve marks a steady fall in religious tone. In some countries the interest in religion is higher than in others. But in those countries where the interest is relatively high, it still falls as the generations pass. Religion is tending to degenerate into a decent formula wherewith to embellish a comfortable life. A great historical movement on this scale results from the convergence of many causes. I wish to suggest two of them which lie within the scope of this chapter for consideration.

In the first place for over two centuries religion has been on the defensive, and on a weak defensive. The period has been one of unprecedented intellectual progress. In this way a series of novel situations have been produced for thought. Each such occasion has found the religious thinkers unprepared. Something, which has been proclaimed to be vital, has finally, after struggle, distress, and anathema, been modified and otherwise interpreted. The next generation of religious apologists then congratulates the religious world on the deeper insight which has been gained. The result of the continued repetition of this undignified retreat, during many generations, has at last almost entirely destroyed the intellectual authority of religious thinkers. Consider this contrast: when Darwin or Einstein proclaim theories which modify our ideas, it is a triumph for science. We do not go about saying that there is another defeat for science, because its old ideas have been abandoned. We know that another step of scientific insight has been gained.

Religion will not regain its old power until it can face change in the same spirit as does science. Its principles may be eternal, but the expression of those principles requires continual development. This evolution of religion is in the main a disengagement of its own proper ideas from the adventitious notions which have crept into it by reason of the expression of its own ideas in terms of the imaginative picture of the world entertained in previous ages. Such a release of religion from the bonds of imperfect science is all to the good. It stresses its own genuine message. The great point to be kept in mind is that normally an advance in science will show that statements of various religious beliefs require some sort of modification. It may be that they have to be expanded or explained, or indeed entirely restated. If the religion is a sound expression of truth, this modification will only exhibit more adequately the exact point which is of importance. This process is a gain. In so far, therefore, as any religion has any contact with physical facts, it is to be expected that the point of view of those facts must be continually modified as scientific knowledge advances. In this way, the exact relevance of these facts for religious thought will grow more and more clear. The progress of science must result in the unceasing codification of religious thought, to the great advantage of religion.

The religious controversies of the sixteenth and seventeenth centuries put theologians into a most unfortunate state of mind. They were always attacking and defending. They pictured themselves as the garrison of a fort surrounded by hostile forces. All such pictures express half-truths. That is why they are so popular. But they are dangerous. This particular picture fostered a pugnacious party spirit which really expresses an ultimate lack of faith. They dared not modify, because they shirked the task of disengaging their spiritual message from the associations of a particular imagery.

Let me explain myself by an example. In the early medieval times, Heaven was in the sky, and Hell was underground; volcanoes were the jaws of Hell. I do not assert that these beliefs entered into the official formulations: but they did enter into the popular understanding of the general doctrines of Heaven and Hell. These notions were what everyone thought to be implied by the doctrine of the future state. They entered into the explanations of the influential exponents of Christian belief. For example, they occur in the *Dialogues* of Pope Gregory, the Great, a man whose high official position is surpassed only by the magnitude of his services to humanity. I am not saying what we ought to believe about the future state. But whatever be the right doctrine, in this instance the clash between religion and science, which has relegated the earth to the position of a second-rate planet attached to a second-rate sun, has been greatly to the benefit of the spirituality of religion by dispersing these medieval fancies.

Another way of looking at this question of the evolution of religious thought is to note that any verbal form of statement which has been before the world for some time discloses ambiguities; and that often such ambiguities strike at the very heart of the meaning. The effective sense in which a doctrine has been held in the past cannot be determined by the mere logical analysis of verbal statements, made in ignorance of the logical trap. You have to take into account the whole reaction of human nature to the scheme of thought. This reaction is of a mixed character, including elements of emotion derived from our lower natures. It is here that the impersonal criticism of science and of philosophy comes to the aid of religious evolution. Example after example can be given of this motive force in development. For example, the logical difficulties inherent in the doctrine of the moral cleansing of human nature by the power of religion rent Christianity in the days of Pelagius and Augustine —that is to say, at the beginning of the fifth century. Echoes of that controversy still linger in theology.

So far, my point has been this: that religion is the expression of one type of fundamental experiences of mankind: that religious thought develops into an increasing accuracy of expression, disengaged from adventitious imagery: that the interaction between religion and science is one great factor in promoting this development.

I now come to my second reason for the modern fading of interest in religion. This involves the ultimate question which I stated in my opening sentences. We have to know what we mean by religion. The churches, in their presentation of their answers to this query, have put forward aspects of religion which are expressed in terms either suited to the emotional reactions of bygone times or directed to excite modern emotional interests of nonreligious character. What I mean under the first heading is that religious appeal is directed partly to excite that instinctive fear of the wrath of a tyrant which was inbred in the unhappy populations of the arbitrary empires of the ancient world, and in particular to excite that fear of an all-powerful arbitrary tyrant behind the unknown forces of nature. This appeal to the ready instinct of brute fear is losing its force. It lacks any directness of response, because modern science and modern conditions of life have taught us to meet occasions of apprehension by a critical analysis of their causes and conditions. Religion is the reaction of human nature to its search for God. The presentation of God under the aspect of power awakens every modern instinct of critical reaction. This is fatal; for religion collapses unless its main positions command immediacy of assent. In this respect the old phraseology is at variance with the psychology of modern civilizations. This change in psychology is largely due to science, and is one of the chief ways in which the advance of science has weakened the hold of the old religious forms of expression. The non-religious motive which has entered into modern religious thought is the desire for a comfortable organization of modern society. Religion has been presented as valuable for the ordering of life. Its claims have been rested upon its function as a sanction to right conduct. Also the purpose of right conduct quickly degenerates into the formation of pleasing social relations. We have here a subtle degradation of religious ideas, following upon their gradual purification under the influence of keener ethical intuitions. Conduct is a by-product of religion—an inevitable by-product, but not the main point. Every great religious teacher has revolted against the presentation of religion as a mere sanction of rules of conduct. Saint Paul denounced the Law, and Puritan divines spoke of the filthy rags of righteousness. The insistence upon rules of conduct marks the ebb of religious fervor. Above and beyond all things, the religious life is not a research after comfort. I must now state, in all diffidence, what I conceive to be the essential character of the religious spirit.

Religion is the vision of something which stands beyond, behind, and within, the passing flux of immediate things; something which is real, and yet waiting to be realized; something which is a remote possibility, and yet the greatest of present facts; something that gives meaning to all that passes, and yet eludes apprehension; something whose possession is the final good, and yet is beyond all reach; something which is the ultimate ideal, and the hopeless quest.

The immediate reaction of human nature to the religious vision is worship. Religion has emerged into human experience mixed with the crudest fancies of barbaric imagination. Gradually, slowly, steadily the vision recurs in history under nobler form and with clearer expression. It is the one element in human experience which persistently shows an upward trend. It fades and then recurs. But when it renews its force, it recurs with an added richness and purity of content. The fact of the religious vision, and its history of persistent expansion, is our one ground for optimism. Apart from it, human life is a flash of occasional enjoyments lighting up a mass of pain and misery, a bagatelle of transient experience.

The vision claims nothing but worship; and worship is a surrender to the claim of assimilation, urged with the motive force of mutual love. The vision never overrules. It is always there, and it has the power of love presenting the one purpose whose fulfilment is eternal harmony. Such order as we find in nature is never force—it presents itself as the one harmonious adjustment of complex detail. Evil is the brute motive force of fragmentary purpose, disregarding the eternal vision. Evil is overruling, retarding, hurting. The power of God is the worship He inspires. That religion is strong which in its ritual and its modes of thought evokes an apprehension of the commanding vision. The worship of God is not a rule of safety—it is an adventure of the spirit, a flight after the unattainable. The death of religion comes with the repression of the high hope of adventure.

LIVING RELIGIONS AND A WORLD FAITH [1]

WILLIAM ERNEST HOCKING

IF ONE were still able to travel by train from the New Harbor of Dubrovnik to Serajevo, climbing noisily (and smokily) up the mountain slopes bordering the fine estuary of the Ombla, he would be aware of a swift change of cultural as well as of physical climate. The Dalmatian coast bears everywhere the Roman and Venetian mark in architecture and religion; there are a few Greek Orthodox Churches and numerous Jewish synagogues. But as one reaches Mostar he sees minarets as well as steeples and domes. And at Serajevo it is evident that the religion of Mohammed is a lively factor in the community. Christianity, Judaism, Islam—three religions of Asiatic origin, dominate the Balkan peninsula. At Spalato, Mestrovic's gigantic statue of Bishop Gregory set up in the ruins of the palace of Diocletian symbolizes the almost complete submersion of the religious influence of classical antiquity, both Roman and Greek, under these faiths from the East.

Except in point of proportion the story of the Balkans is repeated everywhere in Europe and America: whatever forms of religion are alive among us we owe to Asia. We are less conscious of the presence of Islam than of Judaism and Christianity, hardly at all aware of Hinduism. Many do not realize that there are (or were) active Moslem missions in England (as at Woking in Surrey), Germany, and France; and that besides the monumental mosque in Paris built to signalize the fact that France was a great Moslem power, there are active mosques in Brooklyn and Chicago; nor that Bahai is an offshoot of Islam, as the Vedanta movement with a dozen American centers is an offshoot of Hinduism.

There are no religions indigenous to Europe and America which compare with these religions from Asia either in their present vitality or in their influence on our civilization. Ths fact has sometimes been taken as a reproach against the religious originality of the Western world. Sometimes it has

1. From William Ernest Hocking in *The Asian Legacy*, ed. by Arthur E. Christy (New York: The John Day Company, 1942), pp. 193–214.

been taken as an argument that religion itself is a peculiar Oriental export, not really suited to our mentality, which we should do well to lay aside quietly, with all due gratitude for its historic services.

To comment on the latter point first, it is not at all certain that these historic services have been finished. What they amount to, in sum, is supplying the fecundity and the backbone for all that we call "Western civilization." This has been chiefly the work of Christianity. The Christian version of Roman-Stoic law, eked out by canon law, and administered by officers of the church, tided Europe over its darker hours of disorder, and laid the foundation for all civil law in Europe. The common law of England and America is an offspring of Anglo-Saxon conscience under the guidance of the church. The whole conception of the rights of man is directly traceable to Christian conceptions of human nature, and with that, all we call individualism, liberalism, democracy in the modern sense. The art of Europe, including architecture, music, painting, sculpture, was shaped by the medieval church; likewise its literature and philosophy. And as for its science, which we are inclined to think of as the result of a revolt against religious authority, and especially as one point which sets us off from everything Oriental—the whole development of scientific method in the seventeenth century, with its spirit of revolt—not against religion nor Christianity but against the authority of Aristotle and the Bible in matters of logic and science, is demonstrably an application of Christian ethics to the study of Nature, and was carried on by men who regarded themselves as more religious than those who criticized them. No historian can explain why and how what we call the modern era arose in Europe and America and nowhere else, who does not recognize the religion of Europe and America as one of the parents of that era.

And though we owe so much to Christianity, it is not at all clear that we yet know what it means. It still seems strange to us—otherworldly, remote, extravagant, impractical—in short "Oriental." Probably the Orient does in fact understand it better than we do. This means that we claim too much when we say we have taken our religion from the East: it has not yet been completely taken. We still have to learn religion from Asia, both in terms of the living religions which are there, and in terms of Asiatic versions of Christianity. Certainly, the learning business has to go in both directions, but our own culture will lack catholicity, poise, and security until we know what we have to do with religion in an age which is rightly committed to the humanistic spirit and the technology which is the gift of science.

As to the other matter—that we ought to be ashamed to take our religion from Asia—there are two things to be said. First, that religion is always original or nothing: nobody can use the religion of anybody else but himself. Whatever he accepts by way of suggestion or teaching from outside has to become his own conviction before it can do him any good. And as he appropriates it, he remolds it and produces his own version, even when he accepts it most humbly as the authoritative word of God. Second, the Western world is not behind in religious fecundity. Every ethnic region of Europe has produced its religious forms, still discernible in the undercurrents of folklore. There have been magnificent pantheons among them, from the urbane Olympians of Greece to the stormy Aesir, denizens of Asgard (from two of whom, Odin and Thor, we derive the words Wednesday and Thursday—our weekday names remaining obstinately pagan). And with these there have come splendid poetic literatures, mythologies, theologies, and parable-wisdoms. There have not been lacking efforts to resuscitate some of these buried cities of the spirit or to recover for use some of their ideas. Lutoslawski, for example, labored over the doctrine of transmigration as found in the Polish epics in order to show that it was an improvement on either the Hindu doctrine, associated with Karma, or Plato's picture of rebirth. But these European religions remain local reminiscences, held in the subconscious mold of peasant usages or absorbed into the framework of the dominant faith. Why, then, have the great Asiatic religions taken their place? The fact, I believe, is neither accidental nor humiliating: it is an inevitable consequence of the nature of religion and its history. I shall try to make this evident.

I

Religion is man's practical dealing with the enduring auspices of his destiny, his communion with what is eternal and total in his world, conceived as a source of direction to right living. By definition, religion reached toward what is universally true, that which concerns all men alike, no matter of what place, color, sex, race, or nation. Its nature is, therefore, to unite men in the consciousness of a common lot and obligation. Wherever it arises, and however it expresses itself, its whole meaning is to find that one reality and that one law which are valid for all mankind. At the same time, every religion, having its local origins, dealing with the less tangible sides of the world, having to use symbols, metaphors, and appeals rather than market-literalities, is steeped in localism. Belonging as it does to the working balance of a culture, it grows with the given culture, and the early religions naturally observe the limits drawn by language and political control. It is this paradoxical union of the local and the universal by which we have to understand the strange facts of religious history and dominance.

The strain between the local and the universal is relieved by the fact that the worshiper is usually unaware of the local quality of his religion. The Arab does not think of his religion as Arabian; it is his way of dealing with Allah, who, in his view, is the God of all men: so far from being felt as local, it is his way of escaping from localism. But he has something specific to do about his faith; he must make his prayers, and in doing so, orient his prayer-rug toward Mecca. He may well be wholly unconscious that in tethering his religion to a particular point in space, he has thereby separated himself from—let us say, a Japanese for whom a certain brass plate in a temple near Nara marks the spot where Amaterasu Omikami began the creation of the world. It is not the Arab but the outsider who finds that this Arab's religion has an "Oriental" flavor, or if he the outsider is a connoisseur, an Arab flavor, racy with the grandeur and masculinity of the imagination of the great peninsula

And let us notice, too, that whatever the strain may be between the local and the universal, it does not amount to a contradiction. No religion is more local than Hinduism: it is steeped in the atmosphere of the land whose name it insists on keeping: it is a vast tree with a thousand branches and a thousand roots, almost oppressive to the European-American taste by the exuberance of its imagery and the fruitiness of its sense of life. Yet it is just Hinduism which distills itself into the most ethereal of all essences: its Brahman, the absolute being, is devoid of all describable attributes, has no temples, is not worshiped, stands one might say for a sort of dark North Pole in the night sky of the mind. It is as if Hinduism, as it strove to give an exact account of its faith, derived from its soil enough energy to reject every trace of the soil, every trace of the earth itself and of human life, everything that could serve as an identifying mark, and in the guise of Vedanta spread everywhere like a religious ether, pervasive and nonresistant.

This case of Hinduism suggests what happens to a religion as it becomes thoughtful. It becomes aware that its *truth* has no national boundaries, and on that ground, it begins to travel.

It is likely to be handicapped in this undertaking by the fact that a religion does not consist of truth alone; if it did, the problem of a world faith might be much easier. A religion is always a truth (embodied in a creed), a ritual, and a code. The moral code is likely, in early stages, to embody much of the common law of the community and therefore to be so characteristic as not to be applicable to other groups: the Hindu sacred law (*The Book of Manu*) could not be practiced in China. And as for the ritual, these symbolic observances belong so much to the special histories and feelings of the groups in which they arise that they are with difficulty so much as understood by others. Primitive peoples hide their rituals, not because they are ashamed of them, but because they do not wish to expose what is so closely bound up with their own feelings to an unsympathetic eye: early ritual is inherently private to its group—which is one reason of course for the exceptional curiosity it awakens in anthropologists and others. It is for this reason that a great Hindu like Ghandhi, whose creed is in many respects coincident with Christianity, has no inclination to identify himself with Christianity. When he says that God has set his lot in India and that he must remain Hindu, he means not that his beliefs are different but that his religion is inseparable from the code, the ritual, and the sacred literature of his people (including their development and reform), and cannot lightly migrate with the universal scope of their thought. The name Rama is to him the most friendly and homely name of God.

Now Gandhi is certainly right about the localism of the whole concrete working of a religion: it has to have roots in the place it lives in. But if this were the last word, we Americans neither ought to be nor could be using Asiatic religions. God knows what religion we would have—possibly Druidism, if we have a Celtic rill in our veins! For a migratory people, localism presents difficulties, and certainly cannot be the determining factor. But there is a state at which *religion itself becomes migratory;* and this stage was reached in India itself. For Buddhism is an Indian product, and Buddhism is inherently a traveling religion. By its own view of its teachings it was incapable of staying at home; and its wandering saved its life, for after a time it died out in India, and lived only in its newer homes—Burma, Ceylon, Siam, Afghanistan, Tibet, China, Japan. Christianity likewise almost abandoned Palestine, spreading to the north and west. Islam, the third among the great traveling religions, has still its central hearth in Arabia and Palestine, but its great mass of adherents lie across southern Asia and northern Africa. What is the peculiar point of view of the traveling religions?

In my judgment it is a matter of religious maturity. It is a phase which was bound to come with full religious self-consciousness, favored by a long history of civilization. (We may leave Islam aside for the moment, since Mohammed was largely influenced by Judaism and Christianity as he met them in Arabia, the other "religions of the Book," as he called them.) The simple reason why we are all using Asiatic religions is that Asia, having a longer consecutive religious history, and producing the men of genius who were able to read the meaning of this history, reached this stage first. What they did was so well conceived that there is no more reason for rejecting it—in the interest of a specious originality—than there would be for rejecting the alphabet or the multiplication table as "Oriental" because these too were first elaborated in Asia. Every part of the world has its indigenous religion; but only in Asia did the local cult have time to come to full flower and send its seeds, detached from the mother plant, to the four winds.

The local religions of Europe have not traveled, because they were not ready to travel when the era of traveling was on. The Germanic and Scandinavian cults had not been ripened by that wide political experience which plays its part in tempering and saddening the human spirit. Not only were they unchastened and unremorseful with respect to their own inherent powers of right living, they had not encountered that experience of political disillusionment which could make a mental distinction between "the world" and "the spirit," or between "the realm of appearance" and "the realm of true being." In brief, the problem of evil, as an accompaniment of high political civilization, could not so much as be formulated by these European cults: they were exuberant, thoughtless, and aggressive; like the Wends of whom Carlyle wrote, their peoples had to be "damped down into Christianity." And if something was extinguished in them—as no doubt it was—they endured the chastening because there was opened to them, at the same moment, a whole new dimension of moral experience which they were able to recognize—

not as Asiatic—but as their own. The West-bound religion of Asia engulfed them only because it showed them their own destiny in the concrete. Those who wish to decry Christianity in Europe call it an "Oriental religion." Those in Asia who wish to decry the Christianity which Europe and America have at times tried to bring back to it have sometimes called it a "Western religion." Very likely it is both, in various details; since a much-traveled religion, like a much-traveled man, will bear traces of all the regions in which he has been at home. But in its original out-push it was neither; it intended to be simply "the way" for men everywhere; its founder never heard the word "Christian"; he considered himself a Jew, calling for a reform or a reconception of the Jewish faith such as would shake off its local restrictions. Five hundred years earlier a young Indian, Siddhartha, whom we now call "The Buddha" or "The Enlightened One," had undertaken a similar liberation of the local religion of his people. He offered his "way" (under the name of of the Noble or Aryan Eightfold Path) not to Indians but to mankind. He never heard the word Buddhism. These religions traveled because they had to: having reached self-consciousness about what a religion has to do, a local boundary became a self-contradiction.

They did not as a rule spread automatically, as science has done, throughout human history, but by propaganda. Of each it is said that the founder "sent forth" disciples to preach the message—a new function in the life of religion. The words attributed to Buddha are these:

> "Go, ye Bhikkus, for the weal of many, for the enlightenment of gods and of men; go not two together; let your abode be the shade of trees, your food what is given you . . ."

Whether words like these were actually uttered is less important than the fact that they expressed what the original groups of believers thought of their duties and acted on. These religions had reached the traveling-point, as water reaches the boiling-point. I suggest that we now test this theory by examining some of the significant circumstances attending the origins of the great traveling faiths.

II

First note the circumstances that these religions (again excepting Islam) arose within a limited period of world history—let us say between the eighth century B.C. and our era. The eighth century we may take as the period of the great Hebrew prophets, who, considering Jehovah as god of the whole earth, laid the foundations for present-day Judaism. About this time, India's forests were yielding an esoteric wisdom, Aranyakas and Upanishads, drawing from the robust polytheism of the Vedas a strict and abstract monism, the basis of the Vedanta. Here, in the sixth and fifth centuries B.C. Buddha appeared (562–482 perhaps). And almost precisely contemporary with him, Confucius in China (550–478); while Lao Tze, founder of Taoism, whose date is uncertain, may have been an older contemporary of both. About the same time, various so-called mystery religions in the Near East and in Greece, symptomatic of the religious unrest of the era, developed traveling propensities. Socrates and Plato (fourth and third centuries B.C.) were not unrelated to the religious concerns of the time. In Palestine, the hill country of Judaea and Galilee offered retreats for reflective spirits, aside from the main travel routes yet not far from them; its rabbis were called philosophers by the Greeks. Alexander paid it little heed, though his teacher, Aristotle, was said to have conversed with one of these wise men from the hills. But when Rome absorbed the small land the stage was set whereby a local disturbance, started by a dreamer from Galilee, could become a world movement.

The greater traveling religions are all products of religious revolt or reform; all of them shake off as unessential some of the local characters of the traditional religion of their several regions; all of them emphasize the universal aspect of religion. All of them make religion an individual matter, and an inward matter, more concerned with motives than with visible conduct. As revolts, they had to be the work of outstanding personalities. And partly on this account they have all come to be identified by the names or titles of their founders; they are "founded" religions, in contrast to the great local background of religious tradition whose authorship (generally speaking) is as little known as the authorship of the several languages. To identify a religion as "the religion of the Buddha" or "the religion of the Christ" or "the religion of the Prophet" does indeed introduce a new localism, a note of partisanship which promises much future trouble in the way of the world faith; but it does, at least, set the religion in question free from the older localism of habitat or race or people.

Was this striking set of similarities among the traveling religions a coincidence, or was there something like a world situation to which these several movements were responses? One suspects that the latter is the case, because no matter how great the genius of a prophet, he can start no historic movement unless the minds of men are asking the questions to which he offers the answers.

Perhaps the world situation was this—that men began to be aware that there *is* a "world." It was a period in which contact, commerce, and conquest within the area of Asia, Egypt, and Greece were destroying cultural isolation without destroying cultures. The "world" began to be thought of as a cultural pluralism, in which it was no longer possible for each one, having grown strong in solitude, to think of itself as the hearth of mankind, the rest being in peripheral twilight as "barbarian" or "gentile." What was taking place was the Copernican revolution of the cultural universe; the center could no longer be securely located at home! When Rome came, it merely finished what had been going on: to all but Rome itself, the political disasters implied by the Roman conquests toppled the easy mental supremacies of all local deities. Local religion had begun to be under suspicion.

More than this: individual men were forced to realize that they could not find complete human satisfaction any longer in their careers as citizens of their own communities. Standing, in the social world, was full of accident and injustice; the problem of happiness or of "salvation" could not be solved within the human social or political order. Religion, which had hitherto gone along with group life, inspiring its codes and sanctioning its loyalties, begins to pull apart from politics and address itself to the individual soul. The other world becomes important, and immortality a desired prospect, if there is any way to secure it. The career of the soul becomes the dominant theme of the religious "way."

This disaffection from the actual world and its natural ambitions does not need to go to the extent of despair, or what Gilbert Murray calls "loss of nerve," in order to present religion with its primary problem, that of the meaning of life. The distinction between the present world and another world is itself a source of profound unhappiness. How can a man wean away his desires and interests from the world in which he must act? He does not do so unless he is compelled to, not merely by circumstances, but by his thinking which convinces him that the separation *has to be made,* alike whether he is personally fortunate or unfortunate: the world of human experience is simply not capable of satisfying the demands of the human soul. Things at their best are finite and man is infinite; this is the root of the "problem of evil" which religion now faces in its full scope.

The great traveling religions are, accordingly, religions of "salvation." Each gives its own analysis of the human dilemma; each offers its own recipe for cure; each gives its teaching as to what men ought to hope for, here and hereafter. These answers are diverse, and this constitutes a part of the problem of the world faith of the future. We shall speak of these differences. For the moment we have been concerned simply to see why religion, arriving at a certain maturity in Asia, naturally came to Europe and America from that source.

At the same time, we can understand why certain other religious movements of the same period did not have the same tendency to universal spread. The Confucian world view had its religious elements; but Confucius was a reformer in this field only in the sense that, leaning against the superstition of his time, he selected and simplified its working elements, and confronted the rest with a prudent pragmatism. For him the working element of religion was a belief in Heaven (Tien) as an appointer of human destiny; every man had his task, and was bound to qualify himself to fulfil it. For the ordinary conduct of life, Confucius' genius was that of clarifying usage, with great loyalty to tradition, and much sensitiveness of conscience. He has given us one of the great religious sayings of all time: "He who offends the gods has no one to whom he can pray"—the self-created moral solitude of the man who holds himself able to defy duty. There was sufficient universality in the Confucian outlook to permit its spread to Korea and Japan; but China was, in the period we have described, still somewhat apart from the main current of Asiatic thought. Confucius reminds us in many ways of Socrates, in his concern for definitions of ethical ideas, and his indisposition to speculate. But through Socrates and Plato, the career of Greek religious thought took a directly opposite turn, emptying itself almost wholly into philosophy. Now philosophy, like mathematics, is universal by its nature, and neither requires nor can use the methods of preaching and propaganda. Socrates remained the inspiration of various schools of classical thought, especially of the Stoics; but he founded no community, and his thought entered namelessly into the body of Platonism, and thus of Western theology.

Judaism toward the beginning of our era was led into the way of spreading by propaganda. Its own dispersed situation, partly compelled and partly chosen, favored this type of activity. But the impulse subsided in favor of another method of advance. The true religion must indeed become the religion of all men; but this may occur either by transmission or by a gathering in. For Judaism the sense of the community on a family pattern was so strong as to decide the issue for the second type. Judaism was not to be given broadcast to the world, but the world was to be absorbed, so far as it could become worthy, within the Jewish community. The appropriate ceremony of acceptance, involving circumcision, resembled a ceremony of adoption. Judaism may thus be included among the traveling religions; but its mode of travel being corporate, its spread is at present limited to the multiplication of the community under its Law.

III

I said that the answers given by the great religions to the problem of man's suffering and moral misery in the best of civilizations were diverse. It will be sufficient to illustrate this point if we contrast the answers given by Buddhism and Christianity.

To Buddha, the outstanding defect of human life is suffering, to Christ it is moral aimlessness. Buddhism accordingly undertakes to save men from suffering; Christianity to save them from "lostness." Buddha finds the escape from suffering in cutting the root of desire. His "Noble Fourfold Truth" runs in substance as follows:

Life in all its aspects is suffering;

The cause of suffering is the root of all desire, which is the craving for individual existence and that separateness from others implied by individual life.

The cure of suffering must therefore be the extirpation of that root, the overcoming of the craving to be, as a separate entity.

The way to achieve this cure (the Noble Eightfold Path) is neither asceticism nor indulgence, but a middle path, in which a union of activity with periods of meditation works steadily to the disenchantment which is Enlightenment and Nirvana—eternal peace, a goal which may be attained while one yet lives.

Christ finds the cure for moral lostness in nothing short of a rebirth, in which the struggling affections of secular human nature are unified in a dominant affection, a love of God and neighbor which brings desire and ambition to heel without killing them off. For both Christ and Buddha, the important thing about any human being is not what he does but what he cares about; both have long anticipated the psychiatry of today by showing that "integration" or peace can only come about by a rulership of natural desire under a single principle which puts first things first. But Buddha could not say "Seek ye first the Kingdom of God and his righteousness," for to Buddha there was no God in the usual sense—there was only the inexorable law of Karma (which carried over an uncured desire into another spell of existence and hence of more suffering) and the equally infallible law, his own discovery, of the escape from Karma, and therefore from further "existence." By the terms of his problem, the hope held out to men might indeed be called an eternal life, but not an eternal "existence," rather an eternity of unseparateness, the overcoming of individuality, Nirvana, the end of striving. For Christ the hope held out to men was also eternal life, but in a positive sense of personal continuance and effect; it took the vague form of an invitation to membership in a "Kingdom of God," an inner cure of the affections and an outer cure of human history, a long work like the slow leavening of an inert lump—at any rate, something to do.

It is easy to draw up handsome oppositions between these two teachings, and say that Buddha's goal is negative, Christ's is positive; Buddha's attitude toward life is pessimistic, Christ's optimistic; Buddha solaces the bewildered individual by getting him to resign all individual claim on life-satisfaction, Christ by making him individually precious in the sight of God, and a cooperator in a divine work. But these differences do not stand in stark contrast as the two systems are more fully understood; since the life of Buddha and his disciples, like that of Jesus, was one of active endeavor for the good of men. And the later history of Buddhism qualified many of the tenets of the early preaching. It is to be noticed, further, that Buddha and Christ were not asking precisely the same question, and hence their answers cannot be directly compared. Christ was not concerned for the cure of suffering; he tried to get men to face the certainty of "tribulation" with joy. Buddha was not concerned with the category of sin; he was rather a psychologist who inquired how man might train himself out of his earth-bound impulsiveness through a sort of sublimation. Hence many of the observations of each might be accepted by the other, within their diverse frame. The valid comparison of Buddhism and Christianity, though there have been many attempts, has yet to be worked out. Especially must it be remembered that Buddhism, in the forms it assumed in China and Japan, taught that every man participates in the "Buddha nature," and that his chief task is to realize that devotion to his kind, that superiority to selffishness, that power which comes from inner control, which were characteristic of the great sage. In this respect, Buddhism has dignified the conception of the human individual for Asia, as Christianity has done in the West.

But when all is said, the world views are surely not identical. The one is personal, the other impersonal; the one lives in a universe whose reality is moral will, the other in a universe whose reality is moral law; the one is aggressive, the other pacific—except, we must add, in Japan, where Buddhism long ago, in two of its sects, acquired a militant flavor. The ultimate world faith, therefore, will have to be one in which these differences must be resolved.

We have, then, a group of religions each of which accepts the responsibility of spreading its way of life to all men. Arising in widely separated centers and moving in different directions, they have in some measure divided the world among themselves, no one of them being effectively universal. The problem of a world faith will raise the practical question of the relations of these religions to one another, and to the local religions which they meet in the course of their expansion.

Nowhere is there a religious vacuum into which the migrant can move. Buddhism encounters Confucianism and Taoism in China, Confucianism and Shinto in Japan. But it came rather as a supplement than as a contestant. Confucianism had no dogmas regarding the other world and the career of the soul after death which it cared to oppose to the new doctrine, rich with metaphysical analysis and imaginative tapestry, supported by vast tomes of esoteric wisdom, and bringing to the human scene a new sense of divine compassion and of moral appeal to the Buddha nature in each one. Buddhism in China released a great wealth of artistic genius, giving it new themes in architecture, painting, sculpture. But chiefly it dignified human life by making it, in its inner struggle with suffering and desire, the central theme of the meaning of the cosmic process. A Chinese could thus be a good Confucianist and a good Buddhist at the same time. There was of course a silent competition on the plane of subsistence; for an organization must have an economic basis: what is given to Taoist priests cannot be given to Buddhist monks. But on the religious plane, there was room for all.

Christianity has been as a rule more belligerent toward the local religions. Professing to supply all the religious needs of mankind, it has called for singleness of allegiance. Buddhism in China presented the paradox of a religion with no God and at the same time with many divine figures, Buddhas, Bodhisattvas, and saints. A multiform system can flexibly add to its number or find cross-identities, whereas a monotheism such as Christianity or Islam must set itself against the whole apparatus of polytheistic worship, especially the images of the gods. The march of Chrisianity has therefore been a demand for Either-Or decisions; the temples and idols of the "heathen" have had to fall. But here also the conflict has not extended to the ground-level of the local structure. The tenacity of folk-custom and festival has led to many local amalgamations, and the sagacity especially of the Catholic missionaries has seen possibilities of conserving rather than destroying many a local observance within the body of the new faith. Hence the Christianities of the German forests, the Druid countries, the Mexican mountains, the old Spanish Southwest, are markedly different in temper: they are variations on a common theme.

In principle, since religion must be both local and universal, there should always be the possibility of uniting the mature, self-conscious superstructure of the traveling religion with elements of code and rite which belong to local feeling and history. But the problem is in each case a special one, since codes and rites are not separable from creeds; and the union, whatever it may be, must be natural and coherent, not an eclectic patchwork.

But the major problem of world faith arises when the great traveling religions encounter one another.

It belongs to the accidents of history that Buddhism and Christianity are themselves the result of a slow selection among various movements of similar nature—Buddhism and Jainism rising together in India; Christianity, Orphism, Mithraism, and other cults finding themselves together in the Empire. But these survivors, spreading in opposite directions, did not encounter one another, so far as we know, for several centuries; and then understood so little of one another that a romanticized Buddha, under the name of Josaphat, an Indian prince who in the tale was converted by the monk Barlaam, was innocently canonized by the Christian Church, both Byzantine and Roman (though later dropped by the Roman church)! In point of fact, their teachings are very unlike, and Buddha (who died about 480 B.C.) had he met the monk Barlaam, would have been from the monk's point of view sadly in need of conversion, and vice versa.

It belongs also to the accidents of history that Buddhism in its eastward progress encountered no other traveling faith. Its extension was pacific. Pandit Das Gupta's statement, at the opening of the new Buddhist temple at Sarnath, to the effect that Buddhism had never used force, nor inspired the use of force in its behalf, is well justified. He drew a damaging contrast between this history and that of Christianity. The early expansion of Islam brought it into Christian territory, in the Near East—Damascus, Jerusalem, Constantinople, the Balkans, Egypt, North Africa, Spain. Islam had its own methods of tolerating the presence of Christians in its precincts, as witness the division of the great church of Saint John at Damascus into two parts, the Christians using one half, while the other was used as a mosque! But the issue of ownership of the "sphere of influence" between these two religions was determined by the sword; and the political element in the establishment of Christianity in Europe and the Near East is one of the least creditable chapters of religious history. It has to be remembered, however, that from the fourth century onward Christianity had become identified with the maintenance of public law in Europe, tiding over a period in which secular authority was in confusion, and that it had created a "Christian" Europe largely through its power over the sources of legislation and teaching. Likewise for Islam, though to an even higher degree, the religion was at the same time a code of law and a government. For neither religion, during the centuries of Islamic growth, was it possible to separate church and state. With this consolidation of authority, a given territory had to be either Moslem or Christian; and the matter could not be settled by either prayer or philosophy.

We have now reached a point in the evolution of both politics and religion at which a degree of mutual independence is seen to be necessary to the health of both. Religion must influence law, if it is of any value at all. And government must have its religious presuppositions. But when they are united as organizations, religion is corrupted by patronage, the "extension of the faith" becomes an undercover pretext for the extension of empire, politics loses the correction of an independent moral judgment, and the relations between nations lose the tempering influence of a religion which is beyond every state, because it is effectively universal. We have not yet realized this ideal of mutuality and detachment between church and state; but we are sufficiently advanced toward it, so that the relations between the great faiths will henceforth be determined more by persuasion, on the ground of intrinsic merit, than by the political complexion of the world—assuming that the world of tomorrow will allow the free intercourse of faiths, and the free play of thought in regard to them.

Meanwhile, we have three or four promising aspirants for the position of world religion. It is hardly correct to call them competitors, for the impulse to spread is not a matter either of self-interest or of pride—though these motives creep into every man-staffed large-scale enterprise—but of duty in the meeting of human need. And since it is the consumer and not the promoter who, in the end, determines whether the need is met, whatever rivalry there is should be of the most frank and generous character, like the rivalry of physicians in the cure of disease. The presence of these many aspirants is itself an anomaly; if the plurality were acquiesced in, that would be equivalent to saying that there is no world religion at all, and is to be none such, but only a group of differing faiths having no way to settle their differences, since each appeals not to reason nor to experience but to the undebatable and uncompromisable finalities of revelation.

On the other hand, the magnitude of the field of dominance of each of the great religions is so great that we must accord to each of them a large measure of success in satisfying the religious craving of men; no other factor could have maintained them over so long a period. We cannot, then, be dealing with three falsehoods and one verity—one revealed and necessary way, and three works of the devil—with the fateful problem in hand of recognizing the true light; what we have is a variety of versions of truth, struggling through media of human expression, vagary, conceit, superstition—with the problem in hand of recognizing and releasing the essence of the matter, and with the large probability that each of the group will have its own unique contribution to that essence.

IV

There are now two questions before us. What are the elements of agreement among these several aspirants? What are the outstanding differences, and what processes are at work to resolve them?

A certain amount of agreement seems implied in the common circumstances of origin of the traveling faiths. All religion accepts the reality of an invisible order of being which in some way both commands and satisfies the root-awareness of life. It implies belief in the extra-natural, which usually takes shape as a belief in divine personal beings. All the mature religions recognize in the human individual a "soul," that is to say, a phase of the self deeper than the current phase of conversation and the day's work, reflecting on and guiding the current excursions in view of the total picture of destiny: the soul is the self in its dealings with the whole, and therefore with the extra-natural world as well as the natural. All the traveling religions see and teach that the soul is in peril, life being an opportunity which may be missed. They teach that the obvious world attracts and blinds the vision so that spiritual things become obscure, and life runs to frustration. They all offer cure, and guidance to what we may call the cosmic success. All of them propose a code of life, which is in part a condition of the cure; and all of them, whatever their other precepts, include in the code a requirement of good will toward the fellow man, and a degree of detachment from the pressures of physical desire and greed and social ambition.

To the extent of this agreement, we may say that a world faith already exists. This does not imply that all the world assents to the items in which all the religions agree. The advance of science and of positivistic logic has carried with it a wide swath of negation of the first assertion of all religion, the invisible order as a moral order. To this wholly secular and this-worldly temper, all religion is "Oriental" in the sense that it assigns reality to something not "verifiable" by physical observation. This secularism now pervades the Orient, and in order to burn off that religious excess we call superstition proposes to burn off religion itself; it aims to reclaim for pressing mundane business the energy drafted off into the fruitless catalepsies of the mystic. If there is soundness in religion it will accept the ordeal, learn its lessons, and hold to what it perceives, seeing that science itself is an extra-natural structure of the soul, responding partially to a demand of the cosmos for truth. The truth about tangible things is not itself a tangible thing; nor is the truth about perishable things itself perishable. To Gandhi, Truth and God are interchangeable terms, and the scientist has but to become more fully self-conscious to see that he also is a worshiper. We need not therefore make secularism an exception to our statement that a world faith already exists.

All the great religions further agree that the soul has a career not limited to the physical life of man; they have their pictures of continuance or of supplementation. The notion of immortality, once vivid and near, burns dim today; but the concern it stands for, as a part of the problem of the meaning of life, is even more insistent as our noble social orders reveal their insecurity. They agree also on another matter, and one which becomes the kernel of disagreement: all give a unique religious position to their founders. The names of Buddha, Jesus Christ, Mohammed, become the party-signs of religious cleavage, and present the most refractory obstacles to mutual understanding. They incorporate in themselves the contemporary problem of world faith in its sharpest form. To many minds, this represents the crowning perversity of the ecclesiastical nostrumizing of religion, and provokes a disposition to reach a common faith, as Professor Dewey does, by discarding once for all the entire specialized apparatus of the religious organizations. My belief is, however, that there is a reason for the apparent perversity, and that we shall move ahead toward religious understanding far faster if we inquire why it is that the great faiths all take this turn.

We may profitably remember that there have been repeated attempts in history to bring men together on the basis of what they already agree upon, discarding their points of difference, as though differences were less important than agreements, only to discover once more that likenesses are abstractions, and are never enough by themselves to constitute a living organism. Why, then, do the traveling religions give a special divine status to their founders?

V

We may approach the answer to our question by asking another. Why do men make holidays of the anniversaries of the advent of an idea? If an idea is true and valuable, it has no mark of time and place about it: it belongs by its nature to all minds who can apprehend it. The announcers of important ideas may not wish to be remembered in connection with the ideas—and most of them have not been—yet science itself strangely rebels against the impersonality of its product, attaches Napier's name to a set of logarithms, Newton's to certain laws of motion, and a motley array of personal roots to the names of various species of plants and animals. This impulse signalizes the fact that however timeless an idea may be, it is only "realized" when it is born in a time-occupied mind. And in proportion to the scope of the idea will men make holidays of such dates of birth. The "Noble Fourfold Truth" would on this score always be Buddha's doctrine. The "Ideas" of Plato have ceased to be merely platonic beings, since they are forever Platonic. Time makes a time-festival of its capture of the eternal. That is the beginning.

Buddh Gaya, the reputed scene of Buddha's Enlightenment, has long been a holy place for Buddhist visitors. As late as 1931 a temple was opened at Sarnath, near Benares, at the site of the ancient Deer Park where the story places the scene of Buddha's First Sermon. Buddha himself taught the doctrine of non-permanence, non-God-substance, non-soul-substance, and the timeless peace of Nirvana as his own portion; contrary to the spirit of his own thought, he has become an object of personal devotion, in the course of the time-changes which his doctrine has suffered. The Buddha-principle is hardly separable from the Buddha-image. The Buddhist initiate professes, "I take refuge in the Buddha." In much the same way, with careful avoidance of any deification of Mohammed, Islam makes its confession of faith: "There is no God but Allah, and Mohammed is his Prophet." This is not intended to be mere grateful reminiscence; it could not on that ground alone enter into the creed.

We come nearer to the secret when we recall that the founders were not merely seers and thinkers but teachers, planting their ideas in living minds as the best way, perhaps the only way, of securing their continuance. They were concerned to make their ideas forces in history, and to this end their concern was "Have they understood? Will they transmit?" Intentionally or not, they begot communities, bound together by the destiny of the faith in a world of opposition. It was not irrelevant that the founders, as reformers—and in the religious sphere which is the most bitterly conservative of all spheres because the landmarks are so few—had to be fighters as well as dreamers. Such communities, which as Royce has well said, will be communities of memory and of hope, have also to be communities of struggle, burdened with the trust of the teaching: the nerving memory of the original founder-fighter was needed as the living spirit of the effort. He would be thought of as present with them; the career of his idea in history would be the continuance of his cosmic career. The full profession of the Buddhist monk is, "I take refuge in the Buddha; I take refuge in the Dharma (the Law); I take refuge in the Samgha (the brotherhood)." By a similar process to that by which corporations in modern law become legal persons, these communities took on quasi-personal life, promoted by but also promoting the lives of their members. In them, something of the divine nature of truth had not alone entered time, but had taken on an historic career. It belonged to the nature of the divine to act in this way in history; and this nature is identical in quality with the nature of the founder, freed by death from bodily limitations. To take refuge in him is equivalent to taking refuge in God-in-history. We now see why the founder's name, with various shadings of the superhuman attribute, enters into the creedal statements of the several faiths. It is because, consciously or not, they all agree on a farther point, that God must have a human and temporal aspect, and that the human scene is ennobled by his working presence there.

Neither Buddha nor Mohammed would have accepted the phrase I used above, "God in history." Not Buddha, for to him there was no Brahman, but only the divine law, saving men from suffering and the misery of endless rebirth. Not Mohammed, for to him the divine majesty is unreachable, ungraspable, unembodied in any finite form: Allah rules all things, inscrutably, but he "neither begets nor is begotten," and with that denial Islam feels a permanent gulf set between itself and the Christian doctrine of the Son of God. But the chief agency in working toward a world faith is to see beyond language to meanings, by the aid of a sympathetic interpretation, aided by psychology. In the sense I have mentioned, it is the idea of incarnation which has given each of the founders his salient place in the creed. It is this idea which Tagore's "Religion of Man" is calling for and which many a movement which regards itself as atheistic is unknowingly using.

As these implicit meanings become slowly emergent into the general consciousness of men, the abstract world faith already present becomes by so much more concrete, and the obstacles of creedal difference melt away, because the truth namelessly persuades. But it is important that differences should be worked through, not abandoned; for men must differ according to their insights in order that their union when it comes may hold *all* their truth.

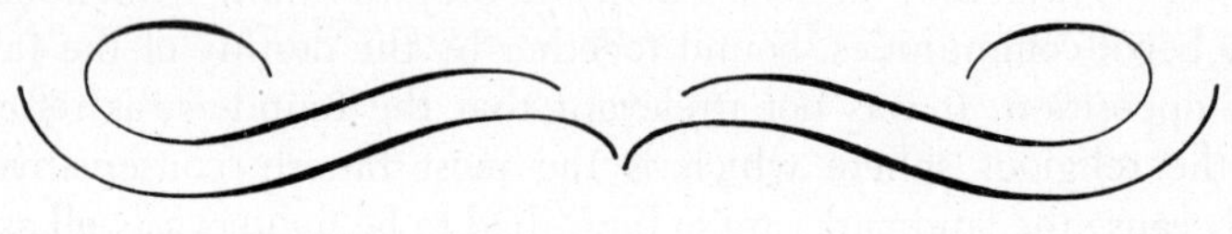

· *THE NATURE OF REALITY* ·

THE ALLEGORY OF THE CAVE [1]

PLATO

Next, said I, here is a parable to illustrate the degrees in which our nature may be enlightened or unenlightened. Imagine the condition of men living in a sort of cavernous chamber underground, with an entrance open to the light and a long passage all down the cave.[2] Here they have been from childhood, chained by the leg and also by the neck, so that they cannot move and can see only what is in front of them, because the chains will not let them turn their heads. At some distance higher up is the light of a fire burning behind them; and between the prisoners and the fire is a track [3] with a parapet built along it, like the screen at a puppet-show, which hides the performers while they show their puppets over the top.

1. From *The Republic,* translated by Francis MacDonald Cornford (Oxford: The Clarendon Press, 1941), pp. 227–231. Reprinted by permission of The Clarendon Press.

2. The *length* of the "way in" (*eisodos*) to the chamber where the prisoners sit is an essential feature, explaining why no daylight reaches them.

3. The track crosses the passage into the cave at right angles, and is *above* the parapet built along it.

I see, said he.

Now behind this parapet imagine persons carrying along various artificial objects, including figures of men and animals in wood or stone or other materials, which project above the parapet. Naturally, some of these persons will be talking, others silent.[4]

It is a strange picture, he said, and a strange sort of prisoners.

Like ourselves, I replied; for in the first place prisoners so confined would have seen nothing of themselves or of one another, except the shadows thrown by the fire-light on the wall of the Cave facing them, would they?

Not if all their lives they had been prevented from moving their heads.

And they would have seen as little of the objects carried past.

Of course.

Now, if they could talk to one another, would they not suppose that their words referred only to those passing shadows which they saw?[5]

Necessarily.

And suppose their prison had an echo from the wall facing them? When one of the people crossing behind them spoke, they could only suppose that the sound came from the shadow passing before their eyes.

No doubt.

In every way, then, such prisoners would recognize as reality nothing but the shadows of those artificial objects.[6]

Inevitably.

Now consider what would happen if their release from the chains and the healing of their unwisdom should come about in this way. Suppose one of them set free and forced suddenly to stand up, turn his head, and walk with eyes lifted to the light; all these movements would be painful, and he would be too dazzled to make out the objects whose shadows he had been used to see. What do you think he would say, if someone told him that what he had formerly seen was meaningless illusion, but now, being somewhat nearer to reality and turned towards more real objects, he was getting a truer view? Suppose further that he were shown the various objects being carried by and were made to say, in reply to questions, what each of them was. Would he not be perplexed and believe the objects now shown him to be not so real as what he formerly saw?

---

4. A modern Plato would compare his Cave to an underground cinema, where the audience watch the play of shadows thrown by the film passing before a light at their backs. The film itself is only an image of "real" things and events in the world outside the cinema. For the film Plato has to substitute the clumsier apparatus of a procession of artificial objects carried on their heads by persons who are merely part of the machinery, providing for the movement of the objects and the sounds whose echo the prisoners hear. The parapet prevents these persons' shadows from being cast on the wall of the Cave.

5. Adam's text and interpretation. The prisoners, having seen nothing but shadows, cannot think their words refer to the objects carried past behind their backs. For them shadows (images) are the only realities.

6. The state of mind called *eikasia* in the previous chapter.

Yes, not nearly so real.

And if he were forced to look at the fire-light itself, would not his eyes ache, so that he would try to escape and turn back to the things which he could see distinctly, convinced that they really were clearer than these other objects now being shown to him?

Yes.

And suppose someone were to drag him away forcibly up the steep and rugged ascent and not let him go until he had hauled him out into the sunlight, would he not suffer pain and vexation at such treatment, and, when he had come out into the light, find his eyes so full of its radiance that he could not see a single one of the things that he was now told were real?

Certainly he would not see them all at once.

He would need, then, to grow accustomed before he could see things in that upper world. At first it would be easiest to make out shadows, and then the images of men and things reflected in water, and later on the things themselves. After that, it would be easier to watch the heavenly bodies and the sky itself by night, looking at the light of the moon and stars rather than the Sun and the Sun's light in the day-time.

Yes, surely.

Last of all, he would be able to look at the Sun and contemplate its nature, not as it appears when reflected in water or any alien medium, but as it is in itself in its own domain.

No doubt.

And now he would begin to draw the conclusion that it is the Sun that produces the seasons and the course of the year and controls everything in the visible world, and moreover is in a way the cause of all that he and his companions used to see.

Clearly he would come at last to that conclusion.

Then if he called to mind his fellow prisoners and what passed for wisdom in his former dwelling-place, he would surely think himself happy in the change and be sorry for them. They may have had a practice of honouring and commending one another, with prizes for the man who had the keenest eye for the passing shadows and the best memory for the order in which they followed or accompanied one another, so that he could make a good guess as to which was going to come next.[7] Would our released prisoner be likely to covet those prizes or to envy the men exalted to honour and power in the Cave? Would he not feel like Homer's Achilles, that he would far sooner "be on earth as a hired servant in the house of a landless man"[8] or endure anything rather than go back to his old beliefs and live in the old way?

7. The empirical politician, with no philosophic insight, but only a "knack of remembering what usually happens" (*Gorg.* 501 A). He has *eikasia* = conjecture as to what is likely (*eikos*).

8. This verse, being spoken by the ghost of Achilles, suggests that the Cave is comparable with Hades.

Yes, he would prefer any fate to such a life.

Now imagine what would happen if he went down again to take his former seat in the Cave. Coming suddenly out of the sunlight, his eyes would be filled with darkness. He might be required once more to deliver his opinion on those shadows, in competition with the prisoners who had never been released, while his eyesight was still dim and unsteady; and it might take some time to become used to the darkness. They would laugh at him and say that he had gone up only to come back with his sight ruined; it was worth no one's while even to attempt the ascent. If they could lay hands on the man who was trying to set them free and lead them up, they would kill him.[9]

Yes, they would.

Every feature in this parable, my dear Glaucon, is meant to fit our earlier analysis. The prison dwelling corresponds to the region revealed to us through the sense of sight, and the fire-light within it to the power of the Sun. The ascent to see the things in the upper world you may take as standing for the upward journey of the soul into the region of the intelligible; then you will be in possession of what I surmise, since that is what you wish to be told. Heaven knows whether it is true; but this, at any rate, is how it appears to me. In the world of knowledge, the last thing to be perceived and only with great difficulty is the essential Form of Goodness. Once it is perceived, the conclusion must follow that, for all things, this is the cause of whatever is right and good; in the visible world it gives birth to light and to the lord of light, while it is itself sovereign in the intelligible world and the parent of intelligence and truth. Without having had a vision of this Form no one can act with wisdom, either in his own life or in matters of state.

9. An allusion to the fate of Socrates.

A DISCOURSE ON METHOD[1]

RENÉ DESCARTES

I WAS then in Germany, attracted thither by the wars in that country, which have not yet been brought to a termination; and as I was returning to the army from the coronation of the emperor, the setting in of winter arrested me in a locality where, as I found no society to interest me, and was besides fortunately undisturbed by any cares or passions, I remained the whole day in seclusion, with full opportunity to occupy my attention with my own

1. From *A Discourse on Method* (1637), by René Descartes, in *The Method, Meditations, and Philosophy of Descartes,* translated by John Veitch (New York: Tudor Publishing Co., n.d.), pp. 155–172, omitting Ch. 3.

thoughts. Of these one of the very first that occurred to me was, that there is seldom so much perfection in works composed of many separate parts, upon which different hands had been employed, as in those completed by a single master. Thus it is observable that the buildings which a single architect has planned and executed, are generally more elegant and commodious than those which several have attempted to improve, by making old walls serve for purposes for which they were not originally built. Thus also, those ancient cities which, from being at first only villages, have become, in course of time, large towns, are usually but ill laid out compared with the regularly constructed towns which a professional architect has freely planned on an open plain; so that although the several buildings of the former may often equal or surpass in beauty those of the latter, yet when one observes their indiscriminate juxtaposition, there a large one and here a small, and the consequent crookedness and irregularity of the streets, one is disposed to allege that chance rather than any human will guided by reason must have led to such an arrangement. And if we consider that nevertheless there have been at all times certain officers whose duty it was to see that private buildings contributed to public ornament, the difficulty of reaching high perfection with but the materials of others to operate on, will be readily acknowledged. In the same way I fancied that those nations which, starting from a semi-barbarous state and advancing to civilization by slow degrees, have had their laws successively determined, and, as it were, forced upon them simply by experience of the hurtfulness of particular crimes and disputes, would by this process come to be possessed of less perfect institutions than those which, from the commencement of their association as communities, have followed the appointment of some wise legislator. It is thus quite certain that the constitution of the true religion, the ordinances of which are derived from God, must be incomparably superior to that of every other. And, to speak of human affairs, I believe that the past pre-eminence of Sparta was due not to the goodness of each of its laws in particular, for many of these were very strange, and even opposed to good morals, but to the circumstance that, originated by a single individual, they all tended to a single end. In the same way I thought that the sciences contained in books (such of them at least as are made up of probable reasonings, without demonstrations), composed as they are of the opinions of many different individuals massed together, are farther removed from truth than the simple inferences which a man of good sense using his natural and unprejudiced judgment draws respecting the matters of his experience. And because we have all to pass through a state of infancy to manhood, and have been of necessity, for a length of time, governed by our desires and preceptors (whose dictates were frequently conflicting, while neither perhaps always counselled us for the best), I farther concluded that it is almost impossible that our judgments can be so correct or solid as they would have been, had our reason been mature from the moment of our birth, and had we always been guided by it alone.

It is true, however, that it is not customary to pull down all the houses of a town with the single design of rebuilding them differently, and thereby rendering the streets more handsome; but it often happens that a private individual takes down his own with the view of erecting it anew, and that people are even sometimes constrained to this when their houses are in danger of falling from age, or when the foundations are insecure. With this before me by way of example, I was persuaded that it would indeed be preposterous for a private individual to think of reforming a state by fundamentally changing it throughout, and overturning it in order to set it up amended; and the same I thought was true of any similar project for reforming the body of the sciences, or the order of teaching them established in the schools: but as for the opinions which up to that time I had embraced, I thought that I could not do better than resolve at once to sweep them wholly away, that I might afterwards be in a position to admit either others more correct, or even perhaps the same when they had undergone the scrutiny of reason. I firmly believed that in this way I should much better succeed in the conduct of my life, than if I built only upon old-foundations, and leaned upon principles which, in my youth, I had taken upon trust. For although I recognized various difficulties in this undertaking, these were not, however, without remedy, nor once to be compared with such as attend the slightest reformation in public affairs. Large bodies, if once overthrown, are with great difficulty set up again, or even kept erect when once seriously shaken, and the fall of such is always disastrous. Then if there are any imperfections in the constitutions of states (and that many such exist the diversity of constitutions is alone sufficient to assure us), custom has without doubt materially smoothed their inconveniences, and has even managed to steer altogether clear of, or insensibly corrected a number which sagacity could not have provided against with equal effect; and, in fine, the defects are almost more tolerable than the change necessary for their removal; in the same manner that highways which wind among mountains, by being much frequented, become gradually so smooth and commodious, that it is much better to follow them than to seek a straighter path by climbing over the tops of rocks and descending to the bottoms of precipices.

Hence it is that I cannot in any degree approve of those restless and busy meddlers who, called neither by birth nor fortune to take part in the management of public affairs, are yet always projecting reforms; and if I thought that this tract contained aught which might justify the suspicion that I was a victim of such folly, I would by no means permit its publication. I have never contemplated anything higher than the reformation of my own opinions, and basing them on a foundation wholly my own. And although my own satisfaction with my work has led me to present here a draft of it, I do not by any means therefore recommend to everyone else to make a similar attempt. Those whom God has endowed with a larger measure of genius will entertain, perhaps, designs still more exalted; but for the many I am much afraid lest even the present undertaking be more than they can safely venture to imitate. The single design to strip one's self of all past beliefs is one that ought not to be taken by every one. The majority of men is composed of two classes, for neither of which would this be at all a befitting resolution: in the first place, of those who with more than a due confidence in their own powers, are precipitate in their judgments and want the patience requisite for orderly and circumspect thinking; whence it happens, that if men of this class once take the liberty to doubt of their accustomed opinions, and quit the beaten highway, they will never be able to thread the byway that would lead them by a shorter course, and will lose themselves and continue to wander for life; in the second place, of those who, possessed of sufficient sense or modesty to determine that there are others who excel them in the power of discriminating between truth and error, and by whom they may be instructed, ought rather to content themselves with the opinions of such than trust for more correct to their own reason.

For my own part, I should doubtless have belonged to the latter class, had I received instruction from but one master, or had I never known the diversities of opinion that from time immemorial have prevailed among men of the greatest learning. But I had become aware, even so early as during my college life, that no opinion, however absurd and incredible, can be imagined, which has not been maintained by some one of the philosophers; and afterwards in the course of my travels I remarked that all those whose opinions are decidedly repugnant to ours are not on that account barbarians and savages, but on the contrary that many of these nations make an equally good, if not a better, use of their reason than we do. I took into account also the very different character which a person brought up from infancy in France or Germany exhibits, from that which, with the same mind originally, this individual would have possessed had he lived always among the Chinese or with savages, and the circumstance that in dress itself the fashion which pleased us ten years ago, and which may again, perhaps, be received into favour before ten years have gone, appears to us at this moment extravagant and ridiculous. I was thus led to infer that the ground of our opinions is far more custom and example than any certain knowledge. And, finally, although such be the ground of our opinions, I remarked that a plurality of suffrages is no guarantee of truth where it is at all of difficult discovery, as in such cases it is much more likely that it will be found by one than by many. I could, however, select from the crowd no one whose opinions seemed worthy of preference, and thus I found myself constrained. as it were, to use my own reason in the conduct of my life.

But like one walking alone and in the dark, I resolved to proceed so slowly and with such circumspection, that if I did not advance far, I would at least guard against falling. I did not even choose to dismiss summarily any of the opinions that had crept in my belief without having been introduced by reason, but first of all took sufficient time carefully to satisfy myself of the general nature of the task I was setting myself, and ascertain the true method by which to arrive at the knowledge of whatever lay within the compass of my powers.

Among the branches of philosophy, I had, at an earlier period, given some attention to logic, and among those of the mathematics to geometrical analysis and algebra,—three arts or sciences which ought, as I conceived, to contribute something to my design. But, on examination, I found that, as for logic, its syllogisms and the majority of its other precepts are of avail rather in the communication of what we already know, or even as the art of Tully, in speaking without judgment of things of which we are ignorant, than in the investigation of the unknown; and although this science contains indeed a number of correct and very excellent precepts, there are, nevertheless, so many others, and these either injurious or superfluous, mingled with the former, that it is almost quite as difficult to effect a severance of the true from the false as it is to extract a Diana or a Minerva from a rough block of marble. Then as to the analysis of the ancients and the algebra of the moderns, besides that they embrace only matters highly abstract, and, to appearance, of no use, the former is so exclusively restricted to the consideration of figures, that it can exercise the understanding only on condition of greatly fatiguing the imagination; and, in the latter, there is so complete a subjection to certain rules and formulas, that there results an art full of confusion and obscurity calculated to embarrass, instead of a science fitted to cultivate the mind. By these considerations I was induced to seek some other method which would comprise the advantages of the three and be exempt from their defects. And as a multitude of laws often only hampers justice, so that a state is best governed when, with few laws, these are rigidly administered; in like manner, instead of the great number of precepts of which logic is composed, I believed that the four following would prove perfectly sufficient for me, provided I took the firm and unwavering resolution never in a single instance to fail to observe them.

The first was never to accept anything for true which I did not clearly know to be such; that is to say, carefully to avoid precipitancy and prejudice, and to comprise nothing more in my judgment than was presented to my mind so clearly and distinctly as to exclude all ground of doubt.

The second, to divide each of the difficulties under examination into as many parts as possible, and as might be necessary for its adequate solution.

The third, to conduct my thoughts in such order that, by commencing with objects the simplest and easiest to know, I might ascend by little and little, and, as it were, step by step, to the knowledge of the more complex; assigning in thought a certain order even to those objects which in their own nature do not stand in a relation of antecedence and sequence.

And the last, in every case to make enumerations so complete, and reviews so general, that I might be assured that nothing was omitted.

The long chains of simple and easy reasonings by means of which geometers are accustomed to reach the conclusions of their most difficult demonstrations, had led me to imagine that all things, to the knowledge of which man is competent, are mutually connected in the same way, and that there is nothing so far removed from us as to be beyond our reach, or so hidden that we cannot discover it, provided only we abstain from accepting the false for the true, and always preserve in our thoughts the order necessary for the deduction of one truth from another. And I had little difficulty in determining the objects with which it was necessary to commence, for I was already persuaded that it must be with the simplest and easiest to know, and, considering that of all those who have hitherto sought truth in the sciences, the mathematicians alone have been able to find any demonstrations, that is, any certain and evident reasons, I did not doubt but that such must have been the rule of their investigations. I resolved to commence, therefore, with the examination of the simplest objects, not anticipating, however, from this any other advantage than that to be found in accustoming my mind to the love and nourishment of truth, and to a distaste for all such reasonings as were unsound. But I had no intention on that account of attempting to master all the particular sciences commonly denominated mathematics: but observing that, however different their objects, they all agree in considering only the various relations or proportions subsisting among those objects, I thought it best for my purpose to consider these proportions in the most general form possible, without referring them to any objects in particular, except such as would most facilitate the knowledge of them, and without by any means restricting them to these, that afterwards I might thus be the better able to apply them to every other class of objects to which they are legitimately applicable. Perceiving further, that in order to understand these relations I should sometimes have to consider them one by one, and sometimes only to bear them in mind, or embrace them in the aggregate, I thought that, in order the better to consider them individually, I should view them as subsisting between straight lines, than which I could find no objects more simple, or capable of being more distinctly represented to my imagination and senses; and on the other hand, that in order to retain them in the memory, or embrace an aggregate of many, I should express them by certain characters the briefest possible. In this way I believed that I could borrow all that was best both in geometrical analysis and in algebra, and correct all the defects of the one by help of the other.

And in point of fact, the accurate observance of these few precepts gave me, I take the liberty of saying, such ease in unravelling all the questions embraced in these two sciences, that in the two or three months I devoted to their examination, not only did I reach solutions of questions I had formerly deemed exceedingly difficult, but even as regards questions of the solution of which I continued ignorant, I was enabled, as it appeared to me, to determine the means whereby, and the extent to which, a solution was possible; results attributable to the circumstance that I commenced with the simplest and most general truths, and that thus each truth discovered was a rule available in the discovery of subsequent ones. Nor in this perhaps shall I appear too vain, if it be considered that, as the truth on any particular points is one, whoever apprehends the truth, knows all that on that point can be known. The child, for example, who has been instructed in the elements of arithmetic, and has made a particular addition, according to rule, may be assured that he has found, with respect to the sum of the numbers before him, all that in this instance is within the reach of human genius. Now, in conclusion, the method which teaches adherence to the true order, and an exact enumeration of all the conditions of the thing sought includes all that gives certitude to the rules of arithmetic.

But the chief ground of my satisfaction with this method, was the assurance I had of thereby exercising my reason in all matters, if not with absolute perfection, at least with the greatest attainable by me: besides, I was conscious that by its use my mind was becoming gradually habituated to clearer and more distinct conceptions of its objects; and I hoped also, from not having restricted this method to any particular matter, to apply it to the difficulties of the other sciences, with not less success than to those of algebra. I should not, however, on this account have ventured at once on the examination of all the difficulties of the sciences which presented themselves to me, for this would have been contrary to the order prescribed in the method, but observing that the knowledge of such is dependent on principles borrowed from philosophy, in which I found nothing certain, I thought it necessary first of all to endeavour to establish its principles. And because I observed, besides, that an inquiry of this kind was of all others of the greatest moment, and one in which precipitancy and anticipation in judgment were most to be dreaded, I thought that I ought not to approach it till I had reached a more mature age (being at that time but twenty-three), and had first of all employed much of my time in preparation for the work, as well by eradicating from my mind all the erroneous opinions I had up to that moment accepted, as by amassing variety of experience to afford materials for my reasonings, and by continually exercising myself in my chosen method with a view to increased skill in its application. . . .

I am in doubt as to the propriety of making my first meditations, in the place above mentioned, matter of discourse; for these are so metaphysical, and so uncommon, as not, perhaps, to be acceptable to every one. And yet, that it may be determined whether the foundations that I have laid are sufficiently secure, I find myself in a measure constrained to advert to them. I had long before remarked that, in relation to practice, it is sometimes necessary to adopt, as if above doubt, opinions which we discern to be highly uncertain, as has been already said; but as I then desired to give my attention solely to the search after truth, I thought that a procedure exactly the opposite was called for, and that I ought to reject as absolutely false all opinions in regard to which I could suppose the least ground for doubt, in order to ascertain whether after that there remained aught in my belief that was wholly indubitable. Accordingly, seeing that our senses sometimes deceived us, I was willing to suppose that there existed nothing really such as they presented to us; and because some men err in reasoning, and fall into paralogisms, even on the simplest matters of geometry, I, convinced that I was as open to error as any other, rejected as false all the reasonings I had hitherto taken for demonstrations; and finally, when I considered that the very same thoughts (presentations) which we experience when awake may also be experienced when we are asleep, while there is at that time not one of them true, I supposed that all the objects (presentations) that had ever entered into my mind when awake, had in them no more truth than the illusions of my dreams. But immediately upon this I observed that, whilst I thus wished to think that all was false, it was absolutely necessary that I, who thus thought, should be somewhat; and as I observed that this truth, I THINK, HENCE I AM, was so certain and of such evidence, that no ground of doubt, however extravagant, could be alleged by the sceptics capable of shaking it, I concluded that I might, without scruple, accept it as the first principle of the philosophy of which I was in search.

In the next place, I attentively examined what I was, and as I observed that I could suppose that I had no body, and that there was no world nor any place in which I might be; but that I could not therefore suppose that I was not; and that, on the contrary, from the very circumstance that I thought to doubt of the truth of other things, it most clearly and certainly followed that I was; while, on the other hand, if I had only ceased to think, although all the other objects which I had ever imagined had been in reality existent, I would have had no reason to believe that I existed; I thence concluded that I was a substance whose whole essence or nature consists only in thinking, and which, that it may exist, has need of no place, nor is dependent on any material thing; so that "I," that is to say, the mind by which I am what I am, is wholly distinct from the body, and is even more easily known than the latter, and is such, that although the latter were not, it would still continue to be all that it is.

After this I inquired in general into what is essential to the truth and certainty of a proposition; for since I had discovered one which I knew to be true, I thought that I must likewise be able to discover the ground of this certitude. And as I observed that in the words *I think, hence I am,* there is nothing at all which gives me assurance of their truth beyond this, that I see very clearly that in order to think it is necessary to exist, I concluded that I might take, as a general rule, the principle, that all the things which we very clearly and distinctly conceive are true, only observing, however, that there is some difficulty in rightly determining the objects which we distinctly conceive.

AN ESSAY CONCERNING HUMAN UNDERSTANDING[1]

JOHN LOCKE

1. Every man being conscious to himself that he thinks; and that which his mind is applied about whilst thinking being the *ideas* that are there, it is past doubt that men have in their minds several ideas,—such as are those expressed by the words *whiteness, hardness, sweetness, thinking, motion, man, elephant, army, drunkenness,* and others: it is in the first place then to be inquired, *How he comes by them?*

I know it is a received doctrine, that men have native ideas, and original characters, stamped upon their minds in their very first being. This opinion I have at large examined already; and, I suppose what I have said in the foregoing Book will be much more easily admitted, when I have shown whence the understanding may get all the ideas it has; and by what ways and degrees they may come into the mind;—for which I shall appeal to every one's own observation and experience.

2. Let us then suppose the mind to be, as we say, white paper, void of all characters, without any ideas:—How comes it to be furnished? Whence comes it by that vast store which the busy and boundless fancy of man has painted on it with an almost endless variety? Whence has it all the *materials* of reason and knowledge? To this I answer, in one word, from EXPERIENCE. In that all our knowledge is founded; and from that it ultimately derives itself. Our observation employed either about external sensible objects, or about the internal operations of our minds perceived and reflected on by ourselves, is that which supplies our understandings with all the *materials* of thinking. These two are the fountains of knowledge, from whence all the ideas we have, or can naturally have, do spring.

3. First, our Senses, conversant about particular sensible objects, do convey into the mind several distinct perceptions of things, according to those various ways wherein those objects do affect them. And thus we come by those *ideas* we have of *yellow, white, heat, cold, soft, hard, bitter, sweet,* and all those which we call sensible qualities; which when I say the senses convey into the mind, I mean, they from external objects convey into the mind what produces there those perceptions. This great source of most of the ideas we have, depending wholly upon our senses, and derived by them to the understanding, I call SENSATION.

4. Secondly, the other fountain from which experience furnisheth the understanding with ideas is,—the perception of the operations of our own mind within us, as it is employed about the ideas it has got;—which, operations, when the soul comes to reflect on and consider, do furnish the under-

1. *An Essay Concerning Human Understanding* (1690), ed., Alexander Campbell Fraser (Oxford: The Clarendon Press, 1894), Book II, Ch. I.

standing with another set of ideas, which could not be had from things without. And such are *perception, thinking, doubting, believing, reasoning, knowing, willing,* and all the different actings of our own minds;—which we being conscious of, and observing in ourselves, do from these receive into our understandings as distinct ideas as we do from bodies affecting our senses. This source of ideas every man has wholly in himself; and though it be not sense, as having nothing to do with external objects, yet it is very like it, and might properly enough be called *internal sense.* But as I call the other Sensation, so I call this REFLECTION, the ideas it affords being such only as the mind gets by reflecting on its own operations within itself. By reflection then, in the following part of this discourse, I would be understood to mean, that notice which the mind takes of its own operations, and the manner of them, by reason whereof there come to be ideas of these operations in the understanding. These two, I say, viz. external material things, as the objects of SENSATION, and the operations of our own minds within, as the objects of REFLECTION, are to me the only originals from whence all our ideas take their beginnings. The term *operations* here I use in a large sense, as comprehending not barely the actions of the mind about its ideas, but some sort of passions arising sometimes from them, such as is the satisfaction or uneasiness arising from any thought.

5. The understanding seems to me not to have the least glimmering of any ideas which it doth not receive from one of these two. *External objects* furnish the mind with the ideas of sensible qualities, which are all those different perceptions they produce in us; and *the mind* furnishes the understanding with ideas of its own operations.

These, when we have taken a full survey of them, and their several modes, [combinations, and relations,] we shall find to contain all our whole stock of ideas; and that we have nothing in our minds which did not come in one of these two ways. Let any one examine his own thoughts, and thoroughly search into his understanding; and then let him tell me, whether all the original ideas he has there, are any other than of the objects of his senses, or of the operations of his mind, considered as objects of his reflection. And how great a mass of knowledge soever he imagines to be lodged there, he will, upon taking a strict view, see that he has not any idea in his mind but what one of these two have imprinted;—though perhaps, with infinite variety compounded and enlarged by the understanding, as we shall see hereafter.

6. He that attentively considers the state of a child, at his first coming into the world, will have little reason to think him stored with plenty of ideas, that are to be the matter of his future knowledge. It is *by degrees* he comes to be furnished with them. And though the ideas of obvious and familiar qualities imprint themselves before the memory begins to keep a register of time and order, yet it is often so late before some unusual qualities come in the way, that there are few men that cannot recollect the beginning of their acquaintance with them. And if it were worth while, no doubt a child might

be so ordered as to have but a very few, even of the ordinary ideas, till he were grown up to a man. But all that are born into the world, being surrounded with bodies that perpetually and diversely affect them, variety of ideas, whether care be taken of it or not, are imprinted on the minds of children. Light and colours are busy at hand everywhere, when the eye is but open; sounds and some tangible qualities fail not to solicit their proper senses, and force an entrance to the mind;—but yet, I think, it will be granted easily, that if a child were kept in a place where he never saw any other but black and white till he were a man, he would have no more ideas of scarlet or green, than he that from his childhood never tasted an oyster, or a pine-apple, has of those particular relishes.

7. Men then come to be furnished with fewer or more simple ideas from without, according as the objects they converse with afford greater or less variety; and from the operations of their minds within, according as they more or less reflect on them. For, though he that contemplates the operations of his mind, cannot but have plain and clear ideas of them; yet, unless he turn his thoughts that way, and considers them *attentively*, he will no more have clear and distinct ideas of all the operations of his mind, and all that may be observed therein, than he will have all the particular ideas of any landscape, or of the parts and motions of a clock, who will not turn his eyes to it, and with attention heed all the parts of it. The picture, or clock may be so placed, that they may come in his way every day; but yet he will have but a confused idea of all the parts they are made up of, till he applies himself with attention, to consider them each in particular.

8. And hence we see the reason why it is pretty late before most children get ideas of the operations of their own minds; and some have not any very clear or perfect ideas of the greatest part of them all their lives. Because, though they pass there continually, yet, like floating visions, they make not deep impressions enough to leave in their mind clear, distinct, lasting ideas, till the understanding turns inward upon itself, reflects on its own operations, and makes them the objects of its own contemplation. Children, when they come first into it, are surrounded with a world of new things, which, by a constant solicitation of their senses, draw the mind constantly to them; forward to take notice of new, and apt to be delighted with the variety of changing objects. Thus the first years are usually employed and diverted in looking abroad. Men's business in them is to acquaint themselves with what is to be found without; and so growing up in a constant attention to outward sensations, seldom make any considerable reflection on what passes within them, till they come to be of riper years; and some scarce ever at all.

WHAT PRAGMATISM IS[1]

WILLIAM JAMES

SOME years ago, being with a camping party in the mountains, I returned from a solitary ramble to find every one engaged in a ferocious metaphysical dispute. The *corpus* of the dispute was a squirrel—a live squirrel supposed to be clinging to one side of a tree-trunk; while over against the tree's opposite side a human being was imagined to stand. This human witness tries to get sight of the squirrel by moving rapidly round the tree, but no matter how fast he goes, the squirrel moves as fast in the opposite direction, and always keeps the tree between himself and the man, so that never a glimpse of him is caught. The resultant metaphysical problem now is this: *Does the man go round the squirrel or not?* He goes round the tree, sure enough, and the squirrel is on the tree; but does he go round the squirrel? In the unlimited leisure of the wilderness, discussion had been worn threadbare. Every one had taken sides and was obstinate; and the numbers on both sides were even. Each side, when I appeared, therefore appealed to me to make it a majority. Mindful of the scholastic adage that whenever you meet a contradiction you must make a distinction, I immediately sought and found one, as follows: "Which party is right," I said, "depends on what you *practically mean* by 'going round' the squirrel. If you mean passing from the north of him to the east, then to the south, then to the west, and then to the north of him again, obviously the man does go round him, for he occupies these successive positions. But if on the contrary you mean being first in front of him, then on the right of him, then behind him, then on his left, and finally in front again, it is quite obvious that the man fails to go round him, for by compensating movements the squirrel makes, he keeps his belly turned towards the man all the time, and his back turned away. Make the distinction, and there is no occasion for any further dispute. You are both right and both wrong, according as you conceive the verb 'to go round' in one practical fashion or the other."

Although one or two of the hotter disputants called my speech a shuffling evasion, saying they wanted no quibbling or scholastic hair-splitting, but meant just plain honest English "round," the majority seemed to think that the distinction had assuaged the dispute.

I tell this trivial anecdote because it is a peculiarly simple example of what I wish now to speak of as *the pragmatic method.* The pragmatic method is primarily a method of settling metaphysical disputes that otherwise might be interminable. Is the world one or many?—fated or free?—material or spiritual? —here are notions either of which may or may not hold good of the world; and disputes over such notions are unending. The pragmatic method in

1. From William James, *Pragmatism* (New York: Longmans, Green & Company, Inc., 1907, 1928), pp. 43–55. Reprinted by permission of Paul R. Reynolds & Son.

such cases is to try to interpret each notion by tracing its respective practical consequences. What difference would it practically make to any one if this notion rather than that notion were true? If no practical difference whatever can be traced, then the alternatives mean practically the same thing, and all dispute is idle. Whenever a dispute is serious, we ought to be able to show some practical difference that must follow from one side or the other's being right.

A glance at the history of the idea will show you still better what pragmatism means. The term is derived from the same Greek word πράγμα, meaning action, from which our words "practice" and "practical" come. It was first introduced into philosophy by Mr. Charles Peirce in 1878. In an article entitled "How to Make Our Ideas Clear," in the *Popular Science Monthly* for January of that year, Mr. Peirce, after pointing out that our beliefs are really rules for action, said that, to develop a thought's meaning, we need only determine what conduct it is fitted to produce: that conduct is for us its sole significance. And the tangible fact at the root of all our thought-distinctions, however subtle, is that there is no one of them so fine as to consist in anything but a possible difference of practice. To attain perfect clearness in our thoughts of an object, then, we need only consider what conceivable effects of a practical kind the object may involve—what sensations we are to expect from it, and what reactions we must prepare. Our conception of these effects whether immediate or remote, is then for us the whole of our conception of the object, so far as that conception has positive significance at all.

This is the principle of Peirce, the principle of pragmatism. It lay entirely unnoticed by any one for twenty years, until I, in an address before Professor Howison's philosophical union at the University of California, brought it forward again and made a special application of it to religion. By that date (1898) the times seemed ripe for its reception. The word "pragmatism" spread, and at present it fairly spots the pages of the philosophic journals. On all hands we find the "pragmatic movement" spoken of, sometimes with respect, sometimes with contumely, seldom with clear understanding. It is evident that the term applies itself conveniently to a number of tendencies that hitherto have lacked a collective name, and that it has "come to stay."

To take in the importance of Peirce's principle, one must get accustomed to applying it to concrete cases. I found a few years ago that Ostwald, the illustrious Leipzig chemist, had been making perfectly distinct use of the principle of pragmatism in his lectures on the philosophy of science, though he had not called it by that name.

"All realities influence our practice," he wrote me, "and that influence is their meaning for us. I am accustomed to put questions to my classes in this way: In what respects would the world be different if this alternative or that were true? If I can find nothing that would become different, then the alternative has no sense."

That is, the rival views mean practically the same thing, and meaning, other than practical, there is for us none. Ostwald in a published lecture gives this example of what he means. Chemists have long wrangled over the inner constitution of certain bodies called "tautomerous." Their properties seemed equally consistent with the notion that an instable hydrogen atom oscillates inside of them, or that they are instable mixtures of two bodies. Controversy raged, but never was decided. "It would never have begun," says Ostwald, "if the combatants had asked themselves what particular experimental fact could have been made different by one or the other view being correct. For it would then have appeared that no difference of fact could possibly ensue; and the quarrel was as unreal as if, theorising in primitive times about the raising of dough by yeast, one party should have invoked a 'brownie,' while another insisted on an 'elf' as the true cause of the phenomenon."

It is astonishing to see how many philosophical disputes collapse into insignificance the moment you subject them to this simple test of tracing a concrete consequence. There can *be* no difference anywhere that doesn't *make* a difference elsewhere—no difference in abstract truth that doesn't express itself in a difference in concrete fact and in conduct consequent upon that fact, imposed on somebody, somehow, somewhere, and somewhen. The whole function of philosophy ought to be to find out what definite difference it will make to you and me, at definite instants of our life, if this world-formula or that world-formula be the true one.

There is absolutely nothing new in the pragmatic method. Socrates was an adept at it. Aristotle used it methodically. Locke, Berkeley, and Hume made momentous contributions to truth by its means. Shadworth Hodgson keeps insisting that realities are only what they are "known as." But these forerunners of pragmatism used it in fragments: they were a prelude only. Not until in our time has it generalized itself, become conscious of a universal mission, pretended to a conquering destiny. I believe in that destiny, and I hope I may end by inspiring you with my belief.

Pragmatism represents a perfectly familiar attitude in philosophy, the empiricist attitude, but it represents it, as it seems to me, both in a more radical and in a less objectionable form than it has ever yet assumed. A pragmatist turns his back resolutely and once for all upon a lot of inveterate habits dear to professional philosophers. He turns away from abstraction and insufficiency, from verbal solutions, from bad *a priori* reasons, from fixed principles, closed systems, and pretended absolutes and origins. He turns towards concreteness and adequacy, towards facts, towards action and towards power. That means the empiricist temper regnant and the rationalist temper sincerely given up. It means the open air and possibilities of nature, as against dogma, artificiality, and the pretence of finality in truth.

At the same time it does not stand for any special results. It is a method only. But the general triumph of that method would mean an enormous change in what I called in my last lecture the "temperament" of philosophy. Teachers of the ultra-rationalistic type would be frozen out, much as the courtier type is frozen out in republics, as the ultra-montane type of priest is frozen out in protestant lands. Science and metaphysics would come much nearer together, would in fact work absolutely hand in hand.

Metaphysics has usually followed a very primitive kind of quest. You know how men have always hankered after unlawful magic, and you know what a great part in magic *words* have always played. If you have his name, or the formula of incantation that binds him, you can control the spirit, genie, afrite, or whatever the power may be. Solomon knew the names of all the spirits, and having their names, he held them subject to his will. So the universe has always appeared to the natural mind as a kind of enigma, of which the key must be sought in the shape of some illuminating or power-bringing word or name. That word names the universe's *principle,* and to possess it is after a fashion to possess the universe itself. "God," "Matter," "Reason," "the Absolute," "Energy," are so many solving names. You can rest when you have them. You are at the end of your metaphysical quest.

But if you follow the pragmatic method you cannot look on any such word as closing your quest. You must bring out of each word its practical cash-value, set it at work within the stream of your experience. It appears less as a solution, then, than as a programme for more work, and more particularly as an indication of the ways in which existing realities may be *changed*

Theories thus become instruments, not answers to enigmas, in which we can rest. We don't lie back upon them, we move forward, and, on occasion, make nature over again by their aid. Pragmatism unstiffens all our theories, limbers them up and sets each one at work. Being nothing essentially new, it harmonizes with many ancient philosophic tendencies. It agrees with nominalism, for instance, in always appealing to particulars; with utilitarianism in emphasizing practical aspects; with positivism in its disdain for verbal solutions, useless questions, and metaphysical abstractions.

All these, you see, are *anti-intellectualist* tendencies. Against rationalism as a pretension and a method pragmatism is fully armed and militant. But, at the outset, at least, it stands for no particular results. It has no dogmas, and no doctrines save its method. As the young Italian pragmatist Papini has well said, it lies in the midst of our theories like a corridor in a hotel. Innumerable chambers open out of it. In one you may find a man writing an atheistic volume; in the next some one on his knees praying for faith and strength; in a third a chemist investigating a body's properties; in a fourth a system of idealistic metaphysics is being excogitated; in a fifth the impossibility of metaphysics is being shown. But they all own the corridor, and all must pass through it if they want a practicable way of getting into or out of their respective rooms.

No particular results then, so far, but only an attitude of orientation, is what the pragmatic method means. *The attitude of looking away from first things, principles, "categories," supposed necessities; and of looking towards last things, fruits, consequences, facts.*

So much for the pragmatic method! You may say that I have been praising it rather than explaining it to you, but I shall presently explain it abundantly enough by showing how it works on some familiar problems. Meanwhile the word pragmatism has come to be used in a still wider sense, as meaning also a certain *theory of truth.* I mean to give a whole lecture to the statement of that theory, after first paving the way, so I can be very brief now. But brevity is hard to follow, so I ask for your redoubled attention for a quarter of an hour. If much remains obscure, I hope to make it clearer in the later lectures.

One of the most successfully cultivated branches of philosophy in our time is what is called inductive logic, the study of the conditions under which our sciences have evolved. Writers on this subject have begun to show a singular unanimity as to what the laws of nature and elements of fact mean when formulated by mathematicians, physicists, and chemists. When the first mathematical, logical, and natural uniformities, the first *laws,* were discovered, men were so carried away by the clearness, beauty, and simplification that resulted that they believed themselves to have deciphered authentically the eternal thoughts of the Almighty. His mind also thundered and reverberated in syllogisms. He also thought in conic sections, squares, and roots and ratios, and geometrized like Euclid. He made Kepler's laws for the planets to follow; he made velocity increase proportionally to the time in falling bodies; he made the law of the sines for light to obey when refracted; he established the classes, orders, families, and genera of plants and animals, and fixed the distances between them. He thought the archetypes of all things, and devised their variations; and when we rediscover any one of these his wondrous institutions, we seize his mind in its very literal intention.

But as the sciences have developed farther, the notion has gained ground that most, perhaps all, of our laws are only approximations. The laws themselves, moreover, have grown so numerous that there is no counting them; and so many rival formulations are proposed in all the branches of science that investigators have become accustomed to the notion that no theory is absolutely a transcript of reality, but that any one of them may from some point of view be useful. Their great use is to summarize old facts and to lead to new ones. They are only a man-made language, a conceptual shorthand, as some one calls them, in which we write our reports of nature; and languages, as is well known, tolerate much choice of expression and many dialects.

Thus human arbitrariness has driven divine necessity from scientific logic. If I mention the names of Sigwart, Mach, Ostwald, Pearson, Milhaud, Poincaré, Duhem, Heymans, those of you who are students will easily identify the tendency I speak of, and will think of additional names.

Riding now on the front of this wave of scientific logic, Messrs. Schiller and Dewey appear with their pragmatistic account of what truth everywhere signifies. Everywhere, these teachers say, "truth" in our ideas and beliefs means the same thing that it means in science. It means, they say, nothing but this, *that ideas (which themselves are but parts of our experience) become true just in so far as they help us to get into satisfactory relation with other parts of our experience,* to summarize them and get about among them by conceptual shortcuts instead of following the interminable succession of particular phenomena. Any idea upon which we can ride, so to speak; any idea that will carry us prosperously from any one part of our experience to any other part, linking things satisfactorily, working securely, simplifying, saving labour—is true for just so much, true in so far forth, true *instrumentally.* This is the "instrumental" view of truth taught so successfully at Chicago, the view that truth in our ideas means their power to "work," promulgated so brilliantly at Oxford.

Messrs. Dewey, Schiller, and their allies, in reaching this general conception of all truth, have only followed the example of geologists, biologists, and philologists. In the establishment of these other sciences, the successful stroke was always to take some simple process actually observable in operation—as denudation by weather, say, or variation from parental type, or change of dialect by incorporation of new words and pronunciations—and then to generalize it, making it apply to all times, and produce great results by summating its effects through the ages.

The observable process which Schiller and Dewey particularly singled out for generalization is the familiar one by which any individual settles into *new opinions.* The process here is always the same. The individual has a stock of old opinions already, but he meets a new experience that puts them to a strain. Somebody contradicts them; or in a reflective moment he discovers that they contradict each other; or he hears of facts with which they are incompatible; or desires arise in him which they cease to satisfy. The result is an inward trouble to which his mind till then had been a stranger, and from which he seeks to escape by modifying his previous mass of opinions. He saves as much of it as he can, for in this matter of belief we are all extreme conservatives. So he tries to change first this opinion, and then that (for they resist change very variously), until at last some new idea comes up which he can graft upon the ancient stock with a minimum of disturbance of the latter, some idea that mediates between the stock and the new experience and runs them into one another most felicitously and expediently.

This new idea is then adopted as the true one. It preserves the older stock of truths with a minimum of modification, stretching them just enough to make them admit the novelty, but conceiving that in ways as familiar as the case leaves possible. An *outrée* explanation, violating all our preconceptions, would never pass for a true account of a novelty. We should scratch round industriously till we found something less eccentric. The most violent revolutions in an individual's beliefs leave most of his old order standing. Time and space, cause and effect, nature and history, and one's own biography remain untouched. New truth is always a go-between, a smoother-over of transitions. It marries old opinion to new fact so as ever to show a minimum of jolt, a maximum of continuity. We hold a theory true just in proportion to its success in solving this "problem of maxima and minima." But success in solving this problem is eminently a matter of approximation. We say this theory solves it on the whole more satisfactorily than that theory; but that means more satisfactorily to ourselves, and individuals will emphasize their points of satisfaction differently. To a certain degree, therefore, everything here is plastic.

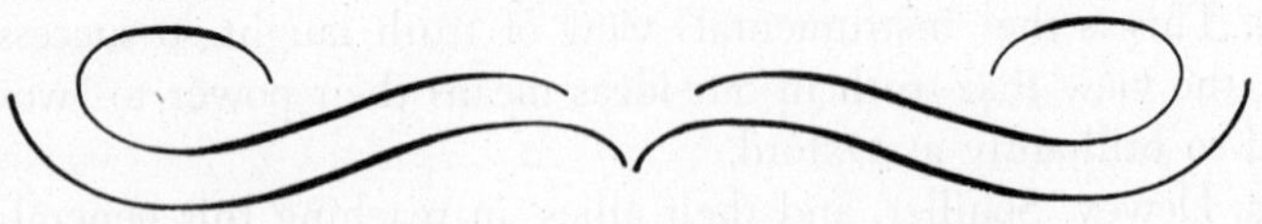

·*CAN PHILOSOPHY SAVE CIVILIZATION?*·

THE BREAKDOWN OF MODERN PHILOSOPHY [1]

ETIENNE GILSON

When Oswald Spengler first published *The Decline of the West,* many readers of his now famous book felt at variance with more than one of its conclusions; yet few among them would have thought of questioning the fact that the West was actually declining. Most of them had already known it for a long time. Not in the least because of the World War; on the contrary, the war had been a time of enthusiasm and complete self-dedication to a sacred cause, when old fears and solicitous misgivings as to the future of Western culture had been forgotten. I know that it is now fashionable to laugh at that sacred cause; yet there are still a few people who remember how they were then trying to redeem war by giving it a meaning and who remember what that meaning was. A certain idea of man and a corresponding ideal of social life were not to be allowed to perish. Yet it now seems clear that even at that time Western culture was steadily following its process of dissolution, and we know it from within, by a sort of immediate and personal experience. For we are the bearers of that culture; it cannot be dying, and dying in us, without our being aware of it.

In its broadest sense, what we call Western culture is essentially the culture of Greece, inherited from the Greeks by the Romans, transfused by the fathers of the church with the religious teachings of Christianity, and pro-

1. From *The Unity of Philosophical Experience* (New York: Charles Scribner's Sons, 1937), pp. 271–277. By permission of Charles Scribner's Sons.

gressively enlarged by countless numbers of artists, writers, scientists, and philosophers from the beginning of the Middle Ages up to the first third of the nineteenth century. It would be a waste of time to look for a turning point in its history—in the continuous stream of historical events every point is a turning point—but it can safely be assumed that the French Revolution marks the time when the more clear-sighted among the representatives of Western culture began to feel that there was something wrong with it. They offered various diagnoses, and they began to suggest remedies. For the reasons we have noted, Comte failed to provide Europe with a living dogma; his new scientific religion was stillborn, and he died, a self-appointed pope, with a very small number of disciples. On the whole, his Reformation was a failure, but Comte had at least seen clearly that the European crisis was essentially a crisis of Western culture: Can a social order, begotten by a common faith in the value of certain principles, keep on living when all faith in these principles is lost?

The meaning of that question will be illustrated best by a summary description of what may be called, for brevity's sake, the Western creed. Its most fundamental feature is a firm belief in the eminent dignity of man. The Greeks of classical times never wavered in their conviction that of all the things that can be found in nature, man is by far the highest, and that of all the things important for man to know, by far the most important is man. When Socrates, after unsuccessful attempts to deal with physical problems, made up his mind to dedicate himself to the exclusive study of man, he was making a momentous decision. "Know thyself" is not only the key to Greek culture but to the classical culture of the Western world as well. What the Greeks left to their successors was a vast body of knowledge, mainly related to man's nature and his various needs: logic, which is the science of how to think; several different philosophies, all of them culminating in ethics and politics, which are the sciences of how to live; remarkable specimens of history and political eloquence, related to the life of the city. As to what we today call positive science, the greatest achievements of the Greek genius were along the lines of mathematics, a knowledge which man draws from his own mind without submitting to the degrading tyranny of material facts, and medicine, whose proper object is to insure the well-being of the human body. And they stopped there, checked by an obscure feeling that the rest was not worth having, at least not at the price which the human mind would have to pay for it; its freedom from matter, its internal liberty.

Of the heirs to Greek culture it can truly be said that while they enlarged and deepened their heritage, they always respected its nature and never thought of displacing its center of gravity. When the Romans added the lofty structure of Roman law to it, man and the betterment of human life still remained their essential interest. As to Christianity, though it be true that God was its ultimate goal and its center of reference, the fact remains that it conceived man, created by God in His own image and likeness, as the most perfect of all earthly beings, with no higher duty than to achieve his own salvation. And why is man an image of God? Because, says St. Augustine, he has a mind. All the Greek philosophers would have gladly subscribed to that statement.

Hence the second fundamental feature of Western culture, which is a definite conviction that reason is the specific difference of man. Man is best described as a rational animal; deprive man of reason, and what is left is not man, but animal. This looks like a very commonplace statement; yet Western culture is dying wherever it has been forgotten, for the rational nature of man is the only conceivable foundation for a rational system of ethics. Morality is essentially normality; for a rational being to act and to behave either without reason or contrary to its dictates is to act and behave, not exactly as a beast, but as a beastly man, which is worse. For it is proper that a beast should act as a beast—that is, according to its own nature—but it is totally unfitting for a man to act as a beast, because that means the complete oblivion of his own nature, and hence his final destruction.

It is hardly possible to realize the continuity that prevails throughout the whole history of Western culture unless one keeps in mind the important part played by the church in the work of its transmission. The Greek and the Latin fathers of the church had so carefully preserved the classical notion of man that when St. Thomas Aquinas, in the thirteenth century, undertook to build up a complete exposition of the Christian truth, he did not scruple to borrow for his technical equipment from the pagan Aristotle, whose logic, physics, biology, ethics, and metaphysics were then transformed by his mediaeval disciple into as many elements of a Christian synthesis.

The Reformation of the sixteenth century was to wreck that stately edifice, whose two component elements then fell apart, Christianity on the one side and Greek culture on the other. Yet not only Catholic humanists such as Erasmus but even Protestants such as Melanchthon immediately set about rebuilding it. Luther himself, despite his fierce attacks upon pagan culture, was fond of Ovid, and he always remained partial to Cicero. The humanists who, more or less consciously, swerved from Christianity to paganism were either going back to what seemed to them the pure doctrine of Aristotle or testing the truth value of the doctrines left by the Stoics and Epicureans. Throughout the Renaissance and until the middle of the nineteenth century, the classical tradition remained the common ground on which both pagans and Christians could still meet and carry on fruitful intellectual intercourse. Even the most brilliant scientific discoveries were made by men who, like Descartes, Pascal, Fermat, Leibniz, and Newton, had learned little more at school than classical Latin, a philosophy which more or less resembled that of St. Thomas or Aristotle, and the elements of mathematics. So long as, and in so far as, science itself kept faith with its own nature, it remained the healthy exercise of reason, reason seeking to know, because knowing is its natural function. Even the most stupendous progress made by the physical and biological sciences entailed no disruption in the continuity of Western culture. While man remained in control of nature, culture could still survive. It was lost from the very moment nature began to control man.

Such a development was by no means inevitable, but the progressive growth of natural science had made it more and more probable. The growing interest taken by men in the practical results of science was in itself both natural and legitimate, but it helped them to forget that science is knowledge, and practical results but its by-products. Moreover, the constant accumulation of hitherto unknown facts and of their recently formulated laws was destroying the old balance between the human and the physical sciences, to the advantage of the latter. This, however, was not the main point. It lay rather in the fact that before their unexpected success in finding conclusive explanations of the material world, men had begun either to despise all disciplines in which such demonstrations could not be found or to rebuild those disciplines after the pattern of the physical sciences. As a consequence, metaphysics and ethics had to be ignored or, at least, replaced by new positive sciences; in either case, they would be eliminated.

A very dangerous move indeed, which accounts for the perilous position in which Western culture has now found itself. The European burned his old ships before making sure that the new ones would float. Moreover, the first article of the scientific creed is the acceptance of nature such as it is. Far from making up for the loss of philosophy, the discovery of the scientific substitutes for it leaves man alone with nature such as it is and obliges him to surrender to natural necessity. Philosophy is the only rational knowledge by which both science and nature can be judged. By reducing philosophy to pure science, man has not only abdicated his right to judge nature and to rule it, but he has also turned himself into a particular aspect of nature, subjected, like all the rest, to the necessary law which regulates its development. A world where accomplished facts are unto themselves their own justification is ripe for the most reckless social adventures. Its dictators can wantonly play havoc with human institutions and human lives, for dictatorships are facts, and they also are unto themselves their own justification.

THE BASIS OF RENEWAL[1]

LEWIS MUMFORD

THE EXTERNAL CRISIS

HENRY ADAMS was right: the last thirty years have been witnessing the active disintegration of Western civilization. In a disintegrating society, decay is its form of life; and all the dynamic forces that are available have worked either to corrupt the human fiber or to multiply the agents of physical destruction. If we go further along the same route we shall fare worse. On our courage in facing this fact and on our promptness in meeting it, all plans for the renewal of personality and community depend. "Bombs educate vigorously," Adams observed, "and even wireless telegraphy or airships might require the reconstruction of society."

Has the destruction yet gone far enough to promote a genuine renewal —or has it already gone so far that it will prevent it? No one can yet answer this question. But only the ability to put the question to ourselves will provide an effectual answer in life and action.

The makers of the New World idolum confidently expected that the older part of the human heritage would disappear: science and technics seemed thoroughly able not merely to reconstruct man's institutions and his personality, but to displace any older forms of art, thought, or practice. If anything, the utilitarians would have been surprised at the persistence of institutions that were manifestly at odds with the utilitarian way of life. But they forgot that the moral and intellectual traditions of Judaea, Greece, and Rome were essential to the development of the New World ideology itself: so that, with the ebbing away of this older tide of culture, the insufficiency of their own creed as a guide to life would become plain. A science that disclaimed all interest in human values, except the satisfaction of curiosity and the increase of manipulative skill, cannot be useful even in its own limited sphere when the general dissolution of values leads to a contempt for science and a deliberate perversion of its results.

Modern civilization has been arrested in mid-flight: its technical advances in saving labor, perfecting automatism, mechanizing the daily processes of life, multiplying the arts of destruction, and dehumanizing the personality, have been responsible for this arrest. The rise of the machine and the fall of man are two parts of the same process: never before have machines been so perfect, and never before have men sunk so low, for the sub-human conduct that the Nazis have exhibited in the torture and extermination of

1. From *The Condition of Man* by Lewis Mumford, copyright, 1944, by Lewis Mumford, pp. 391–423, with omissions. Reprinted by permission of Harcourt, Brace and Company, Inc. With minor changes of the text made by the author.

their victims drops below any level of merely animal brutality. That degradation is shared by those who passively condone this sub-human conduct, by belittling its horror and denying its terrible significance.

This catastrophe and this debasement have no parallels in earlier history; for now, for the first time, the entire world is involved. All consolations that are based on past recoveries are meaningless. What happened to Greece, Rome, China, or India has no parallel in the world today: when those civilizations collapsed, they were surrounded by neighbors that had reached nearly equal levels of culture, whereas if Western civilization should continue its downward course it will spread ruin to every part of the planet; and its going will consume the very forces and ideas within its own tradition that might have given a start to its successor.

The present crisis has long been visible. Jacob Burckhardt observed its early stages in the middle of the nineteenth century: in the series of brilliant essays, now published in English under the title, Force and Freedom, he not merely diagnosed the malady but accurately predicted its outward manifestations. In a letter written to Henry Osborn Taylor in 1905, Henry Adams remarked: "At the present rate of progression since 1600, it will not need another century or half century to tip thought upside down. Law, in that case, would disappear as theory or *a priori* principle and give place to force. Morality would become police. Explosives would reach cosmic violence. Disintegration would overcome integration." Henry Adams did not live to observe fascism: he anticipated it. He knew that the detonators of violence and destruction were present in every part of the social structure of Western society.

Like the die-hards of fourth century Rome, most of our contemporaries are still unaware of the dimensions of the present catastrophe. They were so completely self-hypnotized by pride in man's control over nature that they overlooked all the palpable evidence of the fact that this control did not extend to his own self and his own very life: they were unprepared to believe that a fiendish barbarism could arise in the midst of an advanced scientific country like Germany; and they were unable to analyze in their own reactions to this the characteristic symptoms of decay: a moral inertia, a flight from reality, an unwillingness to face danger or hardship on behalf of an ideal cause. The democratic peoples, inheritors of a universal culture that had actually spread throughout the globe, were willing to barter all their advances for the sake of "peace." When they finally found that the choice was not in their hands, they made ready to fight—but skeptically, reluctantly, stupidly, as men answer an alarm clock when still thick with sleep. This feeble response to the challenge of barbarism was as much a sign of disintegration as the barbarism itself.

The war itself has shocked people into facing the grimmest of realities; but it is not in itself sufficient to promote an understanding of the forces that have promoted this world catastrophe. In its later phases, the war has caused people to accept unthinkable sacrifices: but they have yet to accept the hardest sacrifice of all, and that is, to give up their illusions about this civilization. Modern man is the victim of the very instruments he values most. Every gain in power, every mastery of natural forces, every scientific addition to knowledge, has proved potentially dangerous because it has not been accompanied by equal gains in self-understanding and self-discipline. We have sought to achieve perfection by eliminating the human element. Believing that power and knowledge were by nature beneficent or that man himself was inherently good when freed from external obligations to goodness, we have conjured up a genius capable of destroying our civilization. The disproportionate development of the sciences themselves only hastens this malign end.

The physical victory over the barbarian in war is no answer to the problem that the barbarian's existence has conjured up: it merely clears the way for an answer. Even if valor and skill in war give the democratic peoples a temporary military ascendancy, that in itself will not be sufficient either to secure a lasting peace or to raise up this battered civilization. For the disease that threatens us is an organic one: it is no localized infection that can be lanced, cleaned, bandaged; on the contrary, it requires a re-orientation of our whole life, a change in occupation, a change in regimen, a change in personal relationships, not least, a change in attitude and conscious direction: fundamentally, a change in religion, our total sense of the world and life and time. If we seek salvation more cheaply, we shall not be ready to undertake the heroic feats and sacrifices, the spiritual and practical efforts that will be necessary to create a life-sustaining community and a life-directed personality. To make use of our vitalities and energies—and potentially these were never greater—we must reassert once more the primacy of the person.

The obstacle to renewal does not merely lie in the fact that in so many parts of society the agents of destruction have gained the upper hand, and the organization of destruction has been forced upon us by the barbarian's attempt at world enslavement. Worse than that: organization has become in itself destructive of human values: everywhere the machine holds the center and the personality has been pushed to the periphery: a process which remains sinister even when the intention is benign—as it undoubtedly is, for example, in our overorganized institutions for teaching the young or for healing disease. The only way to renew the forces of life is to begin once again with the repressed and displaced elements: to dismantle a large part of the physical structure, to loosen up the automatisms of habit, to challenge even successful forms of routine, to give time, thought, attention, to all those changes which do not, in their first stages, require the collaboration and support of existing institutions. Our society is now at the stage where conversion—an inner change and redirection—must precede every outer change or transformation.

Here is the benign moment of disintegration: the moment when the old life is sufficiently shattered and broken to make a new life conceivable. When this moment of germination comes, the individual's experience of renewal, or at least his radical readiness for renewal, widens into a collective act. Such a change took place in classic civilization during the fourth century: it occurred again on a similar scale throughout the Western world in the eighteenth century: in both cases responses to disintegration. That inner change, under the pressure of a powerful experience, universally shared, is the prelude to every significant outer change. If rational demonstration cannot bring such a change about, it can nevertheless hasten it and clarify its goals once the personality has made itself ready and the conditions favoring it have come into being.

THE INERTIA OF "PROGRESS"

The Chinese symbol for crisis is composed of two elements: one signifies danger and the other opportunity. If the dangers that the world faces today are greater than the majority yet fully realize, the opportunities are equally great. But these opportunities are of a different order than those of the past. Talk of goods and benefits to be shared among mankind after the war too often has been in the familiar utilitarian terms, and those who have been most confident of technical progress show themselves pitifully incapable of understanding either current dangers or future promises. Such people are the bemused victims of the very values they question least.

In anticipation of the post-war tasks, perhaps the most important thing to remember is that our mission is not the simple one of re-building demolished houses and ruined cities, converting war industries to peacetime manufactures, repairing the broken bodies of the wounded or the broken souls of those who have borne witness to more violence, terror, and misery than the human spirit can endure. All these tasks are essential; but they are only first aid. If the material shell of our society alone needed repair, if only the more obvious human wreckage needed to be restored to the human estate, our designs might follow familiar patterns. But the fact is our task is a far heavier one. In every department of our culture, we must lay the foundations for a new set of purposes, a new drama, a radically different mode of life. The "New World" of the fifteenth century is now the *Old* World: our dawning new world must take in far larger tracts of both the earth and the human personality. The bulk of our institutions no longer corresponds to the needs and possibilities of human life; and this is true, not merely of traditional structures, but of many that boast their unqualified modernity: some of the last, indeed, are already the seediest, the most completely disserviceable, in terms of valid human purposes.

In short, the crisis we are now in the midst of does not admit of a return to our original condition, in the fashion that a crisis in pneumonia, once passed, enables the patient to recover his original health. The fact is that before the war there was spiritually little health in us. Our elaborate mechanical organization of life had resulted in an increasingly purposeless society, in which some of the parts were neatly articulated and ordered, while the whole made little sense in terms of life-satisfactions and life-fulfillments. In its very mechanical elaboration, our civilization had become emptier, because it had not originally been shaped in conformity to the basic needs of human life. Only after the human voice had been transmitted around the world with the speed of light did it become plain that the words so widely disseminated might still be the same words one could hear from the village gossip or the village idiot or the village clown or the village hoodlum.

Man himself did not mirror the perfection of his instruments. Behind this empty technical fabric was an emptier ideology: one which multiplied quantities and forgot qualities: one which centered on the means of life and forgot its consummations.

Western man has exhausted the dream of mechanical power which so long dominated his imagination. If he is to preserve the instruments he has so cunningly created, if he is to continue to refine and perfect the whole apparatus of life, he can no longer let himself remain spellbound in that dream: he must attach himself to more humane purposes than those he has given to the machine. We can no longer live, with the illusions of success, in a world given over to devitalized mechanisms, desocialized organisms, and depersonalized societies: a world that had lost its sense of the ultimate dignity of the person almost as completely as the Roman Empire did at the height of its military greatness and technical facility. All that the Nazis have done has been to bring to a more rapid climax a process that was more slowly, more insidiously, undermining our whole civilization.

But another symptomatic weakness should by now be equally plain: even those who cling to the old drama of expansion and conquest, of mechanical organization and material exploitation, no longer wholly believe in the plot. Georges Sorel observed this fact early in the twentieth century: he compared the new capitalists disparagingly with the American robber barons of the mid-nineteenth century, and he was afraid that the revolutionary élan would disappear in a society whose business men and industrialists had lost their original ruthlessness if not their original greed. The signs of this inner exhaustion multiplied steadily during the last thirty years; one of the most critical of them is the widespread unwillingness to play the game if the player happens to be losing. When people are really interested in a life-theme, they cling to it even under the most adverse conditions; indeed, the pressure of difficulty only intensifies their interest. When the Christian theme was in the making, persecutions welded the faithful together and finally resulted in a unified Church. When the interests of capitalism were dominant, adventurous enterprisers accepted losses and bankruptcies without wincing and began all over again; the Christian did not cease to believe in his religion because it brought personal grief, nor the capitalist in capitalism because it might result in personal ruin.

Now, we have seen just the opposite of these qualities in our time. Capitalists accepted the closing down of the world market for the same reason that democratic peoples accepted without even a timid counter-movement the cancerous spread of fascism. And why? For the sake of peace: for the reason that a counter-movement implied risk and sacrifice; and risk and sacrifice were not accepted, since the faith that would have made them self-justifying had evaporated.

Had the old plot become too complicated to follow? Had the old rewards proved disappointing? Had new motives appeared which cast into disrepute the accepted themes of the old drama? In varying ways all these things had indeed happened; but the main fact to be noted is that the old game no longer thrilled the players: until the war acually was forced upon the anti-fascist powers, neither nationalism nor capitalism had the pride, the self-confidence, the initiative to summon together energies that were still visible as late as 1914. In the course of fighting the war, nationalism and capitalism have both received a powerful stimulant: the nationalist shows a truculent egoism toward allies in victory that might have staved off the war altogether had it been originally present in the face of fascist bluff and bullying; while capitalism, like an old man who has miraculously begotten a baby, actually fancies it has recovered the potencies of youth. Both responses, however, are automatic ones: mere by-products of the war. Examine the motives that are still dominant and they turn out to end up in dreams of escape, escape via the golf-links, the motor highway, the night club, the helicopter, a life of expensive automatism and automatic expense: the tag ends of baroque luxury and baroque futility in a setting of slick machines.

Unlike the rapacious industrialists of the nineteenth century, the leaders today no longer treat the industrial system as an end in itself. Western man demands a special price for further mechanization: bread and shows, physical security, and semi-mental distractions. He must be bribed and coaxed to perform acts his forefathers performed gladly, wholeheartedly, with an almost religious conviction. This applies to both owners and workers, leaders and led. The very economies the machine makes possible bring with them a train of dissipations.

In general, one may say that in the present crisis nothing was real enough to fight for at the beginning because nothing was significant enough to live for at the end.

If technics is the sole key to success, the American cartels that connived with the Nazis to suppress patents essential to democracy's preparation for war might write off their treason to the account of profit. If technics alone constitutes man's desirable future, then the Nazis, who have applied cold technics to the state-controlled copulation of future mothers or to the bestial murder of Jews, were indeed the "wave of the future." But what a future! The danger to human society today does not come solely from the active barbarians: it comes even more perhaps from those who have in their hearts assented to the barbarian's purposes. This lapse was part of a decay of faith in the primacy of the person that people of the most widely assorted convictions succumbed to: the very Churches that had originally sprung from this faith were among its most sinister betrayers.

Unfortunately, the war itself has reawakened a confidence in the future on the basis of a simple restoration of the motives and methods of the past—that very past which has terminated in the present catastrophe. Above all, the capitalist dog has returned to his old vomit. The investor, the organizer, the industrial worker, even the farmer, have once again had a glimpse of that hitherto unattainable heaven which the innocent regard as a practical equivalent of the good life: the heaven of full productivity based on unlimited demand and leading to the hope of unlimited profits. That heaven, it is true, will remain real only until the day of reckoning comes: the day when each country adds up the costs and starts to balance the books. Indeed, no better evidence exists of the mental disorder that is rife in present-day society than the capitalist's confidence in his ability to resume this game on his own terms—when *on his own terms*, that is, on the terms of redeeming the existing debt at par value, and paying to boot the interest charges he has already lost.

Mazzini long ago remarked when he was promoting the national independence of Italy that people were much more willing to sacrifice their lives to the good cause than their pennies. When the time comes to shift from war production to peace production, we shall find that the utopia of full production is a capitalist mirage, as long as the old capitalist super-ego remains in control. Capitalism by nature and principle subordinates public need to private profit. On capitalist terms, there is no satisfactory "moral equivalent of war." That was the illusion of the new capitalism: an illusion that should have been buried forever by the calamitous depression that started in 1929.

But there is far more impressive evidence of the vanity of all these great expectations than I have yet shown. The fact is that most of the current plans for remolding our civilization ignore the vast secular change that has crept up on Western Civilization during the past century, almost unawares. That change is nothing less than the end of the Era of Expansion, and the collapse of the major premises, metaphysical, moral, social, economic, on which it was based.

THE END OF EXPANSION

The world crisis that has existed for the lifetime of a whole generation indicates that a radical shift in the direction of social movement has taken place: this shift began during the last quarter of the nineteenth century and now, directly and indirectly, has affected almost every institution. The crisis has two aspects: an external and an internal one. Here I shall deal mainly with the causes of the external crisis. The external change may be summed up in a brief sentence: an age of expansion is giving place to an age of equilibrium. The achievement of this equilibrium is the task of the next few centuries.

So far this change has been a blind and blundering one. Not merely have the underlying causes themselves been ignored, but the interests and attitudes that were formed by the tradition of expansion have kept every community from meeting by rational means the new conditions of life that open up. Those that have accepted the premises of stabilization have attached the movement itself to regressive purposes and have cut it off from its creative mission. Those who have resisted stabilization have striven to perpetuate a past that is beyond recall: a past that would not be worth recalling even if that were possible. Both the tempo and the direction of our life are about to undergo a profound change: this will prove a change for the better provided we can throw off the fatal temptation to worship our dead selves and perpetuate our past mistakes.

The present period is a painful transition between two eras. The first I have traced in some detail since the fourteenth century: it is associated with the rise of capitalism, militarism, scientism, and mechanization: likewise with the counter-movements of protestantism, romanticism, and democracy. All of these institutions made positive contributions to human culture: even militarism. The total effect of the era of expansion, however, was to increase man's power over nature, and in particular Western man's power over the more amiable or more feebly armed peoples that inhabited the rest of the planet; but the civilization that resulted has been rent by internal conflicts and contradictions which have nullified many of its real triumphs.

The outlines of the period of humanization that approaches are not so easy to describe: many of the characters have still to be invented and their lines have still to be written: at best, some of their costumes and a few odd parcels of scenery indicate what the play is to be about. But by way of broad contrast one may characterize the approaching period as one of dynamic equilibrium, such an equilibrium as the human body maintains at every stage in its growth. The theme for the new period will be neither arms and the man nor machines and the man: its theme will be the resurgence of life, the displacement of the mechanical by the organic, and the re-establishment of the person as the ultimate term of all human effort. Cultivation, humanization, co-operation, symbiosis: these are the watchwords of the new world-enveloping culture.

Many of the miscarriages of the present period are due to the fact that our statesmen, our industrial leaders, our administrators are still trying to apply the ideology of the age of expansion to a social organization that has an entirely different set of requirements: an organization in which the careful timing and spacing of activities, in which the proper diversification of opportunities and the balancing and interlocking of functions must take the place of those spectacular one-sided advances, colossal but incoherent, which were characteristic of the period of expansion. Every department of life will record this change: it will affect the task of education and the procedures of science no less than the organization of industrial enterprises, the planning of cities, the development of regions, the interchange of world resources.

The facts of the present stabilization are familiar to students of history and sociology; but the interpretation of these facts has proved tardy. Yet strangely enough, our present state was accurately forecast by at least one early observer, John Stuart Mill: witness what has become, by force of events, a great chapter in the second volume of his Principles of Political Economy. That chapter is devoted to a theoretical discussion of what Mill misleadingly called the "stationary state." By this he meant an economic order in which the area for new capital investments had dwindled by a natural process of self-limitation, in which, through birth control, the population had become stable, and in which the rates of profit and interest tended, as a result of this twofold curb, to fall toward zero.

This is the chapter that most people know by only a single sentence, one in which Mill doubted whether labor-saving machinery had yet lightened the day's burdens of a single worker. But it was here he made a far more significant observation: namely, that a state of dynamic equilibrium, though it might be dreaded by the profiteer, was precisely the condition required for translating mechanical improvements into social welfare. In restating Mill's observations as history I only accentuate their merit as prophecy.

The era of Western expansion had three overlapping and interacting phases: land expansion, population expansion, and industrial expansion. All three phases have usually been treated as if they were constant phenomena in any healthy society; whereas they were extremely unusual and highly localized changes that had a definite beginning and an inevitable terminus. In our time the whole process has come to an end, or very nearly approaches an end. Other peoples who a hundred years ago existed on a primitive level have fast become masters of Western machines and weapons, producers in their own right. Such people will no longer consent to being treated as packbearers and servants: they properly claim their place as partners, and they reinforce their claim with the Christian doctrine of the infinite worth of the individual, and the democratic doctrine of the freedom and equality of all men as men. We cannot disown either doctrine without betraying our own precious heritage. World trade, world production, world intercourse must now be based upon equivalent advantages for all the regions concerned: it must now be a two-way process: consciously and deliberately so. Meanwhile, equally radical changes are under way in the other departments where expansion has prevailed. I propose to examine these changes and to point out their consequences. . . .

THE INTERNAL CRISIS

The internal crisis in our civilization has been visible for a much longer time than the external crisis; for it grew out of the inadequacy of the New World idolum and the failure of utilitarian man to fulfill the ends of life.

The materialist creed by which a large part of humanity has sought to live during the last few centuries confused the needs of survival with the needs of fulfillment; whereas man's life requires both. For survival, the physiological needs are uppermost; and the most imperative, obviously, are the needs for air and water: then food and shelter against extremes of temperature, and so by degrees one passes to those social needs for communication and co-operation, that never wholly limit themselves to life-preservation in the narrow sense. Within the life-span of a generation, the needs for sexual intercourse and parental care are as imperative as those for air and water.

In terms of life-fulfillment, however, this ascending scale of needs, from bare physical life to social stimulus and personal growth, must be reversed. The most important needs from the standpoint of life-fulfillment are those that foster spiritual activity and promote spiritual growth: the needs for order, continuity, meaning, value, purpose and design—needs out of which language and poesy and music and science and art and religion have grown. The deepest, the most organic, of these higher needs is that for love: all the stronger because it is rooted in survival. Neither group of needs is in a watertight compartment: lovers must eat and even greedy eaters have been known to share their food with the starving. Nevertheless there are conflict and tension between these two sets of needs, as there are between the primitive institutions of the tribe, seeking self-preservation, and the order of an open society, prepared to share its highest values with all other men.

Lured by his elemental needs, man tends to rest content with their satisfaction: instead of using them as the basis of the good life, he often seeks, by merely elaborating and refining them, to use them as a substitute for the good life. Here is one of the chief causes of social fixation and personal arrest. The more complicated and costly the physical and social apparatus for ensuring man's survival, the more likely will it smother the purposes for which it humanly exists. The threat was never stronger than it is today; for the very exquisiteness of our mechanical apparatus, in every department of life, tends to put the non-human process above the human end.

But no matter how primitive the community, and no matter how terrible the pressure of war, pestilence, or natural disaster, there must always be a sufficient margin of time and energy to carry forward the processes that make life-fulfillment possible. No matter how harassed a mother may be, she must give her child the gift of language as well as food. When life-fulfillment is put first, an intensification of activity takes place in all the subordinate needs, for they then have a meaning and a purpose that they do not possess in themselves: they do not merely sustain life but raise it to a higher level.

The emergence of man from his purely animal state consists in the constant increase of the ratio of higher needs to lower needs, and in the fuller contribution of his vitalities and energies to the molding of more richly endowed and more fully expressive personalities. Up to now, the fullest kind of human growth has been possible only to small groups of men: a privileged class, or at best, a city; and the fact that men as a body have not participated fully in man's own highest activities has always undermined and disordered the very growth that even the most fortunate achieved. Only now has mankind itself arrived at the point of inheriting man's whole estate. There lies the meaning and the promise of the democratic ideal.

The great gains that were made in technics during the last few centuries were largely offset by a philosophy that either denied the validity of man's higher needs or that sought to foster only that limited set of interests which enlarged the power of science and gave scope to a power personality. At a moment when a vast surplus was available for the goods of leisure and culture, the very ideals of leisure and culture were cast into disrepute—except when they could be turned to profit. Here lies the core of the inner crisis that has afflicted our civilization for at least two centuries. In the heyday of expansionism, the middle of the nineteenth century, scarcely a single humane voice could be found to defend either the means or the ideals of a power civilization. The wisdom of the race revolted against the inhuman fruits of its knowledge: Blake, Ruskin, Morris, Arnold, Emerson, Whitman, Thoreau, Melville, Dickens, Howells, Hugo, Zola, Mazzini, Tolstoy, Dostoyevsky, Ibsen—almost all the representative minds of Europe and America—denounced the human results of the whole process of mechanization and physical conquest. As with one voice, they protested against the inhuman sacrifices and brutalizations, the tawdry materialisms, the crass neglect of the human personality.

In the course of the last generation, the wisdom of this protest has become plain. As a result, many of the plans and projects that seemed like mere escapist dreams in the nineteenth century have become conditions for renewal; indeed only those who are aware of the importance of man's higher needs will be capable even of providing intelligently for bare food and shelter. This is one of those periods when only the dreamers are practical men. By the same token, the so-called practical men have become makers and perpetuators of nightmares: for it is their attempt to crawl back into the crumbled wreckage of the immediate past that has condemned our society to frustration, to sterility, to savage barbarism.

The inner crisis in our civilization must be resolved before the outer crisis can be effectively met. Our first duty is to revamp our ideas and values and to reorganize the human personality around its highest and most central needs. If we ask ourselves as we face the future, not how to keep our old institutions and organizations running in their accustomed grooves, but how to keep life itself running, with or without the aid of these institutions, our problem immediately clarifies itself. There is no wealth, as Ruskin said, but life; and there is no consummation of life except in the perpetual growth and renewal of the human person: machines, organizations, institutions, wealth, power, culture, cities, landscapes, industries, are all secondary instruments in that process. Whatever nourishes the personality, humanizes it, refines it, deepens it, intensifies its aptitude and broadens its field of action is good: whatever limits it or thwarts it, whatever sends it back into tribal patterns and lessens its capacity for human co-operation and communion must be counted as bad. Nothing that man has created is outside his capacity to change, to remold, to supplant, or to destroy: his machines are no more sacred or substantial than the dreams in which they originated.

In the end, all our contrivances have but one object: the continued growth of human personalities and the cultivation of the best life possible. What sort of personality must we now seek to foster and nourish? What kind of common life? What traits and disciplines are needed in an age of stabilization, co-operation, and balance? What is the order of value in our life needs: do we put babies above motor cars, art above plumbing, the well-being of the worker above the mechanical efficiency or cheapness of his product? If so, we must create a different ego-ideal from that which was the norm in a capitalistic and mechanical civilization: our mode of education and our plan of life must be directed to more humane ends than those that have hitherto governed us.

THE NEED FOR HUMAN BALANCE

As our culture developed during the last five centuries, its center lay more and more outside the human personality: hence a fragment of the personality displaced the whole. In attempting to restore balance in the community and in the personality, we need not be troubled by references to the undoubted existence of individual differences or to the fact, as true in society as in the individual organism, that all equilibrium is necessarily unstable and is constantly upset by the continued act of growth. The first condition makes the effort to achieve a fuller and more balanced development necessary: the second makes it an ideal goal—one always to be aimed at but never, in the nature of things, fully achieved.

Differences in temperament, capacity, aptitude, and interest, differences that have in their origin in diversities of biological inheritance, characterize all men, as they characterize the same men at successive moments in life: Who would doubt it? Who would change it? These differences are the inexhaustible source of the richness of human experience. But no man is an island: every age has a common ideal of personality which represents the goals of living toward which the whole community is more or less set. To the extent that an individual shares in this personality, he is fit for his daily tasks and can co-operate freely with his fellows and make the fullest use of his culture. The more representative the common type, the more it meets the claims of its historic moment, the fewer repressions must be exercised over those whose inner tendency is to depart from it.

If the era of stabilization is to be one devoted to the intensive but balanced cultivation of our natural and social resources, balance and intensity are equally, I believe, the key to the sort of personality that is needed to work effectively within this culture and to create the necessary changes in our disrupted institutions. The age of mechanical specialization produced a quite different ideal: that of the one-sided specialist, the piece worker, the operative conditioned by repetition and reward, as Dr. E. L. Thorndike puts it: the end product of a long period of mechanization in which one by one the higher attributes of the personality have disappeared or have been reduced to mere whims and hobbies. The fatal results of this process were pointed out by Comte a full century ago. "If we have been accustomed to deplore the spectacle, among the artisan class, of a workman occupied during his whole life in nothing but making knife handles or pinheads, we may find something quite as lamentable in the intellectual class, in the exclusive employment of the human brain in resolving equations or classifying insects. The moral effect is, unhappily, analogous in the two cases. It occasions a miserable indifference about the general course of human affairs as long as there are equations to resolve or pins to manufacture."

One of Comte's most able successors in sociology, Dr. Karl Mannheim, has carried this observation even further: he notes the growing irrationality of the personality engaged in production in proportion to the technical refinement and "rationalization" of the process. The dismembered man, whether as engineer or workman, as organizer or salesman, needs less directive insight and intelligence once he is geared to the whole machine than the carpenter or the weaver needed in his workshop. The behaviorist man, with his slot-machine mind, responding mechanically to external stimuli, passive until acted upon, incapable of taking the initiative or choosing his destination, is the typical by-product of current society: fascist minds are thus more common than the conscious philosophy of fascism. Indeed our whole civilization has put a premium upon this primitive kind of automatism and compulsion: the very humanity that quickens the life-like machine leaves the person depleted and empty.

Dr. Mannheim has well pointed out that the chief element in our inner crisis today is the disproportionate development of human faculties: "individuals as well as historical and social groups may, under certain circumstances, suffer from the danger of disintegration because their capacities fail to develop equally and harmoniously." This observation has been reinforced by an experienced psychiatrist and a profound reader of the modern soul, Dr. C. G. Jung, who has sought to combat this unfortunate lopsidedness and disparity by counseling his patients to cultivate their weaker sides. None of our dominant institutions today correct this lack of balance: on the contrary, they encourage it in the name of efficiency, an efficiency which fosters a single function at the expense of the whole life that finally supports it. Only by making the personality itself central, and by drawing forth its repressed or thwarted capacities, can this mischief be cured: balance and autonomy go together.

The ideal of balance itself is an ancient one: common to philosophers as far apart in time and culture as Confucius, Aristotle, and Spencer: the Confucian ideal of the superior man, the Greek ideal of the Golden Mean, and the renascence ideal of the gentleman all embodied this conception.

Behind the notion of balance is the ethical principle laid down by Herbert Spencer: "Strange as the conclusion looks, it is nevertheless a conclusion to be drawn, that the performance of every function is, in general, a moral obligation. It is usually thought that morality requires us only to restrain such vital activities as in our present state are often pushed to excess, or such as conflict with average welfare, special or general; but it also requires us to carry on these vital activities up to their normal limits."

Spencer's doctrine of organic balance was handicapped by the same weakness that crippled Marx's socialism, a defective incarnation: his formulation remained a tissue of abstractions. But it is important to realize how well the deliverances of this nonconformist and individualist expressed the mature beliefs of Marx himself. These indications are significant because the period of formulation almost always anticipates by at least half a century or more the stages of incarnation and fulfillment: so that, if we are to achieve a balanced economy and a balanced community and a balanced personality, it will be with the aid of ideas that have long been in existence: ripened sufficiently to be ready now for assimilation. Hence it is important to realize that Marx, in a brief passage in Capital, anticipated the present argument. He said: "In a socialist society, the 'fragmentary man' would be replaced by the 'completely developed individual,' one for whom different social functions are but alternative forms of activity. Men would fish, hunt, or engage in literary criticism without becoming professional fishermen, hunters, or critics."

In every department of life, man's activity is limited by his capacities for assimilation; and the greater the resources man can potentially use the more disciplined and many-sided must be his response. The difficulty our culture faces was well diagnosed by Shelley: "The accumulations of the materials of external life exceed the quantity of power of assimilating them to the internal laws of human nature." When these accumulations heap up as recklessly as they have in our time and when the internal laws and the internal capacities of human nature are disregarded, the result is to turn each potential gain *against* man: he functions as a distracted atom in a growing chaos, made poor by his wealth, made empty by his fullness, reduced to monotony by his very opportunities for variety, the victim of changes that have in themselves become fixations: all beyond his power to assimilate or control.

Civilizations do not die of old age: they die of the complications of old age. Observing this process long ago, Burckhardt predicted the coming of the "terrible simplifiers": people who would reject all the goods modern man had acquired in order to restore the capacity to act. Those terrible simplifiers have appeared. They are the barbarians who renounce every part of our culture that makes a claim upon man's higher needs: avowed barbarians like the Nazis and more insidious barbarians who, by advertising, propaganda, and education, would turn every part of our life into the mean handiwork of coachman, cook, and groom, of beauty shop, assembly-line, and roadhouse.

We cannot save our culture from these barbarians, external or internal, by clinging to the habits that make us a prey to their corrupt vitality. To recover life and health again we must, like the Christian confronting the classic world, find a benign method of simplification. We must find a method that will assert the primacy of the person and that will re-endow the person with all its attributes, all its heritage, all its potentialities. But unlike the Christian, we must undertake this transformation before the barbarian has finally wrecked our civilization: only thus shall we be able to carry forward the many life-promoting activities that man has created since the breakup of the medieval synthesis.

The task for our age is to decentralize power in all its manifestations. To this end, we must build up balanced personalities: personalities that will be capable of drawing upon our immense stores of energy, knowledge, and wealth without being demoralized by them. On this point, Plato's words in The Laws cannot be improved: "If anyone gives too great power to anything, too large a sail to a vessel, too much food to the body, too much authority to the mind, and does not observe the mean, everything is overthrown, and in the wantonness of excess runs in the one case to disorders, and in the other to injustice, which is the child of excess."

If we are to control machines and organizations, then, we must make men; and our first task is that of self-examination, self-education, self-control. Those who fail at this point will be incapable of contributing to the political, economic, and social transformations that are now so long overdue.

THE ORGANIC PERSON

The ideal personality for the opening age is a balanced personality: not the specialist but the whole man. Such a personality must be in dynamic interaction with every part of his environment and every part of his heritage. He must be capable of treating economic experiences and esthetic experiences, parental experiences and vocational experiences, as the related parts of a single whole, namely, life itself. His education, his discipline, his daily routine must tend toward this wholeness. To achieve this, he must be ready to spurn the easy successes that come, in a dying culture, through self-mutilation.

Such a dynamic balance is not easily achieved: its consummations are precious and its stability is precarious: it demands a vigilance and an athletic readiness for new shifts and stresses that more specialized vocations do not habitually achieve. For balance is not a matter of allotting definite amounts of time and energy to each segment of life that requires attention: even our mechanical partition of functions does that. It means that the whole personality must be constantly at play, at least at ready call, at every moment of its existence and that no one part of life should be segregated from another part, incapable of influencing it or being influenced by it.

But qualitative balance is as important as quantitative balance: many kinds of experience have the role in life that vitamins have in the diet: quantitatively minute elements may be as important for spiritual health as the vitamins and minerals are for bodily health. Most of man's higher activities are in the latter category. No healthy person can look at pictures all day any more than he can make love all day. But for even the humblest person, a day spent without the sight or sound of beauty, the contemplation of mystery, or the search for truth and perfection is a poverty-stricken day; and a succession of such days is fatal to human life. That is why even the most superstitious forms of religion, which have at least kept alive some wraith of beauty or perfection, still contain for the mass of mankind something valuable that a bare scientific positivism has allowed to be lost both in thought and practice.

The importance of balance to both the community and the personality will come out more clearly, perhaps, if we call to mind the patent dangers that will attend stabilization: dangers that are already plainly visible in the bureaucratism and time-serving that have begun to infect every department of life: not alone government but business; and not alone business but education. Those who lack the creative capacity to establish a dynamic balance are already caught by its counterfeit and its negation: Alexandrianism or Byzantinism.

Organizations that have been stabilized for any length of time—the army is an excellent example—become embedded in routine and hostile to change: they are unable to meet fresh challenges, and their very "adjustment" becomes a profound cause of maladjustment. Scientific progress does not alter this fact, for scientific advances themselves tend to follow inflexible institutional forms, and they often seek perfection within a more and more obsolete frame of reference. Stability and security, pursued for their own sake, will result in a caste division of labor and in the denial of any changes that would upset an increasingly sessile routine: forms, precedents, stereotypes would supplant human needs, and the very attributes of life, its capacity for readjustment, for insurgence, for renewal, would be forfeited by these ill-conceived efforts to guard life more effectively.

These regressive forms of stabilization have already taken shape: they have been seized upon by Nazi philosophers and leaders as the basis for enforcing permanent caste divisions. But the danger is not confined to the conscious fascists: many of those who talk loudest about rugged individualism prove themselves in their daily practice the upholders of a Byzantine rigidity and hollowness. The standard examination papers that have appeared in so many departments of American education under the guise of progressive method would, in a short generation, paralyze the acquisition and extension of fresh knowledge: this symbolizes a much wider menace to life and thought.

Precisely because stabilization brings with it these dangers, we must introduce into our conception of the type of personality needed the ability to touch life at many points, to travel light, and to keep every part of experience in a state of constant interplay and interaction: so that fresh challenges will appear at unexpected points, in unforeseeable circumstances. For the age of balance we need a new race of pioneers, of deliberate amateurs, in order to offset the tendency to harden practice into smooth molds and to sacrifice the growing personality to the machine. Such stereotyping of activity as will free the organism for its higher functions—like those human automatisms that put a large part of the burden of behavior on the vertebral column and the cerebellum—must not halt on its way to this destination.

In this respect the varied war experiences that people in many countries have undergone, as soldiers, air raid wardens, fire fighters, nurses, and so forth, must be regarded as essential contributions to the task of peacetime co-operation: typical of a new kind of citizenship and a more vivid routine of life. But we cannot afford to promote a war every generation to break up social fixations: that is burning down the house to roast the pig. We must erect these social and personal counterpoises to rigidity and fixity as the basic requirements for a maturing personality.

The custom of our time is to think no change worth even discussing unless it can be at once organized into a visible movement: the mass enlistment of thousands, preferably millions, of men and women. The very appearance of millions of men in black shirts and brown shirts gave fascism publicity that made its rancid ideas seem important. Many of the actual movements that claim allegiance today are little better than devices of publicity: decorative devices that change nothing and move nothing. Such, even, would be a revolutionary movement, unless those who took part in it remodeled the instruments with which they work: first of all themselves.

Only in one place can an immediate renewal begin: that is, within the person; and a remolding of the self is an inescapable preliminary to the great changes that must be made throughout every community, in every part of the world. Each one, within his or her own field of action—the home, the neighborhood, the city, the region, the school, the church, the factory, the mine, the office, the union—must carry into his immediate day's work a changed attitude toward all his functions and obligations. His collective work cannot rise to a higher level than his personal scale of values. Once a change is effected in the person, every group will record and respond to it.

Today our best plans miscarry because they are in the hands of people who have undergone no inner growth. Most of these people have shrunk from facing the world crisis and they have no notion of the manner in which they themselves have helped to bring it about. Into every new situation they carry only a fossilized self. Their hidden prejudices, their glib hopes, their archaic desires and automatisms—usually couched in the language of assertive modernity—recall those of the Greeks in the fourth century B.C. or those of the Romans in the fourth century A.D. They are in a power dive and their controls have frozen. By closing their eyes they think they can avoid a crash.

Those who look for swift wholesale changes to take place in our institutions under-rate the difficulties we now face: the inroads of barbarism and automatism, those twin betrayers of freedom, have been too deep. In their impatience, in their despair, such people secretly long to cast the burden of their own regeneration upon a savior: a president, a pope, a dictator—vulgar counterparts of a divinity debased or a corruption deified. But such a leader is only the mass of humanity writ small: the incarnation of our resentments, hates, sadisms, or of our cowardices, confusions, and complacencies. There is no salvation through such naked self-worship: God must work within us. Each man and woman must first silently assume his own burden.

We need not wait for bombs and bullets actually to strike us before we strip our lives of superfluities: we need not wait for events to bend our wills to unison. Wherever we are, the worst has already happened and we must meet it. We must simplify our daily routine without waiting for ration cards; we must take on public responsibilities without waiting for conscription; we must work for the unity and effective brotherhood of man without letting further wars prove that the current pursuit of power, profit and all manner of material aggrandizement is treason to humanity: treason and national suicide. Year by year, we must persevere in all these acts, even though the restrictions are lifted and the urgencies of war have slackened. Unless we now rebuild our selves all our external triumphs will crumble.

There is no easy formula for this renewal. It is not enough for us to do all that is possible: we must do that which seems impossible. Our first need is not for organization but for orientation: a change in direction and attitude. We must bring to every activity and every plan a new criterion of judgment: we must ask how far it seeks to further the processes of life-fulfillment and how much respect it pays to the needs of the whole personality.

More immediately we must demand: What is the purpose of each new political and economic measure? Does it seek the old goal of expansion or the new one of equilibrium? Does it work for conquest or co-operation? And what is the nature of this or that industrial or social achievement—does it produce material goods alone or does it also produce human goods and good men? Do our individual life-plans make for a universal society, in which art and science, truth and beauty, religion and sanctity, enrich mankind? Do our public life-plans make for the fulfillment and renewal of the human person, so that they will bear fruit in a life abundant: ever more significant, ever more valuable, ever more deeply experienced and more widely shared?

If we keep this standard constantly in mind, we shall have both a measure for what must be rejected and a goal for what must be achieved. In time, we shall create the institutions and the habits of life, the rituals, the laws, the arts, the morals that are essential to the development of the whole personality, and the balanced community: the possibilities of progress will become real again once we lose our blind faith in the external improvements of the machine alone. But the first step is a personal one: a change in direction of interest *towards* the person. Without that change, no great betterment will take place in the social order. Once that change begins, everything is possible.

QUESTIONS AND BIOGRAPHICAL NOTES

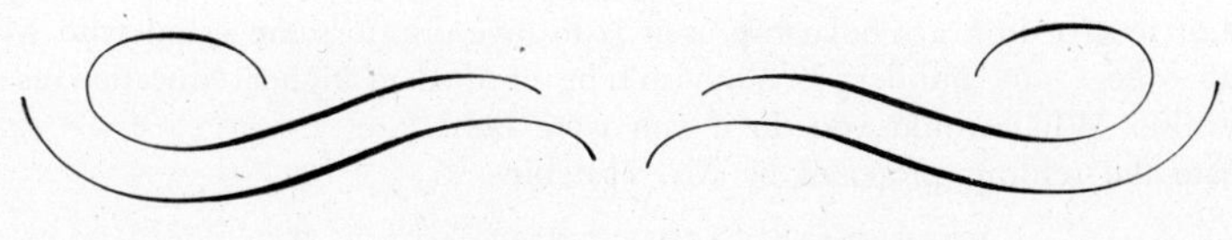

QUESTIONS

I. LEARNING

UNIVERSITY DAYS *by James Thurber*

What criticisms of curriculum, students, teachers, and educational methods lie beneath this delightful account of college life? What elements of satire do you find in it? Have you and your classmates any similar experiences? How typical are the characters that Thurber has portrayed here—with due allowance for humorous exaggeration?

KITTREDGE OF HARVARD *by Rollo Walter Brown*

What is the author's attitude toward his subject? What impression of Kittredge does he give you? One reader has said that Kittredge, as here sketched, is "a disagreeable old eccentric." What do you think of Kittredge?

How do you account, on the basis of this article, for Kittredge's great success as a teacher? What were his classroom methods? How effective do you consider them? Evaluate the elements of respect and fear in the impression he made on undergraduates.

How would you like to study with Kittredge, if he were still living?

To what extent are temper and eccentricity justifiable in a teacher?

What interesting teachers have you known?

HOW AGASSIZ TAUGHT SHALER *by Nathaniel Southgate Shaler*

How do you evaluate Professor Agassiz as a teacher? Account for his effectiveness with Shaler. How well would his methods work with different types of students? with mature ones? with large classes? What do you think you would get out of a course given by a professor who used Agassiz' methods?

NEILSON OF SMITH *by Hubert Herring*

What do you think of Neilson's advice to the girls on behavior? on getting an education? What qualities of mind and temperament made him a great educator?

What kind of intellectual atmosphere did he create at Smith? What similar or dissimilar elements do you note on your campus?

GATE RECEIPTS AND GLORY *by Robert M. Hutchins*

Distinguish between Hutchins' use of "athleticism" and "athletics."

What are the abuses against which Mr. Hutchins is writing? What personal knowledge do you have of them?

Suppose Bob Gulch, who created a state-wide sensation as a quarterback on his high school team but who definitely is not the studious type, receives offers of "scholarships" from five colleges and universities. Why shouldn't he take the best offer? Why isn't it just as fair to give him a scholarship as it is to give one to some grind who will never bring the college any publicity? Why isn't he entitled to higher education as well as anybody else? What would you do if you were Bob?

Evaluate the reforms proposed by Mr. Hutchins.

FRESHMAN ADVISER *by George Boas*

Give a character sketch of Rosburgh Van Stiew. Which of his attitudes do you find represented among your friends and acquaintances?

Of which student does the author approve?

At what is the satire of this essay leveled?

To what extent can all freshman be fitted into Boas's three categories? Are there others which you can suggest? Can you make names and character sketches for them? It might be entertaining to sketch the feminine counterparts of Van Stiew, Hogarth, and Wilkinson.

HONORS COURSES AT SWARTHMORE *by Frank Aydelotte*

Swarthmore is a representative, good, liberal arts college. In its educational philosophy it lies somewhere between the new ultraconservatism of the Chicago or "Great Brooks" plan and the progressivism of Bennington. Here, then, is an example of educational reform which may be considered moderate, for it is imposed upon the framework of the elective system, and the freedom of the elective system is preserved and even enhanced in it.

What faults common in higher education does the Swarthmore Honors plan seek to overcome? How well do you think it succeeds in doing so?

What provisions of the Honors course, if any, could be used in the freshman and sophmore years?

EDUCATION AT BENNINGTON *by Hubert Herring*

Bennington College is a notable example of progressive education in actual practice. Upon what basic assumption does Bennington rest? Explain its underlying philosophy.

If liberal education is defined as the kind which "frees men's souls," to what extent do you think the Bennington plan accomplishes this end? To what extent does it prepare its graduates to make their way in the world?

What features of education at Bennington would you like to see incorporated into your college? In what ways would they improve it?

GENERAL AND SPECIAL EDUCATION *by The Harvard Committee*

Explain what is meant by general education; by special education.

What developments in modern American life have produced a similarity to the slave-owning culture of the ancient Athenians? Why is the education evolved by the Athenian freemen thought to be suited to modern American citizens?

How does democracy make general education obligatory?

State the case for specialism in education. How can general and special education be reconciled? What are the advantages and disadvantages of specialized education?

Distinguish between special education and vocationalism.

What attitude and approach is found in general education? Why are some professors disqualified to give their students a general education?

What is the relation of general education to the free elective system?

What kind of education do you want to get?

For a discussion of educational theory in parable form see J. Abner Peddiwell's "The Saber-Tooth Curriculum." See also Jacques Barzun's "The Ivory Lab" in Section V.

ON THE NEED FOR A QUIET COLLEGE *by Stephen Leacock*

What do you think of Leacock's ideal college? How does it compare with the large American university of today? Why are the small colleges of America no nearer the Leacock ideal than the large ones?

What exaggerations does it contain? At what is the satire leveled?

Do you think professors spend too much of their time in offices, conferences, and committees?

How would you characterize the humor of this essay?

Compare Leacock's remarks with "General and Special Education" and with "The Saber-Tooth Curriculum." What is Leacock's attitude toward Specialism? Vocationalism? Liberal Arts?

What do you think of his remarks about extra-curricular activities? Is he exaggerating here, or is he serious? Is he serious about banning co-eds from the campus, or is he paying the girls a chivalrous compliment?

THE SABER-TOOTH CURRICULUM *by J. Abner Peddiwell*

New-Fist sums up his educational philosophy as follows: "If I could only get these children to do the things that will give more and better food, shelter, clothing, and security . . . I would be helping this tribe to have a better life." What do you think of it? Does it include enough? Which contemporary educators belong to New-Fist's school? What are the modern counterparts of fish-grabbing, woolly-horse-clubbing, and tiger-scaring-with-fire?

What is Peddiwell satirizing when he makes one of the wise old men say in defense of the paleolithic curriculum: "We don't teach fish-grabbing to grab fish; we teach it to develop a generalized agility which can never be developed by mere training"? Does he imply here that all education, even liberal, begins in practical necessity for making a living, but becomes fossilized, and is perpetuated because of a mistaken idea of transfer of values?

The author's sympathies are obviously with the exponents of educational change and of vocationalism. State the arguments on the other side.

Discuss the wise old men's statement: ". . . the essence of true education is timelessness. It is something that endures through changing conditions like a solid rock standing squarely and firmly in the middle of a raging torrent. You must know that there are several eternal verities, and the saber-tooth curriculum is one of them!" Are there qualities of mind, as opposed to subject matters, which are actually "eternal verities"?

INTRODUCTORY LECTURE *by A. E. Housman*

How true is Aristotle's statement that "all men possess by nature a craving for knowledge"? How satisfactory do you find Housman's explanation of the numerous apparent exceptions to Aristotle's dictum?

What implication regarding vocational studies do you find in Housman's essay? regarding the study of the humanities? Are all departments of learning equally valuable? What relation do you see between the elective system and Housman's statement: "If a certain department of knowledge especially attracts a man, let him study that, and study it because it attracts him . . ."? Within what reasonable bounds can this advice be used as a guide in selecting studies?

How convincing do you find Housman's remarks comparing the pleasures of learning with the pleasures of the senses? Why doesn't the acquisition of knowledge and wisdom result in pure unalloyed joy? Compare Housman's statement, "Nay it may be urged on the contrary that the pursuit of truth in some directions is even injurious to happiness, because it compels us to take leave of delusions which were pleasant while they lasted" with the words of *Ecclesiastes*: "For in much wisdom is much grief: and he that increaseth knowledge increaseth sorrow."

What do you consider Housman's strongest arguments for liberal education?

II. READING AND WRITING

OF STUDIES *by Francis Bacon*

Into what three parts does the essay divide? How are they related to each other?

Bacon begins his essay: "Studies serve for delight, for ornament, and for ability." How would you classify, according to these purposes, the selections that you have read so far in this book? Show whether or not this essay by Bacon may be properly said to serve all three purposes.

". . . Else distilled books are, like common distilled waters, flashy [i.e., tasteless] things." After carefully studying the context of this quotation, indicate whether this anthology or *The Reader's Digest* would fare better in Bacon's judgment.

Bacon ends his essay: "So every defect of the mind may have a special receipt." What substitutes from today's store of reading would you propose in place of Bacon's original receipts? for "wandering wit"? for "wit not apt to distinguish"? for a man who cannot easily "call up one thing to prove and illustrate another"?

THE LIBRARY *by Chauncey B. Tinker*

At which of Tinker's three stages does the average freshman find himself? How large and of what quality would you estimate the average freshman's private library to be? Does the average senior's show an improvement?

What "twenty books" should the modern student trying to get a liberal education have in his private library?

Tinker speaks of "larger and grander treatises" in fields of knowledge. Some ways to discover these are the card catalogue, bibliographies in other books, chance remarks in daily reading and conversation, courses in school and college. To what extent does each of these provide knowledge about the scope and quality of such books?

Select some particular field of knowledge and try to discover what the "larger and grander treatises" in it are. Which ones are available in your library?

UNREQUIRED READING *by Irwin Edman*

Edman moves from the phrase "to read not for food but for love" in the earlier part of his essay to the phrase "when the joys of unrequired reading are matched by the profit of wisdom" in the next to the last paragraph. How does he explain and defend this apparent inconsistency?

Is it possible to read a philosophical treatise "for pleasure" in the same way that a poem or novel may be read "for pleasure"? Can a book on cybernetics be read for this or any other kind of pleasure?

What use has Edman's essay for the student or specialist whose reading is nearly all required?

READING *by Henry David Thoreau*

In this essay, by what steps does Thoreau go from a defense of the Latin and Greek classics to a plea for public support of literature?

Is Thoreau's description of the cultural situation in his time still valid for our time? Do you detect contemporary prejudices which detract from the value of his essay?

How close to the purposes of reading presented by Bacon, Tinker, and Edman are those given by Thoreau? Using these four esssays, define your own beliefs about reading.

MR. K*A*P*L*A*N AND SHAKESPEARE *by Leonard Q. Ross*

With the familiar essay as well as the formal essay, an alert reader will find a challenge to understanding as well as a pleasant diversion.

To make application to Ross's essay on a specific level: How do the author's and Mr. Parkhill's attitudes toward Hyman Kaplan differ? What is the significance of such remarks as "Miss Higby, who had once begun a master's thesis on Coventry Patmore" or that Parkhill "had played Polonius in his senior play"?

On a more general level: Does Hyman Kaplan's performance suggest any reflection on the popular saying that "poetry means different things to different people"? What comment on this does Ross seem to make?

THE ART OF PLAIN TALK: LIVE WORDS AND CROWDED WORDS *by Rudolf Flesch*

To achieve plain talk, Flesch elsewhere recommends: 1) short sentences (17 words on the average), 2) few affixes (37 per hundred words), and 3) frequent personal references (6 names, personal pronouns, etc., per 100 words). Besides practicing these three recommendations and the ones made in "Live Words and Crowded Words," how else does Flesch achieve a lively style in his own writing? (For example, study his use of metaphor.)

In the part on crowded words, Flesch does not rewrite his examples as frequently as in the part on live words. This change of method suggests that a different principle is involved. Which has greater justification—"crowding" or "deadening"? What do you make of the sentence, "Mind you, I don't say that this is bad writing; but it isn't plain talk either, by a long shot"?

What does your present handbook of style say about good writing? Does Flesch really disagree? If not, why does his approach seem so startling?

Rewrite some passages by other authors in this book, substituting live words for dead ones. Revise your last essay in the same way.

THE LANGUAGE OF BUSINESS *by the Editors of* Fortune

Describe "businesese" and "reverse gobbledegook." Why, in spite of apparent differences, do they have a great deal in common?

What virtues and vices do the Editors of *Fortune* see in "plain talk"?

List three or four sound principles of style, and show their relationship to principles advanced by Flesch and by the Editors of *Fortune.*

NOTES AND COMMENT *from* The New Yorker

What do the *Fortune* articles and *The New Yorker* note have in common in their treatment of "plain talk"? What differences do they have? As large circulation magazines, what authority or prejudice may they show?

Specifically, what is good or bad about the phrase "How to test Reading-Ease of written matter," the words "personalize" and "ascending," the paragraph from "an early American"?

POLITICS AND THE ENGLISH LANGUAGE *by George Orwell*

To which one of the other essays on writing in this section does Orwell's essay seem closest in its premises? Why?

The Editors of *Fortune* discuss "The Language of Business" and Orwell discusses

"Politics and the English Language." What observations in the *Fortune* article could be extended to politics, and what observations of Orwell could be extended to business?

Examine a recent essay that you have written for dying metaphors, operators, pretentious diction, and meaningless words.

". . . The decadence of our language is probably curable." Discuss the evidence presented by Orwell for its decadence, and evaluate the proposals for its cure.

Reconsider the "three or four sound principles of style" that you listed after reading the first two essays under "Writing." Make a further reconsideration when you have read all the essays in this section.

INTERLUDE: ON JARGON *by Arthur Quiller-Couch*

What would Quiller-Couch probably think of the selection from Rudolf Flesch's book? What common aims and principles does the rewriting of poor English by the two authors show?

Flesch and Quiller-Couch seem little concerned with slang and bad grammar, yet the absence of these is generally associated with good style. What *is* the relative importance in style 1) of jargon and dead and crowded words, 2) of bad grammar and slang?

Can you defend any of the examples of "jargon" (such as "case" or "degree") or any of the passages that Quiller-Couch condemns? If so, how?

ON "ON JARGON" *by Robert J. Geist*

Though Geist addresses himself to teachers, his essay on Quiller-Couch clarifies the difficulties of "On Jargon" for any reader.

What are the main shortcomings of "On Jargon," according to Geist? Can you add any important ones?

Why does Geist regard "On Jargon" as "the greatest single essay on the art of writing"? Do his comments make the reader feel this greatness? Is there irony in his approach?

PLEASANT AGONY *by John Mason Brown*

What light does Brown's essay throw on your own writing practices? To the extent that you enjoy writing, is your work poorly done? If you suffer agony, is it well done?

Has Brown's own writing any touches that suggest a "pleasant agony" in its composition?

Do all skills represent the same labor as Brown ascribes to writing? Do all arts? Does Brown distingush between writing as a skill and art?

THE AMERICAN LANGUAGE *by H. L. Mencken*

Mencken frequently mentions certain widely observed phenomena in language (as clipping). Mark the places where he does this and ask for a fuller explanation in class.

How much does the handbook of style that you use seem to be affected by the "rumblings of revolt" described in the next to the last paragraph? Give instances of words and locutions 1) that it approves but that you have in the past been taught to condemn and 2) that it condemns but that Mencken would probably allow.

How much does Mencken himself seem to be affected? Although he recommends new speech forms, how much does he actually use them? At the level on which he writes are such words as "bounce," "little juice," and "killer" appropriate? These he *uses*, but what about "poppycock," "boloney," "movie," "hoosegow," which he *cites* sympathetically?

As revealed in this selection, what is Mencken's philosophy of usage?

OF THE VANITY OF WORDS *by Michel Eyquem de Montaigne*

Montaigne's essay brings up the moral problem in rhetoric. For example, what use can a selfish but competent student make of the advice in Flesch and Quiller-Couch? Do unscrupulous advertisers and politicians affirm "the vanity of words," or does the real trouble lie with the listener and his standards? (See the last sentence of "Interlude: On Jargon" for possible help in reaching an answer.)

How does the antidemocratic tone affect the whole essay? Here are two views you might take: 1) Reading this essay is a waste of time in a democratic society. 2) The perspective which Montaigne provides is tremendously helpful to a democratic reader. After reducing both views to more concrete terms, decide which is better. Or is some other view sounder than either?

Are the last two paragraphs a whimsical digression or are they structurally essential? Consider especially the final sentence: if it does have a *rhetorical* connection with the essay, is Montaigne's own method ethical or unethical?

III. THINKING

FOUR KINDS OF THINKING *by James Harvey Robinson*

Examine yourself carefully to determine about how much time you spend daily in each of the four kinds of thinking. Give some examples of rationalizing drawn from people of your own acquaintance; from the newspapers. Examine the real reasons, as contrasted with the "good" reasons, for buying a new car, going to college, joining the Rotary Club.

To what extent do you agree with Robinson's evaluation of reverie? What good has ever resulted from reverie?

How much actual necessity for creative thinking is there in the life of a doctor? a lawyer? an insurance agent? a bank teller? a machine-tool worker? a housewife? a writer?

What underlying assumption about progress does this essay contain? What kind of thinking does it represent? creative

THE CASE FOR THE DAYDREAMER *by James Thurber*

Compare Thurber's treatment of reverie with that of James Harvey Robinson. What virtue does Thurber find in daydreaming that Robinson has overlooked? How important is this element?

How harmless, pleasant, and beneficial is daydreaming? What dangers lie in excessive daydreaming?

What would you have done if you had encountered Mr. Bustard at the dog show? What would an extroverted athlete have done?

What imaginary retorts to counterparts of Mr. Bustard do you recall making? What benefit did you derive from them?

LANGUAGE AND THOUGHT *by Suzanne Langer*

What is a sign? What would man's speech be like if it were restricted to signs? How do symbols differ from signs?

What is the relationship of symbolic language to thought? Discuss Miss Langer's statement: "The birth of language is the dawn of humanity."

If language is as important as Miss Langer says it is, ought not students acquire extensive vocabularies? What is the correlation between vocabulary and thinking?

THE FOUR STAGES OF THOUGHT *by Graham Wallas*

What are the four stages, according to Wallas, in the development of a thought? Explain each. What is the role of the conscious and the subconscious in each?

What areas of agreement and of disagreement do you find with James Harvey Robinson's "Four Kinds of Thinking"? What is the relation of incubation to reverie?

What are the dangers of industriousness, so far as the thinker is concerned? of procrastination?

Explain what Wallas means by the habit of "passive reading," and why he considers it dangerous to thought.

How can the thinking processes of most people be improved by an understanding of the four stages of thought as outlined in Wallas's essay? How can you utilize the knowledge presented here? What is the special value of being able to recognize the intimation stage?

CONTEXTS *by S. I. Hayakawa*

How are definitions obtained by the writers of dictionaries? What importance has this method with regard to meaning and thinking? What is the danger of the "One word, one meaning" fallacy? What are the different kinds of contexts?

How well can you rely on a dictionary to give a word's meaning? What should you do about those words for which the dictionary cannot be relied on?

EMOTIONAL MEANINGS *by Robert H. Thouless*

What do you consider the proper areas in which to use emotional words? What is the relation of emotional meanings to connotation and of objective meanings to denotation? Prepare a list made up of pairs of emotionally charged words; for example, *retreat—strategic withdrawal; industrialist—economic royalist; free enterprise—economic exploitation.* Find several examples in your newspaper of slanting the news by the use of emotional meanings.

To what extent is it possible to eliminate the use of emotional meanings from discussion of controversial problems such as race questions, international relations, religious questions, and social and economic problems? What is the principal difficulty involved in eliminating them?

Most people would agree that while science has made phenomenal progress in the last hundred years, knowledge of human relationships has failed to keep pace, and that much of the trouble in our world today can be explained by this lag. To what extent do you believe this lag can be traced to our failure to use unemotional, objective language?

LOGICAL FALLACIES *by Robert Gorham Davis*

Explain each of the thirteen fallacies presented in this essay. Find an example of two of each in your own experience. What examples of name calling in politics can you cite? in labor-management disputes? What examples of *non sequitur* and *post hoc, ergo propter hoc* do you recall in advertisements? Discuss the various logical fallacies you heard in one evening of listening to the radio. Examine the logic of the editorials in today's newspaper.

What are the main areas of agreement between Hayakawa, Thouless, Bacon, and Davis? What major contribution does each make?

OF THE CONDUCT OF THE UNDERSTANDING *by John Locke*

What reasons does Locke give for consulting fully and frequently with all sorts of people? How is broadness of outlook developed?

What, according to Locke, are the greatest enemies of sound reasoning?

What application of this essay can you make to your choice of newspapers and magazines?

Do you think Locke places too great confidence in reason?

REASONING *by William James*

What are the two processes, according to James, by which reasoning takes place? Explain each. Which do you consider more important?

What constitutes genius? What two types of genius are there? How do the minds of geniuses differ from yours? Is the difference in kind or degree?

If you have difficulty in stating your reasons for preferring a painting by Grant Wood to one by Van Gogh, analyze this difficulty in the light of James's remarks.

According to James, much intuition is actually unconscious, unformulated reasoning. Examine in this light some of your hunches which proved to be right. State the actual steps in reasoning which must have taken place.

IDOLS OF THE MIND *by Francis Bacon*

According to Bacon, allegiance of the human mind to the Idols of the Tribe, Cave, Market-place, and Theatre greatly interferes with the processes of genuine reasoning, which alone lead to the discovery of the truth. Explain what he means by each class of idols. Give examples of these idols in contemporary thinking. What connection do you see between the Idols of the Tribe and religious, political, and economic beliefs? Which logical fallacies are included in Idols of the Tribe?

Which sort of idols are race prejudices? class feeling? antilabor bitterness? prejudice against capitalism?

When Walter Reuther talked about "preserving the American way of life" and Senator Bricker used the same phrase in a speech, how much agreement was there in their concepts? What class of idols is here interfering with reason?

Examine your own thinking for examples of the four classes of idols. Or, if this is too painful, examine that of a classmate or acquaintance.

IV. THE ARTS

WHY ABSTRACT? *by Hilaire Hiler*

How does Hiler deal with the problem of partial *vs.* complete abstraction? Is his refusal to argue the problem more fully a sign of inadequacy, of tolerance, or of other interests? Would the Mexicans in Covarrubias' story, after seeing Hiler's painting of the house painters, comment about colic, the proletariat, T.B., or about something else?

According to Hiler, what ought to be the influence of modern culture on painting? He considers specifically the influence of new theories of architecture. What can you add about the possible influences of photography, printing, manufacturing? What qualification in tracing these influences does the presence of abstraction in nearly every historical period suggest?

"Painting was made for man, and not man for painting."

"And you, great sculptor—so you gave
A score of years to Art, her slave,
And that's your Venus, whence we turn
To yonder girl that fords the burn!"

—Browning

What implications do the epigram and the verse have as arguments for or against Hiler?

BOTTICELLI'S *PRIMAVERA* *by Frank Jewett Mather, Jr.*

In concluding with an allusion to Goethe's epigram, "Geniessen ist nachschaffen" (appreciation is re-creating), Mather sums up his own critical approach. It is a method widely, but not unanimously, subscribed to. When Mather writes of "partial but sufficient" re-creating, what qualification of the method does he make? What other qualifications can be suggested? Does Mather, by the way, interpret Goethe's epigram as meaning 1) "Art appreciation is a creative experience," or 2) "Art appreciation is a reconstructing of the artist's creative experience"? Or does he combine these meanings?

Though the essay is an analysis of Botticelli's painting, it is presented as two narratives—the action of Botticelli in creating it and the response of the author on seeing it. What technical reason and what philosophical reason make the second narrative shorter than the first?

Would Hiler, as you gather from his essay, attack Mather primarily, or Botticelli, or both equally? Why are the literary elements of this painting important? Why are the graphic elements more important? What recognition does Mather make of the latter?

Analyze a painting that your teacher may suggest. If it is "representational," how much emphasis should be placed upon its literary elements?

Compare Mather's principles of appreciating painting with Sessions' ideas about the appreciation of music.

MODERN ARCHITECTURE: THE CARDBOARD HOUSE *by Frank Lloyd Wright*

Drawing upon Wright's principles, make a critical description of a house that you know, an automobile, an airplane.

How, if at all, has the organic principle been used in the buildings on your campus? What differentiates classroom units, laboratories, and administrative offices? What use has been made of local materials? What recognition of local climate appears?

Is organic architecture (architecture in which "form follows function") merely materialistic, or does it recognize human values? If the latter, how does it distinguish between vital human values and conventional ones? Which kind of values are symbolized in such campus traditions as collegiate Gothic, colonial Georgian, and Spanish mission? How can organic architecture symbolize values without these traditional forms?

Do you find survivals of convention in Wright's architectural practice as here described? Are some elements in contemporary architecture survivals of conventions begun by Wright?

To what extent can the concept "form follows function" be used in painting?

THE IMPERIAL FAÇADE *by Lewis Mumford*

Mumford uses the word "imperialism" to include several cultural traits. Make these traits as specific as possible from the context, marking those passages that give clearest evidence. What relative weight does Mumford give these aspects of the period in determining its architectural practice? What changes in emphasis, or what additional aspects, do you propose?

A revival of classical architecture also occurred in the early American republic. If you are familiar with this architecture and the period, what comparison in cultural and architectural traits with the later period can you make?

What examples of the imperial façade do you find in your community? What different cultural traits do the public buildings of the last fifteen years suggest?

Mumford's method is also commonly used with other arts. What would Haggin's view of it be for music, Morrison's for literature, Hiler's for painting? Is the method to be regarded as *a)* valid because of the complexity of art; *b)* untrue because art is eternal and above historical considerations; *c)* valid as social criticism only?

MUSIC FOR THE MAN WHO ENJOYS HAMLET *by B. H. Haggin*

If biographical and historical material is unimportant in interpreting music, why is it so frequently used? What difficulties in all music criticism does your answer suggest?

Are Haggin's paragraphs on Shakespeare's sonnet and Cézanne's still-life adequate criticism? What do literature and painting have in common with music? What important differences emerge? How much awareness does Haggin show of these similarities and differences?

Two musical authorities made statements on Haggin's essay (the complete quotations appear in *The American Scholar,* Summer, 1944, XIII, 378–380). Comment upon them:

. . . I find myself substantially in agreement with Haggin's ideas, despite his somewhat labored expression thereof . . . He says, in effect, that the "naïve listener" has only to expose himself to the music and let it "have its way with him" and let all technical matters go hang. In general, that's all right; if it were otherwise, composers would have scant prospects for being heard at all.—ARTHUR SHEPHERD.

. . . There is a very real hurdle to be surmounted between that familiarity which can be gained by repeated playings of the first one and a half inches of a recording and that understanding which is based on having learned "to follow the grammar and logic of thought." This is a high hurdle and only the rare case of native talent can be expected to "take" it, even after repeated attempts, without some sort of guidance.—ARTHUR W. QUIMBY.

THE LISTENER *by Roger Sessions*

What, according to Sessions, are the reasons for our present emphasis on "the listener"?

If the listener has become the consumer, what effect does this have on the programs offered by, say, the Cincinnati Symphony Orchestra?

What does Sessions mean by saying he will not "score" his remarks here? Why do you think he used this word?

Sessions distinguishes four stages of the listener's development. How many, and which, of these stages does Haggin discuss? Evaluate the two essays in these terms.

In view of Sessions' discussion of the third stage of development, "musical understanding," do you think he would consider "understanding Hamlet" of any importance to the listener?

How can you resolve Sessions' paradox that love of music depends on inner security, but inner security depends on the strength of love?

What is the difference between "our musical economy" and "the economics of musical life"?

DIRECTION *by Alfred Hitchcock*

As with most of the other authors discussing "The Modern Folk Arts," Hitchcock recognizes the potential greatness of these forms. But also, along with the others, he sees certain obstacles to their development. What is his emotional and intellectual way of dealing with these obstacles in his own films?

What differences and similarities do you find between Hiler's and Hitchcock's attitude toward their arts? Would you call one "noble and independent," the other "mercenary"? How responsible for the differences is the fact that the movie is a mass medium?

Hitchcock is alert to the special possibilities of the movies. Make a list of the several camera techniques (as the reaction shot) that he mentions. What others can you add from your own observation? How does an awareness of them increase one's appreciation of the movie as an art?

A symbol in art is an object or situation (usually concrete) which stands for something else (usually abstract). Explain how the champagne in *The Ring* functions as a symbol. What examples of symbols have you found in recent movies?

Many such subtleties as those described in *The Ring* are still missed by movie audiences. Probably they are less overlooked than equivalent subtleties by those who go to concerts, look at paintings, or read poetry. To what extent may a movie or these other forms have subtleties without being dependent upon them for general interest? What difference in your answer, if any, is made by whether you are considering sophisticated or popular art?

SOAPLAND *by James Thurber*

What is Thurber's evaluation of the Berg report on soap opera? What parts of his criticism are direct? what parts implied?

As described by Warner and Henry, is the audience response to "Big Sister" any different from its response to a good play or novel? Compare Wylie's essay in regard to this question.

"The producers must give them what they want and demand," writes Thurber. Comment upon this statement as one of the central problems of "The Modern Folk Arts."

WASHBOARD WEEPERS: A SMALL CASE FOR RADIO *by Max Wylie*

According to Wylie, why are soap operas written the way they are? Does Wylie have an axe to grind?

In what way does Wylie's article supplement Hitchcock's on the artistic problems of mass mediums? Which do you think is the sounder, and why?

Compare the critical books in your library on "modern folk arts" with those on the more established arts. Do your findings substantiate the statement that radio is "almost without competent critics"? What is the situation with the movies and detective stories?

Is Wylie's paraphrase of *Macbeth* fair? What does *Macbeth* have that a soap or horse opera with an equivalent story does not have? Is the reply that *Macbeth* is a "classic story and therefore improving" a polite evasion, or can you substantiate the description with specific values?

Pretty frequently readers complain that contemporary novels and stories are "depressing," "sad," or "sordid." Yet radio audiences apparently enjoy this sort of material. How can the paradox be explained? (Your discussion should take into account that large-circulation magazines usually print "inspiring" or "optimistic" stories.)

STRICTLY FROM MARS, OR, HOW TO PHILANDER IN FIVE EASY COLORS *by S. J. Perelman*

Describe Perelman's tone. How does his highly personal style help convey it? What effect does it have on his material?

Though Perelman is making fun of the advertising comic, what broader significance does his sketch have?

Would a Hitchcock, a Wylie, or a Thurber undertake to defend the advertising comic as a modern folk art? Are the differences absolute or of degree?

OOF ! ! (SOB !) EEP ! ! (GULP !) ZOWIE ! ! ! *by E. J. Kahn, Jr.*

Compare the relation of readers to "Li'l Abner" with their relation to "Big Sister."

Al Capp distinguishes three levels of readers of his comic strip. Might the same distinction be made for readers of novels?

Of what kind of culture are such events as the Lena contest and Sadie Hawkins Day symptomatic? Healthy? perverted? or other?

DOVER BEACH REVISITED: A NEW FABLE FOR CRITICS
by Theodore Morrison

Morrison's fable illustrates some of the main critical approaches to literature: the scholarly by the Arnold expert, the aesthetic by Bradley Dewing, the moral by Oliver Twitchell, the psychological by Rudolph Mole, the social by Reuben Hale, and (for want of a better term) the compleat angler's by Peter Lee Prampton. What are the major tenets of each, as they are here reflected more or less satirically?

Do not forget the charm of Morrison's fable as literature in its own right. What evidence is there of Morrison's mingling sympathy and satire? (Note the order of climax and the frequent cross references before you answer this.) Does Prampton's attitude cancel out the rest of the approaches or supplement them? In a word, what is the author's *tone*?

In Volume II, *Introduction to Literature,* an additional interpretation of the poem is printed. To which of the "main critical approaches" does Kirby's interpretation belong? How does it differ from that approach in its reading of the poem?

Indicate specifically the approaches used or suggested in the essays on painting, architecture, music, and the modern folk arts. What bearing have your findings on selecting one of the critical approaches as the soundest?

THE ESSENCE OF TRAGEDY *by Maxwell Anderson*

What is Anderson's prime rule of tragedy? Why is the statement that the hero must be a perfect man considered a corollary? Would you suggest other "elements necessary to a play structure"?

A recent critic of the novel (E. M. Forster) has spoken of "the losing battle that the plot fights with the characters." On what terms does Anderson relate plot and character in the play?

Suggest some points of similarity and difference between Anderson's concept of tragedy and Aristotle's famous definition:

"Tragedy then is an imitation of an action that is serious, complete, and of a certain magnitude; in language embellished with each kind of artistic ornament, the several kinds being found in separate parts of the play; in the form of action, not of narrative; through pity and fear effecting the proper purgation of these emotions."

Apply the criteria of Anderson to one of the plays printed in Volume II, *Introduction to Literature,* or to a recent movie or play that you and some of your classmates have seen. Does the "recognition scene" occur in comedy as well as in tragedy? (And, by the way, how would you explain the treatment of *Hamlet* in paragraphs 6 and 8 of Anderson's essay?)

To which of the approaches in "Dover Beach Revisited" is Anderson's closest? What difference results from Anderson's looking at tragedy as a writer rather than as a critic who has not written plays? Would Anderson agree with Dryden's observation that "to instruct delightfully is the general end of all poetry"?

FENIMORE COOPER'S LITERARY OFFENSES *by Mark Twain*

What are the major faults that Mark Twain finds in Cooper's novel? Describe Twain's order and manner of presentation.

Compare the criteria for narrative set up by Mark Twain with those for drama given by Anderson.

Twain once remarked of Jane Austen's books not being in a library: "Just that one omission alone would make a fairly good library out of a library that hadn't a book in it."

Does the present essay exhibit sound critical method, violent prejudice, or a combination of both?

Yvor Winters has said: "The 7th chapter of *The Deerslayer,* and more properly its first incident, Natty's encounter with the Indian whom he is forced to kill, is probably as great an achievement of its length as one will find in American fiction outside of Melville. . . . Cooper communicates with a power that has rarely been equalled the tremendous and impersonal quiet of the virgin American forest." With this quotation in mind, comment on Twain's sentence: "Counting these out, what is left is Art."

MANNERS, MORALS, AND THE NOVEL *by Lionel Trilling*

What novels that Trilling mentions have you read? How well do they seem to fit his descriptions? How well do other novels that you have read recently bear out his observations?

Midway in the essay, Trilling makes the generalization ". . . that in proportion as we have committed ourselves to our particular idea of reality we have lost our interest in any manners." Show by what steps this generalization has been reached, and in what way Trilling now progresses from it.

With which approach in "Dover Beach Revisited" has this essay most in common? Are the critical standards of this essay in any way similar to those of Mark Twain's essay on Cooper?

POETRY AND ADVERTISING *by S. I. Hayakawa*

In the first section Hayakawa mentions certain techniques and concepts which poetry and advertising have in common. What are the three or four most important?

Point out specifically which of these common concepts are realized in the peanut butter and shoe advertisements described in Perelman's essay. Which are realized in "Dover Beach," or in some other poem in Volume II, *Introduction to Literature*?

What important qualities, not mentioned by Hayakawa but suggested by "Dover Beach Revisited," does poetry have? What qualities other than those mentioned by Hayakawa distinguish advertising from poetry?

Discuss the following statements in the light of Hayakawa's essay: 1) "Modern poetry is defective." 2) "The defects of modern poetry are *caused* by advertising." 3) "Because of advertising, classical poetry can no longer be appreciated by a modern reader." 4) "Advertising creates a difficulty for the writer of poetry, but not necessarily for the reader."

ON READING POETRY *by John Ciardi*

What are Ciardi's seven points? Are they all of the same value or the same kind? Can you group them into two or three larger categories?

Does Ciardi's attitude toward "traditional poetry" underlie all that he says? Just what does he mean by "traditional poetry"? To what extent would Hayakawa agree with him?

Why is "Hickory Dickory Dock" a better poem than "Threnody"?

MAN WILL PREVAIL *by William Faulkner*

What does Faulkner have to say to the writer? Does the occasion of the speech—the awarding of the Nobel prize—influence the value of what Faulkner says? By what means does he transfer his message to all men?

Are the ends and means of literature, as stated here, in accord with those stated or implied in the essays of Morrison, Anderson, Trilling, Hayakawa, and Ciardi?

What is the effect upon you of Faulkner's statement?

V. SCIENCE

CONCERNING ELECTRICITY AND COMBUSTION *by James B. Conant*

Conant, like Jacques Barzun in "The Ivory Lab" (see below), believes that both the student and the layman may most easily arrive at an understanding of science and the scientific method by an historical approach. For whom is he writing here? Why does he choose classical experiments in electricity and combustion?

Dentists know and you may have observed that gold inlays and amalgam fillings which come in contact when the jaws are shut produce at first a definite and slightly irritating sensation in the mouth. What relation does this fact have to Galvani's experiment? What is the "fruitful concept" which Galvani arrived at? How did he, rather than his Dutch predecessor, Swammerdam, come to formulate the concept? What generalization about science and scientific method can you draw from Galvani's work? Name at least one great technological advance and one great field of scientific discovery which would not have been possible without the work of Galvani and Volta.

What *is* the significance of the phlogiston theory, its long persistence, and the relative slowness with which many scientists adopted Lavoisier's new conceptual scheme of combustion? Does this chapter in the history of science alter any of your beliefs about science? if so, how? How likely is it that Lavoisier's explanation of combustion will in the future be found in error and superseded as the phlogiston theory was?

✓THE USEFULNESS OF USELESS KNOWLEDGE *by Abraham Flexner*

What fundamental assumption about human nature does Flexner make in this article? What is the basic paradox he proposes? Is it real or only apparent? In his "Introductory Lecture" (see Section I) Housman makes the same assumption. What is Housman's purpose?

What is the outstanding example in modern times of practical results from a chain of abstract, "pure," and "useless" reasoning and experiment?

Do you agree with the author that scientists are largely not responsible for the wartime uses to which their discoveries and inventions have been put?

What is the difference between science and technology? How does Flexner illustrate this difference? Note that Edison is very often identified in the popular mind with science. Flexner, it is clear, is presenting an argument and wishes us, his readers, to agree with it. State briefly the conclusions he comes to, and state briefly the steps by which he arrives at them. Are they logical? That is, do they follow?

WHAT MAKES THE WEATHER: THE SEVEN AMERICAN AIRS *by Wolfgang Langewiesche*

Which is the most important of the seven American airs? Why?

An airplane pilot trained in the new weather thinking can get quite impatient, Langewiesche asserts, with novelists who attempt to describe the weather instead of labeling it as "Polar Canadian air." What might the novelist reply to the airplane pilot?

With the idea of air mass and of the structure of warm and cold fronts in mind, explain why the radio sonde has been called the biggest thing in weather science since Toricelli invented the barometer. What is the underlying cause of the wave movement of air masses? That is, what makes the weather?

A PRIMER OF ATOMIC ENERGY *by William L. Laurence*

Understanding Laurence's "Primer" depends in large part on understanding his terms.

Define photosynthesis (see Peattie, below), burning, digestion; atom, nucleus, proton, neutron, electron; the periodic table, isotope; fission, fusion, chain reaction; serendipity (see Flexner, above).

Why does Laurence begin his primer with a discussion of photosynthesis? What is the relation between his assertion that "neither matter nor energy can be created" and Einstein's formula "E equals mc ^{2}"? Do thought processes consume energy?

What is the essential difference between burning coal and "burning" atomic nuclei? Between fission and fusion? Between the two types of chain reactions, controlled and uncontrolled?

At what point in his essay does Laurence move from the known and provable to the unknown and speculative? How good an analogy is the recurrent metaphor of banking, bank vaults, and treasure houses? Does it argue prejudice? On what grounds must men decide as to the uses of atomic energy in the future? Some indication of an answer to this last question may be found in the last sentence, which quotes *Revelation.*

Compare Laurence and Eddington (below) as to the origin of the earth. Do you see any resemblance between Laurence's predictions and the attitude of Dr. Faustus in Marlowe's play? (See Vol. II, *Introduction to Literature.*)

THE EVOLUTION OF THE PHYSICAL WORLD
by Arthur Stanley Eddington

What three revolutionary stages of the world as we now know it does the author envision? What rare accident must have taken place in the first stage?

Arnold J. Toynbee, in his *A Study of History,* says, "An encounter between two superhuman personalities is the plot of some of the greatest dramas that the human imagination has conceived," and cites the encounters between Yawweh (Jehovah) and the Serpent; between the Lord and Satan in the Book of Job; between the Lord and Mephistopheles in Goethe's *Faust*; between Danae and Jove, who visited her in a shower of gold; between Semele the Stricken Earth and Zeus the Sky that launches the thunderbolt; and many others. What significance do you find in this ever-recurring myth and Eddington's account of the "birth" of the world?

CHLOROPHYLL: THE SUN TRAP *by Donald Culross Peattie*

In what sense is chlorophyll a "green old alchemist"? What materials does the green leaf use? What does it produce? Where does the fuel or energy for the process of photosynthesis come from?

Is it true, then, as the author asserts, that the light from his desk lamp is the same light that fell two hundred million years ago? Are water and wind power eventually sun-derived?

OF THE QUANTITY OF BLOOD PASSING THROUGH THE HEART
by William Harvey

Harvey's classic experiments and his theory of the circulation of the blood he expounded as early as 1616, but his treatise on the subject was not published until 1628. Why? Harvey gives one important reason here. Can you find in this chapter from Harvey's work a sentence which might do as a motto for the scientist and the liberally educated man?

Earlier in the treatise it was demonstrated that blood is ejected from the ventricle of the heart through the aorta and that it cannot return because of "the valves at the root of the vessel." What is the force then of this argument: ". . . not finding it possible that this [quantity of blood] could be supplied by the juices of the ingested aliment without the veins on the one hand becoming drained, and the arteries on the other getting ruptured through the excessive charge of blood, unless the blood should somehow find its way from the arteries into the veins, and so return to the right side of the heart; I began to think whether there might not be a MOTION, AS IT WERE, IN A CIRCLE."?

The statement, "Respect for antiquity influences all men," embodies good Renaissance doctrine, as well as the idea that the heart is the seat of the "vital spirits." Cite instances here which show that Harvey partially subscribes to the ideas of his time.

CARBON MONOXIDE POISONING *by Claude Bernard*

This short description of the series of experiments which led to the discovery of the cause of carbon monoxide poisoning is worth careful reading and study. What principle in the history of science illustrated by Conant (see above) is again illustrated here? What positive and effective principle in the experimental method, unmentioned by Conant, did Bernard employ here? How serious an omission do you feel this is?

All scientists depend heavily on the observations and discoveries of earlier scientists in widely varied fields. Bernard, clearly, began with the long-known fact that arterial blood is scarlet in color and that venous blood is distinctly darker in color, almost blue. What scientific techniques already perfected did he use in his experiments? what knowledge of the behavior of identified gases? what basic theory of physics?

What essential scientific procedure was followed by Bernard in this experiment? Can you cite other examples to substantiate Karl Pearson's much-quoted assertion that "the unity of all science consists alone in its method, not in its material"?

THE READING MACHINE *by Morris Bishop*

Toward whom or against what is Morris Bishop's good-humored and highly pointed satire directed? faculties? students? energetic pedagogues with no sense of humor? science? technology? modern machine efficiency? a combination of these? or something else? The answer is implicit, of course, in the climactic question, and is driven home by the final twist of the satirical sketch.

What does Professor Entwhistle believe in? How valid or valuable are his "ideals"? (Think twice about this one.) Do they bear any relation to reading? What does the word "read" mean in the text?

What makes "The Reading Machine" effective satire?

THE IVORY LAB *by Jacques Barzun*

Early in his essay, Barzun asserts that aside from the three R's, which are basic and continuing subjects in education, other matters of knowledge both special and general are needful, but that "whereas the special *add* to one's powers, the general *enhance the quality* of all of them." This distinction runs throughout the essay and will serve as an important guide in your reading.

What is wrong, according to Barzun, with the science curriculum in present-day colleges and universities in America? What kind of graduates does such a curriculum produce? What should be done preventively and constructively? That is, how should science be introduced and taught? What evidence is cited to demonstrate the "practical" value of general education for engineers and technicians? What is the special value of teaching sciences in an introductory course historically, or "as humanities," in the author's intentionally provocative phrase?

Is Barzun antiscientific? Why does he lay into the scientists so mightily? Is he presenting a hierarchy of the learnings, or is he attempting to suggest a synthesis of the learnings? What would Barzun think of Conant's proposals (partially embodied in "Concerning Electricity and Combustion" above) for a course in principles of science historically derived for all would-be liberally educated students? To what end is he writing?

What group of present-day scientists are also "responsible, politically and morally active men"?

What general courses in science and the humanities are given in your college or university? What kind of education are you in college for?

THE ANATOMY OF THE MENTAL PERSONALITY *by Sigmund Freud*

After a careful reading of Freud's essay, rereading where necessary, and a study of his diagram at the end, define *super-ego, ego,* and *id*. On what basis does Freud assign to the super-ego the activities of "self-observation, conscience, and the holding up of ideals"? What kinds of evidence does Freud use in developing his description of the human mind? See for example *Oedipus the King,* by Sophocles, in the second volume of this book. What sorts of assumptions does he make about childhood experience, sexuality in children, the study of psychotic people?

What evidence do you find that Freud's psychology, as developed in this essay, is the result of long study? What differences are noted between his earlier and later theory? What effect does this have upon your judgment of the validity of Freudian psychology as a science? What characteristics of the scientist do you find in Freud's attitude, his evidence, and his argument?

It is often asserted that Darwin, Marx, and Freud have exerted the profoundest influence upon twentieth century thought; in what respects, to what extent, does this essay justify the assertion?

Determine so far as you can from this essay what view Freud takes of human nature.

LOOKING FORWARD *by Lewis Mumford*

In what light does Mumford regard the power culture resulting from modern technology, and expansion in land, mechanics, and population? Why, quoting Toynbee, does he present an historical view of this culture and its expansion? What possibilities does he see, "looking forward"? Is his reasoning vitiated by his having written prior to the first explosion of the atomic bomb and the appearance of atomic energy?

What specifically does he mean by the possibility of Western culture's establishing itself on a "much broader human basis"? You will find the answer to this question not only here, but in the essays by Kluckhohn, Toynbee, Cousins, and in the Declaration of Independence, by Jefferson. How does each of these writers deal with the concept of progress?

"The progress of the biological and social sciences will result in a shrinking of the province of the machine." Explain. Compare with Thoreau's chapter on Reading (see Section II); show that Mumford has read Thoreau. Is there a contradiction between Mumford's prediction and the views held by Laurence on the potential uses of atomic energy and by Wiener on the potential uses of machines for running machines? What view, finally, does Mumford hold as to the function of the arts?

VI. SOCIETY

AN ANTHROPOLOGIST LOOKS AT THE UNITED STATES
by Clyde Kluckhohn

The author defines anthropology, in another section of the book from which this chapter is drawn, as the study of "basic anatomical and cultural likenesses and differences." How does the opening paragraph establish the author as an anthropologist? Cite other evidences throughout the essay of "cultural likenesses and differences." Why is travel, in time or space, in different languages, or by means of the written word, "broadening"? What simple condition is necessary for the prospective traveler? (See Thoreau's "Reading" above.)

Make a list of those culture traits which Kluckhohn believes to be peculiarly American. Do you agree in the accuracy of his descriptions? Can you add to his list? How do you account for frequent paradoxes in his enumerations? Do the contradictions mean that his description of American traits is inaccurate? (See Freud and Robinson above.)

What do you regard as the most striking evidence, at the present time, of a gap in American culture between theory and practice? What has been the greatest contribution of America to the world, according to Kluckhohn? To whom finally does he go for a vision of what life might become under "scientific humanism"?

TRENDS IN PERSONAL LIFE *by Margaret Mead*

What basic change has occurred in the American pattern of human relationships, and what dilemma in consequence has resulted for the average American boy or girl?

What groups tend to sever young Americans' family ties at a relatively early age? How strong an attraction do these groups exert, and how much loyalty do they command from their members?

You have read an article by another anthropologist, Clyde Kluckhohn. What is there in the Mead article to show that the writer's viewpoint is anthropological?

Support or attack Margaret Mead's conclusions with evidence from your own knowledge or experience. For example, is it true that most young men and women in college adopt a "line" and use it over and over again on dates? Does the line involve extravagance or "romantic" exaggeration?

COMMON WOMEN *by Philip Wylie*

This chapter from a recent book by Philip Wylie introduced, for the time being, a new word into the American language, "momism." Whether you agree with Wylie's vitriolic attack on idle "middle-aged, middle-class, earth-owning Mrs. America," or whether you feel his punishing "mom" is out of proportion to the crime, or whether you are shocked by his diatribe, you should see that what Wylie is attacking is an American "traditional custom." As a satirist, then, he is attempting to alter unquestioned acceptance by his readers of the uncritical, sentimental attitude of many Americans toward "mom."

What indicates that Wylie does not mean that "mom" is the American mother? How large a proportion of American mothers, then, does he consider are "moms"? Is he right? Your answer will depend partly on your recognition of the traits which Wylie assigns his matriarch. What is the relation of "Mother's Day" to "mom"?

A TALE OF A TUB *by Bergen Evans*

Evans' book *The Natural History of Nonsense,* from which this chapter is drawn, is funny; it is illuminating as well because it not only exposes a long series of American "vulgar errors" but it explains how and why they came to be accepted as fact or truth. Evans is thus a satirist-humorist, with many of the skills of the psychologist, anthropologist, and social historian.

Why do Americans continue to believe as gospel truth Mencken's famous hoax about the bathtub? Are American army officers allowed to carry an umbrella? Why not? Ask your instructor what the saying "the exception proves the rule" means. Read the paragraph about chances in getting any bridge hand; then answer the question, "If a penny flipped in the air turns up heads fifty times in a row, what are the chances that it will turn up heads the fifty-first time?"

Do you believe that hair turns white over night, or that birds live a happy family life, or that oysters are poisonous in months without an R, or that the ant is industrious and the grasshopper lazy, or that orientals have slanting eyes? or that the physical disabilities for which the army rejected hundreds of thousands of Americans in World War II were caused by "soft living"?

If "no error is harmless," what strong intellectual trait must the civilized man acquire and exercise?

PECUNIARY CANONS OF TASTE *by Thorstein Veblen*

Throughout the volume from which this selection is taken, Veblen refers to the "instinct of workmanship." What implications does this phrase have in contrast to "conspicuous consumption" and "invidious comparison"?

Veblen asserts that the "canon of honorific waste may, immediately or remotely, influence the sense of duty, the sense of beauty, the sense of utility, the sense of devotional or ritualistic fitness, and the scientific sense of truth." That is, we tend to try to keep up with the Joneses, or get ahead of them, in owning or expending commodities, and we judge these commodities to be good on the basis of whether they are rarer or more expensive than other peoples'.

Veblen cites as examples the general belief that wealth is the mark of virtue, the satisfaction taken in expensive church decoration, our dislike for the "cheap" machine-made spoon which is a clever imitation of the hand-wrought silver spoon, genuinely beautiful works of art which can be monopolized, women's hats and the rapid change in their fashions, expensive as opposed to common flowers, changing notions as to beauty of figure in women (including the wasp waist, and the deformed foot of the Chinese), and the superiority of costly, slightly crude handmade goods as opposed to inexpensive, finished machine-made goods. Which of these examples still hold good today for most Americans? Which have changed? Can you explain why?

Do Wylie's "Common Women" (see above) have pecuniary canons of taste? Why do most brides want solid silver? Why do people collect antiques or first editions or own purebred dogs? Why is it considered by many people ill-bred to ask the cost of a friend's new possession? Why do many people ask or give such information?

THE BITTER DRINK *by John Dos Passos*

This thumbnail biographical sketch is taken from John Dos Passos' panoramic novel-trilogy of twentieth-century America called *U. S. A.* Thus it presents a kind of writing different in several important respects from the other selections in this part. It should be read along with Veblen (see immediately above).

What attitude does Dos Passos have toward Veblen, and what attitude does he wish you as a reader to have toward Veblen? The answer to this question may be found in the comparison implicit in the title, "The Bitter Drink."

What is the function of the paragraphs on Veblen's family and his early life and environment? How is the socialist point of view of both author and biographical subject presented in the sketch? The prose here is tightly wrought, with some of the characteristics of poetry; point out some of these characteristics.

Why did Veblen drink "the bitter drink"? specifically when? What purpose is served by the paragraph at the end, quoted from Veblen's papers?

THE ILLUSION OF INDIVIDUALITY *by Erich Fromm*

Thoreau (see below) once said that "The mass of men lead lives of quiet desperation." Point to specific evidence in the essay to show that Fromm agrees with this assertion so far as modern man is concerned. What evidence can you adduce from your own experience to support or attack Fromm's conclusion that modern man's unhappiness is deep-seated?

What factors in modern society lead to the individual's sense that he is insignificant and powerless? What attitudes arise in the individual as a result of his feeling lost? What political system thrives on the psychic insecurity of such individuals? Why?

How much do you care about the fraternity or sorority to which you belong? about style in clothing? about having a car? about being popular? What has all this to do with your freedom as an individual? Theodore Dreiser in his novel *An American Tragedy* wrote that people had always told his fictional hero, Clyde Griffiths, what to have—never what to be: what relevance does Clyde Griffiths' tragic situation have to Fromm's argument? Compare Kluckhohn's brief reply to Fromm (above).

Fromm in the section following this one in his book reconciles the uniqueness of the self and the principle of equality, asserting that spontaneous activity is the answer to the problem of freedom. Love and work are the basic components of spontaneous activity; in it, the individual self becomes stronger and more solidified by embracing the world.

APPROACHES TO ECONOMIC REFORM *by Eli Ginzberg*

In the author's view, what degree of development has taken place in the discipline of economics? (Why, by the way, does he use the word discipline? What word might other economists have used?) Over how long a period of time? State briefly the primary points of emphasis of each of the major economists whose views Ginsberg is summarizing. Does he favor the views of any single economist over the others? Why? On what evidence do you base your answer?

Does he despair of economic reform? What significance does he attach to the emotional violence in which current debate on economic issues, such as the "welfare state," goes on? What conclusion does he come to, then, as to the future of economic reform? What sort of man should decide "what kind of world is worthwhile and what are the desired relations between man and government, and man and fellow man?"

Compare what Ginsberg says about Adam Smith and John Maynard Keynes with selections from the writings of these men which follow.

OF THE WAGES OF LABOUR *by Adam Smith*

What differences exist between contemporary American and British combines of "masters" and "workmen" and those of Adam Smith's England? between labor legislation of the two periods?

Benjamin Franklin, by frugality, industry, and a marked ability to persuade others to his point of view, made a fortune in Philadelphia: his contemporary in England, Daniel Defoe, with many of the same talents, was poor throughout his life. Assuming these men were very much alike, how would Smith account for the difference in their financial success?

How much agreement do you find between Adam Smith's discussion of an expanding economy in the British colonies and Turner's frontier thesis (see below)? What is the significance of the liberal reward of the laborer to the state of the national economy?

GOLD-MINING *by John Maynard Keynes*

How does Keynes use the kind of argument known as *reductio ad absurdum* (reduction to absurdity)? What similarities in style and in the use of example do you find between Keynes and Veblen (see above)?

What is the fundamental proposition or assumption on which Keynes bases his judgments in these pages? To what purpose does he find partial justification for investment in gold mines?

CIVIL DISOBEDIENCE *by Henry David Thoreau*

The carefully framed intention of shocking people into thought was practiced by Thoreau long before G. B. Shaw became adept at it. What striking instances of this intention do you find in this essay? Thoreau builds his argument on a series of opposing terms: what are some of these paired opposites?

What reasons for refusing to support American government does Thoreau give? How specifically did he put his refusal into action? On what grounds does he attack Daniel Webster? Was Thoreau right in his belief and action?

How relevant is Thoreau's essay to present issues such as civil rights and the treatment of political, racial, and religious minorities?

THE APOLOGY OF SOCRATES *by Plato*

What are the principal charges brought against Socrates? What counterparts to them do you find in the present world? What accusations are sometimes made against college professors? How well does Socrates' defense serve to defend modern professors from the charges brought against them?

Socrates conceived of himself as "the gadfly of the state." Who are the gadflies of contemporary America? What purpose do they serve?

If you had been in Socrates' place, how would you have defended yourself? If your defense would have been different, explain why.

Socrates said that "the self-examined life is the only life worth living." What are the implications in this statement with regard to vocational subjects and liberal studies? If you agree with the statement, what conclusion must be drawn regarding the lives of many people? If some people live lives which are worthless, according to Socrates, why are they apparently so happy? Compare with what Housman says in his "Introductory Lecture" (above).

THE DECLARATION OF INDEPENDENCE *by Thomas Jefferson*

The philosophy of this document has been a dynamic force in the Western world since its adoption July 4, 1776, by the Continental Congress in Philadelphia. Most of the great reform movements of the nineteenth century—abolition, universal suffrage, labor laws, popular education, and most of the nationalist movements, in Ireland, Finland, Germany in 1848, Czechslovakia, even Sun Yat-sen's China—based their philosophy on it.

What audience did Jefferson and his committee have in mind when they drew up the declaration? How is the dignity and authority of the speakers established? Why is the onus for the revolution placed on George III rather than on the British Parliament? What answer is given to allay fears that anarchy might follow upon the revolution? Which is more important: the paragraph which begins, "We hold these truths to be self-evident," or the list of grievances which follows? Why? What is the significance of Jefferson's substituting the word "happiness" for the traditional word "property"?

Compare the conclusion of Kluckhohn's essay and Thoreau's "Civil Disobedience" (above) with the ideas of the declaration.

THE SIGNIFICANCE OF THE FRONTIER IN AMERICAN HISTORY *by Frederick Jackson Turner*

Turner believed that the historian at his best must understand political, economic, psychological, geographic, and scientific forces at work in the period he studies. To what extent does he interpret his subject in these terms? Find an example of each.

What specifically were the influences created by the frontier on American institutions and on Americans? Do any of these persist in your home town now? If so, what are they? Have they been modified since pioneer days? Have you ever traveled in the West or down the Mississippi? Do you want to? Why?

The American frontier was closed in 1890. Are there geographical frontiers left in the world today? Where? Did the westward movement resemble imperialist conquest in any way? How did it differ from imperialist conquest?

What nongeographical frontiers now opening may prove as historically important as the American frontier?

DOES HISTORY REPEAT ITSELF? *by Arnold J. Toynbee*

Toynbee is the author of *A Study of History,* a brilliant analysis of the twenty-one civilizations of the world, with many insights drawn from a study of some 650 primitive societies known to exist or to have existed. What two meanings does he immediately distinguish for the word *does* in the question? What distinct definitions for the word *history* does he draw? Why? What relationship is brought out between the Civil War and events in the Second German Reich, in Canada, and in Australia, South Africa, and Brazil? Between this pattern and the world situation in the middle of the twentieth century? What conclusion, then, does Toynbee come to in answering the key question of his essay?

What three policies, according to Toynbee, must be followed if history is not to repeat itself disastrously?

On what basic assumptions do Toynbee's reasoning and argument rest? Does he believe in evolution? If so, name the evidence. Does he believe in free will? Is he Christian? On what fundamental concept does he base his belief that history need not repeat itself in the future?

THE FIRST AND THE SECOND INDUSTRIAL REVOLUTION *by Norbert Wiener*

This essay is part of a book on *cybernetics,* or the study of control and communication in the animal and the machine. The thesis of Wiener's book is "that society can only be understood through a study of the messages and the communication facilities which belong to it; and that in the future development of these messages and communication facilities, messages between machine and man, and between machine and machine, are destined to play an ever-increasing part."

What inventions of the first industrial revolution does Wiener choose to describe? Why? What predictions does he make as to the possible future use of electronic computing machines? What evidence does he give to show that a second industrial revolution based on their use is already under way?

What evidence is there that a shortage of manpower exists in the United States which would be aggravated seriously by world war? What economic and social consequences does Wiener predict? On what grounds does he argue his second alternative of "a decade or more of ruin and despair"? Give evidence for the validity, or the lack of it, of his argument.

Compare Wiener's conclusion with the conclusion drawn by Laurence (see above). What factors in American civilization might mitigate the extreme alternatives which each writer sets forth? Compare Toynbee and Mumford, "Looking Forward" (above). How much validity do you find in the often made assertion that the present is an age of anxiety and crisis?

MODERN MAN IS OBSOLETE *by Norman Cousins*

Most of the social sciences, history excepted, are relatively new; they face the bewilderingly complex problem of determining what man is, and by their nature they must provide a basis for saying what man ought to be. The present challenge to these "sciences of man," and to mankind itself, is vigorously made in Cousins' editorial.

How does Cousins set about proving his basic proposition, that all men must act to preserve themselves from destruction because there is so little time?

Granted that Cousins' basic assumption is right, do you think it likely that countries at war would refrain from using the atomic bomb, either from fear of retaliation or for humanitarian reasons? What historical precedent is significant here?

What alternatives, according to Cousins, face men? Compare Toynbee's (above). Are they genuine alternatives? Are any other courses of action possible than world government if men are to survive in any numbers with their civilization relatively unimpaired? How significant to Cousins' argument are the European network of railroads and canals, the federal structure of the United States, the airlines of the world, the radio? What are some of the difficulties implicit in translating Cousins' basic principles for world government into world government?

VII. PHILOSOPHY AND RELIGION

VIRTUE *by Aristotle*

How is moral virtue acquired?

Explain the Aristotelian doctrine of the mean. To what extent do you practice it in your own life? What sort of person do you think you would be if you practiced Aristotle's teachings on virtue for one year?

In what actions and emotions is the idea of the mean inadmissible?

How does Aristotelian virtue differ from Christian?

THE SERMON ON THE MOUNT

The essence of the ethics of Christian religion is contained in this sermon. What standards for conduct does it set up? Judged by them, are Christians Christian?

Is this standard of conduct impossibly idealistic and impractical? Has it ever been given a fair trial by large groups or societies? by individuals? by religious orders? Cite examples.

For an imaginative account of what might happen if the Sermon on the Mount were really taken seriously, see Charles Sheldon's novel, *In His Steps.*

What sort of world do you think would result if most statesmen were activated by the principles of the Sermon on the Mount? what sort, if most of the ordinary people were? Would you feel comfortable in it? Would you prefer it to the world you live in? Why?

THE STOIC CODE *by Marcus Aurelius*

What are the principal qualities of character necessary in the Stoic life? Compare Stoicism with Christianity from the ethical point of view. Name some historical characters whose lives fit this description of the Stoic life. What sort of human character would the practice of Stoicism produce? What elements in Stoicism do you find desirable enough to incorporate in your own living?

THE ENJOYMENT OF LIVING *by Michel Eyquem de Montaigne*

How much of a sensualist is Montaigne? Compare his outlook on life with the philosophies of Aristotle, Marcus Aurelius, and Socrates. In which do you find the most common sense? Which is the most attractive to you? To what extent does this essay serve to counterbalance the asceticism of the others?

To what extent do you agree with Montaigne when he says, "What, have you not lived? That is not only the fundamental but the most honorable of occupations"? What is the effect of Montaigne's philosophy of life upon your ambitions?

How does Montaigne reconcile his views with the teachings of the Church and the practice of saints and mystics?

How closely do the lives of most of your friends conform to the precepts of Montaigne? If Montaigne were an undergraduate in your college, would he be thought a grind, a good all-round fellow, a playboy, or what?

IS HAPPINESS STILL POSSIBLE? *by Bertrand Russell*

How does Russell account for the happiness of scientists?

Why are reformers, even though unsuccessful, usually happy?

What role does belief play in making people happy? What contribution to happiness can a hobby make?

Discuss Russell's statement: "Fundamental happiness depends more than anything else upon what may be called a friendly interest in persons and things." How can you go about developing more of this "friendly interest"?

Does Russell's "secret of happiness" go much beyond the familiar advice to "broaden your interests"?

A FREE MAN'S WORSHIP *by Bertrand Russell*

This is the eloquent statement of a learned atheist's creed. How good is the life which he proposes? To what extent is it possible on the premises that he gives?

George Deeds, a freshman who belongs to the Methodist Church, says: "The trouble with Russell is that he proposes to retain most of the Christian ideals of character and conduct, and even a Christian outlook on life, while denying utterly the validity and power of religion. And I think that religion alone is capable of producing these things. This sort of life just can't be lived when based on atheistic philosophy. He is trying to preserve the framework of Christian civilization, but without God it can be only a hollow shell." Reply to George.

THE NECESSITY OF THE WAGER *by Blaise Pascal*

Why does Pascal differentiate between the unbelievers who make a sincere effort to find God and cannot, and those who are merely indifferent? Why does Pascal feel that this indifference is unnatural—not according to nature? What presuppositions unacceptable to modern materialists and humanists does Pascal make?

How does Pascal make the very incomprehensibility of God an argument in favor of His existence?

What is the wager? Why does everyone have to make it? Do you find this application of the laws of chance and probability to the question of the existence of God flippant? How does Pascal intend it? What are the risks involved? the rewards?

How does Pascal's admission of the uncertainty of religion tend to strengthen his argument?

THE PROVIDENCE OF GOD

List the attributes of God which you find in these psalms. What is the relationship between God and godly men? What has the good man a right to expect of God?

In what ways do the teachings of Jesus differ from these psalms with regard to the providence of God? How do they compare?

MEDITATION XVII *by John Donne*

In this devotional meditation, composed by Donne as he lay stricken by a severe illness, are reflected some of the most important doctrines of the Church, particularly the belief in the fatherhood of God and the brotherhood of man. In what way does he express these ideas? To what extent are they held outside the Church.

If men in earlier centuries felt themselves mystically united in the body of Christ, what comparable bond unites them today?

What ideas in this essay seem typically seventeenth-century or earlier in their difference from twentieth-century religious writing? How have the emphases changed?

What ideas and attitudes of Donne and his contemporaries ought, if possible, to be regained today?

Discuss the excellences of Donne's prose style, of which this devotion is representative.

√For whom was Donne writing? To what end? What elements in Donne's style contribute to his purpose?

IN HIS WILL IS OUR PEACE *by John Woolman*

This brief record of a crucial experience in the life of an eighteenth-century American Quaker is characteristic of Woolman's quietism and his faith. Why did he wait more than two years before writing it down? What virtues are given special dramatic emphasis here? Which virtue above all? Why does the oppression of workers in mines and of slaves seem so grievous to the writer? What was the nature of the experience?

In what respects does this record differ from Dr. John Donne's in "Meditation XVII" (above) from Bertrand Russell's (above)? What similarities, if any, do you find between Woolman and Donne?

THE REASONABLENESS OF CHRISTIANITY *by Theodore M. Greene*

Discuss Greene's defense of God and soul as being not incredible beliefs. What assumptions commonly made by religious apologists does he not make? How do these omissions strengthen his arguments?

What do you think of judging the reality of Christian Revelation by the criteria of (a) coerciveness, (b) coherence, and (c) publicity, which Greene sets up? Are there others in addition? How well do you think the Christian Revelation meets these tests?

How adequate do you consider Greene's definition of faith? Why must Christian faith be, to some extent, a "venture"? Distinguish between dogma and dogmatism.

What, according to Greene, is Original Sin? How well does this doctrine explain the widely experienced feelings of guilt? What would Freudian psychologists say to this?

What are the principal objections that humanists make against the Church? Evaluate the seriousness of each. How well does Greene meet them? Are there others that you can add?

In what ways is Greene's presentation of Christianity more humble than Christian apologies usually encountered? To what extent does he overcome the non-Christian antipathy to the Church?

Define the area of agreement between Pascal and Greene.

RELIGION AND SCIENCE *by Alfred North Whitehead*

What is Whitehead's purpose in giving a number of actual examples of error both from the history of science and from the history of the church?

Explain Whitehead's meaning in this statement: "The clash is a sign that there are wider truths and finer perspectives within which a reconciliation of a deeper religion and a more subtle science will be found." How do you interpret "deeper religion"? "More subtle science"?

How extensive and how important is the clash between science and religion? How does Whitehead de-emphasize the disparity between the two by building up a consciousness of the gradual development of both science and religion?

What, on the other hand, is the necessity for seeking to harmonize the discrepancy?

What has weakened the intellectual authority of religious apologists during the last two centuries? What lesson might religious apologists learn from the advancement of science by the disproving of theories formerly held?

What is meant by the evolution of religion? What is its relation to the progress of science? Why is it a necessity? How does it make possible a reconciliation of religion with science? What connection do you see between the fading of religious interest in modern times and the failure of traditional religion to evolve an expression acceptable to the modern intellect?

Compare Whitehead's view of life with Bertrand Russell's in "A Free Man's Worship." With whom do you find yourself more nearly in agreement? Why?

LIVING RELIGIONS AND A WORLD FAITH *by William Ernest Hocking*

What are the characteristics of the traveling religions? What conditions were common to their origins? What are the similarities between Buddhism and Christianity? What elements of a common faith do the great religions show? What potentialities exist toward the realizing of a world faith?

Would Theodore Greene argue that Hocking omits essentials in dealing with Christianity?

From Hocking's essay what conception do you get of Buddhism? of Islam? of Confucianism?

THE ALLEGORY OF THE CAVE *by Plato*

In the allegory, what does the cave represent? the prison house? the outside world of sunshine? How effectively might Plato's argument be presented in more abstract, nonfigurative language?

If a man's thoughts are based completely on sense perceptions, is he a cave dweller or an inhabitant of the world of light?

To what may the journey from the prison house to the outside world be likened? Who is represented by the person who forcibly frees the cave dwellers?

Where does the man of liberal education live?

A DISCOURSE ON METHOD *by René Descartes*

How does Descartes subdivide the problem of knowing? What is the basis of certitude?

Discuss Descartes's statement that "the ground of our opinions is far more custom and example than any certain knowledge."

According to Descartes, what is the only true method of arriving at any knowledge?

AN ESSAY CONCERNING HUMAN UNDERSTANDING *by John Locke*

What is the importance of Locke's basic premise of the mind as a *tabula rasa*? What use does Locke make of Descartes's foundation?

According to Locke, what are the two sole sources of ideas? To what extent do you agree with him? What ideas can you think of which have other origins?

WHAT PRAGMATISM IS *by William James*

Explain what James means by Pragmatism.

What undesirable consequences can you think of which could result from the use of pragmatic methods? What ethical problems are involved? How well do you agree with the view "that truth in our ideas means their power to 'work'"? Compare this view of truth with that of Descartes or of Locke. According to James, what absolute truth is possible?

THE BREAKDOWN OF MODERN PHILOSOPHY *by Etienne Gilson*

Why, according to Gilson, has Western philosophy broken down? What are the two main tenets of the Western creed? What has undermined them?

Evaluate Gilson's emphasis on the Reformation as a destructive and disintegrative force. What arguments can you think of which place the Reformation in a different light? What, for example, is the relationship between the Reformation and the origin of democracy?

What role has science played in the breakdown? Before deciding finally, perhaps you should re-examine Section V.

THE BASIS OF RENEWAL *by Lewis Mumford*

Describe the nature and the magnitude of the task of reconstruction.

What are some of the signs of the exhaustion of our civilization? How great an area of agreement is there between Mumford and Gilson? between Mumford and Russell? between Mumford and the Christian tradition in general?

What part can liberal education play in the regeneration Mumford envisions?

What is the role of every civilized person in the renewal? In your opinion, how adequate is Mumford's proposal for the crisis? What would you like to add to his "basis for renewal"?

BIOGRAPHICAL NOTES

MAXWELL ANDERSON (1888–) is the author of a number of plays, among them *What Price Glory* (with Laurence Stallings, 1924), *Elizabeth the Queen* (1930), *Winterset* (1935), and *Anne of the Thousand Days* (1947).

ARISTOTLE (384–322 B.C.), versatile Greek philosopher, was a student of Plato. He was appointed by Philip of Macedon to tutor his son, Alexander the Great. Later he returned to Athens where he lectured to many disciples and wrote his numerous works on poetry, logic, natural science, politics, rhetoric, philosophy, and metaphysics. His influence, particularly great during the Middle Ages, continues to this day.

FRANK AYDELOTTE (1880–) was formerly president of the Institute for Advanced Study and, before that, of Swarthmore College. Born in Indiana, he was graduated from Indiana University. He then studied at Oxford as a Rhodes Scholar, taking the degree of B.Litt. In his early career he taught English at Indiana University and at Massachusetts Institute of Technology. Author of many articles and books, he is perhaps best known for *Elizabethan Rogues and Vagabonds* and *The Oxford Stamp*.

FRANCIS BACON (1561–1626), scientist, philosopher, and man of letters, became Lord Chancellor of England. His works, which have influenced the development of human thought and progress, include *The Advancement of Learning* (1605), *Instauratio Magna*, and *Novum Organum* (1627).

JACQUES BARZUN (1907–) was born in Paris and received his early education at a Paris *lycée*. He came to the United States in 1919, and was naturalized in 1933. In 1927, he took his A.B. degree at Columbia and five years later his Ph.D. in history. He has written *The French Race: Theories of its Origins, Of Human Freedom, Darwin, Marx, Wagner, and Teacher in America.* Since 1937 he has taught history at Columbia. His most recent book is *Berlioz and the Romance Century.*

CLAUDE BERNARD (1813–1878), French physiologist and opponent of "vitalism," carried out experimental investigation on nerves and chemical research. He discovered the function of the vasomotor nerves. His theory of the "interior environment" has been of major importance in physiological research. Two of his books are *An Introduction to Experimental Medicine* (1865) and *General Physiology* (1872).

MORRIS GILBERT BISHOP (1893–), scholar and teacher of Romance Languages at Cornell University, is better known as a satirist and humorist. He has published biographical and critical works on Cabeza de Vaca, Pascal, and Ronsard, and a number of volumes of humorous poems and sketches.

GEORGE BOAS (1891–), professor of Philosophy at Johns Hopkins, was educated at Brown, Harvard, and the University of California. He has written for *Harper's* and *The Atlantic* and published many books— among them are *The Happy Beast, Primitivism and Related Ideas in Antiquity, A Primer for Critics,* and *Romanticism in America.*

JOHN MASON BROWN (1900–) served as dramatic critic of the New York *Evening Post* from 1929 to 1941 and of the New York *World-Telegram* from 1941 to 1942. After service in World War II he became dramatic critic and associate editor of *The Saturday Review of Literature,* a position that he still holds. *Seeing Things* (1946) and *Seeing More Things* (1948) are two of several books of dramatic criticism.

ROLLO WALTER BROWN (1880–), author and teacher, was born in Ohio. He has taught English at Carleton College and Harvard, lectured, contributed to the magazines, and written a number of books, among which are *Next Door to a Poet, The Pilgrimage of an Outlander,* and *The Writer's Art.*

JOHN CIARDI (1916–) has taught at the University of Kansas City and is now assistant professor of English at Harvard. Poems by him have been published in four volumes: *Homeward to America, Other Skies, Live Another Day,* and *The Statistician's Eye.*

JAMES BRYANT CONANT (1893–), American scientist and president of Harvard University, was chairman of the National Defense Research Committee in World War II. He is the author of *Organic Chemistry* (1928), *The Chemistry of Organic Compounds* (1933), and *Our Fighting Faith* (1942).

NORMAN COUSINS (1912–), author and journalist, is editor of *The Saturday Review of Literature.* He became consultant to the Overseas Publication Branch of the Office of War Information in 1943. Since 1940 he has edited a number of volumes intended to remind Americans of the wealth and importance of their democratic heritage, such as *The Good Inheritance: The Democratic Chance* (1942).

ROBERT GORHAM DAVIS (1908–) was born in Cambridge, Massachusetts. Since 1943, he has been associate professor of English literature at Smith. He is the author of many critical articles and reviews which have appeared in the *New Republic, Partisan Review, Antioch Review,* and *New York Times Book Review.* His short stories have been published in *The New Yorker* and *Colliers,* and in the *O. Henry Prize Stories* of 1942.

RENÉ DESCARTES (1596–1650), was the French philosopher whose system did much to sweep aside the subtleties of medieval thinkers and thus to influence greatly the formation of the modern mind. A mathematician as well as a philosopher, Descartes aimed at the ideal of mathematical certitude in metaphysical problems. His principal works are *Discours de la Methode, Meditationes de Prima Philosophia,* and *Principia Philosophiae.*

JOHN DONNE (1573–1631), the famous Dean of St. Paul's and metaphysical poet, was born a Roman Catholic. After his conversion to the Anglican Church he took holy orders at the suggestion of King James I, who was pleased to grant him several preferments in the Church, culminating in the Deanship of St. Paul's. Though Donne in early youth was worldly, and wrote some of the most passionate love poetry in English literature, he now became fervent in the spirit and zealous for the Lord. His sermons, many of them preached before Charles I, are among the most eloquent in all English pulpit oratory. His *Devotions,* occasioned by a grave illness, were written in 1623. Donne is considered one of the greatest of English prose writers by many critics.

JOHN DOS PASSOS (1896–) first achieved fame as a novelist with *Three Soldiers* (1921). *U. S. A.* (1938), his panoramic trilogy, embodied a number of new techniques in novel writing including the "thumbnail biography." *The Ground We Stand On* (1941) is an analysis of the foundations of democracy. His most recent novel is *Chosen Country* (1951).

SIR ARTHUR STANLEY EDDINGTON (1882–1944), English physicist and astronomer, made distinguished contributions to astrophysics and the theory of relativity with such books as *Space, Time and Gravitation* (1920), *The Internal Constitution of the Stars* (1926), and *The Expanding Universe* (1933).

IRWIN EDMAN (1896–) has taught at Columbia University since 1918 in the Department of Philosophy, and from Columbia received both his B.A. and Ph.D. He is a philosopher with a lively sense of writing, as his books and essays constantly testify. Two of his best known works are *Philosopher's Holiday* (1938) and *Philosopher's Quest* (1947).

BERGEN EVANS (1904–) teaches English literature at Northwestern University and collects examples of vulgar errors. He has written *The Psychiatry of Robert Burton* (1944).

WILLIAM FAULKNER (1897–), by many readers regarded as the foremost living American novelist, has published about twenty books of fiction. Among these are *Sanctuary* (1931), *Light in August* (1932), *Wild Palms* (1939), and *Intruder in the Dust* (1948). In 1950 he was awarded the Nobel prize for literature.

RUDOLF FLESCH (1911–) took his Ph.D. at Columbia, where he wrote a dissertation entitled *Marks of Readable Style* (1943). *The Art of Plain Talk* (1946), *The Way to Write* (1949), and *The Art of Readable Writing* (1949) further develop the ideas of the first book.

ABRAHAM FLEXNER (1866–), American educator and physician, was director of the Institute for Advanced Studies at Princeton from 1930 to 1939 and is now director emeritus. He has been associated with the General Education Board and has written many books on medical education and higher education in the United States and Europe.

SIGMUND FREUD (1856–1939), Viennese neurologist and psychologist and the founder of psychoanalysis, has exerted a profound influence upon modern art, literature, and philosophy as well as on psychology and medicine. He is best known for such writings as *The Interpretation of Dreams* (1913) and *A General Introduction to Psychoanalysis* (1920).

ERICH FROMM (1900–) was born in Frankfurt, Germany. Trained in psychoanalysis in Munich and at the Psychoanalytic Institute in Berlin, he has devoted his time since 1925 partly to work as a consultant psychologist, and partly to theoretical work especially in the field of the application of psychoanalytic theory to problems of culture and society. In 1934 he settled permanently in America and is now an American citizen. His latest books are *Escape from Freedom* (1941), *Man for Himself* (1947), and *The Forgotten Language.*

ROBERT J. GEIST (1912–) teaches English at Michigan State College and is co-author of *Current English Composition* (1951).

ETIENNE GILSON (1884–), French philosopher and historian, was educated at the Sorbonne, where he has been professor of medieval philosophy. Since 1929 he has been director of the Institute of Medieval Studies at Toronto. A popular lecturer in English as well as French, he has frequently lectured in England and at universities in the United States. He is considered one of the most distinguished medievalists in the world. He is a devout Roman Catholic in religion, and in philosophy he is a follower of St. Thomas Aquinas. Some of his books are *The Philosophy of St. Thomas Aquinas, The Unity of Philosophical Experience, Christianity and Philosophy.*

ELI GINZBERG (1911–) Professor of Economics at Columbia University, is a consultant to the War Department in economic affairs and manpower and the author of an extensive recent report on patterns for hospital care. Among his many books in the field of economics are *Agenda for American Jews* (1950) and *Occupational Choice* (1951).

THEODORE MEYER GREENE (1897–), Professor of Philosophy at Yale, was born in Constantinople. Educated at Amherst and Edinburgh, he taught philosophy for many years at Princeton. He has written *The Arts and the Art of Criticism* and a number of other books, and has contributed widely to journals.

B. H. HAGGIN (1900–) has been music critic for *The Nation* since 1936. His books are *A Book of the Symphony* (1937), *Music on Records* (1938), and *Music for the Man Who Enjoys Hamlet* (1944).

WILLIAM HARVEY (1578–1657), English physiologist and physician to Charles I, was educated at Cambridge and Padua. A series of experiments, now regarded as classic, led to his discovery and description of the circulation of the blood. *On the Motion of the Heart and Blood in Animals* was published under a Latin title in 1628.

S. I. HAYAKAWA (1906–), is a leader in the general semantics movement. He is the editor of *Etc.*, founded in 1943; his *Language in Action* (1941) was distributed by the Book-of-the-Month Club.

HUBERT HERRING (1899–), author and educator, was born in Iowa. He was educated at Oberlin, Columbia, and Union Theological Seminary. Since 1928, he has been executive director of the Committee on Cultural Relationships with South America, Inc. He is author of *The Church and Social Relations, And So To War, Good Neighbors,* and *Renascent Mexico.* He is professor of Latin American civilization at Claremont College.

HILAIRE HILER (1898–) is an artist and psychologist living in Santa Fe. He is the author of several books on painting, of which *Why Expressionism?* (1946) is his most recent.

ALFRED HITCHCOCK (1899–) began his career with the Famous Players Lasky British Studio in 1920. He is now in Hollywood. Some of the pictures that he has directed are: "The 39 Steps" (1935), "Suspicion" (1941), "Spellbound" (1944), and "Rope" (1948).

WILLIAM ERNEST HOCKING (1873–), professor of philosophy emeritus at Harvard, was educated at Harvard and at German universities. Alford Professor of Philosophy at Harvard until his retirement in 1943, Doctor Hocking has also taught at the University of California and Yale. He has lectured at the Universities at Glasgow, Oxford, and Cambridge. Some of his books are *The Meaning of God in Human Experience, Man and the State, Recent Trends in American Philosophy, What Man Can Make of Man,* and *Contemporary Science and the Idea of God.*

ALFRED EDWARD HOUSMAN (1859–1936), distinguished English poet and classical scholar, was educated at Oxford, where he failed to receive honors and took a pass degree. In 1892 he became professor of Latin at University College, London, and in 1911, professor of Latin at Cambridge. His "Introductory Lecture" was delivered upon the occasion of his becoming professor of Latin at University College. He edited Manilius, Juvenal, and Lucan. He ranks among the greatest classical scholars England has produced. But he is more highly esteemed by most readers for his three slender volumes of poems: *A Shropshire Lad* (1896), *Last Poems* (1922), and *More Poems* (1936).

ROBERT MAYNARD HUTCHINS (1899–), ex-president of the University of Chicago, now a Director of the Ford Foundation, was educated at Oberlin and Yale, and holds many honorary degrees. A controversial figure in American education, he undertook significant reforms in the curriculum at Chicago, and has published many articles dealing with educational philosophy and methods. He is one of the most articulate foes of vocationalism and is a firm believer in the "Great Books" curriculum.

WILLIAM JAMES (1842–1910), educated in Europe and at the Harvard Medical School, became an internationally famous psychologist and philosopher. He founded at Harvard the first American psychology laboratory. He was the author of *Principles of Psychology, Pragmatism, The Meaning of Truth.* With Charles S. Peirce, he founded the pragmatic school of philosophy.

THOMAS JEFFERSON (1743–1826) composed his own epitaph: "Here was buried Thomas Jefferson, Author of the Declaration of Independence, of the Statute of Virginia for Religious Freedom, and Father of the University of Virginia."

E. J. KAHN, JR. (1916–) graduated from Harvard in 1937, and in the same year began his career of writer and reporter in New York City. He served with the U. S. Army from 1941 to 1945. Among his books are *The Army Life* (1942) and *Who, Me?* (1949).

JOHN MAYNARD KEYNES (1883–1946), was an English economist and Director of the Bank of England, and is perhaps best known for his volumes *The Economic Consequences of the Peace* (1919) and *A Treatise on Money* (2 vols., 1930). His economic theory has been influential in both Great Britain and the United States.

CLYDE KLUCKHOHN (1905–), Professor of Anthropology at Harvard and Director of Harvard's Russian Research Center, first became interested in anthropology when he began to study the Navajos and other peoples of the Southwest. He has traveled and studied in Europe, was chief of the Policy Division in the Far East of the O. W. I. He is the author of such books as *To the Foot of the Rainbow* (1927) and *Personality in Nature, Society and Culture* (1948).

SUZANNE LANGER (1895–) was born in New York City and educated at Radcliffe College, where she took her A.B., A.M., and Ph.D. degrees. She has taught philosophy at Radcliffe, Wellesley, the University of Delaware, New York University, and at present is teaching at Columbia. Perhaps her best known work is *Philosophy in a New Key* (1942).

WOLFGANG LANGEWIESCHE (1907–) is an authority on weather and on the theory and practice of flight. He has written *Lightplane Flying* (1939), and *Stick and Rudder* (1944).

WILLIAM L. LAURENCE (1888–) is science-news reporter for the *New York Times* and has won the Pulitzer prize twice. He is especially skilled in understanding and interpreting to the everyday reader the complexities of modern science, whether his subject be sulfa drugs, penicillin, cortisone, or atomic fission and atomic power. He is the author of *Dawn over Zero* (1946) and was the only civilian to go along on the mission to bomb Nagasaki.

STEPHEN BUTLER LEACOCK (1869–1944), a native of England, was a famous Canadian economist and humorist. Educated at the University of Toronto and at the University of Chicago, he became professor of economics and head of the economics department at McGill University. He was one of the most popular and best loved contemporary humorists, the author of *Literary Lapses, Frenzied Fiction, Funny Pieces,* and many others.

JOHN LOCKE (1632–1704) was an English philosopher whose writings turned from the subtleties of Aristotle and the Schoolmen and helped point the modern world toward experimental science. Locke has been called the father of English empiricism, and his influence on the development of psychology, philosophy, education, and political science has been tremendous. His principal philosophical work is *An Essay Concerning Human Understanding.* His two *Treatises of Government* denied the divine right of kings and justified the Revolution of 1688, thus indirectly providing justification for the American Revolution. He was probably the most influential English thinker of the seventeenth century, and his influence is still felt in Western democracies.

MARCUS AURELIUS ANTONINUS (121–180), Roman emperor and philosopher, was one of the greatest Stoics. His *Meditations,* written in Greek, consist of twelve books of sage advice on conduct and living. Learned and gentle, he nevertheless opposed Christianity, even to the extent of persecuting Christians.

FRANK JEWETT MATHER, JR. (1868–), Emeritus Professor of Art and Archaeology at Princeton University, has published frequently on art since the appearance in 1912 of *Homer Martin, Poet in Landscape.* His specialty, to which, however, his writings have by no means been confined, is Italian painting.

MARGARET MEAD (1901–) is Associate Curator in the Department of Anthropology at the American Museum of Natural History in New York, and has studied the culture and psychology of many primitive peoples in the Pacific ocean area. *And Keep Your Powder Dry* (1942) is a commentary on American character and its strengths and weaknesses.

H. L. MENCKEN (1880–), critic, editor, and philologist, edited *The American Mercury* from 1924 until 1933, and has long been associated with the Baltimore *Evening Sun.* His six series of *Prejudices* (1919–1927) exemplify his work as a critic, and *The American Language* (1918, with later revisions) is his philological masterpiece.

MICHEL EYQUEM DE MONTAIGNE (1533–1592) was a French courtier and essayist. His *Essais,* important both for their matter and for their style, have exercised a considerable influence on the development of the essay in English literature.

THEODORE MORRISON (1901–), director of English A at Harvard, is the author of several volumes of poetry and of frequent critical papers.

LEWIS MUMFORD (1895–) has written a number of books on American civilization. Though his most distinguished work has concerned architecture (as in *Sticks and Stones,* 1924), he has also made notable contributions in literary and cultural history (as in *The Golden Day,* 1926, and *The Brown Decades,* 1931) and in philosophical analysis (as in *Values for Survival,* 1946, and *The Conduct of Life,* 1951).

GEORGE ORWELL is the pseudonym of Eric Blair (1904–1950), British essayist and novelist. Among his best known books are *Animal Farm* (1945) and *1984* (1949).

BLAISE PASCAL (1623–1662), was a French scientist, mathematician, and philosopher. A child prodigy, he wrote a treatise on conic sections at sixteen. He was the originator (with Fermat) of the mathematical theory of probability. In 1655 he came under the influence of the Jansenists at Port Royal. Aside from his technical treatises, his best known literary works are his *Lettres Provinciales* and *Pensées.*

DONALD CULROSS PEATTIE (1898–) worked in the Department of Agriculture from 1922 to 1925. Since then, writing in the tradition of Agassiz and Thoreau, he has published many books on the natural scene in America, including *Audubon's America* (1940).

J. ABNER PEDDIWELL is the pseudonym of Harold Benjamin (1893–), who is Professor of Education and Dean of the College of Education at the University of Maryland. He is also consulting editor of the education series of McGraw-Hill Book Company.

S. J. PERELMAN (1904–) has written constantly since his graduation from Brown in 1925. An author of plays and a novel, he is best known for his regular contributions to *The New Yorker.* Some titles of his collected essays are *Strictly from Hunger* (1937), *Crazy Like a Fox* (1944), and *Listen to the Mocking Bird* (1949).

PLATO (428–347 B.C.), the Greek philosopher, was a pupil and admirer of Socrates. Most of his adult life was spent in teaching at Athens, his native city, and in the composition of his *Dialogues,* all of which are extant. The *Dialogues* are based on the teachings of Socrates, who figures largely in them as the conductor of the discussions.

SIR ARTHUR QUILLER-COUCH (1863–1944), a minor poet and writer of his generation, was most influential as a lecturer on English literature at Cambridge University (England) and as the editor of *The Oxford Book of English Verse* (1900).

JAMES HARVEY ROBINSON (1863–1936), a native of Illinois, held degrees from Harvard and the University of Freiburg. For many years he was professor of history at Columbia, but resigned in 1917 as a protest against what he considered a suppression of academic freedom in the University. As a historian, his work has done much to change the emphasis of historical writing from wars, territorial changes, and treaties to the development of ideas and beliefs. He is the author of *The Mind in the Making, Introduction to the History of Western Europe,* and many other books.

LEONARD Q. ROSS is the pseudonym of Leo Calvin Rosten (1908–), who, after beginning an academic career as English teacher and student in the social sciences, has been largely associated with motion-picture projects (since 1937). From this latter part of his career has come *Hollywood, the Movie Colony—the Movie Makers* (1941).

BERTRAND RUSSELL (1872–), philosopher and mathematician, was educated at Cambridge. He has taught mathematics and philosophy at Cambridge, Harvard, the University of Chicago, and the University of California at Los Angeles. He is co-author with Alfred North Whitehead of *Principia Mathematica.* Among his other books are *Introduction to Mathematical Philosophy, The Analysis of Matter, Philosophical Essays, Marriage and Morals, Education and the Social Order.* His views on marriage and pacificism have at times involved him in controversies. Though he is an English nobleman, he refuses to use his title.

ROGER SESSIONS (1896–) is a composer and music teacher who is generally recognized to be one of the leading contemporary American practitioners of both arts. His *Symphony No. 1* was first performed by the Boston Symphony in 1927, and this work has been followed by other symphonies and by sonatas, concertos, and chorales, which have been performed by leading ensembles around the world. He now teaches at the University of

California, Berkeley, after eight years of teaching at Princeton University. *The Musical Experience of Composer, Performer, Listener* (1951) is his first book.

NATHANIEL SOUTHGATE SHALER (1841–1906), a Kentuckian by birth, was a distinguished American geologist. During most of his life he was identified with Harvard, and it was there that he studied with the great Louis Agassiz. He was graduated from Lawrence School of Science, Harvard, in 1862. After serving two years as an artillery officer in the Union Army, he taught at Harvard successively zoology, geology, and paleontology, becoming professor of geology in 1888, a position he held until his death. He was director of the Kentucky Geologic Survey, and later geologist in charge of the Atlantic division of the U. S. Geological Survey. He wrote *A First Book in Geology, Aspects of the Earth, The Interpretation of Nature,* and *Man and Death.*

ADAM SMITH (1723–1790) published his *Inquiry into the Nature and Causes of the Wealth of Nations* in 1776. The book revolutionized the economic theories of the day, and has remained a classic statement of the doctrine of "laissez faire."

HENRY DAVID THOREAU (1817–1862) called himself "a mystic, a transcendental philosopher, and a natural philosopher to boot." His dominant individualism is evident in his most famous book, *Walden* (1854). It also appears, but tempered by a belief in acting collectively "according to the spirit of our institutions," in the three John Brown speeches (1859–1860) and *Life without Principle* (1863) as well as in the essay printed here.

ROBERT H. THOULESS (1894–), a British psychologist, has lectured at Cambridge and the University of London. He is the author of *The Control of the Mind, An Introduction to the Psychology of Religion,* and *Straight and Crooked Thinking.*

JAMES THURBER (1894–), one of the best contemporary humorists and cartoonists, was educated at Ohio State University. After working on several newspapers, he joined the staff of *The New Yorker,* where he was for a time managing editor. Later he wrote the "Talk of the Town" for the same magazine. He is now a free-lance writer, but still remains a frequent contributor to *The New Yorker.* He has written *My Life and Hard Times, Let Your Mind Alone, The Male Animal, Fables for Our Times, My World–and Welcome to it!* and others.

CHAUNCEY B. TINKER (1876–) is the Sterling Professor of English Literature emeritus at Yale and keeper of rare books at the library.

ARNOLD JOSEPH TOYNBEE (1889–) is Director of Studies in the Royal Institute of International Affairs. An English historian, he has covered much of the history of East and West in a series of studies, and is now completing the last volumes of *A Study of History* (Vols. I–III, 1934; IV–VI, 1939).

LIONELL TRILLING (1905–) is the author of a novel *The Middle of the Journey* (1947) and of short stories that, though uncollected, have been frequently anthologized. Critical volumes by him are *Matthew Arnold* (1939), *E. M. Forster* (1943), and *The Liberal Imagination* (1950). He teaches English at Columbia University.

FREDERICK JACKSON TURNER (1861–1932) taught history at the University of Wisconsin and at Harvard University. His carefully documented account of the frontiers of the discoverer and explorer, the missionary, soldier, trapper, and farmer constituted a new synthesis and a new point of view in American history.

MARK TWAIN is the pseudonym of Samuel L. Clemens (1835–1910), whose writings and personality have established him as one of our great native Americans. Some of his best books are *Roughing It* (1872), *Life on the Mississippi* (1883), and *The Adventures of Huckleberry Finn* (1885).

THORSTEIN VEBLEN (1857–1929), American teacher and economist, became a leading figure in the "institutional school" of economic theory and was in part responsible for the trend toward social control in the decade 1930–1940. *The Instinct of Workmanship* (1914) and *The Engineers and the Price System* (1921) are important books by him. (See John Dos Passos' "The Bitter Drink" in Part VI of this book.)

GRAHAM WALLAS (1858–1932) was a British political scientist who taught at the London School of Economics and at the University of London. He wrote *Human Nature in Politics* and a number of other works.

ALFRED NORTH WHITEHEAD (1861–1947) was an English philosopher and mathematician. One of the most influential thinkers of the twentieth century, Whitehead taught at Trinity College, Cambridge, the University of London, and at Harvard. Among his books are *Principia Mathematica,* which he wrote with Bertrand Russell in 1910, *The Principles of Natural Knowledge, Science and the Modern World, Adventures of Ideas,* and *Nature and Life.*

NORBERT WIENER (1894–), after receiving his Ph.D. from Harvard, studied at Cornell, Columbia, Cambridge, Gottingen, and Copenhagen. His achievements in mathematics have brought him international recognition. During World War II he devised a method of solving problems of fire control and developed improvements in radar and controlled missiles. He teaches and conducts research in cybernetics at M.I.T..

JOHN WOOLMAN (1720–1772), Quaker preacher and author, was born in New Jersey, where he was apprenticed to a tailor. He traveled widely throughout the Colonies, visiting meetings of the Friends and denouncing slavery. His most famous work is his *Journal,* which gives an account of these activities. It has been frequently reprinted and is much praised for its style. Charles Lamb once suggested that aspiring writers "get Woolman's writings by heart."

FRANK LLOYD WRIGHT (1869–) began his illustrious career in 1893 at Chicago. *An Autobiography—Frank Lloyd Wright* (1932, rev. 1943) tells the long story of his struggle in establishing modern architecture.

MAX WYLIE (1904–) was with the Columbia Broadcasting Company from 1933 to 1940, and for several years has been the radio manager of an advertising agency. He has written a book called *Radio and Television Writing* (1950) and edited several radio annuals.

PHILIP WYLIE (1902–), editor, columnist, and author of the popular "Crunch and Des" fishing stories, is also a satirist and moralist. His virulent criticisms of many aspects of American civilization appear in *Generation of Vipers* (1942), *Night unto Night* (1944), and *An Essay on Morals* (1947).

INDEX

INDEX

Allegory of the Cave, The, 742
American Language, The, 158
An Anthropologist Looks at the United States, 489
Anatomy of the Mental Personality, The, 464
Anderson, Maxwell, 346
Apology of Socrates, The, 585
Approaches to Economic Reform, 560
Aristotle, 649
Arnold, Matthew, 332
Art of Plain Talk: Live Words and Crowded Words, The, 106
Aydelotte, Frank, 45

Bacon, Francis, 83, 237
Barzun, Jacques, 454
Basis of Renewal, The, 766
Bernard, Claude, 450
Bishop, Morris, 452
Bitter Drink, The, 544
Boas, George, 47
Botticelli's *Primavera,* 252
Breakdown of Modern Civilization, The, 762
Brown, John Mason, 153
Brown, Rollo W., 6

Carbon Monoxide Poisoning, 450
Case for the Daydreamer, The, 179
Chlorophyll: The Sun Trap, 442

Ciardi, John, 378
Civil Disobedience, 571
Common Women, 516
Conant, James B., 387
Concerning Electricity and Combustion, 387
Contexts, 199
Cousins, Norman, 640

Davis, Robert G., 215
Declaration of Independence, 605
Descartes, 745
Direction, 295
Discourse on Method, A, 745
Does History Repeat Itself?, 618
Donne, John, 698
Dos Passos, John, 544
Dover Beach, 332
Dover Beach Revisited: A New Fable for Critics, 333

Eddington, Arthur S., 439
Editors of *Fortune,* 115
Edman, Irwin, 87
Education at Bennington, 52
Emotional Meanings, 207
Enjoyment of Living, The, 664
Essay Concerning Human Understanding, An, 753
Essence of Tragedy, The, 346
Evans, Bergan, 523
Evolution of the Physical World, The, 439

Faulkner, William, 385
Fenimore Cooper's Literary Offenses, 352
First and the Second Industrial Revolution, The, 625
Flesch, Rudolf, 106
Flexner, Abraham, 406
Four Kinds of Thinking, 168
Four Stages of Thought, The, 186
Free Man's Worship, A, 683
Freshman Adviser, 41
Freud, Sigmund, 464
Fromm, Erich, 551

Gate Receipts and Glory, 32
Geist, Robert J., 150

General and Special Education, 63
Gilson, Etienne, 762
Ginzberg, Eli, 560
Gold Mining, 569
Greene, Theodore M., 701

Haggin, B. H., 277
Harvard Committee, 63
Harvey, William, 448
Hayakawa, S. I., 199, 372
Herring, Hubert, 19, 52
Hiler, Hilaire, 245
Hitchcock, Alfred, 295
Hocking, William E., 726
Honors Courses at Swarthmore, 45
Housman, A. E., 79
How Agassiz Taught Shaler, 16
Hutchins, Robert M., 32

Idols of the Mind, 237
Illusion of Individuality, The, 551
Imperial Façade, 267
In His Will Is Our Peace, 699
Interlude: On Jargon, 138
Introductory Lecture, 79
Is Happiness Still Possible?, 677
Ivory Lab, The, 454

James, William, 228, 256

Kahn, E. J., Jr., 319
Keynes, John M., 569
Kittredge of Harvard, 6
Kluckhohn, Clyde, 489

Langer, Suzanne, 182
Langewiesche, Wolfgang, 412
Language and Thought, 182
Language of Business, The, 115
Laurence, William L., 424
Leacock, Stephen, 68
Library, The, 84
Listener, The, 284
Living Religions and a World Faith, 726

Locke, John, 224, 753
Logical Fallacies, 215
Looking Forward, 480

Man Will Endure, 385
Manners, Morals, and the Novel, 361
Marcus Aurelius, 660
Mark Twain, 352
Mather, Frank Jewett, Jr., 252
Mead, Margaret, 511
Meditation XVII, 698
Mencken, H. L., 158
Modern Architecture: The Cardboard House, 257
Modern Man Is Obsolete, 640
Montaigne, Michel Eyquem de, 165, 664
Morrison, Theodore, 333
Mr. K*a*p*l*a*n and Shakespeare, 101
Mumford, Lewis, 267, 480, 766
Music for the Man Who Enjoys Hamlet, 277

Necessity of the Wager, The, 689
Neilson of Smith, 19
New Yorker, The, 126
Notes and Comment, 126

Of Studies, 83
Of the Conduct of the Understanding, 224
Of the Quantity of Blood Passing through the Heart, 448
Of the Vanity of Words, 165
Of the Wages of Labour, 564
On "On Jargon," 150
On Reading Poetry, 378
On the Need for a Quiet College, 68
Ooff!! (Sob!) Eep!! (Gulp!) Zowie!!!, 319
Orwell, George, 128

Pascal, Blaise, 689
Peattie, Donald C., 442
Pecuniary Canons of Taste, 533
Peddiwell, J. Abner, 72
Perelman, S. J., 315
Plato, 585, 742
Pleasant Agony, 153
Poetry and Advertising, 372

Politics and the English Language, 128
Primer of Atomic Energy, A, 424
Providence of God, The, 696

Quiller-Couch, Arthur, 138

Reading, 95
Reading Machine, The, 452
Reasonableness of Christianity, The, 701
Reasoning, 228
Religion and Science, 717
Robinson, James Harvey, 168
Ross, Leonard Q., 101
Russell, Bertrand, 677, 683

Saber-Tooth Curriculum, The, 72
Sermon on the Mount, The, 656
Sessions, Roger, 284
Shaler, Nathaniel S., 16
Significance of the Frontier in American History, The, 609
Smith, Adam, 564
Soapland, 302
St. Matthew, 656
Stoic Code, The, 660
Strictly from Mars, or, How to Philander in Five Easy Colors, 315

Tale of a Tub, A, 523
Thoreau, Henry David, 95, 571
Thouless, Robert H., 207
Thurber, James, 1, 179, 302
Tinker, Chauncey B., 84
Toynbee, Arnold, 618
Trends in Personal Life, 511
Trilling, Lionel, 361
Turner, Frederick J., 609

University Days, 1
Unrequired Reading, 87
Usefulness of Useless Knowledge, The, 406

Veblen, Thorstein, 533
Virtue, 649

Wallas, Graham, 186
Washboard Weepers: A Small Case for Radio, 308
What Makes the Weather, 412
What Pragmatism Is, 756
Whitehead, Alfred North, 717
Why Abstract?, 245
Wiener, Norbert, 625
Woolman, John, 699
Wright, Frank Lloyd, 257
Wylie, Max, 308
Wylie, Philip, 516

INTRODUCTION TO LITERATURE

CONTENTS

POEMS

Anonymous

Sir Patrick Spens 1

On *Sir Patrick Spens,* by Mark Van Doren 2

The Three Ravens 4

The Twa Corbies 5

On *The Three Ravens* and *The Twa Corbies,* by Earl Daniels 6

Edward 9

Lord Randal 11

On *Thirty Days Hath September,* by Theodore Spencer 12

Geoffrey Chaucer, 1340–1400

Merciles Beaute, I 15

Lak of Stedfastnesse 15

Sir Thomas Wyatt, 1503–1542

The Lover Complaineth the Unkindness of His Love 16

The Lover Showeth How He Is Forsaken of Such as He Sometime Enjoyed 17

Christopher Marlowe, 1564–1593

The Passionate Shepherd to His Love 18

Sir Walter Ralegh, 1552–1618

The Nymph's Reply 19

Edmund Spenser, 1552–1599

Amoretti, LXXII 19

On Spenser's *Amoretti, LXXII,* by W. B. C. Watkins 20

Sir Philip Sidney, 1554–1586

Come Sleep, O Sleep, the Certain Knot of Peace 21

Leave Me, O Love 21

On Sidney's *Leave Me, O Love,* by Harold S. Wilson 22

Michael Drayton, 1563–1631

Since There's No Help, Come Let Us Kiss and Part 23

William Shakespeare, 1564–1616

Sonnet XXIX 24

Sonnet LXXIII 24

Sonnet CXVI 25

Sonnet CXXIX 25

O Mistress Mine 25

Who Is Silvia? 26

Thomas Campion, 1567–1619

When Thou Must Home 26

Of Corinna's Singing 27

On Campion's *Of Corinna's Singing,* by Rosemond Tuve 27

John Donne, 1572–1631

Song: Go and Catch a Falling Star 28

The Indifferent 29

Death 29

The Anniversary 30

Hymn to God, My God, in My Sickness 31

On Donne's *Hymn to God, My God, in My Sickness,* by Harry M. Campbell 32

Ben Jonson, 1573–1637

Simplex Munditiis 36

Slow, Slow, Fresh Fount 36

Robert Herrick, 1591–1674

Delight in Disorder 37

Upon Julia's Clothes 37

To the Virgins, to Make Much of Time 37

George Herbert, 1593–1633

The Pulley 38

The Collar 38

On Herbert's *The Collar,* by C. Day Lewis 39

Thomas Carew, 1598–1639

A Song: Ask me no more where Jove bestows 41

Edmund Waller, 1606–1687

On a Girdle 41

Go, Lovely Rose 42

John Milton, 1608–1674
Lycidas 42
On Milton's *Lycidas*, by Wayne Shumaker 47
On His Being Arrived to the Age of Twenty-Three 55
On His Blindness 55

Sir John Suckling, 1609–1643
Why So Pale and Wan? 56
The Constant Lover 56

Richard Lovelace, 1618–1658
To Lucasta, Going to the Wars 57
On Lovelace's *To Lucasta, Going to the Wars*, by Norman Holmes Pearson 57

Andrew Marvell, 1621–1678
To His Coy Mistress 59
On Marvell's *To His Coy Mistress*, by John Hawley Roberts 60

John Dryden, 1631–1700
Can Life Be a Blessing? 61
A Song for St. Cecilia's Day, 1687 62

Edward Taylor, 1645–1729
Meditation Eight 64
On Taylor's *Meditation Eight*, by Austin Warren 65

John Wilmot, Earl of Rochester, 1647–1680
Upon His Leaving His Mistress 67
Love and Life, a Song 67

Jonathan Swift, 1667–1745
Stella's Birth-Day, 1720 68

Alexander Pope, 1688–1744
Moral Essay, II 69
On Pope's *Moral Essay, II*, by Hallett D. Smith 76

William Collins, 1721–1759
Ode to Evening 80

Thomas Warton, the Younger, 1728–1790
Sonnet III: Written in a Blank Leaf of Dugdale's Monasticon 82

William Blake, 1757–1827
The Lamb 82
Ah Sunflower 83
The Tiger 83
On Blake's *The Tiger,* by C. M. Bowra 84
To the Accuser Who Is the God of This World 84
Stanzas from Milton 85

Robert Burns, 1759–1796
Tam O'Shanter 85
Ye Flowery Banks 92
On Burns' *Ye Flowery Banks,* by Donald A. Stauffer 92
Mary Morison 94

William Wordsworth, 1770–1850
My Heart Leaps Up When I Behold 95
Composed Upon Westminster Bridge 95
I Wandered Lonely as a Cloud 95
On Wordsworth's *I Wandered Lonely as a Cloud,* by Frederick A. Pottle 96
The World Is Too Much with Us 100

Samuel T. Coleridge, 1772–1834
Kubla Khan; or, A Vision in a Dream 101

George Gordon, Lord Byron, 1788–1824
The Destruction of Sennacherib 102
Don Juan, Canto the Second, 1–23 103

Percy Bysshe Shelley, 1792–1822
Ozymandias 108
Ode to the West Wind 109
To a Skylark 111

John Keats, 1795–1821
On First Looking into Chapman's Homer 114
Ode on a Grecian Urn 114
La Belle Dame Sans Merci 116
To Autumn 117
Bright Star, Would I Were Stedfast as Thou Art 118

Ralph Waldo Emerson, 1803–1882
Days 118
Brahma 119

Elizabeth Barrett Browning, 1806–1861
Sonnet from the Portuguese, XLIII 119
On E. B. Browning's *Sonnet from the Portuguese, XLIII,* by Robert B. Heilman 120

Henry Wadsworth Longfellow, 1807–1832
Snow-Flakes 121
The Tide Rises, the Tide Falls 122

Oliver Wendell Holmes, 1809–1894
Dorothy Q.: A Family Portrait 122
The Peau de Chagrin of State Street 124

Edgar Allan Poe, 1809–1849
The City in the Sea 124
To Helen 126
The Valley of Unrest 126
On Poe's *The Valley of Unrest,* by Roy P. Basler 127

Alfred Lord Tennyson, 1809–1892
Ulysses 128
Tears, Idle Tears 130
On Tennyson's *Tears, Idle Tears,* by Cleanth Brooks 131

Robert Browning, 1812–1889
Soliloquy of the Spanish Cloister 135
My Last Duchess 137
The Bishop Orders His Tomb at St. Praxed's Church 139

Walt Whitman, 1819–1892
One's-Self I Sing 142
When Lilacs Last in the Dooryard Bloom'd 142
On Whitman's *When Lilacs Last in the Dooryard Bloom'd,* by F. O. Matthiessen 149
To a Locomotive in Winter 153
Good-Bye My Fancy! 154

Matthew Arnold, 1822–1888
The Scholar-Gypsy 155
Dover Beach 161
On Arnold's *Dover Beach,* by John P. Kirby 162

George Meredith, 1828–1909
Lucifer in Starlight 163

Emily Dickinson, 1830–1886
A Bird Came Down the Walk 164
The Chariot 164
On Dickinson's *The Chariot,* by Allen Tate 165
Indian Summer 166
'Twas Like a Maelstrom 167

Thomas Hardy, 1840–1928
The Darkling Thrush 168

Gerard Manley Hopkins, 1844–1889
The Windhover (To Christ our Lord) 169
Pied Beauty 169
Spring and Fall: To a Young Child 170
I Wake and Feel the Fell of Dark 170

A. E. Housman, 1859–1936
Be Still, My Soul, Be Still 171
Loveliest of Trees 171
On Wenlock Edge 172
Terence, This Is Stupid Stuff 172
1887 174
On Housman's *1887*, by Charles C. Walcutt 175

W. B. Yeats, 1865–1939
In Memory of Major Robert Gregory 180
On Yeats' *In Memory of Major Robert Gregory,* by Marion Witt 183
Sailing to Byzantium 190
A Prayer for My Daughter 191

E. A. Robinson, 1869–1935
How Annandale Went Out 193
Mr. Flood's Party 194

Stephen Crane, 1871–1900
War Is Kind 195
Should the Wide World Roll Away 196
Well, Then, I Hate Thee 196

Robert Frost, 1875–
Reluctance 197
The Road Not Taken 197

Fire and Ice 198
Stopping by Woods on a Snowy Evening 198
On Frost's *Stopping by Woods on a Snowy Evening*, by John Holmes 200

Carl Sandburg, 1878–
Prayers of Steel 202
Cool Tombs 202

Wallace Stevens, 1879–
Sunday Morning 203
On Stevens' *Sunday Morning*, by Yvor Winters 206
Sea Surface Full of Clouds 210
The Emperor of Ice-Cream 212

Ezra Pound, 1885–
Envoi (1919) 213

T. S. Eliot, 1888–
The Love Song of J. Alfred Prufrock 214
Cousin Nancy 218
Sweeney Among the Nightingales 218
Macavity: the Mystery Cat 219
Burnt Norton 221
On Eliot's *Burnt Norton*, by Elizabeth Drew 225

John Crowe Ransom, 1888–
Here Lies a Lady 232
On Ransom's *Here Lies a Lady*: Two Explications, by Fred H. Stocking and Ellsworth Mason 233
Blue Girls 235

Archibald MacLeish, 1892–
The End of the World 235
You, Andrew Marvell 236

E. E. Cummings, 1894–
Chanson Innocent, I 237
On Cummings' *Chanson Innocent, I,* by R. D. Mayo 238
Space being Curved 241
mr u 241
1 x 1 241

Hart Crane, 1899–1932
At Melville's Tomb 243
On Crane's *At Melville's Tomb*, by Hart Crane and Harriet Monroe 243
Voyages: II 248
The Air Plant 249

Allen Tate, 1899–
Mr. Pope 250
Again the Native Hour 250
On Tate's *Again the Native Hour*: Two Explications, by Samuel Holt Monk and August H. Mason 251

Yvor Winters, 1900–
An Ode on the Despoilers of Learning in an American University 1947 254

Kenneth Fearing, 1902–
Dirge 255

Ogden Nash, 1902–
Very Like a Whale 256
The Purist 257

W. H. Auden, 1907–
Musée des Beaux Arts 258
Petition 258
In Memory of W. B. Yeats 259
Under Which Lyre 261

Stephen Spender, 1909–
The Express 266
The Landscape Near an Aerodrome 266

Karl Shapiro, 1913–
University 267
Auto Wreck 269
Christmas Eve: Australia 270
On Shapiro's *Christmas Eve: Australia*, by David Daiches 270

Dylan Thomas, 1914–
Light Breaks Where No Sun Shines 271
The Force That through the Green Fuse Drives the Flower 272

On Thomas' *The Force That through the Green Fuse Drives the Flower:* Two Explications, by G. Giovannini and S. F. Johnson 273

John Malcolm Brinnin, 1916–
Views of the Favorite Colleges 276

Peter Viereck, 1916–
Blindman's Buff 277

Robert Lowell, 1917–
Where the Rainbow Ends 278
On Lowell's *Where the Rainbow Ends,* by Randall Jarrell 279

SHORT STORIES

Honoré de Balzac, 1799–1850
A Passion in the Desert 281

Nathaniel Hawthorne, 1804–1864
Young Goodman Brown 291
On Hawthorne's *Young Goodman Brown,* by F. O. Matthiessen 301

Edgar Allan Poe, 1809–1849
The Masque of the Red Death 302
On Poe's *The Masque of the Red Death,* by Walter Blair 306

Henry James, 1843–1916
The Real Thing 311
On James' *The Real Thing,* by Clifton Fadiman 330

Guy de Maupassant, 1850–1893
The Jewels 331

Anton Chekhov, 1860–1904
Gooseberries 337

Stephen Crane, 1871–1900
The Bride Comes to Yellow Sky 345

Thomas Mann, 1875–
Gladius Dei 353

Sherwood Anderson, 1876–1941
I'm a Fool 365

E. M. Forster, 1879–

The Celestial Omnibus 373

James Joyce, 1882–1941

A Little Cloud 386

Franz Kafka, 1883–1924

A Country Doctor 396

William Carlos Williams, 1883–

Jean Beicke 400

Katherine Mansfield, 1888–1923

The Fly 406

On Mansfield's *The Fly:* Three Explications, by Robert Wooster Stallman, Willis Jacobs, and Thomas Bledsoe 410

Katherine Anne Porter, 1894–

That Tree 413

James Thurber, 1894–

The Secret Life of Walter Mitty 424

F. Scott Fitzgerald, 1896–1940

Babylon Revisited 428

William Faulkner, 1897–

A Rose for Emily 444

On Faulkner's *A Rose for Emily*, by Cleanth Brooks and Robert Penn Warren 451

Ernest Hemingway, 1898–

The Short Happy Life of Francis Macomber 455

On Hemingway's *The Short Happy Life of Francis Macomber*, by Ray B. West, Jr. 479

Walter Van Tilburg Clark, 1909–

The Portable Phonograph 481

On Clark's *The Portable Phonograph:* The Ghost of an Apprehension, by Walter Van Tilburg Clark 486

Irwin Shaw, 1913–

The Eighty-Yard Run 493

PLAYS

Sophocles, 495–406 B.C.

Oedipus the King, translated by David Grene 505

Christopher Marlowe, 1564–1593

The Tragical History of Doctor Faustus 548

Henrik Ibsen, 1829–1906

Hedda Gabler 587

Jean Cocteau, 1871–

The Infernal Machine, translated by Carl Wildman 653

On Cocteau's *The Infernal Machine*, by Francis Fergusson 710

Eugene O'Neill, 1888–

The Long Voyage Home 720

BIOGRAPHICAL NOTES 733

INDEX 739

INTRODUCTION TO LITERATURE

I

POEMS

ANONYMOUS

SIR PATRICK SPENS

The king sits in Dumferling toune,
Drinking the blude-reid wine:
"O whar will I get a guid sailor,
To sail this schip of mine?"

Up and spak an eldern knicht,
Sat at the kings richt kne:
"Sir Patrick Spens is the best sailor
That sails upon the se."

The king has written a braid letter,
And signd it wi his hand,
And sent it to Sir Patrick Spens,
Was walking on the sand.

The first line that Sir Patrick red,
A loud lauch lauched he;
The next line that Sir Patrick red,
The teir blinded his ee.

"O wha is this has don this deid,
This ill deid don to me,
To send me out this time o' the yeir,
To sail upon the se!

"Mak hast, mak haste, my mirry men all,
Our guid schip sails the morne."
"O say na sae, my master deir,
For I feir a deadlie storme.

"Late late yestreen I saw the new moone,
Wi the auld moone in hir arme,
And I feir, I feir, my deir master,
That we will cum to harme."

O our Scots nobles wer richt laith
To weet their cork-heild schoone,
Bot lang owre a' the play wer playd,
Thair hats they swam aboone.

O lang, lang may their ladies sit,
Wi thair fans into their hand,
Or eir they se Sir Patrick Spens
Cum sailing to the land.

O lang, lang may the ladies stand,
Wi thair gold kems in their hair,
Waiting for thair ain deir lords,
For they'll se thame na mair.

Haf owre, half owre to Aberdour,
It's fiftie fadom deip,
And thair lies guid Sir Patrick Spens,
Wi the Scots lords at his feit.

ON *SIR PATRICK SPENS* [1]

MARK VAN DOREN

SOME versions of this old Scottish ballad are longer than we have it here, and many of them differ in other respects. A popular ballad has no author as we know the term; it may have had one once, but time and repetition have obscured his identity and altered his text—altered it in most cases by shortening it until it contains only the essentials of the tale it originally told. It was a song to be sung, and singers have an immemorial tendency to forget, to improvise, and to improve. The great virtue of any ballad is brevity—assuming, of course, a subject with enough drama in it to invite intensification by abridgement and omission.

The history of the present ballad is not our business here, though it is well to remember that longer versions of it speak of a voyage to Norway to bring back the king's daughter; of Sir Patrick's safe arrival there; of a quarrel be-

1. From *Introduction to Poetry,* by Mark Van Doren (New York, 1951), pp. 127–129. With the permission of William Sloane Associates, Inc. Copyright, 1951, by William Sloane Associates, Inc.

tween his nobles and the nobles of Norway, who accuse the Scots of staying too long and wasting their host's food and drink; of Sir Patrick's resolution to sail for Scotland even though he is advised that the sea is unsafe; of his sailing nevertheless; and of the wreck with which every version ends. The shipwreck was the heart of the ballad, as calamity is likely to be the stuff of any popular narrative.

The present version is the classic one, and serves best to show how a ballad should be constructed, and why it is so difficult for a single author in sophisticated times to capture the secret of the art. Line 41 is the only residue of the return voyage; otherwise we should suppose that the ship was wrecked soon after it first set sail, and indeed most readers do naturally suppose this. We shall suppose it too, and forget everything except the lines before us. They constitute a masterpiece of the ballad art, which is both a lyric and a narrative art since its aim is to sing—briefly, without taking breath—a human action, and to make it as moving as the sweetest song can be.

This song of Sir Patrick Spens is a series of lyric scenes with every transitional or explanatory passage left out. All we are told is that the king asks for a sailor; that an elder knight recommends Sir Patrick; that the king sends him an order and he receives it; that he laughs at first, then weeps at the thought of certain death, and wonders who has brought it on him; that nevertheless he rouses his crew, saying they will sail tomorrow; that one of them protests, foreseeing a storm; that they sail as scheduled; that the ship sinks, leaving only their hats on top of the water; and that their ladies will wait a long time for their return, seeing that they lie fifty fathoms deep, halfway between somewhere and Aberdour. We are told, certainly, a great deal in eleven ballad stanzas; but that is the point. There could have been many more stanzas, and much more detail. As it is there seems to be nothing that we could do without; and everything we are given is musical and moving. Not merely is no mention made of the king's starting to talk as he drinks his blood-red wine, or of his decision to write a letter, or of Sir Patrick's resolution to overlook the danger he faces, or of who it is that has seen the old moon in the new moon's arms, or of the storm itself and the sinking of the ship. A hundred other items are equally ignored—everything, indeed, except that essence which cannot be ignored if the poem is to exist at all.

The genius responsible for our song wastes no time on things we cannot instantly and deeply feel. It is not the facts that matter, or the reasons for the facts; it is the feeling—the pity of it, seeing how well these men were aware that they would die. Twice only does the ballad develop anything at length, and both times it is something to that point: first, the premonition of the men, and last the sorrow of their wives. Out of the forty-four lines as many as sixteen (15–30) are devoted to the one and as many as twelve (33–44) to the other. More than half of the poem, that is to say, concentrates upon the tragedy; less than half provides us with its framework. We have the minimum of deed and the maximum of desolation.

The poet is thus left free to do with his words what words in narrative song can best do—namely, enchant us. The bluff king, the quiet and perhaps cunning old knight, and the courageous crew whose members speak their minds so clearly, create a heroic setting which magnifies the disaster, but it is the disaster that moves us as only things both terrible and beautiful are able to move men. All is beautiful here, but we may not be sure of this until the last three stanzas, whose rhythmical, sweet movement, suggestive of a gentle sea that will bring the king's ship smoothly in, helps also to create the ladies with their fans and their gold combs who wait prettily for what the fair wind and the bright waves have in store. We know, of course, that they will wait forever; and so they seem to be doing as the poem closes. The repetitions in lines 33, 37, and 41 have done their work; they have raised the music of this narrative poem to the lyric level where all poetry, as poetry, is felt. The narrative was necessary, and indeed if it had not been perfect we should not be feeling what we feel in "fiftie fadom deip."

The art of poetry is the art of narrative too; no great lyric but tells its story, regardless of how much action was left out; no poem studied in these pages but somewhere—often in a middle stanza—reveals its concern with humanity in motion. But the final success, as even Homer knew, is when the story sings. That of Sir Patrick Spens sings in the memory of every person who knows it, and sings in the words of the poem itself. This is why there is no greater ballad, and possibly—for its length—no greater poem.

THE THREE RAVENS

1. There were three ravens sat on a tree,
   Downe a downe, hay downe, hay downe
   There were three ravens sat on a tree,
   With a downe
   There were three ravens sat on a tree,
   They were as blacke as they might be.
   With a downe derrie, derrie, derrie, downe, downe.

2. The one of them said to his mate,
   "Where shall we our breakfast take?"

3. "Downe in yonder greene field,
   There lies a knight slain under his shield.

4. "His hounds they lie downe at his feete,
   So well they can their master keepe.

5. "His haukes they flie so eagerly,
There's no fowle dare him come nie."

6. Downe there comes a fallow doe,
As great with yong as she might goe.

7. She lift up his bloudy hed,
And kist his wounds that were so red.

8. She got him up upon her backe,
And carried him to earthen lake.

9. She buried him before the prime,
She was dead herselfe ere even-song time.

10. God send every gentleman,
Such haukes, such hounds, and such a leman.

THE TWA CORBIES

As I was walking all alane,
I herd twa corbies making a mane;
The tane unto the t' other say,
"Where sall we gang and dine to-day?"

"In behint yon auld fail dyke,
I wot there lies a new slain knight;
And naebody kens that he lies there,
But his hawk, his hound, and lady fair.

"His hound is to the hunting gane,
His hawk to fetch the wild-fowl hame,
His lady's ta'en another mate,
So we may mak our dinner sweet.

"Ye'll sit on his white hause-bane,
And I'll pike out his bonny blue een;
Wi ae lock o his gowden hair
We'll theek our nest when it grows bare.

"Mony a one for him makes mane,
But nane sall ken where he is gane;

Oer his white banes when they are bare,
The wind sall blaw for evermair."

ON *THE THREE RAVENS* AND *THE TWA CORBIES* [1]

EARL DANIELS

OPINION will differ on the merits of these two poems, which might almost be subtitled, "Version *A*: By an Optimist" and "Version *B*: By a Pessimist." I have always preferred the corbies over the ravens, for I can recall in literature no love story more sharply etched in bitterness. But it is important to recognize at the start that poles apart as they seem to be, both probably began at the same place, in the same original legend; time, and telling, and variant interests of possibly a long series of narrators have made the difference. The start may have been pure imagination, or an actual murder famous in local history, appropriately headlined, had there been newspapers then, "Knight's Body Found in Field." Crude violence like this is a source for innumerable ballads, most of them tragedies, since comedy seems to have had little interest, at least, little literary interest, for the peoples from whom the ballads came.

Very characteristic of a ballad is the way both of these begin only after almost everything has happened. They are like the fifth act of a five-act play, of which the four preceding acts have somehow been lost. The murder and all that led to it is done and over with. Death is a fact, as the curtain rises on the birds who wait to pick the dead knight's bones. Who he was, who killed him, why—none of that matters, none of a thousand other details of possible interest to a reader matters. We must not try to go behind what is given, except as the poem itself offers suggestion. The poem is not the murder; it is what happened next, presented in a tense last scene. Concentration like this makes for the stark, summary quality to be looked for in a majority of ballads. Attention is not to nonessentials. The result is drama reduced to lowest and, when understood, most moving terms. Nothing else in literature is so stripped as the ballad.

What, here, is the essential thing the ballad is trying to say? What is the story? With "The Three Ravens," true love; with "The Twa Corbies," false love: that and nothing else. True love in "The Three Ravens" is symbolized, made concrete by the hounds, the hawk, and the lady, who refuse to leave the body, the lady with her unborn child, dying herself before the close of day; false love in "The Twa Corbies" by the same hawk, hounds, and lady who have departed, the lady with a speed as indecent as that of Hamlet's mother hurrying to the arms of his uncle, when

The funeral baked-meats
Did coldly furnish forth the marriage tables.

1. Earl Daniels, *The Art of Reading Poetry* (New York: Rinehart & Company, Inc., 1941), pp. 133–137. Copyright, 1941, by Earl Daniels.

She has already "ta'en another mate." This situation is sharpened by the succeeding lines, merely announcing that many mourn for the knight (except those who ought to grieve most); yet nobody knows what has become of him. Nobody, that is, *except* his hawk, his hound, and his wife—and again there seems to be an unpleasant implication.

Downrightness, where all is one thing or the other—love completely true or completely false, superlative heroism or superlative cowardice—blacks or whites without a mitigating gray, is another ballad characteristic. Ballads do not indulge in halfway measures, because the audience to whom they were originally addressed was a forthright, plain-speaking audience, unconcerned about soft nuances of light and shade; they liked directness in their poetry. The interests of that audience were simple. Love and courage were integral to their lives; a supernatural world of ghosts, and spirits of good and evil lay close about them. For these things they made important place in their poetry; because they were dominant in their lives, they are also dominant in their poems, so that all genuine ballads may roughly be classified as (1) ballads of love, (2) ballads of valor, and (3) ballads of the supernatural. There they are—the three great ballad motives, good, if for nothing else, in helping to emphasize the relative meagerness of ballad material, and then, as acquaintance with ballad literature grows, also to emphasize the infinite riches in a little room which these anonymous old poets could provide from what would seem so sparse a beginning. Naturally, more than one motive may appear in a single ballad: love, for example, may be an impulse to courage, or love and courage may together mingle in a supernatural ballad. Both "The Three Ravens" and "The Twa Corbies" are obviously love ballads. Only straining would introduce valor into the former by citing the conduct of the heroine; for the poet's emphasis is on her faithful love, faithful in her own death—a faithfulness which is made concrete in the little sharp details of her activities. He does not say in so many words, "She loved the man; she was true to him." Much more effectively, he *shows* us, and we must be indeed stupid if actions do not lead us to the conclusion he wants us to make.

What other ballad characteristics are illustrated in these two poems? With the regular emphasis on action and nothing else, there is likely to be, in ballads, only meager characterization. Men and women are little more than names; at the best, stock figures with a few elementary attributes like courage, cowardice, or love. And there is usually almost no description. When it is found, either for setting or people, it is in a few stock phrases, occurring over and over again. Heroes are "stout"; heroines are "bonnie," with "milk-white arms," small waists, and golden hair; they wear golden jewels, gowns of silk, with golden girdles. Nor is there psychology or analysis of motive. Stress on action, to the exclusion of almost everything else, is the more marked because of the almost complete objectivity with which ballad material is characteristically handled. The poet does not take sides; he does not comment or moralize. No matter how revolting the crime—and many of them are pretty bad—

he presents it as it was, unconcerned about the ethical implications. Ballads are not moral or immoral; they are simply without morals. Action exists for its own sake, and no one cares about the effect, good or bad, on the individual; social values are non-existent. One does not listen to ballads for education in "the good life." Almost at once "The Three Ravens" declares itself the everlasting exception to the rule, for that last stanza with its moral twist is a pious exhortation to the audience which might make even so earnest a poet as Wordsworth blush. But this kind of thing is rare in the genuine ballad, and when it does appear it justifies suspicion of being a late addition of a later poet. A "modern" has been tampering with the original! As a general thing, modern poets, modern writers of all sorts, cannot keep themselves and their points of view out of their writing. It is almost impossible for them to attain the complete objectivity of the genuine ballad, and this is one reason why the man who knows his ballads is seldom fooled by a modern imitation trying to masquerade as an original. For this telling objectivity "The Twa Corbies" is a vastly better poem, ending suddenly on the bleak forlornness of those last two lines, made even bleaker by the slowness of movement imposed upon them by the long vowels:

> Oer his white banes when they are bare,
> The wind sall blaw for evermair.

Read them again, aloud, with a distinct pause after *banes* and *blaw,* drawing out the sound of *bare* and *mair*.

Other ballad conventions will be illustrated by other ballads. . . . But the ravens and the corbies should not be left without some attention to qualities not at all peculiar to ballads, qualities which are part of the effectiveness of poems of all sorts. There is that frame of the gossiping birds. Talking animals are a favorite literary convention, at least as old as Aesop, popular enough to be frequently overworked and grossly misused. Have they any working validity in these poems? Do they serve any purpose other than that of providing a picturesque setting? I should call them highly important, even vital birds, for they establish and make poignant a central irony which the reader cannot miss without missing a good deal of the poems. Birds of prey of a mild sort, they perch there, ominously, at the opening of the poem, ready to pick the knight's bones for their breakfast, to plunder his body for the necessities of their housekeeping. They suggest the premonitory shudder a sensitive reader ought to feel. In one poem, the faithfulness of those associated with the knight is accentuated by the implied contrast; in the other, the desertion of the murdered warrior and the utter faithlessness of those about him is dramatized by the same foreboding contrast. Here, it seems to me, the effect is even more powerful, so that we almost believe the birds, gross as they are, preferable to the lady, who ought to be a symbol for loyalty, who ought to have remained on the scene. Observe, too, the force of "*new slain* knight," contributing in this connection its own little additional touch to our appalled sense of the too hasty indecency of the knight's betrayal. The birds are, moreover, looking for breakfast, or for means to repair a roof that they may rear their young—domestic details which contribute to the final irony of the contrast. The corbies are loyal to their bird-nature; they are not nearly so rapacious as the hawk, the hound, and the lady. How they accentuate, as they sit there, the loneliness of the knight's situation. *Naebody kens,* and we are left in a wide field, with a desolate human body, and two black crows perching on a near-by tree.

For "The Twa Corbies," one final suggestion will not down, though I cannot be sure, mentioning it, that I am not guilty of reading in what is not part of the poem. But those implications for *new slain,* together with the sudden and complete abandonment of the knight, and the fact that

> . . . næbody kens that he lies there,
> But his hawk, his hound, and lady fair . . . .

—all these have a way with my imagination whenever I read the poem. *Is the lady as innocent as she may seem?* Love may have turned to more than indifference; we may be on the edge, here, of psychological depths in an ugly, involved human situation for which hasty marriage is a culminating touch of horror. Such deeps of tortured human nature are not foreign to the ballad. . . . But the ballad poet never lingers over them. For the sake of action, he is content to leave them in stark suggestion. Quite possibly, they are more powerful when handled in this way, for a sensitive reader, than when analyzed in detail, lingered over. In the ballad, in any good literature, for that matter, analytic minutiae of a clinical laboratory are never mistaken for the pleasures of poetry.

EDWARD

1. "Why dois your brand sae drap wi bluid,
   Edward, Edward,
   Why dois your brand sae drap wi bluid,
   And why sae sad gang yee O?"
   "O I hae killed my hauke sae guid,
   Mither, mither,
   O I hae killed my hauke sae guid,
   And I had nae mair bot hee O."

2. "Your haukis bluid was nevir sae reid,
   Edward, Edward,
   Your haukis bluid was nevir sae reid,

My deir son I tell thee O."
"O I hae killed my reid-roan steid,
Mither, mither,
O I hae killed my reid-roan steid,
That erst was sae fair and frie O."

3. "Your steid was auld, and ye hae gat mair,
Edward, Edward,
Your steid was auld, and ye hae gat mair,
Sum other dule ye drie O."
"Oh I hae killed my fadir deir,
Mither, mither,
O I hae killed my fadir deir,
Alas, and wae is mee O!"

4. "And whatten penance wul ye drie for that,
Edward, Edward,
And whatten penance wul ye drie for that?
My deir son, now tell me O."
"Ile set my feit in yonder boat,
Mither, mither,
Ile set my feit in yonder boat,
And Ile fare ovir the sea O."

5. "And what wul ye doe wi your towirs and your ha,
Edward, Edward?
And what wul ye doe wi your towirs and your ha,
That were sae fair to see O?"
"Ile let thame stand tul they doun fa,
Mither, mither,
"Ile let thame stand tul they doun fa,
For here nevir mair maun I bee O."

6. "And what wul ye leive to your bairns and your wife,
Edward, Edward?
And what wul ye leive to your bairns and your wife,
Whan ye gang ovir the sea O?"
"The warldis room, late them beg thrae life,
Mither, mither,
The warldis room, late them beg thrae life,
For thame nevir mair wul I see O."

7. "And what wul ye leive to your ain mither deir,
Edward, Edward?

And what wul ye leive to your ain mither deir?
My deir son, now tell me O."
"The curse of hell frae me sall ye beir,
Mither, mither,
"The curse of hell frae me sall ye beir,
Sic counseils ye gave to me O."

LORD RANDAL

"O where hae ye been, Lord Randal, my son?
O where hae ye been, my handsome young man?"
"I hae been to the wild wood; mother, make my bed soon,
For I'm weary wi' hunting, and fain wald lie down."

"Where gat ye your dinner, Lord Randal, my son?
Where gat ye your dinner, my handsome young man?"
"I dined wi' my true-love; mother, make my bed soon,
For I'm weary wi' hunting, and fain wald lie down."

"What gat ye to your dinner, Lord Randal, my son?
What gat ye to your dinner, my handsome young man?"
"I gat eels boiled in broo; mother, make my bed soon,
For I'm weary wi' hunting, and fain wald lie down."

"What became of your bloodhounds, Lord Randal, my son?
What became of your bloodhounds, my handsome young man?"
"O they swelld and they died; mother, make my bed soon,
For I'm weary wi' hunting, and fain wald lie down."

"O I fear ye are poisoned, Lord Randal, my son!
O I fear ye are poisoned, my handsome young man!"
"O yes! I am poisoned; mother, make my bed soon,
For I'm sick at the heart, and I fain wald lie down."

ON *THIRTY DAYS HATH SEPTEMBER* [1]

THEODORE SPENCER

I PROPOSE to examine the following poem:

Thirty days hath September,
April, June and November:
All the rest have thirty-one,
Excepting February alone,
Which has only eight and a score
Till leap-year gives it one day more.

2

The previous critics who have studied this poem, Coleridge among them, have failed to explain what we may describe as its fundamental *dynamic*. This I now propose to do. The first thing to observe is the order in which the names (or verbal constructs) of the months are presented. According to the prose meaning—what I shall henceforth call the prose-*demand*—"September" should not precede, it should follow "April," as a glance at the calendar will show. Indeed "September" should follow not only "April," it should also follow "June" if the prose-demand is to be properly satisfied. The prose order of the first two lines should therefore read: "Thirty days hath April, June, September and November." That is the only sequence consonant with prose logic.

3

Why then, we ask ourselves, did the poet violate what educated readers know to be the facts? Was he ignorant of the calendar, believing that September preceded April in the progress of the seasons? It is difficult to imagine that such was the case. We must find another explanation. It is here that the principle of dynamic analysis comes to our aid.

4

Dynamic analysis proves that the most successful poetry achieves its effect by producing an *expectation* in the reader's mind before his sensibility is fully prepared to receive the full impact of the poem. The reader makes a *proto-response* which preconditions him to the total response toward which his fully equilibrized organs of appreciation subconsciously tend. It is this proto-response which the poet has here so sensitively manipulated. The ordinary reader, trained only to prose-demands, expects the usual order of the months. But the poet's sensibility knows that poetic truth is more immediately effective than the truth of literal chronology. He does not *state* the inevitable sequence;

1. Theodore Spencer, "How to Criticize a Poem (In the Manner of Certain Contemporary Critics)," *New Republic* (December 6, 1943). Reprinted by permission of *New Republic*.

he *prepares* us for it. In his profound analysis of the two varieties of mensual time, he puts the *gentlest* month first. (Notice how the harsh sound of "pt" in "September" is softened by the "e" sound on either side of it.) It is the month in which vegetation first begins to fade, but which does not as yet give us a sense of tragic fatality.

5

Hence the poet prepares us, dynamically, for what is to follow. By beginning his list of the months *in medias res,* he is enabled to return later to the beginning of the series of contrasts which is the subject of his poem. The analogy to the "Oedipus Rex" of Euripides and the "Iliad" of Dante at once becomes clear. Recent criticism has only too often failed to observe that these works also illustrate the dynamic method by beginning in the middle of things. It is a striking fact, hitherto (I believe) unnoticed, that a Latin poem called the "Aeneid" does much the same thing. We expect the author of that poem to begin with the departure of his hero from Troy, just as we expect the author of our poem to begin with "April." But in neither case is our expectation fulfilled. Cato, the author of the "Aeneid," creates dynamic suspense by beginning with Aeneas in Carthage; our anonymous poet treats his readers' sensibilities in a similar fashion by beginning with "September," and then *going back* to "April" and "June."

6

But the sensibility of the poet does not stop at this point. Having described what is true of *four* months, he disposes of *seven* more with masterly economy. In a series of pungent constructs his sensibility sums up their inexorable limitation: they *All* (the capitalization should be noted) "have thirty-one." The poet's sensibility communicates a feeling to the sensibility of the reader so that the sensibility of both, with reference to their previous but independent sensibilities, is fused into that momentary communion of sensibility which is the final sensibility that poetry can give both to the sensibility of the poet and the sensibility of the reader. The texture and structure of the poem have erupted into a major reaction. The ambiguity of equilibrium is achieved.

7

Against these two groups of spatial, temporal and numerical measurements —one consisting of four months, the other of seven—the tragic individual, the sole exception, "February," is dramatically placed. February is "alone," is cut off from communion with his fellows. The tragic note is struck the moment "February" is mentioned. For the initial sound of the word "excepting" is "X," and as that sound strikes the sensibility of the reader's ear a number of associations subconsciously accumulate. We think of the spot, the murderous and lonely spot, which "X" has so frequently marked; we remember the examinations of our childhood where the wrong answers were implacably signaled with "X"; we think of ex-kings and exile, of lonely crossroads and executions, of the inexorable anonymity of those who cannot sign their names. . . .

8

And yet the poet gives us one ray of hope, though it eventually proves to be illusory. The lonely "February" (notice how the "alone" in line four is echoed by the "only" in line five), the solitary and maladjusted individual who is obviously the hero and crucial figure of the poem, is not condemned to the routine which his fellows, in their different ways, must forever obey. Like Hamlet, he has a capacity for change. He is a symbol of individualism, and the rhythm of the lines which are devoted to him signalizes a gayety, however desperate, which immediately wins our sympathy and reverberates profoundly in our sensibility.

9

But (and this is the illusion to which I have previously referred) in spite of all his variety, his capacity for change, "February" cannot quite accomplish (and in this his tragedy consists) the *quantitative* value of the society in which circumstances have put him. No matter how often he may alternate from twenty-eight to twenty-nine (the poet, with his exquisite sensibility, does not actually *mention* those humiliating numbers), he can never achieve the bourgeois, if anonymous, security of "thirty-one," nor equal the more modest and aristocratic assurance of "thirty." Decade after decade, century after century, millennium after millennium, he is eternally frustrated. The only symbol of change in a changeless society, he is continually beaten down. Once every four years he tries to rise, to achieve the high, if delusive, level of his dreams. But he fails. He is always one day short, and the three years before the recurrence of his next effort are a sad interval in which the remembrance of previous disappointment melts into the futility of hope, only to sink back once more into the frustration of despair. Like Tantalus he is forever stretched upon a wheel.

10

So far I have been concerned chiefly with the dynamic *analysis* of the poem. Further study should reveal the *synthesis* which can be made on the basis of the analysis which my thesis has tentatively attempted to bring to an emphasis. This, perhaps, the reader with a proper sensibility can achieve for himself.

GEOFFREY CHAUCER

MERCILES BEAUTE, I

Your yen two wol slee me sodenly;
I may the beautee of hem not sustene,
So woundeth hit thourghout my herte kene.

And but your word wol helen hastily
My hertes wounde, while that hit is grene,
  Your yen two wol slee me sodenly;
  I may the beautee of hem not sustene.

Upon my trouthe I sey you feithfully
That ye ben of my lyf and deeth the quene;
For with my deeth the trouthe shal be sene.
  Your yen two wol slee me sodenly;
  I may the beautee of hem not sustene,
  So woundeth it thourghout my herte kene.

LAK OF STEDFASTNESSE

Balade

Somtyme this world was so stedfast and stable,
That mannes word was obligacioun,
And now hit is so fals and deceivable,
That word and deed, as in conclusioun,
Ben no-thing lyk, for turned up so doun
Is all this world for mede and wilfulnesse,
That al is lost for lak of stedfastnesse.

What maketh this world to be so variable,
But lust that folk have in dissensioun?
For among us now a man is holde unable,
But if he can, by som collusioun,
Don his neighbour wrong or oppressioun.
What causeth this but wilful wrecchednesse,
That al is lost, for lak of stedfastnesse?

Trouthe is put doun, resoun is holden fable;
Vertu hath now no dominacioun,
Pitee exyled, no man is merciable.
Through covetyse is blent discrecioun;
The world hath mad a permutacioun

Fro right to wrong, fro trouthe to fikelnesse,
That al is lost, for lak of stedfastnesse.

Lenvoy to King Richard

O prince, desyre to be honourable,
Cherish thy folk and hate extorcioun!
Suffre no thing, that may be reprevable
To thyn estat don in thy regioun.
Shew forth thy swerd of castigacioun,
Dred God, do law, love trouthe and worthinesse,
And wed thy folk agein to stedfastnesse.

SIR THOMAS WYATT

THE LOVER COMPLAINETH THE UNKINDNESS OF HIS LOVE

My lute, awake, perform the last
Labor that thou and I shall waste,
And end that I have now begun.
And when this song is sung and past,
My lute, be still, for I have done.

As to be heard where ear is none,
As lead to grave in marble stone,
My song may pierce her heart as soon.
Should we then sigh, or sing, or moan?
No, no, my lute, for I have done.

The rocks do not so cruelly
Repulse the waves continually,
As she my suit and affection;
So that I am past remedy,
Whereby my lute and I have done.

Proud of the spoil that thou hast got
Of simple hearts through Lovës shot,
By whom unkind thou hast them won,
Think not he hath his bow forgot,
Although my lute and I have done.

Vengeance shall fall on thy disdain,
That makest but game of earnest pain;
Trow not alone under the sun
Unquit to cause thy lovers plain,
Although my lute and I have done.

May chance thee lie withered and old
In winter nights, that are so cold,
Plaining in vain unto the moon;
Thy wishes then dare not be told:
Care then who list, for I have done.

And then may chance thee to repent
The time that thou hast lost and spent,
To cause thy lovers sigh and swoon:
Then shalt thou know beauty but lent,
And wish and want, as I have done.

Now cease, my lute! This is the last
Labor that thou and I shall waste;
And ended is that we begun:
Now is thy song both sung and past;
My lute, be still, for I have done.

THE LOVER SHOWETH HOW HE IS FORSAKEN OF SUCH AS HE SOMETIME ENJOYED

They flee from me, that sometime did me seek,
With naked foot stalking within my chamber.
Once have I seen them gentle, tame, and meek,
That now are wild, and do not once remember
That sometime they have put themselves in danger
To take bread at my hand; and now they range,
Busily seeking in continual change.
Thanked be fortune it hath been otherwise,
Twenty times better; but once especial,
In thin array, after a pleasant guise,
When her loose gown did from her shoulders fall,
And she me caught in her arms long and small,
And therewithal so sweetly did me kiss
And softly said, Dear heart, how like you this?
It was no dream, for I lay broad awaking.
But all is turned now, through my gentleness,
Into a bitter fashion of forsaking;

And I have leave to go, of her goodness,
And she also to use newfangleness.
But since that I unkindly so am served,
How like you this? what hath she now deserved?

CHRISTOPHER MARLOWE

THE PASSIONATE SHEPHERD TO HIS LOVE

Come live with me, and be my love;
And we will all the pleasures prove
That hills and valleys, dales and fields,
Woods, or steepy mountain yields.

And we will sit upon the rocks,
Seeing the shepherds feed their flocks
By shallow rivers, to whose falls
Melodious birds sing madrigals.

And I will make thee beds of roses,
And a thousand fragrant posies;
A cap of flowers, and a kirtle
Embroidered all with leaves of myrtle;

A gown made of the finest wool
Which from our pretty lambs we pull;
Fair-lined slippers for the cold,
With buckles of the purest gold;

A belt of straw and ivy-buds,
With coral clasps and amber studs;
And if these pleasures may thee move,
Come live with me, and be my love.

The shepherd-swains shall dance and sing
For thy delight each May morning;
If these delights thy mind may move,
Then live with me, and be my love.

SIR WALTER RALEGH

THE NYMPH'S REPLY

If all the world and love were young,
And truth in every shepherd's tongue,
These pretty pleasures might me move
To live with thee and be thy love.

Time drives the flocks from field to fold
When rivers rage and rocks grow cold,
And Philomel becometh dumb;
The rest complains of cares to come.

The flowers do fade, and wanton fields
To wayward winter reckoning yields;
A honey tongue, a heart of gall,
Is fancy's spring, but sorrow's fall.

Thy gowns, thy shoes, thy beds of roses,
Thy cap, thy kirtle, and thy posies
Soon break, soon wither, soon forgotten,—
In folly ripe, in reason rotten.

Thy belt of straw and ivy buds,
Thy coral clasps and amber studs,
All these in me no means can move
To come to thee and be thy love.

But could youth last and love still breed,
Had joys no date nor age no need,
Then these delights my mind might move
To live with thee and be thy love.

EDMUND SPENSER

AMORETTI, LXXII

Oft when my spirit doth spred her bolder winges,
In mind to mount up to the purest sky,
It down is weighd with thoght of earthly things,
And clogd with burden of mortality:
Where, when that soverayne beauty it doth spy,

Resembling heavens glory in her light
Drawne with sweet pleasures bayt, it back doth fly,
And unto heaven forgets her former flight.
There my fraile fancy, fed with full delight,
Doth bath in blisse, and mantleth most at ease;
Ne thinks of other heaven, but how it might
Her harts desire with most contentment please.
Hart need not wish none other happinesse,
But here on earth to have such hevens blisse.

ON SPENSER'S *AMORETTI, LXXII* [1]

W. B. C. WATKINS

SPENSER, so counter to present taste, might appear in the stocks more often if he seemed to our critics important enough. Only Mr. William Van O'Connor has recently troubled to pillory him:

In the first four lines Spenser presents the theme. . . . In the next four lines the reader expects to find some exploration of the theme, but finds, instead, simply further statement. . . . In the well constructed lyric one would expect in the last lines to discover the intellectual resolution. Here, however, there is no dramatic emotional situation to be resolved. There is merely further explanation couched in terms of graceful tribute. . . . The difference between the poems of Herrick and Stevens and Spenser is the distinction between the poetry of exploration and the poetry of exposition. Herrick and Stevens present material for the reader to *work* through; Spenser presents an imagined experience unequivocally stated. There is in the first two poems an intellectual and emotional problem to be settled in terms of the materials presented. Spenser, as a Christian, represents and illustrates a Christian attitude; he does not *re-experience* it. He does not *earn* his attitude. ("Tension and Structure of Poetry," *Sewanee Review,* Autumn 1943.)

This does not arouse spirited defense of the *Amoretti,* of all Spenser's mature poems the least exciting, especially if one agrees that Herrick's *Mad Maid's Song* and Stevens' *Peter Quince at the Clavier* are finer poems than this particular sonnet. The sonnet, however, is in its way well constructed and contains more of the qualities which Mr. O'Connor demands than he seems to realize. It is not dramatic, yet there is more sinew in the convolutions of its neo-Platonic thought than casually appears; there is even more surprise and tension, since underlying the whole sonnet is the pull between heaven and earth. The first four lines express the soul's aspirations heavenward defeated by mortality; the next four are statement, but "exploratory statement" essential

1. Reprinted from *The Hudson Review,* II (Autumn, 1949), 343–344, by permission of the Editors and the Princeton University Press.

to particularize "mortality," showing the soul, snared by desire, accepting a substitute heaven. The octave leaves us with a sense of true heaven forgotten in earthly illusion. The opening lines of the sestet, expatiating on this earthly bliss, are the only part of the poem which can be dismissed as merely "further explanation," since the concluding couplet suddenly reverses the neo-Platonism and the *substitute* nature of earthly love, proclaiming the paradox of heaven on earth. In thus forcing a system of philosophy to bow to his mistress Spenser shows no intense spiritual conflict; he stays, as he intends to stay, within the bounds of graceful, playful tribute. Is there no room in poetry for this?

SIR PHILIP SIDNEY

COME SLEEP, O SLEEP, THE CERTAIN KNOT OF PEACE

Come, Sleep! O Sleep, the certain knot of peace,
The baiting-place of wit, the balm of woe,
The poor man's wealth, the prisoner's release,
Th' indifferent judge between the high and low;
With shield of proof shield me from out the prease
Of those fierce darts despair at me doth throw;
O make in me those civil wars to cease;
I will good tribute pay, if thou do so.
Take thou of me smooth pillows, sweetest bed,
A chamber deaf to noise and blind to light,
A rosy garland and a weary head;
And if these things, as being thine in right,
Move not thy heavy grace, thou shalt in me,
Livelier than elsewhere, Stella's image see.

LEAVE ME, O LOVE

Leave me, O love which reachest but to dust;
And thou, my mind, aspire to higher things;
Grow rich in that which never taketh rust,
Whatever fades but fading pleasure brings.
Draw in thy beams, and humble all thy might
To that sweet yoke where lasting freedoms be;
Which breaks the clouds and opens forth the light,
That doth both shine and give us sight to see.

O take fast hold; let that light be thy guide
In this small course which birth draws out to death,
And think how evil becometh him to slide,
Who seeketh heav'n, and comes of heav'nly breath.
Then farewell, world; thy uttermost I see;
Eternal Love, maintain thy life in me.

ON SIDNEY'S *LEAVE ME, O LOVE* [1]

HAROLD S. WILSON

Though the Christian feeling of the poem has often been noticed, the Christian thought and Biblical allusions have not, so far as I know, been made clear. The poem has been associated with Petrarch's "solemn and impressive renunciation of love's empire" (Lee, *Elizabethan Sonnets,* 1904, p. xlvi), and more often with Renaissance Platonism (Pearson, *Elizabethan Love Conventions,* 1933, pp. 99-100). But these associations are vague and conjectural, while the Biblical background of the sonnet is unmistakable and the Christian meaning paramount.

The contrast emphasized throughout the sonnet is between the brevity of the things of this world and the duration of things heavenly (cf. the thought and contrasting mood of *Astrophel and Stella*: sonnet 5). In lines 1-2, the renunciation of earthly love is sufficiently contrasted with the aspiration toward Heavenly Love, despite the generality of "higher things," by the phrase "which reachest but to dust." All the things of this world must pass and return to the dust of which God made man, even the love of a man for a woman (*Matthew,* XXII, 30). The allusion to *Matthew,* VI, 19-21 in line 3 is apparent. The image of "fading" in line 4 may be suggested by *Matthew,* VI, 22-24, where the idea of "darkness" is associated with self-seeking and worldliness, and "light" with the stedfast aspiration of the Christian soul toward eternal salvation. This thought is likewise suggested by the first quatrain of Sidney's poem.

"Draw in thy beams . . ." The association in lines 1-4 of worldly love and its objects with the lustrelessness of that "which moth and rust doth corrupt," of that which "fades" and brings "fading pleasures," may suggest that the mind of the worldly man bent upon worldly pleasures tries to emit its own light (dark though this be in comparison with the light of God), to live by this false light, competing, as it were, with God's light (cf. *John,* I, 4 ff.). The true penitent will want to forsake the feeble "light" of his own mind (which is really the darkness of willfulness and sin) and will submit himself in all humility to God's light (cf. *Acts,* IX, 3 ff.). The act of submission and the accompanying mood of humility are further enforced from two other texts.

1. From *The Explicator,* II (April, 1944), 47. Reprinted by permission of the author and of the Editors of *The Explicator.*

Jesus said: "Take my yoke upon you, and learn of me; for I am meek and lowly in heart: and ye shall find rest unto your souls. For my yoke is easy, and my burden is light" (*Matthew,* XI, 29-30). And Jesus also said: "I am the light of the world: he that followeth me shall not walk in darkness, but shall have the light of life" (*John,* VIII, 12). The reason for associating "that sweet yoke where lasting freedoms be" with the breaking forth of light "that doth both shine and give us sight to see" in lines 6-8 is now clear and indeed compelling. Sidney has brought into conjunction two of the most memorable texts in the Gospels, and they are beautifully consistent with each other. We may then paraphrase lines 5-8 somewhat as follows: Cease to follow the pitiful illumination of your own mind in its worldliness, for its light is but darkness. Submit humbly to the yoke that Jesus lays upon men; for He has promised that by assuming this yoke you will find the only lasting freedom, freedom to follow the path that leads to eternal life by the light of Jesus who is the light of the world.

"O take fast hold . . ." Of what? The answer is, of Christian faith and eternal life. The image is a favorite of St. Paul's, though it also occurs elsewhere in the Scriptures. The imagery and allusions of the first two quatrains are all related to the Gospels. In the third quatrain the mood and imagery become predominantly Pauline. The Pauline texts *I Timothy,* VI, 12 and *II Timothy,* IV, 7 suggest the image, in lines 9-10, of the Christian who takes fast hold upon his faith as running a course, the brief course of human life, which only God can light to a successful end. The image of "sliding" in lines 11-12 is not, I think, Pauline. A parallel may be found in the *Psalms,* XXXVI, 1; XXXVII, 31). The concluding couplet is a prayer, to the eternal God who is love (*I John,* IV, 8, 16); for it is by the grace of the Eternal Love that the Christian finds salvation (*John,* III, 16; *I John,* IV, 9-10).

The sonnet is thus a very careful and beautiful expression of Christian doctrine and Christian feeling. It is an important commentary upon Sidney's Christian experience and attitude.

MICHAEL DRAYTON

SINCE THERE'S NO HELP, COME LET US KISS AND PART

Since there's no help, come let us kiss and part;
Nay, I have done, you get no more of me,
And I am glad, yea glad with all my heart
That thus so cleanly I myself can free;
Shake hands forever, cancel all our vows,
And when we meet at any time again,
Be it not seen in either of our brows

That we one jot of former love retain.
Now at the last gasp of love's latest breath,
When, his pulse failing, passion speechless lies,
When faith is kneeling by his bed of death,
And innocence is closing up his eyes,
    Now if thou wouldst, when all have given him over,
    From death to life thou mightst him yet recover.

WILLIAM SHAKESPEARE

SONNET XXIX

When, in disgrace with fortune and men's eyes,
I all alone beweep my outcast state,
And trouble deaf heaven with my bootless cries
And look upon myself and curse my fate,
Wishing me like to one more rich in hope,
Featured like him, like him with friends possess'd,
Desiring this man's art and that man's scope,
With what I most enjoy contented least;
Yet in these thoughts myself almost despising,
Haply I think on thee,—and then my state,
Like to the lark at break of day arising
From sullen earth, sings hymns at heaven's gate;
    For thy sweet love remembered such wealth brings
    That then I scorn to change my state with kings.

SONNET LXXIII

That time of year thou mayst in me behold
When yellow leaves, or none, or few, do hang
Upon those boughs which shake against the cold,
Bare ruin'd choirs, where late the sweet birds sang.
In me thou see'st the twilight of such day
As after sunset fadeth in the west,
Which by and by black night doth take away,
Death's second self, that seals up all in rest.
In me thou see'st the glowing of such fire
That on the ashes of his youth doth lie,
As the death-bed whereon it must expire
Consum'd with that which it was nourish'd by.
    This thou perceivest, which makes thy love more strong,
    To love that well which thou must leave ere long.

SONNET CXVI

Let me not to the marriage of true minds
Admit impediments. Love is not love
Which alters when it alteration finds,
Or bends with the remover to remove:
O, no! it is an ever-fixed mark
That looks on tempests and is never shaken;
It is the star to every wandering bark,
Whose worth's unknown, although his height be taken.
Love's not Time's fool, though rosy lips and cheeks
Within his bending sickle's compass come;
Love alters not with his brief hours and weeks,
But bears it out even to the edge of doom.
    If this be error and upon me proved,
    I never writ, nor no man ever loved.

SONNET CXXIX

Th' expense of spirit in a waste of shame
Is lust in action; and till action, lust
Is perjur'd, murd'rous, bloody, full of blame,
Savage, extreme, rude, cruel, not to trust;
Enjoy'd no sooner but despisèd straight;
Past reason hunted, and no sooner had,
Past reason hated, as a swallowed bait
On purpose laid to make the taker mad;
Mad in pursuit, and in possession so;
Had, having, and in quest to have, extreme;
A bliss in proof—and prov'd, a very woe;
Before, a joy propos'd; behind, a dream.
    All this the world well knows; yet none knows well
    To shun the heaven that leads men to this hell.

O MISTRESS MINE

O mistress mine, where are you roaming?
O, stay and hear, your true love's coming,
    That can sing both high and low:
Trip no further, pretty sweeting,
Journeys end in lovers meeting,
    Every wise man's son doth know.

What is love? 'Tis not hereafter;
Present mirth hath present laughter;
What's to come is still unsure:
In delay there lies no plenty;
Then come kiss me, sweet and twenty,
Youth's a stuff will not endure.

WHO IS SILVIA?

Who is Silvia? what is she,
That all our swains commend her?
Holy, fair, and wise is she;
The heaven such grace did lend her,
That she might admired be.

Is she kind as she is fair?
For beauty lives with kindness.
Love doth to her eyes repair
To help him of his blindness,
And, being helped, inhabits there.

Then to Silvia let us sing,
That Silvia is excelling;
She excels each mortal thing
Upon the dull earth dwelling:
To her let us garlands bring.

THOMAS CAMPION

WHEN THOU MUST HOME

When thou must home to shades of underground,
And there arrived, a new admirèd guest,
The beauteous spirits do engirt thee round,
White Iöpe, blithe Helen, and the rest,
To hear the stories of thy finished love
From that smooth tongue whose music hell can move;
Then wilt thou speak of banqueting delights,
Of masques and revels which sweet youth did make,
Of tourneys and great challenges of knights,

And all these triumphs for thy beauty's sake:
When thou hast told these honors done to thee,
Then tell, O tell, how thou didst murder me.

OF CORINNA'S SINGING

When to her lute Corinna sings,
Her voice revives the leaden strings,
And doth in highest notes appear
As any challenged echo clear;
But when she doth of mourning speak,
E'en with her sighs the strings do break.

And as her lute doth live or die,
Led by her passion, so must I:
For when of pleasure she doth sing,
My thoughts enjoy a sudden spring;
But if she doth of sorrow speak,
E'en from my heart the strings do break.

ON CAMPION'S *OF CORINNA'S SINGING* [1]

ROSEMOND TUVE

ONE WOULD expect, despite Sidney's notorious defense even of the lyric on moral grounds, that songs would be most likely to show images used simply to assist the representation of a state of mind. This ought to fit love songs at least, which permit "the many moodes and pangs of lovers, throughly to be discovered" (Puttenham, I, xxii, [1589]). Suppose one reads through Bullen's *Lyrics from Elizabethan Song-Books,* for example, with this natural expectation. One finds few poems which can have been chiefly intended to show us just how their writers felt, and few images which fit in with modern notions of the function of sensuous imagery in lyrics. Interestingly enough, the examples which I believe would come nearest to modern expectations turn out to be Campion's.

They do not come very near. The climax of "When to her Lute Corrina Sings" is the announcement "And as her lute doth live or die,/Led by her passion, so must I," but Campion leaves to us all particular elucidation of that element of dependence in a lover's state of mind—nor does the poem lead us on to any such private pursuit. He confines himself to an image whose parallelisms can evoke only the most general notion of the speaker's feelings, as

1. From *Elizabethan and Metaphysical Imagery,* by Rosemond Tuve (Chicago, 1947), pp. 14–16. Copyright, 1947, University of Chicago Press.

though he were interested rather in praise of Corinna neatly elucidated through the parallel he draws. The emotion is so little particularized that Corinna might indeed be the Elizabethan analogue of the latest Carnegie Hall concert sensation, if it were not that we know enough about the conventions of Elizabethan love poetry to deduce another state of mind in the speaker than musical enthusiasm. The images reveal a man moved, but writing what the rhetorics call "a praise" of the lady and the music, rather than examining the nature of his emotional experience. The ambiguity in "My thoughts enjoy a sudden *spring*," picking up the suggestions of "Her voice *revives* the leaden strings," the worn unparticularized image of heartstrings (its nature probably governed by the identity of the musical phrase to which lines 6 and 12 were sung), less metrically felicitous than its musical parallel, "Ev'n with her sighs the strings do break"—these do not describe; rather they invest with new interest a perceived analogy, cunningly patterned to make the most of the repeated musical pattern.

JOHN DONNE

SONG

Go and catch a falling star,
    Get with child a mandrake root,
Tell me where all past years are,
    Or who cleft the devil's foot,
Teach me to hear mermaids singing,
Or to keep off envy's stinging,
        And find
        What wind
Serves to advance an honest mind.

If thou be'st born to strange sights,
    Things invisible to see,
Ride ten thousand days and nights
    Till age snow white hairs on thee,
Thou, when thou return'st, wilt tell me
All strange wonders that befell thee,
        And swear
        No where
Lives a woman true and fair.

If thou find'st one, let me know;
    Such a pilgrimage were sweet.

Yet do not; I would not go,
Though at next door we might meet.
Though she were true when you met her,
And last till you write your letter,
Yet she
Will be
False, ere I come, to two or three.

THE INDIFFERENT

I can love both fair and brown;
Her whom abundance melts, and her whom want betrays;
Her who loves loneness best, and her who masks and plays;
Her whom the country formed, and whom the town;
Her who believes, and her who tries;
Her who still weeps with spongy eyes,
And her who is dry cork and never cries,
I can love her, and her, and you, and you;
I can love any, so she be not true.

Will no other vice content you?
Will it not serve your turn to do as did your mothers?
Or have you all old vices spent, and now would find out others?
Or doth a fear that men are true torment you?
Oh, we are not; be not you so;
Let me, and do you, twenty know.
Rob me, but bind me not, and let me go.
Must I, who came to travail thorough you,
Grow your fixed subject because you are true?

Venus heard me sigh this song,
And by love's sweetest part, variety, she swore
She heard not this till now, and that it should be so no more.
She went, examined, and returned ere long,
And said, "Alas! some two or three
Poor heretics in love there be,
Which think to 'stablish dangerous constancy.
But I have told them, 'Since you will be true,
You shall be true to them who are false to you.' "

DEATH

Death, be not proud, though some have called thee
Mighty and dreadful, for thou art not so;
For those whom thou think'st thou dost overthrow

Die not, poor Death; nor yet canst thou kill me.
From Rest and Sleep, which but thy pictures be,
Much pleasure, then from thee much more must flow;
And soonest our best men with thee do go,
Rest of their bones and souls' delivery!
Thou art slave to fate, chance, kings, and desperate men,
And dost with poison, war, and sickness dwell;
And poppy or charms can make us sleep as well
And better than thy stroke. Why swell'st thou then?
One short sleep past, we wake eternally,
And Death shall be no more: Death, thou shalt die!

THE ANNIVERSARY

All kings and all their favorites,
All glory of honors, beauties, wits,
The sun itself, which makes times as they pass,
Is elder by a year now than it was
When thou and I first one another saw;
All other things to their destruction draw;
Only our love hath no decay;
This no to-morrow hath, nor yesterday;
Running, it never runs from us away,
But truly keeps his first, last, everlasting day.

Two graves must hide thine and my corse;
If one might, death were no divorce.
Alas, as well as other princes, we,
Who prince enough in one another be,
Must leave at last in death these eyes and ears,
Oft fed with true oaths, and with sweet salt tears;
But souls where nothing dwells but love,
All other thoughts being inmates, then shall prove
This, or a love increased there above,
When bodies to their graves, souls from their graves, remove.

And then we shall be throughly blest,
But we no more than all the rest;
Here upon earth we are kings, and none but we
Can be such kings, nor of such subjects be.
Who is so safe as we, where none can do
Treason to us, except one of us two?
True and false fears let us refrain;
Let us love nobly, and live, and add again

Years and years unto years, till we attain
To write threescore; this is the second of our reign.

HYMN TO GOD, MY GOD, IN MY SICKNESS

Since I am coming to that holy room
Where with thy choir of saints for evermore
I shall be made thy music, as I come
I tune the instrument here at the door,
And what I must do then, think here before.

Whilst my physicians by their love are grown
Cosmographers, and I their map, who lie
Flat on this bed, that by them may be shown
That this is my Southwest discovery
Per fretum febris, by these straits to die,

I joy that in these straits I see my West.
For though their currents yield return to none,
What shall my West hurt me? As West and East
In all flat maps (and I am one) are one,
So death doth touch the resurrection.

Is the Pacific Sea my home? Or are
The Eastern riches? Is Jerusalem?
Anian and Magellan and Gibraltar,
All straits, and none but straits, are ways to them,
Whether where Japhet dwelt, or Cham or Shem.

We think that Paradise and Calvary,
Christ's Cross and Adam's tree, stood in one place.
Look, Lord, and find both Adams met in me;
As the first Adam's sweat surrounds my face,
May the last Adam's blood my soul embrace.

So in his purple wrapp'd, receive me, Lord,
By these his thorns give me his other crown;
And as to others' souls I preach'd thy word,
Be this my text, my sermon to mine own:
Therefore that he may raise, the Lord throws down.

ON DONNE'S *HYMN TO GOD, MY GOD, IN MY SICKNESS* [1]

HARRY M. CAMPBELL

THIS poem, which first appeared on March 23, 1631, eight days before the death of Donne, is one of his best, and one of the finest religious poems ever written.

The general plan of Donne's "Hymn to God, My God, in My Sickness" advances logically, although there is a receding of the tension after the third stanza. The poet is approaching death in the opening stanza. In the second and third stanzas he is so close that he can see his "west" and discover joyfully that it is united to the "east." In the fourth stanza he glances back at the world he is leaving but, grand as it is, finds it less attractive than the one he is entering. In the next stanza he prays that, especially in this last journey, he may be protected by the blood of Christ, the Redeemer. Finally, his prayer answered, he is ready to depart. Absolutely no rhetorical repetitions or emotional outbursts retard this simple movement from idea to idea.

The first stanza is a metaphysical conceit "of kind." The dying man, who is, of course, Donne, is approaching the "holy room" of eternity, in which, as a musical instrument, he will be made part of the celestial music of God's saints. He is tuning the instrument at the door so that it will be ready for the touch of the Master Musician. It is interesting to note that here on earth, rather anti-Calvinistically, the sufferer does his own tuning and even plans for some further individual action which seems necessary in heaven before the rest can be with God.

The second and third stanzas form another, far more effective, metaphysical conceit "of kind." The physicians "by their love are grown cosmographers," and the poet, their patient, is a map lying flat on the bed. They show him that death on this map is his "southwest discovery." The selection of this phrase, I believe, was dictated by the romantic associations attached to the fabled Northwest Passage. For Donne's audience in the seventeenth century such a phrase in this powerful context would carry all the emotional impact of the geographical Renaissance intensified by extension to the spiritual realm—a device which Whitman in the nineteenth century was to try, less successfully, in his "Passage to India." But, to continue the conceit, this passage must be through straits; and sailing in straits, as the ancients knew, too often is endangered by both Scylla and Charybdis. There is an echo, too, of the biblical "Strait is the gate, and narrow is the way which leadeth unto life, and few there be that find it." Specifically, in the conceit the straits are the fever, expressed in the Latin *per fretum febris,* which serves several purposes. In the first place, Donne, wishing to make his poem more concrete and at the same time as far as possible to avoid any suggestion of a plea for sympathy, reveals the nature of his malady as casu-

1. From *College English,* V (January, 1944), 192–196. Reprinted by permission of the author and the Editors of *College English.*

ally as if he were merely quoting learnedly from a classical author. The Latin *fretum* carries a double meaning here—both "Straits" and "raging," "swelling," "heat," "violence." Again, the use of *fretum* may serve to avoid overrepetition of the word "straits," which otherwise would appear three times in two lines.

The entire second stanza is a very involved compound dependent clause, the two main parts of which are: "Whilst my physicians . . . . are grown cosmographers" and "I [am grown] their map." The relative "who"-clause, of course, modifies "I" and, figuratively, "map." "That by them may be shown . . . . to die" may be considered a purpose clause but is more probably a result clause, modifying "are grown" and the verb understood before "map." "That this is my Southwest discovery" is a gerund clause used as a subject of "may be shown." The last line of the stanza is in apposition with "discovery."

The main clause on which the whole of the second stanza is grammatically dependent is the first line of the third: "I joy, that in these straits I see my West." "West" is, of course, death, the way to which must be the straits whose "currents yield return to none." The intensity of this passage is increased through its union with the childlike faith of "What shall my West hurt me?" The climax of the whole figure comes in an analogy dependent upon the metaphor:

As West and East
In all flat maps (and I am one) are one,
So death doth touch the resurrection.

The analogy here is rather difficult because we must remember that east and west in a flat map are one only after the map is no longer flat but has been fitted over a globe so that the east and west edges touch each other. That Donne had this in mind is indicated by the word "touch" in the last line. In this stanza, again, we have very simple language, nothing even approaching rhetorical eloquence until "Death doth touch the resurrection," which sounds grand enough to have been thundered, as it probably was, from the pulpit of St. Paul's. Thus at white heat the whole figure has been welded together—a supreme example of wit made up of tough reasonableness joined to intense emotion. Such a fusion is more difficult than that defined by Eliot because there is a greater initial divergence between tough reasonableness and deep emotion than between tough reasonableness and slight lyric grace. This poem has as much emotion as "Crossing the Bar," but wit saves Donne from Tennyson's repetitions, rhetoric, and mixed figure.

In the next stanza the poet looks back to different parts of the world he is leaving and considers their attractiveness. When Donne mentions the "Pacific Sea" as a possible home, we must remember that he and his audience in the seventeenth century probably thought with more emotion than did Keats about the great discovery of the explorer who stood silent upon a peak in Darien. They were close enough, also, to the Renaissance and the Middle Ages to consider "Eastern riches" a product of the land of heart's desire. The third alternative for a worldly home is Jerusalem, the center of a great civilization, as it was, Donne probably means, when Christ spoke of it in tears: "O Jerusalem, Jerusalem, which killest the prophets, and stonest them that are sent unto thee; how often would I have gathered thy children together, as a hen doth gather her brood under her wings, and ye would not!"

In his usual manner of presenting the abstract through the concrete, the poet mentions three particular straits through which these three parts of the world had to be approached, according to the geography of his time. The Strait of Anian (later Bering) was the route to the "Eastern riches," the Magellan Strait led to the Pacific, and the Strait of Gibraltar to Jerusalem. We must remember that "Magellan" was another name that was far more than a geographical location to the seventeenth century, and the significance of these other names had been greatly enhanced by the Renaissance explorations. But the poet wishes also to emphasize the continuity of tradition associated with these parts of the world. He does so, again specifically, by mentioning the names of the traditional ancestors of the races inhabiting these parts of the world. Cham, or Ham, was the youngest son of Noah, whose descendants founded the first great empires of Assyria and Egypt and the republics of Tyre, Sidon, and Carthage. Cham would then be associated here with the land of "Eastern riches." Shem, the eldest son of Noah, was father of the race whose holy city is still Jerusalem. Japhet, or Japheth, another son of Noah, is traditionally credited with being the father of certain races part of whom moved eastward through Asia and on to what is now the Pacific Ocean; hence the association here with the "Pacific sea." This whole stanza, I believe, indicates that neither the world of ancient traditions nor the new world of the Renaissance explorers can tempt him to hold back from his own "Southwest discovery."

The fifth stanza is a specific development of what has already been implicit in the poem—the unity and beneficence of God's plan. Adam's tree made Christ's cross necessary, and they stood in one place, because Christ, on the human side, was descended from Adam, in fulfilment of the prophecy that Eve's seed should "bruise the head" of the serpent. The meeting of both Adams in the dying man is made possible only by the last Adam's death upon the cross. But even here, when the body is almost ready to yield completely to spirit, Donne cannot get away from a strong sense of the physical (characteristic of most of his poetry): "As the first Adam's sweat surrounds my face," he says, describing the effect of the fever, "May the last Adam's blood my soul embrace."

The first line of the last stanza indicates that this prayer has been answered. Wrapped in Christ's purple, he is at last ready to be received into the presence of the Lord. "Purple" here is surely not the regal color of imperial Rome, which would not be appropriate for Christ even when he sits at the right hand of the Father, but the "purple" which is an incorrect translation of a color (probably crimson) admired by the ancient Hebrews. "In his purple wrapp'd," then, would be similar to "washed in the blood." The suffering of the sick man is analogous also to Christ's crown of thorns, after enduring which he feels that he can plead for the other crown. The poem ends in simple, homely language, justifying the ways of God to man: "Therefore that he may raise, the Lord throws down."

Donne in this poem uses five-line stanzas of iambic pentameter, rhyming a b a b b. The rhymes are sometimes rather loose, as, for example, "lie" and "discovery." Trochees are frequently, and dactyls less often, substituted for iambs—trochees like "Whilst my" or "Is the"; dactyls like the last three syllables of "Cosmographers" or of "Jerusalem." Runover lines allow the pauses to fit the thought rather than the meter. These runover lines and the metrical variations within the iambic-pentameter pattern give the effect of a combination of unity with variety—one aspect (we have already discussed others) of the "reconcilement of discordant qualities," which Coleridge demanded of a poem.

Still another aspect of this *discordia concors* appears in the judicious mingling of simple, homely, short words like "What shall my West hurt me?" with long, sonorous words like "Cosmographers," "discovery," "Jerusalem," "evermore," and "resurrection," which in their context add an element of ecclesiastical dignity. More specifically antithetical collocation of words appears in "West and East," "Paradise and Calvary," "Christ's cross and Adam's tree," "first Adam" and "last Adam," "thorns" and "crown."

The serenity of Donne's "Hymn" has a different quality from that of other poems on the same subject. The conclusion to "Thanatopsis," for example, attains a certain kind of serenity, and yet Bryant's rhetoric seems almost to shout at us that we should die in a quiet way. Tennyson's limitations we have mentioned. Shakespeare, in a still different way, stresses the horrible aspects of "dusty death" or of flight "from this vile world with vilest worms to dwell." Even the followers of Donne wear the metaphysical shroud with a difference. Bishop King strikes the note of terror in his famous conceit:

> But hark! my pulse like a soft drum
> Beats my approach, tells thee I come.

Marvell must dwell on his mistress' death, when "worms shall try that long preserved virginity."

Donne, in his valedictory poems at least, certainly has a different emphasis. In view of these poems we can well believe that the picture of the saintly Donne given by Walton is really not inaccurate for one side of this strange poet-preacher—the side that became more and more uppermost as he grew older. Mr. Williamson says that Donne's having his picture painted while he wore his shroud in his last illness indicates morbidity. Perhaps so—but Mr. Williamson ought to make a distinction between this kind of morbidity and that which during the greater part of his life kept Donne from "allaying the fever of the bone." Such a fever has in this poem (written at the same time the shroud picture was painted) given way to a joyful contemplation of the central theme of Christian faith: that "death doth touch the resurrection." Such serenity, reached artistically through a combination of religious intensity with metaphysical wit, makes this one of the finest religious poems ever written.

BEN JONSON

SIMPLEX MUNDITIIS[1]

Still to be neat, still to be drest,
As you were going to a feast;
Still to be powdered, still perfumed:
Lady, it is to be presumed,
Though art's hid causes are not found,
All is not sweet, all is not sound.
Give me a look, give me a face
That makes simplicity a grace;
Robes loosely flowing, hair as free:
Such sweet neglect more taketh me
Than all th' adulteries of art;
They strike mine eyes, but not my heart.

SLOW, SLOW, FRESH FOUNT

Slow, slow, fresh fount, keep time with my salt tears;
Yet slower yet, oh faintly, gentle springs;
List to the heavy part the music bears,
Woe weeps out her division when she sings.
Droop herbs and flowers,
Fall grief in showers;
Our beauties are not ours;
Oh, I could still,
Like melting snow upon some craggy hill,
Drop, drop, drop, drop,
Since nature's pride is now a withered daffodil.

1. The title, from Horace, Book I, Ode 5, means "in simple elegance."

ROBERT HERRICK

DELIGHT IN DISORDER

A sweet disorder in the dress
Kindles in clothes a wantonness;
A lawn about the shoulders thrown
Into a fine distraction,
An erring lace, which here and there
Enthralls the crimson stomacher,
A cuff neglectful, and thereby
Ribands to flow confusedly,
A winning wave, deserving note,
In the tempestuous petticoat,
A careless shoe-string, in whose tie
I see a wild civility,
Do more bewitch me than when art
Is too precise in every part.

UPON JULIA'S CLOTHES

Whenas in silks my Julia goes,
Then, then (methinks) how sweetly flows
The liquefaction of her clothes.
Next, when I cast mine eyes and see
That brave vibration each way free,
O how that glittering taketh me!

TO THE VIRGINS, TO MAKE MUCH OF TIME

Gather ye rose-buds while ye may,
    Old Time is still a-flying:
And this same flower that smiles today,
    Tomorrow will be dying.

The glorious lamp of heaven, the Sun,
    The higher he's a-getting
The sooner will his race be run,
    And nearer he's to setting.

That age is best which is the first,
    When youth and blood are warmer;
But being spent, the worse, and worst
    Times still succeed the former.

Then be not coy, but use your time,
And while ye may, go marry;
For having lost but once your prime,
You may for ever tarry.

GEORGE HERBERT

THE PULLEY

When God at first made man,
Having a glass of blessings standing by,
Let us, said he, pour on him all we can.
Let the world's riches, which dispersèd lie,
Contract into a span.

So strength first made a way,
Then beauty flowed, then wisdom, honor, pleasure.
When almost all was out, God made a stay,
Perceiving that alone of all his treasure
Rest in the bottom lay.

For if I should, said he,
Bestow this jewel also on my creature,
He would adore my gifts instead of me,
And rest in nature, not the God of nature;
So both should losers be.

Yet let him keep the rest,
But keep them with repining restlessness.
Let him be rich and weary, that at least,
If goodness lead him not, yet weariness
May toss him to my breast.

THE COLLAR

I struck the board, and cried, "No more; I will abroad!
What! shall I ever sigh and pine?
My lines and life are free; free as the road,
Loose as the wind, as large as store.
Shall I be still in suit?
Have I no harvest but a thorn

To let me blood, and not restore
What I have lost with cordial fruit?
Sure there was wine
Before my sighs did dry it; there was corn
Before my tears did drown it.
Is the year only lost to me?
Have I no bays to crown it,
No flowers, no garlands gay? all blasted,
All wasted?
Not so, my heart, but there is fruit,
And thou hast hands.
Recover all thy sigh-blown age
On double pleasures; leave thy cold dispute
Of what is fit and not; forsake thy cage,
Thy rope of sands,
Which petty thoughts have made; and made to thee
Good cable, to enforce and draw,
And be thy law,
While thou didst wink and wouldst not see.
Away! take heed!
I will abroad.
Call in thy death's-head there, tie up thy fears.
He that forbears
To suit and serve his need
Deserves his load."
But as I raved, and grew more fierce and wild
At every word,
Methought I heard one calling, "Child";
And I replied, "My Lord."

ON HERBERT'S *THE COLLAR* [1]

C. DAY LEWIS

This is not to say that poems have never been composed on lines of imagery laid down in advance. George Herbert surely did it time and again; and his great poem, *The Collar,* shows how successful this method may be. It is an example of the strictly functional use of images; their use, that is, to point a theme already defined. The central image, the spiritual rope by which the Christian is tied to his God, would represent an idea so familiar to Herbert's contemporaries that the boldest exploration of it could hardly take them far

1. From *The Poetic Image,* by C. Day Lewis (New York, 1947), pp. 80–81. Reprinted by permission of Oxford University Press, Inc.

out of their depth. At first Herbert subtly hints at the tie, by seeming to deny its existence:

I struck the board, and cried, "No more; I will abroad.
What! shall I ever sigh and pine?
My lines and life are free: free as the road
  Loose as the wind, as large as store.
      Shall I be still in suit?

After that delicate hint, a variation of the theme appears. The Tempter's voice within continues,

  Have I no harvest but a thorn
  To let me blood, and not restore
What I have lost with cordial fruit?
      Sure there was wine
  Before my sighs did dry it: there was corn
      Before my tears did drown it.

The images are still conventional, symbols only: but notice how cleverly the Tempter has used these Christian symbols, thorn and blood, bread and wine, for his own nefarious purpose. Next, the full theme appears: but the rope between Christ and Christian is diabolically contorted into

. . . leave thy cold dispute
Of what is fit, and not; forsake thy cage,
      Thy rope of sands,
Which petty thoughts have made, and made to thee
  Good cable, to enforce and draw
      And be thy law,
  While thou did'st wink and would'st not see.

Then, with a master-stroke of cynicism, the Tempter gives one more twist to the rope:

Call in thy death's head there: tie up thy fears.

But Christ has the last word: and it is consonant with the remarkable dialectic skill and dramatic delicacy of the poem that this last word, for all the still, small voice in which it is spoken, should so strike us as a climax noble, thrilling, unanswerable:

But as I raved and grew more fierce and wild
      At every word,
  Methought I heard one calling, "Child";
      And I replied, "My Lord."

THOMAS CAREW

A SONG

Ask me no more where Jove bestows,
When June is past, the fading rose;
For in your beauty's orient deep
These flowers, as in their causes, sleep.

Ask me no more whither doth stray
The golden atoms of the day;
For in pure love heaven did prepare
Those powders to enrich your hair.

Ask me no more whither doth haste
The nightingale when May is past;
For in your sweet dividing throat
She winters, and keeps warm her note.

Ask me no more where those stars light
That downwards fall in dead of night;
For in your eyes they sit, and there
Fixëd become as in their sphere.

Ask me no more if east or west
The phœnix builds her spicy nest;
For unto you at last she flies,
And in your fragrant bosom dies.

EDMUND WALLER

ON A GIRDLE

That which her slender waist confined
Shall now my joyful temples bind;
No monarch but would give his crown
His arms might do what this has done.

It was my heaven's extremest sphere,
The pale which held that lovely deer.
My joy, my grief, my hope, my love,
Did all within this circle move!

A narrow compass, and yet there
Dwelt all that's good and all that's fair;
Give me but what this riband bound,
Take all the rest the sun goes round.

GO, LOVELY ROSE

Go, lovely rose!
Tell her that wastes her time and me,
That now she knows,
When I resemble her to thee,
How sweet and fair she seems to be.

Tell her that's young,
And shuns to have her graces spied,
That hadst thou sprung
In deserts, where no men abide,
Thou must have uncommended died.

Small is the worth
Of beauty from the light retired;
Bid her come forth,
Suffer herself to be desired,
And not blush so to be admired.

Then die! that she
The common fate of all things rare
May read in thee;
How small a part of time they share
That are so wondrous sweet and fair!

JOHN MILTON

LYCIDAS

In This Monody the Author Bewails a Learned Friend, Unfortunately Drowned in His Passage from Chester on the Irish Seas, 1637; and, by Occasion, Foretells the Ruin of Our Corrupted Clergy, Then in Their Height.

Yet once more, O ye laurels, and once more,
Ye myrtles brown, with ivy never sere,
I come to pluck your berries harsh and crude,

And with forced fingers rude
Shatter your leaves before the mellowing year.
Bitter constraint, and sad occasion dear
Compels me to disturb your season due;
For Lycidas is dead, dead ere his prime,
Young Lycidas, and hath not left his peer.
Who would not sing for Lycidas? he well knew
Himself to sing, and build the lofty rhyme.
He must not float upon his watery bier
Unwept, and welter to the parching wind,
Without the meed of some melodious tear.
　Begin, then, Sisters of the sacred well
That from beneath the seat of Jove doth spring;
Begin, and somewhat loudly sweep the string.
Hence with denial vain and coy excuse:
So may some gentle Muse
With lucky words favour my destined urn,
And as he passes turn,
And bid fair peace be to my sable shroud!
For we were nursed upon the self-same hill,
Fed the same flock, by fountain, shade, and rill.
　Together both, ere the high lawns appeared
Under the opening eyelids of the Morn,
We drove a-field, and both together heard
What time the gray-fly winds her sultry horn,
Battening our flocks with the fresh dews of night,
Oft till the star that rose, at evening, bright
Toward heaven's descent had sloped his westering wheel.
Meanwhile the rural ditties were not mute;
Tempered to the oaten flute,
Rough Satyrs danced, and Fauns with cloven heel
From the glad sound would not be absent long;
And old Damoetas loved to hear our song.
　But, oh! the heavy change, now thou art gone,
Now thou art gone and never must return!
Thee, Shepherd, thee the woods and desert caves,
With wild thyme and the gadding vine o'ergrown,
And all their echoes, mourn.
The willows, and the hazel copses green,
Shall now no more be seen
Fanning their joyous leaves to thy soft lays.
As killing as the canker to the rose,
Or taint-worm to the weanling herds that graze,
Or frost to flowers, that their gay wardrobe wear,

When first the white-thorn blows;
Such, Lycidas, thy loss to shepherd's ear.
    Where were ye, Nymphs, when the remorseless deep
Closed o'er the head of your loved Lycidas?
For neither were ye playing on the steep
Where your old bards, the famous Druids, lie,
Nor on the shaggy top of Mona high,
Nor yet where Deva spreads her wizard stream.
Ay me! I fondly dream
"Had ye been there"—for what could that have done?
What could the Muse herself that Orpheus bore,
Whom universal nature did lament,
When, by the rout that made the hideous roar,
His gory visage down the stream was sent,
Down the swift Hebrus to the Lesbian shore?
    Alas! what boots it with uncessant care
To tend the homely, slighted, shepherd's trade,
And strictly meditate the thankless Muse?
Were it not better done, as others use,
To sport with Amaryllis in the shade,
Or with the tangles of Neaera's hair?
Fame is the spur that the clear spirit doth raise
(That last infirmity of noble mind)
To scorn delights, and live laborious days;
But the fair guerdon when we hope to find,
And think to burst out into sudden blaze,
Comes the blind Fury with the abhorrèd shears,
And slits the thin-spun life. "But not the praise,"
Phoebus replied, and touched my trembling ears:
"Fame is no plant that grows on mortal soil,
Nor in the glistering foil
Set off to the world, nor in broad rumour lies,
But lives and spreads aloft by those pure eyes,
And perfect witness of all-judging Jove;
As he pronounces lastly on each deed,
Of so much fame in heaven expect thy meed."
    O fountain Arethuse, and thou honoured flood,
Smooth-sliding Mincius, crowned with vocal reeds,
That strain I heard was of a higher mood.
But now my oat proceeds,
And listens to the Herald of the Sea
That came in Neptune's plea.
He asked the waves, and asked the felon winds,
What hard mishap hath doomed this gentle swain?

And questioned every gust of rugged wings
That blows from off each beakèd promontory.
They knew not of his story;
And sage Hippotades their answer brings;
That not a blast was from his dungeon strayed,
The air was calm, and on the level brine
Sleek Panope with all her sisters played.
It was that fatal and perfidious bark,
Built in the eclipse, and rigged with curses dark,
That sunk so low that sacred head of thine.
    Next, Camus, reverend sire, went footing slow,
His mantle hairy, and his bonnet sedge,
Inwrought with figures dim, and on the edge
Like to that sanguine flower inscribed with woe.
"Ah! who hath reft," quoth he, "my dearest pledge?"
Last came, and last did go,
The Pilot of the Galilean Lake;
Two massy keys he bore of metals twain
(The golden opes, the iron shuts amain).
He shook his mitred locks, and stern bespake:—
"How well could I have spared for thee, young swain,
Enow of such as, for their bellies' sake,
Creep, and intrude, and climb into the fold!
Of other care they little reckoning make
Than how to scramble at the shearers' feast,
And shove away the worthy bidden guest.
Blind mouths! that scarce themselves know how to hold
A sheep-hook, or have learnt aught else the least
That to the faithful herdman's art belongs!
What recks it them? What need they? They are sped;
And, when they list, their lean and flashy songs
Grate on their scrannel pipes of wretched straw;
The hungry sheep look up, and are not fed,
But, swoln with wind and the rank mist they draw,
Rot inwardly, and foul contagion spread;
Besides what the grim wolf with privy paw
Daily devours apace, and nothing said.
But that two-handed engine at the door
Stands ready to smite once, and smite no more."
    Return, Alpheus; the dread voice is past
That shrunk thy streams; return, Sicilian Muse,
And call the vales, and bid them hither cast
Their bells and flowerets of a thousand hues.
Ye valleys low, where the mild whispers use

Of shades, and wanton winds, and gushing brooks,
On whose fresh lap the swart star sparely looks,
Throw hither all your quaint enamelled eyes,
That on the green turf suck the honeyed showers,
And purple all the ground with vernal flowers.
Bring the rathe primrose that forsaken dies,
The tufted crow-toe, and pale jessamine,
The white pink, and the pansy freaked with jet,
The glowing violet,
The musk rose, and the well-attired woodbine,
With cowslips wan that hang the pensive head,
And every flower that sad embroidery wears;
Bid amaranthus all his beauty shed,
And daffadillies fill their cups with tears,
To strew the laureate hearse where Lycid lies.
For so, to interpose a little ease,
Let our frail thoughts dally with false surmise.
Ay me! whilst thee the shores and sounding seas
Wash far away, where'er thy bones are hurled;
Whether beyond the stormy Hebrides,
Where thou perhaps under the whelming tide
Visit'st the bottom of the monstrous world;
Or whether thou, to our moist vows denied,
Sleep'st by the fable of Bellerus old,
Where the great Vision of the guarded mount
Looks toward Namancos and Bayona's hold.
Look homeward, Angel, now, and melt with ruth:
And, O ye dolphins, waft the hapless youth.
Weep no more, woeful shepherds, weep no more,
For Lycidas, your sorrow, is not dead,
Sunk though he be beneath the watery floor.
So sinks the day-star in the ocean bed,
And yet anon repairs his drooping head,
And tricks his beams, and with new-spangled ore
Flames in the forehead of the morning sky:
So Lycidas sunk low, but mounted high,
Through the dear might of Him that walked the waves,
Where, other groves and other streams along,
With nectar pure his oozy locks he laves,
And hears the unexpressive nuptial song,
In the blest kingdoms meek of joy and love.
There entertain him all the Saints above,
In solemn troops, and sweet societies,
That sing, and singing in their glory move,

And wipe the tears for ever from his eyes.
Now, Lycidas, the shepherds weep no more;
Henceforth thou art the Genius of the shore,
In thy large recompense, and shalt be good
To all that wander in that perilous flood.
    Thus sang the uncouth swain to the oaks and rills,
While the still morn went out with sandals grey:
He touched the tender stops of various quills,
With eager thought warbling his Doric lay:
And now the sun had stretched out all the hills,
And now was dropt into the western bay;
At last he rose, and twitched his mantle blue:
To-morrow to fresh woods, and pastures new.

ON MILTON'S *LYCIDAS* [1]

WAYNE SHUMAKER

More insistently, perhaps, than any other poem in English, *Lycidas* raises the purely aesthetic problem of how the emotions may be stirred by lines which at first are much less than perspicuous to the intellect and even after many readings remain obscure at two or three points. Johnson's attack to one side, *Lycidas* has received all but universal praise, couched often in language so high-pitched that it absorbs easily adjectives like "exquisite," "thrilling," "tremendous," and "supreme." Why is the emotional impact so powerful? A reply must be sought (I think) in the affective connotations of words, phrases, and images in formal combination; and it is worth finding because if in one of its aspects literature is history, in another, and not unimportant, aspect it is immediate experience.

In the present paper I shall attempt to make only a small contribution to the complete explanation. I propose, specifically, to extract two of a large number of formal strands and discuss them as musical themes which blend into a total emotional harmony both massive enough and piercing enough to be overpowering.

I must begin by discussing the place of the two strands in the large structure. Three movements are enclosed within a pastoral introduction and conclusion, each movement in turn depending to some extent on pastoral machinery for its organization. I cannot improve on a summary given by Arthur Barker.

> The first movement laments Lycidas the poet-shepherd; its problem, the possible frustration of disciplined poetic ambition by early death, is resolved by the assurance, "Of so much fame in heaven expect thy meed." The second laments Lycidas

1. *PMLA*, LXVI (June, 1951), 485–494. Reprinted with permission of the author and the Modern Language Association of America.

as priest-shepherd; its problem, the frustration of a sincere shepherd in a corrupt church, is resolved by St. Peter's reference to the "two-handed engine" of divine retribution. The third concludes with the apotheosis, a convention introduced by Virgil in *Eclogue* V but significantly handled by Milton. He sees the poet-priest-shepherd worshipping the Lamb with those saints "in solemn troops" who sing the "unexpressive nuptial song" of the fourteenth chapter of *Revelation*. The apotheosis thus not only provides the final reassurance but unites the themes of the preceding movements in the ultimate reward of the true poet-priest.

Barker is almost certainly right in assigning a large part of the poem's impressiveness to the "three successive and perfectly controlled crescendos," culminating in a second triumphal resolution of tensions already half-released in their appropriate sections. The two strands with which I am presently concerned—thematic strands, as will appear shortly—help prepare in the first and second movements for the final resolution in the third.

The third movement begins with the celebrated catalogue of flowers. One function of this passage is to modulate between St. Peter's angry speech about the corruption of the English Church and the exultant description of Edward King's reception into Paradise. The catalogue interposes a little ease, as Milton himself says, which is to lead ultimately into the fuller and less deceptive comfort accessible through the realization that in its largest implications the drowning has not been tragic. It cannot have been tragic, for earthly life is continuous with eternal, in which temporal misfortunes are recompensed. But the image of flowers banking a drowned man's hearse cannot develop immediately into ecstatic and thrilling joy. The notion is too pretty-pretty, too conventionally poetic to carry a heavy emotional weight. Moreover, in this context the thought of floral offerings is consciously and deliberately delusive. Accordingly the next mood is one of profound spiritual depression; and this, by a natural emotional rhythm, illustrated on the abnormal level by the familiar manic-depressive pattern, passes into the final rapture. The three parts of the final movement are thus organically related, the first being emotionally causal to the second, and the second, and through it the first, emotionally causal to the third. The structure is not logically but emotionally inductive. Much of the value of the first two of the three parts lies in their power to entail the third. The first two parts, however, in their turn have been implied by everything that has gone before. The catalogue of flowers that "sad embroidery" wear picks up and utilizes many preceding references to a blight that has been placed on vegetative nature by King's death, and the description of the sounding seas which hurl his body to and fro is the poetically inevitable culmination of many earlier references to water.

I do not know how many readers have noticed the remarkable consistency with which Milton has made every mention of vegetation in the first 132 lines of the elegy suggest a sympathetic frustration in nature to balance the human frustrations about which the poem is built. The technique goes far beyond the use of simple pathetic fallacies. It extends to descriptions of objects which seem not to be conscious of any involvement in the death of the poet-priest-shepherd.

The theme appears at the very beginning and is resumed several times, usually quite briefly and often glancingly, before the climactic enumeration of mournful flowers. The laurels and myrtles invoked in lines 1–5 have berries which are *harsh* and *crude*. The leaves of both laurels and myrtles are to be *shattered* by Milton's singing before they have an opportunity to reach mature exuberance ("before the mellowing year"). The emphasis now shifts to other matters; but when in the fourth verse-paragraph vegetation again comes momentarily into focus, the connotations are similarly depressing. The woods and caves that lament the accident are overgrown with *wild* thyme and *gadding* vines, the adjectives implying, perhaps not quite rationally, a desperate and uncontrolled abandon to grief. The willows and hazel copses have ceased to react with joyous activity to pastoral songs; their leaves, having left off their "fanning," presumably droop in dejection. The rose is subject to canker; early flowers (Lycidas was a young man) succumb to frost. The tree-covered island of Mona mentioned a few lines later is not verdant but *shaggy*. The sixth paragraph offers a slight touch of relief: the *shade* in which the poet contemplates sporting with Amaryllis is thought of as a cool retreat. But Camus, when he appears, is described as wearing a bonnet of inelegant sedge variegated along the borders by figures which resemble "that sanguine flower inscrib'd with woe," and no further relief is offered. The regularity with which natural growth is made to carry lugubrious associations in the introduction and first two movements is remarkable. So pervasive is the blight that as early as line 78, when Phoebus wishes to praise true fame, he is able to do so effectively by simply dissociating it from plants that grow on mortal soil.

All this would seem easily accountable if it were not for the fact that paragraph three recalls the happier times before King's death. Here one might expect attention to be diverted from gloom sufficiently to permit an avowal that for man's gayer hours (as Bryant said) nature has a voice of gladness and a smile and eloquence of beauty. The avowal is there, but it is phrased in terms of sunlight, the sounds of insects, stars, and other non-botanical phenomena. The only exception is in the mention of "high Lawns" in the first line of the description. For the rest, there is a studious avoidance of precisely those faces of nature which one would imagine to be most important to a shepherd. The comparative lightness of the paragraph depends not at all on images of energetic or brilliant growth. The opening eyelids of the morn carry the suggestion of an awakening, a stirring in preparation for the day's chores; the winding of the grayfly's sultry horn is associated with a genially warm air; the brightness of the evening star implies fine weather; the dancing of the satyrs and fauns is indicative of high spirits. The green of the pasturage, however, is hinted only by the single word "lawns," and nothing whatever is said at this point about shade trees or flowers. The flocks, which anywhere else would eat grass, in this setting batten themselves on "the fresh dews of night." The association of plants with depression of the spirit is not compromised.

Against this background the catalogue of flowers takes on strong emotional meaning. It resumes and develops an established theme, which, however, is now partly inverted. Although the emotional connotations set up earlier are not exactly denied, they are subdued to provide a poignant contrast to the ease the poet has announced himself to be seeking. The primrose, we are reminded, dies forsaken; the cowslips hang their pensive heads; the daffodils fill their cups with tears. The floral offerings are in fact meant to include "every flower that sad embroidery wears." On the other hand, the coloring is no longer somber. The myrtles addressed in line 2 were *brown*, and throughout the first two of the three movements the visual imagery has been prevailingly dull. The whiteness of the thorn which blows in early spring and the redness of the sanguine flower have only deepened the general murkiness by contrast. Now, suddenly, we are asked to imagine bells and flowerets *of a thousand hues*. Certain colors are specified—the *purple* of enameled eyes, the *green* of the turf, the *paleness* of the jasmine, the *whiteness* of the pink, the *jet* of the pansy, the glowing *violet*—and others are evoked by the names of flowers like the daffodil, which can hardly be visualized in more than one way. The result is that the grief, while remaining grief, is lifted and brightened. For the moment it is made tolerable by association with beautiful objects. At the same time the reader feels relief of another kind. Up to the present he has been under a constraint to imagine nature in only one of its moods; he has been forced, as it were, to consent to a perversion of what he knows to be the full truth. His conscious mind, which is aware of Milton's elegiac purpose, has assented to the fiction that a human death has lessened the objective beauty of woods and fields. But there is a part of his mind which is not controlled by his will, and this part has perhaps been, hardly perceptibly, uncomfortable, like the part of a father's mind which feels guilty about the answers he has given to his child's questions about the wind and the moon. The injustice is now partly rectified. In the catalogue of flowers Milton says not only, "There is brilliance as well as dullness in nature," but also, more indirectly, "The flowers named here are those poetically associated with sadness. I have made a selection to suit my elegiac theme." He is not, then, unhinged by his grief. He does not really distort. The largeness of his mind permits him to acknowledge a partiality in his descriptions; and his reward is the conquest of a tiny but not wholly insignificant scruple.

The second theme is somewhat less peripheral than the first, though it also lies to one side of the poem's exact center. The description of King's body as it is washed far away by the sounding seas, whether northward, toward or beyond the Hebrides, or southward, toward Cornwall, has been even more elaborately prepared for in advance. The first visual image of the dead poet-priest-shepherd is that of a corpse rocked to and fro on ocean swells swept by a dry wind. From the beginning, accordingly, the sea is in the background of the reader's consciousness. Images of water have considerably greater prominence than images of trees and plants and have frequently been noticed by critics. Sometimes the water moves forward into clear focus; again it flashes rapidly across the margin of attention, half-unnoticed and significant chiefly because the glimpses sustain a theme that must not be allowed to lose continuity.

Some of the references to water carry only a very indirect reminder of the sea, and, with it, the manner of King's death. For example, the invocation in the second paragraph calls up the image of a well: "Begin then, Sisters of the sacred well, / That from beneath the seat of *Jove* doth spring." The well is not, however, quiescent; the word "spring" suggests movement, and the movement of water, though now on a small scale, both carries on the visual motif and, by reducing the image's physical and emotional dimensions, modulates into the calmer passage which follows. A somewhat analogous technique is used at five other points: in the mention of Deva's wizard stream, in the apostrophe to the Fountain Arethuse and smooth-sliding Mincius, in the personification of the River Cam, in the description of St. Peter as pilot of the Galilean lake, and in the reassurance addressed to the River Alpheus. Each of these glancing evocations of water helps keep the theme alive by giving the reader's memory of it a little fillip. In a similar way the fountain, the three rivers, and the Sea of Galilee, by faintly echoing the water motif, prevent the reader from ever quite losing sight of the fact that King died by drowning.

I should like to dwell for a moment on a representative passage, that which contains—and surrounds—the laments of the University and the Church. At the beginning of the paragraph the University is represented, appropriately enough, by the personified figure of the leisurely, rush-lined Cam. I should not like to pretend that every reader has a momentary glimpse of a river sliding among reeds when he comes to these lines; nevertheless the complete dissociation of the river from the figure would be difficult. St. Peter next appears as the "Pilot of the *Galilean* lake," the description providing an ironic contrast to the reader's knowledge that King was *not* rescued from the sea. After this introduction comes a thunderous attack on the state of the English Church; but the attack has no sooner ended in the climactic prediction of the two-handed engine than the water theme is again stated: "Return *Alpheus,* the dread voice is past, / That shrunk thy streams." The transition could hardly be more apt. The hint of timidity in the stream lowers the key from indignation at the same time the words "dread voice" carry the last reverberations of anger. Moreover, the ideas of water and fright have been associated before and will be associated again. The relationship in the present passage is curious, however, for now it is the water that is frightened by the man. The effect is somewhat like that of an inverted musical phrase, which remains recognizable despite the fact that it has been turned upside down.

The address to the Fountain Arethuse and smooth-sliding Mincius performs a somewhat analogous function a little earlier. It too uses water imagery to reassert the pastoral medium just when the need for a reassertion is felt. The mention of Deva's wizard stream is incidental to the fixing of a geographical location, but the motor quality of the verb "spread" adds vividness by making the movement seem the result of an act of will. The Dee spreads its waters as a housewife might spread a tablecloth or a bird its wings.

We have seen, then, that there are six muted statements of the water theme besides the more resonant ones to be noted presently. The sacred well, the River Cam, the Galilean lake, the River Alpheus, the Fountain Areuthuse and smooth-sliding Mincius (I count them as one because they occur in such close juxtaposition), and the River Dee prevent the Irish Sea from ever quite slipping out of the reader's consciousness. Milton's awareness of the manner in which King died is not wholly suppressed even in parts of the elegy in which he is mainly occupied in talking about something else. Formally, the six passages contribute to a massive harmony without themselves being very distinctly heard. It will be approximately accurate to say that their structural function is similar to that of the middle notes of triads struck on the piano. Only the analytic listener pays careful heed to them, but anyone would feel a slight decrease of tonal richness if they were omitted.

The more resonant statements of the theme begin in the description of Lycidas on his watery bier and continue at lines 50, 62, 89, and 154. At each of these points the drowning is specifically mentioned or water is in some other way made to appear menacing. There are also two later passages, at lines 167 and 183, which perform for the water theme the function performed for the flower theme by the catalogue.

The first statement, already once referred to, has evoked the image of a body rocking helplessly on ocean swells. The second is less grisly but in a way even more distressing, for it recreates briefly the exact instant at which a human life succumbed to an indifferent natural force: "Where were ye Nymphs when the remorseless deep / Clos'd o'er the head of your lov'd *Lycidas?*" The visual image is that of a face sinking for the last time beneath water, the motor image that of a rejoining of fluid edges; and there is perhaps induced also a slight muscular strain, as of an effort to fight one's way upward toward air. To describe small things by large, the effect is now rather that of fright than of nausea. (I hope the reader will understand that the only way in which I can make some of my points at all is by overstating them.)

The third statement picks up the nausea and drops the fright—for I should suppose no one to feel personal danger in the sight of a severed and bleeding head being tumbled down a precipitous river bed by the current. The head is that of Orpheus, who, like Lycidas, was a singer.

> by the rout that made the hideous roar,
> His goary visage down the stream was sent,
> Down the swift *Hebrus* to the *Lesbian* shore.

The cold passivity of the second image has been replaced by the movement of the first; but there are in addition angry sound and the blood that is so frequently an accompaniment of violence. The association of water and death, however, has remained constant.

The same association is present in the fourth statement, which recurs to the passivity of the second image and develops it in considerable detail. The herald of the sea

> ask'd the Waves, and ask'd the Fellon winds,
> What hard mishap hath doom'd this gentle swain? . . .
> And sage *Hippotades* their answer brings,
> That not a blast was from his dungeon stray'd,
> The Ayr was calm, and on the level brine,
> Sleek *Panope* with all her sisters play'd.

The drowning and its circumstances are again set in contrast; death is described as having occurred in a peaceful setting. On the other hand, the feeling appropriate to this statement is neither fright nor nausea but perplexity. Within limits, variations in the emotional demands made on the reader increase the affective pull by activating dormant parts of the psyche. At the same time continuity is provided by the maintenance of the association of water and death.

Up to this point the Irish Sea has been described once as weltering and twice—if I do not misread the connotations of lines 50–51—as tranquil. The tranquillity has been insisted on at greater length than the movement and is probably more vividly present in the reader's imagination. Yet the possibility of movement in the Sea has been strongly asserted by the verb "welter" and implied by the swift motion of the Hebrus. In the longest, and climactic, development of the water theme the vastness of the Sea is brought together with the swiftness of the river to produce an impression of great violence.

> Ay me! Whilst thee the shores, and sounding Seas
> Wash far away, where ere thy bones are hurl'd,
> Whether beyond the stormy *Hebrides*,
> Where thou perhaps under the whelming tide
> Visit'st the bottom of the monstrous world . . .

The Irish Sea has become a resistless, unsympathetic force which deals with the body of the poet-priest-shepherd exactly as the Hebrus has dealt with the severed head of Orpheus, tossing it about with the indifference with which it would toss a plank broken from the hull of the wrecked ship. The effect is overwhelming (the word is suggested by the passage), and more than one critic has testified that for him this is the most powerful part of the elegy.

Relief, however, is at hand, for the depressing thought of a tossed and ruined body generates immediately, by contrast, that of a redeemed and joyous soul. The flower and water themes, in direct juxtaposition, thus lead directly into the apotheosis, in which all the tensions are finally resolved. Little more needs to be done with the flower theme. It has served its purpose and will appear only once more, disguised almost beyond recognition, in the last line of all: "To-morrow to fresh Woods, and Pastures new." The water theme, on the other hand, has carried a much heavier emotional weight and cannot be so easily dropped. Moreover, growing nature has already been adequately purged of blight, whereas the sea continues to hold a menace. It too must be purified. The mourners must be reconciled to the physical world as well as to the turnings of human destiny.

Accordingly the transition from despair to hope is made by images drawn from the very water that we have just been led to believe coldly and impersonally fearful:

So sinks the day-star in the Ocean bed,
And yet anon repairs his drooping head,
And tricks his beams, and with new spangled Ore,
Flames in the forehead of the morning sky:
So *Lycidas* sunk low, but mounted high,
Through the dear might of him that walk'd the waves . . .

The sun is not harmed by the sea. Christ walked on its waves. Indeed, the very man who was killed by water on earth can seek out its Heavenly equivalent as a comfort: "other groves, and other streams along, / With *Nectar* pure his oozy Lock's he laves." Even this is not all. The element *water* has been purified, but the Irish Sea must be especially cleared of threat. Hence we are told that travelers on the Sea will gain composure by recalling the "large recompense" which we now realize to have followed the brief torment of drowning.

Now *Lycidas* the Shepherds weep no more;
Hence forth thou art the Genius of the shore,
In thy large recompense, and shalt be good
To all that wander in that perilous flood.

For myself—I do not pretend to speak for others—there is a slight dissatisfaction in the reading of these lines. If the source of composure is to be an understanding of the total meaning of King's death, the word *all* provokes resistance. Calmness of mind will be accessible only to voyagers who, having known King, have been led by reflections on his fate to an acceptance of death similar to that expressed in the poem. If, on the other hand, we are to imagine King's spirit as extending physical protection to voyagers on the Sea, the implication that death is to be avoided as significantly bad contradicts the whole drift and meaning of the elegy. The structural function of the passage, however, is clear. A *formal* means of escape from the last tension has been provided. Not only is the poet-priest-shepherd living after all; the mourners can again face nature courageously and take delight in its external beauty. Everything is as it should be, and daily activities can be taken up at the point where they were dropped.

The two minor themes, then, come into prominence at various places in the first and second movements and at other places are hinted in ways that have been described. In the third movement they are developed side by side in preparation for the apotheosis, in which sorrow is finally transcended and the mind restored to peace. There is a difference, however, both in their intrinsic importance and in their usefulness in preparing for the resolution. The flower theme shows a temporary effect of profound grief, the water theme is intimately related to the cause. The distortion of vision must wear off before adjustment to the irremedial cause becomes possible; hence it is altogether proper that the former of the two themes should be resolved a little in advance of the latter. Yet each has its function, and the emotional impact would be weakened if either were omitted from the third movement. The first paragraph of the final movement, unaccounted for by Barker's explanation of the structure, is thus only less necessary than the apotheosis. It fits not only into a design but also into an emotional pattern; not only into a form but also into a response.

ON HIS BEING ARRIVED TO THE AGE OF TWENTY-THREE

How soon hath Time, the subtle thief of youth,
Stolen on his wing my three and twentieth year!
My hasting days fly on with full career,
But my late spring no bud or blossom shew'th.
Perhaps my semblance might deceive the truth,
That I to manhood am arrived so near,
And inward ripeness doth much less appear,
That some more timely-happy spirits endu'th.
Yet be it less or more, or soon or slow,
It shall be still in strictest measure even
To that same lot, however mean or high,
Toward which Time leads me, and the will of Heaven.
All is, if I have grace to use it so,
As ever in my great Task-master's eye.

ON HIS BLINDNESS

When I consider how my light is spent
Ere half my days in this dark world and wide,
And that one talent which is death to hide
Lodged with me useless, though my soul more bent
To serve therewith my Maker, and present
My true account, lest He returning chide,
"Doth God exact day-labor, light denied?"
I fondly ask. But Patience, to prevent

That murmur, soon replies, "God doth not need
Either man's work or his own gifts. Who best
Bear his mild yoke, they serve him best. His state
Is kingly: thousands at his bidding speed,
And post o'er land and ocean without rest;
They also serve who only stand and wait."

SIR JOHN SUCKLING

WHY SO PALE AND WAN?

Why so pale and wan, fond lover?
Prithee, why so pale?
Will, when looking well can't move her,
Looking ill prevail?
Prithee, why so pale?

Why so dull and mute, young sinner?
Prithee, why so mute?
Will, when speaking well can't win her,
Saying nothing do't?
Prithee, why so mute?

Quit, quit for shame! This will not move,
This cannot take her.
If of herself she will not love,
Nothing can make her:
The devil take her!

THE CONSTANT LOVER

Out upon it, I have loved
Three whole days together!
And am like to love three more,
If it prove fair weather.

Time shall moult away his wings,
Ere he shall discover
In the whole wide world again
Such a constant lover.

But the spite on't is, no praise
Is due at all to me:

Love with me had made no stays,
Had it any been but she.

Had it any been but she,
And that very face,
There had been at least ere this
A dozen dozen in her place.

RICHARD LOVELACE

TO LUCASTA, GOING TO THE WARS

Tell me not, sweet, I am unkind,
That from the nunnery
Of thy chaste breast and quiet mind
To war and arms I fly.

True, a new mistress now I chase,
The first foe in the field;
And with a stronger faith embrace
A sword, a horse, a shield.

Yet this inconstancy is such
As thou too shalt adore:
I could not love thee, dear, so much,
Loved I not honor more.

ON LOVELACE'S *TO LUCASTA, GOING TO THE WARS*[1]

NORMAN HOLMES PEARSON

THAT Lovelace's lyric, "To Lucasta, Going to the Wars," has been attractive there can be no doubt. Its general popularity seems to rest on the epigrammatic quality of its last two lines, considered as a set-piece. Without attacking the absurdity of so confined a view of Lovelace's general achievement, it might be useful to indicate the integrated structure of this Lucasta poem, for something of the same benefit which has come from the realization that Donne's poems have more than brilliant opening lines.

Here the poet is presented with a situation, that of the departure from his

1. From *The Explicator,* VII (June, 1949), 58. Reprinted by permission of the author and of the Editors of *The Explicator*.

mistress of a lover called to the wars. The problem of the lover is that of explaining the motivation of his departure and of anticipating the accusation from her that he is both cruel in so doing and inconstant to his earlier vows of fidelity. He wishes to ease the departure by avoiding sentimentality, that is the display of more emotion than the situation warrants. Faced, then, with a quandary, he offers as solution a paradox (a statement seemingly self-contradictory, though possibly well-founded or essentially true).

The interest of the poem comes from his procedure. He opens his address with an epithet of quality ("sweet"), and urges that she not think him "unkind" (i. e. lacking in natural goodness; contrary to nature; harsh). By his reference to the chaste and sanctified refuge which she provides, as though she herself were a nunnery, he establishes the basis on which the problem can be met not basically as a separation of divisible bodies but as one of indivisible spirit. The path of solution is commonplace in love poetry; the quality of Lovelace's poem arises out of his particular twist to it.

The ambiguity and paradox of the situation is affirmed by the twisted implications of "To war and arms I fly," which so obviously picks up the martial "*Arma virumque cano*" of Virgil. Foreseeing a potential misunderstanding that his true delight will lie in war, the poet proceeds to her expected implication of shifted allegiance, and maintains continuity in the role of lover, as one might with apparent inconstancy leave from a quarrel to pursue the first girl one saw. But any conflicting passion on the level of the flesh is, as he presents the case, subtly omitted, since he does not actually embrace this new mistress, but only his martial accoutrements; and this he does only with "faith," which is non-sensory. This may paradoxically still seem inconstant and inconsistent until we actually understand the nature of the other love. This we see lies in "Honor," a concept of the spirit and not of the body, therefore essentially sexless and genderless, in a situation mutually attractive ("as thou too shalt adore"). Their common adoration of "Honor" is a bond between them of ultimate timelessness, overcoming distance and decay, as "the marriage of true minds" does for Shakespeare, and lunary love (by extension to the compass) does for Donne. Since Lovelace now openly avows his love of Honor, by implication of affinity he pays his mistress the ultimate compliment of extending this inherent superiority to his relationship with her. Any unkindness in his departure can be said to exist only on the sub-lunary level of flesh. It cannot be unnatural except on that plane, and the inconsistency will be resolved by her recognition of the hierarchy of affections, on a higher level of which comes Honor. Perhaps the fullest value of the poem is indicated in the increased density which his final epithet of endearment bears over that of his initial one; for the progress from his opening address to her as "sweet" to that of "dear" cumulatively carries with it, under the circumstances, a final assessment not only of quality but also of value, and of flesh immortalized by ascending spirit.

If there is a question as to the actuality of a shift of tone from beginning to end, one needs only to attempt a simple substitution to understand the incongruity of the alternative:

I could not love thee (sweet) so much,
Loved I not honor more.

ANDREW MARVELL

TO HIS COY MISTRESS

Had we but world enough, and time,
This coyness, Lady, were no crime.
We would sit down and think which way
To walk and pass our long love's day.
Thou by the Indian Ganges' side
Shouldst rubies find; I by the tide
Of Humber would complain. I would
Love you ten years before the Flood,
And you should, if you please, refuse
Till the conversion of the Jews.
My vegetable love should grow
Vaster than empires, and more slow;
An hundred years should go to praise
Thine eyes and on thy forehead gaze;
Two hundred to adore each breast,
But thirty thousand to the rest;
An age at least to every part,
And the last age should show your heart.
For, Lady, you deserve this state,
Nor would I love at lower rate.
But at my back I always hear
Time's winged chariot hurrying near;
And yonder all before us lie
Deserts of vast eternity.
Thy beauty shall no more be found,
Nor, in thy marble vault, shall sound
My echoing song; then worms shall try
That long preserved virginity,
And your quaint honor turn to dust,
And into ashes all my lust:
The grave's a fine and private place,
But none, I think, do there embrace.
Now therefore, while the youthful hue

Sits on thy skin like morning dew,
And while thy willing soul transpires
At every pore with instant fires,
Now let us sport us while we may,
And now, like amorous birds of prey,
Rather at once our time devour
Than languish in his slow-chapped power.
Let us roll all our strength and all
Our sweetness up into one ball,
And tear our pleasures with rough strife
Thorough the iron gates of life:
Thus, though we cannot make our sun
Stand still, yet we will make him run.

ON MARVELL'S *TO HIS COY MISTRESS* [1]

JOHN HAWLEY ROBERTS

THE central intention of the poem is to persuade the speaker's beloved to yield herself to him. His argument is that they have no time to wait. The constant consideration of the time problem gives unity to the whole.

The first twenty lines are in the conditional mode; their tone is ironically patient. The imagery here is developed consistently in terms of infinite time and space, suggesting the delights of endless leisure and deliberation, if such ample time were granted them. The pace of the lines is slow. All the temporal allusions imply a steady *adagio* movement toward a belated consummation of their love, a consummation that is not described physically, as it is to be at the end of the poem, but more reservedly as merely the delayed discovery of the lady's heart. This idea of leisure is stressed by such phrases as "long love's day," "ten years before the Flood," "refuse till the conversion of the Jews," "my vegetable love should grow . . . more slow" [than empires], and the hundreds and thousands of years used to indulge his adoration of her charms. This time element, furthermore, is underscored by references to space: the vast separation between the Ganges and the Humber, and the size of empires. Moreover, in the last couplet of this section (lines 19-20), the word "state" echoes "empires" and suggests size as well as a rich condition; likewise the word "rate" not only suggests the value of the speaker's love but also again emphasizes the tempo. These hyperboles of time and space, phrased conditionally, serve to reduce the lady's reluctance to absurdity. The ironic tone of this section is perhaps best expressed by the word "vegetable" in line 11. It suggests a placid way of love; it connotes a bloodless activity. (You can't get blood out of a turnip.)

1. From *The Explicator,* I (December, 1942), 17. Reprinted by permission of the author and of the Editors of *The Explicator.*

But most of all it is an anticipatory contrast to the fierce actions of the "amorous birds of prey" of the last section.

At line 21 the tone becomes urgent. The pace of line 22 is faster than any earlier line. Time is hurrying them on to death, which is again described in terms of time and space as "deserts of vast eternity," but now such time and space are made meaningless by the images that describe the negations of death. There is a fine irony in the idea that in death only "worms shall try that long-preserved virginity." The syllables here fall together perfectly to make the line invoke the error of her chastity. The last four lines of this section complete the lover's warning. Here the word "quaint" is especially important. It means not only "fastidious" and "out-of-fashion," but in its medieval sense refers to the lady's private parts, with which her honor is so closely associated. This special reference to the "private parts" in the word "quaint" makes the final couplet in this section a superb example of Marvell's wit. The grave, too, is

a fine and private place,
But none, I think, do *there* embrace.

Note how the arrangement of words in this last line forces the emphasis on "there," in contrast to the "place" of her "quaint honor."

In the last section of the poem the argument is positive. Everything from here on is in sharp contrast with what has gone before. The movement of the lines grows broken and rugged. The imagery becomes violently sexual. Moreover, the images that follow must be taken separately by the reader and not allowed to run together. The urgent lover asks that he and the girl may, like "amorous birds of prey" (not like vegetable lovers), devour time (not be slowly munched by it); that they may embrace in the closest physical contact; and that they may fiercely break through the "iron gates of life." This last image for the womb not only repudiates the earlier "quaint honor" and the inactivity of the grave, but positively connotes the life-giving power of the sexual act. In the final couplet the lover argues that by thus seizing love vigorously, they will find the way to defy time: that they can at least make the sun hurry to keep up with their own creative energy.

JOHN DRYDEN

CAN LIFE BE A BLESSING?

1

Can life be a blessing,
Or worth the possessing,
Can life be a blessing if love were away?

Ah no! though our love all night keep us waking,
And though he torment us with cares all the day,
Yet he sweetens, he sweetens our pains in the taking,
There's an hour at the last, there's an hour to repay.

2

In ev'ry possessing,
The ravishing blessing,
In ev'ry possessing the fruit of our pain,
Poor lovers forget long ages of anguish,
What e're they have suffer'd and done to obtain;
'Tis a pleasure, a pleasure to sigh and to languish,
When we hope, when we hope to be happy again.

A SONG FOR ST. CECILIA'S DAY

1687

From harmony, from heav'nly harmony,
This universal frame began;
When Nature underneath a heap
Of jarring atoms lay,
And could not heave her head,
The tuneful voice was heard from high:
"Arise, ye more than dead."
Then cold and hot and moist and dry
In order to their stations leap,
And Music's pow'r obey.
From harmony, from heav'nly harmony,
This universal frame began:
From harmony to harmony
Through all the compass of the notes it ran,
The diapason closing full in man.

What passion cannot Music raise and quell!
When Jubal struck the corded shell,
His listening brethren stood around,
And, wond'ring, on their faces fell
To worship that celestial sound.
Less than a god they thought there could not dwell
Within the hollow of that shell
That spoke so sweetly and so well.
What passion cannot Music raise and quell!

The trumpet's loud clangor
Excites us to arms
With shrill notes of anger
And mortal alarms.
The double, double, double beat
Of the thundering drum
Cries: "Hark! the foes come;
Charge, charge, 'tis too late to retreat!"

The soft complaining flute
In dying notes discovers
The woes of hopeless lovers,
Whose dirge is whispered by the warbling lute.

Sharp violins proclaim
Their jealous pangs and desperation,
Fury, frantic indignation,
Depth of pains, and height of passion,
For the fair, disdainful dame.

But oh! what art can teach,
What human voice can reach
The sacred organ's praise?
Notes inspiring holy love,
Notes that wing their heavenly ways
To mend the choirs above.

Orpheus could lead the savage race;
And trees unrooted left their place,
Sequacious of the lyre;
But bright Cecilia raised the wonder higher:
When to her organ vocal breath was given,
An angel heard, and straight appeared,
Mistaking earth for heaven.

Grand Chorus

As from the power of sacred lays
The spheres began to move,
And sung the great Creator's praise
To all the blessed above;
So when the last and dreadful hour
This crumbling pageant shall devour,
The trumpet shall be heard on high,

The dead shall live, the living die,
And Music shall untune the sky.

EDWARD TAYLOR

MEDITATION EIGHT [1]

John, VI, 52: "I am the living bread."

I kenning through astronomy divine
The world's bright battlement, wherein I spy
A golden path my pencil cannot line
From that bright throne unto my threshold lie.
And while my puzzled thoughts about it pour
I find the bread of life in't at my door.

When that this bird of paradise put in
This wicker cage (my corpse) to tweedle praise
Had pecked the fruit forbid: and so did fling
Away its food: and lost its golden days,
It fell into celestial famine sore:
And never could attain a morsel more.

Alas! alas! poor bird, what wilt thou do?
This creature's field no food for souls e'er gave.
And if thou knock at angels' doors they show
An empty barrel: they no soul bread have.
Alas! poor bird, the world's white loaf is done.
And cannot yield thee here the smallest crumb.

In this sad state, God's tender bowels run
Out streams of grace: And he to end all strife
The purest wheat in heaven, his dear-dear Son
Grinds, and kneads up into this bread of life.
Which bread of life from heaven down came and stands
Dished on thy table up by angels' hands.

Did God mould up this bread in heaven, and bake,
Which from his table came, and to thine goeth?
Doth he bespeak thee thus, this soul bread take;
Come, eat thy fill of this, thy God's white loaf?

1. From *The Poetical Works of Edward Taylor,* edited by Thomas H. Johnson. Copyright, 1939, Rocklands Editions. Copyright, 1943, by Princeton University Press, publishers.

Its food too fine for angels, yet come, take
And eat thy fill. It's heaven's sugar cake.

What grace is this knead in this loaf? This thing
    Souls are but petty things it to admire.
Ye angels, help: this fill would to the brim
    Heav'ns whelm'd-down chrystal meal bowl, yea and higher.
    This bread of life dropped in thy mouth doth cry:
    Eat, eat me, soul, and thou shalt never die.

ON TAYLOR'S *MEDITATION EIGHT* [1]

AUSTIN WARREN

A BETTER than average example of [Taylor's] lyrics is "Meditation Eight," from the Johannine hint, "I am the living bread." Taylor's curious coupling of "thing" and "brim," matched in other poems, shows not only that he did not sound terminal *g* but that he accounted nasals a satisfactory rhyme; and elsewhere he allows loose consonances and assonances to count as rhyme. These latitudes share with his Warwickshire provincialisms, his downright coinages, his inversions and other awkward, sometimes unconstruable constructions (like that in the opening stanza) in giving to this poem and his others a primitive vigor and naïveté irrelevant to the baroque aesthetic and unparalleled in other "metaphysical" verse of the period.

Donne's celebrated prosody in the Satires, like that of other free writers of pentameter iambic, provides its approximate pattern by offering, in a line, either five strong stresses, without calculation of weak syllables, or ten syllables without calculation of stresses, trusting that the two latitudes will balance to a conversational verse. But Taylor, though he had an iambic rhythm in his memory, seems chiefly to have counted the syllables; and his characteristic practice is to write a line slowed up by its extra stresses. "They no soul bread have" requires an equal weight to each syllable. The line of monosyllables, "What grace is this knead in this loaf? This thing," is best read as spondaic. Like other poets, ancient and contemporary, who reduce the flexible music of their rhythms, Taylor compensates by supplying rather copious alliteration—not as structure but as pure and simple phonetic pleasure.

The stiffness of Taylor's lines must not be attributed merely to prosodic awkwardness. Unquestionably he preferred a packed line; like greater poets—Donne, Hopkins, and Crane—he was impatient of space given to prepositions and articles and other poetic neutralities. Taylor's "Heav'ns whelm'd-down chrystal meal bowl" is less rare in kind for him than, for George Herbert, is the "Christ-side-piercing Spear" of "Prayer."

---

1. From *Rage for Order,* by Austin Warren (Chicago, 1948), pp. 12–16. Copyright, 1948, The University of Chicago Press.

The poem, which in spite of its inversions seems modern, has the force of its compression, its density. But its chief character is its metaphorism. Taylor is capable—one sees from "The Ebb and Flow" and "Huswifery"—of working out, neatly and precisely, a conceit: the latter poem tidily analogizes the Christian life to all the instruments and processes of cloth-making—the spinning wheel, the distaff, the reel, the loom, the web, the fulling mills, until the robes of salvation are ready for the pious wearing. Such poems, better called short allegories than extended conceits, are, however, less typical of Taylor and poetically less impressive than the poem before us, of which the method, more bold, is less surely prosecuted.

"Meditation Eight" has the advantage of ending with its two best stanzas. Taylor begins uncertain of direction and with trite locutions (like "golden path" and "bright throne"), locutions bad exactly in the wrong way for baroque poetry. Then the bird figure occurs to him: the soul is bird of Paradise in a double sense—child of heaven and heir of Eden's Adam, who was put in the "cage" of the Garden as the Soul has been put into that of the Body, to sing God's praises, but who (like his descendant soul) has instead eaten of the forbidden fruit. Taylor manages this equivalence neatly for three lines: the "wicker" cage can well stand for the tree-shaded garden; "peckt" properly modifies bird as well as man. But after that he has his difficulties: while, for a stanza more, evoking the soul as bird, he has really ceased thinking in terms of the figure, without knowing how to return to the narrative "I" of the first stanza; and, before he shapes the "I" into a "thou," he takes in transit a scriptural enough figure of God's running bowels which, however scriptural, is too strong a trope to be thrust, briefly and unsignificantly, into a poem with its own central boldness. "To end all strife" seems pure aid to the rhyme, since (though there is famine) no conflict has been mentioned.

Then, happily, Taylor finds his tone and theme, already sounded (under the accidental protection of the "bird") in the third stanza: the translation of Supersubstantial Bread, the *panis angelicus,* into domestic and animistic terms. Even in the last stanzas, the method is too libertine for Donne or Herbert; but the devices associate themselves, in baroque fashion, about surprises—surprises bearing down with a poet's literalness upon the proposition that Christ is the Bread (therefore subject to all the accidents and comparisons to which bread is subject). The total effect of the poem is amateurish but—by virtue of persistent episodic interest and a theme most efficiently defined as the poem nears its end—powerful.

JOHN WILMOT, EARL OF ROCHESTER

UPON HIS LEAVING HIS MISTRESS

I

'Tis not that I am weary grown
Of being yours, and yours alone:
But with what Face can I incline,
To damn you to be only mine?
You, who some kinder Pow'r did fashion,
By Merit, and by Inclination,
The Joy at least of a whole Nation.

II

Let meaner Spirits of your Sex,
With humble Aims their Thoughts perplex:
And boast, if, by their Arts they can
Contrive to make *one* happy Man.
While, mov'd by an impartial Sense,
Favours, like Nature, you dispence,
With universal Influence.

III

See the kind Seed-receiving Earth,
To every Grain affords a Birth:
On her no Show'rs unwelcome fall,
Her willing Womb retains 'em all.
And shall my *Caelia* be confin'd?
No, live up to thy mighty Mind;
And be the Mistress of Mankind.

LOVE AND LIFE, A SONG

All my past life is mine no more;
The flying hours are gone,
Like transitory dreams given o'er,
Whose images are kept in store
By memory alone.

The time that is to come is not;
How can it then be mine?
The present moment's all my lot;
And that, as fast as it is got,
Phillis, is only thine.

Then talk not of inconstancy,
False hearts, and broken vows;
If I by miracle can be
This live-long minute true to thee,
'Tis all that heaven allows.

JONATHAN SWIFT

STELLA'S BIRTH-DAY, 1720

All travellers at first incline
Where-e'er they see the fairest sign;
And, if they find the chambers neat,
And like the liquor and the meat,
Will call again, and recommend
The Angel-inn to ev'ry friend.
What though the painting grows decay'd?
The house will never lose its trade:
Nay, though the treach'rous tapster Thomas
Hangs a new angel two doors from us,
As fine as dauber's hands can make it,
In hopes that strangers may mistake it,
We think it both a shame and sin
To quit the true old Angel-inn.
Now this is Stella's case, in fact:
An *angel's* face, a little crack'd;
(Could poets, or could painters fix
How *angels* look at thirty-six:)
This drew us in at first to find
In such a form an *angel's* mind;
And ev'ry virtue now supplies
The fainting rays of Stella's eyes.
See at her levee crowding swains,
Whom Stella freely entertains
With breeding, humour, wit, and sense;
And puts them but to small expence;
Their mind so plentifully fills,
And makes such reasonable bills,
So little gets for what she gives,
We really wonder how she lives!
And, had her stock been less, no doubt
She must have long ago run out.
Then who can think we'll quit the place,

When Doll hangs out a newer face;
Or stop and light at Cloe's head,
With scraps and leavings to be fed?
Then, Cloe, still go on to prate
Of thirty-six, and thirty-eight;
Pursue your trade of scandal-picking,
Your hints, that Stella is no chicken;
Your innuendos, when you tell us
That Stella loves to talk with fellows:
And let me warn you to believe
A truth, for which your soul should grieve;
That, should you live to see the day
When Stella's locks must all be gray,
When age must print a furrow'd trace
On ev'ry feature of her face;
Though you, and all your senseless tribe,
Could art, or time, or nature bribe,
To make you look like beauty's queen,
And hold for ever at fifteen;
No bloom of youth can ever blind
The cracks and wrinkles of your mind;
All men of sense will pass your door,
And crowd to Stella's at fourscore.

ALEXANDER POPE

MORAL ESSAY, II

To a Lady, of the Characters of Women

Nothing so true as what you once let fall,
"Most Women have no Characters at all."
Matter too soft a lasting mark to bear,
And best distinguished by black, brown, or fair.
How many pictures of one Nymph we view,
All how unlike each other, all how true!
Arcadia's Countess, here, in ermined pride,
Is, there, Pastora by a fountain side.
Here Fannia, leering on her own good man,
And there, a naked Leda with a Swan.
Let then the Fair one beautifully cry,
In Magdalen's loose hair, and lifted eye,
Or drest in smiles of sweet Cecilia shine,
With simp'ring Angels, Palms, and Harps divine;

Whether the Charmer sinner it, or saint it,
If Folly grow romantic, I must paint it.
    Come then, the colours and the ground prepare!
Dip in the Rainbow, trick her off in Air;
Choose a firm Cloud, before it fall, and in it
Catch, ere she change, the Cynthia of this minute.
    Rufa, whose eye quick-glancing o'er the Park,
Attracts each light gay meteor of a Spark,
Agrees as ill with Rufa studying Locke,
As Sappho's diamonds with her dirty smock;
Or Sappho at her toilet's greasy task,
With Sappho fragrant at an evening Masque:
So morning Insects that in muck begun,
Shine, buzz, and fly-blow in the setting-sun.
    How soft is Silia! fearful to offend;
The Frail one's advocate, the Weak one's friend:
To her, Calista proved her conduct nice;
And good Simplicius asks of her advice.
Sudden, she storms! she raves! You tip the wink,
But spare your censure; Silia does not drink.
All eyes may see from what the change arose,
All eyes may see—a Pimple on her nose.
    Papillia, wedded to her am'rous spark,
Sighs for the shades—"How charming is a Park!"
A Park is purchased, but the Fair he sees
All bathed in tears—"Oh, odious, odious Trees!"
    Ladies, like variegated Tulips, show;
'Tis to their Changes half their charms we owe;
Fine by defect, and delicately weak,
Their happy Spots the nice admirer take,
'Twas thus Calypso once each heart alarmed,
Awed without Virtue, without Beauty charmed;
Her tongue bewitched as oddly as her Eyes,
Less Wit than Mimic, more a Wit than wise;
Strange graces still, and stranger flights she had,
Was just not ugly, and was just not mad;
Yet ne'er so sure our passion to create,
As when she touched the brink of all we hate.
    Narcissa's nature, tolerably mild,
To make a wash, would hardly stew a child;
Has even been proved to grant a Lover's prayer,
And paid a Tradesman once to make him stare;
Gave alms at Easter, in a Christian trim,
And made a Widow happy, for a whim.

Why then declare Good-nature is her scorn,
When 'tis by that alone she can be borne?
Why pique all mortals, yet affect a name?
A fool to Pleasure, yet a slave to Fame:
Now deep in Taylor and the Book of Martyrs,
Now drinking citron with his Grace and Chartres:
Now Conscience chills her, and now Passion burns;
And Atheism and Religion take their turns;
A very Heathen in the carnal part,
Yet still a sad, good Christian at her heart.
  See Sin in State, majestically drunk;
Proud as a Peeress, prouder as a Punk;
Chaste to her Husband, frank to all beside,
A teeming Mistress, but a barren Bride.
What then? let Blood and Body bear the fault,
Her Head's untouched, that noble Seat of Thought:
Such this day's doctrine—in another fit
She sins with Poets through pure Love of Wit.
What has not fired her bosom or her brain?
Cæsar and Tall-boy, Charles and Charlemagne.
As Helluo, late Dictator of the Feast,
The Nose of Hautgout, and the Tip of Taste,
Critiqued your wine, and analysed your meat,
Yet on plain Pudding deigned at home to eat;
So Philomedé, lect'ring all mankind
On the soft Passion, and the Taste refined,
Th' Address, the Delicacy—stoops at once,
And makes her hearty meal upon a Dunce.
  Flavia's a Wit, has too much sense to Pray;
To Toast our wants and wishes, is her way;
Nor asks of God, but of her Stars, to give
The mighty blessing, "While we live, to live."
Then all for Death, that Opiate of the soul!
Lucretia's dagger, Rosamonda's bowl.
Say, what can cause such impotence of mind?
A spark too fickle, or a Spouse too kind.
Wise Wretch! with Pleasures too refined to please;
With too much Spirit to be e'er at ease;
With too much Quickness ever to be taught;
With too much Thinking to have common Thought:
You purchase Pain with all that Joy can give,
And die of nothing but a Rage to live.
  Turn then from Wits; and look on Simo's Mate,
No Ass so meek, no Ass so obstinate.

Or her, that owns her Faults, but never mends,
Because she's honest, and the best of Friends.
Or her, whose life the Church and Scandal share,
For ever in a Passion, or a Prayer.
Or her, who laughs at Hell, but (like her Grace)
Cries, "Ah! how charming, if there's no such place!"
Or who in sweet vicissitude appears
Of Mirth and Opium, Ratafie and Tears,
The daily Anodyne, and nightly Draught,
To kill those foes to Fair ones, Time and Thought.
Woman and Fool are two hard things to hit;
For true No-meaning puzzles more than Wit.
        But what are these to great Atossa's mind?
Scarce once herself, by turns all Womankind!
Who, with herself, or others, from her birth
Finds all her life one warfare upon earth:
Shines in exposing Knaves, and painting Fools,
Yet is, whate'er she hates and ridicules.
No Thought advances, but her Eddy Brain
Whisks it about, and down it goes again.
Full sixty years the World has been her Trade,
The wisest Fool much Time has ever made.
From loveless youth to unrespected age,
No passion gratified except her Rage.
So much the Fury still out-ran the Wit,
The Pleasure missed her, and the Scandal hit.
Who breaks with her, provokes Revenge from Hell,
But he's a bolder man who dares be well.
Her every turn with Violence pursued,
Nor more a storm her Hate than Gratitude:
To that each Passion turns, or soon or late;
Love, if it makes her yield, must make her hate:
Superiors? death! and Equals? what a curse!
But an Inferior not dependant? worse.
Offend her, and she knows not to forgive;
Oblige her, and she'll hate you while you live:
But die, and she'll adore you—Then the Bust
And Temple rise—then fall again to dust.
Last night, her Lord was all that's good and great;
A Knave this morning, and his Will a Cheat.
Strange! by the Means defeated of the Ends,
By Spirit robbed of Power, by Warmth of Friends,
By Wealth of Followers! without one distress
Sick of herself through very selfishness!

Atossa, cursed with every granted prayer,
Childless with all her Children, wants an Heir.
To Heirs unknown descends th' unguarded store,
Or wanders, Heaven-directed, to the Poor.
Pictures like these, dear Madam, to design,
Asks no firm hand, and no unerring line;
Some wand'ring touches, some reflected light,
Some flying stroke alone can hit 'em right:
For how should equal Colours do the knack?
Chameleons who can paint in white and black?
"Yet Chloe sure was formed without a spot"–
Nature in her then erred not, but forgot.
"With every pleasing, every prudent part,
Say, what can Chloe want?"—She wants a Heart.
She speaks, behaves, and acts just as she ought;
But never, never, reached one gen'rous Thought.
Virtue she finds too painful an endeavour,
Content to dwell in Decencies for ever.
So very reasonable, so unmoved,
As never yet to love, or to be loved.
She, while her Lover pants upon her breast,
Can mark the figures on an Indian chest;
And when she sees her Friend in deep despair,
Observes how much a Chintz exceeds Mohair.
Forbid it Heaven, a Favour or a Debt
She e'er should cancel—but she may forget.
Safe is your Secret still in Chloe's ear;
But none of Chloe's shall you ever hear.
Of all her Dears she never slandered one,
But cares not if a thousand are undone.
Would Chloe know if you're alive or dead?
She bids her Footman put it in her head.
Chloe is prudent—Would you too be wise?
Then never break your heart when Chloe dies.
One certain Portrait may (I grant) be seen,
Which Heaven has varnished out, and made a *Queen*:
THE SAME FOR EVER! and described by all
With Truth and Goodness, as with Crown and Ball.
Poets heap Virtues, Painters Gems at will,
And shew their zeal, and hide their want of skill.
'Tis well—but, Artists! who can paint or write,
To draw the Naked is your true delight.
That robe of Quality so struts and swells,
None see what Parts of Nature it conceals:

Th' exactest traits of Body or of Mind,
We owe to models of an humble kind.
If Queensbury to strip there's no compelling,
'Tis from a Handmaid we must take a Helen,
From Peer or Bishop 'tis no easy thing
To draw the man who loves his God, or King:
Alas! I copy (or my draught would fail)
From honest Mah'met, or plain Parson Hale.
But grant, in Public Men sometimes are shown,
A Woman's seen in Private life alone:
Our bolder Talents in full light displayed;
Your virtues open fairest in the shade.
Bred to disguise, in Public 'tis you hide;
There, none distinguish 'twixt your Shame or Pride,
Weakness or Delicacy; all so nice,
That each may seem a Virtue, or a Vice.
In Men, we various Ruling Passions find;
In Women, two almost divide the kind;
Those, only fixed, they first or last obey,
The Love of Pleasure, and the Love of Sway.
That, Nature gives; and where the lesson taught
Is but to please, can Pleasure seem a fault?
Experience, this; by Man's oppression curst,
They seek the second not to lose the first.
Men, some to Business, some to Pleasure take;
But every Woman is at heart a Rake:
Men, some to Quiet, some to public Strife;
But every Lady would be Queen for life.
Yet mark the fate of a whole Sex of Queens!
Power all their end, but Beauty all the means:
In Youth they conquer, with so wild a rage,
As leaves them scarce a subject in their Age:
For foreign glory, foreign joy, they roam;
No thought of peace or happiness at home.
But Wisdom's triumph is well-timed Retreat,
As hard a science to the Fair as Great!
Beauties, like Tyrants, old and friendless grown,
Yet hate repose, and dread to be alone,
Worn out in public, weary every eye,
Nor leave one sigh behind them when they die.
Pleasures the sex, as children Birds, pursue,
Still out of reach, yet never out of view;
Sure, if they catch, to spoil the Toy at most,
To covet flying, and regret when lost:

At last, to follies Youth could scarce defend,
It grows their Age's prudence to pretend;
Ashamed to own they gave delight before,
Reduced to feign it, when they give no more:
As Hags hold Sabbaths, less for joy than spite,
So these their merry, miserable Night;
Still round and round the Ghosts of Beauty glide,
And haunt the places where their Honour died.
    See how the World its Veterans rewards!
A Youth of Frolics, an old Age of Cards;
Fair to no purpose, artful to no end,
Young without Lovers, old without a Friend;
A Fop their Passion, but their Prize a Sot;
Alive, ridiculous, and dead, forgot!
    Ah! Friend! to dazzle let the Vain design;
To raise the Thought, and touch the Heart be thine!
That Charm shall grow, while what fatigues the Ring,
Flaunts and goes down, an unregarded thing:
So when the Sun's broad beam has tired the sight,
All mild ascends the Moon's more sober light,
Serene in Virgin Modesty she shines,
And unobserved the glaring Orb declines.
    Oh! blest with Temper, whose unclouded ray
Can make to-morrow cheerful as to-day;
She, who can love a Sister's charms, or hear
Sighs for a daughter with unwounded ear;
She, who ne'er answers till a Husband cools,
Or, if she rules him, never shews she rules;
Charms by accepting, by submitting sways,
Yet has her humour most, when she obeys;
Let Fops or Fortune fly which way they will;
Disdains all loss of Tickets, or Codille:
Spleen, Vapours, or Small-pox, above them all,
And Mistress of herself, though China fall.
    And yet, believe me, good as well as ill,
Woman's at best a Contradiction still.
Heaven, when it strives to polish all it can
Its last best work, but forms a softer Man;
Picks from each sex, to make the Fav'rite blest,
Your love of Pleasure, or desire of Rest:
Blends, in exception to all general rules,
Your Taste of Follies, with our Scorn of Fools:
Reserve with Frankness, Art with Truth allied,
Courage with Softness, Modesty with Pride;

Fixed Principles, with Fancy ever new;
Shakes all together, and produces—You.
Be this a Woman's Fame: with this unblest,
Toasts live a scorn, and Queens may die a jest.
This Phœbus promised (I forget the year)
When those blue eyes first opened on the sphere;
Ascendant Phœbus watched that hour with care,
Averted half your Parents' simple Prayer;
And gave you Beauty, but denied the Pelf
That buys your sex a Tyrant o'er itself.
The gen'rous God, who Wit and Gold refines,
And ripens Spirits as he ripens Mines,
Kept Dross for Duchesses, the world shall know it,
To you gave Sense, Good-humour, and a Poet.

ON POPE'S *MORAL ESSAY, II* [1]

HALLETT D. SMITH

THE SUBTITLE "Of the Characters of Women" describes generally Pope's poem, but the first five-sixths of the epistle is a satirical portrait gallery in verse, and the last part is an enthusiastic favorable portrait—a compliment to the Lady of the title, Martha Blount. Pope contrasts her character, manner, and disposition to an array of eighteenth-century court women. No one in the group is named except the Duchess of Queensbury (line 193), but they are given distinguishing classical names, some of which suggest particular features or qualities.

The poem develops as a series of illustrations of the truth of Martha Blount's remark, "Most women have no characters at all." What this means is that women, unlike men, are not controlled by a ruling passion or principle; they are changeable, self-contradictory, inconsistent. Any definite description you apply to a woman is immediately contradicted by something else in her behavior or temperament. This complaint, by no means original with Pope or Martha Blount, of course, is made fresh and vivid by the metaphor of painting portraits. Most society ladies, says Pope, have to be portrayed in a series of roles—as a countess in court costume and as a shepherdess; as a good and loving wife and as the naked pagan Leda with her swan-lover; as the immoral Magdalen and the pure St. Cecilia. How then is the poet to capture them in a single verse portrait apiece? This is the all but impossible task Pope sets himself, and the answer he gives to the question of how to do it develops the painting metaphor and incidentally characterizes his own style and manner:

1. Reprinted from *The Critical Reader,* edited by Wallace Douglas, Roy Lamson, and Hallett Smith (New York, 1949), pp. 25–31, by permission of W. W. Norton & Company, Inc. Copyright, 1949, by W. W. Norton & Company, Inc.

Come then, the colours and the ground prepare!
Dip in the rainbow, trick her off in air;
Choose a firm cloud, before it fall, and in it
Catch, ere she change, the Cynthia of this minute. (17–20)

The idea that the material itself is evanescent is of course a phrasing of the main theme, but the suggestion that the treatment is to be all delicate and airy is in part a deliberate deception of the reader: he is all the more shocked when he finds that very frequently the ladies are sketched not with cloud-stuff and rainbow tints, but with acid, sharply and firmly etched. But Pope's model in this poem and others like it is Horace, and the epistles of Horace are satires which are never heavy-footed and violent, but witty, urbane, and smooth. The conventional "epistle" or letter gives an air of informality, and the poet is not setting himself up as the formal indignant castigator of the vices and follies of mankind. The instrument of this kind of satirist is the rapier and not the whip.

But neither "rapier" nor "paintbrush" adequately conveys an idea of Pope's technique. It is first of all a kind of thinking, and the intellectual power of the poem should not be underestimated. Take Calypso, for example, she who

once each heart alarm'd,
Awed without virtue, without beauty charm'd; (45–46)

what is the mysterious source of her attractiveness? If she is neither good nor beautiful, what is it that she has? Pope pretends that it is a mystery, but he shows by his manner of describing it that he knows that we are sometimes drawn or attracted by those things that are just this side of the repulsive:

Strange graces still, and stranger flights she had,
Was just not ugly, and was just not mad;
Yet ne'er so sure our passion to create,
As when she touch'd the brink of all we hate. (49–52)

For all the emphasis on female vanity, on social foibles, on fashionable affectations, this epistle is fundamentally a Moral Essay; it probes deeply into the relationship between motives and deeds. Narcissa is not a "bad" woman; she wouldn't stew a child, in the fashion of witches making their broth, just to prepare a cosmetic "wash" for her face; she is even generous, if you recite some of her deeds—but what about the motives? She

Has ev'n been prov'd to grant a lover's pray'r,
And paid a tradesman once to make him stare;
Gave alms at Easter, in a Christian trim,
And made a widow happy, for a whim. (55–58)

As a matter of fact, she is another example of that combination of irreconcilable opposites which constitutes the female character:

Now conscience chills her, and now passion burns;
And atheism and religion take their turns;
A very heathen in the carnal part,
Yet still a sad, good Christian at her heart. (65–68)

Pope's moral insight is exhibited even more impressively in the rhetoric and logical syntax of passages which appear on the surface to be mere wit:

See Sin in state, majestically drunk;
Proud as a peeress, prouder as a punk; (69–90)

Here the paradox in the phrase "majestically drunk" not only expresses contempt for the degradation of majestic qualities in drunkenness; it also prepares the reader's mind for some such phrase as "drunk as a lord." And the phrase follows, satisfyingly: "Proud as a peeress," but by a verbal trick Pope converts what seems like a superlative into a mere positive, and the comparative "prouder as a punk" explodes in a marvelous anticlimax. The rhetorical progression in the description of Flavia, the epicurean, reveals the same degree of profundity:

Wise wretch! with pleasures too refin'd to please;
With too much spirit to be e'er at ease;
With too much quickness ever to be taught;
With too much thinking to have common thought;
You purchase pain with all that joy can give,
And die of nothing but a rage to live. (95–100)

The thrice-repeated "with too much . . ." and the metaphor of purchasing develop a sense of opulence and wealth to give a terrible significance to the word "nothing" in the last line.

To temper this moral seriousness and to keep the poem on the level of the well-bred, cultivated letter from one friend to another, to suggest a tone of gallant frankness rather than zealous misogyny, Pope returns, after one hundred and fifty lines, to a comment on his technique:

Pictures like these, dear Madam, to design,
Asks no firm hand, and no unerring line;
Some wand'ring touches, some reflected light,
Some flying stroke alone can hit 'em right: (151–154)

Any analysis of Pope's style might take this passage as its point of departure. Is there really no firm hand or unerring line in these portraits? Are they really just flying strokes?

The versification of this poem is of course connected with its wit. But the iambic pentameter couplet which Pope so polished and developed, which he made so capable of variety and so fluent in a poem of almost three hundred lines, is not to be considered the source of the wit. It is the sharpening of something which already cuts. So many illustrations offer themselves to show Pope's skill in the technique of versification that it is hard to make a choice. Is he most remarkable for his variation of the normal iambic movement to make a sudden special effect, as in the second line of

> A very heathen in the carnal part,
> Yet still a sad, good Christian at her heart. (67–68)

or is he to be praised for the compactness of his summarizing couplets, when he conveys the matter of an epic in an epigram?

> From loveless youth to unrespected age,
> No passion gratified except her rage. (125–126)

One might point out the extraordinary precision in the choice of the specific detail to contrast with a general emotion:

> She, while her lover pants upon her breast,
> Can mark the figures on an Indian chest;
> And when she sees her friend in deep despair,
> Observes how much a chintz exceeds mohair. (167–170)

This is in reality a perfect realization of balance, intellectually and imaginatively, and the same poise is evident in Pope's prosody. The quotability of his general statements is often due to this balance:

> In men, we various ruling passions find;
> In women, two almost divide the kind;
> Those, only fix'd, they first or last obey,
> The love of pleasure, and the love of sway. (207–210)

Here the unbalance of the third line, in the placing of caesuras, prepares the ear for the satisfaction of the perfect balance of the fourth, and even the parallel structure of the first and second lines, with the early caesura, has its effect on the last line.

The end of the poem, progressing from the character of "Queensbury" through some general reflections on the female sex, leads up to the good advice and gallant compliment paid to Martha Blount. Yet in paying this compliment Pope does not retract his general contention about the contradictions in feminine character; he only makes it clear that one combination of disparate traits, the best from each sex, has resulted in the creation of an ideal woman and friend. As the poet makes his exit, he separates Martha Blount from the women of the world he has been describing. She has beauty but not wealth; hence she is unspoiled. And in the final lines, as he shows the compensations for lack of wealth, he produces the same retarding effect in the last line that we are accustomed to at the end of a piece of music:

> The gen'rous god, who wit and gold refines,
> And ripens spirits as he ripens mines,

Kept dross for duchesses, the world shall know it,
To you gave sense, good-humour, and a poet. (289–292)

Anyone who walks through an art gallery and looks at the portraits of eighteenth-century ladies by Lely, Kneller and Reynolds is not quite satisfied until he goes up to the pictures of the ladies, in their roles as the goddess Diana, the Tragic Muse, or St. Cecilia, to read on the little brass plates the names of the actual subjects of the pictures. So, in Pope's poem, it may be of some interest to know that Philomede is supposed to represent Henrietta, Duchess of Marlborough, in succession to her father, the first Duke; Atossa is traditionally supposed to be Sarah, Duchess of Marlborough, widow of the first Duke; Chloe is thought to be the Countess of Suffolk (Mrs. Howard), a neighbor of Pope's at Twickenham and formerly mistress to King George II. There is some point to "dross for *duchesses*" in the next-to-last line.

WILLIAM COLLINS

ODE TO EVENING

If ought of oaten stop, or pastoral song,
May hope, chaste Eve, to soothe thy modest ear,
Like thy own solemn springs,
Thy springs and dying gales,

O nymph reserved, while now the bright-haired sun
Sits in yon western tent, whose cloudy skirts,
With brede ethereal wove,
O'erhang his wavy bed:

Now air is hushed, save where the weak-eyed bat,
With short shrill shriek flits by on leathern wing,
Or where the beetle winds
His small but sullen horn,

As oft he rises 'midst the twilight path,
Against the pilgrim borne in heedless hum;
Now teach me, maid composed,
To breathe some softened strain,

Whose numbers, stealing through thy darkening vale,
May not unseemly with its stillness suit,
As, musing slow, I hail
Thy genial loved return!

For when thy folding-star arising shows
His paly circlet, at his warning lamp
    The fragrant Hours, and elves
    Who slept in flowers the day,

And many a nymph who wreathes her brows with sedge,
And sheds the freshening dew, and, lovelier still,
    The pensive Pleasures sweet,
    Prepare thy shadowy car.

Then lead, calm votaress, where some sheety lake
Cheers the lone heath, or some time-hallowed pile
    Or upland fallows gray
    Reflect its last cool gleam.

But when chill blustering winds, or driving rain,
Forbid my willing feet, be mine the hut
    That from the mountain's side
    Views wilds, and swelling floods,

And hamlets brown, and dim-discovered spires,
And hears their simple bell, and marks o'er all
    Thy dewy fingers draw
    The gradual dusky veil.

While Spring shall pour his showers, as oft he wont,
And bathe thy breathing tresses, meekest Eve;
    While Summer loves to sport
    Beneath thy lingering light;

While sallow Autumn fills thy lap with leaves;
Or Winter, yelling through the troublous air,
    Affrights thy shrinking train,
    And rudely rends thy robes;

So long, sure-found beneath the sylvan shed,
Shall Fancy, Friendship, Science, rose-lipped Health,
    Thy gentlest influence own,
    And hymn thy favorite name!

THOMAS WARTON, THE YOUNGER

SONNET III

Written in a blank leaf of Dugdale's Monasticon

Deem not devoid of elegance the sage,
By Fancy's genuine feelings unbeguiled,
Of painful Pedantry the poring child;
Who turns, of these proud domes, the historic page,
Now sunk by Time, and Henry's fiercer rage,
Thinkst thou the warbling Muses never smiled
On his lone hours? Ingenuous views engage
His thought, on themes, unclassic falsely styled,
Intent. While cloistered Piety displays
Her mouldering roll, the piercing eye explores
New manners, and the pomp of elder days,
Whence culls the pensive bard his pictured stores,
Nor rough nor barren are the winding ways
Of hoar Antiquity, but strown with flowers.

WILLIAM BLAKE

THE LAMB

Little Lamb, who made thee?
Dost thou know who made thee?
Gave thee life, and bid thee feed,
By the stream and o'er the mead;
Gave thee clothing of delight,
Softest clothing, woolly, bright;
Gave thee such a tender voice,
Making all the vales rejoice?
Little Lamb, who made thee?
Dost thou know who made thee?

Little Lamb, I'll tell thee,
Little Lamb, I'll tell thee:
He is callèd by thy name,
For He calls Himself a Lamb,
He is meek, and He is mild;
He became a little child.
I a child, and thou a lamb,
We are callèd by His name.

Little Lamb, God bless thee!
Little Lamb, God bless thee!

AH SUNFLOWER

Ah Sunflower, weary of time,
Who countest the steps of the sun,
Seeking after that sweet golden clime
Where the traveler's journey is done—

Where the youth pined away with desire,
And the pale virgin, shrouded in snow,
Arise from their graves, and aspire
Where my sunflower wishes to go!

THE TIGER

Tiger! Tiger! burning bright
In the forests of the night,
What immortal hand or eye
Could frame thy fearful symmetry?

In what distant deeps or skies
Burnt the fire of thine eyes?
On what wings dare he aspire?
What the hand dare seize the fire?

And what shoulder, and what art,
Could twist the sinews of thy heart?
And when thy heart began to beat,
What dread hand? and what dread feet?

What the hammer? what the chain?
In what furnace was thy brain?
What the anvil? what dread grasp
Dare its deadly terrors clasp?

When the stars threw down their spears
And watered heaven with their tears,
Did he smile his work to see?
Did he who made the Lamb make thee?

Tiger! Tiger! burning bright
In the forests of the night,

What immortal hand or eye
Dare frame thy fearful symmetry?

ON BLAKE'S *THE TIGER* [1]

C. M. BOWRA

THE poetry of this desire and of what it meant to Blake can be seen in "The Tiger." Here enraptured song conveys in essential vision some themes which Blake presents elsewhere in more detail. This is the pure poetry of his trust in cosmic forces. The images of "The Tiger" recur in the prophetic books, but in the poem, detached from any very specific context, they have a special strength and freedom. The tiger is Blake's symbol for the fierce forces in the soul which are needed to break the bonds of experience. The "forests of the night," in which the tiger lurks, are ignorance, repression, and superstition. It has been fashioned by unknown, supernatural spirits, like Blake's mythical heroes, Orc and Los, prodigious smiths who beat out living worlds with their hammers; and this happened when "the stars threw down their spears," that is, in some enormous cosmic crisis when the universe turned round in its course and began to move from light to darkness—as Urizen says in *The Four Zoas,* when he finds that passion and natural joy have withered under his rule and the power of the spirit has been weakened:

> I went not forth: I hid myself in black clouds of my wrath;
> I call'd the stars around my feet in the night of councils dark;
> The stars threw down their spears and fled naked away.

If we wish to illustrate "The Tiger" from Blake's other works, it is easy to do so, and it adds much to our understanding of its background and its place in Blake's development. But it is first and last a poem. The images are so compelling that for most purposes they explain themselves, and we have an immediate, overwhelming impression of an awful power lurking in the darkness of being and forcing on us questions which pierce to the heart of life.

TO THE ACCUSER WHO IS THE GOD OF THIS WORLD

Truly, My Satan, thou art but a Dunce,
And dost not know the Garment from the Man.
Every Harlot was a Virgin once,
Nor can'st thou ever change Kate into Nan.

Tho' thou art Worship'd by the Names Divine
Of Jesus & Jehovah, thou art still

1. Reprinted by permission of the publishers from *The Romantic Imagination,* by C. M. Bowra, Cambridge, Mass.: Harvard University Press, 1949.

The Son of Morn in weary Night's decline,
The lost Traveller's Dream under the Hill.

STANZAS FROM MILTON

And did those feet in ancient time
Walk upon England's mountain green?
And was the holy Lamb of God
On England's pleasant pastures seen?

And did the Countenance Divine
Shine forth upon our clouded hills?
And was Jerusalem builded here
Among these dark Satanic mills?

Bring me my bow of burning gold!
Bring me my arrows of desire!
Bring me my spear! O clouds, unfold!
Bring me my chariot of fire!

I will not cease from mental fight,
Nor shall my sword sleep in my hand,
Till we have built Jerusalem
In England's green and pleasant land.

ROBERT BURNS

TAM O' SHANTER

A Tale

Of Brownyis and of Bogillis[1] *full is this buke.*
Gawin Douglas

When chapman billies[2] leave the street,
And drouthy neebors neebors meet,
As market-days are wearing late,
An' folk begin to tak the gate;[3]
While we sit bousing at the nappy,[4]

1. specters; hobgoblins.
2. huckster companions, who set up stalls on market days.
3. road (home).
4. drinking the strong ale.

An' getting fou and unco happy,
We think na on the lang Scots miles,[5]
The mosses,[6] waters, slaps,[7] and styles
That lie between us and our hame,
Whare sits our sulky, sullen dame,
Gathering her brows like gathering storm,
Nursing her wrath to keep it warm.

This truth fand honest Tam o' Shanter,
As he frae Ayr ae night did canter,
(Auld Ayr, wham ne'er a town surpasses
For honest men and bonie lasses).

O Tam! had'st thou but been sae wise
As taen thy ain wife Kate's advice!
She tauld thee weel thou was a skellum,[8]
A blethering,[9] blustering, drunken blellum;[10]
That frae November till October,
Ae market-day thou was nae sober;
That ilka melder[11] wi' the miller,
Thou sat as lang as thou had siller;
That ev'ry naig was ca'd a shoe on,[12]
The smith and thee gat roaring fou on;
That at the Lord's house, even on Sunday,
Thou drank wi' Kirkton Jean[13] till Monday.
She prophesied that, late or soon,
Thou would be found deep drowned in Doon;
Or catched wi' warlocks[14] in the mirk[15]
By Alloway's auld haunted kirk.

Ah, gentle dames! it gars me greet[16]
To think how monie counsels sweet,
How monie lengthened sage advices,
The husband frae the wife despises!

But to our tale:—Ae market-night
Tam had got planted unco right,
Fast by an ingle, bleezing finely,

5. formerly somewhat longer than English miles.
6. bogs. 7. gaps in walls or fences. 8. worthless fellow.
9. chattering. 10. idle talker.
11. grist-grinding. 12. every nag that was shod.
13. keeper of an alehouse near the kirk.
14. wizards. 15. dark. 16. makes me weep.

Wi' reaming swats[17] that drank divinely;
And at his elbow, Souter[18] Johnie,
His ancient, trusty, drouthy cronie:
Tam lo'ed him like a very brither;
They had been fou for weeks thegither.
The night drave on wi' sangs and clatter;
And ay the ale was growing better:
The landlady and Tam grew gracious
Wi' secret favors, sweet and precious;
The souter tauld his queerest stories;
The landlord's laugh was ready chorus;
The storm without might rair and rustle,
Tam did na mind the storm a whistle.

Care, mad to see a man sae happy,
E'en drowned himsel amang the nappy:
As bees flee hame wi' lades o' treasure,
The minutes winged their way wi' pleasure;
Kings may be blest, but Tam was glorious,
O'er a' the ills o' life victorious!

But pleasures are like poppies spread;
You seize the flow'r, its bloom is shed:
Or like the snow falls in the river,
A moment white—then melts forever:
Or like the borealis race,
That flit ere you can point their place:
Or like the rainbow's lovely form
Evanishing amid the storm.
Nae man can tether time or tide:
The hour approaches Tam maun ride,—
That hour, o' night's black arch the keystane,
That dreary hour Tam mounts his beast in;
And sic a night he taks the road in,
As ne'er poor sinner was abroad in.

The wind blew as 't wad blawn its last;
The rattling showers rose on the blast;
The speedy gleams the darkness swallowed;
Loud, deep, and lang the thunder bellowed:
That night, a child might understand,
The deil had business on his hand.

17. frothing ale.
18. Cobbler.

Weel mounted on his grey mare, Meg—
A better never lifted leg—
Tam skelpit on thro' dub[19] and mire,
Despising wind and rain and fire;
Whiles holding fast his guid blue bonnet,
Whiles crooning o'er some auld Scots sonnet,
Whiles glow'ring round wi' prudent cares,
Lest bogles[20] catch him unawares:
Kirk-Alloway was drawing nigh,
Whare ghaists and houlets[21] nightly cry.

By this time he was cross the ford,
Whare in the snaw the chapman smoored;[22]
And past the birks[23] and meikle stane,
Whare drunken Charlie brak 's neck-bane;
And thro' the whins,[24] and by the cairn,[25]
Whare hunters fand the murdered bairn;
And near the thorn, aboon the well,
Whare Mungo's mither hanged hersel.
Before him Doon pours all his floods;
The doubling storm roars thro' the woods;
The lightnings flash from pole to pole;
Near and more near the thunders roll:
When, glimmering thro' the groaning trees,
Kirk-Alloway seemed in a bleeze;[26]
Thro' ilka bore[27] the beams were glancing,
And loud resounded mirth and dancing.

Inspiring bold John Barleycorn,
What dangers thou canst make us scorn!
Wi' tippenny[28] we fear nae evil;
Wi' usquebae[29] we'll face the devil!
The swats sae reamed in Tammie's noddle,
Fair play, he cared na deils a boddle.[30]
But Maggie stood right sair astonished,
Till, by the heel and hand admonished,
She ventured forward on the light;
And, vow! Tam saw an unco sight!

Warlocks and witches in a dance:
Nae cotillion brent new[31] frae France,

19. clattered on through puddle. 20. ghosts. 21. owls. 22. smothered.
23. birches. 24. furze; thorny evergreen shrub common on heaths.
25. pile of stones. 26. blaze. 27. crevice. 28. twopenny ale.
29. whisky. 30. small copper coin. 31. brand new.

But hornpipes, jigs, strathspeys,[32] and reels
Put life and mettle in their heels.
A winnock-bunker[33] in the east,
There sat Auld Nick in shape o' beast;
A tousie tyke,[34] black, grim, and large,
To gie them music was his charge;
He screwed the pipes and gart them skirl [35]
Till roof and rafters a' did dirl.[36]
Coffins stood round like open presses,[37]
That shawed the dead in their last dresses;
And, by some devilish cantraip sleight,[38]
Each in its cauld hand held a light,
By which heroic Tam was able
To note upon the haly table[39]
A murderer's banes in gibbet-airns;[40]
Twa span-lang, wee, unchristened bairns;
A thief, new-cutted frae a rape,[41]
Wi' his last gasp his gab[42] did gape;
Five tomahawks wi' bluid red-rusted;
Five scymitars wi' murder crusted;
A garter which a babe had strangled;
A knife a father's throat had mangled—
Whom his ain son o' life bereft—
The grey-hairs yet stack to the heft;
Wi' mair of horrible and awefu',
Which even to name wad be unlawfu'.

As Tammie glowered, amazed, and curious,
The mirth and fun grew fast and furious;
The piper loud and louder blew,
The dancers quick and quicker flew,
They reeled, they set, they crossed, they cleekit,[43]
Till ilka carlin swat and reekit,[44]
And coost her duddies[45] to the wark,
And linket[46] at it in her sark! [47]

Now Tam, O Tam! had thae been queans,[48]
A' plump and strapping in their teens!
Their sarks, instead o' creeshie[49] flannen,

32. like the others named in this line, a vigorous Scottish dance.
33. window seat. 34. shaggy dog. 35. made them scream. 36. vibrate.
37. cupboards. 38. trick of magic. 39. communion table; altar.
40. bones in gibbet irons. 41. rope. 42. mouth.
43. clutched. 44. till each old hag sweated and steamed.
45. threw off her clothes. 46. tripped. 47. shirt. 48. lasses.
49. greasy.

Been snaw-white seventeen hunder linen!—
Thir[50] breeks o' mine, my only pair,
That ance were plush, o' guid blue hair,
I wad hae gi'en them off my hurdies[51]
For ae blink o' the bonie burdies!

But withered beldams, auld and droll,
Rigwoodie[52] hags wad spean[53] a foal,
Louping and flinging on a crummock,[54]
I wonder did na turn thy stomach!

But Tam kend what was what fu' brawlie:[55]
There was ae winsome wench and wawlie,[56]
That night enlisted in the core,[57]
Lang after kend on Carrick shore
(For monie a beast to dead she shot,
An' perished monie a bonie boat,
And shook baith meikle corn and bear,[58]
And kept the country-side in fear).
Her cutty sark,[59] o' Paisley harn,[60]
That while a lassie she had worn,
In longitude tho' sorely scanty,
It was her best, and she was vauntie.[61]
Ah! little kend thy reverend grannie,
That sark she coft[62] for her wee Nannie,
Wi' twa pund Scots ('twas a' her riches),
Wad ever graced a dance of witches!

But here my Muse her wing maun cour,[63]
Sic flights are far beyond her power:
To sing how Nannie lap and flang
(A souple jad she was and strang),
And how Tam stood like ane bewitched,
And thought his very een enriched;
Even Satan glowered, and fidged[64] fu' fain,
And hotched[65] and blew wi' might and main;
Till first ae caper, syne anither,
Tam tint[66] his reason a' thegither,
And roars out: "Weel done, Cutty-sark!"

---

50. these. 51. buttocks. 52. ancient. 53. wean (by disgust).
54. crooked staff. 55. finely. 56. well-built. 57. corps.
58. barley. 59. short smock. 60. coarse cloth. 61. proud.
62. bought. 63. stoop. 64. fidgeted. 65. hitched his arm.
66. lost.

And in an instant all was dark;
And scarcely had he Maggie rallied,
When out the hellish legion sallied.

As bees bizz out wi' angry fyke,[67]
When plundering herds asssail their byke;[68]
As open pussie's[69] mortal foes,
When, pop! she starts before their nose;
As eager runs the market-crowd,
When "Catch the thief!" resounds aloud:
So Maggie runs, the witches follow,
Wi' monie an eldritch[70] skriech and hollo.

Ah, Tam! ah, Tam! thou'll get thy fairin![71]
In hell they'll roast thee like a herrin!
In vain thy Kate awaits thy comin!
Kate soon will be a woefu' woman!
Now, do thy speedy utmost, Meg,
And win the key-stane of the brig;
There, at them thou thy tail may toss,
A running stream they dare na cross!
But ere the key-stane she could make,
The fient[72] a tail she had to shake;
For Nannie, far before the rest,
Hard upon noble Maggie prest,
And flew at Tam wi' furious ettle;[73]
But little wist she Maggie's mettle!
Ae spring brought off her master hale,
But left behind her ain grey tail:
The carlin[74] claught her by the rump,
And left poor Maggie scarce a stump.

Now, wha this tale o' truth shall read,
Ilk man, and mother's son, take heed:
Whene'er to drink you are inclined,
Or cutty sarks run in your mind,
Think! ye may buy the joys o'er dear:
Remember Tam o' Shanter's mare.

---

67. fuss. 68. hive. 69. a hare's. 70. unearthly. 71. reward.
72. devil. 73. aim. 74. witch.

YE FLOWERY BANKS

Ye flowery banks o' bonie Doon,
How can ye blume sae fair?
How can ye chant, ye little birds,
And I sae fu' o' care?

Thou'll break my heart, thou bonie bird,
That sings upon the bough;
Thou minds me o' the happy days
When my fause luve was true!

Thou'll break my heart, thou bonie bird,
That sings beside thy mate;
For sae I sat, and sae I sang,
And wist na o' my fate!

Aft hae I roved by bonie Doon
To see the woodbine twine,
And ilka bird sang o' its luve,
And sae did I o' mine.

Wi' lightsome heart I pu'd a rose
Frae aff its thorny tree;
And my fause luver staw my rose,
But left the thorn wi' me.

ON BURNS' *YE FLOWERY BANKS* [1]

DONALD A. STAUFFER

THE instinctive singers have their own ways of compelling complex states of consciousness in short lyrics. As a final example we might choose a song by Burns. The worn word "little" of the third line suggests in its context a complex state of mind—an expectation of sympathy, a sense of tenderness and sentience in all nature. The fifth line is probably the finest poetically. Burns thought so, for he repeated it. If the poem had gone no further than

Thou'll break my heart, thou bonie bird,

its complexity would already have attained expression through suggestion and inference. The remainder merely keeps the emotion of heartbreak before us by giving in more detail its cause. Yet how this complexity is achieved is hard

1. Reprinted from *The Nature of Poetry,* by Donald A. Stauffer (New York, 1946), pp. 163–166, by permission of W. W. Norton & Company, Inc. Copyright, 1946, W. W. Norton & Company, Inc.

to determine. One remembers another poet who expressed anguish, listening to the song of a bird, and who kept that anguish before his readers by dwelling upon its sources. Keats says "my heart aches"; Burns, "Thou'll break my heart." The difference between *ache* and *break* and the efficacy of each word in its respective poem are almost sufficient proofs of the complexity of poetry. Keats in the "Ode to a Nightingale" goes on:

'Tis not through envy of thy happy lot,
But being too happy in thy happiness.

The idea of the painful transiency of beauty and joy, filling so many of Keats's best poems, here explains his heartache.

Burns's heartbreak, on the other hand, rises not from passing ecstasy but from contrasting moods and times; and although he takes the rest of the poem for amplification, he has already made the antithesis in the first stanza between nature's freshness and his own heaviness (or the heaviness of the girl who perhaps is speaking the poem). Although Burns's lyric centers on a single emotion, that emotion is not simple; furthermore, it is held before the reader not by appealing directly to his emotions, but by presenting pictures and situations to the senses and assuming that their logical relations will be understood. The contrast in the first stanza is between the external joy of flowers and birds and the internal care of the poet. In the second and third stanzas, the joy of nature is associated with the past joy of the poet, so that the contrast develops into an opposition between past happiness and present unhappiness. The theme becomes:

That a sorrow's crown of sorrow is remembering happier things.

The dominant emotion of the poem, therefore, depends upon the interplay between two other emotions—delight in love and anguish at betrayal. The heartbreak would not be so sharp if past joy had never been experienced. Stanza four extends the poet's (or the girl's) past happiness through time and nature and makes it more nearly universal, so that the painful emotion of the moment seems more nearly unbearable; the whole contrast is crystallized in the final stanza, no longer in terms of time, but of space, by the image of the rose and the thorn.

A rose is love; a thorn is betrayal, deceit, falsity, anguish. If one accepts for poetry the laws of concreteness and of significance, poetry is inevitably complex. That is to say, a poem will handle the visibles and tangibles of the world; it will be seeking general significances. At the very least, then, poetry is complex to the extent that it presents ideas in terms of things. The statements of poetry convey their deepest significance obliquely, indirectly. Such poetic thought—and it cannot be simple—is so much a part of us that we must consider closely before we realize that no bonny bird smaller than a vulture could literally break Burns's heart; that we are not supposed to take as an historical fact Burns's plucking a rose which later the false lover stole; that in finding spiritual equivalents for the stealing of a rose and the leaving of the thorn experience almost forces us to think of the poem as spoken by a girl; and that dramatic imagination on Burns's part, rather than actual belief, leads him to suggest that flowers should cease to bloom and birds to sing when he is full of care.

MARY MORISON

1

O Mary, at thy window be!
It is the wished, the trysted hour.
Those smiles and glances let me see,
That make the miser's treasure poor.
How blythely wad I bide the stoure,
A weary slave frae sun to sun,
Could I the rich reward secure—
The lovely Mary Morison!

2

Yestreen, when to the trembling string
The dance gaed thro' the lighted ha',
To thee my fancy took its wing,
I sat, but neither heard or saw:
Tho' this was fair, and that was braw,
And yon the toast of a' the town,
I sighed and said amang them a': —
"Ye are na Mary Morison!"

3

O Mary, canst thou wreck his peace
Wha for thy sake wad gladly die?
Or canst thou break that heart of his
Whase only faut is loving thee?
If love for love thou wilt na gie,
At least be pity to me shown:
A thought ungentle canna be
The thought o' Mary Morison.

WILLIAM WORDSWORTH

MY HEART LEAPS UP WHEN I BEHOLD

My heart leaps up when I behold
    A rainbow in the sky:
So was it when my life began;
So is it now I am a man;
So be it when I shall grow old,
    Or let me die!
The Child is father of the Man;
And I could wish my days to be
Bound each to each by natural piety.

COMPOSED UPON WESTMINSTER BRIDGE

Earth has not anything to show more fair:
Dull would he be of soul who could pass by
A sight so touching in its majesty:
This city now doth, like a garment, wear
The beauty of the morning; silent, bare,
Ships, towers, domes, theaters, and temples lie
Open unto the fields, and to the sky;
All bright and glittering in the smokeless air.
Never did sun more beautifully steep
In his first splendor, valley, rock, or hill;
Ne'er saw I, never felt a calm so deep!
The river glideth at his own sweet will:
Dear God! the very houses seem asleep;
And all that mighty heart is lying still!

I WANDERED LONELY AS A CLOUD

I wandered lonely as a cloud
That floats on high o'er vales and hills,
When all at once I saw a crowd,
A host, of golden daffodils;
Beside the lake, beneath the trees,
Fluttering and dancing in the breeze.

Continuous as the stars that shine
And twinkle on the milky way,
They stretched in never-ending line

Along the margin of a bay:
Ten thousand saw I at a glance,
Tossing their heads in sprightly dance.

The waves beside them danced; but they
Out-did the sparkling waves in glee:
A poet could not but be gay
In such a jocund company:
I gazed—and gazed—but little thought
What wealth the show to me had brought:

For oft, when on my couch I lie
In vacant or in pensive mood,
They flash upon that inward eye
Which is the bliss of solitude;
And then my heart with pleasure fills,
And dances with the daffodils.

ON WORDSWORTH'S *I WANDERED LONELY AS A CLOUD* [1]

FREDERICK A. POTTLE

WHAT are we to make of Wordsworth's boast that he endeavored at all times to look steadily at his subject? I shall try to answer the question by tracing the steps he followed in writing one of his most famous poems, "I Wandered Lonely as a Cloud," commonly (though with no authority from Wordsworth) called "Daffodils." The starting point is the entry in Dorothy's journal for April 15, 1802. That entry is fairly long, but it is all good reading; and I have my reasons for not eliminating any of it.

"It was a threatening, misty morning, but mild. We set off after dinner from Eusemere. Mrs. Clarkson went a short way with us, but turned back. The wind was furious, and we thought we must have returned. We first rested in the large boat-house, then under a furze bush opposite Mr. Clarkson's. Saw the plough going in the field. The wind seized our breath. The Lake was rough. There was a boat by itself floating in the middle of the bay below Water Millock. We rested again in the Water Millock Lane. The hawthorns are black and green, the birches here and there greenish, but there is yet more of purple to be seen on the twigs. We got over into a field to avoid some cows—people working. A few primroses by the roadside—woodsorrel flower, the anemone, scentless violets, strawberries, and that starry, yellow flower which Mrs. C. calls pile wort. When we were in the woods beyond Gowbarrow Park we saw a few

1. Reprinted from *The Yale Review*, XL (Autumn, 1950), 29–35. Copyright, 1950, Yale University Press. Reprinted by permission of the author and the Yale University Press.

daffodils close to the water-side. We fancied that the lake had floated the seeds ashore, and that the little colony had so sprung up. But as we went along there were more and yet more; and at last, under the boughs of the trees, we saw that there was a long belt of them along the shore, about the breadth of a country turnpike road. I never saw daffodils so beautiful. They grew among the mossy stones about and about them; some rested their heads upon these stones as on a pillow for weariness; and the rest tossed and reeled and danced, and seemed as if they verily laughed with the wind, that blew upon them over the lake; they looked so gay, ever glancing, ever changing. This wind blew directly over the lake to them. There was here and there a little knot, and a few stragglers a few yards higher up; but they were so few as not to disturb the simplicity, unity, and life of that one busy highway. We rested again and again. The bays were stormy, and we heard the waves at different distances, and in the middle of the water, like the sea. Rain came on—we were wet when we reached Luff's, but we called in. Luckily all was cheerless and gloomy, so we faced the storm—we *must* have been wet if we had waited—put on dry clothes at Dobson's. I was very kindly treated by a young woman, the landlady looked sour, but it is her way. She gave us a goodish supper, excellent ham and potatoes. We paid 7/– when we came away. William was sitting by a bright fire when I came downstairs. He soon made his way to the library, piled up in a corner of the window. He brought out a volume of Enfield's *Speaker,* another miscellany, and an odd volume of Congreve's plays. We had a glass of warm rum and water. We enjoyed ourselves, and wished for Mary. It rained and blew, when we went to bed. N.B. Deer in Gowbarrow Park like skeletons."

I said this was the starting point, for it is as near the raw matter of the poem as we can get. The true raw matter was certain perceptions—visual, auditory, tactile—which Wordsworth and his sister had on that windy April morning; and those we have no way of recovering. In Dorothy's entry this raw matter has already been grasped and shaped by a powerful imagination, and it has been verbalized. The entry is not a poem, because it contains a good deal of true but inconsequential statement (the rum and water, the volume of Congreve), but much of it is prefabricated material for a poem. And the fact is (though this is doctrine little heard of among men) that Wordsworth made grateful use of prefabricated material whenever he could get it of the right sort. As Professor Lane Cooper showed us long ago, he went regularly to books of travel for material of the right sort, but his best source was his sister's journal.

The function of the Imagination, as Wordsworth and Coleridge insisted, is, at the first level, to make sense out of the undifferentiated manifold of sensation by organizing it into individual objects or things; at the second, and specifically poetic, level, to reshape this world of common perception in the direction of a unity that shall be even more satisfactory and meaningful. Dorothy has made extensive use of the secondary or poetic imagination. Notice the devices by which she has unified and made sense of the experience of the daffodils. First, and most important, she has endowed them with human qualities. They are a social group engaged in busy concerted activity. The notion of the social group, the crowd (she does not actually use the word) is reinforced by her further figure of stragglers. Secondly, besides being active, the crowd of daffodils is happy: they look gay, they toss and reel and dance (their very activity is sport) and seem verily to laugh. And thirdly, some of the crowd have danced so hard that they are tired: they rest their heads upon the stones as on pillows.

Wordsworth recollected the scene in tranquillity and wrote his poem a full two years afterwards. He fixes on Dorothy's fine central perception of "the simplicity, unity, and life of that one busy highway," and condenses it into the one word "crowd." He takes over, too, her impression that the daffodils were "dancing," that they were "gay," that they were even "laughing." Ever since 1807, when Wordsworth published this poem, daffodils have danced and laughed, but there is nothing inevitable about it. The Greek myth of Narcissus is not exactly hilarious; and even Herrick, when he looked at a daffodil, saw something far from jocund:

When a Daffadill I see
Hanging down his head t'wards me,
Guesse I may, what I must be:
First, I shall decline my head;
Secondly, I shall be dead;
Lastly, safely buryed.

The literal, positivistic, "scientific" fact was that Wordsworth and his sister saw a large bed of wild daffodils beside a lake, agitated by a strong, cold spring wind. The rest is all the work of the imagination.

The mark of the poetic imagination is to simplify: to make the manifold of sensation more meaningful by reducing it to a number of objects which can actually be contemplated. Wordsworth continues Dorothy's process of simplification: he eliminates the bitterness of the wind, which is so prominent in her account; reduces the wind, in fact, to a breeze. It may appear here that he has simplified more than was necessary or wise. Shakespeare, in the most famous lines ever written about daffodils, kept the wind:

Daffodils
That come before the swallow dares, and take
The winds of March with beauty.

Admittedly, it is a higher mode. Wordsworth, on some occasions, would have kept the wind, too; but to have kept it here would have made a more complex —if you will, a more tragic—poem than he felt like writing. He felt this poem as something very simple and very pure; when he came to publish it, he put it in a group called "Moods of My Own Mind." But he is impartial; as he throws out matter on the one hand because it is too serious, so he eliminates matter on the other because it is too playful. The prettiest thing in Dorothy's realization —her image of the daffodils pillowing their heads on the stones—drops out. He dispenses too with Dorothy's stragglers. He fastens on her central image of the dancing, laughing crowd, and lets everything else go.

But now the idea of the crowd calls for a modification, and a modification of a fundamental sort. The social glee of the crowd can be made more significant if it is set over against solitary joy; and so in the poem he makes himself solitary, which in literal fact he was not. He now has what for him is a promising situation. The solitariness of the poet and the sociability of the daffodils are set up as poles between which the poem discharges itself. I have said that the situation is for him a promising one. Everyone knows of Wordsworth's love of solitude, his conviction that the highest experiences came to him when he was alone. What we need constantly to remind ourselves of is that his theory assigned an only slightly lower value to the love of men in societies. (The subtitle of Book VIII of "The Prelude" is "Love of Nature Leading to Love of Mankind.") The trouble was that, though he had the best of intentions, he could never handle close-packed, present, human crowds in the mode of Imagination. If he were to grasp the life of a great city imaginatively, it had to be at night or early in the morning, while the streets were deserted; or at least in bad weather, when few people were abroad.

But in the figure of a bed of daffodils endowed with human characteristics, he can handle with feelings of approval and exhilaration the concept of a crowd, of ten thousand individuals packed close together. He begins and ends solitary: at the beginning, we may assume, filled with joy, but a joy somewhat solemn, somewhat cold and remote, as the symbol of the cloud indicates. He is surprised by the sensation of mere unmixed human gaiety and light-heartedness, yields to it, and finds it good; so good that ever after he can derive refreshment from the memory of the experience.

The progress towards explicit identification of the symbol is gradual. In the first stanza the flowers are "fluttering" (literal: the flowers are moved by the breeze); then "dancing" (the flowers are self-moved). By the end of the second stanza they are "tossing their heads in sprightly dance." (The flowers are self-moved and are having a wonderful time. "Dance" is the key-word: it occurs in either the last or the first line of each stanza.) Finally, but not till the third stanza is reached, we get the quite explicit series "glee," "gay," "jocund," "pleasure." Wordsworth is always (or almost always) explicit in this fashion: he tells you just how you are expected to take his figures. Of course it is the figures that do the work. No one can make us joyful by merely using the word "joy" or any of its synonyms. But there is impressive agreement among readers of all periods that by giving us a simple figure, reinforcing it by certain devices of varied iteration, and explicitly interpreting it, Wordsworth does evoke the emotion of joy.

We can now see what Wordsworth meant by looking steadily at his subject.

So far as his subject is expressed in imagery drawn from nature (and that means in all his best poetry), there is implied a lifelong habit of close, detailed, and accurate observation of the objects composing the external universe. By "accurate" I mean something the same thing as "naturalistic," but not entirely so. Wordsworth scorned the merely analytic vision of the naturalist ("One that would peep and botanize Upon his mother's grave"), because in his opinion that kind of apprehension empties the object of life and meaning by detaching it from its ground. "His theme is nature *in solido,*" as Whitehead pointed out, "that is to say, he dwells on that mysterious presence of surrounding things, which imposes itself on any separate element that we set up as an individual for its own sake. He always grasps the whole of nature as involved in the tonality of the particular instance." But, except for those portions of the scientist's vision which require (let us say) dissection and magnification, there is little in the scientist's vision that Wordsworth misses. A *merely* matter-of-fact, an *exclusively* positivistic view of nature fills him with anger, but his own apprehension includes the matter-of-fact view without denying any of it. Dr. Leavis has perhaps put this more intelligibly when he remarks, as the chief virtue of Wordsworth's poetry, a "firm hold upon the world of common perception," though I myself should like to modify it, "in the mode of perception which has been common in Western civilization since some time in the late eighteenth century." In a literal, physiological sense, Wordsworth did look steadily at the natural objects that appear in his poetry.

THE WORLD IS TOO MUCH WITH US

The world is too much with us: late and soon,
Getting and spending, we lay waste our powers:
Little we see in Nature that is ours;
We have given our hearts away, a sordid boon!
This Sea that bares her bosom to the moon;
The winds that will be howling at all hours,
And are up-gathered now like sleeping flowers;
For this, for everything, we are out of tune;
It moves us not.—Great God! I'd rather be
A pagan suckled in a creed outworn;
So might I, standing on this pleasant lea,
Have glimpses that would make me less forlorn;
Have sight of Proteus rising from the sea;
Or hear old Triton blow his wreathèd horn.

SAMUEL T. COLERIDGE

KUBLA KHAN; OR, A VISION IN A DREAM

A Fragment

In Xanadu did Kubla Khan
A stately pleasure-dome decree:
Where Alph, the sacred river, ran
Through caverns measureless to man
Down to a sunless sea.
So twice five miles of fertile ground
With walls and towers were girdled round:
And here were gardens bright with sinuous rills,
Where blossomed many an incense-bearing tree;
And here were forests ancient as the hills,
Enfolding sunny spots of greenery.

But oh! that deep romantic chasm which slanted
Down the green hill athwart a cedarn cover!
A savage place! as holy and enchanted
As e'er beneath a waning moon was haunted
By woman wailing for her demon-lover!
And from this chasm, with ceaseless turmoil seething,
As if this earth in fast thick pants were breathing,
A mighty fountain momently was forced:
Amid whose swift half-intermitted burst
Huge fragments vaulted like rebounding hail,
Or chaffy grain beneath the thresher's flail:
And 'mid these dancing rocks at once and ever
It flung up momently the sacred river.
Five miles meandering with a mazy motion
Through wood and dale the sacred river ran,
Then reached the caverns measureless to man,
And sank in tumult to a lifeless ocean:
And 'mid this tumult Kubla heard from far
Ancestral voices prophesying war!

The shadow of the dome of pleasure
Floated midway on the waves;
Where was heard the mingled measure
From the fountain and the caves.
It was a miracle of rare device,
A sunny pleasure-dome with caves of ice!

A damsel with a dulcimer
In a vision once I saw:
It was an Abyssinian maid,
And on her dulcimer she played,
Singing of Mount Abora.
Could I revive within me,
Her symphony and song,
To such a deep delight 'twould win me,
That with music loud and long,
I would build that dome in air,
That sunny dome! those caves of ice!
And all who heard should see them there,
And all should cry, Beware! Beware!
His flashing eyes, his floating hair!
Weave a circle round him thrice,
And close your eyes with holy dread,
For he on honey-dew hath fed,
And drunk the milk of Paradise.

GEORGE GORDON, LORD BYRON

THE DESTRUCTION OF SENNACHERIB

The Assyrian came down like the wolf on the fold,
And his cohorts were gleaming in purple and gold;
And the sheen of their spears was like stars on the sea,
When the blue wave rolls nightly on deep Galilee.

Like the leaves of the forest when Summer is green,
That host with their banners at sunset were seen:
Like the leaves of the forest when Autumn hath blown,
That host on the morrow lay withered and strown.

For the Angel of Death spread his wings on the blast,
And breathed in the face of the foe as he passed;
And the eyes of the sleepers waxed deadly and chill,
And their hearts but once heaved, and for ever grew still!

And there lay the steed with his nostril all wide,
But through it there rolled not the breath of his pride;
And the foam of his gasping lay white on the turf,
And cold as the spray of the rock-beating surf.

And there lay the rider distorted and pale,
With the dew on his brow, and the rust on his mail:
And the tents were all silent, the banners alone,
The lances unlifted, the trumpet unblown.

And the widows of Ashur are loud in their wail,
And the idols are broke in the temple of Baal;
And the might of the Gentile, unsmote by the sword,
Hath melted like snow in the glance of the Lord!

DON JUAN

Canto the Second

1

Oh ye! who teach the ingenuous youth of nations,
Holland, France, England, Germany, or Spain,
I pray ye flog them upon all occasions,
It mends their morals, never mind the pain:
The best of mothers and of educations
In Juan's case were but employ'd in vain,
Since, in a way that's rather of the oddest, he
Became divested of his native modesty.

2

Had he but been placed at a public school,
In the third form, or even in the fourth,
His daily task had kept his fancy cool,
At least, had he been nurtured in the north;
Spain may prove an exception to the rule,
But then exceptions always prove its worth—
A lad of sixteen causing a divorce
Puzzled his tutors very much, of course.

3

I can't say that it puzzles me at all,
If all things be consider'd; first, there was
His lady-mother, mathematical,
A——never mind;—his tutor, an old ass;
A pretty woman —(that's quite natural,
Or else the thing had hardly come to pass)
A husband rather old, not much in unity
With his young wife—a time, and opportunity.

4

Well—well; the world must turn upon its axis,
And all mankind turn with it, heads or tails,
And live and die, make love and pay our taxes,
And as the veering wind shifts, shift our sails;
The king commands us, and the doctor quacks us,
The priest instructs, and so our life exhales,
A little breath, love, wine, ambition, fame,
Fighting, devotion, dust,—perhaps a name.

5

I said, that Juan had been sent to Cadiz—
A pretty town, I recollect it well—
'Tis there the mart of the colonial trade is,
(Or was, before Peru learn'd to rebel,)
And such sweet girls—I mean, such graceful ladies,
Their very walk would make your bosom swell;
I can't describe it, though so much it strike,
Nor liken it—I never saw the like:

6

An Arab horse, a stately stag, a barb
New-broke, a cameleopard, a gazelle,
No—none of these will do—and then their garb,
Their veil and petticoat—Alas! to dwell
Upon such things would very near absorb
A canto—then their feet and ankles,—well,
Thank Heaven I've got no metaphor quite ready,
(And so, my sober Muse—come, let's be steady—

7

Chaste Muse!—well, if you must, you must)—the veil
Thrown back a moment with the glancing hand,
While the o'erpowering eye, that turns you pale,
Flashes into the heart:—All sunny land
Of love! when I forget you, may I fail
To——say my prayers—but never was there plann'd
A dress through which the eyes give such a volley,
Excepting the Venetian Fazzioli.

8

But to our tale: the Donna Inez sent
Her son to Cadiz only to embark;
To stay there had not answer'd her intent,

But why?—we leave the reader in the dark—
'Twas for a voyage the young man was meant,
As if a Spanish ship were Noah's ark,
To wean him from the wickedness of earth,
And send him like a dove of promise forth.

9

Don Juan bade his valet pack his things
According to direction, then received
A lecture and some money: for four springs
He was to travel; and though Inez grieved
(As every kind of parting has its stings),
She hoped he would improve—perhaps believed:
A letter, too, she gave (he never read it)
Of good advice—and two or three of credit.

10

In the mean time, to pass her hours away,
Brave Inez now set up a Sunday school
For naughty children, who would rather play
(Like truant rogues) the devil, or the fool;
Infants of three years old were taught that day,
Dunces were whipt, or set upon a stool:
The great success of Juan's education
Spurr'd her to teach another generation.

11

Juan embark'd—the ship got under way,
The wind was fair, the water passing rough;
A devil of a sea rolls in that bay,
As I, who've cross'd it oft, know well enough;
And, standing upon deck, the dashing spray
Flies in one's face, and makes it weather-tough:
And there he stood to take, and take again,
His first—perhaps his last—farewell of Spain.

12

I can't but say it is an awkward sight
To see one's native land receding through
The growing waters; it unmans one quite,
Especially when life is rather new:
I recollect Great Britain's coast looks white,
But almost every other country's blue,

When gazing on them, mystified by distance,
We enter on our nautical existence.

13

So Juan stood, bewilder'd on the deck:
The wind sung, cordage strain'd, and sailors swore,
And the ship creak'd, the town became a speck,
From which away so fair and fast they bore.
The best of remedies is a beef-steak
Against sea-sickness; try it, sir, before
You sneer, and I assure you this is true,
For I have found it answer—so may you.

14

Don Juan stood, and, gazing from the stern,
Beheld his native Spain receding far:
First partings form a lesson hard to learn,
Even nations feel this when they go to war;
There is a sort of unexprest concern,
A kind of shock that sets one's heart ajar:
At leaving even the most unpleasant people
And places, one keeps looking at the steeple.

15

But Juan had got many things to leave,
His mother, and a mistress, and no wife,
So that he had much better cause to grieve
Than many persons more advanced in life;
And if we now and then a sigh must heave
At quitting even those we quit in strife,
No doubt we weep for those the heart endears—
That is, till deeper griefs congeal our tears.

16

So Juan wept, as wept the captive Jews
By Babel's waters, still remembering Sion:
I'd weep,—but mine is not a weeping Muse,
And such light griefs are not a thing to die on;
Young men should travel, if but to amuse
Themselves; and the next time their servants tie on
Behind their carriages their new portmanteau,
Perhaps it may be lined with this my canto.

17

And Juan wept, and much he sigh'd and thought,
While his salt tears dropp'd into the salt sea,
"Sweets to the sweet;" (I like so much to quote;
You must excuse this extract,—'t is where she,
The Queen of Denmark, for Ophelia brought
Flowers to the grave;) and, sobbing often, he
Reflected on his present situation,
And seriously resolved on reformation.

18

"Farewell, my Spain! a long farewell!" he cried,
"Perhaps I may revisit thee no more,
But die, as many an exiled heart hath died,
Of its own thirst to see again thy shore:
Farewell, where Guadalquivir's waters glide!
Farewell, my mother! and, since all is o'er,
Farewell, too, dearest Julia!—(here he drew
Her letter out again, and read it through.)

19

"And oh! if e'er I should forget, I swear—
But that's impossible, and cannot be—
Sooner shall this blue ocean melt to air,
Sooner shall earth resolve itself to sea,
Than I resign thine image, oh, my fair!
Or think of anything, excepting thee;
A mind diseased no remedy can physic—
(Here the ship gave a lurch, and he grew sea-sick.)

20

"Sooner shall heaven kiss earth—(here he fell sicker)
Oh, Julia! what is every other woe?—
(For God's sake let me have a glass of liquor;
Pedro, Battista, help me down below.)
Julia, my love—(you rascal, Pedro, quicker)—
Oh, Julia!—(this curst vessel pitches so)—
Beloved Julia, hear me still beseeching!"
(Here he grew inarticulate with retching.)

21

He felt that chilling heaviness of heart,
Or rather stomach, which, alas! attends,
Beyond the best apothecary's art,

The loss of love, the treachery of friends,
Or death of those we dote on, when a part
Of us dies with them as each fond hope ends:
No doubt he would have been much more pathetic,
But the sea acted as a strong emetic.

22

Love's a capricious power: I've known it hold
Out through a fever caused by its own heat,
But be much puzzled by a cough and cold,
And find a quinsy very hard to treat;
Against all noble maladies he's bold,
But vulgar illnesses don't like to meet,
Nor that a sneeze should interrupt his sigh,
Nor inflammations redden his blind eye.

23

But worst of all is nausea, or a pain
About the lower region of the bowels;
Love, who heroically breathes a vein,
Shrinks from the application of hot towels,
And purgatives are dangerous to his reign,
Sea-sickness death: his love was perfect, how else
Could Juan's passion, while the billows roar,
Resist his stomach, ne'er at sea before?

PERCY BYSSHE SHELLEY

OZYMANDIAS

I met a traveller from an antique land
Who said: "Two vast and trunkless legs of stone
Stand in the desert. Near them, on the sand,
Half sunk, a shattered visage lies, whose frown,
And wrinkled lip, and sneer of cold command,
Tell that its sculptor well those passions read
Which yet survive, stamped on these lifeless things,
The hand that mocked them, and the heart that fed:
And on the pedestal these words appear:
'My name is Ozymandias, king of kings:
Look on my works, ye Mighty, and despair!'
Nothing beside remains. Round the decay

Of that colossal wreck, boundless and bare
The lone and level sands stretch far away."

ODE TO THE WEST WIND

1

O wild West Wind, thou breath of Autumn's being,
Thou, from whose unseen presence the leaves dead
Are driven, like ghosts from an enchanter fleeing,

Yellow, and black, and pale, and hectic red,
Pestilence-stricken multitudes: O thou,
Who chariotest to their dark wintry bed

The wingèd seeds, where they lie cold and low,
Each like a corpse within its grave, until
Thine azure sister of the spring shall blow

Her clarion o'er the dreaming earth, and fill
(Driving sweet buds like flocks to feed in air)
With living hues and odors plain and hill:

Wild Spirit, which art moving everywhere;
Destroyer and preserver; hear, oh hear!

2

Thou on whose stream, 'mid the steep sky's commotion,
Loose clouds like earth's decaying leaves are shed,
Shook from the tangled boughs of Heaven and Ocean,

Angels of rain and lightning: there are spread
On the blue surface of thine airy surge,
Like the bright hair uplifted from the head

Of some fierce Maenad, even from the dim verge
Of the horizon to the zenith's height
The locks of the approaching storm. Thou dirge

Of the dying year, to which this closing night
Will be the dome of a vast sepulchre,
Vaulted with all thy congregated might

Of vapours, from whose solid atmosphere
Black rain, and fire, and hail will burst: O, hear!

3

Thou who didst waken from his summer dreams
The blue Mediterranean, where he lay,
Lulled by the coil of his crystalline streams,

Beside a pumice isle in Baiæ's bay,
And saw in sleep old palaces and towers
Quivering within the wave's intenser day,

All overgrown with azure moss and flowers
So sweet, the sense faints picturing them! Thou
For whose path the Atlantic's level powers

Cleave themselves into chasms, while far below
The sea-blooms and the oozy woods which wear
The sapless foliage of the ocean, know

Thy voice, and suddenly grow gray with fear,
And tremble and despoil themselves: O hear!

4

If I were a dead leaf thou mightest bear;
If I were a swift cloud to fly with thee;
A wave to pant beneath thy power, and share

The impulse of thy strength, only less free
Than thou, O, uncontrollable! If even
I were as in my boyhood, and could be

The comrade of thy wanderings over heaven,
As then, when to outstrip thy skiey speed
Scarce seemed a vision; I would ne'er have striven

As thus with thee in prayer in my sore need,
Oh! lift me as a wave, a leaf, a cloud!
I fall upon the thorns of life! I bleed!

A heavy weight of hours has chained and bowed
One too like thee: tameless, and swift, and proud.

5

Make me thy lyre, even as the forest is:
What if my leaves are falling like its own!
The tumult of thy mighty harmonies

Will take from both a deep, autumnal tone,
Sweet though in sadness. Be thou, Spirit fierce,
My spirit! Be thou me, impetuous one!

Drive my dead thoughts over the universe
Like withered leaves to quicken a new birth!
And, by the incantation of this verse,

Scatter, as from an unextinguished hearth
Ashes and sparks, my words among mankind!
Be through my lips to unawakened earth

The trumpet of a prophecy! O, Wind,
If Winter comes, can Spring be far behind?

TO A SKYLARK

Hail to thee, blithe spirit!
  Bird thou never wert,
That from heaven, or near it,
  Pourest thy full heart
In profuse strains of unpremeditated art.

Higher still and higher
  From the earth thou springest
Like a cloud of fire;
  The blue deep thou wingest,
And singing still dost soar, and soaring ever singest.

In the golden lightning
  Of the sunken sun,
O'er which clouds are bright'ning,
  Thou dost float and run;
Like an unbodied joy whose race is just begun.

The pale purple even
  Melts around thy flight;
Like a star of heaven
  In the broad daylight
Thou art unseen, but yet I hear thy shrill delight,

Keen as are the arrows
  Of that silver sphere,
Whose intense lamp narrows

In the white dawn clear,
Until we hardly see, we feel that it is there.

All the earth and air
With thy voice is loud,
As, when night is bare,
From one lonely cloud
The moon rains out her beams, and heaven is overflowed.

What thou art we know not;
What is most like thee?
From rainbow clouds there flow not
Drops so bright to see
As from thy presence showers a rain of melody.

Like a poet hidden
In the light of thought,
Singing hymns unbidden,
Till the world is wrought
To sympathy with hopes and fears it heeded not:

Like a highborn maiden
In a palace tower,
Soothing her love-laden
Soul in secret hour
With music sweet as love, which overflows her bower:

Like a glowworm golden
In a dell of dew,
Scattering unbeholden
Its aërial hue
Among the flowers and grass which screen it from the view:

Like a rose embowered
In its own green leaves,
By warm winds deflowered,
Till the scent it gives
Makes faint with too much sweet these heavy-wingèd thieves.

Sound of vernal showers
On the twinkling grass,
Rain-awakened flowers,
All that ever was
Joyous and clear and fresh, thy music doth surpass.

Teach us, sprite or bird,
What sweet thoughts are thine;
I have never heard
Praise of love or wine
That panted forth a flood of rapture so divine.

Chorus Hymeneal,
Or triumphal chaunt,
Matched with thine would be all
But an empty vaunt,
A thing wherein we feel there is some hidden want.

What objects are the fountains
Of thy happy strain?
What fields, or waves, or mountains?
What shapes of sky or plain?
What love of thine own kind? what ignorance of pain?

With thy clear keen joyance
Languor cannot be:
Shadow of annoyance
Never came near thee:
Thou lovest, but ne'er knew love's sad satiety.

Waking or asleep,
Thou of death must deem
Things more true and deep
Than we mortals dream,
Or how could thy notes flow in such a crystal stream?

We look before and after,
And pine for what is not:
Our sincerest laughter
With some pain is fraught;
Our sweetest songs are those that tell of saddest thought.

Yet if we could scorn
Hate and pride and fear;
If we were things born
Not to shed a tear,
I know not how thy joy we ever should come near.

Better than all measures
Of delightful sound,
Better than all treasures

That in books are found,
Thy skill to poet were, thou scorner of the ground!

Teach me half the gladness
That thy brain must know,
Such harmonious madness
From my lips would flow,
The world should listen then, as I am listening now.

JOHN KEATS

ON FIRST LOOKING INTO CHAPMAN'S HOMER

Much have I travelled in the realms of gold,
And many goodly states and kingdoms seen;
Round many western islands have I been
Which bards in fealty to Apollo hold.
Oft of one wide expanse had I been told,
That deep-browed Homer ruled as his demesne:
Yet did I never breathe its pure serene
Till I heard Chapman speak out loud and bold:
Then felt I like some watcher of the skies
When a new planet swims into his ken;
Or like stout Cortez when with eagle eyes
He stared at the Pacific—and all his men
Looked at each other with a wild surmise—
Silent, upon a peak in Darien.

ODE ON A GRECIAN URN

1

Thou still unravished bride of quietness,
Thou foster-child of silence and slow time,
Sylvan historian, who canst thus express
A flowery tale more sweetly than our rhyme:
What leaf-fringed legend haunts about thy shape
Of deities or mortals, or of both,
In Tempe or the dales of Arcady?
What men or gods are these? What maidens loth?
What mad pursuit? What struggle to escape?
What pipes and timbrels? What wild ecstasy?

2

Heard melodies are sweet, but those unheard
Are sweeter; therefore, ye soft pipes, play on;
Not to the sensual ear, but, more endeared,
Pipe to the spirit ditties of no tone:
Fair youth, beneath the trees, thou canst not leave
Thy song, nor ever can those trees be bare;
Bold Lover, never, never canst thou kiss,
Though winning near the goal—yet, do not grieve;
She cannot fade, though thou hast not thy bliss,
Forever wilt thou love, and she be fair!

3

Ah, happy, happy boughs! that cannot shed
Your leaves, nor ever bid the Spring adieu:
And, happy melodist, unwearied,
Forever piping songs forever new;
More happy love! more happy, happy love!
Forever warm and still to be enjoyed,
Forever panting, and forever young;
All breathing human passion far above,
That leaves a heart high-sorrowful and cloyed,
A burning forehead, and a parching tongue.

4

Who are these coming to the sacrifice?
To what green altar, O mysterious priest,
Lead'st thou that heifer lowing at the skies,
And all her silken flanks with garlands dressed?
What little town by river or sea shore,
Or mountain-built with peaceful citadel,
Is emptied of this folk, this pious morn?
And, little town, thy streets for ever more
Will silent be; and not a soul to tell
Why thou are desolate, can e'er return.

5

O Attic shape! Fair attitude! with brede
Of marble men and maidens overwrought,
With forest branches and the trodden weed;
Thou, silent form, dost tease us out of thought
As doth eternity: Cold Pastoral!
When old age shall this generation waste,

Thou shalt remain, in midst of other woe
Than ours, a friend to man, to whom thou say'st,
"Beauty is truth, truth beauty,"—that is all
Ye know on earth, and all ye need to know.

LA BELLE DAME SANS MERCI

Oh, what can ail thee, knight-at-arms,
Alone and palely loitering?
The sedge has withered from the lake,
And no birds sing.

Oh, what can ail thee, knight-at-arms,
So haggard and so woe-begone?
The squirrel's granary is full,
And the harvest's done.

I see a lily on thy brow,
With anguish moist and fever dew;
And on thy cheeks a fading rose
Fast withereth too.

"I met a lady in the meads,
Full beautiful—a faery's child;
Her hair was long, her foot was light,
And her eyes were wild.

"I made a garland for her head,
And bracelets too, and fragrant zone;
She looked at me as she did love,
And made sweet moan.

"I set her on my pacing steed,
And nothing else saw all day long;
For sideways would she lean, and sing
A faery's song.

"She found me roots of relish sweet,
And honey wild, and manna-dew,
And sure in language strange she said,
'I love thee true.'

"She took me to her elfin grot,
And there she wept, and sighed full sore,

And there I shut her wild, wild eyes,
With kisses four.

"And there she lullèd me asleep,
And there I dreamed—ah! woe betide!—
The latest dream I ever dreamed
On the cold hill side.

"I saw pale kings and princes too,
Pale warriors, death-pale were they all,
They cried—'La Belle Dame sans Merci
Hath thee in thrall!'

"I saw their starved lips in the gloam,
With horrid warning gapèd wide;
And I awoke, and found me here
On the cold hill's side.

"And this is why I sojourn here
Alone and palely loitering,
Though the sedge is withered from the lake,
And no birds sing."

TO AUTUMN

Season of mists and mellow fruitfulness,
Close bosom-friend of the maturing sun;
Conspiring with him how to load and bless
With fruit the vines that round the thatch-eaves run;
To bend with apples the mossed cottage-trees,
And fill all fruit with ripeness to the core;
To swell the gourd, and plump the hazel shells
With a sweet kernel; to set budding more,
And still more, later flowers for the bees,
Until they think warm days will never cease,
For Summer has o'er-brimmed their clammy cells.

Who hath not seen thee oft amid thy store?
Sometimes whoever seeks abroad may find
Thee sitting careless on a granary floor,
Thy hair soft-lifted by the winnowing wind;
Or on a half-reaped furrow sound asleep,
Drowsed with the fume of poppies, while thy hook
Spares the next swath and all its twinèd flowers:

And sometimes like a gleaner thou dost keep
Steady thy laden head across a brook;
Or by a cider-press, with patient look,
Thou watchest the last oozings hours by hours.

Where are the songs of Spring? Ay, where are they?
Think not of them, thou hast thy music too,—
While barrèd clouds bloom the soft-dying day,
And touch the stubble-plains with rosy hue;
Then in a wailful choir the small gnats mourn
Among the river sallows, borne aloft
Or sinking as the light wind lives or dies;
And full-grown lambs loud bleat from hilly bourn;
Hedge-crickets sing; and now with treble soft
The red-breast whistles from a garden-croft;
And gathering swallows twitter in the skies.

BRIGHT STAR, WOULD I WERE STEDFAST AS THOU ART

Bright star, would I were stedfast as thou art—
Not in lone splendor hung aloft the night,
And watching, with eternal lids apart,
Like nature's patient sleepless Eremite,
The moving waters at their priest-like task
Of pure ablution round earth's human shores,
Or gazing on the new soft fallen mask
Of snow upon the mountains and the moors:
No—yet still stedfast, still unchangeable,
Pillowed upon my fair love's ripening breast
To feel for ever its soft fall and swell,
Awake for ever in a sweet unrest;
Still, still to hear her tender-taken breath,
And so live ever—or else swoon to death.

RALPH WALDO EMERSON

DAYS

Daughters of Time, the hypocritic Days,
Muffled and dumb like barefoot dervishes,
And marching single in an endless file,

Bring diadems and fagots in their hands.
To each they offer gifts after his will,
Bread, kingdoms, stars, and sky that holds them all.
I, in my pleachèd garden, watched the pomp,
Forgot my morning wishes, hastily
Took a few herbs and apples, and the Day
Turned and departed silent. I, too late,
Under her solemn fillet saw the scorn.

BRAHMA

If the red slayer thinks he slays,
    Or if the slain think he is slain,
They know not well the subtle ways
    I keep, and pass, and turn again.

Far or forgot to me is near;
    Shadow and sunlight are the same;
The vanished gods to me appear;
    And one to me are shame and fame.

They reckon ill who leave me out;
    When me they fly, I am the wings;
I am the doubter and the doubt,
    And I the hymn the Brahmin sings.

The strong gods pine for my abode,
    And pine in vain the sacred Seven;
But thou, meek lover of the good!
    Find me, and turn thy back on heaven.

ELIZABETH BARRETT BROWNING

SONNET FROM THE PORTUGUESE, XLIII

How do I love thee? Let me count the ways.
I love thee to the depth and breadth and height
My soul can reach, when feeling out of sight
For the ends of Being and ideal Grace.
I love thee to the level of every day's
Most quiet need, by sun and candlelight.
I love thee freely, as men strive for Right;

I love thee purely, as they turn from Praise.
I love thee with the passion put to use
In my old griefs, and with my childhood's faith.
I love thee with a love I seemed to lose
With my lost saints,—I love thee with the breath,
Smiles, tears, of all my life!—and, if God choose,
I shall but love thee better after death.

ON E. B. BROWNING'S *SONNET FROM THE PORTUGUESE, XLIII* [1]

ROBERT B. HEILMAN

"How DO I love thee?" is a theme on which both Elizabeth Barret Browning and Goneril, daughter of Lear, expressed themselves in pentameters—with certain recognizable similarities. Goneril says (*King Lear,* I, i, 56-62):

> Dearer than eye-sight, space, and liberty;
> Beyond what can be valued, rich or rare;
> No less than life, with grace, health, beauty, honour . . . .

E.B.B. says (*Sonnets from the Portuguese,* XLIII):

> I love thee to the depth and breadth and height
> My soul can reach, when feeling out of sight
> For the ends of Being and ideal Grace . . . .
> I love thee freely, as men strive for Right;
> I love thee purely, as they turn from Praise.

There is a notable insistence on spaciousness in each protestation; Goneril disdains even the rich and rare, and E.B.B. conspicuously selects intangibles to express degree; both find a measure in Grace; and presumably striving for Right and turning from Praise are the equivalent of honor. Health and beauty are perhaps a bit more pretentious than "the level of every day's/Most quiet need." But Goneril loves "As much as child e'er loved," and E.B.B., "with my childhood's faith." Goneril's love "makes breath poor and speech unable"; E.B.B. loves "with the breath,/ Smiles, tears of all my life!" and anticipates loving "better after death." Goneril likewise hyperbolizes; she loves "more than words can wield the matter" and "Beyond all matter of so much. . . ."

Goneril wished to give the unperceptive Lear an impression of sincerity; E.B.B., no doubt, looked in her heart and wrote. Yet, except for a detail or two added by E.B.B., both said much the same thing. What comes out of this is a lesson in verse-technique: the piling up of abstractions and generalizations

1. From *The Explicator,* IV (October, 1945), 3. Reprinted by permission of the author and of the Editors of *The Explicator.*

not only does not carry conviction but gives a positive effect of insincerity. E.B.B.'s sonnet is as embarrassing as all platform rhetoric; she can find no images to realize, to prove, her experience. Ironically, she relies upon personal sincerity to give body to her words, whereas Goneril relies upon comparable words to suggest a body of sincerity. Shakespeare succeeded in his intention, for Goneril took in only Lear; in days of sharp awareness of poetic techniques, E.B.B. should not be taking in anybody. Shakespeare's method in Goneril's speech underlines a basic tenet of modern poetic criticism.

With the gusty protestations quoted above, compare Cordelia's single image and understatement (with the real emphasis ironically concealed in *bond,* a word which Lear fails entirely to understand):

I cannot heave
My heart into my mouth: I love your majesty
According to my bond . . . .

Shakespeare knew precisely what kind of language to use for each sister. E.B.B. could have learned from him.

HENRY WADSWORTH LONGFELLOW

SNOW-FLAKES

Out of the bosom of the Air,
Out of the cloud-folds of her garments shaken,
Over the woodlands brown and bare,
Over the harvest-fields forsaken,
Silent, and soft, and slow
Descends the snow.

Even as our cloudy fancies take
Suddenly shape in some divine expression,
Even as the troubled heart doth make
In the white countenance confession,
The troubled sky reveals
The grief it feels.

This is the poem of the air,
Slowly in silent syllables recorded;
This is the secret of despair,
Long in its cloudy bosom hoarded,
Now whispered and revealed
To wood and field.

THE TIDE RISES, THE TIDE FALLS

The tide rises, the tide falls,
The twilight darkens, the curlew calls;
Along the sea-sands damp and brown
The traveller hastens toward the town,
  And the tide rises, the tide falls.

Darkness settles on roofs and walls,
But the sea, the sea in the darkness calls;
The little waves, with their soft, white hands,
Efface the footprints in the sands,
  And the tide rises, the tide falls.

The morning breaks; the steeds in their stalls
Stamp and neigh, as the hostler calls;
The day returns, but nevermore
Returns the traveller to the shore,
  And the tide rises, the tide falls.

OLIVER WENDELL HOLMES

DOROTHY Q.

A Family Portrait

Grandmother's mother: her age, I guess,
Thirteen summers, or something less;
Girlish bust, but womanly air;
Smooth, square forehead with uprolled hair;
Lips that lover has never kissed;
Taper fingers and slender wrist;
Hanging sleeves of stiff brocade;
So they painted the little maid.

On her hand a parrot green
Sits unmoving and broods serene.
Hold up the canvas full in view,—
Look! there's a rent the light shines through,
Dark with a century's fringe of dust,—
That was a Red-Coat's rapier-thrust!
Such is the tale the lady old,
Dorothy's daughter's daughter, told.

Who the painter was none may tell,—
One whose best was not over well;
Hard and dry, it must be confessed,
Flat as a rose that has long been pressed;
Yet in her cheek the hues are bright,
Dainty colors of red and white,
And in her slender shape are seen
Hint and promise of stately mien.

Look not on her with eyes of scorn,—
Dorothy Q. was a lady born!
Ay! since the galloping Normans came,
England's annals have known her name;
And still to the three-hilled rebel town
Dear is that ancient name's renown,
For many a civic wreath they won,
The youthful sire and the gray-haired son.

O Damsel Dorothy! Dorothy Q.!
Strange is the gift that I owe to you;
Such a gift as never a king
Save to daughter or son might bring,—
All my tenure of heart and hand,
All my title to house and land;
Mother and sister and child and wife
And joy and sorrow and death and life!

What if a hundred years ago
Those close-shut lips had answered No,
When forth the tremulous question came
That cost the maiden her Norman name,
And under the folds that look so still
The bodice swelled with the bosom's thrill?
Should I be I, or would it be
One tenth another, to nine tenths me?

Soft is the breath of a maiden's Yes:
Not the light gossamer stirs with less;
But never a cable that holds so fast
Through all the battles of wave and blast,
And never an echo of speech or song
That lives in the babbling air so long!
There were tones in the voice that whispered then
You may hear to-day in a hundred men.

O lady and lover, how faint and far
Your images hover,—and here we are,
Solid and stirring in flesh and bone,—
Edward's and Dorothy's—all their own,—
A goodly record for Time to show
Of a syllable spoken so long ago!—
Shall I bless you, Dorothy, or forgive
For the tender whisper that bade me live ?

It shall be a blessing, my little maid!
I will heal the stab of the Red-Coat's blade,
And freshen the gold of the tarnished frame,
And gild with a rhyme your household name;
So you shall smile on us brave and bright
As first you greeted the morning's light,
And live untroubled by woes and fears
Through a second youth of a hundred years.

THE PEAU DE CHAGRIN OF STATE STREET

How beauteous is the bond
In the manifold array
Of its promises to pay,
While the eight per cent it gives
And the rate at which one lives
Correspond!

But at last the bough is bare
Where the coupons one by one
Through their ripening days have run,
And the bond, a beggar now,
Seeks investment anyhow,
Anywhere!

EDGAR ALLAN POE

THE CITY IN THE SEA

Lo! Death has reared himself a throne
In a strange city lying alone
Far down within the dim West,

Where the good and the bad and the worst and the best
Have gone to their eternal rest.
There shrines and palaces and towers
(Time-eaten towers that tremble not!)
Resemble nothing that is ours.
Around, by lifting winds forgot,
Resignedly beneath the sky
The melancholy waters lie.

No rays from the holy heaven come down
On the long night-time of that town;
But light from out the lurid sea
Streams up the turrets silently—
Gleams up the pinnacles far and free—
Up domes—up spires—up kingly halls—
Up fanes—up Babylon-like walls—
Up shadowy long-forgotten bowers
Of sculptured ivy and stone flowers—
Up many and many a marvelous shrine
Whose wreathèd friezes intertwine
The viol, the violet, and the vine.

Resignedly beneath the sky
The melancholy waters lie.
So blend the turrets and shadows there
That all seem pendulous in air,
While from a proud tower in the town
Death looks gigantically down.
There open fanes and gaping graves
Yawn level with the luminous waves;
But not the riches there that lie
In each idol's diamond eye—
Not the gaily-jeweled dead
Tempt the waters from their bed;
For no ripples curl, alas!
Along that wilderness of glass—
No swellings tell that winds may be
Upon some far-off happier sea—
No heavings hint that winds have been
On seas less hideously serene.

But lo, a stir is in the air!
The wave—there is a movement there!
As if the towers had thrust aside,

In slightly sinking, the dull tide—
As if their tops had feebly given
A void within the filmy Heaven.
The waves have now a redder glow—
The hours are breathing faint and low—
And when, amid no earthly moans,
Down, down that town shall settle hence,
Hell, rising from a thousand thrones,
Shall do it reverence.

TO HELEN

Helen, thy beauty is to me
Like those Nicèan barks of yore,
That gently, o'er a perfumed sea,
The weary, way-worn wanderer bore
To his own native shore.

On desperate seas long wont to roam,
Thy hyacinth hair, thy classic face,
Thy Naiad airs have brought me home
To the glory that was Greece
And the grandeur that was Rome.

Lo! in yon brilliant window-niche
How statue-like I see thee stand,
The agate lamp within thy hand!
Ah, Psyche, from the regions which
Are Holy Land!

THE VALLEY OF UNREST

Once it smiled a silent dell
Where the people did not dwell;
They had gone unto the wars,
Trusting to the mild-eyed stars,
Nightly, from their azure towers,
To keep watch above the flowers,
In the midst of which all day
The red sun-light lazily lay.
Now each visitor shall confess
The sad valley's restlessness.
Nothing there is motionless—
Nothing save the airs that brood

Over the magic solitude.
Ah, by no wind are stirred those trees
That palpitate like the chill seas
Around the misty Hebrides!
Ah, by no wind those clouds are driven
That rustle through the unquiet Heaven
Uneasily, from morn till even,
Over the violets there that lie
In myriad types of the human eye—
Over the lilies there that wave
And weep above a nameless grave!
They wave:—from out their fragrant tops
Eternal dews come down in drops.
They weep:—from off their delicate stems
Perennial tears descend in gems.

ON POE'S *THE VALLEY OF UNREST* [1]

ROY P. BASLER

THE IMAGERY and music of the poem, as well as the definitive significance of the word "unrest" in the title, suggest symbolism of a psychic state or condition. The general emotional import of the poem has been recognized even by orthodox commentators who tend to identify the valley in supernatural terms as the "place of departed spirits" (Campbell). Although the symbolism is not as explicitly allegorical as in "The Haunted Palace," instructive comparison may be made of the contrasting psychic states symbolized in each: sanity and insanity on the conscious level in "The Haunted Palace," expression and repression on the unconscious level in "The Valley of Unrest."

In the first part (*"Once"*), the silent peaceful valley where the people did not dwell because they had gone into the outer world to war against their enemies, we have a symbol of the psychic state in which emotion, finding an objective, conscious activity under the approval of the superego, is *expressed.* The silent dell is the psyche's secret retreat, safe because unknown to the "enemy" in the outer world, but open to discovery by an "enemy" who defeats hate by turning it to love.

In the second part (*"Now"*), the troubled and restless valley, haunted by revenants of its former inhabitants (*i. e.,* dream images), symbolized appropriately as motion without apparent cause, we have a symbol of the unconscious when emotion, denied objective play by the disapproval of the

1. From *The Explicator,* V (Dec., 1946), 25. Reprinted by permission of the author and of the Editors of *The Explicator.* The above article also appears in the author's book *Sex, Symbolism, and Psychology in Literature,* published by Rutgers University Press, 1948.

superego, is *repressed*. In the symbol of fear (eternal watchfulness) presented in "the violets there that lie/ In myriad types of the human eye," and the symbol of sorrow in "the lilies there that wave/ And weep above a nameless grave," we have the dual reaction of the psyche to repression—eternal sorrow for the dead (repressed) emotion whose betrayal of the secret valley made a martyrdom necessary, and eternal fear that the valley may be discovered again. The grave is nameless, because as key symbol of the act of repression (to repress is simply to will the censored feeling out of existence so far as consciousness is concerned) it is not consciously recognized for what it is. Poe presents the mysterious valley and grave as seen by "each visitor" (*i.e.*, perceptions on the part of the conscious ego, which occasionally under emotional stress penetrate the realm of the id; note that in the 1831 version "each visitor" is merely "the unhappy," and that in "Ulalume" and other poems of the unconscious Poe presents similar transient, halfway glimpses of the meaning of dreamland under emotional stress). The valley is perceived, but not understood, by the stranger to the realm.

The final version of the poem has an almost purely psychological symbolism where the earlier versions convey a suggestion of traditional moralistic myth. The introductory lines of the 1831 version, which Poe abandoned, link the story of the valley to a hypothetical Syriac myth with suggestions of "Satan's dart" and a "broken heart" as more or less specific hints of guilt related not to a "nameless grave," but merely to "a grave" in the 1831 version, and to "the old forgotten grave" in the *Southern Literary Messenger* version. In the final version the sense of guilt underlying the symbolism is left entirely to the reader's inference, and the imagery conveys primarily the sense of repression and psychic unrest. This shift parallels in interesting fashion Poe's changes of "The Doomed City" to "The City of Sin" to "The City in the Sea," and I believe indicates a growing awareness on Poe's part of the primarily psychological import of his symbols.

The nameless grave contains buried love, and the haunting awareness of this truth, vaguely apprehended by almost any reader, is grounded in universal human experience that repression creates in the unconscious a psychic "place of departed spirits" troubled by an intolerably real though undefined unrest.

ALFRED LORD TENNYSON

ULYSSES

It little profits that an idle king,
By this still hearth, among these barren crags,
Matched with an agèd wife, I mete and dole

Unequal laws unto a savage race
That hoard and sleep and feed, and know not me.
I cannot rest from travel; I will drink
Life to the lees. All times I have enjoyed
Greatly, have suffered greatly, both with those
That loved me, and alone; on shore, and when
Thro' scudding drifts the rainy Hyades
Vext the dim sea. I am become a name;
For always roaming with a hungry heart
Much have I seen and known—cities of men
And manners, climates, councils, governments,
Myself not least, but honored of them all—
And drunk delight of battle with my peers,
Far on the ringing plains of windy Troy.
I am a part of all that I have met;
Yet all experience is an arch wherethro'
Gleams that untravelled world, whose margin fades
For ever and for ever when I move.
How dull it is to pause, to make an end,
To rust unburnished, not to shine in use!
As though to breathe were life! Life piled on life
Were all too little, and of one to me
Little remains; but every hour is saved
From that eternal silence, something more,
A bringer of new things; and vile it were
For some three suns to store and hoard myself,
And this grey spirit yearning in desire
To follow knowledge like a sinking star,
Beyond the utmost bound of human thought.
    This is my son, mine own Telemachus,
To whom I leave the sceptre and the isle—
Well-loved of me, discerning to fulfil
This labor, by slow prudence to make mild
A rugged people, and through soft degrees
Subdue them to the useful and the good.
Most blameless is he, centered in the sphere
Of common duties, decent not to fail
In offices of tenderness, and pay
Meet adoration to my household gods,
When I am gone. He works his work, I mine.
    There lies the port; the vessel puffs her sail;
There gloom the dark, broad seas. My mariners,
Souls that have toiled, and wrought, and thought with me—
That ever with a frolic welcome took

The thunder and the sunshine, and opposed
Free hearts, free foreheads—you and I are old;
Old age has yet his honor and his toil.
Death closes all; but something ere the end,
Some work of noble note, may yet be done,
Not unbecoming men that strove with gods.
The lights begin to twinkle from the rocks;
The long day wanes; the slow moon climbs; the deep
Moans round with many voices. Come, my friends,
'Tis not too late to seek a newer world.
Push off, and sitting well in order smite
The sounding furrows; for my purpose holds
To sail beyond the sunset, and the baths
Of all the western stars, until I die.
It may be that the gulfs will wash us down;
It may be we shall touch the Happy Isles,
And see the great Achilles, whom we knew.
Though much is taken, much abides; and though
We are not now that strength which in old days
Moved earth and heaven; that which we are, we are—
One equal temper of heroic hearts,
Made weak by time and fate, but strong in will
To strive, to seek, to find, and not to yield.

TEARS, IDLE TEARS

Tears, idle tears, I know not what they mean,
Tears from the depth of some divine despair
Rise in the heart, and gather to the eyes,
In looking on the happy Autumn-fields,
And thinking of the days that are no more.

Fresh as the first beam glittering on a sail,
That brings our friends up from the underworld,
Sad as the last which reddens over one
That sinks with all we love below the verge;
So sad, so fresh, the days that are no more.

Ah, sad and strange as in dark summer dawns
The earliest pipe of half-awaken'd birds
To dying ears, when unto dying eyes
The casement slowly grows a glimmering square;
So sad, so strange, the days that are no more.

Dear as remember'd kisses after death,
And sweet as those by hopeless fancy feign'd
On lips that are for others; deep as love,
Deep as first love, and wild with all regret;
O Death in Life, the days that are no more!

ON TENNYSON'S *TEARS, IDLE TEARS*[1]

CLEANTH BROOKS

Any account of the poem may very well begin with a consideration of the nature of the tears. Are they *idle* tears? Or are they not rather the most meaningful of tears? Does not the very fact that they are "idle" (that is, tears occasioned by no immediate grief) become in itself a guarantee of the fact that they spring from a deeper, more universal cause?

It would seem so, and that the poet is thus beginning his poem with a paradox. For the third line of the poem indicates that there is no doubt in the speaker's mind about the origin of the tears in some divine despair. They "rise in the heart"—for all that they have been first announced as "idle."

But the question of whether Tennyson is guilty of (or to be complimented upon) a use of paradox may well wait upon further discussion. At this point in our commentary, it is enough to observe that Tennyson has chosen to open his poem with some dramatic boldness—if not with the bold step of equating "idle" with "from the depth of some divine despair," then at least with a bold and violent reversal of the speaker's first characterization of his tears.

The tears "rise in the heart" as the speaker looks upon a scene of beauty and tranquillity. Does looking on the "happy Autumn-fields" bring to mind the days that are no more? The poet does not say so. The tears rise to the eyes in looking on the happy "Autumn-fields" *and* thinking on the days that are no more. The poet himself does not stand responsible for any closer linkage between these actions, though, as a matter of fact, most of us will want to make a closer linkage here. For, if we change "happy Autumn-fields," say, to "happy April-fields," the two terms tend to draw apart. The fact that the fields are autumn-fields which, though happy, point back to something which is over —which is finished—*does* connect them with the past and therefore properly suggests to the observer thoughts about that past.

To sum up: the first stanza has a unity, but it is not a unity which finds its sanctions in the ordinary logic of language. Its sanctions are to be found in the dramatic context, and, to my mind, there alone. Indeed, the stanza suggests the play of the speaker's mind as the tears unexpectedly start, tears for which there is no apparent occasion, and as he searches for an explanation of them. He calls them "idle," but, even as he says "I know not what they mean," he

1. From *The Well Wrought Urn*, copyright, 1947, by Cleanth Brooks. Reprinted by permission of the author and Reynal & Hitchcock, Inc., publishers.

realizes that they must spring from the depths of his being—is willing, with his very next words, to associate them with "some divine despair." Moreover, the real occasion of the tears, though the speaker himself comes to realize it only as he approaches the end of the stanza, is the thought about the past. It is psychologically and dramatically right, therefore, that the real occasion should be stated explicitly only with the last line of the stanza.

This first stanza, then, recapitulates the surprise and bewilderment in the speaker's own mind, and sets the problem which the succeeding stanzas are to analyze. The dramatic effect may be described as follows: the stanza seems, not a meditated observation, but a speech begun impulsively—a statement which the speaker has begun before he knows how he will end it.

In the second stanza we are not surprised to have the poet characterize the days that are no more as "sad," but there is some shock in hearing him apply to them the adjective "fresh." Again, the speaker does not pause to explain: the word "fresh" actually begins the stanza. Yet the adjective justifies itself.

The past is fresh as with a dawn freshness—as fresh as the first beam glittering on the sail of an incoming ship. The ship is evidently expected; it brings friends, friends "up from the underworld." On the surface, the comparison is innocent: the "underworld" is merely the antipodes, the world which lies below the horizon—an underworld in the sense displayed in old-fashioned geographies with their sketches illustrating the effects of the curvature of the earth. The sails, which catch the light and glitter, will necessarily be the part first seen of any ship which is coming "up" over the curve of the earth.

But the word "underworld" will necessarily suggest the underworld of Greek mythology, the realm of the shades, the abode of the dead. The attempt to characterize the freshness of the days that are no more has, thus, developed, almost imperceptibly, into a further characterization of the days themselves as belonging, not to our daylight world, but to an "underworld." This suggestion is, of course, strengthened in the lines that follow in which the ship metaphor is reversed so as to give us a picture of sadness: evening, the last glint of sunset light on the sail of a ship

> That sinks with all we love below the verge. . . .

The conjunction of the qualities of sadness and freshness is reinforced by the fact that the same basic symbol—the light on the sails of a ship hull down—has been employed to suggest both qualities. With the third stanza, the process is carried one stage further: the two qualities (with the variant of "strange" for "fresh") are explicitly linked together:

> Ah, sad and strange as in dark summer dawns . . . .

And here the poet is not content to suggest the qualities of sadness and strangeness by means of two different, even if closely related, figures. In this third stanza the special kind of sadness and strangeness is suggested by one and the same figure.

It is a figure developed in some detail. It, too, involves a dawn scene, though ironically so, for the beginning of the new day is to be the beginning of the long night for the dying man. The dying eyes, the poem suggests, have been for some time awake—long enough to have had time to watch the

> . . . casement slowly [grow] a glimmering square . . . .

The dying man, soon to sleep the lasting sleep, is more fully awake than the "half-awaken'd birds" whose earliest pipings come to his dying ears. We know why these pipings are sad; but why are they *strange?* Because to the person hearing a bird's song for the last time, it will seem that he has never before really heard one. The familiar sound will take on a quality of unreality—of strangeness.

If this poem were merely a gently melancholy reverie on the sweet sadness of the past, Stanzas II and III would have no place in the poem. But the poem is no such reverie: the images from the past rise up with a strange clarity and sharpness that shock the speaker. Their sharpness and freshness account for the sudden tears and for the psychological problem with which the speaker wrestles in the poem. If the past would only remain melancholy but dimmed, sad but worn and familiar, we should have no problem and no poem. At least, we should not have *this* poem; we should certainly not have the intensity of the last stanza.

That intensity, if justified, must grow out of a sense of the apparent nearness and intimate presence of what is irrevocably beyond reach: the days that are no more must be more than the conventional "dear, dead days beyond recall." They must be beyond recall, yet alive—tantalizingly vivid and near. It is only thus that we can feel the speaker justified in calling them

> Dear as remember'd kisses after death,
> And sweet as those by hopeless fancy feign'd
> On lips that are for others. . . .

It is only thus that we can accept the culminating paradox of

> O Death in Life, the days that are no more.

We have already observed, in the third stanza, how the speaker compares the strangeness and sadness of the past to the sadness of the birds' piping as it sounds to dying ears. There is a rather brilliant ironic contrast involved in the comparison. The speaker, a living man, in attempting to indicate how sad and strange to him are the days of the past, says that they are as sad and strange as is the natural activity of the awakening world to the man who is dying: the dead past seems to the living man as unfamiliar and fresh in its sadness as the living present seems to the dying man. There is more here, however, than a mere, ironic reversal of roles; in each case there is the sense of being irrevocably barred out from the known world.

This ironic contrast, too, accounts for the sense of desperation which runs through the concluding lines of the poem. The kisses feigned by "hopeless fancy" are made the more precious because of the very hopelessness; but memory takes on the quality of fancy. It is equally hopeless—the kisses can as little be renewed as those "feign'd / On lips that are for others" can be obtained. The realized past has become as fabulous as the unrealizable future. The days that are no more are as dear as the one, as sweet as the other, the speaker says; and it does not matter whether we compare them to the one or to the other or to both: it comes to the same thing.

But the days that are no more are not merely "dear" and "sweet"; they are "deep" and "wild." Something has happened to the grammar here. How can the days be "deep as love" or "wild with all regret"? And what is the status of the exclamation "O Death in Life"? Is it merely a tortured cry like "O God! the days that are no more"? Or is it a loose appositive: "the days that are no more are a kind of death in life?"

The questions are not asked in a censorious spirit, as if there were no justification for Tennyson's license here. But it is important to see how much license the poem requires, and the terms on which the reader decides to accord it justification. What one finds on closer examination is not muddlement but richness. But it is a richness achieved through principles of organization which many an admirer of the poet has difficulty in allowing to the "obscure" modern poet.

For example, how can the days of the past be *deep?* Here, of course, the problem is not very difficult. The past is buried within one: the days that are no more constitute the deepest level of one's being, and the tears that arise from thinking on them may be said to come from the "depth of some divine despair." But how can the days be "wild with all regret"? The extension demanded here is more ambitious. In matter of fact, it is the speaker, the man, who is made wild with regret by thinking on the days.

One can, of course, justify the adjective as a transferred epithet on the model of Vergil's *maestum timorem;* and perhaps this was Tennyson's own conscious justification (if, indeed, the need to justify it ever occurred to him). But one can make a better case than a mere appeal to the authority of an established literary convention. There is a sense in which the man and the remembered days are one and the same. A man is the sum of his memories. The adjective which applies to the man made wild with regret can apply to those memories which make him wild with regret. For, does the man charge the memories with his own passion, or is it the memories that give the emotion to him? If we pursue the matter far enough, we come to a point where the distinction lapses. Perhaps I should say, more accurately, adopting the metaphor of the poem itself, we *descend* to a depth where the distinction lapses. The days that are no more are *deep* and *wild,* buried but not dead—below the surface and unthought of, yet at the deepest core of being, secretly alive.

The past *should* be tame, fettered, brought to heel; it is not. It is capable of breaking forth and coming to the surface. The word "wild" is bold, therefore, but justified. It reasserts the line of development which has been maintained throughout the earlier stanzas: "fresh," "strange," and now "wild"—all adjectives which suggest passionate, irrational life. The word "wild," thus, not only pulls into focus the earlier paradoxes, but is the final stage in the preparation for the culminating paradox, "O Death in Life."

The last stanza evokes an intense emotional response from the reader. The claim could hardly be made good by the stanza taken in isolation. The stanza leans heavily upon the foregoing stanzas, and the final paradox draws heavily upon the great metaphors in stanzas II and III. This is as it should be. The justification for emphasizing the fact here is this: the poem, for all its illusion of impassioned speech—with the looseness and *apparent* confusion of unpremeditated speech—is very tightly organized. It represents an organic structure; and the intensity of the total effect is a reflection of the total structure.

The reader, I take it, will hardly be disposed to quarrel with the general statement of the theme of the poem as it is given in the foregoing account; and he will probably find himself in accord with this general estimate of the poem's value. But the reader may well find that the amount of attention given to the structure of the poem is irrelevant, if not positively bad. In particular, he may find the emphasis on paradox, ambiguity, and ironic contrast displeasing. He has not been taught to expect these in Tennyson, and he has had the general impression that the presence of these qualities represents the intrusion of alien, "unpoetic" matter.

I have no wish to intellectualize the poem—to make conscious and artful what was actually spontaneous and simple. Nevertheless, the qualities of ironic contrast and paradox *do* exist in the poem; and they *do* have a relation to the poem's dramatic power.

ROBERT BROWNING

SOLILOQUY OF THE SPANISH CLOISTER

Gr-r-r—there go, my heart's abhorrence!
    Water your damned flower-pots, do!
If hate killed men, Brother Lawrence,
    God's blood, would not mine kill you!
What? your myrtle-bush wants trimming?
    Oh, that rose has prior claims—
Needs its leaden vase filled brimming?
    Hell dry you up with its flames!

At the meal we sit together:
    Salve tibi! I must hear

Wise talk of the kind of weather,
 Sort of season, time of year:
Not a plenteous cork-crop; scarcely
 Dare we hope oak-galls, I doubt;
What's the Latin name for "parsley"?
 What's the Greek name for Swine's Snout?

Whew! We'll have our platter burnished,
 Laid with care on our own shelf!
With a fire-new spoon we're furnished,
 And a goblet for ourself,
Rinsed like something sacrificial
 Ere 'tis fit to touch our chaps—
Marked with L for our initial!
 (He-he! There his lily snaps!)

Saint, forsooth! While brown Dolores
 Squats outside the Convent bank
With Sanchicha, telling stories,
 Steeping tresses in the tank,
Blue-black, lustrous, thick like horsehairs
 —Can't I see his dead eye glow,
Bright as 'twere a Barbary corsair's?
 (That is, if he'd let it show!)

When he finishes refection,
 Knife and fork he never lays
Cross-wise, to my recollection,
 As do I, in Jesu's praise.
I the Trinity illustrate,
 Drinking watered orange-pulp—
In three sips the Arian frustrate;
 While he drains his at one gulp.

Oh, those melons! If he's able
 We're to have a feast! so nice!
One goes to the Abbot's table,
 All of us get each a slice.
How go on your flowers? None double?
 Not one fruit-sort can you spy?
Strange!—And I, too, at such trouble
 Keep them close-nipped on the sly!

There's a great text in Galatians,
Once you trip on it, entails
Twenty-nine distinct damnations,
One sure, if another fails:
If I trip him just a-dying,
Sure of heaven as sure can be,
Spin him round and send him flying
Off to hell, a Manichee?

Or, my scrofulous French novel
On gray paper with blunt type!
Simply glance at it, you grovel
Hand and foot in Belial's gripe;
If I double down its pages
At the woeful sixteenth print,
When he gathers his greengages,
Ope a sieve and slip it in 't?

Or, there's Satan!—one might venture
Pledge one's soul to him, yet leave
Such a flaw in the indenture
As he'd miss till, past retrieve,
Blasted lay that rose-acacia
We're so proud of! *Hy, Zy, Hine* . . .
'St, there's Vespers! *Plena gratiâ,*
Ave, Virgo! Gr-r-r—you swine!

MY LAST DUCHESS

Ferrara

That's my last Duchess painted on the wall,
Looking as if she were alive. I call
That piece a wonder, now: Frà Pandolf's hands
Worked busily a day, and there she stands.
Will't please you sit and look at her? I said
"Frà Pandolf" by design, for never read
Strangers like you that pictured countenance,
The depth and passion of its earnest glance
But to myself they turned (since none puts by
The curtain I have drawn for you, but I)
And seemed as they would ask me, if they durst,
How such a glance came there; so, not the first

Are you to turn and ask thus. Sir, 'twas not
Her husband's presence only, called that spot
Of joy into the Duchess' cheek: perhaps
Frà Pandolf chanced to say, "Her mantle laps
Over my lady's wrist too much," or "Paint
Must never hope to reproduce the faint
Half-flush that dies along her throat": such stuff
Was courtesy, she thought, and cause enough
For calling up that spot of joy. She had
A heart—how shall I say?—too soon made glad,
Too easily impressed: she liked whate'er
She looked on, and her looks went everywhere.
Sir, 'twas all one! My favor at her breast,
The dropping of the daylight in the West,
The bough of cherries some officious fool
Broke in the orchard for her, the white mule
She rode with round the terrace—all and each
Would draw from her alike the approving speech,
Or blush, at least. She thanked men,—good! but thanked
Somehow—I know not how—as if she ranked
My gift of a nine-hundred-years-old name
With anybody's gift. Who'd stoop to blame
This sort of trifling? Even had you skill
In speech—(which I have not)—to make your will
Quite clear to such an one, and say, "Just this
Or that in you disgusts me; here you miss,
Or there exceed the mark"—and if she let
Herself be lessoned so, nor plainly set
Her wits to yours, forsooth, and made excuse,
—E'en then would be some stooping; and I choose
Never to stoop. Oh sir, she smiled, no doubt,
Whene'er I passed her; but who passed without
Much the same smile? This grew; I gave commands;
Then all smiles stopped together. There she stands
As if alive. Will't please you rise? We'll meet
The company below, then. I repeat,
The Count your master's known munificence
Is ample warrant that no just pretence
Of mine for dowry will be disallowed;
Though his fair daughter's self, as I avowed
At starting, is my object. Nay, we'll go
Together down, sir. Notice Neptune, though,
Taming a sea-horse, thought a rarity,
Which Claus of Innsbruck cast in bronze for me!

THE BISHOP ORDERS HIS TOMB AT ST. PRAXED'S CHURCH

Rome, 15—

Vanity, saith the preacher, vanity!
Draw round my bed: is Anselm keeping back?
Nephews—sons mine . . . ah God, I know not! Well—
She, men would have to be your mother once,
Old Gandolf envied me, so fair she was!
What's done is done, and she is dead beside,
Dead long ago, and I am Bishop since,
And as she died so must we die ourselves,
And thence ye may perceive the world's a dream.
Life, how and what is it? As here I lie
In this state-chamber, dying by degrees,
Hours and long hours in the dead night, I ask
"Do I live, am I dead?" Peace, peace seems all.
Saint Praxed's ever was the church for peace;
And so, about this tomb of mine. I fought
With tooth and nail to save my niche, ye know:
—Old Gandolf cozened me, despite my care;
Shrewd was that snatch from out the corner South
He graced his carrion with, God curse the same!
Yet still my niche is not so cramped but thence
One sees the pulpit o' the epistle-side,
And somewhat of the choir, those silent seats,
And up into the aery dome where live
The angels, and a sunbeam's sure to lurk:
And I shall fill my slab of basalt there,
And 'neath my tabernacle take my rest,
With those nine columns round me, two and two,
The odd one at my feet where Anselm stands:
Peach-blossom marble all, the rare, the ripe
As fresh-poured red wine of a mighty pulse.
—Old Gandolf with his paltry onion-stone,
Put me where I may look at him! True peach,
Rosy and flawless: how I earned the prize!
Draw close: that conflagration of my church
—What then? So much was saved if aught were missed!
My sons, ye would not be my death? Go dig
The white-grape vineyard where the oil-press stood,
Drop water gently till the surface sink,
And if ye find . . . Ah God, I know not, I! . . .
Bedded in store of rotten fig-leaves soft,

And corded up in a tight olive-frail,
Some lump, ah God, of *lapis lazuli,*
Big as a Jew's head cut off at the nape,
Blue as a vein o'er the Madonna's breast . . .
Sons, all have I bequeathed you, villas, all,
That brave Frascati villa with its bath,
So, let the blue lump poise between my knees,
Like God the Father's globe on both his hands
Ye worship in the Jesu Church so gay,
For Gandolf shall not choose but see and burst!
Swift as a weaver's shuttle fleet our years:
Man goeth to the grave, and where is he?
Did I say basalt for my slab, sons? Black—
'Twas ever antique-black I meant! How else
Shall ye contrast my frieze to come beneath?
The bas-relief in bronze ye promised me,
Those Pans and Nymphs ye wot of, and perchance
Some tripod, thyrsus, with a vase or so,
The Saviour at his sermon on the mount,
Saint Praxed in a glory, and one Pan
Ready to twitch the Nymph's last garment off,
And Moses with the tables . . . but I know
Ye mark me not! What do they whisper thee,
Child of my bowels, Anselm? Ah, ye hope
To revel down my villas while I gasp
Bricked o'er with beggar's mouldy travertine
Which Gandolf from his tomb-top chuckles at!
Nay, boys, ye love me—all of jasper, then!
'Tis jasper ye stand pledged to, lest I grieve
My bath must needs be left behind, alas!
One block, pure green as a pistachio-nut,
There's plenty jasper somewhere in the world—
And have I not Saint Praxed's ear to pray
Horses for ye, and brown Greek manuscripts,
And mistresses with great smooth marbly limbs?
—That's if ye carve my epitaph aright,
Choice Latin, picked phrase, Tully's every word,
No gaudy ware like Gandolf's second line—
Tully, my masters? Ulpian serves his need!
And then how I shall lie through centuries,
And hear the blessed mutter of the mass,
And see God made and eaten all day long,
And feel the steady candle-flame, and taste
Good strong thick stupefying incense-smoke!

For as I lie here, hours of the dead night,
Dying in state and by such slow degrees,
I fold my arms as if they clasped a crook,
And stretch my feet forth straight as stone can point,
And let the bedclothes, for a mort-cloth, drop
Into great laps and folds of sculptor's-work:
And as yon tapers dwindle, and strange thoughts
Grow, with a certain humming in my ears,
About the life before I lived this life,
And this life too, popes, cardinals and priests.
Saint Praxed at his sermon on the mount,
Your tall pale mother with her talking eyes,
And new-found agate urns as fresh as day,
And marble's language, Latin pure, discreet,
—Aha, ELUCESCEBAT quoth our friend?
No Tully, said I, Ulpian at the best!
Evil and brief hath been my pilgrimage.
All *lapis,* all sons! Else I give the Pope
My villas! Will ye ever eat my heart?
Ever your eyes were as a lizard's quick,
They glitter like your mother's for my soul,
Or ye would heighten my impoverished frieze,
Piece out its starved design, and fill my vase
With grapes, and add a visor and a Term,
And to the tripod ye would tie a lynx
That in his struggle throws the thyrsus down,
To comfort me on my entablature
Whereon I am to lie till I must ask
"Do I live, am I dead?" There, leave me, there!
For ye have stabbed me with ingratitude
To death—ye wish it—God, ye wish it! Stone—
Gritstone, a-crumble! Clammy squares which sweat
As if the corpse they keep were oozing through—
And no more *lapis* to delight the world!
Well, go! I bless ye. Fewer tapers there,
But in a row: and, going, turn your backs
—Ay, like departing altar-ministrants,
And leave me in my church, the church for peace,
That I may watch at leisure if he leers—
Old Gandolf—at me, from his onion-stone,
As still he envied me, so fair she was!

WALT WHITMAN

ONE'S-SELF I SING[1]

One's-self I sing, a simple separate person,
Yet utter the word Democratic, the word En-Masse.

Of physiology from top to toe I sing,
Not physiognomy alone nor brain alone is worthy for the Muse,
I say the Form complete is worthier far,
The Female equally with the Male I sing.

Of Life immense in passion, pulse, and power,
Cheerful, for freest action form'd under the laws divine,
The Modern Man I sing.

WHEN LILACS LAST IN THE DOORYARD BLOOM'D[1]

1

When lilacs last in the dooryard bloom'd,
And the great star early droop'd in the western sky in the night,
I mourn'd, and yet shall mourn with ever-returning spring.

Ever-returning spring, trinity sure to me you bring,
Lilac blooming perennial and drooping star in the west,
And thought of him I love.

2

O powerful western fallen star!
O shades of night—O moody, tearful night!
O great star disappear'd—O the black murk that hides the star!
O cruel hands that hold me powerless—O helpless soul of me!
O harsh surrounding cloud that will not free my soul.

3

In the dooryard fronting an old farm-house near the white-wash'd palings,
Stands the lilac-bush tall-growing with heart-shaped leaves of rich green,
With many a pointed blossom rising delicate, with the perfume strong I love,
With every leaf a miracle—and from this bush in the dooryard,
With delicate-color'd blossoms and heart-shaped leaves of rich green,
A sprig with its flower I break.

---

1. From *Leaves of Grass* by Walt Whitman, copyright, 1924, by Doubleday & Company, Inc.

4

In the swamp in secluded recesses,
A shy and hidden bird is warbling a song.
Solitary the thrush,
The hermit withdrawn to himself, avoiding the settlements,
Sings by himself a song.

Song of the bleeding throat,
Death's outlet song of life, (for well dear brother I know,
If thou wast not granted to sing thou would'st surely die.)

5

Over the breast of the spring, the land, amid cities,
Amid lanes and through old woods, where lately the violets peep'd from the ground spotting the gray debris,
Amid the grass in the fields each side of the lanes, passing the endless grass,
Passing the yellow-spear'd wheat, every grain from its shroud in the dark-brown fields uprisen,
Passing the apple-tree blows of white and pink in the orchards,
Carrying a corpse to where it shall rest in the grave,
Night and day journeys a coffin.

6

Coffin that passes through lanes and streets,
Through day and night with the great cloud darkening the land,
With the pomp of the inloop'd flags with the cities draped in black,
With the show of the States themselves as of crape-veil'd women standing,
With processions long and winding and the flambeaus of the night,
With the countless torches lit, with the silent sea of faces and the unbared heads,
With the waiting depot, the arriving coffin, and the sombre faces,
With dirges through the night, with the thousand voices rising strong and solemn,
With all the mournful voices of the dirges pour'd around the coffin,
The dim-lit churches and the shuddering organs—where amid these you journey,
With the tolling, tolling bells' perpetual clang,
Here, coffin that slowly passes,
I give you my sprig of lilac.

7

(Nor for you, for one alone,
Blossoms and branches green to coffins all I bring,
For fresh as the morning, thus would I chant a song for you, O sane and sacred death.

All over bouquets of roses,
O death, I cover you over with roses and early lilies,
But mostly and now the lilac that blooms the first,
Copious I break, I break the sprigs from the bushes,
With loaded arms I come, pouring for you,
For you and the coffins all of you, O death.)

8

O western orb sailing the heaven,
Now I know what you must have meant as a month since I walk'd,
As I walk'd in silence the transparent shadowy night,
As I saw you had something to tell as you bent to me night after night,
As you droop'd from the sky low down as if to my side, (while the other stars all look'd on,)
As we wander'd together the solemn night, (for something I know not what kept me from sleep,)
As the night advanced, and I saw on the rim of the west how full you were of woe,
As I stood on the rising ground in the breeze in the cool transparent night,
As I watch'd where you pass'd and was lost in the netherward black of the night,
As my soul in its trouble dissatisfied sank, as where yon sad orb,
Concluded, dropt in the night, and was gone.

9

Sing on there in the swamp,
O singer bashful and tender, I hear your notes, I hear your call,
I hear, I come presently, I understand you,
But a moment I linger, for the lustrous star has detain'd me,
The star my departing comrade holds and detains me.

10

O how shall I warble myself for the dead one there I loved?
And how shall I deck my song for the large sweet soul that has gone?
And what shall my perfume be for the grave of him I love?

Sea-winds blown from east and west,
Blown from the Eastern sea and blown from the Western sea, till there on the prairies meeting,
These and with these and the breath of my chant,
I'll perfume the grave of him I love.

11

O what shall I hang on the chamber walls?
And what shall the pictures be that I hang on the walls,
To adorn the burial-house of him I love?

Pictures of growing spring and farms and homes,
With the Fourth-month eve at sundown, and the gray smoke lucid and bright,
With floods of the yellow gold of the gorgeous, indolent, sinking sun, burning, expanding the air,
With the fresh sweet herbage under foot, and the pale green leaves of the trees prolific,
In the distance the flowing glaze, the breast of the river, with a wind-dapple here and there,
With ranging hills on the banks, with many a line against the sky, and shadows,
And the city at hand with dwellings so dense, and stacks of chimneys,
And all the scenes of life and the workshops, and the workmen homeward returning.

12

Lo, body and soul—this land,
My own Manhattan with spires, and the sparkling and hurrying tides, and the ships,
The varied and ample land, the South and the North in the light, Ohio's shores and flashing Missouri,
And ever the far-spreading prairies cover'd with grass and corn.

Lo, the most excellent sun so calm and haughty,
The violet and purple morn with just-felt breezes,
The gentle soft-born measureless light,
The miracle spreading bathing all, the fulfill'd noon,
The coming eve delicious, the welcome night and the stars,
Over my cities shining all, enveloping man and land.

13

Sing on, sing on you gray-brown bird,
Sing from the swamps, the recesses, pour your chant from the bushes,
Limitless out of the dusk, out of the cedars and pines.

Sing on dearest brother, warble your reedy song,
Loud human song, with voice of uttermost woe.
O liquid and free and tender!
O wild and loose to my soul—O wondrous singer!

You only I hear—yet the star holds me, (but will soon depart,)
Yet the lilac with mastering odor holds me.

14

Now while I sat in the day and look'd forth,
In the close of the day with its light and the fields of spring, and the farmers preparing their crops,
In the large unconscious scenery of my land with its lakes and forests,
In the heavenly aerial beauty (after the perturb'd winds and the storms,)
Under the arching heavens of the afternoon swift passing, and the voices of children and women,
The many-moving sea-tides, and I saw the ships how they sail'd,
And the summer approaching with richness, and the fields all busy with labor,
And the infinite separate houses, how they all went on, each with its meals and minutia of daily usages,
And the streets how their throbbings throbb'd, and the cities pent—lo, then and there,
Falling upon them all and among them all, enveloping me with the rest,
Appear'd the cloud, appear'd the long black trail,
And I knew death, its thought, and the sacred knowledge of death.

Then with the knowledge of death as walking one side of me,
And the thought of death close-walking the other side of me,
And I in the middle as with companions, and as holding the hands of companions,
I fled forth to the hiding receiving night that talks not,
Down to the shores of the water, the path by the swamp in the dimness,
To the solemn shadowy cedars and ghostly pines so still.

And the singer so shy to the rest receiv'd me,
The gray-brown bird I know receiv'd us comrades three,
And he sang the carol of death, and a verse for him I love.

From deep secluded recesses,
From the fragrant cedars and the ghostly pines so still
Came the carol of the bird.
And the charm of the carol rapt me,
As I held as if by their hands my comrades in the night,
And the voice of my spirit tallied the song of the bird.

Come lovely and soothing death,
Undulate round the world, serenely arriving, arriving,
In the day, in the night, to all, to each,
Sooner or later delicate death.

Prais'd be the fathomless universe,
For life and joy, and for objects and knowledge curious,
And for love, sweet love—but praise! praise! praise!
For the sure-enwinding arms of cool-enfolding death.

Dark mother always gliding near with soft feet,
Have none chanted for thee a chant of fullest welcome?
Then I chant it for thee, I glorify thee above all,
I bring thee a song that when thou must indeed come, come unfalteringly.

Approach, strong deliveress,
When it is so, when thou hast taken them I joyously sing the dead,
Lost in the loving floating ocean of thee,
Laved in the flood of thy bliss O death.

From me to thee glad serenades,
Dances for thee I propose saluting thee, adornments and feastings for thee,
And the sights of the open landscape and the high-spread sky are fitting,
And life and the fields, and the huge and thoughtful night.

The night in silence under many a star,
The ocean shore and the husky whispering wave whose voice I know,
And the soul turning to thee O vast and well-veil'd death,
And the body gratefully nestling close to thee.

Over the tree-tops I float thee a song,
Over the rising and sinking waves, over the myriad fields and the prairies wide,
Over the dense-pack'd cities all and the teeming wharves and ways,
I float this carol with joy, with joy to thee O death.

15

To the tally of my soul,
Loud and strong kept up the gray-brown bird,
With pure deliberate notes spreading filling the night.

Loud in the pines and cedars dim,
Clear in the freshness moist and the swamp-perfume,
And I with my comrades there in the night.
While my sight that was bound in my eyes unclosed,
As to long panoramas of visions.
And I saw askant the armies,
I saw as in noiseless dreams hundreds of battle-flags,
Borne through the smoke of the battles and pierc'd with missiles I saw them,

And carried hither and yon through the smoke, and torn and bloody,
And at last but a few shreds left on the staffs, (and all in silence,)
And the staffs all splinter'd and broken.

I saw battle-corpses, myriads of them,
And the white skeletons of young men, I saw them,
I saw the debris and debris of all the slain soldiers of the war,
But I saw they were not as was thought,
They themselves were fully at rest, they suffer'd not,
The living remain'd and suffer'd, the mother suffer'd,
And the wife and the child and the musing comrade suffer'd,
And the armies that remain'd suffer'd.

16

Passing the visions, passing the night,
Passing, unloosing the hold of my comrades' hands,
Passing the song of the hermit bird and the tallying song of my soul,
Victorious song, death's outlet song, yet varying ever-altering song,
As low and wailing, yet clear the notes, rising and falling, flooding the night,
Sadly sinking and fainting, as warning and warning, and yet again bursting with joy,
Covering the earth and filling the spread of the heaven,
As that powerful psalm in the night I heard from recesses,
Passing, I leave thee lilac with heart-shaped leaves,
I leave thee there in the door-yard, blooming, returning with spring.

I cease from my song for thee,
From my gaze on thee in the west, fronting the west, communing with thee,
O comrade lustrous with silver face in the night.

Yet each to keep and all, retrievements out of the night,
The song, the wondrous chant of the gray-brown bird,
And the tallying chant, the echo arous'd in my soul,
With the lustrous and drooping star with the countenance full of woe,
With the holders holding my hand nearing the call of the bird,
Comrades mine and I in the midst, and their memory ever to keep, for the dead I loved so well,
For the sweetest, wisest soul of all my days and lands—and this for his dear sake,
Lilac and star and bird twined with the chant of my soul,
There in the fragrant pines and the cedars dusk and dim.

ON WHITMAN'S *WHEN LILACS LAST IN THE DOORYARD BLOOM'D* [1]

F. O. MATTHIESSEN

WHITMAN's power of giving mythical proportions to his material was best sustained in his tribute to Lincoln. The controlling idea for his other poems about the Civil War, as he had outlined it in his letter to O'Connor only three months before the President's assassination, was the time's "large conflicting fluctuations of despair and hope," "the unprecedented anguish of wounded and suffering," and yet also, sounding through lulls in the chaos like the steady beat of a drum, the "clear notes of faith and triumph." That confidence was now put to its severest test, and the result was "When Lilacs Last in the Door-Yard Bloom'd." Like all of *Drum-Taps* this was written so much under the stress of a dominant emotion that it was not revised, except in the slightest details, after its first printing in 1865. In this period of his most intense feeling Whitman also reverted to the hackneyed cadences and imagery of his first newspaper verse in producing "O Captain! My Captain!" That this ballad, wholly untypical of his poems, should have been the only one to have found its way to the great world of grammar school readers is ample and ironic comment on how far Whitman's authentic idiom was from even the rudimentary means by which a wide audience is reached.

In his later reminiscent lecture about the President (1879), he said that "to the complete limning of this man's future portrait" there will be needed "the eyes and brains and finger-touch of Plutarch and Aeschylus and Michel Angelo, assisted by Rabelais." His poem enlisted no such powers, but was composed as an elegy "for the sweetest, wisest soul of all my days and lands." Whitman was not concerned with the expression of merely personal emotion; he wanted to give it an objective existence as broad as the country over which the coffin passed on its journey to Illinois. We are able to glimpse in a different context some of the original impressions that lay behind his symbols here —a rare thing with Whitman's poems, since he kept no regular journal. He had written down, a month before, what he had experienced on the day of Lincoln's second inauguration. He noted that the President looked very worn and tired, the lines "of vast responsibilities . . . and demands of life and death, cut deeper than ever upon his dark brown face; yet all the old goodness, tenderness, sadness, and canny shrewdness, underneath the furrows. (I never see that man without feeling that he is one to become personally attach'd to, for his combination of purest, heartiest tenderness, and native western form of manliness.)"

In another paragraph Whitman wandered along about the weather, which he thought to have been unusually bad during the past several months, and

1. From *American Renaissance* by F. O. Matthiessen. Copyright, 1941, by Oxford University Press.

wondered whether there might not be some strange correspondence between its tempestuous violence and the upheaval of war. Then he noted that in the afternoon, just before the President had come out on the portico of the Capitol, the deluging rain of the morning had let up, leaving the air "so calm, so bathed with flooding splendor from heaven's most excellent sun, with atmosphere of sweetness; so clear, it show'd the stars, long, long before they were due." This led him on to remember that, in spells of sharpest contrast with the storms, "nor earth nor sky ever knew spectacles of superber beauty than some of the nights lately here. The western star, Venus, in the earlier hours of evening, has never been so large, so clear; it seems as if it told something, as if it held rapport indulgent with humanity, with us Americans." He ended his account of the day by saying that he had been looking up at the "dark blue, the transparent night" when he had heard a bugle sounding tattoo in one of the army hospitals, where the wounded were "lying in their cots, and many a sick boy come down to the war from Illinois, Michigan, Wisconsin, Iowa, and the rest."

There is no description of Lincoln in the poem itself, for it is entirely given up to "sane and sacred death." Yet Whitman asked, in lines whose rhythmical repetitions were all but Biblical,

> O what shall I hang on the chamber walls?
> And what shall the pictures be that I hang on the walls,
> To adorn the burial-house of him I love?

And the pictures that ensued, of "growing spring" on the farms with "the gray smoke lucid and bright," of the breast of a river with "a wind-dapple here and there," of Manhattan's spires and Ohio's shores, were crowned with the light of "the most excellent sun so calm and haughty . . . enveloping man and land," both South and North. The poet may there have been unconsciously repeating a phrase, the broad sound of which had appealed to him. But he made an explicit reference back to his feelings on the day of the inauguration in the section that began:

> O western orb sailing the heaven,
> Now I know what you must have meant as a month since I walk'd,
> As I walk'd in silence the transparent shadowy night,
> As I saw you had something to tell as you bent to me night after night.

Those lines may be adulterated with some of the least satisfactory elements of the poem, in the use of "orb," an orator's word, which seems always to have pleased Whitman as it rolled from his mouth; and particularly in the pathetic fallacy. But as he continued the passage, the poet freed himself from the stilted fancy of the star's bending to him, and saw it in its own motion:

> As my soul in its trouble dissatisfied sank, as where yon sad orb,
> Concluded, dropt in the night, and was gone.

What has taken place through the fusion of Whitman's materials is that the planet whose radiance had so impressed him a month before has become for him now "O powerful western fallen star!" It has become the symbol, in its disappearance into the dark, for the President himself.

Whitman does not handle his subject primarily by objective descriptions, but by thematic use of three primary symbols—the lilac, the star, and the song of the thrush—which are repeated with the most subtle ordonnance that he ever managed. They are introduced in the brief opening section:

> When lilacs last in the dooryard bloom'd,
> And the great star early droop'd in the western sky in the night,
> I mourn'd, and yet shall mourn with ever-returning spring.
>
> Ever-returning spring, trinity sure to me you bring,
> Lilac blooming perennial and drooping star in the west,
> And thought of him I love.

They are then successively extended in the next three sections. The "black murk" that engulfed the star is immediately equated with the "harsh surrounding cloud that will not free my soul." The lilacs "fronting an old farm-house near the white-wash'd palings" are lent a special relevance by their "heart-shaped leaves of rich green." They have come to Whitman from his Long Island childhood, and their use in the poem may unconsciously have been suggested to him by his having been at home in Brooklyn on the day of the assassination, alone with his mother. (". . . we heard the news very early in the morning. Mother prepared breakfast—and other meals afterward—as usual; but not a mouthful was eaten all day by either of us. We each drank half a cup of coffee; that was all. Little was said. We got every newspaper morning and evening . . . and pass'd them silently to each other.") The delicately colored blossoms grew close to nearly every country home. The bush was right by the windows at Whitman's birthplace at West Hills, and its absence in Mount's Long Island scene is exceptional. In fact the lilac is almost as native a symbol as the common grass itself.

The "thought of him I love" is given symbolic concretion by being merged with song, with the note of the solitary hermit-thrush from the swamp-cedars, which had always meant so much to Whitman. Here its painful ecstasy becomes "death's outlet song of life,"

> for well dear brother I know,
> If thou wast not granted to sing thou would'st surely die.

Thus it merges also with the poet's song of grief, through the release of which he finds his way back to acceptance and peace.

The fifth and sixth sections present the picture of the coffin in its night and day journey past depots and streets and over the breast of the land, met everywhere by solemn crowds. Standing among these in his imagination, as the train slowly passes, the poet bestows his "sprig of lilac." But not "for you, for one alone," he says, as he again develops this symbol's theme. He would bring signs of the rebirth of the year to no one man but to all in his chant "for you O sane and sacred death." It is notable that, in deep fulfilment of his instinct for universality, Whitman nowhere in the poem mentions Lincoln by name, not even in the next section (the eighth) where, in the middle of his song, he introduces his reminiscence of the star a month ago. Then he completes his round of symbols for the second time by telling the thrush to sing on in the swamp, that he will come there presently, but that the star, "my departing comrade holds and detains me."

At this point he breaks off to ask,

> O how shall I warble myself for the dead one there I loved?
> And how shall I deck my song for the large sweet soul that has gone?
> And what shall my perfume be for the grave of him I love?

Having bid the sea-winds from both east and west to meet on the prairies, he asks, in like form, his question about the pictures, and decks the burial house with them in the twenty lines of his eleventh and twelfth sections. He then turns once more to the thrush, to its "reedy song, loud human song." The poet's voice now matches that of the bird, as, in the longest section, he launches into his aria to "the sure-enwinding arms of cool-enfolding death," and urges, "When thou must indeed come, come unfalteringly." But before this, in addition to declaring his carol a brother to that of the thrush, he has felt all three of his symbols coalesce into an organic whole:

> O liquid and free and tender!
> O wild and loose to my soul—O wondrous singer!
> You only I hear—yet the star holds me, (but will soon depart,)
> Yet the lilac with mastering odor holds me.

He has blended the impressions of his different senses, of hearing, sight, and smell, as they do blend in an individual's full impression of a moment. Moreover, in "liquid" he has suggested the kind of touch and movement that most appealed to him, just as in "wild and loose" he has characterized the kind of form he felt at home with, and in "free and tender" the emotional range he could encompass best. The symbolists were to carry much farther the merging of sensations, to the point of transference of one into another, as of color into sound or smell. But Whitman's greatest act of pioneering was in helping the modern sensibility feel at home in the natural world. He was able to suggest the interdependence of man and nature since his "trinity" of symbols sprang from the forces of earth, no matter what spiritual implications they could rise to in his hymn to rebirth through fertility. In the closing lines of the poem the three are resumed again, but it is the poet's "powerful psalm" of tribute that now emerges transcendent over the others:

Lilac and star and bird twined with the chant of my soul,
There in the fragrant pines and the cedars dusk and dim.

One other strain had been given development in the penultimate section. The "unprecedented anguish of wounded and suffering" that Whitman had declared to be central to the design of his war poems had found very little foreshadowing in the optimistic glow of the earlier *Leaves*. Among other war poets of the day, despite Lowell's set rhetorical piece in the Commemoration Ode for the Harvard dead, only Melville stressed the tragic purification through terror and pity that could be gained from the disaster of war. Whitman showed humanity as broad as Melville's in his concern for equal treatment for the South. He expressed it in "Reconciliation":

Word over all, beautiful as the sky,
Beautiful that war and all its deeds of carnage must in time be utterly lost . . .
For my enemy is dead, a man divine as myself is dead . . .

In his grief for Lincoln he understood where the real anguish lay:

I saw the debris and debris of all the slain soldiers of the war,
But I saw they were not as was thought,
They themselves were fully at rest, they suffer'd not,
But the living remain'd and suffer'd, the mother suffer'd,
And the wife and the child and the musing comrade suffer'd
And the armies that remained suffer'd.

TO A LOCOMOTIVE IN WINTER[1]

Thee for my recitative,
Thee in the driving storm even as now, the snow, the winter-day declining,
Thee in thy panoply, thy measur'd dual throbbing and thy beat convulsive,
Thy black cylindric body, golden brass and silvery steel,
Thy ponderous side-bars, parallel and connecting rods, gyrating, shuttling at thy sides,
Thy metrical, now swelling pant and roar, now tapering in the distance,
Thy great protruding head-light fix'd in front,
Thy long, pale, floating vapor-pennants, tinged with delicate purple,
The dense and murky clouds out-belching from thy smoke-stack,
Thy knitted frame, thy springs and valves, the tremulous twinkle of thy wheels,
Thy train of cars behind, obedient, merrily following,
Through gale or calm, now swift, now slack, yet steadily careering;
Type of the modern—emblem of motion and power—pulse of the continent,
For once come serve the Muse and merge in verse, even as here I see thee,

1. From *Leaves of Grass* by Walt Whitman, copyright, 1924, by Doubleday & Company, Inc.

With storm and buffeting gusts of wind and falling snow,
By day thy warning ringing bell to sound its notes,
By night thy silent signal lamps to swing.

Fierce-throated beauty!
Roll through my chant with all thy lawless music, thy swinging lamps at
night,
Thy madly-whistled laughter, echoing, rumbling like an earthquake, rousing
all,
Law of thyself complete, thine own track firmly holding,
(No sweetness debonair of tearful harp or glib piano thine,)
Thy trills of shrieks by rocks and hills return'd,
Launch'd o'er the prairies wide, across the lakes,
To the free skies unpent and glad and strong.

GOOD-BYE MY FANCY![1]

Good-bye my Fancy!
Farewell dear mate, dear love!
I'm going away, I know not where,
Or to what fortune, or whether I may ever see you again,
So Good-bye my Fancy.

Now for my last—let me look back a moment;
The slower fainter ticking of the clock is in me,
Exit, nightfall, and soon the heart-thud stopping.

Long have we lived, joy'd, caress'd together;
Delightful!—now separation—Good-bye my Fancy.

Yet let me not be too hasty,
Long indeed have we lived, slept, filter'd, become really blended into one;
Then if we die we die together, (yes, we'll remain one,)
If we go anywhere we'll go together to meet what happens,
May-be we'll be better off and blither, and learn something,
May-be it is yourself now really ushering me to the true songs, (who knows?)
May-be it is you the mortal knob really undoing, turning—so now finally,
Good-bye—and hail! my Fancy.

1. From *Leaves of Grass* by Walt Whitman, copyright, 1924, by Doubleday & Company, Inc.

MATTHEW ARNOLD

THE SCHOLAR-GYPSY

Go, for they call you, shepherd, from the hill;
Go, shepherd, and untie the wattled cotes!
No longer leave thy wistful flock unfed,
Nor let thy bawling fellows rack their throats,
Nor the cropped herbage shoot another head.
But when the fields are still,
And the tired men and dogs all gone to rest,
And only the white sheep are sometimes seen
Cross and recross the strips of moon-blanched green,
Come, shepherd, and again begin the quest!

Here, where the reaper was at work of late—
In this high field's dark corner, where he leaves
His coat, his basket, and his earthen cruse,
And in the sun all morning binds the sheaves,
Then here, at noon, comes back his stores to use—
Here will I sit and wait,
While to my ear from uplands far away
The bleating of the folded flocks is borne,
With distant cries of reapers in the corn—
All the live murmur of a summer's day.

Screened is this nook o'er the high, half-reaped field,
And here till sun-down, shepherd! will I be.
Through the thick corn the scarlet poppies peep,
And round green roots and yellowing stalks I see
Pale pink convolvulus in tendrils creep;
And air-swept lindens yield
Their scent, and rustle down their perfumed showers
Of bloom on the bent grass where I am laid,
And bower me from the August sun with shade;
And the eye travels down to Oxford's towers.

And near me on the grass lies Glanvil's book—
Come, let me read the oft-read tale again!
The story of the Oxford scholar poor,
Of pregnant parts and quick inventive brain,
Who, tired of knocking at preferment's door,
One summer-morn forsook
His friends, and went to learn the gypsy-lore,

And roamed the world with that wild brotherhood,
And came, as most men deemed, to little good,
But came to Oxford and his friends no more.

But once, years after, in the country-lanes,
Two scholars, whom at college erst he knew,
Met him, and of his way of life inquired;
Whereat he answered that the gypsy-crew,
His mates, had arts to rule as they desired
The workings of men's brains,
And they can bind them to what thoughts they will.
"And I," he said, "the secret of their art,
When fully learned, will to the world impart;
But it needs heaven-sent moments for this skill."

This said, he left them, and returned no more.—
But rumors hung about the country-side,
That the lost scholar long was seen to stray,
Seen by rare glimpses, pensive and tongue-tied,
In hat of antique shape, and cloak of gray,
The same the gypsies wore.
Shepherds had met him on the Hurst in spring;
At some lone alehouse in the Berkshire moors,
On the warm ingle-bench, the smock-frocked boors
Had found him seated at their entering.

But, 'mid their drink and clatter, he would fly.
And I myself seem half to know thy looks,
And put the shepherds, wanderer! on thy trace;
And boys who in lone wheatfields scare the rooks
I ask if thou hast passed their quiet place;
Or in my boat I lie
Moored to the cool bank in the summer-heats,
'Mid wide grass meadows which the sunshine fills,
And watch the warm, green-muffled Cumner hills,
And wonder if thou haunt'st their shy retreats.

For most, I know, thou lov'st retired ground!
Thee at the ferry Oxford riders blithe,
Returning home on summer-nights, have met
Crossing the stripling Thames at Bab-lock-hithe,
Trailing in the cool stream thy fingers wet,
As the punt's rope chops round;
And leaning backward in a pensive dream,

And fostering in thy lap a heap of flowers
Plucked in shy fields and distant Wychwood bowers,
And thine eyes resting on the moonlit stream.

And then they land, and thou art seen no more!—
Maidens, who from the distant hamlets come
To dance around the Fyfield elm in May,
Oft through the darkening fields have seen thee roam,
Or cross a stile into the public way.
Oft thou hast given them store
Of flowers—the frail-leafed, white anemone,
Dark bluebells drenched with dews of summer eves.
And purple orchises with spotted leaves—
But none hath words she can report of thee.

And, above Godstow Bridge, when hay-time's here
In June, and many a scythe in sunshine flames,
Men who through those wide fields of breezy grass
Where black-winged swallows haunt the glittering Thames,
To bathe in the abandoned lasher pass,
Have often passed thee near
Sitting upon the river bank o'ergrown;
Marked thine outlandish garb, thy figure spare,
Thy dark vague eyes, and soft abstracted air—
But, when they came from bathing, thou wast gone!

At some lone homestead in the Cumner hills,
Where at her open door the housewife darns,
Thou hast been seen, or hanging on a gate
To watch the threshers in the mossy barns.
Children, who early range these slopes and late
For cresses from the rills,
Have known thee eying, all an April-day,
The springing pastures and the feeding kine;
And marked thee, when the stars come out and shine,
Through thc long dewy grass move slow away.

In autumn, on the skirts of Bagley Wood—
Where most the gypsies by the turf-edged way
Pitch their smoked tents, and every bush you see
With scarlet patches tagged and shreds of gray,
Above the forest-ground called Thessaly—
The blackbird, picking food,
Sees thee, nor stops his meal, nor fears at all;

So often has he known thee past him stray,
Rapt, twirling in thy hand a withered spray,
And waiting for the spark from heaven to fall.

And once, in winter, on the causeway chill
Where home through flooded fields foot-travelers go,
Have I not passed thee on the wooden bridge,
Wrapped in thy cloak and battling with the snow,
Thy face tow'rd Hinksey and its wintry ridge?
And thou hast climbed the hill,
And gained the white brow of the Cumner range;
Turned once to watch, while thick the snowflakes fall,
The line of festal light in Christ-Church hall—
Then sought thy straw in some sequestered grange.

But what—I dream! Two hundred years are flown
Since first thy story ran through Oxford halls,
And the grave Glanvil did the tale inscribe
That thou wert wandered from the studious walls
To learn strange arts, and join a gypsy tribe;
And thou from earth art gone
Long since, and in some quiet churchyard laid—
Some country-nook, where o'er thy unknown grave
Tall grasses and white flowering nettles wave,
Under a dark, red-fruited yew-tree's shade.

—No, no, thou hast not felt the lapse of hours!
For what wears out the life of mortal men?
'Tis that from change to change their being rolls;
'Tis that repeated shocks, again, again,
Exhaust the energy of strongest souls
And numb the elastic powers,
Till having used our nerves with bliss and teen,
And tired upon a thousand schemes our wit,
To the just-pausing Genius we remit
Our worn-out life, and are—what we have been.

Thou hast not lived, why should'st thou perish, so?
Thou hadst *one* aim, *one* business, *one* desire;
Else wert thou long since numbered with the dead!
Else hadst thou spent, like other men, thy fire!
The generations of thy peers are fled,
And we ourselves shall go;
But thou possessest an immortal lot,

And we imagine thee exempt from age
And living as thou liv'st on Glanvil's page,
Because thou hadst—what we, alas! have not.

For early didst thou leave the world, with powers
Fresh, undiverted to the world without,
Firm to their mark, not spent on other things;
Free from the sick fatigue, the languid doubt,
Which much to have tried, in much been baffled, brings.
O life unlike to ours!
Who fluctuate idly without term or scope,
Of whom each strives, nor knows for what he strives,
And each half lives a hundred different lives;
Who wait like thee, but not, like thee, in hope.

Thou waitest for the spark from heaven! and we,
Light half-believers of our casual creeds,
Who never deeply felt, nor clearly willed,
Whose insight never has borne fruit in deeds,
Whose vague resolves never have been fulfilled;
For whom each year we see
Breeds new beginnings, disappointments new;
Who hesitate and falter life away,
And lose tomorrow the ground won today—
Ah! do not we, wanderer! await it too?

Yes, we await it!—but it still delays,
And then we suffer! and amongst us one,
Who most hast suffered, takes dejectedly
His seat upon the intellectual throne;
And all his store of sad experience he
Lays bare of wretched days;
Tells us his misery's birth and growth and signs,
And how the dying spark of hope was fed,
And how the breast was soothed, and how the head,
And all his hourly varied anodynes.

This for our wisest! and we others pine,
And wish the long unhappy dream would end,
And waive all claim to bliss, and try to bear;
With close-lipped patience for our only friend,
Sad patience, too near neighbor to despair—
But none has hope like thine!
Thou through the fields and through the woods dost stray,

Roaming the country-side, a truant boy,
Nursing thy project in unclouded joy,
And every doubt long blown by time away.

O born in days when wits were fresh and clear,
And life ran gayly as the sparkling Thames;
Before this strange disease of modern life,
With its sick hurry, its divided aims,
Its head o'ertaxed, its palsied hearts, was rife—
Fly hence, our contact fear!
Still fly, plunge deeper in the bowering wood!
Averse, as Dido did with gesture stern
From her false friend's approach in Hades turn,
Wave us away, and keep thy solitude!

Still nursing the unconquerable hope,
Still clutching the inviolable shade,
With a free, onward impulse brushing through,
By night, the silvered branches of the glade—
Far on the forest-skirts, where none pursue,
On some mild pastoral slope
Emerge, and resting on the moonlit pales
Freshen thy flowers as in former years
With dew, or listen with enchanted ears,
From the dark dingles, to the nightingales!

But fly our paths, our feverish contact fly!
For strong the infection of our mental strife,
Which, though it gives no bliss, yet spoils for rest;
And we should win thee from thy own fair life,
Like us distracted, and like us unblest.
Soon, soon thy cheer would die,
Thy hopes grow timorous, and unfixed thy powers,
And thy clear aims be cross and shifting made;
And then thy glad perennial youth would fade,
Fade, and grow old at last, and die like ours.

Then fly our greetings, fly our speech and smiles!
—As some grave Tyrian trader, from the sea,
Descried at sunrise an emerging prow
Lifting the cool-haired creepers stealthily,
The fringes of a southward-facing brow
Among the Ægæan isles;
And saw the merry Grecian coaster come,

Freighted with amber grapes, and Chian wine,
Green, bursting figs, and tunnies steeped in brine—
And knew the intruders on his ancient home,

The young light-hearted masters of the waves—
And snatched his rudder, and shook out more sail;
And day and night held on indignantly
O'er the blue Midland waters with the gale,
Betwixt the Syrtes and soft Sicily,
To where the Atlantic raves
Outside the western straits; and unbent sails
There, where down cloudy cliffs, through sheets of foam,
Shy traffickers, the dark Iberians come;
And on the beach undid his corded bales.

DOVER BEACH

The sea is calm to-night.
The tide is full, the moon lies fair
Upon the straits; on the French coast, the light
Gleams and is gone; the cliffs of England stand,
Glimmering and vast, out in the tranquil bay.
Come to the window, sweet is the night-air!
Only, from the long line of spray
Where the sea meets the moon-blanched land,
Listen! you hear the grating roar
Of pebbles which the waves draw back, and fling,
At their return, up the high strand,
Begin and cease, and then again begin,
With tremulous cadence slow, and bring
The eternal note of sadness in.

Sophocles long ago
Heard it on the Aegean, and it brought
Into his mind the turbid ebb and flow
Of human misery; we
Find also in the sound a thought,
Hearing it by this distant northern sea.

The sea of faith
Was once, too, at the full, and round earth's shore
Lay like the folds of a bright girdle furled.
But now I only hear
Its melancholy, long, withdrawing roar,

Retreating, to the breath
Of the night-wind, down the vast edges drear
And naked shingles of the world.

Ah, love, let us be true
To one another! for the world, which seems
To lie before us like a land of dreams,
So various, so beautiful, so new,
Hath really neither joy, nor love, nor light,
Nor certitude, nor peace, nor help for pain;
And we are here as on a darkling plain
Swept with confused alarms of struggle and flight,
Where ignorant armies clash by night.

ON ARNOLD'S *DOVER BEACH* [1]

JOHN P. KIRBY

Professors Tinker and Lowry in *The Poetry of Matthew Arnold* (pp. 173–175) have pointed out the evidence that establishes the writing of the last nine lines as previous to the rest of the poem—the separate draft of the first 28 lines from the library of T. G. Wise, and the shift in metaphor from the sea and the tides to the "darkling plain."

As critics we accept these findings, however, without inferring that the commentators meant necessarily to suggest a serious lack of organic unity in the poem, or a lamentable lapse in the continuity of the theme in lines 29–30, sometimes deemed an inappropriate shift in emphasis.

It seems unnecessary to examine in detail the especially happy wedding of the imagery, rhythm, and alliteration to the theme in the first 28 lines (see, for example, Theodore Morrison's "Dover Beach Revisited"). The irony of the poem lies essentially in the contrast between the calm sea, the tranquil moonlight scene, and the restless incertitude of the speaker. If this contrast be kept in mind, it will be evident that the lines of the last stanza, "for the world,/Which lies before us like a land of dreams" refers to the moonlit cliffs of the first stanza. In line 33, the assertion that the world has "neither joy, nor love, nor light" closes significantly with a reference to *light,* a return not only upon the "land of dreams" and the earlier description of the moonlit cliffs, but even to the "bright girdle" of line 23. The "Ah, love" of line 29 may well be anticipated in the directive of line 6, "Come to the window."

The simile of the armies struggling confusedly is not really a discontinuity in image, for the "darkling plain" continues the contrast between the bright land- and seascape and the gloomy moral chaos of the world. Still more sig-

1. From *The Explicator,* I (April, 1943), 42. Reprinted by permission of the author and of the Editors of *The Explicator.*

nificantly, it develops Arnold's imagery further: the "sea of faith" has *retreated,* its "bright girdle" has been dissipated, and only the "naked shingles of the world" are left in darkness; that is, a dark plain of detritus remains where "ignorant armies clash by night." It is even possible that Arnold had some geological phenomena in mind (his use of "shingles"). The more recurrent rhymes of the last stanza are the poetical device for focusing the reader's attention upon the "message" of the poem.

It may be worth noting that the last stanza illustrates a method Arnold uses in other poems: a conclusion which first states the theme explicitly (cf. lines 221–230 in "The Scholar-Gypsy") and then closes with a striking figure of speech, the "end note of relief." Surely no one would ever assert a lack of organic unity in "The Scholar-Gypsy" because Arnold shifts his figurative language from the Oxford countryside to the Mediterranean Sea; yet there the change may seem less justified than in "Dover Beach."

GEORGE MEREDITH

LUCIFER IN STARLIGHT[1]

On a starred night Prince Lucifer uprose.
Tired of his dark dominion swung the fiend
Above the rolling ball in cloud part screened,
Where sinners hugged their specter of repose.
Poor prey to his hot fit of pride were those.
And now upon his western wing he leaned,
Now his huge bulk o'er Afric's sands careened,
Now the black planet shadowed Arctic snows.
Soaring through wider zones that pricked his scars
With memory of the old revolt from Awe,
He reached a middle height, and at the stars,
Which are the brain of heaven, he looked, and sank.
Around the ancient track marched, rank on rank,
The army of unalterable law.

1. Reprinted from *Poems* by George Meredith; copyright, 1897, by George Meredith, 1925 by W. M. Meredith; used by permission of the publishers, Charles Scribner's Sons.

EMILY DICKINSON

A BIRD CAME DOWN THE WALK[1]

A bird came down the walk:
He did not know I saw;
He bit an angle-worm in halves
And ate the fellow, raw.

And then he drank a dew
From a convenient grass,
And then hopped sidewise to the wall
To let a beetle pass.

He glanced with rapid eyes
That hurried all abroad,—
They looked like frightened beads, I thought
He stirred his velvet head

Like one in danger; cautious,
I offered him a crumb,
And he unrolled his feathers
And rowed him softer home

Than oars divide the ocean,
Too silver for a seam,
Or butterflies, off banks of noon,
Leap, plashless, as they swim.

THE CHARIOT[1]

Because I could not stop for Death,
He kindly stopped for me;
The carriage held but just ourselves
And Immortality.

We slowly drove, he knew no haste,
And I had put away
My labor, and my leisure too,
For his civility.

We passed the school where children played
At wrestling in a ring;

1. From *Poems by Emily Dickinson,* edited by Martha Dickinson Bianchi and Alfred Leete Hampson. Reprinted by permission of Little, Brown and Company.

We passed the fields of gazing grain,
We passed the setting sun.

We paused before a house that seemed
A swelling of the ground;
The roof was scarcely visible,
The cornice but a mound.

Since then 'tis centuries; but each
Feels shorter than the day
I first surmised the horses' heads
Were toward eternity.

ON DICKINSON'S *THE CHARIOT* [1]

ALLEN TATE

ONE of the perfect poems in English is *The Chariot,* and it exemplifies better than anything else [Emily Dickinson] wrote the special quality of her mind. I think it will illuminate the tendency of this discussion. If the word great means anything in poetry, this poem is one of the greatest in the English language; it is flawless to the last detail. The rhythm charges with movement the pattern of suspended action back of the poem. Every image is precise and, moreover, not merely beautiful, but inextricably fused with the central idea. Every image extends and intensifies every other. The third stanza especially shows Miss Dickinson's power to fuse, into a single order of perception, a heterogeneous series: the children, the grain, and the setting sun (time) have the same degree of credibility; the first subtly preparing for the last. The sharp *gazing* before *grain* instils into nature a kind of cold vitality of which the qualitative richness has infinite depth. The content of death in the poem eludes forever any explicit definition. He is a gentleman taking a lady out for a drive. But note the restraint that keeps the poet from carrying this so far that it is ludicrous and incredible; and note the subtly interfused erotic motive, which the idea of death has presented to every romantic poet, love being a symbol interchangeable with death. The terror of death is objectified through this figure of the genteel driver, who is made ironically to serve the end of Immortality. This is the heart of the poem: she has presented a typical Christian theme in all its final irresolution, without making any final statement about it. There is no solution to the problem; there can be only a statement of it in the full context of intellect and feeling. A construction of the human will, elaborated with all the abstracting powers of the mind, is put to the concrete test of experience: the idea of immortality is confronted with the

1. From *Reactionary Essays on Poetry and Ideas* by Allen Tate, pp. 13–16. Reprinted by permission of Charles Scribner's Sons, publishers.

fact of physical disintegration. We are not told what to think; we are told to look at the situation.

The framework of the poem is, in fact, the two abstractions, mortality and eternity, which are made to associate in perfect equality with the images: she sees the ideas, and thinks the perceptions. She did, of course, nothing of the sort; but we must use the logical distinctions, even to the extent of paradox, if we are to form any notion of this rare quality of mind. She could not in the proper sense think at all, and unless we prefer the feeble poetry of moral ideas that flourished in New England in the eighties, we must conclude that her intellectual deficiency contributed at least negatively to her great distinction. Miss Dickinson is probably the only Anglo-American poet of her century whose work exhibits the perfect literary situation—in which is possible the fusion of sensibility and thought. Unlike her contemporaries, she never succumbed to her ideas, to easy solutions, to her private desires.

INDIAN SUMMER[1]

These are the days when birds come back,
A very few, a bird or two,
To take a backward look.

These are the days when skies put on
The old, old sophistries of June,—
A blue and gold mistake.

Oh, fraud that cannot cheat the bee,
Almost thy plausibility
Induces my belief,

Till ranks of seeds their witness bear,
And softly through the altered air
Hurries a timid leaf!

Oh, sacrament of summer days,
Oh, last communion in the haze,
Permit a child to join,

Thy sacred emblems to partake,
Thy consecrated bread to break,
Taste thine immortal wine!

1. From *Poems of Emily Dickinson,* edited by Martha Dickinson Bianchi and Alfred Leete Hampson. Reprinted by permission of Little, Brown & Company.

'TWAS LIKE A MAELSTROM[1]

'Twas like a maelstrom, with a notch
That nearer every day
Kept narrowing its boiling wheel
Until the agony

Toyed coolly with the final inch
Of your delirious hem,
And you dropped, lost, when something broke
And let you from a dream

As if a goblin with a gauge
Kept measuring the hours,
Until you felt your second weigh
Helpless in his paws,

And not a sinew, stirred, could help,
And sense was getting numb,
When God remembered, and the fiend
Let go then, overcome;

As if your sentence stood pronounced,
And you were frozen led
From dungeon's luxury of doubt
To gibbets and the dead;

And when the film had stitched your eyes,
A creature gasped "Reprieve!"
Which anguish was the utterest then,
To perish, or to live?

1. "'Twas Like a Maelstrom" from *Bolts of Melody* by Emily Dickinson. Edited by Mabel Loomis Todd and Millicent Todd Bingham. Copyright, 1945, by Millicent Todd Bingham. Reprinted by permission of Harper & Brothers.

THOMAS HARDY

THE DARKLING THRUSH[1]

I leant upon a coppice gate
    When Frost was specter-gray,
And Winter's dregs made desolate
    The weakening eye of day.
The tangled bine-stems scored the sky
    Like strings of broken lyres,
And all mankind that haunted night
    Had sought their household fires.

The land's sharp features seemed to be
    The Century's corpse outleant,
His crypt the cloudy canopy,
    The wind his death-lament.
The ancient pulse of germ and birth
    Was shrunken hard and dry,
And every spirit upon earth
    Seemed fervorless as I.

At once a voice arose among
    The bleak twigs overhead
In a full-hearted evensong
    Of joy illimited;
An aged thrush, frail, gaunt, and small,
    In blast-beruffled plume,
Had chosen thus to fling his soul
    Upon the growing gloom.

So little cause for carolings
    Of such ecstatic sound
Was written on terrestrial things
    Afar or nigh around,
That I could think there trembled through
    His happy good-night air
Some blessed Hope, whereof he knew
    And I was unaware.

1. From *The Collected Poems of Thomas Hardy*. Copyright, 1925, by The Macmillan Company. By permission of the Macmillan Company, publishers.

GERARD MANLEY HOPKINS

THE WINDHOVER[1]

To Christ our Lord

I caught this morning morning's minion, kingdom of daylight's dauphin,
dapple-dawn-drawn Falcon, in his riding
Of the rolling level underneath him steady air, and striding
High there, how he rung upon the rein of a wimpling wing
In his ecstasy! then off, off forth on swing,
As a skate's heel sweeps smooth on a bow-bend: the hurl and gliding
Rebuffed the big wind. My heart in hiding
Stirred for a bird,—the achieve of, the mastery of the thing!

Brute beauty and valor and act, oh, air, pride, plume, here
Buckle! AND the fire that breaks from thee then, a billion
Times told lovelier, more dangerous, O my chevalier!

No wonder of it: shéer plód makes plow down sillion
Shine, and blue-bleak embers, ah my dear,
Fall, gall themselves, and gash gold-vermilion.

PIED BEAUTY[1]

Glory be to God for dappled things—
For skies of couple-color as a brinded cow;
For rose-moles all in stipple upon trout that swim;
Fresh-firecoal chestnut-falls; finches' wings;
Landscape plotted and pieced—fold, fallow, and plow;
And áll trádes, their gear and tackle and trim.

All things counter, original, spare, strange;
Whatever is fickle, freckled (who knows how?)
With swift, slow; sweet, sour; adazzle, dim;
He fathers-forth whose beauty is past change:
Praise him.

1. From *Poems of Gerard Manley Hopkins*. By permission of the Oxford University Press, London, publishers.

SPRING AND FALL: TO A YOUNG CHILD[1]

Márgarét, are you gríeving
Over Goldengrove unleaving?
Leáves, líke the things of man, you
With your fresh thoughts care for, can you?
Áh! ás the heart grows older
It will come to such sights colder
By and by, nor spare a sigh
Though worlds of wanwood leafmeal lie;
And yet you wíll weep and know why.
Now no matter, child, the name:
Sórrow's spríngs áre the same.
Nor mouth had, no nor mind, expressed
What heart heard of, ghost guessed:
It ís the blight man was born for,
It is Margaret you mourn for.

I WAKE AND FEEL THE FELL OF DARK[1]

I wake and feel the fell of dark, not day.
What hours, O what black hoürs we have spent
This night! what sights you, heart, saw; ways you went!
And more must, in yet longer light's delay.
    With witness I speak this. But where I say
Hours I mean years, mean life. And my lament
Is cries countless, cries like dead letters sent
To dearest him that lives alas! away.

    I am gall, I am heartburn. God's most deep decree
Bitter would have me taste: my taste was me;
Bones built in me, flesh filled, blood brimmed the curse.
    Selfyeast of spirit a dull dough sours. I see
The lost are like this, and their scourge to be
As I am mine, their sweating selves; but worse.

1. From *Poems of Gerard Manley Hopkins*. By permission of the Oxford University Press, London, publishers.

A. E. HOUSMAN

BE STILL, MY SOUL, BE STILL[1]

Be still, my soul, be still; the arms you bear are brittle,
  Earth and high heaven are fixt of old and founded strong.
Think rather,—call to thought, if now you grieve a little,
  The days when we had rest, O soul, for they were long.

Men loved unkindness then, but lightless in the quarry
  I slept and saw not; tears fell down, I did not mourn;
Sweat ran and blood sprang out and I was never sorry:
  Then it was well with me, in days ere I was born.

Now, and I muse for why and never find the reason,
  I pace the earth, and drink the air, and feel the sun.
Be still, be still, my soul; it is but for a season:
  Let us endure an hour and see injustice done.

Ay, look: high heaven and earth ail from the prime foundation;
  All thoughts to rive the heart are here, and all are vain:
Horror and scorn and hate and fear and indignation—
  Oh why did I awake? when shall I sleep again?

LOVELIEST OF TREES[1]

Loveliest of trees, the cherry now
Is hung with bloom along the bough,
And stands about the woodland ride
Wearing white for Eastertide.

Now, of my threescore years and ten,
Twenty will not come again,
And take from seventy springs a score,
It only leaves me fifty more.

And since to look at things in bloom
Fifty springs are little room,
About the woodlands I will go
To see the cherry hung with snow.

---

1. From *A Shropshire Lad* by A. E. Housman. Reprinted by permission of Henry Holt and Company, Inc., and The Society of Authors as the Literary Representative of the Trustees of the Estate of the late A. E. Housman, and Messrs. Jonathan Cape, Ltd., publishers of A. E. Housman's *Collected Poems*.

ON WENLOCK EDGE[1]

On Wenlock Edge the wood's in trouble;
His forest fleece the Wrekin heaves;
The gale, it plies the saplings double,
And thick on Severn snow the leaves.

'Twould blow like this through holt and hanger
When Uricon the city stood:
'Tis the old wind in the old anger,
But then it threshed another wood.

Then, 'twas before my time, the Roman
At yonder heaving hill would stare:
The blood that warms an English yeoman,
The thoughts that hurt him, they were there.

There, like the wind through woods in riot,
Through him the gale of life blew high;
The tree of man was never quiet:
Then 'twas the Roman, now 'tis I.

The gale, it plies the saplings double,
It blows so hard, 'twill soon be gone:
To-day the Roman and his trouble
Are ashes under Uricon.

TERENCE, THIS IS STUPID STUFF[1]

"Terence, this is stupid stuff:
You eat your victuals fast enough;
There can't be much amiss, 'tis clear,
To see the rate you drink your beer.
But oh, good Lord, the verse you make,
It gives a chap the belly-ache.
The cow, the old cow, she is dead;
It sleeps well, the hornèd head:
We poor lads, 'tis our turn now
To hear such tunes as killed the cow.
Pretty friendship 'tis to rhyme

1. From *A Shropshire Lad* by A. E. Housman by permission of the publishers, Henry Holt and Company, Inc., and The Society of Authors as the Literary Representative of the Trustees of the Estate of the late A. E. Housman and Messrs. Jonathan Cape, Ltd., publishers of A. E. Housman's *Collected Poems.*

Your friends to death before their time
Moping melancholy mad:
Come, pipe a tune to dance to, lad."

Why, if 'tis dancing you would be,
There's brisker pipes than poetry.
Say, for what were hop-yards meant,
Or why was Burton built on Trent?
Oh, many a peer of England brews
Livelier liquor than the Muse,
And malt does more than Milton can
To justify God's ways to man.
Ale, man, ale's the stuff to drink
For fellows whom it hurts to think:
Look into the pewter pot
To see the world as the world's not.
And faith, 'tis pleasant till 'tis past:
The mischief is that 'twill not last.
Oh, I have been to Ludlow fair
And left my necktie God knows where,
And carried half-way home, or near,
Pints and quarts of Ludlow beer:
Then the world seemed none so bad,
And I myself a sterling lad;
And down in lovely muck I've lain,
Happy till I woke again.
Then I saw the morning sky:
Heigho, the tale was all a lie;
The world, it was the old world yet,
I was I, my things were wet,
And nothing now remained to do
But begin the game anew.

Therefore, since the world has still
Much good, but much less good than ill,
And while the sun and moon endure
Luck's a chance, but trouble's sure,
I'd face it as a wise man would,
And train for ill and not for good.
'Tis true, the stuff I bring for sale
Is not so brisk a brew as ale:
Out of a stem that scored the hand
I wrung it in a weary land.
But take it: if the smack is sour,

The better for the embittered hour;
It should do good to heart and head
When your soul is in my soul's stead;
And I will friend you, if I may,
In the dark and cloudy day.

There was a king reigned in the East:
There, when kings will sit to feast,
They get their fill before they think
With poisoned meat and poisoned drink.
He gathered all that springs to birth
From the many-venomed earth;
First a little, thence to more,
He sampled all her killing store;
And easy, smiling, seasoned sound,
Sate the king when healths went round.
They put arsenic in his meat
And stared aghast to watch him eat;
They poured strychnine in his cup
And shook to see him drink it up:
They shook, they stared as white's their shirt:
Them it was their poison hurt.
—I tell the tale that I heard told.
Mithridates, he died old.

1887[1]

From Clee to heaven the beacon burns,
The shires have seen it plain,
From north and south the sign returns,
And beacons burn again.

Look left, look right, the hills are bright,
The dales are light between,
Because 'tis fifty years tonight
That God has saved the Queen.

Now, when the flame they watch not towers
About the soil they trod,
Lads, we'll remember friends of ours
Who shared the work with God.

1. From *A Shropshire Lad* by A. E. Housman by permission of the publishers, Henry Holt and Company, Inc., and The Society of Authors as the Literary Representative of the Trustees of the Estate of the late A. E. Housman and Messrs. Jonathan Cape, Ltd., publishers of A. E. Housman's *Collected Poems.*

To skies that knit their heartstrings right,
    To fields that bred them brave,
The saviors come not home tonight:
    Themselves they could not save.

It dawns in Asia, tombstones show
    And Shropshire names are read;
And the Nile spills his overflow
    Beside the Severn's dead.

We pledge in peace by farm and town
    The Queen they served in war,
And fire the beacons up and down
    The land they perished for.

"God save the Queen" we living sing,
    From height to height 'tis heard;
And with the rest your voices ring,
    Lads of the Fifty-third.

Oh, God will save her, fear you not:
    Be you the men you've been,
Get you the sons your fathers got,
    And God will save the Queen.

ON HOUSMAN'S *1887* [1]

CHARLES CHILD WALCUTT

THE statement and experience of this poem are deceptively simple. The deception depends upon the fact that the obvious and accessible meaning satisfies the reader so completely that he may not feel an impulse to investigate further; or, to put it less subjectively, the various levels of meaning in "1887" do not come through with equal ease. Let us, then, first consider what I take to be the poem's most accessible meaning, from which we may turn to some of its less obvious aspects.

A dominant characteristic of "1887" is grandeur. "From Clee to heaven" opens land and sky out broadly. Later the flame "towers about the soil." We turn easily to Asia and the Nile and back with a stride to the Severn; and from Housman's country lads to the Queen. We conceive the British Empire, socially and spatially. Burners of bonfires in rural England are aware of their

1. Charles Child Walcutt, "Housman and the Empire: An Analysis of '1887.'" *College English,* V (February, 1944), 255–258. A paper read at The English Institute. Reprinted here by permission of the author and the Editors of *College English.*

broad Empire. The fiftieth year of Victoria's reign, which they are celebrating, expands with security and permanence.

With the third stanza, however, and just as the vigor and bright exuberance of the lines are reaching a climax, comes the first bitter dash of irony; it is introduced by an abrupt shift of tone and takes advantage of this feeling of spaciousness that has been established:

Now, when the flame they watch not towers
About the soil they trod,
Lads, we'll remember friends of ours
Who shared the work with God.

"Shared," of course, mocks the conception of God's saving the Queen: it does not mock the so casually mentioned "friends" who shared that work. But grief triumphs immediately; irony is abandoned, and the question of who should have credit is swept aside as the lads are praised without reserve in terms both homespun and heroic:

To skies that knit their heartstrings right,
To fields that bred them brave,

And now even the irony of the third stanza is obliterated by the brilliant, audacious stroke of identifying the soldiers who have died abroad with the Christ who as a part of the Trinity would rightfully "share the work with God." The irony, of course, is not forgotten, nor is the bitterness mitigated by the reference to the forment of the crucifixion; but the latter enormously magnifies the heroic proportions of the soldiers and their task:

The saviors come not home tonight:
Themselves they could not save.

We recall: "In like manner also the chief priests mocking him among themselves with the scribes said, He saved others, himself he cannot save" (Mark 15:18).

I have been emphasizing the grandeur which swells through this poem because I believe that Emerson's statement, "The axioms of physics translate the laws of ethics," applies to poetry. Action is equaled by reaction. The power of the irony and bitterness corresponds to the magnitude of the situation. When Housman has sufficiently enlarged our perceptions, he achieves a countermovement of similar intensity. The scale is maintained now, as we are taken with giant strides across the world:

It dawns in Asia, tombstones show
And Shropshire names are read;
And the Nile spills his overflow
Beside the Severn's dead.

"Spills" suggests plenitude, opulence, the superabundance of the Empire's power. It also suggests an extravagance and lavishness of power. We are entirely in the realm of grandeur until we come to "overflow," which adds to the sense of abundant power a recognition of the attitude of, I presume, unspecified empire-builders. To them soldiers are extra men, common people, idle, hungry mouths—overflow legitimately to be spilled in Asia for the profits of empire. This conception of wanton plenitude arises from the whole poem; it does not compete with, but rather builds upon, the expansion of consciousness from Shropshire to the Nile. And the latter is needed to carry us on to the supreme and relieved bitterness of the final stanza:

> Oh, God will save her, fear you not:
> Be you the men you've been,
> Get you the sons your fathers got,
> And God will save the Queen.

This answers the hypocrisy of those who glibly thank God for what has consumed the lives of uncounted Shropshire lads—and the deeper hypocrisy of pretending that God has anything to do with such business.

So far I have presented "1887" as satire on the hypocrisy of empire. This is only one level. It is also complacent, heroic, elegiac, remorseful, sad, and pastoral. It is heroic, with something of the complacency inevitable to an Englishman writing in 1887. The protest is made from the vantage of peace, power, and security. If lads have died, they have not done so in vain. The grandeur which serves as a foil for the irony is also a rock in itself; its impression of national well-being remains unshaken. There are many living for a few dead. It is almost ungrateful to weigh the cost, for the Empire flourishes and brave lads now pursue the arts of peace. The historical past is always a part of the texture of life in the present, which it colors with many sorts of meanings. Traditions of valor are thus an essential part of Victoria's golden jubilee. Without them there would be no impulse to fire the beacons of celebration. What this all comes to is that Housman does not imply through his final bitterness against the hypocrisy that the entire process is intolerable. On the contrary, the historical process is an inevitable one, of which all the celebrants are a part. Britain's might is destined, like an aspect of nature. And so the complacency which I have defined shades off into the elegiac tone. What has happened must have happened, to bc observed with pride and despair and resignation. The poet is sad and bitter, yes, but not indignant. He accepts the situation, sharply though he may wish to reinterpret it.

Close to these levels, yet distinct from them, is a sense of guilt. It appears first in the sharp antithesis of the sixth stanza. There has been a full stop and rest as the reader dwells upon the finality and opulence of

> And the Nile spills his overflow
> Beside the Severn's dead.

The word "dead" is the first direct statement of what had previously been given metaphorically or merely suggested. We resume after this pause on a lower key:

We pledge in peace by farm and town
The Queen they served in war.

The pronounced alliteration on "pledge in peace" underlines the deprecatory, almost apologetic, note: It is easy enough to pledge devotion in peace, by homely farm and town. The words suggest a comfortable littleness which in contrast to Asia and the Nile shrinks the moral stature of the home-stayers. With the next two lines the contrast is sharpened:

And fire the beacons up and down
The land they perished for.

Lighting bonfires is scarcely heroic; it makes a sad contrast with the deeds of the dead, and the futility of the celebration reflects a further irony on the futility of the sacrifice. The alliteration of "perished" with "pledge in peace" emphasizes the distance between the two. Bitterness here becomes self-condemning: the celebrants are shamefaced; and the idea is given again with contrasting words as we go from "perished" to the next stanza:

"God save the Queen" we living sing;

The saviors have perished; we living sing "God save the Queen"; and we cringe from our own brisk hypocrisy. I believe some of this feeling is concentrated, with added meanings, in the rich ambiguity of "ring." In the first place, we cannot be sure whether its mood is indicative or imperative—a statement of fact or a derisive command. The statement would convey awareness of the folly of those surviving soldiers who do not realize how they have been duped; also the accusation that they participate morally in empire by lending it their support; also the indication that "with the rest" they are like the rest; also a tone of fatalistic, elegiac acceptance and pity for these "innocents"; and, finally, a thought for the dead lads of the Fifty-third Regiment, who speak through the situation. The derisive command conveys the same ideas with an ironical accent, adding to the texture of the situation by causing the reader to dwell upon the various possible meanings.

The meter contributes to the quality I have noticed in stanzas VI and VII. We resume, I said, with a lower key in VI; but, though muted, the movement of

We pledge in peace by farm and town
The Queen they served in war,

is also almost orotund in its firm regularity. It comes out too easily and emphasizes the complacency in security, the pomp and circumstance underlying the ceremony in which they are engaged. Thus its pronounced beat sounds hollow rather than stately because it comes so close after the grandeur of the two previous lines. In the next two lines the pace quickens with the thought, and the reader races from beacon to beacon; but, needing a heavy beat to confirm the pattern, he comes down hard on "perished," and the mock pomp of the first two lines is abruptly exposed.

We have, then, condemnation balanced by a sense of guilt; complacency in power balanced by hatred of hypocrisy; the elegiac recognition of the inevitability of historical processes balanced by contempt and pity for the folly of the participants. I must even raise the question here as to whether Housman's feeling for this final irony is not rendered—or enriched—by his use, in lines 15 and 16, of a myth of sacrifice which he probably did not accept any more literally than the pagan myths he knew so well. Perhaps the figure is not, in every respect, audacious.

These tensions are what maintain the psychic or aesthetic objectivity of "1887." It is not propaganda because, far from inciting the reader to action, it does not even suggest a solution to the "evil" upon which it turns. And yet, for all my weighing of these balancing tendencies, the poem does not, actually, balance. Folly and stupidity glow darkly through it and the further conviction that man is doomed ever to be his own worst enemy—that the inadequacy of life to great spirits is due to the inadequacy of most men, a failing which the great spirits share by virtue of their inability ever to change it. The poem ends with a bitterness so direct and intense as to be almost painful. An earnest Anglophobe might take it for a tract, but he would be mistaking Housman's dissatisfaction with mankind for an attack on Britain.

I should like, in closing, to consider some of the respects in which "1887" is a version of pastoral. It employs the convention of expressing the complex through the simple. It implies that these matters are too intricate for the simple man at the same time that it demonstrates his natural ability to cut through the verbiage and ceremony of the upper classes. It identifies the poet with the country soldier and yet makes us aware that this identification is the elaborate pretense of a man who is actually far above the moral level of the ruling caste. It employs the heroic-pastoral device of making the simple man seem absolutely right and good by associating natural rightness and goodness with the simple aspects of his being that are revealed in the poem. The simplicity of the language, likewise, while it suits the pastoral mode, has striking heroic qualities that depend upon the noble directness of the diction and the earthiness of the figures. Only the combined humility and impertinence of the pastoral swain, for example, could carry off the reference to the Savior, surmounting the initial distrust and incredulity that such an image excites and then building the tone up to unequivocal grandeur. (Again I raise the question of whether there is not also an element of mockery and cynicism in this figure.) This image is prepared for by reference to "skies that knit their heartstrings right." "Knit" suggests hardihood, homespun directness, essentially physical qualities, which are transferred to the moral sphere by the force of the common man's uncritical "right." We must feel that he has nature on his side and that his simple "right" springs from his direct access to truth. The verse, finally, contributes here. The ballad stanza is by nature direct and unsophisticated, and its use establishes such a tone. Yet Housman employs it with an ease and flexibility that laugh at his pretense of humility. After the facile iambics of the first two stanzas we see an abrupt shift:

> Now, when the flame they watch not towers.

Here the accent on "now" is dramatic, thoughtful, and in a sense innocent in its obviousness. There is also in this line a lowering of the main vowels ("watch," "towers," "about," "trod") that complements the deepening of the tone. The bitterness of the final stanza is sharpened by the heavy initial accents on "Be" and "Get" in lines 2 and 3; and the brusque alliteration of "God" and "get" contributes powerfully to the idea which receives its most forceful statement here. Such expert metrical effects, in conjunction with the pretended naïveté of the ballad measure, are merely a further instance of the pastoral vein which so much enriches the ironic texture of "1887."

W. B. YEATS

IN MEMORY OF MAJOR ROBERT GREGORY[1]

I

Now that we're almost settled in our house
I'll name the friends that cannot sup with us
Beside a fire of turf in th' ancient tower,
And having talked to some late hour
Climb up the narrow winding stair to bed:
Discoverers of forgotten truth
Or mere companions of my youth,
All, all are in my thoughts to-night being dead.

II

Always we'd have the new friend meet the old
And we are hurt if either friend seem cold,
And there is salt to lengthen out the smart
In the affections of our heart,
And quarrels are blown up upon that head;
But not a friend that I would bring
This night can set us quarrelling,
For all that come into my mind are dead.

1. From *The Collected Poems of W. B. Yeats* (New York, 1933), pp. 150–154. Last copyright holder (1940), Bertha Georgie Yeats. Reprinted by permission of The Macmillan Company and The Macmillan Company of Canada.

III

Lionel Johnson comes the first to mind,
That loved his learning better than mankind,
Though courteous to the worst; much falling he
Brooded upon sanctity
Till all his Greek and Latin learning seemed
A long blast upon the horn that brought
A little nearer to his thought
A measureless consummation that he dreamed.

IV

And that enquiring man John Synge comes next,
That dying chose the living world for text
And never could have rested in the tomb
But that, long travelling, he had come
Towards nightfall upon certain set apart
In a most desolate stony place,
Towards nightfall upon a race
Passionate and simple like his heart.

V

And then I think of old George Pollexfen,
In muscular youth well known to Mayo men
For horsemanship at meets or at racecourses,
That could have shown how pure-bred horses
And solid men, for all their passion, live
But as the outrageous stars incline
By opposition, square and trine;
Having grown sluggish and contemplative.

VI

They were my close companions many a year,
A portion of my mind and life, as it were,
And now their breathless faces seem to look
Out of some old picture-book;
I am accustomed to their lack of breath,
But not that my dear friend's dear son,
Our Sidney and our perfect man,
Could share in that discourtesy of death.

VII

For all things the delighted eye now sees
Were loved by him; the old storm-broken trees
That cast their shadows upon road and bridge;

The tower set on the stream's edge;
The ford where drinking cattle make a stir
Nightly, and startled by that sound
The water-hen must change her ground;
He might have been your heartiest welcomer.

VIII

When with the Galway foxhounds he would ride
From Castle Taylor to the Roxborough side
Or Esserkelly plain, few kept his pace;
At Mooneen he had leaped a place
So perilous that half the astonished meet
Had shut their eyes; and where was it
He rode a race without a bit?
And yet his mind outran the horses' feet.

IX

We dreamed that a great painter had been born
To cold Clare rock and Galway rock and thorn,
To that stern colour and that delicate line
That are our secret discipline
Wherein the gazing heart doubles her might.
Soldier, scholar, horseman, he,
And yet he had the intensity
To have published all to be a world's delight.

X

What other could so well have counselled us
In all lovely intricacies of a house
As he that practised or that understood
All work in metal or in wood,
In moulded plaster or in carven stone?
Soldier, scholar, horseman, he,
And all he did done perfectly
As though he had but that one trade alone.

XI

Some burn damp faggots, others may consume
The entire combustible world in one small room
As though dried straw, and if we turn about
The bare chimney is gone black out
Because the work had finished in that flare.
Soldier, scholar, horseman, he,

As 'twere all life's epitome.
What made us dream that he could comb gray hair?

XII

I had thought, seeing how bitter is that wind
That shakes the shutter, to have brought to mind
All those that manhood tried, or childhood loved
Or boyish intellect approved,
With some appropriate commentary on each;
Until imagination brought
A fitter welcome; but a thought
Of that late death took all my heart for speech.

ON YEATS'S *IN MEMORY OF MAJOR ROBERT GREGORY*[1]

MARION WITT

WHEN Major Robert Gregory was killed leading his air squadron on January 23, 1918, Yeats was moved to write at once of the son of his old and dear friend. His note of appreciation was printed in the *Observer,* February 17, 1918, and reprinted in America in the *Little Review* in November of the same year. This almost unknown tribute, later to be concentrated into the praise of the dead soldier in the last six stanzas of "In Memory of Major Robert Gregory," shows Yeats in his frequent habit of writing first in prose and then transmuting his concept into poetry. The opening of the eulogy cites Gregory's many gifts, " painter, classical scholar, scholar in painting and in modern literature, boxer, horseman, airman"—a variety so great that, Yeats said, "his very accomplishment hid from many his genius."

To Yeats, Gregory was "a great painter in the immaturity of his youth," a genius the poet had first recognized in the young man's designs of costumes and scenery for the Abbey Theatre, "decorations which, obtaining their effect from the fewest possible lines and colours, had always the grave distinction of his own imagination." Gregory's paintings long perplexed Yeats by what seemed neglect of detail. "But," he wrote, "in a few years I came to care for his paintings of the Clare coast, with his cloud shadows upon blue-grey stony hills, . . . more than for any contemporary landscape painting." This admiration for Gregory's painting persisted, and in Yeats's home in his last years space was made between the books in his study for one of Gregory's landscapes. The climax of the tribute to the painter's art follows:

A man of letters may perhaps find in work such as this, or in old Chinese painting, in the woodcuts and etchings of Calvert and Palmer, in Blake's woodcuts to Thornton's Virgil, in the landscape background of Mr. Ricketts' "Wise and Foolish

1. From "The Making of an Elegy," *Modern Philology,* XLVIII (Nov., 1950), 112-121. Abridged by the author.

Virgins," something that he does not find in the great modern masters, and that he cares for deeply. Is it merely that these men share certain moods with great lyric poetry, with, let us say, the "Leach Gatherer" of Wordsworth; or that their moods, unlike those of men with more objective curiosity, are a part of the traditional expression of the soul?

In the final paragraph Yeats said that, though Gregory was often led away from his painting by some other gift, "his attitude to life and art never lost intensity," and concluded:

I have noticed that men whose lives are to be an ever-growing absorption in subjective beauty . . . seek through some lesser gift, or through mere excitement, to strengthen that self which unites them to ordinary men. It is as though they hesitated before they plunged into the abyss. Major Gregory told Mr. Bernard Shaw, who visited him in France, that the months since he joined the army had been the happiest of his life. I think they brought him peace of mind, an escape from that shrinking, which I sometimes saw upon his face, before the growing absorption of his dream, the loneliness of his dream, as from his constant struggle to resist those other gifts that brought him ease and friendship. Leading his squadron in France or in Italy, mind and hand were at one, will and desire.

John Butler Yeats put the final statement about Gregory's war experience more simply in a letter to his son in June, 1918: "The way to be happy is to forget yourself. That is why Robert Gregory was happy." And he added that ways of forgetting yourself are in war, "seeing nothing but its vastness," in social reform, "in games of violent self-exertion," or, best of all, in art and beauty. To Yeats himself perhaps Gregory became in his death a heroic, happy figure because, like the Irish hero, Cuchullain, "he was creative joy separated from fear." Certainly, this was to be a basic concept of the lyric, "An Irish Airman Foresees His Death," in which the flyer (Gregory) is moved not by hate or love, anger or patriotism, but entirely by "a lonely impulse of delight."

A few months after Gregory's death the old Norman castle of Ballylee in the west of Ireland became Yeats's home. He had bought the building in 1917 after Gregory and an architect had advised that it might be made livable. This ancient building was thus closely associated with the dead artist, who had made a charming sepia drawing of the tower, the encircling river, the bridge, and the storm-twisted trees. The tower itself was in no way new to Yeats's experience. As early as 1899 he had described "the old square castle, Baile-laoi . . . and old ash trees throwing green shadows upon a little river and great stepping-stones." In this early work, tower and disappearing river form a mere romantic background for a touching love story; but when the tower, closely linked with Gregory, became, in the very year of the young man's death, what Yeats thought would be his permanent home, disparate material fused into a new complex, a highly personal symbol. Gregory's death defeated one of Yeats's happiest expectations for his new home in the old tower: that the young man would be neighbor, counselor, friend. A tower had long been a symbol Yeats loved and used; but now an old tower stands in a new configuration. From this point in his experience, the tower—not any tower but his own—suggests, as had Shelley's, "the mind looking outward upon men and things," with its winding stair as the gyres of history on which the generations of men climb. Gregory's death may have crystallized these symbols in Yeats's mind. The objects themselves continued to stimulate him to creation, for in 1926 he wrote to a friend, "We are at our tower and I am writing poetry as I always do here. . . ." Though tower and winding stair are presented in the elegy as concrete setting for the experience, they fill it with overtones for the readers of Yeats's later work, where as dominant symbols they serve as titles for two of his greatest volumes.

Technically, the poem is flawless. Yeats always showed power in the use of old metrical forms and skill in creating new stanzas for special purposes. Here the style, even the devices of meter, prove, as the poet wished his technique to be, "sufficiently flexible for expression of the emotions of life as they arise." For this elegy he chose an eight-line stanza, which he was to use again in "A Prayer for my Daughter," in Part II of "The Tower," and with modifications in "Byzantium":

> Now that we're almost settled in our house
> I'll name the friends that cannot sup with us
> Beside a fire of turf in th' ancient tower,
> And having talked to some late hour
> Climb up the narrow winding stair to bed:
> Discoverers of forgotten truth
> Or mere companions of my youth,
> All, all are in my thoughts to-night being dead.

Though this opening stanza echoes "For Lycidas is dead, dead ere his prime," or "I weep for Adonais—he is dead!" the pattern is Yeats's own and combines the majesty of traditional elegy with the simplicity of personal conversation. Largely this dual effect comes from the swift, natural language of the poem. Dr. Gogarty noted in his elegy on Yeats that the dead poet preferred Burns's "straight lines" on Matthew Henderson, "For Matthew was a queer man," to "Adonais," "Shelley's cosmic sermon." The language of "In Memory of Major Robert Gregory" has Burns's direct honesty, the "great voice" that Yeats found in Burns's lines on Henderson. Meter serves well, too, as a "pattern so seeming old that it may seem all men's speech." The four beats of the fourth line break the heroic couplet just as it is to be established in the second couplet; tetrameters in lines six and seven give a gentle, conversational tone, while the pentameters slow the movement; and the enclosed *cddc* rhyme keeps structure and emotion taut. Throughout the poem Yeats used slant rhymes to put into minor key the ordinarily strong major chord of the couplet. Thus in the opening couplets of several stanzas are such approximations as *house, us* (repeated); *he, sanctity; tomb, come; racecourses, horses; year, were; bridge, edge; line, discipline; wind, mind.* The stanza is by these various means exquisitely adjusted to the double effect of intimate personal talk and heroic elegy.

The dead friends summoned in the poem had been hinted at but not named in "Shepherd and Goatherd," an unsuccessful pastoral elegy about Gregory, which Yeats had shortly before completed. In the earlier poem the Goatherd (Yeats himself) said:

> You sing as always of the natural life,
> And I that made like music in my youth
> Hearing it now have sighed for that young man
> And certain lost companions of my own.

The lost companions become the subject of the first half of the new elegy, losses now paid as if not paid before. The originality in Yeats's use of this ancient element in elegies lies in the fact that each of the men he summons carries a facet or facets of Robert Gregory's personality and achievements. "Lionel Johnson comes the first to mind," classical scholar and dreamer, in Yeats's earlier phrase, possessed of "ecstatic stoicism." Of Gregory's painting Yeats had said, "One always understood by something in his selection of line and colour that he had read his Homer and his Virgil and his Dante; that they, while giving something of themselves, had freed him from easy tragedy and trivial comedy." Scholars, dreamers, "courteous to the worst," were Johnson and Gregory, too. "And that enquiring man John Synge comes next," who toward nightfall "in a most desolate stony place" came upon a people "passionate and simple like his heart." Gregory, too, loved all natural life, yet preferred the stony places and, Yeats said, "painted the Burren Hills, and thereby found what promised to grow into a great style." In his *Autobiography* Yeats tells how Synge wanted to combine "ecstasy, asceticism, and austerity," and Gregory's paintings he called "full of austerity and sweetness." George Pollexfen, horseman in youth, astrologist in age, is a man of action "grown sluggish and contemplative." "In muscular youth well known to Mayo men/For horsemanship," Pollexfen combined, as in a much subtler way Gregory did, great skill in sports, a love of natural things, a mind full of pictures, and a mystical concern for the inner life. At this point, with perfect simplicity and justice Yeats first mentions Gregory himself, in one line fusing in him all the qualities of older lost friends, "our perfect man," comparable in the twentieth century to the hero of a great elegy of the Renaissance, also warrior and artist, "Our Sidney":

> They were my close companions many a year,
> A portion of my mind and life, as it were,
> And now their breathless faces seem to look

Out of some old picture-book;
I am accustomed to their lack of breath,
But not that my dear friend's dear son,
Our Sidney and our perfect man,
Could share in that discourtesy of death.

The phrasing of the last line, Elizabethan in tone and magic, links the whole concept of Gregory as hero with the pattern of the Renaissance hero and the poem with the tradition.

The succeeding stanza lists natural beauties around Ballylee of which Gregory might have been the "heartiest welcomer." This scene, which Gregory had drawn, leads directly to a consideration in stanza nine of the great painter and the secret of art. The interpolation of stanza eight, with its adolescent praise of Gregory's foolhardy horsemanship, is, therefore, puzzling:

At Mooneen he had leaped a place
So perilous that half the astonished meet
Had shut their eyes; and where was it,
He rode a race without a bit?

These lines are an almost childish elaboration of the final member of the repeated triad, "Soldier, scholar, horseman." The reason Yeats used the stanza at all is made clear by his comment on an early manuscript of the elegy: "The following stanza was added in proof as Mrs. Gregory did not think I had said enough of Robert's courage." Fortunately, the emotional flow of the poem is so strong, what Joseph Hone called "the intricacy of its passion" so great, that the unhappy eighth stanza is only a ripple in the current.

The climactic ninth stanza considers Gregory's place among artists:

We dreamed that a great painter had been born
To cold Clare rock and Galway rock and thorn,
To that stern colour and that delicate line
That are our secret discipline
Wherein the gazing heart doubles her might.
Soldier, scholar, horseman, he,
And yet he had the intensity
To have published all to be a world's delight.

Every concept of art in these highly charged lines has an immediate source in the writings of Samuel Palmer and Edward Calvert, nineteenth-century disciples of Blake. During the month or so after Gregory's death, Yeats's table at the Bodleian was covered with the etchings and woodcuts of Palmer and Calvert, which had for years been the subject of his admiring study. He had long quoted Calvert and Palmer on art and was to do so to the end of his life; for only a few months before his death he wrote in "Under Ben Bulken":

Calvert and Wilson, Blake and Claude,
Prepared a rest for the people of God,
Palmer's phrase, but after that
Confusion fell upon our thought.

Both Calvert and Palmer emphasized, as had their master Blake, the expression of the soul rather than the realistic representation of the body or of the landscape. "Palmer's phrase" belongs to his praise of Blake, whose woodcuts for Thornton's *Virgil,* he found "like all that wonderful artist's works, the drawing aside of the fleshly curtain, and the glimpse which all the most holy, studious saints and sages have enjoyed, of that rest which remaineth to the people of God." Often as Yeats referred to Calvert and Palmer, to their concern for the expression in art of the visionary soul of man, the ninth stanza of "In Memory of Major Robert Gregory" forms what appears nowhere else in his work: a synthesis and intensification of what the two men said about painting and poetry.

Both Palmer and Calvert chose to paint or draw primitive landscapes, austere and delicate. In their painting and in their theories about their art, color is less important than line; and Yeats finds "stern colour" and "delicate line" the "secret discipline" of poets and painters alike. Power comes, these artists believed, in asceticism, and Yeats had long before written: "All art is, indeed, a monotony in external things for the sake of an interior variety, a sacrifice of gross effects to subtle effects, an asceticism of the imagination." Neither Calvert nor Palmer conceived of such art as pallid but rather as intense. Calvert wrote: *"Only paint what you love in what you see,* and discipline yourself to separate this essence from its dumb accompaniments, so that the accents fall upon the points of passion." The artist's self-discipline in accenting the points of passion becomes in Yeats's words "the secret discipline /Wherein the gazing heart doubles her might." Palmer found the full mystery and might of line in the tiny figures of Blake's woodcuts, which have, he said, "that intense, soul-evidencing attitude and action, and that elastic, nervous spring which belongs to uncaged immortal spirits." In Gregory, Yeats found this power, this mystery and might in an ascetic and delicate art, "the intensity/To have published all to be a world's delight." The final phrase suggests again that Gregory is "Our Sidney"; for Yeats could hardly have forgotten the line from one of the Astrophel poems, "Sidney is dead, dead is my friend, dead is the world's delight." Of such artistic power as the stanza both describes and exemplifies, Calvert wrote, "I know that there is a mastery and a music which shall command truth itself to look as we would have it, and to echo the pulses of the heart. Physical truth being translated into musical truth." If ever in his poetry, Yeats in this ninth stanza achieved the transmutation into musical truth of both the physical and the metaphysical.

In the last stanzas Yeats returns to Gregory's personality, his talents, the terrible loss to his survivors. At the time of Synge's death in 1909, he had written:

One does not feel that death is evil when one meets it,—evil, I mean, for the one who dies. . . . The wildest sorrow that comes at the thought of death is, I think, "Ages will pass over and no one ever again look on that nobleness or that beauty."

Nor was warfare repugnant to Yeats, for in 1910 he said:

I think that all noble things are the result of warfare; great nations and classes, of warfare in the visible world, great poetry and philosophy, of invisible warfare, the division of a mind within itself, a victory, the sacrifice of a man to himself.

Yeats could understand the ecstasy of Gregory's life in war and even that, for the dead man, the end was happy. Because Gregory had epitomized both visible and invisible warfare, the division of his soul made his early death inevitable.

Always Yeats had envied the man of action and as poet had brooded for years on the possibility of one man's achieving unity of being, a state very difficult but, as he long believed, not impossible. Years earlier he had quoted Calvert's exultant cry, "I go inward to God, outward to the gods," Calvert's philosophy of myth, of divine truth in man's heart and the no less divine images created to embody it. Greek myths became to Calvert mysteries on which to ponder, impersonations of moral powers, of gods, of divine attributes, all embodied in the life we love in the natural world. Calvert's dichotomy, which he fused into unity, of subjective brooding on the One, objective concern with the many, Yeats felt as the basic division in Gregory between the absorbing inner dream and the easier external action. Unity of being, Yeats once thought, is perhaps most nearly possible in an age of complexity for a man of action who is also a man of loneliness and of dreams. Charles Stewart Parnell seemed to him such a man, and of Parnell he wrote: "Perhaps unmotivated self-immolation, were that possible, . . . were as great evidence as such a man could give of power over self and so of the expression of the self." Yeats saw Gregory's death as a kind of self-immolation, to which the young man moved as he increasingly realized that the disparate elements of his being could never form a final unity. "I joined up," he had said, "out of friendship." Leaving his absorption in subjective beauty behind him, he went for a few months from the artist's vision to battle. Solitary brooding fosters the "lonely impulse of delight" which made the Irish airman foresee his death and go to meet it, filled with "creative joy separated from fear." Thus for a moment only—and such a moment cannot endure—unity of being is achieved.

In the eleventh stanza of "In Memory of Major Robert Gregory" all this complex of thought and feeling is reduced to its simplest terms. Gregory's work was finished, his death certain:

Some burn damp faggots, others may consume
The entire combustible world in one small room

. . . .

Because the work had finished in that flare.
Soldier, scholar, horseman, he,
As 'twere all life's epitome.
What made us dream that he could comb grey hair?

The final stanza, with its unfulfilled wish to say more of

All those that manhood tried, or childhood loved
Or boyish intellect approved,

ends brokenly:

. . . But a thought
Of that late death took all my heart for speech.

Here none of Yeats's elaborate and unorthodox views of the life of the soul after death distracts the mind and feeling from human loss. The elemental simplicity of concept and expression in this final stanza forms a coda of pure tone to echo and reinforce the surface simplicity of the whole elegy. All complexities are dissolved in grief without comfort. Such a stanza, powerful as it is in its position, gains intensity from these very complexities, "the continuous indefinable symbolism" which pervades all that has gone before and which Yeats had declared to be "the substance of all style."

SAILING TO BYZANTIUM[1]

That is no country for old men. The young
In one another's arms, birds in the trees,
—Those dying generations—at their song,
The salmon-falls, the mackerel-crowded seas,
Fish, flesh, or fowl, commend all summer long
Whatever is begotten, born, and dies.
Caught in that sensual music all neglect
Monuments of unaging intellect.

An aged man is but a paltry thing,
A tattered coat upon a stick, unless
Soul clap its hands and sing, and louder sing
For every tatter in its mortal dress,
Nor is there singing school but studying

1. From *The Collected Poems of W. B. Yeats*. Copyright, 1933. By permission of The Macmillan Company, publishers.

Monuments of its own magnificence;
And therefore I have sailed the seas and come
To the holy city of Byzantium.

O sages standing in God's holy fire
As in the gold mosaic of a wall,
Come from the holy fire, perne in a gyre,
And be the singing-masters of my soul.
Consume my heart away, sick with desire
And fastened to a dying animal
It knows not what it is; and gather me
Into the artifice of eternity.

Once out of nature I shall never take
My bodily form from any natural thing,
But such a form as Grecian goldsmiths make
Of hammered gold and gold enamelling
To keep a drowsy Emperor awake;
Or set upon a golden bough to sing
To lords and ladies of Byzantium
Of what is past, or passing, or to come.

A PRAYER FOR MY DAUGHTER[1]

Once more the storm is howling, and half hid
Under this cradle-hood and coverlid
My child sleeps on. There is no obstacle
But Gregory's wood and one bare hill
Whereby the haystack- and roof-levelling wind,
Bred on the Atlantic, can be stayed;
And for an hour I have walked and prayed
Because of the great gloom that is in my mind.

I have walked and prayed for this young child an hour
And heard the sea-wind scream upon the tower,
And under the arches of the bridge, and scream
In the elms above the flooded stream;
Imagining in excited reverie
That the future years had come,
Dancing to a frenzied drum,
Out of the murderous innocence of the sea.

---

1. From *The Collected Poems of W. B. Yeats.* Copyright, 1933. By permission of The Macmillan Company, publishers.

May she be granted beauty and yet not
Beauty to make a stranger's eye distraught,
Or hers before a looking-glass for such,
Being made beautiful overmuch,
Consider beauty a sufficient end,
Lose natural kindness and maybe
The heart-revealing intimacy
That chooses right, and never find a friend.

Helen being chosen found life flat and dull
And later had much trouble from a fool,
While that great Queen, that rose out of the spray,
Being fatherless could have her way
Yet chose a bandy-leggèd smith for man.
It's certain that fine women eat
A crazy salad with their meat
Whereby the Horn of Plenty is undone.

In courtesy I'd have her chiefly learned;
Hearts are not had as a gift but hearts are earned
By those that are not entirely beautiful;
Yet many, that have played the fool
For beauty's very self, has charm made wise,
And many a poor man that has roved,
Loved and thought himself beloved,
From a glad kindness cannot take his eyes.

May she become a flourishing hidden tree
That all her thoughts may like the linnet be,
And have no business but dispensing round
Their magnanimities of sound.
Nor but in merriment begin a chase,
Nor but in merriment a quarrel.
O may she live like some green laurel
Rooted in one dear perpetual place.

My mind, because the minds that I have loved,
The sort of beauty that I have approved,
Prosper but little, has dried up of late,
Yet knows that to be choked with hate
May well be of all evil chances chief.
If there's no hatred in a mind
Assault and battery of the wind
Can never tear the linnet from the leaf.

An intellectual hatred is the worst,
So let her think opinions are accursed.
Have I not seen the loveliest woman born
Out of the mouth of Plenty's horn,
Because of her opinionated mind
Barter that horn and every good
By quiet natures understood
For an old bellows full of angry wind?

Considering that, all hatred driven hence,
The soul recovers radical innocence
And learns at last that it is self-delighting,
Self-appeasing, self-affrighting,
And that its own sweet will is Heaven's will;
She can, though every face should scowl
And every windy quarter howl
Of every bellows burst, be happy still.

And may her bridegroom bring her to a house
Where all's accustomed, ceremonious;
For arrogance and hatred are the wares
Peddled in the thoroughfares.
How but in custom and in ceremony
Are innocence and beauty born?
Ceremony's name for the rich horn,
And custom for the spreading laurel tree.

E. A. ROBINSON

HOW ANNANDALE WENT OUT[1]

"They called it Annandale—and I was there
To flourish, to find words, and to attend:
Liar, physician, hypocrite, and friend,
I watched him; and the sight was not so fair
As one or two that I have seen elsewhere:
An apparatus not for me to mend—
A wreck, with hell between him and the end,
Remained of Annandale; and I was there.

1. Reprinted from *The Town Down the River* by Edwin Arlington Robinson; copyright, 1910, by Charles Scribner's Sons; 1938 by Ruth Niveson; used by permission of the publishers.

"I knew the ruin as I knew the man;
So put the two together, if you can,
Remembering the worst you know of me.
Now view yourself as I was, on the spot—
With a slight kind of engine. Do you see?
Like this . . . You wouldn't hang me? I thought not."

MR. FLOOD'S PARTY[1]

Old Eben Flood, climbing alone one night
Over the hill between the town below
And the forsaken upland hermitage
That held as much as he should ever know
On earth again of home, paused warily.
The road was his with not a native near;
And Eben, having leisure, said aloud,
For no man else in Tilbury Town to hear:

"Well, Mr. Flood, we have the harvest moon
Again, and we may not have many more;
The bird is on the wing, the poet says,
And you and I have said it here before.
Drink to the bird." He raised up to the light
The jug that he had gone so far to fill,
And answered huskily: "Well, Mr. Flood,
Since you propose it, I believe I will."

Alone, as if enduring to the end
A valiant armor of scarred hopes outworn,
He stood there in the middle of the road
Like Roland's ghost winding a silent horn.
Below him, in the town among the trees,
Where friends of other days had honored him,
A phantom salutation of the dead
Rang thinly till old Eben's eyes were dim.

Then, as a mother lays her sleeping child
Down tenderly, fearing it may awake,
He set the jug down slowly at his feet
With trembling care, knowing that most things break,
And only when assured that on firm earth
It stood, as the uncertain lives of men
Assuredly did not, he paced away,
And with his hand extended paused again:

1. From *Avon's Harvest* by E. A. Robinson. Copyright, 1921, by The Macmillan Company. By permission of the Macmillan Company, publishers.

"Well, Mr. Flood, we have not met like this
In a long time; and many a change has come
To both of us, I fear, since last it was
We had a drop together. Welcome home!"
Convivially returning with himself,
Again he raised the jug up to the light;
And with an acquiescent quaver said:
"Well, Mr. Flood, if you insist, I might.

"Only a very little, Mr. Flood—
For auld lang syne. No more, sir; that will do."
So, for the time, apparently it did,
And Eben evidently thought so too;
For soon amid the silver loneliness
Of night he lifted up his voice and sang,
Secure, with only two moons listening,
Until the whole harmonious landscape rang—

"For auld lang syne." The weary throat gave out,
The last word wavered; and the song being done,
He raised again the jug regretfully
And shook his head, and was again alone.
There was not much that was ahead of him,
And there was nothing in the town below—
Where strangers would have shut the many doors
That many friends had opened long ago.

STEPHEN CRANE

WAR IS KIND[1]

Do not weep, maiden, for war is kind.
Because your lover threw wild hands toward the sky
And the affrighted steed ran on alone,
Do not weep.
War is kind.

Hoarse, booming drums of the regiment,
Little souls who thirst for fight,
These men were born to drill and die.
The unexplained glory flies above them,

1. Reprinted from *Collected Poems of Stephen Crane* by permission of Alfred A. Knopf, Inc. Copyright 1895, 1922 by W. H. Crane.

Great is the battle-god, great, and his kingdom—
A field where a thousand corpses lie.

Do not weep, babe, for war is kind.
Because your father tumbled in the yellow trenches,
Raged at his breast, gulped and died,
Do not weep.
War is kind.

Swift blazing flag of the regiment,
Eagle with crest of red and gold,
These men were born to drill and die.
Point for them the virtue of slaughter,
Make plain to them the excellence of killing
And a field where a thousand corpses lie.

Mother whose heart hung humble as a button
On the bright splendid shroud of your son,
Do not weep.
War is kind.

SHOULD THE WIDE WORLD ROLL AWAY[1]

Should the wide world roll away,
Leaving black terror,
Limitless night,
Nor God, nor man, nor place to stand
Would be to me essential
If thou and thy white arms were there,
And the fall to doom a long way.

WELL, THEN, I HATE THEE[1]

"And the sins of the fathers shall be visited upon the heads of the children, even unto the third and fourth generation of them that hate me."

Well, then, I hate Thee, unrighteous picture;
Wicked image, I hate Thee;
So, strike with Thy vengeance
The heads of those little men
Who come blindly.
It will be a brave thing.

1. Reprinted from *Collected Poems of Stephen Crane* by permission of Alfred A. Knopf, Inc. Copyright 1895, 1922 by W. H. Crane.

ROBERT FROST

RELUCTANCE[1]

Out through the fields and the woods
    And over the walls I have wended;
I have climbed the hills of view
    And looked at the world, and descended;
I have come by the highway home,
    And lo, it is ended.

The leaves are all dead on the ground,
    Save those that the oak is keeping
To ravel them one by one
    And let them go scraping and creeping
Out over the crusted snow,
    When others are sleeping.

And the dead leaves lie huddled and still,
    No longer blown hither and thither;
The last lone aster is gone;
    The flowers of the witch-hazel wither;
The heart is still aching to seek,
    But the feet question "Whither?"

Ah, when to the heart of man
    Was it ever less than a treason
To go with the drift of things,
    To yield with a grace to reason,
And bow and accept the end
    Of a love or a season?

THE ROAD NOT TAKEN[1]

Two roads diverged in a yellow wood,
And sorry I could not travel both
And be one traveler, long I stood
And looked down one as far as I could
To where it bent in the undergrowth;

Then took the other, as just as fair,
And having perhaps the better claim,
Because it was grassy and wanted wear;

1. From *Collected Poems of Robert Frost.* Copyright, 1930, 1939, by Henry Holt and Company, Inc. Copyright, 1936, by Robert Frost.

Though as for that the passing there
Had worn them really about the same,

And both that morning equally lay
In leaves no step had trodden black.
Oh, I kept the first for another day!
Yet knowing how way leads on to way,
I doubted if I should ever come back.

I shall be telling this with a sigh
Somewhere ages and ages hence:
Two roads diverged in a wood, and I—
I took the one less traveled by,
And that has made all the difference.

FIRE AND ICE[1]

Some say the world will end in fire;
Some say in ice.
From what I've tasted of desire
I hold with those who favor fire.
But if it had to perish twice,
I think I know enough of hate
To know that for destruction ice
Is also great
And would suffice.

STOPPING BY WOODS ON A SNOWY EVENING[2]

Whose woods these are I think I know.
His house is in the village though;
He will not see me stopping here
To watch his woods fill up with snow.

My little horse must think it queer
To stop without a farmhouse near
Between the woods and frozen lake
The darkest evening of the year.

He gives his harness bells a shake
To ask if there is some mistake.

---

1. From *Complete Poems of Robert Frost*. Copyright, 1930, 1949, by Henry Holt and Company, Inc. Used by permission of the publishers.
2. From *Collected Poems of Robert Frost*. Copyright, 1930, 1939, by Henry Holt and Company Inc. Copyright, 1936, by Robert Frost.

The only other sound's the sweep
Of easy wind and downy flake.

The woods are lovely, dark and deep.
But I have promises to keep,
And miles to go before I sleep,
And miles to go before I sleep.

~~The steaming horses think it queer~~
To
The ~~horse~~ little horse must ~~begins~~ to think it queer
~~We~~ To stop without a farm house near
Between a ~~forest and a~~ the woods and frozen lake
The darkest evening of the year

~~He~~ She gives her harness bells a shake
To ask if there is some mistake
The only other sound's the sweep
Of easy wind and ~~fallen~~ downy flake.

The woods are lovely dark and deep
But I have promises to keep
~~That bid me give the reins a shake~~ me on and there are miles
And miles to go before I sleep
And miles to go before I sleep

Facsimile of the last three stanzas of "Stopping by Woods on a Snowy Evening" by Robert Frost. By permission of Henry Holt and Company, Inc.

ON FROST'S *STOPPING BY WOODS ON A SNOWY EVENING*[1]

JOHN HOLMES

THIS facsimile is a reproduction of the last three stanzas of "Stopping by Woods on a Snowy Evening" as Robert Frost worked it out. We know from the poet that he had just written the long poem, "New Hampshire," in one all-night unbroken stretch of composition, and that he then turned a page of his workbook and wrote this short poem without stopping. This fact has interesting implications. "New Hampshire" is a discourse in the idiomatic blank verse that is so peculiarly Frost's own style—the rhythms of natural speech matched to the strict but inconspicuous iambic pentameter, the beat always discernible but never formal. It is reasonable to suppose that after the hours spent in writing the long poem, in its loosened but never loose manner, he was ready, unconsciously, for a poem in strict pattern. He had also obviously had in his head for some time the incident on which the short poem was to be based, as well as the use he wished to make of it. He committed himself, as he has said, to the four-stress iambic line and to the *aaba* rime-scheme, in the first stanza, which he wrote rapidly and did not revise. He knew what he had seen, and he knew how he wanted to write it.

Whose woods these are I think I know.
His house is in the village though;
He will not see me stopping here
To watch his woods fill up with snow.

"That went off so easily I was tempted into the added difficulty of picking up my 3 for my 1–2–4 to go on with in the second stanza. I was amused and scared at what that got me into," Frost says. The facsimile shows what it got him into, how he got out of it, and how he achieved the poem as it meant itself to be written.

It began with what was the actual experience of stopping at night by some dark woods in winter, and the fact that there were two horses. He remembered what he saw then. "The steaming horses think it queer." But the poem needs truth more than fact, and he cancels the line, and begins again, "The horse begins to think it queer," but doesn't like the word "begins," needing in the allowed space a word that will particularize the horse, so writes "The little horse must think it queer." Now he runs into a grammatical difficulty, which must somehow be solved before he gets on into the poem he already feels sure of. "I launched into the construction 'My little horse must think it queer that we should stop.' I didn't like omitting the 'that' and I had no room for 'should.' I had the luck to get out of it with the

1. From *Preface to Poetry* by Charles W. Cooper and John Holmes, copyright, 1946, by Harcourt, Brace and Company, Inc.

infinitive." This groping and warming-up has a kind of impatience, an urgency to get on with the poem, but not until all the parts are right. At this point the poet knew and did not know how the poem would end. He knew the feel, and the sense, and almost everything about the form—certainly enough to know when he got off the track.

Whether he revised the third line here or later we cannot know. But we can see in several places in this poem his changes toward particularization. The line "Between a forest and a lake" is a notation, and "Between the woods and frozen lake" is a finished line of poetry. "A forest" is too big, too vague, but "the woods" is definite, and bounded; you get lost in a forest, but you can walk through and out of the woods, and probably you know who owns it—Vermonters do, as he has said in the first stanza. "A lake" has not the specific condition or picture of "frozen lake." This sort of revision, or what Frost calls, "touching up," is what makes a poem—this, plus the first inspiration. Either one, without the other, is unlikely to make a good poem.

The next stanza comes easier, because the rime-scheme has been determined, and one unexpected obstacle has been overcome. But once more there is a delay, as the poet makes a decision as to the "he" or "she"—and the more important and more interesting about the falling snow. In writing "downy flake" for "fall of flake" the gain is great not only for accuracy of feeling and fact, but also for the music of the lines. The simple alliteration in "fall of flake" is canceled in favor of the word, one word, "downy," which blends with the vowel-chords a poet half-consciously makes and modulates as he goes. In this instance, it half-chimes with "sounds" and adds a rounder, fuller, and yet quieter tone.

Now the carry-over rime is "sweep," a fortunate one, really, and important to the final solution of the rime-scheme. It is not too much to assume, knowing all we know about the circumstances of the writing of this poem—the all-night composition of "New Hampshire," and the sudden urge to catch and shape still another saved idea—that the darker, more confident, more rapid strokes of the pen show the poet's growing excitement. The end is in sight. The thing he believed could happen will happen, surely now, and he must hurry to get it onto the page. This is the real moment of power, and any poet's greatest satisfaction.

"The woods are lovely dark and deep/But I have promises to keep." The first two lines of the last stanza come fast, and flow beautifully, the crest of the poem's emotion and its music. We cannot know whether he had held them in his head, or had swept up to and into them as he felt the destined pattern fulfilling itself.

Then, with success in sight, there comes an awkward and unexpected stumble. He writes, "That bid me give the reins a shake," which may have been the fact and the action. But the rime is wrong. Not only has the rime been used in the previous stanza, but so has the image of the horse shaking his head and reins. Things are moving fast now, no doubt impatiently, but certainly with determination, shown in the heavy black lines of abrupt cancellation. He strikes out "me give the reins a shake," and writes above it, so the line will read, "That bid me on, and there are miles," and then the whole thing comes through! Of course! "Miles to go . . ."

That's what it was supposed to be—the feeling of silence and dark, almost overpowering the man, but the necessity of going on. "And miles to go before I sleep." Then the triumph in the whole thing, the only right and perfect last line, solving the problem of the carried-over rime, keeping the half-tranced state, and the dark, and the solitude, and man's great effort to be responsible man . . . the repetition of that line.

"Stopping by Woods on a Snowy Evening" can be studied as perfected structure, with the photostat manuscript to show that art is not, though it must always appear to be, effortless. It can be thought of as a picture: the whites, grays, and blacks of the masses and areas of lake, field, and woods, with the tiny figure of the man in the sleigh, and the horse. And it can be thought of as a statement of man's everlasting responsibility to man; though the dark and nothingness tempt him to surrender, he will not give in. It is interesting to compare this poem with two later pieces of Frost's, in which he uses the same image, "Desert Places," and "Come In," none alike, all on the first level of his poetry, and all three built on the image of the pull of wildness and lawlessness against man's conscious will and the promises he has made to be kept.

CARL SANDBURG

PRAYERS OF STEEL[1]

Lay me on an anvil, O God.
Beat me and hammer me into a crowbar.
Let me pry loose old walls.
Let me lift and loosen old foundations.

Lay me on an anvil, O God.
Beat me and hammer me into a steel spike.
Drive me into the girders that hold a skyscraper together.
Take red-hot rivets and fasten me into the central girders.
Let me be the great nail holding a skyscraper through blue nights into white
    stars.

COOL TOMBS[1]

When Abraham Lincoln was shovelled into the tombs, he forgot the copper-
    heads and the assassin . . . in the dust, in the cool tombs.

1. From *Cornhuskers* by Carl Sandburg. Copyright, 1918, by Henry Holt and Company. Copyright, 1945, by Carl Sandburg. By permission of the publishers.

And Ulysses Grant lost all thought of con men and Wall Street, cash and collateral turned ashes . . . in the dust, in the cool tombs.

Pocahontas' body, lovely as a poplar, sweet as a red haw in November or a pawpaw in May, did she wonder? does she remember? . . . in the dust, in the cool tombs?

Take any streetful of people buying clothes and groceries, cheering a hero or throwing confetti and blowing tin horns . . . tell me if the lovers are losers . . . tell me if any get more than the lovers . . . in the dust . . . in the cool tombs.

WALLACE STEVENS

SUNDAY MORNING[1]

Complacencies of the peignoir, and late
Coffee and oranges in a sunny chair,
And the green freedom of a cockatoo
Upon a rug mingle to dissipate
The holy hush of ancient sacrifice.
She dreams a little, and she feels the dark
Encroachment of that old catastrophe,
As a calm darkens among water-lights.
The pungent oranges and bright, green wings
Seem things in some procession of the dead,
Winding across wide water, without sound.
The day is like wide water, without sound,
Stilled for the passing of her dreaming feet
Over the seas, to silent Palestine,
Dominion of the blood and sepulchre.

2

Why should she give her bounty to the dead?
What is divinity if it can come
Only in silent shadows and in dreams?
Shall she not find in comforts of the sun,
In pungent fruit and bright, green wings, or else
In any balm or beauty of the earth,
Things to be cherished like the thought of heaven?
Divinity must live within herself:

1. Reprinted from *Harmonium* by Wallace Stevens, by permission of Alfred A. Knopf, Inc. Copyright, 1923, 1931, by Alfred A. Knopf, Inc.

Passions of rain, or moods in falling snow;
Grieving in loneliness, or unsubdued
Elations when the forest blooms; gusty
Emotions on wet roads on autumn nights;
All pleasures and all pains, remembering
The bough of summer and the winter branch.
These are the measures destined for her soul.

3

Jove in the clouds had his inhuman birth.
No mother suckled him, no sweet land gave
Large-mannered motions to his mythy mind.
He moved among us, as a muttering king,
Magnificent, would move among his hinds,
Until our blood, commingling, virginal,
With heaven, brought such requital to desire
The very hinds discerned it, in a star.
Shall our blood fail? Or shall it come to be
The blood of paradise? And shall the earth
Seem all of paradise that we shall know?
The sky will be much friendlier then than now,
A part of labor and a part of pain,
And next in glory to enduring love,
Not this dividing and indifferent blue.

4

She says, "I am content when wakened birds,
Before they fly, test the reality
Of misty fields, by their sweet questionings;
But when the birds are gone, and their warm fields
Return no more, where, then, is paradise?"
There is not any haunt of prophecy,
Nor any old chimera of the grave,
Neither the golden underground, nor isle
Melodious, where spirits gat them home,
Nor visionary south, nor cloudy palm
Remote on heaven's hill, that has endured
As April's green endures; or will endure
Like her remembrance of awakened birds,
Or her desire for June and evening, tipped
By the consummation of the swallow's wings.

5

She says, "But in contentment I still feel
The need of some imperishable bliss."
Death is the mother of beauty; hence from her,
Alone, shall come fulfilment to our dreams
And our desires. Although she strews the leaves
Of sure obliteration on our paths,
The path sick sorrow took, the many paths
Where triumph rang its brassy phrase, or love
Whispered a little out of tenderness,
She makes the willow shiver in the sun
For maidens who were wont to sit and gaze
Upon the grass, relinquished to their feet.
She causes boys to pile new plums and pears
On disregarded plate. The maidens taste
And stray impassioned in the littering leaves.

6

Is there no change of death in paradise?
Does ripe fruit never fall? Or do the boughs
Hang always heavy in that perfect sky,
Unchanging, yet so like our perishing earth,
With rivers like our own that seek for seas
They never find, the same receding shores
That never touch with inarticulate pang?
Why set the pear upon those river-banks
Or spice the shores with odors of the plum?
Alas, that they should wear our colors there,
The silken weavings of our afternoons,
And pick the strings of our insipid lutes!
Death is the mother of beauty, mystical,
Within whose burning bosom we devise
Our earthly mothers waiting, sleeplessly.

7

Supple and turbulent, a ring of men
Shall chant in orgy on a summer morn
Their boisterous devotion to the sun,
Not as a god, but as a god might be,
Naked among them, like a savage source.
Their chant shall be a chant of paradise,
Out of their blood, returning to the sky;
And in their chant shall enter, voice by voice,
The windy lake wherein their lord delights,

The trees, like serafin, and echoing hills,
That choir among themselves long afterward.
They shall know well the heavenly fellowship
Of men that perish and of summer morn.
And whence they came and whither they shall go
The dew upon their feet shall manifest.

8

She hears, upon that water without sound,
A voice that cries, "The tomb in Palestine
Is not the porch of spirits lingering.
It is the grave of Jesus, where he lay."
We live in an old chaos of the sun,
Or old dependency of day and night,
Or island solitude, unsponsored, free,
Of that wide water, inescapable.
Deer walk upon our mountains, and the quail
Whistle about us their spontaneous cries;
Sweet berries ripen in the wilderness;
And, in the isolation of the sky,
At evening, casual flocks of pigeons make
Ambiguous undulations as they sink,
Downward to darkness, on extended wings.

ON STEVENS' *SUNDAY MORNING*[1]

YVOR WINTERS

His fundamental ideas are stated in *Sunday Morning,* an early poem, and in some ways his greatest. The poem consists of eight stanzas in blank verse, each containing fifteen lines, and it presents a clear and fairly coherent argument.

The first stanza sets the stage and identifies the protagonist. We are given a woman, at home on a Sunday morning, meditating on the meaning of death. The second stanza asks the question which provides the subject of the poem; it asks what divinity this woman may be thought to possess as a recompense for her ultimate surrender to death; and having asked the question, it replies that her divinity, which must live within herself, consists wholly in her emotions—not in her understanding of the emotions, but in the emotions as a good in themselves. This answer is not quite the orthodox romantic answer, which would offer us in the emotions either a true guide to virtue or a more or less mystical experience leading to some kind of

1. From Yvor Winters, *The Anatomy of Nonsense.* Copyright, 1948, by New Directions, 333 Sixth Avenue, New York.

union with some kind of deity. Any philosophy which offers the cultivation of the emotions as an end in itself, I suppose, is a kind of hedonism. In any event, that is the kind of philosophy which we find here.

The third stanza, by means of the allegory of Jove and his human loves, through his union with whom he crossed the heavenly strain upon the human, implies that man has a capacity which may at least figuratively be termed divine; the stanza is a subordinate commentary on the one preceding; and does not really advance the argument.

In the fourth stanza, however, the argument moves forward. The protagonist objects to the concept which has been offered her; she states that the beauties of this life are transient and that she longs to believe in a Paradise beyond them. The remainder of the stanza, and the greater part of it, is the poet's reply: in a passage of great rhetorical power, he denies the possibility of Paradise, at the same time that he communicates through the feeling of his language a deep nostalgic longing to accept the ideas which he is rejecting. In the first two lines of the fifth stanza, the woman repeats her objection, and the poet then replies with an explanation of the function of death: it is our awareness of the imminence of death which heightens our emotions and sharpens our perceptions; our knowledge of life's transience stimulates our perception of life's beauty.

In the sixth stanza the poet considers an hypothetical paradise, and, since he can imagine it only in terms of a projection of the good life as the hedonist understands the good life, he deduces that paradise would become tedious and insipid: we have in this stanza the first sharp vision of the ennui which is to obsess the later work of the poet and which is ultimately to wreck his talent, an ennui arising from the fact that emotion is not a good in itself, but that if cultivated for itself alone is merely a pleasant diversion so long as the novelty of a given experience endures, at most as long as new experiences can give us the illusion of novel excitement, and then becomes a disease of the spirit, a state of indifferency in which there is neither novelty nor significance.

The seventh stanza presents a vision of a future race of men engaged in a religious ritual, the generating principle of which is their joy in the world as it is given them and their sense of brotherhood as "men that perish." The stanza contains suggestions of a pantheism which goes beyond the bounds of a strict hedonism, but they are merely suggestions and they appear nowhere else. The eighth and last stanza begins by denying the immortality of Jesus, and by implication, of man; and it places the protagonist finally and irretrievably on a small but beautiful planet, floating like a tropical island in boundless space, "in an old chaos of the sun."

This summary, even as summaries go, is extremely skeletalized. It has been my intention, here, merely to isolate the hedonistic theme for future consideration; the theme is not thus isolated in the poem, but is complicated by its inter-connections with other human problems from which not even a hedonist can escape. Whatever the defects of the hedonistic theme, and with the possible but by no means certain exception of a few short poems by Stevens and of two or three poems by E. A. Robinson, *Sunday Morning* is probably the greatest American poem of the twentieth century and is certainly one of the greatest contemplative poems in English: in a blank verse which differs, in its firmness of structure and incalculable sensitivity of detail, from all other blank verse of our time save that of a few poems by Hart Crane which were in some measure modeled upon it, it renders the acute uncertainty of what we are inclined to consider the modern mind, but it does so with no uncertainty of method or of statement; it renders an acute consciousness of the imminence of death, of the sensory and emotional richness of life on this bewildering planet, and of the heroic magnificence of the religious myths which are lost to the poet and to many of the rest of us, except as memories of things long past. If Stevens' career had stopped with this poem, or a few years thereafter, it might seem an unnecessary unkindness to insist upon the limitations of understanding which the poem discloses; but those limitations appear very obviously in a few later poems, and they seem to me to be very clearly related to the rapid and tragic decay of the poet's style. As a poet in early maturity, Stevens brought to this subject a style which was the result of a fine native gift enriched by the study of English blank verse; the subject, once formulated, and accepted as a guide to life and to expression, destroyed the style in less than two decades. In *Sunday Morning* itself, we detect the limitations of the subject only by rational analysis; in the later work we see the effect of those limitations.

Some of the virtues of *Sunday Morning* I have indicated in very general terms, but one cannot turn from the poem that may be the greatest American work of our century without considering briefly some of its more haunting beauties, if it be only as an act of piety.

I have already quoted the final stanza of the poem, and its beauty should be obvious; yet as removed from its context, the stanza loses much of its complexity. The "water without sound," and "wide water inescapable," is not only an image representing infinite space; it is an image, established in the first stanza, representing a state of mind, a kind of bright and empty beatitude, over which the thought of death may darken suddenly and without warning:

> She dreams a little, and she feels the dark
> Encroachment of that old catastrophe,
> As a calm darkens among water-lights.

The language has the greatest possible dignity and subtlety, combined with perfect precision. The imminence of absolute tragedy is felt and recorded, but the integrity of the feeling mind is maintained. The mind perceives, as by a kind of metaphysical sense, the approach of invading impersonality, yet knowing the invasion to be inevitable and its own identity, while that identity lasts, the only source of any good whatever, maintains that identity in its full calm and clarity, that nothing may be sacrificed without need. This combination of calm and terror, in dealing with this particular theme, will be found in only one other poet in English, in Shakespeare as one finds him in a few of the more metaphysical sonnets. The calm clarity of tone enables the poet to deal with a variety of kinds of feeling which would be impossible were the terror emphasized for a moment at any point, were the complete and controlled unity of the experiencing mind for a moment disordered by its own perceptions. The same poem, for example, is able to contain the following lines, of a sweetness and of an illusory simplicity which again are scarcely less than Shakespearean:

> She says, "I am content when wakened birds,
> Before they fly, test the reality
> Of misty fields, by their sweet questionings;
> But when the birds are gone, and their warm fields
> Return no more, where, then, is paradise?"

And out of this passage proceeds the great lament for the lost myths, which I have already mentioned. This passage and others similar, though beautiful in themselves, are a preparation for the descriptive lines in the last stanza, and when we finally come to those lines, they are weighted with meaning and feeling accumulated from all that has gone before. It is difficult for this reason to quote from the poem for the purpose of illustrating its beauty.

One aspect of the poem may perhaps be mentioned, however, with some small profit, and it may best be indicated, I believe, through a brief comparison with Bryant's *Thanatopsis*. Bryant's poem is a great poem and is worthy of the comparison, and its resemblance to Stevens' poem in certain ways is both surprising and illuminating. Both poems are semididactic meditations on death, written in a firm but simplified Miltonic blank verse, the verse of Stevens, possibly, being somewhat smoothed and softened by the intervention of Tennyson. Both poems are pagan in their view: but that of Bryant, the New Englander of the early 19th century, is essentially stoical, whereas that of Stevens, the Pennsylvanian of the 20th century, is Epicurean. Both poems find man, a spiritual being, isolated in a physical universe: but for Bryant that universe is the Earth, hairy, vast, and almost against the eye; for Stevens it is the tropical Pacific of infinity, in which the earth appears as an infinitesimal floating island.

SEA SURFACE FULL OF CLOUDS[1]

I

In that November off Tehuantepec,
The slopping of the sea grew still one night
And in the morning summer hued the deck

And made one think of rosy chocolate
And gilt umbrellas. Paradisal green
Gave suavity to the perplexed machine

Of ocean, which like limpid water lay.
Who, then, in that ambrosial latitude
Out of the light evolved the moving blooms,

Who, then, evolved the sea-blooms from the clouds
Diffusing balm in that Pacific calm?
C'était mon enfant, mon bijou, mon âme.

The sea-clouds, whitened far below the calm
And moved, as blooms move, in the swimming green
And in its watery radiance, while the hue

Of heaven in an antique reflection rolled
Round those flotillas. And sometimes the sea
Poured brilliant iris on the glistening blue.

II

In that November off Tehuantepec
The slopping of the sea grew still one night.
At breakfast jelly yellow streaked the deck

And made one think of chop-house chocolate
And sham umbrellas. And a sham-like green
Capped summer-seeming on the tense machine

Of ocean, which in sinister flatness lay.
Who, then, beheld the rising of the clouds
That strode submerged in that malevolent sheen,

Who saw the mortal massives of the blooms
Of water moving on the water-floor?
C'était mon frère du ciel, ma vie, mon or.

The gongs rang loudly as the windy blooms
Hoo-hooed it in the darkened ocean-blooms.
The gongs grew still. And then blue heaven spread

Its crystalline pendentives on the sea
And the macabre of the water-glooms,
In an enormous undulation fled.

III

In that November off Tehuantepec,
The slopping of the sea grew still one night,
And a pale silver patterned on the deck

Made one think of porcelain chocolate
And pied umbrellas. An uncertain green,
Piano-polished, held the tranced machine

Of ocean, as a prelude holds and holds.
Who, seeing silver petals of white blooms
Unfolding in the water, feeling sure

Of the milk within the saltiest spurge, heard, then,
The sea unfolding in the sunken clouds?
Oh! C' était mon extase et mon amour.

So deeply sunken were they that the shrouds,
The shrouding shadows, made the petals black
Until the rolling heaven made them blue,

A blue beyond the rainy hyacinth,
And smiting the crevasses of the leaves
Deluged the ocean with a sapphire hue.

IV

In that November off Tehuantepec
The night-long slopping of the sea grew still.
A mallow morning dozed upon the deck

And made one think of musky chocolate
And frail umbrellas. A too-fluent green
Suggested malice in the dry machine

Of ocean, pondering dank stratagem.
Who then beheld the figures of the clouds,
Like blooms secluded in the thick marine?

Like blooms? Like damasks that were shaken off
From the loosed girdles in the spangling must.
C'était ma foi, la nonchalance divine.

The nakedness would rise and suddenly turn
Salt masks of beard and mouths of bellowing,
Would— But more suddenly the heaven rolled

Its bluest sea-clouds in the thinking green
And the nakedness became the broadest blooms,
Mile-mallows that a mallow sun cajoled.

V

In that November off Tehuantepec
Night stilled the slopping of the sea. The day
Came, bowing and voluble, upon the deck,

Good clown. . . . One thought of Chinese chocolate
And large umbrellas. And a motley green
Followed the drift of the obese machine

Of ocean, perfected in indolence.
What pistache one, ingenious and droll,
Beheld the sovereign clouds as jugglery

And the sea as turquoise-turbaned Sambo, neat
At tossing saucers—cloudy-conjuring sea?
C'était mon esprit bâtard, l'ignominie.

The sovereign clouds came clustering. The conch
Of loyal conjuration trumped. The wind
Of green blooms turning crisped the motley hue

To clearing opalescence. Then the sea
And heaven rolled as one and from the two
Came fresh transfigurings of freshest blue.

THE EMPEROR OF ICE-CREAM[1]

Call the roller of big cigars,
The muscular one, and bid him whip
In kitchen cups concupiscent curds.

1. Reprinted from *Harmonium* by Wallace Stevens, by permission of Alfred A. Knopf, Inc. Copyright, 1923, 1931, by Alfred A. Knopf, Inc.

Let the wenches dawdle in such dress
As they are used to wear, and let the boys
Bring flowers in last month's newspapers.
Let be be finale of seem.
The only emperor is the emperor of ice-cream.

Take from the dresser of deal,
Lacking the three glass knobs, that sheet
On which she embroidered fantails once
And spread it so as to cover her face.
If her horny feet protrude, they come
To show how cold she is, and dumb.
Let the lamp affix its beam.
The only emperor is the emperor of ice-cream.

EZRA POUND

ENVOI (1919)[1]

Go, dumb-born book,
Tell her that sang me once that song of Lawes:
Hadst thou but song
As thou hast subjects known,
Then were there cause in thee that should condone
Even my faults that heavy upon me lie,
And build her glories their longevity.

Tell her that sheds
Such treasure in the air,
Recking naught else but that her graces give
Life to the moment,
I would bid them live
As roses might, in magic amber laid,
Red overwrought with orange and all made
One substance and one color
Braving time.

Tell her that goes
With song upon her lips
But sings not out the song, nor knows

1. From *Personae: The Collected Poems of Ezra Pound,* copyright, 1926, by Boni & Liveright. Reprinted by permission of New Directions, 333 Sixth Avenue, New York.

The maker of it, some other mouth
May be as fair as hers,
Might, in new ages, gain her worshippers
When our two dusts with Waller's shall be laid,
Siftings on siftings in oblivion,
Till change hath broken down
All things save Beauty alone.

T. S. ELIOT

THE LOVE SONG OF J. ALFRED PRUFROCK[1]

S'io credesse che mia risposta fosse
A persona che mai tornasse al mondo,
Questa fiamma staria senza piu scosse.
Ma perciocche giammai di questo fondo
Non torno vivo alcun, s'i' odo il vero,
Senza tema d'infamia ti rispondo.[2]

Let us go then, you and I,
When the evening is spread out against the sky
Like a patient etherized upon a table;
Let us go, through certain half-deserted streets,
The muttering retreats
Of restless nights in one-night cheap hotels
And sawdust restaurants with oyster-shells:
Streets that follow like a tedious argument
Of insidious intent
To lead you to an overwhelming question. . . .
Oh, do not ask, "What is it?"
Let us go and make our visit.

In the room the women come and go
Talking of Michelangelo.

---

1. From *Collected Poems 1909–1935* by T. S. Eliot, copyright, 1934, 1936, by Harcourt, Brace and Company, Inc.

2. "If I thought my answer were to one who ever could return to the world, this flame should shake no more; but since none ever did return alive from this depth, if what I hear be true, without fear of infamy I answer thee."—*Inferno,* xxvii, 61–66.

The yellow fog that rubs its back upon the window-panes,
The yellow smoke that rubs its muzzle on the window-panes
Licked its tongue into the corners of the evening,
Lingered upon the pools that stand in drains,
Let fall upon its back the soot that falls from chimneys,
Slipped by the terrace, made a sudden leap,
And seeing that it was a soft October night,
Curled once about the house, and fell asleep.
And indeed there will be time
For the yellow smoke that slides along the street
Rubbing its back upon the window-panes;
There will be time, there will be time
To prepare a face to meet the faces that you meet;
There will be time to murder and create,
And time for all the works and days of hands
That lift and drop a question on your plate;
Time for you and time for me,
And time yet for a hundred indecisions,
And for a hundred visions and revisions,
Before the taking of a toast and tea.

In the room the women come and go
Talking of Michelangelo.

And indeed there will be time
To wonder, "Do I dare?" and, "Do I dare?"
Time to turn back and descend the stair,
With a bald spot in the middle of my hair—
(They will say: "How his hair is growing thin!")
My morning coat, my collar mounting firmly to the chin,
My necktie rich and modest, but asserted by a simple pin—
(They will say: "But how his arms and legs are thin!")
Do I dare
Disturb the universe?
In a minute there is time
For decisions and revisions which a minute will reverse.

For I have known them all already, known them all:
Have known the evenings, mornings, afternoons,
I have measured out my life with coffee spoons;
I know the voices dying with a dying fall
Beneath the music from a farther room.
  So how should I presume?

And I have known the eyes already, known them all—
The eyes that fix you in a formulated phrase,
And when I am formulated, sprawling on a pin,
When I am pinned and wriggling on the wall,
Then how should I begin
To spit out all the butt-ends of my days and ways?
    And how should I presume?

And I have known the arms already, known them all—
Arms that are braceleted and white and bare
(But in the lamplight, downed with light brown hair!)
Is it perfume from a dress
That makes me so digress?
Arms that lie along a table, or wrap about a shawl.
    And should I then presume?
    And how should I begin?

Shall I say, I have gone at dusk through narrow streets
And watched the smoke that rises from the pipes
Of lonely men in shirt-sleeves, leaning out of windows? . . .

I should have been a pair of ragged claws
Scuttling across the floors of silent seas.

And the afternoon, the evening, sleeps so peacefully!
Smoothed by long fingers,
Asleep . . . tired . . . or it malingers,
Stretched on the floor, here beside you and me.
Should I, after tea and cakes and ices,
Have the strength to force the moment to its crisis?
But though I have wept and fasted, wept and prayed,
Though I have seen my head (grown slightly bald) brought in upon a platter,
I am no prophet—and here's no great matter;
I have seen the moment of my greatness flicker,
And I have seen the eternal Footman hold my coat, and snicker,
And in short, I was afraid.

And would it have been worth it, after all,
After the cups, the marmalade, the tea,
Among the porcelain, among some talk of you and me,
Would it have been worth while,
To have bitten off the matter with a smile,
To have squeezed the universe into a ball

To roll it toward some overwhelming question,
To say: "I am Lazarus, come from the dead,
Come back to tell you all, I shall tell you all"—
If one, settling a pillow by her head,
    Should say: "That is not what I meant at all;
    That is not it, at all."

And would it have been worth it, after all,
Would it have been worth while,
After the sunsets and the dooryards and the sprinkled streets,
After the novels, after the teacups, after the skirts that trail along the floor—
And this, and so much more?—
It is impossible to say just what I mean!
But as if a magic lantern threw the nerves in patterns on a screen:
Would it have been worth while
If one, settling a pillow or throwing off a shawl,
And turning toward the window, should say:
    "That is not it at all,
    That is not what I meant, at all."

No! I am not Prince Hamlet, nor was meant to be;
Am an attendant lord, one that will do
To swell a progress, start a scene or two,
Advise the prince; no doubt, an easy tool,
Deferential, glad to be of use,
Politic, cautious, and meticulous;
Full of high sentence, but a bit obtuse;
At times, indeed, almost ridiculous—
Almost, at times, the Fool.

I grow old. . . . I grow old. . . .
I shall wear the bottoms of my trousers rolled.

Shall I part my hair behind? Do I dare to eat a peach?
I shall wear white flannel trousers, and walk upon the beach.
I have heard the mermaids singing, each to each.

I do not think that they will sing to me.

I have seen them riding seaward on the waves
Combing the white hair of the waves blown back
When the wind blows the water white and black.

We have lingered in the chambers of the sea
By sea-girls wreathed with seaweed red and brown
Till human voices wake us, and we drown.

COUSIN NANCY[1]

Miss Nancy Ellicott
Strode across the hills and broke them,
Rode across the hills and broke them—
The barren New England hills—
Riding to hounds
Over the cow-pasture.

Miss Nancy Ellicott smoked
And danced all the modern dances;
And her aunts were not quite sure how they felt about it,
But they knew that it was modern.

Upon the glazen shelves kept watch
Matthew and Waldo, guardians of the faith,
The army of unalterable law.

SWEENEY AMONG THE NIGHTINGALES[1]

ὤμοι, πεπληγμαι καιρίαν πληγὴν ἔσω.[2]

Apeneck Sweeney spreads his knees
Letting his arms hang down to laugh,
The zebra stripes along his jaw
Swelling to maculate giraffe.

The circles of the stormy moon
Slide westward toward the River Plate,
Death and the Raven drift above
And Sweeney guards the horned gate.

Gloomy Orion and the Dog
Are veiled; and hushed the shrunken seas;
The person in the Spanish cape
Tries to sit on Sweeney's knees

1. From *Collected Poems 1909–1935* by T. S. Eliot, copyright, 1934, 1936, by Harcourt, Brace and Company, Inc.
2. "Woe's me, I'm stricken a mortal blow within."—*Agamemnon,* line 1341.

Slips and pulls the table cloth
Overturns a coffee-cup,
Reorganised upon the floor
She yawns and draws a stocking up;

The silent man in mocha brown
Sprawls at the window-sill and gapes;
The waiter brings in oranges
Bananas figs and hothouse grapes.

The silent vertebrate in brown
Contracts and concentrates, withdraws;
Rachel *née* Rabinovitch
Tears at the grapes with murderous paws;

She and the lady in the cape
Are suspect, thought to be in league;
Therefore the man with heavy eyes
Declines the gambit, shows fatigue,

Leaves the room and reappears
Outside the window, leaning in,
Branches of wisteria
Circumscribe a golden grin;

The host with someone indistinct
Converses at the door apart,
The nightingales are singing near
The Convent of the Sacred Heart,

And sang within the bloody wood
When Agamemnon cried aloud,
And let their liquid siftings fall
To stain the stiff dishonoured shroud.

MACAVITY: THE MYSTERY CAT[1]

Macavity's a Mystery Cat: he's called the Hidden Paw—
For he's the master criminal who can defy the Law.
He's the bafflement of Scotland Yard, the Flying Squad's despair:
For when they reach the scene of crime—*Macavity's not there!*

1. From *Old Possum's Book of Practical Cats,* copyright, 1939, by T. S. Eliot. Reprinted by permission of Harcourt, Brace and Company, Inc.

Macavity, Macavity, there's no-one like Macavity,
He's broken every human law, he breaks the law of gravity.
His powers of levitation would make a fakir stare,
And when you reach the scene of crime—*Macavity's not there!*
You may seek him in the basement, you may look up in the air—
But I tell you once and once again, *Macavity's not there!*

Macavity's a ginger cat, he's very tall and thin;
You would know him if you saw him, for his eyes are sunken in.
His brow is deeply lined with thought, his head is highly domed;
His coat is dusty from neglect, his whiskers are uncombed.
He sways his head from side to side, with movements like a snake;
And when you think he's half asleep, he's always wide awake.

Macavity, Macavity, there's no-one like Macavity,
For he's a fiend in feline shape, a monster of depravity.
You may meet him in a by-street, you may see him in the square—
But when a crime's discovered, then *Macavity's not there!*

He's outwardly respectable. (They say he cheats at cards.)
And his footprints are not found in any file of Scotland Yard's.
And when the larder's looted, or the jewel-case is rifled,
Or when the milk is missing, or another Peke's been stifled,
Or the greenhouse glass is broken, and the trellis past repair—
Ay, there's the wonder of the thing! *Macavity's not there!*

And when the Foreign Office find a Treaty's gone astray,
Or the Admiralty lose some plans and drawings by the way,
There may be a scrap of paper in the hall or on the stair—
But it's useless to investigate—*Macavity's not there!*
And when the loss has been disclosed, the Secret Service say:
'It *must* have been Macavity!'—but he's a mile away.
You'll be sure to find him resting, or a-licking of his thumbs,
Or engaged in doing complicated long division sums.

Macavity, Macavity, there's no-one like Macavity,
There never was a Cat of such deceitfulness and suavity.
He always has an alibi, and one or two to spare:
At whatever time the deed took place—MACAVITY WASN'T THERE!
And they say that all the Cats whose wicked deeds are widely known
(I might mention Mungojerrie, I might mention Griddlebone)
Are nothing more than agents for the Cat who all the time
Just controls their operations: the Napoleon of Crime!

BURNT NORTON[1]

I

Time present and time past
Are both perhaps present in time future,
And time future contained in time past.
If all time is eternally present
All time is unredeemable.
What might have been is an abstraction
Remaining a perpetual possibility
Only in a world of speculation.
What might have been and what has been
Point to one end, which is always present.
Footfalls echo in the memory
Down the passage which we did not take
Towards the door we never opened
Into the rose-garden. My words echo
Thus, in your mind.
                                        But to what purpose
Disturbing the dust on a bowl of rose-leaves
I do not know.
                              Other echoes
Inhabit the garden. Shall we follow?
Quick, said the bird, find them, find them,
Round the corner. Through the first gate,
Into our first world, shall we follow
The deception of the thrush? Into our first world.
There they were, dignified, invisible,
Moving without pressure, over the dead leaves,
In the autumn heat, through the vibrant air,
And the bird called, in response to
The unheard music hidden in the shrubbery,
And the unseen eyebeam crossed, for the roses
Had the look of flowers that are looked at.
There they were as our guests, accepted and accepting.
So we moved, and they, in a formal pattern,
Along the empty alley, into the box circle,
To look down into the drained pool.
Dry the pool, dry concrete, brown-edged,
And the pool was filled with water out of sunlight,
And the lotos rose, quietly, quietly,
The surface glittered out of heart of light,

1. From *Four Quartets,* copyright, 1943, by T. S. Eliot. Reprinted by permission of Harcourt, Brace and Company, Inc.

And they were behind us, reflected in the pool,
Then a cloud passed, and the pool was empty.
Go, said the bird, for the leaves were full of children,
Hidden, excitedly, containing laughter.
Go, go, go, said the bird: human kind
Cannot bear very much reality.
Time past and time future
What might have been and what has been
Point to one end, which is always present.

II

Garlic and sapphires in the mud
Clot the bedded axle-tree.
The trilling wire in the blood
Sings below inveterate scars
And reconciles forgotten wars.
The dance along the artery
The circulation of the lymph
Are figured in the drift of stars
Ascend to summer in the tree
We move above the moving tree
In light upon the figured leaf
And hear upon the sodden floor
Below, the boarhound and the boar
Pursue their pattern as before
But reconciled among the stars.

At the still point of the turning world. Neither flesh nor fleshless;
Neither from nor towards; at the still point, there the dance is,
But neither arrest nor movement. And do not call it fixity,
Where past and future are gathered. Neither movement from nor towards,
Neither ascent nor decline. Except for the point, the still point,
There would be no dance, and there is only the dance.
I can only say, *there* we have been: but I cannot say where.
And I cannot say, how long, for that is to place it in time.

The inner freedom from the practical desire,
The release from action and suffering, release from the inner
And the outer compulsion, yet surrounded
By a grace of sense, a white light still and moving,
Erhebung without motion, concentration
Without elimination, both a new world
And the old made explicit, understood
In the completion of its partial ecstasy,

The resolution of its partial horror.
Yet the enchainment of past and future
Woven in the weakness of the changing body,
Protects mankind from heaven and damnation
Which flesh cannot endure.
Time past and time future
Allow but a little consciousness.
To be conscious is not to be in time
But only in time can the moment in the rose-garden,
The moment in the arbour where the rain beat,
The moment in the draughty church at smokefall
Be remembered; involved with past and future.
Only through time time is conquered.

III

Here is a place of disaffection
Time before and time after
In a dim light: neither daylight
Investing form with lucid stillness
Turning shadow into transient beauty
With slow rotation suggesting permanence
Nor darkness to purify the soul
Emptying the sensual with deprivation
Cleansing affection from the temporal.
Neither plenitude nor vacancy. Only a flicker
Over the strained time-ridden faces
Distracted from distraction by distraction
Filled with fancies and empty of meaning
Tumid apathy with no concentration
Men and bits of paper, whirled by the cold wind
That blows before and after time,
Wind in and out of unwholesome lungs
Time before and time after.
Eructation of unhealthy souls
Into the faded air, the torpid
Driven on the wind that sweeps the gloomy hills of London,
Hampstead and Clerkenwell, Campden and Putney,
Highgate, Primrose and Ludgate. Not here
Not here the darkness, in this twittering world.

Descend lower, descend only
Into the world of perpetual solitude,
World not world, but that which is not world,
Internal darkness, deprivation

And destitution of all property,
Desiccation of the world of sense,
Evacuation of the world of fancy,
Inoperancy of the world of spirit;
This is the one way, and the other
Is the same, not in movement
But abstention from movement; while the world moves
In appetency, on its metalled ways
Of time past and time future.

IV

Time and the bell have buried the day,
The black cloud carries the sun away.
Will the sunflower turn to us, will the clematis
Stray down, bend to us; tendril and spray
Clutch and cling?
Chill
Fingers of yew be curled
Down on us? After the kingfisher's wing
Has answered light to light, and is silent, the light is still
At the still point of the turning world.

V

Words move, music moves
Only in time; but that which is only living
Can only die. Words, after speech, reach
Into the silence. Only by the form, the pattern,
Can words or music reach
The stillness, as a Chinese jar still
Moves perpetually in its stillness.
Not the stillness of the violin, while the note lasts,
Not that only, but the co-existence,
Or say that the end precedes the beginning,
And the end and the beginning were always there
Before the beginning and after the end.
And all is always now. Words strain,
Crack and sometimes break, under the burden,
Under the tension, slip, slide, perish,
Decay with imprecision, will not stay in place,
Will not stay still. Shrieking voices
Scolding, mocking, or merely chattering,
Always assail them. The Word in the desert
Is most attacked by voices of temptation,
The crying shadow in the funeral dance,
The loud lament of the disconsolate chimera.

The detail of the pattern is movement,
As in the figure of the ten stairs.
Desire itself is movement
Not in itself desirable;
Love is itself unmoving,
Only the cause and end of movement,
Timeless, and undesiring
Except in the aspect of time
Caught in the form of limitation
Between un-being and being.
Sudden in a shaft of sunlight
Even while the dust moves
There rises the hidden laughter
Of children in the foliage
Quick now, here, now, always—
Ridiculous the waste sad time
Stretching before and after.

ON ELIOT'S *BURNT NORTON* [1]

ELIZABETH DREW

The poem opens with a passage of musing commentary on the nature of experience in time, with three self-contained propositions, and then a statement of what is really the substance and conclusion of all four poems [the *Four Quartets*]. First there is the usual concept of time as progression, and events as a sequence of cause and effect:

> Time present and time past
> Are both perhaps present in time future,
> And time future contained in time past.

Then there is the concept of time as "eternally present," with the comment that if that is so, it makes time "unredeemable"; nothing can be altered, we can't bring back the past. This statement is left as it is for the moment: it is developed in the later poems and shown to be a half truth only. Finally there is a third category of experience "what might have been"—the potential. This is "perpetual," but exists only "in a world of speculation." The three aspects of time are then reduced to the central truth:

> What might have been and what has been
> Point to one end, which is always present.

---

1. Reprinted from *T. S. Eliot: The Design of His Poetry* (New York, 1950), pp. 151–162, by Elizabeth Drew; copyright 1949 by Charles Scribner's Sons; used by permission of the publishers.

This is the first entrance of subtle ambiguity in the language, with its two-faced meanings of *point, end* and *present.* As a summing up of time as progression, it says that what has been (the past) and what might have been (the potentialities of the past) point to the present as their conclusion: that is what they have produced. As a summing up of the second idea of the eternal present as a "point," it says that what that points to is both that the present moment is the only actuality, and that what to do in the present is an *aim* or purpose which is always present with us.

Then the pure abstraction modulates into a transition passage. "What might have been" is translated into the sensuous embodiment of the echoing footfalls down the imaginary passage to the closed door into the rose-garden. "My words echo / Thus in your mind," says the poet. He may be addressing the reader and suggesting that such experiences are common to all; or the echoes may be in the mind of the woman in the imaginary scene. Then he returns to the symbolic presentation of the past as "dust on a bowl of rose-leaves." What *purpose* can such disturbing memories have, since the past is unredeemable, its pattern unalterable?

The rhythm quickens to a sense of breathless expectancy and creates the sense of the mind darting about, confusing the logic of temporal and spatial happenings in its own spontaneous flight into "the garden." The interpretation of the lovely scene in the rose-garden itself must depend on personal readings. Many people seem to feel it as a memory of childhood, taking "our first world" to mean that. I interpret the whole passage in the light of the line between the conclusion of the development of all the themes and the final recapitulation at the end of *Little Gidding*: "With the drawing of this Love and the voice of this Calling." That transfigures the bird and the roses of *Burnt Norton* into the dove of *Little Gidding* and the rose of fire and light at the end of that poem: that is, nature becomes a symbol of a spiritual truth which transcends it. By the end of the poems "our first world" and the children in the leaves hold a suggestion of the age of innocence in the Garden of Eden, before the pattern of perfect relationship between God, man and nature was clouded and darkened. Here, in *Burnt Norton,* a transcendence of nature is brought about by the experience being "an airy nothing" given "a local habitation," and by its fusion of nature and man into perfect inter-relationship. But the experience itself—that of *this* love and *this* calling—seems to me to be that of love as a part of the natural world, the "first world" of our development as human beings, the first "gate" on the way. The voice of the thrush is "deception," partly because the whole thing is unseen and unheard by the outward senses, and partly because the experience, though it is one of the moments of "reality," contains only a partial revelation of it, since its centre is in the sense world.

The vision is created in flowing, free and melodious rhythms, its invisible and inaudible quality mysteriously carried by the clearest pictures and verse music. The actual setting in place and time is an autumn scene, but the echoing footfalls of memory and might-have-been enter the deserted rose-garden and people it with life from an inner world. The voice of the bird calls in response to "unheard music" in the shrubbery; the unseen figures *must* be there "for the roses had the look of flowers that are looked at." The roses (the emblems of earthly love) and the dream figures from the past are blended into an inseparable union of giving and receiving, "accepted and accepting." With that the scene groups itself round a symbolic centre "in a formal pattern." The roses and the figures move, concentrating the "point" of vision from the garden to the evergreen "box circle" and thence to the pool and the lotos. The actual deserted drained pool, and its emotional counterpart in the hardness and dryness and neutral shades of the actuality of life, are suddenly transformed into the exquisite moment:

> And the pool was filled with water out of sunlight,
> And the lotos rose, quietly, quietly,
> The surface glittered out of heart of light,
> And they were behind us, reflected in the pool.

Here in natural terms, in the autumn "vibrant air" is the parallel with what in *Little Gidding* is the "mid-winter spring" of the pentecostal fire, which is "not in the scheme of generation." Here, nature and man seem part of an indestructible unity and harmony which *is* within the scheme of generation; the golden cup of the lotos and the surface of the pool receiving their glittering light from the physical sun; the human figures and the roses reflected in the water; the fading leaves full of children "hidden excitedly, containing laughter." The vision is that of an ecstasy of fulfilment at the human and natural level, which is a beautiful "reality," though not the ultimate one. It is blotted out by the cloud, the bird says "Go, go, go"—leave *that* garden—and we are brought back from the vision to the grave statement of the opening, that all things "point to one end, which is always present."

The lovely dancing lyric at the opening of the second movement is obviously based on the Heraclitean idea of the perpetual strife which resolves itself into beautiful harmony. The apparently conflicting and the apparently static are all part of an eternal moving pattern, existing simultaneously in all the elements in nature and linking them in a dynamic whole. The only inanimate thing is "the bedded axle-tree," maybe a relic of some chariot or gun-carriage in a "forgotten war," but reminding us of the symbol of the wheel. From the bright stones under it and the bright flowers around it, from under the "sodden floor" up to the stars, there streams up and down this uninterrupted energy of strife, forming itself into harmonious living patterns; singing, dancing, circulating, and having their final meaning in "the stars," the reflection of the Heraclitean "fire." Even the rather horrible strife of pursuer and pursued, the boarhound and the boar, is constellated (like the warring of the Olympian gods?) into an eternally subsisting order.

But then there is a complete change of rhythm. Heraclitus' system had no still point, which makes his dance very different. His concept of reconciliation is that of perpetual sustaining tension between opposites and not of a centre of resolution. How then define this centre dispassionately, rationally? In place of the crowding, swift images creating the ever-changing configurations of natural forces, the rhythm becomes slow, the vocabulary abstract, the method analytical. But the poet finds the language of logic inadequate here. The still point can be approached only through paradox and negation. It is nothing that can be measured in terms of time, or of movement and fixity, of body or spirit, of ascent and descent. And yet it cannot be detached from these things, because though it is the point where there is no movement, it controls all the movement, and it is only through the measured movements that its presence can be known. It exists, but cannot be captured in a *where* or *when*.

Breaking off the effort at definition by negation and exclusion, the next sequence, continuing the analytical approach, describes in positive terms the *quality* of the experience, which has been given direct sensuous revelation in the vision in the rose-garden. It is a feeling of detachment from the ego and its conflicts, with a sense of grace and illumination and combined stillness and movement; a keeping of personal identity, and of the world of human experience, and yet an expansion beyond it and an elevation above it. Above all a sense of *wholeness,* in which the fragmentary nature of human experience, its partial ecstasy, and its partial horror, are completed and resolved and given *meaning*. Yet man, because he is human, cannot live at the level of the apprehension of wholeness. "Woven in the weakness of the changing body" are the inextricable strands which chain him to time and change. But the chains protect him too. They protect him from more than glimpses of absolute good or evil, ecstasy or agony, "which flesh cannot endure"—whose *duration* would cost man his humanity, since time and change are the laws of his being. He has these moments of ecstasy when he seems to transcend time and conquer it, but it is only within the pattern of time that they can be seen to be a part of a timeless pattern.

The third movement introduces the theme which is in absolute contrast to that of life as part of an ordered natural process, and of life as a pattern of inner relationships centred in the still point, and pointed towards it. It is that of life with no centre, no ordered direction, no organic relationships. Eliot creates these antitheses into a passage where images of them and the language in which they are described produce the most immediate and concrete sensations. On the one hand we feel the true emotional oppositions, by any of which the still point may be reached and which are as patterned as the natural images which symbolize them; on the other all the confusion and fragmentariness and negative neutrality of the dim "place of disaffection." That word itself at once condenses a complex of ideas of the cause and effect of the condition. It carries connotations of discontent; of the diminution and alienation of affection; and of disorder. The next lines contrast the oppositions which are rendered *lucid* by the sense of pattern, with the disaffection and dimness, which are

> neither daylight
> Investing form with lucid stillness
> Turning shadow into transient beauty
> With slow rotation suggesting permanence
> Nor darkness to purify the soul
> Emptying the sensual with deprivation
> Cleansing affection from the temporal.
> Neither plenitude nor vacancy.

The London scene which follows continues the parallels. Instead of creative tension there is *strain* on the "time-ridden faces / Distracted from distraction by distraction." Instead of light or dark, a *flicker* and *faded air* and *gloomy hills;* instead of plenitude or vacancy, the faces "filled with fancies and empty of meaning"; instead of wholeness, *unwholesome* lungs, *unhealthy* souls; instead of permanence and lucid stillness, the *tumid apathy* of the *torpid;* instead of measured movement the "men and bits of paper, whirled by the cold wind."

From all "this twittering world" of dim light and dim humanity, the poet turns to the creative "way down" into the inner darkness and isolation and silence, to the vacancy which is not "empty of meaning," but empty of self. It is "deprivation / And destitution of all property," the active forsaking of the ego, the way of withdrawal from the worlds of both sense and spirit, the disciplined "abstention from movement";

> while the world moves
> In appetency, on its metalled ways
> Of time past and time future.

Here again in *appetency* there is a great concentration of meaning. Not only the sense of conscious and unconscious compulsive drives, but the reminder of the Lamarckian doctrine that changes in the desires and needs of an organism result in adaptive modifications of its structure. So that the "metalled ways" on which the urban world now moves, suggest not only a picture of it as a vast network of roads and railways leading nowhere, but the whole quality of the mechanistic culture of today and its possible consequences for the future of the race.

After the formal declaration and loaded latinized language of the third movement, the short lyric of the fourth takes us back to the memory of the vision in the garden, but in a very different mood. There, there was the ecstatic assurance of lucid pattern uniting nature and man. This was reinforced by the lyric emphasizing the dynamic order of the natural world and the passages of analysis describing the order of the world of spirit. Against this was the disorder of the modern city. From this the poet turned to a discipline of spiritual negation and a conquest of sense. But that is a voluntary darkness and emptiness; there is a return from it to the world which had been renounced. What of the involuntary defeat of the darkness and silence of death, which is the inevitable end of "the changing body"? With mingled horror and hope the poet questions its meaning.

> Time and the bell have buried the day,
> The black cloud carries the sun away.

The day and all that daylight brought, "investing form with lucid stillness" and the sense of permanent moving pattern, is "buried"; its lucid stillness destroyed by the black cloud and the death knell. The only sense of movement is the carrying away of the sun by the cloud, not only obscuring but *removing* the unmoving centre of the universe as we know it. This fact brings at one level sensations of pure terror. The words *bury, cloud, clutch, cling, curled fingers,* and the isolation of *chill* as a line in itself, suggest obliteration, dark cold extinction, strangulation by forces against which man is helpless. Will the only centre of life then be the nourishment our rotting bodies supply to the loveliness of flowers and trees? But there is another tone of gentler questioning. To pass into the pattern of nature expressed in the turning of the sunflower; in the tendrils and sprays of the clematis straying down, bending, clutching and clinging; in the curled fingers of the yew, has its own beauty. But will it be all? The tones of both horror and tender regret in the question are answered by the flashing image of the kingfisher in relation to the source of natural light, and its parallel in terms of the spirit.

> After the kingfisher's wing
> Has answered light to light, and is silent, the light is still
> At the still point of the turning world.

The opposition of the movement of the kingfisher's wing and silence, in the last image, leads on to the next subject, the union of movement and stillness in a work of art and its parallel with the worlds of time and the still point. The poet shifts again to analytical discourse, this time in flowing speech rhythms. Again we have the two worlds of the temporal and the unchanging contrasted. The actuality of poetry and music to eye and ear is a series of progressions in a temporal sequence. But if they existed only in that dimension they would die like the flower and the kingfisher. Their "reality" is a matter of dynamic relationships, a structure where every part is involved with every other part to form an indivisible whole. The temporal sequence is co-existent with the unchanging pattern, all held together in a vital tension of sound and meaning. Carrying on the image of the whole as a system of tensions, he says:

> Words strain,
> Crack and sometimes break, under the burden,
> Under the tension, slip, slide, perish,

Decay with imprecision, will not stay in place,
Will not stay still. Shrieking voices
Scolding, mocking, or merely chattering,
Always assail them.

We shift almost imperceptibly from the abstract discussion of an intellectual aesthetic to the immediate reminder that this is by way of illustration of something else. The theme is not primarily a matter of aesthetics or physics. The *burden* is not only the weight on a word. The *imprecision* is linked with the concrete *decay,* the loss of tension with the concrete *slip, slide, perish.* The abstract stillness and movement of poetic "form" is invaded by the discordant, irrelevant "voices." In the last image the sense of *dis*order is suddenly intensified and its menace as the enemy of pattern and permanence is created in the word *assail.* Then "words" become the Word and we are translated from art to life.

The Word in the desert
Is most attacked by voices of temptation,
The crying shadow in the funeral dance,
The loud lament of the disconsolate chimera.

The temptation, the *attack* on creative order, becomes the wonderful complex imagery of the last two lines, where the harmonious dance is disturbed by "the funeral dance," and where noise, darkness, self-pity and self-deception invade the stillness. "The disconsolate chimera" is another of those strokes of genius where the words absorb and radiate implications. *Disconsolate,* recalling the earlier *disaffection,* carries the meaning of comfortless and melancholy, while *chimera* is both an empty, meaningless fancy and the incongruously composed monster slain by Bellerophon. Every aspect of the meanings fuse, and the *loud lament* and the *crying shadow* again enforce the sense of discord, pain and confused darkness of the temptation.

The recapitulation of the whole poem moves in a measure of short fluent lines, which is used again at the conclusion of *The Dry Salvages* and *Little Gidding.* The pattern of dynamic tensions sustaining life, which in the natural world was "figured in the drift of stars" and down to the garlic and the mud, is, in the world of spirit "the figure of the ten stairs." This is a reference to St. John of the Cross, who pictured the discipline of contemplation as a ladder of ten steps "which the soul is ascending and descending continually in ecstasy and humiliation until it has acquired perfect habits." The summit of the ladder and what it rests upon is God as Love, and for a moment we are taken outside of both the turning world and the pattern whose centre is the still point, to the unmoved mover who exists untouched by the temporal, by the "form of limitation" decreed by life. Love in its human aspect cannot rid itself entirely of the element of desire. It can reach only to the moment of "reality" in the rose-garden, when, for a brief instant, nature and spirit glittered together "out of heart of light." Swiftly we are transported back to that ecstasy—

> Sudden in a shaft of sunlight
> Even while the dust moves
> There rises the hidden laughter
> Of children in the foliage
> Quick now, here, now, always—

The "purpose" of the disturbance of the dust on the bowl of rose-leaves is now clear. It is a reminder that every moment of time can be transfigured by the apprehension of the timeless pattern and the sharing of its vitality. The release, the "grace of sense," the spontaneous, joyous illumination, comes like the "dancing arrow" of bird flight, flashes in the here and now—and is gone—leaving the sense of the combined unimportance and unworthiness and mockery of "the aspect of time."

> Ridiculous the waste sad time
> Stretching before and after.

JOHN CROWE RANSOM

HERE LIES A LADY[1]

Here lies a lady of beauty and high degree.
Of chills and fever she died, of fever and chills,
The delight of her husband, her aunts, an infant of three,
And of medicos marveling sweetly on her ills.

For either she burned, and her confident eyes would blaze,
And her fingers fly in a manner to puzzle their heads—
What was she making? Why, nothing; she sat in a maze
Of old scraps of laces, snipped into curious shreds.

Or this would pass, and the light of her fire decline
Till she lay discouraged and cold as a thin stalk white and blown,
And would not open her eyes, to kisses, to wine.
The sixth of these states was her last; the cold settled down.

Sweet ladies, long may ye bloom, and toughly I hope ye may thole,
But was she not lucky? In flowers and lace and mourning,

1. Reprinted from *Chills and Fever* by John Crowe Ransom, by permission of Alfred A. Knopf, Inc. Copyright, 1924, 1945, by Alfred A. Knopf, Inc.

In love and great honor we bade God rest her soul
After six little spaces of chill, and six of burning.

ON RANSOM'S *HERE LIES A LADY* [1]

FRED H. STOCKING

THE most controversial feature of this poem is the attitude of the speaker toward the aristocratic lady who has died. The tone of the opening line is detached and factual. As we read farther, however, we realize that this objectivity is owing not to a lack of feeling, but to the kind of feeling—or rather, to a blend of several feelings: (1) genuine sorrow induced by this lady's death, (2) respect for the values cherished by all ladies of high degree, and (3) at the same time an awareness that these values *can* be seen as superficial, even mildly comical.

Genuine grief is reflected in his tribute to the affection the lady inspired in her husband, aunts, and child, in the pathos of the image of the "thin stalk white and blown," in the rhetorical grimness of the words, "the cold settled down," and in his report that "in love and great honor we bade God rest her soul."

The poem's central focus, however, is on his appreciation of the values to which all aristocratic ladies adhere: their love of manners, ceremony, and behavior that is controlled, self-conscious, formally patterned. Such ladies put a great premium on lace and fine dress; they delight in symmetry and balance, neatness and precision. And what most impresses the speaker in the poem is the ceremonious way—the almost mannered way—in which she has died. The symmetrical pattern of her chills and fever is emphasized by the repetition, with inversion, in the second line, by the nicely balanced organization of the poem itself (with the second stanza devoted to her fevers and the third to her chills), and by the last line of the poem. In the fourth stanza the speaker says that he hopes sweet ladies will not die; but if they must die, he hopes their dying may be as appropriate as hers. The question in the second line of this stanza is not completely ironic. In one special sense the lady *was* lucky: not only because her friends and neighbors paid their respects in an elaborately ceremonious funeral (with flowers, lace, mourning, love, great honor, and prayer), but also because of the *way* in which she died, "after six little spaces of chill, and six of burning." Her illness, albeit tragic, was nevertheless symmetrical; and it was orderly, neat, and precise in form. Hence the lady's sickness is presented as a symbol of her whole set of values (her "art of living"); her way of death symbolizes her way of life.

There are two ways of reacting to this symbolical death: you can respect it, or you can find it rather silly. Evidence of the speaker's basic attitude—

1. From *The Explicator,* VIII (October, 1949), 1. Reprinted by permission of the authors and of the Editors of *The Explicator.*

genuine respect—has already been cited; but there is also evidence of his awareness that others might find all these goings on rather comical,—that others might, indeed, find the lady's death, like her life, mildly ridiculous. There is the jaunty rhythm of line 2, written as though the speaker, intrigued by the very sounds of "chills and fever, fever and chills," playfully makes the illness sound like a jig; there is a comic tumbling down the scale of importance from the husband in line 3 to the smiling, incompetent medicos of line 4; there is a touch of grim humor in the description of her fevers ("What was she making? Why nothing;"); and there is implied comedy in the very conception of her disease as a piece of complicated ritual. These occasional light touches in the speaker's manner or pose (as distinct from his basic feeling) do not satirize the lady, but they do enable the speaker to suggest that he knows there can be other attitudes than his own; he says, in effect: "Despite my genuine grief and my deep respect for the lady's values, I understand that it might be possible to regard the lady as an inconsequential creature whose death was as cluttered with pointless activity as her life had been."

ELLSWORTH MASON

Ransom's "Here Lies a Lady" reveals the modern fear of sentimentality in that the speaker covers up his really intense grief under layers of a detached, epitaphic manner and of qualifying irony. But the grief appears in his dwelling on the unsightly aspects of the lady's fatal disease and in his contrast of the richness of her life with her sudden death from a superficially trivial ailment.

Stanza 1 contrasts the lady's life with the triviality of her disease. The speaker's emotions are completely under control as he alternates the serious lines 1 and 3 with the jingling rhythm of line 2 and the semi-humorous criticism of the doctors in line 4.

Stanzas 2 and 3 contain the emotional center of the poem. In stanza 2 the speaker's real feelings begin to come to the surface in the emphasis he places on the deranged, uncontrollable actions of the fevered lady. But this emphasis is qualified in line 3. "Why nothing" has a semi-comic effect because it comes as a surprise, but the surprise itself indicates that we should have expected some purposeful action and points up the tragedy of the lady's derangement.

The emotion of stanza 3 is almost completely unqualified. The speaker's deep compassion is emphasized by the details and length of line 2, is intensified by the intimacy of the attempts to revive the lady in line 3, and is justified by the grim finality with which line 4 ends.

Having almost openly revealed his emotions in stanza 3, the speaker immediately covers them up in line 1 of stanza 4. He contrasts the endurance of the sweet ladies with the death of his lady, and the contrast reminds him so deeply of his loss that he nearly falls over backwards in his use of archaic language to appear casual. The question in line 2 is completely ironic. The poem ends, as it began, with a contrast between the richness of the lady's life and the seeming triviality of her disease. The parallel of the details with stanza 1 is exact: "flowers"—"beauty," "lace"—"high degree," love of the mourners—love of her family. But now, the irony is deepened by presenting her life implicitly in the details of her funeral and by emphasizing the triviality of the disease in the added detail "little spaces."

BLUE GIRLS[1]

Twirling your blue skirts, traveling the sward
Under the towers of your seminary,
Go listen to your teachers old and contrary
Without believing a word.

Tie the white fillets then about your lustrous hair
And think no more of what will come to pass
Than bluebirds that go walking on the grass
And chattering on the air.

Practice your beauty, blue girls, before it fail;
And I will cry with my loud lips and publish
Beauty which all our power shall never establish,
It is so frail.

For I could tell you a story which is true:
I know a lady with a terrible tongue,
Blear eyes fallen from blue,
All her perfections tarnished—and yet it is not long
Since she was lovelier than any of you.

ARCHIBALD MacLEISH

THE END OF THE WORLD[2]

Quite unexpectedly as Vasserot
The armless ambidextrian was lighting
A match between his great and second toe
And Ralph the lion was engaged in biting

---

1. Reprinted from *Selected Poems* by John Crowe Ransom, by permission of Alfred A. Knopf, Inc. Copyright, 1924, 1945, by Alfred A. Knopf, Inc.
2. From Archibald MacLeish, *Poems 1924–1933*. By permission of Houghton Mifflin Company, publishers.

The neck of Madame Sossman while the drum
Pointed, and Teeny was about to cough
In waltz-time swinging Jocko by the thumb—
Quite unexpectedly the top blew off:

And there, there overhead, there, there, hung over
Those thousands of white faces, those dazed eyes,
There in the starless dark, the poise, the hover,
There with vast wings across the canceled skies,
There in the sudden blackness, the black pall
Of nothing, nothing, nothing—nothing at all.

YOU, ANDREW MARVELL[1]

And here face down beneath the sun
And here upon earth's noonward height
To feel the always coming on
The always rising of the night

To feel creep up the curving east
The earthly chill of dusk and slow
Upon those under lands the vast
And ever climbing shadow grow

And strange at Ecbatan the trees
Take leaf by leaf the evening strange
The flooding dark about their knees
The mountains over Persia change

And now at Kermanshah the gate
Dark empty and the withered grass
And through the twilight now the late
Few travelers in the westward pass
And Baghdad darken and the bridge
Across the silent river gone
And through Arabia the edge
Of evening widen and steal on

And deepen on Palmyra's street
The wheel rut in the ruined stone
And Lebanon fade out and Crete
High through the clouds and overblown

1. From Archibald MacLeish, *Poems 1924–1933*. By permission of Houghton Mifflin Company, publishers.

And over Sicily the air
Still flashing with the landward gulls
And loom and slowly disappear
The sails above the shadowy hulls

And Spain go under and the shore
Of Africa the gilded sand
And evening vanish and no more
The low pale light across that land

Nor now the long light on the sea
And here face downward in the sun
To feel how swift how secretly
The shadow of the night comes on . . .

E. E. CUMMINGS [1]

CHANSON INNOCENT, I

in Just-
spring when the world is mud-
luscious the little
lame baloonman

whistles far and wee

and eddieandbill come
running from marbles and
piracies and it's
spring

when the world is puddle-wonderful

the queer
old baloonman whistles
far and wee
and bettyandisbel come dancing

from hop-scotch and jump-rope and

1. From *Collected Poems of E. E. Cummings,* published by Harcourt, Brace and Company, Inc. Copyright, 1923, by E. E. Cummings.

it's
spring
and
        the

            goat-footed

baloonMan   whistles
far
and
wee

ON CUMMINGS' *CHANSON INNOCENT, I* [1]

ROBERT MAYO

Subject and the point of view. This is the first of three poems published by Cummings under the heading "Chansons Innocentes" in *Tulips and Chimneys* (1923). The title is an important clue to the poet's intention. *Innocent* in French means *simple* and *childlike,* and on its primary level the poem may be construed as a "song" in which the world is seen through a child's eyes at the moment when winter first gives way to spring—that is, *Just-spring.* The word is one which a child might invent, and the fact that it is capitalized (the only one, excepting *baloonMan*) may mean that *Just-spring* is the subject of the poem, although admittedly this is not Cummings' practice in other poems.

All detail in the poem is selected to create the feeling of a child's world—the *queer old baloonman, eddieandbill, marbles and piracies, bettyandisbel, hopscotch and jump-rope,* and so on.

The imagery likewise is expressive of a child's point of view. *Mud-luscious* suggests not only the season of frequent rains, but the sensuous pleasure which he takes in soft mud; and *puddle-wonderful,* the magic of a world reflected in reverse. Similarly the baloonman is first described as *little* and *lame,* next as *queer* and *old,* and last of all as *goat-footed.* Thus his infirmity is seen not as pathetic—as a sign of misfortune and suffering—but purely as an eccentricity, the twisted leg of the little man, with its built-up shoe (possibly), reminding the child of a goat's foot.

Organization. Some of Cummings' other poems are "abstract" in form—that is, they try to express feeling directly, without representing speech or thought in the conventional manner. But this poem can best be interpreted

1. From *English "A" Analyst,* No. 2 (May, 1947), Northwestern University. By permission of the author.

within a dramatic or psychological framework, as a kind of monologue or thought-stream. The movement is cyclic:

in Just-spring . . . world . . . baloonman . . . eddieandbill. . . . marbles . . .
and it's spring . . . world . . . baloonman . . . bettyandisbel . . . hopscotch . . .
and it's spring . . . . . . baloonMan . . .

The "song" therefore, describes two whole turns and two arcs of a third before it ends abruptly. The organization suggests the rambling discourse or singsong of a child. The paean of *Just-spring* comes in unpremeditated spurts, and breaks off as suddenly as it begins. Perhaps the speaker's attention is diverted elsewhere, or his daydream ends as he falls asleep.

Typography. The unconventional typography—besides being designed, as in Cummings' other poems, to give freshness to the reading experience—seems also to serve more specific functions. In this poem, at least, it is used to enhance the feeling of childlike naïveté, to suggest sound effects, and to support the "action" of the poem in other ways.

1. Most obviously, *eddieandbill* and *bettyandisbel* are attempts to suggest a child's running of words together breathlessly (note the suggestive elision in *is(a)bel*). On the other hand the curious form *baloonMan* in line 21 shows the same process in reverse, the breaking up of a single word into its significant components. Here it may represent a naive qualification by the speaker. This queer, little being—he may wish to remind us—may be *goat-footed,* but he's a *Man* just the same.

2. At first sight the wide spacing and the line-breaks in the poem may seem to be pure freakishness, but with study one discovers a regularity in the irregularity which suggests some method in the poet's oddity. For example, there is after *Just-spring* or *spring* each time either a space or a line-break. These can be interpreted as dramatic pauses—suggestive of the speechless wonder of the child. Every time the subject recurs, he stops to take it in, as it were.

3. In the passages just cited the spacing seems to have been used for emphasis—as exclamation points *in absentia,* so to speak. Elsewhere quite the opposite effect may have been intended. For example, each time the baloonman whistles, the line is either broken or extended by wide spacing.

whistles far and wee	(line 5)
whistles / far and wee	(lines 12–13)
whistles / far / and / wee	(lines 21–24)

It may be that this is intended to convey to the eye the impression of distance, and attenuation. The whistle, that is, is heard by the children *far* off—faintly but sharply (*wee*)—whereupon they come running and skipping from their games.

4. Undoubtedly the most cryptic typographical feature of the poem is found in the last nine lines. The first fifteen are grouped for the eye in

"stanzas" of five lines each, consisting of a "quatrain" and a "refrain." The arrangement is quite arbitrary, it would seem, since the meter is free, the lines are irregular in length, and the grouping bears no observable relation to the sense. After three "regular stanzas," however, the sight pattern dwindles: ten words now occupy nine lines, the margin slips to the right, and the poem breaks off between the "quatrain" and the "refrain."

The disintegration after "stanza" 3, of course, can be interpreted simply as the diversion of the child's thoughts to something else—the poem "runs down," so to speak. But a close reading of the third "stanza" would seem to suggest a more specific cause. It is a striking fact, at any rate, that the *hop-scotch and jump-rope* of line 15 is followed by three hops forward in the verse, two diagonal, a double-hop, and three singles. The game breaks up the poem, just as the baloonman breaks up the game.

The second level of the poem. So much for Cummings' "child's song" on its primary level. The poem should be read, first of all, on the naturalistic plane, as an attempt to create the illusion of a children's world, and to express the joyous exuberance of the "singer" at the first coming of spring.

On the second level, which may be termed the *symbolic,* the poem has a further meaning for the reader which it does not have for the child. Briefly, the baloonman is identified with the god Pan, whose pipings from afar signal the first stirrings of spring and set all the creatures of nature to dancing. The discovery is not immediate, but gradual; the effect is cumulative. Paraphrasing, and underlining key words:

> In Just-*spring* . . . the *little* lame baloonman *whistles far* off and sets the children to *running,* and when it's *spring* the *queer old* baloonman *whistles* and the children come *dancing,* and when it's *spring* the *goat-footed* (!) baloonman *whistles far and wee.*

With the last epithet—*goat-footed*—comes the act of recognition on the part of the reader, at the precise moment when on the first level, as we have observed, the poem seems to be running down. Thus the two planes of meaning in the poem—the one descending, the other ascending, so to speak—intersect at line 20, where the modern child's world of marbles and hop-scotch is linked with the timeless spirit of the spring season, and acquires a kind of extra dimension.

The total meaning of the poem. The double level of meaning in "Just-spring" makes the search for the total meaning somewhat perplexing. In rising from the specific to the general in this poem, at just what point ought one to stop? What was Cummings' intention in overlaying the general detail of American life with the symbolism of pagan antiquity? Exactly how eternal is his *baloon Man?* Is he a primeval force, or just a pantheistic pun?

If we take into account the main body of Cummings' poetry, certainly, there would seem to be no mystical intention—no serious allegory. On the contrary, judging from the other poems in the group the title, the detail and the imagery, the organization of the poem, its typographical oddities, the colloquial tone, and the general air of nostalgia which it breathes, "Just-spring" would seem to be more scintillation than anything else—a kind of witty reminder of the ageless qualities of awakening spring, and an amused glance at the unconscious paganism and animal spirits of childhood.

SPACE BEING CURVED[1]

Space being(don't forget to remember)Curved
(and that reminds me who said o yes Frost
Something there is which isn't fond of walls)
an electromagnetic(now I've lost
the)Einstein expanded Newton's law preserved
conTinuum(but we read that beFore)

of Course life being just a Reflex you
know since Everything is Relative or

to sum it All Up god being Dead(not to

mention inTerred)
LONG LIVE that Upwardlooking
Serene Illustrious and Beatific
Lord of Creation,MAN:
at a least crooking
of Whose compassionate digit,earth's most terrific

quadruped swoons into billiardBalls!

MR U[2]

mr u will not be missed
who as an anthologist
sold the many on the few
not excluding mr u

1 x 1[2]

if everything happens that can't be done
(and anything's righter
than books
could plan)
the stupidest teacher will almost guess
(with a run

1. From W(VIVA) in *Collected Poems,* published by Harcourt, Brace & Company. Copyright, 1931, by E. E. Cummings.
2. From *1 x 1,* published by Henry Holt and Company. Copyright, 1944, by E. E. Cummings.

skip
around we go yes)
there's nothing as something as one

one hasn't a why or because or although
(and buds know better
than books
don't grow)
one's anything old being everything new
(with a what
which
around we come who)
one's everyanything so

so world is a leaf so tree is a bough
(and birds sing sweeter
than books
tell how)
so here is away and so your is a my
(with a down
up
around again fly)
forever was never till now

now i love you and you love me
(and books are shuter
than books
can be)
and deep in the high that does nothing but fall
(with a shout
each
around we go all)
there's somebody calling who's we

we're anything brighter than even the sun
(we're everything greater
than books
might mean)
we're everyanything more than believe
(with a spin
leap
alive we're alive)
we're wonderful one times one

❦

HART CRANE

AT MELVILLE'S TOMB[1]

Often beneath the wave, wide from this ledge
The dice of drowned men's bones he saw bequeath
An embassy. Their numbers as he watched,
Beat on the dusty shore and were obscured.

And wrecks passed without sound of bells,
The calyx of death's bounty giving back
A scattered chapter, livid hieroglyph,
The portent wound in corridors of shells.

Then in the circuit calm of one vast coil,
Its lashings charmed and malice reconciled,
Frosted eyes there were that lifted altars;
And silent answers crept across the stars.

Compass, quadrant and sextant contrive
No farther tides . . . High in the azure steeps
Monody shall not wake the mariner.
This fabulous shadow only the sea keeps.

ON CRANE'S *AT MELVILLE'S TOMB*[2]

HART CRANE AND HARRIET MONROE

APROPOS of the poem *At Melville's Tomb,* printed in the verse section of this number, the following correspondence between its author and the editor, printed with the consent of both, may be of interest to our readers.

From the editor to Mr. Crane:

Take me for a hard-boiled unimaginative unpoetic reader, and tell me how *dice* can *bequeath an embassy* (or anything else); and how a calyx *(of death's bounty* or anything else) can give back a *scattered chapter, livid hieroglyph;* and how, if it does, such a *portent* can be *wound in corridors* (of shells or anything else).

And so on. I find your image of *frosted eyes lifting altars* difficult to

1. From *The Collected Poems of Hart Crane,* published by the Liveright Publishing Corp., N. Y. Copyright, Liveright, Inc., 1933.

2. From *Poetry: A Magazine of Verse,* XXIX (Oct., 1926), 34–41. Whole article, "A Discussion with Hart Crane." Reprinted by permission of the authors and the publisher.

visualize. Nor do compass, quadrant and sextant *contrive* tides, they merely record them, I believe.

All this may seem impertinent, but is not so intended. Your ideas and rhythms interest me, and I am wondering by what process of reasoning you would justify this poem's succession of champion mixed metaphors, of which you must be conscious. The packed line should pack its phrases in orderly relation, it seems to me, in a manner tending to clear confusion instead of making it worse confounded.

But pardon me—you didn't ask for criticism. Of course, I should not venture upon these remarks if I were not much interested.

From Mr. Crane to the editor:

Your good nature and manifest interest in writing me about the obscurities apparent in my Melville poem certainly prompt a wish to clarify my intentions in that poem as much as possible. But I realize that my explanations will not be very convincing. For a paraphrase is generally a poor substitute for any organized conception that one has fancied he has put into the more essentialized form of the poem itself.

At any rate, and though I imagine us to have considerable differences of opinion regarding the relationship of poetic metaphor to ordinary logic (I judge this from the angle of approach you use toward portions of the poem), I hope my answers will not be taken as a defense of merely certain faulty lines. I am really much more interesting in certain theories of metaphor and technique involved generally in poetics, than I am concerned in vindicating any particular perpetrations of my own.

My poem may well be elliptical and actually obscure in the ordering of its content, but in your criticism of this very possible deficiency you have stated your objections in terms that allow me, at least for the moment, the privilege of claiming your ideas and ideals as theoretically, at least, quite outside the issues of my own aspirations. To put it more plainly, as a poet I may very possibly be more interested in the so-called illogical impingements of the connotations of words on the consciousness (and their combinations and interplay in metaphor on this basis) than I am interested in the preservation of their logically rigid significations at the cost of limiting my subject matter and perceptions involved in the poem.

This may sound as though I merely fancied juggling words and images until I found something novel, or esoteric; but the process is much more predetermined and objectified than that. The nuances of feeling and observation in a poem may well call for certain liberties which you claim the poet has no right to take. I am simply making the claim that the poet does have that authority, and that to deny it is to limit the scope of the medium so considerably as to outlaw some of the richest genius of the past.

This argument over the dynamics of metaphor promises as active a future as has been evinced in the past. Partaking so extensively as it does of the issues involved in the propriety or non-propriety of certain attitudes toward subject matter, etc., it enters the critical distinctions usually made between "romantic," "classic" as an organic factor. It is a problem that would require many pages to state adequately—merely from my own limited standpoint on the issues. Even this limited statement may prove onerous reading, and I hope you will pardon me if my own interest in the matter carries me to the point of presumption.

Its paradox, of course, is that its apparent illogic operates so logically in conjunction with its context in the poem as to establish its claim to another logic, quite independent of the original definition of the word or phrase or image thus employed. It implies (this *inflection* of language) a previous or prepared receptivity to its stimulus on the part of the reader. The reader's sensibility simply responds by identifying this inflection of experience with some event in his own history or perceptions—or rejects it altogether. The logic of metaphor is so organically entrenched in pure sensibility that it can't be thoroughly traced or explained outside of historical sciences, like philology and anthropology. This "pseudo-statement," as I. A. Richards calls it in an admirable essay touching our contentions in last July's *Criterion,* demands completely other faculties of recognition than the pure rationalistic associations permit. Much fine poetry may be completely rationalistic in its use of symbols, but there is much great poetry of another order which will yield the reader very little when inspected under the limitation of such arbitrary concerns as are manifested in your judgment of the Melville poem, especially when you constitute such requirements of ordinary logical relationship between word and word as irreducible.

I don't wish to enter here defense of the particular symbols employed in my own poem, because, as I said, I may well have failed to supply the necessary emotional connectives to the content featured. But I would like to counter a question or so of yours with a similar question. Here the poem is less dubious in quality than my own, and as far as the abstract pertinacity of question and its immediate consequences are concerned the point I'm arguing about can be better demonstrated. Both quotations are familiar to you, I'm sure.

You ask me how a *portent* can possibly be wound in a *shell.* Without attempting to answer this for the moment, I ask you how Blake could possibly say that "a *sigh* is a *sword* of an Angel King." You ask me how *compass, quadrant and sextant "contrive"* tides. I ask you how Eliot can possibly believe that "Every street *lamp* that I pass *beats* like a fatalistic *drum!*" Both of my metaphors may fall down completely. I'm not defending their actual value in themselves; but your criticism of them in each case was leveled at an illogicality of relationship between symbols, which similar fault you must have either overlooked in case you have ever admired the Blake and Eliot lines, or have there condoned them on account of some more ultimate convictions pressed on you by the impact of the poems in their entirety.

It all comes to the recognition that emotional dynamics are not to be confused with any absolute order of rationalized definitions; ergo, in poetry the *rationale* of metaphor belongs to another order of experience than science, and is not to be limited by a scientific and arbitrary code of relationships either in verbal inflections or concepts.

There are plenty of people who have never accumulated a sufficient series of reflections (and these of a rather special nature) to perceive the relation between a *drum* and a *street lamp—via* the *unmentioned* throbbing of the heart and nerves in a distraught man which *tacitly* creates the reason and "logic" of the Eliot metaphor. They will always have a perfect justification for ignoring those lines and to claim them obscure, excessive, etc., until by some experience of their own the words accumulate the necessary connotations to complete their connection. It is the same with the "patient etherized upon a table," isn't it? Surely that line must lack all eloquence to many people who, for instance, would delight in agreeing that the sky was like a dome of many-colored glass.

If one can't count on some such bases in the reader now and then, I don't see how the poet has any chance to ever get beyond the simplest conceptions of emotion and thought, of sensation and lyrical sequence. If the poet is to be held completely to the already evolved and exploited sequences of imagery and logic—what field of added consciousness and increased perceptions (the actual province of poetry, if not lullabyes) can be expected when one has to relatively return to the alphabet every breath or so? In the minds of people who have sensitively read, seen and experienced a great deal, isn't there a terminology something like short-hand as compared to usual description and dialectics, which the artist ought to be right in trusting as a reasonable connective agent toward fresh concepts, more inclusive evaluations? The question is more important to me than it perhaps ought to be; but as long as poetry is written, an audience, however small, is implied, and there remains the question of an active or an inactive imagination as its characteristic.

It is of course understood that a street-lamp simply can't beat with a sound like a drum; but it oftens happens that images, themselves totally dissociated, when joined in the circuit of a particular emotion located with specific relation to both of them, conduce to great vividness and accuracy of statement in defining that emotion.

Not to rant on forever, I'll beg your indulgence and come at once to the explanations you requested on the Melville poem:

> The dice of drowned men's bones he saw bequeath
> An embassy.

Dice bequeath an embassy, in the first place, by being ground (in this connection only, of course) in little cubes from the bones of drowned men by the action of the sea, and are finally thrown up on the sand, having "numbers" but no identification. These being the bones of dead men who never completed their voyage, it seems legitimate to refer to them as the only surviving evidence of certain messages undelivered, mute evidence of certain things, experiences that the dead mariners might have had to deliver. Dice as a symbol of chance and circumstance is also implied.

The calyx of death's bounty giving back, etc.

This calyx refers in a double ironic sense both to a cornucopia and the vortex made by a sinking vessel. As soon as the water has closed over a ship this whirlpool sends up broken spars, wreckage, etc., which can be alluded to as *livid hieroglyphs,* making a *scattered chapter* so far as any complete record of the recent ship and her crew is concerned. In fact, about as much definite knowledge might come from all this as anyone might gain from the roar of his own veins, which is easily heard (haven't you ever done it?) by holding a shell close to one's ear.

Frosted eyes lift altars.

Refers simply to a conviction that a man, not knowing perhaps a definite god yet being endowed with a reverence for deity—such a man naturally postulates a deity somehow, and the altar of that deity by the very *action* of the eyes *lifted* in searching.

Compass, quadrant and sextant contrive no farther tides.

Hasn't it often occurred that instruments originally invented for record and computation have inadvertently so extended the concepts of the entity they were invented to measure (concepts of space, etc.) in the mind and imagination that employed them, that they may metaphorically be said to have extended the original boundaries of the entity measured? This little bit of "relativity" ought not to be discredited in poetry now that scientists are proceeding to measure the universe on principles of pure *ratio,* quite as metaphorical, so far as previous standards of scientific methods extended, as some of the axioms in *Job.*

I may have completely failed to provide any clear interpretation of these symbols in their context. And you will no doubt feel that I have rather heatedly explained them for anyone who professes no claims for their particular value. I hope, at any rate, that I have clarified them enough to suppress any suspicion that their obscurity derives from a lack of definite intentions in the subject-matter of the poem. The execution is another matter, and you must be accorded a superior judgment to mine in that regard.

From the editor to Mr. Crane:

No doubt our theories and ideals in the art differ more or less fundamentally, yet I would not deny to the poet the right to take certain of the liberties you claim. I think he can take as many as he succeeds with without mystifying his particular audience; for mystery is good, but not mystification.

I think that in your poem certain phrases carry to an excessive degree the "dynamics of metaphor"—they telescope three or four images together by mental leaps (I fear my own metaphors are getting mixed!) which the poet, knowing his ground, can take safely, but which the most sympathetic reader cannot take unless the poet leads him by the hand with some such explanation as I find in your letter. I refer to such phrases as my letter quoted, except that I think I was over-exacting in criticizing the "quadrant and sextant" line. Accepting as I do much of what you say about "the illogical impingements of the connotations of words on the consciousness, and their combinations and interplay in metaphor," I must admit that these phrases in your poem are for me too elliptical to produce any effect but mystification (this until you explained them).

I don't get this effect from Blake or Eliot in the lines you quote or others that I have read. I am not familiar with Blake's symbolic poems but now, opening Prof. Pierce's volume of selections from them, I find in their use of metaphor a singular simplicity and clarity. He deals with magnificent mysteries, but presents them in flaming images like

what time I bound my sandals
On to walk forward through eternity.

I find here no crowded and tortured lines.

My argument comes down, I suppose, rather to your practice than your theory. Or, more specifically, your practice strains your theory by carrying it, with relentless logic, to a remote and exaggerated extreme. You find me testing metaphors, and poetic concept in general, too much by logic, whereas I find you pushing logic to the limit in a painfully intellectual search for emotion, for poetic motive. Your poem reeks with brains—it is thought out, worked out, sweated out. And the beauty which it seems entitled to is tortured and lost.

In all this I may be entirely wrong, and I am aware that a number of poets and critics would think so. Yvor Winters, for example, in a recent letter, speaks of your *Marriage of Faustus and Helen* in *Secession* 7 as "one of the great poems of our time, as great as the best of Stevens or Pound or Eliot." Well, I cannot grant it such a rank.

The editor would rather not have the last word, but as Mr. Crane contributes no further to the discussion, we must pass it on to our readers.

VOYAGES: II[1]

—And yet this great wink of eternity,
Of rimless floods, unfettered leewardings,
Samite sheeted and processioned where

1. From *The Collected Poems of Hart Crane,* published by the Liveright Publishing Corp., N. Y. Copyright, Liveright, Inc., 1933.

Her undinal vast belly moonward bends,
Laughing the wrapt inflections of our love;

Take this Sea, whose diapason knells
On scrolls of silver snowy sentences,
The sceptered terror of whose sessions rends
As her demeanors motion well or ill,
All but the pieties of lovers' hands.

And onward, as bells off San Salvador
Salute the crocus lusters of the stars,
In these poinsettia meadows of her tides,—
Adagios of islands, O my Prodigal,
Complete the dark confessions her veins spell.

Mark how her turning shoulders wind the hours,
And hasten while her penniless rich palms
Pass superscription of bent foam and wave,—
Hasten, while they are true,—sleep, death, desire,
Close round one instant in one floating flower.

Bind us in time, O seasons clear, and awe.
O minstrel galleons of Carib fire,
Bequeath us to no earthly shore until
Is answered in the vortex of our grave
The seal's wide spindrift gaze toward paradise.

THE AIR PLANT[1]

Grand Cayman, W. I.

This tuft that thrives on saline nothingness,
Inverted octopus with heavenward arms
Thrust parching from a palm-bole hard by the cove—
A bird almost—of almost bird alarms,

Is pulmonary to the wind that jars
Its tentacles, horrific in the lurch.
The lizard's throat, held bloated for a fly,
Balloons but warily from this throbbing perch.

1. From *The Collected Poems of Hart Crane,* published by the Liveright Publishing Corp., N. Y. Copyright: Liveright, Inc., 1933.

The needles and hacksaws of cactus bleed
A milk of earth when stricken off the stalk;
But this—defenseless, thornless, sheds no blood,
Scarce shadow even—but the air's thin talk.

Angelic Dynamo! Ventriloquist of the Blue!
While beachward creeps the shark-swept Spanish Main.
By what conjunctions do the winds appoint
Its apotheosis, at last—the hurricane!

ALLEN TATE

MR. POPE[1]

When Alexander Pope strolled in the city
Strict was the glint of pearl and gold sedans.
Ladies leaned out, more out of fear than pity;
For Pope's tight back was rather a goat's than man's.

One often thinks the urn should have more bones
Than skeletons provide for speedy dust;
The urn gets hollow, cobwebs brittle as stones
Weave to the funeral shell a frivolous rust.

And he who dribbled couplets like the snake
Coiled to a lithe precision in the sun,
Is missing. The jar is empty; you may break
It only to find that Mr. Pope is gone.

What requisitions of a verity
Prompted the wit and rage between his teeth
One cannot say: around a crooked tree
A mortal climbs whose name should be a wreath.

AGAIN THE NATIVE HOUR[2]

Again the native hour lets down the locks
Uncombed and black, but gray the bobbing beard;
Ten years ago His eyes, fierce shuttlecocks,

1. Reprinted from *Poems 1928–1931* by Allen Tate; copyright, 1931, 1932, by Charles Scribner's Sons; used by permission of the publishers.
2. Reprinted from *Poems 1922–1947*, by Allen Tate; copyright 1932, 1948 by Charles Scribner's Sons; used by permission of the publishers.

Pierced the close net of what I failed: I feared
The belly-cold, the grave-clout, that betrayed
Me dithering in the rift of cordial seas;
Ten years is time enough to be dismayed
By mummy Christ, head crammed between his knees.

Suppose I take an arrogant bomber, stroke
By stroke, up to the frazzled sun to hear
Sun-ghostlings whisper: Yes, the capital yoke—
Remove it and there's not a ghost to fear
This crucial day, whose decapitate joke
Languidly winds into the inner ear.

ON TATE'S *AGAIN THE NATIVE HOUR* [1]

SAMUEL HOLT MONK

ALTHOUGH this complex sonnet should be read in relation to all of Tate's writings (which are remarkably unified and consistent) it can be considered separately, for it is a topical poem, commenting with characteristic irony on the observation of Christmas in 1942. Despite the traditionally personal sonnet form and the use of the pronoun "I," it is not necessary to assume that the speaker is the poet: he is the poet, but he is also any contemporary man of sensibility and intelligence brought up in the Christian tradition, who faced the implications of Christmas in war time. In fact, he is modern man, and the sonnet is thus a comment on the dilemma of the twentieth century, in which incapacity for belief in myth and subservience to abstraction and technological skills have brought the human race to the verge of self-destruction.

The first two lines establish an ironic contrast between the perennial and spontaneous emotions that center in the Christmas myth and the changes that time and events have brought about in the speaker's capacity to respond to that myth. The "native hour," of course, is the hour of the birth of Christ; the "locks Uncombed and black" suggest the eternal and unaging aspects of the Christmas myth, in contrast to the sphere of the temporal, in which the beard has turned gray and "bobs," because of the loss of muscular control that accompanies age. Moreover there is a vivid suggestion here of the general ebbing away of spiritual energy in our civilization.

This contrast is made explicit in the rest of the octave: ten years ago (a reference to *Sonnets at Christmas*) the gaze of Christ had been like shuttle-cocks that the will of the speaker sought to "return" or to ward off, but that none the less pierced the net of his consciousness and even, perhaps, threat-

1. From *The Explicator,* VI (June, 1948), 58; VII (Dec., 1948), 23. Reprinted by permission of the authors and of the Editors of *The Explicator.*

ened to win the match. The effort to return the fierce shuttlecocks was due to fear, a fear that is given first a physical expression in "belly-cold" and then a psychological expression in "grave-clout." This fear is implicit in the acceptance of the Christian myth, for to accept the full implications of Christianity is to accept also the fact of death and its significance and to be betrayed to the "rift of cordial seas." Here the word "cordial" operates powerfully because it emphasizes the concept of the sea as the source of life (*cor*), because it has overtones of vitality and warmth, despite the fact that the surface meaning of "sea" conveys symbolically the vast impersonality of death and the consequent obliteration of the self. The last two lines of the octave refer to the interval between *Sonnets at Christmas* and *More Sonnets*: a decade of dismay because it had witnessed the disturbing influence of the grief-stricken Christ ("head crammed between his knees") and even of the dead and meaningless Christ ("mummy") on a mind that could neither accept nor reject the Christian tradition.

Irony is emphasized in the sharp contrast between the octave and the sestet: it is 1942, a year of war, a year of the denial of Christianity and of the freeing of man from the "capital yoke" of a now admittedly dead myth. The "arrogant bomber" is played off against the static and mummified image of Christ in the octave, for it is dynamic, purposeful, proud of its functional precision. Modern man, having rejected Christian civilization, fulfills himself in the application of science and technical skills to the work of destruction. The phrase "stroke By stroke" refers, of course, to the strokes of the aircraft's engines. "Frazzled" is both a visual and an intellectual image: the rays of the sun and the sense of dying energy are both realized. The ghostlings of the frazzled sun whisper that the work of this day (a bombing mission), of this "crucial" day (a pun on Cross), can be carried on without the sort of fear with which the octave dealt. The Christian revelation is irrelevant and meaningless in 1942: it is seen now as having been merely a "capital yoke" (a pun on the primary meaning of "capital"—*caput*), a matter of intellectual assent that can be laid aside as easily as it was assumed; it is now only a "decapitate joke"—a reference back to "capital yoke"; the head that believed abstractly is no longer in control, for man is committed to violence and the meanings of the old myth wind languidly (without conviction) into the inner ear. Without doubt the phrase "capital yoke" also points to Tate's antagonism to the financial industrial system that has enslaved modern man, and thus relates the poem at another level to his general view of the modern world.

AUGUST H. MASON

This sonnet, as Professor Monk has indicated, is one of a double group of Christmas sonnets, and is a topical poem, "commenting with characteristic irony on the observation of Christmas in 1942." All these sonnets argue the difficult case of an intelligent, sensitive man in our time who is anxiously aware of disparity between the living Word and the mummified body of Christian ethics that is carefully preserved in modern capitalistic societies, and who on each recurring Christmas feels himself punished by the consciousness of his own crimes. And as Professor Monk has also capably said: "the sonnet is . . . a comment on the dilemma of the twentieth century, in which incapacity for belief in myth and subservience to abstraction and technological skills have brought the human race to the verge of self-destruction."

It is important to note what the image structure of this sonnet is, and to find out what, and possibly how, the metaphors composing it, both fundamental and subsidiary, contribute severally and reciprocally to the fulfillment of the writer's intention, which has been stated, already. The principal metaphor in the octave, elaborated, or extended by association to include smaller related metaphors, illuminates the humility of Christ, possibly the grief, in conjunction with his aspect of sternness. The metaphor of the sestet lights up the arrogance of a person and a nation. The locks, the beard (apparently older than the locks), the eyes, and the appurtenances are of the Christ, his image, dead as a mummy, yet living to pierce the conscience of the frivolous celebrant of his ancient rites. The bomber taken sunward represents martial progress as well as the personal desire for life, and the frazzled sun may represent the sun's photographic image and so be akin to the medieval portraiture of the Christ alluded to in the preceding sonnet: a painting with deteriorating surface, which has some correspondence to what is expressed in "the crackle of the Christ's deep gaze." Again, depth of gaze may be equivalent to intensity, the intensity of a burning glance, perhaps. A ghostling of the sun would be a little light phenomenon, a glance from the disintegrating sun, whose great energy is being dispersed in the forms of heat and light. Ghostling: glance: syllable from the source of life and light. Fierce shuttlecocks are glances fit to pierce the net that is necessary, and apparently protective, to the player of a well-known game: a game that corresponds in metaphor to strife with the consciousness of failure-guilt, that rests languidly with the player, or plays languidly, behind the veil of sense deficiency until some fierceness penetrates the veil. "The rift of cordial seas" one dithers in is another representation of complacency roughened: warmth and comfort broken.

The play and interplay of words is notable throughout this sonnet. The word *native* is obvious in Nativity. The word *head* and the words *capital* and *decapitate* have related multiple meanings; the word *cordial* belongs to heart, and *crucial,* which is of the cross and crucifixion, has connotations of risk and crisis. Just how the continuous fabric of language which constitutes this poem is adequately woven out of the elements of vocabulary, syntax, rhetoric, rhyme, and the modulating effects of metrical arrangement is a matter too subtle to be made perfectly patent by the craft of explication. Then, of course, it may be questionable whether this difficult kind of poem permits the reader to apprehend imaginatively, and readily enough, the experience it is intended to afford him.

To return to the first verse: The locks are down when the head is crammed between the knees. Think perhaps of the posture of the buried dead, as in Philip Freneau's poem. See also an illustration from Blake's *Jerusalem,* reproduced in Mark Schorer's *William Blake.*

YVOR WINTERS

AN ODE ON THE DESPOILERS OF LEARNING IN AN AMERICAN UNIVERSITY 1947[1]

This was our heritage:
In Learning's monument
To study, and teach the young,
Until our days were spent;
To reëmbody mind
In age succeeding age,
That some few men might see,
Though, mostly, men were blind;
To hold what men had wrung
From struggle to atone
For man's stupidity,
In labor and alone.

But now the insensate, calm
Performers of the hour,
Cold, with cold eye and palm,
Desiring trivial power,
And terror-struck within
At their own emptiness,
Move in. As they move in,
Slow and invidious,
They pause and calculate,
Then, as such beings use,

1. *Poetry,* October 1947, LXXI, 12–13. Copyright, 1947, by Yvor Winters. Revised by author and reprinted by permission of author.

With long-perfected hate,
Strike the immortal Muse.

What art of prose or verse
Should bring their like to book?
What consecrated curse
And pious rhetoric?
Not one: we need but look.
For these have come too far:
They stand here, coarse and lined,
And permanent as stone,
In the final light of mind.
The body politic
Of Learning is its own
Inscrutable old Bar.

KENNETH FEARING

DIRGE[1]

1–2–3 was the number he played but today the number came 3–2–1; bought
his Carbide at 30 and it went to 29; had the favorite at Bowie but the
track was slow—
O, executive type, would you like to drive a floating power, knee-action, silk-
upholstered six? Wed a Hollywood star? Shoot the course in 58? Draw
to the ace, king, jack?
O, fellow with a will who won't take no, watch out for three cigarettes on the
same, single match; O democratic voter born in August under Mars,
beware of liquidated rails—
Denouement to denouement, he took a personal pride in the certain, certain
way he lived his own, private life,
but nevertheless, they shut off his gas; nevertheless, the bank foreclosed;
nevertheless, the landlord called; nevertheless the radio broke,
And twelve o'clock arrived just once too often,
just the same, he wore one grey tweed suit, bought one straw hat, drank
one straight Scotch, walked one short step, took one long look, drew
one deep breath,
just one too many
And wow he died as wow he lived,

---

1. From Kenneth Fearing, *Poems* (Dynamo Press, 1935). Reprinted by permission of the author.

going whop to the office and blooie home to sleep and biff got married
and bam had children and oof got fired,
zowie did he live and zowie did he die.
With who the hell are you at the corner of his casket
and where the hell are we going on the right hand
silver knob, and who the hell cares walking second
from the end with an American Beauty wreath
from why the hell not.
Very much missed by the circulation staff of the New York Evening Post;
deeply, deeply mourned by the B.M.T.,
Wham, Mr. Roosevelt; pow, Sears Roebuck; awk, big dipper; bop, summer rain;
bong, Mr., bong, Mr., bong, Mr., bong.

OGDEN NASH

VERY LIKE A WHALE[1]

One thing that literature would be greatly the better for
Would be a more restricted employment by authors of simile and metaphor.
Authors of all races, be they Greeks, Romans, Teutons or Celts,
Can't seem just to say that anything is the thing it is but have to go out of their way to say that it is like something else.
What does it mean when we are told
That the Assyrian came down like a wolf on the fold?
In the first place, George Gordon Byron had had enough experience
To know that it probably wasn't just one Assyrian, it was a lot of Assyrians.
However, as too many arguments are apt to induce apoplexy and thus hinder longevity,
We'll let it pass as one Assyrian for the sake of brevity.
Now then, this particular Assyrian, the one whose cohorts were gleaming in purple and gold,
Just what does the poet mean when he says he came down like a wolf on the fold?
In heaven and earth more than is dreamed of in our philosophy there are a great many things,
But I don't imagine that among them there is a wolf with purple and gold cohorts or purple and gold anythings.
No, no, Lord Byron, before I'll believe that this Assyrian was actually like a wolf I must have some kind of proof;

1. From *Many Long Years Ago,* by Ogden Nash, by permission of Little, Brown & Co.

Did he run on all fours and did he have a hairy tail and a big red mouth and
big white teeth and did he say Woof woof woof?
Frankly I think it very unlikely, and all you were entitled to say, at the
very most,
Was that the Assyrian cohorts came down like a lot of Assyrian cohorts
about to destroy the Hebrew host.
But that wasn't fancy enough for Lord Byron, oh dear me no, he had to
invent a lot of figures of speech and then interpolate them.
With the result that whenever you mention Old Testament soldiers to
people they say Oh yes, they're the ones that a lot of wolves dressed
up in gold and purple ate them.
That's the kind of thing that's being done all the time by poets, from
Homer to Tennyson;
They're always comparing ladies to lilies and veal to venison,
And they always say things like that the snow is a white blanket after a
winter storm.
Oh it is, is it, all right then, you sleep under a six-inch blanket of snow
and I'll sleep under a half-inch blanket of unpoetical blanket
material and we'll see which one keeps warm,
And after that maybe you'll begin to comprehend dimly
What I mean by too much metaphor and simile.

THE PURIST[1]

I give you now Professor Twist,
A conscientious scientist.
Trustees exclaimed, "He never bungles!"
And sent him off to distant jungles.
Camped on a tropic riverside,
One day he missed his loving bride.
She had, the guide informed him later,
Been eaten by an alligator.
Professor Twist could not but smile.
"You mean," he said, "a crocodile."

1. From *I'm a Stranger Here Myself* by Ogden Nash. Copyright, 1938, by Ogden Nash. Reprinted by permission of Little, Brown and Company.

W. H. AUDEN

MUSÉE DES BEAUX ARTS[1]

About suffering they were never wrong,
The Old Masters: how well they understood
Its human position; how it takes place
While someone else is eating or opening a window or just walking dully along;
How, when the aged are reverently, passionately waiting
For the miraculous birth, there always must be
Children who did not specially want it to happen, skating
On a pond at the edge of the wood:
They never forgot
That even the dreadful martyrdom must run its course
Anyhow in a corner, some untidy spot
Where the dogs go on with their doggy life and the torturer's horse
Scratches its innocent behind on a tree.

In Brueghel's *Icarus,* for instance: how everything turns away
Quite leisurely from the disaster; the ploughman may
Have heard the splash, the forsaken cry,
But for him it was not an important failure; the sun shone
As it had to on the white legs disappearing into the green
Water; and the expensive delicate ship that must have seen
Something amazing, a boy falling out of the sky,
Had somewhere to get to and sailed calmly on.

PETITION[2]

Sir, no man's enemy, forgiving all
But will his negative inversion, be prodigal:
Send to us power and light, a sovereign touch
Curing the intolerable neural itch,
The exhaustion of weaning, the liar's quinsy,
And the distortions of ingrown virginity.
Prohibit sharply the rehearsed response
And gradually correct the coward's stance;
Cover in time with beams those in retreat
That, spotted, they turn though the reverse were great;

---

1. From *Another Time.* Copyright, 1940, by W. H. Auden. Reprinted by permission of Random House, Inc.

2. From *Collected Poetry of W. H. Auden.* Copyright, 1945, by W. H. Auden. Reprinted by permission of Random House, Inc.

Publish each healer that in city lives
Or country houses at the end of drives;
Harrow the house of the dead; look shining at
New styles of architecture, a change of heart.

IN MEMORY OF W. B. YEATS[1]

d. Jan. 1939

I

He disappeared in the dead of winter:
The brooks were frozen, the air-ports almost deserted,
And snow disfigured the public statues;
The mercury sank in the mouth of the dying day.
O all the instruments agree
The day of his death was a dark cold day.

Far from his illness
The wolves ran on through the evergreen forests,
The peasant river was untempted by the fashionable quays;
By mourning tongues
The death of the poet was kept from his poems.

But for him it was his last afternoon as himself,
An afternoon of nurses and rumours;
The provinces of his body revolted,
The squares of his mind were empty,
Silence invaded the suburbs,
The current of his feeling failed: he became his admirers.

Now he is scattered among a hundred cities
And wholly given over to unfamiliar affections;
To find his happiness in another kind of wood
And be punished under a foreign code of conscience
The words of a dead man
Are modified in the guts of the living.

But in the importance and noise of to-morrow
When the brokers are roaring like beasts on the floor of the Bourse,
And the poor have the sufferings to which they are fairly accustomed,
And each in the cell of himself is almost convinced of his freedom;
A few thousand will think of this day
As one thinks of a day when one did something slightly unusual.

1. Copyright, 1945, by W. H. Auden. Reprinted by permission of Random House, Inc.

O all the instruments agree
The day of his death was a dark cold day.

II

You were silly like us: your gift survived it all;
The parish of rich women, physical decay,
Yourself; mad Ireland hurt you into poetry.
Now Ireland has her madness and her weather still,
For poetry makes nothing happen: it survives
In the valley of its saying where executives
Would never want to tamper; it flows south
From ranches of isolation and the busy griefs,
Raw towns that we believe and die in; it survives,
A way of happening, a mouth.

III

Earth, receive an honoured guest;
William Yeats is laid to rest:
Let the Irish vessel lie
Emptied of its poetry.

Time that is intolerant
Of the brave and innocent,
And indifferent in a week
To a beautiful physique,

Worships language and forgives
Everyone by whom it lives;
Pardons cowardice, conceit,
Lays its honours at their feet.

Time that with this strange excuse
Pardoned Kipling and his views,
And will pardon Paul Claudel,
Pardons him for writing well.

In the nightmare of the dark
All the dogs of Europe bark,
And the living nations wait,
Each sequestered in its hate;

Intellectual disgrace
Stares from every human face,
And the seas of pity lie
Locked and frozen in each eye.

Follow, poet, follow right
To the bottom of the night,
With your unconstraining voice
Still persuade us to rejoice;

With the farming of a verse
Make a vineyard of the curse,
Sing of human unsuccess
In a rapture of distress;

In the deserts of the heart
Let the healing fountain start,
In the prison of his days
Teach the free man how to praise.

UNDER WHICH LYRE[1]

A Reactionary Tract for the Times
Phi Beta Kappa Poem. Harvard. 1946

Ares at last has quit the field,
The bloodstains on the bushes yield
To seeping showers,
And in their convalescent state
The fractured towns associate
With summer flowers.

Encamped upon the college plain
Raw veterans already train
As freshman forces;
Instructors with sarcastic tongue
Shepherd the battle-weary young
Through basic courses.

Among bewildering appliances
For mastering the arts and sciences
They stroll or run,
And nerves that never flinched at slaughter
Are shot to pieces by the shorter
Poems of Donne.

1. From *Nones*. Copyright, 1946, by W. H. Auden. Reprinted by permission of Random House, Inc.

Professors back from secret missions
Resume their proper eruditions,
Though some regret it;
They like their dictaphones a lot,
They met some big wheels, and do not
Let you forget it.

But Zeus' inscrutable decree
Permits the will-to-disagree
To be pandemic,
Ordains that vaudeville shall preach
And every commencement speech
Be a polemic.

Let Ares doze, that other war
Is instantly declared once more
'Twixt those who follow
Precocious Hermes all the way
And those who without qualms obey
Pompous Apollo.

Brutal like all Olympic games,
Though fought with smiles and Christian names
And less dramatic,
This dialectic strife between
The civil gods is just as mean,
And more fanatic.

What high immortals do in mirth
Is life and death on Middle Earth;
Their a-historic
Antipathy forever gripes
All ages and somatic types,
The sophomoric

Who face the future's darkest hints
With giggles or with prairie squints
As stout as Cortez,
And those who like myself turn pale
As we approach with ragged sail
The fattening forties.

The sons of Hermes love to play,
And only do their best when they
Are told they oughtn't;

Apollo's children never shrink
From boring jobs but have to think
Their work important.

Related by antithesis,
A compromise between us is
Impossible:
Respect perhaps but friendship never:
Falstaff the fool confronts forever
The prig Prince Hal.

If he would leave the self alone,
Apollo's welcome to the throne,
Fasces and falcons;
He loves to rule, has always done it;
The earth would soon, did Hermes run it,
Be like the Balkans.

But jealous of our god of dreams,
His common-sense in secret schemes
To rule the heart;
Unable to invent the lyre,
Creates with simulated fire
Official art.

And when he occupies a college,
Truth is replaced by Useful Knowledge;
He pays particular
Attention to Commercial Thought,
Public Relations, Hygiene, Sport,
In his curricula.

Athletic, extrovert and crude,
For him, to work in solitude
Is the offence,
The goal a populous Nirvana:
His shield bears this device: *Mens sana*
Qui mal y pense.

Today his arms, we must confess,
From Right to Left have met success,
His banners wave
From Yale to Princeton, and the news
From Broadway to the Book Reviews
Is very grave.

His radio Homers all day long
In over-Whitmanated song
That does not scan,
With adjectives laid end to end,
Extol the doughnut and commend
The Common Man.

His, too, each homely lyric thing
On sport or spousal love or spring
Or dogs or dusters,
Invented by some court-house bard
For recitation by the yard
In filibusters.

To him ascend the prize orations
And sets of fugal variations
On some folk-ballad,
While dietitians sacrifice
A glass of prune-juice or a nice
Marsh-mallow salad.

Charged with his compound of sensational
Sex plus some undenominational
Religious matter,
Enormous novels by co-eds
Rain down on our defenceless heads
Till our teeth chatter.

In fake Hermetic uniforms
Behind our battle-line, in swarms
That keep alighting,
His existentialists declare
That they are in complete despair,
Yet go on writing.

No matter; He shall be defied;
White Aphrodite is on our side:
What though his threat
To organize us grow more critical?
Zeus willing, we, the unpolitical,
Shall beat him yet.

Lone scholars, sniping from the walls
Of learned periodicals,
Our facts defend,

Our intellectual marines,
Landing in little magazines
Capture a trend.

By night our student Underground
At cocktail parties whisper round
From ear to ear;
Fat figures in the public eye
Collapse next morning, ambushed by
Some witty sneer.

In our morale must lie our strength:
So, that we may behold at length
Routed Apollo's
Battalions melt away like fog,
Keep well the Hermetic Decalogue,
Which runs as follows:—

Thou shalt not do as the dean pleases,
Thou shalt not write thy doctor's thesis
On education,
Thou shalt not worship projects nor
Shalt thou or thine bow down before
Administration.

Thou shalt not answer questionnaires
Or quizzes upon World-Affairs,
Nor with compliance
Take any test. Thou shalt not sit
With statisticians nor commit
A social science.

Thou shalt not be on friendly terms
With guys in advertising firms,
Nor speak with such
As read the Bible for its prose,
Nor, above all, make love to those
Who wash too much.

Thou shalt not live within thy means
Nor on plain water and raw greens.
If thou must choose

Between the chances, choose the odd;
Read *The New Yorker,* trust in God;
And take short views.

STEPHEN SPENDER

THE EXPRESS[1]

After the first powerful plain manifesto
The black statement of pistons, without more fuss
But gliding like a queen, she leaves the station.
Without bowing and with restrained unconcern
She passes the houses which humbly crowd outside,
The gasworks and at last the heavy page
Of death, printed by gravestones in the cemetery.
Beyond the town there lies the open country
Where, gathering speed, she acquires mystery,
The luminous self-possession of ships on ocean.
It is now she begins to sing—at first quite low
Then loud, and at last with a jazzy madness—
The song of her whistle screaming at curves,
Of deafening tunnels, brakes, innumerable bolts.
And always light, aerial, underneath
Goes the elate metre of her wheels.
Streaming through metal landscape on her lines
She plunges new eras of wild happiness
Where speed throws up strange shapes, broad curves
And parallels clean like the steel of guns.
At last, further than Edinburgh or Rome,
Beyond the crest of the world, she reaches night
Where only a low streamline brightness
Of phosphorus on the tossing hills is white.
Ah, like a comet through flame she moves entranced
Wrapt in her music no bird song, no, nor bough
Breaking with honey buds, shall ever equal.

THE LANDSCAPE NEAR AN AERODROME[1]

More beautiful and soft than any moth
With burring furred antennae feeling its huge path
Through dusk, the air-liner with shut-off engines

Glides over suburbs and the sleeves set trailing tall
To point the wind. Gently, broadly, she falls,
Scarcely disturbing charted currents of air.

Lulled by descent, the travelers across sea
And across feminine land indulging its easy limbs
In miles of softness, now let their eyes trained by watching
Penetrate through dusk the outskirts of this town
Here where industry shows a fraying edge.
Here they may see what is being done.

Beyond the winking masthead light
And the landing-ground, they observe the outposts
Of work: chimneys like lank black fingers
Or figures frightening and mad: and squat buildings
With their strange air behind trees, like women's faces
Shattered by grief. Here where few houses
Moan with faint light behind their blinds
They remark the unhomely sense of complaint, like a dog
Shut out and shivering at the foreign moon.

In the last sweep of love, they pass over fields
Behind the aerodrome, where boys play all day
Hacking dead grass: whose cries, like wild birds,
Settle upon the nearest roofs
But soon are hid under the loud city.

Then, as they land, they hear the tolling bell
Reaching across the landscape of hysteria
To where, larger than all the charcoaled batteries
And imaged towers against the dying sky,
Religion stands, the church blocking the sun.

KARL SHAPIRO

UNIVERSITY[1]

To hurt the Negro and avoid the Jew
Is the curriculum. In mid-September
The entering boys, identified by hats,

1. Reprinted from *Person, Place and Thing,* copyright, 1942, by Karl Jay Shapiro. Reprinted by permission of Harcourt Brace and Company, Inc.

Wander in a maze of mannered brick
Where boxwood and magnolia brood
And columns with imperious stance
Like rows of ante-bellum girls
Eye them, outlanders.

In whited cells, on lawns equipped for peace,
Under the arch, and lofty banister,
Equals shake hands, unequals blankly pass;
The exemplary weather whispers, "Quiet, quiet"
And visitors on tiptoe leave
For the raw North, the unfinished West
As the young, detecting an advantage,
Practice a face.

Where, on their separate hill, the colleges,
Like manor houses of an older law,
Gaze down embankments on a land in fee,
The Deans, dry spinsters over family plate,
Ring out the English name like coin,
Humor the snob and lure the lout.
Within the precincts of this world
Poise is a club.

But on the neighboring range, misty and high,
The past is absolute; some luckless race
Dull with inbreeding and conformity
Wears out its heart, and comes barefoot and bad
For charity or jail. The scholar
Sanctions their obsolete disease;
The gentleman revolts with shame
At his ancestor.

And the true nobleman, once a democrat,
Sleeps on his private mountain. He was one
Whose thought was shapely and whose dream was broad;
This school he held his art and epitaph.
But now it takes from him his name,
Falls open like a dishonest look,
And shows us, rotted and endowed,
Its senile pleasure.

AUTO WRECK[1]

Its quick soft silver bell beating, beating,
And down the dark one ruby flare
Pulsing out red light like an artery,
The ambulance at top speed floating down
Past beacons and illuminated clocks
Wings in a heavy curve, dips down,
And brakes speed, entering the crowd.
The doors leap open, emptying light;
Stretchers are laid out, the mangled lifted
And stowed into the little hospital.
Then the bell, breaking the hush, tolls once,
And the ambulance with its terrible cargo
Rocking, slightly rocking, moves away,
As the doors, an afterthought, are closed.

We are deranged, walking among the cops
Who sweep glass and are large and composed.
One is still making notes under the light.
One with a bucket douches ponds of blood
Into the street and gutter.
One hangs lanterns on the wrecks that cling,
Empty husks of locusts, to iron poles.

Our throats were tight as tourniquets,
Our feet were bound with splints, but now
Like convalescents intimate and gauche,
We speak through sickly smiles and warn
With the stubborn saw of common sense,
The grim joke and the banal resolution.
The traffic moves around with care,
But we remain, touching a wound
That opens to our richest horror.

Already old, the question Who shall die?
Becomes unspoken Who is innocent?
For death in war is done by hands;
Suicide has cause and still birth, logic.
But this invites the occult mind,
Cancels our physics with a sneer,
And spatters all we knew of dénouement
Across the expedient and wicked stones.

1. From *Person, Place and Thing,* copyright, 1942, by Karl Jay Shapiro. Reprinted by permission of Harcourt, Brace and Company, Inc.

CHRISTMAS EVE: AUSTRALIA[1]

The wind blows hot. English and foreign birds
And insects different as their fish excite
The would-be calm. The usual flocks and herds
Parade in permanent quiet out of sight,
And there one crystal like a grain of light
Sticks in the crucible of day and cools.
A cloud burnt to a crisp at some great height
Sips at the dark condensing in deep pools.

I smoke and read my Bible and chew gum,
Thinking of Christ and Christmas of last year,
And what those quizzical soldiers standing near
Ask of the war and Christmases to come,
And sick of causes and the tremendous blame
Curse lightly and pronounce your serious name.

ON SHAPIRO'S *CHRISTMAS EVE: AUSTRALIA*

DAVID DAICHES[2]

"Christmas Eve: Australia," a sonnet with a most impressive manipulation of imagery, adroit and effective variation of pauses within the line, and that combination of classical gravity with irrepressible modernity that is one of Shapiro's most attractive characteristics, is a remarkable little poem. Rarely in modern poetry is the cadence handled as well as it is here, the rise and fall of the phrases matching and countering each other with self-concealing skill. It has to be read aloud before this quality is fully appreciated. The changes in tempo (not a modern virtue, nor one conspicuous in the run of Shapiro's work) are equally impressive. The following few lines may bear out some of my points:

The wind blows hot. English and foreign birds
And insects different as their fish excite
The would-be calm. The usual flocks and herds
Parade in permanent quiet out of sight . . .

The most attractive thing here is that "usual." The air almost of negligence which that adjective gives the sentence explains in part its poetic effectiveness. And then there is the ironic gravity of "parade," the institutional finality of "permanent," and the almost-humorous, almost paradoxical "out of

1. From *V-Letter and Other Poems*, copyright, 1944, Karl Shapiro. Reprinted by permission of Harcourt, Brace and Company, Inc.
2. "The Poetry of Karl Shapiro," *Poetry: A Magazine of Verse*, LXVI (August, 1945), 267–269. Copyright, 1945, by David Daiches.

sight." And if the reader thinks that the pauses in these lines are as unvaried as they seem to the eye, I would ask him to read these lines aloud. He would then discover the important difference between

> And insects different as their fish excite
> The would-be calm

and

> Parade in permanent quiet out of sight

with its continuous movement, its stately motion in the first half and its sudden burst of speed, done, one might perhaps say, with a suppressed giggle, at "out of sight." The parade is of interest because you *don't* see it—but you are aware of its presence. The turn in the sestet is worth attention:

> I smoke and read my Bible and chew gum
> Thinking of Christ and Christmas of last year,
> And what those quizzical soldiers standing near
> Ask of the war and Christmases to come,
> And sick of causes and the tremendous blame
> Curse lightly and pronounce your serious name.

This is skillful stuff. One scarcely needs to point out the double effect of the last line, both drawing the poem to a personal resolution—in the best tradition of the sonnet form, which ought to stand balanced on its concluding line, or couplet, depending on the rhyme-scheme—and at the same time epitomizing the mood of the whole poem by juxtaposing in the one line the two poles of that mood: "curse lightly" and "*serious* name." The Bible and chewing gum and (ironically but significantly) "Christ and Christmas of last year" are earlier aspects of that contrast here resolved.

DYLAN THOMAS

LIGHT BREAKS WHERE NO SUN SHINES[1]

Light breaks where no sun shines;
Where no sea runs, the waters of the heart
Push in their tides;
And, broken ghosts with glowworms in their heads,
The things of light
File through the flesh where no flesh decks the bones.

1. From *Selected Writings.* Copyright, 1939, 1946, by New Directions, 333 Sixth Avenue, New York.

A candle in the thighs
Warms youth and seed and burns the seeds of age;
Where no seed stirs,
The fruit of man unwrinkles in the stars,
Bright as a fig;
Where no wax is, the candle shows its hairs.

Dawn breaks behind the eyes;
From poles of skull and toe the windy blood
Slides like a sea;
Nor fenced, nor staked, the gushers of the sky
Spout to the rod
Divining in a smile the oil of tears.

Night in the sockets rounds,
Like some pitch moon, the limit of the globes;
Day lights the bone;
Where no cold is, the skinning gales unpin
The winter's robes;
The film of spring is hanging from the lids.

Light breaks on secret lots,
On tips of thought where thoughts smell in the rain;
When logics die,
The secret of the soil grows through the eye,
And blood jumps in the sun;
Above the waste allotments the dawn halts.

THE FORCE THAT THROUGH THE GREEN FUSE DRIVES THE FLOWER[1]

The force that through the green fuse drives the flower
Drives my green age; that blasts the roots of trees
Is my destroyer.
And I am dumb to tell the crooked rose
My youth is bent by the same wintry fever.

The force that drives the water through the rocks
Drives my red blood; that dries the mouthing streams
Turns mine to wax.
And I am dumb to mouth unto my veins
How at the mountain spring the same mouth sucks.

1. From *Selected Writings.* Copyright, 1939, 1946, by New Directions, 333 Sixth Avenue, New York.

The hand that whirls the water in the pool
Stirs the quicksand; that ropes the blowing wind
Hauls my shroud sail.
And I am dumb to tell the hanging man
How of my clay is made the hangman's lime.

The lips of time leech to the fountain head;
Love drips and gathers, but the fallen blood
Shall calm her sores.
And I am dumb to tell a weather's wind
How time has ticked a heaven round the stars.
And I am dumb to tell the lover's tomb
How at my sheet goes the same crooked worm.

ON THOMAS' *THE FORCE THAT THROUGH THE GREEN FUSE DRIVES THE FLOWER* [1]

G. GIOVANNINI

THOMAS' POEM has a highly wrought and closely knit metaphorical surface carefully disguising meaning, and in such poetry what is extracted as basic meaning may be only another surface disguising a meaning felt rather than understood conceptually. The explication which follows attempts to uncover the meaning next to the metaphorical surface of Thomas' poem, and it leaves to one side the felt implications, largely Freudian, which commentators have found in his early verse.

The character speaking in the poem is a youth ("my green age") who discovers that life predicates death, and stands bewildered and inarticulate ("I am dumb") before man and nature informed by a paradoxical principle. The meaning is a variation on an old theme: life (and love) cankered by death (cf. Blake's "The Sick Rose"). The variation consists of the predication that life and death issue from the same cause—"The force" in the poem, a force in an obscure way associated with God; for in the first line of stanza 2 there is an oblique allusion to *Exodus,* XVII, 6, where God draws water out of a rock, and in the first line of stanza 3 an allusion to *John,* v, 4, where the angel of God stirs the water in the pool of Bethesda. The theme may be seen developed in the first three lines of each of the first three stanzas in a powerful manner by a statement immediately followed, after the semicolon, by a counterstatement. The life-giving force driving through the stem ("green fuse") of the flower and the youth's body also "blasts" the tree (the verb echoes "fuse" now understood in its literal sense) and kills the man. The

1. From *The Explicator,* VIII (June, 1950), 59–60. By permission of the authors and of the Editors of *The Explicator*.

syntactic pattern of the first three lines carries the paradoxical meaning; for the counterstatement (death) is grammatically a coordinate and integral part of the statement (life), a conjunction of a meaningful kind seen in small in the phrases (e.g., the oxymoron "wintry fever"). This same pattern and meaning are repeated exactly in the next two stanzas. The force driving the water, traditionally a symbol of life, and the blood also dries the streams at their source ("mouthing") and congeals in death the speaker's life-streams ("turns mine to wax"). In the third stanza the dynamism of the force, now "The hand," is in terms of rapid movement (whirlpool), and of swift time; for "The hand that whirls" seems to suggest a clock, and "quicksand" the swift passage of time as in an hourglass. But the same force checks ("ropes") the movement of the wind and kills ("Hauls my shroud sail"). In the fourth stanza the syntactic pattern is varied a little, and so is the meaning, the paradox of life-death being here translated as love-death. The theme is developed in its cosmic aspects: creation ("The lips of time") passionately sucks ("leech") its being from a source, and love "gathers," possibly in the sense in which Hopkins uses the verb in "God's Grandeur": "The world is charged with the grandeur of God . . . It gathers to a greatness." But with reference to the counterstatement, where death ("fallen blood") again appears, "gathers" has an appropriate medical sense: love is imaged as a swollen suppurating wound, from which the issue of blood signifies the stillness of death ("Shall calm her sores").

The refrain, "And I am dumb," functions as illustration everywhere except in the fourth stanza: the speaker carries death within him; for though he is young and avidly experiences life ("at the mountain spring the same mouth sucks"), his body bends toward death, it is attacked by the "crooked worm" and is the making of the quicklime of the grave ("hangman's lime"). The refrain in the fourth stanza refers not to death, but to the ecstasy of love ticking "a heaven round the stars"; but the meaning here is countered by death in the final refrain which immediately follows, and the poem ends effectively with the two sides of the thematic paradox formally and precisely juxtaposed. All the refrains have in common the sense of the speaker's isolation, of his inability to communicate and establish a sympathetic contact with an inexplicable universe. The isolation is intense; for in the second refrain the young man is unable to communicate even with himself ("dumb to mouth unto my veins"). The theme of this poem is more succinctly and abstractly stated in a passage from Thomas' "A Process in the Weather": "the womb Drives in a death as life leaks out"—a theme which can be glossed by Donne's sermon *Death's Duell* (cf. J. L. Sweeney, Intro., Thomas' *Selected Writings*): "wee celebrate our own funeralls with cries, even at our birth."

S. F. JOHNSON

Thomas' "force" is a generalized *élan vital,* the natural vitality that both creates and destroys us. Human change is but a small part of the great cycle of natural change and is effected by the same simple cause. The opening lines of each stanza present four variations on this implied theme; the two-line refrains stress the limits of human communication by detailing the senses in which even a poet is "dumb."

I. The force is an explosive. Stalks of plants are fuses through which the explosive power is driven; flowers and foliage are products of an explosion which creates on condition of mortality. The poet is "green" (young) and, unlike non-human organisms, is aware that birth is the beginning of death. The refrain emphasizes his humanity, his ability to communicate complex meanings only to other humans. Here the explosive image is translated into human terms (fever). Fever is wintry since it hastens human age and death just as the first frost hastens vegetative age and death.

II. The vitality of growing things is extended to inanimate nature, where again the same force drives and dries (the omission of a phoneme is the difference between life and death). The poet's streams are blood-streams; the pliability and stickiness of wax applies equally to the coagulation of the blood at death and to the drying-up of mud in a stream-bed. Refrain: the force is personified as a mouth (connecting with "leech" in stanza 4). "Mouth" is used in three ways here ("tell" is altered in this refrain alone in order to give scope to the play on words): streams "mouth" into larger streams, into the sea; the poet "mouths" (declaims) to those who can (will) hear him; the "mouth," adapted to giving out and taking in, symbolizes the elemental force that creates and destroys.

III. The force, here as the hand of God, keeps the elements in motion: water, earth, and air, connecting with fire in stanza 1. Of course it controls the poet, now a ship, consistent with the sea imagery of the stanza; the sail, the activated part, is the libido. Refrain: the poet can communicate only with the living, part of whose clay, in various excremental forms, has long since re-entered the natural cycle and helped compose its products.

IV. The force is time itself. The mouth symbol is developed in the verb "leech." The reduction of the life-force from anthropomorphic God to a voracious, blind mouth emphasizes the naturalistic attitude in the poem. Time's leeching lips are juxtaposed with love, the only emotion named in the poem. Love acts in such a way as to place it, with the life-force, at the very pulse of life; it drips and gathers, like blood at a leech wound, subject to the involuntary pulsation of all nature. The supposedly beneficial effects of blood-letting are paralleled with the calming effect of the sexual manifestation of love. The refrain contrasts chillingly with the warmth of love and emphasizes man's small place in the well-integrated, clockwork universe.

Refrain: The facts of death support the poet's consistent view of man's place in nature. The refrain tightens the poem by drawing on the power of earlier elements (lover's tomb and hanging man, crooked worm and crooked rose, worm and leech, sheet and shroud sail) and by reiterating the central notion that everything is subject to decay.

The poem is saved from sentimentality, a risk it runs, by its tightly consistent attitude, which unifies images drawn from widely disparate spheres. The vocabulary, as in most of Thomas' poems, is largely restricted to common Anglo-Saxon words, predominantly monosyllabic, arranged in a pattern so slowly paced that the reader is forced to explore the range of meanings of these words, revitalized by their unusual contexts. The poet is not dumb to tell his readers what he is about: "from the first declension of the flesh I learnt man's tongue . . . To shade and knit anew the patch of words Left by the dead who . . . Need no word's warmth" (from "Love's First Fever"); "I write . . . Not for the towering dead . . . But for the lovers . . . Who pay no praise or wages Nor heed my craft or art" ("In My Craft").

JOHN MALCOLM BRINNIN

VIEWS OF THE FAVORITE COLLEGES[1]

Approaching by the gate, (Class of '79,
All dead) the unimpressed new scholars find
Halls of archaic brick and, if it is April
Three dazzling magnolias behind bars, like lions.

Unsettling winds among the pillars of wisdom
Assure them of harmonious extremes,
However academic. The bells, in key,
Covered with singing birds, ring on the hour.

Towering, but without aspiration, the campanile
Is known to sway an inch in a high wind;
But that, like the statue's changeable complexion,
Is natural. To find the unnatural,

Gradually absorb the industry
Of ten o'clock: the embryo pig slit through
With the proper instruments by embryos;
And Sophocles cut, for speed, with a blue pencil.

1. Reprinted from *No Arch, No Triumph,* by John Malcolm Brinnin; by permission of Alfred A. Knopf, Inc. Copyright, 1945, by John Malcolm Brinnin.

Prehensile sophomores in the tree of learning
Stare at the exiled blossoming trees, vaguely puzzled,
The lecturer, especially if bearded,
Enhances those druidical undertones.

What is the terminus of books? sing the birds.
Tell us about Sophocles! cry the trees.
And a crazy child on roller-skates skates through
The campus like a one-man thunderstorm.

PETER VIERECK

BLINDMAN'S BUFF[1]

Night-watchmen think of dawn and things auroral.
Clerks wistful for Bermudas think of coral.
The poet in New York still thinks of laurel.
(But lovers think of death and touch each other
As if to prove that love is still alive.)

The Martian space-crew, in an Earthward dive,
Think of their sweet unearthly earth Up There,
Where darling monsters romp in airless air.
(Two lovers think of death and touch each other,
Fearing that day when only one's alive.)

We think of cash, but cash does not arrive.
We think of fun, but fate will not connive.
We never mention death. Do we survive?
(The lovers think of death and touch each other
To live their love while love is still alive.)

Prize-winners are so avid when they strive;
They race so far; they pile their toys so high
Only a cad would trip them. Yet they die.
(The lovers think of death and touch each other;
Of all who live, these are the most alive.)

When all the lemming-realists contrive
To swim—where to?—in life's enticing tide,
Only a fool would stop and wait outside.

1. Reprinted from *Terror and Decorum* by Peter Viereck; copyright, 1948, by Peter Viereck; used by permission of the publishers, Charles Scribner's Sons.

(The lovers stop and wait and touch each other.
Who twinly think of death are twice alive.)

Plump creatures smack their lips and think they thrive;
The hibernating bear, but half alive,
Dreams of free honey in a stingless hive.
He thinks of life at every lifeless breath.
(The lovers think of death.)

ROBERT LOWELL

WHERE THE RAINBOW ENDS[1]

I saw the sky descending, black and white,
Not blue, on Boston where the winters wore
The skulls to jack-o'-lanterns on the slates,
And Hunger's skin-and-bone retrievers tore
The chickadee and shrike. The thorn tree waits
Its victim and tonight
The worms will eat the deadwood to the foot
Of Ararat: the scythers, Time and Death,
Helmed locusts, move upon the tree of breath;
The wild ingrafted olive and the root

Are withered, and a winter drifts to where
The Pepperpot, ironic rainbow, spans
Charles River and its scales of scorched-earth miles
I saw my city in the Scales, the pans
Of judgment rising and descending. Piles
Of dead leaves char the air—
And I am a red arrow on this graph
Of Revelations. Every dove is sold.
The Chapel's sharp-shinned eagle shifts its hold
On serpent-Time, the rainbow's epitaph.

In Boston serpents whistle at the cold.
The victim climbs the altar steps and sings:
"Hosannah to the lion, lamb, and beast

1. From *Lord Weary's Castle,* copyright, 1944, 1946, by Robert Lowell. Reprinted by permission of Harcourt, Brace and Company, Inc.

Who fans the furnace-face of IS with wings:
I breathe the ether of my marriage feast."
At the high altar, gold
And a fair cloth. I kneel and the wings beat
My cheek. What can the dove of Jesus give
You now but wisdom, exile? Stand and live,
The dove has brought an olive branch to eat.

ON LOWELL'S *WHERE THE RAINBOW ENDS*[1]

RANDALL JARRELL

"Where the Rainbow Ends" describes in apocalyptic terms the wintry, Calvinist, capitalist—Mr. Lowell has Weber's belief in the connection of capitalism and Calvinism—dead end of God's covenant with man, a frozen Boston where even the cold-blooded serpents "whistle at the cold." (The poems often use cold as a plain and physically correct symbol for what is constricted or static.) There "the scythers, Time and Death, / Helmed locusts, move upon the tree of breath," of the spirit of man; a bridge curves over Charles River like an ironic parody of the rainbow's covenant; both "the wild ingrafted olive and its root / Are withered" [these are Paul's terms for the Judaism of the Old Law and the Gentile Christianity grafted upon it]; "every dove [the Holy Ghost, the bringer of the olive leaf to the Ark] is sold" for commercialized, legalized sacrifice. The whole system seems an abstract, rationalized "graph of Revelations," of the last accusation and judgment brought against man now that "the Chapel's sharp-shinned eagle shifts its hold / On serpent-Time, the rainbow's epitaph." This last line means what the last line in "The Quaker Graveyard"—"The Lord survives the rainbow of His will"—means; both are inexpressibly menacing, since they show the covenant as something that binds only us, as something abrogated merely by the passage of time, as a closed system opening not into liberation but into infinite and overwhelming possibility; they have something of the terror, but none of the pity, of Blake's "Time is the mercy of Eternity."

Then the worshipper, like a victim, climbs to the altar of the terrible I AM, to breathe there the rarefied and intolerable ether of his union with the divinity of the Apocalypse; he despairs even of the wings that beat against his cheek: "What can the dove of Jesus give / You now but wisdom, exile?" When the poem has reached this point of the most extreme closure, when the infinite grace that atones and liberates is seen as no more than the bitter and useless wisdom of the exile, it opens with a rush of acceptant joy into: "Stand and live, / The dove has brought an olive branch to eat." The

1. From *The Nation,* CLXIV (Jan. 18, 1947), 74–75. Reprinted by permission of Randall Jarrell.

dove of Jesus brings to the worshipper the olive branch that shows him that the flood has receded, opening the whole earth for him; it is the olive branch of peace and reconciliation, the olive branch that he is "to eat" as a symbol of the eaten flesh of Christ, of atonement, identification, and liberation. Both the old covenant and the new still hold, nothing has changed: here as they were and will be are life and salvation.

II

SHORT STORIES

A PASSION IN THE DESERT[1]

HONORÉ DE BALZAC

"That show is dreadful," she cried, coming out of the menagerie of M. Martin. She had just been looking at that daring speculator "working with his hyena"—to speak in the style of the program.

"By what means," she continued, "can he have tamed these animals to such a point as to be certain of their affection for——."

"What seems to you a problem," said I, interrupting, "is really quite natural."

"Oh!" she cried, letting an incredulous smile wander over her lips.

"You think that beasts are wholly deprived of passion?" I asked her. "Quite the reverse; we may attribute to them all the vices arising in our own state of civilization."

She looked at me with an air of astonishment.

"Nevertheless," I continued, "the first time I saw M. Martin, I admit, that I, like you, did give an exclamation of surprise. I found myself next to an old soldier whose right leg was amputated, who had come in with me. His face had struck me. He had one of those fearless heads, stamped with the seal of warfare, and on which the battles of Napoleon are written. He had that frank good-humored expression which always impresses me favorably. He was without doubt one of those troopers who are surprised at nothing, who find matter for laughter in the contortions of a dying comrade, who bury or plunder him quite light-heartedly, who stand without flinching in the way of bullets; in fact, one of those men who waste no time in deliberation, and would not hesitate to make friends with the devil himself. After looking very attentively at the proprietor of the menagerie getting out of his box, my companion pursed up his lips with an air of mockery and contempt, with that peculiar and expressive twist which superior people assume to show that they are not to be taken in. Then when I was expatiating on the courage of M. Martin, he smiled, shook his head knowingly, and said, 'That's an old story.' "

1. Translation revised by Marion E. Porter.

"What do you mean 'an old story'?" I said. "If you would explain to me the mystery I should be very obliged."

"After a few minutes, during which we got to know each other, we went to dine at the first *restaurateur's* whose shop caught our eye. At dessert a bottle of champagne completely refreshed and brightened up the memories of this odd old soldier. He told me his story, and I saw he had every reason to exclaim, 'That's an old story!' "

When she got home, she teased me to such an extent and made so many promises, that I consented to write up for her the old soldier's confidences. Next day she received the following episode of an epic which might be entitled "The French in Egypt."

During the expedition in Upper Egypt under General Desaix,[2] a Provençal soldier fell into the hands of the Moors, and was taken by these Arabs into the deserts beyond the falls of the Nile.

In order to place a comfortable distance between themselves and the French army, the Moors made forced marches, and stopped only at night. They camped round a well hidden by palm trees under which they had previously concealed a store of provisions. Never thinking that the notion of flight would occur to their prisoner, they contented themselves with binding his hands, and after eating a few dates, and giving provender to their horses, they went to sleep.

When the brave Provençal saw that his enemies were no longer watching him, he made use of his teeth to steal a scimitar, fixed the blade between his knees, and cut the cords which prevented use of his hands; in a moment he was free. He at once seized a rifle and dagger, then taking the precaution to provide himself with a supply of dried dates, barley, and powder and shot, he fastened a scimitar to his waist, leaped onto a horse, and spurred on vigorously in the direction where he thought to find the French army. Being impatient to see a bivouac again, he pressed on the already tired horse at such speed that at last the poor animal died, its flanks lacerated, leaving the Frenchman alone in the desert.

After walking some time in the sand with all the courage of an escaping convict, the soldier was obliged to stop, as the day had already ended. In spite of the beauty of an oriental sky at night, he felt he had not strength enough to go on. Fortunately he had been able to find a small hill, on the summit of which a few palm trees shot up into the air; it was their verdure seen from afar which had brought hope and consolation to his heart. His fatigue was so great that he lay down upon a rock of granite, cut out by a whim of nature like a camp-bed; there he fell asleep without taking any precaution to defend himself while he slept. He had made the sacrifice of his life. His last thought was one of regret. He repented having left the Moors, whose nomad life seemed agreeable to him now that he was far from them and without help. He was

2. Louis Charles Antoine Desaix de Noygoux (1768–1800) conquered Upper Egypt and saved the day for Napoleon at Marengo, where he lost his life.

awakened by the sun, whose pitiless rays fell straight down on the granite and produced an intolerable heat—for he had had the stupidity to place himself inversely to the shadow thrown by the green and majestic heads of the palm trees. He looked at the solitary trees and shuddered—they reminded him of the graceful shafts crowned with foliage which characterize the Saracen columns in the cathedral of Arles.

But when, after counting the palm trees, he cast his eye around him, the most horrible despair swooped down upon his soul. Before him stretched an ocean without limit. The dark sand of the desert spread farther than sight could reach in every direction, and glittered like a sword-blade of steel struck with a bright light. It might have been a sea of looking-glass, or lakes melted together like a mirror. A fiery vapor rising in sheets made a perpetual whirlwind over the quivering land. The sky was lighted with an oriental splendor of hopeless purity, leaving naught for the imagination to desire. Heaven and earth were on fire.

The silence was awful in its wild and terrible majesty. Infinity, immensity, closed in upon the soul from every side. Not a cloud in the sky, not a breath in the air, not a break in the bosom of the sand, ever moving in diminutive waves; the horizon ended as at sea on a clear day, with one line of light, as clear as the cut of a sword.

The Provençal threw his arms around the trunk of one of the palm trees, as though it were the body of a friend, and then in the shelter of the thin straight shadow that the palm cast upon the granite, he wept. Then sitting down he remained as he was, contemplating with profound sadness the implacable scene, which was all he had to look upon. He cried aloud, to measure the solitude. His voice, lost in the hollows of the hill, sounded faintly, and aroused no echo—the echo was in his own heart. The Provençal was twenty-two years old—he loaded his carbine.

"There'll be time enough," he said to himself, laying on the ground the weapon which alone could bring him deliverance.

Looking by turns at the black expanse and the blue expanse, the soldier dreamed of France—he smelt with delight the gutters of Paris—he remembered the towns through which he had passed, the faces of his fellow-soldiers, the most minute details of his life. In his southern fancy he caught a glimpse of the stones of his beloved Provence in the play of the heat which waved over the spread sheet of the desert. Fearing the danger of this cruel mirage, he went down the side of the hill opposite to that by which he had come up the day before. His joy was great when he discovered a sort of grotto carved by nature into the immense fragments of granite which made up the base of the hill. The remains of a rug showed that this place of refuge had at one time been inhabited; at a short distance he saw some palm trees full of dates. Then the instinct which binds us to life awoke again in his heart. He hoped to live long enough to await the passing of some Arabs, or perhaps he might hear the sound of cannon; for at this time Bonaparte was traversing Egypt.

This thought gave him new life. The palm tree seemed to bend with the weight of the ripe fruit. He shook some of it down. When he tasted this unhoped-for manna, he felt sure that the palms had been cultivated by a former inhabitant—the savory, fresh meat of the dates was proof of the care of his predecessor. He passed suddenly from dark despair to an almost insane joy. He went up again to the top of the hill, and spent the rest of the day in cutting down one of the sterile palm trees, which the night before had served him for shelter. A vague memory made him think of the animals of the desert; and in case they might come to drink at the spring, visible from the base of the rocks but lost farther down, he resolved to guard himself from their visits by placing a barrier at the entrance of his hermitage.

In spite of his diligence, and the strength which the fear of being devoured asleep gave him, he was unable to cut the palm in pieces, though he succeeded in cutting it down. When at eventide the king of the desert fell, the sound of its fall resounded far and wide, like a moan in the solitude; the soldier shuddered as though he had heard some voice predicting woe.

But like an heir who does not long bewail a deceased parent, he tore off from this beautiful tree the tall broad green leaves which are its poetic adornment, and used them to mend the mat on which he was to sleep.

Fatigued by the heat and his work, he fell asleep under the red curtains of his wet cave. In the middle of the night his sleep was troubled by an extraordinary noise. He sat up, and the deep silence around him allowed him to distinguish the alternative accents of a breathing whose savage energy could not belong to a human creature.

A profound terror, increased still further by the darkness, the silence, and his waking image, froze his heart within him. He felt his hair almost stand on end, when by straining his eyes to their utmost he perceived through the shadows two faint yellow lights. At first he attributed these lights to the reflection of his own pupils, but soon the vivid brilliance of the night aided him gradually to distinguish the objects around him in the cave, and he beheld a huge animal lying but two steps from him. Was it a lion, a tiger, or a crocodile? The Provençal was not educated enough to know to what species his enemy belonged; but his fright was all the greater, as his ignorance led him to imagine all terrors at once. He endured a cruel torture, noting every variation of the breathing close to him without daring to make the slightest movement. An odor, pungent like that of a fox, but more penetrating, profounder—so to speak—filled the cave, and when the Provençal became aware of this, his terror reached its height, for he could not longer doubt the proximity of a terrible companion, whose royal dwelling served him for shelter.

Presently the reflection of the moon, descending on the horizon, lit up the den, rendering gradually visible and resplendent the spotted skin of a panther.

This lion of Egypt slept, curled up like a big dog, the peaceful possessor of a sumptuous niche at the gate of a hotel; its eyes opened for a moment and closed again; its face was turned toward the man. A thousand confused thoughts passed through the mind of the panther's prisoner; first the thought of killing it with a bullet from his gun, but he saw there was not enough distance between them for him to take proper aim—the barrel of the gun extended beyond the animal. And if it were to wake!—the thought made his limbs rigid. He listened to his own heart beating in the midst of the silence, and cursed the too violent pulsations which the flow of blood brought on, fearing to disturb that sleep which allowed him time to think of some means of escape.

Twice he placed his hand on his scimitar, intending to cut off the head of his enemy; but the difficulty of cutting the stiff, short hair compelled him to abandon this daring project. To miss would be to die for certain, he thought; he preferred the chances of fair fight, and made up his mind to wait till morning, which was not far off.

The Frenchman could now examine the panther at ease; its muzzle was smeared with blood.

"She's had a good dinner," he thought, without troubling himself as to whether her feast might have been on human flesh. "She won't be hungry when she gets up."

It was a female. The fur on her belly and flanks was glistening white; many small marks like velvet formed beautiful bracelets round her feet; her sinuous tail was also white, ending with black rings; the overpart of her dress, yellow like old gold, very sleek and soft, had the characteristic blotches shading off from the center like roses, which distinguish the panther from every other feline species.

This tranquil and formidable hostess snored in an attitude as graceful as that of a cat lying on the cushion of an ottoman. Her bloodstained paws, nervous and well-armed, were stretched out before her face, which rested upon them, and from which radiated her straight, slender whiskers, like threads of silver.

If she had been like that in a cage, the Provençal would doubtless have admired the grace of the animal, and the vigorous contrasts of vivid color which gave her robe an imperial splendor; but just then his sight was troubled by her sinister appearance. The presence of the panther, even asleep, could not fail to produce the effect which the magnetic eyes of the serpent are said to have on the nightingale.

For a moment the courage of the soldier began to fail before this danger, though no doubt it would have risen at the mouth of a cannon vomiting forth grapeshot. Nevertheless, a bold thought brought daylight to his soul and dried up the source of the cold sweat which sprang forth on his brow. Like men who, driven to bay by misfortune, defy death and offer their body to its blows, so he, seeing in this merely a tragic episode, resolved to play his part with honor to the last.

"The day before yesterday the Arabs would have killed me perhaps," he said. So considering himself as good as dead already, he waited bravely, with excited curiosity, for his enemy's awakening.

When the sun appeared, the panther suddenly opened her eyes; then she put out her paws with energy, as if to stretch them and get rid of cramp. At last she yawned, showing the formidable apparatus of her teeth and forked tongue, rough as a file.

"A regular coquette," thought the Frenchman, seeing her roll herself about so softly and kittenishly. She licked off the blood which stained her paws and muzzle, and scratched her head with reiterated gestures full of prettiness. "All right, make yourself pretty," the Frenchman said to himself, beginning to recover his gaiety with his courage; "we'll say good morning to each other presently," and he seized the small, short dagger which he had taken from the Moors.

At this moment the panther turned her head toward the man and looked at him fixedly without moving. The rigidity of her metallic eyes and their insupportable luster made him shudder, especially when the animal walked toward him. But he looked at her caressingly, staring into her eyes in order to magnetize her, and let her come quite close to him; then with a movement both gentle and amorous, as though he were caressing the most beautiful of women, he passed his hand over her whole body, from the head to the tail, scratching the flexible vertebrae which divided the panther's yellow back. The animal waved her tail voluptuously, and her eyes grew gentle; and when for the third time the Frenchman accomplished this flattery in which there was a purpose, she gave forth one of those purrings by which our cats express their pleasure; but this murmur issued from a throat so powerful and so deep, that it resounded through the cave, like the last vibrations of an organ in a church. The man, understanding the importance of his caresses, redoubled them in such a way as to surprise and stupefy his imperious courtesan. When he felt sure of having extinguished the ferocity of his capricious companion, whose hunger had so fortunately been satisfied the day before, he got up to go out of the cave; the panther let him go out, but when he had reached the summit of the hill she sprang with the lightness of a sparrow hopping from twig to twig, and rubbed herself against his legs, arching her back after the manner of all the race of cats. Then regarding her guest with eyes whose glare had softened a little, she gave vent to that wild cry which naturalists compare to the grating of a saw.

"She is exacting," said the Frenchman, smilingly.

He was bold enough to play with her ears; he caressed her belly and scratched her head as hard as he could. When he saw that he was successful, he tickled her skull with the point of his dagger, watching for the right moment to kill her, but the hardness of her bones made him tremble for his success.

The sultana of the desert graciously manifested her acceptance of the attentions of her slave by lifting her head, stretching out her neck, and showing her delight by the tranquility of her attitude. It suddenly occurred to the soldier that to kill this savage princess with one blow he must poignard her in the throat.

He was raising the blade, when the panther, satisfied no doubt, laid herself gracefully at his feet, and cast up at him glances in which, in spite of their natural fierceness, was mingled confusedly a kind of good-will. The poor Provençal ate his dates, leaning against one of the palm trees, and casting his eyes alternately on the desert in quest of some liberator and on his terrible companion to watch her uncertain clemency.

The panther watched the place where the date stones fell, and every time that he threw one down her eyes expressed an incredible mistrust. She examined the man with an almost commercial prudence. However, this examination was favorable to him, for when he had finished his meager meal she licked his boots with her powerful rough tongue, brushing off with marvellous skill the dust gathered in the creases.

"Ah, but when she's really hungry!" thought the Frenchman. In spite of the shudder this thought caused him, the soldier began to measure curiously the proportions of the panther, certainly one of the most splendid specimens of its race. She was three feet high and four feet long without counting her tail. This powerful weapon, rounded like a cudgel, was nearly three feet long. Her head, large as that of a lioness, was distinguished by a rare expression of refinement. The old cruelty of a tiger was dominant, it was true, but there was also a vague resemblance to the face of a coquettish woman. Indeed, the face of this solitary queen had something of the gaiety of a drunken Nero: she had satiated herself with blood, and she wanted to play.

The soldier tried to walk up and down; the panther left him free, contenting herself with following him with her eyes, less like a faithful dog than a big Angora cat, disturbed at everything, even at the movements of her master.

When he looked around, he saw, by the spring, the remains of his horse; the panther had dragged the carcass all that way. About two-thirds of it had been devoured already. The sight reassured him.

It was easy then to explain the panther's absence, and the respect she had had for him while he slept. This first piece of good luck emboldened him to try the future, and he conceived the wild hope of continuing on good terms with the panther during the entire day, neglecting no means of taming her, and of winning her good graces.

He returned to her, and had the indescribable joy of seeing her wag her tail with an almost imperceptible movement at his approach. He sat down then, without fear, by her side, and they began to play together; he took her paws and muzzle, played with her ears, rolled her over on her back, stroked her warm, silky flanks. She let him do whatever he liked, and when he began to stroke the hair on her feet she drew her claws in carefully.

The Frenchman, keeping one hand on his dagger, was still thinking about plunging it into the belly of the too-confiding panther, but he was afraid that he would be immediately strangled in her last conclusive struggle. Besides, he felt in his heart a sort of remorse which bade him respect a creature that had done him no harm. He seemed to have found a friend, in a boundless desert. Half unconsciously he thought of his first sweetheart, whom he had nicknamed "Mignonne" by way of contrast, because she was so atrociously jealous that all the time of their love he was in fear of the knife with which she had always threatened him.

This memory of his early days suggested to him the idea of making the young panther answer to this name, now that he began to admire with less terror her swiftness, suppleness, and softness. Toward the end of the day he had familiarized himself with his perilous position; he now almost liked the painfulness of it. At last his companion had got into the habit of looking up at him whenever he cried in a falsetto voice, "Mignonne."

At the setting of the sun Mignonne gave, several times running, a profound melancholy cry. "She's been well brought up," said the light-hearted soldier; "she says her prayers." But this mental joke only occurred to him when he noticed what a pacific attitude his companion remained in. "Come, *ma petite blonde*, I'll let you go to bed first," he said to her, counting on the activity of his own legs to run away as quickly as possible, directly she was asleep, and seek another shelter for the night.

The soldier waited with impatience the hour of his flight, and when it had arrived he walked vigorously in the direction of the Nile; but hardly had he done a quarter of a league in the sand when he heard the panther bounding after him, crying with that saw-like cry more dreadful even than the sound of her leaping.

"Ah!" he said, "then she's taken a fancy to me; she has never met any one before, and it is really quite flattering to have her first love." That instant the man fell into one of those movable quicksands so terrible to travellers and from which it is impossible to save oneself. Feeling himself caught, he gave a shriek of alarm; the panther seized him with her teeth by the collar, and, springing vigorously backward, drew him as if by magic out of the whirling sand.

"Ah, Mignonne!" cried the soldier, caressing her enthusiastically; "we're bound together for life and death—but no jokes, mind!" and he retraced his steps.

From that time the desert seemed inhabited. It contained a being to whom the Frenchman could talk, and whose ferocity was rendered gentle by him, though he could not explain to himself the reason for their strange friendship. Great as was the soldier's desire to stay upon guard, he slept.

On awakening he could not find Mignonne; he mounted the hill, and in the distance saw her springing toward him after the habit of these animals, who cannot run on account of the extreme flexibility of the vertebral column. Mignonne arrived, her jaws covered with blood; she received the wonted caress of her companion, showing with much purring how happy it made her. Her eyes, full of languor, turned still more gently than the day before toward the Provençal who talked to her as one would to a tame animal.

"Ah! Mademoiselle, you are a nice girl, aren't you? Just look at that! so we like to be made much of, don't we? Aren't you ashamed of yourself? So you have been eating some Arab or other, have you? that doesn't matter. They're animals just the same as you are; but don't you take to eating Frenchmen, or I shan't like you any longer."

She played like a dog with its master, letting herself be rolled over, knocked about, and stroked, alternately; sometimes she herself would provoke the soldier, putting up her paw with a soliciting gesture.

Some days passed in this manner. This companionship permitted the Provençal to appreciate the sublime beauty of the desert; now that he had a living thing to think about, alternations of fear and quiet, and plenty to eat, his mind became filled with contrast and his life began to be diversified.

Solitude revealed to him all her secrets, and enveloped him in her delights. He discovered in the rising and setting of the sun sights unknown to the world. He knew what it was to tremble when he heard over his head the hiss of a bird's wing, so rarely did they pass, or when he saw the changing clouds, many-colored travellers, one melting into another. He studied in the night time the effect of the moon upon the ocean of sand, where the simoon made waves swift of movement and rapid in their change. He lived the life of the Eastern day, marvelling at its wonderful pomp; then, after having revelled in the sight of a hurricane over the plain where the whirling sands made red, dry mists and death-bearing clouds, he would welcome the night with joy, for then fell the healthful freshness of the stars, and he listened to imaginary music in the skies. Then solitude taught him to unroll the treasures of dreams. He passed whole hours in remembering mere nothings and comparing his present life to his past.

At last he grew passionately fond of the panther; for some sort of affection was a necessity. Whether it was that his will powerfully projected had modified the character of his companion, or whether, because she found abundant food in her predatory excursions in the desert, she respected the man's life, he began to fear for it no longer, seeing her so well tamed.

He devoted the greater part of his time to sleep, but he was obliged to watch like a spider in its web that the moment of his deliverance might not escape him, if any one should pass the line marked by the horizon. He had sacrificed his shirt to make a flag with, which he hung at the top of a palm tree, whose foliage he had torn off. Taught by necessity, he found the means of keeping it spread out, by fastening it with little sticks; for the wind might not be blowing at the moment when the passing traveller was looking through the desert.

It was during the long hours, when he had abandoned hope, that he amused himself with the panther. He had come to learn the different inflections of her voice, the expressions of her eyes; he had studied the capricious patterns of all the rosettes which marked the gold of her robe. Mignonne was not even angry when he took hold of the tuft at the end of her tail to count her rings, those graceful ornaments which glittered in the sun like precious stones. It gave him pleasure to contemplate the supple, fine outlines of her form, the whiteness of her belly, the graceful pose of her head. But it was especially when she was playing that he felt most pleasure in looking at her; the agility and youthful lightness of her movements were a continual surprise to him; he wondered at the supple way in which she jumped and climbed, washed herself and arranged her fur, crouched down and prepared to spring. However rapid her spring might be, however slippery the stone she was on, she would always stop short at the word "Mignonne."

One day, in a bright mid-day sun, an enormous bird hovered above in the air. The man left his panther to look at this new guest; but after waiting a moment the deserted sultana growled deeply.

"My goodness! I do believe she's jealous," he cried, seeing her eyes become hard again; "the soul of Virginie must have passed into her body."

The eagle disappeared into the air, while the soldier admired the curved contour of the panther.

But there was such youth and grace in her form! she was beautiful as a woman! The blond fur of her robe mingled well with the delicate tints of dull white which marked her flanks.

The profuse light cast down by the sun made this living gold, these russet markings, to burn in a way to give them an indefinable attraction.

The man and the panther looked at one another with a look full of meaning; the coquette quivered when she felt her friend stroke her head; her eyes flashed like lightning—then she shut them tightly.

"She has a soul," he said, looking at the stillness of this queen of the sands, golden like them, white like them, solitary and burning like them.

"Well," she said, "I have read your plea in favor of beasts; but how did two so well adapted to understand each other end?"

"Ah, well! you see, they ended as all great passions do end—by a misunderstanding. For some reason one suspects the other of treason; because of pride they don't come to an explanation. They quarrel and part from sheer obstinancy."

"Yet sometimes at the best moments a single word or a look is enough—but anyhow go on with your story."

"It's horribly difficult, but you will understand, after what the old villain told me over his champagne. He said—'I don't know if I hurt her, but she turned round, as if enraged, and with her sharp teeth caught hold of my leg—gently, I daresay; but I, thinking she would devour me, plunged my dagger into her throat. She rolled over, giving a cry that froze my heart; and I saw her dying, still looking at me without anger. I would have given all the world —my Legion of Honor cross even, which I had not got then—to have brought her to life again. It was as though I had murdered a real person. And the soldiers who had seen my flag, and had come to my assistance, found me in tears. 'Well sir,' he said, after a moment of silence, 'since then I have been in war in Germany, in Spain, in Russia, in France; I've certainly carried my carcass about a good deal, but never have I seen anything like the desert. Ah! yes, it is very beautiful!'

"'What did you feel there?'" I asked him.

"'Oh! that can't be described, young man. Besides, I am not always regretting my palm trees and my panther. I should have to be very melancholy for that. In the desert, you see, there is everything, and nothing.'"

"'Yes, but explain——'"

"'Well,' he said, with an impatient gesture, 'it is God without mankind.'"

YOUNG GOODMAN BROWN [1]

NATHANIEL HAWTHORNE

Young Goodman Brown came forth at sunset into the street at Salem village; but put his head back, after crossing the threshold, to exchange a parting kiss with his young wife. And Faith, as the wife was aptly named, thrust her own pretty head into the street, letting the wind play with the pink ribbons of her cap while she called to Goodman Brown.

"Dearest heart," whispered she, softly and rather sadly, when her lips were close to his ear, "prithee put off your journey until sunrise and sleep in your own bed to-night. A lone woman is troubled with such dreams and such thoughts that she's afeard of herself sometimes. Pray tarry with me this night, dear husband, of all nights in the year."

"My love and my Faith," replied young Goodman Brown, "of all nights in the year, this one night must I tarry away from thee. My journey, as thou callest it, forth and back again, must needs be done 'twixt now and sunrise. What, my sweet, pretty wife, dost thou doubt me already, and we but three months married?"

"Then God bless you!" said Faith, with the pink ribbons; "and may you find all well when you come back."

"Amen!" cried Goodman Brown. "Say thy prayers, dear Faith, and go to bed at dusk, and no harm will come to thee."

So they parted; and the young man pursued his way until, being about to turn the corner by the meeting-house, he looked back and saw the head of

1. First printed in the *New-England Magazine,* 1835.

Faith still peeping after him with a melancholy air, in spite of her pink ribbons.

"Poor little Faith!" thought he, for his heart smote him. "What a wretch am I to leave her on such an errand! She talks of dreams, too. Methought as she spoke there was trouble in her face, as if a dream had warned her what work is to be done to-night. But no, no; 'twould kill her to think it. Well, she's a blessed angel on earth; and after this one night I'll cling to her skirts and follow her to heaven."

With this excellent resolve for the future, Goodman Brown felt himself justified in making more haste on his present evil purpose. He had taken a dreary road, darkened by all the gloomiest trees of the forest, which barely stood aside to let the narrow path creep through, and closed immediately behind. It was all as lonely as could be; and there is this peculiarity in such a solitude, that the traveller knows not who may be concealed by the innumerable trunks and the thick boughs overhead; so that with lonely footsteps he may yet be passing through an unseen multitude.

"There may be a devilish Indian behind every tree," said Goodman Brown to himself; and he glanced fearfully behind him as he added, "What if the devil himself should be at my very elbow!"

His head being turned back, he passed a crook of the road, and, looking forward again, beheld the figure of a man, in grave and decent attire, seated at the foot of an old tree. He arose at Goodman Brown's approach and walked onward side by side with him.

"You are late, Goodman Brown," said he. "The clock of the Old South was striking as I came through Boston, and that is full fifteen minutes agone."

"Faith kept me back a while," replied the young man, with a tremor in his voice, caused by the sudden appearance of his companion, though not wholly unexpected.

It was now deep dusk in the forest, and deepest in that part of it where these two were journeying. As nearly as could be discerned, the second traveller was about fifty years old, apparently in the same rank of life as Goodman Brown, and bearing a considerable resemblance to him, though perhaps more in expression than features. Still they might have been taken for father and son. And yet, though the elder person was as simply clad as the younger, and as simple in manner too, he had an indescribable air of one who knew the world, and who would not have felt abashed at the governor's dinner table or in King William's court, were it possible that his affairs should call him thither. But the only thing about him that could be fixed upon as remarkable was his staff, which bore the likeness of a great black snake, so curiously wrought that it might almost be seen to twist and wriggle itself like a living serpent. This, of course, must have been an ocular deception, assisted by the uncertain light.

"Come, Goodman Brown," cried his fellow-traveler, "this is a dull place for the beginning of a journey. Take my staff, if you are so soon weary."

"Friend," said the other, exchanging his slow pace for a full stop, "having kept covenant by meeting thee here, it is my purpose now to return whence I came. I have scruples touching the matter thou wot'st of."

"Sayest thou so?" replied he of the serpent, smiling apart. "Let us walk on, nevertheless, reasoning as we go; and if I convince thee not thou shalt turn back. We are but a little way in the forest yet."

"Too far! too far!" exclaimed the goodman, unconsciously resuming his walk. "My father never went into the woods on such an errand, nor his father before him. We have been a race of honest men and good Christians since the days of the martyrs; and shall I be the first of the name of Brown that ever took this path and kept—"

"Such company, thou wouldst say," observed the elder person, interpreting his pause. "Well said, Goodman Brown! I have been as well acquainted with your family as with ever a one among the Puritans; and that's no trifle to say. I helped your grandfather, the constable, when he lashed the Quaker woman so smartly through the streets of Salem; and it was I that brought your father a pitch-pine knot, kindled at my own hearth, to set fire to an Indian village, in King Philip's war. They were my good friends, both; and many a pleasant walk have we had along this path, and returned merrily after midnight. I would fain be friends with you for their sake."

"If it be as thou sayest," replied Goodman Brown, "I marvel they never spoke of these matters; or, verily, I marvel not, seeing that the least rumor of the sort would have driven them from New England. We are a people of prayer, and good works to boot, and abide no such wickedness."

"Wickedness or not," said the traveller with the twisted staff, "I have a very general acquaintance here in New England. The deacons of many a church have drunk the communion wine with me; the selectmen of divers towns make me their chairman; and a majority of the Great and General Court are firm supporters of my interest. The governor and I, too—But these are state secrets."

"Can this be so?" cried Goodman Brown, with a stare of amazement at his undisturbed companion. "Howbeit, I have nothing to do with the governor and council; they have their own ways, and are no rule for a simple husbandman like me. But, were I to go on with thee, how should I meet the eye of that good old man, our minister, at Salem village? Oh, his voice would make me tremble both Sabbath day and lecture day."

Thus far the elder traveller had listened with due gravity; but now burst into a fit of irrepressible mirth, shaking himself so violently that his snake-like staff acutally seemed to wriggle in sympathy.

"Ha! ha! ha!" shouted he again and again; then composing himself, "Well, go on, Goodman Brown, go on; but, prithee, don't kill me with laughing."

"Well, then, to end the matter at once," said Goodman Brown, considerably nettled, "there is my wife, Faith. It would break her dear little heart; and I'd rather break my own."

"Nay, if that be the case," answered the other, "e'en go thy ways, Goodman

Brown. I would not for twenty old women like the one hobbling before us that Faith should come to any harm."

As he spoke he pointed his staff at a female figure on the path, in whom Goodman Brown recognized a very pious and exemplary dame, who had taught him his catechism in youth, and was still his moral and spiritual adviser, jointly with the minister and Deacon Gookin.

"A marvel, truly, that Goody Cloyse should be so far in the wilderness at nightfall," said he. "But with your leave, friend, I shall take a cut through the woods until we have left this Christian woman behind. Being a stranger to you, she might ask whom I was consorting with and whither I was going."

"Be it so," said his fellow-traveller. "Betake you to the woods, and let me keep the path."

Accordingly the young man turned aside, but took care to watch his companion, who advanced softly along the road until he had come within a staff's length of the old dame. She, meanwhile, was making the best of her way, with singular speed for so aged a woman, and mumbling some indistinct words—a prayer, doubtless—as she went. The traveller put forth his staff and touched her withered neck with what seemed the serpent's tail.

"The devil!" screamed the pious old lady.

"Then Goody Cloyse knows her old friend?" observed the traveller, confronting her and leaning on his writhing stick.

"Ah, forsooth, and is it your worship indeed?" cried the good dame. "Yea, truly it is, and in the very image of my old gossip, Goodman Brown, the grandfather of the silly fellow that now is. But—would your worship believe it?—my broomstick hath strangely disappeared, stolen, as I suspect, by that unhanged witch, Goody Cory, and that, too, when I was all anointed with the juice of smallage, and cinquefoil, and wolf's bane—"

"Mingled with fine wheat and the fat of a new-born babe," said the shape of old Goodman Brown.

"Ah, your worship knows the recipe," cried the old lady, cackling aloud. "So, as I was saying, being all ready for the meeting, and no horse to ride on, I made up my mind to foot it; for they tell me there is a nice young man to be taken into communion to-night. But now your good worship will lend me your arm, and we shall be there in a twinkling."

"That can hardly be," answered her friend. "I may not spare you my arm, Goody Cloyse; but here is my staff, if you will."

So saying, he threw it down at her feet, where, perhaps, it assumed life, being one of the rods which its owner had formerly lent to the Egyptian magi. Of this fact, however, Goodman Brown could not take cognizance. He had cast up his eyes in astonishment, and, looking down again, beheld neither Goody Cloyse nor the serpentine staff, but his fellow-traveller alone, who waited for him as calmly as if nothing had happened.

"That old woman taught me my catechism," said the young man; and there was a world of meaning in this simple comment.

They continued to walk onward, while the elder traveller exhorted his companion to make good speed and persevere in the path, discoursing so aptly that his arguments seemed rather to spring up in the bosom of his auditor than to be suggested by himself. As they went, he plucked a branch of maple to serve for a walking stick, and began to strip it of the twigs and little boughs, which were wet with evening dew. The moment his fingers touched them they became strangely withered and dried up as with a week's sunshine. Thus the pair proceeded, at a good free pace, until suddenly, in a gloomy hollow of the road, Goodman Brown sat himself down on the stump of a tree and refused to go any farther.

"Friend," said he, stubbornly, "my mind is made up. Not another step will I budge on this errand. What if a wretched old woman do choose to go to the devil when I thought she was going to heaven: is that any reason why I should quit my dear Faith and go after her?"

"You will think better of this by and by," said his acquaintance, composedly. "Sit here and rest yourself a while; and when you feel like moving again, there is my staff to help you along."

Without more words, he threw his companion the maple stick, and was as speedily out of sight as if he had vanished into the deepening gloom. The young man sat a few moments by the roadside, applauding himself greatly, and thinking with how clear a conscience he should meet the minister in his morning walk, nor shrink from the eye of good old Deacon Gookin. And what calm sleep would be his that very night, which was to have been spent so wickedly, but so purely and sweetly now, in the arms of Faith! Amidst these pleasant and praiseworthy meditations, Goodman Brown heard the tramp of horses along the road, and deemed it advisable to conceal himself within the verge of the forest, conscious of the guilty purpose that had brought him thither, though now so happily turned from it.

On came the hoof tramps and the voices of the riders, two grave old voices, conversing soberly as they drew near. These mingled sounds appeared to pass along the road, within a few yards of the young man's hiding-place; but, owing doubtless to the depth of the gloom at that particular spot, neither the travellers nor their steeds were visible. Though their figures brushed the small boughs by the wayside, it could not be seen that they intercepted, even for a moment, the faint gleam from the strip of bright sky athwart which they must have passed. Goodman Brown alternately crouched and stood on tiptoe, pulling aside the branches and thrusting forth his head as far as he durst without discerning so much as a shadow. It vexed him the more, because he could have sworn, were such a thing possible, that he recognized the voices of the minister and Deacon Gookin, jogging along quietly, as they were wont to do, when bound to some ordination or ecclesiastical council. While yet within hearing, one of the riders stopped to pluck a switch.

"Of the two, reverend sir," said the voice like the deacon's, "I had rather miss an ordination dinner than to-night's meeting. They tell me that some of our community are to be here from Falmouth and beyond, and others from Connecticut and Rhode Island, besides several of the Indian powwows, who, after their fashion, know almost as much deviltry as the best of us. Moreover, there is a goodly young woman to be taken into communion."

"Mighty well, Deacon Gookin!" replied the solemn old tones of the minister. "Spur up, or we shall be late. Nothing can be done, you know, until I get on the ground."

The hoofs clattered again; and the voices, talking so strangely in the empty air, passed on through the forest, where no church had ever been gathered or solitary Christian prayed. Whither, then, could these holy men be journeying so deep into the heathen wilderness? Young Goodman Brown caught hold of a tree for support, being ready to sink down on the ground, faint and overburdened with the heavy sickness of his heart. He looked up to the sky, doubting whether there really was a heaven above him. Yet there was the blue arch, and the stars brightening in it.

"With heaven above and Faith below, I will yet stand firm against the devil!" cried Goodman Brown.

While he still gazed upward into the deep arch of the firmament and had lifted his hands to pray, a cloud, though no wind was stirring, hurried across the zenith and hid the brightening stars. The blue sky was still visible, except directly overhead, where this black mass of cloud was sweeping swiftly northward. Aloft in the air, as if from the depths of the cloud, came a confused and doubtful sound of voices. Once the listener fancied that he could distinguish the accents of townspeople of his own, men and women, both pious and ungodly, many of whom he had met at the communion table, and had seen others rioting at the tavern. The next moment, so indistinct were the sounds, he doubted whether he had heard aught but the murmur of the old forest, whispering without a wind. Then came a stronger swell of those familiar tones, heard daily in the sunshine at Salem village, but never until now from a cloud of night. There was one voice, of a young woman, uttering lamentations, yet with an uncertain sorrow, and entreating for some favor, which, perhaps, it would grieve her to obtain; and all the unseen multitude, both saints and sinners, seemed to encourage her onward.

"Faith!" shouted Goodman Brown, in a voice of agony and desperation; and the echoes of the forest mocked him, crying, "Faith! Faith!" as if bewildered wretches were seeking her all through the wilderness.

The cry of grief, rage, and terror was yet piercing the night, when the unhappy husband held his breath for a response. There was a scream, drowned immediately in a louder murmur of voices, fading into far-off laughter, as the dark cloud swept away, leaving the clear and silent sky above Goodman Brown. But something fluttered lightly down through the air and caught on the branch of a tree. The young man seized it, and beheld a pink ribbon.

"My Faith is gone!" cried he, after one stupefied moment. "There is no good on earth; and sin is but a name. Come, devil; for to thee is this world given."

And, maddened with despair, so that he laughed loud and long, did Goodman Brown grasp his staff and set forth again, at such a rate that he seemed to fly along the forest path rather than to walk or run. The road grew wilder and drearier and more faintly traced, and vanished at length, leaving him in the heart of the dark wilderness, still rushing onward with the instinct that guides mortal man to evil. The whole forest was peopled with frightful sounds—the creaking of the trees, the howling of wild beasts, and the yell of Indians; while sometimes the wind tolled like a distant church bell, and sometimes gave a broad roar around the traveller, as if all Nature were laughing him to scorn. But he was himself the chief horror of the scene, and shrank not from its other horrors.

"Ha! ha! ha!" roared Goodman Brown when the wind laughed at him. "Let us hear which will laugh loudest. Think not to frighten me with your deviltry. Come witch, come wizard, come Indian powwow, come devil himself, and here comes Goodman Brown. You may as well fear him as he fear you."

In truth, all through the haunted forest there could be nothing more frightful than the figure of Goodman Brown. On he flew among the black pines, brandishing his staff with frenzied gestures, now giving vent to an inspiration of horrid blasphemy, and now shouting forth such laughter as set all the echoes of the forest laughing like demons around him. The fiend in his own shape is less hideous than when he rages in the breast of man. Thus sped the demoniac on his course, until, quivering among the trees, he saw a red light before him, as when the felled trunks and branches of a clearing have been set on fire, and throw up their lurid blaze against the sky, at the hour of midnight. He paused, in a lull of the tempest that had driven him onward, and heard the swell of what seemed a hymn, rolling solemnly from a distance with the weight of many voices. He knew the tune; it was a familiar one in the choir of the village meeting-house. The verse died heavily away, and was lengthened by a chorus, not of human voices, but of all the sounds of the benighted wilderness pealing in awful harmony together. Goodman Brown cried out, and his cry was lost to his own ear by its unison with the cry of the desert.

In the interval of silence he stole forward until the light glared full upon his eyes. At one extremity of an open space, hemmed in by the dark wall of the forest, arose a rock, bearing some rude, natural resemblance either to an altar or a pulpit, and surrounded by four blazing pines, their tops aflame, their stems untouched, like candles at an evening meeting. The mass of foliage that had overgrown the summit of the rock was all on fire, blazing high into the night and fitfully illuminating the whole field. Each pendent twig and leafy festoon was in a blaze. As the red light arose and fell, a numerous congregation alternately shone forth, then disappeared in shadow, and again grew, as it were, out of the darkness, peopling the heart of the solitary woods at once.

"A grave and dark-clad company," quoth Goodman Brown.

In truth they were such. Among them, quivering to and fro between gloom and splendor, appeared faces that would be seen next day at the council board of the province, and others which, Sabbath after Sabbath, looked devoutly heavenward, and benignantly over the crowded pews, from the holiest pulpits in the land. Some affirm that the lady of the governor was there. At least there were high dames well known to her, and wives of honored husbands, and widows, a great multitude, and ancient maidens, all of excellent repute, and fair young girls, who trembled lest their mothers should espy them. Either the sudden gleams of light flashing over the obscure field bedazzled Goodman Brown, or he recognized a score of the church members of Salem village famous for their especial sanctity. Good old Deacon Gookin had arrived, and waited at the skirts of that venerable saint, his revered pastor. But, irreverently consorting with these grave, reputable, and pious people, these elders of the church, these chaste dames and dewy virgins, there were men of dissolute lives and women of spotted fame, wretches given over to all mean and filthy vice, and suspected even of horrid crimes. It was strange to see that the good shrank not from the wicked, nor were the sinners abashed by the saints. Scattered also among their pale-faced enemies were the Indian priests, or powwows, who had often scared their native forest with more hideous incantations than any known to English witchcraft.

"But where is Faith?" thought Goodman Brown; and, as hope came into his heart, he trembled.

Another verse of the hymn arose, a slow and mournful strain, such as the pious love, but joined to the words which expressed all that our nature can conceive of sin, and darkly hinted at far more. Unfathomable to mere mortals is the lore of fiends. Verse after verse was sung; and still the chorus of the desert swelled between like the deepest tone of a mighty organ; and with the final peal of that dreadful anthem there came a sound, as if the roaring wind, the rushing streams, the howling beasts, and every other voice of the unconcerted wilderness were mingling and according with the voice of guilty man in homage to the prince of all. The four blazing pines threw up a loftier flame, and obscurely discovered shapes and visages of horror on the smoke wreaths above the impious assembly. At the same moment the fire on the rock shot redly forth and formed a glowing arch above its base, where now appeared a figure. With reverence be it spoken, the figure bore no slight similitude, both in garb and manner, to some grave divine of the New England churches. "Bring forth the converts!" cried a voice that echoed through the field and rolled into the forest.

At the word, Goodman Brown stepped forth from the shadow of the trees and approached the congregation, with whom he felt a loathful brotherhood by the sympathy of all that was wicked in his heart. He could have well-nigh sworn that the shape of his own dead father beckoned him to advance, looking downward from a smoke wreath, while a woman, with dim features of despair, threw out her hand to warn him back. Was it mother? But he had no power to retreat one step, nor to resist, even in thought, when the minister and good old Deacon Gookin seized his arms and led him to the blazing rock. Thither came also the slender form of a veiled female, led between Goody Cloyse, that pious teacher of the catechism, and Martha Carrier, who had received the devil's promise to be queen of hell. A rampant hag was she. And there stood the proselytes beneath the canopy of fire.

"Welcome, my children," said the dark figure, "to the communion of your race. Ye have found thus young your nature and your destiny. My children, look behind you!"

They turned; and flashing forth, as it were, in a sheet of flame, the fiend worshippers were seen; the smile of welcome gleamed darkly on every visage.

"There," resumed the sable form, "are all whom ye have reverenced from youth. Ye deemed them holier than yourselves, and shrank from your own sin, contrasting it with their lives of righteousness and prayerful aspirations heavenward. Yet here are they all in my worshipping assembly. This night it shall be granted you to know their secret deeds: how hoary-bearded elders of the church have whispered wanton words to the young maids of their households; how many a woman, eager for widows' weeds, has given her husband a drink at bedtime and let him sleep his last sleep in her bosom; how beardless youths have made haste to inherit their fathers' wealth; and how fair damsels—blush not, sweet ones—have dug little graves in the garden, and bidden me, the sole guest, to an infant's funeral. By the sympathy of your human hearts for sin ye shall scent out all the places—whether in church, bedchamber, street, field, or forest—where crime has been committed, and shall exult to behold the whole earth one stain of guilt, one mighty blood spot. Far more than this. It shall be yours to penetrate, in every bosom, the deep mystery of sin, the fountain of all wicked arts, and which inexhaustibly supplies more evil impulses than human power—than my power at its utmost—can make manifest in deeds. And now, my children, look upon each other."

They did so; and, by the blaze of the hell-kindled torches, the wretched man beheld his Faith, and the wife her husband, trembling before that unhallowed altar.

"Lo, there ye stand, my children," said the figure, in a deep and solemn tone, almost sad with its despairing awfulness, as if his once angelic nature could yet mourn for our miserable race. "Depending upon one another's hearts, ye had still hoped that virtue were not all a dream. Now are ye undeceived. Evil is the nature of mankind. Evil must be your only happiness. Welcome again, my children, to the communion of your race."

"Welcome," repeated the fiend worshippers, in one cry of despair and triumph.

And there they stood, the only pair, as it seemed, who were yet hesitating on the verge of wickedness in this dark world. A basin was hollowed, naturally, in the rock. Did it contain water, reddened by the lurid light? or was it blood? or, perchance, a liquid flame? Herein did the shape of evil dip his hand and prepare to lay the mark of baptism upon their foreheads, that they might be partakers of the mystery of sin, more conscious of the secret guilt of others, both in deed and thought, than they could now be of their own. The husband cast one look at his pale wife, and Faith at him. What polluted wretches would the next glance show them to each other, shuddering alike at what they disclosed and what they saw!

"Faith! Faith!" cried the husband, "look up to heaven, and resist the wicked one."

Whether Faith obeyed he knew not. Hardly had he spoken when he found himself amid calm night and solitude, listening to a roar of the wind which died heavily away through the forest. He staggered against the rock, and felt it chill and damp; while a hanging twig, that had been all on fire, besprinkled his cheek with the coldest dew.

The next morning young Goodman Brown came slowly into the street of Salem village, staring around him like a bewildered man. The good old minister was taking a walk along the graveyard to get an appetite for breakfast and meditate his sermon, and bestowed a blessing, as he passed, on Goodman Brown. He shrank from the venerable saint as if to avoid an anathema. Old Deacon Gookin was at domestic worship, and the holy words of his prayer were heard through the open window. "What God doth the wizard pray to?" quoth Goodman Brown. Goody Cloyse, that excellent old Christian, stood in the early sunshine at her own lattice, catechizing a little girl who had brought her a pint of morning's milk. Goodman Brown snatched away the child as from the grasp of the fiend himself. Turning the corner by the meeting-house, he spied the head of Faith, with the pink ribbons, gazing anxiously forth, and bursting into such joy at sight of him that she skipped along the street and almost kissed her husband before the whole village. But Goodman Brown looked sternly and sadly into her face, and passed on without a greeting.

Had Goodman Brown fallen asleep in the forest and only dreamed a wild dream of a witch-meeting?

Be it so if you will; but, alas! it was a dream of evil omen for young Goodman Brown. A stern, a sad, a darkly meditative, a distrustful, if not a desperate man did he become from the night of that fearful dream. On the Sabbath day, when the congregation were singing a holy psalm, he could not listen because an anthem of sin rushed loudly upon his ear and drowned all the blessed strain. When the minister spoke from the pulpit with power and fervid eloquence, and, with his hand on the open Bible, of the sacred truths of our religion, and of saint-like lives and triumphant deaths, and of future bliss or misery unutterable, then did Goodman Brown turn pale, dreading lest the roof should thunder down upon the gray blasphemer and his hearers. Often, awaking suddenly at midnight, he shrank from the bosom of Faith; and at morning or eventide, when the family knelt down at prayer, he scowled and muttered to himself, and gazed sternly at his wife, and turned away. And when he had lived long, and was borne to his grave a hoary corpse, followed by Faith, an aged woman, and children and grandchildren, a goodly procession, besides neighbors not a few, they carved no hopeful verse upon his tombstone, for his dying hour was gloom.

ON HAWTHORNE'S *YOUNG GOODMAN BROWN* [1]

F. O MATTHIESSEN

When young Goodman Brown leaves his wife Faith at home, and is deluded into attending a witch's sabbath in the forest, Hawthorne has the kind of situation where his moral perception and imaginative resources are able to coalesce. The conception of the dark and evil-haunted wilderness came to him from the days of Cotton Mather, who held that "the New Englanders are a people of God settled in those which were once the devil's territories." The fact that so many other strained religious minds had thus dramatized the heroic act of colonizing, had contributed to leave traces of awe in the presence of the lonely Maine woods even for a Pan-worshipper like Thoreau. Hawthorne's main concern with this material is to use it to develop the theme that mere doubt of the existence of good, the thought that all other men are evil, can become such a corrosive force as to eat out the life of the heart. In handling the question of what the young man really saw during his night in the forest, Hawthorne's imagination is at its most delicately masterful. In the sound of the rising wind it seemed to Brown that he heard the tune of a familiar hymn, sung to the most blasphemous words. Then, to his horrified gaze, four tall pines suddenly sprang into flame at the top, like candles at an evening meeting. "Each pendent twig and leafy festoon was in a blaze. As the red light arose and fell, a numerous congregation alternately shone forth, then disappeared in shadow, and again grew, as it were, out of the darkness, peopling the heart of the solitary woods at once."

But when he had turned his eyes upward just before, doubting whether there was a heaven above him, yet lifting his hands to pray, "there was the blue arch, and the stars brightening in it," except where a "black mass of cloud was sweeping swiftly northward."

> Aloft in the air, as if from the depths of the cloud, came a confused and doubtful sound of voices. . . .
>
> "My Faith is gone!" cried he, after one stupefied moment. "There is no good on earth; and sin is but a name. Come, devil, for to thee is this world given."

The intensity of the situation is sustained by all the devices Hawthorne had learned from the seventeenth century, for just as the heavens groaned in Milton's fall of the angels, the winds are made to whisper sadly at the loss of this man's faith. As long as what Brown saw is left wholly in the realm of hallucination, Hawthorne's created illusion is compelling. For the symbolical truth of

1. From *American Renaissance* by F. O. Matthiessen. Copyright, 1941, by Oxford University Press.

what the young man had conjured up in his bewildered vision is heightened by the fact that when he staggered against one of the burning trees, its twigs were cold with dew. The dramatization of his spiritual loss in the form of the agonized struggle and disappearance of his wife allows the description of the inner experience to become concrete, and also doubles its application. Only the literal insistence on that damaging pink ribbon obtrudes the labels of a confining allegory, and short-circuits the range of association.

THE MASQUE OF THE RED DEATH [1]

EDGAR ALLAN POE

THE "Red Death" had long devastated the country. No pestilence had ever been so fatal, or so hideous. Blood was its avatar and its seal—the redness and the horror of blood. There were sharp pains, and sudden dizziness, and then profuse bleeding at the pores, with dissolution. The scarlet stains upon the body, and especially upon the face, of the victim were the pest ban which shut him out from the aid and from the sympathy of his fellow-men. And the whole seizure, progress, and termination of the disease were the incidents of half an hour.

But the Prince Prospero was happy and dauntless and sagacious. When his dominions were half depopulated, he summoned to his presence a thousand hale and lighthearted friends from among the knights and dames of his court, and with these retired to the deep seclusion of one of his castellated abbeys. This was an extensive and magnificent structure, the creation of the Prince's own eccentric yet august taste. A strong and lofty wall girdled it in. This wall had gates of iron. The courtiers, having entered, brought furnaces and massy hammers, and welded the bolts. They resolved to leave means neither of ingress or egress to the sudden impulses of despair or of frenzy from within. The abbey was amply provisioned. With such precautions the courtiers might bid defiance to contagion. The external world could take care of itself. In the meantime it was folly to grieve, or to think. The Prince had provided all the appliances of pleasure. There were buffoons, there were improvisatori, there were ballet dancers, there were musicians, there was Beauty, there was wine. All these and security were within. Without was the "Red Death."

It was toward the close of the fifth or sixth month of his seclusion, and while the pestilence raged most furiously abroad, that the Prince Prospero entertained his thousand friends at a masked ball of the most unusual magnificence.

It was a voluptuous scene, that masquerade. But first let me tell of the rooms in which it was held. There were seven—an imperial suite. In many palaces,

1. First printed in *Graham's Magazine*, 1842.

however, such suites form a long and straight vista, while the folding-doors slide back nearly to the walls on either hand, so that the view of the whole extent is scarcely impeded. Here the case was very different, as might have been expected from the Prince's love of the bizarre. The apartments were so irregularly disposed that the vision embraced but little more than one at a time. There was a sharp turn at every twenty or thirty yards, and at each turn a novel effect. To the right and left, in the middle of each wall, a tall and narrow Gothic window looked out upon a closed corridor which pursued the windings of the suite. These windows were of stained glass, whose color varied in accordance with the prevailing hue of the decorations of the chamber into which it opened. That at the eastern extremity was hung, for example, in blue—and vividly blue were its windows. The second chamber was purple in its ornaments and tapestries, and here the panes were purple. The third was green throughout, and so were the casements. The fourth was furnished and lighted with orange, the fifth with white, the sixth with violet. The seventh apartment was closely shrouded in black velvet tapestries that hung all over the ceiling and down the walls, falling in heavy folds upon a carpet of the same material and hue. But, in this chamber only, the color of the windows failed to correspond with the decorations. The panes here were scarlet—a deep blood-color. Now in no one of the seven apartments was there any lamp or candelabrum, amid the profusion of golden ornaments that lay scattered to and fro or depended from the roof. There was no light of any kind emanating from lamp or candle within the suite of chambers. But in the corridors that followed the suite there stood, opposite to each window, a heavy tripod, bearing a brazier of fire, that projected its rays through the tinted glass and so glaringly illumined the room. And thus were produced a multitude of gaudy and fantastic appearances. But in the western or black chamber the effect of the firelight that streamed upon the dark hangings through the blood-tinted panes was ghastly in the extreme, and produced so wild a look upon the countenances of those who entered that there were few of the company bold enough to set foot within its precincts at all.

It was in this apartment, also, that there stood against the western wall a gigantic clock of ebony. Its pendulum swung to and fro with a dull, heavy, monotonous clang; and when the minute hand made the circuit of the face, and the hour was to be stricken, there came from the brazen lungs of the clock a sound which was clear and loud and deep and exceedingly musical, but of so peculiar a note and emphasis that, at each lapse of an hour, the musicians of the orchestra were constrained to pause, momentarily, in their performance to hearken to the sound; and thus the waltzers perforce ceased their evolutions; and there was a brief disconcert of the whole gay company; and, while the chimes of the clock yet rang, it was observed that the giddiest grew pale, and the more aged and sedate passed their hands over their brows as if in confused revery or meditation. But when the echoes had fully ceased, a light laughter at once pervaded the assembly; the musicians looked at each other and smiled as if at their own nervousness and folly, and made whispering vows, each to the other, that the next chiming of the clock should produce in them no similar emotion; and then, after the lapse of sixty minutes (which embrace three thousand and six hundred seconds of the Time that flies) there came yet another chiming of the clock, and then were the same disconcert and tremulousness and meditation as before.

But, in spite of these things, it was a gay and magnificent revel. The tastes of the Prince were peculiar. He had a fine eye for colors and effects. He disregarded the *decora* of mere fashion. His plans were bold and fiery, and his conceptions glowed with barbaric luster. There are some who would have thought him mad. His followers felt that he was not. It was necessary to hear and see and touch him to be *sure* that he was not.

He had directed, in great part, the movable embellishments of the seven chambers, upon occasion of this great *fête*; and it was his own guiding taste which had given character to the masqueraders. Be sure they were grotesque. There were much glare and glitter and piquancy and phantasm—much of what has been since seen in *Hernani*. There were arabesque figures with unsuited limbs and appointments. There were delirious fancies such as the madman fashions. There was much of the beautiful, much of the wanton, much of the bizarre, something of the terrible, and not a little of that which might have excited disgust. To and fro in the seven chambers there stalked, in fact, a multitude of dreams. And these—the dreams—writhed in and about, taking hue from the rooms, and causing the wild music of the orchestra to seem as the echo of their steps. And, anon, there strikes the ebony clock which stands in the hall of the velvet. And then, for a moment, all is still, and all is silent save the voice of the clock. The dreams are stiff-frozen as they stand. But the echoes of the chime die away—they have endured but an instant—and a light, half-subdued laughter floats after them as they depart. And now again the music swells, and the dreams live, and writhe to and fro more merrily than ever, taking hue from the many tinted windows through which stream the rays from the tripods. But to the chamber which lies most westwardly of the seven, there are now none of the maskers who venture; for the night is waning away, and there flows a ruddier light through the blood-colored panes; and the blackness of the sable drapery appalls; and to him whose foot falls upon the sable carpet, there comes from the near clock of ebony a muffled peal more solemnly emphatic than any which reaches *their* ears who indulge in the more remote gayeties of the other apartments.

But these other apartments were densely crowded, and in them beat feverishly the heart of life. And the revel went whirlingly on, until at length there commenced the sounding of midnight upon the clock. And then the music ceased, as I have told; and the evolutions of the waltzers were quieted; and there was an uneasy cessation of all things as before. But now there were twelve strokes to be sounded by the bell of the clock; and thus it happened, perhaps, that more of thought crept, with more of time, into the meditations of the thoughtful among those who reveled. And thus, too, it happened, perhaps, that before the last echoes of the last chime had utterly sunk into silence, there were many individuals in the crowd who had found leisure to become aware of the presence of a masked figure which had arrested the attention of no single individual before. And the rumor of this new presence having spread itself whisperingly around, there arose at length from the whole company a buzz, or murmur, expressive of disapprobation and surprise—then, finally, of terror, of horror, and of disgust.

In an assembly of phantasms such as I have painted, it may well be supposed that no ordinary appearance could have excited such sensation. In truth the masquerade license of the night was nearly unlimited; but the figure in question had out-Heroded Herod, and gone beyond the bounds of even the Prince's indefinite decorum. There are chords in the hearts of the most reckless which cannot be touched without emotion. Even with the utterly lost, to whom life and death are equally jests, there are matters of which no jest can be made. The whole company, indeed, seemed now deeply to feel that in the costume and bearing of the stranger neither wit nor propriety existed. The figure was tall and gaunt, and shrouded from head to foot in the habiliments of the grave. The mask which concealed the visage was made so nearly to resemble the countenance of a stiffened corpse that the closest scrutiny must have had difficulty in detecting the cheat. And yet all this might have been endured, if not approved, by the mad revelers around. But the mummer had gone so far as to assume the type of the Red Death. His vesture was dabbed in *blood*—and his broad brow, with all the features of the face, was besprinkled with the scarlet horror.

When the eyes of Prince Prospero fell upon this spectral image (which with a slow and solemn movement, as if more fully to sustain its *rôle*, stalked to and fro among the waltzers) he was seen to be convulsed, in the first moment, with a strong shudder either of terror or distaste; but, in the next, his brow reddened with rage.

"Who dares?" he demanded hoarsely of the courtiers who stood near him—"who dares insult us with this blasphemous mockery? Seize him and unmask him—that we may know whom we have to hang at sunrise, from the battlements."

It was in the eastern or blue chamber in which stood the Prince Prospero as he uttered these words. They rang throughout the seven rooms loudly and clearly—for the Prince was a bold and robust man, and the music had become hushed at the waving of his hand.

It was in the blue room where stood the Prince, with a group of pale courtiers by his side. At first, as he spoke, there was a slight rushing movement of this group in the direction of the intruder, who at the moment was also near at hand, and now, with deliberate and stately step, made closer approach to the speaker. But from a certain nameless awe with which the mad assumptions of the mummer had inspired the whole party, there were found none who put forth hand to seize him; so that, unimpeded, he passed within a yard of the Prince's person; and while the vast assembly, as if with one impulse, shrank from the centers of the rooms to the walls, he made his way uninterruptedly, but with the same solemn and measured step which had distinguished him from the first, through the blue chamber to the purple—through the purple to the green—through the green to the orange—through this again to the white—and even thence to the violet, ere a decided movement had been made to arrest him. It was then, however, that the Prince Prospero, maddening with rage and the shame of his own momentary cowardice, rushed hurriedly through the six chambers, while none followed him, on account of a deadly terror that had seized upon all. He bore aloft a drawn dagger, and had approached, in rapid impetuosity, to within three or four feet of the retreating figure, when the latter, having attained the extremity of the velvet apartment, turned suddenly and confronted his pursuer. There was a sharp cry—and the dagger dropped gleaming upon the sable carpet, upon which, instantly afterwards, fell prostrate in death the Prince Prospero. Then, summoning the wild courage of despair, a throng of the revelers at once threw themselves into the black apartment, and, seizing the mummer, whose tall figure stood erect and motionless within the shadow of the ebony clock, gasped in unutterable horror at finding the grave cerements and corpse-like mask, which they handled with so violent a rudeness, untenanted by any tangible form.

And now was acknowledged the presence of the Red Death. He had come like a thief in the night. And one by one dropped the revelers in the blood-bedewed halls of their revel, and died each in the despairing posture of his fall. And the life of the ebony clock went out with that of the last of the gay. And the flames of the tripods expired. And Darkness and Decay and the Red Death held illimitable dominion over all.

ON POE'S *THE MASQUE OF THE RED DEATH* [1]

WALTER BLAIR

POE's theories about incident and tone in the tale suggest a way of considering how, in his own stories, he achieved the kind of reconciliation he believed inevitable between theory and practice. Let us consider, for instance, in the light of these theories, one of his most famous tales, "The Masque of the Red Death."

A change of the sort typical of Poe—one in the feelings of the characters—occurs in this story. At the beginning the courtiers are "hale and light hearted," but they shortly manifest uneasiness by retiring to the secluded abbey and barring the door to "the sudden impulses of despair or of frenzy."

1. From "Poe's Conception of Incident and Tone in the Tale," *Modern Philology,* XLI (May, 1944), 236–240. Reprinted by permission of the University of Chicago Press.

In the final pages they are inspired by "nameless awe," and their only act is prompted by "the wild courage of despair." The prince is so characterized that his growing fright contributes to the graduation of this climactic development: he is "happy and dauntless," "bold and robust," capable of making "bold and fiery plans." Yet, near the end, even this courageous man suffers "momentary cowardice"; and, when he is overcome by the terrible Red Death, the courtiers are "grasped in unutterable horror."

Paralleling this development, characteristically enough, are a series of backgrounds and happenings so selected and arranged as to account for these mounting fears. The raging plague, though it is apparently shut out when the prince and his friends bar the doors of the abbey, nevertheless contributes its element of menace from the start. But the chief scene (in the theatrical sense of the word), beginning in the third paragraph, is the masque during which, by degrees, feverish gaiety gives way to abject terror. This part of the narrative falls into three divisions, in which are inspired, respectively, physical disquiet, fear of the aberrations of the mind, and, finally, horror aroused by the supernatural.

Poe tells first of the decorative scheme—the seven rooms, so arranged as to play upon any claustrophobia the reader may feel as he identifies himself with characters whose vision is limited by walls of single rooms which themselves are in an abbey shut off from the world by welded iron doors. Light and color in each of these rooms are abnormal and disquieting, and into the seventh room—most disquieting of all—"few of the company are bold enough to set foot." Hearing as well as sight is disturbed: the sound which issues from the ebony clock as its pendulum swings is a "dull, heavy, monotonous clang"; and, when the hour strikes, the "peculiar note and emphasis" of the chime stops the music and makes even the giddiest courtiers momentarily turn pale.

From such purely physical details, the account moves to the rumored madness of the prince by a neat transition: "It was necessary to hear and see and touch him to be *sure* that he was not mad." Mad or not, when Prospero makes plans for the ball, mental as well as physical distortion is suggested. "Grotesque," "phantasm," "arabesque," "delirious fancies such as the madman fashions," "much of the *bizarre*, something of the terrible, and not a little of that which might have excited disgust"—such words as these tell of the dreamlike figures moving through the rooms. And, now, "there are none of the masquers who venture" into the seventh room.

For in this room, says the author, introducing the supernatural note to prevail until the end, "the night is waning. . . . and there flows a ruddier light through the blood-colored panes. . . . and to him whose foot falls upon the sable carpet, there comes from the near clock a muffled peal more solemnly emphatic than any which reaches *their* ears who indulge in the more remote gayeties of the other apartments." The ruddier light can have only a supernatural explanation, since the time is not yet midnight; and there is no natural reason for the change in the sound of the clock. Now the clock strikes twelve, and, during the time it strikes, many first see the strange figure who causes the company to feel and voice "disapprobation and surprise," then "terror. . . . horror. . . . disgust." Seeing this figure habited as the Red Death, the pale courtiers shrink back, and even the brave prince is paralyzed by momentary cowardice. Prospero in time, though, finds courage enough to follow the figure to the seventh room; and there he dies. "Summoning the wild courage of despair," the courtiers follow and seize the figure. Finding "the grave-cerements and corpse-like mask . . . untenanted by any tangible form," they "gasp in unutterable horror." But even this high mark in the depiction of the supernatural is surpassed by the final paragraph as it tells of the death not only of animate beings but of inanimate objects as well: "And the life of the ebony clock went out with that of the last of the gay. And the flames of the tripods expired. And Darkness and Decay and the Red Death held illimitable dominion over all."

Since this is a tale of mounting terror, it is so wrought, Poe probably would say, as to excite the heart. The selection and arrangement of incidents, as has been shown, is such as to achieve this effect. Variety in the tone helps make the concluding terror impressive. As in "The Raven," the author avails himself of the force of contrast: he does this by portraying the figures at the masque in terms of the grotesque, thus heightening the effect of the more serious tone at the conclusion. The tone, too, in portions of the story, is such as to present many details with appropriate "homeliness." Consider the particularized description of the mysterious figure:

> . . . . tall and gaunt and shrouded from head to foot in the habiliments of the grave. The mask . . . . was made so nearly to resemble the countenance of a stiffened corpse that the closest scrutiny must have had difficulty detecting the cheat. . . . . His vesture was dabbled in *blood*—and his broad brow, with all the features of the face, was besprinkled with the scarlet horror.

Such vivid details, reminiscent in their particularity of lines in "The Wreck of the Hesperus," bring, to use Poe's words in his criticism of Longfellow, "if not positive disgust," "thrilling horror."

But elsewhere in most of the tale there is that indefiniteness, that suggestiveness—of image, of sensation, and of meaning—calculated to elevate the soul. The use in the tale, after the business-like diction of the opening paragraphs, of "the quaint in phraseology"—may be expected to have an effect similar to that of the archaic diction of the old English poets, which creates in admirers of such poets "a sense of dreamy, wild, indefinite, and . . . indefinable delight." And when the rooms in which the revel is held are described only in terms of color and light, their only mentioned furnishing being the ebony clock, the omission of so many details "stirs the spirit more pleasantly than the most elaborate picture." And often the author, like Margaret Fuller, describes rather by showing effect than by depicting directly, as in the portrayal of the bizarre figures as "delirious fancies" and "a multitude of dreams," or in calling blood "the scarlet horror."

Such phrases serve also, of course, to portray sensations suggestively, since they are attached not to the courtiers but to what they see. Other devices are helpful to the achievement of the same end. The fear stirred by the clock is hinted in words which link human qualities with this inanimate thing: when it chimes, the hour is "stricken," and the "voice of the clock" comes from its "brazen lungs" in a "solemnly emphatic" fashion. Actions suggest emotions indirectly, as when the courtiers weld shut the iron door; when few, then none, of the masquers venture into the seventh chamber; when, after "a slight rushing movement" toward the intruder, none of the courtiers puts forth a hand to seize him. The resemblance of the seventh room to a coffin is simply hinted at in the first description and in subsequent references to the "most westerly" chamber, "the hall of velvet," "the velvet apartment," and "the black apartment." And, at the very end of the story, emotions are vaguely denoted—"a certain nameless awe" and "unutterable horror."

The soul will also be stirred, presumably, by the undercurrent of meaning which runs half-hidden through "The masque of the Red Death." An allegorical signification, suggested by the tone, may be articulated. In such a signification the seven chambers progressing from east to west—from blue to black—connote the seven ages of man from the blue of the dawn of life to the black of its night. The prince and the courtiers stand for the living, who vainly seek to bar out and forget death by being gay and carefree, imagining "it is folly to grieve or to think." But death walks the earth like a plague, certain, in the end, to conquer all, and the courtiers are deceived when they believe that "with such precautions they may bid defiance to contagion." Like all men, they cannot repeat the opening words of the old saw, "Eat, drink and be merry," without adding the conclusion.

The tone, then, implies analogies which are suggestive of hidden meanings. But to say, as one very discerning critic of Poe does, that the tale "reproduces in a synthetic vision the inevitable victory of Death over Humanity," is to formulate a meaning more definitely than Poe would consider proper in the tale itself. In accordance with Poe's demand for ambiguity, he allows such a "moral" to be nothing more than a generally hidden undercurrent, and the last paragraph ends on a note inconsistent with such a meaning—a note which Poe doubtless would hold is suggestive of implications which cannot be made explicit this side of eternity.

However, it is improper, in an important sense, thus to consider separately incident and tone, since in Poe's opinion, if a tale is well constructed, they will be so integrated as to co-operate from the beginning to carry the tale inevitably to its denouement. It should be noticed, therefore, that the opening paragraphs not only introduce the incidents by setting forth the initial situation: they also introduce the word-symbols which are to have cumulative analogical significance—death and inexorable time, on the one hand, and life and the gaiety which seeks to kill time by forgetting it, on the other. The whole story which follows shows these two forces at grips and more and more definitely points forward to the inevitable and meaningful triumph of one of the forces.

The second paragraph shows Prospero and his party apparently successful in their escape from the plague: "buffoons, ... improvisatori, ... ballet-dancers, ... musicians, ... Beauty, ... wine. All these and security were within." But the last short sentence of the long paragraph again mentions the lurking enemy: "Without was the 'Red Death.'" Then, as the scene of the ball is described, the vague hint emerges that the escape is a wish rather than an actuality. The black velvet curtains, the blood-red light, and the clock which ticks the time in the seventh room, and the fear engendered in the hearts of the courtiers by the room, initiate the connotation by that room of the inescapable Red Death.

With such analogies ambiguously suggested, the incidents and tone operate simultaneously in a fashion comparable to that of a ballet. There are moments of gaiety, and then the clock strikes in the seventh room, and, inevitably, the courtiers are constrained to remember Death and Time, which are more and more definitely identified with that room:

> The musicians . . . . were constrained to pause, momentarily, in their performance, to hearken to the sound; and thus the waltzers perforce ceased their evolutions; and there was a brief disconcert of the whole gay company, and, while the chimes of the clock yet rang . . . . the giddiest grew pale, and the more aged and sedate passed their hands over their brows as if in confused reverie and meditation.

When the chimes cease, the musicians vow that they will not allow the clock again to disturb them. However, "after the lapse of sixty minutes (which embrace three thousand and six hundred seconds of the Time that flies)," there comes another chiming of the clock, and "the same disconcert and tremulousness and meditation as before." The parenthetical expression suggests more clearly than before an analogical significance for the clock, and the action and inaction of the dancers acquire accordant significance. The dance resumes, this time with the bizarre figures conjured up by Prospero moving through the rooms. But, when the clock chimes, even these do not bring forgetfulness. And the pause which now follows is, more clearly than in previous pauses, like an instant of death: "for a moment, all is still, and all is silent save the voice of the clock. The dreams are stiff-frozen as they stand." "And now again," continues the story, "the music swells, and the dreams live, and writhe to and fro more merrily than ever. . . . But . . . ." and again the story turns to the room of the clock. The coming of midnight, the hour associated with death and with the walking of the earth by uneasy spirits, is made to coincide with the discovery of the shrouded figure:

> The music ceased . . . . ; and the evolutions of the waltzers were quieted; and there was an uneasy cessation of all things. . . . . But now there were twelve strokes . . . . ; and thus . . . . more of thought crept, with more of time, into the meditations of the thoughtful among those who revelled. And thus, too, it happened, perhaps, that before the last echoes . . . . had utterly sunk into silence, ... many . . . . had found leisure to become aware of the presence of a masked figure who had arrested the attention of no single individual before.

The figure, thus appearing during a pause in music and motion and unwillingly acknowledged as a presence by the courtiers, is the Red Death. He is first viewed in the room most remote from the velvet chamber—the blue room. At first the revelers who have sought to forget and avoid death, as well as the brave prince, shrink from this explicitly symbolical masked figure. Then, when he moves with "solemn and measured step" more appropriate for a funeral than for a dance—when he moves through the seven chambers, the prince and courtiers, as if drawn by fate, follow him to "the black apartment." They see the prince die "within the shadow of the ebony clock," and now is "acknowledged the presence of the Red Death." And "the life of the ebony clock goes out with that of the last of the gay." Thus incident and tone work together from the start of the tale to its inevitable conclusion to achieve a unified effect.

THE REAL THING [1]

HENRY JAMES

WHEN the porter's wife, who used to answer the house-bell, announced "A gentleman and a lady, sir," I had, as I often had in those days—the wish being father to the thought—an immediate vision of sitters. Sitters my visitors in this case proved to be; but not in the sense I should have preferred. There was nothing at first however to indicate that they mightn't have come for a portrait. The gentleman, a man of fifty, very high and very straight, with a moustache slightly grizzled and a dark grey walking-coat admirably fitted, both of which I noted professionally—I don't mean as a barber or yet as a tailor—would have struck me as a celebrity if celebrities often were striking. It was a truth of which I had for some time been conscious that a figure with a good deal of frontage was, as one might say, almost never a public institution. A glance at the lady helped to remind me of this paradoxical law: she also looked too distinguished to be a "personality." Moreover one would scarcely come across two variations together.

Neither of the pair immediately spoke—they only prolonged the prelimi-

1. From Henry James, *The Real Thing*. Copyright, 1893, by Macmillan and Co. Copyright, 1921, by Henry James. By permission of The Macmillan Company, publishers.

nary gaze suggesting that each wished to give the other a chance. They were visibly shy; they stood there letting me take them in—which, as I afterwards perceived, was the most practical thing they could have done. In this way their embarrassment served their cause. I had seen people painfully reluctant to mention that they desired anything so gross as to be represented on canvas; but the scruples of my new friends appeared almost insurmountable. Yet the gentleman might have said "I should like a portrait of my wife," and the lady might have said "I should like a portrait of my husband." Perhaps they weren't husband and wife—this naturally would make the matter more delicate. Perhaps they wished to be done together—in which case they ought to have brought a third person to break the news.

"We come from Mr. Rivet," the lady finally said with a dim smile that had the effect of a moist sponge passed over a "sunk" piece of painting, as well as of a vague allusion to vanished beauty. She was as tall and straight, in her degree, as her companion, and with ten years less to carry. She looked as sad as a woman could look whose face was not charged with expression; that is her tinted oval mask showed waste as an exposed surface shows friction. The hand of time had played over her freely, but to an effect of elimination. She was slim and stiff, and so well-dressed, in dark blue cloth, with lappets and pockets and buttons, that it was clear she employed the same tailor as her husband. The couple had in indefinable air of prosperous thrift—they evidently got a good deal of luxury for their money. If I was to be one of their luxuries it would behoove me to consider my terms.

"Ah Claude Rivet recommended me?" I echoed; and I added that it was very kind of him, though I could reflect that, as he only painted landscape, this wasn't a sacrifice.

The lady looked very hard at the gentleman, and the gentleman looked round the room. Then, staring at the floor a moment and stroking his moustache, he rested his pleasant eyes on me with the remark: "He said you were the right one."

"I try to be, when people want to sit."

"Yes, we should like to," said the lady anxiously.

"Do you mean together?"

My visitors exchanged a glance. "If you could do anything with *me* I suppose it would be double," the gentleman stammered.

"Oh yes, there's naturally a higher charge for two figures than for one."

"We should like to make it pay," the husband confessed.

"That's very good of you," I returned, appreciating so unwonted a sympathy—for I supposed he meant pay the artist.

A sense of strangeness seemed to dawn on the lady. "We mean for the illustrations—Mr. Rivet said you might put one in."

"Put in—an illustration?" I was equally confused.

"Sketch her off, you know," said the gentleman, colouring.

It was only then that I understood the service Claude Rivet had rendered me; he had told them how I worked in black-and-white, for magazines, for storybooks, for sketches of contemporary life, and consequently had copious employment for models. These things were true, but it was not less true—I may confess it now; whether because the aspiration was to lead to everything or to nothing I leave the reader to guess—that I couldn't get the honours, to say nothing of the emoluments, of a great painter of portraits out of my head. My "illustrations" were my pot-boilers; I looked to a different branch of art—far and away the most interesting it had always seemed to me—to perpetuate my fame. There was no shame in looking to it also to make my fortune; but that fortune was by so much further from being made from the moment my visitors wished to be "done" for nothing. I was disappointed; for in the pictorial sense I had immediately *seen* them. I had seized their type—I had already settled what I would do with it. Something that wouldn't absolutely have pleased them, I afterwards reflected.

"Ah you're—you're—a—?" I began as soon as I had mastered my surprise. I couldn't bring out the dingy word "models": it seemed so little to fit the case.

"We haven't had much practice," said the lady.

"We've got to *do* something, and we've thought that an artist in your line might perhaps make something of us," her husband threw off. He further mentioned that they didn't know many artists and that they had gone first, on the off-chance—he painted views of course, but sometimes put in figures; perhaps I remembered—to Mr. Rivet, whom they had met a few years before at a place in Norfolk where he was sketching.

"We used to sketch a little ourselves," the lady hinted.

"It's very awkward, but we absolutely *must* do something," her husband went on.

"Of course we're not so *very* young," she admitted with a wan smile.

With the remark that I might as well know something more about them the husband had handed me a card extracted from a neat new pocket-book—their appurtenances were all of the freshest—and inscribed with the words "Major Monarch." Impressive as these words were they didn't carry my knowledge much further; but my visitor presently added: "I've left the army and we've had the misfortune to lose our money. In fact our means are dreadfully small."

"It's awfully trying—a regular strain," said Mrs. Monarch.

They evidently wished to be discreet—to take care not to swagger because they were gentlefolk. I felt them willing to recognize this as something of a drawback, at the same time that I guessed at an underlying sense—their consolation in adversity—that they *had* their points. They certainly had; but these advantages struck me as preponderantly social; such for instance as would help to make a drawing-room look well. However, a drawing-room was always, or ought to be, a picture.

In consequence of his wife's allusion to their age Major Monarch observed:

"Naturally it's more for the figure that we thought of going in. We can still hold ourselves up." On the instant I saw that the figure was indeed their strong point. His "naturally" didn't sound vain, but it lighted up the question. "*She* has the best one," he continued, nodding at his wife with a pleasant after-dinner absence of circumlocution. I could only reply, as if we were in fact sitting over our wine, that this didn't prevent his own from being very good; which led him in turn to make answer: "We thought that if you ever have to do people like us we might be something like it. *She* particularly—for a lady in a book, you know."

I was so amused by them that, to get more of it, I did my best to take their point of view; and though it was an embarrassment to find myself appraising physically, as if they were animals on hire or useful blacks, a pair whom I should have expected to meet only in one of the relations in which criticism is tacit, I looked at Mrs. Monarch judicially enough to be able to exclaim after a moment with conviction: "Oh yes, a lady in a book!" She was singularly like a bad illustration.

"We'll stand up, if you like," said the Major; and he raised himself before me with a really grand air.

I could take his measure at a glance—he was six feet two and a perfect gentleman. It would have paid any club in process of formation and in want of a stamp to engage him at a salary to stand in the principal window. What struck me at once was that in coming to me they had rather missed their vocation; they could surely have been turned to better account for advertising purposes. I couldn't of course see the thing in detail, but I could see them make somebody's fortune—I don't mean their own. There was something in them for a waistcoat-maker, an hotel-keeper or a soap-vendor. I could imagine "We always use it" pinned on their bosoms with the greatest effect; I had a vision of the brilliancy with which they would launch a table d'hôte.

Mrs. Monarch sat still, not from pride but from shyness, and presently her husband said to her: "Get up, my dear, and show how smart you are." She obeyed, but she had no need to get up to show it. She walked to the end of the studio and then came back blushing, her fluttered eyes on the partner of her appeal. I was reminded of an incident I had accidentally had a glimpse of in Paris—being with a friend there, a dramatist about to produce a play, when an actress came to him to ask to be entrusted with a part. She went through her paces before him, walked up and down as Mrs. Monarch was doing. Mrs. Monarch did it quite as well, but I abstained from applauding. It was very odd to see such people apply for such poor pay. She looked as if she had ten thousand a year. Her husband had used the word that described her: she was in the London current jargon essentially and typically "smart." Her figure was, in the same order of ideas, conspicuously and irreproachably "good." For a woman of her age her waist was surprisingly small; her elbow moreover had the orthodox crook. She held her head at the conventional angle, but why did she come to *me*? She ought to have tried on jackets at a big shop. I feared my visitors were not only destitute but "artistic"—which would be a great complication. When she sat down again I thanked her, observing that what a draughtsman most valued in his model was the faculty of keeping quiet.

"Oh *she* can keep quiet," said Major Monarch. Then he added jocosely: "I've always kept her quiet."

"I'm not a nasty fidget, am I?" It was going to wring tears from me, I felt, the way she hid her head, ostrich-like, in the other broad bosom.

The owner of this expanse addressed his answer to me. "Perhaps it isn't out of place to mention—because we ought to be quite business-like, oughtn't we?—that when I married her she was known as the Beautiful Statue."

"Oh dear!" said Mrs. Monarch ruefully.

"Of course I should want a certain amount of expression," I rejoined.

"Of *course!*"—and I had never heard such unanimity.

"And then I suppose you know that you'll get awfully tired."

"Oh we *never* get tired!" they eagerly cried.

"Have you had any kind of practice?"

They hesitated—they looked at each other. "We've been photographed—*immensely,*" said Mrs. Monarch.

"She means the fellows have asked us themselves," added the Major.

"I see—because you're so good-looking."

"I don't know what they thought, but they were always after us."

"We always got our photographs for nothing," smiled Mrs. Monarch.

"We might have brought some, my dear," her husband remarked.

"I'm not sure we have any left. We've given quantities away," she explained to me.

"With our autographs and that sort of thing," said the Major.

"Are they to be got in the shops?" I enquired as a harmless pleasantry.

"Oh yes, *hers*—they used to be."

"Not now," said Mrs. Monarch with her eyes on the floor.

II

I could fancy the "sort of thing" they put on the presentation copies of their photographs, and I was sure they wrote a beautiful hand. It was odd how quickly I was sure of everything that concerned them. If they were now so poor as to have to earn shillings and pence they could never have had much of a margin. Their good looks had been their capital, and they had good-humouredly made the most of the career that this resource marked out for them. It was in their faces, the blankness, the deep intellectual repose of the twenty years of country-house visiting that had given them pleasant intonations. I could see the sunny drawing-rooms, sprinkled with periodicals she didn't read, in which Mrs. Monarch had continuously sat; I could see the wet shrubberies in which she had walked, equipped to admiration for either exercise. I could see the rich covers the Major had helped to shoot and the wonderful garments in which, late at night, he repaired to the smoking-room to talk about them. I could imagine their leggings and waterproofs, their knowing tweeds and rugs, their rolls of sticks and cases of tackle and neat umbrellas; and I could evoke the exact appearance of their servants and the compact variety of their luggage on the platforms of country stations.

They gave small tips, but they were liked; they didn't do anything themselves, but they were welcome. They looked so well everywhere; they gratified the general relish for stature, complexion and "form." They knew it without fatuity or vulgarity, and they respected themselves in consequence. They weren't superficial; they were thorough and kept themselves up—it had been their line. People with such a taste for activity had to have some line. I could feel how even in a dull house they could have been counted on for the joy of life. At present something had happened—it didn't matter what, their little income had grown less, it had grown least—and they had to do something for pocket-money. Their friends could like them, I made out, without liking to support them. There was something about them that represented credit—their clothes, their manners, their type; but if credit is a large empty pocket in which an occasional chink reverberates, the chink at least must be audible. What they wanted of me was help to make it so. Fortunately they had no children—I soon divined that. They would also perhaps wish our relations to be kept secret: this was why it was "for the figure"—the reproduction of the face would betray them.

I liked them—I felt, quite as their friends must have done—they were so simple; and I had no objection to them if they would suit. But somehow with all their perfections I didn't easily believe in them. After all they were amateurs, and the ruling passion of my life was the detestation of the amateur. Combined with this was another perversity—an innate preference for the represented subject over the real one: the defect of the real one was so apt to be a lack of representation. I like things that appeared; then one was sure. Whether they *were* or not was a subordinate and almost always a profitless question. There were other considerations, the first of which was that I already had two or three recruits in use, notably a young person with big feet, in alpaca, from Kilburn, who for a couple of years had come to me regularly for my illustrations and with whom I was still—perhaps ignobly—satisfied. I frankly explained to my visitors how the case stood, but they had taken more precautions than I supposed. They had reasoned out their opportunity, for Claude Rivet had told them of the projected *édition de luxe* of one of the writers of our day—the rarest of the novelists—who, long neglected by the multitudinous vulgar and dearly prized by the attentive (need I mention Philip Vincent?) had had the happy fortune of seeing, late in life, the dawn and then the full light of a higher criticism; an estimate in which on the part of the public there was something really of expiation. The edition preparing, planned by a publisher of taste, was practically an act of high reparation; the wood-cuts with which it was to be enriched were the homage of English art to one of the most independent representatives of English letters. Major and Mrs. Monarch confessed to me they had hoped I might be able to work *them* into my branch of the enterprise. They knew I was to do the first of the books, "Rutland Ramsay," but I had to make clear to them that my participation in the rest of the affair—this first book was to be a test—must depend on the satisfaction I should give. If this should be limited my employers would drop me with scarce common forms. It was therefore a crisis for me, and naturally I was making special preparations, looking about for new people, should they be necessary, and securing the best types. I admitted however that I should like to settle down to two or three good models who would do for everything.

"Should we have often to—a—put on special clothes?" Mrs. Monarch timidly demanded.

"Dear yes—that's half the business."

"And should we be expected to supply our own costumes?"

"Oh no; I've got a lot of things. A painter's models put on—or put off—anything he likes."

"And you mean—a—the same?"

"The same?"

Mrs. Monarch looked at her husband again.

"Oh she was just wondering," he explained, "if the costumes are in *general* use." I had to confess that they were, and I mentioned further that some of them—I had a lot of genuine greasy last-century things—had served their time, a hundred years ago, on living world-stained men and women; on figures not perhaps so far removed, in that vanished world, from *their* type, the Monarchs', *quoi!* of a breeched and bewigged age. "We'll put on anything that *fits*," said the Major.

"Oh I arrange that—they fit in the pictures."

"I'm afraid I should do better for the modern books. I'd come as you like," said Mrs. Monarch.

"She has got a lot of clothes at home: they might do for contemporary life," her husband continued.

"Oh I can fancy scenes in which you'd be quite natural." And indeed I could see the slipshod rearrangements of stale properties—the stories I tried to produce pictures for without the exasperation of reading them—whose sandy tracts the good lady might help to people. But I had to return to the fact that for this sort of work—the daily mechanical grind—I was already equipped: the people I was working with were fully adequate.

"We only thought we might be more like *some* characters," said Mrs. Monarch mildly, getting up.

Her husband also rose; he stood looking at me with a dim wistfulness that was touching in so fine a man. "Wouldn't it be rather a pull sometimes to have—a—to have—?" He hung fire; he wanted me to help him by phrasing what he meant. But I couldn't—I didn't know. So he brought it out awkwardly: "The *real* thing; a gentleman, you know, or a lady." I was quite ready to give a general assent—I admitted that there was a great deal in that. This encouraged Major Monarch to say, following up his appeal with an unacted gulp: "It's awfully hard—we've tried everything." The gulp was communicative; it proved too much for his wife. Before I knew it Mrs. Monarch had dropped again upon a divan and burst into tears. Her husband sat down beside her, holding one of her hands; whereupon she quickly dried her eyes with the other, while I felt embarrassed as she looked up at me. "There isn't a confounded job I haven't applied for—waited for—prayed for. You can fancy we'd be pretty bad first. Secretaryships and that sort of thing? You might as well ask for a peerage. I'd be *anything*—I'm strong; a messenger or a coal-heaver. I'd put on a gold-laced cap and open carriage-doors in front of the haberdasher's; I'd hang about a station to carry portmanteaux; I'd be a postman. But they won't *look* at you; there are thousands as good as yourself already on the ground. *Gentlemen*, poor beggars, who've drunk their wine, who've kept their hunters!"

I was as reassuring as I knew how to be, and my visitors were presently on their feet again while, for the experiment, we agreed on an hour. We were discussing it when the door opened and Miss Churm came in with a wet umbrella. Miss Churm had to take the omnibus to Maida Vale and then walk half a mile. She looked a trifle blowsy and slightly splashed. I scarcely ever saw her come in without thinking afresh how odd it was that, being so little in herself, she should yet be so much in others. She was a meagre little Miss Churm, but was such an ample heroine of romance. She was only a freckled cockney, but she could represent everything, from a fine lady to a shepherdess; she had the faculty as she might have had a fine voice or long hair. She couldn't spell and she loved beer, but she had two or three "points," and practice, and a knack, and mother-wit, and a whimsical sensibility, and a love of the theatre, and seven sisters, and not an ounce of respect, especially for the *h*. The first thing my visitors saw was that her umbrella was wet, and in their spotless perfection they visibly winced at it. The rain had come on since their arrival.

"I'm all in a soak; there *was* a mess of people in the 'bus. I wish you lived near a stytion," said Miss Churm. I requested her to get ready as quickly as possible, and she passed into the room in which she always changed her dress. But before going out she asked me what she was to get into this time.

"It's the Russian princess, don't you know?" I answered; "the one with the 'golden eyes,' in black velvet, for the long thing in the *Cheapside*."

"Golden eyes? I *say!*" cried Miss Churm, while my companions watched her with intensity as she withdrew. She always arranged herself, when she was late, before I could turn round; and I kept my visitors a little on purpose, so that they might get an idea, from seeing her, what would be expected of themselves. I mentioned that she was quite my notion of an excellent model—she was really very clever.

"Do you think she looks like a Russian princess?" Major Monarch asked with lurking alarm.

"When I make her, yes."

"Oh if you have to *make* her—!" he reasoned, not without point.

"That's the most you can ask. There are so many who are not makeable."

"Well now, *here's* a lady"—and with a persuasive smile he passed his arm into his wife's—"who's already made!"

"Oh I'm not a Russian princess," Mrs. Monarch protested a little coldly. I could see she had known some and didn't like them. There at once was a complication of a kind I never had to fear with Miss Churm.

The young lady came back in black velvet—the gown was rather rusty and very low on her lean shoulders—and with a Japanese fan in her red hands. I reminded her that in the scene I was doing she had to look over some one's head. "I forget whose it is; but it doesn't matter. Just look over a head."

"I'd rather look over a stove," said Miss Churm; and she took her station near the fire. She fell into position, settled herself into a tall attitude, gave a certain backward inclination to her head and a certain forward droop to her fan, and looked, at least to my prejudiced sense, distinguished and charming, foreign and dangerous. We left her looking so while I went downstairs with Major and Mrs. Monarch.

"I believe I could come about as near it as that," said Mrs. Monarch.

"Oh, you think she's shabby, but you must allow for the alchemy of art."

However, they went off with an evident increase of comfort founded on their demonstrable advantage in being the real thing. I could fancy them shuddering over Miss Churm. She was very droll about them when I went back, for I told her what they wanted.

"Well, if *she* can sit I'll tyke to book-keeping," said my model.

"She's very ladylike," I replied as an innocent form of aggravation.

"So much the worse for *you*. That means she can't turn round."

"She'll do for the fashionable novels."

"Oh yes, she'll *do* for them!" my model humorously declared. "Ain't they bad enough without her?" I had often sociably denounced them to Miss Churm.

III

It was for the elucidation of a mystery in one of these works that I first tried Mrs. Monarch. Her husband came with her, to be useful if necessary—it was sufficiently clear that as a general thing he would prefer to come with her. At first I wondered if this were for "propriety's" sake—if he were going to be jealous and meddling. The idea was too tiresome, and if it had been confirmed it would speedily have brought our acquaintance to a close. But I soon saw there was nothing in it and that if he accompanied Mrs. Monarch it was—in addition to the chance of being wanted—simply because he had nothing else to do. When they were separate his occupation was gone and they never *had* been separate. I judged rightly that in their awkward situation their close union was their main comfort and that this union had no weak spot. It was a real marriage, an encouragement to the hesitating, a nut for pessimists to crack. Their address was humble—I remember afterwards thinking it had been the only thing about them that was really professional—and I could fancy the lamentable lodgings in which the Major would have been left alone. He could sit there more or less grimly with his wife—he couldn't sit there anyhow without her.

He had too much tact to try and make himself agreeable when he couldn't be useful; so when I was too absorbed in my work to talk he simply sat and waited. But I liked to hear him talk—it made my work, when not interrupting it, less mechanical, less special. To listen to him was to combine the excitement of going out with the economy of staying at home. There was only one hindrance—that I seemed not to know any of the people this brilliant couple had known. I think he wondered extremely, during the term of our intercourse, whom the deuce I *did* know. He hadn't a stray sixpence of an idea to fumble for, so we didn't spin it very fine; we confined ourselves to questions of leather and even of liquor—saddlers and breeches-makers and how to get excellent claret cheap—and matters like "good trains" and the habits of small game. His lore on these last subjects was astonishing—he managed to interweave the station-master with the ornithologist. When he couldn't talk about greater things he could talk cheerfully about smaller, and since I couldn't accompany him into reminiscences of the fashionable world he could lower the conversation without a visible effort to my level.

So earnest a desire to please was touching in a man who could so easily have knocked one down. He looked after the fire and had an opinion on the draught of the stove without my asking him, and I could see that he thought many of my arrangements not half knowing. I remember telling him that if I were only rich I'd offer him a salary to come and teach me how to live. Sometimes he gave a random sigh of which the essence might have been: "Give me even such a bare old barrack as *this*, and I'd do something with it!" When I wanted to use him he came alone; which was an illustration of the superior courage of women. His wife could bear her solitary second floor, and she was in general more discreet; showing by various small reserves that she was alive to the propriety of keeping our relations markedly professional—not letting them slide into sociability. She wished it to remain clear that she and the Major were employed, not cultivated, and if she approved of me as a superior, who could be kept in his place, she never thought me quite good enough for an equal.

She sat with great intensity, giving the whole of her mind to it, and was capable of remaining for an hour almost as motionless as before a photographer's lens. I could see she had been photographed often, but somehow the very habit that made her good for that purpose unfitted her for mine. At first

I was extremely pleased with her ladylike air, and it was a satisfaction, on coming to follow her lines, to see how good they were and how far they could lead the pencil. But after a little skirmishing I began to find her too insurmountably stiff; do what I would with it my drawing looked like a photograph or a copy of a photograph. Her figure had no variety of expression—she herself had no sense of variety. You may say that this was my business and was only a question of placing her. Yet I placed her in every conceivable position and she managed to obliterate their differences. She was always a lady certainly, and into the bargain was always the same lady. She was the real thing, but always the same thing. There were moments when I rather writhed under the serenity of her confidence that she *was* the real thing. All her dealings with me and all her husband's were an implication that this was lucky for *me*. Meanwhile I found myself trying to invent types that approached her own, instead of making her own transform itself—in the clever way that was not impossible for instance to poor Miss Churm. Arrange as I would and take the precautions I would, she always came out, in my pictures, too tall—landing me in the dilemma of having represented a fascinating woman as seven feet high, which (out of respect perhaps to my own very much scantier inches) was far from my idea of such a personage.

The case was worse with the Major—nothing I could do would keep *him* down, so that he became useful only for the representation of brawny giants. I adored variety and range, I cherished human accidents, the illustrative note; I wanted to characterise closely, and the thing in the world I most hated was the danger of being ridden by a type. I had quarrelled with some of my friends about it; I had parted company with them for maintaining that one *had* to be, and that if the type was beautiful—witness Raphael and Leonardo—the servitude was only a gain. I was neither Leonardo nor Raphael—I might only be a presumptuous young modern searcher; but I held that everything was to be sacrificed sooner than character. When they claimed that the obsessional form could easily *be* character I retorted, perhaps superficially, "Whose?" It couldn't be everybody's—it might end in being nobody's.

After I had drawn Mrs. Monarch a dozen times I felt surer even than before that the value of such a model as Miss Churm resided precisely in the fact that she had no positive stamp, combined of course with the other fact that what she did have was a curious and inexplicable talent for imitation. Her usual appearance was like a curtain which she could draw up at request for a capital performance. This performance was simply suggestive; but it was a word to the wise—it was vivid and pretty. Sometimes even I thought it, though she was plain herself, too insipidly pretty; I made it a reproach to her that the figures drawn from her were monotonously (*bêtement*, as we used to say) graceful. Nothing made her more angry; it was so much her pride to feel she could sit for characters that had nothing in common with each other. She would accuse me at such moments of taking away her "reputytion."

It suffered a certain shrinkage, this queer quantity, from the repeated visits of my new friends. Miss Churm was greatly in demand, never in want of employment, so I had no scruple in putting her off occasionally, to try them more at my ease. It was certainly amusing at first to do the real thing—it was amusing to do Major Monarch's trousers. They *were* the real thing, even if he did come out colossal. It was amusing to do his wife's back hair—it was so mathematically neat—and the particular "smart" tension of her tight stays. She lent herself especially to positions in which the face was somewhat averted or blurred; she abounded in ladylike back views and *profils perdus*. When she stood erect she took naturally one of the attitudes in which court-painters represent queens and princesses; so that I found myself wondering whether, to draw out this accomplishment, I couldn't get the editor of the *Cheapside* to publish a really royal romance, "A Tale of Buckingham Palace." Sometimes however the real thing and the make-believe came into contact; by which I mean that Miss Churm, keeping an appointment or coming to make one on days when I had much work in hand, encountered her invidious rivals. The encounter was not on their part, for they noticed her no more than if she had been the housemaid; not from intentional loftiness, but simply because as yet, professionally, they didn't know how to fraternise, as I could imagine they would have liked—or at least the Major would. They couldn't talk about the omnibus—they always walked; and they didn't know what else to try—she wasn't interested in good trains or cheap claret. Besides, they must have felt—in the air—that she was amused at them, secretly derisive of their ever knowing how. She wasn't a person to conceal the limits of her faith if she had had a chance to show them. On the other hand Mrs. Monarch didn't think her tidy; for why else did she take pains to say to me—it was going out of the way, for Mrs. Monarch—that she didn't like dirty women?

One day when my young lady happened to be present with my other sitters—she even dropped in, when it was convenient, for a chat—I asked her to be so good as to lend a hand in getting tea, a service with which she was familiar and which was one of a class that, living as I did in a small way, with slender domestic resources, I often appealed to my models to render. They liked to lay hands on my property, to break the sitting, and sometimes the china—it made them feel Bohemian. The next time I saw Miss Churm after this incident she surprised me greatly by making a scene about it—she accused me of having wished to humiliate her. She hadn't resented the outrage at the time, but had seemed obliging and amused, enjoying the comedy of asking Mrs. Monarch, who sat vague and silent, whether she would have cream and sugar, and putting an exaggerated simper into the question. She had tried intonations—as if she too wished to pass for the real thing—till I was afraid my other visitors would take offence.

Oh they were determined not to do this, and their touching patience was the measure of their great need. They would sit by the hour, uncomplaining, till I was ready to use them; they would come back on the chance of being wanted and would walk away cheerfully if it failed. I used to go to the door with them to see in what magnificent order they retreated. I tried to find other employment for them—I introduced them to several artists. But they didn't "take," for reasons I could appreciate, and I became rather anxiously aware that after such disappointments they fell back upon me with a heavier weight. They did me the honour to think me most *their* form. They weren't romantic enough for the painters, and in those days there were few serious workers in black-and-white. Besides, they had an eye to the great job I had mentioned to them—they had secretly set their hearts on supplying the right essence for my pictorial vindication of our fine novelist. They knew that for this undertaking I should want no costume-effects, none of the frippery of past ages—that it was a case in which everything would be contemporary and satirical and presumably genteel. If I could work them into it their future would be assured, for the labour would of course be long and the occupation steady.

One day Mrs. Monarch came without her husband—she explained his absence by his having had to go to the City. While she sat there in her usual relaxed majesty there came at the door a knock which I immediately recognised as the subdued appeal of a model out of work. It was followed by the entrance of a young man whom I at once saw to be a foreigner and who proved in fact an Italian acquainted with no English word but my name, which he uttered in a way that made it seem to include all others. I hadn't then visited his country, nor was I proficient in his tongue; but as he was not so meanly constituted—what Italian is?—as to depend only on that member for expression he conveyed to me, in familiar but graceful mimicry, that he was in search of exactly the employment in which the lady before me was engaged. I was not struck with him at first, and while I continued to draw I dropped few signs of interest or encouragement. He stood his ground however—not importunately, but with a dumb dog-like fidelity in his eyes that amounted to innocent impudence, the manner of a devoted servant—he might have been in the house for years—unjustly suspected. Suddenly it struck me that this very attitude and expression made a picture; whereupon I told him to sit down and wait till I should be free. There was another picture in the way he obeyed me, and I observed as I worked that there were others still in the way he looked wonderingly, with his head thrown back, about the high studio. He might have been crossing himself in Saint Peter's. Before I finished I said to myself "The fellow's a bankrupt orange-monger, but a treasure."

When Mrs. Monarch withdrew he passed across the room like a flash to open the door for her, standing there with the rapt pure gaze of the young Dante spellbound by the young Beatrice. As I never insisted, in such situations, on the blankness of the British domestic, I reflected that he had the making of a servant—and I needed one, but couldn't pay him to be only that—as well as of a model; in short I resolved to adopt my bright adventurer if he would agree to officiate in the double capacity. He jumped at my offer, and in the event my rashness—for I had really known nothing about him—

wasn't brought home to me. He proved a sympathetic though a desultory ministrant, and had in a wonderful degree the *sentiment de la pose*. It was uncultivated, instinctive, a part of the happy instinct that had guided him to my door and helped him to spell out my name on the card nailed to it. He had had no other introduction to me than a guess, from the shape of my high north window, seen outside, that my place was a studio and that as a studio it would contain an artist. He had wandered to England in search of fortune, like other itinerants, and had embarked, with a partner and a small green handcart, on the sale of penny ices. The ices had melted away and the partner had dissolved in their train. My young man wore tight yellow trousers with reddish stripes and his name was Oronte. He was sallow but fair, and when I put him into some old clothes of my own he looked like an Englishman. He was as good as Miss Churm, who could look, when requested, like an Italian.

IV

I thought Mrs. Monarch's face slightly convulsed when, on her coming back with her husband, she found Oronte installed. It was strange to have to recognise in a scrap of a lazzarone a competitor to her magnificent Major. It was she who scented danger first, for the Major was anecdotically unconscious. But Oronte gave us tea, with a hundred eager confusions—he had never been concerned in so queer a process—and I think she thought better of me for having at last an "establishment." They saw a couple of drawings that I had made of the establishment, and Mrs. Monarch hinted that it never would have struck her he had sat for them. "Now the drawings you make from *us*, they look exactly like us," she reminded me, smiling in triumph; and I recognised that this was indeed just their defect. When I drew the Monarchs I couldn't anyhow get away from them—get into the character I wanted to represent; and I hadn't the least desire my model should be discoverable in my picture. Miss Churm never was, and Mrs. Monarch thought I hid her, very properly, because she was vulgar; whereas if she was lost it was only as the dead who go to heaven are lost—in the gain of an angel the more.

By this time I had got a certain start with "Rutland Ramsay," the first novel in the great projected series; that is I had produced a dozen drawings, several with the help of the Major and his wife, and I had sent them in for approval. My understanding with the publishers, as I have already hinted, had been that I was to be left to do my work, in this particular case, as I liked, with the whole book committed to me; but my connexion with the rest of the series was only contingent. There were moments when, frankly, it *was* a comfort to have the real thing under one's hand; for there were characters in "Rutland Ramsay" that were very much like it. There were people presumably as erect as the Major and women of as good a fashion as Mrs. Monarch. There was a great deal of country-house life—treated, it is true, in a fine fanciful ironical generalised way—and there was a considerable implication of knickerbockers and kilts. There were certain things I had to settle at the outset; such things for instance as the exact appearance of the hero and the particular bloom and figure of the heroine. The author of course gave me a lead, but there was a margin for interpretation. I took the Monarchs into my confidence, I told them frankly what I was about, I mentioned my embarrassments and alternatives. "Oh take *him!*" Mrs. Monarch murmured sweetly, looking at her husband; and "What could you want better than my wife?" the Major enquired with the comfortable candour that now prevailed between us.

I wasn't obliged to answer these remarks—I was only obliged to place my sitters. I wasn't easy in mind, and I postponed a little timidly perhaps the solving of my question. The book was a large canvas, the other figures were numerous, and I worked off at first some of the episodes in which the hero and the heroine were not concerned. When once I had set *them* up I should have to stick to them—I couldn't make my young man seven feet high in one place and five feet nine in another. I inclined on the whole to the latter measurement, though the Major more than once reminded me that *he* looked about as young as any one. It was indeed quite possible to arrange him, for the figure, so that it would have been difficult to detect his age. After the spontaneous Oronte had been with me a month, and after I had given him to understand several times over that his native exuberance would presently constitute an insurmountable barrier to our further intercourse, I waked to a sense of his heroic capacity. He was only five feet seven, but the remaining inches were latent. I tried him almost secretly at first, for I was really rather afraid of the judgment my other models would pass on such a choice. If they regarded Miss Churm as little better than a snare what would they think of the representation by a person so little the real thing as an Italian streetvendor of a protagonist formed by a public school?

If I went a little in fear of them it wasn't because they bullied me, because they had got an oppressive foothold, but because in their really pathetic decorum and mysteriously permanent newness they counted on me so intensely. I was therefore very glad when Jack Hawley came home: he was always of such good counsel. He painted badly himself, but there was no one like him for putting his finger on the place. He had been absent from England for a year; he had been somewhere—I don't remember where—to get a fresh eye. I was in a good deal of dread of any such organ, but we were old friends; he had been away for months and a sense of emptiness was creeping into my life. I hadn't dodged a missile for a year.

He came back with a fresh eye, but with the same old black velvet blouse, and the first evening he spent in my studio we smoked cigarettes till the small hours. He had done no work himself, he had only got the eye; so the field was clear for the production of my little things. He wanted to see what I had produced for the *Cheapside*, but he was disappointed in the exhibition. That at least seemed the meaning of two or three comprehensive groans which, as he lounged on my big divan, his leg folded under him, looking at my latest drawings, issued from his lips with the smoke of the cigarette.

"What's the matter with you?" I asked.

"What's the matter with *you?*"

"Nothing save that I'm mystified."

"You are indeed. You're quite off the hinge. What's the meaning of this new fad?" And he tossed me, with visible irreverence, a drawing in which I happened to have depicted both my elegant models. I asked if he didn't think it good, and he replied that it struck him as execrable, given the sort of thing I had always represented myself to him as wishing to arrive at; but I let that pass—I was so anxious to see exactly what he meant. The two figures in the picture looked colossal, but I supposed this was *not* what he meant, inasmuch as, for aught he knew to the contrary, I might have been trying for some such effect. I maintained that I was working exactly in the same way as when he last had done me the honour to tell me I might do something some day. "Well, there's a screw loose somewhere," he answered; "wait a bit and I'll discover it." I depended on him to do so: where else was the fresh eye? But he produced at last nothing more luminous than "I don't know—I don't like your types." This was lame for a critic who had never consented to discuss with me anything but the question of execution, the direction of strokes and the mystery of values.

"In the drawings you've been looking at I think my types are very handsome."

"Oh they won't do!"

"I've been working with new models."

"I see you have. *They* won't do."

"Are you very sure of that?"

"Absolutely—they're stupid."

"You mean *I* am—for I ought to get round that."

"You *can't*—with such people. Who are they?"

I told him, so far as was necessary, and he concluded heartlessly: "Ce sont des gens qu'il faut mettre à la porte."

"You've never seen them; they're awfully good"—I flew to their defence.

"Not seen them? Why all this recent work of yours drops to pieces with them. It's all I want to see of them."

"No one else has said anything against it—the *Cheapside* people are pleased."

"Every one else is an ass, and the *Cheapside* people the biggest asses of all. Come, don't pretend at this time of day to have pretty illusions about the public, especially about publishers and editors. It's not for *such* animals you work—it's for those who know, *coloro che sanno*; so keep straight for *me* if you can't keep straight for yourself. There was a certain sort of thing you used to try for—and a very good thing it was. But this twaddle isn't *in* it." When I talked with Hawley later about "Rutland Ramsay" and its possible successors he declared that I must get back into my boat again or I should go to the bottom. His voice in short was the voice of warning.

I noted the warning, but I didn't turn my friends out of doors. They bored me a good deal; but the very fact that they bored me admonished me not to sacrifice them—if there was anything to be done with them—simply to irritation. As I look back at this phase they seem to me to have pervaded my life not a little. I have a vision of them as most of the time in my studio, seated against the wall on an old velvet bench to be out of the way, and resembling the while a pair of patient courtiers in a royal antechamber. I'm convinced that during the coldest weeks of the winter they held their ground because it saved them fire. Their newness was losing its gloss, and it was impossible not to feel them objects of charity. Whenever Miss Churm arrived they went away, and after I was fairly launched in "Rutland Ramsay" Miss Churm arrived pretty often. They managed to express to me tacitly that they supposed I wanted her for the low life of the book, and I let them suppose it, since they had attempted to study the work—it was lying about the studio—without discovering that it dealt only with the highest circles. They had dipped into the most brilliant of our novelists without deciphering many passages. I still took an hour from them, now and again, in spite of Jack Hawley's warning: it would be time enough to dismiss them, if dismissal should be necessary, when the rigour of the season was over. Hawley had made their acquaintance—he had met them at my fireside—and thought them a ridiculous pair. Learning that he was a painter they tried to approach him, to show him too that they were the real thing; but he looked at them, across the big room, as if they were miles away: they were a compendium of everything he most objected to in the social system of his country. Such people as that, all convention and patent-leather, with ejaculations that stopped conversation, had no business in a studio. A studio was a place to learn to see, and how could you see through a pair of feather-beds?

The main inconvenience I suffered at their hands was that at first I was shy of letting it break upon them that my artful little servant had begun to sit to me for "Rutland Ramsay." They knew I had been odd enough—they were prepared by this time to allow oddity to artists—to pick a foreign vagabond out of the streets when I might have had a person with whiskers and credentials; but it was some time before they learned how high I rated his accomplishments. They found him in an attitude more than once, but they never doubted I was doing him as an organ grinder. There were several things they never guessed, and one of them was that for a striking scene in the novel, in which a footman briefly figured, it occurred to me to make use of Major Monarch as the menial. I kept putting this off, I didn't like to ask him to don the livery—besides the difficulty of finding a livery to fit him. At last, one day late in the winter, when I was at work on the despised Oronte, who caught one's idea on the wing, and was in the glow of feeling myself go very straight, they came in, the Major and his wife, with their society laugh about nothing (there was less and less to laugh at); came in like country-callers—they always reminded me of that—who have walked across the park after church and are presently persuaded to stay to luncheon. Luncheon was over, but they could stay to tea—I knew they wanted it. The fit was on me, however, and I couldn't let my ardour cool and my work wait, with the fading daylight, while my model prepared it. So I asked Mrs. Monarch if she would mind laying it out —a request which for an instant brought all the blood to her face. Her eyes were on her husband's for a second, and some mute telegraphy passed between them. Their folly was over the next instant; his cheerful shrewdness put an end to it. So far from pitying their wounded pride, I must add, I was moved to give it as complete a lesson as I could. They bustled about together and got out the cups and saucers and made the kettle boil. I knew they felt as if they were waiting on my servant, and when the tea was prepared I said: "He'll have a cup, please—he's tired." Mrs. Monarch brought him one where he stood, and he took it from her as if he had been a gentleman at a party squeezing a crush-hat with an elbow.

Then it came over me that she had made a great effort for me—made it with a kind of nobleness—and that I owed her a compensation. Each time I saw her after this I wondered what the compensation could be. I couldn't go on doing the wrong thing to oblige them. Oh it *was* the wrong thing, the stamp of the work for which they sat—Hawley was not the only person to say it now. I sent in a large number of the drawings I had made for "Rutland Ramsay," and I received a warning that was more to the point than Hawley's. The artistic adviser of the house for which I was working was of opinion that many of my illustrations were not what had been looked for. Most of these illustrations were the subjects in which the Monarchs had figured. Without going into the question of what *had* been looked for, I had to face the fact that at this rate I shouldn't get the other books to do. I hurled myself in despair on Miss Churm—I put her through all her paces. I not only adopted Oronte publicly as my hero, but one morning when the Major looked in to see if I didn't require him to finish a *Cheapside* figure for which he had begun to sit the week before, I told him I had changed my mind—I'd do the drawing from my man. At this my visitor turned pale and stood looking at me. "Is *he* your idea of an English gentleman?" he asked.

I was disappointed, I was nervous, I wanted to get on with my work; so I replied with irritation: "Oh my dear Major—I can't be ruined for *you*!"

It was a horrid speech, but he stood another moment—after which, without a word, he quitted the studio. I drew a long breath, for I said to myself that I shouldn't see him again. I hadn't told him definitely that I was in danger of having my work rejected, but I was vexed at his not having felt the catastrophe in the air, read with me the moral of our fruitless collaboration, the lesson that in the deceptive atmosphere of art even the highest respectability may fail of being plastic.

I didn't owe my friends money, but I did see them again. They reappeared together three days later, and, given all the other facts, there was something tragic in that one. It was a clear proof they could find nothing else in life to do. They had threshed the matter out in a dismal conference—they had digested the bad news that they were not in for the series. If they weren't useful to me even for the *Cheapside* their function seemed difficult to determine, and I could only judge at first that they had come, forgivingly, decorously, to take a last leave. This made me rejoice in secret that I had little leisure for scene; for I had placed both my other models in position together and I was pegging away at a drawing from which I hoped to derive glory. It had been suggested by the passage in which Rutland Ramsay, drawing up a chair to Artemisia's piano-stool, says extraordinary things to her while she ostensibly fingers out a difficult piece of music. I had done Miss Churm at the piano before—it was an attitude in which she knew how to take on an absolutely poetic grace. I wished the two figures to "compose" together with intensity, and my little Italian had entered perfectly into my conception. The pair were vividly before me, the piano had been pulled out; it was a charming show of blended youth and murmured love, which I had only to catch and keep. My visitors stood and looked at it, and I was friendly to them over my shoulder.

They made no response, but I was used to silent company and went on with my work, only a little disconcerted—even though exhilarated by the sense that *this* was at least the ideal thing—at not having got rid of them after all. Presently I heard Mrs. Monarch's sweet voice beside or rather above me: "I wish her hair were a little better done." I looked up and she was staring with a strange fixedness at Miss Churm, whose back was turned to her. "Do you mind my just touching it?" she went on—a question which made me spring up for an instant as with the instinctive fear that she might do the young lady a harm. But she quieted me with a glance I shall never forget—I confess I should like to have been able to paint *that*—and went for a moment to my model. She spoke to her softly, laying a hand on her shoulder and bending over her; and as the girl, understanding, gratefully assented, she disposed her rough curls, with a few quick passes, in such a way as to make Miss Churm's head twice as charming. It was one of the most heroic personal services I've ever seen rendered. Then Mrs. Monarch turned away with a low sigh and, looking about her as if for something to do, stooped to the floor with a noble humility and picked up a dirty rag that had dropped out of my paint-box.

The Major meanwhile had also been looking for something to do, and, wandering to the other end of the studio, saw before him my breakfast-things neglected, unremoved. "I say, can't I be useful *here?*" he called out to me with an irrepressible quaver. I assented with a laugh that I fear was awkward, and for the next ten minutes, while I worked, I heard the light clatter of china and the tinkle of spoons and glass. Mrs. Monarch assisted her husband

—they washed up my crockery, they put it away. They wandered off into my little scullery, and I afterwards found that they had cleaned my knives and that my slender stock of plate had an unprecedented surface. When it came over me, the latent eloquence of what they were doing, I confess that my drawing was blurred for a moment—the picture swam. They had accepted their failure, but they couldn't accept their fate. They had bowed their heads in bewilderment to the perverse and cruel law in virtue of which the real thing could be so much less precious than the unreal; but they didn't want to starve. If my servants were my models, then my models might be my servants. They would reverse the parts—the others would sit for the ladies and gentlemen and *they* would do the work. They would still be in the studio—it was an intense dumb appeal to me not to turn them out. "Take us on," they wanted to say—"we'll do *anything*."

My pencil dropped from my hand; my sitting was spoiled and I got rid of my sitters, who were also evidently rather mystified and awestruck. Then, alone with the Major and his wife I had a most uncomfortable moment. He put their prayer into a single sentence: "I say, you know—just let *us* do for you, can't you?" I couldn't—it was dreadful to see them emptying my slops; but I pretended I could, to oblige them, for about a week. Then I gave them a sum of money to go away, and I never saw them again. I obtained the remaining books, but my friend Hawley repeats that Major and Mrs. Monarch did me a permanent harm, got me into false ways. If it be true I'm content to have paid the price—for the memory.

ON JAMES' *THE REAL THING* [1]

CLIFTON FADIMAN

With "The Real Thing" we meet a James story concerned specifically with the dilemmas of the artist class. . . . "The Real Thing," though its key is that of light comedy, deals with the serious problem any artist can pose to himself: the nature of reality. James's conclusion is not in the least original. Every writer, painter, sculptor who has the root of the matter in him has come to it. Goethe expresses it with lucidity when he says something to the effect that Life and Art are two different things, and that is why we call one Life and the other Art. It is a truth which the journalists writing our modern novels deny.

James came to write "The Real Thing" very much as he came to write "The Liar." He was talking one day to George du Maurier (at that time "Punch" was du Maurier). The artist told him about a couple whose reduced circumstances had compelled them to propose themselves as models for his weekly illustrations of upper-class English life. They were impeccable in back-

1. "A Note," *The Short Stories of Henry James,* pp. 216–217. Copyright, 1945, by Random House, Inc. Reprinted by permission of the publishers.

ground and appearance. They wouldn't have to pose to "make believe." They were "the real thing." But hiring them would have meant the dismissal of his two professional models. These had not a drop of blue blood in their veins but they nevertheless "had had, for dear life, to *know how* (which was to have learned how) to do something." "The question," James goes on to recall, "struck me as exquisite, and out of a momentary fond consideration of it 'The Real Thing' sprang at a bound."

The story, then, expresses amusingly (and no more than that) the old truth that art is a *transformation* of reality, not a mere reflection of the thing itself. Mrs. Monarch is a true lady, but for that very reason she cannot be a fine model of a true lady. "She was the real thing, but always the same thing." The vulgar Miss Churm, on the other hand, can represent anything, including the gentility she lacks. The Monarchs are amateurs; Miss Churm and the little Italian are professionals.

James's sympathy for his shabby-elegant pair precludes his making the point too explicitly, but it soon becomes apparent to the attentive reader, I think, that the real trouble with the Monarchs is that they are dead. They have not enough life in them to furnish a base on which the transforming power of art may work. James says it amiably enough, but he says it: "It was in their faces, the blankness, the deep intellectual repose of the twenty years of country-house visiting which had given them pleasant intonations." Whereas Miss Churm and the Italian, though social outsiders, obviously have the principle of life active in them. They cannot be lady and gentleman for twenty years, but it is within the scope of their talent to be lady and gentleman, if need be, for half an hour. It is not alone their faculty of mimesis the artist draws on; it is their vitality, their flexibility, their humor, their understanding, crude as it may be, of the sinuous, protean, evasive nature of human character.

Thus "The Real Thing" can be seen, like all of James's stories, to be a moral, as well as esthetic, comment. Or, as he would maintain, the two are one and the same.

THE JEWELS [1]

GUY DE MAUPASSANT

M. LANTIN met the girl at a party given by the assistant to the head of his office and fell in love with her.

She was the daughter of a provincial tax-collector who had died several years previously. After his death she had come to Paris with her mother, who often visited in several bourgeois families in her quarter in the hope of getting her daughter married off. They were poor and honorable, quiet and gentle.

1. Translated by Marion E. Porter and Louis G. Locke.

The girl seemed to be the perfect type of respectable young woman to whom every wise young man dreams of entrusting his future. Her unassuming beauty had a charm of angelic modesty, and the imperceptible smile which never left her lips seemed to be a reflection of the purity of her heart.

Everyone sang her praises: all of those who knew her kept repeating: "Happy will be the man who wins her. He could never find a better wife."

M. Lantin, at that time, was chief clerk in the Ministry of the Interior, with an annual salary of three thousand five hundred francs. He asked for her hand and married her.

He was unbelievably happy with her. She managed his household with such clever economy that they seemed to live in luxury. There were no attentions, no blandishments, no caresses which she did not lavish on her husband; and the attraction of her person was so great that, even six years after their first meeting, he loved her still more than he did in the first days.

He found only two faults with her: her love for the theatre and her great fondness for imitation jewelry.

Her friends (she was acquainted with the wives of several petty functionaries) always procured for her loges for the fashionable plays and sometimes even for the premières; and she dragged along her husband to these amusements whether he wanted to go or not. They tired him frightfully after his day of work at the office. Then he began to beg her to go to the theatre with some lady of her acquaintance who might be willing to accompany her home afterwards. It took a long time for her to give in, since she did not think that was the proper thing to do. Finally, to please her husband, she gave in, and he was infinitely grateful.

Now, her love for the theatre soon made her feel the need of adorning herself. Her gowns remained quite simple, it is true, and, though unpretentious, in good taste; and her gentle, irresistible grace, humble and smiling, seemed to be enhanced by the simplicity of these dresses. She, however, acquired the habit of wearing two large rhinestone ear-rings which simulated diamonds, and she wore necklaces of false pearls, bracelets of imitation gold, and combs set with various cut glasses designed to play the rôle of precious stones.

Her husband, who was somewhat shocked by this love for costume jewelry, often said: "My dear, when one does not have the means of paying for real jewels, one does not go in public ornamented with anything except one's own beauty and grace. Those are the rarest jewels."

But she smiled gently and said: "What does it matter? I like them. They are my vice. Of course, you are right; but one cannot remake oneself. I would have adored jewels!"

And she rolled over her fingers the pearl necklaces, flashed the facets of cut crystals in the light, repeating: "Just look how well made this is. You might swear that it is the real thing."

He smiled as he said: "You have Bohemian tastes."

Sometimes, in the evening when they were alone before the fire, she would bring to the table where they were having tea, the leather box in which she kept her "baubles," as M. Lantin called them; and she would examine the imitation jewelry with passionate attention as if she were tasting some secret and profound joy; and she would insist on putting a necklace around her husband's neck, after which she would laugh heartily and cry: "How funny you are!" Then she would throw herself into his arms and kiss him recklessly.

After going to the Opera one winter night, she returned home shivering with cold. The next morning she was coughing. A week later she died of pneumonia.

Lantin almost followed her into the tomb. His despair was so terrible that his hair turned white within a month. He wept from morning to evening, his soul rent by an intolerable suffering, haunted by the memory, by the smile, the voice, the charm of the dead woman.

Time did not soften his grief. Often during the hours at his office, when his colleagues came to chat about the affairs of the day, one might see his cheeks suddenly swell, his nose wrinkle up, and his eyes fill with tears; he would make a frightful face and begin to sob.

He had kept his wife's room intact and every day he would shut himself up in it to think about her; all the furniture, even her clothes, remained in their places as they had been on her last day.

But life was becoming hard for him. His pay, which, when managed by his wife, had been adequate for all the needs of his household, was now becoming insufficient for him alone. And he wondered with helpless amazement how she had always managed to provide him with excellent wines and delicate foods which he could no longer obtain with his modest resources.

He made a few debts and chased money in the manner of people who are reduced to living by their wits. Finding himself without a sou one morning an entire week before the end of the month, he thought of selling something; and all at once the thought came to him that he might dispose of his wife's "baubles," for he had kept in the bottom of his heart a kind of grudge against these "eye-deceivers" which used to irritate him so much. The very sight of them each day somewhat spoiled his memory of his beloved.

He sought a long time in the pile of tawdry jewelry which she had left behind, for she had obstinately kept on buying these things up to the last days of her life, bringing home some new piece almost every evening. Finally he decided on the great necklace which she seemed to prefer and which he thought might be worth, at least six or eight francs, for it was really very carefully made for artificial jewelry.

He put it in his pocket and left for the office, following the boulevards on which he hoped to find a jeweler's shop which he might feel confident enough to enter.

He finally saw one and went in, a bit ashamed at displaying his poverty by trying to sell a thing of so little value.

"Sir," he said to the merchant, "I would like to know at what you value this piece."

The man took the object, examined it, turned it over, tried its weight, looked at it through his glass, called his clerk, said something to him in a low voice, placed the necklace back on the counter and looked at it from a distance in order to judge its effect better.

M. Lantin, disturbed by all this ceremony, was about to open his mouth to declare: "Oh! I know it is of no value," when the jeweler delivered his pronouncement:

"Sir, that is worth between twelve and fifteen thousand francs; but I could buy it only upon the condition that you inform me as to exactly where it comes from."

The widower opened his eyes wide in amazement and gaped in astonishment, not understanding. He finally stammered: "You say . . . ? You are sure?" The other failed to understand the cause of his astonishment, and said drily: "You can try elsewhere to see if anyone will give you more. As far as I am concerned, that is worth fifteen thousand, at the most. You can come back to see me if you can not find anything better."

M. Lantin, completely stupefied, took up his necklace and left, obeying a confused need to be alone and to think.

But as soon as he was in the street, he was seized by a need to laugh, and he thought: "That fool! Oh, the fool! What if I had taken him at his word? There's a jeweler who can't distinguish between the false and the real."

And he went to another merchant at the entrance of the rue de la Paix. As soon as he saw the jewel, the goldsmith cried:

"Ah! indeed; I am well acquainted with that necklace; it comes from my shop."

Lantin, very disturbed, asked:

"How much is it worth?"

"Sir, I sold it for twenty-five thousand. I am ready to buy it back for eighteen thousand as soon as you have indicated to me just how it happens to be in your possession. I need that information in order to obey the law."

This time M. Lantin sat down paralyzed with amazement. He answered: "Why . . . . why, examine it carefully, sir. I had thought until now that it was . . . artificial."

The jeweler replied: "Will you tell me your name, sir?"

"Certainly. My name is Lantin, I am an employee at the Ministry of the Interior, and I live at 16, rue des Martyrs."

The merchant opened his registers, looked in them, and said: "This necklace was in fact sent to the address of Mme. Lantin at 16, rue des Martyrs, on the 20th of July 1876."

And the two men looked into each other's eyes, the government employee dumb with amazement and the jeweler sensing a thief.

The latter replied, "Will you leave this piece with me for just twenty-four hours? I will give you a receipt for it."

Lantin stammered: "Why yes, certainly." And he departed, folding the receipt which he placed in his pocket.

Then he crossed the street, went up it, saw that he had gone the wrong way, went back down to the Tuileries, crossed the Seine, recognized that he had made another error, returned to the Champs Elysées. His head was completely void of clear ideas. He tried to reason, to understand. His wife had not been able to buy an object of such value. No, certainly not. Why then it was a gift! A gift! A gift from whom? Why?

He had stopped in the middle of the avenue and stood there. A horrible doubt came over him. She? Why then all the other jewels were also gifts! It seemed to him that the earth was shaking; that a tree in front of him was falling; he stretched out his arms and collapsed, unconscious.

He regained consciousness in a pharmacist's shop where some passers-by had carried him. He got somebody to take him home and he shut himself up.

He wept desperately until night, biting a handkerchief to keep from crying out. Then he went to bed overwhelmed with fatigue and sorrow, and he slept soundly and dreamlessly.

A ray of sunlight awakened him and he got up slowly to go to the office. It was hard to work after such shattering experiences. He thought then that he might apologize to his chief; and he wrote to him. Then he thought that he must return to the jeweler's; and shame made him blush. He thought it over for a long time. He could not leave the necklace at that man's shop; he dressed and went out.

It was a beautiful day, the blue sky covering the city seemed to smile. Idlers were strolling about with their hands in their pockets.

Lantin said to himself as he watched them pass: "How happy a person must be who has money. With money one can even shake off grief; one can go where one wants; one can travel, have a good time. Oh! if I were only rich!"

He realized that he was hungry since he had not eaten for forty-eight hours. But his pockets were empty. "Eighteen thousand francs! *That* was a sum!"

He reached the rue de la Paix and began to pace back and forth on the sidewalk across from the shop. Eighteen thousand francs! Twenty times he tried to enter, but shame stopped him.

He was hungry, however, very hungry and did not have a *sou*. All of a sudden he made up his mind, crossed the street at a run, so as not to give himself time to think, and dashed into the jeweler's shop.

As soon as the merchant saw him he rushed forward, offered him a chair with a kind of smiling politeness. The clerks came forward, giving Lantin sidewise glances, with gaiety in their eyes and on their lips.

The jeweler declared: "I have made the necessary inquiries, sir, and if you are still willing, I am prepared to pay you the sum which I proposed to you."

The government employee stammered: "Why certainly."

The jeweler took eighteen large banknotes from a drawer, counted them, handed them to Lantin who signed a receipt and tremblingly placed the money in his pocket.

Then, as he was about to leave, he turned toward the merchant, who was still smiling and, lowering his eyes, said: "I . . . . I have other jewels . . . . which came to me . . . . from the same source. Would you care to buy them also?"

The merchant bowed: "Why certainly, sir."

One of the clerks left the room in order to laugh more freely; another blew his nose loudly.

Lantin, impassive, blushing and serious, said: "I shall bring them to you."

And he took a cab in order to go and get the jewels.

When he came back to the merchant's an hour later, he had not yet had lunch. They began to examine the jewelry piece by piece, evaluating each one. Almost all of them came from that shop.

Lantin was now disposed to argue about the evaluation, he would become angry, he demanded that he be shown the ledgers, and spoke louder as the sum increased.

The large diamond earrings were worth twenty thousand francs, the bracelets thirty-five thousand, the brooches, rings and lockets sixteen thousand, an emerald and sapphire necklace fourteen thousand; a diamond solitaire on a gold chain forty thousand—the lot reached the figure of a hundred and ninety-six thousand francs.

The jeweler declared with bantering good humor: "All that comes from a person whose savings were put in jewels."

Lantin said seriously: "That is as good a way as any of investing money." And he left after deciding with the purchaser that another evaluation would be made the next day.

When he was in the street, he looked at the Colonne Vendôme with the desire to climb it in high good spirits. He felt that he was light enough to play leap frog with the statue of Napoleon which is on top of it.

He went to Voisin's for lunch and drank wine which cost twenty francs per bottle.

Then he took a cab and had a ride through the Bois de Boulogne. He looked at the other carriages somewhat scornfully, assailed with the desire to cry out to all whom he passed: "I, too, am rich. I have two hundred thousand francs!"

He remembered the office. He had the driver take him there, entered his chief's office deliberately, and announced:

"I come, sir, to hand you my resignation. I have inherited three hundred thousand francs." He shook hands with his former colleagues and told them confidentially of his plans for his new life; then he dined at the café Anglais.

Finding himself beside a gentleman who seemed distinguished, he could not resist the desire to confide in him, with a certain coquettishness, that he had just inherited four hundred thousand francs.

For the first time in his life he was not bored at the theater and he spent the night with some girls.

Six months later he remarried. His second wife was very respectable, but of a difficult disposition. She made him suffer a lot.

GOOSEBERRIES [1]

ANTON CHEKHOV

THE SKY had been overcast since early morning; it was a still day, not hot, but tedious, as it usually is when the weather is gray and dull, when clouds have been hanging over the fields for a long time, and you wait for the rain that does not come. Ivan Ivanych, a veterinary, and Burkin, a high school teacher, were already tired with walking, and the plain seemed endless to them. Far ahead were the scarcely visible windmills of the village of Mironositzkoe; to the right lay a range of hills that disappeared in the distance beyond the village, and both of them knew that over there were the river, and fields, green willows, homesteads, and if you stood on one of the hills, you could see from there another vast plain, telegraph poles, and a train that from afar looked like a caterpillar crawling, and in clear weather you could even see the town. Now, when it was still and when nature seemed mild and pensive, Ivan Ivanych and Burkin were filled with love for this plain, and both of them thought what a beautiful land it was.

"Last time when we were in Elder Prokofy's barn," said Burkin, "you were going to tell me a story."

"Yes; I wanted to tell you about my brother."

Ivan Ivanych heaved a slow sigh and lit his pipe before beginning his story, but just then it began to rain. And five minutes later there was a downpour, and it was hard to tell when it would be over. The two men halted, at a loss; the dogs, already wet, stood with their tails between their legs and looked at them feelingly.

"We must find shelter somewhere," said Burkin. "Let's go to Alyohin's; it's quite near."

"Let's."

They turned aside and walked across a mown meadow, now going straight ahead, now bearing to the right, until they reached the road. Soon poplars came into view, a garden, then the red roofs of barns; the river gleamed, and

1. From *The Portable Chekhov,* translated, selected, and edited by Avrahm Yarmolinsky.

the view opened on a broad expanse of water with a mill and a white bathing-cabin. That was Sofyino, Alyohin's place.

The mill was going, drowning out the sound of the rain; the dam was shaking. Wet horses stood near the carts, their heads drooping, and men were walking about, their heads covered with sacks. It was damp, muddy, dreary; and the water looked cold and unkind. Ivan Ivanych and Burkin felt cold and messy and uncomfortable through and through; their feet were heavy with mud and when, having crossed the dam, they climbed up to the barns, they were silent as though they were cross with each other.

The noise of a winnowing-machine came from one of the barns, the door was open, and clouds of dust were pouring from within. On the threshold stood Alyohin himself, a man of forty, tall and rotund, with long hair, looking more like a professor or an artist than a gentleman farmer. He was wearing a white blouse, badly in need of washing, that was belted with a rope, and drawers, and his high boots were plastered with mud and straw. His eyes and nose were black with dust. He recognized Ivan Ivanych and Burkin and was apparently very glad to see them.

"Please go up to the house, gentlemen," he said, smiling; "I'll be there directly, in a moment."

It was a large structure of two stories. Alyohin lived downstairs in what was formerly the stewards' quarters: two rooms that had arched ceilings and small windows; the furniture was plain, and the place smelled of rye bread, cheap vodka, and harness. He went into the showy rooms upstairs only rarely, when he had guests. Once in the house, the two visitors were met by a chambermaid, a young woman so beautiful that both of them stood still at the same moment and glanced at each other.

"You can't imagine how glad I am to see you, gentlemen," said Alyohin, joining them in the hall. "What a surprise! Pelageya," he said, turning to the chambermaid, "give the guests a change of clothes. And, come to think of it, I will change, too. But I must go and bathe first, I don't think I've had a wash since spring. Don't you want to go into the bathing-cabin? In the meanwhile things will be got ready here."

The beautiful Pelageya, with her soft, delicate air, brought them bath towels and soap, and Alyohin went to the bathing-cabin with his guests.

"Yes, it's a long time since I've bathed," he said, as he undressed. "I've an excellent bathing-cabin, as you see—it was put up by my father—but somehow I never find time to use it." He sat down on the steps and lathered his long hair and neck, and the water around him turned brown.

"I say—" observed Ivan Ivanych significantly, looking at his head.

"I haven't had a good wash for a long time," repeated Alyohin, embarrassed, and soaped himself once more; the water about him turned dark-blue, the color of ink.

Ivan Ivanych came out of the cabin, plunged into the water with a splash and swam in the rain, thrusting his arms out wide; he raised waves on which white lilies swayed. He swam out to the middle of the river and dived and a minute later came up in another spot and swam on and kept diving, trying to touch bottom. "By God!" he kept repeating delightedly, "by God!" He swam to the mill, spoke to the peasants there, and turned back and in the middle of the river lay floating, exposing his face to the rain. Burkin and Alyohin were already dressed and ready to leave, but he kept on swimming and diving. "By God!" he kept exclaiming. "Lord, have mercy on me."

"You've had enough!" Burkin shouted to him.

They returned to the house. And only when the lamp was lit in the big drawing room upstairs, and the two guests, in silk dressing-gowns and warm slippers, were lounging in armchairs, and Alyohin himself, washed and combed, wearing a new jacket, was walking about the room, evidently savoring the warmth, the cleanliness, the dry clothes and light footwear, and when pretty Pelageya, stepping noiselessly across the carpet and smiling softly, brought in a tray with tea and jam, only then did Ivan Ivanych begin his story, and it was as though not only Burkin and Alyohin were listening, but also the ladies, old and young, and the military men who looked down upon them, calmly and severely, from their gold frames.

"We are two brothers," he began, "I, Ivan Ivanych, and my brother, Nikolay Ivanych, who is two years my junior. I went in for a learned profession and became a veterinary; Nikolay at nineteen began to clerk in a provincial branch of the Treasury. Our father was a *kantonist,*[1] but he rose to be an officer and so a nobleman, a rank that he bequeathed to us together with a small estate. After his death there was a lawsuit and we lost the estate to creditors, but be that as it may, we spent our childhood in the country. Just like peasant children we passed days and nights in the fields and the woods, herded horses, stripped bast from the trees, fished, and so on. And, you know, whoever even once in his life has caught a perch or seen thrushes migrate in the autumn, when on clear, cool days they sweep in flocks over the village, will never really be a townsman and to the day of his death will have a longing for the open. My brother was unhappy in the government office. Years passed, but he went on warming the same seat, scratching away at the same papers, and thinking of one and the same thing: how to get away to the country. And little by little this vague longing turned into a definite desire, into a dream of buying a little property somewhere on the banks of a river or a lake.

"He was a kind and gentle soul and I loved him, but I never sympathized with his desire to shut himself up for the rest of his life on a little property of his own. It is a common saying that a man needs only six feet of earth. But six feet is what a corpse needs, not a man. It is also asserted that if our educated class is drawn to the land and seeks to settle on farms, that's a good thing. But these farms amount to the same six feet of earth. To retire from the city, from the struggle, from the hubbub, to go off and hide on one's own farm—that's

1. The son of a private, registered at birth in the army and trained in a military school.

not life, it is selfishness, sloth, it is a kind of monasticism, but monasticism without works. Man needs not six feet of earth, not a farm, but the whole globe, all of Nature, where unhindered he can display all the capacities and peculiarities of his free spirit.

"My brother Nikolay, sitting in his office, dreamed of eating his own *shchi*, which would fill the whole farmyard with a delicious aroma, of picnicking on the green grass, of sleeping in the sun, of sitting for hours on the seat by the gate gazing at field and forest. Books on agriculture and the farming items in almanacs were his joy, the delight of his soul. He liked newspapers too, but the only things he read in them were advertisements of land for sale, so many acres of tillable land and pasture, with house, garden, river, mill, and millpond. And he pictured to himself garden paths, flowers, fruit, bird-houses with starlings in them, crucians in the pond, and all that sort of thing, you know. These imaginary pictures varied with the advertisements he came upon, but somehow gooseberry bushes figured in every one of them. He could not picture to himself a single country-house, a single rustic nook, without gooseberries.

"'Country life has its advantages,' he used to say. 'You sit on the veranda having tea, and your ducks swim in the pond, and everything smells delicious and—the gooseberries are ripening.'

"He would draw a plan of his estate and invariably it would contain the following features: a) the master's house; b) servants' quarters; c) kitchen-garden; d) a gooseberry patch. He lived meagerly: he deprived himself of food and drink; he dressed God knows how, like a beggar, but he kept on saving and salting money away in the bank. He was terribly stingy. It was painful for me to see it, and I used to give him small sums and send him something on holidays, but he would put that away too. Once a man is possessed by an idea, there is no doing anything with him.

"Years passed. He was transferred to another province, he was already past forty, yet he was still reading newspaper advertisements and saving up money. Then I heard that he was married. Still for the sake of buying a property with a gooseberry patch he married an elderly, homely widow, without a trace of affection for her, but simply because she had money. After marrying her, he went on living parsimoniously, keeping her half-starved, and he put her money in the bank in his own name. She had previously been the wife of a postmaster, who had got her used to pies and cordials. This second husband did not even give her enough black bread. She began to sicken, and some three years later gave up the ghost. And, of course, it never for a moment occurred to my brother that he was to blame for her death. Money, like vodka, can do queer things to a man. Once in our town a merchant lay on his deathbed; before he died, he ordered a plateful of honey and he ate up all his money and lottery tickets with the honey, so that no one should get it. One day when I was inspecting a drove of cattle at a railway station, a cattle dealer fell under a locomotive and it sliced off his leg. We carried him in to the infirmary, the blood was gushing from the wound—a terrible business, but he kept begging us to find his leg and was very anxious about it: he had twenty rubles in the boot that was on that leg, and he was afraid they would be lost."

"That's a tune from another opera," said Burkin.

Ivan Ivanych paused a moment and then continued:

"After his wife's death, my brother began to look around for a property. Of course, you may scout about for five years and in the end make a mistake, and buy something quite different from what you have been dreaming of. Through an agent my brother bought a mortgaged estate of three hundred acres with a house, servants' quarters, a park, but with no orchard, no gooseberry patch, no duck-pond. There was a stream, but the water in it was the color of coffee, for on one of its banks there was a brickyard and on the other a glue factory. But my brother was not at all disconcerted: he ordered a score of gooseberry bushes, planted them, and settled down to the life of a country gentleman.

"Last year I paid him a visit. I thought I would go and see how things were with him. In his letter to me my brother called his estate 'Chumbaroklov Waste, or Himalaiskoe' (our surname was Chimsha-Himalaisky). I reached the place in the afternoon. It was hot. Everywhere there were ditches, fences, hedges, rows of fir trees, and I was at a loss as to how to get to the yard and where to leave my horse. I made my way to the house and was met by a fat dog with reddish hair that looked like a pig. It wanted to bark, but was too lazy. The cook, a fat, barelegged woman, who also looked like a pig, came out of the kitchen and said that the master was resting after dinner. I went in to see my brother, and found him sitting up in bed, with a quilt over his knees. He had grown older, stouter, flabby; his cheeks, his nose, his lips jutted out: it looked as though he might grunt into the quilt at any moment.

"We embraced and dropped tears of joy and also of sadness at the thought that the two of us had once been young, but were now gray and nearing death. He got dressed and took me out to show me his estate.

" 'Well, how are you getting on here?' I asked.

" 'Oh, all right, thank God. I am doing very well.'

"He was no longer the poor, timid clerk he used to be but a real landowner, a gentleman. He had already grown used to his new manner of living and developed a taste for it. He ate a great deal, steamed himself in the bathhouse, was growing stout, was already having a lawsuit with the village commune and the two factories and was very much offended when the peasants failed to address him as 'Your Honor.' And he concerned himself with his soul's welfare too in a substantial, upper-class manner, and performed good deeds not simply, but pompously. And what good works! He dosed the peasants with bicarbonate and castor oil for all their ailments and on his name day he had a thanksgiving service celebrated in the center of the village, and then treated the villagers to a gallon of vodka, which he thought was the thing to do. Oh, those horrible gallons of vodka! One day a fat landowner hauls the peasants up before the rural police officer for trespassing, and the next, to mark a feast day, treats them to a gallon of vodka, and they drink and shout 'Hurrah' and when they are drunk bow down at his feet. A higher standard of living, overeating and idleness develop the most insolent self-conceit in a Russian. Nikolay Ivanych, who when he was a petty official was afraid to have opinions of his own even if he kept them to himself, now uttered nothing but incontrovertible truths and did so in the tone of a minister of state: 'Education is necessary, but the masses are not ready for it; corporal punishment is generally harmful, but in some cases it is useful and nothing else will serve.'

"'I know the common people, and I know how to deal with them,' he would say. 'They love me. I only have to raise my little finger, and they will do anything I want.'

"And all this, mark you, would be said with a smile that bespoke kindness and intelligence. Twenty times over he repeated: 'We, of the gentry,' 'I, as a member of the gentry.' Apparently he no longer remembered that our grandfather had been a peasant and our father just a private. Even our surname, 'Chimsha-Himalaisky,' which in reality is grotesque, seemed to him sonorous, distinguished, and delightful.

"But I am concerned now not with him, but with me. I want to tell you about the change that took place in me during the few hours that I spent on his estate. In the evening when we were having tea, the cook served a plateful of gooseberries. They were not bought, they were his own gooseberries, the first ones picked since the bushes were planted. My brother gave a laugh and for a minute looked at the gooseberries in silence, with tears in his eyes—he could not speak for excitement. Then he put the one berry in his mouth, glanced at me with the triumph of a child who has at last been given a toy he was longing for and said: 'How tasty!' And he ate the gooseberries greedily, and kept repeating: 'Ah, how delicious! Do taste them!'

"They were hard and sour, but as Pushkin has it,

> The falsehood that exalts we cherish more
> Than meaner truths that are a thousand strong.

I saw a happy man, one whose cherished dream had so obviously come true, who had attained his goal in life, who had got what he wanted, who was satisfied with his lot and with himself. For some reason an element of sadness had always mingled with my thoughts of human happiness, and now at the sight of a happy man I was assailed by an oppressive feeling bordering on despair. It weighed on me particularly at night. A bed was made up for me in a room next to my brother's bedroom, and I could hear that he was wakeful, and that he would get up again and again, go to the plate of gooseberries and eat one after another. I said to myself: how many contented, happy people there really are! What an overwhelming force they are! Look at life: the insolence and idleness of the strong, the ignorance and brutishness of the weak, horrible poverty everywhere, overcrowding, degeneration, drunkenness, hypocrisy, lying— Yet in all the houses and on all the streets there is peace and quiet; of the fifty thousand people who live in our town there is not one who would cry out, who would vent his indignation aloud. We see the people who go to market, eat by day, sleep by night, who babble nonsense, marry, grow old, good-naturedly drag their dead to the cemetery, but we do not see or hear those who suffer, and what is terrible in life goes on somewhere behind the scenes. Everything is peaceful and quiet and only mute statistics protest: so many people gone out of their minds, so many gallons of vodka drunk, so many children dead from malnutrition—And such a state of things is evidently necessary; obviously the happy man is at ease only because the unhappy ones bear their burdens in silence, and if there were not this silence, happiness would be impossible. It is a general hypnosis. Behind the door of every contented, happy man there ought to be someone standing with a little hammer and continually reminding him with a knock that there are unhappy people, that however happy he may be, life will sooner or later show him its claws, and trouble will come to him—illness, poverty, losses, and then no one will see or hear him, just as now he neither sees nor hears others. But there is no man with a hammer. The happy man lives at his ease, faintly fluttered by small daily cares, like an aspen in the wind—and all is well."

"That night I came to understand that I too had been contented and happy," Ivan Ivanych continued, getting up. "I too over the dinner table or out hunting would hold forth on how to live, what to believe, the right way to govern the people. I too would say that learning was the enemy of darkness, that education was necessary but that for the common people the three R's were sufficient for the time being. Freedom is a boon, I used to say, it is as essential as air, but we must wait awhile. Yes, that's what I used to say, and now I ask: Why must we wait?" said Ivan Ivanych, looking wrathfully at Burkin. "Why must we wait, I ask you? For what reason? I am told that nothing can be done all at once, that every idea is realized gradually, in its own time. But who is it that says so? Where is the proof that it is just? You cite the natural order of things, the law governing all phenomena, but is there law, is there order in the fact that I, a living, thinking man, stand beside a ditch and wait for it to close up of itself or fill up with silt, when I could jump over it or throw a bridge across it? And again, why must we wait? Wait, until we have no strength to live, and yet we have to live and are eager to live!

"I left my brother's place early in the morning, and ever since then it has become intolerable for me to stay in town. I am oppressed by the peace and the quiet, I am afraid to look at the windows, for there is nothing that pains me more than the spectacle of a happy family sitting at table having tea. I am an old man now and unfit for combat, I am not even capable of hating. I can only grieve inwardly, get irritated, worked up, and at night my head is ablaze with the rush of ideas and I cannot sleep. Oh, if I were young!"

Ivan Ivanych paced up and down the room excitedly and repeated, "If I were young!"

He suddenly walked up to Alyohin and began to press now one of his hands, now the other.

"Pavel Konstantinych," he said imploringly, "don't quiet down, don't let yourself be lulled to sleep! as long as you are young, strong, alert, do not cease to do good! There is no happiness and there should be none, and if life has a meaning and a purpose, that meaning and purpose is not our happiness but something greater and more rational. Do good!"

All this Ivan Ivanych said with a pitiful, imploring smile, as though he were asking a personal favor.

Afterwards all three of them sat in armchairs in different corners of the drawing room and were silent. Ivan Ivanych's story satisfied neither Burkin nor Alyohin. With the ladies and generals looking down from the golden frames, seeming alive in the dim light, it was tedious to listen to the story of the poor devil of a clerk who ate gooseberries. One felt like talking about elegant people, about women. And the fact that they were sitting in a drawing room where everything—the chandelier under its cover, the armchairs, the carpets underfoot—testified that the very people who were now looking down from the frames had once moved about here, sat and had tea, and the fact that lovely Pelageya was noiselessly moving about—that was better than any story.

Alyohin was very sleepy; he had gotten up early, before three o'clock in the morning, to get some work done, and now he could hardly keep his eyes open, but he was afraid his visitors might tell an interesting story in his absence, and he would not leave. He did not trouble to ask himself if what Ivan Ivanych had just said was intelligent or right. The guests were not talking about groats, or hay, or tar, but about something that had no direct bearing on his life, and he was glad of it and wanted them to go on.

"However, it's bedtime," said Burkin, rising. "Allow me to wish you good night."

Alyohin took leave of his guests and went downstairs to his own quarters, while they remained upstairs. They were installed for the night in a big room in which stood two old wooden beds decorated with carvings and in the corner was an ivory crucifix. The wide cool beds which had been made by the lovely Pelageya gave off a pleasant smell of clean linen.

Ivan Ivanych undressed silently and got into bed.

"Lord forgive us sinners!" he murmured, and drew the bedclothes over his head.

His pipe, which lay on the table, smelled strongly of burnt tobacco, and Burkin, who could not sleep for a long time, kept wondering where the unpleasant odor came from.

The rain beat against the window panes all night.

THE BRIDE COMES TO YELLOW SKY [1]

STEPHEN CRANE

I

THE GREAT Pullman was whirling onward with such dignity of motion that a glance from the window seemed simply to prove that the plains of Texas were pouring eastward. Vast flats of green grass, dull-hued spaces of mesquite and cactus, little groups of frame houses, woods of light and tender trees, all were sweeping into the east, sweeping over the horizon, a precipice.

A newly married pair had boarded this coach at San Antonio. The man's face was reddened from many days in the wind and sun, and a direct result of his new black clothes was that his brick-colored hands were constantly performing in a most conscious fashion. From time to time he looked down respectfully at his attire. He sat with a hand on each knee, like a man waiting in a barber's shop. The glances he devoted to other passengers were furtive and shy.

The bride was not pretty, nor was she very young. She wore a dress of blue cashmere, with small reservations of velvet here and there, and with steel buttons abounding. She continually twisted her head to regard her puff sleeves, very stiff, straight, and high. They embarrassed her. It was quite apparent that she had cooked, and that she expected to cook, dutifully. The blushes caused by the careless scrutiny of some passengers as she had entered the car were strange to see upon this plain, under-class countenance, which was drawn in placid, almost emotionless lines.

They were evidently very happy. "Ever been in a parlor-car before?" he asked, smiling with delight.

"No," she answered; "I never was. It's fine, ain't it?"

"Great! And then after a while we'll go forward to the diner, and get a big lay-out. Finest meal in the world. Charge a dollar."

"Oh, do they?" cried the bride. "Charge a dollar? Why, that's too much—for us—ain't it, Jack?"

"Not this trip, anyhow," he answered bravely. "We're going to go the whole thing."

Later he explained to her about the trains. "You see, it's a thousand miles from one end of Texas to the other; and this train runs right across it, and never stops but four times." He had the pride of an owner. He pointed out to her the dazzling fittings of the coach; and in truth her eyes opened wider as she contemplated the sea-green figured velvet, the shining brass, silver, and glass, the wood that gleamed as darkly brilliant as the surface of a pool of oil.

1. Reprinted from *Twenty Stories* by Stephen Crane by permission of Alfred A. Knopf, Inc. Copyright, 1925, by William H. Crane.

At one end a bronze figure sturdily held a support for a separated chamber, and at convenient places on the ceiling were frescos in olive and silver.

To the minds of the pair, their surroundings reflected the glory of their marriage that morning in San Antonio; this was the environment of their new estate; and the man's face in particular beamed with an elation that made him appear ridiculous to the negro porter. This individual at times surveyed them from afar with an amused and superior grin. On other occasions he bullied them with skill in ways that did not make it exactly plain to them that they were being bullied. He subtly used all the manners of the most unconquerable kind of snobbery. He oppressed them; but of this oppression they had small knowledge, and they speedily forgot that infrequently a number of travellers covered them with stares of derisive enjoyment. Historically there was supposed to be something infinitely humorous in their situation.

"We are due in Yellow Sky at 3:42," he said, looking tenderly into her eyes.

"Oh, are we?" she said, as if she had not been aware of it. To evince surprise at her husband's statement was part of her wifely amiability. She took from a pocket a little silver watch; and as she held it before her, and stared at it with a frown of attention, the new husband's face shone.

"I bought it in San Anton' from a friend of mine," he told her gleefully.

"It's seventeen minutes past twelve," she said, looking up at him with a kind of shy and clumsy coquetry. A passenger, noting this play, grew excessively sardonic, and winked at himself in one of the numerous mirrors.

At last they went to the dining-car. Two rows of negro waiters, in glowing white suits, surveyed their entrance with the interest, and also the equanimity, of men who had been forewarned. The pair fell to the lot of a waiter who happened to feel pleasure in steering them through their meal. He viewed them with the manner of a fatherly pilot, his countenance radiant with benevolence. The patronage, entwined with the ordinary deference, was not plain to them. And yet, as they returned to their coach, they showed in their faces a sense of escape.

To the left, miles down a long purple slope, was a little ribbon of mist where moved the keening Rio Grande. The train was approaching it at an angle, and the apex was Yellow Sky. Presently it was apparent that, as the distance from Yellow Sky grew shorter, the husband became commensurately restless. His brick-red hands were more insistent in their prominence. Occasionally he was even rather absent-minded and far-away when the bride leaned forward and addressed him.

As a matter of truth, Jack Potter was beginning to find the shadow of a deed weigh upon him like a leaden slab. He, the town marshal of Yellow Sky, a man known, liked, and feared in his corner, a prominent person, had gone to San Antonio to meet a girl he believed he loved, and there, after the usual prayers, had actually induced her to marry him, without consulting

Yellow Sky for any part of the transaction. He was now bringing his bride before an innocent and unsuspecting community.

Of course people in Yellow Sky married as it pleased them, in accordance with a general custom; but such was Potter's thought of his duty to his friends, or of their idea of his duty, or of an unspoken form which does not control men in these matters, that he felt he was heinous. He had committed an extraordinary crime. Face to face with this girl in San Antonio, and spurred by his sharp impulse, he had gone headlong over all the social hedges. At San Antonio he was like a man hidden in the dark. A knife to sever any friendly duty, any form, was easy to his hand in that remote city. But the hour of Yellow Sky—the hour of daylight—was approaching.

He knew full well that his marriage was an important thing to his town. It could only be exceeded by the burning of the new hotel. His friends could not forgive him. Frequently he had reflected on the advisability of telling them by telegraph, but a new cowardice had been upon him. He feared to do it. And now the train was hurrying him toward a scene of amazement, glee, and reproach. He glanced out of the window at the line of haze swinging slowly in toward the train.

Yellow Sky had a kind brass band, which played painfully, to the delight of the populace. He laughed without heart as he thought of it. If the citizens could dream of his prospective arrival with his bride, they would parade the band at the station and escort them, amid cheers and laughing congratulations, to his adobe home.

He resolved that he would use all the devices of speed and plains-craft in making the journey from the station to his house. Once within that safe citadel, he could issue some sort of vocal bulletin, and then not go among the citizens until they had time to wear off a little of their enthusiasm.

The bride looked anxiously at him. "What's worrying you, Jack?"

He laughed again. "I'm not worrying, girl; I'm only thinking of Yellow Sky."

She flushed in comprehension.

A sense of mutual guilt invaded their minds and developed a finer tenderness. They looked at each other with eyes softly aglow. But Potter often laughed the same nervous laugh; the flush upon the bride's face seemed quite permanent.

The traitor to the feelings of Yellow Sky narrowly watched the speeding landscape. "We're nearly there," he said.

Presently the porter came and announced the proximity of Potter's home. He held a brush in his hand, and, with all his airy superiority gone, he brushed Potter's new clothes as the latter slowly turned this way and that way. Potter fumbled out a coin and gave it to the porter, as he had seen others do. It was a heavy and muscle-bound business, as that of a man shoeing his first horse.

The porter took their bag, and as the train began to slow they moved forward to the hooded platform of the car. Presently the two engines and their long string of coaches rushed into the station of Yellow Sky.

"They have to take water here," said Potter, from a constricted throat and in mournful cadence, as one announcing death. Before the train stopped his eye had swept the length of the platform, and he was glad and astonished to see there was none upon it but the station-agent, who, with a slightly hurried and anxious air, was walking toward the water-tanks. When the train had halted, the porter alighted first, and placed in position a little temporary step.

"Come on, girl," said Potter, hoarsely. As he helped her down they each laughed on a false note. He took the bag from the Negro, and bade his wife cling to his arm. As they slunk rapidly away, his hang-dog glance perceived that they were unloading the two trunks, and also that the station-agent, far ahead near the baggage-car, had turned and was running toward him, making gestures. He laughed, and groaned as he laughed, when he noted the first effect of his marital bliss upon Yellow Sky. He gripped his wife's arm firmly to his side, and they fled. Behind them the porter stood, chuckling fatuously.

II

The California express on the Southern Railway was due at Yellow Sky in twenty-one minutes. There were six men at the bar of the Weary Gentleman saloon. One was a drummer who talked a great deal and rapidly; three were Texans who did not care to talk at that time; and two were Mexican sheep-herders, who did not talk as a general practice in the Weary Gentleman saloon. The barkeeper's dog lay on the board walk that crossed in front of the door. His head was on his paws, and he glanced drowsily here and there with the constant vigilance of a dog that is kicked on occasion. Across the sandy street were some vivid green grass-plots, so wonderful in appearance, amid the sands that burned near them in a blazing sun, that they caused a doubt in the mind. They exactly resembled the grass mats used to represent lawns on the stage. At the cooler end of the railway station, a man without a coat sat in a tilted chair and smoked his pipe. The fresh-cut bank of the Rio Grande circled near the town, and there could be seen beyond it a great plum-colored plain of mesquite.

Save for the busy drummer and his companions in the saloon, Yellow Sky was dozing. The new-comer leaned gracefully upon the bar, and recited many tales with the confidence of a bard who has come upon a new field.

"—and at the moment that the old man fell downstairs with the bureau in his arms, the old woman was coming up with two scuttles of coal, and of course—"

The drummer's tale was interrupted by a young man who suddenly appeared in the open door. He cried: "Scratchy Wilson's drunk, and has turned loose with both hands." The two Mexicans at once set down their glasses and faded out of the rear entrance of the saloon.

The drummer, innocent and jocular, answered: "All right, old man. S'pose he has? Come in and have a drink, anyhow."

But the information had made such an obvious cleft in every skull in the room that the drummer was obliged to see its importance. All had become instantly solemn. "Say," said he, mystified, "what is this?" His three companions made the introductory gesture of eloquent speech; but the young man at the door forestalled them.

"It means, my friend," he answered, as he came into the saloon, "that for the next two hours this town won't be a health resort."

The barkeeper went to the door, and locked and barred it; reaching out of the window, he pulled in heavy wooden shutters, and barred them. Immediately a solemn, chapel-like gloom was upon the place. The drummer was looking from one to another.

"But say," he cried, "what is this, anyhow? You don't mean there is going to be a gun-fight?"

"Don't know whether there'll be a fight or not," answered one man, grimly; "but there'll be some shootin'—some good shootin'."

The young man who had warned them waved his hand. "Oh, there'll be a fight fast enough, if any one wants it. Anybody can get a fight out there in the street. There's a fight just waiting."

The drummer seemed to be swayed between the interest of a foreigner and a perception of personal danger.

"What did you say his name was?" he asked.

"Scratchy Wilson," they answered in chorus.

"And will he kill anybody? What are you going to do? Does this happen often? Does he rampage around like this once a week or so? Can he break in that door?"

"No; he can't break down that door," replied the barkeeper. "He's tried it three times. But when he comes you'd better lay down on the floor, stranger. He's dead sure to shoot at it, and a bullet may come through."

Thereafter the drummer kept a strict eye upon the door. The time had not yet been called for him to hug the floor, but, as a minor precaution, he sidled near to the wall. "Will he kill anybody?" he said again.

The men laughed low and scornfully at the question.

"He's out to shoot, and he's out for trouble. Don't see any good in experimentin' with him."

"But what do you do in a case like this? What do you do?"

A man responded: "Why, he and Jack Potter—"

"But," in chorus the other men interrupted, "Jack Potter's in San Anton'."

"Well, who is he? What's he got to do with it?"

"Oh, he's the town marshal. He goes out and fights Scratchy when he gets on one of these tears."

"Wow!" said the drummer, mopping his brow. "Nice job he's got."

The voices had toned away to mere whisperings. The drummer wished to ask further questions, which were born of an increasing anxiety and bewilderment; but when he attempted them, the men merely looked at him in irritation and motioned him to remain silent. A tense waiting hush was upon them. In the deep shadows of the room their eyes shone as they listened for sounds from the street. One man made three gestures at the barkeeper; and the latter, moving like a ghost, handed him a glass and a bottle. The man poured a full glass of whisky, and set down the bottle noiselessly. He gulped the whisky in a swallow, and turned again toward the door in immovable silence. The drummer saw that the barkeeper, without a sound, had taken a Winchester from beneath the bar. Later he saw this individual beckoning to him, so he tiptoed across the room.

"You better come with me back of the bar."

"No, thanks," said the drummer, perspiring; "I'd rather be where I can make a break for the back door."

Whereupon the man of bottles made a kindly but peremptory gesture. The drummer obeyed it, and, finding himself seated on a box with his head below the level of the bar, balm was laid upon his soul at sight of various zinc and copper fittings that bore a resemblance to armor-plate. The barkeeper took a seat comfortably upon an adjacent box.

"You see," he whispered, "this here Scratchy Wilson is a wonder with a gun—a perfect wonder; and when he goes on the wartrail, we hunt our holes—naturally. He's about the last one of the old gang that used to hang out along the river here. He's a terror when he's drunk. When he's sober he's all right—kind of simple—wouldn't hurt a fly—nicest fellow in town. But when he's drunk—whoo!"

There were periods of stillness. "I wish Jack Potter was back from San Anton'," said the barkeeper. "He shot Wilson up once—in the leg—and he would sail in and pull out the kinks in this thing."

Presently they heard from a distance the sound of a shot, followed by three wild yowls. It instantly removed a bond from the men in the darkened saloon. There was a shuffling of feet. They looked at each other. "Here he comes," they said.

III

A man in a maroon-colored flannel shirt, which had been purchased for purposes of decoration, and made principally by some Jewish women on the East Side of New York, rounded a corner and walked into the middle of the main street of Yellow Sky. In either hand the man held a long, heavy, blue-black revolver. Often he yelled, and these cries rang through a semblance of a deserted village, shrilly flying over the roofs in a volume that seemed to have no relation to the ordinary vocal strength of a man. It was as if the surrounding stillness formed the arch of a tomb over him. These cries of ferocious challenge rang against walls of silence. And his boots had red tops with gilded imprints, of the kind beloved in winter by little sledding boys on the hillsides of New England.

The man's face flamed in a rage begot of whiskey. His eyes, rolling, and yet keen for ambush, hunted the still doorways and windows. He walked with the creeping movement of the midnight cat. As it occurred to him, he roared menacing information. The long revolvers in his hands were as easy as straws; they were moved with an electric swiftness. The little fingers of each hand played sometimes in a musician's way. Plain from the low collar of the shirt, the cords of his neck straightened and sank, straightened and sank, as passion moved him. The only sounds were his terrible invitations. The calm adobes preserved their demeanor at the passing of this small thing in the middle of the street.

There was no offer of fight—no offer of fight. The man called to the sky. There were no attractions. He bellowed and fumed and swayed his revolvers here and everywhere.

The dog of the barkeeper of the Weary Gentleman saloon had not appreciated the advance of events. He yet lay dozing in front of his master's door. At sight of the dog, the man paused and raised his revolver humorously. At sight of the man, the dog sprang up and walked diagonally away, with a sullen head, and growling. The man yelled, and the dog broke into a gallop. As it was about to enter an alley, there was a loud noise, a whistling, and something spat the ground directly before it. The dog screamed, and, wheeling in terror, galloped headlong in a new direction. Again there was a noise, a whistling, and sand was kicked viciously before it. Fear-stricken, the dog turned and flurried like an animal in a pen. The man stood laughing, his weapons at his hips.

Ultimately the man was attracted by the closed door of the Weary Gentleman saloon. He went to it and, hammering with a revolver, demanded drink.

The door remaining imperturbable, he picked a bit of paper from the walk, and nailed it to the framework with a knife. He then turned his back contemptuously upon this popular resort and, walking to the opposite side of the street and spinning there on his heel quickly and lithely, fired at the bit of paper. He missed it by a half-inch. He swore at himself, and went away. Later he comfortably fusilladed the windows of his most intimate friend. The man was playing with this town; it was a toy for him.

But still there was no offer of fight. The name of Jack Potter, his ancient antagonist, entered his mind, and he concluded that it would be a glad thing if he should go to Potter's house, and by bombardment induce him to come out and fight. He moved in the direction of his desire, chanting Apache scalp-music.

When he arrived at it, Potter's house presented the same still front as had the other adobes. Taking up a strategic position, the man howled a challenge. But this house regarded him as might a great stone god. It gave no sign. After a decent wait, the man howled further challenges, mingling with them wonderful epithets.

Presently there came the spectacle of a man churning himself into deepest rage over the immobility of a house. He fumed at it as the winter wind attacks a prairie cabin in the North. To the distance there should have gone the sound of a tumult like the fighting of two hundred Mexicans. As necessity bade him, he paused for breath or to reload his revolvers.

IV

Potter and his bride walked sheepishly and with speed. Sometimes they laughed together shamefacedly and low.

"Next corner, dear," he said finally.

They put forth the efforts of a pair walking bowed against a strong wind. Potter was about to raise a finger to point the first appearance of the new home when, as they circled the corner, they came face to face with a man in a maroon-colored shirt, who was feverishly pushing cartridges into a large revolver. Upon the instant the man dropped his revolver to the ground and, like lightning, whipped another from its holster. The second weapon was aimed at the bridegroom's chest.

There was a silence. Potter's mouth seemed to be merely a grave for his tongue. He exhibited an instinct to at once loosen his arm from the woman's grip, and he dropped the bag to the sand. As for the bride, her face had gone as yellow as old cloth. She was a slave to hideous rites, gazing at the apparitional snake.

The two men faced each other at a distance of three paces. He of the revolver smiled with a new and quiet ferocity.

"Tried to sneak up on me," he said. "Tried to sneak up on me!" His eyes grew more baleful. As Potter made a slight movement, the man thrust his revolver venomously forward. "No; don't you do it, Jack Potter. Don't you move a finger toward a gun just yet. Don't you move an eyelash. The time has come for me to settle with you, and I'm goin' to do it my own way, and loaf along with no interferin'. So if you don't want a gun bent on you, just mind what I tell you."

Potter looked at his enemy. "I ain't got a gun on me, Scratchy," he said. "Honest, I ain't." He was stiffening and steadying, but yet somewhere at the back of his mind a vision of the Pullman floated: the sea-green figured velvet, the shining brass, silver, and glass, the wood that gleamed as darkly brilliant as the surface of a pool of oil—all the glory of the marriage, the environment of the new estate. "You know I fight when it comes to fighting, Scratchy Wilson; but I ain't got a gun on me. You'll have to do all the shootin' yourself."

His enemy's face went livid. He stepped forward, and lashed his weapon to and fro before Potter's chest. "Don't you tell me you ain't got no gun on you, you whelp. Don't tell me no lie like that. There ain't a man in Texas ever seen you without no gun. Don't take me for no kid." His eyes blazed with light, and his throat worked like a pump.

"I ain't takin' you for no kid," answered Potter. His heels had not moved an inch backward. "I'm takin' you for a damn fool. I tell you I ain't got a gun, and I ain't. If you're goin' to shoot me up, you better begin now; you'll never get a chance like this again."

So much enforced reasoning had told on Wilson's rage; he was calmer. "If you ain't got a gun, why ain't you got a gun?" he sneered. "Been to Sunday-school?"

"I ain't got a gun because I've just come from San Anton' with my wife. I'm married," said Potter. "And if I'd thought there was going to be any galoots like you prowling around when I brought my wife home, I'd had a gun, and don't you forget it."

"Married!" said Scratchy, not at all comprehending.

"Yes, married. I'm married," said Potter, distinctly.

"Married?" said Scratchy. Seemingly for the first time, he saw the drooping, drowning woman at the other man's side. "No!" he said. He was like a creature allowed a glimpse of another world. He moved a pace backward, and his arm, with the revolver, dropped to his side. "Is this the lady?" he asked.

"Yes; this is the lady," answered Potter.

There was another period of silence.

"Well," said Wilson at last, slowly, "I s'pose it's all off now."

"It's all off if you say so, Scratchy. You know I didn't make the trouble." Potter lifted his valise.

"Well, I 'low it's off, Jack," said Wilson. He was looking at the ground. "Married!" He was not a student of chivalry; it was merely that in the presence of this foreign condition he was a simple child of the earlier plains. He picked up his starboard revolver, and, placing both weapons in their holsters, he went away. His feet made funnel-shaped tracks in the heavy sand.

GLADIUS DEI[1]

THOMAS MANN

MUNICH was radiant. Above the gay squares and white columned temples, the classicistic monuments and the baroque churches, the leaping fountains, the palaces and parks of the Residence there stretched a sky of luminous

1. Reprinted from *Stories of Three Decades* by Thomas Mann by permission of Alfred A. Knopf, Inc. Copyright 1936 by Alfred A. Knopf, Inc. Translated from German by H. T. Lowe-Porter.

blue silk. Well-arranged leafy vistas laced with sun and shade lay basking in the sunshine of a beautiful day in early June.

There was a twittering of birds and a blithe holiday spirit in all the little streets. And in the squares and past the rows of villas there swelled, rolled, and hummed the leisurely, entertaining traffic of that easy-going, charming town. Travellers of all nationalities drove about in the slow little droshkies, looking right and left in aimless curiosity at the house-fronts; they mounted and descended museum stairs. Many windows stood open and music was heard from within: practising on piano, cello, or violin—earnest and well-meant amateur efforts; while from the Odeon came the sound of serious work on several grand pianos.

Young people, the kind that can whistle the Nothung motif, who fill the pit of the Schauspielhaus every evening, wandered in and out of the University and Library with literary magazines in their coat pockets. A court carriage stood before the Academy, the home of the plastic arts, which spreads its white wings between the Türkenstrasse and the Siegestor. And colourful groups of models, picturesque old men, women and children in Albanian costume, stood or lounged at the top of the balustrade.

Indolent, unhurried sauntering was the mode in all the long streets of the northern quarter. There life is lived for pleasanter ends than the driving greed of gain. Young artists with little round hats on the backs of their heads, flowing cravats and no canes—carefree bachelors who paid for their lodgings with colour-sketches—were strolling up and down to let the clear blue morning play upon their mood, also to look at the little girls, the pretty, rather plump type, with the brunette bandeaux, the too large feet, and the unobjectionable morals. Every fifth house had studio windows blinking in the sun. Sometimes a fine piece of architecture stood out from a middle-class row, the work of some imaginative young architect; a wide front with shallow bays and decorations in a bizarre style very expressive and full of invention. Or the door to some monotonous facade would be framed in a bold improvisation of flowing lines and sunny colours, with bacchantes, naiads, and rosy-skinned nudes.

It was always a joy to linger before the windows of the cabinetmakers and the shops for modern articles *de luxe*. What a sense for luxurious nothings and amusing, significant line was displayed in the shape of everything! Little shops that sold picture-frames, sculptures, and antiques there were in endless number; in their windows you might see those busts of Florentine women of the Renaissance, so full of noble poise and poignant charm. And the owners of the smallest and meanest of these shops spoke of Mino da Fiesole and Donatello as though he had received the rights of reproduction from them personally.

But on the Odeonsplatz, in view of the mighty loggia with the spacious mosaic pavement before it, diagonally opposite to the Regent's palace, people were crowding round the large windows and glass show-cases of the big art-shop owned by M. Blüthenzweig. What a glorious display! There were reproductions of the masterpieces of all the galleries in the world, in costly decorated and tinted frames, the good taste of which was precious in its very simplicity. There were copies of modern paintings, works of a joyously sensuous fantasy, in which the antiques seemed born again in humorous and realistic guise; bronze nudes and fragile ornamental glassware; tall, thin earthenware vases with an iridescent glaze produced by a bath in metal steam; *éditions de luxe* which were triumphs of modern binding and presswork, containing the works of the most modish poets, set out with every possible advantage of sumptuous elegance. Cheek by jowl with these, the portraits of artists, musicians, philosophers, actors, writers, displayed to gratify the public taste for personalities.—In the first window, next the book-shop, a large picture stood on an easel, with a crowd of people in front of it, a fine sepia photograph in a wide old-gold frame, a very striking reproduction of the sensation at this year's great international exhibition, to which public attention is always invited by means of effective and artistic posters stuck up everywhere on hoardings among concert programmes and clever advertisements of toilet preparations.

If you looked into the windows of the book-shop, your eye met such titles as *Interior Decoration Since the Renaissance, The Renaissance in Modern Decorative Art, The Book as Work of Art, The Decorative Arts, Hunger for Art,* and many more. And you would remember that these thought-provoking pamphlets were sold and read by the thousand and that discussions on these subjects were the preoccupation of all the salons.

You might be lucky enough to meet in person one of the famous fair ones whom less fortunate folk know only through the medium of art; one of those rich and beautiful women whose Titian-blond colouring Nature's most sweet and cunning hand did *not* lay on, but whose diamond parures and beguiling charms had received immortality from the hand of some portrait-painter of genius and whose love-affairs were the talk of the town. These were the queens of the artist balls at carnival-time. They were a little painted, a little made up, full of haughty caprices, worthy of adoration, avid of praise. You might see a carriage rolling up the Ludwigstrasse, with such a great painter and his mistress inside. People would be pointing out the sight, standing still to gaze after the pair. Some of them would curtsy. A little more and the very policemen would stand attention.

Art flourished, art swayed the destinies of the town, art stretched above it her rose-bound sceptre and smiled. On every hand obsequious interest was displayed in her prosperity, on every hand she was served with industry and devotion. There was a downright cult of line, decoration, form, significance, beauty. Munich was radiant.

A youth was coming down the Schellingstrasse. With the bells of cyclists ringing about him he strode across the wooden pavement towards the broad facade of the Ludwigskirche. Looking at him it was as though a shadow passed across the sky, or cast over the spirit some memory of melancholy hours. Did he not love the sun which bathed the lovely city in its festal light? Why did he walk wrapped in his own thoughts, his eyes directed on the ground?

No one in that tolerant and variety-loving town would have taken offence at his wearing no hat; but why need the hood of his ample black cloak have been drawn over his head, shadowing his low, prominent, and peaked forehead, covering his ears and framing his haggard cheeks? What pangs of conscience, what scruples and self-tortures had so availed to hollow out these cheeks? It is frightful, on such a sunny day, to see care sitting in the hollows of the human face. His dark brows thickened at the narrow base of his hooked and prominent nose. His lips were unpleasantly full, his eyes brown and close-lying. When he lifted them, diagonal folds appeared on the peaked brow. His gaze expressed knowledge, limitation, and suffering. Seen in profile his face was strikingly like an old painting preserved at Florence in a narrow cloister cell whence once a frightful and shattering protest issued against life and her triumphs.

Hieronymus walked along the Schellingstrasse with a slow, firm stride, holding his wide cloak together with both hands from inside. Two little girls, two of those pretty, plump little creatures with the bandeaux, the big feet, and the unobjectionable morals, strolled towards him arm in arm, on pleasure bent. They poked each other and laughed, they bent double with laughter, they even broke into a run and ran away still laughing, at his hood and his face. But he paid them no heed. With bent head, looking neither to the right nor to the left, he crossed the Ludwigstrasse and mounted the church steps.

The great wings of the middle portal stood wide open. From somewhere within the consecrated twilight, cool, dank, incense-laden, there came a pale red glow. An old woman with inflamed eyes rose from a prayer-stool and slipped on crutches through the columns. Otherwise the church was empty.

Hieronymus sprinkled brow and breast at the stoup, bent the knee before the high altar, and then paused in the centre nave. Here in the church his stature seemed to have grown. He stood upright and immovable; his head was flung up and his great hooked nose jutted domineeringly above the thick lips. His eyes no longer sought the ground, but looked straight and boldly into the distance, at the crucifix on the high altar. Thus he stood awhile, then retreating he bent the knee again and left the church.

He strode up the Ludwigstrasse, slowly, firmly, with bent head, in the centre of the wide unpaved road, towards the mighty loggia with its statues. But arrived at the Odeonsplatz, he looked up, so that the folds came out on his peaked forehead, and checked his step, his attention being called to the crowd at the windows of the big art-shop of M. Blüthenzweig.

People moved from window to window, pointing out to each other the treasures displayed and exchanging views as they looked over one another's shoulders. Hieronymus mingled among them and did as they did, taking in all these things with his eyes, one by one.

He saw the reproductions of masterpieces from all the galleries in the world, the priceless frames so precious in their simplicity, the Renaissance sculpture, the bronze nudes, the exquisitely bound volumes, the iridescent vases, the portraits of artists, musicians, philosophers, actors, writers; he looked at everything and turned a moment of his scrutiny upon each object. Holding his mantle closely together with both hands from inside, he moved his hood-covered head in short turns from one thing to the next, gazing at each awhile with a dull, inimical, and remotely surprised air, lifting the dark brows which grew so thick at the base of the nose. At length he stood in front of the last window, which contained the startling picture. For a while he looked over the shoulders of people before him and then in his turn reached a position directly in front of the window.

The large red-brown photograph in the choice old-gold frame stood on an easel in the centre. It was a Madonna, but an utterly unconventional one, a work of entirely modern feeling. The figure of the Holy Mother was revealed as enchantingly feminine and beautiful. Her great smouldering eyes were rimmed with darkness, and her delicate and strangely smiling lips were half-parted. Her slender fingers held in a somewhat nervous grasp the hips of the Child, a nude boy of pronounced, almost primitive leanness. He was playing with her breast and glancing aside at the beholder with a wise look in his eyes.

Two other youths stood near Hieronymus, talking about the picture. They were two young men with books under their arms, which they had fetched from the Library, or were taking thither. Humanistically educated people, that is, equipped with science and with art.

"The little chap is in luck, devil take me!" said one.

"He seems to be trying to make one envious," replied the other. "A bewildering female!"

"A female to drive a man crazy! Gives you funny ideas about the Immaculate Conception."

"No, she doesn't look exactly immaculate. Have you seen the original?"

"Of course; I was quite bowled over. She makes an even more aphrodisiac impression in colour. Especially the eyes."

"The likeness is pretty plain."

"How so?"

"Don't you know the model? Of course he used his little dressmaker. It is almost a portrait, only with a lot more emphasis on the corruptible. The girl is more innocent."

"I hope so. Life would be altogether too much of a strain if there were many like this *mater amata*."

"The Pinakothek has bought it."

"Really? Well, well! They knew what they were about, anyhow. The treatment of the flesh and the flow of the linen garment are really first-class."

"Yes, an incredibly gifted chap."

"Do you know him?"

"A little. He will have a career, that is certain. He has been invited twice by the Prince Regent."

This last was said as they were taking leave of each other.

"Shall I see you this evening at the theatre?" asked the first. "The Dramatic Club is giving Machiavelli's *Mandragola*."

"Oh, bravo! That will be great, of course. I had meant to go to the Variété, but I shall probably choose our stout Niccolò after all. Good-bye."

They parted, going off to right and left. New people took their places and looked at the famous picture. But Hieronymus stood where he was, motionless, with his head thrust out; his hands clutched convulsively at the mantle as they held it together from inside. His brows were no longer lifted with that cool and unpleasantly surprised expression; they were drawn and darkened; his cheeks, half-shrouded in the black hood, seemed more sunken than ever and his thick lips had gone pale. Slowly his head dropped lower and lower, so that finally his eyes stared upwards at the work of art, while the nostrils of his great nose dilated.

Thus he remained for perhaps a quarter of an hour. The crowd about him melted away, but he did not stir from the spot. At last he turned slowly on the balls of his feet and went hence.

But the picture of the Madonna went with him. Always and ever, whether in his hard and narrow little room or kneeling in the cool church, it stood before his outraged soul, with its smouldering, dark-rimmed eyes, its riddling smiling lips—stark and beautiful. And no prayer availed to exorcize it.

But the third night it happened that a command and summons from on high came to Hieronymus, to intercede and lift his voice against the frivolity, blasphemy, and arrogance of beauty. In vain like Moses he protested that he had not the gift of tongues. God's will remained unshaken; in a loud voice He demanded that the faint-hearted Hieronymus go forth to sacrifice amid the jeers of the foe.

And since God would have it so, he set forth one morning and wended his way to the great art-shop of M. Blüthenzweig. He wore his hood over his head and held his mantle together in front from inside with both hands as he went.

The air had grown heavy, the sky was livid and thunder threatened. Once more crowds were besieging the show-cases at the art-shop and especially the window where the photograph of the Madonna stood. Hieronymus cast one brief glance thither; then he pushed up the latch of the glass door hung with placards and art magazines. "As God wills," said he, and entered the shop.

A young girl was somewhere at the desk writing in a big book. She was a pretty brunette thing with bandeaux of hair and big feet. She came up to him and asked pleasantly what he would like.

"Thank you," said Hieronymus in a low voice and looked her earnestly in the face, with diagonal wrinkles in his peaked brow. "I would speak not to you but to the owner of this shop, Herr Blüthenzweig."

She hesitated a little, turned away, and took up her work once more. He stood there in the middle of the shop.

Instead of the single specimens in the show-windows there was here a riot and a heaping-up of luxury, a fullness of colour, line, form, style, invention, good taste, and beauty. Hieronymus looked slowly round him, drawing his mantle close with both hands.

There were several people in the shop besides him. At one of the broad tables running across the room sat a man in a yellow suit, with a black goat's-beard, looking at a portfolio of French drawings, over which he now and then emitted a bleating laugh. He was being waited on by an under-nourished and vegetarian young man, who kept on dragging up fresh portfolios. Diagonally opposite the bleating man sat an elegant old dame, examining art embroideries with a pattern of fabulous flowers in pale tones standing together on tall perpendicular stalks. An attendant hovered about her too. A leisurely Englishman in a travelling-cap, with his pipe in his mouth, sat at another table. Cold and smooth-shaven, of indefinite age, in his good English clothes, he sat examining bronzes brought to him by M. Blüthenzweig in person. He was holding up by the head the dainty figure of a nude young girl, immature and delicately articulated, her hands crossed in coquettish innocence upon her breast. He studied her thoroughly, turning her slowly about. M. Blüthenzweig, a man with a short, heavy brown beard and bright brown eyes of exactly the same colour, moved in a semicircle round him, rubbing his hands, praising the statuette with all the terms his vocabulary possessed.

"A hundred and fifty marks, sir," he said in English. "Munich art—very charming, in fact. Simply full of charm, you know. Grace itself. Really extremely pretty, good, admirable, in fact." Then he thought of some more and went on: "Highly attractive, fascinating." Then he began again from the beginning.

His nose lay a little flat on his upper lip, so that he breathed constantly with a slight sniff into his moustache. Sometimes he did this as he approached a customer, stooping over as though he were smelling at him. When Hieronymus entered, M. Blüthenzweig had examined him cursorily in this way, then devoted himself again to his Englishman.

The elegant old dame made her selection and left the shop. A man entered. M. Blüthenzweig sniffed briefly at him as though to scent out his capacity to buy and left him to the young bookkeeper. The man purchased a faïence bust of young Piero de' Medici, son of Lorenzo, and went out again. The Englishman began to depart. He had acquired the statuette of the young girl and left amid bowings from M. Blüthenzweig. Then the art-dealer turned to Hieronymus and came forward.

"You wanted something?" he said, without any particular courtesy.

Hieronymus held his cloak together with both hands and looked the other in the face almost without winking an eyelash. He parted his big lips slowly and said:

"I have come to you on account of the picture in the window there, the big photograph, the Madonna." His voice was thick and without modulation.

"Yes, quite right," said M. Blüthenzweig briskly and began rubbing his hands. "Seventy marks in the frame. It is unfadable—a first-class reproduction. Highly attractive and full of charm."

Hieronymus was silent. He nodded his head in the hood and shrank a little into himself as the dealer spoke. Then he drew himself up again and said:

"I would remark to you first of all that I am not in the position to purchase anything, nor have I the desire. I am sorry to have to disappoint your expectations. I regret if it upsets you. But in the first place I am poor and in the second I do not love the things you sell. No, I cannot buy anything."

"No? Well, then?" asked M. Blüthenzweig, sniffing a good deal. "Then may I ask—"

"I suppose," Hieronymus went on, "that being what you are you look down on me because I am not in a position to buy."

"Oh—er—not at all," said M. Blüthenzweig. "Not at all. Only—"

"And yet I beg you to hear me and give some consideration to my words."

"Consideration to your words. H'm—may I ask—"

"You may ask," said Hieronymus, "and I will answer you. I have come to beg you to remove that picture, the big photograph, the Madonna, out of your window and never display it again."

M. Blüthenzweig looked awhile dumbly into Hieronymus's face—as though he expected him to be abashed at the words he had just uttered. But as this did not happen he gave a violent sniff and spoke himself:

"Will you be so good as to tell me whether you are here in any official capacity which authorizes you to dictate to me, or what does bring you here?"

"Oh, no," replied Hieronymus, "I have neither office nor dignity from the state. I have no power on my side, sir. What brings me hither is my conscience alone."

M. Blüthenzweig, searching for words, snorted violently into his moustache. At length he said:

"Your conscience . . . well, you will kindly understand that I take not the faintest interest in your conscience." With which he turned round and moved quickly to his desk at the back of the shop, where he began to write. Both attendants laughed heartily. The pretty Fräulein giggled over her account-book. As for the yellow gentleman with the goat's beard, he was evidently a foreigner, for he gave no sign of comprehension but went on studying the French drawings and emitting from time to time his bleating laugh.

"Just get rid of the man for me," said M. Blüthenzweig shortly over his shoulder to his assistant. He went on writing. The poorly paid young vegetarian approached Hieronymus, smothering his laughter, and the other salesman came up too.

"May we be of service to you in any other way?" the first asked mildly. Hieronymus fixed him with his glazed and suffering eyes.

"No," he said, "you cannot. I beg you to take the Madonna picture out of the window, at once and forever."

"But—why?"

"It is the Holy Mother of God," said Hieronymus in a subdued voice.

"Quite. But you have heard that Herr Blüthenzweig is not inclined to accede to your request."

"We must bear in mind that it is the Holy Mother of God," said Hieronymus again and his head trembled on his neck.

"So we must. But should we not be allowed to exhibit any Madonnas—or paint any?"

"It is not that," said Hieronymus, almost whispering. He drew himself up and shook his head energetically several times. His peaked brow under the hood was entirely furrowed with long, deep cross-folds. "You know very well that it is vice itself that is painted there—naked sensuality. I was standing near two simple young people and overheard with my own ears that it led them astray upon the doctrine of the Immaculate Conception."

"Oh, permit me—that is not the point," said the young salesman, smiling. In his leisure hours he was writing a brochure on the modern movement in art and was well qualified to conduct a cultured conversation. "The picture is a work of art," he went on, "and one must measure it by the appropriate standards as such. It has been very highly praised on all hands. The state has purchased it."

"I know that the state has purchased it," said Hieronymus. "I also know that the artist has twice dined with the Prince Regent. It is common talk—and God knows how people interpret the fact that a man can become famous by such work as this. What does such a fact bear witness to? To the blindness of the world, a blindness inconceivable, if not indeed shamelessly hypocritical. This picture has its origin in sensual lust and is enjoyed in the same—is that true or not? Answer me! And you too answer me, Herr Blüthenzweig!"

A pause ensued. Hieronymus seemed in all seriousness to demand an answer to his question, looking by turns at the staring attendants and the round back M. Blüthenzweig turned upon him, with his own piercing and anguishing brown eyes. Silence reigned. Only the yellow man with the goat's beard, bending over the French drawings, broke it with his bleating laugh.

"It is true," Hieronymus went on in a hoarse voice that shook with his profound indignation. "You do not dare deny it. How then can honour be done to its creator, as though he had endowed mankind with a new ideal possession? How can one stand before it and surrender unthinkingly to the base enjoyment which it purveys, persuading oneself in all seriousness that one is yielding to a noble and elevated sentiment, highly creditable to the human race? Is this reckless ignorance or abandoned hypocrisy? My understanding falters, it is completely at a loss when confronted by the absurd fact that a man can achieve renown on this earth by the stupid and shameless exploitation of the animal instincts. Beauty? What is beauty? What forces are they which use beauty as their tool today—and upon what does it work? No one can fail to know this, Herr Blüthenzweig. But who, understanding it clearly, can fail to feel disgust and pain? It is criminal to play upon the ignorance of the immature, the lewd, the brazen, and the unscrupulous by elevating beauty into an idol to be worshipped, to give it even more power over those who know not affliction and have no knowledge of redemption. You are unknown to me, and you look at me with black looks—yet answer me! Knowledge, I tell you, is the profoundest torture in the world; but it is the purgatory without whose purifying pangs no soul can reach salvation. It is not infantile, blasphemous shallowness that can save us, Herr Blüthenzweig; only knowledge can avail, knowledge in which the passions of our loathsome flesh die away and are quenched."

Silence.—The yellow man with the goat's beard gave a sudden little bleat.

"I think you really must go now," said the underpaid assistant mildly.

But Hieronymus made no move to do so. Drawn up in his hooded cape, he stood with blazing eyes in the centre of the shop and his thick lips poured out condemnation in a voice that was harsh and rusty and clanking.

"Art, you cry; enjoyment, beauty! Enfold the world in beauty and endow all things with the noble grace of style!—Profligate, away! Do you think to wash over with lurid colours the misery of the world? Do you think with the sounds of feasting and music to drown out the voice of the tortured earth? Shameless one, you err! God lets not Himself be mocked, and your impudent deification of the glistering surface of things is an abomination in His eyes. You tell me that I blaspheme art. I say to you that you lie. I do not blaspheme art. Art is no conscienceless delusion, lending itself to reinforce the allurements of the fleshly. Art is the holy torch which turns its light upon all the frightful depths, all the shameful and woeful abysses of life; art is the godly fire laid to the world that, being redeemed by pity, it may flame up and dissolve altogether with its shames and torments.—Take it out, Herr Blüthenzweig, take away the work of that famous painter out of your window—you would do well to burn it with a hot fire and strew its ashes to the four winds—yes, to all the four winds—"

His harsh voice broke off. He had taken a violent backwards step, snatched one arm from his black wrappings, and stretched it passionately forth, gesturing towards the window with a hand that shook as though palsied. And in this commanding attitude he paused. His great hooked nose seemed to jut more than ever, his dark brows were gathered so thick and high that folds crowded upon the peaked forehead shaded by the hood; a hectic flush mantled his hollow cheeks.

But at this point M. Blüthenzweig turned round. Perhaps he was outraged by the idea of burning his seventy-mark reproduction; perhaps Hieronymus's speech had completely exhausted his patience. In any case he was a picture of stern and righteous anger. He pointed with his pen to the door of the shop, gave several short, excited snorts into his moustache, struggled for words, and uttered with the maximum of energy those which he found: "My fine fellow, if you don't get out at once I will have my packer help you—do you understand?"

"Oh, you cannot intimidate me, you cannot drive me away, you cannot silence my voice!" cried Hieronymus as he clutched his cloak over his chest with his fists and shook his head doughtily. "I know that I am single-handed and powerless, but yet I will not cease until you hear me, Herr Blüthenzweig! Take the picture out of your window and burn it even today! Ah, burn not it alone! Burn all these statues and busts, the sight of which plunges the beholder into sin! Burn these vases and ornaments, these shameles revivals of paganism, these elegantly bound volumes of erotic verse! Burn everything in your shop, Herr Blüthenzweig, for it is a filthiness in God's sight. Burn it, burn it!" he shrieked, beside himself, describing a wild, all-embracing circle with his arm. "The harvest is ripe for the reaper, the measure of the age's shamelessness is full—but I say unto you—"

"Krauthuber!" Herr Blüthenzweig raised his voice and shouted towards a door at the back of the shop. "Come in here at once!"

And in answer to the summons there appeared upon the scene a massive overpowering presence, a vast and awe-inspiring, swollen human bulk, whose limbs merged into each other like links of sausage—a gigantic son of the people, malt-nourished and immoderate, who weighed in, with puffings, bursting with energy, from the packing-room. His appearance in the upper reaches of his form was notable for a fringe of walrus beard; a hide apron fouled with paste covered his body from the waist down, and his yellow shirt-sleeves were rolled back from his heroic arms.

"Will you open the door for this gentleman, Krauthuber?" said M. Blüthenzweig; "and if he should not find the way to it, just help him into the street."

"Huh," said the man, looking from his enraged employer to Hieronymus and back with his little elephant eyes. It was a heavy monosyllable, suggesting reserve force restrained with difficulty. The floor shook with his tread as he went to the door and opened it.

Hieronymus had grown very pale. "Burn—" he shouted once more. He was about to go on when he felt himself turned round by an irresistible power, by a physical preponderance to which no resistance was even thinkable. Slowly and inexorably he was propelled towards the door.

"I am weak," he managed to ejaculate. "My flesh cannot bear the force . . . it cannot hold its ground, no . . . but what does that prove? Burn—"

He stopped. He found himself outside the art-shop. M. Blüthenzweig's giant packer had let him go with one final shove, which set him down on the stone threshold of the shop, supporting himself with one hand. Behind him the door closed with a rattle of glass.

He picked himself up. He stood erect, breathing heavily, and pulled his cloak together with one fist over his breast, letting the other hang down inside. His hollow cheeks had a grey pallor; the nostrils of his great hooked nose opened and closed; his ugly lips were writhen in an expression of hatred and despair and his red-rimmed eyes wandered over the beautiful square like those of a man in a frenzy.

He did not see that people were looking at him with amusement and curiosity. For what he beheld upon the mosaic pavement before the great loggia were all the vanities of this world: the masked costumes of the artist balls, the decorations, vases and art objects, the nude statues, the female busts, the picturesque rebirths of the pagan age, the portraits of famous beauties by the hands of masters, the elegantly bound erotic verse, the art brochures—all these he saw heaped in a pyramid and going up in crackling flames amid loud exultations from the people enthralled by his own frightful words. A yellow background of cloud had drawn up over the Theatinerstrasse, and from it issued wild rumblings; but what he saw was a burning fiery sword, towering in sulphurous light above the joyous city.

"Gladius Dei super terram . . ." [2] his thick lips whispered; and drawing himself still higher in his hooded cloak while the hand hanging down inside it twitched convulsively, he murmured, quaking: *"cito et velociter!"* [2]

---

2. "O Sword of the Lord, [smite] the earth . . . swiftly and sharply!"

I'M A FOOL[1]

SHERWOOD ANDERSON

IT WAS a hard jolt for me, one of the most bitterest I ever had to face. And it all came about through my own foolishness, too. Even yet sometimes, when I think of it, I want to cry or swear or kick myself. Perhaps, even now, after all this time, there will be a kind of satisfaction in making myself look cheap by telling of it.

It began at three o'clock one October afternoon as I sat in the grand stand at the fall trotting and pacing meet at Sandusky, Ohio.

To tell the truth, I felt a little foolish that I should be sitting in the grand stand at all. During the summer before I had left my home town with Harry Whitehead and, with a nigger named Burt, had taken a job as swipe with one of the two horses Harry was campaigning through the fall race meets that year. Mother cried and my sister Mildred, who wanted to get a job as a schoolteacher in our town that fall, stormed and scolded about the house all during the week before I left. They both thought it something disgraceful that one of our family should take a place as a swipe with race horses. I've an idea Mildred thought my taking the place would stand in the way of her getting the job she'd been working so long for.

But after all I had to work, and there was no other work to be got. A big lumbering fellow of nineteen couldn't just hang around the house and I had got too big to mow people's lawns and sell newspapers. Little chaps who could get next to people's sympathies by their sizes were always getting jobs away from me. There was one fellow who kept saying to every one who wanted a lawn mowed or a cistern cleaned that he was saving money to work his way through college, and I used to lay awake nights thinking up ways to injure him without being found out. I kept thinking of wagons running over him and bricks falling on his head as he walked along the street. But never mind him.

I got the place with Harry and I liked Burt fine. We got along splendid together. He was a big nigger with a lazy sprawling body and soft, kind eyes, and when it came to a fight he could hit like Jack Johnson. He had Bucephalus, a big black pacing stallion that could do 2.09 or 2.10 if he had to, and I had a little gelding named Doctor Fritz that never lost a race all fall when Harry wanted him to win.

We set out from home late in July, in a box car with the two horses and after that, until late November, we kept moving along to the race meets and the fairs. It was a peachy time for me, I'll say that. Sometimes now I think that boys who are raised regular in houses, and never have a fine nigger

1. From *Horses and Men,* The Viking Press, Inc. Copyright, 1932, by Eleanor Anderson. Reprinted by permission of Harold Ober.

like Burt for best friend, and go to high schools and college, and never steal anything, or get drunk a little, or learn to swear from fellows who know how, or come walking up in front of a grand stand in their shirt sleeves and with dirty horsy pants on when the races are going on and the grand stand is full of people all dressed up—What's the use of talking about it? Such fellows don't know nothing at all. They've never had no opportunity.

But I did. Burt taught me how to rub down a horse and put the bandages on after a race and steam a horse out and a lot of valuable things for any man to know. He could wrap a bandage on a horse's leg so smooth that if it had been the same color you would think it was his skin, and I guess he'd have been a big driver, too, and got to the top like Murphy and Walter Cox and the others if he hadn't been black.

Gee whizz, it was fun. You got to a county-seat town, maybe say on a Saturday or Sunday, and the fair began the next Tuesday and lasted until Friday afternoon. Doctor Fritz would be, say, in the 2.25 trot on Tuesday afternoon and on Thursday afternoon Bucephalus would knock 'em cold in the "free-for-all" pace. It left you a lot of time to hang around and listen to horse talk, and see Burt knock some yap cold that got too gay, and you'd find out about horses and men and pick up a lot of stuff you could use all the rest of your life, if you had some sense and salted down what you heard and felt and saw.

And then at the end of the week when the race meet was over, and Harry had run home to tend up to his livery-stable business, you and Burt hitched the two horses to carts and drove slow and steady across country, to the place for the next meeting, so as to not overheat the horses, etc., etc., you know.

Gee whizz, Gosh amighty, the nice hickory-nut and beechnut and oaks and other kinds of trees along the roads, all brown and red, and the good smells, and Burt singing a song called "Deep River," and the country girls at the windows of houses and everything. You can stick your colleges up your nose for all me. I guess I know where I got my education.

Why, one of those little burgs of towns you came to on the way, say now on a Saturday afternoon, and Burt says, "Let's lay up here." And you did.

And you took the horses to a livery stable and fed them, and you got your good clothes out of a box and put them on.

And the town was full of farmers gaping, because they could see you were racehorse people, and the kids maybe never see a nigger before and was afraid and run away when the two of us walked down their main street.

And that was before prohibition and all that foolishness, and so you went into a saloon, the two of you, and all the yaps come and stood around, and there was always some one pretended he was horsy and knew things and spoke up and began asking questions, and all you did was to lie and lie all you could about what horses you had, and I said I owned them, and then some fellow said, "Will you have a drink of whisky?" and Burt knocked his eye out the way he could say, offhand like, "Oh, well, all right, I'm agreeable to a little nip. I'll split a quart with you." Gee whizz.

But that isn't what I want to tell my story about. We got home late in November and I promised mother I'd quit the race horses for good. There's a lot of things you've got to promise a mother because she don't know any better.

And so, there not being any work in our town any more than when I left there to go to the races, I went off to Sandusky and got a pretty good place taking care of horses for a man who owned a teaming and delivery and storage and coal and real-estate business there. It was a pretty good place with good eats, and a day off each week, and sleeping on a cot in a big barn, and mostly just shoveling in hay and oats to a lot of big good-enough skates of horses that couldn't have trotted a race with a toad, I wasn't dissatisfied and I could send money home.

And then, as I started to tell you, the fall races come to Sandusky and I got the day off and I went. I left the job at noon and had on my good clothes and my new brown derby hat I'd bought the Saturday before, and a stand-up collar.

First of all I went downtown and walked about with the dudes. I've always thought to myself, "Put up a good front," and so I did it. I had forty dollars in my pocket and so I went into the West House, a big hotel, and walked up to the cigar stand. "Give me three twenty-five-cent cigars," I said. There was a lot of horsemen and strangers and dressed-up people from other towns standing around in the lobby and in the bar, and I mingled amongst them. In the bar there was a fellow with a cane and a Windsor tie on, that it made me sick to look at him. I like a man to be a man and dress up, but not to go put on that kind of airs. So I pushed him aside, kind of rough, and had me a drink of whisky. And then he looked at me, as though he thought maybe he'd get gay, but he changed his mind and didn't say anything. And then I had another drink of whisky, just to show him something, and went out and had a hack out to the races, all to myself, and when I got there I bought myself the best seat I could get up in the grand stand, but didn't go in for any of these boxes. That's putting on too many airs.

And so there I was, sitting up in the grand stand as gay as you please and looking down on the swipes coming out with their horses, and with their dirty horsy pants on and the horseblankets swung over their shoulders, same as I had been doing all the year before. I liked one thing about the same as the other, sitting up there and feeling grand and being down there and looking up at the yaps and feeling grander and more important, too.

One thing's about as good as another, if you take it just right. I've often said that.

Well, right in front of me, in the grand stand that day, there was a fellow with a couple of girls and they was about my age. The young fellow was a nice guy, all right. He was the kind maybe that goes to college and then comes to be a lawyer or maybe a newspaper editor or something like that, but he wasn't stuck on himself. There are some of that kind are all right and he was one of the ones.

He had his sister with him and another girl and the sister looked around over his shoulder, accidental at first, not intending to start anything—she wasn't that kind—and her eyes and mine happened to meet.

You know how it is. Gee, she was a peach! She had on a soft dress, kind of a blue stuff, and it looked carelessly made, but was well sewed and made and everything. I knew that much. I blushed when she looked right at me and so did she. She was the nicest girl I've ever seen in my life. She wasn't stuck on herself and she could talk proper grammar without being like a schoolteacher or something like that. What I mean is, she was O.K. I think maybe her father was well-to-do, but not rich to make her chesty because she was his daughter, as some are. Maybe he owned a drug store or a dry-goods store in their home town, or something like that. She never told me and I never asked.

My own people are all O.K. too, when you come to that. My grandfather was Welsh and over in the old country, in Wales he was—But never mind that.

The first heat of the first race come off and the young fellow setting there with the two girls left them and went down to make a bet. I knew what he was up to, but he didn't talk big and noisy and let everyone know he was a sport, as some do. He wasn't that kind. Well, he come back and I heard him tell the two girls what horse he'd bet on, and when the heat was trotted they all half got to their feet and acted in the excited, sweaty way people do when they've got money down on a race, and the horse they bet on is up there pretty close at the end, and they think maybe he'll come on with a rush, but he never does because he hasn't got the old juice in him, come right down to it.

And then, pretty soon, the horses came out for the 2.18 pace and there was a horse in it I knew. He was a horse Bob French had in his string but Bob didn't own him. He was a horse owned by a Mr. Mathers down at Marietta, Ohio.

This Mr. Mathers had a lot of money and owned some coal mines or something, and he had a swell place out in the country, and he was stuck on race horses, but was a Presbyterian or something, and I think more than likely his wife was one, too, maybe a stiffer one than himself. So he never raced his horses hisself, and the story round the Ohio race tracks was that when one of his horses got ready to go to the races he turned him over to Bob French and pretended to his wife he was sold.

So Bob had the horses and he did pretty much as he pleased and you can't blame Bob, at least I never did. Sometimes he was out to win and sometimes he wasn't. I never cared much about that when I was swiping a horse. What I did want to know was that my horse had the speed and could go out in front, if you wanted him to.

And, as I'm telling you, there was Bob in this race with one of Mr. Mathers' horses, was named "About Ben Ahem" or something like that, and was fast as a streak. He was a gelding and had a mark of 2.21, but could step in .08 or .09.

Because when Burt and I were out, as I've told you, the year before, there was a nigger, Burt knew, worked for Mr. Mathers and we went out there one day when we didn't have no race on at the Marietta Fair and our boss Harry was gone home.

And so everyone was gone to the fair but just this one nigger and he took us all through Mr. Mathers' swell house and he and Burt tapped a bottle of wine Mr. Mathers had hid in his bedroom, back in a closet, without his wife knowing, and he showed us this Ahem horse. Burt was always stuck on being a driver but didn't have much chance to get to the top, being a nigger, and he and the other nigger gulped that whole bottle of wine and Burt got a little lit up.

So the nigger let Burt take this About Ben Ahem and step him a mile on a track Mr. Mathers had all to himself, right there on the farm. And Mr. Mathers had one child, a daughter, kinda sick and not very good looking, and she came home and we had to hustle and get About Ben Ahem stuck back in the barn.

I'm only telling you to get everything straight. At Sandusky, that afternoon I was at the fair, this young fellow with the two girls was fussed, being with the girls and losing his bet. You know how a fellow is that way. One of them was his girl and the other his sister. I had figured that out. "Gee whizz," I says to myself, "I'm going to give him the dope."

He was mighty nice when I touched him on the shoulder. He and the girls were nice to me right from the start and clear to the end. I'm not blaming them.

And so he leaned back and I gave him the dope on About Ben Ahem. "Don't bet a cent on his first heat because he'll go like an oxen hitched to a plow, but when the first heat is over go right down and lay on your pile." That's what I told him.

Well, I never saw a fellow treat any one sweller. There was a fat man sitting beside the little girl, that had looked at me twice by this time, and I at her, and both blushing, and what did he do but have the nerve to turn and ask the fat man to get up and change places with me so I could set with his crowd.

Gee whizz, craps amighty. There I was. What a chump I was to go and get gay up there in the West House bar, and just because that dude was standing there with a cane and that kind of a necktie on, to go and get all balled up and drink that whisky, just to show off.

Of course she would know, me setting right beside her and letting her smell of my breath. I could have kicked myself right down out of that grand stand and all around that race track and made a faster record than most of the skates of horses they had there that year.

Because that girl wasn't any mutt of a girl. What wouldn't I have give right then for a stick of chewing gum to chew, or a lozenger, or some liquorice, or most anything. I was glad I had those twenty-five-cent cigars in my pocket and right away I give that fellow one and lit one myself. Then that fat man got up and we changed places and there I was, plunked right down beside her.

They introduced themselves and the fellow's best girl, he had with him, was named Miss Elinor Woodbury, and her father was a manufacturer of barrels from a place called Tiffin, Ohio. And the fellow himself was named Wilbur Wessen and his sister was Miss Lucy Wessen.

I suppose it was their having such swell names got me off my trolley. A fellow, just because he has been a swipe with a race horse, and works taking care of horses for a man in the teaming, delivery, and storage business, isn't any better or worse than any one else. I've often thought that, and said it, too.

But you know how a fellow is. There's something in that kind of nice clothes, and the kind of nice eyes she had, and the way she had looked at me, a while before, over her brother's shoulder, and me looking back at her, and both of us blushing.

I couldn't show her up for a boob, could I?

I made a fool of myself, that's what I did. I said my name was Walter Mathers from Marietta, Ohio, and then I told all three of them the smashingest lie you ever heard. What I said was that my father owned the horse About Ben Ahem and that he had let him out to this Bob French for racing purposes, because our family was proud and had never gone into racing that way—in our own name, I mean. Then I had got started and they were all leaning over and listening, and Miss Lucy Wessen's eyes were shining, and I went the whole hog.

I told about our place down at Marietta, and about the big stables and the grand brick house we had on a hill, up above the Ohio River, but I knew enough not to do it in no bragging way. What I did was to start things and then let them drag the rest out of me. I acted just as reluctant to tell as I could. Our family hasn't got any barrel factory, and, since I've known us, we've always been pretty poor, but not asking anything of any one at that, and my grandfather, over in Wales—But never mind that.

We set there talking like we had known each other for years and years, and I went and told them that my father had been expecting maybe this Bob French wasn't on the square, and had sent me up to Sandusky on the sly to find out what I could.

And I bluffed it through I had found out all about the 2.18 pace, in which About Ben Ahem was to start.

I said he would lose the first heat by pacing like a lame cow and then he would come back and skin 'em alive after that. And to back up what I said I took thirty dollars out of my pocket and handed it to Mr. Wilbur Wessen and asked him would he mind, after the first heat, to go down and place it on About Ben Ahem for whatever odds he could get. What I said was that I didn't want Bob French to see me, and none of the swipes.

Sure enough, the first heat came off and About Ben Ahem went off his stride, up the back stretch, and looked like a wooden horse or a sick one, and come in to be last. Then this Wilbur Wessen went down to the betting place under the grand stand and there I was with the two girls, and when that Miss Woodbury was looking the other way once, Lucy Wessen kinda, with her shoulder you know, kinda touched me. Not just tucking down, I don't mean. You know how a woman can do. They get close, but not getting gay, either. You know what they do. Gee whizz.

And then they give me a jolt. What they had done, when I didn't know, was to get together, and they had decided Wilbur Wessen would bet fifty dollars, and the two girls had gone and put in ten dollars each, of their own money, too. I was sick then, but I was sicker later.

About the gelding. About Ben Ahem, and their winning their money, I wasn't worried a lot about that. It come out O.K. Ahem stepped the next three heats like a bushel of spoiled eggs going to market before they could be found out, and Wilbur Wessen had got nine to two for the money. There was something else eating at me.

Because Wilbur come back, after he had bet the money, and after that he spent most of his time talking to that Miss Woodbury, and Lucy Wessen and I was left alone together like on a desert island. Gee, if I'd only been on the square or if there had been any way of getting myself on the square. There ain't any Walter Mathers, like I said to her and them, and there hasn't ever been one, but if there was, I bet I'd go to Marietta, Ohio, and shoot him tomorrow.

There I was, big boob that I am. Pretty soon the race was over, and Wilbur had gone down and collected our money, and we had a hack downtown, and he stood us a swell supper at the West House, and a bottle of champagne beside.

And I was with that girl and she wasn't saying much, and I wasn't saying much, either. One thing I know. She wasn't stuck on me because of the lie about my father being rich and all that. There's a way you know. . . . Craps amighty. There's a kind of a girl you see just once in your life, and if you don't get busy and make hay, then you're gone for good and all, and might as well go jump off a bridge. They give you a look from inside of them somewhere, and it ain't no vamping, and what it means is—you want that girl to be your wife, and you want nice things around her like flowers and swell clothes, and you want her to have the kids you're going to have, and you want good music played and no ragtime. Gee whizz.

There's a place over near Sandusky, across a kind of bay, and it's called Cedar Point. And after we had supper we went over to it in a launch, all by ourselves. Wilbur and Miss Lucy and that Miss Woodbury had to catch a ten-o'clock train back to Tiffin, Ohio, because when you're out with girls like that you can't get careless and miss any trains and stay out all night, like you can with some kind of Janes.

And Wilbur blowed himself to the launch and it cost him fifteen cold plunks, but I wouldn't never have knew if I hadn't listened. He wasn't no tin-horn kind of a sport.

Over at the Cedar Point place, we didn't stay around where there was a gang of common kind of cattle at all.

There was big dance halls and dining places for yaps, and there was a beach you could walk along and get where it was dark, and we went there.

She didn't talk hardly at all, and neither did I, and I was thinking how glad I was my mother was all right, and always made us kids learn to eat with a fork at table, and not swill soup, and not be noisy and rough like a gang you see around a race track that way.

Then Wilbur and his girl went away up the beach and Lucy and I sat down in a dark place, where there was some roots of old trees the water had washed up, and after that the time, till we had to go back in the launch and they had to catch their train, wasn't nothing at all. It went like winking your eye.

Here's how it was. The place we were setting in was dark, like I said, and there was the roots from that old stump sticking up like arms, and there was a watery smell, and then the night was like—as if you could put your hand out and feel it—so warm and soft and dark and sweet like an orange.

I most cried and I most swore and I most jumped up and danced, I was so mad and happy and sad.

When Wilbur came back from being alone with his girl, and she saw him coming, Lucy she says, "We got to go to the train now," and she was most crying, too, but she never knew nothing I knew, and she couldn't be so all busted up. And then, before Wilbur and Miss Woodbury got up to where we was, she put her face up and kissed me and she was all quivering and—Gee whizz.

Sometimes I hope I have cancer and die. I guess you know what I mean. We went in the launch across the bay to the train like that, and it was dark, too. She whispered and said it was like she and I could get out of the boat and walk on the water, and it sounded foolish, but I knew what she meant.

And then quick we were right at the depot, and there was a big gang of yaps, the kind that goes to the fairs, and crowded and milling around like cattle, and how could I tell her? "It won't be long because you'll write and I'll write to you." That's all she said.

I got a chance like a hay barn afire. A swell chance I got!

And maybe she would write me, down at Marietta that way, and the letter would come back, and stamped on the front of it by the U.S.A. "There ain't any such guy," or something like that, whatever they stamp on a letter that way.

And me trying to pass myself off for a bigbug and a swell—to her, as decent a little body as God ever made. Craps amighty—a swell chance I got!

And then the train come in, and she got on, and Wilbur Wessen he come shook hands with me, and that Miss Woodbury was nice too and bowed to me, and I at her, and the train went and I busted out and cried like a kid.

Gee, I could have run after that train and made Dan Patch look like a freight train after a wreck but, socks amighty, what was the use? Did you ever see such a fool?

I'll bet you what—if I had an arm broke right now or a train had run over my foot—I wouldn't go to no doctor at all. I'd go set down and let her hurt and hurt—that's what I'd do.

I'll bet you what—if I hadn't a drunk that booze I'd never been such a boob as to go tell such a lie—that couldn't never be made straight to a lady like her.

I wish I had that fellow right here that had on a Windsor tie and carried a cane. I'd smash him for fair. Gosh darn his eyes. He's a big fool—that's what he is.

And if I'm not another you just go find me one and I'll quit working and be a bum and give him my job. I don't care nothing for working, and earning money, and saving it for no such boob as myself.

THE CELESTIAL OMNIBUS[1]

E. M. FORSTER

THE BOY who resided at Agathox Lodge, 28, Buckingham Park Road, Surbiton, had often been puzzled by the old sign-post that stood almost opposite. He asked his mother about it, and she replied that it was a joke, and not a very nice one, which had been made many years back by some naughty young men, and that the police ought to remove it. For there were two strange things about this sign-post; firstly, it pointed up a blank alley, and, secondly, it had painted on it, in faded characters, the words, "To Heaven."

"What kind of young men were they?" he asked.

"I think your father told me that one of them wrote verses, and was expelled from the University and came to grief in other ways. Still, it was a

1. Reprinted from *The Celestial Omnibus* by E. M. Forster, by permission of Alfred A. Knopf, Inc., and Sedgwick & Jackson Ltd., of London, England.

long time ago. You must ask your father about it. He will say the same as I do, that it was put up as a joke."

"So it doesn't mean anything at all?"

She sent him upstairs to put on his best things, for the Bonses were coming to tea, and he was to hand the cakestand.

It struck him, as he wrenched on his tightening trousers, that he might do worse than ask Mr. Bons about the sign-post. His father, though very kind, always laughed at him—shrieked with laughter whenever he or any other child asked a question or spoke. But Mr. Bons was serious as well as kind. He had a beautiful house and lent one books, he was a churchwarden, and a candidate for the County Council; he had donated to the Free Library enormously, he presided over the Literary Society, and had Members of Parliament to stop with him—in short, he was probably the wisest person alive.

Yet even Mr. Bons could only say that the sign-post was a joke—the joke of a person named Shelley.

"Of course!" cried the mother; "I told you so, dear. That was the name."

"Had you ever heard of Shelley?" asked Mr. Bons.

"No," said the boy, and hung his head.

"But is there no Shelley in the house?"

"Why, yes!" exclaimed the lady, in much agitation. "Dear Mr. Bons, we aren't such Philistines as that. Two at the least. One a wedding present, and the other, smaller print, in one of the spare rooms."

"I believe we have seven Shelleys," said Mr. Bons, with a slow smile. Then he brushed the cake crumbs off his stomach, and, together with his daughter, rose to go.

The boy, obeying a wink from his mother, saw them all the way to the garden gate, and when they had gone he did not at once return to the house, but gazed for a little up and down Buckingham Park Road.

His parents lived at the right end of it. After No. 39 the quality of the houses dropped very suddenly, and 64 had not even a separate servants' entrance. But at the present moment the whole road looked rather pretty, for the sun had just set in splendour, and the inequalities of rent were drowned in a saffron afterglow. Small birds twittered, and the breadwinners' train shrieked musically down through the cutting—that wonderful cutting which has drawn to itself the whole beauty out of Surbiton, and clad itself, like any Alpine valley, with the glory of the fir and the silver birch and the primrose. It was this cutting that had first stirred desires within the boy—desires for something just a little different, he knew not what, desires that would return whenever things were sunlit, as they were this evening, running up and down inside him, up and down, up and down, till he would feel quite unusual all over, and as likely as not would want to cry. This evening he was even sillier, for he slipped across the road towards the sign-post and began to run up the blank alley.

The alley runs between high walls—the walls of the gardens of "Ivanhoe" and "Bella Vista," respectively. It smells a little all the way, and is scarcely twenty yards long, including the turn at the end. So not unnaturally the boy soon came to a standstill. "I'd like to kick that Shelley," he exclaimed, and glanced idly at a piece of paper which was pasted on the wall. Rather an odd piece of paper, and he read it carefully before he turned back. This is what he read:

S. AND C.R.C.C.

ALTERATION IN SERVICE

Owing to lack of patronage the Company are regretfully compelled to suspend the hourly service, and to retain only the

Sunrise and Sunset Omnibuses,

which will run as usual. It is to be hoped that the public will patronize an arrangement which is intended for their convenience. As an extra inducement, the Company will, for the first time, now issue

Return Tickets!

(available one day only), which may be obtained of the driver. Passengers are again reminded that *no tickets are issued at the other end,* and that no complaints in this connection will receive consideration from the Company. Nor will the Company be responsible for any negligence or stupidity on the part of Passengers, nor for Hailstorms, Lightning, Loss of Tickets, nor any Act of God.

For the Direction.

Now he had never seen this notice before, nor could he imagine where the omnibus went to. S. of course was for Surbiton, and R.C.C. meant Road Car Company. But what was the meaning of the other C.? Coombe and Malden, perhaps, or possibly "City." Yet it could not hope to compete with the South-Western. The whole thing, the boy reflected, was run on hopelessly unbusiness-like lines. Why no tickets from the other end? And what an hour to start! Then he realized that unless the notice was a hoax, an omnibus must have been starting just as he was wishing the Bonses goodbye. He peered at the ground through the gathering dusk, and there he saw what might or might not be the marks of wheels. Yet nothing had come out of the alley. And he had never seen an omnibus at any time in the Buckingham Park Road. No: it must be a hoax, like the sign-post, like the fairy tales, like the dreams upon which he would wake suddenly in the night. And with a sigh he stepped from the alley—right into the arms of his father.

Oh, how his father laughed! "Poor, poor Popsey!" he cried. "Diddums! Diddums! Diddums think he'd walky-palky up to Evink!" And his mother, also convulsed with laughter, appeared on the steps of Agathox Lodge.

"Don't Bob!" she gasped. "Don't be so naughty! Oh, you'll kill me! Oh, leave the boy alone!"

But all that evening the joke was kept up. The father implored to be taken too. Was it a very tiring walk? Need one wipe one's shoes on the door-mat? And the boy went to bed feeling faint and sore, and thankful for only one thing—that he had not said a word about the omnibus. It was a hoax, yet through his dreams it grew more and more real, and the streets of Surbiton, through which he saw it driving, seemed instead to become hoaxes and shadows. And very early in the morning he woke with a cry, for he had had a glimpse of its destination.

He struck a match, and its light fell not only on his watch but also on his calendar, so that he knew it to be half-an-hour to sunrise. It was pitch dark, for the fog had come down from London in the night, and all Surbiton was wrapped in its embraces. Yet he sprang out and dressed himself, for he was determined to settle once for all which was real: the omnibus or the streets. "I shall be a fool one way or the other," he thought, "until I know." Soon he was shivering in the road under the gas lamp that guarded the entrance to the alley.

To enter the alley itself required some courage. Not only was it horribly dark, but he now realized that it was an impossible terminus for an omnibus. If it had not been for a policeman, whom he heard approaching through the fog, he would never have made the attempt. The next moment he had made the attempt and failed. Nothing. Nothing but a blank alley and a very silly boy gaping at its dirty floor. It *was* a hoax. "I'll tell papa and mamma," he decided. "I deserve it. I deserve that they should know. I am too silly to be alive." And he went back to the gate of Agathox Lodge.

There he remembered that his watch was fast. The sun was not risen; it would not rise for two minutes. "Give the bus every chance," he thought cynically, and returned into the alley.

But the omnibus was there.

II

It had two horses, whose sides were still smoking from their journey, and its two great lamps shone through the fog against the alley's walls, changing their cobwebs and moss into tissues of fairyland. The driver was huddled up in a cape. He faced the blank wall, and how he had managed to drive in so neatly and so silently was one of the many things that the boy never discovered. Nor could he imagine how ever he would drive out.

"Please," his voice quavered through the foul brown air, "please, is that an omnibus?"

"Omnibus est," said the driver, without turning round. There was a moment's silence. The policeman passed, coughing, by the entrance of the alley. The boy crouched in the shadow, for he did not want to be found out. He was pretty sure, too, that it was a Pirate; nothing else, he reasoned, would go from such odd places and at such odd hours.

"About when do you start?" He tried to sound nonchalant.

"At sunrise."

"How far do you go?"

"The whole way."

"And can I have a return ticket which will bring me all the way back?"

"You can."

"Do you know, I half think I'll come." The driver made no answer. The sun must have risen, for he unhitched the brake. And scarcely had the boy jumped in before the omnibus was off.

How? Did it turn? There was no room. Did it go forward? There was a blank wall. Yet it was moving—moving at a stately pace through the fog, which had turned from brown to yellow. The thought of warm bed and warmer breakfast made the boy feel faint. He wished he had not come. His parents would not have approved. He would have gone back to them if the weather had not made it impossible. The solitude was terrible; he was the only passenger. And the omnibus, though well-built, was cold and somewhat musty. He drew his coat round him, and in so doing chanced to feel his pocket. It was empty. He had forgotten his purse.

"Stop!" he shouted. "Stop!" And then, being of a polite disposition, he glanced up at the painted notice-board so that he might call the driver by name. "Mr. Browne! stop; oh, do please stop!"

Mr. Browne did not stop, but he opened a little window and looked in at the boy. His face was a surprise, so kind it was and modest.

"Mr. Browne, I've left my purse behind. I've not got a penny. I can't pay for the ticket. Will you take my watch, please? I am in the most awful hole."

"Tickets on this line," said the driver, "whether single or return, can be purchased by coinage from no terrene mint. And a chronometer, though it had solaced the vigils of Charlemagne, or measured the slumbers of Laura, can acquire by no mutation the double-cake that charms the fangless Cerberus of Heaven!" So saying, he handed in the necessary ticket, and, while the boy said "Thank you," continued, "Titular pretensions, I know it well, are vanity. Yet they merit no censure when uttered on a laughing lip, and in an homonymous world are in some sort useful, since they do serve to distinguish one Jack from his fellow. Remember me, therefore, as Sir Thomas Browne."

"Are you a Sir? Oh, sorry!" He had heard of these gentlemen drivers. "It *is* good of you about the ticket. But if you go on at this rate, however does your bus pay?"

"It does not pay. It was not intended to pay. Many are the faults of my equipage; it is compounded too curiously of foreign woods; its cushions tickle erudition rather than promote repose; and my horses are nourished not on the evergreen pastures of the moment, but on the dried bents and clovers of Latinity. But that it pays!—that error at all events was never intended and never attained."

"Sorry again," said the boy rather hopelessly. Sir Thomas looked sad, fearing that, even for a moment, he had been the cause of sadness. He invited the boy to come up and sit beside him on the box, and together they journeyed on through the fog, which was now changing from yellow to white. There were no houses by the road; so it must be either Putney Heath or Wimbledon Common.

"Have you been a driver always?"

"I was a physician once."

"But why did you stop? Weren't you good?"

"As a healer of bodies I had scant success, and several score of my patients preceded me. But as the healer of the spirit I have succeeded beyond my hopes and my deserts. For though my draughts were not better nor subtler than those of other men, yet, by reason of the cunning goblets wherein I offered them, the queasy soul was ofttimes tempted to sip and be refreshed."

"The queasy soul," the boy murmured; "if the sun sets with trees in front of it, and you suddenly come strange all over, is that a queasy soul?"

"Have you felt that?"

"Why, yes."

After a pause he told the boy a little, a very little, about the journey's end. But they did not chatter much, for the boy, when he liked a person, would as soon sit silent in his company as speak, and this, he discovered, was also the mind of Sir Thomas Browne and of many others with whom he was to be acquainted. He heard, however, about the young man Shelley, who was now quite a famous person, with a carriage of his own, and about some of the other drivers who are in the service of the Company. Meanwhile the light grew stronger, though the fog did not disperse. It was now more like mist than fog, and at times would travel quickly across them, as if it was part of a cloud. They had been ascending, too, in a most puzzling way; for over two hours the horses had been pulling against the collar, and even if it were Richmond Hill they ought to have been at the top long ago. Perhaps it was Epsom, or even the North Downs; yet the air seemed keener than that which blows on either. And as to the name of their destination, Sir Thomas Browne was silent.

Crash!

"Thunder, by Jove!" said the boy, "and not so far off either. Listen to the echoes! It's more like mountains."

He thought, not very vividly, of his father and mother. He saw them sitting down to sausages and listening to the storm. He saw his own empty place. Then there would be questions, alarms, theories, jokes, consolations. They would expect him back at lunch. To lunch he would not come, nor to tea, but he would be in for dinner, and so his day's truancy would be over. If he had had his purse he would have bought them presents—not that he should have known what to get them.

Crash!

The peal and the lightning came together. The cloud quivered as if it were alive, and torn streamers of mist rushed past. "Are you afraid?" asked Sir Thomas Browne.

"What is there to be afraid of? Is it much farther?"

The horses of the omnibus stopped just as a ball of fire burst up and exploded with a ringing noise that was deafening but clear, like the noise of a blacksmith's forge. All the cloud was shattered.

"Oh, listen, Sir Thomas Browne! No, I mean look; we shall get a view at last. No, I mean listen; that sounds like a rainbow!"

The noise had died into the faintest murmur, beneath which another murmur grew, spreading stealthily, steadily, in a curve that widened but did not vary. And in widening curves a rainbow was spreading from the horses' feet into the dissolving mists.

"But how beautiful! What colours! Where will it stop? It is more like the rainbows you can tread on. More like dreams."

The colour and the sound grew together. The rainbow spanned an enormous gulf. Clouds rushed under it and were pierced by it, and still it grew, reaching forward, conquering the darkness, until it touched something that seemed more solid than a cloud.

The boy stood up. "What is that out there?" he called. "What does it rest on, out at that other end?"

In the morning sunshine a precipice shone forth beyond the gulf. A precipice—or was it a castle? The horses moved. They set their feet upon the rainbow.

"Oh, look!" the boy shouted. "Oh, listen! Those caves—or are they gateways? Oh, look between those cliffs at those ledges. I see people! I see trees!"

"Look also below," whispered Sir Thomas. "Neglect not the diviner Acheron."

The boy looked below, past the flames of the rainbow that licked against their wheels. The gulf also had cleared, and in its depths there flowed an everlasting river. One sunbeam entered and struck a green pool, and as they passed over he saw three maidens rise to the surface of the pool, singing, and playing with something that glistened like a ring.

"You down in the water—" he called.

They answered, "You up on the bridge—" There was a burst of music. "You up on the bridge, good luck to you. Truth in the depth, truth on the height."

"You down in the water, what are you doing?"

Sir Thomas Browne replied: "They sport in the mancipiary possession of their gold"; and the omnibus arrived.

III

The boy was in disgrace. He sat locked up in the nursery of Agathox Lodge, learning poetry for a punishment. His father had said, "My boy! I can pardon anything but untruthfulness," and had caned him, saying at each stroke, "There is *no* omnibus, *no* driver, *no* bridge, *no* mountain; you are a *truant*, a *gutter snipe*, a *liar*." His father could be very stern at times. His mother had begged him to say he was sorry. But he could not say that. It was the greatest day of his life, in spite of the caning and the poetry at the end of it.

He had returned punctually at sunset—driven not by Sir Thomas Browne, but by a maiden lady who was full of quiet fun. They had talked of omnibuses and also of barouche landaus. How far away her gentle voice seemed now! Yet it was scarcely three hours since he had left her up the alley.

His mother called through the door. "Dear, you are to come down and to bring your poetry with you."

He came down, and found that Mr. Bons was in the smoking-room with his father. It had been a dinner party.

"Here is the great traveller!" said his father grimly. "Here is the young gentleman who drives in an omnibus over rainbows, while young ladies sing to him." Pleased with his wit, he laughed.

"After all," said Mr. Bons, smiling, "there is something a little like it in Wagner. It is odd how, in quite illiterate minds, you will find glimmers of Artistic Truth. The case interests me. Let me plead for the culprit. We have all romanced in our time, haven't we?"

"Hear how kind Mr. Bons is," said his mother, while his father said, "Very well. Let him say his Poem, and that will do. He is going away to my sister on Tuesday, and *she* will cure him of this alley-slopering." (Laughter.) "Say your Poem."

The boy began. "'Standing aloof in giant ignorance.'"

His father laughed again—roared. "One for you, my son! 'Standing aloof in giant ignorance!' I never knew these poets talked sense. Just describes you. Here, Bons, you go in for poetry. Put him through it, will you, while I fetch up the whisky?"

"Yes, give me the Keats," said Mr. Bons. "Let him say his Keats to me."

So for a few moments the wise man and the ignorant boy were left alone in the smoking-room.

"'Standing aloof in giant ignorance, of thee I dream and of the Cyclades, as one who sits ashore and longs perchance to visit—'"

"Quite right. To visit what?"

"'To visit dolphin coral in deep seas,'" said the boy, and burst into tears.

"Come, come! why do you cry?"

"Because—because all these words that only rhymed before, now that I've come back they're me."

Mr. Bons laid the Keats down. The case was more interesting than he had expected. *"You?"* he exclaimed. "This sonnet, *you?"*

"Yes—and look further on: 'Aye, on the shores of darkness there is light, and precipices show untrodden green.' It *is* so, sir. All these things are true."

"I never doubted it," said Mr. Bons, with closed eyes.

"You—then you believe me? You believe in the omnibus and the driver and the storm and that return ticket I got for nothing and—"

"Tut, tut! No more of your yarns, my boy. I meant that I never doubted the essential truth of Poetry. Some day, when you have read more, you will understand what I mean."

"But, Mr. Bons, it *is* so. There *is* light upon the shores of darkness. I have seen it coming. Light and a wind."

"Nonsense," said Mr. Bons.

"If I had stopped! They tempted me. They told me to give up my ticket—for you cannot come back if you lose your ticket. They called from the river for it, and indeed I was tempted, for I have never been so happy as among those precipices. But I thought of my mother and father, and that I must fetch them. Yet they will not come, though the road starts opposite our house. It has all happened as the people up there warned me, and Mr. Bons has disbelieved me like everyone else. I have been caned. I shall never see that mountain again."

"What's that about me?" said Mr. Bons, sitting up in his chair very suddenly.

"I told them about you, and how clever you were, and how many books you had and they said 'Mr. Bons will certainly disbelieve you.'"

"Stuff and nonsense, my young friend. You grow impertinent. I—well—I will settle the matter. Not a word to your father. I will cure you. Tomorrow evening I will myself call here to take you for a walk, and at sunset we will go up this alley opposite and hunt for your omnibus, you silly little boy."

His face grew serious, for the boy was not disconcerted, but leapt about the room singing, "Joy! joy! I told them you would believe me. We will drive together over the rainbow. I told them that you would come." After all, could there be anything in the story? Wagner? Keats? Shelley? Sir Thomas Browne? Certainly the case was interesting.

And on the morrow evening, though it was pouring with rain, Mr. Bons did not omit to call at Agathox Lodge.

The boy was ready, bubbling with excitement, and skipping about in a way that rather vexed the President of the Literary Society. They took a turn down Buckingham Park Road, and then—having seen that no one was watching them—slipped up the alley. Naturally enough (for the sun was setting) they ran straight against the omnibus.

"Good heavens!" exclaimed Mr. Bons. "Good gracious heavens!"

It was not the omnibus in which the boy had driven first, nor yet that in which he had returned. There were three horses—black, gray, and white, the gray being the finest. The driver, who turned round at the mention of goodness and of heaven, was a sallow man with terrifying jaws and sunken eyes. Mr. Bons, on seeing him, gave a cry as if of recognition, and began to tremble violently.

The boy jumped in.

"Is it possible?" cried Mr. Bons. "Is the impossible possible?"

"Sir; come in, sir. It is such a fine omnibus. Oh, here is his name—Dan someone."

Mr. Bons sprang in too. A blast of wind immediately slammed the omnibus door, and the shock jerked down all the omnibus blinds, which were very weak on their springs.

"Dan . . . Show me. Good gracious heavens! We're moving."

"Hooray!" said the boy.

Mr. Bons became flustered. He had not intended to be kidnapped. He could not find the door-handle nor push up the blinds. The ominbus was quite dark, and by the time he had struck a match, night had come on outside also. They were moving rapidly.

"A strange, a memorable adventure," he said, surveying the interior of the omnibus, which was large, roomy, and constructed with extreme regularity, every part exactly answering to every other part. Over the door (the handle of which was outside) was written "Lasciate ogni baldanza voi che entrate" —at least, that was what was written, but Mr. Bons said that it was Lashy arty something, and that baldanza was a mistake for speranza. His voice sounded as if he was in church. Meanwhile, the boy called to the cadaverous driver for two return tickets. They were handed in without a word. Mr. Bons covered his face with his hand and again trembled. "Do you know who that is!" he whispered, when the little window had shut upon them. "It is the impossible."

"Well, I don't like him as much as Sir Thomas Browne, though I shouldn't be surprised if he had even more in him."

"More in him?" He stamped irritably. "By accident you have made the greatest discovery of the century, and all you can say is that there is more in this man. Do you remember those vellum books in my library, stamped with red lilies? This—sit still, I bring you stupendous news!—*this is the man who wrote them.*"

The boy sat quite still. "I wonder if we shall see Mrs. Gamp?" he asked, after a civil pause.

"Mrs—?"

"Mrs. Gamp and Mrs. Harris. I like Mrs. Harris. I came upon them quite suddenly. Mrs. Gamp's handboxes have moved over the rainbow so badly. All the bottoms have fallen out, and two of the pippins off her bedstead tumbled into the stream."

"Out there sits the man who wrote my vellum books!" thundered Mr. Bons, "and you talk to me of Dickens and of Mrs. Gamp?"

"I know Mrs. Gamp so well," he apologized. "I could not help being glad to see her. I recognized her voice. She was telling Mrs. Harris about Mrs. Prig."

"Did you spend the whole day in her elevating company?"

"Oh, no. I raced. I met a man who took me out beyond to a race-course. You run, and there are dolphins out at sea."

"Indeed. Do you remember the man's name?"

"Achilles. No; he was later. Tom Jones."

Mr. Bons sighed heavily. "Well, my lad, you have made a miserable mess of it. Think of a cultured person with your opportunities! A cultured person would have known all these characters and known what to have said to each. He would not have wasted his time with a Mrs. Gamp or a Tom Jones. The creations of Homer, of Shakespeare, and of Him who drives us now, would alone have contented him. He would not have raced. He would have asked intelligent questions."

"But, Mr. Bons," said the boy humbly, "you will be a cultured person. I told them so."

"True, true, and I beg you not to disgrace me when we arrive. No gossiping. No running. Keep close to my side, and never speak to these Immortals unless they speak to you. Yes, and give me the return tickets. You will be losing them."

The boy surrendered the tickets, but felt a little sore. After all, he had found the way to this place. It was hard first to be disbelieved and then to be lectured. Meanwhile, the rain had stopped, and moonlight crept into the omnibus through the cracks in the blinds.

"But how is there to be a rainbow?" cried the boy.

"You distract me," snapped Mr. Bons. "I wish to meditate on beauty. I wish to goodness I was with a reverent and sympathetic person."

The lad bit his lip. He made good resolutions. He would imitate Mr. Bons all the visit. He would not laugh, or run, or sing, or do any of the vulgar things that must have disgusted his new friends last time. He would be very careful to pronounce their names properly, and to remember who knew whom. Achilles did not know Tom Jones—at least, so Mr. Bons said. The Duchess of Malfi was older than Mrs. Gamp—at least, so Mr. Bons said. He would be self-conscious, reticent, and prim. He would never say he liked anyone. Yet, when the blind flew up at a chance touch of his head, all these good resolutions went to the winds, for the omnibus had reached the summit of a moonlit hill, and there was the chasm, and there, across it, stood the old precipices, dreaming, with their feet in the everlasting river. He exclaimed, "The mountain! Listen to the new tune in the water! Look at the camp fires in the ravines," and Mr. Bons, after a hasty glance, retorted, "Water?

Camp fires? Ridiculous rubbish. Hold your tongue. There is nothing at all."

Yet, under his eyes, a rainbow formed, compounded not of sunlight and storm, but of moonlight and the spray of the river. The three horses put their feet upon it. He thought it the finest rainbow he had seen, but did not dare to say so, since Mr. Bons said that nothing was there. He leant out—the window had opened—and sang the tune that rose from the sleeping waters.

"The prelude of Rhinegold?" said Mr. Bons suddenly. "Who taught you these *leit motifs?*" He, too, looked out of the window. Then he behaved very oddly. He gave a choking cry and fell back onto the omnibus floor. He writhed and kicked. His face was green.

"Does the bridge make you dizzy?" the boy asked.

"Dizzy!" gasped Mr. Bons. "I want to go back. Tell the driver."

But the driver shook his head.

"We are nearly there," said the boy. "They are asleep. Shall I call? They will be so pleased to see you, for I have prepared them."

Mr. Bons moaned. They moved over the lunar rainbow, which ever and ever broke away behind their wheels. How still the night was! Who would be sentry at the Gate?

"I am coming," he shouted, again forgetting the hundred resolutions. "I am returning—I, the boy."

"The boy is returning," cried a voice to other voices, who repeated, "The boy is returning."

"I am bringing Mr. Bons with me."

Silence.

"I should have said Mr. Bons is bringing me with him."

Profound silence.

"Who stands sentry?"

"Achilles."

And on the rocky causeway, close to the springing of the rainbow bridge, he saw a young man who carried a wonderful shield.

"Mr. Bons, it is Achilles, armed."

"I want to go back," said Mr. Bons.

The last fragment of the rainbow melted, the wheels sang upon the living rock, the door of the omnibus burst open. Out leapt the boy—he could not resist—and sprang to meet the warrior, who, stooping suddenly, caught him on his shield.

"Achilles!" he cried, "let me get down, for I am ignorant and vulgar, and I must wait for that Mr. Bons of whom I told you yesterday."

But Achilles raised him aloft. He crouched on the wonderful shield, on heroes and burning cities, on vineyards graven in gold, on every dear passion, every joy, on the entire image of the Mountain that he had discovered, encircled, like it, with an everlasting stream. "No, no," he protested, "I am not worthy. It is Mr. Bons who must be up here."

But Mr. Bons was whimpering, and Achilles trumpeted and cried, "Stand upright upon my shield!"

"Sir, I did not mean to stand! something made me stand. Sir, why do you delay? Here is only the great Achilles, whom you knew."

Mr. Bons screamed, "I see no one. I see nothing. I want to go back." Then he cried to the driver, "Save me! Let me stop in your chariot. I have honoured you. I have quoted you. I have bound you in vellum. Take me back to my world."

The driver replied, "I am the means and not the end. I am the food and not the life. Stand by yourself, as that boy has stood. I cannot save you. For poetry is a spirit; and they that would worship it must worship in spirit and in truth."

Mr. Bons—he could not resist—crawled out of the beautiful omnibus. His face appeared, gaping horribly. His hands followed, one gripping the step, the other beating the air. Now his shoulders emerged, his chest, his stomach. With a shriek of "I see London," he fell—fell against the hard, moonlit rock, fell into it as if it were water, fell through it, vanished, and was seen by the boy no more.

"Where have you fallen to, Mr. Bons? Here is a procession arriving to honour you with music and torches. Here come the men and women whose names you know. The mountain is awake, the river is awake, over the race-course the sea is awaking those dolphins, and it is all for you. They want you—"

There was the touch of fresh leaves on his forehead. Someone had crowned him.

ΤΕΛΟΣ [2]

From the *Kingston Gazette, Surbiton Times,* and *Raynes Park Observer.*

The body of Mr. Septimus Bons has been found in a shockingly mutilated condition in the vicinity of the Bermondsey gas-works. The deceased's pockets contained a sovereign-purse, a silver cigar-case, a bijou pronouncing dictionary, and a couple of omnibus tickets. The unfortunate gentleman had apparently been hurled from a considerable height. Foul play is suspected, and a thorough investigation is pending by the authorities.

2. End.

A LITTLE CLOUD[1]

JAMES JOYCE

EIGHT YEARS before he had seen his friend off at the North Wall and wished him godspeed. Gallaher had got on. You could tell that at once by his travelled air, his well-cut tweed suit, and fearless accent. Few fellows had talents like his and fewer still could remain unspoiled by such success. Gallaher's heart was in the right place and he had deserved to win. It was something to have a friend like that.

Little Chandler's thoughts ever since lunchtime had been of his meeting with Gallaher, of Gallaher's invitation and of the great city London where Gallaher lived. He was called Little Chandler because, though he was but slightly under the average stature, he gave one the idea of being a little man. His hands were white and small, his frame was fragile, his voice was quiet and his manners were refined. He took the greatest care of his fair silken hair and moustache and used perfume discreetly on his handkerchief. The half-moons of his nails were perfect and when he smiled you caught a glimpse of a row of childish white teeth.

As he sat at his desk in the King's Inns he thought what changes those eight years had brought. The friend whom he had known under a shabby and necessitous guise had become a brilliant figure on the London Press. He turned often from his tiresome writing to gaze out of the office window. The glow of a late autumn sunset covered the grass plots and walks. It cast a shower of kindly golden dust on the untidy nurses and decrepit old men who drowsed on the benches; it flickered upon all the moving figures—on the children who ran screaming along the gravel paths and on everyone who passed through the gardens. He watched the scene and thought of life; and (as always happened when he thought of life) he became sad. A gentle melancholy took possession of him. He felt how useless it was to struggle against fortune, this being the burden of wisdom which the ages had bequeathed to him.

He remembered the books of poetry upon his shelves at home. He had bought them in his bachelor days and many an evening, as he sat in the little room off the hall, he had been tempted to take one down from the bookshelf and read out something to his wife. But shyness had always held him back; and so the books had remained on their shelves. At times he repeated lines to himself and this consoled him.

When his hour had struck he stood up and took leave of his desk and of his fellow-clerks punctiliously. He emerged from under the feudal arch of

1. From *Dubliners,* included in *The Portable James Joyce.* Copyright, 1946, 1947, by The Viking Press, Inc. Reprinted by permission of The Viking Press, Inc., New York.

the King's Inns, a neat modest figure, and walked swiftly down Henrietta Street. The golden sunset was waning and the air had grown sharp. A horde of grimy children populated the street. They stood or ran in the roadway or crawled up the steps before the gaping doors or squatted like mice upon the thresholds. Little Chandler gave them no thought. He picked his way deftly through all that minute vermin-like life and under the shadow of the gaunt spectral mansions in which the old nobility of Dublin had roystered. No memory of the past touched him, for his mind was full of a present joy.

He had never been in Corless's but he knew the value of the name. He knew that people went there after the theatre to eat oysters and drink liqueurs; and he had heard that the waiters there spoke French and German. Walking swiftly by at night he had seen cabs drawn up before the door and richly dressed ladies, escorted by cavaliers, alight and enter quickly. They wore noisy dresses and many wraps. Their faces were powdered and they caught up their dresses, when they touched earth, like alarmed Atalantas. He had always passed without turning his head to look. It was his habit to walk swiftly in the street even by day and whenever he found himself in the city late at night he hurried on his way apprehensively and excitedly. Sometimes, however, he courted the causes of his fear. He chose the darkest and narrowest streets and, as he walked boldly forward, the silence that was spread about his footsteps troubled him, the wandering, silent figures troubled him; and at times a sound of low fugitive laughter made him tremble like a leaf.

He turned to the right towards Capel Street. Ignatius Gallaher on the London Press! Who would have thought it possible eight years before? Still, now that he reviewed the past, Little Chandler could remember many signs of future greatness in his friend. People used to say that Ignatius Gallaher was wild. Of course, he did mix with a rakish set of fellows at that time, drank freely and borrowed money on all sides. In the end he had got mixed up in some shady affair, some money transaction: at least, that was one version of his flight. But nobody denied him talent. There was always a certain . . . something in Ignatius Gallaher that impressed you in spite of yourself. Even when he was out at elbows and at his wits' end for money he kept up a bold face. Little Chandler remembered (and the remembrance brought a slight flush of pride to his cheek) one of Ignatius Gallaher's sayings when he was in a tight corner:

"Half time now, boys," he used to say lightheartedly. "Where's my considering cap?"

That was Ignatius Gallaher all out; and, damn it, you couldn't but admire him for it.

Little Chandler quickened his pace. For the first time in his life he felt himself superior to the people he passed. For the first time his soul revolted against the dull inelegance of Capel Street. There was no doubt about it: if you wanted to succeed you had to go away. You could do nothing in Dublin. As he crossed Grattan Bridge he looked down the river towards the lower quays and pitied the poor stunted houses. They seemed to him a band of tramps, huddled together along the river-banks, their old coats covered with dust and soot, stupefied by the panorama of sunset and waiting for the first chill of night to bid them arise, shake themselves and begone. He wondered whether he could write a poem to express his idea. Perhaps Gallaher might be able to get it into some London paper for him. Could he write something original? He was not sure what idea he wished to express but the thought that a poetic moment had touched him took life within him like an infant hope. He stepped onward bravely.

Every step brought him nearer to London, farther from his own sober inartistic life. A light began to tremble on the horizon of his mind. He was not so old—thirty-two. His temperament might be said to be just at the point of maturity. There were so many different moods and impressions that he wished to express in verse. He felt them within him. He tried to weigh his soul to see if it was a poet's soul. Melancholy was the dominant note of his temperament, he thought, but it was a melancholy tempered by recurrences of faith and resignation and simple joy. If he could give expression to it in a book of poems perhaps men would listen. He would never be popular: he saw that. He could not sway the crowd but he might appeal to a little circle of kindred minds. The English critics, perhaps, would recognise him as one of the Celtic school by reason of the melancholy tone of his poems; besides that, he would put in allusions. He began to invent sentences and phrases from the notice which his book would get. *"Mr. Chandler has the gift of easy and graceful verse."* . . . *"A wistful sadness pervades these poems."* . . . *"The Celtic note."* It was a pity his name was not more Irish-looking. Perhaps it would be better to insert his mother's name before the surname: Thomas Malone Chandler, or better still: T. Malone Chandler. He would speak to Gallaher about it.

He pursued his revery so ardently that he passed his street and had to turn back. As he came near Corless's his former agitation began to overmaster him and he halted before the door in indecision. Finally he opened the door and entered.

The light and noise of the bar held him at the doorway for a few moments. He looked about him, but his sight was confused by the shining of many red and green wine-glasses. The bar seemed to him to be full of people and he felt that the people were observing him curiously. He glanced quickly to right and left (frowning slightly to make his errand appear serious), but when his sight cleared a little he saw that nobody had turned to look at him: and there, sure enough, was Ignatius Gallaher leaning with his back against the counter and his feet planted far apart.

"Hallo, Tommy, old hero, here you are! What is it to be? What will you have? I'm taking whisky: better stuff than we get across the water. Soda? Lithia? No mineral? I'm the same. Spoils the flavour. . . . Here, *garçon,* bring us two halves of malt whisky, like a good fellow. . . . Well, and how have you been pulling along since I saw you last? Dear God, how old we're getting! Do you see any signs of aging in me—eh, what? A little grey and thin on the top—what?"

Ignatius Gallaher took off his hat and displayed a large closely cropped head. His face was heavy, pale and clean-shaven. His eyes, which were of bluish slate-colour, relieved his unhealthy pallor and shone out plainly above the vivid orange tie he wore. Between these rival features the lips appeared very long and shapeless and colourless. He bent his head and felt with two sympathetic fingers the thin hair at the crown. Little Chandler shook his head as a denial. Ignatius Gallaher put on his hat again.

"It pulls you down," he said, "press life. Always hurry and scurry, looking for copy and sometimes not finding it: and then, always to have something new in your stuff. Damn proofs and printers, I say, for a few days. I'm deuced glad, I can tell you, to get back to the old country. Does a fellow good, a bit of a holiday. I feel a ton better since I landed again in dear dirty Dublin. . . . Here you are, Tommy. Water? Say when."

Little Chandler allowed his whisky to be very much diluted.

"You don't know what's good for you, my boy," said Ignatius Gallaher. "I drink mine neat."

"I drink very little as a rule," said Little Chandler modestly. "An odd half-one or so when I meet any of the old crowd: that's all."

"Ah, well," said Ignatius Gallaher, cheerfully, "here's to us and to old times and old acquaintance."

They clinked glasses and drank the toast.

"I met some of the old gang today," said Ignatius Gallaher. "O'Hara seems to be in a bad way. What's he doing?"

"Nothing," said Little Chandler. "He's gone to the dogs."

"But Hogan has a good sit, hasn't he?"

"Yes; he's in the Land Commission."

"I met him one night in London and he seemed to be very flush. . . . Poor O'Hara! Boose, I suppose?"

"Other things, too," said little Chandler shortly.

Ignatius Gallaher laughed.

"Tommy," he said, "I see you haven't changed an atom. You're the very same serious person that used to lecture me on Sunday mornings when I had a sore head and a fur on my tongue. You'd want to knock about a bit in the world. Have you never been anywhere even for a trip?"

"I've been to the Isle of Man," said Little Chandler.

Ignatius Gallaher laughed.

"The Isle of Man!" he said. "Go to London or Paris: Paris, for choice. That'd do you good."

"Have you seen Paris?"

"I should think I have! I've knocked about there a little."

"And is it really so beautiful as they say?" asked Little Chandler.

He sipped a little of his drink while Ignatius Gallaher finished his boldly.

"Beautiful?" said Ignatius Gallaher, pausing on the word and on the flavour of his drink. "It's not so beautiful, you know. Of course, it is beautiful. . . . But it's the life of Paris; that's the thing. Ah, there's no city like Paris for gaiety, movement, excitement. . . ."

Little Chandler finished his whisky and, after some trouble, succeeded in catching the barman's eye. He ordered the same again.

"I've been to the Moulin Rouge," Ignatius Gallaher continued when the barman had removed their glasses, "and I've been to all the Bohemian cafés. Hot stuff! Not for a pious chap like you, Tommy."

Little Chandler said nothing until the barman returned with two glasses: then he touched his friend's glass lightly and reciprocated the former toast. He was beginning to feel somewhat disillusioned. Gallaher's accent and way of expressing himself did not please him. There was something vulgar in his friend which he had not observed before. But perhaps it was only the result of living in London amid the bustle and competition of the Press. The old personal charm was still there under this new gaudy manner. And, after all, Gallaher had lived, he had seen the world. Little Chandler looked at his friend enviously.

"Everything in Paris is gay," said Ignatius Gallaher. "They believe in enjoying life—and don't you think they're right? If you want to enjoy yourself properly you must go to Paris. And, mind you, they've a great feeling for the Irish there. When they heard I was from Ireland they were ready to eat me, man."

Little Chandler took four or five sips from his glass.

"Tell me," he said, "is it true that Paris is so . . . immoral as they say?"

Ignatius Gallaher made a catholic gesture with his right arm.

"Every place is immoral," he said. "Of course you do find spicy bits in Paris. Go to one of the students' balls, for instance. That's lively, if you like, when the *cocottes* begin to let themselves loose. You know what they are, I suppose?"

"I've heard of them," said Little Chandler.

Ignatius Gallaher drank off his whisky and shook his head.

"Ah," he said, "you may say what you like. There's no woman like the Parisienne—for style, for go."

"Then it is an immoral city," said Little Chandler, with timid insistence—"I mean, compared with London or Dublin?"

"London!" said Ignatius Gallaher. "It's six of one and half-a-dozen of the other. You ask Hogan, my boy. I showed him a bit about London when he was over there. He'd open your eye. . . . I say, Tommy, don't make punch of that whisky: liquor up."

"No, really. . . ."

"O, come on, another one won't do you any harm. What is it? The same again, I suppose?"

"Well . . . all right."

"*François*, the same again. . . . Will you smoke, Tommy?"

Ignatius Gallaher produced his cigar-case. The two friends lit their cigars and puffed at them in silence until their drinks were served.

"I'll tell you my opinion," said Ignatius Gallaher, emerging after some time from the clouds of smoke in which he had taken refuge, "it's a rum world. Talk of immorality! I've heard of cases—what am I saying?—I've known them: cases of . . . immorality. . . ."

Ignatius Gallaher puffed thoughtfully at his cigar and then, in a calm historian's tone, he proceeded to sketch for his friend some pictures of the corruption which was rife abroad. He summarised the vices of many capitals and seemed inclined to award the palm to Berlin. Some things he could not vouch for (his friends had told him), but of others he had had personal experience. He spared neither rank nor caste. He revealed many of the secrets of religious houses on the Continent and described some of the practices which were fashionable in high society and ended by telling, with details, a story about an English duchess—a story which he knew to be true. Little Chandler was astonished.

"Ah, well," said Ignatius Gallaher, "here we are in old jog-along Dublin where nothing is known of such things."

"How dull you must find it," said Little Chandler, "after all the other places you've seen!"

"Well," said Ignatius Gallaher, "it's a relaxation to come over here, you know. And, after all, it's the old country, as they say, isn't it? You can't help having a certain feeling for it. That's human nature. . . . But tell me something about yourself. Hogan told me you had . . . tasted the joys of connubial bliss. Two years ago, wasn't it?"

Little Chandler blushed and smiled.

"Yes," he said. "I was married last May twelve months."

"I hope it's not too late in the day to offer my best wishes," said Ignatius Gallaher. "I didn't know your address or I'd have done so at the time."

He extended his hand, which Little Chandler took.

"Well, Tommy," he said, "I wish you and yours every joy in life, old chap, and tons of money, and may you never die till I shoot you. And that's the wish of a sincere friend, an old friend. You know that?"

"I know that," said Little Chandler.

"Any youngsters?" said Ignatius Gallaher.

Little Chandler blushed again.

"We have one child," he said.

"Son or daughter?"

"A little boy."

Ignatius Gallaher slapped his friend sonorously on the back.

"Bravo," he said, "I wouldn't doubt you, Tommy."

Little Chandler smiled, looked confusedly at his glass and bit his lower lip with three childishly white front teeth.

"I hope you'll spend an evening with us," he said, "before you go back. My wife will be delighted to meet you. We can have a little music and—"

"Thanks awfully, old chap," said Ignatius Gallaher, "I'm sorry we didn't meet earlier. But I must leave tomorrow night."

"Tonight, perhaps . . . ?"

"I'm awfully sorry, old man. You see I'm over here with another fellow, clever young chap he is too, and we arranged to go to a little card-party. Only for that. . . ."

"O, in that case. . . ."

"But who knows?" said Ignatius Chandler considerately. "Next year I may take a little skip over here now that I've broken the ice. It's only a pleasure deferred."

"Very well," said Little Chandler, "the next time you come we must have an evening together. That's agreed now, isn't it?"

"Yes, that's agreed," said Ignatius Gallaher. "Next year if I come, *parole d'honneur."*

"And to clinch the bargain," said Little Chandler, "we'll just have one more now."

Ignatius Gallaher took out a large gold watch and looked at it.

"Is it to be the last?" he said. "Because you know, I have an a.p."

"O, yes, positively," said Little Chandler.

"Very well, then," said Ignatius Gallaher, "let us have another one as a *deoc an doruis*—that's good vernacular for a small whisky, I believe."

Little Chandler ordered the drinks. The blush which had risen to his face a few moments before was establishing itself. A trifle made him blush at any time: and now he felt warm and excited. Three small whiskies had gone to his head and Gallaher's strong cigar had confused his mind, for he was a delicate and abstinent person. The adventure of meeting Gallaher after eight years, of finding himself with Gallaher in Corless's surrounded by lights and noise, of listening to Gallaher's stories and of sharing for a brief space Gallaher's vagrant and triumphant life, upset the equipoise of his sensitive nature. He felt acutely the contrast between his own life and his friend's, and it seemed to him unjust. Gallaher was his inferior in birth and education. He was sure that he could do something better than his friend had ever done, or could ever do, something higher than mere tawdry journalism if he only got the chance. What was it that stood in his way? His unfortunate timidity! He wished to vindicate himself in some way, to assert his manhood. He saw behind Gallaher's refusal of his invitation. Gallaher was only patronising him by his friendliness just as he was patronising Ireland by his visit.

The barman brought their drinks. Little Chandler pushed one glass towards his friend and took up the other boldly.

"Who knows?" he said, as they lifted their glasses. "When you come next year I may have the pleasure of wishing long life and happiness to Mr. and Mrs. Ignatius Gallaher."

Ignatius Gallaher in the act of drinking closed one eye expressively over the rim of his glass. When he had drunk he smacked his lips decisively, set down his glass and said:

"No blooming fear of that, my boy. I'm going to have my fling first and see a bit of life and the world before I put my head in the sack—if I ever do."

"Some day you will," said Little Chandler calmly.

Ignatius Gallaher turned his orange tie and slate-blue eyes full upon his friend.

"You think so?" he said.

"You'll put your head in the sack," repeated Little Chandler stoutly, "like everyone else if you can find the girl."

He had slightly emphasised his tone and he was aware that he had betrayed himself; but, though the colour had heightened in his cheek, he did not flinch from his friend's gaze. Ignatius Gallaher watched him for a few moments and then said:

"If ever it occurs, you may bet your bottom dollar there'll be no mooning and spooning about it. I mean to marry money. She'll have a good fat account at the bank or she won't do for me."

Little Chandler shook his head.

"Why, man alive," said Ignatius Gallaher, vehemently, "do you know what it is? I've only to say the word and tomorrow I can have the woman and the cash. You don't believe it? Well, I know it. There are hundreds—what am I saying?—thousands of rich Germans and Jews, rotten with money, that'd only be too glad. . . . You wait a while, my boy. See if I don't play my cards properly. When I go about a thing I mean business, I tell you. You just wait."

He tossed his glass to his mouth, finished his drink and laughed loudly. Then he looked thoughtfully before him and said in a calmer tone:

"But I'm in no hurry. They can wait. I don't fancy tying myself up to one woman, you know."

He imitated with his mouth the act of tasting and made a wry face.

"Must get a bit stale, I should think," he said.

. . . . .

Little Chandler sat in the room off the hall, holding a child in his arms. To save money they kept no servant but Annie's young sister Monica came for an hour or so in the morning and an hour or so in the evening to help. But Monica had gone home long ago. It was a quarter to nine. Little Chandler had come home late for tea and, moreover, he had forgotten to bring Annie home the parcel of coffee from Bewley's. Of course she was in a bad humour and gave him short answers. She said she would do without any tea but when it came near the time at which the shop at the corner closed she decided to go out herself for a quarter of a pound of tea and two pounds of sugar. She put the sleeping child deftly in his arms and said:

"Here. Don't waken him."

A little lamp with a white china shade stood upon the table and its light fell over a photograph which was enclosed in a frame of crumpled horn. It was Annie's photograph. Little Chandler looked at it, pausing at the thin tight lips. She wore the pale blue summer blouse which he had brought her home as a present one Saturday. It had cost him ten and elevenpence; but what an agony of nervousness it had cost him! How he had suffered that day, waiting at the shop door until the shop was empty, standing at the counter and trying to appear at his ease while the girl piled ladies' blouses before him, paying at the desk and forgetting to take up the odd penny of his change, being called back by the cashier, and finally, striving to hide his blushes as he left the shop by examining the parcel to see if it was securely tied. When he brought the blouse home Annie kissed him and said it was very pretty and stylish; but when she heard the price she threw the blouse on the table and said it was a regular swindle to charge ten and elevenpence for it. At first she wanted to take it back but when she tried it on she was delighted with it, especially with the make of the sleeves, and kissed him and said he was very good to think of her.

Hm! . . .

He looked coldly into the eyes of the photograph and they answered coldly. Certainly they were pretty and the face itself was pretty. But he found something mean in it. Why was it so unconscious and ladylike? The composure of the eyes irritated him. They repelled him and defied him: there was no passion in them, no rapture. He thought of what Gallaher had said about rich Jewesses. Those dark Oriental eyes, he thought, how full they are of passion, of voluptuous longing! . . . Why had he married the eyes in the photograph?

He caught himself up at the question and glanced nervously round the room. He found something mean in the pretty furniture which he had bought for his house on the hire system. Annie had chosen it herself and it reminded him of her. It too was prim and pretty. A dull resentment against his life awoke within him. Could he not escape from his little house? Was it too late for him to try to live bravely like Gallaher? Could he go to London? There was the furniture still to be paid for. If he could only write a book and get it published, that might open the way for him.

A volume of Byron's poems lay before him on the table. He opened it cautiously with his left hand lest he should waken the child and began to read the first poem in the book:

"Hushed are the winds and still the evening gloom,
Not e'en a Zephyr wanders through the grove,
Whilst I return to view my Margaret's tomb
And scatter flowers on the dust I love."

He paused. He felt the rhythm of the verse about him in the room. How melancholy it was! Could he, too, write like that, express the melancholy of his soul in verse? There were so many things he wanted to describe: his sensation of a few hours before on Grattan Bridge, for example. If he could get back again into that mood. . . .

The child awoke and began to cry. He turned from the page and tried to hush it: but it would not be hushed. He began to rock it to and fro in his arms but its wailing cry grew keener. He rocked it faster while his eyes began to read the second stanza:

"Within this narrow cell reclines her clay,
That clay where once . . ."

It was useless. He couldn't read. He couldn't do anything. The wailing of the child pierced the drum of his ear. It was useless, useless! He was a prisoner for life. His arms trembled with anger and suddenly bending to the child's face he shouted:

"Stop!"

The child stopped for an instant, had a spasm of fright and began to scream. He jumped up from his chair and walked hastily up and down the room with the child in his arms. It began to sob piteously, losing its breath for four or five seconds, and then bursting out anew. The thin walls of the room echoed the sound. He tried to soothe it but it sobbed more convulsively. He looked at the contracted and quivering face of the child and began to be alarmed. He counted seven sobs without a break between them and caught the child to his breast in fright. If it died! . . .

The door was burst open and a young woman ran in, panting.

"What is it? What is it?" she cried.

The child, hearing its mother's voice, broke out into a paroxysm of sobbing.

"It's nothing, Annie . . . it's nothing. . . . He began to cry . . ."

She flung her parcels on the floor and snatched the child from him.

"What have you done to him?" she cried, glaring into his face.

Little Chandler sustained for one moment the gaze of her eyes and his heart closed together as he met the hatred in them. He began to stammer:

"It's nothing. . . . He . . . he began to cry. . . I couldn't . . . I didn't do anything. . . . What?"

Giving no heed to him she began to walk up and down the room, clasping the child tightly in her arms and murmuring:

"My little man! My little mannie! Was 'ou frightened, love? . . . There now, love! There now! . . . Lambabaun! Mamma's little lamb of the world! . . . There now!"

Little Chandler felt his cheeks suffused with shame and he stood back out of the lamplight. He listened while the paroxysm of the child's sobbing grew less and less; and tears of remorse started to his eyes.

A COUNTRY DOCTOR[1]

FRANZ KAFKA

I WAS in great perplexity; I had to start on an urgent journey; a seriously ill patient was waiting for me in a village ten miles off; a thick blizzard of snow filled all the wide spaces between him and me; I had a gig, a light gig with big wheels, exactly right for our country roads; muffled in furs, my bag of instruments in my hand, I was in the courtyard all ready for the journey; but there was no horse to be had, no horse. My own horse had died in the night, worn out by the fatigues of this icy winter; my servant girl was now running round the village trying to borrow a horse; but it was hopeless, I knew it, and I stood there forlornly, with the snow gathering more and more thickly upon me, more and more unable to move. In the gateway the girl appeared, alone, and waved the lantern; of course, who would lend a horse at this time for such a journey? I strode through the courtway once more; I could see no way out; in my confused distress I kicked at the dilapidated door of the yearlong uninhabited pigsty. It flew open and flapped to and fro on its hinges. A steam and smell as of horses came out of it. A dim stable lantern was swinging inside from a rope. A man, crouching on his hams in that low space, showed an open blue-eyed face. "Shall I yoke up?" he asked, crawling out on all fours. I did not know what to say and merely stooped down to see what else was in the sty. The servant girl was standing beside me. "You never know what you're going to find in your own house," she said, and we both laughed. "Hey there, Brother, hey there, Sister!" called the groom, and two horses, enormous creatures with powerful flanks, one after the other, their legs tucked close to their bodies, each well-shaped head lowered like a camel's, by sheer strength of buttocking squeezed out through the door hole which they filled entirely. But at once they were standing up, with their long legs and their bodies steaming thickly. "Give him a hand," I said, and the willing girl hurried to help the groom with the harnessing. Yet hardly was she beside him when the groom clipped hold of her and pushed his face against hers. She screamed and fled back to me;

1. From *The Penal Colony* by Franz Kafka by permission of Schocken Books, New York. (Translated by Willa and Edwin Muir.)

on her cheek stood out in red the marks of two rows of teeth. "You brute," I yelled in fury, "do you want a whipping?" but in the same moment reflected that the man was a stranger; that I did not know where he came from, and that of his own free will he was helping me out when everyone else had failed me. As if he knew my thoughts he took no offense at my threat but, still busied with the horses, only turned round once towards me. "Get in," he said then, and indeed: everything was ready. A magnificent pair of horses, I observed, such as I had never sat behind, and I climbed in happily. "But I'll drive, you don't know the way," I said. "Of course," said he, "I'm not coming with you anyway, I'm staying with Rose." "No," shrieked Rose, fleeing into the house with a justified presentiment that her fate was inescapable; I heard the door chain rattle as she put it up; I heard the key turn in the lock; I could see, moreover, how she put out the lights in the entrance hall and in further flight all through the rooms to keep herself from being discovered. "You're coming with me," I said to the groom, "or I won't go, urgent as my journey is. I'm not thinking of paying for it by handing the girl over to you." "Gee up!" he said; clapped his hands; the gig whirled off like a log in a freshet; I could just hear the door of my house splitting and bursting as the groom charged at it and then I was deafened and blinded by a storming rush that steadily buffeted all my senses. But this only for a moment, since, as if my patient's farmyard had opened out just before my courtyard gate, I was already there; the horses had come quietly to a standstill; the blizzard had stopped; the moonlight all around; my patient's parents hurried out of the house, his sister behind them; I was almost lifted out of the gig; from their confused ejaculations I gathered not a word; in the sick room the air was almost unbreathable; the neglected stove was smoking; I wanted to push open a window; but first I had to look at my patient. Gaunt, without any fever, not cold, not warm, with vacant eyes, without a shirt, the youngster heaved himself up from under the feather bedding, threw his arms around my neck, and whispered in my ear: "Doctor, let me die." I glanced round the room; no one had heard it; the parents were leaning forward in silence waiting for my verdict; the sister had set a chair for my handbag; I opened the bag and hunted among my instruments; the boy kept clutching at me from his bed to remind me of his entreaty; I picked up a pair of tweezers, examined them in the candlelight and laid them down again. "Yes," I thought blasphemously, "in cases like this the gods are helpful, send the missing horse, add to it a second because of the urgency, and to crown everything bestow even a groom—" And only now did I remember Rose again; what was I to do, how could I rescue her, how could I pull her away from under that groom at ten miles' distance, with a team of horses I couldn't control. These horses, now, they had somehow slipped the reins loose, pushed the window open from the outside, I did not know how; each of them had stuck a head in at a window and, quite unmoved by the startled cries of the family, stood eyeing the patient. "Better go back at once," I thought, as if the horses were summoning me to the return journey, yet I permitted the patient's sister, who fancied that I was dazed by the heat, to take my fur coat from me. A glass of rum was poured out for me, the old man clapped me on the shoulder, a familiarity justified by this offer of his treasure. I shook my head; in the narrow confines of the old man's thoughts I felt ill; that was my only reason for refusing the drink. The mother stood by the bedside and cajoled me towards it; I yielded, and, while one of the horses whinnied loudly to the ceiling, laid my head to the boy's breast, which shivered under my wet beard. I confirmed what I already knew; the boy was quite sound, something a little wrong with his circulation, saturated with coffee by his solicitous mother, but sound and best turned out of bed with one shove. I am no world reformer and so I let him lie. I was the district doctor and I did my duty to the uttermost, to the point where it became almost too much. I was badly paid and yet generous and helpful to the poor. I had still to see that Rose was all right, and then the boy might have his way and I wanted to die too. What was I doing there in that endless winter! My horse was dead, and not a single person in the village would lend me another. I had to get my team out of the pigsty; if they hadn't chanced to be horses I should have had to travel with swine. That was how it was. And I nodded to the family. They knew nothing about it, and, had they known, would not have believed it. To write prescriptions is easy, but to come to an understanding with people is hard. Well, this should be the end of my visit, I had once more been called out needlessly, I was used to that, the whole district made my life a torment with my night bell, but that I should have to sacrifice Rose this time as well, the pretty girl who had lived in my house for years almost without my noticing her—that sacrifice was too much to ask, and I had somehow to get it reasoned out in my head with the help of what craft I could muster, in order not to let fly at this family, which with the best will in the world could not restore Rose to me. But as I shut my bag and put an arm out for my fur coat, the family meanwhile standing together, the father sniffing at the glass of rum in his hand, the mother, apparently disappointed in me—why, what do people expect?—biting her lips with tears in her eyes, the sister fluttering a blood-soaked towel, I was somehow ready to admit conditionally that the boy might be ill after all. I went towards him, he welcomed me smiling as if I were bringing him the most nourishing invalid broth—ah, now both horses were whinnying together; the noise, I suppose, was ordained by heaven to assist my examination of the patient—and this time I discovered that the boy was indeed ill. In his right side, near the hip, was an open wound as big as the palm of my hand. Rose-red, in many variations of shade, dark in the hollows, lighter at the edges, softly granulated, with irregular clots of blood, open as a surface mine to the daylight. That was how it looked from a distance. But on a closer inspection there was another complication. I could not help a low whistle of surprise. Worms, as thick and as long as my little finger, themselves rose-red and blood-spotted as well, were wriggling from their fastness in the interior of the wound towards the light, with small white heads and many little legs. Poor boy, you were past helping. I had discovered your great wound; this blossom in your side was destroying you. The family was pleased; they saw me busying myself; the sister told the mother, the mother the father, the father told several guests who were coming in, through the moonlight at the open door, walking on tiptoe, keeping their balance with outstretched arms. "Will you save me?" whispered the boy with a sob, quite blinded by the life within his wound. That is what people are like in my district. Always expecting the impossible from the doctor. They have lost their ancient beliefs; the parson sits at home and unravels his vestments, one after another; but the doctor is supposed to be omnipotent with his merciful surgeon's hand. Well, as it pleases them; I have not thrust my services on them; if they misuse me for sacred ends, I let that happen to me too; what better do I want, old country doctor that I am, bereft of my servant girl! And so they came, the family and the village elders, and stripped my clothes off me; a school choir with the teacher at the head of it stood before the house and sang these words to an utterly simple tune:

Strip his clothes off, then he'll heal us,
If he doesn't, kill him dead!
Only a doctor, only a doctor.

Then my clothes were off and I looked at the people quietly, my fingers in my beard and my head cocked to one side. I was altogether composed and equal to the situation and remained so, although it was no help to me, since they now took me by the head and feet and carried me to the bed. They laid me down in it next to the wall, on the side of the wound. Then they all left the room; the door was shut; the singing stopped; clouds covered the moon; the bedding was warm around me; the horses' heads in the opened windows wavered like shadows. "Do you know," said a voice in my ear, "I have very little confidence in you. Why, you were only blown in here, you didn't come on your own feet. Instead of helping me, you're cramping me on my death bed. What I'd like best is to scratch your eyes out." "Right," I said, "it's a shame. And yet I am a doctor. What am I to do? Believe me, it is not too easy for me either." "Am I supposed to be content with this apology? Oh, I must be, I can't help it. I always have to put up with things. A fine wound is all I brought into the world; that was my sole endowment." "My young friend," said I, "your mistake is: you have not a wide enough view. I have been in all the sickrooms, far and wide, and I tell you: your wound is not so bad. Done in a tight corner with two strokes of the ax. Many a one proffers his side and can hardly hear the ax in the forest, far less that it is coming nearer to him." "Is that really so, or are you deluding me in my fever?" "It is really so, take the word of honor of an official doctor." And he took it and lay still. But now it was time for me to think of escaping. The horses were still standing faithfully in their places. My clothes, my fur coat, my bag were quickly collected; I didn't want to waste time dressing; if the horses raced home as they had come, I should only be springing, as it were, out of this bed into my own. Obediently a horse backed away from the window; I threw my bundle into the gig; the fur coat missed its mark and was caught on a hook only by the sleeve. Good enough. I swung myself on to the horse. With the reins loosely trailing, one horse barely fastened to the other, the gig swaying behind, my fur coat last of all in the snow. "Geeup!" I said, but there was no galloping; slowly, like old men, we crawled through the snowy wastes; a long time echoed behind us the new but faulty song of the children:

O be joyful, all you patients,
The doctor's laid in bed beside you!

Never shall I reach home at this rate; my flourishing practice is done for; my successor is robbing me, but in vain, for he cannot take my place; in my house the disgusting groom is raging; Rose is the victim; I do not want to think about it any more. Naked, exposed to the frost of this most unhappy of ages, with an earthly vehicle, unearthly horses, old man that I am, I wander astray. My fur coat is hanging from the back of the gig, but I cannot reach it, and none of my limber pack of patients lifts a finger. Betrayed! Betrayed! A false alarm on the night bell once answered—it cannot be made good, not ever.

JEAN BEICKE [1]

WILLIAM CARLOS WILLIAMS

DURING A TIME like this, they kid a lot among the doctors and nurses on the obstetrical floor because of the rushing business in new babies that's pretty nearly always going on up there. It's the Depression, they say, nobody has any money so they stay home nights. But one bad result of this is that in the children's ward, another floor up, you see a lot of unwanted children.

The parents get them into the place under all sorts of pretexts. For instance, we have two premature brats, Navarro and Cryschka, one a boy and one a girl; the mother died when Cryschka was born, I think. We got them within a few days of each other, one weighing four pounds and one a few ounces more. They dropped down below four pounds before we got

1. From *Make Light of It,* by William Carlos Williams. Reprinted by permission of Random House, Inc. Copyright, 1933, by William Carlos Williams.

them going but there they are; we had a lot of fun betting on their daily gains in weight but we still have them. They're in pretty good shape though now. Most of the kids that are left that way get along swell. The nurses grow attached to them and get a real thrill when they begin to pick up. It's great to see. And the parents sometimes don't even come to visit them, afraid we'll grab them and make them take the kids out, I suppose.

A funny one is a little Hungarian Gypsy girl that's been up there for the past month. She was about eight weeks old maybe when they brought her in with something on her lower lip that looked like a chancre. Everyone was interested but the Wassermann was negative. It turned out finally to be nothing but a peculiarly situated birthmark. But that kid is still there too. Nobody can find the parents. Maybe they'll turn up some day.

Even when we do get rid of them, they often come back in a week or so—sometimes in terrible condition, full of impetigo, down in weight—everything we'd done for them to do over again. I think it's deliberate neglect in most cases. That's what happened to this little Gypsy. The nurse was funny after the mother had left the second time. I couldn't speak to her, she said. I just couldn't say a word I was so mad. I wanted to slap her.

We had a couple of Irish girls a while back named Cowley. One was a red head with beautiful wavy hair and the other a straight haired blonde. They really were good looking and not infants at all. I should say they must have been two and three years old approximately. I can't imagine how the parents could have abandoned them. But they did. I think they were habitual drunkards and may have had to beat it besides on short notice. No fault of theirs maybe.

But all these are, after all, not the kind of kids I have in mind. The ones I mean are those they bring in stinking dirty, and I mean stinking. The poor brats are almost dead sometimes, just living skeletons, almost, wrapped in rags, their heads caked with dirt, their eyes stuck together with pus and their legs all excoriated from the dirty diapers no one has had the interest to take off them regularly. One poor little pot we have now with a thin purplish skin and big veins standing out all over its head had a big sore place in the fold of its neck under the chin. The nurse told me that when she started to undress it it had on a shirt with a neckband that rubbed right into that place. Just dirt. The mother gave a story of having had it in some sort of home in Paterson. We couldn't get it straight. We never try. What the hell? We take 'em and try to make something out of them.

Sometimes, you'd be surprised, some doctor has given the parents a ride before they bring the child to the clinic. You wouldn't believe it. They clean 'em out, maybe for twenty-five dollars—they maybe had to borrow—and then tell 'em to move on. It happens. Men we all know too. Pretty bad. But what can you do?

And sometimes the kids are not only dirty and neglected but sick, ready to die. You ought to see those nurses work. You'd think it was the brat of their best friend. They handle those kids as if they were worth a million dollars. Not that some nurses aren't better than others but in general they break their hearts over those kids, many times, when I, for one, wish they'd never get well.

I often kid the girls. Why not? I look at some miserable specimens they've dolled up for me when I make the rounds in the morning and I tell them: Give it an enema, maybe it will get well and grow up into a cheap prostitute or something. The country needs you, brat. I once proposed that we have a mock wedding between a born garbage hustler we'd saved and a little female with a fresh mug on her that would make anybody smile.

Poor kids! You really wonder sometimes if medicine isn't all wrong to try to do anything for them at all. You actually want to see them pass out, especially when they're deformed or—they're awful sometimes. Every one has rickets in an advanced form, scurvy too, flat chests, spindly arms and legs. They come in with pneumonia, a temperature of a hundred and six, maybe, and before you can do a thing, they're dead.

This little Jean Beicke was like that. She was about the worst you'd expect to find anywhere. Eleven months old. Lying on the examining table with a blanket half way up her body, stripped, lying there, you'd think it a five months baby, just about that long. But when the nurse took the blanket away, her legs kept on going for a good eight inches longer. I couldn't get used to it. I covered her up and asked two of the men to guess how long she was. Both guessed at least half a foot too short. One thing that helped the illusion besides her small face was her arms. They came about to her hips. I don't know what made that. They should come down to her thighs, you know.

She was just skin and bones but her eyes were good and she looked straight at you. Only if you touched her anywhere, she started to whine and then cry with a shrieking, distressing sort of cry that no one wanted to hear. We handled her as gently as we knew how but she had to cry just the same.

She was one of the damnedest looking kids I've ever seen. Her head was all up in front and flat behind, I suppose from lying on the back of her head so long the weight of it and the softness of the bones from the rickets had just flattened it out and pushed it up forward. And her legs and arms seemed loose on her like the arms and legs of some cheap dolls. You could bend her feet up on her shins absolutely flat—but there was no real deformity, just all loosened up. Nobody was with her when I saw her though her mother had brought her in.

It was about ten in the evening, the interne had asked me to see her because she had a stiff neck, and how! and there was some thought of meningitis—perhaps infantile paralysis. Anyhow, they didn't want her to go through the night without at least a lumbar puncture if she needed it. She had a fierce cough and a fairly high fever. I made it out to be a case of broncho-pneumonia with meningismus but no true involvement of the central nervous system. Besides she had inflamed ear drums.

I wanted to incise the drums, especially the left, and would have done it only the night superintendent came along just then and made me call the ear man on service. You know. She also looked to see if we had an operative release from the parents. There was. So I went home, the ear man came in a while later and opened the ears—a little bloody serum from both sides and that was that.

Next day we did a lumbar puncture, tapped the spine that is, and found clear fluid with a few lymphocytes in it, nothing diagnostic. The X-ray of the chest clinched the diagnosis of broncho-pneumonia, there was an extensive involvement. She was pretty sick. We all expected her to die from exhaustion before she'd gone very far.

I had to laugh every time I looked at the brat after that, she was such a funny looking one but one thing that kept her from being a total loss was that she did eat. Boy! how that kid could eat! As sick as she was she took her grub right on time every three hours, a big eight ounce bottle of whole milk and digested it perfectly. In this depression you got to be such a hungry baby, I heard the nurse say to her once. It's a sign of intelligence, I told her. But anyway, we all got to be crazy about Jean. She'd just lie there and eat and sleep. Or she'd lie and look straight in front of her by the hour. Her eyes were blue, a pale sort of blue. But if you went to touch her, she'd begin to scream. We just didn't, that's all, unless we absolutely had to. And she began to gain in weight. Can you imagine that? I suppose she had been so terribly run down that food, real food, was an entirely new experience to her. Anyway she took her food and gained on it though her temperature continued to run steadily around between a hundred and three and a hundred and four for the first eight or ten days. We were surprised.

When we were expecting her to begin to show improvement, however, she didn't. We did another lumbar puncture and found fewer cells. That was fine and the second X-ray of the chest showed it somewhat improved also. That wasn't so good though, because the temperature still kept up and we had no way to account for it. I looked at the ears again and thought they ought to be opened once more. The ear man disagreed but I kept after him and next day he did it to please me. He didn't get anything but a drop of serum on either side.

Well, Jean didn't get well. We did everything we knew how to do except the right thing. She carried on for another two—no I think it was three—weeks longer. A couple of times her temperature shot up to a hundred and eight. Of course we knew then it was the end. We went over her six or eight times, three or four of us, one after the other, and nobody thought to take an X-ray of the mastoid regions. It was dumb, if you want to say it, but there wasn't a sign of anything but the history of the case to point to it.

The ears had been opened early, they had been watched carefully, there was no discharge to speak of at any time and from the external examination, the mastoid processes showed no change from the normal. But that's what she died of, acute purulent mastoiditis of the left side, going on to involvement of the left lateral sinus and finally the meninges. We might, however, have taken a culture of the pus when the ear was first opened and I shall always, after this, in suspicious cases. I have been told since that if you get a virulent bug like the streptococcus mucosus capsulatus it's wise at least to go in behind the ear for drainage if the temperature keeps up. Anyhow she died.

I went in when she was just lying there gasping. Somehow or other, I hated to see that kid go. Everybody felt rotten. She was such a scrawny, misshapen, worthless piece of humanity that I had said many times that somebody ought to chuck her in the garbage chute—but after a month watching her suck up her milk and thrive on it—and to see those alert blue eyes in that face—well, it wasn't pleasant. Her mother was sitting by the bed crying quietly when I came in, the morning of the last day. She was a young woman, didn't look more than a girl, she just sat there looking at the child and crying without a sound.

I expected her to begin to ask me questions with that look on her face all doctors hate—but she didn't. I put my hand on her shoulder and told her we had done everything we knew how to do for Jean but that we really didn't know what, finally, was killing her. The woman didn't make any sign of hearing me. Just sat there looking in between the bars of the crib. So after a moment watching the poor kid beside her, I turned to the infant in the next crib to go on with my rounds. There was an older woman there looking in at that baby also—no better off than Jean, surely. I spoke to her, thinking she was the mother of this one, but she wasn't.

Before I could say anything, she told me she was the older sister of Jean's mother and that she knew that Jean was dying and that it was a good thing. That gave me an idea—I hated to talk to Jean's mother herself—so I beckoned the woman to come out into the hall with me.

I'm glad she's going to die, she said. She's got two others home, older, and her husband has run off with another woman. It's better off dead—never was any good anyway. You know her husband came down from Canada about a year and a half ago. She seen him and asked him to come back and live with her and the children. He come back just long enough to get her pregnant with this one then he left her again and went back to the other woman. And I suppose knowing she was pregnant, and suffering, and having no money and nowhere to get it, she was worrying and this one never was formed right. I seen it as soon as it was born. I guess the condition she was in was the cause. She's got enough to worry about now without this one. The husband's gone to Canada again and we can't get a thing out of him. I been keeping them, but we can't do much more. She'd work if she could find anything but what can you do with three kids in times like this? She's got a boy nine years old but her mother-in-law sneaked it away from her and now he's with his father in Canada. She worries about him too, but that don't do no good.

Listen, I said, I want to ask you something. Do you think she'd let us do an autopsy on Jean if she dies? I hate to speak to her of such a thing now but to tell you the truth, we've worked hard on that poor child and we don't exactly know what is the trouble. We know that she's had pneumonia but that's been getting well. Would you take it up with her for me, if—of course —she dies.

Oh, she's gonna die all right, said the woman. Sure, I will. If you can learn anything, it's only right. I'll see that you get the chance. She won't make any kick, I'll tell her.

Thanks, I said.

The infant died about five in the afternoon. The pathologist was dog-tired from a lot of extra work he'd had to do due to the absence of his assistant on her vacation so he put off the autopsy till next morning. They packed the body in ice in one of the service hoppers. It worked perfectly.

Next morning they did the postmortem. I couldn't get the nurse to go down to it. I may be a sap, she said, but I can't do it, that's all. I can't. Not when I've taken care of them. I feel as if they're my own.

I was amazed to see how completely the lungs had cleared up. They were almost normal except for a very small patch of residual pneumonia here and there which really amounted to nothing. Chest and abdomen were in excellent shape, otherwise, throughout—not a thing aside from the negligible pneumonia. Then he opened the head.

It seemed to me the poor kid's convolutions were unusually well developed. I kept thinking it's incredible that that complicated mechanism of the brain has come into being just for this. I never can quite get used to an autopsy.

The first evidence of the real trouble—for there had been no gross evidence of meningitis—was when the pathologist took the brain in his hand and made the long steady cut which opened up the left lateral ventricle. There was just a faint color of pus on the bulb of the choroid plexus there. Then the diagnosis all cleared up quickly. The left lateral sinus was completely thrombosed and on going into the left temporal bone from the inside the mastoid process was all broken down.

I called up the ear man and he came down at once. A clear miss, he said. I think if we'd gone in there earlier, we'd have saved her.

For what? said I. Vote the straight Communist ticket.

Would it make us any dumber? said the ear man.

THE FLY[1]

KATHERINE MANSFIELD

"Y'ARE very snug in here," piped old Mr. Woodifield, and he peered out of the great, green leather armchair by his friend, the boss's desk, as a baby peers out of its pram. His talk was over; it was time for him to be off. But he did not want to go. Since he had retired, since his . . . stroke, the wife and the girls kept him boxed up in the house every day of the week except Tuesday. On Tuesday he was dressed up and brushed and allowed to cut back to the City for the day. Though what he did there the wife and girls couldn't imagine. Made a nuisance of himself to his friends, they supposed. . . . Well, perhaps so. All the same, we cling to our last pleasures as the tree clings to its last leaves. So there sat old Woodifield, smoking a cigar and staring almost greedily at the boss, who rolled in his office chair, stout, rosy, five years older than he, and still going strong, still at the helm. It did one good to see him.

Wistfully, admiringly, the old voice added, "It's snug in here, upon my word!"

"Yes, it's comfortable enough," agreed the boss, and he flipped *The Financial Times* with a paper knife. As a matter of fact he was proud of his room; he liked to have it admired, especially by old Woodifield. It gave him a feeling of deep, solid satisfaction to be planted there in the midst of it in full view of that frail old figure in the muffler.

"I've had it done up lately," he explained, as he had explained for the past—how many?—weeks. "New carpet," and he pointed to the bright red carpet with a pattern of large white rings. "New furniture," and he nodded towards the massive bookcase and the table with legs like twisted treacle. "Electric heating!" He waved almost exultantly towards the five transparent, pearly sausages glowing so softly in the tilted copper pan.

But he did not draw old Woodifield's attention to the photograph over the table of a grave-looking boy in uniform standing in one of those spectral photographers' parks with photographers' storm clouds behind him. It was not new. It had been there for over six years.

"There was something I wanted to tell you," said old Woodifield, and his eyes grew dim remembering. "Now what was it? I had it in mind when I started out this morning." His hands began to tremble, and patches of red showed above his beard.

Poor old chap, he's on his last pins, thought the boss. And, feeling kindly, he winked at the old man, and said jokingly, "I tell you what. I've got a little drop of something here that'll do you good before you go out into the cold again. It's beautiful stuff. It wouldn't hurt a child." He took a key off his

1. Reprinted from *The Short Stories of Katherine Mansfield* by Katherine Mansfield, by permission of Alfred A. Knopf, Inc. Copyright, 1922, by Alfred A. Knopf, Inc.

watch-chain, unlocked a cupboard below his desk, and drew forth a dark, squat bottle. "That's the medicine," said he. "And the man from whom I got it told me on the strict Q.T. it came from the cellars at Windsor Castle."

Old Woodifield's mouth fell open at the sight. He couldn't have looked more surprised if the boss had produced a rabbit.

"It's whisky, ain't it?" he piped, feebly.

The boss turned the bottle and lovingly showed him the label. Whisky it was.

"D'you know," said he, peering up at the boss wonderingly, "they won't let me touch it at home." And he looked as though he was going to cry.

"Ah, that's where we know a bit more than the ladies," cried the boss, swooping across for two tumblers that stood on the table with the water bottle, and pouring a generous finger into each. "Drink it down. It'll do you good. And don't put any water with it. It's sacrilege to tamper with stuff like this. Ah!" He tossed off his, pulled out his handkerchief, hastily wiped his mustaches, and cocked an eye at old Woodifield, who was rolling his in his chaps.

The old man swallowed, was silent a moment, and then said faintly, "It's nutty!"

But it warmed him; it crept into his chill old brain—he remembered.

"That was it," he said, heaving himself out of his chair. "I thought you'd like to know. The girls were in Belgium last week having a look at poor Reggie's grave, and they happened to come across your boy's. They are quite near each other, it seems."

Old Woodifield paused, but the boss made no reply. Only a quiver of his eyelids showed that he heard.

"The girls were delighted with the way the place is kept," piped the old voice. "Beautifully looked after. Couldn't be better if they were at home. You've not been across, have yer?"

"No, no!" For various reasons the boss had not been across.

"There's miles of it," quavered old Woodifield, "and it's all as neat as a garden. Flowers growing on all the graves. Nice broad paths." It was plain from his voice how much he like a nice broad path.

The pause came again. Then the old man brightened wonderfully.

"D'you know what the hotel made the girls pay for a pot of jam?" he piped. "Ten francs! Robbery, I call it. It was a little pot, so Gertrude says, no bigger than a half-crown. And she hadn't taken more than a spoonful when they charged her ten francs. Gertrude brought the pot away with her to teach 'em a lesson. Quite right, too; it's trading on our feelings. They think because we're over there having a look around we're ready to pay anything. That's what it is." And he turned towards the door.

"Quite right, quite right!" cried the boss, though what was quite right he hadn't the least idea. He came round by his desk, followed the shuffling footsteps to the door, and saw the old fellow out. Woodifield was gone.

For a long moment the boss stayed, staring at nothing, while the gray-haired office messenger, watching him, dodged in and out of his cubbyhole like a dog that expects to be taken for a run: "I'll see nobody for half an hour, Macey," said the boss. "Understand? Nobody at all."

"Very good, sir."

The door shut, the firm, heavy steps recrossed the bright carpet, the fat body plumped down in the spring chair, and leaning forward, the boss covered his face with his hands. He wanted, he intended, he had arranged to weep. . . .

It had been a terrible shock to him when old Woodifield sprang that remark upon him about the boy's grave. It was exactly as though the earth had opened and he had seen the boy lying there with Woodifield's girls staring down at him. For it was strange. Although over six years had passed away, the boss never thought of the boy except as lying unchanged, unblemished in his uniform, asleep for ever. "My son!" groaned the boss. But no tears came yet. In the past, in the first months and even years after the boy's death, he had only to say those words to be overcome by such grief that nothing short of a violent fit of weeping could relieve him. Time, he had declared then, he had told everybody, could make no difference. Other men perhaps might recover, might live their loss down, but not he. How was it possible? His boy was an only son. Ever since his birth the boss had worked at building up this business for him; it had no other meaning if it was not for the boy. Life itself had come to have no other meaning. How on earth could he have slaved, denied himself, kept going all these years without the promise for ever before him of the boy's stepping into his shoes and carrying on where he left off?

And that promise had been so near being fulfilled. The boy had been in the office learning the ropes for a year before the war. Every morning they had started off together; they had come back by the same train. And what congratulations he had received as the boy's father! No wonder; he had taken to it marvelously. As to his popularity with the staff, every man jack of them down to old Macey couldn't make enough of the boy. And he wasn't in the least spoiled. No, he was just his bright, natural self, with the right word for everybody, with that boyish look and his habit of saying, "Simply splendid!"

But all that was over and done with as though it never had been. The day had come when Macey had handed him the telegram that brought the whole place crashing about his head. "Deeply regret to inform you . . ." And he had left the office a broken man, with his life in ruins.

Six years ago, six years . . . How quickly time passed! It might have happened yesterday. The boss took his hands from his face; he was puzzled. Something seemed to be wrong with him. He wasn't feeling as he wanted to feel. He decided to get up and have a look at the boy's photograph. But it wasn't a favorite photograph of his; the expression was unnatural. It was cold, even stern-looking. The boy had never looked like that.

At that moment the boss noticed that a fly had fallen into his broken inkpot, and was trying feebly but desperately to clamber out again. Help! help! said those struggling legs. But the sides of the inkpot were wet and slippery; it fell back again and began to swim. The boss took up a pen, picked the fly out of the ink, and shook it onto a piece of blotting paper. For a fraction of a second it lay still on the dark patch that oozed round it. Then the front legs waved, took hold, and, pulling its small sodden body up it began the immense task of cleaning the ink from its wings. Over and under, over and under, went a leg along a wing, as the stone goes over and under the scythe. Then there was a pause, while the fly, seeming to stand on the tips of its toes, tried to expand first one wing and then the other. It succeeded at last, and, sitting down, it began, like a minute cat, to clean its face. Now one could imagine that the little front legs rubbed against each other lightly, joyfully. The horrible danger was over; it had escaped; it was ready for life again.

But just then the boss had an idea. He plunged his pen back into the ink, leaned his thick wrist on the blotting paper, and as the fly tried its wings down came a great heavy blot. What would it make of that? What indeed! The little beggar seemed absolutely cowed, stunned, and afraid to move because of what would happen next. But then, as if painfully, it dragged itself forward. The front legs waved, caught hold, and, more slowly this time, the task began from the beginning.

"He's a plucky little devil," thought the boss, and he felt a real admiration for the fly's courage. That was the way to tackle things; that was the right spirit. Never say die; it was only a question of . . . But the fly had again finished its laborious task, and the boss had just time to refill his pen, to shake fair and square on the new-cleaned body yet another dark drop. What about it this time? A painful moment of suspense followed. But behold, the front legs were again waving; the boss felt a rush of relief. He leaned over the fly and said to it tenderly, "You artful little b. . . ." And he actually had the brilliant notion of breathing on it to help the drying process. All the same, there was something timid and weak about its efforts now, and the boss decided that this time should be the last, as he dipped the pen into the inkpot.

It was. The last blot fell on the soaked blotting paper, and the draggled fly lay in it and did not stir. The back legs were stuck to the body; the front legs were not to be seen.

"Come on," said the boss. "Look sharp!" And he stirred it with his pen—in vain. Nothing happened or was likely to happen. The fly was dead.

The boss lifted the corpse on the end of the paper knife and flung it into the wastepaper basket, but such a grinding feeling of wretchedness seized him that he felt positively frightened. He started forward and pressed the bell for Macey.

"Bring me some fresh blotting paper," he said, sternly, "and look sharp about it." And while the old dog padded away he fell to wondering what it was he had been thinking about before. What was it? It was . . . He took out his handkerchief and passed it inside his collar. For the life of him he could not remember.

ON KATHERINE MANSFIELD'S *THE FLY*[1]

ROBERT WOOSTER STALLMAN

THE experiment with the Fly by the Boss, so named because he appears to be the boss of his little world and of the little life of the Fly who has fallen into his inkpot, the boss as well over his employees Woodifield and Macey and over his dead son (all are as flies to him), dramatizes both the plot (the conflict between time and grief) and the theme (time conquers grief). At the first stage of the experiment the Boss is to be equated with the Fly. He is, ironically then, at once both boss and fly. How cleverly Mansfield inverts her symbol!

He is the boss of the fly Woodifield, whose wife keeps him "boxed up in the house [like a fly] every day of the week except Tuesday." On Tuesday he is brushed off (like a fly) "and allowed to cut back to the City for the day." On this Tuesday he visits the Boss, who is shocked (as a fly is shocked at a drop of ink) by old Woodifield's remark about the boy's grave. The remark —it causes the Boss "a quiver of his eyelids" (a quiver, so to speak, of his fly-wings)—reverses the relationship between the fly Woodifield and the Boss.

The Boss, like the Fly, conquers the first drop of ink—the grief he suffers "when Macey handed him the telegram that brought the whole place crashing about his head." Both survive, survive the danger of being drowned in grief. The "new-cleaned body" of the Fly, "ready for life again," compares with the new-furnished office of the Boss. . . . For the second time the Fly survives his grief. But the Fly and the Boss can no longer be equated. This second stage in the experiment reveals the disparity between them: the Fly survives his grief, but the Boss no longer has any grief to conquer—his sensibility for grief . . . has been blotted up by Time.

"He wanted, he intended, he had arranged to weep. . . ." But no tears came. Time's blotting-pad has soaked up the last tear he will ever shed. "Time, he had declared then [when first he lost his boy], he had told everybody, could make no difference. Other men perhaps might recover, might live their loss down, but not he. How was it possible?" Time makes it possible —inevitable—that man does not succumb to his grief but, to the contrary, recovers from it. "How quickly time passed! It might have happened yesterday." So short a time for grieving. "But all *that* [his grief] was over and done with as though it had never been." Now pride, not grief, is his only emotion. . . . For the Boss to survive his grief and for the Fly to succumb to his suffering, "it was only a question of . . ." [*time*]. The third and final drop of ink marks out the difference between them. The Fly dies—dies from too much grief. So the Boss, who in the beginning seemed to be a fly, is not a fly after all. . . . The discovery holds a double irony: he is neither fly nor boss. *Time*, in the form of the blotting-paper brought in by Macey, *is the boss*.

1. From *The Explicator,* III (April, 1945), 49; V (February, 1947), 32; V (May, 1947), 53. By permission of the authors and the Editors of *The Explicator*.

WILLIS D. JACOBS

The interpretation of Katherine Mansfield's *The Fly* by Professor Stallman is at once ingenious and recherché. That the surface theme of the story is the conquest of time over grief—that in time even a slight distraction can banish the truest emotion from the mind—is certain enough. But in its explanation of the fly itself that previous account violates a wise rule known as Morgan's Canon. Of a number of possibilities, declares this maxim of psychology, first choose the simplest. Once introduced into the story, the fly may well have become a symbol. But a symbol of what? Mr. Stallman rapidly affirms that the fly equates seriatim with the Boss, Woodifield, Macey, the dead son, and even the new-furnished office of the Boss; indeed with everything at all handy. Here indeed is God's plenty. The result surely is that the symbolism cancels itself out. At the end moreover we are told summarily that, after all, the fly is not the Boss. Well, then, just what is the fly?

The answer, I believe, is both different from such whirling alternatives and at once more significant and poignant. When the fly entered the story, it began to represent to Katherine Mansfield a true image of her own fate. The fly is Katherine Mansfield herself. During her last years of life K. M. struggled constantly, bravely, and vainly (like the fly) against the tuberculosis which was beating her, blow by blow, into the grave. In "The Fly" the Boss becomes a heavy-handed, unmeaning instrument which destroys the fly, fight for life as it may; he becomes, on K. M.'s level, the inexorable and equally unmeaning illness which is destroying her, fight for life as she may. Like the Boss, the tuberculosis which killed her is blind, callous, and persistent. As the Boss slays the fly, without malice, so does her illness slay her. Both fly and K. M. fight painfully for life. Both lose.

This explication is not visionary. It is supported by two witnesses. First is the evidence of Mrs. Thomas Moult, friend and confidante of K. M. (For the warmth of their friendship, see as an example *The Letters of Katherine Mansfield,* 1929, II, 428). On the basis of Mrs. Moult's contemporary correspondence and conversation with K. M., Mrs. Moult has stated to this writer that she considers *The Fly* a completely personal story. For K. M. herself, Mrs. Moult said, it had two facets: (1) K. M. is the fly, beaten in her struggle with tuberculosis by a careless, blind fate; (2) K. M. realized, as she wrote, that she too would soon be forgotten, slain by her disease.

Another witness establishes reasonable certainty of this view. *That* is the very circumstances surrounding the writing of *The Fly*. They are as follows: In the words of Frank Swinnerton, K. M. "had always been delicate . . . in 1917 she caught a chill which led to tuberculosis . . . the two constant features of her pilgrimages were increasing illness and unfailing bravery" (*The Georgian Scene,* 1934, p. 249). In late 1921 and early 1922 the disease became rapacious. On February 1, 1922, K. M. confided to her Journal:

"Here I try and fail, and the fact of consciousness makes each separate failure very important." Two weeks later, on February 13, she added: "Felt ill all day. Feeling of violent confusion in my body and head. I feel more ill now than ever, so it seems. . . . The worst of it is I have again lost hope. I don't, I can't believe this will change." (*Journal*, II, 229; 234.)

On February 14, K. M. wrote to Dorothy Brett: "I can do nothing but get up and lie down . . . I must begin work. Seven stories sit on the doorstep. One has a foot inside. It is called *The Fly*" (*Letters*, 1929, II, 446). Under such circumstances was this story written, for as she wrote to Miss Brett twelve days later: "I have just finished a queer story called *The Fly*. About a fly that falls into an inkpot and a Bank Manager" (*Letters*, II, 459). Significantly *The Fly* is the only one of those projected seven stories she wrote, and her writing career came to a complete halt within a few months. The fly struggled, but was killed; so too the spirit of K. M. She died in 1923.

These parallels are too immediate to be disregarded. So too is another. Lover of Shakespeare as she was, in this story of a fly K. M. must surely have had in mind his strikingly similar image. As flies to wanton boys—she is repeating with special meaning to herself—are we to the gods; they kill us for their sport.

THOMAS A. BLEDSOE

I believe that Katherine Mansfield's *The Fly* can be explained without recourse either to a devious symbolism, as by Professor Stallman, or to biographical reference, as by Professor Jacobs. Though the former was pro-
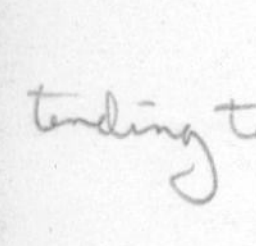
vocative and the latter cogent, both of the writers seem to me to have missed the woods for the trees. They agree that this is a story of the conquest of time over grief, which it is not; they are therefore inevitably led into irreconcilable conflicts of symbols and significances.

While the boss toys with the fly he escapes his grief. But it is not time that cures him, nor does time release the fly from its suffering. The boss murders the fly with wanton and amicable cruelty, the same tender cruelty he shows toward Woodifield, the cruelty with which an inexorable fate has already broken his own life and his son's.

The fly is Katherine Mansfield; but the boss, and Woodifield, and the son are also flies. The whole movement of the story explicates a central theme: "As flies to wanton boys are we to the gods; they kill us for their sport." The tragic irony of *The Fly* is the murderous finality with which other lives are wrecked by powers indifferent to any sorrows but their own. The boss's grief is important only because it absorbs him. To escape it he plays a game of benevolent cruelty, whose end is not to murder but to divert. His pleasure with old Woodifield is sadistic. The sick man's feebleness cheers him; to display the newly furnished office (another diversion) to this broken down hack is comforting, and he gives him a drink, cheerfully indifferent to the old man's health. When the ritual of self-indulgent grief no longer suffices to lay the sorrow Woodifield has unwittingly aroused, he discovers the struggling fly. He accords it the same godlike malice. He admires the fly but he needs diversion; he murders it. The katharsis is a movement of subconscious revulsion, but it is quickly gone. Sport has been good. The boss has forgotten his grief.

Only so viewed is the story an organic whole. Now the long scene with old Woodifield is not merely an elaborate device to introduce the boss's grief, but an integral part of the development of the theme. The boss's bland callousness toward Woodifield is matched by the cheerful indifference with which the old man rambles on toward the boss's innermost grief; while he raises the specter of the boss's bereavement, Woodifield meditates pleasantly about the wide walks of the cemetery (safe for stumbling old feet), and cackles over his daughter's misadventures at the inn. Even the son, in whose last picture the boss sees a strange withdrawal, reflects this eternal selfishness. The game with the fly repeats it: the boss must kill the fly because only killing can show the wantonness of indifferent selfishness. In this brief act the horror which overhangs the whole story becomes explicit.

The world of *The Fly* is one of intermingled and unending cruelties, of monstrous and indifferent egotisms. It is filled with the sheer cruelty of existence, the inevitable savagery which the boss, Woodifield, the son, Katherine Mansfield, and we ourselves alike suffer under and practice. The symbolism of *The Fly* is elaborate but in no wise contradictory. Within the framework of a beautifully planned story, it proclaims the final selfishness of living.

THAT TREE[1]

KATHERINE ANNE PORTER

HE HAD really wanted to be a cheerful bum lying under a tree in a good climate, writing poetry. He wrote bushel basketsful of poetry and it was all no good and he knew it, even while he was writing it. Knowing his poetry was no good did not take away much from his pleasure in it. He would have enjoyed just that kind of life: no respectability, no responsibility, no money to speak of, wearing worn-out sandals and a becoming, if probably ragged, blue shirt, lying under a tree writing poetry. That was why he had come to Mexico in the first place. He had felt in his bones that it was the country for him. Long after he had become quite an important journalist, an authority on Latin-American revolutions and a best seller, he confessed to any friends

1. From *Flowering Judas and Other Stories* by Katherine Anne Porter, copyright, 1930, 1935, by Katherine Anne Porter. Reprinted by permission of Harcourt, Brace and Company, Inc.

and acquaintances who would listen to him—he enjoyed this confession, it gave him a chance to talk about the thing he believed he loved best, the idle free romantic life of a poet—that the day Miriam kicked him out was the luckiest day of his life. She had left him, really, packing up suddenly in a cold quiet fury, stabbing him with her elbows when he tried to get his arms around her, now and again cutting him to the bone with a short sentence expelled through her clenched teeth; but he felt that he had been, as he always explained, kicked out. She had kicked him out and it had served him right.

The shock had brought him to himself as if he had been surprised out of a long sleep. He had sat quite benumbed in the bare clean room, among the straw mats and the painted Indian chairs Miriam hated, in the sudden cold silence, his head in his hands, nearly all night. It hadn't even occurred to him to lie down. It must have been almost daylight when he got up stiff in every joint from sitting still so long, and though he could not say he had been thinking yet he had formed a new resolution. He had started out, you might almost say that very day, to make a career for himself in journalism. He couldn't say why he had hit on that, except that the word would impress his wife, the work was just intellectual enough to save his self-respect, such as it was, and even to him it seemed a suitable occupation for a man such as he had suddenly become, bent on getting on in the world of affairs. Nothing ever happens suddenly to anyone, he observed, as if the thought had just occurred to him; it had been coming on probably for a long time, sneaking up on him when he wasn't looking. His wife had called him "Parasite!" She had said "Ne'er-do-well!" and as she repeated these things for what proved to be the last time, it struck him she had said them often before, when he had not listened to her with the ear of his mind. He translated these relatively harmless epithets instantly into their proper synonyms of Loafer! and Bum! Miriam had been a schoolteacher, and no matter what her disappointments and provocations may have been, you could not expect her easily to forget such discipline. She had got into a professional habit of primness; besides, she was a properly brought-up girl, not a prissy bore, not at all, but a—well, there you are, a nicely brought-up Middle-Western girl, who took life seriously. And what can you do about that? She was sweet and gay and full of little crazy notions, but she never gave way to them honestly, or at least never at the moment when they might have meant something. She was never able to see the amusing side of a threatening situation which, taken solemnly, would ruin everything. No, her sense of humor never worked for salvation. It was just an extra frill on what would have been a good time anyhow.

He wondered if anybody had ever thought—oh, well, of course everybody else had, he was always making marvelous discoveries that other people had known all along—how impossible it is to explain or to make other eyes see the special qualities in the person you love. There was such a special kind of beauty in Miriam. In certain lights and moods he simply got a clutch in the pit of his stomach when he looked at her. It was something that could happen at any hour of the day, in the midst of the most ordinary occupations. He thought there was something to be said for living with one person day and night the year round. It brings out the worst, but it brings out the best, too, and Miriam's best was pretty damn swell. He couldn't describe it. It was easy to talk about her faults. He remembered all of them, he could add them up against her like rows of figures in a vast unpaid debt. He had lived with her for four years, and even now sometimes he woke out of a sound sleep in a sweating rage with himself, asking himself again why he had ever wasted a minute on her. She wasn't beautiful in his style. He confessed to a weakness for the kind that knocks your eye out. Her notion of daytime dress was a tailored suit with a round-collared blouse and a little felt hat like a bent shovel pulled down over her eyes. In the evening she put on a black dinner dress, positively disappeared into it. But she did her hair well and had the most becoming nightgowns he ever saw. You could have put her mind in a peanut shell. She hadn't temperament of the kind he had got used to in the Mexican girls. She did not approve of his use of the word temperament, either. She thought it was a kind of occupational disease among artists, or a trick they practiced to make themselves interesting. In any case, she distrusted artists and she distrusted temperament. But there was something about her. In cold blood he could size her up to himself, but it made him furious if anyone even hinted a criticism against her. His second wife had made a point of being catty about Miriam. In the end he could almost be willing to say this had led to his second divorce. He could not bear hearing Miriam called a mousy little nitwit—at least not by *that* woman. . . .

They both jumped nervously at an explosion in the street, the backfire of an automobile.

"Another revolution," said the fat scarlet young man in the tight purplish suit, at the next table. He looked like a parboiled sausage ready to burst from its skin. It was the oldest joke since the Mexican Independence, but he was trying to look as if he had invented it. The journalist glanced back at him over a sloping shoulder. "Another of those smart-cracking newspaper guys," he said in a tough voice, too loudly on purpose, "sitting around the Hotel Regis lobby wearing out the spittoons."

The smart-cracker swelled visibly and turned a darker red. "Who do you think you're talking about, you banjo-eyed chinless wonder, you?" he asked explicitly, spreading his chest across the table.

"Somebody way up, no doubt," said the journalist, in his natural voice, "somebody in with the government, I'll bet."

"Dyuhwana fight?" asked the newspaper man, trying to unwedge himself from between the table and his chair, which sat against the wall.

"Oh, I don't mind," said the journalist, "if you don't."

The newspaper man's friends laid soothing paws all over him and held him down. "Don't start anything with that shrimp," said one of them, his wet pink eyes trying to look sober and responsible. "For crisesake, Joe, can't you see he's about half your size and a feeb to boot? You wouldn't hit a feeb, now, Joe, would you?"

"I'll feeb him," said the newspaper man, wiggling faintly under restraint.

"Señores'n, señores'n," urged the little Mexican waiter, "there are respectable ladies and gentlemen present. Please, a little silence and correct behavior, please."

"Who the hell are *you*, anyhow?" the newspaper man asked the journalist, from under his shelter of hands, around the thin form of the waiter.

"Nobody you'd wanta know, Joe," said another of his pawing friends. "Pipe down now before these greasers turn in a general alarm. You know how liable they are to go off when you least expect it. Pipe down, now, Joe, now you just remember what happened the last time, Joe. Whaddayah *care*, anyhow?"

"Señores'n," said the little waiter, working his thin outspread mahogany-colored hands up and down alternately as if they were on sticks, "it is necessary it must cease or the *señores'n* must remove themselves."

It did cease. It seemed to evaporate. The four newspaper men at the next table subsided, cluttered in a circle with their heads together, muttering into their highballs. The journalist turned back, ordered another round of drinks, and went on talking, in a low voice.

He had never liked this café, never had any luck in it. Something always happened here to spoil his evening. If there was one brand of bum on earth he despised, it was a newspaper bum. Or anyhow the drunken illiterates the United Press and Associated Press seemed to think were good enough for Mexico and South America. They were always getting mixed up in affairs that were none of their business, and they spent their time trying to work up trouble somewhere so they could get a story out of it. They were always having to be thrown out on their ears by the government. He just happened to know that the bum at the next table was about due to be deported. It had been pretty safe to make that crack about how he was no doubt way up in Mexican official esteem. . . . He thought that would remind him of something, all right.

One evening he had come here with Miriam for dinner and dancing, and at the very next table sat four fat generals from the North, with oxhorn mustaches and big bellies and big belts full of cartridges and pistols. It was in the old days just after Obregón had taken the city, and the town was crawling with generals. They infested the steam baths, where they took off their soiled campaign harness and sweated away the fumes of tequila and fornication, and they infested the cafés to get drunk again on champagne, and pick up the French whores who had been imported for the festivities of the presidential inauguration. These four were having an argument very quietly, their mean little eyes boring into each other's faces. He and his wife were dancing within arm's length of the table when one of the generals got up suddenly, tugging at his pistol, which stuck, and the other three jumped and grabbed him, all without a word; everybody in the place saw it at once. So far there was nothing unusual. The point was, every right-minded Mexican girl just seized her man firmly by the waist and spun him around until his back was to the generals, holding him before her like a shield, and there the whole roomful had stood frozen for a second, the music dead. His wife Miriam had broken from him and hidden under a table. He had to drag her out by the arm before everybody. "Let's have another drink," he said, and paused, looking around him as if he saw again the place as it had been on that night nearly ten years before. He blinked, and went on. It had been the most utterly humiliating moment of his whole blighted life. He had thought he couldn't survive to pick up their things and get her out of there. The generals had all sat down again and everybody went on dancing as though nothing had happened. . . . Indeed, nothing had happened to anyone except himself.

He tried, for hours that night and on and on for nearly a year, to explain to her how he felt about it. She could not understand at all. Sometimes she said it was all perfect nonsense. Or she remarked complacently that it had never occurred to her to save her life at his expense. She thought such tricks were all very well for the Mexican girls who had only one idea in their heads, and any excuse would do to hold a man closer than they should, but she could not, could *not*, see why he should expect her to imitate them. Besides, she had felt safer under the table. It was her first and only thought. He told her a bullet might very well have gone through the wood; a plank was no protection at all, a human torso was as good as a feather pillow to stop a bullet. She kept saying it simply had not occurred to her to do anything else, and that it really had nothing at all to do with him. He could never make her see his point of view for one moment. It should have had something to do with him. All those Mexican girls were born knowing what they should do and they did it instantly, and Miriam had merely proved once for all that her instincts were out of tune. When she tightened her mouth to bite her lip and say "Instincts!" she could make it sound like the most obscene word in any language. It was a shocking word. And she did not stop there. At last she said, she hadn't the faintest interest in what Mexican girls were born for, but she had no intention of wasting her life flattering male vanity. "Why should I trust you in anything?" she asked. "What reason have you given me to trust you?"

He was surprised at the change in her since he had first met her in Minneapolis. He chose to believe this change had been caused by her teaching school. He told her he thought it the most deadly occupation there was and a law should be passed prohibiting pretty women under thirty-five years of age from taking it up. She reminded him they were living on the money she had earned at it. They had been engaged for three years, a chaste long-distance engagement which he considered morbid and unnatural. Of course he had to do something to wear away the time, so while she was in Minneapolis saving her money and filling a huge trunk with household linen, he had been living in Mexico City with an Indian girl who posed for a set of painters he knew. He had a job teaching English in one of the technical schools—damned odd, he had been a schoolteacher too, but he never thought of it just that way until this minute—and he lived very comfortably with the Indian girl on his wages, for naturally the painters did not pay her for posing. The Indian girl divided her time cheerfully between the painters, the cooking pot, and his bed, and she managed to have a baby without interrupting any of these occupations for more than a few days. Later on she was taken up by one of the more famous and successful painters, and grew very sophisticated and a "character," but at that time she was still simple and nice. She took, later on, to wearing native art-jewelry and doing native dances in costume, and learned to paint almost as well as a seven-year-old child; "you know," he said, "the primitive style." Well, by that time, he was having troubles of his own. When the time came for Miriam to come out and marry him—the whole delay, he realized afterward, was caused by Miriam's expansive notions of what a bride's outfit should be—the Indian girl had gone away very cheerfully, too cheerfully, in fact, with a new man. She had come back in three days to say she was at last going to get married honestly, and she felt he should give her the furniture for a dowry. He had helped her pile the stuff on the backs of two Indian carriers, and the girl had walked away with the baby's head dangling out of her shawl. For just a moment when he saw the baby's face, he had an odd feeling. "That's mine," he said to himself, and added at once, "perhaps." There was no way of knowing, and it certainly looked like any other little shock-haired Indian baby. Of course the girl had not got married; she had never even thought of it.

When Miriam arrived, the place was almost empty, because he had not been able to save a peso. He had a bed and a stove, and the walls were decorated with drawings and paintings by his Mexican friends, and there was a litter of painted gourds and carved wood and pottery in beautiful colors. It didn't seem so bad to him, but Miriam's face, when she stepped into the first room, was, he had to admit, pretty much of a study. She said very little, but she began to be unhappy about a number of things. She cried intermittently for the first few weeks, for the most mysterious and far-fetched causes. He would wake in the night and find her crying hopelessly. When she sat down to coffee in the morning she would lean her head on her hands and cry. "It's nothing, nothing really," she would tell him. "I don't know what is the matter. I just want to cry." He knew now what was the matter. She had come all that way to marry after three years' planning, and she couldn't see herself going back and facing the music at home. This mood had not lasted, but it made a fairly dreary failure of their honeymoon. She knew nothing about the Indian girl, and believed, or professed to believe, that he was virgin as she was at their marriage. She hadn't much curiosity and her moral standards were severe, so it was impossible for him ever to take her into his confidence about his past. She simply took it for granted in the most irritating way that he hadn't any past worth mentioning except the three years they were engaged, and that, of course, they shared already. He had believed that all virgins, however austere their behavior, were palpitating to learn about life, were you might say hanging on an eyelash until they arrived safely at initiation within the secure yet libertine advantages of marriage. Miriam upset this theory as in time she upset most of his theories. His intention to play the rôle of a man of the world educating an innocent but interestingly teachable bride was nipped in the bud. She was not at all teachable and she took no trouble to make herself interesting. In their most intimate hours her mind seemed elsewhere, gone into some darkness of its own, as if a prior and greater shock of knowledge had forestalled her attention. She was not to be won, for reasons of her own which she would not or could not give. He could not even play the rôle of a poet. She was not interested in his poetry. She preferred Milton, and she let him know it. She let him know also that she believed their mutual sacrifice of virginity was the most important act of their marriage, and this sacred rite once achieved, the whole affair had descended to a pretty low plane. She had a terrible phrase about "walking the chalk line" which she applied to all sorts of situations. One walked, as never before, the chalk line in marriage; there seemed to be a chalk line drawn between them as they lay together. . . .

The thing that finally got him down was Miriam's devilish inconsistency. She spent three mortal years writing him how dull and dreadful and commonplace her life was, how sick and tired she was of petty little conventions and amusements, how narrow-minded everybody around her was, how she longed to live in a beautiful dangerous place among interesting people who painted and wrote poetry, and how his letters came into her stuffy little world like a breath of free mountain air, and all that. "For God's sake," he said to his guest, "let's have another drink." Well, he had something of a notion he was freeing a sweet bird from a cage. Once freed, she would perch gratefully on his hand. He wrote a poem about a caged bird set free, dedicated it to her and sent her a copy. She forgot to mention it in her next letter. Then she came out with a two-hundred-pound trunk of linen and enough silk underwear to last her a lifetime, you might have supposed, expecting to settle down in a modern steam-heated flat and have nice artistic young couples from the American colony in for dinner Wednesday evenings. No wonder her face had changed at the first glimpse of her new home. His Mexican friends had scattered flowers all over the place, tied bunches of carnations on the door knobs, almost carpeted the floor with red roses, pinned posies of small bright blooms on the sagging cotton curtains, spread a coverlet of gardenias on the lumpy bed, and had disappeared discreetly, leaving gay reassuring messages scribbled here and there, even on the white plastered walls. . . . She had walked through with a vague look of terror in her eyes, pushing back the wilting flowers with her advancing feet. She swept the gardenias aside to sit on the edge of the bed, and she had said not a word. Hail, Hymen! What next?

He had lost his teaching job almost immediately. The Minister of Education, who was a patron of the school superintendent, was put out of office suddenly, and naturally every soul in his party down to the school janitors went out with him, and there you were. After a while you learn to take such things calmly. You wait until your man gets back in the saddle or you work up an alliance with the new one. . . . Whichever. . . . Meanwhile the change and movement made such a good show you almost forgot the effect it had on your food supply. Miriam was not interested in politics or the movements of local history. She could see nothing but that he had lost his job. They lived on Miriam's savings eked out with birthday checks and Christmas checks from her father, who threatened constantly to come for a visit, in spite of Miriam's desperate letters warning him that the country was appalling, and the climate would most certainly ruin his health. Miriam went on holding her nose when she went to the markets, trying to cook wholesome civilized American food over a charcoal brasier, and doing the washing in the patio over a stone tub with a cold water tap; and everything that had seemed so jolly and natural and inexpensive with the Indian girl was too damnifying and costly for words with Miriam. Her money melted away and they got nothing for it.

She would not have an Indian servant near her; they were dirty and besides how could she afford it? He could not see why she despised and resented housework so, especially since he offered to help. He had thought it rather a picnic to wash a lot of gayly colored Indian crockery outdoors in the sunshine, with the bougainvillea climbing up the wall and the heaven tree in full bloom. Not Miriam. She despised him for thinking it a picnic. He remembered for the first time his mother doing the housework when he was a child. There were half a dozen assorted children, her work was hard and endless, but she went about it with a quiet certainty, a happy absorbed look on her face, as if her hands were working automatically while her imagination was away playing somewhere. "Ah, your mother," said his wife, without any particular emphasis. He felt horribly injured, as if she were insulting his mother and calling down a curse on her head for bringing such a son into the world. No doubt about it, Miriam had force. She could make her personality, which no one need really respect, felt in a bitter, sinister way. She had a background, and solid earth under her feet, and a point of view and a strong spine: even when she danced with him he could feel her tense controlled hips and her locked knees, which gave her dancing a most attractive strength and lightness without any yielding at all. She had her points, all right, like a good horse, but she had missed being beautiful. It wasn't in her. He began to cringe when she reminded him that if he were an invalid she would cheerfully work for him and take care of him, but he appeared to be in the best of health, he was not even looking for a job, and he was still writing that poetry, which was the last straw. She called him a failure. She called him worthless and shiftless and trifling and faithless. She showed him her ruined hands and asked him what she had to look forward to, and told him again, and again, that she was not used to associating with the simply indescribably savage and awful persons who kept streaming through the place. Moreover, she had no intention of getting used to it. He tried to tell her that these persons were the best painters and poets and what-alls in Mexico, that she should try to appreciate them; these were the artists he had told her about in his letters. She wanted to know why Carlos never changed his shirt. "I told her," said the journalist, "it was because probably he hadn't got any other shirt." And why was Jaime such a glutton, leaning over his plate and wolfing his food? Because he was famished, no doubt. It was precisely that she could not understand. Why didn't they go to work and make a living? It was no good trying to explain to her his Franciscan notions of holy Poverty as being the natural companion for the artist. She said, "So you think they're being poor on purpose? Nobody but you would be such a fool." Really, the things that girl said. And his general impression of her was that she was silent as a cat. He went on in his pawky way trying to make clear to her his mystical faith in these men who went ragged and hungry because they had chosen once for all between what he called in all seriousness their souls, and this world. Miriam knew better. She knew they were looking for the main chance. "She was abominably, obscenely right. How I hate that woman, I hate her as I hate no one else. She assured me they were not so stupid as I thought; and I lived to see Jaime take up with a rich old woman, and Ricardo decide to turn film actor, and Carlos sitting easy with a government job, painting revolutionary frescoes to order, and I asked myself, Why shouldn't a man survive in any way he can?" But some fixed point of feeling in him refused to be convinced, he had a sackful of romantic notions about artists and their destiny and he was left holding it. Miriam had seen through them with half an eye, and how he wished he might have thought of a trick to play on her that would have finished her for life. But he had not. They all in turn ran out on him and in the end he had run out too. "So you see, I don't feel any better about doing what I did finally do, but I can say I am not unusual. That I can say. The trouble was that Miriam was right, damn her. I am not a poet, my poetry is filthy, and I had notions about artists that I must have got out of books. . . . You know, a race apart, dedicated men much superior to common human needs and ambitions. . . . I mean I thought art was a religion. . . . I mean that when Miriam kept saying . . ."

What he meant was that all this conflict began to damage him seriously. Miriam had become an avenging fury, yet he could not condemn her. Hate her, yes, that was almost too simple. His old-fashioned respectable middle class hard-working American ancestry and training rose up in him and fought on Miriam's side. He felt he had broken about every bone in him to get away from them and live them down, and here he had been overtaken at last and beaten into resignation that had nothing to do with his mind or heart. It was as if his blood stream had betrayed him. The prospect of taking a job and being a decent little clerk with shiny pants and elbows—for he couldn't think of a job in any other terms—seemed like a kind of premature death which would not even compensate him with loss of memory. He didn't do anything about it at all. He did odd jobs and picked up a little money, but never enough. He could see her side of it, at least he tried hard to see it. When it came to a showdown, he hadn't a single argument in favor of his way of life that would hold water. He had been trying to live and think in a way that he hoped would end by making a poet of him, but it hadn't worked. That was the long and short of it. So he might have just gone on to some unimaginably sordid end if Miriam, after four years: four years? yes, good God, four years and one month and eleven days, had not written home for money, packed up what was left of her belongings, called him a few farewell names, and left. She had been shabby and thin and wild-looking for so long he could not remember ever having seen her any other way, yet all at once her profile in the doorway was unrecognizable to him.

So she went, and she did him a great favor without knowing it. He had fallen into the cowardly habit of thinking their marriage was permanent, no matter how evil it might be, that they loved each other, and so it did not matter what cruelties they committed against each other, and he had developed a real deafness to her words. He was unable, towards the end, either to see her or hear her. He realized this afterward, when remembered phrases and expressions of her eyes and mouth began to eat into his marrow. He was grateful to her. If she had not gone, he might have loitered on, wasting his time trying to write poetry, hanging around dirty picturesque little cafés with a fresh set of clever talkative poverty-stricken young Mexicans who were painting or writing or talking about getting ready to paint or write. His faith had renewed itself; these fellows were pure artists—they would never sell out. They were not bums, either. They worked all the time at something to do with Art. "Sacred Art," he said, "our glasses are empty again."

But try telling anything of the kind to Miriam. Somehow he had never got to that tree he meant to lie down under. If he had, somebody would certainly have come around and collected rent for it, anyhow. He had spent a good deal of time lying under tables at Dinty Moore's or the Black Cat with a gang of Americans like himself who were living a free life and studying the native customs. He was rehearsing, he explained to Miriam, hoping for once she would take a joke, for lying under a tree later on. It didn't go over. She would have died with her boots on before she would have cracked a smile at that. So then. . . . He had gone in for a career in the hugest sort of way. It had been easy. He hardly could say now just what his first steps were, but it had been easy. Except for Miriam, he would have been a lousy failure, like those bums at Dinty Moore's, still rolling under the tables, studying the native customs. He had gone in for a career in journalism and he had made a good thing of it. He was a recognized authority on revolutions in twenty-odd Latin-American countries, and his sympathies happened to fall in exactly right with the high-priced magazines of a liberal humanitarian slant which paid him well for telling the world about the oppressed peoples. He could really write, too; if he did say so, he had a prose style of his own. He had made the kind of success you can clip out of newspapers and paste in a book, you can count it and put it in the bank, you can eat and drink and wear it, and you can see it in other people's eyes at tea and dinner parties. Fine, and now what? On the strength of all this he had got married again. Twice, in fact, and divorced twice. That made three times, didn't it? That was plenty. He had spent a good deal of time and energy doing all sorts of things he didn't care for in the least to prove to his first wife, who had been a twenty-three-year-old schoolteacher in Minneapolis, Minnesota, that he was not just merely a bum, fit for nothing but lying under a tree—if he had ever been able to locate that ideal tree he had in his mind's eye—writing poetry and enjoying his life.

Now he had done it. He smoothed out the letter he had been turning in his hands and stroked it as if it were a cat. He said, "I've been working up to the climax all this time. You know, good old surprise technique. Now then, get ready."

Miriam had written to him, after these five years, asking him to take her back. And would you believe it, he was going to break down and do that very thing. Her father was dead, she was terribly lonely, she had had time to think everything over, she believed herself to blame for a great many things, she loved him truly and she always had, truly; she regretted, oh, everything, and hoped it was not too late for them to make a happy life together once more. . . . She had read everything she could find of his in print, and she loved all of it. He had that very morning sent by cable the money for her to travel on, and he was going to take her back. She was going to live again in a Mexican house without any conveniences and she was not going to have a modern flat. She was going to take whatever he chose to hand her, and like it. And he wasn't going to marry her again, either. Not he. If she wanted to live with him on these terms, well and good. If not, she could just go back once more to that school of hers in Minneapolis. If she stayed, she would walk a chalk line, all right, one she hadn't drawn for herself. He picked up a cheese knife and drew a long sharp line in the checkered tablecloth. She would, believe him, walk *that*.

The hands of the clock pointed half past two. The journalist swallowed the last of his drink and went on drawing more cross-patches on the table-cloth with a relaxed hand. His guest wished to say, "Don't forget to invite me to your wedding," but thought better of it. The journalist raised his twitching lids and swung his half-focused eyes upon the shadow opposite and said, "I suppose you think I don't know—"

His guest moved to the chair edge and watched the orchestra folding up for the night. The café was almost empty. The journalist paused, not for an answer, but to give weight to the important statement he was about to make. "I don't know what's happening, this time," he said, "don't deceive yourself. This time, I know." He seemed to be admonishing himself before a mirror.

THE SECRET LIFE OF WALTER MITTY[1]

JAMES THURBER

"We're going through!" The Commander's voice was like thin ice breaking. He wore his full-dress uniform, with the heavily braided white cap pulled down rakishly over one cold gray eye. "We can't make it, sir. It's spoiling for a hurricane, if you ask me." "I'm not asking you, Lieutenant Berg," said the Commander. "Throw on the power lights! Rev her up to 8,500! We're going through!" The pounding of the cylinders increased; ta-pocketa-pocketa-pocketa-*pocketa-pocketa*. The Commander stared at the ice forming on the pilot window. He walked over and twisted a row of complicated dials. "Switch on No. 8 auxiliary!" he shouted. "Switch on No. 8 auxiliary!" repeated Lieutenant Berg. "Full strength in No. 3 turret!" shouted the Commander. "Full strength in No. 3 turret!" The crew, bending to their various tasks in the huge, hurtling eight-engined Navy hydroplane, looked at each other and grinned. "The Old Man'll get us through," they said to one another. "The Old Man ain't afraid of Hell!" . . .

"Not so fast! You're driving too fast!" said Mrs. Mitty. "What are you driving so fast for?"

"Hmm?" said Walter Mitty. He looked at his wife, in the seat beside him, with shocked astonishment. She seemed grossly unfamiliar, like a strange woman who had yelled at him in a crowd. "You were up to fifty-five," she said. "You know I don't like to go more than forty. You were up to fifty-five." Walter Mitty drove on toward Waterbury in silence, the roaring of the SN-202 through the worst storm in twenty years of Navy flying fading in the remote, intimate airways of his mind. "You're tensed up again," said Mrs. Mitty. "It's one of your days. I wish you'd let Dr. Renshaw look you over."

Walter Mitty stopped the car in front of the building where his wife went to have her hair done. "Remember to get those overshoes while I'm having my hair done," she said. "I don't need overshoes," said Mitty. She put her mirror back into her bag. "We've been all through that," she said, getting out of the car. "You're not a young man any longer." He raced the engine a little. "Why don't you wear your gloves? Have you lost your gloves?" Walter Mitty reached in a pocket and brought out the gloves. He put them on, but after she had turned and gone into the building and he had driven on to a red light, he took them off again. "Pick it up, brother!" snapped a cop as the light changed, and Mitty hastily pulled on his gloves and lurched ahead. He drove around the streets aimlessly for a time, and then he drove past the hospital on his way to the parking lot.

. . . "It's the millionaire banker, Wellington McMillan," said the pretty

1. Reprinted by permission of the author. Copyright, 1939, by James Thurber. Originally published in *The New Yorker*.

nurse. "Yes?" said Walter Mitty, removing his gloves slowly. "Who has the case?" "Dr. Renshaw and Dr. Benbow, but there are two specialists here, Dr. Remington from New York and Dr. Pritchard-Mitford from London. He flew over." A door opened down a long, cool corridor and Dr. Renshaw came out. He looked distraught and haggard. "Hello, Mitty," he said. "We're having the devil's own time with McMillan, the millionaire banker and close personal friend of Roosevelt. Obstreosis of the ductal tract. Tertiary. Wish you'd take a look at him." "Glad to," said Mitty.

In the operating room there were whispered introductions: "Dr. Remington, Dr. Mitty. Dr. Pritchard-Mitford, Dr. Mitty." "I've read your book on streptothricosis," said Pritchard-Mitford, shaking hands. "A brilliant performance, sir." "Thank you," said Walter Mitty. "Didn't know you were in the States, Mitty," grumbled Remington. "Coals to Newcastle, bringing Mitford and me up here for a tertiary." "You are very kind," said Mitty. A huge, complicated machine, connected to the operating table, with many tubes and wires, began at this moment to go pocketa-pocketa-pocketa. "The new anaesthetizer is giving away!" shouted an interne. "There is no one in the East who knows how to fix it!" "Quiet, man!" said Mitty, in a low, cool voice. He sprang to the machine, which was now going pocketa-pocketa-queep-pocketa-queep. He began fingering delicately a row of glistening dials. "Give me a fountain pen!" he snapped. Someone handed him a fountain pen. He pulled a faulty piston out of the machine and inserted the pen in its place. "That will hold for ten minutes," he said. "Get on with the operation." A nurse hurried over and whispered to Renshaw, and Mitty saw the man turn pale. "Coreopsis has set in," said Renshaw nervously. "If you would take over, Mitty?" Mitty looked at him and at the craven figure of Benbow, who drank, and at the grave, uncertain faces of the two great specialists. "If you wish," he said. They slipped a white gown on him; he adjusted a mask and drew on thin gloves; nurses handed him shining . . .

"Back it up, Mac! Look out for that Buick!" Walter Mitty jammed on the brakes. "Wrong lane, Mac," said the parking-lot attendant, looking at Mitty closely. "Gee. Yeh," muttered Mitty. He began cautiously to back out of the lane marked "Exit Only." "Leave her sit there," said the attendant. "I'll put her away." Mitty got out of the car. "Hey, better leave the key." "Oh," said Mitty, handing the man the ignition key. The attendant vaulted into the car, backed it up with insolent skill, and put it where it belonged.

They're so damn cocky, thought Walter Mitty, walking along Main Street; they think they know everything. Once he had tried to take his chains off, outside New Milford, and he had got them wound around the axles. A man had had to come out in a wrecking car and unwind them, a young, grinning garageman. Since then Mrs. Mitty always made him drive to a garage to have the chains taken off. The next time, he thought, I'll wear my right arm in a sling; they won't grin at me then. I'll have my right arm in a sling and they'll see I couldn't possibly take the chains off myself. He kicked at the slush on the sidewalk. "Overshoes," he said to himself, and he began looking for a shoe store.

When he came out into the street again, with the overshoes in a box under his arm, Walter Mitty began to wonder what the other thing was his wife had told him to get. She had told him twice before they set out from their house for Waterbury. In a way he hated these weekly trips to town—he was always getting something wrong. Kleenex, he thought, Squibb's, razor blades? No. Toothpaste, toothbrush, bicarbonate, carborundum, initiative and referendum? He gave up. But she would remember it. "Where's that what's-its-name?" she would ask. "Don't tell me you forgot the what's-its-name." A newsboy went by shouting something about the Waterbury trial.

. . . "Perhaps this will refresh your memory." The District Attorney suddenly thrust a heavy automatic at the quiet figure on the witness stand. "Have you ever seen this before?" Walter Mitty took the gun and examined it expertly. "This is my Webley-Vickers 50.80," he said calmly. An excited buzz ran around the courtroom. The Judge rapped for order. "You are a crack shot with any sort of firearms, I believe?" said the District Attorney, insinuatingly. "Objection!" shouted Mitty's attorney. "We have shown that the defendant could not have fired the shot. We have shown that he wore his right arm in a sling on the night of the fourteenth of July." Walter Mitty raised his hand briefly and the bickering attorneys were stilled. "With any known make of gun," he said evenly, "I could have killed Gregory Fitzhurst at three hundred feet *with my left hand*." Pandemonium broke loose in the courtroom. A woman's scream rose above the bedlam and suddenly a lovely, dark-haired girl was in Walter Mitty's arms. The District Attorney struck at her savagely. Without rising from his chair, Mitty let the man have it on the point of the chin. "You miserable cur!" . . .

"Puppy biscuit," said Walter Mitty. He stopped walking and the buildings of Waterbury rose up out of the misty courtroom and surrounded him again. A woman who was passing laughed. "He said 'Puppy biscuit,'" she said to her companion. "That man said 'Puppy biscuit' to himself." Walter Mitty hurried on. He went into an A. & P., not the first one he came to but a smaller one farther up the street. "I want some biscuit for small, young dogs," he said to the clerk. "Any special brand, sir?" The greatest pistol shot in the world thought a moment. "It says 'Puppies Bark for It' on the box," said Walter Mitty.

His wife would be through at the hairdresser's in fifteen minutes, Mitty saw in looking at his watch, unless they had trouble drying it; sometimes they had trouble drying it. She didn't like to get to the hotel first; she would want him to be there waiting for her as usual. He found a big leather chair in the lobby, facing a window, and he put the overshoes and the puppy biscuit on the floor beside it. He picked up an old copy of *Liberty* and sank down into the chair. "Can Germany Conquer the World Through the Air?" Walter Mitty looked at the pictures of bombing planes and of ruined streets.

. . . "The cannonading has got the wind up in young Raleigh, sir," said the sergeant. Captain Mitty looked up at him through tousled hair. "Get him to bed," he said wearily, "with the others. I'll fly alone." "But you can't, sir," said the sergeant anxiously. "It takes two men to handle that bomber and the Archies are pounding hell out of the air. Von Richtman's circus is between here and Saulier." "Somebody's got to get the ammunition dump," said Mitty. "I'm going over. Spot of brandy?" He poured a drink for the sergeant and one for himself. War thundered and whined around the dugout and battered at the door. There was a rending of wood, and splinters flew through the room. "A bit of a near thing," said Captain Mitty carelessly. "The box barrage is closing in," said the sergeant. "We only live once, Sergeant," said Mitty, with his faint, fleeting smile. "Or do we?" He poured another brandy and tossed it off. "I never see a man could hold his brandy like you, sir," said the sergeant. "Begging your pardon, sir." Captain Mitty stood up and strapped on his huge Webley-Vickers automatic. "It's forty kilometers through hell, sir," said the sergeant. Mitty finished one last brandy. "After all," he said softly, "what isn't?" The pounding of the cannon increased; there was the rat-tat-tatting of machine guns, and from somewhere came the menacing pocketa-pocketa-pocketa of the new flame-throwers. Walter Mitty walked to the door of the dugout humming "Auprès de Ma Blonde." He turned and waved to the sergeant. "Cheerio!" he said. . . .

Something struck his shoulder. "I've been looking all over this hotel for you," said Mrs. Mitty. "Why do you have to hide in this old chair? How did you expect me to find you?" "Things close in," said Walter Mitty vaguely. "What?" Mrs. Mitty said. "Did you get the what's-its-name? The puppy biscuit? What's in that box?" "Overshoes," said Mitty. "Couldn't you have put them on in the store?" "I was thinking," said Walter Mitty. "Does it ever occur to you that I am sometimes thinking?" She looked at him. "I'm going to take your temperature when I get you home," she said.

They went out through the revolving doors that made a faintly derisive whistling sound when you pushed them. It was two blocks to the parking lot. At the drugstore on the corner she said, "Wait here for me. I forgot something. I won't be a minute." She was more than a minute. Walter Mitty lighted a cigarette. It began to rain, rain with sleet in it. He stood up against the wall of the drugstore, smoking. . . . He put his shoulders back and his heels together. "To hell with the handkerchief," said Walter Mitty scornfully. He took one last drag on his cigarette and snapped it away. Then, with that faint, fleeting smile playing about his lips, he faced the firing squad; erect and motionless, proud and disdainful. Walter Mitty the Undefeated, inscrutable to the last.

BABYLON REVISITED[1]

F. SCOTT FITZGERALD

"And where's Mr. Campbell?" Charlie asked.

"Gone to Switzerland. Mr. Campbell's a pretty sick man, Mr. Wales."

"I'm sorry to hear that. And George Hardt?" Charlie inquired.

"Back in America, gone to work."

"And where is the Snow Bird?"

"He was in here last week. Anyway, his friend, Mr. Schaeffer, is in Paris."

Two familiar names from the long list of a year and a half ago. Charlie scribbled an address in his note book and tore out the page.

"If you see Mr. Schaeffer, give him this," he said. "It's my brother-in-law's address. I haven't settled on a hotel yet."

He was not really disappointed to find Paris was so empty. But the stillness in the Ritz bar was strange and portentous. It was not an American bar any more—he felt polite in it, and not as if he owned it. It had gone back into France. He felt the stillness from the moment he got out of the taxi and saw the doorman, usually in a frenzy of activity at this hour, gossiping with a *chasseur* by the servants' entrance.

Passing through the corridor, he heard only a single, bored voice in the once-clamorous women's room. When he turned into the bar he travelled the twenty feet of green carpet with his eyes fixed straight ahead by old habit; and then, with his foot firmly on the rail, he turned and surveyed the room, encountering only a single pair of eyes that fluttered up from a newspaper in the corner. Charlie asked for the head barman, Paul, who in the latter days of the bull market had come to work in his own custom-built car—disembarking, however, with due nicety at the nearest corner. But Paul was at his country house today and Alix giving him information.

"No, no more," Charlie said, "I'm going slow these days."

Alix congratulated him: "You were going pretty strong a couple of years ago."

"I'll stick to it all right," Charlie assured him. "I've stuck to it for over a year and a half now."

"How do you find conditions in America?"

"I haven't been to America for months. I'm in business in Prague, representing a couple of concerns there. They don't know about me down there."

Alix smiled.

"Remember the night of George Hardt's bachelor dinner here?" said Charlie. "By the way, what's become of Claude Fessenden?"

Alix lowered his voice confidentially: "He's in Paris, but he doesn't come

1. Reprinted from *Taps at Reveille* by F. Scott Fitzgerald; copyright, 1935, by Charles Scribner's Sons; used by permission of the publishers.

here any more. Paul doesn't allow it. He ran up a bill of thirty thousand francs, charging all his drinks and his lunches, and usually his dinner, for more than a year. And when Paul finally told him he had to pay, he gave him a bad check."

Alix shook his head sadly.

"I don't understand it, such a dandy fellow. Now he's all bloated up—" He made a plump apple of his hands.

Charlie watched a group of strident queens installing themselves in a corner.

"Nothing affects them," he thought. "Stocks rise and fall, people loaf or work, but they go on forever." The place oppressed him. He called for the dice and shook with Alix for the drink.

"Here for long, Mr. Wales?"

"I'm here for four or five days to see my little girl."

"Oh-h! You have a little girl?"

Outside, the fire-red, gas-blue, ghost-green signs shone smokily through the tranquil rain. It was late afternoon and the streets were in movement; the *bistros* gleamed. At the corner of the Boulevard des Capucines he took a taxi. The Place de la Concorde moved by in pink majesty; they crossed the logical Seine, and Charlie felt the sudden provincial quality of the Left Bank.

Charlie directed his taxi to the Avenue de l'Opera, which was out of his way. But he wanted to see the blue hour spread over the magnificent façade, and imagine that the cab horns, playing endlessly the first few bars of *Le Plus que Lent,* were the trumpets of the Second Empire. They were closing the iron grill in front of Brentano's Book-store, and people were already at dinner behind the trim little bourgeois hedge of Duval's. He had never eaten at a really cheap restaurant in Paris. Five-course dinner, four francs fifty, eighteen cents, wine included. For some odd reason he wished that he had.

As they rolled on to the Left Bank and he felt its sudden provincialism, he thought, "I spoiled this city for myself. I didn't realize it, but the days came along one after another, and then two years were gone, and everything was gone, and I was gone."

He was thirty-five, and good to look at. The Irish mobility of his face was sobered by a deep wrinkle between his eyes. As he rang his brother-in-law's bell in the Rue Palatine, the wrinkle deepened till it pulled down his brows; he felt a cramping sensation in his belly. From behind the maid who opened the door darted a lovely little girl of nine who shrieked "Daddy!" and flew up, struggling like a fish, into his arms. She pulled his head around by one ear and set her cheek against his.

"My old pie," he said.

"Oh, daddy, daddy, daddy, daddy, dads, dads, dads!"

She drew him into the salon, where the family waited, a boy and girl his daughter's age, his sister-in-law and her husband. He greeted Marion with his voice pitched carefully to avoid either feigned enthusiasm or dislike, but her response was more frankly tepid, though she minimized her expression of unalterable distrust by directing her regard toward his child. The two men clasped hands in a friendly way and Lincoln Peters rested his for a moment on Charlie's shoulder.

The room was warm and comfortably American. The three children moved intimately about, playing through the yellow oblongs that led to other rooms; the cheer of six o'clock spoke in the eager smacks of the fire and the sounds of French activity in the kitchen. But Charlie did not relax; his heart sat up rigidly in his body and he drew confidence from his daughter, who from time to time came close to him, holding in her arms the doll he had brought.

"Really extremely well," he declared in answer to Lincoln's question. "There's a lot of business there that isn't moving at all, but we're doing even better than ever. In fact, damn well. I'm bringing my sister over from America next month to keep house for me. My income last year was bigger than it was when I had money. You see, the Czechs——"

His boasting was for a specific purpose; but after a moment, seeing a faint restiveness in Lincoln's eye, he changed the subject:

"Those are fine children of yours, well brought up, good manners."

"We think Honoria's a great little girl too."

Marion Peters came back from the kitchen. She was a tall woman with worried eyes, who had once possessed a fresh American loveliness. Charlie had never been sensitive to it and was always surprised when people spoke of how pretty she had been. From the first there had been an instinctive antipathy between them.

"Well, how do you find Honoria?" she asked.

"Wonderful. I was astonished how much she's grown in ten months. All the children are looking well."

"We haven't had a doctor for a year. How do you like being back in Paris?"

"It seems very funny to see so few Americans around."

"I'm delighted," Marion said vehemently. "Now at least you can go into a store without their assuming you're a millionaire. We've suffered like everybody, but on the whole it's a good deal pleasanter."

"But it was nice while it lasted," Charlie said. "We were a sort of royalty, almost infallible, with a sort of magic around us. In the bar this afternoon"—he stumbled, seeing his mistake—"there wasn't a man I knew."

She looked at him keenly. "I should think you'd have had enough of bars."

"I only stayed a minute. I take one drink every afternoon, and no more.

"Don't you want a cocktail before dinner?" Lincoln asked.

"I take only one drink every afternoon, and I've had that."

"I hope you keep to it," said Marion.

Her dislike was evident in the coldness with which she spoke, but Charlie

only smiled; he had larger plans. Her very aggressiveness gave him an advantage, and he knew enough to wait. He wanted them to initiate the discussion of what they knew had brought him to Paris.

At dinner he couldn't decide whether Honoria was most like him or her mother. Fortunate if she didn't combine the traits of both that had brought them to disaster. A great wave of protectiveness went over him. He thought he knew what to do for her. He believed in character; he wanted to jump back a whole generation and trust in character again as the eternally valuable element. Everything wore out.

He left soon after dinner, but not to go home. He was curious to see Paris by night with clearer and more judicious eyes than those of other days. He bought a *strapontin* for the Casino and watched Josephine Baker go through her chocolate arabesques.

After an hour he left and strolled toward Montmartre, up the Rue Pigalle into the Place Blanche. The rain had stopped and there were a few people in evening clothes disembarking from taxis in front of cabarets, and *cocottes* prowling singly or in pairs, and many Negroes. He passed a lighted door from which issued music, and stopped with the sense of familiarity; it was Bricktop's, where he had parted with so many hours and so much money. A few doors farther on he found another ancient rendezvous and incautiously put his head inside. Immediately an eager orchestra burst into sound, a pair of professional dancers leaped to their feet and a maître d'hôtel swooped toward him, crying, "Crowd just arriving, sir!" But he withdrew quickly.

"You have to be damn drunk," he thought.

Zelli's was closed, the bleak and sinister cheap hotels surrounding it were dark; up in the Rue Blanche there was more light and a local, colloquial French crowd. The Poet's Cave had disappeared, but the two great mouths of the Café of Heaven and the Café of Hell still yawned—even devoured, as he watched, the meagre contents of a tourist bus—a German, a Japanese, and an American couple who glanced at him with frightened eyes.

So much for the effort and ingenuity of Montmartre. All the catering to vice and waste was on an utterly childish scale, and he suddenly realized the meaning of the word "dissipate"—to dissipate into thin air; to make nothing out of something. In the little hours of the night every move from place to place was an enormous human jump, an increase of paying for the privilege of slower and slower motion.

He remembered thousand-franc notes given to an orchestra for playing a single number, hundred-franc notes tossed to a doorman for calling a cab.

But it hadn't been given for nothing.

It had been given, even the most wildly squandered sum, as an offering to destiny that he might not remember the things most worth remembering, the things that now he would always remember—his child taken from his control, his wife escaped to a grave in Vermont.

In the glare of a *brasserie* a woman spoke to him. He bought her some eggs and coffee, and then, eluding her encouraging stare, gave her a twenty-franc note and took a taxi to his hotel.

II

He woke upon a fine fall day—football weather. The depression of yesterday was gone and he liked the people on the streets. At noon he sat opposite Honoria at Le Grand Vatel, the only restaurant he could think of not reminiscent of champagne dinners and long luncheons that began at two and ended in a blurred and vague twilight.

"Now, how about vegetables? Oughtn't you to have some vegetables?"

"Well, yes."

"Here's *épinards* and *chou-fleur* and carrots and *haricots*."

"I'd like *chou-fleur*."

"Wouldn't you like to have two vegetables?"

"I usually only have one at lunch."

The waiter was pretending to be inordinately fond of children. *"Qu'elle est mignonne la petite? Elle parle exactement comme une française."*

"How about dessert? Shall we wait and see?"

The waiter disappeared. Honoria looked at her father expectantly.

"What are we going to do?"

"First, we're going to that toy store in the Rue Saint-Honoré and buy you anything you like. And then we're going to the vaudeville at the Empire."

She hesitated. "I like it about the vaudeville, but not the toy store."

"Why not?"

"Well, you brought me this doll." She had it with her. "And I've got lots of things. And we're not rich any more, are we?"

"We never were. But today you are to have anything you want."

"All right," she agreed resignedly.

When there had been her mother and a French nurse he had been inclined to be strict; now he extended himself, reached out for a new tolerance; he must be both parents to her and not shut any of her out of communication.

"I want to get to know you," he said gravely. "First let me introduce myself. My name is Charles J. Wales, of Prague."

"Oh, daddy!" her voice cracked with laughter.

"And who are you, please?" he persisted, and she accepted a rôle immediately: "Honoria Wales, Rue Palatine, Paris."

"Married or single?"

"No, not married. Single."

He indicated the doll. "But I see you have a child, madame."

Unwilling to disinherit it, she took it to her heart and thought quickly: "Yes, I've been married, but I'm not married now. My husband is dead."

He went on quickly, "And the child's name?"

"Simone. That's after my best friend at school."

"I'm very pleased that you're doing so well at school."

"I'm third this month," she boasted. "Elsie"—that was her cousin—"is only about eighteenth, and Richard is about at the bottom."

"You like Richard and Elsie, don't you?"

"Oh, yes. I like Richard quite well and I like her all right."

Cautiously and casually he asked: "And Aunt Marion and Uncle Lincoln—which do you like best?"

"Oh, Uncle Lincoln, I guess."

He was increasingly aware of her presence. As they came in, a murmur of ". . . adorable" followed them, and now the people at the next table bent all their silences upon her, staring as if she were something no more conscious than a flower.

"Why don't I live with you?" she asked suddenly. "Because mamma's dead?"

"You must stay here and learn more French. It would have been hard for daddy to take care of you so well."

"I don't really need much taking care of any more. I do everything for myself."

Going out of the restaurant, a man and a woman unexpectedly hailed him!

"Well, the old Wales!"

"Hello there, Lorraine. . . . Dunc."

Sudden ghosts out of the past: Duncan Schaeffer, a friend from college. Lorraine Quarrles, a lovely, pale blonde of thirty; one of a crowd who had helped them make months into days in the lavish times of three years ago.

"My husband couldn't come this year," she said, in answer to his question. "We're poor as hell. So he gave me two hundred a month and told me I could do my worst on that. . . . This your little girl?"

"What about coming back and sitting down?" Duncan asked.

"Can't do it." He was glad for an excuse. As always, he felt Lorraine's passionate, provocative attraction, but his own rhythm was different now.

"Well, how about dinner?" she asked.

"I'm not free. Give me your address and let me call you."

"Charlie, I believe you're sober," she said judicially. "I honestly believe he's sober, Dunc. Pinch him and see if he's sober."

Charlie indicated Honoria with his head. They both laughed.

"What's your address?" said Duncan sceptically.

He hesitated, unwilling to give the name of his hotel.

"I'm not settled yet. I'd better call you. We're going to see the vaudeville at the Empire."

"There! That's what I want to do," Lorraine said. "I want to see some clowns and acrobats and jugglers. That's just what we'll do, Dunc."

"We've got to do an errand first," said Charlie. "Perhaps we'll see you there."

"All right, you snob. . . . Good-by, beautiful little girl."

"Good-by."

Honoria bobbed politely.

Somehow, an unwelcome encounter. They liked him because he was functioning, because he was serious; they wanted to see him, because he was stronger than they were now, because they wanted to draw a certain sustenance from his strength.

At the Empire, Honoria proudly refused to sit upon her father's folded coat. She was already an individual with a code of her own, and Charlie was more and more absorbed by the desire of putting a little of himself into her before she crystallized utterly. It was hopeless to try to know her in so short a time.

Between the acts they came upon Duncan and Lorraine in the lobby where the band was playing.

"Have a drink?"

"All right, but not up at the bar. We'll take a table."

"The perfect father."

Listening abstractedly to Lorraine, Charlie watched Honoria's eyes leave their table, and he followed them wistfully about the room, wondering what they saw. He met her glance and she smiled.

"I liked that lemonade," she said.

What had she said? What had he expected? Going home in a taxi afterward, he pulled her over until her head rested against his chest.

"Darling, do you ever think about your mother?"

"Yes, sometimes," she answered vaguely.

"I don't want you to forget her. Have you got a picture of her?"

"Yes, I think so. Anyhow, Aunt Marion has. Why don't you want me to forget her?"

"She loved you very much."

"I loved her too."

They were silent for a moment.

"Daddy, I want to come and live with you," she said suddenly.

His heart leaped; he had wanted it to come like this.

"Aren't you perfectly happy?"

"Yes, but I love you better than anybody. And you love me better than anybody, don't you, now that mummy's dead?"

"Of course I do. But you won't always like me best, honey. You'll grow up and meet somebody your own age and go marry him and forget you ever had a daddy."

"Yes, that's true," she agreed tranquilly.

He didn't go in. He was coming back at nine o'clock and he wanted to keep himself fresh and new for the thing he must say then.

"When you're safe inside, just show yourself in that window."

"All right. Good-bye, dads, dads, dads, dads."

He waited in the dark street until she appeared, all warm and glowing, in the window above and kissed her fingers out into the night.

III

They were waiting. Marion sat behind the coffee service in a dignified black dinner dress that just faintly suggested mourning. Lincoln was walking up and down with the animation of one who had already been talking. They were as anxious as he was to get into the question. He opened it almost immediately:

"I suppose you know what I want to see you about—why I really came to Paris."

Marion played with the black stars on her necklace and frowned.

"I'm awfully anxious to have a home," he continued. "And I'm awfully anxious to have Honoria in it. I appreciate your taking in Honoria for her mother's sake, but things have changed now"—he hesitated and then continued more forcibly—"changed radically with me, and I want to ask you to reconsider the matter. It would be silly for me to deny that about three years ago I was acting badly——"

Marion looked up at him with hard eyes.

"—but all that's over. As I told you, I haven't had more than a drink a day for over a year, and I take that drink deliberately, so that the idea of alcohol won't get too big in my imagination. You see the idea?"

"No," said Marion succinctly.

"It's a sort of stunt I set myself. It keeps the matter in proportion."

"I get you," said Lincoln. "You don't want to admit it's got any attraction for you."

"Something like that. Sometimes I forget and don't take it. But I try to take it. Anyhow, I couldn't afford to drink in my position. The people I represent are more than satisfied with what I've done, and I'm bringing my sister over from Burlington to keep house for me, and I want awfully to have Honoria too. You know that even when her mother and I weren't getting along well we never let anything that happened touch Honoria. I know she's fond of me and I know I'm able to take care of her and—well, there you are. How do you feel about it?"

He knew that now he would have to take a beating. It would last an hour or two hours, and it would be difficult, but if he modulated his inevitable resentment to the chastened attitude of the reformed sinner, he might win his point in the end.

Keep your temper, he told himself. You don't want to be justified. You want Honoria.

Lincoln spoke first: "We've been talking it over ever since we got your letter last month. We're happy to have Honoria here. She's a dear little thing, and we're glad to be able to help her, but of course that isn't the question——"

Marion interrupted suddenly. "How long are you going to stay sober, Charlie?" she asked.

"Permanently, I hope."

"How can anybody count on that?"

"You know I never did drink heavily until I gave up business and came over here with nothing to do. Then Helen and I began to run around with——"

"Please leave Helen out of it. I can't bear to hear you talk about her like that."

He stared at her grimly; he had never been certain how fond of each other the sisters were in life.

"My drinking only lasted about a year and a half—from the time we came over until I—collapsed."

"It was time enough."

"It was time enough," he agreed.

"My duty is entirely to Helen," she said. "I try to think what she would have wanted me to do. Frankly, from the night you did that terrible thing you haven't really existed for me. I can't help that. She was my sister."

"Yes."

"When she was dying, she asked me to look out for Honoria. If you hadn't been in a sanitarium then, it might have helped matters."

He had no answer.

"I'll never in my life be able to forget the morning when Helen knocked at my door, soaked to the skin and shivering, and said you'd locked her out."

Charlie gripped the sides of the chair. This was more difficult than he expected; he wanted to launch out into a long expostulation and explanation, but he only said: "The night I locked her out—" and she interrupted, "I don't feel up to going over that again."

After a moment's silence Lincoln said: "We're getting off the subject. You want Marion to set aside her legal guardianship and give you Honoria. I think the main point for her is whether she has confidence in you or not."

"I don't blame Marion," Charlie said slowly, "but I think she can have entire confidence in me. I had a good record up to three years ago. Of course, it's within human possibilities I might go wrong any time. But if we wait much longer I'll lose Honoria's childhood and my chance for a home." He shook his head, "I'll simply lose her, don't you see?"

"Yes, I see," said Lincoln.

"Why didn't you think of all this before?" Marion asked.

"I suppose I did, from time to time, but Helen and I were getting along badly. When I consented to the guardianship, I was flat on my back in a sanitarium and the market had cleaned me out. I knew I'd acted badly, and I thought if it would bring any peace to Helen, I'd agree to anything. But now it's different. I'm functioning, I'm behaving damn well, so far as——"

"Please don't swear at me," Marion said.

He looked at her, startled. With each remark the force of her dislike became more and more apparent. She had built up all her fear of life into one wall and faced it toward him. This trivial reproof was possibly the result of some trouble with the cook several hours before. Charlie became increasingly alarmed at leaving Honoria in this atmosphere of hostility against himself; sooner or later it would come out, in a word here, a shake of the head there, and some of that distrust would be irrevocably implanted in Honoria. But he pulled his temper down out of his face and shut it up inside him; he had a point, for Lincoln realized the absurdity of Marion's remark and asked her lightly since when she had objected to the word "damn."

"Another thing," Charlie said: "I'm able to give her certain advantages now. I'm going to take a French governess to Prague with me. I've got a lease on a new apartment——"

He stopped, realizing that he was blundering. They couldn't be expected to accept with equanimity the fact that his income was again twice as large as their own.

"I suppose you can give her more luxuries than we can," said Marion. "When you were throwing away money we were living along watching every ten francs. . . . I suppose you'll start doing it again."

"Oh, no," he said. "I've learned. I worked hard for ten years, you know—until I got lucky in the market, like so many people. Terribly lucky. It didn't seem any use working any more, so I quit. It won't happen again."

There was a long silence. All of them felt their nerves straining, and for the first time in a year Charlie wanted a drink. He was sure now that Lincoln Peters wanted him to have his child.

Marion shuddered suddenly; part of her saw that Charlie's feet were planted on the earth now, and her own maternal feeling recognized the naturalness of his desire; but she had lived for a long time with a prejudice—a prejudice founded on a curious disbelief in her sister's happiness, and which, in the shock of one terrible night, had turned to hatred for him. It had all happened at a point in her life where the discouragement of ill health and adverse circumstances made it necessary for her to believe in tangible villainy and a tangible villain.

"I can't help what I think!" she cried out suddenly. "How much you were responsible for Helen's death, I don't know. It's something you'll have to square with your own conscience."

An electric current of agony surged through him; for a moment he was almost on his feet, an unuttered sound echoing in his throat. He hung on to himself for a moment, another moment.

"Hold on there," said Lincoln uncomfortably. "I never thought you were responsible for that."

"Helen died of heart trouble," Charlie said dully.

"Yes, heart trouble." Marion spoke as if the phrase had another meaning for her.

Then, in the flatness that followed her outburst, she saw him plainly and she knew he had somehow arrived at control over the situation. Glancing at her husband, she found no help from him, and as abruptly as if it were a matter of no importance, she threw up the sponge.

"Do what you like!" she cried, springing up from her chair. "She's your child. I'm not the person to stand in your way. I think if it were my child I'd rather see her—" She managed to check herself. "You two decide it. I can't stand this. I'm sick. I'm going to bed."

She hurried from the room; after a moment Lincoln said:

"This has been a hard day for her. You know how strongly she feels—" His voice was almost apologetic: "When a woman gets an idea in her head."

"Of course."

"It's going to be all right. I think she sees now that you—can provide for the child, and so we can't very well stand in your way or Honoria's way."

"Thank you, Lincoln."

"I'd better go along and see how she is."

"I'm going."

He was still trembling when he reached the street, but a walk down the Rue Bonaparte to the quais set him up, and as he crossed the Seine, fresh and new by the quai lamps, he felt exultant. But back in his room he couldn't sleep. The image of Helen haunted him. Helen whom he had loved so until they had senselessly began to abuse each other's love, tear it into shreds. On that terrible February night that Marion remembered so vividly, a slow quarrel had gone on for hours. There was a scene at the Florida, and then he attempted to take her home, and then she kissed young Webb at a table; after that there was what she had hysterically said. When he arrived home alone he turned the key in the lock in wild anger. How could he know she would arrive an hour later alone, that there would be a snowstorm in which she wandered about in slippers, too confused to find a taxi? Then the aftermath, her escaping pneumonia by a miracle, and all the attendant horror. They were "reconciled," but that was the beginning of the end, and Marion, who had seen with her own eyes and who imagined it to be one of many scenes from her sister's martyrdom, never forgot.

Going over it again brought Helen nearer, and in the white, soft light that steals upon half sleep near morning he found himself talking to her again. She said that he was perfectly right about Honoria and that she wanted Honoria to be with him. She said she was glad he was being good and doing better. She said a lot of other things—very friendly things—but she was in a swing in a white dress, and swinging faster and faster all the time, so that at the end he could not hear clearly all that she said.

IV

He woke up feeling happy. The door of the world was open again. He made plans, vistas, futures for Honoria and himself, but suddenly he grew sad, remembering all the plans he and Helen had made. She had not planned to die. The present was the thing—work to do and someone to love. But not to love too much, for he knew the injury that a father can do to a daughter or a mother to a son by attaching them too closely: afterward, out in the world, the child would seek in the marriage partner the same blind tenderness and, failing probably to find it, turn against love and life.

It was another bright, crisp day. He called Lincoln Peters at the bank where he worked and asked if he could count on taking Honoria when he left for Prague. Lincoln agreed that there was no reason for delay. One thing—the legal guardianship. Marion wanted to retain that a while longer. She was upset by the whole matter, and it would oil things if she felt that the situation was still in her control for another year. Charlie agreed, wanting only the tangible, visible child.

Then the question of a governess. Charlie sat in a gloomy agency and talked to a cross Bernaise and to a buxom Breton peasant, neither of whom he could have endured. There were others whom he would see tomorrow.

He lunched with Lincoln Peters at Griffons, trying to keep down his exultation.

"There's nothing quite like your own child," Lincoln said. "But you understand how Marion feels too."

"She's forgotten how hard I worked for seven years there," Charlie said. "She just remembers one night."

"There's another thing," Lincoln hesitated. "While you and Helen were tearing around Europe throwing money away, we were just getting along. I didn't touch any of the prosperity because I never got ahead enough to carry anything but my insurance. I think Marion felt there was some kind of injustice in it—you not even working toward the end, and getting richer and richer."

"It went just as quick as it came," said Charlie.

"Yes, a lot of it stayed in the hands of *chasseurs* and saxophone players and maîtres d'hôtel—well, the big party's over now. I just said that to explain Marion's feeling about those crazy years. If you drop in about six o'clock tonight before Marion's too tired, we'll settle the details on the spot."

Back at his hotel, Charlie found a *pneumatique* that had been redirected from the Ritz bar where Charlie had left his address for the purpose of finding a certain man.

> DEAR CHARLIE: You were so strange when we saw you the other day that I wondered if I did something to offend you. If so, I'm not conscious of it. In fact, I have thought about you too much for the last year, and it's always been in the back of my mind that I might see you if I came over here. We *did* have such good times that crazy spring, like the night you and I stole the butcher's tricycle, and the time we tried to call on the president and you had the old derby rim and the wire cane. Everybody seems so old lately, but I don't feel old a bit. Couldn't we get together some time today for old time's sake?

I've got a vile hang-over for the moment, but will be feeling better this afternoon and will look for you about five in the sweat-shop at the Ritz.

Always devotedly,

LORRAINE.

His first feeling was one of awe that he had actually, in his mature years, stolen a tricycle and pedalled Lorraine all over the Etoile between the small hours and dawn. In retrospect it was a nightmare. Locking out Helen didn't fit in with any other act of his life, but the tricycle incident did—it was one of many. How many weeks or months of dissipation to arrive at that condition of utter irresponsibility?

He tried to picture how Lorraine had appeared to him then—very attractive; Helen was unhappy about it, though she said nothing. Yesterday, in the restaurant, Lorraine had seemed trite, blurred, worn away. He emphatically did not want to see her, and he was glad Alix had not given away his hotel address. It was a relief to think, instead, of Honoria, to think of Sundays spent with her and of saying good morning to her and of knowing she was there in his house at night, drawing her breath in the darkness.

At five he took a taxi and bought presents for all the Peters—a piquant cloth doll, a box of Roman soldiers, flowers for Marion, big linen handkerchiefs for Lincoln.

He saw, when he arrived in the apartment, that Marion had accepted the inevitable. She greeted him now as though he were a recalcitrant member of the family rather than a menacing outsider. Honoria had been told she was going; Charlie was glad to see that her tact made her conceal her excessive happiness. Only on his lap did she whisper her delight and the question "When?" before she slipped away with the other children.

He and Marion were alone for a minute in the room, and on an impulse he spoke out boldly:

"Family quarrels are bitter things. They don't go according to any rules. They're not like aches or wounds; they're more like splits in the skin that won't heal because there's not enough material. I wish you and I could be on better terms."

"Some things are hard to forget," she answered. "It's a question of confidence." There was no answer to this and presently she asked, "When do you propose to take her?"

"As soon as I can get a governess. I hoped the day after tomorrow."

"That's impossible. I've got to get her things in shape. Not before Saturday."

He yielded. Coming back into the room, Lincoln offered him a drink.

"I'll take my daily whisky," he said.

It was warm here, it was a home, people together by a fire. The children felt very safe and important; the mother and father were serious, watchful. They had things to do for the children more important than his visit here. A spoonful of medicine was, after all, more important than the strained relations between Marion and himself. They were not dull people, but they were very much in the grip of life and circumstances. He wondered if he couldn't do something to get Lincoln out of his rut at the bank.

A long peal at the door-bell; the *bonne de toute faire* passed through and went down the corridor. The door opened upon another long ring, and then voices, and the three in the salon looked up expectantly; Richard moved to bring the corridor within his range of vision, and Marion rose. Then the maid came back along the corridor, closely followed by the voices, which developed under the light into Duncan Schaeffer and Lorraine Quarrles.

They were gay, they were hilarious, they were roaring with laughter. For a moment Charlie was astounded; unable to understand how they ferreted out the Peters' address.

"Ah-h-h!" Duncan wagged his finger roguishly at Charlie. "Ah-h-h!"

They both slid down another cascade of laughter. Anxious and at a loss, Charlie shook hands with them quickly and presented them to Lincoln and Marion. Marion nodded, scarcely speaking. She had drawn back a step toward the fire; her little girl stood beside her, and Marion put an arm about her shoulder.

With growing annoyance at the intrusion, Charlie waited for them to explain themselves. After some concentration Duncan said:

"We came to invite you out to dinner. Lorraine and I insist that all this shishi, cagy business 'bout your address got to stop."

Charlie came closer to them, as if to force them backward down the corridor.

"Sorry, but I can't. Tell me where you'll be and I'll phone you in half an hour."

This made no impression. Lorraine sat down suddenly on the side of a chair, and focusing her eyes on Richard, cried, "Oh, what a nice little boy! Come here, little boy." Richard glanced at his mother, but did not move. With a perceptible shrug of her shoulders, Lorraine turned back to Charlie:

"Come and dine. Sure your cousins won' mine. See you so sel'om. Or solemn."

"I can't," said Charlie sharply. "You two have dinner and I'll phone you."

Her voice became suddenly unpleasant. "All right, we'll go. But I remember once when you hammered on my door at four A.M. I was enough of a good sport to give you a drink. Come on, Dunc."

Still in slow motion, with blurred, angry faces, with uncertain feet, they retired along the corridor.

"Good night," Charlie said.

"Good night!" responded Lorraine emphatically.

When he went back into the salon Marion had not moved, only now her son was standing in the circle of her other arm. Lincoln was still swinging Honoria back and forth like a pendulum from side to side.

"What an outrage!" Charlie broke out. "What an absolute outrage!"

Neither of them answered. Charlie dropped into an arm chair, picked up his drink, set it down again and said:

"People I haven't seen for two years having the colossal nerve——"

He broke off. Marion had made the sound "Oh!" in one swift, furious breath, turned her body from him with a jerk and left the room.

Lincoln set down Honoria carefully.

"You children go in and start your soup," he said, and when they obeyed, he said to Charlie:

"Marion's not well and she can't stand shocks. That kind of people make her really physically sick."

"I didn't tell them to come here. They wormed your name out of somebody. They deliberately——"

"Well, it's too bad. It doesn't help matters. Excuse me a minute."

Left alone, Charlie sat tense in his chair. In the next room he could hear the children eating, talking in monosyllables, already oblivious to the scene between their elders. He heard a murmur of conversation from a farther room and then the ticking bell of a telephone receiver picked up, and in a panic he moved to the other side of the room and out of earshot.

In a minute Lincoln came back. "Look here, Charlie. I think we'd better call off dinner for tonight. Marion's in bad shape."

"Is she angry with me?"

"Sort of," he said, almost roughly. "She's not strong and——"

"You mean she's changed her mind about Honoria?"

"She's pretty bitter right now. I don't know. You phone me at the bank tomorrow."

"I wish you'd explain to her I never dreamed these people would come here. I'm just as sore as you are."

"I couldn't explain anything to her now."

Charlie got up. He took his coat and hat and started down the corridor. Then he opened the door of the dining room and said in a strange voice, "Good night, children."

Honoria rose and ran around the table to hug him.

"Good night, sweetheart," he said vaguely, and then trying to make his voice more tender, trying to conciliate something, "Good night, dear children."

V

Charlie went directly to the Ritz bar with the furious idea of finding Lorraine and Duncan, but they were not there, and he realized that in any case there was nothing he could do. He had not touched his drink at the Peters', and now he ordered a whisky-and-soda. Paul came over to say hello.

"It's a great change," he said sadly. "We do about half the business we did.

So many fellows I hear about back in the States lost everything, maybe not in the first crash, but then in the second. Your friend George Hardt lost every cent, I hear. Are you back in the States?"

"No, I'm in business in Prague."

"I heard that you lost a lot in the crash."

"I did," and he added grimly, "but I lost everything I wanted in the boom."

"Selling short."

"Something like that."

Again the memory of those days swept over him like a nightmare—the people they had met travelling; then people who couldn't add a row of figures or speak a coherent sentence. The little man Helen had consented to dance with at the ship's party, who had insulted her ten feet from the table; the women and girls carried screaming with drink or drugs out of public places——

—The men who locked their wives out in the snow, because the snow of twenty-nine wasn't real snow. If you didn't want it to be snow, you just paid some money.

He went to the phone and called the Peter's apartment; Lincoln answered.

"I called up because this thing is on my mind. Has Marion said anything definite?"

"Marion's sick," Lincoln answered shortly. "I know this thing isn't altogether your fault, but I can't have her go to pieces about it. I'm afraid we'll have to let it slide for six months; I can't take the chance of working her up to this state again."

"I see."

"I'm sorry, Charlie."

He went back to his table. His whisky glass was empty, but he shook his head when Alix looked at it questioningly. There wasn't much he could do now except send Honoria some things; he would send her a lot of things tomorrow. He thought rather angrily that this was just money—he had given so many people money. . . .

"No, no more," he said to another waiter. "What do I owe you?"

He would come back some day; they couldn't make him pay forever. But he wanted his child, and nothing was much good now, beside that fact. He wasn't young any more, with a lot of nice thoughts and dreams to have by himself. He was absolutely sure Helen wouldn't have wanted him to be so alone.

A ROSE FOR EMILY[1]

WILLIAM FAULKNER

When Miss Emily Grierson died, our whole town went to her funeral: the men through a sort of respectful affection for a fallen monument, the women mostly out of curiosity to see the inside of her house, which no one save an old manservant—a combined gardener and cook—had seen in at least ten years.

It was a big, squarish frame house that had once been white, decorated with cupolas and spires and scrolled balconies in the heavily lightsome style of the seventies, set on what had once been our most select street. But garages and cotton gins had encroached and obliterated even the august names of that neighborhood; only Miss Emily's house was left, lifting its stubborn and coquettish decay above the cotton wagons and the gasoline pumps—an eyesore among eyesores. And now Miss Emily had gone to join the representatives of those august names where they lay in the cedar-bemused cemetery among the ranked and anonymous graves of Union and Confederate soldiers who fell at the battle of Jefferson.

Alive, Miss Emily had been a tradition, a duty, and a care; a sort of hereditary obligation upon the town, dating from that day in 1894 when Colonel Sartoris, the mayor—he who fathered the edict that no Negro woman should appear on the streets without an apron—remitted her taxes, the dispensation dating from the death of her father on into perpetuity. Not that Miss Emily would have accepted charity. Colonel Sartoris invented an involved tale to the effect that Miss Emily's father had loaned money to the town, which the town, as a matter of business, preferred this way of repaying. Only a man of Colonel Sartoris' generation and thought could have invented it, and only a woman could have believed it.

When the next generation, with its more modern ideas, became mayors and aldermen, this arrangement created some little dissatisfaction. On the first of the year they mailed her a tax notice. February came, and there was no reply. They wrote her a formal letter, asking her to call at the sheriff's office at her convenience. A week later the mayor wrote her himself, offering to call or to send his car for her, and received in reply a note on paper of an archaic shape, in a thin, flowing calligraphy in faded ink, to the effect that she no longer went out at all. The tax notice was also enclosed, without comment.

They called a special meeting of the Board of Aldermen. A deputation waited upon her, knocked at the door through which no visitor had passed since she ceased giving china-painting lessons eight or ten years earlier. They were admitted by the old Negro into a dim hall from which a stairway

1. From *These Thirteen.* Copyright, 1931, by William Faulkner. Reprinted by permission of Random House, Inc.

mounted into still more shadow. It smelled of dust and disuse—a close, dank smell. The Negro led them into the parlor. It was furnished in heavy, leather-covered furniture. When the Negro opened the blinds of one window, they could see that the leather was cracked; and when they sat down, a faint dust rose sluggishly about their thighs, spinning with slow motes in the single sun-ray. On a tarnished gilt easel before the fireplace stood a crayon portrait of Miss Emily's father.

They rose when she entered—a small, fat woman in black, with a thin gold chain descending to her waist and vanishing into her belt, leaning on an ebony cane with a tarnished gold head. Her skeleton was small and spare; perhaps that was why what would have been merely plumpness in another was obesity in her. She looked bloated, like a body long submerged in motionless water, and of that pallid hue. Her eyes, lost in the fatty ridges of her face, looked like two small pieces of coal pressed into a lump of dough as they moved from one face to another while the visitors stated their errand.

She did not ask them to sit. She just stood in the door and listened quietly until the spokesman came to a stumbling halt. Then they could hear the invisible watch ticking at the end of the gold chain.

Her voice was dry and cold. "I have no taxes in Jefferson. Colonel Sartoris explained it to me. Perhaps one of you can gain access to the city records and satisfy yourselves."

"But we have. We are the city authorities, Miss Emily. Didn't you get a notice from the sheriff, signed by him?"

"I received a paper, yes," Miss Emily said. "Perhaps he considers himself the sheriff. . . . I have no taxes in Jefferson."

"But there is nothing on the books to show that, you see. We must go by the—"

"See Colonel Sartoris. I have no taxes in Jefferson."

"But, Miss Emily—"

"See Colonel Sartoris." (Colonel Sartoris had been dead almost ten years.) "I have no taxes in Jefferson. Tobe!" The Negro appeared. "Show these gentlemen out."

II

So she vanquished them, horse and foot, just as she had vanquished their fathers thirty years before about the smell. That was two years after her father's death and a short time after her sweetheart—the one we believed would marry her—had deserted her. After her father's death she went out very little; after her sweetheart went away, people hardly saw her at all. A few of the ladies had the temerity to call, but were not received, and the only sign of life about the place was the Negro man—a young man then—going in and out with a market basket.

"Just as if a man—any man—could keep a kitchen properly," the ladies said;

so they were not surprised when the smell developed. It was another link between the gross, teeming world and the high and mighty Griersons.

A neighbor, a woman, complained to the mayor, Judge Stevens, eighty years old.

"But what will you have me do about it, madam?" he said.

"Why send her word to stop it," the woman said. "Isn't there a law?"

"I'm sure that won't be necessary," Judge Stevens said. "It's probably just a snake or a rat that nigger of hers killed in the yard. I'll speak to him about it."

The next day he received two more complaints, one from a man who came in diffident deprecation. "We really must do something about it, Judge. I'd be the last one in the world to bother Miss Emily, but we've got to do something." That night the Board of Aldermen met—three graybeards and one younger man, a member of the rising generation.

"It's simple enough," he said. "Send her word to have her place cleaned up. Give her a certain time to do it in, and if she don't . . ."

"Dammit, sir," Judge Stevens said, "will you accuse a lady to her face of smelling bad?"

So the next night, after midnight, four men crossed Miss Emily's lawn and slunk about the house like burglars, sniffing along the base of the brickwork and at the cellar openings while one of them performed a regular sowing motion with his hand out of a sack slung from his shoulder. They broke open the cellar door and sprinkled lime there, and in all the outbuildings. As they recrossed the lawn, a window that had been dark was lighted and Miss Emily sat in it, the light behind her, and her upright torso motionless as that of an idol. They crept quietly across the lawn and into the shadow of the locusts that lined the street. After a week or two the smell went away.

That was when people had begun to feel really sorry for her. People in our town, remembering how old lady Wyatt, her great-aunt, had gone completely crazy at last, believed that the Griersons held themselves a little too high for what they really were. None of the young men were quite good enough for Miss Emily and such. We had long thought of them as a tableau; Miss Emily a slender figure in white in the background, her father a spraddled silhouette in the foreground, his back to her and clutching a horsewhip, the two of them framed by the back-flung front door. So when she got to be thirty and was still single, we were not pleased exactly, but vindicated; even with insanity in the family she wouldn't have turned down all of her chances if they had really materialized.

When her father died, it got about that the house was all that was left to her; and in a way, people were glad. At last they could pity Miss Emily. Being left alone, and a pauper, she had become humanized. Now she too would know the old thrill and the old despair of a penny more or less.

The day after his death all the ladies prepared to call at the house and offer condolence and aid, as is our custom. Miss Emily met them at the door, dressed as usual and with no trace of grief on her face. She told them that her father was not dead. She did that for three days, with ministers calling on her, and the doctors, trying to persuade her to let them dispose of the body. Just as they were about to resort to law and force, she broke down, and they buried her father quickly.

We did not say she was crazy then. We believed she had to do that. We remembered all the young men her father had driven away, and we knew that with nothing left, she would have to cling to that which had robbed her, as people will.

III

She was sick for a long time. When we saw her again, her hair was cut short, making her look like a girl, with a vague resemblance to those angels in colored church windows—sort of tragic and serene.

The town had just let the contracts for paving the sidewalks, and in the summer after her father's death they began the work. The construction company came with niggers and mules and machinery, and a foreman named Homer Barron, a Yankee—a big, dark, ready man, with a big voice and eyes lighter than his face. The little boys would follow in groups to hear him cuss the niggers, and the niggers singing in time to the rise and fall of picks. Pretty soon he knew everybody in town. Whenever you heard a lot of laughing anywhere about the square, Homer Barron would be in the center of the group. Presently we began to see him and Miss Emily on Sunday afternoons driving in the yellow-wheeled buggy and the matched team of bays from the livery stable.

At first we were glad that Miss Emily would have an interest, because the ladies all said, "Of course a Grierson would not think seriously of a Northerner, a day laborer." But there were still others, older people, who said that even grief could not cause a real lady to forget *noblesse oblige*—without calling it *noblesse oblige*. They just said, "Poor Emily. Her kinsfolk should come to her." She had some kin in Alabama; but years ago her father had fallen out with them over the estate of old lady Wyatt, the crazy woman, and there was no communication between the two families. They had not even been represented at the funeral.

And as soon as the old people said, "Poor Emily," the whispering began. "Do you suppose it's really so?" they said to one another. "Of course it is. What else could . . ." This behind their hands; rustling of craned silk and satin behind jalousies closed upon the sun of Sunday afternoon as the thin, swift clop-clop-clop of the matched team passed: "Poor Emily."

She carried her head high enough—even when we believed that she was fallen. It was as if she demanded more than ever the recognition of her dignity as the last Grierson; as if it had wanted that touch of earthiness to reaffirm her imperviousness. Like when she bought the rat poison, the arsenic.

That was over a year after they had begun to say "Poor Emily," and while the two female cousins were visiting her.

"I want some poison," she said to the druggist. She was over thirty then, still a slight woman, though thinner than usual, with cold, haughty black eyes in a face the flesh of which was strained across the temples and about the eyesockets as you imagine a lighthouse-keeper's face ought to look. "I want some poison," she said.

"Yes, Miss Emily. What kind? For rats and such? I'd recom—"

"I want the best you have. I don't care what kind."

The druggist named several. "They'll kill anything up to an elephant. But what you want is—"

"Arsenic," Miss Emily said. "Is that a good one?"

"Is . . . arsenic? Yes, ma'am. But what you want—"

"I want arsenic."

The druggist looked down at her. She looked back at him, erect, her face like a strained flag. "Why, of course," the druggist said. "If that's what you want. But the law requires you to tell what you are going to use it for."

Miss Emily just stared at him, her head tilted back in order to look him eye for eye, until he looked away and went and got the arsenic and wrapped it up. The Negro delivery boy brought her the package; the druggist didn't come back. When she opened the package at home there was written on the box, under the skull and bones: "For rats."

IV

So the next day we all said, "She will kill herself"; and we said it would be the best thing. When she had first begun to be seen with Homer Barron, we had said, "She will marry him." Then we said, "She will persuade him yet," because Homer himself had remarked—he liked men, and it was known that he drank with younger men in the Elk's Club—that he was not a marrying man. Later we said, "Poor Emily," behind the jalousies as they passed on Sunday afternoon in the glittering buggy, Miss Emily with her head high and Homer Barron with his hat cocked and a cigar in his teeth, reins and whip in a yellow glove.

Then some of the ladies began to say that it was a disgrace to the town and a bad example to the young people. The men did not want to interfere, but at last the ladies forced the Baptist minister—Miss Emily's people were Episcopal—to call upon her. He would never divulge what happened during that interview, but he refused to go back again. The next Sunday they again drove about the streets, and the following day the minister's wife wrote to Miss Emily's relations in Alabama.

So she had blood-kin under her roof again and we sat back to watch developments. At first nothing happened. Then we were sure that they were to be married. We learned that Miss Emily had been to the jeweler's and ordered a man's toilet set in silver, with the letters H.B. on each piece. Two days later we learned that she had bought a complete outfit of men's clothing, including a nightshirt, and we said, "They are married." We were really glad. We were glad because the two female cousins were even more Grierson than Miss Emily had ever been.

So we were not surprised when Homer Barron—the streets had been finished some time since—was gone. We were a little disappointed that there was not a public blowing-off, but we believed that he had gone on to prepare for Miss Emily's coming, or to give her a chance to get rid of the cousins. (By that time it was a cabal, and we were all Miss Emily's allies to help circumvent the cousins.) Sure enough, after another week they departed. And, as we had expected all along, within three days Homer Barron was back in town. A neighbor saw her Negro man admit him at the kitchen door at dusk one evening.

And that was the last we saw of Homer Barron. And of Miss Emily for some time. The Negro man went in and out with the market basket, but the front door remained closed. Now and then we would see her at a window for a moment, as the men did that night when they sprinkled the lime, but for almost six months she did not appear on the streets. Then we knew that this was to be expected too; as if that quality of her father which had thwarted her woman's life so many times had been too virulent and too furious to die.

When we next saw Miss Emily, she had grown fat and her hair was turning gray. During the next few years it grew grayer and grayer until it attained an even pepper-and-salt iron-gray, when it ceased turning. Up to the day of her death at seventy-four it was still that vigorous iron-gray, like the hair of an active man.

From that time on her front door remained closed, save for a period of six or seven years, when she was about forty, during which she gave lessons in china-painting. She fitted up a studio in one of the downstairs rooms, where the daughters and granddaughters of Colonel Sartoris' contemporaries were sent to her with the same regularity and in the same spirit that they were sent on Sundays with a twenty-five cent piece for the collection plate. Meanwhile her taxes had been remitted.

Then the newer generation became the backbone and the spirit of the town, and the painting pupils grew up and fell away and did not send their children to her with boxes of color and tedious brushes and pictures cut from the ladies' magazines. The front door closed upon the last one and remained closed for good. When the town got free postal delivery Miss Emily alone refused to let them fasten the metal numbers above her door and attach a mailbox to it. She would not listen to them.

Daily, monthly, yearly we watched the Negro grow grayer and more stooped, going in and out with the market basket. Each December we sent her a tax notice, which would be returned by the post office a week later, unclaimed. Now and then we would see her in one of the downstairs windows—she had evidently shut up the top floor of the house—like the carven torso of an idol in a niche, looking or not looking at us, we could never tell which. Thus she passed from generation to generation—dear, inescapable, impervious, tranquil, and perverse.

And so she died. Fell ill in the house filled with dust and shadows, with only a doddering Negro man to wait on her. We did not even know she was sick; we had long since given up trying to get any information from the Negro. He talked to no one, probably not even to her, for his voice had grown harsh and rusty, as if from disuse.

She died in one of the downstairs rooms, in a heavy walnut bed with a curtain, her gray head propped on a pillow yellow and moldy with age and lack of sunlight.

V

The Negro met the first of the ladies at the front door and let them in, with their hushed, sibilant voices and their quick, curious glances, and then he disappeared. He walked right through the house and out the back and was not seen again.

The two female cousins came at once. They held the funeral on the second day, with the town coming to look at Miss Emily beneath a mass of bought flowers, with the crayon face of her father musing profoundly above the bier and the ladies sibilant and macabre; and the very old men—some in their brushed Confederate uniforms—on the porch and the lawn, talking of Miss Emily as if she had been a contemporary of theirs, believing that they had danced with her and courted her perhaps, confusing time with its mathematical progression, as the old do, to whom all the past is not a diminishing road, but, instead, a huge meadow which no winter ever quite touches, divided from them now by the narrow bottleneck of the most recent decade of years.

Already we knew that there was one room in that region above stairs which no one had seen in forty years, and which would have to be forced. They waited until Miss Emily was decently in the ground before they opened it.

The violence of breaking down the door seemed to fill this room with pervading dust. A thin, acrid pall as of the tomb seemed to lie everywhere upon this room decked and furnished as for a bridal: upon the valance curtains of faded rose color, upon the rose-shaded lights, upon the dressing table, upon the delicate array of crystal and the man's toilet things backed with tarnished silver, silver so tarnished that the monogram was obscured. Among them lay a collar and tie, as if they had just been removed, which, lifted, left upon the surface a pale crescent in the dust. Upon the chair hung the suit, carefully folded; beneath it the two mute shoes and the discarded socks.

The man himself lay in the bed.

For a long while we just stood there, looking down at the profound and fleshless grin. The body had apparently once lain in the attitude of an embrace, but now the long sleep that outlasts love, that conquers even the grimace of love, had cuckolded him. What was left of him, rotted beneath what was left of the nightshirt, had become inextricable from the bed in which he lay; and upon him and upon the pillow beside him lay that even coating of the patient and biding dust.

Then we noticed that in the second pillow was the indentation of a head. One of us lifted something from it, and leaning forward, that faint and invisible dust dry and acrid in the nostrils, we saw a long strand of iron-gray hair.

ON FAULKNER'S *A ROSE FOR EMILY* [1]

CLEANTH BROOKS AND ROBERT PENN WARREN

THIS story, like Poe's "The Fall of the House of Usher," is a story of horror. In both stories we have a decaying mansion in which the protagonist, shut away from the world, grows into something monstrous, and becomes as divorced from the human as some fungus growing in the dark on a damp wall. Roderick Usher and Miss Emily Grierson remain in voluntary isolation (or perhaps fettered by some inner compulsion) away from the bustle and dust and sunshine of the human world of normal affairs. As we have seen, Poe closes his story with a melodramatic gesture in which the house falls into the lake, carrying with it its dead master. The ending of Faulkner's story is not so spectacular, but what is found in the upstairs room gives perhaps a sense of more penetrating and gruesome horror than ever Poe has achieved.

It has been indicated that, in the case of Poe, the sense of horror had been conjured up for its own sake. Is this true of Faulkner's story? If it is not, then why has he contrived to insert so much of the monstrous into the story? In other words, does the horror contribute to the theme of Faulkner's story? Is the horror meaningful?

In order to answer this question, we shall have to examine rather carefully some of the items earlier in the story. In the first place, why does Miss Emily commit her monstrous act? Is she supplied with a proper motivation—a matter which we concluded was handled rather weakly in "The Fall of the House of Usher." Faulkner has been rather careful to prepare for his *dénouement*. Miss Emily, it becomes obvious fairly early in the story, is one of those persons for whom the distinction between reality and illusion has blurred out. For example, she refuses to admit that she owes any taxes. When the mayor protests, she does not recognize him as mayor. Instead, she refers the committee to Colonel Sartoris, who, as the reader is told, has been dead for nearly ten years. For Miss Emily apparently, Colonel Sartoris is still alive. Most specific preparation of all, when her father dies, she denies to the townspeople for

1. From *Understanding Fiction,* by Cleanth Brooks, Jr., and Robert Penn Warren. Copyright, 1943, by F. S. Crofts & Co., Inc. Published by F. S. Crofts & Co., Inc.

three days that he is dead: "Just as they were about to resort to law and force, she broke down, and they buried her father quickly."

Miss Emily is obviously a pathological case. The narrator indicates plainly enough that people felt that she was crazy. All this explanation prepares us for what Miss Emily does in order to hold her lover—the dead lover is in one sense still alive for her—the realms of reality and appearance merge. But having said this, we have got no nearer to justifying the story: for, if Faulkner is merely interested in relating a case history of abnormal psychology, the story lacks meaning and justification as a story. His interest in this case is as "clinical" as is the interest of Poe in Roderick Usher. If the story is to be justified, there must be what may be called a moral significance, a meaning in moral terms—not merely psychological terms.

Incidentally, it is very easy to misread the story as merely a horrible case history, presented in order to titillate the reader. Faulkner has been frequently judged to be doing nothing more than this in his work.

The lapse of the distinction between illusion and reality, between life and death, is important, therefore, as helping supply the motivation for the story, but a definition of this in itself is not a complete definition of the author's intention. We shall have to go behind it if we are to understand what Faulkner is about.

Suppose we approach the motivation again in these terms: what is Miss Emily like? What are the mainsprings of her character? What causes the distinction between illusion and reality to blur out for her? She is obviously a woman of tremendous firmness of will. In the matter of the taxes, crazed though she is, she is never at a loss. She is utterly composed. She dominates the rather frightened committee of officers who sees her. In the matter of her purchase of the poison, she completely overawes the clerk. She makes no pretenses. She refuses to tell him what she wants the poison for. And yet this firmness of will and this iron pride have not kept her from being thwarted and hurt. Her father has run off the young men who came to call upon her, and for the man who tells the story, Miss Emily and her father form a tableau: "Miss Emily a slender figure in white in the background, her father a spraddled silhouette in the foreground, his back to her and clutching a horse-whip, the two of them framed by the back-flung front door." Whether the picture is a remembered scene, or merely a symbolical construct, this is the picture which remains in the storyteller's mind.

We have indicated that her pride is connected with her contempt for public opinion. This comes to the fore, of course, when she rides around about the town with the foreman who everybody believes is beneath her. And it is her proud refusal to admit an external set of codes, or conventions, or other wills which contradict her own will, which makes her capable at the end of keeping her lover from going away. Confronted with his jilting her, she tries to override not only his will and the opinion of other people, but the laws of death and decay themselves.

But this, still, hardly gives the meaning of the story. For in all that has been said thus far, we are still merely dealing with a case history in abnormal psychology. In order to make a case for the story as "meaningful," we shall have to tie Miss Emily's thoughts and actions back into the normal life of the community, and establish some sort of relationship between them. And just here one pervasive element in the narration suggests a clue. The story is told by one of the townspeople. And in it, as a constant factor, is the reference to what the community thought of Miss Emily. Continually through the story it is what "we" said, and then what "we" did, and what seemed true to "us," and so on. The narrator puts the matter even more sharply still. He says, in the course of the story, that to the community Miss Emily seemed "dear, inescapable, impervious, tranquil, and perverse." Each of the adjectives is important and meaningful. In a sense, Miss Emily because of her very fact of isolation and perversity belongs to the whole community. She is even something treasured by it. Ironically, because of Emily's perversion of an aristocratic independence of mores and because of her contempt for "what people say," her life is public, even communal. And various phrases used by the narrator underline this view of her position. For example, her face looks "as you imagine a lighthouse-keeper's face ought to look," like the face of a person who lives in the kind of isolation imposed on a lighthouse-keeper, who looks out into the blackness and whose light serves a public function. Or, again, after her father's death, she becomes very ill, and when she appears after the illness, she has "a vague resemblance to those angels in colored church windows—sort of tragic and serene." Whatever we make of these descriptions, certainly the author is trying to suggest a kind of calm and dignity which is supermundane, unearthly, or "over-earthly," such as an angel might possess.

Miss Emily, then, is a combination of idol and scapegoat for the community. On the one hand, the community feels admiration for Miss Emily—she represents something in the past of the community which the community is proud of. They feel a sort of awe of her, as is illustrated by the behavior of the mayor and the committee in her presence. On the other hand, her queerness, the fact that she cannot compete with them in their ordinary life, the fact that she is hopelessly out of touch with the modern world—all of these things make them feel superior to her, and also to that past which she represents. It is, then, Miss Emily's complete detachment which gives her actions their special meaning for the community.

Miss Emily, since she is the conscious aristocrat, since she is consciously "better" than other people, since she is above and outside their canons of behavior, can, at the same time, be worse than other people; and she *is* worse, horribly so. She is worse than other people, but at the same time, as the narrator implies, she remains somehow admirable. This raises a fundamental question: why is this true?

Perhaps the horrible and the admirable aspects of Miss Emily's final deed arise from the same basic fact of her character: she insists on meeting the world on her own terms. She never cringes, she never begs for sympathy, she refuses to shrink into an amiable old maid, she never accepts the community's ordinary judgments or values. This independence of spirit and pride can, and does in her case, twist the individual into a sort of monster, but, at the same time, this refusal to accept the herd values carries with it a dignity and courage. The community senses this, as we gather from the fact that the community carries out the decencies of the funeral before breaking in the door of the upper room. There is, as it were, a kind of secret understanding that she has won her right of privacy, until she herself has entered history. Furthermore, despite the fact that, as the narrator says, "already we knew that there was one room in that region above stairs which no one had seen in forty years, and which would have to be forced," her funeral is something of a state occasion, with "the very old men—some in their brushed Confederate uniforms—on the porch and the lawn, talking of Miss Emily as if she had been a contemporary of theirs, believing that they had danced with her and courted her perhaps . . ." In other words, the community accepts her into its honored history. All of this works as a kind of tacit recognition of Miss Emily's triumph of will. The community, we are told earlier, had wanted to pity Miss Emily when she had lost her money, just as they had wanted to commiserate over her when they believed that she had actually become a fallen woman, but she had triumphed over their pity and commiseration and condemnation, just as she had triumphed over all their other attitudes.

But, as we have indicated earlier, it may be said that Miss Emily is mad. This may be true, but there are two things to consider in this connection. First, one must consider the special terms which her "madness" takes. Her madness is simply a development of her pride and her refusal to submit to ordinary standards of behavior. So, because of this fact, her "madness" is meaningful after all. It involves issues which in themselves are really important and have to do with the world of conscious moral choice. Second, the community interprets her "madness" as meaningful. They admire her, even if they are disappointed by her refusals to let herself be pitied, and the narrator, who is a spokesman for the community, recognizes the last grim revelation as an instance of her having carried her own values to their ultimate conclusion. She would marry the common laborer, Homer Barron, let the community think what it would. She would not be jilted. And she would hold him as a lover. But it would all be on her own terms. She remains completely dominant, and contemptuous of the day-to-day world.

It has been suggested by many critics that tragedy implies a hero who is completely himself, who insists on meeting the world on his own terms, who wants something so intensely, or lives so intensely, that he cannot accept any compromise. It cannot be maintained that this story is comparable to any of the great tragedies, such as *Hamlet* or *King Lear*, but it can be pointed out that this story, in its own way, involves some of the same basic elements. Certainly, Miss Emily's pride, isolation, and independence remind one of factors in the character of the typical tragic hero. And it can be pointed out that, just as the horror of her deed lies outside the ordinary life of the community, so the magnificence of her independence lies outside their ordinary virtues.

THE SHORT HAPPY LIFE OF FRANCIS MACOMBER[1]

ERNEST HEMINGWAY

It was now lunch time and they were all sitting under the double green fly of the dining tent pretending that nothing had happened.

"Will you have lime juice or lemon squash?" Macomber asked.

"I'll have a gimlet," Robert Wilson told him.

"I'll have a gimlet too. I need something," Macomber's wife said.

"I suppose it's the thing to do," Macomber agreed. "Tell him to make three gimlets."

The mess boy had started them already, lifting the bottles out of the canvas cooling bags that sweated wet in the wind that blew through the trees that shaded the tents.

"What had I ought to give them?" Macomber asked.

"A quid would be plenty," Wilson told him. "You don't want to spoil them."

"Will the headman distribute it?"

"Absolutely."

Francis Macomber had, half an hour before, been carried to his tent from the edge of the camp in triumph on the arms and shoulders of the cook, the personal boys, the skinner and the porters. The gun-bearers had taken no part in the demonstration. When the native boys put him down at the door of his tent, he had shaken all their hands, received their congratulations, and then gone into the tent and sat on the bed until his wife came in. She did not speak to him when she came in and he left the tent at once to wash his face and hands in the portable wash basin outside and go over to the dining tent to sit in a comfortable canvas chair in the breeze and the shade.

"You've got your lion," Robert Wilson said to him, "and a damned fine one too."

Mrs. Macomber looked at Wilson quickly. She was an extremely handsome and well-kept woman of the beauty and social position which had, five years before, commanded five thousand dollars as the price of endorsing, with photographs, a beauty product which she had never used. She had been married to Francis Macomber for eleven years.

"He is a good lion, isn't he?" Macomber said. His wife looked at him now.

---

1. Reprinted from *The Fifth Column and the First Forty-Nine Stories* by Ernest Hemingway; copyright, 1938, by Ernest Hemingway; used by permission of the publisher, Charles Scribner's Sons.

She looked at both these men as though she had never seen them before.

One, Wilson, the white hunter, she knew she had never truly seen before. He was about middle height with sandy hair, a stubby mustache, a very red face and extremely cold blue eyes with faint white wrinkles at the corners that grooved merrily when he smiled. He smiled at her now and she looked away from his face at the way his shoulders sloped in the loose tunic he wore with the four big cartridges held in loops where the left breast pocket should have been, at his big brown hands, his old slacks, his very dirty boots and back to his red face again. She noticed where the baked red of his face stopped in a white line that marked the circle left by his Stetson hat that hung now from one of the pegs of the tent pole.

"Well, here's to the lion," Robert Wilson said. He smiled at her again and, not smiling, she looked curiously at her husband.

Francis Macomber was very tall, very well built if you did not mind that length of bone, dark, his hair cropped like an oarsman, rather thin-lipped, and was considered handsome. He was dressed in the same sort of safari clothes that Wilson wore except that his were new, he was thirty-five years old, kept himself very fit, was good at court games, had a number of big-game fishing records, and had just shown himself, very publicly, to be a coward.

"Here's to the lion," he said. "I can't ever thank you for what you did."

Margaret, his wife, looked away from him and back to Wilson.

"Let's not talk about the lion," she said.

Wilson looked over at her without smiling and now she smiled at him.

"It's been a very strange day," she said. "Hadn't you ought to put your hat on even under the canvas at noon? You told me that, you know."

"Might put it on," said Wilson.

"You know you have a very red face, Mr. Wilson," she told him and smiled again.

"Drink," said Wilson.

"I don't think so," she said. "Francis drinks a great deal, but his face is never red."

"It's red today," Macomber tried a joke.

"No," said Margaret. "It's mine that's red today. But Mr. Wilson's is always red."

"Must be racial," said Wilson. "I say, you wouldn't like to drop my beauty as a topic, would you?"

"I've just started on it."

"Let's chuck it," said Wilson.

"Conversation is going to be so difficult," Margaret said.

"Don't be silly, Margot," her husband said.

"No difficulty," Wilson said. "Got a damn fine lion."

Margot looked at them both and they both saw that she was going to cry. Wilson had seen it coming for a long time and he dreaded it. Macomber was past dreading it.

"I wish it hadn't happened. Oh, I wish it hadn't happened," she said and started for her tent. She made no noise of crying but they could see that her shoulders were shaking under the rose-colored, sun-proofed shirt she wore.

"Women upset," said Wilson to the tall man. "Amounts to nothing. Strain on the nerves and one thing'n another."

"No," said Macomber. "I suppose that I rate that for the rest of my life now."

"Nonsense. Let's have a spot of giant killer," said Wilson. "Forget the whole thing. Nothing to it anyway."

"We might try," said Macomber. "I won't forget what you did for me though."

"Nothing," said Wilson. "All nonsense."

So they sat there in the shade where the camp was pitched under some wide-topped acacia trees with a boulder-strewn cliff behind them, and a stretch of grass that ran to the bank of a boulder-filled stream in front with forest beyond it, and drank their just-cool lime drinks and avoided one another's eyes while the boys set the table for lunch. Wilson could tell that the boys all knew about it now and when he saw Macomber's personal boy looking curiously at his master while he was putting dishes on the table he snapped at him in Swahili. The boy turned away with his face blank.

"What were you telling him?" Macomber asked.

"Nothing. Told him to look alive or I'd see he got about fifteen of the best."

"What's that? Lashes?"

"It's quite illegal," Wilson said. "You're supposed to fine them."

"Do you still have them whipped?"

"Oh, yes. They could raise a row if they chose to complain. But they don't. They prefer it to the fines."

"How strange!" said Macomber.

"Not strange, really," Wilson said. "Which would you rather do? Take a good birching or lose your pay?"

Then he felt embarrassed at asking it and before Macomber could answer he went on, "We all take a beating every day, you know, one way or another."

This was no better. "Good God," he thought. "I am a diplomat, aren't I?"

"Yes, we take a beating," said Macomber, still not looking at him. "I'm awfully sorry about that lion business. It doesn't have to go any further, does it? I mean no one will hear about it, will they?"

"You mean will I tell it at the Mathaiga Club?" Wilson looked at him now coldly. He had not expected this. So he's a bloody four-letter man as well as a bloody coward, he thought. I rather liked him too until today. But how is one to know about an American?

"No," said Wilson. "I'm a professional hunter. We never talk about our clients. You can be quite easy on that. It's supposed to be bad form to ask us not to talk though."

He had decided now that to break would be much easier. He would eat, then, by himself and could read a book with his meals. They would eat by themselves. He would see them through the safari on a very formal basis—what was it the French called it? Distinguished consideration—and it would be a damn sight easier than having to go through this emotional trash. He'd insult him and make a good clean break. Then he could read a book with his meals and he'd still be drinking their whisky. That was the phrase for it when a safari went bad. You ran into another white hunter and you asked, "How is everything going?" and he answered, "Oh, I'm still drinking their whisky," and you knew everything had gone to pot.

"I'm sorry," Macomber said and looked at him with his American face that would stay adolescent until it became middle-aged, and Wilson noted his crew-cropped hair, fine eyes only faintly shifty, good nose, thin lips and handsome jaw. "I'm sorry I didn't realize that. There are lots of things I don't know."

So what could he do, Wilson thought. He was all ready to break it off quickly and neatly and here the beggar was apologizing after he had just insulted him. He made one more attempt. "Don't worry about me talking," he said. "I have a living to make. You know in Africa no woman ever misses her lion and no white man ever bolts."

"I bolted like a rabbit," Macomber said.

Now what in hell were you going to do about a man who talked like that, Wilson wondered.

Wilson looked at Macomber with his flat, blue, machine-gunner's eyes and the other smiled back at him. He had a pleasant smile if you did not notice how his eyes showed when he was hurt.

"Maybe I can fix it up on buffalo," he said. "We're after them next, aren't we?"

"In the morning if you like," Wilson told him. Perhaps he had been wrong. This was certainly the way to take it. You most certainly could not tell a damned thing about an American. He was all for Macomber again. If you could forget the morning. But, of course, you couldn't. The morning had been about as bad as they come.

"Here comes the Memsahib," he said. She was walking over from her tent looking refreshed and cheerful and quite lovely. She had a very perfect oval face, so perfect that you expected her to be stupid. But she wasn't stupid, Wilson thought, no, not stupid.

"How is the beautiful red-faced Mr. Wilson? Are you feeling better, Francis, my pearl?"

"Oh, much," said Macomber.

"I've dropped the whole thing," she said, sitting down at the table. "What importance is there to whether Francis is any good at killing lions? That's not his trade. That's Mr. Wilson's trade. Mr. Wilson is really very impressive killing anything. You do kill anything, don't you?"

"Oh, anything," said Wilson. "Simply anything." They are, he thought, the hardest in the world; the hardest, the cruelest, the most predatory and the most attractive and their men have softened or gone to pieces nervously as they have hardened. Or is it that they pick men they can handle? They can't know that much at the age they marry, he thought. He was grateful that he had gone through his education on American women before now because this was a very attractive one.

"We're going after buff in the morning," he told her.

"I'm coming," she said.

"No, you're not."

"Oh, yes, I am. Mayn't I, Francis?"

"Why not stay in camp?"

"Not for anything," she said. "I wouldn't miss something like today for anything."

When she left, Wilson was thinking, when she went off to cry, she seemed a hell of a fine woman. She seemed to understand, to realize, to be hurt for him and for herself and to know how things really stood. She is away for twenty minutes and now she is back, simply enamelled in that American female cruelty. They are the damnedest women. Really the damnedest.

"We'll put on another show for you tomorrow," Francis Macomber said.

"You're not coming," Wilson said.

"You're very mistaken," she told him. "And I want *so* to see you perform again. You were lovely this morning. That is if blowing things' heads off is lovely."

"Here's the lunch," said Wilson. "You're very merry, aren't you?"

"Why not? I didn't come out here to be dull."

"Well, it hasn't been dull," Wilson said. He could see the boulders in the river and the high bank beyond with the trees and he remembered the morning.

"Oh, no," she said. "It's been charming. And tomorrow. You don't know how I look forward to tomorrow."

"That's eland he's offering you," Wilson said.

"They're the big cowy things that jump like hares, aren't they?"

"I suppose that describes them," Wilson said.

"It's very good meat," Macomber said.

"Did you shoot it, Francis?" she asked.

"Yes."

"They're not dangerous, are they?"

"Only if they fall on you," Wilson told her.

"I'm so glad."

"Why not let up on the bitchery just a little, Margot," Macomber said, cutting the eland steak and putting some mashed potato, gravy and carrot on the down-turned fork that tined through the piece of meat.

"I suppose I could," she said, "since you put it so prettily."

"Tonight we'll have champagne for the lion," Wilson said. "It's a bit too hot at noon."

"Oh, the lion," Margot said. "I'd forgotten the lion!"

So, Robert Wilson thought to himself, she *is* giving him a ride, isn't she? Or do you suppose that's her idea of putting up a good show? How should a woman act when she discovers her husband is a bloody coward? She's damn cruel but they're all cruel. They govern, of course, and to govern one has to be cruel sometimes. Still, I've seen enough of their damn terrorism.

"Have some more eland," he said to her politely.

That afternoon, late, Wilson and Macomber went out in the motor car with the native driver and the two gun-bearers. Mrs. Macomber stayed in the camp. It was too hot to go out, she said, and she was going with them in the early morning. As they drove off Wilson saw her standing under the big tree, looking pretty rather than beautiful in her faintly rosy khaki, her dark hair drawn back off her forehead and gathered in a knot low on her neck, her face as fresh, he thought, as though she were in England. She waved to them as the car went off through the swale of high grass and curved around through the trees into the small hills of orchard bush.

In the orchard bush they found a herd of impala, and leaving the car they stalked one old ram with long, wide-spread horns and Macomber killed it with a very creditable shot that knocked the buck down at a good two hundred yards and sent the herd off bounding wildly and leaping over one another's backs in long, leg-drawn-up leaps as unbelievable and as floating as those one makes sometimes in dreams.

"That was a good shot," Wilson said. "They're a small target."

"Is it a worth-while head?" Macomber asked.

"It's excellent," Wilson told him. "You shoot like that and you'll have no trouble."

"Do you think we'll find buffalo tomorrow?"

"There's a good chance of it. They feed out early in the morning and with luck we may catch them in the open."

"I'd like to clear away that lion business," Macomber said. "It's not very pleasant to have your wife see you do something like that."

I should think it would be even more unpleasant to do it, Wilson thought, wife or no wife, or to talk about it having done it. But he said, "I wouldn't think about that any more. Any one could be upset by his first lion. That's all over."

But that night after dinner and a whisky and soda by the fire before going to bed, as Francis Macomber lay on his cot with the mosquito bar over him and listened to the night noises it was not all over. It was neither all over nor was it beginning. It was there exactly as it happened with some parts of it indelibly emphasized and he was miserably ashamed at it. But more than shame he felt cold, hollow fear in him. The fear was still there like a cold slimy hollow in all the emptiness where once his confidence had been and it made him feel sick. It was still there with him now.

It had started the night before when he had wakened and heard the lion roaring somewhere up along the river. It was a deep sound and at the end there were sort of coughing grunts that made him seem just outside the tent, and when Francis Macomber woke in the night to hear it he was afraid. He could hear his wife breathing quietly, asleep. There was no one to tell he was afraid, nor to be afraid with him, and, lying alone, he did not know the Somali proverb that says a brave man is always frightened three times by a lion; when he first sees his track, when he first hears him roar and when he first confronts him. Then while they were eating breakfast by lantern light out in the dining tent, before the sun was up, the lion roared again and Francis thought he was just at the edge of camp.

"Sounds like an old-timer," Robert Wilson said, looking up from his kippers and coffee. "Listen to him cough."

"Is he very close?"

"A mile or so up the stream."

"Will we see him?"

"We'll have a look."

"Does his roaring carry that far? It sounds as though he were right in camp."

"Carries a hell of a long way," said Robert Wilson. "It's strange the way it carries. Hope he's a shootable cat. The boys said there was a very big one about here."

"If I get a shot, where should I hit him," Macomber asked, "to stop him?"

"In the shoulders," Wilson said. "In the neck if you can make it. Shoot for bone. Break him down."

"I hope I can place it properly," Macomber said.

"You shoot very well," Wilson told him. "Take your time. Make sure of him. The first one in is the one that counts."

"What range will it be?"

"Can't tell. Lion has something to say about that. Don't shoot unless it's close enough so you can make sure."

"At under a hundred yards?" Macomber asked.

Wilson looked at him quickly.

"Hundred's about right. Might have to take him a bit under. Shouldn't chance a shot at much over that. A hundred's a decent range. You can hit him wherever you want at that. Here comes the Memsahib."

"Good morning," she said. "Are we going after that lion?"

"As soon as you deal with your breakfast," Wilson said. "How are you feeling?"

"Marvellous," she said. "I'm very excited."

"I'll just go and see that everything is ready," Wilson went off. As he left the lion roared again.

"Noisy beggar," Wilson said. "We'll put a stop to that."

"What's the matter, Francis?" his wife asked him.

"Nothing," Macomber said.

"Yes, there is," she said. "What are you upset about?"

"Nothing," he said.

"Tell me," she looked at him. "Don't you feel well?"

"It's that damned roaring," he said. "It's been going on all night, you know."

"Why didn't you wake me," she said. "I'd love to have heard it."

"I've got to kill the damned thing," Macomber said, miserably.

"Well, that's what you're out here for, isn't it?"

"Yes. But I'm nervous. Hearing the thing roar gets on my nerves."

"Well then, as Wilson said, kill him and stop his roaring."

"Yes, darling," said Francis Macomber. "It sounds easy, doesn't it?"

"You're not afraid, are you?"

"Of course not. But I'm nervous from hearing him roar all night."

"You'll kill him marvellously," she said. "I know you will. I'm awfully anxious to see it."

"Finish your breakfast and we'll be starting."

"It's not light yet," she said. "This is a ridiculous hour."

Just then the lion roared in a deep-chested moaning, suddenly guttural, ascending vibration that seemed to shake the air and ended in a sigh and a heavy, deep-chested grunt.

"He sounds almost here," Macomber's wife said.

"My God," said Macomber. "I hate that damned noise."

"It's very impressive."

"Impressive. It's frightful."

Robert Wilson came up then carrying his short, ugly, shockingly big-bored .505 Gibbs and grinning.

"Come on," he said. "Your gun-bearer has your Springfield and the big gun. Everything's in the car. Have you solids?"

"Yes."

"I'm ready," Mrs. Macomber said.

"Must make him stop that racket," Wilson said. "You get in front. The Memsahib can sit back here with me."

They climbed into the motor car and, in the gray first daylight, moved off up the river through the trees. Macomber opened the breech of his rifle and saw he had metal-cased bullets, shut the bolt and put the rifle on safety. He saw his hand was trembling. He felt in his pocket for more cartridges and moved his fingers over the cartridges in the loops of his tunic front. He turned back to where Wilson sat in the rear seat of the doorless, box-bodied motor car beside his wife, them both grinning with excitement, and Wilson leaned forward and whispered.

"See the birds dropping. Means the old boy has left his kill."

On the far bank of the stream Macomber could see, above the trees, vultures circling and plummeting down.

"Chances are he'll come to drink along here," Wilson whispered. "Before he goes to lay up. Keep an eye out."

They were driving slowly along the high bank of the stream which here cut deeply to its boulder-filled bed, and they wound in and out through big trees as they drove. Macomber was watching the opposite bank when he felt Wilson take hold of his arm. The car stopped.

"There he is," he heard the whisper. "Ahead and to the right. Get out and take him. He's a marvellous lion."

Macomber saw the lion now. He was standing alone almost broadside, his great head up and turned toward them. The early morning breeze that blew toward them was just stirring his dark mane, and the lion looked huge, silhouetted on the rise of bank in the gray morning light, his shoulders heavy, his barrel of a body bulking smoothly.

"How far is he?" asked Macomber, raising his rifle.

"About seventy-five. Get out and take him."

"Why not shoot from where I am?"

"You don't shoot them from cars," he heard Wilson saying in his ear. "Get out. He's not going to stay there all day."

Macomber stepped out of the curved opening at the side of the front seat, onto the step and down onto the ground. The lion still stood looking majestically and coolly toward this object that his eyes showed only in silhouette, bulking like some super-rhino. There was no man smell carried toward him and he watched the object, moving his great head a little from side to side. Then watching the object, not afraid, but hesitating before going down the bank to drink with such a thing opposite him, he saw a man figure detach itself from it and he turned his heavy head and swung away toward the cover of the trees as he heard a cracking crash and felt the slam of a .30-06 220-grain solid bullet that bit his flank and ripped in sudden hot scalding nausea through his stomach. He trotted, heavy, big-footed, swinging wounded full-bellied, through the trees toward the tall grass and cover, and the crash came again to go past him ripping the air apart. Then it crashed again and he felt the blow as it hit his lower ribs and ripped on through, blood sudden hot and frothy in his mouth, and he galloped toward the high grass where he could crouch and not be seen and make them bring the crashing thing close enough so he could make a rush and get the man that held it.

Macomber had not thought how the lion felt as he got out of the car. He only knew his hands were shaking and as he walked away from the car it was almost impossible for him to make his legs move. They were stiff in the thighs, but he could feel the muscles fluttering. He raised the rifle, sighted on the junction of the lion's head and shoulders and pulled the trigger. Nothing happened though he pulled until he thought his finger would break. Then he knew he had the safety on and as he lowered the rifle to move the safety over he moved another frozen pace forward, and the lion seeing his silhouette now clear of the silhouette of the car, turned and started off at a trot, and, as Macomber fired, he heard a whunk that meant that the bullet was home; but the lion kept on going. Macomber shot again and every one saw the bullet throw a spout of dirt beyond the trotting lion. He shot again, remembering to lower his aim, and they all heard the bullet hit, and the lion went into a gallop and was in the tall grass before he had the bolt pushed forward.

Macomber stood there feeling sick at his stomach, his hands that held the Springfield still cocked, shaking, and his wife and Robert Wilson were standing by him. Beside him too were the two gun-bearers chattering in Wakamba.

"I hit him," Macomber said. "I hit him twice."

"You gut-shot him and you hit him somewhere forward," Wilson said without enthusiasm. The gun-bearers looked very grave. They were silent now.

"You may have killed him," Wilson went on. "We'll have to wait a while before we go in to find out."

"What do you mean?"

"Let him get sick before we follow him up."

"Oh," said Macomber.

"He's a hell of a fine lion," Wilson said cheerfully. "He's gotten into a bad place though."

"Why is it bad?"

"Can't see him until you're on him."

"Oh," said Macomber.

"Come on," said Wilson. "The Memsahib can stay here in the car. We'll go to have a look at the blood spoor."

"Stay here, Margot," Macomber said to his wife. His mouth was very dry and it was hard for him to talk.

"Why?" she asked.

"Wilson says so."

"We're going to have a look," Wilson said. "You stay here. You can see even better from here."

"All right."

Wilson spoke in Swahili to the driver. He nodded and said, "Yes, Bweano."

Then they went down the steep bank and across the stream, climbing over and around the boulders and up the other bank, pulling up by some projecting roots, and along it until they found where the lion had been trotting when Macomber first shot. There was dark blood on the short grass that the gun-bearers pointed out with grass stems, and that ran away behind the river bank trees.

"What do we do?" asked Macomber.

"Not much choice," said Wilson. "We can't bring the car over. Bank's too steep. We'll let him stiffen up a bit and then you and I'll go in and have a look for him."

"Can't we set the grass on fire?" Macomber asked.

"Too green."

"Can't we send beaters?"

Wilson looked at him appraisingly. "Of course we can," he said. "But it's just a touch murderous. You see we know the lion's wounded. You can drive an unwounded lion—he'll move on ahead of a noise—but a wounded lion's going to charge. You can't see him until you're right on him. He'll make himself perfectly flat in cover you wouldn't think would hide a hare. You can't very well send boys in there to that sort of a show. Somebody bound to get mauled."

"What about the gun-bearers?"

"Oh, they'll go with us. It's their *shauri*. You see, they signed on for it. They don't look too happy though, do they?"

"I don't want to go in there," said Macomber. It was out before he knew he'd said it.

"Neither do I," said Wilson very cheerily. "Really no choice though." Then, as an afterthought, he glanced at Macomber and saw suddenly how he was trembling and the pitiful look on his face.

"You don't have to go in, of course," he said. "That's what I'm hired for, you know. That's why I'm so expensive."

"You mean, you'd go in by yourself? Why not leave him there?"

Robert Wilson, whose entire occupation had been with the lion and the problem he presented, and who had not been thinking about Macomber except to note that he was rather windy, suddenly felt as though he had opened the wrong door in a hotel and seen something shameful.

"What do you mean?"

"Why not just leave him?"

"You mean pretend to ourselves he hasn't been hit?"

"No. Just drop it."

"It isn't done."

"Why not?"

"For one thing, he's certain to be suffering. For another, some one else might run onto him."

"I see."

"But you don't have to have anything to do with it."

"I'd like to," Macomber said. "I'm just scared, you know."

"I'll go ahead when we go in," Wilson said, "with Kongoni tracking. You keep behind me and a little to one side. Chances are we'll hear him growl. If we see him we'll both shoot. Don't worry about anything. I'll keep you backed up. As a matter of fact, you know, perhaps you'd better not go. It might be much better. Why don't you go over and join the Memsahib while I just get it over with?"

"No, I want to go."

"All right," said Wilson. "But don't go in if you don't want to. This is my *shauri* now, you know."

"I want to go," said Macomber.

They sat under a tree and smoked.

"Want to go back and speak to the Memsahib while we're waiting?" Wilson asked.

"No."

"I'll just step back and tell her to be patient."

"Good," said Macomber. He sat there, sweating under his arms, his mouth dry, his stomach hollow feeling, wanting to find courage to tell Wilson to go on and finish off the lion without him. He could not know that Wilson was furious because he had not noticed the state he was in earlier and sent him back to his wife. While he sat there Wilson came up. "I have your big gun," he said. "Take it. We've given him time, I think. Come on."

Macomber took the big gun and Wilson said:

"Keep behind me and about five yards to the right and do exactly as I tell you." Then he spoke in Swahili to the two gun-bearers who looked the picture of gloom.

"Let's go," he said.

"Could I have a drink of water?" Macomber asked. Wilson spoke to the older gun-bearer, who wore a canteen on his belt, and the man unbuckled it, unscrewed the top and handed it to Macomber, who took it noticing how heavy it seemed and how hairy and shoddy the felt covering was in his hand. He raised it to drink and looked ahead at the high grass with the flat-topped trees behind it. A breeze was blowing toward them and the grass rippled gently in the wind. He looked at the gun-bearer and he could see the gun-bearer was suffering too with fear.

Thirty-five yards into the grass the big lion lay flattened out along the ground. His ears were back and his only movement was a slight twitching up and down of his long, black-tufted tail. He had turned at bay as soon as he had reached this cover and he was sick with the wound through his full belly, and weakening with the wound through his lungs that brought a thin foamy red to his mouth each time he breathed. His flanks were wet and hot and flies were on the little openings the solid bullets had made in his tawny hide, and his big yellow eyes, narrowed with hate, looked straight ahead, only blinking when the pain came as he breathed, and his claws dug in the soft baked earth. All of him, pain, sickness, hatred and all of his remaining strength, was tightening into an absolute concentration for a rush. He could hear the men talking and he waited, gathering all of himself into this preparation for a charge as soon as the men would come into the grass. As he heard their voices his tail stiffened to twitch up and down, and, as they came into the edge of the grass, he made a coughing grunt and charged.

Kongoni, the old gun-bearer, in the lead watching the blood spoor, Wilson watching the grass for any movement, his big gun ready, the second gun-bearer looking ahead and listening, Macomber close to Wilson, his rifle cocked, they had just moved into the grass when Macomber heard the blood-choked coughing grunt, and saw the swishing rush in the grass. The next thing he knew he was running; running wildly, in panic in the open, running toward the stream.

He heard the *ca-ra-wong!* of Wilson's rifle, and again in a second crashing *carawong!* and turning saw the lion, horrible-looking now, with half his head seeming to be gone, crawling toward Wilson in the edge of the tall grass while the red-faced man worked the bolt on the short ugly rifle and aimed carefully as another blasting *carawong!* came from the muzzle, and the crawling, heavy, yellow bulk of the lion stiffened and the huge, mutilated head slid forward and Macomber, standing by himself in the clearing where he had run, holding a loaded rifle, while two black men and a white man looked back at him in contempt, knew the lion was dead. He came toward Wilson, his tallness all seeming a naked reproach, and Wilson looked at him and said:

"Want to take pictures?"

"No," he said.

That was all any one had said until they reached the motor car. Then Wilson had said:

"Hell of a fine lion. Boys will skin him out. We might as well stay here in the shade."

Macomber's wife had not looked at him nor he at her and he had sat by her in the back seat with Wilson sitting in the front seat. Once he had reached over and taken his wife's hand without looking at her and she had removed her hand from his. Looking across the stream to where the gun-bearers were skinning out the lion he could see that she had been able to see the whole thing. While they sat there his wife had reached forward and put her hand on Wilson's shoulder. He turned and she had leaned forward over the low seat and kissed him on the mouth.

"Oh, I say," said Wilson, going redder than his natural baked color.

"Mr. Robert Wilson," she said. "The beautiful red-faced Mr. Robert Wilson."

Then she sat down beside Macomber again and looked away across the stream to where the lion lay, with uplifted, white-muscled, tendon-marked naked forearms, and white bloating belly, as the black men fleshed away the skin. Finally the gun-bearers brought the skin over, wet and heavy, and climbed in behind with it, rolling it up before they got in, and the motor car started. No one had said anything more until they were back in camp.

That was the story of the lion. Macomber did not know how the lion had felt before he started his rush, nor during it when the unbelievable smash of the .505 with a muzzle velocity of two tons had hit him in the mouth, nor what kept him coming after that, when the second dripping crash had smashed his hind quarters and he had come crawling on toward the crashing, blasting thing that had destroyed him. Wilson knew something about it and only expressed it by saying, "Damned fine lion," but Macomber did not know how

Wilson felt about things either. He did not know how his wife felt except that she was through with him.

His wife had been through with him before but it never lasted. He was very wealthy, and would be much wealthier, and he knew she would not leave him ever now. That was one of the few things that he really knew. He knew about that, about motorcycles—that was earliest—about motor cars, about duck-shooting, about fishing, trout, salmon and big-sea, about sex in books, many books, too many books, about all court games, about dogs, not much about horses, about hanging on to his money, about most of the other things his world dealt in, and about his wife not leaving him. His wife had been a great beauty and she was still a great beauty in Africa, but she was not a great enough beauty any more at home to be able to leave him and better herself and she knew it and he knew it. She had missed the chance to leave him and he knew it. If he had been better with women she would probably have started to worry about him getting another new, beautiful wife; but she knew too much about him to worry about him either. Also, he had always had a great tolerance which seemed the nicest thing about him if it were not the most sinister.

All in all they were known as a comparatively happily married couple, one of those whose disruption is often rumored but never occurs, and as the society columnist put it, they were adding more than a spice of *adventure* to their much envied and ever-enduring *Romance* by a *Safari* in what was known as *Darkest Africa* until the Martin Johnsons lighted it on so many silver screens where they were pursuing *Old Simba* the lion, the buffalo, *Tembo* the elephant and as well collecting specimens for the Museum of Natural History. This same columnist had reported them *on the verge* at least three times in the past and they had been. But they always made it up. They had a sound basis of union. Margot was too beautiful for Macomber to divorce her and Macomber had too much money for Margot ever to leave him.

It was now about three o'clock in the morning and Francis Macomber, who had been asleep a little while after he had stopped thinking about the lion, wakened and then slept again, woke suddenly, frightened in a dream of the bloody-headed lion standing over him, and listening while his heart pounded, he realized that his wife was not in the other cot in the tent. He lay awake with that knowledge for two hours.

At the end of that time his wife came into the tent, lifted her mosquito bar and crawled cozily into bed.

"Where have you been?" Macomber asked in the darkness.

"Hello," she said. "Are you awake?"

"Where have you been?"

"I just went out to get a breath of air."

"You did, like hell."

"What do you want me to say, darling?"

"Where have you been?"

"Out to get a breath of air."

"That's a new name for it. You *are* a bitch."

"Well, you're a coward."

"All right," he said. "What of it?"

"Nothing as far as I'm concerned. But please let's not talk, darling, because I'm very sleepy."

"You think that I'll take anything."

"I know you will, sweet."

"Well, I won't."

"Please, darling, let's not talk. I'm so very sleepy."

"There wasn't going to be any of that. You promised there wouldn't be."

"Well, there is now," she said sweetly.

"You said if we made this trip that there would be none of that. You promised."

"Yes, darling. That's the way I meant it to be. But the trip was spoiled yesterday. We don't have to talk about it, do we?"

"You don't wait long when you have an advantage, do you?"

"Please let's not talk. I'm so sleepy, darling."

"I'm going to talk."

"Don't mind me then, because I'm going to sleep." And she did.

At breakfast they were all three at the table before daylight and Francis Macomber found that, of all the men that he had hated, he hated Robert Wilson the most.

"Sleep well?" Wilson asked in his throaty voice, filling a pipe.

"Did you?"

"Topping," the white hunter told him.

You bastard, thought Macomber, you insolent bastard.

So she woke him when she came in, Wilson thought, looking at them both with his flat, cold eyes. Well, why doesn't he keep his wife where she belongs? What does he think I am, a bloody plaster saint? Let him keep her where she belongs. It's his own fault.

"Do you think we'll find buffalo?" Margot asked, pushing away a dish of apricots.

"Chance of it," Wilson said and smiled at her. "Why don't you stay in camp?"

"Not for anything," she told him.

"Why not order her to stay in camp?" Wilson said to Macomber.

"You order her," said Macomber coldly.

"Let's not have any ordering, nor," turning to Macomber, "any silliness, Francis," Margot said quite pleasantly.

"Are you ready to start?" Macomber asked.

"Any time," Wilson told him. "Do you want the Memsahib to go?"

"Does it make any difference whether I do or not?"

The hell with it, thought Robert Wilson. The utter complete hell with it. So this is what it's going to be like. Well, this is what it's going to be like, then.

"Makes no difference," he said.

"You're sure you wouldn't like to stay in camp with her yourself and let me go out and hunt the buffalo?" Macomber asked.

"Can't do that," said Wilson. "Wouldn't talk rot if I were you."

"I'm not talking rot. I'm disgusted."

"Bad word, disgusted."

"Francis, will you please try to speak sensibly?" his wife asked.

"I speak too damned sensibly," Macomber said. "Did you ever eat such filthy food?"

"Something wrong with the food?" asked Wilson quietly.

"No more than with everything else."

"I'd pull yourself together, laddybuck," Wilson said very quietly. "There's a boy waits at table that understands a little English."

"The hell with him."

Wilson stood up and puffing on his pipe strolled away, speaking a few words in Swahili to one of the gun-bearers who was standing waiting for him. Macomber and his wife sat on at the table. He was staring at his coffee cup.

"If you make a scene I'll leave you, darling," Margot said quietly.

"No, you won't."

"You can try it and see."

"You won't leave me."

"No," she said. "I won't leave you and you'll behave yourself."

"Behave myself? That's a way to talk. Behave myself."

"Yes. Behave yourself."

"Why don't *you* try behaving?"

"I've tried it so long. So very long."

"I hate that red-faced swine," Macomber said. "I loathe the sight of him."

"He's really *very* nice."

"Oh, *shut up,*" Macomber almost shouted. Just then the car came up and stopped in front of the dining tent and the driver and the two gun-bearers got out. Wilson walked over and looked at the husband and wife sitting there at the table.

"Going shooting?" he asked.

"Yes," said Macomber, standing up. "Yes."

"Better bring a woolly. It will be cool in the car," Wilson said.

"I'll get my leather jacket," Margot said.

"The boy has it," Wilson told her. He climbed into the front with the driver and Francis Macomber and his wife sat, not speaking, in the back seat.

Hope the silly beggar doesn't take a notion to blow the back of my head off, Wilson thought to himself. Women *are* a nuisance on safari.

The car was grinding down to cross the river at a pebbly ford in the gray daylight and then climbed, angling up the steep bank, where Wilson had ordered a way shovelled out the day before so they could reach the parklike wooded rolling country on the far side.

It was a good morning, Wilson thought. There was a heavy dew and as the wheels went through the grass and low bushes he could smell the odor of the crushed fronds. It was an odor like verbena and he liked this early morning smell of the dew, the crushed bracken and the look of the tree trunks showing black through the early morning mist, as the car made its way through the untracked, parklike country. He had put the two in the back seat out of his mind now and was thinking about buffalo. The buffalo that he was after stayed in the daytime in a thick swamp where it was impossible to get a shot, but in the night they fed out into an open stretch of country and if he could come between them and their swamp with the car, Macomber would have a good chance at them in the open. He did not want to hunt buff with Macomber in thick cover. He did not want to hunt buff or anything else with Macomber at all, but he was a professional hunter and he had hunted with some rare ones in his time. If they got buff today there would only be rhino to come and the poor man would have gone through his dangerous game and things might pick up. He'd have nothing more to do with the woman and Macomber would get over that too. He must have gone through plenty of that before by the look of things. Poor beggar. He must have a way of getting over it. Well, it was the poor sod's own bloody fault.

He, Robert Wilson, carried a double size cot on safari to accommodate any windfalls he might receive. He had hunted for a certain clientele, the international, fast, sporting set, where the women did not feel they were getting their money's worth unless they had shared that cot with the white hunter. He despised them when he was away from them although he liked some of them well enough at the time, but he made his living by them; and their standards were his standards as long as they were hiring him.

They were his standards in all except the shooting. He had his own standards about the killing and they could live up to them or get some one else to hunt them. He knew, too, that they all respected him for this. This Macomber was an odd one though. Damned if he wasn't. Now the wife. Well, the wife. Yes, the wife. Hm, the wife. Well he'd dropped all that. He looked around at them. Macomber sat grim and furious. Margot smiled at him. She looked younger today, more innocent and fresher and not so professionally beautiful. What's in her heart God knows, Wilson thought. She hadn't talked much last night. At that it was a pleasure to see her.

The motor car climbed up a slight rise and went on through the trees and then out into a grassy prairie-like opening and kept in the shelter of the trees along the edge, the driver going slowly and Wilson looking carefully out across the prairie and all along its far side. He stopped the car and studied the opening with his field glasses. Then he motioned to the driver to go on and the car moved slowly along, the driver avoiding wart-hog holes and driving around the mud castles ants had built. Then, looking across the opening, Wilson suddenly turned and said,

"By God, there they are!"

And looking where he pointed, while the car jumped forward and Wilson spoke in rapid Swahili to the driver, Macomber saw three huge, black animals looking almost cylindrical in their long heaviness, like big black tank cars, moving at a gallop across the far edge of the open prairie. They moved at a stiff-necked, stiff bodied gallop and he could see the upswept wide black horns on their heads as they galloped heads out; the heads not moving.

"They're three old bulls," Wilson said. "We'll cut them off before they get to the swamp."

The car was going a wild forty-five miles an hour across the open and as Macomber watched, the buffalo got bigger and bigger until he could see the gray, hairless, scabby look of one huge bull and how his neck was a part of his shoulders and the shiny black of his horns as he galloped a little behind the others that were strung out in that steady plunging gait; and then, the car swaying as though it had just jumped a road, they drew up close and he could see the plunging hugeness of the bull, and the dust in his sparsely haired hide, the wide boss of horn and his outstretched, wide-nostrilled muzzle, and he was raising his rifle when Wilson shouted, "Not from the car, you fool!" and he had no fear, only hatred, of Wilson, while the brakes clamped on and the car skidded, plowing sideways to an almost stop and Wilson was out on one side and he on the other, stumbling as his feet hit the still speeding-by of the earth, and then he was shooting at the bull as he moved away, hearing the bullets whunk into him, emptying his rifle at him as he moved steadily away, finally remembering to get his shots forward into the shoulder, and as he fumbled to re-load, he saw the bull was down. Down on his knees, his big head tossing, and seeing the other two still galloping he shot at the leader and hit him. He shot again and missed and he heard the *carawonging* roar as Wilson shot and saw the leading bull slide forward onto his nose.

"Get that other," Wilson said. "Now you're shooting!"

But the other bull was moving steadily at the same gallop and he missed, throwing a spout of dirt, and Wilson missed and the dust rose in a cloud and Wilson shouted, "Come on. He's too far!" and grabbed his arm and they were in the car again, Macomber and Wilson hanging on the sides and rocketing swayingly over the uneven ground, drawing up on the steady, plunging, heavy-necked, straight-moving gallop of the bull.

They were behind him and Macomber was filling his rifle, dropping shells onto the ground, jamming it, clearing the jam, then they were almost up with the bull when Wilson yelled "Stop," and the car skidded so that it almost swung over and Macomber fell forward onto his feet, slammed his bolt forward and fired as far forward as he could aim into the galloping, rounded black back, aimed and shot again, then again, then again and the bullets, all of them hitting, had no effect on the buffalo that he could see. Then Wilson shot, the roar deafening him, and he could see the bull stagger. Macomber shot again, aiming carefully, and down he came, onto his knees.

"All right," Wilson said. "Nice work. That's the three."

Macomber felt a drunken elation.

"How many times did you shoot?" he asked.

"Just three," Wilson said. "You killed the first bull. The biggest one. I helped you finish the other two. Afraid they might have got into cover. You had them killed. I was just mopping up a little. You shot damn well."

"Let's go to the car," said Macomber. "I want a drink."

"Got to finish off that buff first," Wilson told him. The buffalo was on his knees and he jerked his head furiously and bellowed in pig-eyed, roaring rage as they came toward him.

"Watch he doesn't get up," Wilson said. Then, "Get a little broadside and take him in the neck just behind the ear."

Macomber aimed carefully at the center of the huge, jerking, rage-driven neck and shot. At the shot the head dropped forward.

"That does it," said Wilson. "Got the spine. They're a hell of a looking thing, aren't they?"

"Let's get the drink," said Macomber. In his life he had never felt so good.

In the car Macomber's wife sat very white faced. "You were marvellous, darling," she said to Macomber. "What a ride."

"Was it rough?" Wilson asked.

"It was frightful. I've never been more frightened in my life."

"Let's all have a drink," Macomber said.

"By all means," said Wilson. "Give it to the Memsahib." She drank the neat whisky from the flask and shuddered a little when she swallowed. She handed the flask to Macomber who handed it to Wilson.

"It was frightfully exciting," she said. "It's given me a dreadful headache. I didn't know you were allowed to shoot them from cars though."

"No one shot from cars," said Wilson coldly.

"I mean chase them."

"Wouldn't ordinarily," Wilson said. "Seemed sporting enough to me while we were doing it. Taking more chance driving that way across the plain full of holes and one thing and another than hunting on foot. Buffalo could have charged us each time we shot if he liked. Gave him every chance. Wouldn't mention it to any one though. It's illegal if that's what you mean."

"It seemed very unfair to me," Margot said, "chasing those big helpless things in a motor car."

"Did it?" said Wilson.

"What would happen if they heard about it in Nairobi?"

"I'd lose my licence for one thing. Other unpleasantnesses," Wilson said, aking a drink from the flask. "I'd be out of business."

"Really?"

"Yes, really."

"Well," said Macomber, and he smiled for the first time all day. "Now she has something on you."

"You have such a pretty way of putting things, Francis," Margot Macomber said. Wilson looked at them both. If a four-letter man marries a five-letter woman, he was thinking, what number of letters would their children be? What he said was, "We lost a gun-bearer. Did you notice it?"

"My God, no," Macomber said.

"Here he comes," Wilson said. "He's all right. He must have fallen off when we left the first bull."

Approaching them was the middle-aged gun-bearer, limping along in his knitted cap, khaki tunic, shorts and rubber sandals, gloomy-faced and disgusted looking. As he came up he called out to Wilson in Swahili and they all saw the change in the white hunter's face.

"What does he say?" asked Margot.

"He says the first bull got up and went into the bush," Wilson said with no expression in his voice.

"Oh," said Macomber blankly.

"Then it's going to be just like the lion," said Margot, full of anticipation.

"It's not going to be a damned bit like the lion," Wilson told her. "Did you want another drink, Macomber?"

"Thanks, yes," Macomber said. He expected the feeling he had had about the lion to come back but it did not. For the first time in his life he really felt wholly without fear. Instead of fear he had a feeling of definite elation.

"We'll go and have a look at the second bull," Wilson said. "I'll tell the driver to put the car in the shade."

"What are you going to do?" asked Margot Macomber.

"Take a look at the buff," Wilson said.

"I'll come."

"Come along."

The three of them walked over to where the second buffalo bulked blackly in the open, head forward on the grass, the massive horns swung wide.

"He's a very good head," Wilson said. "That's close to a fifty-inch spread."

Macomber was looking at him with delight.

"He's hateful looking," said Margot. "Can't we go into the shade?"

"Of course," Wilson said. "Look," he said to Macomber, and pointed. "See that patch of bush?"

"Yes."

"That's where the first bull went in. The gun-bearer said when he fell off the bull was down. He was watching us helling along and the other two buff galloping. When he looked up there was the bull up and looking at him. Gun-bearer ran like hell and the bull went off slowly into that bush."

"Can we go in after him now?" asked Macomber eagerly.

Wilson looked at him appraisingly. Damned if this isn't a strange one, he thought. Yesterday he's scared sick and today he's a ruddy fire-eater.

"No, we'll give him a while."

"Let's please go into the shade," Margot said. Her face was white, and she looked ill.

They made their way to the car where it stood under a single, wide-spreading tree and all climbed in.

"Chances are he's dead in there," Wilson remarked. "After a little we'll have a look."

Macomber felt a wild unreasonable happiness that he had never known before.

"By God, that was a chase," he said. "I've never felt any such feeling. Wasn't it marvellous, Margot?"

"I hated it."

"Why?"

"I hated it," she said bitterly. "I loathed it."

"You know I don't think I'd ever be afraid of anything again," Macomber said to Wilson. "Something happened in me after we first saw the buff and started after him. Like a dam bursting. It was pure excitement."

"Cleans out your liver," said Wilson. "Damn funny things happen to people."

Macomber's face was shining. "You know something did happen to me," he said. "I feel absolutely different."

His wife said nothing and eyed him strangely. She was sitting far back in the seat and Macomber was sitting forward talking to Wilson who turned sideways talking over the back of the front seat.

"You know, I'd like to try another lion," Macomber said. "I'm really not afraid of them now. After all, what can they do to you?"

"That's it," said Wilson. "Worst one can do is kill you. How does it go? Shakespeare. Damned good. See if I can remember. Oh, damned good. Used to quote it to myself at one time. Let's see. 'By my troth, I care not; a man can die but once; we owe God a death and let it go which way it will he that dies this year is quit for the next.' Damned fine, eh?"

He was very embarrassed, having brought out this thing he had lived by, but he had seen men come of age before and it always moved him. It was not a matter of their twenty-first birthday.

It had taken a strange chance of hunting, a sudden precipitation into action without opportunity for worrying beforehand, to bring this about with Macomber, but regardless of how it had happened it had most certainly happened. Look at the beggar now, Wilson thought. It's that some of them stay little boys so long, Wilson thought. Sometimes all their lives. Their figures stay boyish when they're fifty. The great American boy-men. Damned strange people. But he liked this Macomber now. Damned strange fellow. Probably meant the end of cuckoldry too. Well, that would be a damned good thing.

Damned good thing. Beggar had probably been afraid all his life. Don't know what started it. But over now. Hadn't had time to be afraid with the buff. That and being angry too. Motor car too. Motor cars made it familiar. Be a damn fire eater now. He'd seen it in the war work the same way. More of a change than any loss of virginity. Fear gone like an operation. Something else grew in its place. Main thing a man had. Made him into a man. Women knew it too. No bloody fear.

From the far corner of the seat Margaret Macomber looked at the two of them. There was no change in Wilson. She saw Wilson as she had seen him the day before when she had first realized what his great talent was. But she saw the change in Francis Macomber now.

"Do you have that feeling of happiness about what's going to happen?" Macomber asked, still exploring his new wealth.

"You're not supposed to mention it," Wilson said, looking in the other's face. "Much more fashionable to say you're scared. Mind you, you'll be scared too, plenty of times."

"But you *have* a feeling of happiness about action to come?"

"Yes," said Wilson. "There's that. Doesn't do to talk too much about all this. Talk the whole thing away. No pleasure in anything if you mouth it up too much."

"You're both talking rot," said Margot. "Just because you've chased some helpless animals in a motor car you talk like heroes."

"Sorry," said Wilson. "I have been gassing too much." She's worried about it already, he thought.

"If you don't know what we're talking about why not keep out of it?" Macomber asked his wife.

"You've gotten awfully brave, awfully suddenly," his wife said contemptuously, but her contempt was not secure. She was very afraid of something.

Macomber laughed, a very natural hearty laugh. "You know I *have,*" he said. "I really have."

"Isn't it sort of late?" Margot said bitterly. Because she had done the best she could for many years back and the way they were together now was no one person's fault.

"Not for me," said Macomber.

Margot said nothing but sat back in the corner of the seat.

"Do you think we've given him time enough?" Macomber asked Wilson cheerfully.

"We might have a look," Wilson said. "Have you any solids left?"

"The gun-bearer has some."

Wilson called in Swahili and the older gun-bearer, who was skinning out one of the heads, straightened up, pulled a box of solids out of his pocket and brought them over to Macomber, who filled his magazine and put the remaining shells in his pocket.

"You might as well shoot the Springfield," Wilson said. "You're used to it.

We'll leave the Mannlicher in the car with the Memsahib. Your gun-bearer can carry your heavy gun. I've this damned cannon. Now let me tell you about them." He had saved this until the last because he did not want to worry Macomber. "When a buff comes he comes with his head high and thrust straight out. The boss of the horns covers any sort of a brain shot. The only shot is straight into the nose. The only other shot is into his chest or, if you're to one side, into the neck or the shoulders. After they've been hit once they take a hell of a lot of killing. Don't try anything fancy. Take the easiest shot there is. They've finished skinning out that head now. Should we get started?"

He called to the gun-bearers, who came up wiping their hands, and the older one got into the back.

"I'll only take Kongoni," Wilson said. "The other can watch to keep the birds away."

As the car moved slowly across the open space toward the island of brushy trees that ran in a tongue of foliage along a dry water course that cut the open swale, Macomber felt his heart pounding and his mouth was dry again, but it was excitement, not fear.

"Here's where he went in," Wilson said. Then to the gun-bearer in Swahili, "Take the blood spoor."

The car was parallel to the patch of bush. Macomber, Wilson and the gun-bearer got down. Macomber, looking back, saw his wife, with the rifle by her side, looking at him. He waved to her and she did not wave back.

The brush was very thick ahead and the ground was dry. The middle-aged gun-bearer was sweating heavily and Wilson had his hat down over his eyes and his red neck showed just ahead of Macomber. Suddenly the gun-bearer said something in Swahili to Wilson and ran forward.

"He's dead in there," Wilson said. "Good work," and he turned to grip Macomber's hand and as they shook hands, grinning at each other, the gun-bearer shouted wildly and they saw him coming out of the bush sideways, fast as a crab, and the bull coming, nose out, mouth tight closed, blood dripping, massive head straight out, coming in a charge, his little pig eyes bloodshot as he looked at them. Wilson, who was ahead, was kneeling shooting, and Macomber, as he fired, unhearing his shot in the roaring of Wilson's gun, saw fragments like slate burst from the huge boss of the horns, and the head jerked, he shot again at the wide nostrils and saw the horn jolt again and fragments fly, and he did not see Wilson now and, aiming carefully, shot again with the buffalo's huge bulk almost on him and his rifle almost level with the on-coming head, nose out, and he could see the little wicked eyes and the head started to lower and he felt a sudden white-hot, blinding flash explode inside his head and that was all he ever felt.

Wilson had ducked to one side to get in a shoulder shot. Macomber had stood solid and shot for the nose, shooting a touch high each time and hitting the heavy horns, splintering and chipping them like hitting a slate roof, and

Mrs. Macomber, in the car, had shot at the buffalo with the 6.5 Mannlicher as it seemed about to gore Macomber and had hit her husband about two inches up and a little to one side of the base of his skull.

Francis Macomber lay now, face down, not two yards from where the buffalo lay on his side and his wife knelt over him with Wilson beside her.

"I wouldn't turn him over," Wilson said.

The woman was crying hysterically.

"I'd get back in the car," Wilson said. "Where's the rifle?"

She shook her head, her face contorted. The gun-bearer picked up the rifle.

"Leave it as it is," said Wilson. Then, "Go get Abdulla so that he may witness the manner of the accident."

He knelt down, took a handkerchief from his pocket, and spread it over Francis Macomber's crew-cropped head where it lay. The blood sank into the dry, loose earth.

Wilson stood up and saw the buffalo on his side, his legs out, his thinly-haired belly crawling with ticks. "Hell of a good bull," his brain registered automatically. "A good fifty inches, or better. Better." He called to the driver and told him to spread a blanket over the body and stay by it. Then he walked over to the motor car where the woman sat crying in the corner.

"That was a pretty thing to do," he said in a toneless voice. "He *would* have left you too."

"Stop it," she said.

"Of course it's an accident," he said. "I know that."

"Stop it," she said.

"Don't worry," he said. "There will be a certain amount of unpleasantness but I will have some photographs taken that will be very useful at the inquest. There's the testimony of the gun-bearers and the driver too. You're perfectly all right."

"Stop it," she said.

"There's a hell of a lot to be done," he said. "And I'll have to send a truck off to the lake to wireless for a plane to take the three of us into Nairobi. Why didn't you poison him? That's what they do in England."

"Stop it. Stop it. Stop it," the woman cried.

Wilson looked at her with his flat blue eyes.

"I'm through now," he said. "I was a little angry. I'd begun to like your husband."

"Oh, please stop it," she said. "Please, please stop it."

"That's better," Wilson said. "Please is much better. Now I'll stop."

ON HEMINGWAY'S
THE SHORT HAPPY LIFE OF FRANCIS MACOMBER[1]

RAY B. WEST, JR.

GERTRUDE STEIN called Ernest Hemingway the spokesman for the "lost generation," and critics have consistently pointed to his early novels as documents of despair and insisted that his early themes stressed the absence of all moral values except the isolated and subjective codes of the individual. "Morals are what you feel good after" is a famous statement from *Death in the Afternoon*. All general statements concerning morality are doubtful. As Frederic Henry says in *A Farewell to Arms;*

> I was always embarrassed by the words sacred, glorious, and sacrifice and the expression in vain . . . and I had seen nothing sacred, and the things that were glorious had no glory and sacrifices were like the stockyards at Chicago if nothing was done with the meat except to bury it.

In the same novel, Frederic sees human life as comparable to ants on the log of a burning campfire. In an early essay, Hemingway wrote:

> The first thing you found out about the dead was that, hit badly enough, they died like animals. Some quickly from a little wound you would not think would kill a rabbit. . . . Others would die like cats; a skull broken in and iron in the brain, they lie alive two days like cats that crawl into the coal bin with a bullet in the brain and will not die until you cut their heads off. Maybe cats do not die then. They say they have nine lives. I do not know, but most men die like animals, not men.

Now a concern with how men die is a concern with human morality. In the image of the ants and in the statement above, it would seem that Ernest Hemingway denies any *human* value to the act of dying. All men die like animals. There is nothing glorious about death in war. Yet the themes of two of the best-known short stories, one early ("The Undefeated") and one late ("The Short Happy Life of Francis Macomber"), express almost the exact opposite. If we examine the latter, we discover that the death of Francis Macomber becomes the symbol of a final victory of Man over Death—a symbolic portrayal of the difference between the death of a man and the death of an animal, and that this concept is clothed in terms of the action through which the characters move.

The action is both simple and complex. It is complex in the sense that it does not begin at the actual beginning of the action but breaks into the middle, then flashes back to the earlier scenes, then picks up and continues to the end. It is simple in that the full course of events can be restated briefly,

1. From "Three Methods of Modern Fiction," *College English* (January, 1951), XII, 194–196. Reprinted by permission of the author and the editor of *College English.*

as follows: Francis Macomber, an American sportsman hunting with his wife in Africa, has earned the contempt of his wife through a display of cowardice on a lion hunt. The situation, however, brings the wife pleasure, because she is no longer in love with her husband, and his violation of the code of the hunter serves to justify her in her desire to violate their marriage contract; that is, it gives her a "moral" advantage over him by releasing her from the conventional obligation of marital fidelity. It also releases the guide, who becomes a party to her infidelity, from his obligation to his own code. When, however, Francis Macomber redeems himself by standing up to a charging water buffalo, the situation is reversed. Macomber regains his advantage over his wife; and she, in her frustration at losing and under the pretense of shooting at the animal, sends a bullet into his brain. Francis Macomber dies at the moment of his victory.

Retold thus, the story retains no remnant of its original power. It is the bare skeleton stripped of raiment. But it is with the skeleton that we are here primarily concerned. As in all successful stories, the framework (the action) is of the proper size and shape and density to fit the raiment (the tone, the style, and the characterization) which adorns it. Unsuccessful stories might be said to give the impression of bodies dressed in unsuitable garments—the sleeves and skirts too long or too short, of the wrong color or combination of colors, or patched with remnants or nonmatching materials to cover holes or to extend to proper lengths.

The details of "The Short Happy Life" fit like the parts of a pattern to form the whole. The action is, to use the term of Eliot, an "objective correlative." To state it another way, the theme is adequately embodied in the action, and it is properly intensified by the other elements. The dominant tone is ironic, and this includes, of course, the famous Hemingway style, by means of which the characters are given depth. The supreme irony appears in the facts of Macomber's death. It comes at the moment of his victory over his wife, as we have said, but this is depicted (expressed through the act itself)—not stated. We are not told that it represents a victory, but we know it as a result of the scene in which the man and the animal are seen lying together in death. For the buffalo, the combat was a mere gesture of self-preservation. For the man it was an attempt to prove his manhood, a conscious and deliberate subjecting of himself to danger, a rational disciplining of his urge to flee. As for Margot Macomber, her final act—the shooting of her husband—is an intuitive recognition of defeat. As a matter of fact, we are not told that she intended to shoot him when she raised the rifle or even that she did do it intentionally. The fine line between intuition and reason is drawn carefully. Our clue to the full meaning of the act is given by the guide, who, in a sense, shares her guilt because of his participation in her act of infidelity, but who, we can be sure, would have acknowledged his error if Francis had survived the hunt: "'That was a pretty thing to do,' he said in a toneless voice. 'He would have left you too.'"

We can restate the action, then, in the following manner: The situation consists of a state of tension between two characters—husband and wife. At the moment when we are first introduced, the wife is shown in a position of dominance over her husband, and this condition is explained through a depiction of the unsuccessful lion hunt and the incident portraying the unfaithfulness of the wife. During the ensuing scenes the situation is reversed by the successful enactment of the buffalo hunt and the final act of murder. On the level of pure action, we might say that Margot Macomber is the victor: she is alive, her husband dead by her hand. The ironic method of the author has, however, made us increasingly aware of a separate and distinct set of values which are presented in ironic counterpoint to the level of actual combat. We are shown the emergence of a value which transcends that of simply existing on the animal level. The final clue is obtained from the title: "The Short Happy Life." Why "short" and why "happy"? The implication is clear—Francis Macomber never really lived until that final moment when he had overcome his own fear of death. Margot Macomber and the buffalo both acted instinctively, that is, like animals. Francis Macomber died the death of a Man.

THE PORTABLE PHONOGRAPH[1]

WALTER VAN TILBURG CLARK

THE RED SUNSET, with narrow, black cloud strips like threats across it, lay on the curved horizon of the prairie. The air was still and cold, and in it settled the mute darkness and greater cold of night. High in the air there was wind, for through the veil of the dusk the clouds could be seen gliding rapidly south and changing shapes. A queer sensation of torment, of two-sided, unpredictable nature, arose from the stillness of the earth air beneath the violence of the upper air. Out of the sunset, through the dead, matted grass and isolated weed stalks of the prairie, crept the narrow and deeply rutted remains of a road. In the road, in places, there were crusts of shallow, brittle ice. There were little islands of an old oiled pavement in the road too, but most of it was mud, now frozen rigid. The frozen mud still bore the toothed impress of great tanks, and a wanderer on the neighboring undulations might have stumbled, in this light, into large, partially filled-in and weed-grown cavities, their banks channelled and beginning to spread into badlands. These pits were such as might have been made by falling meteors, but they were not. They were the scars of gigantic bombs, their rawness already made a little natural by rain, seed, and time. Along the road, there

1. From *The Watchful Gods,* by Walter Van Tilburg Clark. Copyright, 1941, by Walter Van Tilburg Clark. Reprinted by permission of Random House, Inc.

were rakish remnants of fence. There was also, just visible, one portion of tangled and multiple barbed wire still erect, behind which was a shelving ditch with small caves, now very quiet and empty, at intervals in its back wall. Otherwise there was no structure or remnant of a structure visible over the dome of the darkling earth, but only, in sheltered hollows, the darker shadows of young trees trying again.

Under the wuthering arch of the high wind a V of wild geese fled south. The rush of their pinions sounded briefly, and the faint, plaintive notes of their expeditionary talk. Then they left a still greater vacancy. There was the smell and expectation of snow, as there is likely to be when the wild geese fly south. From the remote distance, towards the red sky, came faintly the protracted howl and quick yap-yap of a prairie wolf.

North of the road, perhaps a hundred yards, lay the parallel and deeply intrenched course of a small creek, lined with leafless alders and willows. The creek was already silent under ice. Into the bank above it was dug a sort of cell, with a single opening, like the mouth of a mine tunnel. Within the cell there was a little red of fire, which showed dully through the opening, like a reflection or a deception of the imagination. The light came from the chary burning of four blocks of poorly aged peat, which gave off a petty warmth and much acrid smoke. But the precious remnants of wood, old fence posts and timbers from the long-deserted dugouts, had to be saved for the real cold, for the time when a man's breath blew white, the moisture in his nostrils stiffened at once when he stepped out, and the expansive blizzards paraded for days over the vast open, swirling and settling and thickening, till the dawn of the cleared day when the sky was thin blue-green and the terrible cold, in which a man could not live for three hours unwarmed, lay over the uniformly drifted swell of the plain.

Around the smoldering peat, four men were seated cross-legged. Behind them, traversed by their shadows, was the earth bench, with two old and dirty army blankets, where the owner of the cell slept. In a niche in the opposite wall were a few tin utensils which caught the glint of the coals. The host was rewrapping in a piece of daubed burlap four fine, leather-bound books. He worked slowly and very carefully, and at last tied the bundle securely with a piece of grass-woven cord. The other three looked intently upon the process, as if a great significance lay in it. As the host tied the cord, he spoke. He was an old man, his long, matted beard and hair gray to nearly white. The shadows made his brows and cheekbones appear gnarled, his eyes and cheeks deeply sunken. His big hands, rough with frost and swollen by rheumatism, were awkward but gentle at their task. He was like a prehistoric priest performing a fateful ceremonial rite. Also his voice had in it a suitable quality of deep, reverent despair, yet perhaps at the moment, a sharpness of selfish satisfaction.

"When I perceived what was happening," he said, "I told myself, 'It is the end. I cannot take much; I will take these.' "

"Perhaps I was impractical," he continued. "But for myself, I do not regret, and what do we know of those who will come after us? We are the doddering remnant of a race of mechanical fools. I have saved what I love; the soul of what was good in us is here; perhaps the new ones will make a strong enough beginning not to fall behind when they become clever."

He rose with slow pain and placed the wrapped volumes in the niche with his utensils. The others watched him with the same ritualistic gaze.

"Shakespeare, the Bible, *Moby Dick, The Divine Comedy,*" one of them said softly. "You might have done worse, much worse."

"You will have a little soul left until you die," said another harshly. "That is more than is true of us. My brain becomes thick, like my hands." He held the big, battered hands, with their black nails, in the glow to be seen. "I want paper to write on," he said. "And there is none."

The fourth man said nothing. He sat in the shadow farthest from the fire, and sometimes his body jerked in its rags from the cold. Although he was still young, he was sick and coughed often. Writing implied a greater future than he now felt able to consider.

The old man seated himself laboriously, and reached out, groaning at the movement, to put another block of peat on the fire. With bowed heads and averted eyes, his three guests acknowledged his magnanimity.

"We thank you, Doctor Jenkins, for the reading," said the man who had named the books.

They seemed then to be waiting for something. Doctor Jenkins understood, but was loath to comply. In an ordinary moment he would have said nothing. But the words of *The Tempest,* which he had been reading, and the religious attention of the three made this an unusual occasion.

"You wish to hear the phonograph," he said grudgingly.

The two middle-aged men stared into the fire, unable to formulate and expose the enormity of their desire.

The young man, however, said anxiously, between suppressed coughs, "Oh, please," like an excited child.

The old man rose again in his difficult way, and went to the back of the cell. He returned and placed tenderly upon the packed floor, where the firelight might fall upon it, an old portable phonograph in a black case. He smoothed the top with his hand, and then opened it. The lovely green-felt-covered disk became visible.

"I have been using thorns as needles," he said. "But tonight, because we have a musician among us"—he bent his head to the young man, almost invisible in the shadow—"I will use a steel needle. There are only three left."

The two middle-aged men stared at him in speechless adoration. The one with the big hands, who wanted to write, moved his lips, but the whisper was not audible.

"Oh, don't!" cried the young man, as if he were hurt. "The thorns will do beautifully."

"No," the old man said. "I have become accustomed to the thorns, but they are not really good. For you, my young friend, we will have good music tonight."

"After all," he added generously, and beginning to wind the phonograph, which creaked, "they can't last forever."

"No, nor we," the man who needed to write said harshly. "The needle, by all means."

"Oh, thanks," said the young man. "Thanks," he said again in a low, excited voice, and then stifled his coughing with a bowed head.

"The records, though," said the old man when he had finished winding, "are a different matter. Already they are very worn. I do not play them more than once a week. One, once a week, that is what I allow myself.

"More than a week I cannot stand it; not to hear them," he apologized.

"No, how could you?" cried the young man. "And with them here like this."

"A man can stand anything," said the man who wanted to write, in his harsh, antagonistic voice.

"Please, the music," said the young man.

"Only the one," said the old man. "In the long run, we will remember more that way."

He had a dozen records with luxuriant gold and red seals. Even in that light the others could see that the threads of the records were becoming worn. Slowly he read out the titles and the tremendous dead names of the composers and the artists and the orchestras. The three worked upon the names in their minds, carefully. It was difficult to select from such a wealth what they would at once most like to remember. Finally, the man who wanted to write named Gershwin's "New York."

"Oh, no," cried the sick young man, and then could say nothing more because he had to cough. The others understood him, and the harsh man withdrew his selection and waited for the musician to choose.

The musician begged Doctor Jenkins to read the titles again, very slowly, so that he could remember the sounds. While they were read, he lay back against the wall, his eyes closed, his thin, horny hand pulling at his light beard, and listened to the voices and the orchestras and the single instruments in his mind.

When the reading was done he spoke despairingly. "I have forgotten," he complained; "I cannot hear them clearly.

"There are things missing," he explained.

"I know," said Doctor Jenkins. "I thought that I knew all of Shelley by heart. I should have brought Shelley."

"That's more soul than we can use," said the harsh man. "*Moby Dick* is better."

"By God, we can understand that," he emphasized.

The Doctor nodded.

"Still," said the man who had admired the books, "we need the absolute if we are to keep a grasp on anything.

"Anything but these sticks and peat clods and rabbit snares," he said bitterly.

"Shelley desired an ultimate absolute," said the harsh man. "It's too much," he said. "It's no good; no earthly good."

The musician selected a Debussy nocturne. The others considered and approved. They rose to their knees to watch the Doctor prepare for the playing, so that they appeared to be actually in an attitude of worship. The peat glow showed the thinness of their bearded faces, and the deep lines in them, and revealed the condition of their garments. The other two continued to kneel as the old man carefully lowered the needle onto the spinning disk, but the musician suddenly drew back against the wall again, with his knees up, and buried his face in his hands.

At the first notes of the piano the listeners were startled. They stared at each other. Even the musician lifted his head in amazement, but then quickly bowed it again, strainingly, as if he were suffering from a pain he might not be able to endure. They were all listening deeply, without movement. The wet, blue-green notes tinkled forth from the old machine, and were individual, delectable presences in the cell. The individual, delectable presences swept into a sudden tide of unbearably beautiful dissonance, and then continued fully the swelling and ebbing of that tide, the dissonant inpourings, and the resolutions, and the diminishments, and the little, quiet wavelets of interlude lapping between. Every sound was piercing and singularly sweet. In all the men except the musician, there occurred rapid sequences of tragically heightened recollection. He heard nothing but what was there. At the final, whispering disappearance, but moving quietly so that the others would not hear him and look at him, he let his head fall back in agony, as if it were drawn there by the hair, and clenched the fingers of one hand over his teeth. He sat that way while the others were silent, and until they began to breathe again normally. His drawn-up legs were trembling violently.

Quickly Doctor Jenkins lifted the needle off, to save it and not to spoil the recollection with scraping. When he had stopped the whirling of the sacred disk, he courteously left the phonograph open and by the fire, in sight.

The others, however, understood. The musician rose last, but then abruptly, and went quickly out at the door without saying anything. The others stopped at the door and gave their thanks in low voices. The Doctor nodded magnificently.

"Come again," he invited, "in a week. We will have the 'New York.'"

When the two had gone together, out towards the rimed road, he stood in the entrance, peering and listening. At first, there was only the resonant boom of the wind overhead, and then far over the dome of the dead, dark plain, the wolf cry lamenting. In the rifts of clouds the Doctor saw four stars flying. It impressed the Doctor that one of them had just been obscured by the beginning of a flying cloud at the very moment he heard what he had been listening for, a sound of suppressed coughing. It was not near-by, however. He believed that down against the pale alders he could see the moving shadow.

With nervous hands he lowered the piece of canvas which served as his door, and pegged it at the bottom. Then quickly and quietly, looking at the piece of canvas frequently, he slipped the records into the case, snapped the lid shut, and carried the phonograph to his couch. There, pausing often to stare at the canvas and listen, he dug earth from the wall and disclosed a piece of board. Behind this there was a deep hole in the wall, into which he put the phonograph. After a moment's consideration, he went over and reached down his bundle of books and inserted it also. Then, guardedly, he once more sealed up the hole with the board and the earth. He also changed his blankets, and the grass-stuffed sack which served as a pillow, so that he could lie facing the entrance. After carefully placing two more blocks of peat upon the fire, he stood for a long time watching the stretched canvas, but it seemed to billow naturally with the first gusts of a lowering wind. At last he prayed, and got in under his blankets, and closed his smoke-smarting eyes. On the inside of the bed, next the wall, he could feel with his hand the comfortable piece of lead pipe.

ON CLARK'S *THE PORTABLE PHONOGRAPH:* THE GHOST OF AN APPREHENSION[1]

WALTER VAN TILBURG CLARK

SINCE the story took place in my mind somewhat as a play might, the intention producing the scene, the scene and the intention selecting the cast, and all three, by means of certain guiding principles which developed with them, dictating the action, and since its approach has occured often with me, in novels as well as in stories, it will help both to shape the discussion to follow and in a measure to widen its application, if we put the synopsis itself into something like dramatic form. To brief the brief, then (the story is only eight pages long):

THE SCENE. Interior of a dugout above a creek thinly lined with alders. A small, smoky, peat fire in the center. In one wall a niche containing a few battered cooking utensils. In the opposite wall an earth bunk with two old army blankets on it. Above the entrance, a rolled canvas, which is the door. Outside (the back-drop, so to speak) a desolate prairie, pitted by craters and

1. Reprinted from *The Pacific Spectator* by permission of the author.

grooved by the frozen ruts of huge wheels and caterpillar treads. Here and there a remnant of highway pavement, a spidery entanglement of barbed wire, and, in the depressions, a few small, shadowy trees. On the far horizon, a red sunset with bars of black cloud across it. Overhead, changing clouds gliding rapidly south before a high, booming wind. A single wedge of wild geese passes over, going southward more swiftly than the clouds and conversing faintly among themselves. A prairie wolf yaps in the distance. There is no other sound or motion. The air near the ground is still and full of the cold promise of winter.

THE CAST. Four men, all dirty, ragged, and bearded: Dr. Jenkins, a former professor and the host, and three visitors: a powerful, sardonic man, once a writer; a polite, conciliatory soul, whose past is not revealed; and a very thin, nervous young man with a bad cough, who has been a musician. The writer and the conciliatory soul have evidently been here before, though not often, but the musician is making his first call.

THE ACTION. Dr. Jenkins has just finished reading *The Tempest* aloud, and while he wraps up his library, Shakespeare, the Bible, *The Divine Comedy,* and *Moby Dick,* is discussing with the writer and the anonymous one, the present, and possibly future, worth of the books. When he has put the books into the niche with the pots, there is a brief, coercive silence, after which he reluctantly produces an old portable phonograph and twelve records. They may hear one record; one record, once a week, is his rule. He reads the titles. A Gershwin named by the writer is rejected as too sharp a reminder. The musician is given the choice, and after hearing the titles again, and complaining that there are parts he can't remember, he selects a Debussy nocturne. Dr. Jenkins, in a sudden, penitent gesture, takes out one of his three remaining steel needles, though he has been using thorns himself. The visitors rise to their knees in a reverent semicircle to watch him insert the needle and set the record on. At the first note of the piano, however, the musician shrinks back against the wall, where he struggles silently against his cough and the agony of hearing music again.

When the record is finished, the visitors rise. The musician is the last to rise, but then he goes out at once, without a word. The other two leave more slowly and formally. Dr. Jenkins lingers in the doorway, peering down into the dusk and listening. At last, just as a cloud erases one of four visible stars, he hears a faint cough from down among the alders. He lowers the canvas and pegs it down, and puts the phonograph and records, and then the books too, into a hole above the bunk and seals them in. After changing his blankets around so that he will lie facing the door, and putting more fuel on the fire, he stands watching the canvas again. Still only the wind, which has at last come down to earth, moves it. He prays and gets under his blankets, where, "On the inside of the bed, next the wall, he could feel with his hand the comfortable piece of lead pipe."

Even so brief a retelling, when we remember that the story first appeared in the fall of 1941, suggests fully enough all we need to know about the apprehension which was the source of the idea. It also brings us at once to the crux of the writing problem, for it was just the very universality of that apprehension which placed the severest strictures upon the design of the story, and so compelled me, in the first stage, to formulate the guiding principles already mentioned.

Clearly I could justify the use of such a theme only by bringing that universal apprehension into sharp focus, by so heightening the reader's reaction to what he already knew and feared as to make the vaguely possible into the concretely probable. Gradually it became evident that the means to such a concentration and heightening must be three. First, if I were to avoid the flavor of Wellsian prophecy, the great apprehension itself must be touched upon lightly and indirectly, must be little more than a taken-for-granted backdrop. Secondly, the incident played against that backdrop, and the characters engaged in it, had to be highly credible, not in terms of their situation, but in terms of an everyday American life. In short, it didn't seem to me that the desired tone could be achieved in the key of either the incident or the scene alone, but that it must arise out of the dissonant juxtaposition of the two. And finally, the manner of the story had to convey the same contrast, had to be fiddle light on the surface and bass viol deep beneath, which is to say, it had to be satirical. One cannot afford to speak seriously of the end of the world. All of these necessities, the minor and credible activity, presented against a background of doom, in a manner calculated to sustain the dissonance, added up, of course, to a very short story. One does not strain a joke about the end of the world, either.

I didn't, naturally, start with a notion of saying something about the finality of modern war, and out of that melancholy fog evolve a set of rules, and out of them a story. The process was not that orderly. First, I just began to write. I can't remember exactly what set me off. Probably it was some intensifying item of the day's news, stirring me when I had time to sit and brood on it until I had to get rid of the emotion it built up, and the first, suggestive images began to appear. Almost always, whatever may have been working up to it in my mind, recognized and unrecognized, it is some image suddenly coming alive and suggesting more to follow, or to precede, that makes me reach for a pencil. In this case it was the prairie, the vast, desolated backdrop of the dugout, which first appeared, accompanied by a feeling that such a scene implied in itself all that one could afford to say directly about a final war. In short, the critical process began with the creative, and by the time I had completed the introductory description (a slow procedure, involving much cutting, rewriting, and rearranging) the controlling principles, more or less as I have stated them, were already in full operation, the cast had appeared and been approved, and the incident had arisen out of their gathering. The story was finished, except for putting it down, which meant little more than keeping an ear open for that desirable dissonance.

The prairie first appeared blackened by old fires, full of shell craters, deeply scored everywhere by the tracks of enormous tank battles and the vestiges of hopeless entrenchment, and devoid of all present signs of human life. There were no houses, or even shells of houses, no barns, no windmills, no fences, no recognizable fields or even stubs of groves or orchards. It was bare as the moon. It suggested a warfare of almost cosmic proportions (since Hiroshima, we can delete the "almost") which was what I wanted, and it suggested also, that a good deal of time had passed since the battle. That hint of time softening the edges of all detail, but unable to restore anything, made the destruction even more final, and sufficiently indicated, it seemed to me, that the survivors necessary to the story must be so few, and so far set back, as to be without hope or use. But then I saw that the mooniness was too complete, and could just as well mean a region that had always been desert as it could the ruin of a productive region. Yet it seemed wrong to name the place, and I still didn't want any skeletons of building against the sky. I preferred that tundralike emptiness stretching away to the western horizon. (I was looking west, perhaps because Americans have that habit, perhaps because the war we most dreaded was raging in Europe, and so, in the story, would have gone across America westward, but probably just because the scene had first appeared in an end-of-day light, and one would naturally be looking toward the sunset.) So there appeared the broken remnants of a highway as unobtrusive tokens of the past. Clearer signs of time elapsed since the fighting were also needed, yet signs which would not too much relieve the sterility of the earth, so there grew up the sparse lines of willows and alders in the trenches and creek beds, and the stunted, new trees in the craters.

Sometime during its first viewing, though I avoided the narrowing effect of a name (the nature of the land, and the fact that the four men were unquestionably American, seemed enough in the way of location) the region became definitely the American Middle West, because it spread the devastation over the whole world to show the heart of the most isolated major power swept over, and the grain lands gone in a warfare which concentrated on cities. It made the place not only a field of the final war, but the final field as well.

Late autumn became the necessary time of year, the last season before the complete death and the somehow healing secrecy of winter, just as sunset, the last hour of vision before the secrecy of night, was the proper time of day. To begin with, the sky had been cloudless, the sunset one of those infinitely penetrable, green-gold fadings that come with cold, but now such a horizon seemed too peaceful, and even suggestive of hope. There had to be some motion in that inert landscape, some threat in the sky. So that clouds formed, moving in a wintry wind, and the sunset turned red, and then, although that came as an afterthought, in part because the professor had to hear that last faint cough down in the alders, the unmoving lower air settled in. The chief intent was that the dissonance of the two regions of air should furnish a physical lead into the moral dissonance of the action, and also that it should reinforce the threat of the black clouds across the sunset, suggest apprehension by ear and skin as well as by eye. Finally, for by now the story was fully in view, some touch of conscious life was needed, by which to move from the backdrop into the play. Hence, as also maintaining the mood, the far-off yapping of the wolf, unheard in those parts for generations, and the brief, almost invisible passage of the geese, unconcerned with the land except as a distance to get over.

The action of the story, prepared all during the arranging and rearranging of this backdrop, moved forward so swiftly, almost automatically, in its details, as to be now largely beyond recall. I do remember the vital factors of the preparation, however. I remember that the cast first appeared to me as three in number, the three who became the professor, the writer, and the musician; that they were all men because even one woman might imply a future; and that they became men of highly mental pasts because that rendered them more nearly helpless, increased their recession, and made it more likely that they would retain the necessary surface of polite conduct. I remember also that the three men first came together in the open, around a wood fire down by the creek, but that somehow nothing would happen among them there. The size and finality of the setting shrank them and paralyzed them with futility. I could not even seem to discover any reason for their bothering to get together, save an animal loneliness which had no dramatic potential except through a much longer development than I could afford. When at last it became clear that it was the scene which rendered them so unusable, the dugout, as in keeping with the tank tracks and the barbed wire, appeared in the bank behind me, and we moved into it. That was all it took. The men not only came alive, but swelled to more than life-size, filling the little cave enormously, assuming the importance for me that they had for each other, and setting the lifeless prairie away into its proper backdrop perspective. The vestigial touches of homemaking effort became possible: the few and battered utensils, kept in a niche, like a saint; the peat fire and the earthen bunk, hinting of a nearly woodless world; the army blankets and the canvas. Also, the home made necessary the host, and the professor, as likely to be the most provident and the most chairmanly, at once assumed that role, and with it his manner and his more numerous years. Indeed it was only then that he certainly became a professor, a kind of epitome of civilized man in his most familiar form, suggesting thereby a great deal through his mere presence in a cave.

When the fragments of possible conversation among the three men, the professor, the writer, and a third who was for a time alternately a painter and a musician, began to occur in the midst of the backdrop details, I shortly felt the need of a fourth man, not only because I sensed that the musician-painter was going to be nearly inarticulate, and, for the sake of variety and interplay, three speakers were preferable to two, but also because the trio was a bit too patly symbolic, and so likely to resist the individualization without which they couldn't convince. (The writer was first seen as a sculptor—which has something to do with the physical characteristics he retained—but changed his profession, partly for the same reason, to break up the rigid one-two-three alignment by drawing nearer to the professor's interests, making a one-two grouping, and partly because it better suited the intent of the tale that he should be thwarted by an absence of that so-common commodity, paper. Of clay there would still be aplenty.) So the fourth man joined the group, the man with the unknown past, the representative of the great, departed audience whose need had produced the specialists. He was a real help, for not only did he relieve the stiffness of the allegory, but he also furnished a contrasting attitude, a second psychological level, being a trifle deferential in the presence of the more specific abilities of the others, but also more resigned because his individual needs were less acute. He was, in short, different in kind, whereas the other three, all upon one level of bolder individuality, were different only in particulars: the harsh cynicism of the frustrated writer; the advanced tuberculosis which makes time so important to the musician; the grave, reluctant, orderly air of the professor. Furthermore, I believe that I had found in him another sufficiently concealed means to irony, for his deference was, of course, wholly pointless in that place and time, a mere hang-over from an irrecoverable social pattern, and yet it was just that trace of deference, that touch of the conciliatory, that held together, by its remnant of drawing-room conduct, a group that otherwise would almost certainly have broken into an undesirable violence.

Once we were in the dugout, and the anonymous fourth had entered, there seemed to be only one thing lacking, that precipitating agent which would settle the whole narrative out in visible form, the reason for the gathering. I cannot remember how many reasons I fleetingly considered off the top of my mind while I completed the backdrop and caught unusable but suggestive glimpses of the civilized pasts of the men. (The professor, for instance, had taught English in a Midwestern college, specializing in Victorian Literature, but had a wide range of interests beyond that. He had lived in a small, white, frame house, with vines on the front porch, and a dark, somewhat stuffy study in it, with heavy rugs, too much furniture, and the walls lined with books, mostly old and worn, but here and there in bright, new bindings or dust jackets. He had two children, but both were grown and away from home, and he was rather lonely, because he had retired just a couple of years before the war, and his wife, a plump, bespectacled woman, although a fine mother and housekeeper, did not share any of his intellectual interests.) I remember very clearly, however, that the happiest moment of the whole preliminary came with the discovery of the portable phonograph. Beyond question it was the very object, the key symbol, for which I'd been hunting ever since my first dusky glimpse of the prairie. It was portable, which was important. It would seem valuable enough to such a man as the professor, to be worth carrying off in a crisis. It was a universally familiar object, and so would derive its dramatic virtue entirely from its present rarity. In its combined material inconsequence—for certainly it was one of the lesser gadgets of our abundantly gadgeted civilization—and spiritual consequence, as the only remaining vehicle of perhaps the highest achievement of mind and emotion of that same civilization, it became the very centerpiece of the desired dissonance, the touchstone for action and language. The title arrived with it, of course. In its presence, the relationships of the cast were rapidly established. It became evident that the small, suppressed element of conflict that was needed must spring from it and from the music it produced. As a result, the musician at once assumed the brief future that would make him desperate, and became certainly a musician rather than a painter, and also the newcomer, the stranger in the group, the man in whom the restraint of association would play the smallest part and the hunger for music the greatest. At once, also, the professor, as the owner of the treasure, became the antagonist. To all intents the story was complete.

There remained only to discover a valid and contributory means of prolonging, though backwards, into the hours before the tale opens, a meeting which would otherwise be incredibly brief, and which could not, obviously, be extended by eating and drinking. Books were beyond question the means, and certainly, in this context, the reasons for selecting the four the professor had brought with him are equally clear, at least by the time the writer has spoken of *Moby Dick* as something they can all understand now (he might usefully have dropped a word about Ishmael's coffin-boat) and added that Shelley had too much soul, and was "no earthly good." Nor is there any mystery about his selecting *The Tempest* for the reading, once we realize that Caliban and Ariel are at it again over the portable phonograph. The act of reading and the reverence accorded the books serve also as a kind of induction to the high sacrament of the music, in which the professor becomes the priest of a doomed faith and the visitors literally assume kneeling positions around the phonograph.

It is intended that the conclusion should leave with the reader a sense of unity, of the opening dissonance resolved, though not into peace, but rather by means, gently, gently, of almost entirely reducing the professor to the cave man, blending him, as it were, into the terrible landscape. As he stands suspiciously in the doorway, after the guests have departed, he sees, at the very instant he hears the coughing down in the alders, one of four bright stars suddenly hidden by a cloud. It is a sufficient sign to the primitive credulity revived in him, and indirectly, we hope, in the reader. Then also, as he stands watching the canvas he has pegged down, it is moved by "the first gusts of a lowering wind." The opening dissonance between the wuthering upper air and the still ground air is also resolved, and again, as in the case of the human dissonance, by suggesting an end, by bringing winter to the door. Yet, in the last line, as the professor lies on the earth bench, facing the billowing canvas, "On the inside of the bed, next the wall, he could feel with his hand the comfortable piece of lead pipe." His weapon still comes from that lost world of gadgets. He cannot bring even violence to the level of the new—the very old—world in which he now lives. And of course futility, in any but the meanest and most temporary sense, attends the defense for which he is prepared.

It seemed to me that sentence plucked the proper closing note, one that might linger for a time with a tenuous but moving reminder of the whole intention. If so, it was so, happily, by means of the very last phrase, and particularly by means of the one word "comfortable." Nothing in the phrase was considered, not "comfortable" any more than the rest, but even as it came, that "comfortable" tickled me, not so much because of its immediate implication, in which the paradox was clear enough, as for some more remote, redoubling connotation which I could not, at the moment, catch hold of. Then, a few seconds after I had poked home the final period, it came to me. I had done a bit of lucky thieving from Bill of Avon. (Perhaps the professor's volume of Shakespeare had put it out handy for the borrowing.) Remember how Juliet, waking in the tomb, and not yet aware that Romeo is dead, murmurs drowsily to the gentle Friar Lawrence, "Oh, comfortable Friar—"? Oh, poor professor, with only his lead pipe. And I was sure that at least the ghost of that old, warm, trusting "comfortable" would lurk to trouble the reader as it had troubled me. Nor could I feel, considering the grim little twist I had given it, that Bill would begrudge me his word. After all, he was no mean shakes of a borrower himself.

THE EIGHTY-YARD RUN[1]

IRWIN SHAW

THE PASS was high and wide and he jumped for it, feeling it slap flatly against his hands, as he shook his hips to throw off the halfback who was diving at him. The center floated by, his hands desperately brushing Darling's knee as Darling picked his feet up high and delicately ran over a blocker and an opposing linesman in a jumble on the ground near the scrimmage line. He had ten yards in the clear and picked up speed, breathing easily, feeling his thigh pads rising and falling against his legs, listening to the sound of cleats behind him, pulling away from them, watching the other backs heading him off toward the sideline, the whole picture, the men closing in

1. From *Welcome to the City* (New York: Random House, Inc., 1942). Copyright, 1938, by Irwin Shaw. Reprinted by permission of the author.

onimata poeta

on him, the blockers fighting for position, the ground he had to cross, all suddenly clear in his head, for the first time in his life not a meaningless confusion of men, sounds, speed. He smiled a little to himself as he ran, holding the ball lightly in front of him with his two hands, his knees pumping high, his hips twisting in the almost-girlish run of a back in a broken field. The first halfback came at him and he fed him his leg, then swung at the last moment, took the shock of the man's shoulder without breaking stride, ran right through him, his cleats biting securely into the turf. There was only the safety man now, coming warily at him, his arms crooked, hands spread. Darling tucked the ball in, spurted at him, driving hard, hurling himself along, his legs pounding, knees high, all two hundred pounds bunched into controlled attack. He was sure he was going to get past the safety man. Without thought, his arms and legs working beautifully together, he headed right for the safety man, stiff-armed him, feeling blood spurt instantaneously from the man's nose onto his hand, seeing his face go awry, head turned, mouth pulled to one side. He pivoted away, keeping the arm locked, dropping the safety man as he ran easily toward the goal line, with the drumming of cleats diminishing behind him.

How long ago? It was autumn then and the ground was getting hard because the nights were cold and leaves from the maples around the stadium blew across the practice fields in gusts of wind and the girls were beginning to put polo coats over their sweaters when they came to watch practice in the afternoons . . . Fifteen years. Darling walked slowly over the same ground in the spring twilight, in his neat shoes, a man of thirty-five dressed in a double-breasted suit, ten pounds heavier in the fifteen years, but not fat, with the years between 1925 and 1940 showing in his face.

The coach was smiling quietly to himself and the assistant coaches were looking at each other with pleasure the way they always did when one of the second stringers suddenly did something fine, bringing credit to them, making their $2,000 a year a tiny bit more secure.

Darling trotted back, smiling, breathing deeply but easily, feeling wonderful, not tired, though this was the tail end of practice and he'd run eighty yards. The sweat poured off his face and soaked his jersey and he liked the feeling, the warm moistness lubricating his skin like oil. Off in a corner of the field some players were punting and the smack of leather against the ball came pleasantly through the afternoon air. The freshmen were running signals on the next field and the quarterback's sharp voice, the pound of the eleven pairs of cleats, the "Dig, now, *dig!*" of the coaches, the laughter of the players all somehow made him feel happy as he trotted back to midfield, listening to the applause and shouts of the students along the sidelines, knowing that after that run the coach would have to start him Saturday against Illinois.

Fifteen years, Darling thought, remembering the shower after the workout, the hot water steaming off his skin and the deep soapsuds and all the young voices singing with the water streaming down and towels going and managers running in and out and the sharp sweet smell of oil of wintergreen and everybody clapping him on the back as he dressed and Packard, the captain, who took being captain very seriously, coming over to him and shaking his hand saying, "Darling, you're going to go places in the next two years."

The assistant manager fussed over him, wiping a cut on his leg with alcohol and iodine, the little sting making him realize suddenly how fresh and whole and solid his body felt. The manager slapped a piece of adhesive tape over the cut and Darling noticed the sharp clean white of the tape against the ruddiness of the skin, fresh from the shower.

He dressed slowly, the softness of his shirt and the soft warmth of his wool socks and his flannel trousers a reward against his skin after the harsh pressure of the shoulder harness and thigh and hip pads. He drank three glasses of cold water, the liquid reaching down coldly inside of him, soothing the harsh dry places in his throat and belly left by the sweat and running and shouting of practice.

Fifteen years.

The sun had gone down and the sky was green behind the stadium and he laughed quietly to himself as he looked at the stadium, rearing above the tree, and knew that on Saturday when the 70,000 voices roared as the team came running out onto the field, part of that enormous salute would be for him. He walked slowly, listening to the gravel crunch satisfactorily under his toes in the still twilight, feeling his clothes swing lightly against his skin, breathing the thin evening air, feeling the wind move softly in his damp hair, wonderfully cool behind his ears and at the nape of his neck.

Louise was waiting for him at the road, in her car. The top was down and he noticed all over again, as he always did when he saw her, how pretty she was, the rough blonde hair and the large, inquiring eyes and the bright mouth, smiling now.

She threw the door open. "Were you good today?" she asked.

"Pretty good," he said. He climbed in, sank luxuriously into the soft leather, stretched his legs far out. He smiled, thinking of the eighty yards. "Pretty damn good."

She looked at him seriously for a moment, then scrambled around, like a little girl, kneeling on the seat next to him, grabbed him, her hands along his ears, and kissed him as he sprawled, head back, on the seat cushion. She let go of him, but kept her head close to his, over his. Darling reached up slowly and rubbed the back of his hand against her cheek, lit softly by a street lamp a hundred feet away. They looked at each other, smiling.

Louise drove down to the lake and they sat there silently, watching the moon rise behind the hills on the other side. Finally he reached over, pulled her gently to him, kissed her. Her lips grew soft, her body sank into his, tears formed in her eyes. He knew, for the first time, that he could do whatever he wanted with her.

"Tonight," he said. "I'll call for you at seven-thirty. Can you get out?"

She looked at him. She was smiling, but the tears were still full in her eyes. "All right," she said. "I'll get out. How about you? Won't the coach raise hell?"

Darling grinned. "I got the coach in the palm of my hand," he said. "Can you wait till seven-thirty?"

She grinned back at him. "No," she said.

They kissed and she started the car and they went back to town for dinner. He sang on the way home.

Christian Darling, thirty-five years old, sat on the frail spring grass, greener now than it ever would be again on the practice field, looked thoughtfully up at the stadium, a deserted ruin in the twilight. He had started on the first team that Saturday and every Saturday after that for the next two years, but it had never been as satisfactory as it should have been. He never had broken away, the longest run he'd ever made was thirty-five yards, and that in a game that was already won, and then that kid had come up from the third team, Diederich, a blank-faced German kid from Wisconsin, who ran like a bull, ripping lines to pieces Saturday after Saturday, plowing through, never getting hurt, never changing his expression, scoring more points, gaining more ground than all the rest of the team put together, making everybody's All-American, carrying the ball three times out of four, keeping everybody else out of the headlines. Darling was a good blocker and he spent his Saturday afternoons working on the big Swedes and Polacks who played tackle and end for Michigan, Illinois, Purdue, hurling into huge pile-ups, bobbing his head wildly to elude the great raw hands swinging like meat-cleavers at him as he went charging in to open up holes for Diederich coming through like a locomotive behind him. Still, it wasn't so bad. Everybody liked him and he did his job and he was pointed out on the campus and boys always felt important when they introduced their girls to him at their proms, and Louise loved him and watched him faithfully in the games, even in the mud, when your own mother wouldn't know you, and drove him around in her car keeping the top down because she was proud of him and wanted to show everybody that she was Christian Darling's girl. She bought him crazy presents because her father was rich, watches, pipes, humidors, an icebox for beer for his room, curtains, wallets, a fifty-dollar dictionary.

"You'll spend every cent your old man owns," Darling protested once when she showed up at his room with seven different packages in her arms and tossed them onto the couch.

"Kiss me," Louise said, "and shut up."

"Do you want to break your poor old man?"

"I don't mind. I want to buy you presents."

"Why?"

"It makes me feel good. Kiss me. I don't know why. Did you know that you're an important figure?"

"Yes," Darling said gravely.

"When I was waiting for you at the library yesterday two girls saw you coming and one of them said to the other, 'That's Christian Darling. He's an important figure.'"

"You're a liar."

"I'm in love with an important figure."

"Still, why the hell did you have to give me a forty-pound dictionary?"

"I wanted to make sure," Louise said, "that you had a token of my esteem. I want to smother you in tokens of my esteem."

Fifteen years ago.

They'd married when they got out of college. There'd been other women for him, but all casual and secret, more for curiosity's sake, and vanity, women who'd thrown themselves at him and flattered him, a pretty mother at a summer camp for boys, an old girl from his home town who'd suddenly blossomed into a coquette, a friend of Louise's who had dogged him grimly for six months and had taken advantage of the two weeks when Louise went home when her mother died. Perhaps Louise had known, but she'd kept quiet, loving him completely, filling his rooms with presents, religiously watching him battling with the big Swedes and Polacks on the line of scrimmage on Saturday afternoons, making plans for marrying him and living with him in New York and going with him there to the nightclubs, the theatres, the good restaurants, being proud of him in advance, tall, white-teethed, smiling, large, yet moving lightly, with an athlete's grace, dressed in evening clothes, approvingly eyed by magnificently dressed and famous women in theatre lobbies, with Louise adoringly at his side.

Her father, who manufactured inks, set up a New York office for Darling to manage and presented him with three hundred accounts and they lived on Beekman Place with a view of the river with fifteen thousand dollars a year between them, because everybody was buying everything in those days, including ink. They saw all the shows and went to all the speakeasies and spent their fifteen thousand dollars a year and in the afternoons Louise went to the art galleries and the matinees of the more serious plays that Darling didn't like to sit through and Darling slept with a girl who danced in the chorus of *Rosalie* and with the wife of a man who owned three copper mines. Darling played squash three times a week and remained as solid as a stone barn and Louise never took her eyes off him when they were in the same room together, watching him with a secret, miser's smile, with a trick of coming over to him in the middle of a crowded room and saying gravely, in a low voice, "You're the handsomest man I've ever seen in my whole life. Want a drink?"

Nineteen twenty-nine came to Darling and to his wife and father-in-law, the maker of inks, just as it came to everyone else. The father-in-law waited until 1933 and then blew his brains out and when Darling went to Chicago to see what the books of the firm looked like he found out all that was left were debts and three or four gallons of unbought ink.

"Please, Christian," Louise said, sitting in their neat Beekman Place apartment, with a view of the river and prints of paintings by Dufy and Braque and Picasso on the wall, "please, why do you want to start drinking at two o'clock in the afternoon?"

"I have nothing else to do," Darling said, putting down his glass, emptied of its fourth drink. "Please pass the whiskey."

Louise filled his glass. "Come take a walk with me," she said. "We'll walk along the river."

"I don't want to walk along the river," Darling said, squinting intensely at the prints of paintings by Dufy, Braque and Picasso.

"We'll walk along Fifth Avenue."

"I don't want to walk along Fifth Avenue."

"Maybe," Louise said gently, "you'd like to come with me to some art galleries. There's an exhibition by a man named Klee—"

"I don't want to go to any art galleries. I want to sit here and drink Scotch whiskey," Darling said. "Who the hell hung those goddam pictures on the wall?"

"I did," Louise said.

"I hate them."

"I'll take them down," Louise said.

"Leave them there. It gives me something to do in the afternoon. I can hate them." Darling took a swallow. "Is that the way people paint these days?"

"Yes, Christian. Please don't drink any more."

"Do you like painting like that?"

"Yes, dear."

"Really?"

"Really."

Darling looked carefully at the prints once more. "Little Louise Tucker. The middle-western beauty. I like pictures with horses in them. Why should you like pictures like that?"

"I just happen to have gone to a lot of galleries in the last few years . . ."

"Is that what you do in the afternoon?"

"That's what I do in the afternoon," Louise said.

"I drink in the afternoon."

Louise kissed him lightly on the top of his head as he sat there squinting at the pictures on the wall, the glass of whiskey held firmly in his hand. She put on her coat and went out without saying another word. When she came back in the evening, she had a job on a woman's fashion magazine.

They moved downtown and Louise went out to work every morning and

Darling sat home and drank and Louise paid the bills as they came up. She made believe she was going to quit work as soon as Darling found a job, even though she was taking over more responsibility day by day at the magazine, interviewing authors, picking painters for the illustrations and covers, getting actresses to pose for pictures, going out for drinks with the right people, making a thousand new friends whom she loyally introduced to Darling.

"I don't like your hat," Darling said once, when she came in in the evening and kissed him, her breath rich with Martinis.

"What's the matter with my hat, Baby?" she asked, running her fingers through his hair. "Everybody says it's very smart."

"It's too damned smart," he said. "It's not for you. It's for a rich, sophisticated woman of thirty-five with admirers."

Louise laughed. "I'm practicing to be a rich, sophisticated woman of thirty-five with admirers," she said. He stared soberly at her. "Now, don't look so grim, Baby. It's still the same simple little wife under the hat." She took the hat off, threw it into a corner, sat on his lap. "See? Homebody Number One."

"Your breath could run a train," Darling said, not wanting to be mean, but talking out of boredom, and sudden shock at seeing his wife curiously a stranger in a new hat, with a new expression in her eyes under the little brim, secret, confident, knowing.

Louise tucked her head under his chin so he couldn't smell her breath. "I had to take an author out for cocktails," she said. "He's a boy from the Ozark mountains and he drinks like a fish. He's a Communist."

"What the hell is a Communist from the Ozarks doing writing for a woman's fashion magazine?"

Louise chuckled. "The magazine business is getting all mixed up these days. The publishers want to have a foot in every camp. And anyway, you can't find an author under seventy these days who isn't a Communist."

"I don't think I like you to associate with all those people, Louise," Darling said. "Drinking with them."

"He's a very nice, gentle boy," Louise said. "He reads Ernest Dobson."

"Who's Ernest Dobson?"

Louise patted his arm, stood up, fixed her hair. "He's an English poet."

Darling felt that somehow he had disappointed her. "Am I supposed to know who Ernest Dobson is?"

"No, dear. I'd better go in and take a bath."

After she had gone, Darling went over to the corner where the hat was lying and picked it up. It was nothing, a scrap of straw, a red flower, a veil, meaningless on his big hand, but on his wife's head a signal of something . . . big city, smart and knowing women drinking and dining with men other than their husbands, conversation about things a normal man wouldn't know much about, Frenchmen who painted as though they used their elbows instead of brushes, composers who wrote whole symphonies without a single melody in them, writers who knew all about politics and women who knew all about writers, the movement of the proletariat, Marx, somehow mixed up with five-dollar dinners and the best looking women in America and fairies who made them laugh and half-sentences immediately understood and secretly hilarious and wives who called their husbands "Baby." He put the hat down, a scrap of straw and a red flower, and a little veil. He drank some whiskey straight and went into the bathroom where his wife was lying deep in her bath, singing to herself and smiling from time to time like a little girl, paddling the water gently with her hands, sending up a slight spicy fragrance from the bath-salts she used.

He stood over her, looking down at her. She smiled up at him, her eyes half closed, her body pink and shimmering in the warm, scented water. All over again, with all the old suddenness, he was hit deep inside him with the knowledge of how beautiful she was, how much he needed her.

"I came in here," he said, "to tell you I wish you wouldn't call me 'Baby.'"

She looked up at him from the bath, her eyes quickly full of sorrow, half-understanding what he meant. He knelt and put his arms around her, his sleeves plunged heedlessly in the water, his shirt and jacket soaking wet as he clutched her wordlessly, holding her crazily tight, crushing her breath from her, kissing her desperately, searchingly, regretfully.

He got jobs after that, selling real estate and automobiles, but somehow, although he had a desk with his name on a wooden wedge on it, and he went to the office religiously at nine each morning, he never managed to sell anything and he never made any money.

Louise was made assistant editor and the house was always full of strange men and women who talked fast and got angry on abstract subjects like mural paintings, novelists, labor unions. Negro short-story writers drank Louise's liquor, and a lot of Jews, and big solemn men with scarred faces and knotted hands talked slowly but clearly about picket lines and battles with guns and leadpipe at mine shaft-heads and in front of factory gates. And Louise moved among them all, confidently, knowing what they were talking about, with opinions that they listened to and argued about just as though she were a man. She knew everybody, condescended to no one, devoured books that Darling had never heard of, walked along the streets of the city, excited, at home, soaking in all the million tides of New York without fear, with constant wonder.

Her friends liked Darling and sometimes he found a man who wanted to get off in the corner and talk about the new boy who played fullback for Princeton, and the decline of the double wing-back, or even the state of the stock market, but for the most part he sat on the edge of things, solid and quiet in the high storm of words. "The dialectics of the situation . . . the theatre has been given over to expert jugglers . . . Picasso? What man has a right to paint old bones and collect ten thousand dollars for them? . . . I stand firmly behind Trotsky . . . Poe was the last American critic. When he died they put lilies on the grave of American criticism. I don't say this because they panned my last book, but . . ."

Once in a while he caught Louise looking soberly and consideringly at him through the cigarette smoke and the noise and he avoided her eyes and found an excuse to get up and go into the kitchen for more ice or to open another bottle.

"Come on," Cathal Flaherty was saying, standing at the door with a girl, "you've got to come down and see this. It's down on Fourteenth Street, in the old Civic Repertory, and you can only see it on Sunday nights and I guarantee you'll come out of the theatre singing." Flaherty was a big young Irishman with a broken nose who was the lawyer for a longshoreman's union, and he had been hanging around the house for six months on and off, roaring and shutting everybody else up when he got in an argument. "It's a new play, *Waiting for Lefty*, it's about taxi-drivers."

"Odets," the girl with Flaherty said. "It's by a guy named Odets."

"I never heard of him," Darling said.

"He's a new one," the girl said.

"It's like watching a bombardment," Flaherty said. "I saw it last Sunday night. You've got to see it."

"Come on, Baby," Louise said to Darling, excitement in her eyes already. "We've been sitting in the Sunday *Times* all day, this'll be a great change."

"I see enough taxi-drivers every day," Darling said, not because he meant that, but because he didn't like to be around Flaherty, who said things that made Louise laugh a lot and whose judgment she accepted on almost every subject. "Let's go to the movies."

"You've never seen anything like this before," Flaherty said. "He wrote this play with a baseball bat."

"Come on," Louise coaxed, "I bet it's wonderful."

"He has long hair," the girl with Flaherty said. "Odets. I met him at a party. He's an actor. He didn't say a goddam thing all night."

"I don't feel like going down to Fourteenth Street," Darling said, wishing Flaherty and his girl would get out. "It's gloomy."

"Oh, hell!" Louise said loudly. She looked coolly at Darling, as though she'd just been introduced to him and was making up her mind about him, and not very favorably. He saw her looking at him, knowing there was something new and dangerous in her face and he wanted to say something, but Flaherty was there and his damned girl, and anyway, he didn't know what to say.

"I'm going," Louise said, getting her coat. "I don't think Fourteenth Street is gloomy."

"I'm telling you," Flaherty was saying, helping her on with her coat, "it's the Battle of Gettysburg, in Brooklynese."

"Nobody could get a word out of him," Flaherty's girl was saying as they went through the door. "He just sat there all night."

The door closed. Louise hadn't said good-night to him. Darling walked around the room four times, then sprawled out on the sofa, on top of the Sunday *Times*. He lay there for five minutes looking at the ceiling, thinking of Flaherty walking down the street talking in that booming voice, between the girls, holding their arms.

Louise had looked wonderful. She'd washed her hair in the afternoon and it had been very soft and light and clung close to her head as she stood there angrily putting her coat on. Louise was getting prettier every year, partly because she knew by now how pretty she was, and made the most of it.

"Nuts," Darling said, standing up. "Oh, nuts."

He put on his coat and went down to the nearest bar and had five drinks off by himself in a corner before his money ran out.

The years since then had been foggy and downhill. Louise had been nice to him, and in a way, loving and kind, and they'd fought only once, when he said he was going to vote for Landon. ("Oh, Christ," she'd said, "doesn't *anything* happen inside your head? Don't you read the papers? The penniless Republican!") She'd been sorry later and apologized for hurting him, but apologized as she might to a child. He'd tried hard, had gone grimly to the art galleries, the concert halls, the book-shops, trying to gain on the trail of his wife, but it was no use. He was bored, and none of what he saw or heard or dutifully read made much sense to him and finally he gave it up. He had thought, many nights as he ate dinner alone, knowing Louise would come home late and drop silently into bed without explanation, of getting a divorce, but he knew the loneliness, the hopelessness, of not seeing her again would be too much to take. So he was good, completely devoted, ready at all times to go anyplace with her, do anything she wanted. He even got a small job, in a broker's office and paid his own way, bought his own liquor.

Then he'd been offered the job of going from college to college as a tailor's representative. "We want a man," Mr. Rosenberg had said, "who as soon as you look at him, you say 'There's a university man.'" Rosenberg had looked approvingly at Darling's broad shoulders and well-kept waist, at his carefully brushed hair and his honest, wrinkleless face. "Frankly, Mr. Darling, I am willing to make you a proposition. I have inquired about you, you are favorably known on your old campus. I understand you were in the backfield with Alfred Diederich."

Darling nodded. "What happened to him?"

"He is walking around in a cast for seven years now. An iron brace. He played professional football and they broke his neck for him."

Darling smiled. That, at least, had turned out well.

"Our suits are an easy product to sell, Mr. Darling," Mr. Rosenberg said. "We have a handsome, custom-made garment. What has Brooks Brothers got that we haven't got? A name. No more."

"I can make fifty, sixty dollars a week," Darling said to Louise that night. "And expenses. I can save some money and then come back to New York and really get started here."

"Yes, Baby," Louise said.

"As it is," Darling said carefully, "I can make it back here once a month, and holidays and the summer. We can see each other often."

"Yes, Baby." He looked at her face, lovelier now at thirty-five than it had ever been before, but fogged over now as it had been for five years with a kind of patient, kindly, remote boredom.

"What do you say?" he asked. "Should I take it?" Deep within him, he hoped fiercely, longingly, for her to say, "No, Baby, you stay right here," but she said, as he knew she'd say, "I think you'd better take it."

He nodded. He had to get up and stand with his back to her, looking out the window, because there were things plain on his face that she had never seen in the fifteen years she'd known him. "Fifty dollars is a lot of money," he said. "I never thought I'd ever see fifty dollars again." He laughed. Louise laughed, too.

Christian Darling sat on the frail green grass of the practice field. The shadow of the stadium had reached out and covered him. In the distance the lights of the university shone a little mistily in the light haze of evening. Fifteen years. Flaherty even now was calling for his wife, buying her a drink, filling whatever bar they were in with that voice of his and that easy laugh. Darling half-closed his eyes, almost saw the boy fifteen years ago reach for the pass, slip the halfback, go skittering lightly down the field, his knees high and fast and graceful, smiling to himself because he knew he was going to get past the safety man. That was the high point, Darling thought, fifteen years ago, on an autumn afternoon, twenty years old and far from death, with the air coming easily into his lungs, and a deep feeling inside him that he could do anything, knock over anybody, outrun whatever had to be outrun. And the shower after and the three glasses of water and the cool night air on his damp head and Louise sitting hatless in the open car with a smile and the first kiss she ever really meant. The high point, an eighty-yard run in the practice and a girl's kiss and everything after that a decline. Darling laughed. He had practiced the wrong thing, perhaps. He hadn't practiced for 1929 and New York City and a girl who would turn into a woman. Somewhere, he thought, there must have been a point where she moved up to me, was even with me for a moment, when I could have held her hand, if I'd known, held tight, gone with her. Well, he'd never known. Here he was on a playing field that was fifteen years away and his wife was in another city having dinner with another and better man, speaking with him a different, new language, a language nobody had ever taught him.

Darling stood up, smiled a little, because if he didn't smile he knew the tears would come. He looked around him. This was the spot. O'Connor's pass had come sliding out just to here . . . the high point. Darling put up his hands, felt all over again the flat slap of the ball. He shook his hips to throw off the halfback, cut back inside the center, picked his knees high as he ran gracefully over two men jumbled on the ground at the line of scrimmage, ran easily, gaining speed, for ten yards, holding the ball lightly in his two hands, swung away from the halfback diving at him, ran, swinging his hips in the almost-girlish manner of a back in a broken field, tore into the safety man, his shoes drumming heavily on the turf, stiff-armed, elbow locked, pivoted, raced lightly and exultantly for the goal line.

It was only after he had sped over the goal line and slowed to a trot that he saw the boy and girl sitting together on the turf, looking at him wonderingly.

He stopped short, dropping his arms. "I . . ." he said, gasping a little though his condition was fine and the run hadn't winded him, ". . .Once I played here."

The boy and the girl said nothing. Darling laughed embarrassedly, looked hard at them sitting there, close to each other, shrugged, turned and went toward his hotel, the sweat breaking out on his face and running down into his collar.

III

PLAYS

OEDIPUS THE KING

SOPHOCLES

TRANSLATED BY DAVID GRENE[1]

Characters in the Play

OEDIPUS, *King of Thebes*
JOCASTA, *Queen of Thebes; wife of Oedipus; widow of Laius, the late King*
PRIEST OF ZEUS
CREON, *brother of Jocasta*
TEIRESIAS, *a blind prophet*
A MESSENGER, *from Corinth*
A HERDSMAN, *formerly in the service of Laius*
SECOND MESSENGER
CHORUS *of Theban elders*
A CROWD *of suppliants, men, women, and children*

(SCENE: *In front of the palace of* OEDIPUS *at Thebes. To the right of the stage near the altar stands the* PRIEST *with a crowd of suppliants of all ages.* OEDIPUS *emerges from the central door.*)

OEDIPUS. Children, young sons and daughters of old Cadmus,
why do you sit here with your suppliant crowns?
The town is heavy with a mingled burden
of sounds and smells, of groans and hymns and incense;
I did not think it fit that I should hear
of this from messengers but came myself,—
I Oedipus whom all men call the Great.

[*He turns to the* PRIEST.]

You're old and they are young; come, speak for them.
What do you fear or want, that you sit here

1. David Grene, *Three Greek Tragedies*. Copyright, 1942, by The University of Chicago Press. Used by permission.

suppliant? Indeed I'm willing to give all
that you may need; I would be very hard
should I not pity suppliants like these.
PRIEST. O ruler of my country, Oedipus,
you see our company around the altar;
you see our ages; some of us, like these,
who cannot yet fly far, and some of us
heavy with age; these children are the chosen
among the young, and I the priest of Zeus.
Within the market place sit others crowned
with suppliant garlands, at the double shrine
of Pallas and the temple where Ismenus
gives oracles by fire. King, you yourself
have seen our city reeling like a wreck
already; it can scarcely lift its prow
out of the depths, out of the bloody surf.
A blight is on the fruitful plants of the earth,
a blight is on the cattle in the fields,
a blight is on our women that no children
are born to them; a God that carries fire,
a deadly pestilence, is in our town,
strikes us and spares not, and the house of Cadmus
is emptied of its people while black Death
grows rich in groaning and in lamentation.
We have not come as suppliants to this altar
because we thought of you as of a God,
but rather judging you the first of men
in all the chances of this life and when
we mortals have to do with more than man.
You came and by your coming saved our city,
freed us from tribute which we paid of old
to the Sphinx, cruel singer. This you did
in virtue of no knowledge we could give you,
in virtue of no teaching; it was God
that aided you, men say, and you are held
with God's assistance to have saved our lives.
Now Oedipus, whom all men call the Greatest,
here falling at your feet we all entreat you,
find us some strength for rescue.
Perhaps you'll hear a wise word from some God,
perhaps you will learn something from a man
(for I have seen that for the skilled of practice
the outcome of their counsels live the most).
Noblest of men, go, and raise up our city,

go,—and give heed. For now this land of ours
calls you its savior since you saved it once.
So, let us never speak about your reign
as of a time when first our feet were set
secure on high, but later fell to ruin.
Raise up our city, save it and raise it up.
Once you have brought us luck with happy omen;
be no less now in fortune.
If you will rule this land, as now you rule it,
better to rule it full of men than empty.
For neither town nor ship is anything
when empty, and none live in it together.

OEDIPUS. Poor children! You have come to me entreating,
but I have known the story before you told it
only too well. I know you are all sick,
yet there is not one of you, sick though you are,
that is as sick as I myself.
Your several sorrows each have single scope
and touch but one of you. My spirit groans
for city and myself and you at once.
You have not roused me like a man from sleep;
know that I have given many tears to this,
gone many ways wandering in thought,
but as I thought I found only one remedy
and that I took. I sent Menoeceus' son
Creon, Jocasta's brother, to Apollo,
to his Pythian temple,
that he might learn there by what act or word
I could save this city. As I count the days,
it vexes me what ails him; he is gone
far longer than he needed for the journey.
But when he comes, then, may I prove a villain,
if I shall not do all the God commands.

PRIEST. Thanks for your gracious words. Your servants here
signal that Creon is this moment coming.

OEDIPUS. His face is bright. O holy Lord Apollo,
grant that his news too may be bright for us
and bring us safety.

PRIEST. It is happy news,
I think, for else his head would not be crowned
with sprigs of fruitful laurel.

OEDIPUS. We will know soon,
he's within hail. Lord Creon, my good brother,
what is the word you bring us from the God?

[CREON *enters.*]

CREON. A good word,—for things hard to bear themselves
if in the final issue all is well
I count complete good fortune.

OEDIPUS. What do you mean?
What you have said so far
leaves me uncertain whether to trust or fear.

CREON. If you will hear my news before these others
I am ready to speak, or else to go within.

OEDIPUS. Speak it to all;
the grief I bear, I bear it more for these
than for my own heart.

CREON. I will tell you, then,
what I heard from the God.
King Phoebus in plain words commanded us
to drive out a pollution from our land,
pollution grown ingrained within the land;
drive it out, said the God, not cherish it,
till it's past cure.

OEDIPUS. What is the rite
of purification? How shall it be done?

CREON. By banishing a man, or expiation
of blood by blood, since it is murder guilt
which holds our city in this storm of death.

OEDIPUS. Who is this man whose fate the God pronounces?

CREON. My Lord, before you piloted the state
we had a king called Laius.

OEDIPUS. I know of him by hearsay. I have not seen him.

CREON. The God commanded clearly: let some one
punish with force this dead man's murderers.

OEDIPUS. Where are they in the world? Where would a trace
of this old crime be found? It would be hard
to guess where.

CREON. The clue is in this land;
that which is sought is found;
the unheeded thing escapes:
so said the God.

OEDIPUS. Was it at home,
or in the country that death came upon him,
or in another country travelling?

CREON. He went, he said himself, upon an embassy,
but never returned when he set out from home.

OEDIPUS. Was there no messenger, no fellow traveller

who knew what happened? Such a one might tell
something of use.

CREON. They were all killed save one. He fled in terror
and he could tell us nothing in clear terms
of what he knew, nothing, but one thing only.

OEDIPUS. What was it?
If we could even find a slim beginning
in which to hope, we might discover much.

CREON. This man said that the robbers they encountered
were many and the hands that did the murder
were many; it was no man's single power.

OEDIPUS. How could a robber dare a deed like this
were he not helped with money from the city,
money and treachery?

CREON. That indeed was thought.
But Laius was dead and in our trouble
there was none to help.

OEDIPUS. What trouble was so great to hinder you
inquiring out the murder of your king?

CREON. The riddling Sphinx induced us to neglect
mysterious crimes and rather seek solution
of troubles at our feet.

OEDIPUS. I will bring this to light again. King Phoebus
fittingly took this care about the dead,
and you too fittingly.
And justly you will see in me an ally,
a champion of my country and the God.
For when I drive pollution from the land
I will not serve a distant friend's advantage,
but act in my own interest. Whoever
he was that killed the king may readily
wish to dispatch me with his murderous hand;
so helping the dead king I help myself.
Come children, take your suppliant boughs and go;
up from the altars now. Call the assembly
and let it meet upon the understanding
that I'll do everything. God will decide
whether we prosper or remain in sorrow.

PRIEST. Rise, children—it was this we came to seek,
which of himself the king now offers us.
May Phoebus who gave us the oracle
come to our rescue and stay the plague.

[*Exeunt. Enter* CHORUS OF THEBAN ELDERS.]

Strophe 1

CHORUS. What is the sweet spoken word of God from the shrine of Pytho rich in gold
that has come to glorious Thebes?
I am stretched on the rack of doubt, and terror and trembling hold
my heart, O Delian Healer, and I worship full of fears
for what doom you will bring to pass, new or renewed in the revolving years.
Speak to me, immortal voice,
child of golden Hope.

Antistrophe 1

First I call on you, Athene, deathless daughter of Zeus,
and Artemis, Earth Upholder,
who sits in the midst of the market place in the throne which men call Fame,
and Phoebus, the Far Shooter, three averters of Fate,
come to us now, if ever before, when ruin rushed upon the state,
you drove destruction's flame away
out of our land.

Strophe 2

Our sorrows defy number;
all the ship's timbers are rotten;
taking of thought is no spear for the driving away of the plague.
There are no growing children in this famous land;
there are no women staunchly bearing the pangs of childbirth.
You may see them one with another, like birds swift on the wing,
quicker than fire unmastered,
speeding away to the coast of the Western God.

Antistrophe 2

In the unnumbered deaths
of its people the city dies;
those children that are born lie dead on the naked earth
unpitied, spreading contagion of death; and grey haired mothers and wives
everywhere stand at the altar's edge, suppliant, moaning;
the hymn to the healing God rings out but with it the wailing voices are blended.
From these our sufferings grant us, O golden Daughter of Zeus,
glad-faced deliverance.

Strophe 3

There is no clash of brazen shields but our fight is with the War God,
a War God ringed with the cries of men, a savage God who burns us;
grant that he turn in racing course backwards out of our country's bounds

to the great palace of Amphitrite or where the waves of the Thracian sea
deny the stranger safe anchorage.
Whatsoever escapes the night
at last the light of day revisits;
so smite the War God, Father Zeus,
beneath your thunderbolt,
for you are the Lord of the lightning, the lightning that
carries fire.

Antistrophe 3

And your unconquered arrow shafts, winged by the golden corded bow,
Lycean King, I beg to be at our side for help;
and the gleaming torches of Artemis with which she scours the Lycean hills,
and I call on the God with the turban of gold, who gave his name to this
country of ours,
the Bacchic God with the wine flushed face,
Evian One, who travel
with the Maenad company,
combat the God that burns us
with your torch of pine;
for the God that is our enemy is a God unhonoured among the Gods.

[OEDIPUS *returns.*]

OEDIPUS. For what you ask me—if you will hear my words,
and hearing welcome them and fight the plague,
you will find strength and lightening of your load.

Hark to me; what I say to you, I say
as one that is a stranger to the story
as stranger to the deed. For I would not
be far upon the track if I alone
were tracing it without a clue. But now,
since after all was finished, I became
a citizen among you, citizens—
now I proclaim to all the men of Thebes:
whoso among you knows the murderer
by whose hand Laius, son of Labdacus,
died—I command him to tell everything
to me,—yes, though he fears himself to take the blame
on his own head; for bitter punishment
he shall have none, but leave this land unharmed.
Or if he knows the murderer, another,
a foreigner, still let him speak the truth.
For I will pay him and be grateful, too.

his own insistence leads to his doom.

But if you shall keep silence, if perhaps
some one of you, to shield a guilty friend,
or for his own sake shall reject my words—
hear what I shall do then:
I forbid that man, whoever he be, my land,
my land where I hold sovereignty and throne;
and I forbid any to welcome him
or cry him greeting or make him a sharer
in sacrifice or offering to the Gods,
or give him water for his hands to wash.
I command all to drive him from their homes,
since he is our pollution, as the oracle
of Pytho's God proclaimed him now to me.
So I stand forth a champion of the God
and of the man who died.
Upon the murderer I invoke this curse—
whether he is one man and all unknown,
or one of many—may he wear out his life
in misery to miserable doom!
If with my knowledge he lives at my hearth
I pray that I myself may feel my curse.

Even were this no matter of God's ordinance
it would not fit you so to leave it lie,
unpurified, since a good man is dead
and one that was a king. Search it out.
Since I am now the holder of his office,
and have his bed and wife that once was his,
and had his line not been unfortunate
we would have common children—(fortune leaped
upon his head)—because of all these things,
I fight in his defence as for my father,
and I shall try all means to take the murderer
of Laius the son of Labdacus
the son of Polydorus and before him
of Cadmus and before him of Agenor.
Those who do not obey me, may the Gods
grant no crops springing from the ground they plough
nor children to their women! May a fate
like this, or one still worse than this consume them!
For you whom these words please, the other Thebans,
may Justice as your ally and all the Gods
live with you, blessing you now and for ever!

CHORUS. As you have held me to my oath, I speak:

I neither killed the king nor can declare
the killer; but since Phoebus set the quest
it is his part to tell who the man is.

OEDIPUS. Right; but to put compulsion on the Gods
against their will—no man has strength for that.

CHORUS. May I then say what I think second best?

OEDIPUS. If there's a third best, too, spare not to tell it.

CHORUS. I know that what the Lord Teiresias
sees, is most often what the Lord Apollo
sees. If you should inquire of this from him
you might find out most clearly.

OEDIPUS. Even in this my actions have not been sluggard.
On Creon's word I have sent two messengers
and why the prophet is not here already
I have been wondering.

CHORUS. His skill apart
there is besides only an old faint story.

OEDIPUS. What is it?
I seize on every story.

CHORUS. It was said
that he was killed by certain wayfarers.

OEDIPUS. I heard that, too, but no one saw the killer.

CHORUS. Yet if he has a share of fear at all,
his courage will not stand firm, hearing your curse.

OEDIPUS. The man who in the doing did not shrink
will fear no word.

CHORUS. Here comes his prosecutor:
led by your men the godly prophet comes
in whom alone of mankind truth is native.

[*Enter* TEIRESIAS, *led by a little boy.*]

OEDIPUS. Teiresias, you are versed in everything,
things teachable and things not to be spoken,
things of the heaven and earth-creeping things.
You have no eyes but in your mind you know
with what a plague our city is afflicted.
My lord, in you alone we find a champion,
in you alone one that can rescue us.
Perhaps you have not heard the messengers,
but Phoebus sent in answer to our sending
an oracle declaring that our freedom
from this disease would only come when we
should learn the names of those who killed King Laius,
and kill them or expel from our country.

Do not begrudge us oracles from birds,
or any other way of prophecy
within your skill; save yourself and the city,
save me; redeem the debt of our pollution
that lies on us because of this dead man.
We are in your hands; it is the finest task
to help another when you have means and power.

TEIRESIAS. Alas, how terrible is wisdom when
it brings no profit to the man that's wise!
This I knew well, but had forgotten it,
else I would not have come here.

OEDIPUS. What is this?
How sad you are now you have come!

TEIRESIAS. Let me
go home. It will be easiest for us both
to bear our several destinies to the end
if you will follow my advice.

OEDIPUS. You'd rob us
of this your gift of prophecy? You talk
as one who had no care for law nor love
for Thebes who reared you.

TEIRESIAS. Yes, but I see that even your own words
miss the mark; therefore I must fear for mine.

OEDIPUS. For God's sake if you know of anything,
do not turn from us; all of us kneel to you,
all of us here, your suppliants.

TEIRESIAS. All of you here know nothing. I will not
bring to the light of day my troubles, mine—
rather than call them yours.

OEDIPUS. What do you mean?
You know of some thing but refuse to speak.
Would you betray us and destroy the city?

TEIRESIAS. I will not bring this pain upon us both,
neither on you nor on myself. Why is it
you question me and waste your labour? I
will tell you nothing.

OEDIPUS. You would provoke a stone! Tell us, you villain,
tell us, and do not stand there quietly
unmoved and balking at the final issue.

TEIRESIAS. You blame my temper but you do not see
your own that lives within you; it is me
you chide.

OEDIPUS. Who would not feel his temper rise
at words like these with which you shame our city?

TEIRESIAS. Of themselves things will come, although I hide them
and breathe no word of them.

OEDIPUS. Since they will come
tell them to me.

TEIRESIAS. I will say nothing further.
Against this answer let your temper rage
as wildly as you will.

OEDIPUS Indeed I am
so angry I shall not hold back a jot
of what I think. For I would have you know
I think you were complotter of the deed
and doer of the deed save in so far
as for the actual killing. Had you had eyes
I would have said alone you murdered him.

TEIRESIAS. Yes? Then I warn you faithfully to keep
the letter of your proclamation and
from this day forth to speak no word of greeting
to these nor me; you are the land's pollution.

OEDIPUS. How shamelessly you started up this taunt!
How do you think you will escape?

TEIRESIAS. I have.
I have escaped; the truth is what I cherish
and that's my strength.

OEDIPUS. And who has taught you truth?
Not your profession surely!

TEIRESIAS. You have taught me,
for you have made me speak against my will.

OEDIPUS. Speak what? Tell me again that I may learn it better.

TEIRESIAS. Did you not understand before or would you
provoke me into speaking?

OEDIPUS. I did not grasp it,
not so to call it known. Say it again.

TEIRESIAS. I say you are the murderer of the king
whose murderer you seek.

OEDIPUS. Not twice you shall not
say calumnies like this and stay unpunished.

TEIRESIAS. Shall I say more to tempt your anger more?

OEDIPUS. As much as you desire; it will be said
in vain.

TEIRESIAS. I say that with those you love best
you live in foulest shame unconsciously
and do not see where you are in calamity.

OEDIPUS. Do you imagine you can always talk
like this, and live to laugh at it hereafter?

TEIRESIAS. Yes, if the truth has anything of strength.
OEDIPUS. It has, but not for you; it has no strength
for you because you are blind in mind and ears
as well as in your eyes.
TEIRESIAS. You are a poor wretch
to taunt me with the very insults which
everyone soon will heap upon yourself.
OEDIPUS. Your life is one long night so that you cannot
hurt me or any other who sees the light.
TEIRESIAS. It is not fate that I should be your ruin,
Apollo is enough; it is his care
to work this out.
OEDIPUS. Was this your own design
or Creon's?
TEIRESIAS. Creon is no hurt to you,
but you are to yourself.
OEDIPUS. Wealth, sovereignty and skill outmatching skill
for the contrivance of an envied life,
great store of jealousy fill your treasury chests,
if my friend Creon, friend from the first and loyal,
thus secretly attacks me, secretly
desires to drive me out and secretly
suborns this juggling, trick devising quack,
this wily beggar who has only eyes
for his own gains, but blindness in his skill.
For, tell me, where have you seen clear, Teiresias,
with your prophetic eyes? When the dark singer,
the Sphinx, was in your country, did you speak
word of deliverance to its citizens?
And yet the riddle's answer was not the province
of a chance comer. It was a prophet's task
and plainly you had no such gift of prophecy
from birds nor otherwise from any God
to glean a word of knowledge. But I came,
Oedipus, who knew nothing, and I stopped her.
I solved the riddle by my wit alone.
Mine was no knowledge got from birds. And now
you would expel me,
because you think that you will find a place
by Creon's throne. I think you will be sorry,
both you and your accomplice, for your plot
to drive me out. And did I not regard you
as an old man, some suffering would have taught you
that what was in your heart was treason.

CHORUS. We look at this man's words and yours, my king,
and we find both have spoken them in anger.
We need no angry words but only thought
how we may best hit the God's meaning for us.

TEIRESIAS. If you are king, at least I have the right
no less to speak in my defence against you.
Of that much I am master. I am no slave
of yours, but Loxias', and so I shall not
enroll myself with Creon for my patron.
Since you have taunted me with being blind,
here is my word for you.
You have your eyes but see not where you are
in sin, nor where you live, nor whom you live with.
Do you know who your parents are? Unknowing
you are an enemy to kith and kin
in death, beneath the earth, and in this life.
A deadly-footed, double-striking curse,
from father and mother both, shall drive you forth
out of this land, with darkness on your eyes,
that now have such straight vision. Shall there be
a place will not be harbour to your cries,
a corner of Cithaeron will not ring
in echo to your cries, soon, soon,—
when you shall learn the secret of your marriage,
which steered you to a haven in this house,—
haven no haven, after lucky voyage?
And of the multitude of other evils
establishing a grim equality
between you and your children, you know nothing.
So, muddy with contempt my words and Creon's!
there is no man shall perish as you shall.

OEDIPUS. Is it endurable that I should hear
such words from him? Go and a curse go with you!
Quick, home with you! Out of my house at once!

TEIRESIAS. I would not have come either had you not called me.

OEDIPUS. I did not know then you would talk like a fool—
or it would have been long before I called you.

TEIRESIAS. I am a fool then, as it seems to you—
but to the parents who have bred you, wise.

OEDIPUS. What parents? Stop! Who are they of all the world?

TEIRESIAS. This day will show your birth and bring your ruin.

OEDIPUS. How needlessly your riddles darken everything.

TEIRESIAS. But it's in riddle-answering you are strongest.

OEDIPUS. Yes. Taunt me where you will find me great.

TEIRESIAS. It is this very luck that has destroyed you.
OEDIPUS. I do not care, if it has served this city.
TEIRESIAS. Well, I will go. Come, boy, lead me away.
OEDIPUS. Yes, lead him off. So long as you are here,
you'll be a stumbling block and a vexation;
once gone, you will not trouble me again.
TEIRESIAS. I have said
what I came here to say not fearing your
countenance: there is no way you can hurt me.
I tell you, king, this man, this murderer
(whom you have long declared you are in search of,
indicting him in threatening proclamation
as murderer of Laius)—he is here.
In name he is a stranger among citizens
but soon he will be shown to be a citizen
true native Theban, and he'll have no joy
of the discovery: blindness for sight
and beggary for riches his exchange,
he shall go journeying to a foreign country
tapping his way before him with a stick.
He shall be proved father and brother both
to his own children in his house; to her
that gave him birth, a son and husband both;
a fellow sower in his father's bed
with that same father that he murdered.
Go within, reckon that out, and if you find me
mistaken, say I have no skill in prophecy.

[*Exeunt separately* TEIRESIAS *and* OEDIPUS.]

Strophe 1

CHORUS. Who is the man proclaimed
by Delphi's prophetic rock
as the bloody-handed murderer,
the doer of deeds that none dares name?
Now is the time for him to run
with a stronger foot
than Pegasus
for the child of Zeus leaps in arms upon him
with fire and the lightning bolt,
and terribly close on his heels
are the Fates that never miss.

Antistrophe 1

Lately from snowy Parnassus

clearly the voice flashed forth,
bidding each Theban track him down,
the unknown murderer.
In the savage forests he lurks and in
the caverns like
the mountain bull.
He is sad and lonely, and lonely his feet
that carry him far from the navel of earth;
but its prophecies, ever living,
flutter around his head.

Strophe 2

The augur has spread confusion
terrible confusion;
I do not approve what was said
nor can I deny it.
I do not know what to say;
I am in a flutter of foreboding;
I never heard in the present
nor past of a quarrel between
the sons of Labdacus and Polybus,
that I might bring as proof
in attacking the popular fame
of Oedipus, seeking
to take vengeance for undiscovered
death in the line of Labdacus.

Antistrophe 2

Truly Zeus and Apollo are wise
and in human things all-knowing;
but amongst men there is no
distinct judgment, between the prophet
and me—which of us is right.
One man may pass another in wisdom
but I would never agree
with those that find fault with the king
till I should see the word
proved right beyond doubt. For once
in visible form the Sphinx
came on him and all of us
saw his wisdom and in that test
he saved the city. So he will not be condemned by my mind.

[*Enter* CREON.]

CREON. Citizens, I have come because I heard
deadly words spread about me, that the king
accuses me. I cannot take that from him.
If he believes that in these present troubles
he has been wronged by me in word or deed
I do not want to live on with the burden
of such a scandal on me. The report
injures me doubly and most vitally—
for I'll be called a traitor to my city
and traitor also to my friends and you.

CHORUS. Perhaps it was a sudden gust of anger
that forced that insult from him, and no judgment.

CREON. But did he say that it was in compliance
with schemes of mine that the seer told him lies?

CHORUS. Yes, he said that, but why, I do not know.

CREON. Were his eyes straight in his head? Was his mind right
when he accused me in this fashion?

CHORUS. I do not know; I have no eyes to see
what princes do. Here comes the king himself.

[*Enter* OEDIPUS.]

OEDIPUS. You, sir, how is it you come here? Have you so much
brazen-faced daring that you venture in
my house although you are proved manifestly
the murderer of that man, and though you tried,
openly, highway robbery of my crown?
For God's sake, tell me what you saw in me,
what cowardice or what stupidity,
that made you lay a plot like this against me?
Did you imagine I should not observe
the crafty scheme that stole upon me or
seeing it, take no means to counter it?
Was it not stupid of you to make the attempt,
to try to hunt down royal power without
the people at your back or friends? For only
with the people at your back or money can
the hunt end in the capture of a crown.

CREON. Do you know what you're doing? Will you listen
to words to answer yours, and then pass judgment?

OEDIPUS. You're quick to speak, but I am slow to grasp you,
for I have found you dangerous,—and my foe.

CREON. First of all hear what I shall say to that.

OEDIPUS. At least don't tell me that you are not guilty.

CREON. If you believe you cherish something fine
in obstinacy without brains, you're wrong.
OEDIPUS. And you are wrong if you believe that one,
a criminal, will not be punished only
because he is my kinsman.
CREON. This is but just—
but tell me, then, of what offense I'm guilty?
OEDIPUS. Did you or did you not urge me to send
to this prophetic mumbler?
CREON. I did indeed,
and I shall stand by what I told you.
OEDIPUS. How long ago is it since Laius. . . .
CREON. What about Laius? I don't understand.
OEDIPUS. Vanished—died—was murdered?
CREON. It is long,
a long, long time to reckon.
OEDIPUS. Was this prophet
in the profession then?
CREON. He was, and honoured
as highly as he is today.
OEDIPUS. At that time did he say a word about me?
CREON. Never, at least when I was near him.
OEDIPUS. You never made a search for the dead man?
CREON. We searched, indeed, but never learned of anything.
OEDIPUS. Why did our wise old friend not say this then?
CREON. I don't know; and when I know nothing, I
usually hold my tongue.
OEDIPUS. You know this much,
and can declare this much if you are loyal.
CREON. What is it? If I know I'll not deny it.
OEDIPUS. That he would not have said that I killed Laius
had he not met you first.
CREON. You know yourself
whether he said this, but I demand that I
should hear as much from you as you from me.
OEDIPUS. Then hear,—I'll not be proved a murderer.
CREON. Well, then. You're married to my sister.
OEDIPUS. Yes,
that I am not disposed to deny.
CREON. You rule
this country giving her an equal share
in the government?
OEDIPUS. Yes, everything she wants
she has from me.

CREON. And I, as thirdsman to you,
am rated as the equal of you two?

OEDIPUS. Yes, and it's there you've proved yourself false friend.

CREON. Not if you will reflect on it as I do.
Consider, first, if you think anyone
would choose to rule and fear rather than rule
and sleep untroubled by a fear if power
were equal in both cases. I, at least,
I was not born with such a frantic yearning
to be a king—but to do what kings do.
And so it is with every one who has learned
wisdom and self-control. As it stands now,
the prizes are all mine—and without fear.
But if I were the king myself, I must
do much that went against the grain.
How should despotic rule seem sweeter to me
than painless power and an assured authority?
I am not so besotted yet that I
want other honours than those that come with profit.
Now every man's my pleasure; every man greets me;
now those who are your suitors fawn on me,—
success for them depends upon my favour.
Why should I let all this go to win that?
My mind would not be traitor if it's wise;
I am no treason-lover, of my nature,
nor would I ever dare to join a plot.
Prove what I say. Go to the oracle
at Pytho and inquire about the answers,
if they are as I told you. For the rest,
if you discover I laid any plot
together with the seer, kill me, I say,
not only by your vote but by my own.
But do not charge me on obscure opinion
without some proof to back it. It's not just
lightly to count your knaves as honest men,
nor honest men as knaves. To throw away
an honest friend is, as it were, to throw
your life away, which a man loves the best.
In time you will know all with certainty;
time is the only test of honest men,
one day is space enough to know a rogue.

CHORUS. His words are wise, king, if one fears to fall.
Those who are quick of temper are not safe.

OEDIPUS. When he that plots against me secretly
moves quickly, I must quickly counterplot.
If I wait taking no decisive measure
his business will be done, and mine be spoiled.

CREON. What do you want to do then? Banish me?

OEDIPUS. No, certainly; kill you, not banish you.

CREON. I do not think that you've your wits about you.

OEDIPUS. For my own interests, yes.

CREON. But for mine, too,
you should think equally.

OEDIPUS. You are a rogue.

CREON. Suppose you do not understand?

OEDIPUS. But yet
I must be ruler.

CREON. Not if you rule badly.

OEDIPUS. O, city, city!

CREON. I too have some share
in the city; it is not yours alone.

CHORUS. Stop, my lords! Here—and in the nick of time
I see Jocasta coming from the house;
with her help lay the quarrel that now stirs you.

[*Enter* JOCASTA.]

JOCASTA. For shame! Why have you raised this foolish squabbling
brawl? Are you not ashamed to air your private
griefs when the country's sick? Go in, you, Oedipus,
and you, too, Creon, into the house. Don't magnify
your nothing troubles.

CREON. Sister, Oedipus,
your husband, thinks he has the right to do
terrible wrongs—he has but to choose between
two terrors: banishing or killing me.

OEDIPUS. He's right, Jocasta; for I find him plotting
with knavish tricks against my person.

CREON. That God may never bless me! May I die
accursed, if I have been guilty of
one tittle of the charge you bring against me!

JOCASTA. I beg you, Oedipus, trust him in this,
spare him for the sake of this his oath to God,
for my sake, and the sake of those who stand here.

CHORUS. Be gracious, be merciful,
we beg of you.

OEDIPUS. In what would you have me yield?

CHORUS. He has been no silly child in the past.
He is strong in his oath now.
Spare him.

OEDIPUS. Do you know what you ask?

CHORUS. Yes.

OEDIPUS. Tell me then.

CHORUS. He has been your friend before all men's eyes; do not cast him away dishonoured on an obscure conjecture.

OEDIPUS. I would have you know that this request of yours
really requests my death or banishment.

CHORUS. May the Sun God, king of Gods, forbid! May I die without
God's blessing, without friends' help, if I had any such
thought. But my spirit is broken by my unhappiness for my
wasting country; and this would but add troubles amongst
ourselves to the other troubles.

OEDIPUS. Well, let him go then—if I must die ten times for it,
or be sent out dishonoured into exile.
It is your lips that prayed for him I pitied,
not his; wherever he is, I shall hate him.

CREON. I see you sulk in yielding and you're dangerous
when you are out of temper; natures like yours
are justly heaviest for themselves to bear.

OEDIPUS. Leave me alone! Take yourself off, I tell you.

CREON. I'll go, you have not known me, but they have,
and they have known my innocence.

[*Exit*]

CHORUS. Won't you take him inside, lady?

JOCASTA. Yes, when I've found out what was the matter.

CHORUS. There was some misconceived suspicion of a story, and on the other side the sting of injustice.

JOCASTA. So, on both sides?

CHORUS. Yes.

JOCASTA. What was the story?

CHORUS. I think it best, in the interests of the country, to leave it where it ended.

OEDIPUS. You see where you have ended, straight of judgment although you are, by softening my anger.

CHORUS. Sir, I have said before and I say again—be sure that I would
have been proved a madman, bankrupt in sane council, if I
should put you away, you who steered the country I love
safely when she was crazed with troubles. God grant that
now, too, you may prove a fortunate guide for us.

JOCASTA. Tell me, my lord, I beg of you, what was it
that roused your anger so?
OEDIPUS. Yes, I will tell you.
I honour you more than I honour them.
It was Creon and the plots he laid against me.
JOCASTA. Tell me—if you can clearly tell the quarrel—
OEDIPUS. Creon says
that I'm the murderer of Laius.
JOCASTA. Of his own knowledge or on information?
OEDIPUS. He sent this rascal prophet to me, since
he keeps his own mouth clean of any guilt.
JOCASTA. Do not concern yourself about this matter;
listen to me and learn that human beings
have no part in the craft of prophecy.
Of that I'll show you a short proof.
There was an oracle once that came to Laius,—
I will not say that it was Phoebus' own,
but it was from his servants—and it told him
that it was fate that he should die a victim
at the hands of his own son, a son to be born
of Laius and me. But, see now, he,
the king, was killed by foreign highway robbers
at a place where three roads meet—so goes the story;
and for the son—before three days were out
after his birth King Laius pierced his ankles
and by the hands of others cast him forth
upon a pathless hillside. So Apollo
failed to fulfill his oracle to the son,
that he should kill his father, and to Laius
also proved false in that thing he feared,
death at his son's hands, never came to pass.
So clear in this case were the oracles,
so clear and false. Give them no heed, I say;
what God discovers need of, easily
he shows to us himself.
OEDIPUS. O dear Jocasta,
as I hear this from you, there comes upon me
a wandering of the soul—I could run mad.
JOCASTA. What trouble is it, that you turn again
and speak like this?
OEDIPUS. I thought I heard you say
that Laius was killed at a crossroads.
JOCASTA. Yes, that was how the story went and still
that word goes round.

OEDIPUS. Where is this place, Jocasta,
where he was murdered?

JOCASTA. Phocis is the country
and the road splits there, one of two roads from Delphi,
another comes from Daulia.

OEDIPUS. How long ago is this?

JOCASTA. The news came to the city just before
you became king and all men's eyes looked to you.
What is it, Oedipus, that's in your mind?

OEDIPUS. Don't ask me yet—tell me of Laius—
how did he look? How old or young was he?

JOCASTA. He was a tall man and his hair was grizzled
already—nearly white—and in his form
not unlike you.

OEDIPUS. O God, I think I have
called curses on myself in ignorance.

JOCASTA. What do you mean? I am terrified
when I look at you.

OEDIPUS. I have a deadly fear
that the old seer had eyes. You'll show me more
if you can tell me one more thing.

JOCASTA. I will.
I'm frightened,—but if I can understand,
I'll tell you all you ask.

OEDIPUS. How was his company?
Had he few with him when he went this journey,
or many servants, as would suit a prince?

JOCASTA. In all there were but five, and among them
a herald; and one carriage for the king.

OEDIPUS. It's plain—it's plain—who was it told you this?

JOCASTA. The only servant that escaped safe home.

OEDIPUS. Is he at home now?

JOCASTA. No, when he came home again
and saw you king and Laius was dead,
he came to me and touched my hand and begged
that I should send him to the fields to be
my shepherd and so he might see the city
as far off as he might. So I
sent him away. He was an honest man,
as slaves go, and was worthy of far more
than what he asked of me.

OEDIPUS. O, how I wish that he could come back quickly!

JOCASTA. He can. Why is your heart so set on this?

OEDIPUS. O dear Jocasta, I am full of fears

that I have spoken far too much; and therefore
I wish to see this shepherd.

JOCASTA. He will come;
but, Oedipus, I think I'm worthy too
to know what is it that disquiets you.

OEDIPUS. It shall not be kept from you, since my mind
has gone so far with its forebodings. Whom
should I confide in rather than you, who is there
of more importance to me who have passed
through such a fortune?
Polybus was my father, king of Corinth,
and Merope, the Dorian, my mother.
I was held greatest of the citizens
in Corinth till a curious chance befell me
as I shall tell you—curious, indeed,
but hardly worth the store I set upon it.
There was a dinner and at it a man,
a drunken man, accused me in his drink
of being bastard. I was furious
but held my temper under for that day.
Next day I went and taxed my parents with it;
they took the insult very ill from him,
the drunken fellow who had uttered it.
So I was comforted for their part, but
still this thing rankled always, for the story
crept about widely. And I went at last
to Pytho, though my parents did not know.
But Phoebus sent me home again unhonoured
in what I came to learn, but he foretold
other and desperate horrors to befall me,
that I was fated to lie with my mother,
and show to daylight an accursed breed
which men would not endure, and I was doomed
to be murderer of the father that begot me.
When I heard this I fled, and in the days
that followed I would measure from the stars
the whereabouts of Corinth—yes, I fled
to somewhere where I should not see fulfilled
the infamies told in that dreadful oracle.
And as I journeyed I came to the place
where, as you say, this king met with his death.
Jocasta, I will tell you the whole truth.
When I was near the branching of the crossroads,
going on foot, I was encountered by

a herald and a carriage with a man in it,
just as you tell me. He that led the way
and the old man himself wanted to thrust me
out of the road by force. I became angry
and struck the coachman who was pushing me.
When the old man saw this he watched his moment,
and as I passed he struck me from his carriage,
full on the head with his two pointed goad.
But he was paid in full and presently
my stick had struck him backwards from the car
and he rolled out of it. And then I killed them
all. If it happened there was any tie
of kinship twixt this man and Laius,
who is then now more miserable than I,
what man on earth so hated by the Gods,
since neither citizen nor foreigner
may welcome me at home or even greet me,
but drive me out of doors? And it is I,
I and no other have so cursed myself.
And I pollute the bed of him I killed
by the hands that killed him. Was I not born evil?
Am I not utterly unclean? I had to fly
and in my banishment not even see
my kindred nor set foot in my own country,
or otherwise my fate was to be yoked
in marriage with my mother and kill my father,
Polybus who begot me and had reared me.
Would not one rightly judge and say that on me
these things were sent by some malignant God?
O no, no, no—O holy majesty
of God on high, may I not see that day!
May I be gone out of men's sight before
I see the deadly taint of this disaster
come upon me.

CHORUS. Sir, we too fear these things. But until you see this man face to face and hear his story, hope.

OEDIPUS. Yes, I have just this much of hope—to wait until the herdsman comes.

JOCASTA. And when he comes, what do you want with him?

OEDIPUS. I'll tell you; if I find that his story is the same as yours, I at least will be clear of this guilt.

JOCASTA. Why what so particularly did you learn from my story?

OEDIPUS. You said that he spoke of highway *robbers* who killed Laius. Now if he uses the same number, it was not I who killed him. One man cannot be the same as many. But if he speaks of a man travelling alone, then clearly the burden of the guilt inclines towards me.

JOCASTA. Be sure, at least, that this was how he told the story. He cannot unsay it now, for every one in the city heard it—not I alone. But, Oedipus, even if he diverges from what he said then, he shall never prove that the murder of Laius squares rightly with the prophecy—for Loxias declared that the king should be killed by his own son. And that poor creature did not kill him surely,—for he died himself first. So as far as prophecy goes, henceforward I shall not look to the right hand or the left.

OEDIPUS. Right. But yet, send some one for the peasant to bring him here; do not neglect it.

JOCASTA. I will send quickly. Now let me go indoors. I will do nothing except what pleases you.

[*Exeunt.*]

Strophe 1

CHORUS. May destiny ever find me
pious in word and deed
prescribed by the laws that live on high:
laws begotten in the clear air of heaven,
whose only father is Olympus;
no mortal nature brought them to birth,
no forgetfulness shall lull them to sleep;
for God is great in them and grows not old. passage of time

Antistrophe 1

Insolence breeds the tyrant, insolence
if it is glutted with a surfeit, unseasonable, unprofitable,
climbs to the roof-top and plunges
sheer down to the ruin that must be,
and there its feet are no service.
But I pray that the God may never
abolish the eager ambition that profits the state.
For I shall never cease to hold the God as our protector.

Strophe 2

If a man walks with haughtiness
of hand or word and gives no heed
to Justice and the shrines of Gods
despises—may an evil doom
smite him for his ill-starred pride of heart!—
if he reaps gains without justice
and will not hold from impiety

and his fingers itch for untouchable things.
When such things are done, what man shall contrive
to shield his soul from the shafts of the God?
When such deeds are held in honour,
why should I honour the Gods in the dance?

Antistrophe 2

No longer to the holy place,
to the navel of earth I'll go
to worship, nor to Abae
nor to Olympia,
unless the oracles are proved to fit,
for all men's hands to point at.
O Zeus, if you are rightly called
the sovereign lord, all-mastering,
let this not escape you nor your ever-living power!
The oracles concerning Laius
are old and dim and men regard them not.
Apollo is nowhere clear in honour; God's service perishes.

[*Enter* JOCASTA, *carrying garlands.*]

JOCASTA. Princes of the land, I have had the thought to go
to the Gods' temples, bringing in my hand
garlands and gifts of incense, as you see.
For Oedipus excites himself too much
at every sort of trouble, not conjecturing,
like a man of sense, what will be from what was,
but he is always at the speaker's mercy,
when he speaks terrors. I can do no good
by my advice, and so I came as suppliant
to you, Lycaean Apollo, who are nearest.
These are the symbols of my prayer and this
my prayer: grant us escape free of the curse.
Now when we look to him we are all afraid;
he's pilot of our ship and he is frightened.

[*Enter a* MESSENGER.]

MESSENGER. Might I learn from you, sirs, where is the house of Oedipus? Or best of all, if you know, where is the king himself?

CHORUS. This is his house and he is within doors. This lady is his wife and mother of his children.

MESSENGER. God bless you, lady, and God bless your household! God bless Oedipus' noble wife!

JOCASTA. God bless you, sir, for your kind greeting! What do you want of us that you have come here? What have you to tell us?

MESSENGER. Good news, lady. Good for your house and for your husband.

JOCASTA. What is your news? Who sent you to us?

MESSENGER. I come from Corinth and the news I bring will give you pleasure. Perhaps a little pain too.

JOCASTA. What is this news of double meaning?

MESSENGER. The people of the Isthmus will choose Oedipus to be their king. That is the rumour there.

JOCASTA. But isn't their king still old Polybus?

MESSENGER. No. He is in his grave. Death has got him.

JOCASTA. Is that the truth? Is Oedipus' father dead?

MESSENGER. May I die myself if it be otherwise!

JOCASTA (*to a servant*). Be quick and run to the King with the news! O oracles of the Gods, where are you now? It was from this man Oedipus fled, lest he should be his murderer! And now he is dead, in the course of nature, and not killed by Oedipus.

[*Enter* OEDIPUS.]

OEDIPUS. Dearest Jocasta, why have you sent for me?

JOCASTA. Listen to this man and when you hear reflect what is the outcome of the holy oracles of the Gods.

OEDIPUS. Who is he? What is his message for me?

JOCASTA. He is from Corinth and he tells us that your father Polybus is dead and gone.

OEDIPUS. What's this you say, sir? Tell me yourself.

MESSENGER. Since this is the first matter you want clearly told: Polybus has gone down to death. You may be sure of it.

OEDIPUS. By treachery or sickness?

MESSENGER. A small thing will put old bodies asleep.

OEDIPUS. So he died of sickness, it seems,—poor old man!

MESSENGER. Yes, and of age—the long years he had measured.

OEDIPUS. Ha! Ha! O dear Jocasta, why should one
look to the Pythian hearth? Why should one look
to the birds screaming overhead? They prophesied
that I should kill my father! But he's dead,
and hidden deep in earth, and I stand here
who never laid a hand on spear against him,—
unless perhaps he died of longing for me,
and thus I am his murderer. But they,
the oracles, as they stand—he's taken them
away with him, they're dead as he himself is,
and worthless.

JOCASTA. That I told you before now.

OEDIPUS. You did, but I was misled by my fear.

JOCASTA. Then lay no more of them to heart, not one.

OEDIPUS. But surely I must fear my mother's bed?

JOCASTA. Why should man fear since chance is all in all
for him, and he can clearly foreknow nothing?
Best to live lightly, as one can, unthinkingly.
As to your mother's marriage bed,—don't fear it.
Before this, in dreams too, as well as oracles,
many a man has lain with his own mother.
But he to whom such things are nothing bears
his life most easily.

OEDIPUS. All that you say would be said perfectly
if she were dead; but since she lives I must
still fear, although you talk so well, Jocasta.

JOCASTA. Still in your father's death there's light of comfort?

OEDIPUS. Great light of comfort; but I fear the living.

MESSENGER. Who is the woman that makes you afraid?

OEDIPUS. Merope, old man, Polybus' wife.

MESSENGER. What about her frightens the queen and you?

OEDIPUS. A terrible oracle, stranger, from the Gods.

MESSENGER. Can it be told? Or does the sacred law
forbid another to have knowledge of it?

OEDIPUS. O no! Once on a time Loxias said
that I should lie with my own mother and
take on my hands the blood of my own father.
And so for these long years I've lived away
from Corinth; it has been to my great happiness;
but yet it's sweet to see the face of parents.

MESSENGER. This was the fear which drove you out of Corinth?

OEDIPUS. Old man, I did not wish to kill my father.

MESSENGER. Why should I not free you from this fear, sir,
since I have come to you in all goodwill?

OEDIPUS. You would not find me thankless if you did.

MESSENGER. Why, it was just for this I brought the news,—
to earn your thanks when you had come safe home.

OEDIPUS. No, I will never come near my parents.

MESSENGER. Son,
it's very plain you don't know what you're doing.

OEDIPUS. What do you mean, old man? For God's sake, tell me.

MESSENGER. If your homecoming is checked by fears like these.

OEDIPUS. Yes, I'm afraid that Phoebus may prove right.

MESSENGER. The murder and the incest?

OEDIPUS. Yes, old man;
that is my constant terror.

MESSENGER. Do you know
that all your fears are empty?

OEDIPUS. How is that,
if they are father and mother and I their son?

MESSENGER. Because Polybus was no kin to you in blood.

OEDIPUS. What, was not Polybus my father?

MESSENGER. No more than I but just so much.

OEDIPUS. How can
my father be my father as much as one
that's nothing to me?

MESSENGER. Neither he nor I
begat you.

OEDIPUS. Why then did he call me son?

MESSENGER. A gift he took you from these hands of mine.

OEDIPUS. Did he love so much what he took from another's hand?

MESSENGER. His childlessness before persuaded him.

OEDIPUS. Was I a child you bought or found when I
was given to him?

MESSENGER. On Cithaeron's slopes
in the twisting thickets you were found.

OEDIPUS. And why
were you a traveller in those parts?

MESSENGER. I was
in charge of mountain flocks.

OEDIPUS. You were a shepherd?
A hireling vagrant?

MESSENGER. Yes, but at least at that time
the man that saved your life, son.

OEDIPUS. What ailed me when you took me in your arms?

MESSENGER. In that your ankles should be witnesses.

OEDIPUS. Why do you speak of that old pain?

MESSENGER. I loosed you;
the tendons of your feet were pierced and fettered,—

OEDIPUS. My swaddling clothes brought me a rare disgrace.

MESSENGER. So that from this you're called your present name.

OEDIPUS. Was this my father's doing or my mother's?
For God's sake, tell me.

MESSENGER. I don't know, but he
who gave you to me has more knowledge than I.

OEDIPUS. You yourself did not find me then? You took me
from someone else?

MESSENGER. Yes, from another shepherd.

OEDIPUS. Who was he? Do you know him well enough
to tell?

MESSENGER. He was called Laius' man.

OEDIPUS. You mean the king who reigned here in the old
days?

MESSENGER. Yes, he was that man's shepherd.

OEDIPUS. Is he alive
still, so that I could see him?

MESSENGER. You who live here
would know that best.

OEDIPUS. Do any of you here
know of this shepherd whom he speaks about
in town or in the fields? Tell me. It's time
that this was found out once for all.

CHORUS. I think he is none other than the peasant
whom you have sought to see already; but
Jocasta here can tell us best of that.

OEDIPUS. Jocasta, do you know about this man
whom we have sent for? Is he the man he mentions?

JOCASTA. Why ask of whom he spoke? Don't give it heed;
nor try to keep in mind what has been said.
It will be wasted labour.

OEDIPUS. With such clues
I could not fail to bring my birth to light.

JOCASTA. I beg you—do not hunt this out—I beg you,
if you have any care for your own life.
What I am suffering is enough.

OEDIPUS. Keep up
your heart, Jocasta. Though I'm proved a slave,
thrice slave, and though my mother is thrice slave,
you'll not be shown to be of lowly lineage.

JOCASTA. O be persuaded by me, I entreat you;
do not do this.

OEDIPUS. I will not be persuaded to let be
the chance of finding out the whole thing clearly.

JOCASTA. It is because I wish you well that I
give you this counsel—and it's the best counsel.

OEDIPUS. Then the best counsel vexes me, and has
for some while since.

JOCASTA. O Oedipus, God help you!
God keep you from the knowledge of who you are!

OEDIPUS. Here, some one, go and fetch the shepherd for me;
and let her find her joy in her rich family!

JOCASTA. O Oedipus, unhappy Oedipus!
that is all I can call you, and the last thing
that I shall ever call you. [*Exit*]

CHORUS. Why has the queen gone, Oedipus, in wild
grief rushing from us? I am afraid that trouble
will break out of this silence.

OEDIPUS. Break out what will! I at least shall be
willing to see my ancestry, though humble.
Perhaps she is ashamed of my low birth,
for she has all a woman's high-flown pride.
But I account myself a child of Fortune,
beneficent Fortune, and I shall not be
dishonoured. She's the mother from whom I spring;
the months, my brothers, marked me, now as small,
and now again as mighty. Such is my breeding,
and I shall never prove so false to it,
as not to find the secret of my birth.

Strophe

CHORUS. If I am a prophet and wise of heart
you shall not fail, Cithaeron,
by the limitless sky, you shall not!—
to know at tomorrow's full moon that Oedipus honours you as native to him
and mother and nurse at once;
and that you are honoured in dancing by us, as finding favour in sight of our
king.
Apollo, to whom we cry, find these things pleasing!

Antistrophe

Who was it bore you, child? One of
the long-lived nymphs who lay with Pan—
the father who treads the hills?
Or was she a bride of Loxias, your mother? The grassy slopes
are all of them dear to him. Or perhaps Cyllene's king
or the Bacchants' God that lives on the tops
of the hills received you a gift from some
one of the Helicon Nymphs, with whom he mostly plays?

[*Enter an old man, led by* OEDIPUS' *servants.*]

OEDIPUS. If some one like myself who never met him
may make a guess,—I think this is the herdsman,
whom we were seeking. His old age is consonant
with the other. And besides, the men who bring him
I recognize as my own servants. You
perhaps may better me in knowledge since
you've seen the man before.

CHORUS. You can be sure
I recognize him. For if Laius
had ever an honest shepherd, this was he.

OEDIPUS. You, sir, from Corinth, I must ask you first,
is this the man you spoke of?

MESSENGER. This is he
before your eyes.

OEDIPUS. Old man, look here at me
and tell me what I ask you. Were you ever
a servant of King Laius?

HERDSMAN. I was,—
no slave he bought but reared in his own house.

OEDIPUS. What did you do as work? How did you live?

HERDSMAN. Most of my life was spent among the flocks.

OEDIPUS. In what part of the country did you live?

HERDSMAN. Cithaeron and the places near to it.

OEDIPUS. And somewhere there perhaps you knew this man?

HERDSMAN. What was his occupation? Who?

OEDIPUS. This man here,
have you had any dealings with him?

HERDSMAN. No—
not such that I can quickly call to mind.

MESSENGER. That is no wonder, master. But I'll make him remember what he does not know. For I know, that he well knows the country of Cithaeron, how he with two flocks, I with one kept company for three years—each year half a year—from spring till autumn time and then when winter came I drove my flocks to our fold home again and he to Laius' steadings. Well—am I right or not in what I said we did?

HERDSMAN. You're right—although it's a long time ago.

MESSENGER. Do you remember giving me a child
to bring up as my foster child?

HERDSMAN. What's this?
Why do you ask this question?

MESSENGER. Look, old man,
here he is—here's the man who was that child!

HERDSMAN. Death take you! Won't you hold your tongue?

OEDIPUS. No, no,
do not find fault with him, old man. Your words
are more at fault than his.

HERDSMAN. O best of masters,
how do I give offense?

OEDIPUS. When you refuse
to speak about the child of whom he asks you.

HERDSMAN. He speaks out of his ignorance, without meaning.
OEDIPUS. If you'll not talk to gratify me, you
will talk with pain to urge you.
HERDSMAN. O please, sir,
don't hurt an old man, sir.
OEDIPUS (*to the servants*). Here, one of you,
twist his hands behind him.
HERDSMAN. Why, God help me, why?
What do you want to know?
OEDIPUS. You gave a child
to him,—the child he asked you of?
HERDSMAN. I did.
I wish I'd died the day I did.
OEDIPUS. You will
unless you tell me truly.
HERDSMAN. And I'll die
far worse if I should tell you.
OEDIPUS. This fellow
is bent on more delays, as it would seem.
HERDSMAN. O no, no! I have told you that I gave it.
OEDIPUS. Where did you get this child from? Was it your own
or did you get it from another?
HERDSMAN. Not
my own at all; I had it from some one.
OEDIPUS. One of these citizens? or from what house?
HERDSMAN. O master, please—I beg you, master, please
don't ask me more.
OEDIPUS. You're a dead man if I
ask you again.
HERDSMAN. It was one of the children
of Laius.
OEDIPUS. A slave? Or born in wedlock?
HERDSMAN. O God, I am on the brink of frightful speech.
OEDIPUS. And I of frightful hearing. But I must hear.
HERDSMAN. The child was called his child; but she within,
your wife would tell you best how all this was.
OEDIPUS. *She* gave it to you?
HERDSMAN. Yes, she did, my lord.
OEDIPUS. To do what with it?
HERDSMAN. Make away with it.
OEDIPUS. She was so hard—its mother?
HERDSMAN. Aye, through fear
of evil oracles.

OEDIPUS. Which?

HERDSMAN. They said that he
should kill his parents.

OEDIPUS. How was it that you
gave it away to this old man?

HERDSMAN. O master,
I pitied it, and thought that I could send it
off to another country and this man
was from another country. But he saved it
for the most terrible troubles. If you are
the man he says you are, you're bred to misery.

OEDIPUS. O, O, O, they will all come,
all come out clearly! Light of the sun, let me
look upon you no more after today!
I who first saw the light bred of a match
accursed, and accursed in my living
with them I lived with, cursed in my killing.

[*Exeunt all but the* CHORUS.]

Strophe 1

CHORUS. O generations of men, how I
count you as equal with those who live
not at all!
what man, what man on earth wins more
of happiness than a seeming
and after that turning away?
Oedipus, you are my pattern of this,
Oedipus, you and your fate!
Luckless Oedipus, whom of all men
I envy not at all.

Antistrophe 1

Inasmuch as he shot his bolt
beyond the others and won the prize
of happiness complete—
O Zeus—and killed and reduced to nought
the hooked taloned maid of the riddling speech,
standing a tower against death for my land:
hence he was called my king and hence
was honoured the highest of all
honours; and hence he ruled
in the great city of Thebes.

Strophe 2

But now whose tale is more miserable?

Who is there lives with a savager fate?
Whose troubles so reverse his life as his?

O Oedipus, the famous prince
for whom a great haven
the same both as father and son
sufficed for generation,
how, O how, have the furrows ploughed
by your father endured to bear you, poor wretch,
and hold their peace so long?

Antistrophe 2

Time who sees all has found you out
against your will; judges your marriage accursed,
begetter and begot at one in it.

O child of Laius,
would I had never seen you,
I weep for you and cry
a dirge of lamentation.
To speak directly, I drew my breath
from you at the first and so now I lull
my mouth to sleep with your name.

[*Enter a* SECOND MESSENGER.]

SECOND MESSENGER. O Princes always honoured by our country,
what deeds you'll hear of and what horrors see
what grief you'll feel, if you as true born Thebans
care for the house of Labdacus's sons.
Phasis nor Ister cannot purge this house,
I think, with all their streams, such things
it hides, such evils shortly will bring forth
into the light, whether they will or not;
and troubles hurt the most
when they prove self-inflicted.

CHORUS. What we had known before did not fall short
of bitter groaning's worth; what's more to tell?

SECOND MESSENGER. Shortest to hear and tell—our glorious queen
Jocasta's dead.

CHORUS. Unhappy woman! How?

SECOND MESSENGER. By her own hand. The worst of what was done
you cannot know. You did not see the sight.
Yet in so far as I remember it
you'll hear the end of our unlucky queen.

When she came raging into the house she went
straight to her marriage bed, tearing her hair
with both her hands, and crying upon Laius
long dead—Do you remember, Laius,
that night long past which bred a child for us
to send you to your death and leave
a mother making children with her son?
And then she groaned and cursed the bed in which
she brought forth husband by her husband, children
by her own child, an infamous double bond.
How after that she died I do not know,—
for Oedipus distracted us from seeing.
He burst upon us shouting and we looked
to him as he paced frantically around,
begging us always: Give me a sword, I say,
to find this wife no wife, this mother's womb,
this field of double sowing whence I sprang
and where I sowed my children! As he raved
some god showed him the way—none of us there.
Bellowing terribly and led by some
invisible guide he rushed on the two doors,—
wrenching the hollow bolts out of their sockets,
he charged inside. There, there, we saw his wife
hanging, the twisted rope around her neck.
When he saw her, he cried out fearfully
and cut the dangling noose. Then, as she lay,
poor woman, on the ground, what happened after,
was terrible to see. He tore the brooches—
the gold chased brooches fastening her robe—
away from her and lifting them up high
dashed them on his own eyeballs, shrieking out
such things as: they will never see the crime
I have committed or had done upon me!
Dark eyes, now in the days to come look on
forbidden faces, do not recognize
those whom you long for—with such imprecations
he struck his eyes again and yet again
with the brooches. And the bleeding eyeballs gushed
and stained his beard—no sluggish oozing drops
but a black rain and bloody hail poured down.

So it has broken—and not on one head
but troubles mixed for husband and for wife.
The fortune of the days gone by was true

good fortune—but today groans and destruction
and death and shame—of all ills can be named
not one is missing.

CHORUS. Is he now in any ease from pain?

SECOND MESSENGER. He shouts
for some one to unbar the doors and show him
to all the men of Thebes, his father's killer,
his mother's—no I cannot say the word,
it is unholy—for he'll cast himself,
out of the land, he says, and not remain
to bring a curse upon his house, the curse
he called upon it in his proclamation. But
he wants for strength, aye, and some one to guide him;
his sickness is too great to bear. You, too,
will be shown that. The bolts are opening.
Soon you will see a sight to waken pity
even in the horror of it.

[*Enter the blinded* OEDIPUS.]

CHORUS. This is a terrible sight for men to see!
I never found a worse!
Poor wretch, what madness came upon you!
What evil spirit leaped upon your life
to your ill-luck—a leap beyond man's strength!
Indeed I pity you, but I cannot
look at you, though there's much I want to ask
and much to learn and much to see.
I shudder at the sight of you.

OEDIPUS. O, O,
where am I going? Where is my voice
borne on the wind to and fro?
Spirit, how far have you sprung?

CHORUS. To a terrible place whereof men's ears
may not hear, nor their eyes behold it.

OEDIPUS. Darkness!
Horror of darkness enfolding, resistless, unspeakable visitant sped by an ill wind in haste!
madness and stabbing pain and memory
of evil deeds I have done!

CHORUS. In such misfortunes it's no wonder
if double weighs the burden of your grief.

OEDIPUS. My friend,
you are the only one steadfast, the only one that attends on me;
you still stay nursing the blind man.

Your care is not unnoticed. I can know
your voice, although this darkness is my world.

CHORUS. Doer of dreadful deeds, how did you dare
so far to do despite to your own eyes?
what spirit urged you to it?

OEDIPUS. It was Apollo, friends, Apollo,
that brought this bitter bitterness, my sorrows to completion.
But the hand that struck me
was none but my own.
Why should I see
whose vision showed me nothing sweet to see?

CHORUS. These things are as you say.

OEDIPUS. What can I see to love?
What greeting can touch my ears with joy?
Take me away, and haste—to a place out of the way!
Take me away, my friends, the greatly miserable,
the most accursed, whom God too hates
above all men on earth!

CHORUS. Unhappy in your mind and your misfortune,
would I had never known you!

OEDIPUS. Curse on the man who took
the cruel bonds from off my legs, as I lay in the field.
He stole me from death and saved me,
no kindly service.
Had I died then
I would not be so burdensome to friends.

CHORUS. I, too, could have wished it had been so.

OEDIPUS. Then I would not have come
to kill my father and marry my mother infamously.
Now I am godless and child of impurity,
begetter in the same seed that created my wretched self.
If there is any ill worse than ill,
that is the lot of Oedipus.

CHORUS. I cannot say your remedy was good;
you would be better dead than blind and living.

OEDIPUS. What I have done here was best done—don't tell me
otherwise, do not give me further counsel.
I do not know with what eyes I could look
upon my father when I die and go
under the earth, nor yet my wretched mother—
those two to whom I have done things deserving
worse punishment than hanging. Would the sight
of children, bred as mine are, gladden me?
No, not these eyes, never. And my city,

its towers and sacred places of the Gods,
of these I robbed my miserable self
when I commanded all to drive *him* out,
the criminal since proved by God impure
and of the race of Laius.
To this guilt I bore witness against myself—
with what eyes shall I look upon my people?
No. If there were a means to choke the fountain
of hearing I would not have stayed my hand
from locking up my miserable carcase,
seeing and hearing nothing; it is sweet
to keep our thoughts out of the range of hurt.

Cithaeron, why did you receive me? why
having received me did you not kill me straight?
And so I had not shown to men my birth.

O Polybus and Corinth and the house,
the old house that I used to call my father's—
what fairness you were nurse to, and what foulness
festered beneath! Now I am found to be
a sinner and a son of sinners. Crossroads,
and hidden glade, oak and the narrow way
at the crossroads, that drank my father's blood
offered you by my hands, do you remember
still what I did as you looked on, and what
I did when I came here? O marriage, marriage!
you bred me and again when you had bred
bred children of your child and showed to men
brides, wives and mothers and the foulest deeds
that can be in this world of ours.

Come—it's unfit to say what is unfit
to do.—I beg of you in God's name hide me
somewhere outside your country, yes, or kill me,
or throw me into the sea, to be forever
out of your sight. Approach and deign to touch me
for all my wretchedness, and do not fear.
No man but I can bare my evil doom.

CHORUS. Here Creon comes in fit time to perform
or give advice in what you ask of us.
Creon is left sole ruler in your stead.

OEDIPUS. Creon! Creon! What shall I say to him?
How can I justly hope that he will trust me?

In what is past I have been proved towards him
an utter liar.

[*Enter* CREON.]

CREON. Oedipus, I've come
not so that I might laugh at you nor taunt you
with evil of the past. But if you still
are without shame before the face of men
reverence at least the flame that gives all life,
our Lord the Sun, and do not show unveiled
to him pollution such that neither land
nor holy rain nor light of day can welcome.

[*To a servant*]

Be quick and take him in. It is most decent
that only kin should see and hear the troubles
of kin.

OEDIPUS. I beg you, since you've torn me from
my dreadful expectations and have come
in a most noble spirit to a man
that has used you vilely—do a thing for me.
I shall speak for your own good, not for my own.

CREON. What do you need that you would ask of me?

OEDIPUS. Drive me from here with all the speed you can to where I may
not hear a human voice.

CREON. Be sure, I would have done this had not I
wished first of all to learn from the God the course
of action I should follow.

OEDIPUS. But his word
has been quite clear to let the parricide,
the sinner, die.

CREON. Yes, that indeed was said.
But in the present need we had best discover
what we should do.

OEDIPUS. And will you ask about
a man so wretched?

CREON. Now even you will trust
the God.

OEDIPUS. So. I command you—and will beseech you—
to her that lies inside that house give burial
as you would have it; she is yours and rightly
you will perform the rites for her. For me—
never let this my father's city have me
living a dweller in it. Leave me live

in the mountains where Cithaeron is, that's called
my mountain, which my mother and my father
while they were living would have made my tomb.
So I may die by their decree who sought
indeed to kill me. Yet I know this much:
no sickness and no other thing will kill me.
I would not have been saved from death if not
for some strange evil fate. Well, let my fate
go where it will.
Creon, you need not care
about my sons; they're men and so wherever
they are, they will not lack a livelihood.
But my two girls—so sad and pitiful—
whose table never stood apart from mine,
and everything I touched they always shared—
O Creon, have a thought for them! And most
I wish that you might suffer me to touch them
and sorrow with them.

[*Enter* ANTIGONE *and* ISMENE, OEDIPUS' *two daughters.*]

O my lord! O true noble Creon! Can I
really be touching them, as when I saw?
What shall I say?
Yes, I can hear them sobbing—my two darlings!
and Creon has had pity and has sent me
what I loved most?
Am I right?

CREON. You're right: it was I gave you this
because I knew from old days how you loved them
as I see now.

OEDIPUS. God bless you for it, Creon,
and may God guard you better on your road
than he did me!
O children,
where are you? Come here, come to my hands,
a brother's hands which turned your father's eyes,
those bright eyes you knew once, to what you see,
a father seeing nothing, knowing nothing,
begetting you from his own source of life.
I weep for you—I cannot see your faces—
I weep when I think of the bitterness
there will be in your lives, how you must live
before the world. At what assemblages
of citizens will you make one? to what

gay company will you go and not come home
in tears instead of sharing in the holiday?
And when you're ripe for marriage, who will he be,
the man who'll risk to take such infamy
as shall cling to my children, to bring hurt
on them and those that marry with them? What
curse is not there? "Your father killed his father
and sowed the seed where he had sprung himself
and begot you out of the womb that held him."
These insults you will hear. Then who will marry you?
No one, my children; clearly you are doomed
to waste away in barrenness unmarried.
Son of Menoeceus, since you are all the father
left these two girls, and we, their parents, both
are dead to them—do not allow them wander
like beggars, poor and husbandless.
They are of your own blood.
And do not make them equal with myself
in wretchedness; for you can see them now
so young, so utterly alone, save for you only.
Touch my hand, noble Creon, and say yes.
If you were older, children, and were wiser,
there's much advice I'd give you. But as it is,
let this be what you pray: give me a life
wherever there is opportunity
to live, and better life than was my father's.

CREON. Your tears have had enough of scope; now go within the house.

OEDIPUS. I must obey, though bitter of heart.

CREON. In season, all is good.

OEDIPUS. Do you know on what conditions I obey?

CREON. You tell me them,
and I shall know them when I hear.

OEDIPUS. That you shall send me out
to live away from Thebes.

CREON. That gift you must ask of the God.

OEDIPUS. But I'm now hated by the Gods.

CREON. So quickly you'll obtain your prayer.

OEDIPUS. You consent then?

CREON. What I do not mean, I do not use to say.

OEDIPUS. Now lead me away from here.

CREON. Let go the children, then, and come.

OEDIPUS. Do not take them from me.

CREON. Do not seek to be master in everything,
for the things you mastered did not follow you throughout your life.

[*As* CREON *and* OEDIPUS *go out.*]

CHORUS. You that live in my ancestral Thebes, behold this Oedipus,—
him who knew the famous riddles and was a man most masterful;
not a citizen who did not look with envy on his lot—
See him now and see the breakers of misfortune swallow him!
Look upon that last day always. Count no mortal happy till
he has passed the final limit of his life secure from pain.

THE TRAGICAL HISTORY OF DOCTOR FAUSTUS

CHRISTOPHER MARLOWE

Dramatis Personae

THE POPE
CARDINAL OF LORRAINE
CHARLES V, *Emperor of Germany*
DUKE OF VANHOLT
FAUSTUS
VALDES } *friends to Faustus*
CORNELIUS } *friends to Faustus*
WAGNER, *servant to Faustus*
CLOWN
ROBIN
RALPH
VINTNER
HORSE-COURSER[1]
KNIGHT
OLD MAN
SCHOLARS, FRIARS, AND ATTENDANTS
DUCHESS OF VANHOLT
LUCIFER
BELZEBUB
MEPHISTOPHILIS
GOOD ANGEL
EVIL ANGEL
THE SEVEN DEADLY SINS
DEVILS
Spirits in the shape of ALEXANDER THE GREAT, *of his Paramour, and of* HELEN OF TROY
CHORUS

ACT I

[*Enter* CHORUS.]

CHORUS. Not marching now in fields of Thrasimene,
Where Mars did mate[2] the Carthaginians;
Nor sporting in the dalliance of love,
In courts of kings where state is overturn'd;
Nor in the pomp of proud, audacious deeds,
Intends our Muse to vaunt his heavenly verse:—
Only this, gentlemen: we must perform
The form of Faustus' fortunes, good or bad.
To patient judgments we appeal our plaud,[3]
And speak for Faustus in his infancy.
Now is he born, his parents base of stock,
In Germany, within a town call'd Rhodes;[4]

The text and footnotes are based on Hazelton Spencer, *Elizabethan Plays* (Boston: Little, Brown, 1933) modified by the textual readings of W. W. Greg, *Marlowe's Doctor Faustus* (Oxford University Press, 1950).

1. Horse trader.
2. Defeat. But Hannibal won this battle. The author may be confused; and the whole speech may be non-Marlovian.
3. For our applause.
4. Roda, in the Duchy of Saxe-Altenburg.

Of riper years to Wittenberg he went,
Whereas his kinsmen chiefly brought him up.
So soon he profits in divinity,
The fruitful plot of scholarism grac'd,[5]
That shortly he was grac'd [6] with doctor's name,
Excelling all whose sweet delight disputes
In heavenly matters of theology;
Till, swol'n with cunning,[7] of a self-conceit,
His waxen[8] wings did mount above his reach,
And melting Heavens conspir'd his overthrow;
For, falling to a devilish exercise,
And glutted more with learning's golden gifts,
He surfeits upon cursed necromancy.
Nothing so sweet as magic is to him,
Which he prefers before his chiefest bliss.
And this the man that in his study sits. [*Exit.*]

ACT I: SCENE 1 [9]

[*Enter* FAUSTUS *in his Study.*]

FAUSTUS. Settle thy studies, Faustus, and begin
To sound the depth of that thou wilt profess.
Having commenc'd,[10] be a divine in show;
Yet level [11] at the end of every art,
And live and die in Aristotle's works.
Sweet Analytics,[12] 'tis thou hast ravish'd me,
Bene disserere est finis logices.
Is to dispute well logic's chiefest end?
Affords this art no greater miracle?
Then read no more; thou hast attain'd the end—
A greater subject fitteth Faustus' wit.
Bid ὂν καὶ μὴ ὂν[13] farewell, Galen come;
Seeing *Ubi desinit Philosophus, ibi incipit Medicus;*[14]
Be a physician, Faustus, heap up gold,

---

5. Full of graces. (Cf. *Macbeth,* III, iv, 41.)
6. Punning on the official "grace" (at Cambridge) by virtue of which a candidate took his degree.
7. Puffed up with knowledge. 8. *I.e.,* insecure, like the wings of Icarus.
9. Wittenberg. Faustus is "discovered" on the inner stage.
10. Taken a degree. 11. Aim. 12. Aristotelian logic.
13. Aristotle's "being and not being"; emend. Bullen.
14. Where the philosopher leaves off, there the physician begins. (Adapted from Aristotle, as is the third line following.)

And be eterniz'd for some wondrous cure.
Summum bonum medicinae sanitas:
The end of physic is our body's health.
Why, Faustus, hast thou not attain'd that end?
Is not thy common talk sound Aphorisms?[15]
Are not thy bills[16] hung up as monuments,
Whereby whole cities have escap'd the plague,
And thousand desp'rate maladies been eas'd?
Yet art thou still but Faustus and a man.
Wouldst thou make men to live eternally,
Or, being dead, raise them to life again?
Then this profession were to be esteem'd.
Physic, farewell.—Where is Justinian? [*Reads.*]
Si una eademque res legatur duobus, alter rem, alter valorem rei, &c.[17]
A pretty case of paltry legacies! [*Reads.*]
Exhœreditare filium non potest pater nisi. . .[18]
Such is the subject of the Institute
And universal body of the law.
His[19] study fits a mercenary drudge,
Who aims at nothing but external trash;[20]
Too servile and illiberal for me.
When all is done, divinity is best;
Jerome's Bible,[21] Faustus, view it well. [*Reads.*]
Stipendium peccati mors est. Ha! *Stipendium, &c.:*
The reward of sin is death. That's hard. [*Reads.*]
Si peccasse negamus, fallimur, et nulla est in nobis veritas:
If we say that we have no sin we deceive ourselves, and there's no truth in us. Why then, belike we must sin and so consequently die.
Ay, we must die an everlasting death.
What doctrine call you this, *Che sera, sera:*
"What will be, shall be"? Divinity, adieu!
These metaphysics of magicians
And necromantic books are heavenly;
Lines, circles, scenes, letters, and characters,
Ay, these are those that Faustus most desires.
O what a world of profit and delight,
Of power, of honor, of omnipotence
Is promis'd to the studious artisan!

15. Medical memoranda, so called from the Aphorisms of Hippocrates. (Ward.)
16. Prescriptions. (Wheeler).
17. If one and the same thing is bequeathed to two persons, one shall take the thing and the other its value. (An incorrect version of a rule in the *Institutes.*) (Boas.)
18. A father cannot disinherit his son, except . . . (Adapted from the *Institutes* of Justinian, codifier of the Roman law.)
19. Its. 20. *I.e.*, money. 21. The Vulgate.

All things that move between the quiet[22] poles
Shall be at my command. Emperors and kings
Are but obey'd in their several provinces,
Nor can they raise the wind or rend the clouds;
But his dominion that exceeds[23] in this
Stretcheth as far as doth the mind of man.
A sound magician is a mighty god:
Here, Faustus, try thy brains to gain a deity.

[*Enter* WAGNER.]

Wagner, commend me to my dearest friends,
The German Valdes and Cornelius;
Request them earnestly to visit me.

WAGNER. I will, sir. [*Exit.*]

FAUSTUS. Their conference[24] will be a greater help to me
Than all my labors, plod I ne'er so fast.

[*Enter* GOOD ANGEL *and* EVIL ANGEL.]

GOOD ANGEL. O Faustus! lay that damned book aside,
And gaze not on it lest it tempt thy soul
And heap God's heavy wrath upon thy head.
Read, read the Scriptures; that is blasphemy.

EVIL ANGEL. Go forward, Faustus, in that famous art,
Wherein all Nature's treasury is contain'd;
Be thou on earth as Jove is in the sky,
Lord and commander of these elements. [*Exeunt* ANGELS.]

FAUSTUS. How am I glutted with conceit of this![25]
Shall I make spirits fetch me what I please,
Resolve me of all ambiguities,
Perform what desperate enterprise I will?
I'll have them fly to India[26] for gold,
Ransack the ocean for orient pearl,
And search all corners of the new-found world
For pleasant fruits and princely delicates.
I'll have them read me strange philosophy
And tell the secrets of all foreign kings;
I'll have them wall all Germany with brass,
And make swift Rhine circle fair Wittenberg;
I'll have them fill the public schools[27] with silk,[28]

22. *I.e.,* fixed. 23. Excels. 24. Conversation.
25. How am I filled with this notion. 26. Probably, the West Indies, America.
27. University lecture-halls.
28. Emend. Dyce; old eds. *skill.* Brooke cites Cambridge regulations which forbade the wearing of silk by the students.

Wherewith the students shall be bravely clad;
I'll levy soldiers with the coin they bring,
And chase the Prince of Parma[29] from our land,
And reign sole king of all our provinces;
Yea, stranger engines for the brunt of war
Than was the fiery keel[30] at Antwerp's bridge,
I'll make my servile spirits to invent.
Come, German Valdes and Cornelius,
And make me blest with your sage conference.

[*Enter* VALDES *and* CORNELIUS.]

Valdes, sweet Valdes, and Cornelius,
Know that your words have won me at the last
To practise magic and concealed arts;
Yet not your words only, but mine own fantasy,
That will receive no object;[31] for my head
But ruminates on necromantic skill.
Philosophy is odious and obscure;
Both law and physic are for petty wits;
Divinity is basest of the three,
Unpleasant, harsh, contemptible, and vile:
'Tis magic, magic, that hath ravish'd me.
Then, gentle friends, aid me in this attempt;
And I that have with concise syllogisms
Gravell'd the pastors of the German church,
And made the flow'ring pride of Wittenberg
Swarm to my problems,[32] as the infernal spirits
On sweet Musæus, when he came to hell,
Will be as cunning as Agrippa was,
Whose shadows[33] made all Europe honor him.

VALDES. Faustus, these books, thy wit, and our experience
Shall make all nations to canonize us.
As Indian Moors[34] obey their Spanish lords,
So shall the subjects of every element
Be always serviceable to us three;
Like lions shall they guard us when we please;
Like Almain rutters[35] with their horsemen's staves,

---

29. The Spanish governor-general (1579–1592) of the Netherlands, nominally a part of the Empire.
30. A Dutch "devil-ship" (filled with explosives) which damaged Parma's bridge at the siege of Antwerp.
31. *I.e.*, my own fancy, which will entertain no regular academic subject—or anything else but necromancy.
32. Mathematical and logical lectures. (Ward.)
33. Shades raised from the dead.
34. American Indians.
35. German troopers.

Or Lapland giants, trotting by our sides;
Sometimes like women or unwedded maids,
Shadowing more beauty in their airy brows
Than have the white breasts of the queen of love:
From Venice shall they drag huge argosies,
And from America the golden fleece
That yearly stuffs old Philip's treasury;
If learned Faustus will be resolute.

FAUSTUS. Valdes, as resolute am I in this
As thou to live; therefore object it not.

CORNELIUS. The miracles that magic will perform
Will make thee vow to study nothing else.
He that is grounded in astrology,
Enrich'd with tongues, well seen[36] in minerals,
Hath all the principles magic doth require.
Then doubt not, Faustus, but to be renown'd,
And more frequented for this mystery
Than heretofore the Delphian Oracle.
The spirits tell me they can dry the sea
And fetch the treasure of all foreign wracks,
Ay, all the wealth that our forefathers hid
Within the massy entrails of the earth;
Then tell me, Faustus, what shall we three want?

FAUSTUS. Nothing, Cornelius! O, this cheers my soul!
Come show me some demonstrations magical,
That I may conjure in some lusty grove,
And have these joys in full possession.

VALDES. Then haste thee to some solitary grove,
And bear wise Bacon's[37] and Albanus' [38] works,
The Hebrew Psalter and New Testament;
And whatsoever else is requisite
We will inform thee ere our conference cease.

CORNELIUS. Valdes, first let him know the words of art;
And then, all other ceremonies learn'd,
Faustus may try his cunning by himself.

VALDES. First I'll instruct thee in the rudiments,
And then wilt thou be perfecter than I.

FAUSTUS. Then come and dine with me, and after meat
We'll canvass every quiddity[39] thereof;
For ere I sleep I'll try what I can do:
This night I'll conjure though I die therefore. [*Exeunt.*]

36. Versed. 37. Roger Bacon's.
38. Possibly Pietro d'Albano, a thirteenth-century alchemist; or misprinted, Albertus Magnus, the German Dominican of the same century, supposed to be a magician.
39. Essential point.

ACT I: SCENE 2[40]

[*Enter two* SCHOLARS.]

FIRST SCHOLAR. I wonder what's become of Faustus, that was wont to make our schools ring with *sic probo?*[41]

SECOND SCHOLAR. That shall we know, for see here comes his boy.

[*Enter* WAGNER.]

FIRST SCHOLAR. How now, sirrah! Where's thy master?

WAGNER. God in heaven knows!

SECOND SCHOLAR. Why, dost not thou know?

WAGNER. Yes, I know. But that follows not.

FIRST SCHOLAR. Go to, sirrah! Leave your jesting, and tell us where he is.

WAGNER. That follows not necessary by force of argument, that you, being licentiate,[42] should stand upon't; therefore acknowledge your error and be attentive.

SECOND SCHOLAR. Why, didst thou not say thou knew'st?

WAGNER. Have you any witness on't?

FIRST SCHOLAR. Yes, sirrah, I heard you.

WAGNER. Ask my fellow if I be a thief.

SECOND SCHOLAR. Well, you will not tell us?

WAGNER. Yes, sir, I will tell you; yet if you were not dunces, you would never ask me such a question; for is not he *corpus naturale?*[43] and is not that *mobile?* Then wherefore should you ask me such a question? But that I am by nature phlegmatic, slow to wrath, and prone to lechery (to love, I would say), it were not for you to come within forty foot of the place of execution, although I do not doubt to see you both hang'd the next sessions. Thus having triumph'd over you, I will set my countenance like a precisian,[44] and begin to speak thus:—Truly, my dear brethren, my master is within at dinner, with Valdes and Cornelius, as this wine, if it could speak, it would inform your worships; and so the Lord bless you, preserve you, and keep you, my dear brethren, my dear brethren. [*Exit.*]

FIRST SCHOLAR. Nay, then, I fear he has fall'n into that damned Art, for which they two are infamous through the world.

SECOND SCHOLAR. Were he a stranger, and not allied to me, yet should I grieve for him. But come, let us go and inform the Rector, and see if he by his grave counsel can reclaim him.

FIRST SCHOLAR. O, I fear me nothing can reclaim him.

SECOND SCHOLAR. Yet let us try what we can do. [*Exeunt.*]

---

40. Before Faustus' house.
41. Thus I prove (a scholastic formula).
42. Licensed to ascend to a Master's or Doctor's degree. (Boas.)
43. "'Corpus naturale seu mobile' is the current scholastic expression for the subject-matter of physics." (Ward.)
44. Puritan.

ACT I: SCENE 3 [45]

[*Enter* FAUSTUS *to conjure.*]

FAUSTUS. Now that the gloomy shadow of the earth
Longing to view Orion's drizzling look,
Leaps from th' antarctic world unto the sky,
And dims the welkin with her pitchy breath,
Faustus, begin thy incantations,
And try if devils will obey thy hest,
Seeing thou hast pray'd and sacrific'd to them.
Within this circle is Jehovah's name,
Forward and backward anagrammatiz'd,
The breviated names of holy saints,
Figures of every adjunct to[46] the Heavens,
And characters of signs and erring stars,[47]
By which the spirits are enforc'd to rise.
Then fear not, Faustus, but be resolute,
And try the uttermost magic can perform.

Sint mihi Dei Acherontis propitii! Valeat numen triplex Jehovæ! Ignei, œrii, aquatani spiritus, salvete! Orientis princeps Belzebub, inferni ardentis monarcha, et Demogorgon, propitiamus vos, ut appareat et surgat Mephistophilis. Quid tu moraris? Per Jehovam, Gehennam, et consecratam aquam quam nunc spargo, signumque crucis quod nunc facio, et per vota nostra, ipse nunc surgat nobis dicatus Mephistophilis![48]

[*Enter* MEPHISTOPHILIS, *a* DEVIL.]

I charge thee to return and change thy shape;
Thou art too ugly to attend on me.
Go, and return an old Franciscan friar;
That holy shape becomes a devil best. [*Exit* DEVIL.]
I see there's virtue in my heavenly words;
Who would not be proficient in this art?
How pliant is this Mephistophilis,
Full of obedience and humility!
Such is the force of magic and my spells.
Now, Faustus, thou art conjuror laureate;
Thou canst command great Mephistophilis:
Quin regis Mephistophilis fratris imagine.[49]

45. A grove. 46. Every star joined to. 47. Planets.
48. Unto me be the gods of Acheron propitious. May the triple name of Jehovah prevail. Spirits of fire, air, and water, hail! Belzebub, Prince of the East, Sovereign of burning Hell, and Demogorgon, we propitiate you, that Mephistophilis may appear and rise. Why delayest thou? By Jehovah, Gehenna, and the holy water which now I sprinkle, and the sign of the cross which now I make, and by our prayer, may Mephistophilis, by us summoned, now arise.
49. Indeed thou rulest Mephistophilis in his likeness of a friar.

[*Re-enter* MEPHISTOPHILIS, *like a Franciscan* FRIAR.]

MEPHISTOPHILIS. Now, Faustus, what would'st thou have me do?

FAUSTUS. I charge thee wait upon me whilst I live,
To do whatever Faustus shall command,
Be it to make the moon drop from her sphere,
Or the ocean to overwhelm the world.

MEPHISTOPHILIS. I am a servant to great Lucifer,
And may not follow thee without his leave;
No more than he commands must we perform.

FAUSTUS. Did he not charge thee to appear to me?

MEPHISTOPHILIS. No, I came hither of mine own accord.

FAUSTUS. Did not my conjuring speeches raise thee? Speak.

MEPHISTOPHILIS. That was the cause, but yet per accident;
For when we hear one rack[50] the name of God,
Abjure the Scriptures and his Savior Christ,
We fly in hope to get his glorious soul;
Nor will we come, unless he use such means
Whereby he is in danger to be damn'd.
Therefore the shortest cut for conjuring
Is stoutly to abjure the Trinity,
And pray devoutly to the Prince of Hell.

FAUSTUS. So Faustus hath
Already done, and holds this principle:
There is no chief but only Belzebub,
To whom Faustus doth dedicate himself.
This word "damnation" terrifies not him,
For he confounds hell in Elysium;[51]
His ghost be with the old philosophers!
But, leaving these vain trifles of men's souls,
Tell me what is that Lucifer, thy lord?

MEPHISTOPHILIS. Arch-regent and commander of all spirits.

FAUSTUS. Was not that Lucifer an angel once?

MEPHISTOPHILIS. Yes, Faustus, and most dearly lov'd of God.

FAUSTUS. How comes it then that he is prince of devils?

MEPHISTOPHILIS. O, by aspiring pride and insolence,
For which God threw him from the face of Heaven.

FAUSTUS. And what are you that live with Lucifer?

MEPHISTOPHILIS. Unhappy spirits that fell with Lucifer,
Conspir'd against our God with Lucifer,
And are for ever damn'd with Lucifer.

FAUSTUS. Where are you damn'd?

MEPHISTOPHILIS. In hell.

---

50. Torture into anagrams. 51. Makes no distinction between hell and.

FAUSTUS. How comes it then that thou art out of hell?

MEPHISTOPHILIS. Why this is hell, nor am I out of it!
Think'st thou that I who saw the face of God,
And tasted the eternal joys of Heaven,
Am not tormented with ten thousand hells,
In being depriv'd of everlasting bliss?
O Faustus, leave these frivolous demands,
Which strike a terror to my fainting soul.

FAUSTUS. What, is great Mephistophilis so passionate
For being deprived of the joys of Heaven?
Learn thou of Faustus manly fortitude,
And scorn those joys thou never shalt possess.
Go bear these tidings to great Lucifer:
Seeing Faustus hath incurr'd eternal death
By desp'rate thoughts against Jove's[52] deity,
Say he surrenders up to him his soul,
So he will spare him four and twenty years,
Letting him live in all voluptuousness,
Having thee ever to attend on me,
To give me whatsoever I shall ask,
To tell me whatsoever I demand,
To slay mine enemies, and aid my friends,
And always be obedient to my will.
Go, and return to mighty Lucifer,
And meet me in my study at midnight,
And then resolve me of thy master's mind.

MEPHISTOPHILIS. I will, Faustus. [*Exit.*]

FAUSTUS. Had I as many souls as there be stars,
I'd give them all for Mephistophilis.
By him I'll be great Emp'ror of the world,
And make a bridge through the moving air,
To pass the ocean with a band of men;
I'll join the hills that bind the Afric shore,
And make that country continent[53] to Spain,
And both contributory to my crown.
The Emperor shall not live but by my leave,
Nor any potentate of Germany.
Now that I have obtain'd what I desire,
I'll live in speculation[54] of this art
Till Mephistophilis return again. [*Exit.*]

52. Common in Elizabethan literature for the Christian God.
53. Adjoining. 54. Contemplative study.

ACT I: SCENE 4 [55]

[*Enter* WAGNER *and the* CLOWN.]

WAGNER. Sirrah, boy, come hither.

CLOWN. How, boy! Swowns,[56] boy! I hope you have seen many boys with such pickadevaunts[57] as I have. Boy, quotha!

WAGNER. Tell me, sirrah, hast thou any comings in?

CLOWN. Ay, and goings out too. You may see else.

WAGNER. Alas, poor slave! See how poverty jesteth in his nakedness! The villain is bare and out of service, and so hungry that I know he would give his soul to the devil for a shoulder of mutton, though it were blood-raw.

CLOWN. How? My soul to the devil for a shoulder of mutton, though 'twere blood-raw! Not so, good friend. By'r Lady, I had need have it well roasted and good sauce to it, if I pay so dear.

WAGNER. Well, wilt thou serve me, and I'll make thee go like *Qui mihi discipulus?*[58]

CLOWN. How, in verse?

WAGNER. No, sirrah; in beaten silk[59] and stavesacre.[60]

CLOWN. How, how, Knave's acre! [61] Ay, I thought that was all the land his father left him. Do you hear? I would be sorry to rob you of your living.

WAGNER. Sirrah, I say in stavesacre.

CLOWN. Oho! Oho! Stavesacre! Why, then, belike, if I were your man I should be full of vermin.

WAGNER. So thou shalt, whether thou beest with me or no. But, sirrah, leave your jesting, and bind yourself presently unto me for seven years, or I'll turn all the lice about thee into familiars, and they shall tear thee in pieces.

CLOWN. Do you hear, sir? You may save that labor; they are too familiar with me already. Swowns! they are as bold with my flesh as if they had paid for my meat and drink.

WAGNER. Well, do you hear, sirrah? Hold, take these guilders.

[*Gives money.*]

CLOWN. Gridirons! what be they?

WAGNER. Why, French crowns.

CLOWN. Mass, but for the name of French crowns, a man were as good have as many English counters. And what should I do with these?

WAGNER. Why, now, sirrah, thou art at an hour's warning, whensoever or wheresoever the Devil shall fetch thee.

CLOWN. No, no. Here, take your gridirons again.

WAGNER. Truly, I'll none of them.

---

55. Unlocated; perhaps a field or wood near Wittenburg. 56. Zounds, God's wounds.
57. Pointed beards.
58. You shall be my pupil.
59. Silk with metal embroidery hammered into it.
60. A kind of larkspur, used to kill lice.
61. Poultney Street, Soho, where junk-dealers were established.

CLOWN. Truly, but you shall.

WAGNER. Bear witness I gave them him.[62]

CLOWN. Bear witness I give them you again.

WAGNER. Well, I will cause two devils presently to fetch thee away—Baliol [63] and Belcher.

CLOWN. Let your Baliol and your Belcher come here, and I'll knock them, they were never so knockt since they were devils. Say I should kill one of them, what would folks say? "Do you see yonder tall fellow in the round slop? [64]—he has kill'd the devil." So I should be call'd Kill-devil all the parish over.

[*Enter two* DEVILS: *the* CLOWN *runs up and down crying.*]

WAGNER. Baliol and Belcher! Spirits, away! [*Exeunt* DEVILS.]

CLOWN. What, are they gone? A vengeance on them, they have vile long nails! There was a he-devil, and a she-devil! I'll tell you how you shall know them: all he-devils has horns, and all she-devils has clifts and cloven feet.

WAGNER. Well, sirrah, follow me.

CLOWN. But, do you hear—if I should serve you, would you teach me to raise up Banios and Belcheos?

WAGNER. I will teach thee to turn thyself to anything; to a dog, or a cat, or a mouse, or a rat, or anything.

CLOWN. How? a Christian fellow to a dog or a cat, a mouse or a rat? No, no, sir. If you turn me into anything, let it be in the likeness of a little pretty frisking flea, that I may be here and there and everywhere. Oh, I'll tickle the pretty wenches' plackets;[65] I'll be amongst them, i' faith.

WAGNER. Well, sirrah, come.

CLOWN. But, do you hear, Wagner?

WAGNER. How!—Baliol and Belcher!

CLOWN. O Lord! I pray, sir, let Banio and Belcher go sleep.

WAGNER. Villain—call me Master Wagner, and let thy left eye be diametarily fixt upon my right heel, with *quasi vestigias nostras insistere*.[66]

CLOWN. God forgive me, he speaks Dutch fustian. Well, I'll follow him, I'll serve him, that's flat. [*Exit.*]

ACT II: SCENE 1

[*Enter* FAUSTUS *in his study.*]

FAUSTUS. Now, Faustus, must
Thou needs be damn'd, and canst thou not be sav'd:
What boots it then to think of God or Heaven?
Away with such vain fancies, and despair:
Despair in God, and trust in Belzebub.

62. To the audience. 63. Belial. 64. Loose breeches.
65. Slits in skirts and petticoats. 66. As if to tread my tracks.

Now go not backward; no, Faustus, be resolute,
Why waverest thou? O, something soundeth in mine ears
"Abjure this magic; turn to God again!"
Ay, and Faustus will turn to God again.
To God?—He loves thee not—
The God thou serv'st is thine own appetite,
Wherein is fix'd the love of Belzebub;
To him I'll build an altar and a church,
And offer lukewarm blood of new born babes.

[*Enter* GOOD ANGEL *and* EVIL ANGEL.]

GOOD ANGEL. Sweet Faustus, leave that execrable art.
EVIL ANGEL. Go forward, Faustus, in that famous art.
FAUSTUS. Contrition, prayer, repentance! What of them?
GOOD ANGEL. O, they are means to bring thee unto Heaven.
EVIL ANGEL. Rather illusions, fruits of lunacy,
That makes men foolish that do trust them most.
GOOD ANGEL. Sweet Faustus, think of Heaven, and heavenly things.
EVIL ANGEL. No, Faustus, think of honor and of wealth.

[*Exeunt* ANGELS.]

FAUSTUS. Of wealth!
Why, the signiory of Emden[1] shall be mine.
When Mephistophilis shall stand by me,
What God can hurt thee, Faustus? Thou art safe;
Cast[2] no more doubts. Come, Mephistophilis,
And bring glad tidings from great Lucifer!—
Is't not midnight? Come, Mephistophilis:
Veni, veni, Mephistophile!

[*Enter* MEPHISTOPHILIS.]

Now tell me, what says Lucifer thy lord?
MEPHISTOPHILIS. That I shall wait on Faustus whilst he lives,
So he will buy my service with his soul.
FAUSTUS. Already Faustus hath hazarded that for thee.
MEPHISTOPHILIS. But, Faustus, thou must bequeath it solemnly
And write a deed of gift with thine own blood,
For that security craves great Lucifer.
If thou deny it, I will back to hell.
FAUSTUS. Stay, Mephistophilis! and tell me what good
Will my soul do thy lord.
MEPHISTOPHILIS. Enlarge his kingdom.
FAUSTUS. Is that the reason why he tempts us thus?

---

1. Then a great port. 2. Reckon up.

MEPHISTOPHILIS. *Solamen miseris socios habuisse doloris.*[3]

FAUSTUS. Why, have you any pain, that tortures others?

MEPHISTOPHILIS. As great as have the human souls of men.
But tell me, Faustus, shall I have thy soul?
And I will be thy slave, and wait on thee,
And give thee more than thou hast wit to ask.

FAUSTUS. Ay, Mephistophilis, I give it to thee.

MEPHISTOPHILIS. Then Faustus, stab thine arm courageously,
And bind thy soul that at some certain day
Great Lucifer may claim it as his own;
And then be thou as great as Lucifer.

FAUSTUS. [*Stabbing his arm*]: Lo, Mephistophilis, for love of thee,
I cut mine arm, and with my proper blood
Assure my soul to be great Lucifer's,
Chief lord and regent of perpetual night.
View here the blood that trickles from mine arm,
And let it be propitious for my wish.

MEPHISTOPHILIS. But, Faustus, thou must
Write it in manner of a deed of gift.

FAUSTUS. Ay, so I will. [*Writes.*] But, Mephistophilis,
My blood congeals, and I can write no more.

MEPHISTOPHILIS. I'll fetch thee fire to dissolve it straight. [*Exit.*]

FAUSTUS. What might the staying of my blood portend?
Is it unwilling I should write this bill?
Why streams it not that I may write afresh?
"Faustus gives to thee his soul." Ah, there it stay'd.
Why should'st thou not? Is not thy soul thine own?
Then write again, "Faustus gives to thee his soul."

[*Re-enter* MEPHISTOPHILIS *with a chafer of coals.*]

MEPHISTOPHILIS. Here's fire. Come, Faustus, set it[4] on.

FAUSTUS. So; now the blood begins to clear again;
Now will I make an end immediately. [*Writes.*]

MEPHISTOPHILIS. O what will not I do to obtain his soul! [*Aside.*]

FAUSTUS. *Consummatum est:* this bill is ended,
And Faustus hath bequeath'd his soul to Lucifer—
But what is this inscription on mine arm?
Homo, fuge! Whither should I fly?
If unto God, he'll throw me down to hell.
My senses are deceiv'd; here's nothing writ:—
I see it plain; here in this place is writ
Homo, fuge! Yet shall not Faustus fly.

---

3. *I.e.,* misery loves company.

4. The dish of blood.

MEPHISTOPHILIS. [*Aside.*] I'll fetch him somewhat to delight his mind.

[*Exit.*]

[*Re-enter* MEPHISTOPHILIS *with* DEVILS, *giving crowns and rich apparel to* FAUSTUS, *and dance, and then depart.*]

FAUSTUS. Speak, Mephistophilis, what means this show?
MEPHISTOPHILIS. Nothing, Faustus, but to delight thy mind withal,
And to show thee what magic can perform.
FAUSTUS. But may I raise up spirits when I please?
MEPHISTOPHILIS. Ay, Faustus, and do greater things than these.
FAUSTUS. Then there's enough for a thousand souls.
Here, Mephistophilis, receive this scroll,
A deed of gift of body and of soul;
But yet conditionally that thou perform
All articles prescribed between us both.
MEPHISTOPHILIS. Faustus, I swear by hell and Lucifer
To effect all promises between us made.

FAUSTUS. Then hear me read them: *On these conditions following. First, that Faustus may be a spirit in form and substance. Secondly, that Mephistophilis shall be his servant, and at his command. Thirdly, that Mephistophilis shall do for him and bring him whatsoever. Fourthly, that he shall be in his chamber or house invisible. Lastly, that he shall appear to the said John Faustus, at all times, in what form or shape soever he please. I, John Faustus, of Wittenberg, Doctor, by these presents do give both body and soul to Lucifer, Prince of the East, and his minister, Mephistophilis; and furthermore grant unto them, that twenty-four years being expired, the articles above written inviolate, full power to fetch or carry the said John Faustus, body and soul, flesh, blood, or goods, into their habitation wheresoever. By me, John Faustus.*

MEPHISTOPHILIS. Speak, Faustus, do you deliver this as your deed?
FAUSTUS. Ay, take it, and the Devil give thee good on't.
MEPHISTOPHILIS. Now, Faustus, ask what thou wilt.
FAUSTUS. First will I question with thee about hell.
Tell me where is the place that men call hell?
MEPHISTOPHILIS. Under the heavens.
FAUSTUS. Ay, so are all things else; but whereabouts?
MEPHISTOPHILIS. Within the bowels of these elements,
Where we are tortur'd and remain for ever;
Hell hath no limits, nor is circumscrib'd
In one self place; for where we are is hell,
And where hell is there must we ever be;
And, to conclude, when all the world dissolves,
And every creature shall be purified,
All places shall be hell that is not Heaven.
FAUSTUS. Come, I think hell's a fable.

MEPHISTOPHILIS. Ay, think so still, till experience change thy mind.
FAUSTUS. Why, think'st thou then that Faustus shall be damn'd?
MEPHISTOPHILIS. Ay, of necessity; for here's the scroll
Wherein thou hast given thy soul to Lucifer.
FAUSTUS. Ay, and body too; but what of that?
Think'st thou that Faustus is so fond[5] to imagine
That, after this life, there is any pain?
Tush; these are trifles, and mere old wives' tales!
MEPHISTOPHILIS. But, Faustus, I am an instance to prove the contrary,
For I am damn'd, and am now in hell.
FAUSTUS. How! now in hell!
Nay, an this be hell, I'll willingly be damn'd here;
What, walking, disputing, &c.?
But, leaving off this, let me have a wife,
The fairest maid in Germany;
For I am wanton and lascivious,
And cannot live without a wife.
MEPHISTOPHILIS. How, a wife?
I prithee, Faustus, talk not of a wife.
FAUSTUS. Nay, sweet Mephistophilis, fetch me one, for I will have one.
MEPHISTOPHILIS. Well, thou wilt have one. Sit there till I come;
I'll fetch thee a wife in the Devil's name. [*Exit.*]

[*Re-enter* MEPHISTOPHILIS *with a* DEVIL *dressed like a woman, with fire-works.*]

MEPHISTOPHILIS. Tell me, Faustus, how dost thou like thy wife?
FAUSTUS. A plague on her for a hot whore!
MEPHISTOPHILIS. Tut, Faustus,
Marriage is but a ceremonial toy;
And if thou lovest me, think no more of it.
I'll cull thee out of the fairest courtesans,
And bring them ev'ry morning to thy bed;
She whom thine eye shall like, thy heart shall have,
Be she as chaste as was Penelope,
As wise as Saba, or as beautiful
As was bright Lucifer before his fall.
Hold, take this book, peruse it thoroughly: [*Gives a book.*]
The iterating of these lines brings gold;
The framing of this circle on the ground
Brings whirlwinds, tempests, thunder and lightning;
Pronounce this thrice devoutly to thyself,
And men in armor shall appear to thee,
Ready to execute what thou desir'st.

5. Foolish.

FAUSTUS. Thanks, Mephistophilis; yet fain would I have a book wherein I might behold all spells and incantations, that I might raise up spirits when I please.

MEPHISTOPHILIS. Here they are, in this book. [*Turns to them.*]

FAUSTUS. Now would I have a book where I might see all characters and planets of the Heavens, that I might know their motions and dispositions.

MEPHISTOPHILIS. Here they are too. [*Turns to them.*]

FAUSTUS. Nay, let me have one book more, and then I have done, wherein I might see all plants, herbs, and trees that grow upon the earth.

MEPHISTOPHILIS. Here they be.

FAUSTUS. O, thou art deceived.

MEPHISTOPHILIS. Tut, I warrant thee. [*Turns to them. Exeunt.*]

ACT II: SCENE 2[6]

[*Enter* FAUSTUS *and* MEPHISTOPHILIS.]

FAUSTUS. When I behold the Heavens, then I repent,
And curse thee, wicked Mephistophilis,
Because thou hast depriv'd me of those joys.

MEPHISTOPHILIS. Why, Faustus,
Thinkest thou Heaven is such a glorious thing?
I tell thee 'tis not half so fair as thou,
Or any man that breathes on earth.

FAUSTUS. How provest thou that?

MEPHISTOPHILIS. It was made for man, therefore is man more excellent.

FAUSTUS. If it were made for man, 'twas made for me!
I will renounce this magic and repent.

[*Enter* GOOD ANGEL *and* EVIL ANGEL.]

GOOD ANGEL. Faustus, repent; yet God will pity thee.

EVIL ANGEL. Thou art a spirit; God cannot pity thee.

FAUSTUS. Who buzzeth in mine ears I am a spirit?
Be I a devil, yet God may pity me;
Ay, God will pity me if I repent.

EVIL ANGEL. Ay, but Faustus never shall repent. [*Exeunt* ANGELS.]

FAUSTUS. My heart's so hard'ned I cannot repent.
Scarce can I name salvation, faith, or heaven,
But fearful echoes thunder in mine ears
"Faustus, thou art damn'd!" Then swords and knives,
Poison, gun, halters, and envenom'd steel
Are laid before me to despatch myself,
And long ere this I should have slain myself,

6. The same.

Had not sweet pleasure conquer'd deep despair.
Have I not made blind Homer sing to me
Of Alexander's love and Œnon's death?
And hath not he that built the walls of Thebes
With ravishing sound of his melodious harp,
Made music with my Mephistophilis?
Why should I die then, or basely despair?
I am resolv'd: Faustus shall n'er repent.
Come, Mephistophilis, let us dispute again,
And argue of divine astrology.
Tell me, are there many heavens above the moon?
Are all celestial bodies but one globe,
As is the substance of this centric earth?

MEPHISTOPHILIS. As are the elements, such are the spheres
Mutually folded in each other's orb,
And, Faustus,
All jointly move upon one axletree
Whose terminine is term'd the world's wide pole;
Nor are the names of Saturn, Mars, or Jupiter
Feign'd, but are erring stars.

FAUSTUS. But tell me, have they all one motion, both *situ et tempore?*[7]

MEPHISTOPHILIS. All jointly move from east to west in four and twenty hours upon the poles of the world, but differ in their motion upon the poles of the zodiac.

FAUSTUS. Tush! These slender trifles Wagner can decide;
Hath Mephistophilis no greater skill?
Who knows not the double motion of the planets?
The first is finish'd in a natural day;
The second thus: as Saturn in thirty years; Jupiter in twelve; Mars in four; the Sun, Venus, and Mercury in a year; the moon in twenty-eight days. Tush, these are freshmen's suppositions. But tell me, hath every sphere a dominion or *intelligentia?*

MEPHISTOPHILIS. Ay.

FAUSTUS. How many heavens, or spheres, are there?

MEPHISTOPHILIS. Nine: the seven planets, the firmament, and the empyreal heaven.

FAUSTUS. Well, resolve me in this question: Why have we not conjunctions, oppositions, aspects, eclipses, all at one time, but in some years we have more, in some less?

MEPHISTOPHILIS. *Per inœqualem motum respectu totius.*[8]

FAUSTUS. Well, I am answered. Tell me who made the world.

MEPHISTOPHILIS. I will not.

---

7. In both the direction and the duration of their revolutions.
8. On account of their unequal motion in relation to the whole.

FAUSTUS. Sweet Mephistophilis, tell me.

MEPHISTOPHILIS. Move me not, for I will not tell thee.

FAUSTUS. Villain, have I not bound thee to tell me anything?

MEPHISTOPHILIS. Ay, that is not against our kingdom; but this is.
Think thou on hell, Faustus, for thou art damn'd.

FAUSTUS. Think, Faustus, upon God that made the world.

MEPHISTOPHILIS. Remember this. [*Exit.*]

FAUSTUS. Ay, go, accursed spirit, to ugly hell;
'Tis thou hast damn'd distressed Faustus' soul.
Is't not too late?

[*Re-enter* GOOD ANGEL *and* EVIL ANGEL.]

EVIL ANGEL. Too late.

GOOD ANGEL. Never too late, if Faustus can repent.

EVIL ANGEL. If thou repent, devils shall tear thee in pieces.

GOOD ANGEL. Repent, and they shall never raze thy skin.

[*Exeunt* ANGELS.]

FAUSTUS. Ah, Christ, my Savior,
Seek to save distressed Faustus' soul.

[*Enter* LUCIFER, BELZEBUB, *and* MEPHISTOPHILIS.]

LUCIFER. Christ cannot save thy soul, for he is just;
There's none but I have int'rest in the same.

FAUSTUS. O, who art thou that look'st so terrible?

LUCIFER. I am Lucifer,
And this is my companion prince in hell.

FAUSTUS. O Faustus, they are come to fetch away thy soul!

LUCIFER. We come to tell thee thou dost injure us;
Thou talk'st of Christ, contrary to thy promise;
Thou should'st not think of God: think of the Devil,
And of his dam, too.[9]

FAUSTUS. Nor will I henceforth: pardon me in this,
And Faustus vows never to look to Heaven,
Never to name God, or to pray to him,
To burn his Scriptures, slay his ministers,
And make my spirits pull his churches down.

LUCIFER. Do so, and we will highly gratify thee.
Faustus, we are come from hell to show thee some pastime. Sit down, and thou shalt see all the Seven Deadly Sins appear in their proper shapes.

FAUSTUS. That sight will be as pleasing unto me,
As Paradise was to Adam the first day
Of his creation.

---

9. Evidently an actor's gag.

LUCIFER. Talk not of Paradise nor creation, but mark this show: talk of the Devil, and nothing else.—Come away!

[*Enter the* SEVEN DEADLY SINS.]

Now, Faustus, examine them of their several names and dispositions.

FAUSTUS. What art thou—the first?

PRIDE. I am Pride. I disdain to have any parents. I am like to Ovid's flea: I can creep into every corner of a wench; sometimes, like a periwig, I sit upon her brow; or like a fan of feathers, I kiss her lips; indeed I do—what do I not? But, fie, what a scent is here! I'll not speak another word, except the ground were perfum'd, and covered with cloth of arras.

FAUSTUS. What art thou—the second?

COVETOUSNESS. I am Covetousness, begotten of an old churl in an old leathern bag; and might I have my wish I would desire that this house and all the people in it were turn'd to gold, that I might lock you up in my good chest. O, my sweet gold!

FAUSTUS. What art thou—the third?

WRATH. I am Wrath. I had neither father nor mother: I leapt out of a lion's mouth when I was scarce half an hour old; and ever since I have run up and down the world with this case[10] of rapiers wounding myself when I had nobody to fight withal. I was born in hell; and look to it, for some of you shall be my father.[11]

FAUSTUS. What art thou—the fourth?

ENVY. I am Envy, begotten of a chimney sweeper and an oyster-wife. I cannot read, and therefore wish all books were burnt. I am lean with seeing others eat. O that there would come a famine through all the world, that all might die, and I live alone! then thou should'st see how fat I would be. But must thou sit and I stand? Come down with a vengeance!

FAUSTUS. Away, envious rascal! What art thou—the fifth?

GLUTTONY. Who, I, sir? I am Gluttony. My parents are all dead, and the devil a penny they have left me, but a bare pension, and that is thirty meals a day and ten bevers[12]—a small trifle to suffice nature. O, I come of a royal parentage! My grandfather was a Gammon of Bacon, my grandmother a Hogshead of Claret-wine; my godfathers were these, Peter Pickleherring, and Martin Martlemas-beef. O, but my godmother, she was a jolly gentlewoman, and well beloved in every good town and city; her name was Mistress Margery March-beer. Now, Faustus, thou hast heard all my progeny,[13] wilt thou bid me to supper?

FAUSTUS. No, I'll see thee hanged; thou wilt eat up all my victuals.

GLUTTONY. Then the Devil choke thee!

FAUSTUS. Choke thyself, glutton! Who art thou—the sixth?

SLOTH. I am Sloth. I was begotten on a sunny bank, where I have lain

---

10. Pair. 11. One of you devils is doubtless.
12. Between-meal refreshments. 13. Lineage.

ever since; and you have done me great injury to bring me from thence: let me be carried thither again by Gluttony and Lechery. I'll not speak another word for a king's ransom.

FAUSTUS. What are you, Mistress Minx,—the seventh and last?

LECHERY. Who, I, sir? I am one that loves an inch of raw mutton[14] better than an ell of fried stockfish;[15] and the first letter of my name begins with Lechery.

LUCIFER. Away to hell, to hell! [*Exeunt the* SINS.]
—Now, Faustus, how dost thou like this?

FAUSTUS. O, this feeds my soul!

LUCIFER. Tut, Faustus, in hell is all manner of delight.

FAUSTUS. O might I see hell, and return again. How happy were I then!

LUCIFER. Thou shalt; I will send for thee at midnight. In meantime take this book; and peruse it thoroughly, and thou shalt turn thyself into what shape thou wilt.

FAUSTUS. Great thanks, mighty Lucifer!
This will I keep as chary as my life.

LUCIFER. Farewell, Faustus, and think on the Devil.

FAUSTUS. Farewell, great Lucifer! Come, Mephistophilis.

[*Exeunt omnes.*]

ACT II: SCENE 3[16]

[*Enter* ROBIN *the Ostler with a book in his hand.*]

ROBIN. O, this is admirable! Here I ha' stolen one of Dr. Faustus' conjuring books, and i' faith I mean to search some circles[17] for my own use. Now will I make all the maidens in our parish dance at my pleasure, stark naked before me; and so by that means I shall see more than e'er I felt or saw yet.

[*Enter* RALPH *calling* ROBIN.]

RALPH. Robin, prithee come away; there's a gentleman tarries to have his horse, and he would have his things rubb'd and made clean. He keeps such a chafing with my mistress about it; and she has sent me to look thee out. Prithee come away.

ROBIN. Keep out, keep out, or else you are blown up; you are dismemb'red, Ralph: keep out, for I am about a roaring piece of work.

RALPH. Come, what dost thou with that same book? Thou canst not read.

ROBIN. Yes, my master and mistress shall find that I can read, he for his forehead,[18] she for her private study; she's born to bear with me, or else my art fails.

---

14. Punning on "mutton" meaning wench, harlot. 15. Salted or dried fish.
16. An inn-yard. 17. Common with a double meaning in these plays.
18. Innumerable jests in the plays of this time allude to the horns which were supposed to grow in the brows of a deceived husband.

RALPH. Why, Robin, what book is that?

ROBIN. What book! Why, the most intolerable book for conjuring that e'er was invented by any brimstone devil.

RALPH. Canst thou conjure with it?

ROBIN. I can do all these things easily with it: first I can make thee drunk with ippocras[19] at any tavern in Europe for nothing; that's one of my conjuring works.

RALPH. Our Master Parson says that's nothing.

ROBIN. True, Ralph; and more, Ralph, if thou hast any mind to Nan Spit, our kitchen-maid, then turn her and wind her to thy own use as often as thou wilt, and at midnight.

RALPH. O brave Robin, shall I have Nan Spit, and to mine own use? On that condition I'll feed thy devil with horsebread as long as he lives, of free cost.

ROBIN. No more, sweet Ralph: let's go and make clean our boots, which lie foul upon our hands, and then to our conjuring in the Devil's name.

[*Exeunt.*]

ACT III

[*Enter* WAGNER.]

WAGNER. Learned Faustus,
To know the secrets of astronomy
Graven in the book of Jove's high firmament,
Did mount himself to scale Olympus' top,
Being seated in a chariot burning bright,
Drawn by the strength of yoky dragons' necks.
He now is gone to prove cosmography,
And, as I guess, will first arrive at Rome,
To see the Pope and manner of his court,
And take some part of holy Peter's feast,
That to this day is highly solemniz'd. [*Exit.*]

ACT III: SCENE 1[1]

[*Enter* FAUSTUS *and* MEPHISTOPHILIS.]

FAUSTUS. Having now, my good Mephistophilis,
Past with delight the stately town of Trier,[2]
Environ'd round with airy mountain-tops,
With walls of flint, and deep entrenched lakes,

19. Sugared and spiced wine.
1. Rome. The Pope's privy-chamber.
2. Treves.

Not to be won by any conquering prince;
From Paris next, coasting the realm of France,
We saw the river Maine fall into Rhine,
Whose banks are set with groves of fruitful vines;
Then up to Naples, rich Campania,
Whose buildings fair and gorgeous to the eye,
The streets straight forth, and pav'd with finest brick,
Quarter the town in four equivalents.
There saw we learned Maro's[3] golden tomb,
The way he cut, an English mile in length,
Thorough a rock of stone in one night's space;
From thence to Venice, Padua, and the rest,
In one of which a sumptuous temple stands,[4]
That threats the stars with her aspiring top,
Thus hitherto has Faustus spent his time:
But tell me, now, what resting-place is this?
Hast thou, as erst I did command,
Conducted me within the walls of Rome?

MEPHISTOPHILIS. Faustus, I have; and because we will not be unprovided, I have taken up his Holiness' privy-chamber for our use.

FAUSTUS. I hope his Holiness will bid us welcome.

MEPHISTOPHILIS. Tut, 'tis no matter, man, we'll be bold with his good cheer.
And now, my Faustus, that thou may'st perceive
What Rome containeth to delight thee with,
Know that this city stands upon seven hills
That underprop the groundwork of the same.
Just through the midst runs flowing Tiber's stream,
With winding banks that cut it in two parts;
Over the which four stately bridges lean,
That make safe passage to each part of Rome:
Upon the bridge call'd Ponto Angelo
Erected is a castle passing strong,
Within whose walls such store of ordnance are,
And double cannons, fram'd of carved brass,
As match the days within one complete year;
Besides the gates and high pyramides,
Which Julius Caesar brought from Africa.

FAUSTUS. Now by the kingdoms of infernal rule,
Of Styx, of Acheron, and the fiery lake
Of ever-burning Phlegethon, I swear
That I do long to see the monuments

3. Virgil's. A tunnel near it was supposed to be the work of his magic.
4. St. Mark's, at Venice.

And situation of bright-splendent Rome:
Come therefore, let's away.

MEPHISTOPHILIS. Nay, Faustus, stay; I know you'd fain see the Pope,
And take some part of holy Peter's feast,
Where thou shalt see a troop of bald-pate friars,
Whose *summum bonum* is in belly-cheer.

FAUSTUS. Well, I'm content to compass then some sport,
And by their folly make us merriment.
Then charm me, Mephistophilis, that I
May be invisible, to do what I please
Unseen of any whilst I stay in Rome. [MEPHISTOPHILIS *charms him.*]

MEPHISTOPHILIS. So, Faustus, now
Do what thou wilt, thou shalt not be discern'd.

[*Sound a sennet.*[5] *Enter the* POPE *and the* CARDINAL *of* LORRAINE *to the banquet, with* FRIARS *attending.*]

POPE. My Lord of Lorraine, wilt please you draw near?

FAUSTUS. Fall to, and the devil choke you an you spare!

POPE. How now! Who's that which spake?—Friars, look about.

FIRST FRIAR. Here's nobody, if it like your Holiness.

POPE. My lord, here is a dainty dish was sent me from the Bishop of Milan.

FAUSTUS. I thank you, sir. [*Snatches it.*]

POPE. How now! Who's that which snatch'd the meat from me? Will no man look? My Lord, this dish was sent me from the Cardinal of Florence.

FAUSTUS. You say true; I'll ha't. [*Snatches it.*]

POPE. What, again! My lord, I'll drink to your Grace.

FAUSTUS. I'll pledge your Grace. [*Snatches the cup.*]

CARDINAL. My lord, it may be some ghost newly crept out of purgatory, come to beg a pardon of your Holiness.

POPE. It may be so. Friars, prepare a dirge to lay the fury of this ghost. Once again, my lord, fall to. [*The* POPE *crosses himself.*]

FAUSTUS. What, are you crossing of yourself?
Well, use that trick no more I would advise you. [*The* POPE *crosses himself again.*]
Well, there's the second time. Aware the third,
I give you fair warning.

[*The* POPE *crosses himself again, and* FAUSTUS *hits him a box of the ear; and they all run away.*]

Come on, Mephistophilis, what shall we do?

MEPHISTOPHILIS. Nay, I know not. We shall be curs'd with bell, book, and candle.

FAUSTUS. How? bell, book, and candle,—candle, book, and bell,

5. Fanfare of trumpets.

Forward and backward to curse Faustus to hell!
Anon you shall hear a hog grunt, a calf bleat, and an ass bray,
Because it is Saint Peter's holiday.

[*Re-enter all the* FRIARS *to sing the Dirge.*]

FIRST FRIAR. Come, brethren, let's about our business with good devotion.

[*They sing*]:

Cursed be he that stole away his Holiness' meat from the table! *Maledicat Dominus!*[6]
Cursed be he that struck his Holiness a blow on the face! *Maledicat Dominus!*
Cursed be he that took Friar Sandelo a blow on the pate! *Maledicat Dominus!*
Cursed be he that disturbeth our holy dirge! *Maledicat Dominus!*
Cursed be he that took away his Holiness' wine! *Maledicat Dominus! Et omnes sancti!*[7] *Amen!*

ACT III: SCENE 2[8]

[*Enter* ROBIN *and* RALPH *with a silver goblet.*]

ROBIN. Come, Ralph, did not I tell thee we were for ever made by this Doctor Faustus' book? *Ecce signum,* here's a simple purchase[9] for horse-keepers; our horses shall eat no hay as long as this lasts.

[*Enter the* VINTNER.]

RALPH. But, Robin, here comes the vintner.

ROBIN. Hush! I'll gull him supernaturally. Drawer, I hope all is paid: God be with you. Come, Ralph.

VINTNER. Soft, sir; a word with you. I must yet have a goblet paid from you, ere you go.

ROBIN. I, a goblet, Ralph; I, a goblet! I scorn you, and you are but a &c.[10] I, a goblet! Search me.

VINTNER. I mean so, sir, with your favor. [*Searches him.*]

ROBIN. How say you now?

VINTNER. I must say somewhat to your fellow. You, sir!

RALPH. Me, sir! me, sir! search your fill. [VINTNER *searches him.*] Now, sir, you may be ashamed to burden honest men with a matter of truth.[11]

VINTNER. Well, t' one of you hath this goblet about you.

ROBIN. [*Aside*]: You lie, drawer, 'tis afore me.—Sirrah you, I'll teach ye to impeach honest men; stand by;—I'll scour you for a goblet!—stand aside you had best, I charge you in the name of Belzebub. Look to the goblet, Ralph.

---

6. May the Lord curse him. 7. And all the Saints. 8. An inn.
9. Piece of loot.
10. The low comedian was expected to supply a string of racy invective.
11. A question of honesty.

[*Aside to* RALPH.]

VINTNER. What mean you, sirrah?

ROBIN. I'll tell you what I mean. [*Reads from a book.*] *Sanctobulorum, Periphrasticon*—Nay, I'll tickle you, vintner. Look to the goblet, Ralph. [*Aside to* RALPH.] *Polypragmos Belseborams framanto pacostiphos tostu, Mephistophilis, &c.* [*Reads.*]

Enter MEPHISTOPHILIS. [*Sets squibs at their backs, and then exit. They run about.*]

VINTNER. *O nomine Domini!* [12] what meanest thou, Robin? Thou hast no goblet.

RALPH. *Peccatum peccatorum!* [13] Here's thy goblet, good vintner.

ROBIN. *Misericordia pro nobis!* [14] What shall I do? Good Devil, forgive me now, and I'll never rob thy library more.

[*Re-enter to them* MEPHISTOPHILIS.]

MEPHISTOPHILIS. Vanish, villains!
Th' one like an ape, another like a bear, the third an ass, for doing this enterprise. [*Exit* VINTNER.]
Monarch of hell, under whose black survey
Great potentates do kneel with awful fear,
Upon whose altars thousand souls do lie,
How am I vexed with these villains' charms!
From Constantinople am I hither come
Only for pleasure of these damned slaves.

ROBIN. How, from Constantinople? You have had a great journey. Will you take sixpence in your purse to pay for your supper, and begone?

MEPHISTOPHILIS. Well, villains, for your presumption, I transform thee into an ape, and thee into a dog; and so begone. [*Exit.*]

ROBIN. How, into an ape? That's brave! I'll have fine sport with the boys. I'll get nuts and apples enow.

RALPH. And I must be a dog.

ROBIN. I' faith thy head will never be out of the pottage pot. [*Exeunt.*]

ACT IV

[*Enter* CHORUS.]

CHORUS. When Faustus had with pleasure ta'en the view
Of rarest things, and royal courts of kings,
He stay'd his course, and so returned home;
Where such as bear his absence but with grief,

12. The Vintner's imperfect Latin for "in the name of the Lord."
13. Sin of sins. 14. Mercy on us.

I mean his friends and near'st companions,
Did gratulate his safety with kind words,
And in their conference of what befell,
Touching his journey through the world and air,
They put forth questions of Astrology,
Which Faustus answer'd with such learned skill,
As they admir'd and wond'red at his wit.
Now is his fame spread forth in every land;
Amongst the rest the Emperor is one,
Carolus the Fifth, at whose palace now
Faustus is feasted 'mongst his noblemen.
What there he did in trial of his art,
I leave untold—your eyes shall see perform'd. [*Exit.*]

ACT IV: SCENE 1[1]

[*Enter* EMPEROR, FAUSTUS, MEPHISTOPHILIS, *and a* KNIGHT *with attendants.*]

EMPEROR. Master Doctor Faustus, I have heard strange report of thy knowledge in the black art, how that none in my empire nor in the whole world can compare with thee for the rare effects of magic; they say thou hast a familiar spirit, by whom thou canst accomplish what thou list. This, therefore, is my request, that thou let me see some proof of thy skill, that mine eyes may be witnesses to confirm what mine ears have heard reported; and here I swear to thee, by the honor of mine imperial crown, that, whatever thou doest, thou shalt be no ways prejudiced or endamaged.

KNIGHT. I' faith he looks much like a conjuror. [*Aside.*]

FAUSTUS. My gracious sovereign, though I must confess myself far inferior to the report men have published, and nothing answerable[2] to the honor of your imperial majesty, yet for that love and duty binds me thereunto, I am content to do whatsoever your majesty shall command me.

EMPEROR. Then, Doctor Faustus, mark what I shall say.
As I was sometime solitary set
Within my closet, sundry thoughts arose
About the honor of mine ancestors,
How they had won by prowess such exploits,
Got such riches, subdued so many kingdoms,
As we that do succeed, or they that shall
Hereafter possess our throne, shall
(I fear me) ne'er attain to that degree
Of high renown and great authority;
Amongst which kings is Alexander the Great,

1. A room in the imperial palace (at Innsbruck).
2. In no respect adequate.

Chief spectacle of the world's pre-eminence,
The bright shining of whose glorious acts
Lightens the world with his reflecting beams,
As, when I heard but motion[3] made of him,

It grieves my soul I never saw the man.
If, therefore, thou by cunning of thine art
Canst raise this man from hollow vaults below,
Where lies entomb'd this famous conqueror,
And bring with him his beauteous paramour,
Both in their right shapes, gestures, and attire
They us'd to wear during their time of life,
Thou shalt both satisfy my just desire,
And give me cause to praise thee whilst I live.

FAUSTUS. My gracious lord, I am ready to accomplish your request so far forth as by art, and power of my spirit, I am able to perform.

KNIGHT. I' faith that's just nothing at all. [*Aside.*]

FAUSTUS. But, if it like your Grace, it is not in my ability to present before your eyes the true substantial bodies of those two deceased princes, which long since are consumed to dust.

KNIGHT. Ay, marry, Master Doctor, now there's a sign of grace in you, when you will confess the truth. [*Aside.*]

FAUSTUS. But such spirits as can lively resemble Alexander and his paramour shall appear before your Grace in that manner that they best liv'd in, in their most flourishing estate; which I doubt not shall sufficiently content your imperial majesty.

EMPEROR. Go to, Master Doctor, let me see them presently.[4]

KNIGHT. Do you hear, Master Doctor? You bring Alexander and his paramour before the Emperor!

FAUSTUS. How then, sir?

KNIGHT. I' faith that's as true as Diana turn'd me to a stag!

FAUSTUS. No, sir, but when Actæon died, he left the horns for you. Mephistophilis, begone. [*Exit* MEPHISTOPHILIS.]

KNIGHT. Nay, an you go to conjuring, I'll be gone. [*Exit.*]

FAUSTUS. I'll meet with you anon for interrupting me so. Here they are, my gracious lord.

[*Re-enter* MEPHISTOPHILIS *with* ALEXANDER *and his* PARAMOUR.]

EMPEROR. Master Doctor, I heard this lady while she liv'd had a wart or mole in her neck: how shall I know whether it be so or no?

FAUSTUS. Your Highness may boldly go and see. [*Exeunt Spirits.*]

EMPEROR. Sure these are no spirits, but the true substantial bodies of those two deceased princes.

---

3. Mention.
4. At once.

FAUSTUS. Will't please your Highness now to send for the knight that was so pleasant with me here of late?

EMPEROR. One of you call him forth. [*Exit* ATTENDANT.]

[*Re-enter the* KNIGHT *with a pair of horns on his head.*]

How now, sir knight! why I had thought thou had'st been a bachelor; but now I see thou hast a wife, that not only gives thee horns, but makes thee wear them. Feel on thy head.

KNIGHT. Thou damned wretch and execrable dog,
Bred in the concave of some monstrous rock,
How darest thou thus abuse a gentleman?
Villain, I say, undo what thou hast done!

FAUSTUS. O, not so fast, sir; there's no haste; but, good, are you remem-b'red how you crossed me in my conference with the Emperor? I think I have met with you for it.

EMPEROR. Good Master Doctor, at my entreaty release him; he hath done penance sufficient.

FAUSTUS. My gracious lord, not so much for the injury he off'red me here in your presence, as to delight you with some mirth, hath Faustus worthily re-quited this injurious knight; which being all I desire, I am content to release him of his horns: and, sir knight, hereafter speak well of scholars. Meph-istophilis, transform him straight. [MEPHISTOPHILIS *removes the horns.*] Now, my good lord, having done my duty I humbly take my leave.

EMPEROR. Farewell, Master Doctor; yet, ere you go,
Expect from me a bounteous reward. [*Exeunt.*]

ACT IV: SCENE 2

[*Enter* FAUSTUS *and* MEPHISTOPHILIS.]

FAUSTUS. Now, Mephistophilis, the restless course
That Time doth run with calm and silent foot,
Short'ning my days and thread of vital life,
Calls for the payment of my latest years;
Therefore, sweet Mephistophilis, let us
Make haste to Wittenberg.

MEPHISTOPHILIS. What, will you go on horseback or on foot?

FAUSTUS. Nay, till I'm past this fair and pleasant green,[5]
I'll walk on foot.

---

5. A green; afterwards Faustus' house. The wreckage of several scenes probably con-fronts the reader here; most of this is rubbish, but note the Marlovian column still standing in the five lines which begin, "What art thou, Faustus . . ."

[*Enter a* HORSE-COURSER.]

HORSE-COURSER. I have been all this day seeking one Master Fustian: mass, see where he is! God save you, Master Doctor!

FAUSTUS. What, horse-courser! You are well met.

HORSE-COURSER. Do you hear, sir? I have brought you forty dollars for your horse.

FAUSTUS. I cannot sell him so; if thou likest him for fifty, take him.

HORSE-COURSER. Alas, sir, I have no more.—I pray you speak for me.

MEPHISTOPHILIS. I pray you let him have him; he is an honest fellow, and he has a great charge, neither wife nor child.

FAUSTUS. Well, come, give me your money. [HORSE-COURSER *gives* FAUSTUS *the money*.] My boy will deliver him to you. But I must tell you one thing before you have him; ride him not into the water at any hand.

HORSE-COURSER. Why, sir, will he not drink of all waters?

FAUSTUS. O yes, he will drink of all waters, but ride him not into the water: ride him over hedge or ditch, or where thou wilt, but not into the water.

HORSE-COURSER. Well, sir.—Now am I made man for ever. I'll not leave my horse for forty. If he had but the quality of hey-ding-ding, hey-ding-ding, I'd make a brave living on him: he has a buttock as slick as an eel. [*Aside*.] Well, God b' wi' ye, sir, your boy will deliver him me: but hark ye, sir; if my horse be sick or ill at ease, if I bring his water to you, you'll tell me what it is? [*Exit* HORSE-COURSER.]

FAUSTUS. Away, you villain; what, dost think I am a horse-doctor?
What art thou, Faustus, but a man condemn'd to die?
Thy fatal time doth draw to final end;
Despair doth drive distrust unto my thoughts,
Confound these passions with a quiet sleep:
Tush, Christ did call the thief upon the cross;
Then rest thee, Faustus, quiet in conceit. [*Sleeps in his chair*.]

[*Re-enter* HORSE-COURSER, *all wet, crying*.]

HORSE-COURSER. Alas, alas! Doctor Fustian, quotha? Mass, Doctor Lopus[6] was never such a doctor. Has given me a purgation has purg'd me of forty dollars; I shall never see them more. But yet, like an ass as I was, I would not be ruled by him, for he bade me I should ride him into no water. Now I, thinking my horse had had some rare quality that he would not have had me known of, I, like a venturous youth, rid him into the deep pond at the town's end. I was no sooner in the middle of the pond, but my horse vanish'd away, and I sat upon a bottle[7] of hay, never so near drowning, in my life. But I'll

6. Queen Elizabeth's physician, Roderigo Lopez, a Spaniard, charged with conspiring to poison her and executed in 1594—nearly a year after Marlowe's death.
7. Bale.

seek out my Doctor, and have my forty dollars again, or I'll make it the dearest horse!—O, yonder is his snipper-snapper.[8]—Do you hear? You hey-pass,[9] where's your master?

MEPHISTOPHILIS. Why, sir, what would you? You cannot speak with him.

HORSE-COURSER. But I will speak with him.

MEPHISTOPHILIS. Why, he's fast asleep. Come some other time.

HORSE-COURSER. I'll speak with him now, or I'll break his glass windows about his ears.

MEPHISTOPHILIS. I tell thee he has not slept this eight nights.

HORSE-COURSER. An he have not slept this eight weeks, I'll speak with him.

MEPHISTOPHILIS. See where he is, fast asleep.

HORSE-COURSER. Ay, this is he. God save you, Master Doctor! Master Doctor, Master Doctor Fustian!—Forty dollars, forty dollars for a bottle of hay!

MEPHISTOPHILIS. Why, thou seest he hears thee not.

HORSE-COURSER. So ho, ho!—so ho, ho! [*Hollas in his ear.*] No, will you not awake? I'll make you wake ere I go. [*Pulls* FAUSTUS *by the leg, and pulls it away.*] Alas, I am undone! What shall I do?

FAUSTUS. O my leg, my leg! Help, Mephistophilis! call the officers! My leg, my leg!

MEPHISTOPHILIS. Come, villain, to the constable!

HORSE-COURSER. O lord, sir, let me go, and I'll give you forty dollars more.

MEPHISTOPHILIS. Where be they?

HORSE-COURSER. I have none about me. Come to my ostry[10] and I'll give them you.

MEPHISTOPHILIS. Begone quickly. [HORSE-COURSER *runs away.*]

FAUSTUS. What, is he gone? Farewell he! Faustus has his leg again, and the horse-courser, I take it, a bottle of hay for his labor. Well, this trick shall cost him forty dollars more.

[*Enter* WAGNER.]

How now, Wagner, what's the news with thee?

WAGNER. Sir, the Duke of Vanholt doth earnestly entreat your company.

FAUSTUS. The Duke of Vanholt! an honorable gentleman, to whom I must be no niggard of my cunning. Come, Mephistophilis, let's away to him.

[*Exeunt.*]

---

8. Whippersnapper.
9. Juggler, since this was his cry. (Dyce, Ward.)
10. Hostelry, inn.

ACT IV: SCENE 3[11]

[*Enter the* DUKE *of* VANHOLT, *the* DUCHESS, FAUSTUS *and* MEPHISTOPHILIS.]

DUKE. Believe me, Master Doctor, this merriment hath much pleased me.

FAUSTUS. My gracious lord, I am glad it contents you so well.—But it may be, madam, you take no delight in this. I have heard that great-bellied women do long for some dainties or other. What is it, madam? Tell me, and you shall have it.

DUCHESS. Thanks, good Master Doctor; and for I see your courteous intent to pleasure me, I will not hide from you the thing my heart desires; and were it now summer, as it is January and the dead time of the winter, I would desire no better meat than a dish of ripe grapes.

FAUSTUS. Alas, madam, that's nothing! Mephistophilis, begone. [*Exit* MEPHISTOPHILIS.] Were it a greater thing than this, so it would content you, you should have it.

[*Re-enter* MEPHISTOPHILIS *with the grapes.*]

Here they be, madam; wilt please you taste on them?

DUKE. Believe me, Master Doctor, this makes me wonder above the rest, that being in the dead time of winter, and in the month of January, how you should come by these grapes.

FAUSTUS. If it like your Grace, the year is divided into two circles over the whole world, that, when it is here winter with us, in the contrary circle it is summer with them, as in India, Saba, and farther countries in the East; and by means of a swift spirit that I have, I had them brought hither, as ye see.—How do you like them, madam; be they good?

DUCHESS. Believe me, Master Doctor, they be the best grapes that e'er I tasted in my life before.

FAUSTUS. I am glad they content you so, madam.

DUKE. Come, madam, let us in, where you must well reward this learned man for the great kindness he hath show'd to you.

DUCHESS. And so I will, my lord; and whilst I live, rest beholding for this courtesy.

FAUSTUS. I humbly thank your Grace.

DUKE. Come, Master Doctor, follow us and receive your reward.

[*Exeunt.*]

ACT V: SCENE 1[1]

[*Enter* WAGNER, *solus.*]

WAGNER. I think my master means to die shortly,
For he hath given to me all his goods;
And yet, methinks, if that death were near,

11. A residence of the Duke of Vanholt.
1. Wittenberg. A room in Faustus' house.

He would not banquet and carouse and swill
Amongst the students, as even now he doth,
Who are at supper with such belly-cheer
As Wagner ne'er beheld in all his life.
See where they come! Belike the feast is ended. [*Exit.*]

[*Enter* FAUSTUS, *with two or three* SCHOLARS *and* MEPHISTOPHILIS.]

FIRST SCHOLAR. Master Doctor Faustus, since our conference about fair ladies, which was the beautifullest in all the world,[2] we have determined with ourselves that Helen of Greece was the admirablest lady that ever lived: therefore, Master Doctor, if you will do us that favor, as to let us see that peerless dame of Greece, whom all the world admires for majesty, we should think ourselves much beholding unto you.

FAUSTUS. Gentlemen,
For that I know your friendship is unfeigned,
And Faustus' custom is not to deny
The just requests of those that wish him well,
You shall behold that peerless dame of Greece,
No otherways for pomp and majesty
Than when Sir Paris cross'd the seas with her,
And brought the spoils to rich Dardania.
Be silent, then, for danger is in words.

[*Music sounds, and* HELEN *passeth over the stage.*]

SECOND SCHOLAR. Too simple is my wit to tell her praise,
Whom all the world admires for majesty.

THIRD SCHOLAR. No marvel though the angry Greeks pursu'd
With ten years' war the rape[3] of such a queen,
Whose heavenly beauty passeth all compare.

FIRST SCHOLAR. Since we have seen the pride of Nature's works,
And only paragon of excellence,

[*Enter an* OLD MAN.]

Let us depart; and for this glorious deed
Happy and blest be Faustus evermore.

FAUSTUS. Gentlemen, farewell—the same I wish to you.

[*Exeunt* SCHOLARS *and* WAGNER.]

OLD MAN. Ah, Doctor Faustus, that I might prevail
To guide thy steps unto the way of life,
By which sweet path thou may'st attain the goal
That shall conduct thee to celestial rest!
Break heart, drop blood, and mingle it with tears,

2. Simpson notes the survival of a Marlovian line, beginning "which" indicating that this prose is an adapter's work.
3. Capture.

Tears falling from repentant heaviness
Of thy most vile and loathsome filthiness,
The stench whereof corrupts the inward soul
With such flagitious crimes of heinous sins
As no commiseration may expel,
But mercy, Faustus, of thy Saviour sweet,
Whose blood alone must wash away thy guilt.

FAUSTUS. Where art thou, Faustus? Wretch, what hast thou done?
Damn'd art thou, Faustus, damn'd; despair and die!
Hell calls for right, and with a roaring voice
Says "Faustus! come! thine hour is almost come!"
And Faustus now will come to do thee right. [MEPHISTOPHILIS *gives him a dagger.*]

OLD MAN. Ah stay, good Faustus, stay thy desperate steps!
I see an angel hovers o'er thy head,
And, with a vial full of precious grace,
Offers to pour the same into thy soul:
Then call for mercy, and avoid despair.

FAUSTUS. Ah, my sweet friend, I feel
Thy words do comfort my distressed soul.
Leave me a while to ponder on my sins.

OLD MAN. I go, sweet Faustus, but with heavy cheer,
Fearing the ruin of thy hopeless soul. [*Exit.*]

FAUSTUS. Accursed Faustus, where is mercy now?
I do repent; and yet I do despair;
Hell strives with grace for conquest in my breast:
What shall I do to shun the snares of death?

MEPHISTOPHILIS. Thou traitor, Faustus, I arrest thy soul
For disobedience to my sovereign lord;
Revolt, or I'll in piecemeal tear thy flesh.

FAUSTUS. Sweet Mephistophilis, entreat thy lord
To pardon my unjust presumption,
And with my blood again I will confirm
My former vow I made to Lucifer.

MEPHISTOPHILIS. Do it now then quickly, with unfeigned heart,
Lest danger do attend thy drift. [FAUSTUS *stabs his arm and writes on a paper with his blood.*]

FAUSTUS. Torment, sweet friend, that base and crooked age,[4]
That durst dissuade me from my Lucifer,
With greatest torments that our hell affords.

MEPHISTOPHILIS. His faith is great, I cannot touch his soul;
But what I may afflict his body with
I will attempt, which is but little worth.

4. Old man.

FAUSTUS. One thing, good servant, let me crave of thee,
To glut the longing of my heart's desire,
That I might have unto my paramour
That heavenly Helen, which I saw of late,
Whose sweet embracings may extinguish clean
These thoughts that do dissuade me from my vow,
And keep mine oath I made to Lucifer.

MEPHISTOPHILIS. Faustus, this or what else thou shalt desire
Shall be perform'd in twinkling of an eye.

[*Re-enter* HELEN.]

FAUSTUS. Was this the face that launch'd a thousand ships,
And burnt the topless towers of Ilium?
Sweet Helen, make me immortal with a kiss. [*Kisses her.*]
Her lips suck forth my soul; see where it flies!—
Come, Helen, come, give me my soul again.
Here will I dwell, for Heaven be in these lips,
And all is dross that is not Helena.

[*Enter* OLD MAN.]

I will be Paris, and for love of thee,
Instead of Troy, shall Wittenberg be sack'd;
And I will combat with weak Menelaus,
And wear thy colors on my plumed crest;
Yea, I will wound Achilles in the heel,
And then return to Helen for a kiss.
Oh, thou art fairer than the evening air
Clad in the beauty of a thousand stars;
Brighter art thou than flaming Jupiter
When he appear'd to hapless Semele:
More lovely than the monarch of the sky
In wanton Arethusa's azur'd arms:
And none but thou shalt be my paramour. [*Exeunt.*]

OLD MAN. Accursed Faustus, miserable man,
That from thy soul exclud'st the grace of Heaven,
And fly'st the throne of his tribunal seat!

[*Enter* DEVILS.]

Satan begins to sift me with his pride:[5]
As in this furnace God shall try my faith,
My faith, vile hell, shall triumph over thee.
Ambitious fiends, see how the heavens smiles
At your repulse, and laughs your state to scorn!
Hence, hell! for hence I fly unto my God. [*Exeunt.*]

5. Display (of power).

ACT V: SCENE 2[6]

[*Enter* FAUSTUS *with the* SCHOLARS.]

FAUSTUS. Ah, gentlemen!

FIRST SCHOLAR. What ails Faustus?

FAUSTUS. Ah, my sweet chamber-fellow, had I lived with thee, then had I lived still! but now I die eternally. Look, comes he not? comes he not?

SECOND SCHOLAR. What means Faustus?

THIRD SCHOLAR. Belike he is grown into some sickness by being over solitary.

FIRST SCHOLAR. If it be so, we'll have physicians to cure him. 'Tis but a surfeit, never fear, man.

FAUSTUS. A surfeit of deadly sin that hath damn'd both body and soul.

SECOND SCHOLAR. Yet, Faustus, look up to Heaven; remember God's mercies are infinite.

FAUSTUS. But Faustus' offence can ne'er be pardoned: the serpent that tempted Eve may be sav'd, but not Faustus. Ah, gentlemen, hear me with patience, and tremble not at my speeches! Though my heart pants and quivers to remember that I have been a student here these thirty years, oh, would I had never seen Wittenberg, never read book! And what wonders I have done, all Germany can witness, yea, all the world; for which Faustus hath lost both Germany and the world, yea Heaven itself, Heaven, the seat of God, the throne of the blessed, the kingdom of joy; and must remain in hell for ever, hell, ah, hell, for ever! Sweet friends! what shall become of Faustus, being in hell for ever?

THIRD SCHOLAR. Yet, Faustus, call on God.

FAUSTUS. On God, whom Faustus hath abjur'd! on God, whom Faustus hath blasphemed! Ah, my God, I would weep, but the Devil draws in my tears. Gush forth blood instead of tears! Yea, life and soul, Oh, he stays my tongue! I would lift up my hands, but see, they hold them, they hold them!

ALL. Who, Faustus?

FAUSTUS. Lucifer and Mephistophilis. Ah, gentlemen, I gave them my soul for my cunning!

ALL. God forbid!

FAUSTUS. God forbade it indeed; but Faustus hath done it. For vain pleasure of twenty-four years hath Faustus lost eternal joy and felicity. I writ them a bill with mine own blood: the date is expired; the time will come, and he will fetch me.

FIRST SCHOLAR. Why did not Faustus tell us of this before, that divines might have prayed for thee?

FAUSTUS. Oft have I thought to have done so; but the Devil threat'ned to tear me in pieces if I nam'd God; to fetch both body and soul if I once gave

6. The same.

ear to divinity; and now 'tis too late. Gentlemen, away! lest you perish with me.

SECOND SCHOLAR. Oh, what shall we do to save Faustus?

FAUSTUS. Talk not of me, but save yourselves, and depart.

THIRD SCHOLAR. God will strengthen me. I will stay with Faustus.

FIRST SCHOLAR. Tempt not God, sweet friend; but let us into the next room, and there pray for him.

FAUSTUS. Ay, pray for me, pray for me! and what noise soever ye hear, come not unto me, for nothing can rescue me.

SECOND SCHOLAR. Pray thou, and we will pray that God may have mercy upon thee.

FAUSTUS. Gentlemen, farewell! If I live till morning, I'll visit you: if not —Faustus is gone to hell.

ALL. Faustus, farewell. [*Exeunt* SCHOLARS. *The clock strikes eleven.*]

FAUSTUS. Ah, Faustus,
Now hast thou but one bare hour to live,
And then thou must be damn'd perpetually!
Stand still, you ever-moving spheres of Heaven,
That time may cease, and midnight never come;
Fair Nature's eye, rise, rise again and make
Perpetual day; or let this hour be but
A year, a month, a week, a natural day,
That Faustus may repent and save his soul!
O lente, lente, currite noctis equi! [7]
The stars move still,[8] time runs, the clock will strike,
The Devil will come, and Faustus must be damn'd.
O, I'll leap up to my God! Who pulls me down?
See, see where Christ's blood streams in the firmament!
One drop would save my soul—half a drop: ah, my Christ!
Ah, rend not my heart for naming of my Christ!
Yet will I call on him: O spare me, Lucifer!
Where is it now? 'Tis gone; and see where God
Stretcheth out his arm, and bends his ireful brows!
Mountain and hills come, come and fall on me,
And hide me from the heavy wrath of God!
No! no!
Then will I headlong run into the earth;
Earth gape! O no, it will not harbor me!
You stars that reign'd at my nativity,
Whose influence hath allotted death and hell,
Now draw up Faustus like a foggy mist

7. Run slowly, slowly, steeds of the night. (Ovid, *Amores*, I, xiii, 40.)
8. Unceasingly.

Into the entrails of yon laboring clouds,
That when you vomit forth into the air,
My limbs may issue from their smoky mouths,
So[9] that my soul may but ascend to Heaven. [*The watch strikes the half hour.*]
Ah, half the hour is past! 'Twill all be past anon!
O God,
If thou wilt not have mercy on my soul,
Yet for Christ's sake whose blood hath ransom'd me,
Impose some end to my incessant pain;
Let Faustus live in hell a thousand years—
A hundred thousand, and at last be sav'd!
O, no end is limited to damned souls!
Why wert thou not a creature wanting soul?
Or why is this immortal that thou hast?
Ah, Pythagoras' metempsychosis! were that true,
This soul should fly from me, and I be chang'd
Unto some brutish beast! All beasts are happy,
For, when they die,
Their souls are soon dissolv'd in elements;
But mine must live, still to be plagu'd in hell.
Curst be the parents that engend'red me!
No, Faustus, curse thyself, curse Lucifer
That hath depriv'd thee of the joys of Heaven. [*The clock striketh twelve.*]
O, it strikes, it strikes! Now, body, turn to air,
Or Lucifer will bear thee quick[10] to hell. [*Thunder and lightning.*]
O soul, be changed into little water-drops,
And fall into the ocean—ne'er be found.
My God! my God! look not so fierce on me!

[*Enter* DEVILS.]

Adders and serpents, let me breathe awhile!
Ugly hell, gape not! come not, Lucifer!
I'll burn my books!—Ah Mephistophilis! [11] [*Exeunt* DEVILS *with* FAUSTUS.]

[*Enter* CHORUS.]

CHORUS. Cut is the branch that might have grown full straight,
And burned is Apollo's laurel bough,
That sometime grew within this learned man.
Faustus is gone; regard his hellish fall,

---

9. Provided that.
10. Alive.
11. The quarto of 1616 adds 18 lines, in which the scholars discover Faustus' dismembered body.

Whose fiendful fortune may exhort the wise
Only to wonder at unlawful things,
Whose deepness doth entice such forward wits
To practise more than heavenly power permits. [*Exit.*]

Terminat hora diem, terminat author opus.[12]

12. The hour ends the day; the author ends his work.

HEDDA GABLER

HENRIK IBSEN

TRANSLATED FROM THE NORWEGIAN BY EDMUND GOSSE AND WILLIAM ARCHER

Characters

GEORGE TESMAN
HEDDA TESMAN, *his wife*
MISS JULIANA TESMAN, *his aunt*
MRS. ELVSTED
JUDGE BRACK
EILERT LÖVBORG
BERTA, *servant at the Tesmans'*

SCENE: *The action is Tesman's villa, in the west end of Christiania.*

ACT I

SCENE: *A spacious, handsome and tastefully furnished drawing-room, decorated in dark colors. In the back, a wide doorway with curtains drawn back, leading into a smaller room decorated in the same style as the drawing-room. In the right-hand wall of the front room, a folding door leading out to the hall. In the opposite wall, on the left, a glass door, also with curtains drawn back. Through the panes can be seen part of a veranda outside, and trees covered with autumn foliage. An oval table, with a cover on it, and surrounded by chairs, stands well forward. In front, by the wall on the right, a wide stove of dark porcelain, a high-backed arm-chair, a cushioned foot-rest, and two footstools. A settee, with a small round table in front of it, fills the upper right-hand corner. In front, on the left, a little way from the wall, a sofa. Farther back than the glass door, a piano. On either side of the doorway at the back a whatnot with terra-cotta and majolica ornaments.—Against the back wall of the inner room a sofa, with a table, and one or two chairs. Over the sofa hangs the portrait of a handsome elderly man in a General's uniform. Over the table a hanging lamp, with an opal glass shade.—A number of bouquets are arranged about the drawing-room, in vases and glasses. Others lie upon the tables. The floors in both rooms are covered with thick carpets.—Morning light. The sun shines in through the glass door.*

MISS JULIANA TESMAN, *with her bonnet on and carrying a parasol, comes in from the hall, followed by* BERTA, *who carries a bouquet wrapped in paper.* MISS TESMAN *is a comely and pleasant-looking lady of about sixty-five. She is nicely but simply dressed in a gray walking-costume.* BERTA *is a middle-aged woman of plain and rather countrified appearance.*

MISS TESMAN. [*Stops close to the door, listens, and says softly.*] Upon my word, I don't believe they are stirring yet!

BERTA. [*Also softly.*] I told you so, Miss. Remember how late the steamboat got in last night. And then, when they got home!—good Lord, what a lot the young mistress had to unpack before she could get to bed.

MISS TESMAN. Well, well—let them have their sleep out. But let us see that they get a good breath of the fresh morning air when they do appear. [*She goes to the glass door and throws it open.*]

BERTA. [*Beside the table, at a loss what to do with the bouquet in her hand.*] I declare, there isn't a bit of room left. I think I'll put it down here, Miss. [*She places it on the piano.*]

MISS TESMAN. So you've got a new mistress now, my dear Berta. Heaven knows it was a wrench to me to part with you.

BERTA. [*On the point of weeping.*] And do you think it wasn't hard for me, too, Miss? After all the blessed years I've been with you and Miss Rina.

MISS TESMAN. We must make the best of it, Berta. There was nothing else to be done. George can't do without you, you see—he absolutely can't. He has had you to look after him ever since he was a little boy.

BERTA. Ah, but, Miss Julia, I can't help thinking of Miss Rina lying helpless at home there, poor thing. And with only that new girl, too! She'll never learn to take proper care of an invalid.

MISS TESMAN. Oh, I shall manage to train her. And, of course, you know I shall take most of it upon myself. You needn't be uneasy about my poor sister, my dear Berta.

BERTA. Well, but there's another thing, Miss. I'm so mortally afraid I shan't be able to suit the young mistress.

MISS TESMAN. Oh, well—just at first there may be one or two things——

BERTA. Most like she'll be terrible grand in her ways.

MISS TESMAN. Well, you can't wonder at that—General Gabler's daughter! Think of the sort of life she was accustomed to in her father's time. Don't you remember how we used to see her riding down the road along with the General? In that long black habit—and with feathers in her hat?

BERTA. Yes, indeed—I remember well enough!—But, good Lord, I should never have dreamt in those days that she and Master George would make a match of it.

MISS TESMAN. Nor I.—But by the by, Berta—while I think of it: in future you mustn't say Master George. You must say Dr. Tesman.

BERTA. Yes, the young mistress spoke of that, too—last night—the moment they set foot in the house. Is it true then, Miss?

MISS TESMAN. Yes, indeed it is. Only think, Berta—some foreign university has made him a doctor—while he has been abroad, you understand. I hadn't heard a word about it, until he told me himself upon the pier.

BERTA. Well, well, he's clever enough for anything, he is. But I didn't think he'd have gone in for doctoring people, too.

MISS TESMAN. No, no, it's not that sort of doctor he is. [*Nods significantly.*] But let me tell you, we may have to call him something still grander before long.

BERTA. You don't say so! What can that be, Miss?

MISS TESMAN. [*Smiling.*] H'm—wouldn't you like to know! [*With emotion.*] Ah, dear, dear—if my poor brother could only look up from his grave now, and see what his little boy has grown into! [*Looks around.*] But bless me, Berta—why have you done this? Taken the chintz covers off all the furniture?

BERTA. The mistress told me to. She can't abide covers on the chairs, she says.

MISS TESMAN. Are they going to make this their everyday sitting-room then?

BERTA. Yes, that's what I understood—from the mistress. Master George—the doctor—he said nothing.

[GEORGE TESMAN *comes from the right into the inner room, humming to himself, and carrying an unstrapped empty portmanteau. He is a middle-sized, young-looking man of thirty-three, rather stout, with a round, open, cheerful face, fair hair and beard. He wears spectacles, and is somewhat carelessly dressed in comfortable indoor clothes.*]

MISS TESMAN. Good morning, good morning, George.

TESMAN. [*In the doorway between the rooms.*] Aunt Julia! Dear Aunt Julia! [*Goes up to her and shakes hands warmly.*] Come all this way—so early! Eh?

MISS TESMAN. Why, of course I had to come and see how you were getting on.

TESMAN. In spite of your having had no proper night's rest?

MISS TESMAN. Oh, that makes no difference to me.

TESMAN. Well, I suppose you got home all right from the pier? Eh?

MISS TESMAN. Yes, quite safely, thank goodness. Judge Brack was good enough to see me right to my door.

TESMAN. We were so sorry we couldn't give you a seat in the carriage. But you saw what a pile of boxes Hedda had to bring with her.

MISS TESMAN. Yes, she had certainly plenty of boxes.

BERTA. [*To* TESMAN.] Shall I go in and see if there's anything I can do for the mistress?

TESMAN. No thank you, Berta—you needn't. She said she would ring if she wanted anything.

BERTA. [*Going towards the right.*] Very well.

TESMAN. But look here—take this portmanteau with you.

BERTA. [*Taking it.*] I'll put it in the attic.

[*She goes out by the hall door.*]

TESMAN. Fancy, Auntie—I had the whole of that portmanteau chock full of copies of documents. You wouldn't believe how much I have picked up from all the archives I have been examining—curious old details that no one has had any idea of——

MISS TESMAN. Yes, you don't seem to have wasted your time on your wedding trip, George.

TESMAN. No, that I haven't. But do take off your bonnet, Auntie. Look here! Let me untie the strings—eh?

MISS TESMAN. [*While he does so.*] Well, well—this is just as if you were still at home with us.

TESMAN. [*With the bonnet in his hand, looks at it from all sides.*] Why, what a gorgeous bonnet you've been investing in!

MISS TESMAN. I bought it on Hedda's account.

TESMAN. On Hedda's account? Eh?

MISS TESMAN. Yes, so that Hedda needn't be ashamed of me if we happened to go out together.

TESMAN. [*Patting her cheek.*] You always think of everything, Aunt Julia. [*Lays the bonnet on a chair beside the table.*] And now, look here—suppose we sit comfortably on the sofa and have a little chat, till Hedda comes. [*They seat themselves. She places her parasol in the corner of the sofa.*]

MISS TESMAN. [*Takes both his hands and looks at him.*] What a delight it is to have you again, as large as life, before my very eyes, George! My George—my poor brother's own boy!

TESMAN. And it's a delight for me, too, to see you again, Aunt Julia! You, who have been father and mother in one to me.

MISS TESMAN. Oh yes, I know you will always keep a place in your heart for your old aunts.

TESMAN. And what about Aunt Rina? No improvement—eh?

MISS TESMAN. Oh no—we can scacely look for any improvement in her case, poor thing. There she lies, helpless, as she has lain for all these years. But heaven grant I may not lose her yet awhile. For if I did, I don't know what I should make of my life, George—especially now that I haven't you to look after any more.

TESMAN. [*Patting her back.*] There, there, there——!

MISS TESMAN. [*Suddenly changing her tone.*] And to think that here you are a married man, George!—And that you should be the one to carry off Hedda Gabler—the beautiful Hedda Gabler! Only think of it—she, that was so beset with admirers!

TESMAN. [*Hums a little and smiles complacently.*] Yes, I fancy I have several good friends about town who would like to stand in my shoes—eh?

MISS TESMAN. And then this fine long wedding-tour you have had! More than five—nearly six months——

TESMAN. Well, for me it has been a sort of tour of research as well. I have had to do so much grubbing among old records—and to read no end of books too, Auntie.

MISS TESMAN. Oh yes, I suppose so. [*More confidentially, and lowering her voice a little.*] But listen now, George,—have you nothing—nothing special to tell me?

TESMAN. As to our journey?

MISS TESMAN. Yes.

TESMAN. No, I don't know of anything except what I have told you in my letters. I had a doctor's degree conferred on me—but that I told you yesterday.

MISS TESMAN. Yes, yes, you did. But what I mean is—haven't you any—any—expectations——?

TESMAN. Expectations?

MISS TESMAN. Why you know, George—I'm your old auntie!

TESMAN. Why, of course I have expectations.

MISS TESMAN. Ah!

TESMAN. I have every expectation of being a professor one of these days.

MISS TESMAN. Oh yes, a professor——

TESMAN. Indeed, I may say I am certain of it. But my dear Auntie—you know all about that already!

MISS TESMAN. [*Laughing to herself.*] Yes, of course I do. You are quite right there. [*Changing the subject.*] But we were talking about your journey. It must have cost a great deal of money, George?

TESMAN. Well, you see—my handsome traveling-scholarship went a good way.

MISS TESMAN. But I can't understand how you can have made it go far enough for two.

TESMAN. No, that's not so easy to understand—eh?

MISS TESMAN. And especially travelling with a lady—they tell me that makes it ever so much more expensive.

TESMAN. Yes, of course—it makes it a little more expensive. But Hedda had to have this trip, Auntie! She really had to. Nothing else would have done.

MISS TESMAN. No, no, I suppose not. A wedding-tour seems to be quite indispensable nowadays.—But tell me now—have you gone thoroughly over the house yet?

TESMAN. Yes, you may be sure I have. I have been afoot ever since daylight.

MISS TESMAN. And what do you think of it all?

TESMAN. I'm delighted! Quite delighted! Only I can't think what we are to do with the two empty rooms between this inner parlor and Hedda's bedroom.

MISS TESMAN. [*Laughing.*] Oh my dear George, I daresay you may find some use for them—in the course of time.

TESMAN. Why of course you are quite right, Aunt Julia! You mean as my library increases—eh?

MISS TESMAN. Yes, quite so, my dear boy. It was your library I was thinking of.

TESMAN. I am specially pleased on Hedda's account. Often and often, before we were engaged, she said that she would never care to live anywhere but in Secretary Falk's villa.

MISS TESMAN. Yes, it was lucky that this very house should come into the market, just after you had started.

TESMAN. Yes, Aunt Julia, the luck was on our side, wasn't it—eh?

MISS TESMAN. But the expense, my dear George! You will find it very expensive, all this.

TESMAN. [*Looks at her, a little cast down.*] Yes, I suppose I shall, Aunt!

MISS TESMAN. Oh, frightfully!

TESMAN. How much do you think? In round numbers?—Eh?

MISS TESMAN. Oh, I can't even guess until all the accounts come in.

TESMAN. Well, fortunately, Judge Brack has secured the most favorable terms for me,—so he said in a letter to Hedda.

MISS TESMAN. Yes, don't be uneasy, my dear boy.—Besides, I have given security for the furniture and all the carpets.

TESMAN. Security? You? My dear Aunt Julia—what sort of security could you give?

MISS TESMAN. I have given a mortgage on our annuity.

TESMAN. [*Jumps up.*] What! On your—and Aunt Rina's annuity!

MISS TESMAN. Yes, I knew of no other plan, you see.

TESMAN. [*Placing himself before her.*] Have you gone out of your senses, Auntie! Your annuity—it's all that you and Aunt Rina have to live upon.

MISS TESMAN. Well, well—don't get so excited about it. It's only a matter of form you know—Judge Brack assured me of that. It was he that was kind enough to arrange the whole affair for me. A mere matter of form, he said.

TESMAN. Yes, that may be all very well. But nevertheless——

MISS TESMAN. You will have your own salary to depend upon now. And, good heavens, even if we did have to pay up a little——! To eke things out a bit at the start——! Why, it would be nothing but a pleasure to us.

TESMAN. Oh Auntie—will you never be tired of making sacrifices for me!

MISS TESMAN. [*Rises and lays her hands on his shoulders.*] Have I any other happiness in this world except to smooth your way for you, my dear boy? You, who have had neither father nor mother to depend on. And now we have reached the goal, George! Things have looked black enough for us, sometimes; but, thank heaven, now you have nothing to fear.

TESMAN. Yes, it is really marvelous how everything has turned out for the best.

MISS TESMAN. And the people who opposed you—who wanted to bar the way for you—now you have them at your feet. They have fallen, George. Your most dangerous rival—his fall was the worst.—And now he has to lie on the bed he has made for himself—poor misguided creature.

TESMAN. Have you heard anything of Eilert? Since I went away, I mean.

MISS TESMAN. Only that he is said to have published a new book.

TESMAN. What! Eilert Lövborg! Recently—eh?

MISS TESMAN. Yes, so they say. Heaven knows whether it can be worth anything! Ah, when your new book appears—that will be another story, George! What is it to be about?

TESMAN. It will deal with the domestic industries of Brabant during the Middle Ages.

MISS TESMAN. Fancy—to be able to write on such a subject as that!

TESMAN. However, it may be some time before the book is ready. I have all these collections to arrange first, you see.

MISS TESMAN. Yes, collecting and arranging—no one can beat you at that. There you are my poor brother's own son.

TESMAN. I am looking forward eagerly to setting to work at it; especially now that I have my own delightful home to work in.

MISS TESMAN. And, most of all, now that you have got a wife of your heart, my dear George.

TESMAN. [*Embracing her.*] Oh yes, yes, Aunt Julia. Hedda—she is the best part of it all! [*Looks towards the doorway.*] I believe I hear her coming—eh?

[HEDDA *enters from the left through the inner room. She is a woman of nine-and-twenty. Her face and figure show refinement and distinction. Her complexion is pale and opaque. Her steel-gray eyes express a cold, unruffled repose. Her hair is of an agreeable medium brown, but not particularly abundant. She is dressed in a tasteful, somewhat loose-fitting morning gown.*]

MISS TESMAN. [*Going to meet* HEDDA.] Good morning, my dear Hedda! Good morning, and a hearty welcome!

HEDDA. [*Holds out her hand.*] Good morning, dear Miss Tesman! So early a call! That is kind of you.

MISS TESMAN. [*With some embarrassment.*] Well—has the bride slept well in her new home?

HEDDA. Oh yes, thanks. Passably.

TESMAN. [*Laughing.*] Passably! Come, that's good, Hedda! You were sleeping like a stone when I got up.

HEDDA. Fortunately. Of course one has always to accustom one's self to new surroundings, Miss Tesman—little by little. [*Looking towards the left.*] Oh—there the servant has gone and opened the veranda door, and let in a whole flood of sunshine.

MISS TESMAN. [*Going towards the door.*] Well, then we will shut it.

HEDDA. No, no, not that! Tesman, please draw the curtains. That will give a softer light.

TESMAN. [*At the door.*] All right—all right.—There now, Hedda, now you have both shade and fresh air.

HEDDA. Yes, fresh air we certainly must have, with all these stacks of flowers——. But—won't you sit down, Miss Tesman?

MISS TESMAN. No, thank you. Now that I have seen that everything is all right here—thank heaven!—I must be getting home again. My sister is lying longing for me, poor thing.

TESMAN. Give her my very best love, Auntie; and say I shall look in and see her later in the day.

MISS TESMAN. Yes, yes, I'll be sure to tell her. But by the by, George—[*Feeling in her dress pocket.*]—I had almost forgotten—I have something for you here.

TESMAN. What is it, Auntie? Eh?

MISS TESMAN. [*Produces a flat parcel wrapped in newspaper and hands it to him.*] Look here, my dear boy.

TESMAN. [*Opening the parcel.*] Well, I declare!—Have you really saved them for me, Aunt Julia! Hedda! isn't this touching—eh?

HEDDA. [*Beside the whatnot on the right.*] Well, what is it?

TESMAN. My old morning-shoes! My slippers.

HEDDA. Indeed. I remember you often spoke of them while we were abroad.

TESMAN. Yes, I missed them terribly. [*Goes up to her.*] Now you shall see them, Hedda!

HEDDA. [*Going towards the stove.*] Thanks, I really don't care about it.

TESMAN. [*Following her.*] Only think—ill as she was, Aunt Rina embroidered these for me. Oh you can't think how many associations cling to them.

HEDDA. [*At the table.*] Scarcely for me.

MISS TESMAN. Of course not for Hedda, George.

TESMAN. Well, but now that she belongs to the family, I thought—

HEDDA. [*Interrupting.*] We shall never get on with this servant, Tesman.

MISS TESMAN. Not get on with Berta?

TESMAN. Why, dear, what puts that in your head? Eh?

HEDDA. [*Pointing.*] Look there! She has left her old bonnet lying about on a chair.

TESMAN. [*In consternation, drops the slippers on the floor.*] Why, Hedda——

HEDDA. Just fancy, if any one should come in and see it!

TESMAN. But Hedda—that's Aunt Julia's bonnet.

HEDDA. Is it!

MISS TESMAN. [*Taking up the bonnet.*] Yes, indeed it's mine. And, what's more, it's not old, Madam Hedda.

HEDDA. I really did not look closely at it, Miss Tesman.

MISS TESMAN. [*Trying on the bonnet.*] Let me tell you it's the first time I have worn it—the very first time.

TESMAN. And a very nice bonnet it is too—quite a beauty!

MISS TESMAN. Oh, it's no such great thing, George. [*Looks around her.*] My parasol——? Ah, here. [*Takes it.*] For this is mine too—[*mutters*]—not Berta's.

TESMAN. A new bonnet and a new parasol! Only think, Hedda!

HEDDA. Very handsome indeed.

TESMAN. Yes, isn't it? Eh? But Auntie, take a good look at Hedda before you go! See how handsome she is!

MISS TESMAN. Oh, my dear boy, there's nothing new in that. Hedda was always lovely. [*She nods and goes towards the right.*]

TESMAN. [*Following.*] Yes, but have you noticed what splendid condition she is in? How she has filled out on the journey?

HEDDA. [*Crossing the room.*] Oh, do be quiet——!

MISS TESMAN. [*Who has stopped and turned.*] Filled out?

TESMAN. Of course you don't notice it so much now that she has that dress on. But I, who can see——

HEDDA. [*At the glass door, impatiently.*] Oh, you can't see anything.

TESMAN. It must be the mountain air in the Tyrol——

HEDDA. [*Curtly, interrupting.*] I am exactly as I was when I started.

TESMAN. So you insist; but I'm quite certain you are not. Don't you agree with me, Auntie?

MISS TESMAN. [*Who has been gazing at her with folded hands.*] Hedda is lovely—lovely—lovely. [*Goes up to her, takes her head between both hands, draws it downwards, and kisses her hair.*] God bless and preserve Hedda Tesman—for George's sake.

HEDDA. [*Gently freeing herself.*] Oh—! Let me go.

MISS TESMAN. [*In quiet emotion.*] I shall not let a day pass without coming to see you.

TESMAN. No you won't, will you, Auntie? Eh?

MISS TESMAN. Good-bye—good-bye!

[*She goes out by the hall door.* TESMAN *accompanies her. The door remains half open.* TESMAN *can be heard repeating his message to* AUNT RINA *and his thanks for the slippers. In the meantime,* HEDDA *walks about the room, raising her arms and clenching her hands as if in desperation. Then she flings back the curtains from the glass door, and stands there looking out. Presently* TESMAN *returns and closes the door behind him.*]

TESMAN. [*Picks up the slippers from the floor.*] What are you looking at, Hedda?

HEDDA. [*Once more calm and mistress of herself.*] I am only looking at the leaves. They are so yellow—so withered.

TESMAN. [*Wraps up the slippers and lays them on the table.*] Well you see, we are well into September now.

HEDDA. [*Again restless.*] Yes, to think of it!—Already in—in September.

TESMAN. Don't you think Aunt Julia's manner was strange, dear? Almost solemn? Can you imagine what was the matter with her? Eh?

HEDDA. I scarcely know her, you see. Is she not often like that?

TESMAN. No, not as she was to-day.

HEDDA. [*Leaving the glass door.*] Do you think she was annoyed about the bonnet?

TESMAN. Oh, scarcely at all. Perhaps a little, just at the moment——

HEDDA. But what an idea, to pitch her bonnet about in the drawing-room! No one does that sort of thing.

TESMAN. Well you may be sure Aunt Julia won't do it again.

HEDDA. In any case, I shall manage to make my peace with her.

TESMAN. Yes, my dear, good Hedda, if you only would.

HEDDA. When you call this afternoon, you might invite her to spend the evening here.

TESMAN. Yes, that I will. And there's one thing more you could do that would delight her heart.

HEDDA. What is it?

TESMAN. If you could only prevail on yourself to say *du*[1] to her. For my sake, Hedda? Eh?

HEDDA. No, no, Tesman—you really mustn't ask that of me. I have told you so already. I shall try to call her "Aunt"; and you must be satisfied with that.

TESMAN. Well, well. Only I think now that you belong to the family, you——

HEDDA. H'm—I can't in the least see why——[*She goes up towards the middle doorway.*]

TESMAN. [*After a pause.*] Is there anything the matter with you, Hedda? Eh?

HEDDA. I'm only looking at my old piano. It doesn't go at all well with all the other things.

TESMAN. The first time I draw my salary, we'll see about exchanging it.

HEDDA. No, no—no exchanging. I don't want to part with it. Suppose we put it there in the inner room, and then get another here in its place. When it's convenient, I mean.

TESMAN. [*A little taken aback.*] Yes—of course we could do that.

HEDDA. [*Takes up the bouquet from the piano.*] These flowers were not here last night when we arrived.

TESMAN. Aunt Julia must have brought them for you.

HEDDA. [*Examining the bouquet.*] A visiting-card. [*Takes it out and reads.*] "Shall return later in the day." Can you guess whose card it is?

TESMAN. No. Whose? Eh?

HEDDA. The name is "Mrs. Elvsted."

TESMAN. Is it really? Sheriff Elvsted's wife? Miss Rysing that was.

HEDDA. Exactly. The girl with the irritating hair, that she was always showing off. An old flame of yours I've been told.

---

1. The familiar form of the pronoun, used only between persons who are on a footing of intimacy; hence its significance here and later.

TESMAN. [*Laughing.*] Oh, that didn't last long; and it was before I knew you, Hedda. But fancy her being in town!

HEDDA. It's odd that she should call upon us. I have scarcely seen her since we left school.

TESMAN. I haven't seen her either for—heaven knows how long. I wonder how she can endure to live in such an out-of-the-way hole—eh?

HEDDA. [*After a moment's thought, says suddenly.*] Tell me, Tesman—isn't it somewhere near there that he—that—Eilert Lövborg is living?

TESMAN. Yes, he is somewhere in that part of the country.

[BERTA *enters by the hall door.*]

BERTA. That lady, ma'am, that brought some flowers a little while ago, is here again. [*Pointing.*] The flowers you have in your hand, ma'am.

HEDDA. Ah, is she? Well, please show her in.

[BERTA *opens the door for* MRS. ELVSTED, *and goes out herself.*—MRS. ELVSTED *is a woman of fragile figure, with pretty, soft features. Her eyes are light blue, large, round, and somewhat prominent, with a startled, inquiring expression. Her hair is remarkably light, almost flaxen, and unusually abundant and wavy. She is a couple of years younger than* HEDDA. *She wears a dark visiting dress, tasteful, but not quite in the latest fashion.*]

HEDDA. [*Receives her warmly.*] How do you do, my dear Mrs. Elvsted? It's delightful to see you again.

MRS. ELVSTED. [*Nervously, struggling for self-control.*] Yes, it's a very long time since we met.

TESMAN. [*Gives her his hand.*] And we too—eh?

HEDDA. Thanks for your lovely flowers——

MRS. ELVSTED. Oh, not at all—— I would have come straight here yesterday afternoon; but I heard that you were away——

TESMAN. Have you just come to town? Eh?

MRS. ELVSTED. I arrived yesterday, about midday. Oh, I was quite in despair when I heard that you were not at home.

HEDDA. In despair! How so?

TESMAN. Why, my dear Mrs. Rysing—I mean Mrs. Elvsted——

HEDDA. I hope that you are not in any trouble?

MRS. ELVSTED. Yes, I am. And I don't know another living creature here that I can turn to.

HEDDA. [*Laying the bouquet on the table.*] Come—let us sit here on the sofa——

MRS. ELVSTED. Oh, I am too restless to sit down.

HEDDA. Oh no, you're not. Come here. [*She draws* MRS. ELVSTED *down upon the sofa and sits at her side.*]

TESMAN. Well? what is it, Mrs. Elvsted——?

HEDDA. Has anything particular happened to you at home?

MRS. ELVSTED. Yes—and no. Oh—I am so anxious you should not misunderstand me——

HEDDA. Then your best plan is to tell us the whole story, Mrs. Elvsted.

TESMAN. I suppose that's what you have come for—eh?

MRS. ELVSTED. Yes, yes—of course it is. Well then, I must tell you—if you don't already know—that Eilert Lövborg is in town, too.

HEDDA. Lövborg——!

TESMAN. What! Has Eilert Lövborg come back? Fancy that, Hedda!

HEDDA. Well, well—I hear it.

MRS. ELVSTED. He has been here a week already. Just fancy—a whole week! In this terrible town, alone! With so many temptations on all sides.

HEDDA. But, my dear Mrs. Elvsted—how does he concern you so much?

MRS. ELVSTED. [*Looks at her with a startled air, and says rapidly.*] He was the children's tutor.

HEDDA. Your children's?

MRS. ELVSTED. My husband's. I have none.

HEDDA. Your step-children's, then?

MRS. ELVSTED. Yes.

TESMAN. [*Somewhat hesitatingly.*] Then was he—I don't know how to express it—was he—regular enough in his habits to be fit for the post? Eh?

MRS. ELVSTED. For the last two years his conduct has been irreproachable.

TESMAN. Has it indeed? Fancy that, Hedda!

HEDDA. I hear it.

MRS. ELVSTED. Perfectly irreproachable, I assure you! In every respect. But all the same—now that I know he is here—in this great town—and with a large sum of money in his hands—I can't help being in mortal fear for him.

TESMAN. Why did he not remain where he was? With you and your husband? Eh?

MRS. ELVSTED. After his book was published he was too restless and unsettled to remain with us.

TESMAN. Yes, by the by, Aunt Julia told me he had published a new book.

MRS. ELVSTED. Yes, a big book, dealing with the march of civilization—in broad outline, as it were. It came out about a fortnight ago. And since it has sold so well, and been so much read—and made such a sensation——

TESMAN. Has it indeed? It must be something he has had lying by since his better days.

MRS. ELVSTED. Long ago, you mean?

TESMAN. Yes.

MRS ELVSTED. No, he has written it all since he has been with us—within the last year.

TESMAN. Isn't that good news, Hedda? Think of that.

MRS. ELVSTED. Ah yes, if only it would last!

HEDDA. Have you seen him here in town?

MRS. ELVSTED. No, not yet. I have had the greatest difficulty in finding out his address. But this morning I discovered it at last.

HEDDA. [*Looks searchingly at her.*] Do you know, it seems to me a little odd of your husband—h'm—

MRS. ELVSTED. [*Starting nervously.*] Of my husband! What?

HEDDA. That he should send you to town on such an errand—that he does not come himself and look after his friend.

MRS. ELVSTED. Oh no, no—my husband has no time. And besides, I—I had some shopping to do.

HEDDA. [*With a slight smile.*] Ah, that is a different matter.

MRS. ELVSTED. [*Rising quickly and uneasily.*] And now I beg and implore you, Mr. Tesman—receive Eilert Lövborg kindly if he comes to you! And that he is sure to do. You see you were such great friends in the old days. And then you are interested in the same studies—the same branch of science—so far as I can understand.

TESMAN. We used to be, at any rate.

MRS. ELVSTED. That is why I beg so earnestly that you—you too—will keep a sharp eye upon him. Oh, you will promise me that, Mr. Tesman—won't you?

TESMAN. With the greatest of pleasure, Mrs. Rysing——

HEDDA. Elvsted.

TESMAN. I assure you I shall do all I possibly can for Eilert. You may rely upon me.

MRS. ELVSTED. Oh, how very, very kind of you! [*Presses his hands.*] Thanks, thanks, thanks! [*Frightened.*] You see, my husband is so very fond of him!

HEDDA. [*Rising.*] You ought to write to him, Tesman. Perhaps he may not care to come to you of his own accord.

TESMAN. Well, perhaps it would be the right thing to do, Hedda? Eh?

HEDDA. And the sooner the better. Why not at once?

MRS. ELVSTED. [*Imploringly.*] Oh, if you only would!

TESMAN. I'll write this moment. Have you his address, Mrs.—Mrs. Elvsted?

MRS. ELVSTED. Yes. [*Takes a slip of paper from her pocket, and hands it to him.*] Here it is.

TESMAN. Good, good. Then I'll go in—— [*Looks about him.*] By the by—my slippers? Oh, here. [*Takes the packet, and is about to go.*]

HEDDA. Be sure you write him a cordial, friendly letter. And a good long one too.

TESMAN. Yes, I will.

MRS. ELVSTED. But please, please don't say a word to show that I have suggested it.

TESMAN. No, how could you think I would? Eh? [*He goes out to the right, through the inner room.*]

HEDDA. [*Goes up to* MRS. ELVSTED, *smiles and says in a low voice.*] There! We have killed two birds with one stone.

MRS. ELVSTED. What do you mean?

HEDDA. Could you not see that I wanted him to go?

MRS. ELVSTED. Yes, to write the letter——

HEDDA. And that I might speak to you alone.

MRS. ELVSTED. [*Confused.*] About the same thing?

HEDDA. Precisely.

MRS. ELVSTED. [*Apprehensively.*] But there is nothing more, Mrs. Tesman! Absolutely nothing!

HEDDA. Oh yes, but there is. There is a great deal more—I can see that. Sit here—and we'll have a cosy, confidential chat. [*She forces* MRS. ELVSTED *to sit in the easy-chair beside the stove, and seats herself on one of the foot-stools.*]

MRS. ELVSTED. [*Anxiously, looking at her watch.*] But, my dear Mrs. Tesman—I was really on the point of going.

HEDDA. Oh, you can't be in such a hurry.—Well? Now tell me something about your life at home.

MRS. ELVSTED. Oh, that is just what I care least to speak about.

HEDDA. But to me, dear——? Why, weren't we schoolfellows?

MRS. ELVSTED. Yes, but you were in the class above me. Oh, how dreadfully afraid of you I was then!

HEDDA. Afraid of me?

MRS. ELVSTED. Yes, dreadfully. For when we met on the stairs you used always to pull my hair.

HEDDA. Did I, really?

MRS. ELVSTED. Yes, and once you said you would burn it off my head.

HEDDA. Oh, that was all nonsense, of course.

MRS. ELVSTED. Yes, but I was so silly in those days.—And since then, too—we have drifted so far—far apart from each other. Our circles have been so entirely different.

HEDDA. Well then, we must try to drift together again. Now listen! At school we said *du*[2] to each other; and we called each other by our Christian names——

MRS. ELVSTED. No, I am sure you must be mistaken.

HEDDA. No, not at all! I can remember quite distinctly. So now we are going to renew our old friendship. [*Draws the footstool closer to* MRS. ELVSTED.] There now! [*Kisses her cheek.*] You must say *du* to me and call me Hedda.

MRS. ELVSTED. [*Presses and pats her hands.*] Oh, how good and kind you are! I am not used to such kindness.

HEDDA. There, there, there! And I shall say *du* to you, as in the old days, and call you my dear Thora.

MRS. ELVSTED. My name is Thea.

2. See note, p. 596.

HEDDA. Why, of course! I meant Thea. [*Looks at her compassionately.*] So you are not accustomed to goodness and kindness, Thea? Not in your own home?

MRS. ELVSTED. Oh, if I only had a home! But I haven't any; I have never had a home.

HEDDA. [*Looks at her for a moment.*] I almost suspected as much.

MRS. ELVSTED. [*Gazing helplessly before her.*] Yes—yes—yes.

HEDDA. I don't quite remember—was it not as housekeeper that you first went to Mr. Elvsted's?

MRS. ELVSTED. I really went as governess. But his wife—his late wife—was an invalid,—and rarely left her room. So I had to look after the housekeeping as well.

HEDDA. And then—at last—you became mistress of the house.

MRS. ELVSTED. [*Sadly.*] Yes, I did.

HEDDA. Let me see—about how long ago was that?

MRS. ELVSTED. My marriage?

HEDDA. Yes.

MRS. ELVSTED. Five years ago.

HEDDA. To be sure; it must be that.

MRS. ELVSTED. Oh those five years——! Or at all events the last two or three of them! Oh, if you[3] could only imagine——

HEDDA. [*Giving her a little slap on the hand.*] *De*? Fie, Thea!

MRS. ELVSTED. Yes, yes, I will try—— Well, if—you could only imagine and understand——

HEDDA. [*Lightly.*] Eilert Lövborg has been in your neighborhood about three years, hasn't he?

MRS. ELVSTED. [*Looks at her doubtfully.*] Eilert Lövborg? Yes—he has.

HEDDA. Had you known him before, in town here?

MRS. ELVSTED. Scarcely at all. I mean—I knew him by name of course.

HEDDA. But you saw a good deal of him in the country?

MRS. ELVSTED. Yes, he came to us every day. You see, he gave the children lessons; for in the long run I couldn't manage it all myself.

HEDDA. No, that's clear.—And your husband——? I suppose he is often away from home?

MRS. ELVSTED. Yes. Being sheriff, you know, he has to travel about a good deal in his district.

HEDDA. [*Leaning against the arm of the chair.*] Thea—my poor, sweet Thea—now you must tell me everything—exactly as it stands.

MRS. ELVSTED. Well then, you must question me.

HEDDA. What sort of a man is your husband, Thea? I mean—you know—in everyday life. Is he kind to you?

3. Instead of *du,* Mrs. Elvsted uses *De,* the formal pronoun. After being rebuked, she says *du.*

MRS. ELVSTED. [*Evasively.*] I am sure he means well in everything.

HEDDA. I should think he must be altogether too old for you. There is at least twenty years' difference between you, is there not?

MRS. ELVSTED. [*Irritably.*] Yes, that is true, too. Everything about him is repellent to me! We have not a thought in common. We have no single point of sympathy—he and I.

HEDDA. But is he not fond of you all the same? In his own way?

MRS. ELVSTED. Oh I really don't know. I think he regards me simply as a useful property. And then it doesn't cost much to keep me. I am not expensive.

HEDDA. That is stupid of you.

MRS. ELVSTED. [*Shakes her head.*] It cannot be otherwise—not with him. I don't think he really cares for any one but himself—and perhaps a little for the children.

HEDDA. And for Eilert Lövborg, Thea.

MRS. ELVSTED. [*Looking at her.*] For Eilert Lövborg? What puts that into your head?

HEDDA. Well, my dear—I should say, when he sends you after him all the way to town—— [*Smiling almost imperceptibly.*] And besides, you said so yourself, to Tesman.

MRS. ELVSTED. [*With a little nervous twitch.*] Did I? Yes, I suppose I did. [*Vehemently, but not loudly.*] No—I may just as well make a clean breast of it at once! For it must all come out in any case.

HEDDA. Why, my dear Thea——?

MRS. ELVSTED. Well, to make a long story short: My husband did not know that I was coming.

HEDDA. What! Your husband didn't know it!

MRS. ELVSTED. No, of course not. For that matter, he was away from home himself—he was traveling. Oh, I could bear it no longer, Hedda! I couldn't indeed—so utterly alone as I should have been in future.

HEDDA. Well? And then?

MRS. ELVSTED. So I put together some of my things—what I needed most—as quietly as possible. And then I left the house.

HEDDA. Without a word?

MRS. ELVSTED. Yes—and took the train straight to town.

HEDDA. Why, my dear, good Thea—to think of you daring to do it!

MRS. ELVSTED. [*Rises and moves about the room.*] What else could I possibly do?

HEDDA. But what do you think your husband will say when you go home again?

MRS. ELVSTED. [*At the table, looks at her.*] Back to him?

HEDDA. Of course.

MRS. ELVSTED. I shall never go back to him again.

HEDDA. [*Rising and going towards her.*] Then you have left your home—for good and all?

MRS. ELVSTED. Yes. There was nothing else to be done.

HEDDA. But then—to take flight so openly.

MRS. ELVSTED. Oh, it's impossible to keep things of that sort secret.

HEDDA. But what do you think people will say of you, Thea?

MRS. ELVSTED. They may say what they like, for aught *I* care. [*Seats herself wearily and sadly on the sofa.*] I have done nothing but what I had to do.

HEDDA. [*After a short silence.*] And what are your plans now? What do you think of doing?

MRS. ELVSTED. I don't know yet. I only know this, that I must live here, where Eilert Lövborg is—if I am to live at all.

HEDDA. [*Takes a chair from the table, seats herself beside her, and strokes her hands.*] My dear Thea—how did this—this friendship—between you and Eilert Lövborg come about?

MRS. ELVSTED. Oh it grew up gradually. I gained a sort of influence over him.

HEDDA. Indeed?

MRS. ELVSTED. He gave up his old habits. Not because I asked him to, for I never dared do that. But of course he saw how repulsive they were to me; and so he dropped them.

HEDDA. [*Concealing an involuntary smile of scorn.*] Then you have reclaimed him—as the saying goes—my little Thea.

MRS. ELVSTED. So he says himself, at any rate. And he, on his side, has made a real human being of me—taught me to think, and to understand so many things.

HEDDA. Did he give you lessons too, then?

MRS. ELVSTED. No, not exactly lessons. But he talked to me—talked about such an infinity of things. And then came the lovely, happy time when I began to share in his work—when he allowed me to help him!

HEDDA. Oh he did, did he?

MRS. ELVSTED. Yes! He never wrote anything without my assistance.

HEDDA. You were two good comrades, in fact?

MRS. ELVSTED. [*Eagerly.*] Comrades! Yes, fancy, Hedda—that is the very word he used!—Oh, I ought to feel perfectly happy; and yet I cannot; for I don't know how long it will last.

HEDDA. Are you no surer of him than that?

MRS. ELVSTED. [*Gloomily.*] A woman's shadow stands between Eilert Lövborg and me.

HEDDA. [*Looks at her anxiously.*] Who can that be?

MRS. ELVSTED. I don't know. Some one he knew in his—in his past. Some one he has never been able wholly to forget.

HEDDA. What has he told you—about this?

MRS. ELVSTED. He has only once—quite vaguely—alluded to it.

HEDDA. Well! And what did he say?

MRS. ELVSTED. He said that when they parted, she threatened to shoot him with a pistol.

HEDDA. [*With cold composure.*] Oh, nonsense! No one does that sort of thing here.

MRS. ELVSTED. No. And that is why I think it must have been that red-haired singing-woman whom he once——

HEDDA. Yes, very likely.

MRS. ELVSTED. For I remember they used to say of her that she carried loaded firearms.

HEDDA. Oh—then of course it must have been she.

MRS. ELVSTED. [*Wringing her hands.*] And now just fancy, Hedda—I hear that this singing-woman—that she is in town again! Oh, I don't know what to do——

HEDDA. [*Glancing towards the inner room.*] Hush! Here comes Tesman. [*Rises and whispers.*] Thea—all this must remain between you and me.

MRS. ELVSTED. [*Springing up.*] Oh yes—yes! For heaven's sake——!

[GEORGE TESMAN, *with a letter in his hand, comes from the right through the inner room.*]

TESMAN. There now—the epistle is finished.

HEDDA. That's right. And now Mrs. Elvsted is just going. Wait a moment—I'll go with you to the garden gate.

TESMAN. Do you think Berta could post the letter, Hedda dear?

HEDDA. [*Takes it.*] I will tell her to.

[BERTA *enters from the hall.*]

BERTA. Judge Brack wishes to know if Mrs. Tesman will receive him.

HEDDA. Yes, ask Judge Brack to come in. And look here—put this letter in the post.

BERTA. [*Taking the letter.*] Yes, ma'am.

[*She opens the door for* JUDGE BRACK *and goes out herself.* BRACK *is a man of forty-five; thick-set, but well-built and elastic in his movements. His face is roundish with an aristocratic profile. His hair is short, still almost black, and carefully dressed. His eyes are lively and sparkling. His eyebrows thick. His moustaches are also thick, with short-cut ends. He wears a well-cut walking-suit, a little too youthful for his age. He uses an eyeglass, which he now and then lets drop.*]

JUDGE BRACK. [*With his hat in his hand, bowing.*] May one venture to call so early in the day?

HEDDA. Of course one may.

TESMAN. [*Presses his hand.*] You are welcome at any time. [*Introducing him.*] Judge Brack—Miss Rysing——

HEDDA. Oh——!

BRACK. [*Bowing.*] Ah—delighted——

HEDDA. [*Looks at him and laughs.*] It's nice to have a look at you by daylight, Judge!

BRACK. Do you find me—altered?

HEDDA. A little younger, I think.

BRACK. Thank you so much.

TESMAN. But what do you think of Hedda—eh? Doesn't she look flourishing? She has actually——

HEDDA. Oh, do leave me alone. You haven't thanked Judge Brack for all the trouble he has taken——

BRACK. Oh, nonsense—it was a pleasure to me——

HEDDA. Yes, you are a friend indeed. But here stands Thea all impatience to be off—so *au revoir,* Judge. I shall be back again presently.

[*Mutual salutations.* MRS. ELVSTED *and* HEDDA *go out by the hall door.*]

BRACK. Well,—is your wife tolerably satisfied——

TESMAN. Yes, we can't thank you sufficiently. Of course she talks of a little rearrangement here and there; and one or two things are still wanting. We shall have to buy some additional trifles.

BRACK. Indeed!

TESMAN. But we won't trouble you about these things. Hedda says she herself will look after what is wanting.—Shan't we sit down? Eh?

BRACK. Thanks, for a moment. [*Seats himself beside the table.*] There is something I wanted to speak to you about, my dear Tesman.

TESMAN. Indeed? Ah, I understand! [*Seating himself.*] I suppose it's the serious part of the frolic that is coming now. Eh?

BRACK. Oh, the money question is not so very pressing; though, for that matter, I wish we had gone a little more economically to work.

TESMAN. But that would never have done, you know! Think of Hedda, my dear fellow! You, who know her so well——. I couldn't possibly ask her to put up with a shabby style of living!

BRACK. No, no—that is just the difficulty.

TESMAN. And then—fortunately—it can't be long before I receive my appointment.[4]

BRACK. Well, you see—such things are often apt to hang fire for a time.

TESMAN. Have you heard anything definite? Eh?

BRACK. Nothing exactly definite—— [*Interrupting himself.*] But by the by—I have one piece of news for you.

TESMAN. Well?

BRACK. Your old friend, Eilert Lövborg, has returned to town.

TESMAN. I know that already.

BRACK. Indeed! How did you learn it?

TESMAN. From that lady who went out with Hedda.

BRACK. Really? What was her name? I didn't quite catch it.

TESMAN. Mrs. Elvsted.

BRACK. Aha—Sheriff Elvsted's wife? Of course—he has been living up in their regions.

---

4. As professor.

TESMAN. And fancy—I'm delighted to hear that he is quite a reformed character!

BRACK. So they say.

TESMAN. And then he has published a new book—eh?

BRACK. Yes, indeed he has.

TESMAN. And I hear it has made some sensation!

BRACK. Quite an unusual sensation.

TESMAN. Fancy—isn't that good news! A man of such extraordinary talents——. I felt so grieved to think that he had gone irretrievably to ruin.

BRACK. That was what everybody thought.

TESMAN. But I cannot imagine what he will take to now! How in the world will he be able to make his living? Eh?

[*During the last words,* HEDDA *has entered by the hall door.*]

HEDDA. [*To* BRACK, *laughing with a touch of scorn.*] Tesman is for ever worrying about how people are to make their living.

TESMAN. Well you see, dear—we were talking about poor Eilert Lövborg.

HEDDA. [*Glancing at him rapidly.*] Oh, indeed? [*Seats herself in the arm-chair beside the stove and asks indifferently.*] What is the matter with him?

TESMAN. Well—no doubt he has run through all his property long ago; and he can scarcely write a new book every year—eh? So I really can't see what is to become of him.

BRACK. Perhaps I can give you some information on that point.

TESMAN. Indeed!

BRACK. You must remember that his relations have a good deal of influence.

TESMAN. Oh, his relations, unfortunately, have entirely washed their hands of him.

BRACK. At one time they called him the hope of the family.

TESMAN. At one time, yes! But he has put an end to all that.

HEDDA. Who knows? [*With a slight smile.*] I hear they have reclaimed him up at Sheriff Elvsted's——

BRACK. And then this book that he has published——

TESMAN. Well, well, I hope to goodness they may find something for him to do. I have just written to him. I asked him to come and see us this evening, Hedda dear.

BRACK. But my dear fellow, you are booked for my bachelors' party this evening. You promised on the pier last night.

HEDDA. Had you forgotten, Tesman?

TESMAN. Yes, I had utterly forgotten.

BRACK. But it doesn't matter, for you may be sure he won't come.

TESMAN. What makes you think that? Eh?

BRACK. [*With a little hesitation, rising and resting his hands on the back of his chair.*] My dear Tesman—and you too, Mrs. Tesman—I think I ought not to keep you in the dark about something that—that——

TESMAN. That concerns Eilert——?

BRACK. Both you and him.

TESMAN. Well, my dear Judge, out with it.

BRACK. You must be prepared to find your appointment deferred longer than you desired or expected.

TESMAN. [*Jumping up uneasily.*] Is there some hitch about it? Eh?

BRACK. The nomination may perhaps be made conditional on the result of a competition——

TESMAN. Competition! Think of that, Hedda!

HEDDA. [*Leans further back in the chair.*] Aha—aha!

TESMAN. But who can my competitor be? Surely not——?

BRACK. Yes, precisely—Eilert Lövborg.

TESMAN. [*Clasping his hands.*] No, no—it's quite inconceivable! Quite impossible! Eh?

BRACK. H'm—that is what it may come to, all the same.

TESMAN. Well but, Judge Brack—it would show the most incredible lack of consideration for me. [*Gesticulates with his arms.*] For—just think—I'm a married man! We have married on the strength of these prospects, Hedda and I; and run deep into debt; and borrowed money from Aunt Julia too. Good heavens, they had as good as promised me the appointment. Eh?

BRACK. Well, well, well—no doubt you will get it in the end; only after a contest.

HEDDA. [*Immovable in her arm-chair.*] Fancy, Tesman, there will be a sort of sporting interest in that.

TESMAN. Why, my dearest Hedda, how can you be so indifferent about it?

HEDDA. [*As before.*] I am not at all indifferent. I am most eager to see who wins.

BRACK. In any case, Mrs. Tesman, it is best that you should know how matters stand. I mean—before you set about the little purchases I hear you are threatening.

HEDDA. This can make no difference.

BRACK. Indeed! Then I have no more to say. Good-bye! [*To* TESMAN.] I shall look in on my way back from my afternoon walk, and take you home with me.

TESMAN. Oh yes, yes—your news has quite upset me.

HEDDA. [*Reclining, holds out her hand.*] Good-bye, Judge; and be sure you call in the afternoon.

BRACK. Many thanks. Good-bye, good-bye!

TESMAN. [*Accompanying him to the door.*] Good-bye, my dear Judge! You must really excuse me——

[JUDGE BRACK *goes out by the hall door.*]

TESMAN. [*Crosses the room.*] Oh Hedda—one should never rush into adventures. Eh?

HEDDA. [*Looks at him, smiling.*] Do you do that?

TESMAN. Yes, dear—there is no denying—it was adventurous to go and marry and set up house upon mere expectations.

HEDDA. Perhaps you are right there.

TESMAN. Well—at all events, we have our delightful home, Hedda! Fancy, the home we both dreamed of—the home we were in love with, I may almost say. Eh?

HEDDA. [*Rising slowly and wearily.*] It was part of our compact that we were to go into society—to keep open house.

TESMAN. Yes, if you only knew how I had been looking forward to it! Fancy—to see you as hostess—in a select circle! Eh? Well, well, well—for the present we shall have to get on without society, Hedda—only to invite Aunt Julia now and then.—Oh, I intended you to lead such an utterly different life, dear——!

HEDDA. Of course I cannot have my man in livery just yet.

TESMAN. Oh no, unfortunately. It would be out of the question for us to keep a footman, you know.

HEDDA. And the saddle-horse I was to have had——

TESMAN. [*Aghast.*] The saddle-horse!

HEDDA. ——I suppose I must not think of that now.

TESMAN. Good heavens, no!—that's as clear as daylight.

HEDDA. [*Goes up the room.*] Well, I shall have one thing at least to kill time with in the meanwhile.

TESMAN. [*Beaming.*] Oh thank heaven for that! What is it, Hedda? Eh?

HEDDA. [*In the middle doorway, looks at him with covert scorn.*] My pistols, George.

TESMAN. [*In alarm.*] Your pistols!

HEDDA. [*With cold eyes.*] General Gabler's pistols. [*She goes out through the inner room, to the left.*]

TESMAN. [*Rushes up to the middle doorway and calls after her.*] No, for heaven's sake, Hedda darling—don't touch those dangerous things! For my sake, Hedda! Eh?

ACT II

SCENE: *The room at the* TESMANS' *as in the first act, except that the piano has been removed, and an elegant little writing-table with book-shelves put in its place. A smaller table stands near the sofa on the left. Most of the bouquets have been taken away.* MRS. ELVSTED'S *bouquet is upon the large table in front.—It is afternoon.* HEDDA, *dressed to receive callers, is alone in the room. She stands by the open glass door, loading a revolver. The fellow to it lies in an open pistol-case on the writing-table.*

HEDDA. [*Looks down the garden, and calls.*] So you are here again, Judge!

BRACK. [*Is heard calling from a distance.*] As you see, Mrs. Tesman!

HEDDA. [*Raises the pistol and points.*] Now I'll shoot you, Judge Brack!

BRACK. [*Calling unseen.*] No, no, no! Don't stand aiming at me!

HEDDA. This is what comes of sneaking in by the back way. [*She fires.*]

BRACK. [*Nearer.*] Are you out of your senses!——

HEDDA. Dear me—did I happen to hit you?

BRACK. [*Still outside.*] I wish you would let these pranks alone!

HEDDA. Come in then, Judge.

[JUDGE BRACK, *dressed as though for a men's party, enters by the glass door. He carries a light overcoat over his arm.*]

BRACK. What the deuce—haven't you tired of that sport, yet? What are you shooting at?

HEDDA. Oh, I am only firing in the air.

BRACK. [*Gently takes the pistol out of her hand.*] Allow me, Madam! [*Looks at it.*] Ah—I know this pistol well! [*Looks around.*] Where is the case? Ah, here it is. [*Lays the pistol in it, and shuts it.*] Now we won't play at that game any more to-day.

HEDDA. Then what in heaven's name would you have me do with myself?

BRACK. Have you had no visitors?

HEDDA. [*Closing the glass door.*] Not one. I suppose all our set are still out of town.

BRACK. And is Tesman not at home either?

HEDDA. [*At the writing-table, putting the pistol-case in a drawer which she shuts.*] No. He rushed off to his aunt's directly after lunch; he didn't expect you so early.

BRACK. H'm—how stupid of me not to have thought of that!

HEDDA. [*Turning her head to look at him.*] Why stupid?

BRACK. Because if I had thought of it I should have come a little—earlier.

HEDDA. [*Crossing the room.*] Then you would have found no one to receive you; for I have been in my room changing my dress ever since lunch.

BRACK. And is there no sort of little chink that we could hold a parley through?

HEDDA. You have forgotten to arrange one.

BRACK. That was another piece of stupidity.

HEDDA. Well, we must just settle down here—and wait. Tesman is not likely to be back for some time yet.

BRACK. Never mind; I shall not be impatient.

[HEDDA *seats herself in the corner of the sofa.* BRACK *lays his overcoat over the back of the nearest chair, and sits down, but keeps his hat in his hand. A short silence. They look at each other.*]

HEDDA. Well?

BRACK. [*In the same tone.*] Well?

HEDDA. I spoke first.

BRACK. [*Bending a little forward.*] Come, let us have a cosy little chat, Mrs. Hedda.

HEDDA. [*Leaning further back in the sofa.*] Does it not seem like a whole eternity since our last talk? Of course I don't count those few words yesterday evening and this morning.

BRACK. You mean since our last confidential talk? Our last *tête-à-tête?*

HEDDA. Well, yes—since you put it so.

BRACK. Not a day has passed but I have wished that you were home again.

HEDDA. And I have done nothing but wish the same thing.

BRACK. You? Really, Mrs. Hedda? And I thought you had been enjoying your tour so much!

HEDDA. Oh, yes, you may be sure of that!

BRACK. But Tesman's letters spoke of nothing but happiness.

HEDDA. Oh, Tesman! You see, he thinks nothing so delightful as grubbing in libraries and making copies of old parchments, or whatever you call them.

BRACK. [*With a spice of malice.*] Well, that is his vocation in life—or part of it at any rate.

HEDDA. Yes, of course; and no doubt when it's your vocation——. But *I!* Oh, my dear Mr. Brack, how mortally bored I have been.

BRACK. [*Sympathetically.*] Do you really say so? In downright earnest?

HEDDA. Yes, you can surely understand it——! To go for six whole months without meeting a soul that knew anything of our circle, or could talk about the things we are interested in.

BRACK. Yes, yes—I, too, should feel that a deprivation.

HEDDA. And then, what I found most intolerable of all—

BRACK. Well?

HEDDA. ——was being everlastingly in the company of—one and the same person——

BRACK. [*With a nod of assent.*] Morning, noon, and night, yes—at all possible times and seasons.

HEDDA. I said "everlastingly."

BRACK. Just so. But I should have thought, with our excellent Tesman, one could——

HEDDA. Tesman is—a specialist, my dear Judge.

BRACK. Undeniably.

HEDDA. And specialists are not at all amusing to travel with. Not in the long run at any rate.

BRACK. Not even—the specialist one happens to love?

HEDDA. Faugh—don't use that sickening word!

BRACK. [*Taken aback.*] What do you say, Mrs. Hedda?

HEDDA. [*Half laughingly, half irritated.*] You should just try it! To hear of nothing but the history of civilization morning, noon, and night——

BRACK. Everlastingly.

HEDDA. Yes, yes, yes! And then all this about the domestic industry of the middle ages——! That's the most disgusting part of it!

BRACK. [*Looks searchingly at her.*] But tell me—in that case, how am I to understand your——? H'm——

HEDDA. My accepting George Tesman, you mean?

BRACK. Well, let us put it so.

HEDDA. Good heavens, do you see anything so wonderful in that?

BRACK. Yes and no—Mrs. Hedda.

HEDDA. I had positively danced myself tired, my dear Judge. My day was done—— [*With a slight shudder.*] Oh, no—I won't say that; nor think it, either!

BRACK. You have assuredly no reason to.

HEDDA. Oh, reasons—— [*Watching him closely.*] And George Tesman—after all, you must admit that he is correctness itself.

BRACK. His correctness and respectability are beyond all question.

HEDDA. And I don't see anything absolutely ridiculous about him.—Do you?

BRACK. Ridiculous? N—no—I shouldn't exactly say so——

HEDDA. Well—and his powers of research, at all events, are untiring.—I see no reason why he should not one day come to the front, after all.

BRACK. [*Looks at her hesitatingly.*] I thought that you, like every one else, expected him to attain the highest distinction.

HEDDA. [*With an expression of fatigue.*] Yes, so I did—And then, since he was bent, at all hazards, on being allowed to provide for me—I really don't know why I should not have accepted his offer?

BRACK. No—if you look at it in that light——

HEDDA. It was more than my other adorers were prepared to do for me, my dear Judge.

BRACK. [*Laughing.*] Well, I can't answer for all the rest; but as for myself, you know quite well that I have always entertained a—a certain respect for the marriage tie—for marriage as an institution, Mrs. Hedda.

HEDDA. [*Jestingly.*] Oh, I assure you I have never cherished any hopes with respect to you.

BRACK. All I require is a pleasant and intimate interior, where I can make myself useful in every way, and am free to come and go as—as a trusted friend——

HEDDA. Of the master of the house, do you mean?

BRACK. [*Bowing.*] Frankly—of the mistress first of all; but, of course, of the master, too, in the second place. Such a triangular friendship—if I may call it so—is really a great convenience for all parties, let me tell you.

HEDDA. Yes, I have many a time longed for some one to make a third on our travels. Oh—those railway-carriage *tête-à-têtes*——!

BRACK. Fortunately your wedding journey is over now.

HEDDA. [*Shaking her head.*] Not by a long—long way. I have only arrived at a station on the line.

BRACK. Well, then the passengers jump out and move about a little, Mrs. Hedda.

HEDDA. I never jump out.

BRACK. Really?

HEDDA. No—because there is always some one standing by to——

BRACK. [*Laughing.*] To look at your legs, do you mean?

HEDDA. Precisely.

BRACK. Well, but, dear me——

HEDDA. [*With a gesture of repulsion.*] I won't have it. I would rather keep my seat where I happen to be—and continue the *tête-à-tête*.

BRACK. But suppose a third person were to jump in and join the couple.

HEDDA. Ah—that is quite another matter!

BRACK. A trusted, sympathetic friend——

HEDDA. ——with a fund of conversation on all sorts of lively topics——

BRACK. ——and not the least bit of a specialist!

HEDDA. [*With an audible sigh.*] Yes, that would be a relief, indeed.

BRACK. [*Hears the front door open, and glances in that direction.*] The triangle is completed.

HEDDA. [*Half aloud.*] And on goes the train.

[GEORGE TESMAN, *in a gray walking-suit, with a soft felt hat, enters from the hall. He has a number of unbound books under his arm and in his pockets.*]

TESMAN. [*Goes up to the table beside the corner settee.*] Ouf—what a load for a warm day—all these books. [*Lays them on the table.*] I'm positively perspiring, Hedda. Hallo—are you there already, my dear Judge? Eh? Berta didn't tell me.

BRACK. [*Rising.*] I came in through the garden.

HEDDA. What books have you got there?

TESMAN. [*Stands looking them through.*] Some new books on my special subjects—quite indispensable to me.

HEDDA. Your special subjects?

BRACK. Yes, books on his special subjects, Mrs. Tesman.

[BRACK *and* HEDDA *exchange a confidential smile.*]

HEDDA. Do you need still more books on your special subjects?

TESMAN. Yes, my dear Hedda, one can never have too many of them. Of course, one must keep up with all that is written and published.

HEDDA. Yes, I suppose one must.

TESMAN. [*Searching among his books.*] And look here—I have got hold of Eilert Lövborg's new book, too. [*Offering it to her.*] Perhaps you would like to glance through it, Hedda? Eh?

HEDDA. No, thank you. Or rather—afterwards perhaps.

TESMAN. I looked into it a little on the way home.

BRACK. Well, what do you think of it—as a specialist?

TESMAN. I think it shows quite remarkable soundness of judgment. He never wrote like that before. [*Putting the books together.*] Now I shall take all these into my study. I'm longing to cut the leaves——! And then I must change my clothes. [*To* BRACK.] I suppose we needn't start just yet? Eh?

BRACK. Oh, dear, no—there is not the slightest hurry.

TESMAN. Well, then, I will take my time. [*Is going with his books, but stops in the doorway and turns.*] By the by, Hedda—Aunt Julia is not coming this evening.

HEDDA. Not coming? Is it that affair of the bonnet that keeps her away?

TESMAN. Oh, not at all. How could you think such a thing of Aunt Julia? Just fancy——! The fact is, Aunt Rina is very ill.

HEDDA. She always is.

TESMAN. Yes, but to-day she is much worse than usual, poor dear.

HEDDA. Oh, then it's only natural that her sister should remain with her. I must bear my disappointment.

TESMAN. And you can't imagine, dear, how delighted Aunt Julia seemed to be—because you had come home looking so flourishing!

HEDDA. [*Half aloud, rising.*] Oh, those everlasting Aunts!

TESMAN. What?

HEDDA. [*Going to the glass door.*] Nothing.

TESMAN. Oh, all right. [*He goes through the inner room, out to the right.*]

BRACK. What bonnet were you talking about?

HEDDA. Oh, it was a little episode with Miss Tesman this morning. She had laid down her bonnet on the chair there—[*Looks at him and smiles.*]—and I pretended to think it was the servant's.

BRACK. [*Shaking his head.*] Now, my dear Mrs. Hedda, how could you do such a thing? To that excellent old lady, too!

HEDDA. [*Nervously crossing the room.*] Well, you see—these impulses come over me all of a sudden; and I cannot resist them. [*Throws herself down in the easy-chair by the stove.*] Oh, I don't know how to explain it.

BRACK. [*Behind the easy-chair.*] You are not really happy—that is at the bottom of it.

HEDDA. [*Looking straight before her.*] I know of no reason why I should be—happy. Perhaps you can give me one?

BRACK. Well—amongst other things, because you have got exactly the home you had set your heart on.

HEDDA. [*Looks up at him and laughs.*] Do you, too, believe in that legend?

BRACK. Is there nothing in it, then?

HEDDA. Oh, yes, there is something in it.

BRACK. Well?

HEDDA. There is this in it, that I made use of Tesman to see me home from evening parties last summer——

BRACK. I, unfortunately, had to go quite a different way.

HEDDA. That's true. I know you were going a different way last summer.

BRACK. [*Laughing.*] Oh fie, Mrs. Hedda! Well, then—you and Tesman——?

HEDDA. Well, we happened to pass here one evening; Tesman, poor fellow, was writhing in the agony of having to find conversation; so I took pity on the learned man——

BRACK. [*Smiles doubtfully.*] You took pity? H'm——

HEDDA. Yes, I really did. And so—to help him out of his torment—I happened to say, in pure thoughtlessness, that I should like to live in this villa.

BRACK. No more than that?

HEDDA. Not that evening.

BRACK. But afterwards?

HEDDA. Yes, my thoughtlessness had consequences, my dear Judge.

BRACK. Unfortunately that too often happens, Mrs. Hedda.

HEDDA. Thanks! So you see it was this enthusiasm for Secretary Falk's villa that first constituted a bond of sympathy between George Tesman and me. From that came our engagement and our marriage, and our wedding journey, and all the rest of it. Well, well, my dear judge—as you make your bed so you must lie, I could almost say.

BRACK. This is exquisite! And you really cared not a rap about it all the time?

HEDDA. No, heaven knows I didn't.

BRACK. But now? Now that we have made it so homelike for you?

HEDDA. Ugh—the rooms all seem to smell of lavender and dried roseleaves. —But perhaps it's Aunt Julia that has brought that scent with her.

BRACK. [*Laughing.*] No, I think it must be a legacy from the late Mrs. Secretary Falk.

HEDDA. Yes, there is an odor of mortality about it. It reminds me of a bouquet—the day after the ball. [*Clasps her hands behind her head, leans back in her chair and looks at him.*] Oh, my dear Judge—you cannot imagine how horribly I shall bore myself here.

BRACK. Why should not you, too, find some sort of vocation in life, Mrs. Hedda?

HEDDA. A vocation—that should attract me?

BRACK. If possible, of course.

HEDDA. Heaven knows what sort of a vocation that could be. I often wonder whether—— [*Breaking off.*] But that would never do, either.

BRACK. Who can tell? Let me hear what it is.

HEDDA. Whether I might not get Tesman to go into politics, I mean.

BRACK. [*Laughing.*] Tesman? No, really now, political life is not the thing for him—not at all in his line.

HEDDA. No, I daresay not.—But if I could get him into it all the same?

BRACK. Why—what satisfaction could you find in that? If he is not fitted for that sort of thing, why should you want to drive him into it?

HEDDA. Because I am bored, I tell you! [*After a pause.*] So you think it quite out of the question that Tesman should ever get into the ministry?

BRACK. H'm—you see, my dear Mrs. Hedda—to get into the ministry, he would have to be a tolerably rich man.

HEDDA. [*Rising impatiently.*] Yes, there we have it! It is this genteel poverty I have managed to drop into——! [*Crosses the room.*] That is what makes life so pitiable! So utterly ludicrous!—For that's what it is.

BRACK. Now *I* should say the fault lay elsewhere.

HEDDA. Where, then?

BRACK. You have never gone through any really stimulating experience.

HEDDA. Anything serious, you mean?

BRACK. Yes, you may call it so. But now you may perhaps have one in store.

HEDDA. [*Tossing her head.*] Oh, you're thinking of the annoyances about this wretched professorship! But that must be Tesman's own affair. I assure you I shall not waste a thought upon it.

BRACK. No, no, I daresay not. But suppose now that what people call—in elegant language—a solemn responsibility were to come upon you? [*Smiling.*] A new responsibility, Mrs. Hedda?

HEDDA. [*Angrily.*] Be quiet! Nothing of that sort will ever happen!

BRACK. [*Warily.*] We will speak of this again a year hence—at the very outside.

HEDDA. [*Curtly.*] I have no turn for anything of the sort, Judge Brack. No responsibilities for me!

BRACK. Are you so unlike the generality of women as to have no turn for duties which——?

HEDDA. [*Beside the glass door.*] Oh, be quiet, I tell you!—I often think there is only one thing in the world I have any turn for.

BRACK. [*Drawing near to her.*] And what is that, if I may ask?

HEDDA. [*Stands looking out.*] Boring myself to death. Now you know it. [*Turns, looks towards the inner room, and laughs.*] Yes, as I thought! Here comes the Professor.

BRACK. [*Softly, in a tone of warning.*] Come, come, come, Mrs. Hedda!

[GEORGE TESMAN, *dressed for the party, with his gloves and hat in his hand, enters from the right through the inner room.*]

TESMAN. Hedda, has no message come from Eilert Lövborg? Eh?

HEDDA. No.

TESMAN. Then you'll see he'll be here presently.

BRACK. Do you really think he will come?

TESMAN. Yes, I am almost sure of it. For what you were telling us this morning must have been a mere floating rumor.

BRACK. You think so?

TESMAN. At any rate, Aunt Julia said she did not believe for a moment that he would ever stand in my way again. Fancy that!

BRACK. Well, then, that's all right.

TESMAN. [*Placing his hat and gloves on a chair on the right.*] Yes, but you must really let me wait for him as long as possible.

BRACK. We have plenty of time yet. None of my guests will arrive before seven or half-past.

TESMAN. Then meanwhile we can keep Hedda company, and see what happens. Eh?

HEDDA. [*Placing* BRACK'S *hat and overcoat upon the corner settee.*] And at the worst Mr. Lövborg can remain here with me.

BRACK. [*Offering to take his things.*] Oh, allow me, Mrs. Tesman!—What do you mean by "at the worst"?

HEDDA. If he won't go with you and Tesman.

TESMAN. [*Looks dubiously at her.*] But, Hedda, dear—do you think it would quite do for him to remain with you? Eh? Remember, Aunt Julia can't come.

HEDDA. No, but Mrs. Elvsted is coming. We three can have a cup of tea together.

TESMAN. Oh, yes, that will be all right.

BRACK. [*Smiling.*] And that would perhaps be the safest plan for him.

HEDDA. Why so?

BRACK. Well, you know, Mrs. Tesman, how you used to gird at my little bachelor parties. You declared they were adapted only for men of the strictest principles.

HEDDA. But no doubt Mr. Lövborg's principles are strict enough now. A converted sinner——

[BERTA *appears at the hall door.*]

BERTA. There's a gentleman asking if you are at home, ma'am——

HEDDA. Well, show him in.

TESMAN. [*Softly.*] I'm sure it is he! Fancy that!

[EILERT LÖVBORG *enters from the hall. He is slim and lean; of the same age as* TESMAN, *but looks older and somewhat worn-out. His hair and beard are of a blackish brown, his face long and pale, but with patches of color on the cheek-bones. He is dressed in a well-cut black visiting suit, quite new. He has dark gloves and a silk hat. He stops near the door, and makes a rapid bow, seeming somewhat embarrassed.*]

TESMAN. [*Goes up to him and shakes him warmly by the hand.*] Well, my dear Eilert—so at last we meet again!

EILERT LÖVBORG. [*Speaks in a subdued voice.*] Thanks for your letter, Tesman. [*Approaching* HEDDA.] Will you, too, shake hands with me, Mrs. Tesman?

HEDDA. [*Taking his hand.*] I am glad to see you, Mr. Lövborg. [*With a motion of her hand.*] I don't know whether you two gentlemen——?

LÖVBORG. [*Bowing slightly.*] Judge Brack, I think.

BRACK. [*Doing likewise.*] Oh, yes,—in the old days——

TESMAN. [*To* LÖVBORG, *with his hands on his shoulders.*] And now you must make yourself entirely at home, Eilert! Mustn't he, Hedda?—For I hear you are going to settle in town again? Eh?

LÖVBORG. Yes, I am.

TESMAN. Quite right, quite right. Let me tell you, I have got hold of your new book; but I haven't had time to read it yet.

LÖVBORG. You may spare yourself the trouble.

TESMAN. Why so?

LÖVBORG. Because there is very little in it.

TESMAN. Just fancy—how can you say so?

BRACK. But it has been very much praised, I hear.

LÖVBORG. That was what I wanted; so I put nothing into the book but what every one would agree with.

BRACK. Very wise of you.

TESMAN. Well, but, my dear Eilert——!

LÖVBORG. For now I mean to win myself a position again—to make a fresh start.

TESMAN. [*A little embarrassed.*] Ah, that is what you wish to do? Eh?

LÖVBORG. [*Smiling, lays down his hat, and draws a packet, wrapped in paper, from his coat pocket.*] But when this one appears, George Tesman, you will have to read it. For this is the real book—the book I have put my true self into.

TESMAN. Indeed? And what is it?

LÖVBORG. It is the continuation.

TESMAN. The continuation? Of what?

LÖVBORG. Of the book.

TESMAN. Of the new book?

LÖVBORG. Of course.

TESMAN. Why, my dear Eilert—does it not come down to our own days?

LÖVBORG. Yes, it does; and this one deals with the future.

TESMAN. With the future! But, good heavens, we know nothing of the future!

LÖVBORG. No; but there is a thing or two to be said about it all the same. [*Opens the packet.*] Look here——

TESMAN. Why, that's not your handwriting.

LÖVBORG. I dictated it. [*Turning over the pages.*] It falls into two sections. The first deals with the civilizing forces of the future. And here is the second —[*Running through the pages towards the end.*]—forecasting the probable line of development.

TESMAN. How odd now! I should never have thought of writing anything of that sort.

HEDDA. [*At the glass door, drumming on the pane.*] H'm—— I daresay not.

LÖVBORG. [*Replacing the manuscript in its paper and laying the packet on *the table.*] I brought it, thinking I might read you a little of it this evening.

TESMAN. That was very good of you, Eilert. But this evening——? [*Looking at* BRACK.] I don't quite see how we can manage it——

LÖVBORG. Well, then, some other time. There is no hurry.

BRACK. I must tell you, Mr. Lövborg—there is a little gathering at my house this evening—mainly in honor of Tesman, you know——

LÖVBORG. [*Looking for his hat.*] Oh—then I won't detain you——

BRACK. No, but listen—will you not do me the favor of joining us?

LÖVBORG. [*Curtly and decidedly.*] No, I can't—thank you very much.

BRACK. Oh, nonsense—do! We shall be quite a select little circle. And I assure you we shall have a "lively time," as Mrs. Hed—as Mrs. Tesman says.

LÖVBORG. I have no doubt of it. But nevertheless——

BRACK. And then you might bring your manuscript with you, and read it to Tesman at my house. I could give you a room to yourselves.

TESMAN. Yes, think of that, Eilert,—why shouldn't you? Eh?

HEDDA. [*Interposing.*] But, Tesman, if Mr. Lövborg would really rather not! I am sure Mr. Lövborg is much more inclined to remain here and have supper with me.

LÖVBORG. [*Looking at her.*] With you, Mrs. Tesman?

HEDDA. And with Mrs. Elvsted.

LÖVBORG. Ah—— [*Lightly.*] I saw her for a moment this morning.

HEDDA. Did you? Well, she is coming this evening. So you see you are almost bound to remain, Mr. Lövborg, or she will have no one to see her home.

LÖVBORG. That's true. Many thanks, Mrs. Tesman—in that case I will remain.

HEDDA. Then I have one or two orders to give the servant——

[*She goes to the hall door and rings.* BERTA *enters.* HEDDA *talks to her in a whisper, and points towards the inner room.* BERTA *nods and goes out again.*]

TESMAN. [*At the same time, to* LÖVBORG.] Tell me, Eilert—is it this new subject—the future—that you are going to lecture about?

LÖVBORG. Yes.

TESMAN. They told me at the bookseller's that you are going to deliver a course of lectures this autumn.

LÖVBORG. That is my intention. I hope you won't take it ill, Tesman.

TESMAN. Oh no, not in the least! But——?

LÖVBORG. I can quite understand that it must be disagreeable to you.

TESMAN. [*Cast down.*] Oh, I can't expect you, out of consideration for me, to——

LÖVBORG. But I shall wait till you have received your appointment.

TESMAN. Will you wait? Yes, but—yes, but—are you not going to compete with me? Eh?

LÖVBORG. No; it is only the moral victory I care for.

TESMAN. Why, bless me—then Aunt Julia was right after all! Oh, yes—I knew it! Hedda! Just fancy—Eilert Lövborg is not going to stand in our way!

HEDDA. [*Curtly.*] Our way? Pray leave me out of the question.

[*She goes up towards the inner room, where* BERTA *is placing a tray with decanters and glasses on the table.* HEDDA *nods approval, and comes forward again.* BERTA *goes out.*]

TESMAN. [*At the same time.*] And you, Judge Brack—what do you say to this? Eh?

BRACK. Well, I say that a moral victory—h'm—may be all very fine——

TESMAN. Yes, certainly. But all the same——

HEDDA. [*Looking at* TESMAN *with a cold smile.*] You stand there looking as if you were thunderstruck——

TESMAN. Yes—so I am—I almost think——

BRACK. Don't you see, Mrs. Tesman, a thunderstorm has just passed over?

HEDDA. [*Pointing towards the inner room.*] Will you not take a glass of cold punch, gentlemen?

BRACK. [*Looking at his watch.*] A stirrup-cup? Yes, it wouldn't come amiss.

TESMAN. A capital idea, Hedda! Just the thing! Now that the weight has been taken off my mind——

HEDDA. Will you not join them, Mr. Lövborg?

LÖVBORG. [*With a gesture of refusal.*] No, thank you. Nothing for me.

BRACK. Why bless me—cold punch is surely not poison.

LÖVBORG. Perhaps not for every one.

HEDDA. I will keep Mr. Lövborg company in the meantime.

TESMAN.. Yes, yes, Hedda dear, do.

[*He and* BRACK *go into the inner room, seat themselves, drink punch, smoke cigarettes, and carry on a lively conversation during what follows.* EILERT LÖVBORG *remains standing beside the stove.* HEDDA *goes to the writing-table.*]

HEDDA. [*Raising her voice a little.*] Do you care to look at some photographs, Mr. Lövborg? You know Tesman and I made a tour in the Tyrol on our way home?

[*She takes up an album, and places it on the table beside the sofa, in the further corner of which she seats herself.* EILERT LÖVBORG *approaches, stops, and looks at her. Then he takes a chair and seats himself to her left, with his back towards the inner room.*]

HEDDA. [*Opening the album.*] Do you see this range of mountains, Mr. Lövborg? It's the Ortler group. Tesman has written the name underneath. Here it is: "The Ortler group near Meram."

LÖVBORG. [*Who has never taken his eyes off her, says softly and slowly.*] Hedda—Gabler!

HEDDA. [*Glancing hastily at him.*] Ah! Hush!

LÖVBORG. [*Repeats softly.*] Hedda Gabler!

HEDDA. [*Looking at the album.*] That was my name in the old days—when we two knew each other.

LÖVBORG. And I must teach myself never to say Hedda Gabler again—never, as long as I live.

HEDDA. [*Still turning over the pages.*] Yes, you must. And I think you ought to practise in time. The sooner the better, I should say.

LÖVBORG. [*In a tone of indignation.*] Hedda Gabler married? And married to—George Tesman!

HEDDA. Yes—so the world goes.

LÖVBORG. Oh, Hedda, Hedda—how could you[5] throw yourself away!

HEDDA. [*Looks sharply at him.*] What? I can't allow this!

LÖVBORG. What do you mean?

[TESMAN *comes into the room and goes towards the sofa.*]

HEDDA. [*Hears him coming and says in an indifferent tone.*] And this is a view from the Val d'Ampezzo, Mr. Lövborg. Just look at these peaks! [*Looks affectionately up at* TESMAN.] What's the name of these curious peaks, dear?

TESMAN. Let me see. Oh, those are the Dolomites.

HEDDA. Yes, that's it!—Those are the Dolomites, Mr. Lövborg.

TESMAN. Hedda, dear,—I only wanted to ask whether I shouldn't bring you a little punch after all? For yourself, at any rate—eh?

HEDDA. Yes, do, please; and perhaps a few biscuits.

TESMAN. No cigarettes?

HEDDA. No.

TESMAN. Very well.

[*He goes into the inner room and out to the right.* BRACK *sits in the inner room, and keeps an eye from time to time on* HEDDA *and* LÖVBORG.]

LÖVBORG. [*Softly, as before.*] Answer me, Hedda—how could you go and do this?

HEDDA. [*Apparently absorbed in the album.*] If you continue to say *du* to me I won't talk to you.

LÖVBORG. May I not say *du* even when we are alone?

HEDDA. No. You may think it; but you mustn't say it.

LÖVBORG. Ah, I understand. It is an offence against George Tesman, whom you[6] love.

HEDDA. [*Glances at him and smiles.*] Love? What an idea!

LÖVBORG. You don't love him then!

HEDDA. But I won't hear of any sort of unfaithfulness! Remember that.

LÖVBORG. Hedda—answer me one thing——

HEDDA. Hush!

[TESMAN *enters with a small tray from the inner room.*]

TESMAN. Here you are! Isn't this tempting?

[*He puts the tray on the table.*]

---

5. Lövborg uses the familiar *du*.
6. From here on Lövborg uses the formal *De*.

HEDDA. Why do you bring it yourself?

TESMAN. [*Filling the glasses.*] Because I think it's such fun to wait upon you, Hedda.

HEDDA. But you have poured out two glasses. Mr. Lövborg said he wouldn't have any——

TESMAN. No, but Mrs. Elvsted will soon be here, won't she?

HEDDA. Yes, by the by—Mrs. Elvsted——

TESMAN. Had you forgotten her? Eh?

HEDDA. We were so absorbed in these photographs. [*Shows him a picture.*] Do you remember this little village?

TESMAN. Oh, it's that one just below the Brenner Pass. It was there we passed the night——

HEDDA. ——and met that lively party of tourists.

TESMAN. Yes, that was the place. Fancy—if we could only have had you with us, Eilert! Eh?

[*He returns to the inner room and sits beside* BRACK.]

LÖVBORG. Answer me this one thing, Hedda——

HEDDA. Well?

LÖVBORG. Was there no love in your friendship for me, either? Not a spark—not a tinge of love in it?

HEDDA. I wonder if there was? To me it seems as though we were two good comrades—two thoroughly intimate friends. [*Smilingly.*] You especially were frankness itself.

LÖVBORG. It was you that made me so.

HEDDA. As I look back upon it all, I think there was really something beautiful, something fascinating—something daring—in—in that secret intimacy—that comradeship which no living creature so much as dreamed of.

LÖVBORG. Yes, yes, Hedda! Was there not?—When I used to come to your father's in the afternoon—and the General sat over at the window reading his papers—with his back towards us——

HEDDA. And we two on the corner sofa——

LÖVBORG. Always with the same illustrated paper before us——

HEDDA. For want of an album, yes.

LÖVBORG. Yes, Hedda, and when I made my confessions to you—told you about myself, things that at that time no one else knew! There I would sit and tell you of my escapades—my days and nights of devilment. Oh, Hedda—what was the power in you that forced me to confess these things?

HEDDA. Do you think it was any power in me?

LÖVBORG. How else can I explain it? And all those—those roundabout questions you used to put to me——

HEDDA. Which you understood so particularly well——

LÖVBORG. How could you sit and question me like that? Question me quite frankly——

HEDDA. In roundabout terms, please observe.

LÖVBORG. Yes, but frankly nevertheless. Cross-question me about—all that sort of thing?

HEDDA. And how could you answer, Mr. Lövborg?

LÖVBORG. Yes, that is just what I can't understand—in looking back upon it. But tell me now, Hedda—was there not love at the bottom of our friendship? On your side, did you not feel as though you might purge my stains away—if I made you my confessor? Was it not so?

HEDDA. No, not quite.

LÖVBORG. What was your motive, then?

HEDDA. Do you think it quite incomprehensible that a young girl—when it can be done—without any one knowing——

LÖVBORG. Well?

HEDDA. ——should be glad to have a peep, now and then, into a world which——

LÖVBORG. Which——?

HEDDA. ——which she is forbidden to know anything about?

LÖVBORG. So that was it?

HEDDA. Partly. Partly—I almost think.

LÖVBORG. Comradeship is the thirst for life. But why should not that, at any rate, have continued?

HEDDA. The fault was yours.

LÖVBORG. It was you that broke with me.

HEDDA. Yes, when our friendship threatened to develop into something more serious. Shame upon you, Eilert Lövborg! How could you think of wronging your—your frank comrade?

LÖVBORG. [*Clenching his hands.*] Oh, why did you not carry out your threat? Why did you not shoot me down?

HEDDA. Because I have such a dread of scandal.

LÖVBORG. Yes, Hedda, you are a coward at heart.

HEDDA. A terrible coward. [*Changing her tone.*] But it was a lucky thing for you. And now you have found ample consolation at the Elvsteds'.

LÖVBORG. I know what Thea has confided to you.

HEDDA. And perhaps you have confided to her something about us?

LÖVBORG. Not a word. She is too stupid to understand anything of that sort.

HEDDA. Stupid?

LÖVBORG. She is stupid about matters of that sort.

HEDDA. And I am cowardly. [*Bends over towards him, without looking him in the face, and says more softly.*] But now I will confide something to you.

LÖVBORG. [*Eagerly.*] Well?

HEDDA. The fact that I dared not shoot you down——

LÖVBORG. Yes!

HEDDA. ——that was not my most arrant cowardice—that evening.

LÖVBORG. [*Looks at her a moment, understands, and whispers passionately.*] Oh, Hedda! Hedda Gabler! Now I begin to see a hidden reason beneath our comradeship! You[7] and I——! After all, then, it was your craving for life——

HEDDA. [*Softly, with a sharp glance.*] Take care! Believe nothing of the sort!

[*Twilight has begun to fall. The hall door is opened from without by* BERTA.]

HEDDA. [*Closes the album with a bang and calls smilingly.*] Ah, at last! My darling Thea,—come along!

[MRS. ELVSTED *enters from the hall. She is in evening dress. The door is closed behind her.*]

HEDDA. [*On the sofa, stretches out her arms towards her.*] My sweet Thea —you can't think how I have been longing for you!

[MRS. ELVSTED, *in passing, exchanges slight salutations with the gentlemen in the inner room, then goes up to the table and gives* HEDDA *her hand.* EILERT LÖVBORG *has risen. He and* MRS. ELVSTED *greet each other with a silent nod.*]

MRS. ELVSTED. Ought I to go in and talk to your husband for a moment?

HEDDA. Oh, not at all. Leave those two alone. They will soon be going.

MRS. ELVSTED. Are they going out?

HEDDA. Yes, to a supper-party.

MRS. ELVSTED. [*Quickly, to* LÖVBORG.] Not you?

LÖVBORG. No.

HEDDA. Mr. Lövborg remains with us.

MRS. ELVSTED. [*Takes a chair and is about to seat herself at his side.*] Oh, how nice it is here!

HEDDA. No, thank you, my little Thea! Not there! You'll be good enough to come over here to me. I will sit between you.

MRS. ELVSTED. Yes, just as you please.

[*She goes round the table and seats herself on the sofa on* HEDDA'S *right.* LÖVBORG *re-seats himself on his chair.*]

LÖVBORG. [*After a short pause, to* HEDDA.] Is not she lovely to look at?

HEDDA. [*Lightly stroking her hair.*] Only to look at?

LÖVBORG. Yes. For we two—she and I—we are two real comrades. We have absolute faith in each other; so we can sit and talk with perfect frankness——

HEDDA. Not round about, Mr. Lövborg?

LÖVBORG. Well——

MRS. ELVSTED. [*Softly clinging close to* HEDDA.] Oh, how happy I am, Hedda! For, only think, he says I have inspired him, too.

HEDDA. [*Looks at her with a smile.*] Ah! Does he say that, dear?

---

7. *Du* once more. Hedda uses *De* consistently.

LÖVBORG. And then she is so brave, Mrs. Tesman!

MRS. ELVSTED. Good heavens—am I brave?

LÖVBORG. Exceedingly—where your comrade is concerned.

HEDDA. Ah, yes—courage! If one only had that!

LÖVBORG. What then? What do you mean?

HEDDA. Then life would perhaps be livable, after all. [*With a sudden change of tone.*] But now, my dearest Thea, you really must have a glass of cold punch.

MRS. ELVSTED. No, thanks—I never take anything of that kind.

HEDDA. Well, then, you, Mr. Lövborg.

LÖVBORG. Nor I, thank you.

MRS. ELVSTED. No, he doesn't, either.

HEDDA. [*Looks fixedly at him.*] But if I say you shall?

LÖVBORG. It would be no use.

HEDDA. [*Laughing.*] Then I, poor creature, have no sort of power over you?

LÖVBORG. Not in that respect.

HEDDA. But seriously, I think you ought to—for your own sake.

MRS. ELVSTED. Why, Hedda——!

LÖVBORG. How so?

HEDDA. Or rather on account of other people.

LÖVBORG. Indeed?

HEDDA. Otherwise people might be apt to suspect that—in your heart of hearts—you did not feel quite secure—quite confident in yourself.

MRS. ELVSTED. [*Softly.*] Oh, please, Hedda——!

LÖVBORG. People may suspect what they like—for the present.

MRS. ELVSTED. [*Joyfully.*] Yes, let them!

HEDDA. I saw it plainly in Judge Brack's face a moment ago.

LÖVBORG. What did you see?

HEDDA. His contemptuous smile, when you dared not go with them into the inner room.

LÖVBORG. Dared not? Of course I preferred to stop here and talk to you.

MRS. ELVSTED. What could be more natural, Hedda?

HEDDA. But the Judge could not guess that. And I saw, too, the way he smiled and glanced at Tesman when you dared not accept his invitation to this wretched little supper-party of his.

LÖVBORG. Dared not? Do you say I dared not?

HEDDA. *I* don't say so. But that was how Judge Brack understood it.

LÖVBORG. Well, let him.

HEDDA. Then you are not going with them?

LÖVBORG. I will stay here with you and Thea.

MRS. ELVSTED. Yes, Hedda—how can you doubt that?

HEDDA. [*Smiles and nods approvingly to* LÖVBORG.] Firm as a rock! Faithful to your principles, now and forever! Ah, that is how a man should be!

[*Turns to* MRS. ELVSTED *and caresses her.*] Well, now, what did I tell you, when you came to us this morning in such a state of distraction——

LÖVBORG. [*Surprised.*] Distraction!

MRS. ELVSTED. [*Terrified.*] Hedda—oh, Hedda——!

HEDDA. You can see for yourself! You haven't the slightest reason to be in such mortal terror—— [*Interrupting herself.*] There! Now we can all three enjoy ourselves!

LÖVBORG. [*Who has given a start.*] Ah—what is all this, Mrs. Tesman?

MRS. ELVSTED. Oh, my God, Hedda! What are you saying? What are you doing?

HEDDA. Don't get excited! That horrid Judge Brack is sitting watching you.

LÖVBORG. So she was in mortal terror! On my account!

MRS. ELVSTED. [*Softly and piteously.*] Oh, Hedda—now you have ruined everything!

LÖVBORG. [*Looks fixedly at her for a moment. His face is distorted.*] So that was my comrade's frank confidence in me?

MRS. ELVSTED. [*Imploringly.*] Oh, my dearest friend—only let me tell you——

LÖVBORG. [*Takes one of the glasses of punch, raises it to his lips, and says in a low, husky voice.*] Your health, Thea!

[*He empties the glass, puts it down, and takes the second.*]

MRS. ELVSTED. [*Softly.*] Oh, Hedda, Hedda—how could you do this?

HEDDA. *I* do it? *I*? Are you crazy?

LÖVBORG. Here's to your health, too, Mrs. Tesman. Thanks for the truth. Hurrah for the truth!

[*He empties the glass and is about to re-fill it.*]

HEDDA. [*Lays her hand on his arm.*] Come, come—no more for the present. Remember you are going out to supper.

MRS. ELVSTED. No, no, no!

HEDDA. Hush! They are sitting watching you.

LÖVBORG. [*Putting down the glass.*] Now, Thea—tell me the truth——

MRS. ELVSTED. Yes.

LÖVBORG. Did your husband know that you had come after me?

MRS. ELVSTED. [*Wringing her hands.*] Oh, Hedda—do you hear what he is asking?

LÖVBORG. Was it arranged between you and him that you were to come to town and look after me? Perhaps it was the Sheriff himself that urged you to come? Aha, my dear—no doubt he wanted my help in his office. Or was it at the card-table that he missed me?

MRS. ELVSTED. [*Softly, in agony.*] Oh, Lövborg, Lövborg——!

LÖVBORG. [*Seizes a glass and is on the point of filling it.*] Here's a glass for the old Sheriff, too!

HEDDA. [*Preventing him.*] No more just now. Remember, you have to read your manuscript to Tesman.

LÖVBORG. [*Calmly, putting down the glass.*] It was stupid of me all this, Thea—to take it in this way, I mean. Don't be angry with me, my dear, dear comrade. You shall see—both you and the others—that if I was fallen once—now I have risen again! Thanks to you, Thea.

MRS. ELVSTED. [*Radiant with joy.*] Oh, heaven be praised——!

[BRACK *has in the meantime looked at his watch. He and* TESMAN *rise and come into the drawing room.*]

BRACK. [*Takes his hat and overcoat.*] Well, Mrs. Tesman, our time has come.

HEDDA. I suppose it has.

LÖVBORG. [*Rising.*] Mine too, Judge Brack.

MRS. ELVSTED. [*Softly and imploringly.*] Oh, Lövborg, don't do it!

HEDDA. [*Pinching her arm.*] They can hear you!

MRS. ELVSTED. [*With a suppressed shriek.*] Ow!

LÖVBORG. [*To* BRACK.] You were good enough to invite me.

BRACK. Well, are you coming after all?

LÖVBORG. Yes, many thanks.

BRACK. I'm delighted——

LÖVBORG. [*To* TESMAN, *putting the parcel of MS. in his pocket.*] I should like to show you one or two things before I send it to the printers.

TESMAN. Fancy—that will be delightful. But, Hedda dear, how is Mrs. Elvsted to get home? Eh?

HEDDA. Oh, that can be managed somehow.

LÖVBORG. [*Looking towards the ladies.*] Mrs. Elvsted? Of course, I'll come again and fetch her. [*Approaching.*] At ten or thereabouts, Mrs. Tesman? Will that do?

HEDDA. Certainly. That will do capitally.

TESMAN. Well, then, that's all right. But you must not expect me so early, Hedda.

HEDDA. Oh, you may stop as long—as long as ever you please.

MRS. ELVSTED. [*Trying to conceal her anxiety.*] Well, then, Mr. Lövborg—I shall remain here until you come.

LÖVBORG. [*With his hat in his hand.*] Pray do, Mrs. Elvsted.

BRACK. And now off goes the excursion train, gentlemen! I hope we shall have a lively time, as a certain fair lady puts it.

HEDDA. Ah, if only the fair lady could be present unseen——!

BRACK. Why unseen?

HEDDA. In order to hear a little of your liveliness at first hand, Judge Brack.

BRACK. [*Laughing.*] I should not advise the fair lady to try it.

TESMAN. [*Also laughing.*] Come, you're a nice one, Hedda! Fancy that!

BRACK. Well, good-bye, good-bye, ladies.

LÖVBORG. [*Bowing.*] About ten o'clock, then.

[BRACK, LÖVBORG, *and* TESMAN *go out by the hall door. At the same time,* BERTA *enters from the inner room with a lighted lamp, which she places on the drawing-room table; she goes out by the way she came.*]

MRS. ELVSTED. [*Who has risen and is wandering restlessly about the room.*] Hedda—Hedda—what will come of all this?

HEDDA. At ten o'clock—he will be here. I can see him already—with vine-leaves[8] in his hair—flushed and fearless——

MRS. ELVSTED. Oh, I hope he may.

HEDDA. And then, you see—then he will have regained control over himself. Then he will be a free man for all his days.

MRS. ELVSTED. Oh, God!—if he would only come as you see him now!

HEDDA. He will come as I see him—so, and not otherwise! [*Rises and approaches* THEA.] You may doubt him as long as you please; *I* believe in him. And now we will try——

MRS. ELVSTED. You have some hidden motive in this, Hedda!

HEDDA. Yes, I have. I want for once in my life to have power to mould a human destiny.

MRS. ELVSTED. Have you not the power?

HEDDA. I have not—and have never had it.

MRS. ELVSTED. Not your husband's?

HEDDA. Do you think that is worth the trouble? Oh, if you could only understand how poor I am. And fate has made you so rich! [*Clasps her passionately in her arms.*] I think I must burn your hair off, after all.

MRS. ELVSTED. Let me go! Let me go! I am afraid of you, Hedda!

BERTA. [*In the middle doorway.*] Tea is laid in the dining-room, ma'am.

HEDDA. Very well. We are coming.

MRS. ELVSTED. No, no, no! I would rather go home alone! At once!

HEDDA. Nonsense! First you shall have a cup of tea, you little stupid. And then—at ten o'clock—Eilert Lövborg will be here—with vine-leaves in his hair.

[*She drags* MRS. ELVSTED *almost by force towards the middle doorway.*]

ACT III

SCENE: *The room at the* TESMANS'. *The curtains are drawn over the middle doorway, and also over the glass door. The lamp, half turned down, and with a shade over it, is burning on the table. In the stove, the door of which stands open, there has been a fire, which is now nearly burnt out.* MRS. ELVSTED, *wrapped in a large shawl, and with her feet upon a foot-rest, sits close to the stove, sunk back in the armchair.* HEDDA, *fully dressed, lies sleeping upon the sofa, with a sofa-blanket over her.*

MRS. ELVSTED. [*After a pause, suddenly sits up in her chair, and listens eagerly. Then she sinks back again wearily, moaning to herself.*] Not yet! —Oh, God—oh, God—not yet!

8. Bacchus (Greek god of wine) wore vine-leaves in his hair. For Hedda, the vine-leaves symbolize triumphantly courageous unconventionality.

[BERTA *slips cautiously in by the hall door. She has a letter in her hand.*]

MRS. ELVSTED. [*Turns and whispers eagerly.*] Well—has any one come?

BERTA. [*Softly.*] Yes, a girl has just brought this letter.

MRS. ELVSTED. [*Quickly, holding out her hand.*] A letter! Give it to me!

BERTA. No, it's for Dr. Tesman, ma'am.

MRS. ELVSTED. Oh, indeed.

BERTA. It was Miss Tesman's servant that brought it. I'll lay it here on the table.

MRS. ELVSTED. Yes, do.

BERTA. [*Laying down the letter.*] I think I had better put out the lamp. It's smoking.

MRS. ELVSTED. Yes, put it out. It must soon be daylight now.

BERTA. [*Putting out the lamp.*] It is daylight already, ma'am.

MRS. ELVSTED. Yes, broad day! And no one come back yet——!

BERTA. Lord bless you, ma'am—I guessed how it would be.

MRS. ELVSTED. You guessed?

BERTA. Yes, when I saw that a certain person had come back to town—and that he went off with them. For we've heard enough about that gentleman before now.

MRS. ELVSTED. Don't speak so loud. You will waken Mrs. Tesman.

BERTA. [*Looks towards the sofa and sighs.*] No, no—let her sleep, poor thing. Shan't I put some wood on the fire?

MRS. ELVSTED. Thanks, not for me.

BERTA. Oh, very well.

[*She goes softly out by the hall door.*]

HEDDA. [*Is awakened by the shutting of the door, and looks up.*] What's that——?

MRS. ELVSTED. It was only the servant——

HEDDA. [*Looking about her.*] Oh, we're here——! Yes, now I remember. [*Sits erect upon the sofa, stretches herself, and rubs her eyes.*] What o'clock is it, Thea?

MRS. ELVSTED. [*Looks at her watch.*] It's past seven.

HEDDA. When did Tesman come home?

MRS. ELVSTED. He has not come.

HEDDA. Not come home yet?

MRS. ELVSTED. [*Rising.*] No one has come.

HEDDA. Think of our watching and waiting here till four in the morning——

MRS. ELVSTED. [*Wringing her hands.*] And how I watched and waited for him!

HEDDA. [*Yawns, and says with her hand before her mouth.*] Well, well—we might have spared ourselves the trouble.

MRS. ELVSTED. Did you get a little sleep?

HEDDA. Oh, yes; I believe I have slept pretty well. Have you not?

MRS. ELVSTED. Not for a moment. I couldn't, Hedda!—not to save my life.

HEDDA. [*Rises and goes towards her.*] There, there, there! There's nothing to be so alarmed about. I understand quite well what has happened.

MRS. ELVSTED. Well, what do you think? Won't you tell me?

HEDDA. Why, of course, it has been a very late affair at Judge Brack's——

MRS. ELVSTED. Yes, yes—that is clear enough. But all the same——

HEDDA. And then, you see, Tesman hasn't cared to come home and ring us up in the middle of the night. [*Laughing.*] Perhaps he wasn't inclined to show himself either—immediately after a jollification.

MRS. ELVSTED. But in that case—where can he have gone?

HEDDA. Of course, he has gone to his aunts' and slept there. They have his old room ready for him.

MRS. ELVSTED. No, he can't be with them; for a letter has just come for him from Miss Tesman. There it lies.

HEDDA. Indeed? [*Looks at the address.*] Why, yes, it's addressed in Aunt Julia's own hand. Well, then, he has remained at Judge Brack's. And as for Eilert Lövborg—he is sitting, with vine-leaves in his hair, reading his manuscript.

MRS. ELVSTED. Oh, Hedda, you are just saying things you don't believe a bit.

HEDDA. You really are a little blockhead, Thea.

MRS. ELVSTED. Oh, yes, I suppose I am.

HEDDA. And how mortally tired you look.

MRS. ELVSTED. Yes, I am mortally tired.

HEDDA. Well, then, you must do as I tell you. You must go into my room and lie down for a little while.

MRS. ELVSTED. Oh, no, no—I shouldn't be able to sleep.

HEDDA. I am sure you would.

MRS. ELVSTED. Well, but your husband is certain to come soon now; and then I want to know at once——

HEDDA. I shall take care to let you know when he comes.

MRS. ELVSTED. Do you promise me, Hedda?

HEDDA. Yes, rely upon me. Just you go in and have a sleep in the meantime.

MRS. ELVSTED. Thanks; then I'll try to.

[*She goes off through the inner room.* HEDDA *goes up to the glass door and draws back the curtains. The broad daylight streams into the room. Then she takes a little hand-glass from the writing-table, looks at herself in it and arranges her hair. Next she goes to the hall door and presses the bell-button.* BERTA *presently appears at the hall door.*]

BERTA. Did you want anything, ma'am?

HEDDA. Yes; you must put some more wood in the stove. I am shivering.

BERTA. Bless me—I'll make up the fire at once. [*She rakes the embers together and lays a piece of wood upon them; then stops and listens.*] That was a ring at the front door, ma'am.

HEDDA. Then go to the door. I will look after the fire.

BERTA. It'll soon burn up.

[*She goes out by the hall door.* HEDDA *kneels on the foot-rest and lays some more pieces of wood in the stove. After a short pause,* GEORGE TESMAN *enters from the hall. He looks tired and rather serious. He steals on tip-toe towards the middle doorway and is about to slip through the curtains.*]

HEDDA. [*At the stove, without looking up.*] Good morning.

TESMAN. [*Turns.*] Hedda! [*Approaching her.*] Good heavens—are you up so early? Eh?

HEDDA. Yes, I am up very early this morning.

TESMAN. And I never doubted you were still sound asleep! Fancy that, Hedda!

HEDDA. Don't speak so loud. Mrs. Elvsted is resting in my room.

TESMAN. Has Mrs. Elvsted been here all night?

HEDDA. Yes, since no one came to fetch her.

TESMAN. Ah, to be sure.

HEDDA. [*Closes the door of the stove and rises.*] Well, did you enjoy yourselves at Judge Brack's?

TESMAN. Have you been anxious about me? Eh?

HEDDA. No, I should never think of being anxious. But I asked if you had enjoyed yourself.

TESMAN. Oh, yes,—for once in a way. Especially the beginning of the evening; for then Eilert read me part of his book. We arrived more than an hour too early—fancy that! And Brack had all sorts of arrangements to make—so Eilert read to me.

HEDDA. [*Seating herself by the table on the right.*] Well? Tell me, then——

TESMAN. [*Sitting on a footstool near the stove.*] Oh, Hedda, you can't conceive what a book that is going to be! I believe it is one of the most remarkable things that have ever been written. Fancy that!

HEDDA. Yes, yes; I don't care about that—

TESMAN. I must make a confession to you, Hedda. When he had finished reading—a horrid feeling came over me.

HEDDA. A horrid feeling?

TESMAN. I felt jealous of Eilert for having had it in him to write such a book. Only think, Hedda!

HEDDA. Yes, yes, I am thinking!

TESMAN. And then how pitiful to think that he—with all his gifts—should be irreclaimable, after all.

HEDDA. I suppose you mean that he has more courage than the rest?

TESMAN. No, not at all—I mean that he is incapable of taking his pleasures in moderation.

HEDDA. And what came of it all—in the end?

TESMAN. Well, to tell the truth, I think it might best be described as an orgy, Hedda.

HEDDA. Had he vine-leaves in his hair?

TESMAN. Vine-leaves? No, I saw nothing of the sort. But he made a long, rambling speech in honor of the woman who had inspired him in his work—that was the phrase he used.

HEDDA. Did he name her?

TESMAN. No, he didn't; but I can't help thinking he meant Mrs. Elvsted. You may be sure he did.

HEDDA. Well—where did you part from him?

TESMAN. On the way to town. We broke up—the last of us at any rate—all together; and Brack came with us to get a breath of fresh air. And then, you see, we agreed to take Eilert home; for he had had far more than was good for him.

HEDDA. I daresay.

TESMAN. But now comes the strange part of it, Hedda; or, I should rather say, the melancholy part of it. I declare I am almost ashamed—on Eilert's account—to tell you——

HEDDA. Oh, go on——!

TESMAN. Well, as we were getting near town, you see, I happened to drop a little behind the others. Only for a minute or two—fancy that!

HEDDA. Yes, yes, yes, but——?

TESMAN. And then, as I hurried after them—what do you think I found by the wayside? Eh?

HEDDA. Oh, how should I know!

TESMAN. You mustn't speak of it to a soul, Hedda! Do you hear! Promise me, for Eilert's sake. [*Draws a parcel, wrapped in paper, from his coat pocket.*] Fancy, dear—I found this.

HEDDA. Is not that the parcel he had with him yesterday?

TESMAN. Yes, it is the whole of his precious, irreplaceable manuscript! And he had gone and lost it, and knew nothing about it. Only fancy, Hedda! So deplorably——

HEDDA. But why did you not give him back the parcel at once?

TESMAN. I didn't dare to—in the state he was then in——

HEDDA. Did you not tell any of the others that you had found it?

TESMAN. Oh, far from it! You can surely understand that, for Eilert's sake, I wouldn't do that.

HEDDA. So no one knows that Eilert Lövborg's manuscript is in your possession?

TESMAN. No. And no one must know it.

HEDDA. Then what did you say to him afterwards?

TESMAN. I didn't talk to him again at all; for when we got in among the streets, he and two or three of the others gave us the slip and disappeared. Fancy that!

HEDDA. Indeed! They must have taken him home then.

TESMAN. Yes, so it would appear. And Brack, too, left us.

HEDDA. And what have you been doing with yourself since?

TESMAN. Well, I and some of the others went home with one of the party, a jolly fellow, and took our morning coffee with him; or perhaps I should rather call it our night coffee—eh? But now, when I have rested a little, and given Eilert, poor fellow, time to have his sleep out, I must take this back to him.

HEDDA. [*Holds out her hand for the packet.*] No—don't give it to him! Not in such a hurry, I mean. Let me read it first.

TESMAN. No, my dearest Hedda, I mustn't, I really mustn't.

HEDDA. You must not?

TESMAN. No—for you can imagine what a state of despair he will be in when he wakens and misses the manuscript. He has no copy of it, you must know! He told me so.

HEDDA. [*Looking searchingly at him.*] Can such a thing not be reproduced? Written over again?

TESMAN. No, I don't think that would be possible. For the inspiration, you see——

HEDDA. Yes, yes—I suppose it depends on that—— [*Lightly.*] But, by the by—here is a letter for you.

TESMAN. Fancy——!

HEDDA. [*Handing it to him.*] It came early this morning.

TESMAN. It's from Aunt Julia! What can it be? [*He lays the packet on the other footstool, opens the letter, runs his eye through it, and jumps up.*] Oh, Hedda—she says that poor Aunt Rina is dying!

HEDDA. Well, we were prepared for that.

TESMAN. And that if I want to see her again, I must make haste. I'll run in to them at once.

HEDDA. [*Suppressing a smile.*] Will you run?

TESMAN. Oh, my dearest Hedda—if you could only make up your mind to come with me! Just think!

HEDDA. [*Rises and says wearily, repelling the idea.*] No, no, don't ask me. I will not look upon sickness and death. I loathe all sorts of ugliness.

TESMAN. Well, well, then——! [*Bustling around.*] My hat——? My overcoat——? Oh, in the hall——. I do hope I mayn't come too late, Hedda! Eh?

HEDDA. Oh, if you run——

[BERTA *appears at the hall door.*]

BERTA. Judge Brack is at the door, and wishes to know if he may come in.

TESMAN. At this time! No, I can't possibly see him.

HEDDA. But I can. [*To* BERTA.] Ask Judge Brack to come in.

[BERTA *goes out.*]

HEDDA. [*Quickly, whispering.*] The parcel, Tesman!

[*She snatches it up from the stool.*]

TESMAN. Yes, give it to me!

HEDDA. No, no, I will keep it till you come back.

[*She goes to the writing-table and places it in the bookcase.* TESMAN *stands in a flurry of haste, and cannot get his gloves on.* JUDGE BRACK *enters from the hall.*]

HEDDA. [*Nodding to him.*] You are an early bird, I must say.

BRACK. Yes, don't you think so? [*To* TESMAN.] Are you on the move, too?

TESMAN. Yes, I must rush off to my aunts'. Fancy—the invalid one is lying at death's door, poor creature.

BRACK. Dear me, is she indeed? Then on no account let me detain you. At such a critical moment——

TESMAN. Yes, I must really rush—— Good-bye! Good-bye!

[*He hastens out by the hall door.*]

HEDDA. [*Approaching.*] You seem to have made a particularly lively night of it at your rooms, Judge Brack.

BRACK. I assure you I have not had my clothes off, Mrs. Hedda.

HEDDA. Not you, either?

BRACK. No, as you may see. But what has Tesman been telling you of the night's adventures?

HEDDA. Oh, some tiresome story. Only that they went and had coffee somewhere or other.

BRACK. I have heard about that coffee-party already. Eilert Lövborg was not with them, I fancy?

HEDDA. No, they had taken him home before that.

BRACK. Tesman too?

HEDDA. No, but some of the others, he said.

BRACK. [*Smiling.*] George Tesman is really an ingenuous creature, Mrs. Hedda.

HEDDA. Yes, heaven knows he is. Then is there something behind all this?

BRACK. Yes, perhaps there may be.

HEDDA. Well then, sit down, my dear Judge, and tell your story in comfort.

[*She seats herself to the left of the table.* BRACK *sits near her, at the long side of the table.*]

HEDDA. Now then?

BRACK. I had special reasons for keeping track of my guests—or rather of some of my guests—last night.

HEDDA. Of Eilert Lövborg among the rest, perhaps?

BRACK. Frankly—yes.

HEDDA. Now you make me really curious——

BRACK. Do you know where he and one or two of the others finished the night, Mrs. Hedda?

HEDDA. If it is not quite unmentionable, tell me.

BRACK. Oh no, it's not at all unmentionable. Well, they put in an appearance at a particularly animated *soirée.*

HEDDA. Of the lively kind?

BRACK. Of the very liveliest——

HEDDA. Tell me more of this, Judge Brack——

BRACK. Lövborg, as well as the others, had been invited in advance. I knew all about it. But he had declined the invitation; for now, as you know, he has become a new man.

HEDDA. Up at the Elvsteds', yes. But he went after all, then?

BRACK. Well, you see, Mrs. Hedda—unhappily the spirit moved him at my rooms last evening——

HEDDA. Yes, I hear he found inspiration.

BRACK. Pretty violent inspiration. Well, I fancy that altered his purpose; for we menfolk are unfortunately not always so firm in our principles as we ought to be.

HEDDA. Oh, I am sure you are an exception, Judge Brack. But as to Lövborg——?

BRACK. To make a long story short—he landed at last in Mademoiselle Diana's rooms.

HEDDA. Mademoiselle Diana's?

BRACK. It was Mademoiselle Diana that was giving the *soirée,* to a select circle of her admirers and her lady friends.

HEDDA. Is she a red-haired woman?

BRACK. Precisely.

HEDDA. A sort of a—singer?

BRACK. Oh yes—in her leisure moments. And moreover a mighty huntress—of men—Mrs. Hedda. You have no doubt heard of her. Eilert Lövborg was one of her most enthusiastic protectors—in the days of his glory.

HEDDA. And how did all this end?

BRACK. Far from amicably, it appears. After a most tender meeting, they seem to have come to blows——

HEDDA. Lövborg and she?

BRACK. Yes. He accused her or her friends of having robbed him. He declared that his pocket-book had disappeared—and other things as well. In short, he seems to have made a furious disturbance.

HEDDA. And what came of it all?

BRACK. It came to a general scrimmage, in which the ladies as well as the gentlemen took part. Fortunately the police at last appeared on the scene.

HEDDA. The police too?

BRACK. Yes. I fancy it will prove a costly frolic for Eilert Lövborg, crazy being that he is.

HEDDA. How so?

BRACK. He seems to have made a violent resistance—to have hit one of the constables on the head and torn the coat off his back. So they had to march him off to the police-station with the rest.

HEDDA. How have you learnt all this?

BRACK. From the police themselves.

HEDDA. [*Gazing straight before her.*] So that is what happened. Then he had no vine-leaves in his hair.

BRACK. Vine-leaves, Mrs. Hedda?

HEDDA. [*Changing her tone.*] But tell me now, Judge—what is your real reason for tracking out Eilert Lövborg's movements so carefully?

BRACK. In the first place, it could not be entirely indifferent to me if it should appear in the police-court that he came straight from my house.

HEDDA. Will the matter come into court then?

BRACK. Of course. However, I should scarcely have troubled so much about that. But I thought that, as a friend of the family, it was my duty to supply you and Tesman with a full account of his nocturnal exploits.

HEDDA. Why so, Judge Brack?

BRACK. Why, because I have a shrewd suspicion that he intends to use you as a sort of blind.

HEDDA. Oh, how can you think such a thing!

BRACK. Good heavens, Mrs. Hedda—we have eyes in our head. Mark my words! This Mrs. Elvsted will be in no hurry to leave town again.

HEDDA. Well, even if there should be anything between them, I suppose there are plenty of other places where they could meet.

BRACK. Not a single home. Henceforth, as before, every respectable house will be closed against Eilert Lövborg.

HEDDA. And so ought mine to be, you mean?

BRACK. Yes. I confess it would be more than painful to me if this personage were to be made free of your house. How superfluous, how intrusive, he would be, if he were to force his way into——

HEDDA. ——into the triangle?

BRACK. Precisely. It would simply mean that I should find myself homeless.

HEDDA. [*Looks at him with a smile.*] So you want to be the one cock in the basket [9]—that is your aim.

BRACK. [*Nods slowly and lowers his voice.*] Yes, that is my aim. And for that I will fight—with every weapon I can command.

HEDDA. [*Her smile vanishing.*] I see you are a dangerous person—when it comes to the point.

BRACK. Do you think so?

HEDDA. I am beginning to think so. And I am exceedingly glad to think—that you have no sort of hold over me.

9. A proverbial saying in Norway.

BRACK. [*Laughing equivocally.*] Well, well, Mrs. Hedda—perhaps you are right there. If I had, who knows what I might be capable of?

HEDDA. Come, come now, Judge Brack! That sounds almost like a threat.

BRACK. [*Rising.*] Oh, not at all! The triangle, you know, ought, if possible, to be spontaneously constructed.

HEDDA. There I agree with you.

BRACK. Well, now I have said all I had to say; and I had better be getting back to town. Good-bye, Mrs. Hedda. [*He goes towards the glass door.*]

HEDDA. [*Rising.*] Are you going through the garden?

BRACK. Yes, it's a short cut for me.

HEDDA. And then it is a back way, too.

BRACK. Quite so. I have no objection to back ways. They may be piquant enough at times.

HEDDA. When there is shooting practice going on, you mean?

BRACK. [*In the doorway, laughing to her.*] Oh, people don't shoot their tame poultry, I fancy.

HEDDA. [*Also laughing.*] Oh no, when there is only one cock in the basket——

[*They exchange laughing nods of farewell. He goes. She closes the door behind him.* HEDDA, *who has become quite serious, stands for a moment looking out. Presently she goes and peeps through the curtain over the middle doorway. Then she goes to the writing-table, takes* LÖVBORG'S *packet out of the bookcase, and is on the point of looking through its contents.* BERTA *is heard speaking loudly in the hall.* HEDDA *turns and listens. Then she hastily locks up the packet in the drawer, and lays the key on the ink-stand.* EILERT LÖVBORG, *with his greatcoat on and his hat in his hand, tears open the hall door. He looks somewhat confused and irritated.*]

LÖVBORG. [*Looking towards the hall.*] And I tell you I must and will come in! There!

[*He closes the door, turns, sees* HEDDA, *at once regains his self-control, and bows.*]

HEDDA. [*At the writing-table.*] Well, Mr. Lövborg, this is rather a late hour to call for Thea.

LÖVBORG. You mean rather an early hour to call on you. Pray pardon me.

HEDDA. How do you know that she is still here?

LÖVBORG. They told me at her lodgings that she had been out all night.

HEDDA. [*Going to the oval table.*] Did you notice anything about the people of the house when they said that?

LÖVBORG. [*Looks inquiringly at her.*] Notice anything about them?

HEDDA. I mean, did they seem to think it odd?

LÖVBORG. [*Suddenly understanding.*] Oh yes, of course! I am dragging her down with me! However, I didn't notice anything.—I suppose Tesman is not up yet?

HEDDA. No—I think not——

LÖVBORG. When did he come home?

HEDDA. Very late.

LÖVBORG. Did he tell you anything?

HEDDA. Yes, I gathered that you had had an exceedingly jolly evening at Judge Brack's.

LÖVBORG. Nothing more?

HEDDA. I don't think so. However, I was so dreadfully sleepy——

[MRS. ELVSTED *enters through the curtains of the middle doorway.*]

MRS. ELVSTED. [*Going towards him.*] Ah, Lövborg! At last——!

LÖVBORG. Yes, at last. And too late!

MRS. ELVSTED. [*Looks anxiously at him.*] What is too late?

LÖVBORG. Everything is too late now. It is all over with me.

MRS. ELVSTED. Oh no, no—don't say that!

LÖVBORG. You will say the same when you hear——

MRS. ELVSTED. I won't hear anything!

HEDDA. Perhaps you would prefer to talk to her alone? If so, I will leave you.

LÖVBORG. No, stay—you too. I beg you to stay.

MRS. ELVSTED. Yes, but I won't hear anything, I tell you.

LÖVBORG. It is not last night's adventures that I want to talk about.

MRS. ELVSTED. What is it then——?

LÖVBORG. I want to say that now our ways must part.

MRS. ELVSTED. Part!

HEDDA. [*Involuntarily.*] I knew it!

LÖVBORG. You can be of no more service to me, Thea.

MRS. ELVSTED. How can you stand there and say that! No more service to you! Am I not to help you now, as before? Are we not to go on working together?

LÖVBORG. Henceforward I shall do no work.

MRS. ELVSTED. [*Despairingly.*] Then what am I to do with my life?

LÖVBORG. You must try to live your life as if you had never known me.

MRS. ELVSTED. But you know I cannot do that!

LÖVBORG. Try if you cannot, Thea. You must go home again——

MRS. ELVSTED. [*In vehement protest.*] Never in this world! Where you are, there will I be also! I will not let myself be driven away like this! I will remain here! I will be with you when the book appears.

HEDDA. [*Half aloud, in suspense.*] Ah yes—the book!

LÖVBORG. [*Looks at her.*] My book and Thea's; for that is what it is.

MRS. ELVSTED. Yes, I feel that it is. And that is why I have a right to be with you when it appears! I will see with my own eyes how respect and honor pour in upon you afresh. And the happiness—the happiness—oh, I must share it with you!

LÖVBORG. Thea—our book will never appear.

HEDDA. Ah!

MRS. ELVSTED. Never appear!

LÖVBORG. Can never appear.

MRS. ELVSTED. [*In agonized foreboding.*] Lövborg—what have you done with the manuscript?

HEDDA. [*Looks anxiously at him.*] Yes, the manuscript——?

MRS. ELVSTED. Where is it?

LÖVBORG. Oh Thea—don't ask me about it!

MRS. ELVSTED. Yes, yes, I will know. I demand to be told at once.

LÖVBORG. The manuscript——. Well then—I have torn the manuscript into a thousand pieces.

MRS. ELVSTED. [*Shrieks.*] Oh no, no——!

HEDDA. [*Involuntarily.*] But that's not——

LÖVBORG. [*Looks at her.*] Not true, you think?

HEDDA. [*Collecting herself.*] Oh well, of course—since you say so. But it sounded so improbable——

LÖVBORG. It is true, all the same.

MRS. ELVSTED. [*Wringing her hands.*] Oh God—oh God, Hedda—torn his own work to pieces!

LÖVBORG. I have torn my own life to pieces. So why should I not tear my life-work too——?

MRS. ELVSTED. And you did this last night?

LÖVBORG. Yes, I tell you! Tore it into a thousand pieces—and scattered them on the fjord—far out. There there is cool sea-water at any rate—let them drift upon it—drift with the current and the wind. And then presently they will sink—deeper and deeper—as I shall, Thea.

MRS. ELVSTED. Do you know, Lövborg, that what you have done with the book—I shall think of it to my dying day as though you had killed a little child.

LÖVBORG. Yes, you are right. It is a sort of child-murder.

MRS. ELVSTED. How could you, then——! Did not the child belong to me too?

HEDDA. [*Almost inaudibly.*] Ah, the child——

MRS. ELVSTED. [*Breathing heavily.*] It is all over then. Well, well, now I will go, Hedda.

HEDDA. But you are not going away from town?

MRS. ELVSTED. Oh, I don't know what I shall do. I see nothing but darkness before me. [*She goes out by the hall door.*]

HEDDA. [*Stands waiting for a moment.*] So you are not going to see her home, Mr. Lövborg?

LÖVBORG. I? Through the streets? Would you have people see her walking with me?

HEDDA. Of course I don't know what else may have happened last night. But is it so utterly irretrievable?

LÖVBORG. It will not end with last night—I know that perfectly well. And the thing is that now I have no taste for that sort of life either. I won't begin it anew. She has broken my courage and my power of braving life out.

HEDDA. [*Looking straight before her.*] So that pretty little fool has had her fingers in a man's destiny. [*Looks at him.*] But all the same, how could you treat her so heartlessly?

LÖVBORG. Oh, don't say that it was heartless!

HEDDA. To go and destroy what has filled her whole soul for months and years! You do not call that heartless!

LÖVBORG. To you I can tell the truth, Hedda.

HEDDA. The truth?

LÖVBORG. First promise me—give me your word—that what I now confide to you Thea shall never know.

HEDDA. I give you my word.

LÖVBORG. Good. Then let me tell you that what I said just now was untrue.

HEDDA. About the manuscript?

LÖVBORG. Yes. I have not torn it to pieces—nor thrown it into the fjord.

HEDDA. No, no——. But—where is it then?

LÖVBORG. I have destroyed it none the less—utterly destroyed it, Hedda!

HEDDA. I don't understand.

LÖVBORG. Thea said that what I had done seemed to her like a child-murder.

HEDDA. Yes, so she said.

LÖVBORG. But to kill his child—that is not the worst thing a father can do to it.

HEDDA. Not the worst?

LÖVBORG. No. I wanted to spare Thea from hearing the worst.

HEDDA. Then what is the worst?

LÖVBORG. Suppose now, Hedda, that a man—in the small hours of the morning—came home to his child's mother after a night of riot and debauchery, and said: "Listen—I have been here and there—in this place and in that. And I have taken our child with me—to this place and to that. And I have lost the child—utterly lost it. The devil knows into what hands it may have fallen—who may have had their clutches on it."

HEDDA. Well—but when all is said and done, you know—this was only a book——

LÖVBORG. Thea's pure soul was in that book.

HEDDA. Yes, so I understand.

LÖVBORG. And you can understand, too, that for her and me together no future is possible.

HEDDA. What path do you mean to take then?

LÖVBORG. None. I will only try to make an end of it all—the sooner the better.

HEDDA. [*A step nearer him.*] Eilert Lövborg—listen to me.—Will you not try to—to do it beautifully?

LÖVBORG. Beautifully? [*Smiling.*] With vine-leaves in my hair, as you used to dream in the old days——?

HEDDA. No, no. I have lost my faith in the vine-leaves. But beautifully nevertheless! For once in a way!—Good-bye! You must go now—and do not come here any more.

LÖVBORG. Good-bye, Mrs. Tesman. And give George Tesman my love. [*He is on the point of going.*]

HEDDA. No, wait! I must give you a memento to take with you.

[*She goes to the writing-table and opens the drawer and the pistol-case; then returns to* LÖVBORG *with one of the pistols.*]

LÖVBORG. [*Looks at her.*] This? Is this the memento?

HEDDA. [*Nodding slowly.*] Do you recognize it? It was aimed at you once.

LÖVBORG. You should have used it then.

HEDDA. Take it—and do you use it now.

LÖVBORG. [*Puts the pistol in his breast pocket.*] Thanks!

HEDDA. And beautifully, Eilert Lövborg. Promise me that!

LÖVBORG. Good-bye, Hedda Gabler.

[*He goes out by the hall door.* HEDDA *listens for a moment at the door. Then she goes up to the writing-table, takes out the packet of manuscript, peeps under the cover, draws a few of the sheets half out, and looks at them. Next she goes over and seats herself in the arm-chair beside the stove, with the packet in her lap. Presently she opens the stove door, and then the packet.*]

HEDDA. [*Throws one of the quires into the fire and whispers to herself.*] Now I am burning your child, Thea!—Burning it, curly-locks! [*Throwing one or two more quires into the stove.*] Your child and Eilert Lövborg's. [*Throws the rest in.*] I am burning—I am burning your child.

ACT IV

SCENE: *The same rooms at the* TESMANS'. *It is evening. The drawing-room is in darkness. The back room is lighted by the hanging lamp over the table. The curtains over the glass door are drawn close.* HEDDA, *dressed in black, walks to and fro in the dark room. Then she goes into the back room and disappears for a moment to the left. She is heard to strike a few chords on the piano. Presently she comes in sight again, and returns to the drawing-room.* BERTA *enters from the right, through the inner room, with a lighted lamp, which she places on the table in front of the corner settee in the drawing-room. Her eyes are red with weeping, and she has black ribbons in her cap. She goes quietly and circumspectly out to the right.* HEDDA *goes up to the glass door, lifts the curtain a little aside, and looks out into the darkness. Shortly afterwards,* MISS TESMAN, *in mourning, with a bonnet and veil on, comes in from the hall.* HEDDA *goes towards her and holds out her hand.*

MISS TESMAN. Yes, Hedda, here I am, in mourning and forlorn; for now my poor sister has at last found peace.

HEDDA. I have heard the news already, as you see. Tesman sent me a card.

MISS TESMAN. Yes, he promised me he would. But nevertheless I thought that to Hedda—here in the house of life—I ought myself to bring the tidings of death.

HEDDA. That was very kind of you.

MISS TESMAN. Ah, Rina ought not to have left us just now. This is not the time for Hedda's house to be a house of mourning.

HEDDA. [*Changing the subject.*] She died quite peacefully, did she not, Miss Tesman?

MISS TESMAN. Oh, her end was so calm, so beautiful. And then she had the unspeakable happiness of seeing George once more—and bidding him good-bye.—Has he not come home yet?

HEDDA. No. He wrote that he might be detained. But won't you sit down?

MISS TESMAN. No thank you, my dear, dear Hedda. I should like to, but I have so much to do. I must prepare my dear one for her rest as well as I can. She shall go to her grave looking her best.

HEDDA. Can I not help you in any way?

MISS TESMAN. Oh, you must not think of it! Hedda Tesman must have no hand in such mournful work. Nor let her thoughts dwell on it either—not at this time.

HEDDA. One is not always mistress of one's thoughts—

MISS TESMAN. [*Continuing.*] Ah yes, it is the way of the world. At home we shall be sewing a shroud; and here there will soon be sewing too, I suppose —but of another sort, thank God!

[GEORGE TESMAN *enters by the hall door.*]

HEDDA. Ah, you have come at last!

TESMAN. You here, Aunt Julia? With Hedda? Fancy that!

MISS TESMAN. I was just going, my dear boy. Well, have you done all you promised?

TESMAN. No; I'm really afraid I have forgotten half of it. I must come to you again to-morrow. To-day my brain is all in a whirl. I can't keep my thoughts together.

MISS TESMAN. Why, my dear George, you mustn't take it in this way.

TESMAN. Mustn't——? How do you mean?

MISS TESMAN. Even in your sorrow you must rejoice, as I do—rejoice that she is at rest.

TESMAN. Oh yes, yes—you are thinking of Aunt Rina.

HEDDA. You will feel lonely now, Miss Tesman.

MISS TESMAN. Just at first, yes. But that will not last very long, I hope. I daresay I shall soon find an occupant for poor Rina's little room.

TESMAN. Indeed? Who do you think will take it? Eh?

MISS TESMAN. Oh, there's always some poor invalid or other in want of nursing, unfortunately.

HEDDA. Would you really take such a burden upon you again?

MISS TESMAN. A burden! Heaven forgive you, child—it has been no burden to me.

HEDDA. But suppose you had a total stranger on your hands—

MISS TESMAN. Oh, one soon makes friends with sick folk; and it's such an absolute necessity for me to have some one to live for. Well, heaven be praised, there may soon be something in *this* house, too, to keep on old aunt busy.

HEDDA. Oh, don't trouble about anything here.

TESMAN. Yes, just fancy what a nice time we three might have together, if——?

HEDDA. If——?

TESMAN. [*Uneasily.*] Oh, nothing. It will all come right. Let us hope so—eh?

MISS TESMAN. Well, well, I daresay you two want to talk to each other. [*Smiling.*] And perhaps Hedda may have something to tell you too, George. Good-bye! I must go home to Rina. [*Turning at the door.*] How strange it is to think that now Rina is with me and with my poor brother as well!

TESMAN. Yes, fancy that, Aunt Julia! Eh? [MISS TESMAN *goes out by the hall door.*]

HEDDA. [*Follows* TESMAN *coldly and searchingly with her eyes.*] I almost believe your Aunt Rina's death affects you more than it does your Aunt Julia.

TESMAN. Oh, it's not that alone. It's Eilert I am so terribly uneasy about.

HEDDA. [*Quickly.*] Is there anything new about him?

TESMAN. I looked in at his rooms this afternoon, intending to tell him the manuscript was in safe keeping.

HEDDA. Well, did you not find him?

TESMAN. No. He wasn't at home. But afterwards I met Mrs. Elvsted, and she told me that he had been here early this morning.

HEDDA. Yes, directly after you had gone.

TESMAN. And he said that he had torn his manuscript to pieces—eh?

HEDDA. Yes, so he declared.

TESMAN. Why, good heavens, he must have been completely out of his mind! And I suppose you thought it best not to give it back to him, Hedda?

HEDDA. No, he did not get it.

TESMAN. But of course you told him that we had it?

HEDDA. No. [*Quickly.*] Did you tell Mrs. Elvsted?

TESMAN. No; I thought I had better not. But you ought to have told him. Fancy, if, in desperation, he should go and do himself some injury! Let me have the manuscript, Hedda! I will take it to him at once. Where is it?

HEDDA. [*Cold and immovable, leaning on the arm-chair.*] I have not got it.

TESMAN. Have not got it? What in the world do you mean?

HEDDA. I have burnt it—every line of it.

TESMAN. [*With a violent movement of terror.*] Burnt! Burnt Eilert's manuscript!

HEDDA. Don't scream so. The servant might hear you.

TESMAN. Burnt! Why, good God——! No, no, no! It's impossible!

HEDDA. It is so, nevertheless.

TESMAN. Do you know what you have done, Hedda? It's unlawful appropriation of lost property. Fancy that! Just ask Judge Brack, and he'll tell you what it is.

HEDDA. I advise you not to speak of it—either to Judge Brack, or to any one else.

TESMAN. But how could you do anything so unheard-of? What put it into your head? What possessed you? Answer me that—eh?

HEDDA. [*Suppressing an almost imperceptible smile.*] I did it for your sake, George.

TESMAN. For my sake!

HEDDA. This morning, when you told me about what he had read to you——

TESMAN. Yes, yes—what then?

HEDDA. You acknowledged that you envied him his work.

TESMAN. Oh, of course I didn't mean that literally.

HEDDA. No matter—I could not bear the idea that any one should throw you into the shade.

TESMAN. [*In an outburst of mingled doubt and joy.*] Hedda! Oh, is this true? But—but—I never knew you show your love like that before. Fancy that!

HEDDA. Well, I may as well tell you that—just at this time—— [*Impatiently, breaking off.*] No, no; you can ask Aunt Julia. She will tell you, fast enough.

TESMAN. Oh, I almost think I understand you, Hedda! [*Clasps his hands together.*] Great heavens! do you really mean it? Eh?

HEDDA. Don't shout so. The servant might hear.

TESMAN. [*Laughing in irrepressible glee.*] The servant! Why, how absurd you are, Hedda. It's only my old Berta! Why, I'll tell Berta myself.

HEDDA. [*Clenching her hands together in desperation.*] Oh, it is killing me,—it is killing me, all this!

TESMAN. What is, Hedda? Eh?

HEDDA. [*Coldly, controlling herself.*] All this—absurdity—George.

TESMAN. Absurdity! Do you see anything absurd in my being overjoyed at the news! But after all—perhaps I had better not say anything to Berta.

HEDDA. Oh——why not that too?

TESMAN. No, no, not yet! But I must certainly tell Aunt Julia. And then that you have begun to call me George too! Fancy that! Oh, Aunt Julia will be so happy—so happy!

HEDDA. When she hears that I have burnt Eilert Lövborg's manuscript—for your sake?

TESMAN. No, by the by—that affair of the manuscript—of course nobody must know about that. But that you love me so much, Hedda—Aunt Julia must really share my joy in that! I wonder, now, whether this sort of thing is usual in young wives? Eh?

HEDDA. I think you had better ask Aunt Julia that question too.

TESMAN. I will indeed, some time or other. [*Looks uneasy and downcast again.*] And yet the manuscript—the manuscript! Good God! It is terrible to think what will become of poor Eilert now.

[MRS. ELVSTED, *dressed as in the first act, with hat and cloak, enters by the hall door.*]

MRS. ELVSTED. [*Greets them hurriedly, and says in evident agitation.*] Oh, dear Hedda, forgive my coming again.

HEDDA. What is the matter with you, Thea?

TESMAN. Something about Eilert Lövborg again—eh?

MRS. ELVSTED. Yes! I am dreadfully afraid some misfortune has happened to him.

HEDDA. [*Seizes her arm.*] Ah,—do you think so?

TESMAN. Why, good Lord—what makes you think that, Mrs. Elvsted?

MRS. ELVSTED. I heard them talking at my boarding-house—just as I came in. Oh, the most incredible rumors are afloat about him to-day.

TESMAN. Yes, fancy, so I heard too! And I can bear witness that he went straight home to bed last night. Fancy that!

HEDDA. Well, what did they say at the boarding-house?

MRS. ELVSTED. Oh, I couldn't make out anything clearly. Either they knew nothing definite, or else——. They stopped talking when they saw me; and I did not dare to ask.

TESMAN. [*Moving about uneasily.*] We must hope—we must hope that you misunderstood them, Mrs. Elvsted.

MRS. ELVSTED. No, no; I am sure it was of him they were talking. And I heard something about the hospital or——

TESMAN. The hospital?

HEDDA. No—surely that cannot be!

MRS. ELVSTED. Oh, I was in such mortal terror! I went to his lodgings and asked for him there.

HEDDA. You could make up your mind to that, Thea!

MRS. ELVSTED. What else could I do? I really could bear the suspense no longer.

TESMAN. But you didn't find him either—eh?

MRS. ELVSTED. No. And the people knew nothing about him. He hadn't been home since yesterday afternoon, they said.

TESMAN. Yesterday! Fancy, how could they say that?

MRS. ELVSTED. Oh, I am sure something terrible must have happened to him.

TESMAN. Hedda dear—how would it be if I were to go and make inquiries——?

HEDDA. No, no—don't mix yourself up in this affair.

[JUDGE BRACK, *with his hat in his hand, enters by the hall door, which* BERTA *opens, and closes behind him. He looks grave and bows in silence.*]

TESMAN. Oh, is that you, my dear Judge? Eh?

BRACK. Yes. It was imperative I should see you this evening.

TESMAN. I can see you have heard the news about Aunt Rina?

BRACK. Yes, that among other things.

TESMAN. Isn't it sad—eh?

BRACK. Well, my dear Tesman, that depends on how you look at it.

TESMAN. [*Looks doubtfully at him.*] Has anything else happened?

BRACK. Yes.

HEDDA. [*In suspense.*] Anything sad, Judge Brack?

BRACK. That, too, depends on how you look at it, Mrs. Tesman.

MRS. ELVSTED. [*Unable to restrain her anxiety.*] Oh! it is something about Eilert Lövborg!

BRACK. [*With a glance at her.*] What makes you think that, Madam? Perhaps you have already heard something——?

MRS. ELVSTED. [*In confusion.*] No, nothing at all, but——

TESMAN. Oh, for heaven's sake, tell us!

BRACK. [*Shrugging his shoulders.*] Well, I regret to say Eilert Lövborg has been taken to the hospital. He is lying at the point of death.

MRS. ELVSTED. [*Shrieks.*] Oh God! oh God——!

TESMAN. To the hospital! And at the point of death!

HEDDA. [*Involuntarily.*] So soon then——

MRS. ELVSTED. [*Wailing.*] And we parted in anger, Hedda!

HEDDA. [*Whispers.*] Thea—Thea—be careful!

MRS. ELVSTED. [*Not heeding her.*] I must go to him! I must see him alive!

BRACK. It is useless, Madam. No one will be admitted.

MRS. ELVSTED. Oh, at least tell me what has happened to him? What is it?

TESMAN. You don't mean to say that he has himself—— Eh?

HEDDA. Yes, I am sure he has.

TESMAN. Hedda, how can you——?

BRACK. [*Keeping his eyes fixed upon her.*] Unfortunately you have guessed quite correctly, Mrs. Tesman.

MRS. ELVSTED. Oh, how horrible!

TESMAN. Himself, then! Fancy that!

HEDDA. Shot himself!

BRACK. Rightly guessed again, Mrs. Tesman.

MRS. ELVSTED. [*With an effort at self-control.*] When did it happen, Mr. Brack?

BRACK. This afternoon—between three and four.

TESMAN. But, good Lord, where did he do it? Eh?

BRACK. [*With some hesitation.*] Where? Well—I suppose at his lodgings.

MRS. ELVSTED. No, that cannot be; for I was there between six and seven.

BRACK. Well then, somewhere else. I don't know exactly. I only know that he was found——. He had shot himself—in the breast.

MRS. ELVSTED. Oh, how terrible! That he should die like that!

HEDDA. [*To* BRACK.] Was it in the breast?

BRACK. Yes—as I told you.

HEDDA. Not in the temple?

BRACK. In the breast, Mrs. Tesman.

HEDDA. Well, well—the breast is a good place, too.

BRACK. How do you mean, Mrs. Tesman?

HEDDA. [*Evasively.*] Oh, nothing—nothing.

TESMAN. And the wound is dangerous, you say—eh?

BRACK. Absolutely mortal. The end has probably come by this time.

MRS. ELVSTED. Yes, yes, I feel it. The end! The end! Oh, Hedda——!

TESMAN. But tell me, how have you learnt all this?

BRACK. [*Curtly.*] Through one of the police. A man I had some business with.

HEDDA. [*In a clear voice.*] At last a deed worth doing!

TESMAN. [*Terrified.*] Good heavens, Hedda! what are you saying?

HEDDA. I say there is beauty in this.

BRACK. H'm, Mrs. Tesman——

TESMAN. Beauty! Fancy that!

MRS. ELVSTED. Oh, Hedda, how can you talk of beauty in such an act!

HEDDA. Eilert Lövborg has himself made up his account with life. He has had the courage to do—the one right thing.

MRS. ELVSTED. No, you must never think that was how it happened! It must have been in delirium that he did it.

TESMAN. In despair!

HEDDA. That he did not. I am certain of that.

MRS. ELVSTED. Yes, yes! In delirium! Just as when he tore up our manuscript.

BRACK. [*Starting.*] The manuscript? Has he torn that up?

MRS. ELVSTED. Yes, last night.

TESMAN. [*Whispers softly.*] Oh, Hedda, we shall never get over this.

BRACK. H'm, very extraordinary.

TESMAN. [*Moving about the room.*] To think of Eilert going out of the world in this way! And not leaving behind him the book that would have immortalized his name——

MRS. ELVSTED. Oh, if only it could be put together again!

TESMAN. Yes, if it only could! I don't know what I would not give——

MRS. ELVSTED. Perhaps it can, Mr. Tesman.

TESMAN. What do you mean?

MRS. ELVSTED. [*Searches in the pocket of her dress.*] Look here. I have kept all the loose notes he used to dictate from.

HEDDA. [*A step forward.*] Ah——!

TESMAN. You have kept them, Mrs. Elvsted! Eh?

MRS. ELVSTED. Yes, I have them here. I put them in my pocket when I left home. Here they still are——

TESMAN. Oh, do let me see them!

MRS. ELVSTED. [*Hands him a bundle of papers.*] But they are in such disorder—all mixed up.

TESMAN. Fancy, if we could make something out of them, after all! Perhaps if we two put our heads together——

MRS. ELVSTED. Oh yes, at least let us try——

TESMAN. We will manage it! We must! I will dedicate my life to this task.

HEDDA. You, George? Your life?

TESMAN. Yes, or rather all the time I can spare. My own collections must wait in the meantime. Hedda—you understand, eh? I owe this to Eilert's memory.

HEDDA. Perhaps.

TESMAN. And so, my dear Mrs. Elvsted, we will give our whole minds to it. There is no use in brooding over what can't be undone—eh? We must try to control our grief as much as possible, and——

MRS. ELVSTED. Yes, yes, Mr. Tesman, I will do the best I can.

TESMAN. Well then, come here. I can't rest until we have looked through the notes. Where shall we sit? Here? No, in there, in the back room. Excuse me, my dear Judge. Come with me, Mrs. Elvsted.

MRS. ELVSTED. Oh, if only it were possible!

[TESMAN *and* MRS. ELVSTED *go into the back room. She takes off her hat and cloak. They both sit at the table under the hanging lamp, and are soon deep in an eager examination of the papers.* HEDDA *crosses to the stove and sits in the arm-chair. Presently* BRACK *goes up to her.*]

HEDDA. [*In a low voice.*] Oh, what a sense of freedom it gives one, this act of Eilert Lövborg's.

BRACK. Freedom, Mrs. Hedda? Well, of course, it is a release for him——

HEDDA. I mean for me. It gives me a sense of freedom to know that a deed of deliberate courage is still possible in this world,—a deed of spontaneous beauty.

BRACK. [*Smiling.*] H'm—my dear Mrs. Hedda——

HEDDA. Oh, I know what you are going to say. For you are a kind of specialist, too, like—you know!

BRACK. [*Looking hard at her.*] Eilert Lövborg was more to you than perhaps you are willing to admit to yourself. Am I wrong?

HEDDA. I don't answer such questions. I only know that Eilert Lövborg has had the courage to live his life after his own fashion. And then—the last great act, with its beauty! Ah! that he should have the will and the strength to turn away from the banquet of life—so early.

BRACK. I am sorry, Mrs. Hedda,—but I fear I must dispel an amiable illusion.

HEDDA. Illusion?

BRACK. Which could not have lasted long in any case.

HEDDA. What do you mean?

BRACK. Eilert Lövborg did not shoot himself—voluntarily.

HEDDA. Not voluntarily!

BRACK. No. The thing did not happen exactly as I told it.

HEDDA. [*In suspense.*] Have you concealed something? What is it?

BRACK. For poor Mrs. Elvsted's sake I idealized the facts a little.

HEDDA. What are the facts?

BRACK. First, that he is already dead.

HEDDA. At the hospital?

BRACK. Yes—without regaining consciousness.

HEDDA. What more have you concealed?

BRACK. This—the event did not happen at his lodgings.

HEDDA. Oh, that can make no difference.

BRACK. Perhaps it may. For I must tell you—Eilert Lövborg was found shot in—in Mademoiselle Diana's boudoir.

HEDDA. [*Makes a motion as if to rise, but sinks back again.*] That is impossible, Judge Brack! He cannot have been there again to-day.

BRACK. He was there this afternoon. He went there, he said, to demand the return of something which they had taken from him. Talked wildly about a lost child——

HEDDA. Ah—so that was why——

BRACK. I thought probably he meant his manuscript; but now I hear he destroyed that himself. So I suppose it must have been his pocketbook.

HEDDA. Yes, no doubt. And there—there he was found?

BRACK. Yes, there. With a pistol in his breast-pocket, discharged. The ball had lodged in a vital part.

HEDDA. In the breast—yes.

BRACK. No—in the bowels.

HEDDA. [*Looks up at him with an expression of loathing.*] That, too! Oh, what curse is it that makes everything I touch turn ludicrous and mean?

BRACK. There is one point more, Mrs. Hedda—another disagreeable feature in the affair.

HEDDA. And what is that?

BRACK. The pistol he carried——

HEDDA. [*Breathless.*] Well? What of it?

BRACK. He must have stolen it.

HEDDA. [*Leaps up.*] Stolen it! That is not true! He did not steal it!

BRACK. No other explanation is possible. He must have stolen it—— Hush!

[TESMAN *and* MRS. ELVSTED *have risen from the table in the back room, and come into the drawing-room.*]

TESMAN. [*With the papers in both his hands.*] Hedda, dear, it is almost impossible to see under that lamp. Think of that!

HEDDA. Yes, I am thinking.

TESMAN. Would you mind our sitting at your writing-table—eh?

HEDDA. If you like. [*Quickly.*] No, wait! Let me clear it first!

TESMAN. Oh, you needn't trouble, Hedda. There is plenty of room.

HEDDA. No, no, let me clear it, I say! I will take these things in and put them on the piano. There!

[*She has drawn out an object, covered with sheet music, from under the bookcase, places several other pieces of music upon it, and carries the whole into the inner room, to the left.* TESMAN *lays the scraps of paper on the writing-table, and moves the lamp there from the corner table. He and* MRS. ELVSTED *sit down and proceed with their work.* HEDDA *returns.*]

HEDDA. [*Behind* MRS. ELVSTED'S *chair, gently ruffing her hair.*] Well, my sweet Thea,—how goes it with Eilert Lövborg's monument?

MRS. ELVSTED. [*Looks dispiritedly up at her.*] Oh, it will be terribly hard to put in order.

TESMAN. We must manage it. I am determined. And arranging other people's papers is just the work for me.

[HEDDA *goes over to the stove, and seats herself on one of the footstools.* BRACK *stands over her, leaning on the arm-chair.*]

HEDDA. [*Whispers.*] What did you say about the pistol?

BRACK. [*Softly.*] That he must have stolen it.

HEDDA. Why stolen it?

BRACK. Because every other explanation ought to be impossible, Mrs. Hedda.

HEDDA. Indeed?

BRACK. [*Glances at her.*] Of course, Eilert Lövborg was here this morning. Was he not?

HEDDA. Yes.

BRACK. Were you alone with him?

HEDDA. Part of the time.

BRACK. Did you not leave the room whilst he was here?

HEDDA. No.

BRACK. Try to recollect. Were you not out of the room a moment?

HEDDA. Yes, perhaps just a moment—out in the hall.

BRACK. And where was your pistol-case during that time?

HEDDA. I had it locked up in——

BRACK. Well, Mrs. Hedda?

HEDDA. The case stood there on the writing-table.

BRACK. Have you looked since, to see whether both the pistols are there?

HEDDA. No.

BRACK. Well, you need not. I saw the pistol found in Lövborg's pocket, and I knew it at once as the one I had seen yesterday—and before, too.

HEDDA. Have you it with you?

BRACK. No, the police have it.

HEDDA. What will the police do with it?

BRACK. Search till they find the owner.

HEDDA. Do you think they will succeed?

BRACK. [*Bends over her and whispers.*] No, Hedda Gabler—not so long as I say nothing.

HEDDA. [*Looks frightened at him.*] And if you do not say nothing,—what then?

BRACK. [*Shrugs his shoulders.*] There is always the possibility that pistol was stolen.

HEDDA. [*Firmly.*] Death rather than that.

BRACK. [*Smiling.*] People say such things—but they don't do them.

HEDDA. [*Without replying.*] And supposing the pistol was not stolen, and the owner is discovered? What then?

BRACK. Well, Hedda—then comes the scandal.

HEDDA. The scandal!

BRACK. Yes, the scandal—of which you are so mortally afraid. You will, of course, be brought before the court—both you and Mademoiselle Diana. She will have to explain how the thing happened—whether it was an accidental shot or murder. Did the pistol go off as he was trying to take it out of his pocket, to threaten her with? Or did she tear the pistol out of his hand, shoot him, and push it back into his pocket? That would be quite like her; for she is an able-bodied young person, this same Mademoiselle Diana.

HEDDA. But *I* have nothing to do with all this repulsive business.

BRACK. No. But you will have to answer the question: Why did you give Eilert Lövborg the pistol? And what conclusions will people draw from the fact that you did give it to him?

HEDDA. [*Lets her head sink.*] That is true. I did not think of that.

BRACK. Well, fortunately, there is no danger, so long as I say nothing.

HEDDA. [*Looks up at him.*] So I am in your power, Judge Brack. You have me at your beck and call, from this time forward.

BRACK. [*Whispers softly.*] Dearest Hedda—believe me—I shall not abuse my advantage.

HEDDA. I am in your power none the less. Subject to your will and your demands. A slave, a slave then! [*Rises impetuously.*] No, I cannot endure the thought of that! Never!

BRACK. [*Looks half-mockingly at her.*] People generally get used to the inevitable.

HEDDA. [*Returns his look.*] Yes, perhaps. [*She crosses to the writing-table. Suppressing an involuntary smile, she imitates* TESMAN'S *intonations.*] Well? Are you getting on, George? Eh?

TESMAN. Heaven knows, dear. In any case it will be the work of months.

HEDDA. [*As before.*] Fancy that! [*Passes her hands softly through* MRS. ELVSTED'S *hair.*] Doesn't it seem strange to you, Thea? Here are you sitting with Tesman—just as you used to sit with Eilert Lövborg?

MRS. ELVSTED. Ah, if I could only inspire your husband in the same way!

HEDDA. Oh, that will come, too—in time.

TESMAN. Yes, do you know, Hedda—I really think I begin to feel something of the sort. But won't you go and sit with Brack again?

HEDDA. Is there nothing I can do to help you two?

TESMAN. No, nothing in the world. [*Turning his head.*] I trust to you to keep Hedda company, my dear Brack.

BRACK. [*With a glance at* HEDDA.] With the very greatest of pleasure.

HEDDA. Thanks. But I am tired this evening. I will go in and lie down a little on the sofa.

TESMAN. Yes, do, dear—eh?

[HEDDA *goes into the back room and draws the curtains. A short pause. Suddenly she is heard playing a wild dance on the piano.*]

MRS. ELVSTED. [*Starts from her chair.*] Oh—what is that?

TESMAN. [*Runs to the doorway.*] Why, my dearest Hedda—don't play dance-music to-night! Just think of Aunt Rina! And of Eilert, too!

HEDDA. [*Puts her head out between the curtains.*] And of Aunt Julia. And of all the rest of them.—After this, I will be quiet. [*Closes the curtains again.*]

TESMAN. [*At the writing-table.*] It's not good for her to see us at this distressing work. I'll tell you what, Mrs. Elvsted,—you shall take the empty room at Aunt Julia's, and then I will come over in the evenings, and we can sit and work there—eh?

HEDDA. [*In the inner room.*] I hear what you are saying, Tesman. But how am *I* to get through the evenings out here?

TESMAN. [*Turning over the papers.*] Oh, I daresay Judge Brack will be so kind as to look in now and then, even though I am out.

BRACK. [*In the arm-chair, calls out gaily.*] Every blessed evening, with all the pleasure in life, Mrs. Tesman! We shall get on capitally together, we two!

HEDDA. [*Speaking loud and clear.*] Yes, don't you flatter yourself we will, Judge Brack? Now that you are the one cock in the basket——

[*A shot is heard within.* TESMAN, MRS. ELVSTED, *and* BRACK *leap to their feet.*]

TESMAN. Oh, now she is playing with those pistols again.

[*He throws back the curtains and runs in, followed by* MRS. ELVSTED. HEDDA *lies stretched on the sofa, lifeless. Confusion and cries.* BERTA *enters in alarm from the right.*]

TESMAN. [*Shrieks to* BRACK.] Shot herself! Shot herself in the temple! Fancy that!

BRACK. [*Half-fainting in the arm-chair.*] Good God!—people don't do such things.

THE INFERNAL MACHINE[1]

JEAN COCTEAU

ENGLISH VERSION (REVISED FOR THIS EDITION) BY CARL WILDMAN

Characters (in order of appearance)

THE VOICE
THE YOUNG SOLDIER
THE SOLDIER
THE CAPTAIN
JOCASTA, *the queen, widow of Laïus*
TIRESIAS, *a soothsayer, nearly blind*
THE GHOST OF LAÏUS, *the dead king*
THE SPHINX
ANUBIS, *Egyptian God of the Dead*
THE THEBAN MATRON
A LITTLE BOY
A LITTLE GIRL
OEDIPUS, *son of Laïus*
CREON, *brother of Jocasta*
THE MESSENGER FROM CORINTH
THE SHEPHERD OF LAÏUS
ANTIGONE, *daughter of Oedipus*

ACT I

THE GHOST OF LAÏUS

THE VOICE: *'He will kill his father. He will marry his mother.'*

To thwart this oracle of Apollo, Jocasta, Queen of Thebes, leaves her son on the mountain side with his feet pierced and bound. A shepherd of Corinth finds the nursling and carries it to Polybius. Polybius and Merope, king and queen of Corinth, were bemoaning a sterile marriage. The child, Oedipus, or *Pierced-feet,* respected by bears and wolves, is to them a heaven-sent gift. They adopt him.

When a young man, Oedipus questions the oracle of Delphi.

The god speaks: *You will murder your father and marry your mother.* He must therefore fly from Polybius and Merope. The fear of parricide and incest drives him on towards his fate.

One evening, arriving at the cross-roads of Delphi and Daulis, he meets an escort. A horse jostles him; a quarrel starts; a servant threatens him; he replies with a blow from his stick. The blow misses the servant and kills the master. This dead man is Laïus, the old king of Thebes. Parricide!

The escort, fearing an ambush, took to its heels. Oedipus, unsuspecting,

1. Reprinted from *International Modern Plays* (New York: E. P. Dutton & Co., Inc., 1950). This play is fully protected by copyright. Any applications for professional or amateur performances as well as for transmission by radio or television should be directed to the authors' agent, Dr. Jan van Loewen, of 2, Jason's Court, Wigmore Street, London, W. 1, England.

La Machine Infernale was first performed at the Comédie des Champs-Elysées (Théâtre Louis Jouvet) on 10th April 1934, with scenery and costumes by Christian Bérard.

passed on. Besides, he is young, enthusiastic; this accident is soon forgotten.

During one of his halts he learns of the scourge of the Sphinx. The Sphinx, 'the Winged Virgin,' 'the Singing Bitch,' is killing off the young men of Thebes. This monster asks a riddle and kills those who do not guess it. Queen Jocasta, widow of Laïus, offers her hand and her crown to the conqueror of the Sphinx.

Like the young Siegfried to come, Oedipus hurries on. He is consumed with curiosity and ambition. The meeting takes place. What was the nature of this meeting? Mystery. Be that as it may, Oedipus enters Thebes a conqueror, he marries the queen. Incest!

For the gods really to enjoy themselves, their victim must fall from a great height. Years come and go in prosperity. Two daughters and two sons complicate the monstrous union. The people love their king. But the plague suddenly descends upon them. The gods accuse an anonymous criminal of infecting the country and demand that he shall be driven out. Going from one discovery to another, and as if intoxicated by misfortune, Oedipus, in the end, finds himself cornered. The trap shuts. All becomes clear. With her red scarf Jocasta hangs herself. With the golden brooch of the hanging woman Oedipus puts out his eyes.

Spectator, this machine, you see here wound up to the full in such a way that the spring will slowly unwind the whole length of a human life, is one of the most perfect constructed by the infernal gods for the mathematical destruction of a mortal.

ACT I[1]

The Ghost

SCENE: *A patrol path round the ramparts of Thebes. High walls. A stormy night. Summer lightning. The din and bands of the popular district can be heard.*

YOUNG SOLDIER. They 're having a good time!

SOLDIER. Trying to.

YOUNG SOLDIER. Well, anyway, they dance all night.

SOLDIER. They can't sleep, so they dance.

YOUNG SOLDIER. Never mind, they 're getting tight and going with women, and spending their nights in all sorts of dives, while I am here tramping up and down with you. Well I, for one, can't stick it any longer! I can't stick it! I can't! That 's clear enough, isn't it? I 've had my bellyful!

1. The four scenes should be planted on a little platform in the centre of the stage, surrounded by nocturnal curtains. The slope of the platform varies according to the requirements of the scenes. Besides the lighting of details, the four acts should be flooded in the livid mythical light of quicksilver.

SOLDIER. Desert then.

YOUNG SOLDIER. Oh, no! I 've made up my mind. I 'm going to put my name down for the Sphinx.

SOLDIER. What for?

YOUNG SOLDIER. What for? Why, to do something, of course. To put an end to all this creepy business and ghastly hanging about.

SOLDIER. You wouldn't get scared, though?

YOUNG SOLDIER. Scared? How d'you mean?

SOLDIER. Oh, just scared, you know! I 've seen brighter and tougher lads than you who got the wind up. Unless this gent is going to kill the Sphinx and draw the first prize.

YOUNG SOLDIER. And why not? Oh, I know the only man who came back alive from the Sphinx had become a gibbering idiot. But supposing what he gibbers is true? What if it is a riddle? What if I guess the answer? What——

SOLDIER. Now listen here, you poor bastard. Don't you realize that hundreds upon hundreds of chaps who 've been to the stadium and college and everything have left their carcasses behind there, and you, a poor little private soldier like you wants to——

YOUNG SOLDIER. I shall go! I shall, because I can't bear any longer counting the stones of this wall, hearing that band, and seeing your rotten mug, and—— [*He stamps.*]

SOLDIER. That 's the stuff, my hero! I was waiting for this explosion. I like it better that way. Now . . . now . . . enough blubbering. . . . Take it easy . . . there, there, there . . .

YOUNG SOLDIER. To hell with you! [*The* SOLDIER *bangs his spear against the wall behind the* YOUNG SOLDIER *who becomes rigid.*]

SOLDIER. What 's up?

YOUNG SOLDIER. Didn't you hear anything?

SOLDIER. No . . . where?

YOUNG SOLDIER. Ah! . . . I seemed to . . . I thought for a moment——

SOLDIER. You 're like a sheet. . . . What 's the matter? Are you going to pass out?

YOUNG SOLDIER. It 's silly . . . I seemed to hear a knock. I thought it was him!

SOLDIER. The Sphinx?

YOUNG SOLDIER. No, him, the ghost, the phantom, you know!

SOLDIER. The ghost? Our dear old ghost of Laïus? And is that what turns your stomach over? Really!

YOUNG SOLDIER. I 'm sorry.

SOLDIER. You 're sorry, mate? What are you talking about? To start with, there 's a good chance that our ghost will not appear again after last night's business. So that 's that. And besides, what are you sorry about? Look at things squarely. We can hardly say this ghost scared us. Oh, well . . . the first time perhaps! . . . But, after that, eh? . . . He was a decent old ghost, almost a pal, a relief. Well, if the idea of this ghost makes you jumpy, it 's because you 're in a real state of nerves, like me, like everybody in Thebes, rich or poor alike, except a few big pots who make something out of everything. There 's not much fun in war, anyway, but we don't know a blind thing about the enemy we 're up against. We 're beginning to get fed up with oracles, happy deaths, and heroic mothers. Do you think I should pull your leg as I do if my nerves weren't on edge, and do you think you 'd start blubbering, and that lot over there 'd get tight and dance? No, they 'd be in bed and fast asleep, and we 'd be playing dice while waiting for friend phantom.

YOUNG SOLDIER. I say . . .

SOLDIER. Well? . . .

YOUNG SOLDIER. What d' you think it 's like . . . the Sphinx?

SOLDIER. Oh! give the Sphinx a rest. If I knew what it was like I shouldn't be here doing guard duty with you to-night.

YOUNG SOLDIER. Some make out it 's no bigger than a hare, and is timid, and has a tiny little face, like a woman's. But I think it has a woman's head and breasts, and sleeps with the young men.

SOLDIER. Oh, turn it up! Shut up and forget it!

YOUNG SOLDIER. Perhaps it doesn't ask anything and doesn't even touch you. You meet it, look at it, and die of love.

SOLDIER. All we needed was for you to go and fall in love with the public scourge. After all, public scourge . . . between ourselves, do you know what I think about this public scourge? . . . It 's a vampire! Yes, a common or garden vampire! Someone in hiding from the police, and who they can't lay their hands on.

YOUNG SOILDER. A vampire with a woman's head?

SOLDIER. Can't you turn it up? No, not him! A real old vampire with a beard and moustache, and a belly. He sucks your blood and that 's how it is they bring corpses back home, all with the same wound in the same place: the back of the neck! And now, go and see for yourself if you 're still keen.

YOUNG SOLDIER. You say that . . .

SOLDIER. I say that . . . I say that . . . Hi! . . . The captain. [*They stand up to attention. The* CAPTAIN *enters and folds his arms.*]

CAPTAIN. Easy! . . . Well, my lads. . . . Is this where we see ghosts?

SOLDIER. Sir——

CAPTAIN. Silence! You will speak when I ask you. Which of you two has dared——

YOUNG SOLDIER. I did, sir!

CAPTAIN. Good Lord! Whose turn to speak is it? Are you going to keep quiet? I was asking: which of you two has dared to make a report about a service matter, without it passing through the normal channels? Right over my head. Answer.

SOLDIER. It wasn't his fault, sir, he knew——

CAPTAIN. Was it you or him?

YOUNG SOLDIER. Both of us, but *I*——

CAPTAIN. Silence! I want to know how the high priest came to hear of what happens at night at this post, while I myself heard nothing.

YOUNG SOLDIER. It 's my fault, sir, my fault. My comrade here didn't want to say anything about it. But I thought I ought to speak and, as this incident didn't concern the service . . . and, well . . . I told his uncle everything; because his uncle's wife is sister to one of the queen's linen-maids, and his brother-in-law is in Tiresias's temple.

SOLDIER. That 's why I said it was my fault, sir.

CAPTAIN. All right! Don't burst my ear-drums. So . . . this incident doesn't concern the service. Very good, oh, very good! . . . And it seems . . . this famous incident which doesn't concern the service is a ghost story?

YOUNG SOLDIER. Yes, sir.

CAPTAIN. A ghost appeared to you one night when you were on guard duty, and this ghost said to you . . . Just what did this ghost say to you?

YOUNG SOLDIER. He told us, sir, he was the spectre of King Laïus, and he had tried to appear several times since his murder, and he begged us to find some way of warning Queen Jocasta and Tiresias with all speed.

CAPTAIN. With all speed! Fancy that! What a nice old ghost he must be! And . . . didn't you ask him, say, why *you* had the honour of this visit and why he doesn't appear directly before the queen or Tiresias?

SOLDIER. Yes, sir, I asked him, I did. His answer was that he wasn't free to put in an appearance anywhere, and that the ramparts were the most favourable spot for people who had died violent deaths, because of the drains.

CAPTAIN. Drains?

SOLDIER. Yes, sir. He said drains, meaning because of the fumes which rise there.

CAPTAIN. Hoho! A very learned spectre, and he doesn't hide his light under a bushel. Did he scare you much? And what did he look like? What was his face like? What clothes did he wear? Where did he stand, and what language did he speak? Are his visits long or short? Have you seen him on different occasions? Although this business doesn't concern the service, I must say I am curious to learn from your lips a few details about the manners and customs of ghosts.

YOUNG SOLDIER. Well, he did scare us a bit the first night, I admit. You see, sir, he appeared very suddenly, like a lamp lighting up, there in the thickness of the wall.

SOLDIER. We both saw him.

YOUNG SOLDIER. It was hard to make out the face and the body; the mouth, when it was open, was clearer, and a white tuft of his beard, and a large red stain, bright red, near the right ear. He spoke with difficulty and couldn't somehow manage to get out more than one sentence at a time. But you 'd better ask my comrade here about that, sir. He explained to me how it was the poor fellow couldn't manage to get it over.

SOLDIER. Oh! you know, sir, there 's nothing very complicated about it! He spent all his energy in the effort to appear, that is, in leaving his new shape and taking on the old, so that we could see him. That 's the reason why each time he spoke a little better, he began to disappear, became transparent like, and you could see the wall through him.

YOUNG SOLDIER. And as soon as he spoke badly you could see him very well. But you saw him badly as soon as he spoke well, and began saying the same thing over again. 'Queen Jocasta. You must . . . you must . . . Queen . . . Queen . . . Queen Jocasta. . . . You must. . . . You must warn the queen. . . . You must warn Queen Jocasta. . . . I ask you, gentlemen, I ask you, I . . . I . . . Gentlemen . . . I ask . . . you must . . . you must . . . I ask you, gentlemen, to warn . . . I ask you . . . The queen . . . Queen Jocasta . . . to warn, gentlemen, to warn . . . Gentlemen . . . Gentlemen . . .' That 's how he went on.

SOLDIER. And you could see he was afraid of disappearing before he 'd said his piece right to the end.

YOUNG SOLDIER. Oh yes, and then, you know, remember, eh? Every time the same business. The red stain went last. Just like a ship's light on the wall, it was, sir.

SOLDIER. But the whole thing was over in a minute!

YOUNG SOLDIER. He has appeared in the same place five times, every night, a little before dawn.

SOLDIER. But last night it was different, we . . . well, we had a bit of a fight, and my comrade here decided to tell the royal house everything.

CAPTAIN. Well! Well! And how was this night 'different', which, if I 'm not mistaken, caused a dispute between you . . . ?

SOLDIER. It was like this, sir. . . . You know, guard duty isn't exactly all beer and skittles.

YOUNG SOLDIER. So really we were waiting for the ghost to turn up, like.

SOLDIER. And we laid the odds.

YOUNG SOLDIER. Will come . . .

SOLDIER. Won't . . .

YOUNG SOLDIER. Will come . . .

SOLDIER. Won't . . . and it may seem a funny thing to say, but it was a comfort to see him.

YOUNG SOLDIER. A habit, as you might say.

SOLDIER. We ended by imagining we saw him when he wasn't there. We 'd say to each other: 'It 's moving! The wall is lighting up. Don't you see anything? No. But you must do. Over there, I tell you. . . . The wall isn't the same. Don't you see, look, look!'

YOUNG SOLDIER. And we looked and stared our eyes out. We didn't dare move.

SOLDIER. We watched for the least change.

YOUNG SOLDIER. And when, at last, he turned up, we could breathe again, and weren't the least bit afraid.

SOLDIER. The other night we watched and watched and stared ourselves nearly blind; we thought he 'd never show up, but he appeared stealthily . . . not at all quickly like on the first nights. And once he was visible, he said new things and told us as well as he could that something fearful had happened, a thing of death which he couldn't explain to the living. He spoke of places where he could go and places where he couldn't go, and that he had been where he shouldn't and knew a secret which he shouldn't know, and that he would be discovered and punished, and afterwards he wouldn't be allowed to appear, he wouldn't be able to appear any more. [*Solemn voice.*] 'I shall die my last death,' he said, 'and it will be finished, finished. You see, gentlemen, there is not a moment to lose. Run! Warn the queen! Find Tiresias! Gentlemen! Gentlemen, have pity! . . .' He was begging away and day was breaking. And there he stuck!

YOUNG SOLDIER. Suddenly we thought he 'd go mad.

SOLDIER. We understood from sentences without beginning or end that he had left his post, as it were, . . . didn't know how to disappear, and was lost. We saw him going through the same performance to disappear as to appear, and he couldn't manage it. So then he asked us to swear at him, because, he said, swearing at ghosts is the way to make them go. The silliest thing about it was that we hadn't the guts to do it. The more he repeated 'Come on! young men, insult me! Let yourselves go, do your best. . . . Oh, come on!'—the softer we looked.

YOUNG SOLDIER. And the less we could lay our tongue to! . . .

SOLDIER. Yes, that was the limit! And yet, it 's not for lack of blackguarding our superiors.

CAPTAIN. Very nice of you, men, I 'm sure! Thank you on behalf of the superiors.

SOLDIER. Oh! I didn't mean that, sir. . . . I meant . . . I meant the princes, crowned heads, ministers, the government, what . . . the powers that be. In fact, we 'd often talked over wrongs which are done. . . . But he was such a decent sort, the ghost of poor old King Laïus, the swear-words wouldn't come. There he was, urging us on and we kept dithering: 'Go on then! Buzz off, you old bastard!' In short, we gave him bouquets!

YOUNG SOLDIER. Because, you see, sir, 'you old bastard' is a kind of friendly way of speaking among soldiers.

CAPTAIN. It 's as well to know.

SOLDIER. Go on! Go on then! . . . you bleeding . . . you old . . . poor ghost. He hung there between life and death and he was beside himself with fear because of the cocks and the sun. When, all of a sudden, we saw the wall become the wall again, and the red stain go out. We were dog-tired.

YOUNG SOLDIER. It was after that night that I decided to speak to his uncle as he refused to speak himself.

CAPTAIN. Your ghost doesn't seem to be very punctual.

SOLDIER. Oh, you know, sir, he may not show himself again.

CAPTAIN. I am in his way, no doubt.

SOLDIER. No, sir, I mean after last night . . .

CAPTAIN. But I understand from what you say that your ghost is very polite. He will appear, I 'm quite sure. In the first place, the politeness of kings is punctuality, and the politeness of ghosts consists in taking on human form, according to your ingenious theory.

SOLDIER. Possibly, sir, but it 's also possible that with ghosts there are no more kings, and they may mistake a century for a minute. So if the ghost appears in a thousand years instead of this evening . . .

CAPTAIN. You 're a clever sort of chap, but patience has its limits. I tell you this ghost will appear. I tell you my presence is upsetting him, and I tell you that no one outside the service must come along this patrol path.

SOLDIER. Yes, sir.

CAPTAIN. [*In an outburst.*] So, ghost or no ghost, you are to stop any one turning up here without the password. Those are orders. Is that clear?

SOLDIER. Yes, sir.

CAPTAIN. And don't forget to patrol. Dismiss!

[*The two soldiers stand stiffly at the slope.*]

[*False exit.*] Don't try any clever tricks! I 've got my eye on you.

[*He disappears. Long silence.*]

SOLDIER. As you were!

YOUNG SOLDIER. He thought we were trying to pull his leg.

SOLDIER. Don't you believe it! He thought someone was trying to pull ours.

YOUNG SOLDIER. Ours?

SOLDIER. Yes, chum. I get to know lots of things, I do, through my uncle. The queen is nice, you know, but she isn't really liked; they think she 's . . . [*He taps his head.*] They say she is eccentric and has a foreign accent, and is under the influence of Tiresias. This Tiresias advises the queen to do everything that will harm her. Do this . . . and do that. . . . She tells him her dreams, and asks him if she ought to get up right foot or left foot first; he leads her by the nose and licks her brother's boots, and plots with him against his sister. They are a low lot there. I wouldn't mind betting the captain thought our ghost was out of the same bag as the Sphinx. A priest's trick to attract Jocasta and make her believe anything they want.

YOUNG SOLDIER. No?

SOLDIER. Shakes you, doesn't it? But that 's how it is. . . . [*In a very low voice.*] Listen, I believe in the ghost myself, take it from me. But, for that very reason, because I believe in him and they don't, I advise you to keep your mouth shut. You 've already succeeded in making a fine hash of things. Take down this report: 'Has given proof of an intelligence well above his rank. . . .'

YOUNG SOLDIER. Still, if our king . . .

SOLDIER. Our king! . . . Our king! . . . Steady on! . . . A dead king isn't a living king. It's like this, if King Laïus were living, well, between ourselves, he would manage on his own and wouldn't come looking for you to act as his A.D.C. [*They move off towards the right by the patrol path.*]

VOICE OF JOCASTA. [*At the bottom of the steps. She has a very strong accent: the international accent of royalty.*] Still another flight! I hate steps! Why all these steps? We can see nothing! Where are we?

VOICE OF TIRESIAS. But, Majesty, you know what I think of this escapade, and *I* didn't——

VOICE OF JOCASTA. Stop it, Zizi. You only open your mouth to say silly things. This is not the time for moral lessons.

VOICE OF TIRESIAS. You should have taken another guide. I am nearly blind.

VOICE OF JOCASTA. What is the use of being a soothsayer, I wonder! Why, you don't even know where the steps are. I shall break my leg! It will be your fault, Zizi, your fault, as usual.

VOICE OF TIRESIAS. My fleshly eyes have gone out to the advantage of an inner eye which has other uses than counting steps.

VOICE OF JOCASTA. And now he 's cross all over his eye! There, there! We love you, Zizi; but these flights of steps upset me so. We had to come, Zizi, we simply had to!

VOICE OF TIRESIAS. Majesty——

VOICE OF JOCASTA. Don't be obstinate. I had no idea there were all these wretched steps. I am going to go up backwards. You will steady me. Don't be afraid. *I* am leading you. But if I looked at the steps, I should fall. Take my hands. Forward! [*They appear on the set.*]

There . . . there . . . there . . . four, five, six, seven . . .

[JOCASTA *arrives on the platform and moves to the right.* TIRESIAS *treads on the end of her scarf. She utters a cry.*]

TIRESIAS. What is it?

JOCASTA. It 's your foot, Zizi! You 're walking on my scarf.

TIRESIAS. Forgive me . . .

JOCASTA. Ah! he 's cross! But it isn't you that I am annoyed with, it 's the scarf! I am surrounded by objects which hate me! All day long this scarf is strangling me. At one time it catches in the branches, at another it gets wound on to the hub of a carriage, another time you tread on it. It 's a positive fact. And I am afraid of it, but I dare not be separated from it! Awful! It will be the death of me.

TIRESIAS. Look what a state your nerves are in.

JOCASTA. And what is the use of your third eye, I should like to know? Have you found the Sphinx? Have you found the murderers of Laïus? Have you calmed the people? Guards are stationed at my door and I am left with things that hate me, that want my death!

TIRESIAS. From mere hearsay——

JOCASTA. I feel things. I feel things better than all of you! [*She puts her hand on her belly.*] I feel them there! Was every possible effort made to discover the murderers of Laïus?

TIRESIAS. Majesty, you know very well the Sphinx made further searches impossible.

JOCASTA. Well, I for one don't care a jot about your fowls' entrails. . . . I feel, there . . . that Laïus is suffering and wants to be heard. I am determined to get to the bottom of this story, and to hear this young guard for myself; and I *shall* hear him. I am your queen, Tiresias, don't you forget it.

TIRESIAS. My dear child, you must try and understand a poor blind man who adores you, watches over you, and wishes you were sleeping in your room instead of running after a shadow on the ramparts.

JOCASTA. [*With mystery.*] I do not sleep.

TIRESIAS. You don't sleep?

JOCASTA. No, Zizi, I don't sleep. The Sphinx and the murder of Laïus have put my nerves all on edge. You were right there. And I am glad in a way, because if I fall asleep for so much as a minute I have a dream, always the same, and I am ill for the whole day.

TIRESIAS. Isn't it my business to interpret dreams? . . .

JOCASTA. The place of the dream is rather like this platform, so I 'll tell you. I am standing in the night, cradling a kind of nursling. Suddenly this nursling becomes a sticky paste which runs through my fingers. I shriek and try to throw this paste away, but . . . oh! Zizi . . . if only you knew, it 's foul. . . . This thing, this paste stays hanging on to me, and when I think I 'm free of it the paste flies back and strikes me across the face. And this paste is living. It has a kind of mouth which fixes itself on mine. And it creeps everywhere, it feels after my belly, and my thighs. Oh! Horrible!

TIRESIAS. Calm yourself.

JOCASTA. I don't want to sleep any more, Zizi . . . I don't want to sleep any more. Listen to that music. Where is it? They don't sleep either. It 's lucky for them that they have that music. They are afraid, Zizi . . . and rightly. They must dream horrible things, and they don't want to sleep. And while I think of it, why this music? Why is it allowed? Do I have music to keep me from sleeping? I didn't know these places stayed open all night. How is it there is this scandal, Zizi? Creon must send out orders! This music must be forbidden! This scandal must stop at once.

TIRESIAS. Majesty, I implore you to calm yourself and to give up this idea. You 're beside yourself for lack of sleep. We have authorized these bands so that the people don't become demoralized, to keep up their courage. There would be crimes . . . and worse than that if there were no dancing in the crowded parts of town.

JOCASTA. Do I dance?

TIRESIAS. That 's different. You are in mourning for Laïus.

JOCASTA. So are they all, Zizi. All of them! Every one! And yet they can dance and I can't. It 's too unfair . . . I shall—

TIRESIAS. Someone coming, madam.

JOCASTA. I say, Zizi, I 'm shaking. I have come out with all my jewels.

TIRESIAS. There 's nothing to fear. You won't meet prowlers on the patrol path. It must be the guards.

JOCASTA. Perhaps the soldier I am looking for?

TIRESIAS. Don't move. We 'll find out.

[*The* SOLDIERS *enter. They see* JOCASTA *and* TIRESIAS.]

YOUNG SOLDIER. Steady, looks like somebody.

SOLDIER. Where have they sprung from? [*Aloud.*] Who goes there?

TIRESIAS. [*To the* QUEEN.] This is going to be awkward. . . . [*Aloud.*] Listen, my good men . .

YOUNG SOLDIER. Password.

TIRESIAS. You see, madam, we ought to have the password. You 're getting us into an awful mess.

JOCASTA. Password? Why? What password? How silly, Zizi. I shall go and speak to him myself.

TIRESIAS. Madam, I implore you. They have instructions. These guards might not recognize you, nor believe me. It 's very dangerous.

JOCASTA. How romantic you are! You see dramas everywhere.

SOLDIER. They 're whispering together. Perhaps they 're going to spring on us.

TIRESIAS. [*To the* SOLDIERS.] You have nothing to fear. I am old and nearly blind. Let me explain my presence on these ramparts, and the presence of the person who accompanies me.

SOLDIER. No speeches. The password!

TIRESIAS. One moment. Just a moment. Listen, my good men, have you seen any gold coins?

SOLDIER. Attempted bribery.

[*He goes towards the right to guard the patrol path and leaves the* YOUNG SOLDIER *opposite* TIRESIAS.]

TIRESIAS. You 're wrong. I meant: have you seen the queen's portrait on a gold coin?

YOUNG SOLDIER. Yes!

TIRESIAS. [*Stepping aside and showing the queen, who is counting the stars, in profile.*] And . . . don't you recognize . . . ?

YOUNG SOLDIER. If you 're trying to make out there 's a connection, I don't get it. The queen is so young, and this . . . er . . . lady . . . well! . . .

JOCASTA. What does he say?

TIRESIAS. He says he finds madam very young to be the queen. . . .

JOCASTA. How entertaining!

TIRESIAS. [*To the* SOLDIER.] Fetch your officer.

SOLDIER. No need. I have my orders. Clear off! Look sharp!

TIRESIAS. You 'll hear more of this!

JOCASTA. Zizi, what is it now? What does he say?

[*The* CAPTAIN *enters.*]

CAPTAIN. What 's going on here?

YOUNG SOLDIER. Two people without the password, sir.

CAPTAIN. [*Going towards* TIRESIAS.] Who are you? [*He suddenly recognizes* TIRESIAS.] My lord! [*He bows.*] My profoundest apologies.

TIRESIAS. Whew! Thanks, Captain. I thought this young warrior was going to run us through.

CAPTAIN. I am extremely sorry, my lord! [*To the* YOUNG SOLDIER.] Idiot! Leave us.

[*The* YOUNG SOLDIER *goes to his comrade on the extreme right.*]

SOLDIER. [*To the* YOUNG SOLDIER.] What a brick!

TIRESIAS. Don't scold him! He was obeying orders. . . .

CAPTAIN. Such a visit . . . in such a place! What can I do for your lordship?

TIRESIAS. [*Standing back to show the queen.*] Her Majesty!

[*The* CAPTAIN *starts back.*]

CAPTAIN. [*Bows at a respectful distance.*] Majesty! . . .

JOCASTA. No ceremony, please! I should like to know which guard saw the ghost.

CAPTAIN. Oh, the sorry young specimen who ill-used my lord Tiresias, and if Your Majesty . . .

JOCASTA. See, Zizi. What luck! I was right in coming. . . . [*To the* CAPTAIN.] Tell him to approach.

CAPTAIN. [*To* TIRESIAS.] My lord, I don't know if the queen fully realizes that this young soldier would explain himself better through his officer; and that, if he speaks for himself, Her Majesty will be in danger of——

JOCASTA. What now, Zizi? . . .

TIRESIAS. The Captain was pointing out that he is used to the men and he might serve as a kind of interpreter.

JOCASTA. Send the Captain away! Has the boy a tongue, or not? Let him come near.

TIRESIAS. [*Aside to the* CAPTAIN.] Don't insist, the queen is overwrought. . . .

CAPTAIN. Very well. . . . [*He goes to his* SOLDIERS. *To the* YOUNG SOLDIER.] The queen wants to speak to you. And control your tongue. I 'll pay you out for this, young fellow-me-lad.

JOCASTA. Come here! [*The* CAPTAIN *pushes the* YOUNG SOLDIER *forward.*]

CAPTAIN. Go along then! Go on, booby, forward. You won't be eaten. Excuse him, Your Majesty. Our lads are scarcely familiar with court ways.

JOCASTA. Ask that man to leave us alone with the soldier.

TIRESIAS. But, Majesty——

JOCASTA. And no 'but Majestys.' . . . If this Captain stays a moment longer I shall kick him.

TIRESIAS. Listen, officer. [*He leads him aside.*] The queen wants to be alone with the guard who has seen something. She has her whims. She might have your record blotted for you, you know, and I couldn't do anything about it.

CAPTAIN. Right. I 'll leave you. . . . If I stayed it was because . . . well . . . I don't mean to give you advice, my lord. . . . But, between you and me, be on your guard about this ghost story. [*He bows.*] My lord. . . . [*A long salute to the queen. He passes near the* SOLDIER.] Hi! The queen wishes to stay alone with your comrade.

JOCASTA. Who is the other soldier? Has he seen the ghost?

YOUNG SOLDIER. Yes, Your Majesty, we were on guard duty together.

JOCASTA. Then let him stop. Let him stay there! I 'll call him if I want him. Good evening, Captain, you are free.

CAPTAIN. [*To the* SOLDIER.] We 'll have this out later! [*He goes out.*]

TIRESIAS. [*To the* QUEEN.] You have mortally offended that officer.

JOCASTA. About time, too! Generally it 's the men who are mortally offended and never the officers. [*To the* YOUNG SOLDIER.] How old are you?

YOUNG SOLDIER. Nineteen.

JOCASTA. Exactly his age! He would be his age. . . . He looks splendid! Come nearer. Look, Zizi, what muscles! I adore knees. You can tell the breed by the knees. He would look like that too. . . . Isn't he fine, Zizi. Feel these biceps, like iron. . . .

TIRESIAS. I am sorry, madam, but you know . . . I 'm no authority. I can scarcely see what they 're like.

JOCASTA. Then feel. . . . Test them. Thighs like a horse! He steps away! Don't be afraid. . . . The old grandpa is blind. Heaven knows what he 's imagining, poor lad. He 's quite red! He 's adorable! And nineteen!

YOUNG SOLDIER. Yes, Your Majesty!

JOCASTA. [*Mocking him.*] Yes, Your Majesty! Isn't he just too delicious! Ah! what a shame! Perhaps he doesn't even know he 's handsome. [*As one speaks to a child.*] Well . . . did you see the ghost?

YOUNG SOLDIER. Yes, Your Majesty!

JOCASTA. The ghost of King Laïus?

YOUNG SOLDIER. Yes, Your Majesty! The king told us he was the king.

JOCASTA. Zizi . . . what do you know with all your fowls and stars? Listen to this boy. . . . And what did the king say?

TIRESIAS. [*Leading the* QUEEN *away.*] Majesty! Be careful. These young people are hot-headed, credulous . . . pushful. . . . Be on your guard. Are you certain this boy has seen the ghost, and, even if he has seen it, was it really the ghost of your husband?

JOCASTA. Gods! How unbearable you are! Unbearable and a spoil-sport. Every time you come and break the spell you stop miracles with your intelligence and incredulity. Please let me question this boy on my own. You can preach afterwards. [*To the* YOUNG SOLDIER.] Listen. . . .

YOUNG SOLDIER. Your Majesty! . . .

JOCASTA. [*To* TIRESIAS.] I 'll find out straight away whether he has seen Laïus. [*To the* YOUNG SOLDIER.] How did he speak?

YOUNG SOLDIER. He spoke quickly and a lot, Your Majesty, ever such a lot, and he got mixed up, and he didn't manage to say what he wanted to.

JOCASTA. That 's he! Poor dear! But why on these ramparts? The stench. . . .

YOUNG SOLDIER. That 's it, Your Majesty. . . . The ghost said it was because of the swamps and the rising fumes that he could appear.

JOCASTA. How interesting! Tiresias, you would never learn that from your birds. And what did he say?

TIRESIAS. Madam, madam, you must at least question him with some order. You 'll muddle this youngster's head completely.

JOCASTA. Quite right, Zizi, quite right. [*To the* YOUNG SOLDIER.] What was he like? How did you see him?

YOUNG SOLDIER. In the wall, Your Majesty. A sort of transparent statue, as you might say. You could see the beard most clearly, and the black hole of the mouth as he spoke, and a red stain on the temple, bright red.

JOCASTA. That 's blood!

YOUNG SOLDIER. Fancy! We didn't think of that.

JOCASTA. It's a wound! How dreadful! [LAÏUS *appears.*] And what did he say? Did you understand anything?

YOUNG SOLDIER. It wasn't easy, Your Majesty. My comrade noticed that he had to make a big effort to appear, and each time he made an effort to express himself clearly he disappeared; then he was puzzled as to how to set about it.

JOCASTA. Poor dear!

GHOST. Jocasta! Jocasta! My wife! Jocasta! [*They neither hear nor see him during the whole of the scene.*]

TIRESIAS. [*Addressing the* SOLDIER.] And were you not able to grasp anything intelligible?

GHOST. Jocasta!

SOLDIER. Well, yes, my lord. We understood he wanted to warn you of a danger, put you on your guard, both the queen and you, but that 's all. The last time he explained he knew some secrets he ought not to have known, and if he was discovered he would not be able to appear again.

GHOST. Jocasta! Tiresias! Can't you see me? Can't you hear me?

JOCASTA. And didn't he say anything else? Didn't he say anything particular?

SOLDIER. Ah, well, Your Majesty! Perhaps he didn't want to say anything particular in our presence. He was asking for you. That is why my comrade tried to let you know about it.

JOCASTA. Dear boys! And I have come. I knew it all the time. I felt it there! You see, Zizi, with all your doubts. And tell us, Young Soldier, where the ghost appeared. I want to touch the exact spot.

GHOST. Look at me! Listen to me, Jocasta! Guards, you always saw me before. Why not see me now? This is torture! Jocasta! Jocasta! [*While these words are being uttered the* SOLDIER *goes to the place where the* GHOST *is. He touches it with his hand.*]

SOLDIER. There. [*He strikes the wall.*] There, in the wall.

YOUNG SOLDIER. Or in front of the wall. It was difficult to make out.

JOCASTA. But why doesn't he appear to-night? Do you think he will still be able to appear?

GHOST. Jocasta! Jocasta! Jocasta!

SOLDIER. I am sorry, Your Majesty, I don't think so, after what happened last night. I 'm afraid there was a spot of bother and Her Majesty may be too late.

JOCASTA. What a shame! Always too late. Zizi, I am always the last person in the whole kingdom to be informed. Think of the time we have wasted with your fowls and oracles! We ought to have run, to have guessed. We shall learn absolutely nothing! And there will be disasters, terrible disasters. And it will be your fault, Zizi, your fault, as usual.

TIRESIAS. Madam, the queen is speaking in front of these men.

JOCASTA. Yes, I am speaking in front of these men! I suppose I ought to restrain myself? When King Laïus, the dead King Laïus, has spoken in front of these men. But he has not spoken to you, Zizi, nor to Creon. He hasn't been to the temple to show himself. He showed himself on the patrol path to these men, to this boy of nineteen who is so handsome and looks like——

TIRESIAS. I implore you——

JOCASTA. Yes, I am overwrought, you must try to understand. These dangers, this spectre, this music, this pestilential smell. . . . And there 's a storm about. I can feel it in my shoulder. I am stifling, Zizi, stifling.

GHOST. Jocasta! Jocasta!

JOCASTA. I think I hear my name. Didn't you hear anything?

TIRESIAS. My poor lamb. You 're worn out. Day is breaking. You are dreaming where you stand. Are you even sure this ghost business hasn't come from the fatigue of these young men on the watch who force themselves not to sleep and who live in this depressing, swampy atmosphere?

GHOST. Jocasta! For pity's sake, listen to me! Look at me! Gentlemen, you are kind. Keep the queen. Tiresias! Tiresias!

TIRESIAS. [*To the* YOUNG SOLDIER.] Step aside a moment, I want to speak to the queen. [*The* YOUNG SOLDIER *goes to his comrade.*]

SOLDIER. Well, old son! You 've clicked! She 's fallen for you! Petted by the queen, eh!

YOUNG SOLDIER. Look here! . . .

SOLDIER. You 're made for life. Don't forget your pals.

TIRESIAS. . . . Listen! Cockcrow. The ghost will not return. Let us go home.

JOCASTA. Did you see how handsome he is?

TIRESIAS. Don't recall those sad things, my lamb. If you had a son . . .

JOCASTA. If I had a son, he would be handsome, brave, he would guess the riddle and kill the Sphinx. He would return victor.

TIRESIAS. And you would go without a husband.

JOCASTA. Little boys always say: 'I want to become a man so that I can marry mother.' It 's not such a bad idea, you know, Tiresias. Is there a sweeter union, a union that is sweeter and more cruel, and prouder, than that couple: a son and a young mother? Listen, Zizi, just now, when I touched that young guard, heaven alone knows what he must have thought, the poor lad, and I myself nearly fainted. He would be nineteen, Tiresias, nineteen! The same age as this soldier. Can we be sure Laïus did not appear to him because of his likeness?

[*Cock crows.*]

GHOST. Jocasta! Jocasta! Jocasta! Tiresias! Jocasta!

TIRESIAS. [*To the* SOLDIERS.] My friends, do you think it is any use waiting?

GHOST. For pity's sake!

SOLDIER. Frankly, no, my lord. The cocks are crowing. He will not appear now.

GHOST. Gentlemen! Mercy! Am I invisible? Can't you hear me?

JOCASTA. Come along! I will be obedient. But I am very glad I questioned the boy. You must find out his name and where he lives. [*She goes towards the steps.*] I had forgotten these steps, Zizi! . . . That band is making me ill. Listen, we can go back through the higher town by the side streets, and we can see the night life.

TIRESIAS. Madam, you don't mean it.

JOCASTA. Oh! now he 's beginning again! He 'll send me simply raving! Mad and off my head. I 've got my veils on, Zizi, how do you expect I should be recognized?

TIRESIAS. My child, you said yourself you have come out wearing all your jewels. Your brooch alone has pearls as large as an egg.

JOCASTA. I am a martyr! Others can laugh and dance and amuse themselves. Do you imagine I am going to leave this brooch at the palace where it 's simply asking to be taken? Call the guard. Tell him to help me down these steps. And you can follow us.

TIRESIAS. But, madam, since the presence of this young man affects you so strongly . . .

JOCASTA. He is young and strong. He will help me, and I shan't break my neck. Obey your queen for once, at least.

TIRESIAS. Hi! . . . No, he. . . . Yes, you. . . . Help the queen down the steps. . . .

SOLDIER. You see, old man!

YOUNG SOLDIER. [*Approaching.*] Yes, my lord.

GHOST. Jocasta! Jocasta! Jocasta!

JOCASTA. He 's shy! And flights of steps hate me. Steps, hooks, and scarves. Oh! yes, they do, they hate me! They 're after my death. [*A cry.*] Ho!

YOUNG SOLDIER. Has the queen hurt herself?

TIRESIAS. No, silly! Your foot! Your foot!

YOUNG SOLDIER. What foot?

TIRESIAS. Your foot on the end of the scarf. You nearly strangled the queen.

YOUNG SOLDIER. Ye gods!

JOCASTA. Zizi, you are utterly ridiculous. Poor darling. There you go calling him a murderer because he walks, as you did, on this scarf. Don't upset yourself, my boy. My lord is absurd. He never misses an opportunity of hurting people's feelings.

TIRESIAS. But, madam——

JOCASTA. You are the one who is clumsy. Come along. Thank you, my boy. Send your name and address to the temple. One, two, three, four. . . . Marvellous! Zizi! Do you see how well I 'm getting down. Eleven, twelve. . . . Zizi, are you following? Two more steps. [*To the* SOLDIER.] Thank you. I can manage now. Help grandpa! [JOCASTA *disappears left, with* TIRESIAS. *Cocks are heard.*]

VOICE OF JOCASTA. Through your fault I shall never know what my poor Laïus wanted.

GHOST. Jocasta!

VOICE OF TIRESIAS. That story is all very vague.

VOICE OF JOCASTA. What? very vague? What do you mean, vague? It 's you who are vague with your third eye. That boy knows what he has seen, and he has seen the king. Have you seen the king?

VOICE OF TIRESIAS. But——

VOICE OF JOCASTA. Have you seen him? . . . No. . . . Well . . . It 's amazing . . . it 's like . . . [*The voices die away.*]

GHOST. Jocasta! Tiresias! Have pity!

[*The two* SOLDIERS *turn to each other and see the* GHOST.]

THE SOLDIERS. Oh! the Ghost!

GHOST. Gentlemen, at last! I am saved! I kept calling, begging. . . .

SOLDIER. You were there?

GHOST. During the whole of your talk with the queen and Tiresias. Then why was I invisible?

YOUNG SOLDIER. I 'll run and fetch them!

SOLDIER. Halt!

GHOST. What? You stop him?

YOUNG SOLDIER. Let me go . . .

SOLDIER. When the joiner comes the chair stops wobbling; when you get to the shoemender your sandal stops hurting you; when you get to the doctor you no longer feel the pain. Fetch them! That would only make him disappear.

GHOST. Alas! Do these simple souls then know what the priests cannot divine?

YOUNG SOLDIER. I shall go.

GHOST. Too late. . . . Stay. It is too late. I am discovered. They are coming; they are going to take me. Ah! they 're here! Help! Help! Quick! Tell the queen a young man is approaching Thebes, and on no account . . . No! No! Mercy! Mercy! They 've got me! Help! Ended! I . . . I. . . . Mercy . . . I . . . I . . .

[*Long silence. The two* SOLDIERS, *back to the audience, contemplate endlessly the place in the wall where the* GHOST *disappeared.*]

SOLDIER. Good God!

YOUNG SOLDIER. Poor devil!

SOLDIER. These things are beyond us, old man.

YOUNG SOLDIER. But it 's clear that, in spite of death, that fellow wanted, at all costs, to warn his wife of a danger which is threatening her. My duty is to overtake the queen and the high priest and repeat to them word for word what we have just heard.

SOLDIER. You want the queen badly, don't you? [*The* YOUNG SOLDIER *shrugs his shoulders.*] Well . . . he only had to appear to them and talk to them, they were there. We saw him all right ourselves and they didn't. But, to crown all, they even prevented *us* from seeing him. So there you have it! Dead kings become ordinary people. Poor Laïus! Now he knows how easy it is to get into touch with the great of the earth.

YOUNG SOLDIER. But us?

SOLDIER. Oh, us! It 's easy enough to get into touch with men, you coon. . . . But, when it comes to officers, queens, and high priests . . . they always go before it happens, or come when it 's all over.

YOUNG SOLDIER. What 's 'it'?

SOLDIER. How should I know? . . . I understand myself, that 's the chief thing.

YOUNG SOLDIER. And you wouldn't go and warn the queen?

SOLDIER. A word of advice: let princes deal with princes, ghosts with ghosts, and soldiers with soldiers. [*Flourish.*]

ACT II

The Meeting of Oedipus and the Sphinx

THE VOICE: Spectators, let us imagine we can recall the minutes we have just lived through together and relive them elsewhere. For, while the Ghost of Laïus was trying to warn Jocasta on the ramparts of Thebes, the Sphinx and Oedipus met on a hill overlooking the town. The bugle-calls, moon, stars, and crowing cocks will be the same.

SCENE: *An unpeopled spot on a hill overlooking Thebes, by moonlight. The road to Thebes (from right to left) passes over the fore-stage. It gives the impression of rounding a high leaning stone whose base is fixed at the lower end of the platform and forms the support for the wings on the right. Behind the ruins of a little temple is a broken wall. In the middle of the wall stands a complete pedestal which used to indicate the entrance to the temple and bears the trace of a chimera: a wing, a foot, a haunch. Broken and overturned columns. For the Shades of Anubis and Nemesis at the end, a record by the actors can declaim the dialogue, whilst the actress mimes the part of the dead girl with the head of a jackal.*

ACT II

The Meeting of Oedipus and the Sphinx

SCENE: *When the curtain rises a girl in a white dress is seen sitting among the ruins. The head of a jackal lies in her lap, its body remaining hidden behind her. Distant bugle calls.*

SPHINX. Listen.

JACKAL. Well?

SPHINX. That 's the last call. We 're free.

[ANUBIS *gets up, and the* JACKAL'S *head is seen to belong to him.*]

JACKAL, ANUBIS. It 's the first. There 'll be two more before the gates are closed.

SPHINX. It 's the last. I 'm quite sure it 's the last.

ANUBIS. You 're sure because you want the gates closed, but I 'm sorry duty forces me to contradict you; we 're not free. That was the first bugle call. We 'll wait.

SPHINX. I may have been mistaken, but——

ANUBIS. May have been mistaken! You were. . . .

SPHINX. Anubis!

ANUBIS. Sphinx?

SPHINX. I 've had enough of killing, enough of dealing out death.

ANUBIS. We must obey. There are mysteries within mystery, gods above gods. We have our gods and they have theirs. That 's what is called infinity.

SPHINX. You see, Anubis, there is no second call. It 's you who are mistaken, let us go. . . .

ANUBIS. Do you mean you would like this night to pass without any deaths?

SPHINX. Yes! I do, indeed! Yes! Although it 's growing late, I tremble to think someone may still come by.

ANUBIS. You 're getting sensitive.

SPHINX. That 's my business.

ANUBIS. Don't get cross.

SPHINX. Why must we always be acting without aim, without end, without understanding? Why, for example, should you have a dog's head, Anubis? Why have the god of the dead in the shape given to him by credulous people? Why must we have an Egyptian god in Greece and why must he have a dog's head?

ANUBIS. It 's marvellous, how like a woman you look when it comes to asking questions.

SPHINX. That is no answer!

ANUBIS. Well, my answer is: that logic forces us to appear to men in the shape in which they imagine us; otherwise, they would see only emptiness. Moreover, neither Egypt nor Greece nor death, neither the past nor the future has any meaning for us. Further, you know only too well to what use I must put this jaw. And finally, our masters prove their wisdom by giving me a material form which is not human and so preventing me from losing my head, however beastly it may be; for I am your keeper, remember. I can see that if they had given you a mere watchdog we should already be in Thebes with me on a leash and you sitting in the middle of a band of young men.

SPHINX. How stupid you are!

ANUBIS. Then try and remember that these victims who touch the girl-figure you have assumed are no more than noughts wiped off a slate, even if each of these noughts were an open mouth calling for help.

SPHINX. That may be. But here the calculations of gods are hard to follow. . . . Here we kill. Here the dead really die. Here I do kill.

[*While the* SPHINX *was speaking with her eyes on the ground* ANUBIS *pricked up his ears, looked round, and moved silently off over the ruins where he disappears. When the* SPHINX *raises her eyes, she looks for* ANUBIS, *and finds herself face to face with a small group of people who enter down stage right, and whom* ANUBIS *had scented. The group is composed of a Theban* MATRON, *her little boy and girl. The* MATRON *is dragging her daughter along. The boy is walking ahead.*]

MATRON. Look where you 're going! Get along now! Don't look behind you! Leave your sister alone! Go on. . . . [*She sees the* SPHINX *as the little boy stumbles into her.*] Look out! I told you to look where you 're going! Oh! I 'm so sorry, miss. . . . He never looks where he 's going. . . . He hasn't hurt you, has he?

SPHINX. No! not at all.

MATRON. I didn't expect to meet any one on my path at such an hour.

SPHINX. I 'm new in these parts, I haven't been long in Thebes; I was on my way to a relative who lives in the country and got lost.

MATRON. Poor dear! And where does your relative live?

SPHINX. . . . Near the twelfth milestone.

MATRON. The very part I come from! I had lunch with my family, at my brother's place, you know. He made me stay to dinner. And then, you know, you begin gossiping and don't notice the time, and so here I am going home after curfew with my brats half asleep already.

SPHINX. Good night.

MATRON. Good night. [*She makes to go.*] And . . . I say . . . don't linger on the way. I know the likes of you and me haven't much to fear . . . but I wouldn't be too bold, if I were you, till I was inside the walls.

SPHINX. Are you afraid of thieves?

MATRON. Thieves! Ye gods, what could they get out of me? Oh, no, my dear! Where *do* you come from? Any one can see you 're not from the town. Thieves! I should think so! I mean the Sphinx!

SPHINX. Do you really, honestly and truly, believe in that nonsense yourself?

MATRON. That nonsense indeed! How young you are. Young people are so disbelieving these days. Oh, yes, they are! That 's how disasters happen. Let alone the Sphinx, I 'll give you a case from my family. . . . My brother that I 've just left. . . . [*She sits down and lowers her voice.*] He married a beautiful tall blonde from the north. One night he wakes up and what does he find? His wife in bed without head or entrails. She was a vampire. When he 'd got over the first fright what does my brother do? without a moment's hesitation he finds an egg and lays it on the pillow in the place of his wife's head. That 's how you stop vampires getting back into their body. All at once he hears a moaning. It was the head and entrails flying wildly across the room and begging my brother to take away the egg. My brother wouldn't, and the head went from moans to anger, from anger to tears, from tears to kisses. To cut a long story short, my idiot brother takes away the egg and lets his wife get back into her body. Now he knows his wife is a vampire and my sons make fun of their uncle. They maintain that he made up this entire vampire story to disguise the fact that his wife really did go out, but with her body, and that he let her come back, and that he 's a coward and ashamed of himself. But *I* know very well my sister-in-law is a vampire. . . . And my sons are in danger of marrying fiends from the underworld, all because they are obstinate and *disbelieving.*

And the same with the Sphinx—I 'm sorry if I hurt your feelings, but it 's only the likes of my sons and you who don't believe in it.

SPHINX. Your sons . . . ?

MATRON. Not the little brat who just bumped into you. I mean my boy of seventeen. . . .

SPHINX. You have several sons, have you?

MATRON. I had four. Now I have three. Seven, sixteen, and seventeen. And I can tell you ever since that wicked beast appeared the house has been impossible.

SPHINX. Your sons quarrel . . . ?

MATRON. I mean, my dear, that it 's impossible to live under the same roof. The one who 's sixteen is only interested in politics. According to him the Sphinx is a bugbear used to scare the poor and to impose on them. There may have been something like your old Sphinx at one time—that 's how my son speaks—but now the old Sphinx is dead; and he 's merely a priest's demon and an excuse for police jobbery. They fleece and loot and terrorize the masses, and then blame it all on the Sphinx. It 's a good thing the Sphinx has broad shoulders. Whose fault is it that we starve to death, that prices go up, and that bands of looters swarm over the countryside? Why, the Sphinx's, of course. And the Sphinx is to blame because business is bad, and the government 's weak and one crash follows another; because the temples are glutted with rich offerings whilst mothers and wives are losing the bare necessities of life, and because foreigners with money to spend are leaving town. . . . Ah, you should see him, miss, how he gets up on the table, shouting, waving his arms, and stamping his feet; and then he denounces those who are responsible for it all, preaches revolt, eggs on the anarchists, shouting at the top of his voice names that are enough to get us all hanged. And between ourselves, miss . . . I know . . . you can take it from me . . . the Sphinx exists all right, but they 're making the most of it. You can be sure of that. What we want is a man, a dictator!

SPHINX. And . . . what about the brother of your young dictator?

MATRON. Oh! he 's another kettle of fish. He despises his brother, he despises me, he despises the gods, he despises everything. He makes you wonder where he can get hold of all he comes out with. He says, if you please, that the Sphinx would interest him if it killed for killing's sake, but that this Sphinx of ours is in league with the oracles, and so it doesn't interest him.

SPHINX. And your fourth son? When was it . . . ?

MATRON. I lost him nearly a year ago. He was just nineteen.

SPHINX. Poor woman. . . . What did he die of?

MATRON. Sphinx.

SPHINX. [*Gloomily.*] Ah! . . .

MATRON. It 's all very well for his younger brother to maintain he was a victim of police intrigues. . . . Oh, no! There 's no mistake, he died through the Sphinx. Ah, my dear! . . . if I live to be a hundred I 'll never forget that scene. One morning (he hadn't been home that night) I thought I heard him knock; I opened the front door and saw the underneath of his poor feet and then there followed a long way off, ever so far away, his poor little face, and in the back of his neck—look, just here—a large wound from which the blood had already stopped flowing. They brought him to me on a stretcher. Then I went: Ho! and fell, all of a heap. . . . A blow like that, you know, you don't get over in a hurry. You may be thankful you don't come from Thebes, thankful if you have no brothers. . . . You 're lucky. . . . My other boy, the orator, wants to avenge him. What 's the good? But he hates the priests, and my poor son was one of a series of human offerings.

SPHINX. Human offerings?

MATRON. To be sure. During the first months of the Sphinx the soldiers were sent to avenge the fine young men who were found dead all over the place, and they returned empty-handed. The Sphinx couldn't be found. Then, as there was a rumour that the Sphinx asked riddles, young people from the schools were sacrificed; and then the priests stated that the Sphinx demanded human offerings. At that, the youngest and weakest and fairest were chosen.

SPHINX. Poor woman!

MATRON. I tell you, my dear, what we want is a man of action. Queen Jocasta is still young. At a distance you would say she was twenty-nine or thirty. What we want is a ruler to fall from the sky, marry her, and kill the beast; someone to make an end of corruption, lock up Creon and Tiresias, improve the state of finance and liven up the people, someone who would care for the people and save us, yes, that 's it, save us. . . .

SON. Mummy!

MATRON. Sh!

SON. Mummy . . . I say, mummy, what does the Sphinx look like?

MATRON. I don't know. [*To the* SPHINX.] And what d' you think is the latest? They 're asking us to contribute our last farthings for a monument to those killed by the Sphinx! Will that bring them back to us, I should like to know?

SON. Mummy . . . what is the Sphinx like?

SPHINX. Poor little chap! His sister 's asleep. Come along. . . .

[*The son clings to the skirt of the* SPHINX.]

MATRON. Now don't worry the lady.

SPHINX. He 's all right. [*She strokes his neck.*]

SON. I say, mummy, is this lady the Sphinx?

MATRON. Little silly. [*To the* SPHINX.] I hope you don't mind. At that age children don't know what they 're saying. . . . [*She gets up.*] Oh my! [*She takes the little girl who is asleep in her arms.*] Come along now! Off we go, lazy-bones!

SON. Mummy, is that lady the Sphinx? I say, mummy, is the Sphinx that lady? Is that the Sphinx, mummy?

MATRON. Sh! Don't be silly. [*To the* SPHINX.] Well, good evening. Excuse my gossiping to you. I was glad to stop for a breather. . . . And . . . take care. [*Fanfare.*] Quickly. There 's the second bugle. After the third we 'll be shut out.

SPHINX. Go along, quickly. I 'll hurry my way. You 've put me on my guard.

MATRON. Believe me, we 'll not feel safe until there comes a man who will rid us of this scourge. [*She goes out left.*]

SON'S VOICE. I say, mummy, what 's the Sphinx look like? Why wasn't it that lady? Then what 's he like?

SPHINX. A scourge!

ANUBIS. [*Coming from among the ruins.*] That woman *would* have to come along here just now.

SPHINX. I 've been unhappy for the past two days, for two days now I 've been carrying on in this miserable way in the hope that this massacre would come to an end.

ANUBIS. Don't worry. You 're all right.

SPHINX. Listen. This is my secret wish and these the circumstances which would allow me to mount my pedestal for a last time. A young man will climb the hill, I shall fall in love with him. He 'll have no fear. And when I ask my question he will answer as to an equal. He will give *the answer,* d' you hear, Anubis, and I shall fall dead.

ANUBIS. Make no mistake: only your mortal form will fall dead.

SPHINX. And isn't that the form I should want to live in to make him happy!

ANUBIS. It 's nice to see that human form doesn't make a great goddess become a little woman.

SPHINX. You see how right I was. That bugle we heard was the last after all!

ANUBIS. Daughter of men! One is never finished with you. I tell you no! No! [*He leaves her side and mounts an overturned column.*] That was the second. When I 've heard another one you can go. Oh!

SPHINX. What is it?

ANUBIS. Bad news.

SPHINX. Someone coming?

ANUBIS. Yes. [*The* SPHINX *gets up beside* ANUBIS *and looks into the wings, right.*]

SPHINX. I can't! I can't and I won't question this young man. You needn't ask me to.

ANUBIS. I should say, if you 're like a young mortal, he 's like a young god.

SPHINX. What grace, Anubis, and what shoulders! He 's coming.

ANUBIS. I 'll hide. Don't forget you are the Sphinx. I 'm keeping my eye on you. I 'll be with you at the first sign.

SPHINX. Anubis, listen . . . quickly. . . .

ANUBIS. Sh! . . . He 's here. [ANUBIS *hides.*]

[*Oedipus enters up stage right. He is walking along with his eyes on the ground. He starts.*]

OEDIPUS. Oh! I 'm sorry. . . .

SPHINX. I startled you.

OEDIPUS. Well . . . no . . . I was dreaming, I was miles away, and suddenly, before me——

SPHINX. You took me for an animal.

OEDIPUS. Almost.

SPHINX. Almost? Almost an animal, that 's the Sphinx.

OEDIPUS. Yes, I know.

SPHINX. You admit you took me for the Sphinx. Thank you.

OEDIPUS. Oh! I soon realized my mistake.

SPHINX. Too kind. The truth of the matter is it can't be so amusing to find yourself suddenly face to face with the Sphinx, if you 're a young man.

OEDIPUS. And . . . if you 're a girl?

SPHINX. He doesn't attack girls.

OEDIPUS. Because girls avoid his haunts and are not supposed to go out alone when the light is failing.

SPHINX. You 'd do well to mind your own business, young man, and let me go my way.

OEDIPUS. Which way?

SPHINX. You 're simply amazing. Must I give my reasons for being out to a complete stranger?

OEDIPUS. And suppose I guessed your reason?

SPHINX. You amuse me.

OEDIPUS. Aren't you moved by curiosity, the curiosity which is raging amongst all modern young women, the curiosity to know what the Sphinx looks like? If he has claws, or a beak, or wings, and whether he takes after the tiger or the vulture?

SPHINX. Oh, come, come!

OEDIPUS. The Sphinx is the criminal of the day. Who 's seen him? No one. Fabulous rewards are promised to the first person who discovers him. The faint of heart tremble. Young men die. . . . But a girl, couldn't she venture into the forbidden area, setting orders at defiance, and dare what no reasonable person would dare, to unearth the monster, surprise him in his lair, get a view of him?

SPHINX. You 're on the wrong track, I tell you. I'm going back to a relative who lives in the country, and as I had forgotten the very existence of a Sphinx and that the outskirts of Thebes are not safe, I was resting a moment on the stones of these old ruins. You see how far you 're out.

OEDIPUS. What a pity! For some time now I 've only run across people as dull as ditch water; so I hoped for something more unusual. Pardon me.

SPHINX. Good evening!

OEDIPUS. Good evening!

[*They pass each other. But* OEDIPUS *turns back.*]

I say! I may appear unpleasant, but I honestly can't bring myself to believe you. Your presence in these ruins still intrigues me enormously.

SPHINX. You 're simply incredible.

OEDIPUS. Because if you were like other girls you would already have made off as fast as your legs would carry you.

SPHINX. My dear boy, you 're quite absurd.

OEDIPUS. It seemed to me so marvellous to find in a girl a worthy competitor.

SPHINX. A competitor? Then you are looking for the Sphinx?

OEDIPUS. Looking for him? Let me tell you, I 've been on the march for a whole month. Probably that 's why I appeared ill-mannered just now. I was so wild with excitement as I drew near Thebes that I could have shouted my enthusiasm to the merest block of stone, when, instead of a block of stone, what stands in my path but a girl in white? So I couldn't help talking to her about what was uppermost in my mind and thinking she must have the same purpose as myself.

SPHINX. But surely, a moment ago, when you saw me spring out of the shadow, you didn't seem to me very much on the alert for a man who wants to measure his strength with the enemy.

OEDIPUS. That is true. I was dreaming of fame, and the beast would have caught me unawares. To-morrow in Thebes I shall equip myself and the hunt will begin.

SPHINX. You love fame?

OEDIPUS. I'm not sure about that. I like trampling crowds, trumpet calls, flying banners, waving palm branches, the sun, gold and purple, happiness, luck—you know, to live!

SPHINX. Is that what you call living?

OEDIPUS. Don't you?

SPHINX. No, I must say I have quite a different idea of life.

OEDIPUS. What 's that?

SPHINX. To love. To be loved by the one you love.

OEDIPUS. I shall love my people and they me.

SPHINX. The public square is not a home.

OEDIPUS. The public square has nothing to do with it. The people of Thebes are looking for a man. If I kill the Sphinx I shall be that man. Queen Jocasta is a widow; I shall marry her. . . .

SPHINX. A woman who might be your mother!

OEDIPUS. The main thing is that she is not.

SPHINX. Do you imagine that a queen and her people would give themselves up to the first comer?

OEDIPUS. Would you call the vanquisher of the Sphinx a first comer? I know the promised reward is the queen. Don't laugh at me. Please listen. You must. I must prove that my dream isn't merely a dream. My father is King of Corinth. My father and mother were already old when I was born and I lived in a court of gloom. Too much fuss and comfort produced in me a feverish longing for adventure. I began to pine and waste away, when one evening a drunk shouted at me that I was a bastard and that I was usurping the place of a legitimate son. Blows and abuse followed, and the next day, despite the tears of Merope and Polybius, I decided to visit the sanctuaries and question the gods. They all replied with the same oracle: You will murder your father and marry your mother.

SPHINX. What?

OEDIPUS. Yes, I mean it. At first this oracle fills you with horror, but I 'm not so easily imposed on! I soon saw how nonsensical the whole thing was. I took into account the ways of the gods and the priests, and I came to this conclusion: either the oracle hid a less serious meaning which had to be discovered, or the priests who communicate from temple to temple by means of birds found it perhaps to their advantage to put this oracle into the mouth of the gods and to weaken my chances of coming into power. Briefly, I soon forgot my fears, and, I may say, used this threat of parricide and incest as an excuse to flee the court and satisfy my thirst for the unknown.

SPHINX. Now it 's my turn to feel dazed. I 'm sorry I rather made fun of you. Will you forgive me, prince?

OEDIPUS. Give me your hand. May I ask your name? Mine is Oedipus; I 'm nineteen.

SPHINX. Oh, what does it matter about mine, Oedipus? You must like illustrious names. . . . That of a little girl of seventeen wouldn't interest you.

OEDIPUS. That 's unkind.

SPHINX. You adore fame. Yet I should have thought the surest way of foiling the oracle would be to marry a woman younger than yourself.

OEDIPUS. That doesn't sound like you. That 's more like a mother of Thebes where marriageable young men are few.

SPHINX. And that 's not like you either. That was a gross, common thing to say.

OEDIPUS. So, I shall have walked the roads past mountain and stream merely to take a wife who will quickly become a Sphinx, worse than that, a Sphinx with breasts and claws!

SPHINX. Oedipus. . . .

OEDIPUS. No, thank you! I prefer to try my luck. Take this belt: with that you will be able to get to me when I have killed the beast. [*Business.*]

SPHINX. Have you ever killed?

OEDIPUS. Yes, once. At the cross-roads of Delphi and Daulis. I was walking along like a moment ago. A carriage was approaching driven by an old man with an escort of four servants. When I was on a level with the horses one of them reared and knocked me into one of these servants. The fool tried to strike me, I aimed a blow at him with my stick, but he dodged down and I caught the old man on the temple. He fell and the horses bolted, dragging him along. I ran after them, the servants were terrified and fled; I found myself alone with the bleeding body of the old man and the horses who screamed as they rolled about entangled, and broke their legs. It was dreadful . . . dreadful. . . .

SPHINX. Yes, isn't it . . . it 's dreadful to kill.

OEDIPUS. Oh, well, it wasn't my fault and I think no more about it. The thing is to clear all obstacles, to wear blinkers, and not to give way to self-pity. Besides, there is my star.

SPHINX. Then farewell, Oedipus. I am of the sex which is disturbing to heroes. Let us go our ways, we can have little in common.

OEDIPUS. Disturbing to heroes, eh! You have a high opinion of your sex.

SPHINX. And . . . supposing the Sphinx killed you?

OEDIPUS. His death depends, if I 'm not mistaken, on questions which I must answer. If I guess right he won't even touch me, he 'll just die.

SPHINX. And if you do not guess right?

OEDIPUS. Thanks to my unhappy childhood I have pursued studies which give me a great start over the riff-raff of Thebes.

SPHINX. I 'm glad to hear it.

OEDIPUS. And I don't think this simple-minded monster is expecting to be confronted by a pupil of the best scholars of Corinth.

SPHINX. You have an answer to everything. A pity, for, I own, Oedipus, I have a soft spot for weak people, and I should like to have found you wanting.

OEDIPUS. Farewell.

[*The* SPHINX *makes one step as if to rush in pursuit of* OEDIPUS, *stops, but cannot resist the call. Until her* 'I! I!' *the* SPHINX *does not take her eyes off those of* OEDIPUS; *she moves as it were round this immobile, steady, vast gaze from under eyelids which do not flicker.*]

SPHINX. Oedipus!

OEDIPUS. Did you call me?

SPHINX. One last word. For the moment does nothing else occupy your mind, nothing else fire your heart, nothing stir your spirit save the Sphinx?

OEDIPUS. Nothing else, for the moment.

SPHINX. And he . . . or she who brought you into his presence. . . . I mean who would help you. . . . I mean who may perhaps know something to help bring about this meeting . . . would he or she in your eyes assume such prestige that you would be touched and moved?

OEDIPUS. Naturally, but what does all this mean?

SPHINX. And supposing I, I myself, were to divulge a secret, a tremendous secret?

OEDIPUS. You 're joking!

SPHINX. A secret which would allow you to enter into contact with the enigma of enigmas, with the human beast, with the singing bitch, as it is called, with the Sphinx?

OEDIPUS. What! You? You? Did I guess aright, and has your curiosity led you to discover . . . ? No! How stupid of me. This is a woman's trick to make me turn back.

SPHINX. Good-bye.

OEDIPUS. Oh! Forgive me! . . .

SPHINX. Too late.

OEDIPUS. I 'm kneeling; a simple fool who begs forgiveness.

SPHINX. You 're a fatuous young man who is sorry to have lost his chance and is trying to get it back.

OEDIPUS. I am and I 'm ashamed. Look, I believe you, I 'll listen. But if you have played me a trick I shall drag you by the hair and grip you till the blood flows.

SPHINX. Come here. [*She leads him opposite the pedestal.*] Shut your eyes. Don't cheat. Count up to fifty.

OEDIPUS. [*With his eyes shut.*] Take care!

SPHINX. It 's your turn to do that.

[OEDIPUS *counts. One feels that something extraordinary is happening. The* SPHINX *bounds across the ruins, disappears behind a wall and reappears in the real pedestal, that is, she seems to be fastened on to the pedestal, the bust resting on the elbows and looking straight ahead, whereas the actress is really standing, and only lets her bust appear and her arms in spotted gloves with her hands grasping the edge; out of the broken wing suddenly grow two immense, pale, luminous wings and the fragment of statue completes her, prolonging her, and appearing to belong to her.* OEDIPUS *is heard counting:* 'Forty-seven, forty-eight, forty-nine,' *then he makes a pause and shouts:* 'Fifty.' *He turns round.*]

OEDIPUS. You!

SPHINX. [*In a high distant voice, joyous and terrible.*] Yes, I! I, the Sphinx!

OEDIPUS. I 'm dreaming!

SPHINX. You are no dreamer, Oedipus. You know what you want, and did want. Silence. Here I command. Approach.

[OEDIPUS, *with his arms held stiffly by his body as if paralysed, tries frantically to free himself.*]

Come forward. [OEDIPUS *falls on his knees.*] As your legs refuse their help, jump, hop. . . . It 's good for a hero to make himself ridiculous. Come along! Move yourself! Don't worry, there 's nobody to see you.

[OEDIPUS, *writhing with anger, moves forward on his knees.*]

That 's it. Stop! And now. . . .

OEDIPUS. And now, I 'm beginning to understand your methods, what moves you make to lure and slay.

SPHINX. . . . And now, I am going to give you a demonstration, I 'm going to show you what would happen in this place, Oedipus, if you were any ordinary handsome youth from Thebes, and if you hadn't the privilege of pleasing me.

OEDIPUS. I know what your pleasantries are worth.

[*He knits up all the muscles of his body. It is obvious he is struggling against a charm.*]

SPHINX. Yield! Don't try to screw up your muscles and resist. Relax! If you resist you will only make my task more delicate and I might hurt you.

OEDIPUS. I shall resist! [*He shuts his eyes and turns his head away.*]

SPHINX. You need not shut your eyes or turn away your head. For it is not by my look nor by my voice that I work. A blind man is not so dexterous, the net of a gladiator not so swift, nor lightning so fine, nor a coachman so stiff, nor a cow so weighty, nor a schoolboy working at his sums with his tongue out so good, nor a ship so hung with rigging, so spread with sails, secure and buoyant; a judge is not so incorruptible, insects so voracious, birds so bloodthirsty, the egg so nocturnal, Chinese executioners so ingenious, the heart so fitful, the trickster's hand so deft, the stars so fateful, the snake moistening its prey with saliva so attentive. I secrete, I spin, I pay out, I wind, I unwind, I rewind, in such a way that it is enough for me to desire these knots for them to be made, to think about them for them to be pulled tight or slackened. My thread is so fine it escapes the eye, so fluid you might think you were suffering from a poison, so hard a quiver on my part would break your limbs, so highly strung a bow stroked between us would make music in the air; curled like the sea, the column, and the rose, muscled like the octopus, contrived like the settings of our dreams, above all invisible, unseen, and majestic like the blood circulating in statues, my thread coils round you in fantastic patterns with the volubility of honey falling upon honey.

OEDIPUS. Let me go!

SPHINX. And I speak, I work, I wind, I unwind, I calculate, I meditate, I weave, I winnow, I knit, I plait, I cross, I go over it again and again, I tie and untie and tie again, retaining the smallest knots that I shall later on have to untie for you on pain of death; I pull tight, I loosen, I make mistakes and go back, I hesitate, I correct, entangle and disentangle, unlace, lace up and begin afresh; and I adjust, I agglutinate, I pinion, I strap, I shackle, I heap up my effects, till you feel that from the tip of your toes to the top of your head you are wrapped round by all the muscles of a reptile whose slightest breath constricts yours and makes you inert like the arm on which you fall asleep.

OEDIPUS. [*In a weak voice.*] Let me be! Mercy! . . .

SPHINX. And you will cry for mercy, and you won't have to be ashamed of that, for you won't be the first. I have heard prouder than you call for their mothers, and I have seen more insolent than you burst into tears; and the more silent are even weaker than the rest: they faint before the end and I have to minister to them after the fashion of embalmers in whose hands the dead are drunk men no longer able to stand on their feet!

OEDIPUS. Merope! . . . Mother!

SPHINX. Then I should command you to advance a little closer, and I should help you by loosening your limbs. So! And I should question you. I should ask you, for example: What animal is it that goes on four legs in the morning, in the afternoon on two, and in the evening on three? And you would cudgel your brains, till in the end your mind would settle on a little medal you won as a child, or you would repeat a number, or count the stars between these two broken columns; and I should make you return to the point by revealing the enigma.

Man is the animal who walks on four legs when he is a child, on two when he is full-grown, and when he is old with the help of a stick as a third leg.

OEDIPUS. How idiotic!

SPHINX. You would shout: How idiotic! You all say that. Then, since that cry only confirms your failure, I should call my assistant, Anubis. Anubis!

[ANUBIS *appears and stands on the right of the pedestal with folded arms; and his head turned to one side.*]

OEDIPUS. Oh, miss! . . . Oh, Sphinx! . . . Oh, Sphinx, please don't! No! No!

SPHINX. And I should make you go down on your knees. Go on. . . . Go on . . . that 's right. . . . Do as you 're told. And you 'd bend your head . . . and Anubis would bound forward. He would open his wolf-like jaws! [OEDIPUS *utters a cry.*] I said: *would* bend, *would* bound forward, *would* open. . . . Haven't I always been careful to express myself in that mood? Why that cry? Why that horrified expression? It was a demonstration, Oedipus, simply a demonstration. You 're free.

OEDIPUS. Free!

[*He moves an arm, a leg. . . . He gets up, he reels, he puts his hand to his head.*]

ANUBIS. Pardon me, Sphinx, this man cannot leave here without undergoing the test.

SPHINX. But . . .

ANUBIS. Question him.

OEDIPUS. But . . .

ANUBIS. Silence! Question this man.

[*A silence.* OEDIPUS *turns his back and remains motionless.*]

SPHINX. I 'll question him. . . . All right. . . . I 'll question him. . . . [*With a last look of surprise at* ANUBIS.] What animal is it that walks on four legs in the morning, on two in the afternoon, and on three in the evening?

OEDIPUS. Why, man, of course! He crawls along on four legs when he 's little, and walks on two legs when he is big, and when he 's old he helps himself along with a stick as a third leg.

[*The* SPHINX *sways on her pedestal.*]

[*Making his way to the left.*] Victory!

[*He rushes out left. The* SPHINX *slips down into the column, disappears behind the wall, and reappears wingless.*]

SPHINX. Oedipus! Where is he? Where is he?

ANUBIS. Gone, flown. He is running breathlessly to proclaim his victory.

SPHINX. Without so much as a look my way, without a movement betraying feeling, without a sign of gratitude.

ANUBIS. Did you expect anything else?

SPHINX. Oh, you fool! Then he has not understood a single thing.

ANUBIS. Not a single thing.

SPHINX. Kss! Kss! Anubis. . . . Here, here, look, after him, quickly, bite him, Anubis, bite him!

ANUBIS. And now it 's all going to begin afresh. You 're a woman again and I 'm a dog.

SPHINX. I 'm sorry. I lost my head, I 'm mad. My hands are trembling. I 'm like fire. I wish I could catch him again in one bound, I 'd spit in his face, claw him with my nails, disfigure him, trample on him, castrate him, and flay him alive!

ANUBIS. That 's more like yourself.

SPHINX. Help me! Avenge me! Don't stand there idle!

ANUBIS. Do you really hate this man?

SPHINX. I do.

ANUBIS. The worst that could happen to him would seem too good to you?

SPHINX. It would.

ANUBIS. [*Holding up the* SPHINX'S *dress.*] Look at the folds in this cloth. Crush them together. Now if you pierce this bundle with a pin, remove the pin, smooth the cloth till all trace of the old creases disappears, do you think a simple country loon would believe that the innumerable holes recurring at intervals result from a single thrust of a pin?

SPHINX. Certainly not.

ANUBIS. Human time is a fold of eternity. For us time does not exist. From his birth to his death the life of Oedipus is spread flat before my eyes, with its series of episodes.

SPHINX. Speak, speak, Anubis, I 'm burning to hear. What d' you see?

ANUBIS. In the past Jocasta and Laïus had a child. As the oracle gave out that this child would be a scourge. . . .

SPHINX. A scourge!

ANUBIS. A monster, an unclean beast. . . .

SPHINX. Quicker, quicker!

ANUBIS. Jocasta bound it up and sent it into the mountains to get lost. A shepherd of Polybius found it, took it away, and, as Polybius and Merope were lamenting a sterile marriage . . .

SPHINX. I can't contain myself for joy.

ANUBIS. They adopted it. Oedipus, son of Laïus, killed Laïus where the three roads cross.

SPHINX. The old man.

ANUBIS. Son of Jocasta, he will marry Jocasta.

SPHINX. And to think I said to him: 'She might be your mother.' And he replied: 'The main thing is that she is not.' Anubis! Anubis! It 's too good to be true. . . .

ANUBIS. He will have two sons who will kill each other, and two daughters, one of whom will hang herself. Jocasta will hang herself. . . .

SPHINX. Stop! What more could I hope for? Think, Anubis: the wedding of Jocasta and Oedipus! The union of mother and son. . . . And will he know soon?

ANUBIS. Soon enough.

SPHINX. What a moment to live! I have a foretaste of its delights. Oh, to be present!

ANUBIS. You will be.

SPHINX. Is that true? . . .

ANUBIS. I think the moment has come to remind you who you are and what a ridiculous distance separates you from this little body which is listening to me. You who have assumed the role of Sphinx! You, the Goddess of Goddesses! You, the greatest of the great! The implacable! Vengeance! Nemesis! [ANUBIS *prostrates himself.*]

SPHINX. Nemesis. . . . [*She turns her back to the audience and remains a while erect, making a cross with her arms. Suddenly she comes out of this hypnotic state and rushes up stage.*] Once more, if he is in sight, I should like to feed my hatred, I want to see him run from one trap to another like a stunned rat.

ANUBIS. Is that the cry of the awakening goddess or of the jealous woman?

SPHINX. Of the goddess, Anubis, of the goddess. Our gods have cast me for the part of the Sphinx, and I shall show myself worthy of it.

ANUBIS. At last!

[*The* SPHINX *looks down on the plain, leaning over to examine it. Suddenly she turns round. The last trace of the greatness and fury which had transformed her has disappeared.*]

Dog! you lied to me.

ANUBIS. I?

SPHINX. Yes, you! Liar! Liar! Look along the road. Oedipus is coming back, he 's running, he 's flying, he loves me, he has understood!

ANUBIS. You know very well of what goes with his success and why the Sphinx is not dead.

SPHINX. Look how he jumps from rock to rock, just as my heart leaps in my breast.

ANUBIS. Convinced of his triumphs and your death this young fool has just realized that in his haste he 's forgotten the most important thing.

SPHINX. Mean wretch! Do you mean to tell me he wants to find me dead?

ANUBIS. Not you, my little fury: the Sphinx. He thinks he 's killed the Sphinx; he will have to prove it. Thebes won't be satisfied with a fisherman's yarn.

SPHINX. You 're lying. I 'll tell him everything. I 'll warn him. I 'll save him. I 'll turn him away from Jocasta, from that miserable town. . . .

ANUBIS. Take care.

SPHINX. I shall speak.

ANUBIS. He 's coming. Let him speak first.

[OEDIPUS, *out of breath, comes in down stage left. He sees the* SPHINX *and* ANUBIS *standing side by side.*]

OEDIPUS. [*Saluting.*] I 'm glad to see what good health the immortals enjoy after their death.

SPHINX. What brings you back here?

OEDIPUS. The collecting of my due.

[*Angry movement on the part of* ANUBIS *towards* OEDIPUS, *who steps back.*]

SPHINX. Anubis! [*With a gesture she orders him to leave her alone. He goes behind the ruins. To* OEDIPUS.] You shall have it. Stay where you are. The loser is a woman. She asks one last favour of her master.

OEDIPUS. Excuse me for being on my guard, but you 've taught me to distrust your feminine wiles.

SPHINX. Ah! I was the Sphinx. No, Oedipus. . . . You will bear my mortal remains to Thebes and the future will reward you . . . according to your deserts. No . . . I ask you merely to let me disappear behind this wall so that I may take off this body in which, I must confess, I have, for some little while, felt rather . . . cramped.

OEDIPUS. Very well. But be quick. At the last bugles . . . [*The bugles are heard.*] You see, I speak of them and they are sounded. I must waste no time.

SPHINX. [*Hidden.*] Thebes will not leave a hero standing at her gates.

VOICE OF ANUBIS. [*From behind the ruins.*] Hurry, hurry. It looks as though you 're inventing excuses and dawdling on purpose.

SPHINX. [*Hidden.*] Am I the first, God of the Dead, whom you 've had to drag by the clothes?

OEDIPUS. You 're trying to gain time, Sphinx.

SPHINX. [*Hidden.*] So much the better for you, Oedipus. My haste might have served you ill. A serious difficulty occurs to me. If you bear into Thebes the body of a girl instead of the monster which the people expect, the crowd will stone you.

OEDIPUS. That 's true! Women are simply amazing; they think of everything.

SPHINX. [*Hidden.*] They call me: The virgin with the claws. . . . The singing bitch. . . . They will want to identify my fangs. Don't be alarmed. Anubis! My faithful dog! Listen, since our faces are only shadows, I want you to give me your jackal's head.

OEDIPUS. Splendid idea!

ANUBIS. [*Hidden.*] Do what you like, so long as this shameful play-acting may come to an end and you may become yourself once more.

SPHINX. [*Hidden.*] I shan't be long.

OEDIPUS. I shall count up to fifty as I did before. I 'll have my own back.

ANUBIS. [*Hidden.*] Sphinx, Sphinx, what are you waiting for?

SPHINX. Now I 'm ugly, Anubis. A monster! . . . Poor boy . . . supposing I frighten him. . . .

ANUBIS. Don't worry, he won't even see you.

SPHINX. Is he blind then?

ANUBIS. Many men are born blind and only realize it the day a home-truth hits them between the eyes.

OEDIPUS. Fifty.

ANUBIS. [*Hidden.*] Go on. . . . Go on. . . .

SPHINX. [*Hidden.*] Farewell, Sphinx.

[*From behind the wall comes the staggering figure of a girl with a jackal's head. She waves her arms in the air and falls.*]

OEDIPUS. About time too! [*He rushes forward, not stopping to look, lifts the body, and takes a stand down stage right. He carries the body before him on his outstretched arms.*] No, not like that! I should look like that tragedian I saw in Corinth playing the part of a king carrying the body of his son. The pose was pompous and moved no one. [*He tries holding the body under his left arm; behind the ruins on the mound appear two giants forms covered with rainbow veils: the gods.*] No! I should be ridiculous. Like a hunter going home empty-handed after killing his dog.

ANUBIS. [*The form on the right.*] To free your goddess's body of all human contamination, perhaps it might be as well for this Oedipus to disinfect you by bestowing on himself at least a title of demigod.

NEMESIS. [*The form on the left.*] He is so young. . . .

OEDIPUS. Hercules! Hercules threw the lion over his shoulder! . . . [*He puts the body over his shoulder.*] Yes, over my shoulder. Over my shoulder! Like a demigod!

ANUBIS. [*Veiled.*] Isn't he simply *incredible!*

OEDIPUS. [*Moving off towards the left, taking two steps after each of his thanksgivings.*] I have killed the unclean beast.

NEMESIS. [*Veiled.*] Anubis . . . I feel very ill at ease.

ANUBIS. We must go.

OEDIPUS. I have saved the town!

ANUBIS. Come along, mistress, let us go.

OEDIPUS. I shall marry Queen Jocasta!

NEMESIS. [*Veiled.*] Poor, poor, poor mankind! . . . I can stand no more, Anubis. . . . I can't breathe. Let us leave the earth.

OEDIPUS. I shall be king!

[*A murmur envelops the two huge forms. The veils fly round them. Day breaks. Cocks crow.*]

ACT III

The Wedding Night

THE VOICE: The coronation and nuptial celebrations have been going on since dawn. The crowd has just acclaimed the queen and the conqueror of the Sphinx for the last time.

Every one goes home. In the little square of the royal palace now rises only the slight murmur of a fountain. Oedipus and Jocasta find privacy at last in the nuptial chamber. They are very tired and heavy with sleep. In spite of a few hints and civilities on the part of destiny, sleep will prevent them from seeing the trap which is closing on them for ever.

ACT III

THE WEDDING NIGHT

SCENE: *The platform represents* JOCASTA'S *bedroom, which is as red as a little butcher's shop amid the town buildings. A broad bed covered with white furs. At the foot of the bed an animal's skin. On the right of the bed a cradle. On the right fore-stage a latticed bay window, looking on to the square of Thebes. On the left fore-stage a movable mirror of human size.* OEDIPUS *and* JOCASTA *are wearing their coronation costumes. From the moment the curtain rises they move about in the slow motion induced by extreme fatigue.*

JOCASTA. Phew! I 'm done! You are so full of life, dear! I am afraid, for you, this room will become a cage, a prison.

OEDIPUS. My dear love! A scented bedroom, a woman's room, yours! After this killing day, those processions, that ceremonial, that crowd which still clamoured for us under our very windows. . . .

JOCASTA. Not clamoured for us . . . for you, dear.

OEDIPUS. Same thing.

JOCASTA. You must be truthful, my young conqueror. They hate me. My dress annoys them, my accent annoys them, they are annoyed by my blackened eyelashes, my rouge, and my vivaciousness!

OEDIPUS. It 's Creon who annoys them! The cold, hard, inhuman Creon! I shall make your star rise again. Ah! Jocasta! What a magnificent programme!

JOCASTA. It was high time you came. I 'm exhausted.

OEDIPUS. Your room a prison! Your room, dear . . . and our bed.

JOCASTA. Do you want me to remove the cradle? After the death of the child I had to have it near me, I couldn't sleep. . . . I was too lonely. . . . But now . . .

OEDIPUS. [*In an indistinct voice.*] But now . . .

JOCASTA. What?

OEDIPUS. I said . . . I said . . . that it 's he . . . he . . . the dog . . . I mean . . . the dog who won't . . . the dog . . . the fountain dog. . . . [*His head droops.*]

JOCASTA. Oedipus! Oedipus!

OEDIPUS. [*Awakens, startled.*] What?

JOCASTA. You were falling asleep, dear!

OEDIPUS. Me? Never.

JOCASTA. Oh, yes, you were, dear. You were telling me about a dog who won't . . . a fountain dog. And I was listening.

[*She laughs and herself seems to be becoming vague.*]

OEDIPUS. Nonsense!

JOCASTA. I was asking you if you wanted me to remove the cradle, if it worries you.

OEDIPUS. Am I such a kid as to fear this pretty muslin ghost? On the contrary it will be the cradle of my luck. My luck will grow in it beside our love until it can be used for our first son. So you see! . . .

JOCASTA. My poor love. . . . You 're dropping with fatigue and here we stand . . . [*Same business as with* OEDIPUS.] . . . stand on this wall. . . .

OEDIPUS. What wall?

JOCASTA. This rampart wall. [*She starts.*] A wall. . . What? I . . . I . . . [*Haggard.*] What 's happening?

OEDIPUS. [*Laughing.*] Well, this time it 's you dreaming. We 're tired out, my poor sweet.

JOCASTA. I was asleep? Did I talk?

OEDIPUS. We *are* a pretty pair! Here I go telling you about fountain-dogs, and you tell me about rampart walls: and this is our wedding night! Listen, Jocasta, if I happen to fall asleep again (Are you listening?), do please awaken me, shake me, and if you fall asleep I 'll do the same for you. This one night of all must not founder in sleep. That would be too sad.

JOCASTA. You crazy darling you, why? We have all our life before us.

OEDIPUS. Maybe, but I don't want sleep to spoil the miracle of passing this joyous night alone, unutterably alone with you. I suggest we remove these heavy clothes, and as we 're not expecting any one——

JOCASTA. Listen, my darling boy, you 'll be cross . . .

OEDIPUS. Jocasta, don't tell me there 's still some official duty on the programme!

JOCASTA. While my women are doing my hair, etiquette demands that you receive a visit.

OEDIPUS. A visit? At this hour?

JOCASTA. A visit . . . a visit . . . a purely formal visit.

OEDIPUS. In this room?

JOCASTA. In this room.

OEDIPUS. From whom?

JOCASTA. Now don't get cross. From Tiresias.

OEDIPUS. Tiresias? I refuse!

JOCASTA. Listen, dear. . . .

OEDIPUS. That 's the limit! Tiresias playing the part of the family pouring out their farewell advice. How comic! I shall refuse his visit.

JOCASTA. You crazy dear, *I* am asking you to. It 's an old custom in Thebes that the high priest must in some way bless the royal marriage bonds. And besides, Tiresias is our old uncle, our watch-dog. I am very fond of him, Oedipus, and Laïus adored him. He is nearly blind. It would be unfortunate if you hurt his feelings and set him against our love.

OEDIPUS. That 's all very well . . . in the middle of the night. . . .

JOCASTA. Do! Please, for our sake and the sake of the future. It 's essential. See him for five minutes, but see him and listen to him. I ask you to. [*She kisses him.*]

OEDIPUS. I warn you I shan't let him sit down.

JOCASTA. I love you, dear. [*Long kiss.*] I shall not be long. [*At the right-hand exit.*] I am going to let him know he can come. Be patient. Do it for my sake. Think of me. [*She goes out.*]

[OEDIPUS, *alone, looks at himself in the mirror and tries attitudes.* TIRESIAS *comes in left, unheard.* OEDIPUS *sees him in the middle of the room and turns about face.*]

OEDIPUS. I am listening.

TIRESIAS. Steady, my lord. Who told you I had saved up a sermon for your especial benefit?

OEDIPUS. No one, Tiresias, no one. But I don't suppose you find it pleasant acting as kill-joy. I suggest you are waiting for me to pretend I have heard your words of counsel. I shall bow, and you will give me the accolade. That would be enough for us in our tired state and at the same time custom would be satisfied. Have I guessed right?

TIRESIAS. It is perhaps correct that there is at the bottom of this procedure a sort of custom, but for that, it would be necessary to have a royal marriage with all the dynastic, mechanical, and, I admit, even irksome business which that entails. No, my lord. Unforeseen events bring us face to face with new problems and duties. And you will agree, I think, that your coronation, and your marriage, appear in a form which is difficult to classify, and does not fit into any code.

OEDIPUS. No one could say more graciously that I have crashed on Thebes like a tile from a roof.

TIRESIAS. My lord!

OEDIPUS. Let me tell you that things fitting neatly into categories reek of death. What we want, Tiresias, is not to fit, but to make a new departure. That 's the sign of masterpieces and heroes. And that 's the way to astonish and to rule.

TIRESIAS. Right! Then you will admit that I myself, by playing a part outside the ceremonial sphere, am also making a new departure.

OEDIPUS. To the point, Tiresias, to the point.

TIRESIAS. Very well. I shall come straight to the point and speak with all frankness. My lord, your auguries look black, very black. I must put you on your guard.

OEDIPUS. There! Just as I expected! Anything else would have surprised me. This is not the first time the oracles have been violently against me and my audacity has thwarted them.

TIRESIAS. Do you believe they can be thwarted?

OEDIPUS. I am the living proof of it. And even if my marriage upsets the gods, what about your promises, your freeing of the town, and the death of the Sphinx? And why should the gods have pushed me on as far as this room if this marriage displeases them?

TIRESIAS. Do you think you can solve the problem of free will in a minute! Ah, power, I fear, is going to your head!

OEDIPUS. You mean, power is slipping from your hands.

TIRESIAS. Take care! You are speaking to a high priest.

OEDIPUS. Take care yourself, high priest. Must I remind you that you are speaking to your king?

TIRESIAS. To the husband of my queen, my lord.

OEDIPUS. Jocasta notified me a little while ago that her power is to pass into my hands, in full. Run and tell that to your master.

TIRESIAS. I serve only the gods.

OEDIPUS. Well, if you prefer that way of putting it, say that to the person who is awaiting your return.

TIRESIAS. Headstrong youth! You don't understand me.

OEDIPUS. I understand perfectly well: an adventurer is in your way. I expect you hope I found the Sphinx dead on my path. The real conqueror must have sold it to me, like those hunters who buy the hare from a poacher. And supposing I have paid for the mortal remains, whom will you find ultimately as the conqueror of the Sphinx? The same type of person who has been threatening you every minute and preventing Creon from sleeping: a poor private soldier whom the crowd will bear in triumph and who will claim his due . . . [*Shouting.*] *his due!*

TIRESIAS. He would not dare.

OEDIPUS. Ah, you see! I have made you say it. That 's the secret of the intrigue. There go your beautiful promises. That is what you were counting on.

TIRESIAS. The queen is more to me than my own daughter. I must watch over her and defend her. She is weak, credulous, romantic. . . .

OEDIPUS. You are insulting her.

TIRESIAS. I love her.

OEDIPUS. She is in need of no one's love but mine.

TIRESIAS. About this love, Oedipus, I demand an explanation. Do you love the queen?

OEDIPUS. With all my being.

TIRESIAS. I mean: do you love to take her in your arms?

OEDIPUS. I love most of all to be taken in her arms.

TIRESIAS. I appreciate that delicate distinction. You are young, Oedipus, very young. Jocasta might be your mother. I know, oh, I know, you are going to reply——

OEDIPUS. I am going to reply that I have always dreamed of such a love, an almost motherly love.

TIRESIAS. Oedipus, aren't you confusing love and love of glory? Would you love Jocasta if she were not on a throne?

OEDIPUS. A stupid question which is always being asked. Would Jocasta love me if I was old, ugly, and had not appeared out of the unknown? Do you fancy you cannot be infected by love through touching purple and gold? Are not the privileges of which you speak of the very substance of Jocasta, an organic part of her? We have been each other's from all eternity. Within her body lie fold after fold of a purple mantle which is much more regal than the one she fastens on her shoulders. I love and adore her, Tiresias. At her side I seem to occupy at last my proper place. She is my wife, she is my queen. I possess her, I shall keep her, I shall find her again, and neither by prayers nor threats can you drag from me obedience to orders from heaven knows where.

TIRESIAS. Think it over again, Oedipus. The omens and my own wisdom give me every reason to fear this wild marriage. Think it over.

OEDIPUS. Rather late, don't you think?

TIRESIAS. Have you had experience of women?

OEDIPUS. Not the slightest. And to complete your astonishment and cover myself with ridicule in your eyes, I am a virgin.

TIRESIAS. You!

OEDIPUS. The high priest of a capital is astonished that a country boy should put all his pride in keeping himself pure for a single offering. You would, no doubt, have preferred a degenerate prince, a puppet, so that Creon and the priests could work the strings.

TIRESIAS. You are going too far!

OEDIPUS. Must I order you again? . . .

TIRESIAS. Order? Has pride sent you mad?

OEDIPUS. Don't put me into a rage! My patience is at an end, my temper is ungovernable, and I am capable of any unpremeditated act.

TIRESIAS. What arrogance! . . . Weak and arrogant!

OEDIPUS. You will have brought it on yourself.

[*He throws himself upon* TIRESIAS, *seizing him by the neck.*]

TIRESIAS. Let me go. . . . Have you no shame? . . .

OEDIPUS. You are afraid that I could, from your face, there, there, close up, and in your blind man's eyes, read the real truth about your behaviour.

TIRESIAS. Murderer! Sacrilege!

OEDIPUS. Murderer! I ought to be. . . . One day I shall probably have to repent for this foolish respect, and if I dared . . . Oh, oh! Why! Gods, look here . . . here . . . in his blind man's eyes, I had no idea it was possible.

TIRESIAS. Let me go! Brute!

OEDIPUS. The future! My future, as in a crystal bowl.

TIRESIAS. You will repent. . . .

OEDIPUS. I see, I see. . . . Soothsayer, you have lied! I shall marry Jocasta. . . . A happy life, rich, prosperous, two sons . . . daughters . . . and Jocasta still as beautiful, still the same, in love, a mother in a palace of happiness. . . . Now it 's not so clear, not clear. I want to see! It 's your fault, soothsayer. . . . I want to see! [*He shakes him.*]

TIRESIAS. Accursed!

OEDIPUS. [*Suddenly recoiling, letting* TIRESIAS *go, and putting his hands over his eyes.*] Oh, filthy wretch! I am blind. He 's thrown pepper at me. Jocasta! Help! Help! . . .

TIRESIAS. I threw nothing, I swear. You are punished for your sacrilege.

OEDIPUS. [*Writhing on the ground.*] You lie!

TIRESIAS. You wanted to read by force the secrets my diseased eyes hold and that I myself have not yet interpreted; and you are punished.

OEDIPUS. Water, water, quickly, it 's burning me. . . .

TIRESIAS. [*Laying his hands over* OEDIPUS'S *face.*] There, there. . . . Keep quiet. . . . I forgive you. Your nerves are on edge. Come, keep still. Your sight will return, I swear. I expect you got to the point which the gods wish to keep in darkness, or they may be punishing you for your impudence.

OEDIPUS. I can see a little . . . I think.

TIRESIAS. Are you in pain?

OEDIPUS. Less . . . the pain is going. Ah! . . . it was like fire, red pepper, a thousand pinpoints, a cat's paw scrabbling in my eye. Thank you. . . .

TIRESIAS. Can you see?

OEDIPUS. Not clearly, but I can see, I can see. Phew! I really thought I was blind for good and that it was one of your kind of tricks. In any case, I deserved it.

TIRESIAS. We like to believe in miracles when miracles suit us, and when they don't we like to believe in them no longer, but say it is a trick on the part of the soothsayer.

OEDIPUS. Forgive me. I am of a violent and vindictive disposition. I love Jocasta. I was waiting for her, impatiently, and this extraordinary phenomenon, all those images of the future in the pupil of your eyes bewitched me, fuddled me, as it were, and made me mad.

TIRESIAS. Can you see better now? It is an almost blind man asking you.

OEDIPUS. Quite, and I have no more pain. I 'm really ashamed of my conduct towards you, a blind man and a priest. Will you accept my apologies?

TIRESIAS. I was only speaking for your own good and Jocasta's.

OEDIPUS. Tiresias, in a way I owe you something in return, a confession that is difficult to make, and which I had promised myself I would make to no one.

TIRESIAS. A confession?

OEDIPUS. I noticed during the coronation ceremony that you and Creon had some understanding between you. Do not deny it. Well, I wished to keep my identity secret; but I give it up. Listen carefully, Tiresias. I am not a wanderer. I come from Corinth. I am the only child of King Polybius and Queen Merope. A nobody will not soil this marriage bed. I am a king and son of a king.

TIRESIAS. My lord. [*He bows.*] A word from you would have cleared the atmosphere of the uneasiness created by your incognito. My little girl will be so glad. . . .

OEDIPUS. But wait! I ask you as a favour to safeguard at least this last night. Jocasta still loves in me the wanderer dropped out of the clouds, the young man stepping suddenly out of the shadows. It will unfortunately be only too easy to destroy this mirage to-morrow. In the meantime, I hope the queen will become sufficiently submissive for her to learn without disgust that Oedipus is not a prince fallen from the sky, but merely a prince.

I wish you good evening, Tiresias. Jocasta will be on her way back. I am dropping with fatigue . . . and we want to remain alone together. That is our desire.

TIRESIAS. My lord, excuse me.

[OEDIPUS *makes a sign to him with his hand.* TIRESIAS *stops at the left-hand exit.*]

One last word.

OEDIPUS. [*Loftily.*] What is it?

TIRESIAS. Forgive my boldness. This evening, after the closing of the temple, a beautiful young girl came into the private chapel where I work and, without a word of excuse, handed me this belt and said: 'Give it to Lord Oedipus and repeat word for word this sentence: Take this belt: with that you will be able to get to me when I have killed the beast.' I had scarcely tucked away the belt when the girl burst out laughing and disappeared, I don't know how.

OEDIPUS. [*Snatching away the belt.*] And that 's your trump card. You have already built up a whole system in order to destroy my hold on the queen's head and heart. How should I know? A previous promise of marriage. . . . A girl takes her revenge. . . . The temple scandal. . . . Tell-tale find. . . .

TIRESIAS. I was fulfilling my commission. That 's all.

OEDIPUS. Miscalculation and bad policy. Go . . . and carry this bad news with all speed to Prince Creon. [TIRESIAS *stays on the threshold.*] He reckoned he was going to scare me! But in point of fact, it is I who scare you, Tiresias, *I* scare you. I can see it written in large letters on your face. It wasn't so easy to terrorize the child. Confess that the child terrifies you, grandpa! Confess, grandpa! Confess I terrify you! Confess at least I make you afraid! [OEDIPUS *is lying face down on the animal skin.* TIRESIAS *is standing like a bronze statue. Silence. Then thunder.*]

TIRESIAS. Yes. Very afraid. [*He leaves, walking backwards. His prophetic voice can be heard.*] Oedipus! Oedipus, listen to me! You are pursuing classic glory. There is another kind: obscure glory, the last resource of the arrogant person who persists in opposing the stars.

[OEDIPUS *remains looking at the belt. When* JOCASTA *comes in, in her night-dress, he quickly hides the belt under the animal skin.*]

JOCASTA. Well now? What did the old ogre say? Did he torment you?

OEDIPUS. Yes . . . no. . . .

JOCASTA. He 's a monster. Did he prove to you that you are too young for me?

OEDIPUS. You are beautiful, Jocasta! . . .

JOCASTA. That I am old?

OEDIPUS. He rather gave me to understand that I loved your pearls, and your diadem.

JOCASTA. Always spoiling everything! Ruining everything! Doing harm!

OEDIPUS. But you can take it from me, he didn't manage to scare me. On the contrary, I scared him. He admitted that.

JOCASTA. Well done! My love! You, dear, after my pearls and diadem!

OEDIPUS. I am happy to see you again without any pomp, without your jewels and orders, white, young, and beautiful, in our own room.

JOCASTA. Young! Oedipus! . . . You mustn't tell lies. . . .

OEDIPUS. Again! . . .

JOCASTA. Don't scold me.

OEDIPUS. Yes, I shall scold you! I shall scold you because a woman like you ought to be above such nonsense. A young girl's face is as boring as a white page on which my eyes can read nothing moving; whereas your face! . . . I must have the scars, the tattooing of destiny, a beauty which has weathered tempests. Why should you be afraid of crows' feet, Jocasta? What would a silly schoolgirl's look or smile be worth beside the remarkable sacred beauty of your face; slapped by fate, branded by the executioner, and tender, tender and . . . [*He notices that* JOCASTA *is weeping.*] Jocasta! my dear little girl, you 're crying! What ever 's the matter? . . . All right, then. . . . What have I done now? Jocasta! . . .

JOCASTA. Am I so old . . . so very old?

OEDIPUS. My dear crazy girl! It 's you who persist in——

JOCASTA. Women say things to be contradicted. They always hope it isn't true.

OEDIPUS. My dear Jocasta! . . . What a fool I am! What a great brute! . . . Darling. . . . Don't cry. Kiss me. . . . I meant——

JOCASTA. Never mind. . . . I am being ridiculous. [*She dries her eyes.*]

OEDIPUS. It 's all my fault.

JOCASTA. It isn't. . . . There . . . the black is running into my eye now. [OEDIPUS *coaxes her.*] It 's all over.

OEDIPUS. Quick, a smile. [*Slight rumbling of thunder.*] Listen.

JOCASTA. My nerves are bad because of the storm.

OEDIPUS. But look at the sky! It is full of stars, and clear.

JOCASTA. Yes, but there is a storm brewing somewhere. When the fountain makes a still murmur like silence, and my shoulder aches, there is always a storm about and summer lightning. [*She leans against the bay window. Summer lightning.*]

OEDIPUS. Come here, quickly. . . .

JOCASTA. Oedipus! . . . come here a moment.

OEDIPUS. What is it? . . .

JOCASTA. The sentry . . . look, lean out. On the bench on the right, he 's asleep. Don't you think he 's handsome, that boy? with his mouth wide open.

OEDIPUS. I 'll throw some water in it! I 'll teach him to sleep!

JOCASTA. Oedipus!

OEDIPUS. How dare he sleep when guarding the queen!

JOCASTA. The Sphinx is dead and you 're alive. Let him sleep in peace! May all the town sleep in peace! May they all sleep every one!

OEDIPUS. Lucky sentry!

JOCASTA. Oedipus! Oedipus! I should like to make you jealous, but it isn't that. . . . This young guard——

OEDIPUS. What is so extraordinary about this young guard then?

JOCASTA. During that famous night, the night of the Sphinx, while you were encountering the beast, I had an escapade on the ramparts with Tiresias. I had heard that a young soldier had seen the ghost of Laïus, and that Laïus was calling for me to warn me of a threatening danger. Well . . . that soldier was the very sentry who is guarding us.

OEDIPUS. Who is guarding us! . . . Anyway . . . Let him sleep in peace, my kind Jocasta. I can guard you all right on my own. Of course, not the slightest sign of the ghost of Laïus?

JOCASTA. Not the slightest, I 'm sorry to say. . . . Poor lad! I touched his shoulders and legs, and kept saying to Zizi, 'Touch, touch,' and I was in a state . . . because he was like you. And it 's true, you know, Oedipus, he was like you.

OEDIPUS. You say: 'This guard was like you.' But, Jocasta, you didn't know me then; it was impossible for you to know or to guess. . . .

JOCASTA. Yes, indeed, that 's true. I expect I meant to say my son would be about his age. [*Silence.*] Yes . . . I am getting muddled. It 's only now that this likeness strikes me. [*She shakes off this uneasy feeling.*] You 're a dear, you 're good-looking, I love you. [*After a pause.*] Oedipus!

OEDIPUS. My goddess!

JOCASTA. I approve of your not telling the story of your victory to Creon or to Tiresias, or to everybody [*With her arms round his neck.*], but to me . . . to me!

OEDIPUS. [*Freeing himself.*] I had your promise! . . . And but for that boy——

JOCASTA. Is the Jocasta of yesterday the Jocasta of now? Haven't I a right to share your memories without anybody else knowing anything about it?

OEDIPUS. Of course.

JOCASTA. And do you remember you kept saying: 'No, no, Jocasta, later, later when we are in our own room.' Well, aren't we in our own room? . . .

OEDIPUS. Persistent monkey! Charmer! She always ends by getting what she wants. Now lie still. . . . I am beginning.

JOCASTA. Oh, Oedipus! Oedipus! What fun! What fun! I 'm quite still.

[JOCASTA *lies down, shuts her eyes, and keeps still.* OEDIPUS *begins lying, hesitating, inventing, accompanied by the storm.*]

OEDIPUS. Now. I was nearing Thebes. I was following the goat track which rounds the hill to the south of the town. I was thinking of the future, of you whom I imagined less beautiful than you are in reality, but still, very beautiful, painted, and sitting on a throne in the centre of a group of ladies-in-waiting. Supposing you do kill it, I said to myself, would you, Oedipus, dare to ask for the promised reward? Should I dare to go near the queen? . . . And I kept walking and worrying. All of a sudden I stopped dead. My heart was beating hard. I had just heard a sort of song. The voice that sang it was not of this world. Was it the Sphinx? My haversack contained a knife. I slipped the knife under my tunic and crept along. Do you know those ruins of a little temple on the hill, with a pedestal and the hind quarters of a chimera? [*Silence.*] Jocasta . . . Jocasta. . . . Are you asleep?

JOCASTA. [*Awaking with a start.*] What? Oedipus. . . .

OEDIPUS. You were asleep.

JOCASTA. I wasn't.

OEDIPUS. Oh, yes, you were. There 's a fickle little girl for you! She wants me to tell her a story and then goes and falls asleep in the middle of it, instead of listening.

JOCASTA. I heard it all. You 're mistaken. You were speaking of a goat track.

OEDIPUS. I 'd got a long way past the goat track! . . .

JOCASTA. Don't be angry, darling. Are you cross with me? . . .

OEDIPUS. Me?

JOCASTA. Yes, you are cross with me, and rightly. What a stupid silly I am! That 's what age does for you.

OEDIPUS. Don't be sad. I 'll start the story again, I promise you, but first of all you and I must lie down and sleep a little, side by side. After that, we shall be clear of this sticky paste, this struggle against sleep which is spoiling everything. The first one to wake up will wake the other. Promise.

JOCASTA. Promised. Poor queens know how to snatch a moment's sleep where they sit, between two audiences. But give me your hand. I am too old. Tiresias was right.

OEDIPUS. Perhaps so for Thebes, where girls are marriageable at thirteen.

But what about me? Am I an old man? My head keeps dropping and my chin hitting my chest wakes me up.

JOCASTA. You? That 's quite different, it 's the dustman, as children say! But as for me . . . You begin to tell me the most marvellous story in the world, and I go and doze away like a grandma beside the fire. And you will punish me by never beginning it over again, and finding excuses. . . . Did I talk in my sleep?

OEDIPUS. Talk? No. I thought you were being very attentive. You naughty girl, have you some secrets you are afraid you might give away?

JOCASTA. No, only those foolish things we sometimes say when sleeping.

OEDIPUS. You were lying as good as gold. Till soon, my little queen.

JOCASTA. Very soon, my king, my love.

[*Hand in hand, side by side, they shut their eyes and fall into the heavy sleep of people who struggle against sleep. A pause. The fountain soliloquizes. Slight thunder. Suddenly the lighting becomes the lighting of dreams. The dream of* OEDIPUS. *The animal skin is pushed up. It is lifted by the head of* ANUBIS. *He shows the belt at the end of his outstretched arm.* OEDIPUS *tosses about and turns over.*]

ANUBIS. [*In a slow mocking voice.*] Thanks to my unhappy childhood, I have pursued studies which give me a great start over the riff-raff of Thebes, and I don't think this simple-minded monster is expecting to be confronted by a pupil of the best scholars of Corinth. But if you have played a trick on me I shall drag you by the hair. [*Up to a howl.*] I shall drag you by the hair, I shall drag you by the hair, I shall grip you till the blood flows! . . . I shall grip you till the blood flows! . . .

JOCASTA. [*Dreaming.*] No, not that paste, not that foul paste! . . .

OEDIPUS. [*In a distant, muffled voice.*] I shall count up to fifty: one, two, three, four, eight, seven, nine, ten, ten, eleven, fourteen, five, two, four, seven, fifteen, fifteen, fifteen, fifteen, three, four. . . .

ANUBIS. And Anubis would bound forward. He would open his wolf-like jaws!

[*He disappears under the platform. The animal skin resumes its normal appearance.*]

OEDIPUS. Help! Help! I 'm here! Help me! Everybody! Come here!

JOCASTA. What? What is it? Oedipus, my darling! I was in a dead sleep! Wake up! [*She shakes him.*]

OEDIPUS. [*Struggling and talking to the* SPHINX.] Oh, miss! No! No, miss! Please don't! No! Let me go, miss! No! No! No!

JOCASTA. My pet, don't scare me so. It 's a dream. This is me, me, Jocasta, your wife, Jocasta.

OEDIPUS. No, no! [*He awakens.*] Where was I? How ghastly! Jocasta, is that you? . . . What a nightmare, what a horrible nightmare!

JOCASTA. There, there, it 's all over, you are in our room, dear, in my arms. . . .

OEDIPUS. Didn't you see anything? Of course, how silly of me, it was that animal skin. . . . Phew! I must have talked. What did I say?

JOCASTA. Now it 's your turn. You were shouting: 'Oh no, miss! Please don't, miss! Let me go, miss!' Who was that wicked woman?

OEDIPUS. I don't remember. What a night!

JOCASTA. How about me? Your shouts saved me from an unspeakable nightmare. Look! You're soaked through, swimming in perspiration. It's my fault. I let you go to sleep in all those heavy clothes, golden chains, clasps, and those sandals which cut your heel. . . . [*She lifts him up. He falls back.*] Come along! What a big baby! I can't possibly leave you in this state. Don't make yourself so heavy, help me. . . .

[*She lifts him up, takes off his tunic, and rubs him down.*]

OEDIPUS. [*Still in a vague state.*] Yes, my little darling mother. . . .

JOCASTA. [*Mocking him.*] 'Yes, my little darling mother. . . .' What a child! Now he 's taking me for his mother.

OEDIPUS. [*Awake.*] Oh, forgive me, Jocasta, my love, I am being so silly. You see I 'm half asleep, I mix up everything. I was thousands of miles away with my mother who always thinks I am too cold or too hot. You 're not cross?

JOCASTA. Silly boy! Let me see to you, and sleep away. All the time he's excusing himself and asking forgiveness. My word! What a polite young man! He must have been taken care of by a very kind mother, very kind, and then he goes and leaves her, yes. But I mustn't complain of that. I love with all the warmth of a woman in love, that mother who petted you and kept you and brought you up for me, for us.

OEDIPUS. Sweet.

JOCASTA. I should say so! Your sandals. Raise your left leg. [*She takes off his sandals.*] And now the right.

[*Same business; suddenly she utters a terrible cry.*]

OEDIPUS. Hurt yourself?

JOCASTA. No . . . no. . . .

[*She recoils, and stares like a mad creature at* OEDIPUS'*s feet.*]

OEDIPUS. Ah, my scars! . . . I didn't know they were so ugly. My poor darling, did they upset you?

JOCASTA. Those holes . . . how did you get them? . . . They must come from such serious injuries. . . .

OEDIPUS. From the hunt, it seems. I was in the woods; my nurse was carrying me. Suddenly from a clump of trees a wild boar broke cover and charged her. She lost her head and let me go. I fell and a woodcutter killed the animal while it was belabouring me with its tusks. . . . But she is really as pale as a ghost! My darling! I ought to have warned you. I 'm so used to them myself, those awful holes. I didn't know you were so sensitive. . . .

JOCASTA. It 's nothing. . . .

OEDIPUS. Weariness and sleepiness put us into this state of vague terror . . . you had just come out of a bad dream. . . .

JOCASTA. No, Oedipus. No. As a matter of fact, those scars remind me of something I am always trying to forget.

OEDIPUS. I always strike unlucky.

JOCASTA. You couldn't possibly know. It 's to do with a woman, my foster-sister and linen-maid. She was with child at the same age as myself, at eighteen. She worshipped her husband despite the difference of age and wanted a son. But the oracles predicted so fearful a future for the child, that, after giving birth to a son, she had not the courage to let it live.

OEDIPUS. What?

JOCASTA. Wait. . . . Imagine what strength of mind a poor woman must have to do away with the life of her life . . . the son from her womb, her ideal on earth and love of loves.

OEDIPUS. And what did this . . . woman do?

JOCASTA. With death in her heart, she bored holes in the feet of the nursling, tied them, carried it secretly to a mountain-side, and left it to the mercy of the wolves and bears.

[*She hides her face.*]

OEDIPUS. And the husband?

JOCASTA. Every one thought the child had died a natural death, and that the mother had buried it with her own hands.

OEDIPUS. And . . . this woman . . . still lives?

JOCASTA. She is dead.

OEDIPUS. So much the better for her, for my first example of royal authority would have been to inflict on her, publicly, the worst tortures, and afterwards, to have her put to death.

JOCASTA. The oracles were clear and matter-of-fact. Before those things a woman always feels so stupid and helpless.

OEDIPUS. To kill! [*Recalling* LAIUS.] Of course, it isn't infamous to kill when carried away by the instinct of self-defence, and when bad luck is involved. But basely to kill in cold blood the flesh of one's flesh, to break the chain . . . to cheat in the game!

JOCASTA. Oedipus, let 's talk about something else . . . your furious little face upsets me too much.

OEDIPUS. Yes, let us talk about something else. I should be in danger of loving you less if you tried to defend this miserable wretch.

JOCASTA. You 're a man, my love, a free man and a chief! Try and put yourself in the place of a child-mother who is credulous about the oracles, worn out, disgusted, confined, and terrified by the priests. . . .

OEDIPUS. A linen-maid! That 's her only excuse. Would you have done it?

JOCASTA. [*With a gesture.*] No, of course not.

OEDIPUS. And don't run away with the idea that to fight the oracles requires a herculean determination. I could boast and pose as a wonder; I should be lying. You know, to thwart the oracles I only had to turn my back on my family, my longings, and my country. But the farther I got from my native town, and the nearer I came to yours, the more I felt I was returning home.

JOCASTA. Oedipus, Oedipus, that little mouth of yours which chatters away, that little wagging tongue, those frowning eyebrows and fiery eyes! Couldn't the eyebrows relax a little, Oedipus, and the eyes close gently for once, and that mouth be used for softer caresses than words?

OEDIPUS. I tell you, I 'm just a brute! A wretched, clumsy brute!

JOCASTA. You are a child.

OEDIPUS. I 'm not a child!

JOCASTA. Now he 's off again! There, there, be a good boy.

OEDIPUS. You 're right. I 'm behaving very badly. Calm this talkative mouth with yours, and these feverish eyes with your fingers.

JOCASTA. One moment. I 'll close the grille gate. I don't like that gate being open at night.

OEDIPUS. I 'll go.

JOCASTA. You stay lying down. . . . I 'll take a look in the mirror at the same time. Do you want to embrace a fright? After all this excitement the gods alone know what I look like. Don't make me nervous. Don't look at me. Turn the other way, Oedipus.

OEDIPUS. I 'm turning over. [*He lies across the bed with his head on the edge of the cradle.*] There, I 'm shutting my eyes. I 'm not here.

[JOCASTA *goes to the window.*]

JOCASTA. [*To* OEDIPUS.] The little soldier is still asleep, he 's half-naked . . . and it isn't warm to-night . . . poor lad!

[*She goes to the movable mirror; suddenly she stops, listening in the direction of the square. A drunk is talking very loud with long pauses between his reflections.*]

VOICE OF THE DRUNK. Politics! . . . Pol—i—tics! What a mess! They just tickle me to death! . . . Ho! Look, a dead 'un! . . . Sorry, a mistake: 's a soldier asleep. . . . Salute! Salute the sleeping army!

[*Silence.* JOCASTA *stands on her toes, and tries to see outside.*] Politics! . . . [*Long silence.*] It 's a disgrace . . . a disgrace. . . .

JOCASTA. Oedipus, my dear!

OEDIPUS. [*In his sleep.*] H'm!

JOCASTA. Oedipus! Oedipus. There's a drunk and the sentry doesn't hear him. I hate drunks. I want him sent away, and the soldier woken up. Oedipus! Oedipus! Please!

[*She shakes him.*]

OEDIPUS. I wind, I unwind, I calculate, I meditate, I weave, I winnow, I knit, I plait, I cross . . .

JOCASTA. What 's he saying? How soundly he sleeps! I might die, he wouldn't notice it.

DRUNK. Politics!

[*He sings. As soon as the first lines are sung* JOCASTA *leaves* OEDIPUS, *putting his head back on the edge of the cradle, and goes to the middle of the room. She listens.*]

'Majesty, what ever are you at?
Majesty, what ever are you at?
Your husband's much too young,
Much too young for you, that 's flat! . . . Flat. . . .'

Et cetera. . . .

JOCASTA. Oh! The beasts . . .

DRUNK. 'Majesty, what ever are you at
With this holy marriage?'

[*During what follows* JOCASTA, *bewildered, goes to the window on tiptoe. Then she returns to the bed, and leaning over* OEDIPUS, *watches his face, but still looking from time to time in the direction of the window, where the voice of the* DRUNK *alternates with the murmur of the fountain and the cock-crows. She lulls the sleep of* OEDIPUS *by gently rocking the cradle.*]

Now, if I were in politics . . . I 'd say to the queen: Majesty! . . . a minor can't be your man. . . . Take a husband who 's serious, sober, and strong . . . a husband like me. . . .

VOICE OF THE GUARD. [*Who has just awakened. He gradually recovers his self-assurance.*] Get along, there!

VOICE OF THE DRUNK. Salute the waking army! . . .

GUARD. Get a move on!

DRUNK. You might at least be polite. . . .

[*As soon as the* GUARD *is heard* JOCASTA *leaves the cradle, having first muffled* OEDIPUS'S *head in the muslin.*]

GUARD. D' you want a taste of the cooler?

DRUNK. 'Always politics! What a mess!
Majesty, what ever are you at? . . .'

GUARD. Come on, hop it! Clear off! . . .

DRUNK. I 'm clearing off, I 'm clearing off, but you might be polite about it.

[*During these remarks* JOCASTA *goes to the mirror. She cannot see herself owing to the moonlight conflicting with the dawn. She takes the mirror by its supports and moves it away from the wall. The mirror itself stays fastened to the scenery.* JOCASTA *drags the frame along, trying to get some light, glancing at* OEDIPUS *who sleeps on. She brings the piece of furniture carefully into the foreground, opposite the prompter's box, so that the public becomes her mirror and* JOCASTA *looks at herself in full view of all.*]

DRUNK. [*Very distant.*]
'Your husband 's much too young,
Much too young for you, that 's flat! . . . Flat! . . .'

[*Sound of the sentry's footsteps, bugle-calls, cock-crows, a kind of snoring noise from the rhythmic, youthful breathing of* OEDIPUS. JOCASTA, *with her face up against the empty mirror, lifts her cheeks by handfuls.*]

ACT IV

Oedipus Rex

(Seventeen years later)

THE VOICE: Seventeen years soon pass. The great plague in Thebes seems to be the first set-back to that renowned good luck of Oedipus. For their infernal machine to work properly the gods wanted all ill luck to appear in the guise of good luck. After delusive good fortune the king is to know true misfortune, the supreme consecration, which, in the hands of the cruel gods, makes of this playing-card king, in the end, a man.

ACT IV

Oedipus Rex

(Seventeen years later)

SCENE: *Cleared of the bedroom, the red hangings of which are pulled away into the flies, the platform seems to be surrounded by walls which grow in size. It finally represents an inner courtyard. By a balcony high up* JOCASTA'S *room is made to communicate with this court. One gets to it through an open door below, in the centre. When the curtain rises* OEDIPUS, *aged, and wearing a little beard, stands near to the door.* TIRESIAS *and* CREON *are standing on the right and left of the court. Centre right, a young boy rests one knee on the ground: he is the* MESSENGER *from Corinth.*

OEDIPUS. What have I done to shock people now, Tiresias?

TIRESIAS. You are enlarging on things, as usual. I think, and I 'll say again, it might be more decent to learn of a father's death with less joy.

OEDIPUS. Indeed. [*To the* MESSENGER.] Don't be afraid, boy. Tell me, what was the cause of Polybius's death? Is Merope so very terribly unhappy?

MESSENGER. King Polybius died of old age, my lord, and . . . the queen, his wife, is barely conscious. She is so old she can't fully realize even her misfortune.

OEDIPUS. [*His hand to his mouth.*] Jocasta! Jocasta!

[JOCASTA *appears on the balcony; she parts the curtain. She is wearing her red scarf.*]

JOCASTA. What is it?

OEDIPUS. How pale you are! Don't you feel well?

JOCASTA. Oh, you know, the plague, the heat, and visits to hospitals—I 'm absolutely exhausted. I was resting on my bed.

OEDIPUS. This messenger has brought me great news, worth disturbing you for.

JOCASTA. [*Astonished.*] Good news? . . .

OEDIPUS. Tiresias blames me for finding it good: My father is dead.

JOCASTA. Oedipus!

OEDIPUS. The oracle told me I should be his murderer, and that I should be the husband of my mother. Poor Merope! she is very old, and my father, Polybius, has died a good natural death!

JOCASTA. I never knew the death of a father was a subject for rejoicing!

OEDIPUS. I hate play-acting and conventional tears. To tell the truth, I was so young when I left my father and mother that I no longer have any particular feelings for them.

MESSENGER. Lord Oedipus, if I may . .

OEDIPUS. You may, my boy.

MESSENGER. Your indifference is not really indifference. I can explain it to you.

OEDIPUS. Something new.

MESSENGER. I ought to have begun at the end of the story. On his deathbed the King of Corinth asked me to tell you that you are only his adopted son.

OEDIPUS. What?

MESSENGER. My father, one of Polybius's shepherds, found you on a hill, at the mercy of wild beasts. He was a poor man; he carried his find to the queen who used to weep because she had no children. This is how the honour of performing such an extraordinary mission at the Theban court has fallen to me.

TIRESIAS. This young man must be exhausted after his journey, and he has crossed our town which is full of noxious vapours. Perhaps it would be better if he took some refreshment and rested before being questioned.

OEDIPUS. No doubt, Tiresias, you would like the torture to last. You think my world is tottering. You don't know me well enough. Don't you rejoice too soon. Perhaps I am happy to be a child of fortune.

TIRESIAS. I was only putting you on your guard against your sinister habit of questioning, seeking to know and understand everything.

OEDIPUS. Whether I am a child of the muses or of a common tramp, I shall question without fear; I will know things.

JOCASTA. Oedipus, my love, he is right. You get excited. . . . You get excited . . . and you believe everything you 're told, and then afterwards——

OEDIPUS. What! That 's the last straw! Unflinchingly I withstand the hardest knocks, and you all plot to make me put up with these things and not try to find out where I come from.

JOCASTA. Nobody is plotting . . . my love . . . but I know you. . . .

OEDIPUS. You 're wrong, Jocasta. Nobody knows me at present, neither you, nor I, nor any one else. [*To the* MESSENGER.] Don't tremble, my lad. Speak up. Tell us more.

MESSENGER. That 's all I know, Lord Oedipus, except that my father untied you when you were half dead, hanging by your wounded feet from a short branch.

OEDIPUS. Oh, so that 's how we come by those fine scars!

JOCASTA. Oedipus, Oedipus, dear . . . come up here. . . . Anybody would think you enjoy opening old wounds.

OEDIPUS. And so those were my swaddling clothes! . . . My story of the hunt is . . . false, like so many others. Well, if that 's the way things are . . . I may come of a god of the woods and a dryad, and have been nourished by wolves. Don't you rejoice too soon, Tiresias!

TIRESIAS. You do me an injustice. . . .

OEDIPUS. At any rate I haven't killed Polybius, but . . . now I come to think of it . . . I have killed a man.

JOCASTA. You!

OEDIPUS. Yes! I! Oh, you needn't be alarmed! It was accidental, and sheer bad luck! Yes, I have killed, soothsayer, but as for parricide, you 'd better officially give it up. During a brawl with the serving-men I killed an old man at the cross-roads of Delphi and Daulis.

JOCASTA. At the cross-roads of Delphi and Daulis! . . .

[*She disappears as if drowning.*]

OEDIPUS. There 's marvellous material for you to build up a really fine catastrophe. That traveller must have been my father. 'Heavens, my father!' But incest won't be so easy, gentlemen. What do *you* think, Jocasta? . . . [*He turns round and sees* JOCASTA *has disappeared.*] Splendid! Seventeen years of happiness, and a perfect reign, two sons, two daughters, and then this noble lady only has to learn that I am the stranger whom, by the way, she first loved, and she turns her back on me. Let her sulk! Let her sulk! I shall be left alone with my fate.

CREON. Your wife, Oedipus, is ill. The plague is demoralizing us all. The gods are punishing the town and desire a victim. A monster is hiding in our midst. They demand he shall be found and driven out. Day after day the police have failed and the streets are littered with corpses. Do you realize what an effort you are asking of Jocasta? Do you realize that you are a man and she is a woman, an ageing woman at that, and a mother who is worried about the plague? Instead of blaming Jocasta for a movement of impatience, you might have found some excuse for her.

OEDIPUS. I see what you are getting at, brother-in-law. The ideal victim, the monster in hiding. . . . From one coincidence to another . . . wouldn't it be a pretty job, with the help of the priests and the police, to succeed in muddling the people of Thebes and make them believe *I* am that monster!

CREON. Don't be absurd!

OEDIPUS. I think you 're capable of anything, my friend. But Jocasta, that 's another matter. . . . I am astonished at her attitude. [*He calls her.*] Jocasta! Jocasta! Where are you?

TIRESIAS. She looked all to pieces. She is resting . . . let her be.

OEDIPUS. I am going. . . . [*He goes toward the* MESSENGER.] Now, let us come to the point. . . .

MESSENGER. My lord!

OEDIPUS. Holes in my feet . . . bound . . . on the mountainside. . . . How did I fail to understand at once? . . . And then I wondered why Jocasta . . .

It's very hard to give up enigmas. . . . Gentlemen, I was not the son of a dryad. Allow me to introduce you to the son of a linen-maid, a child of the people, a native product.

CREON. What 's this all about?

OEDIPUS. Poor Jocasta! One day I unwittingly told her what I thought of my mother. . . . I understand everything now. She must be terrified, and utterly desperate. In short . . . wait for me. I must question her at all costs. Nothing must be left in the dark. This horrible farce must come to an end.

[*He leaves by the middle door.* CREON *immediately rushes to the* MESSENGER, *whom he pushes out through the door on the right.*]

CREON. He is mad. What does all this mean?

TIRESIAS. Don't move. A storm is approaching from out of the ages. A thunderbolt is aimed at this man, and I ask you, Creon, to let this thunderbolt follow its capricious course, to wait motionless and not to interfere in the slightest.

[*Suddenly,* OEDIPUS *is seen on the balcony, stranded and aghast. He leans on the wall with one hand.*]

OEDIPUS. You have killed her for me.

CREON. What do you mean, killed?

OEDIPUS. You have killed her for me. . . . There she is, hanging . . . hanging by her scarf. . . . She is dead . . . gentlemen, she is dead. . . . It's all over . . . all over.

CREON. Dead? I 'm coming. . . .

TIRESIAS. Stay here. . . . As a priest I order you to. It 's inhuman, I know; but the circle is closing; we must keep silent and remain here. . . .

CREON. You wouldn't stop a brother from——

TIRESIAS. I would! Let the story be. Don't interfere.

OEDIPUS. [*At the door.*] You have killed her for me . . . she was romantic . . . weak . . . ill . . . you forced me to say I was a murderer. . . .Whom did I murder, gentlemen, I ask you? . . . through clumsiness, mere clumsiness . . . just an old man on the road . . . a stranger.

TIRESIAS. Oedipus: through mere clumsiness you have murdered Jocasta's husband, King Laïus.

OEDIPUS. You scoundrels! . . . I can see it now! You are carrying on your plot! . . . It was even worse than I thought. . . . You have made my poor Jocasta believe that I was the murderer of Laïus . . . that I killed the king to set her free and so that I could marry her.

TIRESIAS. Oedipus, you have murdered Jocasta's husband, King Laïus. I have known it for a long time, and you are telling lies. I haven't said a word about it either to you or to her or to Creon or to anyone else. This is how you reward me for my silence.

OEDIPUS. Laïus! . . . So that 's it. . . . I am the son of Laïus and of the linen-maid. The son of Jocasta's foster-sister and Laïus.

TIRESIAS. [*To* CREON.] If you want to act, now 's the time. Quickly. There are limits even to harshness.

CREON. Oedipus, through you, my sister is dead. I kept silence only to protect Jocasta. I think it is useless to prolong unduly the false mystery and the unravelling of a sordid drama whose intrigue I have finally succeeded in discovering.

OEDIPUS. Intrigue?

CREON. The most secret of secrets are betrayed one day or another to the determined seeker. The honest man, sworn to silence, talks to his wife, who talks to an intimate friend, and so on. [*Into the wings.*] Come in, shepherd.

[*An old* SHEPHERD *comes in, trembling.*]

OEDIPUS. Who is this man?

CREON. The man who carried you bleeding and bound on to the mountainside, in obedience to your mother's orders. Let him confess.

SHEPHERD. To speak means death to me. Princes, why haven't I died before so as not to live through this minute?

OEDIPUS. Whose son am I, old man? Strike, strike quickly!

SHEPHERD. Alas!

OEDIPUS. I am near to the sound of something that should not be heard.

SHEPHERD. And I . . . to the saying of something that should not be said.

CREON. You must say it. I wish you to.

SHEPHERD. You are the son of Jocasta, your wife, and of Laïus, killed by you where the three roads cross. Incest and parricide, may the gods forgive you!

OEDIPUS. I have killed whom I should not. I have married whom I should not. I have perpetuated what I should not. All is clear. . . .

[*He goes out.* CREON *drives out the* SHEPHERD.]

CREON. Who was the linen-maid and foster-sister he was talking about?

TIRESIAS. Women cannot hold their tongues. Jocasta must have made out that her crime had been committed by a servant to see what effect it had on Oedipus.

[*He holds his arm and listens with bent head. Forbidding murmur. The little Antigone, with hair dishevelled, appears on the balcony.*]

ANTIGONE. Uncle! Tiresias! Come up, quickly! Hurry, it 's horrible! I heard shrieks inside; mother, my darling mother, doesn't move any more, she has fallen like a log, and my dear, dear father is writhing over her body and stabbing at his eyes with her big golden brooch. There 's blood everywhere. I 'm frightened! I 'm too frightened, come up . . . come up, quickly. . . . [*She goes in.*]

CREON. This time nothing shall prevent me. . . .

TIRESIAS. Yes, I shall. I tell you, Creon, the finishing touches are being put to a masterpiece of horror. Not a word, not a gesture. It would be improper for us to cast over it so much as a shadow of ourselves.

CREON. Sheer insanity!

TIRESIAS. Sheer wisdom. . . . You must admit—

CREON. No! Besides, power falls once more into my hands.

[*He frees himself, and at the very moment when he bounds forward the door opens.* OEDIPUS *appears, blind.* ANTIGONE *is clinging to his clothes.*]

TIRESIAS. Stop!

CREON. I shall go mad! Why, but why has he done that? Better have killed himself.

TIRESIAS. His pride does not desert him. He wanted to be the happiest of men, now he wants to be the most unhappy.

OEDIPUS. Let them drive me out, let them finish me off, stone me, strike down the foul beast!

ANTIGONE. Father!

TIRESIAS. Antigone! My soothsaying staff! Offer it to him from me. It will bring him some luck.

[ANTIGONE *kisses the hand of* TIRESIAS *and carries the staff to* OEDIPUS.]

ANTIGONE. Tiresias offers you his staff.

OEDIPUS. Is he there? . . . I accept it, Tiresias. . . . I accept it. . . . Do you remember, seventeen years ago, I saw in your eyes that I should become blind, and I couldn't understand it? I see it all clearly now, Tiresias, but I am in pain. . . . I suffer. . . . The journey will be hard.

CREON. We must not let him cross the town, it would cause an awful scandal.

TIRESIAS. [*In a low voice.*] In a town of plague? And besides, you know, they saw the king Oedipus wished to be; they won't see the king he is now.

CREON. Do you mean he will be invisible because he is blind?

TIRESIAS. Almost.

CREON. Well, I can tell you I have had enough of your riddles and symbols. *My* head is firmly fixed on my shoulders and my feet planted firmly on the ground. I shall give my orders.

TIRESIAS. Your police may be well organized, Creon; but where this man goes they will not have the slightest power.

CREON. I——

[TIRESIAS *seizes his arm and puts his hand over his mouth. . . . For* JOCASTA *appears in the doorway.* JOCASTA, *dead, white, beautiful, with closed eyes. Her long scarf is wound round her neck.*]

OEDIPUS. Jocasta! You, dear! You alive!

JOCASTA. No, Oedipus. I am dead. You can see me because you are blind; the others cannot see me.

OEDIPUS. Tiresias is blind. . . .

JOCASTA. Perhaps he can see me faintly . . . but he loves me, he won't say anything. . . .

OEDIPUS. Wife, do not touch me! . . .

JOCASTA. Your wife is dead, hanged, Oedipus. I am your mother. It 's your mother who is coming to help you. . . . How would you even get down these steps alone, my poor child?

OEDIPUS. Mother!

JOCASTA. Yes, my child, my little boy. . . . Things which appear abominable to human beings, if only you knew, from the place where I live, if only you knew how unimportant they are!

OEDIPUS. I am still on this earth.

JOCASTA. Only just. . . .

CREON. He is talking with phantoms, he 's delirious. I shall not allow that little girl——

TIRESIAS. They are in good care.

CREON. Antigone! Antigone! I am calling you. . . .

ANTIGONE. I don't want to stay with my uncle! I don't want to, I don't want to stay in the house. Dear father, dear father, don't leave me! I will show you the way, I will lead you. . . .

CREON. Thankless creature.

OEDIPUS. Impossible, Antigone. You must be a good girl. . . . I cannot take you with me.

ANTIGONE. Yes, you can!

OEDIPUS. Are you going to desert your sister Ismene?

ANTIGONE. She must stay with Eteocles and Polynices. Take me away, please! Please! Don't leave me alone! Don't leave me with uncle! Don't leave me at home!

JOCASTA. The child is so pleased with herself. She imagines she is your guide. Let her think she is. Take her. Leave everything to me.

OEDIPUS. Oh! . . . [*He puts his hand to his head.*]

JOCASTA. Are you in pain, dear?

OEDIPUS. Yes, my head, my neck and arms. . . . It 's fearful.

JOCASTA. I 'll give you a dressing at the fountain.

OEDIPUS. [*Breaking down.*] Mother . . .

JOCASTA. Who would have believed it? That wicked old scarf and that terrible brooch. Didn't I say so time and again?

CREON. It 's utterly impossible. I shall not allow a madman to go out free with Antigone. It is my duty to——

TIRESIAS. Duty! They no longer belong to you; they no longer come under your authority.

CREON. And pray whom should they belong to?

TIRESIAS. To the people, poets, and unspoiled souls.

JOCASTA. Forward! Grip my dress firmly . . . don't be afraid.

[*They start off.*]

ANTIGONE. Come along, father dear . . . let 's go. . . .

OEDIPUS. Where do the steps begin?

JOCASTA AND ANTIGONE. There is the whole of the platform yet. . . . [*They disappear . . .* JOCASTA *and* ANTIGONE *speak in perfect unison.*] Careful . . . count the steps. . . . One, two, three, four, five. . . .

CREON. And even supposing they leave the town, who will look after them, who will admit them?

TIRESIAS. Glory.

CREON. You mean rather dishonour, shame. . . .

TIRESIAS. Who knows?

ON COCTEAU'S *INFERNAL MACHINE*[1]

FRANCIS FERGUSSON

THE QUESTION of poetic drama—its possibility in our time—is perhaps *the* question of the contemporary theatre. There is no better way to see into the nature and the limitations of the theatre as we know it, than to ask the perennial question, Why don't we have a living poetic drama?

But this question has occupied some of the best minds of our time and has received a vast variety of answers. It would take a book, at the very least, to handle the matter at all adequately. In a brief paper one can do no more than suggest one approach—expound a sample, more or less arbitrarily chosen from among many—of the attempt to make a modern poetic drama. I have chosen Cocteau's *Infernal Machine* for this purpose. But first of all, I should give a word of explanation of this choice—why Cocteau, who did not even write his play in verse?

When we talk about modern poetic drama in English we think of the long line of poets, beginning with Shelley and Coleridge, and continuing right up to Yeats and Eliot, who have aspired more or less in vain to the stage. But on the continent the picture is quite different. Ibsen and Wagner, Chekhov and Pirandello, Cocteau and Stravinski and Lorca—one can think of many writers who worked directly for the stage and who produced works, whether in verse or not, which could in some sense be called poetic drama and which are certainly "poetic" in the widest meaning of the term. There is no question that they produced viable theatrical pieces, while the work of poets writing in English for the stage is all too likely to be unstageable. The fact is that on the continent the idea of the theatre is even yet not quite lost. The state-supported theatres, the repertory theatres and art theatres, have kept the ancient art of drama alive and provided the means which poets of the theatre would require. But in English-speaking countries the idea of a theatre has succumbed, except for a few undernourished little theatres, to the stereotypes and the mass-production methods of the entertainment industry. In the shallow medium of our commercialized entertainment the poet is lost, however true his inspiration or authentic his dramatic talent.

1. Alan S. Downer, ed., *English Institute Essays, 1949* (New York: Columbia University Press, 1950), pp. 55–72. Reprinted by permission of publisher.

It is for this reason, I think, that contemporary poets in English who wish to write for the stage so often look to the continent for their models of dramatic form—and especially they look to Paris in the twenties, Paris between the Wars; and above all to Jean Cocteau who was one of the leaders of that Paris Theatre. I am thinking of Eliot, from *Sweeney Agonistes* to *Murder in the Cathedral;* of the later Yeats—the Yeats of *Plays for Dancers;* of Thornton Wilder, E. E. Cummings, the Virgil Thompson-Gertrude Stein operas, of the ballet. It is probable that the theatrical dexterity of these more or less poetic theatre-works is largely due to the influence of the Paris Theatre, and, as I say, especially to Cocteau. In other words it is certain that Cocteau is one of the chief sources of contemporary theatre poetry, or poetry in the theatre, even in English.

COCTEAU'S GROWTH; HIS NOTION OF THEATRE POETRY

When Cocteau started to write in Paris just after World War I, he found artists from all over Europe gathered there; and he found a theatrical life nourished from Russia, Italy, Germany, Sweden, as well as a fairly lively native theatre. Copeau's Théâtre du Vieux Colombier for instance, had been in existence since 1912. Paris in the twenties still looks fabulous to us: Bergson and Valéry, Joyce and Picasso and Stravinski; Pirandello and the Moscow Art Theatre, Milhaud and Gide and Maritain and Ezra Pound—if we think over some of the names associated with that time and place, we can see very clearly what an impressive effort was being made, in the center of Europe, to focus and revive the culture which had been so shaken by the war. If there was to be a favorable opportunity in our time to build a poetic drama, it should have been there and then, where the most enlightened audience and greatest talent were concentrated.

When Cocteau began to work, his immediate allies were the young French musicians who were to be called *les six,* a few painters, and the Swedish and Russian Ballets. The collection of his early critical writings, *The Call to Order,* throws a great deal of light upon his labors in this period. He was trying to sort out the extremely rich influences which bore upon him; and to select the elements of a contemporary, and *French,* theatre poetry.

In very general terms, I think one may say that he was trying to fuse two different traditions, one ancient, the other modern. What I call the ancient tradition was that of myth, of ritual, and of primitive or folk art. What I call the modern tradition was French—the classical spirit of intelligence, wit, measure and proportion, which the French are supposed to have at their best—especially the French since Racine and Molière. The formula which Cocteau invented to describe the fusion of these two strands was *une poésie de tous les jours*—an everyday poetry. He was looking for a dramatic or theatrical art which should be poetic as myth, ritual, and the inspired clowning of the Fratellinis is poetic—and yet at the same time acceptable to the shrewd and skeptical Parisians in their most alert moments and as part of their daily lives, like red wine, for instance, as an indispensable part of the diet. He wanted to acclimatize mythopoeia in the most up-to-date, rational, and disillusioned of modern commercial cities.

You will I am sure remember that during this period many other artists were trying to nourish themselves upon myth, upon ritual, and upon primitive and popular forms of art. The painters were studying African and South Pacific sculpture; Stravinski was doing *Petrouchka, Les Noces,* and *Sacre de Printemps;* Eliot was writing *The Wasteland;* Joyce was between *Ulysses* and *Finnegan's Wake*. When Cocteau and his friends began, most of this work was still to come; Cocteau himself was one of the pioneers in the movement. When he looked around for clues to the ancient and perennial theatre art he was seeking, forms which he might imitate or adapt, he found, not the works I have just mentioned, but Wagner and the all-pervasive Wagnerian influence.

Wagner was in a sense a forerunner of this whole movement. He had made use of myth in his operas, elaborated a whole theory of mythic drama, and worked out a singularly potent poetic theatrical form in the very heyday of bourgeois positivism. Cocteau remembered that Baudelaire had greeted Wagner as an ally against the Parisian Philistines of his day. Baudelaire's studies of Wagner remain one of the fundamental documents for any modern theory of poetic drama. Nevertheless Cocteau and his friends found Wagner extremely unsympathetic. The Parisians in Cocteau's day, like the rest of the world, had learned to accept and even to depend on Wagner, as an indulgence whether hypnosis or drug. They had the bad habit of swooning when they heard that kind of music, and this prevented them from listening to the young French composers who were trying to speak to them in their alert, critical, and wakeful moments. Thus for Cocteau and his friends, the Wagnerian taste or habit of mind became the great enemy, in spite of their respect for Wagner's achievement. They saw Wagnerianism as an alien mode of awareness which was impeding the development of native French forms of art. The Wagnerian tradition, Cocteau says in *The Call to Order,* is like "a long funeral procession which prevents me from crossing the street to get home." Probably he felt in Wagner's magic the potent elements which the Nazis were so soon to use for their own purposes—drowning not only the French spirit but the physical life of France also.

However that may be, Cocteau developed his own conception of poetic drama, as it were, in answer to Wagner's. He too wanted to tap the ancient sources of myth and ritual, but without resorting to religiosity, hypnosis, or morose daydreaming. He wanted to bring mythopoeia and some of the ancient myths themselves into the center of the faithless, nimble, modern city—but he sought to establish them there by the clarity and integrity of art.

The Call to Order is a collection of working notes and critical *obiter dicta* from the very beginning of Cocteau's career, between 1918 and 1926. *The Infernal Machine* was published in 1934; and yet that play seems to be exactly the poetic drama which he had planned and foreseen fifteen years earlier. It presents a very ancient myth, the myth of Oedipus, not as a joke, but as a perennial source of insight into human destiny. Yet at the same time the play is addressed to the most advanced, cynical, and even *fashionable* mind of contemporary Paris. It is at one and the same time chic and timeless—rather like the paintings of Picasso's classic period, or his illustrations for Ovid. If one were to try to describe it briefly, one might say it shows the myth behind the modern city: both the mysterious fate of Oedipus and the bright metropolitan intrigues for pleasure and power which go on forever. To have achieved such a fusion of contradictory elements is, of course, an extraordinary feat of virtuosity. And therefore this play illustrates, from one point of view at least, *the* problem of modern poetic drama: that of presentation on the public stage, at a time when poetry has lost almost all public status.

After this prolonged introduction, I wish to look briefly at the play itself, in order to illustrate more concretely what I mean.

THE PLAY: THE MYTH BEHIND THE MODERN CITY

The story of *The Infernal Machine* is the same as that of Sophocles' tragedy, *Oedipus the King*. Before the curtain goes up, a voice reminds us of the main facts.

Jocasta, Queen of Thebes, was told by the oracle of Apollo that her infant son Oedipus would grow up to murder his father and marry his mother. To avoid this terrible fatality she has the infant exposed on Mt. Kitharon with his feet pierced. But a shepherd finds him on the mountain and saves him, and eventually the young Oedipus makes his way to Corinth, where the childless king and queen adopt him as their son. He is brought up to think he is really their son; but in due time he hears the oracle, and to escape his fate he leaves Corinth. At a place where three roads cross, he meets an old man with an escort; gets into a dispute, and kills him. The old man is, of course, his own father Laius. Oedipus continues his journey, and reaches Thebes, where he finds the Sphinx preying on the city. He solves the riddle of the Sphinx and like other young men who make good, marries the boss's daughter, the widowed Queen Jocasta, his own mother. They rule prosperously for years and raise a family; but at last, when Thebes is suffering under the plague, the fate of Oedipus overtakes him. The oracle reports that the plague is sent by the gods, who are angry because Laius' slayer was never found and punished. Oedipus discovers his own identity and his own guilt—but thereby becomes once more, and in a new way, the savior of the city.

Such are the facts, in Cocteau as in Sophocles. But the question is how Cocteau presents them. What attitudes, what dramatic and theatrical forms does he find to bring the ancient tale alive in our time? His dramaturgy is utterly unlike Sophocles'; he presents *both* the mythic tale, and, as it were, the feel, or texture, of contemporary life, in which no myth is supposed to have any meaning.

When the curtain goes up we see the stage hung with nocturnal drapes, as

Cocteau calls them; in the center of the stage there is a lighted platform, set to represent the city wall of Thebes. The play is in four acts, and each act is set upon that lighted platform. Everything that occurs in the set on the lighted platform is in the easy, agile style of the best sophisticated modern comedy—Giraudoux's *Amphitryon,* or the acting of Guitry. In other words Cocteau tells the story in the foreground in a way that his blasé boulevard audience will accept. Thus he achieves the "everyday" part of his formula for "everyday poetry." But the tinkling modern intrigue is itself placed in a wider and darker setting represented by the nocturnal curtains—and in this vaster surrounding area the cruel machine of the gods, Oedipus's fate, is slowly unrolled, almost without the main actors being aware of it at all. Thus the "poetry" part of the formula is ironically hidden; it is to be found in the background, and in the mysterious relation between the hidden shape of the myth and the visible shape of Oedipus's ambitious career.

The first scene on the lighted platform represents the city wall of Thebes. It is the night when Oedipus is approaching the city. Two young soldiers are on guard. They have seen Laius' ghost, who is trying to warn Jocasta not to receive Oedipus when he comes. Queen Jocasta herself has heard rumors of this ghost, and arrives with the high priest Tiresias to investigate. But the ghost cannot appear to Jocasta; he can appear only to the naive, "the innocent, the pure in heart," such as the young soldiers; and Jocasta departs none the wiser.

The second scene shows the suburbs of Thebes, where the Sphinx lies in wait for her prey. Occurring at the same time as the first act, it discloses Oedipus's interview with the Sphinx. The Sphinx is not only a goddess but a very mortal woman, who falls in love with Oedipus and lets him guess her riddle in the hope that he will fall in love with her. But he is more interested in his career than in love; he takes her mortal remains to town as a proof of his victory, while she departs to the realm of the gods, thoroughly disgusted with mortals. She is willing to let him get away with his heroic pretenses because she sees the terrible fate in store for him.

In both of these scenes the most important characters—Jocasta in the first and Oedipus in the second—are unaware of their fate. It is separated from them as by a very thin curtain; they *almost* see what they are doing, but not quite. Moreover, in both scenes the characters and the dialogue are felt as modern, like the scandals in the morning paper.

In the first scene, for instance, Cocteau gives us the atmosphere of Thebes by means of the slangy gossip of the two soldiers. The soldiers, exactly like any GI's, are fed up with military service and especially with the brass hat who commands them. We hear the music, hot or blue, from the cafés and cheap night clubs of the popular quarter, where the people are trying to forget the rising prices, the falling employment, and the threats of war or revolution. We gather that the authorities do not know how to deal with the Sphinx. To explain their failure there are rumors of bribery, corruption and scandal in high places. In other words, Thebes is wholly familiar and acceptable to our worldly understanding—it might be any demoralized modern Mediterranean city of our time or any time. In this atmosphere even the Sphinx and the ghost of Laius are scarcely more surprising or significant than our more commonplace public nightmares. When Jocasta arrives with Tiresias to find out what all this talk of a ghost is about, she, too, is sharply modern: she speaks, Cocteau tells us, with the insolent accent of international royalty. He might have been thinking of Queen Marie of Roumania, or any other Elsa Maxwell character from café society. Jocasta is full of forebodings; she is nervous and overwrought; she complains about everything—but she does not have the naïveté or the "purity of heart" to grasp her real situation, or to see the ghost which appeared to the soldiers.

In the second act the young Oedipus is also a modern portrait, almost a candid-camera picture in the style of Guitry or Noel Coward. He is an ambitious and worldly young Latin—he might be the winner of a bicycle marathon or a politician who managed to stabilize the franc for a day. It is inevitable that he and Jocasta should get together—two shallow careerists, seekers after pleasure and power. The third scene shows their wedding night. It is set in the royal bedroom, and beside the royal bed is the crib which Jocasta kept as a memento of her lost son. In this scene the tenuous curtain of blindness which keeps them from seeing what they are doing is at its thinnest. But they are tired after the ceremonies of the coronation and the marriage; and they proceed sleepwalking toward the fated consummation.

In these first three acts of his play, Cocteau keeps completely separate the mythic fate of Oedipus and the literal story of his undoing, in so far as Oedipus and Jocasta themselves are concerned. The audience is aware of the fact that the terrible machine of the gods is slowly unwinding in the surrounding darkness; but the audience also sees that the victims are winning their victories and building their careers in total ignorance of it. In this respect the plan of *The Infernal Machine* resembles that of Joyce's *Ulysses.* Joyce also shows the lives of the people of a modern city in the form of an ancient legend which they are quite unaware of. Bloom wanders through his Dublin life according to an abstract scheme like that of the *Odyssey;* the reader sees this, but Bloom does not. The audience of *The Infernal Machine* sees Oedipus both as a contemporary politician and as the character in the myth. But at this point the resemblance between Cocteau's play and Joyce's novel ends. For Cocteau proposes to bring the two levels sharply together—to confront the city with the myth, and the myth with the city. This he proceeds to do in the fourth and last act.

We have been prepared all along for the sudden shift in point of view—for the peripety and epiphany of the last act. The naive soldiers saw Laius' ghost, though Jocasta did not. In the second scene the Sphinx saw what was happening to Oedipus, though he did not. And on the wedding night, Tiresias almost guessed who Oedipus was, though the bride and groom themselves could not quite make it out. Moreover, at the beginning of the play, and at the beginning of each of the first three acts, a Voice bids us relish the perfection of the machine which the gods have devised to destroy a mortal. The emphasis is on mortal stupidity and upon the cruelty of the gods. But before the last act, the Voice reminds us of a different meaning in these events; the Voice makes the following proclamation: "After false happiness, the king will learn real unhappiness: the true ritual, which will make out of this playing-card king in the hands of the cruel gods, at long last, a man."

The fourth act, unlike the other three, follows fairly closely the order of events in Sophocles' tragedy. Oedipus feels, like an unsuccessful bluffer in poker, that the jig is up; he receives the evidence of the messenger and the old shepherd which unmistakably reveals him as his mother's husband and his father's killer. Tiresias, who had half-guessed the truth all along, watches this terrible dénouement and explains it to Creon and for the audience. When Oedipus gets the final piece of evidence which convicts him, he runs off to find Jocasta. Tiresias tells Creon, "Do not budge. A storm is coming up from the bottom of time. The lightning will strike this man; and I ask you, Creon, let it follow its whim; wait without moving; interfere with nothing." As in the Sophoclean tragedy, Jocasta kills herself and Oedipus puts out his eyes, while their bewildered child Antigone tries to understand. Cocteau, like Sophocles, imagines these horrors with great intimacy, sparing nothing. But Cocteau brings the play to an end on a different note. In Sophocles the final pathos and enlightenment of Oedipus is presented in a series of steps, and by the time we finally see him blind at the end, the chorus has pretty well digested, or at least accepted, the tragic and purgatorial meaning of it all. But Cocteau ends the play with a *coup de théâtre,* a spectacular effect, a piece of theatrical sleight-of-hand, which visibly presents the tragic paradox on which the whole play is based.

The dead Jocasta appears to Oedipus, who is blind and can therefore see—but she appears not as the corrupt queen and dishonored wife of the sordid tale, but as a sort of timeless mother. "Yes, my child," she says to Oedipus, "my little son. . . . Things which seem abominable to human beings—if you only knew how unimportant they are in the realm where I am dwelling." The blind Oedipus, the child Antigone, and the ghostly Jocasta depart on their endless journey. Creon can see Oedipus and Antigone, if not Jocasta, and he asks Tiresias, "To whom do they belong now?" to which Tiresias replies, "To the people, to the poets, to the pure in heart." "But who," asks Creon, "will take care of them?" To which Tiresias replies, "La Gloire"—glory, or renown.

The effect is to remind us, all of a sudden, that Oedipus, Jocasta, Antigone, are not only literal people as we know people, but legends, figures in a timeless myth. We had in a sense known this all along; but during the first three acts we forgot it—we laughed at Oedipus's youthful vanity, grinned with cynical understanding when we saw his shallow ambition, his bounder-like opportunism. Now he and Jocasta are safe from our irony—as poetry and myth are safe—both more human and less human than the intriguing puppets which we found so familiar in the first three acts.

Cocteau, I think, must have learned a great deal from Pirandello before he wrote this play. The final effect, when Oedipus and Jocasta are suddenly taken up into the legend, like saints receiving the stigmata, is very much like the effect Pirandello contrives for his six characters in search of an author. When the six characters first appear on the stage they have some of the quality of masks, of the achieved and quiet work of art; when they fight with each other about their story, they are all too sharply human; and when they leave at the end, their tragic procession is like the procession of Oedipus, Jocasta, and Antigone—a steady image in the mind's eye, and in the light of the stage, of the tragic human condition in general: they have the eternity, if not of heaven, at least of the poetic image.

Moreover the paradox on which the tragedy is based is very much like Pirandello's favorite paradox—the contradiction between myth or poetry on one side, and the meaningless disorder of contemporary lives on the other. We live in two incommensurable worlds, neither of which we can do without—that of myth-making, and that of literal, unrelated, and therefore meaningless facts.

I do not mean to say that this is the only way to understand tragedy. On the contrary, Pirandello and Cocteau write a particular *kind* of tragedy, which is much more closely akin to the Baroque than it is either to Sophoclean or Shakespearean tragedy. Both of these authors may seem to us artificial; certainly they are Latin, rationalistic, deflated; they work with brilliant images, clear and distinct ideas, sharp contrasts, strong chiaroscuro. If we are used to Shakespeare, the plays of Cocteau like those of Pirandello may seem arbitrary and invented to us,

> Music and philosophy, curiosity,
> The purple bullfinch in the lilac tree,

as Eliot's Thomas of Canterbury says rather scornfully of the refined pleasures of the mind. I do not say that we could ever succeed in making that kind of modernized Baroque tragedy in English—I don't think it fits the genius of our language, or our peculiar habits of mind.

Nevertheless, as I said at the beginning of this paper, many fine playwrights and poets, writing in English, have learned from Cocteau; and I believe that there is much more still to be learned from him, short of direct imitation, about poetic drama in our time. I wish to conclude these remarks with two observations on the dramaturgy of *The Infernal Machine,* which bear upon the problem which concerns us.

The first observation is this: The whole play of *The Infernal Machine,* if properly understood, may be read as a discussion of the most general problem of dramatic poetry in our time: how are we to place upon the public stage, which is formed to reflect only literal snapshots, slogans, and sensationalism, a poetic image of human life? The play, as we have seen, answers this question in its own wonderful way, which cannot be exactly our way in English; but the general question is the same as Wagner answered according to his taste, and Yeats and Eliot according to theirs. *The Infernal Machine* thus takes an important place in the long line of attempts which have been made, for over a hundred years, to build a modern poetic drama.

The other observation has to do with the *nature* of Cocteau's poetry from which, I think, much technical lore is to be learned. The play is not in verse; and though the language is beautifully formed, the poetry is not to be found in the first instance in the language at all. The play is *theatre*-poetry, as Cocteau defines it in his preface to *Les Mariés de la Tour Eiffel:*

> The action of my play is in images, while the text is not. I attempt to substitute a poetry *of* the theatre for poetry *in* the theatre. Poetry *in* the theatre is a piece of lace which it is impossible to see at a distance. Poetry *of* the theatre would be coarse lace; a lace of ropes, a ship at sea. *Les Mariés* should have the frightening look of a drop of poetry under the microscope. The *scenes* are integrated like the *words* of a poem.

Though the language in *The Infernal Machine* is of course more important than it is in *Les Mariés* (essentially a dance pantomime), Cocteau's description of the underlying structure applies also very accurately to *The Infernal Machine*. The poetry is to be found in the relationships of all the main elements: the relationship between the lighted platform in the center of the stage with the darker and vaster area around it; between Oedipus's conscious career with the unseen fatality that governs it; between the first scene and the second, which ironically occurs at the same time; and between the first three acts, when we see Oedipus as a contemporary snapshot, and the last act, when we see him as a legend. In other words, the basic structure, or plot—the primary form of the play as a whole—embodies a poetic idea; and once that is established the language need only realize the poetic vision in detail.

If Cocteau, more than any other contemporary playwright, is thus a master of poetic-dramatic form, it is partly because he has learned from the neighboring arts of music, painting, and ballet, and partly because he found his way back to a root notion of drama itself, that which Aristotle expressed when he said the dramatic poet should be a maker of plots rather than of verses. If Auden and MacNeice do not succeed in making poetic drama, it is because they do not understand the poetry of the theatre—they take an unpoetic well-made plot from the commercial theatre and add, here and there, a pastiche of verses.

This concludes what I have to say about *The Infernal Machine* as a poetic drama. If there is a moral to the tale, it is this: poetic drama, real poetic drama, comparable to the landmarks of the tradition, when the ancient art has really flourished—cannot be invented by an individual or even a small group. If it is to perform its true function it must spring from the whole culture and be nourished by sources which we may perhaps recognize, but can hardly understand. Will such a drama ever reappear? We do not know. In the meantime, all we can do is pick together the pieces, save and cultivate such lesser successes as have been achieved. *The Infernal Machine* is one of these successes —one of the clues, so to say—to the nature and the possibility of poetic drama in our time.

THE LONG VOYAGE HOME[1]

EUGENE O'NEILL

Characters

FAT JOE, *proprietor of a dive*
NICK, *a crimp*
MAG, *a barmaid*
KATE
FREDA
TWO ROUGHS

OLSON
DRISCOLL
COCKY
IVAN
} *Seamen of the British tramp steamer, Glencairn*

SCENE: *The bar of a low dive on the London water front—a squalid, dingy room dimly lighted by kerosene lamps placed in brackets on the walls. On the left, the bar. In front of it, a door leading to a side room. On the right, tables with chairs around them. In the rear, a door leading to the street.*

A slovenly barmaid with a stupid face sodden with drink is mopping off the bar. Her arm moves back and forth mechanically and her eyes are half shut as if she were dozing on her feet. At the far end of the bar stands FAT JOE, *the proprietor, a gross bulk of a man with an enormous stomach. His face is red and bloated, his little piggish eyes being almost concealed by rolls of fat. The thick fingers of his big hands are loaded with cheap rings and a gold watch chain of cable-like proportions stretches across his waistcoat.*

At one of the tables, front, a round-shouldered young fellow is sitting, smoking a cigarette. His face is pasty, his mouth weak, his eyes shifting and cruel. He is dressed in a shabby suit, which must have once been cheaply flashy, and wears a muffler and cap.

It is about nine o'clock in the evening.

JOE. [*Yawning.*] Blimey if bizness ain't 'arf slow to-night. I donnow wot's 'appened. The place is like a bleedin' tomb. Where's all the sailor men, I'd like to know? [*Raising his voice.*] Ho, you Nick! [NICK *turns around listlessly.*] Wot's the name o' that wessel put in at the dock below jest arter noon?

NICK. [*Laconically.*] Glencairn—from Bewnezerry. (Buenos Aires).

JOE. Ain't the crew been paid orf yet?

NICK. Paid orf this arternoon, they tole me. I 'opped on board of 'er an' seen 'em. 'Anded 'em some o' yer cards, I did. They promised faithful they'd 'appen in to-night—them as whose time was done.

JOE. Any two-year men to be paid orf?

NICK. Four—three Britishers an' a square-'ead.

JOE. [*Indignantly.*] An' yer popped orf an' left 'em? An' me a-payin' yer to 'elp an' bring 'em in 'ere!

---

1. Reprinted by permission of Random House, Inc. Copyright 1919, 1946 by Eugene O'Neill.

NICK. [*Grumblingly.*] Much you pays me! An' I ain't slingin' me 'ook abaht the 'ole bleedin' town fur now man. See?

JOE. I ain't speakin' on'y fur meself. Down't I always give yer yer share, fair an' square, as man to man?

NICK. [*With a sneer.*] Yus—b'cause you 'as to.

JOE. 'As to? Listen to 'im! There's many'd be 'appy to 'ave your berth, me man!

NICK. Yus? Wot wiv the peelers li'ble to put me away in the bloody jail fur crimpin', an' all?

JOE. [*Indignantly.*] We down't do no crimpin'.

NICK. [*Sarcastically.*] Ho, now! Not arf!

JOE. [*A bit embarrassed.*] Well, on'y a bit now an' agen when there ain't no reg'lar trade. [*To hide his confusion he turns to the barmaid angrily. She is still mopping off the bar, her chin on her breast, half-asleep.*] 'Ere, me gel, we've 'ad enough o' that. You been a-moppin', an' a-moppin', an' a-moppin' the blarsted bar fur a 'ole 'our. 'Op it aht o' this! You'd fair guv a bloke the shakes a-watchin' yer.

MAG. [*Beginning to sniffle.*] Ow, you do frighten me when you 'oller at me, Joe. I ain't a bad gel, I ain't. Gawd knows I tries to do me best fur you. [*She bursts into a tempest of sobs.*]

JOE. [*Roughly.*] Stop yer grizzlin'! An' 'op it aht of 'ere!

NICK. [*Chuckling.*] She's drunk, Joe. Been 'ittin' the gin, eh, Mag?

MAG. [*Ceases crying at once and turns on him furiously.*] You little crab, you! Orter wear a muzzle, you ort! A-openin' of your ugly mouth to a 'onest woman what ain't never done you no 'arm. [*Commencing to sob again.*] H'abusin' me like a dawg cos I'm sick an' orf me oats, an' all.

JOE. Orf yer go, me gel! Go hupstairs and 'ave a sleep. I'll wake yer if I wants yer. An' wake the two gels when yer goes hup. It's 'arpas' nine an' time as some one was a-comin' in, tell 'em. D'yer 'ear me?

MAG. [*Stumbling around the bar to the door on left—sobbing.*] Yus, yus, I 'ears you. Gawd knows wot's goin' to 'appen to me, I'm that sick. Much you cares if I dies, down't you? [*She goes out.*]

JOE. [*Still brooding over* NICK'*s lack of diligence—after a pause.*] Four two-year men paid orf wiv their bloody pockets full o' sovereigns—an' yer lorst 'em. [*He shakes his head sorrowfully.*]

NICK. [*Impatiently.*] Stow it! They promised faithful they'd come, I tells yer. They'll be walkin' in in 'arf a mo'. There's lots o' time yet. [*In a low voice.*] 'Ave yer got the drops? We might wanter use 'em.

JOE. [*Taking a small bottle from behind the bar.*] Yus; 'ere it is.

NICK. [*With satisfaction.*] Righto! [*His shifty eyes peer about the room searchingly. Then he beckons to* JOE, *who comes over to the table and sits down.*] Reason I arst yer about the drops was 'cause I seen the capt'n of the Amindra this arternoon.

JOE. The Amindra? Wot ship is that?

NICK. Bloody windjammer—skys'l yarder—full rigged—painted white—been layin' at the dock above 'ere fur a month. You knows 'er.

JOE. Ho, yus. I knows now.

NICK. The capt'n says as 'e wants a man special bad—ter-night. They sails at daybreak termorrer.

JOE. There's plenty o' 'ands lyin' abaht waitin' fur ships, I should fink.

NICK. Not fur this ship, ole buck. The capt'n an' mate are bloody slave-drivers, an' they're bound down round the 'Orn. They 'arf starved the 'ands on the larst trip 'ere, an' no one'll dare ship on 'er. [*After a pause.*] I promised the capt'n faithful I'd get 'im one, and ter-night.

JOE. [*Doubtfully.*] An' 'ow are yer goin' to git 'im?

NICK. [*With a wink.*] I was thinkin' as one of 'em from the Glencairn'd do—them as was paid orf an' is comin' 'ere.

JOE. [*With a grin.*] It'd be a good 'aul, that's the troof. [*Frowning.*] If they comes 'ere.

NICK. They'll come, an' they'll all be rotten drunk, wait an' see. [*There is the noise of loud, boisterous singing from the street.*] Sounds like 'em, now. [*He opens the street door and looks out.*] Gawd blimey if it ain't the four of 'em! [*Turning to Joe in triumph.*] Naw, what d'yer say? They're lookin' for the place. I'll go aht an' tell 'em. [*He goes out.* JOE *gets into position behind the bar, assuming his most oily smile. A moment later the door is opened, admitting* DRISCOLL, COCKY, IVAN *and* OLSON. DRISCOLL *is a tall, powerful Irishman;* COCKY, *a wizened runt of a man with a straggling gray mustache;* IVAN, *a hulking oaf of a peasant;* OLSON, *a stocky, middle-aged Swede with round, childish blue eyes. The first three are all very drunk, especially* IVAN, *who is managing his legs with difficulty.* OLSON *is perfectly sober. All are dressed in their ill-fitting shore clothes and look very uncomfortable.* DRISCOLL *has unbuttoned his stiff collar and its ends stick out sideways. He has lost his tie.* NICK *slinks into the room after them and sits down at a table in rear. The seamen come to the table, front.*]

JOE. [*With affected heartiness.*] Ship ahoy, mates! 'Appy to see yer 'ome safe an' sound.

DRISCOLL. [*Turns round, swaying a bit, and peers at him across the bar.*] So ut's you, is ut? [*He looks about the place with an air of recognition.*] 'An the same damn rat's-hole, sure enough. I remimber foive or six years back 'twas here I was sthripped av me last shillin' whin I was aslape. [*With sudden fury.*] God stiffen ye, come none av your dog's thricks on me this trip or I'll—— [*He shakes his fist at* JOE.]

JOE. [*Hastily interrupting.*] Yer must be mistaiken. This is a 'onest place, this is.

COCKY. [*Derisively.*] Ho, yus! An' you're a bleedin' angel, I s'pose?

IVAN. [*Vaguely taking off his derby hat and putting it on again—plaintively.*] I don' li-ike dis place.

DRISCOLL. [*Going over to the bar—as genial as he was furious a moment be-*

fore.] Well, no matther, 'tis all past an' gone an' forgot. I'm not the man to be holdin' harrd feelin's on me first night ashore, an' me dhrunk as a lord. [*He holds out his hand, which* JOE *takes very gingerly.*] We'll all be havin' a dhrink, I'm thinkin'. Whiskey for the three av us—*Irish* whiskey!

COCKY. [*Mockingly.*] An' a glarse o' ginger beer fur our blarsted love-child 'ere. [*He jerks his thumb at* OLSON.]

OLSON. [*With a good-natured grin.*] I bane a good boy dis night, for one time.

DRISCOLL. [*Bellowing, and pointing to* NICK *as* JOE *brings the drinks to the table.*] An' see what that crimpin' son av a crimp'll be wantin'—an' have your own pleasure. [*He pulls a sovereign out of his pocket and slams it on the bar.*]

NICK. Guv me a pint o' beer, Joe. [JOE *draws the beer and takes it down to the far end of the bar.* NICK *comes over to get it and* JOE *gives him a significant wink and nods toward the door on the left.* NICK *signals back that he understands.*]

COCKY. [*Drink in hand—impatiently.*] I'm that bloody dry! [*Lifting his glass to* DRISCOLL.] Cheero, ole dear, cheero!

DRISCOLL. [*Pocketing his change without looking at it.*] A toast for ye: Hell roast that divil av a bo'sun! [*He drinks.*]

COCKY. Righto! Gawd strike 'im blind! [*He drains his glass.*]

IVAN. [*Half-asleep.*] Dot's gude. [*He tosses down his drink in one gulp.* OLSON *sips his ginger ale.* NICK *takes a swallow of his beer and then comes round the bar and goes out the door on left.*]

COCKY. [*Producing a sovereign.*] Ho there, you Fatty! Guv us another!

JOE. The saime, mates?

COCKY. Yus.

DRISCOLL. No, ye scut! I'll be havin' a pint av beer. I'm dhry as a loime kiln.

IVAN. [*Suddenly getting to his feet in a befuddled manner and nearly upsetting the table.*] I don' li-ike dis place! I wan' see girls—plenty girls. [*Pathetically.*] I don't li-ike dis place. I wan' dance with girl.

DRISCOLL. [*Pushing him back on his chair with a thud.*] Shut up, ye Rooshan baboon! A foine Romeo you'd make in your condishun. [IVAN *blubbers some incoherent protest—then suddenly falls asleep.*]

JOE. [*Bringing the drinks—looks at* OLSON.] An' you, matey?

OLSON. [*Shaking his head.*] Noting dis time, thank you.

COCKY. [*Mockingly.*] A-saivin' of 'is money, 'e is! Goin' back to 'ome an' mother. Goin' to buy a bloomin' farm an' punch the blarsted dirt, that's wot 'e is! [*Spitting disgustedly.*] There's a funny bird of a sailor man for yer, Gawd blimey!

OLSON. [*Wearing the same good-natured grin.*] Yust what I like, Cocky. I wus on farm long time when I wus kid.

DRISCOLL. Lave him alone, ye bloody insect! 'Tis a foine sight to see a man wid some sense in his head instead av a damn fool the loike av us. I only wisht I'd a mother alive to call me own. I'd not be dhrunk in this divil's hole this minute, maybe.

COCKY. [*Commencing to weep dolorously.*] Ow, down't talk, Drisc! I can't bear to 'ear you. I ain't never 'ad no mother, I ain't——

DRISCOLL. Shut up, ye ape, an' don't be makin' that squealin'. If ye cud see your ugly face, wid the big red nose av ye all screwed up in a knot, ye'd never shed a tear the rist av your loife. [*Roaring into song.*] We ar-re the byes av We-e-exford who fought wid hearrt an' hand! [*Speaking.*] To hell wid Ulster! [*He drinks and the others follow his example.*] An' I'll strip to any man in the city av London won't dhrink to that toast. [*He glares truculently at* JOE, *who immediately downs his beer.* NICK *enters again from the door on the left and comes up to* JOE *and whispers in his ear. The latter nods with satisfaction.*]

DRISCOLL. [*Glowering at them.*] What divil's thrick are ye up to now, the two av ye? [*He flourishes a brawny fist.*] Play fair wid us or ye deal wid me!

JOE. [*Hastily.*] No trick, shipmate! May Gawd kill me if that ain't troof!

NICK. [*Indicating* IVAN, *who is snoring.*] On'y your mate there was arskin' fur gels an' I thorght as 'ow yer'd like 'em to come dawhn and 'ave a wet wiv yer.

JOE. [*With a smirking wink.*] Pretty, 'olesome gels they be, ain't they, Nick?"

NICK. Yus.

COCKY. Aar! I knows the gels you 'as, not 'arf! They'd fair blind yer, they're that 'omely. None of yer bloomin' gels fur me, ole Fatty. Me an' Drisc knows a place, down't we, Drisc?"

DRISCOLL. Divil a lie, we do. An' we'll be afther goin' there in a minute. There's music there an' a bit av a dance to liven a man.

JOE. Nick, 'ere, can play yer a tune, can't yer, Nick?

NICK. Yus.

JOE. An' yer can 'ave a dance in the side room 'ere.

DRISCOLL. Hurroo! Now you're talkin'. [*The two women,* FREDA *and* KATE, *enter from the left.* FREDA *is a little, sallow-faced blonde.* KATE *is stout and dark.*]

COCKY. [*In a loud aside to* DRISCOLL.] Gawd blimey, look at 'em! Ain't they 'orrible? [*The women come forward to the table, wearing their best set smiles.*]

FREDA. [*In a raspy voice.*] 'Ullo, mates.

KATE. 'Ad a good voyage?

DRISCOLL. Rotten; but no matther. Welcome, as the sayin' is, an' sit down, an' what'll ye be takin' for your thirst? [*To* KATE.] You'll be sittin' by me, darlin'—what's your name?

KATE. [*With a stupid grin.*] Kate. [*She stands by his chair.*]

DRISCOLL. [*Putting his arm around her.*] A good Irish name, but you're

English by the trim av ye, an' be damned to you. But no matther. Ut's fat ye are, Katy dear, an' I never cud endure skinny wimin. [FREDA *favors him with a viperish glance and sits down by* OLSON.] What'll ye have?

OLSON. No, Drisc. Dis one bane on me. [*He takes out a roll of notes from his inside pocket and lays one on the table.* JOE, NICK, *and the women look at the money with greedy eyes.* IVAN *gives a particularly violent snore.*]

FREDA. Waike up your fren'. Gawd, 'ow I 'ates to 'ear snorin'.

DRISCOLL. [*Springing to action, smashes* IVAN'S *derby over his ears.*] D'you hear the lady talkin' to ye, ye Rooshan swab? [*The only reply to this is a snore.* DRISCOLL *pulls the battered remains of the derby off* IVAN'S *head and smashes it back again.*] Arise an' shine, ye dhrunken swine! [*Another snore. The women giggle.* DRISCOLL *throws the beer left in his glass into* IVAN'S *face. The Russian comes to in a flash, spluttering. There is a roar of laughter.*]

IVAN. [*Indignantly.*] I tell you—dot's someting I don' li-ike!

COCKY. Down't waste good beer, Drisc.

IVAN. [*Grumblingly.*] I tell you—dot is not ri-ight.

DRISCOLL. Ut's your own doin', Ivan. Ye was moanin' for girrls an' whin they come you sit gruntin' loike a pig in a sty. Have ye no manners? [IVAN *seems to see the women for the first time and grins foolishly.*]

KATE. [*Laughing at him.*] Cheero, ole chum, 'ows Russha?

IVAN. [*Greatly pleased—putting his hand in his pocket.*] I buy a drink.

OLSON. No; dis one bane on me. [*To* JOE.] Hey, you faller!

JOE. Wot'll it be, Kate?"

KATE. Gin.

FREDA. Brandy.

DRISCOLL. An' Irish whiskey for the rist av us—wid the excipshun av our timperance friend, God pity him!

FREDA. [*To* OLSON.] You ain't drinkin'?

OLSON. [*Half-ashamed.*] No.

FREDA. [*With a seductive smile.*] I down't blame yer. You got sense, you 'ave. I on'y tike a nip o' brandy now an' agen fur my 'ealth. [JOE *brings the drinks and* OLSON'S *change.* COCKY *gets unsteadily to his feet and raises his glass in the air.*]

COCKY. 'Ere's a toff toast for yer: The làdies, Gawd— [*He hesitates—then adds in a grudging tone.*]—bless 'em.

KATE. [*With a silly giggle.*] Oo-er! That wasn't what you was goin' to say, you bad Cocky, you! [*They all drink.*]

DRISCOLL. [*To* NICK.] Where's the tune ye was promisin' to give us?

NICK. Come ahn in the side 'ere an' you'll 'ear it.

DRISCOLL. [*Getting up.*] Come on, all av ye. We'll have a tune an' a dance if I'm not too dhrunk to dance, God help me. [COCKY *and* IVAN *stagger to their feet.* IVAN *can hardly stand. He is leering at* KATE *and snickering to himself in a maudlin fashion. The three, led by* NICK, *go out the door on the left.* KATE *follows them.* OLSON *and* FREDA *remain seated.*]

COCKY. [*Calling over his shoulder.*] Come on an' dance, Ollie.

OLSON. Yes, I come. [*He starts to get up. From the side room comes the sound of an accordion and a boisterous whoop from* DRISCOLL, *followed by a heavy stamping of feet.*]

FREDA. Ow, down't go in there. Stay 'ere an' 'ave a talk wiv me. They're all drunk an' you ain't drinkin'. [*With a smile up into his face.*] I'll think yer don't like me if yer goes in there.

OLSON. [*Confused.*] You wus wrong, Miss Freda. I don't—I mean I do like you.

FREDA. [*Smiling—puts her hand over his on the table.*] An' I likes you. Yer a genelman. You don't get drunk an' hinsult poor gels wot 'as a 'ard an' uneppy life.

OLSON. [*Pleased but still more confused—wriggling his feet.*] I bane drunk many time, Miss Freda.

FREDA. Then why ain't yer drinkin' now? [*She exchanges a quick, questioning glance with* JOE, *who nods back at her—then she continues persuasively.*] Tell me somethin' abaht yeself.

OLSON. [*With a grin.*] There ain't noting to say, Miss Freda. I bane poor devil sailor man, dat's all.

FREDA. Where was you born—Norway? [OLSON *shakes his head.*] Denmark?

OLSON. No. You guess once more.

FREDA. Then it must be Sweden.

OLSON. Yes. I wus born in Stockholm.

FREDA. [*Pretending great delight.*] Ow, ain't that funny! I was born there, too—in Stockholm.

OLSON. [*Astonished.*] You wus born in Sweden?

FREDA. Yes; you wouldn't think it, but it's Gawd's troof. [*She claps her hands delightedly.*]

OLSON. [*Beaming all over.*] You speak Swedish?

FREDA. [*Trying to smile sadly.*] Now. Y'see my ole man an' woman come 'ere to England when I was on'y a baby an' they was speakin' English b'fore I was old enough to learn. Sow I never knew Swedish. [*Sadly.*] Wisht I 'ad! [*With a smile.*] We'd 'ave a bloomin' lark of it if I 'ad, wouldn't we?

OLSON. It sound nice to hear the old talk yust once in a time.

FREDA. Righto! No place like yer 'ome, I says. Are yer goin' up to—to Stockholm b'fore yer ships away agen?

OLSON. Yes. I go home from here to Stockholm. [*Proudly.*] As passenger!

FREDA. An' you'll git another ship up there arter you've 'ad a vacation?

OLSON. No. I don't never ship on sea no more. I got all sea I want for my life—too much hard work for little money. Yust work, work, work on ship. I don't want more.

FREDA. Ow, I see. That's why you give up drinkin'.

OLSON. Yes. [*With a grin.*] If I drink I yust get drunk and spend all money.

FREDA. But if you ain't gointer be a sailor no more, what'll yer do? You been a sailor all yer life, ain't yer?

OLSON. No. I work on farm till I am eighteen. I like it, too—it's nice—work on farm.

FREDA. But ain't Stockholm a city same's London? Ain't no farms there, is there?

OLSON. We live—my brother and mother live—my father iss dead—on farm yust a little way from Stockholm. I have plenty money, now. I go back with two years' pay and buy more land yet; work on farm. [*Grinning.*] No more sea, no more bum grub, no more storms—yust nice work.

FREDA. Ow, ain't that luv'ly! I s'pose you'll be gittin' married, too?

OLSON. [*Very much confused.*] I don't know. I like to, if I find nice girl, maybe.

FREDA. Ain't yer got some gel back in Stockholm? I bet yer 'as.

OLSON. No. I got nice girl once before I go on sea. But I go on ship, and I don't come back, and she marry other faller. [*He grins sheepishly.*]

FREDA. Well, it's nice for yer to be goin' 'ome, anyway.

OLSON. Yes. I tank so. [*There is a crash from the room on left and the music abruptly stops. A moment later* COCKY *and* DRISCOLL *appear, supporting the inert form of* IVAN *between them. He is in the last stage of intoxication, unable to move a muscle.* NICK *follows them and sits down at the table in rear.*]

DRISCOLL. [*As they zigzag up to the bar.*] Ut's dead he is, I'm thinkin', for he's as limp as a blarsted corpse.

COCKY. [*Puffing.*] Gawd, 'e ain't 'arf 'eavy!

DRISCOLL. [*Slapping* IVAN'S *face with his free hand.*] Wake up, ye divil, ye. Ut's no use. Gabriel's trumpet itself cudn't rouse him. [*To* JOE.] Give us a dhrink for I'm perishing wid the thirst. 'Tis harrd worrk, this.

JOE. Whiskey?

DRISCOLL. *Irish* whiskey, ye swab. [*He puts down a coin on the bar.* JOE *serves* COCKY *and* DRISCOLL. *They drink and then swerve over to* OLSON'S *table.*]

OLSON. Sit down and rest for time, Drisc.

DRISCOLL. No, Ollie, we'll be takin' this lad home to his bed. Ut's late for wan so young to be out in the night. An' I'd not trust him in this hole as dhrunk as he is, an' him wid a full pay day on him. [*Shaking his fist at* JOE.] Oho, I know your games, me sonny bye!

JOE. [*With an air of grievance.*] There yer goes again—hinsultin' a 'onest man!

COCKY. Ho, listen to 'im! Guv 'im a shove in the marf, Drisc.

OLSON. [*Anxious to avoid a fight—getting up.*] I help you take Ivan to boarding house.

FREDA. [*Protestingly.*] Ow, you ain't gointer leave me, are yer? An' we 'avin' sech a nice talk, an' all.

DRISCOLL. [*With a wink.*] Ye hear what the lady says, Ollie. Ye'd best stay here, me timperance lady's man. An' we need no help. 'Tis only a bit av a way and we're two strong men if we are dhrunk. Ut's no hard shift to take the remains home. But ye can open the door for us, Ollie. [OLSON *goes to the door and opens it.*] Come on, Cocky, an' don't be fallin' aslape yourself. [*They lurch toward the door. As they go out* DRISCOLL *shouts back over his shoulder.*] We'll be comin' back in a short time, surely. So wait here for us, Ollie.

OLSON. All right. I wait here, Drisc. [*He stands in the doorway uncertainly.* JOE *makes violent signs to* FREDA *to bring him back. She goes over and puts her arm around* OLSON'S *shoulder.* JOE *motions to* NICK *to come to the bar. They whisper together excitedly.*]

FREDA. [*Coaxingly.*] You ain't gointer leave me, are yer, dearie? [*Then irritably.*] Fur Gawd's sake, shet that door! I'm fair freezin' to death wiv the fog. [OLSON *comes to himself with a start and shuts the door.*]

OLSON. [*Humbly.*] Excuse me, Miss Freda.

FREDA. [*Leading him back to the table—coughing.*] Buy me a drink o' brandy, will yer? I'm sow cold.

OLSON. All you want, Miss Freda, all you want. [*To* JOE, *who is still whispering instructions to* NICK.] Hey, Yoe! Brandy for Miss Freda. [*He lays a coin on the table.*]

JOE. Righto! [*He pours out her drink and brings it to the table.*] 'Avin' somethink yeself, shipmate?

OLSON. No. I don't tank so. [*He points to his glass with a grin.*] Dis iss only belly-wash, no? [*He laughs.*]

JOE. [*Hopefully.*] 'Ave a man's drink.

OLSON. I would like to—but no. If I drink one I want drink one tousand. [*He laughs again.*]

FREDA. [*Responding to a vicious nudge from* JOE'S *elbow.*] Ow, tike somethin'. I ain't gointer drink all be meself.

OLSON. Den give me a little yinger beer—small one. [JOE *goes back of the bar, making a sign to* NICK *to go to their table.* NICK *does so and stands so that the sailor cannot see what* JOE *is doing.*]

NICK. [*To make talk.*] Where's yer mates popped orf ter? [JOE *pours the contents of the little bottle into* OLSON'S *glass of ginger beer.*]

OLSON. Dey take Ivan, dat drunk faller, to bed. They come back. [JOE *brings* OLSON'S *drink to the table and sets it before him.*]

JOE. [*To* NICK*—angrily.*] 'Op it, will yer? There ain't no time to be dawdlin'. See? 'Urry!

NICK. Down't worry, ole bird, I'm orf. [*He hurries out the door.* JOE *returns to his place behind the bar.*]

OLSON. [*After a pause—worriedly.*] I tank I should go after dem. Cocky iss very drunk, too, and Drisc——

FREDA. Aar! The big Irish is all right. Don't yer 'ear 'im say as 'ow they'd surely come back 'ere, an' fur you to wait fur 'em?

OLSON. Yes; but if dey don't come soon I tank I go see if dey are in boarding house all right.

FREDA. Where is the boardin' 'ouse?

OLSON. Yust little way back from street here.

FREDA. You stayin' there, too?

OLSON. Yes—until steamer sail for Stockholm—in two day.

FREDA. [*She is alternately looking at* JOE *and feverishly trying to keep* OLSON *talking so he will forget about going away after the others.*] Yer mother won't be arf glad to see yer agen, will she? [OLSON *smiles.*] Does she know yer comin'?

OLSON. No. I tought I would yust give her surprise. I write to her from Bonos Eres but I don't tell her I come home.

FREDA. Must be old, ain't she, yer old lady?

OLSON. She iss eighty-two. [*He smiles reminiscently.*] You know, Miss Freda, I don't see my mother or my brother in—let me tank— [*He counts laboriously on his fingers.*] must be more than ten year. I write once in while and she write many time; and my brother he write me, too. My mother say in all letter I should come home right away. My brother he write same ting, too. He want me to help him on farm. I write back always I come soon; and I mean all time to go back home at end of voyage. But I come ashore, I take one drink, I take many drinks, I get drunk, I spend all money, I have to ship away for other voyage. So dis time I say to myself: Don't drink one drink, Ollie, or, sure, you don't get home. And I want go home dis time. I feel homesick for farm and to see my people again. [*He smiles.*] Yust like little boy, I feel homesick. Dat's why I don't drink noting to-night but dis—belly-wash! [*He roars with childish laughter, then suddenly becomes serious.*] You know, Miss Freda, my mother get very old, and I want see her. She might die and I would never—

FREDA. [*Moved a lot in spite of herself.*] Ow, don't talk like that! I jest 'ates to 'ear any one speakin' abaht dyin'. [*The door to the street is opened and* NICK *enters, followed by two rough-looking, shabbily-dressed men, wearing mufflers, with caps pulled down over their eyes. They sit at the table nearest to the door.* JOE *brings them three beers, and there is a whispered consultation, with many glances in the direction of* OLSON.]

OLSON. [*Starting to get up—worriedly.*] I tank I go round to boarding house. I tank someting go wrong with Drisc and Cocky.

FREDA. Ow, down't go. They kin take care of theyselves. They ain't babies. Wait 'arf a mo'. You ain't 'ad yer drink yet.

JOE. [*Coming hastily over to the table, indicates the men in the rear with a jerk of his thumb.*] One of them blokes wants yer to 'ave a wet wiv 'im.

FREDA. Righto! [*To* OLSON.] Let's drink this. [*She raises her glass. He does the same.*] 'Ere's a toast fur yer: Success to yer bloomin' farm an' may yer live long an' 'appy on it. Skoal! [*She tosses down her brandy. He swallows half his glass of ginger beer and makes a wry face.*]

OLSON. Skoal! [*He puts down his glass.*]

FREDA. [*With feigned indignation.*] Down't yer like my toast?

OLSON. [*Grinning.*] Yes. It iss very kind, Miss Freda.

FREDA. Then drink it all like I done.

OLSON. Well—— [*He gulps down the rest.*] Dere! [*He laughs.*]

FREDA. Done like a sport!

ONE OF THE ROUGHS. [*With a laugh.*] Amindra, ahoy!

NICK. [*Warningly.*] Sssshh!

OLSON. [*Turns around in his chair.*] Amindra? Iss she in port? I sail on her once long time ago—three mast, full rig, skys'l yarder? Iss dat ship you mean?

THE ROUGH. [*Grinning.*] Yus; right you are.

OLSON. [*Angrily.*] I know dat damn ship—worst ship dat sail to sea. Rotten grub and dey make you work all time—and the Captain and Mate wus Bluenose devils. No sailor who know anyting ever ship on her. Where iss she bound from here?

THE ROUGH. Round Cape 'Orn—sails at daybreak.

OLSON. Py yingo, I pity poor fallers make dat trip round Cape Stiff dis time year. I bet you some of dem never see port once again. [*He passes his hand over his eyes in a dazed way. His voice grows weaker.*] Py golly, I feel dizzy. All the room go round and round like I wus drunk. [*He gets weakly to his feet.*] Good night, Miss Freda. I bane feeling sick. Tell Drisc—I go home. [*He takes a step forward and suddenly collapses over a chair, rolls to the floor, and lies there unconscious.*]

JOE. [*From behind the bar.*] Quick, nawh! [NICK *darts forward with* JOE *following.* FREDA *is already beside the unconscious man and has taken the roll of money from his inside pocket. She strips off a note furtively and shoves it into her bosom, trying to conceal her action, but* JOE *sees her. She hands the roll to* JOE, *who pockets it.* NICK *goes through all the other pockets and lays a handful of change on the table.*]

JOE. [*Impatiently.*] 'Urry, 'urry, can't yer? The other blokes'll be 'ere in 'arf a mo'. [*The two roughs come forward.*] 'Ere, you two, tike 'im in under the arms like 'e was drunk. [*They do so.*] Tike 'im to the Amindra—yer knows that, don't yer?—two docks above. Nick'll show yer. An' you, Nick, down't yer leave the bleedin' ship till the capt'n guvs yer this bloke's advance—full month's pay—five quid, d'yer 'ear?

NICK. I knows me bizness, ole bird. [*They support* OLSON *to the door.*]

THE ROUGH. [*As they are going out.*] This silly bloke'll 'ave the s'prise of 'is life when 'e wakes up on board of 'er. [*They laugh. The door closes behind them.* FREDA *moves quickly for the door on the left but* JOE *gets in her way and stops her.*]

JOE. [*Threateningly.*] Guv us what yer took!

FREDA. Took? I guv yer all 'e 'ad.

JOE. Yer a liar! I seen yer a-playin' yer sneakin' tricks, but yer can't fool Joe. I'm too old a 'and. [*Furiously.*] Guv it to me, yer bloody cow! [*He grabs her by the arm.*]

FREDA. Lemme alone! I ain't got no——

JOE. [*Hits her viciously on the side of the jaw. She crumples up on the floor.*] That'll learn yer! [*He stoops down and fumbles in her bosom and pulls out the banknote, which he stuffs into his pocket with a grunt of satisfaction.* KATE *opens the door on the left and looks in—then rushes to* FREDA *and lifts her head up in her arms.*]

KATE. [*Gently.*] Pore dearie! [*Looking at* JOE *angrily.*] Been 'ittin' 'er agen, 'ave yer, yer cowardly swine!

JOE. Yus; an' I'll 'it you, too, if yer don't keep yer marf shut. Tike 'er aht of 'ere! [KATE *carries* FREDA *into the next room.* JOE *goes behind the bar. A moment later the outer door is opened and* DRISCOLL *and* COCKY *come in.*]

DRISCOLL. Come on, Ollie. [*He suddenly sees that* OLSON *is not there, and turns to* JOE.] Where is ut he's gone to?

JOE. [*With a meaning wink.*] 'E an' Freda went aht t'gether 'bout five minutes past. 'E's fair gone on 'er, 'e is.

DRISCOLL. [*With a grin.*] Oho, so that's ut, is ut? Who'd think Ollie'd be sich a divil wid the wimin? 'Tis lucky he's sober or she'd have him stripped to his last ha'penny. [*Turning to* COCKY, *who is blinking sleepily.*] What'll ye have, ye little scut? [*To* JOE.] Give me whiskey, *Irish* whiskey!

BIOGRAPHICAL NOTES

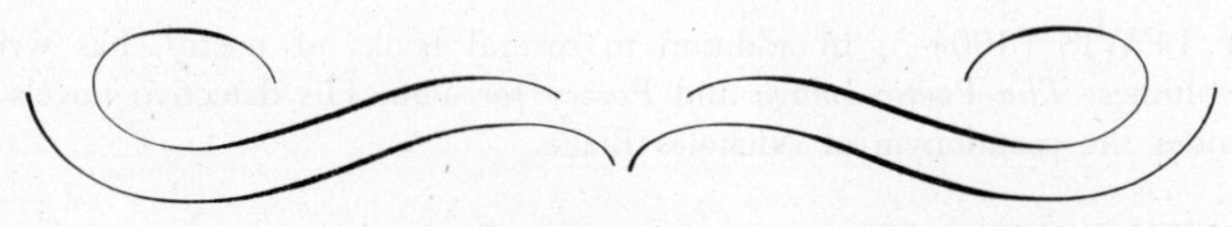

BIOGRAPHICAL NOTES

ROY P. BASLER (1906–) is the author or editor of a number of books on and by Abraham Lincoln. He has been executive secretary of the Abraham Lincoln Association since 1947.

WALTER BLAIR (1900–) is professor of English at the University of Chicago, and is known especially for his studies of American humor.

THOMAS A. BLEDSOE (1914–) formerly taught English at the University of Illinois. He is now editor of the College Department of Rinehart & Company.

C. M. BOWRA (1898–) has been professor of poetry at Oxford University (England) since 1946. In 1948–49 he was the Norton professor of poetry at Harvard.

CLEANTH BROOKS (1906–) now teaches English at Yale. Probably he has been the most influential of the "New Critics" in contemporary letters. From 1935 to 1942 he edited the *Southern Review*. In addition to collaborating on a group of distinguished college textbooks, he has written *Modern Poetry and the Tradition* and *The Well Wrought Urn*.

HARRY M. CAMPBELL (1908–) teaches English at the University of Mississippi. He collaborated with R. E. Foster in writing *William Faulkner: A Critical Appraisal*.

WALTER VAN TILBURG CLARK (1909–) has spent most of his life in Nevada. His novels, *The Ox-Bow Incident* and *The City of Trembling Leaves,* reflect his feeling for the West.

HART CRANE (1899–1932) began his literary career in 1916, and by the time of his death sixteen years later had achieved wide recognition as a poet. *White Buildings* and *The Bridge* were published during his lifetime. *The Collected Poems* appeared in 1933.

DAVID DAICHES (1912–) is professor of English at Cambridge University in England. English by birth and educated in England and Scotland, he has published many studies of literature and literary figures.

EARL DANIELS (1893–) is widely known for his poetry courses at Colgate. In 1941 he published *The Art of Reading Poetry*.

C. DAY LEWIS (1904–), in addition to several books of poetry, has written two critical volumes, *The Poetic Image* and *Poetry for You*. His detective novels are published under the pseudonym of Nicholas Blake.

ELIZABETH DREW (1887–) was educated in England and is now visiting professor of English at Smith College. Among her books are *Discovering Poetry, The Enjoyment of Literature,* and *Directions in Modern Poetry*.

CLIFTON FADIMAN (1904–) reviewed books for *The New Yorker* from 1933 to 1943, and from 1938 to 1948 was master of ceremonies of the radio program "Information Please." Fadiman happily combines a technical interest in literature with feeling for its emotional and moral qualities.

FRANCIS FERGUSSON (1904–), associate professor of literature at Princeton University, is a literary critic with a special interest in the theater. His translations of Greek plays include Sophocles' *Electra*. Among his writings are *The Idea of a Theatre,* poems in *New Directions* and *Partisan Review,* and critical essays in *Hound and Horn, Kenyon Review,* and elsewhere.

G. GIOVANNINI (1906–) teaches at the Catholic University of America, and has contributed to various journals articles on literary theory, on literature and the fine arts, and on Keats, Melville, and Dante.

ROBERT B. HEILMAN (1906–), professor of English at the University of Washington, collaborated with Cleanth Brooks in *Understanding Drama,* and is the author of *This Great Stage: Image and Structure in King Lear*.

JOHN HOLMES (1904–), who teaches at Tufts, has written several volumes of poetry. Two of them are *Address to the Living* and *Map of My Country*.

WILLIS JACOBS (1914–) teaches English and European literature at the University of New Mexico. His short stories and critical articles appear frequently in magazines.

RANDALL JARRELL (1914–), who teaches at the Woman's College of the University of North Carolina, has published three volumes of poetry: *Blood for a Stranger, Little Friend,* and *Losses*.

S. F. JOHNSON (1918–) teaches at New York University and is assistant secretary of the Modern Language Association.

JOHN P. KIRBY (1905–) is professor of English at Randolph-Macon Woman's College. He is a founder and an editor of *The Explicator*.

AUGUST H. MASON (1895–), a professor of English at the University of Alabama, has published poetry in several magazines and edited two collections of poems by Alabama writers.

ELLSWORTH MASON (1917–), who received his Ph.D. from Yale, has taught at Williams College and now lives in Arizona.

F. O. MATTHIESSEN (1902–1950) taught at Harvard. His *The Achievement of T. S. Eliot, American Renaissance,* and *Henry James, the Major Phase* have established him as a contemporary critic able to synthesize cultural history with æsthetic judgments.

R. D. MAYO (1910–) is an assistant professor of English at Northwestern University and editor of the *English "A" Analyst,* a publication of the Department of English for members of the staff and other persons interested in the explication of literary texts.

SAMUEL H. MONK (1902–) is professor of English at the University of Minnesota. His book *The Sublime: A Study of Critical Theories in Eighteenth-Century England* has become a classic in the history of literary criticism.

HARRIET MONROE (1860–1936) founded *Poetry: A Magazine of Verse* in 1912, and remained its editor until her death. Her autobiography, *A Poet's Life,* is an important document in the history of twentieth-century poetry.

NORMAN HOLMES PEARSON (1909–) is director of undergraduate work in the Department of American Studies at Yale University. With W. H. Auden he edited *Poets of the English Language.*

FREDERICK A. POTTLE (1897–) is Sterling professor of English at Yale University. Since the publication of *A New Portrait of James Boswell* in 1927, much of his writing and editing has been concerned with Samuel Johnson's biographer.

JOHN HAWLEY ROBERTS (1897–1949) taught for many years at Williams College and has written numerous articles on nineteenth-century and contemporary English writers, notably Virginia Woolf and E. M. Forster.

WAYNE SHUMAKER (1910–), who teaches English at the University of California, Berkeley, has written a number of critical studies.

HALLETT D. SMITH (1907–) is chairman of the division of humanities at the California Institute of Technology. He is coeditor of *The Golden Hind* and *The Critical Reader.*

THEODORE SPENCER (1902–1949) taught English at Harvard from 1927 until his death. He published a number of books of both poetry and critical essays.

ROBERT WOOSTER STALLMAN (1911–) teaches English at the University of Connecticut and writes critical articles for the periodicals. A contributing editor of *The Western Review,* he collaborated with Ray B. West, Jr., on *The Art of Modern Fiction.* He also edited *The Stephen Crane Reader.*

DONALD A. STAUFFER (1902–), a graduate of Princeton University and a teacher there since 1927, is the author of such recent critical volumes as *The Art of Biography in the Eighteenth Century* and *The Golden Nightingale.*

FRED H. STOCKING (1915–) is associate professor of English at Williams College.

ALLEN TATE (1899–), who began his literary career as a member of the Fugitive group at Nashville, has taught at several colleges and has held various editorial posts. His poetry and criticism show a high regard for metaphysical techniques and neoclassical precision.

ROSEMOND TUVE (1903–), professor of English at Connecticut College, is the author of *Seasons and Month: Studies in a Tradition of Middle English Poetry* and of *Googe's Zodiake of Life.*

MARK VAN DOREN (1894–) has taught at Columbia since 1920. Critic and poet, he received the Pulitzer prize for his *Collected Poems* in 1939.

CHARLES C. WALCUTT (1908–) teaches English at Queens College. He has published frequent essays on naturalism in American fiction.

AUSTIN WARREN (1899–), professor of English at the University of Michigan, is the author of critical volumes on Alexander Pope, Henry James, Sr., and Richard Crashaw. With René Wellek, he wrote *Theory of Literature.*

ROBERT PENN WARREN (1905–) is professor of English at the University of Minnesota. Rhodes scholar, Guggenheim fellow, winner of the Pulitzer prize and many other prizes, he is best known to the layman for his best-selling *All the King's Men.* With Cleanth Brooks he wrote *Understanding Poetry* and *Understanding Fiction.*

W. B. C. WATKINS (1907–), the author of *Perilous Balance* and *Shakespeare and Spenser,* lives in Mississippi.

RAY B. WEST, Jr. (1908–), associate professor of English at the University of Iowa, is an editor of the *Western Review.* His interest in the Far West is reflected in some of the titles of his published works: *Rocky Mountain Reader, Writing in the Rocky Mountains,* and *Rocky Mountain Cities.* With R. W. Stallman he also wrote *The Art of Modern Fiction.*

HAROLD S. WILSON (1904–), associate professor of English at the University of Toronto, edited *Gabriel Harvey's Ciceronianus.*

YVOR WINTERS (1900–), who teaches at Stanford University, has written three books of criticism, now collected in, *In Defense of Reason.* He has also published several volumes of poetry.

MARION WITT (1896–) teaches English at Hunter College and has published numerous studies of the poetry of Yeats.

INDEX

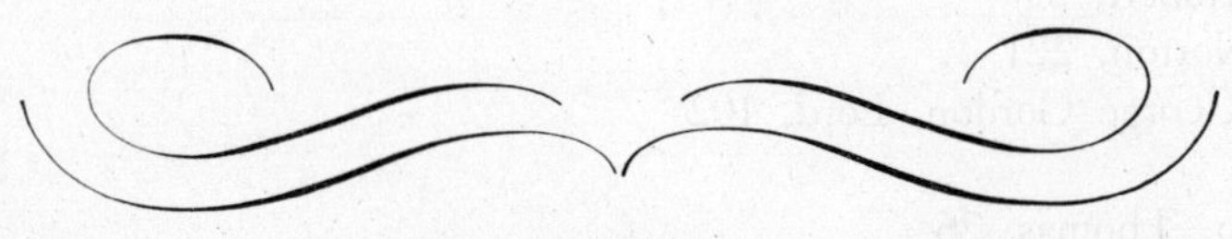

INDEX

Again the Native Hour, 250
Ah Sunflower, 83
Air Plant, The, 248
Amoretti, LXXII, 19
Anderson, Sherwood, 365
Anniversary, The, 30
Arnold, Matthew, 155
At Melville's Tomb, 243
Auden, W. H., 258
Auto Wreck, 269

Babylon Revisited, 428
Balzac, Honoré de, 281
Basler, Roy P., 127
Be Still, My Soul, Be Still, 171
Bird Came Down the Walk, A, 164
Bishop Orders His Tomb at St. Praxed's Church, The, 139
Blair, Walter, 306
Blake, William, 82
Bledsoe, Thomas A., 412
Blindman's Buff, 277
Blue Girls, 235
Bowra, C. M., 84
Brahma, 119
Bride Comes to Yellow Sky, The, 345
Bright Star, Would I Were Stedfast As Thou Art, 118
Brinnin, John Malcolm, 276

Brooks, Cleanth, 131, 451
Browning, Elizabeth Barrett, 119
Browning, Robert, 135
Burns, Robert, 85
Burnt Norton, 221
Byron, George Gordon, Lord, 102

Campion, Thomas, 26
Can Life Be a Blessing?, 61
Carew, Thomas, 41
Celestial Omnibus, The, 373
Chanson Innocent, I, 237
Chariot, The, 164
Chaucer, Geoffrey, 15
Chekhov, Anton, 337
Christmas Eve: Australia, 270
Clark, Walter Van Tilburg, 481, 486
Cocteau, Jean, 653
Coleridge, Samuel T., 101
Collar, The, 38
Collins, William, 80
Come Sleep, O Sleep, the Certain Knot of Peace, 21
Composed upon Westminster Bridge, 95
Constant Lover, The, 56
Cool Tombs, 202
Country Doctor, A, 396
Cousin Nancy, 218
Crane, Hart, 243
Crane, Stephen, 195, 345
Cummings, E. E., 237

Daiches, David, 270
Daniels, Earl, 6
Darkling Thrush, The, 168
Days, 118
Death, 29
Delight in Disorder, 37
Destruction of Sennacherib, The, 102
Dickinson, Emily, 164
Dirge, 255
Don Juan, Canto the Second, 103
Donne, John, 28
Dorothy Q., 122
Dover Beach, 161

Drayton, Michael, 23
Drew, Elizabeth, 225
Dryden, John, 61

Edward, 9
1887, 174
Eighty-Yard Run, The, 493
Eliot, T. S., 214
Emerson, Ralph Waldo, 118
Emperor of Ice-Cream, The, 212
End of the World, The, 235
Envoi (1919), 213
Express, The, 266

Fadiman, Clifton, 330
Faulkner, William, 444
Faustus, 548
Fearing, Kenneth, 255
Fergusson, Francis, 710
Fire and Ice, 198
Fitzgerald, F. Scott, 428
Fly, The, 406
Force That through the Green Fuse Drives the Flower, The, 272
Forster, E. M., 373
Frost, Robert, 197

Ghost of an Apprehension, The, 486
Giovannini, G., 273
Gladius Dei, 353
Go, Lovely Rose, 42
Good-Bye My Fancy!, 154
Gooseberries, 337
Grene, David, 505

Hardy, Thomas, 168
Hawthorne, Nathaniel, 291
Hedda Gabler, 587
Hemingway, Ernest, 455
Herbert, George, 38
Here Lies a Lady, 232
Herrick, Robert, 37
Holmes, John, 200
Holmes, Oliver Wendell, 122
Hopkins, Gerard Manley, 169

Housman, A. E., 171
How Annandale Went Out, 193
Hymn to God, My God, in My Sickness, 31

I Wake and Feel the Fell of Dark, 170
I Wandered Lonely as a Cloud, 95
Ibsen, Henrik, 587
I'm a Fool, 365
In Memory of Major Robert Gregory, 180
In Memory of W. B. Yeats, 259
Indian Summer, 166
Indifferent, The, 29
Infernal Machine, The, 653

Jacobs, Willis D., 411
James, Henry, 311
Jarrell, Randall, 279
Jean Beicke, 400
Jewels, The, 331
Johnson, S. F., 275
Jonson, Ben, 36
Joyce, James, 386

Kafka, Franz, 396
Keats, John, 114
Kirby, John P., 162
Kubla Khan, 101

La Belle Dame Sans Merci, 116
Lak of Stedfastnesse, 15
Lamb, The, 82
Landscape Near an Aerodrome, 266
Leave Me, O Love, 21
Light Breaks Where No Sun Shines, 271
Little Cloud, A, 386
Long Voyage Home, The, 720
Longfellow, Henry Wadsworth, 121
Lord Randal, 11
Love and Life, a Song, 67
Love Song of J. Alfred Prufrock, The, 214
Lovelace, Richard, 57
Loveliest of Trees, 171
Lover Complaineth the Unkindness of His Love, The, 16

Lover Showeth How He Is Forsaken of Such as He Sometime Enjoyed, The, 17
Lowell, Robert, 278
Lucifer in Starlight, 163
Lycidas, 43

Macavity—the Mystery Cat, 219
MacLeish, Archibald, 236
Mann, Thomas, 353
Mansfield, Katherine, 406
Marlowe, Christopher, 18, 548
Marvell, Andrew, 59
Mary Morison, 94
Mason, August H., 252
Mason, Ellsworth, 234
Masque of the Red Death, The, 302
Matthiessen, F. O., 149, 301
Maupassant, Guy de, 331
Mayo, Robert, 238
Meditation Eight, 64
Merciles Beaute, 15
Meredith, George, 163
Milton, John, 42
Mr. Flood's Party, 194
Mr. Pope, 250
mr u, 241
Monk, Samuel Holt, 251
Monroe, Harriet, 243
Moral Essay II, 69
Musée des Beaux Arts, 258
My Heart Leaps Up When I Behold, 95
My Last Duchess, 137

Nash, Ogden, 256
Nymph's Reply, The, 19

O Mistress Mine, 25
Ode on a Grecian Urn, 114
Ode on the Despoilers of Learning in an American University 1947, An, 254
Ode to Evening, 80
Ode to the West Wind, 109
Oedipus the King, 505
Of Corinna's Singing, 27
On a Girdle, 41

On First Looking into Chapman's Homer, 114
On His Being Arrived to the Age of Twenty-Three, 55
On His Blindness, 55
On Wenlock Edge, 172
1 X 1, 241
O'Neill, Eugene, 720
One's-Self I Sing, 142
Ozymandias, 108

Passion in the Desert, A, 281
Passionate Shepherd to His Love, The, 18
Pearson, Norman Holmes, 57
Peau de Chagrin of State Street, The, 124
Petition, 258
Pied Beauty, 169
Poe, Edgar Allan, 124, 302
Pope, Alexander, 69
Pottle, Frederick A., 96
Portable Phonograph, The, 481
Porter, Katherine Anne, 413
Pound, Ezra, 213
Prayer for My Daughter, A, 191
Prayers of Steel, 202
Pulley, The, 38
Purist, The, 257

Ralegh, Sir Walter, 19
Ransom, John Crowe, 232
Real Thing, The, 311
Reluctance, 197
Road Not Taken, The, 197
Roberts, John Hawley, 60
Robinson, E. A., 193
Rochester, Earl of, 67
Rose for Emily, A, 444

Sailing to Byzantium, 190
Sandburg, Carl, 202
Scholar-Gypsy, The, 155
Sea Surface Full of Clouds, 210
Secret Life of Walter Mitty, The, 424
Sidney, Sir Philip, 21
Shakespeare, William, 24
Shapiro, Karl, 267

Shaw, Irwin, 493
Shelley, Percy Bysshe, 108
Short Happy Life of Francis Macomber, The, 455
Should the Wide World Roll Away, 196
Shumaker, Wayne, 47
Simplex Munditiis, 36
Since There's No Help, Come Let Us Kiss and Part, 23
Sir Patrick Spens, 1
Slow, Slow, Fresh Fount, 36
Smith, Hallett D., 76
Snow-Flakes, 121
Soliloquy of the Spanish Cloister, 135
Song, A (Carew), 41
Song (Donne), 28
Song for St. Cecilia's Day, A, 62
Sonnet XXIX, 24
" LXXIII, 24
" CXVI, 25
" CXXIX, 25
Sonnet from the Portuguese, XLIII, 119
Sonnet III Written in a Blank Leaf of Dugdale's Monasticon, 82
Sophocles, 505
Space being Curved, 241
Spencer, Theodore, 12
Spender, Stephen, 266
Spenser, Edmund, 19
Spring and Fall: To a Young Child, 170
Stallman, Robert Wooster, 410
Stanzas from Milton, 85
Stauffer, Donald A., 92
Stella's Birth-Day, 1720, 68
Stevens, Wallace, 203
Stocking, Fred H., 233
Stopping by Woods on a Snowy Evening, 198
Suckling, Sir John, 56
Sunday Morning, 203
Sweeney among the Nightingales, 218
Swift, Jonathan, 68

Tam o'Shanter, 85
Tate, Allen, 165, 250
Taylor, Edward, 64
Tears, Idle Tears, 130
Tennyson, Alfred Lord, 129

Terence, This Is Stupid Stuff, 172
That Tree, 413
Thirty Days Hath September, 12
Thomas, Dylan, 271
Three Ravens, The, 4
Thurber, James, 424
Tiger, The, 83
To a Locomotive in Winter, 153
To a Skylark, 111
To Autumn, 117
To Helen, 126
To His Coy Mistress, 59
To Lucasta, Going to the Wars, 57
To the Accuser Who Is the God of This World, 84
To the Virgins, to Make Much of Time, 37
Tragical History of Doctor Faustus, The, 548
Tuve, Rosemond, 27
Twa Corbies, The, 4
'Twas Like a Maelstrom, 167

Ulysses, 129
Under Which Lyre, 261
University, 267
Upon Julia's Clothes, 37
Upon Leaving His Mistress, 67

Valley of Unrest, The, 126
Van Doren, Mark, 2
Very Like a Whale, 256
Viereck, Peter, 277
Views of the Favorite Colleges, 276

Walcutt, Charles Child, 175
Waller, Thomas, 41
War Is Kind, 195
Warren, Austin, 65
Warren, Robert Penn, 451
Warton, Thomas, the Younger, 82
Watkins, W. B. C., 20
Well, Then, I Hate Thee, 196
West, Ray B., Jr., 479
When Lilacs Last in the Dooryard Bloom'd, 142
When Thou Must Home, 26
Where the Rainbow Ends, 278

Whitman, Walt, 142
Who Is Silvia?, 26
Why So Pale and Wan?, 56
Williams, William Carlos, 400
Wilmot, John, 67
Wilson, Harold S., 22
Windhover, The, 169
Winters, Yvor, 206, 254
Witt, Marion, 183
Wordsworth, William, 95
World Is Too Much with Us, The, 100
Wyatt, Sir Thomas, 16

Ye Flowery Banks, 92
Yeats, W. B., 180
You, Andrew Marvell, 236
Young Goodman Brown, 291

Gooseberries - Checkow
Edipus the King